Air-Britain

TURBOPROP AIRLINERS OF THE WORLD

Including military transport, reconnaissance and surveillance types and variants

4th edition

Edited by Terry Smith

An AIR-BRITAIN Publication

Published in the United Kingdom by
Air-Britain (Historians) Ltd

Registered Office: Victoria House,
Stanbridge Park, Staplefield Lane,
Staplefield, West Sussex RH17 6AS
http://www.air-britain.co.uk

Sales Department: 41 Penshurst Road,
Leigh, Tonbridge, Kent TN11 8HL
e-mail: sales@air-britain.co.uk

Membership Enquiries: 1 Rose Cottages.
179 Penn Road, Hazlemere, Bucks HP15 7NE

ISBN: 0 85130 342 0
EAN: 978 0 85130 342 0

Printed in the United Kingdom by
Bell & Bain Ltd, Glasgow G46 7UQ

VOLUME 1

Front cover:
Air Malawi's ATR-42-320 7Q-YKQ (0236) is seen in a pre-delivery publicity shot. (ATR)

Back cover:

Top: *Beech 1900D YV1372 (UE-331) of Avior Airlines at Caracas on 2.12.07. (Rod Simpson)*
Centre: *RA-09343 Antonov An-22A (043482272) in rather tired Aeroflot titles at Tver-Migalovo in 2002. (via Terry Smith)*
Bottom: *US Navy Lockheed DC-130A Hercules 570496 (3203) was being operated by Flight Systems Inc when seen at Mojave on 6.6.89. (Derek Heley)*

CONTENTS

VOLUME 1

VOLUME 2

MASTER INDEX

INTRODUCTION

This is the fourth edition of this title, the previous edition appearing as long ago as June 2000. Whilst each production list contained herein has been updated completely and much revised data that has come to light been added and corrected, there are bound to be some errors which have not been detected, and some data omitted. We ask readers to submit their additions to the editor, whose details appear below; any items readers might come across, however small, are welcome and will be incorporated into the fifth edition. The new editorial team will also welcome any more general comments on the content of this book.

In this edition, as well as the inclusion of new types which have been constructed since the last edition, we are pleased to have been able to add the DHC-5 Buffalo, Grumman Greyhound and the turbine-powered DC-3s. For the sake of completeness, the piston-engined CL-215s and jet-powered Do328s are also included.

The previous editions of this title were produced under the able leadership of Michael Austen who we must all thank for blazing the trail for the new team, who have assisted in the compilation of this new edition.

As the new compiling editor I must mention specifically and thank in alphabetic order Sue Bushell for the final production work and creation of the Master Index, Chris Chatfield for his unfailing support, Philip Hancock (military type updating), Derek King (updating British types), Steve Mitchell (creation of the Soviet type files), Don Schofield for his superb proof reading and bringing to my attention data discrepancies, and Barrie Towey for much general advice.

In addition to AB-IX, ABN and many other Air-Britain publications, the magazines *Airliner World*, *Aviation Letter* and *Scramble* must be credited whilst Aerodata has provided assistance with last noted data as has the ALST email group. The Aviation Safety Network has provided confirmation of many accident incidents and *Planes.CZ* – LET.410 data. Special credit must be given to the Soviet Transports team and their publication *More than Half a Century of Soviet Transports* by Peter Hillman, Stuart Jessop, Adrian Morgan, Tony Morris, Guus Ottenhof and Michael Roch. Much of the Soviet data has been extracted with kind permission from this book, and from the subsequent updates available from the Dutch Aviation Society website. We encourage all to submit corrections and updates to this website.

The following individuals, without whose assistance you would not have this volume in your hands, must be mentioned: Neil Aird (Beaver Tails), Tony Arbon (Austairdata), Alexandre Avrane (ATDB), Tony Beales (Peruvian data), Martin Best (Buffalo), Jose Santanar Bosch (CASA 212), Richard Bye (accident data), Mike Cain (Anglia Aeronews), Phil Camp (IAF AN-32s), Vladimeiro Cettolo, Mark Checkley, Charles Church, Richard Church (HS.748 & ATP), Paul Compton (Nordic Research), John Davis, Steve Darke (Thai Aviation), Herman Dekker (Dutch Civil Register data), Mike Draper, Malcolm Fillmore, Peter Gerhardt (Dornier), Paul Gehring (Caravan), Grahame Griffiths, Francisco Halbritter (Guarani), Paul Hayes (Airclaims/Ascend Group), Peter Hillman (Nepal), Andrew Hutchings and Ian MacFarlane (Air North), Alan Johnston (Wrecks & Relics), Phil Kemp, Ray Kettle (Viscount), Michael McBurney and Paul McMaster (Ulster Aviation Society SD.3-30 & SD.3-60), Michael Magnusson (Guarani), Stig och Marit Jarlevik, Andy Marden (HAL Do228), Peter Marson, Bernard Martin, Javier Mosquera, Ioannis Mylonas (Greek YS-11s), Mike Ody (Canadian types), Lars Olausson (Hercules), Gary C Orlando (FH-227, www.fh227.rwy.com), Kiyoshi Sato (YS-11), Paul Seymour, Alan Sills, Tom Singfield, Graham Slack and the Graham Slack Collection, Colin R Smith (VNAF C-130), Ton van Soest (Cessna 208), Nev Spalding, Barry Stuart, Terry Sykes (Saunders ST-27/ST-28), Aad van der Voet (www.oldwings.nl), Ron Webster, Dave Wilton (BARG Journal and Cargomaster MASDC park codes), Joerg Windmuller, Luc Wittemans, Phil Yeadon, Frans van

Zelm (editor Fokker News Airnieuws) and to anybody whom I have forgotten and to whom I apologise.

Updating this publication can be achieved by reading the Commercial Scene section of Air-Britain's best-selling monthly magazine *Air-Britain News*, which has recently been enhanced with better print quality and greater topicality. Details of how to subscribe to this magazine are given elsewhere in this book.

October 2012

Terry Smith
28 Summerfields
Ingatestone
Essex CM4 0BS
United Kingdom

Email: turboairliners@air-britain.co.uk (for comments, updates and extra information for inclusion in the next edition)

General User Notes

The layout and data included largely follow that of the previous editions with one major difference. Because of the expansion of the data included the book appears in two volumes – Volume One contains most of the production listings while the smaller Volume Two contains the Air-Britain trademark Master Index. We believe that splitting the book in this manner not only makes the book size more user friendly but it also permits the user to refer to the index at the same time as examining one of the production listings in Volume One. We have also introduced certain refinements which we hope the reader will find enhances the usefulness of the publication.

For both our established and first-time readers we include below a brief explanation of the data layout and the data we have included.

Within each production listing from left to right the reader will find:

c/n (sometimes also known as s/n or msn)
With a very few exceptions, as detailed within the book, all aircraft appear in strict numeric sequence.

Model
Details of sub-models and series are given here. If an aircraft has been converted from one model to another only the latest or last model or series is given.

Last known Owner/Operator
The last known airline, operator or air arm is given here. When the aircraft is in storage or not in use, the name is prefixed by "ex" and when no longer extant the name is bracketed. In cases where the aircraft is owned and preserved by an established museum the name of the museum is given.

Most airline names are presented in the company's marketing style, for example, airBaltic rather than Air Baltic and MASwings rather than MAS Wings. Likewise, in the case of aircraft no longer in service for any reason, the name of the operator at the time of the event is given, rather than any subsequent name.

When aircraft are owned by one operator but are known to be currently operated by another, both names are given separated by a slash with the latter appearing second. We refer readers to Air-Britain's annual publication Airline Fleets (AF) where full airline names and certain other information about the carrier are presented.

The use of Aeroflot without any additional data indicates that either the directorate is unknown, or it was operated by factories with these titles, or it was operated by one of the Soviet republics or (later) a Russian air arm.

Identities/Fate/Comments (where appropriate)
Identities, both civil and military, are given in chronological order with the earliest first. Where marks have been used more than once within a particular type the registration is followed by a number in brackets to indicate how many times the registration concerned has been used. For example (2) means the second use of the mark by that particular type of aircraft. An exception to this rule is manufacturer test or delivery marks such as those used by ATR (French F-Wxxx marks) and Dornier (German marks) where such annotations have not been included.

Except in the case of former United States military aircraft (including USAF, USN and USCG), where a non-current military identity is included there is a note advising readers of the country associated with the serial, but not the name of the actual arm within such a country. The country of a current serial or marking can be ascertained by referring to the operator column.

In the case of aircraft that were operated by the Soviet Air Force and inherited in 1992 by the Russian Air Force, mention is only made of the latter. In the case of aircraft which are known to have been cancelled from the register post 1992, but where the last sighting was prior to 1992, the last operator is still given as being Soviet Air Force unless it has been proved to be in the Russian Air Force inventory. Where it is suspected that an aircraft must have been operated by one of the Soviet air arms, the first identity is shown as "Soviet" in inverted commas, as shown here.

Marks allocated but not taken up appear in brackets. Reserved marks are indicated by the use of the symbol "*". In cases where a note concerning a particular marking appears, the marking in question is followed by the symbol "+". In cases where multi notes are required the symbols "^" and "#" are also used.

In general, military aircraft codes are not quoted as they can change frequently. With the exception of aircraft operated by certain air arms where on occasion the code rather than the serial is quoted, these are separated by a double slash "//" with both being included separately in the Master Index. Where only a single slash "/" is given they appear in the Master Index as a single identity. An example of the latter is the Spanish CASA 212.

In countries such as Colombia and Peru, which on occasion use suffixes such as X or P, the use of these suffixes is only normally quoted once. It must be noted that such prefixes are not normally quoted in the official records and accordingly can only be quoted here if they have been recorded as such by sighting.

The inclusion of a code which appears in brackets after a military serial does not necessarily indicate the code was carried for the whole period it was operated as such. The format of United Nations codes vary; We have included what we understand was painted on the aircraft.

Following the listing of the civil registrations and military markings, comments and remarks appear in square brackets [ ].

Within these square brackets the following data items appear:

- Basic details of all known write-off data
- Other fate data such as details of breaking up including known dates
- Details of aircraft that are in storage including, where known, last-noted details
- For prototype aircraft, known first flight details
- Known codes carried by military aircraft.

Place and country details are given in full except in the case of the USA where only the standard two-letter state codes are given. Standard Australian state and Canadian state/province codes are also used. The name of the country or the place given is the name at the time of the event being described, rather than any later changed name.

The use of "Soviet" as the first identity means that the aircraft's early history is unknown and it has been assumed likely to have been operated by one of the former Soviet air arms. Aircraft may have had a tactical code (01 red etc) or carried unrecorded or unavailable CCCP- marks.

In many cases, in particular with the older Soviet types, the comment "fate unknown" perhaps not surprisingly is given instead of a more detailed remark. We suspect that in the majority of cases the aircraft concerned has been broken up at its final base, although we have no proof of this.

Data that has not been fully confirmed is shown with a following question mark. Where a change of prefix has taken place, for example, CCCP- to RA-, this is only shown when such a change has been confirmed.

Place Names
Generally speaking the Anglicized version of place names has been used. During the past 60+ years country and place names have changed; in some cases more than once. Within this book we have in all cases tried to adopt the name at the time the incident concerned took place. This includes cases where the name of an airport has been changed.

Master Index
Civil aircraft which have flown without a prefix, for example in China prior to the adoption of the B prefix, are normally included in the military section of the index.

Following the break-up of the Soviet Union, many Soviet-built aircraft lost their CCCP- prefixes before taking up the new prefix of the state in which the aircraft was then registered. In such cases the number without prefix is given under the new prefix.

In the case of a Soviet military code where it is known that the same code has been used firstly by a Soviet air arm then by an air arm of the new country, details are only given under the heading of the new country.

SOVIET CONSTRUCTION NUMBERS

The construction numbers used by Soviet airliner types are often complex and require explanation. Within the different aircraft listings, most c/ns are presented with spaces between different parts of the data they represent. Please be aware that the actual c/ns do not have these spaces; they have been included in order to ease use by readers of the book. In addition, and as noted below, we have presented some aircraft types in line number order, to make it easier for readers to use the book.

A dot within a c/n indicates that the character that should appear in that space is not known. Details of the c/n systems used by some selected types follow. Further more detailed explanations of the c/n systems are included in *More than Half a Century of Soviet Transports* and at http://www.scramble.nl/sovdb.htm or alternatively via a link within Air-Britain's Researchers Corner. This document also sets out where c/ns can be found on each type.

Antonov An-8

With the first c/n sequence, the first digit indicates the year built, followed by 34 indicating the factory (the factory number was 84), then a two-digit batch number and then the number in the batch.

From 1960 a new sequence was introduced with the first digit indicating the year built, the second a Cyrillic character indicating the batch number, followed again by 34 and the final two digits indicating the number within the batch.

Antonov An-10

The first digit represents the year built, followed by 4 to indicate the factory number (64) then a three-digit batch number and then two digits for the number within the batch.

Antonov An-12

Irkutsk production: The first digit represents the year built, followed by 9 to indicate the factory number (39) then a three-digit batch number and then two digits for the number within the batch.

Voronezh production: The first digit represents the year built, followed by 4 to indicate the factory number (64) then a three-digit batch number and then two digits for the number within the batch.

Tashkent production: The first digit represents the year built, followed by 34 to indicate the factory number (84) then a two-digit batch number followed by two further digits for the number within the batch.

Antonov An-22

There are two systems; the first consists of the year built (a single digit) followed by the factory code 34 (for 84) then batch number and number within the batch, each of two characters.

The second system has the two digits to indicate the year built, then factory code 34 and lastly an obscure five digit number.

Antonov An-24

Svyatoshino and Ulan Ude production: The first digit indicates the year built followed by either 73 (Svyatoshino) or 99 (Ulan Ude) to indicate the factory number, a three-digit batch number and then two digits for the number within the batch.

Irkutsk An-24T production: Two systems exist, one for export aircraft for which explanation is not totally clear. These start with 102, a factory code for the type of aircraft, a single digit which might indicate the version, another to indicate year of build and then possibly a two-digit sequence number.

Antonov An-26
Most aircraft are known simply by batch number – initially just two digits and then three when batch 100 was reached – followed by two digits being the number within the batch. A fuller version has the year built as a first digit and then 73 derived from the factory code 473.

Antonov An-28/PZL M-28
Construction numbers are prefixed by either 1AJ, AJG or AJE to indicate type and model. These are followed by the batch number (3 digits) and the number within the batch (2 digits).

Antonov An-30
The first two digits are the batch number which is followed by the number in the batch, also two digits.

Antonov An-32
The first two digits are the batch number which is followed by the number in the batch, also two digits.

Antonov An-38
The prototypes have c/ns that give the type number followed by the batch number and the number in the batch. Production aircraft have a complex c/n consisting of 416 (the code for the factory), 38 (type number), quarter of certification and then year of certification (both a single digit), batch number (two digits) and finally number in the batch (four digits).

Antonov An-140
Four different systems, three of which are straightforward. The other consists of the three digits 365 to indicate factory, followed by the product code 253. The last five digits are allocated at random.

Ilyushin Il-18
Product code 18 followed by year of manufacture (one digit), followed by a zero (0) to indicate the factory code. Then a three-digit batch number and a two digit number in the batch.

Ilyushin Il-20
Same as the Il-18 except use of product code 17, rather than 18.

Ilyushin Il-22
New-build aircraft c/ns start with either 039 or 296 indicating at which of two factories it was built, followed by a two-digit product or type code. The final five digits is a random number. Aircraft converted from IL-18s retained their original c/ns.

Ilyushin Il-38
The first two digits 08 indicate the product code, followed by a single digit to indicate year of build, followed by a zero (0) to indicate the factory code. Then a three-digit batch number and two-digit number in the batch.

LET L-410
Production aircraft c/ns consist of year of production (2 digits), then a batch number and number within the batch, each having two digits.

Tupolev Tu-114, Tu-116 and Tu-126
The c/n gives the year of build, followed by a digit to indicate the factory code, then a batch number and number within the batch.

Please note in several cases there are variants to the explanations given above, for example in the case of pre-production aircraft.

Abbreviations

a/p	airport
AF	Air Force
AFB	Air Force Base
Avn	Aviation
b/u	broken up
c/n	construction number
c/s	colour scheme
canx	cancelled
cvtd	converted
dam	damaged
DBF	destroyed by fire
DBR	damaged beyond repair
dest	destroyed
dism	dismantled
ff	first flight
GIA	ground instructional airframe
Govt	Government
Int'l	International
l/n	last noted
NAS	Naval Air Station
nr	near
PWFU	permanently withdrawn from use
regd	registered
scr	scrapped
SOC	Struck off Charge
std	stored
tfd	transferred
TTC	Technical Training Command
UN	United Nations
unkn	unknown
w/o	written off
wfs	withdrawn from service
WFU	withdrawn from use

Any data item followed by a question mark "?" indicates that the data item concerned has not been fully confirmed but in all likelihood is correct.

Meanings of initials used in the operator column of former Soviet types can be found in the previously mentioned book *More than Half a Century of Soviet Transports*.

We are fully aware that the storage facility at Davis-Monthan, Tucson, AZ had been called MASDC – Military Aircraft Storage and Disposition Center, then AMARC – Aerospace Maintenance and Regeneration Center from October 1985 until it became AMARG Aircraft Maintenance and Regeneration Group. As it is well known as AMARC, in common with our sister publication Jet Airliners of the World, we have generally referred to it as that. The exception to this is the C-133 Cargomaster as the aircraft had all been disposed of before AMARC came into being.

AERITALIA/FIAT/ALENIA G.222/C-27J SPARTAN

C/n	Line No.	Model	Last known Owner/Operator	Identities/fates/comments (where appropriate)
4001		TCM	(Italian Air Force)	MM582//RS-06 [prototype ff 18Jly70; b/u Rome-Pratica di Mare, Italy, after Jly03; remains to dump; gone by May07]
4002		TCM	Freizeitpark Irrland	MM583+ I-BOIN I-MARD I-MAXB MM583//RS-07 [+ Italy] [preserved by Dec08 Twisteden, Germany]
4003		TCM	ex Italian Air Force	MM62101//RS-36+ I-CERK MM62101//RS-45 [+ Italy] [wfu Rome-Pratica di Mare, Italy; l/n May07]
4004		TCM	ex Italian Air Force	MM62102//46-20 [stored Pisa-San Giusto, Italy; l/n Aug04]
4005		TCM	ex Italian Air Force	MM62103 I-MARX MM62103//46-37 [wfu Nov98 Pisa-San Giusto, Italy; parts missing by Jun00; l/n Sep03]
4006		TCM	(Dubai Air Force)	321+ 301 [+ Dubai] [wfu in 1989; used for spares Venice, Italy 1992]
4007		TCM	ex Italian Air Force	MM62104//46-91 [stored by May07 Pisa-San Giusto, Italy; l/n 16Dec08 with tail removed; shipped to Warner Robins AFB, GA, as fuselage trainer]
4008		TCM	ex Italian Air Force	MM62105//46-82 [stored Pisa-San Giusto, Italy; l/n Sep03]
4009		TCM	(Italian Air Force)	MM62106//46-84 [w/o 10Jly82 Ponte a Grebe, near Florence, Italy]
4010		TCM	ex Argentine Army	AE-260 [reported wfu Oct96 & stored El Palomar, Argentina; stored by Dec06 Campo Grande, Brazil, due to technical issues]
4011		TCM	ex Argentine Army	AE-261 [wfu or stored by Mar04 Campo de Mayo, Argentina]
4012		VS	Italian Air Force	MM62107
4013		TCM	(Italian Air Force)	MM62108//46-30 [w/o 07Jun96 Pisa-San Giusto, Italy; remains l/n Aug03]
4014		TCM	for Afghanistan	MM62109//46-96 [stored by Oct07 Pisa-San Giusto, Italy; l/n 01Nov09]
4015		TCM	ex Italian Air Force	MM62110//46-81 [stored Pisa-San Giusto, Italy; preserved by Aug08]
4016		TCM	Afghan National Army	MM62111//46-83+ 74016 [+ Italy]
4017		TCM	(Italian Air Force)	MM62113//46-34 [w/o 03Sep92 Mount Zec, near Jasenica, Bosnia-Herzegovina]
4018		TCM	ex Italian Air Force	MM62112//46-85 [wfu for spares Pisa-San Guisto, Italy; l/n Sep03]
4019		TCM	ex Italian Air Force	MM62114//46-80 [stored Pisa-San Giusto, Italy; l/n Nov06]
4020		TCM	for Afghanistan	MM62115//46-22 [Tunisian AF ntu] [stored by Oct07 Pisa-San Giusto, Italy; l/n 01Nov09]
4021		TCM	ex Argentine Army	AE-262 [wfu or stored by Mar04 Campo de Mayo, Argentina]
4022		TCM	(Italian Air Force)	MM62116//46-35 I-MAIR MM62116//46-35 [w/o 08Jan92 Monte Lavello near Prato, Italy]
4023		TCM	for Afghanistan	MM62117//46-25 I-MAIT MM62117//46-25 [stored by Oct07 Pisa-San Giusto, Italy; l/n 01Nov09]
4024		A	Afghan National Army	MM62118//46-24 84024
4025		TCM	for Afghanistan	MM62119//46-21 [stored by Oct07 Pisa-San Giusto, Italy; l/n 01Nov09]
4026		TCM	ex Italian Air Force	MM62120//46-90 [stored by Oct07 Pisa-San Giusto, Italy; l/n 16Dec08]
4027		TCM	ex Italian Air Force	MM62121//RS-46 [stored by Oct07 Pisa-San Giusto, Italy; l/n 16Dec08; reported for Museo Storico dell' Aeronautica Militare, Vigna di Valle, Rome, Italy]
4028		TCM	Afghan National Army	MM62122//46-23+ 84028 [+ Italy]
4029		TCM	ex Italian Air Force	MM62123//46-28 [stored Pisa-San Giusto, Italy; l/n Sep03]
4030		TCM	Italian Air Force	MM62124//46-88
4031		TCM	Afghan National Army	MM62125//46-87+ MM62125//14-24+ 94031
4032		TCM	for Afghanistan	MM62126//46-26 [stored by Oct07 Pisa-San Giusto, Italy; l/n 01Nov09]
4033		J	Alenia Aerospazio	MM62127//46-27 CSX62127 I-RAIC+ [+ not fully confirmed] [conv to C-27J Spartan for type testing]
4034		T	Libyan Arab Republic AF	I-GAIT 221
4035		TCM	(Italian Air Force)	MM62128//RS-46 [w/o 22Aug91 Santa Maria, near Rome, Italy]
4036		TCM	(Italian Air Force)	MM62129//RS-44 [w/o 05Jun91 Rome-Pratica di Mare, Italy; wreck to Parco Ditellandia, Castel Volturno, Italy]
4037		TCM	ex Italian Air Force	MM62130//46-31 [stored Pisa-San Giusto, Italy; l/n May04]
4038		T	Libyan Arab Republic AF	(MM60213//AM93)+ 222 [+ Somali]
4039		L	(Somali Air Force)	MM60214//AM94 [wfu; derelict Mogadishu, Somalia; b/u 1994]
4040		T	Libyan Arab Republic AF	(MM60215//AM95)+ 223 [VIP Aircraft] [+ Somali]
4041		L	(Somali Air Force)	I-RAIG MM60216//AM96 [wfu; stored Sep90 Pisa-San Giusto, Italy; l/n Aug02; probably b/u]
4042		A	ex Venezuelan Air Force	(MM60217//AM97)+ I-CERW EV8227^ 0675 [+ Somali; ^Venezuela] [stored Base Aerea El Libertador, Palo Negro, Venezuela; l/n Aug02]
4043		J	(Alenia Aerospazio)	MM60218//AM98)+ I-CERX EV8228^ I-CERX [+ Somali; ^Venezuela] [converted to C-27J prototype; ff 24Sep99; wfu by Jun03]
4044		TCM	(Italian Air Force)	MM62131//46-92 [w/o 29Aug85 Laconi, Sardinia]

AERITALIA/FIAT/ALENIA G.222/C-27J SPARTAN

C/n	Line No.	Model	Last known Owner/Operator	Identities/fates/comments (where appropriate)
4045		TCM	ex Italian Air Force	MM62132//46-32 [wfu Nov98 Pisa-San Giusto, Italy; parts missing, l/n 22May08]
4046		TCM	Afghan National Army	MM62133//46-93+ (Tunisian AF ntu) 14046 [+ Italy]
4047		TCM	ex Italian Air Force	MM62134//46-33 [stored Pisa-San Giusto, Italy; l/n Sep03]
4048		TCM	Afghan National Army	MM62135//46-94+ 14048 [+ Italy]
4049				[previously reported as being MM62136//46-97, now known to be c/n 4078; nothing known, perhaps not built]
4050		TCM	Afghan National Army	MM62137//46-95+ 14050 [+ Italy]
4051		VS	(Italian Air Force)	MM62138 [believed order cancelled and not built]
4052		T	Libyan Arab Republic AF	224
4053		T	Libyan Arab Republic AF	225
4054		T	Libyan Arab Republic AF	226
4055		A	ex Venezuelan Air Force	1258 [stored Base Aerea El Libertador, Palo Negro, Venezuela; l/n Aug02]
4056		T	Libyan Arab Republic AF	227
4057		RM	ex Italian Air Force	MM62139//14-20 [wfu by Jly03 Pratica di Mare, Italy]
4058		T	Libyan Arab Republic AF	228
4059		T	Libyan Arab Republic AF	229
4060		T	Libyan Arab Republic AF	230
4061		T	Libyan Arab Republic AF	231
4062		T	Libyan Arab Republic AF	232
4063		T	Libyan Arab Republic AF	233
4064		T	Libyan Arab Republic AF	234
4065		T	Libyan Arab Republic AF	235
4066		T	Libyan Arab Republic AF	236
4067		T	ex Libyan Arab Republic AF	237 [stored by 20Nov08, with 7 others, Benghazi, Libya]
4068		T	Libyan Arab Republic AF	238
4069		RM	ex Italian Air Force	MM62140//14-21 [stored Rome-Pratica di Mare, Italy; l/n May 08; Jun11 stored Naples, Italy]
4070		TCM	Nigerian Air Force	NAF-950 [c/n not fully confirmed]
4071		T	Libyan Arab Republic AF	239
4072			Libyan Arab Republic AF	240
4073		A	ex Venezuelan Air Force	2414 [wfu Base Aerea El Libertador, Palo Negro, Venezuela; l/n Aug02]
4074		TCM	Nigerian Air Force	NAF-951
4075		TCM	Nigerian Air Force	NAF-952
4076		RM	ex Italian Air Force	MM62141//14-22 [stored Rome-Pratica di Mare, Italy; l/n May 08; Jun11 stored Naples, Italy]
4077		RM	(Italian Air Force)	MM62142//14-23 [damaged 25Nov01 and stored Rome-Pratica di Mare, Italy; by Aug04 on dump; not noted May07]
4078		TCM	Afghan National Army	MM62136//46-97 54078
4079		TCM	ex Nigerian Air Force	NAF-953 [stored by Apr10 Lagos, Nigeria, fuselage only]
4080		A	ex Venezuelan Air Force	3526 [wfu Base Aerea El Libertador, Palo Negro, Venezuela; l/n Aug02]
4081		A	Museo AMBV	4402 [damaged 17Nov06 Caracas-Maiquetia, Venezuela; May09 preserved Maracay, Venezuela]
4082		A	ex Venezuelan Air Force	5802 [wfu Oct98 Base Aerea El Libertador, Palo Negro, Venezuela; l/n Aug02]
4083		A	ex Venezuelan Air Force	6620 [wfu Oct98 Base Aerea El Libertador, Palo Negro, Venezuela; l/n Jan06]
4084			ex Nigerian Air Force	NAF-954 [stored by Apr10 Lagos, Nigeria]
4085		TCM	ex Protezione Civile	MM62143//46-36 [wfu by Aug01 Pisa, Italy; by Sep05 GIA Bovisio Masciago, Milan, Italy]
4086		J	ex Italian Air Force	MM62144//46-98 CSX62144//RS-44 MM62144 CPX618 [conv to C-27J Spartan] [reported stored by Alenia at Turin-Caselle, Italy]
4087		TCM	Afghan National Army	I-RAIK MM62154//46-54 64087+ [cvtd to TCM] [+ tie-up assumed]
4088		TCM	Afghan National Army	MM62145//46-50 64088+ [cvtd to TCM] [+ tie-up assumed]
4089		TCM	Italian Air Force	MM62146//RS-45 [cvtd to TCM] [re-coded 14-11]
4090		A	Afghan National Army	MM62155//46-53 74090
4091		TCM	Nigerian Air Force	MM62147//46-52 [cvtd to TCM] NAF-955
4092		A	Afghan National Army	MM62152//46-38+ MM62152//RS-45+ 74092^ [+ Italy; [^ Afghanistan] [01Nov09 on rework Naples, Italy; l/n 17Mar10]
4093		A	Afghan National Army	I-RAIS 84093
4094				[for Zaire ntu; probably not built]

AERITALIA/FIAT/ALENIA G.222/C-27J SPARTAN

C/n	Line No.	Model	Last known Owner/Operator	Identities/fates/comments (where appropriate)
4095		TCM	Italian Air Force	MM62153//RS-46 [wfu Rome-Pratica di Mare, Italy; l/n May08]
4096				[for Zaire ntu; probably not built]
4097		A	ex US Dept of State	I-RAI. 90-0170+ N2290E [+ USAF: code DOS-01; stored 11Jan99 AMARC, code AXCC0007; Oct08 fuselage air-freighted Eglin AFB, FL for AC-27J trials]
4098		A	US Dept of State	I-RAIS 90-0171+ N23743 PNC-3003//C-01 N23743 [+ USAF; AMARC, code AXCC0005]
4099		A	ex US Dept of State	I-RAIT 90-0172+ N47612 [+ USAF; code DOS-02] [stored 11Jan99 AMARC, code AXCC0004; l/n Oct06]
4100		A	ex US Dept of State	I-RAIS 90-0173+ N2286K [+ USAF; code DOS-04] [stored 15Sep97 AMARC, code AXCC0002; l/n Oct06]
4101		A	US Dept of State	I-RAIT 90-0174+ N2290J PNC-3004//C-04 N2290J [also wears DOSAW-4; PNC3004 & 174; + USAF; AMARC code AXCC0010]
4102		A	ex US Dept of State	I-RAIS 91-0103+ N22888 [+ USAF; code DOS-03] [stored 14Jan99 AMARC code AXCC0008; moved 21Mar01 to Western International scrapyard, Tucson, AZ; l/n Oct02; by Mar10 rear fuselage only]
4103		A	US Dept of State	I-RAIL 91-0104+ N47892 PNC-3002//C-03 N47892 [+ USAF; AMARC code AXCC0006]
4104		A	ex US Dept of State	[I-RAIL or I-RAIS] 91-0105+ N2286Y [+ USAF; code DOS-05] [stored 14Jly97 AMARC code AXCC0001; reported by 14Jly97 on Celebrity Row, Davis-Monthan AFB, AZ; l/n Mar10]
4105		A	US Dept of State	I-RAIS 91-0106+ N12310 PNC-3001//C-02 N12310 [+ USAF; AMARC code AXCC0009]
4106		A	ex US Dept of State	I-RAIS 91-0107+ N2286Z [+ USAF; code DOS-06] [stored 22Sep97 AMARC code AXCC0003]
4107		TCM	Royal Thai Air Force	I-RAIT BL.14-1/38//60307 [serial followed by code after double forward slash]
4108		TCM	Royal Thai Air Force	BL.14-2/38//60308 [serial followed by code after double forward slash] [by Jly12 preserved Jomtiem, Thaland]
4109		TCM	Royal Thai Air Force	BL.14-3/38//60309 [serial followed by code after double forward slash] [by Jan10 stored Bangkok-Don Muang, Thailand; damaged in floods Oct11; by Jly12 dismantled Jesada Technik Museum, Nakhon Chaisi, Thailand]
4110		TCM	Royal Thai Air Force	BL.14-4/39//60310 [serial followed by code after double forward slash] [by Jan10 wfu Lopburi, Thailand]
4111		TCM	Royal Thai Air Force	BL.14-5/39//60311 [serial followed by code after double forward slash] [by Jan10 stored Bangkok-Don Muang, Thailand; damaged in floods Oct11; by Jly12 dismantled Jesada Technik Museum, Nakhon Chaisi, Thailand]
4112		TCM	ex Royal Thai Air Force	BL.14-6/39//60312 [serial followed by code after double forward slash] [preserved 21Jan09 Tango Squadron, Bangkok-Don Muang, Thailand]
4113		J	Italian Air Force	CSX62214 MM62214//46-84
4114		J	Italian Air Force	CSX62215 MM62215//46-80
4115		J	Lithuanian Air Force	I-FBAX CSX62216 06 blue
4116		J	Italian Air Force	CSX62117 MM62217//46-81
4117		J	Greek Air Force	CSX62231 4117
4118		J	Greek Air Force	CSX62232 4118
4119		J	Italian Air Force	CSX62219//RS-50 MM62219//46-83+ [+ tie up not confirmed; still CSX62219 in Jan10; these marks either another aircraft or ntu]
4120		J	Greek Air Force	CSX62233 4120
4121		J	Greek Air Force	CSX62234 4121
4122		J	Greek Air Force	CSX62235 4122
4123		J	Greek Air Force	CSX62236 4123
4124		J	Greek Air Force	CSX62237 4124
4125		J	Greek Air Force	CSX62238 4125
4126		J	Alena Aermacchi North America	CSX62239 (4126)+ I-EASA N359PL [+ Greece] [JCA testbed]
4127		J	Bulgarian Air Force	CSX62240 071
4128	HA009	J	Mexican Air Force	CSX62241 (4128)+ 3402 [+ Greece]
4129	JCA1	J	USAF	CSX62242 I-RAID N359TA 07-27010 [c/n given as 129 whilst on USCAR]
4130		J	Italian Air Force	CSX62218 MM62218//46-82
4131		J	Italian Air Force	MM62220//46-83
4132		J	Italian Air Force	MM62221//46-85
4133		J	Italian Air Force	MM62222//46-86

AERITALIA/FIAT/ALENIA G.222/C-27J SPARTAN

C/n	Line No.	Model	Last known Owner/Operator	Identities/fates/comments (where appropriate)
4134		J	Italian Air Force	CSX62223//46-88+ MM62223//46-88 [+ not confirmed]
4135		J	Italian Air Force	CSX62224//46-89+ MM62224//46-89 [+ not confirmed]
4136		J	Italian Air Force	CSX62225 MM62225//46-90
4137		J	Italian Air Force	CSX62250 MM62250//46-91
4138	JCA2	J	for USAF	I-RAIF 07-27011* [c/n not confirmed]
4139		J	Lithuanian Air Force	CSX62252 07 blue
4140		J	Bulgarian Air Force	CSX62253 072
4141		J	Romanian Air Force	CSX62256 2701
4142	HA010	J	Mexican Air Force	MM62258 4142+ 3403 [+ Greece]
4143		J	Lithuanian Air Force	08 blue
4144		J	Romanian Air Force	CSX62257 2702
4145		J	Alenia	CSX62254 [for Bulgarian Air Force as 073 but not yet delivered, due to payment problems; l/n 01Sep10]
4146	HA011	J	Mexican Air Force	CSX62259 (4146)+ 3401 [+ Greece ntu]
4147	HA012	A	Mexican Air Force	CSX62260 3404
4148	JCA3	J	USAF	I-RAIF 07-27012
4149	JCA4	J	USAF	I-PTFH 07-27013 [also reported as being c/n 4149]
4150		J	Royal Moroccan Air Force	CSX62272 CNA-MN [coded MN]
4151	JCA5	j	USAF	I-EASA 07-27014
4152		J	Royal Moroccan Air Force	CNA-MO [coded MO]
4153	JCA6	J	USAF	I-PTFJ? 07-27015
4154	JCA7	J	USAF	07-27016
4156		J	Romanian Air Force	2703
4157	JCA8	J	USAF	I-PFTF? 07-27017
4164	JCA10	J	for USAF	I-RAIG [to become 09-27019 but tie up not confirmed]
4165		J	Romanian Air Force	CSX62283 2704
4166	JCA11	J	USAF	I-PTFD? 07-27020
416?	JCA12	J	USAF	09-27021
4169	JCA13?	J	USAF	I-RAIG 09-27022+ [+ tie up not confirmed]
4170				
4171				
4172		J	USAF	I-RAII 10-23023
Unidentified				
unkn		J	Royal Moroccan Air Force	CNA-MP [reported Turin-Caselle, Italy]
unkn		J	Royal Moroccan Air Force	CNA-MQ [reported 22Aug11 Turin-Caselle, Italy; also wearing CSX62778; possibly either c/n 4158, 4161 or 4162]
unkn		J	unknown	CSX62245 [reported 31Jly09 Turin-Caselle, Italy]
unkn		J	unknown	CSX62247 [reported 31Jly09 Turin-Caselle, Italy]
unkn		J	unknown	CSX62259 [reported 31Jly09 Turin-Caselle, Italy]
unkn	JCA7	J	Alenia	I-EASD 08-27016 [reported Oct10 Turin-Caselle, Italy; for USAF as 27016; possibly c/n 4168]
unkn		J	unknown	I-RIAJ [reported 31Jly09 Turin-Caselle, Italy]
unkn		J	Bulgarian Air Force	073 [reported 31Jly09 Turin-Caselle, Italy; ex CSX62254; delivered 31Mar11]
unkn		J	Bulgarian Air Force	074 [reported 21Sep07 Turin-Caselle, Italy, but unlikely]
unkn		J	Romanian Air Force	2706 [reported 16Jun12 Turin-Caselle, Italy]
unkn		J	USAF	I-RAIF 10-27024 [reported ferried 04Jly12 Turin-Caselle, Italy to Keflavik, Iceland]
unkn		J	Greek Air Force	HAF12 [reported 31Jly09 Turin-Caselle, Italy; assumed to be 12th of 12 on order]
unkn		G222		[unmarked stored for many years on east side of Turin-Caselle, Italy believed Zaire Air Force ntu, possibly either c/n 4094 or 4096 – l/n Aug08]

AEROSPATIALE/AERITALIA ATR 42/72

C/n	Model	Last known Owner/Operator	Identities/fates/comments (where appropriate)
001	42-200	(Aerospatiale)	F-WEGA [prototype ff 16Aug84; w/o 17Jun88 Toulouse-Blagnac, France]
002	42-200	AI(R)	F-WEGB [stored since Jan98 Toulouse-Blagnac, France; dismantled; fuselage only l/n 04Dec07]
003	42-320	Top Fly/Flysur	F-WEGC PH-HWJ F-WEGE F-GEGE F-OICG F-WQNE EC-IDG
004	42-300	Aeroperlas	F-WEGD F-GEGD F-WEGD HR-IAX TG-IAX HP-004APP
005	42-300	Danu Oro Transportas	(F-WEGE) F-WWEA OY-CIA F-GEDZ YU-ALM F-WGZH F-GHPZ OY-CIA F-GHPZ EI-SLD LY-OOV
006	42-300	(Air Antilles Express)	F-WWEB OH-LTA F-GGFA B-2206 F-GHPS [dismantled by 12Aug10 Dinard, France; hulk l/n 24Oct10]
007	42-320	Blue Islands	F-WWEC OY-CIB A2-ALJ F-WWEC OY-CIB F-GFLL OY-CIB A2-ALJ F-WWEC OY-CIB G-DRFC
008	42-300	(Soc. Normande d'Entreprise)	F-WWED PH-ATR F-GEQJ [stored Aug05 La Rochelle, France; l/n 21Dec05; canx 18May09 as destroyed; b/u?]
009	42-300	Aerocaribbean	F-WWEE N140DD F-WQGV CU-T1296 CU-T1509
010	42-300	Danu Oro Transportas	F-WDXL F-GDXL F-GLIA N110VV OY-RUM LY-RUM
011	42-300	Colombian National Police	F-WWER F-ODSA D-BAAA(1) F-WQGF SP-EEA F-WVZX F-GVZX HP- F-WCAU PNC-0241
012	42-300	(Si Fly/UN WFP)	F-WWED N420MQ N12MQ F-WQJB F-OHFV [w/o 12Nov99 15km from Kosovska Mitrovica near Pristina, Kosovo]
012A	42-320	Danu Oro Transportas	F-WWEI VH-AQC YU-ALK+ OY-CIF F-WQBT LY-ARI [+ some reports state this was YU-ALL but we consider this to be correct]
013	42-300		[not built]
014	42-300	Aerocaribbean	F-WWEB N421MQ F-WQIE CU-T1297 CU-T1511 PP-PTE CU-T1550
015	42-300	ex Arkas S.A.	F-WWEA N141DD N19AE F-WQIQ CU-T1451 F-WQNO PR-TTA HK-4492X [stored by 02Sep10 Rionegro, Colombia; early 2012 wfu for parts]
016	42-320	Kramer Investment Co	F-WWEE (VH-AQE) DQ-FEJ F-GGBE N42AT F-WHHS N212AZ
017	42-300F	(Bravo Aviation Ltd)	F-WWER N971NA G-IONA SP-KEE G-IONA [arrived 04Jun09 Edinburgh, fully b/u late Sep09; l/n 30Aug09; canx 27Jly09]
018	42-300F	ex Arkas S.A.	F-ODGM F-GIIA TR-LEW F-GPIA HK-4493X [stored by 02Sep10 Rionegro, Colombia; early 2012 wfu for parts]
019	42-320	Atlantique Air Assistance	F-WWEF VH-AQD YU-ALL+ OY-CIG F-WQNE? F-WKVB F-HAAV [+ some reports state this was YU-ALK but we consider this to be correct; marks F-WQNE not confirmed]
020	42-300	MAP Linhas Aereas	F-WWEG I-ATRB (SX-BIA) SX-BIX I-ATRN F-WQNU F-OHOT PR-TTG PR-MPN
021	42-300	TRIP Linhas Aereas	F-WWEH I-ATRC (SX-BIB) SX-BIY I-ATRP F-WQNK F-OHOS EK-42022 F-WQNS PR-TTF
022	42-300	(Nordic Aviation Contractor)	F-WWEI OH-LTB F-GGLK EI-CVR [dismantled for spares Oct/Nov10 Edinburgh, UK & shipment to USA; canx 22Oct10]
023	42-300	FedEx Express	F-WWEA N972NA N908FX
024	42-300F	Jetcraft Aviation Pty Ltd	F-WWEC OY-CIC F-WQJL SP-EEE F-WQNE (F-OHRN) EI-SLE VH-TOX
025	42-300	Overland Airways	F-WWED DQ-FEK F-GHME F-GLIB EC-HVR EC-IYE 5N-BCS
026	42-300	(Total Linhas Aereas)	(F-WWEE) F-OGNE F-GTSM PT-MTS [w/o 14Sep02 Paranapanema, Brazil]
027	42-300	Trigana Air Service	F-WWEF PH-IFH F-WWEF F-GEQK F-OGOE F-GPZB PK-YRE
028	42-300	(Santa Barbara Airlines)	F-WWEJ N422MQ F-WQIO CU-T1452 F-WQNG PR-TTC YV1449 [w/o 21Feb08 Llano del Hato, near Merida in Andes Mountains, Venezuela]
029	42-300	(Pantanal Linhas Aereas)	F-GFJP PT-MFH [used for crash testing by FAA at Egg Harbor, NJ]
030	42-300	Wells Fargo Bank Northwest	F-WWEL N423MQ HR-ARY N330NA
031	42-320	Overland Airways	F-WWEM 3B-NAH F-WQHR 5R-MVU F-OHLA SP-EED F-WQNA TR-LFS F-WQNR 5N-BCR
032	42-320	Solenta Aviation	F-WWEN I-ATRD ZS-OUY PH-RAK ZS-LUC
033	42-310	ex Pantheon Airways	F-WWEO OH-LTC F-WIAF F-GIRC EI-CVS SX-BPA [stored Sep09 Athens, Greece; l/n Mar10]
034	42-300	ex Air Industria	F-WWEP I-ATRF [wfu 06Mar03 following u/c collapse Rome-Fiumicino, Italy; canx 2009; hulk stored l/n Sep11]
035	42-300	TRIP Linhas Aereas	F-WWEQ F-ODUD PP-PTC
036	42-320	Danish Air Transport	F-WWER F-GEGF F-OHFJ 9J-AHJ 9J-HFJ F-WQIS OY-JRJ
037	42-300	(American Eagle)	F-WWES N426MQ N37AE [w/o by hurricane 30Mar01 Freeport International Apt, Bahamas]
038	42-300	SBA Airlines	F-WWET F-ODSG D-BCRM F-WQGK LV-YJA PR-TTD YV2314
039	42-320	Aeromar Airlines	F-WWEU OH-LTD F-WIAQ N71296 XA-SJJ

AEROSPATIALE/AERITALIA ATR 42/72

C/n	Model	Last known Owner/Operator	Identities/fates/comments (where appropriate)
040	42-300	(American Eagle)	F-WWEV N142DD [wfu 31Dec01 for spares by First Air at Ottawa, QC, Canada; canx 02Jan02; fuselage still present 01Jun06]
041	42-320	Antrak Air Ghana	F-ODUE F-OJAM F-ODUE 5Y-INT F-WQNJ TR-LGA F-WQCT (F-GULA) 9G-AAB [stored by 15Jan11 Toulouse-Blagnac, France; l/n 15Mar11]
042	42-300	UTAir Aviation	F-WWEW I-ATRG VP-BCD UR-UTF
043	42-300	ex Pantanal Linhas Aereas	F-GGLR PT-MFV [stored by 22Mar12 Sao Carlos, Brazil]
044	42-320	Air Madagascar	F-WWEX OH-LTE F-WGMN D-BIII F-WQAD 5R-MVT
045	42-300	FedEx Express	F-WWEY N424MQ N911FX
046	42-300	(Aero Trasporti Italiani)	F-WWEZ I-ATRH [w/o 15Oct87 Mount Crezzo, near Lecco, Italy]
047	42-300	FedEx Express	F-WWEC N425MQ N47AE N912FX
048	42-300	(Duntington Ltd/Italair)	F-WWED N4201G F-WQFT EI-COC [w/o 20Jan98 Fertila Airport, Alghero, Italy; canx 10Sep98]
049	42-300	D.G.A.C.	F-GFJH [Calibrator aircraft]
050	42-300F	(Trigana Air Service)	F-WWEE N4202G F-WQIT C-GICB ZS-DHL PK-YRP [w/o 11Feb10 en-route Berau to Samarinda about 40km from Balikpapan, Indonesia]
051	42-300	UTAir Aviation	F-WWEF I-NOWA VP-BCA
052	42-300	Venescar Internacional/DHL	F-WWEG N4203G F-WQBZ EI-COD F-WQNT TG-DHP YV-876C
053	42-320	Israir	F-WWEH F-ODSH D-BCRN(1) F-WQGN 4X-ATN
054	42-300	UTAir Aviation	F-WWEI I-NOWT VP-BCB
055	42-300	Airlinair/Air France	F-WWEJ F-ODSB D-BBBB(1) F-WQGI SP-EEB F-WVZZ F-GVZZ
056	42-300	(American Eagle)	F-WWEK N143DD [w/o 25Oct98 San Juan, PR; used for spares; canx 12Jan99]
057	42-300	UTAir Ukraine	F-WWEL I-ATRJ VP-BCG UR-UTE
058	42-320	Aeromar Airlines	F-WWEM F-OGNF XA-TIC
059	42-300	Indonesia Air Transport	F-OGNS TF-ELK F-OIJJ LY-ARJ PK-TSZ
060	42-320	Solenta Aviation/Gabon Airlines	F-WWEN N47801 F-WQBX PH-XLC ZS-ATR
061	42-300F	Venescar Internacional/DHL	F-WWEO N4204G C-FICO F-WQOE YV-913C YV157T YV2308
062	42-320	Aeromar Airlines	F-WWEP XA-PEP XA-SYH
063	42-300	Danish Air Transport	F-ODUC F-GNPL F-WQOC OY-JRY
064	42-320	ex Israir	F-WWET N23802 F-WQCI F-GPEC 4X-ATO [wfs by Nov11 Sde-Dov, Israel; l/n 29aug12]
065	42-300	Int'l Airline Support Group	F-WWEQ N973NA
066	42-320	Blue Islands	F-WWEU N76803 F-WQBO TG-MWG TG-AFA PH-XLI PJ-XLI F-WQNB D4-CBS F-WQND F-HBSO G-ZEBS
067	42-300F	Danu Oro Transportas/Aviavilsa	F-WWER I-ATRK F-OHFH N42NC (LX-WAC) SE-MAS+ LY-ETM [+ painted on aircraft but not officially regd]
068	42-300	UTAir Aviation	F-WWES I-ATRL VP-BCF UR-UTD
069	42-320	(Israir)	F-WWEV N14804 F-WQCJ 5N-BBI F-WQFS 4X-ATM [ferried Jan11 to Blytheville, AR for possible spares use; canx late 2011 as exported]
070	42-300	Pantanal Linhas Aereas	(I-NOWI) F-WWEW F-GHJE PT-MFU
071	42-320	ex Ethiopian Airlines	F-WWEZ ET-AJC [stored dismantled Addis Ababa, Ethiopia; l/n 17Apr07]
072	42-320	TRIP Linhas Aereas	F-GFES F-WQHH HB-AFB F-WQFU F-GLES XA-TGR F-WQIR LV-ZNV PP-PTF
073	42-320	(Israir)	F-WWEY N34805 F-WQCX 4X-ATK [w/o 18Jun01 Tel Aviv-Ben Gurion; derelict & wfu by 24Jun03; used for emergency training]
074	42-300	(Int'l Airline Support Group)	F-WWEX N144DD [b/u; fuselage stored Macon GA; l/n Sep02]
075	42-320	Solenta Aviation/DHL	F-WWEA N27806 F-WQBS PH-XLD F-WQNU ZS-OVS
076	42-320	ex Ethiopian Airlines	F-WWEB ET-AJD [stored dismantled Addis Ababa, Ethiopia; l/n 17Apr07]
077	42-300	(West Caribbean Airways)	F-WWEC N4205G F-WQBU YR-ATX F-WQJM VP-BBC [wfu Mar05 Medellin, Colombia; sold to Sky Mart Sales, FL for spares; b/u Jan08; fuselage to cabin trainer l/n 03Sep10]
078	42-320	D.G.A.C./Meteo France	F-WWED N31807 F-WQBQ HS-PGG F-WQNI F-WMTO F-HMTO
079	42-300F	Jetcraft Aviation Pty Ltd	F-WWEE D-BATA OY-CID EI-SLB VH-TOQ
080	42-300	Airlinair	F-WWEF D-BCCC F-WQID SP-EEC F-WVZY F-GVZY EC-KGS OY-PCG F-GVZO SP-KTG* [* marks reserved 2011 for OLT Jet Air]
081	42-320	Trans Am/DHL	F-WWEG N4206G (C-) F-WQJI C-FICW F-WQNX YV-914C HC-CDX
082	42-300F	(Air Contractors)	F-WWEH D-BATB OY-CIE EI-SLC [wfu 19Aug11 Edinburgh, UK; canx 09Sep11; b/u by 09Oct11]
083	42-300F	(ATR)	F-WWEI N4207G F-WQBV YR-ATY F-WQJN [w/o 26Dec99 Dinard, France; fuselage to Cimber Air, Sonderborg, Denmark]
084	42-320	(Air Botswana)	F-WWEJ B-2201 F-WIYA TC-AGB F-WQAI OK-TFE F-WQCR F-OIET A2-AJD [w/o 11Oct99 Gaborone, Botswana; see c/n 101]

AEROSPATIALE/AERITALIA ATR 42/72

C/n	Model	Last known Owner/Operator	Identities/fates/comments (where appropriate)
085	42-300	White Eagle Aviation	F-WWEK C-FLCP F-WQNY SP-KCA [stored by 07Dec11 Katowice, Poland]
086	42-300F	Antrak Air Ghana	F-WWEL N4208G F-WQHK C-FICP F-WQOB ZS-ORE F-WQNM 9G-ANT
087	42-320	Farnair Switzerland	F-WWEM B-2202 F-WIYB TC-AGC F-WQAF OK-TFF F-WQCS F-OICA F-WQLF TR-LEZ F-WQLF HB-AFC
088	42-300	Solenta Aviation/DHL	F-WWEN C-FNCP F-WQOK F-WQNG ZS-OVP
089	42-320	ex Israir	F-WWEO N17808 F-WQCY 4X-ATL [wfu May09 Tel Aviv-Sde Dov, Israel; parts to ATR in France; hulk l/n 03Nov09]
090	42-320	Dutch Antilles Express	F-WWEP N18809 F-WQBR PH-XLE F-WQNN PJ-SLH N190NA PJ-DAH
091	42-320	MAP Linhas Aereas	F-WWEQ F-GFIN N427MQ F-WQIB SU-BML F-WQNS PP-PTD PR-MPO* [PR-PPT was worn under wing while stored; * marks reserved Jly12]
092	42-300	OLT Jet Air	F-WWER 9J-AFC N92BN D-BAAA(2) SP-KTR
093	42-320	Regourd Aviation	F-WWES N17810 F-WQCZ TG-MWA TG-AGA PH-XLK F-WQNO (CS-DTN) F-GVZJ
094	42-320	(Continental Express)	F-WWET N25811 [stored Aug02 Roswell, NM & b/u; canx 15Jun04; by 17Jan07 fuselage only at Walnut Ridge, AR]
095	42-300	Airlinair Portugal	F-ODUL F-GKYN (OY-FKA) F-GKYN CS-DTO
096	42-320	Hevilift	F-WWEU 9J-AFD N96BN D-BBBB(2) PK-VSX 8Q-ATN VH-FLH (P2-HLB)? P2-KSJ
097	42-320	Trigana Air Service	F-ODGN PK-YRH
098	72-600	AI(R)	F-WWEY [prototype ff 27Oct88] [2008 rebuilt with wings from c/n 721; late 2008 converted to ATR72-600 prototype]
099	42-320	(Continental Express)	F-WWEV N19812 [stored Aug02 Roswell NM; canx 21Jun04; b/u Walnut Ridge, AR for spares; fuselage only remains; l/n 17Jan07]
100	42-320	(Continental Express)	F-WWEX N14813 [stored Aug02 Roswell NM; canx 20Aug04 used by Cloud Partners for spares; l/n 09Oct04]
101	42-320	(Air Botswana)	F-WWEY A2-ABB [w/o 11Oct99 Gaborone, Botswana; pilot committed suicide; crashed into c/ns 084 and 111]
102	42-300	Trigana Air Service	F-WWEZ F-GFTO N421TE PK-YRN
103	42-320	(Continental Express)	F-WWEA N18814 [stored Aug02 Roswell, NM; to Cloud Partners for spares; l/n 02Oct05]
104	42-320	(Continental Express)	F-WWEB N14815 [stored Sep02 Roswell, NM; to Cloud Partners for spares; canx 14Mar06; l/n 02Oct05]
105	42-320	(Continental Express)	F-WWEC N15816 [stored Aug02 Roswell, NM; to Cloud Partners for spares; canx 17Aug04; l/n 02Oct05]
106	42-300	Trigana Air Service	F-WWED N422TE PK-YRK
107	42-300	Danish Air Transport	F-WWEE EI-BXR F-GHPX TF-ELI F-GHPX OY-CIR
108	72-201F	Farnair Switzerland	F-WWEZ F-GIGO F-OMAR F-WQOA F-WQNA HB-AFG
109	42-300	Wells Fargo Bank Northwest	F-WWEF DQ-FEP G-BUPS TG-RYM N283CS
110	42-320	Linea Aerea Aerotuy	F-WWEG D-BDDD F-WQKQ LN-FAP YV382T
111	42-320	(Air Botswana)	F-WWEH A2-ABC [w/o 11Oct99 Gaborone, Botswana; see c/n 101]
112	42-300	Danish Air Transport	F-WWEI C-FIQB OY-CIU
113	42-300	Inter-Transportes Aereos Inter/ TACA Regional	F-WWEJ DQ-FEQ EI-CIQ G-ZAPJ TG-MYH
114	42-300	(Air Sicilia)	F-WWEK I-ATRM [b/u after May06 for spares Palermo, Sicily, Italy]
115	42-320	Canary Fly Canarias	F-WWEL XA-MAR (HK-4205) XA-TPZ PT-MTO CS-TLR EI-SLI 5Y-BVD EI-SLI EC-LMX
116	42-300F	Solenta Aviation	F-WWEM C-FCQP F-WQOD F-WQNB ZS-OVR
117	42-300	ASECNA	F-WWEN 6V-AFW
118	42-300	Indonesia Air Transport	F-WWEO C-FIQN TF-ELJ LY-ARY PK-TSY
119	42-300	First Air	F-WWEP N423TE C-FTJB
120	42-300	Aeroperlas	F-WWEQ F-GFYN F-WQHM HR-IAY HP-1679APP
121	42-320F	Farnair Switzerland	F-WWER D-BEEE F-WQNA LZ-ATA+ HB-AFD [+ these marks are not fully confirmed for this aircraft]
122	42-300QC	Pescan Express	F-WWES D-BCRO LN-HTC D-BCRO C-GPEB
123	42-300	First Air	F-WWET C-GHCP
124	42-300	(Trans States Airlines)	F-WWEU N424TE [stored 22Feb03 Opa-locka, FL; b/u by Jly04]
125	42-300	First Air	F-WWEV N425TE OY-MUH C-GSRR
126	72-201	Air Contractors	F-WWEJ (OH-LTN) OH-KRA ES-KRA EI-REJ
127	42-300	(Royal Air Maroc)	F-WWEX CN-CDT [w/o 21Aug94 Tizounine, Atlas Mountains, nr Agadir, Morocco]

AEROSPATIALE/AERITALIA ATR 42/72

C/n	Model	Last known Owner/Operator	Identities/fates/comments (where appropriate)
128	42-320	TRIP Linhas Aereas	F-WWEA N428MQ F-WQIA SU-BMU F-WQNT VT-ADB F-WQNA PP-PTG
129	42-320	Necon Air	F-WWEB N4209G C-FICG F-WQNR 9N-AGP
130	42-300	Hemus Air	F-WWEC D-BFFF F-WQLG LZ-ATB F-WQNE YV-1074C F-WQNO LZ-ATS
131	42M-200	Gabon Government	F-WWEB (TR-KGP) TR-KJD
132	42-320	Bradley Air Services/First Air	F-WWED B-2203 F-WQGA 5R-MVK 5R-MJC C-GUNO
133	42-300	First Air	F-WWEE C-FIQR
134	42-300	ex Regional Airlines Morocco	F-WWEF CN-CDU [by Apr12 Casablanca, Morocco]
135	42-310F	Morningstar Air Express	F-WWEG N429MQ N135MQ N923FX C-GATK
136	42-300	Aerocaribbean	F-WWEH N430MQ F-WQIJ CU-T1298 CU-T1512
137	42-300	ex Regional Airlines Morocco	F-WWEI CN-CDV [by Apr12 Casablanca, Morocco]
138	42-300	First Air	F-WWEK C-FIQU
139	42-320	Calm Air International	F-WWEL C-GXCP ZS-OSN PH-RAQ ZS-OSN C-FCIJ(2)
140	72-201	JAT Airways	F-WWER (OH-LTO) OH-KRB ES-KRB YU-ALS
141	42-300F	Swiftair/FedEx Express	F-WWEM N431MQ N141AE (N928FX) EI-FXF EC-KAI
142	42-320	Calm Air International	F-WWEN EI-BXS HK-3943 N142GP C-FMAK
143	42-300	First Air	F-WWEO C-FTCP
144	42-320	Necon Air	F-WWEP N432MQ F-WQIH 9N-AFU
145	72-201	ex Airlinair	F-WWES (OH-LTP) OH-KRC G-HERM (F-GVZV) F-GVZG [stored by 28Mar12 Toulouse, France]
146	42-300	(Intair)	F-WWEQ C-GIQD [stored Nov99 Montreal-Dorval, QC, Canada; to Werner Corp, NJ for parts]
147	72-211F	Swiftair	F-WWET (N974NA) EI-CBC EC-GQS PH-SCY EI-CBC OY-CIP SE-LVK EC-JQF
148	42-320	Regourd Aviation?	F-WWEU D-BGGG F-WQKX LN-FAO LY-LWH F-HAEK TR-LIW
149	42-300F	Air Contractors/Mistral Air	F-WWEV N4210G G-WFEP F-WQNP (9N-AGP) SE-LST EI-SLA
150	72-201F	Swiftair	F-WWEI (N975NA) EI-CBD EC-GUL PH-SCZ EI-CBD OY-CIV EC-JXF
151	42-300	Tropical Air	F-WWEW (N148DD) N433MQ F-WQII CU-T1453 F-WQNC LZ-ATR 5H-AMI
152	42-320	Air Bagan	F-WWEX N34817 XY-AID [reported stored by 23Apr11 Yangon, Myanmar]
153	42-320	(Continental Express)	F-WWEA N15818 [stored Aug02 Roswell, NM; canx 04Nov04 as destroyed; probably b/u; l/n 25Apr04]
154	72-200F	Farnair Switzerland	F-WWEK EC-383 EC-ESS F-WQNF OY-RTE HB-AFJ
155	42-320	Bradley Air Services/First Air	F-WWEC B-2205 F-WQGB 5R-MVX 5R-MJD C-GULU
156	42-320	ex Continental Express	F-WWED N14819 [stored 04Mar03 Roswell, NM; l/n 26Oct05]
157	72-202	Air Contractors	F-WWEL EC-384 EC-EUJ F-WQNH OY-RTG EI-SLH
158	42-300QC	Pescan Express	F-WWEE D-BCRP LN-HTE D-BCRP C-GPEA
159	42-320	Air Bagan	F-WWEF N34820 XY-AIC
160	42-320	(Continental Express)	F-WWEG N14821 [stored Oct02 Roswell, NM; canx 04Nov04 as destroyed; probably b/u; l/n 25Apr04]
161	42-300	Aer Arann	F-WWEH EI-BYO OY-CIS EI-BYO
162	72-201	Danish Air Transport	F-WWEM (OH-LTR) OH-KRD ES-KRD LY-ATR OY-RUD
163	42-320	(Continental Express)	F-WWEN N14822 [stored 10Sep02 Roswell, NM; canx 04Nov04 as destroyed; probably b/u; l/n 25Apr04]
164	72-201	Nok Air	F-WWEO HS-TRA
165	42-320	UTAir Aviation	F-WWEP N15823 VP-BPJ
166	42-320	UTAir Aviation	F-WWEQ N16824 VP-BPK
167	72-201	Nok Air	F-WWEU HS-TRB
168	42-320	(USA Aviation Sales)	F-WWEV XA-RQY N168WA (N342TJ) [stored Jun03 Springfield-Branson, MO; canx 27Oct05 for spares; l/n 06Nov05; fuselage only 24Jly08]
169	42-320	(Olympic Aviation)	F-WWEW SX-BIA [stored by 20Nov09 Athens, Greece; b/u late 2011]
170	42-320	FedEx Express	F-WWEX N14825 N900FX
171	72-202	Swiftair	F-WWEA F-GKPC EC-KAD
172	42-320	FedEx Express	F-WWEC N26826 N901FX
173	42-320	Regourd Aviation/Equaflight	F-WWED D-BHHH F-WQNE OK-VFI F-WEKF F-HEKF
174	72-201	UTAir Aviation	F-WWEE (OH-LTS) OH-KRE ES-KRE VP-BYW
175	42-320	(FedEx Express)	F-WWEF N15827 N902FX [w/o 27Jan09 Lubbock, TX; canx 01Apr09]
176	42-300	(Danu Oro Transportas)	F-WWEG (N426TE) EI-CBF OY-MUK LY-DOT [w/o 08Aug10 Pori Airport, Pori, Finland; b/u by 04Dec10; fuselage to Copenhagen, Denmark; canx]
177	72-202	Danube Wings	F-WWEH F-GKPD OM-VRD

AEROSPATIALE/AERITALIA ATR 42/72

C/n	Model	Last known Owner/Operator	Identities/fates/comments (where appropriate)
178	42-320	Myanmar Airways	F-WWEK N4211G C-GICX F-WQNJ F-OHRP EK-42043 F-WQNM XY-AIB
179	42-320	FedEx Express	F-WWEN N14828 N903FX
180	72-202	JAT Airways	F-WWEP YU-ALN
181	42-320	(Continental Express)	F-WWEQ N14829 [b/u May02 for spares Opa-locka, FL; canx 30Apr02]
182	42-320	West Air Sweden	F-WWER SX-BIB SE-MGE
183	72-202	Air Contractors	F-WWES EC-515 EC-EYK F-WQNI EI-SLG
184	42-320	ex Continental Express	F-WWET N14830 [stored 08Apr03 Roswell, NM; l/n 30Oct05; to be b/u for spares by BAC Leasing]
185	42-320	ex Continental Express	F-WWEV N17831 [stored 08Apr03 Roswell, NM; l/n 30Oct05; to be b/u for spares by BAC Leasing]
186	72-202	JAT Airways	F-WWEW YU-ALO
187	42-320	ex Continental Express	F-WWEJ N14832 [stored Aug02 Roswell, NM; l/n 30Oct05]
188	42-320	ex Continental Express	F-WWEC N14833 [stored Aug02 Roswell, NM; l/n 30Oct05]
189	72-202	JAT Airways	F-WWED YU-ALP
190	42-320	Trigana Air Service	F-WWEF HS-TRK G-BYHA I-RIMS G-BYHA PK-YRV
191	42-300	Aer Arann	F-WWEA C-GIQS (ZS-NYP) C-GIQS EI-CPT (SE-KCX) EI-CPT
192	72-202	Swiftair/SAS	F-WWEE F-GKPE EC-KAE F-WKVC PR-AZZ EC-LSN
193	42-320	Cape Air	F-WWEG N14834
194	42-320	Hevilift PNG	F-WWEH N11835 8Q-ATM VH-FLE (P2-HLA) P2-KSR
195	72-201F	Farnair/Islas Airways	F-WWEI B-22701 F-WQGO PH-XLH F-WQND EC-JNK F-WKVC HB-AFR
196	42-300	Aer Arann	F-WWEK C-GITI C-FZVZ OY-CIT G-SSEA EI-EHH
197	42-320	Calm Air International	F-WWEE SX-BIC C-GKKR
198	72-201F	Farnair Switzerland	F-WWEL B-22702 F-WQGC EC-GQU F-WQJU SX-BSX F-WQOG F-WQND EC-IKK F-WKVJ HB-AFS
199	42-300	Aer Arann/Aer Lingus Regional	F-WWEM EI-CBK
200	42-320	Cape Air	F-WWEN N42836
201	72-202	Trigana Air Service	F-GKOA EI-REF F-WQAL PK-YRY
202	42-320	Kalstar Aviation	F-WWEO N11737 N21837 PK-KSO
203	42-320	Calm Air International	F-WWEQ C-GIQV F-WQNB F-OHRQ 5H-PAK F-WNUG C-FECI
204	72-202F	Swiftair	F-WWER (N7270) F-WWER ZS-NDI F-WQAG F-GKJK (XU-RAC) F-ORAC F-GPOA EC-KIZ
205	42-320	Fly540.com	F-WWET XA-RME N521JS XA-RME 5Y-LNT N521JS ZS-OZX 5Y-BUN
206	42-320	Linea Aerea Aerotuy	F-WWEU HS-TRL G-BYHB I-RIML G-BYHB LN-FAR YV383T
207	72-202F	Swiftair	F-WWEF (N7271) F-WWEF ZS-NDJ F-WQAH (XU-RAN) F-ORAN F-GPOB EC-KJA
208	42-320	(Intertrade Ltd)	F-WWEV 3B-NAP F-WQNN VT-ADD F-WQNL CN-RLF N9621C [wfu for parts & b/u Jun11 Casablanca, Morocco]
209	42-300	West Wind Aviation	F-WWEA N209AT C-GWWL
210	72-201F	Air Contractors	F-WWEH B-22703 F-WQGE EC-GQV F-WQJT (SX-BSY) OY-RUA EI-SLF
211	42-300	West Wind Aviation	F-WWEP N211AM N213AT C-GWWD
212	72-201	Danu Oro Transportes	F-WWEB B-22705 F-WQIU OH-KRH ES-KRH HL5232 SE-MCA LY-MCA
213	42-320	Aeromaster del Peru	F-WWEA XA-RNP OY-PCD EY-321 EX-42301 OB-2010P
214	42-300	Trigana Air Service	F-WWEB F-GHPI PK-YRR
215	72-201	Calm Air International	F-WWEK (N7272) F-WWEK F-OKVN VN-B202 F-WNUE C-FULE
216	42-300	Calm Air International	F-WWEI N216AT C-FJYV
217	72-202	FedEx Express	F-WWEM N721TE N809FX
218	42-300	Swiftair	F-WWEC F-GHPK EC-JBN
219	42-320	West Air Sweden	F-WWEG SX-BID SE-MGG
220	72-202	Swiftair	F-WWEN F-OGQP N722TE N810FX
221	42-320	Tiko Air	F-ODYD (5R-TIK) 5R-MJT
222	72-202	Farnair Switzerland	F-GKPF HB-AFL
223	42-300	ex Air Vanuatu	F-WWEL N223AT YJ-AV42 [arrived 05Oct09 Baltimore, MD; wings & tail used to rebuild c/n 247; fuselage only noted 17Oct09]
224	72-202	Air Contractors/FedEx Express	F-WWEQ D-ANFA (N814FX) EI-FXG
225	42-300	(Pantanal Linhas Aereas)	F-GKNA PT-MFK [DBR 16Jly07 Sao Paulo-Congonhas, Brazil; b/u mid Nov09; hulk noted Sao Carlos, Brazil 22Mar12; reported to downtown Sao Carlos for use at a hotel]

AEROSPATIALE/AERITALIA ATR 42/72

C/n	Model	Last known Owner/Operator	Identities/fates/comments (where appropriate)
226	42-300	Airlinair	F-GKNB
227	72-201F	West Air Luxembourg	F-GHPU (F-GHPH) OY-RUC LX-WAB
228	42-300F	Solenta Aviation	F-WWEJ N426TE N422WA XA-RCA N422WA ZS-XCD
229	72-202	Air Contractors/FedEx Express	F-WWEX D-ANFB N815FX EI-FXH
230	42-300	Airlinair/Air France	F-GKNC
231	42-300	Swiftair	F-GKND EC-IVP
232	72-202	Farnair Switzerland	F-GKOB HB-AFK
233	42-300	UTAir Aviation	F-WWEO D-BCRQ VP-BLI
234	72-201	ex OLT Express	F-GHPV EC-JDX SP-OLL [airline suspended operations 27Jly12]
235	42-300	Calm Air International	F-WWEU N235RM N233RM C-FJYW
236	42-320	Air Malawi	F-WWES (EI-BYP) 7Q-YKQ
237	72-202	Avanti Air	F-WWEG D-ANFC
238	42-300	West Wind Aviation	F-WWEC OY-CIH G-RHUM C-GWWR
239	72-202	West Air Sweden	F-WWED SX-BIE SE-MGH (SP-OLT)
240	42-320	West Wind Aviation	(F-GHPX) F-WWEG XA-RUC N240JS XA-RUC 5Y-JNT N240JS (ZS-OWU) 5Y-BRB ZS-OVL 5Y-BUT D2-FLA C-GWEA
241	72-202	West Air Sweden	F-WWEA SX-BIF SE-MGI
242	42-300	Swiftair	F-WWEW N242AT EC-ISX
243	42-300	Air Contractors/FedEx Express	F-WWEQ N243AT N246AE (N924FX) EI-FXB
244	72-212	ex American Eagle	F-WWEK N244AT N4AE [stored 12Jan12 Myrtle Beach, SC; l/n 01Jun12; canx 13Sep12 fate/status unknown]
245	42-300	Tunisair Express	F-WWET (EI-BYQ) TS-LBA G-BXBV TS-LBA
246	72-202	Eurolot	F-WWEM SP-LFA
247	42-320	Blue Ridge Aero Services	F-WWEV N106LM N470JF [rebuilt Nov/Dec09 with wings & tail from c/n 223]
248	72-212	FedEx Express	F-WWEN N248AT N820FX [parked 07Aug07 Kinston, NC; basic American Eagle c/s]
249	42-300	(Empire Airlines)	F-WWEB N249AS [stored late 2002 Calgary, AB, Canada; moved by road to Coeur d'Alene, ID for parts use; canx 05Oct06; by 25 Jan09 fuselage at San Antonio, TX]
250	42-320	FedEx Express	F-WWEU N250AA N251AE N913FX
251	72-201	UTAir Aviation	F-WWEV B-22706 OH-KRK ES-KRK VP-BYX
252	42-320	Blue Ridge Aviation Services	F-WWEE N315CR
253	72-212	FedEx Express	F-WWED N253AT N252AM N821FX [parked 07Aug07 Kinston, NC; basic American Eagle c/s]
254	42-300	Swiftair	F-WWEJ N254AT N255AE EC-JBX
255	42-300	UTAir Aviation	F-WWEC D-BCRR VP-BLJ
256	72-202	Air Contractors/FedEx Express	F-WWEE D-ANFD N817FX EI-FXK
257	42-320	Kirk Aviation	F-WWEO XA-RXC OY-PCE SP-KTF OY-PCE [stored 26Jly12 Billund, Denmark]
258	72-202	(Tuninter)	F-WWLE TS-LBB [w/o 06Aug05 Tyrrhenian Sea, nr Palermo, Sicily; mid/rear fuselage stored on airfield; l/n Apr06]
259	42-320	(FedEx Express)	F-WWEP (N15840) N99838 HK-4035X N99838 N904FX [DBR 08May08 by tornado at Greensboro, NC; canx 15Aug08]
260	72-201	Aer Arann	F-WWEH EC-873 EC-FIV F-WQNB OY-RTA EI-REH
261	42-320	(Calm Air International)	F-WWEI HK-3678X HK-3678 N261RT C-FCIJ(1) [as at 21Feb08 San Antonio, TX still marked as HK-3678; US & Canadian marks probably ntu; 2008 to Aviation Inventory Resources for spares use; canx 18Nov08 as sold in USA]
262	42-300	FedEx Express	F-WWEL N262AT N918FX
263	72-212	(American Eagle)	F-WWEX N263AT N260AE [stored 12Jan12 Myrtle Beach, SC; canx 14May12 for parts; b/u 01Jun12]
264	42-320	Farnair Switzerland	F-WWLG N99839 F-WQCH F-SEBK F-GOBK HB-AFF
265	72-202	Eurolot	F-WWEJ SP-LFB
266	42-300	FedEx Express	F-WWEB N266AT N265AE N919FX
267	72-201	Aer Arann	F-WWEM EC-874 EC-FJX F-WQNI OY-RTB EI-REI
268	42-320	ex Air Mandalay	F-WWEW G-BUEA F-WQNF F-OHRN XY-AIJ [reported stored by 23Apr11 Yangon, Myanmar missing many parts]
269	42-320	FedEx Express	F-WWEA N269AT (N267AE) N915FX
270	72-212	ex American Eagle	F-WWEL N270AT [stored 07Feb12 Myrtle Beach, SC; l/n 01Jun12]
271	42-320	(FedEx Express)	F-WWLH N93840 N905FX [DBR 08May08 by tornado at Greensboro, NC; canx 14Aug08]
272	72-202	Eurolot	F-WWEH SP-LFC
273	42-300	Air Contractors	F-WWEQ N273AT N271AT (N927FX) EI-FXD
274	72-212	Swiftair	F-WWLC N274AT EC-INV

AEROSPATIALE/AERITALIA ATR 42/72

C/n	Model	Last known Owner/Operator	Identities/fates/comments (where appropriate)
275	42-300	FedEx Express	F-WWEG N275BC N909FX
276	72-201	ex ConViasa	F-WWLB EC-935 EC-FKQ F-WQNE YV1850 F-WQNO [reported stored by 23Oct11Caracas, Venezuela still as YV1850]
277	42-300	FedEx Express	F-WWLA N277AT
278	42-300	UTAir Aviation	F-WWEC D-BJJJ VP-BLN
279	72-202	Eurolot	F-WWLD SP-LFD
280	42-320	FedEx Express	F-WWLF N97841 N906FX
281	72-202	Tunisair Express	F-WWLK TS-LBC
282	42-300	Air Contractors/FedEx Express	F-WWLI N282AT (N281AE) EI-FXA
283	72-202	FedEx Express	F-WWLM N723TE N811FX
284	42-320	TRIP Linhas Aereas	F-WWLJ HK-3684X C-GZMV CX-PUC PP-PTJ
285	72-202	Helitt Linhas Aereas	F-WWLO OK-XFA EC-LNP
286	42-320	FedEx Express	F-WWLY N86842 N907FX
287	42-300	UTAir Aviation	F-WWLL D-BCRS VP-BLU
288	72-212	American Eagle	F-WWLP N288AM
289	42-300	UTAir Aviation	F-WWLN D-BCRT VP-BLO
290	72-202	West Air Sweden	F-WWLQ SX-BIG SE-MGJ
291	42-320	Islena Airlines	F-WWLZ EP-ATR F-WQNZ SX-BIN OY-EDF D-BZZS HR-AXH
292	72-202	Air Contractors/FedEx Express	F-WWLT D-ANFF N813FX EI-FXJ
293	42-300	FedEx Express	F-WWLR N293AT N914FX
294	72-202F	Air Contractors/FedEx Express	F-WWLS D-ANFE N818FX EI-FXI
295	42-300	Pantanal Linhas Aereas	F-WWLU (F-OHLA) F-WWLU PT-MFE
296	42-320	Halcyon Air	F-WWLV (OY-CIJ) VR-BNH VP-BNH F-WQNC (D4-CBQ) J2-GZZ D4-CBQ
297	72-202	Eurolot	F-WWLW OK-XFB SP-EFI
298	42-300	Atlantico Brazil	F-WWLA C-GICY F-GIVG PP-ATV (F-WQHA)
299	72-202	Eurolot	F-WWLX OK-XFC SP-EFK
300	42-320	SBA Airlines	F-WWLD ZS-NGF F-WQGR F-WQKT PP-PSG YV-1017C YV1421
301	72-202	Danish Air Transport/Skyways	F-WWLY F-OHAG F-WQGJ G-BXXA F-WQNS OY-RUB
302	42-320	Pantanal Linhas Aereas	F-WWEA (F-GKNG) F-OKNG (9N-ADA) PT-MFI [abandoned at Mucuri, Bahia, Brazil, following accident 16Mar99 & further damage on 01Jun99]
303	72-201	Helitt Linhas Aereas	F-WWLB OK-XFD EC-LNQ
304	42-320	Asia Pacific Aerospace Pty Ltd	F-WWLE G-BUEB F-WQJZ F-OHRO P2-ALA VH-AVV [stored Aug05 Cairns, QLD, Australia; regd VH-AVV on 11Mar09; l/n Aug10]
305	72-202	(Olympic Aviation)	F-WWLC SX-BIH (SE-MGK) [stored by 07Nov09 Athens, Greece; l/n 10Sep11; b/u late 2011]
306	42-320	ex Pantanal Linhas Aereas	F-WWEF F-OGQV VR-BOQ G-BXEH PT-MFT [stored by 22Mar12 Sao Carlos, Brazil]
307	72-202	Danube Wings/NextJet	F-WWEG F-GKOC EC-IPJ OM-VRC
308	42-320	Precision Air	F-WWEE N983MA F-WQCL F-WQHB 5H-PAA
309	72-212	(American Eagle)	F-WWEB N309AM N308AE [stored 12Jan12 Myrtle Beach, SC; wfu for parts & canx 26Jun12]
310	42-300	Air Contractors/FedEx Express	F-WWEC N310DK (N925FX) EI-FXC
311	72-202F	Airlinair/Air France	F-WWED B-22707 F-GPOC
312	42-300QC	AVIATECA/TACA Regional	F-WWEK 9A-CTS TG-TRA
313	72-202	QuickJet Cargo Airlines	F-WWEI F-GKOD SX-BFK F-GJKP HB-AFH VT-FQA
314	42-300	FedEx Express	F-WWEK N314AM (N315AE) N916FX
315	42-300	Alliance Air	F-WWEN G-BVED F-WQNL (S2-ADK) D-BOOM F-WQNB VT-ABC
316	72-202	ex AZUL Linhas Aereas Brasilerias	F-WWEJ (F-GKOE) (F-OHFA) F-OHOB RDPL-34137 F-WKVF PR-AZW
317	42-300QC	AVIATECA/TACA Regional	F-WWEO 9A-CTT TG-TRB
318	72-202	(Air Gabon)	F-WWEL F-GKOF F-WKOF F-OHOC [w/o 08Dec94 Oyem Airport, Gabon; canx 14Apr95]
319	42-300	FedEx Express	F-WWER N319AM (N318AE) N921FX
320	72-212	American Eagle	F-WWEM N320AT N322AC
321	42-300	Swiftair	F-WWES F-GHPY EC-JAD
322	72-202	(Trans Asia)	F-WWEQ B-22708 G-BXYV B-22708 [w/o 21Dec02 over Taiwan Strait, SW of Makung, Taiwan]
323	42-320	La Costena	F-WWET F-OHGL YN-CHG
324	72-201	Air Contractors	F-WWEU OH-KRF ES-KRF HL5233 LY-PTK EI-SLJ
325	42-300	FedEx Express	F-WWLK N325AT N920FX
326	72-202	Trigana Air Service	F-WWLI F-GKOG SX-BAO F-GJKQ F-WQUF PK-YRI

AEROSPATIALE/AERITALIA ATR 42/72

C/n	Model	Last known Owner/Operator	Identities/fates/comments (where appropriate)
327	72-212	Air Contractors/FedEx Express	F-WWLM N327AT (N926FX) EI-FXE
328	72-202	Eurolot	F-WWLJ SP-LFE
329	42-300	Avanti Air/InterSky	F-WWLO (F-GKNE) F-WQAB ZS-NKY G-BXEG PT-MFX G-WLSH D-BCRN(2)
330	72-202	Swiftair	F-WWLL F-GKOH SX-BAP F-GJKR F-WQUI EC-IYH
331	42-300	Bradley Air Services/First Air	F-WWLP (F-GKNF) G-BVEF LN-FAI G-CDFF C-GKLB
332	72-201	(UTAir Aviation)	F-WWLN B-22710 OH-KRL ES-KRL VP-BYZ [w/o 02Apr12 Tyumen, Russia]
333	42-320	Alliance Air	F-WWLR (N333SG) VR-BOG VP-BOG F-WQNO D-BVIP F-WQNJ VT-ADC F-WQNF VT-ABE
334	72-212	Iran Aseman Airlines	F-WWLQ EP-ATA
335	42-320	Guinea Ecuatoriale	F-WWLW F-ODYE 3C-LLG
336	72-212	FedEx Express	F-WWLS N630AS N800FX
337	42-320	Islena Airlines	F-WWLB N984MA (F-WQHC) F-OGXO TR-LFD F-WQNQ HC-CDC F-WQNQ SX-BIM OY-EDH D-BZZV HR-AXA [first painted as HR-AWA, a Let 410, in error]
338	72-212	FedEx Express	F-WWLT N632AS N801FX
339	72-212	Iran Aseman Airlines	F-WWLU EP-ATH
340	42-320	SBA Airlines	F-WWLE F-WEBB (ZS-NGW) F-OGQX ZS-NKW F-WQGU F-WQIK PP-PSF F-WQNH YV-1018C YV1422
341	72-202F	Farnair Switzerland	F-WW.. F-OKVM VN-B204 F-WKVJ HB-AFV
342	72-202	Trigana Air Service	F-WWLX F-GKOI F-WWEW G-BVTJ EI-REE F-WQRY PK-YRX
343	42-320	ex Pantanal Linhas Aereas	F-WWED ZS-NKZ F-GKNG F-OHFI PK-HJF F-OHFI F-WQHV PT-MFJ [stored by 22Mar12 Sao Carlos, Brazil]
344	72-212	FedEx Express	F-WWLC N633AS N802FX
345	72-212	American Eagle	F-WWLE N345AT N342AT
346	42-300	ex ConViasa	F-WWEI G-ORFH G-KNNY F-WQNB YV1008 [reported stored by 23Oct11Caracas, Venezuela]
347	72-212	FedEx Express	F-WWEC D-AEWG N816FX
348	42-300	Kalstar Aviation	F-WWEL B-22207 HR-ARO N38AN PK-KSI
349	72-212	ex American Eagle	F-WWEF N349AT N348AE N941WP* [stored 04May12 Myrtle Beach, SC; l/n 01Jun12: * marks reserved 06Sep12]
350	72-202	West Air Sweden	F-WWEG SX-BIK SE-MGM
351	42-320	Alliance Air/Air India Regional	F-WWER F-OHFC F-WQOM YV-1023C F-WQNB VT-ADF F-WQNC VT-ABF
352	72-202	AZUL Linhas Aereas Brasileras	F-WWEJ F-GKPH PP-PTK F-WKVI PR-AZX
353	72-202	West Air Sweden	F-WWEK SX-BII SE-MGL
354	42-300	FedEx Express	F-WWEU N354AT N351AT N917FX
355	72-212	American Eagle	F-WWEQ N355AT
356	42-320	Alliance Air	F-WWEW G-BVEC F-WQOJ F-WQNF VT-ABD
357	72-202	Calm Air International	F-GKOJ F-WWEW G-BVTK YU-ALR F-WDHA C-FCRZ
358	42-320F	US Dept of Justice	F-WWLV N985MA F-WQHD F-GREG YV-1016C F-WQNP N215BB N313CG [operated by Drug Enforcement Administration]
359	72-212F	FedEx Express	F-WWEV D-AEWH N819FX
360	42-320	SBA Airlines	F-WWLX N986MH F-WQHF F-GMGI YV-1015C YV1423
361	72-202	Airlinair/Air France	F-WWEX B-22711 F-GPOD
362	72-212	FedEx Express	F-WWEZ N631AS N803FX
363	42-320	Overland Airways	F-WWLC F-OHFA F-WQNV YV-1019C (F-WQNA) 5H-PAP F-WKVD 5N-BND
364	72-202F	Farnair Switzerland	F-WWEA B-22712 HB-AFM
365	72-202	AZUL Linhas Aereas Brasileras	F-WWEM F-OHAT F-WQIX F-GMGK PP-PTH F-WKVB PR-AZY
366	42-320	Regional Airlines Morocco	F-WWLE F-OHFB YV-1036C F-WQNC PH-XLQ F-WQNM CN-RLG
367	72-202	Danube Wings	F-WWEX F-GKOK F-WQAJ HS-PGB F-GJRQ EC-IMH F-WQRK EI-REG OM-VRB
368	42-320	SBA Airlines	F-WWLH N987MH F-WSFB YV-1014C YV-1424
369	72-212	ex American Eagle	F-WWEC N369AT [wfs; 28-30Jan12 ferried to Toulouse, France]
370	72-212	FedEx Express	F-WWEF N634AS N804FX
371	42-300	(ConViasa)	F-WWLN G-BVJP G-TAWE F-WQNC YV1010 [w/o 13Sep10 near Puerto Ordaz Airport, Venezuela]
372	72-212	FedEx Express	F-WWEF N635AS N805FX
373	72-202	VIP Air/Danube Wings	F-WWEU F-GKOL F-WQAK HS-PGA F-GJRX EI-RED F-WAGR OM-VRA

AEROSPATIALE/AERITALIA ATR 42/72

C/n	Model	Last known Owner/Operator	Identities/fates/comments (where appropriate)
374	42-320	TRIP Linhas Aereas	F-WWLQ F-OHFD PH-XLL PJ-XLL F-WQNP PP-PTI
375	72-212	FedEx Express	F-WWLW N636AS N806FX
376	42-300	Pantanal Linhas Aereas	(F-WWLR) F-GKNH PT-MFM
377	72-212	ex American Eagle	F-WWLA N377AT [stored 07Feb12 Myrtle Beach, SC; l/n 01Jun12]
378	42-320	Islena Airlines	F-WWLA F-OHFE PH-XLM PJ-XLM N378NA HR-AXN
379	72-212	United Airways	F-WWLD N69901 D-ACCC ZK-JSY D-ACCC 5H-PAQ D-ACCC N379FA PK-MFA S2-AFN
380	42-300	TRIP Linhas Aereas	F-WWLU N988MA PT-TTL
381	72-201F	Farnair Switzerland	F-WWEG B-22715 HB-AFP
382	42-300	UTair Ukraine	F-WWEA D4-CBE VP-BLP UR-UTA
383	72-212	FedEx Express	F-WWEB N637AS N807FX
384	42-320	Precision Air	F-WWEG PT-MFF F-WQJO 5H-PAG
385	72-212	United Airways	F-WWLF N69902 D-ADDD ZK-JSZ F-WQHC SU-BPT XU-U4G+ 5H-PAU N385FA S2-AFE [+ marks applied to aircraft but ntu]
386	42-300	UTair Ukraine	F-WWEK D4-CBF VP-BLQ UR-UTB
387	72-212	Air Arann/Aer Lingus Regional	F-WWLG N641AS EI-SLL
388	42-320	Buddha Air	F-WWLA PT-MFG F-WQJP VP-BOI F-WQNV VT-ADA F-WQNF 9N-AIM
389	72-202F	Farnair Switzerland	F-WWEH B-22716 HB-AFN
390	42-320	Alliance Air	F-WWLD EC-853 EC-GBJ F-WQHY HR-ARN F-WQNK VT-ABA
391	72-212	Iran Aseman Airlines	F-WWED EP-ATS
392	42-320	Alliance Air	F-WWLF EC-854 EC-GBK F-WQIF HR-ARM F-WQNL VT-ABB
393	72-212	Air Mandalay	F-WWLI F-OHFS XY-AEY
394	42-300QC	Aviateca/TACA Regional	F-WWLJ 9A-CTU HR-AUX TG-AUX
395	72-212	Air Contractors	F-WWLJ N642AS EI-SLK
396	72-202	ex AZUL Linhas Aereas Brasileras	F-WWEJ F-OLAO RDPL-34132 F-WNUA PR-AZV F-WKVD
397	42-320	Islena Airlines	F-WWLK YV-950C F-WQNF VT-ADG F-WQNC HR-AVA
398	72-212	Iran Aseman Airlines	F-WWEK EP-ATZ
399	72-212	ex American Eagle	F-WWLK N399AT [stored 07Feb12 Myrtle Beach, SC; l/n 01Jun12]
400	42-300	TRIP Linhas Aereas	F-WWLA YV-951C F-WQNG PR-TTE
401	72-212	(American Eagle)	F-WWLL N401AM [w/o 01Nov94 near Roselawn, IN]
402	72-202	Eurolot	F-WWLM SP-LFF
403	42-320	Buddha Air	F-WWLD F-OIAM+ F-WQNA 9N-AIN [+ canx 04Jan08 to India]
404	72-212	FedEx Express	F-WWLO D-AEWI N812FX
405	72-212	Aer Arann/Aer Lingus Regional	F-WWLP N640AS EI-SLN
406	42-320	Air India Regional	F-WWLY EC-123 EC-GFY F-WQHZ VP-BOH F-WQNE VT-ADE F-WQNE VT-ABO
407	72-212	American Eagle	F-WWEL N407AT
408	72-212	American Eagle	F-WWEM N408AT
409	42-320	Buddha Air	F-WWEA F-OKMR OK-BFG F-WQNJ SP-KCN F-WKVF 9N-AIT
410	72-212	American Eagle	F-WWLS N410AT
411	72-202	Eurolot	F-WWEO SP-LFG
412	42-320	Aeromar Airlines	F-WWEC F-OKMS OK-BFH F-WQNH XA-UFA
413	72-212	(Air Contractors/Aer Lingus)	F-WWLC N643AS EI-SLM [w/o 17Jly11 Shannon, Ireland; canx 12Mar12 as wfu]
414	72-212	American Eagle	F-WWLD N414WF
415	42-320	Kalstar Aviation	F-WWLA D4-CBH N415AN PK-KSE
416	72-202	Swiftair/UN	F-WWLE VN-B208 F-WNUH EC-LHV
417	72-212	American Eagle	F-WWIT N417AT
418	42-300		[not built]
419	72-202F	Farnair Switzerland	F-WWLW VN-B206 F-WNUD HB-AFW
420	72-212	American Eagle	F-WWLY N420AT
421	42-300		[allocated to American Eagle with marks N421AT reserved but aircraft not built]
422	72-212	Myanma Airways	F-WWLZ F-OHLB HS-PGJ F-WQNR OY-CIW F-WQNQ XY-AIA
423	72-212F	Bradley Air Services/First Air	F-WWEB EI-CLB I-ATRO EI-CLB C-GLHR
424	42-300		[not built]
425	72-212	American Eagle	F-WWEC N425MJ
426	72-212	American Eagle	F-WWED N426AT
427	42-300		[not built]
428	72-212	Helitt Linhas Aereas	F-WWEF EI-CLC I-ATRQ EC-LNR
429	72-212	American Eagle	F-WWEH N429AT

AEROSPATIALE/AERITALIA ATR 42/72

C/n	Model	Last known Owner/Operator	Identities/fates/comments (where appropriate)
430	42-300		[not built]
431	72-212	American Eagle	F-WWEI N431AT
432	72-212	Bradley Air Services/First Air	F-WWLE F-WWEL EI-CLD I-ATRR EI-CLD C-GRMZ
433	42-300		[not built]
434	72-212	ex American Eagle	F-WWEM N434AT [stored 07Feb12 Myrtle Beach, SC; l/n 01Jun12]
435	72-202	(Transasia Airways)	F-WWEN B-22717 [w/o 30Jan95 Kuei Shan Hsiang, near Taipei-Sung Shan, Taiwan]
436	42-300		[not built]
437	72-202	West Air Sweden	F-WWLC SX-BIL SE-MGN SP-OLH SE-MGN
438	72-212	(American Eagle)	F-WWEO N438AT [w/o 09May04 San Juan, PR]
439	42-300		[not built]
440	72-212	ex American Eagle	F-WWEP N440AM [stored 07Feb12 Myrtle Beach, SC; l/n 01Jun12]
441	72-202	Royal Air Maroc Express	F-WWLG G-BWTL F-WQOF F-WQNC EI-REA F-WKVB CN-COA
442	42-300		[not built]
443	42-500	Eurolot	F-WWEZ SP-EDE [prototype ATR 42-500; ff 16Sep94]
444	72-202	Royal Air Maroc Express	F-WWEQ G-BWDA (9M-AMB) F-WQNG G-BWDA F-WKVD CN-COB
445	42-500	Danu Oro Transportas/YLNG Co	F-WWER F-GJMV F-WWLZ F-OHFM I-ADLH F-WQNO VT-ADO F-WKVF LY-DAT
446	72-212	Swiftair/UN	F-WWEA D-AEWK EC-JRP
447	72-212	American Eagle	F-WWEC N447AM
448	72-212	American Eagle	F-WWED N448AM
449	72-202	Aurigny Air Services/Flybe	F-WWEE G-BWDB (9M-AMA) G-BWDB F-WQNI G-BWDB
450	72-212	AZUL Linhas Aereas Brasileras	F-WWEH HS-PGE F-WQNF VN-B216 F-WKVE PR-AZT
451	72-212	American Eagle	F-WWES N451AT
452	72-202	Islas Airways	F-WWEW HS-PGC F-WQND EC-JCD
453	72-212	Aerocaribbean	F-WWLB ZK-MCQ F-WQLC N530AS F-WQNQ CU-T1548
454	72-212	ex TRIP Linhas Aereas	F-WWLI ZK-MCS F-WQLH N531AS PR-TTI [w/o 21Feb11 Altamira Airport, Brazil; fuselage possibly to GIA]
455	72-202F	Deccan Cargo & Express	F-WWLM HS-PGD F-WQNN 5H-PAM F-WQNA HL5230 F-WKVH VT-DEA
456	72-202F	Deccan Cargo & Express	F-WWLN F-OHJA T3-ATR F-WQNE HL5229 F-WKVG VT-DEB
457	42-500	Airlinair/Air France	F-WWET (G-ZAPJ) F-WWET F-GPYA
458	72-212	(Air Bagan)	F-WWLO ZK-MCW(1) F-WQLK N532AS F-WQNB XY-AIE [w/o 19Feb08 Putao Airport, Myanmar]
459	72-212	(Aerocaribbean)	F-WWLE N12903 EC-HBU F-WQND CU-T1549 [w/o 04Nov10 en-route in mountains near Sancti Spiritus, Cuba]
460	72-212	Solenta Aviation/Senegal Airlines	F-WWLH ZK-MCX F-WQLL N533AS F-WQNA 5H-PAR F-WNUC ZS-XCB
461	72-212	Islas Airways	F-WWLP F-OGXF F-GVZF EC-LKK
462	42-500	Aeromar Airlines	F-WWLL F-OHFF I-ADLF XA-UAU
463	72-212	Total Linhas Aereas	F-WWLQ ZK-MCY F-WQLM N534AS PR-TTJ
464	72-212	B & H Airlines	F-WWLR ZK-MCC F-WQKS N535AS F-WQNF T9-AAD E7-AAD
465	72-212	B & H Airlines	F-WWLT ZK-MCL F-WQLB N536AS F-WQNG T9-AAE E7-AAE
466	42-400MP	Italian Coast Guard	F-WWEX F-WQJC CS-X-62170 MM62170 [code 10-01]
467	72-212	Air Mandalay	F-WWLU EI-CMJ I-ATRS EI-CMJ XY-AIR
468	72-212A	Cimber Air	F-WWLV (B-3021) OY-CIM EC-JCR OY-CIM
469	72-212	Air Bagan	F-WWLW F-OHLC HS-PGH F-WQNE F-OHFZ XY-AIH
470	72-202	Fly540 Angola	F-WWED G-BWTM F-WQOL F-WQNH EI-REB F-WKVI CN-COC M-ABEF D2-FLB
471	42-500	Aeromar Airlines	F-WWLS XA-TAH
472	72-212	Aerocaribbean	F-WWEJ G-OILA G-BYTO F-WQNG CU-T1544
473	72-212	Aerocaribbean	F-WWEG G-OILB G-BYTP F-WQNI CU-T1545
474	42-500	Aeromar Airlines	F-WWLF XA-TAI
475	72-212	Myanma Airways	F-WWEH F-OGUO XY-AEZ
476	42-500	Aeromar Airlines	F-WWLX I-ADLG XA-UAV
477	72-202	Islas Airways	F-WWEI HS-PGF F-WQNM EC-IKQ
478	72-202	(Eurolot)	F-WWEK SP-LFH [w/o 14Jly11 Warsaw, Poland; dismantled & fuselage to Monchengladbach, Germany; canx 18Jan12]
479	72-212	Yangon Airways	F-WWEL F-OIYA XY-AIM [stored by 23Apr11 Yangon, Myanmar]
480	42-500	Airlinair	F-WWLZ F-GPYB
481	72-212	Yangon Airways	F-WWEQ F-OIYB XY-AIN [stored by 23Apr11 Yangon, Myanmar]
482	72-212	ConViasa	F-WWES YV-1004C YV1929 F-WQNB YV2421

AEROSPATIALE/AERITALIA ATR 42/72

C/n	Model	Last known Owner/Operator	Identities/fates/comments (where appropriate)
483	72-202	Fly540 Angola	F-WWEV G-BXTN F-WQNR G-BXTN F-WKVC CN-COD M-ABEG D2-FLC
484	42-500	Airlinair	F-WWEB F-GPYC
485	72-212	Aerocaribbean	F-WWLE YV-1005C F-WQNB CU-T1547
486	72-212	ConViasa	F-WWLG YV-1073C F-WQNA YV2422
487	42-400	ConViasa	F-WWEF OK-AFE F-WQNL YV1009
488	72-202	Naysa Aerotaxis/Binter Canarias	F-WWLI EC-GRP
489	72-202	Naysa Aerotaxis/Binter Canarias	F-WWLJ EC-GQF
490	42-500	Airlinair	F-WWLJ F-GPYD
491	42-420	ex ConViasa	F-WWLC OK-AFF F-WQNK YV1005 [reported stored by 23Oct11Caracas, Venezuela]
492	42-500	ex.Air Littoral	F-WWLK F-GPYE [w/o 30Jly97 Florence-Peretola Airport, Italy]
493	72-202	Naysa Aerotaxis/Binter Canarias	F-WWLN EC-GRU
494	72-212A	ex American Eagle	F-WWLS N494AE [ferried 28Jan/02Feb12 to Toulouse, France]
495	42-500	Airlinair	F-WWLM F-GPYF
496	72-202	Cimber Sterling	F-WWLT G-UKTN F-WQNL OY-RTF
497	42-500	Cimber Sterling	F-WWLR OY-CIJ A4O-AL OY-CIJ
498	72-212A	ex American Eagle	F-WWLW N498AT [wfs & ferried 04-06Feb12 to Monchengladbach, Germany
499	72-212A	ex American Eagle	F-WWLY N499AT
500	42-400MP	Guardia di Finanza	F-WWEW MM62165 [code GF-13]
501	42-500	ex Cimber Sterling	F-WWEE OY-CIK A4O-LM OY-CIK [stored Copenhagen, Denmark; l/n 17Aug12]
502	42-400MP	Guardia di Finanza	F-WWEM CM-X-62166 MM62166 [code GF-14]
503	42-500	TRIP Linhas Aereas	F-WWEN N14445 F-WQLJ F-GVZA VT-ADI F-WNUA PP-PTV
504	42-500	TRIP Linhas Aereas	F-WWEO N19446 F-WQLI VP-BOE F-WQNH PH-XLO F-WQNK PR-TTK
505	42-500	(ACES Colombia)	F-WWEP N15447 F-WQND VP-BOF [w/o 11Oct00 Bogota, Colombia]
506	42-500	TRIP Linhas Aereas	F-WWER N17448 F-WQNN VP-BOD F-WQNQ PH-XLP PR-TTH
507	42-500	Air Botswana	F-WWEU N33449 F-WQNG A2-ABN
508	72-202	ex Cimber Sterling	F-WWLU G-UKTM F-WQNK OY-RTC [stored Copenhagen, Denmark; l/n 17Aug12]
509	72-202	Danish Air Transport	F-WWLC G-UKTJ VN-B242 G-UKTJ F-WQNH F-OHFQ OY-RTD OY-RUG
510	42-500	TRIP Linhas Aereas	F-WWLB N16450 F-WQNM VP-BVE F-WQNJ VT-ADH F-WNUB PP-PTW
511	42-500	Air Botswana	F-WWLF N19452 F-WQNC A2-ABO
512	42-500	Air Botswana	F-WWLH N14451 F-WQNI A2-ABP
513	42-500	SATENA	F-WWLL F-OHJB PH-XLN PJ-XLN N513NA HK-4806 FAC1184// HK-4806 [dual marks]
514	42-500	ex Cimber Air	F-WWLO OY-CIL [stored Sonderborg, Denmark; l/n 17Aug12]
515	42-500	Danish Air Transport/ Maldivian Air Taxi	F-WWLP F-OHFN I-ADLI F-WQNN VT-ADP F-WKVK F-GVIJ OY-RUF
516	42-500	Airlinair/Air France	F-WWLU F-GPYG SP-EDA F-WNUA F-GVZC
517	72-212A	Transasia Airways	F-WWLK B-22801
518	42-500	flyMe	F-WWLX (I-ADLL) F-OHFP I-ADLL 8Q-VAR
519	72-202	AZUL Linhas Aereas Brasileras	F-WWLQ G-UKTK F-WQND VN-B248 F-WKVB PR-AZR
520	42-500	Airlinair	F-WWLR F-GPYM
521	72-212A	Fuerza Aerea Colombiana	F-WWED B-3022 N521NA HK-4828X FAC1186
522	42-500	SATENA	F-WWLC F-GPYH SP-EDB F-WNUB OY-PCB HK-4748X FAC1183// HK-4748 [dual marks]
523	72-202	AZUL Linhas Aereas Brasileras	F-WWLD G-UKTL VN-B246 F-WNUE PR-AZS
524	42-500	Airlinair	F-WWEF F-OHQL F-GVZB
525	72-212A	Transasia Airways	F-WWLB B-22802
526	42-500	SATENA	F-WWLM F-GPYI SP-EDC F-WNUI OY- HK-4747X FAC1182// HK-4747 [dual marks]
527	72-212A	Transasia Airways	F-WWLC B-22803
528	42-500	Solenta Aviation (Pty) Ltd	F-WWLF F-OHJC PH-XLS F-WQNJ F-GHNS F-WQNE VT-ADQ F-WKVI ZS-XCC
529	72-212A	ex American Eagle	F-WWLR N529AM
530	42-500	Airlinair	F-WWLH F-GPYJ SP-EDD F-WNUJ F-GVZD
531	72-212A	Buddha Air	F-WWLK B-3023 9N-AJS

AEROSPATIALE/AERITALIA ATR 42/72

C/n	Model	Last known Owner/Operator	Identities/fates/comments (where appropriate)
532	42-500	Fuerza Aerea Colombiana	F-WWLP D-BKKK PH-ISA (D4-CBW) N532FA D4-CBW N532FA HK-4827X FAC1185
533	72-212A	ex American Eagle	F-WWLO N533AT
534	42-500	Pacific Sun	F-WWLF 3B-NBA DQ-PSB
535	72-212A	Buddha Air	F-WWEC F-OHJN F-WQNE VT-DKQ F-WNUF 9N-AJO
536	72-212A	ex American Eagle	F-WWLZ N536AT
537	42-500	Airlinair/Air France	F-WWLC F-GPYK
538	72-212A	ex American Eagle	F-WWEA N538AT
539	42-500	Airlinair	F-WWLO F-GPYN
540	72-212A	ex American Eagle	F-WWLJ N540AM
541	72-212A	ex American Eagle	F-WWLA N541AT
542	42-500	Airlinair	F-WWLH F-GPYL
543	72-212A	Air Kanbawza	F-WWLB I-ADLM OY-PCK XY-AIT [badly damaged 17Feb12 Thandwe, Myanmar]
544	42-500	Airlinair/Air France	F-WWLH F-GPYO
545	72-212A	ex American Eagle	F-WWLE N545AT
546	42-500	Blue Islands	F-WWLE D-BMMM G-ISLF
547	72-212A	Air Kanbawza?	F-WWLO B-3025 N547NA XY-AIY
548	72-212A	ex American Eagle	F-WWLI N548AT [stored 08Feb12 Myrtle Beach, SC; 01Jun12]
549	42-500	US Dept of Justice	F-WWLB D-BLLL OY-RTH N366FM
550	72-212A	Nordic Aviation Contractor	F-WWLK N550LL [stored 07Feb12 Myrtle Beach, SC; 01Jun12; ferried across Atlantic 04Jly12]
551	42-500	Total Linhas Aereas	F-WWLL D-BNNN PR-TTM
552	72-212A	SATENA	F-WWLP B-3026 N550NA HK-4863X F-WTDB
553	72-212A	Airlinair/Air France	F-WWLC F-OHJO F-GVZL
554	42-500	Pacific Sun Airways	F-WWLL 3B-NBB DQ-PSA
555	72-212A	Nordic Aviation Contractor	F-WWLL B-3027 N155NK [stored 17Jun12 Billund, Denmark]
556	42-500	TRIP Linhas Aereas	F-WWLM F-OHJD VT-ADM F-WKVC PR-TKE
557	72-212A	Asian Wings	F-WWLV I-ADLN XY-AIU
558	72-212A	Transasia Airways	F-WWLN F-WQIU B-22805
559	42-500	Eurolot	F-WWLM D-BOOO SP-EDF
560	72-212A	Transasia Airways	F-WWED F-WQIY B-22806
561	42-500	Aeromar Airlines	F-WWLW XA-TKJ
562	72-212A	Passaredo Transportes Aereos	F-WWLZ (F-OIRA) EC-HJI F-WKVE (PR-TKO) PR-PDD
563	72-212A	Airlinair/Air France	F-WWEA F-OHJU F-GVZN
564	42-500	Aeromar Airlines	F-WWEC XA-TLN
565	72-212A	Air Nostrum	F-WWEE (VT-) EC-HEJ
566	42-500	TAROM	F-WWLF YR-ATA
567	72-212A	Transasia Airways	F-WWEF F-WQIZ B-22807
568	72-212A	Cimber Air	F-WWEH OY-CIN
569	42-500	TAROM	F-WWLH YR-ATB
570	72-212A	Air Nostrum	F-WWEG (VT-) EC-HEI
571	42-500	SATENA	F-WWEM F-OHQV VH-UYJ OY-EDL HK-4862X
572	72-212A	Jet Airways	F-WWEI F-WQKD VT-JCA
573	72-212A	Iran Aseman Airlines	F-WWEK F-OIRB EP-ATX+ [+ marks not fully confirmed]
574	42-500	Oman Air	F-WWEO A4O-AS VT-ADL A4O-AS
575	72-212A	Jet Airways	F-WWEJ F-WQKE VT-JCB
576	42-500	Oman Air	F-WWEP A4O-AT VT-AND A4O-AT
577	72-212A	Arkia Israel Airlines	F-WWEN 4X-AVZ
578	72-212A	ex Air Nostrum	F-WWEA EC-HBY F-WNUB
579	42-500	TRIP Linhas Aereas	F-WWEZ F-WWLF F-WWEA F-OIJB PR-TKF
580	72-212A	TRIP Linhas Aereas	F-WWEC EC-HCG PR-TKN
581	42-500	TRIP Linhas Aereas	F-WWEY XA- F-WWLE D-BPPP PR-TKG
582	72-212A	Air Kanbawza,	F-WWEL EC-HEZ XY-AIW
583	72-212A	Arkia Israel Airlines	F-WWER 4X-AVW
584	42-500	TRIP Linhas Aereas	F-WWEP D-BQQQ PR-TKH
585	72-212A	Air Dolomiti	F-WWEQ F-WQJH I-ADLO
586	42-500	Aeromar Airlines	F-WWEA XA-TPR
587	72-212A	Arkia Israel Airlines	F-WWES 4X-AVU
588	72-212A	Borajet/AnadoluJet	F-WWED I-ATMC G-CGFT TC-YAB
589	42-500	TAROM	F-WWLR YR-ATC
590	72-212A	Airlinair/Air France	F-WWET F-OHJT F-GVZM
591	42-500	TAROM	F-WWLS YR-ATD

AEROSPATIALE/AERITALIA ATR 42/72

C/n	Model	Last known Owner/Operator	Identities/fates/comments (where appropriate)
592	72-212A	Air Bagan	F-WWEM F-WQKA I-ATSL XY-AIK
593	72-212A	Jet Airways	F-WWEN F-WQKP VT-JCC
594	42-500	Aeromar Airlines	F-WWEX XA-TPS
595	72-212A	Cimber Sterling	F-WWEB OY-CIO EC-JCF OY-CIO 3B-NBK OY-CIO [stored 03May12 Copenhagen, Denmark; l/n 25May12]
596	42-500	TAROM	F-WWLY YR-ATE
597	72-212A	Air New Zealand Link	F-WWED F-WQKC ZK-MCA
598	72-212A	Air New Zealand Link	F-WWEU F-WQKG ZK-MCB
599	42-500	TAROM	F-WWEB YR-ATF
600	72-212A	Air New Zealand Link	F-WWEV F-WQKH ZK-MCF
601	42-500	Gatari Air Service	F-WWEC D-BRRR PK-TSQ PK-HNS
602	42-500	Eurolot	F-WWLA D-BSSS SP-EDH
603	42-500	Eurolot	F-WWLD D-BTTT SP-EDG
604	42-500	TRIP Linhas Aereas	F-WWLH F-WQKY I-ADLP PR-TKD
605	42-500	TAROM	F-WWLG YR-ATG
606	42-500	flyMe	F-WWLK F-WQMA I-ADLQ 8Q-VAQ
607	42-500	Aeromar Airlines	F-WWEA XA-TRI
608	42-500	Aeromar Airlines	F-WWEB XA-TRJ
609	42-500	TRIP Linhas Aereas	F-WWLP I-ADLU PR-TKC
610	42-500	TRIP Linhas Aereas	F-WWLQ F-WQMI (I-ADLV) F-OHJI I-ADLV PR-TKB
611	42-500	Indonesia Air Transport	F-WWLR F-WQMI I-ADLZ PK-THT
612	42-500	Simplifly Deccan	F-WWLS VP-BOU N612VX VT-ADJ
613	42-500	Simplifly Deccan	F-WWLT N316VX F-WQNH VT-ADK
614	42-500	Gatari Air Service	F-WWLU F-OHJJ F-WKVB OY-EDE PK-HNT
615	42-500MP	Italian Coast Guard	F-WWLV F-WQMJ CSX62208 MM62208 [code 10-02]
616	42-500	Aerogaviota	F-WWLA CU-T1454
617	42-500	Aerogaviota/Cubana	F-WWLB CU-T1240 [VIP aircraft]
618	42-500	Aerogaviota	F-WWLC CU-T1455
619	42-500	Aerogaviota	F-WWLD CU-T1456
620	42-500	Italian Coast Guard	F-WWLA F-WQMU CSX62230 MM62230 [code GF-15]
621	42-500	Air Tahiti	F-WWLB F-OIQB
622	42-500	Druk Air	F-WWLC F-WQMT F-OITQ A5-RGH
623	42-500	CSA Czech Airlines/Flybe Nordic	F-WWLD OK-JFJ
624	72-212A	Air New Zealand Link	F-WWEW F-WQKI ZK-MCJ
625	42-500	CSA Czech Airlines	F-WWLF OK-JFK
626	72-212A	Asian Wings	F-WWLC F-WQKZ I-ATPA XY-AIS
627	42-500	Air Tahiti	F-WWLH F-OIQC
628	72-212A	Air New Zealand Link	F-WWLB F-WQKJ ZK-MCO
629	42-500	CSA Czech Airlines	F-WWLJ OK-JFL
630	72-212A	Air New Zealand Link	F-WWLI F-WQKK ZK-MCP
631	42-500	Air Tahiti	F-WWLL F-OIQD
632	72-212A	Air New Zealand Link	F-WWLJ F-WQKL ZK-MCU
633	42-500	CSA Czech Airlines	F-WWLL F-WWLN OK-KFO
634	72-212A	Air Dolomiti	F-WWLL F-WQMB I-ADLS
635	42-500	(CSA Czech Airlines)	F-WWLP OK-KFM DBF 09Jun12 Prague, Czech Republic]
636	72-212A	Jet Airways	F-WWLM F-WQMC VT-JCD
637	42-500	CSA Czech Airlines	F-WWLR OK-KFN
638	72-212A	Air Dolomiti	F-WWLN F-WQME I-ADLT [600th ATR delivery]
639	42-500	CSA Czech Airlines	F-WWLT OK-KFP
640	72-212A	(Jet Airways)	F-WWLO F-WQMD VT-JCE [w/o 01Jly07 Indore, India; canx 12Aug08]
641	42-500	NordStar	F-WWLV OH-ATA VQ-BPE
642	72-212A	Transasia Airways	F-WWED F-WQMF B-22810
643	42-500	Finncomm Airlines	F-WWLA OH-ATB
644	72-212A	Air Algerie	F-WWEE F-OHGM 7T-VUI
645	42-500	Pakistan International Airlines	F-WWLE (F-OIPI) F-WWLE AP-BHH
646	72-212A	Air New Zealand Link	F-WWEG F-WQMG ZK-MCW(2)
647	42-500	Air Caledonie	F-WWLC F-WWLE F-OIPI
648	72-212A	Air Algerie	F-WWEF F-OHGN 7T-VUJ
649	42-500	Air Madagascar	F-WWLG 5R-MJG
650	72-212A	Air Austral	F-WWEC F-OHSF
651	42-500	Finncomm Airlines	F-WWLI OH-ATC
652	72-212A	Air Algerie	F-WWEH F-OHGO 7T-VUK
653	42-500	Pakistan International Airlines	F-WWLK AP-BHI

AEROSPATIALE/AERITALIA ATR 42/72

C/n	Model	Last known Owner/Operator	Identities/fates/comments (where appropriate)				
654	72-212A	Airlinair	F-WWEI	F-OIJG	F-HAPL		
655	42-500	Finncomm Airlines	F-WWLM	OH-ATD			
656	72-212A	Arkia Israel Airlines	F-WWEJ	4X-AVX			
657	42-500	Pakistan International Airlines	F-WWLO	AP-BHJ			
658	72-212A	Air Dolomiti	F-WWEL	D-ANFG	I-ADCA		
659	42-500	Pakistan International Airlines	F-WWLQ	AP-BHM			
660	72-212A	Air Dolomiti	F-WWEM	D-ANFH	I-ADCB		
661	42-500	Pakistan International Airlines	F-WWLS	AP-BHN			
662	72-212A	Air Dolomiti	F-WWEN	D-ANFI	I-ADCC		
663	42-500	Pakistan International Airlines	F-WWLU	AP-BHO			
664	72-212A	Air Dolomiti	F-WWEO	D-ANFJ	I-ADCD		
665	42-500	Pakistan International Airlines	F-WWLW	AP-BHP			
666	72-212A	TRIP Linhas Aereas	F-WWEP	D-ANFK	F-WKVE	PP-PTX	
667	42-500	Azerbaijan Airlines	F-WWLA	4K-AZ52			
668	72-212A	Air Dolomiti	F-WWEQ	D-ANFL	I-ADCE		
669	42-500	Transportes Aereos de Cabo Verde	F-WWLC	D4-CBV			
670	72-212A	(Bangkok Airways)	F-WWER	HS-PGL	[w/o 04Aug09 Koh Samui Airport, Thailand; wreck still present Nov11]		
671	42-500	Guinea Ecuatoriale	F-WWLE	3C-LLH			
672	72-212A	Air Algerie	F-WWES	F-OHGP	7T-VUL		
673	42-500	Silk Way Airlines	F-WWLG	4K-AZ808			
674	72-212A	Safair/Jet Airways	F-WWET	F-WQMK	VT-JCF		
675	42-500MP	Italian Coast Guard	F-WWLI	CSX62251+	MM62251+	[+ code GF-16]	
676	72-212A	Air Algerie	F-WWEA	7T-VVQ			
677	72-212A	Air Algerie	F-WWEA+	F-WWEB	F-OHGQ	7T-VUM	[+ painted in error]
678	72-212A	Vietnam Airlines	F-WWET	VN-B210			
679	72-212A	Safair/Jet Airlines	F-WWEC	VT-JCG	F-WQML	VT-JCG	
680	72-212A	Bangkok Airways/Siem Reap Air	F-WWEV	HS-PGK			
681	72-212A	CSA Czech Airlines	F-WWED	F-WQMM	VT-JCH	OK-GFR	
682	72-212A	Air Caraibes	F-WWEE	F-OIJH			
683	72-212A	Air Algerie	F-WWEF	7T-VVR			
684	72-212A	Air Algerie	F-WWEG	F-OHGR	7T-VUN		
685	72-212A	Vietnam Air Service Co	F-WWEH	VN-B212			
686	72-212A	Air Dolomiti	F-WWEI	F-WQMO	I-ADLJ		
687	72-212A	Air New Zealand Link	F-WWEJ	F-WQMN	ZK-MCX		
688	72-212A	Vietnam Airlines	F-WWEK	VN-B214			
689	42-500	Azerbaijan Airlines	F-WWLK	4K-AZ53			
690	72-212A	Air Mauritius	F-WWEM	3B-NBG			
691	42-500	Libyan Airlines	F-WWLM	F-WKVD	F-WWLM	5A-LAF	
692	72-212A	Bangkok Airways/Siem Reap Air	F-WWEO	HS-PGG			
693	42-500	Nigerian Air Force	F-WWLO	F-WKVD	CSX62262	NAF-930	
694	72-212A	Air Madagascar	F-WWEQ	(7T-VVS)	F-WWEQ	5R-MJE	
695	42-500	Air Antilles Express	F-WWLQ	F-OIXD			
696	72-212A	Air Tahiti	F-WWES	F-OHJS			
697	72-212A	Iran Aseman Airlines	F-WWET	F-OIRA	EP-ATU		
698	72-212A	Air Madagascar	F-WWEU	(F-OHGT)	F-WWEU	5R-MJF	
699	72-212A	KF Aero	F-WWEV	(7T-VVT)	F-WWEV	VT-KAA	M-ABFC
700	72-212A	Bangkok Airways/Siem Reap Air	F-WWEW	HS-PGF			
701	72-212A	Borajet/AnadoluJet	F-WWEA	I-ATLR	OY-EDC	TC-YAC	
702	72-212A	Borajet	F-WWEX	I-ATSM	OY-EDD	TC-YAD	
703	72-212A	Air New Zealand Link	F-WWEB	F-WQMR	ZK-MCY		
704	72-212A	Bangkok Airways/Siem Reap Air	F-WWEC	HS-PGM			
705	72-212A	Borajet	F-WWED	I-ATPM	G-CGFX	TC-YAE	
706	72-212A	Air Dolomiti	F-WWEF	I-ADLK			
707	72-212A	Air Dolomiti	F-WWEG	I-ADLW			
708	72-212A	Bangkok Airways	F-WWEH	HS-PGB			
709	72-212A	Binter Canarias	F-WWEI	EC-IYC			
710	72-212A	Bangkok Airways/Siem Reap Air	F-WWEJ	HS-PGA			
711	72-212A	Canair/Binter Canarias	F-WWEK	EC-IZO			
712	72-212A	Binter Canarias	F-WWEL	EC-JAH			
713	72-212A	Canair	F-WWEM	EC-JBI			
714	72-212A	Air New Zealand Link	F-WWIJ	F-WWEN	F-WQMV	ZK-MCC	

AEROSPATIALE/AERITALIA ATR 42/72

C/n	Model	Last known Owner/Operator	Identities/fates/comments (where appropriate)			
715	72-212A	Bangkok Airways/Siem Reap Air	F-WWEO	HS-PGC		
716	72-212A	Canair/Binter Canarias	F-WWET	EC-JEH		
717	72-212A	Binter Canarias/Canair	F-WWER	EC-JEV		
718	72-212A	Plateau Aviation	F-WWES	F-WQMW	VT-DKA	M-ABFI
719	72-212A	Air Tahiti	F-WWET	F-OIQN		
720	72-212A	Plateau Aviation	F-WWEA	F-WQMX	VT-DKB	M-ABFJ
721	72-212A	(Air Deccan)	F-WWEB	VT-DKC	[w/o 11Mar06 Bangalore, India; canx11Mar06; fuselage returned to France 16Aug06 for use as spares by Airlinair; wings in rebuild of c/n 098]	
722	72-212A	Air Corsica	F-WWEC	F-GRPI		
723	72-212A	Hubli Aircraft Leasing	F-WWED	(F-OIJK)	VT-DKE	M-ABEV
724	72-212A	Air Corsica	F-WWEE	F-GRPJ		
725	72-212A	Hubli Aircraft Leasing	F-WWEF	F-WQNG	VT-DKD	M-ABEW
726	72-212A	Binter Canarias	F-WWEG	EC-JQL		
727	72-212A	Air Corsica	F-WWEH	F-GRPK		
728	72-212A	KF Aero	F-WWEI	VT-KAB	M-ABFD	
729	72-212A	ex Kingfisher Airlines	F-WWEJ	VT-KAC	[w/o 10Nov09 Mumbai Airport, India; damaged remains l/n 27Jan10]	
730	72-212A	KF Aero	F-WWEK	VT-KAD	M-ABFE	
731	72-212A	Air Tahiti	F-WWEL	F-OIQO		
732	72-212A	Simplifly Deccan	F-WWEM	VT-DKI	[700th ATR delivery]	
733	72-212A	Simplifly Deccan	F-WWEN	VT-DKJ		
734	72-212A	Air Corsica	F-GRPX	F-WWEO	F-GRPX	
735	72-212A	Air Caledonie	F-WWEP	F-OIPN		
736	72-212A	Air Caraibes	F-WWEQ	F-OIJK		
737	72-212A	Kingfisher Airlines	F-WWER	VT-KAE		
738	72-212A	Kingfisher Airlines	F-WWES	VT-KAF		
739	72-212A	Simplifly Deccan	F-WWET	VT-DKH		
740	72-212A	Simplifly Deccan	F-WWEU	VT-DKK		
741	72-212A	Finncomm Airlines	F-WWEB	OH-ATE		
742	72-212A	Air Corsica	F-WWEC	F-GRPY		
743	72-212A	Kingfisher Airlines	F-WWED	VT-KAG		
744	72-212A	Finncomm Airlines	F-WWEE	OH-ATF		
745	72-212A	Air Corsica/Air France	F-WWEF	F-GRPZ		
746	72-212A	Kingfisher Airlines	F-WWEG	VT-KAH		
747	72-212A	Transportes Aereos de Cabo Verde	F-WWEH	D4-CBT		
748	72-212A	Aer Arann/Aer Lingus	F-WWEI	EI-REL		
749	72-212A	Transasia Airways	F-WWEJ	F-WQNC	B-22811	
750	72-212A	Kingfisher Airlines	F-WWEK	VT-KAI		
751	72-212A	Air Tahiti	F-WWEL	F-OIQU		
752	72-212A	Naysa Aerotaxis/Binter Canarias	F-WWEM	EC-KGI		
753	72-212A	Naysa Aerotaxis/Binter Canarias	F-WWEN	EC-KGJ		
754	72-212A	Kingfisher Airlines	F-WWEO	VT-KAJ		
755	72-212A	Transportes Aereos de Cabo Verde	F-WWEP	D4-CBU		
756	72-212A	Sevenair	F-WWEQ	TS-LBD		
757	72-212A	Finncomm Airlines	F-WWER	OH-ATG		
758	72-212A	Kingfisher Airlines	F-WWES	VT-KAK		
759	72-212A	Kingfisher Airlines	F-WWEV	VT-KAL		
760	72-212A	Aer Arann/Aer Lingus	F-WWEW	EI-REM		
761	72-212A	Azerbaijan Airlines	F-WWEX	4K-AZ64		
762	72-212A	Kingfisher Airlines	F-WWEZ	VT-KAM		
763	72-212A	Swiftair	F-WWEB	EC-KKQ		
764	72-212A	Air Caledonie	F-WWEC	F-OIPS		
765	72-212A	Myanma Airways	F-WWED	XY-AIF	[operates VIP flights for Air Force]	
766	72-212A	Islas Airways	F-WWEE	EC-KKZ		
767	72-212A	Kingfisher Airlines	F-WWEF	VT-KAN		
768	72-212A	for Turkish Navy	F-WWEG	F-WQNB	TCB-701??	[ATR72-500ASW]
769	72-212A	Finncomm Airlines	F-WWEH	OH-ATH		
770	72-212A	Islas Airways	F-WWEI	EC-KNO		
771	72-212A	Jet Airways	F-WWEJ	VT-JCJ		
772	72-212A	Kingfisher Airlines	F-WWEK	VT-KAO		
773	72-212A	TRIP Linhas Aereas	F-WWEL	PP-PTL		

AEROSPATIALE/AERITALIA ATR 42/72

C/n	Model	Last known Owner/Operator	Identities/fates/comments (where appropriate)				
774	72-212A	Transasia Airways	F-WWEM	B-22812			
775	72-212A	Jet Airways	F-WWEN	VT-JCK			
776	72-212A	Kingfisher Airlines	F-WWEO	VT-KAP			
777	72-212A	Kingfisher Airlines	F-WWEP	VT-KAQ			
778	72-212A	Golden Air	F-WWEQ	EI-REN	SE-MDA		
779	72-212A	Cebu Pacific Air	F-WWER	RP-C7250			
780	72-212A	Precision Air	F-WWES	5H-PWA			
781	72-212A	Myanma Airways	F-WWET	XY-AIG			
782	72-212A	Kingfisher Airlines	F-WWEX	VT-KAR			
783	72-212A	Finncomm Airlines	F-WWEB	OH-ATI			
784	72-212A	Cebu Pacific Air	F-WWEC	RP-C7251			
785	72-212A	TRIP Linhas Aereas	F-WWED	(VT-KAS)	(VT-DKL)	PP-PTR	
786	72-212A	Air Botswana	F-WWEE	(VT-KAS)	A2-ABR		
787	72-212A	Aer Arann/Aer Lingus	F-WWEF	EI-REO			
788	72-212A	Air Botswana	F-WWEG	(VT-KAT)	A2-ABS		
789	72-212A	Azerbaijan Airlines	F-WWEH	4K-AZ65			
790	72-212A	Guinea Ecuatoriale	F-WWEJ	3C-LLI			
791	72-212A	Jet Airways	F-WWEK	VT-JCL			
792	72-212A	Finncomm Airlines	F-WWEM	OH-ATJ			
793	72-212A	Jet Airways	F-WWEN	VT-JCM			
794	72-212A	Sevenair	F-WWEU	TS-LBE			
795	72-212A	Naysa Aerotaxis/Binter Canarias	F-WWEV	EC-KRY			
796	72-212A	Naysa Aerotaxis/Binter Canarias	F-WWEW	EC-KSG			
797	72-212A	Aer Arann/Aer Lingus	F-WWEZ	EI-REP			
798	72-212A	TRIP Linhas Aereas	F-WWEO	PP-PTM			
799	72-212A	Azerbaijan Airlines	F-WWEP	4K-AZ66			
800	42-500MP	Nigerian Air Force	F-WWLS	F-WKVE	CSX62289+	NAF-931	[+ Italy]
801	42-500	Air St. Pierre	F-WWLT	F-OFSP			
802	42-500	Libyan Airlines	F-WWLU	5A-LAG			
803	42-500	Italian Coast Guard	F-WWLV	F-WNUH	MM62270	[code 10-03]	
804	42-500MP	Libyan Ministry of Interiors	F-WWLW	F-WNUC	CSX62271	5A-DTN	
805	72-212A	BQB Lineas Aereas	F-WWEQ	(VT-KAU)	CX-JCL		
806	72-212A	Air Tahiti	F-WWER	F-OIQV			
807	42-500	Air Antilles Express	F-WWLX	F-OIXE			
808	72-212A	Islas Airways	F-WWES	EC-KUR			
809	72-212A	Swiftair	F-WWET	EC-KUL			
810	72-212A	Guinea Ecuatoriale	F-WWEX	3C-LLM			
811	42-600	ATR	F-WWLY				
812	72-212A	Firefly	F-WWEB	9M-FYA			
813	72-212A	Air Austral	F-WWEC	F-OZSE			
814	72-212A	Firefly	F-WWED	9M-FYB			
815	42-500	Precision Air	F-WWLZ	5H-PWE			
816	72-212A	BQB Lineas Aereas	F-WWEF	CX-JPL			
817	72-212A	MASwings	F-WWEG+	9M-MWA	[+ painted on one side as F-WWGE, assumed in error]		
818	72-212A	Azerbaijan Airlines	F-WWEH	4K-AZ67			
819	42-500	Precision Air	F-WWLA	5H-PWF			
820	72-212A	Cebu Pacific Air	F-WWEJ	RP-C7252			
821	72-212A	Firefly	F-WWEK	9M-FYC			
822	72-212A	Golden Air/Blue 1	F-WWEL	(EI-RER)	SE-MDB		
823	42-500	Airline Taimyr/NordStar, Russia	F-WWLB	F-WNUB	VQ-BKO		
824	72-212A	Swiftair/Antrak Air Ghana	F-WWEM	EC-KVI			
825	72-212A	Jet Airways	F-WWEN	VT-JCN			
826	72-212A	Fly540.com – Angola	F-WWEU	F-WKVD	D2-FLY		
827	42-500	Airline Taimyr/NordStar, Russia	F-WWLC	F-WNUC	VQ-BKN		
828	72-212A	Cebu Pacific Air	F-WWEV	RP-C7253			
829	72-212A	Air Tahiti	F-WWEW	F-OIQT			
830	72-212A	Firefly	F-WWEE	(OH-)	9M-FYD		
831	42-500	Air Guyane	F-WWLD	F-OIXH			
832	72-212A	TRIP Linhas Aereas	F-WWEI	PP-PTN			
833	72-212A	Bangkok Airways	F-WWEZ	HS-PGD			
834	72-212A	Precision Air	F-WWEB	5H-PWB			
835	42-500	Airline Taimyr/NordStar, Russia	F-WWEL+	F-WWLE	VQ-BKP	[+ painted in error]	
836	72-212A	Syrianair	F-WWEC	YK-AVA			

AEROSPATIALE/AERITALIA ATR 42/72

C/n	Model	Last known Owner/Operator	Identities/fates/comments (where appropriate)			
837	72-212A	TRIP Linhas Aereas	F-WWEO	PP-PTO		
838	72-212A	(Cebu Pacific Air)	F-WWEP	RP-C7254	[w/o 18Jly10 Manila, Philippines]	
839	42-500	Airline Taimyr/NordStar, Russia	F-WWLF	VQ-BKQ		
840	72-212A	Firefly	F-WWER	9M-FYE		
841	72-212A	Jet Airways	F-WWES	VT-JCP		
842	72-212A	Cebu Pacific Air	F-WWEH	RP-C7255		
843	72-212A	Jet Airways	F-WWEJ	VT-JCQ		
844	42-500	TAME Ecuador	F-WWLG	HC-CLT		
845	72-212A	Syrianair	F-WWEK	YK-AVB		
846	72-212A	TRIP Linhas Aereas	F-WWEL	(PP-PTS)	PP-PTT	
847	72-212A	Cebu Pacific Air	F-WWEI	RP-C7256		
848	72-212A	Finnish Commuter	F-WWEN	OH-ATK		
849	42-500	TAME Ecuador	F-WWLH	HC-CMB		
850	72-212A	Naysa Aerotaxis/Binter Canarias	F-WWET	EC-KYI		
851	72-212A	Flybe Nordic	F-WWEU	OH-ATL		
852	72-212A	Aurigny Air Services	F-WWEV	G-COBO		
853	72-212A	Aurigny Air Services	F-WWEW	G-VZON		
854	42-500	TAME Ecuador	F-WWLI	HC-CMH		
855	72-212A	Air Austral	F-WWEI	F-OMRU		
856	72-212A	MASwings	F-WWEX	9M-MWB		
857	72-212A	Cebu Pacific Air	F-WWEB	RP-C7257		
858	72-212A	Berjaya Air	F-WWEC	9M-TAG		
859			[not built]			
860	72-212A	Firefly	F-WWEF	9M-FYF		
861	72-212A	TAROM	F-WWEH	YR-ATH		
862	72-212A	Air Tahiti	F-WWEJ	F-OIQR		
863	72-212A	MASwings	F-WWEL	9M-MWC		
864	72-212A	Naysa Aerotaxis/Binter Canarias	F-WWEM	EC-LAD		
865	72-212A	TRIP Linhas Aereas	F-WWEO	PP-PTP		
866	72-212A	Precision Air	F-WWEP	5H-PWC		
867	72-212A	TAROM	F-WWER	YR-ATI		
868	72-212A	Firefly	F-WWES	9M-FYG		
869	72-212A	Wings Abadi Air	F-WWET	PK-WFF		
870	72-212A	Lao Aviation	F-WWEU	F-WNUD	RDPL-34173	
871	72-212A	Wings Abadi Air	F-WWEV	PK-WFI		
872	72-212A	Royal Thai Air Force	F-WWEW	L16-01/52//22-222	[serial followed by code after double slash; the code is only assumed and not carried]	
873	72-212A	MASwings	F-WWEX	9M-MWD		
874	72-212A	TRIP Linhas Aereas	F-WWEZ	PP-PTQ		
875	72-212A	Berjaya Air/Airlines of PNG	F-WWEB	PK-TAQ		
876	72-212A	Air Vanuatu	F-WWED	F-WNUG	YJ-AV72	
877	72-212A	Vietnam Airlines	F-WWEE	VN-B218		
878	72-212A	Lao Aviation	F-WWEG	F-WNUF	RDPL-34174	
879	72-212A	Belle Air	"F-WWHE"+ F-WWEH	ZA-ARB^	F-ORAA	[+ painted in error] [^ painted under wing, but marks on MD80]
880	72-212A	Precision Air	F-WWEI	5H-PWD		
881	72-212A	Royal Thai Air Force	F-WWEJ	L16-02/52//60314	[serial followed by code after double slash; badly damaged 30Apr12 Dhaka-Zia, Bangladesh]	
882	72-212A	Wings Abadi Air	F-WWEL	PK-WFG		
883	72-212A	Wings Abadi Air	F-WWEM	PK-WFH		
884	72-212A	Arkia Israel Airlines	F-WWEN	4X-AVT		
885	72-212A	MASwings	F-WWEO	9M-MWE		
886	72-212A	Vietnam Airlines	F-WWEP	VN-B219		
887	72-212A	Royal Thai Air Force	F-WWER	F-WNUG	L16-03/52//60315	[serial followed by code after double slash]
888	72-212A	Air Caraibes	F-WWES	F-OIXL		
889	72-212A	MASwings	F-WWET	9M-MWF		
890	72-212A	Vietnam Airlines	F-WWEV	VN-B220		
891	72-212A	TRIP Linhas Aereas	F-WWEW	PP-PTU		
892	72-212A	Vietnam Airlines	F-WWEX	VN-B221		
893	72-212A	Royal Thai Air Force	F-WWEZ	L16-04/52//60316	[serial followed by code after double slash]	
894	72-212A	Erik Thun AB/ Golden Air	F-WWED	SE-MDC		
895	72-212A	MASwings	F-WWEE	9M-MWG		

AEROSPATIALE/AERITALIA ATR 42/72

C/n	Model	Last known Owner/Operator	Identities/fates/comments (where appropriate)			
896	72-212A	Vietnam Airlines	F-WWEG	VN-B223		
897	72-212A	Vietnam Airlines	F-WWEH	VN-B225		
898	72-212A	Wings Abadi Air	F-WWEI	PK-WFJ		
899	72-212A	Vietnam Airlines/Cambodia Angkor	F-WWEJ	VN-B227		
900	72-212A	MASwings	F-WWEO	9M-MWH		
901	72-212A	Air Algerie	F-WWEP	7T-VUO		
902	72-212A	Binter Canarias	F-WWER	EC-LFA		
903	72-212A	Air Algerie	F-WWES	7T-VUP		
904	72-212A	MASwings	F-WWET	9M-MWI		
905	72-212A	Wings Adabi Air	F-WWEV	PK-WFK		
906	72-212A	Vietnam Airlines/Cambodia Angkor	F-WWEW	VN-B231		
907	72-212A	Naysa Aerotaxis	F-WWEX	EC-LGF		
908	72-212A	Belle Air	F-WWEZ	F-ORAB	I-LZAN	F-ORAI
909	72-212A	Air Algerie	F-WWEB	7T-VUQ		
910	72-212A	MASwings	F-WWEH	9M-MWJ		
911	72-212A	TRIP Linhas Aereas	F-WWEE	PP-PTY		
912	72-212A	Vietnam Airlines	F-WWEG	VN-B233		
913	72-212A	Air Algerie	F-WWEI	7T-VUS		
914	72-212A	Vietnam Airlines	F-WWEJ	VN-B236		
915	72-212A	Wings Abadi Air	F-WWEM	PK-WFL		
916	72-212A	Finnish Commuter	F-WWEN	OH-ATM		
917	72-212A	Golden Air	F-WWEO	SE-MDH		
918	72-212A	TRIP Linhas Aereas	F-WWEP	PT-PTZ		
919	72-212A	Jet Airways	F-WWER	VT-JCR		
920	72-212A	Jet Airways	F-WWES	VT-JCS		
921	72-212A	Air Mauritius	F-WWET	3B-NBN		
922	72-212A	Wings Adabi Air	F-WWEV	PK-WFM		
923	72-212A	Precision Air	F-WWEW	5H-PWG		
924	72-212A	Jet Airways	F-WWEX	VT-JCT		
925	72-212A	Vietnam Airlines	F-WWEZ	VN-B237		
926	72-212A	TRIP Linhas Aereas	F-WWEB	PR-TKA		
927	72-212A	Vietnam Airlines	F-WWEC	VN-B239		
928	72-212A	Jet Airways	F-WWED	VT-JCU		
929	72-212A	Lao Airlines	F-WWEE	F-WKVF	RDPL-34175	
930	72-212A	Golden Air	F-WWEF	SE-MDI		
931	72-212A	Israir	F-WWEG+	(YK-AVC)	4X-ATH	[+ for time painted as F-WWGE in error]
932	72-212A	Jet Airways	F-WWEH	VT-JCV		
933	72-212A	Jet Airways	F-WWEI	VT-JCW		
934	72-212A	Firefly	F-WWEJ	9M-FYH		
935	72-212A	Firefly	F-WWEK	9M-FYI		
936	72-212A	Wings Abadi Air	F-WWEL	PK-WFO		
937	72-212A	Wings Abadi Air	F-WWEM	PK-WFP		
938	72-212A	Lao Airlines	F-WWEN	F-WKVJ	RDPL-34176	
939	72-212A	Vietnam Airlines	F-WWEO	VN-B240		
940	72-600	Alenia/Italian Navy	F-WWLN	F-WKVD	CSX62279	MM62279*
941	72-212A	Firefly	F-WWEQ	9M-FYJ		
942	72-212A	UTAir Aviation	F-WWER	VQ-BLC		
943	72-212A	Wings Abadi Air	F-WWES	PK-WFQ		
944	72-212A	Cebu Pacific Air	F-WWET	RP-C7258		
945	72-212A	UTAir Aviation	F-WWEV	VQ-BLD		
946	72-212A	Wings Abadi Air	F-WWEW	PK-WFR		
947	72-212A	Firefly	F-WWEX	9M-FYK		
948	72-212A	Firefly	F-WWEZ	9M-FYL		
949	72-212A	Fly540.com Ghana	F-WWEB	9G-FLY		
950	72-212A	UTAir Aviation	F-WWEC	VQ-BLE		
951	72-212A	UTAir Aviation	F-WWED	VQ-BLF		
952	72-212A	UTAir Aviation	F-WWEE	VQ-BLG		
953	72-212A	UTAir Aviation	F-WWEF	VQ-BLH		
954	72-212A	Skywest/Virgin Australia	F-WWEG	VH-FVH		
955	72-212A	Skywest/Virgin Australia	F-WWEH	VH-FVI		
956	72-212A	Skywest/Virgin Australia?	[not built]			

AEROSPATIALE/AERITALIA ATR 42/72

C/n	Model	Last known Owner/Operator	Identities/fates/comments (where appropriate)		
957	72-212A	Wings Abadi Air	F-WWEJ	PK-WFS	
958	72-600	Royal Air Maroc Express	F-WWLO	CN-COF	
959	72-212A	Flybe Nordic	F-WWEL	OH-ATN	
960	72-600	Royal Air Maroc Express	F-WWLP	CN-COE	
961	72-212A	Wings Abadi Air	F-WWEN	(4X-ATH)	PK-WFT
962	72-212A	Israir	F-WWEO	4X-ATI	
963	72-212A	UTAir Aviation	F-WWEP	VQ-BLI	
964	72-212A	Wings Abadi Air	F-WWEQ	PK-WFU	
965	72-212A	UTAir Aviation	F-WWER	VQ-BLJ	
966	72-600	AZUL Linhas Aereas	F-WWLQ	PR-ATR	
967	72-600	TRIP Linhas Aereas	F-WWLR	F-WKVB	PR-TKI
968	72-600	Caribbean Airlines	F-WWLS	9Y-TTA	
969	72-600	AZUL Linhas Aereas	F-WWLT+	PR-ATB	[+ rolled out marked as F-WWTL]
970	72-600	Alenia	F-WWLU	[reported for Italian Navy as MM62282]	
971	72-600	TRIP Linhas Aereas	F-WWLV	PR-TKJ	
972	72-212A	AZUL Linhas Aereas	F-WWLW	PR-ATE	
973	72-212A	Caribbean Airlines	F-WWLX	9Y-TTB	
974	72-212A	Skywest/Virgin Australia	F-WWES	VH-FVL	
975	72-212A	UTAir Aviation	F-WWET	VQ-BLK	
976	72-212A	UTAir Aviation	F-WWEU	VQ-BLL	
977	72-212A	Flybe Nordic	F-WWEV	OH-ATO	
978	72-212A	Skywest/Virgin Australia	F-WWEW	OY-CJU	VH-FVU
979	72-212A	Skywest/Virgin Australia	F-WWEX	VH-FVM	
980	72-212A	UTAir Aviation	F-WWEZ	VQ-BLM	
981	72-212A	UTAir Aviation	F-WWEB	VQ-BLN	
982	72-212A	BoraJet	F-WWEC	TC-YAF	
983	72-212A	UTAir Aviation	F-WWED	VQ-BMA	
984	72-212A	UTAir Aviation	F-WWEE	VQ-BMB	
985	72-212A	Wings Abadi Air	F-WWEF	PK-WFV	
986	72-212A	Skywest/Virgin Australia	F-WWEG	OY-CJV	VH-FVX
987	72-600	TRIP Linhas Aereas	F-WWLN	PR-TKK	
988	72-600	AZUL Linhas Aereas	F-WWLO	PR-ATG	
989	72-600	Caribbean Airlines	F-WWLP	9Y-TTC	
990	72-212A	UTAir Aviation	F-WWEH	VQ-BMD	
991	72-600	AZUL Linhas Aereas	F-WWLQ	PR-ATH	
992	72-600	TRIP Linhas Aereas	F-WWLR	PR-TKL	
993	72-600	for Caribbean Airlines	F-WWLS	9Y-TTD*	
994	72-212A	UTair Ukraine	F-WWEI	(VQ-BME)	UR-UTH
995	72-600	Air Nostrum/Iberia Regional	F-WWLT	EC-LQV	
996	72-600	AZUL Linhas Aereas	F-WWLU	PR-ATJ	
997	72-600	for Caribbean Airlines	F-WWLV	9Y-TTE*	
998	72-600	TRIP Linhas Aereas	F-WWLW	PR-TKM	
999	72-600	Air Nostrum/Iberia Regional	F-WWLX	EC-LRH	
1000	72-212A	UTAir Aviation	F-WWEJ	UR-UTI	
1001					
1002					
1003					
1004					
1005					
1006					
1007					
1008					
1009					
1010					
1011					
1012					
1013					
1014					
1015					
1016					
1017					
1018					
1019					

AEROSPATIALE/AERITALIA ATR 42/72

C/n	Model	Last known Owner/Operator	Identities/fates/comments (where appropriate)		
1020	72-600	AZUL Linhas Aereas	F-WWLN	PR-ATK	
1021	72-600	for Caribbean Airlines	F-WWLO		
1022	72-600	Passaredo Transportes Aereos	F-WWLP	F-WWEW	PR-PDA
1023	72-600	Air Nostrum	F-WWLQ	EC-LRR	
1024	72-212A	Wings Abadi Airlines	F-WWEK	PK-WFW	
1025	72-600	Skywest/Virgin Australia	F-WWLR	VH-FVP	
1026	72-600	AZUL Linhas Aereas	F-WWLS	PR-ATP	
1027	72-600	AZUL Linhas Aereas	F-WWLT	PR-ATQ	
1028	72-600	Passaredo Transportes Aereos	F-WWLU	PR-PDB	
1029	72-212A	UT Air Aviation	F-WWEL	UR-UTJ	
1030	72-600	for Caribbean Airlines	F-WWEO	9Y-TTG?	
1031	72-600	ATR	F-WWEP	[reported for Italian Navy]	
1032	72-600	Air Nostrum	F-WWEQ	EC-LRU	
1033	72-600	AZUL Linhas Aereas	F-WWER	PR-ATU	
1034	72-600	Royal Air Maroc Express	F-WWES	CN-COH	
1035	72-600	Royal Air Maroc Express	F-WWET	CN-COG	
1036	72-212A	UT Air Aviation	F-WWEM	UR-UTK	
1037	72-212A	UT Air Aviation	F-WWEN	UR-UTL	
1038	72-600	for Caribbean Airlines			
1039	72-600	Skywest/Virgin Australia	F-WWEB	VH-FVN	
1040	72-212A	Passaredo Transportes Aereos	F-WWEC	PR-PDC	
1041	72-600	for Air Nostrum			
1042	72-600	for Caribbean Airlines			
1043	72-600	for AZUL Linhas Aereas	F-WWEF	PR-ATV*	
1044	72-600	for UnI Airways, Taiwan	F-WWEG	B-17001*	
1045	72-600		F-WWEH		
1046	72-600	for AZUL Linhas Aereas	F-WWEI	PR-ATW*	
1047	72-600	for AZUL Linhas Aereas			
1048	72-212A	for Wings Abadi Airlines	F-WWEU		
1049	72-600	for Carpatair			
1050	72-212A	for Flybe Nordic			
1051	72-600	for Air New Zealand/Mount Cook			
1052					
1053	72-600	for Skywest/Virgin Australia			
1054	72-600	for Passaredo Transportes			
1055					
1056					
1057					
1058					
1059					
1060					
1061					
1062					
1063					
1064					
1065					
Unidentified					
unkn	42-400MP	for Libyan Ministry of Interiors	CSX62271	[reported Jun10 Naples, Italy; probably c/n 804]	
unkn	42-500		F-WNUA	[reported 12May10 Montpellier, France]	
unkn	42-500		F-WNUB	[reported 22Jun10 Montpellier, France; possibly either c/n 516 or 530]	
unkn	42-500		F-WNUJ	[reported stored by 27Apr10 Montpellier, France; probably either c/n 522 or c/n 530]	
unkn	42-300		F-WQNE	[flew St. Brieuc-Rhodes-Muscat 15Dec/16Dec07[	
unkn	72		F-WQNE	[flew Toulouse-St. Brieuc 28Sep07 – possibly either c/n 351 or 406]	
unkn	42-320		F-WQNG	[flew Toulouse-Paphos-Dubai 18May06/19May06]	
unkn	42		F-WQNY	[reported St. Brieuc, France 29Jun08]	
unkn	42		F-WTCD	[offered for sale Apr08 with t/t 27,086 hours; 1987 built aircraft]	
unkn	42-300	UTAir Aviation	UR-UTF	[reported in Sep11 in Ukraine]	

1506 8Q-RAZ

AEROSPATIALE/VFW C.160 TRANSALL

Note: The c/n prefixes of D, F or R, which are not shown, match those letters given in the model column.
As required codes and call signs used by French aircraft are shown after a double slash

C/n	Model	Last known Owner/Operator	Identities/fates/comments (where appropriate)
V-1		(French Air Force)	D-9507 D-ABEX F-ZWWV F-ZWWV F-ZADK//DK F-SDBJ//DK F-ZADK//373C [prototype ff 25Feb63; wfu 23Jly74; GIA Rochefort-St Agnant, France; was reported to be V-2 whilst in French service]
V-2		(French Air Force)	D-9508 F-ZADH//DH (50+01)^ F-ZADH//DH 50+01^ F-ZJYD [^ West Germany] [b/u in 1982 Clermont Ferrand-Aulnat, France]
V-3		Aerospatiale	D-9509 F-ZADI//DI KA+200^ 50+02^ TR-LWE F-WESE [^ West Germany] [b/u in 1982 Clermont Ferrand-Aulnat, France]
V-4			[static test airframe; b/u Lemwerder, West Germany]
V-5			[static test airframe; b/u Toulouse, France]
A-01	D	(West German Air Force)	D-9524 YA+051^ 50+03^ [^ West Germany] [wfu & b/u Wunstorf, Germany 1979]; fuselage to Altenstadt, Hessen, Germany as GIA]
A-02	R	French Air Force	D-9526 F-ZWWS//ZS F-SDBS//118-BS A-02//61-MI RA-02//61-MI [stored Apr12 Orleans-Bricy, France]
A-03	D	(West German Air Force)	D-9525 YA+052^ (50+04)^ D-ABYG HB-ILN D-ABYG 50+04 [^ West Germany] [b/u 1975 Hohn, West Germany]
A-04	R	ex French Air Force	D-9527 F-ZWWT//WT F-SDBT//118-BT A-04//61-ZA F-ZABI RA-04//61-MS [wfu Nov07 Orleans-Bricy, France; 24Apr08 to Chateaudun, France]
A-05	D	(West German Air Force)	D-9528 YA+053^ 50+05 [^ West Germany] [b/u 1975 Wunstorf, West Germany]
A-06	R	ex French Air Force	D-9529 F-ZWWU//WU F-SDBU//118-BU A-06//61-ZB RA-06//61-ZB [wfu Nov07 Orleans-Bricy, France & stored Chateaudun, France; Jun10 moved onto dump]
1	R	French Air Force	KM+101^ F1//340-YE F1//61-MA R1//61-MA [wfu May11 Orleans-Bricy, France to Chateaudun, France for store] [^ West Germany]
2	R	French Air Force	KA+201^ F2//61-MB R2//61-MB [^ West Germany]
3	R	ex French Air Force	F-ZJYF//340-YF F3//61-MC R3//61-MC [stored 2011 Orleans-Bricy, France; reported will be preserved at Le Bourget, France]
4	R	French Air Force	KM+104^ F4//61-MD R4//61-MD [^ West Germany]
5	R	ex French Air Force	KA+202^ F5//61-ME R5//61-ME [^ West Germany] [wfu Aug05, to GIA Toulouse-Francazal, France; l/n 09Aug06]
6	D	ex German Air Force	50+06 [wfu 10Jan12 Hohn, Germany; to GIA]
7	D	German Air Force	KM+102^ 50+07 [^ West Germany]
8	D	German Air Force	50+08
9	D	German Air Force	50+09
10	D	German Air Force	KM+103^ 50+10 [^ West Germany]
11	R	ex French Air Force	KA+203^ F11//61-MF R11//F-RAMF//61-MF [^ West Germany] [wfu 03May12 Orleans-Bricy, France]
12	R	ex French Air Force	F12//F-RAMG//61-MG R12//61-MG [wfu Orleans-Bricy, France]
13	R	ex French Air Force	KM+105^ F13//61-MH R13//61-MH [^ West Germany] [wfu Orleans-Bricy, France; moved 30May08 Chateaudun, France]
14	F	(French Air Force)	KA+204^ F14//61-MI [^ West Germany] [w/o 23May68 Flores, Azores]
15	R	ex French Air Force	F15//61-MJ F15//330-IR F15//61-MJ R15//61-MJ [wfu & stored 01Jly11 Orleans-Bricy, France]
16	F	ex French Air Force	KM+106^ F16//61-MK F-WUFP F-BUFP F16//61-MK [^ West Germany] [wfu Chateaudun, France, no tail by May03; l/n 18Sep07]
17	R	ex French Air Force	KA+205^ F17//61-ML R17//61-ML [^ West Germany] [wfu Orleans-Bricy, France; l/n 02Jun07; 2010 to Chateaudun, France]
18	R	ex French Air Force	F18//61-MM R18//61-MM [wfs & preserved Aug12 Le Bourget, France]
19	D	Turkish Air Force	KM+107^ 50+11^ 019# 12-019 [^ West Germany; # Turkey]
20	D	Turkish Air Force	50+12^ 020# 12-020 [^ West Germany; # Turkey]
21	D	Turkish Air Force	50+13^ 021# 12-021 [^ West Germany; # Turkey]
22	D	ex Turkish Air Force	50+14^ 022# 12-022 [^ West Germany; # Turkey] [preserved Havacilik Muzesi, Istanbul-Ataturk, Turkey with code 022; l/n 17Feb10]
23	D	Turkish Air Force	50+15^ 023# 12-023 [^ West Germany; # Turkey]
24	D	Turkish Air Force	50+16^ 024# 12-024 [^ West Germany; # Turkey]
25	D	German Air Force	50+17
26	D	Turkish Air Force	50+18^ 026# 12-026 [^ West Germany; # Turkey]
27	D	Turkish Air Force	50+19^ 027# 12-027 [^ West Germany; # Turkey]

AEROSPATIALE/VFW C.160 TRANSALL

C/n	Model	Last known Owner/Operator	Identities/fates/comments (where appropriate)
28	D	ex Turkish Air Force	50+20^ 028# 12-028 [^ West Germany; # Turkey] [by Jun11 GIA Izmir-Gaziemir, Turkey]
29	D	Turkish Air Force	50+21^ 029# 12-029 [^ West Germany; # Turkey]
30	D	(Turkish Air Force)	50+22^ 030# ETI-030 [^ West Germany; # Turkey] [w/o 14Nov88 Kayseri, Turkey]
31	D	Turkish Air Force	50+23^ 031# 12-031 [^ West Germany; # Turkey]
32	D	Turkish Air Force	50+24^ 032# 12-032 [^ West Germany; # Turkey]
33	D	Turkish Air Force	50+25^ 033# 12-033 [^ West Germany; # Turkey]
34	D	Turkish Air Force	50+26^ 034# 12-034 [^ West Germany; # Turkey]
35	D	Turkish Air Force	50+27^ 035# 12-035 [^ West Germany; # Turkey]
36	D	Turkish Air Force	50+28^ 036# 12-036 [^ West Germany; # Turkey]
37	D	German Air Force	50+29
38	D	Turkish Air Force	50+30^ 038# 12-038 [^ West Germany; # Turkey]
39	D	ex Turkish Air Force	50+31^ 039# 12-039 [^ West Germany; # Turkey] [wfs Dec03 preserved Ankara-Etimesgut, Turkey]
40	D	Turkish Air Force	50+32^ 040# 12-040 [^ West Germany; # Turkey]
41	D	German Air Force	50+33
42	R	French Air Force	KA+206^ F42//61-MN R42//61-MN [^ West Germany]
43	R	ex French Air Force	KM+108^ F43//61-MO R43//61-MO [^ West Germany] [stored Feb08 Orleans-Bricy, France]
44	R	(French Air Force)	KA+207^ F44//61-MP R44//61-MP [^ West Germany] [wfu by Jun07 Orleans-Bricy, France; dismantled Feb08 & taken by road 29Feb08 to Chateaudun, France]
45	R	ex French Air Force	F45//61-MQ R45//61-MQ [wfu Orleans-Bricy, France; 2010 to Chateaudun, France]
46	R	(French Air Force)	KM+109^ F46//61-MR R46//61-MR [^ West Germany] [wfu Orleans-Bricy, France; dismantled Mar08 & taken by road 27Mar08 to Chateaudun, France]
47	F	(French Air Force)	F47?//61-MS F-WUFQ F-BUFQ F47? [reported to Cazaux, Gironde, France fire school; l/n 1993; probably b/u]
48	R	ex French Air Force	F48//61-MT R48//61-MT [retired 26May08; stored Orleans-Bricy, France]
49	R	ex CEV KA+208^	R48?//61-MU F-WUFR F-BUFR R49//F-RAMU/59-MU [^ West Germany] [stored Nov08 Orleans-Bricy, France]
50	F	CEAT KM+110^	F50?//61-MV F-WUFS F-BUFS [^ West Germany] [b/u Paris-Orly, France; hulk to Centre D'Essais Aeronautique de Toulouse as GIA; l/n 13Oct07]
51	R	French Air Force	F51//61-MW R51//61-MW
52	R	ex French Air Force	KM+111^ F52//61-MX R52//61-MX [^ West Germany] [wfu 2007 Orleans-Bricy, France; l/n Nov07; 2010 to Chateaudun, France]
53	R	ex French Air Force	KA+209^ F53//61-MY R53//61-MY [^ West Germany] [wfu Orleans-Bricy, France; l/n 02Jun07]
54	R	French Air Force	F54//61-MZ R54//61-MZ
55	R	French Air Force	F55//61-ZC R55//61-ZC
56	D	German Air Force	50+34
57	D	German Air Force	50+35
58	D	German Air Force	50+36
59	D	ex German Air Force	50+37 [wfs 20Mar12 & preserved Damme, Germany]
60	D	German Air Force	50+38^ D-AMBB PK-PTA 50+38 [^ West Germany]
61	D	(West German Air Force)	50+39 [w/o 11May90 near Lohr, West Germany]
62	D	German Air Force	50+40
63	D	German Air Force	50+41
64	D	German Air Force	50+42
65	D	(German Air Force)	50+43 [w/o 23Oct95 Ponta Delgada, Azores]
66	D	German Air Force	50+44
67	D	German Air Force	50+45
68	D	German Air Force	50+46
69	D	German Air Force	50+47
70	D	German Air Force	50+48
71	D	German Air Force	50+49
72	D	ex German Air Force	50+50 [damaged unknown date Wunstorf, Germany; wings removed & fuselage stored]
73	D	Luftwaffen Museum	50+51 [preserved 19Sep11 Berlin-Gatow, Germany]
74	D	German Air Force	50+52 [wfu Jun10 Landsberg, Germany & b/u]
75	D	German Air Force	50+53
76	D	German Air Force	50+54
77	D	German Air Force	50+55
78	D	ex German Air Force	50+56 [preserved by 2011 Gatow, Germany]

AEROSPATIALE/VFW C.160 TRANSALL

C/n	Model	Last known Owner/Operator	Identities/fates/comments (where appropriate)
79	D	German Air Force	50+57
80	D	German Air Force	50+58
81	D	German Air Force	50+59
82	D	German Air Force	50+60
83	D	German Air Force	50+61
84	D	German Air Force	50+62
85	D	(West German Air Force)	50+63 [w/o 09Feb75 near Souda, Crete, Greece]
86	R	French Air Force	KA+210^ F86//61-ZD R86//61-ZD [^ West Germany]
87	R	French Air Force	F87//61-ZE R87//61-ZE
88	R	ex French Air Force	KA+211^ F88//61-ZF R88//61-ZF [^ West Germany] [wfu Aug08 Orleans-Bricy, France; 2010 to Evreux, France]
89	R	French Air Force	F89//61-ZG R89//61-ZG
90	R	French Air Force	KA+212^ F90//61-ZH R90//61-ZH [^ West Germany]
91	R	French Air Force	KM+112^ F91//61-ZI R91//61-ZI [^ West Germany]
92	R	ex French Air Force	KA+213^ F92//61-ZJ R92//61-ZJ [^ West Germany] [wfu & stored 15Jan11 Orleans-Bricy, France; by May11 Chateaudun, France]
93	R	French Air Force	F93//61-ZK R93//61-ZK
94	R	French Air Force	KM+113^ F94//61-ZL R94//61-ZL [^ West Germany]
95	R	French Air Force	KM+214^ F95//61-ZM R95//61-ZM [^ West Germany]
96	R	French Air Force	F96//61-ZN R96//61-ZN
97	R	French Air Force	KM+114^ F97//61-ZO R97//61-ZO [^ West Germany]
98	R	ex French Air Force	KA+215^ F98//61-ZP R98//61-ZP [wfu & stored 17Mar11 Orleans-Bricy, France; ^ West Germany]
99	R	French Air Force	F99//61-ZQ R99//61-ZQ
100	R	(French Air Force)	KM+115^ F100//61-ZR R100//61-ZR [^ West Germany] [DBF 06May04 Le Lamentin, Fort-de-France, Martinique; b/u; fuselage to Chateaudun, France 2007; l/n 18Sep07]
101	D	German Air Force	50+64
102	D	German Air Force	50+65
103	D	German Air Force	50+66
104	D	German Air Force	50+67^ D-AMBA PK-PTC 50+67 [^ West Germany]
105	D	German Air Force	50+68
106	D	German Air Force	50+69
107	D	German Air Force	50+70
108	D	German Air Force	50+71
109	D	German Air Force	50+72
110	D	German Air Force	50+73
111	D	German Air Force	50+74
112	D	German Air Force	50+75
113	D	German Air Force	50+76
114	D	German Air Force	50+77
115	D	German Air Force	50+78
116	D	German Air Force	50+79
117	D	(West German Air Force)	50+80 [w/o 02Jly88 Bordeaux-Merignac, France]
118	D	German Air Force	50+81
119	D	German Air Force	50+82
120	D	German Air Force	50+83
121	D	(German Air Force)	50+84 [reported 2011 b/u, location not stated]
122	D	German Air Force	50+85
123	D	German Air Force	50+86
124	D	German Air Force	50+87
125	D	German Air Force	50+88
126	D	German Air Force	50+89
127	D	ex German Air Force	50+90 [stored Landsberg, Germany]
128	D	German Air Force	50+91
129	D	German Air Force	50+92^ D-ACTR 50+92 [^ West Germany]
130	D	German Air Force	50+93
131	D	ex German Air Force	50+94 [preserved May12 Graz-Thalrhof, Austria]
132	D	German Air Force	50+95
133	D	German Air Force	50+96
134	D	German Air Force	50+97
135	D	ex German Air Force	50+98 [wfu 06Dec11 Weeze, Germany; 06Dec11 Baarlo, Netherlands]
136	D	Technik Museum	50+99 [wfu 13Apr11 & preserved Speyer, Germany]

AEROSPATIALE/VFW C.160 TRANSALL

C/n	Model	Last known Owner/Operator	Identities/fates/comments (where appropriate)
137	D	German Air Force	51+00
138	D	German Air Force	51+01
139	D	German Air Force	51+02
140	D	German Air Force	51+03
141	D	German Air Force	51+04
142	D	German Air Force	51+05
143	D	German Air Force	51+06
144	D	Interessengemeinschaft Ju52	51+07 [preserved by Aug11 Wundorf, Germany]
145	D	German Air Force	51+08
146	D	German Air Force	51+09
147	D	German Air Force	51+10
148	D	German Air Force	51+11 [wfu Aug10 Landsberg, Germany]
149	D	German Air Force	51+12^ D-AMBV 51+12 [^ West Germany]
150	D	German Air Force	51+13
151	D	German Air Force	51+14
152	D	German Air Force	51+15
153	R	French Air Force	F153//61-ZS R153//61-ZS
154	R	French Air Force	F154//61-ZT R154//61-ZT
155	R	(French Air Force)	F155//61-ZU R155//61-ZU [w/o 09Dec96 near Chevilly, France; cockpit to GIA at Evreux-Fauville, France Sep99; gate guardian at Orleans-Bricy, France; l/n 24Sep05; front fuselage preserved Collection de la Base Aerienne d'Orleans-Bricy, France; l/n 29Sep05]
156	F	(French Air Force)	F156//61-ZV [w/o 23Nov84 near Castres, France, mid-air collision with F209 c/n 209]
157	R	French Air Force	F157//61-ZW R157//61-ZW
158	R	French Air Force	F158//61-ZX R158//61-ZX
159	R	French Air Force	F159//61-ZY R159//61-ZY
160	R	French Air Force	F160//61-ZZ R160//61-ZZ
201	R	French Air Force	F-ZJUA F201//64-GA R201//64-GA
202	R	French Air Force	F-ZJUB F202//64-GB R202//64-GB
203	R	French Air Force	F-ZJUC F203//64-GC F-ZVLK R203//64-GC
204	R	French Air Force	F-ZJUD F204//64-GD R204//64-GD
205	P	Manunggal Air Service	F-WZCZ PK-PTX [CofA expired 07Feb97; status/fate unknown]
206	R	French Air Force	F-ZJUE F205//64-GE R205//64-GE
207	P	Manunggal Air Service	F-WZLM PK-PTY PK-VTS
208	P	Manunggal Air Service	F-WZLN PK-PTZ PK-VTZ [CofA expired; status/fate unknown]
209	R	French Air Force	F-ZJUF F206//64-GF R206//64-GF
210	R	French Air Force	F-ZJUG F207//64-GG R207//64-GG
211	R	French Air Force	F-ZJUH F208//64-GH R208//64-GH
212	NG	(French Air Force)	F-ZJUI F209//64-GI [w/o 23Nov84 near Castres, France, mid-air collision with F156 c/n 156]
213	R	French Air Force	F-ZJUJ F210//64-GJ R210//64-GJ
214	R	French Air Force	F-ZJUK F211//64-GK R211//64-GK
215	R	French Air Force	F-ZJUL F212//64-GL R212//64-GL
216	R	French Air Force	F-ZJUM F213//64-GM R213//64-GM
217	R	French Air Force	F-ZJUN F214//64-GN R214//64-GN
218	R	French Air Force	F-ZJUO F215//64-GO R215//64-GO
219	G	French Air Force	F-ZJUP F216//64?-GT
220	R	French Air Force	F-ZJUQ F217//64-GQ R217//64-GQ
221	R	French Air Force	F-ZJUR F218//64-GR R218//64-GR
222	H	ex French Air Force	F-ZJUS H01//59-BA [wfu Chateaudun, France; l/n 10Jun06]
223	H	ex French Air Force	F-ZJUT H02//59-BB [wfu Chateaudun, France; l/n 10Jun06]
224	G	French Air Force	F-ZJUU F221//64?-GS
225	NG	ex French Air Force	F-ZJUV F222//64-GV [w/o 06Apr95 near Calvi, Corsica, France; fuselage to GIA with Army at Calvi, France; l/nJun96]
226	R	French Air Force	F-ZJUW F223//64-GW R223//64-GW
227	R	French Air Force	F-ZJUX F224//64-GX R224//65-GX
228	R	French Air Force	F-ZJUY F225//64-GY R225//64-GY
229	R	French Air Force	F-ZJUZ F226//64-GZ R226//64-GZ
230	NG	(French Air Force)	F-ZJUA F227//64-GP [DBF 17Mar93 Evreux, France; l/n on dump 22Jun03]
231	H	ex French Air Force	F-ZJUB H03//59-BC [wfu Chateaudun, France; l/n 10Jun06]
232	H	ex French Air Force	F-ZJUC H04//59-BD [wfu Chateaudun, France; l/n 10Jun06]
233	P	Manunggal Air Service	F-WDQK PK-PTO PK-VTR

AEROSPATIALE/VFW C.160 TRANSALL

C/n	Model	Last known Owner/Operator	Identities/fates/comments (where appropriate)
234	P	Manunggal Air Service	F-WDQL PK-PTP PK-VTP
235	P	(Manunggal Air Service)	F-WDQM PK-PTQ PK-VTQ [w/o 06Mar08 Wamena Airport, Indonesia]
Z-1	Z	(South African Air Force)	331 [stored circa 1993 Waterkloof, South Africa; l/n 15May07; early 2009 stripped of useful parts and b/u]
Z-2	Z	(South African Air Force)	333 [stored circa 1993 Waterkloof, South Africa ; l/n 15May07; early 2009 stripped of useful parts and b/u]
Z-3	Z	(South African Air Force)	335 [stored circa 1993 Waterkloof, South Africa; l/n 15May07; early 2009 stripped of useful parts and b/u]
Z-4	Z	SAAF Museum	337 [wfu Jan93; preserved Swartkop, South Africa by Mar94; l/n 23Sep08]
Z-5	Z	(South African Air Force)	339 [stored circa 1993 Waterkloof, South Africa ;l/n 15May07; early 2009 stripped of useful parts and b/u]
Z-6	Z	(South African Air Force)	332 [stored circa 1993 Waterkloof, South Africa ;l/n 15May07; early 2009 stripped of useful parts and b/u]
Z-7	Z	(South African Air Force)	334 [stored circa 1993 Waterkloof, South Africa ;l/n 15May07; early 2009 stripped of useful parts and b/u]
Z-8	Z	(South African Air Force)	336 [stored circa 1993 Waterkloof, South Africa ;l/n 15May07; early 2009 stripped of useful parts and b/u]
Z-9	Z	(South African Air Force)	338 [stored circa 1993 Waterkloof, South Africa ;l/n 15May07; early 2009 stripped of useful parts and b/u]

Production complete

AIRBUS MILITARY 400M

C/n	Model	Last known Owner/Operator	Identities/fates/comments (where appropriate)
001		Airbus Military	F-WWMT [ff 11Dec09 Seville, Spain]
002		Airbus Military	EC-402 [ff 30Mar10]
003		Airbus Military	F-WWMS [ff 09Jly10]
004		Airbus Military	EC-404 [ff 20Dec10]
005			[not built]
006		Airbus Military	F-WWMZ [for RAF as ZM401]
007		for French Air Force	
008			
009			
010			
011			
012			
013			
014			
015			
016			
017			

ANTONOV An-3

C/n	Line No.	Model	Last known Owner/Operator	Identities/fates/comments (where appropriate)

Note: Only details of aircraft identities post conversion to turbo-prop power are included

379-01	01 01?	Skh	Antonov Design Bureau	CCCP-26700 CCCP-06131 CCCP-37901 UR-37901 UR-BWD [ex An-2 c/n 1G163-21]
9801-00-01		T-06	PO "Polyot"	9801+ [ex An-2 c/n 1G175-46] [+ Russia; dismantled & stored by 05Sep06 "Polyot" factory, Omsk, Russia]
2001	20 01	T	Tura Aviation Enterprise	RA-05889 [ex An-2 c/n 1G211-55]
2002-03-01	20 02	T	Evenkiya	RA-05882 [ex An-2 c/n 1G214-46]
2003-02-01	20 03	T-02	Zapolyarye	RA-05883 [ex An-2 c/n 1G210-19] [stored by Aug08 Norlisk-Valyok, Russia]
2004	20 04	T	Zapolyarye	RA-05884 [ex An-2 c/n 1G109-14] [stored by Aug08 Norlisk-Valyok, Russia]
2005	20 05	T	Kras Avia	2005 RA-05869 [ex An-2 c/n 1G203-24]
2106-06-01	21 06	T-08	Avialesookhrana	RA-05866 [ex An-2 c/n 1G240-21]
2007-07-04	20 07	T	Avialesookhrana	RA-05867 [ex An-2 c/n 1G240-60]
2108	21 08	T	not yet known	RA-05886 UR-AAF [ex An-2 c/n 1G214-32]
2109	21 09	T	not yet known	RA-05885 UR-AAR [ex An-2 c/n 1G214-31]
2112	21 12	T	Blagoveshchensk Airlines	RA-05888 [ex An-2 c/n 1G159-41]
2113	21 13	T	Blagoveshchensk Airlines	RA-05887 [ex An-2 c/n 1G212-56]
2114	21 14	T	Polyarnya Avialinii	RA-05890 [ex An-2 c/n 1G225-11] [stored by 04May09 Batagai, Russia; l/n Jun09]
2115	21 15	T	Polyarnya Avialinii	RA-05891 [ex An-2 c/n 1G187-44] [stored by 04May09 Batagai, Russia; l/n Jun09]
2217	22 17	T	Polyarnya Avialinii	RA-05880 [ex An-2 c/n 1G191-49]
2218-18-01	22 18	T	Polyarnya Avialinii	RA-05881 [w/o 16May03 45km from Sanghar, Pakistan; canx 12May05]
2310	23 10	T	Zapolyarye	RA-05870 [ex An-2 c/n 1G209-08] [stored by Aug08 Norlisk-Valyok, Russia]
2311	23 11	T	Kras Avia	RA-05868 [ex An-2 c/n 1G109-12] [stored by Apr12 Eniseysk, Russia]
2319	23 19	T	Polyarnya Avialinii	319 RA-05871 [ex An-2 c/n 1G204-53]
2221	22 21	T	Tuvinskive Avialinii	RA-05879 [ex An-2 c/n 1G133-15]
2423	24 23	T	Polyarnya Avialinii	RA-05892 [ex An-2 c/n 1G172-07]
2426	24 26	T	MChS Rossii	RF-31225 RF-31120 RF-32773 [ex An-2 c/n 1G204-54]
2525	25 25	T	MChS Rossii	RF-31226+ RF-31130 [+ not fully confirmed] [ex An-2 c/n 1G191-37]
2524	25 24	T	MChS Rossii	RF-31121 RF-32764
2527	25 27	T	Polyarnya Avialinii	RA-05893 [ex An-2 c/n 1G165-22]
2629	26 29	T	PO "Polyot"	629 [ex An-2 c/n 1G183-12]
2629-29-01		T	MirAvia	[ex An-2 1G183-12 offered for sale Apr11 incomplete]
2722-22-01		T	MirAvia	[ex An-2 1G218-22 offered for sale Apr11 incomplete]
2728-28-01		T	MirAvia	[ex An-2 1G215-41 offered for sale Apr11 incomplete]
2731-31-01		T	MirAvia	[ex An-2 1G207-51 offered for sale Apr11 incomplete]
2732-32-01		T	MirAvia	[ex An-2 1G201-17 offered for sale Apr11 incomplete]

ANTONOV An-8

C/n	Model	Last known Owner/Operator	Identities/fates/comments (where appropriate)
unkn		(Antonov OKB)	[prototype built at Kiev-Svyatoshino, Ukraine, USSR; ff 11Feb56; fate unknown]
8 34 01 01			[reported preserved Tashkent, Uzbekistan]
8 34 01 02		(Soviet Air Force)	[nothing known]
8 34 01 03		(Soviet Air Force)	[nothing known]
8 34 01 04		(MAP Koms. na Amure MSZ)	CCCP-48976 [canx 15Nov72]
8 34 01 05		(Soviet Air Force)	[nothing known]
8 34 02 01		(Soviet Air Force)	[nothing known]
8 34 02 02		(Soviet Air Force)	[nothing known]
8 34 02 03		(MAP Koms. na Amure APO)	CCCP-79170 [canx 12Sep79]
9 34 02 04		(MAP Kirov MSZ)	CCCP-83965 [canx 01Nov89]
9 34 02 05		(Soviet Air Force)	[unknown] [w/o 15Oct59 near Tula, USSR]
9 34 03 01		(Soviet Air Force)	[nothing known]
9 34 03 02		(MAP Arsenyev MSZ)	CCCP-69301 [canx date unknown; probably after Jul92]
9 34 03 03		(MAP Koms. na Amure APO)	CCCP-59505 [canx 14Dec88]
9 34 03 04		(Soviet Air Force)	[nothing known]
9 34 03 05		(MAP Arsenyev MSZ)	14+ CCCP-08822 CCCP-78736 [+ Soviet – colour unknown] [canx 16Jan90]
9 34 03 06		(Aviakor Samara)	CCCP-69305 RA-69305 [canx date unknown; probably after Jun94]
9 34 03 07		(Soviet Air Force)	[nothing known]
9 34 03 08		(MAP Omsk Motors)	CCCP-69329 [canx 26Jun89; l/n 12Jun94 wfu Omsk-Fyodorova, Russia]
9 34 03 09		(Soviet Air Force)	[nothing known]
9 34 03 10		(MAP Kirov MSPO)	CCCP-69336 [w/o 15Jun83 Kharkov, USSR; canx 19Dec84]
9 34 04 01		(Soviet Air Force)	[nothing known]
9 34 04 02		(Soviet Air Force)	[nothing known]
9 34 04 03		(Soviet Air Force)	[nothing known]
9 34 04 04		(Soviet Air Force)	[nothing known]
9 34 04 05		(MAP Novosibirsk APO)	CCCP-69347 [canx date unknown; probably after 15Sep87]
9 34 04 06		(MAP Ulyanovsk APO)	CCCP-69352 [canx 17Jan95]
9 34 04 07		(Soviet Air Force)	[nothing known]
9 34 04 08		(Soviet Air Force)	[nothing known]
9 34 04 09		(MAP Koms. na Amure APO)	CCCP-69326 [canx 05Apr96]
9 34 04 10		(MAP Voronezh MeZ)	CCCP-69330 [canx 23Oct92; wfu Voronezh, Russia by Sep94]
9 34 05 01		(Soviet Air Force)	[nothing known]
9 34 05 02		(Soviet Air Force)	16 red
9 34 05 03		(MAP Ulan Ude APO)	CCCP-69348 [canx date unknown; probably after 29Dec87]
9 34 05 04		Central Air Force Museum	10 red + 10 green^ [+ Soviet; ^ Soviet, believed mis-painted by museum; preserved Monino Museum 20May76]
9 34 05 05		(MAP Kazan Motors)	CCCP-79166 CCCP-69344+ RA-79166 [+ this could be another aircraft with incorrect c/n recorded] [wfu Kazan-Borisoglebskoye, Russia by Aug99, canx 06Mar96]
9 34 05 06		(MAP Ulan Ude APO)	CCCP-69337 [canx date unknown; probably after Sep02]
9 34 05 07		(MAP Omsk Motors)	CCCP-69351 [preserved by JUn94 Omsk-Fyodorova, Russia; canx date unknown]
9 34 05 08		(Soviet Air Force)	[nothing known]
9 34 05 09		(Soviet Air Force)	[nothing known]
9 34 05 10		(Soviet Air Force)	[nothing known]
9 34 06 01		(Soviet Air Force)	[nothing known]
9 34 06 02		(MAP Kirov MSPO)	CCCP-69322 [canx date unknown; probably after 08Dec92]
9 34 06 03		(Rostvertol)	CCCP-69323 RA-69323 [wfu Rostov, Russia by 14 May96; gone by Aug99; canx 12Sep95]
9 34 06 04		(Soviet Air Force)	15 red [preserved 42 km from St Petersburg, Russia Sep06, but due to be broken up; l/n Oct07]
9 34 06 05		(MAP Ulan Ude APO)	CCCP-98110 CCCP-27213 [canx 02Dec86]
9 34 06 06		(Soviet Air Force)	[nothing known]
9 34 06 07		(Soviet Air Force)	[nothing known]
9 34 06 08		(Soviet Air Force)	[nothing known]
9 34 06 09		(Soviet Air Force)	[nothing known]
9 34 06 10		(MAP Moscow OAO)	CCCP-13370 [canx 29Nov90]
9 34 07 01		(MAP Zlatoust MSZ)	CCCP-79163 [canx 24Oct79]
9 34 07 02		(MAP Kazan APO)	CCCP-69339 [canx 14Feb83]
9 34 07 03		(MAP Rostov VPO)	CCCP-13363 [canx 12Sep95; l/n wfu Rostov, Russia 14May96; gone by Aug99]
9 34 07 04		(MAP Koms. na Amure APO)	CCCP-69325 [canx 05Apr96]
9 34 07 05		(Soviet Air Force)	[nothing known]

ANTONOV An-8

C/n	Model	Last known Owner/Operator	Identities/fates/comments (where appropriate)
9 34 07 06		(Rwandan Air Force)	CCCP-27202 RA-27202 EL-RDK TL-ABA TL-ACM+ [+ unofficial marks] [w/o 20Apr00 on take-off Pepa, Congo]
9 34 07 07		(Soviet Air Force)	[nothing known]
9 34 07 08		(Kit Air)	CCCP-69331 RA-69331 [derelict by 29Aug97 Orenburg-Tsentrainly, Russia; canx on unknown date, probably after 29Aug97]
9 34 07 09		(MAP Arsenyev MSZ)	CCCP-27205 [damaged Arsenyev-Varfolomeyevka, USSR Mar80; canx 08Jun81]
9 34 07 10		(MAP Kazan APO)	CCCP-27201 RA-27201 [wfu by Jun94; fuselage l/n Kazan-Borisoglebskoye, Russia 17Aug99; canx date unknown]
0А 34 10		(MAP Koms. na Amure MSZ)	CCCP-48094 [used call sign CCCP-08053] [w/o 30Aug77 10 km from Bratsk, USSR; canx 22Feb78]
0А 34 20		(MAP Orenburg MSZ)	CCCP-69319 [derelict by 29Aug97 by Orenburg-Tsentrainly, Russia; canx date unknown]
0А 34 30		(MAP Arsenyev MSZ)	CCCP-69324 [canx 28May03]
0А 34 40		(MAP Gorki APO)	CCCP-69338 [status/fate unknown]
0А 34 50		(Soviet Air Force)	[nothing known]
0А 34 60		(MAP Arsenyev MSZ)	CCCP-27209 RA-27209 [w/o 30Sep94 Chaibukha, Russia]
0А 34 70		(MAP Arsenyev MSZ)	CCCP-69311 [canx date unknown; probably after 25Sep86]
0А 34 80		(Soviet Air Force)	[nothing known]
0А 34 90		(Soviet Air Force)	[nothing known]
0А 3 401		(Trans Air Congo)	CCCP-69315(2) RA-69315(2) EL-ASA EL-ALE(2) TN-AFN [retired 1998; by summer 04 hulk only Point Noire, People's Republic of Congo]
0Б 34 10		(Soviet Air Force)	[nothing known]
0Б 34 20		(MOM Omsk MSZ)	CCCP-69314 [w/o 09Aug79 Moscow-Domodedovo, USSR; canx 14Nov79]
0Б 34 30		(Mandala Air Cargo)	CCCP-79167 RA-79167 4R-SKJ 3C-DDA [stored Fujairah, UAE by Aug02; l/n Nov05; possibly b/u]
0Б 34 40		(MOMS Zlatoust MSZ)	CCCP-26183 [w/o 20Nov88 Yerevan, USSR]
0Б 34 50		(MAP Koms. na Amure APO)	CCCP-69335 [canx date unknown]
0Б 34 60		(Von Haaf Air)	CCCP-27203 RA-27203 D2-FVB+ [+ not fully confirmed] [l/n Jan95; fate unknown]
0Б 34 70		(MAP Novosibirsk APO)	CCCP-93911 [canx date unknown; probably after 23Jun94]
0Б 34 80		(MAP Kaluga Motors)	CCCP-59504 RA-59504 [w/o 29Sep94 Elista, Russia; canx 29Dec95]
0Б 34 90		(Soviet Air Force)	[nothing known]
0Б 34 01		(MAP Ulan Ude APO)	CCCP-13349 [canx date unknown; probably after 20Apr97]
0В 34 10		(MAP Irkutsk MSZ)	CCCP-13365 [canx date unknown]
0В 34 20		(MAP Novosibirsk APO)	CCCP-69320 [w/o 11Nov90 Novosibirsk-Yeltovka, USSR; canx 19Apr91]
0В 34 30		(Soviet Air Force)	[nothing known]
0В 34 40		(Soviet Air Force)	[nothing known]
0В 34 50		(MAP Moscow OAO)	CCCP-13366 [wfu Krasnodar-Pashkovskaya, Russia by 09Sep94; canx 01Jun94]
0В 34 60		(Soviet Air Force)	[nothing known]
0В 34 70		(MAP Koms. na Amure APO)	CCCP-79165 canx 14Dec88]
0В 34 80		(MAP Kazan APO)	CCCP-69332 [wfu by Jun94; canx date unknown]
0В 34 90		(MAP Gorki APO)	CCCP-93918 [canx 06Dec91]
0В 34 01		ex Air Cess	CCCP-69349 D2-FVC EL-AKT [l/n 26Jan97; fate/status unknown]
0Г 34 10		Kisangani Airlift	CCCP-69343 RA-69343 EL-ALC(1) J2-KBG EL-AKY(1) 9L-LEO S9-DBC [noted 05Mar08 flying Goma, Democratic Republic of Congo; Antonov considered this aircraft has not been airworthy since 23Jun95; l/n 17Aug09 Goma apparently now wfu]
0Г 34 20		(MAP Novosibirsk APO)	CCCP-69316(2) [canx date unknown; probably after 12Jun90]
0Г 34 30		(MAP Novosibirsk APO)	CCCP-69340 RA-69340 [canx date unknown; probably after 27Apr93]
0Г 34 40		(Express – titles)	CCCP-69327 RA-69327 3C-QQE EL-WVA(3) [w/o 22Jan05 near Kongolo, Zaire]
0Г 34 50		(Von Haaf Air)	CCCP-69341 D2-FVA [w/o 06Dec94 Dundo, Angola]
0Г 34 60		(MAP Irkutsk APO)	CCCP-98107 RA-98107 [canx 07Feb96]
0Г 34 70		(MAP Kirov Electrics)	CCCP-98105 [canx date unknown]
0Г 34 80		(MAP Arsenyev MSZ)	CCCP-78731 [canx 1981]
0Г 34 90		(MAP Koms. na Amure MSZ)	19 red + CCCP-19330 [+ Soviet] [w/o 16May91 Irkutsk-2, USSR]
0Г 34 01		(MAP Novosibirsk APO)	CCCP-59500 [l/n 23Jun94; fate/status unknown]
0Д 34 10		(Soviet Air Force)	[nothing known]
0Д 34 20		ex Sky Cabs	CCCP-27215 RA-27215 4R-SKI [stored by Oct01 Colombo, Sri Lanka; l/n Sep08
0Д 34 30		(Yuri Petrov's Airlines)	CCCP-69346 [w/o 29Oct92 Chita, Russia]

ANTONOV An-8

C/n	Model	Last known Owner/Operator	Identities/fates/comments (where appropriate)
0Д 34 40		ex Expo Air	CCCP-69328 RA-69328 3C-ZZO S9-DAJ+ [+ not fully confirmed] [noted 03Oct07 Brazzaville, People's Republic of Congo; l/n there 02Aug10 wfu sitting on tail]
0Д 34 50		(MAP Kaluga Motors)	CCCP-59503 [canx 10Dec91]
0Д 34 60		(MAP Arsenyev APO)	CCCP-69345 [canx date unknown]
0Д 34 70		ex Trans Air Congo	CCCP-69350 RA-69350 EL-ALQ 3D-ADI EL-ALQ [in scrapyard by Mar02 possibly at Kinshasa-N'Djili, Democratic Republic of Congo]
0Д 34 80		(Soviet Air Force)	[nothing known]
0Д 34 90		(MAP Zhukovski)	CCCP-69316(1) [w/o 10Oct75 Sverdlovsk-Koltsovo, USSR; canx 01Jly76]
0Д 34 01		(MAP Kaluga Motors)	CCCP-69303 [canx 06Feb95]
0E 34 10		(MAP Kazan Motors)	CCCP-27217 [wfu 1991; canx 06Mar96]
0E 34 20		(unknown)	CCCP-69353 RA-69353 EL-AKZ [l/n 11Feb03; b/u Sharjah, UAE by Oct04]
0E 34 30		(MAP Kaluga Motors)	CCCP-13323 [w/o 12Dec93 Yerevan, Armenia; hulk still present 16May96; possibly RA-13323 at time of accident]
0E 34 40		(Air Pass)	CCCP-69334 RA-69334 EL-WVA(2) [w/o pre 31May02 Kalemie, Katanga (Congo)]
0E 34 50		ex VAC	CCCP-27204 9Q-CGH+ [canx as CCCP-27204 13Aug04; l/n 27Jun06 stored Rostov-na-Donu, Russia; + no sightings or other proof of existence]
0E 34 60		(MAP Kazan APO)	CCCP-13372 [wfu by Jun94, canx unknown date; possibly hulk noted cut in two at Kazan-Borisoglebskoye , Russia Aug99]
0E 34 70		(MAP Kmos. na Amure MSZ)	76 red + CCCP-13352 [+ Soviet] [canx 28Mar80]
0E 34 80		(Soviet Air Force)	06 red [reportedly w/o Jly62]
0E 34 90		(Soviet Air Force)	[nothing known]
0E 34 01		(MAP Novosibirsk APO)	CCCP-13327 [canx date unknown]
0Ж 34 10		unknown	CCCP-69307 EL-ALC(2) EL-AKY(2) 4R-EXA 3C-QRE S9-GRE+ [+ not fully confirmed] [wfu by Feb08 engineless Fujairah, UAE]
0Ж 34 20		(MAP Koms. na Amure APO)	CCCP-69342 [canx 25Mar99]
0Ж 3 430		(MAP Novosibirsk APO)	CCCP-72615 [canx date unknown]
0Ж 34 40		(Soviet Air Force)	[nothing known]
0Ж 34 50		ex Southern Gateway	CCCP-64457 RA-64457 EL-WVA(1) EL-WHL [l/n active 27Nov00; fate/status unknown]
0Ж 34 60		(Soviet Air Force)	[nothing known]
0Ж 34 70		(MAP Irtutsk MSZ)	CCCP-78738 [w/o 30Sep87 Irkutsk-2, USSR by taxing An-8 CCCP-98107 c/n 0G3460]
0Ж 34 80		(MAP Koms. na Amure APO)	CCCP-69315(1) [was preserved Taru-Yume, Estonia; probably b/u after 1993]
0Ж 34 90		(MAP Moscow OAO)	CCCP-48101 [w/o 27Sep88 3.5 km from Kozyolsk, Kaluga, USSR]
0Ж 34 01		(Soviet Air Force)	[nothing known]
13 34 10		(Soviet Air Force)	[nothing known]
13 34 20		(ex Air Pass c/s)	CCCP-93928 D2-FVE EL-AKM [stored Kigali, Zaire by Apr00, fate/status unknown]
13 34 30		(Soviet Air Force)	[nothing known]
13 34 40		(MAP Moscow OAO)	CCCP-79161 [canx 13Jan91]
13 34 50		(MAP Kirov MSZ)	CCCP-26197 [canx 01Jly81]
13 34 60		ex Air Mark Indo Aviation	CCCP-55502 RA-55502 4R-EXB 3C-KKZ [stored Fujairah, UAE by Mar04; l/n 17May08 very derelict]
13 34 70		(Antonov Design Bureau)	CCCP-55517 [An-8RU testbed for SPRD-159 take-off rockets; w/o 16Sep94 Gostomel, Ukraine]
13 34 80		(MAP Arsenyev)	CCCP-69302 RA-69302 [canx 04Jun03]
13 34 90		(Soviet Air Force)	[nothing known]
13 34 01		(MPA Novosibirsk APO)	CCCP-98109 CCCP-27219 [canx 1979]
1И 34 10		(MOM Voronezh)	CCCP-69333 RA-69333 [canx 18May95]
1И 34 20		(Soviet Air Force)	[nothing known]
1И 34 30		(Volga-Dnepr)	CCCP-13361 RA-13361 [canx 17Jan95]
1И 34 40		(MAP Arsenyev MSZ)	CCCP-13357 [canx 16Jan90]
1И 34 50		(MAP Moscow OAO)	CCCP-13360 [canx 1979]
1И 34 60		(Santa Cruz Imperial)	CCCP-78739 RA-78739 EL-ALE(1) [w/o 12Mar98 Mogadishu, Somalia]
1И 34 70		(MPA Novosibirsk APO)	CCCP-55521 RA-55521 [wfu by 12Dec01 Novosibirsk-Yeltsovka, Russia; by 11Dec02 in use as storage shed; canx date unknown]
1И 34 80		(MAP Zhukovski)	CCCP-83961 [canx 15May73]
1И 34 90		(Soviet Air Force)	[nothing known]
1И 34 01		(Soviet Air Force)	[nothing known]
1K 34 10		(MAP Novosibisrsk SNKh)	CCCP-06190 [last An-8 built; canx 1979]

ANTONOV An-8

C/n	Model	Last known Owner/Operator	Identities/fates/comments (where appropriate)

Production complete

Unidentified – Civil

unkn			CCCP-08770 [probably call-sign only – reported 03Apr74]
unkn			CCCP-55321 [probable mis-read of CCCP-55521;at Leningrad-Pulkovo, USSR 06Jly70]
unkn			CCCP-55322 [probable fake registration]
unkn			CCCP-72401 [probably call-sign only]
unkn			CCCP-72601 [reported in book]
unkn			CCCP-72624 [photo – probably false registration]
unkn			CCCP-72838 [photo – probably false registration]
unkn			CCCP-86725 [photo – probably false registration]
unkn			3X-GDQ 9Q-CXI [latterly Uhuru Airlines; wfu 2006 Kinshasa-N'Djili, Democratic Republic of Congo; not in 2008 register; b/u early 2010]
unkn		(no marks)	[2008 photo – preserved near Avitec factory at Kirov, Russia]

Unidentified – Military

unkn		(Soviet Air Force)	02 red [reported 05Aug68]
unkn		(Soviet Air Force)	03 red [reported 05Aug68]
unkn		(Soviet Air Force)	07 red [reported 05Aug68]
unkn		(Soviet Air Force)	08 red [reported 05Aug68]
unkn		(Soviet Air Force)	09 red [reported 05Aug68]
unkn		(Soviet Air Force)	11 red [reported 05Aug68]
unkn		(Soviet Air Force)	12 red [reported 05Aug68]
unkn		(Soviet Air Force)	13 red [reported 05Aug68]
unkn		(Soviet Air Force)	14 red [reported 05Aug68]
unkn		(Soviet Air Force)	17 red [reported 05Aug68]
unkn		(Soviet Air Force)	20 red [reported 05Aug68]
unkn		(Soviet Air Force)	22 [w/o 16Dec66 Chirchik, USSR; colour of code unknown]
unkn		(Soviet Air Force)	28 red [reported Jly78]
unkn		(Soviet Air Force)	29 red [reported Jly78]
unkn		(Soviet Air Force)	30 red [reported Jly78]
unkn		(Soviet Air Force)	32 red [reported 05Aug68]
unkn		(Soviet Air Force)	33 red [reported Jly78]
unkn		(Soviet Air Force)	34 red [reported Jly78]
unkn		(Soviet Air Force)	36 red [reported 1976]
unkn		(Soviet Air Force)	39 red [reported Jly78]
unkn		(Soviet Air Force)	41 [w/o 13Apr64 in Caucasus mountains, USSR; colour of code unknown]
unkn		(Soviet Air Force)	42 red [reported 05Aug68]
unkn		(Soviet Air Force)	52 red [reported Jly78]
unkn		(Soviet Air Force)	55 red [reported Jly78]
unkn		(Soviet Air Force)	56 red [reported Jly78]
unkn		(Soviet Air Force)	57 red [reported Jly78]
unkn		(Soviet Air Force)	64 red [reported Jly78]
unkn		(Soviet Air Force)	72 red [reported 05Aug68]
unkn		(Soviet Air Force)	74 red [reported 05Aug68]
unkn		(Soviet Air Force)	75 red [reported 05Aug68]
unkn		(Soviet Air Force)	76 red [reported 05Aug68]

ANTONOV An-10

C/n	Model	Last known Owner/Operator	Identities/fates/comments (where appropriate)
?		(Antonov OKB)	CCCP-U1957 CCCP-11170(2) [first prototype ff 07Mar57; displayed 1960s/1970s Economic Achievements Exhibition, Kiev, Ukraine, USSR; possibly then to pioneer camp; fate unknown]
7 4 001 01		Samara Aviation Institute	CCCP-L5723 [fuselage preserved Samara-Smyshlyayevka, Russia; l/n Apr03]
8 40 01 02		(MAP Ramenskoye)	CCCP-L7256+ CCCP-06178 CCCP-64452 [+ not fully confirmed] [canx 20May69]
8 40 01 03		probably ex Soviet Air Force	[nothing known]
8 40 02 01		probably ex Soviet Air Force	[nothing known]
8 40 02 02		(Soviet Air Force)	CCCP-11132 [not confirmed]
8 40 02 03		(Aeroflot/Privolzhsk)	CCCP-11133 [canx 27Aug73]
8 40 03 01		(Soviet Air Force)	CCCP-11134 [fate unknown]
8 40 03 02		(Aeroflot/Ukraine)	CCCP-11135 [canx 27Aug73]
8 40 03 03		(Riga Institute of Civil Aviation)	CCCP-11136 [canx 25Mar61; to GIA Riga, Latvia, USSR; b/u]
8 40 04 01		(Aeroflot/Moldova)	CCCP-11137 [w/o 12Oct72 Kishinev, Moldova, USSR]
8 40 04 02		(Aeroflot/Ukraine)	CCCP-11138 [canx 27Aug73]
8 40 04 03		[Kiev Institute of Civil Aviation)	CCCP-11139 [ex Soviet Air Force to GIA Kiev, Ukraine, USSR; by 1979 in use as cinema in Kiev park; DBF 1993; wreck moved early summer 1994 to Zhulyany for b/u]
8 40 05 01		(Aeroflot/Ukraine)	CCCP-11140 [canx 1969]
8 40 05 02		(Aeroflot/Privolzhsk)	CCCP-11141 [canx date unknown; probably after 19Mar71]
8 40 05 03		(Aeroflot/Ukraine)	CCCP-11142 [canx 1972]
8 40 06 01	S	(Soviet Air Force)	90+ [+ colour unknown] [fate unknown]
8 40 06 02		(MAP Kharkov APO)	CCCP-11143 [canx 05Feb76; preserved in park, Kharkov, Ukraine, USSR 1976; DBF circa 1994 & b/u]
8 40 06 03		(Aeroflot)	CCCP-11144 [details not fully confirmed] [canx 25Mar61]
8 40 07 01		(Aeroflot/Privolzhsk)	CCCP-11145 [w/o 31Mar71 Voroshilovgrad, USSR; canx 1971]
8 40 07 02		(Aeroflot/Privolzhsk)	CCCP-11146 [canx 1971]
8 40 07 03		(MAP Komsomolsk-na-Amure MSZ)	CCCP-11147 [canx 17Feb71]
9 40 08 01		(Aeroflot/Ulyanovsk Higher Flying School)	CCCP-11148 [w/o 27Jan62 Batabtayevka, Ukraine, USSR; canx 29Apr60, which pre-dates w/o]
9 40 08 02		(Aeroflot/Ulyanovsk Higher Flying School)	CCCP-11149 [w/o 15May70 Kishinev, Moldova, USSR]
9 40 08 03		(Aeroflot/Ulyanovsk Higher Flying School)	CCCP-11150 [canx 27Aug73]
9 40 09 01		(Aeroflot/Far East)	CCCP-11151 [canx date unknown, but was later than Mar65]
9 40 09 02		(Aeroflot/Ukraine)	CCCP-11152 [canx 27Aug73]
9 40 09 03		(Aeroflot/Moldova)	CCCP-11153 [canx 1973]
9 40 10 01		(Aeroflot/North Kavkaz)	CCCP-11154 [canx 27Aug73; by Sep92 fuselage only at Ulyanovsk-Tsentrainly, Russia; l/n Jun02]
9 40 10 02		(Aeroflot/Ukraine)	CCCP-11155 [canx 15Jan75]
9 40 10 03		(ex Aeroflot/Ukraine)	CCCP-11156 [preserved recreation centre Burmistrovo, Novosibirsk region, Russia Aug05; l/n decaying Jan07; b/u Jly08]
9 40 11 01		(Aeroflot/Ukraine)	CCCP-11157 [canx 27Aug73]
9 40 11 02		(Aeroflot/Belarus)	CCCP-11158 [not canx from old Soviet register]
9 40 11 03		(Aeroflot/North Kavkaz)	CCCP-11159 [canx 1972]
9 40 12 01		(Aeroflot/Privolzhsk)	CCCP-11160 [canx 1976]
9 40 12 02		(Aeroflot/Moldova)	CCCP-11161 [canx 27Aug73; l/n 1981 playground in Kishinev, Moldova, USSR]
9 40 12 03		(Aeroflot/Moldova)	CCCP-11162 [canx 27Aug73]
9 40 130 1		(MAP Progress Arsenyev MSZ)	CCCP-11163 [canx 19Jan77]
9 40 13 02		(MAP Ulan Ade VPO?)	CCCP-11164 [canx date unknown; by 20Apr97 fuselage only Ulan-Ude East, Russia]
9 40 13 03		(Aeroflot/Privolzhsk)	CCCP-11165 [canx 27Aug73]
9 40 14 01		(Aeroflot/Ukraine)	CCCP-11166 [canx 27Aug73]
9 40 14 02		(Aeroflot/Ukraine)	CCCP-11167 [w/o 16Nov59 Lvov, USSR]
9 40 14 03		(ex Aeroflot/Ukraine)	CCCP-11168 [canx 27Apr62; to Krivoy Rog Aeronautical School, Ukraine, USSR as GIA; b/u]
9 40 15 01		(Aeroflot/East Siberia)	CCCP-11169 [w/o 12Oct69 Mirny, USSR; canx 1969; fuselage only still at Mirny 02Jly92]
9 40 15 02		(Aeroflot/Belarus)	CCCP-11170(1) [canx 1973]
9 40 15 03		(Aeroflot/Belarus)	CCCP-11171 [canx 27Aug73; by Aug93 stored Riga-Spilve, Latvia; b/u by Sep97]
9 40 16 01		probably ex Soviet Air Force	[nothing known]
9 40 16 02		(Aeroflot/East Siberia)	CCCP-11172 [w/o 08Aug68 Mirny, USSR; canx 1969]

ANTONOV An-10

C/n	Model	Last known Owner/Operator	Identities/fates/comments (where appropriate)
9 40 16 03		(Aeroflot/North Kavkaz)	CCCP-11173 [canx 27Aug73]
9 40 17 01		(Aeroflot/Komi)	CCCP-11174 [preserved by 1992 Economic Achievements Exhibition, Kiev, Ukraine; gone by Aug93]
9 40 17 02		(MAP – unit unknown)	CCCP-11175 [canx 20Apr76]
9 40 17 03		(MAP Kuibyshev APO)	CCCP-11176 [canx 19Jan77]
9 40 17 04		(Aeroflot/North Kavkaz)	CCCP-11177 [canx 1975]
9 40 17 05		(Aeroflot/North Kavkaz)	CCCP-11178 [canx 1975]
9 40 17 06		(Aeroflot/Ukraine)	CCCP-11179 [canx 27Aug73]
9 40 18 01		(Aeroflot/Ukraine)	CCCP-11180 [w/o 26Feb60 Lvov, USSR; canx 05Oct60]
9 40 18 02		(Aeroflot/Komi)	CCCP-11181 [canx date unknown]
9 40 18 03		(Aeroflot/Privolzhsk)	CCCP-11182 [canx date unknown; probably after Jun71]
9 40 18 04		(Aeroflot/Belarus)	CCCP-11183 [canx date unknown; photo on unknown dump in 1972]
9 40 18 05		(ex Aeroflot/Far East)	CCCP-11184 [canx 27Aug73]
0 40 18 06	TS	(Soviet Air Force)	[nothing known] [medevac version]
0 40 19 01	TS	(Soviet Air Force)	[nothing known] [medevac version]
0 40 19 02	TS	(Soviet Air Force)	[nothing known] [medevac version]
0 40 19 03	TS	(Soviet Air Force)	[nothing known] [medevac version]
0 40 19 04	VKP?	(Soviet Air Force)	(unknown) CCCP-11854? [regn not confirmed; wfu in 1970s; probably hulk at Wittstock, East Germany firing range in 1980s; l/n 1983]
0 40 19 05	A	(Soviet Navy)	[nothing known]
0 40 19 06	TS	(Soviet Air Force)	[nothing known] [medevac version]
0 40 20 01	TS	(Soviet Air Force)	[Soviet] CCCP-11120 [fate unknown]
0 40 20 02	B	(Soviet Air Force)	CCCP-11185 [fate unknown]
0 40 20 03		(Aeroflot/Ukraine)	CCCP-11186 [w/o 28Jly62 near Sochi-Adler, USSR]
0 40 20 04		(Aeroflot/Belarus)	CCCP-11187 [canx date unknown; probably after 18Jly67]
0 40 20 05		(Aeroflot/Ukraine)	CCCP-11188 [w/o 08Aug70 Kishinev, Moldova, USSR; canx 1970]
0 40 20 06		(Aeroflot/Ukraine)	CCCP-11189 [canx 27Aug73]
0 40 21 01	A	(Aeroflot/Ukraine)	CCCP-11190 [canx 27Aug73]
0 40 21 02	A	(Aeroflot/Ukraine)	CCCP-11191 [canx 27Aug73]
0 40 21 03	A	(Aeroflot/North Kavkaz)	CCCP-11192 [canx 1973]
0 40 21 04	A	(Aeroflot/North Kavkaz)	CCCP-11193 [w/o 08Feb63 Syktyvkar, USSR; canx 1963]
0 40 21 05	A	(Aeroflot/North Kavkaz)	CCCP-11194 [canx 1975]
0 40 21 06	A	(Aeroflot/Privolzhsk)	CCCP-11195 [canx 1975]
0 40 22 01	A	(MAP – unit unknown)	CCCP-11196 [fate unknown]
0 40 22 02	A	(Aeroflot/North Kavkaz)	CCCP-11197 [canx date unknown; probably after 11Jly70]
0 40 22 03	A	(MAP – unit unknown)	CCCP-11198 [canx date unknown]
0 40 22 04	A	(Aeroflot/East Siberia)	CCCP-11199 [canx 27Aug73]
0 40 22 05	A	(Aeroflot/Privolzhsk)	CCCP-11200 [canx 27Aug73; used as cinema in Kuibyshev (Samara), Russia, b/u up after fire Sep96]
0 40 22 06	A	(Aeroflot/Ukraine)	CCCP-11201 [canx 27Aug73; l/n 10Mar74 in repair facility Kharkov-Osnova, Ukraine, USSR]
0 40 23 01	A	(Aeroflot/Ukraine)	CCCP-11202 [canx date unknown; probably after 25Aug71]
0 40 23 02	A	(Aeroflot/Ukraine)	CCCP-11203 [canx 27Aug73]
0 40 23 03	A	(Aeroflot/North Kavkaz)	CCCP-11204 [canx 27Aug73; by 1976 used as cinema Rostov-na-Donu, USSR; removed 1980s & b/u]
0 40 23 04	A	(GosNII GVF)	CCCP-11205 [canx date unknown; post Aug71]
0 40 23 05	A	(Aeroflot/Privolzhsk)	CCCP-11206+ CCCP-34385^ [+ canx 27Aug73; ^ from photo, possibly a fake regn]
0 40 23 06	A	(Aeroflot/Privolzhsk)	CCCP-11207 [canx date unknown; post Feb69]
0 40 24 01	A	(Aeroflot/Syktyvkar)	CCCP-11208 [not canx from old Soviet register]
0 40 24 02	A	(Aeroflot/East Siberia)	CCCP-11209 [canx 27Aug73]
0 40 24 03	A	(MAP – unit unknown)	CCCP-11210 [canx date unknown; probably post 11Jly70]
0 40 24 04	A	(Aeroflot/North Kavkaz)	CCCP-11211 [canx 27Aug73]
0 40 24 05	A	(Aeroflot/Far East)	CCCP-11212 [canx 15May60; Jan72/1981 to Omsk Training School, USSR as GIA; 1982 or 83 displayed Mayakovski Square, Omsk; l/n 1985; b/u]
0 40 240 6	A	Central Russian Air Force Museum	CCCP-11213 [preserved Monino, USSR/Russia; l/n 04Aug08; not canx from old Soviet register]
0 40 25 01	A	(Aeroflot/Ukraine)	CCCP-11214 [canx 27Aug73]
0 40 25 02	A	(Aeroflot/Ukraine)	CCCP-11215 [w/o 18May73 near Kharkov Airport, Ukraine, USSR]
0 40 25 03	A	(Aeroflot/Ukraine)	CCCP-11216 [canx 27Aug73]
0 40 25 04	A	(Aeroflot/North Kavkaz)	CCCP-11217 [canx date unknown; probably post 28Jan71]
0 40 25 05	A	(Aeroflot)	CCCP-11218 [nothing known, possibly a military aircraft]
0 40 25 06	A	(Aeroflot/Ukraine)	CCCP-11219 [canx 27Aug73]

ANTONOV An-10

C/n	Model	Last known Owner/Operator	Identities/fates/comments (where appropriate)
0 40 26 01	A	(Aeroflot/Ukraine)	CCCP-11220 [canx 27Aug73]
0 40 26 02	A	(Aeroflot/Ukraine)	CCCP-11221 [canx 27Aug73]
0 40 26 03	A	(MAP Kiev)	CCCP-11222 [not canx from old Soviet register]
0 40 26 04	A	(Aeroflot/Moldova)	CCCP-11223 [canx date unknown; probably post 29Jly69]
0 40 26 05	A	(Aeroflot/Ukraine)	CCCP-11224 [canx 1973]
0 40 26 06	A	(Aeroflot/Ukraine)	CCCP-11225 [probably last An-10 built] [canx 27Aug73]

Production complete

Unidentified

unkn	A	(Soviet Air Force)	CCCP-11947 [wfu 1976 Tula-Klokovo, USSR; derlict on field until probably b/u in late 1990s]
unkn	VKP?	(ex Soviet Air Force)	CCCP-55501+ [+ not on old register] [preserved by Sep94 in city park Baranovichi, Belarus; b/u circa 1998]
unkn		(Soviet Air Force)	12 blue [noted in photo]
unkn		(Soviet Air Force)	14 blue [noted in photo]
unkn		(Soviet Air Force)	18 [noted in photo; colour unknown]
unkn		(Soviet Air Force)	19 blue [noted in photo]

Note: Civil (airline) operations ceased on 27Aug73 on which day, as can be seen above, several aircraft were cancelled.

ANTONOV An-12

Notes: The term "nothing known" against a c/n does not necessarily indicate that an aircraft with that c/n was actually built; but in most cases it probably was.
Within the first column "Soviet" indicates that the aircraft concerned is considered to have been operated by one of the Soviet/Russian/CIS air arms and no code or other identity, such as CCCP-xxxxx, is known.
Generally, when the first identity is given as Russian Air Force or Navy, the aircraft had been previously operated by the Soviet Air Force or Navy.
Only confirmed model designations have been included, whereas in the past model designations have been wrongly quoted in several publications. One problem has been air force variants being automatically referred to as An12BPs; this is incorrect.

Irkutsk production 1957 to 1962

C/n	Model	Last known Owner/Operator	Identities/fates/comments (where appropriate)
7 9 001 01		(Antonov OKB)	[nothing known] [ff 16Dec57] [damaged 26Jun58 Khodynka, USSR]
7 9 001 02		(Soviet Air Force)	04+ [+ colour not reported; to GIA to Irkutsk-1 with military academy; b/u]
8 9 002 01		(Soviet Air Force)	[unknown] [to GIA to Irkutsk-1 with military academy; b/u]
8 9 002 02		(Soviet Air Force)	[nothing known] [w/o 31Jan59 Vitebsk, USSR]
8 9 002 03		Central Russian Air Force Museum	04 blue+ 04 red+ [+ Soviet] [by 10Jan64 to GIA; by 17Jly83 preserved Monino, Russia]
8 9 002 04		.	[nothing known]
8 9 002 05		.	[nothing known]
8 9 003 01		.	[nothing known]
8 9 003 02		.	[nothing known]
8 9 003 03		.	[nothing known]
8 9 003 04		.	[nothing known]
8 9 003 05		(Antonov OKB)	[nothing known] [trials aircraft 1958 to Jun59; fate unknown]
8 9 004 01		.	[nothing known]
8 9 004 02		.	[nothing known]
8 9 004 03		.	[nothing known]
8 9 004 04	B	(Soviet Air Force)	23 blue [by 06Jly92 GIA at Irkutsk-1 with military academy; l/n Aug07; b/u]
8 9 004 05		.	[nothing known]
8 9 005 01		.	[nothing known] [trials aircraft]
8 9 005 02		.	[nothing known]
8 9 005 03		(Soviet Air Force)	27 blue [by 04Jly04 GIA at Irkutsk-1 with military academy; l/n Aug07]
8 9 005 04		.	[nothing known]
8 9 005 05		.	[nothing known]
8 9 006 01		.	[nothing known]
8 9 006 02		.	[nothing known]
8 9 006 03		.	[nothing known]
8 9 006 04		(Polyarnaya Aviatsiya)	CCCP-04331 [w/o Apr62]
8 9 006 05		(Polyarnaya Aviatsiya)	CCCP-04343 [w/o 14Jan67 Novosibirsk-Tolmachevo, USSR]
8 9 006 06		(Soviet Air Force)	[not known] CCCP-29104+ [w/o 21Nov59 near Belaya, USSR; +regd 18Jly74 with MOMS Omsk; canx 18Jly74; might not be this aircraft]
8 9 006 07		.	[nothing known]
8 9 006 08		(MAP Moscow OAO)	CCCP-11528(1) [canx 16Mar81; fate/status unknown]
8 9 006 09		.	[nothing known]
8 9 006 10		.	[nothing known]
8 9 007 01		ex Soviet Air Force	14 red [status unknown]
8 9 007 02		.	[nothing known]
8 9 007 03		.	[nothing known]
8 9 007 04	BP	(Aviaobshchemash)	CCCP-11795(2) RA-11795 [canx 27Dec95; fate/status unknown]
8 9 007 05		.	[nothing known]
9 9 007 06		(MAP Zhukovski)	CCCP-48114 [canx 18Dec89; fate/status unknown]
9 9 007 07		(MAP Moscow OAO)	CCCP-48108 [canx 26Jan89; wfu by Apr89 Moscow-Domodedovo, USSR; probably b/u]
9 9 007 08		(MAP Omsk APO)	CCCP-11529(1) [canx 28Aug78; fate/status unknown]
9 9 007 09		.	[nothing known]
9 9 007 10		.	[nothing known]
9 9 008 01		.	[nothing known]
9 9 008 02		.	[nothing known]
9 9 008 03		.	[nothing known]
9 9 008 04		(Soviet Air Force)	CCCP-11664 [wfu by Aug93 Kirovograd-Khmelyovoye, Ukraine; l/n Jly99]
9 9 008 05		ex Soviet Air Force	CCCP-11680 [status unknown]
9 9 008 06		.	[nothing known]
9 9 008 07		.	[nothing known]

ANTONOV An-12

C/n	Model	Last known Owner/Operator	Identities/fates/comments (where appropriate)
9 9 008 08		.	[nothing known]
9 9 008 09		.	[nothing known]
9 9 008 10		.	[nothing known]
9 9 009 01		.	[nothing known]
9 9 009 02	LL	(Soviet Air Force)	(unknown) [dbr and later wfu by May93 Mahlwinkel, Germany; b/u1995]
9 9 009 03		.	[nothing known]
9 9 009 04		ex Soviet Air Force	CCCP-72607 [status unknown]
9 9 009 05		ex Soviet Air Force	33 [code colour not reported; might be preserved in museum]
9 9 009 06		ex Soviet Air Force	45 [code not confirmed; status unknown]
9 9 009 07	A	(MAP Irkutsk APO)	CCCP-48977 [canx 24Oct89; fate/status unknown]
9 9 009 08		ex Soviet Air Force	CCCP-79164 [status unknown]
9 9 009 09		(Soviet Air Force)	34 red [derelict by 10May98 Vinnytsa-Gavrishovka, Ukraine; l/n 28Jun99]
9 9 009 10		.	[nothing known]
9 9 010 01		.	[nothing known]
9 9 010 02		.	[nothing known]
9 9 010 03		.	[nothing known]
9 9 010 04		.	[nothing known]
9 9 010 05		.	[nothing known]
9 9 010 06		(MAP Kuibyshev APO)	CCCP-11650(1) [canx 26Jan90; fate/status unknown]
9 9 010 07	UD	(Antonov OKB)	[nothing known] [prototype of long range version; status/fate unknown]
9 9 010 08	A	ex Soviet Air Force	61 blue [status/fate unknown]
9 9 010 09		.	[nothing known]
9 9 010 10	B	(Soviet Air Force)	CCCP-04362 05 red [by Mar97 GIA Chortkov Technical School, Ukraine; b/u Jun99]
9 9 011 01		(MOM Omsk)	CCCP-98116 [canx 18Nov88; fate/status unknown]
9 9 011 02		.	[nothing known]
9 9 011 03	BP	ex Soviet Air Force	09 red [wfu by Jly93 Kirovograd-Khmelyovoye, Ukraine; l/n May02]
9 9 011 04		(MAP Irkutsk APO)	CCCP-48972 [canx 18Jly88]
9 9 011 05		(Soviet Air Force)	CCCP-11384 [canx date unknown; but pre Feb98]
9 9 011 06		.	[nothing known]
9 9 011 07	12B	(Polyarnaya Aviatsiya)	CCCP-04373 [by 11Sep3 burnt on St. Petersburg-Pulkovo, USSR dump]
9 9 011 08		ex Soviet Air Force	36 blue [preserved Vysoke, Ukraine; noted Aug10]
9 9 011 09	BP	(Soviet Air Force)	09 red [fate/status unknown]
9 9 011 10		.	[nothing known]
9 9 012 01		.	[nothing known]
9 9 012 02		.	[nothing known]
9 9 012 03		.	[nothing known]
9 9 012 04		.	[nothing known]
9 9 012 05		.	[nothing known]
9 9 012 06		(MAP Omsk Motors)	CCCP-98115 [canx 18Apr89; by Jly93 fuselage only Omsk-Fyodorovka, Russia; l/n Jun94]
. 9 012 07		(Soviet Air Force)	[not known] [w/o 19Mar66 Tyumen, USSR; used as GIA at unknown location]
. 9 012 08		.	[nothing known]
0 9 012 09		(Soviet Air Force)	64 red [by 14Feb93 on Sperenberg, Germany dump partly b/u; l/n Sep93]
0 9 012 10		.	[nothing known]
0 9 013 01	B	(Soviet Air Force)	CCCP-98119(1) 16 red [dumped by Aug93 Omsk-Fyodorovka, Russia]
0 9 013 02		.	[nothing known]
0 9 013 03		.	[nothing known]
0 9 013 04		ex Lasare Air	[Soviet] 4L-11304 EK-11304 4L-11304 EK-11304 [l/n 05Sep03 Tbilisi-Lochini, Georgia reported grounded; later report at Dubai as EK-11304 considered mis-sighting]
0 9 013 05		.	
0 9 013 06		ex Aero Fret Business	[Soviet] ER-ACL TN-AHA+ [+ reported in documents as TN-AGY but c/n checked as here; l/n 31Jly06 Dzhankoi, Ukraine, reported non-airworthy]
0 9 013 07		.	[nothing known]
0 9 013 08		(Soviet Air Force)	CCCP-04363 01 blue [by Mar97 GIA Chortkov Technical School, Ukraine; b/u by Jun99]
0 9 013 09		(Polyarnaya Aviatsiya)	CCCP-04364 [w/o Apr62 location unknown]
0 9 013 10		.	[nothing known]
0 9 014 01		(Soviet Air Force)	28 red [fate/status unknown]
0 9 014 02		.	[nothing known]
0 9 014 03		.	[nothing known]

ANTONOV An-12

C/n	Model	Last known Owner/Operator	Identities/fates/comments (where appropriate)
0 9 014 04	AP	(Antonov Airlines)	88 red+ UR-21510 [l+ Soviet; l/n 08Jun06 Gostomel, Ukraine; canx 01Oct08]
0 9 014 05		(Soviet Air Force)	CCCP-11822 [l/n wfu 13May95 Yakutsk, Russia]
0 9 014 06		(Soviet Air Force)	[not known] [w/o 23Dec62 nr Norisk-Nezhdanny, USSR; remains still present Jly07]
0 9 014 07		(Soviet Air Force)	87 blue [fate/status unknown]
0 9 014 08		.	[nothing known]
0 9 014 09	P	(Scorpion Air)	CCCP-12777 CCCP-11322 EW-11322 UR-11322 LZ-MNN UR-BYW LZ-MNN [wfu by Aug11 Sofia, Bulgaria; b/u 14Sep11]
9 014 10		.	[nothing known]
9 015 01		.	[nothing known]
. 9 015 02		.	[nothing known]
. 9 015 03		.	[nothing known]
. 9 015 04		.	[nothing known]
. 9 015 05		.	[nothing known]
. 9 015 06		.	[nothing known]
1 9 015 07		ex Russian Air Force	92 red [fate/status unknown]
1 9 015 08		.	[nothing known]
1 9 015 09		.	[nothing known]
1 9 015 10	TP-2	(Polyarnaya Aviatsiya)	CCCP-04366 [w/o 04Jun67 Blagoveshchensk, USSR]
1 9 016 01		.	[nothing known]
1 9 016 02		.	[nothing known]
1 9 016 03		.	[nothing known]
1 9 016 04		.	[nothing known]
1 9 016 05		.	[nothing known]
1 9 016 06		.	[nothing known]
1 9 016 07		.	[nothing known]
1 9 016 08	A	(Soviet Air Force)	06 red [fate/status unknown]
1 9 016 09		.	[nothing known]
1 9 016 10		.	[nothing known]
1 9 017 01		.	[nothing known]
1 9 017 02		(Soviet Air Force)	41 red [by 14Mar97 GIA Chortkov Technical School, Ukraine; l/n 30Jun99 being b/u]
1 9 017 03	B	(Polyarnaya Aviatsiya)	CCCP-04365 [fate unknown]
1 9 017 04		.	[nothing known]
1 9 017 05		.	[nothing known]
1 9 017 06	P	ex Air Cess	CCCP-98101 RA-98101 D2-FVD EL-AKN 3D-SKN 3C-KKO [l/n 15Dec98 Sharijah, UAE; fate/status unknown]
1 9 017 07		.	[nothing known]
1 9 017 08		(MAP Komsomolsk na Amure APO)	CCCP-69321 [w/o en-route 25Sep85 31km from Kharkov-Osnova, USSR; canx 12Jan87]
1 9 017 09		(Soviet Air Force)	84 red [c/n not confirmed] [by 06Jly94 GIA Chortkov Technical School, Ukraine; later b/u]
1 9 017 10		.	[nothing known]
1 9 018 01			[nothing known]
1 9 018 02		.	[nothing known]
1 9 018 03		.	[nothing known]
1 9 018 04		(Soviet Air Force)	85 red [by 06Jly94 GIA Chortkov Technical School, Ukraine; l/n 18Aug97; later b/u]
1 9 018 05		.	[nothing known]
1 9 018 06		.	[nothing known]
1 9 018 07	AP	Russian Air Force	CCCP-12186 RA-12186 [l/n 01Sep01 Pushkin, Russia]
1 9 018 08		.	[nothing known]
1 9 018 09		(Soviet Air Force)	81 red [by 06Jly94 GIA Chortkov Technical School, Ukraine; l/n 09May98; later b/u]
9 018 10		.	[nothing known]
2 9 019 01		ex Soviet Air Force	82 red [by Sep03 in use as club house, Keila, Estonia]
2 9 019 02		.	[nothing known]
2 9 019 03		.	[nothing known]
2 9 019 04		.	[nothing known]
2 9 019 05		unknown	[nothing known]

ANTONOV An-12

C/n	Model	Last known Owner/Operator	Identities/fates/comments (where appropriate)
Irkutsk export production – c/ns unknown but export numbers quoted			
02 4 001		(Indian Air Force)	BL532 [b/u post Feb73]
02 4 002		(Indian Air Force)	BL533 [w/o unknown date & location]
02 4 003		(Indian Air Force)	BL534 [w/o 07Feb68 Chandra Bagga hill range, Northern Himachal Pradesh, India]
02 4 004		(Indian Air Force)	BL535 [b/u; no details]
02 4 005		(Indian Air Force)	BL536 [w/o 05Aug61 Chandigarh, India]
02 4 006		(Indian Air Force)	BL537 [b/u no details]
02 4 007		(Indian Air Force)	BL538 [code Q] [b/u; no details]
02 4 008		(Indian Air Force)	BL539 [b/u no details]
02 4 009		(ex Ghana Airways)	CCCP-75622+ 9G-AAZ CCCP- [+ not confirmed] [returned to USSR 1963]
02 4 010		(Iraqi Air Force)	505 [fate/status unknown]
02 4 011		(Iraqi Air Force)	506 [fuselage only dumped by Sep03 Baghdad-International Airport, Iraq]
02 4 012		(Iraqi Air Force)	507 [fuselage only dumped by Sep03 Baghdad-International Airport, Iraq]
Voronezh production 1961 to 1965			
1 4 001 01	AP	(El Magal Aviation)	CCCP-48975 UR-48975 ST-SIG [w/o 12May04 Dalam, Sudan]
1 4 001 02		.	[nothing known]
1 4 001 03	AP	(MAP Omsk APO)	CCCP-11795(1) [w/o 25Mar86 Omsk-Severny, USSR; canx 07Jly87]
1 4 001 04		(Aviaobshchemash)	CCCP-11327 RA-11327 [DBR 08Nov97 Bryansk, Russia]
1 4 001 05		.	[nothing known]
1 4 001 06	AP	(United Arabian Airlines)	CCCP-12188+ RA-12188 ST-AQE [+ reg not confirmed] [w/o 24Feb07 El Geneina, Sudan; b/u Apr07; remains still present Jly07]
1 4 002 01		Alfa 92 Aviakomp.	[Soviet] RA-11311
1 4 002 02		.	[nothing known]
1 4 002 03		(Soviet Navy)	33 yellow [fate/status unknown]
1 4 002 04		(Indonesian Air Force)	T-120x [not confirmed; fate/status unknown; see unknown listing]
1 4 002 05		(Indonesian Air Force)	T-120x [not confirmed; fate/status unknown; see unknown listing]
1 4 002 06		.	[nothing known]
1 4 002 07		.	[nothing known]
1 4 002 08		(Soviet Air Force)	50 red [not confirmed; c/n hard to read; but were there 8 in this batch?; by 06Jly92 at Irkutsk-1 with military academy; l/n Aug07]
1 4 003 01		Ukraine Air Force	83 red+ 83 blue [+ Soviet]
1 4 003 02	A?	(Aero-Nika)	T-120x+ RA-11790 [+ probably either T-1203/PK-PUC or T-1205/PK-PUE Indonesian AF] [w/o 29Oct94 Ust-Ilimsk, Russia; canx 18Sep97]
1 4 003 03		(Indonesian Air Force)	T-120x [not confirmed; wfu 1970; see unknown listing]
1 4 003 04		Ukraine Air Force	[Soviet] 23 blue
1 4 003 05		Russian Navy	36 yellow
1 4 003 06		.	[nothing known]
2 4 004 01	A	Russian Air Force	02 15 yellow+ [+ not confirmed; considered to be "02" repainted; preserved by 2004 Engels AFB Museum, Russia; l/n Jly06]
2 4 004 02		.	[nothing known]
2 4 004 03			[nothing known] [by May96 derelict Chardzhou, Turkmenistan]
2 4 004 04		.	[nothing known]
2 4 004 05	AP	(Soviet Navy)	35 yellow [b/u between Aug99/Aug02 Moscow-Ostafyevo, Russia]
2 4 004 06	B	(MAP Kuibyshev APO)	CCCP-06155 CCCP-11011 [canx 15May91; fate/status unknown]
2 4 005 01	AP	(Russian Navy)	34 yellow
2 4 005 02	BP	ex 748 Air Services	CCCP-48970 RA-48970 LZ-BFC RA-48970 9L-LFQ [dbr 01Nov06 Lokichoggio, Kenya & stored; canx 08Apr08; l/n May08]
2 4 005 03		(Aeroflot/Polar)	CCCP-11337(1) [w/o 11Sep65 Ulan-Ude-Mukhino, USSR]
2 4 005 04		(Aeroflot/Polar)	CCCP-11338(1) [w/o 02Apr63 Magadan, USSR; canx 03Aug63]
2 4 005 05		Samara Aviation Institute	CCCP-11339(1) [canx 1976; by Apr93 preserved Samara-Smyshlyayevka, Russia; l/n May07]
2 4 005 06		(Russian Navy)	32 yellow [b/u by Mar01 Moscow-Ostafyevo, Russia]
2 4 006 01		Russian Air Force	31 yellow
2 4 006 02	AP	Russian Air Force	47 red [stored by Jly00 Moscow-Ostafyevo, Russia; reported for preservation]
2 4 006 03		.	[nothing known]
2 4 006 04		(Russian Navy)	29 yellow [wfu by 09Jly00; b/u by Mar01 Moscow-Ostafyevo, Russia]
2 4 006 05		.	[nothing known]
2 4 006 06		.	[nothing known]

ANTONOV An-12

C/n	Model	Last known Owner/Operator	Identities/fates/comments (where appropriate)
2 4 007 01		Air Magal	CCCP-11308+ RA-11308 ST-APJ [+ regn assumed]
2 4 007 02	B	DR of Congo Air Force	CCCP-11131 RA-11131 XU-315 9Q-CZD+ [+ not confirmed; in 2008 register without c/n]
2 4 007 03		(Russian Air Force)	CCCP-11965 RA-11965 [canx unknown date; b/u by 2006 Ivanovo-Severny, Russia]
2 4 007 04		.	[nothing known]
2 4 007 05	A	(Aeroflot/East Siberia)	CCCP-11386 [canx 1976; fate/status unknown]
2 4 007 06		.	
2 4 008 01	BP	Russian Air Force?	10 blue RA-13363
2 4 008 02	AP	Africa West Cargo	CCCP-06175 02 blue+ 02 blue^ 11326 UR-11326 S9-DBA [+ Soviet Air Force; ^Ukraine Air Force]
2 4 008 03		.	[nothing known]
2 4 008 04		.	[nothing known]
2 4 008 05		.	[nothing known]
2 4 008 06	B	TAPC Aviatrans	CCCP-11804(1) UK-11804 [canx from register; wfu by 28Mar09 Tashkent-Tuzel AFB, Uzbekistan]
2 4 009 01		(Wimbi Dira Airways)	CCCP-11916 RA-11916 9Q-CWC [w/o 04Oct05 Aru, Democratic Republic of Congo]
2 4 009 02		.	[nothing known]
2 4 009 03		.	[nothing known]
2 4 009 04		.	[nothing known]
2 4 009 05	TA	Russian Air Force	20 blue
2 4 009 06		.	[nothing known]
2 4 010 01		.	[nothing known]
2 4 010 02		.	[nothing known]
2 4 010 03	AP	(Soviet Air Force)	(unknown) [w/o 26May72 near Panevezys, Lithunania, USSR]
2 4 010 04	TA	(Aeroflot/North Kavkaz)	CCCP-11385 [canx 1977; fate/status unknown]
2 4 010 05		.	[nothing known]
2 4 010 06	BP	Russian Air Force	11 blue
2 4 011 01		.	[nothing known]
2 4 011 02		.	[nothing known]
2 4 011 03	BP	(Azerbaijan Air Force)	[Soviet] 4K-12425 [canx between Dec00 and Dec02; fate/status unknown]
2 4 011 04		.	[nothing known]
2 4 011 05	AP	Veteran Airlines	[Soviet] UR-PAS
2 4 011 06		.	[nothing known]
2 4 012 01		.	[nothing known]
2 4 012 02		.	[nothing known]
2 4 012 03		.	[nothing known]
2 4 012 04	A	(Indian Air Force)	BL726 [code S] [broken up]
2 4 012 05	A	Indian Air Force Museum	BL727 [code G] [preserved Palam AFB, Delhi, India; l/n Dec10]
2 4 012 06	A	(Indian Air Force)	BL728 [broken up]
2 4 013 01	A	(Indian Air Force)	BL729 [w/o details unknown]
2 4 013 02	A	(Indian Air Force)	BL730 [broken up]
2 4 013 03	A	(Indian Air Force)	BL731 [codes U, later Z, later Q] [broken up]
2 4 013 04	A	(Indian Air Force)	BL732 [wfu early 1993]
2 4 013 05	A	(Indian Air Force)	BL733 [w/o; details unknown]
2 4 013 06	A	(Indian Air Force)	BL734 [w/o 16Jly63 Delhi-Palam, India]
2 4 014 01	A	(Indian Air Force)	BL735 [broken up]
2 4 014 02	A	(Indian Air Force)	BL736 [codes N, later U] [broken up]
2 4 014 03	A	(Indian Air Force)	BL737 [code B] [w/o details unknown]
2 4 014 04	A	(Indian Air Force)	BL738 [code C] [broken up]
2 4 014 05	A	(Indian Air Force)	BL739 [codes D; call sign VU-FPG] [broken up]
2 4 014 06	A	(Indian Air Force)	BL740 [code L; not confirmed] [w/o details unknown]
2 4 015 01	A	(Indian Air Force)	BL741 [codes Q; later G] [broken up]
2 4 015 02	A	(Indian Air Force)	BL742 [codes E; later T] [broken up]
2 4 015 03	A	(Indian Air Force)	BL743 [wfu early 1993]
4 015 04	A	(Cubana)	CU-T827 [w/o 09Feb67 Mexico City International, Mexico]
2 4 015 05	A	(Indian Air Force)	BL914 [codes M later Z; call sign VU-PGH] [broken up]
2 4 015 06	A	(Indian Air Force)	BL915 [code R] [broken up]
4 016 01	A	(Indian Air Force)	BL916 [broken up]
4 016 02	A	(Indian Air Force)	BL917 [fate unknown]
4 016 03	A	(Indian Air Force)	BL918 [w/o 16Aug71 near Ahmednagar, Pune, India]

ANTONOV An-12

C/n	Model	Last known Owner/Operator	Identities/fates/comments (where appropriate)
4 016 04		(Yemen Air Force)	7O-AAW [not confirmed; fate unknown]
4 016 05	BP	Veteran Airlines	CCCP-11766 RA-11766 UR-CDB
4 016 06	12	(Tyumen Airlines)	CCCP-11973 RA-11973 [possibly wfu Tyumen-Roshchino, Russia; canx 25Jun97]
4 017 01	TB	(Aeroflot/Polar)	CCCP-11340(1) [canx 1976; fate/status unknown]
4 017 02	BP	(Aeroflot/Polar)	CCCP-11341(1) [w/o 17Feb73 Amderma, USSR]
4 017 03	TB	(Aeroflot/Ukraine)	CCCP-11342(1) [canx 1977; fate/status unknown]
4 017 04	BP	ex Russian Air Force	CCCP-11864 RA-11864 [l/n 21Aug07 no engines Novosibirsk-Tolmachovo, Russia]
4 017 05	BP	(Antonov Design Bureau)	CCCP-11765 UR-11765 LZ-SFM UR-11765 [w/o 05Sep04 Kiev-Borispol, Ukraine; b/u by Jun05; remains l/n Aug06; canx 01Oct08]
4 017 06	TB	(Aeroflot/Ukraine)	CCCP-11343(1) [canx 1976; fate/status unknown]
4 017 07	B	ex Aeroflot/North Kavkaz	CCCP-11344(1) [canx 1977; by Jly96 to GIA Krivoy Rog Technical School, Ukraine; l/n Aug08]
4 017 08		SP Air	CCCP-11415 RA-11415
4 017 09		(Soviet Air Force)	CCCP-11865 [CofA canx 01Jun81; derelict by 13May95 Norilsk-Borki, Russia]
4 017 10	BP	ex Sakha Avia	CCCP-11884 RA-11884 [derelict by 26Jun12 Yakutsk, Russia]
4 017 11	BP	(Alada)	CCCP-11421 11421 RA-11421 D2-FBJ [l/n 15Mar01 Luanda, Angola; not in Jan02 fleet list; fate unknown]
4 017 12	BP	(Aeroflot/Yakutsk)	CCCP-11418(1) [w/o 04Oct88 near Deputatski, USSR]
4 018 01	TB	ex S Group Aviation	CCCP-11345 EK-12001 RA-11345 LZ-SFR UN-11012 YU-UIE EX-152 [stored by 16Mar08 Fujairah, UAE; l/n 17Oct09 probably wfu]
4 018 02		Ethiopian Air Force	CCCP-11346 1502
4 018 03	B	(Aeroflot/East Siberia)	CCCP-11347 [w/o 07Dec63 Kirensk, USSR; canx 18Sep64]
4 018 04	B	(Aeroflot/North Kavkaz)	CCCP-11348 [canx 1977; fate/status unknown]
4 018 05	B	(Aeroflot/East Siberia)	CCCP-11349 [w/o 02Nov68 16km from Lensk, USSR; canx 08Dec68]
4 018 06	TB	(Aeroflot/Magadan)	CCCP-11983 [wfu by 1992 Bratsk, USSR; canx by Feb98, date unknown]
4 018 07	BP	(Soviet Air Force)	CCCP-11425 [canx unknown date; fate/status unknown]
4 018 08	B	(Aeroflot/East Siberia)	CCCP-11350 RA-11350 [derelict by May95 Irkutsk-1, Russia; canx 19Sep95]
4 018 09	B	(Aeroflot/Privolzhsk)	CCCP-11351 [canx 1976; by May98 GIA Slavyansk Technical School, Ukraine; l/n Apr99]
4 018 10	TB	(Aeroflot/East Siberia)	CCCP-11352 [canx 1977; fate/status unknown]
4 018 11	TB	(Aeroflot/East Siberia)	CCCP-11353 [canx 1977; fate/status unknown]
4 018 12	B	(Sakha Avia)	CCCP-11354 RA-11354 [not in 2000 Fleet list; derelict by Aug03 Yakutsk, Russia; l/n Jly04]
4 019 01	TB	ex Air Highnesses	CCCP-11986 RA-11986 D2-FCV S9-CDB EX-160 S9-SAJ EK-11986 [canx Sep11; donated to Minsk-Borovaya Aviation Museum]
4 019 02		(Soviet Air Force)	CCCP-12107 [CofA canx 01Jun81; fate/status unknown]
4 019 03		(Russian Air Force)	CCCP-12103 RA-12013 [wfu 1998; by Jun99 derelict Ivanovo-Severny, Russia; canx 16Oct01; b/u by 2006]
4 019 04		(Soviet Air Force)	CCCP-12106 [fate/status unknown]
4 019 05	TB	unknown	CCCP-11863 RA-11863 [canx 25Feb99 to Congo; l/n 05Apr99 Sharjah, UAE; status/fate unknown]
4 019 06	BP	(Sakha Avia)	CCCP-11403 RA-11403 [w/o 24Feb96 near Omsk-Fyodorovo Airport, Russia; canx 18Jun96]
4 019 07	BP	(Azza Air Transport)	CCCP-11234 ST-AQG [canx before Jan07; status/fate unknown]
4 019 08	12	(ACA Air Ancargo)	CCCP-12108(1) 16 red+ RA-11318 D2-FVG(2) TN-AFJ [+ Soviet; disappeared 27Dec98 en-route Luanda to Lucapa, Angola; possibly shot down by missile]
4 019 09	BP	Siberian Aviation Research Institute	[Soviet AF+] CCCP-11767 RA-11767 11767^ [+ code unknown; ^ Russia no prefix]
4 019 10	BP	(Norilsk Avia)	CCCP-11989 RA-11989 [by 07Apr06 fuselage only Norilsk-Alykel, Russia; canx 30Jun97]
4 019 11	12	ex Russian Air Force	CCCP-11227 RA-11227 [canx unknown date; by 18Jly06 preserved Baikonur-Kraini, Kazakhstan]
4 019 12	BP	Avial	CCCP-12121 RA-12121 RA-11372 3X-GDM EX-098 EW-252TI (ER-ACX) EW-252TI RA-11372
4 020 01	BP	(ATMA/InterIsland Airlines)	CCCP-11976(1) LZ-BAE LZ-VEF RDPL-34156 UP-AN216 [w/o 21Apr10 en-route Barangay Laput, Mexico to Pampanga, Philippines]
4 020 02	BP	Avialeasing/SRX Transcontinental	CCCP-12122 RA-12122(1) RA-11373 UK-12002
4 020 03	TB	(Aviaobshchemash)	CCCP-11851 11851 RA-11851 [damaged 01Nov06 Nizhnevartovsk, Russia]
4 020 04	BP	(Soviet Air Force)	CCCP-12123 [canx unknown date by Feb98; fate/status unknown]
4 020 05	BP	ex Soviet Air Force	CCCP-11985 [by Apr93 preserved school Aktyubinsk, Kazakhstan; l/n Jan03]

ANTONOV An-12

C/n	Model	Last known Owner/Operator	Identities/fates/comments (where appropriate)
4 020 06	BP	(Trans Air Congo)	63+ CCCP-11991 RA-11991 LZ-ASY TN-AGK(2) [+ Soviet] [w/o 21Mar11 near Pointe Noire Airport, People's Republic of Congo]
4 020 07	TB	Angolan Air Charter	CCCP-11532 ER-ADB T-306+ D2-MBE^ [+ used call sign D2-MBE; ^ also see aircraft with unknown c/n]
4 020 08	BP	Russian Air Force	[not known] [fate/status unknown]
4 020 09	B	Russian Navy	28 yellow [fate/status unknown]
4 020 10	BP	ex Azza Air Transport	12 yellow+ RA-11374 ST-ASA^ [+ Russian Navy] [^ by 14Oct10 marks painted out Khartoum, Sudan]
4 020 11		.	[nothing known]
4 020 12	BP	(Soviet Air Force)	CCCP-11396 [CofA canx 01Jun81; fate/status unknown]
4 021 01		.	[nothing known]
4 021 02		(Sarit Airlines)	CCCP-11241 RA-11241 4L-11241 4L-CAA ST-SAR [w/o 24Sep03 Wau, Sudan; hulk l/n Apr07]
4 021 03		(Soviet Air Force)	CCCP-12117 [fate/status unknown]
4 021 04		(Soviet Air Force)	CCCP-11411 [CofA canx 01Jun81; fate/status unknown]
4 021 05	BP	(Russian Air Force)	CCCP-11254 21 red [fate/status unknown]
4 021 06		.	[nothing known]
4 021 07	BP	(Soviet Air Force)	CCCP-11265(1) [fate/status unknown]
4 021 08	TBP	(Santa Cruz Imperial)	CCCP-12116 RA-12116 EL-ALB [b/u by early/mid 2000 Sharjah, UAE]
4 021 09	TBP	(North-East Cargo)	CCCP-12119 RA-12119 [canx 04Nov97; fate/status unknown]
4 021 10	BP	(Soviet Air Force)	CCCP-12112 [canx 21Nov83; fate/status unknown]
4 021 11	BP	ex Natalco Air Lines	CCCP-11236 RA-11236 S9-BAN TN-AGQ [wfu by Oct04 Pointe Noire, People's Republic of Congo; l/n 12Nov09]
4 021 12		(Santa Cruz Imperial)	"3D-ALB" "EL-ASJ" [history obscure; in Swaziland register as exported; no reports; could be connected with c/n 4 021 08]
4 022 01		.	[nothing known]
4 022 02		.	[nothing known]
4 022 03		.	[nothing known]
4 022 04		.	[nothing known]
4 022 05		.	[nothing known]
4 022 06		.	[nothing known]
4 022 07	BP	(Soviet Air Force)	8256 [test bed aircraft]
4 022 08	BP	Russian Navy	33 yellow
4 022 09		.	[nothing known]
4 022 10	BK	(Air Mapeko)	CCCP-83962 RA-83962 D2-FBK [missing 26Oct98 en-route Nzaji and Luana, Angola]
4 022 11	BP	(Ukraine Cargo Airways)	[not known] UR-11300 UR-UDN [canx 01Oct08; wfu by 18Sep09 no engines Yevpatoriya, Ukraine]
4 022 12	BP	Kazakhstan Air Force	12 red+ 12 red [+ Soviet]
4 023 01		(Sakhalin)	CCCP-98117 RA-98117 [wfu by Apr04 Moscow-Domodedovo, Russia; l/n Oct08]
4 023 02	BP	(Egyptian Air Force)	1216//SU-AOJ [dual marks] [later reported as 1216//SU-AOS which is unlikely] [fate/status unknown]
4 023 03	BP	(Egyptian Air Force)	1217+ [+ not confirmed; reported destroyed Jun67 by Israeli AF]
4 023 04	BP	(Egyptian Air Force)	1218+ [+ not confirmed; reported destroyed Jun67 by Israeli AF]
4 023 05	BP	(Egyptian Air Force)	1219//SU-AOI [dual marks] [later reported as 1219//SU-AOT which is possible] [fate/status unknown]
4 023 06	BP	(Egyptian Air Force)	1220//SU-AOR [dual marks] [reported b/u; must have been later than Dec76]
4 023 07			[nothing known]
4 023 08	BP	(Egyptian Air Force)	1222//SU-AOJ 1222//SU-APB [dual marks] [reported b/u; must have been later than Aug74]
4 023 09	BP	(Egyptian Air Force)	1223 1223//SU-AOS [dual marks] [reported b/u; must have been later than Oct93]
4 023 10	TB	(Aeroflot/Privolzhsk)	CCCP-11368 [canx 1977; fate/status unknown]
4 023 11	TB	(Aeroflot/Moscow)	CCCP-11369 [canx 1978; fate/status unknown]
4 023 12	TB	(Aeroflot/Ukraine)	CCCP-11370(1) [reported as 1221//SU-AOZ incorrect] [canx 1977; fate/status unknown]
4 024 01	TB	(Aeroflot/Privolzhsk)	CCCP-11371 [canx 1976; fate/status unknown]
4 024 02	TB	(Aeroflot/Moscow)	CCCP-11372 [canx 1977; fate/status unknown]
4 024 03	TB	(Aeroflot/Moscow)	CCCP-11373 [canx 1978; reported preserved until 1987 when hulk dumped Yakutsk, Russia; l/n Jun08]
4 024 04	B	(Aeroflot/Komi)	CCCP-11374 [w/o 16Feb71 Vorkuta, USSR; canx 1971]

ANTONOV An-12

C/n	Model	Last known Owner/Operator	Identities/fates/comments (where appropriate)
4 024 05	TB	(Komiinteravia)	CCCP-11375 RA-11375 [w/o 20Aug93 near Slavograd Airport, Russia]
4 024 06	TB	(Aeroflot/Polar)	CCCP-11376 [w/o 13Nov69 15km from Anderma, USSR; canx 1970]
4 024 07	TB	(Aeroflot/Yakutsk)	CCCP-11377(1) [w/o 08Sep69 Amderma, Russia, USSR when hit by Tu-128 c/n 5035504; canx 11Feb70]
4 024 08	B	ex British Gulf International	CCCP-11768(1) LZ-BAF LZ-BRP S9-SAE EW-291TI EK-12408 [canx 10Jun11 fate/status unknown, but still active]
4 024 09	BP	(Russian Air Force)	[not known] 28 red [c/n sometimes reported as being 44 024 09] [wfu by 09Jan04 Ulyanovsk-Vostochniy/East; 09Feb09 for sale as scrap]
4 024 10	BP	Meridian	CCCP-11959 RA-11959 LZ-RAA LZ-VEE ER-ADQ EW-265TI UR-CGW
4 024 11		(Soviet Air Force)	CCCP-12114 [derelict by Apr94 Asmara, Eritrea; fuselage l/n Jun06 Asmara Expo Park, Eritrea]
4 024 12	BP	(Soviet Air Force)	CCCP-11866 [fate/status unknown]
4 025 01	BP	SirAero	[Soviet] CCCP-11892 RA-11892
4 025 02		(MAP Kiev MSZ)	CCCP-29110 [test aircraft] [w/o 12Dec90 12 km from Kiev-Borispol, Ukraine, USSR]
4 025 03		(Soviet Air Force)	[Soviet] [w/o 23Jun69 en-route Kedainiai to Ryazan, USSR, collided with IL-14M CCCP-52018]
4 025 04	B	Avioleasing/SRX Transcontinental	CCCP-11996 RA-11996 UK-11418(2)
4 025 05	BP	(Russian Air Force)	CCCP-12124 RA-12124(1) [derelict by 15Aug02 Chkalovsky, Russia; l/n 13Aug12]
4 025 06	BP	(Russian Air Force)	CCCP-12125 15 red [reported wfu]
4 025 07	B	(Russian Air Force)	CCCP-12126 RA-12126 [wfu by 14Aug06 Chkalovsky, Russia; l/n 08Sep08]
4 025 08		(Kazakhstan Air Force)	CCCP-11395 UN-11395 [b/u by Jun97 Alamty, Kazakhstan]
4 025 09	BP	(Russian Air Force)	CCCP-12101 RA-12101 [wfu 1998 Ivanovo-Severny, Russia; canx 16Oct01; b/u by 2006]
4 025 10	B	Russian Air Force	[not known] 18 red
4 025 11		Russian Air Force	[not known] 35 red
4 025 12	BP	Russian Air Force	15 yellow
4 026 01	B	(Imtrec Aviation)	CCCP-11899 RA-11899 XU-365(2) [w/o 17Oct07 25km from Phnom Penh, Cambodia en-route to Singapore]
4 026 02	BP	(Russian Air Force)	CCCP-11894 RA-11894 [wfu by 21Aug99 Kubinka, Russia]
4 026 03		.	[nothing known]
4 026 04		(Zenith Air)	CCCP-11992 RA-11992 [canx 02Oct03; fate/status unknown]
4 026 05	BP	(Alada)	514//7T-WAC+ UR-11350^ ER-ACD D2-FAW [+ dual marks] [^ requires confirmation] [wfu by 15Mar01 Luanda, Angola]
4 026 06	BP	unknown	566/7T-WAB+ UR-11351^ ER-ACC [+ dual marks] [^ requires confirmation] [canx 26Dec96; fate/status unknown]
4 026 07	BP	(Algerian Air Force)	560/7T-WAA [fate unknown]
4 026 08	TB	(Aeroflot/Magadan)	CCCP-11378 [possibly w/o 07Feb87 Ekaterinburg-Koltsovo, USSR]
4 026 09	TB	(Aeroflot/Magadan)	CCCP-11379 [canx 1977; fate/status unknown]
4 026 10	TB	(Aeroflot/East Siberia)	CCCP-11380 [w/o 25Jun69 Mirny, USSR; canx 1969]
4 026 11	MGA	(Russian Air Force)	CCCP-11791 RA-11791 [wfu by Aug99 Kubinka, Russia; b/u Aug02]
4 026 12	TB	(Korsar)	CCCP-11008 RA-11008 [w/o 22Nov95 Huambo, Angola; canx 25Jly96]
4 027 01	B	Russian Air Force	CCCP-11792 RA-11792
4 027 02	B	Russian Air Force	CCCP-11652 RA-11652 [damaged 10Sep08 Buturlinovka, Russia; status unknown]
4 027 03	B	Russian Air Force	CCCP-11653 RA-11653
4 027 04	B	(Aeroflot/International)	CCCP-11361 [canx 1977; fate/status unknown]
4 027 05		Russian Air Force	CCCP-11407 [still flying 29Aug95 as CCCP-11407]
4 027 06		(Russian Air Force)	CCCP-11240 RA-11240 [canx unknown date; fate/status unknown]
4 027 07	B	Veteran Airlines	CCCP-11117 RA-11117 UR-CBZ [c/n sometimes reported as 54 027 07]
4 027 08	B	(Russian Air Force)	CCCP-11654 RA-11654 [b/u 2004/2005 Kubinka, Russia; canx]
4 027 09	BP	(Iraqi Air Force)	636 [fate/status unknown]
4 027 10	BP	(Iraqi Air Force)	637 [fate/status unknown]
4 027 11	BP	(Iraqi Air Force)	638 [fate/status unknown]
4 027 12	TB	ex Aeroflot/Magadan	CCCP-11355 [canx 1978; preserved by 1982 Magadan Airport terminal; l/n Jly08]
4 028 01	B	(Aeroflot/Privolzhsk)	CCCP-11356 [canx 1975; fate/status unknown]
4 028 02	TB	(Aeroflot/Ukraine)	CCCP-11357(1) [canx 1977; by Jly96 to GIA Krivoy Rog Technical School, Ukraine; b/u by May02]
4 028 03	TB	Russian Navy	CCCP-11358 RA-11358+ [+ as CCCP-11358 canx 1974; possibly another An-12]
4 028 04	TB	(Aeroflot/International)	CCCP-11359 [canx 1977; fate/status unknown]

ANTONOV An-12

C/n	Model	Last known Owner/Operator	Identities/fates/comments (where appropriate)
4 028 05	TB	(Aeroflot/Moscow)	CCCP-11360 [w/o 21Nov72 Vorkuta, USSR]
4 028 06	B	(Aeroflot/Polar)	CCCP-11365 [canx 1971; fate/status unknown]
4 028 07	PL	(Aeroflot/Polar)	CCCP-11381 [w/o 06Dec69 13km from Khatanga Airport, USSR; canx 1970]
4 028 08	B	ex KAT Cargo	CCCP-11366 RA-11366 TC-KET [stored by Aug94 Istanbul-Ataturk, Turkey; l/n 18Feb10]
4 028 09	BP	(Algerian Air Force)	516/7T-WAH [dual marks] [tie-up not confirmed; fate/status unknown]
4 028 10	BP	(Alada)	560/7T-WAE+ RA-11119 D2-FAR^ [+ dual marks] [^ tie up not fully confirmed] [wfu by Oct03 Pointe Noire, Peoples Republic of Congo; b/u by summaer 2004]
4 028 11	BP	(Algerian Air Force)	590/7T-WAF [dual marks] [by Dec08 GIA Ecole de Techniques Aeronautique, Bilda, Algeria]
4 028 12	BP	(Velocity)	591/7T-WAG+ UR-11352^ ER-ACE# [+ dual marks] [^ not fully confirmed] [# marks used concurrently by An-26 c/n 4304; reported shot down 27Feb96 near Lucapa, Angola, but sighted 16Mar01; repaired or different aircraft?; canx 18Apr96]
4 029 01	B	(Aeroflot/International)	CCCP-11367 [canx 1978; fate/status unknown]
4 029 02	TB	(MAP Rostov VPO)	CCCP-13387 RA-13387 [w/o 25Sep93 Roshino, Russia; canx 09Jly96]
4 029 03		(Indian Air Force)	L450 [c/n not confirmed] [last flight 25May91; fate/status unknown]
4 029 04		.	[nothing known]
4 029 05		.	[nothing known]
4 029 06	BP	(Egyptian Air Force)	1224//SU-AOP [dual marks; 1224 not fully confirmed] [by 28Nov81 fuselage only Cairo, Egypt]
4 029 07	BP	(Egyptian Air Force)	1225//SU-AOJ [dual marks; 1225 not fully confirmed] [reported broken up; post mid1966]
4 029 08	BP	(Egyptian Air Force)	1226//SU-AOT 1226//SU-BAW [dual marks] [reported b/u; post Mar85]
4 029 09	BP	(Egyptian Air Force)	1227//SU-APA [dual marks] [reported b/u 1994]
4 029 10	BP	(Egyptian Air Force)	1228//SU-AOI 1228//SU-APZ [dual marks] [reported b/u; post Mar85]
4 029 11	BP	(Egyptian Air Force)	1229//SU-AOK+ [dual marks] SU-APC+ [+not confirmed] [fate/status unknown]
4 029 12	BP	(Egyptian Air Force)	1231//SU-ARB [dual marks] [reported b/u; post Nov81]
4 029 13	12B	SAT Airlines	CCCP-48984 LZ-SGC LZ-SFC RA-48984 UR-48984 RA-48984

Tashkent production 1961 to 1971

C/n	Model	Last known Owner/Operator	Identities/fates/comments (where appropriate)
1 34 01 01		unknown	CCCP-11923 RA-11923
1 34 01 02		.	[nothing known]
1 34 01 03	A	(Aviatrans)	CCCP-11901 RA-11901 [canx 31Oct96; wfu by Sep98 for spares Moscow Myachkovo, Russia]
1 34 01 04		(Soviet Air Force)	14 blue [preserved by 24Apr03 Baikonur, Kazakhstan]
1 34 01 05	A	(Soviet Air Force)	15 red [fate/status unknown]
1 34 01 06	A	RubyStar	CCCP-11976(2) RA-11976 LZ-VEA UN-11018 EW-269TI UR-DWI EW-338TI
1 34 01 07	A	(Air Cess)	CCCP-48971 RA-48971 4K-48971 RA-48971 EL-AKV 3D-AKV TL-ACJ [w/o 02Sep98 en-route Goma-Kisangani, wreck found 01Aug99 near Lubutu, Democratic Republic of Congo]
1 34 01 08		(Soviet Air Force)	06 yellow [b/u summer 2001 Irtutsk-1, Russia]
1 34 01 09	BP	(Soviet Air Force)	CCCP-11871 [fate/status unknown]
1 34 01 10		.	[nothing known]
1 34 02 01		ex Russian Air Force	[Soviet] RA-12187 [damaged 19Dec93 Lensk, Russia; by Jly08 fuselage only present there]
1 34 02 02		.	[nothing known]
1 34 02 03		.	[nothing known]
1 34 02 04		.	[nothing known]
1 34 02 05		.	[nothing known]
1 34 02 06	AP	(Air Fret Business)	[Soviet] UR-11501 ER-ADC TN-AGV [possibly b/u summer 2004 Poine Noire, People's Republic of Congo]
1 34 02 07		.	[nothing known]
1 34 02 08		(Soviet Air Force)	10 blue [fate/status unknown]
1 34 02 09		Kazakhstan Air Force?	08 blue+ 08 blue [+ Soviet]
. 34 02 10		.	[nothing known]
2 34 03 01		ex Elf Air	CCCP-11855 CCCP-13321 RA-13321
2 34 03 02		(Norislk Avia)	CCCP-11886 RA-11886 [w/o 23Jly98 Pushkin, Russia]
2 34 03 03	B	TAPC Aviatrans	CCCP-58644 UK-58644
2 34 03 04		.	[nothing known]

ANTONOV An-12

C/n	Model	Last known Owner/Operator	Identities/fates/comments (where appropriate)
2 34 03 05		.	[nothing known]
2 34 03 06		.	[nothing known]
2 34 03 07	A	ex Russian Air Force	05 blue (unknown) [handed over to unknown Russian company; left 14Apr00 for the Democratic Republic of Congo in probably non-airworthy state; status unknown]
2 34 03 08	A	(Soviet Air Force)	CCCP-11874 [used call sign CCCP-09524] [fate/status unknown]
2 34 03 09		.	[nothing known]
2 34 03 10	TA	(Soviet Air Force)	CCCP-12970 [canx unknown date; status/fate unknown]
2 34 04 01		.	[nothing known]
2 34 04 02		.	[nothing known]
2 34 04 03	AP	ex Renan	CCCP-11961 ER-ADD [reported wfu by 21Sep03 & to be b/u Kishinyov, Moldova; l/n 28Jun07]
2 34 04 04		Kiev Institute of Civil Aviation	[not known] [GIA by Jly96 Kiev, Ukraine by Jly96]
2 34 04 05		.	[nothing known]
2 34 04 06		.	[nothing known]
2 34 04 07		(Soviet Air Force)	18 yellow [fate/status unknown]
2 34 04 08		.	[nothing known]
2 34 04 09		Angolan Air Force	[Soviet] T-303 [call sign D2-MAW]
2 34 04 10		.	[nothing known]
2 34 05 01		.	[nothing known]
2 34 05 02	TA	(Volga Dnepr)	CCCP-11040 [canx unknown date; fate/status unknown]
2 34 05 03	AP	ex Aerocom	[Soviet] D2-FCU ER-ADE [canx unknown date; fate/status unknown]
2 34 05 04		.	[nothing known]
2 34 05 05	AP	Aerovis Airlines	[Soviet] UR-CCP LZ-CBM UR-CCP
2 34 05 06		(Soviet Air Force)	[not known] [fate/status unknown]
2 34 05 07	A	Aerovis Airlines	CCCP-11936 RA-11936 LZ-SFW UR-CBF
2 34 05 08	BP	Russian Air Force	CCCP-11975 [wfu by Jly02 Novosibirsk-Tolmachovo, Russia; still as CCCP-11975]
2 34 05 09		Kazakhstan Air Force	[Soviet] 19 red
2 34 05 10		.	[not known]
2 34 06 01		(Soviet Air Force)	35 blue [fate/status unknown]
2 34 06 02	AP	British Gulf International	[Soviet Navy?] [Russian Navy] EX-045 S9-SAV
2 34 06 03		.	[not known]
2 34 06 04	TA	unknown	CCCP-11383 11383 ER-ACK(2) D2-FBV [w/o unknown date N'Zaki, Angola]
2 34 06 05	AP	(Pacific Air Express)	CCCP-11382 ER-ADT [w/o 16Oct01 Honiara-Henderson Airport, Solomon Islands; canx 17Sep02]
2 34 06 06	AP	ex Goliaf Air	CCCP-12971(2) S9-DAF [wfu by 07Aug11 Pointe Noire, Peoples Republic of Congo]
2 34 06 07		.	[nothing known]
2 34 06 08	AP	Angolan Air Charter	CCCP-10231 ER-ACB D2-MBD
2 34 06 09	TA	(Soviet Air Force)	CCCP-11277 [canx 16Oct01; fate/status unknown]
2 34 06 10	TA	(Russian Air Force)	CCCP-12978 [l/n 13Aug96 Engels AFB, Russia, still as CCCP-12978; wfu 1998; canx 16Oct01]
2 34 07 01	BP	Russian Air Force	18 red+ 18 red [also wears "09018"] [+ Soviet]
2 34 07 02		.	[nothing known]
2 34 07 03	TA	(Soviet Air Force)	CCCP-11048 [canx unknown date; fate/status unknown]
2 34 07 04		.	[nothing known]
2 34 07 05	BP	ex Russian Air Force	CCCP-11850 [wfu by May95 Yakutsk, Russia, still as CCCP-11850]
2 34 07 06		.	[nothing known]
2 34 07 07		.	[nothing known]
2 34 07 08	BP	Russian Air Force	CCCP-11898 18 blue+ 94 red+ 36 red [+ Soviet AF]
2 34 07 09	AP	ex Anton Air	CCCP-11038(1) RA-11038(1) 7P-ANA [fate/status unknown]
2 34 07 10	BP	Russian Air Force	89 red
2 34 08 01	AP	Goliaf Air?	CCCP-11098 RA-11098 4K-AZ59 EX-085 S9-SAR
2 34 08 02	AP	Avial	CCCP-11906 RA-11906
2 34 08 03	TA	Africa West Cargo	CCCP-11275 RA-11275 S9-BOZ
2 34 08 04	AP	ex Heli Air	CCCP-11039 RA-11370 LZ-CBG [by 07Sep07 stored Sofia, Bulgaria, b/u Oct11]
2 34 08 05	A	(Aerolift)	88 red+ RA-11324 9L-LDW 9Q-CER [+ Soviet/Russia] [w/o 24Jan06 Mbuji Mayi, Democratic Republic of Congo]

ANTONOV An-12

C/n	Model	Last known Owner/Operator	Identities/fates/comments (where appropriate)
2 34 08 06	AP	ATMA	[Soviet] RA-11307 LZ-PHA LZ-FEA LZ-SFN ER-AXM LZ-SFN UN-11015 UP-AN213
2 34 08 07	BP	unknown	CCCP-11880 RA-11880
2 34 08 08	TA	(Soviet Air Force)	CCCP-11041 [canx 16Nov01; fate/status unknown]
2 34 08 09		San Air	CCCP-11734 RA-11734 11734 RA-11734 EL-RDL 3D-RDL TL-ACR+ [+ reported an illegal registration]
2 34 08 10	TA	(Soviet Air Force)	CCCP-11276 [canx unknown date; fate/status unknown]
. 34 09 01		.	[nothing known]
. 34 09 02		.	[nothing known]
3 34 09 03		(Zenith Air)	87 red+ RA-11312 [+Soviet/Russian] [wfu 1999 Zhukovski, Russia; canx 16Oct01]
3 34 09 04		.	[nothing known]
3 34 09 05		Kazakhstan Air Force	[Soviet] 19 red
3 34 09 06	A	(Aeroflot/Krasnoyarsk)	CCCP-11896 [w/o 22Jun92 Norilsk-Alkel. USSR]
3 34 09 07		.	[nothing known]
3 34 09 08	TB	Veteran Airlines	CCCP-11813 UR-11813 RA-11813 UR-CEM
3 34 09 09		(Santa Cruz Int'l/Savanair)	CCCP-11890 RA-11890 3D-ASG EL-ASS+ EY-ASS [+may have been officially regd EL-ASA] [w/o 02Feb99 near Luanda, Angola]
3 34 09 10	BP	(Russian Air Force)	16 red [fate/status unknown]
3 34 10 01	BP	(Russian Navy)	CCCP-11139 RA-11139 [wfu by 09Jly00 Moscow-Ostafyevo, Russia; b/u Aug01]
3 34 10 02		.	[nothing known]
3 34 10 03	A	Norilsk Avia	CCCP-11816 RA-11816
3 34 10 04	BP	(Inter Trans Air)	44 red+ LZ-ITA [+ Ukraine & probably ex Soviet; stored 2002 Gorna-Orechovitsa, Bulgaria; derelict by 30Sep06; b/u by 16Nov06]
3 34 10 05	BP	(Motor Sich/P T Air)	CCCP-11528(2) UR-11528 [dbr 19Aug98 Hang Nadim-Batam Airport, Indonesia]
3 34 10 06	AP	(Avis Amur)	CCCP-11125(2) RA-11125 [w/o 09Aug11 near Omsukchan, Russia, returning with engine fire to Magadan, Russia]
3 34 10 07	BP	(Soviet Air Force)	20 red [fate/status unknown]
3 34 10 08	BP	(MAP Kharkov APO)	CCCP-11833 UR-11833 [canx 13Aug08; probably wfu by 12Sep96 Kharkiv-Sokolniki, Ukraine; l/n 27Apr99]
3 34 10 09	B	Russian Air Force	[Soviet] 17 red
3 34 10 10	BP	(Soviet Air Force)	CCCP-11934 [derelict by 06Jly92 Irkutsk, Russia; l/n 11May95; b/u by summer 2001]
3 34 11 01	BP	ex Russian Navy	[Soviet Navy?] 36 yellow [stored by Aug99 Moscow-Ostafyevo, Russia; l/n Aug02]
3 34 11 02	BP	Russian Air Force	93 red [fate/status unknown]
3 34 11 03	AP	Russian Navy	CCCP-11037 RA-11037 [stored by Aug96 Kaliningrad-Khrabrovo, Russia; sold Jun04; canx date unknown; fate/status known]
3 34 11 04	BP	Russian Air Force	09 yellow
3 34 11 05	BP	(Soviet Air Force)	CCCP-11274 [fate/status unknown]
3 34 11 06	TB	(Russian Air Force)	CCCP-11970 [derelict by Apr97 Vladivostok-Knevichi, Russia by Apr97; canx date unknown]
3 34 11 07	B	(Soviet Air Force)	CCCP-10232 [reported w/o en-route 04Aug84 Nawabshah, Pakistan; canx date unknown]
3 34 11 08	BP	(Galaxi Kavatsi Air)	CCCP-11047 RA-11047 UR-UAF ER-ACP D2-FBS ER-ACP 9XR-MK 4L-SAS [w/o 07Sep07 Goma, Democratic Republic of Congo]
3 34 11 09	TB	(Soviet Air Force)	CCCP-11972 [canx unknown date; fate/status unknown]
3 34 11 10	TB	(Juba Air Cargo)	CCCP-11010 RA-11010 EX-11010 ST-JUA [w/o 11Nov07 Khartoum, Sudan]
3 34 12 01	BP	SCAT	11 blue+ 20 red^ UN-11367 UP-AN202 [+ Soviet; ^Russia; c/n not fully confirmed]
3 34 12 02	BP	Russian Air Force	70 red [offered for sale 09Aug01: fate/status unknown]
3 34 12 03	BP	Russian Air Force	92 red
3 34 12 04	B	(Penza Air Enterprise)	CCCP-11337(2) RA-11337 [w/o 14Mar95 Baku, Azerbaijan]
3 34 12 05	BP	Russian Air Force	CCCP-11507 17 blue
3 34 12 06	BP	ex Santa Cruz Imperial	CCCP-11831 RA-11831 3D-ASC EL-ASC [fate/status unknown]
3 34 12 07	BP	(Russian Air Force)	90 red [wfu by 21Aug99 Kubinka, Russia; no recent reports]
3 34 12 08	B	Russian Air Force	05 white
3 34 12 09	TB	Silk Way	CCCP-11408(2) RA-11408 4K-AZ56 UR-CAF [now painted as a An-12B]
3 34 12 10		.	
3 34 13 01	TB	Ukraine Air Force	[Soviet] 78 red [offered for sale in 2005; fate/status unknown]

ANTONOV An-12

C/n	Model	Last known Owner/Operator	Identities/fates/comments (where appropriate)
3 34 13 02	BP	ex Russian Air Force	15 blue [stored/wfu by 17May99 Kubinka, Russia]
3 34 13 03		Russian Air Force	[Soviet] [not known] [offered for sale in Dec07; fate/status unknown]
3 34 13 04	BP	Russian Air Force	08 yellow+ 08 yellow [+ Soviet] [preserved by Apr06 Ukrainka AFB, Russia]
3 34 13 05	BP	Russian Air Force	09 red
3 34 13 06	BP	(Russian Air Force)	12 red+ 12 red [+ Soviet] [derelict by Jun99 Ivanovo-Severny, Russia; b/u by 2006]
3 34 13 07		.	[nothing known]
3 34 13 08	BP	Russian Air Force	[Soviet AF] 08 yellow+ 33 red [+ Russian AF or Navy] [offered for sale 09Aug01; fate/status unknown]
3 34 13 09		.	[nothing known]
3 34 13 10	B	ex Russian Navy	39 red+ 36 blue [+ Soviet] [offered for sale non-airworthy 30Nov98; l/n 20Apr05 Kaliningrad-Khrabrovo, Russia]
3 34 14 01		.	[nothing known]
3 34 14 02	BP	(Transaviaservice)	70 black+ LZ-MNQ 4L-PAS [+ Soviet/Russian Navy] [canx by 23Mar11; fate/status unknown]
3 34 14 03		.	[nothing known]
3 34 14 04	RR	(Russian Air Force)	21 red [fate/status unknown]
3 34 14 05	BP	ex Tirimavia	[not known] ER-ACT+ D2- [+ canx 26Oct99 to Angola]
3 34 14 06	BP	(North-East Cargo)	CCCP-11242 RA-11242 [canx 23Aug97; fate/status unknown]
3 34 14 07			[nothing known]
3 34 14 08	BP	ex British Gulf International	10 red+ TN-AFT^ D2-FRT^ S9-CAQ EX-162 S9-SAM [+ Soviet; ^not fully confirmed; damaged 02Jan09 Sharjah, UAE, leading to the temporary ban of all An-12s in UAE airspace; by 01Jly09 wfu]
3 34 14 09			[nothing known]
3 34 14 10	PPS	Russian Air Force	33 red+ 33 red^ [+ Soviet] [^not fully confirmed]
3 34 15 01	BP	Akkanat	[not known] UN-11374
3 34 15 02		(Russian Air Force)	[Soviet] [not known] [b/u by 2006 Ivanovo-Severny, Russia]
3 34 15 03		(Russian Air Force)	08 red+ [+Soviet/Russian AF] [wfu by May99 Kubinka, Russia; fate/status unknown]
3 34 15 04		.	[not known]
3 34 15 05	BP	ex Inter Trans Air	CCCP-12174 RA-12174 4R-SKL LZ-ITS [derelict by Sep06 Gorna-Orechovitsa, Bulgaria]
3 34 15 06	B	(Mango Airlines)	[Soviet] CCCP-11338(2) ST-ANL RA-11338 D2-FRC 9U-BHN(2) 9Q-CVT [w/o 13Jly06 20km from Goma, Zaire]
3 34 15 07	BP	(Russian Air Force)	98 red [wfu by 21Aug99 Kubinka, Russia; dismantled l/n Sep05]
3 34 15 08		(Russian Space Forces)	[not known] [b/u prior to Aug08; some parts sold as scrap]
3 34 15 09		Moskoviya/Irkut	CCCP-12162(2) RA-12162 12162
3 34 15 10		.	[nothing known]
3 34 16 01	BP	(Russian Air Force)	16 blue+ 85 red^ 35 red^ 35 blue^ [+Soviet; ^ Russian Air Force]
3 34 16 02		Russian Air Force	[Soviet] 50 red
3 34 16 03		.	[nothing known]
3 34 16 04	BP	Russian Air Force	[Soviet] 21 Red [c/n not confirmed]
3 34 16 05	BP	(Air Sofia)	CCCP-12142 CCCP-11145 LZ-SFG [w/o 04Feb98 Lajes, Azores; canx 30Jan07]
3 34 16 06	BP	ex S Group Aviation	CCCP-11328 RA-11328 ER-ADN LZ-SFI EX-151 [stored 22Mar09 Fujairah, UAE; l/n 17Oct09]
3 34 16 07		.	[nothing known]
3 34 16 08		.	[nothing known]
3 34 16 09		.	[nothing known]
3 34 16 10	B	Ukraine Air Force	[Soviet] 69 red [offered for sale in 2005; fate/status unknown]
3 34 17 01	BP	ex Uzbekistan Air Force	CCCP-12165 12165 [preserved by 30Apr05 Fergana, Uzbekistan; l/n 25Feb06]
3 34 17 02		.	[nothing known]
3 34 17 03	BP	(Soviet Air Force)	CCCP-12184 [canx unknown date; fate/status unknown]
. 34 17 04		.	[nothing known]
4 34 17 05	TB	East Wing	[Soviet] UN-11002+ UN-11004 UP-AN206 [+ not fully confirmed; stored by Jly11 Entebbe, Uganda]
4 34 17 06		.	[nothing known]
4 34 17 07	BP	(Motor Sich)	82 red+ CCCP-13332 UR-13332 [+ Soviet] [l/n 06Aug08 Zaporizhzhya-Vostochny, Ukraine; canx 01Oct08; fate/status unknown]
4 34 17 08	BP	(Russian Air Force)	96 red [wfu by 21Aug99 Kubinka, Russia; b/u Jun01]

ANTONOV An-12

C/n	Model	Last known Owner/Operator	Identities/fates/comments (where appropriate)
4 34 17 09	BP	(Atran)	CCCP-93912 RA-93912 [w/o 29Jly07 Semivragi, near Moscow-Domodedovo, Russia]
4 34 17 10	B	ex Ukraine Cargo Airways	[Soviet] 61 blue+ UR-UDD [+ Ukraine Air Force] [canx 31Dec08; fate/status unknown]
4 34 18 01	BP	(Showa Air)	CCCP-12166 9L-LCR [w/o 27May03 Goma, Democratic Republic of Congo; derelict hulk b/u by Mar05; fuselage to Lake Givu near Goma; l/n Oct08]
4 34 18 02	BP	(Soviet Air Force)	CCCP-12172 [canx as destroyed pre 1994; fate/status unknown]
4 34 18 03		(Aerolift/Uhuru Airlines)	[Soviet] UN-11003(1) 3C-QQL 9L-LEC 9Q-CIH [w/o 08Jan05 near Bukalaza, near Entebbe, Uganda]
4 34 18 04	BP	Russian Air Force	22 blue
4 34 18 05		.	[nothing known]
4 34 18 06		.	[nothing known]
4 34 18 07	BP	(Soviet Air Force)	64+ [+ code colour unknown] [fate/status unknown]
4 34 18 08		.	[nothing known]
4 34 18 09		.	[nothing known]
4 34 18 10		.	[nothing known]
4 34 19 01	BP	ex S Group Aviation	CCCP-11511 LZ-SFK YU-UIC EX-153 [stored 24Oct08 Fujairah, UAE; l/n 17Oct09]
4 34 19 02		ex Uzbekistan Air Force	CCCP-11513 11513 [preserved by 11Mar07 possibly at Fergana, Uzbekistan]
4 34 19 03		.	[nothing known]
4 34 19 04		.	[nothing known]
4 34 19 05	BP	Russian Air Force	CCCP-11537 84 red
4 34 19 06	B	Phoenix Avia	[Soviet] EK-12148 [might not be connected with CCCP-12148; refer to unknown list below]
4 34 19 07		.	[nothing known]
4 34 19 08	BP	(Soviet Air Force)	CCCP-11515 [canx unknown date; fate/status unknown]
4 34 19 09	B	Anteks-Polyus	CCCP-11516 RA-11516
4 34 19 10	BP	ex Panac Cargo	[Soviet] UR-11351 EK-11351 [derelict by Nov07 Malbo, Equatorial Guinea; l/n Jun08]
4 34 20 01	BP	Russian Air Force	17 blue+ 10 red [+Soviet/Russian AF]
4 34 20 02		(Ethiopian Air Force)	[Soviet] 1506 [c/n not confirmed; could be c/n 4 34 20 06] [w/o 15Jan84 Tesenni, Ethiopia]
4 34 20 03		.	[nothing known]
4 34 20 04		.	[nothing known]
4 34 20 05		.	[nothing known]
4 34 20 06	BP	(Soviet Air Force)	CCCP-11229 [see c/n 4 34 20 02 above] [w/o 12Oct89 Kirovabad, USSR when hit by Su-24 that was taking off from the taxiway]
4 34 20 07		Ukraine Air Force	70+ 77 red [+ Soviet, code colour unknown]
4 34 20 08	BP	unknown private company	CCCP-11419 [l/n 08May98 Saky, Ukraine still as CCCP-11419; fate/status unknown]
4 34 20 09		Ethiopian Air Force	[Soviet] 1503 [c/n not confirmed; but image shows barely readable c/n "2104"]
4 34 20 10	BP	(Techaviaservice)	07 yellow+ EW-11368 [+Soviet/Belarus AF] [w/o en-route 26Aug98 80km from Luanda, Angola]
4 34 21 01	BP	ex Galad Air Cargo	CCCP-11521(2) LZ-SFL Z3-AFA LZ-SFL YU-UID EX-154 [stored by 01Nov08 Fujairah, UAE; l/n 17Oct09]
4 34 21 02		.	[nothing known]
4 34 21 03	B	SRX Aero	CCCP-93915 RA-93915 UR-CEX LZ-BRI UK-12005
4 34 21 04		.	
4 34 21 05	BP	(Air Sofia/Mandala Airlines)	2105+ LZ-SFJ [+ Czechoslovakia then Czech Republic] [w/o 29Sep99 Simpang Tiga, Indonesia; canx 30Jan07]
4 34 21 06		Ukraine Air Force	[Soviet] 79 red
4 34 21 07	BP	Russian Air Force	CCCP-11674 [fate/status unknown]
4 34 21 08	BP	ex Techaviaservice	08 yellow+ EW-11371 [+Soviet/Belarus AF] [not on 2001 fleet list; fate/status unknown]
4 34 21 09		.	[nothing known]
4 34 21 10		Ukraine Air Force	[Soviet] 83 Red [fate/status unknown]
4 34 22 01		.	[nothing known]
4 34 22 02	BP	ex Bio Air Company	[Soviet] 84 blue+ UR-11332 T9-CAD UR-11332 [+Ukraine]
4 34 22 03	BP	Russian Air Force	CCCP-12182 91 red
4 34 22 04	BP	ex Afghan Air Force	CCCP-11426 RA-11426 2204+ [+ c/n not confirmed but serial makes it possible] [probably dumped wreck at Kabul, Afghanistan noted Jan04]

ANTONOV An-12

C/n	Model	Last known Owner/Operator	Identities/fates/comments (where appropriate)
4 34 22 05	BP	ex Afghan Air Force	387 [c/n on tail as 2205; serial 2205 reported as wreck Mar02 Kabul, Afghanistan; l/n Jun06 probably same aircraft]
4 34 22 06		.	[nothing known]
4 34 22 07	BP	Ukraine Air Force	[Soviet] [not known] [offered for sale 2005; fate/unknown]
4 34 22 08	BP	Aviast Air	CCCP-11756 RA-11756
4 34 22 09	BP	Angolan Air Force	2209+ 2209+ ER-ACH T-309//D2-MBH [dual marks] [+ Czechoslovak then Slovak Air Force]
4 34 22 10	BP	(Galex Guinea Air)	CCCP-11830 RA-11830 EK-11830 EX-073 EK-11830 EW-284TI 3X-GEQ(1) [w/o 28Jly10 unknown location Helmand Province, Afghanistan]
4 34 23 01		.	[nothing known]
4 34 23 02		.	[nothing known]
4 34 23 03		.	[nothing known]
4 34 23 04	BP	unknown	[Soviet] RA-11313? UR-11313
4 34 23 05		(Aerovista)	[Soviet] 14+ TN-AFW TN-AGC ST-AQP [+ Russia, code colour unknown] [w/o 30Apr02 Heglig, Sudan;canx before Jan07]
4 34 23 06		Ukraine Air Force	[Soviet] 50 red [fate/status unknown]
4 34 23 07	BP	(Antonov Design Bureau)	[Soviet] RA-11315 UR-11315 [l/n 03Oct10 Gostomel, Ukraine; canx 10Jan12 fate/status unknown]
4 34 23 08	B	Veteran Airlines	72+ 61 red^ UR-PLV [+Soviet, code colour unknown; ^ Ukraine] [w/o 10Nov08 Pointe Noire, People's Republic of Congo]
4 34 23 09		.	[nothing known]
4 34 23 10		.	[nothing known]
4 34 24 01		.	[nothing known]
4 34 24 02		.	[nothing known]
4 34 24 03		.	[nothing known]
4 34 24 04	BP	(Victoria Air)	CCCP-11760 RA-11760 7P-ANB EL-ANB+ 3C-QQC TN-AGH EX-11760 9Q-CVG [+ not fully confirmed] [w/o 25May05 Goma, Democratic Republic of Congo]
4 34 24 05	BP	Ukraine Air Force	[Soviet] 79 red [offered for sale 2005; l/n 06Jly10 Saki-Novofedorovka, Ukraine]
4 34 24 06	BP	(Soviet Air Force)	28 blue [fate/status unknown]
4 34 24 07	BP	(Russian Air Force)	99 red [wfu by 21Aug99 Kubinka, Russia; b/u 03Jun01]
4 34 24 08		.	[nothing known]
4 34 24 09	BP	ex Volare	[Soviet] RA-11320 TN-AGE UR-SVG [canx 31Dec08 fate/status unknown; was in 30Sep04 fleet list]
4 34 24 10	BP	Russian Air Force	95 red+ 95 red [+ Soviet]
4 34 25 01	BP	(MOM/Omsk)	CCCP-11399 [damaged 27Feb93 Gyumri, Russia; canx post Feb98; fate/status unknown]
4 34 25 02		Russian Air Force	[Soviet] RA-11406
4 34 25 03		(Soviet Air Force)	CCCP-11433 [canx unknown date; fate/status unknown]
4 34 25 04		(Soviet Air Force)	CCCP-11435 [canx unknown date; fate/status unknown]
4 34 25 05		ex East Wing	[Soviet] 18 red + UN-11008 UP-AN208 [dbr date unknown N'Djamena, Chad; canx late 2008; l/n stored there 14Aug09] [+ Kazakhstan]
4 34 25 06		.	[nothing known]
4 34 25 07	BP	Russian Air Force	10 yellow
4 34 25 08		.	[nothing known]
4 34 25 09	BP	Russian Air Force	14 yellow+ 11 yellow [wfu before 2011] [+Soviet/Russian AF]
4 34 25 10	BP	(Khors Air)	[Soviet] UR-11319 [w/o 14Dec98 shot down near Kuito, Angola]
4 34 26 01		Irkut	[Soviet] RA-11310
4 34 26 02	BP	ex Russian Navy	[Soviet] 10 blue wfu Vladivostok-Knevichi, Russia; l/n Apr12]
4 34 26 03		.	[nothing known]
4 34 26 04	RR	ex Russian Air Force	11 red [possibly derelict by 02Oct08 Levashovo, Russia]
4 34 26 05		.	[nothing known]
4 34 26 06		(Russian Space Forces)	[not known] [b/u prior to Aug08; some parts sold as scrap]
4 34 26 07		.	[nothing known]
4 34 26 08			[nothing known]
4 34 26 09	BP	Atran	CCCP-93913 RA-93913
4 34 26 10	AP	(Inter Transport Congo)	[Soviet] 86 blue+ D2-FBD ER-ADL [+Ukraine] [w/o 15Feb02 Monrovia, Liberia]
4 34 27 01		.	[nothing known]
4 34 27 02	BP	(Soviet Air Force)	CCCP-11247 [fate/status unknown]
4 34 27 03	BP	Russian Air Force	86 red+ 19 red [+ Soviet]
. 34 27 04		.	[nothing known]

ANTONOV An-12

C/n	Model	Last known Owner/Operator	Identities/fates/comments (where appropriate)
5 34 27 05		(Soviet Air Force)	CCCP-11397 [canx unknown date; fate/status unknown]
5 34 27 06	BP	(Russian Air Force)	CCCP-11258 [wfu by May99 Staraya, Russia; l/n Sep02; canx 16Oct01]
5 34 27 07		.	[nothing known]
5 34 27 08	BP	Komosomolsk na Amure Aircraft	CCCP-11230 LZ-SFE LZ-BFA RA-11230
5 34 27 09		.	[nothing known]
5 34 27 10		.	[nothing known]
5 34 28 01	BP	unknown	[Soviet] RA-11325 EL-ALC+ YA-DAB [+ use of these marks by this aircraft in doubt]
5 34 28 02	BP	Air Victory Georgia	CCCP-11905 UN-11005 ER-ADK 4L-ELE
5 34 28 03	BP	(Soviet Air Force)	CCCP-11505 [fate/status unknown]
5 34 28 04		(Soviet Air Force)	CCCP-12118 [canx unknown date; fate/status unknown]
5 34 28 05	12	(IAPO Irkutsk)	CCCP-13391 RA-13391 [canx 07May97; derelict by 06Jun01 Irkutsk-Vostochny, Russia]
5 34 28 06	BP	Russian Air Force	CCCP-11998 16 blue
5 34 28 07		.	[nothing known]
5 34 28 08		(Russian Air Force)	CCCP-12111 RA-12111 [canx unknown date; offered for sale Dec07; fate/status unknown]
5 34 28 09	BP	Russian Air Force	18 red
5 34 28 10		(Russian Air Force)	17 red [b/u Aug99-Jun01 Kubinka, Russia]
5 34 29 01		.	[nothing known]
5 34 29 02		Kazakhstan Air Force	[Soviet] 79 red
5 34 29 03	BP	Taron Avia	CCCP-11772 EK-11772 EK-12129
5 34 29 04		.	[nothing known]
5 34 29 05	BP	(Sarit Airlines)	CCCP-11773 ST-SAA [w/o 17Nov03 Wau, Sudan]
5 34 29 06		.	[nothing known]
5 34 29 07	BP	Ethiopian Air Force	[Soviet] 1505
5 34 29 08	BP	Air Armenia Cargo	CCCP-11810 UR-11810 EK-11810
5 34 29 09		.	[nothing known]
5 34 29 10		.	[nothing known]
5 34 30 01		(Russian Air Force)	CCCP-11431 RA-11431 [wfu 1998; canx 16Oct01]
5 34 30 02	BP	(Russian Air Force)	CCCP-11432 RA-11432 [wfu 1998; canx 16Oct01]
5 34 30 03		.	[nothing known]
5 34 30 04	BP	(ATMA)	CCCP-69314 RA-69314 UN-11003(2) [w/o 25Apr05 Kabul, Afghanistan]
5 34 30 05	BP	Taron Avia	17 yellow+ 29 blue+ 20+^ CCCP-98102 RA-98102 LZ-BFD RA-98102 UN-98102 XU-U4C EK-12005 [+ Soviet; ^ code colour unknown]
5 34 30 06	BP	Democratic Republic of Congo AF	CCCP-11430 4K-AZ32 4L-12005 EX-086(1) EX-092 S9-PSM 9T-TCI
5 34 30 07	BP	Aviast Air	CCCP-11962 RA-11962
5 34 30 08		.	[nothing known]
5 34 30 09		.	[nothing known]
5 34 30 10	BP	Russian Air Force	31 yellow [preserved by 24May06 Tambov, Russia]
5 34 31 01	B	(Indian Air Force)	L2170 [code J] [wfu early 1993; fate unknown]
5 34 31 02		.	[nothing known]
5 34 31 03	BP	Democratic Republic of Congo AF	CCCP-11768(2) RA-11768 4L-12008 S9-GAW 9T-TCH(1) + [marks used concurrently by c/n 8 34 58 07]
5 34 31 04		.	[nothing known]
5 34 31 05		.	[nothing known]
5 34 31 06		.	[nothing known]
5 34 31 07		.	[nothing known]
5 34 31 08		(Russian Air Force)	15 red [wfu by 17May99 Kubinka, Russia]
5 34 31 09	BP	Goliaf Air	09 yellow?+ EW-11365 S9-PSO [+ Soviet]
5 34 31 10		.	[nothing known]
5 34 32 01		.	[nothing known]
5 34 32 02	BP	Avialeasing/SRX Transcontintal	01+ CCCP-11711 UK-12001 [+ Soviet, code colour unknown]
5 34 32 03	B	(Fly Adjara)	CCCP-11357(2) UR-11357 4L-BKN [canx by 23Mar11; fate/status unknown]
5 34 32 04	BP	UKAS	CCCP-12130 UK-11372 ER-ACO YA-KAC 3X-GFT 3X-GHG
5 34 32 05		.	[nothing known]
5 34 32 06	BP	Ethiopian Air Force	1512 [tie-up not confirmed]
5 34 32 07	BP	Russian Air Force	97 red
5 34 32 08	BP	Angola Air Charter	CCCP-11661 661 black+ ER-AXH D2-MBV [+Soviet/Russia]
5 34 32 09	BP	(Aero Service)	CCCP-11660 RA-11660 EK-11660 [w/o 25Jan08 Pointe Noire, People's Republic of Congo]

ANTONOV An-12

C/n	Model	Last known Owner/Operator	Identities/fates/comments (where appropriate)
5 34 32 10		.	
5 34 33 01	BP	Russian Air Force	CCCP-11412 RA-11412
5 34 33 02	B	(Indian Air Force)	L2171 [code K] [wfu 1993; fate/status unknown]
5 34 33 03		.	[nothing known]
5 34 33 04		.	[nothing known]
5 34 33 05	BP	Air Highnesses	CCCP-11667 CCCP-12192 XU-345 D2-FDT S9-BOT EX-161 S9-SAP EW-292TI EK-12335
5 34 33 06	BP	Russian Air Force	CCCP-11932 16 yellow
5 34 33 07	BP	Canair Congo	CCCP-11132 ST-SAD EK-11132 EK-11112 EK-12307
5 34 33 08		.	[nothing known]
5 34 33 09		.	[nothing known]
5 34 33 10		(Russian Air Force)	CCCP-11946 34 red [stored by Aug99 Moscow-Ostafyevo, Russia; l/n Aug01]
5 34 34 01	BP	(Indian Air Force)	L2172 [code L] [fate/status unknown]
5 34 34 02	BP	(Mani Air Freight)	CCCP-11401 RA-11401 EK-11779 EY-404 [b/u Dec11 Tver, Russia]
5 34 34 03		ex Russian Air Force	42 red [last flight 1996; stored by Jun06 Kirzhach, Russia]
5 34 34 04	BP	(Russian Air Force)	CCCP-12105 RA-12105 [w/o 11Dec97 Naryan-Mar, Russia; ran into Mi-8T RA-24247]
5 34 34 05	TB	Angolan Air Charter	CCCP-12388 RA-12388 ER-ADM T-301+ D2-MAZ [+ Angola]
5 34 34 06	BP	(Russian Air Force)	CCCP-12115 RA-12115 [wfu 1998; canx 16Oct01; fate/status unknown]
5 34 34 07	BP	Russian Air Force	81 red
5 34 34 08		East Wing	[Soviet] UN-11001 EX-002 9L-LEA 3C-MIR+ UN-11009 UP-AN209 [possibly wfu by 07Aug11 Ndjamena, Chad; + not fully confirmed]
5 34 34 09	BP	ex Russian Air Force	CCCP-11945 RA-11945 [canx unknown date; l/n 29Aug04 Orenburg-Southeast, Russia]
5 34 34 10	BP	unknown	CCCP-11404 4K-AZ30 EX-083 [canx 15May06 fate/status unknown]
5 34 35 01	BP	(Soviet Air Force)	CCCP-11233 [fate/status unknown]
5 34 35 02	BP	(Sarit Airlines)	CCCP-11424 RA-11424+ ST-SAT [+not fully confirmed] [w/o 26Jun04 Wau, Sudan]
5 34 35 03			[nothing known]
5 34 35 04	BP	Russian Air Force	[Soviet] RA-12574
5 34 35 05	BK	Ukraine Air Force	[Soviet] 72 red [reported wfu 1992; l/n 02May06 Odessa-Tsentrainy, Ukraine with faded markings; offered for sale May06; fate/status unknown]
5 34 35 06	BP	ex Phoenix Avia Gulf	CCCP-11995 RA-11995+ EK-11007 3X-GEQ(2) [+not fully confirmed]
5 34 35 07	BP	Democratic Republic of Congo AF	CCCP-11786 RA-11786 EK-12122 3X-GEO 9T-TCM
5 34 35 08	BP	(Soviet Air Force)	30 red [fate/status unknown]
5 34 35 09		.	[nothing known]
5 34 35 10	BP	Shovkovly Shlyah Airlines	CCCP-11400 RA-11400 4K-AZ60 UR-CGX
5 34 36 01		.	[nothing known]
5 34 36 02		.	[nothing known]
5 34 36 03		(Soviet Air Force)	CCCP-11658 [fate/status unknown]
5 34 36 04	BP	(Russian Air Force)	CCCP-11835 RA-11835 [wfu 1998; canx 16Oct01; fate/status unknown]
5 34 36 05	BP	Russian Air Force	CCCP-11676 38 yellow
5 34 36 06	B	Congo Presidential Flight	CCCP-06105 CIS-06105 UK-06105 EX-001 [canx 26Jun06 but still active 18Nov11 in Democratic Republic of Congo]
5 34 36 07	BP	(Soviet Air Force)	CCCP-11809 [fate/status unknown]
5 34 36 08		.	[nothing known]
5 34 36 09	BP	(Soviet Air Force)	CCCP-11747 [w/o 25Nov85 shot down over Angola]
5 34 36 10	B	(Aeroflot/Komi)	CCCP-11000 [w/o 33Jan71 near Surgut, USSR]
5 34 37 01		.	[nothing known]
5 34 37 02	B	(Magadan Air Leasing)	CCCP-11001 [canx 08Dec98; fate/status unknown]
5 34 37 03	B	not yet known	CCCP-11002 RA-11002 EX-164 S9-SAH 3X-GEV
5 34 37 04	B	ex Air West	CCCP-11003 RA-11003 ST-AWM [canx by Jan07; l/n 04Feb99 Sharjah, UAE; fate/status unknown]
6 34 37 05	BP	Aerovis Airlines	[Soviet] UR-11302 UR-CBG
6 34 37 06		.	[nothing known]
6 34 37 07	BP	Meridian	[Soviet] UR-PWH ER-ACI UR-CAK
6 34 37 08	B	(Air Victory Georgia)	LZ-BAC LZ-CBE 4L-HUS [canx by 23Mar11; fate/status unknown]
6 34 37 09	BP	(Soviet Air Force)	CCCP-11988 [CofA canx 26Feb88; fate/status unknown]
6 34 37 10	B	(Indian Air Force)	L2173 [last flight 21Aug91; fate/status unknown]
6 34 38 01		(Soviet Air Force)	01+ CCCP-11714 [+ Soviet, code colour unknown]
6 34 38 02	BP	Aerovis Airlines	[Soviet] 02 red+ UR-CFB [+ Russia]
6 34 38 03		.	[nothing known]
6 34 38 04		(Afghan Air Force	[unknown] [large parts on dumps Kandahar, Afghanistan; l/n 2011]

ANTONOV An-12

C/n	Model	Last known Owner/Operator	Identities/fates/comments (where appropriate)
6 34 38 05	BP	(Russian Air Force)	CCCP-11265(2) RA-11265 [wfu 1998; canx 16Oct01; b/u by 2006 Ivanovo-Severny, Russia]
6 34 38 06	B	(Indian Air Force)	L2174 [w/o unknown date and location]
6 34 38 07		(Russian Air Force)	CCCP-11287 RA-11287 [canx unknown date; offered for sale Dec07; fate/status unknown]
6 34 38 08	BP	Russian Air Force	CCCP-11755 RA-11755 [stored by 13Aug06 Tver, Russia]
6 34 38 09		(Russian Air Force)	CCCP-11286 RA-11286 [wfu 1998; by 15Jun99 derelict Ivanovo-Severny, Russia; canx 16Oct01; b/u by 2006]
6 34 38 10	B	UKAS	CCCP-11818 UK-11369 ER-ACR YA-KAD 3X-GFU 3X-GHF
6 34 39 01	BK	Russian Air Force	85 red
6 34 39 02		(Russian Air Force)	CCCP-10228 [canx 16Oct01; b/u by 2006 Ivanovo-Severny, Russia]
6 34 39 03		ex Antei	CCCP-11665 RA-11665 [derelict by 30Jun11 Taganrog, Russia]
6 34 39 04		.	[nothing known]
6 34 39 05	BP	Komosomolsk na Amure Aircraft	CCCP-11789 LZ-BFB RA-11789
6 34 39 06	B	(Aeroflot/Ukraine)	CCCP-11004 [canx 1977; fate/status unknown]
6 34 39 07	B	(Aeroflot/Yakutsk)	CCCP-11005(1) [DBR15Dec75 Fergana, USSR; rebuilt with parts from c/n 9 34 64 08 & preserved as "CCCP-11005/CCCP-11064" Fergana, USSR until probably b/u]]
6 34 39 08	B	(Aeroflot/East Siberia)	CCCP-11006 [canx 1977; fate/status unknown]
6 34 39 09	B	(Aeroflot/Polar)	CCCP-11007 [w/o 06Mar67 Salekhard, USSR]
6 34 39 10	B	(Aeroflot/East Siberia)	CCCP-11012 [canx 1978; fate/status unknown]
6 34 40 01	B	(Balkan Bulgarian Airlines)	CCCP-11897 LZ-BAD [w/o 24Aug84 Addis Ababa-Bole Airport, Ethiopia]
6 34 40 02	B	(unknown)	CCCP-11013 RA-11013 S9-CAN [w/o 20Jan99 Lukapa Airport, Angola]
6 34 40 03		.	[nothing known]
6 34 40 04	B	ex Sakha Avia	CCCP-11014 RA-11014 [canx 28Jly94; derelict by 13May95 Yakutsk, Russia by May95]
6 34 40 05	BP	(Russian Air Force)	15 blue [fate/status unknown]
6 34 40 06	B	(Aeroflot/Yakutsk)	CCCP-11015 [w/o 29Jan68 Magan, USSR]
6 34 40 07	B	(Aeroflot/Yakutsk)	CCCP-11016 [DBR date unknown, possibly early 1970s, Batagai, USSR; canx 1978]
6 34 40 08	TB	(Ural Airlines)	CCCP-11017 RA-11017 [canx 29Aug98; probably b/u Sverdlovsk, Russia; cockpit to simulator]
6 34 40 09	BP	Motor Sich	CCCP-11819 UR-11819
6 34 40 10		.	[nothing known]
6 34 41 01		.	[nothing known]
6 34 41 02	BP	(Russian Air Force)	[Soviet] 34 red [b/u by 2006 Ivanovo-Severny, Russia]
6 34 41 03	TB	Kosmos Airlines	CCCP-11025 RA-11025
6 34 41 04		East Wing	[Soviet] EX-11001 UN-11006+ UP-AN210 [c/n quoted elsewhere as 5 34 41 03 but the version here fits into the likely build year of a batch 41 aircraft; + not fully confirmed]
6 34 41 05		.	[nothing known]
6 34 41 06		.	[nothing known]
41 07	BP	(Egyptian Air Force)	1233//SU-ARC [dual marks] [assume full c/n should be 6 34 41 07] [reported as b/u; was l/n 26Oct91 Cairo, Egypt]
6 34 41 08	12BP	(Egyptian Air Force)	1234//SU-AOR 1234//SU-APX [dual marks] [reported as b/u by 1994; was l/n Oct93 Cairo, Egypt]
6 34 41 09	B	RSK MiG	CCCP-11529(2) RA-11529 11529
6 34 41 10		.	[nothing known]
6 34 42 01	B	(Aeroflot/Polar)	CCCP-11018 [w/o 23Aug69 12km from Novosibirsk-Tolmachovo, USSR; canx 1970]
6 34 42 02	TB	unknown	CCCP-11019 RA-11019+ EL- D2-FRJ^ [+ canx 26Nov98 to Liberia;^ not confirmed; derelict by Oct03 Lukapa, Angola; l/n 2009]
6 34 42 03	TB	(Aeroflot/Uralsk)	CCCP-11020 [canx 14Aug72; fate/status unknown]
6 34 42 04	BP	(Ukraine Air Force)	[Soviet] 85 red [wfu by 14Sep02 Kiev-Svyatoshino, Ukraine; l/n 22Jly08 derelict]
42 05	B	(Indian Air Force)	L645 [code H; later S; used call sign VU-PPA at some stage][stored by 05Aug93 Leh AFB, India; fate unknown]
42 06	B	(Indian Air Force)	L646 [code J; later W; later G; used call sign VU-PGB at some stage] [fate/status unknown]
42 07	B	(Indian Air Force)	L647 [code K ;later Q; later X] [b/u after 26Dec85]
42 08	B	(Indian Air Force)	L648 [code B] [b/u after 15Oct81]
42 09	B	(Indian Air Force)	L649 [code X; later J; later Q] [b/u after 24Oct81]
42 10	B	(Indian Air Force)	L650 [code M] [fate/status unknown]

ANTONOV An-12

C/n	Model	Last known Owner/Operator	Identities/fates/comments (where appropriate)
6 34 43 01		Ukraine Air Force	[Soviet] 04 red
6 34 43 02	BP	(Russian Air Force)	11 red
6 34 43 03	BP	(Russian Air Force)	CCCP-11920
6 34 43 04	BP	Aerovis Airlines	CCCP-98118 RA-98118 UR-CEZ
6 34 43 05	B	Air Mark Aviation	685+ YI-AES 351^ CCCP-11650(2) RA-11650 LZ-BAG LZ-BFG RA-11650 11650 UN-11650 UP-AN215 [+ Iraq; ^ Jordan]
43 06	BP	ex Jordanian Air Force	686+ YI-AGD 352^ [+ Iraq; ^ not confirmed] [destroyed in bombing raid by May03 Samarra, Iraq]
6 34 43 07	B	(Polish Air Force)	50+ SP-LZA [+ Poland] [w/o 13May77 Beirut, Lebanon; canx 02Dec77]
6 34 43 08	B	ex Click Airways?	51+ SP-LZB LZ-SFS UN-11014 YU-UIB EX-155 [+ Poland] [stored 08Mar08 Fujairah, UAE; l/n 17Oct09]
6 34 43 09	BP	(Russian Air Force)	CCCP-11393 RA-11393 [wfu 1998; canx 16Oct01; fate/status unknown]
6 34 43 10	B	(Aerolift)	CCCP-11339(2) RA-11339 ER-AXI S9-SVN [w/o 20Feb09 Luxor, Eygpt]
6 34 44 01		.	[nothing known]
6 34 44 02	BP	(China General Aviation)	201+ B-201 B-3151 [+ China] [wfu 1994 Tianjin, China; b/u 1995]
6 34 44 03		.	[nothing known]
6 34 44 04		.	[nothing known]
6 34 44 05		(Russian Air Force)	CCCP-11902 [canx 16Oct01; fate/status unknown]
6 34 44 06	BP	(Russian Air Force)	CCCP-11740 RA-11740 [wfu 1996; canx 16Oct01; fate/status unknown]
6 34 44 07	BP	(Sarit Airlines)	CCCP-11997 EK-11997 [w/o 03Nov03 13 km from Geneina, Sudan]
6 34 44 08	BP	(Russian Air Force)	CCCP-11878 [canx unknown date; fate/status unknown]
6 34 44 09		(Russian Air Force)	CCCP-11912 [wfu 1998; canx 16Oct81; fate/status unknown]
6 34 44 10	BP	Russian Air Force	CCCP-12137 RA-12137(1) [marks used concurrently by c/n 00347605]
6 34 45 01		(Volga Dnepr)	CCCP-11908 RA-11908 [canx unknown date after Feb98; fate/status]
6 34 45 02	B	(Aeroflot/Privolzhsk)	CCCP-11340(2) [w/o 08Feb94 Anadyr, Russia]
6 34 45 03	BP	(GosNII GA)	CCCP-11911 CCCP-11530 RA-11530 [w/o 24Apr99 Sao Tome]
6 34 45 04	BP	ex Russian Air Force	CCCP-11904 RA-11904 [canx unknown date; sold 14Sep07 to TurboArmkom; fate/status unknown]
6 34 45 05	BP	not yet known	CCCP-11930 CCCP-11736 RA-11736 UP-AN214+ [+ not fully confirmed]
6 34 45 06	BP	(Air Nacoia)	CCCP-11531 RA-11531 D2-FVG(1) [w/o 12Mar97 Lupaka, Angola]
6 34 45 07		(Soviet Air Force)	CCCP-11949 [canx 21Oct81; fate/status unknown]
6 34 45 08		(Russian Air Force)	CCCP-11924 RA-11924 [stored by Aug02 Kubinka, Russia; l/n Aug03; canx unknown date; fate/status unknown]
6 34 45 09		(Russian Air Force)	CCCP-11931 RA-11931 [stored by 09Jly08 Sverdlovsk, Russia; canx unknown date]
6 34 45 10	BK	START/Interaviatrans	CCCP-48974 10 red+ CCCP-13331 13331 RA-13331 [+ Soviet]
6 34 46 01	BP	(Russian Air Force)	CCCP-11719 RA-11719(1) [wfu by 15Aug99 Chkalovsky, Russia; canx 16Oct01]
6 34 46 02	PS	Russian Navy	[Soviet] 14 yellow
6 34 46 03	BK	Ukraine Air Force	[Soviet] 89 blue [offered for sale 27May06; l/n 31Oct08 Lvov-Snilow, Ukraine]
6 34 46 04	BP	(Soviet Air Force)	CCCP-11725 [fate/status unknown]
6 34 46 05	BK	(Volare)	[Soviet] 73 blue+ UR-LMI^ [+ Ukraine; ^ canx 20Jly10 fate/status unknown]
6 34 46 06		.	[nothing known]
6 34 46 07	BK	(Aero-Fret Business Aviation)	[Soviet] 86 blue+ TN-AIA [+ Ukraine] [w/o 26Aug09 Nganga Lingolo, near Brazzaville, People's Republic of Congo]
6 34 46 08	PS	Gomelavia	[Soviet] 15 yellow+ EX-096 EW-245TI [+Russian Navy]
6 34 46 09	BK	Kazakhstan Air Force	[Soviet] 18 red
6 34 46 10	BP	Meridian	CCCP-93920 UK-93920 LZ-VEC EW-266TI UR-CGV
6 34 47 01	BP	Africa West Cargo	[Soviet] UR-UAA UR-TSI S9-PSA
7 34 47 02	PS	Russian Navy	16 yellow
7 34 47 03	PS	Russian Navy	[Soviet] 17 yellow
7 34 47 04	BP	(Soviet Air Force)	[Soviet] [fate/status unknown]
7 34 47 05	BP	Click Airways	CCCP-11418(2) UK-11418(1) ER-AXB 3C-QRN EX-022 EX-166 EK-11418
7 34 47 06	PS	ex Russian Navy	[Soviet] 06 blue [wfu by 20Apr11 Vladivostok-Knevichi, Russia; l/n May11]
7 34 47 07	PS	Russian Navy	[Soviet] 02 black
7 34 47 08	PS	Russian Navy	[Soviet] 08 blue

ANTONOV An-12

C/n	Model	Last known Owner/Operator	Identities/fates/comments (where appropriate)
7 34 47 09		.	[nothing known]
7 34 47 10		.	[nothing known]
7 34 48 01	BK	Navette Airlines	CCCP-98119(2) RA-98119 3C-AAG
7 34 48 02		.	[nothing known]
7 34 48 03		.	[nothing known]
7 34 48 04		.	[nothing known]
7 34 48 05		.	[nothing known]
7 34 48 06	B	(Aeroflot/Magadan)	CCCP-11021 [canx 1987; fate/status unknown]
7 34 48 07	B	(Aeroflot/Magadan)	CCCP-11022 [canx 1987; fate/status unknown]
7 34 48 08	B	(Aeroflot/Yakutsk)	CCCP-11023 [canx 1978; fate/status unknown]
7 34 48 09	B	(Aeroflot/Yakutsk)	CCCP-11024 [w/o 25May71 Batagi, USSR; canx 1971]
7 34 48 10	B	ex Ural Airlines	CCCP-11036 RA-11036 A6- [canx 20Dec98 to UAE; fate/status unknown]
7 34 49 01	B	(Aeroflot/East Siberia)	CCCP-11026 [canx 1987; fate/status unknown]
7 34 49 02		.	[nothing known]
7 34 49 03		.	[nothing known]
7 34 49 04		.	[nothing known]
7 34 49 05	BP	Russian Air Force	CCCP-12127 17 yellow
7 34 49 06	BP	(Russian Air Force)	CCCP-12129 RA-12129 [wfu by Jly00 Ostafyevo, Russia; l/n Aug02; canx unknown date]
7 34 49 07	B	(Aeroflot/East Siberia)	CCCP-11028 [canx 1977; fate/status unknown]
7 34 49 08	B	Air Highnesses	CCCP-11029 RA-11029 EK-11029 EK-12908
7 34 49 09	BK	ex Russian Air Force	[Soviet] 35 [semi-derelict by 2011 Aktyubinsk, Russia; serial scrubbed, colour not discernable]
7 34 49 10		.	[nothing known]
7 34 50 01	B	(Air Guinee)	3X-GBC [fate/status unknown]
7 34 50 02	B	(Aeroflot/East Siberia)	CCCP-11030 [w/o 18Oct74 Yenisysk, USSR]
7 34 50 03	B	(Aeroflot/International)	CCCP-11031 [w/o 01Oct70 Mys Kameny, USSR]
7 34 50 04	BP	Aero Charter/Cavok Airlines	CCCP-11032 RA-11032 11032 EK-11032 UR-BXK
7 34 50 05	BP	(Volga Dnepr)	CCCP-11992 [wfu 1998; canx 16Oct01; fate/status unknown]
7 34 50 06		(Soviet Air Force)	CCCP-11875 [w/o 08Jly89 Cam Ranh, South Vietnam; canx 30Jan90]
7 34 50 07	BP	(Russian Air Force)	CCCP-11746 [canx unknown date; offered for sale Dec07; fate/status unknown]
7 34 50 08	BP	(Volga Dnepr)	CCCP-11814 [canx unknown date; fate/status unknown]
7 34 50 09	B	(Aeroflot/Polar)	CCCP-11033 [canx 1977; fate/status unknown]
7 34 50 10	B	(ex Baikal Airlines)	CCCP-11034 RA-11034 [canx 18Feb00 to Lesotho non-airworthy;fate/status unknown]
7 34 51 01	BP	(Soviet Air Force)	CCCP-11815 [w/o pre Apr94 Massawa, (or Asmara?) Eritrea; by Jun06 restaurant at Massawa Bus Station]
7 34 51 02	BP	(Russian Air Force)	CCCP-11780 RA-11780 [wfu/derelict by Aug99 Ivanovo-Severny, Russia; b/u by 2006; canx unknown date]
7 34 51 03		(Russian Air Force)	CCCP-11877 RA-11877 [wfu 1998; canx 16Oct01; fate/status unknown]
7 34 51 04		Russian Air Force	34 red
7 34 51 05		.	[nothing known]
7 34 51 06		.	[nothing known]
7 34 51 07		(Civil Aviation Administration China)	51056+ B-1056 [+ China; not fully confirmed] [preserved by Mar08 Lushan Aviation Museum, China; 28Feb09 fuselage taken away for either scrap or use as a house]
7 34 51 08		.	[nothing known]
7 34 51 09		.	[nothing known]
7 34 51 10		.	[nothing known]
7 34 52 01	BK	Transavia Service	[Soviet] [Uzbek AF] ER-AXE EK-12201 EK-12221 4L-VAS [canx by 01Jan09; fate/status unknown]
7 34 52 02	BK	Russian Air Force	[Soviet] 15 red
7 34 52 03	BK	Silk Way Airlines	[Soviet] 09 red+ UR-CGU 4K-AZ93 [+ Russia]
7 34 52 04		.	[nothing known]
7 34 52 05	BK	Russian Navy	[Soviet] 22 blue 22 red RF-12031 [also wears 22 red]
7 34 52 06	BK	Yermolino Airlines	[Soviet] RA-11356
7 34 52 07		.	
7 34 52 08	BK	(Volare)	84+ 21 blue^ UR-11348 UR-SMA# [+ Soviet, code colour unknown; ^ Ukraine; # canx 20Jly10; status/fate unknown]
7 34 52 09	BK	ex Azza	[Soviet] ER-AXC ST-DAS [canx by Jan07; status/fate unknown]
7 34 52 10	BP	Angolan Air Force?	10 yellow+ 10 yellow^ D2-FRI [+ Soviet; ^ Belarus]
. 34 53 01		.	[nothing known]

ANTONOV An-12

C/n	Model	Last known Owner/Operator	Identities/fates/comments (where appropriate)
. 34 53 02		.	[nothing known]
8 34 53 03	BP	CAAC Aeronautical Institution	203+ B-203 B-3152 [+ China] [GIA by Oct98 Tianjin Technical School; later preserved]
. 34 53 04	BK	Russian Air Force	[Soviet] 10 red
7 34 53 05	BK	UKAS	[Soviet] 27 blue+ EX-130 4L-GLT 3X-GFX [+ Russia]
. 34 53 06		.	[nothing known]
7 34 53 07		China Aviation Museum	1059+ B-1059 [+ China] [preserved by Oct98 Changping, China; l/n 14Oct10]
8 34 53 08		China Aviation Museum	1151+ [+ China] [preserved by Oct98 Changping, China: l/n 14Oct10]
7 34 53 09	BK	(ex V I Panchenko)	[Soviet] [Russia+] RA-11377 [+ code or regn not known] [canx by Jan07; l/n 31Mar09 Khartoum, Sudan]
7 34 53 10	BP	ex Azza Transport	29+ EK-11028 ST-ARV [+ Soviet, code colour unknown] [offered for sale Sep06; l/n 2007 stored Khabarovsk-Bolshoi, Russia]
7 34 54 01	BK	Russian Air Force	[Soviet] 26 blue
7 34 54 02	BK	Russian Air Force	[Soviet] 14 red
7 34 54 03	BK	Aero Fret Business	CCCP-93922 RA-93922 ER-ACZ TN-AGZ EX-124(2)
. 34 54 04		.	[nothing known]
. 34 54 05		.	[nothing known]
7 34 54 06	BK	Russian Air Force	[Soviet] 18 red [offered for sale Nov06; not sold, by Jun12 stored Khabarovsk, Russia]
8 34 54 07	BP	(Special Cargo Airlines)	CCCP-13320 [w/o 23Sep91 Khatanga,USSR; canx date unknown]
8 34 54 08	BK	(Phoenix Avia)	CCCP-46741 RA-46741 EK-46741 [w/o 28Mar06 5km from Payam, Iran; canx 29Mar06]
8 34 54 09		.	[nothing known]
8 34 54 10	BK	(Angolan Air Force)	11 yellow+ 11 yellow^ 9Q-CEN T-311# [+Soviet; ^ Belarus # call sign D2-MBI] [DBR 29Sep08 Luanda, Angola & stored; by 28Mar09 with tail cut off]
8 34 55 01	B	(Aeroflot/Krasnoyarsk)	CCCP-12950 [w/o 01May74 Polar Station SP-22, Arctic; canx 18Jun74]
8 34 55 02	B	(Unknown)	CCCP-12951 RA-12951 TN-AFR [w/o 30Jun99 near Lunda Sul, Angola]
8 34 55 03	B	Mango Airlines	CCCP-12952 RA-12952 ER-ACK(1) 9U-BHN(1) 9U-BHO 9Q-CVM [fate/status unknown]
8 34 55 04	B	Natalco Air Lines	CCCP-12953 RA-12953 ST-AQF TN-AHD+ TN-WHT+ TN-AID [+not fully confirmed]
8 34 55 05	BP	(Volare)	CCCP-12954 RA-12954 UR-LAI [canx 02Oct09; fate/status unknown]
8 34 55 06	B	(Vilyui)	CCCP-12955 RA-12955 [w/o 11Nov98 Krasnoyarsk, Russia]
8 34 55 07	B	ATMA	CCCP-12956 RA-12956 4R-EXC TN-AHZ UP-AN217
8 34 55 08	BP	(Moskovia Airlines)	CCCP-12957 RA-12957 [w/o 26May08 Roshchino, 11km from Chelyabinsk Airport, Russia]
8 34 55 09	B	(Aeroflot/Tyumen)	CCCP-12958 [canx 1978; fate/status unknown]
8 34 55 10	B	Go Cargo	CCCP-12959 RA-12959 EL-ALE D2-FBY ER-ACW LZ-BRC ER-ADY 4L-VPI
8 34 56 01		ex Skycabs	CCCP-13357 RA-13357 [canx 27Nov96 to Zaire; fate/status unknown]
8 34 56 02	BK	Russian Air Force	[Soviet] 25 blue [wfu 1997 Khabarovsk-Bolshoi, Russia; l/n Jan09]
8 34 56 03	BK	Russian Air Force	[Soviet] [not known] [offered for sale Dec07; fate/status unknown]
8 34 56 04	BK	Meridian	87+ 87^ UR-11314 ER-AXX UR-CAH [+ Soviet; ^ Ukraine, both code colour unknown; Sep/Oct11 painted with fake USAF markings as 60026]
8 34 56 05	BK	Silk Way Airlines	CCCP-11715 11715 4K-AZ23+ [+ originally miss-painted as 4KAZ-23]
8 34 56 06	BK	Russian Air Force	12 red
8 34 56 07	BP	Click Airways/Asia Airways	[Soviet] RA-11367 XU-395(1) RDPL-34142 EK-12555 EX-029 EY-401+ [+ not fully confirmed]
8 34 56 08	BK	Russian Air Force	99 red
8 34 56 09	BK	(Silk Way Airlines)	CCCP-11843 4K-AZ21 [w/o 07Nov02 Kome, Chad; b/u Spring 2004]
8 34 56 10	BK	Russian Air Force	19 red [stored by Jan09 Khabarovsk-Bolshoi, Russia]
8 34 57 01		.	[nothing known]
8 34 57 02	BK	unknown	94 red+ 54 red^ UR-11346 ER-ADP [+ Soviet Union; ^ Ukraine]
8 34 57 03	BK	Russian Air Force	{Soviet} 03 red [stored by Jun12 Khabarovsk, Russia]
8 34 57 04		.	[nothing known]
8 34 57 05		.	[nothing known]
8 34 57 06	BK	Russian Air Force	CCCP-11781 RA-11781
8 34 57 07	BP	Ministry of Interior (MVD)	[Soviet] 07 red RF-12042
8 34 57 08	BK	Russian Air Force	[Soviet] CCCP-12504 21 red
8 34 57 09	BK	Russian Air Force	[Soviet] 07 red

ANTONOV An-12

C/n	Model	Last known Owner/Operator	Identities/fates/comments (where appropriate)
8 34 57 10	BK	Aero-Charter	[Soviet] UR-CBH LZ-MNP(2) UR-DWG
8 34 58 01	BK	Russian Air Force	[Soviet] 51 red
8 34 58 02	BK	Meridian	[Soviet] 53 red+ LZ-MNK UR-DWF [+ Ukraine]
8 34 58 03		.	[nothing known]
8 34 58 04	BK	(Ahmed Ould)	[Soviet] ST-AWU 3C-AWU [w/o 10Apr01 Nouadhibou, Mauritania; this accident was earlier reported as being an An-26 with these marks]
8 34 58 05	BK	unknown	CCCP-12153+ ER-AXQ UN-11376 3X-GFO [+ used codes 96 & 17 red, order not certain]
8 34 58 06	BK	Russian Air Force	CCCP-11803 RA-11803
8 34 58 07	BK	Democratic Republic of Congo AF	CCCP-11846 4K-AZ36 EX-084 S9-PSK 9T-TCH(2) [marks used concurrently on c/n 5 34 31 03]
8 34 58 08	BK	Russian Air Force	15 red
8 34 58 09	BP	ex Air Victory Georgia	[Soviet] ER-AXL 4L-ROM [stored by 13Mar10 Fujairah, UAE]
8 34 58 10	BP	Russian Air Force	37 red+ D2-FAY 37 red [+Soviet/Russian AF]
8 34 59 01		.	[nothing known]
8 34 59 02	BK	Russian Air Force	43 red
8 34 59 03		.	[nothing known]
8 34 59 04		.	[nothing known]
8 34 59 05	BP	Russian Air Force	05 red+ 29 blue+ RF-95425 [+ Russia]
8 34 59 06		.	[nothing known]
8 34 59 07	BK	Russian Air Force	48 red+ [+Soviet/Russian AF]
8 34 59 08	BP	(Sudan Air Force)	807+ YI-AER 988 [+Iraq] [derelict by 2001 Wau, Sudan; l/n Apr07]
8 34 59 09	BP	(Sudan Air Force)	805+ YI-AEP ST-ALV+ [+Iraq] [+ marks later reported on unknown Y8F; fate/status unknown]
8 34 59 10	BP	(Iraqi Air Force)	806 YI-AFJ [fate/status unknown; l/n 1987/88 Iran-Iraq war]
8 34 60 01	B	(Balkan Bulgarian Airlines)	LZ-BAA [w/o Dec75 Kufrah, Libya]
8 34 60 02	B	Bourgas Airport Aviaion Expo	LZ-BAB [wfu 06Jly91; preserved by Oct98 Bourgas, Bulgaria]
8 34 60 03	BP	Russian Air Force	[Soviet] RA-11260
8 34 60 04	BK	(Elbrus Air/Sky Cabs)	[Soviet] RA-11302 [w/o 24Mar00 Colombo, Sri Lanka]
8 34 60 05		.	[nothing known]
8 34 60 06	B	Asia Airways	CCCP-11521(1)+ 75 red^ RA-11368 LZ-ITB LZ-BRA EX-12333 EX-031 EY-402 [+not fully confirmed ^ Russia, not fully confirmed]
8 34 60 07		.	[nothing known]
8 34 60 08	BK	Russian Air Force	[Soviet] 28 blue RF-95430+ [+ as of 17Oct11 still carrying 28 blue]
8 34 60 09		.	[nothing known]
8 34 60 10	BK	(Juba Air Cargo)	[Soviet] RA-11329 (EL-AKY) RA-11329 EL-ALF D2-FBZ 3C-QRD EK-11011 ST-ARN [w/o 27Jun08 near Malakal, Sudan]
8 34 61 01	BK	Russian Air Force	[Soviet] RA-11420
8 34 61 02	BK	Russian Air Force	CCCP-11504 22 red
8 34 61 03		ex Russian Air Force	CCCP-12134+ 72 red+ [+ not fully confirmed] [GIA Balashov, Russia Technical School; l/n Jan09]
8 34 61 04	BK	Air Armenia Cargo	CCCP-12110 EX-334 EK-12104
8 34 61 05	BP	unknown	[Soviet] UR-11347 ER-ADO+ ST- [+ canx 15Sep05 to Sudan; fate/status unknown]
8 34 61 06	BK	Meridian	[Soviet] 03 blue+ ER-AXZ UR-CAJ [+ Ukraine]
8 34 61 07	BK	Air Armenia Cargo	CCCP-11244 EK-11001
8 34 61 08		.	[nothing known]
8 34 61 09	TB	ex Minenta Labell Guinee	CCCP-11049 RA-11049 [stored by Aug02 Yermolino, Russia; l/n Aug04]
8 34 61 10	TB	Russian Air Force	CCCP-12968 12968 RA-12968
8 34 62 01	BP	unknown	CCCP-11267 4K-AZ33 4L-12003 4K-AZ33 S9-DBP [substantial damage unknown date somewhere in Africa; photo evidence!]
8 34 62 02	BK	ex Santa Cruz Imperial	CCCP-12147 RA-12191 EL-AKW YA-PAB EL-ALJ [wfu by 14Jan06 Sharjah, UAE; derelict by Nov07; l/n Mar08]
9 34 62 03	BK	Russian Air Force	[Soviet] [Russian AF+] RA-12122(2) [+code/colour unknown]
9 34 62 04	BK	Uzbekistan Air Force	[Soviet] 10 red
9 34 62 05	BK	Angolan Air Force	77 blue+ UR-11306 D2-MBU [+Soviet/Ukraine]
9 34 62 06	12	(Soviet Air Force)	[Soviet] [fate/status unknown]
9 34 62 07	BK	(Soviet Air Force)	33 blue [fate/status unknown]
9 34 62 08	BP	(Ukraine Cargo Airways)	22 blue+ UR-UCM [+Soviet/Ukraine AF; w/o 14Apr00 Kinshasa-N'Djili, Democratic Republic of Congo; canx 02Apr01]
9 34 62 09	TBK	Russian Air Force	98+ 95 red [+Soviet, code colour possibly green]
9 34 62 10		.	[nothing known]

ANTONOV An-12

C/n	Model	Last known Owner/Operator	Identities/fates/comments (where appropriate)
9 34 63 01	BK	Russian Air Force	[Soviet] 34 red
9 34 63 02	BP	Transliz Aviation	[Soviet] UR-11349 UR-YMR S9-KHE
9 34 63 03	BK-IS	Russian Air Force	68 red
9 34 63 04	TBK	(Soviet Air Force)	69+ 19 red [+ Soviet, code colour unknown] [fate/status unknown]
9 34 63 05	TBK	Russian Navy	76+ 26 red [+ Soviet, code colour unknown]
9 34 63 06	TBK-1	(Soviet Air Force)	46 red [fate/status unknown]
9 34 63 07	TBK-1	Russian Air Force	16+ 26 blue^ RF-95682 [+ Soviet, code colour unknown; ^ Russia]
9 34 63 08	TBK	Silk Way Airlines	CCCP-12108(2) RA-12108 LZ-BFE RA-12108 4K-AZ18 UR-CBU 4K-AZ63
9 34 63 09	BK	Scorpion Air	CCCP-12113 LZ-MNP
9 34 63 10	TBK	Atran	CCCP-11868 OB-1448 CCCP-11868 RA-11868
9 34 64 01		.	[nothing known]
9 34 64 02		.	[nothing known]
9 34 64 03	BK	Russian Air Force	[Soviet] 11 red
9 34 64 04	PPS	Russian Air Force	[Soviet] 26 red
9 34 64 05	BK	(Volare)	[Soviet] 24 blue+ UR-LIP [+ Ukraine] [w/o en-route 07Feb02 80km from Agadir, Morocco; canx 31Oct08
9 34 64 06	TB	(Aeroflot/Krasnoyarsk)	CCCP-12962 [w/o 13May86 sank through polar ice near Graham Bell Island, Franz-Joseph-Land]
9 34 64 07	TB	(Aeroflot/Krasnoyarsk)	CCCP-12963 [w/o en-route 23Aug79 18km from Yeniseysk, USSR]
9 34 64 08	TB	(Aeroflot/Yakutsk)	CCCP-12964+ CCCP-11005(2) [+severely damaged in 1976 Yakutsk, USSR; re-built using rear fuselage of c/n 6 34 39 07 using its old marks; canx 1976; fate/status unknown] [canx 1976; fate/status unknown]
9 34 64 09	TB	Donavia	CCCP-12965 RA-12965 5N-BCN 3X-GDR+ [+ not fully confirmed]
9 34 64 10		MAP Komsomolsk na Amure APO	CCCP-48978 RA-48978
9 34 65 01	TB	(Aeroflot/North Kavkaz)	CCCP-12966 [w/o 26Feb70 Beryozovo, USSR; canx 1970]
9 34 65 02	TB	(Aeroflot/Yakutsk)	CCCP-12967 [w/o 02Oct73 Magadan-Sokol, USSR; canx 1973]
9 34 65 03	B	(Aeroflot/Magadan)	CCCP-12971(1) [probably w/o 07Sep87 Omsk, USSR; canx 20Jan88]
9 34 65 04	B	Sudanese State Aviation	CCCP-12972 12972 RA-12972 D2-FCT TN-AGK(1) D2-FCT ER-ACG ST-AQQ
9 34 65 05	B	(Tyumen Airlines)	CCCP-12973 RA-12973 [w/o 11May98 Luanda, Angola; canx 29Dec99]
9 34 65 06	BK	ex Avial	CCCP-12974 RA-12974 [stored by Jan11 & impounded 11Apr11 Tver, Russia; sold 25May11]
9 34 65 07	BK	Russian Air Force	[Soviet] RA-11414+ [+ not fully confirmed]
9 34 65 08	BK	UKAS	[Soviet] 31 blue+ EX-128 ER-ADZ EW- UP-AN203 3X-GGW [+ Russia]
9 34 65 09	B	(RPS Air Freight Company)	CCCP-12975 RA-12975 3C-OOZ UN-11007 [w/o 31Mar05 Al-Rayyan Airport, Mukalia, Yemen]
9 34 65 10	B	(Air Victory Georgia)	CCCP-12976 RA-12976 EX-025 4L-IRA [canx by 23Mar11; fate/status unknown]
9 34 66 01	B	(Sakha Avia)	CCCP-12977 RA-12977 [canx 21Feb96; fate/status unknown]
9 34 66 02	B	(Intertransavia)	CCCP-12960 RA-12960 UN-11006(2) EX-12960 ER-AXD [w/o 11May03 Asmara, Ethiopia; canx 12Sep03]
9 34 66 03		.	[nothing known]
9 34 66 04	BP	Russian Air Force	[Soviet] 21 red
9 34 66 05	PPS	Russian Air Force	[Soviet] 90 red
9 34 66 06		.	
9 34 66 07	BK	Ukraine Air Force	CCCP-11398(2) 86 red
9 34 66 08	BK	Anton Air?	[Soviet] RA-11658 7P-ANC
9 34 66 09		.	[nothing known]
9 34 66 10	PPS	Ministry of Interior (MVD)	08 red+ RF-12043 [+ Soviet/Russian Air Force]
9 34 67 01	BK	Russian Air Force	[Soviet] 06 red
9 34 67 02	BK	(MAP Komsomolsk na Amure APO)	[Soviet] CCCP-12162(1) [w/o 19Oct87 Komsomolsk na Amure, USSR]
9 34 67 03	BK	Uzbekistan Air Force	[Soviet] 09 red
9 34 67 04	BK	UKAS	28 blue+ 28 blue^ EX-131 4L-GLN 3X-GFY [+ Soviet; ^ Russia]
9 34 67 05	BK	(Soviet Air Force)	CCCP-11787 [canx unknown date; fate/status unknown]
67 06	BP	(Egyptian Air Force)	1240//SU-APY [dual marks] [reportedly b/u after Aug74]
67 07	BP	(Egyptian Air Force)	1241//SU-ARA [dual marks] [reportedly b/u after Aug74]
9 34 67 08	BK	Russian Air Force	[Soviet] 23 blue RF-95683+ [+ still wears 23 blue]
67 09	BP	(Egyptian Air Force)	1242//SU-ARE [dual marks] [reportedly b/u after Aug74]

ANTONOV An-12

C/n	Model	Last known Owner/Operator	Identities/fates/comments (where appropriate)
67 10	BP	(Egyptian Air Force)	1243//SU-ARD [dual marks] [reportedly b/u after Aug74]
9 34 68 01	BK	Pamir Air	CCCP-11724 RA-11321 EL-AKR YA-PAA 00406+ [+ reported Kabul, Afghanistan several times since Apr02; latterly also wearing YA-PAA]
9 34 68 02	BK	Russian Air Force	CCCP-11425(2)+ [Ukraine?] RA-11425 [+not fully confirmed]
9 34 68 03	BK	(Skyway)	[Soviet] ER-ACN EX-129 4L-GLU [canx by 23Mar11; fate/status unknown]
9 34 68 04	BK	(Soviet Air Force)	CCCP-11800 [canx unknown date; fate/status unknown]
9 34 68 05	BK	Moskoviya	CCCP-12193 RA-12193
9 34 68 06		.	[nothing known]
9 34 68 07	BK?	(Air Victory Georgia)	[Soviet] RA-11317 LZ-BAH LZ-CBH 4L-VAL [canx by 23Mar11; fate/status unknown]
9 34 68 08	BK	Azza Transport	[Soviet] UR-CFC ST-AZN+ [+ also coded 956 Sudanese Air Force]
9 34 68 09	BK	Angolan Air Force	[Soviet] 87 red+ D2-MBN [+ Ukraine]
9 34 68 10	BK	Motor Sich	[Soviet] RA-11316 UR-11316
9 34 69 01	BP	Russian Air Force	[Soviet] 67 red 17+ 15 red [+ Russia; colour not reported]
9 34 69 02	BK	Russian Air Force	[Soviet] 63 red
9 34 69 03		.	[nothing known]
9 34 69 04	BK	Meridian	CCCP-13341 RA-13341 LZ-SAA LZ-SFT ER-AXY UR-CAG
9 34 69 05	BK	(Ukraine Cargo Airways)	[Soviet] 11304 UR-UCK [canx 03Feb10; fate/status unknown]
00 34 69 06	BK	(Aeroflot)	CCCP-11804(2) [fate/status unknown]
00 34 69 07	BK	KATA	[Soviet] 05 red+ ST-AZM [+ Ukraine]
00 34 69 08	BK	(British Gulf International)	[Soviet] 42 red+ EX-165 S9-SAO [+ Russia] [probably w/o 13Nov08 Al Asab AFB, Iraq]
00 34 69 09	BP	(PT Camar Nusansa As)	[Soviet] RA-11369 LZ-ITC [w/o 25Aug00 Kisangani, Democratic Republic of Congo]
00 34 69 10	B	Tashkent Aircraft Production Corp	65 blue+ CCCP-11807 UK-11807 [+ Soviet]
00 34 70 01		.	[nothing known]
00 34 70 02	MGA	(Russian Air Force)	CCCP-12135 RA-12135 [w/o 22May01 80/100km south of Tver, Russia]
00 34 70 03	TBK	(First Business & Cargo Co)+	CCCP-98103 RA-98103 3C-AAL 9Q-CZB [+ owner/operator obscure] [missing 29Sep07 en-route Kisangani-Goma, Democratic Republic of Congo; no wreck found by Jly08]
00 34 70 04	BK	(Volare)	[Soviet] 20 blue+ UR-BWM [+ Ukraine] [canx 30Apr09; fate/status unknown]
00 34 70 05	BK	Exim Trading	[Soviet] ER-AXK 3X-GEM
00 34 70 06	BK	AZZA Air Transport	[Soviet] 57 blue+ UR-CFD ST-AZH [+ Ukraine]
00 34 70 07	BK	Kush Aviation	[Soviet] 18 red+ RA-11379 ST-KNR [+ Russia]
00 34 70 08	BK	Russian Air Force	[Soviet] 17 red+ [+ Russia]
00 34 70 09	BK	Russian Air Force	[Soviet] 15 red
00 34 70 10	BK	Russian Air Force	[Soviet] 65+ [+ code colour unknown]
00 34 71 01		.	[nothing known]
00 34 71 02	BK	Styron Trading	[Soviet] ER-ACA 4K-AZ35 4L-AIR EX-086(2) S9-DBQ [w/o date unknown Berbera, Somalia; hulk l/n 10Jan10]
00 34 71 03	B	unknown	CCCP-12980 RA-12980 (HK-4308X) RA-12980 [stored/wfu by May02 Villavicencio, Colombia; l/n 07Feb10]
00 34 71 04	B	ex Zapolyarye	CCCP-12981 RA-12981 [DBR 11Apr03 Sredni Island, Arctic; cannibalised & abandoned; l/n Apr07]
00 34 71 05	B	(Aeroflot/Polar)	CCCP-12982 [canx 1978; fate/status unknown]
00 34 71 06	B	(Pulkovo Avia)	CCCP-12983 RA-12983 [canx 16Jan98; b/u]
00 34 71 07	TBK	Asia Airways	[Soviet] 71 red+ RA-11301 LZ-ITD XU-355 4R-AIA EX-042 EY-403 [+ Ukraine]
00 34 71 08	TBK-1	Russian Air Force	14+ 14 red RF-93950^ [+ Soviet, code colour unknown; ^ also with code 14 red]
00 34 71 09	B	Transliz Aviation	CCCP-12984 RA-12984 ER-ADG S9-KHF
00 34 71 10	B	(Aeroflot/East Siberia)	CCCP-12985 [w/o 04Dec74 Ushakovka River, Irkutsk, USSR, following collision with An-2 CCCP-49342]
00 34 72 01	B	ex Volare	CCCP-12986 RA-12986 UR-LTG [canx 08Oct10; l/n 14Aug09 N'Djamena, Chad; fate/status unknown]
00 34 72 02	B	(Alada)	CCCP-12987 RA-12987 D2-FRG [wfu before Jan02; l/n 19Oct03 Pointe Noire, People's Republic of Congo; b/u by summer 2004]
00 34 72 03	BK	Moskoviya	[Soviet] RA-12194
00 34 72 04	BK-1	Russian Air Force	[Soviet] 23 blue
00 34 72 05	BK-1	(Soviet Air Force)	28+ [+ code colour unknown] [fate/status unknown]

ANTONOV An-12

C/n	Model	Last known Owner/Operator	Identities/fates/comments (where appropriate)
00 34 72 06	TB	Kosmos Airlines	CCCP-12988 RA-12988
00 34 72 07	B	(Aeroflot/Privolzhsk)	CCCP-12989 [canx 1985; fate/status unknown]
00 34 72 08	BK	(Russian Navy)	CCCP-11387 RA-11387 [canx unknown date; wfu by 31Aug04 Taganrog, Russia; fate/status unknown]
00 34 72 09	BK	Russian Air Force	[Soviet] 15 red
00 34 72 10	BK	Ruby Star	[Soviet] RA-13392 EW-275TI
00 34 73 01	BK	Russian Air Force	[Soviet] 21 blue
00 34 73 02	BK-1	Russian Air Force	74+ 22 blue^ 25 blue [+ Soviet, code colour unknown; ^ Russia]
00 34 73 03	PPS	Russian Air Force	80+ 80 red [+ Soviet, code colour unknown]
00 34 73 04	B	Atran	CCCP-12990 OB-1448 CCCP-12990 RA-12990
00 34 73 05	BP	ex South Airlines	CCCP-12991 RA-12991 EL-ALA 3C-ZZD EK-12777 ST-SAE EK-12777 EK-12305 [w/o 29Jun06 Bagram, Afghanistan]
00 34 73 06	B	Transliz Aviation	CCCP-12992 RA-12992 ER-ACY S9-KHC
00 34 73 07	B	(Aeroflot/International)	CCCP-12993 [w/o 29Jly71 Calcutta, India; canx]
00 34 73 08	BK	Russian Air Force	09 red+ 27 red [+ Soviet]
00 34 73 09	PPS	(Soviet Air Force)	84+ [+ Soviet, code colour unknown] [fate/status unknown]
00 34 73 10	BK-1	Russian Air Force	62 red+ 16 red [+ Soviet]
00 34 74 01	B	Transliz Aviation	CCCP-12994 RA-12994 ER-ACS S9-KHL
00 34 74 02	B	(Pulkovo Avia)	CCCP-12995 RA-12995 [canx 17Mar99; probably b/u]
00 34 74 03	B	(Aeroflot/Tyumen)	CCCP-12996 [w/o 31Jan71 14km from Surgut, USSR; canx 1971]
00 34 74 04	B	(Aeroflot/Urals)	CCCP-12997 [w/o 13Jan89 Sverdlovsk-Koltovo, USSR; canx 06Apr89]
00 34 74 05		Russian Air Force	[Soviet] 12 red
00 34 74 06	BP	MAP Komsomolsk na Amure APO	22 red+ 22 red^ RA-11371 11371^ RA-11371 [+ Soviet; ^ Russia]
00 34 74 07	BK	(Tiramavia)	12 yellow+ 12 yellow^ ER-AXG [+ Soviet] [^ Belarus] [canx 21Jun07; fate/status unknown]
00 34 74 08	BK	ex Skylink Arabia	CCCP-11038(2) RA-11038(2) 4L-TAS EX-119 ER-ACV UN-11021 UP-AN204 [stored Mar10 Ras el Khaimah, UAE; canx]
00 34 74 09	BP	(Volga Dnepr)	CCCP-11344 (2) RA-11344 [canx unknown date; fate/status unknown]
00 34 74 10	BK	Moskoviya	[Soviet] RA-12195
00 34 75 01	PPS	Russian Air Force	[Soviet] 34+ [+ code colour unknown]
00 34 75 02	BK	Russian Air Force	94+ 24 blue [+ Soviet, code colour unknown]
00 34 75 03	BK	Russian Air Force	CCCP-11343(2) RA-11343
00 34 75 04		(Amuraviatrans)	CCCP-11149 CCCP-13340 RA-13340 [w/o 27Mar95 Bunia, Zaire]
00 34 75 05	BK	Kosmos Airlines	CCCP-11363(2) RA-11363
00 34 75 06	BK	unknown	CCCP-11938 4K-AZ37
00 34 75 07	BKPPS	Russian Air Force	36+ RA-12124(2) [+ Soviet, code colour unknown]
00 34 75 08	BK	Russian Air Force	45+ 45 red [+ Soviet, code colour unknown]
00 34 75 09	BK	Russian Air Force	[Soviet] RA-11245
00 34 75 10	12	Irkut/Gromov Air	[Soviet] RA-11309 11309
00 34 76 01	12BK	SAT Airlines	CCCP-11364 RA-11364
00 34 76 02	BK	Russian Air Force	[Soviet] 02 red+ [+ Russia]
00 34 76 03	BKPPS	Natalco Air Lines	[Soviet] EK-12603 TN-AHY [overhaul abandonned & stored by 09Oct10 Rovno, Ukraine]
00 34 76 04	BK	(Ukraine Cargo Airways)	[Soviet] UR-11303 UR-UCN [l/n 06Oct10 wfu Zaporozhia, Ukraine; canx 07Jly11]
00 34 76 05	BK	Russian Air Force	[Soviet] 27 red+ RA-12137(2) [+ Russia]
00 34 76 06	BK	(Sarit Airlines)	CCCP-11341(2) EK-12222 ST-SAF [w/o 05Oct04 Gajlij, Sudan]
00 34 76 07	BK	(Volga Dnepr)	CCCP-11342(2) [w/o 24Jly92 Mount Liset, 24km S. Skopje, Yugoslavia]
00 34 76 08		(Soviet Air Force)	CCCP-11362(2) [canx unknown date; fate/status unknown]
00 34 76 09	BK	Russian Air Force	[Soviet] 27 red+ 27 blue+ 27 yellow [+ Russia]
01 34 76 10	B	(Tyumen Airlines)	CCCP-12998 RA-12998 [canx 25Jun97; fate/status unknown]
01 34 77 01	B	ATMA	CCCP-12999 12999 CCCP-12999 RA-12999 4K-12999 RA-12999 LZ-VEB UN-11019 UP-AN212
01 34 77 02	TB	ex Norilsk Avia	CCCP-11100 RA-11100 [canx 12Apr99; by Jun06 fuselage used for storage, Norlisk-Alykel, Russia]
01 34 77 03	B	(Sheremetyevo Research Institute)	CCCP-11101 RA-11101 [w/o 06Oct96 Lukapa, Angola]
01 34 77 04	B	Taron Avia	CCCP-11102(2) RA-11102 S9-BOS EX-163 EK-11102 EK-12704
01 34 77 05	B	(Aeroflot/Northern)	CCCP-11103 [canx 1976; fate/status unknown]
01 34 77 06	PPS	Russian Air Force	82+ 82 red [+ Soviet, code colour unknown] [offered for sale Dec07; fate/status unknown]
01 34 77 07	BK-IS	Russian Air Force	32+ 16 red [+ Soviet, code colour unknown]

ANTONOV An-12

C/n	Model	Last known Owner/Operator	Identities/fates/comments (where appropriate)
01 34 77 08	PPS	Russian Air Force	51+ 70 red^ 25 blue^ RF-95685 [+ Soviet, code colour unknown; ^ Russia]
01 34 77 09	PPS	Russian Air Force	70+ RA-12709 19 red [+ Soviet, code colour unknown]
01 34 77 10	B	(Aeroflot/International)	CCCP-11104 [w/o 28Oct80 Mount Vapsi-Karnibaba, Afghanistan; canx 19Nov80]
01 34 78 01	BP	(Pulkovo Avia)	CCCP-11105(2) RA-11105 [canx 16Jan98; b/u]
01 34 78 02	B	(Ariana Afghan Airlines)	CCCP-11106 RA-11106 EL-ALD YA-DAA [reported destroyed late 2001 during US bombing raid]
01 34 78 03	BK	Ridge Airways/Taron Avia	[Soviet] UR-11305 XU-395(2) EK-12803 EK-12835
01 34 78 04		Russian Air Force	[Soviet] 33 red
01 34 78 05	PPS	Russian Air Force	18+ 14 red [+ Soviet, code colour unknown]
01 34 78 06	PPS	Russian Air Force	72+ 72 red [+ Soviet, code colour unknown]
01 34 78 07	PPS	Russian Air Force	38+ 38 red [+ Soviet, code colour unknown]
01 34 78 08	BK	Russian Air Force	42+ RF-12560 [+ Soviet, code colour unknown]
01 34 78 09	B	(Aeroflot/International)	CCCP-11107 [w/o 24Apr82 Novy Urengoi-Yagelnoye, USSR; canx 1982]
01 34 78 10	BP	(Pulkovo Avia)	CCCP-11108(2) LZ-PVK RA-11108 [canx 11Feb97; b/u]
01 34 79 01	BP	(Pulkovo Avia)	CCCP-11109(2) RA-11109 11109 RA-11109 [canx 11Feb97; b/u]
01 34 79 02	B	(Aviakor)	CCCP-11110(2) RA-11110 [w/o 07Aug93 over Sudan]
01 34 79 03		(Soviet Air Force)	54+ [+ Soviet, code colour unknown] [fate/status unknown]
01 34 79 04	BKPPS	610CCT Centre Museum	06 red+ 06 red^ [+ Soviet; ^ Russia] [preserved by Jly02 Ivanovo-Severny, Russia; l/n 2008]
01 34 79 05		.	[nothing known]
01 34 79 06	B	(Magadan Cargo Airlines)	CCCP-11111(2) [w/o 14Jly92 near Irkutsk, USSR]
01 34 79 07	TB	Air Armenia Cargo	CCCP-11112(2) RA-11112 LZ-BRW ER-AXA RDPL-34153 EK-12112
01 34 79 08	BP	Transliz Aviation	CCCP-11113(2) RA-11113 ER-ACQ S9-KHD [reported stored by Aug11 Chisinau, Moldova]
01 34 79 09	TB	East Wing	CCCP-11114 RA-11114 D2-FDC ER-ACJ 3C-QRI UN-11006 UP-AN207
01 34 79 10	PPS	(Soviet Air Force)	44+ [+ Soviet, code colour unknown]
01 34 80 01		.	[nothing known]
01 34 80 02	BP	(Pulkovo Avia)	CCCP-11118 RA-11118 [w/o 24Feb94 Nalchik, Russia; canx 27Jly94]
01 34 80 03	TB	Avial	CCCP-11115 (2) RA-11115
01 34 80 04		Russian Air Force	[Soviet] 08 red
01 34 80 05	BP	Click Airways	10+ UK-11109 XU-365(1) EX-034 EX-169 [+ Soviet, code colour unknown]
01 34 80 06	B	Aero Charter	CCCP-11116 RA-11116 LZ-BRV UR-CGR EK-12006 UR-CJN
01 34 80 07	BP	Miras Cargo	73311//YU-AIC+ LZ-SGA LZ-SFA YU-UIA UP-AN201 [+dual marks]
02 34 80 08	BP	Guinee Air Force	3X-GBA [fate/status?]
02 34 80 09	BP	Guinee Air Force	3X-GBB [full c/n assumed, only 80 09 confirmed; fate/status unknown]
02 34 80 10	BP	(Yugoslav Air Force)	73312//YU-AID+ [+ dual marks] [w/o 12Dec89 Yerevan-Zvarnots, USSR]
02 34 81 01	B	(Aeroflot)	CCCP-11119 [not confirmed; fate/status unknown]
02 34 81 02	BP	(Aeroflot/Yakutsk)	CCCP-11120 [w/o 03Oct91 on unpaved airstrip Cazombo, Angola]
02 34 81 03	B	(Unknown)	CCCP-11121(2)+ D2- [+canx 12Feb93 to Angola; shot down & DBR 26Apr93 in Angola; regn at time unknown]
02 34 81 04	BP	(Avia)	CCCP-11122 RA-11122 [w/o 13Apr97 Verkhneviluisk, Russia]
02 34 81 05	B	(Pulkovo Avia)	CCCP-11123 RA-11123 [canx 04Oct95; b/u]
02 34 81 06	B	ex Aero Service/Veteran	CCCP-11123 RA-11124 UR-CCY [stored by 13Mar10 Fujairah, UAE; canx 08Oct10]
02 34 81 07	BKPPS	Aero-Fret Business	50+ 50 red^ EX-124(1) TN-AHU [+ Soviet, code colour unknown; ^ Russia]
02 34 81 08	BP	(Aeroflot/Yakutsk)	CCCP-11125(1) [canx 1978 following severe internal corrosion caused by leaking cargo]
02 34 81 09	BKPPS	Russian Air Force	52 red+ 52 red^ RF-12556 [+ Soviet; ^ Russia]
02 34 81 10	BK	Russian Air Force	48 red+ RA-11719(2) [+Soviet/Russian AF; code colour unknown]
02 34 82 01	B	(Soviet Air Force)	CCCP-11126 [fate/status unknown]
02 34 82 02	B	(Pulkovo Avia)	CCCP-11127 LZ-PVL RA-11127 [badly damaged 09May95 Lukapa, Angola; repaired(?) then canx 17Mar99]
02 34 82 03	B	(Veteran)	CCCP-11128(2) RA-11128 UR-CEN [DBR 15Sep07 on ground Pointe Noire, People's Republic of Congo; l/n derelict Jan08]
02 34 82 04	BP	(Sigi Air Cargo)	CCCP-11129 [DBR 08Nov91 Janina, Sudan]
02 34 82 05	BP	Avial	CCCP-11130 RA-11130
02 34 82 06	BP	(Khabarovsk Avia)	02 red+ 02 red^ RA-11376 [+ Soviet; ^ Russia] [w/o 21Jly10 Keperveyem, Russia]

ANTONOV An-12

C/n	Model	Last known Owner/Operator	Identities/fates/comments (where appropriate)
02 34 82 07	B	ATMA	CCCP-11526 RA-11526 D2-FDB 3C-QQY LZ-VED UN-11017 UP-AN211
02 34 82 08	B	(Pulkovo Avia)	CCCP-11527 RA-11527 [canx 11Feb97; b/u]
34 82 09	BP	(Egyptian Air Force)	1251//SU-ARY [dual marks] [reportedly b/u; post 28Nov81]
34 82 10	BP	(Egyptian Air Force)	1252//SU-AVA [dual marks] [reportedly b/u; post 21Mar85]
02 34 83 01	BK	Russian Air Force	40+ 27 blue [+ Soviet, code colour unknown]
34 83 02	BP	(Egyptian Air Force)	1253//SU-ARZ [dual marks] [reportedly b/u; post Oct93]
02 34 83 03	BKPPS	Russian Air Force	24 red+ 24 red [+ Soviet]
02 34 83 04	BP	Berkut State Air Company	[Soviet] UN-11373 UP-AN205
34 83 05	BP	(Egyptian Air Force)	1254//SU-AVB [dual marks] [reportedly b/u; post 28Nov93]
02 34 83 06		ex Indian Air Force	L1471+ [+ not fully confirmed] [last flight 16Aug90; reportedly for sale Dec93; fate/status unknown]
02 34 83 07	BK	Russian Air Force	[Soviet] RA-11808 RF-12561
02 34 83 08		ex Indian Air Force	L1472+ [+ not fully confirmed] [last flight 15Dec88; fate/status unknown]
02 34 83 09	PPS	Russian Air Force	[Soviet] 39 red
02 34 83 10		.	[nothing known]

Unidentified – Civil Prefix

unkn		Civil Aviation Administration China	1052 [reported in service during May67]
unkn	BP	Civil Aviation Administration China	1053 [reported Mar75; fate unknown]
unkn		Civil Aviation Administration China	1054 [from photo; fate unknown]
unkn		Civil Aviation Administration China	1055 [in service in 1988; flew mission to Pakistan on 07May88]
unkn		Civil Aviation Administration China	1057 [reported Nov91; fate unknown]
unkn		Civil Aviation Administration China	1058 [reported 08Oct99 Beijing-Nan Yuan, China; later preserved there; l/n Nov08]
unkn		Civil Aviation Administration China	1150 [reported 06Oct09 Lushan, China, in good condition]
unkn		unknown	11259 [reported 11May97 Odessa-Tsentrainly, Ukraine; could be ex CCCP-11259, see below]
unkn		unknown	11474 [reported 08May97 and later Yevpatoriya, Ukraine]
unkn		Russian Navy?	11655 [reported 20Aug00 Engels-2 AFB, Russia; probably not CCCP-11655, see below]
unkn		unknown Ukraine operator	11963 [reported 18Sep96 Mikolayiv, Ukraine; ex CCCP-11963 see below]
unkn	B	Polyarnaya Aviatsiya	CCCP-04341 [reported in 1966; possible mis-sighting]
unkn	B	Polyarnaya Aviatsiya	CCCP-04346 [reported 27Nov82 Leningrad-Pulkovo, USSR; possible mis-sighting]
unkn	BP	Soviet Air Force	CCCP-10212 [reported 20Feb78 Addis Ababa, Ethiopia]
unkn	BP	Soviet Air Force	CCCP-10222 [reported 16Feb78 Addis Ababa, Ethiopia]
unkn	BP	Soviet Air Force	CCCP-11046 [reported 11Apr76 Sperenberg, East Germany]
unkn	BP	Soviet Air Force	CCCP-11083 [reported 03Jly94 Kaliningrad, Russia]
unkn		Soviet Air Force	CCCP-11102(1) [reported 18Aug67 Kano, Nigeria]
unkn		Soviet Air Force	CCCP-11105 1) [reported 18Aug67 Kano, Nigeria]
unkn	BP	Soviet Air Force	CCCP-11108(1) [from photo]
unkn		Soviet Air Force	CCCP-11109(1) [reported 18Aug67 Kano, Nigeria]
unkn	BP	Soviet Air Force	CCCP-11110(1) [reported 26Jly70 London-Heathrow, UK]
unkn		Soviet Air Force?	CCCP-11111(1) [reported 24Jan69 Athens, Greece]
unkn	BP	Soviet Air Force	CCCP-11112(1) [from photo]
unkn	AP?	Soviet Air Force	CCCP-11113(1) [reported 18Aug67 Kano, Nigeria; possibly was An-12 w/o 10Oct73 Aleppo, Syria during Israeli air raid]
unkn		Soviet Air Force	CCCP-11115(1) [reported 18Aug67 Kano, Nigeria]
unkn		Soviet Air Force	CCCP-11121(1) [reported 21Aug68 Hradcany, Czechoslovakia]
unkn		Soviet Air Force	CCCP-11128(1) [reported 21Aug68 Hradcany, Czechoslovakia]
unkn	BP	Soviet Air Force	CCCP-11154 [reported 20Aug92 Moscow-Vnukovo, Russia; these marks used by An-10 requires confirmation]
unkn	BP	Russian Air Force	CCCP-11178 [reported 13Feb89 Kabul, Afghanistan; 02Sep97 Ivanovo-Severny, Russia later there as RA-11178; see below]
unkn	BP	Soviet Air Force	CCCP-11212 [reported Apr85 Addis Ababa, Ethiopia; marks were also used on a An-10]
unkn		Soviet Air Force	CCCP-11217 [reported 18Aug67 Kano, Nigeria; marks were also used on a An-10; full confirmation of this report required]
unkn	BP	Soviet Air Force	CCCP-11222 [reported Sep75 Cairo, Egypt; marks also used on a An-10]
unkn	BP	Russian Air Force	CCCP-11228 [reported 24Aug95 Ivanovo-Severny, Russia and on 24Apr97]
unkn	B	Soviet Air Force	CCCP-11231 [from photo]

ANTONOV An-12

C/n	Model	Last known Owner/Operator	Identities/fates/comments (where appropriate)
unkn	BP	Soviet Air Force	CCCP-11235 [reported 21Oct73 Cairo, Egypt]
unkn	BP	Soviet Air Force	CCCP-11248 [reported 19Oct73 Cairo, Egypt]
unkn		Soviet Air Force	CCCP-11256 [reported 27Apr68 Kano, Nigeria]
unkn	RR	Soviet Air Force	CCCP-11259 [reported 10Jly68 Kano, Nigeria; might have become 11259 see above]
unkn	BP	Soviet Air Force	CCCP-11263 [reported 27Apr68 Kano, Nigeria and 19Oct73 Cairo, Egypt]
unkn	BP	Soviet Air Force	CCCP-11266 [reported 09Mar72 Cairo, Eygpt; see RA-11266 below]
unkn	BP	Soviet Air Force	CCCP-11268 [reported 22Sep80 Sperenberg, East Germany]
unkn	A	Russian Air Force	CCCP-11279 [reported 28Sep02 Staraya, Russia; see RA-11279]
unkn		Aeroflot	CCCP-11362(1) [reported 26Dec68 Amsterdam, Netherlands]
unkn		Soviet Air Force	CCCP-11363(1) [reported 27Mar68 Moscow-Sheremetyevo, USSR]
unkn		Kazakhstan Air Force	CCCP-11377(2) [reported 30Jun99 Almaty, Kazakhstan]
unkn	BP	Soviet Air Force	CCCP-11394? [from photo with only 394 visible in photo]
unkn	BK	Soviet Air Force	CCCP-11398(1) [reported 27Apr68 Kano, Nigeria]
unkn		Soviet Air Force	CCCP-11402 [reported 1978 Asmara, Ethiopia]
unkn	BP	Soviet Air Force	CCCP-11405 [reported 22Jun71 Sperenberg, East Germany; flew 15Oct84 Khost to Kabal, Afghanistan following serious damage by enemy fire at the former]
unkn	BP	Soviet Air Force	CCCP-11409 [from photo]
unkn		Soviet Air Force	CCCP-11413 [reported 18Sep83 Bukhara, Uzbekistan; see RA-11413]
unkn		Soviet Air Force	CCCP-11416 [reported 18Aug67 Kano, Nigeria]
unkn	LL	Soviet Air Force	CCCP-11417 [test aircraft; from photo]
unkn	BP	Soviet Air Force	CCCP-11423 [reported 21Oct73 Cairo, Egypt]
unkn		Soviet Air Force	CCCP-11429 [w/o 18Jan84 40km south of Mazar-i-Sharif, Afghanistan]
unkn	BP	Soviet Air Force	CCCP-11503 [reported 11Jly93 Omsk-Fyodorovka, Russia and 28May01 Chkalovski, Russia, same aircraft?]
unkn		Soviet Air Force	CCCP-11509 [from 1970s photo]
unkn	BP	Soviet Air Force	CCCP-11514 [derelict by Sep88 Kabul, Afghanistan; by Feb06 moved to Kabul scrapyard]
unkn	BP	Soviet Air Force	CCCP-11517 [from photo]
unkn	BP	Soviet Air Force	CCCP-11518 [reported 19Oct73 Cairo, Egypt; see RA-11518]
unkn	BP	Soviet Air Force	CCCP-11519 [reported Jly68 Prague, Czechoslovakia]
unkn	BP	Soviet Air Force	CCCP-11522 [reported 24Dec76 Sperenberg, East Germany]
unkn	BP	Soviet Air Force	CCCP-11535 [reported 1980 Mazar-i-Sharif, Afghanistan]
unkn	BP	Soviet/Russia Air Force	CCCP-11538 [reported 23Sep86 Irkutsk-1 & 19Oct93 Cairo, Egypt]
unkn	BP	Soviet Air Force	CCCP-11595 [reported 18Feb78 Addis Ababa, Ethiopia]
unkn	BP	Aeroflot	CCCP-11601 [reported Jun79 Ulaanbaatar, Mongolia & 28Oct94 Ostend, Belgium; see RA-11601]
unkn	BP	Soviet Air Force	CCCP-11602 [from movie]
unkn	BP	Soviet Air Force	CCCP-11604 [reported 20Aug68 Prague, Czechoslovakia]
unkn	BP	Soviet Air Force	CCCP-11655 [reported 18Aug67 Kano, Nigeria & 29Apr98 Fergana, Uzbekistan probably a different aircraft; also see 11655 above]
unkn	BP	Russian Air Force?	CCCP-11657 [reported 06Aug96 Staraya, Russia]
unkn		Soviet Air Force	CCCP-11659 [reported 18Aug67 Kano, Nigeria]
unkn	BP	Soviet Air Force	CCCP-11663 [reported 18Feb73 Oranienburg, East Germany]
unkn	BP	Soviet Air Force	CCCP-11672 [reported 18Aug74 Cairo, Egypt & 11Jly93 Omsk-Fyodorovka, Russia possibly wfu?]
unkn	BP	Soviet Air Force	CCCP-11673 [reported 30Sep76 Oranienburg, East Germany]
unkn	BP	Russian Air Force	CCCP-11732 [reported 19Sep70 Copenhagen-Kastrup, Denmark; see RA-11732]
unkn		Soviet Air Force	CCCP-11735 [operated from Inanovo-Severny, USSR; no reports]
unkn	BP	Soviet Air Force	CCCP-11748 [reported Apr85 Addis Ababa, Ethiopia]
unkn	BP	Soviet Air Force	CCCP-11758 [reported 10Apr91 Moscow-Sheremetyevo, USSR]
unkn	BP	Soviet Air Force	CCCP-11776 [reported 1978 Asmara, Ethiopia]
unkn	BP	Soviet Air Force	CCCP-11784 [reported 21Oct73 Cairo, Egypt]
unkn	BP	Soviet Air Force	CCCP-11845 [reported 21Oct73 Cairo, Egypt]
unkn	BP	Soviet Air Force	CCCP-11847 [reported 29Mar75 location not recorded & 22Jly92 Rostov-Oktyabrskiv, Russia/USSR]
unkn	BP	Soviet Air Force	CCCP-11852 [reported 02Jly92 Mirny, Russia]
unkn		ex Soviet Air Force	CCCP-11869 [reported Aug9 in housing estate in Minsk, Belarus]
unkn	BP	Soviet Air Force	CCCP-11872 [reported 19Oct73 Cairo, Egypt]
unkn	B	Soviet Air Force	CCCP-11900 [from photo]
unkn	BP	Soviet Air Force	CCCP-11903 [reported 22May77 somewhere in San Salvador]

ANTONOV An-12

C/n	Model	Last known Owner/Operator	Identities/fates/comments (where appropriate)
unkn	BP	Soviet Air Force	CCCP-11907 [reported 23Jan92 Munich, Germany]
unkn	BP	Soviet Air Force	CCCP-11913 [reported 24Jly77 Sperenberg, East Germany; see RA-11913]
unkn	BP	Russian Air Force	CCCP-11928 [reported 20Apr97 Ulan Ude-Vostochny, Russia]
unkn	BP	Soviet Air Force	CCCP-11935 [from photo]
unkn	BP	Soviet Air Force	CCCP-11951 [reported 11Apr92 Kubina, USSR]
unkn	BP	Soviet Air Force	CCCP-11952 [reported 12Oct68; 27Aug93 Paris-Orly, France might be different aircraft]
unkn	BP	Soviet Air Force	CCCP-11954 [reported 03jly76 somewhere in San Salvador]
unkn	BP	Soviet Air Force	CCCP-11955 [reported 18Jun76 Sperenberg, East Germany]
unkn	BP	Soviet Air Force	CCCP-11957 [reported 24Jly76 location not recorded]
unkn	BP	Soviet Air Force	CCCP-11963 [reported 19Oct73 Cairo, Egypt & 1991 Milovice, Czechoslovakia; see 11963 above]
unkn	BP	Soviet Air Force	CCCP-11964 [reported 1980 Istanbul-Ataturk, Turkey]
unkn	BP	Soviet Air Force	CCCP-11981 [reported Jan85 location not recorded]
unkn	BP	Russian Air Force	CCCP-11982 [reported 08Sep93 Taganrog-South, Russia]
unkn	BP	Soviet Air Force	CCCP-11984 [reported wfu by 03Jly92 Yakutsk, Russia]
unkn	BP	Soviet Air Force	CCCP-11987 [w/o 23Jan89 Kandahar, Afghanistan; hulk l/n Jan02]
unkn		Soviet Air Force	CCCP-11994 [hulk at Heiss (Hayes) Island, Franz Josef Land, Russian Arctic; from photo]
unkn	BP	Soviet Air Force	CCCP-12104 [reported 03Jan75 Luanda, Angola]
unkn	BP	Soviet Air Force	CCCP-12109 [from photo]
unkn	BP	Soviet Air Force	CCCP-12128 [reported 10Nov79 Sperenberg, East Germany & 05Aug00 Chkalovski, USSR; see RA-12128]
unkn	BP	Russian Air Force	CCCP-12133 [wreck reported 31Aug03 Kabul, Afghanistan; not RA-12133 see below]
unkn	BP	Soviet Air Force	CCCP-12139 [reported 22Feb78 Addis Ababa, Ethiopia]
unkn	BP	Soviet Air Force	CCCP-12148 [reported 07Sep89 Omsk-Fyodorovka, USSR; possibly not c/n 4 34 19 06]
unkn	BP	Soviet Air Force	CCCP-12159 [reported 09Apr91 Chkalovski, USSR]
unkn	BP	Soviet Air Force	CCCP-12185 [reported 23Sep86 Irkutsk-1, USSR]
unkn	BP	Soviet Air Force	CCCP-12189 [reported 23Sep86 Irkutsk-1, USSR]
unkn		MAP Novosibirsk	CCCP-12380 [from document]
unkn	B	Soviet Air Force	CCCP-12863 [from photo dated 02Dec82 Zaporozhia, Ukraine, USSR]
unkn		Aeroflot	CCCP-12875 [from photo]
unkn	BP	Soviet Air Force	CCCP-12899 [reported 04Apr76 Moscow-Sheremetyevo, USSR]
unkn	BP	Soviet Air Force	CCCP-12900 [reported 04Oct75 Moscow-Sheremetyevo, USSR]
unkn	BP	Soviet Air Force	CCCP-12934 [reported 29Jly69 Moscow-Sheremetyevo, USSR]
unkn	B	Russian Air Force	CCCP-12979 [reported 19Apr97 Vladivostok-Knevichi, Russia & 21May99 Staravia, Russia]
unkn		Soviet Air Force	CCCP-13402 [from photo; avionics test bed; see RA-13402 possibly a different aircraft]
unkn		Aeroflot	CCCP-14531 [1976 in photo at Moscow-Sheremetyevo, USSR]
unkn		Aeroflot	CCCP-31120 [reported 04Oct75 Moscow-Sheremetyevo, USSR; possible mis-sighting of CCCP-11120]
unkn		unknown	CCCP-33688 [Jly60 in photo at Paris-Orly, France]
unkn		Aeroflot	CCCP-71966 [reported 25Sep87 Moscow-Sheremetyevo, USSR; also a report as being a An-26]
unkn	A	Soviet Air Force	CCCP-75617 [from photo]
unkn		Aeroflot	CCCP-75625 [reported in Putnam book]
unkn		Soviet Air Force	CCCP-75890 [photo in newspaper 1963 Skopje, Macedonia, Yugoslavia on relief flight]
unkn		Soviet Air Force	CCCP-75892 [reported 1969 Fergana, Uzbekistan, USSR]
unkn		Aeroflot	CCCP-86721 [reported 01Apr68 Tashkent-Yuzhny South, Uzbekistan, USSR]
unkn		Aeroflot	CCCP-93919 [reported 24Mar86 Moscow-Domodedovo, USSR; possible mis-sighting of CCCP-93912, CCCP-93913 or CCCP-93915?]
unkn		Angolan Government	D2-EAC [reported]
unkn		Angolan Government	D2-EAD [reported w/o 19Sep84]
unkn		Angolan Government	D2-EAE [reported]
unkn		Alada	D2-FAJ [reported 29Apr98 Luanda, Angola; not in Jan02 fleet list]
unkn		Alada	D2-FAO [reported 19Aug99 Luanda, Angola; derelict by Jun03]
unkn		Alada	D2-FAZ [w/o 11Aug98 Saurimo, Angola]
unkn		unknown	D2-FBB [reported 15Apr98 & 16Mar01 Luanda, Angola]
unkn		unknown	D2-FBC [reported 01Apr99 & 22Mar01 Luanda, Angola]

ANTONOV An-12

C/n	Model	Last known Owner/Operator	Identities/fates/comments (where appropriate)
unkn		unknown	D2-FBE [not c/n 4 020 07 T-306; l/n Feb08 Tver-Migalovo, Russia; see T-308 above]
unkn		unknown	D2-FBG [reported 29Apr98 Luanda, Angola; wreck by Jun03]
unkn		unknown	D2-FBI [reported 25May06 & 31Jly06 Dzhankoi, Ukraine]
unkn		unknown	D2-FBM [reported 19Aug99 & 16Mar01 Luanda, Angola]
unkn		Techaviaservice	D2-FBT [reported 19Aug99 Luanda, Angola; see also T-300]
unkn		unknown	D2-FIC [reported 04Oct00 Sharjah, UAE]
unkn		unknown	EX-121 [reported 19Oct06 Ras Al Khaimah, UAE; probable mis-report as regn on 737 in Aug06]
unkn		unknown	EX-12961 [reported Jun02 & 06Dec03 Almaty, Kazakhstan]
unkn		unknown	LZ-BRD [reported 06Jly03 Malabo, Equatorial Guinea]
unkn			PK-PUA [see T-1201 in military section]
unkn			PK-PUB [see T-1202 in military section]
unkn			PK-PUC [see T-1203 in military section]
unkn			PK-PUD [see T-1204 in military section]
unkn			PK-PUE [see T-1205 in military section]
unkn			PK-PUF [see T-1206 in military section]
unkn		Russian Air Force	RA-11178 [ex CCCP-11178 see above; reported Ivanovo-Severny, Russia]
unkn	A	Russian Air Force	RA-11279 [ex CCCP-11279 see above; reported Staraya, Russia]
unkn		Russian Air Force	RA-11290 [reported 07Aug99 Staraya, Russia]
unkn		unknown	RA-11355 [reported 15Aug05 Yermolino, Russia]
unkn		unknown	RA-11413 [possibly ex CCCP-11413, see above; reported 21May99 Staraya, Russia]
unkn	BP	Russian Air Force	RA-11428 [reported 15Aug99 Chkalovskiy, Russia]
unkn	BP?	unknown	RA-11518 [presumably ex CCCP-11518 above; reported 16Jly99 Dubai, UAE]
unkn	BP	unknown	RA-11601 [presumably ex CCCP-11601 above; reported 28Oct94 Ostend, Belgium]
unkn		unknown	RA-11666 [reported 29Apr98 Fergana, Uzbekistan; was the prefix actually RA-?; see next line]
unkn		610CCT Centre Museum	RA-11666 [preserved by 18Aug01 Ivanovo-Severny, Russia; l/n Sep07; presumably ex CCCP-11666 or painted to represent this aircraft; connected with the above?]
unkn	BK	Russian Air Force	RA-11668 [reported 26May99 & Jly02 Ivanovo-Seveny, Russia]
unkn	BP	Russian Air Force	RA-11732 [ex CCCP-11732 above] [reported 17Mar94 Kubinka, Russia]
unkn	BP	Russian Air Force	RA-11742 [reported 25Auq97 Kubinka, Russia]
unkn	BP	Russian Air Force	RA-11861 [reported 13Sep93 Luxembourg-Findel, Luxembourg]
unkn		Russian Air Force	RA-11913 [reported 23Jun06 Sverdlovsk, Russia; see CCCP-11913 above, but possibly not same aircraft]
unkn	BK	Russian Spaces Forces	RA-11943 [reported 16May99 Klin, Russia & Feb08 Kubinka, Russia when carried additional code 15 white; probably to RF-12553, see below]
unkn	BP	Russian Air Force?	RA-11969 [reported 31May93 Moscow-Sheremetyevo, Russia]
unkn	BP	Russian Air Force	RA-12128 [ex CCCP-12128 above; reported 05Aug00 Chkalovskiy, Russia]
unkn	BP	Russian Air Force	RA-12131 [reported 19Jun97 Yerevan-Zvartnots, Armenia & 10Aug99 Rostov-na-Donu, Russia]
unkn	BP	Russian Air Force	RA-12132 [reported 16May96 Tbilisi-Lochini, Georgia & 10Aug99 Rostov-na-Donu, Russia & 05Aug00 Chkalovski, Russia]
unkn	BP	Russian Air Force	RA-12133 [reported 17Aug97 Tibilisi-Lochini, Georgia; not CCCP-12133 above]
unkn	BP	Russian Air Force	RA-12143 [reported 05Aug00 Chkalovski, Russia]
unkn	BP	Russian Air Force	RA-12330 [reported 12May95 overflying Khabarovsk, Russia on approach nearby AFB]
unkn	BP	Aeroflot	RA-12341 [unconfirmed reported 12Jun93 Moscow-Vnukovo, Russia]
unkn		Russian Air Force	RA-13402 [reported 31Aug04 Taganrog, Russia; possibly not same aircraft as CCCP-13402 above]
unkn		Russian Air Force	RF-12553 [possibly ex RA-11943; reported 04Aug08 Chkalovski, Russia with same code 15 white as RA-11943]
unkn		Russian Air Force	RF-12561 [photographed in 2009, location not reported]
unkn		unknown	S9-BOV [reported 16Mar01 Luanda, Angola; by 24Sep02 these marks on An-26 c/n 5610]
unkn		unknown	S9-DBF [reported 20Jun08 Sharjah, UAE; possibly ex TN-AHG]
unkn		unknown	S9-DBO [reported 10May07 Nairobi, Kenya]
unkn		unknown	S9-GRC [reported 19Aug99 & 15Mar01 Luanda, Angola]
unkn		Zanex	S9-SAT(1) [w/o 17Dec98 Saurimo, Angola]

ANTONOV An-12

C/n	Model	Last known Owner/Operator	Identities/fates/comments (where appropriate)	
unkn		Sarit Airlines	S9-SAT(2)	[reported 11Nov02 Sharjah, UAE]
unkn		Data International Aviation	ST-APU	[from airline fleet book, no reports and not on register]
unkn		unknown	ST-AZB	[reported 08May12 Khartoum, Sudan]
unkn	BK	unknown	ST-ZNN	[reported 31Mar10 Khartoum, Sudan; no titles, also wearing serial 9933]
unkn		unknown	TN-ACM	[reported 16Nov99 Sharjah, UAE]
unkn		unknown	TN-AFX	[reported 09Oct99 Brazzaville-Maya Maya, People's Republic of Congo and reported w/o on that date]
unkn		Anton Air	TN-AGF	[reported 21Nov99 Bulawayo, Zimbabwe]
unkn	AP	Aero Fret Business	TN-AGY	[reported 19Oct03 Pointe Noire, People's Republic of Congo; but see c/n 1 34 02 06]
unkn		unknown	TN-AHG	[reported 26Oct05 & 17Feb06 Sharjah, UAE; might have become S9-DBF]
unkn	ex PPS	Natalco Air Lines	TN-AHT	[reported Feb09 Kisangani, Democratic Republic of Congo]
unkn		Natalco Air Lines	TN-AHY	[reported 01Sep09 Rivne, Ukraine in the process of being scrapped]
unkn		Aero Fret Business	TN-AIK	[reported Jun09 Pointe Noire, People's Republic of Congo]
unkn		Aero Fret Business	TN-AIO	[reported 02Aug10 Brazzaville, People's Republic of Congo]
unkn		Natalco Air Lines	TN-ASQ	[reported wfu by 10Oct04 Pointe Noire, People's Republic of Congo]
unkn		unknown	TT-DWZ	[reported wfu by 24Sep00 Almaty, Kazakhstan; l/n 07Jun09]
unkn		Ivory Coast Air Force	TU-VFA	[reported Sep05 Abidjan, Ivory Coast]
unkn		Ivory Coast Air Force	TU-VMA	[reported 23Sep06 Abidjan, Ivory Coast; l/n 23Oct08]
unkn		East Wing	UN-11010	[reported 17Jly07 Kinshasa-N'Djili, DR Congo and 05Mar08 Goma, DR Congo]
unkn		East Wing	UN-11011	[reported 15Jly08 and 25Aug08 N'Djamena, Chad]
unkn		Motul	UN-11016	[reported 08Jan08 through 12Mar09 stored Fujairah, UAE]
unkn		Eastern Express	UN-11020	[reported 08Dec07 Sharjah, UAE]
unkn		unknown	UN-11117	[reported 17Mar08 Kandahar, Afghanistan]
unkn		unknown	UR-11264	[reported 08May98 & 30Apr99 Yevpatoriya, Ukraine]
unkn		United Nations	UR-CBB	[reported 17Nov07 Nairobi, Kenya; regn not fully confirmed]
unkn	BK	Albatros	UR-KAP	[reported 17Dec09 Nikolaev, Ukraine]
unkn		Syrian Air Force	YK-ANC	[old photo shows these marks on an An-12 before being used on An-26 c/n 30 07]
unkn		unknown	3C-HAC	[reported 03Mar03 Fujairah, UAE]
unkn		unknown	3C-JZY	[reported 16Mar01 Luanda, Angola]
unkn	BP	Air Guinee	3X-GBD	[reported in 1988]
unkn		Brise Air?	3X-GDO	[reported 04Apr11 Bost, Afghanistan]
unkn		unknown	3X-GFE	[reported 22Sep10 and 21Feb12 Yevpatoria, Ukraine]
unkn		unknown	4L-BLE	[reported 12Dec09 Entebbe, Uganda; but is not known by the Georgian CAA & Ugandan CAA denies it was there]
unkn	BK	Sky Georgia	4L-FFD	[reported in Mar10 official fleet list; canx between 13Aug10 and 23Mar11]
unkn		South Yemen Air Force	7O-ABH	[reported 06May89 Moscow-Sheremetyevo, USSR]
unkn			7O-ABM	[see 821 in military section]
unkn			7O-ACI	[see 626 in military section]
unkn			7O-ACJ	[see 625 in military section]
unkn	BP	Algerian Air Force	7T-WAD	[from photo]
unkn		unknown	9Q-CCK	[reported Feb04 Kindu, DR Congo]
unkn	B	Great Lakes Business	9Q-CGQ	[reported 09Aug06 Goma, DR Congo; l/n Nov08 wfu/derelict]
unkn		Air Navette	9U-BHS	[mentioned in UN document]

Unidentified – Military (including dual marks)

unkn		Mozambique Air Force	011	[reported returned to USSR]
unkn		Mozambique Air Force	012	[reported returned to USSR]
unkn		Jordanian Air Force	353	[reported Dec84 Hong Kong]
unkn		Pakistan Air Force Museum	380	[preserved Karachi, Pakistan; former Afghan Air Force aircraft]
unkn		Afghan Air Force	381	[reported Feb89 Kabul, Afghanistan]
unkn		Afghan Air Force	382	[reported Feb89 Kabul, Afghanistan]
unkn		Afghan Air Force	384	[reported 13Feb89 Kabul, Afghanistan]
unkn		Afghan Air Force	388	[reported 13Feb89 Kabul, Afghanistan]
unkn		Afghan Air Force	389	[wreck noted 17Oct00 Kandahar, Afghanistan; l/n Nov05]

ANTONOV An-12

C/n	Model	Last known Owner/Operator	Identities/fates/comments (where appropriate)
unkn		Afghan Air Force	390 [reported Jun98 Faizabad, Afghanistan; on 10Feb93 an An-12BK with serial made an emergency landing at Termez, Uzbekistan, USSR]
unkn		Afghan Air Force	393 [reported 12Mar02 Kunduz, Afghanistan]
unkn		Afghan Air Force	397 [wreck noted 25Jly03 Kabul, Afghanistan; by 08Jun06 moved to scrapyard in Kabul]
unkn		Afghan Air Force	398 [reported 21Aug02 Kabul, Afghanistan]
unkn		Afghan Air Force	399 [wreck without cockpit noted 13Jly03 Kabul, Afghanistan; l/n Jun06]
unkn		Afghan Air Force	405 [reported 31Jly03 Kabal-Bagram, Afghanistan; also possibly as wreck Dec04 & Mar06]
unkn		Yemen Air Force	821//7O-ABM [dual marks; reported 09Jan92 Aden, Yemen; l/n 07Aug93; serial might have been 621; marks 7O-ABM known on An26 with serial 616]
unkn		Sudan Air Force	977 [reported 07Aug08 Khartoum, Sudan; serial previously used on unknown An-24]
unkn		Civil Aviation Administration China	1052 [used in hydrogen bomb tests 08May67]
unkn		Civil Aviation Administration China	1055 [in Pakistan 07Mar88]
unkn		Chinese Air Force	1063 [fate unknown]
unkn		Ethiopian Air Force	1501 [not confirmed]
unkn		Ethiopian Air Force	1504 [not confirmed]
unkn		Ethiopian Air Force	1507 [reported Apr81 Addis Ababa, Ethiopia & Feb05 Dzhankoy, Ukraine, operational]
unkn		Ethiopian Air Force	1508 [reported 11Oct80 & 28Aug93 Asmara, Ethiopia]
unkn		Ethiopian Air Force	1509 [w/o prior to May84 during hijack attempt; 06Aug93 wreck still at Addis Ababa, Ethiopia]
unkn		Ethiopian Air Force	1510 [reported Feb86 Dzhankoy, Ukraine & 28Aug93 Bahar Dar, Ethiopia]
unkn		Ethiopian Air Force	1511 [reported 19Jun91 Djibouti-Ambouli, Djibouti]
unkn		Ethiopian Air Force	1513 [reported Feb86 Dzhankoy, Ukraine & 12Mar01 & May02 Asmara, Ethiopia]
unkn		Ethiopian Air Force	1514 [reported w/o Jan87 near Asmara, Ethiopia]
unkn		Ethiopian Air Force	1515 [reported Feb86 Dzhankoy, Ukraine]
unkn		Ethiopian Air Force	1516 [reported Feb86 Dzhankoy, Ukraine]
unkn		Chinese Air Force	4101 [preserved Changping Museum; Beijing, China]
unkn	BP	Egyptian Air Force	4311 [from photo; operated by Soviet AF in Egyptian marks 1972]
unkn	PPS	Egyptian Air Force	4371 [from photo; operated by Soviet AF in Egyptian marks 1972]
unkn	TBK	Egyptian Air Force	4391 [from photo; operated by Soviet AF in Egyptian marks 1972]
unkn		Myanmar Air Force	5812 [reported Jan03 Rangoon, Myanmar; was this a Y-8?]
unkn	BK	Sudan Air Force	9933 [see ST-ZNN above with unknown c/n]
unkn	KJ200	Chinese Air Force	30172 [May06 photo; AWACS version]
unkn	KJ200	Chinese Air Force	30173 [from photo]
unkn		ex Chinese Air Force	32042 [preserved Changping Museum; Beijing, China]
unkn		Chinese Air Force	32045 [reported Aug87 Lhasa, Tibet]
unkn	BP	Russian Air Force	07 red [ex Soviet Air Force; reported 19Apr97 Vladivostok-Knevichi, Russia]
unkn		Egyptian Air Force	1221//SU-AOZ [dual marks; reported 26Apr68 Kano, Nigeria & Dec76/Oct89 Cairo, Egypt; report b/u]
unkn		Yemen Air Force	625//7O-ACJ [dual marks; reported 16Nov85 and later Aden, Yemen, latterly with Yemen AF; l/n 07Aug93]
unkn		Yemen Air Force	626//7O-ACI [dual marks; reported 16Nov85 and later Aden, Yemen, latterly with Yemen AF; l/n 07Aug93]
unkn	PPS	Kazakhstan Air Force	93 red [ex Soviet Air Force; reported 09Mar07 & 14Nov08 Almaty, Kazakhstan]
unkn		Indian Air Force	L451 [reported Dec88;last flight 28Jun91; offered for sale; fate/status unknown]
unkn		Indian Air Force	L452 [reported 09Jun86 Delhi, India; last flight 28Jun91; offered for sale; fate/status unknown]
unkn		Indonesian Air Force	T-1201//PK-PUA [dual marks; w/o unknown date and location]
unkn		Indonesian Air Force	T-1202//PK-PUB [photo just wearing PK- marks; w/o 16Oct64 Palembang, Indonesia]
unkn		Indonesian Air Force	T-1203//PK-PUC [dual marks; reported returned to USSR]
unkn		Indonesian Air Force	T-1204//PK-PUD [dual marks; w/o unknown date and location]
unkn		Indonesian Air Force	T-1205//PK-PUE [photo no visible civil marks; reported returned to USSR]
unkn		Indonesian Air Force	T-1206//PK-PUF [dual marks; w/o unknown date and location]

ANTONOV An-12

C/n	Model	Last known Owner/Operator	Identities/fates/comments (where appropriate)	
unkn		Indonesian Air Force	T-1207	[reported returned to USSR, but report now in some doubt]
unkn		Indonesian Air Force	T-1208	[reported returned to USSR, but report now in some doubt]
unkn		Indonesian Air Force	T-1209	[reported returned to USSR, but report now in some doubt]
unkn		Angolan Air Force	T-300	[ex D2-(FB)T; which see; w/o 07Aug05 Luanda, Angola]
unkn		Angolan Air Force	T-302	[reported 15Mar01 Luanda, Angola]
unkn		Angolan Air Force	T-304	[w/o 27Jan02 Kanyengue, Angola]
unkn		Angolan Air Force	T-305	[reported Jun03 Luanda, Angola]
unkn		Angolan Air Force	T-307	[w/o 16May03 Menongue, Angola]
unkn	BP?	Angolan Air Force	T-308	[reported 06Feb03 Luanda, Angola; possibly stored by 02May06 Odessa-Tsentrainly, Ukraine; to D2-MBE & c/n 4 02 007; but T-308 again on Aug08 Huambo, Angola and 28Mar09 Luanda, Angola; reverted to D2-MBE by 23Jly12]
unkn		Angolan Air Force	T-310	[reported 08May03 Luanda, Angola]
unkn		Angolan Air Force	T-314	[reported 28Mar09 Luanda, Angola]
unkn		Angolan Air Force	T-315	[reported 30Sep08 Luanda, Angola]
unkn		Angolan Air Force	T-316	[reported 30Sep08 Luanda, Angola]

Production continues in China as the Yunshuji Y-8.

ANTONOV An-22

C/n	Line No.	Model	Last known Owner/Operator	Identities/fates/comments (where appropriate)
Prototypes				
5 34 01 01	01 01	PZ	for Antonov OKB Museum	CCCP-46191 40 red+ 01 red+ 10 yellow+ CCCP-180151 CCCP-64459 UR-64459 [+ Soviet] [protoype f/f 27Feb65] [stored 23Oct94 Gostomel, Russia; l/n Sep08; canx 01Oct08]
01 02	01 02		(Antonov Design Bureau)	[static test airframe; tested Sep64 to Dec66]
Production Aircraft				
6 34 01 03	01 03		Technikmuseum Speyer	CCCP-56391 03 red CCCP-56391 41 red CCCP-64460 LZ-SGB LZ-SFD UR-64460 [preserved 29Dec99 Speyer, Germany; l/n 26Apr08]
01 04	01 04		(Antonov Design Bureau)	[fatigue test airframe from Oct69]
7 34 01 05	01 05		(Russian Air Force)	CCCP-76591 CCCP-08822 [wfu 1985; b/u 1997 Ivanovo-Severny, Russia]
7 34 01 06	01 06		(Russian Air Force)	CCCP-67691 CCCP-08837 [wfu 1988; b/u 1997 Ivanovo-Severny, Russia]
7 34 01 07	01 07		(Russian Air Force)	CCCP-08838 [l/n 08Jun96 Ivanovo-Severny, Russia; & b/u 1997]
8 34 01 08	01 08		(Russian Air Force)	08 red CCCP-09317 [+ Soviet] [wfu early 1995; b/u May97 Ivanovo-Severny, Russia; hulk l/n 26Aug97]
8 34 01 09	01 09		(Russian Air Force)	09 red CCCP-09301 [+ Soviet] [wfu 1993; b/u spring 1997 Ivanovo-Severny, Russia; hulk l/n 26Aug97]
8 34 01 10	01 10		(Russian Air Force)	10 red CCCP-09310 [+ Soviet] [wfu 1995 Ivanovo-Severny, Russia; l/n 21Aug96; b/u 1997]
8 34 02 01	02 01		(Russian Air Force)	CCCP-08839 RA-08839 [l/n 24Aug95 Ivanovo-Severny, Russia; b/u 1997]
8 34 02 02	02 02		(Russian Air Force)	CCCP-09302 RA-09302 [b/u up Aug99 Ivanovo-Severny, Russia]
9 34 02 03	02 03	A	(Soviet Air Force)	CCCP-09307(1) [regn not fully confirmed;] [part dismantled 1999 Gostomel, Ukraine; by Jun06 derelict; l/n Sep08]
9 34 02 04	02 04		(Russian Air Force)	CCCP-09304 RA-09304 [l/n 08Jun96 Ivanovo-Severny, Russia; b/u 1997]
0 34 02 05	02 05		(Soviet Air Force)	CCCP-09305(1) [w/o 19Dec70 Panagarh, India]
0 34 02 06	02 06		(Russian Air Force)	CCCP-09306 RA-09306 [wfu 1997; derelict by 15Jun99 Ivanovo-Severny, Russia; b/u Oct99]
00 34 02 07	02 07		(Soviet Air Force)	CCCP-09303(1) [w/o en-route 18Jul70 between Keflavik & Halifax into North Atlantic]
00 34 02 08	02 08		(Russian Air Force)	CCCP-09325 RA-09325 [b/u 1999 Ivanovo-Severny, Russia; hulk l/n Aug99]
00 34 02 09	02 09		Central Russian Air Force Museum	CCCP-09334 [preserved 30Sep87 Monino, USSR/Russia; l/n 04Aug08]
00 34 02 10	02 10		(Russian Air Force)	CCCP-09346 RA-09346 [l/n 24Apr97 Ivanovo-Severny, Russia; b/u spring 1997]
00 34 03 01	03 01		(Russian Air Force)	CCCP-09308 RA-09308 [l/n 26Aug97 Ivanovo-Severny, Russia; b/u Nov99]
00 34 03 03	03 02		(Russian Air Force)	CCCP-09315 RA-09315 [l/n Aug99 Ivanovo-Severny, Russia; b/u 26Sep/03Oct99]
01 34 03 03	03 03		(Russian Air Force)	CCCP-09321 RA-09321 [wfu 1997 Ivanovo-Severny, Russia; l/n 26May99; b/u Jly99]
01 34 03 04	03 04		(Russian Air Force)	CCCP-09323 RA-09323 [wfu mid-1997 Ivanovo-Severny, Russia; l/n Jun99; b/u late 99]
01 34 03 05	03 05		(Russian Air Force)	CCCP-09330 [wfu 1992 used for spares; l/n 26Aug97 Ivanovo-Severny, Russia; b/u spring 1999]
01 34 03 06	03 06		(Russian Air Force)	CCCP-09336 RA-09336 [wfu 1995 Ivanovo-Severny, Russia; l/n 24Aug95; b/u mid 1997]
01 34 03 07	03 07		(Russian Air Force)	CCCP-09313 RA-09313 [lwfu 21Jan98, l/n 26Aug03 Tver-Migalovo, Russia; probably b/u]
01 34 03 08	03 08		(Russian Air Force)	CCCP-09316 RA-09316 [lwfu 21Jan98, l/n 26Aug03 Tver-Migalovo, Russia; probably b/u]
01 34 03 09	03 09		(Russian Air Force)	CCCP-09322 RA-09322 [lwfu 21Jan98, l/n 26Aug03 Tver-Migalovo, Russia; probably b/u]
01 34 03 10	03 10		(Russian Air Force)	CCCP-09326 RA-09326 [b/u May99 Ivanovo-Severny, Russia; hulk only l/n Jun99]
02 34 04 01	04 01		(Russian Air Force)	CCCP-09332 RA-09332 [lwfu 21Jan98, l/n 30Jun03 Tver-Migalovo, Russia; probably b/u]
02 34 04 02	04 02		(Russian Air Force)	CCCP-09333 RA-09333 [b/u 1997 Ivanovo-Severny, Russia]
02 34 04 03	04 03		ex Russian Air Force	CCCP-09335 RA-09335 [wfu Feb98, Tver-Migalovo, Russia; l/n 03Aug09 stored]
02 34 04 04	04 04		ex Russian Air Force	CCCP-09345 RA-09345 [wfu 21Jan98 Tver-Migalovo, Russia; l/n 06Dec08 stored]
02 34 04 05	04 05		(Soviet Air Force)	CCCP-09349 [w/o 08Jun77 Seshcha AFB, USSR]
02 34 04 06	04 06		ex Russian Air Force	CCCP-09319 RA-09319 [stored by 1999 Tver-Migalovo, Russia; l/n 06Dec08]

ANTONOV An-22

C/n	Line No.	Model	Last known Owner/Operator	Identities/fates/comments (where appropriate)
02 34 04 07	04 07		ex Russian Air Force	CCCP-09324 RA-09324 [wfu 21Jan98 Tver-Migalovo, Russia; l/n 06Dec08 stored]
02 34 04 08	04 08		(Russian Air Force)	CCCP-09331 RA-09331 [w/o 19Jan94 Tver-Migalovo, Russia]
03 34 04 09	04 09		ex Russian Air Force	CCCP-09339 RA-09339 [last flight 21Jan1998, l/n 06Dec08 Tver-Migalovo, Russia stored]
03 34 04 10	04 10		(Russian Air Force)	CCCP-09347 RA-09347 [wfu1994 & partly dismantled Tver-Migalovo, Russia; l/n 17Aug05; probably b/u]
03 34 05 01	05 01	A	(Soviet Air Force)	CCCP-09318 [w/o 22Dec76 on test flight from Seshcha AFB, USSR]
03 34 80209	05 02	A	ex Russian Air Force	CCCP-09320 RA-09320 [stored by 13Aug06 Tver-Migalovo, Russia; l/n 03Aug09]
03 34 80212	05 03	A	ex Russian Air Force	CCCP-09327 RA-09327 [stored by Dec07 Tver-Migalovo, Russia; l/n 03Aug09]
03 34 80219	05 04?	A	Russian Air Force	CCCP-09328 RA-09328 [active 03Aug09 Tver-Migalovo, Russia; l/n 18Aug09]
03 34 80225	05 05	A	ex Russian Air Force	CCCP-09337 RA-09337 [stored by 13Aug06 Tver-Migalovo, Russia; l/n 03Aug09]
03 34 80228	05 06	A	ex Russian Air Force	CCCP-09338 RA-09338 [l/n 12Aug12 stored Tver-Migalovo, Russia]
03 34 81234	05 07	A	ex Russian Air Force	CCCP-09340 RA-09340 [stored by Feb08 Tver-Migalovo, Russia; l/n 06Dec08]
04 34 81240	05 08	A	ex Russian Air Force	CCCP-09305(2) RA-09305 [stored by 06Dec08 Tver-Migalovo, Russia]
04 34 81244	05 09	A	Antonov Design Bureau	CCCP-09307(2) UR-09307
04 34 81250	05 10	A	Russian Air Force	CCCP-09309 309+ RA-09309 [+ Soviet] [only camouflaged An-22; l/n 10Dec09 active; Tver-Migalovo, Russia based]
04 34 81251	06 01	A	(Soviet Air Force)	CCCP-09311 [w/o 02Jun80 Moscow-Vnukovo, USSR]
04 34 81256	06 02?	A	ex Russian Air Force	CCCP-09312 RA-09312 [stored by 26Jly07 Tver-Migalovo, Russia; l/n 11Aug09]
04 34 82263	06 03?	A	ex Russian Air Force	CCCP-09314 RA-09314 [l/n 12Aug12 stored Tver-Migalovo, Russia]
04 34 82266	06 04?	A	ex Russian Air Force	CCCP-09341 RA-09341 [l/n 30Jun03 stored by 30Jun03 Tver-Migalovo, Russia; l/n 18Aug09]
04 34 82272	06 05?	A	(Russian Air Force)	CCCP-09343 RA-09343 [w/o 28Dec10 near Krasny Oktyabr, Russia, en-route Voronezh to Tver AFB]
04 34 82276	06 06	A	(Russian Air Force)	CCCP-09329 RA-09329 [l/n 18Aug09 Tver-Migalovo, Russia, operational condition]
04 34 82282	06 07	A	Russian Air Force	CCCP-09342 RA-09342 [airworthy? 18Aug09 Tver-Migalovo, Russia]
05 34 82288	06 08?	A	Russian Air Force	CCCP-09344 RA-09344 [airworthy? 06Dec08 Tver-Migalovo, Russia; l/n 29Aug09 active]
05 34 83292	06 09	A	(Russian Air Force)	CCCP-09348 RA-09348 [b/u spring 2004 Ivanovo-Severny, Russia]
05 34 83299	06 10	A	(Russian Air Force)	CCCP-09303(2) [w/o 11Nov92 Tver-Migalovo, Russia]
05 34 83302	07 01	A	(Russian Air Force)	CCCP-08829 RA-08829 [b/u Jly/Aug04 Ivanovo-Severny, Russia]
05 34 83308	07 02	A	610 CCT Centre Museum	CCCP-08830 RA-08830 [preserved by Aug05 Ivanovo-Severny, Russia; l/n Aug06]
05 34 83311	07 03	A	(Russian Air Force)	CCCP-08831 RA-08831 [b/u autumn 2004 Ivanovo-Severny, Russia]
05 34 84317	07 04?	A	Russian Air Force	CCCP-08832 RA-08832 [serviceable Aug09 Tver-Migalovo, Russia]
05 34 84321	07 05?	A	Russian Air Force	CCCP-08833 RA-08833 [l/n 30Jan12 Ivanovo-Severny, Russia]
05 34 84327	07 06?	A	ex Russian Air Force	CCCP-08834 RA-08834 [stored by 18Aug07 Tver-Migalovo, Russia; l/n 06Dec08]
05 34 84331	07 07?	A	Russian Air Force	CCCP-08835 RA-08835 [l/n 30Jan12 Ivanovo-Severny, Russia]
05 34 85336	07 08?	A	ex Russian Air Force	CCCP-08836 RA-08836 [stored by 06Dec08 Tver-Migalovo, Russia]

Production complete

ANTONOV An-24

C/n	Model	Last known Owner/Operator	Identities/fates/comments (where appropriate)
Kiev-Svyatoshino production			
00 01		(MAP Kiev)	CCCP-L1959 [first prototype; ff 20Dec59; fate unknown]
00 02		(MAP Kazan APO)	CCCP-L1960 CCCP-69313 [canx 19Oct81; fate unknown]
00 03	T	(Samara State Aerospace University)	CCCP-L19603 93 blue+ CCCP-29101 [+ Soviet; prototype An-24T; on register with c/n 19603; canx 22Feb79; by Apr93 GIA; l/n May96]
00 04			[possible static test airframe]
00 05		(MAP Progress Arsenyev)	CCCP-L19605 CCCP-27216 [canx 1978; fate unknown]
00 06		(MAP Kiev)	CCCP-46708 [w/o 29Jly62 Moscow-Sheremetyevo, USSR; canx 19Apr63]
2 73 000 07		(Ukraine NII)	CCCP-46709 [canx 1982; tested to destruction after withdrawal]
2 73 000 08		(Aeroflot/Ukraine)	CCCP-46710 [canx 11May66; tested to destruction after withdrawal]
2 73 000 09		(Aeroflot/Ukraine)	CCCP-46711 [canx 1978; tested to destruction after withdrawal]
2 73 000 10		(NPO Electro Kiev)	CCCP-46712 [canx 11Nov84; tested to destruction after withdrawal]
2 73 001 01		National Aviation University Collection	CCCP-46713(1) UR-46713 [canx 1977; preserved by May89 Kiev Institute of Civil Aviation, Kiev; l/n 29Oct08]
2 73 001 02		(MAP Rostov VPO)	CCCP-46714 [canx 08Apr87; tested to destruction after withdrawal]
2 73 001 03		(Aeroflot/Ukraine)	CCCP-46715 [canx 1970; tested to destruction after withdrawal]
2 73 001 04		(Aeroflot/Ukraine)	CCCP-46716 [canx 1984; fate unknown]
2 73 001 05		(Aeroflot/Ukraine)	CCCP-46717 [canx 1977; fate unknown]
73 002 01		.	[nothing known]
73 002 02		.	[nothing known]
3 73 002 03	B	(Gostomel NII GVF)	CCCP-46718 [derelict by Aug93 Gostomel, Ukraine; canx date unknown]
3 73 002 04		(Aeroflot/Ukraine)	CCCP-46719 [canx 10Jly72; fate unknown]
3 73 002 05		(Samara State Aerospace University)	CCCP-46720 [canx 1977; by Apr93 GIA; l/n May96]
3 73 003 01		(Aeroflot/Kazakhstan)	CCCP-46721 [canx 1979; fate unknown]
3 73 003 02		(Aeroflot/Ukraine)	CCCP-46722 [w/o 17Dec76 near Kiev-Zhulyany, USSR; canx 1976]
3 73 003 03		(Aeroflot/Ukraine)	CCCP-46723 [canx 1975; fate unknown]
3 73 003 04		(AKF Polet)	CCCP-46724 [w/o 26Jun91 into Gulf of Finland, ex Leningrad, USSR]
3 73 003 05		(Aeroflot/Kazakhstan)	CCCP-46725 [canx 1982; fate unknown]
3 73 004 01		.	[nothing known; possible Soviet Air Force aircraft]
3 73 004 02		(Aeroflot/Kazakhstan)	CCCP-46726 [canx 1978; fate unknown]
3 73 004 03		(Gostomel NII GVF)	CCCP-46727 [canx 1976; fate unknown]
3 73 004 04		(Aeroflot/Ukraine)	CCCP-46728 [canx 1977; by Aug99 with Troitsk Technical School, Russia; l/n Aug01]
3 73 004 05		(Aeroflot/Kazakhstan)	CCCP-46729 [canx 1973; fate unknown]
3 73 005 01		(Aeroflot/Moscow Polar)	CCCP-46730 [canx 1977; by Jan77 with Omsk Aviation Technical School, Russia; l/n 2006]
3 73 005 02		(Aeroflot/Uzbekistan)	CCCP-46731 [canx 1981; remains noted Sep93 at Technical School, Minsk-Chizovka, Belarus]
3 73 005 03		.	[nothing known; possible Soviet Air Force aircraft]
3 73 005 04		(Aeroflot/Moscow)	CCCP-46732 [w/o 22Feb72 Lipetsk, USSR; canx 1972]
3 73 005 05		.	[nothing known; possible Soviet Air Force aircraft]
3 73 006 01		(Soviet Air Force)	CCCP-46733 11 black [no reports; fate/status unknown]
3 73 006 02	T		[served as prototype An-24T 1965; but see c/n 0003; fate unknown]
3 73 006 03		(Aeroflot/Kazakhstan)	CCCP-46734 [canx 1979; fate unknown]
3 73 006 04		(Aeroflot/Ukraine)	CCCP-46735 [canx 1979; fate unknown]
3 73 006 05	B	(Aeroflot/Moscow Polar)	CCCP-46736 [canx 1978; fate unknown]
3 73 007 01		.	[nothing known; possible Soviet Air Force aircraft]
3 73 007 02		(Soviet Air Force)	CCCP-46785 [canx 14Apr84; fate unknown possibly to military code]
4 73 007 03		(Aeroflot/Kazakhstan)	CCCP-46749 [canx 1978; noted derelict 07Apr10 Shymkent, Kazakhstan]
4 73 007 04		(Aeroflot/Kazakhstan)	CCCP-46750 [canx 1983; fate unknown]
4 73 007 05		(Aeroflot/Ukraine)	CCCP-46738 [canx 1978; fate unknown]
4 73 008 01		ex Aeroflot/Kirovograd	CCCP-46739 [canx 1984; by Jly93 derelict Kirovograd, Ukraine; l/n May07]
4 73 008 02		(Aeroflot/Moscow Polar)	CCCP-46740 [canx 1971; fate unknown]
4 73 008 03		(MAP Kumertau VPO)	CCCP-46741 [canx 23Mar87; fate unknown]
4 73 008 04	B	ex Omega	CCCP-46742 UR-46742 [wfu by May98 Simferopol-Zavodskoye, Ukraine; canx 13Aug08; l/n May11 in scapping area]
4 73 008 05		(MAP Ramenskoye)	CCCP-46743 [canx 1976; fate unknown]
4 73 009 01		(Aeroflot/Ukraine)	CCCP-46744 [canx 1978; fate unknown]
4 73 009 02		ex Aeroflot/Kazakhstan	CCCP-46745 [canx 1982; by May to Yegoryevsk Technical School, Russia; l/n Aug07]
4 73 009 03		Central Russian Air Force Museum	CCCP-46746 [canx 1979; preserved by Aug87 Monino, Russia; l/n Oct07]
4 73 009 04		(Aeroflot/Moscow Polar)	CCCP-46747 [w/o 31Mar71 Moscow-Bykovo, USSR; canx 1971]
4 73 009 05		(Aeroflot/Kazakhstan)	CCCP-46751 [w/o 24Mar69 Alma-Ata, Kazakhstan, USSR]

ANTONOV An-24

C/n	Model	Last known Owner/Operator	Identities/fates/comments (where appropriate)
4 73 010 01		(MAP Ramenskoye)	CCCP-06184 CCCP-59502 [An-24B titles on rudder; canx 12Dec80; fate unknown]
4 73 010 02		(Aeroflot/Urals)	CCCP-46753 [canx 1982; fate unknown]
4 73 010 03		(Aeroflot/Uzbekistan)	CCCP-46754 [canx 1979; preserved by Apr89 Samarkand, Uzbekistan, USSR]
4 73 010 04		(Aeroflot/Kazakhstan)	CCCP-46755 [canx 1982; fate unknown]
4 73 010 05		.	[nothing known; possible Soviet Air Force aircraft]
4 73 011 01		(Aeroflot/Ukraine)	CCCP-46756 [canx 1978; fate unknown]
4 73 011 02		(Aeroflot/Moscow Polar)	CCCP-46757 [canx 1984; fate unknown]
4 73 011 03		ex Aeroflot/Urals	CCCP-46758 [canx 1983; preserved 1984 Slobodskoy, Kirov region, Russia; l/n 02Mar09; report to be b/u Oct11]
4 73 011 04		(Aeroflot/Urals)	CCCP-46759 [canx 1982?; fate unknown]
4 73 011 05		(Aeroflot/Krasnoyarsk)	CCCP-46760 [canx 1981; fate unknown]
4 73 012 01		Civil Aviation Board Museum	CCCP-46761 [canx 1984; preserved by Sep92 Ulyanovsk, Russia; l/n Jun05]
4 73 012 02	B	(MIAT Mongolia)	BNMAU-1202 [w/o 01May79 Erdenet City, Mongolia]
4 73 012 03		ex Aeroflot/Ukraine	CCCP-46762 [canx 1981; by May98 to Slavyansk Technical School, Ukraine]
4 73 012 04	B	ex MIAT Mongolia	BNMAU-1204 MT-1001 [by Jun01 Ulan Bator city, Mongolia in use as bar; l/n Nov02]
4 73 012 05		(Aeroflot/Moscow Polar)	CCCP-46763 [canx 1983; fate unknown]
4 73 013 01		(Aeroflot/Urals)	CCCP-46764 [w/o 20Mar65 Khanty-Mansiysk, USSR; canx 17Jly65]
4 73 013 02		(Aeroflot/Kazakhstan)	CCCP-46765 [canx 1982; fate unknown]
4 73 013 03		(Aeroflot/Uzbekistan)	CCCP-46766 [canx 1984; fate unknown]
4 73 013 04		(Aeroflot/Krasnoyarsk)	CCCP-46767 [canx 1981; fate unknown]
4 73 013 05		(Aeroflot/Kazakhstan)	CCCP-46768 [canx 1984; fate unknown]
4 73 014 01		(Aeroflot/Krasnoyarsk)	CCCP-46769 [camc 1981; by Aug99 to Troitsk Technical School, Russia; l/n Aug01]
4 73 014 02		(Aeroflot/Kazakhstan)	CCCP-46770 [canx 1982; fate unknown]
4 73 014 03		(Aeroflot/North Kavkaz)	CCCP-46771 [canx 1979; fate unknown]
4 73 014 04		(Kirovograd Flying School)	CCCP-46772 [canx 1977; fate unknown]
4 73 014 05		(Aeroflot/Privolzhsk)	CCCP-46773 [canx 1983; fate unknown]
4 73 015 01		(Aeroflot/Privolzhsk)	CCCP-46774 [canx 1982; fate unknown]
4 73 015 02		(Aeroflot/Central Region)	CCCP-46775 [canx 1983; fate unknown]
4 73 015 03		(Soviet Air Force)	CCCP-46776 [canx 1982; fate unknown]
4 73 015 04	B	ex Avient	CCCP-46777 UR-46777 777 blue+ UR-46777 [+ Ukraine] [canx 13Aug08; l/n 29Sep08 Kiev-Svyatoshino, Ukraine in bare metal]
5 73 015 05		(Kirovograd Flying School)	CCCP-46778 [canx probably on 17May90; fate unknown]
5 73 016 01		(Soviet Government)	CCCP-46779 [canx 1979; preserved Orlyonok Pioneers Camp, 45km NE of Tuapse, Russia; b/u Jly07]
5 73 016 02		(Aeroflot/Urals)	CCCP-46780 [canx 1981; by Jly96 to Kriviy Rig Technical School, Ukraine; l/n May02]
5 73 016 03		(Aeroflot/Uzbekistan)	CCCP-46781 [canx 1978; fate unknown]
5 73 016 04	B	(Air Guinee)	OD-AEN 3X-GAS 3X-GCD [fate/status unknown]
5 73 016 05	B	(Aeroflot/Urals)	CCCP-46782 [canx 1985; by Jly88 to Moscow-Sheremetyevo Technical School, Russia, USSR; b/u by Aug12]
5 73 017 01	B	(Flight State Academy of Ukraine)	CCCP-46783 UR-46783 [not in 2001 fleet list; fate unknown]
5 73 017 02	B	ex Air West Express	YR-AMZ ST-AWS [wfu by Sep95 Bucharest-Otopeni, Romania; l/n Aug01; canx before Jan07]
5 73 017 03		(Aeroflot/North Kavkaz)	CCCP-46784 [canx 1981; fate unknown]
5 73 017 04		(MAP Kazan VPO)	CCCP-46786 [canx 30Jan89; fate unknown]
5 73 017 05		(Aeroflot/Uzbekistan)	CCCP-46787 [canx 1978; fate unknown]
5 73 018 01	B	(Aeroflot/Privolzhsk)	CCCP-46788 [w/o 01Dec71 near Saratov, USSR]
5 73 018 02		(Aeroflot/North Kavkaz)	CCCP-46789 [canx 1979; fate unknown]
5 73 018 03	B	(Aeroflot)	CCCP-46790 3X-GOB CCCP-46790 [canx 1984; fate unknown]
5 73 018 04		Temruyk Military Museum	CCCP-46791 [canx 1987; preserved Temruyk, Russia; report as being painted as 30 red considered incorrect]
5 73 018 05	B	(Egyptair)	SU-ANV [wfu by Aug75 Cairo, Egypt; l/n Sep80; probably b/u]
5 73 019 01		(Aeroflot/Urals)	CCCP-46792 [canx 1983; fate unknown]
5 73 019 02		ex Aeroflot/North Kavkaz	CCCP-46793 [canx 1979; preserved Koktebel, Crimea, Ukraine; l/n Jly06 with "Antosha" titles]
5 73 019 03		(Kirovograd Flying School)	CCCP-46794 3X-GOA CCCP-46794 [canx 1976; fate unknown]
5 73 019 04		(Aeroflot/Kazakhstan)	CCCP-46795 [canx 21Jan88; fate unknown]
5 73 019 05	B	Avialinii Ukrainy	CCCP-46796 RA-46796 UR-46796
5 73 020 01		(Aeroflot/Ukraine)	CCCP-46797 [canx 1979; fate unknown]
5 73 020 02	B	(Egyptair)	SU-ANX [wfu by Aug75 Cairo, Egypt; l/n Sep80; probably b/u]

ANTONOV An-24

C/n	Model	Last known Owner/Operator	Identities/fates/comments (where appropriate)
5 73 020 03	FK	Gos NII GA	CCCP-46389 91 red+ CCCP-46389 [+ Soviet] [ff 21Aug67; to An-24FK prototype; An-30 type nose; fate unknown]
5 73 020 04	B	(Egyptair)	SU-ANY [wfu by Aug75 Cairo, Egypt; l/n Sep80; probably b/u]
5 73 020 05		(Aeroflot?)	CCCP-46798? [not confirmed; possible this was the An-30 prototype]
5 73 020 06		(Aeroflot/Kazakhstan)	CCCP-46799 [canx 1983; byJly94 derelict Rostov-na-Donu, Russia; no recent reports]
5 73 020 07	B	(United Arab Airlines)	SU-ANZ [w/o 19Jly70 Cairo, Egypt]
5 73 020 08		(Aeroflot/North Kavkaz)	CCCP-46800 [canx 1981; wreck noted Aug93 Riga-Spilve, Latvia Aug93; l/n Sep94; b/u by Sep97]
5 73 020 09	B	(United Arab Airlines)	SU-AOA [w/o 18Mar66 near Cairo, Egypt]
5 73 020 10	B	State Aviation Museum	CCCP-46801 [canx 1981; by Aug91 to Kiev Institute of Civil Engineering; preserved Kiev, Ukraine by Oct03]
5 73 021 01	B	(United Arab Airlines)	SU-AOB [w/o 02Feb66 near Luxor, Egypt]
5 73 021 02	B	(Aeroflot/Privolzhsk)	CCCP-46802 [canx 02Apr94; fate unknown]
5 73 021 03	B	(United Arab Airlines)	SU-AOC [w/o 14Mar70 Cairo, Egypt]
5 73 021 04	B	(Buryat Avia)	CCCP-46803 RA-46803 [canx 22Jly98; wfu by 26Nov06 Ulan Ude-Mukhino, Russia]
5 73 021 05	B	(Aeroflot/Kazakhstan)	CCCP-46804 [fate unknown]
5 73 021 06	B	(Izhavia)	CCCP-46805 RA-46805 [canx 11Jan96; fate unknown]
5 73 021 07	B	ex Romavia	YR-AMX 'YR-FEL'+ [+ fake registration;] [canx 16Mar99; by Aug00 to Facultat Electrotechnik, Craovia City, Romania with false regn; l/n Sep08]
6 73 021 08	B	ex Turkmenistan Airlines	CCCP-46806 EZ-46806 [not in 1999 fleet list; for sale 2008; fate/status unknown]
5 73 021 09	B	(Aeroflot/Ukraine)	CCCP-46807 [w/o 15Jan79 Minsk 1, Belarus, USSR]
6 73 021 10		.	[nothing known; possible Soviet Air Force aircraft]
6 73 022 01		China Aviation Museum	50954+ [+ China] [wfu Dec89; preserved by Mar97 Changping, China; l/n 14Oct10]
6 73 022 02		(Aeroflot/Ukraine)	CCCP-46808 [canx 1987; fate unknown]
6 73 022 03	B	ex LOT Polish Airlines	SP-LTA [canx 20Feb92; dumped by Oct94 Warsaw, Poland by Oct94; l/n May08]
6 73 022 04	B	ex Avialinii Ukrainy	CCCP-46813 UR-46813 [stored by Oct96; l/n stored 07Sep96 Lvov, Ukraine]
6 73 022 05	B	(Avialinii Ukrainy)	SP-LTB CCCP-49248 49248 [stored by 28Aug92 Kiev-Zhulyany, Ukraine; l/n 11Sep96 still in basic LOT c/s; assumed b/u]
6 73 022 06	B	Bourgas Airport Aviationexpo	DM-SBA LZ-ANL [preserved by Sep00 Burgas, Bulgaria]
6 73 022 07	B	Air Koryo	P-527
6 73 022 08	B	ex LOT Polish Airlines	SP-LTC [canx 20Feb92, dumped by Jun95 Grodzisko, Poland; then by 02Aug07 Olesno Stare, Poland]
6 73 022 09	B	(LOT Polish Airlines)	SP-LTD [w/o 02Nov88 near Rzeszow, Poland; canx 07Dec88]
6 73 022 10	B	(Vietnam Airlines)	DM-SBD VN-B226 [wfu by Jan91; fate/status unknown]
6 73 023 01	B	(Vietnam Airlines)	DM-SBE VN-B228 [wfu by Jan91; fate/status unknown]
6 73 023 02	B	(Vietnam Airlines)	DM-SBC VN-B224(1) VN-B235 [wfu by Jan91 Saigon, Vietnam; fate/status unknown]
6 73 023 03	B	(Vietnam Airlines)	DM-SBG VN-B230 [wfu by Jan91; fate/status unknown]
6 73 023 04	B	(Vietnam Airlines)	DM-SBF VN-B244 [wfu by Jan91; fate/status unknown]
6 73 023 05		.	[nothing known; possible Soviet Air Force aircraft]
6 73 023 06	B	(Aeroflot/Ukraine)	CCCP-46809 [w/o 12Nov71 Vinnitsa, Ukraine, USSR]
6 73 023 07	B	ex Turkmenistan Airlines	CCCP-46810 EZ-46810 [not in 1999 fleet list; for sale 2008; fate/status unknown]
6 73 023 08	B	(Arkhangelsk Airlines)	CCCP-46811 RA-46811 [canx 30Apr97; fate/status unknown]
6 73 023 09	B	Antonov Design Bureau	CCCP-69308 CCCP-46521 LZ-SFP 46521 [by Aug02 at Gostomel, Ukraine with 46521 under wing only; l/n Jun06 dumped]
6 73 023 10	B	(Independent Carrier)	CCCP-98104 UR-98104 [canx 01Oct08; wfu Kiev-Zhulyany, Ukraine; l/n 26Nov11 marked as 98104]
6 73 024 01	B	(Saravia)	CCCP-46812 RA-46812 [canx 15Apr98; fate/status unknown]
6 73 024 02	B?	(Cubana)	CU-T875 [w/o 29Aug66 Camaguey, Cuba]
6 73 024 03	B?	(Cubana)	CU-T876 [w/o 14May73 Havana, Cuba]
6 73 024 04	B	(Cubana)	CU-T877 [wfu by Jun95 Havana, Cuba; l/n Jly99 in bad condition; assumed b/u]
6 73 024 05	B	(LOT Polish Airlines)	SP-LTE [w/o 24Jan69 Wroclaw, Poland; canx 10Nov69]
6 73 024 06	B	(LOT Polish Airlines)	SP-LTF [w/o 02Apr69 near Podpolice, Poland; canx 23Jly71]
6 73 024 07	B	(unknown)	CCCP-46814 RA-46814 [canx unknown date; fate/status unknown]
6 73 024 08	B	Air Koryo	P-537

ANTONOV An-24

C/n	Model	Last known Owner/Operator	Identities/fates/comments (where appropriate)
6 73 024 09	B	ex Aeroflot/Urals?	CCCP-46815 RA-46815 [canx 13May94; dismantled Jly94 Moscow-Domodedovo, Russia; probably to training facility, Kashira, Russia; l/n Sep07]
6 73 024 10	B	(Cubana)	CU-T878 [b/u post 1996?]
6 73 025 01	B	(Cubana)	CU-T879 [w/o 18Mar76 in mid-air collision with DC-8 CU-T1200 over Cuba]
6 73 025 02	B	ex Cubana	CU-T880 [preserved by Dec95 Lenin Park, Havana, Cuba; l/n Apr02]
6 73 025 03	B	ex Vietnam Airlines	VN-1094 VN-B234 [wfu by Mar96 Saigon, Vietnam; l/n 08Nov09]
6 73 025 04	B	(Avialinii Ukrainy)	SP-LTG CCCP-49249 49249 UR-49249 [not in 1997 fleet list; l/n Jly99 Kiev-Zhulyany, Ukraine; assumed b/u]
6 73 025 05	B	(Avialinii Ukrainy)	SP-LTH CCCP-49250 49250 UR-49250 [not in 1997 fleet list; l/n Jly99 Kiev-Zhulyany, Ukraine; assumed b/u]
6 73 025 06	B	(Avialinii Ukrainy)	SP-LTI CCCP-49251 49251 [not in 1996 fleet list; l/n May98 Kiev-Zhulyany, Ukraine, still in basic LOT c/s; assumed b/u]
6 73 025 07	B	ex Avialinii Ukrainy	SP-LTK CCCP-49252 49252 UR-49252 [wfu by 1997 Kiev-Zhulyany, Ukraine; canx 13Aug08; displayed Ukraine Interior Ministry HQ, Kiev]
6 73 025 08	B	(Soviet Air Force)	CCCP-47769 [canx 14Apr82 but still active 1996; fate/status unknown]
6 73 025 09		.	[nothing known; possible Soviet Air Force aircraft]
6 73 025 10	B	(MIAT Mongolia)	BNMAU-2510 MT-2510 MT-1027 JU-1027 [wfu by Jun01 Ulaanbaatar-Buyant Ukhaa, Mongolia; by Jly07 preserved Mongolian Technical University]
6 73 026 01	B	(Cubana)	CU-T881 [wfu by Nov96 Havana, Cuba; l/n Jly97; assumed b/u]
6 73 026 02	B	(Aerocaribbean)	CU-T882 CU-T1500 [wfu by Apr02 Havana, Cuba; l/n Jan03; assumed b/u]
6 73 026 03	B	(Aeroflot/Kazakhstan)	CCCP-46816 [w/o 09Feb92 Guryev, Kazakhstan, USSR]
6 73 026 04		(Soviet Air Force)	CCCP-47770 [canx 12Mar86; fate unknown]
6 73 026 05	B	(ex Aeroflot/Urals)	CCCP-46817 RA-46817 [canx 07May95; fate unknown]
6 73 026 06		(Aeroflot/Moscow Polar)	CCCP-46818 [canx 1975; fate unknown]
6 73 026 07	B	(Kuban Airlines)	CCCP-46819 RA-46819 [canx 20Jly95; fate unknown]
6 73 026 08	B	Kiev ARP 410 Airlines	CCCP-46820 RA-46820 UR-PWA
6 73 026 09	B	Yoshkar-Ola Air	CCCP-46200 RA-46200
6 73 026 10	B	(Aeroflot/Moscow Polar)	CCCP-46201 [w/o 31Dec67 Voronezh, USSR; canx 1968]
6 73 027 01	B	(Aeroflot/Privolzhsk)	CCCP-46202 [w/o 04Nov72 Kursk, USSR; canx 1973]
6 73 027 02	B	(Kuban Airlines)	CCCP-46203 RA-46203 [canx 20Jly95; fate unknown]
6 73 027 03	B	(Air Guinee)	3X-GAQ [fate unknown]
6 73 027 04	B	(Air Guinee)	3X-GAR [fate unknown]
6 73 027 05	B	ex Somali Air Force	MM60204 [code AM-85] [wfu by 12May09 Nairobi International, Kenya]
6 73 027 06		(Yoshkar-Ola Air)	CCCP-46204 RA-46204 [canx 27Apr98; fate unknown]
6 73 027 07	B	(Balkan Bulgarian Airlines)	LZ-ANA [w/o 22Nov75 near Sofia, Bulgaria]
6 73 027 08	B	(Somali Air Force)	MM60205 [code AM-86] [damaged condition by 09Feb93 Mogadishu, Somalia; fate unknown]
6 73 027 09	B	(Aeroflot?)	MM60206+ CCCP-02709 [+ Somalia; coded AM-87 & GD-87] [Jly96 to Kriviy Rig Technical School, Ukraine; b/u by May02]
6 73 027 10	B	(Balkan Bulgarian Airlines)	LZ-ANB [b/u Sep97 Varna, Bulgaria]
6 73 028 01	B	(Avialinii Ukrainy)	011(1)+ SP-LTO CCCP-49253 49253 UR-49253 [+ Poland] [not in 1997 fleet list; l/n Jly99 Kiev-Zhulyany, Ukraine; assumed b/u; canx 15Nov01]
6 73 028 02	B	(Avialinii Ukrainy)	012(1)+ SP-LTP CCCP-49254 49254 UR-49254 [+ Poland] [not in 1997 fleet list; l/n Jly99 Kiev-Zhulyany, Ukraine; assumed b/u]
6 73 028 03	B	(Ukraine State Flying School)	CCCP-46205 UR-46205 [canx 02Oct09 fate/status unknown]
6 73 028 04	B	ex Turkmenistan Airlines	CCCP-46206 EZ-46206 [not in Nov99 fleet list; for sale 2008; fate/status unknown]
6 73 028 05	B	(United Arab Airlines)	SU-AOK [w/o 30Jan70 Luxor, Egypt]
6 73 028 06	B	(United Arab Airlines)	SU-AOL [w/o 18Aug68 in sea en-route between Port Said, Egypt & Cyprus]
6 73 028 07	B	(Aeroflot/Central Region)	CCCP-46207 RA-46207 [canx 14Jan94; fate unknown]
6 73 028 08	B	ex Aviostart	LZ-ANC [stored by 30Aug06 Sofia-Vrazhdebna, Bulgaria; canx 30Jan07]
6 73 028 09	B	(United Arab Airlines)	SU-AOM [w/o 30Sep66 Cairo, Egypt; hulk still present Aug75]
6 73 028 10	B	(Kurgan Air)	CCCP-46209 RA-46209 [canx 22Apr97; fate unknown]
6 73 029 01	B	(Kirovograd Flying School)	CCCP-46210 [canx 1983; fate unknown]
6 73 029 02	LR	(Aeroflot/Central Region)	CCCP-46211 [wfu by Jun92 Moscow-Bykovo, Russia; canx 12Feb94; l/n Aug95; assumed b/u]
7 73 029 03	B	Gustavo Briceno	2903+ 2903+ YN-CGD YV-2726P^ YV1708 [+ Czechoslovakia then Slovikia; ^ reported false marks]
7 73 029 04	B	Letecke Museum Kbely	2904+ [+ Czechoslovakia/Czech Republic] [stored by Oct05 Kbely, Czech Republic for museum]

ANTONOV An-24

C/n	Model	Last known Owner/Operator	Identities/fates/comments (where appropriate)
7 73 029 05	B	(Balkan Bulgarian Airlines)	SP-LTL LZ-ANM [stored by 30Aug06 Sofia-Vrazhdebna, Bulgaria; canx 30Jan07; b/u Aug11]
6 73 029 06	B	(Balkan Bulgarian Airlines)	CCCP-46212 LZ-ANN [DBR 28Jly92 Sofia-Vrazhdebna, Bulgaria; wreck still there 16Apr95; assumed b/u]
6 73 029 07	B	(Buryat Avia)	CCCP-46213 RA-46213 [not in 2000 fleet list; canx unknown date; fate unknown]
6 73 029 08	B	(Arkhangelsk Airlines)	CCCP-46214 RA-46214 [canx 30Apr97; fate unknown]
6 73 029 09	B	(Aeroflot/Lithuania)	CCCP-46215 [w/o 30Dec67 Liepaya, Latvia, USSR; canx 1969]
6 73 029 10	B	(Uzbekistan Airways)	CCCP-46216 UK-46216 [wfu for spares by Oct97 Samarkand, Uzbekistan; probably b/u by 1999]
6 73 030 01	B	Russian Air Force	CCCP-46457 [based Klin, Russia; l/n 1998 still as CCCP-46497; current status unknown]
6 73 030 02	B	(National Aero Klub Chkalova)	01 red+ 01 red^ RA-49259 [+ Soviet; ^ Russia] [canx 04Dec97; by 16Aug01 derelict Kaluga-Grabtsevo, Russia]
6 73 030 03	B	(Astrakhan Airlines)	CCCP-46208 RA-46208 [canx 04Feb00; fate unknown]
6 73 030 04	B	Ukraine Flight State Academy	CCCP-47791 UR-47791 LZ-MNF (TG-RVS) TG-MNF LZ-MNF UR-47791
6 73 030 05	B	(Aviaobshchemash)	CCCP-47771 RA-47771 [canx 06Jan98; fate unknown]
6 73 030 06	B	CTMA	CCCP-46217 UR-46217 ER-AEL
6 73 030 07	B	(Kirovograd Flying School)	CCCP-46218 [canx 1983; l/n derelict by Jly93 Kirovograd-Khmelyovoye, Ukraine; assumed b/u]
6 73 030 08	B	(Kirovograd Flying School)	CCCP-46219 [canx 1979; fate unknown]
7 73 030 09	B	(Vietnam Airlines)	DM-SBH VN-B232 [wfu by Jan91; fate unknown]
7 73 030 10	B	(Kuban Airlines)	CCCP-46221 RA-46221 [canx 20Oct97; fate unknown]
7 73 031 01	B	(Buryat Avia)	CCCP-46222 RA-46222 [c/n plate reads "77303102"; canx 22Jly98; l/n wfu Nov06 Ulan Ude-Mukhino, Russia]
? 73 031 02	B	Uzbekistan Airways	CCCP-46223 UK-46223 [c/n either 6 73 031 02 or 7 73 031 02; see above]
7 73 031 03	B	(Aeroflot/Moscow Polar)	CCCP-46220 [w/o 18Apr80 Moscow-Bykovo, USSR]
7 73 031 04	B	(Uzbekistan Airways)	CCCP-46224 UK-46224 [wfu 15Aug97 Samarkand, Uzbekistan; used for spares Oct97; canx]
7 73 031 05	B	(Astrakhan Airlines)	CCCP-46225 RA-46225 [not in 1998 fleet list; fate unknown; assumed b/u]
7 73 031 06	B	(Latavio)	CCCP-46226 YL-LCA [canx 13Feb01; wfu by Apr02 Riga-Skulte, Latvia; b/u by Mar08 cockpit only preserved Ciemupe, Latvia]
7 73 031 07	B	(Aeroflot/Moscow Polar)	CCCP-46227 [canx 1974; by Aug99 to Troitsk Technical School, Russia; l/n Aug01]
7 73 031 08	B	ex Turkmenistan Airlines	CCCP-46228 EZ-46228 [not in Nov99 fleet list; for sale 2000; l/n stored 06Nov08 Ashkhabad, Turkmenistan]
7 73 031 09	B	(Komavia)	CCCP-46229 RA-46229 [canx 23Apr97; fate unknown]
7 73 031 10	B	(Kirov Avia)	CCCP-46230 RA-46230 [canx Nov08; fate unknown]
7 73 032 01	B	(Aeroflot/North Kavkaz)	CCCP-47790 [canx 1979; fate unknown]
7 73 032 02	B	(Kirovograd Flying School)	CCCP-47789 [canx 1976; fate unknown]
7 73 032 03	B	National Aviation University Collection	CCCP-46245 [canx 1982; by Jun93 to Kiev Institute of Civil Engineering, by Jun06 preserved Kiev, Ukraine; l/n Aug08]
7 73 032 04	B	(Chita Avia)	CCCP-46246 RA-46246 [canx 03Feb97; wfu by 18Apr97 Chita-Kadala, Russia; assumed b/u]
7 73 032 05	B	(Kuban Airlines)	CCCP-46247 RA-46247 [canx 14Feb97; fate unknown]
7 73 032 06	B	(Aeroflot/Ukraine)	CCCP-46248 [w/o 03Aug69 Preobrazhenskoye, USSR; canx 18Nov69]
7 73 032 07	B	(Lviv Airlines)	CCCP-46249 CCCP-46569(2)+ UR-46569(2)+ UR-46249 [+ may have been painted as such in error; wfu by May07 Lvov-Snilow, Ukraine; canx 13Aug08; b/u 10May12]
7 73 032 08	B	ex Belavia	CCCP-46250 EW-46250 RA-46250 EW-46250 [not in 1998 fleet list; wfu by Aug06 Gomel, Belarus; l/n Jly08 derelict] [not in 1998 fleet list; wfu by Aug06 Gomel, Belarus; l/n Jly08 derelict]
7 73 032 09	B	(Aeroflot/Privolzhsk)	CCCP-46241 [w/o early 1970s in refuelling fire Saratov, USSR; canx 1971]
7 73 032 10	B	(Uzbekistan Airways)	CCCP-46242 UK-46242 [wfu by 15Aug97 Samarkand, Uzbekistan; canx; preserved Soghdiana Park, Samarkand; l/n summer 2009]
7 73 033 01	B	(Balkan Bulgarian Airlines)	LZ-AND [wfu by Apr01 Sofia-Vrazhdeba, Bulgaria; canx 30Jan07; b/u Aug11
7 73 033 02	B	(MIAT Mongolia)	BNMAU-3302 MT-3302 MT-1002 JU-1002 [wfu before 2001; fate unknown]
7 73 033 03	B	ex Avialinii Ukrainy	CCCP-46251 UR-46251 [stored by Apr99 Donetsk, Ukraine; l/n Jun06]
7 73 033 04	B	ex Novosibirsk Avia	CCCP-46252 RA-46252 [canx 18Feb02; wfu by 05Jly04 Novosibirsk-Tolmachovo, Russia; l/n Jly08]

ANTONOV An-24

C/n	Model	Last known Owner/Operator	Identities/fates/comments (where appropriate)
7 73 033 05	B	(Tulpar Avia Service)	CCCP-46253 UN-46253 [stored by Oct08 Karaganda, Kazakhstan; l/n 08May10; b/u Sep10]
7 73 033 06	B	ex Voronezh Avia	CCCP-46243 RA-46243 [canx 29Jly97; by Jun99 roadside attraction in Coca-Cola colours Kon-Kolodez, Russia; l/n 28Jly08]
7 73 033 07		.	[nothing known; possible Soviet Air Force aircraft]
7 73 033 08	B	(Soviet Air Force)	CCCP-47788 [canx 14Apr82; fate unknown]
7 73 033 09	B	(Romavia)	YR-AMR [w/o 13Dec95 Verona, Italy]
7 73 033 10	B	(TAROM)	YR-AMT [w/o 04Feb70 Apuseni Mountains, Romania; canx 09Jun70]
7 73 034 01	B	(Komiavia)	CCCP-46244 RA-46244 [canx 29Dec95; fate unknown]
7 73 034 02	B	(Donbassaero)	CCCP-46254 UR-46254 [canx 31Dec08; l/n 08Sep06 Donesk, Ukraine; fate/status unknown]
7 73 034 03	B	(Saransk Air)	CCCP-46255 RA-46255 [canx 03Oct97; fate unknown]
7 73 034 04	B	(Uzbekistan Airways)	CCCP-46256 UK-46256 [wfu for spares by Aug97 Samarkand, Uzbekistan; canx]
7 73 034 05	B	(unknown)	CCCP-46257 RA-46257 [canx 29Apr96; fate unknown]
7 73 034 06	B	Muzel na Aviatsiyata	LZ-ANE [preserved by 1992 Plovdiv-Krumovo, Bulgaria]
7 73 034 07	B	(Balkan Bulgarian Airlines)	LZ-ANF [b/u Sep97 Varna, Bulgaria; nose section preserved Bourgas Airport Aviaionexpo; l/n 28Jun10]
7 73 034 08	B	(Balkan Bulgarian Airlines)	LZ-ANG [b/u Sep97 Varna, Bulgaria]
7 73 034 09	B	(Astrakhan Airlines)	CCCP-46258 RA-46258 [canx 09Sep98; fate unknown]
7 73 034 10	B	(Bryansk Avia)	CCCP-46259 RA-46259 [canx 29Apr96; fate unknown]
7 73 035 01	B	(Arkhangelsk Airlines)	CCCP-46260 [canx 21Apr98 as to Ukraine; nothing more known]
7 73 035 02	B	(Aeroflot/Kazakhstan)	CCCP-46261 [fate unknown]
7 73 035 03	B	(Federal Border Guard)	CCCP-46262 RA-46262 [canx unknown date; fate unknown]
7 73 035 04	B	(Cheboksary Air Enterprise)	CCCP-46263 RA-46263 UN-46263 RA-46263 [canx 11Aug99; fate unknown]
7 73 035 05	B	(TAROM)	YR-AMP [w/o 17Nov78 near Arad, Romania; canx 05Dec78]
7 73 035 06	B	(Aeroflot/Uzbekistan)	CCCP-46264 [canx 1979; fate unknown]
7 73 035 07	B	(TAROM)	YR-AMV [canx 05Dec78 due to accident; no details known]
7 73 035 08	B	SCAT	CCCP-46265 UN-46265 UP-AN405
7 73 035 09	B	(Uzbekistan Airways)	CCCP-46266 UK-46266 [wfu for spares by Oct97 Samarkand, Uzbekistan; canx]
7 73 035 10	B	(UTair Ekspress)	CCCP-46267 EW-46267 RA-46267 [canx Nov08; by 30Jly12 stored Tyumen, Russia]
7 73 036 01	B	ex Kazakhstan Airlines	CCCP-46268 UN-46268 [derelict by 26Jan03 Aktau, Kazakhstan; l/n 28May04]
7 73 036 02	B	(Aeroflot/Arkhangelsk)	CCCP-46269 [w/o 03Sep79 Anderma, USSR; canx 08Oct79]
7 73 036 03	B	ex Kazakhstan Airlines	CCCP-46270 UN-46270 [wfu by Mar03 & stored outside airfield boundary, Atyrau, Kazakhstan]
7 73 036 04	B	SCAT	CCCP-46271 UN-46271 UP-AN406
7 73 036 05	B	(Bashkirian Airlines)	CCCP-46272 RA-46272 [canx 01May96; fate unknown]
7 73 036 06	B	(Avialinii Tatarstana)	CCCP-46273 RA-46273 [canx 24Sep96; fate unknown]
7 73 036 07	B	ex Turkmenistan Airlines	CCCP-46274 EZ-46274 [not in Nov99 fleet list; for sale 2008; l/n stored 06Nov08 Ashkhabad, Turkmenistan]
7 73 036 08	B	(Arkhangelsk Airlines)	CCCP-46275 RA-46275 [canx 30Apr97; fate unknown]
7 73 036 09	B	(Aeroflot/North Kavkaz)	CCCP-46276 [w/o 22Jan73 Petukhovo 90km from Perm, USSR; canx 07Jun73]
7 73 036 10	B	(Aeroflot/Privolzhsk)	CCCP-46277 [w/o 25Jan74 Rostov, USSR]
7 73 037 01	B	ex Lviv Airlines	CCCP-46278 UR-46278 [wfu by May07 Lviv-Snilow, Ukraine; canx 13Aug08; l/n Nov08]
7 73 037 02	B	ex Chinese Navy	CCCP-46279 028 [preseved by Sep09 Naval Museum, Qingdao, China; c/n not confirmed]
7 73 037 03	B	(Kirovograd Flying School)	CCCP-46281 [canx 1983; 1995 preserved Vinnista, Ukraine; later b/u]
8 73 037 04	B	(Phoenix Avia)	CCCP-46419 RA-46419 EK-46419 [canx 30Dec03; fate unknown]
7 73 037 05	B	(Aeroflot/Moscow Polar)	CCCP-46282 RA-46282 [canx 17Apr95; b/u May96 Moscow-Bykovo, Russia]
7 73 037 06	B	ex Turkmenistan Airlines	CCCP-46284 EZ-46284 [not in Nov99 fleet list; for sale 2008; l/n stored 06Nov08 Ashkhabad, Turkmenistan]
7 73 037 07	B	(Uzbekistan Airways)	CCCP-46285 UK-46285 [wfu for spares by Oct97 Samarkand, Uzbekistan; canx]
7 73 037 08	B	(Kurgan Air)	CCCP-46286 RA-46286 [canx 28Oct97; fate unknown]
7 73 037 09	B	(Kirovograd Flying School)	CCCP-46287 [canx 1983; derelict by Sep94 Kirivograd-Khmelyovoye, Ukraine]
7 73 037 10	B	ex Air Kazakhstan	CCCP-46288 UN-46288 [wfu before Nov02; to roadside attraction Via restaurant, near Seoul, Kimpo, South Korea]
7 73 038 01	B	(unknown)	CCCP-46289 UN-46289 [wfu by 10May98 Shimkent, Kazakstan; l/n Mar04 on blocks]

ANTONOV An-24

C/n	Model	Last known Owner/Operator	Identities/fates/comments (where appropriate)
7 73 038 02	B	(Komiavia)	CCCP-46290 RA-46290 [canx 27Oct97; fate unknown]
7 73 038 03	B	(Aviata)	CCCP-46291 RA-46291 [canx 21Mar00; fate unknown]
7 73 038 04	B	(Daghestan Airlines)	CCCP-46292 RA-46292 [canx 05Nov97; fate unknown]
7 73 038 05	B	Avialini Ukrayiny	CCCP-46293 UR-46293
7 73 038 06	B	(Astrakhan Airlines)	CCCP-46294 RA-46294 [canx 11Mar99; fate unknown]
7 73 038 07	B	(Uzbekistan Airways)	CCCP-46295 UK-46295 [wfu 17Sep97 Samarkand, Uzbekistan; b/u for spares]
7 73 038 08	B	Kurgansk Aviation Museum	CCCP-46296 [canx 30Jun95; preserved by Aug03 Kurgan, Russia]
7 73 038 09	B	Mosphil Aero Inc	CCCP-46297 EW-46297 RA-46297 RP-C7205 [stored by Feb08 Manila, Philippines; wfu by 11Sep09]
7 73 038 10	B	ex Kuban Airlines	CCCP-46298 RA-46298 [canx 14Feb97; wfu Krasnodar-Pashkovskaya, Russia; l/n May08]
7 73 039 01	B	(Aeroflot/Uzbekistan)	CCCP-46299 [w/o 19Dec78 Samarkand, Uzbekistan, USSR; canx 1979]
7 73 039 02	B	Latvijas Aviacijas Technikes Muzejs	CCCP-46400 YL-LCD [canx 13Feb01; preserved by Oct03 Riga-Skulte, Latvia; l/n Mar08]
7 73 039 03		.	[nothing known; possible Soviet Air Force aircraft]
7 73 039 04	B	(Saransk Flight Unit)	CCCP-46401 RA-46401 [w/o 29Dec95 Saransk, Russia; canx 18Apr00]
7 73 039 05	B	ex Astrakhan Airlines	CCCP-46402 RA-46402 [canx 05Apr02; wfu Astrakhan, Russia; l/n 26Mar07]
7 73 039 06	B	(Elektronprylad)	CCCP-46403 UR-46403 [canx 13Aug08; fate/status unknown]
7 73 039 07	B	Magyar Repulestorteneti Muzeum	907+ [+ Hungary] [wfu 03Dec92; preserved Szolnok, Hungary; l/n Aug08]
7 73 039 08	B	Pinter Muvek Hadtorteneti Muzeum	908+ [+ Hungary] [wfu 03Dec92; preserved Tokol, then by May99 Kecel, Hungary; l/n Mar09]
7 73 039 09	B	(Belavia)	CCCP-46404 46404 EW-46404 [not in 1998 fleet list; l/n Jun01 Minsk-1, Belarus; assumed b/u]
7 73 039 10	B	(Nizhny Novgorod Airlines)	CCCP-46405 RA-46405 [canx 27Nov00; fate unknown]
7 73 040 01	B	ex Voronezh Avia	CCCP-46406 46406 RA-46406 [canx 20Feb98; wfu by Aug01 Voronezh, Russia; l/n 27Aug07]
7 73 040 02	B	(Komiavia)	CCCP-46407 RA-46407 [canx 26Aug97; fate unknown]
7 73 040 03	B	Buryata Avia	CCCP-46408 RA-46408
7 73 040 04	B	ex Aeroflot/Moscow Polar	CCCP-46409 RA-46409 [wfu 27Feb95 to Yegoryevsk Technical School, Russia; canx 04May95; l/n Aug07]
7 73 040 05	B	Uzbekistan Airways	CCCP-46410 UK-46410
8 73 040 06	B	(Komiinteravia)	CCCP-46411 RA-46411 [canx 01Jun01; fate unknown]
8 73 040 07	B	(Kazakhstan Airlines)	CCCP-46412 UN-46412 [derelict by 08Mar03 Atyrau, Kazakhstan; assumed b/u]
8 73 040 08	B	(Uzbekistan Airways)	CCCP-46413 UK-46413 [wfu 08Jan98 Samarkand, Uzbekistan; l/n 23Mar99; b/u for spares use; canx]
8 73 040 09	B	(Air Moldova)	CCCP-46414 ER-46414 [canx 16Sep99 as w/o; nothing known]
8 73 040 10	B	ex Kolymaavia	CCCP-46415 RA-46415 [wfu by 28Nov06 Magadan-Sokol, Russia; l/n 04Jly08]
8 73 041 01	B	(Donbassaero)	CCCP-46416 UR-46416 [canx 26Sep02; fate/status unknown]
8 73 041 02	B	ex Air Moldova	CCCP-46417 ER-46417 UR-46417 ER-46417 [reported wfu by 04Apr09 Chisinau, Moldova]
8 73 041 03	B	(Aeroflot/North Kavkaz)	CCCP-46418 [w/o 27Feb72 Mineralnye Vody, USSR; canx 1972]
8 73 041 04	B	(Air Mali)	TZ-ACT [w/o 22Feb85 Timbuktu, Mali]
8 73 041 05	B	(Voronezh Avia)	CCCP-46420 RA-46420 [canx 20Feb98; displayed by Jan00 by road S of Voronezh City, Russia; b/u Nov11]
8 73 041 06	B	SCAT	CCCP-46421 UN-46211 UP-AN411+ [+ regd as such 29Feb08 but as at Jan11 still marked UN-46421]
8 73 041 07	B	(Penza Air)	CCCP-46422 RA-46422 [canx 09Apr98; fate unknown]
8 73 041 08	B	(Aeroflot/Moscow Polar)	CCCP-46423 [w/o 02Mar86 Bulgulma, USSR; canx 02Jun86]
8 73 041 09	B	(ex Arkhangelsk Airlines)	CCCP-46424 RA-46424+ 46424 [+ canx 16Sep98 to Ukraine; l/n bare metal Jly99 Kiev-Zhulyany, Ukraine; assumed b/u]
8 73 041 10	B	(Komiavia)	CCCP-46425 RA-46425 [canx 03Mar99; fate unknown]
8 73 042 01	B	(Baikal Airlines)	CCCP-46426 RA-46426 [canx 21May97; fate unknown]
8 73 042 02	B	ex Air Mali	TZ-ACK [returned 1972 to USSR 1972; by May94 at Yegoryevsk Technical School; l/n Aug07]
8 73 042 03	B	(Syrianair)	YK-ANA [fate unknown; l/n Sep99]
8 73 042 04	B	(Syrianair)	YK-ANB [fate unknown; l/n Aug93]
8 73 042 05	B	(Latavio)	CCCP-46427 YL-LCE [canx 09Dec94; stored Riga-Skulte, Latvia; l/n Sep97; fate unknown]
8 73 042 06	B	(MIAT Mongolia)	BNMAU-4206 [w/o 17Sep73 Hovd Province, Mongolia]
8 73 042 07	B	(Cheboksary Air Enterprise)	CCCP-46428 RA-46428 [canx 15Mar99; fate unknown]

ANTONOV An-24

C/n	Model	Last known Owner/Operator	Identities/fates/comments (where appropriate)
8 73 042 08	B	(MAP Kiev APO)	CCCP-46429(1) [canx 22May72 – derelict Volgograd-Goomrak, Russia by Aug93]
8 73 042 09	B	ex SCAT	CCCP-46430 RA-46430 UN-46430 [not in Jun06 fleet list; fate/status unknown]
8 73 042 10	B	(Air Guinee)	3X-GAU [probably w/o in accident 31Mar80 Conakry, Guinee]
8 73 043 01	B	(Uzbekistan Airways)	CCCP-46431 UK-46431 [wfu 08Jan98 Samarkand, Uzbekistan; b/u for spares; canx]
8 73 043 02	B	(Kurskavia)	CCCP-46432 RA-46432 [canx 08Jun98; fate unknown]
8 73 043 03	B	ex Turkmenistan Airlines	CCCP-46433 EZ-46433 [not in Nov99 fleet list; for sale 2008]
8 73 043 04	B	Avialinii Ukrainy	CCCP-46434 UR-46434
8 73 043 05	B	(Aeroflot/Azerbaijan)	CCCP-46435 [w/o 18Aug73 near Baku, Azerbaijan, USSR; canx 29Nov73]
8 73 043 06	B	(Daghestan Airlines)	CCCP-46436 RA-46436 [canx 13Dec00; fate unknown]
8 73 043 07	B	(Nizhny Novgorod Airlines)	CCCP-46437 RA-46437 [canx 12Sep01; fate unknown]
8 73 043 08		.	[nothing known; possible Soviet Air Force aircraft]
8 73 043 09	B	SCAT	CCCP-46438 UN-46438 UP-AN412
8 73 043 10	B	(Bashkirian Airlines)	CCCP-46439 RA-46439 [canx 26Nov96; wfu Ufa, Russia; l/n Aug99; fate unknown]
8 73 044 01	B	Avialinii Ukrainy	CCCP-46440 UR-46440
8 73 044 02	B	Avialinii Ukrainy	CCCP-46441 UR-46441 [wreck condition by May99 Kiev-Zhulyany, Ukraine; fate unknown]
8 73 044 03	B	(Baikal Airlines)	CCCP-46442 RA-46442 [canx 05Jly95; fate unknown]
8 73 044 04	B	(Republic of Latvia)	CCCP-46443 YL-LCJ [canx 28Jan97; fate unknown]
8 73 044 05	B	Lietuvos Aviacijos Muziejus	CCCP-46444 LY-AAI 06+ [+ Lithuania] [preserved by Jly96 Kaunas, Lithuania; l/n 14Apr08]
8 73 044 06	B	(Palair Macedonian)	SP-LTM LZ-ANO [not in 31Dec99 fleet list; fate unknown]
8 73 044 07	B	(GosNII GA)	CCCP-46445 [fate unknown]
8 73 044 08	B	(Bashkirian Airlines)	CCCP-46446 RA-46446 [wfu by Aug99 Ufa, Russia; l/n 12Aug01; fate unknown]
8 73 044 09	B	ex Bashkirian Airlines	CCCP-46447 RA-46447(1) [canx 30Aug99; preserved by Jun01 downtown Ufa, Russia; l/n May06]
8 73 044 10	B	Tulpar Aviation	CCCP-46448 UN-46448 UP-AN428
8 73 045 01	B	(Bykovo Avia)	CCCP-46449 RA-46449 [canx 01May96; fate unknown]
8 73 045 02	B	(Bykovo Avia)	CCCP-46550 RA-46550 [canx 03Jun96; fate unknown]
8 73 045 03	B	(Aeroflot/North Kavkaz)	CCCP-46551 [w/o 02Jun90 Ken-Kiyak, USSR; canx 28Dec90]
8 73 045 04	B	(Ariana Afghan)	014+ SP-LTZ CCCP-49258 UR-49258 49258 EL-ASA YA-DAG [+ Poland] [probably destroyed late 2001 in hostilities, Afghanistan]
8 73 045 05	B	(Congo Air Force)	TN-KAL TN-101 TN-220 [wfu by Mar96 Brazzaville, Congo; l/n Apr97; fate unknown]
8 73 045 06	B	(Aeroflot/Turkmenistan)	CCCP-46552 [w/o en-route 06Oct68 near Maryy, Turkmenistan, USSR; canx Jan69]
8 73 045 07	B	(Tiramavia)	CCCP-46553 RA-46553 ER-AFS [canx 19Mar99; fate unknown]
8 73 045 08		(Bulgarian Air Force)	035 [w/o 14Apr75 near Sofia, Bulgaria]
8 73 045 09	B	(Bashkirian Airlines)	CCCP-46554 RA-46554 [wfu by 18Aug99 Ufa, Russia; l/n 12Aug01; fate unknown]
8 73 045 10	B	(Kuban Airlines)	CCCP-46555 RA-46555 [canx 20Oct97; fate unknown]
8 73 046 01	B	(Kolymaavia)	CCCP-46556 RA-46556 [canx unknown date; fate unknown]
8 73 046 02	B	(Iraqi Airways)	YI-AEO [w/o 22Apr82 unknown airfield in Iraq]
8 73 046 03	B	(Iraqi Airways)	YI-AEZ [c/n not confirmed; wreck noted May05 Balad, Iraqi]
8 73 046 04	B	(Chita Avia)	CCCP-46557 RA-46557 [canx 08Dec95; wfu by Apr97 Chita-Kadala, Russia]
8 73 046 05	B	Air Urga	CCCP-46558 UR-46558
8 73 046 06	B	unknown	CCCP-46559 UN-46559
8 73 046 07		.	[nothing known; possible Soviet Air Force aircraft]
8 73 046 08	BS	Ukraine Air Force	[Soviet] 19 blue
8 73 046 09	B	(Arkhangelsk Airlines)	CCCP-46560 RA-46560 [canx 30Apr97; fate unknown]
8 73 046 10	B	(Daghestan Airlines)	CCCP-46561 RA-46561(1) [canx 30Sep98; fate unknown]
8 73 047 01	B	ex Avialinii Tatarstana	CCCP-46562 RA-46562 [stored by Aug01 Kazan-Osnovnoi, Russia; l/n Jun05]
8 73 047 02	B	(Daghestan Airlines)	CCCP-46563 RA-46563 [canx 30Sep98; fate unknown]
8 73 047 03	B	(Arkhangelsk Airlines)	CCCP-46564 RA-46564 [w/o 06Feb95 Arkhangelsk, Russia; canx 09Jun95]
8 73 047 04	B	(Dalavia)	CCCP-46565 RA-46565 [canx 02Nov98; fate unknown]
8 73 047 05	B	Air Koryo	P-528 [c/n not confirmed]
8 73 047 06	B	Ukraine Air Force	[Soviet] 40 black+ 01 yellow+ [+ Ukraine] [also recorded as UR-71663; possibly radio call sign]

ANTONOV An-24

C/n	Model	Last known Owner/Operator	Identities/fates/comments (where appropriate)
8 73 047 07	B	(Daghestan Airlines)	CCCP-46566 RA-46566 [canx 30Sep98; fate unknown]
8 73 047 08	B	(Aeroflot/Moscow Polar)	CCCP-46567 [w/o 16Dec82 near Sakanskoe, Ukraine, USSR; canx 1983]
8 73 047 09	B	ex Bashkirian Airlines	CCCP-46568 RA-46568 [wfu by Aug99 Ufa, Russia; canx 09Sep01; preserved by Mar09 Kushnarenkovo, Russia]
8 73 047 10	B	State Aviation Museum	CCCP-46569(1) UR-46569(1) [preserved by Oct03 Kiev, Ukraine; l/n Mar09]
8 73 048 01		.	[nothing known; possible Soviet Air Force aircraft]
8 73 048 02	B	(Russian Navy)	CCCP-47787 RA-47787 [for sale non-airworthy Nov98; fate unknown]
8 73 048 03	B	Russian Air Force	[Soviet] 01 red
8 73 048 04	B	ex Buryat Avia	CCCP-46570 RA-46570 [wfu by Nov06 Ulan Ude-Mukhino, Russia]
8 73 048 05	B	(Novosibirsk Air)	CCCP-46571 RA-46571 [canx 19Sep98; fate unknown]
8 73 048 06	B	(Daghestan Airlines)	CCCP-46572 [canx 30Sep98; fate unknown]
8 73 048 07	B	Uzbekistan Airways	CCCP-46573 UK-46573
8 73 048 08	B	(Kurskavia)	CCCP-46574 RA-46574 [canx 08Jun98; b/u part of fuselage to GIA Rylsk Civil Aviation Centre, Russia; l/n Apr12]
8 73 048 09	B	(Soviet Air Force)	CCCP-47792 [canx 14Apr82; fate unknown]
8 73 048 10	B	(Aeroflot/Moscow Polar)	CCCP-46575 RA-46575 [w/o 17Jly94 Kherston, Russia; canx 30Sep94]
8 73 049 01	B	ex Aeroflot/Northern	CCCP-46576 RA-46576 [canx 15May00; by Sep06 attraction Power Park Amusement Park, Alaharma, Finland]
8 73 049 02	B	Air Urga	CCCP-46577 UR-46577
8 73 049 03		.	[nothing known; possible Soviet Air Force aircraft]
8 73 049 04	B	(FSB/Border Guards)	[Soviet] 02+ [+ Russia; colour unknown] [for sale Jan99; fate unknown]
8 73 049 05	B	(Russian Air Force)	[Soviet] RA-47750(2) [for sale Nov05; fate unknown]
8 73 049 06	B	(FSB/ Border Guards)	[Soviet] [unknown] [b/u post Apr03]
9 73 049 07	B	(Komiavia)	CCCP-46578 RA-46578 [canx 06Aug99; fate unknown]
9 73 049 08	B	(Daghestan Airlines)	CCCP-46579 RA-46579 [canx 30Sep98; fate unknown]
9 73 049 09	B	(Almazy Rossii Sakha)	CCCP-46580 [canx 21Feb96; fate unknown]
9 73 049 10	B	Trade Aero Space/Trast Aero	CCCP-46581 RA-46581 EK-46581 EX-041(2)
9 73 050 01	B	ex Tulpar Aviation	CCCP-46582 46582 UN-46582 UP-AN427 [wfu/stored by 08May10 Karaganda, Kazakhstan]
9 73 050 02	B	Cheboksary Air Enterprise	CCCP-46583 RA-46583
9 73 050 03	B	(Kirovograd Flying School)	CCCP-46584 [canx by 1987; derelict by Jly93 Kirovograd-Khmelyovoye, Ukraine; l/n Sep94]
9 73 050 04	B	Donbassaero	CCCP-46585 UR-46585
9 73 050 05	B	(LOT Polish Airlines)	SP-LTN [w/o 19Apr78 near Rzessznow, Poland; canx 12Jun78]
9 73 050 06	B	(Donbassaero)	CCCP-46586 UR-46586 [stored by 10Jun06 Donesk, Ukraine; canx 01Oct08; fate unknown]
9 73 050 07	B	ex Aeromist Kharkov	CCCP-46587 RA-46587 ER-AFC(2) UR-CAO [canx 01Oct08; fate/status unknown]
9 73 050 08	B	(Arkhangelsk Airlines)	CCCP-46588 RA-46588 [canx 18Apr97; fate unknown]
9 73 050 09	B	Yoshkar-Ola Air	CCCP-46589 RA-46589
9 73 050 10	B	(Komiavia)	CCCP-46590 RA-46590 [canx 06Aug99; fate unknown]
9 73 051 01	B	(Stavropol Avia)	CCCP-46591 RA-46591 [canx 02Feb98; fate unknown]
9 73 051 02	B	Hazar Air Company	CCCP-46592 EZ-46592
9 73 051 03	B	ex Kirovograd Flying School	CCCP-46593 [canx 1979; wfu by Jly93 Kirovograd-Khmelyovoye, Ukraine; l/n derelict May07]
9 73 051 04	B	Uzbekistan Airways	CCCP-46594 UK-46594 [reported stored]
9 73 051 05	B	Tajikistan Airlines	CCCP-46595 EY-46595 UR-46595 EY-46595
9 73 051 06	B	Avialinii Ukrainy	CCCP-46596 UR-46596
9 73 051 07	B	(Orenburg Airlines)	CCCP-46597 RA-46597 [wfu at Orenburg, Russia, wing spar cut; l/n Oct07]
9 73 051 08	B	ex Turkmenistan Airlines	CCCP-46598 EZ-46598 [not in Nov99 fleet list; for sale Jun08]
9 73 051 09	B	ex Air Moldova	CCCP-46599 ER-46599 [wfu by May07 Chisinau, Moldova; l/n 04Apr09]
9 73 051 10	B	(Buryat Avia)	CCCP-46300 RA-46300 [wfu by Nov06 Ulan Ude-Mukhino, Russia]
9 73 052 01	B	(Lviv Airlines)	CCCP-46301 UR-46301 [canx 20Jly10; fate/status unknown]
9 73 052 02	B	(Donbassaero)	CCCP-46302 UR-46302 [canx 13Aug08; fate unknown]
9 73 052 03	B	(Tula Air)	CCCP-46303 [used for spares by 1995 Tula-Klokovo, Russia; canx 20Apr01]
9 73 052 04	B	Gomelavia	CCCP-46304 EW-46304 [stored by 11May08 Gomel, Belarus]
9 73 052 05	B	(Lviv Airlines)	CCCP-46305 UR-46305 [canx 01Oct08; fate/status unknown]
9 73 052 06	B	(Yugavia)	CCCP-46306 RA-46306 [DBR 21Nov92 Krasnodar, Russia; l/n Sep94; canx 09Dec94]
9 73 052 07	B	(Komiinerteravia)	CCCP-46307 RA-46307 [canx 01Jun01; fate unknown]
9 73 052 08	B	(Astrakhan Airlines)	CCCP-46308 RA-46308 [canx 05Sep02; fate unknown]

ANTONOV An-24

C/n	Model	Last known Owner/Operator	Identities/fates/comments (where appropriate)
9 73 052 09	B	ex China United Airlines	50959+ CUA-50959+ [+ China] [stored by Oct99 Beijing-Nan Yuan, China; later preserved; l/n Nov08]
9 73 052 10	B	(China Northern Airlines)	B-420 B-3401 [b/u Mar92 Harbin, China]
9 73 053 01		.	[nothing known; possible Soviet Air Force aircraft]
9 75 053 02	B	(China Northern Airlines)	B-422 B-3402 [b/u May92 Shenyang, China]
9 73 053 03		.	[nothing known; possible Soviet Air Force aircraft]
9 73 053 04	B	(Kirovograd Flying School)	CCCP-46309 [canx by 1978; fate unknown]
9 73 053 05	B	SCAT	CCCP-46310 46310 UN-46310 UP-AN407
9 73 053 06	B	Ukraine Air Force	[Soviet] 777 blue
9 73 053 07	B	Air Urga	CCCP-46311 UR-46311 LZ-MND UR-46311 [used UN code UN-969 in Apr07]
9 73 053 08	B	(Ukraine National)	CCCP-46312 UR-46312 [stored by Jun02 Kiev-Zhulyany, Ukraine; canx 13Aug08; b/u 15Aug11]
9 73 053 09	B	ex Kazakhstan Airlines	CCCP-46313 UN-46313 [stored by Oct02 Astana, Kazakhstan; l/n Apr07]
9 73 053 10	B	ex Turkmenistan Airlines)	CCCP-46314 EZ-46314 [not in 2001 fleet list; for sale Jun08]
9 73 054 01	B	(Orenburg Airlines)	CCCP-46315 RA-46315 [retired by Jan08; reported Aug12 in remote location possibly as a GIA]
9 73 054 02	B	(Balkan Bulgarian Airlines)	CCCP-46316 LZ-ANP [b/u Sep97 Varna, Bulgaria]
9 73 054 03	B	(Kirovograd Flying School)	CCCP-46317 [canx 21Apr88; fate unknown]
9 73 054 04	B	(PMT Air)	CCCP-46318 XU-385 [canx 09Dec09 by Cambodian CAA; l/n 03Apr08 Phnom-Penh, Cambodia; fate/status unknown]
9 73 054 05	B	unknown	CCCP-46319 [unknown] [canx 11Apr73 as sold to Vietnam]
9 73 054 06	B	(Federal Airlines)	CCCP-46320 LY-AAF ST-AOE [wfu by Jan05 Khartoum, Sudan; canx by Jan07]
9 73 054 07	B	ex Novosibirsk Avia	CCCP-46321 RA-46321 [stored by Jly03 Novosibirsk-Severny, Russia; possibly later b/u]
9 73 054 08	B	(Komiavia)	CCCP-46322 [canx 14Jly95; fate unknown]
9 73 054 09	B	(Stavropol Avia)	CCCP-46323 RA-46323 [canx 15Oct97; fate unknown]
9 73 054 10	B	(Stavropol Avia)	CCCP-46324 RA-46324 [canx 02Feb98; fate unknown]
9 73 055 01	B	unknown	CCCP-46325 YL-LCB N93110 OB- [canx 13Jan05 to Peru; l/n 20Nov07 dumped Lima, Peru still as N93110]
9 73 055 02		.	[nothing known; possible Soviet Air Force aircraft]
9 73 055 03	B	ex Lviv Airlines	CCCP-46326 UR-46326 [canx 31Dec08; fate/status unknown]
9 73 055 04	B	(Aeroflot/North Kavkaz)	CCCP-46327 [w/o 23Oct78 in Gulf of Sivash, USSR; canx 1978]
9 73 055 05	B	Tartastan Nizhnekansk Air	CCCP-46328 RA-46328
9 73 055 06	B	(Tula Air)	CCCP-46329 [canx 24Apr01; fate unknown]
9 73 055 07	B	ex Ukraine National	CCCP-46330 UR-46330 [stored Kiev-Zhulyany, Ukraine; canx 13Aug08; l/n 18Apr09]
9 73 055 08	B	ex Saravia	CCCP-46331 RA-46331 [canx 07Jun98; wfu by Aug03 Saratov-Tsentralnyy, Russia; l/n Apr08 dumpted]
9 73 055 09	B	(ex Tyuman Avia Trans)	CCCP-46332 RA-46332 [canx 05Apr00; preserved by mid 2009 Byeloyarski, Russia; no marks but Kompyuterny salon Soyaris titles]
9 73 055 10	B	Polar Airlines	CCCP-46333 RA-46333
9 73 056 01	B	ex Kazakhstan Airlines	CCCP-46334 UN-46334 [wfu Sep94 Astana, Kazakhstan; preserved by Aug01 Astana city, Kazakhstan; l/n Nov07]
9 73 056 02	B	(Aeroflot/Urals)	CCCP-46335 [w/o 21Nov89 Sovietsky, USSR; canx 07Feb90]
9 73 056 03		.	[nothing known; CCCP-46336 was An24T c/n 8 9 107 09]
9 73 056 04	B	(Tyuman Avia Trans)	CCCP-46337 RA-46337 [canx 31Mar99; fate unknown]
9 73 056 05	B	(Slovak Air Force)	5605+ 5605+ [+ Czechoslovakia then Slovakia] [w/o 19Jan06 near Telkibanya, Hungary]
9 73 056 06	B	(Avialinii Tatarstana)	CCCP-46338 RA-46338 [stored by Aug01 Kazan-Osnovoi, Russia; l/n 28Aug05]
9 73 056 07	B	ex Orenburg Airlines	CCCP-46339 RA-46339 [wfu by Oct07 Orenburg-Tsentrainiy, Russia]
9 73 056 08	B	SCAT	CCCP-46340 UN-46340 UP-AN408
9 73 056 09	B	(Ivanovo Air)	CCCP-46341 RA-46341 [stored by Aug97 Ivanovo-Zhukovka, Russia; probably now b/u]
9 73 056 10	B	Kazakhstan Airlines	CCCP-46342 UN-46342
9 73 057 01	B	ex Avialinii Ukrainy	011(2)+ SP-LTT CCCP-49255 49255 UR-49255 [+ Poland] [status/fate unknown]
9 73 057 02	B	(Polish Air Force)	012(2)+ [+ Poland] [w/o 28Feb73 near Goleniow, Poland]
9 73 057 03	B	(Kazakhstan Airlines)	CCCP-46343 UN-46343 [derelict by May04 Atyrau, Kazakhstan by May04]
9 73 057 04	B	(Sakha Avia)	CCCP-46344 RA-46344 [not in 2000 fleet list; wfu by Aug03 Yakutsk, Russia; l/n Jly04]

ANTONOV An-24

C/n	Model	Last known Owner/Operator	Identities/fates/comments (where appropriate)
9 73 057 05	B	(Kirovograd Flying School)	CCCP-46346 [canx 17Apr84; to Riga-Splive, Latvia as GIA by Aug93;b/u by Sep97]
9 73 057 06	B	(Tula Air)	CCCP-46347 [used for spares by 1995 Tula-Klokovo, Russia; canx 20Apr01]
9 73 057 07	B	Hazar Air Company	CCCP-46348 EZ-46348
9 73 057 08	B	(Aeroflot/Belarus)	CCCP-46349 [w/o 20Nov75 near Kharkov, Ukraine, USSR; canx 1976]
9 73 057 09	B	(Aeroflot/Ukraine)	CCCP-46350 [w/o in probably 1977 or 1978 Budyonnovcsk, USSR; canx 1978]
9 73 057 10	B	(Ivanovo Air)	CCCP-46351 RA-46351 [stored by Aug97 Ivanovo-Zhukovka, Russia; probably now b/u]
9 73 058 01	B	(Alrosa)	CCCP-46352 RA-46352? [fate unknown]
0 73 058 02	B	ex Chukotavia	CCCP-46353 RA-46353 [stored by Jun06 Anadyr-Ugolny, Russia]
0 73 058 03	B	Slovak Air Force	5803+ 5803+ [+ Czechoslovakia then Czech Republic before Slovakia]
9 73 058 04	B	ex Novosibirsk Air	CCCP-46354 RA-46354 [stored by Jly03 Novosibirsk-Severny, Russia; possibly later b/u]
0 73 058 05	B	(Ivanovo Air)	CCCP-46355 RA-46355 [stored by Aug97 Ivanovo-Zhukovka, Russia; probably now b/u]
0 73 058 06	B	Air Kazakhstan	CCCP-46356 UN-46356
0 73 058 07	B	(Aeroflot/Ukraine)	CCCP-46357 [w/o 06Jan74 Mukachevo, Ukraine, USSR; canx 30May74]
0 73 058 08	B	Alrosa	CCCP-46358 RA-46358
0 73 058 09	B	ex Air Pabson	CCCP-46359 EW-46359 UR-46539 EW-46539 [derelict by 2008 Isiro-Matari, Democratic Republic of Congo]
0 73 058 10	B	(Dandy Independent Airlines)	040+ LZ-MNI 040+ LZ-CBC [+ Bulgaria] [canx 30Jan07; b/u Aug07 Sofia, Bulgaria]
0 73 059 01	B	Uzbekistan Airways	CCCP-46360 UK-46360
0 73 059 02	B	(Penza Air)	CCCP-46361 [canx 07Apr95; fate unknown]
0 73 059 03	B	Utair	CCCP-46362 RA-46362
0 73 059 04	B	(Stavropol Avia)	CCCP-46363 [canx 30Jan96; fate unknown]
0 73 059 05	B	unknown	CCCP-46364 [canx 11Apr73 to Vietnam; nothing more known]
0 73 059 06	B	(Tajikistan Airlines)	CCCP-46365 EY-46365 [out of fleet by Oct07; fate/status unknown]
0 73 059 07	B	(Kurgan Air)	CCCP-46366 RA-46366 [canx 29May98; fate unknown]
0 73 059 08	B	(Latavio)	CCCP-46367 YL-LCC [canx 24Apr95; fate unknown]
0 73 059 09	B	SCAT	CCCP-46368 UN-46368 UP-AN409
0 73 059 10	B	(Tarco Airlines)	CCCP-46369 RA-46369 EK-46369 ST-ARQ [w/o 11Nov10 Zalingei, Sudan]
0 73 060 01	B	(Balkan Bulgarian Airlines)	CCCP-46370 LZ-ANR [b/u Sep97 Varna, Bulgaria]
0 73 060 02	B	(Uzbekistan Airways)	CCCP-46371 UK-46371 [wfu 08Jan98 Samarkand, Uzbekistan; b/u for spares; canx]
0 73 060 03	B	Avialinii Ukraiiny	CCCP-46372 UR-46372
0 73 060 04	B	Uzbekistan Airways	CCCP-46373 UK-46373
0 73 060 05	B	ex Polar Airlines	CCCP-46374 RA-46374 [wfu by 26Jun12 Yakutsk, Russia]
0 73 060 06	B	ex Balkan Bulgarian Airlines	SP-LTR LZ-ANS [not in Dec99 fleet list; stored Sofia-Vrazhbedna, Bulgaria; l/n 15May08]
0 73 060 07	B	(LOT Polish Airlines)	015+ SP-LTU [+ Poland] [w/o 26Mar81 Slupsk-Redzikowo, Poland; canx 15May81]
0 73 060 08	B	Belavia	CCCP-46375 EW-46375
0 73 060 09	B	(Air Moldova)	CCCP-46376 ER-46376 [canx 16Sep99; fate unknown]
0 73 060 10	B	(Kuban Airlines)	CCCP-46377 RA-46377 [canx 14Feb97; fate unknown]
0 73 061 01	B	(Aeroflot/Ukraine)	CCCP-46378 [w/o 13Nov71 Kerch, Crimea, Ukraine, USSR]
0 73 061 02	B	(Penza Air)	CCCP-46379 RA-46379 [canx 09Aug98; fate unknown]
0 73 061 03	B	(Aquiline)	CCCP-46380 46380 RA-46380 TN-AFL EX-24103 EX-030 [w/o 23Jly07 Shiile, Ethiopia; canx same date]
0 73 061 04	B	SCAT	CCCP-46381 UN-46381 UP-AN410
0 73 061 05	B	(Kirov Avia)	CCCP-46382 RA-46382 [canx 08Jly98; fate unknown]
0 73 061 06	B	ex Lviv Airlines	CCCP-46383 UR-46383 [canx 01Oct08; wfu by 18Nov08 Lviv-Sknilow, Ukraine; l/n 10Mar09]
0 73 061 07	B	(Sibir)	CCCP-46384 RA-46384 [stored by Jly00 Novosibirsk-Severny, Russia; probbaly b/u by 2007]
0 73 061 08	B	(Aeroflot/Uzbekistan)	CCCP-46385 [canx 1985; fate unknown]
0 73 061 09	B	(Kurskavia)	CCCP-46386 [canx 25Mar98; fate unknown]
0 73 061 10	B	Uzbekistan Airways	CCCP-46387 UK-46387 46387 UK-46387
0 73 062 01	B	UTair Express	CCCP-46388 RA-46388
0 73 062 02	LRI	Polar Airlines	CCCP-47195 RA-47195

ANTONOV An-24

C/n	Model	Last known Owner/Operator	Identities/fates/comments (where appropriate)
0 73 062 03	B	(Uzbekistan Airways)	CCCP-46390 UK-46390 [wfu 15Aug97 Samarkand, Uzbekistan; b/u for spares; canx]
0 73 062 04	B	(Chita Avia)	CCCP-46391 RA-46391 [canx 08Dec95; derelict by Apr97 Chita-Kadala, Russia]
0 73 062 05	B	Uzbekistan Airways	CCCP-46392 UK-46392
0 73 062 06	B	(Ivanovo Air)	CCCP-46393 RA-46393 [stored by Aug97 Ivanovo-Zhukovka, Russia; probably now b/u]
0 73 062 07	RV	(MIAT Mongolia)	BNMAU-6207 MT-1003 JU-1003 [wfu & b/u Jan02 for spares]
0 73 062 08	B	(Bryansk Avia)	CCCP-46394 RA-46394 [canx 14Jly99; fate unknown]
0 73 062 09	ALK	Spetsavia	CCCP-46395 RA-46395
0 73 062 10	B	Air Kazakhstan	CCCP-46396 UN-46396
0 73 063 01	B	Podillia Avia	CCCP-46397 RA-46397 UR-46397
0 73 063 02	B	ex Turkmenistan Airlines	CCCP-46398 EZ-46398 [not in Nov99 fleet list; stored by Apr02 Ashkhabat, Turkmenistan; l/n Nov08]
0 73 063 03	B	(Tajikistan Airlines/Trans Air Congo)	CCCP-46399 EY-46399 [w/o 04Mar05 Impfondo, People's Republic of Congo]
0 73 063 04	B	(Ukraine National)	CCCP-47266 UR-47266 [canx 13Aug08; fate/status unknown]
0 73 063 05	B	(Kuban Airlines)	CCCP-47267 RA-47267 [canx 14Apr97; fate unknown]
0 73 063 06	B	ex Dauriya Airlines	CCCP-47268 RA-47268 [airline bankrupt 12May11; for sale; by 26Jun12 stored Irkutsk Technical Institute, Russia with Angara titles]
0 73 063 07	B	Hangard Airlines	CCCP-47269 RA-47269 MT-7048
0 73 063 08	B	SCAT	CCCP-47270 UN-47270 UP-AN420
0 73 063 09	B	(Vietnam Airlines)	VN-B224(2) [wfu by Mar06 Saigon, Vietnam; l/n Mar00]
0 73 063 10		.	[nothing known; possible Soviet Air Force aircraft]
0 73 064 01	B	UTair Express	CCCP-47271 BNMAU-6401 RA-47271
0 73 064 02	B	Alrosa	CCCP-47272 RA-47272
0 73 064 03	B	UTair Express	CCCP-47273 RA-47273
0 73 064 04	B	Uzbekistan Airways	CCCP-47274 UK-47274
0 73 064 05	B	ex Novosibirsk Avia	CCCP-47275 RA-47275 [stored by Aug07 Novosibirsk-Severny, Russia; possibly later b/u]
0 73 064 06	B	(Komiinteravia)	CCCP-47276 RA-47276 [canx 06Aug99; fate unknown]
0 73 064 07	B	SCAT	CCCP-47277 UN-47277 UP-AN421
0 73 064 08	B	ex South Airlines	CCCP-47278 UR-47278 [canx 08Oct10 canx; l/n 04Oct10 stored Kiev-Zhulyani, Ukraine]
0 73 064 09	B	(Pskovia)	CCCP-47279 RA-47279 [canx 14May97; fate unknown]
0 73 064 10	B	(Aeroflot/Urals)	CCCP-47280 [w/o 13Jan76 Smolnoye, USSR; canx 17Feb76]
0 73 065 01	B	Avialinii Ukraiiny	CCCP-47281 UR-47281
0 73 065 02	B	(Omskavia)	CCCP-47282 RA-47282 [canx 24Aug03; fate unknown]
0 73 065 03	B	(South Airlines)	CCCP-47283 RA-47283 ER-AWJ LZ-VVI UR-SLI [canx 02Oct09; stored by 19Jun11 Odessa, Ukraine in poor condition]
0 73 065 04	B	SCAT	CCCP-47284 UN-47284 UP-AN422
0 73 065 05	B	Cheboksary Air Enterprise	CCCP-47285 RA-47285 47285 RA-47285?
0 73 065 06	B	(Uzbekistan Airways)	CCCP-47286 UK-47286 [wfu 15Aug97 Samarkand, Uzbekistan; b/u for spares; canx]
0 73 065 07	B	(Ukraine National)	CCCP-47287 UR-47287 [wfu by Jun02 Kiev-Zhulyany, Ukraine; l/n 09Aug08; canx 13Aug08]
0 73 065 08	B	(Pskovavia)	CCCP-47288 RA-47288 [canx 14May97; fate unknown]
0 73 065 09	B	UTair Express	CCCP-47289 RA-47289
0 73 065 10	B	(Dalavia)	CCCP-47290 RA-47290 [canx 16Jan01; fate unknown]
0 73 066 01	RV	ex Belavia	CCCP-47291 EW-47291 [wfu by Aug07 Minsk-Loshitsa, Belarus; l/n Oct08]
0 73 066 02	RV	(Bakhtar Afghan)	CCCP-47292 YA-BAG [fate unknown]
0 73 066 03	RV	(Air Kazakhstan)	CCCP-47293 UN-47293 [wfu by 22Mar03 Almaty, Kazakhstan]
0 73 066 04	RV	Kiev ARP 410 Airlines	CCCP-47294 RA-47204 UR-47204
0 73 066 05		.	[nothing known; possible Soviet Air Force aircraft]
1 73 066 06	RV	(Congo Air Force)	TN-ABX TN-111 TN-222 [wfu by Mar96 Brazzaville, People's Republic of Congo; l/n Jun97]
1 73 066 07	RV	(Congo Air Force)	TN-ABY TN-224 [wfu by Oct91 Brazzaville, People's Republic of Congo; l/n Jun97]
0 73 066 08	RV	Kirov Air Enterprise/UTAir Express	CCCP-47295 RA-47295 [wore UN code UNO030 at one time]
0 73 066 09	RV	(AeroSvit)	CCCP-47296 UR-47296 [canx 20Jly10; fate/status unknown]
0 73 066 10	RV	Kiev ARP 410 Airlines	CCCP-47297 UR-47297
0 73 067 01	RV	(Almazy Rossii Sakha)	CCCP-47298 RA-47298 [canx 21Feb96; fate unknown]
1 73 067 02	RV	ex Kazakhstan Airlines	CCCP-47299 UN-47299 [derelict by 18Jun02 Astana, Kazakhstan]
1 73 067 03	RV	(Aerokuznetsk)	CCCP-46826 [canx 28Jan97; fate unknown]

ANTONOV An-24

C/n	Model	Last known Owner/Operator	Identities/fates/comments (where appropriate)
1 73 067 04	RV	(Aerokuznetsk)	CCCP-46827 RA-46827 [canx 28May98; b/u by Dec99 location unknown]
1 73 067 05	RV	ex UTair Express	CCCP-46828 RA-46828 [wfu & part dismantled by 18Sep11 Syktyvkar, Russia]
1 73 067 06	RV	ex Kam Air	CCCP-46829 EW-46829 [wrecked condition by late 2005 Kabul, Afghanistan]
1 73 067 07	RV	(Ust-Ilimstk Avia)	CCCP-46830 RA-46830 [canx 09Sep98; fate unknown]
1 73 067 08	RV	(Kirovograd Flying School)	CCCP-46831 [canx 1983; wfu Kirovograd-Khmelyovoye, Ukraine; l/n derelict Mar97]
1 73 067 09	RV	(Bakhtar Afghan)	CCCP-46832 YA-BAH [fate unknown]
1 73 067 10	RV	(Jet Ukrayina)	CCCP-46833 UR-46833 UR-EUR [canx 02Oct09 fate/status; as UR-46833 was reported with only 22 hours left on airframe]
1 73 068 01	RV	Polyarnya Aviation	CCCP-46834 RA-46834
1 73 068 02	RV	ex Gomelavia	CCCP-46835 EW-46385 [wfu 16Jan08 Gomel, Belarus; l/n May08]
1 73 068 03	RV	(Ust-Ilimstk Avia)	CCCP-46836 RA-46836 [canx 25Mar95 or 25Mar96; fate unknown]
1 73 068 04	RV	(Federal Airlines)	CCCP-46837 LY-AAH ST-FAL [canx before Jan07; fate/status unknown]
1 73 068 05	RV	(Med-Air)	CCCP-46838 UR-46838 [wfu by Nov02 Opa-locka, FL, USA; canx 13Aug08; l/n 12Feb09 as "UR-4683" – last digit missing]
1 73 068 06	RV	(MAP Kiev MSZ)	CCCP-46839(1) [canx 09Jan84; fate unknown]
1 73 068 07	RV	(MIAT Mongolia)	BNMAU-6807 MT-1004 JU-1004 [wfu Ulan Bator, Mongolia; b/u for spares 2001; fuselage only noted 27Jan10]
1 73 068 08	RV	Buryat Avia	CCCP-47799 RA-47799
1 73 068 09	RV	UTair Express	CCCP-47800 RA-47800
1 73 068 10	RV	ex Ukraine National	CCCP-47801 UR-47801 [wfu by Jun02 Kiev-Zhulyany, Ukraine; l/n Aug08; canx 13Aug08]
1 73 069 01	RV	Tajikistan Airlines	CCCP-47802 UN-47802 EY-47802
1 73 069 02	RV	ex Baikal Airlines	CCCP-47803 RA-47803 [reported wfu by 04Jly04 Irkutsk-One, Russia]
1 73 069 03	RV	IrAero	CCCP-47804 RA-47804
1 73 069 04	RV	(TAROM)	YR-AMA [w/o 15Nov71 Bucharest-Otopeni, Romania]
1 73 069 05	RV	Katekavia	YR-AMB RA-49279 UN-47279 RA-47279
1 73 069 06	RV	Muzeul Grupul Scolar de Aeronautica	YR-AMC [canx 07May77 after accident Bacau, Romania; preserved by Jly06 Baneasa, Romania; l/n May09]
1 73 069 07	RV	IrAero	CCCP-47805 RA-47805 ER-AWD RA-47805
1 73 069 08	RV	ex Turkmenistan Airlines	CCCP-47806 EZ-47806 [not in Nov99 fleet list; for sale Jun08]
1 73 069 09	RV	(Almazy Rossii Sakha)	CCCP-47807 RA-47807 [canx 21Feb96; fate unknown]
1 73 069 10	RV	Gomelavia	CCCP-47808 EW-47808
1 73 070 01	RV	Kampuchea Airlines	CCCP-47809 XU-314
1 73 070 02	RV	Pecotox Air	CCCP-47810 RA-47810 ER-AZP
1 73 070 03	RV	unknown	CCCP-47811 TC-KHY RA-47811+ 9G- [+ canx 22Jly98 to Ghana; nothing known]
1 73 070 04	RV	(Air Highness/EuroLine)	CCCP-47812 RA-47812 EK-47812 4L-MJX [w/o 18Sep08 Tbilisi, Georgia; hulk l/n 07Mar12]
1 73 070 05	RV	(Palair Macedonian)	LZ-ANK [fate unknown; last reported in 1996; wfu in CIS?]
1 73 070 06	RV	Star Up SA	CCCP-47813 RA-47813 ER-AFC(1) OB-1734 OB-1734-P
1 73 070 07	B	ex Civil Aviation Administration China	B-428 B-3405 [wfu 1990 stored Hohnot, China; May97 to attraction Chingcheng Entertainment Park; l/n Mar04]
1 73 070 08	B	(China Northwest)	B-424 B-3403 [wfu by Mar85 Lanzhou, China; later b/u]
1 73 070 09	B	(China Southwest)	B-426 B-3404 [b/u Jun92 Chengdu, China]
1 73 070 10	RV	(Magnitogorsk Air)	CCCP-47814 [canx 06Feb01; fate unknown]
1 73 071 01	RV	ex Baikal Airlines	CCCP-47815 RA-47815 [wfu by 04Jly04 Irkutsk-One, Russia]
1 73 071 02	RV	ex Kirovograd Flying School	CCCP-47816 [canx 1982; derelict by Jly93 Kirivograd-Khmelyovoye, Ukraine; l/n Sep06]
1 73 071 03	RV	ex Air Baghdad	CCCP-47817 RA-47817 LZ-VPB RA-47817 EX-023 [canx 15May06; by 12Jly12 derelict Erbil, Iraq]
1 73 071 04		China Aviation Museum	71291+ [+ China] [preserved by May99 Changping, near Beijing, China; l/n Oct04]
1 73 071 05	B	(China Eastern)	B-430 B-3406 [wfu by 24Apr00 Shanghai-Longhua, China; marked as SVS-001 by May05; l/n Apr07]
1 73 071 06		.	[nothing known; possible Soviet Air Force aircraft]
1 73 071 07	RV	Angara 403 Airlines	CCCP-47818 RA-47818
1 73 071 08	RV	Yakutia	CCCP-47819 RA-47819
1 73 071 09	B	Letecke Museum Kbely	7109+ [+ Czechoslovakia then Czech Republic] [preserved after Oct05 Kbely, Czech Republic]
1 73 071 10	B	Zruc Air Park	7110+ [+ Czechoslovakia then Czech Republic] [preserved Nov08 Zruc, Czech Republic]

ANTONOV An-24

C/n	Model	Last known Owner/Operator	Identities/fates/comments (where appropriate)
1 73 072 01	RV	UTair Express	CCCP-47820 RA-47820
1 73 072 02	RV	UTair Express	CCCP-47821 RA-47821
1 73 072 03	RV	(Air Kazakhstan)	CCCP-47822 UN-47822 [stored by Oct02 Almaty, Kazakhstan; l/n Jan03]
1 73 072 04	RV	(Aeroflot/Privolzhsk)	CCCP-47823 [w/o 26Oct91 Bugulma, USSR; canx 30Mar92]
1 73 072 05	RV	(JSC National Airlines of Ukraine)	CCCP-47824 UR-47824 [canx 02Oct09; fate/status unknown]
1 73 072 06	B	ex Belavia	CCCP-47825 EW-47825 TC-ANK EW-47825 [wfu by 08Aug06 Minsk-One, Belarus]
1 73 072 07	B	ex Tomsk Avia	CCCP-47826 RA-47826 [preservd by 29Jun11 Tomsk, Russia as CCCP-47826]
1 73 072 08	B	UTair Express	CCCP-47827 RA-47827
1 73 072 09	B	ex South Airlines	CCCP-47828 RA-47828 EK-47828 [canx by 01Jan09; l/n 01Nov08 Fujairah, UAE; fate/status unknown]
1 73 072 10	B	UTair Express	CCCP-47829 RA-47829
1 73 073 01	B	(Sakha Avia)	CCCP-47830 RA-47830 [wfu by Aug03 Yakutsk, Russia]
1 73 073 02	B	(Dalavia)	CCCP-47831 RA-47831 [canx 22Mar99; fate unknown]
1 73 073 03	B	SCAT	CCCP-26196 UN-26196 UP-AN404
1 73 073 04	B	Air Kazakhstan	CCCP-47833 UN-47833
1 73 073 05	B	(Air Kazakhstan)	CCCP-47832 UN-47832 [wfu by Jan03 Almaty, Kazakhstan]
1 73 073 06	B	Mordovia Air	CCCP-47834 RA-47834
1 73 073 07	B	ex Petchabun Airlines	CCCP-47835 RA-47835 47835 EK-47835 [canx 08Dec05; stored by Dec05 Petchabun, Thailand; l/n 03Jly12]
1 73 073 08	B	ex Ukraine National	CCCP-47836 UR-47836 [wfu by Jun02 Kiev-Zhulyany, Ukraine; l/n Aug08; canx 13Aug08]
1 73 073 09	B	ex Ukraine National	CCCP-47837 UR-47837 [wfu by Jun02 Kiev-Zhulyany, Ukraine; l/n Apr09; canx 13Aug08]
1 73 073 10	B	ex Dauria Airlines	CCCP-47838 RA-47838 [airline bankrupt 12May11; for sale]
1 73 074 01	B	Novosibirsk Air	CCCP-47839 RA-47839
1 73 074 02	B	(Alada)	CCCP-47840 RA-47840 D2-FRA [not in Jan02 fleet list; fate unknown]
1 73 074 03	B	(Tyumen Avia Trans)	CCCP-47841 RA-47841 [wreck by Jly01 Rostov-na-Donu, Russia]
1 73 074 04	B	(Kuban Airlines)	CCCP-47842 RA-47842 [not in 2000 fleet list; fate unknown]
1 73 074 05	B	(Kurskavia)	CCCP-47843 RA-47843 [canx 12Jly02; l/n wfu 27Aug07 Kursk-Vostochny, Russia]
1 73 074 06	B	SCAT	CCCP-47844 UN-47844 UP-AN426
1 73 074 07	B	(Sakha Avia)	CCCP-47845 RA-47845 [not in 2000 fleet list; wfu by Aug03 Yakutsk, Russia; l/n Jly04]
1 73 074 08	B	(AeroSvit)	CCCP-47846 UR-47846 [canx 20Jly10 fate/status unknown]
1 73 074 09	B	UTair Express	CCCP-47847 RA-47847
1 73 074 10	B	Angara 403 Airlines	CCCP-47848 RA-47848
1 73 075 01	RV	ex Kirovograd Flying School	CCCP-47849 [canx 1983; derelict by Jly93 Kirovograd-Khmelyovoye, Ukraine; l/n May07]
1 73 075 02	RV	ex MAP LII Zhukovski	CCCP-83968 RA-83968 [canx 27Feb01; but noted flying Sep05; status unknown]
2 73 075 03	RV	Saransk Air	CCCP-46845 RA-46845
2 73 075 04	RV	IrAero	CCCP-46846 RA-46846 ER-AWC RA-46846
2 73 075 05	RV	(Kirovograd Flying School)	CCCP-46847 [w/o 08Jly77 Kirovograd-Khmelyovoye, Ukraine, USSR; canx 09Sep77]
2 73 075 06	RV	UTair Express	CCCP-46848 RA-46848
2 73 075 07	RV	Pecotox Air	CCCP-47690 RA-47690 ER-AZB
2 73 075 08	RV	(Cubana)	CCCP-47691 RA-47691 CU-T1295 [w/o 01Jun03 Nueva Gerona-Rafael Cabrera Airport, Cuba]
2 73 075 09	RV	SCAT	CCCP-47692 UN-47692 UP-AN424
2 73 075 10	RV	Tajikistan Airlines	CCCP-47693 EY-47693 [reported in store as of Oct07]
2 73 076 01	RV	Alrosa	CCCP-47694 RA-47694
2 73 076 02	RV	(Aeroflot/Tyumen)	CCCP-47695 [w/o 09Dec77 Tarko-Saley, USSR; canx 1978]
2 73 076 03	RV	ex Komiinterteravia	CCCP-47696 RA-47696 [canx 15Oct02; wfu by Jun05 Syktyvkar, Russia; l/n Oct07]
2 73 076 04	RV	Gomelavia	CCCP-47697 EW-47697
2 73 076 05	RV	ex Air Moldova	CCCP-47698 ER-47698 [wfu by Jly03 Chisinau, Moldova; l/n Sep07]
2 73 076 06	RV	(TAROM)	YR-AMD [w/o 29Dec74 Lotru Mountains near Sibiu, Romania]
2 73 076 07	RV	Kras Avia	YR-AME RA-49287
2 73 076 08	RV	Motor Sich	CCCP-47699 TC-MOB RA-47699 UR-47699 UR-MSI
2 73 076 09	RV	SCAT	CCCP-47258 RA-47258 UN-47258 UP-AN419
2 73 076 10	RV	(Cubana)	CCCP-47196 CU-T1262 [w/o 11Jun97 Santiago, Cuba]

ANTONOV An-24

C/n	Model	Last known Owner/Operator	Identities/fates/comments (where appropriate)
2 73 077 01	RV	Govt of Democratic Republic of Congo?	CCCP-47197 RA-47197 EL-WTA 3C-KKH 9Q-CYF
2 73 077 02	RV	SAT Airlines	CCCP-47198 RA-47198
2 73 077 03	RV	Nordavia Regional Airlines	CCCP-47199 RA-47199
2 73 077 04	RV	not yet known	CCCP-47252 RA-47252 EX-47252 EX-252
2 73 077 05	RV	(Saransk Air)	CCCP-47253 RA-47253 [wfu by Aug99 Yekaterinburg-Koltsovo, Russia; fate unknown]
2 73 077 06	RV	Tomsk Avia	CCCP-47254 RA-47254
2 73 077 07	RV	Tomsk Avia	CCCP-47255 RA-47255
2 73 077 08	RV	South Airlines	CCCP-47256 UR-47256
2 73 077 09	RV	(Ukraine National)	CCCP-47257 UR-47257 [wfu by Jun02 Kiev-Zhulyany, Ukraine; canx 13Aug08; b/u 11 to 17May12]
2 73 077 10	RV	(MIAT Mongolia)	BNMAU-7710 [w/o 23Jan87 Ulaan Bator, Mongolia; but wreck reported Mar92 Uvurkhangai, Mongolia]
2 73 078 01	RV	(Belavia)	CCCP-47259 EW-47259 [wfu by Aug06 Minsk-One, Belarus by Aug06; b/u Jun08]
2 73 078 02	RV	Polar Airlines	CCCP-47260 RA-47260
2 73 078 03	RV	Kampuchea Airlines	CCCP-47261 XU-311
2 73 078 04	RV	(Trans Amazon)	CCCP-47262 OB-1439 [w/o 22Feb92 Arequipa, Peru]
2 73 078 05	RV	ex Baikal Airlines	CCCP-47263 RA-47263 [stored by Aug03 Irkutsk-One, Russia; l/n 28Aug07]
2 73 078 06	RV	Kirov Air Enterprise/UTair Express	CCCP-47264 RA-47264
2 73 078 07	RV	(Bukovyna)	CCCP-47265 UR-47265 UR-CFO [canx 03Feb10 status/fate unknown]
2 73 078 08	RV	unknown	CCCP-46462 RA-46462+ 9G- [+ canx 22Jly98 to Ghana; nothing known]
2 73 078 09	RV	unknown	CCCP-46463 XU-310 RA-46463 XU-054 UR-ELT [used by United Nations with code UN630]
2 73 078 10	RV	Air Urga/UN	CCCP-46464 UR-46464
2 73 079 01	RV	(Lionair)	CCCP-46465 EW-46465 [w/o 29Sep98 Jaffna, Sri Lanka]
2 73 079 02	RV	(TAROM)	YR-AMF [w/o 05Sep86 Cluj, Romania; canx 28May96]
2 73 079 03	B	(Pamair)	SP-LTS LZ-ANT RA-49290 LZ-ASZ Z3-AAJ YA-PIS [w/o 17May10 Salang Pass en-route Kundaz to Kabul, Afghanistan]
2 73 079 04	RV	Kras Avia	CCCP-46466 RA-46466
2 73 079 05	RV	(Aeroflot/North Kavkaz)	CCCP-46467 [w/o 17Nov75 Mount Apshara 25km from Gali, USSR, en-route Sukhumi; canx 1976]
2 73 079 06	RV	UTair Express	CCCP-46468 RA-46468
2 73 079 07	RV	ex Ukraine National	CCCP-46469 UR-46469 [wfu by 20May04 Kiev-Zhulyany, Ukraine; l/n 09Aug08; canx 13Aug08]
2 73 079 08	RV	Yakutia	CCCP-46470 RA-46470
2 73 079 09	RV	(Federal Airlines)	CCCP-46471 LY-AAG ST-FAG [w/o 06May96 Khartoum-City, Sudan]
2 73 079 10	RV	(Aeroflot/Uzbekistan)	CCCP-46472 [w/o 23Mar91 Nanoi, Uzbekistan, USSR; canx 19Nov91]
2 73 080 01	RV	(Kuban Airlines)	CCCP-46473 RA-46473(1) [w/o 21Dec95 Krasnodar, Russia; canx 14Feb97]
2 73 080 02	RV	(Dalavia)	CCCP-46474 RA-46474 [b/u early 2012 Khabarovsk, Russia]
2 73 080 03	RV	ex Lugansk Aviation	CCCP-46475 UR-46475 [canx 01Oct08; wfs noted 02Aug11 Lugansk, Ukraine]
2 73 080 04	RV	(Aeroflot/Ukraine)	CCCP-46476 [w/o 28Apr75 Poltava, Ukraine, USSR; canx 1975]
2 73 080 05	RV	GoSNii GA	CCCP-46477 UR-46477 4L-GLG RA-46447(2)
2 73 080 06	RV	(Kazakhstan Airlines)	CCCP-46478 46478 [w/o 16Jan93 Kustanay, Kazakhstan; hit military unidentified An-24 which was also w/o]
2 73 080 07	RV	Yakutia	CCCP-46479 RA-46479 ER-AZM RA-46479
2 73 080 08	RV	IrAero	CCCP-46480 RA-46480
2 73 080 09	RV	UTair Express	CCCP-46481 RA-46481
2 73 080 10	RV	Star Up SA	CCCP-46482 RA-46482 ER-AFU OB-1717
2 73 081 01	RV	Pskovavia	CCCP-46483 EW-46483 RA-46473(2)
2 73 081 02	RV	ex Cubana	CCCP-46484 RA-46484 ER-AWH CU-T1236 [by 08Apr09 preserved Air Park in Havana, Cuba; gone by Mar12, probably b/u]
2 73 081 03	RV	(Bashkirian Airlines)	CCCP-46485 RA-46485 [wfu by Aug97 Ufa, Russia; for sale Feb08 for parts recovery]
2 73 081 04	RV	(Magnitogorsk Air)	CCCP-46486 RA-46486+ ER- [+ canx 23Jun99 to Moldova; nothing known]
2 73 081 05	RV	ex Cubana	CCCP-46487 YL-LCF CU-T1294 [impounded 01Apr03 Key West, FL, USA after hijack; still there in 2011]
2 73 081 06	RV	Airosa	CCCP-46488 RA-46488
2 73 081 07	RV	(Regional Airlines)	CCCP-46489 46489 RA-46489 [w/o 16Mar05 5km from Varandei, Russia]

ANTONOV An-24

C/n	Model	Last known Owner/Operator	Identities/fates/comments (where appropriate)
2 73 081 08	RV	Turkmenistan Airlines	CCCP-46490 EZ-46490 UR-46490 EZ-46490 [for sale Jun08]
2 73 081 09	B	(China Northern)	B-432 B-3407 [probably b/u post Nov91 Shenyang, China]
2 73 081 10	B	(Civil Aviation Administration China)	B-434 (B-3408) [w/o 18Jan85 Jinan, China; before new marks were used]
2 73 082 01	B	CAAC Aeronautical Institute	B-436 B-3409 [wfu by Nov86 used by Tianjin Technical School; then preserved; l/n 17Sep09]
2 73 082 02	B	ex China Southwest	B-438 B-3410 [wfu by Sep99 and to Guanghan College, Chengdu, China; l/n Nov08]
2 73 082 03	B	(China Southern)	B-440 B-3411 [b/u 1992 Wuhan-Hankou, China]
2 73 082 04	RV	Katekavia	CCCP-46491 RA-46491 3X-GEB(1) RA-46491
2 73 082 05	RV	Avia Jaynar	CCCP-46492 UN-46492 UP-AN403
2 73 082 06	RV	Katekavia	CCCP-46493 RA-46493
2 73 082 07	RV	UTair Express	CCCP-46494 RA-46494
2 73 082 08	RV	ex Stavropol Avia	CCCP-46495 RA-46495 [wfu by 30Jun12 Stavropol, Russia]
2 73 082 09	RV	Yakutia	CCCP-46496 RA-46496
2 73 082 10	RV	Katekavia	CCCP-46497 RA-46497
2 73 083 01	RV	ex Malift	CCCP-46498 EW-46498 [stored by Jun08 Minsk-One, Belarus; l/n Apr09]
2 73 083 02	RV	Cheboksary Air Enterprise	CCCP-46499 RA-46499 [dbr 05Nov00 Cheboksary, Russia & stored; l/n 27Aug04 later b/u]
2 73 083 03	RV	Transportes Aereos Cielos Andinos	YR-AMG RA-49286 OB-1571 OB-1651
2 73 083 04	RV	Bangladesh Air Force Museum	0001+ [+ Bangladesh] [preserved by Dec98 Dhaka-Tejgoan, Bangladesh; l/n Nov08; c/n not fully confirmed]
2 73 083 05	RV	SCAT	CCCP-46500 UN-46500 UP-AN413
3 73 083 06	RV	(Alrosa)	CCCP-46501 RA-46501 [canx unknown date; fate unknown]
3 73 083 07	RV	Avia Traffic	CCCP-46502 RA-46502 EX-008
3 73 083 08	RV	unknown	CCCP-46504 TC-MOA RA-46504+ D2- [+ canx in 1990s to Angola; nothing more known]
3 73 083 09	RV	Mordovia Air	CCCP-46505 RA-46505
3 73 083 10	RV	UTair Express	CCCP-13344 RA-13344
3 73 084 01	RV	(MIAT Mongolia)	BNMAU-8401 [w/o 25Jun83 Ulaan Baatar, Mongolia]
3 73 084 02	RV	Buryat Avia	CCCP-46506 RA-46506
3 73 084 03	RV	(GR Avia/Jubba Airways)	CCCP-46507 RA-46507 EK-46507 3X-GEB(2) [w/o 28Apr12 Galkayo, Somailand]
3 73 084 04	RV	Air Moldova	CCCP-46508 ER-46508
3 73 084 05	RV	UTair Express	CCCP-46509 RA-46509
3 73 084 06	RV	Yakutia	CCCP-46510 RA-46510
3 73 084 07	RV	(Bryansk Avia)	CCCP-46511 RA-46511+ A6- [+ canx 13Jun97 to UAE; nothing more known]
3 73 084 08	RV	ex Turkmenistan Airlines	CCCP-46512 EZ-46512 [not in 2001 fleet list; for sale Jun08; l/n stored by Nov08 Ashkhabad, Turkmenistan]
3 73 084 09	RV	(South Airlines)	CCCP-46513 RA-46513 UR-46513 EK-46513 [canx by 01Jan09; l/n 05May09 Dijbouti-Ambouil, Dijbouti]
3 73 084 10	RV	ex AeroSvit	CCCP-46514 UR-46514 [canx 20Jly10; fuselage only noted 21Jun12 Lugansk, Ukraine]
3 73 085 01	RV	(Cubana)	CCCP-46515 CU-T1261 [wfu by Jun95 Havana, Cuba; l/n Jly99; probably b/u]
3 73 085 02	RV	(Stavropol Avia)	CCCP-46516 RA-46516 [w/o en-route 18Mar97 near Cherkessk, Russia; canx 08Sep97]
3 73 085 03	RV	ex Lugansk Aviation	CCCP-46517 UR-46517 [canx 20Jly10; by 05Jan12 wfu Lugansk, Ukraine
3 73 085 04	RV	(Aeroflot/Belarus)	CCCP-46518 [w/o 09Sep76 in collision with Yak40 CCCP-87772 near Anapa, USSR over Black Sea; canx 27Sep76]
3 73 085 05	RV	UTair Express	CCCP-46519 RA-46519
3 73 085 06	RV	Katekavia	CCCP-46520 RA-46520
3 73 085 07	RV	(Aeroflot/Central Region)	CCCP-46600 [canx unknown date; fate unknown]
3 73 085 08	RV	(Saravia)	CCCP-46601 RA-46601 [canx 19Oct98; fate unknown]
3 73 085 09	RV	Tajikistan Airlines	CCCP-46602 EY-46602
3 73 085 10	RV	UTair Express	CCCP-46603 RA-46603
3 73 086 01	RV	Katekavia	CCCP-46604 RA-46604
3 73 086 02	RV	ex Aeroflot/Magadan	CCCP-46605 RA-46605 [no reports since Apr93; fate/status unknown]
3 73 086 03	RV	ex Golden Airways	CCCP-46606 RA-46606+ TC-KHT [+ canx 22Jly98 to Ghana; stored by 2000 Kumasi, Ghana; l/n Jun08]
3 73 086 04	RV	ex Aeroflot	CCCP-46607 EW-46607+ [canx 1981; by Sep93 in technical school Minsk-Chizovka, Belarus; + marks only painted on whilst in school]

ANTONOV An-24

C/n	Model	Last known Owner/Operator	Identities/fates/comments (where appropriate)
3 73 086 05	RV	Pamair	CCCP-46608 UR-46608 LZ-MNE ER-AWR YA-CAH [airline suspended operations 19Mar11]
3 73 086 06	RV	UTair Express	CCCP-46609 RA-46609
3 73 086 07	RV	UTair Express	CCCP-46610 RA-46610
3 73 086 08	RV	Avia Jaynar	CCCP-46611 UN-46611 UP-AN402
3 73 086 09	RV	Amur Avia	CCCP-46612 RA-46612
3 73 086 10	RV	(Aeroflot/Privolzhsk)	CCCP-46613 [w/o 10May76 Saratov, USSR; canx 1976]
3 73 087 01	RV	Buryat Avia	CCCP-46614 RA-46614
3 73 087 02	RV	ex Belavia	CCCP-46615 EW-46615 [wfu by Aug07 Minsk-Loshitsa, Belarus; l/n Oct08]
3 73 087 03	RV	Chukotavia	CCCP-46616 RA-46616
3 73 087 04	RV	(Aeroflot/Arkhangelsk)	CCCP-46617 [w/o 24Dec83 Lenhukonskoye, USSR; hulk still present 1993]
3 73 087 05	RV	SAT Airlines	CCCP-46618 RA-46618
3 73 087 06	RV	UTair Express	CCCP-46619 RA-46619
3 73 087 07	RV	Izhavia	CCCP-46620 RA-46620
3 73 087 08	RV	Alrosa	CCCP-46621 RA-46621
3 73 087 09	RV	South Airlines	CCCP-46622 UR-46622 UR-VIK EX-099 UR-WRA
3 73 087 10	RV	Uzbekistan Airways	CCCP-46623 UK-46623
3 73 088 01	RV	Skylink Arabia	CCCP-46624 RA-46624 ER-AZN
3 73 088 02	RV	Transportes Aereos Cielos Andinos	YR-AMH RA-49285 OB-1562 OB-1650 OB-1650-P
3 73 088 03	RV	(Yeniseiski Meridian)	YR-AMI RA-49288 [canx 03Sep99; fate unknown]
3 73 088 04	RV	Angara 403 Airlines	CCCP-46625 RA-46625
3 73 088 05	RV	SCAT	CCCP-46626 UN-46626 UP-AN414
3 73 088 06	RV	Tomsk Avia	CCCP-46627 RA-46627
3 73 088 07	RV	ex Malinas	CCCP-46628 TZ-AJL [stored by Mar03 semi-derelict Tombouctu, Mali]
3 73 088 08	RV	ex Baikal Airlines	CCCP-46629 RA-46629 [wfu by Aug03 Irtusk-One, Russia; l/n 28Aug07]
3 73 088 09	RV	Alfa Airlines	CCCP-46630 UR-46630 EK-46630 ST-ARP
3 73 088 10	RV	Gomelavia	CCCP-46631 EW-46631
3 73 089 01	RV	ex Guinee Paramount	CCCP-46635 RA-46635 3X-GDG [wfu by Jly05 Conakry, Guinea]
3 73 089 02	RV	Motor Sich	CCCP-46636 RA-46636 TC-JUZ TC-MOC RA-46636 UR-46636 UR-BXC
3 73 089 03	RV	Izhavia	CCCP-46637 RA-46637
3 73 089 04	RV	Royal Cambodian Air Force	CCCP-46638 XU-312 RA-46638 XU-312
3 73 089 05	RV	SAT Airlines	CCCP-46639 RA-46639
3 73 089 06	RV	(China Xinjiang Alirlines)	B-442 B-3412 [derelict by May94 Urumqi, China; l/n May01]
3 73 089 07	RV	(Civil Aviation Administration China)	B-444 B-3413 [w/o 15Dec86 Langzhou-Zhongchuang, China]
3 73 089 08	RV	UTair Express	CCCP-46640 RA-46640
3 73 089 09	RV	Cubana	CCCP-46641 RA-46641 CU-T1237
3 73 089 10	RV	Novosibirsk Avia	CCCP-46642 RA-46642
3 73 090 01	RV	Chabavia	CCCP-46643 RA-46643
3 73 090 02	RV	Kazakhstan Airlines	CCCP-46644 UN-46644
3 73 090 03	RV	(China Southern)	B-446 B-3414 [wfu; by Nov93 to Guangzhou Civil Aviation College; l/n 28Oct08]
3 73 090 04	RV	(China Southern)	B-448 B-3415 [fate unknown]
3 73 090 05	RV	(China Eastern)	B-450 B-3416 [fate unknown]
3 73 090 06	RV	(China Eastern)	B-452 B-3417 [w/o 15Aug89 near Shanghai, China]
3 73 090 07	RV	(China Northern)	B-454 B-3418 [preserved by Oct09 Qiqihar, Lonza Park, China]
3 73 090 08	RV	Kam Air	030+ LZ-CBB Z3-AAI YA-KMC [+ Bulgaria]
3 73 090 09	RV	Aviakor	CCCP-46429(2) RA-46429
3 73 090 10	RV	(China Xinjiang Alirlines)	B-456 B-3419 [stored by Jun99 Chengdu, China; fate unknown]
3 73 091 01	RV	(China United Airlines)	B-460 B-4061 [l/n 15Apr97 Beijing-Nan Yuan, China; fate unknown]
4 73 091 02	RV	Tbilaviamsheni	CCCP-46649 RA-46649 EW-224PG 4L-BZG
3 73 091 03		.	[nothing known; possible Soviet Air Force aircraft]
3 73 091 04	RV	ex Cubana	CCCP-46645 RA-46645 CU-T1536 CU-T1257 CU-C1257 [wfu by 07Apr12 & used as restaurant Santa Clara west of Havana, Cuba]
3 73 091 05	RV	ex Novosibirsk Avia	CCCP-46646 RA-46646 [reported sold 15Jun11 to Aviaglobal for possible use as parts; l/n 26Jun12 Yakutsk, Russia]
3 73 091 06	RV	ex China United Airlines	B-466 51051+ B-4064 [+ China] [preserved Bejing-Nan Yuan, China; l/n Nov08]
3 73 091 07	RV	(Donbassaero)	CCCP-46647 UR-46647 [canx 20Jly10 fate/status unknown]
3 73 091 08	RV	ex Cubana	CCCP-46648 RA-46648 CU-T1299 [stored by 31May06 Havana, Cuba]
4 73 091 09		.	[nothing known; possible Soviet Air Force aircraft]
4 73 091 10	RV	Russian Navy	CCCP-46548? RA-46548 [no sightings as CCCP-46548 or on Soviet Register]
4 73 092 01	RV	Tomsk Avia	CCCP-46650 RA-46650

ANTONOV An-24

C/n	Model	Last known Owner/Operator	Identities/fates/comments (where appropriate)
4 73 092 02	RV	Nordavia Regional Airlines	CCCP-46651 RA-46651
4 73 092 03	RV	(Aeroflot/Tyumen)	CCCP-46652 [canx 1976; by Aug99 to Troitsk Technical School, Russia; l/n Aug01]
4 73 092 04	RV	(Aeroflot/Far East)	CCCP-46653 [w/o 24Aug81 in mid-air collision with Tu-16K c/n 6203106 near Zavitinsk, USSR; canx 1981]
4 73 092 05	RV	(Civil Aviation Administration China)	B-462 [not re-regd after 1985; fate unknown]
4 73 092 06	RV	(China Southwest)	B-468 B-3420 [b/u Nov93 Chengdu, China]
4 73 092 07	RV	(China Xingjian Airlines)	B-470 B-3421 [b/u by Jun99 Chengdu, China]
4 73 092 08	RV	(Civil Aviation Administration China)	B-472 B-3422 [wfu by 1993 Hohhot, China; trucked to Hasuhai Holiday Village; l/n Apr00]
4 73 092 09	RV	Daghestan Airlines	CCCP-46654 RA-46654
4 73 092 10	RV	(China Southern)	B-474 B-3423 [fate unknown]
4 73 093 01	RV	(Lionair)	CCCP-46655 UN-46655 [stored by Feb01 Colombo-Ratmalana, Sri Lanka; no recent reports]
4 73 093 02	RV	South Airlines	CCCP-46656 RA-46656 EK-46656 [canx by 01Jan09; l/n 05May09 Dijibouti-Ambouil, Dijibouti]
4 73 093 03	RV	(Aviata)	CCCP-46657 RA-46657 [canx 22Dec00; fate unknown]
4 73 093 04	RV	(Uzbekistan Airways)	CCCP-46658 UK-46658 [reported w/o Aug09 Zarafshan, Uzbekistan]
4 73 093 05	RV	Buryat Avia	CCCP-46661 UR-46661 ST-SHE UR-CDY RA-46661
4 73 093 06	RV	ex Novosibirsk Avia	CCCP-46659 RA-46659 [reported sold 15Jun11 to Aviaglobal for possible use as parts]
4 73 093 07	RV	Kirov Air Enterprise	CCCP-46660 RA-46660
4 73 093 08	RV	(China Northwest)	B-476 B-3424 [derelict by Mar95 Lanzhou, China; l/n May99]
4 73 093 09	RV	Nanjiang University of Aeronautics	B-478 B-3425 [preserved by May92 Nanjing, China; l/n Aug03]
4 73 093 10	RV	unknown	BNMAU-9310 MT-1005 JU-1005 ER-AZY+ EX- [canx 07Apr08 to Kyrgyzstan; nothing more known]
4 73 094 01	RV	(China Southwest)	B-480 B-3426 [retired post Sep87; fate unknown]
4 73 094 02	RV	(China Northwest)	B-482 B-3427 [b/u Mar93 Xian, China]
4 73 094 03	RV	(Civil Aviation Administration China)	B-484 [w/o 20Mar80 Changsha, China]
4 73 094 04	RV	Cubana	CU-T923 CU-T1214
4 73 094 05	RV	Cubana	CU-T924 CU-T1223
4 73 094 06	RV	Daallo Airlines	CCCP-46668 RA-46668 ER-AZL S9-KAS [damaged 13Jan09 Bossaso, Somalia]
4 73 094 07	RV	(China Eastern)	B-488 B-3429 [b/u 1990 Hefei, China]
4 73 094 08	RV	ex China United Airlines	51050+ B-4063 [+ China] [stored by Oct99 Beijing-Nan Yuan, China; l/n Apr07]
4 73 094 09		.	[nothing known; possible Soviet Air Force aircraft]
4 73 094 10	RV	Angara 403 Airlines	CCCP-46662 RA-46662
4 73 095 01	RV	China Aviation Museum	50953+ B-4060 [+ China] [preserved by Feb04 Changping, China; l/n 14Oct10 as just 4060]
4 73 095 02	RV	ex China United Airlines	B-496 B-4062 [stored by Oct99 Beijing-Nan Yuan, China; by Mar06 preserved Oriental Green Boat Park, Shanghai, China]
4 73 095 03	RV	ex China United Airlines	B-498 B-4065 [stored by Oct99 Beijing-Nan Yuan, China; l/n 15Apr07]
4 73 095 04	RV	(Ivanovo Air)	CCCP-46663 RA-46663+ ER- [+ canx 27May99 to Moldova; nothing more known]
4 73 095 05	RV	SCAT	CCCP-46664 UN-46664 UP-AN415
4 73 095 06	RV	Yakutia	CCCP-46665 RA-46665
4 73 095 07	RV	Air Urga/UN	CCCP-46666 YL-LCG UR-46666 UR-ELO [used UN code UN-628 in 2005]
4 73 095 08	RV	Nordavia Regional Airlines	CCCP-46667 RA-46667
4 73 095 09	RV	(Aeroflot/Far East)	CCCP-46669 [w/o 08Jly88 Khabarovsk, USSR; canx 12Sep88]
4 73 095 10	RV	(China Xinjiang Airlines)	B-484 B-3428 [displayed by May94 Urumqi City, China; no recent reports]
4 73 096 01	RV	(Sakha Avia)	CCCP-46670 RA-46670 [w/o 13Jly02 Yakutsk, Russia; wreck srtill present Jly04]
4 73 096 02	RV	ex China United Airlines	51053+ B-4066 [+ China] [stored/preserved by Oct99 Beijing-Nan Yuan, China; l/n Nov08]
4 73 096 03	RV	(Ariana Afghan)	CCCP-46671 RA-46671? TC-KAR RA-46671 EX-46671 YA-DAJ [presumed destroyed late 2001]
4 73 096 04	RV	SCAT	CCCP-46672 UN-46672 UP-AN416
4 73 096 05	RV	Baikal Airlines	CCCP-46673 RA-46673
4 73 096 06	RV	Katekavia	CCCP-46674 RA-46674

ANTONOV An-24

C/n	Model	Last known Owner/Operator	Identities/fates/comments (where appropriate)
4 73 096 07	RV	(Bukovyna)	CCCP-46675 UR-46675 UR-CFN [canx 03Feb10; fate/status unknown]
4 73 096 08	RV	Polet Flight	CCCP-46676 RA-46676
4 73 096 09	RV	(Lugansk Aviation)	CCCP-46677 UR-46677 [l/n 23Sep11 Kiev-Borispol, Ukraine; canx 10Jan12 status/fate unknown]
4 73 096 10	RV	Cubana	CCCP-46678 RA-46678 CU-T1263
4 73 097 01	RV	Tomsk Avia	CCCP-46679 RA-46679
4 73 097 02	RV	ex Turkmenistan Airlines	CCCP-46680 EZ-46680 [not in 2001 fleet list; for sale Jun08; stored by Nov08 Ashkhabad, Turkmenistan]
4 73 097 03	RV	Ocean Air	CCCP-46681 RA-46681 LZ-VPD [reported stored Gan-Seenu, Maldives; l/n 20Nov02; canx reported 30Jan07]
4 73 097 04	RV	Kras Avia	CCCP-46682 RA-46682
4 73 097 05	RV	Aero Fret Business	YR-AMK ER-AEH D2-FVL ER-AEZ 9XR-DB TN-AHH
4 73 097 06	RV	(Katekavia)	CCCP-46683 RA-46683 [damaged 2011 Chita, Russia; canx 29Nov11 as wfu]
4 73 097 07	RV	Air Koryo	P-532
4 73 097 08	RV	Air Koryo	P-533
4 73 097 09	RV	(Aeroflot/Central Region)	CCCP-46684 [canx 07Jly88; by May98 to Slavyansk Technical School, Ukraine; l/n Apr99]
4 73 097 10	RV	Tandem Aero	CCCP-46685 ER-46685
4 73 098 01		.	[nothing known; possible Soviet Air Force aircraft]
4 73 098 02	RV	Air Koryo	P-534
4 73 098 03	RV	(Bashkirian Airlines)	CCCP-46686 RA-46686 [wfu by Aug99 Ufa, Russia; l/n 12Aug01; for sale Feb08 for spares]
4 73 098 04	RV	SkyLink Arabia	CCCP-46687 RA-46687 ER-AZX
4 73 098 05	RV	Hadid International Services	CCCP-46688 EX-46688 EX-038 EX-017
4 73 098 06	RV	Katekavia	CCCP-46689 RA-46689
4 73 098 07	RV	ex MIAT Mongolia	BNMAU-9807 MT-1006 JU-1006 [wfu by Oct05; stored Ulan Bator, Mongolia; l/n 27Jan10]
4 73 098 08	RV	Katekavia	YR-AMJ RA-49278
4 73 098 09	RV	Renan	YR-AMY J5-GBE(2) YR-AMY ER-AFY
4 73 098 10	RV	Avia Traffic	BNMAU-9810 MT-6046 JU-7050 EX-150
4 73 099 01	RV	Polet Flight	CCCP-46690 RA-46690
4 73 099 02	RV	ex Malift	CCCP-46691 RA-46691 9Q-CMK [wfu by 12May09 Kinshasa-N'Djili, Democratic Republic of Congo]
4 73 099 03	RV	UTair Express	CCCP-46692 RA-46692
4 73 099 04	RV	Katekavia	CCCP-46693 RA-46693
4 73 099 05	RV	Yamal	CCCP-46694 RA-46694
4 73 099 06	RV	Yamal	CCCP-46695 RA-46695
4 73 099 07	RV	ex Cubana	CCCP-46696 CU-T1267 [not in 31Dec05 fleet list; l/n 27Mar06 Havana, Cuba]
4 73 099 08	RV	Angara 403 Airlines	CCCP-46697 RA-46697
4 73 099 09	RV	(Aeroflot/Central Region)	CCCP-46698 RA-46698 [b/u May96 Moscow-Bykovo, Russia; was canx 14Feb96]
4 73 099 10	RV	SCAT	CCCP-46699 UN-46699 UP-AN417
4 73 100 01	RV	Dalavia	CCCP-46522 RA-46522
4 73 100 02	RV	(Bykovo Avia)	CCCP-46523 RA-46523 [canx 10Apr96; l/n 21May96 Moscow-Bykovo, Russia]
4 73 100 03	RV	(Katekavia)	CCCP-46524 RA-46524 [w/o 02Aug10 Igarka, Russia]
4 73 100 04	RV	(Aeroflot/Kazakhstan)	CCCP-46525 [w/o 04Oct69 Stepanogorsk, Kazakhstan, USSR; canx 28Jan90]
4 73 100 05	RV	(Avialinii Tatarstana)	CCCP-46526 RA-46526 [stored by Jun02 Kazan-Osnovnoi, Russia; l/n Jun05]
4 73 100 06	RV	ex Ukraine National	CCCP-46527 UR-46527 [wfu by Jun02 Kiev-Zhulyany, Ukraine; canx 13Aug08; l/n Aug08]
4 73 100 07	RV	Khabarovsk Avia?	CCCP-46528 RA-46528 [stored by Mar12 Arkhangelsk, Russia]
5 73 100 08	RV	SAT Airlines	CCCP-46529 RA-46529
5 73 100 09	RV	SAT Airlines	CCCP-46530 RA-46530
5 73 100 10	RV	Taymur	CCCP-46531 RA-46531
5 73 101 01	RV	UTair Express	CCCP-46532 RA-46532
5 73 101 02	RV	ex MIAT Mongolia	BNMAU-10102 MT-1007 JU-1007 [wfu by Oct05; stored Ulan Bator, Mongolia; l/n 27Jan10]
5 73 101 03	RV	(MIAT Mongolia)	BNMAU-10103 (MT-1008) [w/o 21Sep95 Moreon, Mongolia before re-regn; reported 2001 used for spares]
5 73 101 04	RV	ex MIAT Mongolia	BNMAU-10104 MT-1009 JU-1009 [wfu by Oct05; stored Ulan Bator, Mongolia; l/n 27Jan10]
5 73 101 05	RV	Avia Traffic	YR-BMA YR-ARA ER-AZG EX-051+ [+ c/n not fully confirmed]
5 73 101 06	RV	(TAROM)	YR-BMB [wfu by 23Sep98 Bucharest-Baneasa, Romania; fate unknown]
5 73 101 07	RV	(Cubana)	CCCP-46533 CU-T1266 [not in Feb02 fleet list; fate unknown]

ANTONOV An-24

C/n	Model	Last known Owner/Operator	Identities/fates/comments (where appropriate)
5 73 101 08	RV	(Aeroflot/Ukraine)	CCCP-46534 [w/o 15May76 near Chernigov, Ukraine, USSR; canx 20Sep76]
5 73 101 09	RV	Air Urga/UN	CCCP-46535 UN-46535 RA-46535 XU-375 RDPL-34147 UR-ELW
5 73 101 10	RV	Star Up SA	CCCP-46536 46536 UR-46536 OB-1587 UR-46536 ER-AWX OB-1769
5 73 102 01	RV	ex TAROM	YR-BMC [wfu by Sep98 Bucharest-Otopeni, Romania; preserved by Aug06 Pucioasa, Romania]
5 73 102 02	RV	(TAROM)	YR-BMD [w/o 25Jan82 Constanta, Romania]
5 73 102 03	RV	Air Urga	CCCP-47300 UR-47300 UR-ELK
5 73 102 04	RV	(Antares Eyr)	CCCP-13389 RA-13389 [canx 01Jun99 to Congo; l/n 26Jun99 Kiev-Zhulyany, Ukraine; nothing more known]
5 73 102 05	RV	ex Turkmenistan Airlines	CCCP-47301 EZ-47301 [for sale Jun08; stored by Nov08 Ashkhabad, Turkmenistan]
5 73 102 06	RV	ex Air Cess	CCCP-48091 EL-AKO EL-WAC TN-225+ [+ not confirmed] [wfu Poine Noire, People's Republic of Congo; l/n 08Sep09]
5 73 102 07	RV	(MIAT Mongolia)	BNMAU-10207 [w/o Apr85 near Huvsgul, Mongolia; wreck noted Ulaan Baatar, Mongolia Aug94; /n May95]
5 73 102 08	RV	(MIAT Mongolia)	BNMAU-10208 [w/o 26Jan90 near Uvs, Zavkhan, Mongolia]
5 73 102 09	RV	(UM Air)	BNMAU-10209 MT-10209 MT-1010 JU-1010 UR-CDS [canx 20Jly10 fate/status unknown]
5 73 102 10		.	[nothing known; possible Soviet Air Force aircraft]
5 73 103 01	RV	Cubana	BNMAU-10301 MT-1011 JU-1011 CU-T1244
5 73 103 02	RV	(Angara 403 Airlines)	CCCP-47302 RA-47302 [w/o 11Jly11 near Strezhevoy, Russia]
5 73 103 03	RV	ex Expresso Aero	CCCP-47303 OB-1440 CCCP-47303 OB-1583 [wfu by 15Jan02 Lima, Peru]
5 73 103 04	RV	Yakutia	CCCP-47304 RA-47304
5 73 103 05	RV	Nordavia Regional Airlines	CCCP-47305 RA-47305 UR-47305 RA-47305
5 73 103 06	RV	Kras Avia	CCCP-47306 RA-47306
5 73 103 07	RV	Cubana	CCCP-47307 CU-T1260
5 73 103 08	RV	ex South Airlines	CCCP-47308 UR-47308 [canx 08Oct10 canx; l/n 04Oct10 stored Kiev-Zhulyani, Ukraine]
5 73 103 09	RV	(Latavio)	CCCP-47309 YL-LCH [w/o 06Apr93 Stepanakan, Armenia; canx 03Dec03]
5 73 103 10	RV	(TAROM)	YR-BME TC-FBA YR-BME [wfu by Sep98 Bucharest-Baneasea, Romania; reported sold, no details]
5 73 104 01	RV	(Aeroflot/Urals)	CCCP-47310 [w/o 28Feb84 Izhevsk, USSR; canx 1984]
5 73 104 02	RV	(VAT National Airlines of Ukraine)	CCCP-47311 UR-47311 [canx 20Jly10 fate/status unknown]
5 73 104 03	RV	(AeroSvit)	CCCP-47312 UR-47312 [canx 10Jan12 fate/status unknown; l/n 23Sep11 Kiev-Borispol, Ukraine]
5 73 104 04	RV	ex Ariana Afghan	YR-BMF TC-FPA YR-BMF YA-DAM [stored by May05 Kabul, Afghanistan]
5 73 104 05	RV	unknown	YR-BMG YR-RRB ER-AZH+ UR- [+ canx 08Feb05 to Ukraine; l/n 23apr09 Kiev-Zhulyany, Ukraine]
5 73 104 06	RV	IrAero	CCCP-48096 RA-48096
5 73 104 07	RV	(TAROM)	YR-BMH [wfu by May99 Bucharest-Baneasea, Romania; reported sold, no details]
5 73 104 08	RV	Angara 403 Airlines	YR-BMI EX-24408 RA-46712
5 73 104 09	RV	Ariana Afghan	CCCP-48097 UR-48097 YA-DAL
5 73 104 10	RV	Air Urga/UN	CCCP-47313 UR-47313 UR-ELC
5 73 105 01	RV	ex Turkmenistan Airlines	CCCP-47314 EZ-47314 [for sale Jun08; stored by Nov08 Ashkhabad, Turkmenistan]
6 73 105 02	RV	Izhavia	CCCP-47315 RA-47315
6 73 105 03	RV	Air Urga	CCCP-47316 UR-47316 UR-ELL [used UN code UN805]
6 73 105 04	RV	SAT Airlines	CCCP-47317 RA-47317
6 73 105 05	RV	ex South Airlines	CCCP-47318 RA-47318 EK-47318 J2-SHE EK-47218 [canx by 01Jan09; l/n 02Mar09 Fujairah, UAE]
6 73 105 06	RV	Air Urga	CCCP-47319 UR-47319 UR-ELM
6 73 105 07	RV	Yakutia	CCCP-47321 TC-TOR RA-47321
6 73 105 08	RV	ex Turkmenistan Airlines	CCCP-47322 EZ-47322 [for sale Jun08; stored by Nov08 Ashkhabad, Turkmenistan]
6 73 105 09	RV	SCAT	CCCP-47350 UN-47350 UP-AN423
6 73 105 10	RV	Katekavia	CCCP-47351 YL-LCI RA-47351
6 73 106 01	RV	Yakutia	CCCP-47352 RA-47352
6 73 106 02	RV	Yakutia	CCCP-47353 RA-47353
6 73 106 03	RV	Dalavia	CCCP-47354 RA-47354

ANTONOV An-24

C/n	Model	Last known Owner/Operator	Identities/fates/comments (where appropriate)
6 73 106 04	RV	Tomsk Avia	CCCP-47355 RA-47355
6 73 106 05	RV	(Sakha Avia)	CCCP-47356 RA-47356 [w/o 06Nov96 Ust-Nera, Russia; canx 03Jun97]
6 73 106 06	RV	UTair	CCCP-47357 RA-47357
6 73 106 07	RV	Katekavia	CCCP-47358 RA-47358
6 73 106 08	RV	Ryazanaviatrans	CCCP-47359 RA-47359 UR-47359 RA-47359
6 73 106 09	RV	(IrAero)	RDPL-34005 UR-CFU RA-46561(2) [w/o 08Aug11 Blagoveshchensk, Russia]
6 73 106 10	RV	ex Lao Aviation	RDPL-34006 [wfu by Jun97 Vientiane-Wattay, Laos; l/n Apr02; later to Jomtien Waterpark, Thailand]
6 73 107 01	RV	Cubana	RDPL-34007 RDPL-34151 CU-T1706
6 73 107 02	RV	(Lao Aviation)	RDPL-34008 [w/o 22Apr90 Luang Nam Tha, Laos]
6 73 107 03	RV	(Lao Aviation)	RDPL-34009 [not in 2001 fleet list]
6 73 107 04	RV	Yakutia	CCCP-47360 RA-47360
6 73 107 05	RV	Buryat Avia	CCCP-47361 RA-47361
6 73 107 06	RV	Pskov Avia	CCCP-47362 RA-47362 UR-47362 RA-47362
6 73 107 07	RV	ex Nordavia	CCCP-47363 RA-47363 [stored with titles painted out by Mar12 Arkhangelsk, Russia]
6 73 107 08	RV	ex Lao Aviation	RDPL-34010 [wfu by Jun97 Vientiane-Wattay, Laos; l/n Apr02; later to Jomtien Waterpark, Thailand]
7 73 107 09	RV	unknown	CCCP-47364 RA-47364 TC-TRA RA-47364 S9-GRD
7 73 107 10	RV	Avia Traffic	YR-BMO TC-FPB YR-BMO ST-ING EX-019
7 73 108 01	RV	(TAROM)	YR-BMJ [w/o 28Dec99 probably shot-down near Visina 60km west of Bucharest, Romania]
7 73 108 02	RV	Filair	CCCP-47365 RA-47365 TC-TRV? RA-47365 9L-LBQ 9Q-CTR
7 73 108 03	RV	(Romanian Flight Inspectorate)	YR-BMK [w/o 22Feb96 near Baia Mare, Romania]
7 73 108 04	RV	SAT Airlines	CCCP-47366 RA-47366
7 73 108 05	RV	Altyn Air	YR-BML S9-CBA EX-24805
7 73 108 06	RV	Khabarovsk Avia	CCCP-47367 RA-47367
7 73 108 07	RV	Altyn Air	YR-BMM S9-CDA EX-24807 4R-SEL EX-014
7 73 108 08	RV	Alok Air	YR-BMN EX-24808 4L-AVL ST-AWZ
7 73 108 09	RV	Yemen Air Force	4W-ACD 1190
7 73 108 10	RV	(TA Guinee Bissau)	YR-AMW J5-GAE J5-GBE(1) J5-GAE [w/o 07Apr92; unknown location]
8 73 108 10A	RV	(Aviant Kiev Aviation Plant)	CCCP-26175 26175 UR-26175 [canx 20Jly10; fate/status unknown]
8 73 108 10B	RV	Pamair	CCCP-08823 UK-08823 ER-AFB YA-CAJ [airline suspended operations 19Mar11]
9 73 108 10V	RV	Mordovia Air	CCCP-08824 RA-08824
Ulan Ude Production			
99 000 01	B	(MAP Ulan Ade APO)	CCCP-93924 [first An-24 built at Ulan Ude factory;fate unknown]
24 01 01	B	(Aeroflot/West Siberia)	CCCP-47700 [format of c/n unknown;] [wreck by Apr93 Novosibirsk-Severny, Russia; l/n Jun96; canx]
5 99 002 01	B	ex Russian Air Force	101 red [fate/status unknown]
5 99 002 02	B	(Aeroflot/Yakutsk)	CCCP-47701 [w/o 28Jan70 40km from Batagai, USSR; canx 24Mar70?]
5 99 002 03	B	ex Flight State Academy of Ukraine	CCCP-47702 UR-47702 [canx 13Aug08; l/n 31Oct08 Kirovograd-Khmelyovoye, Ukraine]
5 99 002 04		.	[nothing known; c/n not used?]
5 99 002 05		.	[nothing known; c/n not used?]
5 99 003 01	B	(Kirovograd Flying School)	CCCP-47703 [canx 1983; derelict by Jly93 Kirivograd-Khmelyovoye, Ukraine; l/n 20Mar97 derelict]
5 99 003 02	B	(Novosibirsk Avia)	CCCP-47704 RA-47704 [canx 19Aug98; fate unknown]
5 99 003 03	B	ex Flight State Academy of Ukraine	CCCP-47705 UR-47705 [wfu by May02 Kirivograd-Khmelyovoye, Ukraine; l/n 05Aug08; canx 13Aug08]
5 99 003 04	B	(Chita Avia)	CCCP-47706 RA-47706 [derelict by Apr97 Chita-Kadal, Russia; canx 28Aug97]
6 99 003 05		.	[nothing known; possible Soviet Air Force aircraft]
6 99 004 01		.	[nothing known; possible Soviet Air Force aircraft]
6 99 004 02	B	(Aeroflot/Far East)	CCCP-47707 [canx 1974; fate unknown]
6 99 004 03	B	(Sakha Avia)	CCCP-47708 RA-47708 [canx 13Mar96; fate unknown]
6 99 004 04	B	(Aeroflot/Tyumen)	CCCP-47709 [canx 08Aug94; derelict by 14May95 Tuymen-Roschino, Russia]
6 99 004 05	B	unknown	CCCP-47710 UN-47710 [reported damaged 01Nov95 Chimkent, Kazakhstan; possible w/o]
6 99 005 01	Ush	Flight State Academy of Ukraine	CCCP-47711 UR-47711

ANTONOV An-24

C/n	Model	Last known Owner/Operator	Identities/fates/comments (where appropriate)
6 99 005 02	B	(Aeroflot/Kazakhstan)	CCCP-47712 [fate unknown]
6 99 005 03	B	(Uzbekistan Airways)	CCCP-47713 UK-47713 [wfu by 17Sep97 Samarkand, Uzbekistan; used for spares; canx]
6 99 005 04	B	(Cheboksary Air Enterprise)	CCCP-47714 RA-47714 [canx 15Mar99; derelict by 27Aug04 Cheboksary, Russia]
6 99 005 05	B	(Yoshkar-Ola Air)	CCCP-47715 RA-47715 [wfu by 17May12 Yoshkar-Ola, Russia]
6 99 006 01	B	.	[nothing known; possible Soviet Air Force aircraft]
6 99 006 02	B	ex Russian Air Force	50 blue [wfu by Jly92 Irkutsk-One, Russia; l/n Aug07]
6 99 006 03	B	.	[nothing known; possible Soviet Air Force aircraft]
6 99 006 04	B	(Abakan Avia)	CCCP-47716 RA-47716 [canx 25Nov94; fate unknown]
6 99 006 05	B	(Aeroflot/Urals)	CCCP-47717 [canx 26Aug68; fate unknown]
6 99 007 01	B	(Kolymaavia)	CCCP-47718 RA-47718 [w/o 01Feb94 Omsukchan, Russia]
6 99 007 02	B	(Tyumen Airlines)	CCCP-47719 RA-47719 [canx 01Jun96; fate unknown]
6 99 007 03	B	(Sakha Avia)	CCCP-47720 RA-47720 [canx 23Oct96; fate unknown]
6 99 007 04	B	(Kolymaavia)	CCCP-47721 RA-47721 [canx unknown date; fate unknown]
6 99 007 05	B	(Aeroflot/Krasnoyarsk)	CCCP-47722 [canx 1984; fate unknown]
6 99 008 01	B	(Omskavia)	CCCP-47723 RA-47723 [canx 15Nov96; fate unknown]
6 99 008 02	B	(Aeroflot/East Siberia)	CCCP-47724 [canx 1979; fate unknown]
6 99 008 03	B	(Buryat Avia)	CCCP-47725 RA-47725 [derelict by Apr97 Ulan Ude-Mukhino, Russia; l/n 26Nov06; canx 22Jly98]
6 99 008 04	B	(Sakha Avia)	CCCP-47726 RA-47726 [wfu by Aug03 Yakutsk, Russia; used by rescue services; l/n Jly04]
6 99 008 05	B	(Tyumen Airlines)	CCCP-47727 RA-47727 [canx 17Apr98; fate unknown]
6 99 009 01	B	(Dalavia)	CCCP-47728 RA-47728 [canx 12Jan97; fate unknown]
6 99 009 02	B	(Aeroflot/East Siberia)	CCCP-47729 [w/o 01Jun71 Ulan Ude, USSR; canx 1971]
6 99 009 03	B	(Sakha Avia)	CCCP-47730 RA-47730 [not in 1998 fleet list; still current Mar03; fate unknown]
6 99 009 04	B	(Sibair/Sayani)	CCCP-47731 RA-47731 [b/u Jly05 Irkutsk, Russia]
6 99 009 05	B	(Aeroflot/Krasnoyarsk)	CCCP-47732 [w/o 14Apr80 Krasnoyarsk-Severny, USSR; canx 1980]
6 99 010 01	B	(Aeroflot/Yakutsk)	CCCP-47733 [w/o 06Jan68 broke up in mid-air or shot down 92km from Olyokma, USSR; canx 1968]
6 99 010 02	B	(Aeroflot/Kazakhstan)	CCCP-47734 [w/o 13Aug76 Guryev, Kazakhstan, USSR; canx 1976]
6 99 010 03	B	(Aeroflot/East Siberia)	CCCP-47735 [canx 1979; fate unknown]
6 99 010 04	B	(Marshland Aviation)	CCCP-47736 UN-47736 ST-WAL [w/o 02Jun05 Khartoum, Sudan]
6 99 010 05	B	(Aeroflot/Kazakhstan)	CCCP-47737 UN-47737 [displayed by 05Aug02 Atyrau Airport, Kazakhstan; l/n Apr08]
6 99 011 01	B	(Aeroflot/Uzbekistan)	CCCP-47738 [canx 1987; fate unknown]
7 99 011 02	B	(Aeroflot/East Siberia)	CCCP-47739 [canx 03Mar94; b/u between Jly94/May95 Irkutsk-One, Russia]
7 99 011 03	B	ex Turkmenistan Airlines	CCCP-47740 EZ-47740 [not in 1999 fleet list; for sale Jun08]
7 99 011 04	B	(Equatorial Express Airlines)	CCCP-47741 RA-47741 9L-LEP 3C-VQR [w/o 16Jly05 near Malabo, Equatorial Guinea]
7 99 011 05	B	(Aeroflot/Krasnoyarsk)	CCCP-47742 [canx 16May85; fate unknown]
7 99 011 06	Ush	(Flight State Academy of Ukraine)	CCCP-47743 UR-47743 [canx 13Aug08; l/n 05May07 Kirivograd-Khmelyovoye, Ukraine]
7 99 011 07	B	(Tyumen Airlines)	CCCP-47744 RA-47744 [canx 17Apr98; fate unknown]
7 99 011 08	B	(Tyumen Airlines)	CCCP-47745 RA-47745 [canx 15Dec03; fate unknown]
7 99 011 09	B	(Sakha Avia)	CCCP-47746 RA-47746 [not in 1998 fleet list; but still current Mar03]
7 99 011 10	B	(Valan International Cargo)	CCCP-47747 (YL-LCN) YL-LCK ER-AZZ [w/o 23Mar06 Talil, Iraq; canx 11Aug06]
7 99 012 01	B	(Dalavia)	CCCP-47748 RA-47748 [canx 24Jun97; fate unknown]
7 99 012 02	B	(Republic of Latvia)	CCCP-47749 YL-LCL [canx 28Jan97; fate unknown]
7 99 012 03	B	(Aeroflot/East Siberia)	CCCP-47750 RA-47750(1) [canx 03Mar94; fate unknown]
7 99 012 04	B	(Aeroflot/West Siberia)	CCCP-47751 [w/o 01Apr70 near Novosibirsk, USSR; collided with weather balloon; canx 07May70]
7 99 012 05	B	(Abakan Avia)	CCCP-47752 RA-47752 [canx 25Nov94; fate unknown]
7 99 012 06	B	(Kuban Airlines)	CCCP-47753 RA-47753 [canx 20Dec94; fate unknown]
7 99 012 07	B	ex Kirovograd Flying School	CCCP-47754 [canx 15Aug77; by Jly96 to Kriviy Rig Technical School, Ukraine; l/n 05Aug08]
7 99 012 08	B	(Sakha Avia)	CCCP-47755 RA-47755 [not in 2000 fleet list; wfu by Aug03 Yakutsk, Russia; b/u Sep11]
7 99 012 09	B	Permskie Avialinii	CCCP-47756 RA-47756
7 99 012 10	B	ex Turkmenistan Airlines	CCCP-47757 EZ-47757 [not in 1999 fleet list; for sale Jun08]
7 99 013 01	B	(Dalavia)	CCCP-47758 RA-47758 [canx 06Nov97; fate unknown]

ANTONOV An-24

C/n	Model	Last known Owner/Operator	Identities/fates/comments (where appropriate)
7 99 013 02		.	[nothing known; possible Soviet Air Force aircraft]
7 99 013 03	B	(Novosibirsk Air)	CCCP-47759 RA-47759 [canx 08Jly97; fate unknown]
7 99 013 04	B	(Abakan Avia)	CCCP-47760 RA-47760 [canx 15Jly96; fate unknown]
7 99 013 05	B	(Komiavia)	CCCP-47761 RA-47761 [canx 18Nov97; fate unknown]
7 99 013 06	B	(Sakha Avia)	CCCP-47762 RA-47762 [canx 12Jan00; fate unknown]
7 99 013 07	B	SCAT	CCCP-47763 UN-47763 UP-AN425
7 99 013 08	B	(Chita Avia)	CCCP-47764 RA-47764 [canx 03Feb97; fate unknown]
7 99 013 09	B	ex Daghestan Airlines?	CCCP-47765 RA-47765 [canx 03Oct94; by 29Aug09 with Omsk Aviation Technical School, Omsk, Russia, still in Aeroflot c/s]
7 99 013 10	B	Ukraine Air Force	[Soviet] [unknown] [for sale in May06; nothing more known]
7 99 014 01	B	(Dalavia)	CCCP-47766 RA-47766 [canx 02Feb98; fate unknown]
7 99 014 02	B	(Aeroflot/Uzbekistan)	CCCP-47767 [canx 1979; by May94 to Yegoryevsk Technical School, Russia; gone by Aug01]
7 99 014 03	B	(Tyumen Airlines)	CCCP-47768 RA-47768 [canx 17Apr98; b/u by Jly00 Tyumen-Roshchino, Russia]
7 99 014 04	B	(Aeroflot/Tyumen)	CCCP-47772 [w/o 13Oct69 Nizhnevartovsk, USSR; canx 1969]
7 99 014 05		.	[nothing known; possible Soviet Air Force aircraft]
7 99 014 06	B	ex Permskie Avialinii	CCCP-47773 RA-47773 [canx 26Apr99; preserved by Jan07 in park, Perm, Russia]
7 99 014 07	B	(Tyumen Airlines)	CCCP-47774 RA-47774 [derelict by Jly00 Tyumen-Roshchino, Russia; l/n Aug04; canx 14Jly04]
7 99 014 08	B	(Sakha Avia)	CCCP-47775 RA-47775 [not in 2000 fleet list; wfu by Aug03 Yakutsk, Russia; b/u Sep11]
7 99 014 09	B	ex Russian Navy	[Soviet] 01 blue [wfu by 09Apr12 Vladivostok-Knevichi, Russia]
7 99 014 10	B	ex Kirovograd Flying School	CCCP-47776 [canx 1977; used for training in 1980s on banks of Lake Oboznovka, Ukraine; abandoned there l/n Aug07]
7 99 015 01	B	(Sakha Avia)	CCCP-47777 RA-47777 [not in 2000 fleet list; wfu by Aug03 Yakutsk, Russia; b/u Sep11]
7 99 015 02	B	(Tyumen Airlines)	CCCP-47778 RA-47778 [derelict by Jly00 Tyumen-Roshchino, Russia; l/n Aug04; canx 14Jly04]
8 99 015 03		.	[nothing known; possible Soviet Air Force aircraft]
8 99 015 04	B	(Komiavia)	CCCP-47779 RA-47779 [canx 09Mar99; fate unknown]
8 99 015 05	B	ex Tyumen Airlines	CCCP-47780 RA-47780 [wfu by Jly06 Tyumen-Roshchino, Russia; l/n Jly08]
8 99 015 06	B	Trade Links Aviation	CCCP-47781 UR-47781 ER-AEM EX-004 4L-TAS
8 99 015 07	B	(Dalavia)	CCCP-47782 RA-47782 [canx 25Oct96; fate unknown]
8 99 015 08	B	(Aerocom)	CCCP-47783 UR-47783 ER-AFT [w/o en route 17Jan03 near Ndjole, Gabon; canx 20Jan03]
8 99 015 09	B	ex Turkmenistan Airlines)	CCCP-47784 EZ-47784 [not in Nov99 fleet list; for sale Jun08; stored by Apr02 Ashkhabad, Turkmenistan; l/n 06Nov08]
8 99 015 10	B	(Abakan Avia)	CCCP-47785 RA-47785 [canx 25Nov94; fate unknown]
8 99 016 01	B	Polar Airlines	CCCP-47786 RA-47786
8 99 016 02	B	(Novosibirsk Air)	CCCP-47150 [canx 08Jly97; fate unknown]
8 99 016 03	B	(Aeroflot/West Siberia)	CCCP-47151 [canx 1976; fate unknown]
8 99 016 04	B	Permskie Avialinii	CCCP-47152 RA-47152
8 99 016 05	B	Avia Jaynar	CCCP-47153 UN-47153 UP-AN401
8 99 016 06	B	Kirov Air	CCCP-47154 RA-47154 [stored by about 2000 Kirov, Russia; l/n Sep10]
8 99 016 07	B	Air Urga	CCCP-47155 UR-47155 RA-47155 UR-47155 UR-ELN
8 99 016 08	B	Dalavia	CCCP-47156 RA-47156
8 99 016 09	B	(Abakan Avia)	CCCP-47157 RA-47157 [canx 25Nov94; wfu Abakan, Russia; l/n 05May12]
8 99 016 10	B	ex Polar Airlines	CCCP-47158 RA-47158 [wfu by Apr10 Yakutsk, Russia; l/n 26Jun12 derelict]
8 99 017 01	B	Chukotavia	CCCP-47159 RA-47159
8 99 017 02	B	Tyumen Airlines	CCCP-47160 RA-47160
8 99 017 03	B	ex Polar Airlines	CCCP-47161 RA-47161 [wfu Yakutsk, Russia; by 26Jun12 derelict]
8 99 017 04	B	(Abakan Avia)	CCCP-47162 RA-47162 [canx 25Nov94; fate unknown]
8 99 017 05	B	(Aeroflot/East Siberia)	CCCP-47163 [canx 24Jly92; fate unknown]
8 99 017 06	B	(Aeroflot/Far East)	CCCP-47164 [w/o 14Dec90 Shakhtyorsk, USSR; canx 22Mar91]
8 99 017 07	B	(Novosibirsk Air)	CCCP-47165 RA-47165 [canx 30Sep98; fate unknown]
8 99 017 08	B	Tyumen Airlines	CCCP-47166 RA-47166
8 99 017 09	B	(SirAERO)	CCCP-47167 RA-47167 [wfu by Aug03 Yakutsk, Russia; b/u Sep11]
8 99 017 10	B	(Abakan Avia)	CCCP-47168 RA-47168 [canx 15Jly96; fate unknown]
8 99 018 01	B	(Chita Avia)	CCCP-47169 RA-47169 [canx 19Oct98; fate unknown]
8 99 018 02	B	ex Dalavia	CCCP-47170 RA-47170 [canx 28Oct99; wfu by Jun01 Irkutsk-One, Russia; l/n 28Aug07 reported in a technical school]

ANTONOV An-24

C/n	Model	Last known Owner/Operator	Identities/fates/comments (where appropriate)
8 99 018 03	B	(Buryatia)	CCCP-47171 [derelict by 20Apr97 Ulan-Ude-Mukhino, Russia; canx 22Jly98; l/n 26Nov06]
8 99 018 04		.	[nothing known; possible Soviet Air Force aircraft]
8 99 018 05	B	(Novosibirsk Air)	CCCP-47172 [canx 29Dec94; fate unknown]
8 99 018 06	B	(Izhavia)	CCCP-47173 RA-47173 [canx 18Feb99; fate unknown]
8 99 018 07	B	(Kolymaavia)	CCCP-47174 RA-47174 [canx unknown date; wfu by 28Nov06 Magadan-Sokol, Russia; l/n 04Jly08]
8 99 018 08		.	[nothing known; possible Soviet Air Force aircraft]
8 99 018 09	B	(Aeroflot/Kazakhstan)	CCCP-47175 [never canx; fate unknown]
8 99 018 10	B	SCAT	CCCP-47176 UN-47176 UP-AN418
8 99 019 01	RR	(Russian Air Force)	03 blue [l/n 29Apr94 Kubinka AFB, Russia; b/u by Mar97; remains present 23Apr97]
8 99 019 02	B	(Abakan Avia)	CCCP-47177 RA-47177 [canx 15Jly96; fate unknown]
8 99 019 03	B	(Aeroflot/Tyumen)	CCCP-47178 [canx 1977; fate unknown]
9 99 019 04	Ush	(State Flight Academy of Ukraine)	CCCP-47179 UR-47179 [l/n 14Jun07 Kirivograd-Khmelyovoye, Ukraine; canx 13Aug08]
9 99 019 05	B	(Yakutavia)	CCCP-47180 [DBR 03Feb93 Ust'-Kuiga, Russia; canx 01Dec93]
9 99 019 06	B	(Sakha Avia)	CCCP-47181 RA-47181 [wfu by Aug03 Yakutsk, Russia; b/u winter 2008/2009]
9 99 019 07	B	Ural Airlines	CCCP-47182 RA-47182
9 99 019 08	B	(PMT Air)	CCCP-47183 RA-47183 TN-AHB EX-041(1) XU-U4A [w/o en-route 25Jun07 near Bokot mountains, Cambodia]
9 99 019 09	B	(Dalavia)	CCCP-47184 RA-47184 [canx 12May99; fate unknown]
9 99 019 10	B	Novosibirsk Avia	CCCP-47185 RA-47185
9 99 020 01	B	(Air Kazakhstan)	CCCP-47186 UN-47186 [wfu by 02Oct02 Astana. Kazakhstan]
9 99 020 02	B	Ural Airlines	CCCP-47187 RA-47187
9 99 020 03	B	Dalavia	CCCP-47188 RA-47188
9 99 020 04	B	(Novosibirsk Air)	CCCP-47189 RA-47189 [canx 24May00; fate unknown]
9 99 020 05	B	Adygheya Avia	CCCP-47190 RA-47190
9 99 020 06	B	(Chita Avia)	CCCP-47191 RA-47191 [l/n 18Apr97 derelict Chita-Kadala, Russia; canx 09Apr98 or 10Oct98]
9 99 020 07	B	(Baikal Airlines)	CCCP-47192 RA-47192 [canx 23Jun95; fate unknown]
9 99 020 08	B	(Sakha Avia)	CCCP-47193 RA-47193 [not in 2000 fleet list; wfu by Jly03 Yakutsk, Russia; b/u Sep11]
9 99 020 09	B	ex Imtrec Aviation	[unknown] RF-79162 RA-79162 XU-335 [wfu Phnom-Penh, Cambodia; by Jly08 in use as café, Sihanoukhville, Cambodia]
9 99 020 10		.	[nothing known; possible Soviet Air Force aircraft]
9 99 021 01	B	Russian Air Force	[Soviet] 100 red
9 99 021 02		.	[nothing known; possible Soviet Air Force aircraft]
9 99 021 03	B	(Russian Air Force)	[Soviet] 01 red [dumped by May99 Stupino, Russia]
9 99 021 04	B	Kazakhstan Air Force	[Soviet] 01 red
9 99 021 05	B	Russian Air Force	[Soviet] 01 red
9 99 021 06		.	[nothing known; possible Soviet Air Force aircraft]
9 99 021 07	B	ex Sevastopol Avia	[Soviet] 01 blue+ UR-BXA [+ assumed Ukraine] [canx 01Oct08; abandoned Port Sudan, Sudan; l/n 12Jun12]
9 99 021 08	B	(Russian Navy)	[Soviet] [unknown] [offered for sale Dec01; nothing more known]
9 99 021 09	B	Transerviceaero	[unknown] RA-46711 EK-46711 4L-RAS
9 99 021 10		.	[nothing known; possible Soviet Air Force aircraft]
9 99 022 01	B	(Kurgan Air)	CCCP-47194 RA-47194 [canx 11Feb98; fate unknown]
9 99 022 02	B	(Russian Air Force)	01 blue+ 07 blue [+ Soviet] [wfu by 04aug07 Kubinka AFB, Russia; l/n Mar08; probably sold as scrap]
9 99 022 03	B	Belarus Air Force	[Soviet] 01 yellow [l/n 24Aug96 Minsk-Machulishchi, Belarus; current status?]
9 99 022 04		ex Russian Air Force	[Soviet] [unknown] [for sale as scrap Feb09]
9 99 022 05		.	[nothing known; possible Soviet Air Force aircraft]
9 99 022 06	B	(Soviet Air Force)	CCCP-46345 [CofA canx 12Mar80; fate/status unknown]
9 99 022 07		.	[nothing known; possible Soviet Air Force aircraft]
9 99 022 08	B	(Russian Air Force)	CCCP-47794 RA-47794 [canx 12Jan01 as destroyed but was l/n 20Aug01 Klin-5 AFB, Russia]
0 99 022 09	B	(Soviet Air Force)	CCCP-47795 795 black [l/n 24Sep91 Chkalovski, USSR; fate/status unknown]
0 99 022 10	B	(Soviet Air Force)	CCCP-47796 [canx unknown date; fate/status unknown]
0 99 023 01	B	Russian Air Force	CCCP-47797 797 black+ RA-797 [+ Soviet/Russia]
0 99 023 02		.	[nothing known; possible Soviet Air Force aircraft]
0 99 023 03		.	[nothing known; possible Soviet Air Force aircraft]

ANTONOV An-24

C/n	Model	Last known Owner/Operator	Identities/fates/comments (where appropriate)
0 99 023 04	B	ex Russian Air Force	CCCP-47798 798 black+ [+ Soviet/Russia] [for sale as scrap Feb09]
0 99 023 05		.	[nothing known; possible Soviet Air Force aircraft]
0 99 023 06	B	Russian Air Force	[Soviet] 03 red
0 99 023 07	B	Russian Air Force	CCCP-46824 RA-46824 824+ [+ colour?] [l/n 20Aug01 Klin-5 AFB, Russia; for sale Jun09 as scrap metal]
0 99 023 08	B	unknown	CCCP-46825 25 blue+ 02 blue^ RA-49258 [+ Soviet; ^ Russia] [l/n 02Sep97 Moscow-Tushino, Russia; gone by May99; possibly b/u]
1 99 023 09	B	TsSKB Progress	CCCP-26191 RA-26191
0 99 023 10	B	IrAero	CCCP-93934 RA-93934

Irkutsk Production – Freighter versions

It is reported that 164 An-24T were built at Irkutsk; as can been seen below many remain unidentified. Only those c/ns which have been fully identified and those which have not been fully tied up, the latter with a question mark have been included below.

C/n	Model	Last known Owner/Operator	Identities/fates/comments (where appropriate)
102 1 8 01	TV	ex Romanian Air Force	801+ YR-AML 1801 [+ Romania;] [stored by Oct03 Bucharest-Otopeni, Romania; l/n 29Jun07]
102 1 8 02	TV	ex Romanian Air Force	802+ YR-AMM 1802 [+ Romania;] [stored by Oct03 Bucharest-Otopeni, Romania; l/n 29Jun07]
102 1 8 03 ?	RT	(Congo Air Force)	TN-KAN TN-102 TN-221 [wfu by 31Mar06 Brazzaville, Congo]
102 1 8 04 ?	RT	(Congo Air Force)	TN-KAO TN-103 TN-223 [wfu by 31Mar06 Brazzaville, Congo; l/n Apr97]
102 2 8 05 ?	TV	(Iraqi Airways)	[Iraq?] YI-AEM [w/o 24Sep80 near Kirkuk, Iraq]
102 2 8 06 ?	TV	(Iraqi Airways)	[Iraq?] YI-AEN [fate unknown]
102 2 8 07 ?	TV	(Iraqi Airways)	[Iraq?] YI-AFG [fate unknown]
102 2 8 08 ?	TV	(Iraqi Airways)	[Iraq?] YI-ALY [fate unknown]
102 2 8 09 ?	TV	(Iraqi Airways)	[Iraq?] YI-AMB [fate unknown]
102 2 8 10	TV	(Iraqi Airways)	[Iraq?] YI-ALN [w/o 28Aug82 Nasiriya, Iraq; by Jly03 tail section dumped Talili, Iraq; l/n Mar04]
102 1 9 11	TV	(Innovation & Industrial Center)	911+ YR-AMS 1911+ ER-AZD UR-IIC [+ Romania] [stored Kiev-Zhulyani, Ukraine; canx 03Feb10; b/u there 13May12]
102 1 9 12	TV	ex Romanian Air Force	912+ YR-AMU 1912+ [stored by Oct03 Bucharest-Otopeni, Romania; l/n 29Jun07]
102 2 0 15 ?	TV	(Sudan Air Force)	977 [reported Feb85 Khartoum, Sudan; serial later used on a An-12]
102 2 0 16 ?	TV	(North Yemen Air Force)	966+ 2016^ [+ Sudan] [^ not fully confirmed as ex 966; fate unknown]
102 2 0 17 ?	TV	(Sudan Air Force)	955 [fate unknown]
102 5 0 18 ?	RT	(Sudan Air Force)	944 [wfu by Feb88 Khartoum, Sudan; l/n Nov94]
102 5 0 19 ?	RT	(Sudan Air Force)	933 [wfu by Feb88 Khartoum, Sudan; l/n Nov94]
102 5 0 20 ?	RT	(Sudan Air Force)	922 [wfu by Feb88 Khartoum, Sudan; l/n Nov94]
102 5 0 21 ?	RT	(Sudan Air Force)	911 [wfu by Feb88 Khartoum, Sudan; l/n Nov94]
102 5 0 22	RT	ex Romanian Air Force	YR-AMO 5022 [stored by Oct03 Bucharest-Otopeni, Romania; l/n 29Jun07]
102 5 0 23 ?	RT	(Sudan Air Force)	900 [wfu by Feb88 Khartoum, Sudan; l/n Nov94]
102 5 0 24	RT	Romanian Air Force	YR-AMN 5024

C/n	Model	Last known Owner/Operator	Identities/fates/comments (where appropriate)
6 9 1 01 01	T	.	[reported as prototype]
7 9 1 01 04	RT	(Antonov Design Bureau)	CCCP-46280 [w/o 08Mar81 Kursk, USSR]
7 9 1 02 01	T	ex Air Atlantic Cargo	CCCP-46839(2) RA-46839 EK-46839 [canx before 01Jan09; possibly w/o 18May09 Dire Dawa, Ethiopia]
7 9 1 02 02	T	Russian Air Force	[Soviet] 08 red
7 9 1 02 04	T	Russian Air Force	[Soviet] 05 red
7 9 1 03 09	T	(Soviet Air Force)	[Soviet] [used in bombing trials Mar/Apr69]
7 9 1 04 01	T	Bodaibo Air	CCCP-46713(2) RA-46713
7 9 1 04 02	T	ex Bodaibo Air	CCCP-46700(2) RA-46700 [canx 28Jan98; noted derelict Jan09 Bodaibo, Russia]
7 9 1 04 03	T	(Avia Uratu)	CCCP-98116 EK-98116 [canx 15Nov02; b/u Yerevan, Armenia]
7 9 1 04 05	T	ASA Aviation	[unknown] RA-49273 EK-49273 EX-170 [stored Fujairah, UAE; l/n 11Sep10]
8 9 1 05 09	T	ex Russian Air Force	[Soviet] 16 red [wfu 08Jly08 Krasnoyarsk-Yemelyanovo, Russia]
8 9 1 06 07	T	ex Russian Air Force	54 red+ 54 red [+ Soviet] [wfu 1998/1999 Vyazma, Russia; preserved there by 30May09]

ANTONOV An-24

C/n	Model	Last known Owner/Operator	Identities/fates/comments (where appropriate)
8 9 1 06 09	T	(Russian Air Force)	[Soviet] 57 red [preserved by 2004 Engels AFB, Russia Museum; l/n Jly06]
8 9 1 07 01	T	SP Air	[Soviet] RA-46710
89 1 07 04	T	(Russian Air Force)	[Soviet] 60 red [by 2009 GIA Irkutsk Higher Military Training College; probably b/u on closure of college]
8 9 1 07 08	T	Ukraine Air Force	[Soviet] 02 blue [l/n 29Apr99 Saki, Ukraine]
8 9 1 07 09	T	(KhGAPP)	CCCP-46336 RA-46336 UR-46336 [wfu by 05Dec05 Kharkiv-Sokolinki, Ukraine; canx 13Aug08]
8 9 1 08 01	RT	(Ukraine Air Force)	[Soviet] [Ukraine] [offered for sale May06]
9 9 1 08 10	T	(Soviet Air Force)	CCCP-46458 [l/n 28May90 Pushkin, USSR]
9 9 1 09 01	RR	(Soviet Air Force)	03 blue [never reported]
9 9 1 09 07	RT	(Russian Air Force)	[Soviet] [Russia] [offered for sale Apr08]
9 9 1 09 08	T	(Soviet Air Force)	CCCP-47793 [canx unknown date; fate/status unknown]
9 9 1 10 08	T	Kazakhstan Air Force	CCCP-46459 UN-46459 [also has code 03 red]
9 9 1 10 10	T	Congolais	CCCP-49270 UR-49270 RA-01248? N24HM (CX-BRO)? 9Q-CLO+ [+ no reports; fate/status unknown; l/n as N24HM in Dominican Republic]
9 9 1 11 02	T	ASA Aviation	[Soviet] RA-49275 EK-49275 EX-171 [stored Fujiarah, UAE; l/n 11Sep10]
9 9 1 11 04	T	unknown	CCCP-49256 UR-49256
9 9 1 11 10	RT	ZTsLP	35 blue+ 775^ UR-46715 [+ Soviet; ^ Ukraine] [canx 13Aug08; fate unknown]
9 9 1 12 09	RT	(Ukraine Air Force)	[Soviet] 42 blue [offered for sale May2006; l/n 04Aug08 Kiev-Borispol, Ukraine]
9 9 1 13 02	T	(Soviet Navy)	[unknown] [w/o May72 Solnechnogorsk, USSR]
9 9 1 13 03	RT	Russian Air Force	[Soviet] 51 blue
9 9 1 13 04	RT	(Ust-Kutavia)	CCCP-47250 RA-47250 [canx 16Dec01; fate unknown]
9 9 1 13 05	RT	ex Interflight	CCCP-47251 RA-47251 N38LT 3C-ZZA [wfu by Jly99 Nairobi, Kenya: l/n 12May09]
0 9 1 13 07	RT	ex Angolan Air Force	CCCP-26186 RA-26186 ER-AEU T-240+ D2-MAU [+ Angola] [wfu by 28Mar09 Luanda, Angola]
0 9 1 13 08	RT	(IAPO-Irkutsk)	CCCP-26187 [canx 03Oct96; fate unknown]
0 9 1 13 10	RT	ex Peru Aviation	045+ RA-46709 OB-1617 [+ Bulgaria] [wfu by 15Jan02 Lima, Peru]
0 9 1 14 03	T	Russian Air Force	[Soviet] 21 blue
0 9 1 14 04	T	Russian Air Force	[Soviet] 76 red RA-47769
0 9 1 14 05	RT	Ukraine Air Force	[Soviet] 23 blue 47 blue
0 9 1 15 01	T	Russian Air Force	[Soviet] 04 blue [for sale Dec07]
0 9 1 15 02	RT	Russian Air Force	[Soviet] 01 Blue [wfu for several years Ryazan-Dyagilevo, Russia; l/n 27Mar09]
0 9 1 15 04	RT	AK Buryatskie Avialina	CCCP-49264 RA-49264
0 9 1 17 02	RT	(FSB/Russian Border Guards)	[Soviet] 03+ [+ Russia, colour unknown;] [b/u after Apr03]
0 9 1 17 03	RT	(FSB/Russian Border Guards)	[Soviet] 04 [+ Russia, colour unknown;] [b/u after Apr03]
0 9 1 17 08	T	Russian Air Force	[Soviet] 26 red [fate unknown]
1 9 1 18 03	RT	ex Air Cess	CCCP-26189 EL-AKP 3D-SBP 3D-KKM 3C-KKM [fate/status unknown]
1 9 1 18 04	RT	Aerocompany Antey	CCCP-48102 RA-48102
1 9 1 18 05	RT	(MAP Zhukovski)	CCCP-26192 RA-26192 [canx unknown date; fate unknown]

Production complete

Unidentified-Civil Prefix

unkn		(Civil Aviation Administration China)	014	[from photo; fate unknown]
unkn	RV	(Civil Aviation Administration China)	B-458	[reported Apr79 Kunming-Wujiaba, China; canx before 1985]
unkn		(Civil Aviation Administration China)	B-464	[canx before 1985]
unkn		(Civil Aviation Administration China)	B-490	[canx before 1985]
unkn		(Civil Aviation Administration China)	B-492	[w/o 21Jan76 Changsa, China]
unkn		(Civil Aviation Administration China)	B-494	[canx before 1985]
unkn		(Civil Aviation Administration China)	B-500	[reported Apr79 Kunming-Wujiaba, China;fate unknown]
unkn	B	Soviet Air Force	CCCP-09950	[reported 11Aug72 Prague, Czechoslovakia]
unkn		Soviet Air Force	CCCP-46452	[reported 24Oct92 Dijibouti-Ambouli, Dijibouti]

ANTONOV An-24

C/n	Model	Last known Owner/Operator	Identities/fates/comments (where appropriate)
unkn		unknown	CCCP-46456 UR-46456 [l/n 04May99 Kiev-Zhulyany, Ukraine on overhaul; not on register]
unkn	B	Ukraine Air Force	CCCP-46547 46547 [l/n 24May02 Odessa, Ukraine]
unkn	B	(Aeroflot)	CCCP-46700(1) [from postcard; not c/n 7910402 a An-24T; fate/status unknown]
unkn		Soviet Navy	CCCP-46701 [reported 26Aug95 and 21Aug99 Ostafyevo, Russia]
unkn		Soviet Air Force?	CCCP-46823 UR-46823+ [reported 28Mar86 Tashkent, Uzbekistan, USSR; + 06Jly96 Verkhnyaya, Ukraine]
unkn		(Aeroflot)	CCCP-46875 [reported 25Aug92 Moscow-Bykovo, Russia]
unkn		(Aeroflot)	CCCP-46954 [reported 15Sep987 Irkutsk, USSR; possible misreport]
unkn		(Aeroflot)	CCCP-47560 [reported 18Mar92 Moscow-Bykovo, Russia; possible misread]
unkn		(Aeroflot)	CCCP-47861 [reported 05Feb90 Moscow-Sheremetyevo, USSR; possible misread]
unkn	B	(Aeroflot)	CCCP-47874 [reported in 1975 but is possible misread]
unkn		(Aeroflot)	CCCP-47890 [reported 16Jly91 Leningrad-Pulkovo, USSR]
unkn	RV	SAFT Gabon	D2-EPU [reported 15Aug97 Libreville-Leon M'Ba, Gabon]
unkn		unknown	D2-FBQ [reported 16Mar01 Luanda, Angola]
unkn		unknown	D2-FEH [reported 05Sep97Libreville-Leon M'Ba, Gabon; possibly a An-26]
unkn	RV	Santa Cruz	EL-ALF [reported 20May97 & 04Jly01 Sharjah, UAE; between these two dates on An-12 c/n 8346010; not on Liberian register]
unkn		Mongolian Government	JU-7070 [reported 30Aug02 Dalanzadgad, Mongolia & 10Sep05 Ulan Baatar, Mongolia]
unkn		Chosonminhang	P-529 [reported in 1976]
unkn		(Chosonminhang)	P-531 [reported in 1976]
unkn		Chosonminhang	827 [photo late 1960s Kiev-Svyatoshino, Ukraine, USSR; no prefix and out of normal number range]
unkn	B	Russian Air Force	RA-46453 [reported 20Aug01 Klin-5 AFB, Russia]
unkn		Russian Air Force?	RA-46549 [reported 21Aug99 Ivanovo, Russia]
unkn	RV	unknown	RA-47382 [registered by Feb98/Sep01 without c/n]
unkn	RV	unknown	RA-47519 [reported 24May94 Moscow-Bykovo, Russia; possible misread]
unkn		Aeroflot	RA-48256 [reported 04Jly93 Moscow-Sheremetyevo, Russia; possible misread]
unkn		Aeroflot	RA-49276 [reported 30Aug97 Saratov-Tsentrainy, Russia; possible misread]
unkn	RV	Lao Aviation	RDPL-34143 [reported 04Jan04 & 05Apr09 Vientiane, Laos; not c/n 6 73 106 09 as once reported]
unkn		unknown	S9-CAU [reported 22Mar01 Luanda, Angola]
unkn		Air West Express	ST-ART [reported Jan04 & Jan05 Khartoum, Sudan; canx before Jan07 might have been a An-26]
unkn	RV	unknown	TN-AGS [stored Pointe Noire, People's Republic of Congo]
unkn	RV	unknown	UN-47006 [reported 05May03 Sharjah, UAE]
unkn		unknown	UN-47218 [reported probably wfu 10May98 Shymkent, Kazakhstan]
unkn	RV	unknown	UR-AFB [reported 17Dec07 Las Palmas, Gran Canaria, Canary Islands, Spain]
unkn	RV	Air Urga/United Nations	UR-CFU [reported 04Jly07 Istanbul-Sabiha, Turkey; 16Aug07 Mykolaiv, Ukraine; 29Mar08 Entebbe, Uganda; 21Apr09 Kisangani-Bangoka, Democratic Republic of Congo]
unkn		United Nations	UR-LVK [reported 15Jun06 Dubai, UAE]
unkn		unknown	XU-052 [reported 04Aug01 Siem-Reap, Cambodia]
unkn		Air Kampuchea or Air Force	XU-313 [reported Nov95 Phnom-Penh, Cambodia]
unkn		(Pathet Lao)	XW-TCA [w/o 08Mar74 near Hanoi, Vietnam; registration not fully confirmed]
unkn		Air Pamir	YA-CAG [reported 25Mar04 & 24Aug06 Kabul, Afghanistan
unkn		(Ariana Afghan)	YA-DAF [reported Jly99 Sharjah, UAE; probably destroyed end 2001]
unkn		Ariana Afghan	YA-DAH [reported 16Feb99 & 25Feb99 Sharjah, UAE; reported destroyed Oct01 in US Air Raid]
unkn		(Ariana Afghan)	YA-DAI [reported 06Aug03 Kabul, Afghanistan; probably destroyed end 2001; bits noted Feb04]
unkn	RV	Pamir Airways	YR-CAJ [reported 04Apr09 Tarin Kowt, Afghanistan & 31Jly09 Herat, Afghanistan]
unkn	B		3X-GEG [reported arrived 03Jan11 Addis Abada-Bole, Ethiopia]
unkn		Georgian Star International	4L-UCK [mentioned Mar10 in official list and website]
unkn			4R-CAA [reported 2011 in compound at Buddala, Sri Lanka with Civil Aviation Authority titles; assumed false marks]

ANTONOV An-24

C/n	Model	Last known Owner/Operator	Identities/fates/comments (where appropriate)
unkn		(Pan African Air Service)	(5H-MMY) [allocated in 1966 but not delivered]
unkn		(Pan African Air Service)	(5H-MMZ) [allocated in 1966 but not delivered]
unkn		Guinea Government	3C-FMN [reported Aug71 Malabo, Equatorial Guinea; might have become 3C-1GE]
unkn	RV	LA Guinea Equitorianal	3C-IGE [reported mid 1983 Paris-Le Bourget, France; could have been ex 3C-FMN]
unkn		COAGE Airlines	3C-LLM [reported 02Mar00 Malabo, Equatorial Guinea]
unkn	B	unknown	3X-GEG [reported 03Jan11 Addis Ababa, Ethiopia]
unkn		unknown	9XR-SB [reported 31Aug06 Kigali, Rwanda]
Unidentified – Military			
unkn		Bulgarian Air Force	032 [reported Jly78 Sofia-Vrazhdebna, Bulgaria; later report doubtful]
unkn		Bulgarian Air Force	034 [reported Jly78 Sofia-Vrazhdebna, Bulgaria; later report doubtful]
unkn	T	(South Yemen Air Force)	601 [from photo; could be a An-24RT]
unkn	T	(South Yemen Air Force)	602 [from photo; circa Sep81]
unkn		Yemen Air Force	603 [reported 17Mar09 Sanaa International, Yeman]
unkn	T	(South Yemen Air Force)	604 [from 2004 photo damaged condition & dumped Riyan, Yeman; l/n Sep09]
unkn		(Sudan Air Force)	700 [destroyed by rebel action 25Apr03 Al Fasher, Sudan]
unkn	RT	Sudanese Air Force	911 [reported 11Oct80 Khartoum, Sudan & Feb88 & Nov94 as wfu]
unkn		(North Yemen Air Force)	1178 [reported 11Nov85 Sanaa International, North Yeman; possible An-24RT]
unkn	B	Chinese Air Force	4066 [reported stored Beijing-Nan Yuan, China]
unkn		Chinese Air Force	5823 [from photo a possible Y-7]
unkn		Sudan Air Force	7766 [reported 05Feb92 Khartoum, Sudan; possible An-26]
unkn	B	Cuban Air Force	12-46 [reported 28Aug83 Havana, Cuba; reported as a An-24B but possibly a An-26]
unkn		Chinese United Airlines	50950 CUA-50950 [noted in Oct86]
unkn		(Chinese Air Force)	50952 [reported 11Oct88 Wuhan-Tianhe, China; wfu 1989; later preserved Changping; then 1992 to Shane AFB, Beijing, China & b/u]
unkn		(Chinese United Airlines)	50955 CUA-50955 [reported 06Apr86 Nanjing, China]
unkn		Chinese Air Force	50956 [reported Oct93 Beijing-Nan Yuan, China]
unkn		Chinese Air Force	50957 [reported 13Oct88 Nanjing, China]
unkn		Chinese Air Force	50958 [reported 12Nov85 Guangzhou-Baiyan, China & Beijing-Nan Yuan, China]
unkn		Chinese United Airlines	51052 [reported 09Nov93 & 01Jun94 Beijing-Nan Yuan, China]
unkn		Chinese United Airlines	51055 CUA-51055 [reported 08Oct88 Taiyuan-Wusu, China; also a 51055 reported Sep05 as a Y-7 Shahe AFB, China]
unkn	T	Soviet/Russian Air Force	01 red [reported 08Jly94 Yakutsk, Russia]
unkn	RV	(Soviet Air Force)	03 red [from photo showing code on nose]
unkn	T	Russian Air Force	03 red [reported 1992 Moscow-Sheremetyevo, Russia; Sep93/Apr97 Moscow-Tushino, Russia; gone by May99; b/u?]
unkn	RR	(Soviet Air Force)	03 red [reported based at Kubinka, USSR; used as radiation checker following Chernobyl disaster, possibly b/u]
unkn	T	(Soviet Navy)	04 red [reported 05Aug01 Puskin, USSR; as AEW test-bed aircraft]
unkn	RT	Soviet/Russian Air Force	09 red [reported 20Apr94 Yakutsk, Russia]
unkn		Ukraine Border Police	12 yellow [reported 27Mar08 Odessa, Ukraine & 21May09 Kiev-Zhulyany, Ukraine]
unkn	T	Soviet/Russian Air Force	21 blue [reported 21Apr93 Novosibirsk-Tolmachevo, Russia]
unkn	T	Russian Air Force	26 red [reported 24Aug95 Ivanovo-Yasyunikha, Russia]
unkn		Ukraine Air Force	328 black [reported 10May97 and 30Apr99 Mikolayiv-Kulbakino, Ukraine; possibly ex-13328]
unkn		Russian Air Force	51 blue [2010 photo at Khabarovsk-Bolshoy, Russia]
unkn	RT	(Soviet Air Force)	53 blue [from photo]
unkn	T	Russian Air Force	53 blue [based Klin-5 AFB, Russia until b/u during 2000]
unkn	T	Soviet/Russian Air Force	61 red [reported 19Aug91 Moscow-Tushino, USSR]
unkn	T	Russian Air Force	849 black [reported 16Aug96 Klin-5 AFB, Russia; possibly had civil registration CCCP-46849]
unkn			CUA-50950 [see 50950 above]
unkn			CUA-50955 [see 50955 above]
unkn			CUA-51055 [see 51055 above]
unkn		Afghan Air Force	T-005 [reported]

ANTONOV An-26

Note: An Angolan Government An-26 was reported lost on 14Jan87 and another on 14Dec87; identities unknown

C/n	Model	Last known Owner/Operator	Identities/fates/comments (where appropriate)
01 01		(MAP Kiev)	[static test airframe 1969]
02 01		(MAP Kiev)	[no marks] CCCP- 92 red+ CCCP-93913 [+ Soviet] [prototype f/f 21May69; without registration; canx 26Jly82; reported in use for trials until 1993]
02 02		National Aviation University	CCCP-26184 UR-26194 [preserved by 16Aug03 Kiev, Ukraine; l/n 29Oct08]
03 01		(Soviet Air Force)	(unknown)
03 02		(Russian Air Force)	30 red [l/n 28Jun04 Ulyanovsk, Russia; wfu]
04 01		(Russian Air Force)	CCCP-26637 637 black
04 02		unknown	CCCP-26211 RA-26211 [canx unknown date]
04 03		Ministry of Interior (MVD)	[unknown+] RF-56306 [+ had yellow code number not known]
04 04	RT	(Soviet Air Force)	[unknown]
05 01		ex Russian Air Force	[Soviet] (unknown) [offered for sale 31Dec07 as scrap]
05 02		.	[nothing known]
05 03		SCAT	(unknown) UN-26027 UP-AN601
05 04		(Soviet Air Force)	(unknown)
05 05		ex Russian Air Force	CCCP-46704 RA-46704 [reported wfu by 17Aug09 Chkalovsky, Russia]
06 01		(Soviet Air Force)	(unknown)
06 02		.	[nothing known]
06 03		ex Russian Air Force	CCCP-46707 RA-46707 [reported wfu by 17Aug09 Chkalovsky, Russia]
06 04		(Soviet Air Force)	CCCP-46708 [CofA canx 14Apr82; fate unknown]
06 05		Ministry of Interior (MVD)	CCCP-46822 04 yellow+ RF-56309 [+ Russia]
06 06			[nothing known]
06 07	KPA	Russian Air Force	14 red [Soviet/Russia]
06 08		.	[nothing known]
06 09		MRP NPO "Leninets"	CCCP-26648 RA-26648
06 10	KPA	Russian Air Force	[Soviet] (unknown) [reported stored from 2011 Chita, Russia, code not reported]
07 01		Russian Air Force	61 red [Soviet/Russia]
07 02		.	[nothing known]
07 03		.	[nothing known]
07 04		.	[nothing known]
07 05		.	[nothing known]
07 06		.	[nothing known]
07 07		.	[nothing known]
07 08		.	[nothing known]
07 09		.	[nothing known]
07 10		MAP Moscow MSZ	CCCP-26169 RA-26169 [stored by Aug99 Zhukovski, Russia; canx unknown date]
08 01		.	[nothing known]
08 02		(Kosmos I Transport)	CCCP-88286 RA-88286 [w/o 06Nov94 Zyryanka River, Russia]
08 03		.	[nothing known]
08 04		(Antonov Design Bureau)	CCCP-27205 [fate unknown; registration later used on An-30 c/n 0709]
08 05		.	[nothing known]
08 06		ex Ukraine Air Force	61 blue [preserved by 18Apr10 Poltava, Ukraine]
08 07		.	[nothing known]
08 08		Ukraine Air Force	[Soviet] 05 blue
08 09		Russian Air Force	04 red [Soviet/Russia]
08 10		.	[nothing known]
09 01	A	(Russian Air Force)	91 [Soviet/Russia] [b/u by 2006 Ivanovo-Severny, Russia]
09 02		.	[nothing known]
09 03		.	[nothing known]
09 04		ex Russian Air Force	[Soviet] RA-47751 [by 06Nov11 preserved Volsk, Russia with digits 098 added to regn]
09 05		Russian Air Force	[Soviet] (unknown) [offered for sale Dec07; fate unknown]
09 06		.	[nothing known]
09 07		.	[nothing known]
09 08		(Russian Air Force)	[Soviet] 37 red [b/u by 2006 Ivanovo-Severny, Russia]
09 09		(Ukraine Cargo Airways)	04 red+ UR-26241 UR-UDM [+ not confirmed; Soviet/Ukraine; l/n 06Oct10 wfu Zaporizhia, Ukraine; canx 07Jly11]
09 10		Russian Air Force	02 red [Soviet/Russia]
10 01		.	[nothing known]

ANTONOV An-26

C/n	Model	Last known Owner/Operator	Identities/fates/comments (where appropriate)
10 02		.	[nothing known]
10 03		ex Russian Air Force	32 red [Soviet/Russia] [preserved by Aug08 Ukrainka AFB, Russia]
10 04		Ministry of Interior (MVD)	[Soviet] 11 yellow RF-56300
10 05		(Russian Air Force)	[Soviet] (unknown) [b/u by 2006 Ivanovo-Severny, Russia]
10 06		(MAP Kiev)	CCCP-83966 [converted to An-32 c/n 1006]
10 07		.	[nothing known]
10 08		.	[nothing known]
10 09		(Russian Air Force)	[Soviet] (unknown) [offered for sale 09Feb09 as scrap]
10 10		ex Russian Air Force	CCCP-46840 60 yellow [preserved by 27May06 Tambov AFB, Russia]
11 01		Russian Navy	CCCP-46841 04 blue
11 02		(Soviet Air Force)	CCCP-46842 [CofA canx 12Mar80; fate unknown]
11 03		.	[nothing known]
11 04		.	[nothing known]
11 05		Russian Navy	[Soviet] 05 blue
11 06		.	[nothing known]
11 07		.	[nothing known]
11 08		.	[nothing known]
11 09		Kazakhstan Border Guards	[Soviet] 01 white
11 10		Russian Air Force	[Soviet] 03 red
12 01		.	[nothing known]
12 02		.	[nothing known]
12 03		Russian Navy	[Soviet] 04 red
12 04		(Russian Air Force)	[Soviet] 06 yellow [b/u by 2006 Ivanovo-Severny, Russia]
12 05		.	[nothing known]
12 06		(Russian Air Force)	[Soviet] 15 red [b/u by 2006 Ivanovo-Severny, Russia]
12 07		(Russian Air Force)	[Soviet] (unknown) [offered for sale Dec07; fate unknown]
12 08		NAK Rossii	02 red+ CCCP-01208 RA-13339 [+ Soviet]
12 09		.	[nothing known]
12 10		.	[nothing known]
13 01		(MAP LII Zhukovski)	CCCP-29113 29113 RA-29113 [canx 12Apr00; l/n Jan02 stored Zhukovski, Russia]
13 02		748 Air Service	CCCP-21507 RA-21507 9XR-DS 9L-LFW [stored by 06Jly10 Saki-Novofedorovka, Ukraine]
13 03		Somali Air Force	(unknown)
13 04		Russian Air Force	06+ [+ colour of code unknown]
13 05		.	[nothing known]
13 06		Russian Air Force	[Soviet] (unknown) [offered for sale Dec07; fate unknown]
13 07		ex Yakutavia	(unknown) CCCP-26685(2) (RA-26685) [derelict by Jan09 Batagai, Russia; l/n Jun09]
13 08		Yeniselski Meridian	1308+ CCCP-26627(2) RA-26627 [+ Poland]
13 09		AviaExpress	1309+ (unknown) "UR-013-09" UR-26233 LZ-MNL UR-26233 [+ Poland]
13 10		Exin Air	1310+ SP-EKB^ [+ Poland] [^ not yet recoded in register; stored 05Jun11 Katowice-Pyrzowice, Poland; l/n 07Dec11]
14 01		(Soviet Air Force)	CCCP-46843 [CofA canx 01Dec85]
14 02		Exin Air	1402+ SP-EKD^ [+ Poland] [^ stored by 24Aug10 Katowice-Pyrzowice, Poland; marks not yet recorded in register; l/n 07Dec11]
14 03		ex Polish Air Force	1403 [wfu Jan09 Krakow-Balice, Poland; stored for preservation]
14 04		unknown	CCCP-48099 RA-48099 ST-AQM [w/o 28Aug06 El Obeid, Sudan; canx by Jan07; l/n 14Mar07]
14 05		(Russian Air Force)	CCCP-46844 07 red+ [+ Soviet/Russia]
14 06		ex Polish Air Force	1406 [wfu Aug08 Krakow-Balice, Poland; to Luban, Poland for ground training]
14 07		Exin Air	1407+ SP-EKC^ [+ Poland] [wfu & stored 2005 Krakow-Balice, Poland; sold Jan09 to Exin; ^ not on register & no confirmed sightings]
14 08		Kazakhstan Air Force	[Soviet] 09 red
14 09		.	[nothing known]
14 10		.	[trials aircraft; nothing more known]
15 01		Ministry of Interior (MVD)	(unknown) RF-56307
15 02		Belarus Air Force	[Soviet] 22 yellow+ 22 red [+ Belarus; preserved by Sep07 Minsk-Borovaya, Belarus; l/n Jan10]
15 03		Belarus Air Force	[Soviet] 23 yellow

ANTONOV An-26

C/n	Model	Last known Owner/Operator	Identities/fates/comments (where appropriate)
15 04	RTR	Belarus Air Force	24 yellow [ex Soviet Air Force]
15 05		(Tyumen Airlines)	CCCP-46503 RA-46503 [derelict by Jly00 Tyumen-Roschino, Russia; canx 29Oct03; l/n Aug04]
15 06		.	[trials aircraft; nothing more known]
15 07		.	[nothing known]
15 08		Muzeum Lotnictwa Polskiego	1508+ [+ Poland] [wfu & stored 2005 Krakow-Balice, Poland; by May10 preserved Rakowice, Krakow, Poland]
15 09		Exin Air	1509+ SP-EKE^ [+ Poland] [^ stored by 24Aug10 Katowice-Pyrzowice, Poland; marks not yet recorded in register; l/n 07Dec11
15 10		Russian Air Force	06 yellow [Soviet/Russia] [offered for sale Aug08 ex Torzhok, Russia]
16 01	RT	Russian Air Force	[Soviet] (unknown) [offered for sale 19Dec01; fate unknown]
16 02		ex Polish Air Force	1602+ SP-LWC SP-KWC 1602 [reported wfu 2008 & for preservation in Warsaw Military Museum, Poland]
16 03		ex Polish Air Force	1603+ SP-LWB 1603 [+ Poland] [wfu by Aug08 Krakow-Balice, Poland; to Czestochowa, Poland for fire training]
16 04		Exin Air	1604+ SP-LWA 1604 SP-EKF [+ Poland] [stored by 07Dec11 Katowice-Pyrzowice, Poland]
16 05		(Russian Air Force)	[Soviet] 01 blue [b/u by 2006 Ivanovo-Severny, Russia]
16 06		.	[nothing known]
16 07		.	[nothing known]
16 08		Russian Air Force	[Soviet] (unknown) [offered for sale Dec07; fate unknown]
16 09		(Russian Air Force)	[Soviet] 52 red [b/u by 2006 Ivanovo-Severny, Russia]
16 10		.	[nothing known]
17 01		Compagnie Afrique d'Aviation	1701//S3-ABA+ CCCP-58643 CCCP-26009(2) YL-RAB(1) 9Q-CIB [+ Bangladesh; dual marks; later used on An-32 also c/n 1701]
17 02		Bangladesh Air Force	1702//S3-ABB+ [+ dual marks] [stored by Dec98 Dhaka-Teigaon, Bangladesh for museum by Dec98]
17 03	RT	Russian Air Force	[Soviet] (unknown) [offered for sale Dec07; fate unknown]
17 04		.	[nothing known]
17 05		Russian Navy	[Soviet] 07 blue
17 06		.	[nothing known]
17 07		.	[nothing known]
17 08		Belarus Air Force	[Soviet] 02 yellow 02 red [reported sold by 2010 in Africa]
17 09			[nothing known]
17 10		.	[nothing known]
18 01		(Russian Air Force)	CCCP-26699 699 black [wfu 2007; b/u Klin AFB, Russia]
18 02		.	[nothing known]
18 03		.	[nothing known]
18 04	RTR	Russian Air Force	11 red [Soviet/Russia] [wfu by Aug07 Kubinka, Russia]
18 05		Santa Cruz Imperial	(unknown) RA-26004 EL-ALT+ [+ c/n not confirmed]
18 06		Russian Air Force	[Soviet] [unknown] [offered for sale Dec07; fate unknown]
18 07		Russian Air Force	[Soviet] 25 blue+ [+ not fully confirmed]
18 08		MNS Ukrainy	[Soviet] 02 blue+ [+ Ukraine]
18 09		(Baikal Airlines)	CCCP-26533 RA-26533 [not in 1998 fleet list; canx unknown date; b/u Sep03 Irkutsk, Russia]
18 10		(Tyumen Airlines)	CCCP-26534 RA-26534 [canx 05Sep97; derelict by Jly00 Tyumen-Roschino, Russia; l/n 13Aug01]
19 01		.	[nothing known]
19 02		Russian Navy	21 blue+ [Soviet/Russia] [+ later noted with no code]
19 03		.	[nothing known]
19 04		.	[nothing known]
19 05		Russian Air Force	[Soviet] 19 blue
19 06		.	[nothing known]
19 07		(Russian Air Force)	[Soviet] (unknown) [b/u by 2006 Ivanovo-Severny, Russia]
19 08		Russian Air Force	[Soviet] 16 red
19 09			[nothing known]
19 10		(Kosmos I Transport)	CCCP-13371 RA-13371 [canx 17Jan00; stored by Oct00 Moscow-Vnukovo, Russia; fate unknown]
4 73 020 01		El Sam Airlift	CCCP-26535 RA-26535 TN-AGI
20 02		(Soviet Air Force)	02 red [fate/status unknown]
20 03		(Aeroflot/Yakutsk)	CCCP-26536 [w/o 18Aug77 Ust'Kuiga, USSR; canx 1979]
20 04		.	[nothing known]

ANTONOV An-26

C/n	Model	Last known Owner/Operator	Identities/fates/comments (where appropriate)
20 05		Ukraine Air Force	[Soviet] 01 blue
20 06		.	[nothing known]
20 07	RT	Russian Air Force	[Soviet] 09 blue [by 14Aug11 stored Rostov-na-Donu Tsentralny, Russia]
20 08		(Strat Rocket Forces)	[Soviet] 69+ [+ colour unknown; wfu before 2010]
20 09		.	[nothing known]
20 10		ex Magadanaerokontrol	CCCP-26537 RA-26537 [canx 06Aug03 to Armenia; but still stored 04Jly08 Magadan-Sokol, Russia]
21 01	ASLK	Russian Air Force	CCCP-26642 RA-26642 [stored by 04Aug07 Kubinka, Russia]
4 73 021 02	100	Polar Airlines	CCCP-26538 RA-26538
4 73 021 03		(Baikal Airlines)	CCCP-26539 RA-26539 [b/u Jly05 at Irkutsk Technical School, Irkutsk, Russia]
21 04		.	[nothing known]
4 73 021 05	B	(Tyumen Airlines)	CCCP-26540 RA-26540 [canx 05Sep97; fate/status unknown]
4 73 021 06		(Kolymaavia)	CCCP-26541 RA-26541 [w/o 25Jan97 Chokurdah, Russia]
21 07		ex Russian Navy	[Soviet] 03 blue [wfu by 09Apr12 Vladivostok-Knevichi, Russia]
21 08		Russian Air Force	[Soviet] 04 blue
21 09		Kazakhstan Air Force	[Soviet] 54 red
21 10		Russian Air Force	CCCP-48973 [unknown] [offered for sale Dec07; fate unknown]
22 01	RTR	(Russian Air Force)	22 blue [Soviet/Russia] [b/u by 2006 Ivanovo-Severny, Russia]
22 02		Magyar Repulestorteneti Muzeum	202+ [+ Hungary] [wfu 1996; preserved Jun98 Szolnok, Hungary; l/n 26Apr09]
4 73 022 03		ex Scorpion Air/Solenta	203+ LZ-MNS TR-LID [+ Hungary; stored 23Oct11 Sofia, Bulgaria, no marks]
22 04		ex Hungarian Air Force	204+ (HA-TCO) [+ Hungary] [stored by Aug00 Szolnok, Hungary; l/n Dec03]
22 05			[nothing known]
22 06		(Mango Air)	206+ YR-ADD 206+ CCCP-26229 26229 UR-26229 206+ ER-AZE 9U-BHR^ 9Q-CAW [+ Romania; ^ flew in these illegal marks; w/o 29Jun05 Goma, Democratic Republic of Congo; hulk l/n 03Jly05]
22 07		ex Romanian Air Force	207+ YR-ADE 207+ [+ Romania;] [stored by Oct03 Bucharest-Otopeni; l/n 29Jun07]
22 08		Cityline Europe	208+ UR-CEP HA-TCO [+ Hungary]
22 09		ex Solenta Aviation	209+ LZ-MNT TR-LIN^ [+ Hungary;] [^ tie up not fully confirmed; stored 06Nov11 Sofia, Bulgaria]
22 10		(Hungarian Air Force)	210 [w/o 06Dec86 Szentkiralyszabadja, Hungary]
23 01		.	[nothing known]
23 02		Lao Air Force	RDPL-34039 26095+ RDPL-34039 [+ Ukraine]
23 03			[nothing known; this was reported as being ST-APV but this is An-32 c/n 2303]
23 04		.	[nothing known]
23 05		Russian Air Force	[Soviet] 05 blue
23 06		Chinese Air Force	741
23 07		Russian Air Force	[Soviet] 24 black
23 08		Chinese Air Force	742
23 09		(Chinese Air Force)	743 [DBF 16Sep82 on ground at unknown location]
23 10		Chinese Air Force	744
24 01		Chinese Air Force	745
24 02		Chinese Air Force	746
24 03		Chinese Air Force	747
24 04		Chinese Air Force	748
24 05		Chinese Air Force	749
24 06		Russian Air Force	[Soviet] 56+ [+ colour unknown]
24 07			[nothing known]
24 08			[nothing known]
24 09			[nothing known]
24 10		Russian Air Force	[Soviet] [unknown] [offered for sale Dec07; fate unknown]
25 01			[nothing known]
25 02		Chinese Air Force	750
25 03		Chinese Air Force	751
25 04		Lao Air Force	CCCP-26575(1) XW- RDPL-34038
25 05			[nothing known]

ANTONOV An-26

C/n	Model	Last known Owner/Operator	Identities/fates/comments (where appropriate)
25 06		(Lao Air Force/Lao Aviation)	CCCP-26576 RDPL-34037+ [+ tie up not fully confirmed] [damaged 01Sep79 Nam Pard district, Thailand; repaired & ferrried 31Jan80 to Vientiane, Laos & w/o on landing]
25 07		Chinese Air Force	752
25 08		(Romanian Air Force)	508+ YR-ADF 508 [+ Romania] [DBR 1994 Oradea, Romania; later b/u]
25 09		Chinese Air Force	753
25 10		Chinese Air Force	754
26 01		Chinese Air Force	755
26 02		Gorizont	(unknown) RA-26249
26 03			[nothing known]
26 04	RT	Russian Air Force	[Soviet] 11 red [offered for sale Apr08; fate unknown]
26 05		(Antonov Design Bureau)	CCCP-13395 UR-13395 [canx 01Oct08; fate/status unknown]
4 73 026 06	100	(Alfa Airlines)	CCCP-13399 RA-13399 EK-13399 ST-ARL [w/o 19Aug12 Talodi, Southern Sudan]
26 07		Elf Air	CCCP-13398 RA-13398
26 08			[nothing known]
26 09		FSB/Border Guards	(unknown) RF-26275
26 10		Ukraine Air Force	[Soviet] 30 blue
27 01		Russian Air Force	[Soviet] 10 blue+ RF-36071 [+ Russia]
27 02			[nothing known]
27 03			[nothing known]
27 04		Ukraine Air Force	[Soviet] 12 blue [offered for sale Oct07; l/n Aug08 Vinitsa, Ukraine]
27 05			[nothing known]
27 06		ex Meridian	YR-ADC 706+ UR-CHF [+ Romania] [canx 08Oct10; stored Gostomel, Ukraine]
27 07		Romanian Air Force	YR-ADB 707 [stored & for sale Jly05 Bucharest-Otopeni, Romania; l/n 29Jun07]
27 08		(Arkhangelsk Airlines)	CCCP-26542 RA-26542 [canx 16Dec98; fate unknown]
5 73 027 09		Angara 403 Airlines	CCCP-26543 RA-26543
27 10		Ulyanovsk Higher Flying School	CCCP-26544 RA-26544
28 01		Romanian Air Force	YR-ADA 801
28 02			[nothing known]
28 03			[nothing known]
28 04		(Soviet Air Force)	06 [colour unknown] [fate/status unknown]
28 05	RPA	Russian Air Force	[Soviet] 04 [colour unknown] [canx 02Aug04; wfu Magnitogarsk, Russia; l/n mid 2007]
28 06		(Magnitogorsk Air)	CCCP-26545 RA-26545
28 07		Russian Navy	[Soviet] 21 [colour unknown]
28 08		Russian Air Force	[Soviet] (unknown) 06 yellow
5 73 028 09		(Yeniseiski Meridian)	CCCP-26546 RA-26546 [canx unknown date; fate unknown]
28 10		(Aeroflot/Yakutsk)	CCCP-26547 [w/o 09Dec78 Chersky, USSR; canx 1979]
29 01		(Sakhalinsk Air Transport)	CCCP-26548 RA-26548 [canx 13Jan95; hulk status by 2004 Yuzhno-Sakhalinsk, Russia; b/u by 2007]
29 02		Chinese Air Force	756
29 03		Chinese Air Force	757
29 04		China United Airlines	758+ 51054+ [+ China]
29 05		Chinese Air Force	759
29 06		ex Aviant	CCCP-69312 UR-69312 [canx 13Aug08; l/n 29Sep08 Kiev-Svyatoshino, Ukraine]
5 73 029 07		(ex Aeroflot/Urals)	CCCP-26549 RA-26549 [w/o 28Aug93 Donetsk, Russia; canx 14Apr94]
29 08		(Dalavia)	CCCP-26550 [canx 06Jun94; fate unknown]
29 09		ex Russian Navy	[Soviet] 04 blue [wfu by 09Apr12 Vladivostok-Knevichi, Russia]
29 10		ex Russian Navy	[Soviet] 05 blue [wfu by 09Apr12 Vladivostok-Knevichi, Russia]
30 01	B	J.P. Bemba	(unknown) 9Q-CLA
30 02			[nothing known]
30 03		Chinese Air Force	761
30 04		Chinese Air Force	762
30 05		Chinese Air Force	763
30 06			[nothing known]
30 07		Syrianair/Government	YK-ANC
30 08		Syrianair/Government	YK-AND
30 09		unknown	BNMAU-3009 MT-1012 JU-1012 ER-AZS EK-26441 3X-GDI

ANTONOV An-26

C/n	Model	Last known Owner/Operator	Identities/fates/comments (where appropriate)
30 10		ex MIAT Mongolian	BNMAU-3010 MT-1013 JU-1013 [b/u spares 2001 Ulan Baatar, Mongolia; fuselage only noted 27Jan10]
31 01			[nothing known]
31 02	P	(Arkhangelsk Airlines)	CCCP-26551 [canx 21Jun01; sold in Ukraine in non-airworthy condition]
31 03		Syrianair/Government	YK-ANE
31 04		Syrianair/Government	YK-ANF
31 05		Chinese Air Force	760
31 06		Chinese Air Force	765
5 73 031 07		Alrosa	CCCP-26552 RA-26552
31 08		Chinese Air Force	766
31 09		Chinese Air Force	767
31 10		Chinese Air Force	764
32 01		ex Ukraine Flight State Academy	CCCP-26553 RA-26553 UR-26533 26553 [canx 13Aug08 with no CofA; l/n 31Oct08 Kirovograd, Ukraine]
32 02		ex Kras Air	CCCP-26554 RA-26554(1) [canx 19Jly94; by Jly03 in Technical School, Krasnoyarsk-Yemelyanovo, Russia; l/n Jly08]
5 73 032 03		ex Air Kharkiv	CCCP-26555 UR-26555 [canx 13Aug08 with no CofA; by 11Jun06 wfu Kharkov, Ukraine; l/n 10Jly07
32 04	100	Valan International/Sky Link	CCCP-26556 26556 RA-26556 ER-AVB
32 05		ex Ukraine Air Force	[Soviet] (unknown) [offered for sale 27May06 in non-flying condition]
32 06		(Soviet Air Force)	CCCP-26160 [canx 27Mar86; fate/status unknown]
32 07		Ministry of Interior (MVD)	[Soviet] 14 yellow+ RF-56301 [+ Russia]
32 08			[nothing known]
32 09		Ukraine Air Force	[Soviet] 30 blue
32 10			[nothing known]
33 01		(Kras Air)	CCCP-26557 RA-26557 [canx 17Dec97; fate unknown]
33 02		Chinese Air Force	768
33 03		(Mali Air Force)	TZ-347 [w/o 31Aug95 near Thessaloniki, Greece; wreck l/n 08Nov96]
33 04			[nothing known]
33 05		(Magnitogorsk Air)	CCCP-26558 RA-26558 [canx 02Aug04; wfu Magnitogarsk, Russia; l/n mid 2007]
33 06			[nothing known]
33 07	T	Russian Air Force	[Soviet] 07+ [+ code colour not reported]
33 08		Serbian Air Force	71364+ 71364 [+ Yugoslavia then Serbia & Montenegro]
33 09		ex 748 Air Services	CCCP-26559 UN-26559 RA-26559 9L-LFL [canx 08Apr08; l/n Oct08 Lokichogio, Kenya]
5 73 033 10		ex Buryat Avia	CCCP-26560 RA-26560 [canx 22Jly98; wfu by 26Nov06 Ulan Ude-Mukhino, Russia]
34 01		ex Serbian & Montenegro Air Force	71362+ 71362 [+ Yugoslavia] [wfu by 2006; l/n 02Au08 Batajinca, Belgrade, Serbia]
34 02		Serbian Air Force	71371+ 71371 [+ Yugoslavia then Serbia & Montenegro]
34 03		ex Serbian & Montenegro Air Force	71374+ 71374 [+ Yugoslavia] [stored by 2004/06; l/n 01Aug06 Nis, Serbia]
34 04		ex Serbian & Montenegro Air Force	71382+ 71382 [+ Yugoslavia] [wfu by 2006; l/n 02Aug08 Batajnca, Belgrade, Serbia]
34 05		Hungarian Air Force	405
34 06		Hungarian Air Force	406
34 07		Hungarian Air Force	407
34 08		Chinese Air Force	769
34 09		Chinese Air Force	770
34 10			[nothing known]
35 01		Belarus Air Force	03 yellow+ 03 yellow [+ Soviet]
35 02		(Tyumen Airlines)	CCCP-26561 RA-26561 [canx 26Jun97; fate unknown]
35 03		(Soviet Air Force)	CCCP-26161 [canx 27Mar86; fate/status unknown]
35 04	B?	ex Air Highnesses	CCCP-26640 RA-26640 EK-26640 3X-GDF+ [not confirmed]
5 73 035 05		(Dalavia)	CCCP-26562 RA-26562 [canx 01Feb99; fate unknown]
35 06		Sudanese Air Force	CCCP-26563 RA-26563 26563+ 7705 [+ Sudan]
35 07		ex Dalavia	CCCP-26564 RA-26564 [stored by 2005 Khabarovsk-Novy, Russia; wfu for spares; l/n Apr08]
35 08		Alfa	CCCP-58646 RA-58646 ST-AWT
35 09			[nothing known]
35 10			[nothing known]
36 01		Russian Air Force	CCCP-47342 RA-47342

ANTONOV An-26

C/n	Model	Last known Owner/Operator	Identities/fates/comments (where appropriate)
36 02			[nothing known]
36 03		Hungarian Air Force	603
36 04			[nothing known]
36 05		Ukraine Navy	[Soviet] 09 blue 09 yellow
36 06		(Yugoslav Air Force)	71359 [destroyed 1999 Batajnica, Belgrade, Yugoslav by NATO bombing]
36 07			[nothing known]
36 08		ex Serbian & Montenegro Air Force	71366+ 71366 [+ Yugoslavia] [stored by 2004; Batajnica, Belgrade, Serbia; l/n Aug08]
36 09			[nothing known]
36 10		Russian Air Force	19 blue+ 19 red [+ Soviet/Russia]
37 01		Ukraine Air Force	[Soviet] (unknown) [offered for sale 27May06; fate/status unknown]
37 02		(Yugoslav Air Force)	71369 [destroyed 1999 Batajnica, Belgrade, Yugoslav by NATO bombing]
37 03		ex Serbian & Montenegro Air Force	71377+ 71377 [+ Yugoslavia] [stored by 2004; Batajnica, Belgrade, Serbia; l/n Aug08]
37 04			[nothing known]
37 05	B	Yeniseiski Meridian	CCCP-26565 RA-26565
37 06		ex Serbian & Montenegro Air Force	71379+ 71379 [+ Yugoslavia] [wfu by 2006; Batajnica, Belgrade, Serbia; l/n Aug08]
37 07		Russian Air Force	33 red+ [+ Soviet/Russia]
37 08			[nothing known]
37 09		not yet known	23+ (unknown) 4L-BKL [+ Soviet Navy code colour unknown]
37 10		(Tomsk Air)	CCCP-26566 RA-26566 [canx 29Mar97; fate unknown]
38 01		(Aeroflot/Yakutsk)	CCCP-26567 [w/o 23May76 near Khandyga, USSR; canx 1976; by Sep92 derelict Khandyga Airport, Russia]
38 02		ex Russian Navy	[Soviet] 06 blue [wfu by 09Apr12 Vladivostok-Knevichi, Russia]
38 03			[nothing known]
38 04			[nothing known]
38 05		(Cuban Air Force)	12-12+ 14-22+ T-52^ 14-22 [+ Cuba] [^Angola] [w/o 11Sep89 location unknown]
38 06		Aerogaviota	22-22+ CU-T110 14-23+ D2-MIR CU-T1423
38 07		Serbian Air Force	71385+ 71385 [+ Yugoslavia then Serbia & Montenegro;] [damaged 14Aug00 Surcin, Serbia & Monenegro and stored]
6 73 038 08		(Norilsk Air)	CCCP-26568 RA-26568 [w/o 24Aug98 Norilsk, Russia; canx 06Jun00]
6 73 038 09		(Aeroflot/Uralsk)	CCCP-26569 [w/o 25Mar79 Baykit, USSR; canx 1979]
38 10		ex Iraqi Airways	YI-ALA [l/n Dec00 Baghdad International, Iraq; fate/status unknown]
39 01		ex Aerocom	CCCP-26505(2) UR-26505 ER-AFH [seized 29Aug03 by Belize Govt (drug running); sold to USA Jly05 via eBay; l/n 15Mar09 stored Belize City, Belize]
39 02	Sh	Ukraine Air Force	[Soviet] 20 blue
39 03		Chinese Air Force	771
39 04		ex Air Sofia	CCCP-26570 RA-26570 LZ-SFH [stored by 06Nov05 Cox's Bazar, Bangladesh; l/n 04Nov06 bad condition]
39 05		Chinese Air Force	772
39 06		Chinese Air Force	773
39 07		Ukraine Air Force	[Soviet] 07 yellow
39 08		Chinese Air Force	774
6 73 039 09	ASLK	Spetsavia	CCCP-26571 RA-26571
39 10			[nothing known]
40 01		Thom's Airways	[Soviet] 55 blue+ 9Q-CYN [+ Russia]
40 02	100	(Baltika)	[Soviet] 10 red+ UR-VAI [+ Ukraine] [canx 01Oct08]
40 03		Chinese Air Force	775
40 04		Chinese Air Force	776
40 05			[nothing known]
40 06			[nothing known]
40 07		(Soviet Air Force)	CCCP-26153 [canx unknown date; fate/status unknown]
40 08	KPA	Russian Navy	[Soviet] 54 blue
40 09		(Baikal Airlines)	CCCP-26572 RA-26572 [canx 21Dec96; fate unknown]
40 10		(Sakha Avia)	CCCP-26573 RA-26573 [canx 03Jun96; fate unknown]
41 01		Ukraine Air Force	[Soviet] 08 red
41 02		(MRP Solnechnoye)	CCCP-93929 [canx 1984; fate unknown]
6 73 041 03	100	Mordovia Air	CCCP-26247 RA-26247
41 04	B-100	Trast Aero	CCCP-26574 RA-26574 D2-FDA ER-AWV S9-KAV(1) 3X-GET+ [+ identity in doubt as a S9-KAV & a 3X-GET were both reported on 14Feb10 at different airports]

ANTONOV An-26

C/n	Model	Last known Owner/Operator	Identities/fates/comments (where appropriate)
41 05			[nothing known]
41 06	KPA	Russian Air Force	[Soviet] 25 red RF-36017 [also wears code 25 red]
41 07		Chinese Air Force	778
41 08		China United Airlines	779+ [+ China]
41 09		(Kirovograd Flying School)	CCCP-26575(2) [canx 10Apr89; by Jly96 Kriviy Rig Technical School; l/n Aug08]
41 10		Russian Navy	[Soviet] 90 red
42 01		Chinese Air Force	780
42 02		Chinese Air Force	781
42 03		Chinese Air Force	782
42 04			[nothing known]
42 05			[nothing known]
42 06		Itek Air	CCCP-26599 UR-26599 9Q-CTJ 9U-BNO 9U-BHQ 9Q-CMS 3X-GEN
42 07		Chinese Air Force	783
42 08		(Omskavia)	CCCP-26600 RA-26600 [canx 30Dec96; by Nov06 Technical Aviation School, Irkutsk-One, Russia; l/n 28Aug07]
42 09		Ukraine Air Force	[Soviet] 01 red
42 10	Sh	ex Ukraine Air Force	[Soviet] 25 red [wfu by 08Jly07 Zaporozhye-Vostochny, Ukraine; l/n Aug08]
43 01		China United Airlines	784+ [+ China]
43 02		Chinese Air Force	785
43 03		Chinese Air Force	786
43 04		Russian Space Forces	[Soviet] ER-ACE+ RF-36009 [+ marks used on An-12 c/n 402812 at the same time, report in doubt]
43 05			[nothing known]
43 06		Chinese Air Force	787
43 07		Chinese Air Force	788
43 08	Sh	Russian Navy	[Soviet] (unknown) [tender issued 2008 for repair of navigation equipment]
43 09			[nothing known]
43 10		China United Airlines	789+ [+ China]
44 01		Chinese Air Force	790
44 02			[nothing known]
44 03			[nothing known]
44 04			[nothing known]
44 05			[nothing known]
44 06		(Arkhangelsk Airlines)	CCCP-26601 RA-26601 [canx unknown date; fate unknown]
44 07		ex Ukraine Cargo Airways	CCCP-26602 UR-26602 (HA-TCM) UR-UCP [canx 20Jly10 fate/status unknown]
44 08			[nothing known]
44 09		unknown	[Soviet] 20+ UR-TWL [+ Ukraine; colour unknown]
44 10			[nothing known]
45 01			[nothing known]
45 02		Russian Air Force	53 red/white+ 58 blue [+ Soviet/Russia]
45 03		Russian Air Force	[Soviet] 03 blue+ RF-36047^ [+ Russia; ^ also carries 24 red]
45 04			[nothing known]
45 05		(Permskie Avialinii)	CCCP-26603 RA-26603+ 26603 [+ c/n checked as 4603 probably painting error] [wfu by Aug01 Perm-Bolshoye Savino, Russia with tail missing; l/n 22Jun06]
45 06		Polar Airlines	CCCP-26604 UR-26604 RA-26604
45 07		South Airlines	(unknown) ER-AZQ EK-26442 3X-GDP(2) 3X-GFG EK-26819
45 08		Ukraine Border Guards	[Soviet] 11 blue
45 09			[nothing known]
45 10			[nothing known]
46 01		Russian Navy	[Soviet] 22 blue
46 02		Russian Air Force	23 blue+ [+ Soviet/Russia]
46 03			[nothing known]
46 04			[nothing known]
46 05		Russian Air Force	[Soviet] 07 yellow
46 06			[nothing known]
46 07			[nothing known]
46 08			[nothing known]
46 09		Angolan Government	D2-TAD [fate uncertain; l/n 1995 but in 1996 these marks reported on Mi-8]

ANTONOV An-26

C/n	Model	Last known Owner/Operator	Identities/fates/comments (where appropriate)
46 10			[nothing known]
47 01		Ministry of Interior (MVD)	CCCP-48980 06 yellow RF-56302
47 02		SELVA	CCCP-26605 UR-26605 LZ-NHA LZ-RMJ HK-4295X+ [+ also reported without X suffix]
47 03		(Sakhalinsk Air Transport)	CCCP-26606 RA-26606 [canx 01Sep97; fate unknown]
47 04		Alrosa	CCCP-26607 RA-26607
47 05			[nothing known]
47 06		Russian Air Force	[Soviet] 01 blue RF-36129+ [+ also carries 27 red]
47 07		State Aviation Museum	CCCP-78734 CCCP-26215 UR-26215 LZ-NHB UR-26215 [stored by Aug06 Kiev-Zhulyany, Ukraine; l/n Aug08; canx 01Oct08; Jan12 purchased by museum for conversion to restaurant]
47 08	AFS	Belarus Government	21 yellow+ 07^ EW-007DD [+ Soviet/Belarus; ^ Belarus, colour not known]
47 09		MNS Ukrainy	[Soviet] 44+ 04 blue [+ Ukraine; colour unknown]
47 10			[nothing known]
48 01			[nothing known]
48 02		(Afghan Air Force)	234 [w/o 05Apr81 Herat, Afghanistan]
48 03		Russian Air Force	[Soviet] 26 red
48 04			[nothing known]
48 05	B	ex Tyumen Avia Trans	CCCP-26608 [canx 06May96; derelict by 26Jly00 then preserved by 15Nov05 Salekhard-Nepalkovo Airport]
48 06		(Farnas Aviation)	CCCP-26609 RA-26609 ST-FAR [w/o 13Mar96 El Obiad, Sudan]
48 07		Russian Air Force	CCCP-47401 UR-47401 401 black
48 08			[nothing known]
48 09			[nothing known]
48 10			[nothing known]
49 01	B?	ex Taimyr	CCCP-26610 RA-26610 [preserved by summer 2012 near Norilsk-Nadezhda, Russia]
49 02		Russian Air Force	[Soviet] 50 blue+ 05 blue [+ Russia]
49 03		Angolan Air Force	CCCP-26611 RA-26611 T-227+ [+ not fully confirmed]
49 04		(Omskavia)	CCCP-26612 RA-26612 [canx 17Jun96 – to Technical Aviation School, Omsk, Russia by 2006]
49 05			[nothing known]
49 06		Russian Navy	[Soviet] 02 blue
49 07			[nothing known]
49 08			[nothing known]
49 09		Zhigansk Air?	CCCP-26613 RA-26613
7 73 049 10		Baikal Airlines	CCCP-26614 RA-26614 [wfu/stored Jun01 Irkutsk-One, Russia; l/n Apr09]
7 73 050 01		Arkhangelsk Airlines	CCCP-26615 RA-26615
50 02	B	ex Aviavilsa	CCCP-26616 EW-26616 SP-FTI LY-FTL [stored by Sep07 Minsk-Loshitsa, Belarus; l/n Oct08; canx by May10]
50 03		Ukraine Air Force	[Soviet] 72 blue
50 04		unknown	CCCP-26617 RA-26617 [canx 27May98 to Swaziland; fate unknown]
50 05		(Services Air)	CCCP-48092 RA-48092 9Q-CSA [w/o 26May09 near Isiro-Matari, Democratic Republic of Congo]
50 06			[nothing known]
50 07			[nothing known]
50 08		Ukraine Air Force	[Soviet] 34 blue [this might be c/n 50 09, hard to read on aircraft]
50 09			[nothing known]
50 10		ex Lao Air Force	RDPL-34036 [wfu/stored by Apr02 Vientaine-Wattay, Laos]
51 01		(Soviet Air Force)	CCCP-26154 [w/o 30Mar92 near Calcutta, India]
51 02	B	(Kuban Airlines)	CCCP-26618 RA-26618 [canx 20Oct97; fate unknown]
51 03		Transaviaservis	CCCP-26619 RA-26619 [wfu/stored by 22Jun05 Tyumen-Roschino, Russia]
7 73 051 04	B-100	Taimyr	CCCP-26620 RA-26620
51 05		(Soviet Air Force)	CCCP-47404 [canx 13Jly82; fate/status unknown]
51 06		Asia Airways	[Soviet] 32 red+ EY-323 [+ Ukraine]
51 07	B	Russian Air Force	[unknown] RF-46457
7 73 051 08		(Tyumen Avia Trans)	CCCP-26621 RA-26621 [canx 16Jun98; derelict by Jly00 Salekhard-Nepalkovo, Russia]
51 09	B-100	Sadelca	CCCP-26622 YN-CGC HK-4356
51 10		Russian Navy	[Soviet] 04 red
52 01		(Kemerovo Avia Enterprise)	CCCP-26623 [canx 08Dec97; wfu Kermerovo, Russia; l/n 26Aug10]
52 02		(Kuban Airlines)	CCCP-26624 RA-26624 [canx 19Aug97; fate unknown]

ANTONOV An-26

C/n	Model	Last known Owner/Operator	Identities/fates/comments (where appropriate)
52 03	ASLK	Aviastar	CCCP-26625 RA-26625
52 04		(Soviet Air Force)	CCCP-47405 [canx 10Jun82; fate/status unknown]
52 05			[nothing known]
52 06		Russian Air Force	[Soviet] 09 yellow
7 73 052 07		Velocity	CCCP-26626 RA-26626
52 08		(Aeroflot/Turkmenistan)	CCCP-26627(1) [w/o 23Dec82 Rostov-na-Donu, USSR; canx 1983]
52 09		(MAP Kharkov)	CCCP-26198 UR-26198 [not in Jan02 fleet list; fate/status unknown]
7 73 052 10		Centrace Air Services	CCCP-26195 ER-AFX 9Q-CKQ
53 01	T	Galaxy Kavatsi	CCCP-26193 RA-26193 9Q-CVE
53 02		FSB/Border Guards	(unknown)
53 03			[nothing known]
53 04	Sh	ex Ukraine Air Force	[unknown+] 28 red [+ Soviet] [wfu by 08Jly08 Zaporozhye-Vostochny, Ukraine; l/n 06Aug08]
53 05		unknown	[Soviet] 54 yellow+ (ER-AVC) UR-CJS RA-26554(2) [+ Ukraine]
53 06		(Mali Air Force)	TZ-359
53 07			[nothing known]
53 08			[nothing known]
53 09		Alrosa	CCCP-26628 RA-26628
53 10		Russian Navy	[Soviet] 09 blue
54 01		(Kuban Airlines)	CCCP-26629 RA-26629 [canx 19Aug97; fate unknown]
54 02			[nothing known]
54 03		ex Inversija	CCCP-26630 RA-26630+ S9- [+ canx 26Apr99 to Sao Tome; fate/status unknown]
54 04		Russian Air Force	04 blue
54 05		ex Atran	FAP-362+ CCCP-26217 RA-26217 [+ Peru] [stored by Aug02 Moscow-Myachkovo, Russia; l/n Jly06]
54 06		Ukraine Air Force	[Soviet] 25 blue
54 07		Asia Airways	[Soviet] 4L-GST EY-322
54 08		ex Atran	FAP-363+ CCCP-26218(2) RA-26218 [+ Peru] [stored by Aug99 Moscow-Myachkovo, Russia; not in 2001 fleet list; l/n Jly06]
54 09		(Aviant)	FAP-366+ CCCP-26219 UR-79165 [+ Peru] [canx 13Aug08; fate unknown]
54 10	100	Kostroma Airlines	FAP-367+ CCCP-27210 RA-27210 [+ Peru]
55 01		Russian Air Force	02 yellow [Soviet/Russia]
55 02		(Aeroflot c/s)	FAP-374+ CCCP-59501 [+ Peru] [stored by Jly93 Kiev-Zhulyany, Ukraine; l/n Jun06; fate unknown]
55 03	ASLK	Spetsavia	CCCP-26631 RA-26631
55 04		ex Russian Navy	[Soviet] 24 red [wfu by 09Apr12 Vladivostok-Knevichi, Russia]
55 05		Russian Air Force	CCCP-47406 RA-47406
55 06		(Peruvian Air Force)	FAP-375 [fate unknown; this serial later used on An-32]
55 07			[nothing known]
55 08		Ukraine Air Force	[Soviet] 39 red [GIA Novi Petrivtsi, Ukraine]
55 09		Inter Island Air Services	FAP-376+ CCCP-59502 CCCP-26227 RA-26227 ER-AZA EK-26227 RP-C2639 [+ Peru]
55 10	KPA	Russian Air Force	[Soviet] 09 blue
56 01		(Peruvian Air Force)	FAP-377 [w/o 03Jly84 Anacacho Mountains, Peru]
56 02		Marsland Aviation	CCCP-27216 FAP-378+ CCCP-27216 RA-26228 ER-AZC ST-ARJ [+ Peru]
56 03		Aerogaviota	CCCP-47323 12-26+ 14-26+ CU-T1426 [+ Cuba]
56 04			[nothing known]
56 05		ex Companie Afrique d'Aviation	CCCP-26179 RA-26179 9Q-CAB [by Aug10 marks reported on Fokker 50 c/n 20276; fate/status unknown]
56 06			[nothing known]
56 07			[nothing known]
56 08	Sh	Ukraine Air Force	[Soviet] 76 yellow
56 09		Ukraine Air Force	[Soviet] 46 red [offered for sale May06 in non-flying condition]
56 10		British Gulf International	FAP-379+ CCCP-27211 RA-27211 S9-BOV
57 01		(Aeroflot c/s)	FAP-386+ CCCP-58641 [+ Peru] [last flight 29Dec90 to Shannon, Ireland; b/u 16Dec95]
57 02		Russian Space Forces	(unknown)
57 03		Peruvian Air Force	FAP-387 [no recent reports; fate/status unknown]
57 04		(Peruvian Air Force)	FAP-388 [wfu 02Jun95 Havana, Cuba; b/u for spares]
57 05		not yet known	[Soviet] UN-26088 UP-AN605

ANTONOV An-26

C/n	Model	Last known Owner/Operator	Identities/fates/comments (where appropriate)
57 06		Russian Air Force	[Soviet] 60 blue
57 07		unknown	(unknown) UP-AN606
57 08		MRP NPO "Leninets"	(unknown)
57 09		(Soviet Air Force)	CCCP-47408 [canx 01Dec89; fate/status unknown]
57 10	Sh	Ukraine Air Force	[Soviet] 78 yellow+ [+ not fully confirmed]
58 01		(Ukraine Cargo Airways)	[Soviet] 35 red+ UR-UDT [+Ukraine] [canx 01Oct08; fate unknown]
58 02		(Peruvian Air Force)	FAP-389 [wfu 02Jun95 Havana, Cuba; b/u for spares]
58 03		(Aeroflot)	FAP-391 CCCP-58642 [derelict by Jun93 Kiev-Zhulyany, Ukraine; l/n Jun02; fate unknown]
58 04			[nothing known]
58 05		(Peruvian Air Force)	FAP-392 [w/o 18Jun87 near River Jeroche, Saposoa, Peru]
58 06	100	(Podilia Avia)	5806//S3-ABC+ CCCP-58645 UR-26199 LZ-MNO UR-26199 [canx 20Jly10 fate/status unknown] [+ Bangladesh; dual marks]
58 07		Aviatrans Cargo Airlines	5808//S3-SBD+ CCCP-58648 CCCP-26007(2) UR-26007 ST-AVI [+ Bangladesh; dual marks]
58 08		Nuclear, Biological & Chemical Protection Force	CCCP-26641+ A-26641 [+ these marks assumed]
58 09			[nothing known]
58 10		(Soviet Air Force)	CCCP-47409 [canx 01Dec89; fate/status unknown]
59 01		Meridian	[Soviet] [unknown+] UR-VIV UR-CHT [+ Ukraine] [canx 31Dec08; fate unknown]
59 02		Russian Air Force	[Soviet] 25 blue
59 03			[nothing known]
59 04			[nothing known]
59 05		(Benin Government)	TY-AFT [c/n not fully confirmed;] [w/o 1985 Parakou, Benin]
59 06			[nothing known]
59 07			[nothing known]
59 08		ex Soviet Navy?	26+ [+ not confirmed, code colour unknown]
59 09		ex Exin Air	CCCP-26632 EW-26632 SP-FTZ+ LY- [+ canx 25Oct99 to Lithuania; stored by Jun01 Minsk-Lotshisa, Belarus; l/n Oct08]
59 10		Tajikistan Air Force	CCCP-26633 EZ-26633 TJ-26633
60 01			[nothing known]
60 02		Russian Air Force	CCCP-47411 RA-47411 [canx; l/n 28Aug07 Balashov, Russia; status unknown]
60 03		Russian Air Force	CCCP-47410 RA-47410 [canx; l/n 30Aug07 Ivanovo-Severny, Russia; status unknown]
60 04	B	(Success Airlines)	CCCP-26170 RA-26170 ET-AHT+ 9Q-CJI [+ marks reported but doubtful] [probably w/o 12Aug00 64km NW of Tshikapa, Democratic Republic of Congo]
60 05		Russian Air Force	17 blue+ RF-36088^ [+ Russia; ^ as of 27Jun11 still also carrying 17 blue]
60 06		Belarus Air Force	26 yellow+ 26 yellow [+ Soviet]
60 07		Russian Air Force	[Soviet] 26 red [by 12Aug12 stored Ekaterinberg-Koltsovo, Russia]
60 08			[nothing known]
60 09		Russian Air Force	[Soviet] (unknown)
60 10			[nothing known]
61 01		Avia Leasing Asset Management Inc	[Soviet] 57 red+ N5057E [+ Russia]
61 02		Ukraine Air Force	[Soviet] (unknown)
61 03		Russian Air Force	[Soviet] (unknown)
61 04		Russian Air Force	[Soviet] (unknown)
61 05		(Soviet Air Force)	CCCP-26220 [canx unknown date; fate/status unknown]
61 06		Russian Air Force	[Soviet] 57 red
61 07		MNS Ukrainy	[Soviet] 01 blue+ [+ Ukraine]
61 08			[nothing known]
61 09			[nothing known]
61 10			[nothing known]
62 01			[nothing known]
62 02		Russian Air Force	27 blue+ [+ Soviet/Russia]
62 03		Russian Air Force	[Soviet] 19 red
62 04			[nothing known]
62 05		Russian Air Force	CCCP-26165(2) RA-26165
62 06	100	Izhavia	CCCP-26245 RA-26245
62 07		Aero-Charter Airlines	45 blue+ UR-26 UR-BXB UR-DWB [+Soviet/Russia]

ANTONOV An-26

C/n	Model	Last known Owner/Operator	Identities/fates/comments (where appropriate)
62 08		MChS Belarusi	CCCP-26634 EW-26634 SP-FPL [canx 31Jan97; by Oct08 GIA Svetlaya Roshcha, Belarus]
62 09	100	Transportes Aereos Cielos Andinos	[Soviet] [unknown+] UR-VYV OB-1859-P [+ Ukraine]
62 10		East West	TY-AAI CCCP-29107 YL-RAA(1) EL-WAQ
63 01		FSB/Border Guards	[Soviet] 15+ RF-26256 [code colour probably yellow]
8 73 063 02		Sakha Avia	CCCP-26686(2) RA-26686
63 03		Russian Air Force	[Soviet] 41 red
63 04			[nothing known]
63 05		Polyanye Avialinii	CCCP-26635 [stored Cherskly, Russia still in old Aeroflot c/s; l/n 30Mar10]
8 73 063 06	100	UTair Ekspress	CCCP-26636 RA-26636 EP-TPR EP-TQB RA-26636
8 73 063 07		(Dalavia)	CCCP-26500 RA-26500 [canx 30Apr98; fate unknown]
63 08		(Arkhangelsk Airlines)	CCCP-26501 RA-26501 [not in 1997 fleet list; canx unknown date; fate unknown]
63 09		(Kuban Airlines)	CCCP-26502 RA-26502 [canx 01Apr97; fate unknown]
63 10		Museum of Civil Aviation	CCCP-26503 RA-26503 [stored by Aug99 Ulyanovsk-Buyant Ukhaa, Russia; preserved 15Dec08 Ulyanovsk-Tsentraniy, Russia]
64 01		Mango Airlines	[Soviet] [unknown+] 9Q-CGM [+ Ukraine]
64 02		Mozambique Air Force	022
64 03	KPA	Russian Air Force	[Soviet] 147 black
64 04		Russian Air Force	23 blue+ RF-36072^ [+ Soviet/Russia; ^also carries 03 blue]
64 05		Mozambique Air Force	024
64 06		Ukraine Air Force	[Soviet] 35 blue
64 07		South Airlines	CCCP-26504 UR-26504 LZ-MNH YR-ITA LZ-MNH 4L-BKA EK-26407
64 08			[nothing known]
64 09			[nothing known]
64 10			[nothing known]
65 01		Russian Air Force	07+ 03+ 10 red [+ Soviet; colour of codes unknown]
65 02			[nothing known]
65 03		(Meridian)	[Soviet] 40 red+ UR-MMB [+ Ukraine] [canx 01Oct08; fate unknown]
65 04		Yemen Air Force	1188
65 05		Russian Air Force	[Soviet] (unknown)
65 06			[nothing known]
65 07		Yemen Air Force	1177
65 08		Russian Air Force	[Soviet] (unknown)
65 09		Russian Navy	[Soviet] (unknown)
65 10			[nothing known]
66 01		Russian Ministry of the Interior	CCCP-26643 RF-36174
66 02			[nothing known]
66 03			[nothing known]
66 04		Belarus Air Force	[Soviet] 25 yellow+ 04 red+ 09^ [+ Belarus] [^ colour not reported]
66 05		Russian Navy	[Soviet] 15 blue
66 06	100	Amazon Sky	[Soviet] (unknown) UR-VIG OB-1887-P [some reports give c/n as being 8 73 066 06]
8 73 066 07		Aerogaviota	CCCP-47324(1) 12-20+ 14-20+ CU-T1420 [+ Cuba] [status uncertain]
66 08		Russian Navy	[Soviet] 10 red
66 09			[nothing known]
66 10		Aerogaviota	CCCP-47325(1) 12-21+ 14-21+ CU-T1421 [+ Cuba] [status uncertain]
8 73 067 01		(Aeroflot/Krasnoyarsk)	CCCP-26505(1) [w/o 23Dec81 Severo-Yenisseiski, USSR; canx 02Feb82]
67 02		(Kras Air)	CCCP-26506 [canx 23Sep97; fate unknown]
67 03	ASLK	Spetsavia	CCCP-26507 UN-26507 RA-26507
67 04		(Kuban Airlines)	CCCP-26508 RA-26508 [canx 25Mar99; fate unknown]
67 05		ex Yedinaya-Sakha	CCCP-26509 RA-26509 [noted Jun09 Chersky, Russia stored with many parts missing]
8 73 067 06		ex Kemerovskoe Airlines	CCCP-26510 RA-26510+ UR- [+ canx 05Feb99 to Ukraine; l/n 04Jly99 Kiev-Zhulyany, Ukraine]
67 07			[nothing known]
67 08		Russian Air Force	01 yellow [Soviet/Russia]
67 09	Sh	ex Ukraine Air Force	[Soviet] 41 red [by Aug10 to GIF at Lugansk, Ukraine]
67 10		Aero Caribbean	CCCP-47326 12-23+ CU-T1228(1) CU-T110 CU-T1506 [+ Cuba]
68 01			[nothing known]

ANTONOV An-26

C/n	Model	Last known Owner/Operator	Identities/fates/comments (where appropriate)
68 02			[nothing known]
68 03		(Aero Caribbean)	CCCP-47327 12-24+ CU-T115 [+ Cuba] [wfu by 06Jan01 Havana, Cuba]
68 04			[nothing known]
68 05			[nothing known]
68 06		Ukraine Air Force	[Soviet] 08 yellow [stored by 29Sep10 Kiev-Borispol, Ukraine]
68 07		Russian Navy	[Soviet] 59 blue RF-48676 [also wears code 59 blue]
8 73 068 08	100	Angara 403 Airlines	CCCP-26511 RA-26511
68 09		ex Turkmenistan Airlines	CCCP-26512 EZ-26512 [not in 2001 fleet list; for sale Jun08]
68 10		Ulyanovsk Higher Flying School	CCCP-26513 RA-26513 26513 RA-26513
69 01			[nothing known]
69 02	Sh	ex Ukraine Air Force	29 yellow [by Aug10 to GIF at Lugansk, Ukraine]
69 03		Aerogaviota	CCCP-47328 12-08+ 14-08+ CU-T1408 [+ Cuba]
69 04		Aerogaviota	CCCP-47329 12-25+ 14-25+ CU-T1425 [+ Cuba] [status uncertain]
69 05		Russian Navy	16 blue [Soviet/Russia]
69 06		(Cuban Air Force)	CCCP-47330 12-27+ 14-27 [+ Cuba] [w/o Jun84 in sea off Playa Baracoa, Cuba; but could have been w/o in Angola]
69 07		El Magal Aviation Services	CCCP-26514 UR-26514 ST-BEN
69 08		Russian Air Force	[Soviet] 27 red
69 09	KPA	Ukraine Air Force	[Soviet] 57 blue
8 73 069 10		IrAero	CCCP-26515 RA-26515
8 73 070 01		ex Sakha Avia	CCCP-26516 RA-26516 [stored by Aug03 Yakutsk, Russia; l/n Jly04]
70 02		Megaair	CCCP-26517 UN-26517 UP-AN607
70 03		ex Russian Navy	CCCP-26698 RA-26698 [stored by Aug01 Moscow-Ostafyevo, Russia; l/n Aug03]
70 04		(Bentiu Air Transport)	(unknown) RA-49271+ ST-AFT [+ was canx to Ukraine] [canx before Jan07; fate/status unknown]
70 05		Ukraine Ministry of Interior	[Soviet] 07 blue
70 06		Aerogaviota	CCCP-47331 12-29+ 14-29+ CU-T1429 [+ Cuba]
70 07		(Cuban Air Force)	CCCP-47332 12-28+ 14-28 [+ Cuba] [w/o 03Feb83 Playa Baracoa, Cuba]
70 08		Russian Air Force	[Soviet] 28 blue
70 09	100	Tomsk Avia	CCCP-26518 RA-26518 UN-26518 RA-26518
70 10		Turbot Air Cargo	CCCP-26519 UR-26519 UR-CAI 4L-AIL
8 73 071 01	100	UTair Ekspress	CCCP-26520 RA-26520
71 02	ASLK	ex Lyotnye Tehnologii	CCCP-26521 RA-26521 [wfu by 1996 Moscow-Bykovo, Russia; l/n Feb09]
71 03		Sky Test	CCCP-26522 UN-26522 UP-AN602
8 73 071 04		Santa Cruz Imperial	CCCP-26523 RA-26523 EL-ALC
71 05		Turkmenistan Airlines	CCCP-26524 EZ-26524 [for sale early 08]
71 06		Museo Del Aire	CCCP-47412 CU-T1453? T-53+ [+ considerd Angolan rather than Cuban serial] [preserved by Apr96 La Coronela, La Lisa, Havana, Cuba]
71 07			[nothing known]
71 08	100	Meridian	[Soviet] [unknown+] UR-MDA [+ Ukraine]
71 09		Russian Navy	29 blue [Soviet/Russia]
71 10		Russian Air Force	[Soviet] 03 red
72 01		Kazakhstan Border Guards	[Soviet] 02 white
8 73 072 02		Russian Air Force	[Soviet] RA-26081(2)^ 07?+ [report as possibly 81 no colour reported & then later possibly 07 or 08 again no colour reported; ^ see c/n 11703 apparent clash of marks]
72 03			[nothing known]
72 04			[nothing known]
72 05		Russian Air Force	05 red
72 06		ex Magnitogorsk Air	CCCP-26525 RA-26525 [impounded Apr98 & offered for sale; fate/status unknown]
72 07		Solar Cargo	CCCP-47333 12-30+ CU-T1230(1) CU-T111 YV-600C CU-T111 CU-T1501 YV-1110C YV1402 [+ Cuba]
72 08	KPA	(Ukraeorukh)	CCCP-26526 UR-26526 [canx 20Jly10; l/n 12Mar12 Kiev-Zhulyany, Ukraine on probable overhaul]
72 09		ex Turkmenistan Airlines	CCCP-26527 EZ-26527 [not in Jan04 fleet list; for sale Jun08]
72 10	B-100	Trast Aero	CCCP-26528 RA-26528 TN-AGB [some reports give c/n as being 8 73 072 09]
73 01			[nothing known]

ANTONOV An-26

C/n	Model	Last known Owner/Operator	Identities/fates/comments (where appropriate)
73 02		Trast Aero	[Soviet] EX-094 [not on Nov09 register; fate/status unknown]
73 03		(Aero Caribbean)	CCCP-47334 12-31+ CU-T1231 CU-T112 [+ Cuba] [wfu by Apr98 Havana, Cuba; b/u Nov99]
73 04		Chinese Air Force	791
73 05		(Chinese Air Force)	792 [w/o 27Jun89 near Kaifeng, China]
73 06		Aerogaviota	CCCP-47335 12-32+ 14-32+ T-232^ CU-T1432 [+ Cuba;] [^ Angola]
73 07		Chinese Air Force	793
73 08		Chinese Air Force	794
73 09		Aerogaviota	CCCP-47336 12-33+ 14-33+ CU-T1433 [+ Cuba]
73 10		Chinese Air Force	795
74 01		Izhavia	CCCP-26529 RA-26529
74 02		Baikal Airlines	CCCP-26530 RA-26530
74 03		UkSATSE	CCCP-26531 UR-26531
74 04		Russian Navy	[Soviet] 06 blue
74 05			[nothing known]
74 06		(Cuban Air Force)	CCCP-47337 12-36+ 14-36+ CU-T1436 [+ Cuba] [w/o 23Mar90 Santiago del Cuba, Cuba]
74 07		unknown	CCCP-26644 RA-26644+ ST- [canx 24Aug98 to Sudan; fate/status unknown]
74 08		Coza Airways	CCCP-26645 RA-26645 ER-AWN 9Q-CML
74 09		Aero Condor	CCCP-26647 RA-26647 OB-1828-T OB-1828
74 10		IrAero	CCCP-26532 RA-26532
75 01		Kazakhstan Air Force	[Soviet] 06 red [possibly wfu by 25Jan11 Almaty, Kazakhstan]
75 02		Russian Air Force	CCCP-47413 RA-47413 03 gold
75 03		(Russian Air Force)	CCCP-47414 RA-47414 [canx 12Mar01 reportedly as destroyed]
75 04		Scorpion Air	CCCP-26177 RA-26177 LZ-NHC LZ-MNR TR-LIE+ [+ tie up not confirmed]
75 05		G R Avia	CCCP-26171 RA-26171 YA-KAL 3X-GFV+ [+ tie up not confirmed]
8 73 075 06		Burundai Avia	CCCP-26649 UN-26649
75 07		(Airline Cypress)	CCCP-26650 UR-26650 [canx 07Jly11 fate/status unknown]
75 08		ex Air Kharkiv	CCCP-26651 UR-26651 [canx 13Aug08; offered for sale 04Jly09]
75 09		Ukraine Air Force	[Soviet] 39 blue
75 10		Russian Air Force	[Soviet] 19 red+ 19 blue [+ Russia]
76 01		Ministry of Interior (MVD)	[Soviet] 10 yellow RF-56303
76 02		Russian Air Force	[Soviet] 42 red
76 03		Russian Air Force	[Soviet] (unknown) [tender issued 2009 for repair of outer wing]
76 04			[nothing known]
76 05			[nothing known]
76 06		Russian Air Force	[Soviet] 30 blue
76 07	KPA	Russian Air Force	[Soviet] 54 red RF-92954+ [+ still carrying 54 red]
76 08		(Ukraine Cargo Airways)	[Soviet] [unknown+] UR-UDF [+ Ukraine] [canx 01Oct08; fate unknown]
76 09		Gorizont	(unknown) RA-26250
76 10			[nothing known]
77 01		Aerogaviota	CCCP-47338 12-34+ 14-34+ CU-T1434 [+ Cuba]
77 02		Aerogaviota	CCCP-47339 12-35+ 14-35+ CU-T1435 [+ Cuba]
77 03		Russian Air Force	[Soviet] 28 blue
77 04		(Angolan Air Force)	CCCP-47340 12-37+ CU-T1237^ T-237 [+ Cuba] [^ see also An-24RV c/n 37308909] [w/o 27Apr88 shot down Tchahutete, Angola]
77 05	B	Cityline Hungary	[Soviet] 20 blue+ UR-26244 HA-TCN [+ Ukraine]
77 06		Russian Air Force	02 yellow [Soviet/Russia]
77 07		Russian Air Force	07 red [Soviet/Russia]
77 08			[nothing known]
9 73 077 09		(Sakha Avia)	CCCP-26652 RA-26652 [stored by Aug03 Yakutsk, Russia; b/u Sep11]
77 10		Yeniseiski Meridian	CCCP-26653 RA-26653
78 01		(Ural Airlines)	CCCP-26654 RA-26654 [canx 31Aug99; by 19Aug99 derelict Yekaterinburg-Koltsovo, Russia]
9 73 078 02	100	Angara 403 Airlines	CCCP-26655 RA-26655
78 03		Aerogaviota	CCCP-47324(2) 12-38+ CU-T1238 [+ Cuba]
78 04		Angolan Government	D2-EPN
78 05		Sky Wind?	CCCP-49272 45 blue+ 4K-AZ39 [+ Russia]
78 06			[nothing known]

ANTONOV An-26

C/n	Model	Last known Owner/Operator	Identities/fates/comments (where appropriate)
78 07		Turkmenistan Border Guards	[Soviet] 16 blue
78 08	B	ex Ukraine Cargo Airways	[Soviet] [unknown+] UR-UDS [+ Ukraine] [canx 08Oct10; stored Zaporizhe, Ukraine]
78 09		Marshland Aviation	CCCP-26646 RA-26646 ER-AFR EX-26780
9 73 078 10	100	TsSKB Progress AON	CCCP-26180 RA-26180
79 01		Trast Aero	[Soviet] EX-095 [not on Nov09 register; fate/status unknown]
9 73 079 02		(Kuban Airlines)	CCCP-26656 RA-26656 [canx 20Dec99; fate unknown]
79 03	B	(Sakha Avia)	CCCP-26657 RA-26657 [canx 23May97; fate unknown]
79 04		Tajikistan Airlines	CCCP-26658 EY-26658 26658 EY-26658
9 73 079 05		Kirov Air	CCCP-26664 RA-26664 [has used UN codes UNO-962 & UN967]
79 06			[nothing known]
79 07		Aerogaviota	CCCP-47325(2) 12-39+ T-239^ CU-T1239 [+ Cuba] [^ Angola]
79 08			[nothing known]
79 09		BULOG	[Soviet] [Georgian Air Force?] 4L-UCK
79 10		State Aviation Museum	[Soviet] 22 red+ [+ Ukraine] [preserved by Jun06 Kiev, Ukraine; l/n 05Aug08]
80 01			[nothing known]
9 73 080 02		Compangie Afrique d'Aviation	CCCP-26038(2) RA-26038 9Q-CJB
80 03		Russian Air Force	[Soviet] 17 blue+ RF-36070 [+ Russia; also wears 17 blue]
80 04		Skylink	CCCP-26165(1) RA-26246 ER-AWW ER-AUW
80 05		Russian Air Force	(unknown) RA-26696
80 06		Aviaobshchemash	CCCP-26182 RA-26182
80 07	B	(Solenta Aviation/DHL)	CCCP-26659 UR-26659 LZ-CBA? ER-AFF(1) LZ-CBA TR-LII+ [+ c/n tie up not confirmed; w/o 03Jun11 near Libreville, Gabon]
9 73 080 08	100	Yakutia	CCCP-26660 RA-26660
80 09		ex GosNII GA	CCCP-26661 RA-26661+ S9- [+ canx 21Jan97 to Sao Tome; fate/status unknown]
80 10		Ukraine Air Force	[Soviet] 83 blue
9 73 081 01	100	UTair Cargo	CCCP-26662 RA-26662
81 02			[nothing known]
81 03		(Kuban Airlines)	CCCP-26663 RA-26663 [canx 08Sep99; fate unknown]
81 04		Russian Air Force	[Soviet] 10 red [by 12Aug12 stored Ekaterinberg-Koltsovo, Russia]
81 05		Russian Air Force	[Soviet] 43 red
81 06		Russian Air Force	[Soviet] 40 yellow
81 07		(Yaik)	CCCP-26162 [unknown+] RA-26248 [canx 08Apr97; fate unknown]
9 73 081 08		IrAero	CCCP-26665 RA-26665
81 09		ex Sudan Air Force	CCCP-26666 26666 UR-26666 7711 [reported shot down in 1997; hulk reported 20Jly09 Gogrial, Sudan where c/n was checked]
81 10		unknown	CCCP-26667 EW-26667 SP-FPM [canx 31Jan97; by Jun01 stored Minsk-Loshitsa, Belarus; l/n Jun08]
9 73 082 01	100	Alrosa	CCCP-26668 RA-26668
82 02	100	Mirney AE	CCCP-26669 RA-26669
82 03			[nothing known]
82 04			[nothing known]
82 05	B	Aerolinea del Caribe	CCCP-26670 UR-26670 UR-BWY ER-AZR HA-TCY EK-26205 HK-4728
82 06		Ukraine Air Force	[Soviet] 02 blue+ 05 yellow [+ Ukraine]
82 07			[nothing known]
82 08		Ministry of Interior (MVD)	[Soviet] 95 red RF-56308
82 09			[nothing known]
82 10		Yeniseiski Meridian	CCCP-26671 RA-26671
83 01			[nothing known]
83 02	RT	Ukraine Air Force	[Soviet] 20+ [+ colour unknown]
9 73 083 03		South Airlines	CCCP-26185 (unknown) EX-106 3X-GEL 3X-GFH EK-26878
83 04	100	Khabarovsk Avia	CCCP-26174 RA-26174
83 05		Madagascar Air Force	CCCP-26672 RA-26672 5R-MUP "UP/8305"+ [+ painted as just "UP" and "8305"]
83 06		Russian Air Force?	[could possibly be RF-47323; see unknown aircraft below]
83 07		Ministry of Interior (MVD)	[Soviet] 25 red RF-56304
83 08			[nothing known]
83 09		Russian Air Force	03 yellow
83 10	GR	ROSTO?	[Soviet] [unknown+] RF-00714 [+ Russian Air Force] [offered for sale Mar04; fate/status unknown]

ANTONOV An-26

C/n	Model	Last known Owner/Operator	Identities/fates/comments (where appropriate)
84 01		Transportes Aereos Cielos Andinos	[Soviet] 53 yellow+ OB-1893-T OB-1893-P [+ Russia]
84 02		Ukraine Navy	[Soviet] 82 blue+ 10 yellow [+ Ukraine]
84 03			[nothing known]
84 04			[nothing known]
84 05		Russian Navy?	[Soviet] 46 blue+ 05 blue [+ Russia]
84 06		Russian Air Force	[Soviet] 02 blue
84 07		Russian Air Force	[Soviet] 30 blue RF-46878 [also wears code 30 blue]
9 73 084 08	ALSK	Spetsavia	CCCP-26673 RA-26673
84 09			[nothing known]
84 10		Russian Air Force	[Soviet] 09 red
85 01		Ukraine Air Force	[Soviet] 01 blue [has used callsign UR-71500]
85 02			[nothing known]
85 03		Kazakhstan Air Force	[Soviet] 04 red
85 04			[nothing known]
85 05			[nothing known]
85 06		ex Yedinaya-Sakha	CCCP-26674 RA-26674 [noted Jun09 Chersky, Russia stored with many parts missing]
85 07			[nothing known]
85 08			[nothing known]
85 09		Ukraine Air Force	[Soviet] 02 yellow
85 10		ex Russian Air Force	CCCP-46007 RA-46007 [reported wfu by 17Aug09 Chkalovsky, Russia]
86 01	ALSK	GosNII GA	CCCP-26675 UN-26675 UP-AN609 RA-26675
86 02	B	Middlanditracep	CCCP-26676 UR-26676 9Q-CVR 9Q-COR+ [+ report as such doubtful]
86 03		Kirov Air	CCCP-26677 RA-26677
86 04		Russian Air Force	[Soviet] 02 red+ 12 red [+ either Soviet or Russia or both]
86 05			[nothing known]
86 06			[nothing known]
86 07		ex Tyumen Avia Trans	CCCP-26678 RA-26678+ S9- [canx 11Oct99 to Sao Tome; fate/status unknown]
9 73 086 08		Air Sirin	CCCP-26679 RA-26679 ER-AFS UR-AFS 4L-AFS 3X-GHA
86 09		ex Dniproavia	CCCP-26680 UR-26680 [not in 1998 fleet list; fate unknown]
86 10		Santa Cruz Imperial	CCCP-26681 RA-26681 EL-AHO
87 01			[nothing known]
87 02		Russian Air Force	[Soviet] 08 red
87 03			[nothing known]
87 04		Russian Air Force	56 blue [Soviet/Russia]
87 05		Ministry of Interior (MVD)	[Soviet] 55 yellow RF-56305
9 73 87 06	100	Oleg N Rudkin	CCCP-26682 RA-26682
87 07	100	Izhavia	CCCP-26683 RA-26683
87 08		(Kuban Airlines)	CCCP-26684 RA-26684 [canx 20Oct97; fate unknown]
87 09			[nothing known]
87 10			[nothing known]
88 01		(Russian Air Force)	11 red [Soviet/Russia] [hulk by May99 Stupino, Russia]
88 02			[nothing known]
88 03		Russian Air Force	[Soviet] 45 red
88 04			[nothing known]
88 05		(Aeroflot/Yakutsk)	CCCP-26685(1) [w/o 19Jly89 near Kiper Cope, USSR; canx 19Apr90]
88 06		(Aeroflot/Belarus)	CCCP-26686(1) [w/o 14Apr83 Minsk-Lotshita, Belarus, USSR; derelict hulk l/n May08]
88 07		(El Sam Airlift/Malift Air)	[Soviet] [Russia] 9Q-CES 9Q-COS [w/o 04Oct07 Kinshasa, Democratic Republic of Congo]
88 08		(Russian Navy)	CCCP-26697 RA-26697 [canx unknown date; fate/status unknown; l/n 14Aug05 Moscow-Ostafyevo, Russia]
88 09			[nothing known]
88 10		(Russian Air Force)	[Soviet] 31 black [b/u by 2006 Ivanovo-Severny, Russia]
89 01		Russian Air Force	CCCP-46454 RA-46454
89 02	100	Oleg N Rudkin	CCCP-26687 RA-26687
89 03		Chinese Air Force	796
89 04		Russian Air Force	[Soviet] 07 red
89 05			[nothing known]
89 06		Russian Air Force	11 red [Soviet/Russia]
89 07		FSB/Border Guards	[Soviet] 12 red RF-26257
89 08		Chinese Air Force	797

ANTONOV An-26

C/n	Model	Last known Owner/Operator	Identities/fates/comments (where appropriate)
89 09		Chinese Air Force	798
89 10		FSB/Border Guards	[Soviet] RF-26271
90 01			[nothing known]
90 02			[nothing known]
90 03			[nothing known]
9 73 090 04	100	ex Tomsk Air	CCCP-26688 RA-26688 [wfu by 03Mar12 Tomsk, Russia]
90 05	B	(Galaxie)	CCCP-26689 UR-26689 ER-AZT [w/o 05Sep05 Isiro, Democratic Republic of Congo; canx 07Oct05]
90 06		(Kuban Airlines)	CCCP-26690 RA-26690 [canx 17Jly97; fate unknown]
90 07		Chinese Air Force	799
90 08		Chinese Air Force	800
90 09		FSB/Border Guards	[Soviet] RF-26258
90 10		Chinese Air Force	801
91 01			[nothing known]
91 02		Russian Air Force	[Soviet] 01 red
91 03		Chinese Air Force	802
91 04		(SRX Transcontinental)	CCCP-93914 UK-93914 UK-26002 N8038Y [stored since 2005 Opa-locka, FL, USA; l/n Feb09; canx 12Oct11 as wfu; probably b/u]
91 05		ex Atran	CCCP-93916 RA-93916 [wfu by Aug00 Moscow-Myachkovo, Russia; l/n Mar07]
91 06			[nothing known]
91 07		Strat. Rocket Forces	(unknown) RF-90373+ [+ tie up not fully confirmed]
91 08		Russian Air Force	04 yellow [Soviet/Russia]
91 09	100	Petropavlovsk Kamchatsky Air	[unknown+] RA-26251 [+ Soviet/Russia]
91 10		Hungarian Air Force	[Soviet] 32+ 110 [+ Russia; colour unknown]
92 01		(Russian Navy)	[Soviet] (unknown) [offered for sale Feb09 as scrap]
92 02		Russian Air Force	[Soviet] 04 red
92 03			[nothing known]
92 04			[nothing known]
0 73 092 05	B	Nizhny-Novgorod Research Institute	CCCP-26691 RA-26691
92 06			[nothing known]
0 73 092 07		Russian Navy	[Soviet] 14 blue
92 08			[nothing known]
92 09		Russian Navy	[Soviet] 47 blue
92 10		Russian Air Force	[Soviet] 06 red
93 01		Russian Air Force	10 red [Soviet/Russia]
93 02		Russian Air Force	12 red [Soviet/Russia]
93 03		Russian Air Force	15 red [Soviet/Russia]
93 04			[nothing known]
93 05		Russian Air Force	[Soviet] 22 blue
93 06			[nothing known]
93 07		Russian Air Force	[Soviet] 28 blue RF-93999
93 08		Russian Air Force	[Soviet] 02 red
93 09		Russian Air Force	[Soviet] 26 red
93 10			[nothing known]
94 01		Russian Air Force	04 blue+ 04 yellow [+ Soviet/Russia]
94 02	KPA	Russian Air Force	[Soviet] 59 red
94 03			[nothing known]
94 04		Avia-Lizing	[Soviet] [unknown+] [+ sold 20Oct06 by Russian Air Force]
94 05			[nothing known]
94 06			[nothing known]
94 07		Russian Air Force	[Soviet] 03 red
94 08		Russian Air Force	[Soviet] (unknown) [offered for sale Dec07; fate/status unknown]
0 73 094 09	B-100	IrAero	CCCP-26692 RA-26692
94 10		(Soviet Air Force)	05 yellow [fate/status unknown]
95 01			[nothing known]
95 02		Russian Air Force	[Soviet] 044 black
95 03		Yemen Air Force	611 [coded 7O-ABH see also c/n 9507]
0 73 095 04	B	unknown	CCCP-26693 RA-26693 4K-AZ57 EX-091 S9-DBS
95 05		Yemen Air Force	616 [coded 7O-ABM]
95 06		(Soviet Air Force)	101 red [w/o 03May85 Zolochev, USSR mid-air collision with Tu134A CCCP-65856 at which time was using call-sign CCCP-26492]

ANTONOV An-26

C/n	Model	Last known Owner/Operator	Identities/fates/comments (where appropriate)
95 07		(Yemen Air Force)	613 [coded 7O-ABH see also c/n 9503;] [reported wfu by Mar05 Sana'a, Republic of Yemen]
95 08		Ukraine Border Guards	[Soviet] 18 blue
95 09		Yemen Air Force	614+ UR-49262 ST-AOZ 614 [+ South Yemen]
95 10		Aerolinea del Caribe	(unknown) UR-KRB ER-AZF HA-TCX EK-26510 HK-4730
96 01		Russian Air Force	[Soviet] 03 blue+ 01 blue RF-36068^ [+ Russia; ^ still with code 01 blue]
96 02		Russian Air Force	[Soviet] 55 red
96 03			[nothing known]
0 73 096 04		Dalavia	CCCP-26000 RA-26000 [full c/n quoted as 07309604]
96 05		ex Russian Air Force	[Soviet] 20 yellow [wfu by early 2011 Irkutsk, Russia]
96 06			[nothing known]
96 07		ex Russian Air Force	[Soviet] 02 red [wfu by 28Aug07 Balashov Technical School, Russia]
96 08		RAF Avia	(unknown) RA-26242 UR- YL-RAI+ [+ also reported as being c/n 10103]
96 09			[nothing known]
96 10			[nothing known]
97 01		FSB/Border Guards	[Soviet] 50 blue RA-26276 [see also RA-26276P with unknown c/n]
97 02			[nothing known]
0 73 097 03		FSB/Border Guards	55 blue 55 red RF-26277
97 04		Kazakhstan Air Force	[Soviet] 03 red
0 73 097 05		Amuravia	CCCP-26001 RA-26001
97 06		V M Rotar	CCCP-26002 RA-26002
97 07		(Yeniseiski Meridian)	CCCP-26003 RA-26003 [canx unknown date; wfu by Jun01 Krasnoyarsk-Cheremshaka, Russia; l/n Jun02]
97 08		Kazakhstan Air Force	[Soviet] 85 red+ 01 red [+ Kazakhstan]
97 09		(Elmagal Aviation)	[Soviet] UR-49260 RA-49260 TC-ACS ST-MGL [w/o 27Feb02 Heglig, Sudan]
97 10		Ukraine Air Force	[Soviet] 19 blue
98 01			[nothing known]
98 02		(Russian Air Force)	CCCP-47415 RA-47415 [DBR mid-90s Belgorod, Russia; canx 12Mar01 as destroyed]
98 03			[nothing known]
98 04			[nothing known]
98 05		(Air West)	CCCP-79168 UR-79168 ST-APO [canx by Jan07; wfu by Apr07 Wau, Sudan; l/n10Apr07]
98 06		FSB/Border Guards	[Soviet] RF-26283
98 07	100	Air Urga	CCCP-26004 UR-26004 UR-ELR [used code UNO-967 when operated by UN]
98 08		FSB/Border Guards	[Soviet] (unknown)
98 09		Avialesookhrana	CCCP-26005 RA-26005
1 73 098 10		Solar Cargo	CCCP-26006 RA-26006 UN-26006 YV-1101CP YV-1134C YV1403
99 01		(Aeroflot/Tajikistan)	CCCP-26007(1) [w/o 06Mar83 56km from Almaty, Kazakhstan, USSR; canx 22May87]
0 73 099 02	B-100	Evenkiya	CCCP-26008 RA-26008
99 03		RAF Avia/Air Bright	[Soviet] CCCP-79169 YL-RAC
99 04		(Aeroflot/Tyumen)	CCCP-26009(1) [w/o 27Jly84 Krasnoseelskii, USSR; canx 19Oct84]
99 05		Sudanese Air Force	[military?] ST-AQO 7777
99 06	B	UT Air Cargo	CCCP-26010 RA-26010
99 07		ex Vietnam Air Force	VN-B906 [stored by Mar96 Saigon, Vietnam; l/n Mar08]
99 08	B	IrAero	CCCP-26011 RA-26011
99 09			[nothing known]
99 10		Russian Air Force	21 yellow [Soviet/Russia]
100 01		Soviet Air Force	22 yellow [fate/status unknown]
100 02			[nothing known]
100 03		Russian Air Force	[Soviet] 57 yellow 59 red + RF-92950+ [+ wears both marks; but not confirmed for this 59 red]
100 04		Russian Air Force	31 red 51+ [+ colour unknown]
100 05			[nothing known]
100 06		ex Vietnam Air Force	CCCP-26252?+ VN-B906 ["26252" noted on fuselage;] [stored by Mar96 Saigon, Vietnam; l/n Mar08]
100 07	B	(Tyumen Avia Trans)	CCCP-26012 UR-26012 ST-AOF RA-26012 [w/o 09Nov02 Antalya, Turkey]

ANTONOV An-26

C/n	Model	Last known Owner/Operator	Identities/fates/comments (where appropriate)
100 08			[nothing known]
100 09	B	Zapolyare	CCCP-26013 RA-26013
100 10		unknown	(unknown) RA-46261+ UR- [canx to Ukraine unknown date; fate/status unknown]
101 01		Lithuanian Air Force	CCCP-26014 LY-AAJ 04 yellow+ 04 blue [+ Lithuania]
101 02		Russian Air Force	26 blue+ 03 red [+ Soviet/Russia]
101 03	B	Aero-Charter	CCCP-26015 UR-26015 ER-AFF(2) UR-DWD [see c/n 9608]
101 04			[nothing known]
101 05	B	GS Corporation	CCCP-26016 UR-26016
101 06			[nothing known]
101 07		Russian Air Force	[Soviet] 52+ [+ colour unknown]
101 08			[nothing known]
101 09	B	Avialeasing	CCCP-26017 RA-26017 UR-GLS
101 10			[nothing known]
102 01	B	(Chita Avia)	CCCP-26018 RA-26018 [canx 09Apr98; fate unknown]
102 02		Kazakhstan Air Force	[Soviet] 05 red
102 03	B-100	Azza Air Transport	CCCP-26019 RA-26019 EX-003 ST-JAC
102 04		Chinese Air Force	803+ B-803 803 [+ China]
102 05	B	(Ababeel Aviation)	CCCP-26020 UN-26020 ST-ARO [w/o 07Jun04 Geneina, Sudan; hulk l/n Jly07]
102 06		Chinese Air Force	804
102 07		Chinese Air Force	805
102 08	B	Madagascar Government	CCCP-26021 RA-26021 5R-MVP
102 09		Ukraine Air Force	[Soviet] 21 blue
102 10		Russian Strategic Rocket Force	[Soviet] 43 red RF-90321
103 01			[nothing known]
103 02	B	(Norilsk Avia)	CCCP-26022 RA-26022 [wfu by 20May05 Khatanga, Russia; l/n 2006]
103 03		Chinese Air Force	806
103 04	B	ex Valan	CCCP-26023 RA-26023 ER-AEK+ 9XR- [+ canx 05mar02 to Rwanda; fate/status unknown]
103 05		Russian Air Force	[Soviet] 01 red
103 06	B-100	Oleg N Rudkin	CCCP-26024 RA-26024
103 07		Chinese Air Force	807
103 08	B	Ulyanovsk Higher Flying School	CCCP-26025 26025 RA-26025
103 09		China Aviation Museum	808 [preserved by 02Nov10 Changping, China]
103 10	B-100	Dove Air	CCCP-26026 YL-LDA UN-26026 ST-HIS
104 01			[nothing known]
104 02		Chinese Air Force	809
104 03		Ukraine Air Force	[Soviet] 56 yellow
104 04		Sudanese Air Force	371+ DDR-SBE 371+ 52+01^ RA-49264 RA-26240 ST-ZZZ(2) 7706 [+ East Germany; ^ Germany]
0 73 104 05		Air Kasai	372+ DDR-SBG 372+ 52+02^ RA-49265 RA-26235 9Q-CFM
104 06	B	Avialeasing	CCCP-26027 RA-26027 S9-BOW UK-26003
104 07	T	(unknown)	374+ DDR-SBF 374+ 52+03^ RA-49266 RA-26236 ST-ZZZ(1) [shot down & w/o 07Aug06 El Fasher, Sudan; hulk l/n 16Aug08]
104 08	B	(Prestavia)	CCCP-26028 26028 RA-26028 [w/o 02Sep98 in forced landing Malanje province, Angola; probably due to enemy fire]
104 09	T	Technikmuseum Speyer	375+ (DDR-SBN) 52+04^ [+ East Germany; ^ Germany] [preserved by May93 Speyer, Germany; l/n Jan08]
104 10	B	ex Filair/RTL	CCCP-26029 UR-26029 9Q-CEF [derelict by 2004 unknown location in Democratic Republic of Congo]
105 01	B	Polar Airlines	CCCP-26030 RA-26030
105 02			[nothing known]
105 03	B	(Exin Air/DHL)	CCCP-26031 RA-26031 SP-FDO [w/o 18Mar10 in forced landing on frozen Lake Ulemiste, near Tallinn airport, Estonia; canx 26Apr10]
105 04		Russian Air Force	[Soviet] 04 black
105 05	B	Russian Navy	[Soviet] 50 red 53 blue
105 06		Russian Air Force	58 yellow+ 58 red+ RF-92949 [also carries 58 red; +Soviet/Russia]
105 07			[nothing known]
105 08	B	RAF Avia	CCCP-26032 YL-RAB(2)

ANTONOV An-26

C/n	Model	Last known Owner/Operator	Identities/fates/comments (where appropriate)
105 09	T	Schwabisches Bauern Museum	376+ DDR-SBD 376+ 52+05^ [+ East Germany; ^ Germany] [derlict by 2004 unknown location in Democratic Republic of Congo]
105 10		unknown	CCCP-26033 UN-26033 UR-26033
106 01			[nothing known]
106 02	B	(Aerokuznetsk)	CCCP-26034 [canx 17May98; b/u by Dec99]
106 03			[nothing known]
106 04	B	(Tajikistan Airlines)	CCCP-26035 26035+ [+ Tajikistan] [w/o en-route 17Jun93 near Choporti, Georgia]
106 05	B	Air Kasai	364+ DDR-SBC 364+ 52+06^ RA-49267 RA-26237 9Q-CFP [+ East Germany; ^ Germany]
106 06	B	ex Valan	CCCP-26036 EX-26036 ER-AZO EX-26001
106 07		unknown	367+ DDR-SBA 367+ DDR-SBA 367+ 52+07^ RA-49268 RA-26238 YV-965CP? YV1275
106 08	B	(Sakha Avia)	CCCP-26037 RA-26037 [wfu by Aug03 Yakutsk, Russia; l/n Jly04]
106 09		Test Flight Aerographical Center	CCCP-26639 RA-26639 26639
1 73 106 10		Air Sirin	CCCP-93917 RA-93917 ER-AUA UR-AUA 4L-AFL
107 01	B	(Aeroflot/East Siberia)	CCCP-26038(1) [w/o 02Nov89 Nyurba, USSR; canx 25Apr90]
107 02	B-100	Tomsk Air	CCCP-26039 RA-26039
1 73 107 03	B	Angara 403 Airlines	CCCP-26040 RA-26040
107 04	B-100	Star Peru	CCCP-93927 CCCP-26216(2) UR-26216 OB-1772-P
107 05		(Russian Air Force)	(unknown) [destroyed Kabul, Afghanistan; by Feb06 tail section only Pol-e-Charki scrapyard, Kabul]
107 06	T	Flugausstellung Junior Museum	368+ DDR-SBB 368+ DDR-SBB 368+ 50+08^ [+ East Germany; ^ Germany] [preserved 11May93 Hermeskeil, Germany; l/n Apr09]
107 07	B	Pskov Avia	CCCP-26041 RA-26041
107 08			[nothing known]
107 09			[nothing known]
107 10	B	(Ukraine Flight State Academy)	CCCP-26042 UR-26042 [canx 01Oct08; l/n 31Oct08 Kirovograd, Ukraine]
108 01		Russian Air Force	[Soviet] 11 blue+ RF-36075 [+ Russia]
108 02	B	(Dalavia)	CCCP-26043 RA-26043 [canx 20Nov99; fate unknown]
108 03	B-100	(SELVA)	CCCP-26044 RA-26044 3X-GDP(1) RA-26044 LZ-NHD HK-4389X HK-4389 [w/o 22Aug07 Pasto, Colombia]
108 04		Norilsk Avia	CCCP-26045 RA-26045
108 05		Mozambique Air Force	030 [stored by 25May03 Maputo, Mozambique; l/n 25Sep08]
108 06		Mozambique Air Force	032 [tie-up not confirmed]
108 07	B	ex Air Moldova	CCCP-26046 ER-26046 [stored by Apr09 Chisinau, Moldova]
108 08			[nothing known]
108 09			[nothing known]
108 10	B	ex Latavio	CCCP-26047 YL-LDB [impounded 22Dec95 Mumbai, India; b/u by Jly; hulk to GIA with Camellia Institute, Kolkata, India]
109 01	B	Amur Aviakompania	CCCP-26048 RA-26048
109 02		(Ukraine Flight State Academy)	CCCP-26049 UR-26049 [w/o 04Apr95 Palana, Russia]
109 03		unknown	(unknown) RA-26230 9Q-CZK
109 04			[nothing known]
109 05	B	Air Amenia	CCCP-26050 RA-26050 ER-AFE EK-26050
109 06	B	IrAero	CCCP-26051 RA-26051
109 07	B	Syrianair/Government	YK-ANG
109 08	B	Bentiu Air Transport	CCCP-26052 RA-26052 UR-26052 ST-NDC
1 73 109 09	B	ex IrAero	CCCP-26053 RA-26053 [w/o 27Dec02 Ust'-Kuiga, Russia; canx 20Oct03; wreck l/n Aug09]
109 10	B	(Gaesa Air Cargo)	CCCP-26054 UN-26054 3C-CMN [derelict by Nov07 Malabo, Equatorial Guinea; l/n Jun08]
110 01		ex Turkmenistan Airlines	CCCP-26055 EZ-26055 [not in Nov99 fleet list; for sale Jun08]
110 02		FSB/Border Guards	[Soviet] (unknown) RF-26281
110 03			[nothing known]
110 04			[nothing known]
110 05	B	Kras Avia	CCCP-26056 RA-26056
110 06			[nothing known]
110 07			[nothing known]
110 08	B	El Magal Aviation Services	CCCP-26057 RA-26057 EX-26057 ST-AQD
110 09			[nothing known]

ANTONOV An-26

C/n	Model	Last known Owner/Operator	Identities/fates/comments (where appropriate)
110 10			[nothing known]
111 01	B	Dalavia	CCCP-26058 RA-26058
111 02		Turbot Air Cargo	(unknown) 26243 UR-26243
111 03			[nothing known]
111 04	B	Mosphil Aero Inc	CCCP-26059 ER-26059 UR-26059 ER-26059 RP-C7207
111 05			[nothing known]
111 06			[nothing known]
1 73 111 07	B	(World Aero Airways)	CCCP-26060 RA-26060 LY-APC EX-26060 EK-26060 [w/o 04May05 Lubutu, Democratic Republic of Congo]
111 08	B-100	Polar Airlines	CCCP-26061 RA-26061
111 09			[nothing known]
1 73 111 10	B	IrAero	CCCP-26062 RA-26062 [stored by 04Jly04 Irkutsk, Russia; l/n 28Aug07]
112 01		Vietnam Air Force	267
112 02			[nothing known]
1 73 112 03	B	Lithuanian Air Force	CCCP-26063 LY-AAK 05 blue
112 04			[nothing known]
112 05			[nothing known]
1 73 112 06	B	RAF Avia	CCCP-26064 RA-26064 YL-RAA(2)
112 07	B	Sky Way Air	CCCP-26065 RA-26065 EX-016
1 73 112 08		FSB/Border Guards	(unknown) RA-26168 RF-26280+ [tie up not fully confirmed]
112 09	ASLK	Kirov Avia	CCCP-26088 RA-26088
112 10		Aerogaviota	CU-T1240
113 01		Aerogaviota	CU-T1241 "12-41"+ CU-T1241 [painted as such for use in film]
113 02	B	(Polar Airlines)	CCCP-26066 RA-26066 [wfu by Jun01 Krasnoyarsk-Cheremshanka, Russia; canx 15Dec03]
113 03		Aerogaviota	12-53 CU-T1428
113 04		ex Cuban Air Force	12-54 CU-T1254 [damaged & abandoned Dec84 Pearls Harbour, Grenada; l/n Jan06 derelict]
113 05	B	Exin Air/DHL	CCCP-26067 RA-26067 SP-FDR
113 06			[nothing known]
113 07			[nothing known]
113 08	B-100	(Aeriantur-M)	CCCP-26068 ER-26068 [w/o 07Jan07 near Balad AFB, Iraq]
113 09			[nothing known]
113 10			[nothing known]
114 01	B	TCS	CCCP-26069 RA-26069 UR-26069 UR-CBJ
114 02	M	Luftwaffen Museum	369+ (DDR-SBL) 369+ 52+09^ [+ East Germany; ^ Germany] [preserved by 20Apr94 Gatow, Berlin, Germany; l/n 31Mar08]
114 03		Angolan Government	D2-MAB [call sign T-216]
114 04	B	ATI Airlines	CCCP-26070 RA-26070 26070 UR-26070 ER-AWE 4K-AZ20
114 05			[nothing known]
114 06	B	Syrianair/Government	YK-ANH
114 07	B	(Aerokuznetsk)	CCCP-26071 RA-26071 [canx 17Jly98; b/u before Dec99]
114 08			[nothing known]
114 09	B-100	Skylink	CCCP-26072 RA-26072 UR-26072 ER-AVA
1 73 114 10	B-100	unknown	CCCP-26073 RA-26073 UR-26073
115 01			[nothing known]
115 02			[nothing known]
115 03	B	Lithuanian Air Force	CCCP-26074 LY-AAL 03 blue
115 04		Ministry of Interior (MVD)	[Soviet] RF-56310+ [+ tie up not fully confirmed; c/n incorrectly quoted as 1504 in document]
115 05		Kazakhstan Government	CCCP-26167 UN-26167
1 73 115 06	B-100	Transportes Aereoa Ciejos Andinos	CCCP-26090 RA-26090 9Q-CMV EX-063(1) OB-1876-T
115 07			[nothing known]
115 08	B	Sky Way Air	CCCP-26075 UN-26075 EX-126
115 09			[nothing known]
115 10			[nothing known]
116 01	B	unknown	CCCP-26076 RA-26076+ EX- [+canx 16Jly99 to Kyrgyzstan; fate/status unknown]
116 02			[nothing known]
116 03	B	AviaExpress	CCCP-26077 RA-26077 UR-26077
116 04		(Russian Air Force)	[Soviet] (unknown) [offered for sale 31Dec07 as scrap]
116 05		Russian Air Force	[Soviet] 54 red 50 red
116 06	B	(Aerokuznetsk)	CCCP-26078 RA-26078 [canx 17Jly98; b/u before Dec99]

ANTONOV An-26

C/n	Model	Last known Owner/Operator	Identities/fates/comments (where appropriate)
116 07	B	Ukraine Air Force	[Soviet] 22 blue
116 08	B	ex Belavia	CCCP-26079 EW-26079 [wfu by 1998; stored by Nov99 Minsk-Loshitsa, Belarus; l/n Jun08]
116 09	B	(Guinee Air Service)	CCCP-26080 UN-26080 [w/o 26Jan95 Sambailo, Guinea]
116 10			[nothing known]
117 01			[nothing known]
117 02	B	(Afghan National Army Air Corps)	250 [wfu 24Dec10 fate/status unknown]
117 03	B-100	Kostrama Airlines	CCCP-26081 RA-26081(1) UR-BXU RA-26081(1) [see c/n 8 73 072 202, apparent clash of marks]
117 04			[nothing known]
117 05	B-100	Amur Aviakompania	CCCP-26082 RA-26082 ER-AFL EK-26443 ER-AFL EK-26443 RA-26082
117 06			[nothing known]
117 07	B	(Barnaul GAP)	CCCP-26083 RA-26083 [canx 29Jly97; fate unknown]
117 08			[nothing known]
117 09			[nothing known]
117 10			[nothing known]
118 01			[nothing known]
118 02	B	Kam Air	CCCP-06199 RA-06199 EK-26199 YA-KMB
118 03	B	(MAP Moscow OAO)	CCCP-88288 [w/o 07Dec86 Moscow-Bykovo, USSR; canx 26Feb87]
118 04	B	UTAir Cargo	CCCP-88289 88289 RA-88289
118 05		(Sudanese Air Force)	8201+ 5A-DOX 7755//ST-ALU^ [+ Libya] [^ dual marks] [canx before Jan07; derelict by 15Apr07 Raga, Sudan]
118 06	B	(Aeroflot/Cenral Region?)	CCCP-26084 RA-26084 [w/o 16Mar95 near Kossora, Russia]
118 07	B	Bentiu Air Transport	CCCP-08827 RA-08827 ST-SRA
118 08		Libyan Air Force	8202 [tie-up not confirmed]
118 09		Libyan Air Cargo	8203+ 5A-DOW [+ Libya]
118 10	B	(Aeroflot/Belarus)	CCCP-26095 [w/o 06Feb86 Saransk, USSR; canx 27Mar86]
119 01	B	Rainbow Air	CCCP-26096 RA-26096 EX-024
119 02	B	(Tiramavia)	CCCP-26097 UR-26097 ER-AFP [canx 17Mar99; fate unknown]
119 03	B	(Exin Air)	CCCP-26098 RA-26098 SP-FDP [w/o 23Aug10 Tallinn, Estonia; canx 24Mar11]
119 04			[nothing known]
119 05	B-100	Chukotavia	CCCP-26099 RA-26099
119 06			[nothing known]
119 07	B	Badr	CCCP-26100 RA-26100 ST-SAL
119 08	B	Kirov Avia	CCCP-26101 RA-26101
119 09	100	UTair Cargo	CCCP-26102 RA-26102
119 10			[nothing known]
120 01	B	Ministry of Defence	CCCP-26103 RA-26103 UR-26103 ER-AES 9Q-CKT
2 73 120 02	BRL	Arkika	CCCP-26104 RA-26104
120 03	B-100	IrAero	CCCP-26105 RA-26105
120 04	B	(Yeniseiski Meridian)	CCCP-26106 RA-26106 [wfu by 03Jun01Krasnoyarsk-Cheremshanka, Russia; canx 15Dec03]
120 05			[nothing known]
120 06			[nothing known]
120 07	B	Russian Government/FSB?	CCCP-26166 RA-26166 RF-26259
120 08	B	Exin Air	CCCP-26107 RA-26107 LY-LVR RA-26107 SP-EKA
120 09	B	(ACA-Ancargo Air)	CCCP-26108 UR-26108 ER-AFD D2-FDI [w/o en-route 31Oct00 near Mona Quimbundo, Angola; possible action by rebels]
120 10	B	Aviavilsa	CCCP-26109 YL-LDC UR-BXF LY-APN
121 01			[nothing known]
121 02	B	Exin Air	CCCP-26110 RA-26110 SP-FDT
121 03			[nothing known]
121 04			[nothing known]
121 05		Vietnam Air Force	282
121 06			[nothing known]
121 07	B	Kazakhstan Air Force	[Soviet] 02 red
121 08	B	Air Urga/UN	CCCP-26111 UR-26111 UR-ELE
121 09	B	(Belavia)	CCCP-26112 EW-26112 [stored by 18May05 Minsk-Lotshita, Belarus; l/n Oct08 wfu; not noted mid 2011 possibly b/u]
121 10	B-100	Yamal	CCCP-26113 UR-26113 UR-BXV RA-26113
122 01	B	Aviavilsa	CCCP-26114 RA-26114 LY-APK RA-TCV

ANTONOV An-26

C/n	Model	Last known Owner/Operator	Identities/fates/comments (where appropriate)
122 02	RT	Russian Air Force	[Soviet] 09 blue
122 03	B-100	SELVA	CCCP-26089 RA-26089 UR-26089 RA-26089 3X-GFB HK-4706
122 04	B-100	Air Urga/UN	CCCP-26115 UR-26115 UR-ELF
2 73 122 05	B	Exin Air	CCCP-26116 RA-26116 SP-FDS
122 06	B	ex Chukotavia	CCCP-26117 RA-26117 [stored by Jun06 Anadyr-Ugolny, Russia; l/n 24Jly08]
122 07	B-100	Kras Avia	CCCP-26118 RA-26118
122 08	B	Kiev ARP 410 Airlines	CCCP-26119 RA-26119 UR-26119 UR-BWZ
122 09	RT	Russian Air Force	06 blue RF-36078+ [+ still carring code 06 blue]
122 10			[nothing known]
123 01		Libyan Air Cargo	8205+ 5A-DNV 5A-DOP [+ Libya; tie up not fully confirmed;] [wfu 31Oct07 Tripoli-Mitiga; l/n 07Oct09 without wings] [wfu 31Oct07 Tripoli-Mitiga by Oct07; l/n 07Oct09 without wings]
123 02	B	Pskovia	CCCP-26086 RA-26086 [has used UN codes UN962 & UNO961]
123 03		Libyan Air Force	8206+ C9-AUI 8206 [+ Libya]
123 04	B	(unknown)	CCCP-26120 RA-26120 TR-OVA [b/u 18/21Sep11 Sofia, Bulgaria]
123 05	B-100	Kras Avia	CCCP-26121 OB-1347 CCCP-26121 RA-26121 UR-BXT RA-26121
123 06		Libyan Air Cargo	8207+ 5A-DOA^ [+ Libya; ^ Sep11 still also carring 8207]
123 07		Libyan Air Cargo	8208+ 5A-DOB [+ Libya]
123 08		Libyan Air Cargo	8209+ 5A-DOC [+ Libya]
123 09		Libyan Air Force	8210
123 10	B-100	unknown	CCCP-26085 RA-26085 UR-BXP
2 73 124 01	B-100	Petropavlovsk Kamchatsky Air	CCCP-26122 RA-26122
124 02	B-100	SELVA	CCCP-26123 RA-26123 LZ-NHE HK-4388X HK-4388
124 03		Libyan Air Force	8211 [never reported; c/n not confirmed]
124 04		ex Aeronica	YN-BYW [derelict by Dec03 Managua, Nicaragua; l/n Mar08]
124 05		(Aeronica)	YN-BYX [w/o 16Apr90 unknown location]
124 06		Libyan Air Cargo	8212+ 5A-DOD [+ Libya]
124 07		Libyan Air Force	8213
124 08		Czech Air Force	2408+ [+ Czechoslovakia/Czech Republic]
124 09		Czech Air Force	2409+ [+ Czechoslovakia/Czech Republic]
124 10		Russian Air Force	[Soviet] 52+ 57+ [+ colour unknown]
125 01			[nothing known]
125 02			[nothing known]
125 03	B	not yet known	CCCP-26124 UR-26124 ER-AFQ EK-26124 RA-
125 04		(Libyan Air Cargo)	ST-DOZ [also carried Libyan serial 8214;] [w/o in forced landing 31Oct07 in desert at Atiqah, Libya]
125 05			[nothing known]
125 06		Slovakian Air Force	2506+ 2506^ [+ Czechoslovakia; ^ Slovakia]
125 07		Czech Air Force	2507+ [+ Czechoslovakia/Czech Republic]
125 08			[nothing known]
125 09			[nothing known]
125 10			[nothing known]
126 01	B	East Wing	CCCP-26087 GR-26087 4L-26087 UN-26087 UP-AN604
126 02	B	Aerolinea del Caribe	CCCP-26093 RA-26093 TL-ACZ ER-AFN HA-TCW EK-26093 HK-4729
126 03	B	ex Aerocom	CCCP-26125 OB-1348 CCCP-26125 RA-26125 ER-AFU [canx 07Oct07; l/n 09Nov04 Cox's Bazar, Bangladesh]
126 04		Aerogaviota	14-01+ CU-T1401 CU-T1228(2) [+ Cuba]
126 05		Aerogaviota	14-02+ CU-T1402 [+ Cuba]
126 06	B	unknown	YR-ADG 606 UR-CFY+ [+ canx 03Mar12 possibly to Sudanese Air Force]
126 07			[nothing known]
126 08	B	unknown	CCCP-26091 RA-26091 ER-AEY [impounded Jan01 Lanseria, South Africa; canx 03Mar01 to South Africa; fate/status unknown]
126 09	B	(Air Nacoia)	CCCP-26197 UR-26197 [w/o 24Jun96 Cafunfo, Angola]
2 73 126 10	B-100	Suhura Airways	CCCP-26126 RA-26126 UN-26126 RA-26126 EX-021 JY-TWB ET-AMP
127 01	B	Belavia	CCCP-26127 EW-26127
127 02	B-100	Chukotavia	CCCP-26128 RA-26128
127 03	B	Indonesian National Logistics	CCCP-26129 UR-26129 HA-TCP UR-KVI 4L-IFE [reported major damage 28Jan10 Wamena Airport, Indonesia]
2 73 127 04	B-100	TsSKB	CCCP-26130 RA-26130
2 73 127 05		MSM NIIIS Niz.Nov.	CCCP-26092(2) RA-26092

ANTONOV An-26

C/n	Model	Last known Owner/Operator	Identities/fates/comments (where appropriate)
127 06	B	Genex Ltd	CCCP-12706 CCCP-26094 UR-26094 EW-259TG
2 73 127 07	B	IrAero	CCCP-26131 RA-26131
127 08	B	SAT Airlines	CCCP-26132 RA-26132 [stored by Jun99 Yuzhno-Sakhalinsk, Russia; l/n Aug07]
127 09	B-100	Yamal	CCCP-26133 RA-26133
127 10	B	Aeroport Marculesti	YR-ADH 710+ ER-AZU [+ Romania]
128 01		unknown	CCCP-26144 RA-26144 [canx unknown date; fate unknown]
128 02			[nothing known]
128 03		FSB/Border Guards	[Soviet] (unknown) RF-26273
128 04			[nothing known]
128 05	B	Pskovavia	CCCP-26134 OB-1441 RA-26134
128 06	B	Nordavia Regional Airlines	CCCP-26135 RA-26135 [reported Nov11 for Genex, Belarus]
128 07			[nothing known]
128 08	B	Air Armenia	CCCP-26136 RA-26136 XU-325 EK-26112
3 73 128 09	B	unknown	CCCP-26137 RA-26137 ER-AFK
3 73 128 10	B	IrAero	CCCP-26138 RA-26138
129 01	B	(Air Kasai)	CCCP-26139 RA-26139 9Q-CFD [w/o 09Sep05 45km N of Brazzaville, Democratic Republic of Congo]
129 02	B	Air Urga	CCCP-26140 UR-26140 UR-ELG
3 73 129 03	B	(Kuban Airlines)	CCCP-26141 RA-26141 [w/o 26Dec93 Gyumri, Armenia]
129 04	B	Pskovavia	CCCP-26146 OB-1442 RA-26142
129 05		Aerogaviota	14-03+ CU-T1403 [+ Cuba]
129 06		Cuban Air Force	14-04+ CU-T1404 CU-T1235 [+ Cuba]
129 07			[nothing known]
129 08	B	Air Urga	CCCP-26143 UR-26143 UR-ELH
129 09	B	STAG	CCCP-26577 RA-26577 9Q-CFB
129 10			[nothing known]
130 01			[nothing known]
130 02			[nothing known]
130 03		Libyan Air Cargo	8301+ 5A-DOE [+ Libya: tie up not fully confirmed]
130 04		FSB/Border Guards	CCCP-26164 RA-26164 RF-26265+ [+ tie up not fully confirmed]
130 05			[nothing known]
130 06		Ukraine Border Guards	[Soviet] 14 blue
130 07		Libyan Air Cargo	8302+ 5A-DOF [+ Libya: tie up not fully confirmed]
130 08	100	Libyan Air Cargo	8303+ 5A-DOG^ [+ Libya: tie up not fully confirmed; ^ Sep11 also carrying 8303]
130 09		Libyan Air Cargo	8304+ 5A-DON [+ Libya: tie up not fully confirmed]
130 10		FSB/Border Guards	(unknown) RF-26278
131 01			[nothing known]
131 02		Libyan Air Force	8305
131 03		Libyan Air Cargo	8306+ 5A-DOI [+ Libya] [reported 05Oct09 Tripoli-Mitiga, Libya without wings]
131 04		Libyan Air Cargo	8307+ 5A-DOJ [+ Libya]
131 05		Libyan Air Force	8308 [tie up not fully confirmed; reported used for spares]
131 06		(Sin Sad)	8309+ 5A-DOK [before 06Oct08 force landed at Al Jufrah, Libya & dbr] [+ Libya: tie up not fully confirmed]
131 07		Libyan Air Force	8310
131 08		Libyan Air Cargo	8311+ 5A-DOL [+ Libya]
131 09	100	Libyan Air Cargo	8312+ 5A-DOV [+ Libya: tie up not fully confirmed]
131 10		ex Chad Air Force	8313+ TT-LAP [+ Libya] [wfu by 26Oct09 N'Djamena, Chad]
132 01	100	Libyan Air Cargo	8314+ 5A-DOU [+ Libya]
132 02		Libyan Air Cargo	8315+ 5A-DOH 5A-DOQ [+ Libya]
132 03		Yemen Air Force	617 [code 7O-ABN] [w/o 04Mar12 Sana, Yemen]
132 04		Afghan Air Force	256
132 05		Libyan Air Force	8316+ [+ tie up not fully confirmed]
132 06			[nothing known]
132 07			[nothing known]
132 08		Slovak Air Force	3208+ 3208 [Slovakia]
132 09	B-100	Czech Air Force	3209 [Czechoslovakia/Czech Republic]
132 10		Afghan Air Force	257
133 01		Afghan Air Force	258
133 02			[nothing known]
133 03	B	Avialinii Ukrainii	(unknown) UR-26178 [only one report in fleet list 1994]

ANTONOV An-26

C/n	Model	Last known Owner/Operator	Identities/fates/comments (where appropriate)
133 04		Afghan Air Force	261
133 05	M	Russian Air Force	[Soviet] 29 red
133 06	B	Genex	YR-ADI ST-AWC ER-AZV HA-TCZ EW-268TG
133 07	B	Sudanese Air Force	YR-ADJ 307+ UR-CFZ 7715 [+ Romania]
133 08	M	Russian Air Force	[Soviet] 27 red+ RF-36027+ [+ marks not confirmed]
133 09			[nothing known]
133 10	B	ex KAPO Aviakompania	CCCP-26597 RA-26597 UR-CFX [canx 08Oct10; stored/wfu Gostomel, Ukraine]
134 01	B	Kostrama Airlines	CCCP-26595 RA-26595
134 02	B	Blue Airlines	CCCP-26596 RA-26596 UR-26596 9Q-CZO
134 03	B	(Triamavia)	CCCP-26578 26578 UR-26578 ER-AFT [canx 15Mar00; fate unknown]
134 04	B	ex Tulpar Air Service	CCCP-26579 UN-26579 UP-AN603+ [+ possibly ntu as for sale as UN-26579]
134 05	B	Sudanese Air Force	YR-ADK UR-CGA+ 7716 [+ Feb10 test flew marked as 134-05]
134 06			[nothing known]
134 07		Afghan Air Force	275
134 08	B	Air Urga	CCCP-26580 UR-26580 TC-GZT UR-26580 UR-ELP [has used UN codes UN962 & UN626]
134 09			[nothing known]
134 10		(Kiev ARP 410 Airlines)	262+ CCCP-79170 UR-79170 [+ Afghanistan] [w/o 20Mar00 near Anuradhapur, Sri Lanka]
135 01		Cuban Air Force	14-05+ CU-T1405 CU-T1229 [+ Cuba]
135 02	B	Aerogaviota	14-06+ CU-T1406 [+ Cuba]
5 73 135 03	B	TCS	CCCP-26581 RA-26581 26581 UR-26581
5 73 135 04	B	Royal Airlines	CCCP-26582 UN-26582 UP-AN608
135 05	B	Air Urga	CCCP-26583 UR-26583 UR-ELA HA-TCT UR-ELA
135 06		Russian Government/FSB?	[Soviet] [unknown] RF-26274
135 07		Turkmenistan Border Guards	CCCP-26155 26155 RA-26155 26155
135 08			[nothing known]
135 09	B	Azerbaijan Airlines	CCCP-26584 26584 4K-26584
135 10			[nothing known]
136 01			[nothing known]
136 02			[nothing known]
136 03			[nothing known]
136 04			[nothing known]
136 05			[nothing known]
136 06			[nothing known]
136 07		Angolan Government	D2-MOP
136 08			[nothing known]
136 09			[nothing known]
136 10		FSB/Border Guards	CCCP-26157? RA-26157 RF-26266
137 01		FSB/Border Guards	17 red (unknown) RF-26261
137 02			[nothing known]
137 03			[nothing known]
137 04		Angolan Government	D2-MPQ [has used call sign T-223]
137 05			[nothing known]
137 06			[nothing known]
137 07		Afghan Air Force	273
137 08		Bulgarian Air Force	070
137 09		Bulgarian Air Force	075 [c/n not confirmed]
137 10		Bulgarian Air Force	080
138 01		Russian Air Force	[Soviet] 07 blue
138 02	B	ex Azerbaijan Cargo Airlines	CCCP-26585 26585 4K-26585 [derelict by Apr01 Baku-Bina, Azerbaijan; l/n 23Sep01; still current 22Nov05]
138 03			[nothing known]
138 04			[nothing known]
138 05	B	(Air Urga)	CCCP-26586 UR-26586 [reported w/o 19Mar00 Goma, Democratic Republic of Congo]
138 06	D	Russian Air Force	21 red+ 21 yellow+ 21 blue+ RF-36087^ [+ Soviet/Russia; ^ also carring 20 blue]
138 07		Moldovan Air Force	(unknown) ER-AFV 12 black+ [+ tie up not fully confirmed]
138 08		Romanian Air Force	YR-ADL 808
138 09		Romanian Air Force	YR-ADM 809

ANTONOV An-26

C/n	Model	Last known Owner/Operator	Identities/fates/comments (where appropriate)
138 10		Romanian Air Force	YR-ADN 810
139 01			[nothing known]
139 02		(Afghan National Army Air Corps)	278(2) [reported wfu date unknown but before 2011; fate/status unknown]
139 03			[nothing known]
139 04		Serbian Air Force	71386+ 71386 [+ Yugoslavia/Serbia & Montenegro]
139 05	B	RAF Avia	CCCP-26598 UR-26598 UR-DWA HA-TCS UR-DWA YL-RAJ
139 06	B	(Air Angol)	CCCP-26172 RA-26172 EL-ANZ [w/o 04Feb99 Luzamba, Angola]
139 07	B	ex Azerbaijan Airlines	CCCP-26587 26587 4K-26587 [derelict by 17May96 Baku-Bina, Azerbaijan; l/n 23Sep01; still current 22Nov05]
139 08	B	LIATs	CCCP-26588 RA-26588 26588
139 09	B	RAF Avia	CCCP-26589 RA-26589 YL-RAD
139 10	B	Chukotavia	CCCP-26590 RA-26590 [see the unidentified 590 of Vietnam Air Force]
140 01	B	Safat Airlines	CCCP-26591+ EP-SAK [+ canx 26Oct00 to Ukraine as non-airworthy]
140 02	B	Safat Airlines	CCCP-26592 RA-26592+ EP-SAJ [+ canx 26Oct00 to Ukraine as non-airworthy]
140 03	B	Services Air	CCCP-26593 RA-26593 26593 9Q-CFL
140 04	B	RAF Avia	CCCP-26200 YL-RAE
140 05	B	Air Urga	CCCP-26201 UR-26201 UR-ELB [used codes UN963 & UN0687 when operated by UN]
140 06	B	Russian Air Force	[Soviet] 55 yellow+ 55 red [+ Russia]
140 07	B	Mali Air Force	10?+ ER-AWG TZ-399^ [+ Soviet; ^ tie up not fully confirmed]
140 08			[nothing known]
140 09	B	Air Urga	CCCP-26202 UR-26202 UR-ELI HA-TCM UR-ELI
140 10	B	Air Urga	CCCP-26203 UR-26203 UR-ELD
141 01	B-100	Air South	BNMAU-14101 MT-14101 MT-1014 JU-1014 3X-GEV 3X-GFD EK-26818
141 02	B	MIAT Mongolian	BNMAU-14102 [w/o 23Apr93 near Zavkhan, Mongolia]
141 03	B	ex Mosphil Aero	CCCP-26204 ER-26204 UR-26204 RP-C7206 ER-26204
141 04		(Ariana Afghan Airlines)	YA-BAK [w/o 18Jun89 Zabol, Iran]
141 05		(Bakhar Afghan Airlines)	YA-BAL [shot down 11Jun87 near Khost, Afghanistan]
141 06		(Bakhar Afghan Airlines)	YA-BAM [shot down 04Sep85 Kandahar, Afghanistan]
141 07	B	Tajikistan Airlines	CCCP-26205 EY-26205
141 08			[nothing known]
141 09			[nothing known]
141 10		FSB/Border Guards	(unknown) RF-26282
142 01	B-100	Czech Air Force	CCCP-26206 UN-26206 4201
142 02	B	(Avialinii Ukrainii)	CCCP-26207 UR-26207 [shot down 31Jly94 near Saborsko, Croatia on UN flight]
142 03		Nicaraguan Air Force	150?+ YN-CEB FAN150 [+ not fully confirmed; Nicaragua]
142 04		Nicaraguan Air Force	YN-CEA+ 151 [+ tie up not fully confirmed;] [wfu by Dec03 Managua, Nicaragua; l/n Nov07]
142 05	B-100	Transportes Aereos Cielos Andinos	CCCP-26208 RA-26208 OB-1773-T OB-1775-T OB-1777-T OB-1778-P
142 06		Nicaraguan Air Force	152 [possibly w/o 21Jan99 near Bluefields, Nicaragua]
142 07		Nicaraguan Air Force	YN-CBG+ 160 [+ tie up not fully confirmed]
142 08	SM	Schwabisches Bauern Museum	373+ (DDR-SBM) 373+ 52+10^ [+ East Germany; ^ Germany] [damaged 27Feb92 Freidrichshafen; front fuselage preserved by Nov94 Eschach-Seifertshofen, Germany]
142 09		Bulgarian Air Force	087
142 10		FSB/Border Guards	[Soviet] (unknown) RF-26272
5 73 143 01	B	Democratic Republic of Congo AF	CCCP-26210 RA-26210+ ST- 9T- [canx 09Oct98 to Sudan; no new marks known; then Mar10 reported to DRC AF]
5 73 143 02	B-100	Pskov Avia	CCCP-26209 RA-26209
143 03		Bulgarian Air Force	090
143 04		(Ariana Afghan Airlines)	YA-BAN [w/o 28Aug92 on ground in rocket attack Kabul, Afghanistan; hulk l/n Oct94]
143 05		(Ariana Afghan Airlines)	YA-BAO [w/o 01Sep95 near Jalalabad, Afghanistan; hulk l/n 2001]
143 06		Cubana	14-07+ CU-T1407 CU-T1230(2)
143 07	T	Namibian Air Force	359+ DDR-SBK 359+ 52+11^ RA-49269 RA-26239 NAF-3-644 [+ East Germany; ^ Germany]
143 08	T	Tchad Air Force	384+ (DDR-SBH) 384+ 52+12^ RA-49274 RA-26234 TT-LAN [+ East Germany; ^ Germany]

ANTONOV An-26

C/n	Model	Last known Owner/Operator	Identities/fates/comments (where appropriate)
143 09		Russian Navy	[Soviet] 03 blue+ 07 blue+ 03 blue+ RF-36049^ [+ Russia; ^ also wears 03 blue]
143 10	B	unknown	CCCP-26594 RA-26594 ER-AZK+ 5A- [+ canx 12Jly04 to Libya]
144 01	B	unknown	CCCP-26212 RA-26212+ UR- [+ canx 31Mar00 to Ukraine; fate/status unknown]
144 02	B	Avialeasing	CCCP-26213 RA-26213 ST-IPK UN-26213 UK-26001
144 03	B	Genex Ltd	CCCP-26214 UR-26214 EW-246TG
Unidentified – Civil Prefix			
unkn		Air Cargo Liberia	CCCP-04185 [reported 23May90 Athens, Greece]
unkn		Aeroflot c/s	CCCP-13397 [reported 08Sep93 Kiev-Zhulyany, Ukraine]
unkn		Vietnam Air Force	CCCP-26092(1) 240 [reported 24Mar96 Saigon (Ho Chi Minh City) Vietnam; by Mar97 stored there; l/n Jan04; also carries CCCP-26092; see c/n 12705]
unkn		Soviet Air Force	CCCP-26145 145 black [reported 22Sep90 Moscow-Sheremetyevo, USSR and later as 145 black – same aircraft – at Leningrad, USSR]
unkn		FSB/Border Guards	CCCP-26159 RA-26159 [reported 29Apr89 Dushanbe, Tajikistan, USSR & 01Nov05 Engels AFB, Russia as RA-26159]
unkn		Ukraine Air Force	CCCP-26163+ 26163 [+ never reported; reported as 26163 01May99 & 24May02 Odessa, Ukraine]
unkn			CCCP-26216(1) [see Vietnam Air Force 216]
unkn			CCCP-26218(1) [see Vietnam Air Force 218]
unkn			CCCP-26250 [see Vietnam Air Force 250]
unkn			CCCP-26270 [see Vietnam Air Force 270]
unkn			CCCP-26276 [see Vietnam Air Force 276]
unkn		Vietnam Air Force	CCCP-26590+ 590^ [+ see c/n 13910 a different aircraft; ^ reported 15Mar01 & 24Mar08 Saigon (Ho Chi Minh City) Vietnam; also carries CCCP-26590]
unkn		Soviet Air Force	CCCP-26695 [reported 24Mar86 Moscow-Domodedovo, USSR]
unkn		Aeroflot c/s	CCCP-27206 [reported Apr82 Novosibirsk, USSR]
unkn		Aeroflot c/s	CCCP-27223 [reported 31Aug91 Bratsk, USSR]
unkn		Soviet/Russian Air Force	CCCP-46029 RA-46029 [reported Sep90 Moscow-Sheremetyevo, USSR; & as RA-46029 20Aug01 Chkalovski, Russia]
unkn		Aeroflot c/s	CCCP-46879 [photographic evidence]
unkn		Soviet Air Force	CCCP-47341 [regd 17Mar77 without c/n; reported 02Oct78 Addis Ababa, Ethiopia]
unkn		Soviet/Russian Air Force	CCCP-47342+ RA-47342 [+ regd 17Mar77 without c/n; as RA-47342 reported 14May05 Novosibirsk, Russia & 25Nov06 Ulan Ude-Vostochny, Russia]
unkn		Soviet Air Force	CCCP-47347 [reported 29Nov79 Addis Ababa, Ethiopia]
unkn		Soviet Air Force	CCCP-47402 [was on register without c/n]
unkn		610 Combat & Conversion Museum	CCCP-47403 RA-47403 [was on register without c/n; preserved 2005 by Ivanovo-Severny, Russia; l/n Aug06]
unkn		Soviet/Russian Air Force	CCCP-47407 RA-47407 [on register without c/n; reported 12Dec77 & 22Apr93 as CCCP-47407; l/n 21Aug96 Ivanovo-Severny, Russia]
unkn		Aeroflot c/s	CCCP-93417 [reported 07Feb90 Leningrad, USSR]
unkn		Cuban Air Force	CU-T1236 [reported 20Apr02 Havana-Playa Baracoa AFB, Cuba; same marks on An-24RV c/n 27308102 on same day; l/n 27May05 Havana, Cuba]
unkn		Aerogaviota	CU-T1417 [reported 20Apr02 Havana-Playa Baracoa AFB, Cuba & Jan03 Cayo Largo del Sur, Cuba]
unkn		Angolan Government	D2-EFN [reported dumped by 25Apr98 Luanda, Angola; might possibly have been D2-EPN]
unkn		Angolan Government	D2-END [reported 26Jan82 Niamey, Niger]
unkn		Angolan Government	D2-ENI [reported Junn83 Belgrade, Yugoslavia]
unkn			D2-EPN [see D2-EFN above]
unkn		Angolan Government	D2-EPO [reported Jly78 Luanda, Angola]
unkn		Angolan Government	D2-EPP [delivery was scheduled for 20Jly78]
unkn		ex Angolan Government	D2-EPQ [preserved by Mar03 Luanda City fairground, Angola]
unkn		Angolan Government	D2-EPR [delivery was scheduled for 20Jly78]
unkn		Angolan Government	D2-EZG [reported in 1987]
unkn		Angolan Government	D2-EZH [reported in 1987]
unkn		Angolan Government	D2-EZI [reported in 1987; possibly D2-EZJ]
unkn		Angolan Government	D2-FAA [reported delivered Apr77; report as An-32 impossible]
unkn		Angolan Government	D2-FAB [reported delivered Apr77; report as An-32 impossible]

ANTONOV An-26

C/n	Model	Last known Owner/Operator	Identities/fates/comments (where appropriate)
unkn		Angolan Government	D2-FAC [reported delivered Apr77; report as An-32 impossible]
unkn		Angolan Government	D2-FAD [reported 1980 Rome-Fiumicino, Italy; report as An-32 impossible]
unkn		unknown	D2-FBF [reported 19Aug99 Luanda, Angola]
unkn		unknown	D2-FBL [reported 15Apr98 Luanda, Angola & 19Aug99 Lusanga, Zaire]
unkn		unknown	D2-FBN [reported 22Mar01 Luanda, Angola]
unkn		unknown	D2-FBR [disappeared 07Jan00 near border of Malanje and Lunda Norte provinces, Angola]
unkn		unknown	D2-FBX [reported 15Apr98 Luanda, Angola & 07Aug00 Walvis Bay, Namibia]
unkn		Yuno	D2-FCF [reported 19Aug99 Luanda, Angola]
unkn		(Asa Pesada)	D2-FCG [reported w/o 15Nov00 Luanda, Angola]
unkn		Angolan Government	D2-MAD [reported 11Sep87 Kiev-Zhulyany, Ukraine, USSR]
unkn		Angolan Government	D2-MCD [reported 23Dec87 Rome-Fiumicino, Italy]
unkn		Angolan Government	D2-MDE [reported 23Dec87 Rome-Fiumicino, Italy]
unkn		Angolan Air Force	D2-MHI [reported 28Jly96 & 27Apr98 Luanda, Angola; with serial T-214]
unkn		Angolan Air Force	D2-TAE [from photo]
unkn		Trast Aero	ER-AUR [reported 10Oct09 Fujairah, UAE; these marks may be false]
unkn	B-100	Aquiline International	EX-063(2) [reported 17Feb09 Fujairah, UAE; believed second use of marks see c/n 115 06]
unkn		unknown	EX-483 [reported 12Mar09 Fujairah, UAE]
unkn		Air Asia	EY-322 [reported flew 05Jun11 Simferopol, Ukraine to Tabriz, Iran; 18Jun11 at Fujairah, UAE; possibly c/n 5407]
unkn		Balkan Bulgarian Airlines	LZ-ABM [reported 08Aug02 Sofia, Bulgaria]
unkn		Balkan Bulgarian Airlines	LZ-AMM [reported 03Aug02 Sofia, Bulgaria]
unkn	B	DHL	LZ-LVJ [reported 12Oct00 Vilnius, Lithuania]
unkn		FSB/Border Guards	RA-26150 [reported 22Sep90 Moscow-Sheremetyevo, Russia & 08Oct07 Naryan-Mar, Russia]
unkn			RA-26159 [see CCCP-26159 above]
unkn		FSB/Border Guards	RA-26276P [reported 04Aug08 Anadr, Russia & 30Jun11 Chelyabinsk-Shagol, Russia; also has code 50 blue; not c/n 9701 RA-26276 a diffrent aircraft]
unkn		VRKhBZ	RA-26638 [reported 24Sep10 Bagai-Baranovka, Russia]
unkn	B	Ivan Air Cargo	RA-26911 [reported 08Dec97 Split, Croatia]
unkn			RA-46029 [see CCCP-46029]
unkn		Russian Air Force	RA-46455 [reported 2008 Amderma, Russia]
unkn			RA-47342 [see CCCP-47342]
unkn			RA-47403 [see CCCP-47403]
unkn			RA-47407 [see CCCP-47407]
unkn			RA-49260 [see UR-49260]
unkn		FSB/Border Guards	RA-52168 [w/o 06Dec95 Anadyr, Russia]
unkn		Aeroflot c/s	RA-56632 [reported 27Apr93 Moscow-Bykovo, Russia]
unkn		Laotian Air Force	RDPL-34114 [reported 12Sep87 Karachi, Pakistan & 04Jan04 Vientiane, Laos]
unkn		Laotian Air Force	RDPL-34116 [reported 01Apr94 & 30Jun97 with no prefix; possibly in error as regn used on Y-12 c/n 0034 during this period]
unkn		Lao Capricorn Air	RDPL-34161 [reported routed 01Dec08 Luang Prabang, Laos to U-Tapao, Thailand to Saigon, Vietnam]
unkn		ROSTO?	RF-00714 [reported 02Mar08 & 21Dec08 Vladivostok, Russia]
unkn		FSB/Border Guards	RF-26260 [reported 04Apr08 Naryan-Mar Russia]
unkn		FSB/Border Guards	RF-26262 [reported 11Jan10 in tender document]
unkn		FSB/Border Guards	RF-26265 [reported 18Dec10 Sochi-Adler, Russia]
unkn		FSB/Border Guards	RF-26269 [reported 08Jly10 Novosibirsk, Russia]
unkn		FSB/Border Guards	RF-26270 [reported 29Aug07 Novosibirsk, Russia]
unkn		FSB/Border Guards	RF-26276P [reported 04Aug08 Anadyr, Russia; ex 04 red which still carried; not c/n 9701]
unkn		FSB/Border Guards	RF-26281 [reported 14May08 & 25Jun09 Yuzhno-Sakhalinsk, Russia]
unkn		FSB/Border Guards	RF-26310 [reported 26Oct10 Rostov-on Don, Russia]
unkn		Russian Space Forces	RF-36009 [photo 31Mar10 Vyazma-Bryanskaya, Russia]
unkn		Russian Air Force	RF-36010 [reported 22Apr09 Chkalovski, Russia; has been active since at least 2008]
unkn		Russian Space Forces	RF-36013 [reported 07Oct09 Moscow-Vnukovo, Russia]
unkn		Russian Air Force	RF-36017 [reported 06Mar12 Ekaterinburg, Russia]
unkn		Russian Air Force	RF-36022 [reported 2011 Ekaterinburg, Russia; ex 22 red]
unkn		Russian Air Force	RF-36026 [reported 21Jly12 Novosibirsk, Russia also wearing 03 blue]
unkn		Russian Air Force	RF-36028 [reported 2011 Ekaterinburg, Russia; ex 28 red]

ANTONOV An-26

C/n	Model	Last known Owner/Operator	Identities/fates/comments (where appropriate)
unkn		Russian Air Force	RF-36174 [reported 2010 Nizhny Novgorod, Russia]
unkn		Russian Air Force	RF-47323 [reported 23Jun07 Chkalovski, Russia & 25Jun07 Gromovo, Russia; possibly c/n 8306]
unkn		Russian Air Force	RF-47324 [reported Sep10 Gromovo, Russia]
unkn		Russian Air Force	RF-47325 [reported Nov09 Chkalovski, Russia]
unkn		Ministry of Interior (MVD)	RF-56310 [reported 17May09 Vladivostok, Russia; possibly ex 02]
unkn		Russian Air Force	RF-90341 [reported 25May11 Rostov-na-Donu, Russia; also carried code 09 blue]
unkn		Russian Air Force	RF-90342 [reported 07Jun11 Rostov-na-Donu, Russia; also carried code 11 blue, is not c/n 108-01]
unkn		Russian Air Force	RF-90344 [reported 12Sep11 Solovki, Russia; also carrying 02 blue]
unkn		Russian Air Force	RF-90374 [reported 01Aug11 Ivanovo-North, Russia]
unkn		Russian Air Force	RF-92950 [reported 12Aug11 Kubinka, Russia]
unkn		Russian Air Force	RF-92953 [reported Jun12 Chkalovski, Russia]
unkn		Russian Air Force	RF-92955 [reported 29Sep11 Chkalovski, Russia; also carrying 52 red]
unkn		unknown	S9-BON [reported 11Jan01 Sharjah, UAE]
unkn		unknown	S9-GBA [reported 04Mar08 Fujairah, UAE & 10Oct08 Libreville, Gabon]
unkn	B-100	Trast Aero	S9-GBC(1) [reported 25Jly08 & subsequently Fujairah, UAE and active in Iraq/UAE; l/n 04May09; at sometime operated by Aquiline International; concurrent with other "S9-GBC"'s see below and An-32 listing]
unkn	B	Trast Aero	S9-GBC(2) [reported 07Mar09 Fujairah, UAE; not aircraft at 17Mar09 Brazzaville, People's Republic of Congo]
unkn	B	Trast Aero	S9-GBC(3) [reported 17Mar09 Brazzaville, People's Republic of Congo; probably to 3X-GFN(1)]
unkn		unknown	S9-GRB [reported 19Aug99 & 15Mar01 Luanda, Angola]
unkn		unknown	S9-GRG [reported 22Mar01 Luanda, Angola]
unkn		Gulf Aviation Group	S9-GRH [reported 21Nov99 Fujairah, UAE & Sao Tome, Sao Tome Island]
unkn		unknown	S9-KAV(2) [reported 14Feb10 Pointe Noire, People's Republic of Congo; see c/n 41 04 is different aircraft]
unkn		Air Max Gabon	S9-SSA [reported 03Jly03 Sharjah, UAE]
unkn		unknown	S9-SVB [reported 03Aug08 Kherson, Ukraine; ex Uzbekistan 09]
unkn		Air West Express	ST-ARS [reported Jan05 Khartoum, Sudan; canx before Jan07]
unkn		unknown	ST-NNN [reported 01Jan08 Khartoum, Sudan]
unkn		unknown	ST-ZZZ(3) [reported 19Jan07 Khartoum, Sudan; concurrent with ST-ZZZ(2) c/n 10404 also with hulk of ST-ZZZ(1) c/n 10407 still extant!]
unkn		Damal	TL-ABD [reported 20Jan00 and later Sharjah, UAE; l/n 11May00]
unkn		Inter Congo	TN-AGU [reported 19Oct03 Pointe-Noire, People's Republic of Congo]
unkn	M	Tchad Air Force	TT-LAM [reported Jan95 N'Djamena, Republic of Chad]
unkn	M	Tchad Air Force	TT-LAO [reported Mar08 N'Djamena, Republic of Chad & 05Oct09 Tripoli-Mitiga, Libya]
unkn		Tchad Air Force	TT-OAN [reported Feb05 N'Djamena, Republic of Chad]
unkn	B-100	unknown	UN-26089 [reported 15Nov07 and since Fujairah, UAE; l/n 01Nov08]
unkn		unknown	UN-26405 [reported 09May07 Kiev-Zhulyany, Ukraine; later as 26405 for test flight]
unkn		unknown	UR-26847 [reported 08Apr04 Ramstein AFB, Germany; regn not fully confirmed]
unkn		Ukraine Air Force	UR-46146 [reported 08Dec05 Budapest, Hungary]
unkn		unknown	UR-47015 [reported 06Jan99 & later Tatry-Poprad, Slovakia]
unkn		ex Trans Avia	UR-49260+ RA-49260^ [+ reported 30Aug93 Kirovograd, Ukraine; ^ reported Sep94 Istanbul-Ataturk, Turkey; on register without c/n]
unkn		Ukraine Air Force	UR-71488 [reported 16Aug93 Prague, Czech Republic]
unkn		Ukraine Air Force	UR-71815 [reported 03Oct97 Piest'any, Slovakia]
unkn		unknown	UR-CFY [reported 06Jly07 Kiev-Zhulyany, Ukraine & stored 26Sep08 Gostomel, Ukraine]
unkn		Laotian Government	XW-TCC [delivered 09Jun76]
unkn		Laotian Government	XW-TCD [delivered 14Jly76]
unkn		Laotian Government	XW-TCE [delivered 14Jly76]
unkn		Kabul Air	YA-KAL [reported 04May09 Fujairah, UAE; & 01Apr10 Kabul, Afghanistan]
unkn		Baron Congo Mining	3C-BAA [mentioned in UN document]
unkn		unknown	3X-GEI [reported 15Nov07 and since Fujairah, UAE; l/n 02Mar09]
unkn		Galex-Guinee	3X-GEU [reported flew 03Sep09 Ankara, Turkey to Tehran, Iran]
unkn		Trast Aero	3X-GFC [reported 04Jly10 7 14Aug10 Pointe Noire, People's Republic of Congo]

ANTONOV An-26

C/n	Model	Last known Owner/Operator	Identities/fates/comments (where appropriate)
unkn		GR Avia	3X-GFM [reported 13Mar11 Kandahar, Afghanistan & 08Jly11 routed Tbilisi, Georgia to Tehran, Iran]
unkn		Trast Aero?	3X-GFN(1) [see S9-GBC(3) below]
unkn	B	Trast Aero	3X-GFN(2) [reported 22Jan11 Rostov-on-Don, Russia; almost certain ex S9-GBC(3)]
unkn		unknown	3X-GGA [reported 03Feb12 Fujairah, UAE]
unkn		unknown	3X-GGN [reported 18May12 Fujairah, UAE]
unkn	B	unknown	3X-GIV [reported 06Dec09 Sana'a-International, Yemen]
unkn	B	Turbot Air Cargo	4L-26020(1) [first reported 13Jly05 Luqa, Malta & 16Jly05 Dakar, Senegal with Global Georgian; 25Jun06 Las Palmas, Canary Islands, Spain; 03Aug08 Kherson, Ukraine; l/n May10 stored]
unkn		Trast Aero	4L-26020(2) [reported 10Apr10 Dire Dawa, Ethiopia; not 4L-26020(1) which was, as above, still stored in May10]
unkn		unknown	4L-BKL [reported 13Aug08 Vinitsa, Ukraine]
unkn		Air Georgia	4L-GSS [mentioned Dec10 on Georgian CAA website; canx by 23Mar11; possibly became either EY-322 or EY-323]
unkn		Jav Avia	4L-JAV [mentioned Dec10 on Georgian CAA website; canx by 23Mar11]
unkn		unknown	4L-ZUR [reported 27Oct10 Lome, Togo]
unkn		Madagascar Air Force	5R-MUG [reported 21Aug96 Antananarivo, Madagascar]
unkn		Madagascar Air Force	5R-MUK [reported 29Jly80 Antananarivo, Madagascar; stored by 21Aug96; l/n 15Apr01]
unkn		Madagascar Air Force	5R-MUL [reported 1986 Antananarivo, Madagascar; stored by 21Aug96; l/n 15Apr01]
unkn		Madagascar Air Force	5R-MUM [reported stored by Apr96 Antananarivo, Madagascar; not there Oct96; fate unknown]
unkn		Madagascar Air Force	5R-MUN [reported 1986 Antananarivo, Madagascar; stored by 21Aug96; l/n 15Apr01]
unkn		Madagascar Air Force	5R-MUO [reported 1986 Antananarivo, Madagascar; stored by 21Aug96; not there Oct96; fate unknown]
unkn		748 Air Service	9L-LFW [reported routed 14Sep07 Luxor, Egyptt to Heraklion, Greece to Simferopol, Ukraine]
unkn		Defense Nationale	9Q-CBM [reported Jan07 Kinshasa-N'Djili, Democratic Republic of Congo; reservation only on register 2004-2008]
unkn		(Afrique One)	9Q-CMC [reported w/o 26Jly02 Kinshasa-N'Djili, Democratic Republic of Congo; in 2008 register without c/n]
unkn		(Uhuru Airlines?)	9U-BHM [reported w/o 08May04 Beni, Democratic Republic of Congo]
unkn		unknown	9XR-AG [reported derelict 2003 & 2010 Cyanguju, Rwanda]
unkn		Sun Air Charter	9XR-SA [reported 06Jun03 Nairobi, Kenya; 22Feb04 Fortaleza, Brazil; wfu by 10Sep08 Barcelona, Venezuela]
Unidentified – Military			
unkn		(Soviet Air Force)	04 [w/o 20Apr88 Chkalovski, Russia, USSR]
unkn		(Uzbekistan Air Force)	09 [noted under paint on S9-SVB also unidentified]
unkn	RT	(Soviet Air Force)	22 [w/o 26Dec86 shot down 60km from Kabul, Afghanistan]
unkn		Mozambique Air Force	026 [no reported sightings]
unkn		Mozambique Air Force	028 [reported 1986 Wonderboom, South Africa; stored by 25May03 Maputo, Mozambique; l/n 25Sep08]
unkn		(Soviet Air Force)	29 [w/o 24Jun88 Bagram, Afghanistan, following hostile fire]
unkn		Mozambique Air Force	033 [reported stored by Jan04 Maputo, Mozambique]
unkn		Mozambique Air Force	034 [no reported sightings]
unkn		Mozambique Air Force	036 [reported 19Jun85 Maputo, Mozambique; stored by 25May03; l/n 25Sep08]
unkn		Mozambique Air Force	038 [reported 19Jun85 Maputo, Mozambique; by Aug04 derelict in severely damaged condition Quelimanein, Mozambique]
unkn		Bulgarian Air Force	038 [reported 12Jan04 Turany, Czech Republic; sole report, possible mis-sighting]
unkn		Mozambique Air Force	040 [derelict by 1985 Napula, Mozambique]
unkn		Mozambique Air Force	042 [w/o 30Mar86 Pembe, Mozambique]
unkn		(Soviet Air Force)	51 [w/o 15Aug91 near Burevestnik, Russia; code colour not reported]
unkn		Mongolian Air Force	103 [reported Mar92 Ulaanbaatar, Mongolia]
unkn		Mongolian Air Force	107 [reported Mar92 Ulaanbaatar, Mongolia]
unkn		Mongolian Air Force	108 [reported Mar92 Ulaanbaatar, Mongolia]

ANTONOV An-26

C/n	Model	Last known Owner/Operator	Identities/fates/comments (where appropriate)
unkn		Vietnam Air Force	214 [reported 28Jly92 Saigon (Ho Chi Minh City) Vietnam; by Mar96 stored there; l/n Jan07]
unkn		Vietnam Air Force	215 [reported 28Jly92 Saigon (Ho Chi Minh City) Vietnam; by Mar96 stored there; l/n Jan07]
unkn		Vietnam Air Force	216 [reported 25Oct93 Saigon (Ho Chi Minh City) Vietnam; by Mar96 stored there; l/n Jan07; possibly ex CCCP-26216(1)]
unkn		Vietnam Air Force	217 [reported 24Mar96 Saigon (Ho Chi Minh City) Vietnam; by Mar97 stored there; l/n Jan07]
unkn		Vietnam Air Force	218 [reported 28Jly92 Saigon (Ho Chi Minh City) Vietnam; by Mar96 stored there; l/n Jan07; possibly ex CCCP-26218(1)]
unkn		Vietnam Air Force	219 [reported 25Oct93 Saigon (Ho Chi Minh City) Vietnam; by Mar96 stored there; l/n Jan07]
unkn		Afghan Air Force	224 [reported May04 in compound Kabul city, Afghanistan]
unkn		Afghan Air Force	228 [reported became T-004]
unkn		Afghan Air Force	229 [reported Jan77 Kabul, Afghanistan; w/o 17Jun80 Kabul, Afghanistan; hulk l/n Jun06]
unkn		Afghan Air Force	230 [reported Jan77 Kabul, Afghanistan; hulk noted Mar02 & Jun06 Kabul, Afghanistan]
unkn		Afghan Air Force	231 [reported Jan77 Kabul, Afghanistan; hulk noted Mar02 & Jun06 Kabul, Afghanistan]
unkn		Afghan Air Force	232 [reported Jan77 Kabul, Afghanistan]
unkn		Afghan Air Force	233 [no reported sightings]
unkn		Afghan Air Force	235 [w/o 14Jun80 Khost, Afghanistan; wreck cannibalised and abandoned]
unkn		Afghan Air Force	236 [reported 1978 Kabul, Afghanistan]
unkn		Afghan Air Force	238 [reported11Sep87 Kiev-Zhulyany, Ukraine; wreckage noted Mar02 Kabul, Afghanistan; l/n Jun06]
unkn		Afghan Air Force	239 [in UN Dec99 sanction list; dumped by Jan02 Kandahar, Afghanistan]
unkn		Vietnam Air Force	239 [reported 24Mar96 &19Dec08 Saigon (Ho Chi Minh City) Vietnam]
unkn		Afghan Air Force	240 [in UN Dec99 sanction list]
unkn		Afghan Air Force	241 [in UN Dec99 sanction list]
unkn		Vietnam Air Force	241 [reported Nov89 & 28Jly92 Saigon (Ho Chi Minh City) Vietnam]
unkn		Afghan Air Force	242 [in UN Dec99 sanction list]
unkn		Vietnam Air Force	242 [reported Nov89 & 28Jly92 Saiqon (Ho Chi Minh City) Vietnam]
unkn		Afghan Air Force	243 [in UN Dec99 sanction list; hulk reported Apr05 Khost, Afghanistan]
unkn		Vietnam Air Force	243 [reported Nov89 Saigon (Ho Chi Minh City) Vietnam]
unkn		Afghan Air Force	244 [in UN Dec99 sanction list]
unkn		Afghan Air Force	245 [in UN Dec99 sanction list]
unkn		Vietnam Air Force	245 [reported 28Jly92 & 08Jan04 Saigon (Ho Chi Minh City) Vietnam]
unkn		Afghan Air Force	246 [in UN Dec99 sanction list]
unkn		Vietnam Air Force	246 [reported 28Jly92 Saigon (Ho Chi Minh City) Vietnam; by Mar96 stored there; l/n Jan07]
unkn		Afghan Air Force	247 [reported 17Oct00 Kandahar, Afghanistan]
unkn		Vietnam Air Force	248 [reported Nov89 & 24Mar08 Saigon (Ho Chi Minh City) Vietnam; 21Nov09 Hanoi-Gia Lam, Vietnam]
unkn		Vietnam Air Force	249 [reported Nov89 Saigon (Ho Chi Minh City) Vietnam]
unkn		Vietnam Air Force	250 [reported stored 04Apr96 Nha-Trang, Vietnam; l/n Oct02; possibly ex CCCP-26250]
unkn		Vietnam Air Force	251 [reported 07Mar00 & 22Nov08 Saigon (Ho Chi Minh City) Vietnam]
unkn		Afghan Air Force	252 [reported Sep91 Kabul, Afghanistan; hulk reported Aug03 Mazar-i-Sharif, Afghanistan]
unkn		Vietnam Air Force	252 [reported 01Nov02 Hanoi, Vietnam & 08Nov08 Saigon (Ho Chi Minh City) Vietnam]
unkn		Afghan Air Force	253 [reported Feb04 Kabul, Afghanistan]
unkn		Afghan Air Force	254 [reported Sep06 Shindand, Afghanistan]
unkn		Vietnam Air Force	254 [reported 28Jly92 Saigon (Ho Chi Minh City) Vietnam; by Mar96 stored there; l/n Jan07]
unkn		Vietnam Air Force	256 [reported 28Jly92 Saigon (Ho Chi Minh City) Vietnam; by Mar96 stored there; l/n Jan07]
unkn		Vietnam Air Force	257 [reported Nov89 Saigon (Ho Chi Minh City) Vietnam; by Mar96 stored there; l/n Jan07]

ANTONOV An-26

C/n	Model	Last known Owner/Operator	Identities/fates/comments (where appropriate)	
unkn		Vietnam Air Force	258	[reported 28Jly92 Saigon (Ho Chi Minh City) Vietnam; by Mar96 stored there; l/n Mar01 and 10Jan07 not confirmed]
unkn		Vietnam Air Force	259	[reported 28Jly92 Saigon (Ho Chi Minh City) Vietnam; by Mar96 stored there; l/n Jan07]
unkn		Afghan Air Force	260	[wreckage reported Jun06 Kabul, Afghanistan]
unkn		Vietnam Air Force	260	[reported 25Oct93 Saigon (Ho Chi Minh City) Vietnam & 25Mar08 Hanoi-Gia Lam, Vietnam; l/n 21Nov09]
unkn		Vietnam Air Force	261	[reported 31Oct98 Hanoi, Vietnam & 24Mar08 Saigon (Ho Chi Minh City) Vietnam]
unkn		Vietnam Air Force	262	[reported 13Apr96, 25Mar08 & 21Nov09 Hanoi-Gia Lam, Vietnam]
unkn		Afghan Air Force	264	[reported in 1990]
unkn		Vietnam Air Force	264	[reported 07Mar00 & 24Mar08 Saigon (Ho Chi Minh City) Vietnam]
unkn		Afghan Air Force	265	[wreck reported dumped 13Sep09 Ghor Province, Afghanistan]
unkn		Vietnam Air Force	265	[reported 08Jan04 & 24Mar08 Saigon (Ho Chi Minh City) Vietnam; probably w/o 08Apr08 Thana Tri, Hanoi, Vietnam]
unkn		Afghan Air Force	268	[reported 1995 Kabul, Afghanistan]
unkn		Vietnam Air Force	268	[reported 13Apr96 Hanoi, Vietnam & 15Mar01 Saigon (Ho Chi Minh City) Vietnam]
unkn		Vietnam Air Force	269	[reported Nov89 & 24Mar08 Saigon (Ho Chi Minh City) Vietnam]
unkn		Vietnam Air Force	270	[reported Nov89 Saigon (Ho Chi Minh City) Vietnam; possibly ex CCCP-26270]
unkn		Vietnam Air Force	271	[reported Nov89 Saigon (Ho Chi Minh City) Vietnam; 25Mar08 & 21Nov09 Hanoi-Gia Lam, Vietnam]
unkn		Vietnam Air Force	272	[reported 07Mar00 Saigon (Ho Chi Minh City) Vietnam; 25Mar08 & 21Nov09 Hanoi-Gia Lam, Vietnam]
unkn		Vietnam Air Force	274	[reported 13Apr96 Hanoi, Vietnam; by Nov98 stored there; l/n Mar08]
unkn		Vietnam Air Force	276	[reported 25Oct93 & 08Jan04 Saigon (Ho Chi Minh City) Vietnam; possibly ex CCCP-26276]
unkn		Pakistan Air Force Museum	278(1)	[preserved Karachi-Sharea-Faisal AFB, Pakistan; ex Afghan Air Force reportedly hijacked to Pakistan; this might be 276 rather than 278 which is c/n 13902, as painted]
unkn		Vietnam Air Force	279	[reported 13Apr96 Hanoi, Vietnam & 24Mar08 Saigon (Ho Chi Minh City) Vietnam]
unkn		Afghan Air Force	280	[wreckage reported Mar02 Kabul, Afghanistan; l/n Jan04]
unkn		Vietnam Air Force	280	[reported 08Jan04, 24Mar08 & 19Nov09 Saigon (Ho Chi Minh City) Vietnam]
unkn		Vietnam Air Force	281	[reported 31Oct98 & 25Mar08 Hanoi, Vietnam]
unkn		Vietnam Air Force	283	[reported 07Mar00 & 24Mar04 Saigon (Ho Chi Minh City) Vietnam]
unkn		Afghan Air Force	284	[reported 17Oct00 Kandahar, Afghanistan]
unkn		Vietnam Air Force	284	[reported 13Apr96 Hanoi, Vietnam; by Nov98 stored there; l/n Mar08]
unkn		Vietnam Air Force	285	[reported 18Mar99 & 25Mar08 Hanoi, Vietnam]
unkn		Vietnam Air Force	286	[reported 25Oct93 Saigon (Ho Chi Minh City) Vietnam & 25Mar08 Hanoi, Vietnam]
unkn		Vietnam Air Force	287	[reported 13Apr96 Hanoi-Gia Lam, Vietnam & 24Mar08 Saigon (Ho Chi Minh City) Vietnam; again 21Nov09 Hanoi-Gia Lam]
unkn		Vietnam Air Force	291	[serial not fully confirmed was certainly 2?1: reported 25Oct93 Saigon (Ho Chi Minh City) Vietnam]
unkn		Laotian Air Force	505	[first reported 03Apr08 Phnom-Penh, Cambodia; previously from photo]
unkn		Vietnam Air Force	590	[see CCCP-26590]
unkn		Yemen Air Force	612	[reported 07Aug93 Aden, Yemen & 01Sep07 & 04Jan08 Sana'a, Yemen; earlier with South Yemen Air Force]
unkn		Yemen Air Force	615	[reported 16Nov85 Aden, People's Democratic Republic of Yemen (with South Yemen Air Force) & 07Aug93 Aden, Yemen]
unkn		South Yemen Air Force	618	[reported 16Nov85 & 02Apr90 Aden, People's Democratic Republic of Yemen]
unkn		Yemen Air Force	1177	[reported Dec09 Sana'a, Yeman]
unkn		Chinese Air Force	5853	[reported 15May01 Wuhan, China]
unkn		Chinese Air Force	5863	[reported 15May01 Wuhan, China]
unkn		Sudan Air Force	7706	[reported 29Apr10 Nyala, Sudan]
unkn		Sudan Air Force	7722	[photographic evidence on internet]

ANTONOV An-26

C/n	Model	Last known Owner/Operator	Identities/fates/comments (where appropriate)	
unkn		Libyan Air Force	8204	[donated 1990 to Somalia as 6O-204 qv]
unkn		Libyan Air Force	8214	[see 5A-DOZ below]
unkn		Chinese Navy	9112	[preserved in cemetary Jinxiang Yangshan, China; noted Aug10]
unkn		Chinese Navy	9162	[reported 29Apr06 Jiazhou, China & Apr08 Liangxiangzhen AFB, China]
unkn		Yemen Air Force	9503	[reported 13May96 Kiev-Zhulyany, Ukraine]
unkn		Cuban Air Force	12-46	[reported 28Aug83 Havana, Cuba as An-24B, but might be An-26]
unkn		Chinese Air Force	10650	[from photo]
unkn		Chinese Air Force	11259	[reported May12]
unkn		Ukraine Air Force	26163	[see CCCP-26163]
unkn		unknown	26405	[see UN-26405]
unkn		Chinese Air Force	40551	[reported 15Apr07 Beijing-Nan Yuan, China; might be a Y7H, but unlikely]
unkn		Chinese Air Force	40552	[reported May08 Beijing Shahe AFB, China; might be a Y7H, but unlikely]
unkn		Chinese Air Force	40553	[reported May08 Beijing Shahe AFB, China; might be a Y7H, but unlikely]
unkn		Chinese Air Force	70127	[from photo on Chinese website]
unkn		Chinese Air Force	71290	[reported 09Nov93 Beijing-Nan Yuan, China]
unkn		Yugoslav Air Force	71351	[reported 30May90 Luqa, Malta & 03May91 Basel, Switzerland; sold 1996/1997 to "Congo"]
unkn		Yugoslav Air Force	71352	[reported 10Jun80 Zagreb, Yugoslavia]
unkn		Yugoslav Air Force	71356	[reported 10Jun80 Zagreb, Yugoslavia; w/o 1999 Nis, Yugoslavia during NATO bombing raid]
unkn		unknown	71756	[possible military call sign; routed out of 02Jun00 Voronezh, Russia]
unkn		Ukraine Air Force	01 blue	[reported 29Aug93 & 22Sep94 Kiev-Zhulyany, Ukraine; possibly c/n 2005]
unkn		Kazakhstan Air Force	01 red	[reported 20Feb08 & 14Nov08 Almaty, Kazakhstan]
unkn		Uzbekistan Air Force	01 red	[reported 23Nov06 Termez, Uzbekistan]
unkn		Ukraine Air Force	02 red	[reported Nov08 on overhaul Kiev-Zhulyany, Ukraine]
unkn		Ukraine Air Force	03 blue	[reported 02Sep03 Zhukovski, Russia]
unkn		ex Uzbekistan Air Force?	03 red	[reported Aug11 presereved in pioneer camp near Brichmulla, Uzbekistan]
unkn		Kazakhstan Border Guards	03 white	[reported 31May08 & 14Mar09 Almaty, Kazakhstan]
unkn		Kazakhstan Air Force	04 red	[reported 01Jun08, 19Apr09 & 07Jun09 Almaty, Kazakhstan]
unkn		Belarus Air Force	04 red	[reported 23Feb08 & 10May08 Minsk-Machulishchi, Belarus]
unkn		Uzbekistan Air Force	04 red	[reported 02Jun02 Kiev-Zhulyany, Ukraine]
unkn		Kazakhstan Border Guards	04 white	[reported 19May10 Almaty, Kazakhstan]
unkn		Ukraine Air Force	05 blue	[reported 19Jly94, 22Sep94 & 02Jun02 Kiev-Zhulyany, Ukraine; possibly c/n 0808]
unkn		Kazakhstan Air Force	05 red	[reported 12Jly08 Almaty, Kazakhstan]
unkn		Ukraine Air Force	05 red	[reported 20Mar97 Kiev-Zhulyany, Ukraine]
unkn		Russian Air Force	05 red	[reported May08 & Jly09 Levashovo, Russia]
unkn		Ukraine Air Force	06 blue	[reported 20Mar97 Kiev-Zhulyany, Ukraine]
unkn		Russian Navy	06 blue	[reported flew 07Apr11 from Ostafyevo, Russia after storage]
unkn		Kazakhstan Air Force	06 red	[reported 01Apr10 Almaty, Kazakhstan; possibly wfu]
unkn		Russian Navy	06 yellow	[photo Jly05 Saki-Novofedonvka, Russia]
unkn		Russian Navy	07 blue	[reported 09Apr12 Vladivostok-Knevichi, Russia]
unkn		Ukraine Air Force	09 red	[reported 27May02 Mikolayiv-Kulbakino, Ukraine]
unkn		Ukraine Air Force	10 blue	[reported 25Jun99 Nizhyn, Ukraine & 27May02 Mikolayiv-Kulbakino, Ukraine; assumed same aircraft]
unkn		Ukraine Air Force	11 green	[reported 20Mar97 Kiev-Zhulyany, Ukraine]
unkn		Ukraine Air Force	111 red	[see CCCP-26163]
unkn		Soviet Air Force	145 black	[see CCCP-26145]
unkn		Turkmenistan Border Guards	16 blue	[reported 26Dec08 Gostomel, Ukraine]
unkn		Russian Air Force	17 black	[photo 08Jun10 Rostov-na-Donu, Russia]
unkn		Ukraine Air Force	17 blue	[reported 04Aug01 Budapest, Hungary; when used call sign UR-99752]
unkn		Ukraine Air Force	19 blue	[reported 19Jly94 Kiev-Zhulyany, Ukraine & 12Nov08 Kiev-Borispol, Ukraine]
unkn		Ukraine Air Force	22 blue	[reported 23Aug93 & 02Jun02 Kiev-Zhulyany, Ukraine; could have this been c/n 11607?]

ANTONOV An-26

C/n	Model	Last known Owner/Operator	Identities/fates/comments (where appropriate)	
unkn		Ukraine Air Force	23 red	[reported 27May02 Mikolayiv-Kulbakino, Ukraine]
unkn		Ukraine Air Force	30 blue	[reported 29Aug93 & 20Mar97 Kiev-Zhulyany, Ukraine; could this have been c/n 3209?]
unkn		Ukraine Air Force	30 blue	[reported 02Jun02 Kiev-Zhulyany, Ukraine; in ex Aeroflot c/s]
unkn		Ukraine Air Force	32 blue	[reported 29Aug93 & 19Jly94 Kiev-Zhulyany, Ukraine]
unkn		Ukraine Air Force	33 blue	[reported 24May02 Odessa, Ukraine]
unkn		Ukraine Air Force	35 blue	[reported 29Aug93 & 20Mar97 Kiev-Zhulyany, Ukraine; could this have been c/n 6406, but the latter in different c/s?]
unkn		Ukraine Air Force	37 blue	[reported 24May02 Odessa, Ukraine; in ex Aeroflot c/s]
unkn		Ukraine Air Force	41 blue	[reported 16Aug93 Prague, Czech Republic]
unkn		Ukraine Air Force	44 blue	[reported 19May97 Kiev-Borispol, Ukraine & 25Jun99 Nizhyn, Ukraine; same aircraft?]
unkn		Ukraine Air Force	45 blue	[reported 19May97 Kiev-Borispol, Ukraine]
unkn		FSB/Border Guards	50 blue	[reported 21Jly06 Dushanbe, Tajikistan & 03Apr08 Yuzhno-Sakhalinsk, Russia]
unkn		Russian Air Force	59 blue	[reported 20Oct04 Anapa, Russia; c/n 68 07 of Russian Navy with same code might be this aircraft]
unkn		Poltava Aviation Museum	61 blue	[preserved Poltava, Ukraine; l/n 11Nov08]
unkn		Ukraine Air Force	71 blue	[reported 24May02 Odessa, Ukraine]
unkn	SH	Ukraine Air Force	73 yellow	[reported 29Aug09 Chuguev, Ukraine]
unkn		Ukraine Air Force	78 yellow	[reported, via photo, 29Aug09 Chuguyev, Ukraine]
unkn		Ukraine Air Force	80 yellow	[reported 07Sep10 Heraklion, Greece]
unkn		Ukraine Air Force	84 yellow	[reported 26Jun99 Kiev-Borispol, Ukraine]
unkn		Somali Air Force	6O-204	[ex Libyan AF 8204 qv; reported stored Sep03 Nairobi, Kenya; l/n May09 by Jan04; this is not MM60204 which is an An-24]
unkn		Democratic Republic of Congo AF	9T-TAA	[reported Oct02 & 12May09 Kinshasa-N'Djili, Democratic Republic of Congo]
unkn		Democratic Republic of Congo AF	9T-TAB	[reported Sep05 Kolwezi, Democratic Republic of Congo & Jan07 Goma, Democratic Republic of Congo]
unkn		(Democratic Republic of Congo AF)	9T-TAD	[w/o 29Nov03 Boende, Democratic Republic of Congo]
unkn		Congo Air Force	9T-TAE	[reported Sep05 Kolwezi, Democratic Republic of Congo]
unkn	B	Democratic Republic of Congo AF	AT-922	[reported Feb07 & 12May09 Kinshasa, Democratic Republic of Congo]
unkn		Cabo Verde Air Force	FAC-01	[reported in book but no reported sightings; also report of photo showing serial as being FA-C01]
unkn		Cabo Verde Air Force	FAC-02	[reported in book but no reported sightings]
unkn		Pakistan Air Force	J-754	[ex Afghan AF aircraft that crew hijacked 22Sep84 to Miranshah, Pakistan; taken on charge by Pakistan AF; based Islamabad-Chaklala, Pakistan & noted 02Oct88; rarely flew; wfu 7 stored around 1990; l/n 23Apr06]
unkn		Somali Air Force	MM60207	[from photo; coded AM-88; could be c/n 1303]
unkn		Somali Air Force	MM60208	[no reported sightings; could be c/n 1303]
unkn			T-004	[see Afghan Air Force 228]
unkn		Angolan Air Force	T-200	[reported in book but no reported sightings]
unkn		Angolan Air Force	T-201	[reported Jan89 Luanda, Angola; used call sign T-720]
unkn		Angolan Air Force	T-202	[w/o before 27Sep83 no details]
unkn		Angolan Air Force	T-203	[reported 1989 Luanda, Angola]
unkn		Angolan Air Force	T-204	[reported in book but no reported sightings]
unkn		Angolan Air Force	T-205	[reported in book but no reported sightings]
unkn		Angolan Air Force	T-206	[reported in book but no reported sightings]
unkn		Angolan Air Force	T-207	[reported in book but no reported sightings]
unkn		Angolan Air Force	T-208	[reported in book but no reported sightings]
unkn		Angolan Air Force	T-209	[reported in book but no reported sightings]
unkn		Angolan Air Force	T-210	[reported in book but no reported sightings]
unkn		Angolan Air Force	T-211	[reported 16Mar01 Luanda, Angola; later report of this serial on a An-32 questionable]
unkn		Angolan Air Force	T-212	[w/o 30Sep84 no details]
unkn		Angolan Air Force	T-213	[reported in book but no reported sightings]
unkn		Angolan Air Force	T-214	[see D2-MHI]
unkn		Angolan Air Force	T-215	[reported in book but no reported sightings]
unkn		Angolan Air Force	T-217	[reported in book but no reported sightings]
unkn		Angolan Air Force	T-218	[reported in book but no reported sightings]
unkn		Angolan Air Force	T-219	[reported in book but no reported sightings]
unkn		Angolan Air Force	T-221	[reported in book but no reported sightings]

ANTONOV An-26

C/n	Model	Last known Owner/Operator	Identities/fates/comments (where appropriate)	
unkn		Angolan Air Force	T-222	[reported in book but no reported sightings]
unkn		Angolan Air Force	T-223	[photo Oct85 at Cuito Cuanavale, Angola]
unkn		Angolan Air Force	T-224	[w/o 30Jan01 Luena, Angola]
unkn		Angolan Air Force	T-225	[damaged 19Feb01 Luena, Angola; status unknown]
unkn		Angolan Air Force	T-226	[reported in book but no reported sightings]
unkn		Angolan Air Force	T-228	[dumped by Jun03 Luanda, Angola]
unkn		Angolan Air Force	T-229	[reported in book but no reported sightings]
unkn		Angolan Air Force	T-230	[dumped by Jun03 Luanda, Angola]
unkn		Angolan Air Force	T-231	[reported in book but no reported sightings]
unkn		Angolan Air Force	T-233	[reported in book but no reported sightings]
unkn		Angolan Air Force	T-234	[never reported; possibility only]
unkn		Angolan Air Force	T-235	[reported in book but no reported sightings]
unkn		Angolan Air Force	T-236	[reported in book but no reported sightings]
unkn		Angolan Air Force	T-238	[never reported; possibility only]
unkn		Angolan Air Force	T-241	[never reported; possibility only]
unkn		Angolan Air Force	T-242	[never reported; possibility only]
unkn		Angolan Air Force	T-243	[reported in book but no reported sightings]
unkn		Angolan Air Force	T-244	[reported in book but no reported sightings]
unkn		Mali Air Force	TZ-353	[not fully confirmed]
unkn		Yemen Air Force	(unknown)	[an unidentified An-26 was w/o 25Oct11 Al-Anad AFB, Yemen]

Production complete

ANTONOV An-28/PZL M-28

C/n	Model	Last known Owner/Operator	Identities/fates/comments (where appropriate)
01		ex Antonov Design Bureau	CCCP-1968 CCCP-19681 08 red+ CCCP-19681 [+ Soviet; not fully confirmed as this c/n] [prototype f/f 30Apr69; originally designated An-14M; preserved by 13Sep87 Kiev Park of Economic Achievements, Ukraine]
02 ?		(Antonov Design Bureau)	CCCP-19723 CCCP-19753 [fate/status unknown; l/n 02Jly96 Gostomel, Ukraine]
03 ?		ex Antonov Design Bureau	CCCP-48105 CCCP-19754 [wfu by May97 Gostomel, Ukraine; l/n Mar09]
1AJ 001-01		(Antonov Design Bureau)	CCCP-28800 UR-28800 [f/f 22Jly84] [wfu by 03May99 Gostomel, Ukraine; canx 13Aug08; l/n Sep08]
1AJ 001-02			[static test airframe]
1AJ 001-03		(Aeroflot/Komi)	CCCP-28801 [GIA by 14Aug99 Troitsk Technical School, Russia; l/n 12Aug01; canx 13Sep02]
1AJ 001-04		Magdeburg Sky Divers	CCCP-28802 RF-00308 RF-2092K RF-00308
1AJ 001-05		(Aeroflot/Tajikistan)	CCCP-28803 [canx 27Nov90; fate/status unknown]
1AJ 002-01		(Aeroflot/Tajikistan)	CCCP-28804 [GIA by 14Aug99 Troitsk Technical School, Russia; l/n 12Aug01; canx 13Sep02]
1AJ 002-02			[static test airframe]
1AJ 002-03		(Komiavia)	CCCP-28806 [canx 17Dec99; fuselage only by 22Aug01 Moscow-Ostafyevo, Russia; by Feb07 hulk at Kirzhach, Russia]
1AJ 002-04		(Aeroflot/Tajikistan)	CCCP-28805 [probably wfu by 2001; fate/status unknown]
1AJ 002-05		(Aeroflot/Tajikistan)	CCCP-28807 [probably wfu by 2001; fate/status unknown]
1AJ 002-06		(Flying Air Service)	CCCP-28808 UR-28808 ES-NOD ES-ELI [w/o 29Jly04 Beni Mavivi, Democratic Republic of Congo]
1AJ 002-07	PD	not yet known	CCCP-28809 RA-28809 ES-NOW RA-3677K RA-28809 [based 2011 Langar, UK]
1AJ 002-08		Tracep-Congo Aviation	CCCP-28810 EX-28810 9Q-CAX
1AJ 002-09		Middlanditracep	CCCP-28811 EX-28811 9Q-CES+ 9Q-COL [+ not confirmed; might have been an illegal registration]
1AJ 002-10		(WSK-Mielec)	SP-PDA [canx 26Apr89 after accident; used for ground tests; report still stored Sep02 Mielec, Poland]
1AJ 003-01		ex Aeroflot/Tajikistan	CCCP-28812 [canx 27Nov09; derelict by 14Jly93 Dushanbe, Tajikistan; by 28Jan03 on display Aktyubinsk City, Kazakhstan]
1AJ 003-02		ex Komiavia	CCCP-28813 [wfu by Jun94 Syktyvkar, Russia; canx 17Dec99; hulk by Sep08 Jelgava, Latvia]
1AJ 003-03		(Enimex)	CCCP-28814 ES-NOV [w/o 23Nov01 near Kardia, Greece; canx 2003]
1AJ 003-04		ex Aktyubinsk Flying School	CCCP-28740 UN-28740+ UP-AN2803 [+ not confirmed]
1AJ 003-05		(Aeroflot/Komi)	CCCP-28741 [w/o 14Aug87 Ust-Nem, USSR; remains to Troitsk Technical School, Russia; l/n 1999]
1AJ 003-06		ex Aktyubinsk Flying School	CCCP-28742 UN-28742 UP-A2804
1AJ 003-07		(Flightpath)	CCCP-28743 ER-AJA S9-PSB [wfu by Nov08 Lokichogio, Kenya; l/n 31Jan09]
1AJ 003-08		(Komiavia)	CCCP-28744 RA-28744 [canx 28Apr99; reported sold to Rwanda in non-flying condition]
1AJ 003-09		ex Tep Avia Trans	CCCP-28745 ER-AJB [canx 14Jun00; fate/status unknown]
1AJ 003-10		(Komiavia)	CCCP-28746 [canx 04Oct99; fuselage only by 22Aug01 Moscow-Ostafyevo, Russia; fate unknown]
1AJ 003-11		(Komiavia)	CCCP-28747 [canx 29Apr99; reported sold to Rwanda in non-flying condition]
1AJ 003-12		Swala	CCCP-28748 ER-AJC 9Q-CSX
1AJ 003-13		unknown	CCCP-28749 UN-28749 3C-JZX+ UP-A2802 [+ not confirmed]
1AJ 003-14		ex Tajikistan Airlines	CCCP-28750 [wfu by 07Nov04 Dushanbe, Tajikistan; l/n derelict Nov08]
1AJ 003-15		ex Tajikistan Airlines	CCCP-28751 [wfu by 07Nov04 Dushanbe, Tajikistan; fate/status unknown]
1AJ 004-01		ex Tep Avia Trans	CCCP-28752 ER-AJI [canx 10May07 as sold; l/n in poor condition 19Aug09 Bakavu, Democratic Republic of Congo]
1AJ 004-02		Rigas Aeroklubs	CCCP-28753 RA-28753 YL-KAD
1AJ 004-03		Air Excellence	CCCP-28754 UR-28754
1AJ 004-04	M28-B1E	Polish Navy	0404 [originally designed as a An-28T]
1AJ 004-05	M28-B1E	Polish Navy	0405 [originally designed as a An-28T, then An-28M]
1AJ 004-06		African Union Mission in Sudan	SP-GCA ER-AIP ST-AWN
1AJ 004-07		TET	CCCP-28758 ER-AJH ST-AWH
1AJ 004-08		Skydive Venezuela	CCCP-28759 UR-28759 ES-NOA ST-GWA YV-1147CP YV148T
1AJ 004-09		Trans Kasai Air	CCCP-28760 ER-AJG
1AJ 004-10		(Aeroflot/Tajikistan)	CCCP-28761 [probably w/o 18Aug90 Rushan, USSR]
1AJ 004-11		ex Tajikistan Airlines	CCCP-28762 [wfu by 07Nov04 Dushanbe, Tajikistan; fate/status unknown]

ANTONOV An-28/PZL M-28

C/n	Model	Last known Owner/Operator	Identities/fates/comments (where appropriate)
1AJ 004-12		Malliala Airlift	CCCP-28763 9Q-CPG [possibly wfu by 09Feb08 Goma, Democratic Republic of Congo]
1AJ 004-13		unknown	CCCP-28764 UR-28764
1AJ 004-14		(Guinea Equatorial Airlines)	CCCP-28765 UR-28765 3C-JJI [w/o 29Dec99 ditched into Black Sea 50km from Inebolu, Turkey]
1AJ 004-15		TARCO Air	CCCP-28766 RA-28766 UR-28766 28766 UR-ZAN 9XR-KG 9L-LFS EX-916 ST-BRY
1AJ 004-16		ex Kolpashevo Air	CCCP-28767 [fate/status unknown]
1AJ 004-17		TSOU	CCCP-28768 RA-28768 UR-28768 UR-KAMA
1AJ 004-18		Rodina	CCCP-28769 (unknown) RF-01197
1AJ 004-19		ex Kolpashevo Air	CCCP-28770 [fate/status unknown]
1AJ 004-20		ROSTO	CCCP-28771 RA-49808 RF-49808
1AJ 005-01		El Dinder	CCCP-28755 EX-28501 ST-ISG
1AJ 005-02		(Enimex)	CCCP-28756 ES-NOF [w/o 29Nov99 near Szczecin, Poland; wreck still on site May03]
1AJ 005-03		ex Tajikistan Airlines	CCCP-28757 EY-28757 [left fleet by 2001; fate/status unknown]
1AJ 005-04		ex ATI Airlines	CCCP-28772 RA-28772 UR-28772 [canx 13Aug08; fate/status unknown]
1AJ 005-05		ex ATI Airlines	CCCP-28773 RA-28773 UR-28773 [canx 13Aug08; fate/status unknown]
1AJ 005-06		(WSK-PZL)	SP-DDB TC-FEA SP-DDB [canx 04Mar97; converted to M-28 Skytruk prototype c/n AJEP1-01]
1AJ 005-07		ex Peruvian Navy	CCCP-28774 RA-28774 EP-827 [wfs by Jun10]
1AJ 005-08		ex Tajikistan Airlines	CCCP-28775 EY-28775 [left fleet by 01Nov04; fate/status unknown]
1AJ 005-09		ex Blue Lines	CCCP-28776 RA-28776+ 9Q-CZN [+ no reports;] [derelict by 04Mar08 Kinshasa-N'Djili, Democratic Republic of Congo]
1AJ 005-10		Blue Lines	CCCP-28777 9Q-CZM
1AJ 005-11		(Avia Special)	CCCP-28778 RA-28778 HA-LAJ [w/o 28Aug93 Weston-on-the Green, UK; wreck to Farnborough, UK; l/n Sep96]
1AJ 005-12		ex Flightpath	CCCP-28779 ER-AJK S9-CAH [wfu by Nov08 Lokichogio, Kenya; l/n 31Jan09]
1AJ 005-13		T.A. Corporation	CCCP-28780 ES-DAB YV1756
1AJ 005-14		unknown	CCCP-28781 UR-28781 ER-AJL 5R-MJL RA-3560K
1AJ 005-15		unknown	CCCP-28782 TL-ACE
1AJ 005-16		Karakol-Avia	CCCP-28783 EX-28783
1AJ 005-17		Sun Air Services	CCCP-28784 EX-28784 9Q-CMZ
1AJ 005-18		(Komiavia)	CCCP-28785 [w/o 10Oct92 Ust-Nem, Russia]
1AJ 005-19		(Mavivi Air)	CCCP-28786 28786+ 3C-DDB [+ prefix uncertain; by Apr10 derelict Goma, Democratic Republic of Congo]
1AJ 005-20		(Tbilisi Aviation University)	CCCP-28787 RA-28787 UR-28787 4K-AZ58 4L-28001 [canx by 23Mar11 fate/status unknown]
1AJ 005-21		Peruvian Navy	CCCP-28788 RA-28788 EP-826
1AJ 005-22		(Victoria Air)	CCCP-28789 3C-LLA UN-28789+ [+ prefix not noted;] [w/o 23Aug01 20km short of Bukavu, Congo as 3C-LLA; 23Jan03 reported as shown]
1AJ 005-23		(Gran Propellor)	CCCP-28790 3C-KKY UN-28790+ 3C-ZZV [+ prefix not noted;] [w/o 31Mar05 Kampene, Democratic Republic of Congo]
1AJ 005-24		ex Tajikistan Airlines	CCCP-28791 EY-28791 [by 02Oct07 in store; by 17Dec09 derelict Dushanbe, Tajikistan]
1AJ 005-25		ex Tep Avia Trans	CCCP-28792 RA-28792 ER-AJF [canx 27Mar03 to Democratic Republic of Congo; nothing known]
1AJ 006-01		(Blue Lines)	CCCP-28793 RA-28793 9Q-CZL [dbf 14Apr00 Kinshasa-N'Djili, Democratic Republic of Congo]
1AJ 006-02		(El Dinder Aviation)	CCCP-28794 RA-28794 RA-2128K EK-28602 ST-TYB [w/o 06Jul09 Saraf Omra, Darfur, Sudan]
1AJ 006-03		El Dinder	CCCP-28795 EX-28795 3C-KKI 9XR-KI 9Q-CFY ST-OMM
1AJ 006-04		(Enimex)	CCCP-28796 ES-NOY [w/o 10Feb03 Tallinn, Estonia]
1AJ 006-05		(Chukotavia)	CCCP-28797 [w/o 10Feb95 Mys Shmidta Airport, Russia; canx 06Jun95]
1AJ 006-06		Karakol-Avia	CCCP-28798 EX-28798
1AJ 006-07		Air Leone	SP-DDC 9L-LCQ
1AJ 006-08		DOSAAF Rossii	SP-DDD TC-FEB SP-FFN RF-00404 RF-14429+ [+ not confirmed]
1AJ 006-09		(Aeroflot/East Siberia)	CCCP-28703 RA-28703 [canx 29Dec94; l/n 18Apr97 Chita-Kadala, Russia; fate/status unknown]
1AJ 006-10		ex ATI Airlines	CCCP-28799 RA-28799 UR-28799 [canx 13Aug08; fate/status unknown]

ANTONOV An-28/PZL M-28

C/n	Model	Last known Owner/Operator	Identities/fates/comments (where appropriate)
1AJ 006-11		(Tracep Congo)	CCCP-28700 SP-FHR 9XR-IM 9Q-CUN+ [reported w/o 30Jan12 near Namoya, Democratic Republic of Congo; + marks not fully confirmed]
1AJ 006-12		(Air Mark)	CCCP-28701 ER-AJE [w/o 24Dec05 Zalingei, Sudan; canx 11May07]
1AJ 006-13		(Aeroflot/East Siberia)	CCCP-28702 [w/o 16Mar90 Vershyna, USSR; canx 07Dec90]
1AJ 006-14		ex Tajikistan Airlines	CCCP-28704 [derelict by 12Nov06 Dushanbe, Tajikistan; l/n Nov08]
1AJ 006-15		ex Tajikistan Airlines	CCCP-28705 [reported in store by 02Oct07; derelict by Nov08 Dushanbe, Tajikistan]
1AJ 006-16		(Aeroflot/Tajikistan)	CCCP-28706 [w/o 03Jan02 Lyahsh, Tajikistan]
1AJ 006-17		(748 Air Services)	CCCP-28707 RA-28707 9L-LFN [canx 08Apr08; stored by 16May08 Lokichogio, Kenya; l/n Oct08]
1AJ 006-18		ex Aeroflot/East Siberia	CCCP-28708 RA-28708 [canx 29Dec94; wfu by 18Apr97 Chita-Kadala, Russia]
1AJ 006-19		ex Aeroflot/East Siberia	CCCP-28709 RA-28709 [canx 29Dec94; wfu by 18Apr97 Chita-Kadala, Russia]
1AJ 006-20		ex ATI Airlines	CCCP-28710 RA-28710 UR-28710 [canx 13Aug08; fate/status unknown]
1AJ 006-21		Georgian Air Force	CCCP-28711 LY-APB 05 black
1AJ 006-22		ex ATI Airlines	CCCP-28712 RA-28712 UR-28712 [canx 13Aug08; fate/status unknown]
1AJ 006-23		(Koryakavia)	CCCP-28713 [w/o 12May94 Palana, Russia]
1AJ 006-24		Koryakavia	CCCP-28714 RA-28714
1AJ 006-25		Koryakavia	CCCP-28715 RA-28715
1AJ 007-01		Koryakavia	CCCP-28716 RA-28716
1AJ 007-02		ex Aeronautica C.A.	CCCP-28717 RA-28717 YV2157 YV403T [stored mid-2009 Tamiami, FL; l/n 18Feb11]
1AJ 007-03		not yet known	CCCP-28718+ SP-AWR YV^ [+ canx 12Mar03 sold in Latvia; no Russian or other marks known; ^ canx 29Sep09 to Venezuela]
1AJ 007-04		Region Avia	CCCP-28719 28719 RA-28952(2)+ RA-28719 [+ possibly painted in error]
1AJ 007-05		(Aeroflot)	CCCP-28720 [fate unknown, possibly w/o before formally registered]
1AJ 007-06		unknown	CCCP-28721 RA-28721 9XR-SR [wfu by Oct08 Lokichogio, Kenya; used for spares]
1AJ 007-07		Koryakavia	CCCP-28722 RA-28722
1AJ 007-08		IKAR	CCCP-28723 RA-28723
1AJ 007-09		ex Tajikistan Airlines	CCCP-28724 EY-28724 [by 02Oct07 airline reported in store]
1AJ 007-10		(Blue Wings Airlines)	CCCP-28725 SP-FHS RA-28725+ PZ-TSV [+ probable paper registration;] [w/o 15May10 near Poeketi, Suriname]
1AJ 007-11		IKAR	CCCP-28726 RA-28726
1AJ 007-12		unknown	CCCP-28727 RA-28727 YV-1042CP YV1136 [seized 21May11 Barcelona, Venezuela for drug running]
1AJ 007-13		Murmansk Avia	CCCP-28728 28728 RA-28728
1AJ 007-14		Region Avia	CCCP-28729 EX-28729 RA-28900
1AJ 007-15		Raul Helicopters	CCCP-28730 RA-28730 YV-1041CP YV1056
1AJ 007-16		T.A. Corporation	CCCP-28731 ES-DAA YV2032
1AJ 007-17		(Blue Wings Airlines)	CCCP-28732 RA-28732 SP-FHT PZ-TSO [w/o 03Apr08 Lawa-Antino, Netherlands Antilles]
1AJ 007-18		DOSAAF Rossii	CCCP-28733 RA-28733 SP-FHU RF-00418 MSN-00718+RF-14430 [+ based Krasnoyarsk-Manski, Russia, marked as such]
1AJ 007-19		ex Tajikistan Airlines	CCCP-28734 EY-28734 [by 02Oct07 airline reported in store; by 12Mar10 wfu Dushanbe, Tajikistan]
1AJ 007-20		Blue Wings Airlines	SP-FFO SP-FFL YV-578C PZ-TSN
1AJ 007-21		Blue Wings Airlines	SP-FFP SP-FFM YV-592C PZ-TGW PZ-TSA
1AJ 007-22		ex Tajikistan Airlines	CCCP-28735 [by 02Oct07 airline reported in store]
1AJ 007-23		(WSK-Mielec)	SP-PDE [to An-28TD c/n AJBP01-01]
1AJ 007-24		Tajikistan Airlines	CCCP-28736 EY-28736
1AJ 007-25		Georgian Air Force	CCCP-28737 RA-28737 UR-28737 06 black
1AJ 008-01		Region Avia	CCCP-28738 EX-28738 RA-28901
1AJ 008-02		ex ATI Airlines	CCCP-28739 RA-28739 UR-28739 [canx 13Aug08; fate/status unknown]
1AJ 008-03		Region Avia	CCCP-28917 EX-28917 RA-28917+ [+ not confirmed]
1AJ 008-04		(Blue Wings Airlines)	CCCP-28918 RA-28918 SP-FHP PZ-TST [w/o 15Oct09 Kwamalasamutu, Suriname]
1AJ 008-05		Tracep-Congo Aviation	CCCP-28919 RA-28919 SP-FHW 9XR-KV 9Q-CFQ
1AJ 008-06		Vostok Aviakompania	CCCP-28920 RA-28920
1AJ 008-07		Tajikistan Airlines	CCCP-28921 EY-28921
1AJ 008-08		ex Malu Aviation	CCCP-28922 9Q-CRA [reported wfu by 05Aug10 Kinshasa, Democratic Republic of Congo]

ANTONOV An-28/PZL M-28

C/n	Model	Last known Owner/Operator	Identities/fates/comments (where appropriate)
1AJ 008-09		Tracep-Congo Aviation	CCCP-28923 9Q-CJF 9Q-CSP [possibly wfu by 13Apr10 Kavumu, Democratic Republic of Congo]
1AJ 008-10		(WSK-Mielec)	SP-PDC [to An-28B1R c/n AJGP1-01]
1AJ 008-11		(Aeroflot/East Siberia)	CCCP-28924 [w/o 23Oct91 Shelopugino, USSR; canx 23Dec91]
1AJ 008-12		(Aeroflot/East Siberia)	CCCP-28925 RA-28925 [wfu by 18Apr97 Chita-Kadala, Russia; canx 18Mar98]
1AJ 008-13		Ayk Avia	CCCP-28926 RA-28926 ER-AKO S9-PSV EK-28925
1AJ 008-14		ex Aeronavigatslya Yuga	CCCP-28927 RA-28927 RF-38387 [CofA expired 21Sep05; hulk stored Krasnodar, Russia]
1AJ 008-15		Rodina	CCCP-28928 RA-28928 RF-01196
1AJ 008-16		Vostok Aviakompania	CCCP-28929 RA-28929
1AJ 008-17		ex Vostok Aviakompania	CCCP-28930 RA-28930 [canx 16Mar95; wfu by 03Jly04 Khabarovsk-Maly, Russia; l/n 18Jun08]
1AJ 008-18		Vostok Aviakompania	CCCP-28931 RA-28931
1AJ 008-19		(Vladivostok Air)	CCCP-28932 RA-28932 [w/o 29Aug02 Ayan, Russia; canx 10Jun03]
1AJ 008-20		Vladivostok Air	CCCP-28933 RA-28933
1AJ 008-21		(Middlanditracep)	CCCP-28934 UN-28934 EX-28934 EX-018 9Q-COM [w/o 03Aug06 near Bukavu, Democratic Republic of Congo]
1AJ 008-22		unknown	CCCP-28935 UN-28935+ UP-A2805 [+ not confirmed]
1AJ 008-23		Aktyubinsk Flying School	CCCP-28936 UN-28936 UP-A2806
1AJ 008-24			[aircraft ordered for South Africa but not completed]
1AJ 008-25			[aircraft ordered for South Africa but not completed]
1AJ 009-01			[aircraft not completed, customer unknown]
1AJ 009-02			[aircraft not completed, customer unknown]
1AJ 009-03		ex Aeronavigatslya Yuga	CCCP-28937 RA-28937 RF-38388 [CofA expired 21Sep05; hulk stored Krasnodar, Russia]
1AJ 009-04		Aktyubinsk Flying School	CCCP-28938 UN-28001 UP-A2801
1AJ 009-05		Rodina	CCCP-28939 RA-28939 RF-01195
1AJ 009-06		Rodina	CCCP-28940 RA-28940 RF-03555
1AJ 009-07		Vostok Aviakompania	CCCP-28941 RA-28941
1AJ 009-08		Vostok Aviakompania	CCCP-28942 RA-28942
1AJ 009-09		El Dinder	CCCP-28943 YL-KAF ST-TRC
1AJ 009-10		Aktyubinsk Flying School	CCCP-28944 UN-28944
1AJ 009-11		(P A Betancourt)	CCCP-28945 RA-28945 YV-1043CP [w/o 29Jan02 Kavak, near Canaima, Venezuela]
1AJ 009-12		Region Avia	CCCP-28946 EX-28946 RA-28902
1AJ 009-13		ex Aktyubinsk Flying School	CCCP-28947 [status unknown; l/n 29Jan03 Aktyubinsk, Kazakhstan]
1AJ 009-14		ex Djibouti Air Force	CCCP-28948 YL-KAA J2-MAT [has code AT; reported derelict Feb11 Balbala, Djibouti]
1AJ 009-15		Rigas Aeroklubs	CCCP-28949 YL-KAB
1AJ 009-16		(Koryakavia)	CCCP-28950 RA-28950 [w/o 19Sep00 Tigil, Russia]
1AJ 009-17		Tracep-Congo Aviation	CCCP-28951 RA-28951 9Q-CKC
1AJ 009-18		Region Avia	CCCP-28952 RA-28952(1)
1AJ 009-19		Region Avia	CCCP-28953 RA-28953 RA-3072K RA-28903
1AJ 009-20		ex Akhtyrka Air Enterprise	CCCP-28954 RA-28954 [wfu by 09Aug06 Ozero-Kalakrtyrka, Russia]
1AJ 009-21			[aircraft ordered for South Africa but not completed]
1AJ 009-22			[aircraft ordered for South Africa but not completed]
1AJ 009-23			[aircraft ordered for South Africa but not completed]
1AJ 009-24			[aircraft ordered for South Africa but not completed]
1AJ 009-25			[aircraft ordered for South Africa but not completed]
1AJ 010-01		ex Bashkirian Airlines	CCCP-28955 RA-28955 [fate/status unknown]
1AJ 010-02		ex Tep Avia Trans	CCCP-28956 RA-28956 ER-AKA [canx 20Jan00 to Kenya; fate/status unknown]
1AJ 010-03		(WSK-Mielec)	[to M-28TD c/n 1AJGP08-10]
1AJ 010-04		Comair	CCCP-28957 RA-28957 9Q-CCM [engineless by 12Apr10 Kavumu, Democratic Republic of Congo]
1AJ 010-05		(Aeroflot)	CCCP-28958 [stored Mielec 26Apr92; never delivered]
1AJ 010-06		(Aeroflot)	CCCP-28959 [stored Mielec 26Apr92; to c/n AJG001-04]
1AJ 010-07		(Aeroflot)	CCCP-28960 [stored Mielec 26Apr92; to c/n AHJP1-01]
1AJ 010-08		(Aeroflot)	CCCP-28961 [not delivered; to c/n AJG001-02]
1AJ 010-09		(Aeroflot)	CCCP-28962 [not completed; components to c/n 1AJE001-07]
1AJ 010-10		(Aeroflot)	CCCP-28963 [not completed; components to c/n 1AJE001-08]
1AJ 010-11		(Aeroflot)	CCCP-28964 [not completed; components to an M-28?]
1AJ 010-12		(Aeroflot)	CCCP-28965 [not completed; components to c/n 1AJE001-06]

ANTONOV An-28/PZL M-28

C/n	Model	Last known Owner/Operator	Identities/fates/comments (where appropriate)
1AJ 010-13		(Aeroflot)	CCCP-28966 [not completed; components to an M-28?]
1AJ 010-14		(Aeroflot)	CCCP-28967 [not completed; components to an M-28?]
1AJ 010-15		(Aeroflot)	CCCP-28968 [not completed; components to an M-28?]
1AJ 010-16		(Aeroflot)	CCCP-28969 [not completed; components to an M-28?]
1AJ 010-17		(Aeroflot)	CCCP-28970 [not completed; components to c/n AJG001-03]
1AJ 010-18		(Aeroflot)	CCCP-28971 [not completed; components to an M-28?]
1AJ 010-19		Vega Aviation	SP-DDF(1) C5-GAD SP-DFA ER-AJD EK-28019 ST-VGA

PZL-MIELEC M-28 SKYTRUCK

Non-Standard c/ns

C/n	Model	Last known Owner/Operator	Identities/fates/comments (where appropriate)
AJHP1-01	M-28-RM2	(Polish Navy)	SP-PDD 1007 [ex c/n 1AJ 010-07] [w/o 31Mar09 Badie Doly, Poland]
AJBP1-01	TD	Polish Air Force	SP-PDE 0723 [ex c/n 1AJ 007-23]
1AJB001-01	B1R	Polish Navy	SP-PDC 0810 [ex c/n 1AJ 008-10]
1AJGP1-01	M-28	(PZL-Mielec)	SP-PDF SP-DDF(2) [ex c/n 1AJ005-06] [f/f 22Jly93; canx 22Aug01; by Nov05 dismantled Mielec, Poland]
1AJGP08-10	M-28TD	Polish Navy	1003 [ex c/n 1AJ 010-03]

C/n	Model	Last known Owner/Operator	Identities/fates/comments (where appropriate)
AJE 001-01		PZL Sp.	SP-FYV SP-DDA
AJE 001-02		Aerocentro de Servicios Caroni	SP-DDE HK-4066X YV-1016CP YV1769 [damaged 19Oct09 Las Minas, Honduras, whilst on a drug run]
AJE 001-03		Venezuelan National Guard	SP-DFD GN96105
AJE 001-04		Venezuelan National Guard	SP-DFE GN96106
AJE 001-05		Venezuelan National Guard	SP-DFF GN96107
AJE 001-06		Venezuelan National Guard	SP-DFG GN96108
AJE 001-07		Venezuelan National Guard	SP-DFH GN96109
AJE 001-08		Venezuelan National Guard	SP-DFI GN96110+ GNB96110 [+ Venezuela]
AJE 001-09		Venezuelan National Guard	SP-DFB N5091L HP-1416 GN96131+ GNB96131 [+ Venezuela]
AJE 001-10		(Overtec SA)	SP-DFC YV-117CP [w/o 12Jul01 Puerto Cabello, Venezuela]
AJE 001-11			[under construction Sep98 to Jly00; never completed]
AJE 001-12			[under construction Sep98 to Jly00; never completed]
AJE 001-13		Venezuelan National Guard	SP-DFK GN97119+ GNBV97119 [+ Venezuela]
AJE 001-14		Venezuelan National Guard	SP-DFL GN97120+ GNBV97120 [+ Venezuela]
AJE 001-15		(Venezuelan National Guard)	SP-DFM GN97121 [w/o 10Dec04 near Puerto, Venezuela]
AJE 001-16		Venezuelan National Guard	SP-DFN GN97122
AJE 001-17		Venezuelan National Guard	SP-DFO GN97123 GNBV97123 [+ Venezuela]
AJE 001-18		Venezuelan National Guard	SP-DFP GN97124
AJE 001-19		Venezuelan Army	SP-DFR EV9960
AJE 001-20		Venezuelan Army	SP-DFS EV9961
AJE 002-01		Venezuelan Army	SP-DFT EV0062
AJE 002-02		Venezuelan Army	SP-DFU EV0063+ ENBV0063 [+ Venezuela] [w/o 12Jun10 near Caracas-La Carlota, Venezuela]
AJE 002-03		Venezuelan Army	SP-DFW EV0064
AJE 002-04		Venezuelan Army	SP-DFZ EV0065+ ENBV0065 [+ Venezuela]
AJE 002-05		Venezuelan Army	SP-DFY EV0066+ ENBV0066 [+ Venezuela]
AJE 002-06		Venezuelan Army	SP-DFX EV0067+ ENBV0067 [+ Venezuela]
AJE 002-07		Venezuelan Army	SP-DFV EV0068+ ENBV0068 [+ Venezuela]
AJE 002-08		Venezuelan Army	SP-DGA EV0069+ ENBV0069 [+ Venezuela]
AJE 002-09		Venezuelan Army	SP-DGB EV0070
AJE 002-10		Venezuelan Army	SP-DGC EV0071
AJE 003-01		Nepalese Army	SP-DGD RAN-41+ NA-041 [+ Nepal]
AJE 003-02		Nepalese Army	SP-DGE RAN-48+ NA-048 [+ Nepal]
AJE 003-03	M28-05P1	Indonesian Police	SP-DGF P-2036+ P-4201+ [+ c/n not confirmed; Indonesia]
AJE 003-04	M28-05P1	(Indonesian Police)	SP-DGG P-2037+ P-4202 [+ c/n not confirmed; Indonesia] [w/o 02Nov09 near Kanggime en-route Jayapura to Mulia, Indonesia; wreck found 04Nov09]
AJE 003-05		Straight Flight Nevada Commercial Leasing	SP-DGK N305ST
AJE 003-06		Indonesian Police	SP-DGH P-2038+ P-4203+ [+ c/n not confirmed; Indonesia]
AJE 003-07		(Indonesian Police)	SP-DGI P-2039+ P-4204+ [+ c/n not confirmed; Indonesia] [w/o 27Oct10 en-route near Warri, Wanggar, Indonesia]
AJE 003-08	M28-05	Vietnam Air Force	SP-DGL 311
AJE 003-09	M28-05	(Vietnam Air Force)	SP-DGM 312 [w/o 04Nov05 near Dong Zuyen, Vietnam]

ANTONOV An-28/PZL M-28

C/n	Model	Last known Owner/Operator	Identities/fates/comments (where appropriate)
AJE 003-10	M28-05	Air Force Special Operations Command	SP-DGN N310MV
AJE 003-11	M28-05	Polish Border Guard	SP-PDG SN-60YG+ SP-VSB [+ Poland]
AJE 003-12	M28-05	reported for Polish Air Force	
AJE 003-13	M28-05	reported for Polish Air Force	
AJE 003-14	M28-05		[on assembly line Nov05]
AJE 003-15	M28-05	reported for Polish Air Force	
AJE 003-16	M28-05		[on assembly line Nov05]
AJE 003-17	M28-05	Air Force Special Operations Command	SP-DGP N317JG 09-0317
AJE 003-18	M28-05		
AJE 003-19	M28-05	Air Force Special Operations Command	SP-DGO N319TW
AJE 003-20	M28-05	Air Force Special Operations Command	SP-DGR N824KD 09-0320
AJE 003-21	M28-05	Air Force Special Operations Command	SP-DGS N279DH
AJE 003-22	M28-05	Air Force Special Operations Command	SP-DGT N322PW 10-0322 [marked as 00322 and still current on USCAR]
AJE 003-23	M28-05	Air Force Special Operations Command	SP-DGU N323FG SP-DGW N324HA
AJE 003-24	M28-05	Air Force Special Operations Command	
AJE 003-25			
AJE 003-26	M28-05	Air Force Special Operations Command	SP-DGZ N362DD
AJE 003-27			
AJE 003-28			
AJE 003-29	M28-05	Air Force Special Operations Command	SP-DGY N329JD
AJE 003-30			
AJE 003-31	M28	PZL sp	SP-DGV [c/n not fully confirmed]
PZL M-28-B1R Bryza			
AJG 001-01	M28-B1R	Polish Navy	1022 [ex c/n 1AJ 010-22?]
AJG 001-02	M28-B1R	Polish Air Force	1008 [ex c/n 1AJ 010-08]
AJG 001-03	M28-B1R	Polish Navy	1017 [ex c/n 1AJ 010-17]
AJG 001-04	M28-B1R	Polish Navy	1006 [ex c/n 1AJ 010-06]
AJG 001-05	M28-B1R	Polish Navy	1114 [ex c/n 1AJ 011-14]
AJG 001-06	M28-B1R	Polish Navy	1115 [ex c/n 1AJ 011-15]
AJG 001-07	M28-B1R	Polish Navy	1116 [ex c/n 1AJ 011-16]
AJG 002-01	M28-B1TD	Polish Navy	1117 [ex c/n 1AJ 011-17]
AJG 002-02	M28-B1TD	Polish Navy	1118 [ex c/n 1AJ 011-18]
AJG 002-03	M28-B1TD	Polish Air Force	0203
AJG 002-04	M28-B1TD	Polish Air Force	0204
AJG 002-05	M28-B1TD	Polish Air Force	0205
AJG 002-06	M28-B1TD	Polish Air Force	0206
AJG 002-07	M28-BTDII	Polish Air Force	0207
AJG 002-08	M28-BTDII	Polish Air Force	0208
AJG 002-09	M28-BTDII	Polish Air Force	0209
AJG 002-10	M28-BTDII	Polish Air Force	0210
AJG 002-11	M28-BTDII	Polish Air Force	0211
AJG 002-12	M28-BTDII	Polish Air Force	0212
AJG 003-01	M28-BTDII	Polish Air Force	0301+ 0213 [+ Poland]
AJG 003-02	M28-BTDII	Polish Air Force	0302+ 0214 [+ Poland]
AJG 003-03	M28-BTDII	Polish Air Force	0303+ 0215 [+ Poland]
AJG 003-04	M28-BTDII	Polish Air Force	0304+ 0216 [+ Poland]
AJG 003-05	M28-BTDII	Polish Air Force	0305+ 0217 [+ Poland]
AJG 003 06			[reported for Polish Air Force as 0218 now c/n AJG 004 01]
AJG 003 07			[reported for Polish Air Force as 0219 now c/n AJG 004 02]
AJG 004 01	M28-B/PT	Polish Air Force	0218
AJG 004-02	M28-B/PT	Polish Air Force	0219
AJG 004-03	M28-B/PT	Polish Air Force	0220

ANTONOV An-28/PZL M-28

C/n	Model	Last known Owner/Operator	Identities/fates/comments (where appropriate)	
AJG 004-04	M28-B/PT	Polish Air Force	0221	
AJG 004-05	M28-B/PT	Polish Air Force	0222	
Unidentified				
unkn		unknown	FLA-3373	[reported 24Dec05 & 19Feb06 Borki, Russia]
unkn		unknown	LA-3371	[reported 24Dec05 & 19Feb06 Borki, Russia]
unkn		unknown	LA-3372	[reported 05Nov05 Borki, Russia]
unkn		unknown	LY-APB	[mfd 15Jan90; CofA canx 05Apr02]
unkn		unknown	LY-AHU	[mfd 30Oct87; CofA canx 26Oct99; possibly c/n 1AJ004-08]
unkn		unknown	RA-2092K	[reported 28Aug10 Stendal Borstel, Germany]
unkn		unknown	RA-2098K	[reported 12Apr05 Myachkovo, Russia]
unkn		unknown	RA-3012K	[reported 10Apr04 Riga-Skulte, Latvia]
unkn		MA-MA	RA-3072K	[reported 18Aug05 Borki, Russia]
unkn		unknown	RA-3092K	[reported 12Apr05 Myachkovo, Russia]
unkn		unknown	RA-3560K	[reported 06Aug09 Magdeburg, Germany]
unkn		Kuzbassavia	RF-00404	[reported 23Mar10 Tanai, Russia with TsSPK logo]
unkn		unknown	RF-01009	[reported 14May06 & 23Jly06 Rovaniemi, Finland]
unkn		Rodina	RF-01197	[reported 04Feb06 Kirzhach, Russia]
unkn		ROSTO Krasnoyarsk	RF-14430	[based Manski, Russia; l/n 10Feb08 still with damage following accident 26May07]
unkn		unknown	RF-38385	[reported ex registration under military serial]
unkn		unknown	C5-GJD	[reported Sep03 Banjul, Gambia; not confirmed as a An-28]
unkn		unknown	PZ-PSA	[reported 11Nov03 Barbados; was not PZ-TSA c/n 1AJ007-21]
unkn		unknown	TL-ACO	[reported 20Sep99 Ras al Khaimah, UAE]
unkn		unknown	TL-AOG	[reported 27Nov00 Kigali, Rwanda]
unkn		unknown	UP-A2804	[reported in Jan10 Chimkent, Kazakhstan]
unkn		unknown	YV403T	[reported 18Oct09 Tamiami, FL; l/n there Dec09]
unkn		Transmandu	YV1057	[reported 02Mar07 Puerto Ordaz, Venezuela]
unkn		"Peligeo"?	YV2773	[reported in 2012]
unkn		Mavivi Air	3C-DDB	[stored by 29Maro6 Goma, Democratic Republic of Congo; l/n 05Mar08]
unkn		unknown	3C-JJW	[reported 30Jly99 Nairobi, Kenya]
unkn		unknown	3C-KKA	[reported 15Jun99 Chernigov, Ukraine]
unkn		Insolite Travel Fly	5R-MJM	[reported 2010 Ivato, Madagascar]
unkn		Malu Aviation	9Q-COP	[reported 05Mar08 Goma, Democratic Republic of Congo; possible misread of 9Q-CQP]
unkn		(Aigle Aviation)	9U-BHR	[reported 22Sep04 Goma, Democratic Republic of Congo; canx 12Nov04; marks were used illegally on An-26 c/n 2206]
unkn		Franklin Group	9XR-AC	[reported 04Jly99 Kiev-Zhulany, Ukraine]
unkn		unknown	9XR-AE	[reported 06Nov99 Fujairah, UAE]
unkn		unknown	9XR-AG	[reported derelict 2010 Cyanguju, Rwanda]
unkn		unknown	9XR-CM	[mentioned in UN document; canx 17Mar05]
unkn		unknown	9XR-DA	[reported 07mar00 Umm al Quawain, UAE]
unkn		(Regional International Air Services)	9XR-DP	[canx Dec03 sold to South Africa]
unkn		unknown	9XR-KA	[mentioned in UN document; canx 17Mar05]
unkn		Georgian Air Force	05 black	[reported Jly07 Tiblisi, Georgia]
unkn		Georgian Air Force	06 black	[reported Jly07 Tiblisi, Georgia]
unkn		Russian Air Force c/s	"70" red	[reported 09Sep06 Krasnodar-Enem, Russia; is not a military aircraft]
unkn		Tanzanian Air Force	JW9031	[reported 18Oct04 Dar-es-Salaam, Tanzania]
unkn		Tanzanian Air Force	JW9032	[reported 02Oct04 Dar-es-Salaam, Tanzania]

ANTONOV An-30

C/n	Model	Last known Owner/Operator	Identities/fates/comments (where appropriate)

Note: Prototype was An-24FK c/n 5 73 02 003 which please see

01 01		Ukraine Air Force	[Soviet] 01 blue+ 85 blue [+ Ukraine]
02 01		Lukiaviatrans	CCCP-46632 RA-46632
02 02		ex Ukraine National	CCCP-46633 UR-46633 [canx 13Aug08; fate/status unknown]
03 01		(Myachkovo Air Service)	CCCP-46634 RA-46634 [wfu by 01Jly06 Myachkovo, Russia; canx date unknown]
03 02		MNS Ukraiiny	[Soviet] 12 blue+ [+Ukraine]
03 03		Ukraine Air Force	03 red+ 03 red^ 03 blue^ 88 blue^ [+Soviet; ^Ukraine; stored by Sep10 Kiev-Borispol, Ukraine]
03 04		Russian Air Force	[Soviet] 33 yellow
03 05		Russian Air Force	[Soviet] [not known]
04 01		Russian Air Force	09 red+ 41 red [+Soviet]
04 02		Russian Air Force	08 red+ 30 yellow [+Soviet/Russia]
04 03		G-Aisyam	CCCP-30021 RA-30021
04 04		ex Ukraine National	CCCP-30022 UR-30022 [canx 13Aug08; fate/status unknown]
04 05		Russian Air Force	07 red
05 01		(Myachkovo Air Service)	CCCP-30023 RA-30023 [wfu by 29Mar07 Myachkovo, Russia; canx date unknown]
05 02		Polet	CCCP-30024 RA-30024
05 03		ex Ukraine National	CCCP-30025 UR-30025 [canx 13Aug08; fate/status unknown]
05 04		Russian Air Force	06 red+ 32 yellow [+Soviet/Russia]
05 05		ex Ukraine National	CCCP-30026 UR-30026 [canx 13Aug08; noted 28Mar12 stored Kiev-Zhulyany, Ukraine]
05 06		(Myachkovo Air Service)	CCCP-30027 RA-30027 [wfu by 01Jly06 Myachkovo, Russia; canx date unknown]
05 07		Russian Air Force	[Soviet] RA-30078 ["Open Skies"]
05 08		Russian Air Force/UN	[Soviet] 30508
05 09			[nothing known]
05 10		Gromov Air	CCCP-30028 RA-30028
06 01			[nothing known]
06 02		Ukraine Air Force	[Soviet] 06 blue+ 86 blue [+ Ukraine; stored by Jly99 Kiev-Borispol, Ukraine]
06 03		Ministry of Interior (MVD)	[unknown+] RF-30081 [+ code yellow number not known]
06 04		Kazaviaspas	CCCP-30029 UN-30029 UP-AN301
06 05	A-100	Green Flag Aviation	CCCP-30030 UR-30030 ST-GFD
06 06		Kazakhstan Government	CCCP-30031 UN-30031
06 07		(Myachkovo Air Service)	CCCP-30032 RA-30032 [wfu by 29Mar07 Myachkovo, Russia; canx date unknown]
06 08		Ukraine Air Force	[Soviet] 80 gold ["Open Skies"] ["46918" on instrument panel possibly call sign]
06 09	B	Ukraine Air Force	[Soviet] 81 gold ["Open Skies"] [has used call sign "30185"]
06 10		(Myachkovo Air Service)	CCCP-30033 RA-30033 [wfu by 15Aug05 Myachkovo, Russia; canx date unknown; b/u by 29Mar07]
07 01		Novosibirsk Avia	CCCP-30034 RA-30034 [wfu by 08Jly05 Novosibirsk-Severny, Russia; l/n 30Aug07 b/u]
07 02		Myachkovo Air Service	CCCP-30035 RA-30035
07 03		South Airlines	CCCP-30036 UR-30036
07 04	B	(Russian Air Force)	04 red+ 04 black [+Russia] ["Open Skies"] [RA-70167 on instrument panel possibly call sign; w/o 23May12 Caslav, Czech Republic]
07 05			[nothing known]
07 06		Russian Air Force	VN-B378(1) CCCP-26226 RA-26226 ["Open Skies"]
07 07		(Novosibirsk Avia)	CCCP-30037 RA-30037 [wfu by 23Jly00 Novosibirsk-Severny, Russia by Jly00; canx 18Apr02; l/n 30Aug07 b/u]
07 08		Kazaviaspas	CCCP-30038 UN-30038
07 09		Russian Air Force	23+ CCCP-27205 RA-27205 [+ Soviet, colour of code unknown;] ["Open Skies"]
07 10		Lukiaviatrans	CCCP-30039 RA-30039
08 01		Burundai Avia	CCCP-30040 UN-30040
08 02		Bulgarian Air Force	055 ["Open Skies"]
08 03	B	Russian Air Force	83 red
08 04			[nothing known]

ANTONOV An-30

C/n	Model	Last known Owner/Operator	Identities/fates/comments (where appropriate)
08 05		(Novosibirsk Avia)	CCCP-30041 RA-30041 [wfu by Jly01 Novosibirsk-Severny, Russia; l/n 30Aug07 b/u]
08 06		Russian Air Force	86 red
08 07		Russian Air Force	87 red+ 87 black [+Russia] ["Open Skies"]
08 08			[nothing known]
08 09			[nothing known]
08 10		Russian Air Force	[Soviet] 10 red
09 01		Lukiaviatrans	CCCP-30042 RA-30042
09 02		Chinese Air Force	871
09 03		China United Airlines	872
09 04		Russian Air Force	[Soviet] 04 yellow
09 05		ex Myachkovo Air Service	CCCP-30043 RA-30043 [by 22Oct11 preserved Lytkarino, SE of Moscow, Russia]
09 06		ex Kiev ARP 410 Airlines	CCCP-30044 UR-30044 [fate/status unknown]
09 07		(Myachkovo Air Service)	CCCP-30045 RA-30045 [wfu by 29Mar07 Myachkovo, Russia; canx date unknown]
09 08		Burundai Avia	CCCP-30046 UN-30046
09 09		Myachkovo Air Service	CCCP-30047 RA-30047
09 10		Polet Flight	CCCP-30048 RA-30048
10 01		Chinese Air Force	873
10 02		Chinese Air Force	874
10 03		Chinese Air Force	875
10 04		(Novosibirsk Avia)	CCCP-30049 RA-30049 [stored by 03Jly03 Novosibirsk-Severny, Russia; Sep11 b/u for spares]
10 05		(Myachkovo Air Service)	CCCP-30050 RA-30050 [wfu by 29Mar07 Myachkovo, Russia; canx date unknown]
10 06		(Novosibirsk Avia)	CCCP-30051 RA-30051 [stored by 05Jly08 Novosibirsk-Severny, Russia; sold 16Jun11; b/u 20Dec11 for spares]
10 07		(Novosibirsk Avia)	CCCP-30052 RA-30052 [stored by 05Jly08 Novosibirsk-Severny, Russia; b/u Dec11 for spares]
10 08	D	Lukiaviatrans	CCCP-30053 RA-30053
10 09		ex Vietnam Air Services Company	[not known] VN-B376 [wfu by 07Nov09 Ho Chi Minh City, Vietnam; l/n 18Nov09]
10 10		(Myachkovo Air Service)	CCCP-30054 RA-30054 [wfu by 29Mar07 Myachkovo, Russia; canx date unknown]
11 01		(Myachkovo Air Service)	CCCP-30055 RA-30055 [wfu by 15Aug05 Myachkovo, Russia; canx date unknown]
11 02		Novosibirsk Avia	CCCP-30056 RA-30056
11 03	A	Aerop. Marculesti	103+ 1103+ ER-AWZ [+ Romania]
11 04		ex Romanian Air Force	104+ 1104+ [+ Romania] [stored by 28Jly06 Buchaest-Otopeni, Romania; l/n 29Jun07]
11 05		Romanian Air Force	105+ 1105+ [+ Romania] ["Open Skies"]
11 06		Burundai Avia	CCCP-30057 RA-30057 UN-30057
11 07	FG	Letecke Muzeum Kbely	LZ-AEG 1107+ [+ Czech Republic] [preserved by Sep06 Kbely, Czech Republic; Nov09 moved to Zruc Air Park; l/n Apr10]
11 08		Novosibirsk Avia	CCCP-30059 RA-30059
11 09		Burundai Avia	CCCP-30060 UN-30060 [wfu by 29Mar07 Myachkovo, Russia; canx date unknown]
11 10		(Myachkovo Air Service)	CCCP-30061 RA-30061 [wfu by 29Mar07 Myachkovo, Russia; canx date unknown]
12 01		Sudanese Air Force	CCCP-30062 RA-30062 7708+ [+ not confirmed]
12 02	D	ex Novosibirsk Avia	CCCP-30063 RA-30063
12 03	-100	ex Myachkovo Air Service	CCCP-30064 RA-30064 [canx post Aug94 date unknown; but overhauled Oct05 at Kiev-Zhulyany, Ukraine; current owner/status unknown]
12 04		(Myachkovo Air Service)	CCCP-30065 RA-30065 [wfu by 29Mar07 Myachkovo, Russia; canx date unknown]
12 05		ex Vietnam Air Services Company	VN-B378(2) [stored by Nov97 Ho Chi Minh City, Vietnam; l/n derelict by 10Apr12]
12 06		(Myachkovo Air Service)	CCCP-30066 RA-30066 [wfu by 29Mar07 Myachkovo, Russia; canx date unknown]
12 07			[nothing known]
12 08		ex BaltAeroTrans	CCCP-30067 RA-30067 [impounded 22Aug11 Pskov, Russia]

ANTONOV An-30

C/n	Model	Last known Owner/Operator	Identities/fates/comments (where appropriate)
12 09	D	(Novosibirsk Avia)	CCCP-30068 RA-30068 [stored by 05Jly08 Novosibirsk-Severny, Russia; b/u Dec11 for spares]
12 10		(Myachkovo Air Service)	CCCP-30069 RA-30069 [wfu by 29Mar07 Myachkovo, Russia; canx date unknown]
13 01	A-100	Aero Fret Business	CCCP-30070 RA-30070 EX-116 TN-AHJ+ [+ not confirmed]
13 02		Burundai Avia?	CCCP-30071 UN-30071
13 03	A-100	Aero Fret Business	CCCP-30072 RA-30072 EX-118 TN-AHS+ [+ not confirmed]
13 04		Flight Research Aerogeophysical Centre	CCCP-30073 RA-30073 30073
13 05		(Myachkovo Air Service)	CCCP-30074 RA-30074 [wfu by 29Mar07 Myachkovo, Russia; canx date unknown]
13 06	D	Myachkovo Air Service	CCCP-30075 RA-30075
13 07		Russian Air Force	01 red ["Open Skies"]
13 08		Russian Air Force	[Soviet] 31 yellow
13 09		Ukraine Air Force	05 blue+ 87 blue [+ Ukraine]
13 10		MNS Ukraiiny	[Soviet] 11 blue [+ Ukraine]
14 01	A-100	Angolan Air Force	CCCP-30000 UR-30000 D2-MBO T-240+ D2-MBO T-240 [+ Angola]
14 02		Grodno Air	CCCP-30001 RA-30001 EW-281CN+ [+ not fully confirmed]
14 03		(Aeroflot/Central Region)	CCCP-30002 [w/o 22Mar92 53km east of Nizhneyansk, Yakutia, USSR]
14 04		Burundai Avia	CCCP-30003 UN-30003
14 05	D	ex Novosibirsk Avia	CCCP-30004 RA-30004 [for sale 09Feb11 following demise of airline in 2010]
14 06		(Ukraine National)	CCCP-30005 UR-30005 [l/n stored Kiev-Zhulyani, Ukraine; canx 07Jly11 fate/status unknown]
14 07		Geodynamika	CCCP-30006 RA-30006
14 08	D	Lukiaviatrans	CCCP-30007 RA-30007
14 09		(China General Aviation)	876+ B-3301 [+China] [stored by Oct98 Taiyuan, China; b/u by Aug00]
14 10		(China General Aviation)	877+ B-3302 [+China] [stored by Oct98 Taiyuan, China; b/u by Aug00]
15 01		(China General Aviation)	878+ B-3303 [+China] [stored by Oct98 Taiyuan, China; b/u by Aug00]
15 02			[nothing known]
15 03			[nothing known]
15 04		Russian Space Forces	[Soviet] [Russian AF] RF-36014
15 05	R	Russian Air Force	[Soviet] 30080 [operated at times for United Nations, UN 30000 under wing relating to UN and not Kazakhstan]
15 06		ex MIAT Mongolian	BNMAU-1506 (MT-1016) (JU-1016) [wfu by 1995 Ulan Baatar, Mongolia; b/u; fuselage only noted 27Jan10]
15 07		Chinese Air Force	879
15 08		Chinese Air Force	880
15 09		Chinese Air Force	881
15 10		Chinese Air Force	882
16 01		Chinese Air Force	883
Unidentified			
unkn		Afghan Air Force	237 [reported 1978 Kabul, Afghanistan; fate/status unknown; photo proof]
unkn		Cuban Air Force	FAR-1444 [probably ex Soviet/Russian Air Force and to CU-F1444]
unkn		Aerogaviota	CU-F1444 [reported 16Jun98 Camaguey, Cuba & 11Mar00 Santiago de Cuba, Cuba]
unkn		Aerogaviota	CU-T1445 [reported 21Nov97 Havana-Playa Baracoa, Cuba & Jun99 Cayo Largo del Sur, Cuba]
unkn		Russian Air Force	31 yellow [reported 20Aug06 & 28Aug07 Irkutsk One, Russia]
unkn		Russian Air Force	32 yellow [reported 14Aug07 & 28Aug07 Irkutsk One, Russia]
unkn		Russian Air Force	33 yellow [reported summer 2006 & 28Aug07 Irkutsk One, Russia]
unkn		Soviet/Russian Air Force	01 red [reported several times between 01Jly92 & 01Sep97; could be c/n 1307]
unkn		Soviet Air Force	04 red [reported 1984 Kabul, Afghanistan; same code reported 19Aug06 Voronezh-Baltimor, Russia after c/n 0704 became 04 black]
unkn		Soviet Air Force	05 red [w/o 11Mar85 25km N of Kabul, Afghanistan]
unkn		Soviet/Russian Air Force	05 red [reported 01Jly92 Krasnoyarsk-Yemelyanovo, USSR]

ANTONOV An-30

C/n	Model	Last known Owner/Operator	Identities/fates/comments (where appropriate)	
unkn		Soviet Air Force	16	[reported Oct87 Kabul, Afghanistan; colour of code not known; code 01 before and after this mission]
unkn		Soviet Air Force	17	[reported Oct87 Kabul, Afghanistan; colour of code not known]
unkn		Soviet/Russian Air Force	17 red	[reported 13Jly93 Krasnoyarsk-Yemelyanovo, USSR]
unkn		Sudan Air Force	7704	[reported 14Mar07 Geneina, Sudan & 31Mar09 Khartoum, Sudan]
unkn		Soviet Air Force	84	[reported w/o 19/20Oct79 by typhoon "Tip" at Burevestnik, Iturup Island, USSR]
unkn		Ukraine Air Force	89 blue	[noted 21May04 & 10Jun06 Kiev-Borispol, Ukraine]
unkn		Aero Fret Business	TN-AHP	[reported 26Oct08 & 07Jun09 Pointe Noire, Peoples Republic of Congo; earlier report as An-24 incorrect]

Production complete

ANTONOV An-32

Notes: 1) Many of the c/ns of the Indian Air Force aircraft have not been confirmed; such aircraft are shown with a question mark following the c/n in the c/n column.
2) Indian Air Force aircraft carry different single-letter codes from time to time and sometimes no code at all; the quoting of a code or codes above do not constitute a full record of their use.
3) Within the first column "Soviet" indicates aircraft concerned is considered to have operated by one of the Soviet/Russian/CIS air arms and no code or other identity, such as CCCP-xxxxx, is known.
4) A yet to be identified Indian Air Force An-32 was w/o 08Jun09 when it crashed near Mechukla AFB, India.
5) Two Indian Air Force An-32s were w/o on 04Oct88 and 15Jly90; no details known.
6) An Indian Air Force An-32 was w/o 09Jun09 Mechuka, India.

C/n	Model	Last known Owner/Operator	Identities/fates/comments (where appropriate)
1006	An-32	(Antonov Design Bureau)	CCCP-83966 CCCP-46961 [cvtd from An-26 using its original c/n; derelict by 28Aug93 Gostomel, Ukraine; l/n 10Sep96]
001	An-32	ex Antonov Design Bureau	CCCP-380122 CCCP-21508 [wfu or w/o before 12Mar07; dumped by May99 Gostomel, Ukraine; l/n Jun06]
002	An-32	[static test airframe?]	
003	An-32P	(Heliservico)	CCCP-380322 CCCP-21132 UR-48018 [cvtd Oct93 to An-32P fire-fighter; w/o 06Jly94 Sierra Mariola mountain range nr Alicante, Spain]
0101	An-32	ex Indian Air Force	AJ301 K2667 [f/f 23Jun83;] [fate/status unknown]
0102	An-32RE	Indian Air Force	AJ303 K2668
0103?	An-32	(Indian Air Force)	K2669 [code A] [w/o 01Apr92 near Boothgarh, Ludhiana, India collided with An-32 c/n 1710 K3055]
0104	An-32RE	Indian Air Force	K2670 [codes B & A]
0105?	An-32	Indian Air Force	K2671 [codes F & A] [stored/wfu by 08Feb11 Yelahanka AFB, India]
0106	An-32	(Antonov Design Bureau)	(unknown) [w/o before 1990 whilst on test flight]
0107	An-32	Indian Air Force	K2672 [code G]
0108?	An-32	(Indian Air Force)	K2673 [w/o 07Mar99 Delhi, India]
0109?	An-32	Indian Air Force	K2674 [code M]
0110?	An-32	Indian Air Force	K2675 [code C]
0201	An-32RE	Indian Air Force	K2676
0202	An-32RE	Indian Air Force	K2677 [codes E & B; later uncoded]
0203	An-32	Indian Air Force	K2678 [code F]
0204	An-32RE	Indian Air Force	K2679 [codes E & K]
0205	An-32RE	Indian Air Force	K2680
0206	An-32RE	Indian Air Force	K2681 [code B]
0207	An-32RE	Indian Air Force	K2682 [code K]
0208?	An-32	Indian Air Force	K2683 [code M]
0209	An-32	Indian Air Force	K2684
0210?	An-32	Indian Air Force	K2685
0301	An-32RE	Indian Air Force	K2686
0302	An-32RE	Indian Air Force	K2687 [codes M & T]
0303?	An-32	Diamond Jubilee Museum	K2688+ [+ India] [w/o in hard landing at Kalaikunda AFB, India & preserved there by Nov99]
0304	An-32RE	Indian Air Force	K2689 [code H]
0305?	An-32	(Indian Air Force)	K2690 [reported w/o 23Feb00 Vijaynagar, India; by Feb11forward fuselage in use as simulator Yelahanka AFB, India]
0306?	An-32	Indian Air Force	K2691
0307	An-32RE	Indian Air Force	K2692 [code D]
0308	An-32	Indian Air Force	K2693 [codes T & F]
0309	An-32RE	Indian Air Force	K2694 [code W]
0310?	An-32	Indian Air Force	K2695 [code X]
0401	An-32RE	Indian Air Force	K2696 [code C]
0402	An-32	Indian Air Force	K2697
0403	An-32	Indian Air Force	K2698
0404?	An-32	Indian Air Force	K2699
0405?	An-32	Indian Air Force	K2700 [stored/wfu by 08Feb11 Yelahanka AFB, India]
0406?	An-32	Indian Air Force	K2701 [code N]
0407	An-32	(Indian Air Force)	K2702 [w/o 22Mar86 Kishtwar, Jammu, Kashmir, India]
0408	An-32	Indian Air Force	K2703 [codes P & T]
0409	An-32RE	Indian Air Force	K2704 [codes H & E]
0410	An-32	(Indian Air Force)	K2705 [w/o or wfu prior to 12Mar07]

ANTONOV An-32

C/n	Model	Last known Owner/Operator	Identities/fates/comments (where appropriate)
0501	An-32RE	Indian Air Force	K2706 [code J]
0502	An-32RE	Indian Air Force	K2707 [code M]
0503	An-32RE	Indian Air Force	K2708
0504	An-32	Indian Air Force	K2709 [codes J & L & K]
0505?	An-32	(Indian Air Force)	K2710 [w/o or wfu prior to 12Mar07]
0506?	An-32	Indian Air Force	K2711 [code K]
0507	An-32	Indian Air Force	K2712 [codes O & B]
0508?	An-32	(Indian Air Force)	K2713 [w/o or wfu prior to 12Mar07]
0509	An-32	Indian Air Force	K2714 [codes F & K]
0510	An-32RE	Indian Air Force	K2715 [codes N & E]
0601	An-32	Indian Air Force	K2716
0602?	An-32	Indian Air Force	K2717 [code E]
0603?	An-32	Indian Air Force	K2718 [code A]
0604	An-32RE	Indian Air Force	K2719
0605	An-32RE	Indian Air Force	K2720
0606?	An-32	Indian Air Force	K2721 [code O] [seriously damaged 15Dec11 at unknown location in India]
0607?	An-32	Indian Air Force	K2722
0608?	An-32	Indian Air Force	K2723
0609	An-32RE	Indian Air Force	K2724
0610?	An-32	Indian Air Force	K2725
0701?	An-32	Indian Air Force	K2726 [codes E & Y]
0702	An-32	Indian Air Force	K2727 [code B]
0703	An-32P	Libyan Air Cargo	CCCP-48093 UR-48093 5A-DRC [cvtd to fire-fighter version]
0704	An-32	Indian Air Force	K2728
0705?	An-32	(Indian Air Force)	K2729 [w/o 25Mar86 in Indian Ocean 450km off Jamnagar, India; on delivery]
0706	An-32	Indian Air Force	K2730 [codes K & Y]
0707?	An-32	Indian Air Force	K2731
0708?	An-32	Indian Air Force	K2732 [codes N & L]
0709	An-32RE	Indian Air Force	K2733
0710?	An-32	Indian Air Force	K2734 [codes L & D]
0801	An-32RE	Indian Air Force	K2735 [codes L, F & again L]
0802?	An-32	Indian Air Force	K2736 [code D]
0803?	An-32	Indian Air Force	K2737 [codes B & E]
0804?	An-32	Indian Air Force	K2738 [code B]
0805?	An-32	Indian Air Force	K2739
0806	An-32	Indian Air Force	K2740 [code Q]
0807	An-32	Indian Air Force	K2741
0808?	An-32	Indian Air Force	K2742 [code U]
0809?	An-32	Indian Air Force	K2743 [code C]
0810	An-32	Indian Air Force	K2744 [code P]
0901	An-32	Indian Air Force	K2745 [code E]
0902?	An-32A	ex Afghan Air Force	281 [stored by 12Mar03 Mazar-I-Sharif, Afghanistan; l/n Aug03]
0903	An-32	ex Indian Air Force	K2746 [wreckage reported Nov02 Tezpur AFB, India]
0904	An-32	Indian Air Force	K2747 [code P; later no code]
0905?	An-32	Indian Air Force	K2748 [codes Q & F; later no code]
0906?	An-32	ex Afghan Air Force	282 [wreck noted 08Jun06 Khost, Afghanistan]
0907?	An-32	Indian Air Force	K2749 [not fully confirmed]
0908?	An-32A	(Afghan Air Force)	283 [wfu or w/o by 12Mar07]
0909	An-32	ex Peruvian Air Force	362+ OB-1379 362+ [+ Peru] [last flight 04Jun98; wfu because of corrosion; l/n Lima, Peru 06Sep05]
0910	An-32	Colleccion de la Base Aerea de Lima	363+ OB-1380 363+ [+ Peru] [wfu; preserved post Sep05 Callao, Lima, Peru]
1001	An-32	(Peruvian Air Force)	366+ OB-1381 366+ [+ Peru] [reported wfu and probably b/u]
1002	An-32	ex Peruvian Air Force	367+ OB-1382 367+ [+ Peru] [last flight 08Sep97; wfu because of corrosion; l/n Lima, Peru 06Sep05]
1003	An-32	ex Peruvian Air Force	376+ OB-1383 376+ [+ Peru] [last flight 01Sep99; wfu because of corrosion; l/n Lima, Peru 06Sep05]
1004	An-32A	(Afghan Air Force)	284 [wfu or w/o by 12Mar07]
1005?	An-32A	(Afghan Air Force)	285 [wreck noted Sep05 Khost, Afghanistan; l/n 08Jun06]
1006	An-32A	(Afghan Air Force)	286 [wfu or w/o by 12Mar07; see first prototype above which used An-26 c/n 1006; nothing known on this c/n]
1007	An-32	Indian Air Force	K2750 [code H at one time]
1008	An-32	Indian Air Force	K2751 [codes N, D, C & F]

ANTONOV An-32

C/n	Model	Last known Owner/Operator	Identities/fates/comments (where appropriate)
1009	An-32	Indian Air Force	K2752 [codes M & L] [stored/wfu by 08Feb11 Yelahanka AFB, India]
1010?	An-32A	(Afghan Air Force)	287 [wfu or w/o by 12Mar07]
1101?	An-32A	(Afghan Air Force)	288 [wfu or w/o by 12Mar07]
1102?	An-32A	(Afghan Air Force)	289 [wfu or w/o by 12Mar07]
1103?	An-32A	(Afghan Air Force)	290 [wfu or w/o by 12Mar07]
1104	An-32	Indian Air Force	K2753
1105	An-32	Indian Air Force	K2754 [codes N & W & K]
1106	An-32	(Peruvian Air Force)	374+ OB-1384 374+ [+ Peru] [w/o 1990 in jungle]
1107	An-32	ex Peruvian Air Force	378+ OB-1385 378+ [+ Peru] [wfu by Apr03 Lima, Peru; l/n Nov07]
1108	An-32	(Peruvian Air Force)	379+ OB-1386 379+ [+ Peru] [w/o 1997 in jungle]
1109	An-32	(Peruvian Air Force)	386+ OB-1387 386+ [+ Peru] [hard landing summer 2001 Las Palmas AFB, Peru; repaired; l/n 11Aug07 Lima, Peru; wfu by Jly10]
1110	An-32	Indian Air Force	K2755 [codes D & U]
1201	An-32	Indian Air Force	K2756 [code B]
1202?	An-32	Indian Air Force	K2757 [codes D & G]
1203	An-32	ex Peruvian Air Force	388+ OB-1388 388+ [+ Peru] [wfu by 20Nov07 Lima, Peru]
1204?	An-32	Indian Air Force	K2758 [code Z]
1205	An-32	Indian Air Force	K2759 [code B]
1206	An-32RE	Indian Air Force	K2760 [code J]
1207?	An-32	(Indian Air Force)	K2761 [w/o or wfu prior to 12Mar07]
1208	An-32	Indian Air Force	K2762 [codes P & T]
1209?	An-32	Indian Air Force	K2763 [w/o or wfu prior to 12Mar07]
1210?	An-32A	Indian Air Force	K2764 [c/n tie up not confirmed]
1301	An-32	(Peruvian Air Force)	389+ OB-1390^ [reported crashed 1997 nr Colombian border] 382? OB-1398? [+ reported crashed 1997 nr Colombian border; ^ Peru; possibly re-serialed after repair; noted Apr03; the serial 382 used on C-130; wfu before 12Mar07; l/n Nov07; possibly b/u]
1302	An-32	ex Peruvian Air Force	391+ OB-1391 391+ [+ Peru] [wfu by Nov07 Lima, Peru]
1303	An-32	ex Peruvian Air Force	392+ OB-1392 392+ [+ Peru] [wfu by Nov07 Lima, Peru; by Jly09 preserved Parque Tematico de la FAP, Lima-Callao, Peru]
1304	An-32	(Peruvian Air Force)	375+ OB-1389 375+ [+ Peru] [w/o 29Mar98 Piura, Peru]
1305	An-32	(Peruvian Air Force)	387+ OB-1394 387+ [+ Peru] [l/n Mar04; wfu Lima, Peru and probably b/u]
1306	An-32P	Libyan Arab Air Force	CCCP- UR-48004 5A-DRD [fire-fighter version; reportedly de-converted by Sep02]
1307?	An-32A	(Afghan Air Force)	291 [wfu or w/o by 12Mar07]
1308?	An-32A	(Afghan Air Force)	292 [wfu or w/o by 12Mar07]
1309	An-32	(Peruvian Air Force}	377 [w/o 06Mar90 Satipo, Peru]
1310	An-32	Ethiopian Air Force	1551
1401	An-32	(Ethiopian Air Force)	1552? [details not confirmed; del 1989; w/o before 2007 in Ethiopia]
1402?	An-32A	(Afghan Air Force)	293 [wfu or w/o by 12Mar07]
1403?	An-32A	(Afghan Air Force)	294 [wfu or w/o by 12Mar07]
1404?	An-32A	(Afghan Air Force)	295 [wfu or w/o by 12Mar07]
1405?	An-32A	(Afghan Air Force)	296 [wfu or w/o by 12Mar07]
1406?	An-32A	(Afghan Air Force)	297 [wreck noted early00 Bagram AFB, Afghanistan; l/n May04]
1407	An-32B	(Great Lakes Bus)	CCCP-48974 RA-48974 3D-RTB TL-ACH 3C-QQT 9Q-CAC [w/o 26Aug07 nr Kongolo, Democratic Republic of Congo]
1408	An-32A	Aquiline Aero	CCCP-69356 RA-69356 D2-FED 9Q-CJU ST-SMZ 3X-GES(1) 4L-OVE(2) 3X-GES(1) 3X-GHJ
1409	An-32	Angolan Air Force	CCCP-48979 RA-48979 ER-AWU T-255
1410	An-32A	Angolan Air Force	CCCP-69321 RA-69321 ER-AWI D2-FEN T-257
1501?	An-32A	(Afghan Air Force)	298 [wfu or w/o by 12Mar07]
1502?	An-32A	(Afghan Air Force)	299 [wfu or w/o by 12Mar07]
1503?	An-32A	(Afghan Air Force)	300 [reported May04 Begram AFB as wreck & 08JUn08 Kabul, Afghanistan also as wreck]
1504?	An-32A	(Afghan Air Force)	301 [wfu or w/o by 12Mar07]
1505?	An-32A	(Afghan Air Force)	302 [wfu or w/o by 12Mar07]
1506?	An-32A	(Afghan Air Force)	303 [wfu or w/o by 12Mar07]
1507?	An-32A	(Afghan Air Force)	304 [wfu or w/o by 12Mar07]
1508?	An-32A	(Afghan Air Force)	305 [wfu or w/o by 12Mar07]
1509?	An-32A	(Afghan Air Force)	306 [by Feb06 wreck Pol-e-Charki scrap yard, Kabul, Afghanistan; l/n 08Jun06]
1510	An-32A	Alada	CCCP-48115 48115 RA-48115 D2-FAX
1601	An-32	(MAP Ufa Motors)	CCCP-48981 RA-48981 [w/o 25Oct95 Maksimovska, Russia]

ANTONOV An-32

C/n	Model	Last known Owner/Operator	Identities/fates/comments (where appropriate)
1602	An-32A	(Tura Flight Enterprise)	CCCP-48104 RA-48104 [w/o 22Nov96 Baiket, Russia; canx 27Dec96]
1603	An-32	(Trans Charter/Renan)	CCCP-48983 RA-48983 ER-AEQ [w/o 02Apr02 Cafunfo, Angola; canx 12Jun02]
1604	An-32A	Ayk Avia	CCCP-29120 RA-29120 9L-LFO EK-32604 [wfu by 14Sep08 Fujairah, UAE; l/n 02Mar09; canx by 01Jan09]
1605	An-32	Kazan Motors	CCCP-69309 RA-69309
1606	An-32	Kras Avia	CCCP-69354 RA-69354
1607	An-32	Taimyr	CCCP-69355 RA-69355
1608	An-32	(Transportes Aeroes Andahuaylas S.A)	CCCP-48107 OB-1488 [CofA expired 03Apr98; canx 16Jly01; l/n 15Jan02; Lima-Callao, Peru; fate unknown]
1609	An-32	(Equatorial Guinee Air Force)	3C-5GE [w/o 16Apr08 off Annobon Island, Equatorial Guinee]
1610?	An-32A	(Afghan Air Force)	307 [wfu or w/o by 12Mar07]
1701	An-32	Bangladesh Air Force	1701//S3-ACA [dual marks which previously used on An-26 c/n 1701]
1702	An-32	Bangladesh Air Force Museum	1702//S3-ACB [dual marks;] [preserved Dhaka-Tejgaon AFB, Bangladesh]
1703	An-32A	Trast Aero	CCCP-48094 RA-48094 EL-WCB 9Q-CAF S9-GBC 4L-OVE(1) 4L-GSI 3X-GES(2) 4L-GSI 3X-GHC
1704	An-32A	SAEP	CCCP-48976 RA-48976 ER-AEX(2) D2-FDJ ER-AXF HK-4296X HK-4296
1705	An-32	(MAP Moscow)	CCCP-48095 [w/o 28Sep89 nr Semyonovka, USSR; canx 29Nov90]
1706	An-32	unknown	CCCP-48103 RA-48103 ER-AFH+ D2- [+ canx 11Feb00 to Angola]
1707	An-32	Centrafrican	CCCP-48105 RA-48105 3D-RTC 7Q-YWY TL-ACS
1708	An-32	Air Pass	CCCP-48109 RA-48109 3D-RTD
1709	An-32A	not yet known	CCCP-48113 48113 RA-48113 3X-GGS
1710?	An-32	(Indian Air Force)	K3055 [w/o 01Apr92 collided with An-32 c/n 0103 K2669 after t/o Ludhiana, India]
1801	An-32	Indian Air Force	K3056
1802?	An-32	Indian Air Force	K3057 [codes P & Q]
1803?	An-32	Indian Air Force	K3058
1804?	An-32	Indian Air Force	K3059
1805	An-32	Selva	YN-CBU HK-4052X HK-4052 HK-4052G
1806?	An-32A	(Afghan Air Force)	308 [wfu or w/o by 12Mar07]
1807?	An-32A	(Afghan Air Force)	309 [wfu or w/o by 12Mar07]
1808?	An-32A	(Afghan Air Force)	310 [wfu or w/o by 12Mar07]
1809	An-32A	Aer Caribe	YN-CBV HK-4132X YN-CFQ YN-CBV HK-4427X HK-4427
1810	An-32B	unknown	CCCP-69336 RA-69336 ER-AEI D2-FDP [reported wfu by 12Mar07]
1901?	An-32A	(Afghan Air Force)	311 [wfu or w/o by 12Mar07]
1902?	An-32A	(Afghan Air Force)	312 [wfu or w/o by 12Mar07]
1903?	An-32A	(Afghan Air Force)	313 [wfu or w/o by 12Mar07]
1904?	An-32A	(Afghan Air Force)	314 [wfu or w/o by 12Mar07]
1905?	An-32A	(Afghan Air Force)	315 [wfu or w/o by 12Mar07]
1906?	An-32A	(Afghan Air Force)	316 [wfu or w/o by 12Mar07]
1907?	An-32A	(Afghan Air Force)	317 [wfu or w/o by 12Mar07]
1908?	An-32A	(Afghan Air Force)	318 [wfu or w/o by 12Mar07]
1909?	An-32A	(Afghan Air Force)	319 [wfu or w/o by 12Mar07]
1910?	An-32A	(Afghan Air Force)	320 [wfu or w/o by 12Mar07]
2001?	An-32A	(Afghan Air Force)	321 [wfu or w/o by 12Mar07]
2002?	An-32A	(Afghan Air Force)	322 [wfu or w/o by 12Mar07]
2003?	An-32A	(Afghan Air Force)	323 [wfu or w/o by 12Mar07]
2004?	An-32A	(Afghan Air Force)	324 [wreck noted Sep05 Khost, Afghanistan; l/n 08Jun06]
2005?	An-32A	(Afghan Air Force)	325 [wfu or w/o by 12Mar07]
2006?	An-32A	(Afghan Air Force)	326 [wfu or w/o by 12Mar07]
2007?	An-32A	(Afghan Air Force)	327 [wfu or w/o by 12Mar07]
2008?	An-32A	(Afghan Air Force)	328 [wreck noted Sep05 Khost, Afghanistan; l/n 08Jun06]
2009	An-32B	Air Armenia/748 Air Services	CCCP-69344 RA-69344 ST-AQU 9L-LFP EK-32500
2010?	An-32	Indian Air Force	K3060 [code M]
2101?	An-32	Indian Air Force	K3061
2102	An-32	Angolan Air Force	CCCP-48098 RA-48098 ER-AFO T-252+ D2-MAX T-252 [+ Angola]
2103	An-32A	Air Mark	CCCP-48972 RA-48972 ER-AWY EW-262TK
2104	An-32A	Angolan Air Force	CCCP-69306 RA-69306 ER-AEH T-251
2105	An-32A	(unknown)	CCCP-69310 RA-69310 HK-4113X RA-69310 ER-AET 9XR-SN [w/o 01Jun04 Kigali, Rwanda; l/n 15Dec04]
2106	An-32	Angolan Air Force	CCCP-48101 RA-48101 ER-AWT T-254
2107	An-32B	(Avia Trend)	CCCP-66759 66759 4K-66759 [w/o 14Sep98 Lokichogio, Kenya]
2108	An-32B	Goliaf Air	CCCP-66752 UN-66752+ 4K-66752 ER-AEA T-256^ S9-BOH T-256^ S9-BOH [+ used United Nations code UN975; ^ Angola]
2109	An-32B	Tarco Air	CCCP-66756 66756 4K-66756 ER-AEU S9-BOI ER-AZW ST-NSP

ANTONOV An-32

C/n	Model	Last known Owner/Operator	Identities/fates/comments (where appropriate)
2110	An-32A	Airjet	CCCP-64452 LZ-INL 64452 4K-64452 ER-AEV D2-FDQ
2201	An-32A	Gira Globe Aeronautica	CCCP-48116 RA-48116 4L-48116 ER-AFW D2-FDG
2202	An-32	Angolan Air Force	CCCP-69329 T-250
2203?	An-32	Indian Air Force	K3062 [codes N & B]
2204?	An-32	Indian Air Force	K3063 [codes B & F]
2205?	An-32	Indian Air Force	K3064
2206	An-32A	(Afghan Air Force)	CCCP-48117 RA-48117? 9L-LDO 9Q-CLS 9Q-CIP RDPL-34159? 354 [dbr 08Oct09 Kandahar, Afghanistan; wreck l/n Jan10]
2207	An-32	unknown	CCCP-48118 RA-48118 3D-DRO RA-48118
2208	An-32	Alada	CCCP-69313 D2-FRB
2209	An-32	Russian Aircraft Factory MiG	CCCP-48119 RA-48119 48119
2210	An-32B	ex Malift	CCCP-26221 RA-26221 9Q-CMD [reported as non-airworthy]
2301	An-32B	(Moscow Airways)	CCCP-26222 RA-26222 [w/o 08Jan96 Kinshasa-N'dolo, Democratic Republic of Congo; canx 26Feb96]
2302	An-32B	(Southern Gateway)	CCCP-26223 RA-26223 3D-DRV [dbr in forced landing 07May98 grass strip near Vaalwater, South Africa]
2303	An-32	unknown	CCCP-26224 RA-26224 ST-APV [canx before Jan07; fate/status unknown]
2304	An-32	unknown	CCCP-26225 RA-26225+ ER- [+ canx 10Jun97 to Moldova; fate/status unknown]
2305?	An-32	Indian Air Force	K3065 [code J]
2306?	An-32	Indian Air Force	K3066 [code A]
2307?	An-32	Indian Air Force	K3067
2308	An-32	Indian Air Force	K3068 [codes G & J]
2309?	An-32	Indian Air Force	K3069
2310?	An-32A	(Afghan Air Force)	329 [wfu or w/o by 12Mar07]
2401?	An-32A	(Afghan Air Force)	330 [wfu or w/o by 12Mar07]
2402?	An-32A	(Afghan Air Force)	331 [wreck noted Sep05 Khost, Afghanistan; l/n 08Jun06]
2403?	An-32A	(Afghan Air Force)	332 [wfu or w/o by 12Mar07]
2404?	An-32A	(Afghan Air Force)	333 [wfu or w/o by 12Mar07]
2405?	An-32	Afghan Air Force	334 [no reports]
2406?	An-32A	(Afghan Air Force)	335 [wfu or w/o by 12Mar07]
2407?	An-32A	(Afghan Air Force)	336 [wfu or w/o by 12Mar07]
2408?	An-32A	(Afghan Air Force)	337 [wfu or w/o by 12Mar07]
2409?	An-32A	(Afghan Air Force)	338 [by 21Mar02 wreck Pol-e-Charki scrap yard, Kabul, Afghanistan; l/n Feb06]
2410	An-32B	Ayk Avia	CCCP-48121 RA-48121 9L-LFU EK-32410
2501	An-32B	Peruvian National Police	RA-48066 PNP-233+ 345+ PNP-233 [+ Peru]
2502	An-32B	Peruvian National Police	RA-48067 PNP-234
2503?	An-32	Indian Air Force	K3070
2504?	An-32	Indian Air Force	K3071
2505?	An-32	Indian Air Force	K3072
2506?	An-32	Indian Air Force	K3073
2507	An-32	Indian Air Force	K3074 [code G]
2508	An-32A	(Selva)	CCCP-48122 RA-48122 ER-AEM HK-4171X [w/o 19Apr02 Valencia, Colombia; canx 24Jly02]
2509	An-32A	Colombian Army	CCCP-48123 RA-48123 ER-AES YV-1089CP HK-4136X EJC-146+ EJC-052+? EJC-1146 [+ Colombia] [c/n tie-up not confirmed but likely]
2510	An-32A	Guicango	CCCP-48089 RA-48089 ER-AWA ZS-PHP HK-4369X HK-4369 D2-FFV
2601	An-32A	Valan	CCCP-48090 RA-48090 ER-AEW ZS-PHR+ [+ marks reported but not allocated by South African CAA]
2602	An-32A	Transaer R.A.S.A.	CCCP-48084 UR-48084 OB-1962T
2603	An-32	(Imperial Air)	CCCP-48085 UR-48085 OB-1603 [wfu or w/o before 12Mar07; canx 28Mar96]
2604	An-32B	(Imperial Air)	CCCP-48125 UR-48125 OB-1604 [w/o 06Jan96 Chachapoyas, Peru; canx 06Oct98]
2605?	An-32A	(Afghan Air Force)	339 [wfu or w/o by 12Mar07]
2606?	An-32A	(Afghan Air Force)	340 [wfu or w/o by 12Mar07]
2607?	An-32A	(Afghan Air Force)	341 [wfu or w/o by 12Mar07]
2608	An-32A	(Afghan Air Force)	342 [wfu summer 2011; fate/status unknown]
2609?	An-32A	(Afghan Air Force)	343 [report wreck Herat, Afghanistan]
2610?	An-32A	(Afghan Air Force)	344? [no reports]
2701?	An-32A	(Afghan Air Force)	345 [by Jan04 wreck Kundaz, Afghanistan]
2702?	An-32A	(Afghan Air Force)	346 [by Mar01 wreck Faizabad, Afghanistan]
2703?	An-32A	(Afghan Air Force)	347 [wfu or w/o by 12Mar07]
2704?	An-32A	(Afghan Air Force)	348? [no reports]
2705?	An-32A	(Afghan Air Force)	349? [no reports]

ANTONOV An-32

C/n	Model	Last known Owner/Operator	Identities/fates/comments (where appropriate)
2706	An-32A	(Afghan Air Force)	350 [wfu 17Jun11 fate/status unknown; report last Afghan An-32 to be wfu]
2707?	An-32A	(Afghan Air Force)	351? [no reports]
2708?	An-32A	(Afghan Air Force)	352? HZ-TAM 352? [fate/status unknown]
2709	An-32A	(Afghan Air Force)	353 [wfs Nov09 Kabul, Afghanistan; used for spares; l/n 11Apr10]
2710	An-32B	ex Air Pass	CCCP-48032 48032 RA-48082 3D-RTE [canx as exported; fate/status unknown]
2801	An-32B	ex Aero Tumi	OB-1461 [wfu by Jly94 Lima, Peru; l/n 04Feb97]
2802	An-32B	Transaer R.A.S.A.	OB-1462 OB-1868-P
2803	An-32B	Goliaf Air/El Magal	CCCP-48053 UR-48053 S9-PSE
2804	An-32B	(Aviatrans K Airlines)	CCCP-48054 UR-48054 [w/o 07Jun00 Lima-25 airstrip, Sudan]
2805	An-32B	El Magal	CCCP-48055 UR-48055 ER-AZI ST-GSM [by early 2010 stored Zaporihzhya-Vostochny, Ukraine]
2806	An-32B	Air Million Cargo	CCCP-48057 D2-FVI ER-AWB ZS-OWX
2807	An-32B	(Aero Pulse Air Transport School)	CCCP-48058 [w/o 16Apr92 Marromeu, Mozambique; hulk l/n 15Nov00]
2808	An-32B	Valan International Cargo	CCCP-48059 ZS-PSO
2809	An-32B	(Peruvian Air Force)	CCCP-48052 48052 323+ OB-1641 323 [+ Peru] [last flight 06May01; wfu due to corrosion; l/n 06Sep05 Lima, Peru]
2810	An-32B	Croatian Air Force	CCCP-48056 9A-BAC 021+ 727 [+ Croatia]
2901	An-32P	Aviant	CCCP-48086 UR-48086 [fire-fighter conversion]
2902	An-32B	ex Ural Aviakompania	CCCP-48050 RA-48050 [reported wfu or w/o before 12Mar07]
2903	An-32B	Sudan Air Force	CCCP-48051 D2-FAP ST-EIB 7712
2904	An-32B	Kiev Aviation Plant	CCCP-48087 UR-48087
2905	An-32	(Kiev Aviation Plant)	CCCP-48088 [w/o 09Oct92 Mogadishu, Somalia]
2906	An-32	(Peruvian Air Force)	[Soviet] RA-48128 326 OB-1643 [w/o 11May96 near Andoas, Peru; canx 21Dec01]
2907	An-32B	Peruvian Air Force	[Soviet] RA-48129 324+ OB-1642 324 [+ Peru]
2908	An-32B	ex Impulse Aero	CCCP-48070 RA-48070 [canx 19Dec98 to Congo; fate/status unknown]
2909	An-32B	(Selva)	CCCP-48071 48071 RA-48071 HK-4117X HK-4117 [w/o 27Aug07 Mitu, Colombia]
2910	An-32B	Mexican Air Force	CCCP-48060? 48060 RA-48060 UR-48060 3104
3001	An-32B	Jordanian Air Force	CCCP-48083 UR-48083 3010
3002	An-32B	(Peruvian Air Force)	CCCP-48075 48075 ER-48075 TS-LCA 322+ OB-1640 322 [+ Peru] [last flight 21Mar02; wfu because of corrosion; l/n 21Mar05 Lima, Peru]
3003	An-32B	(Air Million Cargo)	CCCP-48061 48061 ER-48061 ER-ADC (ZS-OIT) ER-AEC (ZS-ORG) ZS-PDV [w/o 24Apr06 Lashkar Gar, Afghanistan]
3004	An-32B	Valan	CCCP-48062 48062 UR-48062 ER-ADF 48062 (ZS-OIU) D2-FVK ER-AFG ZS-PEL
3005	An-32B	Mexican Navy	CCCP-48068 LZ-PVM MT-318+ MP-318+ AMT-214 [+ Mexico]
3006	An-32B	Servicaribe Express	CCCP-48069 LZ-PVN MT-319+ MP-319+ AMT-210+ HK-4832X [+ Mexico]
3007	An-32B	Colombian Army	CCCP-48072 HP-1217AAK HP-1217AVL YN-CGA EJC-1147
3008	An-32B	Mexican Air Force	CCCP-48080 UR-48080 3102+ [+ not fully confirmed]
3009	An-32B	(Kata Air Transport)	CCCP-48073 48073 UR-48073 ER-ADB HA-TCL ER-AWM ST-AZL [w/o 11Apr08 nr Kishinev, Russia]
3010	An-32B	(Maibi Air Company/UN)	CCCP-48074 48074 UR-48074 [w/o 18Jan95 Kinshasa-N'Dolo, Democratic Republic of Congo]
3101	An-32B	(Virunga Air Charter)	CCCP-48077 48077 ER-48077 [dbr by Mar96; l/n Klyuchevoye, Russia; canx by Mar04]
3102	An-32B	Peruvian Army	CCCP-48127? RA-48127 EP-831
3103	An-32B	Azerbaijan Airlines	CCCP-48136? 48136 4K-48136
3104	An-32B	Peruvian Army	CCCP-48078 EP-833 [wfu by Apr03 Lima, Peru; l/n Dec08]
3105	An-32B	(Azerbaijan Airlines)	CCCP-48137? 48137 4K-48137 [dumped by Jly07 Baku-Bina, Azerbaijan; l/n Jan09; not noted mid 2011 possibly b/u]
3106	An-32B	(Mexican Air Force)	CCCP-48081 UR-48081 3103 [w/o 17Dec06 nr Pie de la Cuenta, Mexico]
3107	An-32B	Transaer R.A.S.A.	CCCP-48134? UR-48134 HP-1226AAK HP-1226AVL OB-1907-T [derelict by Apr98 Panama City-Tocumen, Panama; l/n Mar08]
3108	An-32B	Peruvian Army	CCCP-48079 EP-835 [stored by 01May10 Lima, Peru]
3109	An-32B	Transaer R.A.S.A.	CCCP-48135? UR-48135 HP-1227AAK HP-1227AVL OB-1924-P [derelict by Apr98 Panama City-Tocumen, Panama; l/n Mar08]
3110	An-32B	Air Taxi Sudan	CCCP-48076 48076 RA-48076 ER-AEX(1) S9-GRL ER-AWL ST-TKO
3201	An-32B	(Great Lakes Bus)	CCCP-48138? RA-48138 ER-AEP EX-48138 9Q-CMG [w/o 26May08 Goma, Democratic Republic of Congo]
3202	An-32B	(Afghan Air Force)	CCCP-48130 UR-48130 OB-1610 ER-AWK N6505 ER-AWK 356 [wfu Jun11; fate/status unknown]

ANTONOV An-32

C/n	Model	Last known Owner/Operator	Identities/fates/comments (where appropriate)
3203	An-32B	Aer Caribe	RA-48139 UR-48139 OB-1669 HK-4257X HK-4257
3204	An-32B	(Afghan Air Force)	UR-48131 OB-1652 HK-4240X HK-4240 RDPL-34162 357 [wfu Jun11; fate/status unknown]
3205	An-32B	ex Alok Air	RA-48140 UR-48140 RA-48140 ER-ADI ER-AFI ST-ATF [damaged 29Jly07 Palouge, Sudan; airline ceased operations 15Aug07; fate/status unknown]
3206	An-32B	Mexican Navy	UR-48016 MT-316+ MP-316+ AMT-212 [+ Mexico]
3207	An-32B	Peruvian Air Force	RA-48063 327+ OB-1686 327 [+ Peru]
3208	An-32B	Sri Lankan Air Force Museum	UR-48007 HK-4011X UR-48007 CR867 [preserved by 13Mar10 Ratmakana, Sri Lanka]
3209	An-32B	Sudan Police Air Wing	EX-48026 203//ST-PAW [dual marks]
3210	An-32B	Mexican Navy	UR-48132 MT-320+ MP-320+ AMT-215 [+ Mexico]
3301	An-32B	(Selva)	RA-48133 HK-3929X [w/o 08Oct94 Mitu, Colombia; canx 13Jun95]
3302	An-32B	Air Manas?	UR-48017 MT-317+ MP-317+ AMT-213^ EX-32100 [+ Mexico; ^ also reported as XB-MKI which could be a radio call-sign]
3303	An-32B	(Caricarga)	UR-48019 HK-4007X [w/o 24Aug98 Alfredo Vasquez Cobo Airport, Letica, Colombia; canx 26May99]
3304	An-32B	unknown	48000 RA-48000 ER-AEL [canx 22Apr99; fate/status unknown]
3305	An-32B	(Afghan Air Force)	RA-48002 HK-4021X ER-ACM ER-AFM OB-1869-T+ 355 [+ possibly ntu; wfu Jun11; fate/status unknown]
3306	An-32B	(Mexican Air Force)	UR-48006 3101 [w/o 24Nov10 Monterrey-International, Mexico]
3307	An-32B	Peruvian National Police	YL-LDD PNP-227+ OB-1624 PNP-227 [+ Peru]
3308	An-32B	Peruvian National Police	YL-LDE PNP-228+ OB-1625 PNP-228 [+ Peru]
3309	An-32B	(Selva)	RA-48015 HK-3930X [w/o 22Dec98 Rionegro, Colombia; canx 30Apr99]
3310	An-32B	Croatian Air Force	UR-48005 9A-BAB 707
3401	An-32B	Filair	RA-48014
3402	An-32B	(Selva)	UR-48020 HK-4008X [w/o 21Dec96 near Rio Negro-Jose Maria Cordova, Colombia; canx 26Sep97]
3403	An-32B	Peruvian Navy	AT-530+ OB-1612 AT-530 [+ Peru]
3404	An-32B	Servicaribe Express	UR-48012 MT-321+ MP-321^ AMT-211^ HK-4833X [+ Mexico, serial assumed; ^ Mexico]
3405	An-32B	ex Ukraine Air Alliance	UR-48008 [delivered to Colombia 31Jly95; fate/status unknown]
3406	An-32B	(Malu Aviation)	UR-48003 ER-ADA ER-AFA [w/o 07Nov00 Luabo, Democratic Republic of Congo; canx 16Feb01]
3407	An-32B	Peruvian Air Force	325+ OB-1685 325 [+ Peru]
3408	An-32B	Peruvian Navy	AT-531+ OB-1613 AT-531 [+ Peru]
3409	An-32B	Sudanese Air Force	UR-48023 HK-4006X UR-48003 ST-ATL 7710+ ST-ATL [+Sudanese Air Force; may have worn ST-ATL at same time]
3410	An-32B	Sri Lankan Air Force	UR-48022 HK-4009X UR-48022 CR868+ SCM-3305 SCM868 [+ Sri Lanka]
3501	An-32B	Sri Lankan Air Force	CR860+ SCM-3301 [+ Sri Lanka]
3502	An-32B	(Sri Lankan Air Force)	CR861 [w/o 12Sep95 shot down Colombo, Sri Lanka]
3503	An-32B	(Sri Lankan Air Force)	CR862 [w/o 22Nov95 shot down Palay, Sri Lanka]
3504	An-32B	Sri Lankan Air Force	UR-48025 HK-4012X UR-48025 CR869+ SCM-3304+ SCM869^ [+ Sri Lanka; ^not confirmed]
3505	An-32B	Bangladesh Air Force	3505//S3-ACD [dual marks]
3506	An-32B	(Peruvian Army)	EP-837 [w/o 04Apr04 Puerto Esperanza, Peru]
3507	An-32P	Libyan Air Cargo	5A-DRE
3508	An-32B	Sri Lankan Air Force	CR863+ SCM-3302+ SCM863^ [+ Sri Lanka; ^not confirmed]
3509	An-32B	Sri Lankan Air Force	CR864+ SCM-3303 [+ Sri Lanka]
3510	An-32B	(Sri Lankan Air Force)	CR865 [w/o 21Feb97 Ratmalana, Sri Lanka; front fuselage to Sri Lanka Air Force Museum, Colombo; l/n 13May10]
3601	An-32B	(Sri Lankan Air Force)	CR866 [w/o before 12Mar07 possibly at Palaly, Sri Lanka
3602	An-32P	Libyan Air Cargo	5A-DRF
3603	An-32B	Equitorial Guinea Air Force	UR-CFS 3C-4GE
3604	An-32B	Iraqi Air Force	YI-401
3605	An-32B	Iraqi Air Force	YI-402
3606	An-32B	Iraqi Air Force	YI-403
3607	An-32B	Iraqi Air Force	YI-404
3608	An-32P	MNS Ukraine	31 black
3609	An-32P	MNS Ukraine	32 black
3610	An-32P	MNS Ukraine	33 black
3701	An-32P	MNS Ukraine	34 black
3702	An-32B	Iraqi Air Force	YI-405
3703	An-32B	Iraqi Air Force	YI-406

ANTONOV An-32

C/n	Model	Last known Owner/Operator	Identities/fates/comments (where appropriate)
3704	An-32B		[reported flying 30Jun12 no regn Kiev-Gostomel, Ukraine]
3705	An-32B	Iraqi Air Force	YI-406
Unidentified Civil Prefix			
unkn	An-32	Aeroflot c/s	CCCP-46019 [reported 16Aug92 Zhukovski, Russia]
unkn	An-32B	Aeroflot c/s	CCCP-48047+ RA-48047^ [+reported Feb93 Nairobi, Kenya;^ reported 20Aug93 Asmara, Eritrea]
unkn	An-32	Alada	D2-FBP [reported 15Apr99 & 19Aug99 Luanda, Angola; not in Alada Jan02 fleet list]
unkn	An-32	Guicango	D2-FDQ [reported 24Apr03 Luanda, Angola; l/n 02Nov11 with Airjet titles]
unkn	An-32	(Air Nave)	D2-FEO [w/o 11Dec01 Luzamba, Angola]
unkn	An-32B	Guicango	D2-FFV [reported 28Mar09 Luanda, Angola; 22Aug09 Pointe-Noire, Congo & 12Sep09 Lanseria, South Africa]
unkn	An-32	unknown	D2-FVF [reported 10Jan96 Luanda, Angola]
unkn	An-32	Angolan Air Force?	D2-MAJ [from photo; reportedly w/o 28Mar00 Huambo, Angola; report of being c/n 3201 incorrect]
unkn	An-32	Angolan Air Force?	D2-MAV [reported Jun03 Luanda, Angola]
unkn	An-32	Angolan Air Force?	D2-MBG [reported 24Apr03 Luanda, Angola]
unkn	An-32	Aviatrans	RA-69326 [reported on register 20Apr95 with no c/n]
unkn	An-32	Sudan Air Force	ST-ATM [see 7709 below]
unkn	An-32	Farnas Aviation	ST-FAS [reported in JP Airline Fleets 1996 to 1999; not on Mar00 register]
unkn	An-32	AYR Aviation	ST-SMZ [reported 21Nov07 Khartoum, Sudan, later Sharjah, UAE & 18Jly08 Fujairah, UAE; l/n there 23Jan09]
unkn	An-32	unknown	S9-GBC [reported 15Apr08 & 25Sep08 Kiev-Zhulyany, Ukraine; three unknown An-26s also reported with this regisration; there is photo proof of An26 & An32 taken on same day; this might be c/n 1408]
unkn	An-32	unknown	S9-KAS [reported 08Jan08 & 29Apr08 Fujairah, UAE; An-24 c/n 473 09 406 also reported with this registration]
unkn	An-32B	Vitair	UR-48005 [reported 04Apr95 Luxembourg-Findel, Luxembourg]
unkn	An-32	United Nations	UR-48009 [reported 09Sep93 Maputo, Mozambique]
unkn	An-32	United Nations	UR-48010 [reported 09Sep93 Maputo, Mozambique]
unkn	An-32B	Transavia Ukraine	UR-48012 [reported several times; l/n 05Nov98 Bratislavia, Slovakia]
unkn	An-32	unknown	3X-GHJ [reported 09Mar12 Lahore, Pakistan]
unkn	An-32	ex Regional International Air Service	9XR-QT [canx Dec03 as exported to South Africa; fate/status unknown]
unkn	An-32	Sun Air Charter	9XR-ST [reported 24Mar05 Kigali, Rwanda & 22May06 Nairobi-Wilson, Kenya]
Unidentified Military			
unkn	An-32	Ethiopian Air Force	1551 [reported 21May93 Axum, Turkey & 10Mar01 Addis Ababa, Ethiopia; later report Feb05 as just "155"]
unkn	An-32	Sudan Air Force?	7707 [reported 31Mar09 Khartoum, Sudan]
unkn	An-32	Aeroflot c/s	48813 [reported 29Aug93 Asmara, Eritrea]
unkn	An-32	Afghan Air Force	357(1) [wreck reported Nov04 Bamiyan, Afghanistan, but type not fully confirmed; serial later used on c/n 3204]
unkn	An-32	Sudan Air Force	7709//ST-ATM [dual marks] [reported 01Jan08 and 07Aug08 Khartoum, Sudan with no mention of civil registration]
unkn	An-32	Sudan Air Force	7710//ST-ATL [dual marks] [reported Jly08 and later Khartoum, Sudan; l/n 26Mar09 & 25Dec09 with no mention of military serial]
unkn	An-32	Colombian Army	EJC-1147 [reported in Nov09]
unkn	An-32	Colombian Army	EJC-131 [reported 08Aug09 Lima, Peru]
unkn	An-32	Peruvian National Police	PNP-323 [reported 08Mar01 Lima, Peru; not FAP-323 c/n 2809 which was there on the same day]
unkn	An-32	Angolan Air Force	T-211 [reported 16Mar01 Luanda, Angola; this serial was earlier confirmed on a An-26 which calls this report into question]
unkn	An-32	Angolan Air Force	T-249 [never reported but known to exist]
unkn	An-32	Angolan Air Force	T-253 [reported 06Aug07 & 28Mar09 Luanda, Angola]
unkn	An-32	Congo Air Force	TN-224 [reported 11Aug04 Brazzaville, Peoples Republic of Congo; but not An-24RV c/n 17306607 with same marks which was wfu there]
unkn	An-32	Congo Air Force	TN-227 [reported 28Aug04 flying in Brazzaville FIR, Peoples Republic of Congo & 02Aug10 at airport]

ANTONOV An-38

C/n	Model	Last known Owner/Operator	Identities/fates/comments (where appropriate)
Pre-Production Aircraft			
38 01 001	120	(NAPO/Aviatrans)	3810001 RA-41900(1) [prototype f/f 23Jun94; canx 19Dec00; fate/status unknown]
38 01 002			[static test airframe]
38 02 003	120	Layang Layang	3810003 RA-41900(2) 41900 RA-41900(2) [c/n quoted in register as 4160381607003]
38 02 002		ex NAPO/Aviatrans	41910 [last noted 15Aug02; fate/status unknown]
Production Aircraft			
4 7 01 0001	100	Vostok Airlines	RA-41901 [full c/n 41638 4 7 01 0001]
4 7 01 0002	120	Vostok Airlines	RA-41902 [full c/n 41638 4 7 01 0002]
3 8 01 0003	100	Vostok Airlines	RA-41903 [full c/n 41638 3 8 01 0003]
3 9 01 0004	100	Airosa	RA-41904 [full c/n 41638 3 9 01 0004]
01 0005	100		RA-41905+ [+ not confirmed; no data] [full c/n 41638 . . 01 0005]
01 0006	100		RA-41906+ [+ not confirmed; no data] [full c/n 41638 . . 01 0006]
2 0 01 0007	100	Airosa	RA-41907 [full c/n 41638 2 0 01 0007]
Unidentified			
unkn		Polyarnaya Avia	RA-05861
unkn		MChS Rossii	RF-32764

ANTONOV An-140

C/n	Line No.	Model	Last known Owner/Operator	Identities/fates/comments (where appropriate)
(01 01)	01 01	100	ex Antonov Design Bureau	UR-NTO [prototype f/f 17Sep97; wfu by 21Oct08 Kiev-Svyatoshino, Ukraine]
(01 02)	01 02			[static test airframe]
(01 03)	01 03		(Antonov Design Bureau)	UR-NTP [damaged 23Dec08 Gostomel, Ukraine; no recent reports; canx 07Jly11]
01 003	01 04		ex Odessa Airlines	(no marks) UR-PWO UR-14001 [stored 2004 at factory; canx 01Oct08]
01 005	01 05			[assembled in Iran with c/n 9001]
02 006	02 01		ex Aeromist Kharkiv	UR-14002 [returned to factory; canx 01Oct08]
365253 02 011	02 02		(Aeromist Kharkiv)	UR-14003 [w/o 23Dec02 Isfahan, Iran]
02 009	02 03			[assembled in Iran with c/n 9002]
365253 02 008	02 04		(Ukrtransleasing/ Motor-Sich)	UR-14004 [damaged 06Sep08 Kiev-Borispol, Ukraine & wfs & stored Mar10 Kiiev-Svyatoshino, Ukraine; l/n Dec10; canx 10Jan12]
02 015	02 05			[assembled in Iran with c/n 9003]
05 016	03 01			[assembled in Iran with c/n 9004]
05 018	03 02			[assembled in Iran with c/n 9005]
05 021	03 03		Motor-Sich	UR-14005
05 022	03 04			[assembled in Iran with c/n 9006]
365253 05 025	03 05		(Ukrtransleasing)	UR-14006 [l/n May11 Zaporizhye, Ukraine; canx 10Jan12 fate/status unknown]
05 027	03 06			[assembled in Iran with c/n 9007]
365253 05 029	03 07	100	(Business Avia)	UR-14007 [canx 07Jly11 fate/status unknown]
05 031	03 08	100		[assembled in Iran with c/n 9008]
05 032	03 09	100	Yakutiya	UR-14008 RA-41253
05 034	03 10	100		[assembled in Iran with c/n 9009]
07 036	04 01	100	(Azerbaijan Airlines)	4K-AZ48 [w/o 23Dec05 shortly after take off from Baku, Azerbaijan]
07 039	04 02	100		[assembled in Iran with c/n 9010]
07 041	04 03	100	ex Azerbaijan Airlines	4K-AZ49 [wfu 22Nov06 Baku, Azerbaijan; 03Dec08 ferried to Kharkov, Ukraine for storage]
(04 04)	04 04	100		[to Iran for assembly]
07 045	04 05	100	ex Azerbaijan Airlines	4K-AZ50 [not delivered & order canx Nov06; stored at factory]
(04 06)	04 06	100		[to Iran for assembly]

ANTONOV An-140

C/n	Line No.	Model	Last known Owner/Operator	Identities/fates/comments (where appropriate)
07 049	04 07	100	ex Azerbaijan Airlines	4K-AZ51 [order canx Nov06, before completion; l/n Sep07]
(04 08)	04 08	100		[to Iran for assembly]
(04 09)	04 09	100		
(04 10)	04 10	100		

line numbers 01-01 to 01-03 were assembled at Kiev-Svyatoshino, the remainder, unless otherwise noted at Kharkov, Ukraine
most c/ns probably prefixed by 365 253

Samara, Russia assembled

C/n	Line No.	Model	Last known Owner/Operator	Identities/fates/comments (where appropriate)
05A001			Yakutiya	RA-14001 41250 RA-41250 [reported May09 stored due to lack of parts; noted 27Jan12 stored Yakutsk, Russia]
002		100		[fatigue test airframe]
003				
004				
005				
006				
007				
008				
009				
010				
011				
07A012		100	Yakutiya	RA-41251 [by 27Jan12 stored Yakutsk, Russia]
013				
09A014		100	Yakutiya	RA-41252
12A015		100	Russian Air Force	RA-41258
11A002		100	Russian Air Force	41254 RA-41254 [VVS Rossii titles]

Iran assembled

C/n	Line No.	Model	Last known Owner/Operator	Identities/fates/comments (where appropriate)
9001	01 05		(Safiran Airlines)	HESA-01+ EP-SFD HESA 90-01+ [+ Iran; w/o 09Nov04 Arak, Iran; rebuilt as prototype maritime version, rolled out 30Apr12]
9002	02 03		Iranian Police Aviation	EP-SFE HESA 90-02+2201 [+ Iran]
9003	02 05		Iranian Police Aviation	EP-SFF HESA 90-03+2202 [+ Iran]
9004	03 01		(Iran Air Tour)	HESA 90-04+[+ Iran] [w/o 15Feb09 Isfahan AFB, Iran]
9005	03 02		HESA Airlines	EP-GPA [c/n originally 36525305018]
9006	03 04		HESA Airlines	HESA 90-06+EP-GPB [+ Iran] [c/n originally 36525305022]
9007	03 06	100	HESA Airlines	EP-GPC [c/n not confirmed but if correct was originally 36525305027; c/n now also reported as 9009]
9008	03 08	100	HESA Airlines	EP-GPD [c/n also reported as 9010]
9009	03 10	100	HESA Airlines	HESA 90-09+EP-GPE [+ Iran] [c/n also reported as 9007; possibly stored Mar12 Tehran, Iran]
9010	04 02		HESA Airlines	EP-GPF [c/n also reported as 9008]
9011?	04 04		unknown	[not completed by Jun09]
9012?	04 06		unknown	[not completed by Jun09]

ARMSTRONG-WHITWORTH AW.650/AW.660 ARGOSY

C/n	Model	Last known Owner/Operator	Identities/fates/comments (where appropriate)
6651	101	Yankee Air Museum	G-AOZZ G-11-1 N896U [prototype ff 08Jan59; wfu; on display 1995 Willow Run, Detroit, MI; canx 20Oct93; l/n 11Oct07]
6652	101	Midland Air Museum	G-APRL N6507R N602Z N890U G-APRL [preserved Feb87 Baginton, Coventry, UK; canx 19Nov87 as wfu]
6653	102	(Field Aircraft Services)	G-APRM [wfu Apr82 Exeter, UK; b/u; canx 12Aug85 as destroyed]
6654	102	(Air Bridge Carriers)	G-APRN G-11-2 G-APRN N897U G-APRN [wfu 17Apr82 Belfast-Aldergrove, UK; b/u; canx 27Aug82]
6655	101	(US Department of Interior)	G-APVH N6504R N891U [w/o 19May74 Campbell Airstrip, nr Anchorage, AK]
6656	101	(IPEC Aviation)	G-1-3 G-APWW N6503R N892U G-APWW VH-BBA N37897 VH-IPD [b/u 04Dec90 Melbourne-Essendon, VIC, Australia]
6657	101	(Air Bridge Carriers)	G-1-4 N6505R N600Z N893U G-AZHN [b/u 23May77 East Midlands Airport, UK; canx 29Nov76 as wfu]
6658	101	(Duncan Aviation)	G-1-5 N6506R N894U [w/o en-route 08Jly74 emergency landing on Interstate 75 nr Port Hope, AK]
6659	101	(Zantop Air Transport)	G-1-6 N6501R N601Z [w/o 14Oct65 nr Pique, OH]
6660	101	East Midlands Aeropark	G-1-7 N6502R N895U G-BEOZ [preserved Dec96 East Midlands Airport, UK; canx 19Nov87; l/n 11Oct08]
6743	E.1	(Royal Air Force)	XN814 [wfu & stored May77 RAF Kemble, UK; Oct77 to R C Hurst for scrap; b/u Nov77]
6744	C.1	(Royal Air Force)	XN815 [wfu Jan71 & stored RAF Shawbury, UK then in Apr72 RAF Kemble, UK; 12Sep75 to Hants & Sussex Aviation; b/u Sep75]
6745	E.1	(Royal Air Force)	XN816 8489M [Mar76 to School of Technical Training, Cosford, UK; 1988 to IPEC Aviation for spares; b/u 1988]
6746	C.1	(UK Defence Research Agency)	XN817 [w/o 01Oct84 RAE West Freugh, UK; by Sep99 fuselage only on fire dump; l/n 15May11]
6747	C.1	(Royal Air Force)	XN818 [wfu Sep70 & stored RAF Shawbury, UK then in Feb72 RAF Kemble, UK; 12Sep75 to Hants & Sussex Aviation; b/u]
6748	C.1	(Royal Air Force)	XN819 (8198M) 8205M [stored 10Aug72 RAF Finningley, UK; to fire dump Sep79; DBF by Sep86 RAF Finningley; Jly93 cockpit section preserved Newark Aircraft Museum, Newark, UK; l/n 04Jly08]
6749	C.1	(Royal Air Force)	XN820 [wfu Nov70 & stored RAF Shawbury, UK then in Feb72 RAF Kemble, UK; 18Aug75 to Hants & Sussex Aviation; b/u]
6750	C.1	(Royal Air Force)	XN821 [wfu & stored Apr71 RAF Kemble, UK; 22May75 to Rolls Royce (1971) Ltd for engine salvage; b/u]
6751	C.1	(Royal Air Force)	XN847 8220M [wfu Jan71 & stored RAF Shawbury, UK; Aug72 to School of Technical Training, RAF St Athan, UK; 10Jan75 to Hants & Sussex Aviation; b/u]
6752	C.1	(Royal Air Force)	XN848 8195M [wfu & stored 09Aug71 RAF Topcliffe, UK; b/u Jun73]
6753	C.1	(Royal Air Force)	XN849 [wfu & stored May70 RAF Kemble, UK; 15Jun73 to Rolls Royce (1971) Ltd for engine salvage; b/u]
6754	C.1	(Royal Air Force)	XN850 [wfu Nov71 & stored RAF Shawbury, UK; then in Dec71 RAF Kemble, UK; 25Apr75 to A J Walter Aviation; b/u]
6755	C.1	(Royal Air Force)	XN851 [conversion to T.2 not completed; Jan72 wfu & stored RAF Kemble; 10Feb76 to Field Aircraft Services; b/u for spares for c/n 6779]
6756	C.1	(Royal Air Force)	XN852 [wfu & stored Dec71 RAF Kemble, UK; 22May75 Field Aircraft Services; b/u]
6757	C.1	(Royal Air Force)	XN853 [wfu Oct71 & stored RAF Shawbury, UK; then in Feb72 RAF Kemble, UK; 18Aug75 to Hants & Sussex Aviation; b/u Sep75]
6758	C.1	(Royal Air Force)	XN854 [wfu Oct71 & stored RAF Shawbury, UK; then in Dec71 RAF Kemble, UK; 22May75 to Rolls Royce (1971) Ltd for engine salvage; b/u]
6759	E.1	(Royal Air Force)	XN855 8556M [wfu May80 RAF Manston, UK; to fire dump, burnt by May92]
6760	C.1	(Royal Air Force)	XN856 [wfu & stored Oct71 RAF Kemble, UK; 18Aug75 to Field Aircraft Services; b/u]
6761	C.1	(Royal Air Force)	XN857 [wfu Nov71 RAF Shawbury, UK; then stored Mar72 RAF Kemble, UK; 18Aug75 to Hants & Sussex Aviation; b/u]
6762	C.1	(Royal Air Force)	XN858 [wfu Nov70 & stored RAF Shawbury, UK; then in Apr72 RAF Kemble, UK; 07Oct75 to Rolls Royce (1971) Ltd for engine salvage; b/u]
6763	C.1	(Royal Air Force)	XP408 [wfu & stored Oct71 RAF Kemble, UK; 15Jun73 to Rolls Royce (1971) Ltd for engine salvage; b/u]
6764	C.1	(Royal Air Force)	XP409 8197M 8221M; [b/u late 1978 RAF Halton, UK; 14Dec78 fuselage to Nuclear Bacteriological & Chemical Centre, Winterbourne Gunner, UK; b/u 1985]
6765	C.1	(Royal Air Force)	XP410 [wfu & stored May71 RAF Kemble, UK; 15Jun73 to Rolls Royce (1971) Ltd for engine salvage; b/u]
6766	T.1	Royal Air Force Museum	XP411 8442M; [preserved Feb97 RAF Cosford, UK as XP411; l/n Nov09]
6767	C.1	(Air Bridge Carriers)	XP412 G-BDCV [wfu Jan78; b/u for spares 1980 East Midlands, UK; canx 02Feb78]
6768	E.1	(Royal Air Force)	XP413 [SOC 01May75 RAF Fairford, UK; Sep76 to fire dump; still extant May80; DBF]

ARMSTRONG-WHITWORTH AW.650/AW.660 ARGOSY

C/n	Model	Last known Owner/Operator	Identities/fates/comments (where appropriate)
6769	C.1	(Royal Air Force)	XP437 [wfu & stored May70 RAF Kemble, UK; 07Oct75 to Rolls Royce (1971) Ltd for engine salvage; b/u]
6770	C.1	(Royal Air Force)	XP438 [wfu & stored Oct71 RAF Kemble, UK; 07Oct75 to Rolls Royce (1971) Ltd for engine salvage; b/u Dec75]
6771	E.1	(Royal Air Force)	XP439 8558M [SOC 13Sep77 RAF Lossiemouth, UK; to fire dump & DBF Jly87]
6772	C.1	(Royal Air Force)	XP440 [wfu & stored Dec71 RAF Kemble, UK; 22May75 to Rolls Royce (1971) Ltd for engine salvage; b/u Jun75]
6773	C.1	(Royal Air Force)	XP441 [w/o 04Jun70 RAF Benson, UK; b/u Mar71]
6774	T.2	(Royal Air Force)	XP442 8454M [used as T.2 mock up; b/u Feb91 RAF Halton, UK]
6775	C.1	(Royal Air Force)	XP443 [wfu Oct71 & stored RAF Shawbury, UK; then in Feb72 RAF Kemble, UK; 18Aug75 to Field Aircraft Services; b/u]
6776	C.1	(Royal Air Force)	XP444 8455M [1988 to IPEC Aviation for spares; b/u Mar89 RAF Cosford, UK]
6777	C.1	(Royal Air Force)	XP445 [wfu & stored May70 RAF Kemble, UK; 15Jun73 to Rolls Royce (1971) Ltd for engine salvage; b/u Aug75]
6778	C.1	(OTRAG Range Air Services)	XP446 9Q-COE [w/o 01Jun79 Lubumbashi, Zaire; hulk b/u 1980]
6779	C.1	Milestones of Flight Museum	XP447 N1430Z [used for T.2 trials; wfu & stored Oct78; preserved Dec91 Lancaster-Fox Field, CA; l/n Feb07]
6780	E.1	(Royal Air Force)	XP448 [SOC 18Jan78 for fire training RAF Catterick; DBF by Apr82]
6781	E.1	(Royal Air Force)	XP449 [wfu Oct70 RAF Shawbury, UK; then stored Mar72 RAF Kemble, UK; 13Oct75 to Hants & Sussex Aviation; b/u]
6782	C.1	(Philippine Airlines)	XP450 RP-C1192 [wfu & stored by Sep81 Manila-International, Philippines; b/u 1983]
6783	C.1	(Royal Air Force)	XR105 [w/o 27Apr76 RAE Boscombe Down, UK]
6784	C.1	(Royal Air Force)	XR106 [wfu & stored Oct71 RAF Kemble, UK; 18Aug75 to Hants & Sussex Aviation; b/u Sep75]
6785	C.1	(Royal Air Force)	XR107 8441M [reported with designation T.1; 1988 to IPEC Aviation for spares; b/u Mar89 RAF Cosford, UK]
6786	C.1	(Royal Air Force)	XR108 [wfu & stored Oct71 RAF Kemble, UK; 25Apr75 to A J Walter Aviation; b/u May/Jun75]
6787	C.1	(Royal Air Force)	XR109 [wfu & stored Oct71 RAF Kemble, UK; 22May75 to Field Aircraft Services; b/u Jun75]
6788	C.1	(Royal Air Force)	XR133 [w/o 07May68 Got-El-Afrag Airstrip, Libya]
6789	C.1	(Royal Air Force)	XR134 [wfu Oct71 RAF Shawbury, UK; then stored Dec72 RAF Kemble, UK; 18Aug75 to Hants & Sussex Aviation; b/u]
6790	C.1	(Royal Air Force)	XR135 [wfu Oct71 RAF Shawbury, UK; then stored Jan72 RAF Kemble, UK; 18Aug75 to Field Aviation Services; b/u]
6791	C.1	(OTRAG Range Air Services)	XR136+ 9Q-COA [+ conversion to T.2 abandoned; wfu & stored 1978 East Midlands Airport, UK; b/u Jun81]
6792	E.1	(Royal Air Force)	XR137 [to GIA 10Jan78 RAF Northolt, UK; to fire section Jun87; DBF Jun87]
6793	C.1	(Royal Air Force)	XR138 [wfu Oct71 RAF Shawbury, UK; then stored Dec72 RAF Kemble, UK; 18Aug75 to Hants & Sussex Aviation; b/u Sep75]
6794	C.1	(Royal Air Force)	XR139 [wfu & stored Dec71 RAF Kemble, UK; 22Sep75 to Hants & Sussex Aviation; b/u Oct75]
6795	E.1	(Royal Air Force)	XR140 8579M [b/u Mar88 RAF Halton, UK; hulk to fire dump Jun88; DBF]
6796	C.1	(Royal Air Force)	XR141 [wfu & stored Dec71 RAF Kemble, UK; 22May75 to Rolls Royce (1971) Ltd for engine salvage; b/u]
6797	C.1	(Royal Air Force)	XR142 [wfu & stored Oct71 RAF Kemble, UK; 18Aug75 to Hants & Sussex Aviation; b/u]
6798	E.1	Mid-America Transportation & Avn Museum	XR143 G-BFVT [canx 17Jly78 as sold in USA; report of marks N1403Z incorrect confirmed by FAA; dismantled 15/16May99 Lincoln, NB and flown under Iowa ANG Chinook helicopters to Sioux City-Gateway Airport; reassembled & preserved; l/nJun05]
6799	220	(Hawker Siddeley Aviation)	G-ASKZ [wfu 24Nov65; b/u Sep67 Bitteswell, UK for spares; canx 11Sep68]
6800	222	(BEA) G-ASXL	[w/o 04Jly65 nr Piacenza, on approach to Milan-Linate, Italy]
6801	222	The Argosy Trust	G-ASXM CF-TAG EI-AVJ CF-TAG ZK-SAF [w/o 01Apr90 Blenheim-Woodbourne, New Zealand; canx 03Oct90; fuselage hulk stored on local farm; l/n 11Oct11]
6802	222	The Argosy Trust	G-ASXN CF-TAJ ZK-SAE [wfu 30Sep90 Blenheim-Woodbourne, New Zealand; canx 03Oct90; preserved 12Mar00 off airport outside "The Argosy Cafe"; l/n 11Oct11]
6803	222	(IPEC Aviation)	G-ASXO CF-TAX TR-LWQ VH-IPA [b/u 04Dec90 Melbourne-Essendon VIC, Australia]
6804	222	(BEA) G-ASXP	[w/o 04Dec67 Stansted Airport, UK]
6805	222	(Mayne Nickless)	G-ATTC CF-TAZ TR-LWR VH-IPB ZK-SAL VH-IPB [b/u 04Dec90 Melbourne-Essendon, VIC, Australia]
6806	222		[uncompleted airframe; b/u by Apr67; reported wore marks G-11-6806]

Production complete

BEECH 99

Note: An asterisk after the model identifier indicates an aircraft converted to a freighter without windows

C/n	Model	Last known Owner/Operator	Identities/fates/comments (where appropriate)
LR-1		(Beech Aircraft Corporation)	N599AT [PD.208 aerodynamic pre-production concept aircraft; b/u Wichita, KS Sep70]
U-1		(Ontario Aircraft Sales)	N7099N N212BH C-FPLX [ff Dec65 as long-fuselage Queen Air; ff Jly66 with turboprops; fuselage Peterborough, ON, Canada in bare metal as N212BH; l/n 18Feb10 in bare metal]
U-2		Trans Northern Aviation	N7199N (N17JC) N201TC N208BH TI-AYM N39TN
U-3		(Bar Harbor Airlines)	N1032C N200WP [w/o 16Aug76 Bar Harbor, ME; canx 22Nov76]
U-4		(Flanagan Enterprises)	N8399N PP-VDY N8399N N133PM N205TC [canx 13Jun11; probably pwfu]
U-5		Ontario Aircraft Sales	N1036C N100WP N203BH [canx 24Jan91 to Canada & wfu & stored for spares Jly94 Peterborough, ON, Canada; l/n 18Feb10]
U-6		Alpine Air Express	N1038C N849NS N19RA N95WA
U-7		(Trans Bharat Aviation)	N1048C N200TC N205BH VT-ESU [stored Chennai, India l/n Aug 03; canx 17May06]
U-8		(Maine Aviation Sales)	N245V N408SA C-GFLW N50PA [b/u Chino, CA; canx 24Nov97]
U-9		(Ameriflight)	N1049C [DBR 03May96; b/u by Dodson International Aircraft Parts at Ratoul KS, late 2005 for spares; canx 18May07]
U-10		Freight Runners Express	N246V N410SA C-GFLN N3984B D-IBSP N99NN (N84SD) N699CZ(2)
U-11		North Wright Airways	N8499N F-BRUN C-FKHD
U-12		Bemidji Airlines	N3757Q VR-UDW N1977G C-GPFF OH-WWT C-GPCE N125DP
U-13		(Beech Aircraft Corporation)	N8899N N312BA N311BA [wfu and on dump at Selma, AL; canx 11Feb89; l/n 30Oct08]
U-14		Bemidji Airlines	N651EX D-IBPF SE-GEO N914Y N70NP
U-15		(Alpine Air Express)	N196HA N199FA N17MV N199GL C-GJEZ N199GL [w/o 18Aug04 Big Baldy Mountain, Great Falls, MT; canx 26Feb08]
U-16		(Air South)	N844NS [w/o 06Jly69 Monroe, LA]
U-17		Wiggins Airways	N845NS N10MV N193WA
U-18		(Kenn Borek Air/Aklak Air)	N3115C F-BSTE N3115C C-GXFC HP-1233APP C-FKBK [DBF 04Nov10 Inuvik, NT, Canada; canx 11May11]
U-19		(Avia Taxi France)	N650EX F-BSRZ [w/o 31Aug73 Auvers, Seine-et-Oise, France]
U-20		ex Alberta Aircraft Leasing	N850SA N299CA [ex Mall A/W; b/u for spares Jly96 Calgary-Springbank Apt, AB, Canada; canx 25Oct01; fuselage still present 03Feb10]
U-21		Aeromarine	N1058C F-BSUK OO-WAY F-GFPE 5R-MKG
U-22		(Bar Harbor Airlines)	N985MA N300WP [w/o 25May85 Auburn-Lewiston, ME]
U-23		Aerodynamics Worldwide Inc	N749A N218BH C-FKCG N899AE
U-24		(Beech Aircraft Corporation)	N315VA [wfu and stored; assumed subsequently b/u; canx 16Feb89]
U-25		(Majestic Air Cargo)	N851SA [inactive since at least Jan96; canx 09Aug12, probably b/u]
U-26		ex Aerolease of America	N538M N538MA N746A EI-BLV OY-BEN TF-ELC C-FRQC N199SD [by 2009 hulk with Westcan Aircraft Sales & Salvage, Kamloops, BC, Canada; still current]
U-27		(Beech Aircraft Corporation)	N7507N N313BA [wfu and stored; assumed subsequently b/u; canx 16Feb89]
U-28		Lake Clark Air Services	N699JM N699AM N42CA C-GSFY N4415L N99TA N33TN N991AK
U-29		Ameriflight	N448MD N7486N N115CA N433BC N800BE N802BA
U-30		Freight Runners Express	N652EX N219BH N3RP N199CZ
U-31		(Beech Aircraft Corporation)	N1071C N316VA [wfu and stored; assumed subsequently b/u; canx 16Feb89]
U-32		Suburban Air Freight	N444T N441T N41NA C-FESU N118SF
U-33		ex SFC Aircraft Corp	N1128H N433SA [ex Majestic A/L; wfu 1992; used for spares Jly96 Calgary-Springbank Apt, AB, Canada; fuselage still present 10Sep08; current; l/n 03Feb10]
U-34		Ameriflight	N852SA N134PM
U-35		Bill Dause	N336PL
U-36		Ameriflight	N949K
U-37		(Columbia Pacific Airlines)	N7530N C-GLFH N199EA [w/o 10Feb78 Richland, WA; canx 12May09]
U-38		Wiggins Airways	N1075C N202TC N202BH N214TA N202BH N195WA
U-39		Arctic Sunwest Charters	N7647N N99LP C-GASW
U-40		Bemidji Airlines	N910JM N910AM C-GQFD N108BA
U-41		(Houston Metro Airlines)	N853SA [w/o 01May74 Galveston, TX]
U-42		(Beech Aircraft Corporation)	N7799R N318VA [wfu and stored; assumed subsequently b/u; canx 16Feb89]

BEECH 99

C/n	Model	Last known Owner/Operator	Identities/fates/comments (where appropriate)
U-43		(Contact Air)	N899JM N37CA C-GSFP [w/o 06Dec96 Fort Chipewyan, AB, Canada; canx Jan98; used for spares at Edmonton, AB, Canada]
U-44		(Monmouth Airlines)	N986MA [w/o 24Oct71 Allentown, PA]
U-45		(Nightexpress)	N854SA C-GGBI N42948 D-IBEX [w/o 29Jun99 4km N of Liege, Belgium]
U-46		Air Service Wildgruber	N855SA SE-FOR LN-SAX D-IEXE (N99LM) D-IEXE
U-47		Suburban Air Freight	N7485N N447SA N204TC N204BH N147SF
U-48		(Holmstrom Flyg)	N7699N N299ME SE-IZO [w/o 08May89 Oskarshamn, Sweden]
U-49		Alaska Air Taxi	N846NS N11MV N846NS N215BH HR-IAL N98RZ HI- N98RZ N31TN
U-50	C	Ameriflight	N7940 N4199C [conv to C99 prototype while regd N7940]
U-51		(Beech Aircraft Corporation)	N1031S [wfu and stored; assumed subsequently b/u; canx 16Feb89]
U-52		(Freight Runners Express)	N847NS N12MV ZK-LLA N399CZ [w/o 16Dec03 Mosinee, WI; canx 20Aug04]
U-53		(Beech Aircraft Corporation)	N1032S N203TC [wfu and stored; assumed subsequently b/u; canx 04Jan90]
U-54		(Skystream Airlines)	N1129H N454SA [wfu and stored; assumed subsequently b/u; canx 04Jan90]
U-55		(Air Ontario)	N3116C N44KC N44KX N13MV C-GFKB [to spares Jly94 Thunder Bay, Ont, Canada; canx Aug94 as wfu]
U-56		(Beech Aircraft Corporation)	N7901R N12HA N20RA N20RG N320BA [wfu and stored; assumed subsequently b/u; canx 16Feb89]
U-57		Northwestern Air	N1173C F-BSUZ OY-BYU TF-ELD C-GNAL
U-58		Jamaica Air Shuttle	N7801R C-GQAH V2-ANU 6Y-JSA
U-59	*	Alpine Air Express	N7834R F-BSUG N7834R N14MV C-FGJT N14MV
U-60		Ameriflight	N7888R N82TC N72TC N164HA
U-61		(Touraine Air Transport)	N8110R (9Y-TDJ)+ N2811B F-BTQE [+marks painted on aircraft; not delivered; w/o 02Jly75 Nantes, France]
U-62		(CARA Express Aviation)	N1178C F-BSUJ OO-WAZ LN-SAZ D-IEXF [wfu and stored 31Mar90 Cologne-Bonn, Germany; dismantled Aug91; reported parts shipped to USA for use as spares]
U-63		(TAT European Airlines)	N995E 9Y-TDI N995E F-BUYG [w/o 04Sep83 Tours, France; canx 07Sep90 as destroyed]
U-64		Wiggins Airways	N1033S N200WP C-FAWX N194WA
U-65		SUDEM PP-FSC	PT-FSC
U-66		(Pilgrim Airlines)	N451C [w/o 01Feb82 Groton, CT]
U-67		Alpine Air Express	N954SM C-GVNQ N24BH
U-68		Freight Runners Express	N1185C N8068R N111PA N220BH N220RH ZK-CIB N900AR N196WA N799CZ
U-69		(Nightexpress)	N8012R C-GGAV N3236V D-IEXA [w/o 25Nov86 Paris-Orly, France]
U-70		Nightexpress	N1191C N8013R C-GESP G-NUIT D-IEXB
U-71		Aerodynamics Worldwide Inc	N1034S N406JB N406UB N216BH N4381Y
U-72		(Beech Aircraft Corporation)	N856SA N317VA [wfu and stored; assumed subsequently b/u; canx 16Feb89]
U-73		Aerodynamics Ltd	N796A N209BH C-FYSJ N899AG G-DLAB
U-74		Freight Runners Express	N7655N C-GQAG N102AF C-FCVJ N299CZ
U-75		ex Air Tindi	N875SA F-BIEM SE-IRE C-FEJL C-FATS+ N [+ canx 13Feb09 to USA]
U-76		Piper East Inc/Wiggins Airways	N983MA N139BA N189WA
U-77		(Air South)	N848NS [w/o 31Mar74 St.Simons Island, GA]
U-78		(Beech Aircraft Corporation)	N7809R N319BA [wfu and stored; assumed subsequently b/u; canx 16Feb89]
U-79		(Skydive Portugal)	N551GP F-BTME [w/o 14Aug09 near Bairro de Almerim, Evora, Portugal; canx 25Sep09]
U-80	A	Bemidji Airlines	N653EX C-GFKN N51PA N130BA
U-81	A	Freight Runners Express	N654EX N832T ZS-JVV N501TF N36AK N499CZ
U-82	A	(Methow Aviation)	N655EX CF-AGQ N4954W [wfu & b/u 1989; canx Mar91]
U-83	A	(Northeast Regional Express)	N656EX N124CA N435BC N802BE N804BA [wfu Jan95 & stored Manchester NH; by 29Feb08 b/u hulk with Alpine Aviation, Provo-Municipal, UT; current]
U-84	A	(Islena Airlines)	N657EX N836T F-BVJL (D-IEXC) F-BVJL HR-IAO [wfu; to spares Nov94 White Industries, Bates City, MO]
U-85	A	Ameriflight	N7862R
U-86		(Compagnie Aerienne Languedoc)	N671GP F-BTMO [w/o 28Apr80 Paris-Orly, France]
U-87	A	Suburban Air Freight	N7902R F-BSTO N98WA N59CA N128SF
U-88		not yet known	N7899R HP- N7899R YV-
U-89	A	Freight Runners Express	N658EX N301MA 5Y-BJW N599CZ
U-90		ex TAT European Airlines	N921GP F-BTMA [wfu Jun91; on display Jun95 Tours town centre, France]

BEECH 99

C/n	Model	Last known Owner/Operator	Identities/fates/comments (where appropriate)
U-91		Freight Runners Express	N19991 N533SK N195WA N399CZ
U-92		National Aerotech Aviation	N931GP F-BTDV N112WA N112PA C-GDSL V2-NEV N612NA+ 8P- 6Y-JSC N450NA [+ canx 16Mar10 to Barbados]
U-93	A	(Sabourin Lake Airways)	ZS-CHH N502TF N35CA C-FHIE [DBF and canx 15Jly92]
U-94		(Majestic Air Cargo)	N981GP F-BVRA F-OGKF N9FH [canx 16Sep09; probably wfu in 2002]
U-95		(Beech Aircraft Corporation)	N9995 N29B [wfu and stored; assumed subsequently b/u; canx 23Aug89]
U-96	A	Freight Runners Express	N1920T ZS-PTF N503TF N199CA N899CZ
U-97	A	(Alberta Aircraft Leasing)	N3990A N327CA N531SK C-FVCM N491BB [w/o 31Dec99 Saint Barthelemy, Guadeloupe; by 19Sep08 Atlanta Air Salvage, Griffin, GA; canx 05Feb02]
U-98		Jamaica Air Shuttle	N991GP C-GPEM V2-DOM 6Y-JSI
U-99		(Trans Bharat Aviation)	N8099R N217BH VT-ERP [canx 17May06, assumed wfu]
U-100		(Beech Aircraft Corporation)	N99100 N321BA [wfu and stored; assumed subsequently b/u; canx 16Feb89]
U-101	A	(Cascade Airways)	N7961R N11HA N13RA N390CA [w/o 20Jan81 near Spokane, WA; canx 14Apr83]
U-102		(Alpine Air Express)	N247V N15MV ZK-JAF N321KB N299GL [w/o 17Oct98 Missoula, MT; current]
U-103		Suburban Air Freight	N7994R
U-104	B	Alpine Air Express	N4155A N1922T N415SA N1922T N899CA
U-105	A	Ameriflight	N4099A N34AK
U-106		(Cascade Airways)	N2550A [w/o 20Jun69 Pasco, WA]
U-107		Northwestern Air	N7986R F-BSTU N7986R N107TJ N207BH C-GNAH
U-108		(Beech Aircraft Corporation)	N8084R [wfu and stored; assumed subsequently b/u; canx 16Feb89]
U-109		Freight Runners Express	N2880A N109CZ
U-110	A	(Transwest Air)	N4212A N396HA C-FDYF [w/o 23Apr03 Prince Albert, SK, Canada; canx 22Aug05]
U-111	A	Ameriflight	N20FW
U-112	A	Alpine Air Express	N195R C-GXAZ N86569 N99GH
U-113	A	Bayview Air Service	N113TM N295R C-GWYD
U-114	A	(Great Lakes Aviation)	N2860A N82NA N699CA [wfu 1997 & stored; canx 21Jly11; possibly was w/o 11Feb87 Oneonta, NY]
U-115	A	Ameriflight	N91FA N24AT N1924T
U-116	A	Freight Runners Express	N860SA N711GL N601CA N430BC N804BE N806BA N116EE N17AL C-GZAM N999CZ
U-117	A	Ameriflight	N21FW
U-118	A	North Wright Airways	N296HA C-FVCE N918BB C-FVCE
U-119	A	(Tilm-Aire Aviation)	N7997R [w/o 16Mar76 Dutchess County, NY; canx 30Jly98]
U-120		Perimeter Airlines	N9018Q 9018+ N47156 C-GFQC [+ Thailand]
U-121		(Air Alpes)	F-BRUF [w/o 15Jan70 Chambery, France]
U-122		(Air Alpes)	F-BRUX [w/o 16Feb78, location not known; CofA suspended 16Feb78]
U-123	A	(SALSA d'Haiti)	N3947A N10HA N18RA C-GDFX V2-SLU N610NA HH-APA [w/o 20Sep11 en-route Port au Prince to Prince-Cap Haiten, Haiti]
U-124	A	Perimeter Airlines	N788C EI-BKY SE-IOG TF-ELB C-FRQI
U-125	A	(Air East)	N3925A N125AE [w/o 06Jan74 Johnson, PA]
U-126	A	ex Flanagan Enterprises (Nevada)	N21AT N12RA N324CA OO-EEE N4302J C-FQCN N126WD+ C- [+ canx 05Sep12 to Canada]
U-127	A*	Alpine Air Express	N22AT N99CA
U-128	A	Flamingo Air USA	N1921T C-GJKO N949CC J6-AAE N955AA
U-129	A	(TAT European Airlines)	LN-LML F-BTMJ [wfu and stored Dinard, France; canx 07Sep90 as destroyed; b/u]
U-130	A	Wiggins Airways	N7971R LN-LMT F-BTMK N130EA C-FOZU N197WA
U-131	A	(Rio Airways)	N12RA [w/o 12Jan71, location not known; canx 03Mar71]
U-132	A	(Precision Air Lease)	N23AT N1923T C-FCRW N1923T [to spares Jly94 Peterborough, ON, Canada; hulk to White Industries, Bates City by Jan01; canx 29Feb12]
U-133	B	(Freight Runners Express)	N2421A N133AE N142CA N434BC N801BE N803BA N27AL N699CZ(1) [serious damage 24Jan07 Milwaukee, MI; canx 03Feb10]
U-134	A	LANHSA	N180Z N140Z N204FW N80275 HR-AXK
U-135	A*	Alpine Air Express	N10RA N326CA
U-136	A	Wiggins Airways	PT-CIK N9PD SE-FNV LN-SAL N114PA N110PA OH-WWS C-GPCF N191WA
U-137	A	Bemidji Airlines	N9073Q CC-EEO FAC-300+ C-GAWW N137BA [+ Chile]
U-138	A	Museo Nacional de Aeronautica	CC-EEP FAC-301+ [+ Chile] [preserved Dec10 Los Cerillos, Chile]
U-139	A	Chilean Air Force	CC-EEQ FAC-302+ [+ Chile]
U-140	A	Chilean Air Force	CC-EER FAC-303+ [+ Chile]

BEECH 99

C/n	Model	Last known Owner/Operator	Identities/fates/comments (where appropriate)
U-141	A	Win Win Aviation	CC-EES FAC-304+ N141WW [+ Chile]
U-142	A	Wiggins Airways	CC-EET FAC-305+ C-GAVV N133BA N198WA [+ Chile]
U-143	A	ex Alpine Air Express – Chile	CC-EEU FAC-306+ CC-PNO N399AA CC-PNO N399AA CC-CAQ [+ Chile] [by late 2007 derelict Puerto Aysen, Chile]
U-144	A	Chilean Air Force	CC-EEV FAC-307+ [+ Chile]
U-145	A	(Aerocord)	CC-EEW FAC-308+ CC-EEW CC-KIW CC-PLL N391MH CC-CFM [+ Chile] [w/o 10Jly08 near Puerto Montt-Marcel Marchant Airport, Chile]
U-146	B	Ameriflight	N4299A
U-147	A	Ameriflight	N147AE N151CA N431BC N803BE N805BA
U-148	B	(Nature Island Express)	N9399Q N42AK [w/o 24Jan92 into sea off Dominica-Cane Field;canx 23Sep92]
U-149	B	Kenn Borek Air/Aklak Air	N3149W ZS-UAS N444JJ N495R N149CJ C-FIRC HP-1230APP C-GKKB
U-150	B	(Prince Edward Air)	N35MW N5SS N999CA C-FJCC [canx 04May05 as wfu]
U-151	B	Keystone Air Service	N1599W N338PL N151CJ C-FBRO N222YL C-FBRO C-FPCD
U-152	B	Wiggins Airways	N16RA C-GEOI N192WA
U-153	B	Skydive UK Ltd	N17RA N17RX C-GHVI N899DZ [based in UK]
U-154	B	Wiggins Airways	N99CH N199WA
U-155	B	(Alpine Air Express)	N99TH [w/o 29Dec06 Rapid City, SD; by 28May07 to MTW Aerospace facility near Montgomery, AL; for spares use; canx 15Jun11]
U-156	B	(Henson Airlines)	N339PL N339HA [w/o 23Sep85 Blue Ridge Mts, Shenandoah Valley, VA; canx]
U-157	B	(Precision Airlease Int'l)	N496HA [wfu by Jan01; to White Industries, Bates City MO for spares; current]
U-158	B	ex Air Kentucky Air Lines	N8558R N38AK [wfu & stored Jly94 Peterborough, ON, Canada; l/n 18Feb10; current]
U-159	B	Alpine Air Express	N133CA N163HA C-FCBU N950AA
U-160	B	(Bearskin Lake Air Services)	N596HA C-GXBE [w/o 4Dec97 Webequie, ON, Canada; canx 30May01]
U-161	B	Ameriflight	N12AK N199AF
U-162	B	Trim-Aire Aviation	N4499S C-FBCH N4499S
U-163	B	(Senpaku Gijutsu Kenkyujo)	N9387S JA8801 [damaged 11Mar11 in Tsunami; canx 26Mar12]
U-164	B	Kenn Borek Air/Aklak Air	SE-GRB C-GKBA
U-165	C	Pineapple Air	N3860D N263SW PT-LUW N42517 C6-HAN
U-166	C	Ameriflight	N106SX
U-167	C	Courtesy Air	N990SB N991SB N167EE C-FNMF
U-168	C	Ameriflight	N18487 N18AK N221BH
U-169	C	Ameriflight	N6199D
U-170	C	(Sunbird Airlines)	(N995SB) N992SB [w/o 28Aug85 near Hickory, NC]
U-171	C	Ameriflight	N63978
U-172	C	Corporate Air	(N996SB) N993SB N172EE
U-173	C	Ameriflight	N6460D N223BH
U-174	C	Ameriflight	N6188D N264SW N399ME (N99CY) N99CJ N174AV
U-175	C	Bemidji Airlines	(N997SB) N994SB N175EE
U-176	C	Ameriflight	N107SX
U-177	C	Ameriflight	N62933 N265SW N103BE N177EE N68TA
U-178	C	(Ameriflight)	N63995 [w/o 16Nov94 near Avenal, CA; canx 09Feb95]
U-179	C	Piper East Inc/Wiggins Airways	(N998SB) N995SB N196WA
U-180	C	Courtesy Air	CP-1804 OY-PAG C-FJMF
U-181	C	Ameriflight	N62936 N225BH
U-182	C	Ameriflight	N6263D N226BH
U-183	C	Ameriflight	N62989
U-184	C	Ameriflight	N6787P N108SX
U-185	C	(GP Express Airlines)	N62995 N118GP [w/o 08Jun92 near Anniston, AL; canx 18Aug92]
U-186	C	(Raytheon Aircraft Company)	N6399X N119GP [wfu Aug96 Las Vegas-Henderson, NV; fuselage only remains by Jan01, no longer present; but re-regd 25Aug08 to Hawker Beechcraft Corp; current]
U-187	C	(Wings West Airlines)	N6399U [w/o 24Aug84 near San Luis Obispo, CA, after mid-air collision with Rockwell 112TC N112SM]
U-188	C	Ameriflight	N64799 N799GL N388AV
U-189	C	Courtesy Air	N516DM N189AV C-FLMF
U-190	C	Ameriflight	N6506V N986RA 6Y-JVB N8226Z
U-191	C	Ameriflight	N6599U (N63978) N191YV C-GFAQ N191BE N191EE VR-CIB N191AV
U-192	C	Ameriflight	N6534A N997SB
U-193	C	Ameriflight	N6599A N193YV C-GFAT N2225Y C-GFAT N193SU
U-194	C	Ameriflight	N6568N N116GP 6Y-JVA N8227P
U-195	C	Ameriflight	N64997 N53RP

BEECH 99

C/n	Model	Last known Owner/Operator	Identities/fates/comments (where appropriate)
U-196	C	(Ameriflight)	N68730 N109SX [wfu and stored; canx 14Aug89; now assumed b/u]
U-197	C	(Frontier Air)	N63984 N197YV C-GFAW [w/o 30Apr90 Ship Sands Island, ON, Canada; canx 05Jly90]
U-198	C	Ameriflight	N64002 N55RP
U-199	C	Colombian Police	HK-3040 PNC-0203+ [+ not fully confirmed]
U-200	C	Air Direct Aircraft	HK-3041 SE-IZX N223CA
U-201	C	Ameriflight	N96AV
U-202	C	Ameriflight	N261SW
U-203	C	Ameriflight	N262SW N203YV C-GFAZ N203TY N541JC N992AF
U-204	C	Ameriflight	N65453 N199ME N575W C6-RMM N575W N204AF
U-205	C	(Ameriflight)	N97AV N987RA 6Y-JVC N205RA [w/o 12Feb99 in mountains near Bishop, CA; canx 04Apr00]
U-206	C	(Ameriflight)	N6612K N206YV N216EE N206AV [w/o 06Jan10 Kearney Regional Airport. NE]
U-207	C	Piper East Inc/Wiggins Airways	C-GGLE N207CS N190WA
U-208	C	Ameriflight	N6628K N102GP (N114GE) N102GP
U-209	C	Air Direct Aircraft	N6645K
U-210	C	Ameriflight	N66305 N52RP
U-211	C	Ameriflight	N66446 N113GP N990AF
U-212	C	Ameriflight	N51RP
U-213	C	Anthem Aircraft Leasing	N6656N N213AV
U-214	C	Ameriflight	N6828K N112GP N991AF
U-215	C	Ameriflight	N6724D
U-216	C	Alpine Air Express	C-GGPP N216CS
U-217	C	(Raytheon Aircraft Credit Corp)	N6728J [DBR 16May86 Laramie WY; wfu and stored Aug87; assumed b/u by Dodson International Parts; current]
U-218	C	(Ameriflight)	N54RP [w/o 18Mar06 near Butte, MT; canx 18May07]
U-219	C	Ameriflight	N7200Z
U-220	C	Bemidji Airlines	N7212P
U-221	C	Ameriflight	N7203L N104BE
U-222	C	Ameriflight	N7205A N818FL N130GP
U-223	C	Bemidji Airlines	N7207E
U-224	C	Ameriflight	N7209W
U-225	C	Ameriflight	N72138 N131GP J6-AAF N131GP
U-226	C	(L'Express Airlines)	N7217L [w/o 10Jly91 Birmingham, AL; canx 19Jly12]
U-227	C	Ameriflight	N7217K C-FWAD N2225H N227AV
U-228	C	(GP Express Airlines)	CP-2106 N29WJ N115GP [w/o 28Apr93 nr Shelton, 28km S.W. of Grand Island, NE; current]
U-229	C	Ameriflight	CP-2107 N3067L N228BH
U-230	C	Ameriflight	N3063W N330AV
U-231	C	Angel Air	N72365 N229BH N141RM C6-RRM C6-DOC
U-232	C	Ameriflight	N7243U N232BH J6-AAG N81820
U-233	C	Ameriflight	N72355 N230BH
U-234	C	Ameriflight	N7243N N234BH N234AV
U-235	C	Ameriflight	N72493 N235BH N235AV
U-236	C	Alpine Air Express	N7250E N237BH VH-OXE N236AL RP-C2317 N236AL
U-237	C	Alpine Air Express	N72520 N240BH VH-OXD N237SL RP-C2370 N237SL
U-238	C	Alpine Air Express	N7249E N227BH VH-OXB N238AL RP-C2380 N238AL
U-239	C	Alpine Air Express	N7257K N239BH VH-OXC N239AL RP-C2390 N239AL

Production complete

BEECH 1900

C/n	Model	Last known Owner/Operator	Identities/fates/comments (where appropriate)

Note: An asterisk after the model identifier indicates an aircraft converted to a freighter without windows

C/n	Model	Last known Owner/Operator	Identities/fates/comments (where appropriate)
UA-1		(Beech Aircraft Corp)	N1900A [prototype ff 03Sep82; wfu & stored 1985 Wichita-Beech Field, KS; canx 07Mar90; still intact 27Apr09]
UA-2		Hawker Beechcraft Corp	N6800J [wfu & stored Apr85, Wichita-Beech Field, KS; canx 05Mar09; still intact 27Apr09]
UA-3		Bolivian Air Force	N1900J SE-KOH N1900J FAB043 [serious damage 30Nov11 La Paz, Bolivia]
Beech 1900C			
UB-1	C	Alpine Air Express	N6667L N1PU N1YW N190GA
UB-2	C	Ameriflight	N121CZ N31701
UB-3	C	Ameriflight	N122CZ N31702
UB-4	C	Aviation Assistance	N6829J N301BH SE-KSX OY-GEN 5Y-DHW OY-GEN [stripped; remains marked "OY-RKE" stored since Jun01 Roskilde, Denmark; l/n 09Jan08]
UB-5	C	Alpine Air Express	N302BH N5ZR N198GA CC-CAS N198GA
UB-6	C	Alpine Air Express	N6778R N125GP N125BA
UB-7	C	Alpine Air Express	N303BH N7ZR N126GP N127BA
UB-8	C	Alpine Air Express	N304BH N8ZR N194GA CC-CAF N194GA
UB-9	C	Pacific Coastal Airlines	N305BH N9ZR N189GA C-FPCV
UB-10	C	Ameriflight	N123CZ N31703
UB-11	C	Alpine Air Express	N306BH N11ZR N172GA
UB-12	C	Ameriflight	N124CZ N31704
UB-13	C	(ex Gulfstream International A/L)	N307BH N13ZR N199GA [b/u Nov02 for spares, Orlando, FL; canx 05Oct04]
UB-14	C	Alpine Aviation Inc	N308BH N14ZR N188GA N219VP
UB-15	C	Qwila Air	N309BH N715GL ZS-PRE
UB-16	C	Alpine Air Express	N311BH N16ZR N197GA
UB-17	C	Alpine Air Express	N72152 N17ZR N192GA
UB-18	C	Rossair	N72154 N18ZR Z-DHS ZS-OLP
UB-19	C	Suburban Air Freight/Pet Airways	N125CZ N314BH N719GL
UB-20	C	Comav Aviation/Air Namibia	N126CZ N101BE ZS-MMN V5-MMN ZS-OUB
UB-21	C	Skylink Express	N127CZ N21YV N61MK C-GSKM
UB-22	C	MTW Aerospace Inc	N7254R
UB-23	C	Suburban Air Freight	N128CZ N23YV N23VK N124GP
UB-24	C	Aviation One of Florida Inc	N7243R N181GA N172TE N218VP
UB-25	C	(Alpine Air Express)	N15RA N315BH N154GA [w/o 23May08 Billings, MT]
UB-26	C	(ex Air Cargo Masters)	N16RA N316BH [b/u for spares by White Inds, Bates City, MO; canx Mar02 as wfu]
UB-27	C	(Skylink Express)	N6929M C-GSKC [w/o 14Sep01 St Johns, NL, Canada; canx 26Apr06; fuselage hulk to Chatham-Kent, ON, Canada; l/n Oct08]
UB-28	C	Ameriflight	N7203C
UB-29	C	Compion Aviation/ALS Ltd	N7212K ZS-LTB V5-LTB ZS-OUC 5Y-BVV
UB-30	C	SERAIR	N7210R EC-GTM
UB-31	C	Southern Air Charter, Bahamas	(N275HK) N331CJ N196GA N378SA
UB-32	C	Skylink Express	N17RA N317BH C-GSKA
UB-33	C	Skylink Express	N18RA N318BH C-GSKW
UB-34	C	Alpine Air Express	N7214R N734GL N153GA
UB-35	C	Skylink Express	N35CJ N735GL C-GSKU
UB-36	C	Corporate Air	N19RA N319BH
UB-37	C	(Dept of the Air Force/ EG & G Group)	(N270HK) N7214K N27RA [w/o 16Mar04 in Nellis area, NV]
UB-38	C	Ameriflight	N805BE N330AF
UB-39	C	Courtesy Air	N7227E N404SS N484SS N2TS N502CG N888MX C-FJTF
UB-40	C	Air Katanga	(N271HK) N809BE N896SC ST-ASG N495KL 9Q-CYD
UB-41	C	(Southern Air Charter Co)	N806BE OB-1694 N79YV [w/o 22Oct04 off South Beach, New Providence, Bahamas; remains dumped on beach; l/n 09Jan05; canx 05Oct06]
UB-42	C	Dept of the Air Force/EG & G Group	(N272HK) N20RA
UB-43	C	Pacific Coastal Airlines	N34GT N565M C-GBPC
UB-44	C	Ameriflight	(N273HK) N807BE N331AF
UB-45	C	Pacific Coastal Airlines	(N274HK) N808BE N1900A C-FYZD C-GPCY
UB-46	C	Ameriflight	(N276HK) N10RA N3071A
UB-47	C	(Ameriflight)	N47RA N3172A [w/o 13Aug97 Seattle, WA; canx 23Mar98; remains to White Inds, Bates City, MO]
UB-48	C	Pineapple Air, Bahamas	N810BE N896FM N800MX

BEECH 1900

C/n	Model	Last known Owner/Operator	Identities/fates/comments (where appropriate)
UB-49	C	(Business Express)	N811BE [w/o 28Dec91 Block Island, RI; canx 12Oct11]
UB-50	C	ex Stratovest (Pty) Ltd/DHL	N812BE ZS-NXX 9G-DHL ZS-NXX+ TZ- [+ canx 13May10 as exported]
UB-51	C	Ameriflight	N3229A
UB-52	C	Pacific Coastal Airlines	N817BE C-GKHB C-FPCO
UB-53	C	SAEREO	N814BE HC-BVN
UB-54	C	Aero Transporte S.A.	N815BE OB-1667 OB-1667-P
UB-55	C	Tropical Transport Services	N3155B N55YV (N57AF) N259AF N155GA N900MX
UB-56	C	Pineapple Air	N7239T D-CESA OK-REA D-CESA OY-JRP N505RH N157PA
UB-57	C	Air Venezuela/Brinks	N816BE YV-687CP
UB-58	C	(Ryan Air Service)	N29951 N401RA [w/o 23Nov87 Homer, AK; canx 21Mar91]
UB-59	C	Freight Runners Express	N72391 D-CARA N191CZ
UB-60	C	Ameriflight	N31705
UB-61	C	Ad-Astral Aviation	N7254E N818BE VH-FWA
UB-62	C	Ad-Astral Aviation	N29995 N819BE VH-IYP ZS-NAV VH-VOA
UB-63	C	Kenya Airlink	N30234 N106BE N63YV N63MK C-FUCB 5Y-LKG
UB-64	C	Craig Air Center Inc	N3039X N820BE N93BD N23BD N191TV
UB-65	C	(Alpine Air Express)	N3113M N65YV N65CJ N195GA CC-CAK N195GA [w/o 23May08 Billings-Logan International, MT; canx 22May09]
UB-66	C	Pacific Coastal Airlines	N3044C N823BE F-OJAS F-GTOT OY-JRF C-FPCX
UB-67	C	Skylink Express	N3067X C-FKAX
UB-68	C	Courtesy Air	N1GT N30CY N521M N60GH N68GH C-FJDF
UB-69	C	Pineapple Air	N3068M N331CR N381CR
UB-70	C	Ameriflight	N3052K
UB-71	C	Pacific Coastal Airlines	N3069K C-GNPG C-GCPZ [before last reregn was reported as wfu & to South Alberta Institute of Technology as GIA]
UB-72	C	Southern Air Charter, Bahamas	N3076N D-CAPA OK-SEB D-CAPA OY-JRS N504RH S7- N504RH N376SA
UB-73	C	ex Jumbo Repairs	N72402 ZS-LTC V5-LTC ZS-OUD+ C- [+ canx 02Mar12 to Canada]
UB-74	C	Air Tropiques	D-CISA S9-CAC 5Y-SEJ ZS-ODR 9Q-CEJ
UC-1	C-1	Marvin Lumber & Cedar	N3114B N640MW
UC-2	C-1	Alaska Central Express	N18263 N19NA N19NG N115AX
UC-3	C-1	(Raytheon Aircraft Credit Corp)	N917RM N34010 [stored Marana,AZ; l/n13Oct03; canx 27Aug04; assumed b/u]
UC-4	C-1	Saudi Arabian CAA	N3078C HZ-PC2
UC-5	C-1	(Republic of China Air Force)	N3186H 1905 [w/o 21Aug90 Yunlin Province, Taiwan]
UC-6	C-1	Republic of China Air Force	N72423 1906
UC-7	C-1	Republic of China Air Force	N72424 1907
UC-8	C-1	Republic of China Air Force	N3179U N7242V 1908
UC-9	C-1	(Raytheon Aircraft Credit Corp)	N918RM N22011 N918RM N38011 YV-575C N38011 (N108GA) [stored Oklahoma City-Wiley Post, OK; l/n 04Nov05; canx 13Dec06 wfu for parts]
UC-10	C-1	Egyptian Air Force	N7242C 4801//SU-BKV [dual marks]
UC-11	C-1	(Raytheon Aircraft Credit Corp)	N31079 N919RM N17012 YV-1095C N17012 [wfu by Dec03 stored in scrapyard of MTW Aerospace near Montgomery, AL; l/n 24Jan06 – Falcon Royal Air titles; canx 02Apr09]
UC-12	C-1	(Raytheon Aircraft Credit Corp)	N31101 N920RM N76013 CP-2350 N76013 [wfu for spares Montgomery-Regional, AL by Dec03; l/n 24Jan06 – Servicio Aereo Vargas Espana, titles; canx 02Apr09]
UC-13	C-1	Aerologistics II LLC	N31121 N921RM N33014 YV-1094C N33014 N413CM
UC-14	C-1	Latina de Aviacion	N922RM N38015 HK-4173X
UC-15	C-1	Egyptian Air Force	N7242D 4803//SU-BKW [dual marks]
UC-16	C-1	Egyptian Air Force	N7242L 4804//SU-BKX [dual marks]
UC-17	C-1*	Alaska Central Express	N31135 N1547C N17ZV CC-COK N17ZV N116AX
UC-18	C-1	Egyptian Air Force	N7242M 4805//SU-BKY [dual marks]
UC-19	C-1	Summer Sun Trading 296 (Pty) Ltd	N31143 N1552C (N341MA) N119CJ N119CU ZS-TAB
UC-20	C-1	(Raytheon Aircraft Credit Corp)	N31187 N1563C [wfu by Feb04 Marana-Pinal Airpark, AZ; l/n 19Apr06; canx 02Apr09; assumed b/u for parts]
UC-21	C-1	Egyptian Air Force	N7242Q 4806//SU-BKZ [dual marks]
UC-22	C-1	Skylink Express	N923RM N19016 C-GSKG
UC-23	C-1	Republic of China Air Force	N3188K 1901
UC-24	C-1	Frontier Alaska	N31226 N1553C
UC-25	C-1	Republic of China Air Force	N3189F 1902

BEECH 1900

C/n	Model	Last known Owner/Operator	Identities/fates/comments (where appropriate)
UC-26	C-1	(Raytheon Aircraft Credit Corp)	N31228 N1562C (N125GA) [to spares use by White Inds, Bates City, MO by Mar04; l/n 26Jly05; canx 02Apr09]
UC-27	C-1	Republic of China Air Force	N31904 1903
UC-28	C-1	(Alaska Central Express)	N31240 (N901YW) N31240 [w/o 11Feb99 St. Mary's, AK; canx 01Jun00]
UC-29	C-1	Republic of China Air Force	N3192E 1904
UC-30	C-1	Republic of China Air Force	N3199H 1911
UC-31	C-1	Colombian National Police	N31079 (VH-MJH) VH-JHP C-FCMV N187GA HK-4355 PNC-0237
UC-32	C-1	Republic of China Air Force	N3206C 1912
UC-33	C-1	Egyptian Air Force	N7242U 4802//SU-BLA [dual marks]
UC-34	C-1	Republic of China Air Force	N3206K 1909
UC-35	C-1	Republic of China Air Force	N3214Z 1910
UC-36	C-1	Alpine Aviation Inc	N15536 N1566C N114AX
UC-37	C-1	National Airways	N32017 ZS-PMF
UC-38	C-1	Colombian National Police	N32018 N38SU HK-4392 PNC-0238
UC-39	C-1	CEM Air (Pty) Ltd	N39019 HK-4143X N39019 ZS-PUD
UC-40	C-1	Falcon Express Cargo A/L	N31101 OY-BVG OH-BPA OY-BVG F-GLPJ A6-FCX
UC-41	C-1	Alaska Central Express	N219GL N41UE N113AX
UC-42	C-1	(Raytheon Aircraft Credit Corp)	N31134 (N902YW) N31134 (N135GA) [wfu by Mar03; stored in scrapyard of MTW Aerospace near Montgomery, AL; l/n 24Jan06 – Gulfstream International A/L c/s; canx 02Apr09]
UC-43	C-1	Alaska Central Express	N31210 JA8863 N31210 N43GP N1900C YV149T N119AX
UC-44	C-1	West Wind Aviation/Pronto Airways	N31261 JA8864 N31261 (N144GP) N31261 SE-KXX OY-JRI (F-HJJJ) F-GJRI C-GWWX
UC-45	C-1	(Alaska Central Express)	N3127M RP-C312 N125PN OY-CCH N45GL N112AX [w/o 22Jan10 Sand Point, AK; canx 21Jan12]
UC-46	C-1	(Aerolift Philippines)	N31827 RP-C314 [w/o 18May90 near Manila Airport, Philippines]
UC-47	C-1	Servicio Pan Americano de Proteccion	N31228 N1501C CC-COJ N1501C 9N-AGA N47UC HK-4325-X HK-4325 YV1674
UC-48	C-1	Solenta Aviation	N31559 9J-AFJ ZS-OHE
UC-49	C-1	Ameriflight	N31495 C-GFAC N80198 C-GCMJ N49UC
UC-50	C-1	ex Aircraft Contracts Africa (Pty) Ltd	N31526 N1568C N550CJ 7Q-NXA ZS-OKU N [canx 25Jly12 to USA]
UC-51	C-1	Egyptian Air Force	N31527 4807//SU-BLS [dual marks]
UC-52	C-1	Egyptian Air Force	N31544 4808//SU-BLT [dual marks]
UC-53	C-1	Suburban Air Freight	N31764 (N903YW) N31764 CC-COD LV-WPH N31764 N253SF
UC-54	C-1	Skylink Express	N31729 C-GSKN
UC-55	C-1	Aviation Assistance/UN	N15031 OY-BVI OK-UEA OY-BVI 5Y-BVI
UC-56	C-1	Vincent Aviation	N1568B VH-AFR (VH-IMP) VH-OST ZK-VAE VH-VNV
UC-57	C-1	Falcon Express Cargo A/L	N15189 N57YV OY-GED A6-FCA
UC-58	C-1	Ameriflight	N15305 N1568G F-GNAD N1568G
UC-59	C-1	(Raytheon Aircraft Credit Corp)	N1568K N120GP (N120GA) [to spares use by White Inds, Bates City, MO by Mar04; l/n 26Jly05; canx 02Apr09]
UC-60	C-1	SEARCA	N15337 N319GL N60UE N901SC (D-CFDL) HK-4210X N901SC HK-4282X HK-4282
UC-61	C-1	Northern Thunderbird Air	N1568L C-GCMZ
UC-62	C-1	Skylink Express	N62YV LV-WSJ N62YV C-GTGA
UC-63	C-1	West Wind Aviation/Pronto Airways	N15394 TR-LEU ZS-ONJ ZS-PDI C-GWWY
UC-64	C-1	SEARCA	N1568W HK-4266X HK-4266
UC-65	C-1	(Southern Sudan Air Connection)	D-CIRB 5Y-ROS ZS-OGZ 5Y-ROS ZS-OGZ 5Y-ROS 5Y-FLX [w/o 02May08 45km from Rumbek, Sudan]
UC-66	C-1	Falcon Express Cargo A/L	N66YV OY-GEI A6-FCB
UC-67	C-1	Craig Air Center Inc	N119GL N67UE N902SC N192TV
UC-68	C-1	Falcon Express Cargo A/L	N68YV OY-GEJ A6-FCC
UC-69	C-1	ex Global Air Charters	N15466 N520LX N69ZR F-GPYS OY-GML 5Y-BSN [reported wfu by 12Jun11 Nairobi-Wilson. Kenya]
UC-70	C-1	(Alpine Air Express)	N15674 N70YV N15674 (N904YW) N410UB CC-COF LV-WPI N410UB [w/o 14Jan08 into sea near Lihu'e, HI; canx 20May09]
UC-71	C-1	Falcon Express Cargo A/L	N15669 (N71YV) OY-GEK A6-FCD
UC-72	C-1	Frontier Alaska	N15503
UC-73	C-1	National Airways	N1570B F-GJTP TJ-AIL N1570B ZS-OZZ
UC-74	C-1	Executive Turbine Aircraft Hire	N15528 F-GLPK TR-LEO F-GOPK TR-LFP N374UC ZS-PHL
UC-75	C-1	Ameriflight	N31228 N521LX N75YV CC-COG LV-WZA N75YV JA190C N19RZ

BEECH 1900

C/n	Model	Last known Owner/Operator	Identities/fates/comments (where appropriate)
UC-76	C-1	West Wind Aviation/Pronto Airways	(N71YV) N76YV CC-COM N76YV ZS-PJM C-GPRZ
UC-77	C-1	ex Aircraft Contracts Africa (Pty) Ltd	N77YV CC-COL N77YV ZS-PJL+ TZ- [+ canx 17Aug10 as to Mali]
UC-78	C-1	Frontier Alaska	N1568D N503RH N121WV N815GV
UC-79	C-1	Farnair Hungary	N619GL N79GL A6-FCE HA-FAJ
UC-80	C-1	(Avirex)	N15337 N522LX N80ZR F-GPYT TR-LFQ [w/o 29Apr03 Kinshasa, Democratic Republic of Congo]
UC-81	C-1	Alaska Central Express	N15189 N5632C N111AX
UC-82	C-1	(Beech Aircraft)	[cvtd on production line to prototype Beech 1900D c/n UE-1 q.v.]
UC-83	C-1	Frontier Alaska	N15625 C-GFAD N80334 N575A
UC-84	C-1	Professional Air Service LLC	N719GL N84GL HI-719CT N719JP
UC-85	C-1	(Dodson's International)	(C-FNCB) N15662 N85YV C-FGOI (N90DL) [w/o 04Jan99 St.Augustin, PQ, Canada; regd N90DL for spares use only by Dodson at Rantoul, KS]
UC-86	C-1	(Raytheon Aircraft Credit Corp)	N15547 N86UE N147GA [stored Marana-Pinal Airpark, AZ; l/n 13Oct03; b/u by Apr04; canx 18Nov08]
UC-87	C-1	(Great Lakes Aviation)	(C-FNCD) N15687 N819GL N87GL [w/o 19Nov96 Quincy, IL; canx 25Oct99]
UC-88	C-1	fly540.com	N31495 N88YV CC-COH N88YV HK-4203X N88YV ZS-PJA 5Y-BSS
UC-89	C-1	(Raytheon Aircraft Credit Corp)	N15536 N89UE N148GA [stored Marana-Pinal Airpark, AZ; l/n 27Nov03; b/u by Apr04; canx 18Nov08]
UC-90	C-1	not yet known	C-FNCL N31226 N90YV 5Y-EOE+ 3X-G [+ canx 18Aug11 to Guinea]
UC-91	C-1	SERAIR	N91YV S9-CAF N91YV EC-JDY
UC-92	C-1	Heliconia Palmair	N15382 F-GLPL CN-TAS
UC-93	C-1	Frontier Alaska	N93YV S9-CAB S9-CAC N93YV N575U
UC-94	C-1	Northern Thunderbird Air	C-GFAF N80346 C-GEFA N80346 C-GEFA
UC-95	C-1	Martinaire Aviation	N80532 C-GFAK N80532 N575P
UC-96	C-1	ex Executive Turbine Kenya	N15680 (N138GL) N15680 N96UE N130GA ZS-PBY 5Y-BTG [reported wfu by 09Dec12 Nairobi-Wilson, Kenya]
UC-97	C-1	Guna Airlines	N15693 N523LX N97YV YV-461C N97YV 9N-AGI
UC-98	C-1	(Raytheon Aircraft Credit Corp)	N5664F N55054 N192GL N98GL [to spares use by MTW Aerospace at Montgomery-Regional, AL by Dec03; l/n 24Jan06; canx 02Apr09]
UC-99	C-1	Martinaire Aviation	N80598 C-GFAN N80598 VQ-THW N80598 N575F
UC-100	C-1	Aircraft Leasing Services/DHL	N15305 5Y-DHL
UC-101	C-1	Corporate Air	(N819GL) N919GL N101UE
UC-102	C-1	Keewatin Air	N15479 (N905YW) N15479 CC-COI N15479 HK-4200X N15479 C-FJXL
UC-103	C-1	Corporate Air	N15031 (N103CJ) C-GZTU N205CA [stored by 01Feb09 Tampa, FL; l/n 17Jly09; canx by Jan12]
UC-104	C-1	ex Sky King Airlines	N55107 N198GL N104GL VQ-TBL
UC-105	C-1	(Raytheon Aircraft Credit Corp)	N191GL N105GL N137GA [wfu by Dec03; stored in scrapyard of MTW Aerospace near Montgomery, AL; l/n 24Jan06 – Gulfstream International c/s; canx 02Apr09]
UC-106	C-1	Ameriflight	(N524LX) N106YV RP-C2318 N106YV JA190B N21RZ
UC-107	C-1	ex Fly Air Ethiopia	N15539 (N906YW) N207CJ ZS-POF 5Y-BTY ET-AMX [reported wfu by Jun11 Addis Ababa, Ethiopia]
UC-108	C-1	Guna Airlines	N15656 PT-MFD N15656 CC-COE N15656 9N-AGL
UC-109	C-1	Hawker Pacific Pty	N109YV F-GPYU N109YV VH-EMI
UC-110	C-1	Pacific Coastal Airlines	(N525LX) N55309 N132GP N210CU C-GIPC
UC-111	C-1	Ameriflight	N111YV F-GPYX N111YV
UC-112	C-1	Ameriflight	N112YV RP-C2319 N112YV VH-AFR N112YV
UC-113	C-1	Solenta Aviation/DHL	N55227 ZS-NPT 5Y-HAC ZS-NPT
UC-114	C-1	Aircraft Leasing Services /UN	(N526LX) N15550 N129GP 5Y-SGL V5-SGL 5Y-SGL
UC-115	C-1	Atlantique Air Assistance	N115YV F-GPYY
UC-116	C-1	CEM Air (Pty) Ltd/UN	N55280 (N907YW) 9G-KFN ZS-OLU
UC-117	C-1	Skylink Express	N527LX N117ZR C-GKGA
UC-118	C-1	Freight Runners Express	N15189 N118YV (LV-PMC) 6Y-JVD N118YV YV-1150C YV219T N439QA N192CZ
UC-119	C-1	JS Focus Air	N119YV YV-1070C N119YV AP-BJC
UC-120	C-1	Northern Thunderbird Air	N15683 C-GCMT
UC-121	C-1	Martinaire Aviation	N528LX N121ZR F-GPYV N121ZR ZS-PKX V5-PKX ZS-PKX N821SF

BEECH 1900

C/n	Model	Last known Owner/Operator	Identities/fates/comments (where appropriate)
UC-122	C-1	Corporate Air	N195GL N122GL
UC-123	C-1	(Corporate Air)	N193GL N123UE [wfu and stored at Billings, MT in basic United Express c/s; l/n 28May06; canx 08Jly09 as wfu]
UC-124	C-1	Keewatin Air	(N529LX) N122GP EC-HCM N124CU C-FJXO
UC-125	C-1	fly540.com	N15248 N196GL N125GL VQ-TPT ZS-POU 5Y-BTT
UC-126	C-1	CTK Network Aviation	N194GL N126UE N139GA ZS-PBZ TZ-PBZ
UC-127	C-1	(Hageland Avn Services)	(N530LX) N127YV [w/o 09Dec02 Eagleton, AR]
UC-128	C-1	ex Sky King Airlines	(N55684) (N908YW) N15553 YV-923C N15553 VQ-TGK [stored by 01Feb09 Tampa, FL; l/n 17Jly09; canx by Jan12]
UC-129	C-1	not yet known	N15615 N129CJ ZS-POK+ TZ- [+ canx 26Sep11 to Mali]
UC-130	C-1	Airport Management Services Inc	N15712 N197GL N130UE C-GFET N130UE VH-EEY N130UE
UC-131	C-1	Aerologistics III LLC	N15486 F-GNAH N15486 N420CM
UC-132	C-1	Niels Birke Bruel/Air Traffic	N55201 OY-GEG 1180+ OY-GEG 5Y-BTF [+ Yemen]
UC-133	C-1	(Avibex)	F-GKST TR-LFK [w/o 17May00 Moanda, Gabon]
UC-134	C-1	Ameriflight	N134YV F-GNYL N134YV JA190D N26RZ
UC-135	C-1	(CommutAir)	(N122GP) N55000 [w/o 03Jan92 Saranac Lake, NY; canx 20Apr92]
UC-136	C-1	Frontier Flying Service	N5685X C-GAAF N21493 N575Z
UC-137	C-1	(CEM Air (Pty) Ltd)	N137YV 9G-FAN ZS-OLV ZS-OLD [w/o en-route 01Sep08 15km NW of Bukavu, Democratic Republic of Congo]
UC-138	C-1	Angola Air Services	N55668 N138GL N138GA ZS-PCA
UC-139	C-1	Propair	N1128M N9331M N500PR N506RH N253RM C-GLPJ
UC-140	C-1	West Wind Aviation/Pronto Airways	N140YV CC-CET N140YV 9N-AGB N140YV C-GPRT
UC-141	C-1	(Raytheon Aircraft Credit Corp)	N55132 N141UE [to spares use by MTW Aerospace at Montgomery-Regional, AL by Dec03; l/n 24Jan06 United Airlines Express c/s; canx 02Apr09]
UC-142	C-1	(SAL Express)	N55456 N142YV S9-CAE [w/o 17Mar01 Quilemba, Angola]
UC-143	C-1	Naturelink Aviation	N143YV N143AM J6-AAI N143AM N152GA ZS-PCC 9J-AWS ZS-PCC
UC-144	C-1	CEM Air (Pty) Ltd	N55426 N144YV 5Y-BND ZS-OKA ZS-OLG
UC-145	C-1	J S Focus Air	N55594 N145GL N143GA ZS-PCD AP-BJS
UC-146	C-1	(Raytheon Aircraft Credit Corp)	N146YV J6-AAH N146YV [canx 11Mar02 as destroyed; b/u by White Industries, Bates City, MO; l/n 25Oct05]
UC-147	C-1	Air Burundi	N8207B 9U-BHD TN-AFK 9U-BHG
UC-148	C-1	(Kaya Airlines)	N148YV 3D-BEE C9-AUO [w/o 03Dec10 Maputo, Mozambique]
UC-149	C-1	Frontier Alaska	N149YV LV-PMB LV-WSM N149YV N575X
UC-150	C-1	Kalahari Air Services	N55872 N150UE N150GA ZS-PCE A2-KAB
UC-151	C-1	Ameriflight	N151YV 6Y-JVE N151YV JA190A N34RZ
UC-152	C-1	Helitaxi, Colombia	N152YV N152GL HK-4208X HK-4208
UC-153	C-1	Chalair Aviation	N153YV F-GNPM N153YV F-GOOB
UC-154	C-1	Frontier Alaska	N154YV N404GV
UC-155	C-1	UAS Transervices/Ameriflight	N155YV N575G
UC-156	C-1	SERAIR	N156YV EC-GUD
UC-157	C-1	(JS Focus Air)	N157YV S9-CAG N157YV AP-BJD [w/o 05Nov10 Karachi-Jinnah, Pakistan]
UC-158	C-1	Solenta Aviation	N55355 N158YV ZS-ODG
UC-159	C-1	Vincent Aviation	N159GL VH-EMK
UC-160	C-1	Frontier Alaska	N160YV N160AM N575Q
UC-161	C-1	SERAIR	N55635 EC-GZG
UC-162	C-1	UAS Transervices/Ameriflight	N162YV LV-WSL N162YV N575Y N718AF
UC-163	C-1	Department of the Air Force/EG & G	N163YV N163AM F-GNAJ N3043L N623RA
UC-164	C-1	Ameriflight	N164YV J6-AAJ N2049K
UC-165	C-1	Leni Overseas Developments	N55456 TC-DRD N55456 YV-1105C N55456 AP-BGH
UC-166	C-1	Summer Sun Trading 296 (Pty) Ltd	N166GL EC-IAH N166GL ZS-DRC
UC-167	C-1	M & N Aviation	N167GL N410MN
UC-168	C-1	JDP France Sal	N55782 N168GL C-GLAL F-GVLC
UC-169	C-1	Royal Thailand Army	N8181E 0169
UC-170	C-1	Royal Thailand Army	N8265K 0170
UC-171	C-1	ex Raytheon Aircraft Credit Corp	N55522 N171GL N151GA [stored Mena-Intermountain Municipal, AR; l/n 06Nov06; canx 02Dec08 presumably wfu]
UC-172	C-1	Flex Air Cargo	F-GHSE OY-GMM 5Y-BSI 5Y-BBI 5Y-BSI
UC-173	C-1	AD Astral Aviation Services Pty Ltd	F-GHSI OY-GMN N371UC N412CM VH-KFN
UC-174	C-1	Eagle Air	N174GL PK-VPC N174GL ZS-PIT 5X- ZS-PIT 5X-EBZ
UD-1	C-1	US Air Force	86-0078 [C-12J]

BEECH 1900

C/n	Model	Last known Owner/Operator	Identities/fates/comments (where appropriate)					
UD-2	C-1	US Army	86-0079	[C-12J]				
UD-3	C-1	US Air Force	86-0080	[C-12J]				
UD-4	C-1	US Air Force	86-0081	[C-12J]				
UD-5	C-1	US Army	86-0082	[C-12J]				
UD-6	C-1	US Air Force	86-0083	[C-12J]				
Beech 1900D								
UE-1	D	(Hawker Beechcraft Corp)	N5584B	[cvtd on production line from Beech 1900C-1 c/n UC-82; prototype ff 01Mar90; wfu Wichita-Beech Field, KS; canx 25Feb09]				
UE-2	D	Sky Bahamas	N2YV	C6-SBF				
UE-3	D	Aircraft Contracts Africa (Pty) Ltd	N3YV	ZS-PKB				
UE-4	D	Air Namibia	N304YV	N4ZV	ZS-OWN	V5-OWN		
UE-5	D	Royal Leasing LLC	N5YV					
UE-6	D	Aircraft Contracts Africa (Pty) Ltd	N6YV	ZS-JAZ	VT-AVJ	ZS-JAZ		
UE-7	D	Swanvest 318 (Pty) Ltd	N136MA	VH-SMH	VH-IMA	ZS-OYA	V5-COY	ZS-OYA
UE-8	D	Wasaya Airways	N55778	D-CBSF	C-FWZK			
UE-9	D	King Air Services Partnership	N9YV	C-FSKO	C-FIGJ	ZS-PEF	V5-PEF	ZS-PEF
UE-10	D	IMP Group/Execaire	N137MA	VH-MML	ZS-OYB	V5-COX	ZS-PUJ	C-GMZE
UE-11	D	North Cariboo Flying Services	N11ZV	C-FSKT	C-FNCL			
UE-12	D	Aerosmith Penny	N138MA	N45AR				
UE-13	D	(ex US Airways Express)	N13ZV	[b/u for spares by White Industries, Bates City, MO; l/n 26Jly05]				
UE-14	D	Aircraft Contracts Africa (Pty) Ltd	(N139MA)	N14YV	(ZS-OPI)	ZS-OUG		
UE-15	D	(ex Air Midwest)	N15YV	[b/u for spares by White Industries, Bates City, MO; l/n 26Jly05]				
UE-16	D	Farnair Europe	(N140MA)	N837CA	N83700	C-GXGX	N16UE	HA-FAM
UE-17	D	SAEREO	N17YV	HC-CBC				
UE-18	D	ACIA Aircraft (Pty) Ltd	N18YV	ZS-OMC				
UE-19	D	Colgan Air/US Airways Express	N830CA	N83005	(ZS-OPP)	N191CJ		
UE-20	D	North Cariboo Flying Service	N831CA	N83103	N220CJ	C-FMCN		
UE-21	D	Bluebird Aviation/Red Cross	N21YV	ZS-OLX	PH-RAE	5Y-RAE	ZS-TIL	
UE-22	D	Aircraft Properties Inc	N832CA	N83206				
UE-23	D	National Airways Corp	N23YV	ZS-OKN	V5-OKN	ZS-OKN		
UE-24	D	ex Colgan Air/US Airways Express	N833CA	N83306	N575D	N124CJ	[to MTW Aerospace for spares use; by 21Sep08 fuselage & detached wings noted in scrapyard near Montgomery, AL]	
UE-25	D	Hawker Beechcraft Corp	N834CA	N83413	(ZS-OPL)			
UE-26	D	Compion Aviation/COMAV	N26YV	ZS-PJF				
UE-27	D	Aerosmith Penny	N46AR					
UE-28	D	Solenta Aviation	N28YV	ZS-NAC				
UE-29	D	Rossair	N29YV	OY-GMP	PH-RAG	ZS-PIR		
UE-30	D	(Raytheon Aircraft Credit Corp)	N835CA	N83511	[to spares use by MTW Aerospace at Montgomery-Regional, AL by Dec03; l/n 24Jan06; canx 02Apr09]			
UE-31	D	Medavia	N31YV	OY-GEP	PH-RAH	9H-AFI		
UE-32	D	Aircraft Africa Contracts (Pty) Ltd	N836CA	N83611	ZS-PZE			
UE-33	D	Rossair Contracts	N33YV	ZS-OLW				
UE-34	D	Wasaya Airways	N838CA	N83801	C-GSWA			
UE-35	D	National Airways/Tullow Air	N35YV	(ZS-OPJ)	ZS-OSF			
UE-36	D	King Air Services Partnership	N839CA	N83901	(ZS-OPM)	N136MJ	ZS-SHH	
UE-37	D	Bering Air	N37YV	F-HCHA	N15GA			
UE-38	D	(Raytheon Aircraft Credit Corp)	N840CA	N84010	[stored Oklahoma City-Wiley Post, OK; l/n 06Nov06 – US Airways Express c/s; b/u for spares, fuselage only to Montgomery, AL; canx 13Dec06]			
UE-39	D	Solenta Aviation/UN	N39ZV	ZS-OLY				
UE-40	D	Colgan Air	N841CA	N84102	N240CJ	[w/o 26Aug03 Nantucket Sound off Hyannis, MA; canx 22Nov03]		
UE-41	D	(US Airways Express)	N842CA	N84204	[b/u post 31Jan04 Fort Lauderdale-International, FL; canx 06Apr07]			
UE-42	D	Air Express, Algeria/UN WFP	N42YV	(ZS-OPK)	ZS-ORV			
UE-43	D	ex Skyline Enterprises Corp	N843CA	N84307	N243CJ	[canx 04Dec09 fate/status unknown]		
UE-44	D	Solenta Aviation/DHL	N80683	D-CBSG	OK-YES	D-CBSG	PH-ACY	ZS-MKE
UE-45	D	Leni Overseas Developments	N844CA	N84413	D-CBCC	N45UE	AP-BII	
UE-46	D	(Raytheon Aircraft Credit Corp)	N46YV	[stored Beech Field, KS; l/n 23Feb05; at Wichita-Mid-Continent, KS by 21Jly07; l/n 05Nov08; canx 10Jly09 as wfu]				
UE-47	D	Air Georgian/Air Alliance	N845CA	N84502	ZS-OKL	N84502	(N147MJ)	C-GORI
UE-48	D	ACIA Aircraft (Pty) Ltd	N48YV	ZS-OKL	5Y-OKL	ZS-OKL		

BEECH 1900

C/n	Model	Last known Owner/Operator	Identities/fates/comments (where appropriate)
UE-49	D	(Colgan Air/US Airways Express)	N846CA N84613 N149CJ [w/o Hartford, CT; canx 21Oct04; remains stored by MTW Aerospace, Montgomery-Regional, AL; l/n 24Jan06]
UE-50	D	Oil Aviation Services Group	N50YV F-GSAH N50YV HK-4557X HK-4557
UE-51	D	Northstar Avlease	N51YV F-GNOA N51YV ZS-PVN C-FNSN
UE-52	D	Air Tindi	N847CA N84703 N152MJ C-GHUE
UE-53	D	Air Link (Pty) Ltd	N848CA N84802 (ZS-OPN) ZK-JNG VH-RUE
UE-54	D	Taxi Aereo de Caldas S.A.	N54YV (F-GNOC) F-GSAN N54YV HK-4634
UE-55	D	Alpine Aviation	N852CA N85230 (ZS-OPO) N155CJ
UE-56	D	(MTW Aerospace Inc)	N853CA N85341 [to spares use by Jly08 at Montgomery-Regional, AL; l/n 24Jan06]
UE-57	D	National Airways	N57ZV ZS-OOW
UE-58	D	North Cariboo Flying Services	N83022 F-OHRV F-GYAB C-GSKY C-FNCP
UE-59	D	Aircraft Africa Contracts (Pty) Ltd	N59YV ZS-PVV [canx 20Jun07; restored 01Aug07, reason unknown]
UE-60	D	Alpine Air Express	N854CA N85445 N60MJ
UE-61	D	US Department of State	N855CA N85516
UE-62	D	fly540.com	N62ZV 5Y-BVG
UE-63	D	Sunwest Aviation	N82890 N166K C-GSWX
UE-64	D	Evergreen Helicopters	N64YV N1900R N105EV
UE-65	D	(Raytheon Aircraft Credit Corp)	N65YV [to spares use by MTW Aerospace at Montgomery-Regional, AL Dec03; l/n 24Jan06; canx 02Apr09]
UE-66	D	(Raytheon Aircraft Credit Corp)	N856CA N85608 [stored Marana-Pinal Airpark, AZ; l/n 07Nov03; canx 18May07 as wfu]
UE-67	D	Maverick Airlines	N67YV N567MA
UE-68	D	Aero Transporte S. A.	N68ZV N168AZ OB-1875
UE-69	D	Twin Jet	N82896 YR-AAK YR-RLA F-GLNF
UE-70	D	Chalair Aviation	N70ZV ZS-PZH PH-RNG F-HBCG
UE-71	D	Evergreen Helicopters	N857CA N85704 N171CJ
UE-72	D	Evergreen Helicopters	N858CA N85804 N172MJ
UE-73	D	Twin Jet	N82923 YR-AAL YR-RLB F-GLNH
UE-74	D	New Order Vehicle Sales/Air Ghana	N74YV ZS-OKM
UE-75	D	Wasaya Airways	N75ZV JA016A N175MH C-FQWA
UE-76	D	Northern Thunderbird Air	N76ZV C-FDTR
UE-77	D	Mobil Producing Nigeria	N82936 5N-MPN
UE-78	D	Confiforce (Pty)	N78YV ZS-SKU V5-SKU ZS-SDH
UE-79	D	Transwest Air	N79SK C-GTWG
UE-80	D	Turbine Air Partnership	N801SK ZS-STE
UE-81	D	CEM Air (Pty) Ltd	N81SK ZS-OMB
UE-82	D	Taxi Aereo de Caldas S.A.	N82YV 6Y-JRH N82YV HK-4610X HK-4610
UE-83	D	Federal Air	N831SK ZS-OXN
UE-84	D	Federal Air/Arik Air	N841SK ZS-PUC
UE-85	D	Awesome Flight Logistics/Air South	N85SK ZS-SER VH-VNT+ VH-ZOA [+ painted in error]
UE-86	D	Maverick Airlines	N86YV N886MA
UE-87	D	Federal Air/Air Express	N87SK ZS-PWY
UE-88	D	Balmoral Central Contracts SA (Pty)	N881SK ZS-JCT
UE-89	D	Summer Sun Trading	N891SK ZS-CCL
UE-90	D	Awesome Aviation Pty Ltd	(N90ZV) N901SK ZS-PRG VH-VAU ZS-PRG
UE-91	D	Vincent Aviation	N91SK ZS-SEM (VH-ZOA) VH-VNT
UE-92	D	Balmoral Central Contracts SA (Pty)	N92SK ZS-MMJ
UE-93	D	SEARCA	N93ZV HK-4630
UE-94	D	Awesome Aviation Pty Ltd	N94UX N94GL ZS-PPX PK-OCW VH-NOA
UE-95	D	SEARCA	N95YV HK-4537
UE-96	D	Awesome Flight Logistics	N96UX VH-NIA ZS-PPK ZS-SNO
UE-97	D	not yet known	N97UX 5Y-BSP ET-ANE
UE-98	D	(Raytheon Aircraft Credit Corp)	N98YV [stored 09Mar07 to Oklahoma City, OK; l/n 30Apr07; canx 31Aug09 presumed wfu]
UE-99	D	SEARCA	N99YV HK-4600
UE-100	D	Great Lakes Aviation	N100UX
UE-101	D	Compion Aviation/ALS Ltd	N101UX ZS-PJG 5Y-BVX
UE-102	D	Solenta Aviation/DHL	N82928 P2-MBX ZS-PJX
UE-103	D	Pan Européene Air Service	N82930 (F-GMSA) F-GOPE
UE-104	D	SEARCA	N104YV HK-4673
UE-105	D	SEARCA	N105YV HK-4512
UE-106	D	Air Service Liege	N15574 F-GMSM TR-LET N6011C F-GJFX N106UE OO-PHB

BEECH 1900

C/n	Model	Last known Owner/Operator	Identities/fates/comments (where appropriate)
UE-107	D	CEM Air (Pty) Ltd/Tunis Air Express	N107YV ZS-PYU
UE-108	D	Tropicana	N118SK D2-FFM
UE-109	D	(ex Florida Gulf Airlines)	N109ZV [wfu & b/u for spares by White Industries, Bates City, MO; fuselage only l/n 25Oct05; canx 20Jun02]
UE-110	D	SEARCA	N110YV HK-4499
UE-111	D	Sonair	N3119U VT-AGB N3119U D2-EVJ
UE-112	D	North-Wright Airways	N112ZV C-FNWH
UE-113	D	SEARCA	(N3193Q) N113YV HK-4563
UE-114	D	GC Air LLC/Evergreen Helicopters	N114YV N191EV
UE-115	D	Vincent Aviation	N15317 P2-MBY ZS-PMD VH-VAZ
UE-116	D	Overland Airways	N116YV 5N-BCP
UE-117	D	Solenta Aviation	N15527 VH-IPB VH-NTL ZS-OYC
UE-118	D	fly540.com	N118ZV N118UX N118GL ZS-PPJ 5Y-BTN
UE-119	D	(Air St.Martin)	N15594 F-OHRK [w/o 07Dec95 Belle Anse, near Port-au-Prince, Haiti; canx 04Apr96]
UE-120	D	SEARCA	N120YV HK-4434
UE-121	D	Sonair	N3221A VT-AGA N3221A D2-EVK
UE-122	D	Great Lakes Aviation	N122YV N122UX
UE-123	D	SEARCA	N123YV HK-4476
UE-124	D	US Department of State	N124YV
UE-125	D	SEARCA	N125YV HK-4424
UE-126	D	Exploits Valley Air Services	N126YV C-FEVA
UE-127	D	MTW Aerospace Inc	N127ZV [ex Mesa Airlines; stored by 15Jly10 Wichita, KS]
UE-128	D	Osprey Wings Ltd	(N128YV) N859CA C-GORJ N128EU C-FBPK
UE-129	D	Air Creebec	C-FTQR
UE-130	D	Airco Aircraft Charters	C-FTOW
UE-131	D	National Airways Corp (Pty) Ltd	N131YV ZS-SNJ
UE-132	D	National Airways Corp (Pty) Ltd	N132YV ZS-SNK
UE-133	D	National Airways Corp (Pty) Ltd	N133YV ZS-SRZ
UE-134	D	Air Georgian/Air Alliance	N134ZV N860CA C-GORZ
UE-135	D	Shine Aviation	N135YV ZS-SSY VH-EKG
UE-136	D	Eros Aircraft Services/Compion Avn	(N136YV) N3212K 9G-AGF ZS-PHM 5Y-BVP
UE-137	D	Silver Airways	N137ZV N81533
UE-138	D	Aero Transporte	N138YV ZS-STJ N239SC OB-1985
UE-139	D	Exploits Valley Air Services	N139ZV C-GSNQ
UE-140	D	SEARCA	N140ZV HK-4709
UE-141	D	Sunwest Aviation	N17534 C-GSWV
UE-142	D	Peruvian Army	N142ZV EP-828
UE-143	D	Air South	N143YV ZS-SSX VH-YOA
UE-144	D	Florida Gulf/US Airways Express	N144ZV
UE-145	D	Turbine Air Partnership	N145SK ZS-PHX
UE-146	D	(Raytheon Aircraft Credit Corp)	N146ZV [ex Mesa Airlines; last reported Mar10 Wichita, KS; canx 07Jly10 fate/status unknown]
UE-147	D	Silver Airways	N81535
UE-148	D	Bering Air	N148SK
UE-149	D	Mobil Producing Nigeria	N3217L VH-IMC N3217L 5N-MPA
UE-150	D	National Airways	N150YV N150UX N150GL ZS-PPM
UE-151	D	(Great Lakes Aviation)	N151ZV N151UX N151GL [w/o 14May02 Grand Island Airport., NB; canx 09Apr12]
UE-152	D	Silver Airways	N81536
UE-153	D	Great Lakes Aviation	N153ZV N153GL
UE-154	D	Great Lakes Aviation	N154ZV N154GL
UE-155	D	SEARCA	N155ZV+ HK-4780
UE-156	D	SEARCA	N3241J C-FVJU N156E HK-4558
UE-157	D	Toyota of Venezuela	N3217P N743SY 3B-NBC N157AX YV-837CP YV1894
UE-158	D	Silver Airways	N38537
UE-159	D	MTW Aerospace Inc	N159YV [ex Mesa Airlines; stored by 24Jly09 Wichita-Mid Continent, KS]
UE-160	D	Petroleum Air Service	N3216S C-FVKC VQ-TEB N877NA HK-4732
UE-161	D	Mustang Leasing LLC	N161YV N690MA
UE-162	D	Exploits Valley Air Services	N162ZV C-GERI
UE-163	D	(MTW Aerospace Inc)	N163YV [ex Mesa Airlines; stored location unknown; canx 09Jun10 assumed used for parts]
UE-164	D	Wasaya Airways	N81538 N861CA C-FWAU

BEECH 1900

C/n	Model	Last known Owner/Operator	Identities/fates/comments (where appropriate)
UE-165	D	Great Lakes Aviation	N165YV
UE-166	D	Evergreen Helicopters	N166YV N104EV
UE-167	D	ex Fargo Jet Center Inc	N167YV+ TZ- [+ canx 26Sep11 to Mali]
UE-168	D	Silver Airways	N82539
UE-169	D	Great Lakes Aviation/North Star Air Cargo	(N169UX)+ N169GL [+ not confirmed]
UE-170	D	Great Lakes Aviation	N170YV N170GL
UE-171	D	Egyptian Air Force	N171ZV SU-BRS [also carries serial 4809]
UE-172	D	Silver Airways	N16540
UE-173	D	National Airways Corp	N173YV ZS-SVI
UE-174	D	MTW Aerospace Inc	N17541 N174YV [ex Mesa Airlines; stored location unknown]
UE-175	D	Blue Bird Aviation	N995WS N61HA 5Y-VVM
UE-176	D	Hill Air Executive Inc	N176YV
UE-177	D	Indonesia Air Transport	N3237H PK-TRW
UE-178	D	Great Lakes Aviation	N47542 N178YV
UE-179	D	Northstar Avlease	N179YV N179GL ZS-PPI C-FNSV
UE-180	D	Kenn Borek Air	N862CA 9N-AHZ C-GSKB
UE-181	D	Skyline Enterprises	N49543
UE-182	D	Cemair	N182YV ZS-CEM
UE-183	D	SEARCA	N48544 HK-4598
UE-184	D	Great Lakes Airlines	N184YV N184UX
UE-185	D	Silver Airways	N53545
UE-186	D	Indonesia Air Transport	N3233J PK-TRX
UE-187	D	Silver Airways	N81546
UE-188	D	Chalair Aviation	N1564J SE-KXV F-HBCA
UE-189	D	Silver Airways	N69547
UE-190	D	MTW Aerospace Inc	N190YV
UE-191	D	National Airways/Air Express Algeria	N191YV N10326 VH-SMH VH-IAR ZS-OYD
UE-192	D	Great Lakes Aviation	N192YV N192GL
UE-193	D	Sonair	N69548 D2-EWR
UE-194	D	Silver Airways	N69549
UE-195	D	Great Lakes Aviation	N195YV N195GL
UE-196	D	Twin Jet	N3234G F-GLND
UE-197	D	Twin Jet	N3234U F-GLNE
UE-198	D	Silver Airways	N47542
UE-199	D	Silver Airways	N81538
UE-200	D	Solenta Aviation/Tullow Air	N3193Q VH-AFR VH-IAV ZS-OYE
UE-201	D	Great Lakes Aviation	N201YQ N201GL
UE-202	D	Great Lakes Aviation	N202YV N202ZK N202UX
UE-203	D	Silver Airways	N17541
UE-204	D	Federal Air/UN	N204YV N204GL ZS-PJY
UE-205	D	ex Silver Airways	N87550+ C- [+ canx 26Jly12 to Canada]
UE-206	D	Silver Airways	N87551
UE-207	D	Air Georgian/Air Alliance	N10625 C-GAAR
UE-208	D	Great Lakes Aviation	N208YV N208GL
UE-209	D	Air Georgian/Air Alliance	N10659 C-GAAS
UE-210	D	Great Lakes Aviation	N210UX N210GL
UE-211	D	Great Lakes Aviation	N211UX N211GL
UE-212	D	Seychelles Coast Guard	N3217U S7-IDC
UE-213	D	SEARCA	N3199Q HK-4681
UE-214	D	ex National Airways Corp	N3230V VH-IMS ZS-OYF XY- [noted 04Oct08 Luanda, Angola without tail; still there 28Mar09; status not reported; cx 18May12 to Myanmar]
UE-215	D	Wings Aviation	N215CJ N850CA 5N-PTL
UE-216	D	Silver Airways	N87552
UE-217	D	Exploits Valley Air Services	N1564J C-GAAT
UE-218	D	ex Specialized Aircraft Services	N218YV+ ZS- [+ canx 20Dec11 to South Africa]
UE-219	D	Great Lakes Aviation	N219YV N219GL
UE-220	D	Great Lakes Aviation	N220YV N220GL
UE-221	D	Sky Jet M.G. Inc	N221CJ C-GHFB
UE-222	D	Korean Air Express	N81553 VQ-TVC N789BL HL5238
UE-223	D	Wasaya Airways	N1123J C-FYSJ N1123J C-GZVJ
UE-224	D	Private Wings	N224YV D-COCA

BEECH 1900

C/n	Model	Last known Owner/Operator	Identities/fates/comments (where appropriate)
UE-225	D	Overland Airways	N229G N225GL 5N-BCO [stored by 11Nov07 Lanseria, South Africa; l/n 22Sep08]
UE-226	D	Parmtro Investments/ALS Ltd	N226YV N226GL ZS-PJZ 5H-SXY 5Y-BVT
UE-227	D	Silver Airways	N87554
UE-228	D	Execaire	N228YV N228GL ZS-PKA C-GMYY
UE-229	D	Tamara	N10675 9G-HNH 5U-TNB
UE-230	D	Aircraft Africa Contracts (Pty) Ltd	N3252M VH-IMH ZS-OYG 5N-BCQ ZS-OYG
UE-231	D	Great Lakes Aviation	N231YV
UE-232	D	Air Georgian/Air Alliance	N10705 C-GAAU
UE-233	D	(Mesa Airlines/Air Midwest)	N233YV [w/o 08Jan03 Charlotte, NC]
UE-234	D	Silver Airways	N87555
UE-235	D	Air Georgian/Air Alliance	N10708 C-GAAV
UE-236	D	Petroleos de Venezuela	SE-KXY SX-BST SE-KXY N901CG+ YV [+ canx 28Oct11 to Venezela]
UE-237	D	(MTW Aerospace Inc)	N237YV [wfu near Montgomery, AL for parts; canx 10Feb12]
UE-238	D	(Proteus Airlines)	N10726 F-GSJM [w/o 30Jly98 in sea off coast of Baie de Quiberon, France]
UE-239	D	Silver Airways	(N239YV) N81556
UE-240	D	Great Lakes Aviation	N240YV N240GL
UE-241	D	Chevron/Wings Aviation	N10876 YV-1152CP YV1106
UE-242	D	Exploits Valley Air Services	N242YV C-GLXV
UE-243	D	Central Mountain Air	N10879 C-GCML
UE-244	D	Egyptian Air Force	N244YV SU-BRT
UE-245	D	Great Lakes Aviation	N245YV N245GL
UE-246	D	Silver Airways	N87557
UE-247	D	Great Lakes Aviation	N247YV N247GL
UE-248	D	Hex' Air	N10882 F-GUPE
UE-249	D	Sonangol	N249YV N249GL D2-EVY
UE-250	D	(Blue Bird Aviation)	N10898 VH-TRW ZS-OYH VH-IAY ZS-OYH 5Y-VVQ [w/o 09Nov09 near Nairobi-Wilson, Kenya; canx 19Jan11]
UE-251	D	Great Lakes Aviation	N251ZV N251GL
UE-252	D	Northern Air Charter	N10907 F-GSFD N10907 JA017A C-GNAR
UE-253	D	Great Lakes Aviation	N253YV N253GL
UE-254	D	Great Lakes Aviation	N10840 N254GL
UE-255	D	Great Lakes Aviation/Scenic Airlines	N10860 N255GL
UE-256	D	US Army	N10931 96-0112 [C-12J]
UE-257	D	Great Lakes Aviation	N257YV N257GL [reported stored by 08Oct08 Albuquerque, NM]
UE-258	D	US Department of State	N10936 F-GLNJ N10936 N28NG N63MW N258AW
UE-259	D	Regional Air Lines/Sophia Airlines	N10863 CN-RLA
UE-260	D	Solenta Aviation	N260YV N260GL ZS-ZED
UE-261	D	Great Lakes Aviation	N261YV N261GL
UE-262	D	(Great Lakes Aviation)	N10746 N262GL [w/o 14May02 Grand Island Airport, NB; canx 14Jly04]
UE-263	D	National Airways Corp/Safari Plus	N10963 CN-RLB ZS-SGH
UE-264	D	Sunwest Aviation	N10759 C-GSLB C-GSLX
UE-265	D	National Airways Corp	N10969 CN-RLC ZS-SET VT-AVR ZS-SET
UE-266	D	Exploits Valley Air Services	N10950 C-GLHO
UE-267	D	Global Airlift/Somali Government	N10999 CN-RLD 5Y-JIA
UE-268	D	Avior Express	N11002 YV-402C YV1365
UE-269	D	Twin Jet	N11017 F-GLNK
UE-270	D	Avior Express	N11024 YV-401C YV1364
UE-271	D	Northern Thunderbird Air	N11037 C-FCMP
UE-272	D	Central Mountain Air	N11079 C-FCMV
UE-273	D	Solenta Aviation	N11187 VH-IMQ ZS-OYJ 5Y-NAC ZS-OYJ
UE-274	D	Sonair	N11015 VT-AGC N11015 D2-ERQ
UE-275	D	Petroleos de Venezuela	N11189 SE-LCX N905CG+ YV [+ canx 19Jan12 to Venezuela]
UE-276	D	Northern Thunderbird Air	C-FCMN
UE-277	D	Central Mountain Air	C-FCME
UE-278	D	Northern Thunderbird Air	C-FCMB
UE-279	D	Avior Express	N11252 YV-403C YV1366
UE-280	D	Sonair	N11284 VT-AGD N11284 D2-EVR
UE-281	D	Northern Thunderbird Air	C-FCMO
UE-282	D	Wanair	N11296 F-OHRX
UE-283	D	Central Mountain Air	N21872 C-FCMR
UE-284	D	Reliance Industries Ltd	N11298 VT-AMA VT-KDA [stored Sep06 Dusseldorf, Germany; l/n 17Jun07]

BEECH 1900

C/n	Model	Last known Owner/Operator	Identities/fates/comments (where appropriate)
UE-285	D	Central Mountain Air	C-FCMU
UE-286	D	Buddha Air	N11194 9N-AEE
UE-287	D	Northern Thunderbird Air	C-GCMY
UE-288	D	Swiss Air Force	N11320 TC-CNK N11320 D-CBIG HB-AEN T-729
UE-289	D	Central Mountain Air	C-GCMA
UE-290	D	Chevron Global Technology Services	N18153 F-GMAD N18153 N659WF+ YV [+ canx 08Jun12 to Venezuela]
UE-291	D	Air Georgian/Air Alliance	N20704 C-GGGA
UE-292	D	Air Georgian	N20707 C-GVGA
UE-293	D	Air Georgian/Air Alliance	N21063 C-GHGA
UE-294	D	Air Traffic	N21334 TC-TON N21334 YV-955CP YV-411CP YV188T N187RL 5Y-BZH
UE-295	D	(Buddha Air)	N21540 9N-AEK [w/o 25Sep11 near Kathmandu-Tribhuvan Airport, Nepal]
UE-296	D	Star Aviation	N21572 (F-GRPM) F-GRMD HB-AEK 7T-VNG
UE-297	D	Wasaya Airways	N21679 C-FWAX
UE-298	D	North Caribou Flying Service	N21693 YV-404C YV1367 C-GNCE
UE-299	D	(Peabody Coal Company)	N305PC [w/o 22Feb08 Kayenta-Peabody Bedard Field, AZ; canx 24Sep08; hulk to United States Aviation Underwriters and then possibly to MTW Aerospace, Montgomery, AL; noted 21Sep08]
UE-300	D	Safari Express Airways/Safari Plus	N22120 F-GRPM EC-IJO 5H-SPB
UE-301	D	Twin Jet	N22161 F-GRYL
UE-302	D	Vincent Aviation	N11197 C-GBPY ZK-JND N11197 ZK-JND ZK-VAB VH-VAQ
UE-303	D	Northrop Grumman Corp	N11249 F-GPSD N11249 N29NG
UE-304	D	Avior Express	N22675 YV-406C YV1368
UE-305	D	Star Aviation	N22546 F-GPBM N22546 7T-WRF 7T-VNB
UE-306	D	Air Georgian/Air Alliance	N22700 C-GZGA
UE-307	D	Niagara Mohawk Power Corp	N22761 F-GREA N22761 N733DC
UE-308	D	Petroleos de Venezuela	N22841 F-GUCB N22841 EC-JBT N803UE PK-TVV N904CG+ YV- [+ canx 24Jly12 to Venezuela]
UE-309	D	Air Georgian/Air Alliance	N22874 C-GWGA
UE-310	D	Curtain Bros (Qld) Pty Ltd	N22873 TR-LFE ZS-ONH VH-VAY VH-VPZ
UE-311	D	Australian Police	N10984 F-GRCD N10984 VH-PSK
UE-312	D	National Airways	N11193 TR-LFA ZS-ONI N312RC D2-EVL ZS-ONI
UE-313	D	Nouvellles Air Affaires Gabon	N11354 ZS-OCV TR-LFO
UE-314	D	Tenax Air Logistics	N22889 VT-AGE N22889 9N-AFW N22889
UE-315	D	Air Georgian/Air Alliance	N22890 C-GMGA
UE-316	D	National Airways	N21716 TR-LFC N21716 ZS-PRH
UE-317	D	Hanseo University/Korean Air Express	N22908 HC-BYO N713UE HL5231
UE-318	D	Solenta Aviation/Tullow Air	N22953 VH-NBN ZS-OYK
UE-319	D	Safari Express Airways/Safari Plus	N23004 9J-MBO ZS-SHA 5H-SPC
UE-320	D	Air Georgian/Air Alliance	N22976 C-GORC
UE-321	D	Nouvellles Air Affaires Gabon	N22978 ZS-OCZ+ ZS-OCX TR-LBV [+ marks probably applied in error]
UE-322	D	(Wings Aviation)	N23045 F-GNPT N23045 5N-JAH [w/o 16Mar08 near Igabu Village, Yala Region en-route Lagos to Obudu Cattle Ranch, Nigeria; wreck not found until 30Aug08]
UE-323	D	Chalair Aviation	N23047 9J-MAS ZS-SHB OY-CHU F-HBCE
UE-324	D	National Airways Corp	N23143 VH-IMR ZS-OYL A6-YST ZS-OYL
UE-325	D	Myanma Airways	N23150 (F-GTKJ) VH-NKN ZS-OYM A2-NAC ZS-OYM+ XY- [+ canx 11Apr12 to Myanmar]
UE-326	D	Air Georgian/Air Alliance	N23164 C-GORA
UE-327	D	Atlantique Air Assistance	N23154 (F-GPBR) F-GNBR
UE-328	D	Buddha Air	N23179 9N-AEW
UE-329	D	Sonair	N23183 TR-LFI ZS-OOX OY-GMY N23183 D2-FFN
UE-330	D	Air Georgian/Air Alliance	N23222 C-GORF
UE-331	D	Avior Express	N534M N2820B YV-660C YV1372
UE-332	D	Menard	N535M
UE-333	D	Menard	N23235 N534M
UE-334	D	Menard	N536M
UE-335	D	PGA Express	N23269 EC-GZL N23369+ N23269 CS-TMU [+ N23369 incorrectly applied]
UE-336	D	Fred's Aviation Svcs of Nevada	N23320 C-GDHE N842E
UE-337	D	Sunwest Aviation	N23159 C-GURG N23159 C-GSWZ

BEECH 1900

C/n	Model	Last known Owner/Operator	Identities/fates/comments (where appropriate)
UE-338	D	ex PT Travira Air	N23381 OY-JRV N338RH PK-TVE PH-RNI* [marks reserved Sep10 for Jetisfaction]
UE-339	D	Fred's Aviation Svcs of Nevada	N23340 C-GDHF N843E
UE-340	D	Sonair	N23317 (F-GSVC) D2-EVX
UE-341	D	PGA Express	N23309 EC-HBG N23309 CS-TMV
UE-342	D	Avior Express	N23369 YV-438C YV1369
UE-343	D	Avior Express	N23373 YV-466C YV1370
UE-344	D	Aeroeste	N23376 YV-503C YV1371 CP-2673
UE-345	D	Air Labrador	N23340 C-GTMB
UE-346	D	Central Mountain Air	N23424 C-GORI C-GFSV
UE-347	D	(Regionnair)	N23427 (C-FLIM) C-FLIH [w/o 12Aug99 nr Sept Iles, Canada; canx 30May00 on sale to USA for parts by White Industries, Bates City, MO]
UE-348	D	Twin Jet	N23406 F-GTKJ
UE-349	D	Twin Jet/French Police	N23430 F-GTVC
UE-350	D	Catovair/Chalair Aviation	N23481 ZS-OOV PH-RAT ZS-OOV 3B-VIP F-HBCC
UE-351	D	Central Mountain Air	N23517 C-GGBY YV-654C C-GGBY
UE-352	D	P T Travira Air	N23519 C-FLWE N23519 HI-717CT N352RA PK-TVJ
UE-353	D	Sunwest Aviation	N23527 D-CSAG VT-TOI C-GHCS
UE-354	D	Meijer Distribution	N30414 N1883M
UE-355	D	Avior Express	N23538 YV-663C YV1373
UE-356	D	Avior Express	N23593 YV-664C YV1374
UE-357	D	Heliang, Angola?	N23598 S9-BAJ D2-EZE
UE-358	D	Heliang, Angola	N23610 S9-BAK D2-EZD
UE-359	D	Central Mountain Air	N31559 C-GGCA
UE-360	D	Oyonnair	N30662 VH-FOZ PK-TVL (PH-RNH) F-HETS
UE-361	D	Futura Travels	N31001 N1865A C-GSKQ VT-ASH
UE-362	D	Red Line Air LLC	N23627 N196NW
UE-363	D	Air New Zealand Link	N31136 N846CA ZK-EAQ
UE-364	D	P T Travira Air	N30469 PK-TVH
UE-365	D	(Tassili Airlines)	N31685 7T-VIN [w/o 28Jan04 Ghardaia, Algeria]
UE-366	D	Tassili Airlines	N30511 7T-VIO
UE-367	D	Pan Européene Air Service	N30515 F-HAPE
UE-368	D	West Wind Aviation	N30535 N368DC C-GWEA C-GDCG
UE-369	D	Tassili Airlines	N30538 7T-VIP
UE-370	D	Sonair	N30539 (F-OHGD) D2-EVN
UE-371	D	Fleet Management Airways	N31712 HC-CAO N371UE CS-DOC F-GUME
UE-372	D	Medavia	N30287 ZS-ONS PH-RAR 9H-AFH
UE-373	D	MHS Aviation	N31110 9M-STL
UE-374	D	MHS Aviation	N31419 9M-STM
UE-375	D	P T Travira Air	N31424 PK-TVK
UE-376	D	EastIndo	N31425 PK-RGA
UE-377	D	Marvin Lumber & Cedar Co	N31477 N833CA N655MW
UE-378	D	US Department of State	N44678 N834CA N165GC N378AW
UE-379	D	Zimex Business Aviation	N31525 F-HALS HB-AEM
UE-380	D	Algerian Air Force	N31557 (F-OHGE) 7T-WSA [tie up not confirmed]
UE-381	D	Tassili Airlines	N31683 7T-VIQ
UE-382	D	Northrop Grumman Corp	N32022 N843CA N27NG
UE-383	D	General Aviation Services LLC	N31686 (F-OHGF) N800CA PH-ACF* [* marks reserved 12Oct11]
UE-384	D	Algerian Air Force	N32345 (F-OHGG) 7T-WSB [tie up not confirmed]
UE-385	D	Solenta Aviation	N32290 N839CA HB-AEL ZS-AEA
UE-386	D	Sunwest Aviation	N40486 N847CA C-GSWB
UE-387	D	ERA Aviation	N44687 N848CA N971EA
UE-388	D	Air New Zealand Link	N32571 N845CA JA018A ZK-EAR VH-EAS ZK-EAR
UE-389	D	ERA Aviation	N40484 N852CA N972EA
UE-390	D	Catovair/Chalair Aviation	N40729 N853CA 3B-VTL F-HBCB
UE-391	D	ERA Aviation	N44810 N841CA N973EA
UE-392	D	Freeport McMoRan Corp	N44102 N855CA N191CS
UE-393	D	Airfast Indonesia	N43939 N830CA PK-OCY
UE-394	D	Schwans Shared Services	N41255 N470MM
UE-395	D	West Wind Aviation LP	N44695 N831CA VH-RUI C-GWWK
UE-396	D	West Wing Aviation Pty Ltd	N43596 N838CA VH-XDY
UE-397	D	Peabody Western Coal Company	N42957 N837CA N305PC
UE-398	D	Helivan/Hawk de Mexico SA de CV	N44118 XA-MVD

BEECH 1900

C/n	Model	Last known Owner/Operator	Identities/fates/comments (where appropriate)				
UE-399	D	Sonair	N44679	N854CA	D2-EWW		
UE-400	D	PT Eastindo Services	N44640	N835CA	PK-RGD		
UE-401	D	Sonair	N44871	N840CA	D2-EWY		
UE-402	D	Petroleum Aviation & Services SA	N43442	N842CA	HK-4564		
UE-403	D	Air Georgian	N44644	N857CA	VH-XDU	N330DH	C-GORN
UE-404	D	Algerian Air Force	N44663	7T-WSC	[tie up not confirmed]		
UE-405	D	Sonair	N44666	N856CA	D2-EWX		
UE-406	D	Republique du Chad	N44703	N832CA	TT-ABB		
UE-407	D	Religare Aviation Pvt Ltd	N44739	N836CA	VT-REQ		
UE-408	D	US Department of State	N44762	N858CA	N408SN		
UE-409	D	Buddha Air	N4192N	9N-AGH			
UE-410	D	Religare Aviation Pvt Ltd	N44812	N844CA	VT-REN		
UE-411	D	Algerian Air Force	N44824	7T-WSD			
UE-412	D	Sonair	N44828	D2-FFJ			
UE-413	D	Algerian Air Force	N44849	7T-WSE	[tie up not confirmed]		
UE-414	D	Algerian Air Force	N44808	7T-WSF	[tie up not confirmed; also reported as being 7T-WRD]		
UE-415	D	not yet known	N44829	PK-	[+ marks canx 27Feb04 to Indonesia; possibly as PK-TVV]		
UE-416	D	Algerian Air Force	N50916	7T-WSG	[tie up not confirmed]		
UE-417	D	Algerian Air Force	N50317	7T-WSH	[tie up not confirmed]		
UE-418	D	Algerian Air Force	N44868	7T-WSI	[tie up not confirmed]		
UE-419	D	Algerian Air Force	N50919	7T-WSJ	[tie up not confirmed]		
UE-420	D	Algerian Air Force	N50220	7T-WSJ	[tie up not confirmed]		
UE-421	D	Algerian Air Force	N50321	7T-WSK	[tie up not confirmed]		
UE-422	D	Tenax Air	N4222A				
UE-423	D	Debswana Diamond Company	N3241X	A2-OLM			
UE-424	D	Air New Zealand Link	N2335Y	ZK-EAA			
UE-425	D	Air New Zealand Link	N2335Z	ZK-EAB			
UE-426	D	Air New Zealand Link	N51226	ZK-EAC			
UE-427	D	Air New Zealand Link	N50127	ZK-EAD			
UE-428	D	Air New Zealand Link	N3188L	ZK-EAE			
UE-429	D	Air New Zealand Link	N50069	ZK-EAF			
UE-430	D	Air New Zealand Link	N50430	ZK-EAG			
UE-431	D	Air New Zealand Link	N51321	ZK-EAH			
UE-432	D	Air New Zealand Link	N5032L	ZK-EAI			
UE-433	D	Air New Zealand Link	N4469Q	ZK-EAJ			
UE-434	D	Air New Zealand Link	N4474P	ZK-EAK			
UE-435	D	Air New Zealand Link	N50815	ZK-EAL			
UE-436	D	Air New Zealand Link	N5016C	ZK-EAM			
UE-437	D	Air New Zealand Link	N50307	ZK-EAN			
UE-438	D	Air New Zealand Link	N4470D	ZK-EAO			
UE-439	D	Air New Zealand Link	N50899	ZK-EAP			

Production complete

Unidentified

unkn	D		C-GERI	[reported 24Aug11 ferried to Canada; probably either c/n UE-162 or UE-242]
unkn			D2-ENF	[reported 23Jan12 Lanseria, South Africa]
unkn	D		F-HBCE	[marks reserved Oct07 Chalair SA]
unkn	D		F-HBCG	[marks reserved Oct07 Chalair SA]
unkn	D		(F-HBCJ to F-HBCZ)	[all marks reserved Oct07 Chalair SA]
unkn	D	Indonesian Police	P-2033	[reported 06Sep03 and Nov07]
unkn	?		P-4301	[reported 20Oct09 Batam-Hang Nadim, Indonesia]
unkn	?		PK-RGD	[reported 05Nov08 Wichita-Mid Continent, KS[
unkn	C-1		YV1734	[reported Apr10 Tamiami, FL]
unkn	C		YV1864	[reported 14Feb09 Caracas, Venezuela]
unkn	C		3X-GGD	[reported 04Oct11 Conakry, Guinea]
unkn	C		3X-GGZ	[reported 04Oct11 Conakry, Guinea]
unkn	C		5Y-BYY	[reported 08Jun10 Mumbai, India]
unkn	D		7T-VNG	[reported 21Mar10 Attenrhein-St Gallen, Switzerland; Zimex badge on tail]
unkn	D	Algerian Air Force	7T-WRB	[reported Aug10]
unkn	D	Algerian Air Force	7T-WRC	[reported Dec10]
unkn	D	Algerian Air Force	7T-WRE	[reported Oct10]

BREGUET 1150/1151 ATLANTIC

Note: Dutch Navy aircraft were designated as SP-13As while Italian aircraft are designated as P-1150s.

C/n	Model	Last known Owner/Operator	Identities/fates/comments (where appropriate)
01		German Navy	01//F-ZWWA UC+301 61+01 [prototype ff 21Oct61] [wfu; GIA Marineflieger Technical School, Westerland-Sylt, Germany]
02		(Breguet)	02//F-ZWWB [w/o 19Apr62 Paris-Le Bourget, France]
03		(French Navy)	03//F-ZWWG [b/u]
04		(French Navy)	04//F-ZWWM [wfu Nimes-Garons, France; l/n Feb05]
1		(French Navy)	1 [b/u, circa 1994]
2		(German Navy)	UC+310 61+01 [wfu; b/u; fuselage to GIA Fassberg, Germany]
3		(French Navy)	3 [b/u Nimes-Garons, France; l/n on dump 08Dec04]
4		(German Navy)	UC+311 61+02 [wfu 1995 Nordholz, Germany]
5		(French Navy)	5 [wfu Nimes-Garons, France; l/n on dump 12May07]
6		German Navy	UC+312 61+03
7		(French Navy)	7 [wfu & preserved Lorient-Lann-Bihoue, France, in base museum]
8		(German Navy)	UC+313 61+04 [wfu & preserved Apr06 Friedrichshafen, Germany, for Dornier museum; l/n 26Sep07]
9		(French Navy)	9 [b/u; fuselage to GIA Peyrelevade, France with Thales]
10		Luftfahrtmuseum Rechlin-Larz	UC+314 61+05 [wfu 2006; preserved Rechlin-Larz, Germany]
11		(French Navy)	11 [b/u circa 1995 Nimes-Garons, France]
12		German Navy	UC+315 61+06
13		(French Navy)	13 [b/u post Sep94, Nimes-Garons, France]
14		(German Navy)	UC+316 61+07 [w/o 25Apr78 Nordholz, West Germany]
15		(French Navy)	15 [b/u and dumped Nimes-Garons, France]
16		(German Navy)	UC+317 61+08 [wfu 2005 Erding, Germany; preserved Lehnin, Germany; l/n Sep11]
17		(French Navy)	17 [b/u Cuers-Pierrefeu, France; fuselage only by 2000]
18		(German Navy)	UC+318 61+09 [b/u Mar06 Westerland-Sylt, Germany; cockpit preserved by Luftfahrt und Technik, Merseburg, Germany]
19		(French Navy)	19 [w/o 18May86 Montagne du Day, 25 miles N of Djibouti]
20		(German Navy)	UC+319 61+10 [wfu 2005 Erding AFB, Germany; preserved Jun06 by Autobedrijf Piet Smedts Collectie, at Kassel, Germany; Jun08 moved to Mill, Netherlands]
21		(French Navy)	21 [b/u post May00 Cuers-Pierrefeu, France]
22		(German Navy)	UC+320 61+11 [wfu Oct06 Nordholz, Germany; reported preserved by Autobedrijf Piet Smedts Collectie, at Baarlo, Netherlands]
23		(French Navy)	23 [b/u and moved to dump Nimes-Garons, France]
24		Flugwelt Altenburg-Nobitz	UC+321 61+12 [wfu Apr07; preserved Altenburg-Nobitz Airport, Germany]
25		(French Navy)	25 [dumped by Mar00 Nimes-Garons, France; b/u by Feb05]
26		(German Navy)	UC+322 61+13 [wfu Oct05 Wunstorf, Germany; used as GIA; part b/u after 17Oct05; fuselage only by 10Sep06]
27		(French Navy)	27 [b/u; sections on display at Geneva airport, Switzerland, using tail from c/n 47]
28		Aeronauticum	UC+323 61+14 [wfu & preserved 2005 Nordholz, Germany]
29		(French Navy)	29 [w/o 10Mar81 near Moroni, Comores Islands]
30		(German Navy)	UC+324 61+15 [wfu 2004 Erding, German; b/u Mar05]
31		(French Navy)	31 [preserved by Sep99 as gate guardian Nimes-Garons, France]
32		(German Navy)	UC+325 61+16 [wfu 2004 Erding, Germany; b/u Mar05]
33		(Pakistan Navy)	33+ 91//AR-NZA [+ France] [w/o 10Aug99 near Rann of Kutch, Pakistan; reported shot down]
34		Luftwaffen Museum	UC+326 61+17 [wfu May05; preserved Berlin-Gatow, Germany; l/n Nov09]
35		(French Navy)	35 [b/u post Jun95 Nimes-Garons, France]
36		(German Navy)	UC+327 61+18 [wfu 2004 Erding, Germany; b/u Mar05]
37		(French Navy)	37 [b/u; l/n at Nimes-Garons, France]
38		(French Navy)	38 [b/u; l/n at Nimes-Garons, France]
39		(French Navy)	39 [w/o 31Aug67 Spitsbergan, Norway]
40		Pakistan Navy	40+ 40//AR-NZB 92//AR-NZB [+ France]
41		(French Navy)	41 [b/u Nimes-Garons, France; l/n May01]
42		(French Navy)	42 [cvtd to Atlantique ATL.2/ANG with c/n 01]
43		(French Navy)	43 [w/o 20Sep68 Farnborough, UK]
44		(French Navy)	44 [b/u post Jun95 Nimes-Garons, France]
45		(French Navy)	45 [dumped by Sep99 Nimes-Garons, France]
46		Pakistan Navy	46+ 46//AR-NZC 93//AR-NZC [+ France]
47		(French Navy)	47 [b/u; tail used on preserved c/n 27; qv]
48		(French Navy)	48 [b/u after Jun05 Nimes-Garons, France]

BREGUET 1150/1151 ATLANTIC

C/n	Model	Last known Owner/Operator	Identities/fates/comments (where appropriate)
49		(French Navy)	49 [dumped Nimes-Garons, France Sep99]
50		(French Navy)	50 [wfu by 14Jun95; subsequently b/u Nimes-Garons, France]
51		(French Navy)	51 [dumped by Sep99 Nimes-Garons, France; l/n 07May04; gone by Feb05]
52		(French Navy)	52 [b/u Nimes-Garons, France]
53		Pakistan Maritime Museum	53 [+ France] [wfu Nimes-Garons, France; believed sold to Pakistan Navy for spares use; preserved 2005 Karachi, Pakistan; l/n 08Apr08]
54		(French Navy)	54 [b/u Nimes-Garons, France]
55		(French Navy)	250+ 55 [+ Netherlands] [b/u post Jun05 Nimes-Garons, France]
56		(French Navy)	251+ F-YELZ 56 [+ Netherlands] [wfu Nimes-Garons, France; believed sold to Pakistan Navy for spares use]
57		(French Navy)	252+ F-YELB 57 [+ Netherlands] [wfu Nimes-Garons, France; believed sold to Pakistan Navy for spares use]
58		(Dutch Navy)	253 [w/o 14Sep78, ditched in Irish Sea]
59		(German Navy)	61+19 [wfu Dec06 preserved Peenemunde, Germany]
60		Militaire Luchtvaart Museum	61+20 [wfu & preserved Jan07 Soesterberg, Netherlands; marked as 250]
61		Musee de l'Air et de l'Espace	254+ F-YELX 61^ [+ Netherlands; ^ France] [preserved Feb97 Paris-Le Bourget, France]
62		(Dutch Navy)	255 [w/o 15Jan81, 190 miles west of Hebrides, Scotland, UK]
63		Pakistan Navy	256+ F-YELY 63^ 94 [+ Netherlands; ^ France]
64		(Dutch Navy)	257 [w/o 15Aug73, ditched off Den Haag and towed to Den Helder, Netherlands]
65		(French Navy)	258+ F-YELY 65 [+ Netherlands] [b/u Lorient-Lann-Bihoue, France]
66		(French Navy)	66 [b/u post Jun96 Lorient-Lann-Bihoue, France]
67		(French Navy)	67 [b/u post Jun96 Lorient-Lann-Bihoue, France]
68		(French Navy)	68 [b/u post Jun96 Lorient-Lann-Bihoue, France]
69		(French Navy)	69 [cvtd to Atlantique ATL.2/ANG with c/n 02]
70		Italian Air Force	MM40108//41-70
71		Italian Air Force	MM40109//30-71 MM40109//41-71
72		Italian Air Force	MM40110//41-72
73		Italian Air Force	MM40111//41-73
74		Italian Air Force	MM40112//30-74
75		Italian Air Force	MM40113//30-75 MM40113//41-75
76		Italian Air Force	MM40114//41-76
77		Italian Air Force	MM40115//41-77
78		Italian Air Force	MM40116//30-78 MM40116//41-01
79		Italian Air Force	MM40117//41-02
80		Italian Air Force	MM40118//30-03 MM40118//41-03
81		Italian Air Force	MM40119//30-04 MM40119//41-04
82		Italian Air Force	MM40120//41-05
83		Italian Air Force	MM40121//41-06
84		Italian Air Force	MM40122//30-07 MM40122//41-07
85		Italian Air Force	MM40123//30-10
86		Italian Air Force	MM40124//41-11
87		Italian Air Force	MM40125//30-12 MM40125//41-12

Production complete

BREGUET 1150 ATLANTIQUE ATL.2/ANG

01		(French Navy)	01 [built from Atlantic c/n 42; reported wfu by 14Jun95 Nimes-Garons, France]
02		(French Navy)	02 [built from Atlantic c/n 69; dumped Nimes-Garons, France by Jun99; l/n 07May04; b/u by Feb05]
03		CEV	03
04		(French Navy)	04 [dumped Nimes-Garons, France Sep99; l/n 08Dec04]
1		French Navy	1 [ff 19Oct88; wfu & stored 10Nov10 Cuers Pierefeu, France]
2		French Navy	2
3		French Navy	3
4		French Navy	4
5		French Navy	5
6		French Navy	6

BREGUET 1150/1151 ATLANTIC

C/n	Model	Last known Owner/Operator	Identities/fates/comments (where appropriate)	
7		French Navy	7	
8		French Navy	8	
9		French Navy	9	
10		French Navy	10	[damaged & stored 22Jan07 Lann Bihoue, France; l/n 2011]
11		French Navy	11	
12		French Navy	12	
13		French Navy	13	
14		French Navy	14	
15		French Navy	15	[reported stored Jun07 Cuers-Pierrefeu, France]
16		French Navy	16	
17		French Navy	17	
18		French Navy	18	[reported stored Jun07 Cuers-Pierrefeu, France]
19		French Navy	19	
20		French Navy	20	[reported stored Jun07 Cuers-Pierrefeu, France]
21		French Navy	21	[reported stored Jun07 Cuers-Pierrefeu, France]
22		French Navy	22	
23		French Navy	23	
24		French Navy	24	
25		French Navy	25	
26		French Navy	26	
27		French Navy	27	
28		French Navy	28	

Production complete

BRISTOL B.175 BRITANNIA

C/n	Model	Last known Owner/Operator	Identities/fates/comments (where appropriate)
12873	100	(Ministry of Supply)	(VX442) (WB470) G-ALBO 7708M [prototype ff 16Aug52] [wfu 31Oct60 RAF St Athan, UK as GIA; b/u 12Jun68 with parts still present to Apr74]
12874	101	Britannia Aircraft Preservation Trust	(VX447) (WB473) G-ALRX [w/o 04Feb54 Littleton-upon-Severn, UK; canx 05Apr54; fuselage used as GIA, Filton, UK; front fuselage preserved Bristol Aircraft Collection, Kemble, UK; l/n 02Nov08]
12875		(Ministry of Supply)	(VX454) [static test airframe; used for functional trials]
12902	102	(Britannia Airways)	G-ANBA [wfu 20Nov69 Luton, UK; b/u Jun70; canx 10Mar70 still regd to BOAC]
12903	102	(Britannia Airways)	G-ANBB [w/o 01Sep66 nr Ljubljana Airport, Yugoslavia; canx 01Sep66]
12904	102	(BOAC)	G-ANBC [w/o 11Nov60 Khartoum, Sudan; canx 15Feb61]
12905	102	(BKS Air Transport)	G-ANBD [wfu Mar69 Southend, UK; b/u by May70; canx 24Apr70]
12906	102	(Britannia Airways)	G-ANBE [wfu Dec70; b/u Jun72 Luton, UK; canx 02Oct81]
12907	102	(Britannia Airways)	G-ANBF [wfu 26Oct69; b/u Apr70 Luton, UK; canx 10Mar70]
12908	102	(BKS Air Transport)	G-ANBG G-APLL [wfu 21Feb69; b/u Sep69 Newcastle UK; canx 24Apr70]
12909	102	(BKS Air Transport)	G-ANBH [wfu 28Oct68; b/u Sep69 Southend, UK; canx 24Apr70]
12910	102	(Britannia Airways)	G-ANBI [wfu 27Sep69; b/u Oct69 Luton, UK; canx 10Apr70]
12911	102	(Britannia Airways)	G-ANBJ [wfu 13Oct70; b/u Feb71 Luton, UK; canx 25Jan71]
12912	102	(Northeast Airlines)	G-ANBK [wfu 31Dec71; b/u Mar72 Newcastle, UK; canx 25Jan72]
12913	102	(Britannia Airways)	G-ANBL [wfu 29Dec70; b/u Jly72 Luton, UK; canx 20Feb73]
12914	102	(Indonesian Angkasa)	G-ANBM PK-ICA [wfu Jun70; b/u Dec71 Jakarta-Soekarno-Hatta, Indonesia; hulk l/n Jun74]
12915	102	(Indonesian Angkasa)	G-ANBN PK-ICB [wfu Jun70; b/u Dec71 Jakarta-Soekarno-Hatta, Indonesia; hulk l/n Jun74]
12916	102	(Britannia Airways)	G-ANBO [wfu 15Oct70; b/u May71 Luton, UK; canx 25Jan71]
12917	300	(Ministry of Supply)	G-ANCA [w/o 06Nov57 Downend, nr Filton, UK; canx 03Aug60]
12918	302	(Aeronaves de Mexico)	G-ANCB G-18-1 XA-MEC [w/o 09Jly65 Tijuana, Mexico; hulk b/u Apr66; canx 30Oct65]
12919	302	(International Aviation Services)	G-ANCC G-18-2 XA-MED G-ANCC [wfu for spares 16Mar70 Biggin Hill, UK; b/u Aug70; canx 27Apr73]
12920	307F	(Allcargo Airlines)	G-18-3 G-ANCD (N6595C) 4X-AGE G-ANCD 5Y-AYR [wfu Aug82 Bournmouth-Hurn; b/u Oct82]
12921	307F	(Aer Turas)	(N6596C) G-ANCE EI-BAA [wfu Apr79; b/u May81 Dublin for spares; canx 27May81]
12922	308F	Britannia Aircraft Preservation Trust	(N6597C) G-ANCF G-18-4 G-14-1 LV-PPJ LV-GJB G-ANCF 5Y-AZP G-ANCF [wfu & stored Oct80, later dismantled Manston, UK; canx 21Feb81; preserved Weybridge, UK, later Kemble, UK then Liverpool Airport, UK; l/n 17Nov08]
12923	308F	(British Eagle Internaional Airlines)	(N6598C) G-ANCG LV-PPL LV-GJC G-ANCG [w/o 20Apr67 Manston, UK; canx 10Jly67]
12924	309	(International Aviation Services)	(N6599C) G-ANCH 9G-AAG G-41+ G-ANCH 9G-AAG^ G-ANCH [+ B class marks used by Aviation Traders; ^ possibly ntu; wfu Dec72 Biggin Hill, UK; b/u Aug73]
12925	312	(Monarch Airlines)	(G-ANCI) G-AOVH [wfu 23Nov71 to GIA Luton, UK; b/u Jun72; canx 26May72]
12926	312	(Monarch Airlines)	(G-ANCJ) G-AOVI [wfu 16Jan72 Luton, UK; b/u Apr72; canx 26May72]
13207	200	(Bristol Aeroplane Co Ltd)	(G-AMYK) [canx 11Mar55 as wfu; not built]
13207	300LR	(Bristol Aeroplane Co Ltd)	(G-AOFA) [canx 01Jan56 as wfu; not built]
13207	319	(Airline Engineering)	G-AOVA 9G-AAH G-AOVA [wfu & b/u for spares Oct71 Baginton, UK; canx 07Jun71]
13208	200	(Bristol Aeroplane Co Ltd)	(G-AMYL) [canx 11Mar55 as wfu; not built]
13208	300LR	(Bristol Aeroplane Co Ltd)	(G-AOFB) [canx 01Jan56 as wfu; not built]
13230	312F	(Aerotransportes Entre Rios)	G-AOVB LV-PNJ LV-JNL [w/o 12Jly70 Buenos Aires-Ezeiza, Argentina; canx 06Apr71]
13231	300LR	(Bristol Aeroplane Co Ltd)	(G-AOFC) [canx 01Jan56 as wfu; not built]
13231	312	(Donaldson Int'l Airways)	G-AOVC [wfu 17Nov70 to fire school, Stansted, UK; DBF 1973; canx 17Nov70]
13232	313	(Globe-Air)	4X-AGA G-ASFV 4X-AGA HB-ITB [w/o 20Apr67 Nicosia, Cyprus]
13233	313	(Air Spain)	4X-AGB G-ARWZ 4X-AGB EC-WFL EC-BFL [wfu 1972; b/u for spares late 1974 Palma, Spain]
13234	250	(Bristol Aeroplane Co Ltd)	(G-ANGK) [canx 11Mar55 as wfu not built]
13234	313	(Monarch Airlines)	4X-AGC G-ARXA 4X-AGC G-ARXA [b/u for spares Nov70 Luton, UK; canx 08Nov68]
13235	300LR	(Bristol Aeroplane Co Ltd)	(G-AOFD) [canx 01Jan56 as wfu; not built]
13235	312	(BOAC)	G-AOVD [w/o 24Dec58 Sopley Farm, near Christchurch, UK; canx 13Jly60]
13236	300LR	(Bristol Aeroplane Co Ltd)	(G-AOFE) [canx 01Jan56 as wfu; not built]

BRISTOL B.175 BRITANNIA

C/n	Model	Last known Owner/Operator	Identities/fates/comments (where appropriate)
13236	312	(Air Spain)	[G-AOVE EC-WFK EC-BFK [wfu mid 1972; b/u winter 1974 for spares Palma, Spain, for International Air Services]
13237	300LR	(Bristol Aeroplane Co Ltd)	(G-AOFF) [canx 01Jan56 as wfu; not built]
13237	312F	Royal Air Force Museum	G-AOVF 9Q-CAZ G-AOVF [preserved Mar86 RAF Museum, Cosford, UK as XM497 which was c/n 13509; canx 21Nov84; l/n 27Sep08]
13238	300LR	(Bristol Aeroplane Co Ltd)	(G-AOFG) [canx 01Jan56 as wfu; not built]
13238	312	(Monarch Airlines)	G-AOVG [wfu 30Jan74 Luton, UK; b/u Aug74; canx 04Apr77]
13393	314	(African Safari Airways)	CF-CZA G-ATGD 5X-UVT 5Y-ALP [wfu Apr71 Biggin Hill, UK; b/u Dec71]
13394	314	(Canadian Pacific Air Lines)	CF-CZB [w/o 22Jly62 Hickham Field, Honolulu, HI]
13395	314	(IAS Cargo Airlines)	CF-CZC G-ATLE [b/u for spares early 1970 Gatwick, UK; hulk to fire training until b/u Mar84; canx 16Mar70]
13396	314	(IAS Cargo Airlines)	CF-CZD G-ATNZ [wfu Apr71 Biggin Hill, UK; b/u Jun71; canx 06May71]
13397	253F	(Young Cargo)	XL635 OO-YCA [b/u Jly77 Stansted, UK]
13398	253F	(Young Cargo)	XL636 OO-YCE [wfu Dec77 Ostend, Belgium; b/u Aug80]
13399	253F	(Domaine de Katale)	XL637 OO-YCH EL-LWH OO-YCH 9Q-CKG [derelict by 1990 Goma, Zaire; b/u by Jan92]
13400	253	(Royal Air Force)	XL638 [w/o 12Oct67 RAF Khormaksar, Aden; blown up on site]
13418	300LR	(Bristol Aeroplane Co Ltd)	(G-AOFJ) [canx 01Jan56 as wfu; not built]
13418	312	(Donaldson Int'l Airways)	G-AOVJ [wfu for spares 17Dec70 Stansted, UK; hulk to fire school until DBF; canx 17Nov70]
13419	312	(Airline Engineering Services)	G-AOVK [wfu & b/u Feb70 Luton, UK; canx 27Feb70]
13420	312	(Monarch Airlines)	G-AOVL [wfu early 1971 Luton, UK; b/u Jly71; canx 26May72]
13421	312F	(Business Cash Flow Aviation)	G-AOVM EC-BSY XX367 9Q-CHY [last airworthy Britannia; wfu 06Jly90 Kinshasa-N'Djili, Zaire; b/u Jan94]
13422	312	(Monarch Airlines)	G-AOVN [wfu Nov73 Luton, UK; b/u Feb74; canx 04Apr77; nose section used by Laker Airways as GIA Gatwick, UK]
13423	312	(British Eagle International)	G-AOVO [w/o 29Feb64 in Alps near Innsbruck, Austria; canx 29Feb64]
13424	312F	(IAS Cargo Airlines)	G-AOVP [wfu for spares 06Aug75 Biggin Hill, UK; later b/u UK; canx 05Dec83]
13425	317	(IAS Cargo Airlines)	G-APNA [wfu for spares May72 Baginton, UK; b/u Jly73, proposed use as cafe abandoned; canx 21Oct72]
13426	317	(Airline Engineering Services)	G-APNB [wfu Mar71 Luton, UK; b/u Nov71 for spares; canx Mar71]
13427	317	Duxford Aviation Society	G-AOVT [preserved 29Jun75 Duxford, UK; canx 21Sep81; l/n 04Oct08]
13428	314	(International Aviation Services)	CF-CZX G-ATMA 5Y-ANS G-ATMA [wfu 01Jun73 Biggin Hill, UK; b/u spring 74; canx 01Jun73]
13429	312	(Air Spain)	G-AOVR EC-WFJ EC-BFJ [ferried Apr73 to Biggin Hill, UK for spares use by IAS Cargo Airlines; b/u Aug75]
13430	312F	(Redcoat Air Cargo)	G-AOVS [b/u Oct79 Luton, UK; canx 07May81; hulk to GIA marked as "G-BRAC" (qv c/n 13448); on fire dump 05Feb81; hulk l/n Dec08]
13431	313	(African Cargo Airways)	4X-AGD G-ASFU 4X-AGD HB-ITC 5X-UVH 5Y-ALT [wfu for spares 22May75 Stansted, UK; hulk to fire school; DBF]
13432	318	(Compania Cubana de Aviacion)	CU-P668 CU-T668 G-APYY CU-T668 OK-MBA CU-T668 [wfu & stored 1983 Havana, Cuba; b/u by 1995]
13433	318	(Aerocaribbean)	CU-P669 CU-T669 CU-T114 [wfu Dec87 Havana, Cuba; b/u by 1997]
13434	253F	(Young Cargo)	XM489 OO-YCC [wfu & stored Jan76 Gosselies, Belgium; b/u 1978]
13435	253F	(Air Faisal)	XM490 G-BDLZ [wfu May79 Luton, UK; b/u Sep79; canx 01Aug83]
13436	253F	(Domaine de Katale)	XM491 EI-BBH 9Q-CMO [b/u Jan92 Goma, Zaire]
13437	318	(Compania Cubana de Aviacion)	CU-P670 CU-T670 [wfu & stored 1978 Havana, Cuba; b/u by 1997]
13448	253F	(Redcoat Air Cargo)	XL639 EI-BDC G-BRAC + [+ these marks also applied to wfu fuselage of c/n 13430; w/o 16Feb80 near Boston-Logan, MA]
13449	253F	(Katale Aero Transport)	XL640 EI-BCI G-BHAU 9Q-CHU [b/u 1986 Kinshasa-N'Djili, Zaire]
13450	252	(Royal Air Force)	G-APPE XN392 [wfu & stored Jly75 RAF St Athan, UK; Dec75 to Baginton, UK for spares use by Aer Turas; b/u May76]
13451	252F	(Zaire Aero Service)	G-APPF XN398 9Q-CPX [wfu Mar84 Goma, Zaire; b/u by Jan91]
13452	252	(Royal Air Force)	G-APPG XN404 [wfu & stored Jly75 RAF St Athan, UK; to Luton, UK for spares use by Air Faisal; b/u Mar77]
13453	314	(Caledonian Airways)	CF-CZW G-ASTF CF-CZW G-ASTF [wfu 17Nov69 Gatwick, UK; b/u Oct70; canx 30Oct70]
13454	253F	(Centre Air Afrique)	XL657 9U-BAD [wfu & stored Feb77 Ostend, Belgium; b/u Apr81]
13455	253F	(Interconair)	XL658 EI-BBY [w/o 30Sep77 nr Shannon, Ireland; canx 12Sep85]
13456	253F	(Young Cargo)	XL659 OO-YCB [wfu & stored Aug76; Ostend, Belgium; b/u 1978 & reported used as cafe; no recent reports]
13457	253F	(Katale Aero Transport)	XL660 G-BEMZ A6-HMS G-BEMZ 9Q-CGP [wfu & later b/u Jan92 Goma, Zaire]

BRISTOL B.175 BRITANNIA

C/n	Model	Last known Owner/Operator	Identities/fates/comments (where appropriate)
13508	253F	Britannia Aircraft Preservation Trust	XM496 G-BDUP CU-T120 9Q-CJH EL-WXA [wfu & preserved Oct97 Kemble, UK as XM496; l/n 01Nov10]
13509	253F	(Young Cargo)	XM497 OO-YCF [wfu & stored 1976 Stansted, UK; b/u Jly77; hulk to fire school; DBF May81]
13510	253F	(Domaine de Katale)	XM498 OO-YCG EL-LWG 9Q-CDT [wfu & stored Jan88 Kinshasa-N'Djili, Zaire; b/u Jan92]
13511	253F	(Airline Engineering Services)	XM517 9Q-CAJ G-BEPX [wfu Apr77 & used as engine test bed until b/u Mar80 Luton, UK; canx 01Jly83]
13512	253F	(Young Cargo)	XM518 OO-YCD [wfu Mar76 Gosselies, Belgium; b/u 1978]
13513	253F	(Aerocaribbean)	XM519 G-BDUR CU-T121 [wfu & stored 1988 Havana, Cuba; used by Trans Air Cargo Zaire for spares & b/u Nov95]
13514	253F	(Domaine de Katale)	XM520 9G-ACE 9Q-CUM [wfu & b/u Jul86 Kinshasa, Zaire]
13515	318	(Compania Cubana de Aviacion)	CU-P671 CU-T671 OK-MBB CU-T671 [wfu & stored 1979 Havana, Cuba; b/u by 1997]
13516	324	(Airline Engineering Services)	G-18-8 CF-CPD G-ARKA (HB-ITF) [wfu & stored Nov69 Baginton, UK; b/u Oct71 for spares; canx 27Jan72]
13517	324	(Airline Engineering Services)	CF-CPE G-ARKB (HB-ITG) [wfu & stored Nov69 Baginton, UK; b/u Oct71 for spares; canx 27Jan72]

Production complete

BRITISH AEROSPACE ATP (Jetstream 61)

Note: Unless indicated by "pax" in the model column are in pure cargo configurations; LFD = Large Freight Door

C/n	Model	Last known Owner/Operator	Identities/fates/comments (where appropriate)
2001		(BAE Systems (Operations) Ltd)	(G-OATP) G-MATP G-PLXI [prototype ff 06Aug86] [stored 28Oct97 Woodford, UK; b/u by 13Aug08 for spares; canx 09Jun09; forward fuselage to RAF Millom Aviation & Military Museum]
2002		West Air Sweden	G-BMYM G-MAUD (G-MANK) SE-MAF LX-WAI* [* marks reserved 2012]
2003	pax	(West Air Sweden)	G-BMYK G-ERIN G-MANL (SE-MAG) [stored 29Sep06 Lidkoping, Sweden; canx 21Dec07; Aug08 used for EFIS cockpit trials; for spares use; b/u Nov09]
2004		West Air Sweden	G-BMYL G-LOGE G-MANJ SE-MAH LX-WAH* [* marks reserved 2012]
2005	LFD	ex AirGo Bulgaria	N375AE G-BZWW G-OATP G-MANM SX-BTK G-MANM SE-MAM SX-BPS LZ-BPS [stored 28Oct11 Coventry, UK; l/n 15Feb12]
2006	LFD	Atlantic Airlines	N376AE G-5-376 G-11-5 G-UIET G-MANO OK-TFN G-MANO SE-MAN G-MANO
2007	LFD	Atlantic Airlines	(N377AE) G-BTPA EC-GYE (G-BTPA) EC-HGC G-BTPA
2008	LFD	Atlantic Airlines	(N378AE) G-11-8 CS-TGA G-BUUP G-MANU G-BUUP
2009	pax	(BAE Systems (Operations) Ltd)	(N379AE) G-11-9 CS-TGB G-BUWM CS-TGB G-BUWM [stored 11Oct95 & wfu Woodford, UK; sold to Atlantic Airlines for spares use; canx 01Jly08; b/u 11Aug08]
2010	LFD	Atlantic Airlines	(N380AE) G-11-10 G-BTPC EC-GYF G-BTPC EC-HGB G-BTPC SE-MAI G-BTPC
2011	LFD	West Air Luxembourg	(N381AE) G-BTPD EC-GYR (G-BTPD) EC-HGD G-BTPD SE-MAO LX-WAT
2012	LFD	Atlantic Airlines	(N382AE) G-BTPE EC-GZH G-BTPE EC-HGE G-BTPE
2013	LFD	Atlantic Airlines	(N383AE) G-BTPF G-11-013 G-BTPF EC-HCY G-BTPF
2014	LFD	Atlantic Airlines	(N384AE) G-BTPG EC-HEH G-BTPG
2015	LFD	Atlantic Airlines	G-BTPH EC-HFM G-BTPH (G-JEMF) G-BTPH
2016	LFD	Deutsche Leasing Sverige AB	G-BTPJ EC-HFR G-BTPJ [stored by late 2008 Coventry, UK; l/n Nov11]
2017	LFD	Atlantic Airlines	G-OLCC G-LOGC G-MANH
2018	pax	ex SATA-Air Acores	G-OLCD G-LOGD G-MANG (ES-NBB) CS-TFJ [stored 08Jun10 Southend, UK; l/n 20Jly11]
2019	pax	NexJet CS-TGL	G-11-19 G-BRTG CS-TGL SE-MEE
2020		West Air Luxembourg	G-WISS G-11-20 (G-WISS) N851AW SE-LHX LX-WAN SE-LHX LX-WAN
2021	LFD	West Air Luxembourg	(G-BRKM) G-11-21 G-11-021 N852AW SE-LGZ LX-WAW
2022		West Air Sweden	G-11-022 N853AW SE-LGU [DBF 23Oct09 Malmo, Sweden; l/n Nov11 stored]
2023		NexJet/Sverigeflyg	G-PEEL G-MANP OK-VFO G-MANP PH-MJP ES-NBA G-MANP ES-NBA G-MANP SE-LLO
2024	LFD	Atlantic Airlines	G-11-024 CS-TGC G-BUUR G-OEDJ EC-GUX G-BUUR
2025	pax	ex SATA-Air Acores	G-BRLY TC-THP G-BRLY CS-TGX [ferried 19Oct09 to Norwich, UK for Regional 1 Airlines; 26Oct09 to Southend, UK; l/n 20Jly11]
2026	LFD	P T Deraya Air	S2-ACX G-11-026 S2-ACX (SE-LHX) G-JEMD PK-DGA
2027	LFD	P T Deraya Air	S2-ACY G-11-027 S2-ACY (SE-LHY) G-JEME PK-DGI
2028	pax	ex PTB (Emerald) Pty Ltd	G-11-028 N854AW G-JEMA [stored 04May06 Blackpool, UK; l/n Aug11]
2029		Atlantic Airlines	G-11-029 N855AW G-JEMB G-OAAF [stored 07Sep10 Coventry, UK; l/n 30Jly12]
2030	pax	(SATA-Air Acores)	G-11-030 G-11-30 CS-TGM [w/o 11Dec99 Pico da Esperanca, Sao Jorge, Azores]
2031	pax	NexJet G-11-031	CS-TGN SE-MEG [stored as CS-TGN Malmo, Sweden; l/n Aug11]
2032	pax	PTB (Emerald) Pty Ltd	G-11-032 G-11-32 N856AW G-JEMC [stored 20Mar09 Coventry, UK; l/n Nov09]
2033	LFD	Atlantic Airlines	G-11-033 (S2-ACZ) G-BTTO TC-THV G-BTTO G-OEDE G-BTTO G-OEDE G-BTTO EC-GJU G-BTTO EC-HNA G-BTTO (PH-MJF)
2034		West Air Sweden	G-11-034 N857AW SE-LGV [stored 28Feb10 Ronaldsway, Isle of Man, UK; l/n 02Dec11]
2035		West Air Sweden	G-11-035 N858AW SE-LGY LX-WAZ* [* marks reserved 2012]
2036		West Air Sweden	G-11-036 N859AW SE-LGX [stored by 05Nov11 Malmo, Sweden]
2037	LFD	West Air Luxembourg	G-11-037 G-BTNK G-11-037 N860AW G-BTNK G-CORP SE-MAP LX-WAE
2038	LFD	West Air Luxembourg	G-SLAM G-BTNI TC-THU G-BTNI (N238JX) G-OEDI EC-GKJ EC-GSE G-BTNI (PH-MJG) SE-MAJ LX-WAD
2039		(Aircraft Maintenance Services Ltd)	G-11-039 G-BTUE G-11-039 G-BTUE TC-THT G-BTUE G-OEDH G-OGVA G-OEDH EC-GKI EC-GSF G-BTUE VT-FFB+ G-BTUE^ [w/o 15Jun07 Chennai, India; +canx 04Jly08; ^ regd for spares use only; b/u 02Aug08 Chennai; India; canx 23Jun09]

BRITISH AEROSPACE ATP (Jetstream 61)

C/n	Model	Last known Owner/Operator	Identities/fates/comments (where appropriate)
2040	pax	NexJet G-LOGA	G-MANF SE-MAK
2041	LFD	West Air Luxembourg	G-11-041 G-BTPK EC-GLC EC-GSG G-BTPK SE-LPV LX-WAV
2042	LFD	European Turboprop Management AB	G-11-042 G-BTPL EC-GLH G-BTPL EC-HES G-BTPL (PH-MJK) G-BTPL (PH-MGB) G-BTPL [stored 24May07 Coventry, UK; l/n 18Feb11; for West Atlantic]
2043	LFD	West Air Luxembourg	G-BTPM G-11-2043 G-BTPM EC-GNI EC-GSH G-BTPM SE-LPS LX-WAO
2044	BLC	West Air Sweden	G-BTPN EC-GNJ EC-GSI G-BTPN SE-MAY
2045	pax	NexJet G-11-045	G-LOGB G-MANE SE-MAL
2046	pax	(Trident Avn Leasing Services (Jersey) Ltd)	(PK-MAA) PK-MTV G-BTZG PK-MTV G-BTZG [stored 14Sep99 Woodford, UK; b/u 11/12Aug08 for spares for West Air Sweden; canx 27Mar09]
2047	pax	(Trident Avn Leasing Services (Jersey) Ltd)	(PK-MAC) G-BTZH PK-MTW G-BTZH [stored 03Apr97 Woodford, UK; b/u 08/12Aug08 for spares for West Air Sweden]
2048	pax	(Merpati Nusantara Airlines)	(PK-MAD) G-BTZI PK-MTX [w/o 19Apr97 Buluh Tumbang Airport, Tanjung, Indonesia]
2049	pax	ex SATA-Air Acores	(PK-MAE) G-BTZJ PK-MTY G-BTZJ CS-TGY [stored 06May10 Southend, UK; l/n 20Jly11]
2050	pax	(Trident Avn Leasing Services (Jersey) Ltd)	(PK-MAF) G-BTZK PK-MTZ G-BTZK [stored 25Apr00 Woodford, UK; b/u 08/13Aug08 for spares for West Air Sweden]
2051		European Turboprop Management AB	G-BTPO G-OBWP (VT-FFA) VT-FFC G-OBWP [stored 28Mar09 Coventry, UK; l/n 11Dec10; for West Atlantic]
2052		ex Trident Avn Leasing Services (Jersey) Ltd	G-BUKJ TC-THZ G-BUKJ G-OEDF EC-GLD G-BUKJ EC-HCO G-BUKJ+ (PH-MJL) (PH-MGC) N [stored 14Sep09 Baneasa, Romania; l/n Dec09; for Regional 1 Airlines, Canada; + canx 21Dec10 to USA]
2053		West Air Sweden	G-11-053 G-BUWP G-OBWR SE-MAR LX-WAG* [* marks reserved 2012]
2054		European Turboprop Management AB	G-11-054 G-LOGF G-MANC (SE-KXO) VT-FFA G-MANC [stored by Nov09 Coventry, UK ex Southend store; l/n 11Dec10; for West Atlantic]
2055	pax	Air Aceh	G-11-055 G-JATP G-LOGG G-MANB RP-C2786 PK- [stored Manila, Philippines in Air Aceh c/s; l/nDec09]
2056	LFD	West Air Luxembourg	G-11-056 G-LOGH G-MANA SE-KXP LX-WAF
2057		West Air Luxembourg	G-11-057 G-OBWL G-11-057 G-OBWL (SE-LNX) SE-LPR LX-WAP
2058		West Air Luxembourg	G-11-058 G-OBWM G-11-058 G-OBWM (SE-LNY) SE-LPT LX-WAS
2059		West Air Luxembourg	G-11-059 G-BVEO G-11-059 G-OBWN SE-LHZ LX-WAL SE-LHZ LX-WAL
2060		West Air Luxembourg	G-11-060 (EI-COS) G-OBWO (SE-LNZ) SE-LPU LX-WAM SE-LPU LX-WAM
2061		West Air Luxembourg	G-11-061 G-BUYW HL5227 G-BUYW OY-SVI SE-LNX LX-WAK
2062		West Air Sweden	G-11-062 OY-SVT SE-LNY LX_WAJ* [* marks reserved 2012]
2063		West Atlantic	G-11-063 HL5228 G-BWYT OY-SVU (SE-LNZ) SE-LPX LX-WAX

JETSTREAM 61 aircraft

C/n	Model	Last known Owner/Operator	Identities/fates/comments (where appropriate)
2064		Jetstream Aircraft	G-JLXI [ff 10May94; dismantled 03Apr97 Prestwick, UK; canx 12Jun97; by Aug04 fuselage at Humberside Airport, UK, with Eastern Airlines]
2065		(British Aerospace)	G-11-065 [ff 26Jly95, last ATP to fly; dismantled 03Apr97 Prestwick, UK]
2066		(British Aerospace)	(G-11-066) [never flown; completed up to engine installation; dismantled by Apr97 Prestwick, UK]
2067		(British Aerospace)	(G-11-067) [never flown; noted 16Sep96 Prestwick, UK without engines, doors or leading edges; dismantled by Apr97 Prestwick, UK]
2068		(British Aerospace)	[dismantled; fuselage, wings not mated; Sep99 to Fire Service Prestwick, UK]
2069		not completed	[fuselage Sep99 to Fire Service Prestwick, UK; moved to fire dump; b/u by Feb04]
2070		not completed	[fuselage Sep96 Chorley International Fire Training Center, Euxton, Chorley, UK; l/n 11Jly08]
2071		not completed	[fuselage Jun96 to Fire Service Woodford, UK; marked as "N-ORAK" as ground evaluation trials airframe; Aug11 moved to Manchester Airport for fire training]
2072		not completed	[fuselage Mar96 to Fire Service Manchester Airport, UK; b/u 15Aug08]
2073		not completed	[fuselage Sep96 to Blackpool, UK for Fire Department – fuselage on dump 25 Aug 07; l/n 18Mar08]
2074		not completed	[fuselage b/u at Prestwick, UK]
2075		not completed	[fuselage Apr96 Chester, UK; fire dump at Hawarden 1998; l/n 13Nov08]
2076		not completed	[fuselage b/u Mar98 Chadderton, UK]

Production complete

BRITISH AEROSPACE JETSTREAM 31/32

C/n	Model	Last known Owner/Operator	Identities/fates/comments (where appropriate)
601	3102	ex Maersk Air Ltd	G-31-601 G-TALL N G-31-601 G-WMCC N [wfu 30Aug96 Birmingham-International, UK; b/u for spares; 11Dec97 fuselage to fire service at Smethwick, UK; canx 26Dec97 as sold in USA]
602	3101	(British Aerospace Asset Management)	G-31-39 G-JBAE N92MA N331J N422MX [wfu 18Mar91 Little Rock, AR; by 03Jan98 fuselage only Kingman, AZ; canx 10Aug99; b/u; l/n 25Jan05]
603	3103	Aircraft Guaranty Corp	G-31-42 G-CONE G-31-42 D-CONE SE-KHB OY-EDA V2-LEZ N603JS D-CJRA N603JS [wfu May03 Kingman, AZ; by 24May04 fuselage only wearing D-CJRA, later removed; gone by 08Sep05]
604	3101	Southern Aircraft Consultancy	G-BKHI SE-IPC G-BKHI SE-IPC OY-CLC LN-FAL N78019 [stored by Sep11, Roskilde, Denmark; l/n Jun12]
605	3101	Sky-High Aircraft	G-31-45 N331JS N331NY N903FH
606	3102	Royal Norwegian Air Force	G-31-46 G-BKKY (SE-IZA) G-BKKY SE-KHA OY-CLB LN-FAV [wfu & canx 19Dec06; to GIA]
607	3102	Premiere Aero	G-31-47 G-OBEA (N) G-OBEA N607BA [stored by Dec07 Fort Lauderdale-Executive, FL; l/n 23Mar11]
608	3102	(White Industries Inc)	G-31-48 G-JSBA (N331BE) G-JSBA N331BJ N608JX [wfu Sep99; canx 04Mar05; b/u Bates City, MO for parts; l/n 04Oct07]
609	3102	Professional Aviation Group	(N331BF) G-31-49 G-CBEA (SE-LGH) G-CBEA N609BA [by 22Oct08 Tamiami, FL with missing parts; l/n 14Jun10]
610	3103	Jetstream Executive Travel	G-31-50 D-CONI SE-KHC OY-EDB SE-KHC D-CNRY G-JXTA [stored by 14Nov08 Inverness, UK; l/n Feb11]
611	3101	(British Aerospace Asset Management)	G-31-611 N155AA N988AX N419MX [wfu Dec97 Kingman, AZ; by 25Oct02 fuselage only; gone by 08Sep05]
612	3102	ex SK Air	G-31-612 G-BKTN HB-AEA OM-NKD [canx 14Jan05; fate unknown]
613	3101	Jetstream VIP	G-31-613 N331BG N331BA N904FH N904EH
614	3104	BAE Systems (Operations)	G-31-614 G-BWWW
615	3101	(British Aerospace Asset Management)	G-31-615 (N93MA) G-BKVU G-31-615 N822JS [wfu Kingman, AZ; fuselage only by Jan97; gone by 08Sep05]
616	3102	(SASCA Servicios Aeronauticos)	G-31-616 G-BKUY (SE-LHY) G-BKUY D-CNRX N430JV YV-1163C YV186T [w/o 13Feb08 Los Roques Airport, Venezuela]
617	3101	(British Aerospace Asset Management)	G-31-617 N156AA N989AX N420MX [wfu Dec97 Kingman, AZ, fuselage only; gone by 08Sep05]
618	3101	KSC Enterprises Inc	G-31-618 N820JS N618JX N618SC
619	3101	(British Aerospace Asset Management)	G-31-619 N821JS N619JX [wfu & b/u by Dec97 Kingman, AZ; canx 10Aug99]
620	3107	(Jetstream Executive Travel)	G-31-620 VH-JSW G-BYYI [canx 13Sep06 and stored Southampton, UK; b/u; fuselage to Alton, UK; l/n 06May07]
621	3102	(Luftforsvarets Skolesenter Kjevik)	G-31-621 (G-BLCY) G-BLDO G-BTXL LN-FAJ [canx 19Dec06 & used as GIA by RNAF at Kristiansand-Kjevik, Norway]
622	3102	Sky Aeronautical	G-31-622 G-BLCB G-31-622 VH-HSW G-LOVB
623	3101	(Jetstream Int'l/Piedmont Commuter)	G-31-623 N823JS [w/o 09Feb88 Springfield, OH; fuselage to White Industries, Bates City, MO; l/n 25Apr07]
624	3101	(Eastern Metro Express)	G-31-624 N400MX [canx 03Oct96; wfu by Oct00 Kingman, AZ; fuselage only by 13Nov07; l/n Oct11]
625	3101	(Eastern Metro Express)	G-31-625 N404MX [b/u Sep96 Kingman, AZ; canx 03Oct96; Jun03 hulk moved to Mena, AR]
626	3103	(Sun-Air of Scandinavia)	G-31-626 D-CONU G-LAKJ D-CONU OY-SVP [w/o 27Jan98 Copenhagen-Kastrup, Denmark]
627	3101	(British Aerospace Asset Management)	G-31-627 N824JS [b/u Dec97 Kingman, AZ; fuselage in USAir Express c/s stored; canx 10Aug99; gone by 08Sep05]
628	3101	(Jet Acceptance Corp)	G-31-628 G-BLFX N401MX [dismantled Sep96 Kingman, AZ; fuselage in Eastern Express c/s stored; canx 03Oct96; b/u 2005]
629	3107	Tango Squadron	G-31-629 VH-OSW ZK-OSW HS-KLB [canx & stored Jly03 Bangkok-Don Muang, Thailand; by 26Nov09 preserved there; l/n 13Jan12]
630	3101	(Jet Acceptance Corp)	G-31-630 N402MX [by Sep96 stored Kingman, AZ in Eastern Express c/s; canx 03Oct96; dismantled Oct00; gone by 08Sep05]
631	3101	(Jet Acceptance Corp)	G-31-631 N406MX [by Sep96 stored Kingman, AZ in Eastern Express c/s; dismantled Oct00; canx 08Aug01; gone by 08Sep05]
632	3101	(Jet Acceptance Corp)	G-31-632 N403MX [by Sep96 stored Kingman, AZ in Eastern Express c/s; canx 03Oct96; dismantled Oct00; gone by 08Sep05]
633	3101	(British Aerospace Asset Management)	G-31-633 N825JS [by Jan97 stored Kingman, AZ in US Air Express c/s; canx 10Aug99; dismantled Oct00; gone by 08Sep05]

BRITISH AEROSPACE JETSTREAM 31/32

C/n	Model	Last known Owner/Operator	Identities/fates/comments (where appropriate)
634	3102	(European Centre for Aerospace Training)	G-31-634 (G-BLEX) G-BLKP [wfu & canx 07Dec06 Humberside, UK; fuselage only to Macclesfield College as GIA]
635	3101	Corporate Flight Management	G-31-635 N405MX N635JX N10UP
636	3101	(European Executive Express)	G-31-636 N407MX G-BVDK N636JX SE-LGA [w/o 30Nov01 Skien, Norway]
637	3102	Cranfield University	G-31-637 G-BLHC G-BRGN G-NFLA
638	3102	ex Air Andaman	G-31-638 N408MX G-BUFL OH-JAC G-BUFL SE-LHP HS-KLA [canx & stored Jly05 Bangkok-Don Muang, Thailand; l/n 10Dec10; probably destroyed in floods Nov11]
639	3101	(Skylease Sweden)	G-31-639 N409MX N639JX SE-LGB G-EDAY [dismantled 31May11 Inverness, UK; fuselage to be used as film prop in London]
640	3102	(Jetstream Executive Travel)	G-31-640 N410MX G-BUFM G-LAKH G-BUFM G-OAKA G-LOVA G-PLAH [wfu by Nov07 & canx 22Jan08 Blackpool, UK; dismantled remains to RAF Millom Aviation & Military Museum; remains b/u 2010]
641	3102	ex Bromma Air Sales	G-31-641 SE-IPD G-REGB SE-IPD OY-SVZ G-MACX OY-SVZ SE-LGC OY-SVZ LN-SVZ+ HI- [+ canx 19Aug11 to Dominican Republic]
642	3101	ex Professional Aviation Group	G-31-642 N402AE N642JX HI- [canx 15Dec08 to Dominican Republic]
643	3101	Jetstream Air	G-31-643 G-BLMH N157AA N990AX N421MX N643JX [stored by 31Oct09 Smyrna, TN; l/n 05Nov11]
644	3101	Aero Ejectiva	G-31-644 N403AE (N411MX) N403AE N644JX CC-CZA
645	3102	SACSA Servicios Aeronauticos	G-31-645 PH-KJA G-BXLM N645JD G-BXLM SE-LGC YV263T YV2211+ [+ ntu? by 20Mar12]
646	3101	Vee Neal Aviation	G-31-646 N404AE N646JX N646SA N646VN
647	T.3	ex Transworld Aviation Trading	G-31-647 ZE438+ N437UH^ [+ code 76] [+ United Kingdom; SOC 11Sep08 RAF Cranwell, UK; ^ stored 02Dec11 Dunsfold , UK; canx 08Feb12 as wfu]
648	3108	ex Downwind Investments	G-31-648 PH-KJB [stored by 2003 Rotterdam, Netherlands; canx 23 Apr04; l/n 18Jly08; reported removed by Jly09 & used in bizarre car race; remains scheduled to go to Hoofddorp as GIA]
649	3102	Quest Aviation	G-31-649 PH-KJC G-31-649 G-BPZJ VH-LJR G-LOGP G-SWAD SP-FTH N554DM N220FN
650	3101	ex Aircraft Maintenance Support	G-31-650 N405AE N650JX [stored by 23Apr10 Dallas-Love Field, TX; l/n 28Aug11; canx 29Sep11 as wfu]
651	3101	Vee Neal Aviation	G-31-651 N406AE N651JX VH-PAJ ZK-JSX N651VN
652	3101	(Boston-Maine Airways/PanAm)	G-31-652 N300PX N515PA [ex storage Kingman, AZ; canx 15Sep09 as wfu; fate/status unknown]
653	3101	ex Aircraft Maintenance Support	G-31-653 N407AE N653JX [stored by 23Apr10 Dallas-Love Field, TX; l/n 28Aug11; canx 30Aug11; canx 30Aug11 as wfu]
654	3101	(Boston-Maine Airways/PanAm)	G-31-654 N301PX N517PA [ex storage Kingman, AZ; canx 15Sep09 as wfu; fate/status unknown]
655	3102	Quest Aviation	G-31-655 PH-KJD G-BRGR G-LOGR G-ENIS SP-FTG N789AA N221FN
656	T.3	ex Transworld Aviation Trading	G-31-656 ZE439+ N437SS^ [+ code 77] [+ United Kingdom; SOC 25Sep08 RAF Cranwell, UK; ^ stored 02Dec11 Dunsfold, UK; b/u by 15Feb12; canx 08Feb12]
657	3101	Jetstream Air	G-31-657 N991AX N412MX N657BA [stored by 31Oct09 Smyrna, TN]
658	3101	(Boston-Maine Airways/PanAm)	G-31-658 N992AX N413MX N658BA N518PA [canx 15Sep09 as wfu; fate/status unknown]
659	T.3	ex Transworld Aviation Trading	G-31-659 ZE440+ N437ZZ [+ code 78] [+ United Kingdom; stored 28Jly06 Shawbury, UK; Mar11 by road to location in West Sussex; canx 08Feb12 as wfu]
660	3101	ACSA-Air Century	G-31-660 N411MX HI-772CT HI772
661	3101	(Finova Capital Corp)	G-31-661 N302PX [wfu Sep98 Kingman, AZ; b/u for parts; canx 22Aug01]
662	3101	(Finova Capital Corp)	G-31-662 N303PX N463CE N303PX [wfu & dismantled Sep98 Kingman, AZ; fuselage in Northwest Airlink c/s stored; gone by 08Sep05]
663	3101	ex Boston-Maine Airways/PanAm	G-31-663 N304PX (HI-) N522PA
664	3101	World Jet of Delaware	G-31-664 N408AE N664JX
665	3107	Tasair Pty Ltd	G-31-665 VH-ESW VH-SMQ
666	3101	Salsa d'Haiti	G-31-666 N305PX N525PA+ HH- [+ canx 25Oct11 to Haiti]
667	T.3	ex Transworld Aviation Trading	G-31-667 ZE441+ N437TH^ [+ United Kingdom; SOC 29Sep08 RAF Cranwell, UK; stored 02Dec11 Dunsfold, UK; canx 08Feb12 as wfu]
668	3101	CSC Trust Co of Delaware	G-31-668 N410AE N668JX N668SA VH-OZD N668MP YV N668MP
669	3101	Northwest Int'l Industries	G-31-669 N409AE N669JX [status unknown]

BRITISH AEROSPACE JETSTREAM 31/32

C/n	Model	Last known Owner/Operator	Identities/fates/comments (where appropriate)
670	3101	(Boston-Maine Airways/PanAm)	G-31-670 N306PX N528PA [canx 15Sep09 as wfu; fate/status unknown]
671	3101	(Chaparral Airlines/American Eagle)	G-31-671 N411AE [w/o en-route 25Mar88 near Decatur, TX]
672	3101	(California Coastal Airways)	G-31-672 N310PX [wfu Dec97 & stored Portsmouth-Pease International, NH; l/n 20Apr04]
673	3101	Pan Am Dominicana	G-31-673 N307PX N507PA HI-817CT
674	3101	Pan Am Dominicana	G-31-674 N308PX N508PA HI841CT
675	3101	(Boston-Maine Airways/PanAm)	G-31-675 N161PC N509PA [ex storage Kingman, AZ; canx 15Sep09 as wfu; fate/status unknown]
676	3101	SAVE-Servicio Aereo Vargas Espana	G-31-676 N309PX CP-2405
677	3101	(Boston-Maine Airways/PanAm)	G-31-677 N162PC N510PA [ex storage Kingman, AZ; canx 15Sep09 as wfu; fate/status unknown]
678	3101	(Boston-Maine Airways/PanAm)	G-31-678 N163PC N512PA [ex storage Kingman, AZ; canx 15Sep09 as wfu; fate/status unknown]
679	3101	ex Mapiex Aero	G-31-679 N311PX HP-1458N? HP-1458MAM HP-1458PS [wfu by 11May09 Panama City, Panama for spares; b/u; hulk l/n 05Sep10]
680	3101	(SAVE-Servicio Aereo Vargas Espana)	G-31-680 N312PX N460CE CP-2404 [w/o 17Jan03 Yacuiba, Bolivia]
681	3101	(Salsa d'Haiti)	G-31-681 N313PX N461CE N536PA HH-ANA [w/o 13Feb11 Port-au-Prince, Haiti]
682	3101	(Boston-Maine Airways/PanAm)	G-31-682 N164PC (N331BN) N164PC N514PA [ex storage Kingman, AZ; canx 15Sep09 as wfu; fate/status unknown]
683	3101	(CC Air/US Air Express)	G-31-683 N165PC (N331BP) N165PC [w/o 12Mar92 Knoxville-McGhee Tyson, TN; canx 29Sep97]
684	3101	(Boston-Maine Airways/PanAm)	G-31-684 N314PX N462CE N537PA [canx 27Mar06; fate unknown]
685	3101	ex US Specialty Insurance Co	G-31-685 N315PX N445PE N685RD [wfu by Oct11 with Dodson International Parts, Rantoul, KS]
686	3108	Sun-Air of Scandinavia	G-31-686 PH-KJF G-BSFG OY-SVF
687	3101	(Boston-Maine Airways/PanAm)	G-31-687 N316PX N535PA [canx 15Sep09 as wfu; fate/status unknown]
688	3101	Paraclete Aviation	G-31-688 N317PX N478XP * [marks reserved 12May08; but 05Feb09 Kingman, AZ, with many parts missing]
689	3101	(Air Solutions)	G-31-689 N318PX N216FN [stored by 05Jly07 Tamiami, FL; l/n 04Feb10; gone by Apr10, probably b/u]
690	3108	University of Glamorgan	G-31-690 PH-KJG G-BSFH G-LOGT PH-KJG (G-JXTC) [dismantled 04/05Dec09 Eindhoven, Netherlands; 08Dec09 to GIA Treforest, Glamorgan, UK still marked as PH-KJG; G-JXTC ntu; canx 07Oct11]
691	3101	Medical Air Rescue Services	G-31-691 N319PX N217FN C6-ASL 3D-MRP ZS-JSL
692	3101	Caribair	G-31-692 N166PC N692JX HI746CA HI-746CT
693	3101	(Avspares International Corp)	G-31-693 N331BK N826JS N693JX [wfu & stored 18Oct98 Kingman AZ; b/u for parts]
694	3101	ACSA-Air Century	G-31-694 N168PC N694AM HI-816CT HI816
695	3101	Murray Air	G-31-695 N169PC N695MA
696	3111	(Royal Saudi Air Force)	G-31-696 (G-WSOC) G-BMNR 2102 [w/o 14Oct89 Dhahran, Saudi Arabia; hulk l/n Apr06]
697	3101	Transportes Aereos Guatemaltecos	G-31-697 N331BL N827JS YV216T TG-TAW
698	3102	ex Flight Ops International	G-31-698 G-BMTV N330PX C-FCCP [stored by 03Dec09 Calgary, AB, Canada; l/n 03Sep11]
699	3101	(Jetstream Aircraft)	G-31-699 N414MX G-BUJT [wfu for spares Nov96 Prestwick, UK, still marked as N414MX; canx 22Jly97]
700	3101	(Express Airlines/Northwest Airlink)	G-31-700 N331PX [w/o 14Dec87 Joplin, MO; canx 29Sep97]
701	3103	Avies Air Company	G-31-701 (PH-KJH) D-CONA OY-SVR ES-LJD ES-PJG
702	3101	(Boston-Maine Airways/PanAm)	G-31-702 N332PX N521PA [ex storage Kingman, AZ; canx 15Sep09 as wfu; fate/status unknown]
703	3103	ex European Air Express	G-31-703 VH-TQJ D-CNRZ [stored 18Aug02 Monchengladbach, Germany; canx 07Apr03; b/u for spares; hulk l/n 17Oct09]
704	3101	Starlink Aviation	G-31-704 N333PX C-GCCN
705	3107	(Eastern Australia Airlines)	G-31-705 VH-TQK [canx 15Nov02; to college in Tamworth, NSW, Australia as GIA; l/n Nov03]
706	3101	(Express Airlines/Northwest Airlink)	G-31-706 N334PX [w/o 01Dec93 Hibbing, MN; wreck to Atlanta Air Salvage, Griffin, GA; gone by 31Jan00]
707	3107	(Eastern Australia Airlines)	G-31-707 VH-TQL [canx 15Nov02; to college in Tamworth, NSW, Australia as GIA; l/n Nov03]
708	3101	(J V Air Maintenance)	G-31-708 N331BN N828JS [by 05Jly07 stored Tamiami, FL; l/n 01Mar09; unconfirmed report sold to El Sol de America, Venezuela, but b/u by Apr10]
709	3111	Royal Saudi Air Force	G-31-709 (G-TWSS) G-BMNS 2101+ 3501 [+ Saudi Arabia]

BRITISH AEROSPACE JETSTREAM 31/32

C/n	Model	Last known Owner/Operator	Identities/fates/comments (where appropriate)
710	3101	(CC Air/US Air Express)	G-31-710 N167PC [w/o 30Mar91 Raleigh-Durham Airport, NC; hulk to White Industries, Bates City, MO; l/n 25Apr07]
711	3101	Links Air/Blue Islands	G-31-711 N415MX G-BTYG OY-SVJ G-OJSA G-JIBO
712	3101	Starlink Aviation	G-31-712 N335PX C-GCCZ
713	3101	(Britannia Aviation Services)	G-31-713 N829JS [wfu & b/u Kingman AZ; canx 03Dec03]
714	3101	(EME Spares Inc)	G-31-714 N830JS(1) [DBR 30Nov86 Erie, PA in ground collision with Cessna 441 N117EA (c/ 0191); b/u for parts Dec86]
715	3101	ex Avient Ltd	G-31-715 N416MX G-BTZT G-IJYS+ TU- [+ canx 30Sep11 to Ivory Coast]
716	3101	HBA LLC	G-31-716 N831JS (N331BQ) N831JS
717	3101	MAS 1 Inc	G-31-717 N170PC
718	3101	Jetstream Executive Travel/Manx 2	G-31-718 N417MX G-OAKI SX-BSR G-OAKI
719	3102	Flyglinjen Vatterbygden	G-31-719 N418MX G-BTXG OY-EEC G-BTXG OK-REJ G-BTXG SE-FVP G-BTXG+ ES- SE-FVP* [+ canx 09Jan11 to Estonia]
720	3102	Starlink Aviation	G-31-720 G-BRGL G-31-720 I-BLUA G-BRGL G-LOGU G-OEDC OK-SEK G-BRGL SE-LHV G-PLAM G-HDGS C-GDFW
721	3101	SASCA Servicios Aeronauticos	G-31-721 N832JS YV-1181C YV176T+ YV314T [+ not fully confirmed] [stored 01Mar09 Tamiami, FL; l/n 14Jun10]
722	3101	Transportes Aereos Guatemaltecos	G-31-722 N331BP N830JS(2) TG-TAN TG-CAO
723	3101	Empower Aviation	G-31-723 N331BQ N107XV N342PF N723VN N723CA
724	3101	ex Air Mikisew	G-31-724 N331BR N106XV N852JS C-FKAM [canx 05Oct11 fate/ status unknown]
725	3101	Aerolineas Sosa	G-31-725 N833JS HR-ATA
726	3101	Aerolineas Sosa	G-31-726 N834JS HR-ATB
727	3112	Gordon Peariso	G-31-727 G-BRUK I-BLUU I-ALKC G-BRUK G-SWAC C-GKGM
728	3101	(CC Air/US Air Express)	G-31-728 N156PC [wfu by 04Oct07 for parts White Industries, Bates City, MO; canx 24Oct07]
729	3101	Venezolana	G-31-729 N331BS N401UE OB-1785-T YV-1085C
730	3101	ex PSA Airlines/US Air Express	G-31-730 N157PC N104XV N853JS [wfu by 04Oct07 for parts White Industries, Bates City, MO; canx 24Oct07]
731	3101	(Guildford Transportation Industries)	G-31-731 N835JS N534PA [canx 22Sep05 as destroyed; fate unknown]
732	3101	ex Boston-Maine Airways/PanAm	G-31-732 N836JS N530PA
733	3112	Chartright Air	G-31-733 N331BT C-GJPC N8000J N733VN C-FREQ
734	3101	Venezolana	G-31-734 N331BU N402UE OB-1784-T YV-1084C
735	3101	Swanberg Air	G-31-735 N158PC N101XV N854JS C-GPSW
736	3101	ex AT Turboprop Eight Corp	G-31-736 N837JS [canx 20Jun06 to Canada; for parts recovery by Mountainwest Air at Fort Smith, NT, Canada]
737	3101	(CC Air/US Air Express)	G-31-737 N331QA N157PC [wfu by 04Oct07 for parts White Industries, Bates City, MO; canx 24Oct07]
738	3102	Skybird	G-31-738 N331QB C-GJPH N2274C G-PLAJ
739	3101	Infinity Flight Services	G-31-739 N331CX N105XV N855JS C-GNGI
740	3112	Eagle Air	G-31-740 (N331QC) C-GJPO (N2247R) LN-FAM G-FARA TF-ORD
741	3101	Boston-Maine Airways	G-31-741 N838JS N539PA
742	3101	(Air New Orleans/Continental Express)	G-31-742 N331CY [w/o 26May87 New Orleans-International, LA; canx 04Apr91]
743	3101	Vol Air	G-31-743 N331QD N403UE N16EN HI877 [stored Tamiami, FL; l/n18Feb12]
744	3101	ex PSA Airlines/US Air Express	G-31-744 N159PC N102XV N856JS [wfu by 04Oct07 for parts White Industries, Bates City, MO; canx 30Oct07]
745	3112	Sky Research	G-31-745 N331QE C-GJPQ N22746
746	3112	(Air Mikisew)	G-31-746 N331QF N404UE (N746JX) N404UE C-FUAM [canx 07Sep11 as wfu; fate unknown]
747	3101	Starlink Aviation	G-31-747 N160PC N103XV C-GEMQ
748	3101	ex Boston-Maine Airways/PanAm	G-31-748 G-BNIC (N161PC) N839JS N531PA
749	3112	ex Spitfire Investments	G-31-749 (N839JS) C-GJPU LN-FAZ G-NOSS+ ES- [+ canx 23Nov11 to Estonia]
750	3102	(Highland Airways)	G-31-750 N840JS (N331QH) N190PC G-UIST [part cut-up 24Feb11 Inverness, UK; remains to Pinewood Film Studios, UK as film prop; canx 05May11]
751	3101	Vale Air USA	G-31-751 N841JS N538PA
752	3101	Vee Neal Aviation	G-31-752 N711PN N752JX N403GJ N120HR N752VN [sold to Jose Rodriguez, Mexico]
753	3101	Caribbean Aircraft	G-31-753 N842JS HH-DMX N12925+ HH-DMX? [+regd 16Mar09 and canx same day on sale in Haiti]

BRITISH AEROSPACE JETSTREAM 31/32

C/n	Model	Last known Owner/Operator	Identities/fates/comments (where appropriate)
754	3101	Northeast Air & Sea Services	G-31-754 N711HH N754JX N404GJ
755	3101	Vee Neal Aviation	G-31-755 N331QG N405UE (N755JX) N755SP N743PE
756	3112	Swanberg Air	G-31-756 C-GJPX N2275S C-GJPX C-GPSO
757	3101	Aerolineas Sosa	G-31-757 N843JS HR-ATO
758	3109	(Sun-Air of Scandinavia)	G-31-758 I-BLUI G-BTAI I-ALKD G-BTAI (OM-SKY) G-BTAI OY-MUE [w/o 12Feb04 Aarhus, Denmark; canx 14Oct04; hulk to local fire service; l/n 16May08]
759	3101	Venezolana	G-31-759 N406UE (N226RJ) N759JS P4-JSA OB-1739 YV-1086C YV179T
760	3101	(Air Panama)	G-31-760 N844JS HP-1477MAM HP-1477PS [w/o 01Jun06 Bocas del Toro Airport, Panama]
761	3102	Air New Zealand Aviation Institute	G-31-761 I-BLUO G-BSZK G-LOGV G-OEDA G-LOGV ZK-JSI [2013 to GIA at either Auckland or Christchurch, New Zealand]
762	3101	(Venezolana)	G-31-762 N407UE (N762JX) N407UE OB-1735 YV-1083C [w/o 18Nov04 Caracas-Simon Bolivar, Venezuela]
763	3101	(CC Air/US Air Express)	G-31-763 N331QL N158PC [stored by 14Jan99 Kingman, AZ; to White Industries, Bates City, MO for parts; l/n 04Oct07; canx 29Apr09]
764	3112	Rollins Air	G-31-764 N331QJ N422AE (N764JX) N422AE N223JL C-FSEW HR-AWG
765	3101	(Boston-Maine Airways/PanAm)	G-31-765 N840JS N532PA [canx 15Sep09 as wfu; fate/status unknown]
766	3112	Rollins Air	G-31-766 N331QN N423AE (N766JX) N423AE N222JF C-GPDC N HR-AWH
767	3112	Northwestern Air	G-31-767 N331QP N424AE N113XV N424AE N767JX C-FNAM
768	3101	(Northwestern Air)	G-31-768 N159PC C-FNAY [w/o 27Nov08 Fort Smith, NT, Canada; canx 30May11]
769	3101	(Caribintair)	G-31-769 N845JS HH-DPL [DBR 28Apr06 Cap Haitien, Haiti; derelict hulk l/n 23Apr10]
770	3101	Venezolana	G-31-770 N408UE N770JX OB-1782-T YV-1093C YV180T
771	3101	Boston-Maine Airways	G-31-771 N846JS N529PA
772	3102	Links Air	G-31-772 C-FAMJ OY-SVK SE-LDH G-JURA G-LNKS
773	3112	Links Air/Blue Islands	G-31-773 C-FAMK OY-SVO SE-LGH LN-BES+ SE-LGH G-EIGG [+ marks painted on but not delivered]
774	3101	(Westair/United Express)	G-31-774 N160PC N426UE [wfu Jun98; stored by 19Dec98 Kingman AZ; to White Industries, Bates City, MO; l/n 04Oct07]
775	3101	(Westair/United Express)	G-31-775 N409UE (N775JX) N409UE [wfu & stored by 18Jun96 Kingman AZ; l/n Mar01 b/u for parts; canx 06Jan11]
776	3101	(North Pacific Airlines/United Express)	G-31-776 N410UE [w/o 26Dec89 Pasco-Tri-Cities Airport, WA; canx 12Apr90]
777	3101	Ultra Motorsports	G-31-777 N425AE N114XV N425AE N777JX N443PE N127UM
778	3112	Integra Air	G-31-778 N426AE N1114X N426AE N778JX C-FMIP C-GGIA
779	3101	Bar XH Air	G-31-779 N331QE N419UE C-FSAS C-FFIA
780	3101	Caribair	G-31-780 N331QG N418UE HI830CT+ HI-830+ [+ marks not fully confirmed]
781	3112	(Eastern Airways)	G-31-781 C-FASJ OY-SVY SE-LGM G-EEST [w/o 18Aug03 Wick, UK; dismantled Feb04; remains to RAF Millom Aviation & Military Museum for rebuild to external display; canx 05Nov07]
782	3101	(Westair/United Express)	G-31-782 N331QH N422UE [wfu & to White Industries, Bates City, MO for parts; l/n 04Oct07; canx 25Oct07]
783	3112	Swanberg Air	G-31-783 C-FCOE HL5224 N837SC C-GHGI C-GPSN
784	3101	not yet known	G-31-784 N331QK N430UE YV-1134CP YV215T YV-1134CP
785	3112	Linkair/Manx2	G-31-785 C-FHOE SE-LDI G-CCPW
786	3112	West Wind Aviation	G-31-786 C-FIOE HL5225 N786SC C-GHGK
787	3101	(Westair/United Express)	G-31-787 N331QB N131CA [w/o 19Apr93 Merced-Municipal, CA; by Jan96 fuselage at White Industries, Bates City, MO; l/n 04Oct07]
788	3101	(Westair/United Express)	G-31-788 N331QC N420UE [stored by 14Jan99 Kingman, AZ; to White Industries, Bates City, MO for parts; l/n 04Oct07; canx 22Jan09]
789	3101	Northwestern Air	G-31-789 N411UE (N789JX) N411UE C-FNAF
790	3201	(UMI International)	G-31-790 G-BOOR N332QA N492UE [by Jly05 stored Tamiami, FL; l/n 14Jun10; canx 22Sep10]
791	3101	LANHSA	G-31-791 N412UE N791JX C-GNRG HR-AXG
792	3101	(PSA Airlines/US Air Express)	G-31-792 N847JS [wfu & canx 22Aug96; to White Industries, Bates City, MO for parts; l/n 04Oct07]
793	3101	ex Skyservice Business Aviation	G-31-793 N331QQ N331CA C-GEOC [canx 27Aug08 fate/status unknown]

BRITISH AEROSPACE JETSTREAM 31/32

C/n	Model	Last known Owner/Operator	Identities/fates/comments (where appropriate)
794	3101	Aeropacifico	G-31-794 N331QM N417UE XA-UEP
795	3202	ex Helitrans	G-31-795 G-BOTJ G-OAKJ G-BOTJ G-OAKJ LN-HTB [canx 05Jun12 fate/reason?]
796	3101	Bar XH Air/Integra Air	G-31-796 N331QR N424UE C-GZOS
797	3101	(United Express)	G-31-797 N413UE (N797JX) N413UE [stored 15Aug95 Kingman AZ; wfu 1996 & to White Industries, Bates City, MO; l/n 25Apr07; canx 22Jan09]
798	3101	Quasar	G-31-798 N331QS N425UE [stored by 08Nov04 Addison, TX; l/n 04Feb11]
799	3101	(Westair/United Express)	G-31-799 N331QT N423UE [wfu & canx 25Oct07; stored Roswell, NM; to White Industries, Bates City, MO for parts; l/n 04Oct07]
800	3201	ProFlight Zambia	G-31-800 (N32SU) (G-BOYJ) N370MT G-31-800 N370MT N290MA 9J-PCU
801	3101	(Westair/United Express)	G-31-801 G-BOJP N414UE (N801JX) N414UE [wfu & stored Jun95 Kingman, AZ; to White Industries, Bates City, MO for parts; l/n 04Oct07]
802	3112	Latitude Air Ambulance	G-31-802 C-FBID
803	3101	(Jet Acceptance Corp)	G-31-803 N415UE N803JX [wfu & stored Jly98 Kingman, AZ; to White Industries, Bates City, MO for parts; l/n 04Oct07; canx 22Jan09]
804	3101	(Westair/United Express)	G-31-804 N331QU N421UE [wfu & stored Jun98 Kingman, AZ; to White Industries, Bates City, MO for parts; l/n 04Oct07; canx 25Oct07]
805	3201	Aerolineas MAS	G-31-805 (N32MT) N371MT N493UE HI-859
806	3101	Aviation College of Sweden	G-31-806 N331QV C-FBII N331QV N428UE [canx 19Feb04 to Sweden; to GIA Vasteras-Hasslo, Sweden; l/n 15Jun09]
807	3101	(Caribbean Eagle)	G-31-807 N331QW N429UE [by 05Jly07 stored Tamiami, FL; l/n 14Jun10 wfu; b/u by Jly11]
808	3101	(Westair/United Express)	G-31-808 N416UE (N808JX) N416UE [wfu & stored Jun95 Kingman, AZ; to White Industries, Bates City, MO for parts; l/n 04Oct07]
809	3101	(PSA Airlines/US Air Express)	G-31-809 N848JS [wfu for spares use Jly96 by White Industries, Bates City, MO; canx 22Aug96; l/n 04Oct07]
810	3201	Aerolineas MAS	G-31-810 (N33MT) N372MT N494UE HI874
811	3101	Sapair	G-31-811 N331QX N427UE TG-TAK HI-819CT HI819
812	3101	Driscoll Health Care Services	G-31-812 N849JS
813	3101	(Sunrise Airlines)	G-31-813 N331QY N431UE [wfu & stored Nov00 Kingman, AZ; canx 9Oct03; b/u for parts, fuselage to White Industries, Bates City, MO]
814	3201	(MTW Aerospace)	G-31-814 N332QB N470UE [wfu for parts Montgomery, AL; canx 15Oct04; l/n 24Jan06 in United Express c/s]
815	3112	(Alberta Citylink)	G-31-815 C-FBIE N215D+ [w/o 20Jan98 Lloydminster, AB, Canada as C-FBIE; roaded to Springbank, AB, Canada; later with Dodson International, Rantoul, KS; l/n 07Nov06] [+reg'd for parts recovery]
816	3112	Swanberg Air	G-31-816 C-FBII C-GPSV
817	3112	(Peace Air)	G-31-817 C-FBIJ [wfu Edmonton International, AB, Canada; canx 25May06; l/n 12Jly08]
818	3201	(Jet Acceptance Corp)	G-31-818 N332QC N495UE [wfu Mar01 Kingman, AZ; b/u & canx 19Jun03 for parts]
819	32EP	ACSA-Air Century	G-31-819 N332QD N3107 N148JH HI840
820	3112	(Peace Air)	G-31-820 C-FBIP [w/o 09Jan07 Fort St John Airport, BC, Canada; canx 03Oct07; by 16Sep08 to Allied Air Parts, Oklahoma-Wiley Post, OK being b/u for spares; l/n 16May11]
821	3201	(Turbine Engine Consultants)	G-31-821 N322QE N471UE [wfu & stored Jun01 Kingman, AZ; b/u and canx 28Feb05]
822	3112	West Wind Aviation	G-31-822 C-FCPD
823	3201	(Atlantic Coast Airlines/United Express)	G-31-823 N332QF N472UE [wfu & stored 15Jun01 Kingman, AZ; to White Industries, Bates City, MO for parts; l/n 04Oct07]
824	3201	ProFlight Zambia	G-31-824 N332QG N3108 9J-PCS
825	3112	Northwestern Air	G-31-825 C-FCPE
826	3101	Volair Taxi	G-31-826 N850JS N16EX HI862 [stored Tamiami, FL; l/n 18Feb12]
827	3112	Bar XH Air	G-31-827 C-FCPF
828	3201	ADA-Aerolinea de Antioquia	G-31-828 N332QH N473UE HK-4398
829	3116	Sky Express	G-31-829 C-FCPG G-31-829 HB-AED G-BSIW G-OAKK G-OEDL G-BSIW C-GMDJ SX-BNJ G-VITO SX-SKY [w/o 12Feb09 Heraklion, Greece]
830	3212	Aero VIP	G-31-830 C-GBDR LV-VEI N22NC [to spares use at Buenos Aires-Aeroparque, Argentina; l/n 28Mar09 minus parts still as LV-VEI; by Oct10 possibly with museum at Moron, Argentina]
831	3212	(Linea Aerea de Entre Rios)	G-31-831 C-GDBR LV-VEJ [wfu Apr02 Kingman, AZ; l/n 03Oct03; later b/u]

BRITISH AEROSPACE JETSTREAM 31/32

C/n	Model	Last known Owner/Operator	Identities/fates/comments (where appropriate)
832	3212	SAVE-SA Vargas Espana	G-31-832 C-FTAR LV-PGO LV-WCZ CP-2441
833	3212	Pascan Aviation	G-31-833 C-FTDB N833JX ZP-PNP N833JX C-FZVY
834	3102	(East Coast Aviation Services)	G-31-834 N851JS N16EJ [w/o 21May00 near Wilkes-Barre/Scranton Airport, PA; canx 17Nov00]
835	3202	Southwest Florida Land Developers	G-31-835 C-GZRT G-BUIO OH-JAB G-BUIO YR-TRG N574SW [stored by Sep07 Smyrna, TN; l/n 05Nov11]
836	3201	SARPA Colombia	G-31-836 N332QJ G-31-836 C-FGLH N836JX OH-JAD G-OEST HK-4350
837	32EP	Northwestern Air	G-31-837 C-FFPA N837JX ZP-CPV N837JX C-FYWY C-FZYB C-GNAQ
838	3102	Vincent Aviation	G-31-838 G-IBLW G-WENT G-OEDD OO-EDA G-IBLW ZK-JSH
839	3102	Air New Zealand Aviation Institute	G-31-839 G-IBLX G-GLAM G-OEDG G-GLAM ZK-JSA [2013 to GIA at either Auckland or Christchurch, New Zealand]
840	3201	SARPA Colombia	G-31-840 N332QK G-31-840 C-GSCS N840JX OH-JAE (G-OESU) G-BYMA HK-4362
841	32EP	Largus Aviation/Direktflyg	G-31-841 N338AE G-BPZL N841AE N841JX SE-LHI
842	3201	ex Jet Air/OLT	G-31-842 N332QL G-31-842 N842AE N842JX SE-LHA G-CBCS SP-KWE [by 04Apr11 stored Bremen, Germany; l/n Jun12]
843	3212	Northwestern Air	G-31-843 (C-GKRW) C-GQRO C-GEAZ C-FNAZ
844	3201	Largus Aviation/Direktflyg	G-31-844 N844AE N844JX SE-LHB
845	3201	ex Jet Air/OLT	G-31-845 (N374MT) N845AE N845JX OH-JAG G-BYRA SP-KWF [by 10Mar12 stored Gdansk-Rebiechowo, Poland]
846	3201	Largus Aviation/Direktflyg	G-31-846 N846AE N846JX SE-LHC
847	3201	ex Jet Air/LOT	G-31-847 N332QN N847AE N847JX OH-JAF G-BYRM SP-KWD [CofA expired 04Dec10; l/n 27Mar09 Warsaw-Okecie, Poland]
848	32EP	Largus Aviation/Direktflyg	G-31-848 N332QP N848AE N848JX SE-LHH
849	3201	SARPA Colombia	G-31-849 N332QQ N474UE HK-4405E
850	3201	(Atlantic Coast Airlines/United Express)	G-31-850 N475UE [wfu & stored 25Mar01 Kingman, AZ; to White Industries, Bates City, MO for parts; l/n 04Oct07]
851	32EP	de Bruin Air Pty Ltd	G-31-851 N851AE N851JX VH-OAB+ VH-OAE [+ mis-painted as such on delivery flight]
852	3200	ex Gecamines	G-31-852 9Q-CFI [reported wfu by Sep03 Kinshasa-Ndolo, Democratic Republic of Congo]
853	32EP	de Bruin Air Pty Ltd	G-31-853 N853AE N853JX VH-OAB
854	3201	Largus Aviation/Direktflyg	G-31-854 N854AE N854JX SE-LHE
855	3201	Largus Aviation/Direktflyg	G-31-855 N855AE N855JX SE-LHF
856	3201	ex Jet Air	G-31-856 N422AM N856TE LN-FAC SP-KWN [stored 01Jun11 Cranfield, UK; l/n 02Jun12]
857	32EP	Largus Aviation/Direktflyg	G-31-857 G-BREV N857AE N857JX SE-LHG
858	3201	Corporate Flight Management	G-31-858 N423AM N858CY [stored ex Kingman, AZ; by 10Jun07 Fort Lauderdale-Executive, FL]
859	3201	de Bruin Air Pty Ltd	G-31-859 N859AE VH-OAM
860	32EP	AIS Active BV	G-31-860 N860AE 4X-CII PH-CCI
861	32EP	Macair Jet	G-31-861 N861AE (N861JX) N861AE LV-ZPW
862	3201	Alternative Air	G-31-862 N862AE N862JX XA-UFT
863	3201	Pascan Aviation	G-31-863 N3126 C-FIBA
864	3201	Helitrans	G-31-864 N864AE Z3-ASA N864AE SE-LHK LN-FAN
865	3201	Aerolineas de Antioquia	G-31-865 N424AM N865CY HK-4792
866	3201	ex Trans States Airlines	G-31-866 N866AE [wfu & stored Dec93 Kingman, AZ; to White Industries, Bates City, MO for parts; l/n 25Jan05; canx 11Feb09 as sold in Mexico]
867	3201	(Trans States Airlines)	G-31-867 N867AE (N867JX) [wfu & stored Dec99 Kingman, AZ; to White Industries, Bates City, MO for parts; l/n 04Oct07]
868	3207	ex Aeropelican Air Services	G-31-868 VH-TQM VH-OTA [moved by road to Bankstown, NSW, Australia; for use as spares; l/n 14Mar11]
869	32EP	Macair Jet	G-31-869 N869AE (N869JX) N869AE LV-ZOW
870	3201	SARPA Colombia	G-31-870 N425AM N870CY HK-4411
871	32EP	Blue Islands	G-31-871 N871AE N871JX G-ISLB
872	32EP	ex Regions Air	G-31-872 N872AE [wfu by 05Nov11 Smyma, TN]
873	32EP	Blue Islands	G-31-873 N873AE N873JX G-ISLC
874	3201	CKU Aviation	G-31-874 N426AM N874CP [stored by 31Oct09 Smyrna, TN]
875	32EP	(Corporate Airlines/American Connection)	G-31-875 N875AE N875JX [w/o 29Sep05 near Kirksville-Regional Airport, MO]
876	3201	Pascan Aviation	G-31-876 N427AM N876CP C-FHQA

BRITISH AEROSPACE JETSTREAM 31/32

C/n	Model	Last known Owner/Operator	Identities/fates/comments (where appropriate)
877	3201	Pascan Aviation	G-31-877 N428AM N877CP C-FKQA
878	32EP	Air National	G-31-878 N878AE (N878JX) N878AE VH-BAE ZK-ECP
879	3201	ex Coast Air	G-31-879 N429AM N879CP LN-VIP [l/n stored Haugesund, Norway & for sale]
880	3201	ex Aircraft Leasing Corp	G-31-880 N430AM N880TE [stored by 31Oct09 Smyrna, TN; wfu by 05Nov11]
881	3201	Northwestern Air	G-31-881 N431AM C-FNAE
882	3216	(Zimex Aviation/UN)	G-31-882 HB-AEB [destroyed 02Sep94 by sabotage on ground at Aden International Airport, Yemen]
883	3201	Tortug'Air	G-31-883 N432AM N883CH HH-JET
884	3201	Transmandu	G-31-884 N476UE YV-2456
885	3201	(Trans States Airlines)	G-31-885 N433AM [wfu & stored 10Apr00 Kingman AZ; b/u by 16Oct06]
886	3201	Pascan Aviation	G-31-886 N3136 N886CP C-GQJT
887	3201	(Corporate Flight Management)	G-31-887 N434AM [stored by Jun07 Smyrna, TN in TWA Express c/s; canx 17Sep09 as wfu]
888	3201	ex Vecolair Leasing	G-31-888 N3137 N888CY+ HK- [+ canx 14Aug12 to Colombia]
889	3201	ex TWA Express	G-31-889 N435AM [wfu & stored 10Apr00 Kingman AZ; canx 09Jan07; l/n 16Sep08 extant]
890	3201	ADA USA Inc	G-31-890 N477UE [status unknown; l/n 18Aug05 stored Kingman, AZ]
891	3201	(TWA Express)	G-31-891 N436AM [wfu & stored 10Apr00 Kingman AZ; l/n 19Mar07; canx 13Feb08 for spares]
892	3201	(Atlantic Coast Airlines/United Express)	G-31-892 N478UE [wfu & stored 20Apr00 Kingman AZ; l/n 18Aug05; canx 06Jun06 for spares]
893	3201	ADA-Aerolinea de Antioquia	G-31-893 N479UE HK-4548
894	3201	ex Kolob Canyons Air Services	G-31-894 N480UE N894KA+ HK- [+ marks canx 20Apr12 to Colombia]
895	3201	ex Kolob Canyons Air Services	G-31-895 N481UE+ HK- [+ marks canx 28Nov11 to Colombia]
896	3201	Aerolineas Sosa	G-31-896 N3140 N896CP C-GQJV HR-AXJ
897	3201	ADA-Aerolinea de Antioquia	G-31-897 N482UE HK-4364-X HK-4364
898	3201	ADA-Aerolinea de Antioquia	G-31-898 N483UE HK-4381-X HK-4381
899	3201	Senegalair	G-31-899 N484UE 6V-AIE
900	3202	ADA-Aerolinea de Antioquia	G-31-900 G-BSMY N3142 N496UE HK-4515X HK-4515
901	3201	(Vecolair Leasing)	G-31-901 N485UE [w/o 27Jun09 in Afghanistan]
902	3201	Pascan Aviation	G-31-902 N3155 N242BM C-GUSC
903	3201	ProFlight Zambia	G-31-903 N3156 N242RH VP-CEX 9J-PCT
904	3201	Corporate Flight Management	G-31-904 N3157 N497UE
905	3201	SARPA Colombia	G-31-905 N486UE HK-4394-E
906	3201	Sisserou Airways/BVI Airways	G-31-906 N487UE
907	3201	Tortug'Air	G-31-907 N488UE N264CA HH-DCT N264CA HH-ZET
908	3201	(Westair/United Express)	G-31-908 N489UE [wfu & stored Dec01 Kingman AZ; canx 29Jun05 for spares; l/n 29Jan05]
909	3201	Sundance Air Venezuela	G-31-909 N490UE YV310T [canx 05Jly07 to Venezuela; impounded 2007 still marked N490UE Valencia-Arturo Michelena, Venezuela; l/n 01Feb08]
910	32EP	Kavok Airlines	G-31-910 N910AE YV2532 YV1200 [badly damaged 19Jly09 Caracas-Metropolitano, Venezuela]
911	3201	Transmandu	G-31-911 N491UE YV1019
912	32EP	(Aerocaribe)	G-31-912 N912FJ [w/o en-route 08Jly00 near Chulum Juarez, Mexico]
913	32EP	Corporate Flight Management	G-31-913 N913AE
914	32EP	Tortug'Air	G-31-914 N914AE HH-YET
915	32EP	Blue Islands	G-31-915 N915AE G-ISLD
916	32EP	AIS Active BV	G-31-916 N916AE 4X-CIJ PH-DCI
917	3201	SARPA Colombia	G-31-917 N917AE HP- HK-4791
918	3201	(Flagship Airlines/American Eagle)	G-31-918 N918AE [w/o 13Dec94 near Raleigh-Durham Airport, NC; canx 17Sep97]
919	3201	Sapair	G-31-919 N919AE (N919CX) N919AE HI856
920	32EP	Skylane Airways	G-31-920 N920AE 6Y-JIC
921	3201	ex Vecolair Leasing	G-31-921 N921AE (N921CX) N921AE+ HK- [+ canx 14Aug12 to Colombia]
922	32EP	Aerolineas MAS	G-31-922 N922AE N922CX+ HI888 [+ canx10Aug09 to Haiti; but new regn reported as here]
923	3217	Royal Star Aviation	G-31-923 JA8876 N938A RP-C2812
924	3201	SARPA Colombia	G-31-924 N924AE HK-4803
925	3217	Ernir Air	G-31-925 JA8877 OY-SVR TF-ORA
926	32EP	ex Vecolair Leasing	G-31-926 N926AE+ HK- [+ canx 15Aug12 to Colombia]

BRITISH AEROSPACE JETSTREAM 31/32

C/n	Model	Last known Owner/Operator	Identities/fates/comments (where appropriate)
927	3201	(Roberto Diaz)	G-31-927 N927AE YV-1467 [w/o 10May09 near Utila Airport, Islas de la Bahia, Honduras; ran out of fuel whist on illegal drug flight]
928	32EP	Macair Jet	G-31-928 N928AE LV-ZRL
929	3201	Infinity Flight Services	G-31-929 N929CG N337TE C-GINL
930	32EP	Pascan Aviation	G-31-930 N930AE C-FPSC
931	32EP	Macair Jet	G-31-931 N931AE (N931CX) N931AE LV-ZPZ
932	3201	Briko Air Services	G-31-932 N338TE 9Y-JET [also reported as 9Y-BKO see c/n 939 below]
933	32EP	SARPA Costa Rica	G-31-933 N933AE N933CX HK-4540X TI-BDF
934	3201	ex Proflight	G-31-934 N934AE N934CX N934AE+ YV- [+ canx 15May08 to Venezuela]
935	3201	ex TWA Express	G-31-935 N339TE [wfu & stored May00 Kingman, AZ; l/n 19Mar07]
936	3201	ex Jet Acceptance Corp	G-31-936 N936AE (N936CX) N936AE [stored 30Jun07 Smyrna TN; canx 03Sep08; wfu by 05Nov11]
937	3201	SARPA Colombia	G-31-937 N937AE (N937CX) N937AE HK-4541
938	3201	SAPSA – Servicios Aereos Profesionales	G-31-938 N938AE (N938CX) N938AE HI858
939	3201	Briko Air Services	G-31-939 N340TE 9Y-BKO [also reported as 9Y-JET see c/n 932 above; stored by Jly11 Tamiami, FL]
940	3201	SAPSA – Servicios Aereos Profesionales	G-31-940 N940AE N940CX N940AE HI851
941	32EP	Macair Jet	G-31-941 N941AE LV-ZST
942	32EP	Macair Jet	G-31-942 N942AE LV-ZSB
943	32EP	not yet known	G-31-943 N943AE C-FIBD CN-TMK
944	3201	Air Century	G-31-944 N944AE HI-860
945	3202	Buraq Air	G-31-945 G-BTYU HL5214 5A-DGR
946	32EP	Airwork Flight Operations	G-31-946 N946AE ZK-REY ZK-TPC ZK-JSU ZK-ECI
947	32EP	Sky Express Airlines	G-31-947 N947AE N149JH SX-IDI
948	32EP	(European Executive Express)	G-31-948 N948AE VH-XFB SE-LNT [w/o 17Sep03 Lulea-Kallax, Sweden]
949	32EP	Avies Air Company	G-31-949 N949AE VH-XFC SE-LNU ES-PJR
950	3201	SARPA Colombia	G-31-950 N341TE HK-4772
951	32EP	Barents AirLink/Nordkalottflyg	G-31-951 N951AE VH-XFD SE-LNV
952	32EP	739 Flight Management	G-31-952 N952AE N569ST
953	32EP	Helitrans	G-31-953 (N953AE) N953LM VH-XFE (SE-LNX) UR-CET HA-LN-FAQ
954	3201	ex Quasar USA Inc	G-31-954 N342TE+ YV- [+ canx 03Dec08 to Venezuela; 14Feb09 Caracas, Venezuela still as N342TE]
955	3201	ex TWA Express	G-31-955 N343TE [wfu & stored Jun00 Kingman, AZ; l/n 13Nov07]
956	3202	(British Aerospace)	G-31-956 G-SUPR [w/o 06Oct92 Prestwick, UK; canx 21Jan93]
957	32EP	Pascan Aviation	G-31-957 N957AE C-GPSJ
958	32EP	Pascan Aviation	G-31-958 N958AE C-GPSK
959	32EP	ex Jetstream Sales	G-31-959 N959AE [stored 13Dec07 Smyrna, TN; l/n 05Nov11]
960	3202	Thailand Dept of Civil Aviation	G-31-960 G-BUDJ (N960AE) (HS-ASD) HS-DCA
961	32EP	Pascan Aviation	G-31-961 N961AE C-GPPS
962	32EP	ex Jet Acceptance Corp	G-31-962 N962AE [stored 08Jan08 Smyrna, TN; l/n 05Nov11]
963	32EP	Pascan Aviation	G-31-963 N963AE C-FPSI
964	32EP	Julian F Rodriguez, Venezuela	G-31-964 N964AE YV2536+ [+ marks not confirmed]
965	32EP	Transmandu	G-31-965 N965AE YV1116
966	32EP	ex J & E Aircraft Company	G-31-966 N966AE YV- [canx 20Jun08 to Venezuela]
967	32EP	Vincent Aviation	G-31-967 N967JS ZK-ECN VH-OTH ZK-VAH
968	32EP	ex Airwork Flight Operations	G-31-968 N968AE ZK-REW ZK-JSQ ZK-ECR+ EK- [+ canx 22Jun12 as exported]
969	32EP	Airwork Flight Operations	G-31-969 N969AE ZK-RES ZK-JSR ZK-ECJ
970	3206	Largus Aviation/Direktflyg	G-31-970 G-BUVC (F-OHFS) F-GLPY G-BUVC F-GMVP G-BUVC SE-LXE
971	3201	International Aircraft Systems	G-31-971 N971AE N971JX YR-KAA N971JX [stored 02Mar08 Kingman, AZ; by 05Feb09 in Angel Air c/s; l/n 06May10]
972	3201	(Professional Air Service)	G-31-972 N972AE N972JX (Z3-ASC) N972JX [stored by 05Dec08 Tamiami, FL; l/n 14Jun10; b/u by Jly11]
973	3201	Kavok Airlines	G-31-973 N973AE N973JX (Z3-ASB) YR-KAB N973JX YV2472
974	3202	Mid-Sea Express	G-31-974 (F-OHFT) G-BURU F-GMVH G-BURU VH-OTP RP-C863
975	3202	Aeropelican Air Services	G-31-975 (F-OHFU) G-BUTW F-GMVI G-BUTW VH-OTQ
976	3202	Vincent Aviation/Lite Flight	G-31-976 (F-OHFV) G-BUUZ F-GMVJ G-BUUZ VH-OTR ZK-LFW
977	3206	Largus Aviation/Direktflyg	G-31-977 (F-OHFW) (F-OHFR) G-BUVD F-GMVK G-BUVD SE-LXD
978	3202	Aeropelican Air Services	G-31-978 (F-OHFX) F-GMVL G-BZYP (YR-KAE) (SE-LJA) VH-OTD

BRITISH AEROSPACE JETSTREAM 31/32

C/n	Model	Last known Owner/Operator	Identities/fates/comments (where appropriate)
979	3206	(International Air Parts)	G-31-979 (F-OHFZ) F-GMVM G-CBEO [canx 08Jun07 sold in Australia for spares use]
980	3206	Aeropelican Air Services	G-31-980 F-GMVN G-CBEP (SE-LJB) VH-OTE
981	3217	Ernir Air	G-31-981 JA8865 OY-SVY TF-ORC
982	3206	Aeropelican Air Services	G-31-982 F-GMVO G-CBER (SE-LJC) VH-OTF
983	3206	Newcastle University	G-31-983 (F-GMVP) [delivered 27May04 from Woodford, UK ex Prestwick, UK store; at Rye Hill Campus, Newcastle upon Tyne, UK as GIA; l/n 13Aug08]
984	32xx	(BAE Systems)	G-31-984 [not delivered; b/u Jan98 Prestwick, UK]
985	3217	Sun-Air of Scandinavia	G-31-985 JA8591 OY-SVB
986	3217	Redstar Airlines	G-31-986 JA8590 G-CBDA TC-RSA
987	32xx		[on production line Nov93; not completed and b/u by 1995 at Prestwick, UK]
988	32xx		[on production line Nov93; not completed and b/u by 1995 at Prestwick, UK]

Unidentified

unkn	unknown	HH-KPS	[reported operational 15Apr10 Port-au-Prince, Haiti]
unkn	not reported	HI541	[reported Oct08 Tamiami, FL]
unkn	SARPA Colombia	HI854	[reported; no further details]
unkn	ACSA-Air Century	HI860	[reported 13Apr09 Punta Cana, Dominican Republic; posibly c/n 944]
unkn	unknown	HI867	[reported 14Aug12 Tamiami, FL]
unkn	SAPSA	HI875	[reported]
unkn	Volair Taxi	HI877	[reported 25May10 San Juan-Isla Grande, PR & 03Dec10 Tamiami, FL]
unkn	Aerolineas MAS	HI880	[reported 11Jun10 Oranjestad, Netherlands Antillies & 29Jan10 Port au Prince, Haiti]
unkn	not reported	HK-4382	[reported; no further details; possible misread of HK-4362?]
unkn	SARPA Colombia	HK-4384	[reported; no further details; possible misread of HK-4394?]
unkn	not reported	HR-AIO	[reported 14Apr11 Roatan, Honduras]
unkn	not reported	TG-SAT	[reported; no further details]
unkn	SACSA Servicios Aeronauticos	YV315T	[reported Tamiami, FL and 19Feb09 Porlamar, Venezuela]
unkn	not reported	YV-1134CP	[reported; no further details]
unkn	Transmandu	YV2272	[reported 07Feb11 Ciudad Bolivar, Venezuela]
unkn	Transmandu	YV2536	[reported 17Feb09 Porlamar, Venezuela]

Production complete

BRITISH AEROSPACE JETSTREAM 41

C/n	Model	Last known Owner/Operator	Identities/fates/comments (where appropriate)
41001	4100	(BAE Systems (Operations))	G-GCJL [prototype ff 25Sep91] [canx 15Nov02; taken by road Aug04 to Humberside Airport, UK for spares use by Eastern Airways; l/n 07Mar09]
41002	4100	(BAE Systems (Operations))	G-PJRT [stored Nov96 Prestwick, UK; canx 27Mar99; then stored Woodford, UK, until b/u]
41003	4100	(Jetstream Aircraft)	G-OXLI [dismantled Jun97 Prestwick, UK; fuselage to FR Aviation, Bournemouth-Hurn, UK for trials use; canx 31Jly97; l/n May99]
41004	4100	The Jetstream Club	G-JXLI G-JAMD G-JMAC [preserved Jan03 Liverpool Airport, Old Terminal, UK; canx 21May03; l/n 17Nov08]
41005	4100	Air Kilroe/Eastern Airways UK	G-LOGJ G-MAJC
41006	4100	Air Kilroe/Eastern Airways UK	G-WAWR G-MAJD
41007	4100	Air Kilroe/Eastern Airways UK	G-LOGK G-MAJE
41008	4100	Air Kilroe/Eastern Airways UK	G-WAWL G-MAJF
41009	4100	Air Kilroe/Eastern Airways UK	G-LOGL G-MAJG
41010	4100	Air Kilroe/Eastern Airways UK	G-WAYR G-MAJH
41011	4100	Air Kilroe/Eastern Airways UK	G-WAND G-MAJI
41012	4101	ex Kirland 41012 LLC	G-4-012 N301UE [stored by May08 Mena-Intermountain Municipal, AR; reported for spares use for Royal Star Aviation; l/n 10Apr10]
41013	4101	Royal Star Aviation	G-4-013 N302UE RP-C8298
41014	4100	Sky Express	G-4-014 OY-SVS G-MAJN G-ISAY SX-SEH
41015	4101	Eastern Airways UK	G-4-015 N303UE G-MAJW
41016	4101	(Atlantic Coast/United Express)	G-4-016 N304UE(1) [w/o 07Jan94 near Port Columbus, OH; canx 11Oct94]
41017	4101	Yeti Airlines	G-4-017 (N139MA) N304UE(2) N324UE G-CDYH 9N-AIB
41018	4101	Air Kilroe/Eastern Airways UK	G-4-018 (N140MA) G-BVKT G-MAJB G-MAJB
41019	4101	Air Kilroe/Eastern Airways UK	G-4-019 N305UE G-CDYI [stored Jun06 Humberside Airport, UK; l/n 11Sep08; to be used for spares; canx 02Jun09; restored 08Oct09]
41020	4101	RAVSA Airlines/Venezolana	G-4-020 N306UE+ YV- [+ canx 19Mar08 to Venezuela]
41021	4101	Milon Air LLC	G-4-021 N307UE
41022	4101	French Navy/AVDEF	G-4-022 N309UE XA- N309UE F-HAVD
41023	4101	Kirland 41023 LLC	G-4-023 N308UE N423KA
41024	4100	Air Kilroe/Eastern Airways UK	G-4-024 G-WAFT G-MAJJ
41025	4101	French Navy/AVDEF	G-4-025 N312UE F-HAVF
41026	4101	ex RAVSA Airlines/Venezolana	G-4-026 N313UE YV293T [by 09Apr10 stored Tamiami, FL; l/n 03Dec10]
41027	4101	ex RAVSA Airlines/Venezolana	G-4-027 N314UE YV280T [stored Tamiami, FL; l/n 22Jan11]
41028	4101	(Atlantic Coast A/L/United Express)	G-4-028 N310UE [w/o 01Jly02 Pittsburgh, PA, towed into hangar door; canx 24Jly02; to Washington-Dulles as GIA; Feb04 moved to Centreville, VA for fire training]
41029	4101	(A & W Aeronautics Services)	G-4-029 N311UE [stored by 13Nov06 Tamiami, FL; by 09Aug08 minus parts & on jacks still in old United Express c/s; wfu for parts, fuselage only by 01Mar09; l/n 04Jun09; gone by 09Apr10 b/u]
41030	4101	ex Acrecent Financial Corp	G-4-030 N410JA N680AS+ (N941H) HK- [stored 28Sep11 Smyma, TN; l/n 05Nov11; canx 24Jly12 to Colombia]
41031	4101	A & W Aeronautics Services	G-4-031 N317UE [stored by 13Nov06 Tamiami, FL; by 09Aug08 minus parts & on jacks still in old United Express c/s; wfu for parts, fuselage only by 01Mar09; l/n 18Feb11]
41032	4100	Air Kilroe/Eastern Airways	G-4-032 G-MAJA
41033	4101	ex RAVSA Airlines/Venezolana	G-4-033 N315UE YV283T [reported stored, location unknown]
41034	4100	ProFlight Zambia	G-4-034 VH-SMH G-BWIH N434JX G-MSKJ ZS-OMF
41035	4100	Midland Aviation/Airlink	G-4-035 VH-IMQ VH-JSX ZS-OMS
41036	4100	Midland Aviation/Airlink	G-4-036 VH-AFR G-BWIC N436JX VH-CCJ ZS-OMY [freighter]
41037	4100	ProFlight Zambia	G-4-037 HL5226 G-BWUI VH-CCW ZS-OMZ
41038	4101	FABCO Equipment	G-4-038 VH-IMR G-BWJF N438JX N514GP N410TJ N602FJ
41039	4100	Easyfly SA	G-4-039 (N502TS) N550HK G-MAJP HK-4775X
41040	4100	Sky Express	G-4-040 N551HK G-MAJT SX-SEC
41041	4101	(Bravo Aviation)	G-4-041 N318UE G-TEXA [reported for parts use at Inverness, UK; but canx 16May11 to Sweden]
41042	4101	Jet Finance Group	G-4-042 N319UE [stored 13Dec06 Smyrna, TN; l/n 05Nov11]
41043	4101	V1 Leasing	G-4-043 N320UE
41044	4100	LAM/Mocambique Expresso	G-4-044 VH-IMS (ZS-SUN) ZS-NUO C9-AUK
41045	4101	A & W Aeronautics Services	G-4-045 N321UE [stored by 13Nov06 Tamiami, FL; by 09Aug08 minus parts & on jacks still in old United Express c/s; wfu for parts, fuselage only by 01Mar09; l/n 18Feb11]
41046	4101	Air Jet	G-4-046 C-FTVI ZK-JSE N146KM D2-FHE
41047	4102	MCC Aviation	G-4-047 G-BVZC OY-SVW G-MAJO ZS-NOM
41048	4121	Midland Aviation/Airlink	G-4-048 ZS-NRE
41049	4112	Air Jet	G-4-049 C-FTVK ZK-JSK N149KM D2-FHF
41050	4121	Midland Aviation/Airlink	G-4-050 ZS-NRF

BRITISH AEROSPACE JETSTREAM 41

C/n	Model	Last known Owner/Operator	Identities/fates/comments (where appropriate)
41051	4121	Midland Aviation/Airlink	G-4-051 ZS-NRG
41052	4112	Nomic 177 (Pty) Ltd	G-4-052 C-FTVN ZK-JSM (SE-LJD) A3-XRH ZK-JSM ZS-JSM
41053	4112	Kirland 41053 LLC	G-4-053 C-FTVP ZK-JSN (SE-LJE) N153KM [stored by 20Jan08 Mena-Intermountain Municipal, AR; l/n 10Apr10]
41054	4121	Midland Aviation/Airlink	G-4-054 ZS-NRH
41055	4101	Agni Air	G-4-055 N316UE 9N-AIO
41056	4112	Northstar Aviation Services	G-4-056 C-FTVQ ZK-JSO (SE-LJF) N156KM N679AS [stored 20Jun08 Fort Lauderdale-Executive, FL; l/n 09Aug08]
41057	4101	Easyfly	G-4-057 N552HK HK-4568X HK-4568
41058	4101	Agni Air	G-4-058 N322UE 9N-AIP
41059	4101	(Atlantic Coast/United Express)	G-4-059 N323UE [w/o 29Dec00 Charlottesville-Albemarle Airport, VA; canx 03Dec01; by Nov02 fuselage to AIM Aviation, Bournemouth, UK; 09Aug03 taken away by road]
41060	4122	Royal Thai Army	G-4-060 G-BWGW 41060
41061	4121	Midland Aviation/Airlink	G-4-061 ZS-NRI
41062	4121	Midland Aviation/Airlink	G-4-062 ZS-NRJ
41063	4101	Jet Finance Group	G-4-063 N325UE [stored 13Sep05 Calgary, AB Canada; 30Jly08 ferried to Smyrna, TN; l/n 05Nov11]
41064	4101	Agni Air	G-4-064 N326UE 9N-AIQ
41065	4121	Swaziland Airlink	G-4-065 ZS-NRK
41066	4101	Yeti Airlines	G-4-066 N553HK 9N-AHY
41067	4101	Easyfly	G-4-067 N554HK HK-4585X
41068	4121	Midland Aviation/Airlink	G-4-068 ZS-NRL
41069	4121	(Midland Aviation/Airlink)	G-4-069 ZS-NRM [w/o 24Sep09 near Durban-Louis Botha Airport, South Africa; canx 27Sep10]
41070	4102	Air Kilroe/Eastern Airways	G-4-070 G-MAJK SX-SEB G-MAJK
41071	4101	Air Kilroe/Eastern Airways	G-4-071 N558HK G-MAJU
41072	4101	Yeti Airlines	G-4-072 N555HK 9N-AHU
41073	4101	Easyfly	G-4-073 N556HK HK-4584X [stored by Jun09 Bogota, Colombia]
41074	4101	Easyfly	G-4-074 N557HK G-MAJV HK-4765X
41075	4101	Sky Express	G-4-075 N559HK G-CEYV SX-DIA
41076	4101	Sky Express	G-4-076 N560HK G-CEYW SX-ROD
41077	4101	Yeti Airlines	G-4-077 N561HK 9N-AHV
41078	4101	Yeti Airlines	G-4-078 N562HK 9N-AHW
41079	4101	Easyfly	G-4-079 N563HK HK-4596X
41080	4101	Semirara Mining Corporation	G-4-080 N327UE RP-C8299
41081	4101	Corporate Flight Management	G-4-081 N564HK [stored by 31Oct09 Smyrna, TN; reported for Agni Air, Nepal]
41082	4101	Brindabella Airlines	G-4-082 N565HK N565EZ N565HK VH-TAI
41083	4101	Kirland 41083 LLC +	G-4-083 N328UE [+ on register as Kirland 41803 LLC, assumed in error; by May08 stored Mena-Intermountain Municipal, AR; reported for Royal Aviation; l/n 10Apr10]
41084	4101	Brindabella Airlines	G-4-084 N566HK VH-TAH
41085	4101	Yeti Airlines	G-4-085 N567HK 9N-AIH
41086	4101	Easyfly	G-4-086 N568HK HK-4522X HK-4522
41087	4102	Air Kilroe/Eastern Airways	G-4-087 G-MAJL
41088	4101	Corporate Flight Management	G-4-088 N569HK [stored Smyrna, TN; l/n 05Nov11]
41089	4101	Easyfly	G-4-089 N570HK G-CEFI N570HK HK-4551X HK-4551
41090	4101	Eastern SkyJets	G-4-090 N571HK G-CEDS A6-ESK
41091	4101	Easyfly	G-4-091 N572HK HK-4502X HK-4502
41092	4101	Easyfly	G-4-092 N573HK HK-4521X HK-4521
41093	4101	Easyfly	G-4-093 N574HK HK-4503X HK-4503
41094	4122	Royal Thai Army	G-4-094 G-BWTZ 41094
41095	4121	Air Jet	G-4-095 ZS-NYK D2-ENG
41096	4100	Yeti Airlines	G-4-096 G-MAJM 9N-AJC
41097	4101	Venezola	G-4-097 N329UE YV270T
41098	4101	Easyfly	G-4-098 N330UE G-MAJX HK-4786X
41099	4101	Eastern Airways	G-4-099 N331UE G-MAJY
41100	4101	Eastern Airways	G-4-100 N332UE G-MAJZ
41101	4101	Delbitur	G-4-101 N333UE CX-CAF
41102	4124	Hong Kong Government Services	G-4-102 G-BXWM B-HRS
41103	4101	Midland Aviation/Airlink	G-4-103 ZS-OEX
41104	4124	Hong Kong Government Services	G-4-104 G-BXWN B-HRT
41105	4103	(for Atlantic Coast Airlines)	[not completed; b/u unflown Jan98 Prestwick, UK; by Jun03 to Humberside Airport for spares use; l/n 07Mar09]

BRITISH AEROSPACE JETSTREAM 41

C/n	Model	Last known Owner/Operator	Identities/fates/comments (where appropriate)
41106	4103	(for Atlantic Coast Airlines)	[not completed – b/u Jan98 Prestwick; reported May98 to Woodford, UK until b/u Jan99; by 2008 nose preserved AeroVenture, Doncaster, UK]
41107	4103	(for Atlantic Coast Airlines)	[not built]
41108	4103	(for Atlantic Coast Airlines)	[not built]
41109	4103	(for Atlantic Coast Airlines)	[not built]
41110	4103	(for Atlantic Coast Airlines)	[not built]

Production complete

CANADAIR CL-44 and CC-106 YUKON

C/n	Model	Last known Owner/Operator	Identities/fates/comments (where appropriate)

Note: The CC-106 was the Canadair CL-44-6 and had the name Yukon whilst in Canadian service.

C/n	Model	Last known Owner/Operator	Identities/fates/comments (where appropriate)
1	CC-106	(Aerocondor Colombia)	15501+ 15921+ 106921+ CF-DSY YS-04C C-FDSY HK-1972 [prototype ff 15Nov59] [+ Canada] [w/o 22Feb75 Alto de Toledo, nr Medellin, Colombia]
2	CC-106	(TRAMACO)	15502+ 15922+ 106922+ 9Q-CWN [+ Canada] [wfu & stored 1978 Kinshasa, Zaire; b/u 13Oct84]
3	CC-106	(Aerolineas Nacionales del Ecuador)(Andes Airways)	15503+ 15923+ 106923+ CF-CHC HC-AYS [+ Canada] [wfu & stored Jan86 Guayaquil, Ecuador; still present Oct94; l/n Oct00; b/u 2001]
4	CC-106	(Aerotransportes Entre Rios)	15504+ 15924+ 106924+ LV-LBS [+ Canada] [wfu & stored in Sep78; b/u 1982 Buenos Aires-Ezeiza, Argentina]
5	CC-106	(Aerotransportes Entre Rios)	15505+ 15925+ 106925+ LV-PQL LV-JSY [+ Canada] [w/o 27Sep75 Miami International, FL]
6	CC-106	(Virunga Air Cargo)	15506+ 15926+ 106926+ LV-JZR OB-R-1005 9Q-CKQ [+ Canada] [wfu Dec83 Kinshasa, Zaire; b/u 1986]
7	CC-106	(Aerotransportes Entre Rios)	15507+ 15927+ 106927+ LV-JYR [+ Canada] [w/o 20Jly72 en-route Montevideo, Uruguay to Santiago, Chile]
8	CC-106	(Atlantida Linea Aerea Sudamericana) (ALAS)	15508+ 15928+ 106928+ LV-PRX LV-JZB CX-BKD [+ Canada] [w/o 10Oct79 Montevideo-Carrasco, Uruguay]
9	CL-44J	(Aer Turas)	CF-MKP-X TF-LLH EI-BGO [cvtd from CL44-D4; wfu 03Jan86 Dublin, Ireland & used for rescue training; b/u began 09Jun86; canx 18Sep86]
10	CC-106	(TRAMACO)	15509+ 15555+ 15929+ 106929+ C-GADY 9Q-CWS [+ Canada] [stored 1978 Kinshasa, Zaire; b/u 01Apr83]
11	CC-106	(Katale Aero Transport)	15510+ 15930+ 106930+ 9Q-CWK [+ Canada] [wfu Goma, Zaire Apr83; some reports state 11Oct85; b/u 1986/87]
12	CC-106	(Aeronaves del Peru)	15511+ 15931+ 106931+ C-GACH OB-R-1104 [+ Canada] [w/o 27Aug76 near Shanisu River, 640kms NE of Lima, Peru; en route Lima to Caracas, Venezuela]
13	CC-106	(Aerolineas Nacionales del Ecuador (Andes Airways))	15512+ 16666+ 15932+ 106932+ CF-JSN HC-AZH [+ Canada] [stored Jan86 Guayaquil, Ecuador; reported for preservation by Ecuadorian AF, but dismantled Nov09; fuselage moved to Cuenca, Ecuador for use as bar "Mayday"; l/n 27Oct10]
14	CL-44D4-1	(Aeroservicios Ecuatorianos CA)	CF-MYO-X N124SW (G-AWUD) TF-CLA TR-LWF HC-BHS [DBR 19Jan82 Miami, FL; b/u for spares Jan82]
15	CL-44D4-2	(Conroy Aircraft/Mobil Oil Corp)	N446T [w/o 01May69 Anchorage, AK]
16	CL-44-0	ex Johnson's Air	N447T EI-BND 4K-GUP (P4-GUP) 9G-LCA (N440CC) RP-C8023 [cvtd from CL-44D4-2 to Conroy CL-44-0; ff 26Nov69; arrived 31Dec02 Bournemouth, UK; test flew 18Apr03; not on end 2007 register; reported 26Jly10 wearing 9G-LCA again & being worked on; l/n 03Jly12]
17	CL-44D4-2	(Tradewinds Int'l A/L)	N448T G-AWWB VR-HHC G-AWWB N908L (N200TK) [wfu Feb93 Greensboro,NC; used for spares; b/u Mar95]
18	CL-44D4-2	(Tradewinds Int'l A/L)	N449T G-AXAA N122AE [wfu Apr94 Greensboro, NC; donated to airport fire dept; b/u 22Sep99; canx 27Sep99]
19	CL-44D4-2	(Bayu Indonesia Air)	CF-NBP-X N450T G-AZIN PK-BAW [wfu & derelict by 1989 Jakarta-Kemayoran, Indonesia; l/n Mar00; b/u 2003; airfield closed in 1985]
20	CL-44D4-2	(Affretair)	CF-NND-X N451T TF-LLJ OO-ELJ TR-LVO [DBF 05Feb82 Harare, Zimbabwe; b/u]
21	CL-44D4-2	(Transmeridian Air Cargo)	CF-NNE-X N452T G-ATZH+ XV196^ [+ in Mar72 initially painted at Southend, UK as G-AZHZ; ^ painted in these false marks for film; w/o 02Sep77 in sea off Kai Tak, Hong Kong; canx 07Dec77]
22	CL-44D4-2	(Flying Tiger Line)	N453T [w/o 21Mar66 nr NAS Norfolk, VA]
23	CL-44D4-1	(Bayu Indonesia Air)	CF-NNM-X N125SW G-AWDK PK-BAZ [derelict by 1989 Jakarta-Halim, Indonesia; still present Nov96; b/u by 2002]
24	CL-44D4-2	Africargo/Congo Government	N454T G-AXUL N104BB 9U-BHI 3C-ZPO [DBR 14Apr00 Kinshasa-N'Djili, Zaire by exploding munitions, together with TN-235 c/n 37]
25	CL-44D4-2	(Skymaster Freight Services)	N455T (G-ATZI) HB-IEN 5A-DHG 5A-DHJ N3951C 9Q-CQU N103BB EL-WLL TN-AFP 9Q-CTS [w/o 14Feb00 en-route Mbuji-Mayi to Kinshasa, Zaire, shortly after take-off; l/n Feb02]
26	CL-44D4-1	(Tradewinds Airways)	N126SW G-AWSC N126SW G-AWSC [w/o 22Dec74 Lusaka, Zambia; canx 28Feb75]
27	CL-44D4-1	(Wrangler Aviation Inc)	N127SW G-AWGS N127SW G-AWGS N907L [b/u 30Apr90 Dallas-Love Field, TX, for spares]

CANADAIR CL-44 and CC-106 YUKON

C/n	Model	Last known Owner/Operator	Identities/fates/comments (where appropriate)
28	CL-44D4-6	(Tradewinds Airways)	CF-NYC-X N602SA VP-LAT N62163 G-BCWJ [w/o 06Jly78 Nairobi-Wilson, Kenya]
29	CL-44D4-6	(Tradewinds Int'l Air Cargo)	N603SA N100BB [w/o 01Dec92 Aguadilla-Borinquen Airport, Puerto Rico; b/u during 1993; canx Jly95]
30	CL-44D4-1	(Cyprus Airways)	N123SW G-AWGT N123SW G-AWGT 5B-DAN [w/o 04Nov80 RAF Akrotiri, Cyprus]
31	CL-44D4-1	(Flying Tiger Line)	CF-OFH-X N228SW [w/o 24Dec66 Da Nang AFB, South Vietnam]
32	CL-44D4-1	(Jamahiriya Air Transport)	N229SW G-AWOV N429SW G-AWOV HB-IEO 5A-DGE [wfu & stored Nov80 Tripoli-Ben Gashir, Libya; reported DBR 15Apr86 in US air raid; reported there 11Nov02 by KLM crew; subsequently b/u; gone by 2007]
33	CL-44D4-6	(Transporte Aereo Rioplatense)	N604SA LV-JZM [wfu & stored May80 Buenos Aires-Ezeiza, Argentina; b/u late 1991]
34	CL-44D4-6	(Transporte Aereo Rioplatense)	N605SA LV-JTN (CX-BML) LV-JTN [shot down 18Jly81 50kms from Yerevan, Armenia, USSR]
35	CL-44J	(Heavylift Cargo Airlines)	CF-PBG-X TF-LLF N4993U 5A-CVB 5A-DGJ 9Q-CQS EI-BRP [cvtd from CL-44D-8 to CL-44J prototype ff 08Nov65; wfu & stored 17Nov90 Southend, UK; b/u Apr92 to Aug92]
36	CL-44J	(Cargolux)	TF-LLG [cvtd from CL-44D4-8; w/o 02Dec70 Dacca, Bangladesh]
37	CL-44D4-2	(Government of Congo)	CF-PZZ-X N1001T G-AZKJ G-BRED N106BB EL-AMC 7Q-YMS (TN-235) TN-AFC+ [+ marks reported but not confirmed; DBR 14Apr00 Kinshasa-N'Djili, Zaire by exploding munitions, together with 3C-ZPO c/n 24]
38	CL-44D4-2	(City Connections/Africargo)	CF-RSL-X N1002T G-AZML N121AE "EL-WLM"+ [b/u 22Sep99 Greensboro, NC, by United Metals; + these marks were allocated after b/u had started]
39	CL-44J	(Atlantida Linea Aerea Sudamericana Colombia)	CF-SEE-X CF-SEE TF-LLI CX-BJV N4998S HK-3148X [w/o 06Jly88 Barranquilla, Colombia; canx 23Jan89]

Production complete

CANADAIR CL-215/CL-215T

C/n	Model	Last known Owner/Operator	Identities/fates/comments (where appropriate)

Note: The piston-powered CL-215 aircraft have been included for completeness.

1001		(Securite Civile)	CF-FEU-X F-ZBBR [prototype ff 23Oct67; code 01; w/o 04Aug83 Marseille, France]
1002		Province of Newfoundland & Labrador	CF-PQQ-X CF-YWP C-FYWP [code 285]
1003		Province of Saskatchewan	CF-PQD-X CF-YWO C-FYWO [code 214]
1004		SOREM/Protezione Civile	CF-PQH CF-YWQ C-FYWQ 9A-CAB 822+ C-FYWQ I-SRMA [code A1] [+ Croatia]
1005		(Securite Civile)	CF-PQJ-X CF-YWN F-ZBBE [code 05] [wfu & b/u; nose preserved Musee de L'Hydraviation, Biscarrosse, France]
1006		Province of Newfoundland & Labrador	(CF-PQN) CF-TXA C-FTXA [code 284]
1007		THK Turk Hava Kurumu	CF-PQR CF-TXB C-FTXB+ TC-TKJ [+ code 298]
1008		Buffalo Airways	(CF-PQI) CF-TXC C-FTXC N215NC C-GNCS
1009		Province of Saskatchewan	CF-PQN CF-YXG C-FYXG [code 215]
1010		Museo del Aire	CF-TXD EC-BXM UD.13-01 [code 43-01] [preserved Cuatro Vientos, Madrid, Spain]
1011		Air Spray (1967) Ltd/THK	CF-PQH CF-TUU C-FTUU+ TC-TKL [+ code 208]
1012		SOREM/Protezione Civile	(CF-PQQ) CF-TXE C-FTXE 9A-CAC 833+ C-FTXE I-SRMB [code A2] [+ Croatia]
1013		(Spanish Air Force)	CF-TXF EC-BXN UD.13-02 [code 413-02] [w/o 02Mar81 unknown location in Spain]
1014		Province of Quebec	CF-TXG C-FTXG [code 228]
1015		(Greek Air Force)	CF-TXH+ 1015 [+ ntu?] [w/o 09Mar84 Elefsis, Greece]
1016		Province of Manitoba	CF-TXI C-FTXI [code 255]
1017		Province of Quebec	CF-TXJ C-FTXJ [code 230]
1018		Province of Quebec	CF-TXK C-FTXK [code 231]
1019		(Securite Civile)	CF-TXM+ F-ZBBM [+ ntu?] [code 19] [w/o 25Jly73 Bastia, France]
1020		Province of Manitoba	CF-TUV C-FTUV [code 256]
1021		Technik Museum Speyer	F-ZBAR [code 21] [preserved Speyer, Germany; l/n Feb08]
1022		(Securite Civile)	CF-YAZ F-ZBAX [code 22] [w/o 04Jly70 off Corsica, France]
1023		Musee de l'Air et de L'Espace	CF-TUW F-ZBAY [code 23] [preserved Paris-Le Bourget, France; as of Mar08 in Dugny store]
1024		Securite Civile	F-ZBBD [code 24] [stored Marseille-Marignane, France]
1025		(Securite Civile)	F-ZBBG [code 25] [w/o 03Sep71 Golfe de Sagone, France]
1026		Auto und Technik Museum	F-ZBBH [code 26] [preserved Sinsheim, Germany; l/n Apr08]
1027		THK Turk Hava Kurumu	F-ZBBI C-GFNF+ TC-TKM [+ code 299]
1028		(Securite Civile)	F-ZBBJ [code 28] [stored by 26Jly04 Marseille-Marignane, France; b/u 2005]
1029		(Securite Civile)	F-ZBBD [code 29] [stored then b/u Marseille-Marignane, France; nose preserved Musee St Victoret, France; l/n 19May08]
1030		Air Spray (1967) Ltd/THK	CF-TUW C-FTUW+ TC-TKK [+ code 209]
1031	T	CEGISA	CF-HNX-X UD.13-03 EC-957 EC-GBP
1032		(Spanish Air Force)	UD.13-04 [w/o 09Sep88 off Santiago de Compostela, Spain; hulk l/n Mar93 Albacete, Spain]
1033	T	CEGISA	UD.13-05 EC-958 EC-GBQ
1034		CEGISA	UD.13-06 I-SISB EC-HET
1035		(Spanish Air Force)	UD.13-07 [w/o 08Sep76 off Santiago de Compostela, Spain]
1036		(Spanish Air Force)	UD.13-08 [w/o 11Apr77 Valencia, Spain]
1037		(Spanish Air Force)	UD.13-09 [w/o 07Mar77 San Sebastian, Spain]
1038		CEGISA	UD.13-10 I-SISC EC-HEU
1039		Greek Air Force	1039
1040		Canadian Bushplane Heritage Centre	F-ZBBT [code 40] [preserved Sault Ste Marie, ON, Canada with false marks CF-GVM]
1041		Greek Air Force	C-GAJN 1041
1042		(Greek Air Force)	C-GAZX 1042 [w/o 26May77 Loutraki, Greece]
1043		Greek Air Force	1043
1044		Province of Manitoba	C-GUMW C-GMAF [code 250]
1045		Greek Air Force	1045
1046		Association un Canadair pour Saint-Victoret	C-GAOS+ F-ZBBV^ [+ ntu?] [code 46] [wfu 24May96; preserved near Marseille Airport, France]
1047		Conservatoire de l'Air et de l'Espace	F-ZBBW [code 47] [wfu 24May96; preserved Bordeaux-Merignac, France; l/n 17Jun08 – carries no regn]
1048		(Greek Air Force)	1048 [w/o 15Jly00 Argalasti mountain, near Athens, Greece]

CANADAIR CL-215/CL-215T

C/n	Model	Last known Owner/Operator	Identities/fates/comments (where appropriate)
1049		(SOREM/Protezione Civile)	C-GUKM I-SRME [code S4] [w/o 04Oct07 Lake Terkos, near Istanbul, Turkey]
1050		(Greek Air Force)	C-GUMW 1050 [w/o 18Jly78 unknown location in Greece]
1051	T	CEGISA	C-GUMW UD.13-11+ EC-983 EC-GBR [+code 413-11?]
1052	T	CEGISA	(C-GVNS) UD.13-12+ EC-984 EC-GBS [+code 413-12?]
1053		(Spanish Air Force)	(C-GVWX) UD.13-13 [code 431-13; w/o 12Dec80 off Beniarres, Spain]
1054	T	CEGISA	C-GUBI UD.13-14 + EC-985 EC-GBT [+code 413-14?]
1055		Greek Air Force	1055
1056	T	Spanish Air Force	UD.13-15 [code 431-15; circa 2000/02 reported used serial UD.13T-15 & code 43-15]
1057	T	Spanish Air Force	UD.13-16 [code 43-16; circa 2000/02 may have used serial UD.13T-16]
1058		Royal Thai Navy	231 2204 2103 [stored U-Tapao, Thailand; l/n 17May06; by Oct09 preserved Royal Thai Navy Museum, Thailand]
1059		Royal Thai Navy	232 2205 2104 [stored U-Tapao, Thailand]
1060		Greek Air Force	C-GUMW 1060
1061	T	Spanish Air Force	(C-GUKM) UD.13-17 [code 431-17; circa 2000/02 may have used serial UD.13T-17]
1062		ex CVG Ferrominera Orinoco	C-GVXD YV-O-CFO-5 YV-O-INC-1 [stored Puerto Ordaz Airport, Venezuela; l/n Sep11]
1063		(CVG Ferrominera Orinoco)	C-GVXG YV-O-CFO-6 YV-O-INC-2 [w/o 22Aug89 Puerto Ordaz Airport, Venezuela]
1064		(Greek Air Force)	1064 [w/o 22Aug93 Ano Rodini, near Patras, Greece]
1065		Province of Manitoba	C-GUMW [code 251]
1066		(Yugoslav Air Force)	C-GKDC 74225+ 72201 [+ Yugoslavia] [w/o 11Jly84 Zadar, Croatia]
1067		Greek Air Force	C-GKDE 74226+ 72202+ YU-BRE 1067 [+ Yugoslavia]
1068		Province of Manitoba	C-GYJB [code 252]
1069		Greek Air Force	C-GKDH 74227+ 72203+ YU-BRF 1069 [+ Yugoslavia]
1070		Greek Air Force	C-GKDL 74228+ 72204+ YU-BRG 1070 [+ Yugoslavia]
1071		(Societa Italiana Servizi Aerei Mediterranea)	C-GKDN I-CFSQ MM62018 I-CFSS [w/o 27Jan89 Quiliana-Vado Ligure, Italy]
1072		THK Turk Hava Kurumu	C-GKDP I-CFSR MM62019 I-CFST+ TC-TKV [+ code S5]
1073		Greek Air Force	C-GKDT 1073
1074		(Societa Italiana Servizi Aerei Mediterranea)	C-GKDV MM62023 I-CFSU [code 2] [w/o 30Jly96 lake near Palermo, Italy]
1075		(Greek Air Force)	C-GKDY 1075 [w/o 15Jly92 Saronic Gulf, Greece; nose section preserved Elefsis,Greece]
1076		THK Turk Hava Kurumu	C-GKEA C-GBXQ I-SRMC+ TC-TKZ^ [+ code S2] [^ code 7; Nov11 pained with fake serial "XP2112" for a film]
1077		(Societa Italiana Servizi Aerei Mediterranea)	C-GKEC MM62024+ I-CFSV^ [+code 15-54; ^ code 3; w/o 06Auq91 Piana Crixia, Savona, Italy]
1078		(Canadair Limited)	C-GKEE [w/o 29Sep83 Montreal-Dorval, QC, Canada]
1079		(Spanish Air Force)	C-GBCE UD.13-18 [code 432-18] [w/o 03Feb87 San Juan, near Madrid, Spain]
1080	T	Spanish Air Force	UD.13-19 [code 43-19; circa 2000/02 may have used serial UD.13T-19]
1081		Aero Flite/Minnesota Dept of Natural Resources	C-GKDN C-GDRS N262NR [code 262]
1082		Aero Flite/Minnesota Dept of Natural Resources	C-GKDP C-GENU N263NR
1083		Buffalo Airways/Legislature of Northwest Territories	C-GKEA C-GBYU [code 290]
1084		Buffalo Airways/Legislature of Northwest Territories	C-GBPD [code 291]
1085		Conair Group/Province of Alberta	C-GKDN C-GFSK [code 201]
1086	T	Conair Group/Province of Alberta	C-GKDP C-GFSL [code 202]
1087		Province of Manitoba	C-GKDY C-GBOW [code 253]
1088		Buffalo Airways/Legislature of Northwest Territories	C-GKEA C-GCSX [code 295]
1089		Buffalo Airways/Legislature of Northwest Territories	C-GKEE C-GDHN [code 296]
1090		A F I Leasing Inc	C-GOFM N264V [probably operated by Minnesota Dept of Natural Resources]
1091		(Province of Quebec)	C-GFQA [code 236] [w/o 19Jun91 Chute-Des-Passes, QC, Canada]
1092		Province of Quebec	C-GKDP C-GFQB [code 237]
1093		Province of Saskatchewan	C-GKDY C-FAFN [code 216]
1094		Province of Saskatchewan	C-GKBO C-FAFO [code 217]
1095		Buffalo Airways	C-GDKW [code 280]
1096		Korea Business Air Services	C-GDKY+ HL2036 [+ code 281]
1097		THK Turk Hava Kurumu	C-GOFN I-SRMD+ TC-TKT [+ code S3]
1098	T	Conair Group/Province of Alberta	C-GFSM [code 203]

CANADAIR CL-215/CL-215T

C/n	Model	Last known Owner/Operator	Identities/fates/comments (where appropriate)
1099		Conair Group/Province of Alberta	C-GFSN [code 204]
1100	T	Province of Saskatchewan	C-GKEA C-FAFP [code 218]
1101	T	Province of Saskatchewan	C-GKEE C-FAFQ [code 219]
1102		Minnesota Dept of Natural Resources	C-GOFO N266NR [code 266]
1103		A F I Leasing Inc/Aero Flite	C-GOFP N267V [code 267] [probably operated by Minnesota Dept of Natural Resources]
1104		THK Turk Hava Kurumu	C-GOFR+ TC-TKH [+ code 268]
1105		Buffalo Airways	C-FAYN [code 282]
1106		Buffalo Airways	C-FAYU [code 283]
1107		Province of Manitoba	C-GMAK [code 254]
1108		THK Turk Hava Kurumu	C-FFYO I-CFSZ+ TC-TKY [+ code S6]
1109	T	Spanish Air Force	UD.13-22 [code 43-22; circa 2000/02 may have used serial UD.13T-22]
1110		Greek Air Force	C-GDAT 72301+ 72205+ YU-BRH 1110 [+ Yugoslavia]
1111		Greek Air Force	C-GKEA 1111
1112		(Greek Air Force)	C-GKON 1112 [w/o 06Jly06 off Patroklos Island, Greece; wreck to Elefsis, Greece & stored; l/n 06Jun06]
1113	T	Spanish Air Force	C-GDRQ UD.13-20 [code 43-20; circa 2000/02 may have used serial UD.13T-20]
1114	T	Province of Quebec	C-GKEX 1114 + C-FASE [+ Greece] [code 238]
1115	T	Province of Quebec	1115 + C-FAWQ [+Greece] [code 239]
1116	T	Spanish Air Force	C-FFDN UD-13-21 [code 43-21; circa 2000/02 may have used serial UD.13T-21]
1117	T	Spanish Air Force	C-FFDO UD.13-23 [code 43-23; circa 2000/02 reported used serial UD.13T-23]
1118	T	Spanish Air Force	UD.13-24 [code 43-24; circa 2000/02 may have used serial UD.13T-24]
1119	T	Spanish Air Force	UD.13-25 [code 43-25; circa 2000/02 may have used serial UD.13T-25]
1120	T	Spanish Air Force	UD.13-26 [code 43-26; circa 2000/02 may have used serial UD.13T-26]
1121	T	Spanish Air Force	C-GKEA C-FIKS UD.13-27 [code 43-27; circa 2000/02 may have used serial UD.13T-27]
1122	T	Spanish Air Force	C-GKEI C-FIKT UD.13-28 [code 43-28; circa 2000/02 may have used serial UD.13T-28]
1123		Greek Air Force	1123
1124	T	(Spanish Air Force)	C-GKEV UD.13-29 [code 43-29; circa 2000/02 may have used serial UD.13T-29; w/o 25Mar03 off Mallorca, Spain; wreck to fire dump Albacete-Los Llanos, Spain; l/n 08May05]
1125	T	Spanish Air Force	UD.13-30 [code 43-30; circa 2000/02 may have used serial UD.13T-30]

Production complete

CANADAIR CL-415

C/n	Model	Last known Owner/Operator	Identities/fates/comments (where appropriate)				
CL-415							
2001		Securite Civile	C-GSCT	F-ZBFS	[prototype f/f 06Dec93]	[code 32]	
2002		Securite Civile	C-FBET	F-ZBFP	[code 31]		
2003		SOREM/Protezione Civile	C-FBPM	C-FTUA	I-DPCD	[code 7]	
2004		SOREM/Protezione Civile	C-GDPU	C-FTUS	I-DPCE	[code 8]	
2005		Province of Quebec	C-GKDN	C-GQBA	[code 240]		
2006		Securite Civile	C-GKDP	C-FVUK	F-ZBFN	[code 33]	
2007		Securite Civile	C-GKDY	C-FVUJ	F-ZBFX	[code 34]	
2008		SOREM/Protezione Civile	C-GKEA	C-FUAK	I-DPCN	[code 9]	[w/o 16Aug03 near Esine, Italy]
2009		SOREM/Protezione Civile	C-GKEE	C-FVRA	I-DPCO	[code 10]	
2010		Securite Civile	C-GKEO	C-FVDY	F-ZBFY	[code 35]	
2011		(Securite Civile)	C-GKEQ	C-FWPD	F-ZBEO	[code 36]	[w/o 01Aug05 near Caalvi, Corsica, France]
2012		Province of Quebec	C-GKET	C-GQBC	[code 241]		
2013		Securite Civile	C-GKEV	C-FWPE	F-ZBFV	[code 37]	
2014		Securite Civile	C-GKEX	C-FWZH	F-ZBFW	[code 38]	
2015		Securite Civile	C-GBPM	C-FXBH	F-ZBEG	[code 39]	
2016		Province of Quebec	C-GBPU	C-GQBD	[code 242]		
2017		Province of Quebec	C-GKEA	C-GQBE	[code 243]		
2018		(Securite Civile)	C-GKEO	C-FXBX	F-ZBEZ	[code 41]	[w/o 08Mar04 Lac Sainte Croix, France]
2019		Province of Quebec	C-FVKV	C-GQBF	[code 244]		
2020		SOREM/Protezione Civile	C-FVLU	C-FYCY	I-DPCP	[code 11]	
2021		SOREM/Protezione Civile	C-FVKW	C-FYDA	I-DPCQ	[code 12]	
2022		Province of Quebec	C-FVLW	C-GQBG	[code 245]		
2023		Province of Quebec	C-FVLI	C-GQBI	[code 246]		
2024		Securite Civile	C-FVLZ	C-FZDE	F-ZBEU	[code 42]	
2025		(Securite Civile)	C-FVLM	C-FZDK	F-ZBFQ	[code 43]	[w/o 17Nov97 off Marseille, France]
2026		Province of Quebec	C-FVLY	C-GQBK	[code 247]		
2027		Croatian Air Force	C-FVLQ	C-FZQZ	9A-CAG	844	
2028		Province of Ontario	C-FVLX	C-GAOI	C-GOGD	[code 270]	
2029		SOREM/Protezione Civile	C-GKDN	C-FZYS	I-DPCT	[code 18]	
2030		SOREM/Protezione Civile	C-GKDP	C-GALV	I-DPCU	[code 14]	
2031		Province of Ontario	C-GKDY	C-GAUR	C-GOGE	[code 271]	
2032		Province of Ontario	C-GKEE	C-GBGE	C-GOGF	[code 272]	
2033		Province of Ontario	C-GKEQ	C-GBFY	C-GOGG	[code 273]	
2034		Province of Ontario	C-GKET	C-GCNO	C-GOGH	[code 274]	
2035		SOREM/Protezione Civile	C-GKEV	C-GCXG	(I-DPCR)	I-DPCV	[code 15]
2036		SOREM/Protezione Civile	C-GKEX	C-GDHW	(I-DPCS)	I-DPCW	[code 16]
2037		Province of Ontario	C-GBPM	C-GOGW	[code 275]		
2038		Province of Ontario	C-GBPU	C-GOGX	[code 276]		
2039	GR	Greek Air Force	C-GELJ	2039			
2040		Province of Quebec	C-GOGY	[code 277]			
2041		Croatian Air Force	C-GEUN	(2041) +	9A-CAH	855	[+ Greece]
2042	GR	Greek Air Force	C-GFBX	2042			
2043		Province of Ontario	C-GOGZ	[code 278]			
2044	GR	Greek Air Force	C-GFOJ	2044			
2045		(SOREM/Protezione Civile)	C-GFPX	I-DPCX	[code 19]	[w/o 23Jly07 near Sant Erasmo, Italy]	
2046		Croatian Air Force	C-GFRQ	9A-CAI	866		
2047		SOREM/Protezione Civile	C-GFUS	I-DPCY	[code 20]		
2048		SOREM/Protezione Civile	C-GFRQ	C-GGCW	I-DPCZ	[code 21]	
2049	GR	Greek Air Force	C-GGIF	2049			
2050	GR	Greek Air Force	C-GGMZ	2050			
2051		(SOREM/Protezione Civile)	C-GHGV	I-DPCK	[code 22]	[w/o 18Mar05 Versilia, Italy]	
2052	GR	Greek Air Force	C-GHMP	2052			
2053	GR	Greek Air Force	C-GHRX	2053			
2054	GR	Greek Air Force	C-GHVB	2054			
2055	MP	(Greek Air Force)	C-GHVX	2055	[w/o 23Jly07 near Dilesos, Greece]		
2056	MP	Greek Air Force	C-GIFE	2056			
2057		Securite Civile	C-GILN	F-ZBME	[code 44]		
2058		SOREM/Protezione Civile	C-GISM	I-DPCI	[code 26]		
2059		SOREM/Protezione Civile	C-GIWU	I-DPCF	[code 23]		
2060		SOREM/Protezione Civile	C-GJHU	I-DPCG	[code 24]		

CANADAIR CL-415

C/n	Model	Last known Owner/Operator	Identities/fates/comments (where appropriate)		
2061		Croatian Air Force	C-GJKZ	877	
2062		SOREM/Protezione Civile	C-GJLB	I-DPCH	[code 25]
2063		Securite Civile	C-FGZT	F-ZBMF	[code 45]
2064		Spanish Air Force	C-FIFG	UD.14-01	[code 43-31]
2065		Securite Civile	C-FLFW	F-ZBMG	[code 48]
2066		SOREM/Protezione Civile	C-FNLH	I-DPCC	[code 27]
2067		Spanish Air Force	C-FQWA	UD.14-02	[code 43-32]
2068	MP	Malaysian Maritime Enforcement Agency	C-FTBZ	M71-01	
2069		Spanish Air Force	C-FUDY	UD.14-03	[code 43-33]
2070		SOREM/Protezione Civile	C-FUEP	I-DPCN	[code 28]
2071	MP	Bombardier Inc	C-FWLK	[for Malaysian Maritime Enforcement Agency as M71-02]	
2072		Croatian Air Force	C-FYOL	888	
2073		SOREM/Protezione Civile	C-FZEG	I-DPCS	[code 29; later code 30]
2074		SOREM/Protezione Civile	C-FZTY	I-DPCR	[code 31]
2075		Croatian Air Force	C-GCUH	811	
2076		Province of Newfoundland & Labrador	C-GDMI	C-FIZU	[code 286]
2077		Province of Newfoundland & Labrador	C-FNJC	[code 287]	
2078		Province of Manitoba	C-GMFY	[code 257]	
2079		Moroccan Air Force	C-GISO	CN-ATM	[code TM]
2080		Moroccan Air Force	C-GKCX	CN-ATN	[code TN]
2081		Province of Newfoundland & Labrador	C-FOFI	[code 288]	
2082		Pronvince of Manitoba	C-GMFW	[code 258]	
2083		Pronvince of Manitoba	C-GMFX		
2084		Province of Newfoundland & Labrador	C-FIGJ		
2085		Bombardier Inc	C-GOJS		
2086		Bombardier Inc	C-GMFZ		
2087					
2088					
2089					
2090					
2091					
2092					
2093					
2094					
2095					
2096					
2097					
2098					
2099					
2100					

CASA/NURTANIO C-212 AVIOCAR

Notes: Spanish Air Force codes follow the serial after double forward slashes.
The c/ns of most CASA built aircraft are prefixed by a customer code followed by a sequential number for the customer concerned.
Line numbers, as shown, were allocated to aircraft assembled in Indonesia by IPTN, now known as P T Dirgantara.

C/n	Line No.	Model	Last known Owner/Operator	Identities/fates/comments (where appropriate)
P1		100	Spanish Air Force	XT.12A-1//54-10 [prototype ff 26Mar71]
P2		100	(Spanish Air Force)	XT.12-2//54-12 [w/o 12Mar98 La Cisterniga, near Villanubla, Spain]
B-1-1		100	Museo del Aire	TR.12A-3//403-01 [wfu Jun99; preserved Cuatro Vientos, Spain]
B-2-2		100	Spanish Air Force	TR.12A-4//403-02 [by Oct05 stored Cuatro Vientos, Spain; l/n Oct09]
B-3-3		100	Spanish Air Force	TR.12A-5//403-03 [stored Jly08 Cuatro Vientos, Spain; l/n Oct09]
B-4-4		100	Spanish Air Force	TR.12A-6//403-04 [stored Oct09 Cuatro Vientos, Spain]
B-5-5		100	ex Spanish Air Force	TR.12A-7//403-05 [wfu Nov99; stored Matacan AFB, Salamanca, Spain; to be used as monument]
B-6-6		100	Spanish Air Force	TR.12A-8//403-06 [by Apr08 stored no engines Cuatro Vientos, Spain; l/n Oct09]
E-1-7		100	Spanish Air Force	TE.12B-9//79-91 T.12B-9//74-83 [stored Mar09 Cuatro Vientos, Spain; l/n Oct09]
E-2-8		100	Spanish Air Force	TE.12B-10//79-92 TE.12B-10//74-85 [stored Seville-San Pablo, Spain; l/n 23Nov10]
TC15-1-9		100	(Medavia)	EC-101 EC-CRV 9H-AAP [wfu for spares; canx Jun12]
TC9-1-10		100	(Eupari Boogie Performance)	EC-102 EC-CRX TC-AOS (F-GOBP) F-GOPB [w/o 22Jun99 La Garenne, France]
A1-1-11		100	(Spanish Air Force)	T.12B-11//461-11 [w/o 01Jun76 Getafe, Madrid, Spain]
A1-2-12		100	ex Spanish Air Force	T.12B-14//46-30 T.12B-14//37-01 [wfu; stored Apr02 Cuatro Vientos, Spain; by Sep05 in use as GIA; by Nov07 reported preserved; l/n 25Apr09]
A1-3-13		100	Portuguese Air Force	6501+ 16501 [+ Portugal] [stored Beja, Alentejo, Portugal; l/n Jun05]
A1-4-14		100	Portuguese Air Force	6502+ 16502 [+ Portugal] [stored Beja, Alentejo, Portugal; l/n Jun05]
A1-5-15		100	(Spanish Air Force)	T.12B-15//37-02 [wfu since 20Oct06; displayed Villanubla AFB, Valladolid, Spain]
A1-6-16		100	ex Spanish Air Force	T.12B-12//74-82 [stored Aug07 Cuatro Vientos, Spain; Jly11 for preservation]
A1-7-17		100	Portuguese Air Force	6503+ 16503 [+ Portugal]
A1-8-18		100	ex Portuguese Air Force	6504+ 16504 [+ Portugal] [wfu Dec11]
A1-9-19		100	Spanish Air Force	T.12B-13//74-70 T.12B-13//72-01
A1-10-20		100	Spanish Air Force	T.12B-16//74-71 [stored by Nov07 Cuatro Vientos, Spain; l/n Oct09]
A1-11-21		100	Spanish Air Force	T.12B-17//37-03 [stored by Nov07 Cuatro Vientos, Spain; l/n Oct09]
A1-12-22		100	East Horizon	T.12B-18//46-31+ YA-EH02 [+ Spain]
A1-13-23		100	Colombian Army	T.12B-19//46-32+ EJC-122^ EJC-065# [+ Spain] [^ Colombia] [# also reported as EJC1122]
A1-14-24		100	Spanish Air Force	T.12B-20//37-04 T.12B-20//72-01 [stored Nov07 Cuatro Vientos, Spain; l/n Oct09]
A2-1-25		100	ex Portuguese Air Force	6505+ 16505 [+ Portugal] [wfu Dec11]
A2-2-26		100	Portuguese Air Force	6506+ 16506 [+ Portugal] [stored by 14Jly08 Sintra, Portugal]
A1-15-27		100	Spanish Air Force	T.12B-21//37-05 T.12B-21//46-05
A2-3-28		100	Portuguese Air Force	6507+ 16507 [+ Portugal] [stored by 14Jly08 Sintra, Portugal; reported for preservation]
A2-4-29		100	Portuguese Air Force	6508+ 16508 [+ Portugal] [stored by May09 Sintra, Portugal]
A1-16-30		100	ex Spanish Air Force	T.12B-22//37-06 T.12B-22//72-02 [stored by Oct10 Cuatro Vientos, Spain]
A1-17-31		100	East Horizon	T.12B-23//72-01+ YA-EH03 [+ Spain]
A2-5-32		100	Portuguese Air Force	6509+ 16509 [+ Portugal] [stored Jly08 Sintra, Portugal; by Aug10 at Montijo, Portugal]
A2-6-33		100	ex Portuguese Air Force	6510+ 16510 [+ Portugal] [wfu Dec11]
C4-1-34	1N	100	Pelita Air Services	PK-PCK PK-PCZ
A2-7-35		100	Portuguese Air Force	6511+ 16511 [+ Portugal] [stored Beja, Alentejo, Portugal; l/n Jun05]
A2-8-36		100	Portuguese Air Force	6512+ 16512 [+ Portugal] [stored by Aug10 Montijo, Portugal]
A2-9-37		100	Portuguese Air Force	6513+ 16513 [+ Portugal] [stored by Aug10 Montijo, Portugal]
A2-10-38		100	Portuguese Air Force	6514+ 16514 [+ Portugal] [dismantled Lajes, Azores, Portugal; by 21Sep10 shipped Beja AFB for storage]
C4-2-39	2N	100	Pelita Air Services	PK-PCL PK-PCY

CASA/NURTANIO C-212 AVIOCAR

C/n	Line No.	Model	Last known Owner/Operator	Identities/fates/comments (where appropriate)
A1-18-40		100	ex Spanish Air Force	T.12B-24//37-07 T.12B-24//54-12 [wfu Jun06; stored Aug07 Cuatro Vientos, Spain; Jly11 for preservation]
A2-11-41		100	Portuguese Air Force	6515+ 16515 [+ Portugal] [stored by Jun05 Lajes, Azores, Portugal; l/n Jun05; dismantled by 21Sep10 for shipment to mainland Portugal for further storage possibly at Beja AFB]
A1-20-42		100	Spanish Air Force	T.12B-26//72-02 [stored by Nov07 Cuatro Vientos, Spain; l/n Oct09]
A1-19-43		100	ex Spanish Air Force	T.12B-25//74-72 [preserved by Mar08 Matacan AFB, Salamanca, Spain]
A3-1-44		100	(Royal Jordanian Air Force)	123+ 323 [+ Jordan] [DBR 1977 after hangar collapse; location unknown]
C4-3-45	3N	100	(Pelita Air Services)	PK-XCX PK-XCE PK-PCX [w/o 23Jan80 Sangga Buana, Indonesia]
A1-21-46		100	Colombian Army	T.12B-27//46-33+ EJC-123 EJC-066^ EJC-1123 [+ Spain; ^ Colombia]
A2-12-47		100	(Portuguese Air Force)	6516 [w/o 19Nov76, flew into mountain in Portugal]
A1-22-48		100	Spanish Air Force	T.12B-28//72-03
A2-13-49		100	ex Portuguese Air Force	6517+ 16517 [+ Portugal] [wfu Dec11]
A2-14-50		100	(Portuguese Air Force)	6518 [w/o 05Jly78 location unknown]
A1-23-51		100	Spanish Air Force	T.12B-29//37-08 [damaged 09Sep05 Gerona Airport, Spain; status uncertain]
A3-2-52		100	ex Southeast Jet Group	124+ 324+ N324SE^ YV- [+ Jordan] [^ marks canx 18Jun08; still wearing US marks 04Dec08]
A2-15-53		100	Portuguese Air Force	6519+ 16519 [+ Portugal] [stored Beja, Alentejo, Portugal; l/n Jun05]
A2-16-54		100	Portuguese Air Force	6520+ 16520 [+ Portugal] [stored Beja, Alentejo, Portugal; l/n Jun05]
A3-3-55		100	(Royal Jordanian Air Force)	125+ 325 [+ Jordan] [w/o 02Jan84 Amman, Jordan]
B2-1-56		100	Portuguese Air Force	6521+ 16521 [+ Portugal] [by Aug10 to GIA Montijo, Portugal]
B2-2-57		100	(Portuguese Air Force)	6522+ 16522 [+ Portugal] [wfu & cannibalised for spares Sintra, Portugal; l/n 03Aug05]
A1-24-58		100	Spanish Air Force	T.12B-30//74-73 [stored Oct07 Cuatro Vientos, Spain]
A1-25-59		100	Bolivian Army	T.12B-31//46-34 EB-51
A4-1-60	4N	100	Sabang Merauke Raya Air	PK-XCC AX-2102+ A-2102+ PK-ZAN [+ Indonesia]
B2-3-61		100	Portuguese Air Force	6523+ 16523 [+ Portugal] [stored Beja, Alentejo, Portugal; l/n Jun05]
B2-4-62		100	Portuguese Air Force	6524+ 16524 [+ Portugal] [stored by Jly08 Sintra, Portugal]
A4-2-63	5N	100	Merpati Nusantara Airlines	PK-XCB PK-NCD
A4-3-64	6N	100	Sabang Merauke Raya Air	PK-XCA AX-2101+ A-2101+ PK-ZAO [+ Indonesia]
A1-26-65		100	(Spanish Air Force)	T.12B-32//352-32 [w/o 02Jan87 off the coast of Equatorial Guinea]
A1-27-66		100	Spanish Air Force	T.12B-33//72-04
A1-28-67		100	Spanish Air Force	T.12B-34//74-74 [stored Oct07 Cuatro Vientos, Spain; l/n Oct09]
AV3-1-68		100	Southeast Jet Group	126+ 326+ N [+ Jordan]
AV1-1-69		100	Spanish Air Force	T.12C-43//46-50 [stored Aug07 Cuatro Vientos, Spain; l/n Oct09]
AV2-2-70		100	Bolivian Air Force	EC-ZAA T.12C-44//37-50+ FAB-86 [+ Spain] [wears TAM titles; c/n also quoted as AV1-2-70]
A1-29-71		100	ex Spanish Air Force	T.12B-35//37-09 [by Sep03 stored Cuatro Vientos, Spain]
A1-30-72		100	Spanish Air Force	T.12B-36//37-10 [stored Feb08 Cuatro Vientos, Spain; l/n Oct09]
A1-31-73		100	Spanish Air Fprce	T.12B-37//72-05
A1-32-74		100	(Spanish Air Force)	T.12B-38//37-10 [w/o 06Jun92 Torrejon, Spain; by Mar97 fuselage only to Montero Scrapyard, Salamanca, Spain; l/n Sep03]
A1-33-75		100	ex Spanish Air Force	T.12B-39//74-75 [stored by Nov07 Cuatro Vientos, Spain; Jly11 for preservation]
E1-1-76		100	Spanish Air Force	TE.12B-40//79-93 TE.12B-40//74-84 [stored Oct09 Cuatro Vientos, Spain]
AV1-3-77		100	Paraguay National Police	T.12C-59//37-51+ A-21 [+ Spain]
A4-4-78	7N	100	Dirgantara Air Service	PK-XCF PK-NCE PK-VSP [CofA expired 28Oct10 fate/status unknown]
E1-2-79		100	Colombian Navy	TE.12B-41//79-94+ ARC-702 [+ Spain]
A7-1-80		100	ex Nicaraguan Air Force	AN-BSV 420+ 222+ AN-BSV [+ Nicaragua] [wfu by 25Nov07 Managua, Nicaragua when noted without wings & other parts]

CASA/NURTANIO C-212 AVIOCAR

C/n	Line No.	Model	Last known Owner/Operator	Identities/fates/comments (where appropriate)
E1-3-81		100	(Spanish Air Force)	TE.12B-42//79-96 [w/o 06Mar91 in mountains near Pinofranqueado, Salamanca, Spain]
A4-5-82	8N	100	ex Bali Airlines	PK-XCG PK-ICD [CofA expired 18Mar89; stored Oct94 Bandung, Indonesia]
A4-6-83	9N	100	ex Bali Airlines	PK-XCH PK-ICE [CofA expired 19Mar89; stored Oct94 Bandung, Indonesia]
A4-7-84	10N	100	Bouraq Airlines	PK-XCI PK-ICF
A4-8-85	11N	100	KASET (Thailand)	PK-XCJ 1511
A4-9-86	12N	100	KASET (Thailand)	PK-XCK 1512
AA1-1-87		100	Senegal Air Force	T.12B-45+ D.3A-01+ 6W-TSA [+ Spain; no code known]
AA1-2-88		100	Spanish Air Force	T.12B-46//74-76 [stored Seville-San Pablo, Spain; l/n 11Nov10]
CB8-1-89		100	Broken Aero Inc	N99TF
A7-3-90		100	Bolivian Air Force	AN-BSX 421+ 221+ TAM-85 [+ Nicaragua] [stored by 2002 La Paz, Bolivia]
A7-4-91		100	(Nicaraguan Air Force)	AN-BSY 422 [w/o 29Jan79 in Nicaragua]
CB9-92		200CB	(Federation Francaise de Parachutisme)	TC-AOC (F-GOBP) F-GOGN [major damage in collision 15Nov09 near St Jean de Turac, France; canx 02Apr12 final fate unknown]
A4-10-93	13N	100	(Deraya Air Taxi)	PK-XCL PK-DCO [wfu by 06Jan07 Jakarta-Halim, Indonesia]
AA1-3-94		100	Spanish Air Force	T.12B-47//72-06 [stored by Feb09 Cuatro Vientos, Spain; l/n Oct09]
A7-5-95		100	(Nicaraguan Air Force)	AN-BSZ 423 [w/o 05Jan79 Managua, Nicaragua]
AA1-11-96		100	East Horizon	T.12B-53//46-36+ YA-EH01 [+ Spain]
A7-2-97		100	(Nicaraguan Air Force)	AN-BSW 424 [w/o 01Jan79 Managua, Nicaragua]
AA1-12-98		100	(Spanish Air Force)	T.12B-54//37-13 T.12B-54//46-37 [w/o 19Oct04 Lanzarote, Gran Canaria, Spain; moved by road 09Feb06; by 24May07 preserved Ingenio, Gran Canaria; l/n 11Oct08]
AA1-4-99		100	East Horizon	T.12B-48//37-11+ YA-EH04 [+ Spain]
AA1-5-100		100	Spanish Air Force	T.12B-49//46-36 T.12B-49//72-07
A4-11-101	14N	100	Nusantara Buana Air	PK-XCM PK-DCP
AA1-6-102		100	ex Spanish Air Force	T.12B-50//74-77 [stored by Oct06 Cuatro Vientos, Spain; l/n 25Apr09; by Oct09 in compound off airfield]
A10-1-103		M-100	Aerovias DAP	E-210+ CC-CLT [+ Chile] [stored since circa 2000 Punta Arenas, Chile; l/n 2006]
AA1-7-104		100	ex Spanish Air Force	T.12B-51//74-78 [preserved San Javier AB, Spain as "TE.12B-10/79-93", with c/n painted on as "AA-1-104"]
AA1-8-105		100	Spanish Air Force	T.12B-52//72-07 T.12B-52//46-35 [stored Seville-San Pablo, Spain, l/n 11Nov10]
A10-2-106		M-100	Chilean Army	E-211
A10-3-107		M-100	(Chilean Army)	E-212 [w/o 23Dec95 near Rancagua, Chile]
A4-12-108	15N	100	(Merpati Nusantara Airlines)	PK-XCN PK-NCF [w/o 25Mar86 near Naha, Sulawesi, Indonesia]
AV1-4-109		100	Spanish Air Force	T.12C-60//37-52 [stored by Feb05 Seville-San Pablo, Spain; l/n 23Nov10]
AA1-13-110		100	Bolivian Air Force	T.12B-57//72-08 FAB-87
AA1-14-111		100	ex Spanish Air Force	T.12B-58//46-38 T.12B-58//74-86 [preserved Aug09 Gando, Spain]
A4-13-112	16N	100	Deraya Air Taxi	PK-XCO PK-DCQ [CofA expired 22Oct10; fate/status unknown]
AA1-9-113		100	Spanish Air Force	T.12B-55//46-37 T.12B//46-38 T.12B-55//72-08
AA1-10-114		100	ex Spanish Air Force	T.12B-56//74-79 T.12B-56//12-56 [by 14Apr07 preserved on roundabout at Perales del Rio, near Madrid-Getafe, Spain]
AV1-5-115		100	ex Spanish Air Force	T.12C-61//37-53 T.12C-61//47-11 [stored by Nov10 Cuatro Vientos, Spain]
A4-14-116	17N	100	(Dirgantara Air Service)	PK-XCP PK-VSM [w/o 25Jun92 Butu Island en-route Singapore to Pontianak, Indonesia]
A10-4-117		M-100	Chilean Army	E-213
A10-5-118		M-100	Chilean Army	E-214
TC15-2-119		100	(Medavia)	ECT-105 9H-AAQ (N505TF) 9H-AAQ [b/u 1990 Benghazi, Libya]
A4-15-120	18N	100	(Sabang Merauke Raya Air)	PK-XCQ PK-ZAI [w/o 12Feb11 whilst on test flight from Batam-Hang Nadim, Indonesia at Bintin Island]
AB1-1-121		100	Spanish Air Force	T.12B-62+ D.3A-02//803-11 [+ no code reported]
AB1-2-122		100	Spanish Air Force	T.12B-63//37-14 T.12B-63//72-14
AB1-3-123		100	ex Spanish Air Force	T.12B-64//46-39 T.12B-64//46-40 [by Sep06 preserved Getafe town, Spain with code 12-64]

CASA/NURTANIO C-212 AVIOCAR

C/n	Line No.	Model	Last known Owner/Operator	Identities/fates/comments (where appropriate)
A4-16-124	19N	100	(Mantrust Asahi Airways)	PK-XCR PK-NCG [wfu; wreck condition by 25Oct06 at Jakarta-Halim, Indonesia]
CB16-1-125		100	Korean Air	HL5253 [preserved Korean Air Museum, Jeju International, South Korea; l/n 30Sep08]
A10-6-126		M-100	ex Chilean Army	E-215 [preserved by Mar10 Rancagua, Chile]
AB1-4-127		100	Spanish Air Force	T.12B-65//37-09 T.12B-65//74-80 T.12B-65//72-11
A4-17-128	20N	100	(Deraya Air Taxi)	PK-XCS PK-DCR [w/o 08Nov82 near Bontang, East Kalimantan, Indonesia]
AB1-5-129		100	Spanish Air Force	T.12B-66//72-09
AB1-6-130		100	Spanish Air Force	T.12B-67//74-81 T.12B-67//72-12
CB38-1-131		100	Louisa Flying Service	N4261X
A4-18-132	21N	100	Pelita Air Services	PK-XCT PK-PCV
TC18-1-133		100	Medavia	9H-AAT 5A-DMJ 9H-AAT [stored Malta-Luqa, Malta; l/n Nov08]
A11-1-134		M-100	Chilean Navy	145
A11-2-135		M-100	Chilean Navy	146
A4-19-136	22N	100	Dirgantara Air Service	PK-XCU PK-VSN
A11-3-137		M-100	Chilean Navy	ARC-147
CC37-1-138		200	Fugro Airborne Services	ECT-103 EC-DHQ VH-KDV P2-CNP VH-TEM
P2-1-139		200	not yet known	ECT-104 EC-DHO 89001+ AS0925 T7-JCR [+Sweden; code 891]
A4-20-140	23N	100	Sabang Merauke Raya Air	PK-XCV PK-ZAB
A11-4-141		M-100	(Chilean Navy)	ARC-148 [w/o 15Oct86 20kms south of Cabildo, Chile]
AB1-7-142		100	Spanish Air Force	T.12B-68//37-15 [by Oct03 stored Cuatro Vientos, Spain; l/n 06Sep08]
AB1-8-143		100	Spanish Air Force	T.12B-69//37-16 T.12B-69//72-15
A4-21-144	24N	100	(Pelita Air Services)	PK-XCW PK-PCW [CofA expired 06Aug87; wfu; fate unknown]
145			not built	
AB1-9-146		100	Spanish Air Force	T.12B-70//37-17 T.12B-70//72-17
AB1-10-147		100	Spanish Air Force	T.12B-71//37-18 T.12B-71//72-10
A4-22-148	25N	100	KASET (Thailand)	PK-XCX 1513
CB14-1-149		100	Aero Stock	F-WEIY EC-DKU F-WEIY F-ODMJ 6V-AFJ TZ-AMM F-ODTH F-GKJP [stored Dec94 Seletar, Singapore; canx 10Jly97 on sale]
CB14-2-150		100	ex Aero Stock	F-WIPE TR-LZJ F-GJRF J5-GZZ
CB13-1-151		100	(Aero Service)	EC-139 HB-LKX TN-AFA [w/o 19Jun10 en-route near Cameroon/People's Republic of Congo border near Avima in unknown circumstances]
A4-23-152	26N	100	(Dirgantara Air Service)	PK-XCY PK-VSO [w/o 07Dec96 Banjarmasin, Indonesia]
CB20-1-153		100	Louisa Flying Service	N124JM
CB20-2-154		100	Williams Aviation FBO	N125JM SE-LDB N214WA
155			not built	
156			not built	
A4-24-157	27N	100	KASET (Thailand)	PK-XCZ 1514
A4-25-158	28N	100	(Sabang Merauke Raya Air)	PK-XAA PK-ZAG [w/o 03Oct95 near Gunung Antara, Aceti, Indonesia]
CC14-1-159		200	(Lutexfo)	F-ODMI F-WCGC F-GCGC TJ-AGH [CofA expired 24Aug83; canx; wfu & stored by Sep97 wingless Paris-Le Bourget, France; l/n 26May12]
CC20-1-160		200	(Fisher Brothers Aviation)	N126JM N160FB [w/o 04Mar87 Detroit-Metropolitan, MI]
CC15-1-161		200	EP Aviation Inc	9H-AAR N602AR
CC15-2-162		200	EP Aviation Inc	9H-AAS N603AR
CC21-1-163		200	(SANSA)	TI-SAB [w/o 15Jan90 Pico Blanco mountain, 10m SW of San Jose-Juan Santamaria, Costa Rica]
CC20-2-164		200	(Sandair)	N37831 N450AM HP-1171 N461CA [canx 06Mar00 as destroyed/scrapped]
CC20-4-165		200	Bighorn Airways	N37834 N451AM N212TH N107BH
CC21-2-166		200	(Ryan Air Inc)	TI-SAC N437CA N437RA (N437WA) [w/o 02Nov08 Toksook Bay, AK; canx 27May11]
CC22-1-167		200	Fayard Enterprises LLC	HB-LMH EL-AJE HB-LMH C9-AST N467CS
CC24-1-168		200	Carolina Sky Sports	LV-OOI N426CA(2)
CC20-3-169		200	(W H Simpson)	N37838 N169FB+ [b/u 1996 Denver, NC; canx Feb97; + marks reserved 18Aug04 after b/u & expired 22Feb11]
AB4-1-170	29N	200	(LPPU)	PK-XAC PK-ABQ [wfu 08Dec82; stored Jakarta-Halim, Indonesia; l/n Dec04]
CC23-1-171		200	Bighorn Airways	N349CA N117BH

CASA/NURTANIO C-212 AVIOCAR

C/n	Line No.	Model	Last known Owner/Operator	Identities/fates/comments (where appropriate)
CC20-5-172		200	ex Evergreen Helicopters	N346CA [wfu Dec91 Marana, AZ; stripped b/u Dec95; l/n 22Mar10]
AB4-2-173	30N	200	Merpati Nusantara Airlines	PK-XAD PK-NCH
CC20-6-174		200	Ryan Air Inc	N347CA N174FB N687MA N440RA [serious damage 14Feb09 Kotzebue, AK]
CC20-7-175		200	Evergreen Helicopters	N3CA
AB4-3-176	31N	200	(Merpati Nusantara Airlines)	PK-XAE PK-NCI [wfu 01Feb86; stored Bandung, Indonesia]
A27-1-177		200	Venezuelan Navy	TR-0204+ ARV-0204+ ARBV-204 [+ Venezuela]
VF25-1-178		200	Ministry of Finance Customs	EC-DNB TR.12D-80//37-64 EC-LSK
AB4-4-179	32N	200	(Merpati Nusantara Airlines)	PK-XAF PK-NCK [wfu 03Nov84; stored location unknown]
CC29-1-180		200	Evergreen Helicopters	TR-LZW N160GA ZS-PRL N437CA
CC20-8-181		200	South African Air Force	N350CA HP-1151 T-300+ 8022 [+ Bophuthatswana]
AB4-5-182	33N	200	(Mantrust Asahi Airways)	PK-XAG PK-ABM [wfu; wreck condition by 24Feb06 Jakarta-Halim, Indonesia; l/n 25Oct06]
AV27-1-183		200	Venezuelan Navy	TR-0206+ ARV-0206+ ARBV-0206 [+ Venezuela]
CC20-9-184		200	(Arlington Leasing)	N351CA HP-1161 N184CA [wfu May89, stored Riverside, CA; b/u 28Jan03]
AB4-6-185	34N	200	(Merpati Nusantara Airlines)	PK-XAH PK-NCL [w/o 05Jun06 Bandanaira, Indonesia]
A45-14-186		200	Zimbabwean Air Force	T-530/CX-BOF+ EC-411(1) 813 [+ dual marks]
CC28-2-187		200	(Uruguayan Air Force/UN)	T-531/CX-BOG+ 531^ [+ dual marks] [^ code UN146] [w/o 09Oct09 Chaine de la Selle, near Fond Verrettes, Haiti]
AB4-7-188	35N	200	Merpati Nusantara Airlines	PK-XAI PK-NCM
A28-1-189		200	Uruguayan Air Force	T-532/CX-BPI [dual marks]
CC40-1-190		200	Ryan Air Inc	N352CA
AB4-8-191	36N	200	Merpati Nusantara Airlines	PK-XAJ PK-NCN
CC35-1-192		200	Bighorn Airways	N437CA LV-WEU N192MA SE-LDG N192PL N109BH
CC41-1-193		200	Fayard Enterprises LLC	VH-ICJ SE-LDC 5Y-TSL N431CA
AB4-9-194	37N	200	(Merpati Nusantara Airlines)	PK-XAK PK-NCO [w/o 13Dec96 Kupang Eltari, Indonesia]
CC34-1-195		200	Fayard Enterprises LLC	HB-LNG EL-AJF HB-LNG C9-ASU N195CS
CC40-2-196		200	(Fugro Aviation/Terra Surveys)	N353CA C-FDKM (PT-WYR) PP-XBJ C-FDKM PT-WZK C-FDKM PR-FAB C-FDKM [w/o 01Apr11 Saskatoon, SK, Canada]
AB4-10-197	38N	200	Merpati Nusantara Airlines	PK-XAL PK-NCP
A28-2-198		200	Uruguayan Air Force	T-533/CX-BPJ [dual marks]
AB4-11-199	39N	200	(Merpati Nusantara Airlines)	PK-XAM PK-NCQ [wfu 17Feb89; stored location unknown]
AB4-12-200	40N	200	(Merpati Nusantara Airlines)	PK-XAN PK-NCR [wfu 09Dec86; stored Surabaya, Indonesia; l/n 12Dec09 derelict]
AB4-13-201	41N	200	(Merpati Nusantara Airlines)	PK-XAO PK-NCS [w/o 10Jly97 Ambon, Eastern Indonesia]
AB4-14-202	42N	200	(Merpati Nusantara Airlines)	PK-XAP PK-NCT [wfu 08Jan87; stored Bandung, Indonesia]
AB4-15-203	43N	200	Pelita Air Services	PK-XAQ PK-PCU
AB4-16-204	44N	200	Pelita Air Services	PK-XAR PK-PCT
AB4-17-205	45N	200	Pelita Air Services	PK-XAS PK-PCS
AB4-18-206	46N	200	Pelita Air Services	PK-XAT PK-PCR
AB4-19-207	47N	200	Pelita Air Services	PK-XAU PK-PCQ
AB4-20-208	48N	200	Pelita Air Services	PK-XAV PK-PCP
CC4-1-209	49N	200	Indonesian Army	PK-XAW PK-NZD PK-ENB PK-RRA PK-AIL PK-ACC [canx 31Jly06; military serial not yet known]
CC4-2-210	50N	200	Airfast Indonesia	PK-XAX T-2103+ PK-NZJ PK-OCC [+ Indonesia]
CC4-3-211	51N	200	KASET (Thailand)	PK-XAY 1521
4-212	52N	M-200	Indonesian Army	PK-XAZ PK-TRG A-9031
4-213	53N	M-200	Indonesian Army	PK-XDA A-9032 [w/o 19Jly06, location unknown]
4-214	54N	M-200	Indonesian Army	PK-XDC A-9035
CC4-7-215	55N	200	Pelita Air Services	PK-XDD PK-PCO

CASA/NURTANIO C-212 AVIOCAR

C/n	Line No.	Model	Last known Owner/Operator	Identities/fates/comments (where appropriate)
CC4-8-216	56N	200	Pelita Air Services	PK-XDE PK-PCN
CC4-9-217	57N	200	(Pelita Air Services)	PK-XDF PK-PCM [w/o 02Jan90 Java Sea, near Pabelokan Island, Indonesia]
CC4-10-218	58N	200	(Pelita Air Services)	PK-XDG PK-PCL [w/o 24Jan84 near Manado, Northern Sulawesi, Indonesia]
4-219	59N	M-200	Indonesian Army	PK-XDH A-9034
4-220	60N	M-200	Indonesian Navy	PK-XDI U-610
4-221	61N	M-200	Indonesian Navy	PK-XDJ U-611
4-222	62N	M-200	Indonesian Navy	PK-XDK U-612
4-223	63N	M-200	(Indonesian Navy)	PK-XDL U-614 [w/o 08Jan01 Silimo, Indonesia]
CC4-16-224	64N	200	Guam Marianas Airlines	PK-XDM N5022
4-225	65N	M-200	Indonesian Air Force	PK-XDN A-2103
4-226	66N	M-200	Indonesian Air Force	PK-XDO PK-NZK A-2104
4-227	67N	M-200	Indonesian Air Force	PK-XDP A-2105
4-228	68N	M-200	(Indonesian Air Force)	PK-XDQ A-2106 [w/o 26Jun08 near Pasir Gaok village, Tenjolaya, West Java, Indonesia]
AS28-1-229		200	Uruguayan Air Force	T-534//CX-BPK+ EC-502 SE-KVG^ FAU534 [+ dual marks; ^ code 587; then Dec09 with UN code UN-147]
A36-1-230		200	(United Arab Emirates Air Force)	EC-DRA 805 [reported SOC; l/n Sep92, fate unknown]
CC40-3-231		200	(Flight International)	N354CA N699MA N203FN N960BW [w/o 27Nov04 Baba Mountains, S of Bamiyan, Bagram, Afghanistan]
CC32-1-232		200	(Aero Chasqui)	OB-T-1218 OB-1218 [w/o 10Jly91 near Bellavista, Peru]
A36-2-233		200	(United Arab Emirates Air Force)	EC-DRB 806 [reported SOC; l/n Sep92, fate unknown]
CC40-4-234		200	(Executive Airlines)	N355CA [w/o 07Jun92 Maria de Hostos, PR]
CC34-2-235		200	(Zaire Air Force)	HB-LNH 9Q-CZC 9T-CBD [wfu Sep93 Kinshasa-N'Dolo, Zaire]
CC30-1-236		200	Air Kiribati	T3-ATC
A31-1-237		200	(Panama Air Force)	215 [w/o 01Feb88 in Panama]
CC40-5-238		200	Evergreen Helicopters	N422CA
S1-1-239		200	Spanish Air Force	D.3B-03 [no code known]
CC40-6-240		200	Evergreen Helicopters	N423CA [reported 19Oct11 Sharajah, UAE on pallet with wings removed]
A31-2-241		200	Panama Air Force	220
CC40-7-242		200	Arctic Transportation Svces	N424CA
A31-3-243		200	Panama Air Force	225
A36-3-244		200	(United Arab Emirates Air Force)	EC-DRH 807 [reported SOC; l/n Sep92, fate unknown]
CC39-1-245		200	(Terra Surveys)	N29004 N426CA (1) HB-LNS C-GILU [w/o 02Aug88 Reykjavik, Iceland; canx 24Oct88]
A36-4-246		200	(United Arab Emirates Air Force)	EC-DRI 808 [reported SOC; l/n Sep92, fate unknown]
VF25-2-247		200	INEAR	EC-DRO TR.12D-81//37-65+ EC-LKJ [+ Spain]
CC40-8-248		200	EP Aviation Inc	N428CA N248MA N202FN N961BW
4-249	69N	M-200	Indonesian Air Force	PK-XDR A-2107
4-250	70N	M-200	Indonesian Air Force	PK-XDS A-2108
4-251	71N	M-200	Indonesian Air Force	PK-XDT A-2109
4-252	72N	M-200	Indonesian Air Force	PK-XDU A-2110
CC4-25-253	73N	200	Guam Marianas Airlines	PK-XDV N5040
CC4-24-254	74N	200	(Merpati Nusantara Airlines)	PK-XDW PK-NCU [w/o 10Mar96 Soroako Airport, Indonesia]
CC4-26-255	75N	200	Merpati Nusantara Airlines	PK-XDX PK-NCV
CC4-27-256	76N	200	Merpati Nusantara Airlines	PK-XDY PK-NCW
CC4-28-257	77N	200	Merpati Nusantara Airlines	PK-XDZ PK-NCX
CC4-29-258	78N	200	(Merpati Nusantara Airlines)	PK-XEA PK-NCY [w/o 30Jan91 Gorontalo, Sulawesi Island, Indonesia]
S1-2-259		200	Mauritanian Air Force	D.3B-04+ 5T-M [+ Spain; no code known]
S1-3-260		200	ex Spanish Air Force	EC-ZZX D.3B-05 [no code known; stored by Oct10 Cuatro Vietos, Spain]

CASA/NURTANIO C-212 AVIOCAR

C/n	Line No.	Model	Last known Owner/Operator	Identities/fates/comments (where appropriate)
CE25-01-261		200	INEAR	ECT-121 LV-PAC LV-AYL EC-FAQ TR.12D-77//37-61+ EC-LJH [+ Spain]
CC50-1-262		200	EP Aviation Inc	N429CA N262MA N969BW
CC50-2-263		200	Samaritan's Purse	N427CA LV-WCV N263MA ZS-OWR 9U-BHL 9Q-CCW (9Q-CHP)? N499SP
A27-2-264		200	(Venezuelan Navy)	ARV-0209 [w/o 10Jan91 in mountains 60 kms S of Merida, Venezuela]
CC50-3-265		200	Fugro Airborne Surveys	N430CA C-GDPP
S1-4-266		200	Spanish Air Force	D.3A-06//803-12 D.3B-06+ [+ no code reported] [stored Sep08 Sevilla-San Pablo, Spain]
267		300	CASA	EC-122 ECT-122
A27-3-268		200	(Venezuelan Navy)	ARV-0210 [w/o 23Jan90 near El Juncal Village, 24 kms W of Caracas, Venezuela]
CC50-4-269		200	(Latin Air Service)	N431CA [w/o 17Dec86 in sea en route Key West, FL, to Panama City, Panama]
CC49-2-270		200	Spanish Air Force	EC-DUQ TR.12D-75//403-07 T.12D-75//403-07 T.12D-75//47-14
CC50-6-271		200	(American Eagle)	N432CA [w/o 08May87 Mayaguez, PR]
CC50-7-272		200	Military Support Services	N433CA TI-AVV N433CA VH-MQD
CC79-1-273		200	Cia Generale Ripresearee	(N434CA) EC-DVD I-MAFE
CC4-30-274	79N	200	Merpati Nusantara Airlines	PK-XEC PK-NCZ [status unknown following accident 03Dec11 Larat-Watidor Airport, Indonesia]
CC4-31-275	80N	200	ex Mantrust Asahi Airways	PK-XED PK-ENA [stored Oct94 Bandung, Indonesia]
CC4-32-276	81N	200	Sabang Merauke Raya Air	PK-XEE PK-ENC PK-JSS PK-ZAV
CC4-33-277	82N	200	Sabang Merauke Raya Air	PK-XEF PK-END PK-JSR PK-ZAQ+ [+ not fully confirmed]
4-278	83N	MP-200	Indonesian Navy	PK-XEG U-615
4-279	84N	MP-200	Indonesian Navy	PK-XEH U-616
4-280	85N	MP-200	Indonesian Navy	PK-XEI U-617
4-281	86N	M-200	Indonesian Navy	PK-XEJ U-618
CC4-38-282	87N	200	Nusantra Buana Air	PK-XEK PK-HJA PK-VSA PK-TLE
CC4-39-283	88N	200	(Nusantara Buana Air)	PK-XEL PK-HJB PK-VSB PK-TLF [w/o 29Sep11 Bukit Barisan range, Sumatra, Indonesia]
S1-5-284		200	Spanish Air Force	D.3B-07//803-13 D.3B-07 [stored by Oct09 Cuatro Vientos, Spain]
S1-6-285		200	Spanish Air Force	D.3B-08//22-92 D.3B-08 [stored by Oct09 Cuatro Vientos, Spain]
CC50-8-286		200	Fayard/Carolina Sky Sports	N434CA
CC50-9-287		200	Ryan Air Inc	N436CA N287MA N439RA
A45-1-288		200	Zimbabwean Air Force	800
CC50-10-289		200	EP Aviation Inc	N435CA N316ST N966BW N604AR
CC44-1-290		200	EP Aviation Inc	YN-BYY N439CA N962BW N605AR
CD63-1-291		200	Fayard/Carolina Sky Sports	ECT-131 EC-DTU OO-FKY C9-ATY ZS-PBM N497CA
CC50-11-292		200	Bighorn Airways	N292CA N311ST N112BH
A45-2-293		200	(Zimbabwean Air Force)	801 [w/o Nov85 Zambesi Valley, Zimbabwe]
CD58-1-294		200	Evergreen Helicopters	VH-SMO ZK-THV A3-CMP N31BR N502FS
A45-3-295		200	(Zimbabwean Air Force)	802 [w/o 11Jan99 near Kinshasa, Congo]
CC50-14-296		200	(US Army)	N296CA 88-0321 [w/o 01Dec89 near Patuxent River NAS, MD]
S1-7-297		200	(Spanish Air Force)	D.3B-09//803-14 [w/o 05Feb98 near Pinilla del Valle, Madrid, Spain]
CC44-2-298		200	(Aeronica)	YN-BYZ [w/o 29Jun83 in Nicaragua]
C212-299				[static test airframe]
A45-4-300		200	Zimbabwean Air Force	803
CC49-1-301		200	Spanish Air Force	ECT-128 EC-DTV T.12D-74//54-11
A48-1-302		200	B & H Airlines	F-ODIT TT-LAL F-GHOX T9-ABA E7-ABA
CD51-1-303		200	(Colombian Air Force)	ECT-136 1150 [w/o 11Nov90 in jungle, 110 kms SW of Medellin, Colombia]
CD51-2-304		200	EP Aviation Inc	1151+ N72405 N203PA N967BW [+ Colombia]
CC54-1-305		200	(Guam Marianas Airlines)	N5069L [wfu Louisa, VA; canx Sep96 as parted out; fuselage Anchorage, AK Aug99]
CD51-3-306		200	(Colombian Air Force)	1152 [w/o 09Sep95 La Macarena, SW Bogata, Colombia]

CASA/NURTANIO C-212 AVIOCAR

C/n	Line No.	Model	Last known Owner/Operator	Identities/fates/comments (where appropriate)
A52-1-307		200	Paraguayan Air Force/ TAM	2027
CC46-1-308		200	(CASC Inc)	F-ODQC TT-LAM F-GELO C9-ATM ZS-PCP N413CA [canx 17Mar11 fate/status unknown]
CD51-4-309		200	EP Aviation Inc	ECT-143 1153+ N72408 N204PA N968BW N2357G N607AR [+ Colombia]
A52-2-310		200	Paraguayan Air Force/ TAM	2029 [in store 2010]
VF25-3-311		200	Ministry of Finance Customs	EC-DTL TR.12D-78//37-62 EC-LSL
AV45-5-312		200	Zimbabwean Air Force	804
DE1-1-313		200ECM	Spanish Air Force	TR.12D-72 (D.3B-10) TM.12D-72//408-01 TM.12D-72//47-12
DE1-2-314		200ECM	(Spanish Air Force)	TR.12D-73 (D.3B-11) TM.12D-73//408-03 [w/o 22Mar00 near Herreria, Guadalajara province, Spain]
A52-3-315		200	Paraguayan Air Force/ TAM	2031 [in store 2010]
AC52-1-316		200	Paraguayan Air Force/ TAM	2033
CD51-5-317		200	(Colombian Air Force)	1154 [w/o 19Mar94 near La Macarena, Colombia]
CD51-6-318		200	Military Support Services	ECT-128 1155+ N7241E VH-MQE [+ Colombia]
A56-1-319		200	Bophuthatswana DF	ECT-133 T-301 [reported to South African Air Force]
CC60-3-320		200	EP Aviation Inc	N214TA 87-0158+ N2129J N204FN N963BW [+ US Army]
A45-13-321		200	Zimbabwean Air Force	ECT-134 812
CC60-01-322		200	[US Drug Enforcement Agency]	N4999U
CE25-02-323		200	INAER	ECT-131 EC-FAP TR.12D-79//37-60+ TR.12D-79^ EC-LJB [+ Spain; ^ Spain uncoded]
CC60-02-324		200	Argentine Army	ECT-145 LV-RBB AE-264
A53-1-325		200	(Angolan Air Force)	T-400//D2-MAC [dual marks] [w/o 02Jan97 near Quiangala, Bengo province, Angola]
A53-2-326		200	(Angolan Air Force)	T-401 [w/o 17Jun95 15km E of Catumbela City, Angola]
S5-1-327		200	Mexican Navy	MP-111
CC60-4-328		200	USAF	N215TA 87-0159
A45-6-329		200	Zimbabwean Air Force	805
A53-3-330		200	Angolan Air Force	T-402
A53-4-331		200	Angolan Air Force	T-403
CC60-5-332		200	USAF	N213TA N618GQ N8005R 90-0177
S5-2-333		200	Mexican Navy	MP-112
A53-5-334		200	(Angolan Air Force)	T-404 [w/o 12May93, details unknown]
S5-3-335		200	Mexican Navy	MP-113+ MP-413 [+ Mexico]
CC60-6-336		200	USAF	N216TA 90-0168
A53-6-337		200	(Angolan Air Force)	T-405 [w/o 24Oct92; details unknown]
S5-4-338		200	Mexican Navy	MP-311
A53-7-339		200	(Angolan Air Force)	T-406 [w/o 04Aug92; details unknown]
A53-8-340		200	Angolan Air Force	T-407/D2-MAE [dual marks]
S5-5-341		200	Mexican Navy	MP-312+ MP-412 [+ Mexico]
S5-6-342		200	Mexican Navy	MP-211+ MT-211 [+ Mexico]
CE61-1-343		200	Uruguayan Air Force	SE-IVE+ FAU535 [+code 583]
S5-7-344		200	Mexican Navy	MP-312
S5-8-345		200	(Mexican Navy)	MP-113 [w/o 19Feb88 near Campeche, Mexico]
CE61-2-346		200	(Swedish Coast Guard)	SE-IVF [w/o 26Oct06 Holvik, near Malmo, Sweden]
CC60-7-347		200	USAF	N217TA N478GQ N8005L 90-0178
CC60-8-348		200	USAF	N218TA 90-0169
CC60-9-349		200	Bering Air	ECT-124 N316CA N349TA [major damage 18Sep09 Savoonga, AK]
350		200	Chilean Air Force	EC-006 960
S43-1-351		200MR	Venezuelan Navy	ARV-0401+ ARBV-0401 [+ Venezuela]
S43-2-352		200	(Venezuelan Navy)	TR-0206+ ARV-0402 [+ Venezuela] [w/o 25Mar87 into sea off Venezuela]
S43-3-353		200MR	Venezuelan Navy	ARV-0403+ ARV-0403 [+ Venezuela]
S43-4-354		200	Venezuelan Navy	ARV-0404+ ARV-0404 [+ Venezuela]
355		200	Chilean Air Force	961
CD67-01-356		200	Air Kiribati	N104CA N398FL T3-ATJ

CASA/NURTANIO C-212 AVIOCAR

C/n	Line No.	Model	Last known Owner/Operator	Identities/fates/comments (where appropriate)
CD67-02-357		200	(US Dept of Justice)	N119CA [w/o 27Aug94 15m N of Puerto Pisana, Peru; canx Jly95]
A45-7-358		200	Zimbabwean Air Force	806 [stored Harare, Zimbabwe; l/n Mar98]
CC25-1-359		200	INAER	EC-ECD TR.12D-76//37-60+ EC-LLN [+ Spain]
S5-9-360		200	Mexican Navy	MP-313
S5-10-361		200	Mexican Navy	MP-411
A62-1-362		200	(Transkei Defence Force)	ECT-125 TDF-01 [w/o 06Jly93 near Umtata, Transkei, South Africa]
A62-2-363		200	South African Air Force	ECT-126 TDF-02+ 8010 [+ Transkei]
A45-8-364		200	Zimbabwean Air Force	EC-411(2) 807
A45-9-365		200	(Zimbabwean Air Force)	808 [w/o 11Feb87 in Mozambique]
A45-10-366		200	(Zimbabwean Air Force)	809 [w/o May87; no further details known]
A45-11-367		200	Zimbabwean Air Force	810
A45-12-368		200	Zimbabwean Air Force	811
MS03-07-369		200	(Bolivian Army)	ECT-130 EB-50 [w/o 21Apr95 near Apolo, Bolivia]
A51-01-370		300	Colombian Air Force/ SATENA	1156
DD65-1-371		300	South African Air Force	040+ 8020 [+ Venda]
A51-02-372		300	Colombian Air Force/ SATENA	1157
DD61-1-373		300	South African Air Force	EC-112 T-310+ 8021 [+ Bophuthatswana]
AA31-01-374		300	Panama Air Force	250+ AN-250 [+ Panama]
AA31-02-375		300	Panama Navy	255+ AN-255 [+ Panama]
AA31-03-376		300	Panama Navy	260+ AN-260 [+ Panama]
A12-01-377		300	French Air Force	377/MO/F-ZVMO
A12-02-378		300	French Air Force	378/MP/F-ZVMP
MS03-08-379		300	EP Aviation Inc	ECT-212 N379CA EB-51+ N379CA N897FL N205FN N964BW N6369C [+ Bolivia]
1-380		M-300	Angolan Air Force	T-408/D2-MKL [dual marks]
2-381		M-300	Angolan Air Force	T-409/D2-MLN [dual marks]
1-382		M-300	Argentine Coast Guard	PA-61
2-383		M-300	Argentine Coast Guard	PA-62
3-384		M-300	(Angolan Air Force)	T-410/D2-MNM [dual marks] [w/o 27Mar90 Kuito, Angola]
4-385		M-300	Angolan Air Force	T-411//D2-MMO [dual marks]
A12-03-386		300	French Air Force	386/MQ/F-ZVMQ
A12-04-387		M-300	CAE Aviation Ltd	387/MR/F-ZVMR F-GIQQ I-DZPO D-CJMP F-HBMP
A12-05-388		M-300	(French Air Force)	388/MS/F-ZVMS [wfu by 20Apr06 Bretigny, France; reported sold as scrap]
A71-1-389		M-300	(Lesotho Defence Force)	RLDF-46 [w/o 10Nov89 Maluti mountains, Lesotho]
A71-2-390		300	Lesotho Defence Force	RLDF-48+ LDF-48 [+ Lesotho] [w/o 16Dec00 Mokhotlong Airport, Lesotho; remains to Dodson International Aircraft, Rantoul KS for parts use; l/n 25Jly10]
A51-1-391		300	Colombian Air Force	1158 1258 [substantial damage 07Feb08 Nugui-Reyes Murillo Airport, Colombia; date also reported as 08Feb08]
392		300	Botswana Defence Force	EC-006 OC-1//Z10
DF-1-393		300	EP Aviation Inc	N393DF 0393+ N393DF N965BW N4399T [+ USCG]
394		300	Botswana Defence Force	OC-2 [also marked with squadron identity Z10]
AA72-1-395		300	KASET (Thailand)	1531
AA72-2-396		300	KASET (Thailand)	1532
DF72-1-397		300	Aero Service	D4-CBA TN-AFC
DF72-2-398		300	Evergreen Helicopters	D4-CBB TN-AFD N392CA
3-399		M-300	Argentine Coast Guard	(PA-63)+ PA-71 [+ Argentina]
4-400		M-300	Argentine Coast Guard	(PA-64)+ PA-72 [+ Argentina]
5-401		M-300	Argentine Coast Guard	(PA-65)+ PA-73 [+ Argentina]
A12-06-402		300	French Air Force	402/MT/F-ZVMT
A12-07-403		300	French Air Force	403//MU//F-ZVMU
404		300		[no details known]
DF-2-405		300	Conoco Phillips Alaska	N405AC N515FL N405CP
406		300		[no details known]
407		300		[no details known]
A71-3-408		300	Lesotho Defence Force	RLDF-45+ LDF-46 [+ Lesotho]
CC4-409	89N	200MPA	Indonesian Navy	PK-XEM AX-2107 P-850 [model NC212-200MPA]
4-410	90N	200	Nusantra Buana Air	PK-XEN PK-HJC PK-VSC PK-BRN PK-TLH
4-411	91N	200	Nusantra Buana Air	PK-XEO PK-HJD PK-VSD PK-BRM PK-TLI

CASA/NURTANIO C-212 AVIOCAR

C/n	Line No.	Model	Last known Owner/Operator	Identities/fates/comments (where appropriate)
4-412	92N	200	(Dirgantara Air Service)	PK-XEP PK-HJE PK-VSE [w/o 26Jan08 near Malinau, Kalimantan, Borneo, Indonesia]
4-413	93N	200	Nusantra Buana Air	PK-XEQ PK-HJI PK-VSF PK-TLG
4-414	94N	200	IPTN-Nurtanio	PK-XER
4-415	95N	200	IPTN-Nurtanio	PK-XES
4-416	96N	200		
4-417	97N	200		
4-418	98N	200		
4-419	99N	200		
4-420	100N	200		
4-421	101N	200		
4-422	102N	200	Transwisata Prima Aviation	PK-XEX PK-TWW
4-423	103N	200		
4-424	104N	200		
4-425	105N	200		
4-426	106N	200		
4-427	107N	200	Indonesian Army	A-9152
4-428	108N	200		
4-429	109N	200		
4-430	110N	200		
4-431	111N	200		
4-432	112N	200		
4-433	113N	200		
4-434	114N	200		
4-435	115N	200		
4-436	116N	200		
4-437	117N	200		
4-438	118N	200		
4-439	119N	200		
4-440	120N	200		
4-441	121N	200		
442		300DF	Chilean Air Force	965
443		300DF	(Chilean Air Force)	966 [w/o 02Sep11 in sea near Isla Robinson Crusoe Airport, Chile]
AA73-1-444		300	KASET (Thailand)	1533
4-445	122N	300		
A83-1-446		300	Royal Thai Army	[Venezuela] EC-144 446 [wfu May06 Bangkok-Don Muang, Thailand]
A83-2-447		300	Royal Thai Army	[Venezuela] 447 [wfu Dec06 Bangkok-Don Muang, Thailand]
4-448	123N	300		
A74-1-449		300	Colombian Air Force	1701+ 1250 [+ Colombia]
A74-2-450		300	(Colombian Air Force)	1702+ 1251 [+ Colombia][w/o 05Dec00 Rio Orteguaza, Colombia]
AA73-2-451		300	KASET (Thailand)	EC-149 1534
AA73-3-452		300	KASET (Thailand)	EC-147 1535
AA73-4-453		300	KASET (Thailand)	EC-148 1536
AB10-1-454		300	(Chilean Army)	E-230 [w/o 06Aug00 18m from Chaiten, near Michimahuida volcano, Chile]
AB10-2-455		300	Chilean Army	E-231
AB10-3-456		300	Chilean Army	E-232
457				
458				
1-459		M-300	ex Portuguese Air Force	IFSP-11 17201 [wfu Dec12]
2-460		M-300	ex Portuguese Air Force	IFSP-12 17202 [wfu Dec12]
461		400	Lesotho Defence Force	EC-212 LDF-52
462		400	Venezuelan Navy	ARV-0216+ ARBV-0216 [+ Venezuela]
463		400EE	Venezuelan Navy	ARV-0217+ ARBV-0217 [+ Venezuela]
464		400	Venezuelan Navy	ARV-0218+ ARBV-0218 [+ Venezuela]
465		MP-400	TRAGSA	EC-011 EC-HAP
466		400	Surinam Air Force	SAF-212 PZ-TJR SAF-212+ [+ not confirmed]
467		400	Surinam Air Force	SAF-214
468		400	Dominican Republic Air Force	3500

CASA/NURTANIO C-212 AVIOCAR

C/n	Line No.	Model	Last known Owner/Operator	Identities/fates/comments (where appropriate)		
469		400	Dominican Republic Air Force	3501	[stored Santo Domingo-San Isidro, Dominican Republic; l/n 03Jly06]	
470		MP-400	TRAGSA	EC-HTU		
471		400	Dominican Republic Air Force	3502		
472		MP-400	Helisureste	EC-INX		
473		400	Paraguayan Air Force	2035		
474		400	Skytraders	VH-VHA		
475		400	Skytraders	VH-VHB	[damaged 15Nov10 landing in Antarctica]	
476		?	Ecuadorian Army	AEE-301		
477		?	Ecuadorian Army	IFSP007	AEE-302	
478		400MP	Korean Coast Guard	EC-212	B702	
479		400	KASET (Thailand)	1541		
480		400	Vietnam Marine Police	EC-212	SE-MGX	8981
481		400MP	Vietnam Marine Police	EC-025	SE-MGY	8982
482						
483		400	KASET (Thailand)	1542		
Unidentified						
unkn			Indonesian Air Force	A-2111		
unkn			Indonesian Air Force	A-2112		
unkn			Indonesian Army	A-9118		
unkn			Indonesian Army	A-9144	[reported 25Oct06 Pondok Cabe, Indonesia]	
unkn			Mexican Navy	AMP-114	[reported w/o 15Nov06 in Gulf of Mexico, near Progresso, Yucatan, Mexico]	
unkn			CASA	EC-131	[displayed at 1989 Paris Air show]	
unkn			CASA	ECT-114	[displayed at 1987 Paris Air show]	
unkn		200	Mexican Navy	MP-510		
unkn			Indonesian Navy	P-851	[reported delivered 29Nov06]	
unkn			Indonesian Navy	P-852	[reported delivered 06Mar07]	
unkn		M-100	Indonesian Police Wing	P-2031		
unkn		M-100	Indonesian Police Wing	P-2032	[w/o 22Feb05 or 24Feb05 Macarena Airport, Sarmi, Papua Provence, Indonesia]	
unkn				PK-DHX	[reported 18Apr09 Jakarta-Halim, Indonesia]	
unkn			Nusantara Buana Air	PK-TLE	[reported 18Dec08 Balikpapan, Indonesia]	
unkn			Nusantara Buana Air	PK-TLH	[reported 18Apr09 Jakarta-Halim; 08Jun10 Banda Aceh; 11Jly10 Pandang-Minangkabau all in Indonesia]	
unkn			Nusantara Buana Air	PK-TLI	[reported May11 Medan, Indonesia]	
unkn		200	Colombian National Police	PNC-238		
unkn			Colombian National Police	PNC-240		
unkn		200	Spanish Air Force	T.12B-82		
unkn		200	Angolan Air Force	T-412		
unkn		M-200	Indonesian Navy	U-619	[ex AX-2103]	
unkn		M-200	Indonesian Navy	U-620	[ex AX-2106]	
unkn		M-200	Indonesian Navy	U-621		
unkn		M-200	Indonesian Navy	U-623		
unkn		M-200	Indonesian Navy	U-625		
unkn			Parsa S.A.	HP-1626PS	[marks reserved 2007]	

CASA/AIRTECH CN-235 TETUKO

C/n	Model	Last known Owner/Operator	Identities/fates/comments (where appropriate)
Spanish production			
991/P1	100MP	CASA	ECT-100 ECT-130 EC-100 [prototype ff 11Nov83]
C001	1	ex South African Air Force	ECT-135 [f/f 02Dec98] T-330+ 8026 [ff 20Aug86] [+ Bophuthatswana] [wfu 17Jly12 Zwartkop AFB, South Africa for preservation there by SAAF Museum]
C002	10	Royal Saudi Air Force	118
C003	10	Royal Saudi Air Force	119
C004	10M	Royal Saudi Air Force	ECT-101 126
C005	10M	Royal Saudi Air Force	127
C006	10	ex Binter Canarias	EC-011 EC-EMO EC-252 EC-EMO [canx; fate/status unknown]
C007	10	EP Aviation LLC	EC-012 EC-233 EC-EMJ ZS-OGF V5-CAN N981BW N2696S
C008	100M	Togo Air Force	OG1(1)+ N820CA 5V-MBM [+ Botswana; also carried squadron identity Z1]
C009	100M	ex Fayard Enterprises LLC	OG2(1)+ N833CA^ ZS- N833CA^ [+ Botswana; also carried squadron identity Z1; ^ canx 25May12 to South Africa & restored 08Jun12; stored at Johannesburg, South Africa]
C010	10	EP Aviation LLC	EC-013 EC-234 EC-EMK ZS-OGE N982BW [stored Johannesburg, South Africa as ZS-OGE; l/n Aug08 in poor condition]
PA01-C011	10M	Mexican Federal Police	FAP-265+ HP-1296 HP-1292 N100FN XC-PFW^ [+ Panama] [^ coded PF-203 then PF-512]
C012	10	EP Aviation LLC	EC-014 EC-EMN ZS-OGG 5R-MKM N983BW N1269J
EA01-1-C013	10M	Spanish Air Force	T.19C-01 T.19A-01//35-60 TR.19A-01//403-01
EA01-2-C014	10M	Spanish Air Force	T.19C-02 T.19A-02//35-61 TR.19A-02//403-02
C015	100M	Ecuadorean Army	EC-016 AEE-502
C016	100M	Ecuadorean Navy	EC-016 AEE-503 ANE-202 AN-202
C017	100M	(Ecuadorean Navy)	ANE-204 [canx; fate/status unknown]
C018	200	ex Binter Mediterraneo	EC-018 EC-FAD [preserved by Jan12 outside Airbus HQ, Seville, Spain]
C019	100M	Chilean Army	EC-330 250+ E-219 [+ Ireland]
C020	100M	Chilean Army	E-216
C021	100M	(Chilean Army)	E-217 [w/o 24Feb92 Teniente Marsh Martin base, Antarctica]
C022	100M	Chilean Army	E-218
AL05-1-C023	100M	Royal Moroccan Air Force	CNA-MA [code 023]
AL05-2-C024	100M	Royal Moroccan Air Force	CNA-MB
AL05-3-C025	100M	Royal Moroccan Air Force	CNA-MC
AL05-4-C026	100M	Royal Moroccan Air Force	CNA-MD
AL05-5-C027	100M	Royal Moroccan Air Force	CNA-ME CN-AME
AL05-6-C028	100M	Royal Moroccan Air Force	CNA-MF
C029	200	Colombian Navy	EC-009 EC-FAC ARC-801
C030	200	APA Leasing Inc	EC-FAE LV-VHM EC-HAU N235TF N5025
C031	100M	Royal Moroccan Air Force	EC-030 CNA-MG
C032	200	Colombian Navy	EC-FBD LV-VGV EC-HAV ARC-802
C033	200	(Binter Mediterraneo)	EC-012 EC-FBC [w/o 29Aug01 near Malaga, Spain]
EA02-01-C034	100M	Jordan Special Operations	EC-014 T.19B-03//35-21+ 3210 [+ Spain]
EA02-02-C035	100M	Jordan Special Operations	T.19B-04//35-22+ 3211 [+ Spain]
EA02-03-C036	100MPA-100	Spanish Air Force	T.19B-05//35-23 D.4-06+ [+ also still marked T.19B-05]
EA02-04-C037	100MPA-100	Spanish Air Force	T.19B-06//35-24 D.4-05+ [+ also still marked T.19B-06]
EA02-05-C038	100M	Spanish Air Force	T.19B-07//35-25 T.19B-07//74-25
EA02-06-C039	100MPA-100	Spanish Air Force	T.19B-08//35-26 D.4-04+ [+ also still marked T.19B-08]
EA02-07-C040	100M	Spanish Air Force	T.19B-09//35-27 T-19B-09//D.4-02
C041	200QC	Mexican Federal Police	N235CA EC-996 EC-GEJ XC-PFH [coded PF-212 then PF-511]
C042	200QC	USAF	EC-764 EC-FSX N235CA N375ET N9858H N385RS 96-6049+ [+ not fully confirmed]
C043	200M	(French Air Force)	43//330-ID+ 43//62-IA//F-RAIA [+ France] [w/o 17Dec03 French Pyrenees, France]
C044	100M	Gabon Air Force	TR-KJE
C045	200M	French Air Force	45//330-IB 45//62-IB//F-RAIB
EA02-08-C046	100MPA-100	Spanish Air Force	T.19B-10//35-28 D.4-03+ [+ also still marked T.19B-10]
EA02-09-C047	100M	Spanish Air Force	T.19B-11//35-29 T.19B-11//74-29
C048	100M	Papua New Guinea DF	P2-0501
C049	100M	Papua New Guinea DF	P2-0502
EA02-10-C050	100MPA-100	Spanish Air Force	T.19B-12//35-30 D.4-01+ [+ also still marked T.19B-12]
C051	100M	Turkish Air Force	051+ 91-051 [+ Turkey]

CASA/AIRTECH CN-235 TETUKO

C/n	Model	Last known Owner/Operator	Identities/fates/comments (where appropriate)			
C052	100M	Turkish Air Force	052+	91-052	[+ Turkey]	
C053	200	Royal Thai Police	EC-235(1)	28053		
EA02-11-C054	100M	Spanish Air Force	T.19B-13//35-31	T.19B-13//74-31		
C055	100M	Turkish Air Force	055+	92-055	[+ Turkey]	
C056	100M	Turkish Air Force	056+	92-056	[+ Turkey]	
C057	100M	Turkish Air Force	057+	93-057	[+ Turkey]	
C058	100M	Turkish Air Force	058+	93-058	[+ Turkey]	
EA02-12-C059	100M	Spanish Air Force	T.19B-14//35-32	T.19B-14//74-32	T.19B-14//74-14	
EA02-13-C060	100MPA	Spanish Air Force	T.19B-15//35-33	T.19B-15//74-33	T-19B-17//74-17	
			D.4-07			
C061	100M	Turkish Air Force	061+	93-061	[+ Turkey]	
C062	100	Oman Police Air Wing	A4O-CU			
C063	100	Oman Police Air Wing	A4O-CV			
C064	100M	Turkish Air Force	064+	93-064	[+ Turkey]	
C065	200M	French Air Force	065//330-IF+	065//62-IC//F-RAIC	[+ France]	
C066	200M	French Air Force	066//330-IG+	066//62-ID//F-RAID	066/52-ID	[+ France]
C067	100M	Turkish Air Force	067+	94-067	[+ Turkey]	
C068	100M	Turkish Air Force	068+	94-068	[+ Turkey]	
C069	100M	Turkish Air Force	069+	94-069	[+ Turkey]	
EA02-14-C070	100M	Spanish Air Force	T.19B-16//35-34	T.19B-16//74-34		
C071	200M	French Air Force	EC-001	71//330-IH	71//62-IE//F-RAIE	
C072	200M	French Air Force	72/330-II	72//62-IF	72//82-IF//F-RAIF	
C073	100M	Turkish Air Force	073+	94-073	[+ Turkey]	
EA02-15-C074	100M	Spanish Air Force	T.19B-17//35-35	T.19B-17//74-35		
EA02-16-C075	100M	Spanish Air Force	T.19B-18//35-36	T.19B-18//74-36		
EA02-17-C076	100M	Spanish Air Force	T.19B-19//35-37	T.19B-19//74-19		
C077	100M	Turkish Air Force	077+	94-077	[+ Turkey]	
C078	100M	South Korean Air Force	5-078+	40-078	[+ South Korea]	
EA02-18-C079	100M	Spanish Air Force	T.19B-20//35-38			
C080	100M	Turkish Air Force	080+	94-080	[+ Turkey]	
C081	100M	South Korean Air Force	5-081			
C082	100M	South Korean Air Force	30-082			
C083	100M	Turkish Air Force	083+	95-083	[+ Turkey]	
C084	100M	South Korean Air Force	30-084			
C085	100MPA	Irish Air Corps	252			
C086	100M	(Turkish Air Force)	086	[w/o 16May01 location unknown]		
C087	100M	South Korean Air Force	EC-564	087+	30-087	[+ South Korea]
C088	100M	South Korean Air Force	5-088+	30-088	[+ South Korea]	
C089	100M	Turkish Air Force	089+	95-089	[+ Turkey]	
C090	100M	South Korean Air Force	EC-555	5-090+	40-090	[+ South Korea]
C091	100M	Turkish Air Force	091+	95-091	[+ Turkey]	
C092	100M	South Korean Air Force	EC-556	5-092+	40-092	[+ South Korea]
C093	100M	Turkish Air Force	093+	95-093	[+ Turkey]	
C094	100MPA	Irish Air Corps	IFP253	253		
C095	100M	Turkish Air Force	095+	95-095	[+ Turkey]	
C096	100M	South Korean Air Force	EC-551	096+	40-096	[+ South Korea]
C097	100M	(Turkish Air Force)	097	[w/o 19Jan01 Kayseri, Turkey]		
C098	100M	South Korean Air Force	EC-552	5-098+	40-098	[+ South Korea]
C099	100M	Turkish Air Force	099+	95-099	[+ Turkey]	
C100	100M	South Korean Air Force	5-100+	40-100	[+ South Korea]	
C101	100M	Turkish Air Force	101+	95-101	[+ Turkey]	
C102	100M	South Korean Air Force	5-102+	40-102	[+ South Korea]	
C103	100M	Turkish Air Force	103+	95-103	[build no.TK118]	[+ Turkey]
C104	100M	Turkish Air Force	104+	95-104	[build no.TK119]	[+ Turkey]
C105	200M	French Air Force	105//62-IG//F-RAIG			
C106	100M	Turkish Air Force	106+	95-106	[build no.TK120]	[+ Turkey]
C107	200M	French Air Force	107//62-IH//F-RAIH	107//52-IH//F-RAIH		
C108	100M	Turkish Air Force	108+	95-108	[build no.TK121]	[+ Turkey]
C109	100	Colombian Air Force	FAC1260			
C110	100M	Turkish Air Force	110+	95-110	[build no.TK122]	[+ Turkey]
C111	200M	French Air Force	111//62-II//F-RAII			
C112	100M	Turkish Air Force	112+	96-112	[build no.TK123]	[+ Turkey]
C113	100M	Turkish Air Force	113+	96-113	[+ Turkey]	

CASA/AIRTECH CN-235 TETUKO

C/n	Model	Last known Owner/Operator	Identities/fates/comments (where appropriate)
C114	200M	French Air Force	114//62-IJ//F-RAIJ
C115	100M	Turkish Air Force	115+ 350^ 96-115 [+ Turkey; ^ Jordan]
C116	100M	Turkish Air Force	116+ 351^ 96-116 [+ Turkey; ^ Jordan]
C117	100M	Turkish Air Force	117+ 96-117 [build no.TK124] [+ Turkey]
C118	100	Colombian Air Force	FAC1261
C119	100M	Turkish Air Force	119+ 96-119 [+ Turkey]
C120	100M	Turkish Air Force	120+ 96-120 [+ Turkey]
C121	100	Colombian Air Force	FAC1262
C122	100M	Turkish Air Force	122+ 96-122 [+ Turkey]
C123	200M	French Air Force	123//62-IM//F-RAIM
C124	100M	Turkish Air Force	124+ 97-124 [+ Turkey]
C125	100M	Turkish Air Force	125+ 97-125 [+ Turkey]
C126	100M	Turkish Air Force	126+ 97-126 [+ Turkey]
C127	100M	Turkish Air Force	127+ 97-127 [+ Turkey]
C128	200M	French Air Force	128//62-IK//F-RAIK
C129	200M	French Air Force	129//F-ZVLY 129//62-IL//F-RAIL
C130	300	Turbo Flite Aviation LLC	EC-101 6T-AA+ N825FA [+ Austria]
C131	100M	Turkish Air Force	131+ 97-131 [+ Turkey]
C132	100M	Turkish Air Force	132+ 97-132 [+ Turkey]
C133	100M	Turkish Air Force	133+ 97-133 [+ Turkey]
C134	100M	Turkish Air Force	134+ 97-134 [+ Turkey]
C135	300	Devon Holding & Leasing	N168D N464HA
C136	100M	Turkish Air Force	136+ 97-136 [+ Turkey]
C137	200M	French Air Force	137//62-IN//F-RAIN
C138	100M	Turkish Air Force	138+ 97-138 [+ Turkey]
C139	300	Devon Holding & Leasing	N196D N589CE
C140	100M	Turkish Air Force	140+ 97-140 [+ Turkey]
C141	200M	French Air Force	141//62-IO//F-RAIO
C142	100M	Turkish Air Force	142+ 98-142 [+ Turkey]
C143	300	Devon Holding & Leasing	N187D N387AB
C144	100M	Turkish Air Force	144+ 98-144 [+ Turkey]
C145	300	Devon Holding & Leasing	N219D N471EB
C146	100M	Turkish Air Force	146+ 98-146 [+ Turkey]
C147	100MPA	Ecuadorian Navy	AN-204 [substantial damage 08Jun11 Manta, Ecuador]
C148	100M	Turkish Air Force	148+ 98-148 [+ Turkey]
C149	100M	Turkish Air Force	149+ 98-149 [+ Turkey]
C150	100	Ecuadorian Army	AEE-503 [substantial damage 16Mar12 Quito, Ecuador]
C151	100MPA	Thales Airborne Systems	F-ZWMP [for Turkish Coast Guard possibly as TCB-654]
C152	200M	French Air Force	152//62-IP//F-R???
C153			
C154	MPA	Turkish Coast Guard	TCSG-552
C155			
C156	200M	French Air Force	156//62-IQ//F-R???
C157	100MPA	Turkish Navy	TCB-651
C158	200M	French Air Force	158//62-IR//F-R???
C159			
C160	200M	French Air Force	160//62-IS//F-R???
C161			
C162			
C163			
C164			
C165	200M	French Air Force	165//62-IT//F-R???
C166	300MPA	Transportes Aereos del Sur	EC-235(2) EC-KEK [coded 101]
C167	300MPA	US Coast Guard	FSP-001+ 2301 [HC-144A] [+ Spain]
C168	300MPA	US Coast Guard	FSP-002+ 2302 [HC-144A] [+ Spain]
C169	300MPA	Transportes Aereos del Sur	EC-027 EC-KEL [coded 102]
C170	300MPA	US Coast Guard	2303 [HC-144A]
C171	300MPA	Transportes Aereos del Sur	EC-021 EC-KEM [coded 103]
C172	300MPA	US Coast Guard	2304 [HC-144A]
C173			
C174	300MPA	US Coast Guard	2305 [HC-144A]
C175	300MPA	US Coast Guard	2306 [HC-144A]
C176	300	Turbo Flite Aviation LLC	N248MD N835CE

CASA/AIRTECH CN-235 TETUKO

C/n	Model	Last known Owner/Operator	Identities/fates/comments (where appropriate)
C177	300	Turbo Flite Aviation LLC	N528LD N383EC [Nov11 possibly to USAF as 96-6045]
C178	300MPA	US Coast Guard	2307 [HC-144A]
C179	300MPA	US Coast Guard	2308 [HC-144A]
C180	300	Spanish Air Force	T.19B-21//09-501
C181	300	Spanish Air Force	T.19B-22//09-502
C182	300	APA Leasing Inc	N768KD
C183	300MPA	US Coast Guard	2310 [HC-144A]
C184	300MPA	US Coast Guard	2311 [HC-144A]
C185		Botswana Defence Force	OG1(2) [second use of serial; see c/n C008] [also carries squadron identity Z10]
C186	300?	Turbo Flite Aviation LLC	N460ES
C187		Botswana Defence Force	OG2(2) [second use of serial; see c/n C009] [also carries squadron identity Z10]
C188		Yemen Air Force	2211
C189	300MPA	Mexican Navy	AMP-120
C190	300MPA	Mexican Navy	AMP-121
C191	300MPA	Mexican Navy	AMP-122
C192	300MPA	Colombian Navy	ARC-803
C193	300	French Air Force	193 [code 62-HA]
C194	300	French Air Force	194 [code 62-HB]
C195	300	French Air Force	195 [code 62-HC]
C196	300	French Air Force	196 [code 62-HD]
C202		US Coast Guard	2313 [HC-144A]
C203		US Coast Guard	2314 [HC-144A]
C204	300MPA	Mexican Navy	AMP-123
C205	300MPA	Mexican Navy	AMP-124
C206	300MPA	Mexican Navy	AMP-125
C207			
C208			
C209			
C210			
C211			
C212			
C213			
C214			

IPTN/NURTANIO CN-235 TETUKO

C/n	Model	Last known Owner/Operator	Identities/fates/comments (where appropriate)
992/01N	200MPA	Nurtanio	PK-XNC [prototype ff 30Dec83] [CofA expired 23Jun10; fate/status unknown]
2/001N	10	Zest Airways	PK-XNA PK-MNA RP-C5000
5/002N	10	ex Merpati Nusantara Airlines	PK-XND PK-MNC [wfu by 01May11 Medan, Indonesia]
7/003N	10	Merpati Nusantara Airlines	PK-XNE PK-MND [stored by 09Mar06 Surabaya, Indonesia; l/n 12Dec09]
9/004N	10	Merpati Nusantara Airlines	PK-XNF PK-MNE [stored by 30Mar04 Surabaya, Indonesia; by 01May11 moved to Medan, Indonesia]
10/005N	200	Merpati Nusantara Airlines	PK-XNG PK-MNF PK-XNG PK-MNF [stored by 09Mar06 Surabaya, Indonesia; l/n 12Dec09]
14/006N	10	Merpati Nusantara Airlines	PK-XNH PK-MNG [stored by 09Mar06 Surabaya, Indonesia]
16/007N	10	Merpati Nusantara Airlines	PK-XNJ PK-MNI [stored by 09Mar06 Surabaya, Indonesia]
18/008N	10	Merpati Nusantara Airlines	PK-XNI PK-MNH
19/009N	10	Merpati Nusantara Airlines	PK-XNK PK-MNJ
20/010N	10	Merpati Nusantara Airlines	PK-XNL PK-MNK [stored Surabaya, Indonesia]
24/011N	10	Merpati Nusantara Airlines	PK-XNM PK-MNL
26/012N	10	Merpati Nusantara Airlines	PK-XNN PK-MNM
28/013N	10	(Merpati Nusantara Airlines)	PK-XNO PK-MNN [w/o 18Oct92 Mount Papandayan, Indonesia]
29/014N	220AT	Senegal Air Force	PK-XNP PK-MNO AX-2337 6W-STA
30/015N	220AT	Senegal Air Force	PK-XNQ PK-MNP AX-2338 6W-STB
/016N	100	(Indonesian Air Force)	PK-XNR AX-2301 A-2301 [w/o 21Jly05 Sumatra, Indonesia]
/017N	100	Indonesian Air Force	PK-XNS AX-2302 A-2302
37/018N	220	(Nurtanio)	PK-XNT [w/o 22May97 Gorda Serang AB, West Java, Indonesia]
/019N	220MPA	Indonesian Air Force	PK-XNU AX-2336 AI-2317
/020N	220	Burkina Faso Air Force	PK-XNV RP-C4000 XT-MBE
19/021N	100	Indonesian Air Force	PK-XNW AX-2314 [to be converted to MPA version]
/022N	100	Indonesian Air Force	PK-XNX AX-2303 A-2303

CASA/AIRTECH CN-235 TETUKO

C/n	Model	Last known Owner/Operator	Identities/fates/comments (where appropriate)
/023N	100	Indonesian Air Force	PK-XNY AX-2304 A-2304
/024N	100	Indonesian Air Force	PK-XNZ AX-2305 A-2305
/025N	100M	Indonesian Air Force	AX-2306 A-2306
/026N	100M-330	United Arab Emirates Air Force	(AX-2307)+ PK-XNA 810 [+ Indonesia]
/027N	100M-330	United Arab Emirates Air Force	(AX-2308)+ 811 [+ Indonesia]
/028N	100M-330	United Arab Emirates Air Force	(AX-2309)+ 812 [+ Indonesia]
/029N	100M-330	United Arab Emirates Air Force	(AX-2310)+ 813 [+ Indonesia]
/030N	100M-330	United Arab Emirates Air Force	(AX-2311)+ 814 [+ Indonesia]
/031N	100M-330	United Arab Emirates Air Force	(AX-2312)+ 815 [+ Indonesia]
/032N	100M-330	United Arab Emirates Air Force	AX-2313+ 816 [+ Indonesia]
/033N	100MPA	Royal Brunei Air Force	(AX-2314)+ ATU-501^ TUDB-501 [+ Indonesia; ^ Brunei]
/034N	220MPA	Malaysian Air Force	(AX-2315)+ M44-01 [+ Indonesia]
/035N	220MPA	Malaysian Air Force	(AX-2316)+ M44-02 [+ Indonesia]
/036N	220MPA	Malaysian Air Force	(AX-2317)+ M44-03 [+ Indonesia]
/037N	220MPA	Malaysian Air Force	(AX-2318)+ M44-04 [+ Indonesia]
/038N	220MPA	Malaysian Air Force	(AX-2319)+ M44-05 [+ Indonesia]
/039N	220MPA	Malaysian Air Force	(AX-2320)+ M44-06 [+ Indonesia]
/040N	220M	for Indonesian Air Force	
/041N	100M	KASET (Thailand)	2221 [possibly wfu by 27Jan11 Nakhon Sawan, Thailand]
/042N	100M	KASET (Thailand)	2222
/043N	220M	Pakistan Air Force	04-043
/044N	220M	South Korean Air Force	AX-2322+ 10-044 [+ Indonesia]
/045N	220M	South Korean Air Force	AX-2323+ 10-045 [+ Indonesia]
/046N	220M	South Korean Air Force	AX-2324+ 5-046^ 20-046 [+ Indonesia; ^ South Korea]
/047N	220M	South Korean Air Force	AX-2325+ 20-047 [+ Indonesia]
/048N	220M	South Korean Air Force	AX-2326+ 20-048 [+ Indonesia]
/049N	220M	South Korean Air Force	AX-2327+ 20-049 [+ Indonesia]
/050N	220M-VIP	South Korean Air Force	AX-2328+ ?-050 [+ Indonesia]
/051N	220M-VIP	South Korean Air Force	AX-2329+ ?-051 [+ Indonesia]
/052N	220M	Pakistan Air Force	04-052
/053N	220M	Pakistan Air Force	04-053
/054N	220M-VIP	Pakistan Air Force	04-054
/055N	220M-VIP	Malaysian Air Force	M44-07
/056N	220M-VIP	Malaysian Air Force	PK-XNE M44-08
/057N	220MPA	South Korean Coast Guard	PK-XNA B-704
/058N?	220MPA	South Korean Coast Guard	B-705
/059N?	220MPA	South Korean Coast Guard	PK-XND B-706
Unidentified			
unkn	220MPA	Indonesian Air Force	AX-2336 A1-2317* [displayed 18Feb08 at Singapore Air Show; serial A1-2317 scrubbed over; no c/n given on c/n plate]
unkn	300MPA	US Coast Guard	2309 [HC-144A] [reported 10Apr10 Seville, Spain]
unkn	300MPA	US Coast Guard	2312 [HC-144A; ferried 03Aug11 to Elizabeth City, NJ]
unkn		USAF	2477 [reported Jly11 Chania, Crete, Greece]
unkn		USAF	96-6042 [reported 29Jan10 Lajes, Azores, Portugal]
unkn		USAF	96-6043 [reported 30Jan10 & 13Nov11 Lajes, Azores, Portugal]
unkn		USAF	66044 [reported 18Sep11 Patrick AFB, FL; assume full serial is 96-6044]
unkn		USAF	96-6046 [noted Sep06 with 427th SOS; plate checked Mar08 "1998 built aircraft, accepted Jly04 CN235 Version L3-02, version no 1]
unkn	400	Secretaria General de Pesca Maritima	EC-HTU

CASA (EADS-CASA) CN-295

C/n	Line No	Model	Last known Owner/Operator	Identities/fates/comments (where appropriate)
P001		AEW	EADS/CASA	EC-295 [prototype ff 28Nov97; converted 2011 to AEW version]
S001	001		EADS/CASA	EC-296 [f/f 02Dec98]
EA03-1-002	002		Spanish Air Force	XT.21-01 T21-01//35-39 [f/f 22Dec98]
EA03-2-003	003		Spanish Air Force	XT.21-02 T.21-02//35-40
EA03-3-004	004		Spanish Air Force	T.21-03//35-41
EA03-4-005	005		Spanish Air Force	T.21-04//35-42
EA03-5-006	006		Spanish Air Force	T.21-05//35-43
007	007		Royal Jordanian Air Force	352
EA03-6-008	008		Spanish Air Force	T.21-06//35-44
PO01-1-009	009		Polish Air Force	011
PO01-2-010	010		Polish Air Force	012
011	011		Royal Jordanian Air Force	353
EA03-7-012	012		Spanish Air Force	T.21-07//35-45 [operator and serial tie up not confirmed, might be line number 013]
PO01-3-013	013		Polish Air Force	013 [operator and serial tie up not confirmed, might be line number 012]
PO01-4-014	014		Polish Air Force	014
PO01-5-015	015		Polish Air Force	015
EA03-8-016	016		Spanish Air Force	T.21-08//35-46
EA03-9-017	017		Spanish Air Force	T.21-09//35-47
PO01-6-018	018		Polish Air Force	016
PO01-7-019	019		Polish Air Force	017
PO01-8-020	020		Polish Air Force	018
021	021		Algerian Air Force	7T-WGA
022	022		Algerian Air Force	7T-WGB
023	023		Algerian Air Force	7T-WGC
024	024		Algerian Air Force	7T-WGD
025	025		Algerian Air Force	7T-WGE
026	026		Algerian Air Force	7T-WGF
EA03-10-027	027		Spanish Air Force	T.21-10//35-48
BR01-4-028	028		Brazilian Air Force	2803 [C-105A] [NOTE: Brazilian c/ns also quoted as BR01-04-0xx etc]
BR01-1-029	029		Brazilian Air Force	2800 [C-105A]
BR01-2-030	030		Brazilian Air Force	2801 [C-105A] [tie-up not confirmed]
BR01-3-031	031		Brazilian Air Force	2802 [C-105A]
EA03-11-032?	032		Spanish Air Force	T.21-11//35-49
033	033		Colombian Air Force	1280
034	034		Colombian Air Force	1281
FI01-1-035	035		Finnish Air Force	CC-1
FI01-2-036	036		Finnish Air Force	CC-2
BR01-5-037	037		Brazilian Air Force	2804 [C-105A]
BR01-6-038	038		Brazilian Air Force	2805 [C-105A]
BR01-7-039	039		Brazilian Air Force	2806 [C-105A] [tie-up not confirmed]
BR01-8-040	040		Brazilian Air Force	2807 [C-105A]
041	041		Portuguese Air Force	16701
042	042		Portuguese Air Force	16702
PO01-9-043	043		(Polish Air Force)	019 [w/o 23Jan08 Miroslawiec, Poland]
PO01-10-044	044		Polish Air Force	020
EA03-11-045	045		Spanish Air Force	T.21-12//35-50
EA03-12-046	046		Spanish Air Force	T.21-13//35-51
047	047		Portuguese Air Force	16703
048	048		Portuguese Air Force	16704
BR01-9-049	049		Brazilian Air Force	2809 [C-105A]
BR01-10-050	050		Brazilian Air Force	2809 [C-105A]
PO01-11-051	051		Polish Air Force	021
052	052	MPA	Portuguese Navy	16708
053	053		Polish Air Force	022
054	054		Colombian Air Force	1282
055	055	MPA	Portuguese Navy	16709
BR01-11-052	056		Brazilian Air Force	2810 [C-105A]
057	057		Portuguese Air Force	16705
BR01-12-058	058		Brazilian Air Force	2811 [C-105A]
059	059		Portuguese Air Force	16706
060	060		Colombian Air Force	1283

CASA (EADS-CASA) CN-295

C/n	Line No	Model	Last known Owner/Operator	Identities/fates/comments (where appropriate)	
061	061		Portuguese Air Force	16707	
062	062		Czech Air Force	0452	
063	063	MPA	Portuguese Navy	16710	
064	064	MPA	Portuguese Navy	16711	
065	065	MPA	Portuguese Navy	16712	
066	066	MPA	Chilean Navy	501	
067	067	MPA	Chilean Navy	502	[wears squadron badge VP-1]
068	068	MPA	Chilean Navy	503	
069	069		Czech Air Force	0453	
070	070		Mexican Navy	AMT-250	
071	071		Mexican Navy	AMT-251	
072	072	M	Mexican Air Force	3201	
073	073	M	Mexican Air Force	3202	
074	074	ASW	Czech Air Force	082	0454
075	075		Czech Air Force	0455	[not confirmed]
076	076	M	Mexican Air Force	3203	
077	077	M	Mexican Air Force	3204	[also reported as c/n 080]
078	078	M	Mexican Air Force	3205	
079	079		Mexican Navy	AMT-252	
080	080	M	Mexican Navy	AMT-253	
081	081		Ghana Air Force	GHF-550	
082	082		Mexican Air Force	3206	
083	083		Egyptian Air Force	SU-BRP	
084	084		Egyptian Air Force	SU-BPQ	
085	085		Egyptian Air Force	SU-BRR	
086	086		Finnish Air Force	CC-3	
087	087	M	Ghana Air Force	GHF-551	
088	088				
089	089	M	Mexican Navy	AMT-255	
090	090	M	Indonesian Air Force	A-9501	
091					
092					
093					
094					
095					
096					
097					
098					
099					
100					

CESSNA 208 CARAVAN

C/n	Model	Last known Owner/Operator	Identities/fates/comments (where appropriate)
699		Cessna Aircraft Co	N208LP [prototype f/f 09Dec82]
700		Cessna Aircraft Co	N208FP [canx 18Apr11 as wfu]

CESSNA 208/208A CARAVAN I/CARGOMASTER

Note: Caravan I c/ns are prefixed with 208 as are those of the 208A, known as Cargomaster, both without a hyphen.

C/n	Model	Last known Owner/Operator	Identities/fates/comments (where appropriate)
00001		(North American Flight Services)	N9157F F-GDRP HB-CLD 5R-MVL N336DN [w/o 15Sep09 near Sheffield, MA]
00002		Interandes	N9182F HK-3226
00003		(A R McVinish)	N9225F A9C-BC N3212D VH-MMV [w/o 29Apr01 near Nagambie, VIC, Australia]
00004		Regional Air Services	(N9229F) N208CC VH-JEE N208CC HB-CLI 5H-MUR 5Y-MAK 5H-MUR
00005		F K Aros Flyg i Vasteras	N9231F SE-LZY [floatplane]
00006		(Hermens Air)	N9241F [w/o 01Nov85 Bethel, AK; canx 02Jun89]
A00007		Aircraft Guaranty Corp	(N9300F) N800FE N208RF
00008		PenAir-Peninsula Airways	N9304F
A00009		Spokane Turbine Skydiving	(N9305F) N801FE N801JA
00010		Missionary Aviation Fellowship	N9314F 9Q-CAU N9314F TZ-CAU N9314F 9Q-CAU
00011		(PenAir-Peninsula Airways)	N9316F [w/o 30Jan98 Port Heiden, AK; canx 11Sep98; hulk to Dodson International Parts, Rantoul, KS for spares]
A00012		Agro Pec de Nova Fronteira	(N9321F) N802FE PT-OGH
00013		(Air Serv International)	N9324F [w/o 28Jun05 Matemo Airport, Mozambique; canx 14Jly07]
00014		Millennium Aviation Transportes	(N9328F) N770TC YV-1122P TG-MMM
A00015		(West Air/FedEx Express)	(N9338F) N803FE [w/o 06Jun90 Fresno-Chandler Executive, CA]
A00016		J A Flight Services	(N9342F) N804FE SE-KRX EI-FEX N835FE(2) N803JA
00017		(Air Carriers Express Services)	(N9344F) N551CC [w/o 29Sep85 near Jenkinsburg, GA]
00018		Mission Aviation Fellowship of Canada	N9346F C-GWOH
A00019		TAF Linhas Aereas	(N9347F) N805FE PT-OGV
A00020		(Transportes Aereos Meridionais – TAM)	(N9348F) N806FE PT-OGN [DBF 26Aug93 following hijacking Sinop Airport, Brazil]
00021		Greystoke Engineering Inc	N9349F YV-10CP YV-434C N9349F 5Y-HAA
00022		Scott Air	N9351F CP-1987 N32009
00023		Business Wings	N9354F D-FALK
00024		Falcon Air Charters	N9358F 5Y-GSV
00025		not yet known	N9359F CP-2019 N9359F C-FGLC C-FTEL C-GBOP 8Q-HID N8CU XB-ALO [floatplane]
A00026		(Martinaire)	(N9360F) N807FE N807LA [w/o 04Sep87 Bulverde, TX; hulk to White Industries, Bates City, MO]
A00027		(Transportes Aereos Meridionais – TAM)	(N9362F) N808FE PT-OGO [w/o 11Apr95 Luziania Airport, Brazil; canx 06Sep95]
00028		Pofolk Aviation Hawaii	(N502BA) N9363F N502BA N502HA N9454F
00029		Parachutisme Atmosphair	N9370F C-GJJM
00030		Fugro Airborne Surveys	(N9373F) N208MH ZS-MSJ A2-AHJ ZS-MSJ
00031		Air Labrador	N9376F D-FLYH N8JM N604MA C-GUYR
A00032		Fretax Taxi Aereo	(N9378F) N809FE PT-OGQ
A00033		Fayard Enterprises	(N9379F) N810FE PT-OGZ ZP-CAR N246CB
A00034		Abaete Aerotaxi	(N9381F) N811FE PT-OGS
00035		Rusty Myers Flying Service	N9382F CP-2089 N9382F C-FKSJ [floatplane]
00036		Fly 540	N9383F ZS-NON 5Y-NON ZS-NON 5Y-NON
00037		(DHL Aviation Africa)	N9384F HB-CKK 5Y-RAN [w/o 26Nov99 Nairobi-Jomo Kenyatta Airport, Kenya]
A00038		Abaete Aerotaxi	(N9386F) N815FE PT-OGT
A00039		(PENTA – Pena Transportes Aereos)	(N9392F) N816FE PT-OGI [w/o 26Apr94 near Jacareacanga, Brazil; canx 03Nov94]
A00040		S Ulrich	(N9401F) N812FE N208NN OY- G-GOHI [floatplane]
A00041		TAF Linhas Aereas	(N9402F) N813FE PT-OGG
A00042		Aeromas	(N9403F) N814FE PT-OGA ZP-TYT CX-MAX
A00043		(P M Air/FedEx Express)	(N9404F) N820FE [w/o 27Feb90 Denver-Stapleton International, CO]
00044		SEC Colombia	N9410F CP-2149 HK-3686X HK-3686
00045		Coton Tchad	N9411F TT-BAU
00046		(Zimex Aviation)	N9413F HB-CKW [w/o 22Jly89 near Mocuba, Mozambique]

CESSNA 208 CARAVAN

C/n	Model	Last known Owner/Operator	Identities/fates/comments (where appropriate)
A00047		Nobel-Paragon Mining	(N9414F) N821FE PT-OGB N8HE V5-NOP
00048		Missionary Aviation Fellowship	(N9418F) N88TJ PK-MAN
00049		Skydiving Productions Over Texas	N9421F VH-TFT N9421F
A00050		Abaete Aerotaxi	(N9424F) N817FE PT-OGP
00051		(Soundsair)	N9426F ZK-SFA [w/o 29Jan96 en-route near Mount Robertson, New Zealand]
00052		(Brazilian Air Force)	N9429F 2701 [C98] [w/o 29Oct09 en-route between villages of Aldeias Aurelio & Rio Novo, Brazil]
00053		Mobile Carpet Cleaning Factory	N9438F VH-XLV [Supervan conversion # 6]
00054		(Phaeton LLC)	N9440F YV-435C N347TC N208RD N702MJ [w/o 12Mar06 Sampson Cay, Bahamas; canx 10Aug07]
00055		(Liberian Air Reconnaissance Unit)	N9447F ARU-021 [w/o 30Jan87 in Atlantic Ocean 65kms SE of Monrovia, Liberia]
A00056		J A Flight Services	(N9451F) N819FE N840JA
00057		Westwind Air	N9452F VH-JEJ N9452F ZS-NIH N208NN(1) N2AV
00058		(Liberian Air Reconnaissance Unit)	N9454F ARU-022 [reportedly w/o during the 1990 Liberian Civil War]
00059		(Outdoor Aviation)	N9461F ZK-SFB [w/o 27Nov87 in sea off Haumuri Bluffs, S of Kaikoura, New Zealand; canx 17May88]
00060		Procuraduria General de la Republica	N9462F YV-436C FAC1121+ XC-AA35^ [+ Colombia; ^ status unclear; these marks were/are known on Cessna T210N c/n 64536]
00061		(Aviation Sans Frontieres)	N9463F F-OHLG [w/o 02Aug02 Pimu Airsrip, Democratic Republic of Congo]
00062		Greystoke Engineering Inc	(N834FE) N9464F PT-WKC N9464F N208GE HH-CAT N208GE [floatplane]
00063		not yet known	N9469F CP-2090
A00064		(TAM Brazil)	(N9472F) N823FE PT-OGC [w/o 18Oct97 near Sao Paulo, Brazil; canx 06Aug98]
A00065		Eagle Air Transport	(N9473F) N807FE C-FEXF N799FE (N805JA) N799FE N40EA
A00066		Abaete Aerotaxi	(N9475F) N826FE PT-OGU
A00067		ex Brasil Central Regional	(N9476F) N822FE PT-OGW [no current CofA; reported retired 12Nov08 its canx date]
00068		Aeronautica Civil	N9478F HK-3200G
A00069		(TAM Express/Helisul)	(N9479F) N824FE PT-OGM [w/o 06Dec93 Tucuma, Brazil; canx 31May94]
00070		PenAir-Peninsula Airways	N9481F
00071		South African Air Force	(N9488F) N437K N35K ZS-LYR 3001
A00072		Something Aviation	(N9491F) N827FE N806JA
A00073		(Union Flights/FedEx Express)	(N9496F) N828FE(1) [w/o 23Oct87 near Fairfield, CA; canx 07Jun90]
00074		Hot Wings	(N9501F) N829FE PT-OGD ZP-TXT N208SC
A00075		B A Jacobs Flight Services	(N9502F) N830FE N807JA
A00076		TAM Express or Brazil Central Regional	(N9510F) N825FE PT-OGX
00077		Budbay Pty Ltd	N9511F VH-UMV
A00078		Abaete Aerotaxi	(N9512F) N831FE C-FEXE(1) N65575 PT-OGK
00079		Avion Capital/Air Net Systems	N9514F
00080		South African Air Force	(N9515F) ZS-LNJ ZS-LZS 3002
A00081		J A Flight Services	(N9518F) N832FE N809JA
00082		(Govt of Canada/Royal Canadian Mounted Police)	(N9521F) C-GMPB [floatplane] [w/o 15Aug00 Teslin Lake, BC, Canada; canx 23Apr03]
00083		Skydive Byron Bay	N9523F D-FLMT HB-CJS N831AM VH-ZMV
A00084		Remote Area Medical Inc	(N9525F) N833FE F-GEOH EI-FDX N833FE N833EB
00085		Roger Wiplinger LLC	N9526F N80RD [floatplane]
00086		Colombian Air Force	N9527F YV-437C+ FAC1120 FAC5050 [+ reported seized 21Dec89 by Colombian Air Force]
A00087		Bill & Ben Investments	(N9528F) N834FE PT-OGJ N899MA VH-NMV
00088		Lake & Peninsula Airlines	N9530F
00089		Windway Capital Corp	N9535F N555HM N94MT
00090		Sunwest Aviation	N9536F C-FNOC
A00091		(P M Air/FedEx Express)	(N9537F) N835FE [w/o 17Jan90 near Leadville, CO; canx 18May90]
00092		Avion Capital/Air Net Systems	N9539F
00093		Skydive Express	N9540F V5-NCA ZS-OAI VH-OAI
A00094		Vera Cruz Taxi Aereo	(N9543F) N836FE PT-OGY
00095		Inversiones Bellavista	N9545F HK-3296W
00096		Budbay Pty Ltd	N9546F C-GLIC N35CA N242SS N89RD 8Q- N89RD VH-MMV [floatplane]
A00097		(TAF Linhas Aereas)	(N9548F) N837FE PT-OHA [w/o 08Dec99 Joao Pessoa, Brazil]

CESSNA 208 CARAVAN

C/n	Model	Last known Owner/Operator	Identities/fates/comments (where appropriate)
00098		Blue Wing Airlines	N9549F HK-3309P XC-HGA HK-3309 N207RM XC-AA90 N207RM PZ-TSB
00099		T & T Capital	N9551F N216TA (C-FRZQ) N399TT
A00100		Abaete Aerotaxi	(N9555F) N838FE PT-OGR
00101		Tessel Air	N9555F N99U PH-LBR [floatplane]
A00102		TAF Linhas Aereas	(N9577F) N839FE PT-OGL
00103		Lake & Peninsula Airlines	N9602F
00104		(Hermens Air/Markair Express)	N9603F VH-JEY N9603 N9444F [w/o 21Dec90 near False Pass, Aleutian Islands, AK; canx 28Jan94]
00105		Utin Lento	N9604F N105YV N9604F (OY-CJL) OY-TCA (LN-PBA) OY-TCA LN-PBD OH-SIS
00106		(California Air Charter)	N9613F [w/o en-route 16Jan87 Cima, CA; canx 06Jly94]
00107		Desert Locust Control Organisation	N9617F 5Y-DLA
00108		(Cape York Air Service)	N9624F JA8224 N9624F D-FAST N977A VH-CYC [w/o 08Feb04 ditched in sea off Green Island, QLD, Australia; canx 25May09]
00109		Sky Aviation	N9628F JA8225 N9628F 5H-NAA 5H-TFC 5H-EWA
00110		Avion Capital/Air Net Systems	N9642F
00111		River Air	N9647F ZS-LXK N9647F C-FFYC
00112		L'Hopitallier Pierre	N9649F D-FILM SE-LER D-FROG F-GPHO
00113		Pacific Aero	N9652F
00114		Australia Skydive	N9653F VH-YMV
00115		(Westchester Air)	(N9659F) N208W [w/o 06Oct89 unknown farm strip in Texas; canx 06Oct89]
00116		Start Skydiving	N9663F C-GMPR N208HF [floatplane]
00117		Skydive Stadtlohn	N9670F 8Q- N9670F N117SA N209JS [floatplane]
00118		Seawings	N9678F (N6KA) TF-SEA A6-SEA [floatplane]
00119		Preferred Airparts	(N9680F) N9635F N275PM
00120		(Planemasters)	(N9681F) N9637F [w/o 26Apr89 Mount Zion, IL; hulk to White Industries, Bates City, MO; l/n 25Apr07]
00121		Umatilla Aviation	N9639F
00122		Speedstar Express	N9641F
00123		Corpjet/Midline Air Freight	N9680F N801TH
00124		Central Coast Aircraft	(N9681F) C-FKAL N65570 A2-AHL N203CA (D-FROG) 4X-CSV N208TS
00125		ex Save the Children Fund	N9690F N1659C JA8227 N51967 VR-BNL 5Y-BKJ [canx by Dec98, fate unknown]
00126		South African Air Force	N9695F PJ-AVY N9695F ZS-MHU 3008
00127		(Country Flyin)	N1660C JA8226 N5197X ZS-NHA N208CP [w/o 25Aug05 by hurricane Katrina at Tamiami, FL; canx 12Dec06; by 03Jly09 fuselage at Kidron-Stoltzfus, OH for spares recovery]
00128		Wilderness Aircraft	N9697F [Supervan conversion # 5]
00129		BP208 LLC	N9698F N9NX [floatplane]
00130		South African Air Force	N9699F ZS-MEF 3004
00131		Access Aviation (Australia)	(N9700F) C-GCAR N777PU VH-OMV VH-DVS
00132		Brazilian Air Force	N9702F 2702 [C98]
00133		Brazilian Air Force	N9704F 2703 [C98]
00134		South African Air Force	N9705F ZS-MHJ 3005
00135		Mike's Oilfield Services	N9706F C-GBIT
00136		South African Air Force	N9707F ZS-MEG 3006
00137		Hankyu Airlines	N9708F N1570C JA8229
00138		South African Air Force	N9709F ZS-MEH 3007
00139		Hubbard Broadcasting	(N9710F) N1662C JA8230 N35NA C-FASP N4195R N35NA PT- N35NA N76AZ
00140		South African Air Force	N9711F ZS-MHL 3003
00141		Watson's Skyways	N1664C JA8211 N40DJ ZS-NLT N208WA N524DB C-GIKP C-GHGV C-GIKP
00142		(R Mary & A Trichot)	HK-3467X HK-3467P N208RM F-OHRM [w/o 18Sep01 N'Djamena Airport, Chad; hulk to Dodson International Parts, Rantoul, KS; l/n Jun06]
00143		(Lineas Aereas de Los Libertadores)	HK-3479X HK-3479 [w/o 29Apr94 El Rosal near Bogota, Colombia]
00144		US Bureau of Immigration	N9720F PNP-020+ N9720F [+ Peru]
00145		(Policia Nacional del Peru)	N9721F PNP-021 [w/o 20May89 Mount Huacranacro, Andes, Peru]
00146		Abateco Inc	N9722F C-GTLT N170JP N177JP

CESSNA 208 CARAVAN

C/n	Model	Last known Owner/Operator	Identities/fates/comments (where appropriate)
00147		not yet known	N9723F HK- N9723F+ HP- [+ first canx 03Oct89 to Aviones de Colombia; probably ntu then on 05Feb92 as sold in Panama; no subsequent identity traced]
00148		Grumeti Reserves	N9724F N77TF N77TZ 5H-PTJ [floatplane]
00149		Guy B Comer	N9725F N996PM N200LF
00150		Dilkara Leasing	N9726F JA8212 N208KM
00151		Tactical Air Operations	N9727F VH-FIG ZK-REY N9727F
00152		ex Landa Aviation	N9728F F-OGPC N9728F VH-PRW N9728F C-GJEM [canx 30Jly12 fate/status unknown]
00153		Sunwest Aviation	N9729F HS-TFF HS-SKT N4118K N7248J N319D N1016M C-GSWO
00154		Policia Nacionales de Colombia	N9730F HK-3510X HK-3510P PNC-0219
00155		G Garcia Calero	N9731F HK-3522X HK-3522P
00156		Air Serv International/Reliance Air	N9732F 5X-ASI [badly damaged 04Mar09 Maridi Airport, Sudan]
00157		Nautilus Aviation Pty	N9733F VH-PSR ZK-REZ N501TA N501P VH-OPH
00158		not yet known	N9734F JA8213 N9734F N242CS C-GAWP N705A 5N-WMB ZS-ORR 5Y-ORR ZS-ORR+ ET- [+ canx 11Jan12 to Ethiopia]
00159		(South African Air Force)	N9735F ZS-MLM 3009 [w/o 23Jly11 near Kei river, Eastern Cape, South Africa]
00160		(South African Air Force)	N9736F ZS-MLP 3010 [w/o 24Feb96 near Bulwer, KwaZulu, Natal, South Africa]
00161		South African Air Force	N9737F ZS-MLT 3011
00162		Missionary Aviation Fellowship	N9738F PK-MAO
00163		Groupe L'Hotel	N9739F JA8214 N9739F ZS-NJL N208JD 5R-MLH
00164		South African Air Force	N9740F ZS-MLR 3012
00165		Aeroexpresso de La Frontera	N9741F HK-3539
00166		Greystoke Engineering	N9743F F-OGOD N208JW 5Y- + HH-CAN N208JW [+ canx 20Apr05 as sold in Kenya; no marks known] [substainal damage 21Apr09 Frederick, MD]
00167		Brazilian Air Force	N9744F 2704 [C98]
00168		(Brazilian Air Force)	N9745F 2705 [C98] [w/o 18Sep98 near Peru border]
00169		Brazilian Air Force	N9746F 2706 [C98]
00170		Brazilian Air Force	N9748F 2707 [C98]
00171		ex Joe Husta Aircraft Corp	N9749F [canx 03Sep91 as sold in Panama; no subsequent identity traced]
00172		Missionary Aviation Fellowship	N9750F JA8217 N9750F ET-ALD
00173		Seair Pacific Gold Coast	N9751F JA8218 N9751F OY-IRP LN-SEA VH-LMZ [floatplane]
00174		Ridgeaire Inc	N9753F JA8216 N999U N134V
00175		Baker Planes	(N9754F) C-GAWJ N711AU N23MB
00176		Brazilian Air Force	N9756F 2708 [C98]
00177		Caravan Air	N9757F ZS-MVY V5-GPX
00178		Nellair Charters & Travel	N9758F A9C-BD N9758F ZS-NKG 5Y-NKG ZS-NKG
00179		not yet known	N9759F YV-523CP
00180		Taxi Aereo del Baudo	N9761F HK-3685X HK-3685 HK-3685G
00181		Skydive Byron Bay	N9762F VH-DZQ
00182		State of Alaska	N9763F C-FKAL(1) N70715
00183		Skydive Tandem	N9764F N50PD N923JC N165TC ZK-PMT
00184		Vera Cruz Taxi Aereo	N9765F PT-OGE
00185		Djibouti Air Force	N9766F J2-MAI
00186		Lardel Trading	F-OGPE N1163Q PT-WOS
00187		Vera Cruz Taxi Aereo	N9768F PT-OGF
00188		Finist'Air	(N9769F) F-GHGZ
00189		Black Sheep Aviation & Cattle	N9770F (C-GPAB) C-FMKP
00190		Missionary Aviation Fellowship-Kajjansi	N9771F ET-AKL N9771F 5X-BIL
00191		US Department of Justice	N9772F N313LL N20373 N50648 [operated by Drug Enforcement Administration]
00192		Rheinbraun	N9773F D-FOTO
00193		(Greystoke Engineering)	(N9774F) N193PP 5X-AVA N193GE [w/o en-route 13Aug99 Hillsborough, NH; canx 03Aug00]
00194		Springview Casualty Company	N9775F N888NT N388NT
00195		Hankyu Airlines	N9776F JA8890
00196		(Air Wemindji)	(N9778F) C-GAWM [w/o 31Aug01 N of La Grande, QC, Canada; canx 04Mar02]
00197		Budbay P/L Ltd	N9779F F-OGPT N708A VH-DZZ

CESSNA 208 CARAVAN

C/n	Model	Last known Owner/Operator	Identities/fates/comments (where appropriate)
00198		Mission Aviation Fellowship (PNG)	N9780F F-OGPU N839MA N466SP PK-MPN P2-MAF
00199		Kyoritsu Koko Satsuei	N9782F JA8891
00200		(Pan African Airlines)	N9783F N208CA N51558 5N-PAN [floatplane] [w/o 25Nov98 Ugborikoko, Nigeria]
00201		Missionary Aviation Fellowship	N9785F 5Y-ZBZ 5H-ZBZ
00202		(Skylink Kenya)	N9786F C-FKMY N208SN(1) 5Y-JAO [w/o 12Jly00 Nairobi-Wilson, Kenya]
00203		Missionary Aviation Fellowship	(N9787F) N133WW 5Y-BOI 5H-BOI 5R-MKD
00204		Thai KASET	N9788F 1911
00205		Thai KASET	N9789F 1912
00206		Thai KASET	N9790F 1913
00207		Business Wings	N208MT N208MC D-FAST(2)
00208		Kyoritsu Koko Satsuei	N9792F JA8895
00209		James R Fox	N9793F N224JW N915JF
00210		Asahi Koku	N9794F F-OGUD N654M JA881A
00211		Cameron Air Service	C-FRHL A6-AKO A6-MEB N211PA C-FKCA
00212		Whistler Air Services	N9828F (OY-) N9828F 8Q-MAT C-GSFA
00213		Queensland Police Service	N9798F VH-PSQ
00214		Vera Cruz Taxi Aereo	N9799F PT-OPA
00215		Aircraft Structures International	N9800F N9829F N9800F N192RA N192AV
00216		Taxi Aereo de Ibague	N9831F HK-3743 HK-3743P
00217		Seair Pacific Gold Coast	N9832F F-GNAA N772A 9M-FBA VH-LMD [floatplane]
00218		Bontrail Pty Ltd	N9813F VH-SJJ
00219		J LF Vilhena	N9815F PT-OQR [serious damage 09Jly12 Sao Paulo, Brazil]
00220		(Kyoritsu Koko Satsuei)	N9816F JA8897 [w/o 11Mar11 in tsunami at Sendai, Japan; canx 01Jun11]
00221		(Andaman & Nicobar Administration)	N9817F VT-AAN [w/o 06Sep93 near Port Blair Airport, India]
00222		Talon Air Service	N9818F N88TW N253TA [Supervan 900 conversion # 3]
00223		West Caribou Air Service	N9819F F-OGUU N899A C-FKLR
00224		Steen Ulrich	(N9820F) N788SR N288SR G-OHPC
00225		C2C Aviation	(N9821F) HB-CJY N248A N8DB N225WA I-SEAB F-GUTS [floatplane]
00226		Paracentrum Texel	(N9823F) PH-JAS
00227		Broome Aviation	N9824F VH-NGD VH-MOX [floatplane]
00228		(TransNorthern Aviation)	N9825F [w/o 30Apr97 near Kampong Chhnang, Cambodia; canx 05Nov99]
00229		Polis Diraja Malaysia (Police)	N9826F 9M-PSL
00230		Polis Diraja Malaysia (Police)	N9829F 9M-PSM
00231		Polis Diraja Malaysia (Police)	N9833F 9M-PSN
00232		Polis Diraja Malaysia (Police)	N9834F 9M-PSO
00233		Polis Diraja Malaysia (Police)	N9835F 9M-PSP
00234		Polis Diraja Malaysia (Police)	N9836F 9M-PSQ
00235		(Necon Air)	N9837F 9N-ADA [w/o 17Jan99 Jumla Airport, Nepal]
00236		Expressair	C-FKAZ [floatplane]
A00237		Gedex	N9840F C-GDEC
00238		Air Korea	N9824F HL5107
00239		not yet known	N5071M N1115V HI-649 HI-649SP XB-MFQ
00240		Sounds Air	N5122X N1289N ZK-PDM
00241		Skydive Spa Center	N241KA EP-857+ N241KA OO-NKA D-FLIZ [+ Peru]
00242		Cameron Air Service	N5131M C-GCGA (A6-CGA) C-GCGA
00243		Wright Caravan	N52670 N1213S
00244		Air Milford 2000	N1286A B-3610 VH-BSX ZK-SKB
00245		EFS European Flight Service	N1006K N622JW SE-KTH [floatplane]
00246		(Peruvian Army Aviation)	N1205A A6-AKA A6-EBI N228PA(2) EP-858 [floatplane] [w/o 09Jan09 Tigre river, Intuto region, Loreto province, Peru]
00247		Skydive The Beach	N5200U N1263V N208TB N208JM VH-PTX
00248		Turk Hava Kurumu	N1123X TC-CAU
00249		Camacho Express	N1288Y 5N-CES N578DD
00250		WDR Inc	N5188N N12666
00251		Fugro Airborne Surveys	N1251V C-GFAV VH-FGQ
00252		not yet known	N1268F ZP-TZB
00253		Royal Canadian Mounted Police	N1126P N208CF(1) C-GMPR
00254		North American Float Plane Service	N1218P EP-859+ OB-1786 [+ Peru]
00255		Guay Inc	N5130J C-GJDP C-GUAY
00256		Turk Hava Kurumu	N1249T TC-CAV

CESSNA 208 CARAVAN

C/n	Model	Last known Owner/Operator	Identities/fates/comments (where appropriate)
00257		Flying Bulls Museum	N5135A N666CS OE-EDM
00258		Air Hotel (titles)	N5162W N1244Z YV-733C N899MA C-GKAS 5R-MKH
00259		Aeroequipos	N5250E LV-PME LV-WST
00260		Sportline Nominees	N5265B N12324 (F-OHQA) VH-KLP HS-BWA VH-KLP VH-FYC [floatplane]
00261		Air Saguenay	N5261R C-GFLN C-GTBY [floatplane]
00262		Mess Aero	N208MA N858MA
00263		KASET (Thailand)	N5250E N1229Q 1914
00264		G.C. Air	N52601 N485JR
00265		KASET (Thailand)	N5200Z N1240T 1915
00266		KASET (Thailand)	N52626 N1240Z 1916
00267		KASET (Thailand)	N5200U N12408 1917
00268		KASET (Thailand)	N5264S N1241A(1) 1918
00269		J A Aero	N5201J N168GC RA-3020K RA-67702 N269JE
00270		Mercuryair	N52609 N1115V 9N-AEF N126V
00271		Big Island Air	N888GC LV-PND LV-WYX N281A
00272		Air Roberval	N5265B 8Q-HIC C-FCPW C-FDGW [floatplane]
00273		Kyoritsu Koko Satsuei	N5267K N1126F JA889A
00274		not yet known	N52609 N12149 D-FLIC
00275		Utin Lento	N52639 OH-USI
00276		Combined Air Ventures	N208MK N998PT (N5623J) N276MA
00277		Riversville Aircraft	(N5265N) N900RG
00278		Kimberley Air	N208GT HS-BWA HC-CCO VH-NRP VH-NRP VH-MBQ [floatplane]
00279		Westlake Marina	(N208GT) N5266F C-FWCS N518KM [floatplane]
00280		Herbold Group	(N208CD) N675CD N1126L
00281		Reynolds Group	N281SA N208JK N208JB N208JK
00282		KLR Enterprises Inc	N5263D N208HB
00283		Lakeview Aviation	N208LB N103AK N103AU C-FBKR
00284		Rico Linhas Aereas	PT-WRU [floatplane]
00285		(Brazilian Air Force)	N5264A FAC5054 [w/o en-route 22Nov06 Siberia, Cunday, Colombia]
00286		Brazilian Air Force	N5263D FAC5055
00287		Brazilian Air Force	N5265N FAC5056
00288		The Booking Company	N208KW 8Q-HIE C-FWBK C-FWTK A2-AKH [floatplane]
00289		Rustair	N675HP N850HP [floatplane]
00290		not yet known	N98FD LV-CAV
00291		Lancelot Development Corp	N5262X C-FHRB
00292		Wheel-Air	N208KW N88TW [floatplane]
00293		Nigel Albert Moore	G-ETHY N1295M G-ETHY
00294		not yet known	N15NH C-FLDC C-GHGV C-FTJK XA-WET
00295		Rotar	N5268V LV-ZOU
00296		Slingair/Aviation Tourism Australia	N208MM VH-HAM
00297		Wamair Service & Outfitting	N1299T N208LA C-FLXY
00298		Slingair/Aviation Tourism Australia	N1316A C-FRHL N94MS VH-LNI
00299		Bank of Utah; trustee	N208KS VP-BFR N208KS [floatplane]
00300		V1 Jet Management/Greg Arnette	N1260V N810GA [floatplane]
00301		BBS Aircraft	N1269J OH-CYP N1269J PK-MPJ N802EA C-GLDX C-FFCL [floatplane]
00302		Wamair Service & Outfitting	N1284N C-GJPX
00303		Aqua Airlines	N1260V N984JD (N728CP) N984J I-SEAA [floatplane]
00304		SCB Aviation	N208KR
00305		Air Tindi	N52627 C-GATY
00306		Kenmore Air	N12656 N426KM [floatplane]
00307		McMurray Aviation	N5264A C-FKEY [floatplane]
00308		Air Bellevue	N12712 C-GABM
00309		Shoreline Aviation	N309SA
00310		(Seair Services 1990)	N5206T C-FGGG [w/o 28Dec99 near Abbotsford, BC, Canada; canx 25Apr00]
00311		(Taxval)	N1229D LV-ZSR [w/o en-route 01Apr00 near Gualeguaychu, Argentina]
00312		Air Whitsunday Seaplanes	N1127W VH-PGA [floatplane]
00313		Travira Air	N51612 C-FAMB PK-TVI [floatplane]
00314		Lale LLC	N126JK N208AV
00315		Enterprise Aviation	N326RM
00316		Hearst Air Service	N5168Y N343EH C-FKAL(2) C-FKAE
00317		Marin Air	N52234 TC-KEU [floatplane]

CESSNA 208 CARAVAN

C/n	Model	Last known Owner/Operator	Identities/fates/comments (where appropriate)
00318		Air Roberval	N5165P TC-CAS N208JL C-FNME
00319		Amik Aviation	N1273E N208JV C-FLDC
00320		Chibougamau Diamond Drilling Ltd	N5181U C-FKAL
00321		Robert S Murray	N5264M N122KW HS-DAA N122KW [floatplane]
00322		North Star	N51869 C-GJAS
00323		Kudik Aviation	N5264S N208AM C-FKGY
00324		Alan R Stahlman	N52627 N324CC
00325		not yet known	N5212M TG-JCB TG-GET
00326		Tokyo Lease	N52682 N12845 JA888P
00327		(Aero Ruta Maya)	N5268E TG-JCS [w/o 24Aug08 near El Puente, Guatemala]
00328		Air Korea	N36964 HL5111
00329		Shelter Air Charter	N5166T N916BB N208LA N822BB
00330		Asas do Socoro	N1128H PR-ADS
00331		(Tokyo Century Lease)	N5262B N12895 JA889B [w/o 11Mar11 in tsunami at Sendai, Japan; canx 16Jun11]
00332		Shandong Airlines/Rainbow Jet	N5264M N1284F B-3632 [floatplane]
00333		Shandong Airlines/Rainbow Jet	N5155G N1228V B-3631 [floatplane]
00334		Broome Aviation	N5163K N1292B N84BD N75FT VH-NRT N76EA VH-NUX
00335		Four Seasons Aviation	N52626 C-GSEG
00336		Loch Lomond Seaplanes	N5263S XA-TSV N208FM G-MDJE [floatplane]
00337		Network Sales & Leasing	N1239K N37JW
00338		Shandong Airlines/Rainbow Jet	N5268M N1321L B-3636
00339		Tourist Development & Investment	N55CH N381A A6-TDB
00340		Tourist Development & Investment	N985SC A6-TDA
00341		Seair Seaplanes	N5154J C-GSAS [floatplane]
00342		Rusty Myers Flying Service	N51744 C-GAGK [floatplane]
00343		Bamaji Air	C-GIPR
00344		Joe C. Pace III	N701DL
00345		Air Whitsunday Seaplanes	N52639 N1133G HB-CYW A6-ELA N208E VH-PGT [floatplane]
00346		Air Whitsunday Seaplanes	N5264U N1128N HB-CYR A6-ELB N209E VH-PGB [floatplane]
00347		Flight Management	N52683+ N1267K N688RP N688RB [+ was current on a Cessna 172S at the time]
00348		Thomas J. Daly	N1458Q
00349		First Pegasus	N64PT
00350		Naka Nihon Koku	N12522 JA818N
00351		Simply Living	N4086L N725LM
00352		Wright Air Service	N52623 N1323Y
00353		White Birch Transportation	N5264A N1236B N84BD
00354		Shandong Airlines/Rainbow Jet	N5263U B-3639 [floatplane]
00355		Seawings Europe	N5264U N444GH A6-SEC LZ-SEC [floatplane]
00356		Amik Aviation	N526GM N208TG(1) VH-MXD N4356 C-FTMO
00357		Seair Seaplanes	N5267J C-FLAC [floatplane]
00358		Travira Air	N5147B N1229N PK-TVN [floatplane]
00359		Blackhawk Modifications	N908KA
00360		Sounds Air Travel & Tourism	N800RA ZK-TZR
00361		Wipaire Inc	N912DS
00362		Underhill Holdings	N52532 N12570 N208JB N208JP
00363		Commuter Duck	N5124F N41145 D-FISH N16CG
00364		Aurora Aircraft	N8PY N14RP (N208GW)
00365		McMurray Aviation	N5152X N675TF C-GKOM
00366		Goldak Airborne Surveys	N5109W N675DE C-FFCL C-GLDX
00367		Aerodynamics	N208KP VH-CXX G-DLAA
00368		Tango Corporation	N675WS N239JR
00369		Paspaley Pearling Co	N5257C VH-MOV
00370		Spectrum Air Service	N675MS
00371		Fisher Wavy	N5168Y C-GCAF
00372		Itabira Agro Industrial	N40446 PR-ITB
00373		not yet known	N4075L PR-ITC
00374		Wipaire Inc	N12615 N208SF
00375		Caravan Aviation	N1265U
00376		Peruvian Army Aviation	N5165T N415GA EP-857
00377		Wyoming Dept of Transportation	N104WY
00378		Fargo Jet Center	N51993 N208LB

CESSNA 208 CARAVAN

C/n	Model	Last known Owner/Operator	Identities/fates/comments (where appropriate)
00379		HRT Oil & Gas Expporacao	N51995 N1282D N307MD PR-HRE
00380		(Rico Taxi Aereo)	N5247N N12717 PR-RTA [floatplane] [w/o 09Oct05 Rio Negro River, near Santa Isabel, Brazil]
00381		not yet known	N5202D N1272V PR-PAZ
00382		Tudor Investment Corp	N5061W N77TF N77NF
00383		Maritime Energy Heli Air Services	N719MS N7890C LN-SEA VT-MHB [floatplane]
00384		Missionary Aviation Fellowship	N12747 S2-AEC [floatplane]
00385		Kyoritsu Koko Satsuei	N51143 N12675 JA889C
00386		Pilot International	N991Y
00387		Nakina Outpost Camp & Air Services	N5148N C-FNQB
00388		Air Alliance	N5125J N68FE D-FLEC
00389		Sandbar Air	N5244W N524DB
00390		Seair Seaplanes	N5254Y C-FJOE [floatplane]
00391		Northway Aviation	N5250P N12784 N675ST N85LF N85EE C-GNWI [floatplane]
00392		Robert B Cassil	N736WD
00393		Alan Rudd	N712WS
00394		Cosmopolitan Broadcasting	N394SF
00395		Nihon Aerospace Corp	N884RW N633PC JA889J
00396		103CQ LLC	N5165T N103CQ
00397		Missionary Aviation Fellowship – PNG	N543TC P2-MAG
00398		Mitsui Lease – Jiygo	N1297B JA889D
00399		AvWest	N5235G N40203 N877AA VH-ZWH
00400		(United Aviation Holdings Inc)	N5132T N208JS (D-FSEA) [sunk 24Mar12 following water landing Abalone Caye, Belize]
00401		Seawings	N5260U N12999 N1000X A6-SEB [floatplane]
00402		Osprey Express	N52235 N13170 ZP-TGH N754MS N719MS N719MZ N887ME [floatplane]
00403		Air Logistics/Pan African Airlines	N5267J N1316N 5N-BIW [floatplane]
00404		Cosmopolitan Broadcasting	N404SF
00405		Sydney Seaplanes	N1122Y VH-SXF [floatplane]
00406		Jetport	C-FMSK
00407		Prokon Airservice	N5262Z D-FUNK
00408		NTT Finance	N1084M JA889E
00409		Cleanwater Fine Foods	N5214J C-GDMH
00410		Queensland Police Service	N52690 N1230Y VH-PSV
00411		Thompson Aviation	N208W C-GHWT
00412		Northway Aviation	N52136 C-GNWG
00413		Shoreline Aviation	N1283T N984JD
00414		Basin Electric Power Corp	N1298L N379BE
00415		Army Parachute Association	N5265N G-OAFF
00416		Scenic Air	HB-TCK
00417		ex Africair	N20718+ ET- [+ marks canx 07Apr08 to Ethiopia]
00418		Travira Air	N20869 PK-TVW [floatplane]
00419		Kalkavan	N5193C TC-KSF
00420		Third Pegasus	N208CY (D-FISH(2)) N208RT
00421		Travira Air	N2098U PK-TVX [floatplane]
00422		Verona Aviation	N208TE
00423		UK Parachute Services	N5148N G-UKPS

Construction numbers 00424 to 00499 not built

Cessna 208s with glass cockpits (Garmin G1000 avionics)

C/n	Model	Last known Owner/Operator	Identities/fates/comments (where appropriate)
00500		Washington Aviation	N776TF
00501		Seair Seaplanes	N52475 C-GURL
00502		Wilderness Air	N52645 C-GNFN
00503		Cessna Finance Corp	N801VW [probably operated by Tom's Aircraft Maintenance Inc]
00504		Peter K Jaffe	N208KJ
00505		Thunderhook Air	N51743 N463DB
00506		Set Air	N5148N N2234Y TC-MAR
00507		Rotkopf	N5076L D-FAAK I-ROTK
00508		Joe B Aday	N208MD N149CD
00509		Gary L Redhead Holdings	N5045W C-GFDD

CESSNA 208 CARAVAN

C/n	Model	Last known Owner/Operator	Identities/fates/comments (where appropriate)			
00510		Manaus Aerotaxi	N5233J	N6144K	PR-MPE	[floatplane]
00511		Victory Aircraft	N208MJ	N5MJ	N208JC	
00512		Joseph M Rieger	N504SB	N77RZ		
00513		Bank of Utah; trustee	N463DB	N968TC		
00514		First Flight LLC	N5207V	N6143P	N828B	[floatplane]
00515		Prince Al Bin Salman Bin Abdulaziz	N257X	HZ-SBS3		
00516		Strange Bird	N915JB	N208JB		
00517		BTE Investments	N215BT			
00518		George J Mandes	N5216A	N75GM		
00519		Dr. Hans Michel Piech	N5045W	D-FAAM	OE-ENI	
00520		Caravan Aviation	N52699	N228GS		
00521		Montauk Air Group	N5264A	N111NV	N521CE	N720QB
00522		Whitsunday Air Services	N5086W	N1027V	VH-WTY	
00523		Ramblers Skydiving	VH-DJV			
00524		Ifly Greece	N5163K	N30183	SX-SKV	
00525		Triad Charters	N51444	N3043V	N539AK	
00526		Ridler Verwaltungs-und Vermittlungs	N52623	N3036A	M-ZELL	
00527		Big Chino Aviation	N5168Y	N3TC		
00528		Seair Seaplanes	N5036Q	C-GMOW		
00529		Challenger Administration	N5166U	N459WM		
00530		2274997 Ontario	N5204D	C-GMSZ		
00531		Nihon Aerospace Corp	N5095N	N30377	JA889G	
00532		Bank of Utah; trustee	N51511	N969TC		
00533		Aerodynamics Worldwide Inc	N533DL			
00534		Cessna Finance Export Corp	N20210			
00535		Wells Fargo Bank Northwest	N2033H	N338RT		
00536		ex Cessna Aircraft Co	N6059Z	PP-RTC	[floatplane]	
00537		Wells Fargo Bank Northwest	N20432	N138RW		
00538		Meiya Air	N2047F	B-9466		
00539		Alfa Trans Dirgantara	N2033V+	PK-	[+ canx 20Jun12 to Indonesia]	
00540		Meiya Air	N20480	B-9469		
00541		Cessna Aircraft Co	N2026G			
00542		Van Bortel Aircraft	N215TX			
00543		Cessna Aircraft Co	N9539Z			
00544						
00545						
00546						
00547						
00548						
00549						
00550						
00551						
00552						
00553						
00554						
00555						
00556						
00557						
00558						

CESSNA 208B CARAVAN/GRAND CARAVAN/SUPER CARGOMASTER

Note: c/ns are prefixed with 208B without a hyphen, but shown here as Bnnnn

B0001		Pacific Coast Group	N9767F	N901FE	N416TT*	[prototype ff 03Mar86; * marks reserved 13Jun12]
B0002		Baron Aviation Services/ FedEx Express	N902FE			
B0003		Corporate Air/FedEx Express	N903FE			
B0004		Corporate Air/FedEx Express	N904FE			
B0005		Mountain Air Cargo/FedEx Express	N905FE			
B0006		CSA Air/FedEx Express	N906FE			
B0007		CSA Air/FedEx Express	N907FE			
B0008		West Air/FedEx Express	N908FE			

CESSNA 208 CARAVAN

C/n	Model	Last known Owner/Operator	Identities/fates/comments (where appropriate)
B0009		Wiggins Airways/FedEx Express	N909FE
B0010		Corporate Air/FedEx Express	N910FE
B0011		Wiggins Airways/FedEx Express	N911FE
B0012		Baron Aviation Services/ FedEx Express	N912FE
B0013		(Mountain Air Cargo/ FedEx Express)	N913FE [w/o 09Jan98 Maiden-Little Mountain, NC; canx 16Nov98; hulk to Atlanta Air Salvage, Griffin, GA; l/n 24Oct06]
B0014		CSA Air/FedEx Express	N914FE
B0015		Empire Airlines/FedEx Express	N915FE C-FEXG N895FE
B0016		Corporate Air/FedEx Express	N916FE
B0017		Mountain Air Cargo/FedEx Express	N917FE
B0018		Empire Airlines/FedEx Express	N918FE
B0019		Wiggins Airways/FedEx Express	N919FE
B0020		West Air/FedEx Express	N920FE
B0021		Mountain Air Cargo/FedEx Express	N921FE
B0022		Baron Aviation Services/ FedEx Express	N922FE
B0023		CSA Air/FedEx Express	N923FE
B0024		Corporate Air/FedEx Express	N924FE
B0025		CSA Air/FedEx Express	N925FE
B0026		Corporate Air/FedEx Express	N926FE
B0027		CSA Air/FedEx Express	N927FE
B0028		Baron Aviation Services/ FedEx Express	N928FE
B0029		Baron Aviation Services/ FedEx Express	N929FE
B0030		West Air/FedEx Express	N930FE
B0031		Wiggins Airways/FedEx Express	N931FE
B0032		Redding Aero Enterprises	N932FE N932C
B0033		Corporate Air/FedEx Express	N933FE
B0034		Baron Aviation Services/ FedEx Express	N934FE
B0035		Wiggins Airways/FedEx Express	N935FE
B0036		Corporate Air/FedEx Express	N936FE
B0037		Wiggins Airways/FedEx Express	N937FE
B0038		Mountain Air Cargo/FedEx Express	N938FE
B0039		Wiggins Airways/FedEx Express	(N939FE) F-GETN N804FE
B0040		Empire Airlines/FedEx Express	N940FE
B0041		Wiggins Airways/FedEx Express	(N941FE) F-GETO N807FE
B0042		Corporate Air/FedEx Express	N942FE C-FEXH N797FE
B0043		Mountain Air Cargo/FedEx Express	N943FE
B0044		(Baron Aviation Services/ FedEx Express)	N944FE [w/o 24Jan03 San Angelo-Ducote Airpark, TX; canx 30Jun03; hulk to Dodson International Parts, Rantoul, KS]
B0045		(Eagle Air Cargo)	(N945FE) N7392B [w/o 23Sep04 near Gwinner-Roger Melroe Field, ND; canx 01Dec04]
B0046		(P M Air/FedEx Express)	(N946FE) N945FE [w/o 05Jan89 near Aspen Airport, CO; canx 23Oct91]
B0047		Skylink Express	(N947FE) N7393B C-FESH C-FHGA
B0048		CSA Air/FedEx Express	(N948FE) N946FE
B0049		(Priority Air Charter)	(N949FE) N7565B C-FESA N2520P N228PA(1) [w/o en-route 15Mar02 near Alma, WI; canx 27Oct04; hulk to Preferred Airparts]
B0050		Wiggins Airways/FedEx Express	(N950FE) N947FE
B0051		Bird of Paradise Inc	(N951FE) N7580B
B0052		(Corporate Air/FedEx Express)	(N952FE) N948FE [w/o 05May01 near Steamboat Springs Airport, CO; canx 11Oct01]
B0053		(Atlantic Aero)	(N953FE) N9330B [w/o 11Jan89 Rockingham County-Shiloh Airport, NC; canx 01Apr91]
B0054		Baron Aviation Services/ FedEx Express	(N954FE) N949FE SE-KLX (F-GJHL) N900FE
B0055		Martinaire Aviation	(N955FE) N9331B
B0056		Baron Aviation Services/ FedEx Express	(N956FE) N950FE
B0057		Skydive the Ranch Inc	(N957FE) N9339B

CESSNA 208 CARAVAN

C/n	Model	Last known Owner/Operator	Identities/fates/comments (where appropriate)
B0058		(Baron Aviation Services/ FedEx Express)	(N958FE) N951FE [w/o 16Nov91 near Destin, FL; canx 06Jan92]
B0059		Pegasus Aircorp Inc	(N959FE) N9347B [reported leased to Aerofly, Portugal]
B0060		Corporate Air/FedEx Express	(N960FE) N952FE
B0061		(Regency Express Air)	(N961FE) N9352B [w/o 23Nov88 near Victoria International Airport, BC, Canada; canx 28Feb01]
B0062		Empire Airlines/Federal Express	(N962FE) N953FE
B0063		(DK & L Co)	(N963FE) N9362B C-FESO N31MG C-FESO N208AD [w/o 15May03 near Loran County Regional Airport, OH; canx 01Jun06]
B0064		CSA Air/FedEx Express	(N964FE) N954FE
B0065		(Union Flights)	(N965FE) N9417B [w/o 22Mar95 near Reno-Tahoe Airport, NV; canx 28Jly95]
B0066		Mountain Air Cargo/FedEx Express	(N966FE) N955FE
B0067		(Fretax Taxi Aereo)	(N967FE) (N9448B) N126HA PR-JOS [w/o 24Jly10 Rio Santana, near Afua, Brazil]
B0068		Empire Airlines/FedEx Express	(N968FE) N956FE
B0069		Redding Aero Enterprises	(N969FE) (N9452B) C-FKEL N6540Q N121HA
B0070		Baron Aviation Services/ FedEx Express	(N970FE) N957FE
B0071		Wiggins Airways/FedEx Express	N958FE
B0072		Airspeed Aviation/Skydive Palatka	N9454B
B0073		Wiggins Airways/FedEx Express	N959FE
B0074		Fly Safari Air Link	N9457B N276PM 5Y-BTM 5H-FOX
B0075		Empire Airlines/FedEx Express	N960FE
B0076		(Martinaire Aviation)	N9461B [w/o 18Jan95 near Lubbock International Airport, TX; hulk to Aircraft Structures International Corp for parts]
B0077		Baron Aviation Services/ FedEx Express	N961FE
B0078		Mountain Air Cargo/FedEx Express	N962FE
B0079		Martinaire Aviation	N9469B
B0080		Wiggins Airways/FedEx Express	N963FE
B0081		Martinaire Aviation	N9471B
B0082		J.R.S. Sky	N9479B [Supervan conversion # 4]
B0083		Corporate Air/FedEx Express	N964FE
B0084		Empire Airlines/FedEx Express	N965FE
B0085		Martinaire Aviation	N9505B
B0086		Wiggins Airways/FedEx Express	N966FE
B0087		Martinaire Aviation	N9525B
B0088		Mountain Air Cargo/FedEx Express	N967FE
B0089		T & T Capital	N9527B C-FESJ N9527B N415TG
B0090		West Air/FedEx Express	N968FE
B0091		Martinaire Aviation	(N9546B) N9529G
B0092		West Air/FedEx Express	N969FE
B0093		Baron Aviation Services/ FedEx Express	N970FE
B0094		Corporate Air/FedEx Express	N971FE
B0095		Suburban Air Freight	N9662B N895SF
B0096		Corporate Air/FedEx Express	N972FE
B0097		Martinaire Aviation	N9738B
B0098		Mountain Air Cargo/FedEx Express	N973FE
B0099		(Wiggins Airways/FedEx Express)	N974FE [w/o 26Apr01 near Plattsburgh, NY; canx 11Oct01]
B0100		Asesoria y Servicios Logisticos de Occidente	N9750B XA-UOH
B0101		Mountain Air Cargo/FedEx Express	N975FE
B0102		Martinaire Aviation	N9760B
B0103		Empire Airlines/FedEx Express	N976FE
B0104		Corporate Air/FedEx Express	N977FE
B0105		(Baron Aviation Services/ FedEx Express)	N978FE [w/o 18Oct05 near Round Rock, TX; canx 29Nov05]
B0106		Pacific Coast Group	N979FE N106BZ* [* marks reserved 13Jun12]
B0107		Martinaire Aviation	N9761B
B0108		Corporate Air/FedEx Express	N980FE
B0109		Martinaire Aviation	N9762B
B0110		Wiggins Airways/FedEx Express	N981FE

CESSNA 208 CARAVAN

C/n	Model	Last known Owner/Operator	Identities/fates/comments (where appropriate)
B0111		Mountain Air Cargo/FedEx Express	N982FE F-GHHC N820FE
B0112		Martinaire Aviation	N9766B
B0113		Empire Airlines/FedEx Express	N983FE
B0114		Dilkara Leasing	N9793B N87RM
B0115		West Air/FedEx Express	N984FE
B0116		Kapowsin Air Sports	N9829B
B0117		West Air/FedEx Express	N985FE
B0118		Arctic Aerospace	(N986FE) C-FPEX N208HW C-GIHM
B0119		Martinaire Aviation	N9956B
B0120		(Provincial Express)	(N987FE) C-FPEX [w/o 08Feb91 Postville Airport, NL, Canada; canx 13Feb91]
B0121		Avion Capital Corp	N9448B
B0122		CSA Air/FedEx Express	N988FE F-GHHD N828FE(2)
B0123		Airspeed Aviation/Skydive Palatka	N9452B
B0124		Wiggins Airways/FedEx Express	N989FE
B0125		Corporate Air/FedEx Express	N990FE
B0126		Martinaire Aviation	N9546B
B0127		Corporate Air/FedEx Express	N991FE
B0128		Empire Airlines/FedEx Express	N992FE
B0129		(Wasaya Airways)	N9552B C-FKSL [w/o 15Oct99 Red Lake, ON, Canada; canx 17May00; hulk to Global Aircraft Industries, Edmonton, Canada, AB; l/n 14Jun08]
B0130		CSA Air/FedEx Express	N993FE
B0131		Atlantic Aero	N9594B
B0132		Baron Aviation Services/ FedEx Express	N994FE
B0133		West Air/FedEx Express	N995FE
B0134		Pofolk Aviation Hawaii Inc	N9608B N208JL N248PA
B0135		Wiggins Airways/FedEx Express	N996FE
B0136		Avion Capital Corp/Paragon Air Express	N9612B
B0137		Martinaire Aviation	(N997FE) N4591B
B0138		Martinaire Aviation	N9623B
B0139		Wiggins Airways/FedEx Express	N998FE
B0140		Martinaire Aviation	(N999FE) N4602B
B0141		Aero Leasing/Union Flights	N9634B
B0142		(Baron Aviation Services/ FedEx Express)	N840FE [w/o 05Mar98 near Clarkesville, TN; canx 16Nov98]
B0143		(Planemasters/UPS)	N9648B N277PM [w/o 17Dec02 Greater Rockford Airport, IL; canx 01Jly04]
B0144		Baron Aviation Services/ FedEx Express	N841FE
B0145		Raven Aero/Union Flights	N9655B
B0146		Mountain Air Cargo/FedEx Express	N842FE
B0147		CSA Air/FedEx Express	N843FE
B0148		Maxim Aviation	N127HA
B0149		West Air/FedEx Express	N844FE
B0150		Catalina Air Transport	N9680B
B0151		Eagle Air Transport	N9697B N220EA
B0152		Baron Aviation Services/ FedEx Express	N845FE
B0153		Martinaire Aviation	N9714B
B0154		Corporate Air/FedEx Express	N846FE
B0155		Flex Air Cargo	N9727B JA8215 N502TA XA-SVN N504TA ZS-ODL 5Y-BOL ZS-ODL V5-ODL 5Y-MJI
B0156		Mountain Air Cargo/FedEx Express	N847FE
B0157		Abaete Aerotaxi	N4615B PT-OZA
B0158		Mountain Air Cargo/FedEx Express	N848FE
B0159		Martinaire Aviation	N4625B
B0160		Martinaire Aviation	N4655B
B0161		Martinaire Aviation	N4662B
B0162		Mountain Air Cargo/FedEx Express	N849FE
B0163		Colombian National Police	N4667B PNC-3019 [probably leased from the US Department of State]
B0164		Empire Airlines/FedEx Express	N850FE
B0165		Avion Capital/Martinaire	N4674B
B0166		Corporate Air/FedEx Express	N851FE

CESSNA 208 CARAVAN

C/n	Model	Last known Owner/Operator	Identities/fates/comments (where appropriate)
B0167		Martinaire Aviation	N4687B
B0168		Mountain Air Cargo/FedEx Express	N852FE
B0169		(Business Air/Airborne Express)	N4688B [w/o 29Jan90 Burlington International Airport, VT; canx 24Jun92]
B0170		Mountain Air Cargo/FedEx Express	N853FE
B0171		Skydive Toronto	N4694B N278PM C-FZDN
B0172		(Wiggins Airways/FedEx Express)	N854FE [w/o 25Jan90 Plattsburgh-Clinton County, NY; canx 05Oct92]
B0173		Skydive Promotion	N4695B OO-JMP
B0174		Corporate Air/FedEx Express	N855FE C-FEDY N798FE
B0175		Atlantic Aero/Martinaire	N4698B
B0176		Empire Airlines/FedEx Express	N856FE
B0177		West Air/FedEx Express	N857FE
B0178		CSA Air/FedEx Express	N858FE
B0179		(Tar Heel Aviation/UPS)	N4700B N802TH [w/o 02Jan97 near Edenton, NC; canx 16Mar98; hulk to White Industries, Bates City, MO; l/n 25Apr07]
B0180		Baron Aviation Services/ FedEx Express	N939FE
B0181		Empire Airlines/FedEx Express	N859FE
B0182		Corporate Air/FedEx Express	N860FE
B0183		Baron Aviation Services/ FedEx Express	N861FE
B0184		Mountain Air Cargo/FedEx Express	N862FE
B0185		Corporate Air/FedEx Express	N885FE
B0186		Corporate Air/FedEx Express	N863FE
B0187		Corporate Air/FedEx Express	N864FE
B0188		Wiggins Airways/FedEx Express	N865FE
B0189		Baron Aviation Services/ FedEx Express	N866FE
B0190		West Air/FedEx Express	N886FE
B0191		Corporate Air/FedEx Express	N867FE
B0192		(Empire Airlines/FedEx Express)	N941FE [w/o en-route 09Oct00 Lummi Island, WA; canx 26Jan01]
B0193		(Corporate Air/FedEx Express)	N868FE [w/o 27Apr98 near Bismarck Airport, ND; canx 16Nov98]
B0194		CSA Air/FedEx Express	N986FE
B0195		Mountain Air Cargo/FedEx Express	N869FE
B0196		Wiggins Airways/FedEx Express	N870FE
B0197		Corporate Air/FedEx Express	N997FE
B0198		CSA Air/FedEx Express	N871FE
B0199		(Arctic Transportation Services)	N4704B [w/o 26Nov96 near Bethel Airport, AK; canx 12Aug97; hulk to Dodson International Parts, Rantoul, KS; l/n 24Oct05]
B0200		West Air/FedEx Express	N872FE
B0201		West Air/FedEx Express	N987FE
B0202		Empire Airlines/FedEx Express	N873FE
B0203		Mountain Air Cargo/FedEx Express	N855FE
B0204		Mountain Air Cargo/FedEx Express	N881FE
B0205		Mountain Air Cargo/FedEx Express	N874FE
B0206		Empire Airlines/FedEx Express	N875FE
B0207		Empire Airlines/FedEx Express	N876FE
B0208		Empire Airlines/FedEx Express	N882FE
B0209		Morningstar Air Express/ FedEx Express	(N877FE) C-FEXX
B0210		(CSA Air/FedEx Express)	N883FE [w/o en-route 09May08 Ada, MI]
B0211		Mountain Air Cargo/FedEx Express	N878FE
B0212		Corporate Air/FedEx Express	(N884FE) C-FEXY N796FE
B0213		West Air/FedEx Express	N879FE
B0214		(Transportes Aereos de Coahuila – TACSA)	N4710B JA8219 N503TA XA-SVM [w/o 31Oct95 near Piedras Negras Airport, Mexico]
B0215		Empire Airlines/FedEx Express	N880FE
B0216		Mountain Air Cargo/FedEx Express	N887FE
B0217		Wiggins Airways/FedEx Express	N888FE
B0218		Baron Aviation Services/ FedEx Express	N889FE
B0219		Corporate Air/FedEx Express	N890FE
B0220		(Gallovents Ten/Kivu Air Services)	N4742B JA8220 N819D F-GROI N819D ZS-ONT [w/o 19Apr00 Kahuzi-Biega National Park, near Bukavu, Democratic Republic of Congo]

CESSNA 208 CARAVAN

C/n	Model	Last known Owner/Operator	Identities/fates/comments (where appropriate)
B0221		West Air/FedEx Express	N891FE
B0222		West Air/FedEx Express	N892FE [substainial damage 18Feb10 Sacramento, CA]
B0223		(CSA Air/FedEx Express)	N893FE N223P+ [w/o 09May08 Ada, MI; + sold 12Dec08 to Preferred Airparts LLC for spares recovery; by 03Jly09 fuselage at Kidron-Stoltzfus, OH; canx 27May10]
B0224		Baron Aviation Services/ FedEx Express	N894FE
B0225		Mountain Air Cargo/FedEx Express	N895FE F-GHHE N831FE
B0226		Morningstar Air Express/ FedEx Express	N896FE C-FEXY
B0227		Empire Airlines/FedEx Express	N897FE
B0228		Wiggins Airways/FedEx Express	N898FE
B0229		LSO Acquisition Corp	N90GL
B0230		Finist'Air	(N4909B) (N899FE) N208GC F-GJFI
B0231		Mountain Air Cargo/FedEx Express	N999FE
B0232		Corporate Air/FedEx Express	N877FE
B0233		CSA Air/FedEx Express	N884FE
B0234		Wright Air Service	(N4909B) C-FKEL N32WA
B0235		Empire Airlines/FedEx Express	N899FE
B0236		(Empire Airlines/FedEx Express)	N746FE [w/o 11Jan95 near Flagstaff-Pulliam Field, AZ; canx 28Mar97]
B0237		Hirata Gakuen	N4965B JA8893
B0238		Mountain Air Cargo/FedEx Express	N747FE
B0239		Nordic Aviation Contractor	(N51108) C-GAWV N242CS 5Y-BUR
B0240		Wasaya Airways	(N5127B) C-FKDL
B0241		Wiggins Airways/FedEx Express	N748FE
B0242		Baron Aviation Services/ FedEx Express	N749FE
B0243		ex Samaritan's Purse Kenya	N5164B N349EA 5Y-SPK [substainially damaged 28Apr08 Doro airstrip, Sudan; fuselage only 03Jly09 Kidron-Stoltzfus, OH reported to be re-built]
B0244		Morningstar Air Express/ FedEx Express	N750FE C-FEXE(2)
B0245		Corporate Air/FedEx Express	N751FE
B0246		Nozaki Sangyo	N5127B JA8899
B0247		CSA Air/FedEx Express	N752FE
B0248		(Empire Airlines/FedEx Express)	N753FE [w/o 24Dec05 Portland International Airport, OR; hulk sold to Metal Innovations Inc, then Wings of Hope; canx 30Aug12]
B0249		(West Air/FedEx Express)	N754FE [w/o 12Jan95 near Pleasanton, CA; canx 14Apr95]
B0250		Pacific Coast Group	N755FE N250BZ* [* marks reserved 13Jun12]
B0251		Baron Aviation Services/ FedEx Express	N756FE
B0252		Corporate Air/FedEx Express	N760FE
B0253		Wright Air Service	N208CC N4365U
B0254		CSA Air/FedEx Express	N761FE
B0255		West Air/FedEx Express	N762FE
B0256		West Air/FedEx Express	N763FE
B0257		Missionary Aviation Fellowship	N5147B F-OGRJ N244D 5Y-BNG
B0258		Mountain Air Cargo/FedEx Express	N764FE
B0259		Baron Aviation Services/ FedEx Express	N765FE
B0260		Corporate Air/FedEx Express	N766FE
B0261		Solenta Aviation	XA-RVQ N41057 ZS-NOM 5Y-NOM 9J-DHL ZS-TIN
B0262		CSA Air/FedEx Express	N767FE
B0263		West Air/FedEx Express	N768FE
B0264		Pacific Coast Group	N769FE N264LB
B0265		Baron Aviation Services/ FedEx Express	N770FE
B0266		Westwind Air	LN-TWD N81U N850VY
B0267		West Air/FedEx Express	N771FE
B0268		West Air/FedEx Express	N772FE
B0269		Baron Aviation Services/ FedEx Express	N773FE
B0270		(Arctic Circle Air Service)	N5187B F-OGRO N5187B [w/o 18Dec07 Bethel, AK; canx 13Apr09]
B0271		Baron Aviation Services/ FedEx Express	N774FE

CESSNA 208 CARAVAN

C/n	Model	Last known Owner/Operator	Identities/fates/comments (where appropriate)
B0272		Empire Airlines/FedEx Express	N775FE
B0273		Pacific Coast Group	N776FE N273LB
B0274		Colombian National Police	HP-1191XI PNC-0216
B0275		Empire Airlines/FedEx Express	N778FE
B0276		Empire Airlines/FedEx Express	N779FE
B0277		Wiggins Airways/FedEx Express	N780FE
B0278		West Air/FedEx Express	N781FE
B0279		Union Flights	N5226B F-OGRU N208N
B0280		West Air/FedEx Express	N782FE
B0281		Wiggins Airways/FedEx Express	N783FE
B0282		CSA Air/FedEx Express	N784FE
B0283		West Air/FedEx Express	N785FE
B0284		Baron Aviation Services/ FedEx Express	N786FE
B0285		Mountain Air Cargo/FedEx Express	N787FE
B0286		Empire Airlines/FedEx Express	N788FE
B0287		Wiggins Airways/FedEx Express	N789FE
B0288		West Air/FedEx Express	N790FE
B0289		David J. Evans	N791FE N208BT
B0290		Mountain Air Cargo/FedEx Express	N792FE
B0291		Baron Aviation Services/ FedEx Express	N793FE
B0292		Corporate Air/FedEx Express	N794FE
B0293		CSA Air/FedEx Express	N795FE
B0294		Federal Air/Airworks Kenya	N5275B ZS-NFY 5Y-NFY
B0295		(Transmile Air Service)	N5327B 9M-PMN [w/o 20Mar95 Tawau, Sabah, Malaysia]
B0296		Federal Air/Airworks Kenya	N5374B OK-XKB N103A ZS-OER 5Y-BNB ZS-OER 5Y-BNB ZS-OER 5Y-OER [reported serious damage 19Jan11 Thar Jath, Sudan]
B0297		Vias Aereas Nacionales	N5444B HK-3734
B0298		Cetty Taxi Aereo Nacional	N5480B XA-EDS XA-SHF XC-CCC
B0299		(Deep South Investments/ One Leasing)	N5512B [w/o 25Mar03 near El Paujil, Colombia, whilst on classified counter drug mission on behalf of the US military; but ownership change 13Oct09 to Aircraft Structures International Corp]
B0300		(Mega Transportes Aereos)	N5516B PT-OSG [w/o 23May11 Barra do Vento, Boa Vista, Brazil]
B0301		Aero Calafia	N5538B XA-SFJ XA-AVT
B0302		Asahi Koku	N1002D (C-FESJ) OY-TCB LN-PBB N4YA JA881B
B0303		DHL Aviation Zimbabwe	N1002H D-FTME N31SE Z-KPS
B0304		Soley	N1002N V3-HFE N2106T N5010Y [Soley Pathfinder conversion]
B0305		(Wasaya Airways)	C-FKAB [w/o 11Sep03 near Summer Beaver Airport, ON, Canada; canx 16Dec03]
B0306		Priority Air Charter	C-FLAQ N218PF N218PA
B0307		Sefofane Air Charter	N1006H N404GE 5Y-BMZ V5-SUN ZS-SUN
B0308		(Air Tindi)	C-GATV [w/o 04Oct11 en-route Utsigi Point, Great Slave Lake, NT, Canada]
B0309		Airstar Aviation	N1114A (N279PM)
B0310		(Hangar 5 Airservices Norway)	N1015E OY-TCC LN-PBC [w/o 04Dec94 Oslo-Gardermoen, Norway; canx 11Sep95]
B0311		Jump Out Now	N1015G YN-CDR 6Y-JRG N104JP
B0312		Savannah Air Services/fly540	N1017V LV-PGD LV-VGE N208PF N208PA 5Y-SAV
B0313		(Nozaki Sanoyo)	N208LS(1) JA8898 [w/o 06Apr94 Saiki-Gun, Hiroshima, Japan; canx 19Apr94]
B0314		TAF Linhas Aereas	N1018X PT-OQT
B0315		Aeroexpresso de la Frontera	N1024A HK-3804X HK-3804 HK-3804P
B0316		Swawek Aviation	V5-JPB
B0317		Nakina Outpost Camps & Air Service	C-GMVB
B0318		Vera Cruz Taxi Aereo	N1025Y PT-OTM
B0319		Avion Capital/Air Net Systems	N1026V
B0320		Helicondor	N1027C HK-3801X HK3801 HK-3801P
B0321		Avion Capital/Air Now	N1027G N803TH
B0322		(Airworks Kenya/UN-WFP	N1027S ZS-NGO 5Y-NGO [DBR 02May12 Yambio, South Sudan]
B0323		Fretax Taxi Aereo	N102Y F-OGUX N807MA N465BA PR-JOH
B0324		ZB Air/Safarilink	N1029P 5Y-ZBI
B0325		Avion Capital	N1029Y
B0326		Kenmore Air Express	N1030N N72KA [floatplane]
B0327		Wasaya Airways	C-FKAD

CESSNA 208 CARAVAN

C/n	Model	Last known Owner/Operator	Identities/fates/comments (where appropriate)
B0328		ex King Air Services/Airworks Kenya	N1031Y ZS-NHB 5Y-NHB 5H-
B0329		AIM Air	N1032G 5Y-XPA
B0330		ZB Air	N1034S 5Y-OPM
B0331		Advanced Aviation	N1036C 9M-PMO N3331 D-FLIP
B0332		(Aviation & Services Europe)	N1037D (F-OGTC) [w/o en-route 16Aug93 Valensole, France; canx 27Jly99]
B0333		TAM – Taxi Aereo Marilia	N1037L PT-MEA
B0334		Aero Leasing/Martinaire	N1037N (C-GWFN)
B0335		TAM – Taxi Aereo Marilia	N1038G PT-MEB
B0336		Secure 120 Investments	N1040W (C-FWSK) D4-CBJ ZS-ORK
B0337		Atlantic Aero/Mid Atlantic Freight	N1041L
B0338		ZB Air	N1042Y 5Y-ZBL
B0339		Broome Aviation	N1045Y P2-TSJ VH-TLD
B0340		Kenya Parks & Wildlife Service	N1043N 5Y-KWT
B0341		(La Costena)	N1044V YN-CED [w/o en-route 20Jly99 Cerro Silva region, Nicaragua]
B0342		TAM – Taxi Aereo Marilia	N1045C PT-MEC
B0343		TAM – Taxi Aereo Marilia	N1052C PT-MED
B0344		ex TAM – Taxi Aereo Marilia	N1054M PT-MEE [considerable damage 01Jly08 Belem-Itiatuba, Brazil; probable w/o; by 22May09 Jundiai, Brazil with wings removed]
B0345		Solenta Aviation/DHL	N1057T 9Q-CDI ZS-OBY 5Y-OBY
B0346		Mombasa Air Safari	N1058C PT-MEF C-FMHD+ N4288T ZS-OHC 5Y-VAN [+ hijacked Sep93; recovered in 1997 wearing these false marks]
B0347		Avion Capital/Mid Atlantic Freight	N1058N
B0348		Adventure Air	N1071G (N208GC) XA-NLK N1288T VH-NTS N208PM N32JA C-GAAX
B0349		Taxi Aereo del Baudo	N1075 HK-3915X HK-3915 HK-3915W
B0350		Skylink Express	N1089V N64AP C-GLGA
B0351		CFA Air Charters	N1114K N100US ZS-ATP
B0352		SETE Taxi Aero	N1114N PT-MEG
B0353		Solenta Aviation/DHL	N1114S ZS-NIZ 5Y-NIZ ZS-NIZ
B0354		SETE Taxi Aero	N1114W PT-MEH
B0355		RCT International /Trackmark	N1114X N9697C 5Y-TVM
B0356		Martinaire Aviation	N1115M
B0357		Federal Air	N1115N ZS-NXZ 5Y-NXZ ZS-NXZ 5Y-NXZ
B0358		SETE Taxi Aero	N1115P PT-MEI
B0359		TAM – Taxi Aereo Marilia	N1115V PT-MEJ
B0360		SETE Taxi Aero	N1115W PT-MEK
B0361		SETE Taxi Aero	N1116G PT-MEL
B0362		Aviles Guzman Jorge Luis	C-GJDI C-GJDM N98LH XA-LKF
B0363		T & T Capital	N1116H F-OGVJ N8RQ N600TG
B0364		(DMC Flying Service)	N208GC N227DM [w/o 03Mar95 near Gainsville-Lee Gilmer Memorial Airport, GA; canx 19Mar97]
B0365		T & T Capital/Air Now	N1116R N208TA N415TT
B0366		(Executive Turbine Kenya)	(N1116V) HI-641SP HI-641CT N6280Q ZS-OAT 5Y-OAT ZS-OAT 5Y-BUQ [w/o 11Feb09 Boma, Sudan]
B0367		ex Titan Air/Save the Children Fund (UK)	(N1116W) HI-642SP HI-642CT N6236G 5Y-BMZ ET-
B0368		(Suburban Air Freight)	N1116Y [w/o 08Feb07 near Alliance, NE; canx 16Mar10]
B0369		(Airworks Kenya/United Nations)	N1117A ZS-NPD A2-NPD ZS-NPD 5Y-NPD [w/o en-route 22Oct06 100km N of Jura, Sudan]
B0370		Brylee Investments Corp	N1117G
B0371		T & T Capital/Air Now	N1117N N207TA N929TG
B0372		Aeroexpresso de la Frontera	N1117P HK-3916X HK-3916 YV204T YV1622 HK-3916
B0373		Government of Canada/Royal Canadian Mounted Police	N1117S N973CC C-FSUJ
B0374		Flightlink	N1117Y ZS-NDV 5Y-NDV ZS-NDV 5H-FLT
B0375		Caravan Air/Airworks Kenya/ UN WFP	N1118N ZS-NLM TZ-NLM ZS-NLM 5Y-NLM
B0376		Conair Aviation	N1118P (HK-3987X) C-GSDG
B0377		Government of Canada/Royal Canadian Mounted Police	N1118V C-FRPH
B0378		Minair	N1118W N208SA ZS-TAS
B0379		Skylink Express	N1119A XA-SQB N1119A C-GEGA

CESSNA 208 CARAVAN

C/n	Model	Last known Owner/Operator	Identities/fates/comments (where appropriate)
B0380		Air Panama	N1119G YN-CEJ HP-1345AR HP-1345PS
B0381		(King Air Services/United Nations)	N1119K 5Y-TAS ZS-ADL [w/o en-route 27Apr06 Margarita Mountain, Uganda]
B0382		Tanganyika Flying Company	N1119N N10YR ZS-NYR 5H-NYR N77NF* [* marks reserved 09May12]
B0383		Aero Leasing/Martinaire	N1119V
B0384		Tropical Airlines	N1120A 7T-VIH 5H-OLA
B0385		Trackmark	N1120G Z-BEN ZS-NYS 5Y-BNH
B0386		Aero Leasing/Martinaire	N1120N
B0387		Federal Air/Airworks Kenya	N1120U ZS-NKV 5Y-BOA ZS-NKV 5Y-NKV
B0388		Aero Leasing/Martinaire	N1120W
B0389		Desert Sand Aircraft Leasing	N1122E (C-GATW) C-FTZF N7581F
B0390		Pleasure Leasing	N1122G LN-TWE N398A
B0391		Air Algerie	N1122N 7T-VIG
B0392		(Telford Aviation)	N1122Y [w/o 25Dec02 Croatan Sound near Manro-Dare County, NC; canx 10Aug04; hulk to Atlanta Air Salvage, Griffin, GA; l/n 12Feb07]
B0393		Air Algerie	N1123G 7T-VII
B0394		HDM Air/Safari Link Aviation	N1123L YV-636C N894MA 5Y-BNS
B0395		Norton Basin Services/Bering Air	N1123R
B0396		(Naturelink Charters/Southern Right Air Charters)	N1123S YV-645C N1123S ZS-POG [w/o 30Jun06 Vilanculos Airport, Mozambique]
B0397		Trans Guyana Airways	N1123T XA-SVI (N208WA) N397TA 8R-GTG
B0398		Gobernacion de la Provincia de Buenos Aires	N1123W LV-PLD LV-WMI
B0399		Aquila del Sur	N5200R N12000 LV-WLY
B0400		Airworks Kenya/Flex Air	N1200V ZS-NLO 5Y-BNR ZS-NLO 5H-PAI ZS-NLO 5Y-BUC
B0401		Air Excel	N12142 N401MC D-FHEW 5H-AXL
B0402		(Deep South Investments/ One Leasing)	N1116G [w/o 13Feb02 near El Paujil, Colombia, whilst on classified counter drug mission on behalf of the US Military; hulk to Atlanta Air Salvage, Griffin, GA; l/n 04Oct06; change of ownership 13Oct09 to Aircraft Structures International Corp]
B0403		Worldwide Aviation	N1119N XB-GCG N403VP 66047+ [+ current as N403VP but also wears these marks believed to be the USAF serial 96-6047; operated by the US Government]
B0404		Avion Capital/Martinaire	N1031P
B0405		TAM – Taxi Aereo Marilia	PT-MEM
B0406		US Army – AMRDEC*	N1114N N124GL [* AMRDEC is the Aviation & Missile Research, Development & Engineering Center]
B0407		Air Services	N1116V V3-HSS 8R-GZR
B0408		TAM – Taxi Aereo Marilia	PT-MEN
B0409		ZB Air	N1115W 5Y-ZBW
B0410		Avion Capital/Mid Atlantic Freight	N9820F
B0411		Avion Capital/Martinaire	N1116W
B0412		TAM – Taxi Aereo Marilia	PT-MEO
B0413		TAM – Taxi Aereo Marilia	PT-MEP
B0414		(TAM – Taxi Aereo Marilia)	PT-MEQ [reported w/o but no details known; was canx 12May97; CofA expired 12Jan94]
B0415		(Kapowsin Air Sports)	N1295A LN-TWF N430A [w/o en-route 07Oct07 55km WSW of Naches, WA]
B0416		Broome Aviation	N1114W VH-NGS
B0417		Aero Leasing/Union Flights	N1116N
B0418		Broome Aviation	N1121M VH-DEX VH-NTC
B0419		Empire Airlines/FedEx Express	N700FX
B0420		Wiggins Airways/FedEx Express	N701FX
B0421		Avion Capital/Air Now	N804TH
B0422		Baron Aviation Services/ FedEx Express	N702FX
B0423		CSA Air/FedEx Express	N703FX
B0424		Tropic Air Commuter	N5192F VH-LSA P2-BEN
B0425		Empire Airlines/FedEx Express	N705FX
B0426		CSA Air/FedEx Express	N706FX
B0427		West Air/FedEx Express	N707FX
B0428		Broome Air Services	N1288D VH-URT VH-CRN
B0429		(Mountain Air Cargo/ FedEx Express)	N708FX [DBR 06Feb10 location unknown; canx 13Dec10 reason unknown]
B0430		Empire Airlines/FedEx Express	N709FX

CESSNA 208 CARAVAN

C/n	Model	Last known Owner/Operator	Identities/fates/comments (where appropriate)
B0431		Corporate Air/FedEx Express	N710FX
B0432		(Scenic Airways)	N12022 [w/o 08Oct97 Uncompahgre Plateau, 23nm SW of Montrose, CO; canx 04Oct01]
B0433		Empire Airlines/FedEx Express	N711FX
B0434		Polar Aviation	N1203D VH-CFL
B0435		CSA Air/FedEx Express	N712FX
B0436		Avion Capital/Air Net Systems	N677SC C-GSKR N3RY
B0437		Federal Air/Nomad Aviation	ZS-PAT A2-SGZ(1) ZS-PAT A2-PAT ZS-FED 5H-FED
B0438		West Air/FedEx Express	N713FX
B0439		Sala Tecnica 90210 CA	N1203S HH-CAB+ N208RK^ YV- [+ not confirmed] [^ canx 07Aug08 to Venezuela]
B0440		Mountain Air Cargo/FedEx Express	N715FX
B0441		Xugana Air	N682GC ZS-OAR A2-AKK
B0442		Corporate Air/FedEx Express	N716FX
B0443		Air Kenya	N1209X 5Y- 5H-REG 5Y-BYO
B0444		Aerovias Caribe Express	N1265C YN-CEQ YV-1088CP YV158T
B0445		CSA Air/FedEx Express	N717FX
B0446		ZB Air	N12922 5Y-ZBR
B0447		Telford Group/USAF	N215TA
B0448		Baron Aviation Services/ FedEx Express	N718FX
B0449		Worldwide Aviation Services	N1229Z N208BB
B0450		Baron Aviation Services/ FedEx Express	N719FX
B0451		not yet known	N1213Z PT-XBB N1213Z PT-FLW
B0452		Empire Airlines/FedEx Express	N5132T N720FX
B0453		Mountain Air Cargo/FedEx Express	N5133E N721FX
B0454		West Air/FedEx Express	N51342 N722FX
B0455		(Gussic Ventures/Hageland Aviation Services)	N5135A N1233B N208GV N408GV [w/o 10Apr97 into frozen ice pack off Wainwright, AK; canx 31Aug98]
B0456		Baron Aviation Services/ FedEx Express	N723FX
B0457		Dick Smith Adventure	N5060P N2648Y VH-SHW
B0458		Corporate Air/FedEx Express	N724FX
B0459		Aeronav	N5187B N2646X F-OGXK ZS-SLT 5Y-MDL
B0460		Wiggins Airways/FedEx Express	N725FX
B0461		Bonn Plant Hire	N1287B ZS-NNK
B0462		Fugro Airborne Surveys	N1241A(2) N90LN C-GRCK PR-FAS
B0463		Priority Air Charter	N5266T XA-TBJ N80195 N209TF 5Y-PAP N885SP
B0464		Istlecote	N13313 VH-OZH
B0465		West Air/FedEx Express	N5267K N726FX
B0466		McNeely Charter Service	N5000R N212SA
B0467		Martinaire Aviation	N5058J N78SA
B0468		CSA Air/FedEx Express	N5121N N727FX
B0469		(International Express/Sonicblue Airways)	N12852 C-GRXZ [w/o en-route 21Jan06 10km from Port Alberni Airport, BC, Canada; canx 23Jan09]
B0470		Air Tindi	N5261R N1294N C-FKAY
B0471		Empire Airlines/FedEx Express	N5061W N728FX
B0472		Solenta Aviation/DHL	N1209Y N9147N 5Y-RAS 5Y-TLC ZS-TLC 5Y-TLC
B0473		Mack Air	N1287N ZS-NVH A2-NVH
B0474		Mountain Air Cargo/FedEx Express	N2617Z N729FX
B0475		Com Aircraft Service	N5094D N1220D 9M-PMT N1202D D-FINA
B0476		Tanganyika Flying Company	N5060K N1132V XA-TFA N208BA ZS-EGG A2-EGG ZS-EGG 5Y-EGG 5H-EGG
B0477		Corporate Air/FedEx Express	N5066U N730FX
B0478		ex Tropic Air Commuter	N5188A N1289Y V3-HFP [not current; status/fate unknown]
B0479		Farm & Harvest Machinery	N5267K N600HM
B0480		Wiggins Airways/FedEx Express	N731FX
B0481		Solenta Aviation/Nomad Aviation	N5156V C-FWVO N72FD ZS-OJF 5H-OJF
B0482		Morningstar Air Express/ FedEx Express	N5124F N738FX C-FEXV
B0483		Thunder Airways	N51246 N1006K+ N51426 C-FWVR [+ marks reported but not confirmed]
B0484		Mountain Air Cargo/FedEx Express	N740FX

CESSNA 208 CARAVAN

C/n	Model	Last known Owner/Operator	Identities/fates/comments (where appropriate)
B0485		Medecins Sans Frontieres	N2647Y F-OGXI ZS-SLO
B0486		Baron Aviation Services/ FedEx Express	N5145P N741FX
B0487		Regional Air Services	N1328K 5Y-BLM 5H-MUA
B0488		Blue Wing Airlines	N1301K PZ-TSK [Supervan 900 conversion # 1]
B0489		Mountain Air Cargo/FedEx Express	N742FX
B0490		GSST LLC	N444FA N9310F
B0491		Frontier Alaska	(N610DK) N208SD
B0492		West Air/FedEx Express	N5148B N744FX
B0493		Sander Geophysics	N5264E N1254Y C-GSGZ A2-SGZ(2) ZS-SGZ C-GSGZ
B0494		British Parachute Schools	N1219G N208BA LV-YJC D-FBPS
B0495		Baron Aviation Services/ FedEx Express	N5162W N745FX
B0496		Lineas Aereas Comerciales	N5165T XB-MIC
B0497		ex Solenta Aviation	N12289 F-OGXJ N497AC ZS-SLR+ 5Y- [+ canx 29Jun12 to Kenya]
B0498		Empire Airlines/FedEx Express	N51743 N746FX
B0499		Amazonaves Taxi Aereo	N5188N PP-ITZ
B0500		ex East African Air Charter	N51001 (N500TH) 9M-PMV 5Y-BOX(1) [fuselage only reported 31May06 in scrapyard of Westcan Aircraft Recovery, Kamloops, BC, Canada & b/u by Aug08; no accident known; but also reported 22Sep09 as in w/o condition at Nairobi-Wilson, Kenya]
B0501		Mountain Air Cargo/FedEx Express	N51017 N747FX
B0502		David J. Evans	N1020K ZS-NUX N208DE
B0503		West Air/FedEx Express	N52609 N748FX
B0504		(Gussic Ventures/Hageland Aviation Services)	N5233G N750GC [w/o 08Nov97 in Arctic Ocean 1 mile NW of Point Barrow Airport, AK; canx 10Jun98]
B0505		Razorbill Properties 249 CC	N1129H YV-734C N813MA N880MA ZS-PFL
B0506		Brazilian Air Force	N5071M+ PT-MER 2726 [C98 later C98A] [+ marks reported but not confirmed]
B0507		TAM – Taxi Aereo Marilia	N5071S+ PT-MES [+ marks reported but not confirmed]
B0508		Morningstar Air Express/ FedEx Express	N5261R N749FX C-FEXF
B0509		Amazonaves Taxi Aereo	N5073G PT-MET
B0510		Brazilian Air Force	N5076J PT-MEU 2727 [C-98]
B0511		West Air/FedEx Express	N5211Q N750FX
B0512		Vera Cruz Taxi Aereo	N5076K PT-MEV
B0513		(Sun Road Trading 10 CC/ Wings Over Africa)	N5079V PT-MEW ZS-OTU V5-CAR ZS-OTU [w/o 15Nov09 Windhoek-Eros Airport, Namibia]
B0514		Baron Aviation Services/FedEx Express	N5262W N751FX
B0515		TAM – Taxi Aereo Marilia	N50280 PT-MEX
B0516		Slingair	N6302B VH-KSA
B0517		Empire Airlines/FedEx Express	N5214J N752FX
B0518		TAM – Taxi Aereo Marilia	PT-MEY
B0519		Trans Guyana Airways	PT-MEZ+ 8R-GHR [+ as such reported w/o 18Mar01 Sao Jose dos Campos, Brazil, whilst operating for TAM – Taxi Aereo Marilia]
B0520		Baron Aviation Services/ FedEx Express	N51942 N753FX
B0521		TAM – Jatos Executivos Marilia	N5058J PT-WIO
B0522		Ministerio Obras Publicas	N5245P N1303T LV-PNA LV-WYZ
B0523		OLT – Ostfriesische Lufttransport	N5197A D-FOLE
B0524		Sander Geophysics	N5201J C-FSDK C-GSGV
B0525		Five Forty Aviation	N5202D XA-TFB N208BC ZS-ORI 5H-YEP 5Y-CAC
B0526		West Air/FedEx Express	N5201M N754FX
B0527		RUTACA	N5283S YV-790C YV1951
B0528		Sustut Air	N5185J N9510W C-FAFV
B0529		Wiggins Airways/FedEx Express	N5264E N755FX
B0530		Air Japan	N51042 N1248D N164SA JA55DZ
B0531		ex Jet Stream LLC	N5105F N212CP+ VH- [+ canx 13Sep12 to Australia]
B0532		Empire Airlines/FedEx Express	N756FX
B0533		Brazilian Air Force	PT-MHA 2724 [C98 later C98A]

CESSNA 208 CARAVAN

C/n	Model	Last known Owner/Operator	Identities/fates/comments (where appropriate)
B0534		(Brazilian Air Force)	PT-MHB 2725 [C98] [w/o 29Oct09 forced landing Itui River near Aurelio, Brazil]
B0535		Morningstar Air Express/ FedEx Express	N757FX C-FEXO
B0536		Bering Air	N1128L
B0537		Desert Sand Aircraft Leasing/ Mario's Air	N1293E
B0538		Federal Air	N5000R C-FKAC ZS-ODS 5Y-ODS ZS-ODS 5Y-ODS
B0539		Morningstar Air Express/ FedEx Express	N758FX C-FEXB
B0540		Wright Air Service	N1329G N540ME
B0541		Northern Thunderbird Air (NT Air)	N1130K N621BB C-GDOX
B0542		(Morningstar Air Express/ FedEx Express)	N759FX C-FEXS [w/o 06Oct05 6.6km SE of Winnipeg Airport, AB, Canada; canx 25Apr06]
B0543		TAM – Taxi Aereo Marilia	PT-MHC
B0544		Twin City Development	PT-MHD ZS-OWC V5-VAN ZS-OWC
B0545		Solenta Aviation/DHL	PT-MHE ZS-OTV 5Y-OTV ZS-OTV
B0546		North Wright Airways	N5262W C-GZIZ
B0547		Industrias Metalicas de Monclova	N5060K XB-MIN XB-AHW
B0548		Aero Leasing/Martinaire	N1219N N162SA
B0549		(Comav Aviation)	PT-MHF ZS-OUR V5-CAS [w/o 26Jun03 near Rooisand, Desert Ranch, Namibia]
B0550		Kaare Remme	N575R
B0551		AMREF Flying Doctor Service	N1277J 5Y-FDA
B0552		Mack Air	(N5133E) N1132M 7T-VIJ 5Y-VIJ A2-AKI
B0553		(Maxfly Aviation)	N5145P YV-735C N812MA [w/o 06Jly01 ditched 32km E of Fort Lauderdale, FL; canx 17Apr02]
B0554		Kato Airline	N51743 N1267A LN-KJK
B0555		RUTACA	N5095N YV-791C YV1950 [substantial damage 15Feb09 Guasdualito-Vare Maria, Venezuela]
B0556		(Agape Flights)	N5136J N954PA [ditched 20Dec07 off Andros Island, Bahamas; canx 09Feb10]
B0557		Ass Aviation Sans Frontieres	N5071M+ N1268M (F-OHXI) F-OGXX [+ marks reported but not confirmed]
B0558		East African Air Charters	(N1220N) N50938 5Y-BLN
B0559		Aero Tucan	N51396 XA-TDS
B0560		TAM – Taxi Aereo Marilia	N1301B PP-ITY
B0561		ex Makalu Air	N5073G N1226X ZK-VAN N919C SE-LPZ C-FWAM 9N-AJM [w/o 21Nov11 Talcha, Nepal; wreck for sale Mar12]
B0562		Aero Leasing/Martinaire	N5188A (C-FKAX) N12155
B0563		Naturelink Charters	N5200K N330AK ZS-OXV
B0564		Planemasters	N5162W N1256P
B0565		McMurray Aviation	N5858J C-GHLI
B0566		Frontier Alaska	N5246Z N1232Y
B0567		ex Megador 126	N52601 ZS-NUU+ 5Y- [canx 31May12 to Kenya]
B0568		SAL-Sociedade de Aviacao Ligeira	N52609 N1215K D2-EDA
B0569		Fugro Aviation Canada	N5264A N1210N C-FZLK
B0570		Coastal Aviation	N5262Z N1024Y TI-LRU YN-CGH N9EU 5H-JOE
B0571		Federal Air	N12030 TI-LRW HP-1392APPN282FV ZS-THR
B0572		Trans Guyana Airways	N1266Z TI-LRY HP-1390APPTI-BBG 8R-GHT
B0573		Leopont 278 Properties	N1009M 7T-VIK A2-AKG ZS-SVP+ [+ reported as A2-AKG w/o 06Jan10 Piajo Airstrip, Chief's Island, Okavango, Botswana, with Mack Air]
B0574		Safari Link	N1207A (F-OHXJ) F-OGXY 5Y-SLA
B0575		(Tropic Air Commuter)	N52623 V3-HFQ [w/o 07Sep08 off-shore Belize City, Belize]
B0576		British Parachute Schools	N52626 N1041F D-FLOH
B0577		Queensland Police Service	N1260G VH-PSY
B0578		Sky Business Rent	N5263S N805TH(1) N555SA D-FLOC
B0579		ex Maya Island Air	N52627 V3-HFS [not current; fate/status unknown]
B0580		(Les Grands Jorasses)	LV-PLZ LV-WSC [w/o en-route 28Apr01 12km from Roque Perez, Argentina]
B0581		Frontier Alaska	N303GV
B0582		(Moremi Air Services)	N5264S N1024V TI-LRZ TG-CDA N9MU ZS-JML A2-AKD [w/o 14Oct11 Xaxanaka, Okavango, Botswana]
B0583		Stichting Nationaal Paracentrum Teuge	N52645 N1115P PH-JMP
B0584		Ben Air	N52642 N1126L G-MART OY-PBF LN-PBF OY-PBF*

CESSNA 208 CARAVAN

C/n	Model	Last known Owner/Operator	Identities/fates/comments (where appropriate)
B0585		Paraclete Aviation	N5264U N1205M TR-LEM N80GE
B0586		Coastal Aviation	N12160 (F-OHXK) F-OGXZ N5QP 5H-BAD
B0587		Skydiving Promotion	N52655 N7229Z N9782X (OY-PBE) LN-PBE OO-SPA
B0588		Precision Shooting Equipment	N5267D N588PS [status unclear]
B0589		Scott Air	N5267J N1229C
B0590		Slingair Pty Ltd	N5267K N590TA VH-LNH
B0591		(ATESA – Aerotaxis Ecuatorianos)	N5267T N12296 HC-BXD [w/o 24Mar06 near Cuenca-Mariscal Lamar Airport, Ecuador]
B0592		Priority Air Charter	N5268A N208CR N208TF
B0593		Federal Air	N5268E N1194F ZS-OJC
B0594		Priority Air Charter	N5268M N179SA
B0595		Arctic One/Everts Air Alaska	N5268V N575JD
B0596		Kavango Air	N52601 ZS-NUV A2-NUV
B0597		Nakina Outpost Camps & Air Service	N52609 C-FZRJ
B0598		Gobernacion Corrientes	N5262W LV-PMX LV-WYR
B0599		Frontier Alaska	N5264E N1219G N169BJ (N877XL) N169BJ N169LJ
B0600		Sander Geophysics	N5217B C-GSGY
B0601		Air Algerie	N5211F N1247H 7T-VIL
B0602		Air Algerie	N52038 N1247K 7T-VIM
B0603		Hageland Aviation Services	N5200R N715HL N715HE
B0604		Air2There.Com	N51993 (D-FLAX) N64BP ZK-MYH
B0605		not yet known	N1116J ZS-BRT 5Y-BOM 9J-NAZ ZS-BRT 9J-NAZ 5X-NAZ
B0606		(Transworld Safaris)	N5263S N1127S 5Y-BNA 5Y-TWI [w/o 19Aug03 Old Fangak, Sudan]
B0607		La Costena	N51817 HP-1400 YN-CGU
B0608		Wells Fargo Bank Northwest – trustee	N580K YV-792C YV1670 N608AG
B0609		Avion Capital/Air Now	N9551F N805TH(2)
B0610		Bursiel Equipment	N5188N N880TT+ N1014X N97HA [+ marks reported but not confirmed]
B0611		La Costena	N5214L N1277Y TI-LRS HP-1407APP YN-CGB
B0612		Youngone	N52613 N1215A S2-ACU
B0613		(Aeroperlas)	N5262Z N1133H TI-LRT HP-1397APP [w/o en-route 16Aug04 Arraijan, Panama]
B0614		Air Services	N52623 N12397 TI-LRV TG-RMM TI-BBL YN-CHA 8R-GCB
B0615		Hinterland Aviation	N51881 N1215S VH-AGS VH-HLL
B0616		Frontier Alaska	N5262X N407GV
B0617		(Union Charter Trust)	N5194J (OY-PBG) ZS-OCZ 5Y-EOA ZS-OCZ [w/o 15Apr01 near Tembo, Democratic Republic of Congo]
B0618		Missionary Aviation Fellowship	N5223D N102VE N28MF
B0619		Glass Eels	N5264M G-EELS
B0620		Northern Air Paradive Club	N5263D N103VE 4X-CSX
B0621		TAM – Taxi Aereo Marilia	N5260Y ZP-CAD PR-MAU
B0622		Aero Ruta Maya	N52601 TG-JFT
B0623		Planemasters	N104VE N279PM
B0624		Random Participacoes	N12191 PT-WRZ
B0625		Quilque	N5262X LV-PMY LV-WYO
B0626		not yet known	(OY-PBH) N1123F 5H-TLT 7Q-ULA ZS-SGG+ 5X- [+ marks canx 23Oct08 to Uganda]
B0627		(PENTA – Pena Transportes Aereos)	N5263D PT-MPA [w/o 29Mar05 Verapaz Farm, Brazil]
B0628		Pen Air-Peninsula Airways	N750PA
B0629		Maxim Aviation	N52639 SE-KYI N850SD
B0630		PENTA – Pena Transportes Aereos	N5264A PT-MPB
B0631		Planemasters	N286PM
B0632		Frontier Alaska	N5264U N410GV
B0633		Weaver Aero International	N52642 N997CP ZS-PIF [not current status/fate unknown]
B0634		Aero Service ASF	N12386 6V-AHF
B0635		(Broome Aviation)	N1216Q VH-NTQ [w/o 14Jan10 Beagle Bay Airport, WA, Australia]
B0636		Air Safaris & Services (NZ)	N1038F TG-ROC N208PR(1) ZK-SRI
B0637		Skydive Academy	N1002Y TG-EAA TI-AZU N208AD N208UP
B0638		STC Aircraft Conversions	N1119B YN-CFG HR-IBI YN-CGI N750TE
B0639		Tanzanair – Tanzanian Air Services	N1132Y TI-LRB HR-IBJ N452NU A6-MRM ZS-PJJ 5H-TZU
B0640		Aerodynamics	N1128P TI-LRA HP-1399APP TI-BAE N208PW G-DLAC
B0641		Sunwest Aviation	N52655 C-FAFJ

CESSNA 208 CARAVAN

C/n	Model	Last known Owner/Operator	Identities/fates/comments (where appropriate)
B0642		Safari Links	N1219N 6Y-JRE N208GJ 5Y-BOP
B0643		Sky Aviation	N522GM HS-GAA PK-ECC
B0644		PENTA – Pena Transportes Aereos	N5267T PT-MPD
B0645		PENTA – Pena Transportes Aereos	N5268A PT-MPG
B0646		Sander Geophysics	N5268E C-GSGW
B0647		Tropic Air Commuter	N5268M V3-HFV
B0648		Broome Aviation	N5268V (F-OHQM) N1253K VH-UZF VH-TWX
B0649		West Wing Aviation	N5269A (F-OHQN) N1253Y VH-UZC VH-TWW P2-TWW VH-TIY
B0650		Avion Capital/Castle Aviation	N5261R N27MG
B0651		Chilean Army	N5262Z E-131
B0652		Chilean Army	N52623 E-132
B0653		Chilean Army	N5264M E-133
B0654		Air Excel	N5260Y N1216J VT-TAP 5H-SMK
B0655		(M & N Aviation)	N1315A [1,000th Caravan built] [w/o 23Dec99 near Adjuntas, Puerto Rico; hulk to Atlanta Air Salvage, Griffin, GA; l/n 24Oct06; canx 13Apr09]
B0656		Missionary Aviation Fellowship	N12284 PK-MPS
B0657		M & N Aviation	N52601 N1241X
B0658		(Georgian Express)	N5262W C-FAGA [w/o 17Jan04 in Lake Erie, 3km from Pelee Island, ON; canx 04Mar04]
B0659		Wright Air Service	N52613 N900WA
B0660		Aerodynamics Worldwide Inc	(N5263U) N12249 N73MM C-GKRM N208AF
B0661		M & N Aviation	N1131G
B0662		Sontair	N5264E C-FFGA
B0663		Alta Flights (Charters)	N5263D N1229A C-FAFC
B0664		Tanzanair – Tanzanian Air Services	N5264U C-GSOW C-FSKX ZS-PSR 5H-TZT
B0665		SAL – Sociedade de Aviacao Ligeira	N1256G D2-EDB
B0666		Alkan Air	N1131S N95NA N939JL C-FAKZ
B0667		Avion Capital Corp	N5263S C-FPNG N162GA
B0668		Tropical Air (Z)	7Q-YKR ZS-OFK 5H-ALO
B0669		SASCA – Servicios Aereos Sucre	YV-657C N51319 YV-1149C YV183T
B0670		ex Aero Condor	N1132D OB-1741 OB-1741-P [canx 06Oct10 to Aircraft Structures International Corp in USA]
B0671		Caravan Air	N211SA N208TW
B0672		Frontier Alaska	N411GV
B0673		Alkan Air	N5268M C-FSKF
B0674		Xstro Opencast Mining	N1286N 5Y-TWG ZS-OUR
B0675		Sanei Shoji	N444BT JA208D
B0676		Hinterland Aviation	N12372 VH-CVN
B0677		Coastal Aviation	N1256N 5H-HOT
B0678		(Brazilian Air Force)	N5263U 2709 [C98] [reported w/o; no details known]
B0679		(Air Charter Botswana)	N5260Y N1239A 7Q-YKU A2-AKL [w/o 27Dec03 Mzuzu, Botswana]
B0680		Eric M Passmore	N105VE
B0681		SANSA	HP-1355APP TI-BAK
B0682		Tropic Air	ZS-ELE 5Y-BRT
B0683		(Blue Nile Ltd/Stellavia)	N1126T 5Y-BNN [missing 14Feb07 between Goma & Walikale, Democratic Republic of Congo; believed w/o, no wreckage found by Mar07]
B0684		Peruvian National Police	N684SA PNP-245
B0685		(Tropic Airlines)	N685SA F-OIXZ [w/o 05Sep10 near Anse-Bertrand, Guadeloupe]
B0686		Aerolineas Paraguayas	ZP-TAZ
B0687		Trollope Mining Services	N955PA ZS-OPE
B0688		D & D Aviation/Airworks Kenya	N12580 ZS-OIH 5Y-TAV
B0689		(Air Carrier)	N499BA [w/o 01Dec01 near Bessemer Airport, AL; still current]
B0690		(Linea Turistica Aereotuy)	N52601 HK-4186X N506C YV-861C YV1183 [ditched 26Aug09 into Caribbean Sea near La Tortuga, Venezuela]
B0691		La Costena	YN-CFK
B0692		Council for Geoscience	N824BT N824BL ZS-JAK
B0693		Regional Air	N90HL N90HE C6-RAS
B0694		Goma Air	N694MA 9N-AJT
B0695		(Linea Turistica Aereotuy)	N5269A HK-4185X N504C YV-862C YV1181 [w/o 17Apr09 near Canaima, Venezuela]
B0696		Vera Cruz Taxi Aereo	PT-WYP
B0697		Frontier Alaska	N5268Z (HK-) N12373
B0698		Vera Cruz Taxi Aereo	PT-WZN

CESSNA 208 CARAVAN

C/n	Model	Last known Owner/Operator	Identities/fates/comments (where appropriate)
B0699		(Carbinair)	YV-658C N5133F HH-CAR N379DW+ [w/o 31Aug07 near Port-au-Prince Airport, Haiti; + regd 30Apr09 to Aircraft Structures International Corp; for either re-build or spares recovery]
B0700		Fretax Taxi Aereo	N700RH PR-MSH [badly damaged 24Nov10 Brotas, Brazil]
B0701		RJR Transport Logistics	N701SE
B0702		(Paragon Air Express)	(N702SE) N702PA [w/o en-route 05Sep07 near Cross City Airport, FL; by Nov08 hulk with Atlanta Air Salvage, Griffin, GA; regd 30Sep10 to Priority Air Charter]
B0703		Air Roberval	N12421 N903DP C-GLIE
B0704		Sefofane Air Charter	N1307P (ZS-TIG) ZS-TSW A2-NAS
B0705		Planemasters	C-GDWY N9183L N274PM
B0706		Desert Air	N1244Y N910HL N910HE V5-MAX
B0707		Tropic Air Commuter	N5264S N23681 V3-HIK
B0708		DLR Flugbetriebe	D-FDLR
B0709		(Aeroperlas/SANSA)	HP-1357APP [w/o en-route 26Aug00 Arenal Volcano, Costa Rica]
B0710		Aerodynamics Worldwide Inc	HP-1358APP TI-BAN HP-1358APP N208AX
B0711		Aerodynamics Worldwide Inc	HP-1359APP TI-BAO HP-1359APP N208AJ(2)
B0712		Fugro Airbourne Surveys	N5246U N1268C I-LSBB D-FLIZ ZS-SSA
B0713		(SASCA – Servicios Aereos Sucre)	YV-1069C [w/o 08Aug03 Tocomita Airport, Venezuela]
B0714		Coastal Aviation	N208FK(1) 5H-VIP
B0715		Take Air Lines	N52627 N1258H F-OHQN
B0716		S.F.I.L.	N5267K TJ-AIK
B0717		Skydive Santa Barbara	TG-APC N10WJ N208DZ
B0718		Transportes Bragado	N51872 LV-POC LV-ZNU
B0719		Guatemalan Air Force	HP-1360AR+ YV193T YV2453 (N718BT)^ 606 [+ marks canx pre Jly05 and became YV2453 in 2008; status during this period unknown; ^ false marks current at time on c/n 208B0881; impounded wearing these marks 28May08]
B0720		Missionary Aviation Fellowship	N702SE ZS-SCO 5H-ERI ZS-SCO 5X-SCO
B0721		Westwind Aviation	N208WW
B0722		Discovery Air Fire Service	N5268M C-FSKS
B0723		Inversiones F.K.	N5183V CC-LLT CC-CFM
B0724		Air Tindi	N997Q C-FAFG
B0725		Africair Inc	N12326 F-OHQU N208LF
B0726		not yet known	F-OHQM D-FTDZ
B0727		Northern Air Charter	N1133L ZS-NAP A2-NAP
B0728		Aerotron Air Adventure	XA-TNI
B0729		Linea Turistica Aereotuy	YV-659C YV1182 [substantial damage 26Aug09 La Tortuga, Venezuela]
B0730		Frontier Alaska	N12328 N215MC
B0731		Aircraft Guaranty Corp	N1263Y N208SV [Supervan conversion # 7]
B0732		(Avion Capital/Air Net Systems)	N28MG [w/o 05Dec07 near Columbus-Rickenbacker, OH; canx 06Jun11]
B0733		Polar Aviation	N5109W N1269N VH-NWT
B0734		Saturno Participacoes	N5268A PT-XIS
B0735		ex Aero Condor	N12652 OB-1740 OB-1740-P
B0736		Xugana Air	N5264U N1309J A2-RAN ZS-OWW A2-AKO
B0737		East African Air Charters	N1266A 5Y-EOC
B0738		Wilken Aviation	N1266B 5Y-EOD ZS-CAT 5Y-LEX
B0739		Wings of Alaska	N5264S N331AK
B0740		Servicios Aereos Milenio	N5265B XA-TOE XA-MUR
B0741		Federal Bureau of Investigation	N1132F
B0742		Airways Airlink	N5262X HK-4201X N878C 9J-CGC
B0743		Take Off Fallschirmsport	D-FUMP
B0744		Fallschirmsportcentrum Albatross	D-FALB
B0745		Wright Air Service	N1323R
B0746		Makalu Air	N998LA 9N-AJG
B0747		ex Sander Geophysics	N1285D C-GSGU+ PK- [+ canx 01Nov11 to Indonesia]
B0748		Aircraft Structures International Corp	N5163K YV-669C N5133W HH-CAW N376JX
B0749		Larkspur Fund	N1279Y N208SM
B0750		Wilderness Air	(N1253M) N52639 P4-SSL YV-1205CP N750LK A2-AEB A2-ZEB
B0751		Frontier Alaska	N28AN
B0752		James D. Rowe/Bering Air	N204BA
B0753		South Aero/Air Now	N29AN
B0754		Coastal Aviation	N1772E 5H-PAF 5H-SUN
B0755		Missionary Aviation Fellowship	N208DW PK-MAE

CESSNA 208 CARAVAN

C/n	Model	Last known Owner/Operator	Identities/fates/comments (where appropriate)
B0756		Frontier Alaska	N1275N
B0757		(Foxtreks/Sky Aviation)	N1307D 5H-NAC+ [+ canx by Jly10 fate/status unknown]
B0758		Air Services	(N1253M) N5264M YN-CFO 8R-BKP
B0759		Skylink Express	N5262W C-GSKT
B0760		Sky Dive M.V.	N333FA D-FIXX
B0761		Far Reaching Ministries Aviation	N5262X HK-4202X N514C 5X-FRM
B0762		Skylink Express	N52623 C-GSKS
B0763		CTA – Cleiton Taxi Aereo	N5165P PT-PTA
B0764		Fugro Aviation Canada	N5172M N208KC C-GNCA
B0765		Airborne Energy Solutions	N5174W C-FARQ
B0766		(CTA – Cleiton Taxi Aereo)	N52086 PT-PTB [w/o 28Feb12 Manaus-Flores, Brazil]
B0767		North Wright Airways	N5151D C-GDLC
B0768		Aero Ruta Maya	N5152X TG-ARM
B0769		Mabena Pty	N51666 N106VE EC-IKU VH-UZB P2-TZZ VH-TUY(1) VH-TOV
B0770		Goma Air	N1299P C-FDON N36SJ N74KA 9N-AJU [floatplane]
B0771		Country Flyin Inc	N208MQ
B0772		Qwila Air/Fortune Air	N208LT ZS-SLG
B0773		Skydiving Promotion	N599BA PH-PPS OO-SEX
B0774		Suburban Air Freight	N5261R N208QC
B0775		(Atlantic Aero/Mid-Atlantic Freight)	N52613 N76U [w/o 23Oct02 Bateau Bay near Mobile Aerospace Field, AL; canx 01Jun06; hulk to Atlanta Air Salvage, Griffin, GA; l/n 24Oct06]
B0776		Paragon Air Express	N5262B N703PA
B0777		Aero Leasing/Martinaire	N5262Z N1324G
B0778		Pennsylvania State Police	N1287G
B0779		Wings of Alaska	N52645 N332AK
B0780		Beaver Air Services/Missinippi Airways	N5265B N308KC C-GOCN
B0781		La Costena	N5268A YV-1126C YV184T YN-CGS
B0782		Blue Skies Aviation	N5262W N1283K N208BS JU-2114
B0783		Sander Geophysics	N5264S C-GOCZ C-GSGL
B0784		(Transworld Safaris)	N52639 N1253M 5Y-TWH [w/o 18Aug04 Nyarigongo Volcano, near Goma Airport, Democratic Republic of Congo]
B0785		Tropicair	N5268M LV-ZSL N785SC P2-AMH
B0786		ex The New Reclamation Group	N52626 YV-924C N208AH(1) ZS-OZE+ Z [+ canx 22Jly10 as exported]
B0787		Rustic Corp	N386AR [status unclear]
B0788		(SANSA – Servicios Aereos Nacionales)	N52623 HP-1405APP [w/o en-route 28Nov01 Cerro Chontales, near Quepos Airport, Costa Rica]
B0789		SANSA – Servicios Aereos Nacionales	N5163K N1318L HP-1402APPTI-BAP
B0790		SANSA – Servicios Aereos Nacionales	N51869 N1318M HP-1403APPTI-BAQ
B0791		(Tropic Air Commuter)	N5262X V3-HFW [w/o 09Mar05 near Belize City Airport, Belize]
B0792		Westwind Aviation	N5267T N785WW
B0793		Avior Airlines	N52627 YV-925C YV1766
B0794		Paracentrum Vlaaderen	N5263D N13047 OO-FUS
B0795		not yet known	N5264U YV-794C YV1979 N795AL 5Y-CBG
B0796		Nouvelles Air Affaires Gabon	N5268E N99FX TR-LFX
B0797		Lake & Peninsula Airlines	N5180C+ N454SF [+ marks also used concurrently by a Cessna 172F]
B0798		Jindal Iron & Steel	N51806 N78HM VT-JSW
B0799		North Star Air	N799B C-FLNB
B0800		Broome Aviation	N5197M N1278M 9M-PMA VH-TLH
B0801		Slingair	N51984 N1278N 9M-PMB VH-LNN
B0802		Air Santo Domingo	N5212M N1326D HI-760CT
B0803		Brazilian Air Force	N5206T 2719 [C98]
B0804		Frontier Alaska	N51612 N12890 N717PA
B0805		Missionary Aviation Fellowship	N52682 N8725B D-FPUL OY-TPC D-FPUL TT-BER
B0806		not yet known	N5263S N1284B N806BF PR-FAM
B0807		Commercial Aerea	N5261R XA-ESV
B0808		L.3 Capital LLC	N12813 (N1274N) (N208BD)
B0809		Caribbean Air Management	N5264E N801FL
B0810		Nord-Flyg	N5262W N1223A D-FROG(2) S5-CAN OY-TPG SE-LSL
B0811		Army Parachute Association	N5196U G-BZAH

CESSNA 208 CARAVAN

C/n	Model	Last known Owner/Operator	Identities/fates/comments (where appropriate)
B0812		Avion Capital/Castle Aviation	N52229 N29MG
B0813		Watermakers Aviation	N5151D N811FL
B0814		Samanja Flight	N5152X N12812 ZS-ORU
B0815		Sefofane Air Charter	N5268A N1285G A2-BUF ZS-BUF A2-BUF
B0816		Avtran	N52609 XA-MTA N900SA
B0817		(NTD Air Cargo)	N5262W SE-KYH [w/o 31Jan05 Helsinki-Vantaa Airport, Finland; canx 06Dec06]
B0818		Sefofane Air Charter	N5263U N1289Y V5-ELE
B0819		Governor of the State of Parana	N52639 PP-JAQ PP-EPV
B0820		Wilderness Air	N52086 N1307A A2-LEO
B0821		Brazilian Air Force	N52626 2720 [C98]
B0822		Cherokee Air	N5265B N822SA C6-SBH
B0823		Western Caravans	N5267T N823SA
B0824		Brazilian Air Force	N5163K 2721 [C98]
B0825		Mokulele Airlines/Go! Express	N5180C N98RR N861MA [substantial damage 15Oct09 Kaunakakai, HI]
B0826		J. C. Relants	N51806 LV-ZTW
B0827		Little Red Air Service	N5147B C-GGUH
B0828		Georgia Skies	N5197M N297DF N305PW
B0829		Missionary Aviation Fellowship	N51984 N12162 9Q-CKC 9Q-CMO
B0830		Trans Guyana Airways	N5261R N408MN 8R-GHS
B0831		L-3 Communications Aeromet	N5206T N208SA
B0832		Skydive Queenstown	N832SA ZK-KPH
B0833		Paraclete Aviation	N52613 N699BA N304PW N477XP
B0834		Paracentrum Vlaaderen	N51612 N1958E OO-FFB
B0835		not yet known	N5262B N715BT+ 5X- [+ canx 14Oct11 to Uganda]
B0836		Brazilian Air Force	N52642 2723 [C98]
B0837		Najaco America	N5269A N837AK
B0838		Frontier Alaska	N5194B XA-ABW N3039G CP-2413 N838FB N838GV
B0839		Urbanizaciones Gamma	N52609 XB-ABC [Supervan 900 conversion # 2]
B0840		Wasaya Airways	N52623 C-FPCC (D-FLUC)
B0841		Microsurvey Aerogeofisica	N5263U N1295G CX-TRA N1295G C6-RAL N51AD PR-MIC
B0842		(Amaszonas Compania de Servicios de Transporte)	N1300N CP-2395 [w/o 10Jly01 Sarija Hill near La Paz-El Alto Airport, Bolivia]
B0843		Priority Air Charter	N5260Y N716BT
B0844		Missionary Aviation Fellowship	N5266F N805AA 5R-MKE 9Q-CMZ
B0845		Brazilian Air Force	N51511 2722 [C98]
B0846		M & N Aviation	N51666 N409MN
B0847		Skylink Express	C-GSKV
B0848		ex Wilderness Air	N52626 N1287Y A2-GNU [canx by Oct10; fate/status unknown]
B0849		Paraclete Aviation	N5265B N588LL
B0850		Avion Capital/Castle Aviation	N5261R N24MG
B0851		AAA Investments	N52627 ZS-PGB Z-YES ZS-PCM
B0852		Missionary Aviation Fellowship	N5264S N1276P PK-MAD
B0853		Superior Airways	N5262Z PNC-0220 N853PA C-FAMK
B0854		A/K Warszaw/Skydive Warsaw	N854BF SP-WAW
B0855		M G Aviation	N208GC N53U
B0856		J.A. Leigh	N5145A+ N20JA XC-AAM N856WE (ZS-CIC) ZS-JMS [+ marks also used concurrentlly by Cessna 172 c/n 28145]
B0857		Soaring Safaris	N5181U N801AA V5-AGS [reported 09Nov10 Arequipa, Peru]
B0858		Missionary Aviation Fellowship	N5165P CX-TRB N5077H 5H-OPE
B0859		(Grant Aviation)	N5188W+ LN-PBJ N207DR [+ marks also used concurrently by a Volksplane; w/o 02Sep11 mid-air collision with Ce207 near Nightmute, AK]
B0860		Fugro Airborne Surveys	N51869 N124AA ZS-SSB PR-SSB ZS-FSB
B0861		Salt Air	N51896 N861CM ZK-MJL
B0862		Sounds Air Travel & Tourism	N5192E N208DG ZK-SAA
B0863		(Corpjet/Baltimore Air Transport)	N5197M N717BT [w/o 22Jly05 San Carlos Apache Airport, Globe, AZ; canx 29Sep05]
B0864		Suburban Air Freight	N864SF
B0865		Hageland Aviation Services/Fly BVI	N5206T N208RL
B0866		(Salmon Air)	NN52613 N13142 N25SA [w/o 06Dec04 near Sun Valley Airport, ID; canx 15Jun07]
B0867		Barragan Villareal Javier Lucio	N5262X XB-LGA
B0868		Rani Air	N1311A N787DM ZS-POH
B0869		O. C. McDonald Co	N52626 N30NE N494Q

CESSNA 208 CARAVAN

C/n	Model	Last known Owner/Operator	Identities/fates/comments (where appropriate)
B0870		TP Air	N208SJ
B0871		(Tropic Air)	N51612 V3-HGB [w/o 20Mar04 near Punta Gorda Airport, Belize]
B0872		Coastal Tours & Travels	N1294K 5H-MAD
B0873		Caribbean Air Management	N802AA
B0874		874 LLC	N40NE
B0875		Aereo Servicio Guerrero	N5261R XA-TSB
B0876		Missionary Aviation Fellowship	N5263D N1301B ZS-EST
B0877		Fugro Airborne Surveys	N208LW ZS-FSA
B0878		518JJ LLC/Rio Grande Air	N52642 N518JJ
B0879		Paracentrum Vlaaderen	N5267J C-GIKG N209AA OO-JEE
B0880		Atlantico Transporte Aereo	PR-ATA
B0881		ex Air Serv International	N718BT+ 5X- [+ canx 07May10 to Uganda] [see c/n B0719]
B0882		African Inland Mission International	N5268E N1133K 5Y-BOY N2NQ N208EA 5Y-PCS
B0883		Shandong Airlines	N51806 N12285 B-3630
B0884		Fugro Airborne Surveys	N51984 N1291K (XA-) N1171 C-GJQV VH-FAY
B0885		Sunshine Aircraft	N885PE
B0886		not yet known	N5223X N1251P HI-754SP
B0887		Samaritan's Purse	N5260Y C-GIKN N250AA N883SP
B0888		M Carrington Ross	N52613 YV-1037C YV2269 N271Z 5Y-MCR
B0889		SBA Airlines	N52677 YV-1038C YV
B0890		Bering Air	N205BA
B0891		Zantas Air Services	N1239B 5H-TAK
B0892		Frontier Alaska	N5181U C-GWCA N405GV
B0893		Jetmax Aviation	N52609 N208GC D-FGAK ZS-JAX
B0894		Tradewind Aviation	N52623 N208SG
B0895		Wasaya Airways	N5265B C-FWAW
B0896		Meint Jes Sun Road Partnership/ Federal Air	N5265N N1128S 5Y-TWJ ZS-FDL
B0897		(Amaszonas Compania de Servicios de Transport)	N5266F CP-2412 [w/o en-route 21Jan05 Mount Huaricollo, Bolivia; fuselage to Preferred Airparts, Kidron, OH for parts recovery]
B0898		ex Air Serv International	N719BT+ 5X- [+ canx 16Dec11 to Uganda]
B0899		Colombian Air Force	FAC5057
B0900		Nature Air	N375WY N181GC TI-BEI
B0901		SBA Airlines	N5267K YV-1039C YV
B0902		Planemasters	N281PM
B0903		Brazilian Police	N5267T PR-AAB
B0904		Inter-Archipelago Airways	N77X
B0905		Gobierno Edo Bolivar	N51511 YV-O-CBL-6 YV0134
B0906		Air Net Systems	N51666 N102AN
B0907		Tropic Air	N5168Y N12171 PR-PMA (PP-PMA) N32211 5Y-BSY
B0908		National Aircraft Leasing/FBI	N51612 N1259Z PR-PMB (PP-PMB) N32212 N324SJ
B0909		Puma Air Linhas Aereas	N12826 PR-PMC
B0910		Maya Island Air	N5180C N12522 V3-HGD
B0911		Aerotech Australasia	N51689 XA-TSJ N747LE (N747EE) VH-ODU
B0912		Jemax Aviation	N5188W N900HL N490CA ZS-JEM
B0913		Vogel Engineers	N208BV
B0914		Ben Air	N5196U LN-PBK OY-PBK*
B0915		Brazilian Police	N5192E PR-AAC
B0916		Chartair	N1254D VH-SMH VH-NGC
B0917		Air Net Systems	N5207V N106AN
B0918		Avion Capital Corp	N104AN
B0919		Sichuan Aolin General Aviation	N52086 N1294D B-3637
B0920		Missionary Aviation Fellowship	N12396 5Y-MAG
B0921		Venezuelan Air Force	N5260Y N2222C N622AL 2406
B0922		ex Southern Aircraft Consultancy	N52601 N786DM+ PK- [+ canx 22May12 to Indonesia]
B0923		Gum Air	N5262B N1132W PZ-TBH
B0924		Arrow Three	N5262X N1129G
B0925		Slingair	N125AR VH-LNO
B0926		(Gobernacional Estado Bolivar)	N5262Z YV-O-CBL-7 [w/o en-route 04May04 in Chimanta Mountains, Venezuela]
B0927		Maya Island Air	N52627 V3-HGF
B0928		Air Net Systems	N103AN
B0929		Africair Inc	N1129K 5H-RJS

CESSNA 208 CARAVAN

C/n	Model	Last known Owner/Operator	Identities/fates/comments (where appropriate)						
B0930		Priority Air Charter	N5264E	V3-HGH	N2418W	N228PA(3)			
B0931		Aero Calafia	N5296M	XA-TWN					
B0932		Veltal Avia	N1228Y	P4-ELA	RA-67701	[badly damaged 02Oct10 in forced landing near Makarovo, Irkutsk, Russia]			
B0933		Flight Team	N5265N	D-FCOM					
B0934		Leis Air/Pacific Air Express	N5267D	D-FOKM	EC-IHD	N108JA	N866MA		
B0935		J. A. Aero	N5263D	G-EORD	EC-JVY	G-EORD	N208PM	N900JA	
B0936		WAS Aircraft Leasing	N40753	EC-IEV	D-FAAH	UR-CEGC	(D-FAMC)	D-FAAH	G-SYLV
B0937		West Wing Aviation	N4057D	EC-IEX	VH-UZY				
B0938		Northridge Associates	N891L						
B0939		Frontier Alaska	N5261R	N1242Y	N124LA	N1242Y			
B0940		Jerry D Clayton/Hawks Nest Resort & Marina	N208G						
B0941		SIASA/United Nations	N52609	XA-TUF	[UN code UN-90W]				
B0942		D.A. & J. F. Camm Pty Ltd	N5155G	N208AR	VH-DJG				
B0943		Bering Air	N806BA						
B0944		Mack Air	N4085S	A2-MEG					
B0945		D P Acquisitions	N830CE						
B0946		Maya Island Air	N52639	V3-HGJ					
B0947		Aereo Servicio Guerrero	N5263S	(XA-TUJ)	N1244Z	XA-TXM			
B0948		ex Lanzarote Aerocargo	D-FMCG	EC-IKM	[deleted from 01Nov09 register; fate/status unknown]				
B0949		not yet known	N5267T	C-GKEC	HL5113				
B0950		Northern Air	N52682	N1130T	5H-SJF				
B0951		Bangladesh Army	N1230A	S3-BMJ					
B0952		Sichuan Aolin General Aviation	N1132X	B-3640					
B0953		Sichuan Aolin General Aviation	N5265B	N1133B	B-3641				
B0954		Helifix Operations	N1242A	P2-HFA					
B0955		Linea Turistica Aereotuy	N5262Z	YV-863C	YV1188				
B0956		Air Net Systems	N105AN						
B0957		Skydive Rotterdam	N5268M	LN-PBM	G-ZOBA	C-GOTA	PH-BSU		
B0958		Icecap LLC	N5264A	N1230G	XA-TVS	N814GV			
B0959		Zulu Charlie Inc	N602ZC	N623ZC					
B0960		32 EL LLC	N32EL						
B0961		Tropic Air Lines	N5262W	N4109K	F-OIJO				
B0962		Aerovic	N602RL	HC-CJH					
B0963		John B. Cashman	N123JK						
B0964		Vieques Air Link	N5260Y	N335VL					
B0965		Coastal Aviation	N1129Y	5H-POA					
B0966		Moroccan Government	N52626	N12297	CN-TSZ				
B0967		Wasaya Airways	N52627	N1229M	VH-KCV	RDPL-34144	N428FC	C-FHWA	
B0968		Henry Moreno Cortazar	N208GB	YV2514	N665DL	HK-4669			
B0969		A.L.S. Trust	N5264E	ZS-VAN					
B0970		Kato Airline	N5268E	N12295	LN-KAT				
B0971		(Brown County Financial Services)	N5269A	N514DB	[w/o en-route 08Nov02 3mls S of Parks, AZ; canx 26May11]				
B0972		not yet known	N52645	N4110D	PR-VAL				
B0973		Maya Island Air	N5264S	N1248G	V3-HGQ				
B0974		Low Country Trading	N1259K						
B0975		South Aero	N108AN						
B0976		Wright Air Service	N5263D	N976E					
B0977		ex F.L. Aviation Group	N5267D	N1266G	N321LM	N180LQ	[sale reported to FAA]		
B0978		Freedom LLC	N662LM						
B0979		not yet known	PR-ITA						
B0980		ex Air Serv International	N8HZ+	5X-	[+ canx 03May12 to Uganda]				
B0981		Planemasters	N282PM						
B0982		Red River Service Corp	N800JG						
B0983		Pacific Wings	N301PW						
B0984		Pacific Wings	N302PW						
B0985		Pacific WingsEcoJet	N303PW						
B0986		Fallshirmsportclub Hohenems (Austria)	N807AA	N208PC					
B0987		Missionary Aviation Fellowship	N52623	N12173	5Y-BRE				
B0988		CAE Aviation	N52655	LN-PBL	T7-VAL	D-FLUC			
B0989		Missionary Aviation Fellowship	N5265B	N1232X	PK-MPF				

CESSNA 208 CARAVAN

C/n	Model	Last known Owner/Operator	Identities/fates/comments (where appropriate)				
B0990		Wings Aviation (Air Guyana)	N5207B	N208KT	8R-WAL		
B0991		Cape Flattery Silca Mines	N52144	N12374	VH-LZK		
B0992		(Servicios Aereos Milenio)	N52178	N1238G	XA-TWK	[w/o 14Jun10 near Felippe Carrillo Puerto, Quintana Roo, Mexico]	
B0993		Air Net Systems	N107AN				
B0994		Africair	N5268V	N1239Z	C6-NFS	N785PA	
B0995		Maya Island Air	N5241Z	N1241G	V3-HGO		
B0996		Leis Air/Pacific Air Express	N5200R	N281WB	N747CG	N865MA	
B0997		SJC Leasing	N5153K	N71SC	N712LA	N71SC	
B0998		Maya Island Air	N5213S	N12419	V3-HGP		
B0999		Zambia Flying Doctor Service	N5260Y	N12383	9J-AGC		
B1000		Khun Suwat Liptapanlob	N52462	N12424	HS-SMC	HS-SMI	HS-SPL
B1001		Low Country Trading	N51881	N583JH			
B1002		Leis Air/Pacific Air Express	N52626	N208EA	N501LA	N687MA	
B1003		Westwind Air	N5079V	N1243D	N850VX		
B1004		Frontier Alaska	N5163K	N126AR			
B1005		US Department of State	N51986	N1243E			
B1006		Hinterland Aviation	N5201M	N1247N	VH-TFS		
B1007		US Department of State	N52234	N1243G			
B1008		Alkan Air	N5108G	N208B	N961TP	C-FAKV	
B1009		Textron Receivables Corp	N5201J	N1244V			
B1010		ex CFA Air Charters	N52086	N208CG	ZS-CTP+	A2-	[+ canx 26Mar12 to Botswana]
B1011		US Department of State	N5155G	N1243Y			
B1012		Nord-Flyg AB	N5236L	SE-LSK			
B1013		Multi-Aero	N5226B	N1248E	N1983X		
B1014		Sivad Holding Corp	N5260M	N304PW	N208CX		
B1015		ITT Industries Space Systems	N5228J	N208CE	N208EK		
B1016		Helifix Operations	N52639	N1242L	P2-HFB		
B1017		Aero Biniza	N52457	N1255L	XA-TVS	XA-UAB	
B1018		Cotia Vitoria Servicos e Comercio	N808BC	N208RR	PR-ARZ		
B1019		Horizon Management Corp	N52144	N787RA			
B1020		ex Africair Aviation Leasing	N52352	N110WY+	5H-	[+ canx 14Oct10 to Tanzania]	
B1021		Mission Aviation Fellowship	N5244W	N208FG			
B1022		Bering Air	N907BA				
B1023		Telnet Software	N208ST	N208B			
B1024		not yet known	G-WIKY	EC-JGQ	G-WIKY	SU-KAH	
B1025		Westwind Aircraft Leasing	N5090V	N122JB			
B1026		Taganyika Flying Company	N1247V	5H-	N1257M	5H-RPF	5H-FEE
B1027		Greenman-Pedersen	N682AC				
B1028		not yet known	N5214K	PR-BBM			
B1029		Zambia Flying Doctor Service	N1257M	9J-FDS			
B1030		ex Coastal Aviation	N12554	5H-BAT+	[+ canx by Jly10 fate/status unknown]		
B1031		AMREF Flying Doctor Service	N1266P	5Y-FDB			
B1032		Del-Air	N4096H	N208TG(2)			
B1033		Wilmar Air/Enggang Air	N688RT	PK-RSW			
B1034		ex US Department of State	N1267X+	HK-	[+ canx 09Nov11 to Colombia]		
B1035		West Wing Aviation	N5058J	N421YC	VH-ZGS	VH-WZY	
B1036		not yet known	N12605	HI-788SP	N788WS+	YV	[+ canx 30Mar06 to Venezuela]
B1037		Northrop Grumman Systems Corp	N51612	N112LT			
B1038		Instituto Cartografico de Catalunya	N5174W	EC-IRV			
B1039		Governor's Aviation	D-FOXI	F-GNYR	CN-TYR	5Y-GCA	
B1040		Colombian Air Force	N5157E	FAC5059			
B1041		Black Ginger 425	N51564	G-OCIT	D-FQSZ	ZS-AGC	
B1042		Wipaire	N208JF(1)	N208WF			
B1043		Van Bortel Inc	N208FL				
B1044		Sartec Corp	N208CE	N617ST			
B1045		Yellow Wings Air Services	N208Y	N575TC	N884AA	5Y-LLO	
B1046		(Aereo Calafia)	N12298	XA-UBC	[w/o 05Nov07 Caliacan Airport, Mexico]		
B1047		Worldwide Aircraft Leasing/FBI	N208EB				
B1048		Hinterland Aviation	N1266V	VH-MRZ			
B1049		Mokulele Airlines/Go! Express	N208LR	N863MA			
B1050		Thai Indo Industries	N40363	9M-MAR+	[+ not fully confirmed]		
B1051		The Castle Kyalami Hotel	N208NJ	ZS-CCC			

CESSNA 208 CARAVAN

C/n	Model	Last known Owner/Operator	Identities/fates/comments (where appropriate)
B1052		(Volga Avia)	N5061P N1283Y P4-OIN [w/o en-route 19Nov05 10km from Stupino, Russia]
B1053		Department of Natural & Environmental Resources	N516PR
B1054		Ozinga Aviation	N819CS N750Z
B1055		1055 LLC	N127AR
B1056		National Aircraft Leasing/FBI	N956D
B1057		Ekspres Transportasi Antarbenua	N5060K N4088Z RP-C2801 PK-RJS
B1058		Avtran/Pacific International Skydiving Center	N5066U N12677 N989BW
B1059		Army Parachute Association	N5075K+ N4024W G-OAKW M-YAKW N208AJ(1) G-CPSS [+ marks used concurrently by a Cessna 305]
B1060		The Point Group	N5206T N610LA
B1061		State of Ohio Department of Transportation	N52136 N850H
B1062		(Aero Tucan)	N5185V XA-UBL [w/o 30Oct06 near Punta Pajaros Airstrip, Mexico]
B1063		Seaport Airlines	N5221Y N208ED(1) N950PA
B1064		MSPL Limited	N5181U N208WD(1) VT-AHB
B1065		Castle Aviation	N31MG
B1066		Pudjiastuti Aviation/Susi Air	N5225K N12690 PK-VVA
B1067		Governor of the State of Parana	N52591 N1275T PP-MMS
B1068		ex Aero Condor	N1266Y OB-1797-T OB-1797-P [canx 06Oct10 fate/status unknown]
B1069		Alta Nea	N5260M N208GP N6XN LV-CKW
B1070		Trans Guyana Airways	N5269Y+ N1271T^ N90HL# 8R- [+ marks used concurrently by a PA-23-250; ^ marks used concurrently by a Columbia LC41-550FG; # canx 20Dec10 to Guyana]
B1071		Worldwide Aircraft Leasing/FBI	N971N
B1072		Tropic Air Commuter	N5185V V3-HGV
B1073		Phelan & Taylor Produce Co	N458PT N107LA N458PT
B1074		AEF L. C. IV	N208FD N92JJ
B1075		Watershed Sciences	N404AT N604MD
B1076		GC Air	N804AT N704MD
B1077		Gateway Canyons Air Tours	N81MJ
B1078		PT ASI (Susi Air)	N5166T N278ST PK-VVH
B1079		AEF XV LLC	N12675 N52JJ
B1080		Parachutisme Adrenaline	N1268R+ N910HL C-FDJN [+ marks used concurrently by a Columbia LC41-550OFG]
B1081		not yet known	N52653 N1272G PR-CMD
B1082		Cessna Aircraft Co	N209LR N773BM
B1083		Multi-Aero	N732MD
B1084		International Trading Co of Yukon	N1269D C-FCYX N841MA
B1085		PT ASI (Susi Air)	N52613 N12722 PK-VVR
B1086		National Aircraft Leasing/FBI	N986W
B1087		(Aero Ruta Maya)	N5000R TG-APG [w/o 26Jly05 near Hierba Buena, Guatemala]
B1088		Aero Biniza	N5066U N817SB XA-GIL
B1089		not yet known	N5060K LN-PBN PR-FAK
B1090		State of Tennessee Department of Transportation	N5058J N910EC
B1091		Wings of Eagles Aircraft Delivery	N5061P N1272N N741VL
B1092		Texas Turbine Conversions	N5095N N611CB
B1093		Aereo Calafia	N5076J XA-UCT XA-BTS
B1094		F.W. Weber	N5076K N12730 ZS-FWW
B1095		Maya Island Air	N51038 N1273Z V3-HGW
B1096		Falcon Air Service	N5120U N777VW N213LA
B1097		Colombian National Police	N12720 PNC-0253
B1098		not yet known	N51444 PR-CPF
B1099		Westwind Aviation	N51743 N12744 N786WW
B1100		Vieques Air Link	N3068B+ N12727 N742VL [+ marks used concurrently by a Beech F35 Bonanza]
B1101		Worldwide Aircraft Leasing/FBI	N301A
B1102		Outback Spirit Tours	N678HC VH-VCW
B1103		Falcon Air Service	N52086 N1285V N688RP N688FA
B1104		Aereo Calafia	N4047W XA-HVB

CESSNA 208 CARAVAN

C/n	Model	Last known Owner/Operator	Identities/fates/comments (where appropriate)
B1105		U C Aviation	N5135A N208WE N987BH VH-UCR
B1106		Caravan Charters	N5135K N713CB
B1107		BHMS Air Charters	N52229 N208ED(2) N666TG N92CC
B1108		West Wing Aviation	N5223D N208JJ VH-WZJ
B1109		ZB Air	N5225K N1275Z 5Y-ZBD
B1110		Hageland Aviation Services/ Frontier Alaska	N5151D XA-UDJ N68EA C-GWKM N208BR N409GV [floatplane]
B1111		ex Eastwest Aircraft Sales	N5066U XA-UDX XA-GMR XB-LJP N412BZ+ PZ- [canx 26Apr10 to Suriname]
B1112		Aero Util	N52352 XA-UDK
B1113		Texas Aviation Ventures	N5061W N1276Y
B1114		(Beaver Air Services/Missinippi Airways)	N1274B (N910PS) C-FMCB [w/o 04Jly11 Pukatawagen, MB, Canada]
B1115		Northway Aviation	N5093D C-GNWV
B1116		ex C J Airways	N5096S G-JCIT N308CJ M-TOMS M-ABDS+ 5X- [+ canx 11Jan11 to Uganda]
B1117		PT ASI (Susi Air)	N5100J N12775 PK-VVS
B1118		Peanut Air	N5101J N937CK
B1119		Worldwide Aircraft Leasing/FBI	N119PL N969PL
B1120		Air Wakaya	N1274X DQ-DHG
B1121		United Arab Emirates Army	N5200Z N12824 2240
B1122		not yet known	N5245L N696PW HL5116
B1123		not yet known	N1278Z N321LM N821LM HL5117
B1124		Nationaal Paracentrum	EC-JHH D-FAAG PH-SWP
B1125		Air Alliance/Slydive Flyzone	EC-JHI D-FAAF
B1126		J. A. Aero	N5263S N1278C N208NR
B1127		Albatros Aircorp	N1278L N208KL N179LV
B1128		Ben Air	LN-PBO OY-PBO*
B1129		Broome Aviation	N1282M OB-1815-T OB-1815-P N229CF VH-NCK
B1130		SERAMI-Servicios Mineros?	N52397 N12838 YV1419
B1131		not yet known	N106JA HL5112
B1132		ex United States Air Force	N2WV N2WQ+ YI- [+ canx 09Aug11 to Iraq; report to L-217 with Lebanese AF assumed incorrect]
B1133		Falcon Air Service	N128ST
B1134		Thai KASET	N12788 1921
B1135		EDELCA	YV-0-TWH-1 YV0113
B1136		Venezuelan Air Force	N208WE N208DT(1) 1708
B1137		(Patagonia Airlines)	N1277K CC-CTR [w/o en-route 07Jun08 18km from La Junta, Chile]
B1138		Mokulele Airlines/Go! Express	N12896 N208ST N115KW N862MA
B1139		Air Alliance	N5264M EC-JKU D-FAAE
B1140		Red Bull	EC-JKV D-FAAD LV-CMD
B1141		Fazza Sky/Dubai Skydive	N5264M EC-JLS D-FAAC DU-SD1
B1142		Air Pack Express	EC-JLT
B1143		Shining Star Equities	N6FF N208PK
B1144		Watermakers Air	N12920+ N1273E^ N208JH [+ marks also used in 2006 by a Cessna 172R; ^ marks used concurrently by a Cessna LC41-550FG]
B1145		Plane Imp. Exp. De Aer Pecas	N12945 PR-FCM
B1146		Aerodynamics Worldwide Inc	N1293Z SX-ARU N208CF(2) N208AY
B1147		PLANO	EC-JLU D-FAAB SP-KON [Supervan conversion # 8]
B1148		Falcon Air Service	N891DF
B1149		not yet known	N1275D+ 5H- [+ canx 28Jun11 to Tanzania]
B1150		Fugro Aviation Canada	N5225K N208ML C-GGRD
B1151		J. B. Lessley Communities	N1297Z N208TR
B1152		United Arab Emirates Army	N4010N 2249
B1153		(Lancton Taverns)	N208EC [w/o 05Jly07 Minna-Connemara Airport, Ireland; canx 22Jan09]
B1154		Vera Cruz Taxi Aereo	PR-SLD
B1155		Missionary Aviation Fellowship	N1307V (5Y-MAS) 5Y-MAE
B1156		Aviation Sans Frontieres	N5216A LN-PBP OY-PBP F-OJJC
B1157		United Arab Emirates Army	N4010P 2252
B1158		Sefofane Air Charter	N1297E ZS-ABR A2-EGL
B1159		Lao Airlines	N12879 RDPL-34149
B1160		United Arab Emirates Air Force	N1276J 2254
B1161		not yet known	N52475 N12979 DQ-JMJ

CESSNA 208 CARAVAN

C/n	Model	Last known Owner/Operator	Identities/fates/comments (where appropriate)
B1162		Tropic Air Commuter	N5108G V3-HGX
B1163		Jindal Steel & Power	N5270E N1308J VT-JIN
B1164		ex Asante Aviation	N52234 N424JP+ 5X- [+ canx 25May11 to Uganda]
B1165		United Arab Emirates Army	N1298H 2256
B1166		Cessna Aircraft Co	N1298N
B1167		United Arab Emirates Army	N1308D 2260
B1168		Geotech	N5270P C-GEOA
B1169		East Lake Aviation	N479DV N95EL
B1170		ZB Air	N52466+ N1308N 5Y-ZBX [+ marks used concurrently on a Cessna 182P]
B1171		(Cessna Aircraft Co)	N208WE [w/o en-route 28Mar06 1.2km of Oak Glen, CA, whilst on demonstration flight; canx 22May06]
B1172		Gobernacional Estado Bolivar	N5145V N208ED(3) YV0147
B1173		Chartair	N51072 N208JJ VH-LWA
B1174		Aeroland	N13080 SX-ARW
B1175		Hinterland Aviation	N5117U N208AZ G-GOTF VH-ETF
B1176		J A Mitsui Lease (Nihon Aerospace)	N5153K N1309F JA01AD
B1177		PT ASI (Susi Air)	N5207V N1307K OB-1844-T N1307K PK-VVF
B1178		Seahan Zio	N48JA HL5119
B1179		Danda Aviation	N427MD N233PC
B1180		Aerobell Air Charters	N5058J TI-BAJ
B1181		Cessna Aircraft Co	N5241Z N4021U
B1182		Aeroland	N1300G SX-ARX
B1183		State of Alabama	N51780 N624AL
B1184		United Arab Emirates Army	N52141 N13006 2264
B1185		NTT Finance	N52446 N406DA JA882B
B1186		Zantas Air Services	N5244W N12998 5H-TAZ
B1187		Sander Geophysics	C-GSGJ
B1188		Northway Aviation	N5183U N471MC C-GNWD
B1189		Shanghai General Aviation	N5066U N806DR B-9328
B1190		Two O Eight LLC	N5061W N13007 N208BK
B1191		Ohio Department of Public Safety	N51038 N717HP
B1192		Gen Air Services/Air Excel	N13162 5H-FAC 5H-XLL
B1193		Interavia Taxi Aereo	N5073G N13189 PR-JAT
B1194		Colombian Army	N5108G N13175 EJC-130+ EJC-031+ EJC-1130 [+ Colombia]
B1195		not yet known	N1318X N610GM TU-GOD
B1196		ex SGA Airlines	N5086W N208WD(2) HS-GAB+ 5X- [+ canx 19Sep11 to Uganda]
B1197		not yet known	N5262B N208WE N208ED(4) N90646 D-FIDT
B1198		Cessna Finance Corp	N1318Q N208ST
B1199		(Colombian Army)	N51984 N1318A EJC-131+ EJC-032+ EJC-1131 [+ Colombia] [w/o 23Jun12 Tocaima, Colombia]
B1200		Slingair	N5264A XA-TOY N599CF VH-TFW VH-TUY(2)
B1201		Motta Internactional	N5091J HP-1611
B1202		Patagonia Airlines	N5270P N13194 CC-CDR
B1203		Skyport /Chartair	N1318P HB-CZE VH-NGK
B1204		Nakina Outpost Camps & Air Service	N208DD C-FUYC
B1205		PT ASI (Susi Air)	N5174W N1320K RP-C2929 PK-VVI
B1206		Naka Nihon Koku	N712GG JA828N
B1207		Sky Bahamas?	C6-SBI
B1208		Istlecote	N51055 N1320B VH-LYT
B1209		North Star Air	C-FIXS
B1210		Nature Air	N5204D N1320U TI-BBC N183GC TI-BBC
B1211		Aereo Calafia	N5166U XA-UGI
B1212		Limbo LLC/Grant Aviation	N25JA
B1213		Gogal Air Services	N208EE C-GAGP
B1214		Air Excel	N50321 N13204 5H-VAN
B1215		KMB Aviation II	N819KM
B1216		Hinterland Aviation	N5048U N5213S N84BP VH-TFQ
B1217		Vera Cruz Taxi Aereo	N52136 PR-CFJ
B1218		Aerobell Air Charters	TI-BAY
B1219		Condor Aviation	N5064M N9208 ZS-XXL
B1220		Peter Collings Holdings	N5214J N1320X N920RD VH-BAM
B1221		ex Ulrich Krell	N5067U N1312X D-FEMU OE-EMU+ [+ canx Feb10 fate/status unknown]

CESSNA 208 CARAVAN

C/n	Model	Last known Owner/Operator	Identities/fates/comments (where appropriate)				
B1222		Africair	N5073F	N1320V	5X-BAT		
B1223		Ll-3 Communications	N97826				
B1224		Fretax Taxi Aereo	PR-SMM				
B1225		Iraqi Air Force	N1321A	YI-112	[model 208B-ISR: missile-equipped]		
B1226		Iraqi Air Force	N13210	YI-111	[model 208B-ISR: missile-equipped]		
B1227		Iraqi Air Force	N13217	YI-113	[model 208B-ISR: missile-equipped]		
B1228		Sander Geophysics	N1084N	C-GSGA			
B1229		McMurray Aviation	N208LC	C-GWRK			
B1230		Coastal Travels	N5203J	N1084Y	5H-LXJ		
B1231		ex Cessna Aircraft Co	N11116+	AP-	[+ marks canx 28Feb07 to Pakistan; but reported with United Arab Emirates Army possibly as 2257]		
B1232		Due-Mor Air	N208ED(5)	N208JG			
B1233		Morukuru Air	N208WD(3)	N208MN	ZS-EPZ		
B1234		Air Services	N1141H	YV336T	N1141H	8R-GAS	
B1235		Flying Fish Airline	N5161J	N1153U	(ZS-PAT)	ZS-UMG	
B1236		Vera Cruz Taxi Aereo	N51511	N208GH	PR-VCB		
B1237		not yet known	N5064M	D-FIFA	LN-AAZ	D-FWZA	
B1238		not yet known	N1156C	D-FSAS			
B1239		Alliant Techsystems	N208JF(2)				
B1240		Delta Wing Equipment/New Mexico Airlines	N52114	N208TD	N306PW		
B1241		SGA Airlines	N5155G	N208AE(1)	HS-SKR		
B1242		SERAMI – Servicios Mineros	N52178	YV2355			
B1243		ZB Air	N5048U	N1226X	5Y-ZBT		
B1244		Air Tindi	N5225K	C-GATH			
B1245		WMK Holdings/McMurray Aviation	N52591	C-GWKO			
B1246		Geosan Airborne Surveys	N12326	JU-9991			
B1247		Northern Air	N1106K	5H-TOM	5H-SUZ		
B1248		Tanzania Game Tracker Safaris	N12686	5H-DAN			
B1249		ex Sefofane Air Charters	N1167L	9J-ELE	ZS-ELE+	Z-	[+ canx 17Feb11 to Zimbabwe]
B1250		Aircraft Guaranty Corp	N950BZ				
B1251		Brazilian Air Force	2728	[C98A]			
B1252		Avemex	XA-UHP				
B1253		Apex Homes	N208Y	N208AH(3)			
B1254		Delta Wing Equipment/New Mexico Airlines	N12959	N307PW			
B1255		Tanzania National Parks	N1203S	5H-TPC			
B1256		Ward Leasing Co	N256ST				
B1257		Ministerio Economia y Finanzas Formosa	N1214V	LV-BIV			
B1258		Multi-Aero	N1314X	N208EP(1)	N14821	CX-MPM	N1258B
B1259		not yet known	N208WP	D-FINK			
B1260		Abyssinian Flight Services	N10966	ET-AMI			
B1261		not yet known	N50612	N1346S	HL5114		
B1262		Sefofane Air Charter	N1239Y	9J-TAU			
B1263		Tropic Air (PNG)	N50549	N41149	P2-SAH		
B1264		Villers Air Services	N5090Y	C-FTVP			
B1265		PT Ekspres Transportasi Antarbenua	N41168	PK-RJV			
B1266		Capital Holdings 191	N208AH(2)	N208E			
B1267		Associated Mission Aviation	N13193	PK-RCC			
B1268		not yet known	N41028	(PR-VIC)	PP-VIC		
B1269		Aereo Calafia	XA-VVT	[test regn either N5253S or N52538]			
B1270		Servicios Empresariales Administrativos	N5026Q	XA-ULH			
B1271		Agro Flight	N5200U	N1358F	LV-BMP		
B1272		ex Cessna Finance Corp	N5206T	N6UE+	CN-	[+ canx 27Dec10 to Morocco]	
B1273		Most Construction	N5194J	N1363D	RA-67707		
B1274		New Mexico Airlines	N5166T	N308PW			
B1275		Mokulele Airlines/Go! Express	N5162W	N4115J	N864MA		
B1276		Brazilian Air Force	N5093L	2729	[C98A]		
B1277		Brighter Days	N5166U	N208BD			
B1278		Aerodiana	N5270M	OB-1870-P	OB-1870-T		
B1279		Air Alliance	N5225K	(ES-MAA)	D-FAAA		

CESSNA 208 CARAVAN

C/n	Model	Last known Owner/Operator	Identities/fates/comments (where appropriate)
B1280		AMREF Flying Doctor Service	N5105F N41132 5Y-FDC
B1281		XP Taxi Aereo	N5249W PR-VXP
B1282		Nihon Aerospace	N52591 N4117E JA282J
B1283		Itealaich Dotair	N5148N N4118K
B1284		Gum Air	N5262Z N4114A PZ-TBS
B1285		PT ASI (Susi Air)	N5188W N4117B PK-VVB
B1286		Vera Cruz Taxi Aereo	N5147B PR-VCE
B1287		(PT ASI (Susi Air))	N5183U N41176 PK-VVE [w/o 09Sep11 near Tangma, Indonesia]
B1288		Peter Bennedsen	N5261R N208PB(1) OY-PBR
B1289		Geotech Aviation South Africa	N5264E C-FGEO PR-MSX C-FGEO PR-MSX C-GEOK ZS-ABN
B1290		Ameriwing II	N5264S N129CG
B1291		ex Cessna Finance Corp	N5264U N41179+ 5X- [+ marks canx 05Mar08 to Uganda]
B1292		Maya Island Air	N5245U N4117D V3-HHA
B1293		Zantas Air Services	N5125J N4115R 5H-NBL
B1294		Iraqi Air Force	N5061W N41143+ YI-114 [+ marks canx 28Mar08 to Kuwait rather than Iraq]
B1295		Africair Inc	N41158 N900HL
B1296		CAE Aviation	N5202D D-FCAE
B1297		Iraqi Air Force	N41144+ YI-115 [+ marks canx 17Apr08 to Kuwait rather than Iraq]
B1298		Iraqi Air Force	N41145+ YI-116 [+ marks canx 27Jun08 to Qatar rather than Iraq]
B1299		Metro Industries	N103FT
B1300		Aereo Servicio Guerrero	XA-UJF
B1301		Aeroland	N5269J N2028N SX-ARY
B1302		Proflight Charters	N5265N N2047V 9J-PCR
B1303		PT ASI (Susi Air)	N20722 PK-VVD
B1304		Sefofane Air Charter	N41138 (ZS-) V5-RNO
B1305		Southwest Aviation Solutions	N435MT
B1306		Aerodiana	OB-1882-P
B1307		Royal Air Charters	N20527 9J-CID
B1308		(PT ASI (Susi Air))	N20840 PK-VVG [w/o 16Nov11 Sugapa, Indonesia]
B1309		Iraqi Air Force	N2125U YI-119 [model 208B-ISR: missile-equipped]
B1310		Lebanese Air Force	N2126P L-401 [also reported as being L-126; model 208B-ISR: missile-equipped]
B1311		Auric Air Services	N2123S 5H-NCS
B1312		Iraqi Air Force	N21420 YI- [canx 09Aug11 to Iraq; model 208B-ISR: missile-equipped; possibly YI-117]
B1313		KASET (Thailand)	N21005 1922
B1314		Doonerak Limited Parnership	N1314X
B1315		Ministry of Natural Resources & Tourism	N21716 5H-TWF
B1316		Patagonia Airlines	N5124F N21424 CC-CTS
B1317		Coastal Tours & Travels	N21738 5H-GUS

Construction numbers B1318 to B1999 not built

Cessna 208Bs with glass cockpits (Garmin G1000 avionics)

C/n	Model	Last known Owner/Operator	Identities/fates/comments (where appropriate)
B2000		Preferred Airparts	N208ED(6) N171CC^ (N301RM) N917KS [^ serious damage 31Mar11 Lakeland, FL]
B2001		Africair	N208GH+ ET-AMV? [+ canx 04Jun09 to Ethiopia; reported 18Dec08 at Lanseria, South Africa with ET-AMV under a sticker but these marks also reported on AS350B c/n 1581]
B2002		Jhonlin Air	N208WD(4) XA- N2248K PK-JBC
B2003		Air Alliance	N208AE(2) D-FAAJ
B2004		Tropic Air	V3-HHC
B2005		Kaam Aviation/Air Excel	N421WF 5H-IKI
B2006		ex Ranchflyers	N2251Z+ RDPL- [+ marks canx 02Jly08 to Laos]
B2007		CMC Aviation	5Y-BVS
B2008		Landesbank Baden-Wurttemberg/ CAE Aviation	N208WV D-FOLI
B2009		Booth Transport	N5262X VH-JXB
B2010		ex Lopez Air	N359JA+ CP- [+ marks canx 16Nov11 to Bolivia]
B2011		Air Korea Company	N22430 HL5115
B2012		N774AT LLC	N774AT
B2013		Industrial Maintenance Services	N424AG
B2014		Iraqi Air Force	N21070+ YI- [+ but marks canx 23Dec08 to Bahrain]
B2015		Conair Group	N5067U C-FDON

CESSNA 208 CARAVAN

C/n	Model	Last known Owner/Operator	Identities/fates/comments (where appropriate)				
B2016		Iraqi Air Force	N21079+	YI-	[+ but marks canx 23Dec08 to Bahrain]		
B2017		Air Excel	N2293Y	5H-MEK			
B2018		Acme Prevost	N22600	N208DH			
B2019		Kamaka Air	N145KA				
B2020		Tigair Aviation	N2282Y	ZS-SKY			
B2021		State Governor of Vera Cruz	XA-GID				
B2022		D. Lund Farms	N21460	ZS-AMA			
B2023		not yet known	N2255K	7Q-ULL			
B2024		Kangaru Enterprises	N208CV				
B2025		(Northeast Shuttle Private)	N23045	VT-NES	[w/o 04May11 Aizwal-Lengpui Airport, Mizoram, India; canx May12; remains to Aircraft Structures International, OK; N23045 allocated]		
B2026		Levis Air	N708RL				
B2027		Boeing Company	N208BA				
B2028		Aircraft Owners & Pilots Association	N4120G	N394GA			
B2029		not yet known	PR-IAL				
B2030		Streak Street Investmants	N2015A	ZS-PGB	ZS-TBB		
B2031		Zantas Air Services	N2326S	5H-ZAI			
B2032		Houston Executive Airport Services	N526V				
B2033		Harvey Black Group	N52038	VH-JOZ			
B2034		Vera Cruz Taxi Aereo	PR-VCI				
B2035		ZanAir	N2327X	5H-CAR			
B2036		Linehan Aviation Services	N208MT				
B2037		ex Sefofane Air Charters	N2193K	V5-ECO	[canx 2009; fate/status unknown]		
B2038		Aircraft Guaranty Corp	D-FDAK	N188GV			
B2039		Deccan Charters	N5079Y	N2077Y	D-FAAI	VT-DCD	
B2040		not yet known	N51575	N2039B+	PR-RJO		
B2041		ex Sebastian S Bennedsen	N52113	N208PB(2)	OY-PBU		
B2042		Brazilian Air Force	N5030U	2730	[C98A]		
B2043		Desmond Equipment	N41211	ZS-LDG			
B2044		not yet known	N20683	C6-ACS			
B2045		SANSA Regional	N5166U	N23045+	VT-	TI-BCU	[+ marks canx 06Oct08 to India]
B2046		Indian Point Aviation	N681TF				
B2047		AA Aircraft Holdings	N5254Y	N41219+	YV	N208AB	[+ canx 18Nov08 to Venezuela; no regn known]
B2048		MNRPA Holdings	N2240U	N423GS	N428GS	C-GPGV	
B2049		Colombian Air Force	N5172M	N20909	FAC5074+	[+ tie up not confirmed]	
B2050		SANSA Regional	N5148B	TI-BCV			
B2051		Tropic Air	N5270K	V3-HHG			
B2052		DG + AG LLC	N228DA				
B2053		Bean Resources	N5117U	N529AB			
B2054		F Muller Apparatebau Ingelfingen	N5069E	N21173	D-FIMI		
B2055		Auric Air Services	N2208Y	5H-TMS			
B2056		BSF Swissphoto	N51984	D-FBSF			
B2057		Aero Transporte (ATSA)	N5264M	OB-1903-T	OB-1903-P		
B2058		SANSA Regional	N5040E	TI-BCX			
B2059		Brazilian Air Force	N5265N	2731	[C98A]		
B2060		Ecole Francaise de Parachutisme	N5260U	N2140X	F-HDNT		
B2061		Brazilian Air Force	N5259Y	2732	[C98A]		
B2062		Tropic Air	N52475	V3-HHE			
B2063		Phoenix Aviation	N2268V	5Y-LEO			
B2064		SANSA Regional	N5214L	TI-BCY			
B2065		not yet known	N5263U	PR-MNS			
B2066		Deccan Charters	N5130J	D-FROB	VT-DCE		
B2067		Southern Aircraft Consultancy	N5151D	N717RD			
B2068		PT ASI (Susi Air)	N51872	N61413	PK-VVT		
B2069		Spirit Air	N5093L	D-FXAA	VT-VAT		
B2070		Maraja LLC	N51143	N516NC			
B2071		Colombian Air Force	N5073F	N365GC	FAC5075+	[+ tie up not confirmed]	
B2072		ZB Air	N5211Q	N2212X	5Y-ZBE		
B2073		Amazonaves Taxi Aereo	N52397	N2210K	PP-AMZ		
B2074		WOC Aviation	N5188W	N208WD(5)	N828DC		
B2075		Colombian Air Force	N5093Y	FAC5064			
B2076		Martin Air	N5244W	N707EM			

CESSNA 208 CARAVAN

C/n	Model	Last known Owner/Operator	Identities/fates/comments (where appropriate)				
B2077		State of West Virginia	N5262B	N2222L	N2WV		
B2078		Sowinitec	N5183U	N2217M	SP-NAT		
B2079		Samaritan's Purse	N51055	N2215V	N375SP		
B2080		Colombian Air Force	N5262X	FAC5065			
B2081		Cam Business Development	N5067U	N984AC			
B2082		Wright Air Service	N5236L	N999WV			
B2083		Colombian Air Force	N5253S	FAC5066			
B2084		Royal Bahamas Defence Force	N5086W	C6-AWO	[code 04]		
B2085		Zuni LLC	N50543	N2232U			
B2086		PT ASI (Susi Air)	N5061W	N2232Y	PK-VVJ		
B2087		Spartan Aviation Industries	N771AL				
B2088		N1950X Inc	N5243K	N208ED(7)	N88NB		
B2089		Bering Air	N52623	N988BA			
B2090		Grey Aviation Advisors & Solutions	N51575	N130GA			
B2091		Safarilink Aviation	N52113	N2234J	5Y-SLE		
B2092		Tropical Air (Zanzibar)	N5155G	N22562	5H-YES		
B2093		PT ASI (Susi Air)	N2154L	PK-VVM			
B2094		T. Erbak (Aeropartner)	N50522	N208AE(3)	OK-DAY		
B2095		Suomen Laskuvarjokerhory	N5101J	OH-DZF			
B2096		Sierra Nevada Corp	N51995	N6147Y			
B2097		SANSA Regional	N52682	N208LD(1)	TI-BDL		
B2098		unknown	N5166U	N2255R	5N-BMJ+	[+ not fully confirmed]	
B2099		Aerodiana	N5090Y	N2360B	OB-1922-T	OB-1922-P	[missing 10Jun10 on flight from Nazca, Peru; possible hijack]
B2100		Stone Oak Management	N50282	N131ST			
B2101		Colombian Air Force	N5151D	FAC5067			
B2102		Colombian Air Force	N5227G	FAC5068			
B2103		ex Cessna Aircraft Co	N52397	N2246G+	JU-	[canx 29May09 to Mongolia]	
B2104		Aereo Servicios Empresariales	N5073F	XA-ULU			
B2105		Hanjin Information Communication	N5163C	N6102L	HL5118		
B2106		Sierra Nevada Corp	N5148B	N6159V			
B2107		Dept of Resources Surveys	N5263U	N6104M	5Y-DRS		
B2108		Severin Air Safaris	N5197M	N6130K	5Y-SXS		
B2109		Colombian Army	N5168W	EJC-1132			
B2110		Cessna Finance Corp	N5264E	PR-IHP			
B2111		PT ASI (Susi Air)	N5257C	N61611	PK-VVO		
B2112		Straight Flight	N5165T	N208EP(2)	N208SN(2)		
B2113		West Wing Aviation	N5244W	XA-XPL	VH-XDU		
B2114		Rio Madeira Aerotaxi	N5161J	PR-RMI	[severely damaged 21Jan11 Rio Branco, Brazil]		
B2115		Royal Jordanian Air Force	N51055	N61084+	143.+	[+ canx 12Nov09 to Jordan; these marks not confirmed]	
B2116		Fred R Lowther	N50715	N208FK(2)			
B2117		St. Barth Commuter	N5263S	N6137Y	F-OSBH		
B2118		Pleasant Aircraft Leasing/Royal Air	N5265B	N208PX	N498GG		
B2119		TAM – Taxi Aereo Marilia	N50776	N61466	PT-MLR		
B2120		Royal Jordanian Air Force	N6111A	1430			
B2121		Aereo Calafia	N5135K	XA-HVT			
B2122		Colombian Army	N5141F	EJC-1133			
B2123		Brazilian Air Force	N5241R	2733+	[C98A; + tie up not confirmed]		
B2124		not yet known	N52591	C6-			
B2125		Albatros Airlines	N52691	YV2484			
B2126		PT ASI (Susi Air)	N5095N	N61905	PK-BVA		
B2127		CMC Aviation	N51780	N2460G+	5Y-	[+ canx 23Oct09 to Kenya]	
B2128		Air Alliance	N5236L	N61882	D-FAAL		
B2129		Brazilian Air Force	N5031E	2734	[C-98A]		
B2130		(Brazilian Air Force)	N5296X	2735	[w/o 02Aug11 near Born Jardin da Sierra, Santa Catarina, Brazil; C-98A]		
B2131		Aero Rio	N	(VH-NQB)	PR-RJZ		
B2132		Albatros Airlines	N5183U	YV2489			
B2133		Royal Jordanian Air Force	N6111B	1432			
B2134		Splendor Air Charters	N52623	N6206W	N159AK		
B2135		Marine Connection Leasing	N5211A	N61729			
B2136		Major Blue Air	N52081	N6251V	A2-MBA		

CESSNA 208 CARAVAN

C/n	Model	Last known Owner/Operator	Identities/fates/comments (where appropriate)			
B2137		Microsurvey Aerog. E Cons. Cient	N5202D	PR-MCY		
B2138		Royal Flying Doctor Service	N52645	VH-NQC		
B2139		Royal Flying Doctor Service	N50756	VH-NQD		
B2140		ex Cessna Aircraft Co	N5250E	[fate/status unknown; these marks later allocated to c/n B2224]		
B2141		PT ASI (Susi Air)	N5058J	N61932	PK-BVD	
B2142		PT ASI (Susi Air)	N5112K	N6194X	PK-BVE	
B2143		PT ASI (Susi Air)	N5260Y	N61983	PK-BVF	
B2144		Japan Aerospace Corp	N5260M	N6204Q	JA315G	
B2145		Associated Mission Aviation	N5061F	N6211C	PK-RCB	
B2146		PT ASI (Susi Air)	N5228Z	N6203C	PK-BVG	
B2147		not yet known	N51817	TI-BDY		
B2148		OB Interationale	N52114	D-FLYE	F-HOBI	
B2149		Tropic Air	N52234	V3-HHI		
B2150		Kenya Police Air Wing	N6185N	5Y-POL		
B2151		PT ASI (Susi Air)	N5235G	N6204C	PK-BVH	
B2152		not yet known	N5066U	LV-CDS		
B2153		Propel Aviation Leasing	N51396	N578GC		
B2154		Hide Investments	N6183B	ZS-DGH		
B2155		Colombian Air Force	N5093D	FAC5079		
B2156		Kenya Police Air Wing	N6178N	5Y-GSU		
B2157		Colombian Air Force	N5200R	[unknown]		
B2158		Lady Lori (Kenya)	N6243N	5Y-JLL		
B2159		Auric Air Services	N62408	5H-DTA	5H-DTS	
B2160		not yet known	N5061P	LV-CCX		
B2161		Zuni LLC	N5032K	N208TM	N379TC	N186GC
B2162		ex Cessna Aircraft Co	N5181U	N208ED(8)+	TG-	[+ canx 14Dec11 to Guatemala]
B2163		PT ASI (Susi Air)	N52627	N208CC	PK-BVB	
B2164		ex Africair	N5214K	N208AE(4)+	PZ-	[+ canx 29Aug12 to Suriname]
B2165		Aero Power Distributing	N52086	N208X		
B2166		Provincia La Pampa	N5060K	LQ-CEB		
B2167		Rift Valley Flying Co	N5168Y	N208WD(6)	N169WD	
B2168		Hainan Asia & Pacific Aviation	N5152X	N24199	B-9425	
B2169		Two Taxi Aereo	N5180K	PR-BAT		
B2170		Shannon No 1	N5076L	N2422J	N406CR	
B2171		Royal Jordanian Air Force	N5196U	N62220	143.?	[full serial not known]
B2172		ex Cessna Finance Corp	N51743	N62173+	PR-	[canx 19Jly11 to Brazil]
B2173		HSG Caravan	N5132T	N208PR(2)	N555HG	
B2174		ex B A Jacobs Flight Services	N5064Q	N208JA+	HP-	[+ canx 18Feb11 to Panama]
B2175		Proimport Brazil	N5203S	N1009T	PR-RAE	
B2176		SANSA Regional	N5109R	N208LD(2)	TI-BDW	
B2177		PT ASI (Susi Air)	N5267D	N1015J	PK-BVI	
B2178		ex Rangeflyers Inc	N5264S	N60352+	RA-	[+ canx 29Nov10 to Russia]
B2179		Amazonaves Taxi Aereo	N5036Q	PP-AMV		
B2180		Colombian Air Force	N5156D	[unknown]		
B2181		Colombian Air Force	N5239J	[unknown]		
B2182		Royal Jordanian Air Force	N51872	N62327	143.?	[full serial not known]
B2183		Alfa Trans Dirgantara	N5093Y	N1014A	PK-ASA	
B2184		Sichuan West China General Aviation Co	N5262X	N9004G	B-9467	
B2185		Brazilian Air Force	N5253S	2736	[C98A]	
B2186		not yet known	N1030X	PR-DNA		
B2187		Colombian Air Force	N52113	[unknown]		
B2188		St. Barth Commuter	N5166U	N1029J	F-OSBC	
B2189		Air Kenya Express	N50282	N1008P	5Y-BXW	
B2190		ex Cessna Aircraft Co	N5151D	N2440G+	ZP-	[+ canx 03May10 to Paraguay]
B2191		Centre Ecole Regional de Parachutisme	N1008G	F-HJMP		
B2192		Pacific Air Center	N5097H	N20194	N619MA	
B2193		Kakuda Air Services	N5204D	N2028N	VH-KNQ	
B2194		PT ASI (Susi Air)	N1016M	PK-BVJ		
B2195		Cessna Aircraft Co	N5153K			
B2196		Zhongshan Eagle	N5200Z	N1035Q	B-9327	
B2197		Cessna Aircraft Co	N51942			

CESSNA 208 CARAVAN

C/n	Model	Last known Owner/Operator	Identities/fates/comments (where appropriate)			
B2198		Susi Air	N5268E	N10200	PK-BVK	
B2199		Zan Air	N1009U	5H-CAT+	[+ not fully confirmed as this aircraft]	
B2200		Caribbean Heli-Jets	N5058J	N2033R	N224HJ	
B2201		Yellow Wings Air Services	N5112K	N1032L	5Y-ELO	
B2202		Shanghai Grand Sea Aviation	N2052G	B-9426		
B2203		Phoenix Aviation	N51072	N2059S	5Y-MJA	
B2204		Promotora Industrial Totolapa	N5095N	XA-UNX		
B2205		Arizona Taxi Aereo	N5152X	PR-ECC		
B2206		Susi Air	N1021S	PK-BVL		
B2207		Auric Air Services	N5076L	N60253	5H-KKC	
B2208		Shanghai General Aviation	N2052A	B-9430		
B2209		Tropical Air (Z)	N51743	N6026F	5H-NOW	
B2210		Zuni LLC	N5214J	N2442H		
B2211		Hainan Asia & Pacific Aviation	N1027B	B-9427		
B2212		Oxford Hill LLC	N28ST			
B2213		Zuni LLC	N209JA	N187GC*	[* marks reserved 22May12]	
B2214		Susi Air	N60059	PK-BVN		
B2215		Broome Aviation	N2056W	VH-NDC		
B2216		Anhui Foreign Economic Construction Co	N5063P	N20564+	B-	[+ canx 09Jly12 to China]
B2217		Susi Air	N1022G	PK-BVO		
B2218		Susi Air	N1022Z	PK-BVP		
B2219		not yet known	N5267J	D-FRTK	I-KOPF	N79PF
B2220		Shanghai Hao Hai General Aviation Co	N5247U	N2057S	B-9468	
B2221		Brazilian Air Force	N5257C	2737	[C98A]	
B2222		Kannithi Aviation/Kan Air	N5200U	N6034P	HS-KAB	
B2223		not yet known	N5168W	N6027Y	9J-FQM	
B2224		Zhong Fei General Aviation Co	N5250E	N60214	B-9457	
B2225		Susi Air	N10225	PK-BVQ		
B2226		Cristatus Investments 11	N51055	N6037J	ZS-MID	
B2227		Two Taxi Aereo	N5260M	PR-CRF		
B2228		Associated Mission Aviation	N5135K	N6037R	PK-RCA	
B2229		ex Rangeflyers	N5141F	N1023Q+	PK-	[+ canx 12May11 to Indonesia]
B2230		Cahil	N52591	N208WB		
B2231		Panama Navy	N60368	AN-040+	[+ tie up not confirmed]	
B2232		Air St Kitts & Nevis/DHL	N920HL	[2000th Caravan]		
B2233		Zhong Fei General Aviation Co	N52646	N5264U?	N30439	B-9458
B2234		Brazilian Air Force	N5236L	2738	[C98A]	
B2235		Zhong Fei General Aviation Co	N5270P	N52446?	N30355	B-9459
B2236		ASTA – America do Sul Taxi Aereo	N5296X	PP-OSP		
B2237		Zhong Fei General Aviation Co	N52081	N6023R	B-9460	
B2238		Air St Kitts & Nevis/DHL	N930HL			
B2239		ex Rangeflyers	N50756	N6032K+	RA-	[+ canx 18Jan11 to Russia]
B2240		Two Taxi Aereo	N5166T	PR-WOT		
B2241		Safarilink Aviation	N5048U	N60259	5Y-SLG	
B2242		Panama Navy	N5207U	N60361	AN-041+	[+ not fully confirmed]
B2243		Heymans Kole	N1025B	ZS-DVL		
B2244		Cia Azucarera Chumbagua	N52235	HR-AWP		
B2245		EDAS Early Detection Alarm	N5185J	N1789M		
B2246		SANSA Regional	N5091J	TI-BDX		
B2247		Fretax Taxi Aereo	N5148B	(PR-SMG)	PR-BAX	PR-SMG
B2248		SANSA Regional	N	TI-BDY		
B2249		Tropic Air	N52038	V3-HHK		
B2250		ex Geotech Aviation	N	C-GSVY	ZS-ABO	
B2251		ex Africair	N60313+	XT-	[canx 01Mar11 to Burkina Faso]	
B2252		Aeroandina	N5073F	OB-1963P		
B2253		Rio Branco Aerotaxi	N5163C	PR-SBR*		
B2254		ex Rangeflyers	N52234	N60336+	PK-	[+ canx 20Mar12 to Indonesia]
B2255		not yet known	N5161J	N6034H+	PK-	[+ canx 23Aug11 to Indonesia]
B2256		Gulf Atlantic Airways	N52144	N208LS(2)		
B2257		Banco Itauleasing	N51881	N6033H+	PR-BUS	[+ canx 08Jun11 to Indonesia; rather than Brazil]
B2258		Susi Air	N5120U	N258CC	PK-BVN	

CESSNA 208 CARAVAN

C/n	Model	Last known Owner/Operator	Identities/fates/comments (where appropriate)			
B2259		Cessna Aircraft Co	N5223P	N259CC		
B2260		Cessna Aircraft Co	N5180K	N260CC		
B2261		George R Teufel	N208DT(2)			
B2262		Conair Group	N5064Q	N262GC	C-GQVC	
B2263		Cargohouse	N5203S	N3042E	RP-C6021	
B2264		Coastal Air	N5156D	N3041Q	5H-BEE	
B2265		North American Float Plane	N5239J	N265CC	OB-1998-T	OB-1998-P
B2266		Jet Eagle International	N5223Y	N30197	RP-C7573	
B2267		Amazonaves Taxi Aereo	N50549	PP-AMX		
B2268		Africair	N5097H	N910HL		
B2269		Ventura Airconnect	N5268E	N9000F	VT-VAM	
B2270		Hainan Asia & Pacific Aviation	N5058J	N30428	B-9428	
B2271		Cessna Aircraft Co	N5112K			
B2272		Cotia Vitoria Servicos e Comercio	N51072	N3043K	PR-BUS	
B2273		Susi Air	N5270E	N3042C+	PK-	[+ canx 02Apr12 to Indonesia]
B2274		ex Cessna Finance Export Corp	N5214J	N30391+	5H-	[+ canx 22Jly11 to Tanzania]
B2275		Wells Fargo Bank Northwest – trustee	N30416	HP-	N30416	
B2276		FedEx Express	N990FX			
B2277		Brazilian Air Force	N	2740	[C98A]	
B2278		Ministry of Environment & Natural Resources	N3041E	5Y-GOK		
B2279		FedEx Express	N991FX			
B2280		not yet known	N	PP-OSL		
B2281		Ventura Airconnect	N90015	VT-VAK		
B2282		Auric Air Services	N3034D	5H-AAA		
B2283		ex Cessna Finance Export Corp	N6019C+	PK-	[+ canx 29Jly11 to Indonesia]	
B2284		Air Excel	N9005N+	5H-	[+ canx 29Sep11 to Tanzania]	
B2285						
B2286		Victory General Aviation Service	N9007C+	B-9463^	[+ canx 08Dec11 to Peoples Republic of China; ^ tie up not confirmed]	
B2287		Afghan National Army Air Force	N3034P	YA12287		
B2288		FedEx Express	N992FX			
B2289		FedEx Express	N993FX			
B2290		not yet known	N9008Q	UR-CRTV		
B2291		not yet known	N	PP-AGP		
B2292		Sky Tech	N9012F			
B2293		Susi Air	N9012S+	PK-	[+ canx 02Apr12 to Indonesia]	
B2294		Royal Joranian Air Force	N9001U+	1435?	[serial only assumed]	
B2295		Afghan National Army Air Force	N3032V	YA12295		
B2296		Pelican Aviation & Tours	N9014K+	5H-	[+ canx 15Nov11 to Tanzania]	
B2297		Cape Chamonix Holdings	N9010Y	ZS-CGH		
B2298		not yet known	N9012U+	4R-	[+ canx 11Jan12 to Sri Lanka]	
B2299		Afghan National Army Air Force	N4123R	YA12299		
B2300		Wells Fargo Bank Northwest – trustee	N9017M			
B2301		Afghan National Army Air Force	N41228	YA12301		
B2302		Flightlink Air Charters	N90151	5H-FLS		
B2303		Afghan National Army Air Force	N6017T	YA12303		
B2304		Afghan National Army Air Force	N60182	YA12304		
B2305		Geotech Aviation	C-GZTB			
B2306		Paraguayan Air Force	N60196	ZP-BDO	0250	
B2307		Safra Leasing	N	PP-TRC		
B2308		Pinnacle Air	N6019U	VT-VTP		
B2309		Wells Fargo Northwest	N9018Z			
B2310		Air Kenya Express	N60200	5Y-BZJ		
B2311		Cessna Aircraft Co	N5166UI			
B2312		Silver Creek Aviation Services	N4751W			
B2313		Aerodiana SAC	N	OB-2001-P		
B2314		ex Cessna Aircraft Co	N9028G+	RA-	[+ canx 16May12 to Russia]	
B2315		Federal Express Corp	N994FX			
B2316		ex Cessna Aircraft Co	N9029K+	RA-	[+ canx 16May12 to Russia]	
B2317		Cessna Aircraft Co	N9023W			

CESSNA 208 CARAVAN

C/n	Model	Last known Owner/Operator	Identities/fates/comments (where appropriate)			
B2318		Boskovic Z Air Charters	N60207+	5Y-	[+ canx 29Nov11 to Kenya]	
B2319		ex Cessna Finance Export Corp	N60208+	PK-	[+ canx 12Jly12 to Indonesia]	
B2320		Guangdong General Aviation Co	N90243	B-9461		
B2321						
B2322						
B2323		ex Cessna Aircraft Co	N9030Q+	RA-	[+ canx 16May12 to Russia]	
B2324						
B2325		Inter Regionale Express	N	F-OIXJ		
B2326		Guangdong General Aviation Co	N9031X	B-9462		
B2327						
B2328		Jet Eagle International	N90237+	PK-	RP-C7574	[+ canx 05Jan12 to Indonesia]
B2329		Daiagi Aviation	N8CA			
B2330		ex Cessna Finance Export Corp	N9025C+	PK-	[+ canx 26Apr12 to Indonesia]	
B2331						
B2332		Cessna Finance Co	N90215	[operated by SAEREO, Ecuador]		
B2333		Ortiz Taxi Aereo	N	PR-OTZ		
B2334						
B2335		Propel Aviation Sales & Service	N6059K			
B2336		Afghan National Army Air Force	N90263	YA-22336		
B2337		Afghan National Army Air Force	N9026Z	YA-22337		
B2338		Cessna Finance Export Corp	N2032C			
B2339		Cessna Aircraft Co	N339GC			
B2340		Cessna Aircraft Co	N234GC			
B2341		Cessna Aircraft Co	N341GC			
B2342		ex Pilot International	N20245+	B-	[+ canx 05Jun12 to China]	
B2343		Cessna Aircraft Co	N343GC			
B2344		Afghan National Army Air Force	N90277	YA-22344		
B2345		Afghan National Army Air Force	N9027Z	YA-22345		
B2346		Pacific Air Center	N701MA			
B2347		Cessna Aircraft Co	N347GC			
B2348		Cessna Aircraft Co	N2025X			
B2349		Cessna Aircraft Co	N985FX			
B2350		Cessna Aircraft Co	N2033Q			
B2351		Cessna Aircraft Co	N351CC			
B2352		Air Kenya	N20269+	5Y-	[+ canx 20Jly12 to Kenya]	
B2353		Pacific Air Center	N272MA			
B2354		Rajawali Megantara Mandiri	N354RM	PK-LTY		
B2355		Africair	N940HL			
B2356		Cessna Aircraft Co	N20168			
B2357		Afghan National Army Air Force	N2001V	YA-22357		
B2358		Afghan National Army Air Force	N2006V	YA-22358		
B2359		Cessna Aircraft Co	N2034F			
B2360		Safarilink Aviation	N2013Q	5Y-	[+ canx 18Jly12 to Kenya]	
B2361						
B2362		Cessna Aircraft Co	N95399			
B2363						
B2364						
B2365		for Fuerza Aerea Paraguaya				
B2366						
B2367		Africair	N20166			
B2368		Pilot International	N2021Y			
B2369		Federal Express Corp	N985FX			
B2370		Cessna Aircraft Co	N6061N			
B2371		Africair	N2021G			
B2372		Cessna Aircraft Co	N20194			
B2373		ex Globeflyers Inc	N5161J	N2032T+	UP-	[canx 24Aug12 to Kazakhstan]
B2374						
B2375						
B2376		Africair	N2019J			
B2377		Federal Express Corp	N986FX			
B2378		Cessna Aircraft Co	N2009F			
B2379		Cessna Aircraft Co	N379BD			
B2380		Pacific Air Center	N508BH			

CESSNA 208 CARAVAN

C/n	Model	Last known Owner/Operator	Identities/fates/comments (where appropriate)		
B2381		Cessna Aircraft Co	N381BB		
B2382		Afghan National Army Air Force	N20461	YA-22382	
B2383		Afghan National Army Air Force	N2043N	YA-22383	
B2384		Cessna Aircraft Co	N20288		
B2385					
B2386		ex Globeflyers	N2010H+	RA-	[+ canx 24Aug12 to Russia]
B2387					
B2388		Cessna Aircraft Co	N9540H		
B2389					
B2390		Federal Express Corp	N987FX		
B2391		Cessna Aircraft Co	N2025M		
B2392					
B2393		Globeflyers Inc	N2015A		
B2394		Globeflyers Inc	N2017J		
B2395		Cessna Export Finance	N20294(2)		
B2396		Cessna Aircraft Co	N2039J		
B2397		Cessna Aircraft Co	N2033T		
B2398		Cessna Aircraft Co	N2001P		
B2399		Cessna Aircraft Co	N20049		
B2400		Cessna Aircraft Co	N988FX		
B2401		Cessna Aircraft Co	N2037G		
B2402		Cessna Aircraft Co	N2038G		
B2403					
B2404		Cessna Aircraft Co	N2039B		
B2405					
B2406					
B2407					
B2408					
B2409		Cessna Aircraft Co	N95416		
B2410		Cessna Aircraft Co	N2034L		
B2411		Cessna Aircraft Co	N9542P		
B2412					
B2413		Cessna Aircraft Co	N9542Y		
B2414		Cessna Aircraft Co	N95421		
B2415		Cessna Aircraft Co	N9543Z		
B2416		Cessna Aircraft Co	N95432		
B2417					
B2418		Cessna Aircraft Co	N9544Z		

Unidentified

C/n	Model	Last known Owner/Operator	Identity	Comments
unkn			C6-AWD	[noted in Bahamas; a 208B]
unkn		Royal Bahamas Police	C6-PFA	[reported 02Mar12 Nassau, Bahamas]
unkn			ET-AOF	[reported 03Dec10 Tamiami, FL]
unkn			HK-3976X	[reported]
unkn			HP-20A	[reported 05Sep10 Panama City-Marcos A Gelabert, Panama]
unkn		Aeroperlas	HP-1320APP	[noted in Mar00 in Central America]
unkn		Islena Airlines	HR-IBD	[reported]
unkn		Islena Airlines	HR-IBH	[reported]
unkn		Cessna Aircraft Co	N5253S	[reported 24Mar10 Wichita, KS in camouflage c/s]
unkn		Cessna Aircraft Co	N5267J	[reported 15Jly10 Wichita, KS]
unkn			PH-OGH	[marks reserved 29Feb08[
unkn			PK-FLM	[reported 12Dec09 Jakarta-Halim, Indonesia[
unkn	208B	AeroGeo	RA-67422	[reported]
unkn			RA-67430	[reported 22Jun12 Wichita, KS]
unkn			RA-67434	[reported 09Jun12 & 22Jun12 Wichita, KS]
unkn			RA-67435	[reported 22Jun12 Wichita, KS]
unkn			TG-IPC	[noted in Mar00 in Central America[
unkn			TU-GOD	[reported 28Feb11 Lanseria, South Africa; possibly c/n B1195]
unkn		Tropic Air	V3-HHL	[reported 16Nov11 Wichita, KS]
unkn		Tropic Air	V3-HHM	[reported 16Nov11 Wichita, KS; also reported as V3-HTM]
unkn		AX Transporter	XA-FTG	[reported 08Jan12 Cancun, Mexico]
unkn			XA-TPF	[reported Feb02 Toluca, Mexico]
unkn		not known	XA-UEJ	[w/o 01Sep06 en-route Cancun to Campeche, Mexico]

CESSNA 208 CARAVAN

C/n	Model	Last known Owner/Operator	Identities/fates/comments (where appropriate)	
unkn		Aeroservicio Guerrero	XA-UJF	[reported]
unkn			XB-JNQ	[reported]
unkn	208B	Iraqi Air Force	YI-120	[reported Mar10 a 208B-ISR]
unkn			YN-CGS	[reported 25Nov07 Managua, Nicaragua]
unkn			YN-CGU	[reported 25Nov07 Managua, Nicaragua]
unkn		J. Rangel	YV164T	[official record states ex "XB-IPW" also unknown]
unkn			YV384T	[reported 26Mar09 Wichita, KS]
unkn			YV2453	[reported 01Dec07 Valencia-International, Venezuela]
unkn			YV467T	[reported 18Aug11 Curacao, Netherlands Antillies]
unkn			ZP-BBN	[reported delivered to Paraguay Air Force as 0251]
unkn		Community Airlines	5H-CAA	[reported 31Jly10 Dar es Salaam, Tanzania]
unkn			5H-FAY	[reported]
unkn		Regional Air	5H-NHB	[reported 14Feb12 Arusha, Tanzania]
unkn			5H-OBY	[reported a 208B]
unkn			5H-SLR	[reported]
unkn			5X-ACE	[reported 2010 based Entebbe, Uganda]
unkn			5X-AMC	[reported 2011 based Entebbe, Uganda]
unkn			5X-NAZ	[reported 21Nov11 Lanseria, South Africa]
unkn			5Y-BOX(2)	[reported 21Sep09 Nairobi-Wilson, Kenya; not c/n B0500]
unkn			5Y-OJF	[reported 19May09 Nairobi-Wilson, Kenya]
unkn			5Y-SAI	[reported 04Sep11 Nairobi, Kenya]
unkn			5Y-YEP	[reported 04Sep11 Nairobi-Wilson, Kenya]
unkn			5Y-ZBB	[reported 24May09 Nairobi-Wilson, Kenya]
unkn			5Y-ZBG	[reported 12Apr12 Nairobi-Wilson, Kenya]
unkn		Air Services	8R-BKP	[reported 08Jly12 Bonaire, Netherlands Antillies]
unkn		Air Services	8R-GFA	[registered in 2009; reported imported from Belize]
unkn		Panama Navy	AN-041	[reported delivered Jan12]
unkn		Colombia Army	EJC-107	[wreck noted Feb95 Guaymaral, Colombia – possibly confiscated aircraft]
unkn		Colombia Army	EJC-1134	[reported delivered 09Nov09 via Veracruz, Mexico]
unkn		Colombia Army	EJC-1135	[reported in Colombia Apr10]
unkn		(Bolivian Air Force)	FAB221	[w/o during 2000 near Mallcu, Bolivia; no other details]
unkn		United Arab Air Force	2247	[reported 26Oct11 Al Ain AFB, UAE]
unkn		United Arab Air Force	2249	[reported Oct11 Al Ain AFB, UAE]
unkn		United Arab Air Force	2253	[reported 31Jan09 Al-Ain AFB, UAE]
unkn		United Arab Air Force	2256	[reported Oct11 in Afganistan]
unkn		United Arab Air Force	2257	[reported delivered Apr10]
unkn		Brazilian Air Force	2739	[ferried 08Apr11 through Orlando International, FL [C98A]]
unkn		Brazilian Air Force	2741	[ferried 17Jun11 through Orlando International, FL [C98A]]
unkn		Colombian Air Force	FAC1128	[possibly a confiscated civilian aircraft]
unkn		Colombian Air Force	FAC1416	[noted during 2002]
unkn		Colombian Air Force	FAC5058	[reported wfu]
unkn		Colombian Air Force	FAC5059	[reported delivered Nov10]
unkn		Colombian Air Force	FAC5060	[reported delivered Nov10]
unkn		Colombian Air Force	FAC5071	[reported Jun10]
unkn		Colombian Air Force	FAC5072	[reported May10]
unkn		Lebanese Air Force	L-217	[possibly c/n 208B1132 ex N2WQ]
unkn	208B	United States Air Force	86022	[reported May12 Prestwick, UK & ferrying 12Jun12 Quimper, France to Prestwick]
unkn	208	United States Air Force	12-1276	[reported 28Aug12 Mildenhall, UK]

CONVAIR TWINS

Notes: Only details of aircraft registrations/serials post conversion to turbo-prop power have been included.
Convair 580 and 5800 conversions – as noted some aircraft were earlier converted to Convair 540s (Eland Convairs) which subsequently reverted to piston power.
+ conversion numbers allocated by PacAero Engineering Corp.
Convair 770 is the unoffical civil designation for the YC-131C, which differ from the later converted 580s.

C/n	Line No.	Model	Last known Owner/Operator	Identities/fates/comments (where appropriate)
2	79	580	Honeywell International	N73102 N116GS N113AP N580AS N580HW
4	155	580	(R & R Holdings)	N73104 [stored by Jun03 Columbus-Rickenbacker, OH; l/n 28Apr08; by 15Sep09 b/u with only front half of fuselage present; l/n 15Mar10; canx 01Dec10]
7	41	580	(Laredo Air)	N73106 [stored by Sep92 Marana, AZ; subsequently b/u; canx 09Jun97 as destroyed]
8	128	580	(JBQ Aviation)	N73107 [DBR 11May92 Opa-Locka, FL on collision with L.188 N360WS (c/n 1112); canx 09May96; hulk b/u Nov96]
11	98	580	(Kelowna Flightcraft)	N73108 HP- HK-3616X C-FRDE+ C-FYTV [+ painted under wing, but not officially regd as such; ferried May97 to Kelowna, BC; l/n 26Dec03; b/u 2004]
12	157	580	(Westates Airlines)	N73109 [wfu Mar95 by Richmor Aviation possibly at Dutchess County Airport, Poughkeepsie, NY; considered b/u]
13	105	580	(Air Venezuela)	N7517U YV-971C [stored Jun99 Caracas-Simon Bolivar, Venezuela; b/u by Apr05]
14	159	580	(Panacarga Nacional)	N73110 HP-615 (FAP-206) [wfs by Feb77; canx 24Jly84]
15	30	580 +	(Charter One)	N73111 N540Z N8424H YV-C-EVS YV-64C C-GNMO N117GT [+ 340 cvtd 540 then to 440 before 580; b/u Apr93 Fort Lauderdale International, FL; canx Aug93]
16	48	580	(Sierra Pacific Airlines)	N73112 [stored Jan91 Marana, AZ; stripped by Oct95; b/u; canx Jly97]
17	61	580F	(Air Freight New Zealand)	N73113 N8428H N5809 C-GKFU ZK-KFU [proposed conversion to 540 not completed; w/o 03Oct03 in sea off Waikanae, North Island, New Zealand]
18	13	580	(SERCA)	N73114 N200A N2004 N328VP N580SC HK-3666X HK-3666 [no reports since 1997; assumed b/u]
19	53	580F +	(World Aviation Services)	N73115 N541Z N8425H N5805 C-GTEM N581HG [+ 340 cvtd 540 then to 440 before 580; stored Mar99 Opa- Locka, FL; l/n 15Feb07; canx 29May08; perhaps b/u]
22	138	580	Kelowna Flightcraft	N90852 N32KA C-GKFG
23	67	580	(Lake Central Airlines)	N791G N73130 [w/o 05Mar67 near Kenton, Hardin County, OH]
24	120	580F	Air Tribe	N5834 N585PL C-FAUF N584E XA-UPL
25	69	580F	ex Skyhaul	N73117 OO-DHG EC-943 ZS-SKG [reported derelict by 18Sep10 Cape Town, South Africa; l/n 29Feb12]
28	70	580	(European Air Transport)	N73118 N5840 C-GDTD OO-VGH [wfu & canx 26Sep91 Brussels, Belgium; b/u 15Dec94]
29	63	580	ex Air Tahoma	N8424H N5810 N581PL C-FBHW N581P [proposed conversion to 540 not completed]
30	170	580	(Royal Aviation Inc)	N4801C (N505GA) C-GQBO [canx 27Oct07; fate unknown; assumed b/u]
33	1	580	(Kelowna Flightcraft)	N5100 N5127 N5127H HR-SAY (XA-IAG) N5599J N771PR [prototype 580 f/f 19Jan60; wfu & stored Aug86 Gainesville, FL; b/u by 2006]
34	38	580	Kelowna Flightcraft	N73120 N538JA [US marks canx 05Jun03 as exported to Canada; stored Kelowna, BC; l/n late 2010; not yet regd in Canada]
35	35	580	(Sierra Pacific Airlines)	N73121 (N115GS) [wfu & b/u location not reported; canx Sep95]
38	164	580	(Hydro-Quebec)	N4802C C-GFHB [canx 10Dec01; fate unknown, assumed wfu]
39	162	580	Heli Logistics (Pty) Ltd	N4803C TAM-70+ N81MR N511GA ZS-LYL [+ Bolivia]
41	115	580	(Compagnie Africaine d'Aviation)	N73122 TAM-72+ N5590L N777TL 9Q-CRS 9Q-CRU [+Bolivia] [w/o 01Apr97 Tshibaka, Democratic Republic of Congo]
42	100	580F	Air Freight New Zealand	N73123 N5843 LN-BWG C-FKFL ZK-KFH
43	116	580	(Allegheny Airlines)	N73124 N5844 [w/o 20Aug71 Pittsburgh, PA]
46	109	580F	(World Aviation Services)	N5827 N534SA OO-EEB C-FHEO N582HG [w/o 06Dec01 ditched off Miami Beach, FL; canx 29May08]
49	131	580	ex JBQ Aviation	N90854 N26KA C-GQBM N352Q [stored Jly95 Roswell, NM; canx 16Oct02; l/n 29Nov10 derelict]
50	147	580	(Conifair Aviation)	N90855 C-GQBN [derelict May92 Quebec City, QC, Canada; b/u by 1994]

CONVAIR TWINS

C/n	Line No.	Model	Last known Owner/Operator	Identities/fates/comments (where appropriate)
51	160	580	Gulf & Caribbean Air	N4804C C-GFHA N5810 N151FL
52	80	580F	Air Tribe	N73125 N5845 C-GDTE OO-DHE EC-HLD N588X XA-TRB
53	27	580	(R & R Holdings)	N73126 [stored May01 Columbus-Rickenbacker, OH; l/n 28Apr08; used for spares, by 15Sep09 only front half of fuselage remained; l/n 15Mar10; canx 01Dec10]
54	28	580	(JBQ Aviation)	N73127 N5822 [stored 1994 Tucson, AZ; b/u Jan03]
55	169	580	(Air Venezuela)	N3430 YV-970C [wfu & stored Jun99 Caracas-Simon Bolivar, Venezuela; b/u by Apr05]
56	2	580	(Partnair)	N5120 N51207 HR-SAX N9012J (N700WC) N770PR C-GKFT LN-PAA [w/o 08Sep89 into Skaggerak, 30kms N of Hirtshals, Denmark]
57	32	580	Conair Aviation	N73129 N117GS N73129 N568JA C-FKFB [code 47]
60	119	580	(Air Venezuela)	N4805C (YV-966C) [stored Oct99 El Paso, TX, still marked as N4805C; l/n 03Nov07 parts missing]
61	127	580	(Air Venezuela)	N3418 YV-972C [wfu & stored Jun99 Caracas-Simon Bolivar, Venezuela; b/u by Apr05]
62	88	580	Colombian Army	N3419 N5820 C-GKFQ N580EH HK-3559X HK-3559 EJC-121 EJC-051 EJC-1121
65	89	580	(World Aviation Services)	N3421 N5821 C-GJEE N583HG [stored Mar03 Opa-Locka, FL; canx 29May08; probably b/u]
67	167	580	(Air Venezuela)	N2728R YV-968C [wfu & stored Jun99 Caracas-Simon Bolivar, Venezuela; b/u by Apr05]
68	122	580F	(Air Tahoma)	N73131 N5841 N535SA OO-DHC EC-HMR N586P [w/o 13Aug04 Covington near Cincinnati, OH; canx 02Oct07]
69	58	580	Kelowna Flightcraft	N73132 N569JA+ [+ canx 05Jun03 as exported to Canada; stored Kelowna, BC; l/n late 2010; not yet regd in Canada]
70	148	580F	Conair Aviation	N73133 C-FKFM [code 54]
72	26	580	Environment Canada	N400J CF-BGY N8EG C-GRSC
77	129	580	(Air Venezuela)	N3423 YV-973C [wfu & stored Jun99 Caracas-Simon Bolivar, Venezuela; b/u by Apr05]
78	76	580F	Conair Aviation	N3424 N5815 C-GKFO [code 53]
79	20	580	(Compagnie Africaine d'Aviation)	N3431 N5128 N5128H N424BJ N53RB N2261N C-GKFZ 9Q-CEJ [w/o 17Nov99 Maramba, Zambia]
80	64	580F	Conair Aviation	N73301 C-FEKF [code 45]
81	81	580	(Clark Equipment)	N3426 N5817 [dismantled Nov81 & b/u Jly83 Detroit-Willow Run, MI]
82	125	580	Kelowna Flightcraft	N90857 C-GKFU
83	156	580	(North Central Airlines)	N90858 [w/o 29Jun72 near Neenah, Appleton, WI, after mid-air collision with DHC-6 N4043B, c/n 13]
85	150	580	(Tex Johnson)	N73135 [w/o 04Nov68 Santa Barbara, CA on its post conversion delivery flight]
86	66	580	Pionair Australia	N73136 C-GKFQ VH-PDW
89	92	580	ex JBQ Aviation	N73138 N5846 C-GDTC N203RA [stored Oct97 Roswell, NM; canx 16Oct02; l/n 01Feb08]
91		770	Kelowna Flightcraft	N5511K 53-7886 N454 N454X N970L N630V N600AB N400AB C-GKFY [stored by late 2010 Kelowna, BC with regn painted out]
94	55	580	Bolivian Air Force	N73140 TAM-70 [stored & wfu Nov96 La Paz-El Alto, Bolivia; l/n Oct08]
98	153	580	(Canair Cargo)	N73141 N25278 C-FICA [w/o 18Sep91 30 miles NE of Burlington, VT]
100	168	580F	Conair Aviation	N4810C C-GFHD N5807 C-FKFA [code 52]
101	154	580	ex Los Pequenos Airlines	N4811C (YV-967C) [not deld; stored by 05Jly98 Waco Regional, TX; l/n 30Jun05 derelict]
109	91	580	(Hydro-Quebec)	N3429 C-GFHH [w/o 27Sep00 La Grande LG-4 airstrip, QC, Canada]
110	42	580	(Kelowna Flightcraft)	N5803 N900WC [wfu May85 Gainesville, FL; l/n 1989 in bad condition; canx 26May99; assumed b/u]
111	57	580F	Gulf & Caribbean Air	N15824 N5119 N302K N141FL
114	106	580F	Air Freight New Zealand	N73159 N5839 LN-BWN C-GKFJ CS-TMG C-GKFJ ZK-KFJ
115	118	580	(Kelowna Flightcraft)	N5833 N584PL C-GKFT N584PL C-FACX+ [+ not included on register; stored May94 Kelowna, BC, Canada; b/u by Dec97]

CONVAIR TWINS

C/n	Line No.	Model	Last known Owner/Operator	Identities/fates/comments (where appropriate)
116	158	580	ex JBQ Aviation	N7530U C-GTAO N362Q OB-1535 N362Q [stored Oct97 Roswell, NM; canx 16Oct02; derelict by 30Mar03; l/n 29Nov10]
119	39	580	(Mexican Government)	N73155 [seized Sep93 for drug running, may have carried marks HK-3616X; stored Santa Lucia AFB, Mexico; b/u mid 1990s for spares by FFV Aerotech]
121	97	580F	RPG Airlift Inc	N5824 N531SA (OO-EEE) C-GJTU C-FMGC N905GA [stored 17Dec04 Daytona Beach, FL; l/n 15Feb09]
126	78	580F	Pionair Australia	N5816 C-FIWN VH-PDX
127	112	580	(Air Ontario)	N73142 N5837 C-GGWJ [stored & wfu Dec93 St Jean, QC, Canada; used for spares; l/n Nov94]
128	82	580	Kelowna Flightcraft	N5818 HK-3616X XA-FOU C-FIWM
129	74	580	(Conair Aviation)	N5814 C-FKFY [code 48] [w/o fire fighting 31Jly10 15km S of Lytton, BC, Canada; canx 23Nov10]
130	72	580F	ex Air Tahoma	N5813 C-GGWG OO-HUB EC-GSJ N590X [stored 20Apr06 Columbus-Rickenbacker, OH still painted as EC-GSJ; l/n 15Mar10]
131		770	(Houston Avn Products)	N8422H 53-7887 N9988Z [cvtd to YC-131C/Convair 770 standard; b/u Jan74 Houston, TX for spares; canx 22Jan74]
132	50	580	Bolivian Air Force	N73143 CP-2212 TAM-72+ FAB-72 [+ Bolivia] [stored by 20Oct07 La Paz-El Alto, Bolivia; l/n Oct08]
135	22	580F	Skyhaul/Sky Congo	CF-ECS N7600 N5812 N582PL N536SA OO-DHD EC-GKH ZS-SKK [stored by 2006 Kinshasa, Democratic Republic of Congo; for sale 2008; l/n 12May09]
137	152	580	Pionair Australia	N7528U C-GQBP N631MW VH-PDL (ZK-PNR)
141	93	580	Heli Logistics (Pty) Ltd	N5822 ZS-KEI
145	102	580	ex Taxsur Colombia	N73145 HK-3740 [wfu & stored Jun00 Bogota, Colombia; l/n Jly01; reported for sale]
147	12	580F	(Skyhaul/LAC-SkyCongo)	N7600 N100A N200A N2006 N73158 N5838 C-GQHA OO-DHF EC-HJU ZS-SKH [w/o 27Apr06 Labutu/Amisi, Democratic Republic of Congo]
150	141	580	(Air Venezuela)	N2729R YV-969C [wfu & stored Jun04 Caracas-Simon Bolivar, Venezuela; b/u by Apr05]
151	95	580	Kelowna Flightcraft	N5823 C-FKFZ
154	59	580F +	Nolinor Aviation	N73146 N542Z N8426H N5807 N580PL N110AS C-FJTW C-FMGB C-FAWV [+ 340 cvtd 540 then to 440 before 580]
155	47	580	Gulf & Caribbean Air	N5804
157	5	580	(AVENSA)	N73147 YV-C-AVG YV-54C N90420 N585GN N587PL N500ME YV-84C [w/o 28May85 Cabimas, near Maracaibo, Venezuela]
160	133	580F	Kelowna Flightcraft	N9067R C-GKFF
161	33	580 +	(Ground Air Transfer)	N73148 N544Z YV-C-AVA YV-53C N4806Q N588PL YV-78C C-GNMQ N118GT [+340 cvtd 540 then to 440 before 580; wfu & b/u Aug93 Fort Lauderdale, FL]
163	161	580F	ex Air Tahoma	N5847 N532SA OO-EEA C-FHEL (N103DE) CS-TMO N718RA N585P [stored by Jan09 Columbus-Rickenbacker, OH; l/n 15Mar10]
168	56	580 +	Air Freight New Zealand	N73150 N543Z N8427H N5806 N590PL C-GKFP ZK-FTA [+ 340 cvtd 540 then to 440 before 580]
169	85	580	ex Cargo Panama Three	N73151 N5836 C-GGWI HP-1221CTH HP-1221CTW TG-TAJ+ HP-1221 [+ not confirmed; stored by Jly03 Panama City, Panama; l/n 28Nov07]
170	46	580	(Bolivian Air Force)	N73152 TAM-73 FAB-73 [w/o 22Feb05 Trinidad Airport, Bolivia]
176	94	580	Aviheco, Colombia	N4634S C-GFHF N631MB HK-4334
179	52	580	Conair Aviation	N73153 C-GEVC C-FFKF [code 44]
180	151	580	(Air Freight New Zealand)	N73154 N14278 (N20H) C-FEDO ZK-FTB [w/o 31Jly89 in Manukau Harbour, Auckland, New Zealand]
186	43	580	Skyhaul/Sky Congo	N73156 OO-DHH EC-255 EC-GHN ZS-SKI [stored by 2006 Kinshasa, Democratic Republic of Congo; for sale 2008; l/n 12May09]
202	25	580	(Province of Saskatchewan)	N270E N278E N331G N60FM N8500 N30ER N30EG C-GSKJ [w/o 14May06 La Ronge, SK, Canada]
214	34	580	(SERCA)	N76Y N200GL YV-86C HK-3675X HK-3675 [w/o 08Apr95 Aguablanca, Colombia]
217	54	580	Province of Saskatchewan	54-2815 CS097+ N7146X PNP-025^ N723ES C-GSKQ [+ AMARC code; ^ Peru]
220	62	580	(E-Systems)	54-2816 [w/o 12May77 Majors Field, Greenville, TX]
221	71	580	(US Navy)	54-2817 [w/o 15Nov85 near Dothan, AL]

CONVAIR TWINS

C/n	Line No.	Model	Last known Owner/Operator	Identities/fates/comments (where appropriate)
234		580	Province of Saskatchewan	C-GYSK [code 474]
238		580	Province of Saskatchewan	C-GVSK [code 473]
276		5800	Gulf & Caribbean Air	C-FKFS(1) N5800 C-FKFS(1) N381FL [prototype 5800, conversion number 001; rolled out 05Nov91; f/f 11Feb92]
277		5800	Air Freight New Zealand	C-FKFS(2) ZK-KFS [5800 conversion number 004]
278		5800	Gulf & Caribbean Air	N8526M C-FNLY C-GKFD N391FL [5800 conversion number 002]
279		5800	Kelowna Flightcraft	N5248N C-FKFS(4) [is a C-131F & not a Convair 580, Convair 5800 conversion number 006]
309		5800	Gulf & Caribbean Air/IFL	C-FMKF N371FL [converted from C-131F, was never a 580; 5800 conversion number 003]
312	103	580	Ecole Nationale d'Aerotechnique	N73157 C-GDBX [wfu 02Dec98 & dismantled; donated as GIA at St Hubert, QC, Canada]
318	6	580F	(Gulf & Caribbean Air)	N300K N171FL [w/o 11May12 Guatemala City-La Aurora, Guatemala]
326	51	580	Gulf & Caribbean Air	55-0299 CS096+ N4276C PNP-026^ N4276C N923DR N191FL [+ AMARC code, ^ Peru]
327A	166	580	Air Chatham's	N8444H TG-MYM N8444H C-FCIB ZK-CIB
334	136	580	Nolinor Aviation	N2041 N580N C-FTAP
336	132	580	(Sierra Pacific Airlines)	N73160 [w/o 20Jan89 Buena Vista, CO]
343	17	5800	Gulf & Caribbean Air/IFL	N105 N90 N3UW C-FKFS(3) N361FL [5800 conversion number 005]
347	143	580	Nolinor Aviation	N2042 C-GKFW N580TA C-GRLQ
348	60	580	(Aspen Airways)	N5808 [w/o 02Feb88 Durango, CO]
352	123	580	(F C Services Inc)	N2044 C-GFHC N5812 [stored Jun95 Kelowna, BC, Canada; b/u by Dec03]
354	134	580F	(Swift Air)	N73161 OO-DHI EC-899 [w/o 19May95 Vitoria, Spain]
361	126	580F	(Air Tahoma)	N73162 OO-DHJ N73162 OO-DHJ HZ-SN14 N587X [w/o 01Sep08 Columbus-Rickenbacker Airport, OH]
366	130	580	ex Renown Aviation	N73163 [wfu Dec03 Roswell, NM; l/n 29Nov10]
367	135	580	Bolivian Air Force	N73164 TAM-74 [stored Sep97 La Paz-El Alto, Bolivia; l/n Oct08]
368	142	580	(European Air Transport)	N73165 [wfu spares May88 Brussels, Belgium; b/u Dec94]
369	140	580	(North Central Airlines)	N2045 [w/o 27Dec68 Chicago-O'Hare, IL]
370	145	580	Bolivian Air Force	N2046 TAM-71 FAB-71 [stored Sep97 La Paz-El Alto, Bolivia; l/n Oct08]
372	21	580F	Air Freight New Zealand	N108G N108GL N114M N114ML SE-IEY C-FKFL ZK-KFL
374	139	580	Conair Aviation	N73166 C-FHKF [code 55]
375	110	580	(Nolinor Aviation)	N5828 N533SA OO-EED C-FHEN CS-TMM C-GNRL [dbr 20Mar11 Boeing Field, WA; b/u Jly11 for parts; canx 15Aug11]
376	113	580	Nolinor Aviation	N5831 N580GN ZS-KRX C-GQHB
377	121	580	(Air Venezuela)	N4822C YV-974C [wfu & stored Jan97 Caracas-Simon Bolivar, Venezuela; b/u by Apr05]
379	108	580	Air Venezuela	N4824C YV-975C [wfu & stored 1998 Caracas-Simon Bolivar, Venezuela; b/u by Apr05]
380	87	580	(North Central Airlines)	N4825C [w/o 25Jly78 Kalamazoo-Battle Creek, MI]
381	146	580	Air Chathams	N73167 N566EA ZK-CIF
382		580	(Air Niagara Express)	N73168 C-FARO [wfu Mar97 Toronto, ON, Canada; b/u by 12Mar00; canx 21Mar12]
383	49	580	IFL Group	N4E N4479 N55H N45LC N51255
384	114	580	(Allegheny Airlines)	N5832 [w/o 07Jun71 New Haven, CT]
385	99	580F	Air Chathams	N5826 ZS-KFA V5-KFA C-FKFA HZ-SN11 ZK-CID [stored by 29Nov08 Palmerston North, New Zealand]
386	104	580	(Allegheny Airlines)	N5825 [w/o 06Jan69 Pine Acres Golf Course, Bradford, PA]
387	24	580F	Gulf & Caribbean Air	N321K N301K N181FL
390	149	580	(Advanced Aviation Industries)	N7743U [derelict Feb94 Carlsbad, CA; b/u for spares Sep96; canx Nov96]
399	19	580	Air Chathams	N98G N98GL N57RD N565EA ZK-CIE
410	40	580	(Allegheny Airlines)	N5802 [w/o 24Dec68 near Bradford, PA]
430	29	580	(Contact Air Cargo)	N5129 N303K N161FL [w/o 04Dec04 McAllen, TX]
445	44	580 +	(AVENSA)	N440EL YV-C-AVZ YV-59C [+440 cvtd 540 then to 440 before 580; wfu before 1990; also reported w/o 04Nov97 San Antonio, TX; assumed b/u]
446	163	580	Nolinor Aviation	YV-C-EVJ YV-63C N4862M N589PL C-GKFP [possibly w/o 03Aug11 Kasba, NT, Canada]
452	7	580	(Union Oil Company of California)	N7601 [w/o 21Dec63 near Midland, TX]

CONVAIR TWINS

C/n	Line No.	Model	Last known Owner/Operator	Identities/fates/comments (where appropriate)
453	84	580	(Evergreen International Airlines)	N5819 [b/u Oct81 Detroit-Willow Run, MI]
454	107	580F +	Nolinor Aviation	CF-LMA 11106^ CF-LMA-X CF-LMA 11162^ N13328 YV-C-AVP YV-56C N90421 N586PL C-GKFR N583P C-FHNM [+ 440 cvtd 540 (CL-60C/CC109) then cvtd to 580 ^ Canada]
455	37	580	Mexican Air Force	N910BS N812PS N123MH N123RP N153WC N318CP N333TN HK-3635+ TE-003^ 3907 [+ seized by Mexican Air Force; wfu Santa Lucia AFB, Mexico; l/n Aug07; ^ Mexico]
458	111	580F	Skyhaul	N5829 N583PL N537SA OO-DHB EC-830 EC-GBF ZS-SKL
459	65	580F	ex Air Tahoma	N5811 C-GGWF OO-DHL EC-HMS N589X + XA- [+ marks canx 21Oct08 to Mexico]
462	96	580 +	(R & R Holdings Inc)	CF-MKO 11107^ 11163^ N968N [+ 440 cvtd 540 (CL-60C/CC109) then cvtd to 580; ^ Canada; wfu Aug97 Tucson, AZ; b/u May03; canx 11Apr07]
465	124	580	Conair Aviation	N5835 C-GGWH ZK-JDQ C-FKFL [code 49]
466	137	580F	(Insumos Alimenticios Prawn)	N21466+ C-GJRP HP-1222CTH HP-1222CTW HK-3969X YV-OTC YV2079 [+ cvtd as in-flight simulator (TIFS) aircraft by the grafting on of a second cockpit; later de-cvtd; l/n Dec98 stored Caracas, Venezuela; no reports since Feb99; assumed b/u]
473	31	580	National Research Council	N920BS N916R CF-NRC C-FNRC
475	101	580 +	ex Air Tahoma	CF-LMN 11161^ N969N N582P [+ 440 cvtd 540 (CL-60C) then cvtd to 580; ^ Canada; wfu by 28Sep07 Columbus-Rickenbacker, OH, no tail; l/n 15Mar10]
477	18	580	(US Dept of The Navy)	N101 N91 N6226M [b/u for spares Jly96, location not recorded; canx 23May97]
478	16	580	Conair Aviation	N102 N92 N8099S C-FJVD [reported 15Jly08 for spares use at Abbotsford, BC, Canada; l/n 26May11]
479	14	580	FAA	N103 N49 [reported wfu by Mar94 Oklahoma City, OK; but also active 27Apr05; still current 2008]
480	15	580	FAA	N104 N30 N74 N39 [reported wfu May96 Fulton, GA; but also active 27Apr05; still current 2008]
485	36	580	(Inter Canadian)	YV-C-EVD YV-61C C-GNMR [wfu & canx Jun89; presumably b/u]
489	8	580	IFL Group	N5121 N51211
496	11	580	Insumos Alimenticios Prawn 7 CA	N5126 N5126N YV-83C HK-3674 YV2348
500	3	580	Raytheon E-Systems	N5122 N580R N580HH [reported re-regd N580ES but still current as N580HH & no reports with these marks]
501	4	580	Conair Group Inc	N5123 N5122 C-GTTA N631AR ZK-PAL VH-PAL C-GYXS [stored by late 2010 Abbotsford, BC, Canada still as VH-PAL; l/n 26May11]
507	9	580	Conair Group Inc	N5124 N8124 C-GTTE ZK-KSA VH-PDV C-GYXC [tanker code 42] [l/n 18May10 Abbotsford, BC, Canada still as VH-PDV]
508	10	580	Gulf & Caribbean Air	N5125 N5126 C-GTTG N991FL
509	23	580	Province of Saskatchewan	N8860 N12F N886Q N12F N12FV N57RD C-GSKR [code 471]
510	45	580	(Theodore L Vallas)	N440M N580HA [wfu & stored Dec86 Carlsbad, CA; derelict by Mar95; b/u for spares; canx 28Aug96]

Unidentified:

unkn		580		YV2380 [reported by Feb09 and subsequently Valencia, Venezuela]
unkn		580		YV2476 [reported 01Feb09 Maracay Boca del Rio AFB, Venezuela]

Convair 600

Note: Trans Texas Airlines undertook the conversion of their own 240s from kits supplied by General Dynamics and allocated unofficial conversion numbers in the TTA sequence; those converted by General Dynamics are in a GD sequence.

10	TTA3	600F	(Rhoades Aviation Inc)	N94205 [stored by 26May01 Columbus Municipal Airport, IN; canx 04Oct01; no later reports; presumably b/u]
13	TTA21	600	(Aerolineas Colonia)	N94207 CX-BOJ-F CX-BOJ [stored by 28Dec86 Colonia, Uruguay; l/n Jly92 in good condition; no longer present assumed b/u]
15	TTA17	600	(International Turbine Service)	N94208 [stored May89 Sherman-Grayson, TX; derelict by Mar91; canx 12May92]
26	TTA4	600	(SMB Stage Line)	N94215 [wfu Tuscon, AZ; b/u between Apr-Oct93]

CONVAIR TWINS

C/n	Line No.	Model	Last known Owner/Operator	Identities/fates/comments (where appropriate)
28	TTA14	600	ex International Turbine Service	N94216 [stored by Mar91 Daytona Beach, FL; canx 16Jly90; derelict by Apr01; l/n 20Feb05]
32	GD?	600	(Rhoades Aviation)	N2008 N331G N278E [conversion number either GD10 or 29; extensively damaged by sabotage on 22Aug68; wfu & b/u Sep68 DuPage County Airport, IL; canx 25Mar11]
43	TTA10	600	(SMB Stage Line)	N94223 [wfu for spares Jly90 Dallas-Love Field, TX; b/u Dec90; canx 03Dec90]
45	TTA8	600	ex SMB Stage Line	N94224 [wfu & stored; b/u Apr-Oct93 Tucson, AZ]
46	GD19	600F	Robert J Trzeciak	N74855 (N855FW) [wfu & stored Feb96 Sherman-Greyson, TX; l/n 02Mar05]
48	TTA11	600F	(Rhoades Aviation)	N94226 [b/u 2004 Columbus, OH; canx 08Mar04]
51		600	(US West Financial Services)	N74854 (N854FW) [wfu & stored Aug89 Tucson, AZ; wings removed by Apr93; b/u Aug93]
56	TTA12	600	(Texas International Airlines)	N94230 [w/o 27Sep73 Rich Mountain, Eagleton, AR]
57	TTA15	600	(SMB Stage Line)	N94231 [wfu & stored Dec88 Fort Worth-Meacham, TX; derelict by Mar90; b/u]
63		600	(International Turbine Service)	N94233 [b/u for spares, location not reported; canx 16Jly90]
68	TTA20	600	(SMB Stage Line)	N94235 [wfu & stored 1990 Tucson, AZ; outer wings removed Apr93; b/u Apr-Oct93]
69	TTA13	600	(SMB Stage Line)	N94236 [wfu & stored May90; b/u Feb93]
74	GD24	600F	(Kitty Hawk Aircargo)	N74850 (N850FW) [b/u 1994 Fort Worth-Meacham, TX; canx 05Aug95]
80		600	(Convair Airframe Associates)	N94239 N2654D [stored Jly81 Tucson, AZ; wfu Jan82; l/n Mar87; b/u]
81	TTA18	600	(Bowen Properties)	N94240 (N942DB) [wfu & stored Jly84 location unknown; assumed b/u]
92		600	ex Aerolineas Colonia	N240R N123SC CX-BJL [wfu & stored Nov86 Laguna De Los Patos, Uruguay; status unknown]
101	TTA7	600F	Aeronaves TSM	N94279 XA-TYF [stored by 10May11 Tapachula, Mexico]
102	TTA2	600F	(Rhoades Aviation Inc)	N94246 [wfu & b/u late 2004 Columbus-Rickenbacker, OH; canx 08Mar04]
105		600	(SMB Stage Line)	N94248 [wfu & b/u Dec90 Dallas-Fort Worth, TX; canx 03Dec90]
106	TTA19	600	(SMB Stage Line)	N94249 [wfu & stored Mar91 Sherman-Grayson, TX; later b/u; canx 04Apr95]
114	TTA1	600	(International Turbine Service)	N94253 (N142RA) [w/o 04Aug89 Augusta Airport, ME]
118		600	(Wright Air Lines)	N74851 [stored 1976 Cleveland-Burke Lakefront, OH; b/u Mar81]
119	TTA9	600F	(Kitty Hawk Aircargo)	N94258 [stored by 26May01 Columbus Municipal Airport, IN; canx 08Mar04; no later reports; presumably b/u]
122		600	(Hamilton Aviation Inc)	N94261 [stored Dec94 Tucson, AZ; later b/u; canx 16Aug96]
136	GD23	600	(SMB Stage Line)	N74852 (N852FW) [wfu & stored Oct91 Tucson, AZ; b/u Apr-Oct93]
137	TTA16	600	(Texas International Airlines)	N94264 [wfu Jun74, b/u Oct76 Houston-Hobby, TX]
138	TTA5	600	(Texas International Airlines)	N94265 [wfu1974; b/u Oct76 Houston-Hobby, TX]
163	TTA6	600	ex International Turbine Service	N94278 [wfu & stored Las Vegas, NV; b/u Nov93]
164	GD9	600F	(Aircraft Leasing Inc)	N74853 (CC-CIK) [stored Mar91 Sherman-Grayson, TX; b/u Nov96; canx 17Jan97]
168	GD11	600	(Bar Harbor Airlines)	N74857 PK-RCQ N74857 N128AJ [wfu & stored 1981; b/u 1989 Bangor, ME]
170	GD14	600F	(S&S Partnership)	N74856 PK-RCR N74856 N129AJ [wfu & stored 1981 Cleveland-Burke Lakefront, OH; derelict by Mar84; b/u]
171	GD2	600	(Mandala-Seulawah Airlines)	N94295 N74858 PK-RCN [wfu 1979 Jakarta/Soekarno-Hatta, Indonesia; derelict by Jan81; canx before 1991]
173	GD7	600	(Mandala-Seulawah Airlines)	N94296 N74860 PK-RCO [wfu 1979 Jakarta/Soekarno-Hatta, Indonesia; derelict by Jan81; canx before 1991]
178		600	(Mandala-Seulawah Airlines)	N94294 N74859 PK-RCP [wfu 1979 Jakarta/Soekarno-Hatta, Indonesia; derelict by Jan81; canx before 1991]
Convair 640				
9		640	(Gambcrest)	N7262 CF-PWT C-FPWT N2691W N862FW C-FCWE N862FW [w/o 09Feb92 Cap Skirring Airport, Senegal]
10		640F	ex Kitty Hawk Aircargo	N7263 CF-PWU C-FPWU N2569D N860FW [wfu 01Mar05 Fort Worth-Meacham Field, TX; stored by Vintage Flying Museum; fuselage only noted 07Nov11]
20	GD4	640	Vintage Flying Museum	N3407 [preserved Feb96 Forth Worth-Meacham Field, TX; fuselage only noted 07Nov11]
21	GD17	640	(Caribair)	N3408 [w/o 23Jan67 San Juan, PR]
27	GD27	640F	(C & M Airways)	N3410 [stored by 23Feb01 El Paso, TX; l/n 15Nov07; canx 08Apr08]
31	GD20	640	(SMB Stage Line)	N3411 [w/o 28Oct87 near Bartlesville, OK; remains to White Industries, Bates City, MO]

CONVAIR TWINS

C/n	Line No.	Model	Last known Owner/Operator	Identities/fates/comments (where appropriate)
32	GD10	640F	(Rhoades Aviation)	N3412 (N278E) [l/n Sep97 Sherman-Grayson, TX; probably b/u; canx 09Aug12]
48	GD15	640F	Aeronaves TSM	N3417 XA-UMI
58	GD16	640F	(Zantop International Airlines)	N7529U [stored by Aug96 Detroit-Willow Run, MI; b/u after May98; canx 27Mar02]
64	GD6	640F	ex C & M Airways	N3420 [stored El Paso, TX; l/n 07Oct11]
66	GD12	640F	(Zantop International Airlines)	N5509K [stored by Oct89 Detroit-Willow Run, MI; b/u after Sep01; canx 27Mar02]
76	GD27	640F	(Zantop International Airlines)	N5510K [stored by Aug96 Detroit-Willow Run, MI; b/u after Sep01; canx 27Mar02]
88		640F	Aeronaves TSM	N73137 XA-UJI
104		640F	ex C & M Airways	PH-CGD N111TA N861FW C-GCWY N640CM [stored El Paso, TX; l/n 07Oct11]
108	GD18	640	(Time Air)	N5514K CF-PWY C-FPWY [wfu & stored Dec91 Springbank, AB, Canada; b/u May05; canx 22Mar93]
133	GD5	640F	(Century Airlines)	N5515K [stored 23Feb01 El Paso, TX; l/n 27Feb05 later b/u; canx 24May06]
134	GD8	640F	(Zantop International Airlines)	N5512K [wfu Dec94 Detroit-Willow Run, MI; b/u after 20Feb04; canx 27Mar02]
171	GD21	640F	(Zantop International Airlines)	N5511K [wfu Dec94 Detroit-Willow Run, MI; b/u before 30Jly00; canx 27Mar02]
332		640	Aeronaves TSM	PH-MAL N640R XA-UNH
408		640	(Air Algerie)	7T-VAH [w/o 02May76 Djanet-Inedbirenne Airport, Algeria]
409		640F	ex Rhoades Aviation	7T-VAO N866TA [stored by 08Aug04 Columbus-Municipal, IN; l/n 29Aug07; canx 16Jan09]
412		640	(SA de Transport Aerien)	HB-IMM [w/o 17Jly73 Tromso, Norway]
440	GD30	640	(Pacific Western Airlines)	N45003 CF-PWR [w/o 17Sep69 Elk Lake Park, Vancouver Island, BC, Canada]
441	GD28	640	(Time Air)	N45004 CF-PWS C-FPWS [wfu & stored 12Jun92 Springbank, AB, Canada; b/u Feb05; canx Mar93]
451		640F	(Hamilton Aviation)	7T-VAR N848TA C-GQCQ (TN-ACW) N55AP [stored Jly96 Tucson, AZ; b/u Sep96]
460		640	(Time Air)	7T-VAY N849TA C-GQCY [wfu & stored Dec91 Springbank, AB, Canada; b/u Feb05; canx 22Mar93]
463		640F	TransAir	N4405 CF-PWO C-FPWO N587CA

Canadair CL-66B Cosmopolitan (Convair 540) (designated CC-109 in Canadian military service)

Notes: with the exception of c/ns 5 and 8 all were converted to Convair 580 standard by PacAero Engineering Corp; conversion nunbers as shown.

All c/ns are prefixed CL66B; the first two identities are Royal Canadian Air Force serials.

1	68	580	Las Vegas Aircraft Sales & Leasing	11151 + 109151 C-FNCI N4AX [+ cvtd 580 21Mar/15Dec66; stored 31Oct00 Calgary, AB, Canada; l/n 12Jly08]
2	73	580	Kelowna Flightcraft	11152 + 109152 C-FNCL C-GLWF [+ cvtd 580 24May/13Dec66]
3	75	580	(Royal Canadian Air Force)	11153 [cvtd 580 Jun66/Dec66; DBF 11Apr69 Montreal, QC, Canada]
4	90	580	ex Bolivian Air Force	11154 + 109154 C-FNCT 9Q-CLU 9XR-NB HP-1468 HP-1468APP YV191T FAB-74 [+ cvtd 580 17Nov66/10Apr67; wfu by Apr08 & stored La Paz-El Alto, Bolivia; l/n 05Jun12]
5		540	(Royal Canadian Air Force)	11155 [wfu & b/u 1972; SOC 09May76]
6	77	580	(Quantum Flight Systems)	11156 109156 C-FNCV C-GNCU N987L 5Y-BNV 9XR-NC 3D-ZOE [+ cvtd 580 19Jly66/09Jan67; w/o 03Apr04 Shabunda, Democratic Republic of Congo]
7	83	580	Kelowna Flightcraft	11157 + 109157 C-FNCW N4FY HP-1445APP(YV192T) C-GPQY [+ cvtd 580 21Sep66/06Feb67; stored by Apr07 Panama-Albrook, Panama; sold 19Apr12 in Canada]
8		540	(Royal Canadian Air Force)	11158 [b/u 09May72]
9	86	580	Kelowna Flightcraft	11159 + 109159 C-GNCB HP-1473APP (YV192T) HP-1473 C-GTVJ [+ cvtd 580 19Oct66/02Mar67]
10	117	580	Kelowna Flightcraft	11160 + 109160 C-GNCM C-GNDK [+ cvtd 580 17Jun67/20Oct67]

CONVAIR TWINS

C/n	Line No.	Model	Last known Owner/Operator	Identities/fates/comments (where appropriate)
Other Convair Turbo Conversions				
1		240-21	(General Motors Corp)	N24501 N112G [cvtd from piston 240 with Allison 501 engines, later used in the Electra, ff 29Dec50; known as Turboliner; Oct63 cvtd back to piston-power]
143		540	(Turbo Conversions Inc)	G-ANVP N340EL [cvtd from 340-42 by D Napier & Son Ltd to Eland power, ff 04Feb56; cvtd back to piston-power as a 440 Aug63]

DE HAVILLAND CANADA DHC-2T TURBO BEAVER

Note: Only details of identities post conversion to turbo-prop power are included.
Many aircraft operate on floats, for at least part of the year.

C/n	Cvtd No.	Conversion	Last known Owner/Operator	Identities/fates/comments (where appropriate)
261		Wipaire	Pilots of the Caribbean	N148KS N215TS
388		Wipaire	Chevron USA	N554BB
615		Wipaire	Flying Fish	N654DF N446PM N754MS C-FZKS
758		Wipaire	Robert D Wiplinger N100KL LLC	N100KL
815		Trace	Trace Inc	C-GGBF N600AX
850		Viking	Fairey Ltd	N63VA
912		Viking	Tarmac Turbo	N72TT
930		Wipaire	James E Schuster	N477JS
969		Viking	Terry Cunningham	N511CM
979		Viking	Pacific Sky Aviation	C-GODH
1026		Viking	Western Forest Products	C-GWFP
1161		Viking	E & L Trucking	N600MC C-GYST
1185		Viking	Northern Uniform Corp	C-FCVS N299WS C-GNTB
1207		Volpar	US Department of the Interior	N754
1300		Viking	North Cariboo Flying Service	SE-LEK S2-ACE C-FMPC
1411		Walleroo	Mobile Carpet Cleaning Factory	VH-AAX
1423		Wipaire	Imel Wheat Jr	N914CW
1476		Wipaire	not yet known	N9063V C6-BIQ
1511		Viking	Curtis Lemieux	N728TB C-GTBV
1525	TB1	DH	Canadian Bushplane Heritage Centre	CF-PSM-X CF-PSM C-FPSM [w/o 03Jly88 Ahmic Lake, ON, Canada; preserved Saulte Ste Marie, ON, Canada]
1543	TB2	DH	Wings Over Kississing	CF-ROM-X CF-ROM N535E N76PF N669EC C-GETH ET-AKI C-FPSM
1548		Viking	1144781 Alberta Ltd	C-FBVR
1562	TB3	DH	Desert Locust Control Organisation	C-FOEA 5Y-DLD
1566	TB4	DH	Charles E Cole	CF-ROC N90135 N478D N30CC
1570	TB5	DH	Alaska West Air	CF-OEB C-FOEB N222RL
1574	TB6	DH	ex Era Helicopters	CF-SCI N7620 [canx Nov86; fate/status unknown]
1578	TB7	DH	Aero Tech	CF-RDA C-FRDA N33DV N1DV C-GDOV N812LT N62DB
1586	TB8	DH	Amphib Air	CF-OEC C-FOEC C-GDZK N522GM N448PM N917WG
1591	TB9	DH	Transwest Air	CF-OED C-FOED
1598	TB10	DH	Hatchet Lake Aviation	CF-OEE C-FOEE
1605	TB11	DH	Heinz Oldach	CF-OEF C-FOEF C-FTCL
1614	TB12	DH	Red Lion & Sun Organisation	EP-RLS [reported w/o 06May67 but also stored intact]
1622	TB13	DH	Barrick Gold Corp	CF-UBN C-FUBN
1623	TB14	DH	Katmai Air	CF-MCM N9631 C-GWQF N45GB G-FNPW N45GB
1625	TB15	DH	Seair Seaplanes	N1805R N1454T C-FPMA
1627	TB16	DH	My Beaver	CF-UKL VH-UKL CF-UKL N81AT N53GB N995TT N995JG
1629	TB17	DH	Skanes Fallskarmsklubb	TI-407L CF-YOD N4482 SE-KKD
1632	TB18	DH	Douglas Aviation	CF-UKK C-FUKK N911CC OY-JRR N338DP N94DN
1634	TB19	DH	Government of Newfoundland & Labrador	CF-GFS C-FGFS
1636	TB20	DH	Bulkley Holdings	HZ-ZAF N4429V C-GXUT
1638	TB21	DH	Eager Beaver	CF-MAB C-FMAB N1638 C-GDTB N14TB
1640	TB22	DH	Telus Communications	CF-ASA C-FASA
1642	TB23	DH	Abraham Holdings	CF-UKQ C-GMET N388N
1644	TB24	DH	Ontario Ministry of Natural Resources	CF-OEH C-FOEH
1646	TB25	DH	Pantechnicon Aviation	N5301 N8307+ HP-468 N53011 [+ marks not fully confirmed]
1647	TB26	DH	Kenmore Air	CF-OEI C-FOEI N1455T
1649	TB27	DH	Eriksson Aviation	CF-OEJ C-FOEJ N69JJ N67EA
1650	TB28	DH	Hearst Air Service	CF-OEK C-FOEK
1652	TB29	DH	Alpha Distributors	CF-OEL C-FOEL N207X N20KA
1653	TB30	DH	Martini Aviation	CF-VON N4478 C-GMNT
1655	TB31	DH	Erik Nielsen	CF-CSA C-FCSA N66TB C-FDJH

DE HAVILLAND CANADA DHC-2T TURBO BEAVER

C/n	Cvtd No.	Conversion	Last known Owner/Operator	Identities/fates/comments (where appropriate)					
1656	TB32	DH	ex Harold J Hansen	CF-OEM	C-FOEM	N4603U	[canx Jun87; fate/status unknown]		
1658	TB33	DH	M & B Beaver	CF-OEN	C-FOEN	N122MC	N249N		
1659	TB34	DH	N906JS LLC	CF-OEO	C-FOEO	N906JS			
1661	TB35	DH	Emo Investments	CF-OEP	C-FOEP	N26584	N8PE	C-GDCN	
1662	TB36	DH	Canadian Kenworth Company	CF-CKW	C-FCKW				
1665	TB37	DH	William Ames Curtright	CF-VPV	C-FVPV	N1459T	N260HC		
1668	TB38	DH	C-FETN Ltd	N501Z	N2699	C-FETN			
1669	TB39	DH	Wallace E Opdycke	CF-CJB	C-FCJB	N967TB			
1670	TB40	DH	Arctic Air	CF-WSC	VP-FAM	CF-BLX			
1671	TB41	DH	Ontario Ministry of Natural Resources	CF-OER	C-FOER				
1672	TB42	DH	Pacific Sky Aviation	CF-WSD	5X-UVU	C-GJZX	C-GDTB		
1673	TB43	DH	CBE Construction	CF-OES	C-FOES				
1674	TB44	DH	Michael K Schilling	CF-OET	C-FOET	N8198Q	N64WG		
1677	TB45	DH	Seair Seaplanes	N6776	CF-WSE	N164WC	C-FDHC		
1678	TB46	DH	Ontario Ministry of Natural Resources	CF-OEU	C-FOEU				
1679	TB47	DH	Eager Beaver	N4491	N1444T	C-GJZZ	N724JR	N329TB	N16TB
1680	TB48	DH	Arctic Sunwest Charters	CF-OEV	C-FOEV				
1681	TB49	DH	Donald M Rogers	CF-XRT	C-FXRT	N450DM	C-FDEM		
1682	TB50	DH	Ontario Ministry of Natural Resources	CF-OEW	C-FOEW				
1683	TB51	DH	Melaire	CF-OMJ	C-FOMJ				
1684	TB52	DH	Northern Adventures	CF-OEX	C-FOEX				
1685	TB53	DH	Aviation Canmex	CF-MPA	C-FMPA	C-GUNF	C-GPMY		
1686	TB54	DH	T B Plane	CF-OEY	C-FOEY	N227N			
1687	TB55	DH	Michael K Schilling	CF-OEZ	C-FOEZ	ET-AKK	N6102Y	N1543	
1688	TB56	DH	Ontario Ministry of Natural Resources	CF-OPA	C-FOPA				
1689	TB57	DH	Pearl Equipment	CF-OPB	C-FOPB	N70346	N97AA	C-GQMP	
				5N-AXN	N70346				
1690	TB58	DH	Clemente Motor	CF-OPD	C-FOPD	N258PA			
1691	TB59	DH	Arctic Sunwest Charters	CF-OPE	C-FOPE				
1692	TB60	DH	Kenmore Air	N1944	N9744T				

DE HAVILLAND CANADA DHC-3T TURBO OTTER

Notes: Only details of identities post conversion to turbo-prop power are included.
Many aircraft operate on floats, for at least part of the year.

C/n	Conversion	Last known Owner/Operator	Identities/fates/comments (where appropriate)
3	Vazar	Harbour Air	C-FODH
7	Texas	Wings of Alaska	N753AK
10	Texas	Black Sheep Aviation & Cattle	C-GDHW
11	Vazar	Kenmore Air	N87KA
13	Texas	Nestor Falls Fly-In Outposts	C-FODK
15	Texas	Kenai River Xpress	N150BA
19	Vazar	Harbour Air	C-GHAZ
21	Vazar	Harbour Air	C-FRNO
22	Vazar	(Harbour Air)	N9707B C-GCMY [w/o 17Aug96 Alliford Bay, BC, Canada; canx 17Sep96]
24	Walter	Huron Air & Outfitters	C-FIOF
28	Vazar	Air Wemindji	C-FSVP N252KA C-FSVP
30	Texas	Ward Air Inc	N63354
37	Vazar	Kenmore Air	N606KA
38	Vazar	(Western Straits Air)	C-FEBX [w/o 27Sep95 Campbell River, BC, Canada; canx 31Jly96]
39	Vazar	Provincial Airlines	C-GOFB
42	Vazar	Harbour Air	N234KA C-GHAR
44	Vazar	Waweig Air	C-FYCX N10704 C-FYCX
46	Texas	Talkeetna Air Taxi	N565TA
52	Vazar	Alaska West Air	N87AW
65	Walter	(Huron Air & Outfitters)	C-GOFF [w/o 16Dec03 near Jellicoe, ON, Canada; canx 07Jun05; hulk to Atlantic Aircraft Salvage, Halifax, NS, Canada]
69	Vazar	Slate Falls Airways (1999)	C-FCZP
74	Texas	Maxwell Ward	C-FMAU
77	Vazar	North Star Air	N129JH C-GCQA
89	Vazar	Harbour Air	C-FITF
90	Walter	Tofino Air	C-FITS
97	Vazar	Vancouver Island Air	C-GGOR C-GVIX
105	Vazar	Harbour Air	C-GVNL
106	Vazar	Kenmore Air	N888KA N707KA
108	Texas	(Black Sheep Aviation & Cattle Co)	C-GMCW [w/o 31Mar11 near Mayo Lake, YK, Canada]
113	Vazar	Osprey Wings	C-GPHD
115	Texas	Prof Fate Inc	N120BA N69JJ
118	Texas	Bald Mountain Air Service	N104BM
119	Vazar	Harbour Air	C-FHAD
125	Walter	Voyage Air	C-GBNA
130	Texas	Blue Water Aviation	CF-KOA
131	Vazar	Kenmore Air	N58JH
135	Vazar	Harbour Air	C-FIUZ
140	Texas	Smaritans Purse	C-FSZS N43SP
142	Vazar	Air Tindi	C-FXUY N214L C-FXUY
144	Texas	Ward Air Inc	N93356
145	Vazar	Wings Over Kississing	C-FFVZ
147	Vazar	Air Roberval	C-FJFJ C-GLPM
152	Vazar	Kenmore Air	N90422
159	Vazar	Promech Air	N959PA
165	Vazar	Hearst Air Service	C-FDDX
172	Vazar	Leuenberger Air Service	C-GLCW
174	Texas	Alpine Lakes Air	C-GFTZ
183	Vazar	Promech Air	C-GIGZ N435B
184	Vazar	Hawk Air	C-FQMN
201	Texas	Rapids Camp Lodge	N205RC
206	Texas	(Wood River Lodge)	N455A [w/o 09Aug10 Muklung Hills, near Aleknagik, AK]
208	Vazar	Wings Over Kississing	C-FWEJ
209	Walter	Blue Water Aviation	C-GBTU
213	Vazar	White River Air Services	C-FWRA
214	Vazar	Harbour Air	C-FJUH 8Q-TMZ 4R-ARA C-GHAG
216	Vazar	Air Saguenay (1980)	C-GLMT
218	Texas	Air Saguenay (1980)	C-FODT
221	Vazar	Kenmore Air	N50KA

DE HAVILLAND CANADA DHC-3T TURBO OTTER

C/n	Conversion	Last known Owner/Operator	Identities/fates/comments (where appropriate)				
225	Vazar	Promech Air	N3952B				
226	Texas	Ultima Thule Lodge	N226UT				
233	Vazar	Waweig Air	C-FQND				
239	Texas	Nestor Falls Fly-In Outposts	C-FSOR				
247	Walter	West Caribou Air Service	C-FYLZ				
250	Vazar	Talkeetna Air Taxi	N373A	VH-OTV	N510PR		
252	Texas	Talon Air Service	N252TA				
254	Texas	Alaskan Wilderness Outfitting Co	N254AW				
258	Vazar	Osprey Wings	C-FXRI				
261	Walter	West Caribou Air Service	C-GKYG				
262	Texas	Wings of Alaska	N338AK				
267	Vazar	Province Of Manitoba	C-FMAX				
270	Vazar	Promech Air	N51KA	N270PA			
273	Vazar	Transwest Air	C-FHPE				
274	Vazar	Misty Fjords Air	N6868B				
284	Vazar	Harbour Air	N84SF	C-FADW	N84SF	C-GHAS	
287	Texas	River Air Limited	C-GYKO				
288	Vazar	Harbour Air	N68086	DQ-GLL	C-GHAQ		
292	Vazar	Northwestern Air	C-FLLL				
296	Walter	Adventure Air	C-FFIJ	N103SY	C-FXZD	C-GRRJ	
300	Vazar	Prof Fate Inc	N79JJ				
302	Vazar	Fort Frances Sportsmen Airways	C-GMDG				
307	Viking	ex Viking Air	C-GITL+	N	[+ canx 01Sep11 to USA; marks N8510T reported]		
310	Texas	Alaska West Air	N49AW				
316	Vazar	Transwest Air	C-FSGD				
324	Vazar	Nakina Outpost Camps & Air Service	C-FMPY				
333	Texas	Wings of Alaska	N336AK				
336	Vazar	Nakina Outpost Camps & Air Service	CF-MIQ				
338	Vazar	K2 Aviation	N424KT				
339	Vazar	Harbour Air	C-FHAX				
348	Vazar	Waweig Air	C-GLAB				
349	Vazar	Liard Air	C-FZDV	C-GUDK			
355	Vazar	Harbour Air	N53KA	C-GOPP			
357	Vazar	Harbour Air	C-FHAA				
359	Vazar	Wilderness North Air	C-GMLB	N10708	C-GMLB		
361	Texas	(Paklook Air)	N361TT	[w/o 23Sep11 Kodiak, AK]			
362	Texas	Tsayta Aviation	N362TT	C-FMZC	[floatplane]		
363	Texas	Blue Water Aviation	C-GSMG				
365	Vazar	Fort Frances Sportsmen Airways	C-GUTL				
371	Vazar	Harbour Air	C-GEND				
376	Walter	West Caribou Air Service	C-GSUV				
382	Vazar	Harbour Air	N382BH	C-FHAS			
385	Viking	Viking Air	C-FDNK				
387	Texas	Flamingo Quay Resort	N443CB				
393	Vazar	Harbour Air	C-GVTO	8Q-	4R-ARB	C-FJHA	
394	Texas	40 Mile Air	N3125N				
397	Vazar	Aircraft Marketing & Leasing	HB-TCM	SX-ARO	N113DG		
398	Vazar	ex Labrador Airways	C-FQOS+	N	[+ canx 26May08; on rebuild by Jly07 Kenai, AK]		
403	Vazar	Jackson Air Services	C-FODW				
405	Vazar	Harbour Air	C-GUTW				
406	Vazar	Harbour Air	SE-KOX	N406H	C-FHAH	9H-AFA	C-FHAJ
407	Vazar	Kenmore Air	N3125S				
409	Vazar	Promech Air	N409PA				
410	Vazar	Air Roberval	C-FVVY				
412	Vazar	Slate Falls Airways	C-FNWX				
418	Texas	Wings of Alaska	N337AK				
419	Vazar	K2 Aviation	N472PM	N727KT			
420	Texas	Air Saguenay (1980)	C-GLCO				
421	Cox	Cox Aircraft Co of Washington	N4247A	[experimental conversion; status/fate unknown]			
422	Vazar	Harbour Air	C-GLCP				
425	Vazar	Rust's Flying Service	N2899J				
427	Vazar	Martini Aviation	N644JJ	C-FODX	C-GTMW		
428	Vazar	Alkan Air	C-GLCS				

DE HAVILLAND CANADA DHC-3T TURBO OTTER

C/n	Conversion	Last known Owner/Operator	Identities/fates/comments (where appropriate)
429	Vazar	Province Of Manitoba	C-FODY
431	Vazar	Katmai Air	N17689
434	Texas	Katmai Air	N491K
437	Vazar	Leuenberger Air Service	C-FSOX
439	Texas	Ookpik Aviation	C-FPEN
440	Vazar	(A D M S E Inc)	N9758N [w/o 01Jly00 Didier la Foret, L'Allier, France; canx 19Sep00]
445	Texas	Kississing Lake Lodge	C-FRHW
447	Texas	(Black Sheep Aviation & Cattle Co)	C-GZCW [w/o 02Jun07 Mayo Airport, YK, Canada; canx 22Mar10]
452	Vazar	Waasheshkun Airways	C-FDIO
454	Texas	Wings of Alaska	N339AK
456	?	Hans W. Munich	N703TH
460	Vazar	Osprey Wings	CF-DIZ
461	Vazar	Rust's Flying Service	N929KT
463	Vazar	Osprey Wings	C-FASZ
465	Vazar	(Liard Air Ltd)	N5010Y N32910 N342KA C-GNNP [DBF 20Jan11 in hangar fire Muncho Lake, BC, Canada; canx 29Mar11]
466	Walter	Kississing Lake Lodge	C-FVQD

DE HAVILLAND CANADA DHC-5 BUFFALO

C/n	Model	Last known Owner/Operator	Identities/fates/comments (where appropriate)

Notes: c/ns 1 to 4 are DHC-5 (no sub-type) and were originally designated CV-7A whilst with the US Army and re-designated C-8As when taken over by the USAF.
The designation CC-115 is used when in service with the Canadian Armed Forces.
In Brazilian service the designation C-115 was used.

DH1		(de Havilland Aircraft of Canada)	63-13686+ NASA 716^ N716NA C-GFIU [+ ff 09Apr64; ^ used for augmentor wing research, as XC-8A, ff 09Apr72; cvtd back to standard configuration; c/n quoted as DH1 whilst regd C-GFIU; b/u 06-09Dec88 Downsview, ON, Canada; canx 11Sep89]
2		ex NASA	63-13687 NASA 715+ N326D N715NA [+ mod as Quiet Short-haul Research Aircraft (QSRA) testbed; stored after Aug86 Moffett Field, CA; canx 24Sep96; l/n Apr08]
3		(Sky Relief/International Red Cross)	63-13688 N13689+ 161546^ N37AU 5Y-SRK [^ USN] [w/o 30Dec06 near Nairobi, Kenya] [+ report of being N13659 in error as in use on Cessna 150]
4		(NASA) 63-13689	[w/o 22Apr96 Moffett Field, CA] [reports of being N13689 are in error]
5	A	Canadian Armed Forces	9451+ 115451+ CF-LAQ 115451^ [+ Canada; ^ used by Bell Aerospace in development of an air-cushion landing system XC-8]
6	A	Canadian Armed Forces	9452+ 115452+ CF-QVA 115452 [+ Canada]
7	A	(Sky Relief/UNHCR)	9453+ 115453+ CF-ABR 115453+ Z-SRD 5Y-SRD 9Q-CSR [+ Canada] [stored by Jun07 Nairobi-Wilson, Kenya; b/u Dec11]
8	A	(Canadian Armed Forces)	9454+ 115454+ [Canada] [b/u 1995 for spares CFB Mountain View, ON, Canada]
9	A	Sky Relief/UNHCR	9455+ 115455+ Z-SRE 5Y-SRE [+ Canada]
10	A	Canadian Armed Forces	9456+ 115456+ CF-YPK 115456 [+ Canada]
11	A	Canadian Armed Forces	9457+ 115457 [+ Canada]
12	A	(Sky Relief or InterAir)	9458+ 115458+ Z-SRF [+ Canada] [b/u for spares by Apr97 Harare-Charles Prince, Zimbabwe]
13	A	(Sky Relief or InterAir)	9459+ 115459+ Z-SRC [+ Canada] [b/u for spares by Sep00 Harare-Charles Prince, Zimbabwe]
14	A	Sky Relief/UNHCR	9460+ 115460+ (CF-AQD) CF-LAQ 115460+ Z-SRB [+ Canada] [l/n stored 21Aug97 Goma, Democratic Republic of Congo; fate/status unknown]
15	A	(Brazilian Air Force)	2350 [w/o 12Nov90 Rio de Janeiro-Galeao AFB, Brazil]
16	A	(Canadian Armed Forces)	9461+ 115461 [+ Canada] [shot down 09Aug74 near Diemas, Syria; preserved c/n 85 painted to represent this aircraft]
17	A	ex Brazilian Air Force	CF-DJU 2351 [wfs 14Mar08; operated last Brazilian AF Buffalo flight; stored Sao Paulo-Campo de Marte AFB, Brazil; l/n 25Oct09]
18	A	ex Brazilian Air Force	2352 [wfs; location/status unknown; no known reports since delivery]
19	A	Canadian Armed Forces	9462+ 115462+ C-GNUZ-X 115462 [+ Canada]
20	A	ex Brazilian Air Force	2353 [wfs; stored Manaus-Ponta Pelada AFB, Brazil; l/n Oct09]
21	A	(Sky Relief)	9463+ 115463+ CF-DJU 115463+ C-GGCM 115463 Z-SRA [b/u Sep00 Harare-Charles Prince, Zimbabwe]
22	A	ex Brazilian Air Force	2354 [wfs; location/status unknown; possibly stored Manaus-Ponta Pelada, AFB, Brazil]
23	A	ex Canadian Armed Forces	CF-XTE 9464+ 115464 [+ Canada] [wfs Jun95 & stored CFB Mountainview, ON, Canada; by Oct97 GIA CFB Borden, ON]
24	A	(Brazilian Air Force)	2355 [w/o 27Nov86 Queria, Brazil]
25	A	Canadian Armed Forces	9465+ 115465 [+ Canada]
26	A	(Brazilian Air Force)	2356 [w/o 18Oct74 Rio de Janeiro-Campos dos Afonsos AFB, Brazil]
27	A	ex Brazilian Air Force	2357 [wfs & b/u Pedra do Leme AFB, Brazil; front fuselage preserved; l/n Apr07]
28	A	(Brazilian Air Force)	2358 [w/o 16Mar78 Rio de Janeiro-Campos dos Afonsos AFB, Brazil]
29	A	ex Brazilian Air Force	2359 [wfs by Oct07 & stored Sao Paulo-Campo de Marte AFB, Brazil; l/n 25Oct09]
30	A	ex Brazilian Air Force	2360 [wfs by Oct07 & stored Sao Paulo-Campo de Marte AFB, Brazil; l/n Oct09 Manaus, Brazil]
31	A	(Brazilian Air Force)	2361 [w/o 15May95 Manaus-Ponta Pelada AFB, Brazil]
32	A	ex Brazilian Air Force	2362 [wfs & stored Sao Paulo-Campo de Marte, Brazil AFB; l/n 25Oct09]
33	A	(Brazilian Air Force)	2363 [wfs Sao Paulo-Campo de Marte AFB, Brazil; by 23Oct05 hulk only in trees]
34	A	ex Brazilian Air Force	2364 [wfs & stored Sao Paulo-Campo de Marte AFB, Brazil; l/n 23Oct05]
35	A	ex Brazilian Air Force	2365 [wfs & stored Sao Paulo-Campo de Marte AFB, Brazil; l/n 25Oct09; reported to be donated to Ecuador]
36	A	(Brazilian Air Force)	2366 [w/o 18Sep74 Ponta Pora, Brazil]
37	A	ex Brazilian Air Force	2367 [wfs & stored Sao Paulo-Campo de Marte AFB, Brazil; Nov11 for preservation at Dos Afonos, Brazil]
38	A	ex Brazilian Air Force	2368 [wfs & stored Sao Paulo-Campo de Marte AFB, Brazil; l/n Apr07; no tail or engines]

DE HAVILLAND CANADA DHC-5 BUFFALO

C/n	Model	Last known Owner/Operator	Identities/fates/comments (where appropriate)
39	A	ex Brazilian Air Force	2369 [wfs & stored Sao Paulo-Campo de Marte AFB, Brazil; l/n Apr07]
40	A	ex Brazilian Air Force	2370 [wfs & stored Sao Paulo-Campo de Marte AFB, Brazil; l/n 25Oct09]
41	A	Museu Aeroespacial	2371+ [+ Brazil] [wfu Dec06; preserved Rio de Janeiro-Campo dos Afonos, Brazil; l/n Oct08]
42	A	(Brazilian Air Force)	2372 [w/o 23Feb72, also quoted as 23Feb73, location uncertain but has been reported as Manaus, Brazil]
43	A	(Brazilian Air Force)	2373 [possibly w/o 04Feb85 at unknown location]
44	A	(Peruvian Air Force)	321 [w/o 22Dec79 near Puerto Esperanza, Peru]
45	A	Museo Aeronautico del Peru	322+ [+ Peru] [wfs; preserved Lima-Las Palmas, Peru; l/n 08Apr08]
46	A	(Peruvian Air Force)	323 [wfu by Aug85 Lima-Callao AFB, Peru; l/n 1990]
47	A	(Peruvian Air Force)	324 [wfs; was based Lima-Callao AFB, Peru; status/fate unknown]
48	A	(Peruvian Air Force)	325 [wfs; was based Lima-Callao AFB, Peru; reported b/u]
49	A	(Peruvian Air Force)	326 [wfs Lima-Callao AFB, Peru; l/n Mar90]
50	A	(Peruvian Air Force)	327 [wfu by Aug85 Lima-Callao AFB, Peru; l/n 1990]
51	A	Coleccion de la Base Aerea de Lima	328 [wfs; preserved Lima-Callao AFB, Peru; l/n 06Sep05]
52	A	(Peruvian Air Force)	329 [w/o 21Jun89 near Tarma, Junin Province, Peru]
53	A	(Peruvian Air Force)	346 [reported w/o date unknown at "Pucialoa"]
54	A	(Peruvian Air Force)	347 [wfs Lima-Callao AFB, Peru; l/n Mar90]
55	A	(Peruvian Air Force)	348 [w/o 22Dec79 "near Ucavail"; note this is the same date as c/n 44 above]
56	A	(Peruvian Air Force)	349 [wfs Lima-Callao AFB, Peru; l/n Mar90]
57	A	(Peruvian Air Force)	350 [reported b/u no other details]
58	A	(Peruvian Air Force)	351 [reported w/o date unknown at Andahuaylas, Peru]
59	A	(Peruvian Air Force)	352 [last reported active Feb85; status/fate unknown]
60	D	unknown	C-GBUF-X 9T-CBA(1) C-GBUF 5T-MAW 9T-CBA(1) 3D-AIR [stored 10Dec99 Liege, Belgium; reported left Liege 24Apr00 to Cairo, Egypt via Bari, Italy; has been reported as becoming 5Y-MEG but see c/n 62 below; to Kenya]
61	D	ex Zambian Air Force	C-GGQA AF314 [wfs & stored Lusaka, Zambia; l/n 19Sep08]
62	D	ex Togo Air Force	5V-MAG [reported stored by May97 Lome, Togo; but also reported w/o 01May89 Kara, Kenya; also reported to 5Y-MEG which on 12Dec07 collided with Cessna 208 5Y-SLA Nairobi-Wilson, Kenya]
63	D	(Ecuadorean Air Force)	(C-GGQB) FAE-063+ HC-BFG [+ Ecuador] [w/o after Apr76 no details; but also reported as in use as a GIA]
64	D	(Ecuadorean Air Force)	(C-GGQC) FAE-064+ HC-BFH [+ Ecuador] [w/o 17Jul90 Calgary, AB, Canada]
65	D	(Zambian Air Force)	C-GGQC AF315 [wfs & stored Lusaka, Zambia; l/n 19Sep08]
66	D	(Zambian Air Force)	C-GGQD AF316 [w/o 1976 unknown location or w/o 27Jly82 Lusaka, Zambia]
67	D	(Zambian Air Force)	C-GGQB AF317 [reported w/o date unknown Mongu, Zambia]
68	D	(Trident Enterprises/UNDP)	C-GGQE AF318+ 5Y-TEL [+ Zambia] [reported w/o 16Feb05 in Southern Sudan]
69	D	(Zambian Air Force)	C-GGQG AF319 [w/o 27Apr93 in Atlantic Ocean off Gabon shortly after t/o from Libreville, Gabon]
70	D	(Zambian Air Force)	C-GGQF AF320 [reported w/o 17Feb90 Ngwerere, Zambia]
71	D	ex Togo Air Force	5V-MAH [stored & wfu 1994 Dinard, France; impounded; l/n 29Jun08]
72	D	Democratic Republic of Congo Air Force	(C-GGQG) 9T-CBA(2)+ [+ some reports reverse last ids of this aircraft & c/n 73; reported stored]
73	D	(Zaire Air Force)	(C-GGQB) 9T-CBB [reported w/o 20Sep93 Kinshasa-N'dola, Zaire; hulk reported May94]
74	D	(Zaire Air Force)	9T-CBC [w/o 17Sep80 Kindu, Zaire]
75	D	(Kenyan Air Force)	C-GQFR 207 [w/o 01May99 Mandera Airport, Kenya]
76	D	Kenyan Air Force	C-GQFS 208
77	D	Kenyan Air Force	C-GQFT 209
78	D	Kenyan Air Force	C-GQFU 210
79	D	Indonesian Navy	306+ AX-5001^ AL-5001^ U-631 [+ United Arab Emirates; ^ Indonesia; might be U-632 see below; stored by Nov05 Surabaya, Indonesia; l/n 15Sep11]
80	D	Indonesian Navy	307+ AX-5002^ AL-5002^ U-632 [+ United Arab Emirates; ^ Indonesia; might be U-631 see below; stored by Nov05 Surabaya, Indonesia]
81	D	Trident Enterprises	308+ AX-5003^ AD-5003^ PK-XNZ 5Y-XNZ [+ United Arab Emirates; ^ Indonesia]
82	D	Indonesian Army	309+ AX-5004^ AD-5004^ A-9121 [stored Bandung, Indonesia; l/n Nov08]
83	D	(Sudan Air Force)	800 [w/o 04Apr86 near Bor, Sudan]
84	D	(Trident Enterprises/Opal Aerospace)	A4O-CD 5Y-OPL [possibly w/o 29Sep08 Lokichoggio, Kenya]

DE HAVILLAND CANADA DHC-5 BUFFALO

C/n	Model	Last known Owner/Operator	Identities/fates/comments (where appropriate)
85	D	Canadian Warplane Heritage Museum	811+ ST-AHP 811+ "ST-AHT"^ "115461" [+ Sudan] [^ marks crudely painted out on aircraft during ferry flight to N America; preserved Hamilton, ON, Canada with false serial, used by c/n 5; l/n 10Jly08]
86	D	Sudan Air Force	822+ ST-AHQ 822 [+ Sudan]
87	D	(Sudan Air Force)	C-GQUT 833 [w/o 14Mar85 near Akobo, Sudan]
88	D	(Mauritanian Air Force)	5T-MAX [w/o 27May79 off Dakar, Senegal]
89	D	Kenyan Air Force	211
90	D	Kenyan Air Force	(C-GQUT) 212
91	D	ex Tanzanian Air Force	C-GTJV JW9019 [wfs & stored by Nov99 Dar es Salaam, Tanzania; l/n 26Sep08]
92	D	ex Tanzanian Air Force	C-GTJW JW9020 [wfs & stored by Nov99 Dar es Salaam, Tanzania; l/n Nov99]
93	D	ex Tanzanian Air Force	C-GTJX JW9021 [wfs & stored by Nov99 Dar es Salaam, Tanzania; l/n Nov99]
94	D	(Trident Enterprises)	C-GTJY JW9022+ 5H-BAF [+ Tanzania] [w/o 12Jun96 Yambio, Sudan]
95A	A	Arctic Sunwest Charters	C-GTZL-X A4O-CE C-FSKO 3B-NAW+ 5Y-BUF 9Q-CTT 5Y-GBA C-FASV [+ quoted as 3B-NAE in some sources]
96	D	(Chilean Air Force)	C-GTLW 920 [w/o Oct81 Punta Arenas, Chile]
97	D	ex Tanzanian Air Force	C-GAVV JW9023 [wfs & stored by Jan98 Dar es Salaam, Tanzania; l/n Nov99]
98	D	(Mexican Air Force)	TP-216+ XC-UTO^ [+ Mexico] [^ also reported with dual mark TP-200; DBR 18May89]
99	D	(Tanzanian Air Force)	C-GAVX JW9024 [w/o 21May94 Bukoba, Tanzania]
100	D	ex Mexican Navy	TP-217+ MT-220+ AMT-237 [+ Mexico] [reported wfs La Paz, Mexico; l/n Jan05]
101	A	(Ethiopian Airlines)	C-GBXI ET-AHI [w/o 8Nov88 Gondar Airport, Ethiopia]
102	A	(Ethiopian Airlines)	C-GBXJ ET-AHJ [fate/status unclear; reported shot down 17Mar83 Degehabur, Ethiopia; then 01Dec99 Addis Ababa, Ethiopia in primer for Ethiopian Air Force]
103	D	(de Havilland Aircraft of Canada)	C-GCTC-X C-GCTC [w/o 04Sep84 Farnborough, UK]
104	D	(Ecuadorian Army)	C-GCTL+ AEE-501 [+ marks not confirmed] [w/o 28May09 location unknown]
105	D	Cameroon Air Force	C-GDAF TJ-XBM
106	D	(Cameroon Air Force)	C-GDAI TJ-XBN [stored by Jun02 Douala, Cameroon; l/n 12Oct07]
107A	A	Arctic Sunwest Charters	(C-GDAU) C-GDNG A4O-CI C-FSKN 5Y-GAA C-FASY
108	E	Trident Enterprises/UNDP	C-GDOB (AEE-502)+ (N4294S) C-GDOB 5Y-TAJ [+ Ecuador]
109	D	Indonesian Army	(AEE-502)+ C-GEOZ-X 310^ AX-5005# AD-5005# A-9122 [+ Ecuador; ^ United Arab Emirates; # Indonesia] [stored by 18Apr08 Pondok Cabe, Indonesia]
110	D	Egyptian Air Force	(AEE-503)+ C-GIBF 1210^ 1161//SU-BFA [dual marks] [+ Ecuador; ^ Egypt]
111	D	Egyptian Air Force	(AEE-504)+ C-GDPY 1211^ 1162//SU-BFB [dual marks] [+ Ecuador; ^ Egypt] [stored by Jan09 Almaza, Egypt]
112	D	Egyptian Air Force	(AEE-505)+ C-GEMU 1212^ 1163//SU-BFC [dual marks] [+ Ecuador; ^ Egypt]
113	D	Egyptian Air Force	C-GFCA 1213+ 1164//SU-BFD [dual marks] [+ Egypt]
114	D	Egyptian Air Force	C-GFCI 1214+ 1165//SU-BFE [dual marks] [+ Egypt]
115	D	Egyptian Air Force	C-GERC 1215+ 1166//SU-BFF [dual marks] [+ Egypt]
116	D	Egyptian Air Force	C-GFCW 1216+ 1167//SU-BFG [dual marks] [+ Egypt]
117	D	Egyptian Air Force	C-GEWI 1217+ 1168//SU-BFH [dual marks] [+ Egypt]
118	D	(Egyptian Air Force)	C-GEVI 1218+ 1169//SU-BFI [dual marks] [w/o 02Apr84 Luxor, Egypt]
119	D	Egyptian Air Force	C-GJWU 1219+ 1170//SU-BFJ [dual marks]
120	D	Cameroon Air Force	C-GEAY TJ-XBR
121	D	(Cameroon Air Force)	C-GDWT TJ-XBS [DBR 26Oct83 & stored Douala, Cameroon; l/n 12Oct07]
122	D	ex Cameroon Air Force	C-GHSV TJ-XBT [wfu by Jun02 Douala, Cameroon]
123	D	(Kenyan Air Force)	C-GFHE+ 214 [+ marks not fully confirmed; w/o 03May99 Mandera Airport, Kenya]
124	D	Kenyan Air Force	C-GFHZ 216
125	D	Kenyan Air Force	C-GJFO 218 [w/o 16Apr92 Kaloleni, Nairobi, Kenya]
126	D	Kenyan Air Force	C-GJFH 220

Unidentified

unkn	U	5Y-CSR	[reported 05Sep08 Nairobi-Wilson, Kenya]
unkn	U		[an unknown Kenyan Air Force aircraft was w/o 25Jly02 Mugumo Coffee farm, Kenya]

Production complete

DE HAVILLAND CANADA DHC-6 TWIN OTTER

Note: An asterisk after the series number indicates a known Vistaliner conversion

C/n	Model	Last known Owner/Operator	Identities/fates/comments (where appropriate)
1	100	Canada Aviation Museum	CF-DHC-X CF-DHC CF-DHC-X CF-DHC [prototype ff 20May65] [preserved Rockcliffe, ON, Canada; canx Nov81]
2	100	Aero Space Museum Association	CF-SJB-X CF-SJB N856AC CF-PAT C-FPAT [wfu Oct1997 Calgary-Springbank, AB, Canada & preserved Calgary; l/n 11Sep08]
3	100	Peruvian Navy	CF-SUL-X CF-SUL N4901 C-GKAZ+ OB-512^ AB-583 [+ canx 19May95 as sold in USA] [^ marks not confirmed] [floatplane]
4	100	NASA/Glenn Research Center	CF-OEG N508NA N607NA
5	100	(Air Central)	CF-UCD N7711+ CF-UCD XA-TUO N7705 [w/o 25Mar73 Savoy, IL] [+ painted as such at Downsview, ON, Canada but not delivered]
6	100	(Trans-Australia Airlines)	N12706 VH-TGR [w/o 28Apr70 near Kainantu, Papua New Guinea]
7	100	Chilean Air Force	935+ 931^ [+ w/o 19Aug98 Cerro Moreno AFB, Antofagasta, Chile] [^ gate guardian by Dec08 El Tepual International, Puerto Montt with fake serial]
8	100	Transwest Air	N12708 VH-TGS CF-CCE C-FCCE [serious damage 04Feb09 La Ronge, SK, Canada]
9	100	Ikhana Group	CF-UXE (VH-TGT) F-OCFJ DQ-FEZ N806RT
10	100	Chilean Air Force	936
11	100	Chilean Air Force	937 [preserved by Dec08 El Tepual International, Puerto Montt, Chile]
12	100	(Kenting Atlas Aviation)	CF-WWP [w/o 15Aug73 near Eureka, NT, Canada]
13	100	(Air Wisconsin)	N4043B [w/o 29Jun72 over Lake Winnebago, WI after colliding with Convair 580 N90858 (c/n 83)]
14	100	Freefall Adventures	N121PM
15	100	Dilkara Leasing	N364MA N122PM (N456PJ)
16	100	(Chilean Air Force)	938 [w/o 17Nov72 Segundo Corral, Chile]
17	100	Transwest Air	(CF-UYL) (CF-SDH) CF-SCA C-FSCA
18	100	(SAESA)	XA-HIL XB-BAS XA-BOP [w/o 09Sep78 near Mexico City, Mexico]
19	100	(AirWest Airlines)	CF-UXP PP-SRV CF-UXP HP-466 CF-AJB C-FAJB [w/o 16Dec76 near Strait of Juan de Fuca, Vancouver Island, BC, Canada]
20	100	Chilean Air Force	939
21	100	Kenn Borek Air	CF-VMD N1370T CF-QHC C-FQHC 8Q-QHC C-FQHC 8Q-QHC C-GBPE
22	100	Twin Otter Support Services	PJ-WIA HP-772 N100AP N122AR* [* marks reserved 11Aug11]
23	100	(GT Air)	CF-INB PK-KBD PK-LTZ [w/o 12Apr05 Enarotali, Indonesia]
24	100	Chilean Air Force	940
25	100	ex Desert Air	VP-LIR N7702 N123PM N525EH [canx 23Aug01 as exported to Canada, but not reg'd there; rear fuselage reported 09Jun04 Calgary-Springbank, AB, Canada; l/n 03Feb10]
26	100	(High Noon Holdings)	CF-VTL C-FVTL [DBF 14May83 Calgary-International, AB, Canada; canx Jly83]
27	100	Fayard/Carolina Sky Sports	VP-LIS CF-DTK "STOL-1" CF-DTK N85113 DQ-FDK ZK-FQK(2) N227CS
28	100	(Chilean Air Force)	941 [w/o 09Sep74 near Puerto Montt, Chile]
29	100	(LLH Services)	CF-CSB C-FCSB N220YK C-FCSB N229YK N225CS [canx 13May11 as wfu; fate/status unknown]
30	100	(Aeralpi Linee Aeree)	I-CLAI [w/o 11Mar67 Mt. Visentin, Borgo Priolo, Italy]
31	100	(General Air)	D-IDHC [w/o 27May72 Heligoland, West Germany]
32	100	(Pace Aviation)	N332MA C-GGNI N332MA [PWFU1994]
33	100	(Chilean Air Force)	942 [w/o 26Sep69 near Puerto Montt, Chile]
34	100	(Labrador Airways)	N582PA N241GW CF-ZUV CF-AUS C-FAUS [w/o 11Oct84 Mealy Mountains, Goose Bay, NL, Canada]
35	100	Transwest Air	CF-VOG C-FVOG
36	100	(Pacific Coastal Airlines)	CF-DMR C-FDMR [w/o 17Sep94 Fish Egg Inlet, BC, Canada but canx 18Jan00 as exported; assumed used as spares by Aviation Quebec Labrador; wings only noted 22Jly08 Calgary-Springbank, AB, Canada]
37	100	Emerald Coast Air	VP-LIT CF-DTJ C-FDTJ N71EC
38	100	(Interior)	N2711H N2711N [w/o 06Sep69 Sagwon, AK]
39	100	(Guyana Airways)	VP-GCP 8R-GCP [w/o 03Dec73 Dhanrai, 300m SW Georgetown, Guyana]
40	100	West Coast Air	5H-MNK CF-GQE C-FGQE
41	100	(Pilgrim Airlines)	N124PM [ditched 10Feb70 Long Island Sound, New London, CT]
42	100	(Pal Air International)	N347MA [b/u Aug87 Winnipeg, MB, Canada; canx Jun91]
43	100	Karratha Flying Services	I-CHAN N935JM SE-FTO VH-TZL VH-ZKF
44	100	Maldivian Air Taxi	CF-OEQ C-FOEQ 8Q-OEQ C-FOEQ 8Q-OEQ

DE HAVILLAND CANADA DHC-6 TWIN OTTER

C/n	Model	Last known Owner/Operator	Identities/fates/comments (where appropriate)
45	100	JHH Aircraft	N4044B N920R HC-BUV N920R HC-BYK N920R [leased Helicopteros Marinos S.A., Buenos Aires, Argentina]
46	200	Servicios Aereos Profesionales	I-FALO N955JM TF-REG(2) TF-VLE N46WJ CS-TFG N46WJ HI-644CT HI-644
47	100	(Wiggins Airways)	N223P N7672 N56AN N656WA [w/o 18Jun08 Hyannis, MA; canx 28May09; to Dodson International Parts Inc for spares]
48	100	The Sky's The Limit	N4914 N202EH
49	100	(Trigana Air Service)	PK-NUA PK-YPG [w/o 08Dec92 Pogapa, Irian Jaya, Indonesia]
50	100	(Rocky Mountain Aircraft)	I-TOFA N965JM N292S N927MA N927BA [canx Jly89; by 30Jly92 fuselage only, Boatman Air Lift titles, at Calgary-Springbank, AB, Canada; l/n 03Feb10]
51	100	West Coast Air	N368MA N51FW CF-MHR C-FMHR
52	200	Kapowsin Air Sports	N369MA N52FW N962 N52FW
53	200	(Quantum Leap Skydiving Center)	N203E [w/o 29Jly06 Sullivan Regional Airport, MO]
54	100	North-Wright Airways	N8081N C-GRDD
55	100	(Trigana Air Service)	PK-NUB PK-NUD PK-BIZ PK-YNM [w/o 04Nov94 in mountains near Nabire, Irian Jaya, Indonesia]
56	100	(Royal Norwegian Air Force)	67-056+ 056 [+ Norway] [w/o 11Jly72 Harstad, Norway]
57	100	(Desert Sand Aircraft Leasing Co)	67-057+ 057+ 7057+ N157KM [+ Norway] [w/o 08Mar11 Clayton County Airport-Tara Field, GA; by 16Mar11 with Atlanta Air Storage, Griffin, GA]
58	100	ex Athabaska Airways	CF-WGE-X CF-WGE C-FWGE [w/o 13Jun87 Maudsley Lake, SK, Canada; canx Feb90; fuselage only at Calgary-Springbank, AB, Canada 30Jly92; by10Sep08 forward fuselage only; l/n 03Feb10]
59	100	Twin Otter International	N512S N512AR
60	100	Kenn Borek Air	JDFT-1+ C-GIAW 8Q-IAW C-GTKB 8Q-TKB 8Q-MAC C-GTKB 8Q-MAC C-GTKB 8Q-MAC C-GTKB [+ Jamaica]
61	100	JST Management	N8082N N204EH
62	100	Forsvarets Flysamling Gardermoen	67-062+ 062+ 7062+ [+ Norway] [preserved Oslo-Gardermoen, Norway]
63	100	(Royal Norwegian Air Force)	67-063+ 063+ [+ Norway] [w/o 29Oct90 Honningsvag, Norway]
64	100	Kenn Borek Air	CF-CSL C-FCSL 8Q-CSL C-FCSL 8Q-CSL C-FCSL 8Q-CSL C-GIKB
65	100	Twin Otter International	N8083N N666PV N98VA
66	100	Sussex Skydive	CF-ARC C-FARC N166DH C-FIED N166DH
67	100	(AirWest Airlines)	N1454T CF-AWF [w/o 22Sep76 Mosher Creek, Bella Coola, BC, Canada]
68	100	(Samoa Aviation)	N374MA N950JM C-GEAW N44693 N202RH [w/o 17Jun88 near Tau, Manua Islands, American Samoa; canx Sep89]
69	100	ex Alaska Aeronautical Industries	N4907 N2714R [by Jly84 fuselage only at Calgary-Springbank, AB, Canada; l/n 03Feb10]
70	100	(Merpati Nusantara Airlines)	PK-NUC [w/o 28Feb73 near Nabire, Irian Jaya, Indonesia]
71	100	South Nahanni Airways	N16430 VH-EWM CF-CIJ C-FCIJ D-IDHC(3) C-GSOL C-GGLE
72	100	(Servicios Aereos Profesionales)	F-BOOH TF-VLD PH-DDC C-GZFP HI-624CT [stored off airport Miami, FL – Jan07; nose used to re-build c/n 691]
73	100	Flanagan Enterprises (Nevada)	390+ (CF-APH) CF-PPD C-FPPD N73WD C-FPPD N73WD [+ Peru]
74	100	(Malu Aviation)	I-ANTE N970JM OO-JFP 9Q-CXK [w/o 03Oct96 Kahemba, Zaire]
75	100	Ayeet Aviation & Tourism	391+ (CF-QQI) CF-CSF C-FCSF 4X-AHP [+ Peru]
76	100	(Mission Aviation Fellowship)	PZ-TAU C-GBKF N3776D PK-MAM [w/o 25May87 near Ilaga, Indonesia]
77	100	North London Parachute Centre	YA-GAS C-GDQY N808PC [as of 14Mar10 still marked as C-GDQY at Chatteris, UK]
78	100	Arctic Sunwest Charters	N4714 N242GW CF-AKM C-FAKM C-FASQ
79	100	Fayard/Carolina Sky Sports	I-NUVO N995JM TF-REI C-GHYH N1022S
80	100	(Aeropelican Air Services)	N1566 VH-MMY [PWFU; canx 15Jun87; fate unknown]
81	100	ex Alaska Aeronautical Industries	N376MA [b/u Jly84; fuselage only at Calgary-Springbank, AB, Canada by 30Jly92; l/n 03Feb10]
82	100	Ikhana Group	392+ CF-SCF C-FSCF 8Q-HIA 8Q-TMA C-GDTO N804RT [+ Peru]
83	100	(Golden West Airlines)	N6383 [w/o 09Jan75 Whittier, CA after colliding with Cessna 120 N11421]
84	100	(Talair)	N1754 VH-TGT P2-TGT (P2-RDE) [w/o 28Feb78 Garaina, Papua New Guinea]
85	100	(Sudan Airways)	ST-ADB [w/o 18Mar75 near Khartoum, Sudan]
86	100	Erwin Aero Industries	N591MA VP-BDC C6-BDC N2228H C-GGAW [w/o 01Nov00 Vancouver Harbour, BC, Canada; Feb07 restored for possible re-build; but by 19Nov09 preserved by Southern Alberta Institute of Technology, Calgary, AB, Canada]

DE HAVILLAND CANADA DHC-6 TWIN OTTER

C/n	Model	Last known Owner/Operator	Identities/fates/comments (where appropriate)
87	100	Ikhana Group	N6384 N64NR N64NB C-GSWK N64NB DQ-FEY N807RT
88	100	Pegasus Air Sports	N1756 VH-TGU P2-TGU P2-RDB N669JW
89	100	Mile Hi Skydiving	N125PM
90	100	(Sydney Skydiving Centre)	N950SA+ N950SM VH-OTA [+marks applied in error; wfu and b/u for spares Wilton, NSW, Australia; canx 18Jly06]
91	100	Rocky Mountain Aircraft	N8084N CF-WIA N8084N N34TC RP-C1153 C-FIBI [stored as RP-C1153 Calgary-Springbank, AB, Canada; l/n 03Feb10, fuselage only]
92	100	ex Rocky Mountain Aircraft	CF-RRH XA-HAC N525N [wfu Jan92; fuselage only at Calgary-Springbank, AB, Canada; l/n 03Feb10]
93	100	Mid Pacific Air/U S Army	N915SA+ N951SM N169TH [+ marks applied in error]
94	100	West Coast Air	PZ-TAV C-GQKN (C-GIAL)
95	100	(Kenn Borek Air)	CF-QBT C-FQBT [w/o 06Mar93 Baffin Island, NWT, Canada]
96	100	West Coast Air	CF-WTE C-FWTE
97	100	Flanagan Enterprises (Nevada)	N2715R TF-REG(1) N203EH C-FLXQ N97DZ
98	100	(Flugfelag Nordurlands)	N1371T PJ-WIB HP-771 HP-791(2) TF-JME(1) N2270D TF-JME(1) [w/o 27Jly79 Daneborg, Greenland]
99	100	Osprey Wings	CF-QBU C-FQBU 8Q-QBU C-FQBU 8Q-QBU C-GSKB N990KD C-GPVQ
100	100	(AirWest Airlines)	ST-ADC C-GPBO [w/o 01Dec77 Saturna Island near Narvaez Bay, BC, Canada; canx]
101	100	ex ERA Aviation	CF-RRX N8085N N205EH [canx Feb92; by 30Jly92 fuselage only at Calgary-Springbank, AB, Canada; l/n 03Feb10]
102	100	(Royal Flight of Nepal)	9N-RFI 9N-RF9 CF-NWV 9N-RF9 [w/o 27Feb70 Jomsom, Nepal]
103	100	Skydive Spaceland	CF-QBV C-FQBV N169BA
104	100	Perris Valley Aviation Services	N454PA N125SA
105	300	(Pilgrim Airlines)	N17132 N244GW N127PM [w/o 21Feb82 Scituate Reservoir near Providence, RI]
106	100	West Coast Air	5H-MNR CF-GQH C-FGQH 8Q-MAF C-FGQH
107	100	(Metroflight)	N17133 XA-CIN N925MA [b/u for spares May86 Opa-locka, FL]
108	100	(Liard Air)	N204E CF-AWC C-FAWC [w/o 08Jly07 Muncho Lake, BC, Canada; canx 24Oct07]
109	100	Vertical Air/Skydive Leland	N7711 N128PM C-FAPZ N C-FBHK N911BX N24HV [May97 advertised for sale as N209TS; marks not allocated or probably carried]
110	100	Freefall Express	N952SM N716NC
111	100	(Bakhtar Afghan Airlines)	YA-GAT [w/o 18Apr73 Bamiyan Airport, Afghanistan]
112	100	not yet known	ST-ADD C-GPBP N80701 N120DA+ V3-HTA N491AL N200DZ TG-JOC [+ no reports, marks probably not carried]
113	100	Rocky Mountain Aircraft	N243P N59AN RP-C1152 C-FJIW [stored Jun04 as RP-C1152 Calgary-Springbank, AB, Canada; by 29Apr07 no regn; l/n 03Feb10 fuselage only]
114	100	Freefall Express	D-IDHA SE-FTE N67CA N129PM
115	100	(Nahanni Air Services)	XA-NAC N526N C-FPPL [w/o 09Oct84 Fort Franklin, NT, Canada]
116	200	National Research Council of Canada	N954MA N594MA (N31TW) CF-POK-X CF-POK C-FPOK
117	200	Blue Wing Airlines	N7252 VH-TGV P2-TGV P2-RDD N7252 RP-C1219 P2-RDD P2-ALT VH-JEA+ PZ-TSD [+ canx to USA but not regd there]
118	200	(Mission Aviation Fellowship)	N63118 P2-MFR [wfu circa 2004 Mount Hagen, Papua New Guinea]
119	200	Twin O Inc	N63119 ZS-PDY N323SJ
120	200	Warren Transportation	N7253 VH-TGW (P2-TGW) (P2-RDF) P2-RDE P2-ALS VH-KEA N120AA N718KW
121	200	Desert Sand Aircraft Leasing	N1372T (CF-OOL) CF-QXW C-FQXW N690MF
122	200	(West Coast Air Services)	CF-WAF C-FWAF [w/o 30Sep79 Porpoise Bay, BC, Canada]
123	200	(Talair)	N7254 VH-TGX P2-TGX P2-RDC [w/o 09Sep91 Mendi, Papua New Guinea; wreck stored Mareeba, QLD, Australia]
124	200	(Corporate Air Services (Pty))	N7255 VH-TGY P2-RDH RP-C1218 P2-RDH P2-MBS (VH-MBX) [canx 12Jly01 wfu; b/u Cairns, QLD, Australia Jun01, still painted as P2-MBS]
125	200	(Arctic Guide)	N7661 N4048B [w/o 13Oct78 Barrow, AK]
126	200	(Aero Servicios Empresariales)	CF-CSG N201E (N870SA) XA-SWJ [w/o 10May96 near Santa Maria de Otalo, Mexico]
127	200	Norsk Luftfartsmuseum	LN-LMN D-IORA N25TC N54AN C-FHNM [w/o 20Jan92 Baie Comeau, PQ, Canada; canx Nov96; on display Apr99 Bodo, Norway as LN-LMN in original Wideroe's c/s]
128	200	Kavalair/Skydive Arizona	N63128 N128WJ

DE HAVILLAND CANADA DHC-6 TWIN OTTER

C/n	Model	Last known Owner/Operator	Identities/fates/comments (where appropriate)
129	200	(Carson Helicopters)	N17134 N245GW PT-WEO N245GW [w/o 09Mar96 near Bagua, Peru; canx 09Apr08]
130	300	(Bradley Air Service)	CF-DHT C-FDHT [w/o 15Mar81 Station Nord, Greenland]
131	200	(Aeroperlas)	N187SA [w/o 14Apr90 in ocean 3m S of Contadora Island, Gulf of Panama]
132	200	Fazza Sky/Dubai Skydive	CF-WZH C-FWZH N501BA RP-C1776 D-IDHB(2) F-GKHM DUSD-444 DU-SD4
133	200	Speedstar Express	N953SM N926MA
134	200	Rocky Mountain Aircraft	N1373T RP-C1155 C-FIBO [stored as RP-C1155 Calgary-Springbank, AB, Canada; by 29Apr07 no regn; l/n 03Feb10 fuselage only]
135	200	(Pace Aviation)	N303GW N53AN C-FBRA [wfu for spares Dodson Aviation, Ottawa, KS Jan96; l/n Jun06]
136	200	Argentine Army	AE-100+ AE-106
137	200	Paraguayan Air Force	ZP-GAS FAP-01+ FAP-02+ 2036 [+ Paraguay]
138	200	Transwest Air	AE-258+ LV-APT C-FGLF [+ Argentina]
139	200	(Michael C. Vinther)	N64139 (N257DP) F-OGKK F-GHSD N711SD N719AS [by 19Oct10 fuselage only Hampton-Tara Field, GA; canx 03Oct11]
140	200	(Argentine Army)	AE-259+ [+ Argentina] [w/o 06Jan75 Mt. Aconquita, Argentina]
141	200	(Bennie E Conatser)	N64141 N257DP N64141 HR-ALE N141PV [w/o 22Apr92 Perris Valley, CA; canx 06Mar03]
142	200	(Northern Thunderbird Air)	N1374T CF-MHU [w/o 30Sep75 Klua Tan Tan, BC, Canada, en-route Prince George to Dease Lake]
143	200	(Gateway Aviation)	N7662 CF-BQJ [w/o 29Jan77 Gomez Nunatak, near King George VI Sound, Antarctica]
144	200	Centre de Parachutisme Sportif	N202E (N871SA) F-GHRK
145	200	Blue Wing Airlines	N1375T D-IBFD C-GGUQ N852KB DQ-FDD VH-TZR PZ-TSH [reported for spares use]
146	200	Maldivian Air Taxi	8R-GDC C-GNTA 8Q-NTA C-GNTA 8Q-NTA 8Q-MAT
147	200	(Curtain Brothers PNG)	CP-845 N9822 XA-BOR CF-MOL C-FMOL(1) P2-OTR [w/o 26Sep89 Kiunga, Papua New Guinea; canx Apr90]
148	200	(Cable Commuter)	N7666 [w/o 23Nov68 Orange County Airport, CA]
149	200	Desert Sand Aircraft Leasing Co	F-OCLV F-GELV F-OHKF ZS-OLD ZS-ORJ 5H-MUW ZS-SBP N469TS
150	200	Perris Valley Aviation	N64150
151	200	Skydive Factory Inc	N4443 CF-JCL C-FJCL N141FS C-FJCL N203SF
152	200	Freefall Express	VP-FAO F-BRPC J2-KAA F-GHXY N40269
153	200	Flanagan Enterprises (Nevada)	N248GW (N33TW) F-BTAU C-GMJV N153KD
154	200	Nakina Outpost Camps & Air Service	N7663 D-IDHD SE-FTX TF-JMD(1) C-FDGV
155	200	Osprey Wings	EC-BPE C-GQOQ
156	200	(La Ronge Aviation Services)	N553MA CF-ZZM C-FZZM [w/o 14Jun86 west of Calgary, AB, Canada; canx Mar97]
157	200	Twin Otter International	5X-UVL N64116
158	200	Argentine AF/LADE	LV-PLM LV-JMD LV-JMP T-87(2) [originally reported as T-88, also reported there never was a T-88]
159	200	(Mountain Air Cargo)	N996SA CF-OOL C-FOOL C-GMKA N996SA [w/o 19Jan88 Charlotte, NC]
160	200	Raeford Aviation	N921HM N921MA N901BS
161	200	(Metroflight)	N922HM N922MA [w/o 01Apr83 Lawton, OK]
162	200	World Jet A/c Int'l Sales & Leasing	N997SA N559MA HC-AVN HC-AXC CF-CHE C-FCHE HR-AKN HR-ALS N162WJ [canx 12Dec94, fate unknown; possibly parted out]
163	200	(Win Win Aviation)	N7664 XA-BOA C-GFAW N201RH [w/o 31Jly00 Umstead State Park, near Raleigh-Durham, NC]
164	200	Helibits Pty	N206E P2-RDG VH-XFH P2-MBU P2-MDK P2-POM VH-XFM
165	200	Argentine AF/LADE	T-81
166	200	(Kar-Air)	N7665 OH-KOA [w/o 05Feb73 Pudasjarvi, Finland]
167	200	Argentine AF/LADE	T-82
168	200	Speedstar Express	N923HM N923MA
169	200	Aviones Taxi Aereo	CF-HMP N65169 N931MA TI-ATZ
170	200	(Argentine AF/LADE)	T-83(1) [w/o 25Mar84 Cordoba, Argentina]
171	200	(TAPSA)	0640+ LV-LNY [+ code 1-G-101 then 1-F-10] [w/o 09Aug96 near Auca Mahuida, Neuquen, Argentina, en-route Cutral Co to Rincon de los Sauces]
172	200	(Argentine Air Force)	T-84(1) [w/o 24Sep91 Base Bernardo O'Higgins, Antarctica]
173	200	Argentine AF/LADE	T-85

DE HAVILLAND CANADA DHC-6 TWIN OTTER

C/n	Model	Last known Owner/Operator	Identities/fates/comments (where appropriate)
174	300	(Mission Aviation Fellowship)	N7667 CF-QSC C-FQSC N9762E N9762J P2-MFQ [w/o 22Feb05 near Bimin, Papua New Guinea]
175	200	(New York Airways)	N558MA [w/o 15Jly69 New York-JFK, NY]
176	200	J R S Sky Inc	CF-QDM XA-BOQ N2261L C-GJAW N137JR
177	200	(Pacific Airways)	N7668 CF-DKK C-FDKK N7668 RP-C1154 [w/o 02Apr96 Manila-Ninoy Aquino, Philippines in ground collision with Boeing 737 EI-BZF]
178	200	Argentine AF/LADE	LV-PLN LV-JMR T-90
179	200	Argentine AF/LADE	LV-PLO LV-JMS T-83(2) [originally reported as T-87; also as T-89] [w/o during 1983 location unknown]
180	200	(Islena Airlines)	N66180 HR-ALH [w/o 04Apr90 near Utila Island Airport, Honduras]
181	200	Fayard Enterprises/ARKEX	5X-UVN CF-GQK C-FGQK 5X-UWV 5Y-BEK N181CS
182	200	Mission Aviation Fellowship	5X-UVP CF-GQL C-FGQL TJ-AHV P2-MFU
183	200	(Kodiak Aviation)	N7669 N103AC N103AQ [w/o 16May82 Hooper Bay, AK]
184	200	Hoppfly	N1455T 73-184+ 7184+ 184+ (LN-HJK) N184KM LN-JMP [+ Norway]
185	200	Argentine AF/LADE	LV-POO LQ-JPX LV-JPX T-89
186	200	13500 Air Express	XA-BON N54539 C-GKNR N985DL C-GKNR N142FS C-GKNR N186AL
187	200	(Mission Aviation Fellowship)	N7670 VH-GKR P2-GKR P2-RDA P2-MFS [w/o 17Dec94 en-route Tabubil-Selbang, Papua New Guinea]
188	200	(Maxfly Aviation)	N997SA CF-AIY 1277//HH-AIY+ N838MA [+ Haiti; dual marks; w/o 05Apr99 near Lantana, FL; canx 15Mar00]
189	200	(Interior Airways)	N6767 [w/o 30Jan72 in hangar fire Fairbanks, AK]
190	200	Kevin McCole/Skydive Chicago	N659E (N872SA) N930MA N220EA N190KM
191	200	Eagle Air Transport/Skydive Chicago	N66191 SE-KOK N30EA
192	200	(Mountain Air Cargo)	N7671 N3257 [w/o 11Oct85 Homer City, PA]
193	200	AerOhio Skydiving	N3434 HK-3643X N3434 [w/o 05Jun05 near Rittman, OH]
194	200	Skydive Arizona	N995SA N206EH C-FLXN N206EH N194LH
195	200	(Fairways Corp)	N7267 [w/o 20Jly88 Chantilly, near Washington-Dulles Apt, VA]
196	200	(Alaska Aeronautical Industries)	N563MA [w/o 06Sep77 Mount Iliamna, AK]
197	200	Transwest Air	N790M CF-PGE C-FPGE
198	200	Carolina Sky Sports	CF-IOH C-FIOH N198AA N30EA C-GFFN N226CS
199	200	Eagle Air Transport/Skydive Chicago	N993SA F-BSUL TF-JME(2) C-FRXU N10EA
200	200	Blue Sky Express	N66200 G-DOSH G-BUOM N123FX
201	200	(Sound Adventures)	N66201 C-GGDZ N851T N851TB [w/o 19Sep89 Sleepy Bay, AK]
202	200	Tactical Air Operations	N711AS
203	200	(Mississippi Valley Airlines)	N954SM+ N956SM [+ painted, delivered & operated as such in error; marks were current on Beech 99 c/n U-67; [w/o 09Nov70 La Crosse, WI]]
204	200	Kavalair/Skydive Arizona	CF-YLC N200EH C-FISO N204BD C-FISO V3-HTB C-FISO N204BD
205	200	Centro de Paracaidismo Costa Brava	LV-PMP LQ-JMM LV-JMM OY-PAE EC-ISV
206	200	Twin Otter International	6Y-JFX C-GNYO N753AF 5A-DCK 5A-DDZ F-GCVR N753AF [+ not fully confirmed]
207	200	(Ted McGill)	N562MA (N32TW) F-BTAO J2-KAB F-GHXZ N37ST [w/o 16Mar95 in Pacific Ocean, 300km NE of Honolulu, HI]
208	200	Sky Team Aviation	6Y-JFY HC-AZM C-GNYP HP-791(1) CP-1395 N852KB N1024A DQ-FCY RP-C663 C-GZXV N116DA C-GZXV N116DA N901ST
209	200	Adlair Aviation	N992SA N915SA C-GFYN
210	200	SSC International	CF-YFT C-FYFT PK-YPF N60619
211	200	Jump Run Aviation	N554MA N932MA V3-HTD N932MA N321CY
212	200	(ERA Helicopters)	N1456T [w/o 02Mar75 Fairbanks, AK]
213	200	(Inuvik Coastal Airways)	N955SM CF-QEH CF-GJK C-FGJK [w/o 17Dec83 Paulatuk, NT, Canada]
214	200	(Argentine AF/LADE)	LV-PMQ LQ-JMN LV-JMN T-84(2) [w/o 04Apr08 Laprida near Comodoro Rivadavia, Argentina]
215	200	(Air West Airlines)	N652MA N916SA CF-AIV C-FAIV [w/o 02Sep78 Coal Harbour, Vancouver, BC, Canada]
216	200	Skydive Arizona	N653MA N653HM N653DA N653MA N924MA
217	200	Osprey Wings	N4901W N201EH C-FLXP
218	200	Airlines of Papua New Guinea	N604MA P2-MBC VH-MBY P2-MBC VH-IPD P2-MCC
219	200	Airlines of Papua New Guinea	N5216 VH-BMG P2-MFY P2-MCR

DE HAVILLAND CANADA DHC-6 TWIN OTTER

C/n	Model	Last known Owner/Operator	Identities/fates/comments (where appropriate)
220	200	(Ashe Aircraft Enterprises)	N654MA (CF-BDA) VP-BDA C6-BDA C-GJLZ [b/u for parts May95 Calgary-Springbank, AB, Canada; wings only noted 22Jly10]
221	200	Win Win Aviation	CF-YTH C-FYTH N800LJ HP-1224XI C-FQIM CU-T130 C-FQIM DQ-FIL N301CL
222	200	(Eastland Air)	VP-BDB C6-BDB C-GSFC N5593K P2-RDF P2-ALU (VH-HEA) [b/u for spares Sep00 Toowoomba, QLD, Australia; by Mar04 remains to Thunder Bay, ON, Canada]
223	200	Parachutisme Nouvel Air	CF-YPP C-FYPP HI-367 C-FYPP N223AL
224	200	ex Maldivian Air Taxi	(N657MA)+ (N110TM)+ XA-BOL C-GENT 8Q-ENT C-GENT 8Q-MAG [+ both sets of marks painted on aircraft, but not delivered; w/o 01Jun09 Halaveli Atoll, Maldives]
225	200	Argentine AF/LADE	T-86
226	200	Air Tindi/Tli Cho Air	N655MA VH-ATK 8Q-HIB N153BU C-FATN
227	200	(Pan-Air)	(N656MA) (N111TM) XA-BOM N54540 VH-PAQ [w/o 13Feb79 Yarra Creek, King Island, TAS, Australia]
228	200	Skydiving Productions Over Texas	CF-PAE C-FPAE N228YK
229	200	(Newcal Aviation/Downeast Airlines)	N659MA N68DE [w/o 30May79 Knox County Airport, Owls Head, ME; not canx until 23Apr09]
230	200	(Argentine Air Force)	T-87(1) [w/o 07Aug77 between Bariloche & Comodoro Rivadavia, Argentina]
231	200	not yet known	N660MA N168SG+ RDPL- [+ canx 22Dec11 to Laos]
232	300	Ontario Ministry of Natural Resources	CF-OPG C-FOPG
233	300	Zimex Aviation	CF-FTC 5N-AMO 8Q-HIK 5N-BBT D-IXXY PK-LTX HB-LUE
234	300	Trans Maldivian Airways	N2711H N3H N279WW N705PV C-FBZN 8Q-TMO
235	300	not yet known	N6868 OY-POF TF-POF+ P2- [+ canx 15Apr11 to Papua New Guinea]
236	300	(Coastair)	(CF-TAX) N774M N76214 [w/o 13Jly78 Candor, NC; fuselage to Calgary-Springbank, AB, Canada; l/n 18Aug99; aft fuselage only by 10Sep08]
237	300	Transportes Aereos Terrestres	XA-TAT
238	300	Zimex Aviation	CF-WAA C-FWAA N5584H ST-AHT C-GHTO HB-LTR
239	300	JHH Aircraft	CF-YZD N13239 N15239 N239Z
240	300	Manitoba Government Air Service	CF-WAH C-FWAH
241	300*	Monarch Enterprises/Scenic Airlines	N385EX N142SA
242	300	Air Service Gabon	CF-NAN C-FNAN TR-LGU
243	300	Ontario Ministry of Natural Resources	CF-OPI C-FOPI [floatplane]
244	310	Compania Minera Atacocha SA	N100AS PZ-TAX C-GBPV VH-TNM P2-IAA N244MV N804AS C-FBLY CC-PQI
245	300	(Newcal Aviation/Air New England)	N383EX [w/o 17Jun79 Barnstable Airport, Cape Cod, MA; not canx until 23Apr09]
246	300	(Bradley Air Services)	CF-QDG VP-BDD CF-QDG C-FQDG [w/o 23Aug78 Frobisher Bay, NU, Canada]
247	300*	Ikhana Group	N384EX C-GOES N224SA
248	300	(Grand Canyon Airlines)	N368EX N76GC [w/o 18Jun86 near Grand Canyon Airport, AZ; canx Jly94]
249	300	SVG Air/Grenadine Airways	N9766 N23RM 5N-BAM N23FL 5N-BAM N15GL 8P-ERK V2-LGF J8-VBS
250	300	(Goroka Air Services)	CF-JCS C-FJCS N250CM ZK-OTR YJ-RV8(1) P2-RDX P2-MMU [w/o 18Jly97 near Goroka, Papua New Guinea]
251	300	(Air America)	N310MA N389EX [w/o 28Apr74 Sala Phou Khoun, Laos; b/u Aug74 Udon Thani, Thailand; canx 22Aug74]
252	300	(Am-Son Drilling Company)	N301MA HC-AXN N252M N252MM HK-1710W [w/o 19Dec79 near Cucuta, Colombia]
253	300*	Monarch Enterprises/Scenic Airlines	N112TM N649MA N699MA N669MA N22RM N54SA N103AC N228SA
254	300	(Air Caraibes)	N302MA F-OGES [w/o 24Mar01 St Barthelemy, Guadeloupe, French West Indies]
255	300	(Air Regional)	N200AS PZ-TAY+ PZ-TCB C-GBNI VH-TNS YJ- VH-TNS P2-IAE PK-WAX [+ often reported with these marks but was probably ntu or guess work; Canadian records state ex PZ-TCB] [w/o 19Jan04 Mulia Airport, Indonesia; 29Aug06 remains to Cairns, QLD, Australia; l/n 29Jly07]
256	300	Maldivian Air Taxi	N661MA HK-3219X N661MA H4-SIB 8Q-MBC
257	300	Sirte Oil Company	CF-TSN N304MA N2005 5A-DKE
258	300	(Air Guadeloupe)	N303MA F-OGFE [w/o 21Dec72 off St.Maarten, Netherlands Antilles]

DE HAVILLAND CANADA DHC-6 TWIN OTTER

C/n	Model	Last known Owner/Operator	Identities/fates/comments (where appropriate)
259	300	Maldivian Air Taxi	(CF-QEI) CF-AJK ZK-CJZ CF-KBI C-FKBI HP-1197APPC-FKBI 8Q-MAO C-FKBI 8Q-MAO
260	300	Osprey Wings	N9767 (CF-JCE) CF-CDM CF-JCH SE-GEG OH-SLK C-FVEG
261	300	(Air Regional)	N305MA CF-IOJ C-FIOJ VH-IAM P2-IAF PK-WAY [w/o 27Mar03 Mulia Airport, Indonesia]
262	300	(Atlantic City Airlines)	N306MA N101AC [w/o 12Dec76 Cape May County Airport, Wildwood, NJ]
263	300*	Grand Canyon Airlines	N310MA N102AC N177GC
264	300*	Grand Canyon Airlines	N13264 N264Z N72GC
265	300	Air Tindi	N93985 (VH-TGE) N94457 AP-AXP C-GABJ N4993X N304PC C-FATM PJ-ATL C-FATM
266	300	Peruvian Air Force	N307MA CF-AKZ 9V-BCE XW-PGV N85TC 308//OB-1157 [dual marks]
267	300*	Nature Air	N387EX N140SA TI-BDZ
268	300	(Bradley Air Services)	N308MA N3526 HC-AUL CF-DIJ [w/o 28Jan74 Carp, ON, Canada]
269	300	Ashe Aircraft Enterprises	N5217 VH-PGS CF-JJF N928MA C-GKBO(2) HP-1283APP (TG-AGD) C-GHKL
270	300	Trans Maldivian Airways	N93995 VH-TGF VH-UQR N270CM 8Q-TMR
271	300	(Solomon Islands Airways)	N5218 VH-PGT CF-JJI AP-AXH N9090Z H4-SIA VH-NIO H4-SIA [w/o 27Sep91 near Honiara, Solomon Islands]
272	300	ex North-Wright Airways	N388EX N272Z C-GBEB 8Q-SUN C-FFGZ+ C-GBEB [+marks not fully confirmed, probably ntu; and no reports as such] [w/o 16Jly08 near Hook Lake, NWT, Canada; by 10Sep08 fuselage only Calgary-Springbank, AB, Canada]
273	300	Maldivian Air Taxi	CF-IOK C-FIOK 8Q-LEN C-FIOK 8Q-LEN C-FIOK 8Q-IOK 8Q-MAD C-FIOK 8Q-MAD C-FAKB 8Q-MAD C-FAKB N12326 C-FAKB 8Q-MAD
274	300	Peruvian Air Force	9V-BCF XW-PHF N86TC 305//OB-1154 [dual marks]
275	300	(Milne Bay Air)	CF-BEL N65308 SE-GTU N126PM P2-MBI [w/o 12Jly95 near Alotau, Papua New Guinea]
276	300	Kenn Borek Air/Sri Lankan Air Taxi	CF-MPB C-FMPB C-FBBA 8Q-MAK C-FBBA 8Q-MAK C-FBBA
277	320	Air Loyaute	N8861 VH-TGG HB-LSU (ZS-OVL) F-OIJI
278	300	(Kenn Borek Air)	CF-ABW C-FABW [w/o 21Dec77 near Nanisivik, NT, Canada]
279	300	Maldivian Air Taxi	N5227 VH-PGU N934MA C-GKBM 8Q-KBM C-GKBM 8Q-MAI
280	300	Airlines of Papua New Guinea	9V-BCJ XW-PHP 9V-BCJ ZS-JEU 7P-AAE VR-CAV VH-AQB P2-RDZ(2)+ P2-GVI VH-FNT H4-FNT VH-FNT H4-FNT P2-MCV [+marks not fully confirmed]
281	320	ex Air Guyane Express	N8336 VH-TGH HB-LSV F-OIJL [stored by Jan12 Berne, Switzerland]
282	300	Servicios Aereos de Los Andes	9V-BCK XW-PHQ+ N2656 C-GGHC J6-SLG J8-VAL F-OGNC C-FGHX P2-RDY VH-XFB C-FFNM CC-PCI C-FFNM CC-PCI OB-1864
283	300	Maldivian Air Taxi	N8339 VH-TGI N616BA HB-LSY SX-BVP D-IBVP 8Q-MBD
284	300	(Panamanian Air Force)	HP-101 FAP-205 [w/o 02Aug81 into jungle in Panama]
285	300	Grand Canyon Airlines	9V-BCL XW-PHS A-060+ XW-PKH 9V-BCL JA8797 N60ME N190GC TI-BDM N190GC TI-BDM N190GC [+ marks believed used whilst being operated by Air America in Laos]
286	300	Neos Argentina S.A.	N8286 F-OCQD P2-RDI VH-FNU F-OAIY VH-FNU N969AC
287	300	Kenn Borek Air	N622MA 5A-DBC F-GBDD N2303X N918MA C-GKBV 8Q-KBV 8Q-MAB C-GKBV 8Q-MAB C-GKBV 8Q-MAB C-GKBV
288	300	Maldivian Air Taxi	HC-ASJ N26TC N288Z C-GFXJ N288Z C-FCUS VH-TGC HB-LSP ZS-OVD TR-LGS N102SK 8Q-MBG
289	300	Mission Aviation Fellowship	N623MA 5A-DBD F-GBDE N48MK N9041Q N127AP C-GOPR N910H N910HD P2-MFB
290	300	(Milne Bay Air)	CF-ZKP C-FZKP N442CA C-FZKP P2-MBB [w/o 09Jly96 Clancys Knob, near Mendi, Papua New Guinea]
291	300	Labrador Airways	AP-AWF F-BTOO+ C-FOPN^ [+ wfu Apr97 Brazzaville, People's Republic of Congo; fuselage remains only noted 26Jly07 Calgary-Springbank, AB, Canada; ^ l/n 03Feb10 on rebuild]
292	300	French Air Force	AP-AWG F-BTOQ 292+ [code CC] [+ also wearing F-RACC in 2011]
293	300	(Pakistan International Airlines)	AP-AWH [w/o 05Dec71 Dacca-Kurmitola Airport, East Pakistan in air raid]
294	300	(Evergreen Helicopters)	LN-BEN C-GBDG N8061V [w/o 03Dec79 en-route Nome to Shishmaref, AK]
295	300*	Grand Canyon Airlines	LN-BEO C-GDJK N50RP N144SA(1) N173GC C-GLAZ N173GC
296	300	Air Labrador	LN-BEP (C-GBDI) HZ-PL5 N5377G C-GLAI
297	300*	Cortez Fisher LLC/Scenic Airlines	LN-BER C-GESV N852TB N297SA

DE HAVILLAND CANADA DHC-6 TWIN OTTER

C/n	Model	Last known Owner/Operator	Identities/fates/comments (where appropriate)
298	300	French Air Force	AP-AWJ F-BTOR 298+ F-RACD^ [+ call sign F-RACD; code CD; ^ by Sep09 only wears these marks and no titles]
299	300	PT Aviastar Mandiri	AP-AWK F-BTOS SE-GRI LN-FAL C-GNTH N321EA C- N321EA C-FPNZ PK-BRS
300	300	SIFORCO	AP-AWL F-BTOT 300+ 9Q-CJD(2) [+ France; code CE]
301	300	(Royal Nepal Airlines)	9N-ABA [w/o 09Jun91 Lukla, Nepal]
302	300	Royal Nepal Airlines	9N-ABB
303	300	Ashe Aircraft Enterprises	13801+ N774A C-FUGP C-FMOL(2) [+ Canada CC-138; by 29Apr07 fuselage only stored Calgary-Springbank, AB, Canada; l/n 03Feb10]
304	300	Canadian Armed Forces	13802 [CC-138]
305	300	Canadian Armed Forces	13803 [CC-138]
306	300	Canadian Armed Forces	13804 [CC-138]
307	300	Canadian Armed Forces	13805 [CC-138]
308	300	Arctic Sunwest Charters	13806+ N776A C-FTXQ [+ Canada CC-138]
309	300	(Canadian Armed Forces)	13807 [CC-138] [w/o 14Jun86 near Calgary, AB, Canada]
310	300	(Canadian Armed Forces)	13808 [CC-138] [w/o 05Dec71 Kashmir, Pakistan in Indian AF air raid]
311	300	Kenn Borek Air	CF-MPC C-FMPC C-FBBV
312	300	Kenn Borek Air	CF-MPF C-FMPF C-GCKB
313	320	(PT Regional Air)	N4977 F-OCQF P2-RDJ VH-FNV PK-WAR [w/o 28Apr03 Mulia Airport, Indonesia]
314	300	(Kenn Borek Air)	300+ (C-GJJL) C-GKBD HK-3538X C-GKBD [+ Peru] [w/o 23Nov94 Rothera Station, Adelaide Island, Antarctica; canx May97]
315	300	(Peruvian Air Force)	303 [w/o 10Jly74 near Andoas, Peru]
316	300	(TA Nationales de la Selva)	304//OB-R1153+ OB-1153 [+ Peru; dual marks; w/o 27Aug92 Peruvian Amazon near Rio Algodon, Iquitos, Peru]
317	300	(Peruvian Air Force)	307//OB-1156 [dual marks] [w/o 18Dec84 Jaen, Peru]
318	300	(Air Madagascar)	5R-MGA [w/o 20Apr86 Ambatondrazaka, Madagascar]
319	300	(Royal Canadian Mounted Police)	CF-MPH C-FMPH [w/o 27May89 Colville Lake, NT, Canada]
320	300	Royal Canadian Mounted Police	CF-MPL C-FMPL
321	300	Kenn Borek Air/Sri Lankan Air Taxi	CF-MPN C-FMPN C-GBBU 8Q-MAL C-GBBU 8Q-MAL C-GLKB
322	300	Peruvian Air Force	312//OB-R1160+ 312//OB-1160+ [+ dual marks]
323	300	(Peruvian Air Force)	313 [w/o in 1980 near Yarinacocha, Peru]
324	300	(Peruvian Air Force)	317//OB-R1161 [dual marks] [w/o 09Mar12 Laguna de Caballocoha, Peru]
325	300	Air Inuit	318//OB-R1162+ OB-1162 (N95NC) C-FTJJ 8Q-MAJ C-FTJJ (N93NC) [+ dual marks]
326	300	(Air America)	N5662 [w/o 25Jly72 north of Vientiane, Laos]
327	300	(Air Madagascar)	5R-MGB [w/o 24Jly81 en-route Toamasina-Andapa, Madagascar]
328	300	Air Madagascar	5R-MGC
329	300	Air Madagascar	5R-MGD
330	300	Airlines of Papua New Guinea	5R-MGE N901WW P2-MCZ [serious damage 15May12 Sasaremi airstrip, Papua New Guinea]
331	300	Ariana Afghan Airlines	YA-GAX
332	300	(Bakhtar Afghan Airlines)	YA-GAY [w/o 08Jan85 Bamiyan, Afghanistan]
333	300	(British Antarctic Survey)	VP-FAP (C-GNYX) [w/o 21Jan77 Gomez Nunatak, near King George VI Sound, Antarctica]
334	300	Fayard Enterprises	CF-TVO C-FTVO F-GUTH ZS-OUJ N344CS
335	300	(Norontair)	CF-TVP C-FTVP [w/o 30Dec77 Kenora, ON, Canada]
336	300	Ashraf	D-IDHB(1) HB-LOI 5Y-JHZ
337	300	Twin Otter International	CF-DHA JA8798 N2886Z N56SP N2886Z N331SA TI-BAF N331SA N331AR
338	300	Kenn Borek Air	CF-DHB C-FDHB
339	300	Kenn Borek Air	CF-KAS N983FL N916MA C-GOKB 8Q-MAM C-GOKB 8Q-MAM C-GOKB
340	300	Arctic Sunwest Charters	CF-TFX C-FTFX
341	300	(Inter Atoll Air)	LN-BEC C-GFLS LN-WFC C-GFLS 8Q-GIA [w/o 07Feb87 in sea off Maldives]
342	300	(Corporate Air)	CF-DJF EC-CAO F-BYAG C-FHPG N242CA [ditched 13Apr97 in Pacific Ocean off Hilo, HI; canx Apr98]
343	300	Washington Corporation	CF-WAG C-FWAG N90WF N86LU N167WC
344	300	Ontario Ministry of Natural Resources	CF-OPJ C-FOPJ
345	300	(Merpati Nusantara Airlines)	PK-NUE [w/o 15Sep89 Bintuni, Indonesia]
346	300	(Merpati Nusantara Airlines)	PK-NUG [w/o 12Aug85 Mulia, Irian Jaya, Indonesia]

DE HAVILLAND CANADA DHC-6 TWIN OTTER

C/n	Model	Last known Owner/Operator	Identities/fates/comments (where appropriate)
347	300	Air Serv International	VP-FAQ (C-GNYY) G-BKBC LN-FKB N899AS [has UN & UNICEF titles]
348	300	Kenn Borek Air	CF-GOG C-FGOG
349	300	(Ptarmigan Airways)	CF-WAB C-FWAB [w/o 06Jun90 Thistle Lake, NT, Canada; canx Apr91]
350	300	Aerotecnia	CF-WAC N90503 N305EH N253SA N258SA YV-1034C N53AR N258SA
351	300	Zimex Aviation	CF-CST C-FCST N353PM J8-VBP N353PM HB-LUC
352	300	Provincial Airlines	CF-CSU C-FCSU N300EH C-GIMK
353	300	(Airlines of Papua New Guinea)	LN-BNX C-FWAX P2-MBA [w/o 29Jly04 en-route Port Moresby – Ononge, Papua New Guinea]
354	300	(Canadian Department of Transport)	CF-CSV C-FCSV [w/o 27Feb81 Galt, ON, Canada]
355	300	Alkan Air	CF-CSW C-FCSW
356	300	PT Aviastar Mandiri	CF-GJT JA8790 N972SW PK-BRP [serious damage 30Jan08 Sugapa, Indonesia]
357	300	ex BBS Aircraft	CF-CSX C-FCSX+ PK- [+ canx 21Mar12 to Indonesia]
358	300	Winair	CF-CSY C-FCSY PJ-WIL
359	300*	Twin Otter International	D-IDHC N149SA N410LP N149SA PJ-TSA N149SA PJ-TSB N149SA PJ-TSC N149SA PJ-TSD N149SA N359AR
360	300	Air Panama	LN-BNY C-FWUL 6Y-JMQ C-FWUL HP-1509PS HP-1509APP HP-1509PS
361	300	(Transwestern)	N361V [w/o 15Feb83 Friedman Memorial Airport, Hailey, ID]
362	300	Air Inuit	CF-ASS N304EH C-FASS C-FAIY
363	300	(YPF Bolivianos)	CP-1018 [w/o 19May87 Santa Cruz-El Trompillo, Bolivia]
364	300	Skydive Airlines	D-IDOT SE-GEE F-GFAH SE-GEE
365	300	Twin Otter International	N544N N144SA(2) N97AR PJ-TSE N97AR
366	300	(Talair)	F-OGGG P2-RDW [w/o 21Jly89 near Porgera, Papua New Guinea]
367	300	(Arctic Sunwest Charters)	N200DA C-GARW [w/o 22Sep11 Yellowknife-Waterdrome, NT, Canada]
368	300	Procuraduria General de la Republica	CP-1019 XA-TTU+ XC-ALA+ [+ both Mexican marks & owner are suspect; however XC-ALA has been reported as a Twin Otter in Mexico]
369	300	Labrador Airways	CF-GON C-FGON
370	300	(Royal Nepal Airlines)	9N-ABG [w/o 15Oct73 Lukla Airport, Nepal]
371	300	Alkan Air	SE-GEA F-GFAG C-FKKV LN-FAP VH-NTO N371AM C-GGMV PJ-TOC HC-CES N371SS C-FCPV
372	300	Alberta Central Airways	N24RM 5N-BAN N17GL C-FTWU
373	300	Hevi-Lift	CF-ASG C-FASG P2-KSP
374	300	Maldivian Air Taxi	SE-GEB F-GFAF C-FMYV P2-MBK C-FMYV 8Q-MAH C-FMYV 8Q-MAH
375	300	Maldivian Air Taxi	SE-GEC F-GFAE C-FKDN TR-LDH F-GJDS C-GHAZ SX-BMG C-GIZQ 8Q-MBF
376	300	(Royal Nepal Airlines)	9N-ABH [w/o 22Dec84 Mount Burj Lek near Bhojpur, Nepal]
377	300	(Kenn Borek Air)	CF-SJB C-FSJB N4901D C-FSJB [w/o sank through ice 92nm N of Alert, NU, Canada; canx 30May11]
378	300	Peruvian Air Force	302//OB-R1152 [dual marks] [302 is now c/n 858; fate/status unknown]
379	300	(Peruvian Air Force)	305//OB-R1155 [dual marks] [w/o 21Oct92 near Lake Caballococha, Peru; to spares use White Industries, Bates City, MO]
380	300	PT Aviastar Mandiri	6V-ADD C-GHBP (F-GUTR) PK-BRT
381	300	Air Work Leasing/Air Caledonie Int'l	TZ-ACD F-GGKA N26KH 6Y-JMV VH-RPZ F-OIAQ
382	300	Seabird Airlines	13809+ C-FSLR 13809+ N677A (P2-KSK) N677A C-FUGT 8Q-MAR C-FUGT TC-SBA [+ Canada; CC-138] [floatplane]
383	300	Merpati Nusantara Airlines	PK-NUH
384	300	(Peruvian Air Force)	309//OB-R-1158 [dual marks] [w/o 28Nov83 Trompeteros, Peru]
385	300	Peruvian Air Force	311//OB-R-1159 [dual marks]
386	300	Merpati Nusantara Airlines	PK-NUI
387	300	(Rocky Mountain Airways)	N25RM [w/o 04Dec78 near Steamboat Springs, CO; canx Apr81]
388	300	Twin Otter International	N529N N245SA N94AR
389	300*	Montecito New York	N24KA N238SA V2-LEY N288SA V2-LEY N288SA [reports of being YN-CHQ incorrect; see c/n 766]
390	300	(Merpati Nusantara Airlines)	PK-NUK [w/o 10Jan95 Molo Strait, East Nusa Tenggara, Indonesia]
391	300	Servicios Aereos de Los Andes	PK-NUL C-GHVV OB-1913-P
392	300	(Royal Nepal Airlines)	9N-ABI [w/o 17Jan95 Kathmandu, Nepal]
393	300	(Air Senegal)	6V-ADE [w/o 09Dec93 near Dakar, Senegal in mid-air collision with YS-11 C5-GAA]
394	300	(Air Mali)	TZ-ACH [w/o 21Jun83 Niela, near Bamako, Mali]
395	300	(Bakhtar Afghan Airlines)	YA-GAZ [w/o 10Mar83 in mountains near Ghazni, Afghanistan]

DE HAVILLAND CANADA DHC-6 TWIN OTTER

C/n	Model	Last known Owner/Operator	Identities/fates/comments (where appropriate)
396	300	(Chilean Air Force)	CC-CAE 943 [w/o 11Jly80 on approach to Santiago-Los Cerrillos, Chile]
397	300	Chilean Air Force	CC-CBB 944
398	300	Chilean Air Force	CC-CBF 945
399	300	Chilean Air Force	CC-CBH 946
400	300	J D Melvin	N25KA N22RM N137AP C-GPPT N35HB C-GPPT N2916N N177TA C-GJAT N707PV N6218T
401	300	Viking Air Ltd	N540N C-FVLT [w/o 12Mar85 near Barter Island, AK; fuselage stored by Newcal Aviation at Teterboro, NJ by Oct00; canx 04Aug11 to Canada probably for parts]
402	300	Kenn Borek Air/Allegiance Airways	N980FL N546N F-GFYE 5N-ATM V3-HFM N546N HP-1308APP C-GHRE N204SA C-FHKB
403	300	ex Aeroperlas	HP-747 HP-747APP [damaged 16May09; by 05Sep10 no wings or tail Panama City-Gelabert, Panama]
404	300	(Chilean Air Force)	CC-CBM 947 [w/o 02Jly08 between Puerto Montt and Cochamo, Chile]
405	300	(Chilean Air Force)	CC-CBU 948 [w/o 12Jly80 40km east of Santiago-Los Cerrillos, Chile]
406	300*	Grand Canyon Airlines	N300SP AP-AYF N300SP N101AC N171GC 8P-JML N171GC J8-VBR N171GC
407	300	Ashe Aircraft Enterprises	LN-BNB C-FVFK HP-1281APPC-GHMV
408	300	(Wideroes Flyveselskap)	LN-BNM [w/o 27Oct93 Namsos, Norway]
409	300*	Zuni LLC/Scenic Airlines	N981FL N548N N148SA
410	300	Pacific Sun Airlines	(JA8796) C-GOAX JA8796 N974SW CC-CHL N974SW VQ-TVG N974SW D2-PSE
411	300	Aerotrans Flugcharter	C-FHBR HK-2950 C-FHBR LN-FKC CS-TFF LN-FKG SE-IYP D-IVER
412	300	Aircalin	F-OCQZ
413	300	Norlandair	D-IDLT SE-GRX C-GIZR TF-JMC TF-NLC
414	300	Pacific Sun Airlines	G-BDHC N38535 VQ-TGW N38535 DQ-PSD
415	300	(Bradley Air Services)	C-GROW [w/o 29Aug79 Frobisher Bay, NT, Canada; canx Nov81]
416	300	(Cameroon Airlines)	TJ-CDA+ TJ-CBC [+ painted on aircraft; reg'n changed before delivery; w/o 31Oct81 Bafoussam, Cameroon]
417	300	(Kenn Borek Air)	C-GBDR C-GKBM [w/o 18Jly88 near John Day, OR]
418	300	(Peruvian Air Force)	333 [w/o 15Dec76 Iquitos, Peru]
419	300	(Servicios Aereos Ejecutivos)	N300JF N303EH HK-2920 [w/o 11Oct87 El Poleo, Colombia; canx 12Dec94]
420	300	Zimex Aviation	C-GOWO JA8799 D-ISKY(2) PK-YRF(1) PK-TWG HB-LUM
421	300*	Fairey Ltd	C-GREN N545N N232SA TI-BBR N821AR
422	300	Aereo Ruta Maya	EC-CJI F-OGJV TI-AYQ TG-JCE
423	300	US Department of Interior	N490AS N49SJ
424	310	Airkenya Express	N26RM HZ-PL3 N999AK 5Y-BHR ZS-OVJ 5Y-BPW ZS-LGN 5Y-GGG ZS-LGN 5Y-PJP
425	300	National Iranian Oil Company	EP-IOE
426	300	Kenn Borek Air	YV-0-MC7+ C-GXXB N97333 C-GXXB 8Q-MAN(1) C-GXXB [+ painted on aircraft; but not delivered]
427	300	(First Air)	C-GNDN VQ-TAN C-GNDN [w/o 12Aug96 Markham Bay, Baffin Island, NU, Canada; canx Dec96 wfu]
428	300	(de Havilland Canada)	C-GDHA [w/o 03May76 near Monze, Zambia]
429	300	Rampart Aviation	N35062 N162DE
430	300	Air Inuit	C-GNDO
431	300	(South Pacific Island Airways)	N23BC [w/o 05Nov79 Tau Island, American Samoa]
432	300	Twin Otter International	8R-GEI N254SA N63AR
433	300*	Nature Air	8R-GEJ N81215 N239SA DQ-AFL N239SA DQ-AFL N239SA TI-AZC
434	400	Viking Air	N26KA G-BHFD N703PV C-FYUS N927MA C-GCGW 8Q-SUM 8Q-TMC C-FDHT [badly damaged 17May04 as 8Q-TMC; 300 series re-built as prototype series 400 by Viking Air; f/f 01Oct08; floatplane]
435	300	Maldivian Air Taxi	N27RM N127RL HK-2625X N127RL TF-ORN TG-JAZ C-FWKZ 8Q-MAN(2)
436	300	(Ecuadorian Air Force)	C-GNSD FAE-450 [w/o 06Apr94 Mount Lozan, Ecuador]
437	300	US Forest Service	D-IDCT N97847 N300LJ 87-0802 N300LJ N143Z
438	300	Air Tindi	N546N C-GMAS
439	300	(Grand Canyon Airlines)	N62145 N300EH N409RA N75GC [w/o 27Sep89 Grand Canyon, AZ; canx Mar94]
440	300	Twin Otter International	N547N N233SA N83AR
441	300	Airlines of Papua New Guinea	C-GNHB P2-MCB [w/o 11Aug09 near Kokoda, Papua New Guinea]
442	310	Solomon Airlines	3B-NAB YJ-RV9(1) VH-XFE P2-RDZ(1) VH-XFE H4-SID

DE HAVILLAND CANADA DHC-6 TWIN OTTER

C/n	Model	Last known Owner/Operator	Identities/fates/comments (where appropriate)
443	300	Merpati Nusantara Airlines	PK-NUM PK-NUZ
444	300	Zuetina Oil	5A-DBJ
445	300	(Maldivian Air Taxi)	LN-BNJ C-FVBH HP-1276APP C-FDKB 8Q-MAS [floatplane; sunk in shallow water 14Jly08 Adaaran Club, Bathala, Maldives]
446	300	(Ecuadorian Air Force/TAME)	FAE-446//HC-BCG [dual marks] [w/o 20Nov84 en-route Loja to Zumba, Ecuador]
447	300	Winair	C-GPAO N5356A C-GPAO PJ-WIS
448	300*	Aerocord	HP-710 FAP-210 N7020J N234SA DQ-AFM N448CS CC-CST CC-PUK CC-CFN
449	300	Maldivian Air Taxi	TG-CAC C-FWKQ 8Q-MAF
450	300	Air Labrador	C-GNQY
451	300	Alberta Central Airways	C-GNWC TN-ACW C-FINM C-FTSU
452	300	(Lina Congo)	C-GNWD TN-ACX [w/o 12Mar92 Etsouali, Congo-Brazzaville]
453	300	(Ecuadorian Air Force/TAME)	FAE-453//HC-BAV [dual marks] [w/o 02Sep80 24 de Mayo Airstrip, Ecuador]
454	300	Trans Maldivian Airways	N301EH N454MG N885EA C-FNBI 8Q-TMT
455	300	Tara Air	N302EH 9N-ABM
456	300	TAPSA Aviacion	LV-PTW LV-LSI
457	300	(Ecuadorian Air Force/TAME)	FAE-457//HC-BAX [dual marks] [w/o 21May81 near Zumba, Ecuador]
458	300	(Trigana Air Service)	LV-PTX LV-LSJ N685RJ PK-YPZ [w/o 25May02 50km from Nabire, Indonesia]
459	300	(Merpati Nusantara Airlines)	PK-NUY [w/o 30Dec87 near Samarinda, Indonesia]
460	300	National Iranian Oil Company	EP-IOD
461	300	(Provincial Airlines/Innu Mikun Airlines)	PK-NUX C-FIZD [damaged 05Apr08 landing on frozen lake 150km from Nain, NL, Canada; a few weeks later whilst being recovered dropped from sling under a helicopter and w/o; regd 10Feb09 to Ashe Aircraft Enterprises Inc for possible rebuild or parts recovery]
462	300	Trigana Air Service	C-GGVX D-ISKY(1) PK-YRF(2)
463	300	(Northern Thunderbird Air)	JA8802+ C-GNTB [+painted on aircraft but not delivered; w/o 14Jan77 near Terrace, BC, Canada]
464	300	Kenn Borek Air	D-IKST SE-GED C-GNXH N92WF C-GNXH N706PV C-FPOQ P2-MBL C-FPOQ 8Q-MAE C-FPOQ 8Q-MAE C-GPOQ
465	300	(Frontier Airlines)	N982FL [w/o 18Jan78 Pueblo Memorial Airport, CO]
466	300	Swiss Federal Office of Topography	C-GPXO-X HB-LID T-741
467	300	ex Air Labrador	N404BG N404X N887EA C- N887EA C-FOIM 8Q-TMU
468	300	Twin Otter International	N214SA N104AC N229SA C-FWCA N229SA J6-AAP N229SA
469	300	(Air Guadeloupe)	F-OGHD [w/o 18Nov78 near Marie Galante Island, West Indies]
470	300	Ikhana Group	F-ODBN N805RT
471	300	Provincial Airlines	C-GMPK C-GJDE
472	300	Merpati Nusantara Airlines	PK-NUV
473	300	(Merpati Nusantara Airlines)	PK-NUT [w/o 17Jly95 Bintuni, Indonesia]
474	300	(Merpati Nusantara Airlines)	PK-NUW [w/o 23May87 near Ruteng, Flores Island, Indonesia]
475	300	Norlandair	C-GDAA TF-JMD(2) TF-NLD
476	310	Winair	5N-AKP PH-STJ 5N-AKP TJ-SAC N476R PJ-WJR
477	300	Grenadine Airways	C-GGAA N7138K HK-3777X HK-3777 8P-MLK J8-SUN
478	300	(Merpati Nusantara Airlines)	PK-NUU [w/o 06Aug99 Irian Jaya, Indonesia]
479	300	Blue Bird Airlines/UNICEF	C-GDVN-X ST-AFP
480	300	Southwest Air	TR-LVW P2-RDL P2-SWE
481	300	Merpati Nusantara Airlines	PK-NUS
482	300	Air Madagascar	5R-MGF
483	300	Peruvian Air Force	303//OB-1336 [dual marks] [w/o 24May07 in mountains en-route Orellana to Pampa Hermosa, Peru]
484	300	Merpati Nusantara Airlines	PK-NUR
485	300	Hevi-Lift	N76PH N117AP C-GPPY HK-2921 CP-2035 P2-HCX VH-RPU P2-KSB
486	300	(Merpati Nusantara Airlines)	PK-NUP [w/o 29Mar77 Bairaha Valley, Sulawesi, Indonesia]
487	300	Merpati Nusantara Airlines	PK-NUO
488	300	Merpati Nusantara Airlines	PK-NUQ [w/o 03Apr90 Laboehan Ree, Indonesia]
489	300	Perris Valley Aviation	C-GDMP N708PV
490	300	(Air Burkina)	N376US XT-AAX [w/o 08Oct88 Dori, Burkina Faso]
491	300	Solomon Airlines	HP-730 HP-730AP YJ-RV1(2) H4-NNP
492	300	Osprey Wings	C-GPBR JA8802 N300BC C-GIGK
493	300	Air Labrador	N72348 N148DE C-GKSN
494	300	Kenn Borek Air	C-GDHC
495	300	US Army	76-22565 [UV-18A]

DE HAVILLAND CANADA DHC-6 TWIN OTTER

C/n	Model	Last known Owner/Operator	Identities/fates/comments (where appropriate)
496	300	US Dept of the Navy	76-22566 [UV-18A] N83NX [also wears serial 762256 at base of tail and code 256 on nose]
497	300	(ACES Colombia)	HK-1910 [w/o 23Jan85 en-route Quibdo-Medellin, Colombia]
498	300	(Trigana Air Service)	F-OGHO N8431H PK-YPQ [w/o 03Sep02 Silimo, Papua, Indonesia]
499	300	Air Seychelles	XY-AEA PH-STB S7-AAJ
500	300	ex Air Moorea	N929MA F-OHJF HB-
501	300	(Burma Airways)	XY-AEB [w/o 12Aug82 near Mindat, Burma]
502	300	Star Aviation	OY-ATB D-IASD F-ODGI N555WJ 5Y-UAU HB-LRS 7T-VND
503	300	Greenwood Group	XY-AEC PH-STC 5Y-SKT N504WJ
504	300	Ethiopian Army	C-GQFE EA-61+ ET-AID EA-61 [+ Ethiopia]
505	300	Zimex Aviation	C-GPJA J6-SLH N505GH F-ODGP N888WJ 5Y-KZT HB-LRR
506	300	Ethiopian Army	C-GQFF EA-62
507	300	Air Loyaute	C-GPJB N720CA P2-KSR F-OIAY
508	300	Ethiopian Army	C-GQFG EA-63
509	300	Hevi-Lift	C-GCSC N502CS VH-WPT P2-KSG
510	300	ex Carib Aviation	HK-1980 V2-LFL J8-GAL
511	300	SonAir	XY-AED PH-STD HB-LOM D2-EVH
512	300	(Burma Airways)	XY-AEE [w/o 08Oct83 near Lonkin Airfield, Burma]
513	300	Safarilink Aviation	HB-LIS G-BLIS 9Q-CBN (N50EW) ZS-OHS 5Y-BOS 5Y-ETA ZS-SCJ 5Y-SLF [badly damaged 16Apr11 Keekorak, Kenya]
514	300*	Zuni LLC/Scenic Airlines	N27RA N146SA
515	300	Twin Otter International	YV-26C YV-526C N75482 N122SA N515AR
516	310	Airlines of Papua New Guinea	G-BTWT PH-STI P2-RDK VH-FNX 5W-PAH P2-MCS
517	300*	Grand Canyon Airlines	N20RA N43SP N227SA
518	300	Unity Group	D-IDWT 5Y-SKA PJ-WIN C-GSOZ
519	300	(Procuraduria General de la Republica)	XC-BOS [w/o 28Oct79 Otay Mesa, San Diego, CA; used for spares for c/n 752]
520	300	Hevi-Lift	YV-27C YV-527C N699WJ 5U-ABU YJ-RV5 P2-KST
521	300	Servicios Aereos de Los Andes.	YV-28C YV-528C (N) C-FSXF OB-1897-P
522	300	Airfast Indonesia	N99110 A6-MBM PK-OCJ
523	300	Zimex Aviation	F-GAMR TR-LAL F-GKTO HB-LRO
524	300*	Montecito New York	YV-29C YV-529C N81708 N251SA
525	310	Air Tindi	(G-BEIR) G-BEJP C-GATU PK-BRA C-FATW
526	300	(Linea Aeropostal Venezolana)	YV-30C [w/o 17Apr78 near Uriman, Venezuela]
527	300	Bald Mountain Air Service	C-GDHA N379WW N9SP P2-RDM RP-C1312 P2-RDM VH-FNY VH-OHP TI-AZV N716JP
528	300	Hevi-Lift	YV-31C YV-531C N528SA P2-HCF P2-KSF
529	300	CHC Cameroon	5N-AKV 9M-MDZ TJ-SAF
530	310	(Trans Maldivian Airlines)	G-BELS ZK-MCO N530JM 8Q-HIG 8Q-TMD [w/o 11Jly11 Bryadhoo Lagoon, Maldivies; fuselage noted Male, Maldivies 20Feb12]
531	300	(Jamaican Defence Force)	JDFT-6 [w/o 30Jun81 Kingston-Up Park Camp Air Base, Jamaica]
532	300	Air Panama	C-GQKZ J6-AAL C-GQKZ 6Y-JMU C-GQKZ HP-1507PS
533	300	Kenn Borek Air	C-GNTD N222BS HK-2821X N222BS HK-3398X N222BS 4X-AHZ N533SW C-FAKB
534	300	Royal Canadian Mounted Police	C-GMPJ
535	300	(Trigana Air Service)	LV-PVF LV-MAH N477AG PK-YPY [w/o 17Nov06 Puncak, Java, Indonesia]
536	300	(Wideroes Flyveselskap)	LN-BNS [w/o 12Apr90 near Vaeroy, Lofoten Islands, Norway; spares use White Industries, Bates City, MO]
537	300*	ex Avro Ltd	N19RA (N19RE) N147SA TI-BBQ N537AR+ P2- [+ canx 23Nov10 to Papua New Guinea; Dec12 still on overhaul Cairns, QLD, Australia]
538	300	(Aero Contractors)	XY-AEF PH-STE 7P-LAK 5N-ATQ [w/o 13Sep94 Karsana, near Abuja, Nigeria]
539	300	Air Seychelles	XY-AEG PH-STF S7-AAR
540	300	(Burma Airways)	XY-AEH [w/o 08Sep77 en-route Monghsat-Keng Tung, Burma]
541	300	(Burma Airways)	XY-AEI [w/o 26Aug78 near Papun, South Burma]
542	300	JAS Aircaft Sales & Leasing	PJ-WIE N34KH [reported wfu Sep07 French Valley, CA, still marked PJ-WIE]
543	300	(Windward Island Airways)	PJ-WIF [wfu Aug02 on reaching design life maximum landings of 132,000; fuselage returned to Canada for tests; by mid-08 dumped at Airdrie, AB, Canada; l/n 10Sep08]
544	300	(Aeroperlas)	HP-759 HP-759APP [hijacked 05Jly90, landed near Viterbo to release passengers, t/o again; has not been seen since; canx 26Jly96]
545	310	(Fairflight)	N302EH N64791 N302EH G-STUD [w/o 20Apr83 Flotta, Orkneys, Scotland, UK]

DE HAVILLAND CANADA DHC-6 TWIN OTTER

C/n	Model	Last known Owner/Operator	Identities/fates/comments (where appropriate)
546	300	(British Antarctic Survey)	VP-FAW [w/o 18Nov81 Rothera Station, Adelaide Island, Antarctica; wreck shipped to UK and used to rebuild c/n 748 VP-FAZ; remains to US for spares use]
547	300	(Kenn Borek Air)	C-GQSO C-GKBO(1) [w/o 15May82 North Pole, Arctic]
548	310	Fry's Electronics	C-GQTJ PH-EMA 9M-AVT PH-EMA B-3510 N548X N622JM N814BC
549	300	Air Labrador	N160CA N61UT C-GIZF
550	300	(Transportes Aereos de Cabo Verde)	C-GQYQ CR-CAX D4-CAX [w/o 28Sep98 Praia, Cape Verde Islands; wreck to Dodson International Aircraft Parts, Rantoul, KS, for spares]
551	300	Merpati Nusantara Airlines	PH-EMB 9M-AVU PH-EMB B-3511 N997D VH-ZRP VH-UQY PK-NVA
552	300	Mobil	C-GQTM 9U-BHA 5N-MPU
553	300	ex Erwin Aero Industries	C-GQTN N888AL 3X-GAY (C-GHOU) C-GIGZ J8-
554	300	USAF	77-0464//N70464 [dual marks] [UV-18B] [some reports suggest i/ds of this aircraft and c/n 555 below are reversed]
555	300	USAF	77-0465//N70465 [dual marks] [UV-18B]
556	300*	Grand Canyon Airlines	N97RA N241SA
557	300	not yet known	C-GQYP YV-184CP N208JE C-FWVV+ PK- [+ canx 26Jly11 to Indonesia; fuselage only reported Airdrie, AB, Canada 10Sep08; no marks]
558	300	Air Tindi	C-GNPS
559	300*	Grand Canyon Airlines	N63RA N74GC 9M-BCP N74GC J8-SVD N74GC (F-OIAV) J6-AAK N74GC
560	300	Ecuadorian Air Force	9U-BHB 9U-BHP N293JM C-GNQK FAE-452
561	300	Maldivian Air Taxi	C-GRZH OY-ATY 8Q-MBE
562	300	Greenwood Group	HK-2050 HK-2050P HK-2050 TI-BAL N562CP
563	300	Cayman Airways Express	C-GNOE 512+ B-3501 N563DH VP-CXB [+ China]
564	300	Bald Mountain Air Service	C-GNZT 510+ B-3504 N564DH [+ China]
565	300	Mission Aviation Fellowship	C-GNOF 514+ B-3502 P2-MFT [+ China]
566	300	(Air Inuit)	F-GBDA N306EH C-GBJE [w/o 26Oct89 Kangiqsujuaq, QC, Canada; fuselage to Calgary-Springbank, AB, Canada by 30Jly92; canx Jan93]
567	300	Waha Oil Company	5A-DAS
568	300	(Wideroes Flyveselskap)	LN-BNK [w/o 11Mar82 80 kms east of North Cape, Norway]
569	300	Waha Oil Company	5A-DAT [stored Altenrhein, Switzerland; l/n 11Oct06]
570	300	(Waha Oil Company)	5A-DAU [w/o Jun08 Waha Oil Camp, Libya; exact date unknown]
571	310	Maldivian Air Taxi	G-BFGP RP-C1217 G-BFGP C-GKBX VP-LVT C-GKBX 8Q-MAP C-FBKX 8Q-MAP C-FKBX 8Q-MAP
572	300	Avmax Aircraft Leasing	C-GSXW PH-SAK 5N-AKY (5B-CJN) TJ-ALL C-GOYX
573	300	ex Seaborne Airlines	N662MA ZK-TFS C-FMUS N41991 N573SA+ P2- [+ canx 23Nov10 to Papua New Guinea; by 22Sep10 fuselage stored Calgary, AB, Canada]
574	300	Airkenya Express	F-GBDB N4226J 5Y-BGH
575	300	Tunisavia	TS-DSF TS-LSF
576	300	Air Born	F-GBDC N57AN N302EH N54LM+ PK- [+ canx 07Feb12 to Indonesia]
577	300	NAFT Airlines (Iranian Air Transport)	EP-IOP
578	300	Nyaman Air	C-GNZJ (G-BFRZ) G-RBLA (PH-DDF) LN-FKA N578SA P2-KSS PK-FUF
579	300	Airkenya Express	5H-MRB 5Y-BIO 5H- 5Y-BIO
580	300	Trans Maldivian Airways	5H-MRC 5Y-BIJ 5H-MUC ZS-PZO 8Q-TAC [floatplane]
581	300	(Air Tanzania)	5H-MRD [w/o 20Dec84 Karege near Dar es Salaam, Tanzania]
582	300	Trans Maldivian Airways	5H-MRE 5Y-BIK 5H-MUG ZS-OVI 5Y-DDD ZS-OVI 5H-MVJ ZS-SAI 8Q-TAB [floatplane]
583	300	Chilean Air Force	932
584	300	Chilean Air Force	933
585	300	Maldivian Air Taxi	934+ N226SA 8Q-MBH [+ Chile]
586	300	Chilean Air Force	938
587	300	Trans Maldivian Airways	C-GOVC A6-FAM C-GASV 8Q-TMB
588	300	Kenn Borek Air	C-GMPX C-FBBW VP-CLC C-FBBW 8Q-KBA C-FBBW
589	300	Chilean Air Force	941
590	300	Chilean Air Force	942
591	300	(Dolphin Express Airlines)	N98RA N143SA [w/o 07Apr96 Virgin Gorda Airport, BVI]
592	300	Airlines of Papua New Guinea	C-GOVG P2-MCD
593	300	Lao Airlines	N663MA N169SG RDPL-34179
594	300	Argentine Army	AE-263
595	300	Occidental Oil of Libya	5A-DCJ

DE HAVILLAND CANADA DHC-6 TWIN OTTER

C/n	Model	Last known Owner/Operator	Identities/fates/comments (where appropriate)
596	300	North-Wright Airways	N596K N596KC N16NA N16NG C-FNWL
597	310	Trans Maldivian Airways	5N-AVD PH-LJK 8Q-HIJ 8Q-TMG
598	300	Solenta Avn/Air Serv International	N403CA ZS-NJK [w/o 31Aug07 near Punia, Democratic Republic of Congo]
599	300	Libyan Dept of Civil Aviation	5A-DCA [reported wfu by 09Oct09 Tripoli, Libya]
600	300	Provincial Airlines	N601KC HI-685CA HI-685CT HI-685CA N612BA (PH-) TJ-SAD N604NA C-GIED
601	300	Transportes Aereos Terrestres	N28SP PZ-TBW N471SC
602	300	Cayman Airways Express	C-GQWJ 516+ B-3503 N602DH VR-CXA [+ China]
603	300	Air Moorea	C-GRQZ 603+ F-OHJG [+ France; code CY then 70-MB]
604	300	SVG Air/Grenadine Airways	C-GQWL JA8808 N604ML 8P-BGC J8-VBQ
605	300	Libyan Ministry of Agriculture	5A-DCP [reported derelict at Benina, Libya]
606	300	(Helicol Colombia)	N46RA HK-2889X [w/o 04Jly91 near El Yopal, Colombia]
607	300	(Bristow Helicopters)	(N984FL) G-BFYY 5N-AJQ [w/o 23Apr95 Lagos, Nigeria when it hit F.27 NAF908 c/n 10656]
608	300	(Air Moorea)	HK-2215X N784DL HK-3523 N228CS F-OIQI [w/o 09Aug07 near Moorea-Temae Airport, French Polynesia]
609	300	(ACES Colombia)	HK-2216X [w/o 18Dec81 San Antero, Colombia]
610	300	ex Sabang Merauke Raya Air	N96RA (N99XV) DQ-FEU P2-MBT P2-MRN PK-ZAP P2-MRN [repossessed mid-2002 ex Indonesia; stored dismantled by 26Feb09 Madang, Papua New Guinea]
611	310	Air Born	G-BFYX 5N-AJR C-FBKB 8Q-MAQ C-FBKB+ PK- [+ canx 16May12 to Indonesia]
612	300	TMK Air Commuter	5N-ALG PH-STK HC-BNY PH-STK 9Q-CRE
613	310	Transportes San Francisco	SE-GEF G-BMXW C-FQOL V3-HTC C-FQOL CC-PII C-GGPM CC-ACH
614	300	Twin Otter International	N933MA N252SA N614AR
615	300	Twin Otter International	C-GTYZ YV-34C YV-530C N220SA V2-LFC N615AR
616	310	Airfast Indonesia	G-BGEN PK-OCK
617	310	Kenn Borek Air	G-BGMC G-JEAC OY-SLA C-GKBR HP-1167APP C-GKBR 8Q-MAU C-GKBR 8Q-MAU C-GKBR 8Q-MAU C-GKBR
618	300*	(Zimex Aviation)	5A-DCR HB-LQX [w/o 30Jun90 in Angola; no further details]
619	300	Yeti Airlines	A2-ABL 7P-LAG ET-AIW C-GBQA 9N-AEM 9N-AET
620	300	Seaborne Airlines	LN-BNA C-FTWV N888PV
621	300	(Libyan Ministry of Agriculture)	5A-DCS [w/o 15Apr86 Tripoli, Libya, in a US air-raid]
622	300	(Lesotho Airways)	7P-LAA [w/o 13Jly84 near Mokhotlong, Lesotho]
623	300	Air Seychelles	7P-LAB 5N-ATN S7-AAO S7-AAF
624	300	(Aeroperlas)	(LN-BNQ) LN-BNH C-FTOT HP-1267APP [w/o 17Mar00 in Pico Carreto mountains en-route Panama City-Puerto Obaldia, Panama]
625	300	Trans Maldivian Airways	C-GTYG N305EH C-GCVI N320EA C-FNBL 8Q-TMV
626	300	(Merpati Nusantara Airlines)	PH-SAY N5467X PH-SAY 9M-MDN 9M-PEG 9M-BMM PK-NVC [w/o en-route 02Aug09 near Ampisibil, Papua, Indonesia]
627	300	Libyan Airlines	5A-DCT
628	300	Zimex Aviation	LN-BNT D-IFLY HB-LTG
629	310	MASwings	G-BGMD ZK-KHA 9M-MDO
630	300	(Austin Airways)	C-GTJA [w/o 01Nov79 Big Trout Lake, ON, Canada]
631	300	Air Inuit	C-GTYX [wings with these marks at Calgary-Springbank, AB, Canada 10Sep08; assumed rebuilt with new wings]
632	300	(Austin Airways)	C-GTLA [w/o 23Nov83 Lansdowne House, ON, Canada]
633	300	Twin Otter Support Services/ US Government	N391AC N6292Q N237JR N6151C N6161Q N633AR
634	310	Hevi-Lift	5N-AVG N933DR PK-LTV P2-KSS
635	310	Viking Air	G-BGPC+ C-FJVT^ [+ w/o 12Jun86 near Port Ellen, Islay, Scotland; fuselage stored circa Oct00 by Newcal Aviation at Teterboro, NJ; ^ regd 29Oct10]
636	310	Zimex Aviation	3B-NAD N636WJ HB-LRN PK-YPE HB-LRN ST-LRN HB-LRN
637	300	Libyan Airlines	5A-DCV
638	300	Nepal Airlines	9N-ABO
639	300	(Libyan Ministry of Agriculture)	5A-DCW [PWFU or w/o 1982]
640	300	Trans Maldivian Airways	C-GBDG HZ-PL4 N664MA N709PV 8Q-TML
641	300	Libyan Airlines	5A-DCX
642	310	Sander Geophysics	OH-KOG C-GSGF
643	300	ex Zimex Aviation	5A-DCY TT-EAI F-GFAJ HB-LQV 5Y-LQV HB-LQV [canx 24Feb12 fate/status unknown]
644	300	Tactical Air Operations	HK-2381 C-GIMG N300DZ

DE HAVILLAND CANADA DHC-6 TWIN OTTER

C/n	Model	Last known Owner/Operator	Identities/fates/comments (where appropriate)
645	300	Libyan Airlines	5A-DCZ
646	300	Gum Air	PZ-TCD N7015A PZ-TBY
647	300	Aero Ruta Maya	N205CA VH-XFC N300WH TG-JCA
648	300	(Air Sao Tome e Principe)	CS-TFD S9-BAL [w/o 23May06, ditched off Sao Tome]
649	300	Libyan Ministry of Agriculture	5A-DDB+ [+ previously quoted as 5A-DDA but Aug08 register gives this version]
650	300	Kenn Borek Air	C-GKBC N55921 C-GKBC [considerable damage 12Apr10 Melville Island, Ice Cap, NWT, Canada]
651	300	(Yeti Airlines)	G-BHCY 9M-SSA 9N-AEA 9M-BDE+ 9N-AFD [+ these marks may have been used prior to 9N-AEA, rather than after; w/o 25May04 Lamjura Pass, near Lukla, Nepal]
652	300	Trans Maldivian Airways	N479WW VH-KZN 8Q-TMP
653	300	Aero Club Libya	5A-DDB
654	300	(Royal Nepal Airlines)	9N-ABP [w/o 27Jly00 Jarayakchali, Nepal; date of accident also reported as being 25Jly00 or 28Jly09]
655	300	Tara Air	9N-ABQ
656	300	Isles of Scilly Skybus	PZ-TCE N70551 G-CEWM
657	300	Trans Maldivian Airways	SE-GXN HB-LPA 8Q-HII 8Q-TMF
658	300	(Zimex Aviation)	D-IASL HB-LOK [w/o 19Nov04 Menzel Lejmant North, Algeria]
659	300	Maldivian Air Taxi	N105AC ZK-FQK(1) A3-FQK VH-AHI 9M-KAT 9M-SSN PK-LTW HB-LUG 8Q-MBB
660	300	Pacific Sun Airlines	PZ-TCF J6-SLP N456RE N933LC DQ-FIE
661	300	Libyan Airlines	9H-AAR C-GELZ 5A-DHY
662	300	Petro Air	5A-DDC TT-LAK TT-EAH 5N-EVS TJ-CQE 5A-DDC
663	300	Trans Maldivian Airways	CR-CAY D4-CAY D-INAC N53GD PK-TWH 8Q-TMS
664	300	Yemenia	CS-TFE OY-SLH HB-LRT 7O-ADI
665	300	Shangri-La Air	N16RP VT-ERV 9N-AFA
666	310	Loganair/Flybe	LN-BEZ G-BVVK
667	300	Ecuadorian Air Force	N49RA N546WA FAE-451
668	300	Trans Maldivian Airways	9H-AAS HK-2439X HK-2439 HK-4194X 8Q-TMH
669	300	(South Pacific Island Airways)	N43SP [w/o 21Jly84 Tau, American Samoa; canx Aug84]
670	300	Libyan Airlines	5A-DDC [previously quoted as 5A-DDD of Tripoli Aero Club/Air Jamahiriya; w/o 30Nov88 Hamada oilfield, Libya; but Aug08 gives this version]
671	300	(Kenn Borek Air/Aklak Air)	C-GCGU HZ-SN4 HZ-F02 C-GZVH VP-CCB C-GZVH [DBF 04Nov10 Inuvik, NT, Canada]
672	300	Seychelles Defence Force	C-GBOX N776BE N776BF 2777+ A6-MBZ 2777+ 2277 S7-007^ [+ United Arab Emirates; not fully confirmed. Possible miss-sighting of 2277?]
673	300	Airlines of Papua New Guinea	C-GHRB P2-MCE
674	300	Air Tindi	A6-MRM C-FATO
675	300	Provincial Airlines	F-OGIZ C-GGKR 5N-BCL TJ-SAE C-GGKR PJ-TOD C-FUMY
676	300	(Aero TACA)	C-GBZF N3760V HK-2486X HK-2486 [w/o 11Jun89 Caribabare, near Tama, Colombia]
677	300	Libyan Airlines	5A-DDE
678	300	(Polynesian Airlines)	N12RA N630DP 5W-FAU [w/o 07Jan97 near Apia, Samoa]
679	300	Air Vanuatu	C-GCJE 9XR-KC OY-SLI YJ-RV10
680	300	US Army	79-23255 [UV-18A]
681	300	US Army	79-23256 [UV-18A]
682	310	Windward Islands Airways International	G-BGZP 5Y-SKS C-GKGQ PJ-WII
683	300	Gloster Ltd	C-GCGN HK-2444X FAP-230+ N7020G N237SA TI-BBF N683AR [+ Panama]
684	300	Trigana Air Service	C-GCGP HK-2445X HK-2445 C-GIEB HB-LTF PK-YPX [considerable damage 08Jly08 Dekai, Indonesia]
685	300	Trigana Air Service	N107AC ZK-FQL A3-FQL VH-VHP PK-YRU [possibly DBR 01Jun07 Mulia, Papua, Indonesia]
686	300	Sopwith Ltd	HP-771 HR-ALG N7172D N225SA
687	300	Procuraduria General de la Republica	C-GCSQ (N549N) XC-DIO
688	310	US Department of Commerce/ NOAA	PH-SSD N9240N (N688CC) HK-3332X N9240N N485RF N57RF
689	300	Airfast Indonesia	OB-M-1182 OB-1152 N689WJ PK-OCL
690	300	Polynesian Airlines	C-GTNO VH-XSW VH-UQW 5W-FAY

DE HAVILLAND CANADA DHC-6 TWIN OTTER

C/n	Model	Last known Owner/Operator	Identities/fates/comments (where appropriate)
691	300	Maldivian Air Taxi	G-BWRB N230BV ZS-MZB N691JM C-FSHJ (SX-BXF) D-IHAI 8Q-MBA [rebuilt with nose of c/n 72]
692	300*	Bristol Ltd	N549N N230SA N692AR
693	300	Kenn Borek Air	C-GKBE HP-1196AP C-GKBE VP-LVS C-GKBE 8Q-KBE C-GKBE 8Q-MAA C-GKBE 8Q-MAA C-GKCS 8Q-MAA C-GKCS
694	310	(Vanair)	C-GBXN (G-BHTO) G-BHXG PH-STG 9M-PEH YJ-RV9(2) [w/o 08May99 into the Pacific Ocean, near Port-Vila, Vanuatu]
695	310	Isles of Scilly Skybus	C-GJZK TR-LZO C-FZSP HB-LSN C-FZSP G-CBML
696	310	Loganair/Flybe	C-GKIQ TR-LZN F-ODUH N696WJ N712PV C-GGNF G-BZFP
697	300*	Grand Canyon Airlines	PH-SSE 7P-LAM N226SA N178GC TI-AZD N178GC
698	300	(Air Inuit)	C-GKCJ (C-GSFT) A6-AMM C-GKCJ [w/o 11Feb07 Berbegamau Airstrip, QC, Canada]
699	310	(RRC Air Service)	G-OJEA ET-AIL [w/o 06Aug89 near Fugnido, Ethiopia]
700	300	Trans Maldivian Airways	LN-WFD TJ-OHN (PH-OHN) 8Q-TMN
701	300	Minera Barrick Misquichilca	N701PV C-GBGC OB-1704
702	300	Alberta Aircraft Leasing	N702PV+ C- [+ canx 06Mar08 to Canada]
703	310	Airlines of Papua New Guinea	(G-BHTO) G-MAIL F-ODGL YJ-RV8(2) (F-OIAV) (ZS-OUL) P2-MCX
704	300	SonAir	C-GDGI PH-SSF 5N-ASP D2-FVQ
705	300	Libyan Airlines	5A-DHN [previously reported as 5A-DBF with Umm Al Jawaby Petroleum Company, but Aug08 register gives this version; see c/n 712]
706	320	Heavilift	F-ODGB YJ-RV1(1) P2-RDV VH-FNZ VH-HPY P2-KSI
707	320	(Hawker Pacific/Australian Army)	4R-UAA (C-GGOX) (VH-SFJ) VH-USW VH-HPT [canx 23Aug05 and stored; for probable spares use by UAE Air Force]
708	310	(Yeti Airlines)	G-BHTK PH-STH 7P-LAO ET-AKJ C-GBQD 9N-AEQ [w/o 21Jun06 Jumla, Nepal]
709	300	Aerovias DAP	G-BHUY+ CC-CHV [+ marks only reserved but were painted on the aircraft]
710	310	(Lumbini Airways)	C-GDGP OY-BYO 5Y-BNT 9N-ACC [w/o 21Aug98 en-route Jomson to Pokhara, Nepal]
711	300	Vulcan Aircraft Inc	C-GDGR A6-AHM N4693H N503CS A6-NHM C-FCSC C-FTEL C-GIFG N711AF
712	300	Veba Oil	5A-DBF [previously reported as 5A-DHN with Air Libya but Aug08 gives this version; see c/n 705]
713	300	(ACES Colombia)	HK-2536X [w/o 29Nov82 Cerro Pan de Azucar, near Villavicencio, Colombia]
714	300	(Aviones Comerciales de Guatemala)	TG-JAK [w/o 16Feb96 El Quiche, Guatemala]
715	300	Air Moorea	N8489H HK-2534X N8489H 5Y-SKL F-OIQP
716	300	Tunisavia	C-GDLD TS-DIB TS-LIB
717	300	Star Aviation	HK-2547X HK-2547 C-GIED HB-LTD 7T-VNE
718	300	ADA-Aerolinea de Antioquia	C-GDIW HK-2548X HK-2548
719	300	Avmax Aircraft Leasing	C-GDKL HK-2553X HK-2553 N719DK ZS-OVN N719DK 9Q-CEL C-GNFZ
720	310	(Yeti Airlines)	G-BIEI 9M-SSH 9N-AEB 9M-BDD+ 9N-AFE [+ marks not fully confirmed; w/o 08Oct08 Lukla, Nepal]
721	300	ex CAAMS LLC	N999PG VH-SHW S7-AAT ZS-OVT ZS-PNT N149WJ+ XA- [+ canx 23Jun10 to Mexico]
722	300	Maldivian Air Taxi	N72DA N3H N3HU TG-JEL C-FWKO 8Q-MAW
723	300	Twin Otter International	N723CA C-FWZA 8R-GHN N255SA N723AR
724	300	(Provincial Airlines)	C-GDKV N914MA C-FWLQ [w/o 19Mar99 Davis Inlet, NL, Canada; canx 06Apr99]
725	300	Kenn Borek Air	C-GDOX (G-BIDR) LN-WFF C-FTYU HP-1273APP C-GKBO(3)
726	310	Airlines of Papua New Guinea	C-GCVZ AP-BCG N726JM P2-EMO
727	300	Colombian National Police	N214FC HK-2777G PNC-201
728	310	SonAir	C-GLIT VP-LMD V2-LDD D2-EVA
729	300	Yeti Airlines	C-GPAZ N722CA C-FWQF P2-MBM C-FWQF 9N-AEV
730	300	French Air Force	730 [code CA; then F-RALF/LF]
731	300	Provincial Airlines	N915MA C-FWLG
732	300	Kenn Borek Air	G-BIEM C-GKBH 8Q-MAV C-GKBH 8Q-MAV C-GKBH 8Q-MAV C-GKBH
733	300	Kenn Borek Air	C-GKBG
734	300	(Aerolatino)	N331CC N942MA XA-TCF [w/o 17Jly96 Playa del Carmen, Mexico]
735	300	(TMK Air Commuter)	N123SL 9Q-CBO [w/o 08Sep05 Goma, Democratic Republic of Congo; by 18Jan12 fuselage noted at Calgary, AB, Canada]
736	300	Iraq Northern Petroleum	YI-AKY

DE HAVILLAND CANADA DHC-6 TWIN OTTER

C/n	Model	Last known Owner/Operator	Identities/fates/comments (where appropriate)
737	300	(Air Benin)	C-GEAY TY-BBL [w/o 24Feb83 Taneka-Koko, near Djougou, Benin]
738	310	Isles of Scilly Skybus	G-BIHO A6-ADB G-BIHO
739	300	Ontario Ministry of Natural Resources	C-GOGA
740	300	US Department of Commerce/ NOAA	G-BIMW N600LJ N48RF
741	300	Airlines of Papua New Guinea	C-GRBY P2-MCF
742	300	French Air Force	742 [code CB; then F-RALG/LG; w/o 06May07 near El-Thamad, Egypt]]
743	300	SonAir	743+ F-WQJG 5Y-TMF D2-FVP [+ France; code F-RAVX/CZ then 070-MA]
744	300	Libyan Airlines	(2027)+ C-GFHQ 5A-DJG [+ Paraguay]
745	300	French Air Force	745 [codes reported as CV; then 745/63-VY & 745/118-IG]
746	300	(ACES Colombia)	C-GEMU HK-2602 [w/o 30Nov96 Mount.Padre Amaya, Medellin, Colombia]
747	300	Libyan Airlines	(2029)+ C-GEOA 5A-DJH [+ Paraguay]
748	300	British Antarctic Survey	C-GEOA VP-FAZ
749	300	ADA-Aerolinea de Antioquia	HK-2603
750	300	Ontario Ministry of Natural Resources	C-GOGC
751	300	Trans Maldivian Airways	C-GERC HZ-PL6 N710PV 8Q-TMK
752	300	Procuraduria General de la Republica	XC-FIT [w/o 15Jan02 Chilpancingo, Mexico; repaired using parts from c/n 519]
753	300	Trans Maldivian Airways	C-GFBS VH-KZO N162AY 8Q-TMQ
754	300	Trans Maldivian Airways	N308EH C-GEOA HK-2739X HK-2739 HK-3021 HK-3021X HK-4018X HK-4168X N107JM 8Q-TMI
755	300	Maldivian Air Taxi	C-FCSG N504CS C-FCSG TG-JAC C-FWKX 8Q-MAX
756	300	(PT Aviastar Mandiri)	N126AS N886EA C- N886EA C-FOIJ PK-BRO [w/o 29Jun09 near Wamena, Indonesia]
757	300	Libyan Airlines	C-GEVI C-GERL 5A-DJI
758	300	(Abu Dhabi Aviation)	C-GFBU VH-KZP A6- [left Australia 10Mar03 & canx 21Mar03; reduced to spares by 2004 Dubai Airport, UAE probably without UAE marks being allocated]
759	300	(Abu Dhabi Aviation)	C-GFBY VH-KZQ A6- [left Australia 10Mar03 & canx 21Mar03; reduced to spares by 2004 Dubai Airport, UAE probably without UAE marks being allocated]
760	300	ADA-Aerolinea de Antioquia	C-GEWI HK-2669X HK-2669
761	300	Ontario Ministry of Natural Resources	C-GOGB
762	310	(Shangri-La Air)	C-GEVL V2-LCK 9M-CHH 9N-AFR [w/o 22Aug02 Pokhara, Nepal]
763	300	Air Inuit	C-GMDC
764	310	Yemenia	N25RM N30BV G-OILY A6-ADC G-GBAC (VQ-TAN) 7O-ADH
765	300	Fazza Sky/Dubai Skydive	ST-AHV DU-SD3
766	300	Unity Group	C-GFCA N304CH PJ-WIH N67SA YN-CHQ C-GKPV [floatplane]
767	300	Tactical Air Operations	C-GFCW HK-2670X HK-2670 N2670X N3PY
768	310	Trans Maldivian Airways	C-GFCI C6-BEL C-GFJC AP-BCH N768JM+ C-FQWE SX-GIK 9H-AFY C-GDQM 8Q-TMW [+ painted as N-768JM in Pakistan and ferried to USA as such by 18Jun07]
769	300	Libyan Airlines	C-GESR 5A-DJJ C-GETI 5A-DJJ
770	300	(ACES Colombia)	C-GESP HK-2758X [w/o 18Feb91 Otu airstrip, Colombia; burnt out by rebels]
771	300	(Aerotaca)	C-GFHT HK-2759X HK-2759 [w/o 06Jun93 near El Yopal, Colombia]
772	300*	Seaborne Airshuttle	PJ-TOA N7033U N235SA 8P-TIB N235SA J8-VBO N235SA N189GC
773	300	Twin Otter International	PJ-TOB N70331 N236SA VR-CTO VP-CTO N236SA N70AR
774	300M	Maldivian Air Taxi	C-GFJQ-X C-GFJQ TG-JAJ C-FWKU 8Q-MAZ
775	300	(Aero Club Libya)	C-GESR 5A-DJK [w/o 19Mar94 Tripoli, Libya]
776	300	ex Libyan Ministry of Agriculture	C-GDCZ 5A-DJL [not on Aug08 register; fate/status unknown]
777	300	(Aerotaca)	C-GETI HK-2760 [w/o 08Apr99 near Malaga, Colombia]
778	300	Arab Mining Company	C-GEVP N1345U HK-2954X N778CC HB-LRE ST-AOQ
779	300	not yet known	C-GERL(1) N1345X N114ES HK-2834X N1345X N779CC N89HP N894S C-GMKW+ 5R- [+ canx 12Oct11 to Madagascar]
780	300	(ACES Colombia)	C-GETI HK-2761X [w/o 27Apr86 near Saravena, Colombia]
781	300	Trans Maldivian Airways	C-GETI (FAE781)+ HK-2970X HK-4019X HK-4169X N781JM 8Q-TMJ [+ fully painted in Ecuador AF c/s except serial]
782	310	Alberta Central Airways	C-GEVP (FAE-782)+ AP-BBR C-FZPQ C-FTMU [+ Ecuador]
783	310	British Antarctic Survey	C-GDKL VP-FBB
784	300	Air Inuit	C-GDFT HK-2762X HK-2762 C-FJFR

DE HAVILLAND CANADA DHC-6 TWIN OTTER

C/n	Model	Last known Owner/Operator	Identities/fates/comments (where appropriate)
785	310	(LIAT)	C-GEOA V2-LCJ [w/o 03Aug86 into sea near Vale, St.Vincent, West Indies]
786	300	(French Air Force)	C-GEOA 786 [code CT then call sign F-RAVV or F-RAVY; w/o 08Nov89 El Gorah, Sanai, Egypt, used as GIA]
787	310	British Antarctic Survey	C-GDIU VP-FBC
788	300	US Dept of Commerce/NOAA	C-GBOD 6V-AFF N788SS C-FMRU N56RF
789	300	(ACES Colombia)	C-GDIU HK-2763 [w/o 27Feb85 El Bagre, Colombia in arson attack]
790	300	French Air Force	C-GERL 790 [code CW then F-RAVW/VW; by Jun07 preserved museum at Chateaudun, France; l/n Jun10]
791	310	(Dodson International Parts)	C-GERL(2) 9M-MDJ N6008E [by Jan99 wfu and stored Rantoul, KS; l/n Jun06]
792	300	MASwings	C-GESR 9M-MDK
793	300	Compania Minera Nevada	C-GDNG C-GDCZ N742CA C-FWZB CC-PQQ
794	300	SonAir	C-GESR N27278 N794CC HB-LRF D2-FVM
795	300	Royal Nepal Airlines/United Nations	C-GDNG N27283 9N-ABS [w/o 20Jun91 Simikot, Nepal]
796	300	(Skyline Airways)	C-GMPY C-GBBY 9N-AFL [w/o 25Dec99 near Simara, Nepal]
797	300	Air Guyane	C-GDIU 9Q-CJD(1) D-IFLY(2) F-OIJY
798	300	Trans Maldivian Airways	C-GERL TR-LAK C-FTJD 5N-BFW 8Q-HIH 8Q-TME
799	310	Regional Air Services	C-GDFT C-GGBE A4O-DA OY-SLD 5Y-KEG 5H-KEG
800	300	US Army	C-GCVT 82-23835 [UV-18A]
801	300	US Army	C-GBXN 82-23836 [UV-18A]
802	300	MASwings	C-GDFT 9M-MDL
803	300	US Forest Service	C-GDNG N141Z
804	300	MASwings	C-GDKL 9M-MDM
805	310	CAAMS LLC	C-GEOA V2-LCN N805AA N805AS TI-AZQ N42729+ N805WJ [w/o 16Dec05 Tamarindo, Costa Rica, whilst reg'd TI-AZQ; US marks reg'd 27Dec07, possibly for spares recovery]
806	310	(Tara Air)	C-GERL V2-LCO N806AA 9N-AFX [w/o 15Dec10 Lamidanda, Nepal]
807	300	Benin Air Force	C-GESR TY-BBS TY-23A
808	300	Veba Oil	C-GDFT 5A-DBH
809	310	SonAir	C-GETI N542N V2-LDG D2-EVC
810	310	SonAir	C-GDCZ N543N V2-LDH D2-EVB
811	300	Sirte Oil Company	C-GDIU N550N HB-LPM 5A-DSC
812	300	(Royal Nepal Airlines)	C-GDCZ C-GHHI 9N-ABT [probably w/o 24Dec08 Kathmandu, Nepal]
813	310	Yemenia	C-GDKL A4O-DB 7O-ADK [w/o 23Jun07 by random gunfire Al-Naeem airstrip, Yemen; canx]
814	300	Nepal Airlines	C-GDNG C-GHHY 9N-ABU
815	300	Polynesie Francaise/Air Moorea	C-GDCZ ET-AIM N45KH F-OIQF
816	300	Caverton Helicopters	C-GDFT ET-AIN HB-LUB 807+ 5N-BJV [+ Ethiopia; but reported use of these marks now in doubt]
817	300	SonAir	C-GGSS B-3505 N817L D2-FVN
818	300	(Ethiopian Airlines)	C-GDIU ET-AIO [w/o 22Oct95 Addis Ababa-Bole, Ethiopia]
819	300	(Ethiopian Airlines)	C-GDKL ET-AIQ [w/o 22Jun86 near Dembidollo, Ethiopia]
820	300	Ethiopian Airlines	C-GDNG ET-AIT
821	300	SonAir	C-GGPB B-3506 N821L D2-FVO
822	300	Ethiopian Airlines	C-GDCZ ET-AIU
823	300	Transport Services LLC	C-GGWA B-3507 N823X
824	300	US Dept of Commerce/NOAA	C-GGWB B-3508 N824X N824ED C-GIUZ N46RF
825	310	Indian Department of Mines	C-GIIG VT-ELX
826	300	Transport Services LLC	C-GGWC B-3509 N826X
827	300	Polynesian Airlines	C-GDFT 9XR-KD N190JM C-FTLQ 5W-FAW
828	300	Skyline Airways	C-FMPW C-FBBO 9N-AGF [w/o 17Jly02 Surkhet, Nepal]
829	300	Colombian National Police	C-GDIU PNC-202
830	300	Nepal Airlines	C-GDKL C-GIQS 9N-ABX [seriously damaged 19Apr10 Kangel Danda, Nepal]
831	300	Caverton Helicopters	C-GDNG VR-BJP B-3512 PK-LTY VH-VHM 5N-BLJ
832	300	(Ecuadorian Air Force)	C-GDCZ FAE-447 [w/o 14Feb91 Mount Paso, Mucuna, Ecuador]
833	300	Ecuadorian Air Force	C-GDFT FAE-448
834	300	(Ecuadorian Air Force)	C-GDIU FAE-449+ N463BA [w/o 20Jan11 near Tena, Ecuador; with marks N463BA reserved at this time]
835	300	Ethiopian Airlines	C-GDFT ET-AIX
836	300	Supreme Commission for Tourism	C-GDCZ HZ-ATO HZ-SCT
837	300	Maldivian Air Taxi	C-GDFT 7P-LAP N565GA C-GJDI C-GJDP+ OY- 8Q-MAJ [+ canx 11Aug09 to Denmark but not regd there]

DE HAVILLAND CANADA DHC-6 TWIN OTTER

C/n	Model	Last known Owner/Operator	Identities/fates/comments (where appropriate)
838	310	Air Kaibu	C-GDIU 7P-LAQ ZS-OEF N6371X A2-OTA N451RA ZS-OEF ZS-PNS N970AS C-GIGZ D2-KVV
839	300	British Antarctic Survey	C-GDCZ VP-FBL
840	300	Air Loyaute	C-GDKL N840ES C-FCVY N721RA PJ-WIM (F-O) C-FZYG F-ONCA
841	300	Regional Air Services	C-GDCZ C-FCZH C-GDCZ N9045S A6-MAR
842	300	Conoco Phillips Alaska	C-FDHA N842AR
843	300	(Royal Nepalese Army)	C-FDKZ RAN-26 [w/o 10Jly91 near Surkhet, Nepal]
844	300	FlyAsianXpress	C-FDQL 9M-MDN [substantial damage 13Sep08 Bakalalan, Malaysia]
VIKING DHC-6-400 TWIN OTTER			
845	400	Zimex Aviation	C-FMJO HB-LUX
846	400	Air Seychelles	C-GLVA(1) S7-CUR
847	400	Peruvian Air Force	C-GNVA(1) (5A-PAC) 301
848	400	Trans Maldivian Airways	(C-GUVA) C-FPPL 8Q-TMX
849	400	Trans Maldivian Airways	C-GVVA C-GLCU 8Q-TMY
850	400	Trans Maldivian Airways	C-GVAQ C-GLTI 8Q-TMZ [floatplane]
851	400	Zimex Aviation	C-FUVA C-FTRO VH-ZZH HB-LPY
852	400	US Army Golden Knights	C-FMJO+ N [+ canx 10Jly12 to USA]
853	400	OK Tedi Mining?	C-GLVA(2) C-GOVN P2-IRM
854	400	Petrolair	C-GUVA 5A-PAC
855	400	Viking Air	C-GFVT(1) C-GNOA [for Air Loyaute]
856	400	ex Viking Air	C-GUVT(1)+ OB- [+ canx 29May12 to Peru]
857	400	Korfez Havacilik/Gozen Air Service	C-GVVA TC-KHC [floatplane]
858	400	Peruvian Air Force	C-GLVA 302
859	400	OK Tedi Mining?	C-GVAQ P2-BFW*
860	400	Vityaz Avia	C-GFVT(2) RA-67281*
861	400	Viking Air	C-GNVA(2) RA-67282*
862	400	Viking Air	C-GLVA(3)
863	400	Viking Air	C-FVAT
864	400	Viking Air	C-GUVA [for Caverton Helicopters as 5N-SHE]
865	400	Viking Air	C-GFAP
866	400	Viking Air	C-FGAL
867	400	Viking Air	C-GUVT(2)
868	400	Viking Air	C-FAFI
869			
870			
871			
872			
873			
874			
875			
876			
877			
878			
879			
880			

Unidentified

unkn	300		HK-3027 [registered circa 1983 and canx 08Oct92]
unkn	200		HK-3677 [registered 22Nov91 and canx 10May95]
unkn		Islena Airlines	HR-IBE [reported]
unkn		SVG Air	J8-GAL [reported 08Jly09 in Barbados]
unkn	?		N5801J [ferried Nice-Cork 16Jun93; at Keflavik, Iceland 18Jun93; to Goose Bay, NL, Canada 19Jun93]
unkn	?	Alpenwings titles	OE-ELX [photo dated 07Aug04 reported on internet; but OE-E only used for single-engined aircraft]
unkn	?	PT Aviastar Mandiri	PK-BRQ [registered 19Feb08, c/n unknown]
unkn	?	Hevi-Lift	PK-LTV [reported 30Mar11 Cairns, QLD, Australia]
unkn	?	Nature Air	TI-BDZ [reported 25Dec10 San Jose, Costa Rica; probably either c/n 267 or 285]
unkn	?	Mexican Air Force	TP200 [noted Apr 88]
unkn	?		XC-BOS [reported Mexico City, Mexico in Mar00, Jan05 and Mar06; is probably not c/n 519]

DE HAVILLAND CANADA DHC-6 TWIN OTTER

C/n	Model	Last known Owner/Operator	Identities/fates/comments (where appropriate)	
unkn	300	Safarilink Aviation	5Y-SLF	[reported 21Sep09 Nairobi-Wilson, Kenya; possibly c/n 513 ex ZS-SCJ canx Jly09]
unkn	?	Malaysian Helicopter Services	9M-SSN	[reported 05Mar90 routing Kerkira-Bournemouth, UK-Plymouth, UK en-route to Scenic Airlines in the USA. This cannot be c/n 659 which used these marks post Nov00]
unkn	300	Kivu Air	9Q-CCX	[reported in Jly07 United Nations sponsored report as being at Goma, Democratic Republic of Congo]
unkn	?	United Arab Air Force	2266	[reported Oct11 Al Ain AFB, UAE]
unkn	?	PT Aviastar Mandiri	[unknown]	[w/o landing at Sugapa Airport, Indonesia]
unkn	?	French Air Force	[unknown]	[aircraft operating for the United Nations; crashed 06May07 near El Thamad, 80km SE of Nakhi in the Sinai desert]
unkn	?	Chilean Air Force	[unknown]	[w/o 02Jly08 near La Lobada, Southern Chile]
unkn	?	Chilean Air Force	949	

DE HAVILLAND CANADA DHC-7

C/n	Model	Last known Owner/Operator	Identities/fates/comments (where appropriate)
001	100	Canadian Aviation Museum	C-GNBX [prototype ff 27Mar75; wfu 26Oct88 & preserved Rockcliffe, ON, Canada]
002	100	(de Havilland Canada)	C-GNCA [wfu Dec88; b/u 22Feb89 Van Nuys, CA]
003	102	(AGES Group)	C-GQIW-X EC-DCB C-GFEL N703WW [canx Mar95; b/u Jly92 Oklahoma City, OK]
004	102	(Pegasus Aviation)	C-GQYX N27RM [wfu & b/u Amarillo, TX; canx Jun00]
005	102	Linea Turistica Aereotuy	C-GNPU N9058P (N17AP) N702AC YV-638C YV1185
006	102	(Pegasus Aviation)	N37RM C-GSEV N926RM N28RN [wfu & b/u Amarillo, TX; canx Jun00]
007	103	(Candler & Associates)	C-GXVF-X C-GXVF N27AP C-GWTG N677MA [b/u Tucson, AZ Jan02]
008	102	(Arkia Israel Airlines)	132001+ C-GJSZ 4X-AHI [+ Canada] [wfu circa 2000 & b/u May04 Tel Aviv-Sde Dov, Israel]
009	103	Trans Capital Air/UN	A6-ALM OY-GRD C-FPBJ+ [+ UN code UN-498]
010	103	Air Tindi	C-GRQB-X OY-CBT C-GUAT
011	103	Trans Capital Air/UN	C-GXVG N791S N210AW C-GJVY N273EP HH-TRO N273EP C-FDTI PK-TVS C-FJHQ [UN code UN-145]
012	103	Trans Capital Air/UN	132002+ C-GILE N678MA C-FWYU [+ Canada] [UN code UN-234]
013	102	(Voyageur Airways)	N890S (N779HA) N890S C-FXFX [b/u Jun98 North Bay, ON, Canada]
014	102	(DPF Airlease)	N170RA [stored Sep95 & b/u Sep98 Kingman, AZ; canx Aug96]
015	103	(Alyemda)	(C-GXVH) 7O-ACK [w/o 09May82 Gulf of Aden]
016	102	(DPF Airlease)	N171RA [stored Sep95 & b/u Sep98 Kingman, AZ; canx Aug96]
017	102	Linea Turistica Aereotuy	N47RM YV-640C [stored Caracas-Simon Bolivar, Venezuela]
018	102	ex Zest Airways	C-GBOZ N895S N701AC RP-C2996 [stored by Dec09 Manila, Philippines; l/n Sep11]
019	103	(Regional A/L Support Group)	N4860J (N486GG) N4860J N701GA [b/u for spares Fort Lauderdale International, FL; canx 12Sep12]
020	103	Air Greenland	OY-CBU
021	102	(Arkia Israel Airlines)	N701GW C-GXPO 4X-AHK [wfu circa 2000 & b/u Oct2000 Tel Aviv-Sde Dov, Israel]
022	102	(Far Airlines)	OE-HLS OE-LLS I-FARB [b/u 29Mar01 Guernsey, Channel Islands, UK]
023	103	Yemenia	7O-ACL [reported wfu at Sana'a, Yemen]
024	102	(Gulfstream International A/L)	HR-AND N234SL TC-JCJ N234SL (PH-SDP) C-FDNR N234SL (N703GA) [wfu by Jan01; sold to Voyageur A/W & b/u circa Oct03 Fort Lauderdale International, FL]
025	102	(AGES Aircraft Sales & Leasing)	N900HA N25AG [stored Jly01 Bangor, ME, and wfu; l/n 16Sep07 as hulk]
026	102	(AGES Aircraft Sales & Leasing)	C-GTAD N726AG HP-1250AHC N8041D YV-640C N2620 [stored Jly01& b/u Dec01 Bangor, ME]
027	102	(AGES Group)	N172RA [stored 19Jly01 & b/u Dec01 Bangor, ME]
028	102	(Wideroes Flyveselskap)	N721S LN-WFN [w/o 06May88 Bronnoysund, Norway]
029	102	(Kaiken Lineas Aereas)	N705ZW LN-WFO C-FTSU LV-PHS LV-WJF [wfu & b/u Feb98 Rio Grande, Tierra del Fuego, Argentina]
030	102	Linea Turistica Aereotuy	C-GTAJ N4309N YV-639C YV1184
031	103	Yemenia	7O-ACM [reported wfu at Sana'a, Yemen]
032	102	ex Air Kenya	4W-ACK 7O-ACZ 5Y-BPD [reported wfu by 12Jun11 Nairobi-Wilson, Kenya]
033	102	Trans Capital Air	N8504A TC-JCG (PH-SDR) N235SL OY-MBF N235SL G-BPDX G-BRYF 4X-AHG G-BRYF N235SL 4X-AHG N330KK C-GNUY
034	102	US Govt/US Army	(N700PR) N703GG LN-WFK ZS-IRS N34HG [US type code RC-7B]
035	102	ex Zest Airways	4W-ACL 7O-ADB RP-C2895 [stored by Dec09 Manila, Philippines; l/n Sep11]
036	102	Fugro Aviation Canada	N702GW C-GJPI
037	102	Voyageur Airways/UN	N703GW N67RM C-GFOF
038	102	White Industries	N173RA [stored Bates City, MO; l/n Jun02; canx 29Apr09]
039	102	Voyageur Airways/UN	N724GW N87RM C-GLOL HB-IVW C-GLOL
040	102	(Aviation Enterprises)	C-GELN N919HA [b/u Jly93-Feb94 Clarksburg, WV]
041	102	ex Kaiken Lineas Aereas	LN-WFE C-FTAW LV-WIN [wfu & b/u Feb98 Rio Grande, Tierra del Fuego, Argentina; hulk l/n Dec10]
042	102	(Wilmington Trust)	N901HA [stored Jly01 & b/u Jan06 Bangor, ME]
043	102	(AGES Aircraft Sales & Leasing)	N705GW (N778HA) VH-UUM N90283 [stored Jly00 & b/u Jan06 Bangor, ME; still marked as VH-UUM]
044	102	ex United States Army	N702GG TC-JCH N702GG (PH-SDS) OY-MBG C-FCOQ N702GG [US type code RC-7B; wfu by Jun10 Hagerstown, MD]
045	102	(Arkia Israel Airways)	(OY-MMZ) OY-MBC C-FDFK N7156J LN-WFC N7156J 4X-AHH [canx early 2010 as sold; dismantled in Israel for sea shipment to USA for part-out]
046	102	Aviones Comerciales (AVCOM)	LN-WFI C-FYMK TG-JAY
047	102	Linea Turistica Aereotuy	N701GG OY-GRA N701GG YV-637C [stored Caracas-Simon Bolivar, Venezuela]

DE HAVILLAND CANADA DHC-7

C/n	Model	Last known Owner/Operator	Identities/fates/comments (where appropriate)
048	102	US Govt/Dept of Army	N705GG [US type code RC-7B]
049	102	Skyline Nigeria	N706ZW LN-WFP ZS-ITT N340JK 4X-AHL 5N-EMP [w/o 07Sep99 Port Harcourt, Nigeria]
050	102	(Arkia Israel Airways)	OE-HLT OE-LLT N8120W G-BRYE 4X-AHJ [canx early 2010 as sold; dismantled in Israel for sea shipment to USA for part-out]
051	102	(Arkia Israel Airways)	N929HA 4X-AHE [wfu Oct01 Tel Aviv-Sde Dov, Israel]
052	102	(AGES Group)	N902HA [stored Jly01 & b/u Jan06 Bangor, ME]
053	102	White Industries	N174RA N706GA [stored Jan02 Bates City, MO]
054	110	Pelita Air Service	C-GFCO-X G-BRYC C-FYXV PK-PKT
055	102	ex Skyline Nigeria	(OY-MMY) OY-MBD (G-BPSF) N8102N 4X-AHD 5N-EMR [wfu Tel Aviv-Sde Dov, Israel; used for spares; hulk l/n 19Jan09]
056	102	US Govt/Dept of Army	N175RA VH-UUX N56HG N566CC [US type code RC-7B]
057	102	Telford Aviation	C-GTAZ N341DS [stored Loring-Limestone, ME; l/n Jan06]
058	102	US Govt/Dept of Army	C-GEWQ C-GFJS (N706GG) N2704J C-GFYI N42RA N158CL [US type code RC-7B]
059	102	US Govt/Dept of Army	C-GFBW N707ZW C-GYMC N59AG [US type code RC-7B]
060	102	(Arkia Israel Airways)	C-GFCF 4X-AHA 5N-BDB 4X-AHA 5N-BDS 4X-AHA 5N-BDS 4X-AHA [canx early 2010 as sold; dismantled in Israel for sea shipment to USA for part-out]
061	102	Voyageur Airways/UN	C-GEWQ N708ZW N903HA C-FZKM
062	110	ex Berjaya Air	C-GFBW G-BRYA 9M-TAO [stored/dumped by 09Sep09 at Kuala Lumpur-Subang, Malaysia; l/n 16Sep10]
063	103	Air Tindi	C-GFCF P2-ANN C-GCEV
064	102	Trans Capital Air	C-GFCF 4X-AHB C-GGXS
065	102	US Govt/Dept of Army	C-GFBW (N706GW) C-GFNN N2655P N765MG [US type code RC-7B]
066	110	ex Voyageur Airways	C-GRLA C-GFMU G-BRYB C-FYXT N66SU C-GGUN [wfu North Bay, ON, Canada; l/n 27Oct09 in poor condition]
067	102	(Trans Capital Air)	C-GFCF C-GFLL N939HA C-GLPP [dbr 01May06 Tchien, Liberia; canx 13May09 probably wfu]
068	100	Conviasa	C-GFBW ARV-0203+ YV-1169C YV1000 [+ Venezuela]
069	102	AGES Group	C-GFBW N709ZW C-GYXC N169AG [stored Jly01 & b/u Jan06 Bangor, ME]
070	102	Voyageur Airways	C-GEWQ N710ZW N905HA (N747BC) N905HA C-GGUL
071	102	(Wilmington Trust)	C-GFCF C-GFNN (N707GW) N2655W C-GFQL N53RA N171CL [wfu circa 94 Fort Lauderdale International, FL; canx Jan95]
072	103	Trans Capital Airways	C-GEWQ (ET-AHS) C-GEWQ P2-ANO C-GJKS P2-ANO C-GJKS N272EP HP-1242AHC N272EP P2-ANO N722A C-FASC HH-TRP N272EP C-GVPP+ [had UN code UN431]
073	102	Arkia Israel Airlines	C-GFCF N720AS 4X-AHM 5N-SKA 4X-AHM
074	102	Air Tindi	C-GEWQ N903HA C-GHRV N6541C A6-ADA A6-ADG C-GFFL HB-IVY C-GFFL
075	103	Pelita Air Service	C-GFCF (ET-AHT) C-GFCF PK-PSZ
076	102	US Govt/Dept of Army	C-GFOD N176RA [US type code RC-7B]
077	102	Trans Capital Air	C-GFCF C-GFQL OY-MBE (G-BPSG) N8110N G-BOAZ N76598 4X-AHF N770DD C-GYTZ
078	102	(Zest Airways)	C-GFRP N60RA (N772HA) RP-C2988 [reported wfu Manila, Philippines; l/n Feb02; hulk by Sep09]
079	102	ex Zest Airways	C-GFUM N949HA RP-C1382 N67DA RP-C2978 [stored by Dec09 Manila, Philippines]
080	102	ex Regional Air Services	C-GFYI N904HA C-GHSL N747BC N780MG 5Y-BMP 5H-BMP [canx from online register; fate/status unknown]
081	103	Air Tindi	C-GFOD P2-ANP C-FWZV
082	102	ex Skyline Nigeria	C-GFUM 4X-AHC 5N-BDT [stored & canx 22Jun03 Tel Aviv-Sde Dov, Israel; wfu & used for spares; hulk l/n 05May08; b/u 09Nov09]
083	102	ex Air Kenya	C-GFQL N721AS 5Y-BMJ [reported wfu by Jly08 Nairobi-Wilson, Kenya; l/n 12Jun11]
084	102	(DNK Aviation Leasing)	C-GEWQ LN-WFL SU-MAB VP-CDY [w/o 28Nov98 near Bickington, Devon, UK]
085	102	US Govt/US Army	C-GFOD N177RA
086	103	Pelita Air Service	C-GFUM PK-PSY
087	102	ex Trans Capital Air	C-GFBW C-GBZR HK-3111X HK-3111G HK-3111W HK-3111 C-GCPP [stored by 01May09 Toronto-Island Airport, ON, Canada; possible parts use; l/n 30Aug09]
088	102	US Govt/Dept of Army	C-GFOD C-GESG HK-3112X HK-3112G N89068 [US type code RC-7B]

DE HAVILLAND CANADA DHC-7

C/n	Model	Last known Owner/Operator	Identities/fates/comments (where appropriate)
089	102	(Asian Spirit)	C-GFQL N62RA (N773HA) RP-C2788 [w/o 04Sep02 Manila, Philippines; l/n Sep11 derelict]
090	102	ex Zest Airways	C-GFRP YU-AIE SL-ACA S5-ACA C-GELW SX-BNA RP-C2955 [stored by 2009 Manila, Philippines; l/n Sep11]
091	102	ex Tassili Airlines/BenAvia	C-GFUM LN-WFG SU-MAC VP-CDZ HB-IVX [canx 21Oct05; stored by Oct03 Luqa, Malta; l/n May10]
092	102	ex Zest Airways	C-GFCF YU-AIF SL-ACB S5-ACB C-GELY (N383BC) RP-C2915 [probably stored by 2009 Manila, Philippines]
093	102	Petroleum Air Services	C-GFYI SU-CBA
094	103	Pelita Air Service	C-GFYI PK-PSX
095	102	(US Govt/Dept of Army)	C-GFQL N905HA C-GGUZ N5382W [US type code RC-7B; w/o 23Jly99 near Puerto Ospina, Colombia]
096	102	ex Petroleum Air Services	C-GEWQ SU-CBB [reported wfu by Sep09 Cairo, Egypt]
097	102	Petroleum Air Services	C-GFQL SU-CBC
098	102	Petroleum Air Services	C-GEWQ SU-CBD
099	102	Petroleum Air Services	C-GFBW SU-CBE
100	103	Pelita Air Service	C-GFCF PK-PSW
101	102	Air Tindi	C-GFQL ZK-NEW G-BNDC OY-CTC C-GCPY
102	150	Transport Canada	C-GCFR
103	102	Conviasa	C-GFRP ZK-NEX G-BNGF N773BE N703MG C-FEDO YV1003 [by 07Apr07 stored North Bay, ON, Canada; l/n 29May08 with parts missing]
104	103	US Govt/Dept of Army	C-GFUM N53993 [US type code RC7B]
105	103	Pelita Air Service	C-GFOD PK-PSV
106	103	Air Greenland	C-GFYI (N53994) N54026 OY-GRE
107	102	Air Guinee	C-GEWQ 3X-GCJ
108	102	Trans Capital Air/UN	C-GFBW HK-3340X HK-3340G HK-3340W C-GVWD [UN code UN-311]
109	110	Berjaya Air	C-GEWQ G-BRYD 9M-TAH
110	110	Berjaya Air	C-GFBW G-BOAW LN-TAW G-BOAW 9M-TAK
111	110	British Antarctic Survey	C-GDNG G-BOAX VP-FBQ
112	110	Berjaya Air	C-GFBW G-BOAY 9M-TAL
113	102	Air Greenland	C-GFCF (G-BOAZ) OE-LLU OY-GRF
114	102		[not completed]

Production complete

DE HAVILLAND CANADA DHC-8

C/n	Model	Last known Owner/Operator	Identities/fates/comments (where appropriate)

Note: In the Canadian Armed Forces service the DHC-8 (Dash 8) is known by the designation CT-142.

C/n	Model	Last known Owner/Operator	Identities/fates/comments (where appropriate)
001	300	(de Havilland Canada)	C-GDNK [prototype series 100 ff 20Jun83; cvtd series 300 May87; wfu Sep89; b/u Aug90 Van Nuys, CA]
002	Q200	Pima Community Avn Center	C-GGMP [series 100 reg'd 18Mar99 as series Q200; wfu & donated to Pima Community Avn Center, Tucson, AZ as GIA]
003	103	Presidential Airways	C-GGOM N810LR
004	101	Skytrans Regional/Marooba A/S	C-GGPJ VH-TQO VH-QQB
005	102	Skytrans Regional/Marooba A/S	C-GGTO N85CL HC-BSX N4229R VH-WZS P2-MCN VH-QQA
006	102	Airlines of Papua New Guinea	C-GJCB P2-MCG
007	102	ALS Ltd	C-GEOA N800MX C-GFQI V2-LFJ C-GFQI TR-LGX C-GFQI 5Y-BVO
008	102	Skytrans Regional	C-GERL C-GHSY N801MX VH-DHD P2-NAY VH-JSZ VH-QQC
009	101	Piedmont/US Airways Express	C-GHRI N906HA
010	103	Kahama Mining Corp	C-GERL C-GIAU OE-HLR C-GIQQ N809MX C-GIQQ OE-LLR P2-RDY OE-LLR C-GTBZ OE-LLR N101AV N802WP 5H-KMC
011	101	Piedmont/US Airways Express	C-GESR N907HA
012	102	Airlines of Papua New Guinea	C-GPYD P2-MCH
013	102	Arctic Sunwest	C-GETI N802MX TJ-AIC C-GAKZ VH-JSY N802MX C-GASB
014	102	Skytrans Regional	C-GCTX(1) N814CL VH-WZI P2-MCO VH-QQF
015	101	Piedmont/US Airways Express	C-GEVP C-GIBQ N908HA
016	102	(Regional Air Support)	C-GEOA N803MX N819EX [stored May03 Springfield, MO; b/u Apr04 for spares; canx 17Jly04]
017	103	Government of Alberta	C-GFSJ
018	102	ex AIRES Colombia	C-GESR N909HA HK-4258X HK-4258 [possibly wfu by 18Sep08 Bangor, ME; probably arrived post Sep07]
019	102	(Regional Air Support)	C-GLOT N804MX N820EX [stored May03 Springfield, MO; b/u Jun04 for spares; canx Jly04]
020	101	Transport Canada	C-GCFJ
021	110	(TYR Aviation Services)	C-GETI C-GIQK V2-LCV C-GOBE [b/u Calgary, AB, Canada; canx Dec02]
022	102	(Regional One)	C-GEVP N910HA [stored May03 Springfield, MO; b/u May06]
023	103	(Willis Lease Finance)	C-GEOA N811PH N807WP [by Oct06 wfu Honolulu, HI; canx 08Feb07]
024	102	Dynamic Avlease Inc/US Army	C-GMOK 5N-MGV C-FZCC N1000 [survey aircraft]
025	101	Air Canada Jazz	C-GABF
026	103	Hawaii Island Air	C-GESR N812PH N808WP
027	102	Airlines of Papua New Guinea	C-FCTE N27CL VH-WZJ P2-MCL
028	101	Transport Canada	C-GCFK
029	110	(TYR Aviation Services)	C-GLOT V2-LCW C-FDDC [b/u Calgary, AB, Canada circa mid Feb02]
030	102	US Department of Justice	C-GEOA N444T N713M
031	110	(TYR Aviation Services)	C-GESR V2-LCX C-FTYR [wfu at Calgary, AB, Canada; b/u for spares Didsbury, AB, Canada; canx 05Oct01]
032	102	Island Air	C-GETI N813PH N813SN N809WP
033	102	Airlines of Papua New Guinea	C-GEVP N805MX VH-TNX P2- VH-QQH P2-MCP
034	101	Piedmont/US Airways Express	C-GEOA N911HA
035	110	ex LIAT – The Caribbean Airline	C-GESR V2-LCY [stored by Oct04 Antigua-VC Bird International, Antigua; l/n 10Feb11 as hulk]
036	102	Skytrans Regional	C-GEVP N806MX VH-TND P2-MCM 5W-FAA VH-QQG P2-MCM* [* marks reserved 01Mar12 for Airlines PNG]
037	102	USAF	C-GLOT N801AP 84-0047 [E-9A] [damaged 01May08 Tallahassee, FL]
038	102	Arctic Sunwest	C-GJBT 142801+ C-GJUZ C-FASC [+ Canada]
039	101	3 Points Aviation Corp	C-FCTA N805LR [by 23Mar08 stored Calgary, AB, Canada; l/n 03Sep11]
040	101	Piedmont/US Airways Express	C-GEOA N912HA
041	102	Airlines of Papua New Guinea	C-GESR N807MX VH-TNG P2-MCK VH-QQD P2-MCK
042	101	Air Canada Jazz	C-GANF
043	102	(Air Jamaica Express)	C-GETI N814PH 6Y-JEC [wfu & b/u Apr05 Calgary, AB, Canada by TYR Aviation Services]
044	102	Air Canada Jazz	C-FABN
045	102	USAF	C-GEVP N802AP 84-0048 [E-9A]
046	102	Transport Canada	C-GIQG 142802+ C-GJVB C-GSUR [+ Canada]
047	103	EP Aviation LLC	C-GAAC N801LR N635AR
048	110	(TYR Aviation Services)	C-GEOA V2-LCZ C-FEML [wfu at Calgary, AB, Canada; b/u for spares Didsbury, AB, Canada; canx 21Dec01]
049	102	Air Canada Jazz	C-FABT

DE HAVILLAND CANADA DHC-8

C/n	Model	Last known Owner/Operator	Identities/fates/comments (where appropriate)
050	102	(Air Jamaica Express)	C-GESR N815PH 6Y-JED [canx 23Dec05; noted 03Jun06 wfu Quebec-Jean Lesage International, QC, Canada missing many parts]
051	103	Presidential Airways	C-GAAN N511AV
052	102	Skippers Aviation	C-GFQL P2-GVA VH-XFT ZK-NEW(1) VH-XFT
053	101	Piedmont/US Airways Express	C-GETI N914HA
054	102	(GMG Airlines)	C-GFOD N816PH S2-ADJ [wfu by May09 & b/u by Nov11 Dhaka, Bangladesh]
055	102	(Ansett New Zealand)	C-GFRP ZK-NEY(1) [w/o 09Jun95 Palmerston North, New Zealand; canx 12Jly95]
056	101	(Volvo Aero Services)	C-GFUM N817PH [b/u for spares circa Mar02 Bangor, ME]
057	102	Air Canada Jazz	C-GANS
058	102	(Volvo Aero Services)	C-GFYI N818PH [b/u for spares circa Mar02 Bangor, ME]
059	102	(Air Creebec)	C-GAAM 6Y-JEB N507CT C-FHRV [wfu Timmins, ON, Canada; never entered service with Air Creebec, used for parts; canx 27Feb07 as b/u]
060	102	Danish Air Transport	C-GEOA ZK-NEZ(1) ZK-VAC OY-RUW
061	101	(Alaska Horizon)	C-GESR N819PH [w/o 16Apr88 near Seattle-Tacoma, WA]
062	103	Bluebird Aviation	C-GJFX D-BEST VH-TQN 5Y-VVN
063	102	AIRES Colombia	C-GLOT N820PH HK-4345X HK-4345
064	102	Air Canada Jazz	C-GANI
065	102	Air Canada Jazz	C-GCTC N65CL C-GCTC
066	102	Air Canada Jazz	C-GTBP
067	102	Airlines of Papua New Guinea	C-GFYI N801AW VH-TQF P2- VH-QQI P2-MCW
068	102	Air Canada Jazz	C-GJIG
069	101	Avmax Group	C-GFUM N915HA C-FCWC [stored Calgary AB, Canada still marked as N915HA; l/n 03Sep11still in US Airways Express c/s; hulk, for spares use]
070	102	3 Points Aviation Corp	C-GWRR N807LR [stored by 23Mar08 Calgary, AB, Canada; l/n 03Sep11; wfu for spares]
071	102	Canadian Armed Forces	C-GESR 142803 [CT-142]
072	102	Westinghouse Aircraft Leasing	C-GEOA N916HA [status unclear, may have been b/u]
073	102	3 Points Aviation Corp	C-GTAE N808LR [stored by 23Mar08 Calgary, AB, Canada; reported will be b/u for spares; canx 17Apr09]
074	102	(3 Points Aviation Corp)	C-GESR N802AW N840PH C-GESC N253P [canx 22Dec04 as sold in Canada, but not reg'd; b/u Calgary, AB, Canada]
075	102	(Westinghouse Aircraft Leasing)	C-GEVP N917HA [b/u in 2004 Calgary, AB, Canada]
076	103	(AIRES Colombia)	C-GLOT OE-LLP N4101Z HK-3946X HK-3946 [wfu 2007; sold to 3 Points Avn Corp for parts; noted as hulk 16Sep07 Bangor, ME]
077	103	Air Canada Jazz	C-GJMI
078	103	Air Canada Jazz	C-GTAI
079	102	Air Canada Jazz	C-GJMO
080	102	Canadian Armed Forces	C-GFRP 142804 [CT-142]
081	102	(3 Points Aviation Corp)	C-GJMK [canx 06Apr05; b/u Apr05 Calgary, AB, Canada]
082	102	(Canadian Metro A/L)	C-GFOD N804AW N841PH (N841SL) [canx 04Mar04 as sold in Canada, but not reg'd; b/u London, ON, Canada]
083	102	Hawkair Aviation Service	C-GTAF N809LR C-FYDH
084	102	(NTE Aviation)	C-GFRP N920HA [canx 24Jly03; b/u Mar03 Nashville, TN]
085	102	Air Canada Jazz	C-GJSV
086	103	EP Aviation LLC	C-GTBU N801WP C-FJFW N986BW N150RN N636AR
087	102	Air Canada Jazz	C-GANK
088	102	Air Canada Jazz	C-GJSX
089	102	(NTE Aviation)	C-GLOT N921HA [canx 24Jly03; b/u Jly03 Nashville, TN]
090	102	Air Canada Jazz	C-GOND
091	102	(3 PoInts Aviation Corp)	C-GFOD OE-LLO C-FATA OE-LLO N102AV C-GESH N926P [canx 01Nov04 as sold in Canada, but not regd; b/u Calgary, AB, Canada]
092	102	Air Canada Jazz	C-FABA
093	102	ex 3 Points Aviation Corp	C-GONH N806LR [stored by 23Mar08 Calgary, AB, Canada; l/n 10Sep08; reported will be b/u for spares; canx 17Apr09]
094	102	Avmax Group	C-GETI N922HA C-FCWE [stored May03 Calgary, AB, Canada still marked N922HA; l/n Jun11 still in US Airways Express c/s]
095	102	Air Canada Jazz	C-GONJ
096	102	Air Canada Jazz	C-FANQ
097	102	Air Canada Jazz	C-FABW
098	102	Frontier Alaska	C-GEVP D-BERT N882EA
099	103	Presidential Airways	C-GEOA N923HA C-GZTC N990AV

DE HAVILLAND CANADA DHC-8

C/n	Model	Last known Owner/Operator	Identities/fates/comments (where appropriate)
100	301	AIRES Colombia	C-FWBB N100CQ HS-SKM N100CQ 9V-RGB N100CQ HK-4030X HK-4030
101	102	Air Canada Jazz	C-GONN
102	102	Air Canada Jazz	C-GONO
103	102	Canadian Armed Forces	C-GDNG 142805+ [CT-142]
104	102	DAC Aviation	C-GEVP N821PH 6Y-JMT 5Y-BTP
105	102	Southern Star Airlines	C-GFOD N924HA RA-67253 C-FOVR 9Q-CWP 5Y-BZI
106	102	ex Caribbean Star	C-GFQL N822PH V2-LFO [wfu & stored Aug06; fuselage only 15Jly09 Calgary, AB, Canada]
107	102	Canadian Armed Forces	C-GFQL 142806+ [CT-142]
108	301	Wings Abadi Air	C-GEVP N108CL B-3353 N108TY PK-WIE
109	102	Air Canada Jazz	C-GONR
110	102	(Trident Aviation)	C-GFUM N823PH 6Y-JMZ 5Y-EMD [w/o 13Jan10 Moba, Democratic Republic of Congo, whilst being operated by DAC East Africa]
111	102	North Cariboo Air	C-GFYI N925HA C-FCWP
112	102	Air Canada Jazz	C-GONW
113	102	LIAT – The Caribbean Airline	C-GEOA C-FCTD EI-BWX V2-LDQ
114	102	fly540 Airlines	C-GETI N926HA C- N926HA C-GRGZ 5Y-BYB
115	102	Air Canada Jazz	C-GONY
116	301	Wings Abadi Air	C-GDNG B-3351 N116TY PK-WID
117	102	Skytrans Regional	C-GEOA N927HA C-GZKH+ N717AV VH-QQI [+ used UN code UN-95W for period]
118	102	Air Canada Jazz	C-GONX
119	102	Air Creebec	C-GTCO
120	102	Perimeter Aviation	C-GFOD N928HA C-GWPS
121	102	Air Creebec	C-GEOA B-15201 C-FWZV (6V-AGZ) 6V-AHD N381BC C-GJOP
122	102	Air Creebec	C-FCSK
123	102	Air Inuit	C-FDAO
124	301	Air Canada Jazz	C-GKTA
125	102	(Airlines of Papua New Guinea)	C-GETI B-15203 ZK-NES(1) P2-MCJ [w/o 13Oct10 near Madang, Papua New Guinea]
126	102	Piedmont/US Airways Express	C-GFQL (N929HA) N930HA
127	102A	Air Canada Jazz	C-GION
128	102	Air Service Gabon	C-FDOJ OB-1768 C-FDOJ TR-LHA
129	102	Wasaya Airways	C-FDND
130	102	Air Canada Jazz	C-GKON
131	301	Air Canada Jazz	C-GMON
132	102	Piedmont/US Airways Express	C-GFOD N931HA
133	102	ex Air Labrador	C-GLON [wfu Summerside, Prince Edward Island, Canada; by 15Sep11 hulk status]
134	102	Piedmont/US Airways Express	C-GFUM N933HA
135	102	Airlines of Papua New Guinea	C-GFQL VH-TQP P2- VH-QQH P2-MCT
136	102	(AIRES Colombia)	C-GFYI OE-LLN N4101T HK-3942X HK-3924 [wfu 2007; sold to 3 Points Avn Corp and/or Hawkair for parts; noted as hulk 16Sep07 Bangor, ME]
137	301	Air Canada Jazz	C-GNON
138	102	Air Creebec	C-FCIZ C-GAIS
139	102	Piedmont/US Airways Express	C-GETI N934HA
140	102	ex Volvo Aero Services	C-GFOD EI-BZC V2-LDP N140LS [stored Nov06 Marana, AZ; ferried 15/16Nov07 to Bangor, ME for parts recovery; hulk l/n 18Sep08; canx 04Dec08]
141	103	Magellan Aviation Services	C-FDNE N803WP [stored by Dec07 Quebec-Jean Lesage International, QC, Canada; to be b/u for spares; canx 20Feb08]
142	102	Piedmont/US Airways Express	C-GLOT N935HA
143	301	Air Canada Jazz	C-GUON
144	103	LIAT – The Caribbean Airline	C-GEOA HS-SKH V2-LEF
145	102	Piedmont/US Airways Express	C-GFQL N936HA
146	102	SN146 LLC	C-GETI N805AW N829EX [stored Goderich, ON, Canada; l/n 17May07]
147	102	(TYR Aviation Services)	C-FABG [b/u Nov05 Terrace Bay, BC, Canada]
148	102	Piedmont/US Airways Express	C-GLOT N937HA
149	301	Air Canada Jazz	C-GVON
150	102	Air Canada Jazz	C-FACD
151	102	Skippers Aviation	C-GFYI N711MS P2-GVB VH-XFU ZK-NEV VH-XFU
152	102	Piedmont/US Airways Express	C-GFUM N938HA
153	102	Air Niugini	C-GFOD D-BOBO P2-ANL(2)+I449
154	301	Air Canada Jazz	C-GLTA

DE HAVILLAND CANADA DHC-8

C/n	Model	Last known Owner/Operator	Identities/fates/comments (where appropriate)
155	102	ex Air Inuit	C-GFQL N806AW N830EX C-GAIW+ XA- [canx 11Jly12 to Mexico]
156	102	Piedmont/US Airways Express	C-GLOT N940HA
157	102	Provincial Airlines	C-GEOA N824PH C-GPAL
158	102	Air Creebec	C-FCJD
159	301	(Bahamasair)	C-GFYI N801XV C6-BFN [w/o 20Apr07 Governor's Harbour/Cape Eleuthera, Bahamas; canx by Jan09]
160	102	ex Air Inuit	C-GEWQ N807AW N831EX C-GAII+ XA- [+ canx 25May12 to Mexico]
161	102	Piedmont/US Airways Express	C-GETI N941HA
162	102	(Mellon Financial Group)	C-FCJI N883CC [wore false marks G-ZPXN for period while in store at Calgary, AB, Canada] [b/u Nov06 Calgary, AB, Canada; canx 22Dec06; remains noted 25Aug07 Airdrie, AB, Canada]
163	102	Piedmont/US Airways Express	C-GFUM N942HA
164	301	Bahamasair	C-GDNG N802XV C6-BFO
165	102	Hawkair Aviation Service	C-FCJE
166	102	Hawkair Aviation Service	C-FDNG
167	102	Piedmont/US Airways Express	C-GFOD N943HA
168	102	(Mellon Financial Group)	C-FDNH N882CC [b/u Nov06 Calgary, AB, Canada; canx 22Dec06; by 05Oct11 fuselage to Toronto-International, ON, Canada]
169	301	AIRES Colombia	C-GFEN (N803XV) C-FGNP N6625A PJ-DHC N169CL HS-SKU N169CL HK-3952X HK-3952
170	103	National Jet Systems	C-GFQL VH-NID VH-NJD VH-JSJ
171	102	Air Canada Jazz	C-FPON
172	102	(Bangkok Airways)	C-GFUM HS-SKI [w/o 21Nov90 en route to Koh Samui Island, Thailand; Jan96 remains to Dodson Aviation, Ottawa, KS]
173	102	Maroomba Airlines	C-GLOT N808AW N821EX VH-QQE
174	301	Air Canada Jazz	C-GMTA
175	102	Air Creebec	C-GFOD OE-HRS OE-LRS N283BC 6Y-JML N283BC C-GYWX N283BC C-GYWX
176	102	Piedmont/US Airways Express	C-GEWQ N975HA
177	102	Air Niugini	C-GFQL D-BOBY P2-ANP
178	102	(Air Canada Jazz)	C-FTON [b/u Aug04 Calgary, AB, Canada; canx 06Apr05; by 07Aug08 fuselage to Kelowna, BC, Canada]
179	102	Common Air Service/UN	C-FCON 5Y-STN
180	301	Air Canada Jazz	C-GFOD (N804XV) C-FGVK C-GTAQ
181	102	(Air Canada Jazz)	C-FVON [b/u Aug04 Calgary, AB, Canada; canx 06Apr05]
182	301	Air Canada Jazz	C-GSTA
183	102	Air Labrador	C-FXON V2-LDZ C-FXON
184	301	not yet known	C-GFUM (N805XV) C-FGVL PJ-DHD N184CL HK-3951X N184AV C-GRGF+ TT- [+ canx 07May12 to Tchad]
185	102	Aircraft Leasing Services – ALS	C-FGQI 5Y-PRV
186	301	Air Canada Jazz	C-GETA
187	102	(Werner Aviation)	C-GDNG N809AW N822EX [canx 18Jun04; b/u Jun04 Springfield, MI]
188	301	Air Canada Jazz	C-FGVT (N806XV) C-FGVT C-GTAT
189	103	Kenyan Air Force	C-GLOT KAF-304
190	301	Air Canada Jazz	C-GVTA
191	102A	(Air Inuit)	C-GFRP N810AW N817EX C-FESG [b/u Sep06 Winnipeg, MB, Canada; canx 12Sep06]
192	301	Regional 1 Airlines	C-GFRP C6-BFL HK-4061X N3554T N192PF
193	102	Air Canada Jazz	C-FGQK
194	301	Wings Abadi Air	C-GFCF B-3352 N194TY PK-WIA [stored by Aug11 Surabaya, Indonesia]
195	102	Air Canada Jazz	C-FGRC
196	301	(Intercontinental de Aviacion)	C-GETI C6-BFM HK-4062X [w/o 14Sep97 Pereira, Colombia]
197	102	Airlines of Papua New Guinea	C-GEOA B-15205 ZK-NET(1) P2-MCI
198	301	Air Canada Jazz	C-GHTA
199	102	Air Canada Jazz	C-FGRM
200	301	Air Canada Jazz	C-GTAG
201	102A	(Air Inuit)	C-GDNG N811AW (N811EX) C-FGQL [canx 11Jly06 as b/u; details unknown]
202	311A	Air Canada Jazz	C-GEWQ
203	102	Air Kenya	C-GLOT OE-LLM VH-TNU 5Y-BTZ
204	102	Bluebird Aviation	C-GFUM VH-TQQ 5Y-VVR

DE HAVILLAND CANADA DHC-8

C/n	Model	Last known Owner/Operator	Identities/fates/comments (where appropriate)
205	102	Aircraft Leasing Services – ALS	C-GABI N802LR C-FLAD 5Y-BXH
206	102	Air Service Gabon	C-FHRA LN- C-FHRA TR-LHF
207	102	Air Canada Jazz	C-FGRP
208	102	Airlines of Papua New Guinea	C-GESR VH-TQR P2- VH-QQJ P2-MCU
209	102	Provincial Airlines	C-FHRC TJ-AIA C-FHRC LN- C-FHRC TR-LGL C-FHRC
210	311A	(Contact Air)	C-GEOA D-BEAT [w/o 06Jan93 near Paris-Charles de Gaulle, France]
211	102	Airlines of Papua New Guinea	C-GABH C-FNCG P2-MCY
212	102	Air Canada Jazz	C-FGRY
213	102	fly540 Airlines	C-GEOA N825PH 5Y-BXB
214	102	(3 Points Aviation Corp)	C-GFUM N826PH [b/u during 2005 Calgary, AB, Canada]
215	103	Wells Fargo Bank/Era Aviation	C-GFCF EI-CBJ C-GZPV RA-67251(1) C-FOVO+ N215AL N886EA [+ reported 02May08 Yuzhno-Sakhalinsk, Russia]
216	311A	CHC Tchad	C-GFRP (N807XV) PH-SDI 5N-EVD PH-SDI 5N-EVD PH-SDI C-GOFW TT-DAC
217	102A	Piedmont/US Airways Express	C-GETI N801EX N976HA N837EX
218	102	Air Marshall Islands	C-GESR B-15207 ZK-NEU(1) V7-0210
219	103	Kenyan Air Force	C-GFCF KAF-305
220	102	Piedmont/US Airways Express	C-GEOA N802EX N977HA N838EX
221	311	Piedmont/US Airways Express	C-GFYI I-ADLB OE-LTC N803SA N333EN
222	102	Medavia	C-GFUM PH-SDH 9H-AEW
223	103	Kenyan Air Force	C-GFBW KAF-306
224	311A	Colombian National Police	C-GESR D-BELT HK-4107X HK-4107 PNC-0259
225	102A	Royal Bengal Airlines	C-GFQL D-BOBL S2-AEL
226	102A	Piedmont/US Airways Express	C-GFOD N803EX N978HA N839EX
227	102A	Piedmont/US Airways Express	C-GFYI N804EX
228	102A	Piedmont/US Airways Express	C-GLOT N805EX
229	103	Asia Pacific Airlines	C-GETI VH-LAR VH-JSI P2-NAX
230	311A	LIAT – The Caribbean Airline	C-GLOT N679MA PT-OKE VT-ETP VT-AKB C-FZVU PJ-DHI PJ-DHL V2-LGN
231	102A	(Bombardier Capital Corp)	C-GFUM N801RM N816MA YJ-RV6 N231ES (SX-BIO) [stored 25May03 Calgary, AB, Canada; l/n Mar07 Abbotsford, BC, Canada; canx 15Jun10 as wfu]
232	311A	Skytrans Regional	C-GFBW HS-SKJ C-FXXU YR-GPZ C-FXXU PH-SDU C-GZTX V2-LGA VH-QQP
233	106	Frontier Alaska	C-GFOD I-ADLC N881EA
234	311	Piedmont/US Airways Express	C-GDNG D-BOBA N386DC N326EN
235	106	Air Inuit	C-GFCF N812AW N818EX C-FAIV
236	311A	Wideroes Flyveselskap	C-GFCF D-BEYT LN-WFC
237	102A	Air Service Gabon	C-GEOA G-BRYG PH-TTA TR-LGR
238	311A	Wideroes Flyveselskap	C-GFYI PH-SDJ C-FZOH LN-WFH
239	103A	Wideroes Flyveselskap	C-GETI OE-LLK C-FXNE LN-WIP
240	311A	Air Canada Jazz	C-FJFM
241	102A	Compagnie Aerienne du Mali	C-GESR G-BRYH PH-TTB TR-LGC
242	311A	(LIAT – The Caribbean Airline)	C-GESR N680MA PT-OKF VT-ETQ VT-NKB C-FZPS PJ-DHE C-FBNA V2-LGH [DBF 10Jun12 V.C. Bird Airport, Antigua]
243	102A	Solomon Airlines	C-GFUM OE-LLI C-GGTO OE-LLI 6V-AGZ OE-LLI D-BFRA VH-TNW P2-MCQ
244	311A	North Cariboo Air	C-GFOD HS-SKK C-FXXV+ C-FEEV YR-GPV C-GCDO 5N-DAP PH-ABQ C-GNCF [+ painted in error]
245	102A	ex GMG Airlines	C-GEOA N802YW N802MA S2-AAA [stored by 22Apr12 Dhaka, Bangladesh]
246	311A	Air Canada Jazz	C-FTAK
247	103	(Wideroes Flyveselskap)	C-GFRP N813AW LN-WIS [w/o 14Jun01, Batsfjord, Norway; shipped to Bodo, Norway for b/u; by 26Jan12 hulk at Rygge, Norway]
248	311A	Air Canada Jazz	C-GABO
249	102A	Air Creebec	C-GFBW N803YW C-GFBW C-FJIO N803YW N817MA S2-ACT N817MA N841EX C-FCLS
250	311	LIAT – The Caribbean Airline	C-GFUM I-ADLC OE-LTB N802SA V2-LFU
251	102A	Dove Air, Sudan	C-GDNG C-FJIR N804YW N819MA S2-ACZ C-GJNZ V2-LFR C-GZAN 5Y-DAC
252	311A	Air Niugini	C-GFCF D-BOBU P2-ANO
253	106	fly540 Airlines	C-GETI OE-LLL D-BDUS N287BC V2-LFH N812LR C-FOBU 5Y-BUZ
254	311A	Waha Oil Co	C-GFYI PH-SDK 5A-DLX

DE HAVILLAND CANADA DHC-8

C/n	Model	Last known Owner/Operator	Identities/fates/comments (where appropriate)
255	102A	Air Canada Jazz	C-FJMG
256	311A	ex Air Kilroe/Eastern Airways	C-GEOA G-BRYI C-FFBG G-WOWE+ C- [+ canx 27Jan12 to Canada]
257	311A	Air Canada Jazz	C-GABP
258	106	Regional 1 Airlines	C-GFRP VH-FNQ EI-CHP C-FEOX N735AG C-GRGO
259	311A	Air Canada Jazz	C-FACF
260	103A	Era Aviation	C-GFOD D-BIRT C-GGEW N883EA
261	311A	Piedmont/US Airways Express	C-GETI B-15209 VH-IVI B-15209 N379DC N327EN
262	311A	Air Canada Jazz	C-FACT
263	102A	Piedmont/US Airways Express	C-GEVP N806EX
264	311A	Air Canada Jazz	C-FTAQ C-FJXZ
265	102A	EP Aviation LLC	C-GDNG N41873 N228H N308RD
266	311A	LIAT – The Caribbean Airline	C-GFCF PT-OKA C-FYPL YR-GPX C-GDBB 4X-ARP C-FWZU C-GFPY 5N-BBM C-GZTB V2-LGB
267	311A	LIAT – The Caribbean Airline	C-GFOD PT-OKB C-FYUP YR-GPW C-GCEF 4X-ARU C-GFPZ V2-LFM
268	106	748 Air Services	C-GFBW OE-LLH N286BC V2-LFG C-FOEN 5Y-IHO
269	311A	Air Canada Jazz	C-FMDW
270	102A	LIAT – The Caribbean Airline	C-GESR EI-CBV V2-LDU
271	311A	Air Canada Jazz	C-FJVV
272	311A	Air Canada Jazz	C-FACU C-FADF
273	103A	Wideroes Flyveselskap	C-GFYI OE-HRT OE-LRT C-FZNU LN-WIR
274	311A	Piedmont/US Airways Express	C-FKCU I-ADLD OE-LTA N805SA C-GFCE N805SA N330EN
275	106	PAL Aerospace Ltd	C-GDNG N827PH C-GPAB [maritime patrol aircraft operated by Dutch Coast Guard in Curacao, Netherlands Antilles]
276	311A	Skytrans Regional	C-GFRP PT-OKC C-FZBL PH-SDT TJ-SAB TT-DAD PH-SDT C-GMOH VH-QQN
277	106	Air Creebec	C-GLOT (N814AW) N880CC C-FDWO
278	311A	Air Canada Jazz	C-FACV
279	311A	Piedmont/US Airways Express	C-GDFT N430AW N806SA N331EN
280	102A	Yemenia Joint Venture	C-GDIU N415AW N832EX C-FMCZ 7O-ADS
281	311A	Piedmont/US Airways Express	C-GDKL B-15211 N380DC N328EN
282	102A	Provincial Airlines	C-GFHZ N416AW N833EX C-GPAU
283	311A	LIAT – The Caribbean Airline	C-GFUM EI-CED PH-SDR V2-LFV
284	311A	Piedmont/US Airways Express	C-GETI N431AW G-BRYK N385DC SU-UAE N337EN
285	102A	North Cariboo Air	C-GFBW N417AW N834EX C-FLSX
286	311A	Skytrans Regional	C-GFCF N432AW C-FXGF JY-RWA N547DS C-FDIY G-WOWD VH-QQM
287	102A	748 Air Services	C-GFYI N828PH 5Y-JGM
288	311A	Bahamasair	C-GESR C6-BFG
289	102A	Olympic Air	C-GEOA N418AW N835EX C-FNZM OE-HWG SX-BIW
290	311A	Piedmont/US Airways Express	C-GDNG OE-LLV SU-UAD N329EN
291	311A	Bahamasair	C-GFOD C6-BFH
292	102A	Piedmont/US Airways Express	C-GFQL N807EX
293	311A	Air Canada Jazz	C-GDIU PT-OKD EI-CIU PH-SDS LN-WFB N2492B C-FRUZ
294	106	North Cariboo Air	C-GEVB N881CC C-FODL
295	311A	(Bahamasair)	C-GFHZ C6-BFI [dbr 10Aug09 on ground Nassau, Bahamas; b/u by Aug10]
296	311A	Air Inuit	C-GFQL D-BKIS PH-SDG G-BRYS C-GZOF G-WOWA C-GIAB
297	102A	Trident Avn/DAC East Africa	C-GDFT N419AW N836EX 5Y-ENA
298	311A	LIAT – The Caribbean Airline	C-GETI N511SK PH-SDM 5N-BFB PH-SDM V2-LGC
299	102A	Piedmont/US Airways Express	C-GDKL N808EX
300	311A	LIAT – The Caribbean Airline	C-GFRP N501DC PH-SDP 5N-BEH PH-SDP V2-LGD
301	311A	(Magellan Aviation Services)	C-GFBW PJ-DHA N341CT [canx 31Dec03; b/u Nov03 Loring, ME]
302	102A	Piedmont/US Airways Express	C-GFYI N809EX
303	311A	(Magellan Aviation Services)	C-GESR PJ-DHB N343CT [canx 26Apr04; b/u Apr04 Bangor, ME; l/n 16Sep07 as hulk]
304	102A	Canadian North	C-GEVP N829PH C-FKCU C-GRGI
305	311A	Hawkair Aviation Service	C-GDFT N433AW G-BRYM (C-GKJY) N305DC V2-LFW C-FIDL
306	106	Skippers Aviation	C-GFOD D-BAGB C-GGEW VH-TQW VH-XFQ
307	311A	ex GMG Airlines	C-GEOA D-BOBE EI-CIT C-FTUX OE-LRW S2-ACT [wfu 2008 for spares Dhaka, Bangledash; l/n Nov11]
308	102A	Piedmont/US Airways Express	C-GDKL N810EX
309	311A	Bahamasair	C-GFHZ OE-LLW N394DC G-JEDA N994DC C6-BFP

DE HAVILLAND CANADA DHC-8

C/n	Model	Last known Owner/Operator	Identities/fates/comments (where appropriate)
310	103A	Wideroes Flyveselskap	C-GFCF OE-LEA D-BIER LN-WIT
311	311A	North Cariboo Air	C-GEVP N434AW G-BRYO N784BC G-WOWC C-GLWN
312	102A	Piedmont/US Airways Express	C-GDNG N812EX
313	314	Skippers Aviation	C-GFOD OE-LEC (D-BSEE) D-BHAM VH-XFX
314	106	PAL Aerospace Ltd	C-GFYI N830PH C-GRNN [maritime patrol aircraft operated by Dutch Coast Guard in Curacao, Netherlands Antilles]
315	311A	Central Mountain Air	C-GFCF N435AW G-BRYP N783BC V2-LFX N315SN C-FJFW
316	106	Asia Pacific Airlines	C-GFUM (OE-LEB) P2-NAZ
317	103A	Perimeter Aviation	C-GDKL OE-HRU OE-LRU OE-LLJ N288BC V2-LFI N288DH C-FOFR
318	102A	Piedmont/US Airways Express	C-GDNG N814EX
319	314	Voyageur Airways/UN	C-GEOA G-BRYJ C-FEXZ
320	311A	Voyageur Airways	C-FDHD (B-15215) N107AV C-FDHD B-15215 N320BC C-FEYG
321	102A	Piedmont/US Airways Express	C-GDFT N815EX
322	106	Era Aviation	C-FADJ N803LR N889EA
323	311A	Bahamasair	C-GFEN OE-LLX N395DC G-JEDB C-GZVN N538DS C6-BFJ
324	106	Canadian North	C-FADK N804LR C-FSQY C-GECN
325	311A	LIAT – The Caribbean Airline	C-FNJD N104AV C-FNJD B-15221 C-FHXB V2-LGI
326	102A	Skytrans Regional	C-GFYI N822MA N960HA N846EX VH-QQK
327	102A	Yemenia Joint Venture	C-GFQL N824MA N840EX 7O-ADU
328	102A	(3 Points Aviation Corp)	C-FWBB N831PH [canx 06Jly06 to Canada, where marks C-FJOW were reported but were never registered; b/u Jly06 Terrace, BC, Canada]
329	102A	Piedmont/US Airways Express	C-GFHZ N816EX
330	102A	Olympic Aviation	C-GEVP N826MA LV-POD LV-ZOD C-GZQZ SX-BIO
331	102A	SafariLink	C-GDKL N827MA N962HA N848EX C-FLPQ 5Y-SLD
332	311A	Air Service Gabon	C-GDNG N106AV TR-LFJ
333	103	Yemenia	C-GEOA N828MA N961HA N847EX C-FJFO N847EX C-FSID 7O-ADY
334	314	Air Inuit	C-GFEN D-BKIR G-BRYT C-GZOU G-WOWB C-FEAI
335	106	Danish Air Transport	C-GFCF N829MA N843EX C-FIZE TF-JMA OY-RUI
336	311A	Piedmont/US Airways Express	C-GFRP N436AW G-BRYR N284BC N336EN
337	102A	(Air Iceland)	C-FWBB N830MA N963HA N849EX C-FHYQ TF-JMB [w/o 04Mar11 Nuuk, Iceland; part hulk noted Dec12 Reykjavik, Iceland]
338	314B	Dynamic Avlease Inc	C-GETI ZS-NLW N8300F
339	106	Bluebird Aviation	C-GDFT N831MA N844EX C-FLPP 5Y-VVP
340	311A	Piedmont/US Airways Express	C-GLOT (N437AW) OE-LLZ N343EN
341	102A	Wells Fargo Bank	C-GHRI N832MA N842EX C-FKDI N842EX
342	311A	Air Canada Jazz	C-GFHZ D-BOBS EI-CIS C-FTUY LN-WFA C-FSOU
343	103	Wideroes Flyveselskap	C-GFBW N833MA N964HA N851EX C-FKDN N851EX C-GJMQ LN-WIV
344	106A	Rwandair Express	C-GFYI N846MA N845EX C-GFKC 5Y-BXU
345	106B	Canadian North	C-GFQL OE-LLG N791BC C-GZKA RA-67255(1) C-GXCN
346	102A	Skippers Aviation Ltd	C-GDIU N848MA VH-TQU VH-XFP
347	102A	Olympic Air	C-GEVP N849MA LV-PIB LV-ZPM C-GZRA SX-BIP
348	314B	Dynamic Avlease Inc	C-GDKL ZS-NLX N8300G
349	102A	Bluebird Aviation	C-GEOA N852MA C-GBSW VH-TQT 5Y-VVS
350	314A	Skippers Aviation	C-GUAY D-BMUC VH-XFV
351	106B	Frontier Alaska	C-FWBB OE-LLF C-GILX N387BC V2-LFN N387BC C-FRIY SX-BVE N887EA
352	314B	Dynamic Avlease Inc	C-GFCF ZS-NLY N8300L
353	102A	Island Air	C-GDNG N853MA N805WP
354	315	North Cariboo Air	C-GFRP ZS-NLZ C-FNSA
355	106B	Trident Aviation/DAC East Africa	C-GFEN OE-LLE C-GFEN OE-LLE SX-BIS OE-LLE SX-BIS 5Y-GRS
356	311A	Skippers Aviation	C-GFOD D-BKIM VH-XFW
357	102A	Island Air	C-GFYI N854MA N806WP
358	314B	Dynamic Avlease Inc	C-GDFT ZS-NMA N8300T
359	103B	Wideroes Flyveselskap	C-GHRI LN-WIA
360	103B	Wideroes Flyveselskap	C-GFBW LN-WIB
361	102A	Olympic Air	C-GFHZ N859MA LV-ZIZ LV-ZLZ C-GZRD SX-BIQ
362	102A	Bluebird Aviation	C-GDIU N861MA C-GCWZ VH-TQV 5Y-VVT
363	103	United Airways Bangladesh	C-GEVP N864MA LV-YTA C-GZRE N810WP S2-AES
364	102A	Olympic Air	C-GFQL N865MA LV-ZGB C-GZRF SX-BIR

DE HAVILLAND CANADA DHC-8

C/n	Model	Last known Owner/Operator	Identities/fates/comments (where appropriate)
365	314	Skippers Aviation	C-FWBB D-BACH VH-TQA D-BACH VH-XFZ
366	102A	United Airways Bangladesh	C-GEOA N866MA LV-YTC C-GZSD N811WP S2-AER
367	103B	Wideroes Flyveselskap	C-GDNG LN-WIC
368	314B	Air Inuit	C-GDIU ZS-NMB C-GJYZ
369	103B	Wideroes Flyveselskap	C-FDHD LN-WID
370	314	Voyageur Airways/UN	C-GFUM OE-LLY C-GHQZ
371	103B	Wideroes Flyveselskap	C-GFYI LN-WIE
372	103B	Wideroes Flyveselskap	C-GFOD LN-WIF
373	102A	Presidential Airways	C-GFQL N979HA
374	315	Trident Aviation	C-GFHZ ZS-NMC C-GBZV (PT-MPM) C-GBZV N374SC ZK-NER(1) N782BC C-FDYW 5Y-MOC
375	311B	Piedmont/US Airways Express	C-GEVP ZS-NMD N804SA N335EN
376	102A	Aircraft Leasing Services – ALS	C-GFBW N980HA C-GRGQ 5Y-BXI
377	106	Northrop Grumman Systems	C-GHRI N823EX N984HA
378	103A	Wideroes Flyveselskap	C-GDNG N981HA C-FZKQ LN-WIU
379	314B	Uni Air	C-GEOA B-15217
380	102A	Skytrans Regional	C-FWBB N982HA VH-QQH
381	314B	Uni Air	C-FDHD B-15219
382	103B	Wideroes Flyveselskap	C-GLOT LN-WIG
383	103B	Wideroes Flyveselskap	C-GFYI LN-WIH
384	103B	Wideroes Flyveselskap	C-GFOD LN-WII
385	314	Voyageur Airways/UN	C-GFUM ZS-NME N383DC LN-WFR C-FEZD
386	103B	Wideroes Flyveselskap	C-GFQL LN-WIJ
387	106	Frontier Alaska	C-GFBW N824EX N884EA
388	102A	Skytrans Regional	C-GHRI N825EX VH-QQL
389	102A	EP Aviation LLC	C-GDNG N826EX N638AR
390	106A	Perimeter Aviation	C-GEOA N827EX C-FPPW
391	202	(BP Exploration Colombia)	C-GFBW HK-3997X HK-3997W HK-3997 [w/o 28Jun08 Bogota, Colombia; l/n 22Feb08 minus engines and with titles painted out]
392	102A	Skytrans Regional	C-GEVP N828EX VH-QQJ
393	311B	Wells Fargo Bank	C-GLOT ZS-NMF N801SA
394	103B	(Wideroes Flyveselskap)	C-GDNG LN-WIK [w/o 01May05 Hammerfest, Norway; remains moved to Bodo, Norway for use as parts; canx 09Apr08]
395	315	Voyageur Airways/UN	C-GEOA ZS-NMG C-GBQZ PT-MPH N511CL N342EN C-FIQT
396	103	Norwegian CAA/Fred Olsen	C-GHRI LN-ILS
397	311	Humanitarian Air Services	C-GETI ZS-NMH C-GBRA PT-MPI N282BC ZK-NEQ(1) N788BC 5Y-PTA
398	103B	Wideroes Flyveselskap	C-GFCF LN-WIL
399	311A	Surveillance Australia	C-GFOD (ZS-NMI) VH-NJT VH-JSQ VH-ZZN
400	311A	Air Inuit	C-GFQL OE-LTD VH-TQB OE-LTD C-FAID
401	311B	Air Niugini	C-GFYI (ZS-NMJ) VH-NJU VH-JSU N7985B JY-RWB P2-ANN
402	311	Uni Air	C-GDFT ZS-NMI C-GDFT B-15233
403	103B	Wideroes Flyveselskap	C-GDIU LN-WIM
404	311B	LIAT – The Caribbean Airline	C-GDKL B-15223 C-FHFY V2-LGG
405	311B	Uni Air	C-GFHZ B-15225
406	311B	DAC East Africa	C-FDHD B-15227 C-FTYU 5Y-BWG
407	311B	Wideroes Flyveselskap	C-GFEN B-15229 C-FSIJ LN-WFD
408	311B	LIAT – The Caribbean Airline	C-FWBB V2-LEU
409	103	Wideroes Flyveselskap	C-GDNG LN-WIN
410	311B	LIAT – The Caribbean Airline	C-GEOA OE-LRZ N285BC V2-LFF
411	202	National Jet Systems	C-GHRI (VT-ETR) VH-JSH VH-ZZP
412	311B	LIAT – The Caribbean Airline	C-GETI V2-LES
413	202	Bombardier Inc	C-GEVP C-FBCS N556PM
414	311B	Uni Air	C-GFBW B-15231
415	315B	Path Corporation	C-GFCF 9M-EKA N600SR C-GEPA N600SR N505LL
416	311B	LIAT – The Caribbean Airline	C-GFOD V2-LET
417	103B	Wideroes Flyveselskap	C-GFQL LN-WIO
418	202	QantasLink	C-GFRP 9M-EKB VH-TQS
419	202MPA	National Jet Systems/Customs	C-FWWU VH-ZZA
420	315B	South African Express	C-GFUM YR-GPM C-GFJZ N477DC ZS-NNJ ZS-NMP C- [canx 18jly12 to Canada]
421	201	Air Niugini	C-GFYI N986HA P2-ANZ
422	311A	Hydro-Quebec	C-GLOT OE-LTE N377DC G-BXPZ C-GJNL

DE HAVILLAND CANADA DHC-8

C/n	Model	Last known Owner/Operator	Identities/fates/comments (where appropriate)						
423	314	Air Inuit	C-GDIU	OE-LTF	VH-TQC	OE-LTF	C-GUAI		
424	202MPA	National Jet Systems/Customs	C-FXBC	VH-ZZB					
425	201	Mesa/US Airways Express	C-GFHZ	N987HA					
426	201	Mesa/US Airways Express	C-FDHD	N988HA					
427	201	Mesa/US Airways Express	C-GFEN	N989HA					
428	201	Regional 1 Airlines	C-GDKL	N990HA	HK-4432X	HK-4432	C-GOSW		
429	202	Island Aviation Services	C-GDKL	8Q-AMD					
430	201	QantasLink	C-GDNG	VH-TQG					
431	201	Mesa/US Airways Express	C-GLOT	N991HA					
432	201	AIRES Colombia	C-GFQL	N992HA	HC-CFK	HK-4618			
433	202MPA	National Jet Systems/Customs	C-FXFK	VH-ZZC					
434	202	US Airways Express	C-GDNG	N434YV					
435	202	Wideroes Flyveselskap	C-GDIU	N759A	LN-WSA	C-GLUD	LN-WSA		
436	202	Mesa/US Airways Express	C-GDNG	N436YV					
437	202	Berry Aviation Inc	C-FDHD	N437YV					
438	Q311	CommutAir	C-GDFT	OE-LTG	N876CA				
439	202	QantasLink	C-GHRI	(9M-PGA)	C-GHRI	PT-TVB	N439SD	VH-TQX	
440	202	Wideroes Flyveselskap	C-GFBW	(N440YV)	N724A	LN-WSB	C-GLUF	LN-WSB	
441	202	Wideroes Flyveselskap	C-GFCF	(N441YV)	N725A	LN-WSC	C-GLUG	LN-WSC	
442	Q314	Air Inuit/Wasaya Airways	C-GFUM	OE-LTH	C-GMWT				
443	Q311B	Uni Air	C-FWBB	B-15235					
444	202	Avmax/L. C. Burse, Peru	C-GFRP	N444YV					
445	202	Air Iceland	C-GFEN	N445YV	C-GLRT	TF-JMG			
446	202	Air Iceland	C-GEOA	N446YV	C-GLSG	TF-JMK			
447	202	Avmax Aircraft Leasing	C-GFYI	N447YV					
448	202	Avmax/L. C. Burse, Peru	C-GLOT	N448YV					
449	202	Berry Aviation Inc	C-GFHZ	N449YV					
450	202	AIRES Colombia	C-GFCF	N450YV	N965HA	HK-4554X	HK-4554		
451	311A	Sakhalin Airlines	C-GDNG	(YR-GPN)	G-NVSA	5N-BJW	C-GAPW	RA-67253	
452	202	AIRES Colombia	C-GETI	(N452YV)	N966HA	HK-4539X	HK4539		
453	202	QantasLink	C-FDHD	9M-PGB(1)	C-FDHD	PT-TVC	N453DS	VH-SDE	
454	202	Avmax/L. C. Burse, Peru	C-GEOA	N454YV					
455	202	Dynamic Avlease Inc	C-GFRP	N455YV	N8200L				
456	202	DAC East Africa	C-GFOD	N456YV	5Y-WJF				
457	201	SAT Airlines	C-GDIU	N993HA	C-FJFW	RA-67257			
458	315	Medavia	C-GFEN	9M-PGC(1)	9M-PGA(1)	C-GFEN	G-BRYU	9H-AFD	
459	201	Avmax Group/Sakhalin Aviation	C-GFYI	N994HA	C-FNOP	RA-67259			
460	202	Air Niugini	C-GFBW	N995HA	C-FNOQ	RA-67261	C-GHQO	P2-PXI	
461	202	Air Niugini	C-GFBW	P2-ANK					
462	311A	(Air Tanzania)	C-GFHZ	(9M-PGD)	9M-PGB(2)	C-GFHZ	G-BRYV	5H-MWG	[w/o 09Apr12 Kigoma, Tanzania]
463	202B	Air Niugini	C-GFOD	(N463YV)	D-BHAL	(VT-VAB)	P2-ANX		
464	311A	ex GMG Airlines	C-FCSG	G-BRYZ	S2-ADX	[stored by 22Apr12 Dhaka, Bangladesh]			
465	202	AIRES Colombia	C-GFBW	(N465YV)	(D-BHAK)	N968HA	HK-4520		
466	Q314	Air Inuit	C-GFQL	OE-LTI	C-FOAI				
467	311A	Uni Air	C-GELN	B-15237					
468	202	AIRES Colombia	C-FDHD	(N468YV)	N969HA	HK-4513X	HK-4513		
469	202	Bluebird Aviation	C-GLOT	(N469YV)	ET-AKZ				
470	202	Government of Quebec	C-GDKL	P2-ANL(1)	C-GQBT				
471	202	Abu Dhabi Aviation	C-GLOT	A6-ADA					
472	103	Ryukyu Air Commuter	C-GDKL	(JA8591)	JA8972				
473	202	Abu Dhabi Aviation	C-GFRP	A6-ADC					
474	311A	Air Tanzania	C-GDIU	9M-PGC(2)	C-GDIU	G-BRYW	5H-MWF		
475	202	Bluebird Aviation	C-GDKL	(N475YV)	ET-AKY	ZK-ECR	ET-ALX		
476	202	SATA Air Azores	C-GFYI	N345PH	C-FXBX	CS-TRB			
477	202	Air Greenland	C-GEOA	N346PH	C-	N346PH	C-GJXW	OY-GRI	
478	201	AIRES Colombia	C-GEMU	(N478YV)	N983HA	HK-4491X	HK-4491		
479	202	AIRES Colombia	C-GEOZ	(N479YV)	N985HA	HK-4473X	HK-4473		
480	202B	SATA Air Azores	C-FWBB	N347PH	C-FXBZ	CS-TRC			
481	Q314	Air Inuit	C-GDOE	OE-LTJ	C-GXAI				
482	202	QantasLink	C-GFQL	VH-SDA					
483	Q314	Air Inuit	C-GDFT	(YR-GPO)	OE-LTK	C-GRAI			
484	202B	Prime Aviation	C-FWBB	N348PH	P4-TCO				

DE HAVILLAND CANADA DHC-8

C/n	Model	Last known Owner/Operator	Identities/fates/comments (where appropriate)
485	Q314	Air Inuit	C-GFYI OE-LTL C-FIAI
486	202B	Win Win Services	C-GEOA N349PH
487	314	Caribbean Airlines	C-GEWI OE-LSA 9Y-WIT
488	202B	Air Greenland	C-GFQL N350PH C-GCTX(2) OY-GRH
489	Q311	Tobago Express	C-GFCW 9Y-WIL
490	202	CommutAir/United Express	C-GFUM N351PH
491	311	Island Aviation Services	C-GFCA LN-WFE 8Q-IAP
492	202	Surveillance Australia	C-GEOA VH-LCL
493	311	Wideroes Flyveselskap	C-GERC (LN-WFP) LN-WFO
494	202B	Dynamic Avlease Inc	C-GHRI N352PH N801VA N8200H+ [reported Feb12 with US Army titles]
495	311	Wideroes Flyveselskap	C-GFUM LN-WFP
496	202	Air Greenland	C-GFRP N353PH C-GLVB OY-GRJ
497	201	AIRES Colombia	C-GDIW PT-TVD C-GDIW N996HA HK-4495X HK-4495
498	202	Air Greenland	C-FCSG N354PH C-GLUZ OY-GRK
499	Q311	Tobago Express	C-GDSG 9Y-WIN
500	202	(Win Win Services)	C-GEMU N355PH 97-0500+ [leased to L-3 Communications Integrated Systems; operating for the USAF (Africa Command) on lease; w/o 19Nov09 near Tarakigne, near Kolokani, Mali; by 22Oct10 fuselage at Kemble, UK for scrapping; l/n 01Nov10; + serial 97-0500 also carried]
501	103	Ryukyu Air Commuter	C-GDLD (JA8592) JA8973
502	202	Straight Flight Nevada	C-GEOZ N356PH [leased to L-3 Communications Integrated Systems]
503	311	InterSky	C-GDLD D-BHAS JY-RWD D-BHAS OE-LIC
504	202	Air Greenland	C-GFRP N357PH C-FXBO OY-GRG
505	311	InterSky	C-GDFT D-BHAT OE-LIA
506	202	CommutAir/United Express	C-FWBB N358PH
507	201	AIRES Colombia	C-GFRP N997HA HK-4509X HK-4509X
508	315	Medavia/Air Vallee	C-GDOE G-BRYX 9H-AEY
509	201	LAN Airlines	C-GFYI N998HA HK-4480X HK-4480
510	202	CommutAir/United Express	C-GELN N366PH
511	202	CommutAir/United Express	C-GDLD N367PH
512	202	CommutAir/United Express	C-GDFT N368PH
513	202	CommutAir/United Express	C-FWBB N369PH
514	202	CommutAir/United Express	C-GEOA N359PH
515	202	CommutAir/United Express	C-GEWI N360PH
516	202	CommutAir/United Express	C-GFOD N361PH
517	314A	Voyageur Airways/UN	C-GHRI G-NVSB C-FNCU
518	202	CommutAir/United Express	C-FDHI N362PH
519	311A	Provincial Airlines	C-FDHO G-BRYY HP-1625PST C-GPAR
520	202	CommutAir/United Express	C-FDHP N363PH
521	314	Regent Airways	C-FDHU D-BLEJ S2-AHA
522	202	Regional 1 Airlines	C-FDHV B-17201 C-GRGK
523	314	Air Niugini	C-FDHW D-BPAD P2-ANM
524	202	CommutAir/United Express	C-FDHX N364PH
525	314	InterSky	C-FDHY OE-LSB
526	202	CommutAir/United Express	C-FDHZ N365PH
527	Q311	CommutAir/United Express	C-FGNP OE-LTM N838CA
528	202	CommutAir/United Express	C-GDIU N374PH
529	202	CommutAir/United Express	C-GDKL N375PH
530	202	CommutAir/United Express	C-GDLK N379PH
531	Q311	CommutAir/United Express	C-GDNK OE-LTN N857CA
532	311A	Wideroes Flyveselskap	C-GEOA G-JEDC C-FATN LN-WFT
533	311A	SAT Airlines	C-GERC G-JEDD C-FCLN OE-HBC C-FWFH RA-67251(2)
534	311A	Aero Contractors	C-GERL G-JEDE C-FFMZ (OE-HBD) LN-WFU C-FLGJ 5N-BJO
535	311	Wideroes Flyveselskap	C-GEWI LN-WFS
536	202	Transportes San Francisco	C-GFCA D-BTHF (VT-VAA) P2-ANY VH-AFF C-GBGC CC-ADX
537	103	Amakusa Airlines	C-FCSG JA81AM
538	311B	BWee Express	C-FDHI 9Y-WIP
539	315	QantasLink	C-FDHO VH-SBB
540	103B	Ryukyu Air Commuter	C-FDHP (JA8593) JA8974
541	201B	Berry Aviation Inc	C-FDHV G-JEDX N541BC C-FEPA OE-HBB C-FSQT N541AV
542	201B	Island Aviation Services	C-FNGB G-JEDY N542BC C-FEGY N542BB C-FIKT 8Q-IAQ
543	314	Regent Airways	C-GFYI D-BEBA S2-AHB
544	314	Island Aviation Services	C-GHRI D-BHOQ 8Q-IAO

DE HAVILLAND CANADA DHC-8

C/n	Model	Last known Owner/Operator	Identities/fates/comments (where appropriate)						
545	314	Air Affaires Gabon	C-FCSG	D-BDTM	TR-CLB				
546	315	Maldivian Airlines	C-FDHD	SU-YAM	HB-JEJ	OE-LIE	8Q-IAS		
547	201B	Cross River State Govt	C-GDIU	G-JEDZ	N544BC	C-FEPB	5N-GRS		
548	311A	North Cariboo Air	C-GDIW	G-JEDF	C-FFBJ	5N-BHW	C-GAQN		
549	315	Travira Air	C-GDKL	SU-YAN	PK-TVM	SU-YAN	JY-RWC	SU-YAN	HB-JEK
			VH-AAY	PK-TVY					
550	202MPA	National Jet Systems/Customs	C-GDLD	VH-ZZI					
551	202MPA	National Jet Systems/Customs	C-FDHI	VH-ZZJ					
552	315	QantasLink	C-FDHP	VH-TQY					
553	314	CommutAir/United Express	C-FWBB	OE-LTO	N839CA				
554	311	CommutAir/United Express	C-GDLK	OE-LTP	N837CA				
555	315	QantasLink	C-GDNK	VH-TQZ					
556	315	Sakhalin Airlines	C-GDSG	6V-AHL	PH-JHB	C-GOJE+	RA-	[+ canx 31Aug12 to	
			Russia]						
557	315	Tobago Express	C-GEMU	9Y-WIZ					
558	202	Banco de Mexico	C-GEOA	XA-BCO	XC-BCO				
559	202	Banco de Mexico	C-GEOZ	XA-AEA	XC-BDM				
560	315	US Department of State	C-GERC	PH-DME	EC-IBS	N560WK			
561	315	Japan Coast Guard	C-FCSG	PH-DMI	EC-IBT	C-FYRQ	JA728A	[code MA728]	
562	315	Provincial Airlines	C-FDHO	PH-DML	EC-ICA	C-FPAE			
563	315	US Department of State	C-FDHU	PH-DMM	EC-ICX	PH-DMM	C-FVTM	D2-EWT	C-GOGN
			N563AW						
564	315	Japan Coast Guard	C-FDHV	PH-DMP	EC-IDK	C-FYRO	JA726A	[code MA726]	
565	314	Cenovus Energy Inc	C-GDFT	JA801K	OY-EDK	C-GBOS			
566	201	Oriental Air Bridge	C-GDNG	JA801B					
567	315	US Department of State	C-GDOE	PH-DMQ	N567WK				
568	315	US Department of State	C-GERL	(PH-DMR)	PH-DMU	N568AW			
569	315	US Department of State	C-GETI	(PH-DMU)	PH-DMR	N569AW			
570	315	US Department of State	C-GEVP	PH-DMV	N570AW				
571	311	Uni Air	C-GEWI	(PH-DMW)	B-15239				
572	202	Mexican Navy	C-GFBW	(PH-DMX)	MTX-05+	AMT-230	[+ Mexico]		
573	315	US Department of State	C-GFCF	(PH-DMY)	PH-DMW	N800AW			
574	315	African Barrick Gold	C-GFEN	(PH-DMZ)	PH-DMX	EC-IFK	PH-DMX	EC-LFU	C-FBLY
			5H-ABG						
575	Q315	QantasLink	C-GSAH	VH-SBG					
576	315	Cenovus Energy Inc	C-FCSG	PH-DMY	EC-IGE	C-GFCD			
577	314	Nordic Aviation Contractor	C-FDHD	JA802K	OY-CLI				
578	315	Eastern Australia Airlines	C-FDHI	VH-SBJ					
579	201	Oriental Air Bridge	C-FDHO	JA802B					
580	315	QantasLink	C-FDHP	VH-SBT					
581	315	SAT Airlines	C-FDHU	PH-DEJ	EC-IOV	C-GLKW	RA-67255(2)		
582	315	Worldwide Aircraft Ferrying	C-FDHV	PH-DMZ	EC-IJP	PH-DMZ	EC-LFG	C-GLWO	
583	314	Air Nippon Network	C-FDHW	JA803K					
584	315	Petroleum Air Services	C-FDHX	SU-CBF					
585	315	Petroleum Air Services	C-FDHY	SU-CBG					
586	315	Bombardier Inc	C-FWBB	(PH-DEI)	EC-IGS	PH-DXA	EC-LFH	C-GNUD	
			[stored reported to be JA727B with code MA727]						
587	Q315	Skippers Aviation	C-GDIU	EC-IIA	C-GKUX	VH-XKI			
588	Q315	Skippers Aviation	C-GDIW	EC-IIB	C-GLPG	VH-XKJ			
589	315	US Department of State	C-GDKL	EC-IJD	PH-DXB	EC-LFE	N589AW		
590	315	Tavira Air	C-GDLD	EC-IKA	PH-DXC	EC-LFF	C-GJTR	PK-TUB	
591	314B	Air Nippon	C-GFUM	JA804K					
592	314B	Wideroes Flyveselskap	C-GFYI	JA805K	OY-CJY	LN-WFU			
593	103	Ryukyu Air Commuter	C-GSAH	JA8935					
594	315B	Petroleum Air Services	C-FPJH	SU-CBH					
595	315B	QantasLink	C-GIHK	VH-SBV					
596	315B	QantasLink	C-GDOE	VH-TQE					
597	315B	QantasLink	C-GZDM	VH-TQH					
598	315B	QantasLink	C-GZDO	VH-TQD					
599	315B	QantasLink	C-GZPN	VH-SBW					
600	315B	QantasLink	C-GZPO	VH-TQK					
601	315B	Denim Air/ Petro Air	C-FDHD	(PH-VOO)	PH-AGR	5A-AGR			
602	315B	QantasLink	C-GZBB	VH-SCE					

DE HAVILLAND CANADA DHC-8

C/n	Model	Last known Owner/Operator	Identities/fates/comments (where appropriate)			
603	315B	QantasLink	C-GZPQ	VH-TQL		
604	315B	QantasLink	C-FZHW	VH-TQM		
605	315B	QantasLink	C-FZKU	VH-SBI		
606	202	Dept of Homeland Security	C-FDHW	N606CS	N801MR	
607	315B	Petroleum Air Services	C-FBNT	SU-CBJ		
608	315B	CHC Global Operations	C-FBOA	5N-BIA	C-FBOA	
609	315B	Government of Quebec	C-FCPM	5N-BIB	C-FLGJ	
610	315MSA	UAE Air Force	C-FCPN	V2-LGJ	A6-ADF	1320
611	311B	Air New Zealand Link	C-FCPO	ZK-NEA		
612	202	Dept of Homeland Security	C-FCPQ	N802MR		
613	315B	Topbrass Aviation	C-FDGW	D2-EYL	5N-TBB	
614	315B	Topbrass Aviation	C-FDHE	D2-EYM	5N-TBC	
615	311B	Air New Zealand Link	C-FDRG	ZK-NEB		
616	311B	Air New Zealand Link	C-FEDG	ZK-NEC		
617	311B	Air New Zealand Link	C-FERB	ZK-NED		
618	311B	Air New Zealand Link	C-FFBY	ZK-NEE		
619	315B	Japan Civil Aviation Bureau	C-FDRJ	JA007G		
620	311B	Air New Zealand Link	C-FFCC	ZK-NEF		
621	311B	Air New Zealand Link	C-FFOZ	ZK-NEG		
622	311B	Swedish Coast Guard	C-FEDJ	501//SE-MAA		[dual marks]
623	311B	Air New Zealand Link	C-FGAI	ZK-NEH		
624	315MSA	UAE Air Force	C-FGNJ	V2-LGK	A6-ADG	1321
625	311B	Air New Zealand Link	C-FFPA	ZK-NEJ		
626	202	Dept of Homeland Security	C-FERE	N803MR		
627	315B	Abu Dhabi Aviation	C-FHED	V2-LGL	A6-ADD	[for conversion to maritime surveillance aircraft for UAE Air Force]
628	315B	Abu Dhabi Aviation	C-FHPW	V2-LGM	A6-ADE	[for conversion to maritime surveillance aircraft for UAE Air Force]
629	311B	Air New Zealand Link	C-FHPZ	ZK-NEK		
630	311B	Air New Zealand Link	C-FHQB	ZK-NEM		
631	311B	Swedish Coast Guard	C-FGJS	502//SE-MAB		[dual marks]
632	315B	Petroleum Air Services	C-FIOY	SU-CBN		
633	311B	Air New Zealand Link	C-FIOS	ZK-NEO		
634	311B	Air New Zealand Link	C-FIOV	ZK-NEP		
635	314B	Ryukyu Air Commuter	C-FIOX	JA8936		
636	311B	Air New Zealand Link	C-FJKL	ZK-NEQ(2)		
637	202	Opticap Aviation LLC	C-FHEF	N637CC		
638	311B	Swedish Coast Guard	C-FHEG	503//SE-MAC		[dual marks]
639	311B	Air New Zealand Link	C-FJKO	ZK-NER(2)		
640	315B	Surveillance Australia	C-FHQG	VH-ZZE		
641	311B	Air New Zealand Link	C-FJKP	ZK-NES(2)		
642	311B	Air New Zealand Link	C-FJKQ	ZK-NET(2)		
643	315B	Surveillance Australia	C-FJKS	VH-ZZF		
644	315B	Surveillance Australia	C-FJKU	VH-ZZG		
645	315B	Heli Malongo Airways	C-FLKI	D2-EYU		
646	202	Opticap Aviation LLC	C-FLKJ	N646CC		
647	311B	Air New Zealand Link	C-FLTZ	ZK-NEU(2)		
648	311B	Air New Zealand Link	C-FLUH	ZK-NEW(2)		
649	202	Opticap Aviation LLC	C-FLKK	N649CC	[operated for Northrop Grumman]	
650	311B	Abu Dhabi Aviation	C-FLUJ	(ZK-NEY(2))	A6-ADB	
651	315B	Japan Coast Guard	C-FMIS	JA720A	[code MA720]	
652	315B	Japan Coast Guard	C-FMTJ	JA721A	[code MA721]	
653	314	AirPhil Express	C-FNEA	RP-C3016		
654	311B	Air New Zealand Link	C-FNPY	ZK-NEZ(2)		
655	202	Dept of Homeland Security	C-FNZS	N368BT	N805MR	
656	315	Japan Coast Guard	C-FOIY	JA722A	[code MA722]	
657	314	Air Philippines Express	C-FOUN	RP-C3017		
658	314	PAL Express	C-FPDR	RP-C3018		
659	311	Air New Zealand Link	C-FPPN	ZK-NFA		
660	314	Icelandic Coast Guard	C-FQWY	TF-SIF		
661	202	Tassili Airlines	C-FRIZ	7T-VCP		
662	315	Dept of Homeland Security	C-FRLH	N806MR		
663	315	Dept of Homeland Security	C-FSRJ	N807MR		

DE HAVILLAND CANADA DHC-8

C/n	Model	Last known Owner/Operator	Identities/fates/comments (where appropriate)
664	202	Tassili Airlines	C-FTGX 7T-VCQ
665	202	Tassili Airlines	C-FTUE 7T-VCR
666	202	Tassili Airlines	C-FUCF 7T-VCS
667	315	Dept of Homeland Security	C-FUOD N808MR
668	315	Japan Coast Guard	C-FURK JA723A [code MA723]
669	315	Japan Coast Guard	C-FVGD JA724A [code MA724]
670	311	Air New Zealand Link	C-FVUF ZK-NFB
671	311	Air New Zealand Link	C-FWGQ ZK-NFI
672	315	Japan Coast Guard	C-FXAP JA725A [code MA725] [last series 100/200/300 aircraft]
Unidentified			
unkn	300	SVG Air	J8-GAL [operating as such since 2009; possibly c/n 553]
BOMBARDIER/DE HAVILLAND CANADA DHC-8-400 SERIES			
4001	401	Bombardier Inc	C-FJJA [prototype; ff 31Jan98]
4002	402	(Bombardier Inc)	C-GCLI [wfu Feb02 to GIA; donated to L'Ecole Nationale d'Aerotechnique (ENA) du College Edouard-Montpetit, St Hubert, QC, Canada; by Jun07 fuselage broken into three parts; no wings present]
4003	402	Augsburg Airways	C-FPJH C-GHQO C-FHUP D-ADHP
4004	402	Hydro-Quebec	C-GIHK C-GHQP
4005	402	(Chang An Airlines)	C-GSAH B-3567 [DBR Feb02 Xian-Xianyang Airport, China; l/n 01Aug03; no further reports, assumed b/u]
4006	402	Alaska Horizon	C-GFEN (B-17401) B-3568 N424QX
4007	402	(Bombardier Inc)	C-GFHZ [canx Feb05 as wfu – never made airworthy; stored 1999 to 2005 Downsview, ON, Canada when b/u]
4008	402PF	Blue Bird Aviation	C-GFOD (SE-LOA) (SE-LRA) OY-KCB LN-RDQ SE-LSM 5Y-VVU
4009	402	Blue Bird Aviation	C-GFQL (SE-LRC) LN-RDD 5Y-VVY
4010	402	Aircraft Solutions	C-GFUM (LN-RDA) N480DC LN-RDJ N404AV
4011	402	Blue Bird Aviation	C-FDHY (SE-LOB) (SE-LRB) LN-RDL 5Y-VVW
4012	402	Aircraft Solutions	C-FWBB (SE-LOC) (SE-LRC) OY-KCA LN-RDP [stored different locations then 30Jun09 Nykoping, Sweden; l/n 21Mar11]
4013	402	Aircraft Solutions	C-GDFT (OY-KCB) (SE-LRA) LN-RDA
4014	402	Austrian Arrows	C-GDNG (LN-RDB) OE-LGA
4015	402	Austrian Arrows	C-GDOE (SE-LOD) (SE-LRD) OE-LGB
4016	402	Lufthansa Regional	C-GELN (SE-LOE) (SE-LRE) LN-WDZ N539DS C-FSPV D-ADHQ
4017	402	Darwin Airline	C-GLOT (SE-LOF) (SE-LRF) LN-RDF (LN-RDO) (B17403) N546DS C-GAFM N814WP C-FJJG HB-JQA
4018	402	Blue Bird Aviation	C-FDHU (OY-KCC) LN-RDB 5Y-VVX
4019	402	Linhas Aereas de Mocambique	C-FDHW (OY-KCD) (SE-LRD) LN-RDC C9-AUL
4020	402	Linhas Aereas de Mocambique	C-FDHX (LN-RDC) (SE-LRC) LN-RDE C9-AUM
4021	402	Linhas Aereas de Mocambique	C-FDHZ (LN-RDD) (SE-LRF) LN-RDF G-ECOW C9-AUY
4022	402	Bombardier Inc	C-FGNP (SE-LRG) LN-RDG (OY-KCC) G-ECOY C-GKZV
4023	402	PAL Express	C-FNGB (SE-LRH) (OY-KCD) LN-RDH RP-C3036
4024	402PF	Blue Bird Aviation	C-GERL (OY-KCE) (LN-RDC) LN-RDI (SE-LSN) 5Y-VVZ
4025	402	(Scandinavian Airlines System)	C-GETI (LN-RDD) LN-RDK [w/o 09Sep07 Aalborg Airport, Denmark; dismantled 10Aug10 for parts]
4026	402	Tyrolean/Brussels Airlines	C-GEVP (SE-LRK) (LN-RDM) OE-LGC
4027	402	Austrian Arrows	C-GEWI OE-LGD
4028	402	Augsburg Airways	C-GFBW D-ADHA
4029	402	Augsburg Airways	C-GFCA D-ADHB
4030	402	Alaska Horizon	C-GFCF (OY-KCF) (LN-RDN) N400QX
4031	402	Alaska Horizon	C-GFCW N401QX
4032	402	Alaska Horizon	C-GFOD N402QX
4033	402	Bombardier Inc	C-GFRP N481DC LN-RDM G-ECOV C-GLPE N33WQ C-GLPE [company shuttle aircraft]
4034	402	Bombardier Inc	C-GFYI N482DC (SE-LRG) LN-RDR G-ECOZ C-GLOZ
4035	402	(Scandinavian Airlines System)	C-GHRI (SE-LRH) LN-RDS [substantially damaged 12Sep07 Vilnius, Lithuania; l/n 26Jly08; canx 08Jun09 for spares]
4036	402	Aircraft Solutions	C-FDHD LN-RDO N436AV
4037	402	Alaska Horizon	C-FDHP N403QX
4038	402	Bombardier Inc	C-FDHW N382BC (OY-KCE) LN-RDT C-GLGV
4039	402	Alaska Horizon	C-FDHX (LN-RDE) B-3569 N425QX
4040	402MR	Securite Civile	C-FDHZ N384BC LN-RDW N532DS C-FBAM F-ZBMC [code 73]

DE HAVILLAND CANADA DHC-8

C/n	Model	Last known Owner/Operator	Identities/fates/comments (where appropriate)
4041	402	Lufthansa Regional	C-FGNP (SE-LRI) N385BC LN-RDX N533DS C-FFUV JY-ASM C-FRGT D-ADHR
4042	402	Austrian Arrows	C-FNGB OE-LGE
4043	402	Securite Civile	C-FWBB LN-RDN N535DS C-FBSG F-ZBMD
4044	402	Lufthansa Regional	C-GDIU LN-RDU N536DS C-FGNV JY-ASN C-FRBO D-ADHS
4045	402	Augsburg Airways	C-GDIW D-ADHC
4046	402	Alaska Horizon	C-GDKL N404QX
4047	402	Alaska Horizon	C-GDLD N405QX
4048	402	Alaska Horizon	C-GDLK N406QX
4049	402	Alaska Horizon	C-GDNK N407QX
4050	402	Alaska Horizon	C-GFCA N408QX
4051	402	Alaska Horizon	C-GFCW N409QX
4052	402	ex Flybe	C-GFOD G-JEDI [returned to lessor Sep11; stored Maastricht, Netherlands; l/n 29Feb12]
4053	402	Alaska Horizon	C-GFQL N410QX
4054	402	SAS Norge AS	C-GFRP (LN-RDY) OY-KCD HA-LQA LN-RDV
4055	402	Alaska Horizon	C-GFUM N411QX
4056	402	Augsburg Airways	C-GFYI D-ADHD
4057	402	ex SAS Norge AS	C-GHRI (LN-RDZ) OY-KCE HA-LQB LN-RDX [canx 24Jly12; reported for spares use Innsbruck, Austria]
4058	402	Bombardier Inc	C-FDHZ G-JEDJ C-GSVY
4059	402	Alaska Horizon	C-FGNP N412QX
4060	402	Alaska Horizon	C-FNGB N413QX
4061	402	Alaska Horizon	C-GDFT N414QX
4062	402	SAS Norge AS	C-GDNG (LN-RNI) OY-KCF HA-LQC LN-RDY
4063	402	SAS Norge AS	C-GDSG (LN-RNK) OY-KCG HA-LQD LN-RDZ
4064	402	PAL Express	C-GELZ (LN-RNL) OY-KCH LN-WDD RP-C3030
4065	402	ex Flybe	C-GEMU G-JEDK [stored by 16Jun12 Maastricht, Netherlands]
4066	402	Lufthansa Regional	C-GEOA D-ADHE
4067	402	Flybe	C-GEOZ G-JEDL
4068	402	Austrian Arrows	C-GERC OE-LGF
4069	402	PAL Express	C-GERL LN-WDA RP-C3031
4070	402	PAL Express	C-GETI LN-WDB RP-C3032
4071	402	PAL Express	C-GEVP LN-WDC RP-C3033
4072	402	Japan Air Commuter	C-GEWI JA841C
4073	402	Japan Air Commuter	C-GFCA JA842C
4074	402	Austrian Arrows	C-GFCF OE-LGG
4075	402	Austrian Arrows	C-GFCW OE-LGH
4076	402	Japan Air Commuter	C-FDHZ JA843C
4077	402	Flybe	C-FGNP G-JEDM
4078	402	Flybe	C-FNGB G-JEDN
4079	402	Flybe	C-GDFT G-JEDO
4080	402	Air Nippon Network	C-GDLK JA841A
4081	402	Alaska Horizon	C-GELN N415QX
4082	402	Air Nippon Network	C-GFOD JA842A
4083	402	Alaska Horizon	C-GDNK N416QX
4084	402	Air Nippon Network	C-GFQL JA843A
4085	402	Flybe	C-FDHO G-JEDP
4086	402	Alaska Horizon	C-FCSG N417QX
4087	402	Flybe	C-FDHI G-JEDR
4088	402	Flybe	C-FDHP G-JEDT
4089	402	Flybe	C-GEMU G-JEDU
4090	402	Flybe	C-FDHX G-JEDV
4091	402	Air Nippon Network	C-GHRI JA844A
4092	402	Japan Air Commuter	C-GFEN JA844C
4093	402	Flybe	C-GFBW G-JEDW
4094	402	Flybe	C-FDHU G-JECE
4095	402	Flybe	C-FDHV G-JECF
4096	402	Air Nippon Network	C-FAQB JA845A
4097	402	Air Nippon Network	C-FAQD JA846A
4098	402	Flybe	C-FAQH G-JECG
4099	402	Air Nippon Network	C-FAQK JA847A
4100	402	Austrian Arrows	C-FAQR OE-LGI

DE HAVILLAND CANADA DHC-8

C/n	Model	Last known Owner/Operator	Identities/fates/comments (where appropriate)				
4101	402	Japan Air Commuter	C-FCPZ	JA845C			
4102	402	Air Nippon Network	C-FCQA	JA848A			
4103	402	Flybe	C-FCQC	G-JECH			
4104	402	Tyrolean Airways	C-FCQH	OE-LGJ			
4105	402	Flybe	C-FCQK	G-JECI			
4106	402	Eznis Airways	C-FCVE	JA849A	C-GDXC	JU-9919	
4107	402	Japan Air Commuter	C-FCVI	JA846C			
4108	402	Air Nippon Network	C-FCVJ	JA850A			
4109	402	Air Nippon Network	C-FCVK	JA851A			
4110	402	Flybe	C-FCVN	G-JECJ			
4111	402	Japan Air Commuter	C-FCVS	JA847C			
4112	402	Sunstate/QantasLink	C-FDNG	VH-QOA			
4113	402	Flybe	C-FDRL	G-JECK			
4114	402	Flybe	C-FDRN	G-JECL			
4115	402	Hydro-Quebec	C-GHQL				
4116	402	Sunstate/QantasLink	C-FERF	VH-QOB			
4117	402	Sunstate/QantasLink	C-FFCD	VH-QOC			
4118	402	Flybe	C-FFCE	G-JECM			
4119	402	LAN Airlines	C-FFCH	HL5251	HK-4726	HK-4726-X	HK-4726
4120	402	Flybe	C-FFCL	G-JECN			
4121	402	Japan Air Commuter	C-FFCO	JA848C			
4122	402	South African Express	C-FFCU	ZS-NMO			
4123	402	Sunstate/QantasLink	C-FFQL	VH-QOD			
4124	402	AIRES Colombia	C-FFQF	HL5252	HK-4725X		
4125	402	Sunstate/QantasLink	C-FFQE	VH-QOE			
4126	402	Flybe	C-FFPT	G-JECO			
4127	402	South African Express	C-FFPH	ZS-NMS			
4128	402	Sunstate/QantasLink	C-FFQM	VH-QOF			
4129	402	AIRES Colombia	C-FGAJ	HL5254	HK-4727		
4130	402	Porter Airlines	C-GLQB				
4131	402	Air Nippon Network	C-FGKC	JA852A			
4132	402	Sunstate/QantasLink	C-FGKH	VH-QOH			
4133	402	Japan Air Commuter	C-FGKJ	JA849C			
4134	402	Porter Airlines	C-GLQC				
4135	402	Air Nippon Network	C-FGKN	JA853A			
4136	402	Flybe	C-FHEL	G-JECP			
4137	402	AIRES Colombia	C-FHQL	HL5255	HK-4724X	HK-4724	
4138	402	Porter Airlines	C-GLQD				
4139	402	Flybe	C-FHQM	G-JECR			
4140	402	Porter Airlines	C-GLQE				
4141	402	(Jeju Air)	C-FHQQ	HL5256	[w/o 12Aug07 Pusan, South Korea; canx 25Feb10]		
4142	402	South African Express	C-FHQV	G-JECS	ZS-YBP		
4143	402	Alaska Horizon	C-FHQX	N418QX			
4144	402	South African Express	C-FHQV	G-JECT	ZS-YBR		
4145	402	Alaska Horizon	C-FHRD	N419QX			
4146	402	South African Express	C-FJKY	G-JECU	ZS-YBT		
4147	402	Alaska Horizon	C-FJLA	N420QX			
4148	402	Olympic Air	C-FJLE	G-JECV	SX-BIT		
4149	402	Alaska Horizon	C-FJLF	N421QX			
4150	402	Alaska Horizon	C-FJLG	N422QX			
4151	402	Air Nippon Network	C-FJLH	JA854A			
4152	402	Olympic Air	C-FJLK	G-JECW	SX-BIU		
4153	402	Alaska Horizon	C-FJLO	N423QX			
4154	402	Alaska Horizon	C-FJLX	N426QX			
4155	402	Flybe	C-FLKO	G-JECX			
4156	402	Alaska Horizon	C-FLKU	N427QX			
4157	402	Flybe/Brussels Airways	C-FLKV	G-JECY			
4158	402	Japan Air Commuter	C-FLKW	JA850C			
4159	402	Luxair	C-FLKX	LX-LGA			
4160	402	Alaska Horizon	C-FLTL	N428QX			
4161	402	Alaska Horizon	C-FLTT	N429QX			
4162	402	Luxair	C-FLTY	LX-LGC			
4163	402	Alaska Horizon	C-FMES	N430QX			

DE HAVILLAND CANADA DHC-8

C/n	Model	Last known Owner/Operator	Identities/fates/comments (where appropriate)			
4164	402	Alaska Horizon	C-FMEU	N431QX		
4165	402	Air Canada Express	C-FMFG	N501LX	C-FSRJ	
4166	402	Alaska Horizon	C-FMFH	N432QX		
4167	402	Tassili Airlines	C-FMIT	7T-VCL		
4168	402	Lynx Aviation/Frontier Airlines	C-FMIU	N502LX		
4169	402	Tassili Airlines	C-FMIV	7T-VCM		
4170	402	Sky Regional Airlines	C-FMIX	N503LX	C-FSRN	
4171	402	Luxair	C-FMJC	LX-LGD		
4172	402	Air Canada Express	C-FMJN	N504LX	C-FSRW	
4173	402	Tassili Airlines	C-FMKF	7T-VCN		
4174	402	Sky Regional Airlines	C-FMKH	N505LX	C-FSRY	
4175	402	Darwin Airline	C-FMKK	HB-JQB		
4176	402	Sky Regional Airlines	C-FMKN	N506LX	C-FSRZ	
4177	402	Japan Air Commuter	C-FMTK	JA851C		
4178	402	Tassili Airlines	C-FMTN	7T-VCO		
4179	402	Flybe	C-FMTY	G-JECZ		
4180	402	Flybe	C-FMUE	G-ECOA		
4181	402	Lynx Aviation/Republic Airlines	C-FMUF	N507LX		
4182	402	Lynx Aviation/Frontier Airlines	C-FMUH	N508LX		
4183	402	Wideroes Flyveselskap	C-FNEC	LN-WDE		
4184	402	Skywork Airlines	C-FNEI	N509LX	C-GARX	HB-JIJ
4185	402	Flybe	C-FNEN	G-ECOB	LN-WDT	G-ECOB
4186	402	Lynx Aviation/Republic Airlines	C-FNER	N510LX		
4187	402	Colgan Air/United Express	C-FNQG	N187WQ		
4188	402	Colgan Air/United Express	C-FNQH	N188WQ		
4189	402	Sunstate/QantasLink	C-FNQL	VH-QOI		
4190	402	Colgan Air/United Express	C-FNQN	N190WQ		
4191	402	Colgan Air/United Express	C-FNQQ	N191WQ		
4192	402	Sunstate/QantasLink	C-FNZU	VH-QOJ		
4193	402	Porter Airlines	C-GLQF			
4194	402	Porter Airlines	C-GLQG			
4195	402	Colgan Air/United Express	C-FOJM	N195WQ		
4196	402	Colgan Air/United Express	C-FOJT	N196WQ		
4197	402	Flybe	C-FOKA	G-ECOC	LN-WDU	G-ECOC
4198	402	Sky Work Airlines	C-FOKB	HB-JGA		
4199	402	Colgan Air/United Express	C-FOUO	N199WQ		
4200	402	(Colgan Air/United Express)	C-FOUQ	N200WQ	[w/o 12Feb09 near Buffalo Airport, NY; canx 02Mar11]	
4201	402	Flybe	C-FOUU	(G-ECOD)	G-KKEV	
4202	402	Colgan Air/United Express	C-FOUY	N202WQ		
4203	402	Colgan Air/United Express	C-FPDY	N203WQ		
4204	402	Colgan Air/United Express	C-FPEF	N204WQ		
4205	402	Croatia Airlines	C-FPEL	9A-CQA		
4206	402	Flybe	C-FPEX	(G-ECOD)	C-FPEX	G-ECOD
4207	402	Arik Air	C-FPPU	5N-BKU		
4208	402	Colgan Air/United Express	C-FPPW	N208WQ		
4209	402	Colgan Air/United Express	C-FPQA	N209WQ		
4210	402	Alaska Horizon	C-FPQB	N433QX		
4211	402	Croatia Airlines	C-FPQD	9A-CQB		
4212	402	Flybe	C-FQXJ	G-ECOE	LN-WDV	G-ECOE
4213	402	Colgan Air/United Express	C-FQXO	N213WQ		
4214	402	Colgan Air/United Express	C-FQXP	N214WQ		
4215	402	Sunstate/QantasLink	C-FQXU	VH-QOK		
4216	402	Flybe	C-FRJU	G-ECOF	LN-WDW	G-ECOF
4217	402	Sunstate/QantasLink	C-FRLL	VH-QOM		
4218	402	Sunstate/QantasLink	C-FRLP	VH-QON		
4219	402	Arik Air	C-FSRN	5N-BKV		
4220	402	Flybe	C-FSRQ	G-ECOG		
4221	402	Flybe/Brussels Airways	C-FSRW	G-ECOH		
4222	402	Abu Dhabi Aviation	C-FTIA	A6-ADK		
4223	402	Air Berlin	C-FTID	D-ABQA		
4224	402	Flybe/Brussels Airways	C-FTIE	G-ECOI		
4225	402	Porter Airlines	C-GLQH			
4226	402	Air Berlin	C-FTUM	D-ABQB		

DE HAVILLAND CANADA DHC-8

C/n	Model	Last known Owner/Operator	Identities/fates/comments (where appropriate)			
4227	402	Alaska Horizon	C-FTUQ	N434MK		
4228	402	Porter Airlines	C-GLQJ			
4229	402	Flybe	C-FTUS	G-ECOJ		
4230	402	Flybe/Brussels Airways	C-FTUT	G-ECOK		
4231	402	Air Berlin	C-FUCI	D-ABQC		
4232	402	Alaska Horizon	C-FUCO	N435QX		
4233	402	Flybe	C-FUCR	G-ECOM		
4234	402	Air Berlin	C-FUCS	D-ABQD		
4235	402	US Department of Justice	C-FUOE	N721AL		
4236	402	Alaska Horizon	C-FUOF	N436QX		
4237	402	Flybe	C-FUOH	G-ECOO		
4238	402	Sunstate/QantasLink	C-FUOI	VH-QOP		
4239	402	Air Berlin	C-FURQ	D-ABQE		
4240	402	Alaska Horizon	C-FUSM	N437QX		
4241	402	Sunstate/QantasLink	C-FUST	VH-QOR		
4242	402	Flybe	C-FUTG	G-ECOP		
4243	402	Alaska Horizon	C-FUTP	N438QX		
4244	402NG	Wideroes Flyveselskap	C-FUTZ	LN-WDF	[first NextGen version]	
4245	402	Air Berlin	C-FVGV	D-ABQF		
4246	402	Alaska Horizon	C-FVGY	N439QX		
4247	402	Porter Airlines	C-GLQK			
4248	402	Bombardier Inc	C-FVUJ	G-ECOR		
4249	402	Porter Airlines	C-GLQL			
4250	402	Air Berlin	C-FVUN	D-ABQG		
4251	402	Flybe	C-FVUV	G-ECOT		
4252	402	Porter Airlines	C-GLQM			
4253	402	Flybe	C-FVVB	G-FLBA		
4254	402	Porter Airlines	C-GLQN			
4255	402	Flybe	C-FWGE	G-FLBB		
4256	402	Air Berlin	C-FWGO	D-ABQH		
4257	402	Flybe	C-FWGY	G-FLBC		
4258	402	Croatia Airlines	C-FWIJ	9A-CQC		
4259	402	Flybe	C-FWZN	G-FLBD		
4260	402	Croatia Airlines	C-FWZU	9A-CQD		
4261	402	Flybe	C-FXAB	G-FLBE		
4262	402	Air Niugini	C-FXAW	(5N-BKW)	P2-PXS	
4263	402	Sunstate/QantasLink	C-FXAZ	VH-QOS		
4264	402	Air Berlin	C-FXIW	D-ABQI		
4265	402	Skywork Airlines	C-FXJC	N511LX	C-GMRX	HB-JIK
4266	402NG	Wideroes Flyveselskap	C-FXJF	LN-WDG		
4267	402	Olympic Air	C-FXJS	(G-FLBF)	G-PTHA	SX-OBA
4268	402	Olympic Air	C-FXKG	(G-FLBG)	G-PTHB	SX-OBB
4269	402	Sunstate/QantasLink	C-FXYP	VH-QOT		
4270	402	Porter Airlines	C-GLQO			
4271	402	Porter Airlines	C-GLQP			
4272	402	Porter Airlines	C-GLQQ			
4273	402NG	Wideroes Flyveselskap	C-FYGI	LN-WDH		
4274	402	Air Berlin	C-FYGN	D-ABQJ		
4275	402	Sunstate/Qantaslink	C-FYGQ	VH-QOU		
4276	402	Olympic Air	C-FYGZ	G-PTHC	SX-OBC	
4277	402	Sunstate/QantasLink	C-FYIC	VH-QOV		
4278	402	Porter Airlines	C-GLQR			
4279	402	Porter Airlines	C-GLQV			
4280	402	Austrian Arrows	C-FYMK	OE-LGK		
4281	402	Lufthansa Regional	C-FYMQ	D-ADHT		
4282	402	Porter Airlines	C-GLQX			
4283	402		[fuselage DBR during shipping; not completed or registered; was for Porter Airlines]			
4284	402	Luxair	C-FXYV	LX-LGE		
4285	402	Sunstate/QantasLink	C-FZFT	VH-QOW		
4286	402NG	Wideroes Flyveselskap	C-FZFX	LN-WDI		
4287	402	Sunstate/QantasLink	C-FZGC	VH-QOX		
4288	402	Sunstate/QantasLink	C-FZGG	VH-QOY		
4289	402NG	Air Baltic	C-FZGL	YL-BAE		

DE HAVILLAND CANADA DHC-8

C/n	Model	Last known Owner/Operator	Identities/fates/comments (where appropriate)		
4290	402NG	Wideroes Flyveselskap	C-GARX	LN-WDJ	
4291	402NG	SATA Air Acores	C-GAUA	CS-TRD	
4292	402	ANA Wings	C-GAUB	JA855A	
4293	402NG	Air Baltic	C-GAUI	YL-BAF	
4294	402NG	Angolan Government	C-GAUK	D2-EEA	
4295	402NG	SATA Air Acores	C-GBIY	CS-TRE	
4296	402NG	Air Baltic	C-GBJA	YL-BAH	
4297	402NG	SATA Air Acores	C-GBJE	CS-TRF	
4298	402NG	Bombardier Inc	C-GBJF	CS-TRG	
4299	402	Ethiopian Airlines	C-GBKC	ET-ANI	
4300	402	Croatia Airlines	C-GBKD	9A-CQE	
4301	402	Croatia Airlines	C-GCKE	9A-CQF	
4302	402NG	Air Baltic	C-GCKV	YL-BAI	
4303	402NG	Ethiopian Airlines	C-GCLU	ET-ANJ	
4304	402NG	Ethiopian Airlines	C-GCPF	ET-ANK	
4305	402NG	Angolan Government	C-GCPQ	D2-EEB	
4306	402NG	Porter Airlines	C-FLQY		
4307	402NG	Ethiopian Airlines	C-GCPY	ET-ANL	
4308	402NG	Porter Airlines	C-GLQZ		
4309	402NG	Air Baltic	C-GCQG	YL-BAJ	
4310	402NG	Austrian Arrows	C-GCQB	OE-LGL	
4311	402NG	Olympic Air	C-GDCD	G-PTHD	SX-OBD
4312	402	AvTrade/Heli Malongo	C-GDCQ	D2-EUO	
4313	402NG	Air Baltic	C-GDDU	YL-BAQ	
4314	402NG	Olympic Air	C-GDEU	G-PTHE	SX-OBE
4315	402	AvTrade/Heli Malongo	C-GDFF	D2-EUP+	[+ not confirmed]
4316	402NG	Air Niugini	C-GEHE	P2-PXU	
4317	402NG	Ethiopian Airlines	C-GEHI	ET-ANV	
4318	402NG	Olympic Air	C-GEHQ	G-PTHF	SX-OBF
4319	402NG	Austrian Arrows	C-GEII	OE-LGM	
4320	402NG	Asky Airlines	C-GEUN	ET-ANW	
4321	402NG	Olympic Air	C-GEUZ	G-PTHG	SX-OBG
4322	402NG	Heli Malongo Airways	C-GEVB	D2-EUQ	
4323	402NG	Colgan Air/United Express	C-GEVP	N323NG	
4324	402NG	Air Baltic	C-GLTI	YL-BAX	
4325	402NG	Heli Malongo Airways	C-GEZN	D2-EUR	
4326	402NG	Austrian Arrows	C-GEZY	OE-LGN	
4327	402NG	Olympic Air	C-GFAK	G-PTHH	SX-OBH
4328	402NG	Colgan Air/United Express	C-GPNN	N328NG	[1,000th DHC-8]
4329	402NG	Air Niugini	C-GNIU	P2-PXT	
4330	402NG	Ethiopian Airlines/ASky Airlines	C-GSNH	ET-ANX	
4331	402NG	Air Baltic	C-GKLC	YL-BAY	
4332	402NG	Colgan Air/United Express	C-GFKK	N332NG	
4333	402NG	Colgan Air/United Express	C-GGFI	N333NG	
4334	402NG	Ethiopian Airlines	C-GGFU	ET-ANY	
4335	402NG	ANA Wings	C-GGHS	JA856A	
4336	402NG	Colgan Air/United Express	C-GGIF	N336NG	[marks N336PN for Colgan Air were also reserved]
4337	402NG	Wideroes Flyveselskap	C-GGIR	LN-WDK	
4338	402NG	Colgan Air/United Express	C-GGQY	N338NG	[marks N338PN for Colgan Air were also reserved]
4339	402NG	Colgan Air/United Express	C-GGRI	N339NG	[marks N339PN for Colgan Air were also reserved]
4340	402NG	Colgan Air/United Express	C-GGSI	N34NG	
4341	402NG	Colgan Air/United Express	C-GGSV	N341NG	[marks N341PN for Colgan Air were also reserved]
4342	402NG	Colgan Air/United Express	C-GGUB	N342NG	[marks N342PN for Colgan Air were also reserved]
4343	402NG	Sunstate/QantasLink	C-GGUK	VH-LQB	
4344	402NG	South African Express	C-GGUX	G-FLBF	ZS-YBU
4345	402NG	Colgan Air/United Express	C-GHCF	N345NG	
4346	402NG	Colgan Air/United Express	C-GHCO	N346NG	
4347	402NG	Alaska Horizon	C-GHCV	N440QX	
4348	402NG	Alaska Horizon	C-GHCY	N441QX	
4349	402NG	Luxair	C-GHDB	LX-LGF	
4350	402NG	South African Express	C-GHVF	G-FLBG	ZS-YBW
4351	402NG	ex Colgan Air/United Express	C-GHVS	N351NG	[stored 23Apr12 Victorville, CA]
4352	402NG	Alaska Horizon	C-GHWA	N442QX	

DE HAVILLAND CANADA DHC-8

C/n	Model	Last known Owner/Operator	Identities/fates/comments (where appropriate)		
4353	402NG	Alaska Horizon	C-GILG	N443QX	
4354	402NG	ex Colgan Air/United Express	C-GHWL	N354NG	[stored 23Apr12 Victorville, CA]
4355	402NG	Alaska Horizon	C-GHYE	N444QX	
4356	402NG	Colgan Air/United Express	C-GILK	N356NG	
4357	402NG	Porter Airlines	C-GKQA		
4358	402NG	Alaska Horizon	C-GILN	N445QX	
4359	402NG	Porter Airlines	C-GKQB		
4360	402NG	Porter Airlines	C-GKQC		
4361	402NG	Porter Airlines	C-GKQD		
4362	402NG	ANA Wings	C-GISU	JA857A	
4363	402NG	Alaska Horizon	C-GISZ	N446QX	
4364	402NG	Alaska Horizon	C-GITK	N447QX	
4365	402NG	Jazz Air/Air Canada Express	C-GGOY		
4366	402NG	South African Express	C-GIUO	G-FLBH	ZS-YBX
4367	402NG	Smartair	C-GJFG	SU-SMH	
4368	402NG	Smartair	C-GJFP	SU-SMI	
4369	402NG	Jazz Air/Air Canada Express	C-GKUK		
4370	402NG	South African Express	C-GJFR	G-FLBJ	ZS-YBY
4371	402NG	Sunstate/QantasLink	C-GJFZ	VH-LQD	
4372	402NG	Jazz Air/Air Canada Express	C-GGOK		
4373	402NG	Spice Jet	C-GJJU	VT-SUA	
4374	402NG	Spice Jet	C-GJKC	VT-SUB	
4375	402NG	Sunstate/QantasLink	C-GJKV	VH-LQF	
4376	402NG	Sunstate/QantasLink	C-GJLE	VH-LQG	
4377	402NG	Spice Jet	C-GKLF	VT-SUC	
4378	402NG	Spice Jet	C-GKLZ	VT-SUD	
4379	402NG	Spice Jet	C-GKMS	VT-SUE	
4380	402NG	Colgan Air/United Express	C-GKNB	N380NG	
4381	402NG	Jazz Air/Air Canada Express	C-GGOI		
4382	402NG	Spice Jet	C-GKOI	VT-SUF	
4383	402NG	Jazz Air/Air Canada Express	C-GGOF		
4384	402NG	Jazz Air/Air Canada Express	C-GGNZ		
4385	402NG	ANA Wings	C-GKVD	JA858A	
4386	402NG	Jazz Air/Air Canada Express	C-GGNY		
4387	402NG	Spice Jet	C-GKVM	VT-SUG	
4388	402NG	Jazz Air/Air Canada Express	C-GGNW		
4389	402NG	Spice Jet	C-GKVP	VT-SUH	
4390	402NG	Porter Airlines	C-GKQE		
4391	402NG	Porter Airlines	C-GKQF		
4392	402NG	Wideroes Flyveselskap	C-GLKA	LN-WDL	
4393	402NG	Jazz Air/Air Canada Express	C-GGNF		
4394	402NG	Jazz Air/Air Canada Express	C-GGND		
4395	402NG	Spice Jet	C-GLEP	VT-SUI	
4396	402NG	Bombardier Inc	C-GLFS	[stored Downsview, ON, Canada; l/n 21Mar12; for Spice Jet as VT-SUJ]	
4397	402NG	Jazz Air/Air Canada Express	C-GGMU		
4398	402NG	Bombardier Inc	C-GLKU	(VT-SUK)	
4399	402NG	Jazz Air/Air Canada Express	C-GGMZ		
4400	402NG	Spice Jet	C-GLUM	VT-SUL	
4401	402NG	ANA Wings	C-GLKE	JA859A	
4402	402NG	Spice Jet	C-GLKV	VT-SUM	
4403	402NG	Jazz Air/Air Canada Express	C-GGMQ		
4404	402NG	Spice Jet	C-GMOU	VT-SUO	
4405	402NG	Jazz Air/Air Canada Express	C-GGMN		
4406	402NG	Eurolot	C-GMXB	SP-EQA	
4407	402NG	Eurolot	C-GMXR	SP-EQB	
4408	402NG	Eurolot	C-GMYD	SP-EQC	
4409	402NG	Alaska Horizon	C-GMYH	N448QX	
4410	402NG	Alaska Horizon	C-GNGZ	N449QX	
4411	402NG	ex Bombardier Inc	C-GNHD	SP-EQD	
4412	402NG	Spice Jet	C-GNHX	VT-SUP	
4413	402NG	Jazz Air/Air Canada Express	C-GGMI		
4414	402NG	Sunstate/QantasLink	C-GNZW	VH-LQJ	
4415	402NG	Sunstate/QantasLink	C-GOAO	VH-LQK	

DE HAVILLAND CANADA DHC-8

C/n	Model	Last known Owner/Operator	Identities/fates/comments (where appropriate)	
4416	402NG	ANA Wings	C-GOBK	JA460A
4417	402NG	Eurolot	C-GOCX	SP-EQE
4418	402NG	Luxair	C-GOEA	LX-LGG
4419	402NG	Bombardier Inc	C-GNKT	[reported for Ethiopian]
4420	402NG	Bombardier Inc	C-GPID	[reported for Luxair as LX-LGH]
4421	402NG	Bombardier Inc	C-GPIZ	
4422	402NG	Eurolot	SP-EQF	
4423	402NG	Bombardier Inc	C-GPYN	[reported for Eurolot as SP-EQG]
4424	402NG	Bombardier Inc	C-GPZF	[reported for Eurolot as SP-EQH]
4425				
4426				
4427				
4428				
4429				
4430				
4431				
4432				
4433				
4434				
4435				
4436				
4437				
4438				

DORNIER Do228

Notes: Production aircraft also have a line number. These run from 0001 to 0245 and the last three digits of the c/n and line number are the same.
Production 100 series aircraft have c/ns starting with 7 whilst 200 series aircraft c/ns start with 8; the two series are intertwined within the same sequence.
Some aircraft were assembled/built in India by Hindustan Industries and were also given a c/n in a separate sequence starting at HAL0001, in addition to the Dornier c/n and line number.
Some reports suggest that the HAL sequence only ran to HAL1007 with subsequent c/n's running from HAL2008.
Registrations in the series D-CBDA to D-CBDZ were used by many aircraft for test flying.

C/n	Cvtd No.	Model	Last known Owner/Operator	Identities/fates/comments (where appropriate)
4358		100	(Dornier Luftfahrt)	(D-ILDO) D-IFNS [ff 28Mar81; w/o 26Mar82 near Egenhausen, Augsburg, Germany]
4359		200	Dornier Museum	D-ICDO [wfu; last flight 30May06 & stored Friedrichshafen, Germany by Mar10 on display there]
7001		100	(Dornier Luftfahrt)	D-ICOG LN-HPG D-ICOG [wfu Mar93 Oberpfaffenhofen, Germany; canx Apr93]
8002		200	LGW-Luftfahrtgesellschaft Walter	D-IDCO 9M-AXB D-IDCO 9M-AXB D-IDCO OY-CHJ D-CBDU D-ILWS
7003		100	Business Wings	D-IDNI LN-HPA SE-KHL D-IROL [by 08Mar10 with 228NG 5-blade props]
7004		100	Kaskazi Aviation	D-ICGO LN-HPE SE-KKX 5Y-BRX
7005		100	FLM Aviation/Manx2	D-IDOM LN-HTB D-ILKA
8006		201	Jagson Airlines	D-IBOO A5-RGB VT-ESQ
8007		200	Solar Aviation	D-IDID JA8835 RP-C2817 D-ISIS HS-SAB
8008		201	(Formosa Airlines)	D-IHIC B-12203 D-CASE B-12208 [w/o 18Jun95 Green Island Airport, Taiwan]
8009		202K	Cobham Leasing Ltd/DEFRA	D-IDON (PH-HAL) SX-BHB D-CATI D-IDON PH-SDO G-MLDO G-OALF G-MAFE
8010		200	(Gorkha Airlines)	D-IHDO SX-BHA 9M-DMF 9M-AXF SE-KTO OY-CHF SE-KTO 9N-AEO [DBR 30Jun05 Lukla Airport, Nepal, and reported stored]
7011		101	Nigerian Border Air Patrol	D-ICIP 5N-AQV 5N-AUV
8012		201	(Afrimex)	D-IDMC (5N-AQU) 5N-ARI [w/o Oct 1990 in Nigeria; fuselage and tail to Dodson International Aircraft Parts, Rantoul, KS]
8013		201	ex Dana Air	(N1339D) D-IDMI (5N-AOH) 5N-ARP [reported wfu by 14May10 Kaduna AFB, Nigeria]
7014		101	Planes for Africa	(N1339U) (D-ICIO) D-IAWI D-CAWI 5Y-BYH
7015		100	(Okada Air)	D-IDOC (5N-AQW) 5N-AOR [w/o 1992 in Nigeria]
8016		201	(Star Air Aviation)	D-IBLH SE-IKY LN-BEQ N228CT D-CBDQ N228CT AP-BGF [w/o 19Feb03 Karachi-Quaid-E-Azam Airport, Pakistan; canx 20May09]
8017		201	Jagson Airlines	D-IBLI A5-RGC VT-ESS
7018		101	Nigerian Border Air Patrol	D-IBLB 5N-AUW
8019		200	Solar Air	D-IBLJ JA8836 RP-C2814 HS-SAA
7020		100	(Royal Oman Police)	D-IBLC A4O-CP [w/o 27Apr87 near Al Jaylah, Oman]
8021		200	Black Ginger 425 (Pty)	D-IBLK 9M-AXD OY-CHK ZS-NRN [reported wfu by 20Apr09 Lanseria, South Africa]
7022		100	ex Cosmic Air	D-IBLD LN-HPG SE-KTM OY-CHG SE-KTM 9N-AGY [stored by 24Oct06 Kathmandu, Nepal; l/n14Apr09]
7023		100	Niemur Aviation (Pty)	D-IBLE 5N-AQX 5N-AUM 3D-DMI ZS-SSO
7024		100	(Gorkha Airlines)	D-IBLF (LN-HPH) LN-NVB SE-KTN (OY-CHI) D-CBDW 9N-ACV(2) [w/o 02Nov00 Lukla Airport, Nepal]
8025		202	General Avn Maintenance Pty	D-IBLL N228RP 5N-DOA VH-VJJ
8026		202	Dana Air	D-IBLM N232RP 5N-DOB
7027		101	Aerocardal	D-IBLG D-CDWM 5N-ARK D-CBDI D-IABE CC-CSA CC-CWX
7028		100	Royal Oman Police	D-IBLN A4O-CQ
7029		101	(Everest Air)	(D-IBLO) D-IASS D-CASS MI-8504 D-CLEX MI-8504 D-CBDK D-CAMI(2) 9N-ACL [w/o 31Jly93 near Bharatpur, Nepal]
8030		201	AP Logistics	D-IDBB SX-BHC 5Y-BTU
8031		201	Nigerian Air Force	D-IDBC NAF-028
7032		101	(Agni Air)	D-IBLP VT-EIX 9N-AHE [w/o 24Aug10 near Bastipur, 18nm SW of Kathmandu, Nepal]
8033		201	Nigerian Air Force	D-IDBD NAF-029

DORNIER Do228

C/n	Cvtd No.	Model	Last known Owner/Operator	Identities/fates/comments (where appropriate)
8034		201	AP Logistics	D-IDBE SX-BHD A6-ZYG 5Y-BUW
8035		200	LGW-Luftfahrtgesellschaft Walter	(D-IDBF) D-IASX D-CDIZ D-ILWB
7036		100	AAS Leasing/Kivu Air	D-IBLQ A2-ABA ZS-NGW [stored by 24Jan11 Libbreville, Gabon]
8037		201	Indian Airlines	D-IDBG VT-EIO
8038		201	(Vayudoot Airlines)	D-IDBH VT-EIP [std by 18Sep01 Delhi, India; derelict by 04Jly02; canx 01Aug03]
7039		100	(DLR Flugbetriebe)	(D-IBLR) D-IGVN [w/o 24Feb85 by missile Argub, nr Dakhla, Western Sahara, Morocco]
8040		202	General Avn Maintenance Pty	D-IDBI N233RP 5N-DOG VH-VJB VH-VJN V7-0811 VH-VJN
8041		202	General Avn Maintenance Pty	D-IDBJ N234RP 5N-DOC VH-VJE
8042		201	(Vayudoot Airlines)	D-IDBK VT-EIQ [stored by 18Sep01 Delhi, India; canx 01Aug03]
7043		101	Nigerian Air Force	D-IBLS NAF-027
8044		201	Wells Fargo Bank Northwest	(D-IDBL) D-COKI HZ-SG1 HZ-NC11? N407VA [stored by 08Mar04 North Las Vegas Airport, NV; l/n 09Oct11 probably wfu]
8045		201	Wells Fargo Bank Northwest	(D-IDBM) D-COKO HZ-SG2 HZ-NC12? N408VA [stored by 08Mar04 North Las Vegas Airport, NV; l/n 09Oct11 probably wfu]
8046		201	FLM Aviation/Manx2	D-IDBN LN-NVC TF-ELF TF-ADB TF-CSF TF-VMF TF-CSF D-IFLM
8047		201	General Avn Maintenance Pty	D-IDBO D-CDWF 5N-ARF VH-VJF [stored minus wings Rand, South Africa, still as 5N-ARF; l/n 01Mar11]
8048		202	(Dana Air)	D-IDBP N235RP 5N-DOD [b/u Jly/Aug12 Kaduna, Nigeria, for spares]
8049		202	(Dana Air)	D-IDBQ N236RP 5N-DOE [b/u Jly/Aug12 Kaduna, Nigeria, for spares]
8050		201	Air Traffic	D-IDBR SX-BHE A6-ZYE 5Y-BUV
7051		101	Natural Enviroment Research Council	D-CALM G-ENVR
8052	HAL1001	201	(Vayudoot Airlines)	D-CAFE(1) VT-EJF [w/o 23Sep89 Lake Indapur, near Poona, India]
7053		101	Indian Coast Guard	D-CILA CG751
8054		201	Orient Flights	D-CALI VT-EJO
8055	HAL1007	201	Indian Air Force	HM671 [code J]
8056		201	Summerset Charters	D-CAMI (1) 7P-LAL F-GPIV F-OGOQ F-GOAH (ZS-STA) ZS-OVM ZS-MJH
8057		201	ex Olympic Aviation	D-CAPO SX-BHF [stored by 18Oct03 Athens-Spata, Greece; l/n 29Feb08; by 2010 stored dismantled Nairobi-Jomo Kenyatta, Kenya; canx]
8058		200	Air Traffic	(D-CERA) D-IERA VH-NSC G-SJAD D-IHKB VH-NSX D-CMIC D-IMIK 5Y-BYC
7059		101	Indian Coast Guard	D-CIRI CG752+ D-CAOT CG752 [+ India]
8060	HAL1002	201	(Indian Airlines)	VT-EJN [w/o 09Jun02 Jaipur-Sanganer Airport, India; by Sep05 to Dodson International Aircraft Parts, Rantoul, KS; l/n Jun06]
8061		201	(Olympic Aviation)	D-COBB SX-BHG [w/o 02May97 Paros, Greece; by Sep00 wreck moved to Athens-Spata, Greece; l/n 29Feb09; gone by early 2009 fate unknown]
7062		101	Indian Coast Guard	D-CAUM CG753+ D-CAOR CG753 [+ India]
8063		202K	LASSA – Linea de Aeroservicios	D-CAOS D-IAOT G-BMMR CC-CNW
8064	HAL1003	201	(Vayudoot Airlines)	VT-EJT [w/o 22Sep88 Aurangabad Airport, India]
8065		202K	FLM Aviation/Manx2	D-CBOL TC-FBM D-CBOL G-BUXT TF-ADC TF-CSG TF-VMG TF-CSG (D-IMNX) D-CMNX
8066		201	LGW-Luftfahrtgesellschaft Walter	D-CECK D-IAHG HB-LPC D-CANA(2) D-CBDR D-IKBA
8067	HAL1004	201	(Vayudoot Airlines)	VT-EJU [stored 18Sep01 Delhi, India; derelict by 04Jly02; canx 01Aug03]
8068		201	Africa's Connection STP	D-CENT 98+78+ D-CPBO TR-LHE S9-RAS [+ West Germany]
8069		200	ex LGW-Luftfahrtgesellschaft Walter	D-CHOF D-ILWD [canx 30Nov11 as sold abroad]
8070		201K	(Landsflug)	D-CLIC LN-NVG SE-KVV TF-ELH SE-KVV TF-ELH G-RGDT TF-ELH TF-ADD [substantial damage 23Jun04 Siglufjordur, Iceland, whilst regd TF-ELH; taken to Reykjavik and reg'd but ultimately assessed dbr; fuselage l/n Sep08 at Akureyri, Iceland; canx 06Dec11]
8071		202	Summit Air Charters	(D-IECA) D-CEBA N71FB N253MC C-FPSH
8072	HAL1005	201	(Vayudoot Airlines)	VT-EJV [l/n Oct94 parked Bombay, later Mumbai, India; canx 01Aug03]
7073		101	(DLR Flugbetriebe)	D-CICE [substantially damaged 25Jan05 British Research Station, Antarctica; shipped back to Oberpfaffenhofen, Germany and in Nov05 assessed dbr; canx 23Feb07; hulk to be auctioned May10]

DORNIER Do228

C/n	Cvtd No.	Model	Last known Owner/Operator	Identities/fates/comments (where appropriate)
8074		201	Escadrille Nationale du Niger	D-CELO 5U-MBI [ferried 09Jly07 Oberpfaffenhofen, Germany for overhaul or storage; l/n 17Nov08]
8075	HAL1006	201	(Alliance Air)	VT-EJW [w/o 30Jly98 Cochin, India]
8076		201	Dana Air	D-CEPT 5N-AUN
8077		202K	Island Aviation Services	D-CESI D-IESI G-BMND VH-NSZ N2255Y F-ODZH RP-C2283
8078		201	ex Cosmic Air	D-CFAN MI-8605 D-CBDJ D-CBMI 9N-ACV(1) D-CDMI VT- D-CBDC D-CBMI 9N-AEP [wfu by 14Apr09 Kathmandu, Nepal] [by 16Feb08 stored Katmandu, Nepal]
8079		201	ex Olympic Aviation	D-CLEC SX-BHH [wfu 18Oct03 Athens-Hellenikon, Greece; by 31Jun06 fuselage only noted; l/n Feb08; by 2010 stored dismantled Jomo Nairobi-Kenyatta, Kenya; canx]
8080		201	Air Traffic	D-COLE SX-BHI 5Y-BUX
8081	HAL2008	201	Indian Air Force	HM667 [code K]
8082	HAL2009	201	Indian Air Force	HM668
7083		101	DLR Flugbetriebe	(D-CEVA) D-CODE
8084		200	Aero VIP	(D-CLAB) D-ILAB G-MAFS VP-FBK CS-AYT
8085		202K	Vision Air	D-CALU F-GGAV D-CBDQ D-CALU CS-AZZ PH-FXB CS-AZZ G-BWEX N402VA
8086		201	Airports Authority of India	D-CANA(1) VT-ENK
8087		202	ex Trans-Jamaican Airlines	D-CAPA N87FB N254MC 6Y-JQL [canx 13Jly92; stored dismantled by Jun02, Oberpfaffenhofen, Germany; l/n Mar03]
8088		202	Summit Air Charters	D-CBUL N88FB N255MC 6Y-JQM C-GJPY
8089	HAL2010	201	Indian Air Force	HM669 [code M]
8090	HAL2016	201	Airports Authority of India	VT-EPU
8091		201	(Cape Verde Coast Guard/TACV)	D-CEDS F-GGGV D-CBDR D-CEDS D4-CBC [w/o 07Aug99 near Santo Antao Airport, Cape Verde]
8092		200	(ExecuJet Aircraft Sales)	D-CEKO MAAW 1+ MAAW T-01^ ZS-CCC [+ Malawi; ^ code 76-01 also reported at this time; canx 16Sep04 fate unknown]
8093		201	American Jet	D-CEMA D-CERA N228BM LV-WTV
8094		202	American Jet	(D-CERO) D-CEYH (PH-FXA) TF-VLI D-CBDL D-CDAL D-ICAT D-CDAL D-ICAT D-CBDR LV-WTD
7095		101	Nigerian Border Police	D-COHU D-CAGE 5N-AUX
8096		201	Jagson Airlines	D-COHA D-IOHA G-CFIN D-CBDN D-CAOT D-IAAL D-CAAL VT-EUM
8097		202	Wells Fargo Bank Northwest	D-COHB D-COCO N228ME N409VA
8098	HAL2011	201	Indian Air Force	HM670
7099	HAL2017	101	(United Breweries)	VT-EPV [w/o 13Sep91 Madras, India]
8100		202	Ten Barrel	D-COHC N228DA N275MC P2-MBO C-FEQZ ZK-VIR PJ-DVA C-GTBN
8101		202	Summit Air Charters	D-COHD N101BB N256MC P2-MBP C-FEQX
8102		202	Bighorn Airways	D-COHE N102BF N257MC C-FVAH N257MC YV-648C N257MC
8103		202	Summit Air Charters	D-COHF N103BY N258MC P2-MBQ C-FEQW
8104		202	Nationale	D-COHG MAAW-2+ D-CBDQ D-CATO MAAW T-02^ ZS-DOC [+ Malawi; ^ code 76-02 also reported at this time]
7105	HAL2013	101	Indian Coast Guard	CG755
7106	HAL2015	101	Indian Coast Guard	CG756
8107		201	Tara Air	D-COHH LN-NVH F-ODZF 9N-AGQ
8108		201	Regourd Aviation	D-COHI D-IOHI G-MLNR D-CBDO D-IABE G-CAYN SE-LHD LN-AAO SE-LHD LN-AAO 5Y-EKA
8109		202	Summit Air Charters/UN	D-CAAA N109HW N276MC C-FNWZ N276MC YV-649C N276MC C-FUCN
8110		202	Wells Fargo Bank Northwest	D-CAAB N110DN N501VA [by 08Aug04 stored North Las Vegas Airport, NV; reported 06Sep08 minus most parts still marked N110DN]
8111		201	(Formosa Airlines)	D-CAAC B-12238 [w/o 28Feb93 Orchid Island Airport, Taiwan; fuselage preserved Taitung City, Taiwan]
8112		202K	Cobham Leasing Ltd/DEFRA	D-CAAD G-OMAF
7113	HAL2012	101	Indian Coast Guard	CG754
7114	HAL2015	101	Indian Coast Guard	CG757 [w/o 02Jan93 off Paradip, India]
8115		202K	Cobham Leasing Ltd/DEFRA	D-CAAE G-MAFI
7116		101	(Nigerian Border Police)	D-CIMA 5N-AUY [stored by 17Mar05 Kaduna, Nigeria; l/n Feb06; canx 26Oct06 with expired CofA]

DORNIER Do228

C/n	Cvtd No.	Model	Last known Owner/Operator	Identities/fates/comments (where appropriate)
8117		203F	Wells Fargo Bank Northwest	D-CIMB N117DN [stored by Feb02 North Las Vegas Airport, NV; l/n 09Oct11 probably wfu]
8118		202	ex Trans-Jamaican Airlines	D-CIMC N121DA N259MC 6Y-JQN [by Mar02 stored dismantled Oberpfaffenhofen, Germany; l/n Apr11]
8119		202	Aerocardal	D-CIMD D-CMUC TC-DBS D-CMUC CS-TGO CC-AAQ
8120		203F	Vision Air	D-IABD N228RM N243RP N279MC N404VA
8121		203F	Wells Fargo Bank Northwest	D-CBDA N260MC [stored 08Jan02 North Las Vegas Airport, NV; l/n 03Apr09 probably wfu]
8122		202	Summit Air Charters	D-CBDB N226PT N278MC D-CBDI VT-KCV D-CLUU(2) C-FPSA
8123		202K	Sita Air	(D-CBDC) D-CEZH VH-NSH N2255E F-ODZG 9H-AHA
8124		202	Solar Aviation	(D-CBDD) D-CFAA D-IAHD JA8866 VH-UJD 5Y-BWN HS-SAE
8125		202	(Dana Air)	D-CBDE N228PT N245RP 5N-DOF [b/u Jly/Aug12 Kaduna, Nigeria, for spares]
8126		202	Summit Air Charters	D-CBDF N227PT N246RP P2-MBR C-FEQV [stored by Feb99 Oberpfaffenhofen, Germany as P2-MBR; reg'd in Canada Mar05; l/n 14Mar11 still as P2-MBR]
8127		202	(KATO Air)	D-CBDG N262MC D-CBDE (VT-) D-CLUU(1) LN-HTA [w/o 04Dec03 Bodo Airport, Norway]
8128		200	National Aerospace Laboratory	D-CBDH N111AL D-CBDU JA8858
8129		201	(Formosa Airlines)	D-CBDI D-CBEA B-12268 [w/o 14Aug90 Orchid Island Airport, Taiwan]
8130		201	Nigerian Border Police	D-CBDJ D-CAOS 5N-ACT 5N-FCT
8131		202	(Somali Airlines)	D-CBDK D-COAA 6O-SCD [circa 1991 stolen; fate not known; also reported wfu & stolen; canx]
8132		202	(Somali Airlines)	D-CBDL D-COAB 6O-SCE [wfu Jly91 Mogadishu, Somalia; canx]
8133		202	(Summit Air Charters)	D-CBDM N261MC C-FYEV N261MC C-FYEV [w/o 14Dec08 near Cambridge Bay, NU, Canada; canx 07May09]
8134		202	Dana Air	D-CBDN N112DN N239RP 5N-DOH [DBR 28Dec00 Benguela, Angola by small arms fire]
8135		202	Wells Fargo Bank Northwest	D-CBDO N229PT N269MC N502VA [by Sep99 stored North Las Vegas Airport, NV; l/n 09Oct11 as N69MC; probably wfu]
8136		202K	(Caraibes Air Transport)	D-CBDP D-CBCA D-CIRA F-OGOJ [CofA expired 06Apr02; canx Feb02; wfu and stored Fort-de-France, Martinique]
8137		202	(Dana Air)	D-CBDQ N113DN N237RP 5N-DOI [b/u Jly/Aug12 Kaduna, Nigeria, for spares]
8138		202	(Dana Air)	D-CBDR N114DN N238RP 5N-DOJ [b/u Jly/Aug12 Kaduna, Nigeria, for spares]
8139		202K	Aero Cuahonte	D-CBDS D-CACC F-OGOL XA-UNB
8140		202	(Dana Air)	D-CBDT N115DN N240RP 5N-DOK [b/u Jly/Aug12 Kaduna, Nigeria, for spares]
8141		202	Bighorn Airways	D-CBDU N116DN N263MC
8142		201	(Formosa Airlines)	D-CBDV D-CALA(1) B-12288 [w/o 15Jun96 Taitung Airport, Taiwan]
8143		202K	JetFly Aviation	D-CBDW D-CBCB F-OGOF TJ-PHT
8144		202	Wells Fargo Bank Northwest	D-CBDX N264MC N405VA
8145		202	Dana Air	D-CBDY N241RP 5N-DOL [reported stored 30Oct07 Abuja, Nigeria; l/n 08Sep08]
8146		201	(National Electric Power Authority)	D-CBDZ D-CALO 5N-MPS [canx 26Oct06 with expired CofA, noted wfu 14May10 Kaduna AFB, Nigeria]
8147		202	(Dana Air)	D-CBDA N242RP 5N-DOM [b/u Jly/Aug12 Kaduna, Nigeria, for spares]
8148		202K	Malawi Air Wing	D-CBDI D-CORN(1) MAAW T-03 [reported also coded 76-03]
8149		202	Wells Fargo Bank Northwest	D-CBDK N265MC N406VA [stored by Oct04 North Las Vegas Airport, NV; l/n 09Oct11 as N265MC; probably wfu]
8150		202	Bighorn Airways	D-CBDL N266MC
8151		201	(Formosa Airlines)	D-CBDB D-CALA(2) B-12298 [w/o 14Jun93 Green Island Airport, Taiwan]
8152		202K	SCD Aviation/Minair	D-CBDC TC-FBX D-CBDO D-CAOT CS-TGH D-CAAL
8153		202	Summit Air Charters/UN	D-CBDD N267MC P2-MBV C-GSAX
8154		202	Sita Air	D-CBDE N268MC P2-MBW C-GSAU 9N-AHR
8155		212	SCD Aviation/Africa Connection	D-CBDG D-CAOS D-CALY D-CDBU TR-LGM PH-IOL TR-LGM D-CALI* [* marks reserved 2012]

DORNIER Do228

C/n	Cvtd No.	Model	Last known Owner/Operator	Identities/fates/comments (where appropriate)
8156		202K	Transportes Aereos Corpativos	D-CBDP D-CORN(2) TC-FBN TF-ELA LN-MOL CP- CC-AAI
8157		202K	General Avn Maintenance Pty	D-CBDF D-CIRC TC-FBM D-CBDV D-CTCB G-BVTZ D-CBDQ D-CBIM D2-EBT VH-VJD
8158		202	ex Mandarin Airlines	D-CBDH D-CAHA B-12252 [reported wfu by 2002]
8159		202K	(Advanced Aviation/RUAG)	D-CBDN D-COBE CS-TGF D-CAAW [w/o 16Aug08 Banjul-Yundum International Airport, Gambia; canx 07Feb11]
8160		202K	Aero VIP	D-CBDQ D-CORA CS-TGG
8161		202K	(Air Caraibes)	D-CBDR F-OGOZ [by 30Apr04 stored derelict Pointe-a-Pitre, Guadeloupe]
8162		202K	Aerocardal	D-CBDS D-CATY PH-FXA D-CBDZ D-CUBI G-BVTY (D-IASD) D-CBDM VH-URU D-CBDN D-CLEE CC-CWC
8163		202K	Aerocon	D-CBDT D-CIKI CP-2176
8164		201	Indian Navy	D-CBDU D-CAFE(2) D-CBDK D-CAFE IN225 [code DAB]
8165		202K	Agni Air	D-CBDV D-CALK G-BVPT D-CALK N419VA 9M-VAA 9N-AIE
8166		202K	Lufttransport AS	D-CBDW D-CBCE TC-FBP D-CBDU D-CTCA LN-LYR
7167		101	(Nigerian Border Police)	D-CBDX D-CAFA 5N-AUZ [canx 26Oct06 with expired CofA, fate unknown]
7168		101	ex Cosmic Air	D-CBDY D-CDOC ZK-TRD D-CDOC D-CCDB 9N-ACE [stored by 08May99 Kathmandu, Nepal; reported DBR by Oct06; l/n 14Apr09] is this Everest Air?
8169		202K	ex Sita Air	D-CBDL D-COCA F-OGPI 9N-AHB [badly damaged & stored 12Oct10 Lukla, Nepal; l/n 21Feb11]
8170		202K	Malawi Air Wing	D-CBDM D-CAOT MAAW T-04 [reported also coded 76-04]
8171		202	Vision Air	D-CBDF D-CDFW (SX-) 9M-BAS N403VA
8172		202K	ex Pelangi Air	D-CBDC D-CATH 9M-PEN [owner ceased operations 2001; abandoned Subang Airport, Selangor, Malaysia; l/n 24Jun06; by Nov09 fuselage only]
8173		202K	Island Aviation Services	D-CBDA F-OGOH N23UA RP-C2282(2)
8174		202K	Island Aviation Services	D-CBDB D-CBCI 9M-PEL VH-YJD RP-C2287
8175		202K	ex Pelangi Air	D-CBDE D-CHTM 9M-PEM [owner ceased operations 2001; abandoned Subang Airport, Selangor, Malaysia; l/n 24Jun06, by Nov09 fuselage only]
8176		212	(Air Caraibes)	D-CBDG D-CDDB F-WGXG F-OGXG [canx 08Jun01 as destroyed; no details known]
8177		212	Island Transvoyager	D-CBDD D-CARI 5Y-HLC D-CBDW D-CPDD B-11150 RP-C2289
8178		212	ex Island Aviation Services	D-CBDN D-COLT 8Q-AMB [wfu 30Jun06; canx before 21May07; stored wingless Male, Maldives; l/n 20Feb12]
8179		212	ex Island Aviation Services	D-CBDO D-CISS 8Q-AMC [stored wingless by Apr04 Male, Maldives; canx before 21May07; l/n 20Feb12]
8180		212	DFLR – Deutsche Forschungsanstalt	D-CFFU
8181		212	Dutch Coast Guard	D-CBDP D-CIBA YV-635C D-CBDG RP-C2282(1) 9N-AFS (OY-BNS) D-CNLA (PH-KWO) PH-CGN
8182		212	(Linea Turistica Aereotuy)	D-CBDQ D-CJRM YV-532C [arrived Dec99 Oberpfaffenhofen, Germany & stored and then dismantled; l/n 08Oct07]
8183		212	Dutch Coast Guard	D-CBDS D-CJPM YV-533C D-CNLB (PH-KWN) PH-CGC
8184		212	ex Linea Turistica Aereotuy	D-CBDT D-CICA YV-534C [stored by Jly01 Oberpfaffenhofen, Germany; l/n 21Apr08]
8185		212	German Navy	D-CBDU 98+77+ 57+01 [+ West Germany]
8186		212	ex Cosmic Air	D-CBDV D-CDOB ZK-TRA D-CDOB 9N-ACG [wfu by 2003 Kathmandu, Nepal; l/n 14Apr09]
8187		212	ex Linea Turistica Aereotuy	D-CBDW D-CDOA ZK-TRB D-CDOA P2-MBH D-CBDD D-CAET YV-647C [stored by Jly01 Oberpfaffenhofen, Germany; l/n Apr11]
8188		212	Royal Thai Navy	D-CBDX D-CAOT 121+ 1109 [+ Thailand]
8189		212	Royal Thai Navy	D-CBDM D-CATS 122+ 1110 [+ Thailand]
8190		212	Royal Thai Navy	D-CBDN D-COTZ 123+ 1111 [+ Thailand]
8191		212	Northeast Shuttles (Pvt)	D-CBDA D-CORK F-ODYB 9N-AIY VT-NER
8192		212	Business Wings	D-CBDB D-CJKM F-ODYC LN-BER D-CULT
8193		212	Island Transvoyager	D-CBDS D-CARD RP-C1008

DORNIER Do228

C/n	Cvtd No.	Model	Last known Owner/Operator	Identities/fates/comments (where appropriate)
8194		212	Air Marshall Islands	D-CBDA D-CAHD MI-9206 V7-9206 [stored by 11Feb08 Majuro, Marshall Islands]
8195		212	National Cartographic Center	D-CBDL D-CNCC EP-TCC
8196		212	(Air Tahiti)	D-CBDD D-CAPE F-OHAB [w/o 18Apr91 nr Nuku Hiva Island, French Polynesia]
8197		212	(Air St Barthelemy)	D-CBDH D-CATS F-ODUN [stored Dec99 Dinard, France; l/n 26Aug01 derelict, missing parts]
8198		212	Agni Air	D-CBDK D-CDWK F-OHAA VH-ATZ 9N-AJH
8199		212	Inter Island Airways	D-CBDZ D-CLOG F-OHAF N229ST
8200		212	Arcus-Air-Logistic	D-CBDC D-CUTT
8201		212	Air Marshall Islands	D-CBDD D-CAHE MI-9207 V7-9207 [stored by 11Feb08 Majuro, Marshall Islands]
8202		212	Italian Army	D-CBDE D-CAOT MM62156 [code EI-101]
8203		212	Italian Army	D-CBDF D-CAOS MM62157 [code EI-102]
8204		212	National Cartographic Center	D-CBDM D-CIMO EP-TKH
8205		212	Arcus-Air-Logistic	D-CBDH D-CAAM
8206		212NG	RUAG	D-CDOQ D-CDIV PH-MNZ D-CNEU [development prototype for upgraded production restart]
8207		212	National Cartographic Center	D-CBDN D-CIME EP-THA
8208		212	National Cartographic Center	D-CBDO D-CIMU EP-TZA
8209		212	Italian Army	D-CBDP D-CLOZ MM62158 [code EI-103]
8210		212	Iran Aircraft Manufacturing Industries	D-CBDQ D-CRAM EP-TAA H-228
8211		212	Arcus-Air-Logistic	D-CBDX 57+02+ D-CAAR [+ Germany]
8212		212	Arcus-Air-Logistic	D-CBDY 57+03+ D-CAAZ [+ Germany]
8213		212	(Pelangi Air/Air Maldives)	D-CBDR D-CIMI 9M-PEQ [w/o 18Oct95 Male, Maldives]
8214		212	German Navy	D-CBDK 57+04
8215		212	Daily Air	D-CBDS D-CJOH B-12253 B-55561
8216		212	(Agni Air)	D-CBDL 9N-NEO N420VA 9M-VAM 9N-AIG [w/o 14May12 near Jomson, Nepal]
8217		212	(Merpati Intan/Royal Brunei Airlines)	D-CBDS 9M-MIA [w/o 06Sep97 in Lambir Hills National Park, near Miri, Malaysia]
8218		212	Gorkha Airlines	D-CBDT 9M-MIB 9M-BOR RP-C2101 9N-AHS
8219		212	Nigerian Air Force	D-CBDB D-CIST D-CBDI NAF-030
8220		212	(Formosa Airlines)	D-CBDT D-CROC (B-12254) B-12256 [w/o 10Aug97 near Matsu Airport, Taiwan]
8221		212	Nigerian Air Force	D-CBDJ D-CICK D-CBDJ NAF-031
8222		212	Cabo Verde Coast Guard	D-CBDX D-CLFA 7Q-YKS D4-CBK
8223		212	(Formosa Airlines)	D-CBDY D-CLFB B-12257 [w/o 05Apr96 10 miles off Matsu Island, Taiwan]
8224		212	Daily Air	D-CLFC B-12259 B-55563
8225		212	Nigerian Air Force	D-CATA D-CBDL NAF-032
8226		212	Royal Thai Navy	D-CBDF 1112
8227		212	Royal Thai Navy	D-CBDG D-CCCP 1113
8228		212	Royal Thai Navy	D-CBDH D-CDDH 1114
8229		212	(Nigerian Air Force)	D-CBDK D-CATZ D-CBDK NAF-033 [w/o 17Sep06 18nm from Obudu Cattle Ranch/ Bebi Airstrip, Nigeria]
8230		212	(Nigerian Air Force)	D-CBDA D-CATB NAF-034 [w/o 12Sep97 Nguru, Nigeria]
8231		212	Nigerian Air Force	D-CBDN D-CATC NAF-035
8232		213	Finnish Frontier Guard	D-CBDS D-CATD OH-MVO
8233		213	Finnish Frontier Guard	D-CBDT D-CATE OH-MVN
8234		212	Daily Air	D-CBDO D-CFLO B-11152 B-55565
8235		212	Daily Air	D-CBDP D-COAX B-11156 B-55567
8236		212	Nature Air	D-CBDB F-OGVA XA-AIR TI-BCS*
8237		212	ex Take Air Lines	D-CBDD F-OGVE+ XA- [+ canx 27Sep10 to Mexico]
8238		212	ex Air Caraibes	D-CBDH F-OHQK+ XA- [+ canx 27Nov09 to Mexico]
8239		212	Sita Air	D-CBDI F-OHQJ 8Q-IAS 9N-AIJ
8240		212	Inter Island Airways	D-CBDJ (N981A) N228ST
8241		212	Royal Thai Navy	D-CBDM (NAF-036)+ D-COTT 1115
8242		212	New Central Air Service	D-CBDO JA31CA
8243		212	New Central Air Service	D-CBDP JA32CA
8244		212	Island Aviation Services	D-CBDX 8Q-IAR
8245		212	New Central Air Service	D-CBDP D-CDRS JA33CA

DORNIER Do228

C/n	Cvtd No.	Model	Last known Owner/Operator	Identities/fates/comments (where appropriate)				
8246		212		[assembled by RUAG Aerospace using fuselage built by Hindustan at Kanpur, India as prototype 228NG; c/n changed to 8300]				
Production by RUAG Aerospace								
8300		212NG	New Central Air Service	(D-CRAP)	D-CRAQ	JA34CA		
8301		212NG	Lufttransport A/S	(D-CRAQ)	D-CNEW	(57+05)+	LN-LTS	[+ Germany]
8302		212NG	RUAG	D-CEWB	98+35	[for German Navy as 57+05]		
8303		212NG	RUAG	D-CREW*	[* marks reserved 03Nov11]			
8304		212NG	RUAG	[on production line May11]				
8305		212NG	RUAG	[on production line May11]				
8306								
8307								
8308								
8309								
Production by Hindustan Industries in India								
DORNIER/HAL 228								
3018		101	Indian Coastguard	CG758				
3019		101	Indian Coastguard	CG759				
3020		101	Mauritius Coast Guard	MP-CG-1				
3021		101	Indian Coastguard	CG761				
3022		101	Indian Coastguard	CG762				
3023		201	Indian Air Force	HM672				
3024		201	Indian Air Force	HM673	[code Q]			
3025		201	Indian Air Force	HM674				
3026		201	Indian Air Force	HM675				
3027		201	Indian Air Force	HM676	[code S]	[possibly wfu by 08Feb11 Yelahanka AFB, India]		
4028		201	Indian Air Force	VT-EQV	HM682			
4029		201	Indian Air Force	VT-EQW	HM683			
4030		201	Indian Air Force	HM677				
4031		201	Indian Air Force	HM678				
4032		201	Indian Air Force	HM679				
4033		201	Indian Air Force	HM680				
4034		201	Indian Air Force	HM681				
4035		201	Indian Navy	IN221				
4036		201	Indian Navy	IN222				
4037		201	Indian Navy	IN223	[code DAB]			
4038		201	Indian Navy	IN224	[code DAB]			
3039		101	Indian Coastguard	CG760				
4040		201	Indian Air Force	HM684				
4041		201	Indian Air Force	HM685				
4042		201	Indian Air Force	HM686				
4043		201	Indian Air Force	HM687				
3044		101	Indian Coastguard	CG763				
4045		201	Indian Air Force	HM688				
4046		201	Indian Air Force	HM689	[code G]			
4047		201	Indian Air Force	HM690				
4048		201	Indian Air Force	HM691	[code H]			
4049		101	Indian Coastguard	CG764				
4050		101	Indian Coastguard	CG765				
4051		101	Indian Coastguard	CG766				
4052		101	Indian Coastguard	CG767				
4053		101	Indian Coastguard	CG768				
4054		201	Indian Navy	IN226	[code COC]			
4055		201	Indian Navy	IN227				
4056		201	Indian Navy	IN228				
4057		201	Indian Navy	IN229	[code COC]			
4058		201	Indian Navy	IN230				
4059		201	Indian Navy	IN231	[surveillance testbed]			
4060		201	Indian Navy	IN232	[code DAB]			
4061		201	Indian Navy	IN233	[code PBR]			
4062		201	Indian Navy	IN234	[code PBR]			
4063		201	Indian Navy	IN235	[code DAB]			

DORNIER Do228

C/n	Cvtd No.	Model	Last known Owner/Operator	Identities/fates/comments (where appropriate)	
4064		201	Indian Coastguard	CG769	
4065		201	Indian Coastguard	CG770	
4066		201	Indian Coastguard	CG771	
4067		201	Indian Coastguard	CG772	
4068		201	Indian Coastguard	CG773	
4069		201	Indian Coastguard	CG774	[leased Feb11 to Seychelles Coast Guard, for 18 months]
4070		201	Indian Coastguard	CG775	
4071		201	Indian Air Force	HM692	
4072		201	Indian Air Force	HM693	
4073		201	Indian Air Force	HM694	
4074		201	Mauritius Coast Guard	MP-CG-3	
4075		201	Indian Navy	IN236	[code DAB]
4076		201	Indian Navy	IN237	[code DAB]
4077		201	Indian Navy	IN238	[code VVZ]
4078		201	Indian Navy	IN239	[code DAB]
4079		201	Indian Navy	IN240	
4080		201	Indian Navy	IN241	
4081		201	Indian Navy	IN242	[code DAB]
4082		201	Indian Navy	IN243	
4083		201	Indian Navy	IN244	
4084		201	Indian Navy	IN245	
4085		201	Indian Navy	IN246	

Unidentified

C/n	Cvtd No.	Model	Last known Owner/Operator	Identities/fates/comments (where appropriate)	
unkn				5Y-BBH	[reported ferried Luxor, Eygpt to Larnaca, Cyprus]]
unkn				9N-AHD	[marks reserved for unspecified Do228 but ntu]
unkn				9N-AHF	[marks reserved for unspecified Do228 believed ntu]
unkn			Indian Coast Guard	CG778	[reported 24Jan12 Callcut, India]
unkn		201	Indian Air Force	HM695	[reported 11Jly09 Delhi, India]
unkn		201	Indian Air Force	HM696	[reported 14Nov09 Delhi, India]
unkn		201	Indian Air Force	HM697	[reported 14Nov09 Delhi, India]
unkn		201	Indian Air Force	HM698	[reported 08Feb11 Yelahanka AFB, India]
unkn		201	Indian Air Force	HM698	[serial reported]
unkn		201	Indian Air Force	HM700	[reported 08Feb11 Yelahanka AFB, India]
unkn		201	Indian Air Force	HM701	[reported 27Jan10 Mumbai, India]
unkn		201	Indian Air Force	HM703	[reported 09Feb11 Yelahanka AFB, India]
unkn		201	Indian Air Force	HM704	[reported 08Feb11 Yelahanka AFB, India]
unkn		201	Indian Air Force	HM705	[reported 20May10 Bangalore, India]
unkn		201	Indian Air Force	HM706	[serial reported]
unkn			Seychelles Defence Force	S7-008	[reported 2011 donated by Indian Government; no sightings reported; could this be c/n 4069 reported to loan to this air arm?]
unkn			Africa's Connection STP	S9-AUN	[reported August 2011 Sao Tome e Principe]

DORNIER Do328

C/n	Model	Last known Owner/Operator	Identities/fates/comments (where appropriate)
Note:			Series 300 aircraft are the jet-powered version and are included here for the sake of completeness
3001	100	(Dornier Luftfahrt/Fairchild)	D-CHIC(1) [prototype ff 06Dec91; stored by Jun96; dismantled parts only noted 19Dec00 Oberpfaffenhofen, Germany]
3002	300	ex Dornier Luftfahrt/Fairchild	D-CATI D-BJET(1) [-100 series cvtd to Do328-300 prototype; ff 20Jan98 permit expired 02Oct02 & preserved Oberpfaffenhofen, Germany; l/n 14Mar11]
3003	110	South East Asian Airlines (SEAIR)	D-CDOL RP-9328
3004	110	Dornier Luftfahrt	D-CITI [stored Jun00 Oberpfaffenhofen, Germany]
3005	110	Cirrus Airlines/Sun Air	D-CITA HB-AEE TF-CSC D-CIRI
3006	120	MHS Helicopter-Flugservice	D-CDIY N328PH N470PS TF-CSD D-CIRP
3007	120	ex Wells Fargo Bank Northwest	D-COCI N329PH N471PS+ (D-C) [sale to Cirrus Aviation fell through; wfu Myrtle Beach, SC; fuselage only by 15Sep08; + canx 03Oct08; l/n 30Sep10]
3008	110	Xpress Air	D-CDAN N330PH N472PS PK-TXR
3009	110	(OLT)	D-CATS [w/o 02Dec01 Bremen, Germany; remains sold for parts]
3010	110	Berry Aviation	D-CFFA N332PH N473PS
3011	110	MHS Aviation	D-CDOG HB-AEG D-CIRD
3012	120	Wells Fargo Bank Northwest	D-CASI N334PH (D-CIRI) (SE-LJU) [reported will be converted to freighter]
3013	110	Sierra Nevada Corp	D-CALT N335PH N645MP* [* marks reserved 10May12]
3014	110	North Park Aviation	D-CANO N336PH N900LH [stored by 12May08 San Marcos Municipal, TX; l/n 02Nov11]
3015	110	Berry Aviation	D-CARR N339PH [stored by 14Feb08 San Marcos Municipal, TX; l/n 02Nov11]
3016	110	USAF Special Operations Command	D-CASU 5N-SAG D-CAAH N941EF 11-3016
3017	110	ex Cirrus Airlines	(D-CERL) D-CDHB HB-AEF D-CIRB [reported imported into Canada Jly12]
3018	110	Vuelos Internos Privados – VIP	D-CDHC N422JS HC-CFC
3019	110	Private Wings	D-CDHD N328DC D-CSUE
3020	120	Wells Fargo Northwest Bank	D-CDHE N337PH [by 14Feb08 stored basic United express c/s San Marcos Municipal, TX; l/n 02Nov11]
3021	110	SkyWork Airlines	D-CDHF D-CDXG VT-VIF D-CDXN D-CAOS D-CDXQ D-CHIC(3) HB-AES
3022	110	Suckling Airways/Flybe	D-CDHG VT-VIG D-CDXO G-BWWT
3023	110	Suckling Airways/City Jet	D-CDHH N328DA D-CDXF G-BWIR
3024	110	Corning Glass Inc	D-CDHI N95CG N28CG
3025	120	for Cirrus Airlines	D-CDHK N328LS (D-CIRO) [stored by 14Feb08 San Marcos Municipal, TX; l/n 09Jun10]
3026	110	Sierra Nevada Corp	D-CDHL 5N-IEP D-CAAG N929EF
3027	110	South East Asian Airlines (SEAIR)	D-CDHM N653PC N653JC RP-C6328
3028	110	VAC1 LLC	D-CDHN (VT-RAK) N431JS [stored by 20Jun07 Las Vegas, NV in basic old US Airways c/s]
3029	110	Lima Delta Co/Katanga Express	D-CDHO N338PH
3030	110	Xpress Air	D-CDHP N328JS PK-TXN [substantial damage 14Jun09 Tanah Merah, Indonesia]
3031	110	USAF Special Operations Command	D-CDHQ 5N-DOZ D-CDXL 5N-DOZ D-CAAF N975EF 11-3031 [painted as 13031]
3032	110	Xpress Air	D-CDHR N423JS (D-CIRQ) PK-TXM
3033	110	ADA USA Inc	D-CDHS N424JS D-CIRU* [stored 2012 Medellin, Colombia]
3034	110	Corning Glass Inc	(D-CDHT) D-CDXA N38CG
3035	120	Cirrus Airlines	D-CDHU N335LS D-CIRJ
3036	110	Air Alps Aviation	(D-CDHV) D-CDXB HB-AEH OE-LKB [stored 14Jan12 Innsbruck, Austria]
3037	110	Xpress Air	(D-CDHW) D-CDXC N425JS (D-CIRV) PK- N425JS+ PK-TXL [+ canx 04Aug08 to Indonesia, restored 26Aug08 and canx again 22Sep08; serious damage 06Nov08 Fakfak Airport, Indonesia]
3038	110	Xpress Air	(D-CDHX) D-CDXD N426JS PK-TXP
3039	110	Vuelos Internos Privados – VIP	(D-CDHY) D-CDXE N427JS HC-CFS
3040	120	Cirrus Airlines	(D-CDHZ) (D-CFUN) D-CDXF N340LS D-CIRG D-CAAI* [stored 2012 Oberpfaffenhofen, Germany;* marks reserved 2012]
3041	110	Cirrus Airlines	D-CDXH HB-AEI D-CIRC [canx 18Apr12 as exported]
3042	120	South East Asian Airlines (SEAIR)	D-CDXI (B-12281) D-CDXI D-CPRT RP-C4328
3043	110	Xpress Air	D-CDXJ N429JS (D-CIRT) PK-TXQ
3044	110	Comtran International	D-CDXK N430JS (D-CIRW)
3045	110	Xpress Air	D-CDXL N432JS PK-TXO
3046	110	South East Asian Airlines (SEAIR)	D-CDXM (B-122..) D-CPRS RP-C5328

DORNIER Do328

C/n	Model	Last known Owner/Operator	Identities/fates/comments (where appropriate)
3047	110	Sun-Air/British Airways	D-CDXN N433JS OY-NCA
3048	110	(Wells Fargo Bank Northwest)	D-CDXP N457PS (D-CIRN) [stored by 14Feb08 San Marcos Municipal, TX; DBF and w/o 27Jun08; canx 17Mar09]
3049	100	Vision Air	D-CDXQ D-CAOS N329MX
3050	120	Cirrus Airlines	(D-CDXR) D-CAOT N350AD G-BYHF N350AD D-CIRK
3051	110	Pearl Aviation/Aero Rescue	D-CDXS N434JS D-CEAD VH-PPQ
3052	110	Pearl Aviation/Aero Rescue	D-CDXT N436JS D-CDAD VH-PPV
3053	110	Pearl Aviation/Aero Rescue	D-CDXU F-GNBS G-BZIF D-CIAB VH-PPG
3054	110	(Minerva Airlines)	D-CDXV D-CPRR [w/o 25Feb99 Genoa, Italy; rear fuselage to Dodson International Parts, Rantoul, KS]
3055	110	Air Alps Aviation	D-CDXW N437JS OY-NCG OE-LKH
3056	110	SkyWork Airlines	D-CDXX N438JS PH-EEV I-IRTI HB-AEV
3057	110	Pearl Aviation/Aero Rescue	D-CDXY N439JS D-CAAD VH-PPF
3058	110	USAF Special Operations Command	D-CDXZ N440JS D-CIRE N570EF 95-3058
3059	110	Pearl Aviation/Aero Rescue	D-CDXA N441JS D-CCAD VH-PPJ
3060	110	Air Service Liege	D-CDXC N442JS PH-SOX OO-ELI D-CAAJ* [* marks reserved Q2 2012]
3061	110	Sky Work Airlines	D-CDXD N460PS OY-NCK HB-AEO
3062	110	Suckling Airways/CityJet	D-CDXE LN-ASK G-BYMK
3063	110	Aerocardal	D-CDXK F-GNPA D-CALP OE-LKE CC-ACG
3064	110	DOTP LLC	D-CDXG N340PH [stored by 30Sep09 Myrtle Beach, SC; l/n 01May10]
3065	110	DOTP LLC	D-CDXJ N341PH [stored Oklahoma City, OK ex United Express; l/n 22Feb05]
3066	110	SkyWork Airlines	D-CDXL D-CPRP HB-AER
3067	120	Vision Air	D-CDXN N330MX
3068	110	USAF Special Operations Command	D-CDXS N458PS (D-CIRM) D-CAAC N565EF 10-3068
3069	110	South East Asian Airlines (SEAIR)	D-CDXT LN-ASL D-CDUL G-BYML RP-C7328
3070	110	DANA Nigeria	D-CDXW N459PS OY-NCS D-CASI 5N-DOW
3071	120	Vision Air	D-CDXX N328MX
3072	110	Aerocardal	D-CDXY HS-PBB OE-LKD CC-AEY
3073	110	Dornier Aviation Nigeria	D-CDXZ F-GNPB D-CDXG D-CHOC OE-LKF 5N-DOX
3074	110	Vision Air	D-CDXA N331MX
3075	110	Sierra Nevada Corp	D-CDXC N461PS D-CIRL N953EF
3076	120	(Vuelos Internos Privados-VIP)	D-CDXE HC-BXO [early 2007 wfu and b/u Opa-locka, FL; hulk l/n 09Aug08]
3077	120	USAF Special Operations Command	D-CDXF HC-BXP D-CHIC(2) N328CP HB-AEJ D-CIRA N577EF 10-3077
3078	110	Welcome Air	D-CDXG OE-GBB
3079	120	Colombian AF/SATENA	D-CDXB 1160+ HK-4531X^ [+ Colombia; ^ dual marks with 1160]
3080	120	Colombian AF/SATENA	D-CDXH 1161+ HK-4523X^ [+ Colombia; ^ by 17Nov08 dual marks with 1161]
3081	120	ex Colombian AF/SATENA	D-CDXM (N332MX) 1163+ HK-4532X^ [+ Colombia; ^ dual marks with 1163; reported wfu Mar12 Bogata-El Dorado, Colombia]
3082	120	Colombian AF/SATENA	D-CDXP 1162+ HK-4524X^ [+ Colombia; ^ by 17Nov08 dual marks with 1162]
3083	110	Botswana Defence Force	D-CDXO 5N-SPC D-CDXO (G-BZUT) 5N-SPC D-CIAC OY-NCC OB2
3084	110	Aerolinea de Antioquia	D-CDXI F-GOAC N328ML N462PS HC-CFI HK-4849
3085	110	Cirrus Airlines	D-CDXR D-COSA [canx 24May12 as exported]
3086	110	Inter Island Airways	D-CDXH 5N-SPD N503CG N328ST
3087	110	Private Wings	D-CDXK F-GOFB N329ML N463PS D-CDAX
3088	110	Suckling Airways	D-CDXU F-GNPR D-CDXN G-BZOG
3089	110	Dornier Aviation Nigeria	D-CDXL F-GTJL D-CGEP OE-LKG 5N-DOY
3090	110	Private Wings	D-CDYY N404SS D-CATZ
3091	110	USAF Special Operations Command	D-CPRU TF-CSA D-CIRQ(2) N391EF 97-3091 [marked as 73091]
3092	120	Colombian AF/SATENA	D-CDXO 1164//HK-4533X [dual marks]
3093	110	USAF Special Operations Command	D-CDXD (F-OHQL) D-CPRV TF-CSB D-CIRT(2) N545EF
3094	110	Central Mountain Air	D-CDX. D-CMTM C-FHVX
3095	120	Dornier 3095 LLC	D-CDX. D-CATI N328FA PH-EVY N309DP
3096	110	Central Mountain Air	D-CDXM D-CMUC C-FDYW+ C-FDYN [+ painted on in error mid 05]
3097	110	Sierra Nevada Corp	D-CDXV D-CPRW N307EF [also wears USAF serial 13097]

DORNIER Do328

C/n	Model	Last known Owner/Operator	Identities/fates/comments (where appropriate)
3098	110	Suckling Airways	D-CDXZ D-CDAE G-BYHG
3099	300	Air Force Research Laboratory	D-BWAL N807LM [first production 328JET; ff 19May98]
3100	130	MHS Helicopter-Flugservice	D-CDXA (B-11131) D-CCIR
3101	120	Suckling Airways	D-CDXR D-CPRX G-CCGS
3102	300	ex Dornier Luftfahrt/Fairchild	D-BEJR [wfu & stored Friedrichshafen, Germany, preserved in Dornier Museum; l/n 07May12]
3103	120	ex Colombian AF/SATENA	D-CDX. 1165+ HK-4534 [+ Colombia; civil marks allocated 07Apr08 but not worn by Oct09; reported wfu Mar12 Bogata-El Dorado, Colombia]
3104	120	USAF Special Operations Command	D-CDXB 5N-BRI D-CDXJ G-BYTY D-CIAA OY-NCD N907EF 11-3104
3105	300	(PAC Jet Acquisitions/Private Jet)	D-BALL N328JT N328PD [w/o 03Jun06 Manassas, VA; to Dodson International Parts, Rantoul, KS for parting out]
3106	110	USAF Special Operations Command	D-CDXC D-CPRY OY-NCE D-CAAB N525EF 99-3106 [has 93106 on tail, still current on USCAR]
3107	110	(Cirrus Airlines)	D-CDXD (I-GANL) D-CGAP OE-LKH D-CTOB [w/o 19Mar08 Mannheim, Germany; canx 07Feb11]
3108	300	Jetran LLC	D-BALU N351SK [stored 06Jun08 Myrtle Beach, SC; l/n 01Jun12]
3109	130	Shell Canada	D-CDXV (V7-9909) C-FSCO
3110	130	Air Alps Aviation	D-CDXI OE-LKA
3111	300	Jetran LLC	D-BALI N352SK [stored by 30Sep09 Myrtle Beach, SC; l/n 01Jun12]
3112	110	Private Wings	D-CDXE D-CGAN D-CFWF D-CPWF
3113	110	Private Wings	D-CDXF D-CGAO D-CREW
3114	300	Tyrolean Jet Services	D-BDXA OE-HTJ
3115	110	Welcome Air	D-CDXG OE-LIR
3116	300	Ultimate Jetcharters	D-BDXM (N328FD) D-BGAD N328WW
3117	110	Medavia	D-CDXV (D-CGAC) D-CDXL D-COMM 9H-MET
3118	300QC	Ktesias Holdings/Aerostar	D-BDXB N873JC 5B- UR-WOG
3119	110	Private Wings Flugcharter	D-CDXK OE-LKC
3120	300	Skybird Air	D-BDXC D-BABA 5N-SPN 5N-BMH
3121	300	Tyrolean Jet Services	D-BDXE D-BMYD D-BDXI (OO-MYD) OE-HMS
3122	300	Jetran LLC	D-BDXD N353SK [stored 05Jun08 Myrtle Beach, SC; l/n 01May10 reported for Sun Air]
3123	300	Tianjin Airlines	D-BDXJ B-3960 [stored by 19Sep11 Tianjin, China]
3124	300	Jetran LLC	D-BDXI N355SK
3125	300	FlyMex/UN	D-BDXF N410Z XA-FAS
3126	300	Jetran LLC	D-BDXG N354SK [stored 03Jun08 Myrtle Beach, SC; l/n 01Jun12]
3127	300	FlyMex/UN	D-BDXH N430Z XA-AAS
3128	300	Tianjin Airlines	D-BDXK B-3961 [reported stored by 17Sep09 Xian, China; l/n 14Apr12]
3129	300	Pratt & Whitney Canada	D-BDXL F-OHJM N129UM N328JT C-GCPW
3130	300	Cirrus Airlines	D-BDXM D-BGAQ
3131	300	Cirrus Airlines	D-BDXN D-BGAL
3132	300	Sun-Air	D-B N328AC OY-NCP(2)
3133	300	ItAli Airlines	D-BDXO D-BGAG I-ACLG
3134	300	(RUAG)	D-BDXP D-BGAB [stored by 14Sep10 Oberpfaffenhofen, Germany; canx 31Mar11 as wfu]
3135	300	Tianjin Airlines	D-BDXQ B-3966 [reported stored by 17Sep09 Xian, China; l/n 22Sep11]
3136	300	Royal Star Aviation	D-BDXR N360SK RP-C8328
3137	300	Dornier 3137 Operating LLC	D-BDXS (D-BGAF) N328BH N328CK [stored by 01May10 Myrtle Beach, SC]
3138	300	Tianjin Airlines	D-BDXT B-3963 [stored by 19Sep11 Tianjin, China]
3139	300	DC Aviation/Cirrus Airlines	D-BDXZ D-BGAS
3140	300	Tianjin Airlines	D-BDXW B-3965 [reported stored by 17Sep09 Xian, China; l/n 14Apr12]
3141	300	Shell Nigeria	D-BDXX (D-BMAA) 5N-SPM
3142	300	Air Vallee	D-BDXS I-AIRX
3143	300	Tianjin Airlines	D-BDXX B-3962 [reported stored by 17Sep09 Xian, China; l/n 22Sep11]
3144	300	Tianjin Airlines	D-BDXB B-3967 [reported stored by 17Sep09 Xian, China; l/n 22Sep11]
3145	310	Aviando Services LLC	D-BDXU N401FJ
3146	300	Cirrus Airlines	D-BDXC D-BGAE
3147	310	RUAG?	D-BDXV N402FJ TF-MIK D-BDTB
3148	300	Tianjin Airlines	D-BDXE B-3968
3149	310	RUAG?	D-BDXY N403FJ TF-MIL D-BDTC
3150	310	LD Services	D-BDXA N404FJ
3151	300	Shell Nigeria	D-BDXT (D-BMAB) 5N-SPE
3152	300	ex ItAli Airlines	D-BDXO D-BGAR I-ACLH [stored by 14Sep10 Oberpfaffenhofen, Germany]

DORNIER Do328

C/n	Model	Last known Owner/Operator	Identities/fates/comments (where appropriate)
3153	300	Tianjin Airlines	D-BDXN B-3969 [reported stored by 17Sep09 Xian, China; l/n 27Apr11]
3154	300	Tianjin Airlines	D-BDXP B-3970 [reported stored by 17Sep09 Xian, China; l/n 14Apr12]
3155	310	Comtran International	D-BDXJ N405FJ
3156	310	Ultimate Jetcharters	D-BDXK N406FJ
3157	310	Ultimate Jetcharters	D-BDXL N407FJ
3158	300	Tianjin Airlines	D-BDXQ (D-BMAC) B-3973 [reported stored by 17Sep09 Xian, China; l/n 14Apr12]
3159	300	Tianjin Airlines	D-BDXU (D-BMAD) B-3975 [reported stored by 19Sep11 Tianjin, China; l/n 19Sep11]
3160	310	Petra Aviation	D-BDXF N408FJ N328CR N821MW
3161	310	RUAG?	D-BDXS N409FJ TF-MIM TF-NPB D-BDTA [reported for Angola Air Services]
3162	300	Avex Air Transport	D-BDXG OE-HTG OY-NCR ZS-AAK
3163	300	Jetran LLC	D-BDXH N356SK [stored 05Jun08 Myrtle Beach, SC; l/n 01May10]
3164	300	Jetran LLC	D-BDX. N357SK [stored 02Jun08 Myrtle Beach, SC; l/n 01May10]
3165	310	Xpress Air	D-BDXV N410FJ N365SK+ PK- [+ canx 22Feb11 to Indonesia]
3166	310	ex Atlantic Coast/Delta Connection	D-BDXW N411FJ [stored Myrtle Beach, SC; l/n 19Nov05]
3167	310	FlyMex	D-BDXA N412FJ N367SK N117LM XA-ALA
3168	310	International Bank of Commerce	D-BDXB N413FJ N328BC N131BC
3169	310	Aerostar	D-BDXC N414FJ N328DP UR-DAV
3170	310	Comtran International	D-BDXZ N415FJ N328VA
3171	310	Comtran International	D-BDXE N416FJ N328DA
3172	300	Tianjin Airlines	D-BDXJ B-3971 [reported stored by 17Sep09 Xian, China; l/n 14Apr12]
3173	310	Air Investors	D-BDXH (D-BMAE) N419FJ
3174	310	CBG LLC/Key Lime Air	D-BDXH N417FJ N38VP N394DC
3175	300	Tianjin Airlines	D-BDXK B-3972 [stored by 22Sep11 Xian, China]
3176	310	Funfite	D-BDXL N418FJ N328DR UR-AER M-BETY
3177	300	Tianjin Airlines	D-BDXY B-3976 [stored by 17Sep09 Xian, China; l/n 22Sep11]
3178	310	Key Lime Air	D-B N420FJ N905HB N395DC
3179	310	Jetran LLC/Vision Air	D-B N421FJ N906HB
3180	310	Private Wings	D-B N422FJ D-BIRD
3181	310	RUAG?	D-BDXF N423FJ TF-MIO D-BDTD
3182	300	Tianjin Airlines	D-B B-3977 [reported stored by 17Sep09 Xian, China]
3183	310	Ultimate Jetcharters	D-B N328FD N328GT
3184	310	Cummins Inc	(D-BMAF) N328PM N804CE
3185	310	Calm Air International	D-BDXH N424FJ C-GBEU
3186	310	Air Vallee	D-B I-AIRJ
3187	310	Tianjin Airlines	D-BDXP B-3978 [stored by 17Sep09 Xian, China; by 19Sep11 at Tianjin, China]
3188	310	Jetran LLC	D-B N358SK [stored 04Jun08 Myrtle Beach, SC; l/n 01May10]
3189	310	Jackson Jet Investors	D-BDXI N425FJ
3190	310	Sun-Air/British Airways	D-BDXU N426FJ OY-NCM
3191	310	Tianjin Airlines	D-BDXT B-3979 [reported stored by 17Sep09 Xian, China; l/n 27Apr11]
3192	310	Sun-Air/British Airways	D-BDXK (D-BMAG) N427FJ OY-NCL
3193	310	Sun-Air/British Airways	D-BDXX N428FJ OY-NCN
3194	310	Ultimate Jetcharters	D-BDXJ N429FJ
3195	310	Tianjin Airlines	D-BDXJ B-3982 [reported stored by 17Sep09 Xian, China; l/n 14Apr12]
3196	310	Wilmington Trust Company	D-B N328FD [stored Myrtle Beach, SC; l/n 21Mar07]
3197	310	Mexican Consulate General	D-BDXA (N430FJ) N500FJ D-BEOL N328PA XC-LLS
3198	310	Tianjin Airlines	D-BDXL N328AB B-3949 [reported stored by 17Sep09 Xian, China; l/n 27Apr11]
3199	310	Sun Air	D-B (I-AIRH) OE-HCM HB-AEU OY-JJB
3200	320	ex Corporate Jet Services/Club 328	(D-BMAH) (V5-NMC) D-BDMO D-BDXN N328BC (G-CJAB) D-BDXN OE-HAA G-CJAB [stored by 14Sep10 Oberpfaffenhofen, Germany]
3201	310	Tianjin Airlines	D-BDXO (V5-NMD) N328CD D-BDXO B-3873 [reported stored by 10Apr12 Tianjin, China]
3202	310	Ultimate Jetcharters	D-B N359SK
3203	310	Tianjin Airlines	D-BDXP (N328DE) D-BXXX B-3947 [reported stored by 17Sep09 Xian, China; l/n 14Apr12]
3204	310	Tianjin Airlines	D-BDXT D-BYYY B-3948 [reported stored by 17Sep09 Xian, China]
3205	310	Thompson Tractor Co	D-BDXX N451FJ N57TT [reported painted UR-DAV but still on USCAR as at 10Jun10]
3206	310	CBG LLC/Key Lime Air	D-BDXY N328EF+ D-BDXY (B-3889) D-BHRJ OE-HRJ N398DC [+ marks not worn]

DORNIER Do328

C/n	Model	Last known Owner/Operator	Identities/fates/comments (where appropriate)
3207	310	Private Wings	D-BDXE N328FG D-BDXE D-BJET(2)
3208	310	Tianjin Airlines	D-BDXI N328GH D-BDXI B-3946 [reported stored by 17Sep09 Xian, China]
3209	310	Aviando Services	D-BDXB D-BDXA N430FJ
3210	310	Sun-Air/British Airways	D-BDXQ N328HJ D-BDXQ (OE-HAB) OY-NCO
3211	310	Tianjin Airlines	D-BDXK N328KL B-3983 [reported stored by 17Sep09 Xian, China; l/n 14Apr12]
3212	310	RUAG?	(D-BMAJ) D-BDXF N328LM D-BDXF [reported for Shaanxi Aviation, China]
3213	310	Sun Air	D-BDXJ OE-LJR OY-NCT
3214	310	Aviando Services	D-BDXC N452FJ [stored Myrtle Beach, SC; l/n 01Jun12]
3215	310	Tianjin Airlines	D-BDXV N328MN D-BHUU B-3985 [stored by 17Sep09 Xian, China; l/n 22Sep11]
3216	310	ADAC	D-BDXD (N454FJ) N328NP D-BADC
3217	310	Tianjin Airlines	D-BDXH (N455FJ) N328FQ B-3986 [stored by 17Sep09 Xian, China; l/n 22Sep11]
3218	310	Tianjin Airlines	D-BDXR (N456FJ) N328QR B-3987 [reported stored by 17Sep09 Xian, China]
3219	310	Sishen Iron Ore Company (Pty)	D-BDXU (N457FJ) N328RS (B-3893) OY-NCP(1) ZS-IOC
3220	310	US Department of State	D-BDXC TF-NPA N3220U [last production aircraft]
3221	300	Easy Aviation	D-BDXA D-BERG VP-CJD [built from stored parts; ff 24Jly08]
3222	310		
3223	310		[fuselage without wings stored Oberpfaffenhofen, Germany; l/n 13Jly07
3224	310	for ADAC but not built	(D-BDXB) (D-BADA)
3225			
3226			
3227			
3228			
3229			
3230			
3231			
3232			
3233			
3234		not built	(D-BDXY) (N502FJ)

Unidentified

unkn		Xpress Air	PK-TXM [reported 30Jun09 Jayapura, Indonesia]
unkn		Xpress Air	PK-TXO [reported Dec10 Ujung Pandang, Indonesia]
unkn			5Y-DUV [reported Jun07 with two others with the Desert Locust Control Organisation at Nairobi-Wilson, Kenya]

DOUGLAS TURBINE DC-3 CONVERSIONS

C/n	Conv No	Series	Last known Owner/Operator	Identities/fates/comments (where appropriate)

Notes: Only details of aircraft identities after conversion to turbo-prop power have been included.

UNITED STATES AIRCRAFT CORP/AEROMODIFICATIONS INTERNATIONAL DC-65TP/C-47TP CONVERSIONS

The initials 'SA' in the series column indicates aircraft was converted in South Africa.

C/n	Conv No	Series	Last known Owner/Operator	Identities/fates/comments (where appropriate)
9766		SA	Missionary Flights International	6879 ZS-MRR 6879 N147RD N200MF
11746		SA	ex South African Air Force	6875 [reported stored by SAAF]
11925		SA	South African Air Force	6877
11986		SA	ex South African Air Force	6811 [stored Snake Valley, South Africa; l/n Jly06; for sale]
11990		SA	South African Air Force	6814
12064		SA	ex South African Air Force	6884 [wfu 08Nov03 Ysterplaat, South Africa; 06Jly08 to GIA Bokrivier Military Base, South Africa]
12073		AMI	(Turbine DC-3 Partnership/Rossair)	ZS-MFY (ZS-DAK) (5Y-DAK)? [converted in South Africa; w/o 09Mar03 Rumbak, Sudan; canx 25Mar09 to Kenya possibly as 5Y-DAK ntu; stored Lanseria, South Africa; l/n 03Apr09]
12112		SA	(South African Air Force)	6816 [w/o 06May94 Bloemspruit, South Africa; by Dec96 wings on dump Ysterplaat, South Africa]
12115		SA	Dodson International Parts	6820 N192RD
12160		SA	South African Air Force	6825
12166		SA	ex Dodson International Parts	6886 N8194Z [conversion not completed; by 1998 stored Wonderboom, South Africa marked as F-1; l/n Jan07; by 18Feb10 moved to Pretoria-Freeway airstrip, South Africa]
12415		SA	South African Air Force	6828
12580		SA	ex South African Air Force	6864 [stored Ysterplaat, South Africa; 20Jly09 to GIA Bokrivier Military Base, South Africa]
12582		SA	ex Dodson International Parts	6876 N81949 [conversion not completed; by 1998 stored Wonderboom, South Africa marked as F-7; l/n 29Nov04; by 18Feb10 moved to Pretoria-Freeway airstrip, South Africa]
12590		SA	ex National Test Pilot School	6834 ZS-OSO N834TP [substantial damage 04Feb09 Mojave, CA; taken to storage area; canx 13Apr09; by Nov09 on trailer dismantled Ottawa, KS for repair & corrosion check]
12596		SA	South African Air Force	6885 [reported stored by SAAF]
12704		SA	ex South African Air Force	6887 [preserved/stored Ysterplaat, South Africa; l/n 20Sep08]
13143		AMI	(Speed Service Couriers)	YV-32CP ZS-NKK [w/o 24Aug98 Wonderboom, South Africa; tail section only l/n Dec01]
13539		SA	South African Air Force	6837
13540		SA	South African Air Force	ZS-MRS 6839
20175		SA	Priority Air Charter	6835 N145RD (N467KA) N467KS
13866/25311		SA	ex South African Air Force	6840 [preserved/stored Ysterplaat, South Africa; l/n Sep08]
14101/25546		SA	Dodson International Parts SA	6880 N330RD ZS-OJL(1) 9U-BHL ZS-OJM N330RD ZS-OJM
14165/25610		SA	Mombasa Air Safari	6844 ZS-OJK 5Y-WOW
14357/25802		AMI	(Wonder Air)	ZS-LYW [w/o 13Apr95 Kikwangala, Zaire; canx 09Feb96; converted in South Africa]
14642/26087		SA	ex South African Air Force	6845 [preserved/stored Ysterplaat, South Africa; l/n Sep08]
14995/26439		SA	not yet known	6892 N195RD ZS-OJI N9562N+ YV2119 [+ probably never applied to aircraft]
15268/26713		AMI	(Space Aviation)	N240GB ZS-KCV [w/o 07Nov03 Lokichoggio, Kenya; canx 22Jly97]
15557/27002		SA	South African Air Force	6852
15602/27047		AMI	Missionary Flights International	N376AS ZS-OBU 5Y-BNK ZS-OBU (N376AS) ZS-OBU N376AS N500MF
15640/27085		AMI	Rossair Kenya	N70BF N887AM N146JR 5Y-RDS
15754/27199		SA	ex Dodson International Parts	6853 N148RD [conversion not completed; by 1998 fuselage stored Wonderboom, South Africa marked as F-2 & DC-3-2; l/n Sep06; by 18Feb10 moved to Pretoria-Freeway airstrip, South Africa]
15887/32635		SA	South African Air Force	6854
15896/32644		SA	National Test Pilot School	6882 ZS-MAP N882TP
15908/32656		AMI	(Professional Aviation Services)	ZS-DHX [converted in South Africa; w/o 31Aug92 Jamba, Angola]
16077/32825		SA	ex Dodson International Parts	6874+ N81952 [+ dismantled Dec97 & stored Waterkloof, South Africa; by 1998 moved to Wonderboom, South

DOUGLAS TURBINE DC-3 CONVERSIONS

C/n	Conv No	Series	Last known Owner/Operator	Identities/fates/comments (where appropriate)
				Africa marked as F-6; l/n Sep06; by 18Feb10 moved to Pretoria-Freeway airstrip, South Africa]
16149/32897		SA	Lee County District Mosquito District	6858 N146RD (N8241T)
16200/32948		SA	Samaritan's Purse	6868 N194RD ZS-OIR N194RD N467SP
16213/32961		SA	Dodson International Parts SA	6855 N8194Q ZS-OJJ [reported stored 08Jly09 near Ottawa Airport, KS; l/n Nov09]
16276/33024		SA	Lee County District Mosquito District	6891 N198RD
16386/33134		SA	ex Dodson International Parts	6846 N8241T [fuselage stored by 1998 Wonderboom, South Africa marked as F-3; l/n Sep06; by 18Feb10 moved to Pretoria-Freeway airstrip, South Africa]
16463/33211		SA	Dodson International Parts	6870 N332RD [reported stored Aug09 Mena Intermountain Municipal, AR; l/n Aug09]
16565/33313		SA	Dodson International Parts	6863 N81907 ZS-OJL(2) N81907
16627/33375		SA	Dodson International Parts	6857 N193RD [reported derelict Aug09 Mena Intermountain Municipal, AR]
16730/33478		SA	ex Dodson International Parts	6865 N8190X [stored by 1998 Wonderboom, South Africa marked as F-4; l/n Sep06; by 18Feb10 moved to Pretoria-Freeway airstrip, South Africa]
16804/33552		SA	ex Dodson International Parts	6890 N149RD [dismantled & stored by 1998 Wonderboom, South Africa marked as F-5; l/n Sep06; by 18Feb10 moved to Pretoria-Freeway airstrip, South Africa]
16965/34225		AMI	Skiya Property Investments	ZS-LJI [converted in South Africa; c/n sometimes quoted as DBL-0047]

BASLER BT-67 CONVERSIONS

C/n	Conv No	Series	Last known Owner/Operator	Identities/fates/comments (where appropriate)
6204	17		(El Salvador Air Force)	119 [w/o 19Nov00 Chilanga-Los Comandos Airport, El Salvador]
9100	12		ex Guatemalan Air Force	580 [reported DBR Mar04 & stored]
9290	18		Royal Thai Air Force	L2k-03/41//46153 [serial followed by code after double forward slash]
9415	40		Basler Turbo Conversions	N400BF
9670	45		Colombian National Police	N840MB 1473+ PNC-0257 [+ Colombia]
12300	54		Kenn Borek Air	N907Z C-GVKB
12543	34		Mauritania Air Force	5T-MAH
13110	9		(Colombian National Police)	PNC-212 PNC-0212 [w/o 30Apr03 Toscana-Aguas Claras, Colombia]
13321	5		(Turbo Power & Marine Systems)	N96BF [w/o 16Dec94 Lobito, Central African Republic]
13383	28		Kenn Borek Air	TZ-391 N167BT C-GJKB
13439	57		Furgo Aviation Canada	N36AP C-FAZO
19052	38		Colombian Air Force	1667
19125	36		(Colombian Air Force)	1670 [reworked as conversion # 41, following accident; see next line]
19125	41		(Colombian Air Force)	1670+ PNC-0214+ 1670 [+ Colombia][w/o 18Feb09 near Palanquero-German Olano AFB, Colombia]
19173	22		Republic of Mali Air Force	TZ-390
19227	50		Kenn Borek Air	N79017 C-GAWI
19446	49		Basler Turbo Conversions	N471DK [still under conversion Oshkosh-Wittman Regional, WI; l/n Jly09]
19560	47		Kenn Borek Air	C-FMKB
19572	27		Royal Thai Air Force	L2k-01/41//46151 [serial followed by code after double forward slash; damaged & stored 2003/04 Phitsanulok, Thailand; l/n Apr06]
19674	15		Guatemalan Air Force	575
19685	43		Colombian National Police	PNC-0256
20031	25		Guatemalan Air Force	530
20082	39		Royal Thai Air Force	L2k-07/45//46157 [serial followed by code after double forward slash]
20494	6		US Dept of Agriculture	N142Z
20507	8		ex Bolivian Air Force	TAM-38 [reported stored Sep97 Santa Cruz, Bolivia]
20875	2		Colombian National Police	N8059P HK-3576 PNC-213 PNC-0213 [earlier conversion by USAC as Turbo Express probably never completed]
13824/25269	32		Royal Thai Air Force	L2k-05/42?//46155 [serial followed by code after double forward slash]

DOUGLAS TURBINE DC-3 CONVERSIONS

C/n	Conv No	Series	Last known Owner/Operator	Identities/fates/comments (where appropriate)
13964/25409	16		El Salvador Air Force	117
13998/25443	24		Colombian Air Force	1686
14064/25509	10		Stevens Express Leasing	N5156T N811RB N845S
14222/25667	14		Colombian National Police	PNC-211 PNC-0211 [destroyed by grenade 18Feb09 Medellin-Olaya Herrera, Colombia]
14229/25674	31		Royal Thai Air Force	L2k-04/41//46154 [serial followed by code after double forward slash]
14308/25753	44		Royal Thai Air Force	L2k-08/47//46-158 [serial followed by code after double forward slash]
14324/25769	55		ALCI Aviation	N56KS C-FTGX
14519/25964	56		Kenn Borek Air/Alfred Wegener	N9923S C-GHGF
14557/26002	21		(Republic of Mali Air Force)	TZ-389(1) [w/o 15Mar97 in mid-air collision with Beech A36 Bonanza N3657A 11kms from Manitowoc, WI]
14675/26120	35		Kenn Borek Air	N40386 C-GEAJ
14823/26268	51		Bell Aerospace	N232GB C-FTGI
14847/26292	26		Colombian Air Force	1654
15070/26515	33		Royal Thai Air Force	L2k-06/42//46156 [serial followed by code after double forward slash]
15299/26744	none		Basler Turbo Conversions	N300BF TZ-389(2) N300BF [earlier USAC conversion; to prototype Basler BT67]
15692/27137	46		Colombian Air Force	1683
15781/32529	48		Colombian National Police	N73CD+ PNC-0258 [+ still registed as such to Department of State]
15793/32541	37		Colombian Air Force	1658
16236/32984	29		(Colombian Air Force)	1659 [w/o 02Sep00 Montezuma, Risaralda, Colombia]
16262/33010	42		Royal Thai Air Force	L2k-09/47//46-159 [serial followed by code after double forward slash]
16298/33046	52		US Department of State	N707BA [for operations in Afghanistan]
16305/33053	1		Kenn Borek Air	N72BF HK-3575 (N177DM) HK-3575X N72BF N200AN C-GEAI
16490/33238	4		El Salvador Air Force	118
16500/33248	23		Colombian Air Force	1681
16534/33282	3		El Salvador Air Force	116
17101/34368	53		Airborne Support Inc	N932H
16751/33499	20		Guatemalan Air Force	555
16794/33542	13		Guatemalan Air Force	"560"+ 590 [possible false ID; could be c/n 16820/33568]
16819/33567	7		US Dept of Agriculture	N115Z
16833/33581	11		Anglo Operations/Spectrum Air	A2-ADL ZS-ASN PT-WXE ZS-ASN PR-MGF ZS-ASN PR-MSY ZS-ASN
17024/34288	30		Royal Thai Air Force	L2k-02/41//46152 [serial followed by code after double forward slash; w/o 24Aug06 Korat, AFB, Thailand; SOC]
17131/34398	19		Guatemalan Air Force	560
OTHER CONVERSIONS				
4903			(Conroy Aircraft Corp)	N4700C N23SA [Conroy Turbo-Three; f/f 13May69; see next line]
4903			(OK Turbines)	N23SA [converted to Specialised Aircraft Tri-Turbo-Three; f/f 02Nov77; wfu & stored 1980 Camarillo, CA, later Santa Barbara, CA, then 1991 Mojave, CA; dismantled fuselage to Basler at Oshkosh, WI for spares; hulk stored off airport; l/n 20Jun10]
14168/25613			(Rolls-Royce)	KJ829 G-AOXI G-37-2(2) G-AOXI [Dart Dakota; ff 15Mar50; dismantled Feb64 & b/u 11Nov64 Usworth, UK by Tyne-Tees Airways; canx 24Mar65]
14178/25623			(Armstrong Siddeley)	KJ839 [Mamba Dakota; ff 27Aug49; 1953 converted back to piston power]
14661/26106			(British European Airways)	G-ALXN G-37-1 G-ALXN [Dart Dakota; 1953 converted back to piston power]
14987/26432			(British European Airways)	G-AMDB G-37-2(1) G-AMDB [Dart Dakota; by 31Aug53 converted back to piston power]
43193			(Pilgrim Aviation & Airlines)	N156WC N156PM [Conroy Super Turbo-Three; f/f May74] [dbr 24Feb84 New London, CT in ground collison with C-130 N15ST; hulk to Roswell, NM]

DOUGLAS C-133 CARGOMASTER

C/n	Model	Last known Owner/Operator	Identities/fates/comments (where appropriate)
44705	A	(USAF)	54-0135 [prototype ff 24Apr56; arrived MASDC 08Mar71, storage code CU004; SOC 18Aug71; b/u by May74]
44706	A	(Cargomaster Corp)	54-0136+ N136AR N133AB [+ arrived 21Jly71 MASDC; code CU030; SOC 07Sep71; by Oct73 stored Mojave, CA, still present Apr98; canx; late 2008 expected to be moved to Travis AFB, CA as spares source for c/n 45164; marks N133AB probably never applied]
44707	A	(DMI Aviation)	54-0137 N2251X [arrived 07Jan71 MASDC, storage code CU002, later 9C001; SOC 22Jan71; by Sep79 to local scrapyard; hulk l/n Oct06]
44708	A	(USAF)	54-0138 [arrived 20Mar71 MASDC; storage code CU009; SOC 19Aug71; b/u by May74]
44709	A	(USAF)	54-0139 [arrived 11Mar71 MASDC, storage code CU005; SOC 18Aug71; b/u by May74]
44710	A	(USAF)	54-0140 [w/o 10Jan65 Wake Island AFB, North Pacific]
44711	A	(USAF)	54-0141 [arrived 15Apr71 MASDC, storage code CU017; SOC 19Aug71; b/u by May74]
44712	A	(USAF)	54-0142 [arrived 13Apr71 MASDC, storage code CU016; SOC 19Aug71; b/u by May74]
44713	A	(USAF)	54-0143 [arrived 22Apr71 MASDC, storage code CU020; SOC 19Aug71; b/u by May74]
44714	A	(USAF)	54-0144 [arrived 10Apr71 MASDC, storage code CU015; SOC 19Aug71; b/u by May74]
44715	A	(USAF)	54-0145 [arrived 13Mar71 MASDC, storage code CU006; SOC 19Aug71; b/u by May74]
44716	A	(USAF)	54-0146 [w/o 13Apr58 26 miles from Dover AFB, DE, whilst on local flight]
45163	A	(FAA)	56-1998 [in use to Oct74 for accident survival tests Atlantic City, NJ; b/u during 1992]
45164	A	Travis Air Museum	56-1999+ N199AR HI-264 N199AB [+arrived 06Apr71 MASDC, storage code CU013; SOC19Aug71] [ferried 28Aug08 Anchorage, AK – McChord AFB, WA & 30Aug08 to Travis AFB, CA; last C-133 flight]
45165	A	(Properties Investment Enterprises)	56-2000+ N200AR [+ arrived 26Jly71 MASDC, storage code CU032; SOC 07Sep71; to Airborne Relief Project; no CofA issued believed b/u Long Beach, CA]
45166	A	Cargomaster Corp	56-2001+ N201AR [+ arrived 08Apr71 MASDC, storage code CU014; SOC 19Aug71; spares use since Oct73 Mojave, CA, still present 2005; expected late 2008 to be moved to Travis AFB, CA as source of spares for c/n 45164]
45167	A	(USAF)	56-2002 [w/o 22Sep63 in sea near Dover AFB, DE; SOC 07Oct63]
45168	A	(USAF)	56-2003 [arrived 14Jly71 MASDC, storage code CU028; SOC 07Sep71; b/u by May74]
45169	A	(USAF)	56-2004 [arrived 23Jly71 MASDC, storage code CU031; SOC 07Sep71; b/u by May74]
45170	A	(USAF)	56-2005 [DBF in ground accident 13Jly63 Dover AFB, DE; SOC 03Sep63; remains to Douglas for fatigue tests]
45171	A	(USAF)	56-2006 [arrived 18Mar71 MASDC, storage code CU008; SOC 19Aug71; b/u by May74]
45172	A	(USAF)	56-2007 [arrived 17Apr71 MASDC, storage code CU018; SOC 19Aug71; b/u by May74]
45245	A	National Museum of US Air Force	56-2008 [SOC & preserved 17Mar71 Wright-Patterson AFB, OH as 62008; l/n Nov07]
45246	GC-133A	Octave Chanute Aerospace Museum	56-2009 [preserved by 24Jun77 Chanute AFB, IL as 0-62009; on loan from USAF Museum; l/n 29Jly06]
45247	A	(USAF)	56-2010 [arrived 03Apr71 MASDC, storage code CU012; SOC 19Aug71; b/u by May74]
45248	A	(FAA)	56-2011 [SOC 15Apr71; in use to Oct74 for accident survival tests Atlantic City, NJ; b/u date unknown; l/n 2005]
45249	A	(USAF)	56-2012 [arrived 06Feb71 MASDC, storage code CU003; SOC 03Mar71; b/u by May74]
45250	A	(USAF)	56-2013 [arrived 21Apr71 MASDC, storage code CU019; SOC 19Aug71; b/u by May74]
45251	A	(USAF)	56-2014 [w/o 07Nov64 near Goose Bay AFB, Nfld (NL), Canada]
45507	A	(USAF)	57-1610 [arrived 11Jun70 MASDC, storage code CU001; SOC 12Jun70; b/u by May74]
45508	A	(USAF)	57-1611 [w/o 27May62 in sea near Dover AFB, DE]
45509	A	(USAF)	57-1612 [arrived 16Mar71 MASDC, storage code CU007; SOC 18Aug71; b/u by May74]
45510	B	(USAF)	57-1613 [arrived 25Mar71 MASDC, storage code CU011; SOC 18Aug71; b/u by May74]
45511	B	(USAF)	57-1614 [w/o 11Jun61 in sea near Tachikawa AFB, Japan]
45512	B	(USAF)	57-1615 [arrived 12Jly71 MASDC, storage code CU027; SOC 07Sep71; b/u by May74]

DOUGLAS C-133 CARGOMASTER

C/n	Model	Last known Owner/Operator	Identities/fates/comments (where appropriate)
45573	B	(USAF)	59-0522 [arrived 01Jun71 MASDC, storage code CU021; SOC 19Aug71; b/u by May74]
45574	B	(USAF)	59-0523 [w/o 10Apr63 near Travis AFB, CA, whilst on a local flight]
45575	B	(USAF)	59-0524 [arrived 16Jun71 MASDC, storage code CU022; SOC 19Aug71; b/u by May74]
45576	B	(USAF)	59-0525 [arrived 07Jly71 MASDC, storage code CU025; SOC 07Sep71; b/u by May74]
45577	B	(USAF)	59-0526 [arrived 02Jly71 MASDC, storage code CU024; SOC 07Sep71; b/u by May74]
45578	B	Pima Air & Space Museum	59-0527 [arrived 30Jun71 MASDC, code CU023; SOC 24Aug71; preserved by May74 Pima, AZ]
45579	B	(USAF)	59-0528 [arrived 16Jly71 MASDC, storage code CU029; SOC 07Sep71; b/u by May74]
45580	B	(Bradley Air Museum)*	59-0529 [preserved 16Mar71; SOC 03Nov71; DBR by tornado 03Oct79 Windsor Locks, CT; * name now New England Air Museum who hold nose section]
45581	B	(USAF)	59-0530 [w/o 06Feb70 near Palisade, NE en-route Travis AFB to Harrisburg Airport, PA]
45582	B	(Cargomaster Corp)	59-0531+ N2276V [arrived Oct73 MASDC, code CU034; stored May76 Tucson Apt, AZ; l/n Sep99; b/u Jan01]
45583	B	(USAF)	59-0532 [arrived 09Jly71 MASDC, storage code CU026; SOC 07Sep71; b/u by May74]
45584	B	(Cargomaster Corp)*	59-0533+ N77152 N133B [arrived 02Aug71 MASDC, storage code CU033; SOC 07Sep71; stored by Oct96 Anchorage, AK; canx 08Nov00 destroyed; b/u 2002; * registered to Maurice Carlson]
45585	B	(USAF)	59-0534 [w/o 30Apr67 80 miles E of Okinawa, Japan]
45586	B	(USAF)	59-0535 [arrived 23Mar71 MASDC, storage code CU010; SOC 18Aug71; b/u by May74]
45587	B	Air Mobility Command Museum	59-0536 [preserved 30Jun71 Offutt AFB, NE; later Dover AFB, DE; SOC 28Dec71; l/n 26Sep07]

Production complete

EMBRAER EMB-110 BANDEIRANTE AND EMB-111 BANDEIRULHA

C/n	Model	Last known Owner/Operator	Identities/fates/comments (where appropriate)
01	YC-95	Museu Aeroespacial	2130 [Brazil] [prototype ff 22Oct68; wfu 15Jun75 & preserved Rio de Janeiro-Campo dos Afonsos, Brazil; l/n 23Aug07]
02	YC-95	Santos Dumont Foundation	2131 [Brazil] [wfu 18Aug78 & preserved Rio de Janeiro-Santos Dumont, Brazil; l/n 23Oct96; restored Sep08 by Embraer and preserved Cotia, Sao Paulo, Brazil]
03	100	CNAE/INPE	PP-ZCN PP-FXC PP-ZDF [stored 1980 Sao Jose dos Campos, Brazil]
110001	C-95	(Brazilian Air Force)	2133 [SOC fate unknown; l/n Dec86]
110002	110C	(Norte Jet Taxi Aereo)	2132+ PT-ODK [+ Brazil] [w/o 14Sep99 near Belem Airport, Brazil; probably rebuilt using spares & preserved as 2132 Sao Jose dos Campos, Brazil; but this has also been reported as being c/n 110002]
110003	C-95	(Brazilian Air Force)	2134 [SOC fate unknown; l/n Dec91]
110004	110C	(Nordeste Linhas Aereas)	PT-TBA [w/o 28Oct76 Petrolina-Pernambuco, Brazil; canx]
110005	110C	(Nordeste Linhas Aereas)	PT-TBB [w/o 03Feb92 into mountains near Caetite, Bahia, Brazil]
110006	110C	Taxi Aereo Ceu Azul	PT-TBC
110007	C-95	(Brazilian Air Force)	2135 [SOC fate unknown; l/n Oct88]
110008	C-95	ex Brazilian Air Force	2136 [wfu & used as GIA, Guaratingueta, Brazil; l/n May05]; by Feb12 stored Dos Afonos, Brazil]
110009	110C	Museu Asas de Um Sonho	(PP-SSA) PP-SBA [wfu Apr93 Sao Paulo-Congonhas, Brazil; fuselage only preserved Sao Carlos, Brazil; l/n 19Mar06]
110010	110C	(TAM Brasil)	PP-SBB [w/o 08Feb89 Bauru-Agudos, Brazil; canx 17Nov89]
110011	110C	(TransBrasil)	PT-TBD [w/o 22Jan76 Chapeco, Santa Catarina, Brazil; canx]
110012	110C	ex Total Linhas Aereas	PT-JHG [stored by Oct01 Belo Horizonte-Pampulha, Brazil]
110013	110C	(TAM Brasil)	PP-SBC [w/o 28Jun84 Sao Pedro d'Aldeia, Brazil; canx]
110014	C-95	(Brazilian Air Force)	2137 [SOC fate unknown; l/n Oct88]
110015	C-95	(Brazilian Air Force)	2138 [SOC fate unknown; l/n Oct88]
110016	110C	Extreme Taxi Aereo	PP-SBD PT-EDO
110017	110C	ex Aero Taxi Poty	PT-TBE [wfu and stored Oct00]
110018	110C	(Nordeste Linhas Aereas)	PT-TBF [w/o 04Nov78 Bocaiuva, Minas Gerais, Brazil; canx]
110019	110C	(Admiral Taxi Aereo)	2139 PT-WBG [wfu circa Nov98 for spares Porto Alegre, Brazil]
110020	C-95	(Brazilian Air Force)	2140 [SOC fate unknown; l/n Oct88]
110021	110C	(VASP)	PP-SBE [w/o 27Feb75 near Sao Paulo-Congonhas, Brazil; canx]
110022	110C	(VOTEC Servicios Aereos Regionais)	PP-SEE [wfu & stored Mar96 Rio de Janeiro-Santos Dumont, Brazil; l/n 11Mar11]
110023	110C	ex Brasil Central	PP-SBF [wfu by 14Dec07; stored by 23Mar09 Sorocaba, Brazil]
110024	110C	Museu Asas de Um Sonho	PP-SBG [wfu by 25Jun03; preserved Sao Carlos, Brazil; l/n 19Mar06]
110025	110C	ex Governo do Estado de Roraima	PT-FVH PP-EOO [wfu Brasilia-International, Brazil; l/n 07Mar11]
110026	110C	(TAM-Transportes Aereos Regionais)	PP-SBH [w/o 07Oct83 Aracatuba, Brazil; canx]
110027	C-95	(Brazilian Air Force)	2141 [SOC fate unknown; l/n Nov91]
110028	C-95	(Brazilian Air Force)	2142 [SOC fate unknown; l/n Aug86]
110029	C-95	(Brazilian Air Force)	2143 [w/o 14Oct80 Sao Paulo-Marte, Brazil; but also reported repaired]
110030	110C	Memorial Aeroespacial Brasileiro	PP-SBI [wfu by 31Mar06; preserved Sao Jose dos Campos, Brazil in Embraer c/s with no regn; l/n 20Apr08]
110031	110E	(Regional Taxi Aereo)	PT-EMB PT-LDD [wfu by 24Apr02 Belo Horizonte-Pampulha, Brazil; fuselage only by 26Dec06]
110032	110E	Governo do Estado de Minas Gerais	PT-GJV PP-EMG
110033	110C	(TAF Linhas Aereas)	PT-GJA PT-FAE PT-LBU [wfu by 30Jun06; fate unknown]
110034	110C	Apui Taxi Aereo	2144+ PT-ODJ [+ Brazil]
110035	110C	(Transportes Aereos Presidente)	2145+ PT-ODG [+ Brazil] [wfu by 31Mar06; fate unknown]
110036	C-95	Policia Militar	2146+ PR-EAP [+ Brazil]
110037	110C	(Oeste Linhas Aereas)	PP-SBJ [w/o 23Mar93 near Cuiaba, Brazil; canx 25Nov94]
110038	110C	ex Governo do Estado de Roraima	PT-KOK PP-EON [wfu by Oct98; stored Brasilia-International, Brazil; l/n 07Mar11]
110039	110C	Apui Taxi Aereo	2147+ PT-ODY [+ Brazil]
110040	110C	Aerotaxi Abaete	2148+ PT-MFN [+ Brazil]
110041	110C	Leticia Sims Corp	2149+ PT-WCM [+ Brazil]
110042	C-95	ex Brazilian Air Force	2150 [stored Nov11 Parque Matrerial Aeronautico Afonsos, Brazil]
110043	C-95	ex Brazilian Air Force	2151 [by Feb12 stored Dos Afonos, Brazil]
110044	110C	Aerotaxi Jacarepagua	2152+ PT-WAP [+ Brazil]
110045	110C	Cruiser Taxi Aereo Brasil	2153+ PT-WBR [+ Brazil]

EMBRAER EMB-110 BANDEIRANTE AND EMB-111 BANDEIRULHA

C/n	Model	Last known Owner/Operator	Identities/fates/comments (where appropriate)
110046	110C	ex VOTEC Servicios Aereos Regionais	PT-GJB [stored Mar96 Rio de Janeiro-Santos Dumont, Brazil; later Belem, Brazil; l/n 19Sep04 in poor condition]
110047	110C	Selva Taxi Aereo	PT-FAD PT-LGB
110048	110C	(Helisul Taxi Aereo)	2154+ PT-WAV [+ Brazil] [w/o 13Sep96 near Joinville, Santa Catarina, Brazil]
110049	110C	ex VOTEC Servicios Aereos Regionais	PT-GJG [stored by Mar96 Rio de Janeiro-Santos Dumont, Brazil]
110050	110C	(Transportes Aereos Presidente)	PT-GJH [wfu 31Mar06 and stored]
110051	110C	Rico Linhas Aereas	2159+ PT-WDB [+ Brazil]
110052	C-95	ex Brazilian Air Force	2155 [by Apr12 preserved Dos Afonos, Brazil]
110053	C-95	Brazilian Air Force	2156
110054	110C	Abaete Linhas Aereas	2160 PT-MFS [+ Brazil]
110055	110E	Rico Taxi Aereo	PT-GJC
110056	110E(J)	TAF Linhas Aereas	PT-GJD
110057	C-95	(Brazilian Air Force)	2157+ [+ Brazil] [w/o 03Jun77 Natal, Brazil]
110058	110C	Abaete Linhas Aereas	2158+ PT-MFO [+ Brazil]
110059	110E(J)	ex Taxi Aereo Rio Amazonas	PT-GJE PT-EPE PT-LFW [wfu and stored after Mar99; status unknown]
110060	C-95	Brazilian Air Force	2161
110061	C-95	Brazilian Air Force	2162
110062	110E(J)	(Marzetti Materials)	PT-GJF [reported canx 12Nov91; probably b/u]
110063	110P	(Transportes Aereos da Bacia Amazonica)	PT-GJN [w/o 23Jun85 near Cuiaba, Brazil; canx]
110064	C-95	Brazilian Air Force	2164
110065	110E(J)	Tavaj Linhas Aereas	PT-GJP
110066	110C	Wee Air Taxi Aereo	2163+ PT-WAM [+ Brazil]
110067	C-95	Brazilian Air Force	2165
110068	C-95	Brazilian Air Force	2166
110069	110E(J)	(Governo do Amapa)	PT-GJO PT-FDL [canx 31Dec00; fate unknown]
110070	110E(J)	Taxi Aereo Itaituba	PT-GJR
110071	110C	(NHR Taxi Aereo)	2167+ PT-WAK [+ Brazil] [w/o 11Dec04 Uberaba, Minas Gerais, Brazil]
110072	110E(J)	(Rico Taxi Aereo)	PT-GJW [w/o 07May94 Sao Gabriel da Cachoeira, Brazil; canx 27Sep94]
110073	C-95	(Brazilian Air Force)	2168 [w/o 10Mar81 Rio de Janeiro, Brazil]
110074	110E(J)	ex Departamento Nacional de Estreades de Rodagem	PT-GJX PT-FRE [wfu by 07Mar11 Brasilia-International, Brazil]
110075	C-95	(Brazilian Air Force)	2169 [w/o 23Apr77 Natal, Brazil]
110076	110C	Uruguayan Air Force	PT-GJI 580/CX-BJJ+ 580 [dual marks]
110077	C-95	ex Brazilian Air Force	2170 [donated Jun11 State of Mato Grosso do Sul]
110078	C-95	Brazilian Air Force	2171
110079	110C	(Uruguayan Air Force)	PT-GJJ 581/CX-BJK [dual marks] [w/o 25Feb91 near Montevideo, Uruguay; b/u May91]
110080	C-95	ex Brazilian Air Force	2172 [Sep11 to GIA at SENAI Sao Jose, Florianopolis, Brazil]
110081	110C	(Uruguayan Air Force)	PT-GJK 582/CX-BJB [dual marks] [wfu Dec94 Montevideo, Uruguay; b/u by Jly95; nose to Escuela Tecnica de Aeronautica as GIA; l/n 24Apr07]
110082	110C	Uruguayan Air Force	PT-GJL 583/CX-BJC 583 [dual marks]
110083	110C	(Uruguayan Air Force)	PT-GJM 584/CX-BJE [dual marks] [w/o 20Jun77 Salto-Nueva Hesperides Airport, Uruguay]
110084	110P	(Transportes Aereos da Bacia Amazonica)	PT-GJQ (YV-246C) [reported w/o 21Jan88 Vilhena, Brazil; also reported wfu 1995]
110085	110P	ex Transportes Aereos da Bacia Amazonica	PT-GJS [airline suspended operations 2001; fate unknown]
110086	110P	ex Transportes Aereos da Bacia Amazonica	PT-GJT [airline suspended operations 2001; fate unknown]
110087	110E(J)	(Purus Aerotaxi)	PT-GJY [w/o 23Sep94 near Feijo, Brazil]
110088	110E(J)	(VOTEC Servicios Aereos Regionais)	PT-GJZ [w/o 18Apr84 near Imperatriz, Maranhao, Brazil, mid-air collision with EMB-110 PT-GKL (c/n 110107); canx Aug84]
110089	110P	ex Transportes Aereos da Bacia Amazonica	PT-GJU [airline suspended operations 2001; fate unknown]
110090	110C	(Nordeste Linhas Aereas)	PT-GKA [w/o 11Oct85 Vitoria da Conquista, Brazil; canx 16Apr90]
110091	110P	Aerocaribbean	PT-GKB CU-T1108 CU-T1540
110092	110P	(Rio-Sul)	PT-GKC [w/o 24May82 Florianopolis, Brazil; canx]
110093	110C	ex Fly Brasil Taxi Aereo	2173+ PT-WDS [+ Brazil] [wfu 2003; by 23Mar09 stored Sorocaba, Brazil]
110094	110C	Taxi Aereo Hercules	2174 PT-WDM [+ Brazil]
110095	C-95	ex Brazilian Air Force	2175 [preserved by Nov10 Fortaleza-Pinto Martins, Brazil]
110096	110B1	Taxi Aereo Itaituba	PT-ZKE PT-GKE

EMBRAER EMB-110 BANDEIRANTE AND EMB-111 BANDEIRULHA

C/n	Model	Last known Owner/Operator	Identities/fates/comments (where appropriate)
110097	EC-95	ex Brazilian Air Force	2176 [w/o 30Aug86 Queluz, Brazil; stored Nov11 Parque Matrerial Aeronautico Afonsos, Brazil]
110098	110P	(Aerotaxi)	PT-GKD CU-T1110 [w/o 06Dec02 Murgas, near Havana Airport, Cuba]
110099	EC-95	Brazilian Air Force	2177
110100	EC-95	ex Brazilian Air Force	2178 stored Nov11 Parque Matrerial Aeronautico Afonsos, Brazil]
110101	110C(N)	ex Chilean Navy	PT-GKF 107 [wfu and preserved Vina Del Mar-Torquemada, Chile]
110102	110C(N)	ex Chilean Navy	PT-GKG 108 [wfu and used for ground training Vina Del Mar-Torquemada, Chile]
110103	110C	(Piquiatuba Taxi Aereo)	2179+ PT-TAF [+ Brazil] [w/o 25Jan10 Senador Jose Porfirio-Wilma Rebelo, Brazil]
110104	110C	Taxi Aereo Itaituba	2180+ PT-WTL [+ Brazil]
110105	110C	Abaete Linhas Aereas	2181+ PT-MFP [+ Brazil]
110106	110P	ex VOTEC Servicios Aereos Regionais	PT-GKI [stored by Nov95 engineless Rio de Janeiro-Santos Dumont, Brazil; l/n 11Mar11]
110107	110P	(VOTEC Servicios Aereos Regionais)	PT-GKL [w/o 18Apr84 nr Imperatriz, Maranhao, Brazil, mid-air collision with EMB-110 PT-GJZ (c/n 110088); canx]
110108	110C(N)	ex Chilean Navy	PT-GKH 109 [stored Vina Del Mar-Torquemada, Chile]
110109	C-95	(Brazilian Air Force)	2182 [w/o 16Nov82 Rio de Janeiro, Brazil]
110110	C-95	Brazilian Air Force	2183
110111	110P	ex Triton Taxi Aereo	PT-GKM [wfu & dismantled Belo Horizonte-Pampulha, Brazil; but reported Jly10 sold to Aerocaribbean, Cuba]
110112	110P	(Arara Taxi Aereo)	PP-ZKJ PT-GKJ [wfu by 31May01; fate unknown]
110113	110C	(Rico Linhas Aereas)	2184+ PT-WDC [+ Brazil] [wfu Jun00; fate unknown]
110114	C-95	(Brazilian Air Force)	2185 [w/o 16Jun87 Manaus, Brazil]
110115	110E(J)	ex Departamento Nacional de Estreades de Rodagem	PT-GKK PT-FRF
110116	110P	Aerotaxi	PT-GKN CU-T1109 CU-T1541
110117	110C	(Komodoro Taxi Aereo)	2186 PT-WDP [+ Brazil] [wfu by 31Dec04; fate unknown]
110118	C-95	Brazilian Air Force	2187
110119	110E(J)	Abaete Linhas Aereas	PT-GKO
110120	110E	(Tavaj Transportes Aereos Regulares)	PT-GKP [wfu by 31Mar06; fate unknown]
110121	110C	Abaete Linhas Aereas	2188+ PT-MFQ [+ Brazil]
110122	110C	NHR Taxi Aereo	2189+ PT-WAW [+ Brazil]
110123	EC-95	ex Brazilian Air Force	2190 [preserved by Nov10 Brasilia, Brazil]
110124	EC-95	Brazilian Air Force	2191
110125	110P	(Taxi Aereo Weiss)	PT-GKQ [w/o 19May10 near Cascavel Airport, Brazil]
110126	110P	(VOTEC Servicios Aereos Regionais)	PT-GKR [report damaged & canx 28Jun90; no further details]
110127	110P	(TAM Express)	PT-GKS [wfu by Feb00 and probably b/u Goiania, Brazil]
110128	110P	(Transportes Aereos da Bacia Amazonica)	PT-GKW [w/o 31Jan78 Eirunepe, Amazonas, Brazil; canx]
110129	110P	Apui Taxi Aereo	PT-GKX
110130	110P	(Rio-Sul)	PT-GKT [w/o 25Jly87 Santo Angelo, Brazil]
110131	110P	ex VOTEC Servicios Aereos Regionais	PT-GKU [wfu & stored Nov95 Rio de Janeiro-Santos Dumont, Brazil]
110132	110P	Aerocaribbean	PT-GKV CU-T1551
110133	R-95	Brazilian Air Force	2240
110134	R-95	Brazilian Air Force	2241
110135	R-95	Brazilian Air Force	2242
110136	110P	Aerotaxi	PT-GKY CU-T1542
110137	110P	ex Transportes Aereos da Bacia Amazonica	PT-GKZ [airline suspended operations 2001; fate unknown]
110138	R-95	(Brazilian Air Force)	2243 [w/o 23Oct92 near Recife, Brazil]
110139	C-95A	ex Brazilian Air Force	2280 stored Nov11 Parque Matrerial Aeronautico Afonsos, Brazil]
110140	R-95	Brazilian Air Force	2244
110141	R-95	Brazilian Air Force	2245
110142	P-95A	ex Brazilian Air Force	2260+ 7050 [+ Brazil] [prototype EMB-111; ff 15Aug77; by Apr12 stored Dos Afonos, Brazil]
110143	C-95A	Brazilian Alr Force	PT-GLA 2283
110144	110P	(VOTEC Servicios Aereos Regionais)	PT-GLB [w/o 24Feb81 Belem, Brazil; canx]

EMBRAER EMB-110 BANDEIRANTE AND EMB-111 BANDEIRULHA

C/n	Model	Last known Owner/Operator	Identities/fates/comments (where appropriate)
110145	110P	ex Tavaj Transportes Aereos Regulares	PT-GLC [wfu Jun01; no further details]
110146	110P2	ex Islena Airlines	PT-GLD PP-ZCY F-GATS N717GA HR-IAV [not active; status unknown]
110147	111A(N)	Museo de la Aviacion Naval de Chile	261+ [+ Chile] [preserved Vina del Mar, Torquemada, Chile; l/n 18Mar04]
110148	C-95A	Brazilian Air Force	2281
110149	C-95A	Brazilian Air Force	2282
110150	111A(N)	Chilean Navy	262
110151	P-95	Brazilian Air Force	2261+ 7051 [+ Brazil]
110152	C-95A	Brazilian Air Force	2284
110153	110P2	(Islena Airlines)	PT-GLA G-BWTV G-BSVT N2932C HR-IAA [wfu for spares 1999 Bennington, VT; l/n 19Jly99; assumed b/u]
110154	111A(N)	Chilean Navy	263
110155	P-95	Brazilian Air Force	2262+ 7052 [+ Brazil]
110156	110P2	(Islena Airlines)	G-FMFC N4764A N890AC HR-IAB [reportedly b/u Mar98; no details]
110157	110P2	ex Airnorth Regional	PT-GLG P2-DKN P2-RDN VH-FNP [canx 04Dec09; wfu Maroochydore, QLD, Australia; l/n 02Jan10 minus parts]
110158	111A(N)	Chilean Navy	264
110159	P-95	(Brazilian Air Force)	2263+ 7053+ PP-ZDT 7053 [+ Brazil] [w/o 27Jun85 Macuari, Brazil]
110160	C-95A	Brazilian Air Force	2285
110161	110P2	Fly Smart	G-CELT N4942S OY-BHT
110162	111A(N)	Chilean Navy	265
110163	P-95	(Brazilian Air Force)	2264+ 7054 [+ Brazil] [w/o 11Jly84 Recife, Brazil]
110164	C-95A	Brazilian Air Force	2286
110165	110P1	(General Aviation Services)	PT-GLF G-BGCR OY-ASL SE-INK N64GA [canx 02Mar93, after being reg'd for less the one month, fate unknown; but possibly b/u for spares at Bennington, VT]
110166	111A(N)	Chilean Navy	266
110167	P-95	Brazilian Air Force	2265+ 7055 [+ Brazil]
110168	C-95A	Brazilian Air Force	2287
110169	C-95A	Brazilian Air Force	2288+ PT-GLE 2288 [+ Brazil]
110170	C-95A	ex Brazilian Air Force	2289 stored Nov11 Parque Matrerial Aeronautico Afonsos, Brazil]
110171	P-95	Brazilian Air Force	2266 7056 [+ Brazil]
110172	C-95A	(Brazilian Air Force)	2290 [w/o 29Oct93 in sea near Angra dos Reis, Brazil]
110173	C-95A	Brazilian Air Force	2291
110174	C-95A	(Brazilian Air Force)	2292 [w/o 26Dec02 near Curitiba-Afonso Pena Airport, Brazil]
110175	C-95A	ex Brazilian Air Force	2293 [by Feb12 stored Dos Afonos, Brazil]
110176	C-95A	Brazilian Air Force	2294
110177	C-95A	Brazilian Air Force	2295
110178	C-95A	Brazilian Air Force	2296
110179	P-95	Brazilian Air Force	2267 7057 [+ Brazil]
110180	C-95A	ex Brazilian Air Force	2297 [by Feb12 stored Dos Afonos, Brazil]
110181	C-95A	Brazilian Air Force	2298
110182	P-95	Brazilian Air Force	2268 7058 [+ Brazil]
110183	C-95A	Brazilian Air Force	2299
110184	110P2	(Tranzair)	PT-GLH VH-MWU ZK-REX [wfu for spares; canx 09Feb96]
110185	P-95	Brazilian Air Force	2269 7059 [+ Brazil]
110186	110P2	(Sabin Air)	F-GBGA (3D-JMC) C9-AUH [w/o 08Feb00 Maputo-International Airport, Mozambique]
110187	110B1	Uruguayan Air Force	585//CX-BKF+ 585 [dual marks]
110188	P-95	Brazilian Air Force	2270 7060 [+ Brazil]
110189	110P2	ex Transportes Aereos da Bacia Amazonica	PT-GLK [airline suspended operations 2001; fate unknown]
110190	110P2	(Air Fiji)	PT-GLJ VH-MWV HS-SKG VH-MWV VH-JAX DQ-AFP [damaged on ground Suva-Nausori, Fiji, by Sun Air DHC-6 and stored; l/n 20Jly06 minus wings and other parts]
110191	P-95	Brazilian Air Force	2271 7061 [+ Brazil]
110192	110P1	(Transporte Aereo Federal)	PT-GLI XC-COX [w/o 31Aug88 near Cerro la Calera, Mexico]
110193	110P2	(Air Burkina)	PT-GLL (XT-ABG) XT-ABJ [not current, fate unknown]

EMBRAER EMB-110 BANDEIRANTE AND EMB-111 BANDEIRULHA

C/n	Model	Last known Owner/Operator	Identities/fates/comments (where appropriate)
110194	110P2	(Transtate Airlines)	PT-GLM VH-MWW P2-RDT VH-XFM VH-UQC [wfu by Jun01 Cairns, QLD, Australia; bought by Aeropelican for spares; canx 21Jly04; trucked 19Jly04 to Newcastle, NSW, Australia; hulk only by 28Jly05]
110195	110P1	Acariza Aviation	PT-GLN TR-LYK ZS-OUM 5Y-FWA
110196	110P2	Knight Aviation	PT-GLO F-GBMF (3D-CAG) C9-AUG 5Y-BPH
110197	110P2	(Air Alma)	PT-GLP F-GBMG N212GA C-FOYJ [canx 21Oct02 sold in USA; to MTW Aerospace, Montgomery, AL for spares; by 13Dec02 only fuselage present]
110198	110P1	LeAir Charter Services	PT-GLQ N522MW PH-FVA G-ONEW C6-CAB
110199	110P2	ex Comed Aviation	(PT-GLR) G-CHEV G-BKWB G-OEAB PH-FVB (G-OEAB) G-OBPL [marked "G-OBWB" on starboard side; b/u Aug03 Southend, UK; remains to Hanningfield Metals, Stock, Essex, UK; canx 27Feb04; by 25Oct09 at paintball site at Abridge, Essex, UK; l/n 20Jan11]
110200	110P2	(Execaire)	PT-GLS G-BFZK N5071N OY-BNM [ferried 06May00 to Bournemouth, UK for spares use; Jly00 remains to Valley Nurseries, Alton, UK]
110201	110P2	Aerolink Air Services	(PT-GLT) (G-YMRU) G-BGNK G-DATA N110PJ G-DATA G-EIIO VH-OZF
110202	110P1	(Ruhe Sales)	PT-GLV N102WJ [stored Nov92 Knoxville, TN; canx 22Mar99; assumed b/u]
110203	110P1	Ruhe Sales	PT-GLT N101WJ
110204	110P1	Marta Corp	PT-GLU (N203MW) N523MW N103VA [not active; status unknown]
110205	110P1	Business Air/AirNow	PT-GLW N524MW N830AC
110206	110P1	(Taxi Aereo el Venado)	PT-GLX N227CH N181AC N227CH HK-2651 [w/o 02Sep81 Paipa, Colombia]
110207	110P1	(Air Alma)	PT-GLZ (G-BGCR) G-BGCS C-GPDI [canx 21Oct02 sold in USA; to MTW Aerospace, Montgomery, AL for spares; by 13Dec02 only fuselage present]
110208	110P1	ex Airlink	PT-GMA VH-AAP P2-RDR VH-FWR VH-UQD P2-ALT [by 23Feb09 stored Madang, Papua New Guinea]
110209	110P2	(General Aviation Services)	PT-GMB F-GBME N121GA [wfu, stripped of spares & dumped by 19Jly99 Bennington, VT; canx 08Dec99]
110210	110P2	(Airlink)	PT-GMC VH-WDF P2-ALX [w/o 17Jun99 20km SE of Goroka, Papua New Guinea]
110211	110P1	Delta Force Paintball	PT-GMD (G-BGCS) G-MOBL G-OFLT [wfu by 01Jan01 & stored Southend, UK; canx 17Aug04; fuselage to Damyns Hall near Upminster, Essex, UK theme park; l/n May09]
110212	110P1	Skydrift	PT-GME F-GCLA F-OGME F-GCLA G-PBAC G-TABS
110213	110P2	(General Aviation Services)	PT-GMF F-GBLE N808GA [not active; probably b/u for spares possibly at Bennington, VT]
110214	110P1	Air South Regional	PT-GMG XC-COY ZK-MAS VH-EQB
110215	110P1	ex Skydrift Air Charter	PT-GMH N711NH G-REGA G-ZUSS G-FLTY [wfu by Aug05; used for spares Southend, UK; canx 11Apr06; hulk l/n 06Mar12]
110216	110P2	ex Transportes Aereos da Bacia Amazonica	PT-GMI [airline suspended operations 2001; fate unknown]
110217	110P1	(Comed Aviation)	PT-GMJ XC-DAB N8536J G-BNIX PH-FVC G-ODUB [wfu by Feb01; canx 09Oct02; l/n 07Sep06 under transport, hulk reported acquired by Aircraft Salvage International, Kemble, UK; fate unknown]
110218	110P1	ex Transportes Aereos Guatemaltecos	PT-GMK (N110HV) PT-GMK N202RA N127JM TG-TAY TG-JCU
110219	110P1	SAS Leasing S.A.	PT-GML G-OBIA G-BKBG N102VN TG-TWO ZS-OOZ N131CS
110220	110P1	Transportes Aereos Guatemaltecos	PT-GMM N101RA TG-TAM
110221	110P1	King Island Airlines	PT-GMN DQ-FCV YJ-RV6 VH-XFD VH-KGQ
110222	110P1	(Atlas Aircraft Corp)	PT-GMO G-OAIR N4582Q N855AC TF-ABZ N855AC [canx Nov97as destroyed; details unknown]
110223	110P1	BAC Charter	PT-GMP G-BNOC G-LOOT [wfu Southend, UK; derelict by Mar93; canx 10May94 as wfu; 14Nov01 fuselage to Hanningfield Metals, Stock, Essex, UK; l/n 03Jly05]
110224	110P2	(EuroAir)	PT-GMQ N614KC SX-BNL [arrived 06Jun04 Kemble, UK; wfu; moved to fire dump marked as "G-FIRE"; l/n 15Mar08]
110225	110P1	ex Airlink	PT-GMR DQ-FCW ZK-FHX P2-ALR [by 26Feb09 stored Madang, Papua New Guinea]
110226	110P1	(Wasa Wings)	PT-GMS OH-EBA [w/o 14Nov88 Ilmajoki, Finland]
110227	110P2	(Airlink)	PT-GMT VH-WDI P2-ALY [stored by Jun98 Brisbane, QLD, Australia; b/u for spares by Nov98]
110228	110P1	(Business Air/AirNow)	PT-GMU OH-EBB C-FZAU N7801Q [w/o 08Nov05 near Manchester, NH]

EMBRAER EMB-110 BANDEIRANTE AND EMB-111 BANDEIRULHA

C/n	Model	Last known Owner/Operator	Identities/fates/comments (where appropriate)
110229	110P2	(Sahakol Air)	PT-GMV (N525MW) N123MS HS-SKL [DBR 25Oct93 Bangkok-Don Muang, Thailand; by Feb95 hulk to Sydney-Bankstown, NSW, Australia; assumed b/u]
110230	110P1	(White Industries)	PT-GMW N615KC [wfu Nov91; b/u for spares; canx Apr95; 31Jan96 fuselage only Bates City, MO; l/n 04Oct07]
110231	110P2	Pacestar Corp	PT-GMX G-BGYS N4578U N865AC [not active, status unknown]
110232	110P2	(Airlink)	PT-GMY VH-KIQ P2-RDW VH-XFO VH-UQF P2-ALU [w/o 30Mar07 near Kandrian, Papua New Guinea]
110233	110P1	ex Airlink	PT-GMZ N202SX VH-HVS P2-ALZ [by 23Feb09 stored Goroka, Papua New Guinea]
110234	110P1	Manx Aviation & Military Museum	PT-SAA G-BGYT N104VA G-BGYT [canx 26Sep06; preserved Ronaldsway, Isle of Man, UK; l/n 07Aug12]
110235	110P1	(Willow Air)	PT-SAB XC-DAI G-OPPP G-OHIG [wfu Southend, UK; b/u Jly98; fuselage to Valley Nurseries, Alton, UK Apr99; nose to Bottle Bar & Café, Bognor Regis, UK; canx 11Apr01]
110236	110P2	ex Airlink	PT-SAC N203SX P2-RDQ VH-XFP VH-UQG P2-ALV [by 23Feb09 stored Goroka, Papua New Guinea]
110237	110P1	Southwest Air	PT-SAD N691RA P2-SWF
110238	110P1	(White Industries)	PT-SAE N616KC [wfu for spares Nov91; fuselage only by 31Jan96 Bates City, MO; canx Mar98; l/n 04Oct07]
110239	110P1	Air Rarotonga	PT-SAF N123MS (N525MW) N107CA ZK-FTS E5-ETS
110240	110P1	(Commercial National Bank)	PT-SAG N692RA [believed wfu and used for spares Dec09 Shreveport, LA; still current]
110241	110P1	(Airtex Aviation)	PT-SAH N108CA VH-CRG VH-OZG VH-XFJ VH-OZG [w/o 25Jun01 Cootamundra Airport, NSW, Australia]
110242	110P1	(Western Air)	PT-SAI XC-DAK N1348B N1348B [w/o 07Jly80 Tepic, Mexico; reg'd in USA post accident for spares recovery; b/u Sep81 Albuquerque, NM]
110243	110P2	(Pacestar)	PT-SAJ G-BGYU N4578Q N875AC [canx 24Jly92; exported to Brazil but believed b/u during 1997]
110244	110P1	ex Transportes Aereos da Bacia Amazonica	PT-SAK G-BHHA N59PB PT-OHE [airline suspended operations 2001; by Oct05 derelict Belem, Brazil]
110245	110P2	Air Rarotonga	PT-SAL VH-MWX VH-XFL VH-UQA E5-TAL
110246	C-95B	Brazilian Air Force	PT-SAM 2300
110247	C-95B	Brazilian Air Force	PT-SAN 2301
110248	110P1	(Eagle Airways)	PT-SAO N301A VH-SBH ZK-REU VH-SBH ZK-KML [wfu & stored Hamilton, New Zealand; canx 21Dec00; l/n Mar01 minus parts; final fate unknown]
110249	110P1	ex Cat Island Air	PT-SAP G-BGYV N105VA G-BGYV G-JBAC C6-BHA C6-CAH [stored by Dec08 Nassau, Bahamas]
110250	110P2	Business Air/AirNow	PT-SAQ N710NH
110251	110P1	(White Industries)	PT-SAR N617KC [wfu for spares Nov91; by 31Jan95 fuselage only at Bates City, MO; canx 03Apr95; l/n Jun06]
110252	110P1	(BAC Leasing)	PT-SAS G-POST G-NBAC [canx 25Jly95 wfu; b/u for spares Bartow, FL; l/n 09Mar97]
110253	110P1	ex Airlink	PT-SAT DQ-FDE VH-FCK VH-XFK VH-UQB P2-ALS [by 23Feb09 stored Madang, Papua New Guinea]
110254	110P1	Taxi Aereo General	PT-SAU DQ-FDF VH-FCE P2-IAJ PR-KIN
110255	C-95B	(Brazilian Air Force)	2302 [w/o 20Oct85 near Galeao AB, Rio de Janeiro, Brazil]
110256	110P2	(Euroair/Knight Air)	PT-SAW G-BHJY G-BTAA G-OEAA [w/o 24May95 near Leeds-Bradford, UK; canx 16Jun95]
110257	110P1	(General Aviation Services)	PT-SAW TR-KGB F-GESB N560GA [not active; probably b/u for spares, possibly at Bennington, VT]
110258	110P1	Taxi Aereo Weiss	PT-SAX OH-EBC CX-VIP PT-TAW
110259	110P1	Air Creebec	PT-SAY N91PB C-FYRH
110260	110P1	(Aviation Quebec Labrador)	PT-SAZ XC-FAB HR-IAE C-FEAS [canx 22Dec03; fate/reason unknown]
110261	110P1	Insel Air International	PT-SBA G-CTLN G-BKWS LN-FAP VH-BWC PJ-VIC
110262	110P2	(Talair)	PT-SBB P2-RDM [w/o 06Feb87 off eastern coast Papua New Guinea]
110263	110P1	(Muk Air)	PT-SBC N431A OY-MUA [wfu May00 Southend, UK; parts to Valley Nurseries, Alton, UK; canx 11Apr01]
110264	C-95B	ex Brazilian Air Force	2303 [by Apr12 stored Dos Afonos, Brazil]
110265	110P1	Rico Linhas Aereas	PT-SBD N92PB PT-OHF PT-WJA
110266	110P1	(White Industries)	PT-SBE N618KC [wfu for spares Nov91; canx 03Apr95; l/n 04Oct07 Bates City, MO]

EMBRAER EMB-110 BANDEIRANTE AND EMB-111 BANDEIRULHA

C/n	Model	Last known Owner/Operator	Identities/fates/comments (where appropriate)
110267	110P1	Tauwhare Military Museum	PT-SBF ZK-ERU [canx 01Aug01 as "destroyed" but preserved Tauwhare, Hamilton, New Zealand]
110268	110P1K	Gabonese Air Force	PT-SBG TR-KMA TR-KNA
110269	C-95B	Brazilian Air Force	2304
110270	110P2	(Willow Air)	PT-SBH G-BHJZ G-OCSI [wfu & stored 02Dec97 Bembridge, Isle of Wight, UK; canx 11Apr01]
110271	110P1	Agape Flights Inc	PT-SBI N101TN N316AF
110272	110P1	(Skyward Aviation)	PT-SBJ XC-DUA PH-FWT N272GA C-FSKJ [wfu by Jun05 to White Industries, Bates City, MO for spares use; l/n 04Oct07; canx 02Feb09]
110273	110P1	Taxi Aereo Vale do Jurua	PT-SBK N90PB PT-OCW
110274	110P1	ex City Jet [New Zealand	PT-SBL VH-KIR P2-NAL ZK-REV ZK-TZO [canx 16Aug00 as destroyed; by Feb10 fuselage only noted at Palmerston North, New Zealand]
110275	110P1	(WestAir Commuter A/L)	PT-SBM N731A [w/o 08Oct91 near.Narsarsuaq, Greenland; canx 05Aug92]
110276	C-95BM	Brazilian Air Force	PP-ZKK 2305
110277	110P2	(Skycraft Air Transport)	PT-SBN G-BHYT C-GHOY [canx Apr94 on sale in USA; reported wfu & stored, fate unknown]
110278	110P1	(Business Air)	PT-SBP (G-BHPP) XA-LES N790RA G-CLAW G-SWAG N790RA [w/o 09Dec05 Orangeburg, SC; wreck to Leipsic-Ruhe's Airport, OH; l/n 27Sep07; canx 19Apr10]
110279	110P1	(Pacific Coast Lease)	PT-SBQ N693RA [wfu & stored Sep93, no details; canx Jun01 as scrapped; fate unknown]
110280	110P1	(Pacific Coast Lease)	PT-SBR N694RA [wfu & stored Sep93, no details; canx Jun01 as scrapped; fate unknown]
110281	110P1	ex Airlink	PT-SBS VH-WPI P2-VAD P2-ALW [by 23Feb09 stored Goroka, Papua New Guinea]
110282	C-95B	Brazilian Air Force	2306
110283	110P1	Skyline Enterprises Corp	PT-SBT (N182AC) N404AS P4-AVE N404AS
110284	110B1	Instituto Nacional de Pesquisas Espaciais	PT-SBO PP-FFV
110285	110P1	(Sowind Air)	PT-SBU N84940 C-GVRO [w/o 09Dec97 Little Grand Rapids, MB, Canada; canx 30Nov98; remains to Dodson Aircraft Parts, Rantoul, KS; l/n 16Apr09]
110286	110P1	Queensland Institute for Aviation Engineering	PT-SBV VH-KIP ZK-KIP [wfu & stored Jun02; 12Mar03 Maroochydore, QLD, Australia; by May07 GIA Caloundra, QLD, Australia; l/n 31Jan09]
110287	110P1	(Twin Air)	PT-SBW N63CZ N360CL [stored Mar00 Opa-locka, FL; b/u Jun04]
110288	110P1	ex Package Delivery Express	PT-SBX G-BIBE N193PB G-BIBE SE-IYZ OO-SKU C6-PDX [reported stored by Dec08 Nassau, Bahamas]
110289	110P1	(Brazilian Air Force)	PT-SBY 2315 [w/o 30Aug96 on Queluz mountain, Brazil]
110290	110P1	(MTW Aerospace)	PT-SBZ C-GDBF [canx 21Oct02; to spares use Montgomery, AL; fuselage only by 13Dec02; l/n 22Oct06]
110291	EC-95B	Brazilian Air Force	2307
110292	110P2	Aerolink Air Services	PT-SCA VH-WBI DQ-WBI VH-WBR
110293	110P1	(RUTACA)	PT-SCB N901A YV-247C [wfu by 2004 Caracas-Simon Bolivar, Venezuela; l/n Apr05; assumed b/u]
110294	110P1	(Euroair)	PT-SCC G-HGGS [w/o 19Nov84 north of Inverness, UK; canx 22Feb85]
110295	110P2	ex Transportes Aereos Presidente	PT-SCD [not active; status unknown]
110296	110P1	ex FUNAI Brasilia	PT-SCE [not active; status unknown]
110297	110P1K	Gabonese Air Force	PT-SCF TR-KNB
110298	110P1	Robert Keys	PT-SCG N124MS VH-LSE ZK-REU ZK-TZN ZK-VJG VH-BQB
110299	C-95B	Brazilian Air Force	2308
110300	110P2	(Talair)	PT-SCH P2-RDL [w/o 04Nov84 Port Moresby, Papua New Guinea]
110301	110P1	(Business Air/AirNow)	PT-SCI N401AS N49BA [w/o 13Jan05 Keene/Dillant-Hopkins Airport, NH; canx 15Nov07]
110302	110P1	(AIRES)	PT-SCJ HK-2593 [w/o 04Aug85 Mocoa, Colombia]
110303	110P2	Star Airways	PT-SCK F-GCMQ ZA-ADA
110304	110P1	Cat Island Air	PT-SCL G-LATC SE-KYE G-BVRT J8-VAZ C6-CAP
110305	110P1	Air New Zealand Technical School	PT-SCM (N712NH) N201AE ZK-JCM [wfu & canx 04Apr03; to GIA Hamilton, New Zealand]
110306	C-95B	Brazilian Air Force	2309
110307	110P2	ex Air Fiji	PT-SCN P2-RDO VH-FNR DQ-YES [stored by Jly09 Suva-Nausori, Fiji; sold May10 to Northern Air Charter Services without engines]
110308	110P1	ex Stenberg Aviation/Benair	PT-SCO OY-ASY EI-BPI OY-ASY [canx 08Aug12 as w/o but by Mar11 hulk stored Stauning, Denmark; l/n Sep11]

EMBRAER EMB-110 BANDEIRANTE AND EMB-111 BANDEIRULHA

C/n	Model	Last known Owner/Operator	Identities/fates/comments (where appropriate)
110309	110P1	ex FUNAI Brasilia	PT-SCP PT-FAS [not active; reported stored May96 Rio de Janeiro-Jacarepagua, Brazil; no recent reports]
110310	110P1	(AIRES)	PT-SCQ HK-2594 [w/o 14Aug95 in moutains en-route Neiva to Cali, Colombia]
110311	110P1	(Naturelink Charters)	PT-SCR N303JA (N119ME) HB-LQE G-DBAC 8P-TIA ZS-OWO [w/o 01Oct04 Douala, Cameroon]
110312	110P1	Beason Simons Ltd	PT-SCS N102TN [canx 15Jly03; reported wfu; fate unknown]
110313	110P1	(TAPSA)	PT-SCT VP-LCH V2-LCH N30DR TG-TPA [w/o 01Nov96 near Tikal, en-route La Aurora to Santa Elena, Guatemala]
110314	110P1	(Nordeste Linhas Aereas)	PT-SCU [w/o 11Nov91 Episepe near Recife, Brazil; canx 22Jan92]
110315	110P1	Apui Taxi Aereo	PT-SCV N695RA PT-LRR
110316	110P1	Tavaj Linhas Aereas	PT-SCW N94PB PT-OCX
110317	C-95B	(Brazilian Air Force)	2310 [w/o 23Jly97 on a mountainside near Guaratingueta, Brazil]
110318	110P2	Business Air/AirNow	PT-SCX F-GBRM N24AN
110319	110P2	FUNCEME	PT-SCY [not active; status unknown]
110320	C-95B	Brazilian Air Force	2311
110321	110P1	Air Sunshine	PT-SCZ N619KC N123HY
110322	110P1	Business Air/AirNow	PT-SDA (N402AS) N403AS N97BA
110323	110P1	(Two Taxi Aereo)	PT-SDB [w/o 22Aug07 near Curitiba, Brazil]
110324	110P1	(Comair)	PT-SDC N75CZ [canx 19Jly94 wfu; hulk to Atlanta Air Salvage, Griffin-Spalding Scrapyard, GA; l/n Oct03]
110325	110P1	(RUTACA)	PT-SDD N103TN YV-245C [wfu by 2004 Caracas-Simon Bolivar, Venezuela; l/n Apr05; assumed b/u]
110326	C-95B	Brazilian Air Force	2312 [stored Oct08 Campo Grande, Brazil]
110327	110P1	(Air Sunshine)	PT-SDE N620KC N327AB [wfu by Jun02 Fort Lauderdale-International, FL; b/u Aug10]
110328	110P1	ex Air Fiji	PT-SDF VH-PGS ZK-REW ZK-TZM ZK-CEF VH-IQB DQ-AFQ [reported DBR in 2006 Savu-Nausori, Fiji; l/n Jly09, no wings; possibly sold May10 to Northern Air Charter]
110329	110P1	(Skyward Aviation)	PT-SDG (N183AC) N9540G N850AC C-GSKD (ZS-PDC) [wfu by Jun05 for spares; 29Jun05 arrived White Industries, Bates City, MO; l/n 04Oct07; canx 02Feb09]
110330	110P1	(Southern Express)	PT-SDH N95PB [w/o 06May89 Mount Pleasant, TN]
110331	110P1	(Skyward Aviation)	PT-SDI N4268R C-GYQT G-BPHN PH-FWS N331GA C-FSKR [wfu by Jun05 for spares; to White Industries, Bates City, MO; l/n 04Oct07; canx 02Feb09]
110332	C-95B	Brazilian Air Force	2313
110333	110P2	(Kyrnair)	PT-SDJ F-GDCI [wfu & stored Dec94 Ajaccio, Corsica; fate unknown; canx 04Jly12 pwfu]
110334	110P1	ex Flight Line Inc	PT-SDK N97121 [wfu for spares Mar96 Guernsey, UK; canx 10 Mar97 as dismantled; donated to fire service; l/n 17Jan08]
110335	110P1	Business Air/AirNow	PT-SDL N621KC
110336	110P1	Skyline Enterprises Corp	PT-SDM N76CZ P4-AVD N76CZ [last reported Nov06 stored Caracas-Simon Bolivar, Venezuela]
110337	C-95B	Brazilian Air Force	2314
110338	110P1	(White Industries)	PT-SDN N622KC [wfu Nov91 for spares & b/u; canx 07Mar95; l/n 04Oct07]
110339	110P1	(Aviation Quebec Labrador)	PT-SDO N696RA C-FGCL [reported grounded 26Jun02; canx to USA but not regd, assumed b/u for spares]
110340	110P1	(Air Creebec)	PT-SDP N4268K N305EB N820AC SE-KEM LN-TDI C-FPCM [canx 08Jly11 PWFU]
110341	110P1	(AIRES)	PT-SDQ HK-2638X [w/o 23Jan85 16km from Buga, Colombia]
110342	110P1	Transportes Aereos Guatemaltecos	PT-SDR (N102VA) N90420 N90492 N304JA N486FS C-GPCQ TG-TAN
110343	110P1	(Selva Linhas Aereas)	PT-SDS (N4268L) HK-2639X PT-LGN [w/o 29Jly98 ditched in Manacapuru river 120 kms west of Manaus, Brazil]
110344	110P1	Governo Estado do Rio Grande do Norte	PT-SDT PT-FAV PP-ERN
110345	110P1	(Aeromil (Aircraft) (Pty) Ltd)	PT-SDU N90427 ZK-LBC [wfu & stored 19May02 Hamilton, New Zealand; ferried 27Mar03 Maroochydore, QLD, Australia for further storage; canx 04Apr03; l/n Apr06]
110346	110P1	META Mesquita Taxi Aereo	PT-SDV N697RA PT-LNW
110347	110P1	Air Shuttle	PT-SDW VH-FCG P2-NAB VH-FCG YJ-AV7 VH-SJP YJ-RV12 VH-CEG 9G-FWD
110348	110P1	Aereo Ruta Maya	PT-SDX (N601A) N57DA TG-JCC
110349	SC-95B	Brazilian Air Force	2315+ 6542 [+ Brazil]

EMBRAER EMB-110 BANDEIRANTE AND EMB-111 BANDEIRULHA

C/n	Model	Last known Owner/Operator	Identities/fates/comments (where appropriate)
110350	110P1	Royal Air Freight	PT-SDY N77CZ N4361Q N34A
110351	110P1	Business Air/AirNow	PT-SDZ N405AS N83BA
110352	110P1	(Manaus Aero Taxi)	PT-SEA [w/o en-route 07Feb09 near Santo Antonio, Rio Manacapuru, Brazil]
110353	110P1	(Skyward Aviation)	PT-SEB N623KC C-FSKL [wfu by Jun05 for spares; to White Industries, Bates City, MO; l/n 04Oct07; canx 02Feb09]
110354	110P1	Aereo Ruta Maya	PT-SEC N102EB TG-JCO
110355	110P1	(Talair)	PT-SED VH-FCJ P2-RDS [w/o 15Apr92 Daulo Pass near Goroka, Papua New Guinea]
110356	SC-95B	Brazilian Air Force	6543
110357	110P1	(Comair)	PT-SEE N79CZ [wfu by 21Oct93 & b/u Long Beach, CA; canx 09Dec96; remains to The Aviation Warehouse, El Mirage, CA; l/n 19May07]
110358	110P1	(GATX Capital Corp)	PT-SEF N78CZ [wfu & b/u Mojave, CA; canx 06Jan97]
110359	110P1	(Rico Linhas Aereas)	PT-SEG N97PB PT-OCV [w/o 21Apr08 Coari-Amazonas, Brazil]
110360	111A	Gabonese Air Force	TR-KNC [stored/wfu LibrevilLe-Leon M'ba, Gabon; l/n 24Jan11]
110361	C-95B	Brazilian Air Force	6544
110362	110P1	(White Industries)	PT-SEH N58DA [wfu for spares Nov91; to Bates City, MO; canx 21Apr95; l/n 04Oct07]
110363	110P1	(RUTACA)	PT-SEI N104TN YV-246C [wfu Caracas-Simon Bolivar, Venezuela; l/n Apr05; assumed b/u]
110364	110P1	Queensland Institute for Aviation Engineering	PT-SEJ G-RLAY G-BLVG SE-KES G-BLVG ZK-DCH [wfu & stored Maroochydore, QLD, Australia; canx 21Mar03; l/n Apr06; by May07, GIA, Caloundra, QLD, Australia; fuselage only l/n 31Jan09]
110365	110P1	(Provincetown-Boston A/L)	PT-SEK N96PB [w/o 06Dec84 nr Jacksonville, FL]
110366	110P1	(TAVINA)	PT-SEL HK-2743 [w/o 29May83 Barranquilla, Colombia]
110367	SC-95B	Brazilian Air Force	6545
110368	110P1	(SUDENE)	PT-SEM PT-FAW [w/o 20Sep90 near Fernando de Noronha, Brazil]
110369	110P1	(Willow Air)	PT-SEN N698RA G-DORK G-OCSZ [wfu & b/u Apr98 Southend, UK; canx 11Apr04]
110370	110P1	(Simmons Airlines)	PT-SEO N1356P [w/o 13Mar86 near Alpena County-Regional Airport, MI; canx 22Aug08]
110371	110P1	Aeroperlas	PT-SEP N61CZ HP-1201AC HP-1201APP
110372	110P1	Business Air/AirNow	PT-SEQ (ZK-TNA) N800AC C-FSXR N31AN
110373	110P1	ex Kenn Borek Air	PT-SER HP-931 HP-931AC HP-931APP C-GANR [stored wfu by 22Jly08 Airdrie, AB, Canada; l/n 13Sep10]
110374	SC-95B	Brazilian Air Force	PP-ZAD 6546
110375	110P1	(Alas Chiricanas)	PT-SES N60CZ HP-1202AC [w/o 19Jly94 near Colon, Panama; canx 26Jly96]
110376	110P1	(RUTACA)	PT-SET N61DA YV-248C [wfu Caracas-Simon Bolivar, Venezuela; l/n Apr05; assumed b/u]
110377	110P1	ex Royal Air Freight	PT-SEU (G-BJCZ) G-RVIP C-GHOV N72RA [wfu by 18Jly09 Pontiac, MI]
110378	110P1	(Aeromil (Aircraft) (Pty) Ltd)	PT-SEV N605W P2-RDU VH-FWI ZK-TZL [wfu & stored Dec00 Hamilton, New Zealand; fate unknown]
110379	110P1	Robert Keys	PT-SEW N62DA G-OJAY ZK-NDC VH-PYA [l/n engineless 25Mar08 Melbourne-Essendon, VIC, Australia]
110380	110P1	(AIRES)	PT-SEX HK-2741 [wfu Oct01; fate unknown]
110381	110P1	Air Shuttle	PT-SEY TR-LAG F-WFYZ F-GFYZ LX-SKS OO-SKW S9-DAI 9G-FWC
110382	110P1	Insel Air International	PT-SEZ N63DA YV-249C PJ-VIP
110383	110P1	Double D Leasing Inc	PT-SFA N135EM PT-LLB SE-KEL ZK-ECM N135EM C-FPCX C-GBYL N383AK
110384	110P1	Tavaj Linhas Aereas	PT-SFB N699RA PT-SFB PT-LRJ
110385	110P1	Royal Air Freight	PT-SFC N64DA
110386	110P1	Payam Airlines	PT-SFD N68DA JA8842 VH-LVH (I5-9851)+ EP-TPG EP-TPK [+ Iran]
110387	110P1	ex Insel Air International	PT-SFE N2734C N134EM (ZK-TRJ) ZK-TAI E5-TAI PJ-VIA [reported wfs, fate/sttaus unknown]
110388	110P1	Piper East/Wiggins Airways	PT-SFF N62CZ N117WA
110389	110P1	(Atlantic Southeast Airlines)	PT-SFG N65DA [wfu for spares by 31Jan96; fuselage to White Industries, Bates City, MO; canx 18May95; l/n 25Apr07]
110390	110P1	Brazilian Air Force	PT-SFH 2316
110391	110P1	(Titan Airways)	PT-SFI N115MQ G-BPDL G-ZAPE [w/o 13Jan93 nr Sellafield, Cumbria, UK; canx 06Sep93]
110392	110P1	ex Arara Taxi Aereo	PT-SFJ N69DA PT-LLD [not active; status unknown]

EMBRAER EMB-110 BANDEIRANTE AND EMB-111 BANDEIRULHA

C/n	Model	Last known Owner/Operator	Identities/fates/comments (where appropriate)
110393	110P1	Aeromas	PT-SFK N91DA CX-MAS
110394	110P1	Taxi Aereo General	PT-SFL G-BJZJ ZS-LGM P2-IAK PR-NHR
110395	110P1	ex Aerolineas SOSA	PT-SFM N2992C HR-AOG [not active; status unknown]
110396	110P1	(Business Air/AirNow)	PT-SFN N900FB N59BA [w/o 04Aug06 near Bennington-William H Morse State Airport, VT; canx 01Jly11]
110397	110P1	Kenn Borek Air	PT-SFO N901FB C-FLKB N903LE C-FLKB
110398	110P1	Aeroperlas	PT-SFP HK-2878 HP-1012 HP-1012APP
110399	110P1	Piper East/Wiggins Airways	PT-SFQ N64CZ N116WA
110400	110P1	Kenn Borek Air	PT-SFR N902FB C-GFKB N902LE C-GFKB 9N-AFF C-GFKB 9N-AFF C-GFKB
110401	110P1	Taxi Aereo Weiss	PT-SFS
110402	110P1	(Bop-Air)	PT-SFT G-BKZX ZS-LGP [w/o 01Mar88 near Germiston, Johannesburg, South Africa]
110403	110P1	(RUTACA)	PT-SFU N2783L N202EB YV-787C [wfu 2004 Caracas-Simon Bolivar, Venezuela; l/n Apr05; assumed b/u]
110404	110P1	Business Air/AirNow	PT-SGB N903FB N51BA
110405	110P1	Transportes Aereos Guatemaltecos	PT-SFV N810AC OY-CPG (SE-KYR) LN-TED C-FPCO TG-TAK
110406	110P1	(AIRES)	PT-SFW HK-2856 [reported wfu Jun00 Bogota, Colombia; fate unknown]
110407	110P1	Aeropro	PT-SFX N92DA C-GTNV N212EB VH-XTL ZK-REX VH-TLH C-FZSN
110408	110P1	Helen N Wilkins Family Trust	PT-SFY N905FB [not active; status unknown]
110409	110P1	Tavaj Linhas Aereas	PT-SFZ N720RA PT-LRB
110410	110P1	ex Air Fiji	PT-SGA P2-RDP VH-XFH P2-RDP VH-XFN DQ-LCM [stored 20Jly06 time expired Suva-Nausori, Fiji; l/n Dec06]
110411	110P1	Helen N Wilkins Family Trust	PT-SGC N904FB [not active; status unknown]
110412	110P1	Taxi Aereo General	PT-SGD G-BJZI ZS-LGN P2-IAL PR-ELT
110413	110P1A	Royal Air Freight	PT-SGE N98PB C-GPNW N73RA
110414	110P1	(AIRES)	PT-SGG N94DA C-GTNW N145EM HK-3195X [DBF 15Dec90 Villa Garzon, Colombia; canx 31May91]
110415	110P1	(Disri Dist Co Prod Alim Beb)	PT-SGH N39174 PT-LRA [wfu & stored Jly00; status unknown]
110416	110P1	(Air Fiji)	PT-SGI N2783S N130EM VH-TFK DQ-AFN [w/o 24Jly99 into high ground near Suva-Nausori, Fiji]
110417	110P1	ex Air Fiji/Airlines Tonga	PT-SGJ N110EA ZK-TRL ZK-REZ VH-TLD DQ-TLC [stored by Jly09 Suva-Nausori, Fiji; sold May10 to Northern Air Charter Services without engines]
110418	110P1	Tavaj Linhas Aereas	PT-SGK N860AC PT-LTN
110419	110P1	ex Air Fiji	PT-SGL N870AC EI-BVX DQ-AFO [stored by Jly09 Suva-Nausori, Fiji; sold May10 to Northern Air Charter Services without engines]
110420	110P1	Aerotaxi	PT-SGM 8R-GFO PT-SGM
110421	110P1	Pacific Island Aviation	PT-SGN N104EB [wfu & b/u Aug03 no details; canx 09Sep03]
110422	110P1	(Air North Regional)	PT-SGO N131EM ZK-TRK VH-LNC [wfu for spares 2003 Port Lincoln, SA, Australia; l/n Nov99; canx 05Feb09 as b/u]
110423	110P1	Payam Airlines	PT-SGP N101EB N110SX VH-LVI (5-9852)+ EP-TPS EP-TPL [+ Iran]
110424	110P1A	Royal Air Freight	PT-SGQ N199PB C-GPRV N49RA
110425	110P1	(Aviation Services International)	PT-SGR F-GEDR N118GA [canx 09Oct02 as destroyed; details unknown]
110426	110P1	ex Aerolink Air Services	PT-SGS N110EM [canx 13Feb04 on sale in Australia; l/n 26Nov04 stored Cairns, QLD, Australia still wearing US marks]
110427	110P1	PENTA – Pena Transportes Aereos	PT-SGT N302EB PT-LLC
110428	110P1	Sao Raimundo Mineracao Alta Floresta	PT-SGU PP-EUO PT-LRE [reported wfu and stored; no details]
110429	C-95B	Brazilian Air Force	PT-SGV 2317
110430	C-95B	Brazilian Air Force	2318
110431	C-95B	Brazilian Air Force	2319
110432	C-95B	Brazilian Air Force	2320
110433	C-95B	(Brazilian Air Force)	2321 [w/o 23apr98 near Resende, Brazil]
110434	C-95B	(Brazilian Air Force)	2322 [w/o 08May98 Barra da Tijuca, Brazil]
110435	C-95B	Brazilian Air Force	2323
110436	110P1	(Eagle Airways)	PT-SGW N132EM ZK-TRM [canx 04Apr03 as exported; fuselage used as ground trainer Hamilton, New Zealand]
110437	C-95B	(Brazilian Air Force)	2324 [w/o 26Mar87 near Rio de Janeiro, Brazil]
110438	110P1A	Payam Airlines	PT-SGX N144EM JA8843 VH-LVJ (5-9853)+ EP-TPA EP-TPI [+ Iran]

EMBRAER EMB-110 BANDEIRANTE AND EMB-111 BANDEIRULHA

C/n	Model	Last known Owner/Operator	Identities/fates/comments (where appropriate)
110439	110P1A	Acariza Aviation	PT-SGY N110EB OH-EBD ZS-OZJ 5Y-FWB
110440	C-95B	Brazilian Air Force	2325
110441	110P1A	Transportes Aereos Guatemaltecos	PT-SGZ N141EM VH-WPE VH-LNB TG-TAG
110442	110P1A	Payam Airlines	PT-SHA N142EM VH-LVK (5-9854)+ EP-TPT EP-TPJ [+ Iran]
110443	C-95B	Brazilian Air Force	2326
110444	110P1A	Kenn Borek Air	PT-SHB N143EM HP-1177AC HP-1177APPC-GBBR [stored wfu by 23Jly08 Airdrie, AB, Canada; l/n 13Sep10]
110445	110P1A	Air Creebec	PT-SHC N217EB SE-KYO LN-TDA C-FPCU
110446	110P1A	(Skypower Express Airways)	PT-SHD (N221PB) 5N-AXM [w/o 17Mar00 near Kaduna, Nigeria]
110447	110P1A	Air Rarotonga	PT-SHE N216EB VH-MWF E5-TAI
110448	110P1A	Air Rarotonga	PT-SHF N219EB VH-LHW VH-KHA ZK-TAK E5-TAK
110449	110P1A	ex Skypower Express Airways	PT-SHG (N212PB) 5N-AXK [derelict by 08Dec07 Malabo, Equatorial Guinea; l/n 19Jun08]
110450	IC-95B	Brazilian Air Force	2327
110451	110P1A	Piper East/Wiggins Airways	PT-SHH N218EB C-GDCQ N36AN N115WA
110452	EC-95B	Brazilian Air Force	2328
110453	110P1A	Payam Airlines	PT-SHI N211EB VH-ABD EP-TPM EP-TPH
110454	C-95B	Brazilian Air Force	2329
110455	110P1A	(Skypower Express Airways)	PT-SHJ 5N-AXL [w/o 05Jan00 near Abuja, Nigeria]
110456	110P1A	Business Air/AirNow	PT-SHK N220EB LN-TDY C-GHCA N42AN
110457	C-95B	Brazilian Air Force	2330
110458	110P1A	(Skypower Express Airways)	PT-SHL 5N-AXS [w/o 31Jan97 Yola, Nigeria]
110459	110P1A	Skypower Express Airways	PT-SHM 5N-AXR
110460	110P1A	GENSA – General Servicos Aereos	PT-SHN
110461	110P1A	Furnas Centrais Eletricas	PT-SHO
110462	110P1A	CIA Hidro Eletrica de San Francisco	PT-SHP
110463	110P1A	ex Sao Raimundo Mineracao Itaituba	PT-SHQ PT-SRM [not active; status unknown]
110464	110P1A	Furnas Centrais Eletricas	PT-SHR
110465	110P1A	Angolan Government	PT-SHT D2-EUT
110466	110P1A	Cia Energetica de Minas Gerais	PT-SHU
110467	110P1A	Angolan Government	PT-SHV D2-EUN
110468	110P1A	Government of Amapa	PT-SHW PP-EIX
110469	110P1A	ex Transportes Aereos da Bacia Amazonica	PT-SHX [airline suspended operations 2001; fate unknown]
110470	110P1A	NHR Taxi Aereo	PT-SHY
110471	IC-95C	Brazilian Air Force	2331
110472	C-95C	Brazilian Air Force	2332
110473	C-95C	(Brazilian Air Force)	2333 [w/o 29Nov91 in high ground near Guaratingueta AFB, Brazil]
110474	110P1A	Brazilian Air Force	7100
110475	110P1A	Brazilian Air Force	PT-SOC 2337
110476	IC-95C	Brazilian Air Force	2334
110477	C-95C	Brazilian Air Force	2335
110478	C-95C	Brazilian Air Force	2336
110479	110P1	Batair Charters	PT-SHZ FAC-03 ZS-CMO ZS-NVB [+ Cape Verde Islands]
110480	C-95C	Brazilian Air Force	PT-SOA 2338
110481	C-95CM	Brazilian Air Force	PT-SOB 2339
110482	C-95C	Brazilian Air Force	PT-SOD 2340
110483	P-95A	Brazilian Air Force	7101
110484	C-95C	Brazilian Air Force	PT-SOE 2341
110485	P-95A	Brazilian Air Force	2342
110486	110P1A	PENTA – Pena Transportes Aereos	PT-SOF
110487	P-95A	(Brazilian Air Force)	7102 [w/o 17Nov96 near Caetano en-route Salvador-Natal, Brazil, in formation with three other aircraft when hit by another member of the formation which landed safely]
110488	P-95A	Brazilian Air Force	7103
110489	P-95A	Brazilian Air Force	7104
110490	110P1A	GENSA – General Servicos Aereos	PT-SOG
110491	C-95C	Brazilian Air Force	2342
110492	C-95C	Brazilian Air Force	2343
110493	C-95C	Brazilian Air Force	2344

EMBRAER EMB-110 BANDEIRANTE AND EMB-111 BANDEIRULHA

C/n	Model	Last known Owner/Operator	Identities/fates/comments (where appropriate)	
110494	110P1K	Colombian Air Force	PT-SOH	1270
110495	C-95C	Brazilian Air Force	2345	
110496	110P1K	Colombian Air Force	PT-SOI	1271
110497	C-95C	Brazilian Air Force	2346	
110498	110P1A	Governo do Estado do Amazonas	PT-SBS	PP-EAM
110499	C-95C	Brazilian Air Force	2347	
110500	C-95C	Brazilian Air Force	2348	

Unidentified

unkn			ET-ANT	[reported stored 28Nov10 Addis Ababa, Ethiopia]

Production complete

EMBRAER EMB-120 BRASILIA

C/n	Model	Last known Owner/Operator	Identities/fates/comments (where appropriate)
120001		Embraer	PT-ZBA [prototype ff 27Jly83; wfu and stored Jun03 Centro Tecnico Aeroespacial, Sao Jose dos Campos, Brazil; l/n Oct08; rebuilt & preserved using hulk of c/n 120167]
120002			[static test airframe; reported b/u mid 1990's]
120003	RT	Brazilian Air Force	PT-ZBB 2000 [YC-97 then VC-97]
120004	RT	ex Rico Linhas Aereas	PT-ZBC PT-SIH PT-ZBC XA-SQN PT-WGE [DBR 13Aug02 Manaus Airport, Brazil & stored; l/n 12Aug08 in hangar]
120005			[fatigue test airframe; reported b/u mid 1990's]
120006	RT(F)	World Aircraft Leasing	PT-ZAS N210AS (EC-HFC) [stored by Jan11 Fort Lauderdale Executive, FL Transcarga c/s; l/n 15Jly11]
120007	RT(F)	Swiftair	PT-SIB N211AS EC-HCF
120008	RT(F)	Swiftair	PT-SIC N212AS EC-HAK
120009	RT(F)	Swiftair	PT-SID N214AS EC-HMY
120010	RT	(Volvo Aero Services)	PT-SIE N215AS [wfu & stored Sep01 Bangor, ME; canx 19Oct01; l/n 13May05; not reported 10May06; assumed b/u]
120011	RT	ex Corporate Air	PT-SIF N217AS [wfu & stored by Oct03 Billings-Logan, MT; l/n 28May06; canx 08Apr10]
120012	RT(F)	Swiftair	PT-SIG N120AM D-CAOB EC-JBD
120013	RT(F)	Swiftair	PT-SII N122AM D-CAOA EC-JBE
120014	RT	Flightline	PT-SIJ F-GFIN F-WQGG OY-JRT (F-HAOC) LX-PTU F-GVBR EC-LFT
120015	RT	(MTW Aerospace)	PT-SIK N218AS [wfu 23Mar08 Montgomery, AL; b/u for spares started 25Apr08; canx 18Jly08]
120016	RT	(Nordic Aviation Contractor)	PT-SIL N124AM (SE-LIZ) SE-LKB OY-PAO [b/u Oct04 Siegerland, Germany; fuselage to training aid Zweibrucken, Germany marked as SE-LKB; l/n 05Sep09]
120017	RT(F)	Transcarga International Airways	PT-SIM N125AM YV2546
120018	RT	Naturelink Charter	PT-SIN N516P C-FPAW N95644 ZS-SRW
120019	RT	(Atlantic Southeast A/L)	PT-SIO (N219AS) [w/o 19Sep86 near Sao Jose dos Campos, Brazil on delivery; canx 01May90]
120020	RT	(Aviation Services of America)	PT-ZBD PT-SIP N221AS [b/u Springfield-Branson National, MO; l/n 28Jun03; canx 08Nov04]
120021	RT(F)	Transcarga International Airways	PT-SIQ N223AS YV2694
120022	RT	(NTE Aviation Management)	PT-SIR (N126AM) N225AS [wfu about Jan04 Springfield-Branson National, MO; l/n 28Jun03; b/u; canx 08Jun04]
120023	RT	(Volvo Aero Leasing)	PT-SIS (N127AM) N227AS [wfu & stored Feb02 Loring near Limestone, ME; l/n 26Jly04; b/u]
120024	RT	(Ibertrans Aerea)	PT-SIT LN-KOC N72157 EC-GTJ [w/o 14Jan02 Santa Marie de la Vieja mountain, near Bilbao, Spain]
120025	RT	(Volvo Aero Leasing)	PT-SIU N228AS [wfu & stored Feb02 Loring near Limestone, ME; l/n 26Jly04; b/u]
120026	RT	(NTE Aviation)	PT-SIV N270UE [stored by Nov98 Victorville, CA; wfu Jun04 for spares b/u; l/n 19May07 still in US Airways Express c/s]
120027	RT(F)	Ibertrans Aerea	PT-SIW LN-KOD N14033 EC-GMT EC-GQA
120028	RT	Air Solutions	PT-SIX D-CEMA PT-SSC N314MC N330JS N336TB [stored by 13May08 Orlando International, FL; l/n 03Aug09; gone by 11Oct10; fate unknown; canx 30Aug11]
120029	RT	(Brazilian Air Force)	PT-SIY 2001 [VC-97] [w/o 08Jly88 Sao Jose dos Campos, Brazil]
120030	ER	Regional Aviation Pty	PT-SIZ N271UE P2-HLA VH-RPX
120031	RT	(Volvo Aero Leasing)	PT-SJA N233AS [wfu & stored Feb02 Loring near Limestone, ME; l/n 26Jly04; b/u]
120032	RT	(Atlantic Southeast A/L)	PT-SJB N230AS [wfu & b/u Hot Springs, AR; post 2004 fuselage to Gulfstream International Airlines, Fort Lauderdale International, FL; canx 17Sep04; l/n 05Jan05]
120033	RT	(Air Littoral)	PT-SJC F-GEGH [w/o 21Dec87 near Bordeaux, France]
120034	ER	Network Aviation Australia	PT-SJD N186SW VH-NHZ
120035	RT	ex Diexim Expresso	PT-SJE D-CEMB PT-SRV N308MC N331JS D2-FFI [reported 23Sep09 on dump at Lanseria, South Africa; l/n 20Jan10, to be b/u by NN Metals]
120036	RT	ex Air Turks & Caicos	PT-SJF N232AS VQ-TAQ [canx by Jan12 fate/status unknown; has also been reported as being VQ-TAG]
120037	ER	Aerojet	PT-SJG N187SW D2-EDF
120038	RT	SAPSA	PT-SJH D-CEMC PT-SSY N317MC N332JS HI-720CT
120039	ER	Aerojet	PT-SJI N188SW D2-EDE
120040	RT	Brazilian Air Force	PT-SJO 2002 [VC-97]
120041	RT	Rico Linhas Aereas	PT-SJJ D-CEMD PT-SSN N316MC PT-SLH PP-ISD PT-WZM

EMBRAER EMB-120 BRASILIA

C/n	Model	Last known Owner/Operator	Identities/fates/comments (where appropriate)
120042	RT	ex Atlantic Southeast A/L	PT-SJK N229AS [traded into Bombardier Feb02 & stored location not recorded; canx 12Aug04 as sold in Canada but not reg'd there]
120043	ER	(Rico Linhas Aereas)	PT-SJL D-CEME PT-SSZ N318MC PT-SLF PT-WRQ [w/o 30Aug02 Rio Branco, Brazil]
120044	ER	META-Mesquita Transportes Aereos	PT-SJM D-CEMF PT-SSB N312MC PT-SLI PT-FLY
120045	ER	Skippers Aviation	PT-SJN N272UE VH-XUA
120046	ER	International Business Air	PT-SJP N273UE SE-LKC
120047	RT	(Atlantic Southeast A/L)	PT-SJQ N235AS [traded into Bombardier Feb02 & stored location not recorded; canx 12Aug04 as sold in Canada but not reg'd there; b/u St Paul-Lake Elmo, MN; cockpit to Flight Solutions as simulator]
120048	RT	Associated Aviation	PT-SJR N189SW 5N-BIU
120049	RT	ex Atlantic Southeast A/L	PT-SJS N236AS [traded into Bombardier & stored location not recorded; canx 13Jun03 as sold in Canada but not reg'd there]
120050	RT	Associated Aviation	PT-SJT N190SW 5N-BIT
120051	RT	America Air Taxi Aereo	PT-SJU N237AS PR-OAN
120052	ER	META-Mesquita Transportes Aereos	PT-SJV D-CEMG PT-LXN
120053	RT	(MTW Aerospace	PT-SJW N238AS [wfu for spares Nov02 Montgomery, AL; b/u; l/n 24Jan06; canx 24Aug07]
120054	ER	Network Aviation Australia	PT-SJX N274UE VH-FNQ VH-NIF VH-NHY
120055	RT	Brazilian Air Force	PT-SJY 2003 [VC-97]
120056	ER	Hardy Aviation (NT) Pty	PT-SJZ D-CEMH PT-SRI N306MC N334JS VH-ASN
120057	RT	ex OceanAir	PT-SKA N239AS PR-OAO [wfu by 21Mar09 Sorocaba, Brazil]
120058	RT	(NTE Aviation)	PT-SKB N275UE [stored May98 Victorville, CA, in United Express c/s; b/u by 13Jan04]
120059	RT	ex Int'l Airline Support Group	PT-SKC D-CEMI PT-SRU N307MC N335JS [wfu for spares 14Sep98 Nashville International, TN; then used for airport fire training; dumped by Feb06]
120060	RT	OceanAir	PT-SKD N240AS PR-OAP
120061	RT	TRIP Linhas Aereas	PT-SKE F-GFEN PP-PTA
120062	RT	Air 26 Linhas Aereas	PT-SKF F-GFEO D2-EYQ
120063	RT(F)	Swiftair	PT-SKG LN-KOE C-FZWF N7215U EC-HFK
120064	RT	TRIP Linhas Aereas	PT-SKH PT-SLA PT-PCA PT-WJG
120065	RT	(Volvo Aero Leasing)	PT-SKI N241AS [stored by Feb02 Loring near Limestone, ME; b/u for spares; l/n 30Nov07]
120066	RT	Brazilian Air Force	PT-SKJ 2004 [VC-97]
120067	RT	ex AVENSA	PT-SKK N276UE YV-100C [stored Jan06 Caracas-Simon Bolivar, Venezuela; l/n 30Nov07; derelict by 14Feb09]
120068	RT	ex Embraer Finance	PT-SKL D-CEMJ PT-STA N319MC PT-SLG PT-MPJ [wfu for spares Jan03 Santarem, Brazil; l/n 12Oct08]
120069	RT	ex Atlantic Southeast A/L	PT-SKM N242AS [traded into Bombardier Oct 02; stored & b/u Billings-Logan, MT; canx 13Jun03 as sold in Canada but not reg'd there; by 13Oct03 only front fuselage noted]
120070	RT	(Rico Linhas Aereas)	PT-SKN PT-SLB PT-WRO [w/o 14May04 in jungle near Manaus, Brazil]
120071	RT	Great Lakes Aviation	PT-SKO G-BRAS LN-KOF G-BRAS PT-LUS N267UE N71GL
120072	RT	(Volvo Aero Leasing)	PT-SKP N243AS [stored by Feb02 Loring near Limestone, ME; b/u for spares; l/n 26Jly04]
120073	RT	ex NTE Aviation	PT-SKQ N244AS [wfu for spares Feb05 Walnut Ridge-Regional, AL; b/u, derelict by 17May07; but re-reg'd 03Jly08 to Universal Asset Management Inc]
120074	RT	Albatros Airlines	PT-SKR D-CEMK PT-SRA N301MC N336JS PT-WKI YV2777
120075	RT	(Atlantic Southeast A/L)	PT-SKS N245AS [traded into Bombardier Apr02; wfu & stored Burlington-International, VT; l/n Nov06; canx 29Feb12]
120076	RT	(Selva Taxi Aereo)	PT-SKT D-CEML PT-SRH N305MC N337JS PT-WKH [w/o 21Oct98 near Fortaleza International-Pinto Martins Airport, Brazil
120077	RT	(Continental Express)	PT-SKU N33701 [w/o 11Sep91 near Eagle Pass, TX; canx 06Nov92]
120078	ER	Royal Daisy Airlines/African Express	PT-SKV N16702 C-GOAB ZS-CAE 5X-TEX 5Y-AXJ
120079	RT	Network Aviation Australia	PT-SKW N277UE VH-XFH DQ-MUM VH-RPA VH-TFX
120080	RT	ex Puma Linhas Aereas	PT-SKX F-GFEP PP-PTB [damaged 24Nov06 Altamira, Brazil; possible w/o]
120081	RT	Angola Air Charter	PT-SKY G-BRAZ F-GFTC G-BRAZ PH-XLA 4L-XLA N103SK D2-FDT
120082	RT	Angola Air Charter	PT-SKZ OO-DTF PH-XLF 4L-XLF N102SK D2-FDO

EMBRAER EMB-120 BRASILIA

C/n	Model	Last known Owner/Operator	Identities/fates/comments (where appropriate)
120083	RT	ex Aircraft Africa Contracts (Pty)	PT-SMA N278UE PH-BRL ZS-OUY [reported wfu by Aug11 Lanseria, South Africa]
120084	FC	Everts Air Cargo	PT-SMB N12703 [stored Fairbanks, AK, still in North-South Airways c/s; l/n 26May09 being used for spares]
120085	RT	(Skippers Aviation)	PT-SMC N279UE N85GL [stored Jun03 Cheyenne, WY; canx 09Dec04 sold in Australia, but not reg'd there; arrived Oct05 Perth, WA, Australia dismantled; possible spares use]
120086	ER	(Starlink Aviation)	PT-SMD N19704 C-GOAD+ N [+ canx 28May12 to USA; stored by Dec07 Montreal-Trudreau, QC, Canada; b/u Jun12]
120087	RT	Skybridge AirOps/UN	PT-SME OO-DTG (F-GTSG) PH-BRS I-SKYB
120088	ER	SAEREO/TAM Cargo	PT-SMF N193SW HC-CDM
120089	ER	Uruguayan Air Force	PT-SMG N12705 CX-BTZ 550 [designated a C-120 by this air force]
120090	RT	ex Metropolis	PT-SMH N280UE PH-BRM [wfu & stored Siegerland, Germany; canx 20Jan04; derelict; l/n 02Apr05]
120091	RT	AIM Group	PT-SMI F-GFTB PH-XLB [canx 23Mar06 for parts; derelict Maastricht, Netherlands; l/n 29Feb12]
120092	RT(F)	Swiftair	PT-SMJ N281UE N92GL OM-SPY EC-JKH
120093	RT	(Continental Express)	PT-SMK N24706 [w/o 29Apr93 Pine Bluff, AR; canx 18Jan94]
120094	RT	(OceanAir)	PT-SML PT-SLC [wfu by 21Mar09 Sorocaba, Brazil]
120095	RT	Associated Aviation	PT-SMM N27707 N138DE 5N-BJZ
120096	RT	Great Lakes Aviation	PT-SMN N452UE N96ZK
120097	RT	Naturelink Charter	PT-SMP F-GFEQ LX-NVL F-GTSO ZS-SSV
120098	RT	ex Nationale	PT-SMQ N59708 C-GOAF ZS-CAB [reported wfu by Aug11 Lanseria, South Africa]
120099	RT	ex Regional CAE/Air France	PT-SMR F-GFER LX-RGI F-GTSN [canx 18Jun09 as wfu; used for spares Clermont-Ferrand, France; hulk l/n 11Sep09]
120100	RT	Ameriflight	PT-SMS N246AS
120101	RT	Brazilian Air Force	PT-SMT N12709 2008 [C-97]
120102	ER	Air 26 Linhas Aereas	PT-SMU N126AM D2-EZZ
120103	RT	Flightline	PT-SMV N127AM EC-HHN
120104	RT	Budapest Aircraft Service	PT-SMW OO-DTH F-GTSH HA-FAN
120105	FC	Everts Air Cargo	PT-SMX N1105G
120106	RT	Brazilian Air Force	PT-SMY N16710 2009 [C-97]
120107	RT	Brazilian Air Force	PT-SMZ N31711 2006 [C-97]
120108	RT	Great Lakes Aviation	PT-SNA N451UE N108UX
120109	RT	Capital Airlines	PT-SNB N128AM F-WQJV F-GMOD N763BC 5N-TUE [stored by Jan08 Lagos, Nigeria; l/n 02May08]
120110	FC	Everts Air Cargo	PT-SNC N1110J
120111	RT	Imetame Metalmecanica	PT-SND N34712 N229CR PP-IAS
120112	RT	Regional CAE/Air France	PT-SNE LN-KOB C-FKOE F-GIVK
120113	RT	(Volvo Aero Leasing)	PT-SNF N247AS [wfu & stored Feb02 Loring near Limestone, ME; l/n 26Jly04; b/u]
120114	RT	(Continental Express)	PT-SNG N15713 [wfu Nov05 Victorville, CA; b/u by NTE Aviation; l/n 19May07]
120115	RT	Skippers Aviation	PT-SNH ZS-MIR VH-XFQ VH-XUE
120116	RT	(Regional Pacific Airlines)	PT-SNI G-EXEL VH-XFX VH-ANB [w/o 22Mar10 near Darwin Airport, NT, Australia; canx 28May10]
120117	FC	ex Pel-Air Aviation	PT-SNJ N1117H VH-EEB [stored 06May09 Wagga Wagga, NSW, Australia]
120118	RT	Passaredo Transportes Aereos	PT-SNK N26714 N500DE N507DM PR-PSD
120119	RT	Capital Airlines	PT-SNL N129AM LX-VDV N762BE 5N-TCE+ PR-GSA* [+ canx 30Jan09; * reserved Nov08 for GENSA]
120120	ER	ex Capital Airlines	PT-SNM N194SW 5N-CCE [wfu by 02May08 Lagos, Nigeria; l/n early 2009 in poor condition]
120121	RT	RCR Air LLC	PT-SNN OO-DTI PH-XLG N331CR
120122	RT	(Atlantic Southeast A/L)	PT-SNO N256AS [w/o 21Aug95 near Carrollton, GA; canx 15Nov95]
120123	RT	Budapest Aircraft Service	PT-SNP OO-DTJ F-GTSI HA-FAI
120124	RT	(NTE Aviation)	PT-SNQ N282UE [stored by Oct99 Victorville, CA; l/n Jly02; b/u for spares by Oct03]
120125	RT	ex Atlant-Soyuz Airlines	PT-SNR N12715 N363AS RA-02581 [status unknown]
120126	RT	Ameriflight	PT-SNS N257AS
120127	RT	ex Capital Airlines	PT-SNT N195SW 5N-LCE+ PR-GSB* [+ canx 30Jan09; * reserved Nov08 for GENSA]
120128	ER	ex Atlant-Soyuz Airlines	PT-SNU N27716 N364AS RA-02852 [stored by 11Jly11 Ljubliana, Slovenia; l/n 31Dec11]

EMBRAER EMB-120 BRASILIA

C/n	Model	Last known Owner/Operator	Identities/fates/comments (where appropriate)
120129	RT	ex Linhas Aereas de Mocambique	PT-SNV F-GGTD OY-PAU 3D-BIN 3D-JGL [repossessed Mar07 by Nordic Aviation Contractor of Denmark; stored Johannesburg-Grand Central, South Africa; l/n 22Sep08]
120130	RT	Albatros Airlines	PT-SNW N130G PR-MGE YV2775
120131	ER	Ameriflight	PT-SNX N258AS
120132	RT	(Atlantic Southeast A/L)	PT-SNY N260AS [traded into Bombardier Apr02; wfu & stored Burlington-International, VT; l/n Dec06; canx 29Feb12]
120133	ER	ex Aviation Starlink	PT-SNZ N40717 N366AS [wfu by Feb12 Montreal-Dorval, Que, Canada]
120134	RT	(NTE Aviation)	PT-SPA N130AM [stored by Apr04 Victorville, CA; b/u for spares]
120135	RT	Air North Regional	PT-SPB ZS-MMB VH-XFR VH-ANZ
120136	ER	ex Atlant-Soyuz Airlines	PT-SPC N16718 N367AS RA-02854 [stored by 11Jly11 Ljubliana, Slovenia; l/n 31Dec11]
120137	RT	Naturelink Charter	PT-SPD N137H ZS-POE [UN code UN331]
120138	RT	Brazilian Air Force	PT-SPE N16719 2007 [C-97]
120139	RT	Kaya Airlines	PT-SPF N283UE 3D-BCI C9-AUQ
120140	ER	Skippers Aviation	PT-SPG D4-CAZ VH-XFZ VH-XUD
120141	ER	NTE Aviation	PT-SPH N261AS [by 10Mar10 wfu for parts at Springfield, MO; canx 23Apr10]
120142	RT	(Continental Express)	PT-SPI N17720 [stored by Sep02 Roswell, NM; not noted 15Apr07 assumed b/u; canx 24Oct07]
120143	RT	Bill Davis Racing	PT-SPJ N161CA N22BD
120144	RT	ex Aparte Taxi Aereo	PT-SPK F-GGTE PT-SPK PT-OZM [stored & wfu Oct00 Sao Jose dos Campos, Brazil; canx; l/n 14Apr10 in poor condition]
120145	RT	Air 26 Linhas Aereas	PT-SPL N284UE D2-EYV
120146	RT	Air 26 Linhas Aereas	PT-SPM N262AS D2-EYP
120147	RT	Air Amazonia	PT-SLD
120148	RT	ex Naturelink Charter	PT-SPN N453UE ZS-PCG [by 23Sep08 on dump Wonderboom, South Africa; l/n Jan12]
120149	ER	Inter Iles Air	PT-SPO OO-DTK PH-MGX F-GLRG D6-HUA
120150	RT	Albatros Airlines	PT-SPP N162CA N789TX PR-GDC YV2776
120151	RT	Naturelink Charter/Swazi Express	PT-SPQ N196SW ZS-PUH
120152	ER	Network Aviation Australia	PT-SPR N152CA VH-TLZ VH-NHC
120153	RT	Air North Regional	PT-SPS N285UE VH-DIL
120154	RT	Runway Asset Management (Pty)	PT-SPT F-GHIA ZS-SRI
120155	RT	Air North Regional	PT-SPU N454UE VH-YDD VH-ANK
120156	RT	Freedom Airline Express	PT-SPV N156CA ZS-PPF 5Y-FAE
120157	RT	(MTW Aerospace)	PT-SPW N263AS [wfu for spares Dec04 Montgomery, AL; canx 23Mar05; l/n 24Jan06 with parts missing]
120158	ER	Swiftair	PT-SPX N131AM (PH-BRR) P4-RAL N312FV EC-IMX
120159	RT	(Comair)	PT-SPY N159A [to White Industries, Bates City, MO, for spares Nov03; canx 24Oct07]
120160	ER	Phoenix EMB120 LLC	PT-SPZ N15721 C-GOAG N132PP N919EM N405PA
120161	RT	Air Amazonia	PT-SLE
120162	RT	Runway Asset Management (Pty)	PT-SQA F-GHIB ZS-SMV
120163	RT	(Air North Regional)	PT-SQB N455UE VH-ANJ [canx 01Nov10 as wfu; by 06Dec11 stored in hanger Darwin, NT, Australia]
120164	RT	(MTW Aerospace)	PT-SQC N164D N120AX [wfu for spares Feb02 Montgomery, AL; canx 12May05; l/n 22Oct06 still with Alaska Central Express]
120165	ER	Air 26 Linhas Aereas	PT-SQD N264AS D2-EYN
120166	RT	(Embraer Finance)	PT-SQE N47722 [wfu & stored May05 Columbus-Rickenbacker, OH; l/n 03May09; canx 07Mar12]
120167	RT	(Linhas Aereas Pantanal)	PT-SQF P4-EMA PT-MFB [stored Mar03 & DBR in 2006 in hangar collapse Sao Jose dos Campos, Brazil; hulk on dump by Jun09; later removed & used in restoration of c/n 120001]
120168	RT	Swiftair	PT-SQG N168CA EC-HTS
120169	RT	(Continental Express)	PT-SQH N16723 [wfu & stored Sep02 Roswell, NM; l/n 30Oct05; gone by 15Apr07 assumed b/u; canx 24Oct07]
120170	RT	ex NTE Aviation	PT-SQI N265AS [wfu and stored late 2004 Walnut Ridge, AR; l/n Mar07 derelict; but re-reg'd 29Jly08 to Universal Asset Management Inc]
120171	RT	Diexim Expresso	PT-SQJ N16724 N221CR D2-FFY
120172	RT	Ronald J Cozad	PT-SQK C-FPOE N340JS HC-CBX N709BC N365AS [stored May06 Tamiami, FL; still as N709BC; l/n Apr10]
120173	RT	(Continental Express)	PT-SQL N15725 [wfu & stored Oct02 Roswell, NM; l/n 30Oct05; gone by 15Apr07; canx 24Oct07]

EMBRAER EMB-120 BRASILIA

C/n	Model	Last known Owner/Operator	Identities/fates/comments (where appropriate)
120174	RT	Associated Aviation	PT-SQM N51726 N388JR 5N-BJY
120175	RT	ex AeroJet	PT-SQN N286UE PH-BRP OM-SKY D2-FET [stored by 29Feb12 Maastricht, Netherlands; l/n 16Jun12]
120176	RT	Budapest Aircraft Service	PT-SQO OO-DTL F-GTSJ HA-FAL
120177	RT	ex Continental Express	PT-SQP N22727 [wfu & stored Oct02 Roswell, NM; l/n 15Apr07; canx 24Oct07]
120178	RT	NTE Aviation	PT-SQQ C-GDOE N341JS HC-CBE N716BC [stored Mar06 Victorville, CA; l/n 19May07]
120179	ER	Ameriflight	PT-SQR N179CA
120180	RT	(NTE Aviation)	PT-SQS N180YV [wfu & l/n Nov05 Grand Junction-Regional, CO; assumed b/u; canx 11Apr06]
120181	RT	Skippers Aviation	PT-SQT VH-XFW VH-XUB
120182	RT	Berry Aviation	PT-SQU N17728 N707TG
120183	RT	ex Rico Linhas Aereos	PT-SQV N287UE PP-ISG [stored by 12Oct08 Manaus, Brazil]
120184	RT	ex Hellas Wings	PT-SQW N288UE LX-EAC N288UE LX-GDE SX-BHW TR-NRT
120185	RT	(Continental Express)	PT-SQX N16729 [wfu & stored Oct02 Roswell, NM; l/n 15Apr07; canx 24Oct07]
120186	ER	Network Aviation Australia	PT-SQY N197SW VH-TWF
120187	RT	(Continental Express)	PT-SQZ N15730 [wfu & stored Sep02 Roswell, NM; l/n 30Oct05; gone by 15Apr07; canx 24Oct07]
120188	RT	Triangle Aviation RDD	PT-SRB N266AS [stored by 10Mar10 Springfield, MO]
120189	RT	Ameriflight	PT-SRC N189CA
120190	RT	MWR Racing	PT-SRD N16731
120191	RT	Capital Airlines	PT-SRE N289UE N593SW ZS-PGZ 5N-BLN [fire damage 02Aug09 Enugu, Nigeria]
120192	RT	ex OceanAir	PT-SRF [wfu & stored by Dec07 Sorocaba, Brazil]
120193	RT	(Bayview Aviation)	PT-SRG N193YV [wfu & stored Oct01; l/n 16Oct06; b/u for spares]
120194	RT	Naturelink Charter	PT-SRJ N269UE ZS-PGY
120195	RT	Phoenix EMB120 LLC	PT-SRK N15732 N109EM N410PA
120196	RT	Naturelink Charter	PT-SRL N196CA ZS-PSB
120197	ER	Charter Air Transport	PT-SRN N58733 N651CT
120198	ER	Charter Air Transport	PT-SRO N267AS N650CT
120199	ER	Air 26 Linhas Aereas	PT-SRP N57734 N652CT D2-EZC
120200	RT	Kaya Airlines?	PT-SRQ N200CD ZS-OEN+ C9- [+ canx 10Feb12 to Mozambique]
120201	RT	Ameriflight	PT-SRR N142EB N201YW
120202	ER	Worldwide Aircraft Services	PT-SRS N268AS [by 10Mar10 wfu for parts at Springfield, MO]
120203	RT	Capiteq	PT-SRT N203YV VH-BRP VH-ANN
120204	RT	ex Pantanal Linhas Aereas	PT-SRW PT-MFA [wfu & stored Jan03 Sao Jose dos Campos, Brazil; l/n 14Apr10 with parts missing]
120205	ER	Region Avia, Russia	PT-SRX N205CA VQ-BBX
120206	RT	(Pantanal Linhas Aereas)	PT-SRY PT-MFC [w/o 03Mar97 Vilhena Airport, Brazil]
120207	ER	Skippers Aviation	PT-SRZ N268UE VH-XUF
120208	RT	Skippers Aviation	PT-SSA VH-XFV VH-XUC
120209	RT	ex Equaflight Service	PT-SSD F-GHEX EC-HUP F-HBBB+ TN- [+ canx 08Jan10 to People's Republic of Congo]
120210	RT	Air 26 Linhas Aereas	PT-SSE N269AS D2-EYO
120211	RT	(Boeing Capital Corp)	PT-SSF N241CA [wfu & stored Feb03 Hot Springs-Memorial Field, AR; canx 16Nov06]
120212	RT	Nationlink Charter/Comores Avn	PT-SSG N243CA ZS-SAU
120213	RT	Flightline	PT-SSH OO-MTD F-GTSK EC-LHY
120214	ER	Premiair	PT-SSI F-GHEY EC-HSO VH-ANV PK-RJC
120215	RT	Runway Asset Management (Pty)	PT-SSJ F-GJAK ZS-STR
120216	ER	(Wells Fargo Bank)	PT-SSK N216YV [b/u Hayward, CA; canx 30Apr09]
120217	RT	(Magellan Aircraft Services)	PT-SSL N244CA [wfu & stored Aug02 Hot Springs-Memorial Field, AR; l/n 29Jun03; assumed b/u]
120218	RT	(Atlantic Southeast A/L)	PT-SSM N270AS [w/o 05Apr91 on landing Brunswick, GA; canx 30Jly91]
120219	ER (QC)	ex InterBrasil Star	PT-SSO PP-ISA [stored 2003 Sao Paulo-Congonhas, Brazil]
120220	RT	ex InterBrasil Star	PT-SSP C-GLOE PT-OQI PP-ISF [stored early 2003 Brasilia, Brazil; l/n 30Apr06]
120221	RT	Bayview Aviation	PT-SSQ N221YV [stored Aug98 Roswell, NM; wfu for spares Jly05; l/n 16Oct06]
120222	RT	(NTE Aviation)	PT-SSR N273AS [stored Mar03 Hot Springs-Memorial Field, AR; l/n 18Dec03; canx 09Apr08]
120223	RT	Air Moldova	PT-SSS N246CA ER-EMA
120224	ER	MTW Aerospace	PT-SST N281AS [stored Jly03 Hot Springs-Memorial Field, AR; l/n Mar07]
120225	ER	Ameriflight	PT-SSU N247CA

EMBRAER EMB-120 BRASILIA

C/n	Model	Last known Owner/Operator	Identities/fates/comments (where appropriate)
120226	ER	(NTE Aviation)	PT-SSV N282AS [by 10Mar10 wfu for parts at Springfield, MO; canx 11May10]
120227	ER	SAEREO	PT-SSW N198SW HC-CEM
120228	RT	MEX Mozambique Express	PT-SSX N248CA ZS-AAB
120229	RT	(NTE Aviation)	PT-STB N274AS [wfu & stored 29Dec04 Marana, AZ; l/n 14Mar05; canx 15Sep05, b/u]
120230	RT	Mouritzen Family Trust	PT-STC N249CA ZS-OTD
120231	RT	RusLine, Russia	PT-STD N280AS VQ-BCB
120232	ER (QC)	ex InterBrasil Star	PT-STE F-GJAO PP-ISB [stored Jan02 Sao Paulo-Congonhas, Brazil; l/n Sep06]
120233	RT	(Magellan Aircraft Services)	PT-STF N254CA [stored Mar01 Hot Springs-Memorial-Field, AR; l/n 29Jun03; assumed b/u; canx 16Apr09]
120234	RT	MTW Aerospace	PT-STG N275AS [stored Mar03 Hot Springs-Memoria-Field, AR; l/n Mar07 in Delta Connection c/s]
120235	ER	Diexim Expresso	PT-STH OO-DTN PH-BRI LX-RCT F-GTSP OM-SAY F-GJTF D2-FFP
120236	RT	(NTE Aviation)	PT-STI N283AS [by 10Mar10 wfu for parts at Springfield, MO; canx 07May10]
120237	ER	(NTE Aviation)	PT-STJ N199SW [wfu & stored Aug04 Marana, AZ; l/n 14Mar05; canx 06Dec05]
120238	RT	(Magellan Aircraft Services)	PT-STK N255CA [stored & wfu Hot Springs-Memorial Field, AR; l/n 29Jun03; assumed b/u]
120239	RT	not yet known	PT-STL LX-LGL F-GIYH OM-FLY F-GTBG TR-LRS S5-BAL TR-LRS+ [+ not confirmed]
120240	RT	ex Atlant-Soyuz Airlines	PT-STM N203SW RA-02856 [stored by 11Jly11 Ljubliana, Slovenia; l/n 31Dec11]
120241	ER	Puma Linhas Areas	PT-STN
120242	ER	Diexim Expresso	PT-STO C-GUOE PT-OQJ N8078V (N140KD) D4-CBM N8078V D2-FFE
120243	ER	Players Air	PT-STP N204SW N653CT
120244	RT	Diexim Expresso	PT-STQ (F-GHEZ) LX-LGM F-GIYI OM-DAY F-GTBH D2-FFU
120245	RT	(Naturelink Charter/Nationale, Gabon)	PT-STR N256CA ZS-PYO [w/o 12Oct11 Port Gentil, Gabon]
120246	ER	PENTA-Pena Transportes Aereos	PT-STS C-FWCP N6222Z PT-OUI N6222Z PP-ISE
120247	RT	not yet known	PT-STT N258CA 5N-BLB
120248	RT	Mouritzen Family Trust	PT-STU N257CA+ ZS- [USCAR shows sale reported to South Africa but not canx; fate/status unknown]
120249	RT	MTW Aerospace	PT-STV N284AS [stored Hot Springs-Memorial Field, AR; l/n Mar07]
120250	ER	Air Minas Linhas Aereas	PT-STW N250YV PR-MDP
120251	ER	Charter Air Transport	PT-STX N251YV N654CT
120252	RT	Sahara African Leasing	PT-STY N259CA ZS-AAG TN-AHV ZS-AAG
120253	RT	ex T Miallier	PT-STZ OO-DTO (PH-BRJ) PH-BRK F-GMMU OM-SHY F-GJTG F-GTVA+ TT- [+ canx 26Nov10 to Tchad]
120254	RT	Allegiance Air	PT-SUA N261CA ZS-OKT
120255	RT	Mouritzen Family Trust	PT-SUB N263CA ZS-AAD
120256	RT	ex MTW Aerospace	PT-SUC N264CA [PWFU Oct06 Montgomery, AL off airport; canx 05Oct06 fuselage only l/n 18Oct06]
120257	RT	(Comair)	PT-SUD N265CA [w/o 10Jan97 Rainsville Township, near Monroe, MI]
120258	RT	(Comair)	PT-SUE N266CA [stored by 29Jun03 Winston-Salem, NC; canx 21Aug12]
120259	RT	ex Imatong Airlines	PT-SUF N267CA 5Y-BVN ZS- [+canx 15Oct08 to South Africa; fate/status unknown]
120260	RT	Nationale	PT-SUG N205SW N223BD ZS-PBT
120261	RT	Interlink Airlines	PT-SUH LX-LGK EC-HFZ ZS-PVF+ [+ for a time used UN code UN-331]
120262	RT	Naturelink Charter/Elysian	PT-SUI N268CA ZS-AAF
120263	RT	Everts Air Cargo	PT-SUJ N269CA [stored & wfu for spares use Oct07 Fairbanks, AK; l/n 26May09 still in Atlantic Southeast c/s]
120264	RT	ex Everts Air Cargo	PT-SUK N462CA [wfu Oct07 for spares Fairbanks, AK; not reported on 16Sep08]
120265	RT	Region Avia, Russia	PT-SUL N285AS VQ-BBY
120266	ER	Network Aviation Australia	PT-SUM N207SW VH-TWZ
120267	RT	Everts Air Cargo	PT-SUN N463CA
120268	RT	Deborah C Aharon	PT-SUO N286AS
120269	ER	Network Aviation Australia	PT-SUP N209SW VH-NHA
120270	ER	Skywest Airlines/United Express	PT-SUQ N270YV
120271	ER	Skywest Airlines	PT-SUR N271YV
120272	RT	Martin R. Weinberg	PT-SUS N500AS XA-UAI N500DN [status/fate unclear; l/n stored Hot Springs, AR]

EMBRAER EMB-120 BRASILIA

C/n	Model	Last known Owner/Operator	Identities/fates/comments (where appropriate)
120273	RT	Deborah C Aharon	PT-SUT N501AS [stored by Mar07 Hot Springs-Memorial Field, AR; Delta Connection c/s]
120274	RT	Air Turks & Caicos	PT-SUU N502AS VQ-TMJ
120275	ER	Air Turks & Caicos	PT-SUV N503AS VQ-TDG
120276	ER	SETE Linhas Aereas	PT-SUW N212SW PR-TUH PR-STI
120277	ER	Allegiance Air	PT-SUX N213SW ZS-ETA
120278	RT	Deborah C Aharon	PT-SUY N504AS
120279	RT	Deborah C Aharon	PT-SUZ N505AS [stored by Mar07 Hot Springs-Memorial Field, AR; Delta Connection c/s]
120280	ER	TAB Air Charter	PT-SVA N214SW PR-UHT ZS-TAA
120281	RT	AeroJet	PT-SVB N215SW D2-FDK+ [+ not confirmed]
120282	RT	Deborah C Aharon	PT-SVC N638AS VQ-T N638AS
120283	ER	Air Turks & Caicos	PT-SVD N639AS VQ-TBC
120284	ER	Skywest Airlines/United Express	PT-SVE N284YV
120285	ER	Skywest Airlines	PT-SVF N216SW
120286	ER	Skywest Airlines	PT-SVG N217SW
120287	ER	(Skywest Airlines/United Express)	PT-SVH N218SW [b/u for spares by 10Mar10 Springfield, MO, engineless hulk present; canx 18Jun10 as wfu]
120288	ER	CBG LLC/Key Lime Air	PT-SVI N220SW N366DC
120289	ER	N652CT LLC	PT-SVJ N289YV N652CT
120290	ER	Skywest Airlines/United Express	PT-SVK N221SW
120291	ER	Skywest Airlines/United Express	PT-SVL N223SW
120292	ER	Royal Air Charter	PT-SVM N292UX 9J-RYL N292UX 9J-RYL
120293	ER	Great Lakes Airlines	PT-SVN N293UX
120294	ER	Skywest Airlines/United Express	PT-SVO N224SW
120295	ER	SETE Linhas Aereas	PT-SVP N295UX PR-STE
120296	ER	Swift Flite	PT-SVQ N226SW ZS-NKE
120297	ER	Great Lakes Airlines	PT-SVR N297UX
120298	ER	(Wells Fargo Bank)	PT-SVS N298YV [stored Sep99 Hayward Executive, CA; l/n Jun07; later b/u; canx 30Apr09]
120299	ER	Great Lakes Airlines	PT-SVT N299UX
120300	ER (QC)	ex InterBrasil Star	PT-SVU PP-ISC [stored Jan02 Sao Paulo-Congonhas, Brazil; l/n 06Mar11]
120301	ER	Skywest Airlines	PT-SVV N301YV
120302	ER	Air Amazonia	PP-PSA
120303	ER	Passaredo Transportes Aereos	PP-PSB
120304	ER	RusLine, Russia	PT-SVW N227SW VQ-BCL
120305	ER	Skywest Airlines/United Express	PT-SVX N229SW
120306	ER	Team Aero	PT-SVY N232SW N597M
120307	ER	Skywest Airlines/United Express	PT-SVZ N233SW
120308	ER	Skywest Airlines/United Express	PT-SXA N234SW
120309	ER	Brazilian Air Force	PT-SXB (N309UX) PT-SRB 2010 [C-97]
120310	ER	Skywest Airlines/United Express	PT-SXC N235SW
120311	ER	Brazilian Air Force	PT-SXD (N311UX) PT-SRC 2011 [C-97]
120312	ER	Skywest Airlines/United Express	PT-SXE N236SW
120313	ER	Brazilian Air Force	PP-PSC 2020 [C-97]
120314	ER	Charter Air Transport	PT-SXG N237SW N659CT
120315	ER	Brazilian Air Force	PT-SXH PT-SRD 2012 [C-97]
120316	ER	Menard	PT-SXI N288SW N591M
120317	ER	Skywest Airlines/United Express	PT-SXJ N290SW
120318	ER	Mauiva-AC2 LLC	PT-SXK N291SW N660CT* [* marks reserved 04Sep12]
120319	ER	Skywest Airlines/United Express	PT-SXL N292SW
120320	ER	(Skywest Airlines/United Express)	PT-SXM N293SW [canx 09Mar09; b/u location unknown]
120321	ER	Skywest Airlines/United Express	PT-SXN N294SW
120322	ER	Skywest Airlines	PT-SXO N295SW
120323	ER	Embraer Finance	PT-SXP
120324	ER	Brazilian Air Force	PT-SXQ PT-SRE 2013 [C-97]
120325	ER	Skywest Airlines	PT-SXR N296SW
120326	ER	Skywest Airlines/United Express	PT-SXS N308SW
120327	ER	Skywest Airlines/United Express	PT-SXT N297SW
120328	ER	Mauiva Air Tours	PT-SXU N298SW N658CT
120329	ER	Skywest Airlines/United Express	PT-SXV N299SW
120330	ER	Aereo Calafia	PT-SXW N393SW XA-JVT

EMBRAER EMB-120 BRASILIA

C/n	Model	Last known Owner/Operator	Identities/fates/comments (where appropriate)						
120331	ER	Brazilian Air Force	PT-SXX	PT-SRG	1175+	PT-SRG	2014	[C-97]	[+ Colombia]
120332	ER	Brazilian Air Force	PT-MNF	2015	[C-97]				
120333	ER	Brazilian Air Force	PT-MNG	2016	[C-97]				
120334	ER	Skywest Airlines/United Express	PT-SZA	N560SW					
120335	ER	Skywest Airlines/United Express	PT-SZB	N561SW					
120336	ER	Skywest Airlines/United Express	PT-SXZ?	N562SW					
120337	ER	Brazilian Air Force	PT-SAD	2005	[C-97]				
120338	ER	Skywest Airlines/United Express	PT-SAB	N563SW					
120339	ER	Skywest Airlines/United Express	PT-SAC	N564SW					
120340	ER	Skywest Airlines/United Express	PT-SAI	N565SW					
120341	ER	Skywest Airlines/United Express	PT-SAF	N566SW					
120342	ER	Skywest Airlines/United Express	PT-SAL	N567SW					
120343	ER	Skywest Airlines/United Express	PT-SAZ	N568SW					
120344	ER	Skywest Airlines/United Express	PT-SBY	N569SW					
120345	ER	Skywest Airlines	PT-SBZ	N576SW					
120346	ER	Skywest Airlines/United Express	PT-SCA	N578SW					
120347	ER	Skywest Airlines/United Express	PT-SCB	N579SW					
120348	ER	Skywest Airlines/United Express	PT-SCC	N580SW					
120349	ER	Skywest Airlines/United Express	PT-SCZ	N581SW					
120350	ER	Skywest Airlines/United Express	PT-SDC	N582SW					
120351	ER	Skywest Airlines/United Express	PT-SEF	N583SW					
120352	ER	Skywest Airlines/United Express	PT-SEG	N584SW					
120353	ER	Skywest Airlines/United Express	PT-SEH	N585SW					
120354	ER	Skywest Airlines/United Express	PT-SEJ	N586SW					
120355	ER	Brazilian Air Force	PT-SGO	YV-667C	PR-EBE	2018	[C-97]		
120356	ER	Brazilian Air Force	PT-SHK	YV-602C	PR-EBC	2019	[C-97]		
120357	ER	Brazilian Air Force	PT-SOJ	T-500(1)+	PT-SOJ	2017	[C-97]	[+ Angolan Air Force ntu]	
120358	ER	Companhia Vale do Rio Doce	PT-SOK	T-501+	PT-SOK	[+ Angolan Air Force ntu]			
120359	ER	(Angolan Air Force)	PT-SOL	T-500(2)	[w/o 14Sep11 Huambo, Angola]				

Unidentified

unkn	Atlant-Soyuz Airlines	RA-02853	[marks reported reserved 2008; assumed ntu]
unkn	Atlant-Soyuz Airlines	RA-02855	[marks reported reserved 2008; assumed ntu]
unkn	Aereo Calafia	XA-JVT	[reported 26Jan12 Cabo San Lucas, Mexico]

FAIRCHILD F-27

C/n	Model	Last known Owner/Operator	Identities/fates/comments (where appropriate)
1		(Fairchild Engine & Airplane Co)	N1027 [prototype ff 12Apr58; w/o 09May58 in ground accident Hagerstown, MD]
1 (A)	A	(AREA Ecuador)	N1027 HC-ADV [reported built from parts of c/n 1; w/o 07Nov60 near Quito, Ecuador]
2		(Med Air International Sales)	N2027 XA-MOT N8687E N4303F N112TA [wfu 1982 Miami Airport, FL; b/u Sep84; canx 24May12]
3		(Mexican Navy)	N2701 N708WA N27CP N27WA MT-203+ MT-0206 [+ Mexico] [reported sold Jun92 to Aero Eslava, Mexico; never reported, assumed b/u]
4		(Air Manila International)	N2700R (PI-C870) PI-C892 (RP-C892) [wfu by 1977; b/u late 1977 Manila, Philippines]
5		(TAC Colombia)	N2702 HK-1492 [w/o 05Mar75 Barranquilla, Colombia]
6		(West Coast Airlines)	N2703 [w/o 17Jan63 Great Salt Lake, near Salt Lake City, UT; not canx until 18Sep09]
7		(Med Air International Sales)	N2704 HK-1493 [wfu 1982 Miami Airport, FL; b/u early 1992]
8		(Air Manila International)	N2701R (PI-C871) PI-C873 [w/o 09May68 Davao Airport, Philippines]
9		(Trans Nusantara Airways)	N2702R PI-C872 PK-EHF [wfu 1979 Jakarta-Kemayoran, Indonesia; probably b/u there]
10		(Air Manila International)	N2703R (PI-C873) PI-C875 [substantial damage 06Sep73 Daet Airport, Philippines; returned to Manila, Philippines & b/u by Sep75]
11		(Airlift International)	CF-QBA C-FQBA N273PH N273RD [wfs 1991; DBR 24Aug92 by Hurricane Andrew at Miami Airport, FL; b/u 1993]
12		(AVENSA)	YV-C-EVH [w/o 25Feb62 near Porlamar, Margarita Island, Venezuela]
13		(Pacific Alaska A/L)	YV-C-EVK N4304F C-GWRR N777DG [w/o 08Oct80 Fairbanks, AK; used to re-build c/n 18, hulk b/u 1982]
14		(International Air Service Establishment)	CF-QBZ C-FQBZ N271PH [b/u Sep1986 Las Vegas-McCarran International, NV]
15		(LASA) N4903	YV-65C [fate/status unknown; probably PWFU or b/u in El Salvador]
16		Aeronics Aircraft Parts	N2705 N707WA N101FG N235KT (PH-FFA) [stored Oct03 Palatka, FL; l/n 19May06; was due to be operated as part of the F.27 Friendship Association]
17		(Air Manila International)	N2704R PI-C874 RP-C874 [w/o 29Mar75 Baguio-Loakan Airport, Philippines; subsequently reported wfu 18Jly73 & stored 18Jly75 Manila; b/u there]
18		(Oceanair)	N2705R (PI-C873) PI-C893 RP-C893 PK-EHG N85084 [wfu 1982; b/u May87 San Juan, PR]
19		(Air Manila International)	N2706R (PI-C876) PI-C871 [w/o 08Mar68 in sea near Ibahay village, en-route Manila-Cebu, Philippines]
20		(Air Manila International)	N2707R (PI-C877) PI-C870 [w/o 14Apr69 Roscas, Philippines; reported b/u 1977 Manila, Philippines]
21		(Wien Air Alaska)	N4904 [w/o 30Aug75 Gambell Airport, St Lawrence Island, AK]
22		(Britt Airways/Air Mike Express)	N2706 N709WA N700BP (N27WA) HZ-TA2 HZ-SN5 N916 N386BA [wfs about 1991, l/n 05Dec88 Bloomington, IL in disrepair; probably b/u]
23	F	ex Aero Cozumel	N5G N27GC XA-CNI XA-RIS [wfu by Jun93; b/u 1994-1995 Merida, Mexico; fuselage only noted 23Mar94]
24		ex Britt Airways/Air Mike Express	YV-C-EVS N4703S N2708 N711TW N78L N444SL N385BA [wfs 14Jun92; ferried 24Jly92 Christchurch, New Zealand and b/u; hulk used by Air New Zealand Technical School; then fire training; l/n 09Feb10]
25		(Mexican Navy)	YV-C-EVP N4305F MT-205+ TP-0205//XC-UTB [dual marks] [+ Mexico] [w/o ??Apr88 Mexico City, Mexico]
26		ex Aeromorelos	YV-C-EVQ N2709 N707JR N555AJ N410BB N555AU TP-0745+ XA-LIW XA-MOR [+ Mexico] [wfs & stored Oaxaca, Mexico circa 1997/98; l/n 29Aug09]
27		(Air Atlantic Uruguay)	N994 CF-QBD C-FQBD N272PH N272RD HR-IAM N98MD (LV-WDM) CX-BRS [w/o Nov96 Guarani Airport, Paraguay; hulk l/n 21Apr06]
28	A	(Air Mauritanie)	N1500 N15001 (N2780R) N2740 N27PX 5T-CJY [w/o 14Mar79 Nouakchott, Mauritania]
29	A	(Bonanza Airlines)	N145L N745L [w/o 15Nov64 near Las Vegas-McCarran International, NV]
30	F	(LADECA)	N2781R XC-CAT AP-0203 N2815J N760L D-BFOK N760L N781R (N2781R) N3NR N9NB HR-IAH LV-WII CU-T129 YN-CER [stored by 30Nov96 Tamiami, FL; b/u by 07May03]
31	F	Museum of Mountain Flying	N1924 C-GJON N54506 N222DG [donated & preserved Mar03, Missoula, MT; canx 26Sep05; l/n 08Sep08]
32		(West Coast Airlines)	N3027 N2707 [w/o 24Aug63 Calgary, AB, Canada; canx 04Nov63]
33	F	Phillippi Equipment Co	N2709R N1004 161628+ N1004 N127HP [+ USN]
34	F	ex Aerosur, Linea Aerea Pampa	N65A HC-BGI CC-CNB LV-WDN [by Jly05 wfu Montevideo-Angel S Adami, Uruguay; l/n 17Oct08 in faded Pampa Linea Aerea c/s]
35	F	Joyce Jackson Ventrice	N1000L N291WX N768RL N432NA [GIA by Feb00 Durant-Eaker Field, OK]

FAIRCHILD F-27

C/n	Model	Last known Owner/Operator	Identities/fates/comments (where appropriate)
36	A	(Pacific Air Lines)	N2770R [w/o 07May64 near San Ramon, CA after both crew had been shot; canx 20Oct65]
37	J	Museo Nacional de Aeronautica	N146L N746L CC-CBS (CC-PKA) [derelict by Feb97 Santiago-Los Cerrillos, Chile; by 01Nov08 preserved fully restored]
38	J	(Hughes Airwest/Saudia)	N147L N747L [w/o 03Mar78 Jeddah, Saudi Arabia]
39	J	(Aeronor Chile)	N2708R CC-CBP [by 1986 stored Santiago-Los Cerrillos, Chile; b/u Jan90 when only fuselage present; l/n Jun91]
40		(Newair Services)	N5095A N2712 N5095A CF-QBE N3225 HK-1137 N3225 (SE-INB) LN-BSD OY-MUF LN-BSD OY-MUF LN-BSD OY-MUF [wfu by 12Sep00; b/u 2002 Billund, Denmark; canx 26Oct03]
41	J	(Rockwell International)	N200KC OB-M-950 N927 N64NR [canx Apr87; b/u Oct87, possibly at Burbank, CA, by Pacific Airmotive for spares]
42	J	(CATA Linea Aerea)	N1823A N184K N7444 N7677 D-BOSS LN-BSC N142TT SE-KLE N102FJ LV-RLB [wfu by Apr02 Moron, Argentina; l/n Oct07 in hangar, no engines]
43	J	(Transport Aerien Transregional)	N2771R EL-AHI N2771R F-GBRU [stored Oct92 Dinard, France; Oct93 used for spares; still current 2009]
44	A	(Transport Aerien Transregional)	N2772R EL-AHJ N2772R F-GBRV [wfu Apr93; b/u circa 1997 Dinard, France; l/n Apr97; canx 07Mar00]
45	F	(Med Air International Sales)	N25JM N258J N20H N20HE [b/u Mar91 Tucson, AZ; canx 26Apr91]
46		(Trans Nusantara Airways)	N5093A N2711 PI-C894 RP-C894 PK-EHJ [wfu 1979 Jakarta-Kemayoran, Indonesia; probably b/u there]
47		(Quebecair)	CF-QBL [w/o 29Mar79 Ancienne Lorette Airport, Quebec, QC, Canada]
48	J	(Ken Robertson Aero Tool)	N2712R N153L N753L C-GEGH N274PH (HR-) (YN-CER) (N48FA) [wfu 1991; b/u by late Apr03 Chino, CA; rear fuselage to El Mirage Hotel in Las Vegas, NV; by 02Mar12 remains to Aviation Warehouses, El Mirage, CA]
49	B	(Wien Consolidated Airlines)	N4905 [w/o 02Dec68 near Foxies Lake, on approach to Iliamna Airport AK, in severe turbulence]
50		(Trans Nusantara Airways)	N5094A N2710 PI-C895 RP-C895 PK-EHK [wfu 1981 Jakarta-Kemayoran, Indonesia; probably b/u there]
51	A	(North American Aircraft)	N2773R CF-GVL SE-IGZ N724US [by 1987 stored Las Vegas-McCarran International, NV; probably b/u]
52	J	ex Kelowna Flightcraft Group	N2774R C-GCRA N3180D C-GCRA [stored May95 Kelowna, BC, Canada; canx 07Apr98; l/n 10Oct04 derelict still with Norcanair titles; later with no reg'n/titles; l/n 07Aug08]
53	J	(Les Ailes de l'Ile)	N2775R CF-GZJ C-FGZJ [stored by Apr04 Toluca, Mexico; wfu Mar06; derelict l/n Jun10]
54	A	(Bonanza Airlines)	N200R N157L N757L [w/o 16Apr65 Las Vegas-McCarran Airport, NV]
55	A	(Aeronor Chile)	N2710R CC-CBR [w/o 20Apr79 Iquique-Cavancha Airport, Chile]
56	F	(Aerogal)	N42N N42NL N28FA HC-BSL [wfu 13Nov03 Quito, Ecuador; l/n Apr07]
57	F	(Aerocaribe)	N270L N27C N46K N79MD N790D D-BDFD N2786J N380BA XA-RUK [wfu Mar00 Flores/Santa Elena, Guatemala; reported b/u]
58		(Wonderair)	N4300F N113TA N113SB N158WC N113AS N158WQ 9Q-CST ZS-LPI [DBF 07Sep84 Omega AFB, Namibia; canx 09Oct84]
59		(Aero Cozumel)	N4301F N49UC N49CC XA-MIL [not active since at least 2002; fate unknown but possibly b/u Cozumel, Mexico]
60		(Donald S Burns)	N4302F [b/u during 1991 Tucson, AZ]
61		(Britt Airways/Air Mike Express)	N27R N2742 N25YC N255C N16FB N382BA [wfu Jun92 Guam; probably b/u there]
62	A	(Aero Cozumel)	N148L N748L 5T-CJT N45611 N500TE XA-NAP [stored 1988 Cozumel, Mexico; wfu by early 90s; probably b/u there]
63	J	(Aeronor Chile)	N149L N749L CC-CJE [w/o 09Dec82 La Serena, Chile]
64	F	(AIRES Colombia)	N270VR HK-3637X [wfu Apr96 Bogota, Colombia; b/u Jun98]
65	J	(CATA Linea Aerea)	N150L N750L 5T-CJU N4798W N280PH LV-PAD LV-AZW [wfu 2002 and b/u; fuselage to La Montaza Technical Institute Buenos Aires-Jorge Newbury, Argentina; l/n 20Apr08]
66	F	(Trygon Ltd)	N42Q CF-PQI C-FPQI 3C-QQB(1) [stored 11Jun00 Southend, UK; b/u between early Jly00 & late Aug00]
67	F	(General Avn Services)	N12500 YV-P-APZ YV-O-CFO-1 N108AS [reported b/u May90 for spares Seattle-King County-Boeing Field, WA; but later fuselage reported off airport at Memphis, TN in fore training area; canx 03Jan11]

FAIRCHILD F-27

C/n	Model	Last known Owner/Operator	Identities/fates/comments (where appropriate)
68	J	(Aero Continente)	N991 N5503L N267AB N276AB N276BT SE-IPE HK-3375X HK-3617X N276BT HK-3735X OB-1589 [stored 09Jun03 Opa-Locka, FL; l/n 16Oct06; assumed later b/u]
69	J	(Aero Continente)	N1027 N31LG N31HG SE-INA HK-3374X N43675 HK-3799X N43675 OB-1591 [wfu Aug97, stored Lima, Peru; canx 08Feb00; l/n circa 2002, assumed b/u]
70	J	(CATA Linea Aerea)	N1X N620M N6200S N758L F-OCZB F-BXAB TR-LVE S9-TAB N279PH LV-AZV [wfu by Apr02 Moron, Argentina; l/n 09Apr04]
71	F	ex Aerogal	N1100L N292WX N906L N870H N870HA HC-BSV [wfu by 13Nov03 Quito, Ecuador; l/n Apr07]
72		(Aerovias de Oaxaquenas)	CF-LWN N225 SE-IEG N225 N311NA N311RD [reported Aug92 stored Oaxaca, Mexico; possibly still present on 29Aug09]
73		(West Coast Airlines)	N5096A N2712 [w/o 10Mar67 Stukel Mountain, near Klamath Falls Airport, OR; canx 25Aug70]
74	F	ex Nexus Aviation	N38N N3802 N2614 5A-DBF N2614 HZ-PL2 F-GEXZ F-WQJQ 5N-CAF [grounded Mar04 by Nigerian CAA; noted wfu 27Jun05 Ibadan, Nigeria; l/n Oct06]
75		(TAC Colombia)	N5097A HL5205 N5097A HK-1139 [w/o 05Feb72 en route to Valledupar, Colombia]
76	J	(Kansas Air Investments)	N2713R N2X N630M N6301 N2709R CC-CBQ N7086J CC-PMP N7068J [wfu by 21Apr95 Ottawa, KS still marked as CC-PMP; b/u Dodson Parts, Rantoul, KS; hulk l/n Jly05]
77	J	(Transportes Aereos Coyhaique)	N151L N751L CC-CJF [wfu by 1987; bare hulk Mar96 Santiago, Chile]
78	J	ex CATA Linea Aerea	N152L N752L N278PH LV-PAG LV-RBO [airline suspended operations early 2004; reported stored in hangar Moron, Argentina]
79	F	(Air Corse)	N2714R (N1911B) N1911G N1823L F-GFHZ [w/o 22Sep89 Toulon-Hyeres, France; hulk moved to Nantes, France; l/n 14Feb99]
80		(TAC Colombia)	N5098A HL5203 N5098A (HK-1140) [wfu Sep70 and b/u 1987 Marana, AZ; Dec91 fuselage to Quartzsite, AZ; by Apr95 at El Mirage, CA; l/n 02Mar12]
81		(THY Turk Hava Yollari)	N2715R TC-KOC [w/o 10May72 Istanbul, Turkey; Jly74 remains to Air International Inc]
82		(Coronado Aircraft Corp)	TC-KOD N90713 EC-CPO+ [wfu 06Sep85 to GIA Valencia, Spain; + false marks; by Mar89 wore both marks N90713/EC-CPO; by 02Nov03 fuselage only at technical school at Cheste near Valencia, Spain]
83		(THY Turk Hava Yollari)	TC-KOP [w/o 08Mar62 Taurus Mountains near Adana-Sakirpasa Airport, Turkey]
84	F	Aerolineas Sosa	N2716R N1410 CF-PQH C-FPQH 3C-QQA HR-ASR
85	J	(Air Service Nantes)	N172C F-GDXY [b/u Jun89 Nantes, France; fuselage only reported Jun92 Paris-Le Bourget, France]
86		(Land Air Sales & Leasing Inc)	TC-KOR N90709 [b/u Apr74 Istanbul, Turkey]
87		ex Aeromorelos	TC-KOZ N90708 9Q-CKH N855TA XA-MOW [by Dec92 stored Cuermavaca, Mexico; by May05 derelict, in use as fire trainer; l/n 24Aug09]
88	F	(Agricultural Investors Corp)	N9090 RP-C890 [wfu by Oct84 Manila, Philippines; l/n 11Apr91, no engines]
89	F	(Westex Airlines)	N27C N472SP CF-SHA N4425B C-FVQE [by 26Sep06 derelict Powell River, BC, Canada; canx 05Jly07 as wfu]
90	F	(Aerocaribe)	N2719R AP-0204+ XC-COX TP-204//XC-UTC+ XA-MCJ [+ Mexico] [b/u Jun93 Merida-Manuel Crescencio Rejon International, Mexico]
91	A	(International Turbine Service)	N154L N754L F-OCVZ N2234U N712AB [stored by 19Sep98 Tamiami, FL; l/n 01Feb99]
92	A	(UNI Air International)	N2719R N155L N755L F-OCVY F-GIPD [stored by Jly91 Toulouse, France; b/u between Apr95 & 1997]
93	J	(Aerocaribe)	N2720R N16R N1689 N27W N27WC HZ-BOF N383BA XA-RJO [wfu by Jan01 Cozumel, Mexico, minus parts; probably b/u]
94	F	Myanmar Air Force	N2721R N227W CF-BNX N88973 RP-C5130 N1353T 5006 [in 1982 wore both marks N1353T/5006; by 1993 stored Mingaladon, Myanmar]
95	F	Atlantic Airlines	N2722R N44R N270E CF-QYP C-FQYP N19FF HR-ATI [possibly w/o 14Dec07 La Ceiba, Honduras]
96	J	(Australian Aircraft Sales)	N2723R N227K N228X PK-VFM [b/u Sep87 to Nov87 Sydney-Kingsford Smith, Australia]
97	F	Idaho State University	N2724R (N9060) N2724R N20W N366SB [by Dec00 stored North Las Vegas Airport, NV; l/n 22Apr06; donated 21Jan09 by Sunbelt Communications as GIA; arrived 26Sep06 Pocatello, ID]
98	J	ex Air Cortez International	N2725R N156L N756L F-OCYA N2708B [wfu Aug88 Ontario, CA; used for fire training; l/n 24Oct07]

FAIRCHILD F-27

C/n	Model	Last known Owner/Operator	Identities/fates/comments (where appropriate)
99	F	Alas Del Sur	N2726R N630TL N630TE CC-CAS N990H CX-BRT CP-2479 [hard landing 03Apr07 Riberalta, Bolivia; by 14Apr07 ferried to Santa Cruz, Bolivia & possibly stored as damage greater than first thought; l/n 29Jun08]
100	F	ex Aerocaribe	N2727R N471SP N384BA (F-GIPB) N384BA XA-RPM [wfu by 1995 Merida-Manuel Crescencio Rejon International, Mexico; used for fire training with titles C.R.E.I. (= Cuerpo de Rescate y Extincion de Incendios); later dumped in trees]
101	F	(Air Service Nantes/AVIACSA)	N2728R N3M N5963R F-GHXA [w/o 10May90 near Tuxtla Gutierrez, Mexico]
102	J	(Aero Sudpacifico)	N2729R N63M N58694 F-GHXB XA-RMB [wfu by Dec95 Mexico City-Benito Juarez International, Mexico; later b/u]
103	J	(Air Guadeloupe)	N2730R N2776R F-BFQQ TR-LWB F-GBRR F-OGJB (SE-KLF) (F-GGZP) [wfu Aug90 Dinard, France; l/n Apr00; probably b/u]
104	A	(North Canada Air)	N2731R N2777R CF-TPA C-FTPA [w/o 29Jun82 Wollaston Lake Airport, SK, Canada; moved late 1980s to Saskatoon Airport, SK, Canada; used for fire training; l/n Jun08]
105	J	(AIRES Colombia)	N2732R N2778R F-OCXI N725US HK-3356X HK-3895X [wfu by 09Sep94 Bogota, Colombia; probably b/u]
106	A	(US Aircraft Sales)	N2733R N2779R F-OCXJ N726US [wfu 1986 Las Vegas-McCarran International, NV; probably b/u; canx 12Jun91]
107	A	(Aero Stock)	N2734R N4306F N1782 F-GBRT F-OGJC [wfu by Jan93 Paris-Le Bourget, France; probably b/u]
108	A	(Transport Aerien Transregional)	N759L F-OCZC F-BXAA TR-LVF F-GBRS [w/o 05Jly79 Paris-Orly, France; removed to Dinard, France; b/u 1980]
109	F	(General Avn Services)	N2700J CF-IOG C-FIOG N550GA [by Oct90 wfu Greenwood, MS; b/u 1993; canx 09Dec96]
110	F	(Spa Aviation)	N966P C-GQCM N19HE 8Q-AEQ 8Q-SPA [canx 06Jan08 fate/status unknown]
111	M	(Lloyd Aereo Boliviano)	N2701J CP-1116 [derelict by Nov94 Cochabamba, Bolivia; l/n 08Apr03; assumed b/u]
112	J	(Air Corse)	N1823G F-GGSZ [stored by 1994 Nantes, France; b/u in 1998]
113	J	(Great Northern Airways)	N2702J CF-GND [w/o 12Jun68 Resolute Bay, NU, Canada]
114	J	(Great Northern Airways)	N2703J CF-GNG [w/o 20Dec69 Inuvik, NT, Canada]
115	J	(ex Cara Express Aviation)	N2704J D-BOOM N381BA (F-GIAP) (9M-SSN) D-BCEA [wfu circa 1992 Cologne/Bonn, Germany; by 2003 used for fire training marked "D-CGN01"; b/u Mar12]
116	J	(Aerolineas Uruguayas)	N2705J HR-LAP N275PH CX-BPP [wfu by Mar96 Montevideo, Uruguay; l/n 15Apr95; gone by 04Jun01; b/u]
117	J	ex UNI Air International	N2706J F-ODBY F-GIHR [by stored Jun96 Dinard, France; canx 16Jly96 as wfu; l/n 27Aug07; not reported 30May10]
118	M	(Lloyd Aereo Boliviano)	N2707J CF-GNJ N2707J CP-1117 [w/o 02Jun80 Tapecua Hills, near Yacuiba Airport, Bolivia]
119	J	(Islena Airlines)	N2708J CP-1176 N277PH N277RD HR-IAN [wfu Dec96 Opa-locka, FL; b/u by 1998]
120	J	(Air Mindanao)	N2709J CF-IJI C-FIJI N2709J N4914M RP-C5138 [b/u circa 1986 Manila, Philippines]
121	M	(Lloyd Aereo Boliviano)	N2710J CP-1175 [DBF and w/o 23Jan80 Yacuma, Bolivia]
122	J	Petroecuador	N994 HC-BHD [wfu by 27Jun10 Quito, Ecuador]
123	F	(Eastex) N27W	[w/o 04May68 Paisano Ranch, near Bruni, TX; canx 17May68]
124	J	(United Air Express)	N516T F-GGKF 5N-ARL [derelict by 1998 Lagos, Nigeria; l/n 05Sep03; probably b/u]
125	F	(Stanair)N?	(N413E) CF-PAP [w/o 08Feb69 Mikaa Lake, near Fort McMurray, AB, Canada]
126	J	ex Afrijet Airlines	N517T F-GDXT 3C-ZZE 5N-FRJ [reported stored Lagos, Nigeria]
127	M	(Lloyd Aereo Boliviano)	N2736R CP-862 [w/o 16Mar84 El Pilon Hill, near San Borja-Capitan G Q Guardia Airport, Bolivia]
128	M	(Airlift International)	N2737R CP-863 N276PH N276RD [stored by Jun91 Miami, FL; b/u 15Oct93]

Production complete

SEE FAIRCHILD FH227 FOR UNIDENTIFIED AIRCRAFT

FAIRCHILD-HILLER FH-227

C/n	Model	Last known Owner/Operator	Identities/fates/comments (where appropriate)
501	E	Myanmar Air Force	N2227L N2657 N2657 0001 [prototype; ff 27Jan66; report w/o 21Jun93 incorrect]
502		(Peruvian Air Force)	N2227F N518T N518TA OB-M-1221 395 (N7171J) [stored by Sep94 Lima, Peru; l/n 23Oct03; probably b/u]
503	E	ex Islena Airlines/Bamiyan Airlines	N7801M HR-IAU [stored by 26Sep99 Tehran, Iran; l/n 07Dec02; report of probably being 6-9704 Iranian Air Force now thought to be false, see c/n 566]]
504	C	(Airlift International)	N374NE N374RD [wfu by Jly91; b/u 15Oct93 Miami, FL]
505	E	(Ireland Airways)	N7802M PP-BUK N7802M CF-NAI C-FNAI SE-KBP EI-CLF [stored by 04Apr99 Dinard, France; b/u; canx 16Apr01]
506	C	ex Aerocaribe	N375NE XA-SDB XA-TIS+ [+ not fully confirmed; aircraft with these marks dumped at Hermosillo, Mexico; l/n 2005]
507	C	(Aerocaribe)	N376NE XA-RUL [wfu by Mar01 Merida-International, Mexico; l/n 11Apr05; b/u]
508	E	(Canadian Airlines International)	N7803M CF-NAJ C-FNAJ [wfu and b/u by 1992 Red Deer, AB, Canada]
509	E	(Transport Aerien Transregional)	N7804M C6-BDV F-GCFC [stored by Oct93 Dinard, France; canx 11Jun97 as wfu; probably b/u]
510	C	(Aerocaribe)	N377NE XA-RSV [damaged 13Mar92 Acapulco, Mexico; temporarily repaired & ferried 13Jun92 to Merida-International, Mexico for spares use; b/u]
511	E	(Petroecuador)	N7805M HC-AYM [w/o 17Jan02 El Tigre region, Ecuador, en-route Quito-Lago Agrio, Ecuador]
512	C	(Aerocaribe)	N378NE XA-RXR [stored Apr93 Merida-International, Mexico; l/n 24Nov98; b/u]
513	B	(Ozark Air Lines)	N4215 [w/o 23Jly73 near St Louis-Lambert International, MO]
514	B	(Servicios Operativos Aereos)	N4216 C-GMAL N4216 XA-RUN [stored by 1995 Monterrey, Mexico; probably b/u by 31Dec98]
515	D	(Lancing Community College)	N7806M [wfu by Aug94 Lansing, MI; to GIA; b/u 27-29Jun02]
516	C	(Aerocaribe)	N379NE XA-RPP [stored by Mar92 Merida-International, Mexico; use of tape to create false marks XA-PPF & XA-PIF at different periods; b/u there]
517	C	(Northeast Airlines)	N380NE [w/o 25Oct68 Moose Mountain, near Lebanon, NH]
518	B	(Bahamasair)	N7807M C6-BDQ [w/o 31Jly78 Berry Islands, Bahamas; 12Oct78 remains to Charlotte Aircraft Corp as N7807M; canx Feb83]
519	D	(Iona National Airways)	(N701U) N2735R CF-NAK C-FNAK SE-KBR EI-CAZ [stored Mar93 Norwich, UK; canx 15Dec94; on fire dump by Oct96; l/n 26Jan06; b/u]
520	B	(United Air Express)	N4217 F-GCLQ 5N-BMK [wfu by Nov03 Abuja, Nigeria; probably b/u]
521	B	(Servicios Operativos Aereos)	N4218 XA-RUM [stored by Jun95 Monterrey, Mexico; probably b/u by 31Dec98; but also reported late 2009 in use as a fire trainer]
522	B	(TABA)	N7808M VP-BDL C6-BDL F-GCFD PT-LCS [w/o 25Jan93 near Altamira, Brazil; canx 24Aug94]
523	B	(Air Service Company)	N702U EP-AMJ [w/o 25Feb78 Abadan, Iran]
524	B	Tehran Aerospace Exhibition Center	N701U EP-AMI EP-SNA [preserved by Mar00 Tehran, Iran; l/n Feb06 in poor condition]
525	B	(Pan Adria Airlines)	N7809M YU-ALA [w/o 18Jun77 Zagreb, Yugoslavia]
526	B	(United Air Express)	N4219 F-GCPV 5N-BMO [wfu by Dec94 Lagos, Nigeria; l/n Mar03 poor condition; probably b/u]
527	B	(United Air Express)	(N703U) N4221 F-GCLN 5N-BKO [wfu by Dec94 Lagos, Nigeria; l/n Mar03 poor condition; probably b/u]
528	B	ex TABA	N7810M YU-ALB N851TA PT-LBF [airline suspended operations 2001; fate unknown]
529	B	ex Atlantic Airlines de Honduras	N4220 HK-1981X HK-1981 F-GDAH C-GNDH SE-KGA OY-EBA N529LE HR-ARZ [probably wfu by 2002, stored La Ceiba Airport, Honduras; l/n Sep07]
530	B	ex ACE Transvalair	(N704U) N703U F-GCJO [stored 22Feb98 Dinard, France; l/n 06Sep10]
531	B	(Mohawk Airlines)	N7811M [w/o 19Nov69 Mount Pilot near Glens Falls, NY]
532	B	(Uni-Air)	N7812M YU-ALC N852TA F-ODMP F-GGDM [w/o 10Apr89 near Valence, France]
533	B	ex Austro Aereo	N7813M YU-ALD N853TA F-ODMR F-GGPN F-WQFK HC-BXC [stored by 23Sep06 Cuenca, Ecuador; l/n 13Feb08]
534	B	(Concord Airlines)	N7814M YU-ALE N854TA OO-DTE F-WFBH 5N-ATL [w/o 01Apr90 Lagos, Nigeria; by Jan92 b/u for spares]
535	B	(Transport Aerien Transregional)	N4222 F-GCPX [stored by Dec92 Dinard, France; l/n Oct93; canx 11Jun97 wfu; probably b/u]
536	B	(TABA)	N7815M G-SKYA PT-LBV [w/o 12Jun82 Tabatinga, Brazil; canx]
537	B	(TABA)	N7816M LN-KAA F-GBRZ PT-LCT [canx 03Sep91 as wfu; fate unknown]
538	B	(Transport Aerien Transregional)	N4223 F-GCPY [stored by Dec92 Dinard, France; canx 11Jun97; l/n 04Apr99 wfu; probably b/u]

FAIRCHILD-HILLER FH-227

C/n	Model	Last known Owner/Operator	Identities/fates/comments (where appropriate)
539	B	(TABA)	N7817M G-SKYB PT-LBG [wfu Belem, Brazil; l/n May04 in very bad condition; probably b/u by 2007]
540	B	(Iran Aseman Airlines)	N704U EP-AMR [probably wfu circa 1993; fate unknown]
541	B	(Mohawk Airlines)	N7818M [w/o 03Mar72 near Albany Airport, NY]
542	B	ex Atlantic Airlines de Honduras	N7819M (G-SKYC) 5T-CJZ N4716Z N101FG N155JB HR-ASK [wfu due to corrosion by 05May05 La Ceiba Airport, Honduras; l/n 26Jly07]
543	B	(United Air Express)	N4224 F-GCGH 5N-BAH [wfu by Dec94 Lagos, Nigeria; l/n Feb03; probably b/u]
544	B	ex Sahara Airlines	(N705U) N4225 F-GCLM 7T-VVJ [airline ceased operations 2003; by 04Dec04 wfu Algiers, Algeria; l/n 05Nov07]
545	B	(Burmese Air Force)	N705U 5002 [w/o 24Jan80 Mandalay, Burma]
546	B	(Transport Aerien Transregional)	N4226 F-GCPS [w/o 04Mar88 Pamfou, near Fontainebleau, France]
547	B	(Transport Aerien Transregional)	(N706U) N4227 F-GCPT [stored by Aug96 Dinard, France; canx 11Jun97 wfu; probably b/u]
548	B	(Transport Aerien Transregional)	N4228 F-GCPU [stored by Jun92 Dinard, France; canx 11Jun97 wfu; probably wfu]
549	B	Myanmar Air Force	N708U 5004
550	B	(ACE Transvalair)	N4229 F-GCLO [CofA expired Nov93; wfu Caen, France; l/n Aug95; canx 12Aug96; probably b/u]
551	B	(Aerolineas Regionales)	(N709U) N4230 OO-DTA CX-BQU [wfu by Jan97 Montevideo-Carrasco, Uruguay; l/n Nov00; b/u by 04Jun01]
552	B	Myanmar Air Force	N709U 5003
553	B	(Aerolineas Regionales)	(N710U) N4231 OO-DTB 7P-LAH OO-DTB CX-BQT [wfu by Jan97 Montevideo-Carrasco, Uruguay; l/n 1999; b/u by 04Jun01]
554	B	Myanmar Air Force	N710U 5005
555	B	(ALM Antillean Airlines)	N4232 OO-DTD PJ-FHB [wfu by Apr92 Curacao, Netherlands Antilles; used for fire training; by May02 only small parts intact; l/n 02Oct04]
556	B	(Paraense Transportes Aereos)	N2737R PP-BUF [w/o 14Mar70 Baia do Guajara Bay near Belem, Brazil; canx]
557	B	(Piedmont Airlines)	N712U [w/o 10Aug68 Charleston, WV]
558	B	ex Air Inter Ivoire	N7820M XC-LPG XA-SQT N7820M 5N-BCB TU-TDC [never entered service; by 09Feb04 stored airworthy Abidjan, Ivory Coast; l/n 30Oct08]
559	B	(ALM Antillean Airlines)	N4233 OO-HTC OO-DTC PJ-FHA [wfu by Apr92 Curacao, Netherlands Antilles; used for fire training; 25Feb07 fuselage sunk near Watamula, Curacao for dive training]
560	B	(Iran Aseman Airlines)	N7821M C-GGHK EP-AMT [probably wfu; reported b/u location not noted]
561	B	(Transport Aerien Transregional)	N4234 F-GCPZ [DBF 23Mar91 Dinard, France; 02Nov93 fuselage reported on pole outside TAT facility; assumed later b/u]
562	B	(Sahara Airlines)	N7822M ZS-SWK F-GBRQ 7T-VVK [airline ceased operations 2003; assumed wfu somewhere in Algeria; no reports]
563	B	ex Angolan Air Force	N7823M ZS-JOZ (G-BEAI) T-40 [reported wfu; status/unknown]
564	B	(Legion Express)	N4235 F-GCLP C-GNDI SE-KGB OY-EBB N564LE [w/o 26Jly98 Keflavik, Iceland, whilst on ferry flight; b/u Nov00]
565	B	(TABA)	N2738R PP-BUG [stored by 27Jly94 Manaus, Brazil; later reported DBF, but no details]
566	B	Iran Army Aviation	N706U EP-AMS 6-9704+ [+ almost certain this serial by Sep99 at Tehran Aerospace Exhibition Center, Tehran, Iran; l/n Aug08; these marks were thought to be on c/n 503]
567	B	(CATA Linea Aereas)	N2739R PP-BUH LV-MGV [w/o 26Oct03 near Buenos Aires-Ezeiza, Argentina]
568	B	ex CATA Linea Aereas	N2742R PP-BUI LV-MGW [wfu by Jan01 Moron, Argentina; l/n 28Mar09 derelict]
569	B	(TABA)	N2740R PP-BUJ [w/o 28Nov95 near Santarem Airport, Brazil]
570	B	(TABA)	N227V N9NL EP-PAR N9NL PT-ICA [w/o 06Jun90 Altamira Airport, Brazil; canx 20Aug90]
571	D	(Transporte Aereo Militar Uruguayo)	N2741R N2744R FAU570 T570//CX-BHX [dual marks] [b/u by 15Apr95 Montevideo, Uruguay]
572	D	(Transporte Aereo Militar Uruguayo)	N2745R FAU571 T-571//CX-BHY [+ dual marks] [w/o 13Oct72 near El Tiburcio, Andes Mountains, Argentina en route Mendoza, Argentina-Santiago, Chile]
573	D	(AeroGal)	N2784R "T-571"+ N2784R HC-BUF [+ painted as T-571 Uruguay Air Force circa Apr92 Boeing Field, WA for film "Alive"; qv c/n 572; w/o 28Oct97 Ambato-Chachoan Airport, Ecuador]

FAIRCHILD-HILLER FH-227

C/n	Model	Last known Owner/Operator	Identities/fates/comments (where appropriate)
574	D	(Transporte Aereo Militar Uruguayo)	N2785R T-572//CX-BIM [dual marks] [wfu by Sep90 Montevideo-Carrasco, Uruguay; by 16Oct03 preserved as gate guardian; l/n 05Apr08; by 17Oct08 only wearing serial 572]
575	D	ex Afrijet Airlines	N2743R HK-1411W HK-1411 5N-BCC [stored by 2003 Lagos, Nigeria]
576	D	(Aerocaribe)	N2781R XC-SOP TP-202+ XC-UTB XA-NJI [+ Mexico] [wfu 24May03 Merida-International, Mexico; probably b/u]
577	D	(Aerocaribe)	N2782R XC-FIL TP-203+ XC-UTC XA-CZA [+ Mexico] [wfu by Mar01 Merida-International, Mexico; probably b/u]
578	D	Mexican Navy	N2783R XB-DOU+ TP-204^ XC-UTZ MT-125^ MT-216^ [+ marks XC-DOU also reported but no photo proof of these marks; ^ Mexico; note the Mexican history in doubt; stored by 1995 Mexico City, Mexico; probably b/u]
579	D	not completed	
Unidentified			
unkn			C-GGWB [reported 17Apr95 stored Las Vegas, NV; but these marks not on CCAR]
unkn		IACI Airlines	EP-SNE [reported 26Sep99 and Nov99 Tehran, Iran]
unkn			XA-TZS [reported 02Apr02 Hermosillo, Mexico]

Production complete

FMA IAe.50 GUARANI G-II

C/n	Model	Last known Owner/Operator	Identities/fates/comments (where appropriate)
00	IAe.50	ex Argentine Air Force	LQ-HER+ LV-X23 LV-X27 T-110(1)^ TX-110 LQ-JNG T-110 TX-01(2) T-121(2)# [+ fictitious marks; to c/n 1 then P-1; f/f 06Feb62 as FA1 Guarani I] [rebuilt as FA2 Guarani II, with c/n 00 and then back to P-1 again] [f/f 23Apr63 as IA-50B; wfu Aug94; displayed Tancacha, Argentina; l/n 2000; ^ assigned in error; # fictitious – painted on after donantion preservation]
01	IAe.50B	ex Argentine Air Force	LV-X30 TX-01(1) T-124 LQ-JLV T-124 + LV-AMC + T-124 + [also known as c/n PPS-1; + coded 293-14; stored in LMAASA factory Cordoba, Argentina; l/n Apr06]
02	IAe.50	(Argentine Air Force)	LV-X32+ T-112 [+ coded 293-02 for time] [also known as c/n PPS-2; w/o 02Dec75 Comodoro-Rivadavia, Argentina]
03	IAe.50	ex Argentine Air Force	T-111(1)+ LQ-JXN T-123(2) [+ coded 293-01 for period; GIA Parana, Argentina; b/u mid 05]
04	IAe.50	(Argentine Air Force)	T-113(1) 5-T-30 T-113 [coded 293-03 for period; w/o 11Oct74 Cutral-Co, Argentina]
05	IAe.50B	Museo de la Industria	T-114+ F-34+ [+ coded 293-04 for period; preserved late 04 Cordoba, Argentina, with early 2005 wings from c/n 13]
06	IAe.50B	Museo Nacional de Aeronautica	F-31 [coded 293-15 for period; last operational flight by type 07Jan07; preserved Moron, Argentina]
07	IAe.50	(Argentine Air Force)	T-115(1) [coded 293-05 for period; SOC Jun91]
08	IAe.50	(Argentine Air Force)	T-116 [coded 293-06 for period; SOC Apr94; displayed Universidad del Litoral, Oro-Verde, Argentina; DBF spring 2009, remains reported to Parana, Argentina for spares]
09	IAe.50B	ex Argentine Air Force	T-117(1) [coded 293-07 for period; SOC 1998; displayed outside Governor's residence, Crespo, Argentina; l/n Nov04]
10	IAe.50A	ex Argentine Air Force	T-118+ T-117(2) [coded 293-08 for period; SOC 1999; preserved on pole outside Aeroclub San Francisco, Cordoba, Argentina; l/n Nov04]
11	IAe.50B	(Argentine Air Force)	T-119 LQ-JZO T-119 [w/o 01Oct93 near Crespo, Argentina]
12	IAe.50	ex Argentine Air Force	T-120 [coded 293-10 for period; SOC 1990?; stored in garden in Cordoba, Argentina as part of private collection; l/n 25Mar04]
13	IAe.50B	(Museo de la Industria)	T-121(1) [coded 293-11 for period; SOC Oct94; DBF Cordoba, Argentina when set on fire by vandals in 2004; wings used in rebuild of c/n 05]
14	IAe.50B	ex Argentine Air Force	T-122 [coded 293-12 for period; SOC Apr99; displayed outside Aeroclub Argentino, San Justo, Argentina; l/n 21Mar12]
15	IAe.50	(Argentine Air Force)	T-123(1) [w/o 27May69 Pajas Blancas, Argentina]
16	IAe.50	(Argentine Air Force)	T-125 [w/o 10Oct83 near Cordoba, Argentina]
17	IAe.50	(Argentine Air Force)	F-32 [coded 293-16 for period; SOC Jun95; used for fire fighting practice at Parana, Argentina until destroyed in Oct00]
18	IAe.50	LMAASA	[static test frame]
19	IAe.50B	(Argentine Air Force)	F-33 [wfu Sep05 to GIA Parana, Argentina by Apr07; wings on dump by Jly09]
20	IAe.50	ex Argentine Air Force	VR-15 T-110(2) [wfu Jun06 & stored Parana, Argentina; l/n Jly09]
21	IAe.50	Museo Nacional de Aeronautica	AE-1001 LQ-JXY LV-JXY [wfu Jun93; initially preserved Buenos Aires-Aeroparque, Argentina then moved to Moron, Argentina; l/n 13Mar06]
22	IAe.50B	Coleccion Estancia Santa Romana	VR-16 T-129 [preserved Santa Romana, Argentina; l/n Apr06]
23	IAe.50B	(Argentine Air Force)	LQ-JZS LV-JZS T-112(2) [Oct94; DBF Aug02 during fire practice Parana, Argentina; hulk b/u mid-05]
24	IAe.50	Ministerio de Salud y Accion Social	LQ-MBS LV-MBS [wfu late 95; to GIA Cordoba, Argentina]
25	IAe.50	(Gobierno Provincia de Salta)	LQ-LAD LV-LAD [wfu following accident on 23Sep83 and used for static testing by LMAASA until b/u circa 1996]
26	IAe.50B	ex Argentine Air Force	T-126 [wfu in 1995; stored Parana, Argentina; Jun05 donated Municipio Diamante; l/n Apr07]
27	IAe.50	(LAER-Linea Aerea Entre Rios)	LQ-LAE LV-LAE [wfu Aug95 Parana, Argentina; by Apr09 on display Aero Club Parana]
28	IAe.50	ex Argentine Air Force	LQ-LAF+ LV-LAF T-114 (2) [+ marks not confirmed; SOC Jun95; on display Cordoba, Argentina; l/n 25Mar04]
29	IAe.50	(LAER-Linea Aerea Entre Rios)	LV-LAI [wfu Aug95; b/u 1997 Parana, Argentina]
30	IAe.50	(Argentine Air Force)	LQ-LAJ LV-LAJ T-113(2) [w/o 13Dec82 Buenos Aires-Aeroparque, Argentina]
31	IAe.50B	ex Argentine Air Force	LV-LAL T-127 [SOC 1995; to fire dump Cordoba, Argentina; l/n Sep05]
32	IAe.50	ex Argentine Air Force	LV-LAM T-111(2) [SOC 1990?; fuselage displayed at holiday camp in Santa Cruz del Lago, Argentina; l/n Jan98]
33	IAe.50B	Museo Nacional de Malvinas	(LV-LAN) T-128 [SOC Oct94; preserved Cordoba, Argentina; l/n Sep99]
34	IAe.50	ex Argentine Air Force	F-35 [preserved as gate guardian Parana, Argentina; l/n 2009]

Production complete

FOKKER F.27 FRIENDSHIP

C/n	Model	Last known Owner/Operator	Identities/fates/comments (where appropriate)
10101	100	Fokker Heritage Trust	PH-NIV [prototype ff 24Nov55; last flight 08Jun61; tt 850 hours; b/u 12Dec62 Amsterdam-Schiphol, Netherlands; Nov97 rear fuselage to Delft Technical University; 2005 preserved on loan to Aviodrome, Lelystad, Netherlands]
10102	100	Fokker Friendship Association	PH-NVF D-BAKI PH-NVF [on loan to Aviodrome, Lelystad, Netherlands]
10103			[static test airframe]
10104			[fatigue test airframe]
10105	100	Stichting Fokker Heritage Flight	PH-FAA EI-AKA PH-FSF ZK-NAH VH-NLS PH-FHF [canx 13Mar08 with expired CofA]
10106	100	(Swetrail Transport)	PH-FAB EI-AKB PI-C530 JY-ADD PH-FSH EC-BNJ D-BOBY(2) G-IOMA G-BMZI D-BAKO [spares use 1993/4; Apr96 used for fire practice Vasteras, Sweden; canx Jly96]
10107	100	(Chon Dal Inc)	PH-FAC EI-AKC PH-SAP EC-BFV N144PM [canx Jly96; b/u Aug96 Hernando County, FL]
10108	100	(Pilgrim Airlines)	PH-FAD LN-SUN EC-BPJ N148PM [w/o 13Jan84 New York-JFK Airport, NY]
10109	100	(White Industries)	PH-FAE EI-AKD PH-YFF D-BAKA(1) PH-YFF EC-BRN N143PM [spares use Hernando County, FL; canx 30Jly96; never reported at Bates City, MO]
10110	100	ex Transportes Aereos da Guinea-Bissau	PH-FAF EI-AKE PH-FSE ZK-NAF TS-LVA 8Q-CA006 206+ 805^ ST-SMM J5-GBA [+ Yemen; ^ Sudan; canx 01May92; derelict by 31Jan05 Algiers, Algeria; l/n 05Nov07]
10111	200	ex Guatemalan Air Force	PH-FAG VH-TFA P2-TFA P2-ANA TG-AIA 1094+ 1093 [+ Guatemala; by 08Feb06 wfu Guatemala City-La Aurora, Guatemala; l/n 23Nov07]
10112	100	(Trans Australia Airlines)	PH-FAH VH-TFB [w/o 10Jun60 near Mackay, QLD, Australia]
10113	100	(Flanders Airlines)	PH-FAI VH-TFC F-BYAP OO-SVL [by stored Feb92 Dinard, France; canx Jun95; l/n 30May10, in poor condition; gone by 06Sep10; probably b/u]
10114	100	ex Air Dabia	PH-FAK VH-TFD N1036P N141PM OB-1644 [derelict by 08Mar02 Banjul, Gambia; l/n Jly05]
10115	200	ex Philippine Air Force	PH-FAM 59-0259 [wfu Jan00 Villamor AFB, Pasay City, Manila, Philippines; l/n Jan01]
10116	100	ex Aerocondor	PH-FAL LN-SUO EC-BPK N145PM YV-929C OB-1627 [reported wfu 2009/2010 Lima, Peru and donated as GIA]
10117			[not built]
10118	100	(Aeronica)	PH-FAN EI-AKF PH-FSA ZK-NAA TS-LVB 8Q-CA007 204+ YN-BZF [+ Yemen; w/o 20Apr85 Kulusuk, Greenland]
10119	100	(Transportes Aereos da Guinea-Bissau)	PH-FAO EI-AKG PH-FSB ZK-NAB TS-LVC 202+ 8Q-CA002 8Q-PNA 866^ ST-EVF J5-GBB [+ Yemen; ^ Sudan; w/o 15Aug91 Don, Burkina Faso]
10120	100	(Air UK)	PH-FAP VH-TFE G-SPUD G-OMAN G-BLFJ [wfu Nov94; b/u Dec96 Norwich, UK; canx 06Jan97]
10121	100	(Trans Oceanic Traders)	PH-FAR VH-TFF N1036U F-GAOT OO-SVM F-WKPX [b/u Apr93 Rotterdam, Netherlands]
10122	100	(Chon-Dal Inc)	PH-FAS VH-TFG N300AS N142PM [stored Miami, FL; canx 01Aug96 as exported to Gambia but not delivered; l/n 27Sep97; probably b/u]
10123	100	(THY – Turk Hava Yollari)	PH-FAT TC-TEZ [w/o 17Feb70 Samsun Airport, Turkey]
10124	100	ex Myanmar Airways	PH-FAU TC-TON N47SB 5001(1)+ XY-AER(2) [+ Myanmar; stored by 18Nov05 Yangon, Myanmar; l/n Apr11]
10125	100	(TAAG Angola Airlines)	PH-FAV TC-TOY PH-FAV N48SB D2-FPH D2-TFK [b/u 01Jly86 Luanda, Angola]
10126	200	(Government of Iran)	PH-FAW EP-MRP [w/o 10Oct62 near Kouche, Iran]
10127	102A	Aviation Rotables Supply	PH-FAX VH-TFN VH-EWA F-BYAO F-WYAO F-BYAO [wfu by Jan04 Dinard, France; l/n Aug07; canx 12Feb10 as wfu; not reported 30May10]
10128			[not built]
10129			[not built]
10130			[not built]
10131	200	(Air UK)	PH-FAY VH-CAV G-STAN [wfu 02Apr96 Norwich, UK; b/u Dec96; canx 20Dec96]
10132	100	South Australian Aviation Museum	PH-FAZ VH-CAT [stored by Nov03 Adelaide-Parafield, SA, Australia; canx 27Jun06; l/n 19Dec07; preserved by 17Sep09 Port Adelaide, SA, Australia; l/n 15Feb10]
10133	200	ex Pakistan International Airlines	PH-FBA VH-FNA P2-ANJ PT-LCX AP-BDS [wfu by Jly05 Karachi, Pakistan; canx 31Mar06]
10134	200	ex Pakistan International Airlines	PH-FBB VH-TFI P2-TFI P2-ANB P2-ANZ N1036S (G-BMAR) PT-LGH AP-BDR [grounded Jly06; canx 18Jly06; reported for Pakistan Air Force for preservation; noted stored 11Dec07 Karachi, Pakistan]

FOKKER F.27 FRIENDSHIP

C/n	Model	Last known Owner/Operator	Identities/fates/comments (where appropriate)
10135	200	(Secretary of State for Scotland)	PH-FBC VH-TFJ P2-TFJ P2-ANC G-BLML G-SOFS [canx 03Dec91 PWFU; b/u Dec91 Southend, UK; remains to Stock Scrapyard, Essex, UK]
10136	200	ex Merpati Nusantara Airlines	PH-FBD VH-FNB PK-MFP [stored by Apr92 Surabaya, Indonesia]
10137	200	(WDL Flugdienst)	PH-FBE D-BATU(2) PH-FSD F-BRHL TN-ACR D-BAKU [b/u Jan94 Essen-Mulheim, Germany; canx Jan94; fuselage only l/n 21Jly96]
10138	200	Bolivian Army	PH-FBF VH-TFK P2-TFK P2-AND VH-TFK PH-FBF CP-2013 EB-91
10139	200	ex Expresso Aereo del Peru	PH-FBG (VH-TFL) VH-MMS OB-1454 [by Dec94 spares use Santiago-Benitez, Chile; l/n Mar96]
10140	300	(National Iranian Oil Co)	PH-IOK EP-IOK [blown up 20Feb86 near Ahvaz, Iran in bizarre re-enactment in front of international press of the reported shooting down of c/n 10554 q.v.]
10141	200	(Balair AG)	PH-IOP HB-AAI [w/o 13Sep64 Malaga, Spain]
10142	100	(Bali International Air Service)	PH-PBF PK-KFR [w/o 04Nov76 Banjarmasin, Indonesia]
10143	200	ex Merpati Nusantara Airlines	PH-FBH VH-FNC PK-MFR [stored by 13May92 Surabaya, Indonesia; l/n 08Nov92]
10144	200	(Comair)	PH-FBI VH-FND ZS-JVA [wfu by 10Sep96 Johannesburg, South Africa; b/u Jly97; canx 22Jly97]
10145	200	(Ansett Airlines of Australia)	PH-FBK VH-FNE [w/o 23Mar71 in hangar fire Melbourne-Essendon, VIC, Australia]
10146	200	(Ansett Airlines of Australia)	PH-FBL VH-FNF VH-MMO [wfu May90 Melbourne, VIC, Australia; canx 30May90; fuselage used by airport fire service; 22Jly99 fuselage removed to Adelaide International Airport, SA, Australia, fire service; l/n 15Feb10]
10147	100	(Philippine Airlines)	PH-FBM PI-C501 [w/o 28Feb67 Mactan-Cebu Airport, Philippines]
10148	200	(Philippine Air Force)	PH-FBN PI-C502 10148 [stored by Jly95 Villamor AFB, Pasay City, Manila, Philippines; b/u 1999; some parts used in repair of c/n 10327]
10149	100	Malaysian Airways Training College	PH-FBO C-2+ 3C-QSJ N32180^ [+ Netherlands; ^ canx 18Sep08 to Malaysia; to GIA Kuala Lumpur-Subang, Malaysia; l/n Oct09]
10150	100	Royal Netherlands AF Historic Flight	PH-FBP C-3+ PH-FBP* [+ Netherlands; stored by 1996 Woensdrecht, Netherlands pending restoration; l/n Sep09]
10151	300	National Iranian Oil Co	(PH-FRA) PH-IOS EP-IOS
10152	100	Air Tropiques	PH-FBR C-1+ ZS-OEH 9Q-CLN(2) [+ Netherlands]
10153	300	ex National Iranian Oil Co	(PH-FRB) PH-IOT EP-IOT [hijacked 29Nov93 to Basra, Iraq; abandoned there; l/n Aug03]
10154	300M	Imatong South Sudan Airlines	PH-FBS C-4+ ZS-OEJ TN-AGX TR-LGH 5Y-BTD [+ Netherlands; stored by Jun07 Nairobi-Wilson, Kenya; by 20Dec07 described as derelict; l/n 25Jly08]
10155	300M	(Safe Air Company)	PH-FBT C-5+ ZS-OEI 5Y-BRN [+ Netherlands; w/o 04Mar10 Bosaso, Somalia]
10156	300M	Africa Air Assistance	PH-FBU C-6+ C-GWXD J5-GBU C-GWXD J5-GIA [+ Netherlands; stored 2006 Dakar, Senegal]
10157	300M	(Royal Netherlands Air Force)	PH-FBV C-7 [b/u by Trygon Oct02; to Woensdrecht, Netherlands for spares; by Nov03 fuselage to Eindhoven, Netherlands for fire service training]
10158	300M	ex Royal Netherlands Air Force	PH-FBW PH-FSC C-8 [by Oct96 gate guardian Eindhoven, Netherlands; replaced 28Aug03 by c/n 10162 qv; to GIA there]
10159	300M	ex Royal Netherlands Air Force	PH-FBX C-9+ PH-KFA C-9 [+ Netherlands; b/u Oct02 by Trygon at Woensdrecht, Netherlands for spares; Apr09 fuselage to Der Kooji then Eindhoven, Netherlands]
10160	300M	Militaire Luchtvaart Museum	PH-FBY C-10 [preserved by 10Feb94 Soesterberg, Netherlands; dismantled Mar10 & moved Jun10 to Hoofdorp, Netherlands, for restoration as GIA]
10161	300M	ex Luft Cargo	PH-FBZ PH-KFB C-11+ PH-KFB C-11+ ZS-OEK [+ Netherlands; stored by 15Jun01 Wonderboom, South Africa; canx 24Jly02; l/n derelict 22Sep10]
10162	300M	ex Royal Netherlands Air Force	PH-FCA C-12 [wfu to GIA Sep96 Eindhoven, Netherlands; at one time marked "F-FICC" with titles "Air Fictief"; 28Aug03 became gate guardian there painted as "C-8"; see c/n 10157; l/n 12Jan10]
10163	200	(Pakistan International Airlines)	PH-FCB AP-ALM [w/o 06Aug70 Islamabad, Pakistan]
10164	200	(Pakistan International Airlines)	PH-FCC AP-ALN [w/o 05Jly94 Dera Ismail Khan Airport, Pakistan]
10165	200	(Pakistan International Airlines)	PH-FCD AP-ALO [w/o 25Jun64 Dhaka, Pakistan]
10166	100	(Burundi BCR Charter)	PH-FCE ZK-BXA PK-MFS ZK-BXA 9V-BLE PK-OBP OO-SVN 9U-BHE [stored by Sep98 Dinard, France; l/n 14Feb09 semi-derelict; former marks OO-SVN visible; not reported 30May10; probably b/u]
10167	100	(Laoag International Airlines)	PH-FCF ZK-BXB NZ2781+ RP-C3888 [+ New Zealand; wfu by Feb03 Manila, Philippines; b/u by May07]

FOKKER F.27 FRIENDSHIP

C/n	Model	Last known Owner/Operator	Identities/fates/comments (where appropriate)
10168	100	(President Airlines)	PH-FCG ZK-BXC NZ2782+ RP-C5888 XU-881 [+ New Zealand; stored by 2005 Phnom-Penh/Pochentong, Cambodia; gone by 21Dec10 presumed b/u]
10169	100	(Laoag International Airlines)	PH-FCH ZK-BXD NZ2783+ RP-C6888 [+ New Zealand; belly landing 06Dec95 Maclan, Philippines; ferried Laoag, Philippines & wfu Mar96; gone by 25Dec10, presumed b/u]
10170	200	(Pakistan International Airlines)	PH-FCI VH-FNG P2-ANK PT-LCY AP-BDP [wfu Oct99 Karachi, Pakistan; b/u for spares]
10171	100	(Indian Airlines)	PH-FCK VT-DMA [hijacked 31Jan71 & flown to Lahore, Pakistan; 02Feb71 blown up there]
10172	100	(Vayudoot Airlines)	PH-FCL VT-DMB [DBR 23Sep93 whilst taxiing Calcutta, (Kolkata) India; by Oct94 derelict no wings; canx 10Dec04]
10173	100	(Vayudoot Airlines)	PH-FCM VT-DMC CG710+ VT-DMC [+ India; w/o 19Oct88 Guwahati-Borjhar Airport, India]
10174	100	(Indian Airlines)	PH-FCN VT-DMD [w/o 24Jly76 Bhubaneswar, India]
10175	100	(Indian Airlines)	PH-FCO VT-DME [w/o 11Aug72 near Delhi-Palam, Airport, India]
10176	700	ex Australian Flyers	PH-FCP LN-SUG PH-FCP VH-TFH D-BEKU TF-FIP TF-FLP N146PM VH-JCC [b/u late 1999 Tamworth, NSW, Australia for spares; canx 22Oct02; hulk l/n 23Feb03]
10177	600P	TAM Museum	PH-FCR (JA8301) JA8601 PK-PFW PH-FCR PT-LAF [wfu & stored Oct00 Sao Paulo-Guarulhos, Brazil; Feb09 moved to Sao Carlos, Brazil for preservation]
10178	600P	ex Tavaj Linhas Aereas	PH-FCS (JA8302) JA8602 PK-PFX PH-FCS PT-LAH [stored by 07Jan06 Brasilia, Brazil; l/n 07Mar11]
10179	600	ex WDL Flugdienst	PH-FCT (JA8303) JA8603 P2-MNE P2-ANE TG-AEA PH-FCT ST-ALG PH-FCT F-GKJC D-BAKD SP-FNF D-BAKD [stored by 03Nov06 Cologne/Bonn, Germany; canx 13Nov08; l/n 03Jly11]
10180	200	(Ansett-ANA)	PH-FCU VH-FNH [w/o 17Mar65 Launceston, TAS, Australia]
10181	200	ex Aerocondor	PH-FCV VH-FNI ZS-KVI N863MA OB-1693 [by 19Apr05 stored Lima, Peru]
10182	100	(THY – Turk Hava Yollari)	PH-FCW TC-TAY [w/o 23Sep61 near Ankara, Turkey]
10183	400MAR	Piet Smedts Collection	PH-FCX TC-TEK PH-FCX [wfu Jan85; purchased Jun03 Autobedrijf Piet Smedts Collectie; by Jan06 fuselage on display Baarlo, Netherlands; l/n 12Jan10]
10184	100	Indian Institute of Aircraft Engineering	PH-FCY ZK-BXE VT-ROY [wfu Mar93 Bombay-Santa Cruz, India; derelict by 2001; 04Nov07 to GIA off airport, Delhi, India]
10185	100	(Laoag International Airlines)	PH-FCZ ZK-BXF RP-C8889 [wfu by 2006 Luang, Philippines; gone by 25Dec10 presumed b/u]
10186	300	(Air West Express)	PH-FDA D-BAKU PH-FSG D-BAKU(1) PH-FSG VH-MMB LN-NPH PH-SFE ST-AWA [w/o 23Mar93 nr Addis Ababa, Ethiopia]
10187	400	(Pakistan International Airlines)	PH-FDB AP-ALW [reported wfu Jan04 location & fate unknown; canx by 2004]
10188	200	(Pakistan International Airlines)	PH-FDC AP-ALX [w/o 12Dec71 near Iranian border, en-route Karachi – Zahedan, Pakistan]
10189	100	Ashburton Aviation Museum	PH-FDD ZK-BXG [wfu 31Mar90; used as office at Wigram, New Zealand Oct93 to Feb07; moved to Ashburton, New Zealand for preservation; l/n 23Nov08]
10190	100	ex Air New Zealand	PH-FDE ZK-BXH VH-EWH ZK-BXH [wfu Jly92; used as GIA Air New Zealand Engineering Training School, Christchurch, New Zealand; l/n 09Feb10]
10191	100	(Philippine Air Lines)	PH-FDF PI-C503 [w/o 12Oct62 nr Manila Airport, Philippines; reported parts used in re-build of c/n 10258 whilst PI-C512]
10192	200	(Sudan Airways)	PH-FDG (ST-AAQ) ST-AAA [w/o 25Mar91 Khartoum, Sudan]
10193	200	(Sudan Airways)	PH-FDH ST-AAR [w/o 02Jly85 Eldebba Airport, Sudan]
10194	200	(Sudan Airways)	PH-FDI ST-AAS [w/o 05Oct82 Merowe, Sudan]
10195	600	(WDL Flugdienst)	PH-FDK JA8605 PK-PFR (PH-KAJ) PH-FDK PT-ODM F-GFJS D-BAKC [wfu & stored Oct99 Cologne/Bonn, Germany; canx 13Nov08; b/u 17Jun11]
10196	600	City of Norwich Aviation Museum	PH-FDL JA8606 PK-PFS (F-GBRV) F-GBDK G-BHMY [CofA expired 02May99; canx 27Feb03 wfu; preserved Norwich, UK; l/n 04Sep07]
10197	600P	ex Tavaj Linhas Aereas	PH-FDM JA8607 PK-PFT PH-FDM PT-LAG [stored by 18Dec05 Curitiba, Brazil; l/n 13Apr09]
10198	100	(WDL Flugdienst)	PH-LIP D-BAKA(2) [stored Jan97 Essen-Mulheim, Germany; canx Jly97; fully b/u by 17Jun99]
10199	100	ex Uruguayan Air Force/TAMU	PH-FDN LN-SUW PH-FDN T-560/CX-BHV [dual marks] [wfu Nov96; b/u Jun99 Montevideo,Uruguay; 14Oct03 remains reported in scrapyard at Neptunia, Uruguay; l/n Sep09]

FOKKER F.27 FRIENDSHIP

C/n	Model	Last known Owner/Operator	Identities/fates/comments (where appropriate)
10200	200	(Business Flight Services)	PH-FDO (LV-PMP) (LV-PTO) D-BAKE(1) HB-AAU PH-KFC A2-ADG OY-BVH [wfu Aug92; b/u Dec95 Roskilde, Denmark; 06Jly96 remains to Copenhagen-Kastrup for use by fire service; l/n Apr03; canx 23Oct03]
10201	200	(Air UK)	PH-FDP (LV-PMR) (LV-PTP) JA8615 PH-OGA G-BCDN [wfs 15Oct95 & stored Norwich, UK; canx 28Jan98, fuselage used as cabin trainer; l/n 28Jun06]
10202	100	(Uruguyan Air Force/TAMU)	PH-FDR (LV-PMS) (LV-PTQ) LN-SUA PH-FDR T-561//CX-BHW [dual marks] [reported w/o or retired before 12Feb99 no details] [reported w/o or retired before 12Feb99 no details]
10203	200	ex Air Comores	PH-FDS (LV-PMT) JA8608 PK-PFU F-GBRX D6-CAI (F-GBRX) [by Apr94 stored Moroni-Hahaya, Comores; by 2012 hulk status]
10204	200	(Brasil Central Linha Aerea Regional)	PH-FDT CR-AIA C9-AIA N379SL PT-LCF [w/o 27Jan87 Varginha, Brazil]
10205	200	(DETA-Linhas Aereas de Mocambique)	PH-FDU CR-AIB [w/o 27Mar70 Lourenco Marques (now Maputo) Airport, Mozambique]
10206	200	(Brasil Central Linha Aerea Regional)	PH-FDV CR-AIC C9-AIC N379SF PT-LCG [w/o 12Feb90 near Bauru Airport, Brazil]
10207	200	(Pakistan International Airlines)	PH-FDW CR-LEO D2-LEO PH-FDW AP-BBF [w/o 25Aug91 in Himalayas near Gilgit, Pakistan]
10208	200	(Zaire Aero Service)	PH-FDX CR-LEP D2-LEP 9Q-CEB [reported wfu 1979; b/u Aug82 Kinshasa-N'Djili, Zaire]
10209	100	(Philippine Airlines)	PH-FDY PI-C504 [w/o 01Jly70 Dumaguete City, Philippines]
10210	200	(Philippine Air Force)	PH-FDZ PI-C506 10210 [reported w/o in 1997 Hukbong-Himpapawid NG, AFB Philippines; also reported crashed into sea]
10211	200	(Rwanda Airlines)	PH-FEA VP-KSA 5Y-AAB 9XR-RD [w/o 27Oct02 in Southern Sudan]
10212	200	ex Mesaba Airlines/Northwest Airlink	PH-FEB VP-KSB 5Y-AAC 5H-MRH G-BMAW N270MA [wfu Feb94; Jun94 to White Industries, Bates City, MO for spares; canx Feb97; l/n 25Apr07]
10213	200	(Kenya Airways)	PH-FEC VP-KSC 5H-AAI 5Y-BBS [w/o 10Jly88 Kisumu, Kenya; derelict fuselage reported 17Oct93 Nairobi, Kenya]
10214	100	(Indian Airlines)	PH-FED VT-DOJ [w/o 21Apr69 Daulatpur, near Khulna Airport, East Pakistan]
10215	100	(Vayudoot Airlines)	PH-FEE VT-DOK [wfu 08Jly90 Calcutta, India; canx 10Dec04; reported b/u 1996]
10216	200	(Nigeria Airways)	PH-FEF 5N-AAV [seized by Biafran Air Force; shot down 07Oct87 on a bombing raid against the Nigerian military headquarters near Ikoyi, Lagos, Nigeria]
10217	200	(Nigeria Airways)	PH-FEG "PH-AAW"+ 5N-AAW [+ painted as such in Schreiner c/s for photographs; w/o 25Apr77 Sokoto Airport, Nigeria]
10218	200	(Nigeria Airways)	PH-FEH 5N-AAX [w/o 04Apr71 Jos Airport, Nigeria]
10219	200	(Vayudoot Airlines)	PH-FEI VT-DOL [wfu 01Jan91 Calcutta, India; canx 10Dec04; reported b/u 1996]
10220	100	(Indian Coast Guard)	PH-FEK VT-DOM CG710 (VT-DOM) [wfu 31Dec93 Calcutta, India; l/n Oct94; b/u 1996]
10221	100	(Indian Coast Guard)	PH-FEL VT-DON CG711 (VT-DON) [wfu Dec93 Calcutta, India; l/n Jun99]
10222	200	(Trigana Air Service)	PH-FEM 5N-AAY PK-GRA PK-MFA PK-ZAF PK-YPU [by 25Oct06 b/u Jakarata-Halim Perdanakusuma, Indonesia]
10223	200	Trigana Air Service	PH-FEN 5N-AAZ PK-GRC PK-MFC (PK-CFY) PK-ZAY PK-YPA
10224	100	(Burlington Engineering)	PH-FEO LX-LGA F-GKPY [stored May93 Dinard, France; reported b/u 2000]
10225	200	ex Jersey European Airways	PH-FEP (VR-RCZ) 9M-AMI 9V-BAP PH-FEP G-BAUR [wfu Oct95; canx 25Jan96; b/u; fuselage only Exeter, UK for cabin services training; dumped on airfield by Jly01; used for fire training; l/n Jan09]
10226	200	(Sempati Air Transport)	PH-FER 9M-AMJ PK-JFK [damaged & stored 07Oct96 Singapore-Seletar; b/u 1998]
10227	200	ex Amazonia Linhas Aereas	PH-FES JA8616 F-OCSH F-BVTA G-BMAS OY-BST ZS-LMZ PT-WNB N877A PT-FPR [reported stored/wfu; status unknown]
10228	200	(Mesaba Airlines/Northwest Airlink)	PH-FET JA8617 F-BUFU 6V-AEG F-GCMA G-RNSY N267MA [canx 16May95; assumed b/u]
10229	200	(WDL Flugdienst)	PH-FEU JA8618 F-BUTA F-OGIF F-BSIF G-BHMW (PH-FFA) G-BHMW D-BAKK [wfu Jan98 Essen-Mulheim, Germany; b/u 17Jun99 for spares]
10230	200	ex Pakistan International Airlines	PH-FEV JA8619 F-OCSI F-BVTE AP-BAO [grounded Jly06 Karachi, Pakistan; canx 19Apr07; sold May07 to Pakistan Navy for spares]
10231	200	(Air UK)	PH-FEW 9M-AML 9V-BAQ PK-KFG G-BLGW [stored Norwich, UK; canx 04Oct95; b/u 03Dec96]
10232	200	(Air UK)	PH-FEX 9M-AMM PH-EXC PH-FEX S2-ABK G-BDVS [wfu 25Sep94; b/u 17Dec96 Norwich, UK; forward fuselage preserved Norfolk & Suffolk Aviation Museum; canx 19Dec96; l/n 04Sep07]

FOKKER F.27 FRIENDSHIP

C/n	Model	Last known Owner/Operator	Identities/fates/comments (where appropriate)
10233	200	(WDL Flugdienst)	PH-FEY 9M-AMN 9V-BAR PH-FEY S2-ABL G-BDVT TF-FLS PH-FEY TT-WAD PH-FEY D-BAKH [wfu Sep96 Essen-Mulheim, Germany; b/u 10Feb05; cockpit & fuselage donated to FS Technical School, Woensdrecht, Netherlands]
10234	200	(KLM UK)	PH-FEZ JA8621 PH-OGB G-BCDO [DBR 19Jly90 Amsterdam, Netherlands; ferried 29Jly90 to Norwich, UK; b/u 1992, fuselage to Air UK Technical College; canx 27Jan95; l/n Dec96]
10235	200	(Burma Airways Corp)	PH-FFA XY-ADK [w/o 25Mar78 Okaraba near Rangoon, Burma]
10236	200	(Union of Burma Airways)	PH-FFB XY-ADL [w/o 25Jun66 Moulmein Airport, Burma]
10237	200	(Burma Airways Corp)	PH-FFC XY-ADM [w/o 30Apr74 Bassein Airport, Burma]
10238	200	(Sudan Airways)	PH-FFD ST-AAY [w/o; ran out of fuel 06Dec71 Tirkaka, Southern Sudan]
10239	200	(Sunshine Aviation)	PH-FFE HL5201 TF-FLS OH-LKA HB-ISG [wfu Feb93 Basle, Switzerland; b/u Jan94; canx Mar94; hulk l/n 17Jly99]
10240	200	(WDL Flugdienst)	PH-FFF HL5202 TF-FLT OH-LKB TF-FLP PH-FFF D-BAKG [stored by Jan97 Essen-Mulheim, Germany; b/u Apr97]
10241	200	(British Midland Airways)	PH-FFG VP-KTK 5X-AAP 5H-MRO G-BMAU [w/o 18Jan87 near East Midlands Airport, UK]
10242	200	(Sempati Air Transport)	PH-FFH JA8622 F-BUFA 9M-MCZ PK-JFN [wfu Oct97 Jakarta-Soekarno-Hatta, Indonesia; b/u Oct01]
10243	200	(Pakistan International Airlines)	PH-FFI JA8623 F-BUFE AP-BAL [w/o 10Jly06 near Multan Airport, Pakistan; canx 19Dec07]
10244	200	(Air UK)	PH-FFK JA8624 PK-PFV F-GBRY G-BHMZ [wfu Mar94 Norwich, UK; canx 04Oct95; b/u 03Dec96]
10245	100	ex Swetrail Transport	PH-FFL LN-SUE SE-KZD [stored Nov96 Woensdrecht, Netherlands; 31Mar03; moved to Oudehaske, Netherlands for use in disaster training; l/n 17Jun06; canx 18Jan07; Feb10 moved to Groningen-Eelde, Netherlands for fire training]
10246	200	ex Philippine Air Force	PH-FFM PI-C507 10246 [stored by Jan00 Clark AFB, Philippines; fuselage only reported 24Jly07; l/n 01Aug08]
10247	100	(Aero Stock)	PH-FFN PI-C508 I-SARK F-BVTO F-OGIM F-BIUK [wfu Dec91 Paris-Le Bourget, France; b/u 29Jun00]
10248	100	Ljungbyhed Technical School	PH-FFO LN-SUL PH-SAF LN-SUL SE-KZE [wfu by 11Aug00 Malmo, Sweden; Dec01 moved to Aviation School, Ljungbyhed, Sweden]
10249	200	(WDL Flugdienst)	PH-FFP I-ATIM PH-KFG D-BAKF [wfu by Apr 98 Cologne/Bonn, Germany; b/u 01Mar99]
10250	200	(Pakistan International Airlines)	PH-FFR AP-ATO [w/o 16Dec78 near Karachi, Pakistan]
10251	200	(Aero Trasporti Italiani)	PH-FFS I-ATIP [w/o 16Apr72 struck high ground near Ardinello di Amaseno, Italy, en-route to Foggia]
10252	200	Pakistan Navy	PH-FFT JA8630 VH-FNV AP-BDG 52//AR-NZQ+ FK73//AR-NZQ+ [+ dual marks]
10253	200	ex Pakistan International Airlines	PH-FFU JA8631 VH-TFW PT-LDJ AP-BDQ [grounded Jly06 Karachi, Pakistan; reported for Pakistan Navy for spares; DBR 17Aug06 crushed by A300 AP-BAZ c/n 099; canx 17Aug06]
10254	200	(Pakistan Air Force)	PH-FFV JA8632 VH-FNW AP-BDF 54//AR-NYA+ 10254 [+ Pakistan; dual marks; w/o 20Feb03 flew into mountain 20miles E of Kohat, Pakistan]
10255	200	(Expresso Aereo del Peru)	PH-FFW JA8633 TF-FIN TF-FLN PH-FFW OB-1484 [wfu Jan94 Mena-Intermountain Municipal, AR; b/u 17Jan98]
10256	200	(Mountain Air Cargo)	PH-FFX I-ATIS PH-KFH G-BMAE N275MA [wfu Dec95 Maiden-Little Mountain Airport, Denver, NC; l/n 13Apr96 missing parts, assumed b/u; canx 29May03]
10257	100	ex WDL Flugdienst	PH-FFY PI-C509 I-SARQ D-BOBY(1) OE-HLA D-BAKE(2) [wfu Sep92 Essen-Mulheim, Germany; by Apr98 b/u; fuselage only noted Bonn-Hangelar, Germany]
10258	100	ex Continental Aviation	PH-FFZ VH-MMU PI-C512 I-SARO F-BVTU F-OGJA F-GCPA LN-NPC N101FJ VT-ERZ [parts of c/n 10191 used in re-build; wfu by 14Aug93; canx 28Mar06; hulk dumped Bhopal, India; l/n 2008]
10259	200	(Air UK)	PH-FGA JA8634 F-BUFO G-BHMX [wfu May94 Norwich, UK; canx 04Oct95; b/u Dec96]
10260	200	(Sunshine Aviation)	PH-FGB JA8635 TF-SYR TF-FLS OH-LKC HB-ISH [wfu Feb93 Basle, Switzerland; canx and b/u Mar94, hulk in use for fire training; l/n Jan07]
10261	600	(WDL Flugdienst)	PH-FGC JA8636 P2-BNF P2-ANF TG-AOA 1093+ PH-FGC ST-ALF PH-FGC F-GHRC D-BAKB [+ Guatemala] [canx 06Aug09 as wfu; b/u Mar12 Cologne-Bonn, Germany]
10262	200MPA	Pakistan Navy	PH-FGD JA8637 ZK-DCG AP-BBG AR-MLF 62//AR-NZE+ FK74//AR-NZE+ 74//AR-NZE+ [+ Pakistan; dual marks]

FOKKER F.27 FRIENDSHIP

C/n	Model	Last known Owner/Operator	Identities/fates/comments (where appropriate)
10263	200	(WDL Flugdienst)	PH-FGE JA8638 TF-FIM TF-FLM PH-FGE D-BAKE(3) [wfu 28Jly96 Essen-Mulheim, Germany; b/u Apr97]
10264	200	ex Comair	PH-FGF VH-FNJ ZS-KVJ [wfu Jan95 Johannesburg, South Africa; canx 25May98 wfu; b/u Dec01; hulk dumped mid-field; l/n Jan07]
10265	100	ex Philippine Air Force	PH-FGG PI-C514 10265 [stored by 2002 Villamor AFB, Pasay City, Manila, Philippines; derelict by 14May07]
10266	100	(Sobel Air)	PH-FGH VH-EWG LN-NPI SE-KZF 9G-AIR [stored by 09Oct06 Accra-Kotoka, Ghana; b/u Mar07]
10267	100	ex Philippine Air Force	PH-FGI PI-C516 10267 [stored by 2002 Villamor AFB, Pasay City, Manila, Philippines; l/n 25Nov09]
10268	400	ex Air Panama	PH-FGK D-BARI PH-ARI F-BRQL HB-AAZ C-GWXC HP-1543PST [canx by May10 presumed wfu; reported 05Sep10 Panama City-Gelabert, Panama]
10269	100	(Trans Oceanic Traders)	PH-FGL LX-LGB LX-OOO [dismantled Nov91 Rotterdam, Netherlands, used by fire service; by 05Jun93 painted wth fake regn'"G-HOST" then by Oct99 "PH-JRM"; l/n Dec07]
10270	400	ex Guatemalan Air Force	PH-FGM D-BARO PH-ARO G-BFDS PH-ARO PK-JFM TG-ACA 1467 [wfu & stored by Sep99 Guatemala City-La Aurora, Guatemala; l/n 10Jan09]
10271	200	(Schreiner Airways/Indian Airlines)	PH-FGN PH-SAB [w/o 07Feb66 Banihal Pass, Pir Panjal Range, India]
10272	200	(Sudamericana de Aviacion)	PH-FGO PH-SAD LV-WEB [wfu and stored Dec96 Buenos Aires-Ezeiza, Argentina; b/u by Jan06]
10273	400M	(Sudan Airways)	PH-FGP 833+ ST-ADX [+ Sudan] [w/o 10May72 near El Obeid, Sudan]
10274	100	Finnish Air Force	PH-FGR TF-FIJ TF-FLJ (OH-LKC) OH-KFA FF-1 [ELINT Aircraft]
10275	400	(Libyan Arab Airlines)	PH-FGS N10625 5A-DBE [w/o 28Nov80 Kufra, Tchad]
10276	200	(Sudamericana de Aviacion)	PH-FGT HB-AAV PH-KFD LV-WEL [wfs Apr97 Buenos Aires-Ezeiza, Argentina; b/u 04Oct03]
10277	400M	(Sudan Airways)	PH-FGU 844+ ST-ADY [+ Sudan] [shot down 16Aug86 near Malakal, Sudan]
10278	200	(Pakistan International Airlines)	PH-FGV AP-ATU [wfu Jan04 location not known; canx by 2004]
10279	200	(Pakistan International Airlines)	PH-FGW AP-ATT [w/o 08Oct65 near Naran, Kaghan Valley, Himalayas, Pakistan]
10280	200	ex 19th Hole Corp, UK	PH-FGX VH-FNK P2-ANL LX-LGK N278MA [b/u Feb06 Daytona Beach, FL; fuselage only dumped; canx 16Jan09; l/n 21Oct09]
10281	200	Pakistan Air Force	PH-FGY AP-ATW J-752+ 77//AR-NZY [dual marks; + Pakistan]
10282	400M	(Sudan Airways)	PH-FGZ 888+ ST-ADW [+ Sudan] [w/o 06Jun77 near El Fasher Airport, Sudan]
10283	400M	(Sudanese Air Force)	PH-FIA 899 [w/o 10Nov69 in Sudan]
10284	200	(Eagle Jet Charter)	PH-FIB VH-TFL PH-FIB N268MA [stored by Apr97 Las Vegas-McCarran, NV; canx Sep97; subsequently b/u]
10285	100	(Philippine Airlines)	PH-FIC PI-C527 [w/o 06Jly67 Bacolod, Negros Island, Philippines]
10286	100	ex Jetlease Inc	PH-FID ZK-BXI [stored 08Apr90 Christchurch, New Zealand; canx 12Jly95; PWFU 15Mar96; b/u by 1997; fuselage in bits used by Air New Zealand Training School; l/n 09Feb10]
10287	100	unknown	PH-FIE VH-EWJ LN-NPM SE-KZG 9G-SOB TL-ADS [wfu by 02Aug10 Brazzaville, People's Republic of Congo]
10288	200	(Pakistan International Airlines)	PH-FIF I-ATIG AP-AXB [canx 25May91; by 16Oct00 wfu without tail Quetta, Pakistan]
10289	200	(Pakistan International Airlines)	PH-FIG I-ATIB LN-DAF G-BDDH AP-BCT [by May05 wfu Karachi, Pakistan; canx 31Mar06]
10290	200	(Royal Nepal Airlines)	PH-FIH 9N-AAR [w/o 25Jan70 Delhi-Palam, India]
10291	200	(Rio-Sul)	PH-FII VH-FNL P2-ANI PT-LCZ [w/o 06Aug84 Rio de Janeiro-Santos Dumont, Brazil; canx Sep84]
10292	200MPA	Pakistan Navy	PH-FIK VH-FNM AP-BDB 76//AR-NZX [dual marks]
10293	200	(Air UK)	PH-FIL 9M-AOJ PH-FIL G-BAKL [wfu by 21Dec95 Norwich, UK; b/u by 03 Dec96; canx 11Dec96]
10294	400	ex Myanma Airways	PH-FIN N710A PH-SFA OY-UEZ (PH-SFL) PH-SFA 5Y-BIP XY-AEQ [stored by 07Jan06 Yangon, Myanmar; derelict by Apr11]
10295	400	Miniliner Malta	PH-FIO N714A PH-SFB HB-ITQ HA-ACK HB-ITQ I-MLQT 9H-MQT
10296	200	(Philippine Air Force)	PH-FIP PI-C528 10296 [wfu May98, b/u Villamor AFB, Pasay City, Manila, Philippines; by Mar00 parts trucked to Clark AFB, Philippines]
10297	200	(Air Panama)	PH-FIR VH-FNN P2-ANM LX-LGJ N279MA HP-1541PST [w/o 31Oct07 Panama City-Albrook/Marcos Gelabert Airport, Panama;hulk l/n 29Nov07; b/u by May09]

FOKKER F.27 FRIENDSHIP

C/n	Model	Last known Owner/Operator	Identities/fates/comments (where appropriate)
10298	100	Flyhistorisk Museum Sola	PH-FIS LN-SUF PH-SAN LN-SUF [wfu Nov92; donated 21Jly93 Flyhistorisk Museum Sola, Stavanger, Norway]
10299	400	ex Trigana Air Service	PH-FIT PK-PFA PK-MFT PK-YPN [PWFU 01Oct01]
10300	100	(Finnish Air Force)	PH-FIU TF-FIK TF-FLK (OH-KFB) OH-KLC FF-2 [wfu 31Mar04; to Pori Lansi College of Technology, Finland; l/n 12Nov07]
10301	200	(Aero Trasporti Italiani)	PH-FIV I-ATIR [w/o 30Oct72 Poggiorsini, Italy]
10302	200	(Mesaba Airlines/Northwest Airlink)	PH-FIW VT-DUT 9N-AAS VT-DUT 9N-AAW VT-DUT S2-ABF G-BMAP N276MA [to White Industries for spares use; wfu 28Apr94 Bates City, MO; b/u between 1996/98; Apr99 cockpit section to Opa-locka, FL; canx Feb97]
10303	200	(Ansett Airlines)	PH-FIX VH-MMR [wfu Jly86, stored Melbourne-Tullamarine, VIC, Australia; Aug92 to GIA Broadlands Technical School, Avondale Heights, Melbourne, VIC, Australia]
10304	400	(Trygon Ltd)	PH-FIY VH-FNO HZ-KA8 (EI-MLA) 3C-AWW [wfu 11Dec99 Southend, UK; b/u by 04Sep00]
10305	200	(Pakistan International Airlines)	PH-FIZ VH-FNP AP-BCZ [canx 07May07; sold to Pakistan Navy for spares use]
10306	400	(Pelita Air Service)	PH-FKA PK-PFB [w/o 27Apr67 Malaybalay, Philippines]
10307	200	(Pakistan International Airlines)	PH-FKB AP-AUR [w/o 16Jun04 Chitral Airport, Pakistan; canx 20Oct04]
10308	200	(Biman Bangladesh Airlines)	PH-FKC VT-DVF 9N-AAT VT-DVF S2-ABG [w/o 18Nov79 Savar Bazar near Dhaka, Bangladesh]
10309	200	(Indian Airlines)	PH-FKD VT-DVG [w/o 07Jun70 Agartala-Singerbhil Airport, India]
10310	200	ex Philippine Air Force	PH-FKE PI-C531 10310 [stored by 31Jly07 Villamor AFB, Pasay City, Manila, Philippines; l/n 25Nov09]
10311	100	(Philippine Airlines)	PH-FKF PI-C532 [w/o 09May70 Iligan-Maria Cristina Airport, Mindanao, Philippines]
10312	400	(Burma Airways Corp)	PH-FKG XY-ADN [w/o 29Jun81 Sandoway, Burma]
10313	400	(Burma Airways Corp)	PH-FKH XY-ADO [w/o 20Aug80 Moulmein, Burma]
10314	600	(Pakistan International Airlines)	PH-FKI AP-AUS [w/o 08Dec72 near Maidan, Pakistan]
10315	600	Queensland Air Museum	PH-FKK VH-FNQ ZK-RTA VH-WAN [stored 2002 Tamworth, NSW, Australia; l/n Jun04; canx 08Jun07 as wfu; preserved 30Oct08 Caloundra, QLD, Australia; to be painted as VH-FNQ]
10316	600	ex WDL Flugdienst	PH-FKL G-AVDN A4O-FN HL5262 A4O-FN PH-SFG OY-BVF D-ADOP [stored Oct04 Cologne/Bonn, Germany; l/n 24Mar07; canx 13Nov08]
10317	600	(Morningstar Air Express)	PH-FKM VH-FNR SE-KGC EC-EUU C-GBWC [wfu & stored Nov93 Marana, AZ; canx Dec93 to USA; assumed subsequently b/u; date unknown]
10318	600	WDL Flugdienst	PH-FKN VH-FNS P2-ANS G-BLMM OY-CCK D-ADEP
10319	100	Sobel Air	PH-FKO VH-EWK PH-FKO LN-NPD SE-KZH 9G-BEL
10320	200	(CNET)	PH-FKP I-ATID F-SEBF [wfu & b/u Dec94 Lannion, France; by 24Mar96 fuselage moved to Dinard, France; l/n Jun07; not reported 30May10]
10321	200	(WDL Flugdienst)	PH-FKR I-ATIF LN-RNX PH-FKR PH-LMP PT-BFZ (PH-FJA) PH-FKR ST-AWB PH-FKR (OY-EBD) D-BAKJ [b/u by 01Feb05 Essen, Germany; fuselage used in "TUI Roadshow" 2005]
10322	600	Peruvian Coast Guard	PH-FKS VH-FNT EC-137 EC-EHG VH-FNT C-FAFE AB-584
10323	600	(WDL Flugdienst)	PH-FKT HB-AAW G-AZFD A4O-FD (AP-BBJ) A4O-FD (PH-XPA) PH-FKT D-AELF [wfu & stored in hangar 2002 Cologne/Bonn, Germany; canx 01Oct03; b/u 02Feb09]
10324	200	(Mesaba Airlines)	PH-FKU I-ATIL OO-PSF F-GCMR G-JRSY N266MA [wfu and canx May95 Wausau, WI; assumed b/u]
10325	600	(Burma Airways Corp)	PH-FKV PH-SAR G-AWFU A4O-FU PH-SAR XY-AEK [w/o 03Feb89 Yangon, Burma]
10326	200	(ACE Aviation Contractors Europe)	PH-FKW CR-LIJ D2-TIJ D2-TFO PT-LAI (PH-FKW) [stored Jan98 Mena-Intermountain Municipal, AR as PT-LAI; b/u for spares]
10327	200	ex Philippine Air Force	PH-FKX PI-C534 10327 [wfu 27Mar07 Villamor AFB, Pasay City, Manila, Philippines; l/n 25Nov09]
10328	200	(Philippine Air Force)	PH-FKY PI-C536 10328 [w/o 14Sep78 Barrio Santo, near Manila, Philippines]
10329	600	(Empire Airlines/FedEx Express)	PH-FKZ VH-TFM SE-IRF PH-FKZ HB-ISJ N740FE [stored 02Oct04 Spokane, WA; canx 02Oct05; b/u, confirmed by airline]
10330	200	(Pakistan International Airlines)	PH-FLA AP-AUV [w/o 30Dec70 Shamshernagar Airport, East Pakistan]
10331	200	(Pakistan International Airlines)	PH-FLB AP-AUW [w/o 28May73 Lyallpur Airport, Pakistan]
10332	600	(Cubana)	PH-FLC EC-BMS CU-T1286 [stored May01 Havana, Cuba; b/u by 03Mar03]
10333	600	(Indian Airlines/Vayudoot)	PH-FLD F-BOOC PH-FLD A2-ZEW VT-EBJ [b/u Oct94 Calcutta, India]

FOKKER F.27 FRIENDSHIP

C/n	Model	Last known Owner/Operator	Identities/fates/comments (where appropriate)
10334	600	(Tavaj Linhas Aereas)	PH-FLE F-BOOD PH-EXC VH-FNU G-BNAL PT-TVA [w/o 20Oct03 Tarauaca, Brazil]
10335	600	(Pakistan International Airlines)	PH-FLF AP-AUX [w/o 23Oct86 near Peshawar, Pakistan]
10336	400	(Indian Airlines)	PH-FLG VT-DWT [w/o 29Aug70 Silchar, India]
10337	400	(Indian Airlines)	PH-FLH VT-DWU [wfu Sep94 Calcutta, India; probably b/u]
10338	600	(ex WDL Flugdienst)	PH-FLI LX-LGD PH-XPS VR-BLZ D-AELG [stored by 03Oct06 Cologne-Bonn, Germany; canx 13Nov08; b/u Mar12]
10339	400	(Pelita Air Service)	PH-FLK PK-PFC [w/o 13Oct80 Misool Islands, Indonesia]
10340	400	ex WDL Flugdienst	PH-FLL OO-SBP F-BYAA A2-AEC PH-SFJ VR-BLX D-AELH [wfu and stored by 03Oct06 Cologne/Bonn, Germany; canx 13Nov08; l/n 19Dec08 basically intact]
10341	500F	ex Farnair Hungary	PH-FLM OY-STO VH-EWO PH-EXM N272FA PT-LAL (PH-LAL) PH-FLM (D-AFGA) HA-FAC [wfu Jan09 Bergamo, Italy; b/u Feb10; hulk l/n 14May12]
10342	600	WDL Flugdienst	PH-FLN OY-DNF PH-FLN OO-HLN F-BYAB D-AELJ
10343	600	ex Myanma Airways	PH-FLO EC-BMT CU-T1287 XY-AEU [stored by 23Oct06 Yangon, Myanmar; l/n Apr11]
10344	100	(East-West Airlines)	PH-FLP VH-EWL [w/o 31May74 Bathurst, NSW, Australia]
10345	600	Argentine Air Force	PH-FLR T-79+ T-41 [+ Argentina]
10346	600	Museo Nacional de Aeronautica	PH-FLS T-80+ T-42 [+ Argentina] [wfu Apr99 Moron, Argentina; donated 2002 to museum for preservation at Moron; l/n Apr06]
10347	600	ex Myanma Airways	PH-FLT EC-BMU CU-T1288 XY-AEV [reported wfu by 07Jan06 Yangon, Myanmar; l/n Apr11]
10348	600	(Cubana)	PH-FLU (EC-BMW) EC-BOA CU-T1289 [wfu & stored Jly96 Havana, Cuba; sale in Feb00 fell through due to bad condition; l/n 29Aug01]
10349	600	Air Maleo	PH-FLV I-ATIC SE-ITH PH-FLV G-FEAE N742FE N19QQ PK-ZMM
10350	600	19th Hole Corp, UK	PH-FLW I-ATIN SE-ITI PH-FLW OO-FEG N702FE N19AQ [stored 26Aug09 Coeur d'Alene, ID]
10351	600	(Channel Express)	PH-FLX HB-AAX PH-KFE G-CEXD [wfu 26Jun02; canx 25Oct04; b/u 26Oct04 Bournemouth, UK; nose saved & to South Cave Scuba Diving Centre, East Yorkshire, UK]
10352	600	ex Myanma Airways	PH-FLY EC-BOB CU-T1290 XY-AEW [stored by Apr11 Yangon, Myanmar]
10353	600	(Cubana)	PH-FLZ EC-BOC CU-T1291 [wfu by Nov96 Havana, Cuba; b/u by Jun97 for spares]
10354	600	(Pakistan International Airlines)	PH-FMA JY-ADF 5N-CLN PH-FMA OO-SCA AP-AXF [w/o 05Jun81 Gilgit Airport, Pakistan]
10355	200	Peruvian Coast Guard	PH-FMB VH-MMV (OB-1505) OB-1510 AB-582
10356	300	(Icelandair)	PH-FMC TF-FIL [w/o 26Sep70 Vagar, Faroe Islands, Denmark]
10357	200	(Burma Airways Corp)	PH-FMD XY-ADP [w/o 21Jun87 near Hopong, Burma]
10358	200	(Zaire Aero Service)	PH-FME 9V-BBF PH-FME CR-LMU VQ-GAC D2-LMU 9Q-CPC 9Q-CPC [wfu & stored by 1984 Kinshasa-Ndolo, Zaire; later b/u]
10359	200	(Zaire Aero Service)	PH-FMF 9M-AOX PH-FMF CR-LMV D2-LMV 9Q-CPI [wfu & stored by 1984 Kinshasa-Ndolo, Zaire; later b/u]
10360	600	(Iberia)	PH-FMG EC-BOD [w/o 05Jan70 Tenerife-Norte-Los Rodeos Airport, Canary Islands, Spain]
10361	600	WDL Flugdienst	PH-FMH EC-BOE F-GCJV D-AELK
10362	600	(Sempati Air Transport)	PH-FMI PK-CFD PK-JFI [wfu Oct97 Jakarta-Soekarno-Hatta, Indonesia; b/u Oct01]
10363	600	(Aero Trasporti Italiani)	PH-FMK I-ATIT [w/o 25May69 Reggio Calabria Airport, Italy]
10364	500	Airwork Flight Operations	PH-FML (PJ-ALB) PJ-FRE 9M-APP 9V-BFK ZK-NAO
10365	500	(Airwork New Zealand/Air Post)	PH-FMM (PJ-ALM) PJ-FRM 9V-BCN ZK-NAN [w/o 27Feb03 Blenheim-Woodbourne Airport, New Zealand; canx 18Sep03; fuselage remains l/n Mar05]
10366	500	(ACL Aircraft Trading)	PH-FMN F-BPNA PT-LZM PH-FMN G-BVOB [stored 30Jly05 Southend, UK with CofA to 06Oct06; by 17Sep09 dumped as hulk; b/u 23Oct09; canx 27Jan11]
10367	500	Hickory Aviation Museum	PH-FMO F-BPNB G-BNZE G-FEDX N705FE [wfu 10Jan08 & preserved Hickory, NC; donated by FedEx 13Feb08; canx 07Jan09]
10368	600	Argentine Air Force	PH-FMP (AP-AUY) N20XY PH-FMP TC-79+ T-45 [+ Argentina] [stored with parts missing 23May07 Comodoro Rivadavia, Argentina; l/n 03Jly09]
10369	500	ex Miniliner	PH-FMR F-BPUA I-MLUT [stored 17Dec09 Paris-Charles de Gaulle, France]

FOKKER F.27 FRIENDSHIP

C/n	Model	Last known Owner/Operator	Identities/fates/comments (where appropriate)
10370	500	Farnair Hungary	PH-FMS F-BPUB HB-ISY HA-FAB A6-FCY HA-FAB A6-FCY [by 06Jly12 stored Tokol, Hungary with UAE marks painted over]
10371	500	(19th Hole Corp, UK)	PH-FMT F-BPNC G-FEBZ N707FE N19XA [l/n 02Oct04 stored Coeur d'Alene, ID; later b/u for spares; canx 16Jan09]
10372	500	Sky Relief Kenya	PH-FMU F-BPND G-BOMV N708FE N19XD 5Y-SRJ [seriously damaged 15Apr12 airsrip in South Sudan]
10373	500	ex Miniliner	PH-FMV F-BPUC I-MLVT [stored by 14May12 Bergamo, Italy]
10374	500	ex Miniliner	PH-FMW F-BPUD I-MLXT [stored 17Dec09 Clermont-Ferrand, France]
10375	500	(Mountain Air Cargo/FedEx Express)	PH-FMX F-BPNE (G-BONI) N709FE [canx 14Mar05 as wfu; assumed b/u, location unknown]
10376	500	(Air Inter)	PH-FMY F-BPNF [w/o by bomb whilst on ground 05Aug74 Quimper, France]
10377	500	ex Miniliner	PH-FMZ F-BPUE I-MLRT [stored 17Dec09 Bergamo, Italy]
10378	500	ex Miniliner	PH-FNA F-BPUF I-MLTT [stored 17Dec09 Limoges, France]
10379	500	ex Miniliner	PH-FNB F-BPUG I-MLGT [stored 17Dec09 Bergamo, Italy; l/n 14May12
10380	500	(Mountain Air Cargo/FedEx Express)	PH-FNC F-BPNG N710FE [canx 14Mar05 as wfu; last reported Kinston Regional Jetport-Stallings Field, NC; probably b/u there]
10381	500	ex Boreal Aviation	PH-FND F-BPNH PT-LZN PH-FND G-BVOM EC-GYL [stored 05Mar02 Madrid, Spain; l/n 09Jly11]
10382	500	Miniliner	PH-FNE F-BPUH I-MLHT [stored 16Jun12 Bergamo, Italy]
10383	500	(19th Hole Corp, UK)	PH-FNF F-BPNI N711FE N19XB [by Jun05 stored Coeur d'Alene, ID; later b/u for spares; canx 16Jan09]
10384	500	(Mountain Air Cargo/FedEx Express)	PH-FNG F-BPNJ G-BOCE G-OFEC N706FE [canx 14Mar05 as wfu; assumed b/u, location unknown]
10385	600	Air Maleo	PH-FNH VH-TQN OY-KAC PH-FNH OO-FEA EI-FEA N729FE N19NN PK-ZMV
10386	600	ex Air Panama	PH-FNI VH-TQO LN-RNZ PH-FNI I-FEAB N730FE+ HP- [+ canx 30Apr08 to Panama; stored by 12Oct08 Panama City-Albrook/Marcos A Gelabert, Panama, still as N730FE; l/n 11May09]
10387	600	ex Empire Airlines/FedEx Express	PH-FNK VH-TQP SE-IRG PH-FNK G-FEAD N741FE [wfs mid-2008 Coeur d'Alene, ID; l/n 08Sep08; canx 13Jan09]
10388	600	(Trans Australia Airlines)	PH-FNL VH-TQQ [w/o 09Jun82 RAAF Amberley, QLD, Australia]
10389	500	(Air France)	PH-FNM F-BPUI [w/o 25Jly74 Nantes, France; rebuilt as c/n 10528 q.v.]
10390	500	(Miniliner)	PH-FNN F-BPUJ [stored Feb02 Bergamo-Orio al Serio, Italy; canx 28Aug08; l/n 14May12]
10391	600	(ex WDL Flugdienst)	PH-FNO 9Q-CLK G-BNTB OY-CCR D-AISY [wfu by Nov06 Colgone-Bonn, Germany; canx 13Nov08; hulk b/u Mar12]
10392	600	Myanmar Air Force	PH-FNP 9Q-CLL G-BNIY OY-SRR XY-AER(1) 5001(2)
10393	600	(Air Zaire)	PH-FNR 9Q-CLM [w/o 07Jan75 Boende Airport, Zaire]
10394	600	ex Air Panama	PH-FNS 9Q-CLN(1) G-BNTA OY-SRB N280EA HP-1606PST [stored Jun06 Panama City-Albrook/Marcos A Gelabert, Panama; l/n 05Sep10 still in Eagle c/s; wfu; qv Fokker 50 c/n 20179]
10395	600	(Air Zaire)	PH-FNT 9Q-CLO [w/o 03Mar76 in ground rocket attack Vila Gago Coutinho, Angola]
10396	600	(Sempati Air Transport)	PH-FNU OY-DHW EC-CAU OY-DHW PK-JFH PH-SFH PK-JFH [wfu Oct97 Jakarta-Soekarno-Hatta, Indonesia; b/u Oct01]
10397	500	Trigana Air Service	PH-FNV F-BPUK PH-FNV (D-AFGB) PK-YRG
10398	500F	ex G T Air	PH-FNW F-BPUL PH-FNW (D-AFGC) PK-LTP [stored by 25Oct06 Jakarta-Halim, Indonesia]
10399	600	(Merpati Nusantara Airlines)	PH-FNX 5N-ABA PK-GRD PK-MFD [w/o 09May91 near Manado Airport, Indonesia]
10400	600	(Trigana Air Service)	PH-FNY 5N-ABB PK-GRE PK-MFE PK-YPO [stored by Jan98 Jakarta-Halim, Indonesia; no recent reports]
10401	600	(Ste Co-operative Aeronautique)	PH-FNZ CR-AMD C9-AMD N379BS PT-LDT PH-FNZ 9Q-CBP F-WQIN+ F-WWUA [+ illegal marks; stored by Sep98 Dinard, France; l/n 29Jun08 in TMK c/s, still wearing F-WQIN; also reported wearing 9Q-CBP; not reported 30May10; probably b/u]
10402	600	(Air Zaire)	PH-FOA 9Q-CLP [w/o 08Feb80 Kinshasa-N'Djili, Zaire]
10403	400M	ex Lineas Aereas Del Estado	PH-FOB TC-71 [stored Nov97 El Palomar, Argentina]
10404	400M	(Lineas Aereas Del Estado)	PH-FOC TC-72(1) [w/o 16Mar75 near San Carlos de Bariloche Airport, Argentina]
10405	600F	MNG Airlines	PH-FOD 9Q-CLQ G-BNIZ OY-SRA G-BNIZ TC-MBF
10406	600	(Air Zaire)	PH-FOE 9Q-CLR [w/o 06Jan78 near Kisangani, Zaire]
10407	400M	(Lineas Aereas Del Estado)	PH-FOF TC-73 [w/o 16Jun95 Jeremie, Haiti]
10408	400M	Lineas Aereas Del Estado	PH-FOG TC-74

FOKKER F.27 FRIENDSHIP

C/n	Model	Last known Owner/Operator	Identities/fates/comments (where appropriate)
10409	600	ex Eureca	PH-FOH PK-GFE PH-FOH (TY-AAG) TY-ATM TY-BBI PH-EXX F-SEBG OY-FCM I-FSTK [stored & wfu by 18Sep03 Bergamo, Italy; canx 13Aug09 as exported; but l/n there wfu 14May12]
10410	600	(Sempati Air Transport)	PH-FOI PK-GFF PK-JFF PT-LLA PK-JFF [w/o 05Jun91 Gresik, Indonesia]
10411	400M	(Lineas Aereas Del Estado)	PH-FOK TC-75 [w/o 10Jun70 near Huaricanga, Peruvian Andes, Peru]
10412	400M	(Lineas Aereas Del Estado)	PH-FOL TC-76 [w/o 17May01 Mendoza, Argentina]
10413	600	(Sempati Air Transport)	PH-FOM PK-GFG PH-FOM (TY-ATM) TY-BBJ F-GBGI TY-BRJ PK-JFG [wfu Oct97 Jakarta-Soekarno Hatta, Indonesia; b/u Oct01]
10414	200	ex WDL Flugdienst	PH-FON HL5209 TF-FLO PH-FON VT-ETE PH-FON D-AELL [wfu by Jan01; preserved Moenchengladbach Airport, Germany; l/n 17Oct09]
10415	600	(Trigana Air Service)	PH-FOO PK-GFH PK-MFH PK-YPM [w/o 17Jly97 Sulaiman AFB, Bandung, Indonesia]
10416	400M	(Lineas Aereas Del Estado)	PH-FOP TC-77 [w/o 02Dec69 Marambio Base, Antarctica]
10417	500	ex ACL Aircraft Trading	PH-FOR (HL5206) HL5210 TF-FLR G-BMXD [last flew Jly05 & stored; Dec07 stripped of parts, to fire service Edinburgh, UK; canx 10Oct08; l/n Feb11]
10418	400M	ex Lineas Aereas Del Estado	PH-FOS TC-78 [wfu & stored 30Seo09 Parana AFB, Argentina; l/n Aug11]
10419	600	(Empire Airlines/FedEx Express)	PH-FOT I-ATIV LN-RNY PH-FOT OO-FEF N701FE [wfu 10Aug04 Spokane, WA; canx 26Oct05; airline reports b/u]
10420	600	19th Hole Corp, UK	PH-FOU I-ATIZ OY-KAD PH-FOU (OO-FEG) D-AFEH N703FE N19AU [wfu 12Sep08 Coeur d'Alene, ID; l/n 26Aug09]
10421	600	(Cubana)	PH-FOV PK-GFI PH-EXT EC-DBM CU-T1292 [wfu for spares use Nov96 Havana, Cuba; no recent reports, probably b/u]
10422	600	(Garuda Indonesia)	PH-FOW PK-GFJ [w/o 07Sep74 Bandar Lampung-Branti Airport, Indonesia]
10423	600	(TAAG Angola Airlines)	PH-FOX PK-GFK PH-EXT PH-EXL PH-FOX D2-TAE D2-TFQ [w/o 30Nov98 Luanda, Angola; some reports state 30Dec98; wreck l/n 14Dec01]
10424	600	(TAAG Angola Airlines)	PH-FOY PK-GFL PH-EXM PH-FTG D2-TAF D2-TFP [w/o 14Apr97 Brazzaville, Zaire]
10425	500	ex Farnair Hungary	PH-FOZ (OY-DKR) OY-APA F-BYAF VH-EWS PH-FOZ 9Q-CBU G-BVZW (PH-TLP) PH-FOZ HB-IVQ HA-FAE [wfu Feb08 for parts Bergamo, Italy; hulk by 17Apr10; l/n 14May12]
10426	500	(Maersk Air)	PH-FPA (OY-DKS) OY-APB [w/o 27Dec69 Bornholm Ronne, Denmark]
10427	500	(Boreal Aviation)	PH-FPB (HL5207) HL5211 PH-FPB G-BVRN EC-GYM [stored 01Nov00 Las Palmas-Gran Canaria, Spain; b/u 18Nov11]
10428	500	(Korean Air)	PH-FPC (HL5208) HL5212 [w/o 23Jan71 near Kaesong, South Korea]
10429	600	(Cubana)	PH-FPD PK-GFM PH-EXD EC-DBN CU-T1293 [wfu Aug96 Havana, Cuba; b/u for spares Dec96; remains l/n Apr98]
10430	600	(Air Kasai)	PH-FPE PK-GFN PK-RFN PK-RFT PK-GFN PH-FTC F-BYAR 5A-DJN TT-AAK TT-WAK 3D-JCP 9Q-CJV [w/o 20Jly10 Lubumbashi, Democratic Republic of Congo]
10431	500	(International Air Parts Australia)	PH-FPF (OY-DKT) OY-APC F-BYAC VH-EWT PH-EXI N4560Z N980MA (VH-EIV) VH-IAV [l/n 17Jan98 Mena-Intermoutain Municipal, AR; b/u by end 1998 in USA]
10432	600	ex Fire SARL	PH-FPG CN-CDA OY-CCM C-FGDS F-ZBFF//71 F-WQVF+ [+ ferry marks only; by 04Mar05 stored Bergamo, Italy; l/n 14may12 still wearing F-ZBFF/71 as hulk]
10433	600	(Myanma Airways)	PH-FPH CN-CDB OY-CCN D-AFTG OY-CCN XY-AET [w/o 24Jly96 near Mergui, Myanmar]
10434	500	(SkyTeam)	PH-FPI OY-STN VH-EWN PH-EXF N271FA N981MA D-ACCS [stored by late 2002 Karlsruhe/Baden-Baden, Germany; b/u Dec04/Jan05]
10435	600	(Trigana Air Service)	PH-FPK PK-GFO PK-MFO PK-YPL [stored by Sep98 Jakarta-Halim, Indonesia; l/n Apr99; no recent reports; assumed b/u]
10436	600	(Libyan Red Crescent)	PH-FPL 5A-DBN [w/o 21Nov90 Labrak AFB, Libya]
10437	600	(Maersk Air)	PH-FPM OY-APD [w/o 15Jan75 Vagar Airport, Faroe Islands, Denmark]
10438	600	(WDL Flugdienst)	PH-FPN (AP-AWN) PH-EXB PH-FPN S2-ABH OY-SLG D-AELC [wfu by Oct02 Cologne/Bonn, Germany; canx 01Oct03; by 08Nov08 fuselage & inner wings mounted on trailer with AELS titles; b/u 02Feb09]
10439	200	(DTA Angola Airlines)	PH-FPO CR-LLD [w/o 21May72 near Lobito, Angola]
10440	600	(Fire SARL)	(PH-FPP) PH-EXB VH-TQR C-FBDY F-ZBFG//72 F-WQVG+ [+ ferry marks only; by 04Mar05 stored Bergamo, Italy; l/n May08 still wearing F-ZBFG/72; b/u during May08]
10441	600	ex Asia Avia Airlines	(PH-FPR) PH-EXB VH-TQS PK-TSK PK-YYA [stored by 25Oct06 Pondok Cabe, Indonesia; l/n 18Apr09 apparently wfu]

FOKKER F.27 FRIENDSHIP

C/n	Model	Last known Owner/Operator	Identities/fates/comments (where appropriate)
10442	600	ex WDL Flugdienst	(PH-FPS) PH-EXA PH-FPR S2-ABP (I-VANA) OY-SLF D-AELD [wfu & stored by Oct02 Cologne/Bonn, Germany; canx 01Oct03; l/n 24Mar07]
10443	600	(Star Air)	(PH-FPT) PH-EXD OY-APE OB-R-1072 OY-APE F-BYAI A4O-FA F-WDFT F-GDFT OY-APE [w/o 26May88 Hanover, West Germany]
10444	200	Pakistan Navy	(PH-FPU) PH-EXE ZK-DCA 44//AR-NZZ+ FK76//AR-NZZ+ [+ Pakistan; dual marks]
10445	200	Pakistan Navy	(PH-FPV) PH-EXF ZK-DCB 45//AR-NZV+ FK72//AR-NZV+ [+ Pakistan; dual marks]
10446	600	ex Lina Congo	(PH-FPW) TN-ABZ [stored Dec94 Woensdrecht, Netherlands; seized Jun98 by Fokker Aircraft Services; l/n derelict Feb08]
10447	500	(Air France)	(PH-FPX) F-BSUM [w/o 11Aug73 Strasbourg, France; rebuilt as c/n 10506]
10448	500	Falcon Express Cargo Airlines	(PH-FPY) F-BSUN (PH-JLN) HB-ITY D-AAAC HB-ITY (PH-ITY) (PH-FNQ) A6-FCZ
10449	500F	ex 19th Hole Corp, UK	(PH-FPZ) F-BSUO PH-JLN D-AAAF PH-JLN (D-AFGD) HA-FAD N19XE [arrived 24Nov11 Amsterdam-Schiphol, Netherlands for preservation at nearby Fokker Logistics Park as "PH-NIV"; canx 09Mar12 to UK]
10450	600	ex WDL Flugdienst	TU-VAJ TU-TIA PH-FTR I-ALML PH-FTR 9M-MCY EC-DSH OY-CCL D-AARS OY-CCL D-AARS OY-CCL D-AELM [stored by 03Nov06 Cologne/Bonn, Germany; canx 13Nov08; to be preserved by Aviation Friends Cologne/Bonn as "D-ACGN" at Cologne/Bonn, Germany]
10451	600	ex Argentine Air Force	PH-EXA T-43 [wfu & stored 30Jun03 Parana AFB, Argentina; l/n Aug11]
10452	600	(Burma Airways Corp)	XY-ADQ [w/o 16Jun88 near Putao, Burma]
10453	600	(Biman Bangladesh Airlines)	PH-EXD PH-FPU (AP-AWM) S2-ABJ [w/o 05Aug84 near Dhaka Airport, Bangladesh]
10454	600	ex Argentine Air Force	PH-EXB T-44 [stored by 11Aug11 Parana, Argentina]
10455	500	(Mountain Air Cargo/FedEx Express)	(PH-FPR) 9V-BCS 9M-ARI 9M-MCA N717FE [canx 14Mar05 as wfu; last reported Kinston Regional Jetport-Stallings Field, NC; probably b/u there]
10456	500	(Air New Zealand)	PH-FPS 9M-APU 9M-MCB ZK-NFC [w/o 17Feb79 Manukau Harbour, near Auckland Airport, New Zealand]
10457	600	ex TAAG Angola Airlines	PH-FPP CR-LMB D2-LMB D2-TMB D2-TFR [wfu by Apr99 Luanda, Angola; l/n Mar01]
10458	600	ex Asia Avia Airlines	(PH-FRI) PH-EXB VH-TQT PK-TSL PK-YYC [stored by 25Oct06 Pondok Cabe, Indonesia; wfu by 26Dec08; l/n 18Apr09]
10459	500	ex MNG Airlines	PH-EXD OY-APF F-BYAH(1) VH-EWR PH-RUA 9Q-CBI OY-APF 9Q-CBI 9Q-CBI G-CEXG TC-MBG [w/o 02Feb08 Edinburgh, Scotland, UK; hulk l/n 02Oct09 with fire service in bad condition]
10460	500	(Mountain Air Cargo/FedEx Express)	9V-BCT 9M-ARJ 9M-MCC N721FE [stored by 06Nov05 Kinston Regional Jetport-Stallings Field NC; probably b/u there; canx 16Aug06]
10461	500	(Mountain Air Cargo/FedEx Express)	9M-APV 9M-MCD N714FE [stored by 06Nov05 Kinston Regional Jetport-Stallings Field NC; probably b/u there; canx 15May06]
10462	600	(Garuda Indonesia)	PK-GFP [w/o 26Sep72 near Jakarta-Kemayoran, Indonesia]
10463	500	(Malaysia-Singapore Airlines)	9V-BCU [w/o 23Nov71 Kota Kinabalu, Sabah, Malaysia]
10464	500	(19th Hole Corp, UK)	9M-APW 9M-MCE N720FE N19XC [stored mid-2005 Coeur d'Alene, ID; later b/u for spares; canx 21Jan09]
10465	600		[built as c/n 10484]
10466	600		[built as c/n 10486]
10467	500	ex Air Panama	9V-BCV 9M-ARK 9M-MCF N719FE HP-1605PST [stored Jun06 Panama City-Albrook/Marcos A Gelabert, Panama; l/n 05Sep10, still in FedEx c/s]
10468	500	(Mountain Air Cargo/FedEx Express)	9M-APX 9M-MCG N715FE [w/o 27Apr04 Melo Airport, Uruguay, following in-flight fire]
10469	400	Pakistan Navy	TU-VAK F-GBDE 5A-DJN HB-AAP PH-SFC VR-BLY 69//AR-NZW+ FK75//AR-NZW+ [+ Pakistan; dual marks]
10470	500	National Museum of Commercial Aviation	9V-BCW 9M-ARL 9M-MCH N718FE [canx 02Oct06 to GIA Atlanta-Hartsfield, GA; dismantled circa 24May11 for preservation in new museum]
10471	500	Air Panama	PH-EXF 9M-ARE 9M-MCI N716FE HP-1604PST
10472	500	Purdue University	PH-EXA PH-EXF 9M-ASF 9M-MCJ N722FE [canx 14Feb07; donated to Purdue University, Camp Atterbury, IN; for anti-terrorist training]
10473	600	(Conair Aviation/Securite Civile)	(NAF-701)+ NAF-901+ 5N-ANL N4449D C-GSFS [+ Nigeria] [w/o 04Sep89 near Arles, France]
10474	600	Iranian Air Force	5-201+ 5-8801+ EP-SHL 5-8801 [+ Iran] [l/n 03Sep08 Tehran-Mehrabad, Iran]
10475	600	Iranian Air Force	5-202+ 5-8802+ EP-SHM 5-8802 [+ Iran] [l/n 02Sep08 Tehran-Mehrabad, Iran]

FOKKER F.27 FRIENDSHIP

C/n	Model	Last known Owner/Operator	Identities/fates/comments (where appropriate)
10476	600	(Myanma Airways)	(NAF-702)+ NAF-902+ 5N-ANM N4449C PH-EXB PH-BAC XY-AEN [+ Nigeria] [w/o 24Aug98 Payakha Mountain, Myanmar]
10477	600	(WDL Flugdienst)	PH-EXB PH-EXC PH-FRB S2-ABO OY-SLE D-AELE [stored Cologne/Bonn, Germany; canx 13Nov08; b/u 04Feb09]
10478	400M	Iranian Air Force	I5-203+ 5-8803 [+ Iran]
10479	400M	Iranian Air Force	I5-204+ 5-8804 [+ Iran] [l/n 02Sep06 Tehran-Mehrabad, Iran]
10480	400M	Iranian Air Force	5-205+ 5-8805+ EP-SHN 5-8805 [+ Iran] [l/n 29Jun08 Zahedan, Iran]
10481	400M	ex Air Bissau	PH-FPV 5-206+ 5-8806+ 201 J5-GBC [+ Iran; ^ Yemen; by 04Dec04 stored Algiers, Algeria; l/n 05Nov07]
10482	400M	Iranian Air Force	5-207+ 5-8807 [+ Iran]
10483	400M	Iranian Air Force	5-208+ 5-8808 [+ Iran] [l/n 11Jly99 Tehran-Mehrabad, Iran]
10484	600	(Iranian Air Force)	5-209 [originally built as c/n 10465][w/o 25Aug73 near Chalus, Iran] [originally built as c/n 10465] [w/o 25Aug73 near Chalus, Iran]
10485	400M	Iranian Air Force	5-210+ 5-209+ 5-8809 [+ Iran]
10486	600	Iranian Air Force	5-211+ 5-210+ 5-8810 [originally built as c/n 10466; + Iran]
10487	400M	ex Equatorial International Airlines	NAF-903+ 5N-ANT S9-TAC [+ Nigeria] [by Aug97 stored engineless Sao Tome; l/n Sep05 derelict]
10488	400M	(Nigerian Air Force)	PH-EXE NAF-904+ PH-FRD NAF-904 [+ Nigeria] [w/o 26May80 Lagos, Nigeria]
10489	400M	(Iranian Air Force)	PH-EXA PH-FPW 5-212+ 5-211 [+ Iran] [w/o 30Sep74 Sahrood, Iran]
10490	400M	ex Nigerian Air Force	PH-EXC NAF-905+ PH-FUD NAF-905 [+ Nigeria] [by Feb88 stored Benin City, Nigeria; l/n Mar96 derelict]
10491	400M	Iranian Air Force	PH-EXA 5-213+ 5-212+ 5-8811 [+ Iran]
10492	400M	Iranian Air Force	PH-EXF 5-214+ 5-213+ 5-8812 [+ Iran]
10493	400M	Guatemalan Air Force	PH-EXA NAF-906+ 5N-ANS N4449E TG-AFA 1093^ 1470^ 1770 [+ Nigeria; ^ Guatemala]
10494	400M	ex Air Algerie	PH-EXB PH-FPX 7T-WAI 7T-VRU [stored by May04 Algiers, Algeria; l/n 31May05]
10495	400M	ex Air Algerie	PH-FPZ 7T-WAK 7T-VRL [stored by May04 Algiers, Algeria; l/n 31May05]
10496	400M	(Air Algerie)	PH-FRA 7T-WAL 7T-VRM [w/o 25Jly91 In Guezzam Airport, Algeria]
10497	400M	Iranian Air Force	PH-EXW (5-215)+ 5-214+ 5-8813+ EP-SHO 5-8813 [+ Iran] [reported wfu by 02Sep06 Tehran-Mehrabad, Iran]
10498	600	Iranian Air Force	PH-EXX (5-216)+ 5-215+ EP-IAJ 5-8814 [+ Iran]
10499	400M	(Iranian Air Force)	PH-EXA (5-217)+ 5-216+ 5-8815 [w/o 26Apr92 near Saveh, Iran]
10500	400M	Iranian Air Force	PH-EXE 5-217+ 5-8816 [+ Iran]
10501	600	(Burma Airways Corp)	PH-EXF XY-ADS [w/o 12Oct85 near Putao, Burma]
10502	400M	Iranian Air Force	PH-EXI 5-218+ 5-8817 [+ Iran] [reported wfu by 02Sep06 Tehran-Mehrabad, Iran]
10503	500CRF	(Channel Express)	PH-EXK N703A G-CEXA [wfu May03; b/u 25Oct04 Bournemouth, UK]
10504	600	Iranian Air Force	PH-EXL 5-219+ EP-IAK 5-8818 [+ Iran]
10505	600	Ghana Air Force	PH-EXM PH-FRF G520 [coded A]
10506	500	(Trigana Air Service)	[rebuild of c/n 10447] F-BSUM HB-ISQ PK-YRA [w/o 16Sep08 during maintenance at Jayapura, Indonesia]
10507	400M	Ghana Air Force	PH-EXR PH-FRE G521+ PH-FRE G521 [coded B] [+ Ghana]
10508	600	(Channel Express)	PH-EXA OB-R-1042 N61AN OY-SRZ G-CHNL [w/o 12Jan99 near Guernsey Airport, Channel Islands; canx 28May99]
10509	400M	Iranian Navy	PH-EXB (5-2601)+ 5-2604 [+ Iran]
10510	400M	Iranian Navy	PH-EXC 5-2602 [reported wfu by 02Sep06 Tehran-Mehrabad, Iran]
10511	600	Iranian Navy	PH-EXD 5-2603 [reported wfu by 02Sep06 Tehran-Mehrabad, Iran; also reported to be b/u]
10512	600	Iranian Navy	PH-EXE PH-FRG 5-2601
10513	600	(Libyan Arab Airlines)	PH-EXG 5A-DBO [reported destroyed 2011 in air strike Bir Durfan AFB, Libya]
10514	600	(WDL Flugdienst)	PH-EXF OB-R-1082 N60AN D-AELI [wfu & stored Dec00 Cologne/Bonn, Germany; canx 01Oct03; b/u 03Feb09]
10515	600	ex Libyan Arab Airlines	PH-EXK 5A-DBP [wfu & stored Jun97 Tripoli International, Libya; l/n 09Oct09 derelict]
10516	400	ex Libyan Arab Airlines	PH-EXU 5A-DBQ [wfu & stored Jly99 Tripoli International, Libya; l/n 02Nov07 derelict]
10517	400	(Libyan Arab Airlines)	PH-EXV 5A-DBR [w/o 26Mar81 Kufra, Libya]
10518	400M	Ghana Air Force	PH-EXW PH-FRH G522 [coded C]

FOKKER F.27 FRIENDSHIP

C/n	Model	Last known Owner/Operator	Identities/fates/comments (where appropriate)
10519	600	ex Libyan Arab Airlines	PH-EXA 5A-DBS [stored Oct93 Tripoli International, Libya; l/n 19Nov08 derelict in compound]
10520	400M	Ghana Air Force	PH-EXX PH-FRI G523+ G525 [coded F] [+ Ghana coded D at this time]
10521	600	ex Libyan Arab Airlines	PH-EXB 5A-DBT [wfu & stored Jun92 Tripoli International, Libya; l/n 31Oct07]
10522	500F	Atlantic Airlines	PH-EXC VH-FCA N280MA N283EA HR-ATL
10523	600	ex Myanmar Airways	PH-EXE XY-ADT [stored by 18Nov05 Yangon, Myanmar; l/n Apr11]
10524	500F	Peruvian Navy	PH-EXD VH-FCB CC-CIS OB-1446 AE-562
10525	500CRF	Indonesian Air Transport	PH-EXF N702A PK-TSJ
10526	400M	ex Air Algerie	PH-EXR PH-FRC 7T-WAO 7T-VRQ [reported wfu by Oct05 Algiers, Algeria]
10527	600	Algerian Government	PH-EXS PH-FRD 7T-WAN 7T-VRN
10528	500	(G T Air)	[rebuild of c/n 10389] F-BPUI HB-ILQ PK-LTQ [b/u Feb10 Jakarta, Indonesia]
10529	400M	Algerian Government	PH-EXT PH-FRK 7T-WAM
10530	500CRF	(Fly540 Uganda)	PH-EXK N737A OK-ABA TC-MBC 5X-FFD [serious damage 27Jan11 Nairobi-Wilson, Kenya]
10531	500CRF	Fly540 Uganda	PH-EXM N739A OK-ABB TC-MBD 5X-FFN
10532	500F	(Friendship Spares)	PH-EXO VH-FCC N282MA [stored by 17Jan98 Mena-Intermountain Municipal, AR; canx 30Oct01 as b/u]
10533	500	(Expresso Aereo del Peru)	PH-EXS VH-FCD CC-CIT OB-1443 [w/o 10Sep92 Bellavista, Peru]
10534	500RF	(Fugro LADS Corp)	PH-EXW VH-EWP [canx 14Apr11 on sale to IAP Group for parts; ferried 27Mar11 to Opa-locka, FL; gone by 17Jly11]
10535	600	(Ghana AF/Ghana Airlink)	PH-EXX G524 [coded E] [w/o 05Jun00 Accra-Kotoka International Airport, Ghana]
10536	400M	Indonesian Air Force	PH-EXA PH-FRL T-2701+ A-2701 [+ Indonesia]
10537	400M	(Indonesian Air Force)	PH-EXB PH-FRM T-2702 [w/o 14Aug86 near Garut, Indonesia]
10538	400M	(Indonesian Air Force)	PH-EXC PH-FRN T-2703+ PK-VFE A-2703 [+ Indonesia] [w/o 06Apr09 Bandung-Husein Sastranegara International, Indonesia]
10539	500F	(TAM-Brazil)	PH-EXY VH-EWQ PH-JBO PT-LAM [w/o 17Jan97 near Uberaba Airport, Brazil; canx 05Jun97]
10540	400M	Indonesian Air Force	PH-EXD PH-FRO T-2704+ A-2704 [+ Indonesia]
10541	400M	Indonesian Air Force	PH-EXE PH-FRP T-2705+ A-2705 [+ Indonesia]
10542	400M	Indonesian Air Force	PH-EXF PH-FRR T-2706+ A-2706 [+ Indonesia]
10543	400M	ex Air Algerie	PH-EXS PH-FRU 7T-WAQ 7T-VRV [reported wfu byMay04 Algiers, Algeria]
10544	400M	Indonesian Air Force	PH-EXB PH-FRS T-2707+ A-2707 [+ Indonesia]
10545	200	Akureyri Museum	PH-EXC TF-SYN [preserved May 2009 Akureyri, Iceland; canx 10Jan12]
10546	400M	(Indonesian Air Force)	PH-EXH PH-FRT T-2708+ A-2708 [+ Indonesia] [w/o 21Jun12 near Jakarta-Halim Airport, Indonesia]
10547	400M	ex Air Algerie	PH-EXG PH-FRV 7T-WAS 7T-VRJ [reported wfu by May04 Algiers, Algeria; l/n Oct05]
10548	400MAR	(Peruvian Navy)	PH-EXD AE-560 [w/o 08Dec87 in Pacific Ocean near Lima, Peru]
10549	400MAR	(Peruvian Navy)	PH-EXE PH-MPA AE-561 [w/o 29Apr86 off Las Salines de Huacho, Peru]
10550	500CRF	MED Airlines	PH-EXF N743A G-CEXB TC-MBH CN-MMA
10551	500F	ex Merpati Nusantara Airlines	PH-EXA ZK-NFA PK-MFF [stored 27Apr04 Surabaya, Indonesia; l/n 13Dec09 poor condition]
10552	500F	ex Merpati Nusantara Airlines	PH-EXB ZK-NFB PK-MFG [stored by 30Jun04 Surabaya, Indonesia; l/n 13Dec09, poor condition]
10553	400M	ex Air Algerie	PH-EXO PH-FRW 7T-WAT 7T-VRK [reported wfu by May04 Algiers, Algeria; l/n Oct05]
10554	600	Tehran Aerospace Exhibition Center	PH-EXK PH-FRZ EP-ANA SN-4101 [used in re-enactment of the shooting down of c/n 10140 q.v.; by Nov04 stored in compound Tehran, Iran; l/n Sep06]
10555	400M	ex Air Algerie	PH-EXT PH-FRX 7T-WAU 7T-VRR [reported wfu by May04 Algiers, Algeria; l/n Oct05]
10556	400M	Algerian Govt	PH-EXS PH-FRY 7T-WAV 7T-VRW
10557	600RF	(Somali Airlines)	PH-EXC PH-FTA 6O-SAY [w/o en-route 20Jly81 near Balad, Somalia]
10558	500F	(Air UK)	PH-EXH VH-FCE G-BNCY [w/o 07Dec97 Guernsey Airport, Channel Islands, UK; canx 19Feb98]
10559	600RF	(Somali Airlines)	PH-EXG PH-FTB 6O-SAZ [w/o 28Jun89 near Hargeisa, Somalia]
10560	500	Air Panama	PH-EXL VH-FCF N284MA HP-1542PST
10561	400	(TAAG Angola Airlines)	PH-EXI PH-FTT D2-EFA T-101+ D2-TFS [+ Angola] [wfu by 01Apr99 Luanda, Angola; no recent reports]

FOKKER F.27 FRIENDSHIP

C/n	Model	Last known Owner/Operator	Identities/fates/comments (where appropriate)
10562	600	(FTG Air Service)	PH-EXK PH-YEM OE-ILB EC-DSS OE-ILB D-AELB [w/o 24Feb90 near Bergisch Gladbach, Germany]
10563	600	(Sudan Airways)	PH-EXM PH-FTH 5U-BAH PH-FTH HB-AAT EC-DSP HB-AAT 7P-LAJ ZS-EDY ST-SSD [w/o 11Jun02 Khartoum, Sudan]
10564	400M	Senegal Air Force	PH-EXA 6W-STA
10565	400M	(Senegal Air Force)	PH-EXB 6W-STB [wfu & stored 31May88 Dakar, Senegal; l/n Oct99, gone by Jly05; presumed b/u]
10566	600RF	(Air Tanzania)	PH-EXC PH-FTD 5H-MPT [w/o 12Dec93 Dar es Salaam, Tanzania; wreck stored & used for spares; l/n Jly97]
10567	600	Iranian Army	PH-EXF PH-FTF 5-4041+ 5-3031 [+ Iran]
10568	400M	Iranian Army	PH-EXG 5-4042+ 5-3032 [Iran]
10569	600RF	(International Aviation)	PH-EXH PH-FTE 5H-MPU [sold in Myanmar for spares use; noted 02Oct02 Yangon, Myanmar basic Air Tanzania c/s; canx post 26Apr03; b/u by Apr11]
10570	500	(Air Rouergue)	PH-EXA F-BYAH(2) [w/o 27Jan79 near Rodez Airport, France]
10571	600	(Laoag International Airlines)	PH-EXB PH-FTF SU-AZN 5X-UAO 5X-UWX 3C-QQB(2) RP-C6888 [w/o 11Nov02 Manila Bay, Philippines; en-route]
10572	600	(Burma Airways Corp)	PH-EXC XY-ADY [w/o 03Oct78 Mandalay, Burma]
10573	600	(Air Ivoire)	PH-EXE TU-TIF [w/o 25Jly86 Tabou Airport, Ivory Coast]
10574	600	ex Myanma Airways	PH-EXF XY-ADZ [wfu by Apr11 Yangon, Myanmar]
10575	400M	Argentine AF/LADE	PH-EXG TC-79
10576	600	(Myanma Airways)	PH-EXH PH-FTI (SU-AZZ) 5X-UAP OY-SRC XY-AES [w/o 27Jan98 Thandwe, Myanmar]
10577	400M	(Air Ivoire)	PH-EXK TU-VAD TU-TIP [w/o 26Jun96 Abidjan, Ivory Coast; remains l/n Aug00]
10578	400M	Bolivian Air Force	PH-EXL PH-FTN TAM-90+ FAB-90 [+ Bolivia]
10579	600	(Air Ivoire)	PH-EXF TU-TIH [wfu Sep92 Abidjan, Ivory Coast; derelict by Jan97; by mid-2004 in use as children's library in park in Abidjan City]
10580	400M	ex Bolivian Air Force	PH-EXM PH-FTO TAM-91+ FAB-91 [+Bolivia] [w/o 16Apr06 Guayaramerin, Bolivia; fuselage dumped La Paz-El Alto, Bolivia; l/n Oct09]
10581	200MAR	Spanish Air Force	PH-EXA PH-FTK D.2-01 [code 801-10]
10582	400M	Senegal Air Force	PH-EXB 6W-STC
10583	400M	(Senegal Air Force)	PH-EXC 6W-STD [stored by Oct99 Dakar, Senegal; late 2000 b/u for spares]
10584	400M	Bolivian Air Force	PH-EXH PH-FTM TAM-92+ FAB-92 [+Bolivia] [badly damaged in forced landing 23Jly08 on road near Beni, Bolivia, en-route to Guayaramerin, Bolivia]
10585	200MAR	Spanish Air Force	PH-EXD D.2-02 [code 801-11]
10586	600	ex Libyan Arab Airlines	PH-EXA 5A-DDU [wfu Nov93; by early 2004 dumped Tripoli International, Libya; l/n 09Oct09]
10587	200MAR	Spanish Air Force	PH-EXB PH-FTL D.2-03 [code 801-12]
10588	600	(Libyan Arab Airlines)	PH-EXC 5A-DDV [w/o 06Jun89 near Zella Airport, Libya]
10589	600RF	(Air Tanzania)	PH-EXD PH-FTP 5H-MRM [wfu 24Nov95 Dar es Salaam, Tanzania; used for spares]
10590	400M	(Senegal Air Force)	PH-EXE 6W-STE [wfu & stored 07Aug90 Dakar, Senegal; b/u 17Jly07]
10591	400M	Senegal Air Force	PH-EXF PH-FTS 6W-STF
10592	600	(Lloyd Aereo Boliviano)	PH-EXG N421SA PH-GDG CP-2165 [w/o 22Dec94 Guayaramerin Airport, Bolivia]
10593	600	(Myanma Airways)	PH-EXH N422SA PH-BKR XY-AEP [w/o 06Oct93 Kawthaung Airport, Myanmar]
10594	600	(Myanma Airways)	PH-EXK N423SA PH-ADJ XY-AEO [w/o 02Jly99 near Sittwe, Myanmar]
10595	200MAR	(TAAG Angola Airlines)	PH-EXL PH-FTU R-301+ T-101+ D2-MEF D2-TFM [+ Angola] [wfu by 01Apr99 Luanda, Angola; l/n Dec01; no recent reports]
10596	500	Airwork Flight Operations	PH-EXM PH-FTX N334MV N272SA PH-FTX CN-CDC PH-FTX TR-LCQ (F-GKEM) PH-FTX F-SEBJ HB-ILJ ZK-PAX
10597	500	(Merpati Nusantara Airlines)	PH-EXA ZK-NFD PK-MFI [w/o 18Jun94 near Pala Mutiara Airport, Indonesia]
10598	500	ex Merpati Nusantara Airlines	PH-EXB ZK-NFE PK-MFJ [by 30Jun04 stored Surabaya, Indonesia; l/n 13Dec09 derelict]
10599	400M	ex Bolivian Air Force	PH-EXC PH-FTT TAM-93+ FAB-93 [+ Bolivia] [by 20Oct07 stored La Paz-El Alto, Bolivia; l/n Oct09]
10600	400M	ex Bolivian Air Force	PH-EXD PH-FTV TAM-94+ FAB-94+ CP-2282 FAB-94 [+ Bolivia] [w/o 22Jan02 Guayaramerin Airport, Bolivia; fuselage dumped La Paz-El Alto, Bolivia; l/n Nov09]
10601	400M	ex Bolivian Air Force	PH-EXE PH-FTW TAM-95 [stored by 07Apr03 La Paz-El Alto, Bolivia; l/n Oct09]

FOKKER F.27 FRIENDSHIP

C/n	Model	Last known Owner/Operator	Identities/fates/comments (where appropriate)
10602	200MAR	(Philippine Air Force)	PH-EXF (TAM-96)+ 10602 [+ Bolivia] [w/o 19Dec88 Catarman, Philippines]
10603	500RF	Wings College of Aviation Technology	(PH-EXG) PH-KFI VT-EWK [stored Jun95 Bombay, India; derelict by Oct05; canx 28Mar06; moved 2006 to Pune, India, as GIA]
10604	500	ex Libyan Arab Airlines	PH-EXG PH-FTZ (N337MV) 5A-DJE [wfu & stored Apr93 Tripoli International, Libya; l/n 03Nov07]
10605	500RF	ex East-West Airlines	PH-KFK VT-EWE [w/o 01Jly95 Vadodara (Baroda), India; canx 28Mar06; hulk still present 19Dec09]
10606	500RF	Wings College of Aviation Technology	PH-KFL VT-EWG [stored Jun95 Bombay, India; derelict by Oct05; canx 28Mar06; moved 2006 to Pune, India, as teaching aid]
10607	500F	ex Merpati Nusantara Airlines	PH-EXH ZK-NFF PK-MFK [by 30Jun04 stored Surabaya, Indonesia; l/n 13Dec09 derelict]
10608	500	(TAAG Angola Airlines)	PH-EXK (N424SA) (G527)+ (D2-ESM) PH-FSK D2-TFW [+ Ghana; code G] [wfu by May01 Luanda, Angola; l/n derelict Dec01, no recent reports; assumed b/u]
10609	500F	(Merpati Nusantara Airlines)	PH-EXI (ZK-NFG) ZK-NFH PK-MFL [w/o 26Mar01 near Surabaya Airport, Indonesia]
10610	500RF	Sonair	PH-EXJ PH-FTY D2-ESN
10611	500	ex Libyan Arab Airlines	PH-EXL (N338MV) 5A-DJF [wfu & stored May93 Tripoli International, Libya; l/n 09Oct09]
10612	200MAR	(Trygon Ltd)	PH-EXC M-1+ 3C-QSB [+ Netherlands] [stored 28Aug02 Southend, UK; b/u for spares 30Jan-03Feb06; by 20Jan11 mid-fuselage at paintball site Abridge, Essex, UK]
10613	500RF	(Mountain Air Cargo/FedEx Express)	PH-EXM 9M-MCK N712FE [stored Kinston Regional Jetport-Stallings Field NC; probably b/u there; canx 14Mar05]
10614	500F	(Merpati Nusantara Airlines)	PH-EXB (ZK-NFH) ZK-NFI PK-MFM [PWFU 01Jly98; stored Surabaya, Indonesia; l/n 13Dec09]
10615	500RF	Canguro Onlus Flights Aid Association	PH-EXD 9M-MCL N713FE N19AY I-MDLT XT-AID
10616	200MAR	(Philippine Air Force)	PH-EXF 10616 [w/o Mar89 Laoag Airport, Philippines]
10617	500	Myanmar Air Force	PH-EXE (N339MV) (N425SA) XY-ADX XY-AEJ 0002
10618	500F	ex Merpati Nusantara Airlines	PH-EXG (ZK-NFI) ZK-NFJ PK-MFN [by 30Jun04 stored Surabaya, Indonesia; l/n 13Dect09 derelict]
10619	400M	(Argentine AF/LADE)	PH-EXH TC-72(2) [w/o 89Nov95 near Valla de Valores, Argentina, en-route]
10620	200MAR	Philippine Air Force	PH-EXI 10620
10621	400M	Argentine AF/LADE	PH-EXM TC-75
10622	200MAR	(Trygon Ltd)	PH-EXD PH-FSI M-2+ 3C-QSC [+ Netherlands] [stored 27Aug02 Southend, UK; b/u for spares Jun-Jly06]
10623	500RF	ex Merpati Nusantara Airlines	PH-EXB PK-GRF PK-MFG PK-GRF PK-MFQ [stored 30Mar06 Surabaya, Indonesia; l/n 13Dec09 derelict]
10624	500RF	ex Merpati Nusantara Airlines	PH-EXC PK-GRG PK-MFI PK-GRG PK-MFU [canx by 2001; stored by 03Mar04 Surabaya, Indonesia; l/n 13Dec09; reported sold in Malaysia for parts]
10625	500RF	ex Merpati Nusantara Airlines	PH-EXJ PK-GRH (PK-MFJ) PK-GRH PK-MFV [stored by 30Jun04 Surabaya, Indonesia; l/n 13Dec09 derelict]
10626	500RF	ex Merpati Nusantara Airlines	PH-EXF PK-GRI (PK-MFK) PK-GRI PK-MFW [stored by 09Mar06 Surabaya, Indonesia; l/n 26Dec08 derelict; reported to be auctioned on 05Jan09]
10627	500	(Fly540.com)	PH-EXL VH-EWU G-JEAD I-FWXB G-JEAD 5Y-BVF [w/o 13Aug08 airstrip K-50 about 50km SW of Mogadishu, Somalia]
10628	500RF	ex Merpati Nusantara Airlines	PH-EXG PK-GRJ (PK-MFL) PK-GRJ PK-MFX [stored by Jun01 Surabaya, Indonesia; l/n 13Dec09; reported sold in Malaysia for parts]
10629	500RF	ex Merpati Nusantara Airlines	PH-EXE PK-GRK (PK-MFM) PK-GRK PK-MFY [stored by 14Jan10 Sentani-Jayapura, Indonesia]
10630	500RF	ex Voyager Airlines	PH-EXH A4O-FB 4R-EXG (AP-BHE) S2-AEM [by 22Apr12 stored Chittagong, Bangladesh]
10631	500RF	Expo Aviation	PH-EXM A4O-FC 4R-EXF 4R-MRA 4R-EXK
10632	500F	Asialink Cargo Express	PH-EXB PH-FSJ PT-LAJ F-WQKM PH-FYC (D-AFGE) HA-FAF N19XF PK-KRA
10633	500F	Knight Aviation	PH-EXC PH-FSO VH-EWV G-JEAE EI-SMF 5Y-BTX [reported stored Sep09 Nairobi-Wilson, Kenya; l/n 09Dec11]
10634	500F	ex 19th Hole Corp, UK	PH-EXJ PH-FSL (N426SA) PT-LAK PH-FHL (D-AFGF) HA-FAH N19XG+ 9Q- [+ canx 09Mar12 to Congo]
10635	600	ex Libyan Arab Airlines	PH-EXD 5A-DLK [wfu & stored Nov94 Tripoli International, Libya; l/n 03Nov07]
10636	600	ex Libyan Arab Airlines	PH-EXB 5A-DLM [wfu & stored Tripoli International, Libya; l/n 31Oct07]

FOKKER F.27 FRIENDSHIP

C/n	Model	Last known Owner/Operator	Identities/fates/comments (where appropriate)
10637	500F	ex Executive Jet Support	PH-EXE VH-EWW G-JEAF OY-SRD G-JEAF I-JEAF G-JEAF I-SIXA G-JEAF [stored as I-SIXA by 29Mar08 Bergamo, Italy; l/n 14May12]
10638	600	ex Libyan Arab Airlines	PH-EXF 5A-DKD [wfu & stored Nov94 Tripoli International, Libya; l/n 03Nov07]
10639	500	MNG Airlines	PH-EXG VH-EWX G-JEAG D-ADAP G-JEAG D-ACCT [w/o 18Jan07 Coventry, UK, stripped of parts & stored; b/u & parts removed 14Jly08]
10640	600	ex Libyan Arab Airlines	PH-EXH 5A-DLN [wfu & stored Feb95 Tripoli International, Libya; l/n 09Oct09 sitting on its tail]
10641	500RF	ex Eagle Air	PH-EXI A4O-FE PH-SFI A4O-FE 5H-HSE 3C-QRZ (RP-C588) [stored/wfu Jly02 Subang, Selangor, Malaysia; l/n 16Sep10]
10642	500RF	Expo Aviation	PH-EXJ A4O-FG 4R-EXH AP-BHF 4R-EXH
10643	500	(Dodson Aviation Inc)	PH-EXK PH-FSN N27SA N982MA [wfu May94 Honolulu, HI; used for spares; l/n 30Jun07]
10644	600	ex Libyan Arab Airlines	PH-EXM 5A-DLO [lstored Jun97 Tripoli International, Libya; l/n 09Oct09 derelict in compound]
10645	600	(Libyan Arab Airlines)	PH-EXB 5A-DLP [w/o 15Apr86 in air raid Benghazi-Benina Airport, Libya; hulk l/n 28May99]
10646	600	ex Libyan Arab Airlines	PH-EXD 5A-DLQ [wfu & stored Jly94 Tripoli International, Libya; l/n 31Oct07]
10647	600	(Libyan Arab Airlines)	PH-EXH 5A-DLR [w/o during 1986 Giallo Airport, Libya]
10648	600	ex Libyan Arab Airlines	PH-EXA 5A-DLS TT-LAA 5A-DLS [wfu & stored Aug91 Tripoli International, Libya; l/n 03Nov07]
10649	400M	(Scibe Airlift)	PH-EXJ PH-EXE 9Q-CBH TR-LDF 9Q-CBH [w/o 13Dec92 nr Goma, Zaire]
10650	400M	Royal Thai Navy	PH-EXI PH-EXK PH-TAI 10650+ 221+ 2211+ 2110 [+ Thailand] [l/n active 08Jan11]
10651	400M	Royal Thai Navy	PH-EXM PH-EXI PH-EXA PH-NAV 10651+ 222+ 2212+ 2111 [+ Thailand] [l/n active 08Jan11]
10652	400M	US Army	PH-EXB PH-FUA 85-1607 [C-31A; Golden Knights Parachute team]
10653	200MAR	(Nigerian Air Force)	PH-EXH PH-FSM NAF-907 [wfu 06Jan88 Benin City, Nigeria; l/n Mar96]
10654	500F	PT Asialink Cargo Express	PH-EXJ SU-GAF G-CEXE TC-MBA PK-KRL
10655	400M	(Scibe Airlift)	PH-EXI PH-FSR 9Q-CBE [DBR 10Sep91 in Uganda by rebel gunfire; wfu Goma, Democratic Republic of Congo; l/n Jan92]
10656	200MAR	(Nigerian Air Force)	PH-EXD PH-FSP NAF-908 [w/o 23Apr95 at Lagos, Nigeria, hit by DHC-6 5N-AJQ (c/n 607) on the ground; l/n derelict 10Dec96]
10657	500	(Mountain Air Cargo/FedEx Express)	PH-EXK N501AW N728FE OO-FEL N728FE [stored by 07Aug07 Kinston Regional Jetport-Stallings Field, NC; canx 08Apr08]
10658	500	Air Panama	PH-EXA N241MA N514AW (OO-FEO) N725FE HP-1631PST
10659	500	(Air Sinai)	PH-EXF SU-GAD [w/o 06Jun86 Cairo, Egypt]
10660	500F	PT Asialink Cargo Express	PH-EXC SU-GAE G-CEXF TC-MBB PK-KRJ
10661	500	(Mountain Air Cargo/FedEx Express)	PH-EXE N502AW N727FE OO-FEM N727FE [stored by 07Aug07 Kinston Regional Jetport-Stallings Field, NC; canx 08Apr08]
10662	400M	Finnish Air Force	PH-EXL FF-3
10663	200MAR	Royal Thai Navy	PH-EXH PH-FSX 10663+ 111+ 1109+ 1202 [+Thailand] [by 10Nov02 stored U-Tapao, Thailand; l/n 01Oct07]
10664	500F	Indian Aerospace & Engineeering	PH-EXG N239MA G-JEAA VT-UPD [CofA expired 24Apr00; stored Rajkot, India; by 2011 GIA Turbhe, Mumbai, India]
10665	200MAR	(Royal Thai Navy)	PH-EXL PH-FSU 10665 [w/o 08Jan85 Bangkok, Thailand]
10666	200MAR	Royal Thai Navy	PH-EXC PH-FSV 10666+ 112+ 1110+ 1109+ 1201+ [+Thailand] [by 10Nov02 stored U-Tapao, Thailand; l/n 10Jan09]
10667	500F	ex UP Air	PH-EXI N240MA G-JEAB VT-UPC [CofA expired 03Jly99, stored derelict Delhi, India; l/n 06May08]
10668	400M	US Army	PH-EXJ PH-FUB 85-1608 [C-31A; Golden Knights Parachute team]
10669	500RF	Philippine Air Force	PH-EXL VH-EWY G-JEAH G-ECAH 10669
10670	200	(Elbee Airlines)	PH-EXU PH-FSY LN-AKA (SE-KXV) VT-SSA [w/o 03Jly97 in sea off Mumbai, India]
10671	500	(NEPC Airways)	PH-EXC N503AW VT-NEA [wfu by 09Jun97 & stored Calcutta, India; l/n derelict 10May08]
10672	500F	ex Euroceltic Airways	PH-EXS VH-EWZ G-JEAI G-ECAT [w/o 02Nov02 Sligo, Ireland; wreck used for fire training; l/n 05Jun07]
10673	200	ex Elbee Airlines	PH-EXY LN-AKB 5N-BAU LN-AKB VT-SSB [wfu by 18Nov98 Chennai (Madras), India; l/n 23Feb06]
10674	200	(Elbee Airlines)	PH-EXG LN-AKC (SE-KXY) LN-AKC VT-SSC (D-ASKY) [wfu by 17Nov98 Mumbai, India; dismantled and taken away by road 03Nov07]

FOKKER F.27 FRIENDSHIP

C/n	Model	Last known Owner/Operator	Identities/fates/comments (where appropriate)
10675	200	Africa Air Assistance	(PH-EXB) PH-EXL LN-AKD (SE-KXZ) OY-EBC 6V-AHS [stored by 14Jly05 Dakar, Senegal; 17Jan07 hangared; l/n Nov07]
10676	200MAR	ex Royal Thai Navy	PH-EXT PH-RTN 10676+ 113+ 1111+ 1203 [+ Thailand; by Sep11 derelict U-Tapao, Thailand]
10677	500	North Carolina Global TransPark	PH-EXP N504AW N729FE OO-FEK N724FE [wfu & canx 18Aug06; donated by FedEx for use as firefighting training Kinston Regional Jetport-Stallings Field, NC]
10678	500	ex NEPC Airways	PH-EXR N242MA N515AW VT-NEE [wfu by 31Jan97; stored Chennai (Madras), India; l/n 17Mar11]
10679	500	ex NEPC Airways	PH-EXV N243MA PH-RTG VT-NEG [wfu by 21Jun97; stored Channai (Madras), lIndia; l/n 17Mar11]
10680	500	Airwork Flight Operations	PH-EXW N244MA PH-RFG VT-NEH ZK-POH
10681	500	Safari Express Cargo	PH-EXN N505AW OE-ILW N19KK 5Y-SXP
10682	500	(Mountain Air Cargo/FedEx Express)	PH-EXA N506AW N730FE OO-FEI N723FE [stored by 06Nov05 Kinston Regional Jetport-Stallings Field, NC; canx 15Apr08; l/n 05Sep10]
10683	500	(Mountain Air Cargo/FedEx Express)	PH-EXX N508AW N726FE (OO-FEN) N726FE [stored by 06Nov05 Kinston Regional Jetport-Stallings Field, NC; canx 21Mar08]
10684	500	ex NEPC Airways	PH-EXM N509AW OE-IGN N509AW VT-NEJ [wfu by 21Jan98; stored Coimbatore, India; l/n 24Mar11]
10685			[prototype Fokker 50]
10686	500	J S Focus Air	PH-EXF N510AW OE-IPN D-ADUP AP-BHZ
10687	500	ex NEPC Airways	PH-EXS 9Q-CBD TR-LCW N8005L VT-NEK [wfu by 21Jan98; stored Chennai (Madras), India; l/n 17Mar11]
10688			[second prototype Fokker 50]
10689	600	(Burma Airways Corp)	PH-EXB PH-EXI PH-FUC XY-AEL [w/o 11Oct87 near Pagan, Burma]
10690	500	ex NEPC Airways	PH-EXO N511AW VT-NEB [wfu by 03Apr97; stored Coimbatore, India; rotting hulk l/n 24Mar11]
10691	500	ex NEPC Airways	PH-EXD N512AW VT-NEC [wfu by 25May97; stored Chennai (Madras), India; l/n 17Mar11]
10692	500	(NEPC Airways)	PH-EXH N513AW VT-NED [wfu 21Nov97 Blenheim-Woodbourne, New Zealand; b/u 02Jun06]

Unidentified

unkn		Peruvian Coast Guard	AB-527 [reported at Lima, Peru during 2007, could be ex AB-582 c/n 10355 but this was seen there 21Aug07]
unkn	200	Pakistan Navy	AR-NZY//77 [reported Mehran, Pakistan; possibly either c/n 10230 or c/n 10305 made airworthy; dual marks]

Production complete

FOKKER 50 and 60 (FOKKER F-27-050 AND F-27-060)

C/n	Model	Last known Owner/Operator	Identities/fates/comments (where appropriate)

Note: With the exception of c/n 20253, 20268, 20269, 20287, 20294 and 20295 which have the certicated designation F27-0502 all Fokker 50s are officially F27-050s. The Fokker 60s are F27-604 but sometimes also known F27-0602s.

C/n	Model	Last known Owner/Operator	Identities/fates/comments (where appropriate)
10685	50	(Fokker)	PH-OSO [f/f 28Dec85; wfu & stored Aug96 Amsterdam, Netherlands, until b/u Jun98]
10688	50	(Fokker)	PH-OSI [last flight 15Nov89; used as non-flying version of proposed maritime & military variant, except fuselage & tail b/u; 01Oct92 fuselage to Fokker Heritage Trust & loaned to Aviodrome Museum, Lelystad, Netherlands & used as "gate guardian"]
20103	50F	Largus Aviation/Amapola Flyg	PH-DMO OO-VLC PH-DMO OY-MBM PH-DMO SX-BTI PH-DMO VT-CAA SE-LJV
20104	50	(VLM Airlines)	PH-EXC (PH-DLT) D-AFKA PH-ARD SX-BSE PH-ARD Z-WPG PH-ARD OO-VLG [b/u Brussels, Belgium circa Oct02; canx 23Oct02]
20105	50	CityJet	PH-EXE D-AFKB PH-ARE SX-BSF PH-ARE Z-WPH PH-ARE OO-VLJ
20106	50	Skywest Airlines	PH-EXG VH-FNA (PH-FZA)
20107	50	Skywest Airlines	PH-EXF VH-FNB
20108	50	ex Skyways Express	PH-EXP VH-FNC SE-LEH [stored 28Jun12 Maastricht, Netherlands]
20109	50	CityJet	PH-EXR (PH-WDL) D-AFKH EC-868 EC-GBG OO-VLS
20110	50	ex Skyways Express	PH-EXL VH-FNE (VT-RAA) SE-LEL [stored 27Jun12 Maastricht, Netherlands]
20111	50	ex Skyways Express	PH-EXV VH-FNF VT-RAB VH-FNF SE-LED [stored 28Jun12 Maastricht, Netherlands]
20112	50	ex Skyways Express	PH-EXW VH-FNG OE-LFX VH-FNG SE-LEC [stored 02Aug12 Maastricht, Netherlands]
20113	50	Skywest Airlines	PH-EXY VH-FNH (VT-RAC)
20114	50	Skywest Airlines	PH-EXZ VH-FNI
20115	50	ex Skyways Express	PH-EXD VH-FNJ OE-LFW VH-FNJ 9M-MGZ SE-LEU [stored 27Jun12 Maastricht, Netherlands]
20116	50	ex Skyways Express	PH-EXJ (VH-FNK) OE-LFY PH-GHK D-AFKX PH-GHK SE-LEA [stored 29Jun12 Maastricht, Netherlands]
20117	50F	(Aircraft Salvage Int'l)	PH-EXA (VH-FNL) OE-LFZ PH-DLT D-AFKY PH-DLT LN-KKA PH-DLT [canx 30Jly04; b/u Kemble, UK]
20118	50F	Amapola Flyg	PH-EXB (VH-FNM) PH-LMA EI-FKA OY-EBB (PH-LCA) PH-LMA SE-MFA
20119	50F	Amapola Flyg	PH-EXC (VH-FNN) PH-LMB EI-FKB OY-EBD (PH-LCD) PH-LMB
20120	50	airBaltic	PH-EXE (VH-FNO) (PH-LMC) PH-JHD D-AFKZ PH-JHD SE-LEB YL-BAA
20121	50	CityJet	PH-EXF D-AFKC PH-ARF (OO-VLJ) PT-SLL PH-ARF OO-VLR
20122	50	Travel Air	PH-EXG OE-LFA PH-FZF OO-VLK PH-FZF P2-TAH
20123	50	Palestinian Airlines	PH-EXH OE-LFB (PH-FXJ) PH-FZJ SU-YAH
20124	50	Amapola Flyg	PH-EXI OY-MMG SE-KTC
20125	50	Amapola Flyg	PH-EXJ OY-MMH SE-KTD
20126	50	airBaltic	PH-EXK OY-MMI ES-AFK PH-AAO YL-LAU
20127	50	CityJet	PH-EXL OY-MMJ ES-AFL OO-VLO
20128	50	ex Skyways Express	PH-PRA SE-LEZ [stored 29Jun12 Malmo-Sturup, Sweden]
20129	50	Skywest Airlines	PH-EXB VH-FND
20130	50	Mid Airlines	PH-EXC (LN-AKE) LN-BBA ST-ARG
20131	50	Mid Airlines	PH-EXE (LN-AKF) LN-BBB ST-ARH
20132	50	ex CityJet	PH-EXF D-AFKD PH-ARG OO-VLE [wfu for parts 17Jly11 Norwich, UK; canx 17Aug11]
20133	50	Bluebird Aviation	PH-EXG D-AFKE PH-FZA EC-771 EC-GAD D-AFFZ 5Y-VVJ
20134	50	Mid Airlines	PH-EXH (LN-AKG) LN-BBC ST-ARZ
20135	50	CityJet	PH-EXI (LN-AKH) LN-BBD OO-VLM PH-VLM OO-VLM
20136	50	Bluebird Aviation	PH-EXJ 5Y-BFM (PH-DMD) EC-GQT (PH-DML) N136NM 5Y-VVF
20137	50	Bluebird Aviation	PH-EXM 5Y-BFN PH-DMK (EC-GUT) EC-HLC N137NM 5Y-VVG
20138	50	Feeder Airlines	PH-PRB SE-LIN PH-PRB ST-NEW
20139	50		[was for Corsair Inc, but order cancelled and aircraft not built]
20140	50		[was for Corsair Inc, but order cancelled and aircraft not built]
20141	50	Indonesian Police	PH-EXN D-AFKF PH-FZB EC-780 EC-GAE D-AFFY PK-TWE P-2035+ P-4401 [+ Indonesia]
20142	50	Riau Airlines	PH-EXO D-AFKG PH-FZC EC-781 EC-GAF D-AFFX PK-TWF PK-RAH
20143	50	Palestinian Airlines	PH-EXP OE-LFC PH-FZI SU-YAI
20144	50	CityJet	PH-EXS OE-LFD (PH-DMI) SE-LEM PH-DMD TF-JMG OO-VLL

FOKKER 50 and 60 (FOKKER F-27-050 AND F-27-060)

C/n	Model	Last known Owner/Operator	Identities/fates/comments (where appropriate)
20145	50	CityJet	PH-EXT (LN-AKI) LN-BBE OO-VLN PH-VLN OO-VLN
20146	50	Skyways Express	PH-PRC SE-LIO
20147	50	Largus Aviation/Amapola Flyg	PH-PRD SE-LIP PH-PRD SE-LIP
20148	50	airBaltic	PH-EXU OY-MMS YL-BAW
20149	50	airBaltic	PH-EXV OY-MMT PH-LVL YL-BAR
20150	50	ex MASwings	PH-EXM (9M-MSA) 9M-MGA [reported sold Aug11 to Werner Aero Services for spares recovery; stored Kuala Lumpur-Sebang, Malaysia; l/n 05Dec11]
20151	50	ex Skyways Express	PH-PRE SE-LIR [stored 28Jun12 Borlange, Sweden]
20152	50	Largus Aviation/Amapola Flyg	PH-PRF SE-LIS
20153	50	airBaltic	PH-EXN OY-MMU G-BYBT OY-MMU ES-AFM YL-BAZ LY-BAZ YL-BAZ
20154	50	(Mid Airlines)	PH-EXO OY-MMV G-BXZW OY-MMV ES-AFN ST-ARA [w/o 16Jun03 Adar Yel Airstrip, Sudan]
20155	50	Sudan Airways	PH-PRG ST-ASF
20156	50	ex MASwings	PH-EXP (9M-MSB) 9M-MGB [stored by 16Sep10 Subang, Malaysia; l/n Jan12 with no engines]
20157	50	(Cargil International)	PH-EXA ST-ALN VP-CSD [believed b/u during 2002 Khartoum, Sudan]
20158	50	Kish Air	PH-EXB ST-ALO VP-CSE EP-LBV
20159	50	CityJet	PH-EXC PH-LBT (ST-ALP) D-AFKI EC-869 EC-GBH OO-VLQ
20160	50	Alliance Airlines	PH-EXD (ST-ALR) (PH-LBV) PH-EXD D-AFKJ EC-871 EC-GDD OO-VLV VH-FKO
20161	50	Alliance Airlines	PH-EXG (9M-MSC) 9M-MGC VH-AHX VH-FKP [reported wfu Jly12 Adelaide, Australia]
20162	50	airBaltic	PH-EXE OY-KAE YL-BAS
20163	50	airBaltic	PH-EXF OY-KAF YL-BAT
20164	50	Werner Aero Services	PH-EXL (9M-MSD) 9M-MGD [by 16Sep10 stored Subang, Malaysia; l/n Jan12; for parts use]
20165	50	(Scandinavian Airlines System)	PH-EXG SE-LFA [stored 06Aug01; b/u Dec02 Linkoping, Sweden]
20166	50	ex MASwings	PH-EXN (9M-MSE) 9M-MGE [stored 2010 Subang, Malaysia; l/n 05Dec11; reported for Travel Air]
20167	50	ex MASwings	PH-EXO (9M-MSF) 9M-MGF [stored Subang, Malaysia; l/n Jan12]
20168	50	Amapola Flyg	PH-EXH LX-LGC SE-LJG
20169	50	(Scandinavian Airlines System)	PH-EXI SE-LFB [stored by 06Jly07; b/u Dec02 Linkoping, Sweden]
20170	50	ex MASwings	PH-EXS (9M-MSG) 9M-MGG [reported purchased by Werner Aero Services for spares: by Mar10 noted stripped of parts Subang, Malaysia]
20171	50	Amapola Flyg	PH-EXJ LX-LGD SE-LJH
20172	50	(SAS Commuter)	PH-EXW LN-RNH [wfs 03May02; stored 04Jun02 Maastricht, Netherlands; canx 11Jly02; b/u 05Mar04, fuselage shipped to Denver-Centennial, CO for use in Fokker 50]
20173	50	(Scandinavian Airlines System)	PH-EXX LN-RNB [stored 22Feb02 Maastricht, Netherlands; canx11Jly02; b/u 05Mar04]
20174	50	(Malaysia Airlines)	PH-EXA (9M-MSH) 9M-MGH [w/o 15Sep95 Tawau, Malaysia]
20175	50	Skyward International	PH-EXB (9M-MSI) 9M-MGI 5Y-CAN
20176	50	Compagnie Africaine d'Aviation	PH-EXY LN-RNC+ 9Q-CCI
20177	50	Travel Air	PH-EXC EI-FKC PH-ZFD OO-VLX PH-ZFD P2-TAG
20178	50	Air Panama	PH-EXZ LN-RND HP-1605PST
20179	50	Air Panama	PH-EXE LN-RNE HP-1606PST [qv Fokker F-27 c/n 10394]
20180	50	Amapola Flyg	PH-EXF LX-LGE SE-LJI
20181	50	CityJet	PH-EXG EI-FKD PH-ZFC OO-VLY
20182	50	(Denim Air/Air Nostrum)	PH-EXH HB-IAN PH-FZE PT-MLA PH-FZE EC-HUB PH-FZE [w/o 17Jan03 Melilla, Spanish Morocco]
20183	50	Mongolian Airlines	PH-EXI LN-RNF JU-8881
20184	50	Mongolian Airlines	PH-EXJ LN-RNG JU-8882
20185	50	Indonesia Air Transport	PH-EXL OY-KAG PH-ZDA PK-TSN
20186	50	Indonesia Air Transport	PH-EXM OY-KAH PH-ZDB PK-TSO
20187	50	ex Air Astana	PH-EXN SE-LFC PH-ZDC HS-KLC PH-ZDC P4-JAS PH-ZDC [stored 18Jun12 Woendrecht, Netherlands]
20188	50	ex Air Astana	PH-EXB SE-LFK PH-ZDD HS-KLD PH-ZDD P4-KAS PH-ZDE [stored 18Jun12 Woendrecht, Netherlands]
20189	50	airBaltic	PH-EXC PH-KVA YL-BAO LY-BAO YL-BAO*
20190	50	airBaltic	PH-EXD PH-KVB YL-BAV LY-BAV YL-BAV*
20191	50F	ex Miniliner	PH-EXF PH-KVC I-MLCT [stored 17Dec09 Bergamo, Italy]
20192	50	Travel Air	PH-EXO PH-LMT HB-IAO PH-LMT PT-MLB PH-LMT EC-HYJ PH-LMT P2-TAF

FOKKER 50 and 60 (FOKKER F-27-050 AND F-27-060)

C/n	Model	Last known Owner/Operator	Identities/fates/comments (where appropriate)
20193	50	Air Astana	PH-EXP SE-LFN PH-ZDE HS-KLE PH-ZDE P4-LAS
20194	50	ex Skyways Express	PH-EXS OY-KAI PH-ZDF SE-LIT [stored 27Jun12 Borlange, Sweden]
20195	50	Air Astana	PH-EXA OY-KAK PH-ZDG P4-LAS
20196	50	Compagnie Africane d'Aviation	PH-EXE PH-LMS JA8875 SE-KXZ PH-LMS (9Q-CAA) PH-LMS 9Q-CJB
20197	50F	Miniliner	PH-KVD I-MLDT
20198	50	Air Astana	PH-EXG SE-LFO PH-ZDH SX-BTJ SE-LFO P4-HAS
20199	50	Minoan Air/Goodfly	PH-EXH SE-LFP PH-ZDI (SX-BTK) (SE-LFP) LN-RNM PH-ZDI SX-BRV
20200	50	Skywest Airlines	PH-PRH VH-FNF
20201	50	Sudan Airways	PH-PRI ST-ARB PH-PRI ST-ASD
20202	50	Travel Air	PH-EXL HB-IAP PH-FZG PT-MLC PH-FZG EC-HZA PH-FZG P2-TAE
20203	50	Bluebird Aviation	PH-EXR (5Y-BHI) 5Y-BHK EC-GTE PH-DMG EC-HKA 5Y-VVH
20204	50	Skyward International	PH-EXM 9M-MGJ 5Y-BYE
20205	50	Air Iceland	PH-EXN D-AFKK TF-JMO
20206	50	Minoan Air	PH-KVE SX-BRS
20207	50	Minoan Air	PH-KVF SX-BRM
20208	50	CityJet	PH-EXA EI-FKE PH-DMT OO-VLF
20209	50	CityJet	PH-EXE EI-FKF PH-DMS OO-VLP
20210	50	Skyways Express	PH-EXB HB-IAR PH-FZH PT-MLD PH-FZH EC-IAD PH-FZH SE-MEI (E3-)
20211	50	Insel Air	PH-KVG PJ-KVG
20212	50	Skywest Airlines	PH-PRJ VH-FNE
20213	50	ex Bluebird Aviation	PH-EXC D-AFKL 5Y-VVK [seriously damaged 10Nov11Guriceel, Somalia; l/n 11Jan12]
20214	50	Air Iceland	PH-EXD D-AFKM TF-JMM
20215	50	(Scandinavian Airlines System)	PH-EXG PH-RRD SE-LFR [wfu 06Jly03; b/u Nov02 Linkoping, Sweden; canx 11Apr03]
20216	50	airBaltic	PH-EXO SE-LFS YL-BAC
20217	50	Insel Air	PH-KVH PJ-KVH+ [+ canx 23Jun11 to Aruba; marks not confirmed]
20218	50	Insel Air	PH-KVI PJ-KVI
20219	50	Insel Air	PH-KVK PJ-KVK
20220	50	NAFT Airlines	PH-EXS PH-RRF HB-IAS PH-RRF PT-MLE PH-RRF EC-HNS PH-RRF EP-NFT
20221	50	(Luxair)	PH-EXU LX-LGB [w/o 06Nov02 Luxembourg-Findel, Luxembourg]
20222	50	NAFT Airlines	PH-EXV PH-LNZ EP-OIL
20223	50	Air Iceland	PH-EXX D-AFKN TF-JMN
20224	50	NAFT Airlines	(PH-EXY) PH-JXA EP-GAS
20225	50	Pelangi Air	(PH-EXZ) PH-JXB 9M-MEQ
20226	50	CityJet	PH-EXC PH-JXC PT-SLQ LN-KKE SE-LTR PH-JXC OO-VLI
20227	50	Samco Aircraft Maintenance	(PH-EXJ) PH-EXY OE-LFE PH-DMC OY-EBG PK-AIY ST-NVA PH-DMC [stored by 14Dec10 Maastricht, Netherlands as ST-NVA; reported for parts use; l/n 26Mar11]
20228	50	Royal Thai Police	PH-JXD 27228
20229	50	Republic of China Air Force	(PH-EXF) PH-JXE 5001
20230	50	Minoan Air	PH-JXF PT-SLR LN-KKD PH-JXF SE-LTS (PH-STU)? 5B-DCB SX-BRT [ferried Jan11 to Maastricht, Netherlands; canx; l/n 26Mar11]
20231	50	Tanzanian Government	PH-JXG 5H-TGF
20232	50	Denim Air	PH-JXJ (PT-OQB) PT-SLJ PH-JXJ
20233	50	Denim Air	PH-JXK (PT-OQA) PH-JXK PT-SLK PH-JXK
20234	50	Aria Air	PH-EXB PH-JXO D-AFKO EP-EAH
20235	50	Aria Air	PH-EXE D-AFKP EP-EAF
20236	50	Kish Air	PH-JXL D-AFKU PH-JXL EP-LCG
20237	50	Air Astana	PH-JXM D-AFKV PH-JXM PT-SLZ PH-JXM PK-PFH PH-JXM (SE-LLO) OO-VLT P4-RAS
20238	50	Republic of China Air Force	PH-JXH 5002
20239	50	Denim Air	PH-JXN D-AFKW PH-JXN (PH-JXW) (PH-JYB) EC-152 EC-GFP PH-JXN
20240	50	TransNusa	PH-EXC PH-RRK D2-ESR PK-TNC
20241	50	Sonangol State Corp/SonAir	PH-EXD PH-RRM D2-ESW [stored Woensdrecht, Netherlands; l/n 03Dec11]
20242	50	Republic of China Air Force	PH-JXI 5003
20243	50	Air Iceland	PH-EXM TF-FIR TF-JMR

FOKKER 50 and 60 (FOKKER F-27-050 AND F-27-060)

C/n	Model	Last known Owner/Operator	Identities/fates/comments (where appropriate)
20244	50	Air Iceland/Skyways Express	PH-EXN TF-FIS TF-JMS
20245	50	Pelangi Air	PH-EXP 9M-MER
20246	50	(Sudan Airways)	PH-KXF G-UKTA ST-ASJ [w/o 12Dec06 Kenana, Sudan]
20247	50	Sudan Airways	PH-KXG G-UKTB ST-ASI
20248	50	Feeder Airlines	PH-EXR 9M-MGK ST-NEX [badly damaged 29Mar12 Wau airport, Sudan]
20249	50	Skywest Airlines	PH-KXH G-UKTC PH-KXH VH-FSL
20250	50	Air Iceland	PH-EXT TF-FIT TF-JMT
20251	50	Aero Mongolia	PH-EXU TF-FIU PH-WXH EC-GQI PH-WXH JU-8251
20252	50	Amapola Flyg	PH-KXM (PT-OQC) PT-SLO PH-KXM SE-MFB
20253	50	ex Royal Netherlands Air Force	PH-KXO U-05 [wfs 08Aug12]
20254	50	Sky Aviation	PH-KXN D-AFFE PH-KXN PT-MLH PH-KXN PR-OAA PH-KXN PK-ECG
20255	50	Sky Aviation	PH-KXS D-AFFF PH-KXS PT-MLI PH-KXS PR-OAB PH-KXS PK-ECH
20256	50	Sudan Airways	PH-KXT G-UKTD ST-ASO
20257	50	Aero Mongolia	PH-KXY D-AFFA PH-KXY EC-282 EC-GHB PH-KXY JA01NV OY-PCI JU-8257
20258	50	Aero Mongolia	PH-KXU D-AFFB PH-KXU EC-284 EC-GJI PH-KXU JU-8258
20259	50F	Amapola Flyg	PH-EXX (JA8894) JA8889 OY-PAA SE-LJY
20260	50	TransNusa	PH-KXV D-AFKT PH-KXV PT-SLY PH-KXV PK-PFJ PH-KXV SE-LLN OB-1829 PK-TND
20261	50	TransNusa	PH-KXW D-AFFC PH-KXW PT-SRA PK-RAS PK-BRX PK-TNA
20262	50	Denim Air/Blue Island	PH-KXX D-AFFD PH-KXX EC-287 EC-GHC PH-KXX PR-OAC PH-KXX
20263	50	Kish Air	PH-LXE D-AFFG EC-GKE PH-LXE EP-LCF
20264	50	CityJet	PH-EXA OE-LFF PH-DMB TF-JMU T9-BBC TF-JMU OO-VLZ
20265	50	Kish Air	PH-LXF (9M-MGL) D-AFFH EC-GJY PH-LXF EP-LCE
20266	50	Avianca	PH-LXW HK-4487X
20267	50	Singapore Air Force	PH-LXX 714 [Fokker 50MPA Enforcer II]
20268	50	Singapore Air Force	PH-LXY 710 [Fokker 50UTA-B]
20269	50	Singapore Air Force	PH-LXZ 711 [Fokker 50UTA-B]
20270	50	Compagnie Africaine d'Aviation	PH-LXJ G-UKTE PH-LXJ 9Q-CBD
20271	50	Sky Aviation	PH-LXK G-UKTF PH-LXK PK-ECD
20272	50	Sky Aviation	PH-LXL D-AFFI PK-TWC PK-RAM
20273	50	(Kish Air)	PH-LXM D-AFFJ EC-GKU EP-LCA [w/o 10Feb04 near Sharjah Airport, UAE; remains l/n 12Feb05]
20274	50	Kish Air	PH-LXN D-AFFK EC-GKV EP-LCB
20275	50	Kish Air	PH-LXO D-AFFL EC-GKX EP-LCC
20276	50	Compagnie Africaine d'Aviation	PH-LXP G-UKTG PH-LXP 9Q-CAB
20277	50	Sky Aviation	PH-LXR G-UKTH PH-LXR PK-ECE
20278	50	Avianca	(PH-LXS) PH-AVG HK-4496X
20279	50	Sky Aviation	PH-LXT G-UKTI PH-LXT PK-ECF
20280	50	Aero Transporte SA	PH-LXU V8-RB1 G-BWZL PH-LXU EC-GRY PH-LXU OB-1770-P N209AC OB-1770-P
20281	50	Avianca	PH-AVH HK-4481X PR-OAW HK-4580
20282	50	TransNusa	PH-MXE V8-RB2 G-BWZM PH-MXE EC-GRZ PH-MXE PK-RAL PK-BRY PK-TNB
20283	50	NAFT Airlines	PH-MXF PT-SLX PH-MXF PK-PFK PH-MXF EP-PET
20284	50	Alliance Airlines	PH-MXG B-12271 VH-FKY
20285	50	Avianca	PH-AVJ HK-4469X
20286	50	Alliance Airlines	PH-MXH B-12272 VH-FKZ
20287	50	ex Royal Netherlands Air Force	PH-MXI U-06 [wfs 08Aug12]
20288	50	Avianca	PH-MXJ HK-4497X
20289	50		[not built]
20290	50		[not built]
20291	50		[not built]
20292	50		[not built]
20293	50	Singapore Air Force	(PH-EXW) PH-JCG 715 [Fokker 50MPA Enforcer II]
20294	50	Singapore Air Force	PH-EXY PH-MXU 712 [Fokker 50UTA-B]
20295	50	Singapore Air Force	PH-EXZ PH-MXV 713 [Fokker 50UTA-B]
20296	50	Avianca	PH-AVN HK-4482X PR-OAX HK-4581
20297	50	Avianca	PH-AVO HK-4470

FOKKER 50 and 60 (FOKKER F-27-050 AND F-27-060)

C/n	Model	Last known Owner/Operator	Identities/fates/comments (where appropriate)
20298	50	Taftan Air	PH-MXT+ (PH-LXR) PH-MXR PT-MNA PH-MXR EP-TFT [+ marks used in error late 1993]
20299	50	Avianca	PH-MXS HK-4501X
20300	50	Avianca	PH-MXT HK-4468X
20301	50	Avianca	PH-MXZ HK-4467
20302	50	Taftan Air	PH-JCE PT-MNB PH-JCE EP-TFN
20303	50	Alliance Airlines	PH-JCF B-12273 VH-FKV
20304			[not built]
20305	50	Singapore Air Force	PH-EXR 716 [Fokker 50MPA Enforcer II]
20306	50	Alliance Airlines	PH-JPB B-12275 VH-FKW
20307	50	TransNusa	(PH-EXT) PH-JCN JA8200 OY-PCJ PK-BRW PK-TNS
20308	50	Singapore Air Force	PH-EXY 717 [Fokker 50MPA Enforcer II]
20309			[not built]
20310			[not built]
20311	50	Singapore Air Force	PH-EXT+ PH-EXZ 718 [Fokker 50MPA Enforcer II; + marks applied while on line]
20312	50	Alliance Airlines	PH-JCR B-12276 VH-FKX
20313	50	Pacifc Royale Airways	PH-LOP ET-AKR PK-PRA
20314	50	ex Fokker	[fuselage stored Jan96 Amsterdam, Netherlands; moved 20Feb98 Venlo, Netherlands, with Piet Smedts Collection; by Apr08 moved to Baarlo, Netherlands; l/n 12Jan10]
20315	50	ex Fokker	[fuselage stored Jan96 Amsterdam, Netherlands]
20316	50	Indonesia Air Transport	PH-EXK PT-MLF B-12270 PK-TWJ PK-TSP
20317	50	Riau Airlines	PH-EXA PT-MLG B-12279 PK-TWR PK-RAR [damaged 07Mar09 Batam, Indonesia]
20318	50	ex Fokker	[fuselage stored Jan96 Amsterdam, Netherlands]
20319			[not built]
20320			[not built]
20321	60	Peruvian Navy	PH-UTL U-01+ AE-563 [first production Fokker 60; ff 02Nov95; Fokker 60UTA-N; + Netherlands]
20322			[not built]
20323			[not built]
20324	60	Peruvian Navy	PH-UTN U-02+ AE-565 [Fokker 60UTA-N; + Netherlands]
20325	50	ex Fokker	[fuselage stored Jan96 Amsterdam, Netherlands]
20326			[not built]
20327	60	Peruvian Navy	PH-UTP U-03+ AE-564 [Fokker 60MPA; + Netherlands]
20328	50	Pacifc Royale Airways	PH-EXB ET-AKS PK-PRB
20329	60	Peruvian Navy	PH-UTR U-04+ AE-566 [Fokker 60UTA-N; + Netherlands]
20330	50		[intended for TAM-Brazil as PT-MLH but not built]
20331	50	Pacific Royale Airways	PH-EXC ET-AKT PK-PRC
20332	50		[intended for TAM-Brazil as PT-MLI but not built]
20333	50	Pacific Royale Airways	PH-EXD ET-AKU PK-
20334	50		[intended for TAM-Brazil as PT-MLJ but not built]
20335	50	Ethiopian Airlines	PH-EXE ET-AKV
Unidentified			
unkn	50	Indonesian Police	P-4401 [reported 12Oct08 and Mar11 Pondok Cabe, Indonesia]
unkn	50	Faraz Qeshm Airlines	EP-FQB [reported May12 Tehran, Iran; possibly ex Kish Air]

Production complete

GOVERNMENT AIRCRAFT FACTORIES N22/N24 NOMAD

Notes: Royal Thai Air Force serials are normally only displayed in Thai script and in very small characters. The five digits that follow are codes which are known to have been used. This has caused these aircraft to be normally recognised by their codes, rather than their serials. With thanks to Steve Darke's Thai Aviation website further unidentified codes of Royal Thai Air Force Nomads have been reported as follows; 40182, 46136, 46146 (Apr06), 4816, 4838, 60142, 60516 & 60508
During 2008 Gippsland Aeronautics acquired the Nomad type certificate and were planning new build aircraft, with updated specification and with production starting in 2011.
Either c/n 75 N4812C or c/n 77 N4817E is reported preserved by the Palm Springs Air Museum, CA.
Some sources show aircraft delivered directly to military air arms have an M-suffix at the end of their c/ns.

C/n	Model	Last known Owner/Operator	Identities/fates/comments (where appropriate)
N2-01	N2	Ballarat Aviation Museum	VH-SUP+ VH-MSF^ [prototype ff 23Jly71; + canx 15Feb76; ^ painted as such for filming of "The Flying Doctors" TV series at Point Cook, VIC, Australia; wfu & preserved Ballarat, VIC, Australia]
N2-02	N2	Flypast Museum	VH-SUR A18-002+ VH-SUR [+ Australia] [preserved as "A18-300" Oakley, QLD, Australia; l/n 26Jly07]
1	N22	(Government Aircraft Factories)	VH-AUI [w/o by hurricane 25Oct75 Mazatlan, Mexico]
2	N22B	(Douglas Airways)	(VH-EPG) VH-ELN P2-DNO [wfu 1981; by Jun88 dismantled Wewak, PNG; remains to Aviation Salvage, Bankstown, NSW, Australia]
3	N22	(Royal Australian Army)	A18-303 [w/o 09Sep91 near Tenterfield, NSW, Australia]
4	N22B	(Hibiscus Air Services)	VH-AUH ZK-NOM [w/o 25Oct93 Franz Josef Glacier, Southern Alps, New Zealand]
5	N22B	Philippine Air Force	5
6	N22B	Philippine Air Force	6 [reported 2010 for sale as scrap]
7	N22B	Sabah Air	9M-AUA
8	N22B	Indonesian Navy	P-801
9	N22B	Indonesian Navy	P-802
10	N24	(Government Aircraft Factories)	VH-DHU(1) [w/o 06Aug76 Avalon, VIC, Australia]
11	N22B	(Philippine Air Force)	11 [w/o 28Dec93 Margosatubig, Zamboanga, Philippines; but reported 2010 for sale as scrap]
12	N22B	ex Philippine Air Force	12 [reported stored by Mar98 Mactan AFB, Cebu, Philippines]
13	N22B	(Philippine Air Force)	13 [reported w/o, no details known]
14	N22B	(Sabah Air)	9M-ATZ [w/o 06Jun76 near Kota Kinabalu, Sabah, Malaysia]
15	N22B	Philippine Air Force	15
16	N22B	Indonesian Navy	P-803
17	N22B	Indonesian Navy	P-804
18	N22B	(Philippine Air Force)	18 [w/o 28Jan10 near Awang Airport, Cotabato City, Philippines]
19	N22B	Philippine Air Force	19 [reported 2010 for sale as scrap]
20	N22B	Philippine Air Force	20 [reported 2010 for sale as scrap]
21	N22B	(Philippine Air Force)	21 [w/o during 1987 off Mapur Island, Riau Islands, Philippines]
22	N22B	Philippine Air Force	22 [reported 2010 for sale as scrap]
23	N22B	Philippine Air Force	23 [reported 2010 for sale as scrap]
24	N22B	Indonesian Navy	P-805
25	N22B	(Sydney Skydive Parachute School)	VH-DNM [w/o 05Apr90 near Leongatha, VIC, Australia; canx 09Jan02]
26	N22B	(Chatteris Aviation Inc)	VH-AUN N5190Y [w/o 09May09 Chatteris, UK; stored there; l/n 14Mar10]
27	N22B	(Australian Aircraft Salvage)	P2-IAT [b/u during 1989 Bankstown, NSW, Australia]
28	N22B	(Mission Aviation Fellowship)	VH-AUF PK-MAJ [w/o 23Jly79 West Irian, Indonesia]
29	N22B	(Douglas Airways)	P2-DNJ [w/o 21May77 Wewak-Boram Airport, Papua New Guinea]
30	N24A	(Great Barrier Airlines)	VH-DHF ZK-NAD [canx 25Mar04 exported; fate/status unknown]
31	N22B	Indonesian Navy	P-806
32	N24A	(Venture Aviation)	VH-DHO ZK-OUT [by Mar00 stored Taupo, New Zealand; canx 21Nov00 as wfu, used for spares; l/n 25Jan05]
33	N22B	ex Aquatic Airways	VH-RCC "VH-MSF" [wfu 08Mar84; painted as VH-MSF at Maryborough, QLD, Australia, to represent the Nomad used in the TV series "The Flying Doctors", flown to Broken Hill, NSW, Australia for display at RFDS base]
34	N24A	Gippsaero	VH-DHP ZK-NMC VH-XGZ [floatplane]
35	N22B	Queensland Air Museum	VH-BFH OY-ATU VH-BFH (N48234) ZK-SAL VH-BFH [DBR 18Jan85 Brisbane Airport, QLD, Australia; donated 26Sep90; preserved by 1999 Caloundra, QLD, Australia]
36	N24A	(Skywest Airlines)	VH-DHQ ZK-NMD(1)+ VH-DHQ^ [+ w/o 20Jly87 Lake Tekapo Airport, New Zealand; canx Oct87; ^ regd 28Jun90 & canx by 12Nov92; used for spares at Lake Tekapo for c/n 60; never returned to Australia]
37	N22B	(Capital Aviation)	P2-IAC VH-HHW ZK-NDB [b/u in 1993 for spares Ardmore, New Zealand; canx Jan94]

GOVERNMENT AIRCRAFT FACTORIES N22/N24 NOMAD

C/n	Model	Last known Owner/Operator	Identities/fates/comments (where appropriate)
38	N24A	(Rollins Air)	VH-DHR N62573 HR-AQY [w/o 24Nov97 La Ceiba-Goloson Airport, Honduras]
39	N22B	(Douglas Airways)	VH-WLG P2-DNL [w/o 23Dec79 Mendi, Papua New Guinea]
40	N22B	ex Indonesian Navy	A18-304 P-822 [wfu by 15Sep11 Surabaya, Indonesia]
41	N22B	ex Royal Australian Army	A18-305 [stored Dec94 Oakey, QLD, Australia; unconfirmed report to Indonesian Navy for spares]
42	N24A	ex Gum Air	VH-WFF ZK-ECN PZ-TBM (D-IUFG) [stored Peenemunde, Germany; l/n 24Jun09]
43	N22B	RAAF School of Technical Training	A18-306 [wfu & stored 1996 Oakey, QLD, Australia; Oct98 to Wagga Wagga AFB, NSW, Australia as GIA; l/n 25Oct05]
44	N24A	(Agape Flights Inc)	VH-AUJ VH-ACQ N8071L [w/o 01Jun91 off Great Inagua, Bahamas; canx 02Jun93]
45	N22B	Flypast Museum	A18-307 [DBR 24Sep86 Bundi, Papua New Guinea; by Feb97 preserved Oakey, QLD, Australia]
46	N24A	Indonesian Navy	VH-BLY HB-LIB VH-FCX ZK-FVX P-842
47	N22B	Indonesian Navy	A18-308 P-823 [stored by 11Apr09 Surabaya-Juanda, Indonesia; l/n 15Sep11]
48	N22B	Indonesian Navy	A18-309 P-824
49	N22B	Indonesian Navy	A18-310 P-825
50	N22B	Australian Aviation Museum	VH-CPX [canx 21Feb86 as wfu for spares; by Nov98 fuselage preserved Bankstown, NSW, Australia]
51	N22B	Indonesian Navy	A18-311 P-826
52	N22B	(Papua New Guinea DF)	P2-DFN P2-011 [w/o 04May81 Kalifas Area, West Sepik Province, Papua New Guinea]
53	N22B	(Philippine Air Force)	VH-CRI 53 [w/o 17Dec02 in sea on approach Zamboanga AFB, Philippines]
54	N22B	Papua New Guinea DF	P2-DFO P2-012
55	N22C	ex Fiordland Travel	(VH-CEI) VH-IIG ZK-FVU [canx 10Dec02 as exported; report to Indonesian Navy]
56	N22B	Aviation Historical Society	VH-WRT [canx 31Aug04 wfu; derelict by 2002 Picton, NSW, Australia; l/n 09Mar08]
57	N22B	(Paraguay Air Services)	VH-FAI CC-CBV ZP-TDZ [w/o 28Aug06 near Cerrillos, Argentina]
58	N22B	Australian Aviation Museum	VH-FZP [wfu 05Sep82; b/u for spares; fuselage painted as "VH-AAM" preserved Bankstown, NSW, Australia, as mobile exhibit; l/n 14Feb04]
59	N22B	(Douglas Airways)	P2-DNM [wfu Port Moresby, Papua New Guinea; used by PNG Defence Force for spares]
60	N24A	Air Safaris & Services (NZ)	VH-DHU(2) ZK-NMD(2)
61	N22B	Rik Luytjes	VH-BLV N59365 N32JW VH-BRQ N22NM [floatplane]
62	N24A	(Haiti Express)	VH-FHS JA8834 N224E [w/o 12Feb96 near Port-au-Prince, Haiti; canx 25Sep96]
63	N22B	Indonesian Navy	A18-312 P-827
64	N24A	(Challenge Air)	VH-COV N4807W F-OGVD [w/o 1995 in hurricane; to Atlanta Air Salvage, Griffin, GA for spares; l/n 24Oct06]
65	N22B	Indonesian Navy	A18-313 P-828 [wfu by 15Sep11 Surabaya, Indonesia]
66	N22B	Gum Air	PZ-TBA
67	N22SB	(Papua New Guinea DF)	P2-DFP P2-013 [wfu Mar98 Jackson Airfield, Papua New Guinea; report sold to Seagull Aviation & b/u for spares]
68	N22C	Philippine Air Force	VH-MSE 68
69	N22B	Layang Layang Aerospace	VH-MSF 9M-LLI
70	N22B	ex Air Safaris & Services (NZ)	5W-FAR ZK-NOL [stored Tekapo, New Zealand for spares use; canx 13Nov95 as wfu; l/n Nov08]
71	N24A	ex Holland Aero Lines	VH-MXI N1022K RP-C1219 (PH-HAK) PH-HAF [wfu 1986; used for spares at Rotterdam, Netherlands; fuselage mounted on pole outside a scrapyard at Geldrop still marked as N1022K; by 28Apr09 moved to Wevelgem, Belgium]
72	N24A	ex Aerospace Ground Equipment	VH-MXL N1037P PH-HAL N871US [wfu by 1998 to Seagull Aviation for spares; fate/status unknown]
73	N24A	(Gum Air)	VH-FHR ZK-NMG PZ-TBP [w/o 10Feb01 near Njoeng Jakob Kondre Airstrip, Suriname]
74FA	N24A	(Karlog Air)	VH-PNF N5579M (PH-DHL) PH-HAG N870US ZK-NMH OY-NMH [canx 15Mar12 as wfu & b/u]
75	N24A	(Hughes Corporation)	VH-IIJ N4812C [wfu 1983; b/u 1994 Davis-Monthan, AZ, remains to Allied Metals, Tucson, AZ; canx 30Oct89]
76FA	N24A	(Air St Barthelemy)	VH-IIK N4816C F-OGVB [wfu & stored Jly95 Opa-locka, FL; May97 fuselage only moved to Tamiami, FL]
77	N24A	(Hughes Corporation)	VH-IIL N4817E [damaged in hurricane, FL & wfu; canx 08Nov89; b/u 1994 Davis-Monthan, AZ; remains to Allied Metals, Tucson, AZ; canx 30Oct89]

GOVERNMENT AIRCRAFT FACTORIES N22/N24 NOMAD

C/n	Model	Last known Owner/Operator	Identities/fates/comments (where appropriate)
78	N24A	(Hughes Corporation)	VH-KKI N420NE [wfu & b/u Nov89 Las Vegas, NV; canx 08Nov89]
79	N24A	(Hughes Corporation)	VH-AIW N421NE [b/u 1994 Davis-Monthan, AZ, for spares; remains to Allied Metals, Tucson, AZ]
80	N24A	(Mobile Carpet Cleaning Factory)	VH-SNF VH-BRP [wfu Bankstown, NSW, Australia; dismantled 1997; canx 28Sep98; to TAFE Aviation Industry Training Centre, Broadmeadows, VIC, Australia, as GIA]
81	N24A	Dolphin Aviation	VH-IIN N4821M HR-ARH N4821M [stored Palm Beach County-Lantana Airport, FL; l/n 14Feb06]
82	N22SL	Aviation Historical Society	VH-FCS [canx 20Oct08; fuselage purchased for preservation or spares use]
83	N22F	(Johnson Wax Company)	(VH-FPP) VH-WOZ N5590M [w/o 04May91 near Bowling Green, KY; to White Industries, Bates City, MO; canx 26Aug95]
84	N22SL	Indonesian Navy	VH-CEK P-820
85	N22B	Indonesian Navy	P-807
86	N22C	(Philippine Air Force)	VH-SBY 86 [w/o 02Jly00 in sea off Cagayancillo Island, Philippines]
87	N22C	Philippine Air Force	VH-SDZ 87
88	N22B	Indonesian Navy	P-808
89	N24A	(Tar Heel Aviation)	VH-IIO N418NE N120CA N418NE [w/o 04May90 Wilmington-New Hanover Airport, NC; canx 06Feb91]
90	N22SB	Royal Australian Army	VH-SFR A18-316 [wfu Nov91; stored Oakey, QLD, Australia; by 23Dec11 with GippsAero, Latrobe Valley, VIC, Australia for use in GA-18 development]
91	N22B	Indonesian Navy	P-809
92	N22SL	Indonesian Navy	VH-CEI P-821
93	N22B	(Sunshine Coast Air Charter)	P2-IAM VH-SMJ N137C VH-SMJ [canx Jun04 as wfu]
94	N22B	(Indonesian Navy)	P-810 [w/o, details unknown]
95	N22SB	Layang Layang Aerospace	VH-SNL 9M-WKU VH-SNL 9M-LLB
96	N24A	Dolphin Aviation	VH-IIP N48213 N60PA [by 2004 stored Saratoga, FL; l/n 13Feb05]
97	N22B	Indonesian Navy	P-811
98	N24A	Air St Barthelemy	VH-IIQ N419NE F-OGVC
99	N24A	(Dolphin Aviation)	VH-IIR N37808 [wfu 1993; dismantled & stored Saratoga, FL; canx 13Aug07]
100	N22B	Indonesian Navy	P-812
101	N24A	(Dolphin Aviation)	VH-AUM MI-8201 N855SC [wfu; dismantled & stored Saratoga, FL; canx 13Aug07]
102	N22B	(Dolphin Aviation)	VH-IIM N4826M [w/o 23Aug95 Jeremie Airport, Haiti; canx 14Nov95]
103	N22C	Australian Avn Heritage Centre	VH-SNX [wfu Jun04; preserved Jan08 Darwin, NT, Australia]
104	N22C	Venture Aviation	VH-SNZ ZK-SNZ
105	N22B	Saratoga Jet Center	VH-UAI N422NE [floatplane] [wfu Nov00 & stored Saratoga, FL; l/n 30May11]
106	N24A	(Dolphin Aviation)	VH-IIS MI-8202 N854SC [stored Saratoga, FL; canx 13Aug07; fate/status unknown]
107FA	N22B	(Alimediterranea)	VH-UFM N423NE I-JALA [floatplane] [w/o 06Jly92 in storm Reggio Calabria-Tito Menniti, Airport, Italy]
108	N22C	Baywater Road Pty	VH-UHL F-ODMX VH-ATO
109	N22B	Royal Thai Air Force	VH-MVZ VH-UVD L9-1/25 46111 [see note below]
110	N22SL	Indonesian Navy	P-813
111	N22SL	ex Indonesian Navy	P-814 [preserved Surabaya Naval Air Base Collection, Surabaya, Indonesia; l/n 13Dec09]
112	N22SL	(Papua New Guinea DF)	P2-DSQ P2-014 [w/o 28Jan83 Darli, Nanango, QLD, Australia]
113	N22SL	(Papua New Guinea DF)	P2-015 [wfu 1998 & to Seagull Aviation for spares; b/u]
114	N22B	Royal Thai Air Force	VH-UVA L9-2/25 46112 [see note below]
115	N24A	Dolphin Aviation	VH-AUP N424NE [wfu & stored Saratoga, FL; reported derelict 2004; canx13Aug07]
116	N22SL	Indonesian Navy	P-815
117	N24A	(Fleet Vandrup)	(VH-AUR) VH-PGW (N415NE) ZK-ECM VH-KNA OY-JRW [w/o 13May02 RAF Weston-on-the-Green, UK; canx 06Jan04]
118	N22SL	Indonesian Navy	P-816
119	N24A	(Rollins Air)	VH-UUB JA8827 N244E [w/o 19Nov97 La Ceiba-Goloson Airport, Honduras]
120	N24A	ex Royal Thai Navy	VH-HBS 120+ 211+ 2206+ 2105 [+ Thailand] [stored by May06 U-Tapao, Thailand; l/n Jan08; preserved by Oct09 Royal Thai Navy Museum, U-Tapao; l/n 31Dec09]
121	N24A	(Royal Thai Navy)	(VH-UHW) VH-HBT (N416NE) 121+ 212 [+ Thailand] [w/o 1994 U-Tapao AFB, Thailand; l/n Aug95; was to have been serialled 2106]
122	N24A	Air Safaris & Services (NZ)	5W-FAT (N417NE) ZK-NME
123	N24A	Royal Thai Navy	(VH-URV) VH-HBU 123+ 213+ 2208+ 2107 [+ Thailand]
124	N24A	Airline Academy of Australia	VH-NOM A18-408 [GIA Brisbane, QLD, Australia; l/n 26Jly07]

GOVERNMENT AIRCRAFT FACTORIES N22/N24 NOMAD

C/n	Model	Last known Owner/Operator	Identities/fates/comments (where appropriate)
125	N22SL	Indonesian Navy	P-817
126	N22SL	Indonesian Navy	P-818
127	N24A	Royal Thai Navy	VH-HBV 127+ 214+ 2210+ 2108 [+ Thailand]
128	N24B	(Royal Australian Air Force)	(VH-AUU) A18-401 [w/o 12Mar90 near Mallala, SA, Australia]
129	N24A	Royal Thai Navy	VH-HBW 129+ 215+ 22xx? 2109 [+ Thailand]
130	N24A	ex Indonesian Navy	VH-HVK A18-402 P-836 [by 2012 preserved on pole Probolinggo, Java, Indonesia]
131	N22B	Indonesian Navy	A18-314 P-829 [wfu by 15Sep11 Surabaya, Indonesia]
132	N22B	Indonesian Navy	A18-315 P-830 [reported stored/wfu by Dec10 Surabaya, Indonesia]
133	N22B	Royal Thai Air Force	VH-UVE L.9-3/25 46121 [see note below] [by 2012 fuselage in use as holiday home Phitsanulok, Thailand]
134	N22B	Royal Thai Air Force	VH-UVG L.9-4/25 46122 [see note below]
135	N24A	(Indonesian Navy)	VH-HVL A18-403 P-837 [w/o 07Sep09 near East Kalimantan, Borneo]
136	N24A	Indonesian Navy	A18-404 P-838
137	N22B	ex Royal Thai Air Force	VH-UVI L.9-5/25? 46231 46131 [see note below; w/o 06Mar09 Lopburi-Khok Kratiem AFB, Thailand & noted dismantled there by Jan12 l/n Jly12]
138	N22B	Royal Thai Air Force	VH-UVJ L.9-6/25 46232 46132 [see note below]
139	N24A	Indonesian Navy	A18-405 P-839
140	N24A	Indonesian Navy	A18-406 P-840 [stored by 11Apr09 Surabaya-Juanda, Indonesia]
141	N22B	Royal Thai Air Force	VH-UVK L.9-7/25 46241 46141 [see note below] [wfu by Apr04; by 2012 fuselage in use as holiday home Phitsanulok, Thailand]
142	N24A	Indonesian Navy	A18-407 P-841
143	N22SB	Papua New Guinea DF	P2-016 [wfu 1998 & to Seagull Aviation for spares & b/u]
144	N22B	Royal Thai Air Force	VH-UVL L.9-8/26 46242 46142 [see note below]
145	N22B	Royal Thai Air Force	VH-UVM L.9-9/26 46113 [see note below] [by 2012 fuselage in use as holiday home Phitsanulok, Thailand]
146	N22B	Royal Thai Air Force	VH-UUF L.9-10/26? 46114 60508 46114 [see note below] [by 2012 fuselage in use as holiday home Phitsanulok, Thailand]
147	N22B	Royal Thai Air Force	VH-UUI L.9-11/26 46123 [see note below]
148	N22B	Royal Thai Air Force	VH-UUK L.9-12/26 46124 [see note below] [by 2012 fuselage in use as holiday home Phitsanulok, Thailand]
149	N22B	Royal Thai Air Force	VH-UUN L.9-13/26? 46233 46133 [see note below]
150	N22B	Royal Thai Air Force	VH-UUO L.9-14/26? 46134 [see note below]
151	N22B	Royal Thai Air Force	VH-UZP L.9-15/26 46143 [see note below] [reported wfu Jan03 & Apr04]
152	N22C	Royal Thai Air Force	VH-XZA JL.9-21/30 46116 [see note below] [by 2012 fuselage in use as holiday home Phitsanulok, Thailand]
153	N22B	Royal Thai Air Force	VH-UUS L.9-16/26 46144 [see note below]
154	N22C	Royal Thai Air Force	VH-XZB JL.9-22/30 46126 [see note below] [preserved by 2012 Nan AFB, Thailand]
155	N22B	Royal Thai Air Force	VH-UUT L.9-17/26? 46115 [see note below]
156	N22B	Royal Thai Air Force	VH-UUV L.9-19/27 46135 [see note below]
157	N22B	Royal Thai Air Force	VH-UUX L.9-18/26 46125 [see note below]
158	N22B	Royal Thai Air Force	VH-UUZ L.9-20/.. ? 46145 [see note below] [by 2012 fuselage in use as holiday home Phitsanulok, Thailand]
159	N22SL	Chatteris Aviation Inc	VH-HWB N6302W
160	N22SL	(US Customs Service)	VH-HTG N6305U [ditched 18Sep98 into Caribbean Sea, 1.5km off Mona Island, PR; canx 18Nov98]
161	N22SL	Dodson International	VH-HQC N6313P [wfu for spares Rantoul, KS; l/n May06]
162	N22SL	Dodson International	VH-HVY N3225F [wfu for spares Rantoul, KS; l/n Jun06]
163	N22SL	Pima Air & Space Museum	VH-HVZ N6328 [preserved Sep98 Pima, Tucson, AZ]
164	N22SL	ex US Customs Service	VH-HMZ N5056D [status/fate unknown]
165	N22S	Dodson International	VH-JQM N6338C [wfu for spares Rantoul, KS; l/n Jun06]
166	N24A	Indonesian Navy	A18-317 P-831
167	N24A	Indonesian Navy	A18-318 P-832
168	N24A	(Indonesian Navy)	A18-319 P-833 [w/o30Dec07 200m off Sabang, Indonesia]
169	N24A	Indonesian Navy	A18-320 P-834
170	N24A	Indonesian Navy	A18-321 P-835

Production complete

GRUMMAN G-123 GREYHOUND (C-2A)

C/n	Model	Last known Owner/Operator	Identities/fates/comments (where appropriate)		
1	C-2A	(Grumman)	148147	[converted from E-2A; ff 18Nov64; w/o 29Apr65 Long Island Sound, CT/NY]	
2	C-2A	(US Navy)	148148	[RW-30]	[converted from E-2A; stored 19Jun87 AMARC, code AN1C0005]
3	C-2A	(US Navy)	152786	[RW-31]	[stored 17Jun87 AMARC, code 1C001; to NAS North Island, CA 15Oct98; l/n Oct06]
4	C-2A	(US Navy)	152787	[JM]	[w/o 16Nov73]
5	C-2A	(US Navy)	152788	[w/o 23Aug71]	
6	C-2A	(US Navy)	152789	[spares recovery NAS North Island, CA by Mar96]	
7	C-2A	(US Navy)	152790	[stored 10Nov86 AMARC, code AN1C0001]	
8	C-2A	(US Navy)	152791	[RW-32]	[stored 17Jun87 AMARC, code AN1C0004]
9	C-2A	(US Navy)	152792	['027]	[GIA NAS Norfolk,VA by Feb92; l/n Oct00]
10	C-2A	(US Navy)	152793	[RG]	[w/o 12Dec71 South China Sea off S Vietnam]
11	C-2A	(US Navy)	152794	[RW-33]	[stored 17Jun87 AMARC, code AN1C0003]
12	C-2A	National Naval Aviation Museum	152795	[RW-30]	[preserved NAS North Island, CA by Aug96; l/n Feb08]
13	C-2A	(US Navy)	152796	[RG-412]	[w/o 02Oct69 60 miles NE of Dong Hoi, N Vietnam]
14	C-2A	(US Navy)	152797	[spares recovery NAS North Island, CA by May90; l/n Mar96]	
15	C-2A	(US Navy)	155120	[RG-414]	[w/o 15Dec70 125 miles E of Dong Hoi, N Vietnam on take-off from "USS Ranger"]
16	C-2A	(US Navy)	155121	[fate unknown]	
17	C-2A	(US Navy)	155122	[JM]	[w/o 30Jan72 near Naples harbour, Italy]
18	C-2A	US Navy – Cargo Handling & Port Group	155123	[RW-34]	[stored 19Jun87 AMARC, code 1C006; to Cheatham Annex, VA 09Oct98]
19	C-2A	(US Navy)	155124	[spares recovery NAS North Island, CA by Mar92; l/n Mar96]	
20	C-2A	US Navy	162140	[RW-34]	
21	C-2A	(US Navy)	162141	[RW-23]	[w/o 26 or 28Apr11on flight from USS Enterprise somewhere in Bahrain]
22	C-2A	US Navy	162142		
23	C-2A	US Navy	162143	[40]	
24	C-2A	US Navy	162144	[41]	
25	C-2A	US Navy	162145	[NF-25]	
26	C-2A	US Navy	162146	[NK-34]	[SOC 07May01; to store NAS North Island, CA by May01; l/n Apr02]
27	C-2A	US Navy	162147	[45]	
28	C-2A	US Navy	162148	[NH-24]	
29	C-2A	US Navy	162149	[RW-33]	
30	C-2A	US Navy	162150	[RW-20]	
31	C-2A	(US Navy)	162151	[44]	[stored 10Aug00 AMARC, code AN1C0007; on display Celebrity Row, Davis-Monthan AFB, AZ]
32	C-2A	US Navy	162152	[NK-32]	
33	C-2A	(US Navy)	162153	[AD]	[w/o 12Mar03 MCAS Cherry Point, NC]
34	C-2A	US Navy	162154	[43]	
35	C-2A	US Navy	162155	[AD-636]	
36	C-2A	(US Navy)	162156	[SOC by 30Sep99; to Grumman for fatigue life testing]	
37	C-2A	US Navy	162157	[47]	
38	C-2A	US Navy	162158	[44]	
39	C-2A	US Navy	162159	[NK-30]	
40	C-2A	US Navy	162160	[50]	
41	C-2A	US Navy	162161	[RW-35]	
42	C-2A	US Navy	162162	[56]	
43	C-2A	US Navy	162163	[AD-633]	
44	C-2A	US Navy	162164	[NG-26]	
45	C-2A	US Navy	162165	[55]	
46	C-2A	US Navy	162166	[AD-635]	
47	C-2A	US Navy	162167	[46]	
48	C-2A	US Navy	162168	[30]	
49	C-2A	US Navy	162169	[NF-27]	
50	C-2A	US Navy	162170	[632]	
51	C-2A	US Navy	162171	[51]	
52	C-2A	US Navy	162172	[NE-22]	
53	C-2A	US Navy	162173	[RW-24]	
54	C-2A	US Navy	162174	[54]	
55	C-2A	US Navy	162175	[52]	
56	C-2A	US Navy	162176	[RW-21]	

GRUMMAN G-123 GREYHOUND (C-2A)

C/n	Model	Last known Owner/Operator	Identities/fates/comments (where appropriate)
57	C-2A	US Navy	162177
58	C-2A	US Navy	162178 [42]

Production complete

HANDLEY PAGE HPR.7 HERALD

C/n	Model	Last known Owner/Operator	Identities/fates/comments (where appropriate)
147	100	(Handley Page Ltd)	G-AODE [ff 25Aug55 as a HPR.3 Herald; ff 11Mar58 as HPR.7 Dart Herald 100; w/o 30Aug58 near Godalming, Surrey, UK]
148	200	(Handley Page Ltd)	G-AODF G-ARTC [ff 03Aug56 as a HPR.3 Herald; cvtd to HPR.7 Dart Herald 100 then to a series 200; wfu & stored May62; canx 23Mar67; b/u 1970 Radlett, UK]
149	100	Museum of Berkshire Aviation	G-APWA PP-ASV G-APWA PP-SDM G-APWA [canx 29Jan87 as wfu; preserved 1993 Woodley, Berkshire, UK; l/n 12Oct08]
150	101	(Lineas Aereas La Urraca)	G-APWB HK-718 [w/o 02Nov73 Villavicencio-La Vanguardia Airport, Colombia]
151	101	(Lineas Aereas La Urraca)	G-APWC HK-715 [damaged 22Jun75 landing La Libertad, Colombia; ferried to Villavicencio-La Vanguardia, Colombia & stored; b/u Oct82; canx 30Jun83]
152	101	(Lineas Aereas La Urraca)	G-APWD HK-721 [w/o 07May72 near Valledupar, Colombia]
153	201	(Air UK (Jersey) Ltd)	G-APWE [wfu Nov82 Norwich, UK; used for fire training; b/u by end Oct85; canx 14Nov84]
154	201	(Air UK)	G-APWF [wfu & stored Jersey, Channel Islands, UK 1981; used for spares 1983; canx 09Feb84; b/u Apr84; nose preserved locally]
155	201	(Air UK)	G-APWG [wfu & stored Jersey, Channel Islands, UK 1981; used for spares 1983; canx 09Feb84; b/u Apr84; nose retained locally]
156	201	(Air UK)	G-APWH [stored 16Oct80 Norwich, UK; canx 01Feb82; b/u Apr82; fuselage to fire service, l/n Apr97]
157	201	(Far Eastern Air Transport)	G-APWI B-2009 [w/o 24Feb69 near Kaohsiung, Taiwan]
158	201	Duxford Aviation Society	G-APWJ [preserved 07Jly85 Duxford, UK; canx 10Jly85; l/n 04Oct08]
159	202	(MMM Aero Service)	CF-NAC G-BCZG 9Q-CAH [w/o 01Sep84 near River Kwango, Bandundu Province, Zaire]
160	211	(Eastern Provincial Airways)	CF-NAF [w/o en-route 17Mar65 Upper Musquodoboit, NS, Canada]
161	211	City of Norwich Aviation Museum	(CF-MCK) (PI-C910) G-ASKK PP-ASU G-ASKK [preserved 30Mar80 Norwich, UK; canx 29Apr85; l/n 17Jun08]
162	210	ex Far Eastern Air Transport	(CF-MCM) HB-AAG G-ATHB B-2001 [wfu & stored Taipei-Songshan, Taiwan; spares recovery May87 for Channel Express; by Oct96 remains preserved Yen Liao, Hualien , Taiwan; l/n semi derelict 11Mar03]
163	204	(Air Manila International)	(G-ASBF) G-ASBP PI-C869 G-ASBP PI-C869 [DBR Nov70 in hangar collapse Manila, Philippines; b/u 1978]
164	203	(Air UK)	G-ASBG I-TIVA G-ASBG [stored Sep81 Norwich, UK; wfu by Jun83; canx 13Jun83; b/u Aug84]
165	207	(Far Eastern Air Transport)	(CF-EPA) 109 + JY-ACR G-ATHE D-BOBO G-ATHE B-2011 [+ Jordon] [wfu 1979; Taipei-Songshan, Taiwan; May87 b/u by Channel Express for spares]
166	206	(Aerovias de Mexico)	CF-EPI G-BCWE TG-ASA [stored by Oct98 Guatemala City-La Aurora, Guatemala; reported b/u early 1998 but also l/n Nov01; not present 23Nov07]
167	206	(MMM Aero Service)	CF-EPC VP-BCG CF-EPC G-BDFE 9Q-CAA [wfu Apr86 Kinshasa-N'Djili, Zaire; b/u Mar87]
168	203	(Itavia)	I-TIVE [w/o 04Nov71 Rome-Ciampino, Italy]
169	210	(City of Norwich Aviation Museum)	HB-AAH G-AVEZ PP-ASW G-AVEZ [wfu Sep81 Norwich, UK; canx 04Jan83; preserved Apr84 but by Apr85 to fire dump; b/u Jun08]
170	207	(Royal Jordanian Airlines)	110 + JY-ACQ [+ Jordan] [w/o en-route 10Apr65 near Damascus, Syria]
171	401	(Panavia Air Cargo)	FM1020 + G-BEYD [+ Malaysia] [stored May83 Southend, UK; b/u Oct84; canx 12Nov84]
172	401	(Panavia Air Cargo)	FM1021+ G-BEYE [+ Malaysia] [stored 1983 Southend, UK; b/u Dec84; canx 05Mar87]
173	210	(Channel Express (Air Services))	(HB-AAI) G-ASPJ HB-AAK F-OCLY F-BLOY G-SCTT [wfu 19Jan97 Bournemouth, UK; on fire dump 05Mar97; canx 08Apr97; b/u by Sep00]
174	209	(Channel Express (Air Services))	G-8-2 4X-AHS G-BEZB [wfu & stored Nov87 Bournemouth, UK; canx 08Mar88; b/u by 24Jan92]
175	401	(Parkhouse Aviation)	FM1022 + G-BEYF [+ Malaysia] [wfu 09Apr99, last Herald flight; preserved Bournemouth, UK; canx 18Nov99; b/u 30Jun08; remains to Parkhouse Aviation, Booker, UK; l/n 30Aug08]
176	213	Yorkshire Air Museum	(HB-AAK) D-BIBI G-AVPN I-TIVB G-AVPN [wfu 20Oct97 & preserved Elvington, UK; canx 08Dec97; l/n 24Aug08]
177	214	(Nordic Oil Services/BAC Express)	G-ATIG PP-SDI G-ATIG [wfu & stored 05Apr95 Norwich, UK; canx 29Oct96; moved to fire dump 1996; l/n 19Dec06; fully b/u Jun08]
178	401	(LACOL Colombia)	FM1023 + G-BEYG HK-2701X HK-2701 [+ Malaysia] [w/o 16Sep91 Barranquilla, Colombia]
179	213	(Channel Express (Air Services))	D-BEBE G-AYMG [wfu 07Jly92 Bournemouth, UK; b/u 04Aug94; canx 10Jan97]
180	401	(Aerosucre Colombia)	FM1024 + G-BEYH HK-2702X HK-2702 [+ Malaysia] [w/o 05Nov89 at Tolima, 300 kms SW of Bogota, Colombia]

HANDLEY PAGE HPR.7 HERALD

C/n	Model	Last known Owner/Operator	Identities/fates/comments (where appropriate)
181	401	(Bembridge Air Hire Ltd)	FM1025 + G-BEYI [+ Malaysia] [DBR in belly landing probably at Kuala Lumpur, Malaysia whilst in Royal Malaysian Air Force service; purchased by British Air Ferries & b/u Jan78 for spares locally]
182	401	(Aerovias de Mexico)	FM1026 + G-BEYJ TG-ALE [wfu Oct85 Guatemala City-La Aurora, Guatemala; stripped of parts by Oct96; hulk by Oct98, gone by May01]
183	209	(Air UK)	G-8-1 4X-AHR G-BAZJ [wfu 31Oct84 Guernsey, Channel Islands, UK & placed on fire dump; canx 04Jan85; l/n 21Oct08]
184	203	(Air UK)	I-TIVU G-BBXI [w/o 11Jun84 when struck by lorry Bournemouth, UK; b/u Jly84 for spares; canx 09Jly84]
185	214	(Channel Express (Air Services))	G-8-3 G-ASVO PP-SDG G-ASVO [w/o 08Apr97 taxied into floodlight Bournemouth, UK; canx 25Sep01; b/u front fuselage to Alton, UK; 05May99 moved to Shoreham; by 2003 with Highland Aviation Museum, Dalcross, Inverness, UK]
186	214	(Channel Express (Air Services))	PP-SDH G-BEBB G-CEAS [wfu Jan97 Bournemouth, UK; canx 23Jun97; b/u Nov97]
187	401	(Trygon Ltd)	FM1027 + G-BEYK [+ Malaysia] [wfu & stored Aug97 Southend, UK; b/u Jan98; canx 26Feb98; reported nose section saved]
188	210	(Channel Express (Air Services))	HB-AAL F-OCLZ F-BOIZ G-STVN [b/u Apr97 Bournemouth, UK; canx 08Apr97]
189	209	(Channel Express (Air Services))	G-ATDS 4X-AHT G-ATDS [wfu 10Jan91 Bournemouth, UK; Feb93 to fire service; wings removed by Mar96; canx 07Feb96; gone by Jan97]
190	214	(SADIA)	PP-SDJ [w/o 03Nov67 Marumbi Peak, near Curitiba Airport, Brazil]
191	214	(Aerovias de Mexico)	PP-SDL G-BDZV F-BVFP TG-AZE [wfu Dec95 Guatemala City-La Aurora, Guatemala; derelict by Oct98; not present May01; report hulk to a tourist centre at Zacapa, Guatemala]
192	215	(Air Manila International)	PI-C866 RP-C866 [wfu & stored 1981 Manila, Philippines; l/n 28May83; no further reports, probably b/u]
193			[airframe used for water tank pressure testing; b/u in 1970]
194	214	(Channel Express (Air Services))	PP-SDN G-BAVX G-DGLD [wfu Feb96 Exeter, UK; canx 19Jun96; b/u during 1996]
195	209	ex Channel Express (Air Services)	4X-AHO G-BFRJ I-ZERC G-CEXP [wfu 08Mar96; canx 22Mar96; preserved Mar98 terminal roof London-Gatwick, UK; 12Sep03 moved & stored on field; l/n 27Feb09]
196	203	(British Island Airways)	I-TIVI G-BBXJ [w/o 24Dec74 Jersey Airport, Channel Islands, UK; canx 10May83; Nov95 fuselage to fire dump]
197	209	(Channel Express (Air Services))	4X-AHN G-BFRK I-ZERD G-GNSY [wfu Dec96 Bournemouth, UK; b/u Jan97; canx 08Apr97]
252	700	(VASP)	[canx in 1966; components only; airframe not completed]
253	700	(VASP)	[canx in 1966; components only; airframe not completed]
254	700	(VASP)	[canx in 1966; components only; airframe not completed]
255	700	(VASP)	[canx in 1966; components only; airframe not completed]
256	700	(VASP)	[canx in 1966; components only; airframe not completed]
257	700	(VASP)	[canx in 1966; components only; airframe not completed]

Production complete

HANDLEY PAGE HP.137 JETSTREAM

C/n	Line No.	Model	Last known Owner/Operator	Identities/fates/comments (where appropriate)
198	01	200	(Handley Page Aircraft Ltd)	G-ATXH [ff 18Aug67; wfu & stored Feb70 Filton, UK; canx 22Apr71; b/u Oct72; nose preserved AeroVenture, Doncaster, UK]
199	02	3M	(Handley Page Aircraft Ltd)	G-ATXI [b/u Dec70 Radlett, UK; canx 17Jan74; nose used for fire training Stansted, UK]
200	03	200	(Handley Page Aircraft Ltd)	G-ATXJ [canx 11Apr72 as sold in USA; airframe found non-acceptable and returned to BAe; used as Jetstream 31 then J41 mock-up ; Feb95 to Cardiff Airport Fire Service, UK]
201	04	1	(Apollo Airways)	G-ATXK N2958F (N2201) [wfu for spares Nov79 Santa Barbara-Municipal, CA; hulk l/n 14Apr85]
202	1	1	Regionaal Opleidings Centrum	G-AWSE N1039S N14RJ N114CP TF-ODM [donated as GIA Oct97, Hoofddorp, Netherlands; l/n 22Jan11]
203	2	1	(South Central Air Transport)	G-8-4 G-AXEK N1FY N103SC [wfu & stored 1985 Natchez, MO; later b/u for spares]
204	3	1	(Air Illinois)	G-AWVI N1040S N11DH N11DN [wfu & stored Oct83 Springfield, IL; b/u 1988]
205	4	1	(Bavaria Fluggesellschaft)	G-8-5 G-AXEM D-INAH [w/o 06Mar70 Samedan, Switzerland]
206	5	T.2	Northbrook College	G-AWVJ N1036S XX475 [wfu before 30Nov05; GIA Shoreham, UK painted as G-AWVJ but not reg'd; l/n Dec08]
207	6	1	(British Steel Corporation)	G-8-6 G-AXEL [w/o en-route 29Sep69 Courtyard Farm, near Hunstanton, UK; canx 06Jan70]
208	7	200	ex Cranfield University	G-AWVK N1035S G-AWVK G-RAVL [wfu to GIA Cranfield, UK; canx 30Jan01; l/n 20Jan11]
209	8	1	(Newair of Denmark)	G-8-7 G-AXEP N5V N74169 N5VP N5VH N2209 OY-CRP [wfu Sep 90 Esbjerg, Denmark; b/u spares Sep96; hulk l/n Nov98]
210	9	1	(Odin Air)	G-AWYM N62BS N2MG N2MQ TF-ODI [wfu & stored 1994 Roskilde, Denmark; b/u 1997; nose preserved Vliegend Museum, Seppe, Netherlands]
211	10	T.2	Everett Aero	G-8-8 G-AXFV 9Q-CTC ZA111 [code CU/565]
212	11	1	(Northwest Int'l Industries)	G-AWYN N340 N2212 [canx 10Aug12 probably b/u]
213	12	1	(Barron Thomas Aviation)	G-AWYP N137HP N666AE N1213 [canx Oct93; fate unknown]
214	13	1	Regionaal Opleidings Centrum	G-AXHB CF-QJB N17RJ TF-ODN "PH-HAN" [preseved Aug97 Hoofddorp, Netherlands in false marks; l/n 22Jan11]
215	15	200	(Ibis Investments)	G-AXGK N200PA (OO-BIS) OO-IBJ [wfu Antwerp, Belgium 12Sep97; canx 23Oct97; b/u Dec97]
216	16	T.2	ex Royal Navy	G-AXGL N1037S XX476 [code CU/561; 31Jan11 & sold; fuselage to museum at Hermeskeil, Germany]
217	17	1	(Newair of Denmark)	G-AXHJ N12217 OY-CRR [wfu Dec95 Esbjerg, Denmark; by Aug03 reported derelict at Roskilde, Denmark; canx 24Oct03; by 06Apr07 reported at Ishoj, Denmark]
218	18	III	Malaysian Institute of Avn Technology	G-AXGM N12218 85-24688 + [+ US Army] [Century III conversion; wfu 1999 Houston-Hobby, TX used as GIA painted as "N12218"; by Aug04 moved to Dengkil, Malaysia; l/n Nov09 all white]
219	14	C-10A	(USAF)	(68-10378) [first for USAF; order canx Oct69, not completed; b/u Jan72 Cove, UK]
220	19	1	(D.H.Gayne & Associates)	G-AXGN N1038S N651KE N16RJ [wfu for spares Feb83 Santa Barbara-Municipal, CA; b/u]
221	21	III	(TAAN – Transporte Aereo Andino)	G-AXIK N12221 YV-626C [Century III conversion; wfu & canx by 2002; fate unknown]
222	22	1	Perth College	G-8-9 G-AXUI G-NFLC [ferried 15Jly04 Cranfield to Perth, UK; wfu & canx 03Aug04; used as GIA; l/n 28Nov08]
223	24	1	(California Capital Corp Leasing)	G-AXIL N12223 N1044S N12223 [wfu & stored by1988, Santa Barbara-Municipal, CA; l/n Dec90; assumed b/u; canx 12Jun12]
224	25	III	(Federal Aviation Administration)	G-AXIM N12224 N1041S N12224 85-24687 + N12224 [+ US Army] [Century III conversion; wfu & stored Mar83; used as GIA by Purdue University, IN; preserved by Aug11 Daytona Beach, FL]
225	26	1	(Newair of Denmark)	G-8-10 G-AXON N10AB N12225 OY-CRS [wfu Jun90 Esbjerg, Denmark; by Nov01 fuselage in field near airport]
226	23	C-10A	(USAF)	(68-10379) [order canx Oct69, not completed; b/u Jan72 Cove, UK]
227	28	1	National Museum of Flight	G-AXJZ N12227 N510E N510F G-JSSD [converted to BAe3100 prototype ff 28Mar80; canx 30Jan96; preserved Aug96 East Fortune, UK; l/n 12Oct08]
228	27	C-10A	(USAF)	(68-10380) [order canx Oct69, not completed; b/u Jan72 Cove, UK]
229	29	1	(Kurt W Simon)	G-AXKG N10EA N229 [wfu by 1988; probably b/u Los Angeles-Whiteman, CA; l/n Nov88; canx 14Aug12]
230	30	1	(Andrew, Fred & Myrna Molnar)	G-8-11 G-AXVF N14230 N85230 N9033Z [wfu by 1988, probably b/u Del Rey, CA]

HANDLEY PAGE HP.137 JETSTREAM

C/n	Line No.	Model	Last known Owner/Operator	Identities/fates/comments (where appropriate)
231	32	1	(Jetstream Inc)	G-AXLO N10DG N7RJ (N7RS) N7RJ [reported wfu Oct83 Springfield IL; still reg'd Nov09]
232	31	C-10A	(USAF)	(68-10381) [order canx Oct69, not completed; b/u Jan72 Cove, UK]
233	33	1	(Newair of Denmark)	G-AXLP N8943 N815M (N2ES) N815M N33233 OY-CRT [wfu Dec95 Esbjerg, Denmark; b/u 1999; canx 24Oct03]
234	34	1	National Museum of Flight	G-8-12 G-BBBV (N1BE) N200SE N1BE N102SC N14234 [wfu Oct86; bought by BAe & fuselage used as static demonstrator for Jetstream 31; May94 fuselage preserved East Fortune, UK; l/n 12Oct08]
235	36	III	Aerovias Caribe SA de CV?	G-AXRE (N71AS) N10GA YV-625C YV-690CP + YV1878 [Century III conversion; + marks in doubt as YV-690C used by Cessna 206] [by 13Oct09 stored Tamiami, FL; 04Feb10]
236	35	C-10A	(USAF)	(68-10382) [order canx Oct69, not completed; b/u Jan72 Cove, UK]
237	37	1	California Partners in Flight	G-AXRF N2527 N666WB [wfu by 1988; possibly b/u Culver City, CA]
238	38	III	(Air US)	G-AXRG N11360 (N72AS?) N11360 [Century III conversion; w/o 17Apr81 Loveland, CO after mid-air collision with Cessna 206G N4862F]
239	39	C-10A	(USAF)	(68-10383) [order canx Oct69, not completed; b/u Jan72 Cove, UK]
240	40	III	Technical Education Services	G-AXRH (N10JA) N4770 (N73AS) 85-24689 + N4770 [+ US Army] [Century III conversion; wfu by May87 Daytona Beach, FL; 2007 to Lawrenceville-Gwinnett County, GA; in use as GIA; l/n 19Oct10]
241	41	200	(IBIS Investments BV)	G-AXRI G-BCGU G-GLOS OO-IBL [wfu & stored by 23May99 Antwerp, Belgium; canx 24Sep07, l/n 11Aug10 complete]
242	43	C-10A	(USAF)	(68-10384) [order canx Oct69, not completed; b/u Jan72 Cove, UK]
243	42	200	Newcastle Aviation Academy	G-8-13 G-AYWR G-BBYM [preserved by May00 Cosford, UK; canx07Jun00; moved to Newcastle, UK; l/n 25Jun08]
244	47	C-10A	(USAF)	(68-10385) [order canx Oct69, not completed; b/u Jan72 Cove, UK]
245	44	1	Thales Universite Cooperation	G-AXUM [wfu Jan99 & used as GIA, near Paris-Le Bourget, France; l/n Jly08]
246	45	200	(Centrax)	G-AXUN G-BCWW G-CTRX [wfu 29May91 Guernsey, UK; b/u Jly95; canx 25Sep95; May97 fuselage to Antwerp, Belgium for spares; nose preserved at Eindhoven Aviation Shop]
247		C-10A	(USAF)	(68-10386) [order canx Oct69, not completed; b/u Jan72 probably at Cove, UK]
248	46	T.2	ex Royal Navy	G-AXUO F-BTMI ZA110 [code CU/563] [wfu & stored 29Oct10 Culdrose, UK]
249	48	T.1	(Royal Air Force)	G-8-14 G-AXXS XX477+ 8462M [+ code 31] [w/o 01Nov74 Little Rissington, UK; to RAF Finningley, UK as GIA; by Apr05 fuselage at Church Farm Strip, Askern, Yorks; 01Nov08 fuselage preserved AeroVenture, Doncaster, UK]
250		C-10A	(USAF)	(68-10387) [order canx Oct69, not completed; b/u Jan72 probably at Cove, UK]
251	49	T.2	Everett Aero	G-AXUP XX481 [code CU/560; wfu 31Jan11Culdrose, UK; 24May11 to Sproughton, UK]
258	05	3M	(Handley Page Aircraft Ltd)	G-AWBR [wfu Oct69 Radlett, UK; b/u May70; canx 17Jan74]
259	50	T.2	Royal Navy Fire School	G-AXUR XX479 A2611 [code CU/563] [19Feb97 fuselage used as GIA FAA Predannack, UK; l/n 16Apr08]
260		C-10A	(USAF)	(68-10388) [order canx Oct69, not completed; b/u Jan72 probably at Cove, UK]
261	52	T.2	Everett Aero	G-AXXT XX478 [code CU/564; wfu 31Jan11 Culdrose, UK; 03Jun11 to Sproughton, UK]
262	53	T.2	(Royal Navy)	G-AXXU XX480 [code CU/561] [stored Sep97 RAF Shawbury, UK; b/u May 99, hulk to Mil-Ver Metals, Coventry, UK]
263	54	T.1	(Air & Ground Aviation Ltd)	XX482 [code J] [wfu 12Dec03; b/u Mar06, fuselage stored Hixon, UK]
264	56	T.2	(Royal Navy)	XX483 [code CU/562] [stored Sep97 RAF Shawbury; b/u Feb98, hulk to Mil-Ver Metals, Coventry, UK; nose section preserved Dumfries & Galloway Museum, Dumfries, UK]
265	57	T.2	Everett Aero	XX486 [codes CU/569 and later CU/567; wfu 31Jan11 Culdrose, UK; 16May11 to college near Ipswich, UK as GIA]
266	58	T.2	Royal Navy	XX484 [code CU/566; reported wfu 31Jan11 and for sale]
267	60	T.2	(Royal Navy)	XX488 [code CU/562] [by Aug10 wfu for spares Culdrose, UK; b/u 24Jan11]
268	61	T.2	Uruguayan Navy	XX485 + 875 [+ Royal Navy; code CU/567; reported stored by 07Feb10 Laguna del Sauce, Uruguay]
269	62	T.2	Royal Navy	XX487 [code CU/568; reported wfu 31Jan11 and for sale]
270		C-10A	(USAF)	(68-10389) [order canx Oct69, not completed; wings to Scottish Aviation]
271	64	T.2	Uruguayan Navy	(XX495) XX490 + 876 [+ Royal Navy; code CU/570]
272		C-10A	(USAF)	(68-10390) [order canx Oct69, not completed]
273		C-10A	(USAF)	(68-10391) [order canx Oct69, not completed]

HANDLEY PAGE HP.137 JETSTREAM

C/n	Line No.	Model	Last known Owner/Operator	Identities/fates/comments (where appropriate)
274	67	T.1	Newark Air Museum	(XX491) XX492 [code A] [wfu 22Mar04 to FAA Culdrose for spares; preserved 09Dec04 Winthorpe, UK]
275	68	T.1	Northbrook College	(XX490) XX491 [code K] [SOC by Dec03 for spares; 10Nov05 by road to Shoreham, UK as GIA]
276	69	T.1	Royal Air Force Museum	(XX493) XX496 [code D] [wfu 22Mar04 & preserved Cosford, UK; l/n Nov09]
277		C-10A	(USAF)	(68-10392) [order canx Oct69, not completed]
278	71	T.1	(Royal Air Force)	(XX492) XX493 [code L] [SOC 12Apr04 RAF Cranwell, UK; moved 24May04 Spur Scrapyard North Scarle, UK]
279	72	T.2	(Royal Navy)	XX489 [code CU/575] [w/o 08May89 in Portland Harbour, Dorset, UK]
280	73	T.1	(Air & Ground Aviation Ltd)	(XX494) XX497 [code E] [wfu & stored 17Dec03; b/u May05; fuselage stored Hixon, UK]
281		200		[components only, parts used for later production]
282		200		[components only, parts used for later production]
283		200		[components only, parts used for later production]
284		200		[components only, parts used for later production]
285		200		[components only, parts used for later production]
286		200		[components only, parts used for later production]
287		200		[components only, parts used for later production]

Production continued with Scottish Aviation

SCOTTISH AVIATION HP.137 JETSTREAM

C/n	Line No.	Model	Last known Owner/Operator	Identities/fates/comments (where appropriate)
422		T.1	University of Nottingham?	(XX496) XX494 [code B] [SOC 22Mar04, dismantled Apr05; stored Sep05 Sproughton, UK; l/n 04Sep07; by 04Jly09 moved to Gamston, UK as GIA; by Aug11 to Bruntingthorpe, UK]
423		T.1	Bedford College	(XX497) XX495 [code C] [SOC 22Mar04 to GIA Bedford, UK; l/n 25Jun06]
424		T.1	(Royal Air Force)	XX498 [code F] [SOC 22Mar04, b/u Sep05 Stafford; by Jun06 hulk to Spur Scrapyard, North Scarle, UK]
425		T.1	Brooklands Museum	XX499 [code G] [SOC 22Mar04; preserved 21May08 Brooklands, UK]
426		T.1	Everett Aero	XX500 [code H] [SOC 22Mar04, dismantled Apr05; stored Sep05 Sproughton, UK; l/n 04Sep07]

Production continued with British Aerospace (q.v.)

HARBIN (AVIC II) Y-12

C/n	Model	Last known Owner/Operator	Identities/fates/comments (where appropriate)
0001	I	(China Flying Dragon Aviation)	B-3822 [w/o 21Jun96 Changhai, China]
0002	I	(China Flying Dragon Aviation)	B-3802 [w/o 28Oct90 near Sishou City, China]
0003	I	China Flying Dragon Aviation	B-3803 [fate/status unknown]
0004	II	China Flying Dragon Aviation	B-3819
0005	II	China Flying Dragon Aviation	B-3805
0006	II	China Flying Dragon Aviation	B-3801
0007			[not known] [seen in Harbin factory Oct88]
0008	II	China Flying Dragon Aviation	B-3806
0009	II	ex Yeti Airlines	B-3810 9N-AFB [derelict by Oct06 Kathmandu, Nepal; l/n 04Feb09]
0010			[nothing known]
0011	II	China Flying Dragon Aviation	B-3804
0012	II	Shuangyang General Aviation	B-3811
012B	II	Zuhai Avia	B-3809(1) B-3859
0013	II	(Sri Lankan Air Force)	CR851 [w/o 20Jan97 in sea off Palaly, Sri Lanka]
0014	II	Sri Lankan Air Force	CR852+ SCL-3201+ SCL852 [+ Sri Lanka] [report of being SCL-3200 probably an error]
0015	II	Sri LankanAir Force	CR853+ SCL-3204+ SCL853 [+ Sri Lanka]
0016	II	China Flying Dragon Aviation	B-3807
0017	II	China Flying Dragon Aviation	B-3808
0018	II	Sri Lankan Air Force	CR854+ SCL-3202+ SCL854 [+ Sri Lanka]
0019	II	Sri Lankan Anir Force	CR855+ SCL-3203 [+ Sri Lanka]
0020	II	(Sri Lankan Air Force)	CR856 [w/o 06Mar97 Vavunative Army Base, Sri Lanka]
0021	II	Sri Lankan Air Force	CR857+ SCL-3205 [+ Sri Lanka]
0022	II	Sri Lankan Air Force	CR858+ SCL-3206 [+ Sri Lanka]
0023	II	Xinjiang General Aviation	B-3815
0024	II	Zhuhai AVIC General Aviation	B-3812
0025	II	Zhuhai Air General Aviation	B-3813
0026	II	Shuangyang General Aviation	B-3814
0027	II	Sri Lankan Air Force	CR859+ SCL-3207 [+ Sri Lanka]
0028	II	ex Yeti Airlines	B-3816 9N-AFO [derelict by Oct06 Kathmandu, Nepal; l/n 04Feb09]
0029	II	Xinjiang General Aviation	B-3817
0030	II	Xinjiang General Aviation	B-3818
0031	II	China Zhong Fei General Aviation	B-3820
0032	II	Jiangnan University Aviation	D-0066(2)+ JU-1019 B-3821 [+ MIAT Mongolia]
0033	II	(Lao Aviation)	B-512L RDPL-34115 [wfu by 2000 Vientiane-Wattay, Laos; l/n Apr02; canx; Jan07 noted in Vientiane City, Laos]
0034	II	(Lao Aviation)	RDPL-34116 [canx post 12Feb04; noted Dec09 in used car compound Vientiane City, Laos]
0035	II	Pakistan Air Force	96-035
0036	II	Iranian Revolutionary Guard	15-2241
0037	II	Iranian Revolutionary Guard	15-2243
0038	II	China National Aero-Technology Corp	[not known]
0039	II	Iranian Revolutionary Guard	15-2245
0040	II	Iranian Revolutionary Guard	15-2248
0041	II	Iranian Revolutionary Guard	15-2254
0042	II	(Lao Aviation)	RDPL-34117 [w/o 14Dec93 Phongsavah, Laos]
0043	II	(Lao Aviation)	RDPL-34118 [w/o 14Feb02 Xam Neua, Laos]
0044	II	(Nepal Airways)	9N-ACS [w/o 08Nov93 Jomsom, Nepal]
0045	II	Pakistan Army	045
0046	II	Eritrean Government	B-534L ER800+ ST-ALY [+ Eritrea]
0047	II	ex Airlines Tonga	B-531L (1) DQ-FHF [stored by Jly09 Suva-Nausori, Fiji]
0048	II	(Air Fiji)	DQ-FSC VH-LLK DQ-FSC [stored by Jly09 Suva-Nausori, Fiji; b/u by Aug10; cockpit section to Archerfield, QLD, Australia]
0049	II	(TANS)	333+ OB-1498 [+ Peru] [w/o 04Apr95 Iquitos, Peru]
0050	II	(TANS)	334+ OB-1499 [+ Peru] [w/o 14May93 Atalaya, Peru]
0051	II	Peruvian Air Force?	335+ OB-1500 335^ [+ Peru] [^ not fully confirmed]
0052	II	Peruvian Air Force	336+ OB-1501 336 [+ Peru] [stored by 19Nov07 Lima-Las Palmas, AFB, Peru]
0053	II	Peruvian Air Force	337+ OB-1502 337 [+ Peru]
0054	II	(TANS)	338+ OB-1503 [+ Peru] [w/o 04Jun92 Oxapampa, Peru]
0055	II	(Yeti Airways)	9N-ACD 9N-AEB [wfu by Jan02 Kathmandu, Nepal; not noted 04Feb09]
0056	II	ex Airlines Tonga	DQ-FHC [stored by Jly09 Suva-Nausori, Fiji]

HARBIN (AVIC II) Y-12

C/n	Model	Last known Owner/Operator	Identities/fates/comments (where appropriate)
0057	II	ex Berjaya Air	9M-TAB [wfu by summer 2006 Subang, Malaysia]
0058	II	ex Berjaya Air	9M-TAE [w/o 02Feb95 Kuala Lumpur, Malaysia; reported 25Dec96 Sabang, Malaysia; l/n summer 06]
0059	II	Red Sea Air	ER802+ E3-AAI [+ Eritrea]
0060	II	Eritrean Air Force	ER801 [not fully confirmed]
0061	II	ex Flying Dragon Airlines, Nepal	DQ-FHI B-539L S2-AAQ B-531L(2) 9N-AHP [fate/status unknown]
0062	II	Flying Dragon Airlines	B-550L S2-AAR B-532L 9N-AHQ B-3842
0063	II	Shuangyang General Aviation	9N-ACF B-3827
0064	II	(MIAT Mongolia)	D-0064+ JU-1017 [+ MIAT Mongolia; w/o 26May98 Erdenet, Mongolia]
0065	II	China Zhong Fei General Aviation	D-0065+ JU-1018 B-3829 [+ MIAT Mongolia]
0066	II	(MIAT Mongolia)	D-0066(1)+ [+ MIAT Mongolia; w/o 05Dec92 Dornod, Mongolia; by Aug94 hulk at Ulan Bator, Mongolia; l/n May95]
0067	II	(MIAT Mongolia)	D-0067+ JU-1020 [+ MIAT Mongolia; w/o 10Jun97 Dundgovi, Mongolia]
0068	II	Jiangnan University Aviation	D-0068+ JU-1021 B-3823 [+ MIAT Mongolia]
0069	II	(Nepal Airways)	9N-ACI [w/o 26Sep92 Lukla, Nepal]
0070	II	Tung Wah Group	B-579L RP-C1518 B-3838
0071	II	Shuangyang General Aviation	9N-ADB B-3828
0072	II	(Peruvian Police)	OB-1621 PNP-224 [w/o 04Mar95 Bon Jesus, Peru]
0073	II	Peruvian Police	OB-1622 PNP-225
0074	II	Peruvian Police	OB-1623 PNP-226
0075	II	Zambian Air Force	AF213
0076	II	Zambian Air Force	AF214 [also reported as c/n 0075]
0077	II	Air Kiribati	T3-ATI
0078	II	Eritrean Air Force	ER803
0079	II	Tanzanian Air Force	B-580L JW9029
0080	II	Tanzanian Air Force	B-581L JW9030
0081	II	Tung Wah Group	B-582L RP-C1519 B-3839
0082	II	Guyana Defence Force	B-590L RP-C1520 B-596L 8R-GDS
0083	II	ex Cambodian Air Force	XU-701 XU-016 [wfu by 19Nov05 Phnom Penh, Cambodia; not noted 14Dec09]
0084	II	Cambodian Air Force	XU-702 XU-017
0085	II	ex Lao Aviation	RDPL-34129 [retired end 2006 & stored Vientiane-Wattay, Laos; l/n 05Apr08]
0086	II	(Lao Aviation)	RDPL-34130 [w/o 20Oct00 near Sam Neua, Laos]
0087	II	ex Lao Aviation	RDPL-34131 [retired end 2006 & stored Vientiane-Wattay, Laos; l/n 05Apr08; by Jun10 in car museum Wat Hua Krabue, Thailand; l/n 21Sep10]
0088	II	(Zambian Air Force)	AF215 [w/o 16Oct10 Mukinge Airport, Zambia]
0089	II	(Zambian Air Force)	B-600L AF216 [w/o 18May05 Mongu Airport, Zambia]
0090	II	Zambian Air Force	B-601L AF217
0091	II	Pakistan Air Force	96-091
0092			[nothing known]
0093	II	Kenyan Air Force	KAF120 [c/n not confirmed]
0094	II	Kenyan Air Force	KAF124
0095	II	Kenyan Air Force	KAF126
0096	II	Kenyan Air Force	KAF128 [c/n not confirmed]
0097	II	Kenyan Air Force	KAF130 [c/n not confirmed]
0098	II	Kenyan Air Force	KAF132 [c/n not confirmed] [w/o 10Apr06 near Marsabit, Kenya]
0099	II	Pakistan Army	099
0100			[nothing known]
0101			[nothing known]
0102	II	Iranian Revolutionary Guard	15-2244
0103			[nothing known]
0104	II	Namibian Air Force	NDF97-600
0105	II	Namibian Air Force	NDF97-639
0106			[nothing known]
0107			[nothing known]
0108			[nothing known]
0109			[nothing known]
0110			[nothing known]
0111			[nothing known]
0112	II	Pakistan Army	112
0113	II	Pakistan Army	113
001	IV	Harbin Aircraft Company	B-569L [prototype MK4; c/n not confirmed]
002	IV	CATIC	B-573L B-3826 B-620L+ [+ c/n not fully confirmed]

HARBIN (AVIC II) Y-12

C/n	Model	Last known Owner/Operator	Identities/fates/comments (where appropriate)
003	IV	China Flying Dragon Aviation	B-3830
004	12E	China Flying Dragon Aviation	B-3831
005	12E	Yunnan Dacite GA	B-3833
006	12E	China Heilongjiang Nongken General Avn2)	B-620L B-3809(
007	?	China Flying Dragon Aviation	B-3825
008	IV	Xinjiang General Aviation	B-3850
009	?	China Flying Dragon Aviation	B-3835
010	?	Baicheng General Aviation	B-3836
011	12E	Ying'an Airlines	B-3832
012	?	China Flying Dragon Aviation	B-3837
013	IV	China Flying Dragon Aviation	B-+ DQ-AFR B-3846 [+ delivery reg'n B-744L or B-745L]
014			[nothing known]
015	IV	ex Air Fiji	B-+ DQ-AFS^ [+ delivery reg'n B-744L or B-745L; ^ canx by 2011 possibly returned to China]
016			
017			
018			
019	12E	Tri Star General Aviation	B-3840
020			
021	IV	Uganda Air Cargo	5X-UYZ+ [+ ex Ugandan Air Force, serial unknown]
022			
023			
024			
025			
026	IV	Uganda Air Cargo	5X-UYX+ [+ ex Ugandan Air Force, serial unknown]
027	IV	Uganda Air Cargo	5X-UXZ+ [+ ex Ugandan Air Force, serial unknown]
028	IV	Air Vanuatu	B-958L YJ-AV4
029		Air Vanuatu	B-978L YJ-AV5
030			
031			
032		Air Vanuatu	B-979L YJ-AV6
033	IV	Ordos City General Aviation	B-3851
034			
035	IV	Xinjiang General Aviation	B-3849
036	IV	China Flying Dragon Aviation	B-3852
037	IV	Sri Lankan Air Force	B-1097L SCL-3209 SCL-3124+ [+tie up not confirmed]
038	IV	Sri Lankan Air Force	B-1098L SCL-3210 SCL-3125+ [+tie up not confirmed]
039	IV	China Flying Dragon Aviation	B-3858
040	IV	China Flying Dragon Aviation	B-3856
041			
042			
043	IV	Jiangnan General Aviation	B-3853
044			
045	IV	Xinjiang General Aviation	B-3847
046			
047	IV	China Flying Dragon Aviation	B-3855
048	IV	Erdos City General Aviation	B-3848
049	IV	China Flying Dragon Aviation	B-3857
050			
051			
052			
053			
054			
055			
056			
057			
058			
Unidentified			
unkn	II	Mauritanian Air Force	B-530L 5T-MAE [not c/n 0081 as once reported]
unkn	?		B-548L [demonstrator aircraft]
unkn	IV	for Kenyan Air Force	B-552L [reported 08Sep00 Muscat, UAE on delivery]

HARBIN (AVIC II) Y-12

C/n	Model	Last known Owner/Operator	Identities/fates/comments (where appropriate)	
unkn	IV	for Kenyan Air Force	B-554L	[reported 08Sep00 Muscat, UAE on delivery]
unkn	IV	for Kenyan Air Force	B-556L	[reported 08Sep00 Muscat, UAE on delivery]
unkn	IV		B-578L	[reported 01Nov01 Zhuhai, China]
unkn	II	Mauritanian Air Force	B-599L	5T-MAD [not c/n 0070 as once reported]
unkn	IV	for Zambian Air Force	B-801L	[reported 22Jan07 Tianjin, China on delivery; possibly to AF221]
unkn	IV	for Zambian Air Force	B-802L	[reported 22Jan07 Tianjin, China on delivery; possibly to AF222]
unkn	MK5?	for Ugandan Air Force	B-983L	[reported 12Dec08 Kunming, China on delivery]
unkn	F		B-1233L	[new model with name Aircar Y12F with retractable undercarriage; f/f Dec12]; c/n 001 reported]
unkn	IV		B-1234L	[reported 20Mar11 Kunming, China; 107 on nose]
unkn	II	(China Flying Dragon Aviation)	B-3841	[w/o 15Jun08 45 km from Chifeng, China; not c/n 0066 as once reported]
unkn	II	Zhuhai China National	B-3859	[on register with incorrect c/n 01213]
unkn	IV	Civil Aviation Administration of China	6016	[reported 12Oct09 Hanzhong-Chenggu, China; a survey aircraft]
unkn	IV	Civil Aviation Administration of China?	6017	[from photo dated Feb10; a survey aircraft based at Hanzhong-Chenggu, China]
unkn	IV	Civil Aviation Administration of China	6020	[from photo at Hanzhong-Chenggu, China; a survey aircraft]
unkn	?	Iranian Revolutionary Guard	15-2239	[reported 05Mar08 Tehran-Mehrabad, Iran]
unkn	?	Iranian Revolutionary Guard	15-2240	
unkn	?	Iranian Revolutionary Guard	15-2242	
unkn	II	Iranian Revolutionary Guard	15-2246	[reported 25Feb07 Bandar Abbas, Iran]
unkn	?	Iranian Revolutionary Guard	15-2247	
unkn	II	Kenyan Air Force	KAF110	[reported 12Mar10 Laikipia AFB, Kenya]
unkn	II	Kenyan Air Force	KAF114	[reported 26Mar10 Laikipia AFB, Kenya]
unkn	II	Kenyan Air Force	KAF134	[reported 21Sep09 Nairobi-Wilson, Kenya with a possible c/n of 0096 which is reported as KAF128]
unkn	II	Kenyan Air Force	KAF136	[reported 22Jun11 Nairobi-Wilson, Kenya]
unkn	II	Kenyan Air Force	KAF138	
unkn	II	Kenyan Air Force	KAF140	[reported 14Apr11 Nairobi-Wilson, Kenya]
unkn	IV	Zambian Air Force	AF218	[reported 17Sep08 Luanda, Zambia]
unkn	IV	Zambian Air Force	AF219	[reported 30Mar07 Lunada, Zambia]
unkn	IV	Zambian Air Force	AF220	[reported 12Sep06 Luanda, Zambia]
unkn	IV	Zambian Air Force	AF222	[reported 30Mar07 Lunada, Zambia]
unkn	II	Cambodian Air Force	RCAF-602	[reported 14Dec09 Phnom Penh, Cambodia; possibly either c/n 0083 or 0084]
unkn		Sri Lankan Air Force	SCL-3200	[reported 13May10 Colombo-Ratmalana, Sri Lanka; prefix not confirmed]
unkn		Sri Lankan Air Force	SCL-3201	[reported Sep10 Colombo-Ratmalana, Sri Lanka]
unkn	E	Seychelles Defence Force	SY-008	[delivered 16Jun11]
unkn	E	Seychelles Defence Force	SY-009?	[delivered 16Jun11]
unkn	IV	Pakistan Air Force	Y-4106	[reported Mar12]
unkn	II	Mauritanian Air Force	[an unidentified Mauritanian Air Force Y12 was w/o 12Jly12 Nouakchott, Mauritania]	

AVRO/ HAWKER SIDDELEY HS.748

C/n	Line No.	Model	Last known Owner/Operator	Identities/fates/comments (where appropriate)

Notes: LFD – Large Freight Door
At different times in service with the Indian Air Force the serials have been applied with and without the hyphen.

C/n	Line No.	Model	Last known Owner/Operator	Identities/fates/comments (where appropriate)
1534		1/100	(AV Roe & Co Ltd)	G-APZV [prototype ff 24Jun60; wfu Jly62 & converted to HS748/748MF prototype with c/n 1548; marks canx 09May63]
1535		1A/200	(Dan-Air Services)	G-ARAY YV-C-AMC G-ARAY PP-VJQ G-ARAY VP-LIO G-ARAY PI-C784 G-ARAY G-11 OY-DFV G-ARAY [wfu 17Oct89 Lasham, UK; b/u May90; nose section to Hillside Nurseries, Alton, UK; canx 02Nov92]
1536	1	1/101	(Skyways Coach Air)	G-ARMV [w/o 11Jly65 Lympne, Kent, UK; canx 18Nov65]
1537	15	1A/101	ex Necon Air	G-ARMW VP-LII G-ARMW VP-LVO G-ARMW G-FBMV G-ARMV G-ERMV 9N-ACH [wfs 06Nov94 Kathmandu,Nepal; derelict by Oct99; l/n 14Mar08]
1538	18	1A/101	(Dan-Air Services)	G-ARMX VP-LVN (G-ARMX) [b/u Sep90 Manchester, UK; fuselage donated to airport fire service; on dump by 1998, gone by summer 2000]
1539	3	1/105	(Aerolineas Argentinas)	LV-PIZ LV-HGW [w/o 04Feb70 Loma Alta, Corrientes, Argentina]
1540	4	1/105	(Yacimientos Petroliferos Fiscales)	LV-PJA LV-HHB [w/o en-route 14Apr76 near Neuquen, 35km N of Cutral Airport, Argentina]
1541	5	1/105	(Dan-Air Services)	LV-PJR LV-PRJ LV-HHC G-BEKC [wfu 21Nov87 Manchester, UK; b/u May92, but another report suggests b/u in 1989; nose section to Florida USA for use as ATP simulator; canx 21Oct92 as exported to USA]
1542	7	1/105	(Dan-Air Services)	LV-PUC LV-HHD G-BEKF [w/o 31Jly79 Sumburgh, UK; canx 14Dec79]
1543	10	1/105	ex PTB (Emerald) Pty Ltd	LV-PUF LV-HHE G-BEJD [stored 13Mar05 Blackpool, UK; Cof A expired 29Mar06; l/n 06Dec08; dismantled Apr09 for possible museum collection]
1544	12	1/105	ex Ryanair	LV-PUM LV-HHF G-BEKD EC-DTP EI-BSF [wfs Jan87 Dublin, Ireland; b/u Mar91; canx 26Jly94; used as cabin trainer until Mar05; to Irish Air Corps, Baldonnel, Ireland – used by fire service in non-destructive role; l/n 21Jly08]
1545	13	1/105	(Emerald Airways)	LV-PUP LV-HHG G-BEKE [wfu 26Jly93 Liverpool, UK for spares use; b/u Oct93; canx 10Sep96]
1546	16	1/105	(Aerolineas Argentinas)	LV-PVH LV-HHH [damaged 19Jan70 Colonia Catriel, Argentina; ferried Buenos Aires, subsequently declared w/o]
1547	17	1/105	(Aerolineas Argentinas)	LV-PVF LV-HHI [w/o 27Nov69 Santa Rosa Airport, La Pampa, Argentina]
1548		HS780	(Royal Air Force)	G-ARRV+ 8669M^ [rebuild of c/n 1534] [+ wore pseudo Russian AF marks 57 for film; ^ GIA Benson, UK; by 1985 on fire dump; b/u May90; by Oct90 hulk to Coley's scrap yard, Egham, UK]
1549	25	1A/106	(Necon Air)	G-ARRW EI-BSE G-ARRW G-MRRV 9N-ACM [w/o 06Nov97 Pokhara, Nepal]
1550	19	2/204	ex Brazilian Air Force	(VR-AAU) C-91-2500 [stored by Jun01 Rio de Janeiro-Galeao, Brazil; SOC 01Oct01; l/n Jun04]
1551	22	2/205	ex Brazilian Air Force	(VR-AAV) C-91-2501 [stored by Jun01 Rio de Janeiro-Galeao, Brazil; SOC 01Oct01; l/n 26May08]
1552	21	2/205	ex Brazilian Air Force	(VR-AAW) C-91-2502 [stored by Jun01 Rio de Janeiro-Galeao, Brazil; SOC 01Oct01; by Nov03 gate guardian; l/n 26May08]
1553	23	2/205	ex Brazilian Air Force	C-91-2503 [stored by Jun01 Rio de Janeiro-Galeao, Brazil; SOC 01Oct01; l/n Jun04]
1554	24	2/205	Museu Aeroespacial	C-91-2504 [SOC 01Oct01; 25Oct01 preserved Campo dos Afonsos, Rio de Janeiro, Brazil; l/n 23Aug07]
1555	30	2/205	ex Brazilian Air Force	C-91-2505 [stored by Jun01 Rio de Janeiro-Galeao, Brazil; SOC 01Oct01; l/n 26May08]
1556	26	1/105	(Emerald Airways)	LV-PXD LV-IDV G-BEJE [wfs 17Jan97; b/u 1997 Blackpool, UK; canx 16May97]
1557	27	1A/105	(Emerald Airways)	LV-PXH LV-IEE G-BEKG VR-CBH G-VAJK G-BEKG G-DAAL [wfs 05Oct96; b/u Jan97 Blackpool, UK; canx 18Mar97]
1558	28	1/105	(Aerolineas Argentinas)	LV-PXP LV-IEV [w/o 15Jly69 Bahia Blanca-Comandante, Argentina]
1559	29	1/107	Aerospace Trust Management	G-ASJT XW750 G-ASJT N748D(1) [wfu as GIA 25Jan07 Finningley, UK; canx 29May07; restored 11Dec08 & ferried 20Dec08

AVRO/ HAWKER SIDDELEY HS.748

C/n	Line No.	Model	Last known Owner/Operator	Identities/fates/comments (where appropriate)
				Southend, UK; canx again 26Mar09; l/n b/u by 03Nov09, left by lorry to unknown location]
1560	37	2A/108	(Dan-Air Services)	G-ASPL [w/o 26Jun81 Nailstone, near East Midlands Airport, UK; canx 19May83]
1561	34	2A/206	ITAB Cargo	XS789 D2-MAG 9L-LBF 9Q-CLL(2) [built as Andover CC Mk. 2]
1562	35	2A/206	(Defence Evaluation & Research Establishment)	XS790 [built as Andover CC Mk. 2; wfu 28Jly97; b/u Nov98 Boscombe Down, UK; cockpit section preserved by Boscombe Down Aviation Collection; l/n 20Jly08]
1563	46	2/206	(Royal Air Force)	XS791 [Andover CC Mk. 2; wfu Dec93 Northolt, UK; b/u fuselage to Bruntingthorpe, UK; by 27Mar05 to Hanningfield Metals Scrapyard, Stock, UK]
1564	49	2/206	(African Commuter Services)	XS792 G-BVZS 5Y-IAK 9XR-AB [built as Andover CC Mk. 2; w/o during Feb05 Old Fangak, Sudan]
1565	50	2A/206	(Gabon Express)	XS793 9178M EL-AIF 3C-KKP [built as Andover CC Mk. 2; wfu Libreville-Leon M'ba International, Gabon; l/n May03; airline ceased ops Jun04]
1566	54	2/206	(748 Air Services)	XS794 D2-MAF 9L-LBG [built as Andover CC Mk. 2; w/o 14Feb99 Foxtrot airstrip, Sudan]
1567	44	2A/207	(Airfast Indonesia)	HS-THA PK-OBW [w/o en-route 25Jan90 Mount Rinjani, Lombok Island, Indonesia]
1568	38	2/207	(Thai Airways)	HS-THB [w/o 27Apr80 15km NE of Bangkok-Don Muang Airport, Thailand]
1569	39	2/207	Royal Thai Air Force	HS-THC L5-3/26+ 60203^ 60303# [+ serial not carried externally; ^ code; # recoded]
1570	48	2/208	Royal Thai Air Force	"HS-RTAF"+ HS-TAF L5-1/08 11-111^ 60301# [+ marks applied in error; ^ code; # re-coded; serial not carried externally; damaged in floods Oct11 Don Muang, Thailand]
1571	20	2/212	(Air Ceylon)	4R-ACJ [w/o by sabotage 07Sep78 Colombo-Ratmalana Airport, Sri Lanka]
1572				[built as Andover C. Mk 1 set number 1]
1573				[built as Andover C. Mk 1 set number 2]
1574				[built as Andover C. Mk 1 set number 3]
1575				[built as Andover C. Mk 1 set number 4]
1576	14	2A/214LFD	Wasaya Airways	G-ATAM XA-SEI G-ATAM PI-C1020 G-ATAM 9G-ABV G-ATAM OY-DFS G-ATAM 9J-ABL G-ATAM ZS-HSA G-ATAM TR-LQY C-GMAA
1577	36	2A/215	(Bradley Air Services/First Air)	YV-C-AME YV-04C C-GDUI [wfu 25Sep87; b/u 30Mar91 Carp, ON, Canada; canx 24Jun01]
1578	40	2A/215	(Bradley Air Services/First Air)	YV-C-AMI YV-05C FAV6201+ YV-05C C-GDUL [+ Venezuela] [stored by 05May04 Carp, ON, Canada; canx 09Oct07 as wfu; by 06Sep10 fuselage in scrapyard Arnprior, ON, Canada; l/n late 2010]
1579	47	2A/215	(Air Creebec)	YV-C-AMO YV-06C TR-0203+ C-GFFU [+ Venezuela] [stored 28Jan92; canx 29Mar04; reported Jly95 stripped of parts and wings Timmins, ON, Canada]
1580	57	2/215	(Linea Aeropostal Venezolana)	YV-C-AMY [w/o 20Aug68 near Maturin-Quiriquire Airport, Venezuela]
1581	59	2A/215	(Bradley Air Services/First Air)	YV-C-AMF YV-07C VP-LAX YV-07C C-GDUN [wfu 12Dec01 Carp, ON, Canada; b/u Oct02; canx 23Dec02]
1582	61	2A/215	(Bradley Air Services)	YV-C-AMC YV-08C C-GDOV [w/o 12Jan89 James M Cox Dayton International, OH; canx 06Sep89]
1583	45	2/217	(Airfast Indonesia)	VP-LIK V2-LIK N43AZ [b/u for spares Mar87 Seletar, Singapore by Aviation Consultants; canx 17Jly89; hulk l/n Nov95]
1584	71	2/217	(British Aerospace)	VP-LIP V2-LIP RP-C1042 G-11-4 (G-BPNW) [canx 05Nov90; dismantled Aug/Sep91 Exeter, UK; Sep91 moved by road to Woodford, UK & used as a structural airframe]
1585	55	2A/222	(Airfast Indonesia)	G-ATEH HP-416 G-ATEH VP-LIW PK-OBV [w/o 07Sep93 Tanah Merah, Indonesia]
1586	56	2/222	(Philippine Airlines)	G-ATEI VP-LIN G-ATEI CF-TAX G-ATEI PI-C1029 RP-C1029 [w/o 10May75 near Manila, Philippines]
1587	60	2/222	Sri Lankan Air Force Museum	G-ATEJ CF-MAL TG-MAL C-GCZY 4R-ACR CR831 [wfu Mar94 Ratmalana AFB, Colombo, Sri Lanka; preserved there by Dec09]
1588	58	2/222	(STH Sales Ltd)	G-ATEK VP-LIV V2-LIV RP-C1041 G-ATEK CS-TAV 6V-AFX (G-ATEK) [b/u 11Jly91 Southend, UK; canx 17Jun92]

AVRO/ HAWKER SIDDELEY HS.748

C/n	Line No.	Model	Last known Owner/Operator	Identities/fates/comments (where appropriate)
1589	64	2A/226	(Northland Air Manitoba)	OE-LHS G-AXVG RP-C1031 G-AXVG C-FGGE [wfu & b/u Oct95 Winnipeg, MB, Canada; canx 17Feb97]
1590	66	2/226	(Philippine Airlines)	OE-LHT PI-C1028 RP-C1028 [w/o 03Feb75 near Manila International Airport, Philippines]
1591	68	2/223	(Linea Aeropostal Venezolana)	0111 (G-BIOV) YV-39C+ [+ regn not confirmed; these marks were used by a DC-6B; photo seen taken Mar87 at Caracas, Venezuela in Aeropostal c/s but no regn; also reported w/o there; these marks and latter history of this airframe remain a mystery]
1592	62	2A/225	(Emerald Airways)	G-ATMI VP-LIU G-ATMI VP-LIU G-ATMI VP-LIU G-ATMI VP-LIU G-ATMI [CofA expired 18May00; b/u Mar01 Blackpool, UK; canx 30Jly01]
1593	63	2A/225	(PTB (Emerald) Pty Ltd)	G-ATMJ 6Y-JFJ G-ATMJ VP-LAJ G-ATMJ [wfu & stored 04May06 Blackpool, UK; l/n 06Dec08; b/u & canx 15Jun09]
1594	70	2A/227	(Macavia International)	HP-432 C-GEPI G-BNJK [Macavia 748 Turbine Tanker conversion; wfu 1995 Chateauroux, France, later b/u; canx 29Feb96 by CAA]
1595	76	2A/229	(West Air Sweden)	A10-595+ SE-LIE [+ Australia] [wfu 22Sep06 Lidkoping, Sweden; b/u by Dec06; canx 06Dec06]
1596	77	2A/229	(Air Creebec)	A10-596+ SE-LIF C-FLJC [+ Australia] [ferried 29Jan08 to Timmins, ON, Canada & wfu; canx 15Jly08; b/u Nov11]
1597	75	2A/221	ex Air Creebec	(LV-PGG) T-01+ T-02+ T-03+ C-GQWO [+ Argentina] [ferried 10Jly08 to Timmins, ON, Canada & wfu: Nov11 donanted to Canadian Armed Forces for emergency training; canx 20Feb12]
1598	72	2A/230	(SAESA)	G-11 XA-SEV [w/o en-route 06Jan72 Chetumal, 25m N of Bacalar, Mexico]
1599	73	2A/230	(Quebecair)	G-11 XA-SEY (G-BFUA) C-GAPC [wfu & b/u Jun87 Montreal-Dorval, QC, Canada; canx 26Feb88]
1600	90	2/231	(Zambian Air Force)	AF601 [w/o 26Aug69 Lusaka, Zambia]
1601	108	2/228	RAAF Museum	G-AVZD A10-601 [preserved 20Jan04 Point Cook, VIC, Australia; l/n 17Aug07]
1602	121	2/228	Guinee Air Cargo	A10-602+ VH-POZ 3D-POZ 3X-GEE [+ Australia]
1603	124	2/228	ex Ross M Hornblower	A10-603+ VH-AMQ(2)^ N [+ Australia] [stored 20Feb05 Southend, UK; ^ marks canx 25Sep08 to USA; l/n 21Jly09 still wearing VH-AMQ; engines removed by 07Feb09; moved off airport 19Jly10 to Skylark Hotel for preservation]
1604	127	2/228	(Horizon Airlines)	A10-604+ VH-IMG [+ Australia] [did not enter service, b/u for spares 06Jly04 Bankstown, NSW, Australia; canx 12May05; nose preserved Australian Aviation Museum, Bankstown, NSW, Australia]
1605	130	2/228	(IAP Group (Australia)	A10-605+ VH-AMQ(1) [+ Australia] [ferried 18Sep04 to Bankstown, NSW, Australia & b/u for spares; canx 15Dec04]
1606	133	2/228	ex Ross M Hornblower	A10-606+ VH-AHL^ N [Australia] [stored 03Mar05 Southend, UK; ^ marks canx 25Sep08 to USA; l/n 21Jly09 still wearing VH-AHL; engines removed by 07Feb09; moved off airport 19Jly10 to Skylark Hotel for preservation]
1607	136	2/228	(Horizon Airlines)	A10-607+ [+ Australia] [taken by road Jan01 to Bankstown NSW, Australia; b/u by 16Nov01; fuselage remains l/n Jly02]
1608	139	2/228	ex Ross M Hornblower	A10-608+ VH-AYS^ N [+ Australia] [^ marks canx 30Aug08 to USA; stored 14Mar05 Southend, UK; l/n 11Oct08 still wearing VH-AYS; engines removed by 07Feb09; b/u commenced 09May09]
1609	74	2/232	(Philippine Airlines)	VP-BCJ PI-C1027 [w/o 28Nov72 Bislig, Philippines]
1610	81	2/232	(Mandala Airlines)	VP-BCK PK-RHQ PK-RHS [w/o 18Oct77 Manila International Airport, Philippines]
1611	82	2A/232	(Gabon Express)	VP-BCL "LF-INE" + CF-INE A2-ABA C-FINE F-OSPM 9L-LBH TN-AGA 3D-BAE TR-LFW [+ marks incorrectly painted; w/o 08Jun04 near Libreville, Gabon]
1612	83	2A/232	(Air Provence)	VP-BCM G-AZSU A2-ABB G-AZSU F-GPDC [stored by Jan03 Marseille-Marignane, France; b/u Feb04]
1613	100	2A/233LFD	(V Kelner Airways)	VQ-FAL DQ-FAL G-BEBA RP-C1032 G-BEBA C-FKTL(1) [dbf 14Aug91 Big Trout Airport, ON, Canada; ferried 16Aug91 to Bar River, ON; declared w/o & canx 19Nov91]
1614	87	2A/234	(Bouraq Indonesia Airlines)	CC-CEC PK-IHA [w/o 04Jan89 Banjarmasin-Sjamsudin Noor Airport, Indonesia]

AVRO/ HAWKER SIDDELEY HS.748

C/n	Line No.	Model	Last known Owner/Operator	Identities/fates/comments (where appropriate)
1615	92	2A/234	(Bouraq Indonesia Airlines)	CC-CED PK-IHB PK-IHS [wfu Feb91 Jakarta-Halim, Indonesia; b/u by May04]
1616	102	2A/234	(Bouraq Indonesia Airlines)	CC-CEE PK-IHC [wfu Feb91 Jakarta-Halim, Indonesia; b/u by May04]
1617	106	2A/234	(Northland Air Manitoba)	CC-CEF C-GQTH OY-MBH C-GQTH [w/o 10Nov93 Sandy Lake Airport, ON, Canada; canx 12Dec94]
1618	114	2A/234	(Air Creebec)	CC-CEG C-GQSV OY-MBY C-GQSV [w/o 03Dec88 Waskaganish, QC, Canada; canx 30Jan89]
1619	132	2A/234	(Air Creebec)	CC-CEH C-GQTG [wfu 29Oct01; canx 09May02 wfu; fuselage reported Sep06 Skywagon City, ON, Canada; site of b/u not known]
1620	125	2A/234	(Bouraq Indonesia Airlines)	CC-CEI HK-1698X CC-CEI PK-IHE [w/o 09Jan93 Surabaya-Juanda, Indonesia]
1621	149	2A/234	(Air Creebec)	CC-CEJ C-GOUT OY-APT C-GOUT [wfu 09Jan01; canx 29Mar94; by Jly94 stripped of parts and wings Timmins, ON, Canada]
1622	120	2A/234	(Bouraq Indonesia Airlines)	CC-CEK PK-IHF [wfu Feb91 Jakarta-Halim, Indonesia; b/u by May04]
1623	122	2A/238	(Emerald Airways)	G-AVXI [wfu 22Sep98 Southend, UK; canx 24Oct01; dismantled 05/08Nov01; fuselage to Hanningfield Metals, Stock, Essex & b/u Oct04]
1624	137	2A/238	(Emerald Airways)	G-AVXJ [stored 01Aug98 Exeter, UK; canx 17Jan03; b/u 14May04; fuselage sunk in quarry Mells, Somerset, UK as diving attraction]
1625	101	2A/235	(VARIG)	PP-VDN [w/o 17Jun75 Pedro Afonso Airport, Brazil]
1626	105	2A/235	(Bouraq Indonesia Airlines)	PP-VDO PK-IHI [w/o 10Dec82 Manado-Sam Ratulangi Airport, Indonesia]
1627	109	2A/235	(Bouraq Indonesia Airlines)	PP-VDP PK-IHG [CofA expired 30Sep98 – wfu; location not known]
1628	110	2/235	(VARIG)	PP-VDQ [w/o 14Dec69 Uberlandia, Brazil]
1629	111	2A/235	ex Bali Air	PP-VDR PK-IHH [stored 06Oct05 Jakarta-Soekarno-Hatta, Indonesia; l/n 25Dec08]
1630	112	2A/235	ex Bali Air	PP-VDS PK-IHJ "EX-DLT" [stored 2005 Surabaya-Juanda, Indonesia; l/n 13Dec09; by Jan11 painted with bogus reg'n]
1631	113	2A/235	(West Air Sweden)	PP-VDT LN-FOM SE-LEY [wfu 24Nov00 Lidkoping, Sweden; canx 03Sep01; b/u, hulk to local fire service]
1632	115	2A/235	(VARIG)	PP-VDU [w/o 09Feb72 Porto Alegre, Brazil]
1633	116	2A/235	(Bouraq Indonesia Airlines)	PP-VDV PK-IHK [w/o 09Feb77 Ujung Pandang (now Makassar), Indonesia]
1634	117	2A/235	(Bouraq Indonesia Airlines)	PP-VDX PK-IHM [wfu Feb91 Jakarta-Halim, Indonesia; b/u by May04]
1635	88	2A/239	(Eastern Provincial Airways)	G-AVRR CF-YQD G-AVRR ZS-IGI G-AVRR 9J-ABM G-AVRR ZS-HSI G-AVRR TR-LQJ C-GEPH [w/o 29Dec81 Sydney Airport, NS, Canada]
1636	89	2/209	(Philippine Airlines)	PI-C1014 RP-C1014 [w/o 11Jly82 Jolo Airport, Sulu, Philippines]
1637	91	2/209	(Philippine Airlines)	PI-C1015 RP-C1015 [w/o 26Jun87 Mount Ugo, near Baguio, Philippines]
1638	93	2A/209	(Airfast Indonesia)	PI-C1016 RP-C1016 PK-OBQ [wfu & stored Jun02 Jakarta-Halim, Indonesia by International Air Parts; l/n 06Jun07 in poor condition; b/u Apr08]
1639	103	2/209	(LBC Airways)	PI-C1017 RP-C1017 [wfu Jan97 Manila-Ninoy Aquino, Philippines; b/u by May07]
1640	104	2A/209	ex Bradley Air Services/First Air	PI-C1018 RP-C1018 C-GJVN [highest-timed 748 30Apr07 TT 62,521, landings 56,413; wfu & retired 30Apr07 Trois-Rivieres, QC, Canada; l/n 08Sep10; canx 28Aug12]
1641	107	2/209	(Philippines Bureau of Air Transportation)	PI-C1019 RP-C1019 RP-122 RP-211 (RP-2000) RP-2001 [b/u Mar03 Manila-Ninoy Aquino, Philippines by International Air Parts for spares]
1642	118	2/209	(Trans Service Airlift)	PI-C1021 RP-C1021 9Q-CST [no reports since 2000, believed b/u location unknown]
1643	119	2/209	(Philippine Airlines)	PI-C1022 [w/o en-route 21Apr70 N of Manila, Philippines; internal explosion]
1644	123	2/243LFD	Royal Thai Air Force	HS-THD L5-4/26 60204+ 60304^ [+ code; ^ re-coded; serial not carried externally]
1645	135	2/243	Royal Thai Air Force	HS-THE L5-6/26 60206+ 60306^ [+ code; ^ re-coded; serial not carried externally; damaged in floods Oct11 Don Muang, Thailand]

AVRO/ HAWKER SIDDELEY HS.748

C/n	Line No.	Model	Last known Owner/Operator	Identities/fates/comments (where appropriate)
1646	138	2/243	Royal Thai Air Force	HS-THF L5-5/26 60205+ 60305^ [+ code; ^ re-coded; serial not carried externally]
1647	131	2A/242	Bismillah Airlines	ZK-CWJ ZS-OCF (G-CLEW) G-ORCP S2-AEE
1648		2/240	(Argentine Air Force)	(TC-71) [not built]
1649		2/240	(Argentine Air Force)	(TC-72) [not built]
1650		2/240	(Argentine Air Force)	(TC-73) [not built]
1651		2/240	(Argentine Air Force)	(TC-74) [not built]
1652		2/240	(Argentine Air Force)	(TC-75) [not built]
1653		2/240	(Argentine Air Force)	(TC-76) [not built]
1654		2/240	(Argentine Air Force)	(TC-77) [not built]
1655		2/240	(Argentine Air Force)	(TC-78) [not built]
1656	146	2A/244	Wasaya Airways	D-AFSD N57910 C-GLTC
1657	129	2A/245	(AVIANCA)	HK-1408 [w/o 05Jly73 Bucaramanga-Gomez Nino Airport, Colombia]
1658	134	2A/245	(Best Air/Astral Aviation)	HK-1409 G-BFLL F-GODD S2-ABE [w/o early Nov06 Alek, Southern Sudan; b/u Feb07 on site by International Air Parts for spares]
1659	126	2/209	(Air ADS/LBC Air Cargo)	PI-C1023 RP-C1023 [CofA expired 09Oct97; wfu for spares Jun98 Manila-Ninoy Aquino , Philippines; l/n May99; b/u by May07]
1660	128	2/209	(LBC Air Cargo)	PI-C1024 RP-C1024 [derelict by May99 Manila-Ninoy Aquino, Philippines; b/u by May07]
1661	140	2A/233	Air North Charter	VQ-FBH DQ-FBH ZK-MCJ C-FYDY
1662	143	2A/210	ex Calm Air International	HP-484 G-BCDZ G-11-3 C-GSBF [wfu 26Sep06 Thompson, MB, Canada]
1663	141	2A/209LFD	Wasaya Airways	CF-TAZ PI-C1025 RP-C1025 G-BHCJ RP-C1030 G-BHCJ C-FFFS
1664	148	2/209	(Trans Service Airlift)	CF-TAG PI-C1026 RP-C1026 9Q-CSR [l/n 31Jly01; believed b/u location unknown; marks later used on DHC-5 Buffalo c/n 7]
1665	150	2A/233	(Bradley Air Services/First Air)	VQ-FBK DQ-FBK C-GYMX [wfu 21Mar03 Carp, ON, Canada, used for spares; Dec03 fuselage to Royal Canadian Mounted Police as anti-terrorist trainer; canx 20Apr04]
1666	158	2A/256	(Air BVI)	7Q-YKA VP-LVQ [b/u Aug89 Timmins, ON, Canada]
1667	159	2A/256	Clewer Aviation	7Q-YKB G-BPNK G-BURJ 9N-ACP G-BURJ [stored since 13May02 Johannesburg-OR Tambo, South Africa; l/n 26Sep08 with no reg'n]
1668	142	2A/257	(Calm Air International)	G-11 CF-MAK C-FMAK [wfu 17Nov02; b/u late Dec07 Thompson, MB, Canada; canx 21Dec07]
1669	144	2A/258LFD	Calm Air International	CF-AMO C-FAMO
1670	145	2/217	(STH Sales Ltd)	9Y-TDH VP-LAA V2-LAA RP-C1043 G-BORM [canx 18Jun92; wfu & used for spares 28Jun97 Exeter, UK; hulk to local fire service until b/u Dec05]
1671	161	2A/253	ex Royal Nepal Airlines	9N-AAU G-AXVZ 9N-AAU [wfu & stored 1991 Kathmandu, Nepal; derelict by 2000; l/n 06Feb09]
1672	162	2A/253	(Royal Nepal Airlines)	9N-AAV G-11 9N-AAV [wfu & stored 2000 Kathmandu, Nepal; canx by Nov03; b/u 16/17Nov09 for spares]
1673	151	2A/259	(SAESA)	XA-SAB [w/o 27Jly73 Acapulco-Alvarez International Airport, Mexico]
1674	152	2A/259	(Air Creebec)	XA-SAC C-GSXS [wfu 28Sep94; b/u for spares Timmins, ON, Canada; canx 18Jun99 as wfu]
1675	153	2A/259	(Austin Airways)	XA-SAF C-GPAA [DBF & w/o 15Jly79 on ground Moosonee Airport, ON, Canada; canx]
1676	163	2A/263	(Air Senegal)	9J-ABJ (G-BHRG) 6V-AET [wfu Jun96 Dakar, Senegal; derelict by Dec97; dismantled in 1998]
1677	166	2A/263	ex KelAir	9J-ABK G-BPNK F-GHKL [wfu Jun95 St Rambert d'Albon Airport, France; canx 27Feb97; by 28Aug97 hulk in Auto-Pieces Scrapyard, Le Creux de la Thine, France; l/n Sep09]
1678	147	2A/264	(Aerocontracts)	G-11-2 G-AYDH F-BSRA G-AYDH [wfu 1992 Dinard, France; b/u Aug92 for spares; canx 25Nov92]
1679	164	2A/269	Air North Charter	G-11 G-11-1 G-AYFL CF-CSE C-FCSE
1680	165	2A/263	(PTB (Emerald) Pty Ltd)	G-11-4 9J-ABW G-BPNJ F-GHKA ZS-ODJ G-BPNJ [by 19Mar04 stored Blackpool, UK; to fire dump Jun06 still marked ZS-ODJ; l/n 06Dec08; b/u by Jun09; canx 15Jun09]
1681	154	2A/264	(Wasaya Airways)	G-11-3 G-AYIR CS-TAF F-BSRU A2-ABC ZS-LHN 7P-LAI ZS-LHN G-AYIR C-FTTW [DBF 12Jun12 Sandy Lake, ON, Canada]

AVRO/ HAWKER SIDDELEY HS.748

C/n	Line No.	Model	Last known Owner/Operator	Identities/fates/comments (where appropriate)
1682	168	2A/246	Museo Aeronautico de la Fuerza Aerea Ecuatoriana	FAE-682//HC-AUD [dual marks for operation by TAME; preserved by 1997]
1683	169	2A/246	(Fuerza Aerea Ecuatoriana)	FAE-683//HC-AUF [dual marks for operation by TAME; w/o 20Jan76 en route Loja-Guayaquil, in Andes, Ecuador]
1684	155	2A/267	Fuerza Aerea Ecuatoriana	FAE-684//HC-AUK FAE-001//HC-AUK FAE684//HC-AUK+ [all dual marks for operation by TAME; + noted 01Apr09 with 001 on nose]
1685	157	2A/254	(Ghana Airways)	9G-ABW [w/o 22Jan71 Accra-Kotoka Airport, Ghana]
1686	156	2A/254	ex Calm Air International	9G-ABX C-GEPB [wfu & stored 30Jun09 Thompson, MB, Canada; by Oct09 outer wings & tailplane cut off]
1687	167	2A/270	ex Janes Aviation Ltd	G-11-5 G-AYIM CS-TAG G-11-687 G-AYIM N687AP
1688	160	2A/265	Zambian Air Force	AF602
1689	186	2A/242	Aerospace Trust Management	ZK-DES G-SOEI N748D(2) [wfu & stored 04May06 Blackpool, UK; l/n 22Jun09; canx 29Jun09 to USA for ferry flight 17Aug09 to Southend, UK; l/n 27Apr11]
1690	172	2A/272	(Bradley Air Services/First Air)	ZS-SBU C-GGNZ [stored 21Jun05 Carp, ON, Canada; canx 09Oct07 as wfu; l/n Jun08; by Nov10 possibly to paintball park Gatineau, QC, Canada]
1691	173	2A/272	ex Sri Lankan Air Force	A2-ZFT ZS-SBW C-GGOB CR830+ SCM-3101 [+ Sri Lanka] [wfu & stored 15Mar94 Ratmalana AFB, Colombo, Sri Lanka; l/n 11Feb11]
1692	174	2A/272	(Air Creebec)	ZS-SBV C-GGOO ZS-SBV C-GGOO [w/o 27Nov91 Riviere-au-Saumon, QC, Canada; canx 10Sep92]
1693	170	2/243	(Thai Airways)	HS-THG [w/o 21Jun80 Chiang Rai Airport, Thailand]
1694	171	2A/273	Air North Charter	AMB-110+ AMDB-110+ VR-UEH VS-UEH V8-UEH ZK-MCP C-FYDU [+ Brunei]
1695	176	2A/274	(Merpati Nusantara Airlines)	PK-MHD G-11-10 G-AZAE PK-MHM [wfu & stored Nov92 Surabaya-Juanda, Indonesia; l/n Dec94; b/u 1999]
1696	180	2A/274	(Merpati Nusantara Airlines)	PK-MHR [wfu & stored Nov92 Surabaya-Juanda, Indonesia; l/n Dec94; b/u 1999]
1697	179	2A/275	Janes Aviation Ltd	G-11-9 G-AYYG ZK-MCF G-AYYG ZK-MCF G-AYYG ZK-MCF G-AYYG ZK-MCF C-GRCU ZK-MCF G-AYYG G-OSOE
1698	190	2A/271LFD	Royal Nepal Army Air Wing	G-AZJH 9N-RAC RAN-20+ NA-020 [+ Nepal]
1699	175	2A/276	Air North Charter	G-11-6 CF-AGI C-FAGI
1700	177	2A/216	(Bouraq Indonesia Airlines)	G-11-7 G-AYVR PK-IHD G11-5 G-AYVR PK-IHD [w/o 23Jan76 Palu-Mutiara Airport, Sulawesi, Indonesia]
1701	178	2A/266LFD	Avro Express	G-11-8 G-AYYH 5W-FAN G-BIUV 3X-GEW 5Y-BXI
1702	181	2A/260	(SATENA)	G-11-1 FAC1101+ [+ Colombia] [w/o 22Aug79 Bogota-El Dorado, Colombia]
1703	182	2A/260	(West Air Sweden)	G-11-2 FAC1102+ (SE-LIC) [+ Colombia] [wfu Sep97 for spares Lidkoping, Sweden; l/n 21Jan99; b/u Oct00]
1704	183	2A/260	(SATENA)	G-11-3 FAC1103+ [+ Colombia] [w/o 09Jan74 near Florencia-Capitolio Airport, Colombia]
1705	184	2A/260	(SATENA)	G-11-4 FAC1104+ [+ Colombia] [w/o 07Aug83 Pasto-Cano Airport, Colombia]
1706	185	2A/263	(Zambia Airways)	G-11-5 A2-ZGF 9J-ADM [badly damaged 04Jly83 Kasaba Bay Airport, Zambia; b/u for spares]
1707	187	2/243	ex Thai Airways/Bangkok A/W	G-11-6 HS-THH [w/o 07Dec87 Udon-Thani Airport, Thailand; later displayed Mekong Hotel, Nong Khai; taken by road to Jomtien, Thailand and painted as "ZS-AGB" Lion Air c/s, then in fake USAF c/s as "208"; by 31Dec09 no sign of fake serial; l/n May11 gone by Aug11 fate unknown]
1708	189	2/243	ex Thai Airways	HS-THI [w/o 28Apr87 Chiang Rai, Thailand; later displayed Siam Country Club, Pattaya, Thailand; l/n 11Dec09 – marked on one side only as "HS-TH"]
1709	201	2/268	Australian Aviation Museum	N15-709+ 3C-QQP [+ Australia coded 800; Jly01 to Horizon Airlines for spares use; 19May04 loaned Australian Aviation Museum & preserved Bankstown, NSW, Australia]
1710	202	2/268	(Royal Australian Navy)	N15-710 [code 801] [wfu 23Jun00 RAAF East Sale, VIC, Australia; b/u May01]
1711	209	2A/244	Air Inuit	D-AFSE TF-GMB C-GEGJ
1712	188	2A/242	(PTB (Emerald) Pty Ltd)	G11-7 ZK-MCA A3-MCA G-OTBA [wfu 03Feb06 & stored Blackpool, UK; l/n 06Dec08; b/u by Jun09; canx 15Jun09 as wfu; by Nov09 nose held by West Yorkshire Fire Service, Birkenshaw near Bradford, UK]
1713	191	2A/248	Republic of Korea Air Force	G11-8 G-BBGY 1713

AVRO/ HAWKER SIDDELEY HS.748

C/n	Line No.	Model	Last known Owner/Operator	Identities/fates/comments (where appropriate)
1714	193	2A/266	ex PTB (Emerald) Pty Ltd	G11-10 5W-FAO G-BMFT VR-BFT VP-BFT G-BMFT G-OPFW [wfu & stored 05May06 Blackpool, UK; l/n 06Dec08; b/u started Apr09; canx 15Jun09 as wfu; b/u by Jun09, nose section to RAF Milton collection for preservation]
1715	198	2/208	ex Royal Thai Air Force	HS-RTAF+ HS-TAF L5-2/16^ 99-999# 60302~ [+ painted in error; ^ serial not carried externally; # code; ~ re-coded; DBR 22Nov04 Bangkok-Don Muang, Thailand; wfu & SOC 10Apr06; May07 preserved Crown Prince Taweewattana Palace, Bangkok, Thailand]
1716	199	2A/FAA	(Air Illinois)	G11-3 G-BAFY (N666) N748LL [w/o en-route 11Oct83 near Pinckneyville, IL]
1717	192	2A/264	ex West Air Sweden	G11-9 G-BASZ F-BUTR ZS-JAY F-GFYM SE-LIA (F-GMHT) [wfu 20Apr04 Linkoping, Sweden; Sep05 by road to Skavsta, Sweden as non-destructive rescue trainer; canx 08May06]
1718	194	2A/248	Republic of Korea Air Force	G11-1 G-BABJ 1718
1719	195	2A/278	(Transportes Aereos de Cabo Verde)	G11-2 G-BBLN CR-CAV D4-CAV [wfu 05Nov94; b/u 23Jan98 for spares Praia, Cabo Verde for Emerald Airways]
1720	196	2A/278	(International Aviation Parts)	G11-4 CR-CAX+ CR-CAW G-BBPT CR-CAW D4-CAW N339C VH-IMJ (1) [+ painted in error; wfu 21Sep97 Bankstown, NSW, Australia; b/u 04Jly99; canx 05Jun00; fuselage hulk to fire training at RAAF Amberley, QLD, Australia; l/n 04Oct08 still marked as N339C]
1721	197	2A/270	(PTB (Emerald) Pty Ltd)	G11-6 CS-TAH G-BVOU [stored 04May06 Blackpool, UK; l/n 06Dec08; b/u started Apr09]
1722	200	2A/216	ex Bradley Air Services/First Air	G11-6 PK-IHR G-BBTA PK-IHR CG-TLD+ C-GTLD [+ painted in error; wfu & stored 09Oct07 Trois-Rivieres, QB, Canada; canx 23Dec08; l/n 08Sep10]
1723	215	2A/244LFD	Air Creebec	D-AFSF SE-LEG C-FLIY
1724	218	2A/244	ex Air Inuit	D-AFSG C-FGET [wfs 22Jly10 location unknown]
1725	219	2A/244	Air Creebec	D-AFSH SE-LEK C-FPJR
1726	216	2A/244	(West Air Sweden)	D-AFSI SE-LEO [w/o 13Dec01 Lidkoping, Sweden; b/u spares, l/n 25Apr02; canx 12Sep02]
1727	217	2A/244	(West Air Sweden)	D-AFSJ SE-LEX [wfu 23Dec05 Lidkoping, Sweden; l/n 17Jun05; canx 12Apr06; b/u early Oct06]
1728	203	2A/282	(Tanzanian Government)	5H-MPG 5H-STZ (5H-RJN) [wfu & stored May94 Dar es Salaam, Tanzania; CofA expired 10Aug98; derelict by Oct99; l/n 27Sep08; canx]
1729	205	2A/281LFD	Fuerza Aerea Ecuatoriana	C-91-2506+ FAE-743 [+ Brazil]
1730	206	2A/281LFD	(Brazilian Air Force)	C-91-2507 [wfu 31Dec05; donated to Fuerza Aerea Ecuatoriana for spares use; b/u May06 Campo dos Afonsos, Brazil]
1731	207	2A/281LFD	Fuerza Aerea Ecuatoriana	C-91-2508+ FAE-741 [+ Brazil]
1732	208	2A/281LFD	(Brazilian Air Force)	C-91-2509 [w/o 09Feb98 Navegantes Airport, Brazil]
1733	211	2A/281LFD	Fuerza Aerea Ecuatoriana	C-91-2510+ VU-91-2510+ FAE-742 [+ Brazil; no proof ever carried VU-91-2510]
1734	212	2A/281LFD	Fuerza Aerea Ecuatoriana	C-91-2511+ FAE-740 [+ Brazil]
1735	204	2A/216	(Bouraq Indonesia Airlines)	G-11-7 G-BCDM PK-KHL [w/o 09Aug95 Mount Komawa, near Kaimana Airport, Indonesia]
1736	210	2B/287LFD	Fulloutput 191 (Pvt)	G-BCOE 9N-ACN G-BCOE VH-IMI (SE-LIA) ZS-DBM 9G-MKV 5Y-HVS ZS-DBM
1737	213	2B/287LFD	(Timbis Air Services)	G-BCOF VH-IMK (SE-LIB) ZS-OEO ZS-DBL 5Y-BZR [w/o 02Apr12 Doro, Southern Sudan]
1738	214	2A/285LFD	Museo Aeronautico de la Fuerza Aerea Ecuatoriana	FAE-738//HC-BAZ [dual marks] [preserved by early 1992 Quito-Mariscal Sucre Airport, Ecuador]
1739	220	2A/285LFD	Fuerza Aerea Ecuatoriana/TAME	FAE-739//HC-BEY [dual marks]
1740	221	2A/286LFD	(Trackmark Cargo)	5H-WDL ZS-XGZ 5Y-TCA [w/o 17Mar06 Old Fangak, Sudan]
1741	222	2A/288LFD	Force Aerienne Populaire de Benin	CS-01+ TY-21A [+ Belgium]
1742	223	2A/288LFD	Force Aerienne Populaire de Benin	CS-02+ TY-22A [+ Belgium] [stored by Oct08 Cotonou, Benin; l/n Aug09]
1743	224	2A/288LFD	(Belgian Air Force)	CS-03 G-BEEM CS-03 [dismantled Weelde, Belgium; 02Oct03 transported to Antwerp docks for shipment to Benin for spares use by Force Aerienne Populaire de Benin; hulk at Cotonou, Benin; l/n Oct08]
1744	225	2A/283	(Linea Aeropostal Venezolana)	(YV-09C) YV-45C [w/o 03Mar78 Caracas-Maiquetia Airport, Venezuela]
1745	226	2A/283	Calm Air International	(YV-10C) YV-46C C-GDOP F-ODQQ C-GDOP [wfu & used as ground engine testbed 13Dec08 Thompson, MB, Canada]

AVRO/ HAWKER SIDDELEY HS.748

C/n	Line No.	Model	Last known Owner/Operator	Identities/fates/comments (where appropriate)
1746	228	2A/301LFD	ex Sri Lanka Air Force	G-BDVH C6-BEA G-BDVH C6-BEA G-BDVH 5R-MJS G-BDVH CR833 [wfu 23Aug02; stored Ratmalana AFB, Colombo, Sri Lanka; l/n 11Feb11]
1747	230	2A/309LFD	(Guyana Airways)	8R-GEU [stored 1987 Georgetown, Guyana; sold to Calm Air in Canada for spares 1999; assumed b/u in situ]
1748	232	2A/309LFD	(Guyana Airways)	8R-GEV [stored 1987 Georgetown, Guyana; sold to Calm Air in Canada for spares 1999; assumed b/u in situ; rear fuselage to South Alberta Institute of Technology, Calgary, AB, Canada; l/n 19Nov09]
1749	231	2A/310LFD	Air Inuit	TJ-XAF TJ-AAN TJ-CCD C-FDOX
1750	235	2A/310LFD	(Wasaya Airways)	TJ-XAH TJ-AAO TJ-CCE G-11-2 5N-ARJ CS-TAU G-JHLN C-GTAD [w/o 06Aug98 Kasabonika Airport, ON, Canada; canx 11May00]
1751	236	2A/314LFD	(Tanzania People's DF)	G-BETZ JW9008 [w/o 1987 Lake Manyara Airport, Tanzania; b/u for spares by International Air Parts; by 01Jun02 remains at Bankstown, NSW, Australia]
1752	237	2A/314LFD	(Tanzania People's DF)	G-BETY JW9009 [w/o 01Jly85 Mbeya, Tanzania]
1753	239	2A/314LFD	ex Tanzania People's DF	G-BETX JW9010 [w/o 07Feb91 Dar es Salaam Airport, Tanzania; remains stored, l/n 26Sep08]
1754	229	2A/320LFD	Burkina Faso Air Force	XT-MAL
1755	240	2A/329LFD	(Air Liberia)	EL-AIH [w/o 16Apr83 near Khartoum Airport, Sudan]
1756	227	2A/334	(PTB (Emerald) Pty Ltd)	G-11-8 9Y-TFS G-GLAS G-BPDA G-ORAL [stored 04May06 Blackpool, UK; l/n 06Dec08; b/u by Jun09; canx 15Jun09 as wfu; nose section preserved for display at events, stored Wirral, UK]
1757	233	2A/334	(Sri Lankan Air Force/Helitours)	9Y-TFT VP-LCG V2-LCG 9Y-TFT G-EDIN G-BPFU G-OMDS CR835 + 4R-HVB ^ [+ Sri Lanka] [^ probably carried its military serial as well at this time; w/o 28Apr95 Palay AFB, Sri Lanka]
1758	234	2A/335LFD	Air North Charter & Training	9Y-TFX C-GFNW C-GANA
1759	238	2A/335LFD	(Bradley Air Services/First Air)	9Y-TGD C-FBNW [w/o 03Dec98 Iqaluit, NU, Canada; canx 21Apr99]
1760	241	2A/333	(West Air Sweden)	G11-9 G-BFVR J5-GAT SE-LID [wfu 29Sep04; b/u May06 Lidkoping, Sweden; canx 08May06; forward fuselage preserved near Malmo Airport, Sweden; l/n 14Apr04]
1761	244	2A/344	(Air Manitoba)	G-11-10 C6-BEA+ C6-BEB C-FQPE [+ painted in error; wfu Oct95 Winnipeg, MB, Canada; b/u Apr05; canx 04Apr05]
1762	245	2A/343LFD	ex Air Inuit	VP-LAZ V2-LAZ C-GCUK [wfs 07Sep10 location unknown]
1763	242	2A/348LFD	(Bahamasair)	C6-BEC+ C6-BED [+ allocated in error; stored 1993 or 1994 Nassau, Bahamas; w/o 12Oct98 by Hurricane Mitch, when tail broke off; no reports after Dec98; assumed b/u]
1764	248	2A/344	(Intensive Air)	(C6-BED) C6-BEE F-ODTX 5Y-SAL HR-AQV TN-AFI ZS-XGY [wfu & stored 08Apr02 Johannesburg-OR Tambo, South Africa]
1765	254	2A/344	(Bahamasair)	(C6-BEE) C6-BEF [wfu by 1993 Nassau, Bahamas; l/n Oct98; assumed b/u]
1766	250	2A/347	Bismillah Airlines	9Y-TGH G-BGMN 9Y-TGH G-BGMN PK-OCH G-BGMN S2-ADW [stored by 15Nov11 Dhaka, Bangledash]
1767	256	2A/347	Easy Fly Express	G-BGMO 9Y-TGI V2-LDB 9Y-TGI G-BGMO ZK-MCB G-BGMO "S2-AXX"+ S2-AAX [+ marks painted in error]
1768	243	2B/357LFD	(Sri Lanka Air Force/Helitours)	G-BGJV MI-GJV G-BGJV CR834+ 4R-HVA [+ Sri Lanka] [w/o 29Apr95, shot down by SAM missile near Palay AFB, Sri Lanka]
1769	246	2A/353	(Air Senegal)	G11-11 6V-AEO [w/o 01Feb97 Tambacounda, Senegal]
1770	252	2A/351	Best Air	G-BGPR ZS-XGE S2-AAT
1771	247	2A/352LFD	(Royal Nepal Airlines)	9N-ABR [w/o 25Apr96 Meghuli, Nepal; b/u 1998 by International Air Parts for spares]
1772	249	2B/360LFD	Safe Air Kenya Ltd	5R-MJA VH-IPA 5Y-TCO
1773	251	2B/360LFD	International Air Parts	5R-MJB VH-IPB S2-ADL VH-DQY [repossessed from Zoom Airways by 17Oct08; ferried 23Oct08 to Nairobi-Wilson, Kenya for maintenance prior to sale; l/n Jun11]
1774	253	2B/401LFD	(Bouraq Indonesia Airlines)	G-11-12 G-BKLD PK-IHO [damaged in heavy landing Yogyakarta, Indonesia & grounded; l/n 26Nov06]
1775	255	2A/369LFD	ex Burkina Faso Air Force	G-11-13 XT-MAN [stored by 25Jan09 Ouagadougou, Burkina Faso]
1776	257	2B/371LFD	748 Air Services	G-11-14 FAC-1108+ SE-LIB (5Y-YKN) 5Y-HAJ [+ Colombia]
1777	258	2A/372	ex PTB (Emerald) Pty Ltd	G-11-4 CS-TAO G-BVOV [stored 04May06 Blackpool, UK; dismantled & 26May09 to Jackdaw Quarry, Carnforth, UK for use as diving feature at Capernwray Diving School; sunk 29Mar10; canx 04Dec09]

AVRO/ HAWKER SIDDELEY HS.748

C/n	Line No.	Model	Last known Owner/Operator	Identities/fates/comments (where appropriate)
1778	259	2B/399LFD	748 Air Services	G-11-20 5U-BAS C-FKTL(2) SE-LIC (5Y-YKO) 5Y-BVQ
1779	260	2B/398	(748 Air Services)	G-11-19 5U-BAR C-GDTD 5Y-YKM [w/o 20Dec09 (some reports state 19Dec09) Tonj, Southern Sudan]
1780	261	2B/362	(Madagascar Government)	G-11-16 5R-MTI 5R-MUT [stored Dec95 Rand/Germiston, South Africa; derelict by Oct97; l/n Oct02; not noted Jan07]
1781	262	2B/FAA	(Bradley Air Services/First Air)	G-11-15 G-BIRF N117CA C-GBFA [stored 05Nov02 Carp, ON, Canada; canx 18Nov04; by 06Sep10 fuselage in scrapyard Arnprior, ON, Canada; late 2010]
1782	263	2B/FAA	AirQuarius Aviation	G-BICK N748AV G-11-3 CS-TAP G-11-782 G-BICK C-GHSF ZS-OJU [w/o 01Jun02 in Outeniqua Mountains, near George Airport, South Africa]
1783	264	2B/FAA	ex Executive Aerospace	N749LL N748BA C-GRXE G-11-10 C-GRXE V2-LDA G-11-1 G-BMJU ZS-LSO [stored by 11Jly07 Johannesburg-OR Tambo, South Africa]
1784	265	2B/378	ex Executive Aerospace	D-AHSA G-BOHY 9N-ADE (ZS-KLC) ZS-TPW [stored by Jly07 Johannesburg-OR Tambo, South Africa; l/n 03Mar11 report 2012 for Avro Express of Kenya]
1785	266	2B/378	ex Executive Aerospace	G-11-17 D-AHSB G-BOHZ (VT-WAY) ZS-NNW [stored 27 Nov 97 Durban, South Africa; l/n Dec06]
1786	269	2B/378	ex Executive Aerospace	G-11-18 D-AHSC G-HDBC (VT-GOA) ZS-NWW [stored by 22 Aug 07 Johannesburg-OR Tambo, South Africa; l/n 03Mar11 wfu]
1787	267	2B/402	(Bouraq Indonesia Airlines)	G-11-22 G-BKLE PK-IHP [wfu Oct91 Jakarta-Halim, Indonesia; b/u by May04]
1788	268	2B/402	(Bouraq Indonesia Airlines)	G-BKLF PK-IHW [wfu Mar89 Jakarta-Halim, Indonesia; b/u by May04]
1789	270	2B/FAA	(Bradley Air Services)	G-BJGI N118CA C-GFFA [w/o 15Sep88 Cheney near Ottawa-Macdonald-Cartier International Airport, ON, Canada; canx 30Nov88]
1790	271	2B/FAALFD	Calm Air International	G-BJTL N749AV G-11-6 G-BJTL G-11-6 CS-TAQ G-11-790 G-BJTL C-GHSC
1791	272	2B/378	(Emerald Airways)	(N119CA) G-BKAL D-AHSD V2-LDK G-BKAL (9N-ADF) G-BKAL ZK-MCH G-OJEM [w/o 30Mar98 Stansted, UK; b/u late Jun98 for spares; canx 27Jly98]
1792	273	2B/378	ex West Wind Aviation	G-BJTM (N750AV) D-AHSE G-SSFS C-FQVE [wfu 28Jan04 Saskatoon-Diefenbaker, SK, Canada; canx 28Apr06; 16May06 after spares recovery hulk to Cory Russell and preserved in garden 40km from airport; l/n 18Aug06]
1793	274	2B/402	ex Bali Air	G-11-23 G-BKLG PK-IHT [stored 06Oct05 Jakarta-Soekarno-Hatta, Indonesia; l/n 25Dec08]
1794	275	2B/402	(Bouraq Indonesia Airlines)	G-11-24 G-BKLH PK-IHN [w/o 11Jly96 Ambon-Pattimura, Indonesia]
1795	276	2B/402	ex Bali Air	G-BKLI PK-IHV [stored by 08Oct05 Surabaya-Juanda, Indonesia; l/n 13Dec09]
1796	277	2B/400	(AirQuarius Aviation)	MI-8203 G-BKIG MI-8203 V7-8203 (ZS-OJU) ZS-OLE [w/o 16Apr02 Pilanesberg, South Africa; 21Jun02 fuselage via Lanseria to Johannesburg-Jan Smuts; then to Chartwell, Johannesburg as GIA with Cranwell Aviation; l/n Jan12]
1797	278	2B/378	ex Executive Aerospace	G-11-2 D-AHSF G-11-1 CS-TAR G-11-747 G-HDBD G-EMRD ZS-PLO [stored early 2007 Johannesburg-OR Tambo, South Africa; l/n 11Jly07]
1798	279	2B/426	(Nepal Airlines)	G-HDBA A6-GRM G-HDBA 9N-ACW [wfu 23Nov96 Pokhara, Nepal; w/o 06Nov97 struck on ground by HS748 9N-ACM c/n 1549; b/u locally 1999 for parts by International Air Parts]
1799	280	2B/426	Ivoirienne de Transportes/ East Horizon Airways	G-HDBB A6-ABM G-HDBB 9N-ACX VH-IMJ (2) 4R-SER TU-PAD [operates in Afghanistan]
1800	281	2B/424	ex Bengal Air	G-BLGJ V2-LCQ C-GBCN VT-DOA VT-BAA [stored by Nov98 Kolkata (Calcutta)-Chandra Bose International, India; l/n 10May08]
1801	282	2B/424	Aerocaribe Honduras	G-11-4 V2-LCR C-GBCS VT-BAB HR-ATC C-GBCS HR-ATC
1802	283	2B/424	ex LIAT	G-11-5 G-BLYL V2-LCS (VT-BAC) [wfu May96 St John's, Antigua; l/n Aug99; by Dec04 ferried Saulte Ste Marie, ON, Canada; sold to Wasaya Airways for spares in situ]
1803	284	2B/424	ex Wasaya Airways	G-11-9 V2-LCT (VT-BAD) C-GBCY [ferried 02Sep05 Thunder Bay, ON, Canada, for spares recovery; still intact Feb07]

AVRO/ HAWKER SIDDELEY HS.748

C/n	Line No.	Model	Last known Owner/Operator	Identities/fates/comments (where appropriate)
1804	285	2B/435	(Cameroon Airlines)	G-11-10 TJ-CCF [w/o 28Jun89 Yaounde, Cameroon]
1805	286	2B/435	ex Cameroon Airlines	G-11-11 TJ-CCG [stored Sep97 Douala, Cameroon; derelict by Oct07]
1806	287	2B/501	(Necon Air)	G-11-1 G-BPEP B-1771 9N-AEG [w/o en-route 05Sep99 near Ramkot, 25km W of Kathmandu, Nepal]
1807	288	2B/501	ex Executive Aerospace	G-11-2 G-BPIW B-1773 9N-AEH ZS-AGB 4R-AGB 4R-LPV ZS-AGB [stored 22Jly05 Johannesburg-OR Tambo, South Africa; l/n 19Apr09 wfu with missing parts]
1808	289		not completed	[27Apr89 incomplete airframe to Hatfield, UK; forward fuselage to Chester, UK 1993; reported remains b/u Hatfield Jly95]
1809	290		not completed	[Sep94 incomplete fuselage b/u Woodford, UK; remains to Maxi Haulage, Irving, Scotland, UK]
Unidentified				
unkn				3D-BAG [reported 09May00 Rand-Germiston, South Africa]

Production complete

HAWKER SIDDELEY HS.780 ANDOVER

1		C.Mk.1	(Royal Air Force)	XS594 [also c/n 1572; f/f 09Jly65; stored 1970; SOC 24Jan80; b/u Aug88; hulk to Otterburn Ranges, UK; b/u 1994]
2		C.Mk.1	(Royal Air Force)	XS595 [also c/n 1573; stored 1970; SOC 28Jan80; used for fire practice RAF Brize Norton, UK; b/u 1992]
3		C.Mk.1(PR)	QinetiQ	XS596 [also c/n 1574; stored since Feb08 Boscombe Down, UK; wfu 19Dec11 for scrapping]
4		C.Mk.1	ex Malu Aviation/Air Aid	XS597 G-BVNJ 3D-ATS 9Q-CMJ [also c/n 1575] [stored Kinshasa-N'Djili, Zaire; l/n Aug96; current status unknown]
5		C.Mk.1	ex Royal Air Force	XS598 [w/o 05Jly67 Abingdon, UK; SOC 01Aug67; reported used as GIA at Brize Norton, UK; Feb94 to The Fire College, Moreton-in-Marsh for non-destructive testing; l/n Feb07]
6		C.Mk.1	(748 Air Services)	XS599 NZ7620+ 9Q-CYG EL-VDD 3C-JJX 5Y-SFE [+ New Zealand] [w/o 10Jun05 Lokichoggio, Kenya; suffered undercarriage collapse on runway then hit by landing Hercules S9-BAS c/n 472; reported b/u Mar07]
7		C.Mk.1	Air Force Museum	XS600 NZ7621 [preserved 28Jun96 Wigram, Christchurch, New Zealand; l/n 11Dec08]
8		C.Mk.1	(Royal Air Force)	XS601 [stored 28May75; 22Mar82 Otterburn Ranges, UK; SOC 29Mar83; b/u 1994]
9		C.Mk.1	(748 Air Services)	XS602 NZ7622+ 3C-KKB [+ New Zealand] [w/o 15Aug03 Rumbek, Sudan]
10		E.Mk.3	Air Transport Office	XS603 P4-PVS 9Q-CVS EL-WCP [status unknown]
11		C.Mk.1	ex Eureka Aviation	XS604 NZ7623+ 9Q-CDY [+ New Zealand] [stored/wfu Jan98 Antwerp-Duerne, Belgium; moved by 31May98 to Antwerp, Belgium; l5Sep06 fuselage only to National Fire Academy, Ranst, Belgium as non-destructive trainer; l/n 27Jun07]
12		E.Mk.3	(RAF/Hunting Avn Services)	XS605 [SOC 12Oct94 Northolt, UK; sold to Hunting Air Services & b/u Oct97]
13		C.Mk.1	QinetiQ/ETPS	XS606
14		C.Mk.1	Waltair	XS607 G-BEBY XS607 9Q-CPW [stored by Sep03 Kinshasa-N'Djili, Democratic Republic of Congo; report 17Jly07 on overhaul; status unknown]
15		C.Mk.1	(Royal New Zealand Air Force)	XS608 NZ7624 [wfu 1992; b/u for spares 1993 Whenuapai, New Zealand; fuselage to fire trainer l/n 14Oct11]
16		C.Mk.1	(Royal Air Force)	XS609 [w/o 08Apr72 Ampugnano AFB near Siena, Italy; SOC 01Jly72]
17		E.Mk.3	(Aero Services Corp)	XS610 P4-BLL 9Q-CVK [w/o Jun05 Kapoeta, Sudan]
18		C.Mk.1	(748 Air Services)	XS611 NZ7625+ 3C-KKC [+ New Zealand] [w/o 14Jly01 Lokichoggio, Kenya; b/u Mar07]
19		C.Mk.1	(Malu Aviation)	XS612 NZ7626+ 9Q-CJR EL-AFY 3C-CPX 3D-MKX [+ New Zealand] [wfu by Mar03 Kinshasa-N'Djili. Democratic Republic of Congo; no reports perhaps b/u]

AVRO/ HAWKER SIDDELEY HS.748

C/n	Line No.	Model	Last known Owner/Operator	Identities/fates/comments (where appropriate)
20		C.Mk.1	ex 748 Aero Services	XS613 NZ7627 + 3C-KKS 9Q-COE(2) 3C-KKS 9Q-COE(2) 5Y-BSX [+ New Zealand] [wfu 01Jun07 Lokichoggio, Kenya]
21		C.Mk.1	(ITAB Cargo)	XS637 G-BVNK 9Q-CJJ 9Q-CLL(1) [l/n 02Jun97 Rand-Germiston, South Africa; reportedly wfu by Jun98, location unknown]
22		C.Mk.1	ITAB Cargo	XS638 NZ7628 + 9Q-CYB [+ New Zealand] [l/n 18Jun05 Manono, Democratic Republic of Congo]
23		E.Mk.3A	RAF Museum, Cosford	XS639 9241M [preserved 13Jly94 RAF Cosford, UK as XS639; l/n Nov09]
24		E.Mk.3	(Air Traffic Office)	XS640 P4-TBL 9Q-CVC(1) [w/o Apr99 unknown location Katanga Region, Democratic Republic of Congo; b/u on site]
25		C.Mk.1(PR)	(Royal Air Force)	XS641 9198M [wfu 18Feb92; Jun93 to GIA RAF Cosford, UK; b/u 30Nov05 hulk to Sandbach Car & Commercial Dismantlers, Elworth, Sandbach, UK; Jun07 & Jun08 used at Glastonbury Music Festival & back to Sandbach; l/n 30Aug12]
26		C.Mk.1	(Royal Air Force)	XS642 8785M [SOC 18Jan83 RAF Benson, UK; by 13Jly91 on fire dump; b/u Jly94]
27		E.Mk.3A	(Royal Air Force)	XS643 9278M [wfu Aug96 Boscombe Down, UK; 18Mar98 to Manston fire school; b/u nose section to Hanningfield Metals, Stock, Essex, UK]
28		E.Mk.3A	(ITAB Cargo/Air Aid)	XS644 VR-BOI 9Q-COE(1) [w/o Apr99 unknown location Katanga Region, Democratic Republic of Congo; b/u on site; had been flown in to pick up recovered spares from SET # 24]
29		C.Mk.1	Air Katanga	XS645 NZ7629 + 3C-KKT 9Q-CVC(2) 3C-KKT 9Q-CVC(2) [+ New Zealand] [l/n 10Mar06 Lanseria, South Africa]
30		C.Mk.1	QinetiQ/ETPS	XS646
31		C.Mk.1	(BAe Systems)	XS647 [SOC Jan81; fuselage used as ATP design rig; later used as ATP cabin/cockpit mock-up for trial installation of interior fittings; 15Aug88 to Hatfield, UK; 1994 to Wales Aircraft Museum, Cardiff, Wales; Feb96 to Enstone Airfield, Oxon, UK]

Unidentified

unkn	Democratic Republic of Congo AF	9T-TCO	[reported in service by 2009; no sightings]
unkn	Democratic Republic of Congo AF	9T-TCP	[reported in service by 2009; no sightings]

Production complete

HINDUSTAN AERONAUTICS HAL 748

HAL/K/500	2	1/103	Hindustan Aeronautics	BH-572 VT-DRF BH-572
HAL/K/501	8	2/104	Indian Air Force	BH-573 [no reports for several years; status?]
HAL/K/502	9	2/104	Indian Air Force	BH-574 [no reports for several years; status?]
HAL/K/503	11	2/104	Indian Air Force	BH-575 BH-1047 [reportedly wfu, location unknown]
HAL/K/504	31	2/203	Indian Air Force	BH-576 BH-1048 [code L]
HAL/K/505	32	2/203	Indian Air Force	BH-1010 VT-DTR BH-1010 [code Y]
HAL/K/506	33	2/224	(Indian Airlines)	VT-DUO [w/o 05Mar84 Hyderabad-Begumpet Airport, India]
HAL/K/507	41	2/203	Indian Air Force	BH-1011 [code A then H]
HAL/K/508	42	2/203	Indian Air Force	BH-1012 [code K] [wfu Feb01 Delhi-Palam, India]
HAL/K/509	43	2/203	Indian Air Force	BH-1013
HAL/K/510	51	2/203	Indian Air Force	H-913 [code A then D]
HAL/K/511	52	2/224	(Indian Airlines)	VT-DXF [w/o 19Aug81 Mangalore Airport, India]
HAL/K/512	53	2/224	(Indian Airlines)	VT-DXG [w/o en-route 09Dec71 Chinnamanur, near Madurai Airport, India]
HAL/K/513	65	2/224	ex Indian Border Security Force	VT-DXH [stored by Sep98 Delhi, India; l/n 24Nov05]
HAL/K/514	67	2/224	(Indian Airlines)	VT-DXI [w/o 16Jun81 Tirupati Airport, India]
HAL/K/515	69	2/224	(Indian Airlines)	VT-DXJ [w/o 04Aug79 near Panvel, Kiroli Hills, near Pune Airport, India]
HAL/K/516	78	2/218	Indian Air Force	H-914 [code D] [no reports for several years; status?]
HAL/K/517	79	2/218	Indian Air Force	H-915 [code G]
HAL/K/518	80	2/224	(Indian Airlines)	VT-DXK [wfu & stored Dec93 Hyderabad-Begumpet Airport; b/u 1996/97; canx 10Dec04]
HAL/K/519	84	2/224	(Indian Airlines)	VT-DXL [wfu & stored Dec93 Hyderabad-Begumpet Airport; b/u 1996/97; canx 10Dec04]
HAL/K/520	85	2/224	(Indian Airlines)	VT-DXM [wfu & stored Dec93 Hyderabad-Begumpet Airport; b/u 1996/97; canx 10Dec04]

AVRO/ HAWKER SIDDELEY HS.748

C/n	Line No.	Model	Last known Owner/Operator	Identities/fates/comments (where appropriate)
HAL/K/521	86	2/224	(Indian Airlines)	VT-DXN [wfu & stored Dec93 Hyderabad-Begumpet Airport; b/u 1996/97; canx 10Dec04]
HAL/K/522	94	2/224	(Indian Airlines)	VT-DXO [wfu & stored Dec93 Hyderabad-Begumpet Airport; b/u 1996/97; canx 10Dec04]
HAL/K/523	95	2/224	(Indian Airlines)	VT-DXP [wfu & stored Dec93 Hyderabad-Begumpet Airport; b/u 1996/97; canx 10Dec04]
HAL/K/524	96	2/224	(Indian Airlines)	VT-DXQ [wfu & stored Dec93 Hyderabad-Begumpet Airport; b/u 1996/97; canx 10Dec04]
HAL/K/525	97	2/224	(Indian Airlines)	VT-DXR [wfu & stored Dec93 Hyderabad-Begumpet Airport; b/u 1996/97; canx 10Dec04]
HAL/K/526	98	2/219	Indian Air Force	H-1030 [code A]
HAL/K/527	99	2/219	Indian Air Force	H-1031
HAL/K/528		2/219	(Indian Air Force)	H-1032 [code C] [w/o 24Dec96 Peddareddy Palem, near Nellore, Andhra Pradesh State, India]
HAL/K/529		2/219	Indian Air Force	H-1033 [code D]
HAL/K/530		2/219	Indian Air Force	H-1034
HAL/K/531		2/219	Indian Air Force	H-1175
HAL/K/532		2M LFD	Indian Air Force	H-1176
HAL/K/533		2/218	Indian Air Force	H-1177 [code E]
HAL/K/534		2/218	Indian Air Force	H-1178 [code F then B]
HAL/K/535		2/218	Indian Air Force	H-1179 [code I then K]
HAL/K/536		2/220	Indian Air Force	H-1180
HAL/K/537		2/220	Indian Air Force	H-1181 [carried codes B, E & H]
HAL/K/538		2/220	Indian Air Force	H-1182
HAL/K/539		2/220	Indian Air Force	H-1386 [no reports for several years; status?]
HAL/K/540		2/224	Indian Border Security Force	VT-EAT [reported stored 2012]
HAL/K/541		2/224	(Indian Airlines)	VT-EAU [w/o 15Mar73 Hyderabad-Begumpet Airport, India]
HAL/K/542		2/224	Indian Border Security Force	VT-EAV [reported stored 2012]
HAL/K/543		2/224	Indian Air Force	(VT-EAW) H-2064 [code G then B]
HAL/K/544		2/224	Indian Air Force	VT-EAX H-2065 [code H] [photo reconnaissance version]
HAL/K/545		2/224	Indian Air Force	(VT-EAY) H-2066 [code P]
HAL/K/546		2/224	ex Indian Civil Aviation Dept	(VT-EAZ) VT-EFQ [wfu by 24Sep00 Delhi, India; Aug07 to VSM Aerospace School, Yelahanka AFB, Bangalore, India as GIA]
HAL/K/547		2/224	(National Airports Authority)	(VT-EBA) VT-EFR [wfu & stored by 24Sep00 Delhi, India; removed in 2010, possibly b/u]
HAL/K/548		2/224	Indian National Remote Sensing	VT-EBB VT-EFN [wfu stored location not reported; canx 02Sep96]
HAL/K/549		2/224	Indian Border Security Force	VT-EBC VT-EHL
HAL/K/550		2/218	Indian Air Force	H-1512 [code J]
HAL/K/551		2M LFD	Indian Air Force	H-1513 [w/o 25Mar91 Yelahanka AFB, Bangalore, India]
HAL/K/552		2M LFD	Indian Air Force	H-1514 [code A then B]
HAL/K/553		2/247	Indian Air Force	H-1515 [code B]
HAL/K/554		2/247	Indian Air Force	H-1516 [code F then C]
HAL/K/555		2M LFD	Indian Air Force	H-1517
HAL/K/556		2/247	Indian Air Force	H-1518 [code B]
HAL/K/557		2/247	Indian Air Force	H-1519 [code G]
HAL/K/558		2/247	Indian Air Force	H-1520 [w/o 27Apr75 Yelahanka AFB, Bangalore, India]
HAL/K/559		2M LFD	Indian Air Force	H-1521
HAL/K/560		2M LFD	Indian Air Force	H-1522 [code H]
HAL/K/561		2M LFD	Indian Air Force	H-1523 [code E]
HAL/K/562		2M LFD	Indian Air Force	H-1524 [reported stored by 08Feb11 Yelanhaka AFB, India]
HAL/K/563		2M LFD	Indian Air Force	H-1525 [code D then C]
HAL/K/564		2/247	Indian Air Force	H-1526 [code E]
HAL/K/565		2/247	Indian Air Force	H-1527
HAL/K/566		2/247	Indian Air Force	H-1528 [code G]
HAL/K/567		2M LFD	Indian Air Force	H-1529 [code A]
HAL/K/568		2M LFD	Indian Air Force	H-1530 [code J]
HAL/K/569		2M LFD	(Defence Research & Development)	H-2175 [cvtd to AEW test-bed; w/o 11Jan99 near Arakonam Naval Air Station, 50km from Chennai, India]]
HAL/K/570		2M LFD	DRDO/CABS	H-2176 [radar flying test bed]
HAL/K/571		2M LFD	Indian Air Force	H-2177 [code A then I]
HAL/K/572		2M LFD	Indian Air Force	H-2178 [w/o 07Jun79 Leh, India]
HAL/K/573		2M LFD	Indian Air Force	H-2179 [code D]

AVRO/ HAWKER SIDDELEY HS.748

C/n	Line No.	Model	Last known Owner/Operator	Identities/fates/comments (where appropriate)		
HAL/K/574		2M LFD	Indian Air Force	H-2180		
HAL/K/575		2M LFD	Indian Air Force	H-2181		
HAL/K/576		2M LFD	Indian Air Force	H-2182	[code G]	
HAL/K/577		2M LFD	Indian Air Force	H-2183		
HAL/K/578		2M LFD	Indian Air Force	H-2184		
HAL/K/579		2M LFD	Indian Air Force	H-2372	[code F]	
HAL/K/580		2M LFD	Indian Air Force	H-2373		
HAL/K/581		2M LFD	Indian Air Force	H-2374		
HAL/K/582		2M LFD	Indian Air Force	H-2375	[code C]	
HAL/K/583		2M LFD	Indian Air Force	H-2376		
HAL/K/584		2M LFD	Indian Air Force	H-2377	[code K]	
HAL/K/585		2M LFD	Indian Air Force	H-2378	[code Q]	
HAL/K/586		2M LFD	Indian Air Force	H-2379	[code R]	
HAL/K/587		2M LFD	Indian Border Security Force	H-2380	VT-EIR	[stored Sep98 Delhi, India; l/n 19Sep07]
HAL/K/588		2M LFD	Indian Air Force	H-2381	[code A]	

Production complete

ILYUSHIN Il-18 and Il-20, Il-22 and Il-38

C/n	Model	Last known Owner/Operator	Identities/fates/comments (where appropriate)
187 0000 01	18	(MAP Ramenskoye)	CCCP-L5811 CCCP-75420 [ff 04Jly57; first prototype; fate unknown]
187 0000 02	18I	(Ilyushin OKB)	CCCP-L5812 CCCP-75888 [second prototype; fate unknown]
187 0001 01	18A	State Aviation Museum	001 red CCCP-L5818 CCCP-75634 [ff 26Oct57; first production aircraft] [canx 18May66; GIF then preserved Kiev-Zhuliany, Ukraine; l/n Mar09]
187 0001 02	18A	(Kharkov Aviation Institute)	CCCP-L5819 [wfu 06Nov59 to GIA Kharkov, Ukraine, USSR; fate unknown]
187 0001 03	18A	(Ilyushin OKB)	CCCP-L5820 CCCP-75636+ [canx 28May62; to GIA Krivoy Rog, Ukraine, USSR, fate unknown; + marks never worn]
187 0001 04	18A	(Soviet Air Force)	002 red [c/n not confirmed but only option; w/o 07May58 on test flight while attempting to reach Moscow-Sheremetyevo, USSR; used call sign CCCP-33569 which at one time was worn on airframe]
187 0001 05	18A	(Aeroflot/Moscow-MUTA)	CCCP-75748 [canx 24Sep73; preserved by Sep77 Sverdlovsk in park, USSR; gone by 1993]
188 0002 01	18LL	(MAP LII Zhukovski)	CCCP-L5821 CCCP-75637 [fate unknown]
188 0002 02	18A	(Aeroflot/Tajikistan)	CCCP-75638 [canx 1973; fuselage used as store Dushanbe, Tajikistan; l/n 22Nov08]
188 0002 03	18A	(Aeroflot/Moscow)	CCCP-75639 [canx 1973; fate unknown]
188 0002 04	18A	(Aeroflot/Moscow)	CCCP-75640 [canx 25Mar61; fate unknown]
188 0002 05	18A	(Aeroflot/Turkmenistan)	CCCP-75641 [canx 24Sep73; fate unknown]
188 0003 01	18A	(Krivoy Rog Aeronautical School)	CCCP-75642 [canx 24Sep73; preserved Krivoiy Rog, Ukraine; b/u by Apr99]
188 0003 02	18SL	(MRP NPO Leninets)	CCCP-75643 [canx 28Jan88; preserved by 07Sep92 Pushkin in town, Russia; b/u summer 1998]
188 0003 03	18A	(NII VVS)	CCCP-75644 [canx unknown date; fate unknown]
188 0003 04	18A	(Riga Aviation Institute)	CCCP-75645 [canx 24Sep73; by 1983 GIA Riga Aviation Institute, Skulte, Latvia; b/u by late 1994]
188 0003 05	18A	(Aeroflot/Kazakhstan)	CCCP-75646 [canx 24Sep73, by Mar90 fuselage with Sheremetyevo Technical School, Moscow, Russia; l/n Sep95]
188 0004 01	20RT	(LII Zhukovski)	CCCP-75647 CCCP-06180 CCCP-27220 [canx 26Jly82; by Aug92 derelict Zhukovsky, Russia; l/n Sep93; assumed b/u]
188 0004 02	18A	(Aeroflot/Urals)	CCCP-75648 [w/o 27Apr60 nr Sverdlovsk, USSR; canx 11Jun60]
188 0004 03	18A	(Ulyanovsk Higher Flying School)	CCCP-75649 [canx 24Sep 73; fate unknown]
188 0004 04	18A	(Ulyanovsk Higher Flying School)	CCCP-75650 [canx 1973; fate unknown]
188 0004 05	18A	(Ulyanovsk Higher Flying School)	CCCP-75651 [w/o 26Dec60 Ulyanovsk, USSR; canx 14Feb61]
188 0005 01	18B	(Soviet Air Force)	(CCCP-75652) CCCP-75473 [canx; fate/status unknown]
188 0005 02	18B	(Aeroflot/Moscow)	CCCP-75653 [w/o 13Aug61 Riga, Latvia, USSR]
188 0005 03	18B	(Aeroflot/Moscow)	CCCP-75654 [w/o 17Dec61 en-route near Millerovo, USSR]
188 0005 04	18B	(Aeroflot/Moscow)	CCCP-75655 [canx 1978; fate unknown]
188 0005 05	18B	(Aeroflot/Azerbaijan)	CCCP-75656 [canx 1976; fate unknown]
188 0006 01	18B	.	[nothing known but CCCP-75657 would fit into registration sequence]
188 0006 02	18B	(Aeroflot/Ukraine)	CCCP-75658 [canx 1978; preserved by May98 Zaporozhye in park, Ukraine; l/n Apr99]
188 0006 03	18B	ex Ulyanovsk Higher Flying School	CCCP-75659 [canx 1980; preserved by 1995 Lutsk, Ukraine; l/n 19Feb10]
188 0006 04	18B	(LNPO Leninets)	CCCP-75660 CCCP-06187 CCCP-48093 [canx 1981; preserved pioneer camp Losevo, Russia; l/n May08; b/u by Aug12]
188 0006 05	18B	(Aeroflot/Moscow)	CCCP-75661 [w/o 02Jly64 Krasnodar, USSR; rear fuselage to Kiev Institute of Civil Engineering, Kiev Ukraine; l/n Aug08]
188 0007 01	18B	(Aeroflot/Moscow)	CCCP-75662 [canx 1977; fate unknown]
188 0007 02	18B	(Aeroflot/Northern)	CCCP-75663 [w/o 26Aug72 Archangelsk, USSR; canx 1973]
188 0007 03	18B	(Aeroflot/Azerbaijan)	CCCP-75664 [canx 1976; fate unknown]
188 0007 04	18B	(Aeroflot/Kazakhstan)	CCCP-75665 [w/o 22Nov66 Alma Ata, Kazakhstan, USSR; canx 08Dec66]
188 0007 05	18D	(Soviet Air Force)	CCCP-75666 [canx 1989; fate/status unknown]
188 0008 01	18B	(Aeroflot/Ukraine)	CCCP-04330 CCCP-75479 [canx 30Nov78; fate unknown]
188 0008 02	18B	(Aeroflot/Moscow)	CCCP-75668(1) [canx 25Mar61; fate unknown]
188 0008 03	18B	(Aeroflot/Moscow)	CCCP-75669 [w/o 11Dec69 after flight through heavy turbulence; canx 1977]
189 0008 04	18B	(Ulyanovsk Higher Flying School)	CCCP-75670 [canx 1974; fate unknown]
189 0008 05	18B	(Ulyanovsk Higher Flying School)	CCCP-75671 [canx 1976; by Sep91 derelict Moscow-Sheremtyevo, Russia; l/n Apr97]
189 0009 01	18B	(Riga Aviation Institute)	CCCP-75672 [dbr 22Jun61 near Bogoroditsk, USSR; ferried to Riga Aviation Institute, Riga, Latvia, USSR & to GIA]
189 0009 02	18B	(Aeroflot/Ukraine)	CCCP-75673 [canx 1979; fate unknown]
189 0009 03	18B	(GosNII GVF)	CCCP-75674 [canx 1979; fate unknown]
189 0009 04	18B	(Aeroflot/Azerbaijan)	CCCP-75675 [canx 14Jan77; fate unknown]
189 0009 05	18B	(Aeroflot/Moscow)	CCCP-75676(1) [w/o 02Sep59 location unknown; canx 25Mar61]
189 0010 01	18B	(Aeroflot/Moscow)	CCCP-75749 [canx 1977; fate unknown]

ILYUSHIN Il-18 and Il-20, Il-22 and Il-38

C/n	Model	Last known Owner/Operator	Identities/fates/comments (where appropriate)
189 0010 02	18B	(SibNIA)	CCCP-75677 [canx 14Jan77; fate unknown]
189 0010 03	18B	(Aeroflot/Azerbaijan)	CCCP-75678 [canx 14Jan77; fate unknown]
189 0010 04	18B	(Aeroflot/Northern)	CCCP-75679 [canx 1977; fate unknown]
189 0010 05	18B	(Aeroflot/Kyrgyzstan)	CCCP-75680 [canx 1978; b/u – by May95 rear fuselage only at Frunze, Russia; l/n Sep04]
189 0011 01	18B	(Aeroflot/Moscow)	CCCP-75681 [canx 1969; fate unknown]
189 0011 02	18B	(Aeroflot/Kazakhstan)	CCCP-75682 [canx 1977; fate unknown]
189 0011 03	18B	(Aeroflot/Moscow)	CCCP-75683 [canx 1977; fate unknown]
189 0011 04	18B	(Aeroflot/East Siberia)	CCCP-75684 [canx 1977; fate unknown]
189 0011 05	18B	(Aeroflot/Kazakhstan)	CCCP-75685 [w/o 03Jan65 Alma Ata, Kazakhstan, USSR; canx 1965]
189 0012 01	18B	(Aeroflot/Moscow)	CCCP-75686 [w/o 10Nov63 Kuibyshev, USSR; canx 29Dec63]
189 0012 02	18B	(Aeroflot/Azerbaijan)	CCCP-75687 [w/o in mid-air disintegration 11May73 Semipalatinsk, Kazakhstan, USSR; canx 15Aug73]
189 0012 03	18B	(Aeroflot/Moscow)	CCCP-75688 [w/o 23Dec65 Magadan, USSR; canx 1971]
189 0012 04	18B	(Aeroflot/Kazakhstan)	CCCP-75689 [by 13Apr78 in use as cinema Gagarin Park, Simferopol, USSR; b/u by 2000]
189 0012 05	18B	(Aeroflot/Kyrgyzstan)	CCCP-75690 [canx 1978; assumed b/u Bishkek-Manas, Kyrgyzstan where 09May95 fuselage part noted]
189 0013 01	18B	(Aeroflot/Kazakhstan)	CCCP-75691 [canx 1977; fate unknown]
189 0013 02	18V	(Aeroflot/Uzbekistan)	CCCP-75710 [Il-18V prototype; ff 10Dec59; canx 24Oct78; fate unknown]
189 0013 03	18B	(Aeroflot/Kyrgyzstan)	CCCP-75693 [canx 1978; fate unknown]
189 0013 04	18B	(Aeroflot/Latvia)	CCCP-75694 [canx 1977; fate unknown]
189 0013 05	18B	(Aeroflot/Northern)	CCCP-75695 [canx 1973; fate unknown]
189 0014 01	18B	(Civil Aviation Administration China)	202+ B-202 [+ China] [w/o 24Dec82 Canton, China]
189 0014 02	18B	(Aeroflot/Urals)	CCCP-75699 [w/o 11Dec69 possibly Leningrad-Pulkovo, USSR; canx 1971]
189 0014 03	18B	(Aeroflot/Urals)	CCCP-75696 [canx 1978; fate unknown]
189 0014 04	18B	(Aeroflot/Turkmenistan)	CCCP-75697 [canx 1979; fate unknown]
189 0014 05	18B	(Aeroflot/Kazakhstan)	CCCP-75698 [canx 1977; fate unknown]
189 0015 01	18B	(Aeroflot/Urals)	CCCP-75700 [canx 1978; preserved & used as cinema in Oryol, Russia until b/u in 1985]
189 0015 02	18B	(Aeroflot/Turkmenistan)	CCCP-75701 [canx 1978; fate unknown]
189 0015 03	18B	(Aeroflot/Magadan)	CCCP-75702 [canx 1979; fate unknown]
189 0015 04	18B	ex Civil Aviation Administration China	B-200 208(1) 240+ B-240+ 240 [+ China; not confirmed; preserved by 02Sep03 Liu Shaoqi memorial, Huaminglou, Huhan province, China; l/n Nov07]
189 0015 05	18B	(Bykovo ARZ-402)	CCCP-75703 RA-75703 [canx; wfu Bykovo, Russia by Aug02; gone by Jly04; assumed b/u]
189 0016 01	18B	(Civil Aviation Administration China)	206+ B-206 [+ China] [wfu Apr84 Tianjin, China; l/n 02Nov86 Chengdu, China; fate unknown]
189 0016 02	18B	(Civil Aviation Administration China)	204+ B-204 [+ China] [w/o Feb77 Shanyang, China]
189 0016 03	18B	(Aeroflot/Turkmenistan)	CCCP-75704 [canx 1979; fate unknown]
189 0016 04	18V	Letecke Museum Kbely	OK-NAA [DBR 02Jan77 Prague, Czechoslovakia hit by landing CSA Tu134, OK-CFD; preserved Kbely Czech Republic]
189 0016 05	18V	(CSA)	OK-NAB [w/o 28Jly76 Bratislava, Czechoslovakia]
189 0017 01?	18B	(Aeroflot)	CCCP-75601 [nothing known; possibly a military aircraft]
189 0017 02	18B	(Soviet Government)	CCCP-75705 [w/o 17Aug60 Tarasovichi near Kiev, USSR; canx 03Dec60]
189 0017 03	18B	(Aeroflot/Moscow)	CCCP-75706 [canx 1975; fate unknown]
189 0017 04	18B	(Aeroflot/Moscow)	CCCP-75707 [canx 1979; fate unknown]
189 0017 05	18B	(Aeroflot/Moscow)	CCCP-75708 [w/o 26Aug69 Moscow-Vnukovo; canx 1969]
189 0018 01	18B	(Aeroflot/Tajikistan)	CCCP-75709 [canx 1980; fate unknown]
189 0018 02	18V	(Aeroflot/Urals)	CCCP-75711 [canx 1977; by Sep81 wfu Moscow-Sheremetyevo, USSR]
180 0018 03	18V	(Aeroflot/Tajikistan)	CCCP-75712 [orginally reported as c/n 189 0018 03; w/o 24Feb73 Buston near Leninabad, USSR; canx 18Jly73]
180 0018 04	18V	(GosNII GVF)	CCCP-75713(1) [canx 17Apr74; fate unknown]
189 0018 05	18V	(Aeroflot/Moscow)	CCCP-75714 [canx 1979; fate unknown]
180 0019 01	18V	(Aeroflot/Moscow)	CCCP-75715 [canx 1977; fate unknown]
180 0019 02	18V	(Ulyanovsk Higher Flying School)	CCCP-75716 [w/o summmer 1975 Chelyabinsk, Russia, USSR; canx 1976]
180 0019 03	18V	Hungarian Museum of Transport	HA-MOA [wfu 19Feb87; preserved Jun92 Budapest-Ferihegy, Hungary]
180 0019 04	18V	(Aeroflot/Latvia)	CCCP-75717 [w/o summer 1975 Chelyabinsk, USSR; canx 1976]
180 0019 05	18V	Flughafen Leipzig-Halle	DM-STA DDR-STA DM-STA [canx 26Sep88; preserved by Mar90 Leipzig Airport, Germany; by mid 2009 re-painted in original Deutsche Lufthansa c/s with its original registration DM-STA; l/n 31Oct10]

ILYUSHIN Il-18 and Il-20, Il-22 and Il-38

C/n	Model	Last known Owner/Operator	Identities/fates/comments (where appropriate)
180 0020 01	18V	Rubesan's Da Capo Museum	DM-STB DDR-STB [wfu 18Oct87; canx 05Nov87; preserved different locations; now at Plagwitz, Germany; l/n May08]
180 0020 02	18V	(MALEV)	HA-MOD [w/o 23Nov62 near Paris Le Bourget, France]
180 0020 03	18Gr	(Compagnie Africaine d'Aviation)	CCCP-75431 RA-75431 9Q-CHB [CofA expired Oct07; b/u Mar08 Kinshasa-N'Djili, Democratic Republic of Congo]
180 0020 04	18V	(Aeroflot/Turkmenistan)	CCCP-75719 3X-NZE(1) CCCP-75719 [canx 1980; fate unknown]
180 0020 05	18V	(Aeroflot/Moscow)	CCCP-75718 [canx 1978; wfu dumped Moscow-Domodedovo, USSR; l/n Sep95]
180 0021 01	18V	(CSA)	OK-OAC [wfu 30May80; destroyed 19/20Nov84 in Semtex tests]
180 0021 02	18V	(CSA)	OK-OAD [w/o 28Mar61 near Nürnberg, West Germany]
180 0021 03	18V	(Aeroflot/Moscow)	CCCP-04356 CCCP-75422 [canx 1978; fate unknown]
180 0021 04	18V	(Aeroflot/Northern)	CCCP-75720 [canx 1976; fate unknown]
180 0021 05	18V	(Aeroflot/Moscow)	CCCP-75721 [canx 1977; fate unknown]
180 0022 01	18V	(Aeroflot/Latvia)	CCCP-75722 [canx Feb76; fate unknown]
180 0022 02	18LL	(VZLU)	DM-STC DDR-STC OK-018 [stored Kbely, Czech Republic; b/u Jan96]
180 0022 03	18V	(Aeroflot/Azerbaijan)	CCCP-75723 [canx 14Jan77; fate unknown]
180 0022 04	18V	(Aeroflot/Urals)	CCCP-75724 [canx 1977; reported preserved Perm park; b/u by 1997]
180 0022 05	18V	(Aeroflot/Latvia)	CCCP-75725 [canx 1978; fate unknown]
189 0023 01	18V	(Aeroflot/Kazakhstan)	CCCP-75726 [canx 1978; fate unknown]
180 0023 02	18V	ex Interflug	493+ DM-STD DDR-STD [+ E Germany] [wfu 26Oct86; canx 24Nov88; dismantled 1991; preserved different locations; 24Apr09 at Teuge, Netherlands to become a hotel]
180 0023 03	18V	(GosNII GVF)	CCCP-75727 [w/o 21Jan71 Rostov-on-Don, USSR; canx 1971]
180 0023 04	18V	(Aeroflot/Moscow)	CCCP-75728 [canx 1977; fate unknown]
180 0023 05	18V	(Aeroflot/Urals)	CCCP-75729 [canx 1978; fate unknown]
180 0024 01	18V	(Aeroflot/Moscow)	CCCP-75730 [canx 1977; fate unknown]
180 0024 02	18V	(Aeroflot/Ukraine)	9G-AAI CCCP-75534 [canx 1979; fate unknown]
180 0024 03	18Gr	(LOT)	SP-LSA [wfu 20Oct88 Warsaw-Okecie, Poland; canx 16Jun89; b/u Feb90]
180 0024 04	18V	(LOT)	SP-LSB [wfu 02Nov88 Warsaw-Okecie, Poland; canx 24Aug89; b/u Feb90]
180 0024 05	18V	(Aeroflot/Northern)	9G-AAJ CCCP-75535 [wfu 16Feb84 Moscow-Bykovo, USSR; b/u]
180 0025 01	18V	(Aeroflot/Uzbekistan)	9G-AAK CCCP-75532 [canx 1978; fate unknown]
180 0025 02	18V	(Aeroflot/Uzbekistan)	9G-AAL CCCP-75533 [w/o 05Jun70 Samarkand, USSR; canx 1970]
180 0025 03	18V	(GosNII GVF)	[static test airframe]
180 0025 04	18V	(LOT)	101(1) + SP-LSE [+ Poland] [wfu 28Nov89; canx 29Dec89; preserved until destroyed 26Sep95 by vandals, Warsaw, Poland]
180 0025 05	18V	(Aeroflot/Moscow)	CCCP-75731 [canx 1980; fate unknown]
181 0026 01	18V	(Polyarnaya Aviatrans)	CCCP-75732 [w/o 26Feb63 nr Cape Schmidt, USSR; canx 06Apr63]
181 0026 02	18V	(Aeroflot/Krasnoyarsk)	CCCP-75733 [canx 1978; fate unknown]
181 0026 03	18V	(Aeroflot/Azerbaijan)	CCCP-75734 [canx 1977; fate unknown]
181 0026 04	18V	(Aeroflot/Kyrgyzstan)	CCCP-75735 [canx 1978; fate unknown]
181 0026 05	18V	(Aeroflot/Urals)	CCCP-75736 [canx 1982; fate unknown]
181 0027 01	18Gr	(LOT)	102(1) + SP-LSH [+ Poland] [wfu 30Apr89; canx 22Nov89 preserved different locations; by 09Aug97 Strumien, Poland; l/n Feb09]
181 0027 02	18V	Central Air Force Museum	CCCP-75737 [canx 1977; preserved 12Jly77 Monino, Russia; l/n Aug08]
181 0027 03	18V	(Aeroflot/Urals)	CCCP-75738 [canx 1977; preserved by Sep77 Sverdlovsk park, USSR; DBF post 1977]
181 0027 04	18V	(Aeroflot/Kyrgyzstan)	CCCP-75739 [canx 1978; fate unknown]
181 0027 05	18V	(Aeroflot/Turkmenistan)	CCCP-75740 [canx 1978; fate unknown]
181 0028 01	18V	(Aeroflot/Krasnoyarsk)	CCCP-75741 [canx 1977; preserved in park Abakan, USSR; b/u mid 90s]
181 0028 02	18V	(Soviet Government)	CCCP-75742 [canx 1977; fate unknown]
181 0028 03	18V	(Aeroflot/West Siberia)	9G-AAX CCCP-75426 [canx 1979; fate unknown]
181 0028 04	18V	(Aeroflot/Krasnoyarsk)	9G-AAY CCCP-75421 [canx 1979; fate unknown]
181 0028 05	18Gr	(Balkan)	SP-LSC LZ-BEI [wfu by Sep97 Varna, Bulgaria; l/n Jun99; b/u]
181 0029 01	18V	(Aeroflot/Moscow)	CCCP-75743 [canx 1979; dumped by 16Aug92 Zhukovski, Russia; assumed b/u]
181 0029 02	18V	Zruc Air Park	OK-PAE [wfu 18May80; preserved by Mar82 latterly at Zruc, Czech Republic; l/n May08]
181 0029 03	18V	(MALEV)	HA-MOC [w/o 28Aug71 Copenhagen-Kastrup, Denmark]
181 0029 04	18V	(CSA)	OK-PAF [w/o 12Jly62 nr Casablanca, Morocco]
181 0029 05	18D	(Aeroflot/Krasnoyarsk)	CCCP-75744 [canx Mar83, preserved 1983 Abkhazia, Georgia, l/n Oct06; b/u by 2008]
181 0030 01	18V	(Aeroflot/Krasnoyarsk)	CCCP-75745 [canx 1977; fate unknown]

ILYUSHIN Il-18 and Il-20, Il-22 and Il-38

C/n	Model	Last known Owner/Operator	Identities/fates/comments (where appropriate)
181 0030 02	18V	(Aeroflot/Krasnoyarsk)	CCCP-75746 [canx 1977; fate unknown]
181 0030 03	18V	(Aeroflot/Kazakhstan)	CCCP-75747 [canx 1977; fate unknown]
181 0030 04	18V	(Aeroflot/Latvia)	CCCP-75750 [canx 1978; fate unknown]
181 0030 05	18V	Sochi-Adler Museum	CCCP-75751 [canx 1978; preserved by Aug84 Sochi Adler park, USSR; DBF Jly99]
181 0031 01	18T	(Aeroflot/Magadan)	CCCP-75752 [canx 1983; fate unknown]
181 0031 02	18V	(Aeroflot/Krasnoyarsk)	CCCP-75753 [canx 1977; fate unknown]
181 0031 03	18V	(Aeroflot/Armenia)	CCCP-75754 [canx 1979; by 10Aug89 to fire trainer Krasnodar, USSR; by 14May96 to Sochi-Adler, Russia by 1996; b/u post Jly07]
181 0031 04	18V	(Aeroflot/East Siberia)	CCCP-75755 [canx 1983; fate unknown]
181 0031 05	18V	Auto & Technik Museum	OK-BYP OK-PAI [wfu 15Dec97; ferried 29Jan90 to Nurnberg, Germany; preserved Sinsheim, Germany; l/n Jun07]
181 0032 01	18V	(Aeroflot/Tajikistan)	CCCP-75756 [canx 1979; fate unknown]
181 0032 02	18V	(Aeroflot/Armenia)	CCCP-75757 [w/o 31Dec61 Mineralnye Vody, USSR; canx 06Feb62]
181 0032 03	18V	(Soviet Government)	CCCP-75758 [canx 1976; fate unknown]
181 0032 04	18V	(Aeroflot/Urals)	CCCP-75759 [canx 1977; fate unknown]
181 0032 05	18V	(Aeroflot/Latvia)	CCCP-75760 [canx 1977; fate unknown]
181 0033 01	18V	(Aeroflot/Uzbekistan)	CCCP-75761 [canc 1978; fate unknown]
181 0033 02	18V	(Aeroflot/Kazakhstan)	CCCP-75762 [canx 1977; fate unknown]
181 0033 03	18V	(Aeroflot/Moscow)	TZ-ABD CCCP-75477 [canx 1979; fate unknown]
181 0033 04	18V	(Air Mali)	TZ-ABE [w/o 11Aug74 Lingomin, Upper Volta]
181 0033 05	18V	(Aerflot/Northern)	9G-AAM CCCP-75424 [canx 1980; preserved by 02Jly83 "Lininski Komsomol" park, Tashkent, USSR]
181 0034 01	18V	(Soviet Government)	CCCP-75763 [canx 1976; fate unknown]
181 0034 02	18V	(Algerian Government)	CCCP-75764 7T-VRA [canx 1989; fate unknown]
181 0034 03	18V	(Aeroflot/Urals)	9G-AAN CCCP-75425 [w/o 09May74 Ivano-Frankovsk, USSR; canx 30May74]
181 0034 04	18V	(Aeroflot/Turkmenistan)	CCCP-75765 [w/o 05Mar63 Ashkhabad, Turkmenistan, USSR; canx 04Apr63]
181 0034 05	18V	(Ilyushin OKB)	CCCP-75766 [w/o 28Jly61 Tretyakovo, USSR, before delivery]
181 0035 01	18V	ex Aeroflot/Armenia	CCCP-75767 [canx 1979; ferried May81 to Stavropol-Grushovy, USSR & preserved as café, in park Pobedy, Stavropol, Russia; l/n 08May05]
181 0035 02	18V	(Aeroflot/Uzbekistan)	CCCP-75768 [canx 1979; fate unknown]
181 0035 03	18V	(Aeroflot/Urals)	CCCP-75769 [canx 1977; fate unknown]
181 0035 04	18V	(Aeroflot/Kazakhstan)	CCCP-75770 [canx 1977; fate unknown]
181 0035 05	18V	(Aeroflot/Krasnoyarsk)	CCCP-75771 [canx 1977; fate unknown]
181 0036 01	18V	(Aeroflot/Kyrgyzstan)	CCCP-75772 [canx 1978; fate unknown]
181 0036 02	18V	(TAROM)	YR-IMA B-230(1) YR-IMA [wfu 07Aug91; canx 01Feb96; by 23Sep98 fire trainer at Bucharest-Otepeni Airport, Romania]
181 0036 03	18V	(Aeroflot/Armenia)	CCCP-75773 [w/o 31Dec70 Moscow-Pulkovo, USSR; canx 1971]
181 0036 04	18V	(Aeroflot/Armenia)	CCCP-75774 [canx 1979; by 1980 used as cafe Yerevan, Armenia, USSR; destroyed by explosives 01Apr90 & b/u]
181 0036 05	18V	(Aeroflot/Uzbekistan)	CCCP-75775 [canx 1978; fate unknown]
181 0037 01	18V	(Aeroflot/Moscow)	CCCP-75776 [canx 1978; fate unknown]
181 0037 02	18V	(TAROM)	YR-IMB [damaged 24Feb62 Paphos, Cyprus; to Moscow-Vnukovo, USSR, but not repaired; after 1977 to Ivanovo, USSR as GIA]
181 0037 03	18V	(Air Guinee)	3X-KKN 3X-GAB [w/o 09Jlul67 Casablanca, Morocco; hulk still present 1992]
181 0037 04	18V	(Aeroflot/Uzbekistan)	3X-NZE(2) 3X-GAC CCCP-75428 [canx 1980; preserved by Jly93 Petropavlovsk, Kazakhstan]
181 0037 05	18V	(Aeroflot/Moscow)	3X-LBE 3X-GAA CCCP-74299 [canx 08Oct81; derelict by Aug92 Moscow-Domodedovo, Russia; l/n Sep95]
181 0038 01	18V	(Aeroflot/Krasnoyarsk)	CCCP-75777 [canx 1977; fate unknown]
181 0038 02	18V	(Aeroflot/Uzbekistan)	CCCP-75778 [canx 27Dec77; fate unknown]
181 0038 03	18V	(Aeroflot/Tajikistan)	CCCP-75779 [canx 1979; fate unknown]
181 0038 04	18V	(Aeroflot)	CCCP-75780(1) [nothing known]
181 0038 05	18V	ex Aeroflot/Turkmenistan	CCCP-75781 CCCP-190979+ [+ fake registration applied after preservation; canx Nov81; Nov/Dec81 preserved Brest, Belarus, USSR; l/n 15Jun09; by 23Jly09 in museum Borovaya, Belarus]
181 0039 01	18V	(Aeroflot/Azerbaijan)	CCCP-75782 [canx 1977; fate unknown]
181 0039 02	18V	(Aeroflot/Krasnoyarsk)	CCCP-75783 [canx 1977; fate unknown]
181 0039 03	18V	(Aeroflot/Kazakhstan)	CCCP-75784 [canx 1979; fate unknown was reported preserved Adler, Russia; but this is thought to be CCCP-75751]
181 0039 04	18V	(Aeroflot/Moscow)	CCCP-75785 [last flight 23Dec81; b/u Moscow-Bykovo, USSR; canx 1982]

ILYUSHIN Il-18 and Il-20, Il-22 and Il-38

C/n	Model	Last known Owner/Operator	Identities/fates/comments (where appropriate)
181 0039 05	18V	ex MRP NPO	CCCP-75786 RA-75786 75786 [wfu & no engines by 25Aug01 Pushkin, Russia, l/n May06]
181 0040 01	18V	(Aeroflot/Turkmenistan)	CCCP-75787 [canx 1986; fate unknown]
181 0040 02	18T	(Aeroflot/Krasnoyarsk)	CCCP-75788 [canx 1983; fate unknown]
181 0040 03	18V	(Aeroflot/Northern)	CCCP-75789 [canx 1977; fate unknown]
181 0040 04	18V	(Aeroflot/Azerbaijan)	CCCP-75790 [canx 1977; fate unknown]
181 0040 05	18V	(Aeroflot/Krasnoyarsk)	CCCP-75791 [w/o 10Sep69 Yakutsk, USSR; canx 1970]
181 0041 01	18V	(Aeroflot/Kazakhstan)	CCCP-75792 [canx 1977; fate unknown]
181 0041 02	18V	(Aeroflot/Krasnoyarsk)	CCCP-75793 [canx 1977; fate unknown]
181 0041 03	18V	(LII Zhukovski)	CCCP-78732 RA-78732 [canx 23Nov01; l/n 23Nov01 wfu Zhukovski, Russia]
181 0041 04	18V	(Aeroflot/Krasnoyarsk)	CCCP-75797 [canx 1982; fate unknown]
181 0041 05	18V	(Aeroflot/Krasnoyarsk)	CCCP-75796 DM-STF(1) CCCP-75475 [wfu & canx 1979; fate unknown]
181 0042 01	18V	(CSA)	OK-PAG [wfu 21Feb80; 25May82 to restaurant near Slusovice, Czechoslovakia; l/n Sep96; later to Lensa, Czech Republic, until b/u 2001]
181 0042 02	18V	(CSA)	OK-PAH [wfu 31Oct79 Prague, Czechoslovakia; b/u Aug81]
182 0042 03	18V	(Russian Air Force)	CCCP-75602 RA-75602 [wfu 1998; canx 12Mar01; reported destroyed]
182 0042 04	18V	(Aeroflot/Far East)	CCCP-75799 [canx 1982; fate unknown]
182 0042 05	18V	(Aeroflot/Moscow)	CCCP-75800 75800 CCCP-75800 [canx 1978; fate unknown]
182 0043 01	18V	(Aeroflot/Moscow)	CCCP-75801 [w/o 12Dec75 Krasnoyarsk, USSR; canx 1976]
182 0043 02	18V	(Aeroflot/Latvia)	CCCP-75802 [canx 1978; fate unknown]
182 0043 03	18V	(Aeroflot/Uzbekistan)	CCCP-75798 [w/o 06Feb70 near Samarkand, USSR; canx 10Mar70]
182 0043 04	18V	(Aeroflot/Krasnoyarsk)	CCCP-75803 75803 CCCP-75803 [canx 1983; fate unknown]
182 0043 05	18V	ex NPP-MIR	CCCP-75804 75804 RA-75804 75804+ [+ prefix totally faded; wfu by 07Jly06 Pushkin, Russia; 21May11 fuselage cut off forward wings]
182 0044 01	18V	(Ulyanovsk Higher Flying School)	CCCP-75805 [canx 1978; fate unknown]
182 0044 02	18V	Flughafen Erfurt	DM-STG DDR-STG [wfu 09Nov88; 18Nov88 to rescue trainer Erfurt, Germany; l/n May08]
182 0044 03	18V	(Aeroflot/Azerbaijan)	CCCP-75807 [canx 1977; fate unknown]
182 0044 04	18V	(Aeroflot/Kazakhstan)	CCCP-75806 [canx 1978; fate unknown]
182 0044 05	18V	(Russian Air Force)	CCCP-75606 RA-75606 [wfu 1998 Chkalovski, Russia; l/n 05Aug00; canx 12Mar01 reportedly as destroyed]
182 0045 01	18V	(Aeroflot/Northern)	CCCP-75808 [canx 1978; fate unknown]
182 0045 02	18V	(Aeroflot/Urals)	CCCP-75809 [canx 1977; fate unknown]
182 0045 03	18V	(Aeroflot/Moscow)	CCCP-75810 [canx 1982; fate unknown]
182 0045 04	18V	(Sevastopol Avia)	CCCP-75811 RA-75811 EX-028 UR-CEV [wfu by Jun07 7 b/u Jly08 Sevastopol, Ukraine]
182 0045 05	18V	(Aeroflot/Kazakhstan)	TZ-ABY CCCP-74298 [w/o 31Aug72 near Magnitogorsk, USSR; canx 19Feb73]
182 0046 01	18V	(Balkan)	LZ-BEL [DBF Dec76 Tashkent, Uzbekistan, USSR]
182 0046 02	18T	(Aeroflot/Kazakhstan)	CCCP-75812 [canx 1983; derelict fuselage Jly94 Khabarovsk, Russia; l/n May95]
182 0046 03	18V	(Balkan)	LZ-BEK [b/u circa 1985 Varna, Bulgaria; some parts l/n 1992]
182 0046 04	18V	(Aeroflot/Kazakhstan)	CCCP-75813 [canx 1980; 2011 found preserved Merke, Kazakhstan]
182 0046 05	18V	(Aeroflot/Urals)	CCCP-75814 [canx 1979; fate unknown]
182 0047 01	18V	(Aeroflot/Krasnoyarsk)	CCCP-75815 [canx 1982; fate unknown]
182 0047 02	18V	(Soviet Government)	CCCP-75816 [canx 1979; fate unknown]
182 0047 03	18V	(Aeroflot/Krasnoyarsk or Moscow)	CCCP-75817 [canx 1982; fate unknown]
182 0047 04	18V	(Aeroflot/Moscow)	CCCP-75818 [canx 1978; derelict by Jly93 Aktyubinsk, Kazakhstan]
182 0047 05	18V	(Aeroflot/Urals)	CCCP-75819 [canx 1985; fate unknown]
182 0048 01	18V	Aquiline?	CCCP-75894 RA-75894 EX-059 [stored Fujairah, UAE; canx 19Mar09; fate/status unknown; l/n 17Oct09; b/u by Mar10]
182 0048 02	18V	(TAROM)	YR-IMC [preserved by 1992 Banasti, Romania; l/n Jun00 bad condition; canx 01Feb96]
182 0048 03	18V	(Aeroflot/Northern)	CCCP-75821 [canx 1978; fate unknown]
182 0048 04	18V	Aerovista	YR-IMD 3D-ALQ EL-ADV EX-7504 ER-ICM EX-011
182 0048 05	18V	(Aeroflot/Tajikistan)	CCCP-75820 [canx 1979; fate unknown]
182 0049 01	18T	(Aeroflot/Krasnoyarsk)	CCCP-75822 [canx 1983; fate unknown]
182 0049 02	18V	(Aeroflot/Far East)	CCCP-75823 [w/o 23Aug70, but also quoted 23Aug71, Yuzhno-Sakhalinsk, USSR]
182 0049 03	18V	(Aeroflot/Moscow)	CCCP-75824 [w/o 03Aug64 Magadan, USSR; canx 01Nov64]
182 0049 04	18V	(Phoenix)	CCCP-75825 RA-75825 EL-ALW EX-75825 EX-904 [possibly w/o 15Sep02 Neghazi, Angola]
182 0049 05	18V	(Cubana)	CCCP-75826 CU-T830 [w/o 10Jly66 nesr Cienfuegos, Cuba]
182 0050 01	18T	(Aeroflot/Magadan)	CCCP-75827 [canx Oct82; fate unknown]

ILYUSHIN Il-18 and Il-20, Il-22 and Il-38

C/n	Model	Last known Owner/Operator	Identities/fates/comments (where appropriate)
182 0050 02	18T	(Aeroflot/Krasnoyarsk)	CCCP-75828 [canx 1983; fate unknown]
182 0050 03	18V	(Aeroflot/Turkmenistan)	CCCP-75829 [canx 1978; fate unknown]
182 0050 04	18V	(Aeroflot/Moscow)	CCCP-75830 [canx 1982; fate unknown]
182 0050 05	18V	(Aeroflot/Tajikistan)	CCCP-75831 [canx 1979; fate unknown]
182 0051 01	18V	Hans Grade Museum	DM-STE DDR-STE [canx 24Nov89; preserved Birkenheide, Germany; l/n May06]
182 0051 02	18V	(Aeroflot/Northern)	CCCP-75832 [canx 1977; fate unknown]
182 0051 03	18V	(Aeroflot/Far East)	CCCP-75833 [canx 1982; fate unknown]
182 0051 04	18V	ex AstAir	CCCP-75834 RA-75834 [wfu by Jun06 Moscow-Domodedovo, Russia; l/n 06Aug11; gone by 16Aug11 b/u?]
182 0051 05	18V	(Aeroflot/Ukraine)	CCCP-75835 [canx 1983; fate unknown]
182 0052 01	18V	(Aeroflot/Leningrad)	CCCP-75842 [last flight 26May81; canx 1982; fate unknown]
182 0052 02	18V	(Cubana)	CCCP-75836 CU-T831 [wfu by Sep84 Havana, Cuba]
182 0052 03	18V	(Aeroflot/Latvia)	CCCP-75837 [canx 1977; fate unknown]
182 0052 04	18V	(Aeroflot/Tajikistan)	CCCP-75838 [canx 1980; fate unknown]
182 0052 05	18V	(Aeroflot/Uzbekistan)	CCCP-75839 [canx 1978; fate unknown]
182 0053 01	18V	(IRS-Aero)	CCCP-75840 RA-75840 [w/o 19Nov01 nr Kalyazin, Russia]
182 0053 02	18V	(Aeroflot/Kazakhstan)	CCCP-75481 75841 CCCP-75481 [canx 1980; fate unknown]
182 0053 03	18V	(Aeroflot/Moscow)	CCCP-75843 [w/o 29Nov62 location unknown; canx same date]
182 0053 04	18V	(Aeroflot/Moscow)	CCCP-75844 [canx 1978; preserved by Jly96 Nikolayev town, Ukraine; b/u after May02]
182 0053 05	18V	(Aeroflot/Moscow)	CCCP-75845 [canx 1983; fate unknown]
182 0054 01	18V	(Aeroflot/Uzbekistan)	CCCP-75846 [canx 1984; fate unknown]
182 0054 02	18V	(Aeroflot/Magadan)	CCCP-75847 [canx 1983; fuselage extant Jly94-May95 Magadan, Russia; gone by Aug96]
182 0054 03	18V	(Aeroflot/Far East)	CCCP-75848 [canx 1982; fate unknown]
182 0054 04	18V	(Aeroflot/Krasnoyarsk)	CCCP-75849 [canx 1977; fate unknown]
182 0054 05	18V	(Aeroflot/Uzbekistan)	CCCP-75850(1) [canx 1977; fate unknown]
182 0055 01	18Gr	(Expo Aviation)	CCCP-75851 CU-T832 CCCP-75851 RA-75851 EX-026 UR-CEV UR-CFR [stored 27Nov07 Fujairah, UAE; l/n 10Apr09 being b/u; canx 03Feb10]
182 0055 02	18V	(Aeroflot/West Siberia)	CCCP-75852 [canx 1982; fate unknown]
182 0055 03	18V	(Aeroflot/Kazakhstan)	CCCP-75853 [canx 1978; derelict by Apr93 Aktyubinsk, Kazakhstan; l/n Jan03]
182 0055 04	18V	(Aeroflot/Far East)	CCCP-75854 [canx 1982; fate unknown]
182 0055 05	18Gr	Magyar Repulestorteneti Muzeum	HA-MOE [preserved 22Apr87 Szolnok, Hungary; l/n Aug08]
182 0056 01	18V	ex Trast Aero	CCCP-06160 CCCP-75423 RA-75423 EX-603 [canx 19Mar09; l/n wfu 19Aug09 Zhukovski, Russia]
182 0056 02	18V	(Balkan)	LZ-BEM [w/o 03Mar73 near Moscow-Sheremetyevo, USSR]
182 0056 03	18V	(Aeroflot/Northern)	CCCP-75856 [canx 1978; fate unknown]
182 0056 04	18V	(Aeroflot/Urals)	CCCP-75857 [canx 1978; derelict by Apr93 Sverdlovsk-Koltsovo, Russia; l/n Jly06; gone by Aug07]
182 0056 05	18V	(Aeroflot/Kazakhstan)	CCCP-75877 [canx 1978; fate unknown]
182 0057 01	18V	(Aeroflot/Krasnoyarsk)	CCCP-75878 [canx 1977; fate unknown]
182 0057 02	18V	(Aeroflot/Azerbaijan)	CCCP-75858 [canx 1977; fate unknown]
182 0057 03	18V	(Aeroflot/Northern)	CCCP-75859 [canx 1978; was preserved Rzhevka, USSR, remains noted between 1991 & 2002]
183 0057 04	18V	(Soviet Air Force)	CCCP-75668(2) [w/o 19Oct64 Mount Avala, nr Belgrade, Yugoslavia]
183 0057 05	18V	(Aeroflot/West Siberia)	CCCP-75860 [canx 1982; fate unknown]
183 0058 01	18V	(Aeroflot/Krasnoyarsk)	CCCP-75861 [canx 1978; fate unknown]
183 0058 02	18V	(Aeroflot/Azerbaijan)	CCCP-75862 [canx 1977; fate unknown]
183 0058 03	18V	(Aeroflot/Northern)	CCCP-75863 [canx 1978; fate unknown]
183 0058 04	18V	(Aeroflot/Kyrgyzstan)	CCCP-75864 [canx 1978; fate unknown]
183 0058 05	18V	(Aeroflot/Urals)	CCCP-75865 [canx 1982; fate unknown]
183 0059 01	18V	(Aeroflot/Krasnoyarsk)	CCCP-75866 [w/o 04Apr63 near Urakhcha, Tatarstan, USSR; canx 28Apr64]
183 0059 02	18V	(Aeroflot/Uzbekistan)	CCCP-75867 [canx 1977; fate unknown]
183 0059 03	18V	(Aeroflot/Urals)	CCCP-75868 [canx 1984; fate unknown]
183 0059 04	18V	(Aeroflot/Tajikistan)	CCCP-75869 [last flight 07May76 & to GIA; canx1979; then preserved by 1990s Khujand, Tajikistan; l/n Oct07, poor condition]
183 0059 05	18V	G-R Avia	CCCP-75870 YE-AYE 4W-ABO LZ-BEU LZ-BFU EX-75427 3X-GEZ [l/n 17Apr09 Fujairah, UAE; sitting on its tail]
183 0060 01	18T	(Aeroflot/Azerbaijan)	CCCP-75871 [canx 1976; fate unknown]
183 0060 02	18V	(Aeroflot/Kazakhstan)	CCCP-75872 [canx 1978; fate unknown]
183 0060 03	18V	(Aeroflot/Krasnoyarsk)	CCCP-75873 [canx 1982; b/u post Jun83 Moscow-Bykovo, USSR]

ILYUSHIN Il-18 and Il-20, Il-22 and Il-38

C/n	Model	Last known Owner/Operator	Identities/fates/comments (where appropriate)
183 0060 04	18V	(Aeroflot/Turkmenistan)	CCCP-75874 [canx 1984; by 18May96 dumped Ashgabat, Turkmenistan]
183 0060 05	18V	(Aeroflot/Krasnoyarsk)	CCCP-75875 [canx 1978; fate unknown]
183 0061 01	18V	(Aeroflot/Armenia)	CCCP-75876 [canx 1979; fate unknown]
183 0061 02	18V	(Aeroflot/Kazakhstan)	CCCP-75879 [canx 1982; by Oct05 preserved Chimkent City, Kazakhstan]
183 0061 03	18V	(Aeroflot/Kyrgyzstan)	CCCP-75880 [canx 1983; fate unknown]
183 0061 04	18V	(Aeroflot/Moscow)	CCCP-75881 [canx 1978; fate unknown]
183 0061 05	18V	(Aeroflot/Moscow)	CCCP-75882 [canx 1983; fate unknown]
183 0062 01	18V	(Aeroflot/Far East)	CCCP-75883 [canx 1983; fate unknown]
183 0062 02	18V	(Aeroflot/Moscow)	CCCP-75884 [canx 1981; dumped by Sep93 Zhukovsky, Russia ; l/n Aug99]
183 0062 03	18V	(Aeroflot/Latvia)	CCCP-75885 [canx 1978 fate unknown]
183 0062 04	18V	(Aeroflot/Moscow)	CCCP-75886 [canx 1983; fate unknown]
183 0062 05	18V	(Southern Cross)	YR-IME B-232 YR-IME 3D-AHO EL-AHO [fate unknown was to be preserved post May98 Muzeul Aviatiei, Bucharest-Otopeni, Romania]
183 0063 01	18V	(MALEV)	HA-MOF [w/o 23Nov77 Bucharest-Otopeni, Romania]
183 0063 02	18V	(Aeroflot/Moscow)	CCCP-75887 [canx 1983; fate unknown]
183 0063 03	18V	(Soviet Navy)	CCCP-75500 [canx 1983, but possibly still active in 1995; fate/status unknown]
183 0063 04	18V	(Aeroflot/West Siberia)	CCCP-75501 [canx Jan78; fate unknown]
183 0063 05	18V	(Aeroflot/Urals)	CCCP-75502 [canx 1984; fate unknown]
183 0064 01	18V	(Aeroflot/West Siberia)	CCCP-75503 [canx 1982; fate unknown]
183 0064 02	18V	(Aeroflot/Latvia)	CCCP-75504 [canx 1978; fate unknown]
183 0064 03	18V	(Aeroflot/Latvia)	CCCP-75505 [canx 1977; fate unknown]
183 0064 04	18V	(Aeroflot/Armenia)	CCCP-75506 [canx 1979; last flight 08May79 & b/u Moscow-Bykovo, USSR]
183 0064 05	18V	(Aeroflot/Moscow)	CCCP-75507 [w/o 01Oct72 near Sochi-Adler, USSR; canx 19Feb73]
183 0065 01	18V	(Aeroflot/Leningrad)	CCCP-75508 [last flight 11Apr83; canx 1983; fate unknown]
183 0065 02	18V	(Aeroflot/West Siberia)	CCCP-75509 [canx 1978; fate unknown]
183 0065 03	18V	(Aeroflot/Latvia)	CCCP-75510 [canx 1978; fate unknown]
183 0065 04	18V	(Aeroflot/Magadan)	CCCP-75511 [canx 17Jan83; fate unknown]
183 0065 05	18V	(Aeroflot/Northern)	CCCP-75512 [canx 1978; fate unknown]
183 0066 01	18V	Vologda Museum	CCCP-75518 [last flight 20Oct84; canx 1984; preserved Vologda-Grishino, Russia; l/n Aug08]
183 0066 02	18V	(Aeroflot/Krasnoyarsk)	CCCP-75514 [canx 1982; b/u Moscow-Bykovo, USSR]
183 0066 03	18V	(Aeroflot/Moscow)	CCCP-75515 [canx 1982; fate unknown]
183 0066 04	18V	Russian Air Force	CCCP-75516 RA-75516
183 0066 05	18V	(Aeroflot/Magadan)	CCCP-75517 [canx 1983; fate unknown]
183 0067 01	18V	(SIBNIA)	[static test frame]
183 0067 02	18V	(Aeroflot/Northern)	CCCP-75519 [w/o 09Jan68 Karaganda, Kazakhstan, USSR; canx 1968]
183 0067 03	18V	(Aeroflot/Uzbekistan)	CCCP-75520 [w/o 15Feb77 Mineralnye Vody, USSR; canx 1977]
183 0067 04	18V	(Aeroflot/Magadan)	CCCP-75521 [canx 1983; fate unknown]
183 0067 05	18V	(Aeroflot/Far East)	CCCP-75522 [canx 1985; fate unknown]
183 0068 01	18V	(Aeroflot/Moscow)	CCCP-75523 [canx 13Nov91; derelict by Aug92 Moscow-Domodedovo, Russia;l/n Sep93]
183 0068 02	18V	(Aeroflot/Urals)	CCCP-75524 [last flight Feb83; canx 1983; b/u Moscow-Bykovo, USSR]
183 0068 03	18V	(Aeroflot/Northern)	CCCP-75525 [last flight 14Sep79; canx; displayed in park, Pereyaslav-Khmelnitski, near Kiev, Ukraine; b/u circa 2008/2009]
183 0068 04	18V	(Aeroflot/Moscow)	CCCP-75526 [w/o 22Apr68 Moscow-Domodedovo, USSR; canx 1968]
183 0068 05	18V	(Aeroflot/Moscow)	CCCP-75527 [canx 18Aug83; displayed by 1984 or 1985 in park Sergiyev Posad (Zagorsk) Russia; DBF around 2004]
183 0069 01	18RT	Russian Navy	CCCP-75528 RA-75528
183 0069 02	18V	(Aeroflot/Moscow)	CCCP-75529 [canx 1983; fate unknown]
183 0069 03	18V	Mega Aircompany?	CCCP-75530 LZ-AZC 3D-SBC 3C-KKJ UN-75003 UP-I1803
183 0069 04	18V	(Aeroflot/Krasnoyarsk)	CCCP-75531 [w/o 02Sep64 Vuzhno Sakhalinsk, USSR; canx 24Dec64]
183 0069 05	18V	(Aeroflot/Urals)	CCCP-75536 [canx 1981; fate unknown]
184 0070 01	18V	(Aeroflot/Turkmenistan)	CCCP-75537 [canx 1983; fate unknown]
184 0070 02	18V	(Aeroflot/Urals)	CCCP-75538 [w/o 16Nov67 Sverdlovsk-Koltsovo, USSR; canx 1968]
184 0070 03	18V	(Aeroflot/Leningrad)	CCCP-75539 [canx 1982; fate unknown]
184 0070 04	18V	(Aeroflot/Urals)	CCCP-75540 [canx 1981; preserved by Nov81 in Saratov square, USSR; DBF & b/u in 1988]
184 0070 05	18V	(Aeroflot/Kazakhstan)	CCCP-75541 [canx 21Jun81; fate unknown]
184 0071 01	18V	(TABSO)	LZ-BEN [w/o 24Nov66 Bratislava, Czechoslovakia]
184 0071 02	18V	(LOT)	SP-LSD [canx 21Sep90; used as restaurant at various sites latterly in 1999 Koscielec, Poland; l/n Apr09]
184 0071 03	18V	ex MALEV	HA-MOG [wfu 06Dec88; preserved Budapest-Ferihegy, Hungary; l/n Feb09]
184 0071 04	18V	(MALEV)	HA-MOH [w/o 15Jan75 Budapest-Ferihegy, Hungary]

ILYUSHIN Il-18 and Il-20, Il-22 and Il-38

C/n	Model	Last known Owner/Operator	Identities/fates/comments (where appropriate)
184 0071 05	18GrM	ex Air GVG Company	YR-IMF B-234 YR-IMF UN-75111 [stored by summer 2004 Moscow-Domodedovo, Russia; l/n Jun08]
184 0072 01	18V	(Aeroflot/Krasnoyarsk)	CCCP-75543 [canx 1983; fate unknown]
184 0072 02	18V	(Aeroflot/Moscow)	CCCP-75544 [canx 1984; fate unknown]
184 0072 03	18V	(Aeroflot/Urals)	LZ-BER CCCP-74297 [canx 1980; fate unknown]
184 0072 04	18V	(Aeroflot/Krasnoyarsk)	CCCP-75545 [last flight 25Nov80; b/u Moscow-Bykovo, USSR; canx 1983]
184 0072 05	18V	(Aeroflot/Moscow)	CCCP-75546 [canx 1983; fate unknown]
184 0073 01	18V	ex Renan	YR-IMG ER-ICG [stored by Feb05 Sana'a, Yemen; canx 01Feb06; l/n Sep07]
184 0073 02	18V	(Aeroflot/Northern)	CCCP-75547 [canx 1979; fate unknown]
184 0073 03	18V	(Aeroflot/Turkmenistan)	CCCP-75548 [canx 1986; fate unknown]
184 0073 04	18V	(Aeroflot/Turkmenistan)	CCCP-75549 [canx 27Jan86; fate unknown]
184 0073 05	18V	Flugausstellung Junior Museum	DM-STH DDR-STH [wfs 29Apr90; last flight 05May90; canx 11Jun90; preserved spring 1994 Hermeskeil, Germany; l/n May08]
184 0074 01	18V	Alada	497+ DM-STP DDR-STP D-AOAQ UR-75475 3D-SEP^ D2-FAM [+ E Germany] [^ probable illegal regn underwing; not noted since 2003 status unclear]
184 0074 02	18V	(Aeroflot/Far East)	CCCP-75550 [canx 1983; fate unknown]
184 0074 03	18V	(Aeroflot/Kyrgyzstan)	CCCP-75551 [canx 1983; by May95 derelict Manas-Bishkek, Kyrgyzstan; l/n Nov04]
184 0074 04	18V	(Aeroflot/Latvia)	CCCP-75552 [w/o 27Aug66 Arkhangelsk-Talagi, Latvia, USSR; canx 1966]
184 0074 05	18V	Anikay Air	CCCP-75553 DM-STF(2) DDR-STF D-AOAO RA-75553 LZ-AZO EL-ADY T9-ABB EX-405
184 0075 01	18V	(Aeroflot/Moscow)	CCCP-75554 [canx Apr79; presever 20Apr79 Moscow-Sheremetyevo, Russia; dismantled May12 moved to Khimki, Russia for further preservation by Lavochkin]
184 0075 02	18T	(Aeroflot/Urals)	CCCP-75555 [canx 1985; fate unknown]
184 0075 03	18V	(Aeroflot/Latvia)	CCCP-75556 [canx 1978; to cabin trainer 12Sep87 Leningrad-Pulkovo, Russia; l/n Nov94]
184 0075 04	18V	(Aeroflot/Krasnoyarsk)	CCCP-75557 [canx 1983; fate unknown]
184 0075 05	18V	(Aeroflot/Kyrgyzstan)	CCCP-75558 [w/o 30Jan76 Frunze-Manas, Kyrgyzstan, USSR; canx 16Mar76]
184 0076 01	18V	(CAAC)	208(2)+ 218+ B-218 [+ China] [wfu 29Jun90; Nov91 at Xian, China; 1998 to Langzhou City, China]
184 0076 02	18V	CAAC Aeronautical Institute	210+ B-210 [+ China] [wfu 1988; by May94 to Tianjin Technical School; l/n preserved 17Sep09]
184 0076 03	18V	(Aeroflot/Far East)	CCCP-75564 [canx 1983; derelict by Jly94 Khabarosk-Novyy, Russia; l/n May95]
184 0076 04	18V	(Ulyanovsk Higher Flying School)	CCCP-75574 [canx 1976; fate unknown]
184 0076 05	18V	China Aviation Museum	50852+ B-230(2) "232" [+ China] [preserved Mar96 Changping, Beijing, China; painted as 232; l/n 14Oct10]
184 0077 01	18T	(Aeroflot/Krasnoyarsk)	CCCP-75569 [canx 1984; fate unknown]
184 0077 02	18V	(CAAC)	212+ B-212 [+ China] [l/n 09Oct88 Xian, China; fate/status unknown]
184 0077 03	18V	(Aeroflot/Northern)	CCCP-75559 [w/o 27Apr74 Leningrad-Pulkovo, USSR; canx 15Jly74]
184 0077 04	18V	(Soviet Government)	CCCP-75560 [w/o 24Feb68 Donetsk, USSR; canx 1986]
184 0077 05	18V	(Aeroflot/Far East)	CCCP-75561 [canx 1983; fate unknown]
184 0078 01	18V	(Aerocaribbean)	CCCP-75562 CU-T1269 [wfu & b/u Nov99 Havana, Cuba]
184 0078 02	18V	(Soviet Government)	CCCP-75563 [w/o 06Apr67 Moscow-Domodedovo, USSR; canx 19Sep67]
185 0078 03	18D	(Aeroflot/Ukraine)	CCCP-75581 [prototype Il-18D; canx 1984; fate unknown]
184 0078 04	18V	(Aeroflot/West Siberia)	CCCP-75565 [canx 1983; fate unknown]
184 0078 05	18V	(Chinese Air Force)	50851 [preserved by 1995 Han Cuhne park, south of Beijing, China; l/n May08]
184 0079 01	18V	(Aeroflot/Magadan or Krasnoyarsk)	CCCP-75566 [canx 1984; fate unknown]
184 0079 02	18V	(Aeroflot/Kazakhstan)	CCCP-75567 [canx 1982; preserved Yevpatoriva, Ukraine until b/u]
185 0079 03	18V	(Aeroflot/Leningrad)	CCCP-75568 [canx 17Jan83; fate unknown]
185 0079 04	18V	(Aeroflot/Far East)	CCCP-75570 [canx 1983; fate unknown]
185 0079 05	18V	(Aeroflot/Far East or Krasnoyarsk)	CCCP-75571 [canx 1984; fate unknown]
185 0080 01	18D	(Aeroflot/Turkmenistan)	CCCP-75572 [canx 24Oct89; but was reported operational 15Mar90; fate unknown]
185 0080 02	18V	(Soviet Army)	CCCP-75573 [canx 1985; fate unknown]
185 0080 03	18V	Russian Air Force	CCCP-75591 RA-75591 RF-91821
185 0080 04	18V	(Aeroflot/Uzbekistan)	CCCP-75575 [w/o 30Oct76 Tashkent, Uzbekistan, USSR; canx 1977]
185 0080 05	18V	(Aeroflot/Far East)	CCCP-75576 [canx 1984; fate unknown]
185 0081 01	18V	(Aeroflot/Urals)	CCCP-75577 [canx 1981; fate unknown]

ILYUSHIN Il-18 and Il-20, Il-22 and Il-38

C/n	Model	Last known Owner/Operator	Identities/fates/comments (where appropriate)
185 0081 02	18V	(Aeroflot/Armenia)	CCCP-75578 [w/o 16Oct70 Simferopol, Ukraine, USSR; canx 1970]
185 0081 03	18V	(Aeroflot/Leningrad)	CCCP-75579 [canx 17Jan83 ; used as café by Sep94 on Moscow-Kashira, Russia]
185 0081 04	18V	(Bulair)	LZ-BES [w/o 21Dec71 Sofia, Bulgaria]
185 0081 05	18V	(Balkan)	LZ-BEP [w/o 16Jun84 Sana'a, Yemen]
185 0082 01	18V	ex Balkan	LZ-BEV [preserved in a playground in Sofia, Bulgaria; DBF 1992; l/n Aug92]
185 0082 02	18V	(Aeroflot/Far East)	CCCP-75580 [canx 1984; fate unknown]
185 0082 03	18V	(Aeroflot/Far East)	CCCP-75582 [canx 1984; fate unknown]
185 0082 04	18GrM	Air Koryo	836+ P-836 [+ North Korea]
185 0082 05	18V	(Aeroflot/Uzbekistan)	CCCP-75583 [canx 1983; fate unknown]
185 0083 01	18V	(TAROM)	YR-IMH [w/o 13Aug91 Carpathian Mountains, Romania; canx 01Feb96]
185 0083 02	18V	(TAROM)	YR-IMI [w/o 21Apr77 Bucharest-Otopeni, Romania; canx 13Feb81]
185 0083 03	18V	(Aeroflot/Krasnoyarsk)	CCCP-75584 [canx 1983; fate unknown]
185 0083 04	18V	(Aeroflot/Far East)	CCCP-75585 [canx 1982; fate unknown]
185 0083 05	18V	(Aeroflot/Magadan)	101(2)+ CCCP-75593 [+ Poland] [canx 1984; fate unknown]
185 0084 01	18V	(Aeroflot/Ukraine)	CCCP-75586 [canx 1985; fate unknown]
185 0084 02	18V	(Aeroflot/West Siberia)	CCCP-75587 [canx 1981; fate unknown]
185 0084 03	18V	(Aeroflot/Ukraine)	CCCP-75588 [canx 1983; fate unknown]
185 0084 04	18GrM	(Ramaer)	DM-STI DDR-STI D-AOAP RA-75554 [w/o 17Dec97 Johannesburg, South Africa; b/u Apr00; canx 23Nov01]
185 0084 05	18V	(Aeroflot/Urals)	CCCP-75589 [canx 1984; fate unknown]
185 0085 01	18V	(Aeroflot/West Siberia)	CCCP-75590 [canx 1984; fate unknown]
185 0085 02	18E	(Aeroflot/Moscow)	CCCP-75592 [canx 1987; fate unknown]
185 0085 03	18E	ex Alada	101(3)+ SP-LSK 75711 CCCP-75850(2) UR-75850 RA-75850 UR-75850 D2-FDY [+ Poland] [wfu by 08Mar09 Luanda, Angola]
185 0085 04	18E	(Aeroflot/Ukraine)	CCCP-75594 [canx 1983; fate unknown]
185 0085 05	18D	(CAAC)	B-214 [fate/status unknown]
185 0086 01	18E	Galaxy Air?	SP-LSF LZ-BEW 3D-ALD EL-ALD EX-601
185 0086 02	18D	(Aeroflot/Urals)	YR-IMZ(1) CCCP-75445 [canx 1984; fate unknown]
185 0086 03	18E	IRBIS	SP-LSG LZ-BEZ EY-ADY+ EL-ARK 3C-KKR UN-75002 UN-I1802+ [+ not fully confirmed]
185 0086 04	18D	(Chinese Air Force)	50850 [fate/status unknown]
185 0086 05	18E	Russian Air Force	CCCP-75676(2) RA-75676
185 0087 01	18D	(CAAC)	208(3)+ B-208 [l/n 09Oct88 Xian, China; b/u post Oct88]
185 0087 02	18D	(China Agricultural Museum)	50855+ B-228 [preserved by late 1995 Beijing, China; l/n May06; gone by Sep07; b/u?]
185 0087 03	18E	(North Korean Government)	825+ 525 [+ North Korea] [fate/status unknown]
185 0087 04	18D	ex CAAC	216 B-216 [preserved by Nov91 Tun Fu Park, Chengdu, China, in China Southwest c/s]
185 0087 05	18E	(Aeroflot/Kazakhstan)	CCCP-75595 [canx 1984; wfu Karaganda, Kazakhstan; b/u by 18Sep10]
186 0088 01	18E	(Aeroflot/Moscow)	CCCP-75596 [canx 1985; fate unknown]
186 0088 02	18D	(Aerocaribbean)	CCCP-75598 RA-75598 CU-T1546 [by 16Sep09 preserved Havana Airpark, Cuba; gone by Mar12, presumably b/u]
186 0088 03	18E	(Aeroflot/Krasnoyarsk)	CCCP-75597 [canx 1984; fate unknown]
186 0088 04	18D	(Hang Khong Vietnam)?	[unknown] [possibly Hang Khong Vietnam; w/o 04Jan67 Nanking, China?]
186 0088 05	18E	(Aeroflot/Urals)	CCCP-75599 [canx 1985; by Aug95 GIA Chelyabinsk, Russia; b/u before Aug99]
186 0089 01	18E	(Aeroflot/West Siberia)	CCCP-75400 [canx 1983; fate unknown]
186 0089 02	18D	(Aeroflot/Ukraine)	CCCP-75401 [canx 1985; fate unknown]
186 0089 03	18E	(Aeroflot/Magadan)	CCCP-75402 [canx 1982; fate unknown]
186 0089 04	18D	(Balkan)	LZ-BET [wfu & in poor condition by May92 Sofia, Bulgaria; l/n Apr96]
186 0089 05	18Gr	ex Phoenix	102(2)+ SP-LSI LZ-BEH LZ-ZAH EX-75905 [+ Poland] [by 03Apr12 wfu in poor condition Djibouti]
186 0090 01	18E	(Aeroflot/Krasnoyarsk)	CCCP-75403 [canx 1986; fate unknown]
186 0090 02	18D	(Bulair)	LZ-BED [w/o 18Jan71 Zurich, Switzerland]
186 0090 03	18E	(Aeroflot/Krasnoyarsk)	CCCP-75404 [canx 1983; fate unknown]
186 0090 04	18D	(CSA)	OK-BYZ OK-VAF [wfu 23Jan90 Nurnberg, Germany; l/n 11May90; later DBF]
186 0090 05	18E	(Aeroflot/Uzbekistan)	CCCP-75405 [w/o 24Apr74 Tashkent, USSR; canx 16Jly74]
186 0091 01	18E	(TABSO)	LZ-BEG [w/o 03Sep68 Burgas, Bulgaria]
186 0091 02	18D	(Renan)	YR-IMJ ER-ICJ EL-ALY ER-ICJ [w/o 27Jan04 Luena, Angola on flight to Luanda, Angola; canx 30Mar05]
186 0091 03	18E	(Aeroflot/Moscow)	CCCP-75406 [canx 1986; fate unknown]

ILYUSHIN Il-18 and Il-20, Il-22 and Il-38

C/n	Model	Last known Owner/Operator	Identities/fates/comments (where appropriate)
186 0091 04	18D	(TAROM)	YR-IMK [w/o 09Dec74 en-route Jeddah-Cairo into Red Sea; canx 28Jly77]
186 0091 05	18E	(Aeroflot/Azerbaijan)	CCCP-75407 [canx 1978; preserved 30Aug79 Baku-Bina, Azberaijan, USSR; b/u 1980s]
186 0092 01	18E	(Aeroflot/Armenia)	CCCP-75408 [w/o en-route 06Mar76 Verkhnyaya Khava, USSR; canx 1976]
186 0092 02	18Gr	Mega Air Co	DM-STK DDR-STK D-AOAR SP-FNB SP-FNW 3D-SBW 3C-KKK UN-75004 UP-I1804
186 0092 03	18E	(Aeroflot/Far East)	CCCP-75409 [canx 1984; fate unknown]
186 0092 04	18E	(Aeroflot/Urals)	CCCP-75410 [canx 1983; fate unknown]
186 0092 05	18E	(NPP-MIR)	CCCP-75411 RA-75411 [wfu by Jun08 Pushkin, Russia; noted in poor condition]
186 0093 01	18D	(Aeroflot/Moscow)	CCCP-75412 [canx 1985; by Apr92 remains used as workman's hut Moscow-Domodedovo, Russia; l/n Sep97]
186 0093 02	18D	(Aeroflot/Urals)	CCCP-75413 [canx 1985; fate unknown]
186 0093 03	18D	(Aeroflot/Urals)	CCCP-75414 [w/o 10May79 Sochi, USSR; canx 1979]
186 0093 04	18D	(Aeroflot/Ukraine)	CCCP-75415 [canx 1982; fate unknown]
186 0093 05	18D	(Aeroflot/Krasnoyarsk)	CCCP-75416 [canx 1984; fate unknown]
186 0094 01	18D	(Aeroflot/Kazakhstan)	CCCP-75417 [canx 1983; fate unknown]
186 0094 02	18D	(Interflug)	DM-STL [w/o 26Mar79 Luanda, Angola]
186 0094 03	18D	NPP-MIR	[Soviet] CCCP-75713(2) 75713 RA-75713 75713 [Il-20 prototype ff 25Mar68; cvtd late 1992 to Il-18D]
186 0094 04	18D	(Aeroflot/Ukraine)	CCCP-75418 [canx 1984; fate unknown]
186 0094 05	18D	(Aeroflot/Tajikistan or Krasnoyarsk)	CCCP-75419 [canx 1983; fate unknown]
186 0095 01	18D	(Aeroflot/Moscow)	CCCP-75432 [canx 1983; fate unknown]
186 0095 02	18D	(Aeroflot/Turkmenistan)	CCCP-75433 [canx 1985; fate unknown]
186 0095 03	18D	(Ulyanovsk Higher Flying School)	CCCP-75434 [canx 1977; fate unknown]
186 0095 04	18D	(Aeroflot/Moscow)	CCCP-75435 [canx 1984; fate unknown]
186 0095 05	18D	(Aeroflot/West Siberia)	CCCP-75436 [w/o 20Oct68 nr Krasnoyarsk, USSR; canx 21May69]
186 0096 01	18D	(Aeroflot/Ukraine)	CCCP-75437 3X-GOD CCCP-75437 [canx 1984; fate unknown]
186 0096 02	18D	(Balkan)	CCCP-75438 LZ-BEO [wfu; after 1985 to cafe 75 km from Sofia, road Bourgas/Zlatitca; gone by Aug02]
186 0096 03	18D	(Aeroflot/Magadan)	CCCP-75439 [canx 1983; fate unknown]
187 0096 04	18D	(Aeroflot/Turkmenistan)	CCCP-75440 [canx 1985; fate unknown]
187 0096 05	18D	(CAAC)	B-220 [l/n May87; fate unknown]
187 0097 01	18D	(Aeroflot/Moscow)	CCCP-75441 [canx 1984; fate unknown]
187 0097 02	18D	Comp. Afrique d'Aviation	CCCP-75442 RA-75442 EX-75442 9Q-CAA [CofA expired Dec08; l/n 16May08 Kinshasa-N'Djili, Democratic Republic of Congo; possibly b/u]
187 0097 03	18D	China Aviation Museum	50854+ B-224 "208"+ [+ China] [preserved by Mar92 Changping, China; painted by May99 to represent Chairman Mao's aircraft; l/n 14Oct10]
187 0097 04	18D	(China United Airlines)	50853+ [+ China] [wfu Jun94 Beijing-Nan Yuan, China; Jun94; fuselage only by Oct99]
187 0097 05	18D	(CSA)	OK-WAI [w/o 05Sep67 Gander, Newfoundland]
187 0098 01	18D	(Aeroflot/West Siberia)	CCCP-75444 [canx 1983; fate unknown]
187 0098 02	18GrM	ExpoAir	YR-IMZ(2) 4R-EXD
187 0098 03	18D	(Air Guinee)	YU-AIB 7502+ YU-AIB 3X-GAX [+ Yugoslavia] [w/o 03Sep78 Conakry, Guinea]
187 0098 04	18D	Russian Navy	CCCP-75498 RA-75498
187 0098 05	18D	(Aeroflot/Krasnoyarsk)	YU-AIA 7501+ 73201+ CCCP-75780(2) [+ Yugoslavia] [cvtd Apr83 to Il-22M-II c/n 29640 09805]
187 0099 01	18D	(China Southwest Airlines)	222+ B-222 [+ China] [w/o 18Jan88 Chongqing, China]
187 0099 02	18D	China Aviation Museum	50856+ B-226 [+ China] [preserved circa 1986 Changping, China; l/n 14Oct10 as 226]
187 0099 03	18D	Grixona	YR-IML ER-ICL UR-TMD UR-CEO ER-ICS
187 0099 04	18D	Trast Aero	YR-IMM UN-75001 EX-115 EX-18001 EX-18005 3X-GGU
187 0099 05	18D	(Aeroflot/Northern or Krasnoyarsk)	CCCP-75446 [canx 1984; fate unknown]
187 0100 01	18D	(Aeroflot/Ukraine)	CCCP-75447 [canx 1983; fate unknown]
187 0100 02	18Gr	(MALEV)	HA-MOI [last flight 29Aug89 to Papa, Hungary; used as restaurant nr Györ-Ottevény, Hungary; l/n 31May08]
187 0100 03	22M-11	(Soviet Air Force)	CCCP-75448 CCCP-75928 [cvtd May84 from Il-18D; wfu by 07Jly94 Pushkin, Russia]
187 0100 04	18D	Intal Air	CCCP-75449 RA-75449 ST-APZ RA-75449 EX-75449
187 0100 05	18D	(Aeroflot/Krasnoyarsk)	CCCP-75450 [canx 1983; fate unknown]

ILYUSHIN Il-18 and Il-20, Il-22 and Il-38

C/n	Model	Last known Owner/Operator	Identities/fates/comments (where appropriate)
187 0101 01	18D	ex CSA	OK-WAJ [wfu 25Nov84, preserved by 17Sep86 Bakov nad Jizerou, Czech Republic, l/n Jan08]
187 0101 02	18D	(Aeroflot/Tajikistan or Krasnoyarsk)	CCCP-75452 [canx May86; fate unknown]
187 0101 03	18D	(Rossiya)	CCCP-75453 3X-GOF CCCP-75453 RA-75453 [b/u Mar08 Moscow-Vnukovo, Russia]
187 0101 04	18D	Rossiya	CCCP-75454 RA-75454
187 0101 05	18D	Russian Air Force	T-001+ CCCP-75451 CCCP-75917^ RA-75917^ [+ Afghanistan; ^ cvtd Mar83 to Il-22M-11; c/n 29640 17103 reported but checked with this c/n]
187 0102 01	18T	(Aeroflot/Krasnoyarsk)	CCCP-75455 [canx 01Feb89; fate unknown]
187 0102 02	18D	(Aeroflot/Moscow)	CCCP-75456 [canx 1983; fate unknown]
187 0102 03	18D	(Aeroflot/Moscow)	CCCP-75457 [canx 1985; fate unknown]
187 0102 04	18D	IRBIS	CCCP-75497 RA-75497 EL-AKQ 3D-SBQ 3C-KKL UN-75005 UP-I1801
187 0102 05	18D	(Aeroflot/Ukraine)	CCCP-75458 [canx 1983; fate unknown]
187 0103 01	18D	(Aerocaribbean)	CCCP-75459 TZ-ADF CCCP-75459 CU-T1270 [w/o 15Nov92 in Dominican Republic]
187 0103 02	18D	(Aeroflot/Tajikistan or Krasnoyarsk)	CCCP-75460 [canx 1986; reported displayed 1986-1993 Ashkhabad airport; later fire trainer]
187 0103 03	18D	(Aeroflot/Moscow)	CCCP-75461 [canx 1985; fate unknown]
187 0103 04	18D	(Domodedovo Airlines)	CCCP-75462 RA-75462 [canx 01Mar96; wfu by Aug96; b/u Jan/Feb98 Moscow-Domodedovo, Russia]
187 0103 05	22M-11	ex Russian Air Force	CCCP-75463 CCCP-75923 RA-75923(1) [cvtd from Il-18D with same c/n but new marks; wfu by Aug03 Chkalovski, Russia; l/n 17Aug09]
187 0104 01	18D	Rossiya	CCCP-75464 RA-75464
187 0104 02	18D	(Vietnam Airlines)	CCCP-75465 VN-B196 [wfu by 1990 Hanoi, Vietnam; canx 03Dec91]
187 0104 03	18GrM	S Group Aviation	CCCP-75466 RA-75466 EX-75466
187 0104 04	18D	(Aeroflot/Moscow)	CCCP-75467 [canx 17Apr84; fate unknown]
187 0104 05	18D	(Aeroflot/Northern or Krasnoyarsk)	CCCP-75468 [canx 1984; fate unknown]
187 0105 01	18D	(Aeroflot/Ukraine)	CCCP-75469 [canx 1984; fate unknown]
187 0105 02	18D	(Aeroflot/Moscow)	CCCP-75470 [canx 1984; fate unknown]
187 0105 03	18D	(Aeroflot/Ukraine)	CCCP-75471 [canx 1984; fate unknown]
187 0105 04	18D	Civil Aviation Board Museum	CCCP-74250 [canx 1983; preserved by Jun86 Ulyanovsk, Russia; l/n Jun05]
187 0105 05	18D	Vichi Air Company	CCCP-74251 CCCP-75929 ER-75929 [cvtd to Il-22M-II c/n unknown & back to Il-18D; by 04Apr09 at Chisinau, Moldova possibly wfu; l/n Sep09]
187 0106 01	18D	(Aeroflot/Far East)	CCCP-74252 [w/o en-route 29Feb68 160km from Bratsk, USSR; canx 1968]
187 0106 02	18D	(Russian Air Force)	CCCP-75472? CCCP-74295 RA-74295 [w/o 25Oct00 Mount Mtirala, near Batumi, Russia; canx 25Oct00]
188 0106 03	18D	NPP-MIR	CCCP-74296 RA-74296 ER-ICB RA-74296+ [+ reported 06Mar12 without a prefix]
188 0106 04	18D	(Air Guinea)	834+ 3X-GAT [+ North Korea] [reported wfu by 1986 Conakry, Guinea]
188 0106 05	18D	(Aeroflot/Moscow)	CCCP-74253 [canx 1983; fate unknown]
188 0107 01	18D	(Aeroflot/West Siberia)	CCCP-74254 [canx 1983; dumped by Jly92 Novosibirsk, Russia; l/n Jly93]
188 0107 02	18D	(Aeroflot/Magadan)	CCCP-74255 [canx 1984; forward fuselage to simulator by Jun97 Susuman, Russia; l/n Jun07]
188 0107 03	18D	(Vietnam Airlines)	VN-B190+ [+ tie up not confirmed; w/o 26Mar81 Hoa Bin, Vietnam]
188 0107 04	18D	(Aerocaribbean)	CCCP-74256 CU-T1268 CU-T1517 [wfu by 11Jan03 Havana, Cuba; probably l/n May06]
188 0107 05	18D	(Aeroflot/Moscow)	CCCP-74257 [canx 1985: fate unknown]
188 0108 01	18D	(Aeroflot/Krasnoyarsk)	CCCP-74258 [canx 1985; fate unknown]
188 0108 02	18Gr	(Balkan)	LZ-BEA [wfu by 23Sep97 Varna, Bulgaria; b/u]
188 0108 03	18D	(Aeroflot/Ukraine)	CCCP-74259 [canx 1984; fate unknown]
188 0108 04	18D	(Aeroflot/Magadan)	CCCP-74260 [canx 1984; reported as workman's hut 03Sep07 Moscow-Domodedovo, Russia, but not since]
188 0108 05	18GrM	Aerocaribbean	DM-STM DDR-STM D-AOAS LZ-AZZ CU-T132 CU-C132 CU-C1515
188 0109 01	18D	(Aeroflot/West Siberia)	CCCP-74261 [canx 1986; reported b/u 2001 Novosibirsk-Tolmachovo, Russia]
188 0109 02	18D	(Aeroflot/Moscow)	CCCP-74262 [canx 1984; fate unknown]
188 0109 03	18Gr	(Air Cess)	DM-STN DDR-STN D-AOAT SP-FNC SP-FNZ 3D-SBZ [canx as exported; derelict by Jly02 Kalemie, Congo; reported damaged by air attack 23Nov98; l/n Dec04]
188 0109 04	18D	ex Aerocaribbean	DM-STO DDR-STO D-AOAU LZ-AZR CU-T131 CU-T1532 [DBR 06Mar04 Holguin-Frank Pais Airport, Cuba; hulk l/n 10Mar08]

ILYUSHIN Il-18 and Il-20, Il-22 and Il-38

C/n	Model	Last known Owner/Operator	Identities/fates/comments (where appropriate)
188 0109 05	18D	(Aeroflot/Kazakhstan)	CCCP-74263 [canx 25Jan84; possibly cvtd to Il-22M-II]
188 0110 01	18D	(Aeroflot/Moscow)	CCCP-74264 [canx 1984; fate unknown]
188 0110 02	18D	(Aeroflot/Krasnoyarsk)	CCCP-74265 [canx 1984; fate unknown]
188 0110 03	18D	(Egyptair)	SU-AOV [w/o 29Jan73 Nicosia, Cyprus]
188 0110 04	18D	Russian Air Force	CCCP-75499 RA-75499
188 0110 05	18D	(Aeroflot/Turkmenistan)	SU-AOX CCCP-75430 [canx 1986; fate unknown]
188 0111 01	18D	(Aeroflot/Moscow)	SU-AOY CCCP-75429 [canx 1984; used as workman's hut by 03Sep97 Moscow-Domodedovo, Russia]
188 0111 02	18D	(Cubana)	CU-T899 [w/o 19Jan85 near San Jose de los Lajas, Cuba]
188 0111 03	18D	(Aeroflot/Magadan)	CCCP-74266 [canx 1984; fate unknown]
188 0111 04	18Gr	(Aerocaribbean)	CU-T900 CU-C900 [wfu by Apr98 Havana, Cuba; reported to become restaurant but no reports]
188 0111 05	18GrM	(Phoenix)	CCCP-74267 RA-74267 EX-105 EX-005 [w/o 04Feb04 Colombo, Sri Lanka; hulk l/n May04; gone by Nov05]
188 0112 01	18D	Central Asian Aviation	CCCP-74268 RA-74268 EX-201 EX-786 EX-505 [Kyrghyz records give registation order as EX-786 to EX-201 then EX-505, but this can be proved incorrect]
188 0112 02	18D	(Aeroflot/Magadan)	CCCP-74269 [canx 1985; fate unknown]
188 0112 03	22M-11	Russian Air Force	CCCP-74270 CCCP-75926+ [+ IL-22M-11] [cvtd post Mar85 from Il-18D; no new c/n issued but at one time c/n 29640 11203 painted on aircraft, probably in error]
188 0112 04	18D	(Hang Khong Vietnam)	VN-195+ VN-B195+ [+ c/n tie-up not confirmed; wfu by 15Dec89 Hanoi, Vietnam; canx 31Dec89]
188 0112 05	18D	Air Koryo	835+ P-835 [+ North Korea]
188 0113 01	18D	(United Arab Airlines)	SU-APC [w/o 20Mar69 Aswan, Egypt]
189 0113 02	18D	Russian Air Force	CCCP-75478 RA-75478 RF-75478
189 0113 03	18D	Russian Air Force	CCCP-75496 RA-75496
189 0113 04	18D	ex Vietnam Airlines	5T-CJL VN-B198 [wfu by Apr96 Hanoi, Vietnam; l/n 24Mar12 in very poor condition]
113 05	20		[nothing known possibly 2nd prototype IL-20]

IL-20 PRODUCTION AIRCRAFT

C/n	Model	Last known Owner/Operator	Identities/fates/comments (where appropriate)
172 0114 01	18D	Air Sirin	CCCP- UR-BXD 3X-GGQ [assumed cvtd from IL-20]
172 0114 02	18D	Russian Air Force	CCCP-75903(2) RA-75903(2)+ RF-93954 [cvtd from IL-20; + marks used concurrently on Il-22 c/n 03936 10235]
173 0114 03	20	(Russian Air Force)	[unknown] [reported w/o 07Dec95 – possibly call sign RA-54460]
173 0114 04	20	Russian Air Force	88 white
173 0114 05	20RT	ex Soviet Navy	CCCP-75480 [offered for sale Mar04 and Sep06]
173 0115 01	20M	Russian Air Force	90 red RA-75923(2) [reported with no marks 17Aug09 Chkalovski, Russia]
173 0115 02	20M	Russian Air Force	20 red
173 0115 03	20RT	Russian Navy	CCCP-75481 RA-75481
173 0115 04	20M	Russian Air Force	21 red+ RF-93610 [+ Russia]
173 0115 05	20RT	Russian Navy	CCCP-75482 RA-75482
174 0116 01	20		[nothing known]
174 0116 02	20	Russian Air Force	[no code] [noted Aug03 Puskin, Russia with no code]
174 0116 03	20	Russian Air Force	[no code] [noted 23May01 Puskin, Russia with no code]
174 0116 04	20M	Russian Air Force	[unknown] [noted 24May99 Puskin, Russia in primer; & Dec10 Rostov-na Donu AFB, Russia]
175 0116 05	20RT	Russian Navy	CCCP-75483 RA-75483 [c/n not confirmed; reported Jun12 Puskin, Russia with no code]
175 0117 01	20	Russian Air Force	[no code] [noted 03Sep93 Kubinka AFB, Russia]
17* 0117 02	20		[nothing known]
17* 0117 03	20		[nothing known]
17* 0117 04	20		[nothing known]
17* 0117 05	20		[nothing known]
175 0117 06	20M	Russian Air Force	[unknown]
176 0117 07	20	Russian Air Force	07+ RF-75931^ [+colour unknown; ^ not confirmed]
176 0117 08	20		[nothing known; perhaps not built]
176 0117 09	20		[nothing known; perhaps not built]

ILYUSHIN Il-18 and Il-20, Il-22 and Il-38

IL-22 PRODUCTION AIRCRAFT

C/n	Model	Last known Owner/Operator	Identities/fates/comments (where appropriate)
03936 07050	22	ex Russian Air Force	CCCP-75895 RA-75895 [wfu by Aug07 Chkalovski, Russia; l/n 08Sep08]
03936 07150	18D	Alada	CCCP-75896 75896 UR-75896 D2-FFR+ [+ cvtd from Il-22]
03936 07430	22	Russian Air Force	CCCP-75897 RA-75897
03936 07950	22	Russian Air Force	CCCP-75898 [c/n also reported as 03936 07930; still as CCCP-75898 02Nov08]
03936 09306	22	Russian Air Force	CCCP-75899 RA-75899
03936 09681	22	Russian Air Force	CCCP-75900 RA-75900
03936 09935	22	Russian Air Force	CCCP-75901 RA-75901
03936 10226	22	Russian Air Force	CCCP-75902 75902 RA-75902
03936 10235	22PP	Russian Air Force	CCCP-75903(1) RA-75903(1) [marks used concurrently on Il-18 c/n 172 0114 02]
unkn	22	ex Soviet Air Force	CCCP-75904 [no sightings since 1988; fate/status unknown]
03936 10270	22	Russian Air Force	CCCP-75905 RA-75905
03936 10501	22M-II	Russian Air Force	CCCP-75906 RA-75906 RF-95673
unkn	22	(Soviet Air Force)	CCCP-75907 [probably w/o 02Dec81 Domma AFB, USSR]
03940 11091	22M-II	Russian Air Force	CCCP-75908? RA-75908
03940 11092	22M-II	Russian Air Force	CCCP-75909 RA-75909
03940 11094	22M-II	Russian Air Force	CCCP-75910 RA-75910 RF-94417
03940 11096	22M-II	Russian Air Force	CCCP-75911? 75911 RA-75911
03940 11097	22M-II	Russian Air Force	CCCP-75912 RA-75912 RF-95675
03940 11098	22M-II	Russian Air Force	CCCP-75913 RA-75913
03940 17100	22M-II	Russian Air Force	CCCP-75914 RA-75914
29640 17101	22M	(Kazakhstan Government)	CCCP-75915 UN-75915 [w/o Jan95 Almaty, Kazakhstan, ground collision with an An-12; by May96 hulk to local scrapyard; l/n May04]
29640 17102	18D	(Aero Caribbean)	CCCP-75916 YL-LAO+ CU-T1539 [+ cvtd from Il-22M-II; w/o 28Mar05 Caracas, Venezuela]
29640 17103	22M-II	Russian Air Force	CCCP-75917 RA-75917 [uses Il-18D c/n 187 0101 05]
29640 17104	22M-II	Ukraine Air Force	CCCP-75918 75918
29640 09805	22M-II	Russian Air Force	CCCP-75919 [cvtd from Il-18D 187 0098 05; still CCCP-75919 16May99]
29640 17551	22M-II	Russian Air Force	CCCP-75920 RA-75920
29640 10905	22M-II	(Russian Air Force)	CCCP-75921? [registration surmised; b/u between 1998 & 2006 Akhtubinsk, Russia]
29640 17552	22M-II	Russian Air Force	CCCP-75922 RA-75922
29640 17554	22M-II	Russian Air Force	CCCP-75924 RA-75924
29640 17557	22M-II	Russian Air Force	CCCP-75925 RA-75925
29640 11203	22M-II	(Soviet Air Force)	CCCP-75926 [see c/n 100 01 1203]
29640 17558	22M-II	Russian Air Force	CCCP-75927 RA-75927 [stored by May01 Levashovo, Russia; l/n Nov08]

IL-38 PRODUCTION AIRCRAFT

C/n	Model	Last known Owner/Operator	Identities/fates/comments (where appropriate)
**** 101 06	38	ex Soviet Navy	10 red [reported has line number 1] [preserved by Apr99 Lugansk, Ukraine; l/n Jly08]
**** 101 07	38	ex Soviet Navy?	[nothing known] [reported line number 2]
**** 101 08	38	ex Soviet Navy?	[nothing known] [reported line number 3]
**** 101 09	38	ex Russian Navy	02 red [reported line number 4][stored by 11Apr12]
**** 101 10	38	ex Soviet Navy?	[nothing known] [reported line number 5]
**** 102 06	38	ex Soviet Navy?	[nothing known] [reported line number 6]
**** 102 07	38	ex Soviet Navy?	[nothing known] [reported line number 7]
**** 102 08	38	ex Soviet Navy?	[nothing known] [reported line number 8]
**** 102 09	38	ex Soviet Navy?	[nothing known] [reported line number 9]
**** 102 10	38	ex Soviet Navy?	[nothing known] [reported line number 10]
**** 103 06	38	ex Soviet Navy?	[nothing known] [reported line number 11]
**** 103 07	38	ex Soviet Navy?	[nothing known] [reported line number 12]
**** 103 08	38	ex Soviet Navy?	[nothing known] [reported line number 13]
**** 103 09	38	ex Soviet Navy?	[nothing known] [reported line number 14]
**** 103 10	38	ex Soviet Navy?	[nothing known] [reported line number 15]
**** 104 06	38	ex Soviet Navy?	[nothing known] [reported line number 16]
8900 104 07	38N	Russian Navy	15 yellow [reported line number 17]
8900 104 08	38	Russian Navy	[unknown] [reported line number 18]
**** 104 09	38	Ukraine Air Force	09 red+ [reported line number 19] [+ c/n tie-up only possible; 14-09 on nose wheel door]
**** 104 10	38	ex Soviet Navy	[unknown] [reported line number 20] [possible Ukraine Air Force aircraft]
**** 105 06	38	Russian Navy	06 red [reported line number 21]
**** 105 07	38	Russian Navy	07 red [reported line number 22]

ILYUSHIN Il-18 and Il-20, Il-22 and Il-38

C/n	Model	Last known Owner/Operator	Identities/fates/comments (where appropriate)
**** 105 08	38	ex Soviet Navy?	[nothing known] [reported line number 23]
**** 105 09	38	ex Soviet Navy?	[nothing known] [reported line number 24]
**** 105 10	38	ex Soviet Navy?	[nothing known] [reported line number 25]
**** 106 06	38	ex Soviet Navy?	[nothing known] [reported line number 26]
**** 106 07	38	ex Soviet Navy?	[nothing known] [reported line number 27]
**** 106 08	38	ex Soviet Navy?	[nothing known] [reported line number 28]
**** 106 09	38	ex Soviet Navy?	[nothing known] [reported line number 29]
**** 106 10	38	ex Soviet Navy?	[nothing known] [reported line number 30]
**** 107 06	38N	Russian Navy	19 red [reported line number 31] [prototype Il-38N; ff 04Apr01]
**** 107 07	38	ex Soviet Navy?	[nothing known] [reported line number 32]
**** 107 08	38	Russian Navy	01 red+ [reported line number 33; + tie up not fully confirmed]
**** 107 09	38	ex Soviet Navy?	[nothing known] [reported line number 34]
**** 107 10	38	ex Soviet Navy?	[nothing known] [reported line number 35]
0800 108 06	38	ex Soviet Navy?	[nothing known] [reported line number 36]
**** 108 07	38	ex Soviet Navy?	[nothing known] [reported line number 37]
**** 108 08	38	Russian Navy	21 red [reported line number 38]
**** 108 09	38	ex Soviet Navy?	[nothing known] [reported line number 39]
0810 108 10	38	Russian Navy	23 red [reported line number 40]
0810 109 06	38	Russian Navy	24 red [reported line number 41; c/n painted as 080110906 in error]
081 0109 07	38	Russian Navy	25 red [reported line number 42]
081 0109 08	38	Russian Navy	26 red [reported line number 43] [stored by 11Apr12 Nikolayeka, Russia]
**** 109 09	38	ex Soviet Navy?	[nothing known] [reported line number 44]
081 0109 10	38	Russian Navy	21 red [reported line number 45]
**** 110 06	38	Russian Navy	22 red [reported line number 46]
**** 110 07	38	ex Soviet Navy?	[nothing known] [reported line number 47]
**** 110 08	38	ex Soviet Navy?	[nothing known] [reported line number 48]
08* 0110 09	38	Russian Navy	77 red [reported line number 49] [stored by 11Apr12 Nikolayeka, Russia]
**** 110 10	38	ex Soviet Navy?	[nothing known] [reported line number 50]
082 0111 06	38	(Russian Navy)	79 red [reported line number 51] [wfu by May01 Puskin, Russia; b/u by 2006]
082 0111 07	38	Russian Navy	73 red+ [reported line number 52] [+ tie up not confirmed]
082 0111 08	38	Russian Navy	74 red [reported line number 53] [stored by 11Apr12 Nikolayeka, Russia]
082 0111 09	38	Russian Navy	75 red [reported line number 54] [stored by 11Apr12 Nikolayeka, Russia]
082 0111 10	38	Russian Navy	76 red [reported line number 55] [wfu by 09Apr12 Vladivostok-Knevostok, Russia]
082 0112 06	38	Russian Navy	72 red [reported line number 56] [stored by 11Apr12 Nikolayka, Russia]
082 0112 07	38	Russian Navy	71 red [reported line number 57]
082 0112 08	38	Russian Navy	70 red [reported line number 58] [last built Il-38] [+ tie up not confirmed]
082 0112 09	38	ex Russian Navy	73 red [stored 11Apr12]
Unidentified			
unkn	38	(Soviet Navy)	11 red [dbr 09Mar84 Asmara, Eritrea; hit by shells]
unkn	38	(Soviet Navy)	28 red [dbr 09Mar84 Asmara, Eritrea; hit by shells]
unkn	38	Russian Navy	05 red [from photo]
unkn	38	Russian Navy	06 red [reported 07Jly94 Pushkin, Russia; based mid 1990s Ostrov, Russia]
unkn	38	Russian Navy	08 red [reported 07Jly94 Pushkin, Russia; stored there Sep02/Jan09]
unkn	38	Russian Navy	09 red [reported 07Jly94 Pushkin, Russia; based mid 1990s Severomorsk-1, Russia; l/n 09Aug06]
unkn	38	(Russian Navy)	09 red [w/o 03Feb94 on night training flight from Severomorsk, Russia]
unkn	38	Russian Navy	10 red [reported 07Jly94 & 25Aug99 Pushkin, Russia; probably the same aircraft]
unkn	38	Russian Navy	11 red [reported 07Aug99 Pushkin, Russia]
unkn	38	Russian Navy	12 red [from photo]
unkn	38	Russian Navy	15 red [from photo]
unkn	38	Russian Navy	15 yellow [reported 17Aug09 Zhukovsky, Russia]
unkn	38	Russian Navy	16 red [based Severomorsk-1, Russia and reported there 09Aug06]
unkn	38	Russian Navy	17 red [based mid 1990s Severomorsk-1, Russia]
unkn	38	Russian Navy	20 red [based mid 1990s Ostrov, Russia]
unkn	38	Russian Navy	23 red [reported 05Aug01 Pushkin, Russia; same aircraft as c/n 0810 108 10 above?]
unkn	38	Russian Navy	24 red [reported 17Jun06 Petrozavodsk, Russia]
unkn	38	Ukraine Air Force	74 red [reported]

ILYUSHIN Il-18 and Il-20, Il-22 and Il-38

C/n	Model	Last known Owner/Operator	Identities/fates/comments (where appropriate)	
unkn	18	Chinese Air Force	230	[reported 12Apr63 Jakarta-Soekarno Hatta, Indonesia; note c/n 184007605 now painted with these marks]
unkn	18	Chinese Air Force	232(1)	reported 21Jly67 flew Hankou to Shanghai, China; also see c/n 184007605]
unkn	18	Chosonminghang (North Korea)	824	[from old photo]
unkn	38	Egyptian Air Force	38	[operated by Soviet Navy 1971/1972 from Mersah Matruh, Egypt; from drawing; returned to USSR]
unkn	38	Egyptian Air Force	4299	[operated by Soviet Navy 1971/1972 from Mersah Matruh, Egypt; from photo; returned to USSR]
unkn	38	Egyptian Air Force	4399	[possibly misreading of 4299]
unkn	38SD	Indian Navy	IN301	[ex Soviet Navy; based by Jun78 Goa-Dabolim, India; l/n 12Feb09]
unkn	38	(Indian Navy)	IN302	[ex Soviet Navy; based by Jun78 Goa-Dabolim, India; w/o 01Oct02 over Goa in mid-air collision with Il-38 IN304]
unkn	38SD	Indian Navy	IN303	[ex Soviet Navy; based by Jun78 Goa-Dabolim, India; l/n 12Feb09]
unkn	38	(Indian Navy)	IN304	[ex Soviet Navy; based by Oct84 Goa-Dabolim, India; w/o 01Oct02 over Goa in mid-air collision with Il-38 IN302]
unkn	38SD	Indian Navy	IN305	[ex Soviet Navy; based by Oct84 Goa-Dabolim, India; l/n 09Feb09]
unkn	38SD	Indian Navy	IN306	[ex Russian Navy, attrition replacement; delvered 03Dec09]
unkn	38SD	Indian Navy	IN307	[ex Russian Navy, attrition replacement; noted 19Dec09 Zhukovsky, Russia]
unkn	18	Aeroflot/Polar	CCCP-04350	[delivered 1964]
unkn	18	Aeroflot/Polar	CCCP-04770	[delivered 1964]
unkn	18	Russian Air Force	RA-42246	[reported May06 on Russian AFB]
unkn	18D	ex Soviet Air Force	74626	[reported Girua, Papua New Guinea]
unkn	18	Soviet Air Force	CCCP-75474	[reported 16Nov75 Eberswalde, East Germany & 1978 Moscow-Vnukovo, USSR]
unkn	18V	Aeroflot	CCCP-75855	[reported 02Oct72 Moscow-Vnukovo, USSR]
unkn	18	Russian Air Force	RA-75490	[reported 04Jly11 Pushkin, Russia]
unkn	18	Alada	D2-FDL	[reported 05Feb03 Luanda, Angola; possible error for D2-FDY]
unkn	18	Congo Air Force	TN-105	[reported]
unkn	18D	Air Guinee	3X-GOC	[local report leased from Aeroflot]
unkn	18D	Air Guinee	3X-GOE	[local report leased from Aeroflot]
unkn	20	Soviet Air Force	08	[reported 01Sep81 Moscow-Sheremetyevo, USSR]

Production complete

ILYUSHIN Il-114

C/n	Line No.	Model	Last known Owner/Operator	Identities/fates/comments (where appropriate)
(01 01)	01 01		Ilyushin OKB	CCCP-54000 RA-54000 [prototype ff 29Mar90; stored by Aug03 Zhukovski, Russia; l/n Aug07]
(01 02)	01 02		Ilyushin OKB	[static test airframe]
(01 03)	01 03		(Ilyushin OKB)	CCCP-54001 RA-54001 [w/o 05Jly93 Zhukovski, Russia]
(01 04)	01 04		Ilyushin OKB	[fatigue test airframe]
(01 05)	01 05		ex Ilyushin OKB	CCCP-54002 RA-54002 [derelict by Aug97 Zhukovski, Russia; l/n Aug07]
23024	01 06		Vyborg	UK-91001 RA-91014 [c/n 10238 23024] [reported for Pskovavia]
28025	01 07		Vyborg	UK-91000 RA-91015 [c/n 10338 28025] [reported for Pskovavia]
30030	01 08		ex Ilyushin OKB	RA-91002 [c/n 10338 30030] [survey aircraft; wfu by Aug01 Zhukovski, Russia; l/n Aug07]
109	01 09	LL	Russian Navy	RA-91003 [c/n 20538 00109] [flying laboratory]
00110?	01 10			[nothing known] [c/n 10.38 00110?]
00201?	02 01		ex Uzbekistan Airways	UK-91006 [c/n 10.38 00201?] [stored by 28Feb05 Tashkent-Vostochny, Uzbekistan; canx by Dec07]
00202	02 02		Uzbekistan Airways	UK-91009 UK-91102 [c/n 10638 00202]
00203?	02 03			[nothing known] [c/n 10.38 00203?]
00204	02 04	100	Uzbekistan Airways	UK-91104 [c/n 20938 00204]
00205	02 05	100	Uzbekistan Airways	91105 UK-91105 [c/n 20638 00205]
00206	02 06	100	Uzbekistan Airways	91106 UK-91106 [c/n 20838 00206]
00207	02 07	100	Uzbekistan Airways	UK-91107 [c/n .21038 00207]
00208?	02 08		Uzbekistan Airways	91108 UK-91108 [c/n 10.38 00208?]
00209?	02 09		for Uzbekistan Airways	91109 [c/n 10.38 00209?] [for 2012 delivery]
00210?	02 10			[c/n 10.38 00210?] [reported 28Feb05 Tashkent-Vostochny, Uzbekistan]
00301	03 01	T	Ilyushin OKB	RA-91005 UK-91005 [c/n 10638 00301] [stored Tashkent-Vostochny, Uzbekistan]
00302?	03 02			[c/n 10.38 00302?] [nothing known]
00303?	03 03			[c/n 10.38 00303?] [nothing known]
00304?	03 04			[c/n 10.38 00304?] [nothing known]
00305	03 05	T	(Tashkent Aircraft Production Organisation)	UK-91004 [c/n 10838 00305] [w/o 04Dec99 Moscow-Domodedovo, Russia]
Unidentified				
unkn			ex Uzavialeasing/Vyborg	UK-91011 RA-91011 [not delivered & stored Mar09 Tashkent-Vostochny, Uzbekistan]

ISRAEL AIRCRAFT INDUSTRIES IAI-101 ARAVA

Note: Unidentified Mexican Aravas were w/o as follows: 31May89 nr Mexico City, 25Jun93 Chihuahua State, 16Sep98 Chiapas State, plus one other in 1998.

C/n	Model	Last known Owner/Operator	Identities/fates/comments (where appropriate)
0001			[Static test airframe]
0002	101	(Israel Aircraft Industries)	4X-IAI [prototype ff 27Nov69; [w/o 19Nov70 Tulkarm, Central Palestine]]
0003	201	(Israel Defence Force Air Force)	4X-IAA 4X-FDA [b/u Feb80]
0004	101A	ex Guatemalan Air Force	4X-IAB 04+ 4X-IAB TG-SAB 897 [+ Israel] [stored Guatemala City-La Aurora, Guatemala; l/n 28Nov11; yet to enter service]
0005	201	(Mexican Air Force)	4X-IAC BRE-01//XC-GAW BRE-2001 [w/o 26Feb94 in Culiacan State, Mexico]
0006	201	(Nicaraguan Air Force)	4X-IAD AN-BIR 419+ 223 [+ Nicaragua] [w/o 14Aug82 near Managua-Sandino Airport, Nicaragua]
0007	201	(Mexican Air Force)	4X-IAE BRE-02//XC-GAX BRE-2002 [w/o see note below*]
0008	201	Mexican Air Force	4X-IAF BRE-03//XC-GEB BRE-2003+ 3003 [+ Mexico]
0009	201	(Mexican Air Force)	4X-IAG BRE-04//XC-GEC BRE-2004 [w/o see note below*]
0010	201	Mexican Air Force	4X-IAH BRE-05//XC-GED BRE-2005+ 3005 [+ Mexico]
0011	201	(Ecuadorian Army)	4X-IAJ T-201 [probably w/o details unclear; one report suggests w/o 23Mar91 near Marcas, Morona Santiago, Ecuador; this is a similar fate to c/n 0023 qv]
0012	201	Ecuadorian Army	4X-IAK T-202+ AEE-202 [+ Ecuador]
0013	201	ex El Salvador Air Force	4X-IAL 801 [returned Sep02 to Israel via the UK; nothing more known]
0014	201	(El Salvador Air Force)	4X-IAM 802 [w/o 1980, no further details]
0015	201	Ecuadorian Army	4X-IAN T-203+ AEE-203 [+ Ecuador]
0016	102	ex Guatemalan Air Force	4X-IAO HK-2870X CP-1946 4X-IAO 4X-FDB 4X-IAO 816 [stored Guatemala City-La Aurora, Guatemala; fuselage only noted 28Oct11]
0017	201	ex El Salvador Air Force	4X-IAP 803 [returned Sep02 to Israel via the UK; nothing more known]
0018	201	ex El Salvador Air Force	4X-IAQ 804 [returned Sep02 to Israel via the UK; nothing more known]
0019	201	(Ecuadorian Army)	4X-IAR T-204+ AEE-204 [+Ecuador] [w/o 27Jun95 Pastaza-Shell AFB, Ecuador]
0020	201	(Ecuadorian Navy)	4X-IAS ANE-402 ANE-202 [+Ecuador] [w/o 08/09Jun88 near Aroma, Manabi, Ecuador]
0021	201	(Bolivian Air Force)	4X-IAT TAM-75 [wfu & dismantled by Oct94 La Paz, Bolivia]
0022	201	(Guatemalan Air Force)	4X-IAU 808 [w/o by 1983; later b/u Guatemala City-La Aurora, Guatemala]
0023	201	(Ecuadorian Army)	4X-IAV T-205+ AEE-205 [+Ecuador] [w/o 23/25Mar91 near Marcas, Morona Santiago, Ecuador]
0024	201	(Bolivian Air Force)	4X-IAW TAM-76 [w/o 02Mar76 in jungle, en-route Cameri-Itaguasurenda, Bolivia]
0025	201	Guatemalan Air Force	4X-IAX 816 [stored Guatemala City-La Aurora, Guatemala; l/n 23Nov07]
0026	201	(Bolivian Air Force)	4X-IAY TAM-77 [w/o 16Mar77 unknown location, Bolivia]
0027	201	(Guatemalan Air Force)	4X-IAZ 824 [w/o 1981 Poptun, Guatemala; wreck recovered to Guatemala City-La Aurora, Guatemala; l/n 28Oct11]
0028	201	Guatemalan Air Force	4X-IBA 832
0029	201	Guatemalan Air Force	4X-IBB 840 [stored Guatemala City-La Aurora, Guatemala; fuselage only noted 28Oct11]
0030	201	Bolivian Air Force	4X-IBC TAM-78 [l/n 04May76; status?]
0031	201	Honduran Air Force	4X-IBD 316 [w/o 09Jan01; by 2003 wreck dumped Toncontin AFB, Honduras; l/n 24Nov07]
0032	201	Bolivian Air Force	4X-IBE TAM-79 [l/n 21Jun76; status?]
0033	201	Guatemalan Air Force	4X-IBF 848 [stored Guatemala City-La Aurora, Guatemala; fuselage only noted 28Oct11]
0034	201	Honduran Air Force	4X-IBG 317
0035	201	Mexican Air Force	4X-IBH XC-BIY BRE-2008+ 3008 [+ Mexico]
0036	201	Mexican Air Force	4X-IBI XC-BIW BRE-2006+ 3006 [+ Mexico]
0037	201	Mexican Air Force	4X-IBJ XC-BIZ BRE-2009+ 3009 [+ Mexico]
0038	201	(Guatemalan Air Force)	4X-IBK 856 [w/o post Aug83]
0039	201	(Mexican Air Force)	4X-IBL XC-BIX BRE-2007 [w/o see note below*]
0040	201	(Mexican Air Force)	4X-IBM XC-BOA BRE-2010 3010 [w/o 20Apr12 El Zorrillo, Mexico]
0041	102	Gobierno de la Provincia de Salta	4X-IBN LV-PZU LV-MHP
0042	201	Bolivian Air Force	4X-IBO TAM-80 [l/n 10Nov76, status?]
0043	201	ex Aviacion de Chiapas	4X-IBP VR-CAF XA-LON [possibly to Mexican Air Force 1993 or 1994 & used for spares]
0044	201	(Ecuadorian Navy)	4X-IBQ ANE-234 [w/o 29Apr79 Eastern Ecuador]
0045	201	Guatemalan Air Force	4X-IBR 864 [status unknown; not noted on maintenance board 23Nov07]

ISRAEL AIRCRAFT INDUSTRIES IAI-101 ARAVA

C/n	Model	Last known Owner/Operator	Identities/fates/comments (where appropriate)
0046	102	Joint Aviation Distribution	4X-IBS LV-PIJ LV-OLS N307CL N302CL [stored Fort Lauderdale Executive, FL; l/n 12Nov11]
0047	201	Guatemalan Air Force	4X-IBT 872 [stored Guatemala City-La Aurora, Guatemala; l/n 28Oct11]
0048	201	Guatemalan Air Force	4X-IBU 880 [stored 2006 Guatemala City-La Aurora, Guatemala; l/n 28Oct11]
0049	201	Venezuelan National Guard	4X-IBV GN7952 [status unknown]
0050	102	Venezuelan Army	4X-IBW YV-O-MAR-3 EV9959
0051	201	(Venezuelan National Guard)	4X-IBX GN7953 [w/o 23Jly79 Matthews Ridge, Venezuela en-route Ciudad Bolviar Airport to Santa Elena Airport]
0052	102	ex Owl Aerospace Inc	4X-IBY LV-PAP LV-MRR LQ-MRR N30299 [canx 30May02 as sold in Mexico; no reports]
0053	102	Mexican Air Force	4X-IBZ LV-PAR LV-MRS N30682 3015
0054	102	(Secretaria de Gobernacion)	4X-ICA LV-PBN LV-MRX [w/o 21Nov79 Navarino Island, Chile]
0055	102	Mexican Air Force	4X-ICB LV-PBO LV-MRY N58590 3016
0056	201	Royal Thai Air Force	4X-ICC 40456+ 60509+ BTL7-1/22//40203 [+ Thailand; serial followed by code after double slash]
0057	201	Royal Thai Air Force	4X-ICD 40457+ 60510+ BTL7-2/22//40204 [+ Thailand; serial followed by code after double slash]
0058	201	Royal Thai Air Force	4X-ICE 40458+ 60511+ BTL7-3/22//40205 [+ Thailand; serial followed by code after double slash]
0059	102	ex Swaziland Government	4X-ICF 3D-DAA [wfu 2006 Matsapha, Swaziland for spares; hulk l/n 25Oct10]
0060	102	(Swaziland Government)	4X-ICG 3D-DAB [w/o 15Jan80 Songe, Malawi]
0061	102	Gob.TNAC.de Tierra del Fuego	4X-ICH LV-PCP LV-MTP [status unknown]
0062	201	(Venezuelan Army)	4X-ICI EV8012 [w/o 24Oct99 San Carlos, Cojedes State, Venezuela]
0063	201	Venezuelan Army	4X-ICJ EV8014
0064	201	(Venezuelan National Guard)	4X-ICK GN7960 [w/o 28Feb90 near La Carlota Airport, Avila mountains, Venezuela]
0065	201	(Colombian Air Force)	4X-ICL 951 [w/o 02Jun82 Puerto Rondon, Colombia]
0066	201	Colombian Air Force	4X-ICM FAC952+ FAC1952 [Colombia]
0067	102	(Provincia de Formosa)	4X-ICN LV-PGB 4X-CUA LV-POA LV-ASZ [b/u Jun07]
0068	201	(Colombian Air Force)	4X-ICO 953 [w/o before Aug90; wreck noted Bogota-Eldorado, Colombia Aug90]
0069	102	ex Aviacion de Chiapas	4X-ICP XC-CUO XA-PUG XA-DUG+ XC-HIU XA-MIS [+ marks in question as also used on DC-10; possibly to Mexican Air Force 1993 or 1994 and used for spares]
0070	102	(Swaziland Government)	4X-ICQ 3D-DAC [w/o 20Nov04 strip in SE Swaziland]
0071	201	(Venezuelan National Guard)	4X-ICS GN8168 [w/o 05May06 12 miles N of Caracas-Simon Bolivar Airport, Venezuela]
0072	101B	Israel Defence Air Force	4X-ICT N525MW 4X-ICT 4X-JUA//101 [stored Tel Aviv; Israel; end 2007 for sale by tender; l/n 04May08]
0073	101B	Mexican Air Force	4X-ICU NI81AC XA-RAA XB-FPN 3011
0074	101B	Mexican Air Force	4X-ICV N601AE XA-RAB XB-FPO 3012
0075	101B	(Mexican Air Force)	4X-ICW N701AE XA-RAC XB-FPP + 3013 [w/o see note below*]
0076	101B	Mexican Air Force	4X-CUA N801AE XA-RAD XB-FPQ + 3014
0077	101B	Liberian Army	4X-CUD EL-AJG
0078	101B	(Liberian Army)	4X-CUJ EL-AJH [w/o 08Oct89 Sasstown Airport, Liberia]
0079	101B	(Venezuelan Air Force)	4X-CVA 4X-CUT (EL-AJI) 4X-CUU 4X-CST 6944 [w/o 23Mar94 Buena Vista, Venezuela]
0080	101B	Israel Defence Air Force	303//4X-JUC [reported re-built as c/n 100] [stored Tel Aviv; Isreal; end 2007 for sale by tender; l/n 04May08]
0081	101B	Cameroon Government	4X-IAC 4X-CUP TJ-AAS
0082	201	Papua New Guinea DF	4X-CUQ P2-021 [stored by Dec89]
0083	201	Papua New Guinea DF	4X-CUR P2-022 [stored by Dec89]
0084	201	Papua New Guinea DF	4X-CUS P2-023 [stored by Dec89]
0085	201	Haitian Air Force	4X-CUT 1283
0086	201		[nothing known]
0087	201	(Venezuelan Army)	4X-CUG EV9047 [wfu by Dec07 Caracas-Charallave, Venezuela]
0088	201	Venezuelan National Guard	4X-CUE GN8575
0089	201	Venezuelan National Guard	4X-CUF GN8578
0090	201	Ecuadorian Army	4X-CUG T-206 AEE-206
0091	201	Ecuadorian Army	4X-CUH T-207 AEE-207
0092			[reported for Israel Defence Force Air Force; aircraft but built]
0093			[reported for Israel Defence Force Air Force; aircraft but built]

ISRAEL AIRCRAFT INDUSTRIES IAI-101 ARAVA

C/n	Model	Last known Owner/Operator	Identities/fates/comments (where appropriate)
0094			[reported for Israel Defence Force Air Force; aircraft but built]
0095			[reported for Israel Defence Force Air Force; aircraft but built]
0096			[reported for Israel Defence Force Air Force; aircraft but built]
0097			[reported for Israel Defence Force Air Force; aircraft but built]
0098			[reported for Israel Defence Force Air Force; aircraft but built]
0099	201	Venezuelan National Guard	4X-CST GN8595
0100			[reported built as, or re-build of, c/n 0080]
0101	202	Israel Air Force Museum	4X-ICR 4X-CUC 4X-ICU 203//4X-JUB [dual marks] [preserved Hatzerim AFB, Israel; l/n 09Dec08]
0102	202	Venezuelan Army	4X-CVC EV8118
0103	202	Venezuelan Army	4X-CVD EV8119
0104	202	El Salvador Air Force	4X-CUL 205//4X-FDD+ YS-07N 801 [+ dual marks]
0105	102	Cameroon Air Force	4X-CUH TJ-XCA
0106	202	Israel Defence Force Air Force	209//4X-JUE+ [dual marks] [wfu; for sale by tender end 2007; l/n 04May08]
0107	202	El Salvador Air Force	211//4X-JUF+ YS-08N 802^ [+ dual marks; ^ not confirmed]
0108	202	Israel Defence Force Air Force	212//4X-JUG+ [dual marks] [wfu; for sale by tender end 2007; l/n 04May08]
0109	202	Israel Defence Force Air Force	215//4X-JUH+ [dual marks] [wfu; for sale by tender end 2007; l/n 04May08]
0110	202	El Salvador Air Force	217//4X-JUI+ YS-09N 803^ [+ dual marks; ^ not confirmed]

Production complete

LET 410 AND 420 TURBOLET

Notes: Many aircraft used test marks in the OK-120 to OK-178 range.
The c/ns of late production aircraft do not include the first two characters, indicating the year built.

NON UVP PRODUCTION

C/n	Model	Last known Owner/Operator	Identities/fates/comments (where appropriate)
001	XL-410	ex Letecke Zavodu (LET Aircraft Factory)	OK-60 OK-61 OK-YKE [f/f 16Apr69] [wfu by end 1983; preserved different locations until renovated for display at LET Factory Museum, Kunovice, Czech Republic; l/n May10]
002			[static test airframe; wfu 15Sep96]
003	XL-410	Letecke Muzeum Kbely	OK-63 OK-YKF OK-20 [canx 1974; preserved in store Kbely, Czech Republic; l/n May11]
004	XL-410	Slovacke Letecke Muzeum	OK-ZKA [preserved by Oct90 Kunovice, Czech Republic]
00-01			[static test airframe]
00-02	AB	Blue Bird Aviation	OK-178(1) OK-AKF OK-AZB OK-ADR 5Y-HHF
00-03	A	Autobedrijf Piet Smedts Collectie	OK-176 OK-AKG OK-AZA OK-ADQ [canx 23Jun02; stored by Sep03 Baarlo, Holland; l/n 12Jan10]
00-04	A	Aero Muzeum	OK-ADN(1) [preserved by Sep01 Martin Airfield, Slovakia]
00-05	A	Slovacke Letecke Muzeum	OK-ADO [preserved by Sep94 Kunovice, Czech Republic]
71 01 01	A	Slovacke Letecke Muzeum	OK-ADP [preserved by Jly96 Kunovice, Czech Republic]
72 01 02	A	(Czechoslovakian Air Force)	OK-ADT(1) [canx; wfu Apr82 as GIA]
72 01 03	AS	(Gos. NII GA)	OK-174 OK-CKA CCCP-67251 [canx 07Aug85; fate/status unknown]
72 01 04	AS	Civil Aviation Board Museum	CCCP-67252 [preserved by Sep92 Ulyanovsk, Russia; l/n Sep08]
72 01 05	AS	(Aeroflot/Yakutsk)	CCCP-67253 [canx 07Aug85; fate/status unknown]
72 01 06	AS	(Aeroflot/Yakutsk)	CCCP-67254 [canx 07Aug85; fate/status unknown]
72 02 01	AS	(Aeroflot/Yakutsk)	CCCP-67255 [canx 07Aug85; fate/status unknown]
72 02 02	A	(Czechoslovakian Air Force)	OK-CDO OK-CDR [canx & wfu by Sep82 as GIA, Kosice, Czechoslovakia]
72 02 03	A	Eagle Aviation	OK-CDN OK-CDS 5Y-HNT
72 02 04	A	Blue Bird Aviation	OK-DKC OK-DDU 5Y-HHC
72 02 05	A	(LET Factory)	OK-DKD(1) [w/o by fire after 15Dec75]
73 02 06	M	(VZLU)	OK-018 OK-DZB [wfu 15Jun83 – believed b/u Lviv, Ukraine]
73 02 07	MA	Slovacky Aeroklub	OK-144 OK-158 OK-DZA
73 02 08	A	(Eagle Uganda)	OK-DKD(2) 5X-CNF [w/o 14Dec01 near Geti, Democratic Republic of Congo]
73 02 09	AB	Busy Bee Congo	OK-DDV 5Y-HHB 9Q-CSW [this c/n on DRC register as 9Q-CSX which is a An-28 c/n 1AJ0033-12]
73 02 10	A	Eagle Aviation	OK-DDW 5Y-FNT
73 03 01	A	ex Blue Sky Aviation	OK-DDX 5Y-GNT [wfu & dismantled by 08Oct10 fuselage only Mombasa, Kenya]
73 03 02	A	ex Eagle Aviation	OK-DDY 5Y-ENT [wfu & dismantled by 08Oct10 fuselage only Mombasa, Kenya]
74 03 03	AF	(Air Service Hungary)	HA-YFA [w/o 05Aug77 into Lake Balaton, Hungary]
74 03 04	AS	(Aeroflot/Yakutsk)	OK-EXA CCCP-67256 [canx 07Aug85; fate/status unknown]
74 03 05	AS	(Aeroflot/Yakutsk)	CCCP-67257 [canx 07Aug85; fate/status unknown]
74 03 06	AS	(Aeroflot/Yakutsk)	CCCP-67258 [canx 07Aug85; fate/status unknown]
74 03 07	AS	(Aeroflot/Yakutsk)	CCCP-67259 [canx 07Aug85; fate/status unknown]
74 03 08	AS	(Aeroflot/Yakutsk)	CCCP-67260 [canx 07Aug85; fate/status unknown]
74 03 09	A	Zruc Air Park	OK-EKB (OK-EDB) OK-EKB [wfu 1997; preserved 02Oct02 Zruc, Czech Republic]
74 03 10	M		[fatigue static test airframe; by 15Sep74 at Zruc Airpark, Czech Republic]]
75 04 01	M	Slovacke Letecke Muzeum	OK-022(1) [preserved by Oct90 Kunovice, Czech Republic]
75 04 02	MA	Luftfahrtsammlung Sanner	0402+ [+ Czechoslovakia later Czech Republic; preserved by Oct02 Bensheim-Auerbach, Germany]]
75 04 03	MA	Sky-Diving For Fun	0403+ OM-PGD [+ Czechoslovakia later Czech Republic]
75 04 04	M	ex Slovak Air Force	0404+ 0404 [+ Czechoslovakia; wfu by Jly99 Piestany, Slovakia; l/n Jun08]]
75 04 05	M	Dubnica Air	0405+ 0405^ OM-SAB [+ Czechoslovakia; ^ Slovakia]
75 04 08	M	Museo dell'Aviazione	OK-FDC [preserved by Oct95 Cerbaiola, Rimini, Italy]
75 04 09	AB	ex Solinair	OK-FDE S5-BAG [wfu by 27Aug99 Portoroz, Slovenia with broken tail; reported to become a cafe]
75 04 10	MU	(Aeroflot/Central Region)	CCCP-67200 [canx 04Dec90; fate/status unknown]
75 05 01	MA	ex Czech Air Force	OK-160(1) 0501+ [+ Czechoslovakia later Czech Republic; sold 2000 in Germany; by Aug05 stored Rothenburg, Germany; l/n May06]]
75 05 02	MA	(Zruc Air Park)	0502+ [+ Czechoslovakia later Czech Republic; preserved by Sep94 Zruc, Czech Republic; destroyed in film making 16Jly06 in Prague]
76 05 03	MA	ex Czech Air Force	0503+ [+ Czechoslovakia later Czech Republic; sold 2000 in Germany; by Aug05 stored Rothenburg, Germany; l/n May06]]

LET 410 AND 420 TURBOLET

C/n	Model	Last known Owner/Operator	Identities/fates/comments (where appropriate)	
76 05 04	MU	(Aeroflot/Central Region)	CCCP-67201	[canx 25Oct90; fate/status unknown]
76 05 05	MU	(Aeroflot/Central Region)	CCCP-67202	[canx 04Dec90; fate/status unknown]
76 05 06	MU	(Aeroflot/Central Region)	CCCP-67203	[canx 17Oct90; fate/status unknown]
76 05 07	MU	(Aeroflot/Central Region)	CCCP-67204	[canx 08Aug90; fate/status unknown]
76 05 08	MU	(Aeroflot/Central Region)	CCCP-67205	[canx 08Jly90; fate/status unknown]
76 05 09	M	(Aeroflot/Central Region)	CCCP-67206	[w/o 03Aug79 on approach Leningrad-Rzhevka, USSR; canx 12Oct79]
76 05 10	MU	(Aeroflot/Central Region)	CCCP-67207	[canx 16Oct90; fate/status unknown]
76 05 11	MU	(Aeroflot/Central Region)	CCCP-67208	[canx 17Oct90; fate/status unknown]
76 05 12	M	ex Gos. NII GA	CCCP-67209	[canx 24Apr89; by Aug99 Kirsanov Technical School, Russia; l/n Sep07]
76 05 13	M	(Aeroflot/Central Region)	CCCP-67210	[w/o 18Jan79 near Belgorod, USSR; canx 1979]
76 05 14	MU	(Aeroflot/Central Region)	CCCP-67211	[canx 30Nov88; fate/status unknown]
76 05 15	MU	(Aeroflot/Central Region)	CCCP-67212	[canx 28Feb89; fate/status unknown]
76 06 01	MU	(Aeroflot/Central Region)	CCCP-67213	[canx 30Nov88; fate/status unknown]
76 06 02	MU	(Aeroflot/Central Region)	CCCP-67214	[canx 28Feb89; fate/status unknown]
77 06 03	MU	(Aeroflot/Central Region)	CCCP-67215	[canx 04Dec88; reported 22Aug96 Kostroma, Russia; status unknown]
77 06 04			[built as Let 410UVP c/n X-01]	
77 06 05	MU	(Aeroflot/Central Region)	CCCP-67216	[canx 04Dec89; fate/status unknown]
77 06 06	MU	(Aeroflot/Central Region)	CCCP-67217	[canx 04Dec89; fate/status unknown]
77 06 07			[not built]	
77 06 08			[not built]	
77 06 09	MU	(Aeroflot/Central Region)	CCCP-67218	[canx 10May90; fate/status unknown]
77 06 10	MU	(Aeroflot/Central Region)	CCCP-67219	[canx 13Sep89; fate/status unknown]
77 07 01	MU	(Aeroflot/Central Region)	CCCP-67220	[canx 04Dec89; fate/status unknown]
77 07 02	MU	(Aeroflot/Central Region)	CCCP-67221	[canx 29Jun89; fate/status unknown]
77 07 03	MU	(Aeroflot/Central Region)	CCCP-67222	[canx 19Feb90; fate/status unknown]
77 07 04	MU	(Aeroflot/Central Region)	CCCP-67223	[canx 13Sep89; fate/status unknown]
77 07 05	MU	(Aeroflot/Central Region)	CCCP-67224	[canx 29Jun89; fate/status unknown]
77 07 06	MA	(Aeroflot/Central Region)	CCCP-67225	[w/o 04Dec84 near Kostroma, USSR; canx 18Apr85]
77 07 07	MU	(Aeroflot/Central Region)	CCCP-67226	[canx 28Feb89; fate/status unknown]
77 07 08	MU	(Aeroflot/Central Region)	CCCP-67227	[canx 05May89; reported 14Mar90 Moscow-Vnukovo, USSR probably wfu; l/n 05Jun92]
77 07 09	MU	(Aeroflot/Central Region)	CCCP-67228	[canx 04Dec89; fate/status unknown]
77 07 10	MU	(Aeroflot/Central Region)	CCCP-67229	[canx 04Dec89; wfu by Aug96 Kostrama, Russia]
77 07 11	MU	(Aeroflot/Central Region)	CCCP-67230	[canx 05May89; fate/status unknown]
77 07 12	MU	(Aeroflot/Central Region)	CCCP-67231	[canx 10May90; fate/status unknown]
77 07 13	MU	(Aeroflot/Central Region)	CCCP-67232	[canx 10Apr90; fate/status unknown]
77 07 14	MU	(Aeroflot/Central Region)	CCCP-67233	[canx 05May89; reported ended days in garden of a house]
77 07 15	MU	(Aeroflot/Central Region)	CCCP-67234	[fate/status unknown; never canx]
77 08 01	M	(Aeroflot/Yakutsk)	CCCP-67235	[w/o 26Aug88 on approach to Irkutsk, USSR; canx 26Nov88]
77 08 02	M	(Aeroflot/Yakutsk)	CCCP-67236	[canx 10Apr91; derelict by 05Jly92 Batagai, USSR]
77 08 03	M	(Aeroflot/Yakutsk)	CCCP-67237	[w/o 10Feb82 Yakutsk, USSR, when An-2 CCCP-70439 ran into it; canx 1986]
77 08 04	M	(Aeroflot/Yakutsk)	CCCP-67238	[canx 11Nov90; fate/status unknown]
77 08 05	M	(Aeroflot/Yakutsk)	CCCP-67239	[w/o 13Jun87 in ground incident involving An-2s CCCP-70129 & CCCP-84655; canx 1987]
77 08 06	M	(Aeroflot/Yakutsk)	CCCP-67240	[probably w/o 09Nov83 at Ust Nera, Russia, USSR; canx 29Jan91]
77 08 07	M	(Aeroflot/Yakutsk)	CCCP-67241	[canx 29Jan91; fate/status unknown]
77 08 08	M	(Aeroflot/Yakutsk)	CCCP-67242	[canx 30Dec91; fate/status unknown]
77 08 09	M	(Aeroflot/Yakutsk)	CCCP-67243	[canx 29Jan91; fate/status unknown]
77 08 10	M	(Aeroflot/Yakutsk)	CCCP-67244	[canx 25Dec91; wfu by 02Jly92 Nyurba, USSR]
77 08 11	M	(Aeroflot/Yakutsk)	CCCP-67245	[canx 30Dec91; fate/status unknown]
77 08 12	M	(Aeroflot/Yakutsk)	CCCP-67246	[canx 25Dec91; wfu by Jly92 Yakutsk-Magan, Russia; l/n Jly04]
77 08 13	M	(Aeroflot/Yakutsk)	CCCP-67247	[canx 23Nov90; wfu by Jly92 Yakutsk-Magan, Russia; l/n Jly04]
77 08 14	M	(Aeroflot/Yakutsk)	CCCP-67248	[canx 25Dec90; derelict by 02Jly92 Nyurba, USSR]
77 08 15	M	(Aeroflot/Yakutsk)	CCCP-67249	[w/o 24Sep87 Yakutsk-Magan, USSR; canx 31Mar88]
78 09 01	M	National Aviation University Collection	CCCP-67250	[by Sep93 GIA with Kiev Institute of Civil Aviation; later preserved Kiev, Ukraine; l/n Aug08]
78 09 02	M	(Aeroflot/Yakutsk)	CCCP-67261	[canx 25Dec91; wfu by 02Jly92 Nyurba, USSR]
78 09 03	M	(Aeroflot/Yakutsk)	CCCP-67262	[canx 23Nov90; wfu Yakutsk-Magan, Russia; l/n Jly04]
78 09 04	M	(Aeroflot/Yakutsk)	CCCP-67263	[canx 16Oct91; fate/status unknown]
78 09 05	M	(Aeroflot/Yakutsk)	CCCP-67264	[w/o 14Oct86 near Ust-Maya, USSR; canx 21Feb87]
78 09 06	M	(Aeroflot/Yakutsk)	CCCP-67265	[canx 1986; fate/status unknown]
78 09 07	M	(Aeroflot/Yakutsk)	CCCP-67266	[canx 11Nov90; fate/status unknown]

LET 410 AND 420 TURBOLET

C/n	Model	Last known Owner/Operator	Identities/fates/comments (where appropriate)
78 09 08	M	(Aeroflot)	CCCP-67267 RA-67267 [canx date unknown; fate/status unknown]
78 09 09	M	(Aeroflot/Yakutsk)	CCCP-67268 [canx 14Jul91; fate/status unknown]
78 09 10	M	(Aeroflot/Yakutsk)	CCCP-67269 [canx 06Mar91; fate/status unknown]
78 10 01	M	(Aeroflot/Yakutsk)	CCCP-67270 [canx 09Jly91; wfu by Jly92 Irtursk-one, USSR]
78 10 02	M	(Aeroflot/Yakutsk)	CCCP-67271 [canx 06Mar91; fate/status unknown]
78 10 03	M	(Aeroflot/Yakutsk)	CCCP-67272 [canx 25Dec90; wfu by 02Jly92 Nyurba, Russia]
78 10 04	M	(Aeroflot/Yakutsk)	CCCP-67273 [DBF 18Feb81 location not reported; canx 1981]
78 10 05	M	(Aeroflot/Yakutsk)	CCCP-67274 [canx 11Nov90; fate/status unknown]
78 10 06	M	(Aeroflot/Yakutsk)	CCCP-67275 [canx 17May91; derelict by 05Jly92 Batagai, Russia]
78 10 07	M	(Aeroflot/Yakutsk)	CCCP-67276 [w/o 04Jly84 Neryungri-Culman, USSR; canx 1985]
78 10 08	M	(Aeroflot/Yakutsk)	CCCP-67277 [canx 05Jun91; fate/status unknown]
78 10 09	M	(Aeroflot/Yakutsk)	CCCP-67278 [canx 25Dec90; derelict by 02Jly92 Nyurba, USSR]
78 10 10	M	(Aeroflot/Yakutsk)	CCCP-67279 [canx 25Dec90; derelict by 02Jly92 Nyurba, USSR]
78 10 11	M	(Aeroflot/West Siberia)	CCCP-67280 [stored by Aug93 Kharkov-Osnova, Ukraine; never canx]
78 10 12	M	(Aeroflot)	CCCP-67281 RA-67281 [canx date unknown; fate/status unknown]
78 10 13	M	(Aeroflot/West Siberia)	CCCP-67282 [stored by Aug93 Kharkov-Osnova, Ukraine; never canx]
78 10 14	MU	(Aeroflot/West Siberia)	CCCP-67283 [never canx; fate/status unknown]
78 10 15	M	ex Aeroflot/West Siberia)	CCCP-67284 [canx 31Jly91; wfu by Novosibirsk-Severny, USSR; restored & 16Sep11 to Omsk, Russia by road for preservation]
78 10 16	M	(Aeroflot/West Siberia)	CCCP-67285 [never canx; dumped by 17Aug01 Morshansk, Russia]
78 10 17	M	(Aeroflot/West Siberia)	CCCP-67286 [never canx; fate/status unknown]
78 10 18	M	(Aeroflot/West Siberia)	CCCP-67287 [canx 13Jun91; l/n 21Apr93 Novosibirsk-Severny, Russia; fate/status unknown]
78 10 19	M	(Aeroflot/West Siberia)	CCCP-67288 [canx 13Jun91; l/n 21Apr93 Novosibirsk-Severny, Russia; fate/status unknown]
78 10 20	M	(Sasovo Flying School)	CCCP-67289 [canx 24Apr89; fate/status unknown]
78 11 01	M	(Aeroflot/Georgia)	CCCP-67290 [w/o 07Jan82 near Gelendzhik, USSR]
78 11 02	MU	(Exin)	CCCP-67291 SP-FTN(1) [canx 11Jan93; by Mar96 used as bar at Biala Blota, Poland; by summer 2001 as cafe/bar at Charzykowskie, Poland; l/n Aug06]
78 11 03	M	(Sasovo Flying School)	CCCP-67292 [canx 24Apr89; fate/status unknown]
78 11 04	M	(Aeroflot/West Siberia)	CCCP-67293 [canx 13Jun91; l/n 21Apr93 Novosibirsk-Severny, Russia; fate/status unknown]
78 11 05	M	(Aeroflot/West Siberia)	CCCP-67294 [never canx; fate/status unknown]
78 11 06	M	(Aeroflot/West Siberia)	CCCP-67295 [canx 13Jun91; l/n 21Apr93 Novosibirsk-Severny, Russia; fate/status unknown]
78 11 07	M	(Aeroflot/West Siberia)	CCCP-67296 [canx 13Jun91; l/n 21Apr93 Novosibirsk-Severny, Russia; fate/status unknown]
78 11 08	M	(Aeroflot/West Siberia)	CCCP-67297 [never canx; fate/status unknown]
78 11 09	M	(Aeroflot/West Siberia)	CCCP-67298 [canx 13Jun91; l/n 21Apr93 Novosibirsk-Severny, Russia; fate/status unknown]
78 11 10	MU	Aeroklub Borki	CCCP-67299 FLARF-02181 2181K+ [+ Russia]
78 11 11	MU	(Aeroflot/West Siberia)	CCCP-67182 [canx date unknown; fate/status unknown]
78 11 12	MU	(Aeroflot/West Siberia)	CCCP-67183 [canx date unknown; fate/status unknown]
78 11 13	MU	(Aeroflot/West Siberia)	CCCP-67184 [canx date unknown; stored by 30Aug93 Kharkov-Osnova, Ukraine]
78 11 14	MU	(Aeroflot/West Siberia)	CCCP-67185 [canx date unknown; fate/status unknown]
78 11 15	MU	ex Exin	CCCP-67186 SP-FTS [canx 11Jan93; preserved as restaurant Okuninka, Poland]
78 11 16	MU	(Safe Air Company)	CCCP-67187 FLA-02155 RA-02155 TN-AGD 9Q-COA [w/o 15Jun10 Shabunda, Democratic Republic of Congo]
78 11 17	MU	ex Exin	CCCP-67188 SP-FTT [canx 11Jan93; by May04 hulk at Stary Uscimow, Poland]
78 11 18	MU	ex Exin	CCCP-67189 SP-FTM(1) [canx 11Jan93; by May96 near Chelm, Poland as restaurant; l/n Oct05]
78 11 19	M	(Aeroflot/Georgia)	CCCP-67190 [w/o 29Mar83 near Poti, Georgia, USSR; canx 1983]
78 11 20	M	(Aeroflot/Georgia)	CCCP-67191 [w/o 14Aug82 hit by Tu-134 CCCP-65836 Sukhumi, Georgia, USSR]

LET L-410UVP SERIES PRODUCTION

X-01	UVP	Slovacke Letecke Muzeum	OK-166 OK-030 [formerly c/n 76 06 04] [f/f 01Nov76; preserved by Oct90 Kunovice, Czech Republic]
X-02	UVP		[static test airframe; preserved by Apr93 in private collection Druztova, Czech Republic]
X-03	UVP	Zruc Air Park	OK-162(1) [w/o 07Jly77 Nedakonice, Czechoslovakia; by Aug98 preserved Zruc, Czech Republic]

LET 410 AND 420 TURBOLET

C/n	Model	Last known Owner/Operator	Identities/fates/comments (where appropriate)
X 01 01	UVP	(Tracep Congo Aviation)	OK-160(2) OK-IYA OK-026 OK-IYA 3C-FFK 9L-LFE+ 9L-LFR 9Q-CUA [+ regn not confirmed] [w/o 21Oct10 Mount Kahuzi near Bugulumisa, Democratic Republic of Congo]
X 01 02	UVP	Zruc Air Park	OK-162(2) OK-IYB [preserved by 1993 Zruc, Czech Republic]
X 01 03	UVP	ex LET Factory	OK-164(1) OK-IYC OK-164(1) "OK-LET" [wfu by Aug98 Kunovice, Czech Republic; by 24Jun11 painted with fictitious marks OK-LET]
79 02 01	UVP	(Aeroflot/Privolzhsk)	CCCP-67165 RA-67165 [canx 14Nov88; by 29Dec02 in Omsk Aviation Technical School, Russia; l/n 2006]
79 02 02	UVP	(Kazan 2nd Aviation Enterprise)	OK-150 OK-JYD CCCP-67166 RA-67166 [canx 11Jly97; fate/status unknown]
79 02 03	UVP	(Kazan 2nd Aviation Enterprise)	CCCP-67167 [wfu by 15Jly94 Krasnodar-Pashkovskaya, Russia; canx 11Sep96]
79 02 04	UVP	(Peruvian Army)	CCCP-67168 LY-ABO OB-1709 EP-830 [w/o 28Apr05 near Pisco, Peru]
79 02 05	UVP	Cetraca Aviation Service	CCCP-67169 UR-67169 9Q-CAZ
79 02 06	UVP	ex Kazan 2nd Aviation Enterprise	CCCP-67170 RA-67170 [canx 11Jly97; noted 11Jly12 preserved Bazarnyy Karabulak, Russia]
79 02 07	UVP	ex Kazan 2nd Aviation Enterprise	CCCP-67171 RA-67171 [stored by Nov01 Kazan-Osnovno, Russia; l/n 26Jun05]
79 02 08	UVP	ex Kazan 2nd Aviation Enterprise	CCCP-67172 RA-67172 [canx 14Jan98; preserved Vsevolodchino, Russia; noted 13Jun09]
79 02 09	UVP	Concors	CCCP-67173 RA-67173 YL-KAE
79 02 10	UVP	(Aeroflot/Privolzhsk)	CCCP-67174 [fate/status unknown]
79 02 11	UVP	(Kazan 2nd Aviation Enterprise)	CCCP-67175 RA-67175 [canx 11Nov97; fate/status unknown]
79 02 12	UVP	Mesoamerica Air Service	CCCP-67176 UR-67176 TG-AGZ TG-AGV
79 02 13	UVP	(Aeroflot/Privolzhsk)	CCCP-67177 [canx 11Sep96; fate/status unknown]
79 02 14	UVP	ex Aeroflot/Privolzhsk	CCCP-67178 [canx 11Sep96; wfu by 04May98 Kharkov-Osnova, Ukraine; l/n Jly08]
79 02 15	UVP	ex Aeroflot/Privolzhsk	CCCP-67179 [canx 18Nov90; GIA by 18Aug98 Kirsanov Technical School, Russia]
79 02 16	UVP	ex Congo Fret Espoir	CCCP-67180 LZ-MNP 9L-LCP 9XR-EJ [derelict by Aug06 Goma, Democratic Republic of Congo; l/n Jly10]
79 02 17	UVP	(Aeroflot/Ukraine)	CCCP-67181 [wfu by 30Aug93 Kharkov-Osnova, Ukraine]
79 02 18	UVP	(Aeroflot/Ukraine)	CCCP-67192 [wfu by 30Aug93 Kharkov-Osnova, Ukraine]
79 02 19	UVP	ex Aeroflot/North Kavkaz	CCCP-67193 [canx date unknown; reported 19Sep10 Poltava-MVS barracks, Ukraine]
79 02 20	UVP	(Aeroflot/Ukraine)	CCCP-67194 UR-67194 [wfu by 12Sep99 Rivne, Ukraine; canx 17Mar00]
79 03 01	UVP	(Avialinii Ukraïny)	CCCP-67195 UR-67195 [not in 1998 fleet list; fate/status unknown]
79 03 02	UVP	(Aeroflot/North Kavkaz)	CCCP-67196 [wfu by 15Jly94 Krasnodar-Pashkovskaya, Russia; canx 14Feb97]
79 03 03	UVP	Cetraca Aviation Service	CCCP-67197 UR-67197 ER-LIB 9Q-CKX
79 03 04	UVP	ex Avialinii Ukraïny	CCCP-67198 UR-67198 [not in 1998 fleet list; by 22Jun99 stored Poltava-Suprunovka, Ukraine; by 22Mar09 on display in local MVS training centre]
79 03 05	UVP	Aviaexpress	CCCP-67199 UR-67199
79 03 06	UVP	(Aeroflot/North Kavkaz)	CCCP-67110 [wfu by 15Jly94 Krasnodar-Pashkovskaya, Russia; canx 14Feb97]
79 03 07	UVP	Rainbow Air	CCCP-67111 YV308T
79 03 08	UVP	(Aeroflot/North Kavkaz)	CCCP-67112 [wfu by 15Jly94 Krasnodar-Pashkovskaya, Russia; canx 14Feb97]
79 03 09	UVP	(Aeroflot/North Kavkaz)	CCCP-67113 [wfu by 15Jly94 Krasnodar-Pashkovskaya, Russia; canx 14Feb97; possibly by Nov99 preserved Yermish, Russia]
79 03 10	UVP	(ex Aeroflot/ North Kavkaz)	CCCP-67114 UR-67114 [derelict by 12Sep96 Poltava-Suprunovka, Ukraine]
79 03 11	UVP	(Avialinii Ukraïny)	CCCP-67115 UR-67115 [w/o 23Jan95 Provideniya, Ukraine]
79 03 12	UVP	(ex Aeroflot/ North Kavkaz)	CCCP-67116 UR-67116 [wfu by Sep96 Rivne, Ukraine; canx 01Apr98]
79 03 13	UVP	(ex Aeroflot/ North Kavkaz)	CCCP-67117 UR-67117 [derelict by 12Sep96 Poltava-Suprunovka, Ukraine]
79 03 14	UVP	(Aeroflot/North Kavkaz)	CCCP-67118 [wfu by 15Jly94 Krasnodar-Pashkovskaya, Russia; canx 14Feb97]
79 03 15	UVP	(Aeroflot/North Kavkaz)	CCCP-67119 [wfu by 15Jly94 Krasnodar-Pashkovskaya, Russia; canx 14Feb97]
79 03 16	UVP	(Abakan Avia)	CCCP-67120 RA-67120 [w/o 20Jan95 Krasnoyarsk, Russia; canx 31May95]
79 03 17	UVP	Yeniseisk Air	CCCP-67121 RA-67121
79 03 18	UVP	ex Ukraine Flight State Academy	CCCP-67122 UR-67122 [wfu by 2001 Kirovograd, Ukraine; derelict by May07; canx 13Aug08]
79 03 19	UVP	(Yeniseiski Meridian)	CCCP-67123 RA-67123 [canx 15Jly96; fate/status unknown]
79 03 20	UVP	(Yeniseiski Meridian)	CCCP-67124 RA-67124 [wfu by 09Jly94 Krasnoyarsk-Cheremshanka, Russia; canx 08Nov94]
79 03 21	UVP	(Yeniseiski Meridian)	CCCP-67125 RA-67125 [canx 15Jly96; fate/status unknown]
79 03 22	UVP	Yeniseisk Air	CCCP-67126 RA-67126
79 03 23	UVP	(Aeroflot/Krasnoyarsk)	CCCP-67127 [w/o 07Dec88 Kodinsk, USSR; canx 30Dec88]
79 03 24	UVP	ex Ukraine Flight State	CCCP-67128 UR-67128 [wfu by 2001 Kirovograd, Ukraine; l/n Nov07; canx 13Aug08]

LET 410 AND 420 TURBOLET

C/n	Model	Last known Owner/Operator	Identities/fates/comments (where appropriate)
		Academy	
79 03 25	UVP	Safe Air Company	CCCP-67129 UR-67129 3D-ERS 9Q-CUB
80 03 26	UVP	(Kamchatavia)	CCCP-67130 [w/o 04Apr92 Baykovo, Kuril Islands, Russia]
80 03 27	UVP	Samara State Aerospace University Museum	CCCP-67131 [preserved by Apr93 Samara-Smyshlyayevka, Russia; l/n May07; canx date unknown]
80 03 28	UVP	(Petropavlovsk-Kamchatsky Air)	CCCP-67132 RA-67132 [canx 04Aug97; fate/status unknown]
80 03 29	UVP	Patriot Air	CCCP-67133 TU-TCS [for sale Jly09 at Kharkov, Ukraine]
80 03 30	UVP	(Aeroflot/Privolzhsk)	CCCP-67134 [canx 26Sep89; fate/status unknown]
80 04 01	UVP	(Aeroflot/Privolzhsk)	CCCP-67135 [wfu & stored by 04May98 Kharkov-Osnova, Ukraine; canx 11Sep96; preserved by 02Jly11 Kharkov-Sokolniki, no marks]
80 04 02	UVP	ex Aeroflot/Privolzhsk	CCCP-67136 RA-67136 [canx 11Jly97; preserved 1997 Alexandrov-Gai, Saratov, Russia; l/n Apr12]
80 04 03	UVP	ex Aeroflot/Privolzhsk	CCCP-67137 [canx 26Sep89; GIA by Aug99 Kirsanov Technical School, Russia; l/n Aug07]
80 04 04	UVP	(Aeroflot/North Kavkaz)	CCCP-67138 [wfu by 15Jly94 Krasnodar-Pashkovskaya, Russia; canx 14Apr97]
80 04 05	UVP	ex Aeroflot/North Kavkaz	CCCP-67139 [preserved by 1997 Shepsi, Russia; canx 14Apr97; l/n Jun06]
80 04 06	UVP	(Aeroflot/North Kavkaz)	CCCP-67140 [w/o 29Dec84 forced landing 76km from Astrakhan, USSR; canx 1987]
80 04 07	UVP	Rainbow Air	CCCP-67141 (UR-67141) YV307T
80 04 08	UVP	Rainbow Air	CCCP-67142 RA-67142 YV309T
80 04 09	UVP	(Kostrama Air)	CCCP-67143 [canx 21Oct98; fate/status unknown]
80 04 10	UVP	(Aeroflot/Privolzhsk)	CCCP-67144 [canx 23Mar94; wfu by 14Jly94 Kazan-Osnovnoi, Russia]
80 04 11	UVP	(Aeroflot/Privolzhsk)	CCCP-67145 [w/o 17Feb91 Muslyumovo, USSR; by Nov01 fuselage dumped at Kazan-Osnovnoi, Russia; canx 30Mar92]
80 04 12	UVP	(Aeroflot/Privolzhsk)	CCCP-67146 [canx 23Mar94; by Nov01 fuselage dumped at Kazan-Osnovnoi, Russia]
80 04 13	UVP	ex Tortug' Air	CCCP-67147 RA-67147 YL-PAJ N41431 HI-671CA HI-671CT HH-CRB [stored by Feb12 Puerto Ordaz, Venezuela]
80 04 14	UVP	Krasnoyarsk-Yemelyanovo Technical School	CCCP-67148 RA-67148 [canx 08Nov94; by Jun01 GIA at Krasnoyarsk-Yemelyanovo, Russia]
80 04 15	UVP	(Cheremshanka Airlines)	CCCP-67149 RA-67149 [canx 15Jly96; fate/status unknown]
80 04 16	UVP	ex Sasovo Flying School	CCCP-67150 RA-67150 [canx 21Aug98; by Nov08 preserved on poles in Ryazan Region, Russia]
80 04 17	UVP	(Sasovo Flying School)	CCCP-67151 [canx 06Aug99; fate/status unknown]
80 04 18	UVP	ex Petropavlovsk-Kamchatsky Air	CCCP-67152 RA-67152 [canx 04Aug97; wfu by Jun06 Petropavlovsk-Kamchatskiy-Yelizovo, Russia; l/n Jun08]
80 04 19	UVP	Avion Express	CCCP-67153 RA-67153 3X-GDK
80 04 20	UVP	Avion Express	CCCP-67154 RA-67154 3X-GDL
80 04 21	UVP	(Nizhneudinsk Air)	CCCP-67155 RA-67155 [canx 23Mar04; fate/status unknown]
80 04 22	UVP	(Aeroflot/East Siberia)	CCCP-67156 [canx 07Jly94; fate/status unknown]
80 04 23	UVP	(Aeroflot/East Siberia)	CCCP-67157 [canx 26Dec94; derelict by 20Apr97 Ulan Ude-Mukhino, Russia]
80 04 24	UVP	Rollins Air	CCCP-67158 RA-67158 HR-ARW [stored by Dec02 on airfield in Honduras]
80 04 25	UVP	Poltava Aviation Museum	CCCP-67159 UR-67159 HA-LAG(2) [preserved by 2005 Poltava, Ukraine]
80 04 26	UVP	(Aeroflot/North Kavkaz)	CCCP-67160 [wfu by 15Jly94 Krasnodar-Pashkovskaya, Russia; canx 14Apr97]
80 04 27	UVP	ex Ukraine Flight State Academy	CCCP-67161 UR-67161 [canx 13Aug08; wfu by 2001 Kirovograd, Ukraine; l/n Aug08]
80 04 28	UVP	ex Sasovo Flying School	CCCP-67162 RA-67162 [canx 21Oct00; wfu by 29Aug07 Sasovo, Russia]
80 04 29	UVP	(Aeroflot/North Kavkaz)	CCCP-67163 [wfu by 15Jly94 Krasnodar-Pashkovskaya, Russia; canx 14Apr97]
80 04 30	UVP	(Aeroflot/North Kavkaz)	CCCP-67164 [wfu by 15Jly94 Krasnodar-Pashkovskaya, Russia; canx 14Apr97]
80 05 01	UVP	ex Ukraine Flight State Academy	CCCP-67030 UR-67030 [canx 13Aug08; wfu by 2001 Kirovograd, Ukraine; l/n Aug08]
80 05 02	UVP	(Aeroflot/Krasnoyarsk)	CCCP-67031 [canx date unknown; fate/status unknown]
80 05 03	UVP	(Petropavlovsk-Kamchatsky Air)	CCCP-67032 [canx 04Aug97; fate/status unknown]
80 05 04	UVP	(Aeroflot/Krasnoyarsk)	CCCP-67033 [canx date unknown; fate/status unknown]
80 05 05	UVP	(Aeroflot/Krasnoyarsk)	CCCP-67034 [canx date unknown; fate/status unknown]
80 05 06	UVP	ex Islena Airlines	CCCP-67035 TG-TJF HR-IAR [status unknown]
80 05 07	UVP	Rainbow Air	CCCP-67036 LZ-MNO YV322T
80 05 08	UVP	(Abakan Avia)	CCCP-67037 [canx 23Sep94; fate/status unknown]
80 05 09	UVP	(Aeroflot/Krasnoyarsk)	CCCP-67038 [canx date unknown; fate/status unknown]
80 05 10	UVP	(Yeniseisk Air)	CCCP-67039 [canx 23Sep94; fate/status unknown]
80 05 11	UVP	(Yeniseiski Meridian)	CCCP-67040 RA-67040 [wfu by 09Jly94 Krasnoyarsk-Cheremshanka, Russia; canx 08Nov94]

LET 410 AND 420 TURBOLET

C/n	Model	Last known Owner/Operator	Identities/fates/comments (where appropriate)
80 05 12	UVP	(Mayair SA)	CCCP-67041 TG-TJR XA-SXX(2) [w/o 24Oct05 by Hurricane Wilma at Fort Lauderdale-Executive, USA; hulk b/u by Aug08]
80 05 13	UVP	(Abakan Avia)	CCCP-67042 [canx 23Sep94; fate/status unknown]
80 05 14	UVP	(Yeniseiski Meridian)	CCCP-67043 RA-67043 [wfu by 09Jly94 Krasnoyarsk-Cheremshanka, Russia; canx 08Nov94]
80 05 15	UVP	(Aeroflot/East Siberia)	CCCP-67044 [canx 26Dec94; derelict by 20Apr97 Ulan Ude-Mukhino, Russia]
80 05 16	UVP	(Aeroflot/East Siberia)	CCCP-67045 [canx 07Jly94; fate/status unknown]
80 05 17	UVP	(Aeroflot/East Siberia)	CCCP-67046 [canx 07Jly94; fate/status unknown]
80 05 18	UVP	(Aeroflot/East Siberia)	CCCP-67047 [canx 07Jly94; fate/status unknown]
80 05 19	UVP	(Aeroflot/East Siberia)	CCCP-67048 [canx 07Jly94; fate/status unknown]
80 05 20	UVP	(Aeroflot/East Siberia)	CCCP-67049 [canx 26Dec94; derelict by 20Apr97 Ulan Ude-Mukhino, Russia]
80 05 21	UVP	(Aeroflot/East Siberia)	CCCP-67050 [canx 07Jly94; fate/status unknown]
80 05 22	UVP	Inversiones	CCCP-67051 RA-67051 HR-ARX YV2358
80 05 23	UVP	(Petropavlovsk-Kamchatsky Air)	CCCP-67052 [derelict by 08Jly94 Petropavlovsk-Kamchatskiy-Yelizovo, Russia; canx 04Aug97]
80 05 24	UVP	not yet known	OK-162(3) 317+ 53+09^ 9L-LBW(1) 9L-LCE 9L-LFT 3X-GEK [+ E Germany; ^ Germany]
80 05 25	UVP	Luftwaffen Museum	OK-164(2) 318+ 53+10^ [+ E Germany; ^ Germany; preserved 12Dec00 Gatow, Berlin, Germany; l/n Mar07]
80 05 26	UVP	Comores Aviation	OK-168 319+ 53+11^ N229DB HA-LAB(2) D6-CAL [+ East Germany; ^ Germany]
80 05 27	UVP	ex TA Guatemaltecos	OK-165 320+ 53+12^ N26RZ TG-TAJ HR-AUT# [+ East Germany; ^ Germany; # canx 09Mar12 fate/status unknown]
80 05 28	UVP	(Petropavlovsk-Kamchatsky Air)	CCCP-67053 RA-67053 [canx 04Aug97; stored by Jun04 Petropavlovsk-Kamchatskiy-Yelizovo, Russia; l/n Jun06]
80 05 29	UVP	(Petropavlovsk-Kamchatsky Air)	CCCP-67054 RA-67054 [canx 04Aug97; stored by Jun04 Petropavlovsk-Kamchatskiy-Yelizovo, Russia; l/n 02Sep09]
80 05 30	UVP	ex Rollins Air	CCCP-67055 RA-67055 HR-ARV [stored by Dec02 on airfield in Honduras]
81 06 01	UVP	ex Ukraine Flight State Academy	CCCP-67000 UR-67000 [wfu by 2001 Kirovograd, Ukraine; l/n Nov07; left for overhaul early 2008]
81 06 02	UVP	Tengeriin Elch	CCCP-67001 UR-67001 JU-2032
81 06 03	UVP	ex Aeroflot/Privolzhsk	CCCP-67002 [canx date unknown; preserved by Jun99 Oleksandrivka, Ukraine then by Oct07 Chubinskoye, Ukraine; l/n Jly11]
81 06 04	UVP	(Ukraine Flight State Academy)	CCCP-67003 [canx; fate/status unknown]
81 06 05	UVP	ex Ukraine Flight State Academy	CCCP-67004 UR-67004 UR-CJG
81 06 06	UVP	ex Aeroflot/Privolzhsk	CCCP-67005 RA-02641
81 06 07	UVP	(Kazan 2nd Aviation Enterprise)	CCCP-67006 [canx date unknown; fate/status unknown]
81 06 08	UVP	(Aeroflot/West Siberia)	CCCP-67007 [canx 31Oct94; fate/status unknown]
81 06 09	UVP	(Aeroflot/West Siberia)	CCCP-67008 [canx 15Dec93; fate/status unknown]
81 06 10	UVP	(Aeroflot)	CCCP-67009 RA-67009 [canx 03Oct94: fate/status unknown]
81 06 11	UVP	Sierra Leone Airways	CCCP-67010 UR-67010 C5-LES 9L-LCD 9XR-RC [emergency landing 11Oct04 Kivu, Democratic Republic of Congo; status unknown]
81 06 12	UVP	(Sasovo Flying School)	CCCP-67011 RA-67011 [canx 21Oct00; fate/status unknown]
81 06 13	UVP	(Sasovo Flying School)	CCCP-67012 [canx 21Aug98; fate/status unknown]
81 06 14	UVP	Sasovo Flying School	CCCP-67013 RA-67013
81 06 15	UVP	(Aeroflot/Privolzhsk)	CCCP-67014 [wfu by 14Jly94 Kazan-Osnovnoi, Russia; canx 23Mar94]
81 06 16	UVP	(Kazan 2nd Aviation Enterprise)	CCCP-67015 [canx date unknown; fate/status unknown]
81 06 17	UVP	(Free Airlines)	CCCP-67016 UR-67016 9Q-CVL [w/o 24Sep07 Malemba-N'Kulu, Democratic Republic of Congo]
81 06 18	UVP	Universal Avia	CCCP-67017 UR-67017
81 06 19	UVP	(Aeroflot/West Siberia)	CCCP-67018 RA-67018 [canx 03Oct94; fate/status unknown]
81 06 20	UVP	ex Sasovo Flying School	CCCP-67019 RA-67019 [wfu by 29Aug07 Sasovo, Russia]
81 06 21	UVP	(Universal Avia)	CCCP-67020 UR-67020 [stored by 04Jly07 Rivne, Ukraine; canx 13Aug08]
81 06 22	UVP	unknown	CCCP-67021 LY-MMR [stored/wfu by Sep95 Plovdiv-Krumovo, Bulgaria; l/n Sep09; canx]
81 06 23	UVP	(ACS Ltd)	CCCP-67022 UR-67022 ER-LIA 9XR-AL [w/o 14Sep03 Lankien, Sudan]
81 06 24	UVP	ex Universal Avia	CCCP-67023 (UR-67023) [derelict by May02 Voroniv, Ukraine; canx 13Aug08; l/n 14Jly11 still as CCCP-67023]
81 06 25	UVP	Zruc Air Park	OK-028 [preserved by Jly02 Zruc, Czech Republic; l/n Mar06]

LET 410 AND 420 TURBOLET

C/n	Model	Last known Owner/Operator	Identities/fates/comments (where appropriate)
81 06 26	UVP	(Universal Avia)	CCCP-67024 RA-67024 UR-67024 [derelict by May02 Cherkasy, Ukraine; l/n Aug08; canx 13Aug08]
81 06 27	UVP	ex Sasovo Flying School	CCCP-67025 RA-67025 [wfu by 29Aug07 Sasovo, Russia]
81 06 28	UVP	ex Sasovo Flying School	CCCP-67026 RA-67026 [wfu by 29Aug07 Sasovo, Russia]
81 06 29	UVP	ex Sasovo Flying School	CCCP-67027 [wfu by 22Aug95 Sasovo, Russia; l/n 29Aug07]
81 06 30	UVP	ex Sasovo Flying School	CCCP-67028 [wfu by 22Aug95 Sasovo, Russia; l/n 29Aug07]
81 06 31	UVP	ex Sasovo Flying School	CCCP-67029 RA-67029 [wfu by 29Aug07 Sasovo, Russia]
81 06 32	UVP	ex Sasovo Flying School	CCCP-67056 RA-67056 [wfu by 29Aug07 Sasovo, Russia]
81 06 33	UVP	ex Sasovo Flying School	CCCP-67057 [wfu by 22Aug95 Sasovo, Russia; l/n 29Aug07]
81 06 34	UVP	unknown	CCCP-67058 LY-MAA [stored by Sep95 Plovdiv-Krumovo, Bulgaria; l/n May08; canx by May10]
81 06 35	UVP	(Universal Avia)	CCCP-67059 UR-67059 [derelict by May02 Cherkasy, Ukraine; l/n Aug08; canx 13Aug08]
81 06 36	UVP	(Ocean Airlines)	CCCP-67060 UR-67060 9L-LBO 9XR-RB [w/o 27Dec02 Anjouan-Ouani, Comores Islands]
81 06 37	UVP	unknown	CCCP-67061 UR-67061 9L-LBL(1) [reported dumped by Apr01 Lokichoggio, Kenya]
81 06 38	UVP	(Aeroflot/Ukraine)	CCCP-67062 [fate/status unknown]
81 06 39	UVP	ex Sasovo Flying School	CCCP-67063 RA-67063 [preserved by Sep09 Sasovo, Russia in old Aeroflot c/s]
81 06 40	UVP	Comeravia	CCCP-67064 UR-67064 YV1232
81 07 01	UVP	ex Trans Airways	CCCP-67065 3C-KKU(1) 9Q-CGU 9Q-CUG+ C9-STG(3) [+ possible mis-painting; no longer operated; fate/status unknown]
81 07 02	UVP	CIACA	CCCP-67066 YV-978C
81 07 03	UVP	ex Omskavia	CCCP-67067 RA-67067 67067+ [+ prefix painted out; canx 06Mar95; stored by Sep05 off airfield, Omsk, Russia]
81 07 04	UVP	ex Universal Avia	CCCP-67068 UR-67068 RA-67068 UR-67068 [derelict by May02 Cherkasy, Ukraine; l/n Aug08; canx 13Aug08]
81 07 05	UVP	ex Ukraine Pilot School	CCCP-67069 UR-VTV [stored May08 Kiev-Chaika, Ukraine; canx 08Oct10]
81 07 06	UVP	ex Rollins Air	CCCP-67070 UR-67070 HR-AQJ [fate/status unknown]
81 07 07	UVP	(Lexus Air)	CCCP-67071 XT-FAS 9XR-JT [w/o 12Aug03 Rumbek, Sudan]
81 07 08	UVP	(Aeroflot/East Siberia)	CCCP-67072 [canx 26Dec94; derelict by 20Apr97 Ulan Ude-Mukhino, Russia]
81 07 09	UVP	(Aeroflot/East Siberia)	CCCP-67073 [canx 26Dec94; derelict by 20Apr97 Ulan Ude-Mukhino, Russia]
81 07 10	UVP	(Aeroflot/East Siberia)	CCCP-67074 [canx 26Dec94; derelict by 20Apr97 Ulan Ude-Mukhino, Russia]
81 07 11	UVP	(Aeroflot/East Siberia)	CCCP-67075 [canx 26Dec94; derelict by 20Apr97 Ulan Ude-Mukhino, Russia]
81 07 12	UVP	Sky Diving for Fun	0712+ OM-PGB [+ Czechoslovakia later Czech Republic]
81 07 13	UVP	(Aeroflot/East Siberia)	CCCP-67076 [canx 26Dec94; derelict by 20Apr97 Ulan Ude-Mukhino, Russia]
81 07 14	UVP	(Aeroflot/East Siberia)	CCCP-67077 [canx 26Dec94; derelict by 20Apr97 Ulan Ude-Mukhino, Russia; by 2002 in garden of house]
81 07 15	UVP	(Aeroflot/East Siberia)	CCCP-67078 [canx 26Dec94; derelict by 20Apr97 Ulan Ude-Mukhino, Russia]
81 07 16	UVP	ex Aeroflot/East Siberia	CCCP-67079 [canx 09Apr96; by early 2009 preserved Nizhneudinsk, Russia]
81 07 17	UVP	(Nizhneudinsk Air)	CCCP-67080 [canx 07Jly94; fate/status unknown]
81 07 18	UVP	(KVS Air Club)	CCCP-67081 RA-67081 FLARF-01192 [derelict Jun03 following accident Moscow-Myachkovo, Russia; l/n May04]
81 07 19	UVP	ex Universal Avia	CCCP-67082 [converted to boat, in use Puzha near Rivne, Ukraine; l/n 04Jly07]
81 07 20	UVP	not yet known	CCCP-67083 UR-67083 3D-NIK
81 07 21	UVP	(Skaiden)	CCCP-67084 UR-67084 UR-SKD [w/o 10Jun12 Borodyanka, Ukraine]
81 07 22	UVP	(Universal Avia)	CCCP-67085 [wfu by 12Sep99 Rivne, Ukraine; fate/status unknown; canx 13Aug08]
81 07 23	UVP	ex Rollins Air	CCCP-67086 HR-AQK [stored Honduras by Dec02]
81 07 24	UVP	Cotair	CCCP-67087 UR-67087 3D-NVE(2)+ UR-67087 EL-GPZ 9U-BHK 3D-BHK TU-TBS [+illegal marks c/n 84 12 19 used legal marks]
81 07 25	UVP	ex Sakha Avia	CCCP-67088 [canx 27May95; by Jun09 derelict Batagai, Russia]
81 07 26	UVP	Estonian Border Guards	313+ 53+01^ ES-EPA ES-PLW [+ E Germany; ^ Germany]
81 07 27	UVP	Estonian Border Guards	316+ 53+02^ ES-EPI ES-PLY [+ E Germany; ^ Germany]
81 07 28	UVP	(Vostok Aviakompania)	CCCP-67089 RA-67089 [canx 25Oct95; fate/status unknown]
81 07 29	UVP	(Vostok Aviakompania)	CCCP-67090 RA-67090 [canx 07Oct95; fate/status unknown]
81 07 30	UVP	ex Slovak Air Force	0730+ 0730 [+ Czechoslovakia; stored Sep06 Malacky, Slovakia; l/n Oct08; by 2011 wfu GIA Holesov, Czech Republic]
81 07 31	UVP	Czech Air Force	0731+ [+ Czechoslovakia later Czech Republic]
81 07 32	UVP	(Aeroflot/Far East)	CCCP-67091 [w/o 21Aug91 Polina-Osipenko, USSR; canx 03Feb95]
82 07 33	UVP	ex Sasovo Flying School	CCCP-67092 RA-67092 [wfu by 29Aug07 Sasovo, Russia]
82 07 34	UVP	ex Sasovo Flying School	CCCP-67093 RA-67093 [wfu by 29Aug07 Sasovo, Russia]
82 07 35	UVP	ex Sasovo Flying School	CCCP-67094 RA-67094 [wfu by 29Aug07 Sasovo, Russia]
82 07 36	UVP	unknown	CCCP-67095 RA-3131K
82 07 37	UVP	Latvian Air Force	321+ 53+03^ 45# 145 [+ E Germany; ^ Germany; # Latvia]

LET 410 AND 420 TURBOLET

C/n	Model	Last known Owner/Operator	Identities/fates/comments (where appropriate)
82 07 38	UVP	Lithuanian Air Force	323+ 53+04^ 01 [+ E Germany; ^ Germany]
82 07 39	UVP	Lithuanian Air Force	324+ 53+05^ 02 [+ E Germany; ^ Germany]
82 07 40	UVP	(Aeroflot/West Siberia)	OK-MYD CCCP-67300 [canx 04Oct96; fate/unknown]
82 08 01	UVP	ex Job Air	CCCP-67301 RA-67301 OM-MDF(2) [stored 2005 Thumama, Saudi Arabia; l/n 21Dec11]
82 08 02	UVP	(Novosibirsk Air)	CCCP-67302 RA-67302 [canx 21Dec98; wfu Novosibirsk-Severny, Russia; b/u Nov02]
82 08 03	UVP	(Novosibirsk Air)	CCCP-67303 RA-67303 [canx 21Dec98; wfu Novosibirsk-Severny, Russia; b/u Nov02]
82 08 04	UVP	Sokol-Nizhi Novgorod Aviation Factory	CCCP-67304 RA-67304 RA-3156K RF-01010
82 08 05	UVP	ex Novosibirsk Air	CCCP-67305 RA-67305 [wfu by Jly00 Novosibirsk-Severny, Russia; derelict by Jly05; l/n 07Jly08]
82 08 06	UVP	(Vostok Aviakompania)	CCCP-67306 RA-67306 [wfu by 12May95 Khabarovsk-Two, Russia; canx 25Oct95]
82 08 07	UVP	(Vostok Aviakompania)	CCCP-67307 RA-67307 [wfu by 12May95 Khabarovsk-Two, Russia; canx 25Oct95]
82 08 08	UVP	Vostok Aviakompania	CCCP-67308 RA-67308
82 08 09	UVP	unknown	CCCP-67309 RA-3132K
82 08 10	UVP	(ex Tomsk Air)	CCCP-67310 RA-67310 [canx 27Mar95; preserved by 15Sep99 Tomsk City, Russia; l/n Oct07; b/u Sep/Oct09]
82 08 11	UVP	(Novosibirsk Air)	CCCP-67311 RA-67311 [wfu by Jly00 Novosibirsk-Severny, Russia; l/n Jun03; canx 04Dec03]
82 08 12	UVP	ex Tomsk Air	CCCP-67312 [wfu Tomsk-Bogashevo, Russia; l/n Nov08; canx 27Mar95]
82 08 13	UVP	(Aeroflot/Krasnoyarsk)	CCCP-67313 [canx 13Apr95; fate/status unknown]
82 08 14	UVP	(Aeroflot/Krasnoyarsk)	CCCP-67314 [canx 30Oct95; fate/status unknown]
82 08 15	UVP	(Aeroflot/Krasnoyarsk)	CCCP-67315 [w/o 19Oct83 Kransk, USSR; canx 1984]
82 08 16	UVP	(Novosibirsk Air)	CCCP-67316 RA-67316 [wfu by Jly00 Novosibirsk-Severny, Russia; l/n Jun03; canx 04Dec03]
82 08 17	UVP	(Aeroflot/West Siberia)	CCCP-67317 [wfu by Jly04 Tomsk-Bogashevo, Russia; l/n Nov08; canx 27Mar95]
82 08 18	UVP	(Novosibirsk Air)	CCCP-67318 RA-67318 [wfu by Jly00 Novosibirsk-Severny, Russia; l/n Jun03; canx 21Dec98]
82 08 19	UVP	(Tomsk Air)	CCCP-67319 [canx 27Mar95; fate/status unknown]
82 08 20	UVP	(Omskavia)	CCCP-67320 [canx 15Jun98; fate/status unknown]
82 08 21	UVP	(Tomsk Air)	CCCP-67321 [canx 27Mar95; fate/status unknown]
82 08 22	UVP	(Omskavia)	CCCP-67322 RA-67322 [canx 28Sep95; fate/status unknown]
82 08 23	UVP	(Tomsk Air)	CCCP-67323 [canx 27Mar95; fate/status unknown]
82 08 24	UVP	(Omskavia)	CCCP-67324 [canx 28Sep95; fate/status unknown]
82 08 25	UVP	(Kez Shemskogo Air Enterprise)	CCCP-67325 [canx 30Oct95; fate/status unknown]
82 08 26	UVP	(Kez Shemskogo Air Enterprise)	CCCP-67326 [canx 30Oct95; fate/status unknown]
82 08 27	UVP	(Aeroflot/East Siberia)	CCCP-67327 [canx 09Apr96; fate/status unknown]
82 08 28	UVP	(Aeroflot/East Siberia)	CCCP-67328 [canx 09Apr96; fate/status unknown]
82 08 29	UVP	(STASA)	CCCP-67329 C9-STG(1) [fate/status unknown; not current]
82 08 30	UVP	Trans Air Congo	CCCP-67330 UR-67330 UR-MLD TN-AHM
82 08 31	UVP	(Aeroflot/Ukraine)	CCCP-67331 [w/o 12Oct90 Odessa-Tsentralnyi, Ukraine, USSR; canx 12May91]
82 08 32	UVP	Avia Soyuz	CCCP-67332 UR-67332 UR-ASM
82 08 33	UVP	(ex Aeroflot/North Kavkaz)	CCCP-67333 [canx 16Oct96; fate/status unknown]
82 08 34	UVP	(Aeroflot/Privolzhsk)	CCCP-67334 [w/o 18Oct87 Saratov, USSR; canx 05Feb88]
82 08 35	UVP	unknown	CCCP-67335 HA-LAB(1) 3C-JJG YV-991C [stored by Mar01 Charalleve, Venezuela; l/n 21Mar04]
82 08 36	UVP	(Aeroflot/North Kavkaz)	CCCP-67336 RA-67336 [canx 12Sep97; fate/status unknown]
82 08 37	UVP	Air Tropiques	CCCP-67337 UR-67337 3D-NVI 9U-BHE 5R-MGZ 9Q-CEO
82 08 38	UVP	Kostroma Air	CCCP-67338 RA-67338 [canx 21Oct98; fate/status unknown]
82 08 39	UVP	(Aeroflot/Privolzhsk)	CCCP-67339 [canx 18Jan90; GIA by Aug99 Kirsanov Technical School, Russia; l/n Aug07]
82 08 40	UVP	unknown	CCCP-67340 HA-LAC(1) UR-67340 YV-861C YV-861CP YV1515
82 09 01	UVP	(Aeroflot/Privolzhsk)	CCCP-67341 [canx 19Jun91; fate/status unknown]
82 09 02	UVP	ex Ryazanaviatrans	CCCP-67342 HA-LAG(1) RA-67342 [canx 14Aug98; wfu by 28Aug03 Turlatvo, Russia; l/n Aug07]
82 09 03	UVP	ex Apatas Airlines	CCCP-67343 RA-67343 LY-ASN [not current; fate/status unknown]
82 09 04	UVP	Olimpic Skydive	CCCP-67344 UR-67344 EW-215PA UR-OLM
82 09 05	UVP	(Aeroflot/Far East)	CCCP-67345 RA-67345 [derelict by 20Apr97 Blagoveshchensk-Ignatyevo, Russia; canx 11Nov97]
82 09 06	UVP	(Aeroflot/Far East)	CCCP-67346 RA-67346 [derelict by 20Apr97 Blagoveshchensk-Ignatyevo, Russia; canx 11Nov97]
82 09 07	UVP	(Aeroflot/East Siberia)	CCCP-67347 [canx 09Apr96; fate/status unknown]
82 09 08	UVP	(Novosibirsk Air)	CCCP-67348 RA-67348 [wfu by Jly00 Novosibirsk-Severny, Russia; canx 21Dec98]

LET 410 AND 420 TURBOLET

C/n	Model	Last known Owner/Operator	Identities/fates/comments (where appropriate)
82 09 09	UVP	(Tepavia Trans)	CCCP-67349 RA-67349 EW-215KB ER-LIC [canx 10May07 fate/status unknown; l/n 28Jun07 Kishinev-Chisinau, Moldova]
82 09 10	UVP	(Novosibirsk Air)	CCCP-67350 [wfu by Aug01 Abakan, Russia; canx 15May95]
82 09 11	UVP	(Abakan Avia)	CCCP-67351 [canx 15May95; fate/status unknown]
82 09 12	UVP	(Abakan Avia)	CCCP-67352 [canx 15May95; fate/status unknown]
82 09 13	UVP	(Aeroflot/Far East)	CCCP-67353 [derelict by 20Apr97 Blagoveshchensk-Ignatyevo, Russia; canx 11Nov97]
82 09 14	UVP	(Aeroflot/Far East)	CCCP-67354 [derelict by 20Apr97 Blagoveshchensk-Ignatyevo, Russia; canx 11Nov97]
82 09 15	UVP	(Aeroflot/Far East)	CCCP-67355 [derelict by 20Apr97 Blagoveshchensk-Ignatyevo, Russia; canx 11Nov97]
82 09 16	UVP	(Abakan Avia)	CCCP-67356 [canx 15May95; fate/status unknown]
82 09 17	UVP	Ukraine Flight State Academy	CCCP-67357 UR-67357
82 09 18	UVP	(Nizhneudinsk Air)	CCCP-67358 [canx 09Apr96; fate/status unknown]
82 09 19	UVP	(Nizhneudinsk Air)	CCCP-67359 [canx 09Apr96; fate/status unknown]
82 09 20	UVP	(ex Aeroflot/North Kavkaz)	CCCP-67360 RA-67360 [canx 14Apr97; fate/status unknown]
82 09 21	UVP	ex Lamac Collection	CCCP-67365 (OK-NDN) (OM-NDN) CCCP-67365 [wfu for spares; then preserved Lamac, near Bratislava, Slovakia; gone by early 2009, fate unknown]
82 09 22	UVP	Companie Aer. Maouene	CCCP-67366 UR-67366 TN-AHF
82 09 23	UVP	(Aerolineas SOSA)	DDR-SXA D-COXA S9-TAQ HR-AQG [w/o 07Mar98 near La Ceiba, Honduras]
82 09 24	UVP	Air Space Agency Magellan	DDR-SXB D-COXB UR-MAG
82 09 25	UVP	Team Aviation	DDR-SXC D-COXC S9-TBT D-COXC OK-LEB 3D-LEB
82 09 26	UVP-T	(Czech Air Force)	0906+ [+ Czechoslovakia later Czech Republic; wfu by 1999 after unknown incident]
82 09 27	UVP-T	ex Slovak Air Force	0927+ 0927 [+ Czechoslovakia; wfu by Jun10 & to GIA Kunovice, Czech Republic; later painted as 002 with Kunovial Air Force titles; l/n 24Jun11]
82 09 28	UVP-T	Czech Air Force	0928+ [+ Czechoslovakia later Czech Republic]
82 09 29	UVP-T	not yet known	0929+ OM-DAA OM-PGA HA-KDZ [+ Czechoslovakia later Czech Republic]
82 09 30	UVP-T	Slovak Air Force	0930+ 0930
82 09 31	UVP-T	(Libyan Air Force)	OK-MXH 0931 [w/o by 1990]
82 09 32	UVP-T	Libyan Air Force	OK-MXI 0932
82 09 33	UVP-T	Libyan Air Force	OK-MXJ 0933
82 09 34	UVP-T	Libyan Air Force	OK-MXK 0934
83 09 35	UVP	(Cargo Bull Aviation)	CCCP-67367 (OK-NDO) (OM-NDO) CCCP-67367 9Q-CIM [w/o 18Jun07 Bandaka Airport, Democratic Republic of Congo]
83 09 36	UVP	Lukoil c/s	CCCP-67368 UR-67368 UR-SEW+ [+ c/n not fully confirmed]
83 09 37	UVP	(Aeroflot/Krasnoyarsk)	CCCP-67369 [wfu by Aug01 Abakan, Russia; canx 12Nov99]
83 09 38	UVP	(Yeniseiski Meridian)	CCCP-67370 RA-67370 [wfu by 09Jly94 Krasnoyarsk-Cheremshanka, Russia; canx 08Nov94]
83 09 39	UVP	Transaven	CCCP-67371 YV-980C YV1417
83 09 40	UVP	Universal Avia	CCCP-67372 UR-67372
83 10 01	UVP	(Abakan Avia)	CCCP-67373 [wfu by Aug01 Abakan, Russia; canx 12Nov99]
83 10 02	UVP	(Yeniseiski Meridian)	CCCP-67374 RA-67374 [canx 08Nov94; fate/status unknown]
83 10 03	UVP	ex Sakha Avia	CCCP-67375 [canx 21Feb96; by Jun09 derelict Batagai, Russia]
83 10 04	UVP	(Barnaul Airlines)	CCCP-67376 [canx 02Aug95; fate/status unknown]
83 10 05	UVP	(Vostok Aviakompania)	CCCP-67377 RA-67377 [wfu by 12May95 Khabarovsk-Two, Russia; l/n Jly06]
83 10 06	UVP	(Barnaul Airlines)	CCCP-67378 [canx 02Aug95; fate/status unknown]
83 10 07	UVP	(Aeroflot/Privolzhsk)	CCCP-67379 [canx 14Nov88; fate/status unknown]
83 10 08	UVP	(Amuravia)	CCCP-67380 RA-67380 [derelict by 20Apr97 Blagoveshchensk-Ignatyevo, Russia; canx 11Nov97]
83 10 09	UVP	Yeniseisk Air	CCCP-67381 RA-67381
83 10 10	UVP	Sundance Air	CCCP-67382 RA-67382 YV-1025C YV2063
83 10 11	UVP	(Berkut)	CCCP-67383 [awaiting scrapping by Dec00 Oral-Ak Zhol, Kazakhstan; l/n 01Aug03]
83 10 12	UVP	(Amuravia)	CCCP-67384 RA-67384 [derelict by 20Apr97 Blagoveshchensk-Ignatyevo, Russia; canx 11Nov97]
83 10 13	UVP	Berkut	CCCP-67385 [awaiting overhaul Oral-Ak Zhol, Kazakhstan; l/n 27May04]
83 10 14	UVP	(Amuravia)	CCCP-67386 [derelict by 20Apr97 Blagoveshchensk-Ignatyevo, Russia; canx 11Nov97]
83 10 15	UVP	Centre Industrial Aeronautical	CCCP-67387 YV-984C(2)
83 10 16	UVP	(Tomsk Air)	CCCP-67388 [canx 21Dec98; fate/status unknown]
83 10 17	UVP	(El Amrion Plus Corp)	CCCP-67389 UR-67389 D2-FEY 9XR-KL [w/o en-route 09Oct04 in bush, Democratic Republic of Congo]
83 10 18	UVP	(Aeroflot/Kazakhstan)	CCCP-67390 [never canx; fate/status unknown]
83 10 19	UVP	(Aeroflot/Kazakhstan)	CCCP-67391 [never canx; fate/status unknown]

LET 410 AND 420 TURBOLET

C/n	Model	Last known Owner/Operator	Identities/fates/comments (where appropriate)
83 10 20	UVP	ex Safair	CCCP-67392 UR-67392 9L-LDP D2-FEX 9Q-CIY [wfu & dismantled; by 05Oct10 fuselage only Nairobi-Wilson, Kenya]
83 10 21	UVP	ex Ukraine Flight State Academy	CCCP-67393 UR-67393 [wfu by 2001 Kirovograd, Ukraine; l/n Aug08; canx 13Aug08]
83 10 22	UVP	(Sakha Avia)	CCCP-67394 [wfu by Jly92 Yakutsk-Magan, Russia; l/n Apr94; canx 30Jun97]
83 10 23	UVP	Free Airlines	CCCP-67395 UR-67395 9Q-CET 9Q-COT
83 10 24	UVP	(Yeniseiski Meridian)	CCCP-67396 RA-67396 [wfu by 09Jly94 Krasnoyarsk-Cheremshanka, Russia; canx 08Nov94]
83 10 25	UVP	ex Sakha Avia	CCCP-67397 RA-67397 [wfu by 1998; l/n 01Jun04 Yakutsk-Magan, Russia]
83 10 26	UVP	ex Aeroflot/Kazakhstan	OK-NZB(1) CCCP-67398 [reported preserved Arkalyk, Kazakhstan]
83 10 27	UVP	Sundance Air	CCCP-67399 RA-67399 LY-ANR PZ-TGR YV-1029C
83 10 28	UVP	Comeravia	CCCP-67400 OK-NDP OM-NDP S9-TBP TI-AXX YV-906C YV1332
83 10 29	UVP	unknown	CCCP-67401 RA-67401 RA-1256K
83 10 30	UVP	unknown	CCCP-67402 RA-67402 FLARF-02736 RA-2736K 2736K+ [+ Russia]
83 10 31	UVP	(Yeniseiski Air)	CCCP-67403 RA-67403 [canx 30Nov95; fate/status unknown]
83 10 32	UVP	Sundance Air	CCCP-67404 YV-983CP YV-1114C YV1544
83 10 33	UVP	Trans Air Ways	CCCP-67405 RA-67405 5Y-BLC 3D-NVC
83 10 34	UVP	(Kazan 2nd Aviation Enterprise)	CCCP-67406 RA-67406 [wfu by 25Aug01 Kazan-Two, Russia; canx 23Mar04]
83 10 35	UVP	ex Aeroflot/Kazakhstan	CCCP-67407 UN-67407 [preserved by early 2008 Zhezkazgan Airport, Kazakhstan]
83 10 36	UVP	Alicea	CCCP-67408 UR-67408 C5-LET 9L-LCI 3D-ALC
83 10 37	UVP	ex Ukraine Flight State Academy	CCCP-67409 UR-67409 [wfu by 2001 Kirovograd, Ukraine; l/n Aug08; canx 13Aug08]
83 10 38	UVP	not yet known	CCCP-67410 UN-67410
83 10 39	UVP	Air J Michael	CCCP-67411 UR-67411 D2-FDR
83 10 40	UVP	Aerotaxi/Oleg Chemical	CCCP-67412 OK-SAS
83 11 01	UVP	Berkut	CCCP-67413 [awaiting overhaul by 22Dec02; l/n Mar08 Ostrava-Mosnov, Czech Republic]
83 11 02	UVP	(Aeroflot/East Siberia)	CCCP-67414 [canx 09Apr96; fate/status unknown]
83 11 03	UVP	(Aeroflot/Kazakhstan)	CCCP-67415 [never canx; fate/status unknown]
83 11 04	UVP	(Air Max)	CCCP-67416 UR-67416 LZ-RMF [not in 2003 fleet list; fate/status unknown]
83 11 05	UVP	ex Tropical Airways	DDR-SXD D-COXD S9-TAZ HI-670CT HH-TAH [derelict by 08Oct11 Port au Prince, Haiti, with no markings]
83 11 06	UVP	ex SA Profesionales	DDR-SXE D-COXE S9-TAR HI-690CT HI-690 [hulk only by Dec06 at Santo Domingo-Herrara, Dominican Republic]
83 11 07	UVP	SA Profesionales	DDR-SXF D-COXF S9-TAW HI-691CT
83 11 08	UVP	Ukraine Flight State Academy Museum	CCCP-67417 UR-67417 [preserved by 29May02 Kirovograd-Khmelyovoye, Ukraine by 29May02; l/n Aug08]
83 11 09	UVP	(Borki Air Club)	CCCP-67418 RA-67418 FLARF-01032 [painted as 01032-FLARF; w/o 01Mar03 near Borki Airfield, Russia]
83 11 10	UVP	CHC Stellavia	CCCP-67419 UR-67419 9L-LFM 9Q-CUC
83 11 11	UVP	(Barnaul Airlines)	CCCP-67420 [canx 06Jun96; fate/status unknown]
83 11 12	UVP	(Barnaul Airlines)	CCCP-67421 [canx 06Jun96; fate/status unknown]
83 11 13	UVP	(Air Max)	CCCP-67422 UR-67422 LZ-RMI [stored by 15May08 Sofia-Vrazhdebna, Bulgaria; b/u Sep11]
83 11 14	UVP	Turismo Air Iglesias	CCCP-67423 3C-KKU(2) YV-953C YV1844
83 11 15	UVP	unknown	CCCP-67424 3C-DLH YV-831CP YV2075 [impounded 21May11 Barcelona, Venezuela]
83 11 16	UVP	(Barnaul Airlines)	CCCP-67425 [canx 06Jun96; fate/status unknown]
83 11 17	UVP	(Barnaul Airlines)	CCCP-67426 [canx 30Aug96; fate/status unknown]
83 11 18	UVP	(Aeroflot/Krasnoyarsk)	CCCP-67427 [canx 29Nov94; preserved in children's camp Krasny Zavod, Russia]
83 11 19	UVP	(Aeroflot/Krasnoyarsk)	CCCP-67428 [w/o 31Dec86 Chernenko, USSR; canx 1987]
83 11 20	UVP	(Aeroflot/Krasnoyarsk)	CCCP-67429 RA-67429 [canx 29Nov94; reported wfu Omsk-Maryanovka, Russia]
83 11 21	UVP	(Aeroflot/Krasnoyarsk)	CCCP-67430 [canx 29Nov94; fate/status unknown]
83 11 22	UVP	(Aeroflot/East Siberia)	CCCP-67431 [w/o 19Apr88 Ulan Ude, USSR; canx 09Apr96]
83 11 23	UVP	(Nikolayevsk na Amure Airlines)	CCCP-67432 [canx 26Feb96; fate/status unknown]
83 11 24	UVP	ex Planar	CCCP-67433 UR-67433 ES-LLF UR-67433 D2-FFD [wfu by 25Jun12 Luanda, Angola]
83 11 25	UVP	(Doren Air Africa)	CCCP-67434 RA-67434 9L-LBK(1) [wfu by 16Jly05 Conakry, Guinea]
83 11 26	UVP	Libyan Air Force	OK-NZA 1126
83 11 27	UVP	Libyan Air Force	OK-NZB(2) 1127
83 11 28	UVP	Libyan Air Force	OK-NZC 1128
83 11 29	UVP	Libyan Air Force	OK-NZD 1129
83 11 30	UVP	Libyan Air Force	OK-NZE 1130

LET 410 AND 420 TURBOLET

C/n	Model	Last known Owner/Operator	Identities/fates/comments (where appropriate)
83 11 31	UVP	Libyan Air Force	OK-NZF 1131
83 11 32	UVP-T	Czech Air Force	1132+ [+ Czechoslovakia later Czech Republic]
83 11 33	UVP-T	Slovak Air Force	1133+ 1133 [+ Czechoslovakia]
83 11 34	UVP-T	Czech Air Force	1134+ [+ Czechoslovakia later Czech Republic]
83 11 35	UVP	(Latvian Air Force)	325+ 53+06^ 46# 146 [+ E Germany; ^ Germany; # Latvia; w/o 07Jun95 near Lielvarde, Latvia]
83 11 36	UVP	(Atlantic Airways)	326+ 53+07^ YS-406 TG-TJC XA-TDN N7962V HI-674CT HR-IBB YS-04C HR-ASF [+ E Germany; ^ Germany; w/o in Honduras between Sep01 & Aug02; hulk l/n Sep08 La Cieba, Honduras]
83 11 37	UVP	E.G. Figueroa	327+ 53+08^ YS-407 TG-TJB HR-AQQ HR-IAZ TG-AGW HR-ASS TG-AGW [+ E Germany; ^ Germany]
83 11 38	UVP	Praga Aviation	OK-178(2) OK-OZG OK-NZG OK-NDG SP-KPS OK-PRH
84 11 39	UVP	(Trans Air)	CCCP-67435 RA-67435 S9-CAD S9-CIO 3C-QRU [wfu for spares by Oct04 Peoples Republic of Pointe-Noire, Congo]
84 11 40	UVP	(Kostrama Air)	CCCP-67436 HA-LAH RA-67436 [damaged 02Dec96 Nyagan, Russia; canx 12Nov97]
84 12 01	UVP	Doren Air Congo	CCCP-67437 RA-67437 EL-LBL 9L-LBL(2) 9Q-CXZ [these marks noted 24Jan10 on An-74 c/n 36547098956, not confirmed]
84 12 02	UVP	ex West Coast Airways	CCCP-67438 HA-LAI 9L-LBJ(1) [fate/status unknown]
84 12 03	FG	ex Slovak Air Force	1203+ 1203 [+ Czechoslovakia; [preserved by Jun08 Piestany, Slovakia]]
84 12 04	UVP	Universal Avia	CCCP-67439 UR-67439 HA-LAU YL-KAH UR-67439
84 12 05	UVP	Djibouti Air Force	CCCP-67440 3D-NVH 3D-HVR J2-MBA
84 12 06	UVP	Djibouti Air Force	CCCP-67441 3D-NVG 3D-MCG J2-MBB
84 12 07	UVP	(Aeroflot/North Kavkaz)	CCCP-67442 RA-67442 [canx 20Oct97; fate/status unknown]
84 12 08	UVP	(Kostrama Air)	CCCP-67443 SP-FTP RA-67443 [canx 20Oct97; fate/status unknown]
84 12 09	UVP	ex Sasovo Flying School	CCCP-67444 RA-67444 [wfu by Jly02 Sasovo, Russia; l/n 29Aug07]
84 12 10	UVP	ex Sasovo Flying School	CCCP-67445 RA-67445 [wfu by 29Aug07 Sasovo, Russia]
84 12 11	UVP	ex Sasovo Flying School	CCCP-67446 [wfu by 22Aug95 Sasovo, Russia; canx 21Aug98; dumped by 17Aug01 Morshansk, Russia; later preserved Civil Aviation Technical College, Rylsk, Russia]
84 12 12	UVP	ex Sasovo Flying School	CCCP-67447 RA-67447 [wfu by 29Aug07 Sasovo, Russia]
84 12 13	UVP	(TsSPK)	CCCP-67448 RA-67448 RF-01152 [reported Aug10 Tanay, Russia; w/o 17Feb12 Tanay, Russia]
84 12 14	UVP	Avia Soyuz	CCCP-67449 UR-67449
84 12 15	UVP	unknown	CCCP-67450 UR-67450 ER-LIE 9L-LCT [derelict by 23Nov08 Lokichoggio, Kenya; l/n Mar12]
84 12 16	UVP	Oswaldo Cancines	CCCP-67451 YV-1071C YV1962
84 12 17	UVP	(Karibu Airways)	CCCP-67452 3D-NVF 9U-BHH 5R-MVW 5R-MGO 9Q-CEU [w/o 21Jun07 Kamina, Democratic Republic of Congo]
84 12 18	UVP	(Kezhemskogo Air Enterprise)	CCCP-67453 [fate/status unknown]
84 12 19	UVP	(Comores Aviation)	CCCP-67454 RA-67454 (3D-RAB) 3D-NVE(1) D6-TGH D6-CAK [w/o 09Apr07 Anjouan, Comores Islands]
84 12 20	UVP	(Nikolayevsk na Amure Airlines)	CCCP-67455 [canx 18Jly97; fate/status unknown]
84 12 21	UVP	(Nikolayevsk na Amure Airlines)	CCCP-67456 [canx 22Feb96; fate/status unknown]
84 12 22	UVP	(Nikolayevsk na Amure Airlines)	CCCP-67457 [canx 22Feb96; fate/status unknown]
84 12 23	UVP	(Aeroflot/East Siberia)	CCCP-67458 [canx 09Apr96; fate/status unknown]
84 12 24	UVP	Aero Caribe	CCCP-67459 S9-TBE N408LT(1) HH-PRO YV-595C YV1427
84 12 25	UVP	Muzel Aviatsiyata Voennovazdushni Sili	CCCP-67460 062+ [+ Bulgaria; preserved by Mar08 Krumovo-Plovdiv, Bulgaria]
84 12 26	UVP	Bulgarian Air Force	CCCP-67461 063
84 12 27	UVP	Berkut Z.K.	CCCP-67462 UP-L4106
84 12 28	UVP	(Berkut)	CCCP-67463 [fate/status unknown]
84 12 29	UVP	Air Aktobe	OK-ODA CCCP-67464 UN-67464 UP-L4101
84 12 30	UVP	(Aeroflot/Kazakhstan)	CCCP-67465 [never canx; fate/status unknown]
84 12 31	UVP	ex Aeroflot/Kazakhstan	CCCP-67466 [reported preserved Kustanay, Kazakhstan]
84 12 32	UVP	(Aeroflot/Krasnoyarsk)	CCCP-67467 [canx 23Dec98; fate/status unknown]
84 12 33	UVP	(Nizhneudinsk Air)	CCCP-67468 RA-67468 [canx 04Sep96; fate/status unknown]
84 12 34	UVP	(Aeroflot/East Siberia)	CCCP-67469 [canx 09Apr96; fate/status unknown]
84 12 35	UVP	(Aeroflot)	CCCP-67470 RA-67470 [damaged 14Jun94 Blagoveshchensk-Ignatyevo, Russia; hulk noted 20Apr97; canx 11Nov97]
84 12 36	UVP	(Aeroflot/East Siberia)	CCCP-67471 [canx date unknown; fate/status unknown]
84 12 37	UVP	SBA	CCCP-67472 UR-67472
84 12 38	UVP	(Kezhemskogo Air Enterprise)	CCCP-67473 [canx 30Oct95; fate/status unknown]

LET 410 AND 420 TURBOLET

C/n	Model	Last known Owner/Operator	Identities/fates/comments (where appropriate)
84 12 39	UVP	Aqua Limpa	CCCP-67474 RA-67474 S9-BAP+ [+ not confirmed; as RA-67474 was canx 26Sep97 following accident that day at Khabarovsk, Russia]
84 12 40	UVP	(Nikolayevsk na Amure Airlines)	CCCP-67475 [canx 29Dec95; fate/status unknown]
84 13 01	UVP	(Aeroflot/East Siberia)	CCCP-67476 [canx 09Apr96; fate/status unknown]
84 13 02	UVP	(Universal Avia)	CCCP-67477 UR-67477 [canx 30Apr09; fate/status unknown]
84 13 03	UVP	unknown	CCCP-67478 HH-OSA YV-981C YV-957C YV-1097CP [by 25Oct11 derelict Charallave, Venezuela]
84 13 04	UVP	(Avialinii Ukraïny)	CCCP-67479 UR-67479 [derelict by May02 Cherkasy, Ukraine; canx 13Aug08]
84 13 05	UVP	(Aeroflot/Central Region)	CCCP-67480 [canx 18Feb91; l/n wfu Kostrama, Russia by22Aug96]
84 13 06	UVP	(Avialinii Ukraïny)	OK-OZB CCCP-67481 UR-67481 [derelict by May02 Cherkasy, Ukraine; canx 13Aug08]
84 13 07	UVP	(Petropavlovsk Airlines)	CCCP-67482 RA-67482 [stored by 17Jun06 Petropavlovsk-Kamchatskiy-Yelizovo, Russia]
84 13 08	UVP	ex Tropical Airways	CCCP-67483 SP-FTR RA-67483 N40252 9L-LCJ N40252 HH-TRA [derelict by 15Apr10 Port-au-Prince, Haiti]
84 13 09	UVP	(Aeroflot/East Siberia)	CCCP-67484 [never canx; fate/status unknown]
84 13 10	UVP	(Kezhemskogo Air Enterprise)	CCCP-67485 [canx 30Oct95; fate/status unknown]
84 13 11	UVP	Yuri M Kabanov	CCCP-67486 RA-67486 FLARF-01841 RF-01841 RF-38386
84 13 12	UVP	Aerolineas SOSA	CCCP-67487 OK-ODD S9-TBL HR-ARE
84 13 13	UVP	(Travelair)	CCCP-67488 SP-FTM(2) TI-AWY [b/u hulk by Jan04 San Jose, Costa Rica; gone by Nov07]
84 13 14	UVP	unknown	CCCP-67489 LY-MRA [stored by Sep95 Plovdiv-Krumovo, Bulgaria; canx date unknown but by May10]
84 13 15	UVP	(Aeroflot/Kazakhstan)	CCCP-67490 [never canx; fate/status unknown]
84 13 16	UVP	ex Air Almaty	CCCP-67491 UN-67491 UP-L4105
84 13 17	UVP	(Universal Avia)	CCCP-67492 HA-LAL ES-LLD UR-67492 [canx 31Dec08; fate/status unknown]
84 13 18	UVP	unknown	CCCP-67493 LY-MJR [stored by Sep95 Plovdiv-Krumovo, Bulgaria; l/n May08; canx date unknown but by May10]
84 13 19	UVP	Turismo Aereo Amazonas	CCCP-67494 3C-KKD N550AG 3C-DDC 9L-LCA YV-1147C YV1219
84 13 20	UVP	Dubnica Air	CCCP-67096 OK-ODQ OM-ODQ
84 13 21	UVP	(Abakan Avia)	CCCP-67097 RA-67097 [canx 30May01; fate/status unknown]
84 13 22	UVP	(Petropavlovsk-Kamchatsky Air)	CCCP-67098 RA-67098 [stored by 02Sep09 Petropavlovsk-Kamchatsky-Yelizovo, Russia]
84 13 23	UVP-E	SEARCA	OK-022(2) OK-PZE OK-022(2) TG-TJT HK-4038
84 13 24	UVP-E9	(United Airlines)	OK-170 OK-OZF OK-ODF J2-KBD OK-ODF 5Y-UAS [w/o 17Apr02 Masai Mara, Kenya]
84 13 25	UVP	(Aeroflot/Kazakhstan)	CCCP-67099 [w/o 27Aug91 42km from Guryev, Kazakhstan, USSR; canx 05Nov91]
84 13 26	UVP	Air Scorpio	CCCP-67100 UR-67100 LZ-MNG HA-LAY LZ-MNG
84 13 27	UVP	(Amuravia)	CCCP-67101 RA-67101 [canx 11Nov97; fate/status unknown]
84 13 28	UVP	(Universal Avia)	CCCP-67102 UR-67102 HA-LAP(1) UR-67102 [canx 01Oct08; fate/status unknown]
84 13 29	UVP	El Sol de America	CCCP-67103 YV-982C YV-982CP? YV-1120C
84 13 30	UVP	(Aeroflot/North Kavkaz)	CCCP-67104 [w/o 28Aug89 near Labinsk, USSR; canx 25Dec89]
84 13 31	UVP	Comores Aviation	CCCP-67105 RA-67105 9L-LCZ D6-CAN
84 13 32	UVP	(Global Para)	HA-YFB 332+ HA-LAQ [+ Hungary] [stored by 14Mar10 Sibson, UK; b/u Feb11]
84 13 33	UVP	Bulgarian Air Force	065
84 13 34	UVP-E20B	SEARCA	OK-120 OK-PDH OK-120 OK-PZH OK-PDH OK-120 CP-2252 HK-4367
85 13 35	UVP	(Trans Air Congo)	CCCP-67106 RA-67106 3C-QRV TN-AHE [w/o 17May07 near Kilambo, Democratic Republic of Congo]
85 13 36	UVP	Comores Aviation	CCCP-67107 RA-67107 OK-PDM RA-67107 RA-02719 3X-GDH D6-GDH D6-CAM
85 13 37	UVP	ex West Coast Airways	CCCP-67108 RA-67108 9L-LBN [damaged 24Aug00; wfu by 11Mar01 Freetown, Sierra Leone; l/n 14Jly09]
85 13 38	UVP	(Doren Air Congo)	CCCP-67109 RA-67109 9L-LBM 9Q-CBQ [w/o 09Nov06 Walikale, Democratic Republic of Congo]
85 13 39	UVP	Doren Air Congo	CCCP-67495 RA-67495 9L-LBS 3X-GDE 9L-LEM 9Q-CQZ
85 13 40	UVP	Caribair	OK-PXM CCCP-67496 N63015 HI-676SP HI-676CA HI-676CT HI-713CA HI-713CT
85 14 01	UVP	Jump Tandem	CCCP-67497 RA-67497 3D-HRS OM-JUM
85 14 02	UVP	(Sky Executive)	CCCP-67498 RA-67498 (3D-RAA) 3D-NVD 9Q-CGX [w/o 22May02 near Akani Obi Oron, Nigeria]

LET 410 AND 420 TURBOLET

C/n	Model	Last known Owner/Operator	Identities/fates/comments (where appropriate)
85 14 03	UVP	Eagle Air Guinee	CCCP-67499 RA-67499 3D-DSI HH-BET 3D-DSI
85 14 04	UVP	Jungle Flying	CCCP-67500 N63020 HI-677SP HI-677CA N63020 HR-IBC TG-AGY
85 14 05	UVP	unknown	CCCP-67501 RA-67501 FLARF-02839 RA-2839K RA-00814 RF-00973
85 14 06	UVP	Air Max	CCCP-67502 UR-67502 LZ-RMK
85 14 07	UVP	ex North Adria Aviation	CCCP-67503 UR-67503 9A-BAN [not on early 2010 register, assumed canx; fate/status unknown]
85 14 08	UVP	(Universal Avia)	CCCP-67504 UR-67504 HA-LAN UR-67504 [canx 01Oct08; fate/status unknown]
85 14 09	UVP	Aero Ferinco	CCCP-67505 RA-67505 N41020 XA-TFG
85 14 10	UVP	ex Universal Avia	CCCP-67506 UR-67506 [derelict by May07 Cherkasy, Ukraine; l/n Aug08; canx 13Aug08]
85 14 11	UVP	(Petr Navratil Aerotaxi & Air School)	CCCP-67507 UR-67507 OK-PDO [stored by 18Jun07 Otrokovice, Czech Republic; & DBF 31Oct10]
85 14 12	UVP	Turismo Aereo Amazonas	CCCP-67508 RA-67508 3C-KKE TI-AYH HH-PRT YV1157
85 14 13	UVP	Avies	CCCP-67509 LY-AVY ES-PLB
85 14 14	UVP	(unknown)	CCCP-67510 ZS-OSC XT-FBD 9XR-AM [w/o May04 at unknown location in Sudan]
85 14 15	UVP	Eric Distava	CCCP-67511 UN-67511 3C-NVE EX-415 9Q-CEI
85 14 16	UVP	ASAS de Mocambique	CCCP-67512 UN-67512 3C-ZZC(2) 3D-KIM [reported 12Sep12 Nelspruit, South Africa with no c/n plate alongside another Let410 registered C9-AUR carring this c/n plate]
85 14 17	UVP	Aerovista	CCCP-67513 EX-417
85 14 18	UVP	(Sky Service)	CCCP-67514 OK-SKY [canx 07Apr08; fate/status unknown]
85 14 19	UVP	ASAS de Mocambique	CCCP-67515 3C-ZZB 3C-ZZC(1) 3C-ZZB 3D-NEB
85 14 20	UVP	Rainbow Air	CCCP-67516 UR-KMA YV301T YV398T
85 14 21	UVP	CM Airlines	CCCP-67517 TG-TJD HR-AXC
85 14 22	UVP	(Aeroflot/East Siberia)	CCCP-67518 [w/o 19Apr88 Borgadin. USSR; canx 13May88]
85 14 23	UVP	Cotair	CCCP-67519 UR-67519 3D-GAM 9U-BHF 3D-GAM TU-TBG
85 14 24	UVP	unknown	CCCP-67520 9L-LCC
85 14 25	UVP	AviaExpress Air Company	CCCP-67521 UR-UAE YL-KAA UR-LAA
85 14 26	UVP	Transaca	CCCP-67522 RA-67522 LY-ASB YV-922CP
85 14 27	UVP	Comeravia	CCCP-67523 UR-KAM UR-KMD YV1233
85 14 28	UVP-E	Aircraft Industries	CCCP-67551 RA-67551 OK-PDN OK-LEK
85 14 29	UVP-E	(Asian Spirit)	CCCP-67552 RA-67552 RP-C3883 [w/o 07Dec99 Kasibu, Philippines]
85 14 30	UVP-E	Arkhangelsk 2nd Aviation Enterprise	CCCP-67553 RA-67553
85 14 31	UVP	(Rivne Universal Avia)	CCCP-67524 UR-67524 [wfu by 04Jly07 Rivne, Ukraine; canx 13Aug08]
85 14 32	UVP	unknown	CCCP-67525 UN-67525 9U-BHT
85 14 33	UVP	ex Ukraine Flight State Academy	CCCP-67526 UR-67526 [wfu Kirovograd, Ukraine; l/n Aug08; canx 13Aug08]
85 14 34	UVP	ex Ukraine Flight State Academy	CCCP-67527 UR-67527 [wfu by 2001 Kirovograd, Ukraine; l/n Aug08; canx 13Aug08]
85 14 35	UVP	Free Airlines	CCCP-67528 9L-LBR 9Q-CBR [wfu by 12Jly05 Kananga, Democratic Republic of Congo]
85 14 36	UVP	(Aeroflot/Krasnoyarsk)	CCCP-67529 [canx 30May01; fate/status unknown]
85 14 37	UVP	ex Olimex	CCCP-67530 RA-67530 OK-PDP [by 04Jly00 stored Kunovice, Czech Republic; canx 09Sep03; derelict by Oct04; roaded 20Oct11 to Bubovice, Czech Republic]
85 14 38	UVP	GisAir	CCCP-67531 LY-AIL ES-PLI UR-TVA 9Q-CGE
85 14 39	UVP	National Air	CCCP-67532 YL-PAH S9-TBC HI-693CT HH-HAT
85 14 40	UVP	African Air Charter	CCCP-67533 RA-67533 9L-LBI
85 15 01	UVP	(Sakha Avia)	CCCP-67534 [wfu by 11Jun02 Yakutsk-Magan, Russia; l/n Jly04]
85 15 02	UVP	(Sakha Avia)	CCCP-67535 [wfu by 11Jun02 Yakutsk-Magan, Russia; l/n Jly04]
85 15 03	UVP	(Aeroflot/Ukraine)	CCCP-67536 [never canx; fate/status unknown]
85 15 04	UVP	Letecke Muzeum Kbely	CCCP-67537 1504+ [+ Czechoslovakia later Czech Republic; preseved by Sep05 Kbely, Czech Republic; l/n Nov08]
85 15 05	UVP	(Aeroflot/Yakutsk)	CCCP-67538 [damaged 27Sep91 Magadan, USSR; derelict by 03Jly92 Yakutsk-Magan, USSR; canx 28Apr95]
85 15 06	UVP	(Sakha Avia)	CCCP-67539 RA-67539 [derelict by 01Jly04 Yakutsk, Russia; no recent reports]
85 15 07	UVP	Shuttle Bird	CCCP-67540 YL-KAJ UR-SEV TU-TCV
85 15 08	UVP	(Aeroflot/Yakutsk)	CCCP-67541 RA-67541 [wfu by 11Jun02 Yakutsk-Magan, Russia]
85 15 09	UVP	(Sakha Avia)	CCCP-67542 RA-67542 [wfu by 01Jly04 Yakutsk, Russia; no recent reports]
85 15 10	UVP	ex Ukraine Flight State Academy	CCCP-67543 LZ-MNB UR-67543 [wfu Kirovograd, Ukraine; l/n Aug08; canx 13Aug08]
85 15 11	UVP	Zest Airways	CCCP-67544 RA-67544 RP-C3889

LET 410 AND 420 TURBOLET

C/n	Model	Last known Owner/Operator	Identities/fates/comments (where appropriate)
85 15 12	UVP	(Amuravia)	CCCP-67545 RA-67545 [canx 11Nov97; fate/status unknown]
85 15 13	UVP	unknown	CCCP-67546 RA-67546 C9-STG(2) 3D-SPL
85 15 14	UVP	ITAB	CCCP-67547 RA-67547 LY-AVP 3D-AVP 9Q-CMD
85 15 15	UVP	(Edga V Lacruz)	CCCP-67548 YV-956C [w/o en-route 22Apr99 near Caen, France]
85 15 16	UVP	Aerolineas SOSA	CCCP-67549 YL-PAI (1) S9-TBD HR-AQR
85 15 17	UVP	Caribair	CCCP-67550 RA-67550 TG-TJV HI-666CT
85 15 18	UVP	North Adria Aviation	CCCP-67554 9A-BNA
85 15 19	UVP	Ukraine Flight State Academy	CCCP-67555 LZ-MNC UR-67555 LZ-MNC UR-67555
85 15 20	UVP	ex Ukraine Flight State Academy	CCCP-67556 UR-67556 [wfu by 2001 Kirovograd, Ukraine; l/n Aug08; canx 13Aug08]
85 15 21	FG	Slovak Air Force	1521+ 1521 [+ Czechoslovakia]
85 15 22	FG	(Budvai)	1522+ OK-PDB [+ Czechoslovakia later Czech Republic; wfu & b/u by Jan06 Presov, Slovakia]
85 15 23	FG	(Czech Air Force)	1523+ [+ Czechoslovakia later Czech Republic; wfu 2004 Kbely, Czech Republic; 15Oct05 fuselage to Jince, Czech Republic as GIA; b/u by Jan06]]
85 15 24	FG	Doren Air Congo	1524+ OK-PDC 9Q-CZA [+ Czechoslovakia later Czech Republic]
85 15 25	FG	Czech Air Force	1525+ [+ Czechoslovakia later Czech Republic]
85 15 26	FG	Czech Air Force	1526+ [+ Czechoslovakia later Czech Republic]
85 15 27	UVP	(Slovair)	OK-PXI OK-PDI [w/o 13Mar93 Zilina, Czech Republic; dumped by May95 Bratislava, Slovakia]
85 15 28	FG	Turbojet Kft	HA-YFC
85 15 29	UVP	ex Aero Ferinco	CCCP-67557 RA-67557 XA-TAU [w/o 22Oct05 by Hurricane Wilma, Playa del Carmen, Mexico; being used as spares source; l/n 05Mar09]
85 15 30	UVP	Aerolineas SOSA	CCCP-67558 RA-67558 HR-AQO HR-ASZ
85 15 31	UVP	(Eagle Air)	CCCP-67559 YL-KAC 9L-LCG [w/o 23Jan01 Maiduguri, Nigeria]
85 15 32	UVP	(Aero Ferinco)	CCCP-67560 TG-TJQ XA-SYJ [w/o 27Nov01 in Gulf of Mexico, off Playa de Carmen, Mexico]
85 15 33	UVP-T	Libyan Air Force	OK-PXJ 1533
85 15 34	UVP-T	Libyan Air Force	OK-PXK 1534
85 15 35	UVP-T	Libyan Air Force	OK-PXL 1535
86 15 36	UVP-T	Libyan Air Force	OK-RXA 1536
86 15 37	UVP-T	Libyan Air Force	OK-RXB 1537
86 15 38	UVP-T	Libyan Air Force	OK-RXC 1538
86 15 39	UVP-E		[used for static tests on L-410 UVP-E programme]
86 15 40	UVP-E		[used for static tests on L-410 UVP-E programme]
86 16 01	UVP-E	National de Aviacion Colombia	OK-RZI CCCP-67561 TG-TJS HK-4013X HK-4013
86 16 02	UVP-E	ex Arkhangelsk Aviation	CCCP-67562 RA-67562 [wfu by 13Oct11 Arkhangelsk-Vaskovo, Russia, with Air Mali titles]
86 16 03	UVP-E	ex Arkhangelsk Aviation	CCCP-67563 RA-67563 [wfu by 13Oct11 Arkhangelsk-Vaskovo, Russia]
86 16 04	UVP-E	Arkhangelsk Aviation	CCCP-67564 RA-67564
86 16 05	UVP-E	ex Arkhangelsk Aviation	CCCP-67565 RA-67565 [wfu by 13Oct11 Arkhangelsk-Vaskovo, Russia]
86 16 06	UVP-E	Kazair West	CCCP-67566 RA-67566 UN-67566 HA-LAK(2) UN-67566 UP-L4104
86 16 07	UVP-E	Arkhangelsk Aviation	CCCP-67567 RA-67567
86 16 08	UVP-E	(Islena Airlines)	CCCP-67568 TG-NAS HR-IAS [w/o 03Mar97 La Ceiba, Honduras]
86 16 09	UVP-E	ex Arkhangelsk Aviation	CCCP-67569 RA-67569 [wfu by 13Oct11 Arkhangelsk-Vaskovo, Russia]
86 16 10	UVP-E	National de Aviacion Colombia	CCCP-67570 RA-67570 N16100 HK-4151X
86 16 11	UVP-E	Aero Caribe	CCCP-67571 YS-10C HR-ASE
86 16 12	UVP-E	SEARCA	CCCP-67572 N6968L HK-4161X HK-4161 FAC1105 HK-4161
86 16 13	UVP-E	SEARCA	CCCP-67573 N5957N HK-4105X HK-4105
86 16 14	UVP-E	Atlantic Airlines	CCCP-67574 RA-67574 YS-07C [stored by 03Sep08 La Ceiba, Honduras]
86 16 15	UVP-E	Air Santo Domingo	CCCP-67575 N5957P HI-695CA HI-695CT PR-IBD* [* marks reserved 16Sep10 for Alfly Taxi Aereo]
86 16 16	UVP-E	Air Santo Domingo	CCCP-67576 N7874M HI-688CA HI-688CT
86 16 17	UVP-E	Transporte Aereo de Colombia	OK-RXD CCCP-67577 HK-4196X HK-4196
86 16 18	UVP-E	(Heliandes)	CCCP-67578 N5957Q HK-4175X [w/o 16Dec01 near Medellin, Colombia]
86 16 19	UVP-E	(Soviet Air Force)	CCCP-67579 [fate/status unknown]
86 16 20	UVP-E	(Taxis Aereos)	CCCP-67580 YS-09C [w/o 15Jan00 near Tobias Bolanos, Costa Rica]
86 17 01	UVP-E	Atlantic Airlines	CCCP-67581 RA-67581 YS-06C HR-ASN
86 17 02	UVP-E	ex International Jet Centre	CCCP-67582 N5854P HK-4152X N808LT HP-1073 HH-TAD N408LT(2) HH-EIR
86 17 03	UVP-E	Sundance Air	CCCP-67583 RA-67583 N5957J HK-4142 YV2362
86 17 04	UVP-E	(Atlantic Airlines)	CCCP-67584 N5957L YN-CFE TG-CFE [w/o 18Sep01 Aurora, Guatemala]
86 17 05	UVP-E	Atlantic Airways	CCCP-67585 N5956C YN-CFD+ TG-CFD YN-CFR [+ not fully confirmed]

LET 410 AND 420 TURBOLET

C/n	Model	Last known Owner/Operator	Identities/fates/comments (where appropriate)
86 17 06	UVP-E	(MRP LII Gorki)	CCCP-67586 [canx date unknown; fate/status unknown]
86 17 07	UVP-E	(TAC Colombia)	CCCP-67587 N5857T HK-4094 FAC1104+ HK-4094 [+ Colombia] [w/o 26Jun09 Capurgana, Colombia]
86 17 08	UVP-E	South East Asian	CCCP-67588 RP-C5888 RP-C2728
86 17 09	UVP-E	Comeravia	CCCP-67589 YV-985C YV-985CP YV-1108CP YV1333
86 17 10	UVP-E	Atlantic Airlines	CCCP-67590 9L-LBT(1) HR-AJG+ YS-13C+ HR-ASG [+ not fully confirmed]
86 17 11	UVP-E	Atlantic Airlines	1711+ LY-AZA YS-05C HR-ASM [+ Soviet] [stored by Jly08 La Ceiba, Honduras]
86 17 12	UVP-E	unknown	1712+ YV-863CP [+ Soviet]
86 17 13	UVP-E	Aeromed?	1713+ YV-1023CP YV2027 [+ Soviet]
86 17 14	UVP-E	Transhaven	1714+ YV-864CP YV1463 [+ Soviet]
86 17 15	UVP-E	Comercial Hubagi	1715+ YV-865CP YV2109 [+ Soviet]
86 17 16	UVP-E	Atlantic Airlines	1716+ YS-14C HR-ASH [+ Soviet]
86 17 17	UVP-E	CIACA Airlines	1717+ HK-4159X YV-866CP [HK-4159X [+ Soviet] [reported wfu by 08Mar08 Medellin, Colombia; l/n 03Sep10]
86 17 18	UVP-E	unknown	1718+ YV-868CP [+ Soviet; code 04]
86 17 19	UVP-E	Aeroservicios OK	1719+ YV-1004CP YV-1176C YV1752 [+ Soviet]
86 17 20	UVP-E	Balashov Technical School	1720+ [+ Soviet] [by 28Aug07 GIA, Balashov, Russia]
86 17 21	UVP-E	Caribair	1721+ LY-AZF HH-CRT [+ Soviet]
86 17 22	UVP-E	Kiri Avia	1722+ LZ-CCF 3D-CCF 9Q-CKA 3D-CCF 9Q-CKA [+ Soviet]
86 17 23	UVP-E	ex Aerolineas Sosa	1723+ LY-ARC YS-11C [+ Soviet] [stored by 03Sep08 La Ceiba, Honduras]
86 17 24	UVP-E	Atlantic Airlines	1724+ LY-AZO YS-12C HR-ASJ [+ Soviet]
86 17 25	UVP-E	ex SA Profesionales	1725+ LY-AFY N188LT HI-703CT HI-703 [+ Soviet; later codes 51 & 222; hulk by Dec06 Santo Domingo-Herrera, Dominican Republic]
86 17 26	UVP-E	Libyan Air Force	1726+ YL-KAI OM-HLF 1726 [+ Soviet]
86 17 27	UVP-E9	Aero Este	1727+ S9-TBH CP-2382 [+ Soviet; later code 08 red]
86 17 28	UVP-E	Russian Air Force	1728+ 09 red [+ Soviet]
86 17 29	UVP-E	ex SA Profesionales	1729+ LY-AZH HI-722CT HI-722 [+ Soviet] [hulk by Dec06 Santo Domingo-Herrera, Dominican Republic]
86 17 30	UVP-E	ex SA Profesionales	1730+ LY-AZI HI-723CT [+ Soviet] [hulk by Dec06 Santo Domingo-Herrera, Dominican Republic]
86 18 01	UVP-E1	Tengerin Elch	LZ-LSA OM-RDE OK-RDE JU-2030
86 18 02	UVP-E2	Heli Air Services	LZ-LSB [at one time carried code UN523]
86 18 03	UVP-E2	Urzad Morski (Gdansk Maritime Office)	SP-MBA
86 18 04	UVP-E	(Aeroflot/East Siberia)	CCCP-67591 [canx 02Apr97; fate/status unknown]
86 18 05	UVP-E	(Aeroflot/East Siberia)	CCCP-67592 [canx 02Apr97; fate/status unknown]
86 18 06	UVP-E	(Aeroflot/East Siberia)	CCCP-67593 [canx 02Apr97; fate/status unknown]
86 18 07	UVP-E	(Aeroflot/East Siberia)	CCCP-67594 [canx 02Apr97; fate/status unknown]
86 18 08	UVP-E	(Aeroflot/East Siberia)	CCCP-67595 [canx 02Apr97; fate/status unknown]
86 18 09	UVP-E8	Eagle Air	CCCP-67596 5X-JNF
86 18 10	UVP-E	unknown	CCCP-67597 OM-111(1) HK-4002X HK-4002 HK-4285 (YV-661C) HK-4285-X [stored by 10Jly09 Bogota, Colombia]
87 18 11	UVP-E20	Air Excel	CCCP-67598 RA-67598 OK-SDO 5H-PAD 5H-AES
87 18 12	UVP-E20	(Eagle Aviation)	CCCP-67599 OK-SDP OY-PBI(1) OY-PAC 5Y-ONT [w/o 28Nov02 Masai Mara, Kenya]
87 18 13	UVP-E5	ex Van Air/Manx2	OK-RDA OM-RDA OM-RAY OK-RDA HA-YFG OK-RDA [wfu by end 2010 derelict in field near Bratislava, Slovakia]
87 18 14	UVP-E3	Russian Air Force	1814+ [+ earlier Soviet]
87 18 15	UVP-E3	(Soviet Air Force)	1815 [fate/status unknown]
87 18 16	UVP-E3	Tortug'Air	1816+ LZ-CCE 3D-CCE HH-AET [+ Soviet]
87 18 17	UVP-E3	(unknown)	1817+ 97+ 3D-WAS [+ Soviet] [b/u at Bratislava-Ivanka, Slovakia; l/n May04]
87 18 18	UVP-E3	Russian Air Force	1818+ 1818^ 26 red [+ Soviet] [^ Russia]
87 18 19	UVP-E3	DOSAAF Rossii	1819+ 19 blue^ FLARF0195 RF-00195 [+ Soviet] [^ Russia]
87 18 20	UVP-E3	ex Russian Air Force	1820+ 39 red [+ Soviet] [offered for sale in 1998; fate/status unknown]
87 18 21	UVP-E3	Rupashi Bangla Airlines	1821+ RA-67821 RP-C2928 S2-AEI^ [+ Soviet; ^ not imported & remained in Phillipines]
87 18 22	UVP-E3	DOSAAF	1822+ 1822^ 25 blue [+ Soviet] [^ Russia]
87 18 23	UVP-E3	(Soviet Air Force)	1823+ [fate/status unknown]
87 18 24	UVP-E3	Zan Air	1824+ 9L-LBV(2) 5H-ZAP [+ Soviet]
87 18 25	UVP-E3	Russian Air Force	1825+ 54 red [+ Soviet]

LET 410 AND 420 TURBOLET

C/n	Model	Last known Owner/Operator	Identities/fates/comments (where appropriate)
87 18 26	UVP-E3	(Soviet Air Force)	1826+ [fate/status unknown]
87 18 27	UVP-E3	Tortug'Air	1827+ LZ-CCL S9-DIV HH-LOG [+ Soviet] [stored by Sep08 La Ceiba, Honduras]
87 18 28	UVP-E3	ex Air Max	1828+ HA-LAC(2) T9-AAJ LZ-RML [+ Soviet] [canx 09Jan09; no C of A for six months; fate/status unknown]
87 18 29	UVP-E3	Russian Air Force	1829+ 1829 [+ Soviet]
87 18 30	UVP-E3	Aerograd	1830+ 13 red^ FLARF-01731 RA-1731K RF-00964 [+ Soviet] [^ Russia]
87 19 01	UVP-E3	ex Soviet Air Force	1901 [by 2007 GIA at Balashov, Russia]
87 19 02	UVP-E3	Russian Air Force	1902+ 1902 [+ Soviet] [also carries 12 blue]
87 19 03	UVP-E3	DOSAAF	1903+ 1903^ 31 blue [+ Soviet] [^ Russia]
87 19 04	UVP-E20	Aircraft Systems South Africa (Pty)/UN	1904+ OK-SDL 5X-UAG 5H-PAN 5Y-BSV ZS-PNI [+ Soviet]
87 19 05	UVP-E3	Air Tranzit	1905+ 88 red^ FLARF-01953 RA-0144G RA-67678 [+ Soviet] [^ Russia] [stored by 03Nov09 Kunovice, Czech Republic; l/n Jly11]
87 19 06	UVP-E3	Tropical Airways	1906+ 42 red^ YL-PAI(2) N82311 HK-4085 HR-IBA HH-PRN [+ Soviet] [^ Russia]
87 19 07	UVP-E3	ex Soviet Air Force	1907 [fate/status unknown]
87 19 08	UVP-E3	DOSAAF Rossii	1908+ 108 red^ FLARF-01747 FLARF-1747K RF-00132 RF-00138 [+ Soviet] [^ Russia] [dbr 22Jly12 Bolshoe Gryzlovo, Russia]
87 19 09	UVP-E3	ex South East Asian Airlines	1909+ 72^ 3D-DAM RP-C2428 S2-AEJ# [+ Soviet] [^ Russia] [# not imported & remained in Phillipines]
87 19 10	UVP-E3	Atlantic Airlines	1910+ 41 red^ OK-SDE CU-T1193 HR-ASW [+ Soviet] [^ Russia]
87 19 11	UVP-E3	Air Kasai	1911+ 9L-LBJ(2) 5V-TTH 9Q-CFG [+ Soviet]
87 19 12	UVP-E3	Tramas Textiles	1912+ 109 red^ YV395T YV220T# YV1712# [+ Soviet] [^ Russia] [# c/n not fully confirmed]
87 19 13	UVP-E3	Air Tranzit	1913+ FLARF-01751 RF-01050 RA-1106G RA-67681 [+ Soviet] [stored by 03Nov09 Kunovice, Czech Republic; l/n Jly11]
87 19 14	UVP-E3	ex Seagle Air	1914+ 89 red^ OM-HLB OM-CGL [+ Soviet] [^ Russia]
87 19 15	UVP-E3	Atlantic Airlines	1915+ 19 red^ OK-SDF CU-T1194 HR-ASX [+ Soviet] [^ Russia]
87 19 16	UVP-E20	Atlantic Airways	1916+ 43 red^ OK-SDG YN-CFM [+ Soviet] [^ Russia]
87 19 17	UVP-E3	Atlantic Airways	1917 37 black^ OK-SDH YN-CFL [+ Soviet] [^ Russia]
87 19 18	UVP-E3	ex Soviet Air Force	1918 [by 28Aug07 GIA at Balashov, Russia]
87 19 19	UVP-E3	(unknown)	1919+ YV-928CP [+ Soviet] [w/o 14Jan98 Bruno, Czech Republic]
87 19 20	UVP-E20	Air-Tec Africa/Air Express Algeria	1920+ 44 red^ OK-SDB Z-LET ZS-OOF 5H-HSB ZS-OOF 5H-PAJ ZS-OOF [+ Soviet]
87 19 21	UVP-E3	Air Tropiques	1921+ 45 red^ 9L-LBU(2) 9L-LCH# 5V-TTF 9Q-CFA [+ Soviet] [^ Russia] [# not confirmed]
87 19 22	UVP-E20	Citylink	1922+ 33 red^ OK-SDC Z-LNK ZS-OOH Z-OMC 5X-UAZ ZS-OOH 9G-LET [+ Soviet]
87 19 23	UVP-E4	(Farnair Europe)	923+ HA-LAR [+ Hungary] [w/o 27Jan05 Iasi, Romania]
87 19 24	UVP-E4	Farnair Europe	924+ HA-LAS 9A-BAL HA-LAS [+ Hungary]
87 19 25	UVP-E3	Aerolineas SOSA	1925+ 94 red^ OK-SDJ S9-TBW N888LT(2) HR-ASI [+ Soviet] [^ Russia]
87 19 26	UVP-E3	Sky Pasada	1926+ 23 blue^ 9L-LBT(2) 5V-TTG RP-C6868 [+ Soviet] [^ Russia]
87 19 27	UVP-E3	Tortug'Air	1927+ 20^ OK-SDU S9-BAM PT-XCP HH-LET [+ Soviet] [^ Russia; colour unknown]
87 19 28	UVP-E3	Aircraft Systems South Africa (Pty)	1928+ OK-SDS(1) 5A-DMT ST-CAV ZS-ATC [+ Soviet]
87 19 29	UVP-E3	Taxi Aereo Cusiana	1929+ 31^ S9-CBB HK-4225X HK-4225 [+ Soviet] [^ Russia; colour unknown]
87 19 30	UVP-E3	Tortug'Air	1930+ 12^ OK-SDV S9-BAO HH-TOR [+ Soviet] [^ Russia; colour unknown]
87 19 31	UVP-E3	South East Asian Airlines	1931+ RP-C2628 [+ Soviet]
87 19 32	UVP-E3	Kharkov APO	1932+ FLARF-01833 UR-NPO [+ Soviet]
87 19 33	UVP-E3	Taxi Aereo Cusiana	1933+ 56 red^ OK-SDQ HK-4260X HK-4260 [+ Soviet] [^ Russia]
87 19 34	UVP-E3	South East Asian Airlines	1934+ 28 red^ 3C-QRH RP-C3318# [+ Soviet] [^ Russia] [# report as RP-C3118 assumed to be in error]
87 19 35	UVP-E3	Aerograd Kolomna	1935+ RF-00858 [+ Soviet]
87 19 36	UVP-E20	Benair	1936+ OK-SDM OY-PBI(2) [+ Soviet]
87 19 37	UVP-E3	ex Soviet Air Force	1937 [by 28Aug07 GIA at Balashov, Russia]
87 19 38	UVP-E3	AeroDomca	1938+ 21 red^ RA-67780 9L-LCF HI-761CT HI-761 [+ Soviet] [^ Russia]
87 19 39	UVP-E3	Mombasa Air Safari	1939+ S9-TBK 3D-SIG 5Y-BSM [+ Soviet]

LET 410 AND 420 TURBOLET

C/n	Model	Last known Owner/Operator	Identities/fates/comments (where appropriate)
87 19 40	UVP-E3	unknown	1940+ 17 blue^ FLARF-01952 RF-00136 RF-00139 [+ Soviet] [^ Russia]
87 20 01	UVP-E3	(Tropical Airways)	2001+ S9-TBF N888LT(1) HH-PRV N888LT(1) HH-PRV [+ Soviet] [w/o 24Aug03 near Cap-Haitien, Haiti]
87 20 02	UVP-E3	(Easy Link)	2002+ 34 red^ OK-SDR 5N-BEK [+ Soviet] [^ Russia] [wfu/derelict by 10Nov07 Abuja, Nigeria]
87 20 03	UVP-E3	South East Asian Airlines	2003+ 38 red^ RP-C528 RP-C3328 [+ Soviet] [^ Russia]
87 20 04	UVP-E3	South East Asian Airlines	2004+ 20 blue^ RA-67781 S9-BOY RP-C2328 [+ Soviet] [^ Russia]
87 20 05	UVP-E3	Universal Investment Group	2005+ 21 blue^ UR-GNG [+ Soviet] [^ Russia]
87 20 06	UVP-E	KIN Avia	CCCP-67600 OM-SDA 3D-MSC 9Q-CRJ
87 20 07	UVP-E3	Polyarnye Avialinii	2007+ RA-67676 [+ Soviet]
87 20 08	UVP-E3	Libyan Air Force	2008+ RA-67674 OM-HLD 2008 [+ Soviet]
87 20 09	UVP-E3	(Blue Bird Aviation)	2009+ LZ-CCM OK-SDD 5Y-VVD [+ Soviet] [w/o 23May04 near Mwingi, Kenya, collided with Let-410 5Y-VVA c/n 962633]
87 20 10	UVP-E3	unknown	2010+ 100^ YV-867CP [+ Soviet] [^ Russia; colour unknown]
87 20 11	UVP-E20	Air Express Algeria	2011+ RA-67673 ES-LLG OK-SDT 7T-VAE [+ Soviet]
87 20 12	UVP-E3	Noel Rodriguez	2012+ YV-1002CP YV1963 [+ Soviet]
87 20 13	UVP-E3	Kazan 2nd Aviation Enterprise	2013+ RA-67672 [+ Soviet]
87 20 14	UVP-E3	Aero Ejecutivos	2014+ YV-1026CP YV1434 [+ Soviet]
87 20 15	UVP-E3	(Transaven)	2015+ 41 blue^ LY-AVX XA-ABK YV-1119C YV2081 [+ Soviet] [^ Russia] [w/o 04Jan08 off Los Roques archipeligo, Venezuela]
87 20 16	UVP-E3	Transporte Air Checo	2016+ YV-1003CP YV-795CP^ YV2263 [+ Soviet] [^ marks not confirmed]
87 20 17	UVP-E20	Aircraft Systems South Africa (Pty)/UN	2017+ LZ-CCN OK-SDN ZS-OMI 9J-ZSL ZS-OMI 5Y-BRM ZS-ATA [+ Soviet]
87 20 18	UVP E7	Blue Bird Aviation	OK-SDA S2-ADC 5Y-HHL 5Y-VVL
87 20 19	UVP-E6	SLI Slovak Republik	OK-SYI OM-SYI
87 20 20	UVP-E3	Aerocon	2020+ CP-2393 [+ Soviet]
87 20 21	UVP-E3	ex Atlantic Airlines	2021+ LY-AFI TG-COR^ TG-ELJ [+ Soviet] [^ not fully confirmed; wfu/derelict by Apr06 Managua, Nicaragua; l/n Mar08; canx by Jun08]]
88 20 22	UVP-E3	ex Aerofly Monogas	2022+ YV-1028C YV-1028CP YV1518 [+ Soviet] [derelict by 08Oct11 Port au Prince, Haiti]
88 20 23	UVP-E3	Air Santo Domingo	2023+ N16545 HI-679SP HI-679CA HI-679CT [+ Soviet]
88 20 24	UVP-E3	SA Professionale	2024+ N5658G HI-680SP HI-680CA HI-680SP HI-680CT PR-IBB* [+ Soviet] [* marks reserved 16Sep10 for Alfly Taxi Aereo]
88 20 25	UVP-E3	Aero Caribe	2025+ N54637 HI-681SP HI-681CA HI-681CT HR-AWA [+ Soviet]
88 20 26	UVP-E3	CIACA Airlines	2026+ YV-1027C YV-1127CP [+ Soviet]
88 20 27	UVP-E3	not known	2027+ RA-67675 [+ Soviet] [stored by 07Aug07 Kazan-Osnovnoi, Russia]
88 20 28	UVP-E3	(TA Guatemaltecos)	2028+ TG-TAG [+ Soviet] [w/o 03Jun05 Zacapa, Guatemala]
88 20 29	UVP-E3	Aerolineas SOSA	2029+ LY-AZM TG-TAY HR-AUE [+ Soviet]
88 20 30	UVP-E3	Aero Ferinco	2030+ XA-TQC [+ Soviet]
88 20 31	UVP-E3	(Business Aviation of Congo)	2031+ 9Q-CTM [+ Soviet] [w/o en-route 26Jun07 100km from Brazzaville, People's Republic of Congo]
88 20 32	UVP-E3	Air Santo Domingo	2032+ LY-AZN HI-724CT [+ Soviet]
88 20 33	UVP-E3	AP Airlines	2033+ LY-AVT [+ Soviet]
88 20 34	UVP-E3	Atlantic Airlines	2034+ LY-AZK YS-15C HR-ASD [+ Soviet]
88 20 35	UVP-E3	Transairways	2035+ 3D-NVA 3D-ZZM 3D-NVA [+ Soviet]
88 20 36	UVP-E3	AP Airlines	2036+ LY-AVA [+ Soviet]
88 20 37	UVP-E3	ex Aerolineas Sosa	2037+ 9Q-CUS YS-08C [+ Soviet] [stored by 03Sep08 La Ceiba, Honduras]
88 20 38	UVP-E10	North South Airlines	SP-TAA SP-FTV 3D-FTV RP-C8258
88 20 39	UVP-E9A	Caribair	OK-TZA OY-CTE OK-TDB S9-TAU HI-698CT
88 20 40	UVP-E9A	Caribair	OK-TZB OY-CTF OK-TDG S9-TAV HI-697CT
88 21 01	UVP-E3	Sol Linhas Aereas	2101+ 14 red^ OK-TDA PR-VLA [+ Soviet] [^ Russia]
88 21 02	UVP-E3	South East Asian Airlines	2102+ 65 red^ S9-BOX RP-C2128 [+ Soviet] [^ Russia]
88 21 03	UVP-E3	Ambjek Air Services	2103+ 34 red^ OK-TDS 5N-BEB [+ Soviet] [^ Russia]
88 21 04	UVP-E3	Russian Air Force	2104+ 2104^ 94 blue [+ Soviet] [^ Russia]
88 21 05	UVP-E3	Russian Air Force	2105+ 36 red [+ Soviet]
88 21 06	UVP-E3	Russian Air Force	2106+ 2106 38 red [+ Soviet] [^ Russia]
88 21 07	UVP-E3	Russian Air Force	2107+ 2107 [+ Soviet]
88 21 08	UVP-E3	(Soviet Air Force)	2108 [fate/status unknown]
88 21 09	UVP-E3	(Soviet Air Force)	2109 [fate/status unknown]
88 21 10	UVP-E3	Russian Air Force	2110+ 81 red [+ Soviet]
88 21 11	UVP-E3	Russian Air Force	2111+ 11 red [+ Soviet]
88 21 12	UVP-E3	(Soviet Air Force)	2112 [fate/status unknown]

LET 410 AND 420 TURBOLET

C/n	Model	Last known Owner/Operator	Identities/fates/comments (where appropriate)
88 21 13	UVP-E3	Russian Air Force	2113+ 2113 [+ Soviet]
88 21 14	UVP-E3	Russian Air Force	2114+ 61^ 14 blue [+ Soviet/Russia; ^ Russia; colour unknown]
88 21 15	UVP-E3	Russian Air Force	2115+ 2115 [+ Soviet]
88 21 16	UVP-E3	Russian Air Force	2116+ 2116 [+ Soviet] [coded 5 red]
88 21 17	UVP-E3	Russian Air Force	2117+ 2117 [+ Soviet]
88 21 18	UVP-E3	Russian Air Force	2118+ 2118^ 65 blue [+ Soviet] [^ Russia]
88 21 19	UVP-E3	Russian Air Force	2119+ 2119^ [+ Soviet] [^ Russia]
88 21 20	UVP-E3	(Soviet Air Force)	2120 [fate/status unknown]
88 21 21	UVP-E3	Russian Air Force	2121+ 2121^ [+ Soviet] [^ Russia]
88 21 22	UVP-E3	Russian Air Force	2122+ 2122^ 02 red [+ Soviet] [^ Russia]
88 21 23	UVP-E3	Russian Air Force	2123+ 2123^ 59 red [+ Soviet] [^ Russia]
88 21 24	UVP-E3	Russian Air Force	2124+ 2124^ 71 red [+ Soviet] [^ Russia]
88 21 25	UVP-E3	Russian Air Force	2125+ 2125^ 78 blue [+ Soviet] [^ Russia]
88 21 26	UVP-E3	ex Russian Air Force	2126+ 2126^ [+ Soviet] [^ Russia] [wfu by 16Aug11 Kolomna, Russia; also with codes 22 blue and 115 red]
88 21 27	UVP-E3	Russian Air Force	2127+ 116 red 37 red [+ Soviet; ^ Russia; 2127 on rear fuselage]
88 21 28	UVP-E3	Russian Air Force	2128+ 2128 [+ Soviet]
88 21 29	UVP-E3	ex Russian Air Force	2129 2129^ [+ Soviet] [^ Russia] [wfu by 16Aug11 Kolomna, Russia; also with codes 92 blue and 92 red]
88 21 30	UVP-E3	Russian Air Force	2130+ 2130^ 67 red [+ Soviet] [^ Russia]
88 21 31	UVP-E3	Russian Air Force	2131+ 2131^ 93 red [+ Soviet] [^ Russia]
88 21 32	UVP-E3	Russian Air Force	2132+ 2132^ 08 blue [+ Soviet] [^ Russia] [wfu as 2132 by 16Aug11 Kolomna, Russia; also with codes 08 blue and 94 outline]
88 21 33	UVP-E3	Russian Air Force	2133+ 2133^ 96 red [+ Soviet] [^ Russia]
88 21 34	UVP-E3	DZ Yegoryevsk	2134+ 2134^ 87 blue^ RA-94601 [+ Soviet] [^ Russia]
88 21 35	UVP-E3	Russian Air Force	2135+ 2135^ 57 red [+ Soviet] [^ Russia]
88 21 36	UVP-E3	Russian Air Force	2136+ 2136 [+ Soviet] [^ Russia]
88 21 37	UVP-E3	Russian Air Force	2137+ 2137 [+ Soviet]
88 21 38	UVP-E3	Russian Air Force	2138+ 2138^ 48 Blue [+ Soviet] [^ Russia]
88 21 39	UVP-E3	Russian Air Force	2139+ 69 red [+ Soviet]
88 21 40	UVP-E3	Russian Air Force	2140+ 2140^ 80 red [+ Soviet] [^ Russia]
88 22 01	UVP-E3	Russian Air Force	2201+ 2201^ 42 blue [+ Soviet] [^ Russia]
88 22 02	UVP-E3	Russian Air Force	2202+ 2202^ 07 red [+ Soviet] [^ Russia]
88 22 03	UVP-E3	unknown	2203+ RF-49416 [+ Soviet]
88 22 04	UVP-E3	Russian Air Force	2204+ 2204 56 red [+ Soviet] [^ Russia]
88 22 05	UVP-E3	(Soviet Air Force)	2205 [fate/status unknown]
88 22 06	UVP-E3	Russian Air Force	2206+ 2206^ 14 red [+ Soviet] [^ Russia]
88 22 07	UVP-E12	Air Max	LZ-LSC LZ-RMC [stored by 15Mar08 Sofia-Vrazhdebna, Bulgaria; l/n 15May08]
88 22 08	UVP-E3	(Soviet Air Force)	2208 [fate/status unknown]
88 22 09	UVP-E3	Russian Air Force	2209+ 79 red [+ Soviet]
88 22 10	UVP-E3	Russian Air Force	2210+ 2210^ 15 red [+ Soviet] [^ Russia]
88 22 11	UVP-E3	Russian Air Force	2211+ 2211 [+ Soviet]
88 22 12	UVP-E3	Russian Air Force	2212+ 2212^ 52 yellow [+ Soviet] [^ Russia]
88 22 13	UVP-E3	(Soviet Air Force)	2213 [fate/status unknown]
89 22 14	UVP-E	Arkhangelsk 2nd Aviation Enterprise	CCCP-67603 RA-67603
89 22 15	UVP-E	Air Max	CCCP-67604 RA-67604 HA-LAV SP-KTA HA-LAV LZ-RMV
89 22 16	UVP-E	LR Airlines	CCCP-67605 OK-LRA
89 22 17	UVP-E3	Russian Air Force	2217+ 2217^ 01 red [+ Soviet] [^ Russia]
89 22 18	UVP-E3	Russian Air Force	2218+ 2218^ 71 blue [+ Soviet] [^ Russia]
89 22 19	UVP-E3	Russian Air Force	2219+ 2219^ 53 red [+ Soviet] [^ Russia]
89 22 20	UVP-E3	unknown	2220+ YV-869CP [+ Soviet]
89 22 21	UVP-E3	unknown	2221+ RF-49417 [+ Soviet]
89 22 22	UVP-E3	Russian Air Force	2222+ 2222 [+ Soviet]
89 22 23	UVP-E3	Russian Air Force	2223+ 2223^ 15 blue [+ Soviet] [^ Russia]
89 22 24	UVP-E3	Russian Air Force	2224+ 2224^ 76 red [+ Soviet] [^ Russia]
89 22 25	UVP-E3	ex Star Africa Air	2225+ 3D-LEA TL-LCK 3C-UAQ [+ Soviet] [reported derelict by Jan10 Berbera, Somalia]
89 22 26	UVP-E9	Zan Air	2226+ 9L-LBK(2) 5H-LET [+ Soviet]
89 22 27	UVP-E3	Russian Air Force	2227+ 2227 [+ Soviet]
89 22 28	UVP-E	Zest Airways	CCCP-67601 RA-67601 RP-C3880
89 22 29	UVP-E	Arkhangelsk 2nd Aviation Enterprise	CCCP-67602 RA-67602

LET 410 AND 420 TURBOLET

C/n	Model	Last known Owner/Operator	Identities/fates/comments (where appropriate)
89 22 30	UVP-E3	Russian Air Force	2230+ 2230^ [+ Soviet] [^ Russia]
89 22 31	UVP-E3	Russian Air Force	2231+ 2231^ 51 red [+ Soviet] [^ Russia]
89 22 32	UVP-E3	Russian Air Force	2232+ 2232^ 88 blue [+ Soviet] [^ Russia]
89 22 33	UVP-E3	Russian Air Force	2233+ 0? red [+ Soviet]
89 22 34	UVP-E3	Russian Air Force	2234+ 2234^ 44 red [+ Soviet] [^ Russia]
89 22 35	UVP-E3	Russian Air Force	2235+ 2235^ 45 red [+ Soviet] [^ Russia]
89 22 36	UVP-E3	Russian Air Force	2236+ 2236^ 46 red [+ Soviet] [^ Russia]
89 22 37	UVP-E3	Russian Air Force	2237+ 2237^ 82 blue [+ Soviet] [^ Russia]
89 22 38	UVP-E3	Russian Air Force	2238+ 2238^ [+ Soviet] [^ Russia]
89 22 39	UVP-E3	(Soviet Air Force)	2239 [fate/status unknown]
89 22 40	UVP-E3	Russian Air Force/VVS Rossii	2240+ 2240^ RF-892240# RF-94658 [+ Soviet; ^ Russia; # non standard marks]
89 23 01	UVP-E10	Heli Air Services/United Nations	SP-TAB SP-FTX LZ-CCR
89 23 02	UVP-E3	ex Centrafrican	2302+ 71^ 3D-LEC TL-ACI EL-MLC [+ Soviet] [^ Russia; colour unknown; damaged around 2004 Gbadolite, Democratic Republic of Congo; wfu/derelict by 24Mar09, no marks]]
89 23 03	UVP-E3	DOSAAF	2303+ 2303^ RF-49920 [+ Soviet] [^ Russia]
89 23 04	UVP-E3	Russian Air Force	2304+ 2304^ 18 red [+ Soviet] [^ Russia]
89 23 05	UVP-E3	Russian Air Force	2305+ 2305^ 32 red [+ Soviet] [^ Russia]
89 23 06	UVP-E3	Russian Air Force	2306+ 2306^ 84 red [+ Soviet] [^ Russia]
89 23 07	UVP-E3	(United States Air Force)	2307+ 120 red^ S9-TBU N551AG 3C-DDD 9L-LCB 00-0292 [+ Soviet] [^ Russia] [w/o 08Feb02 Fort Bliss, TX; serial possibly not painted on aircraft]
89 23 08	UVP-E3	Russian Air Force	2308+ 78 red^ 05 red [+ Soviet] [^ Russia]
89 23 09	UVP-E3	Russian Air Force	2309+ 2309^ [+ Soviet] [^ Russia]
89 23 10	UVP-E3	Russian Air Force	2310 80 red [2310 on rear fuselage]
89 23 11	UVP-E14	Slovak Air Force	2311+ 2311 [+ Czechoslovakia]
89 23 12	UVP-E14	Czech Air Force	2312+ OK-UDB 2312 [+ Czechoslovakia later Czech Republic]
89 23 13	UVP-E18	ex Aerosur	SP-FGK CP-2246 [stored by Sep97 Santa Cruz-El Trompillo, Bolivia; l/n Apr03]
89 23 14	UVP-E	Transaven	CCCP-67617 LY-AZR N30RZ YV-1113C YV2083
89 23 15	UVP-E	ex Sakha Avia	CCCP-67618 [wfu by Jly92 Yakutsk-Magan, Russia; derelict byJun02; l/n Jly04]
89 23 16	UVP-E	Presidental Flight	CCCP-67619 RA-67619 9L-LBV(1) YU-BYY 3C-RBA
89 23 17	UVP-E10	WCC Aviation Company	SP-TAC SP-FTY 3D-FTY RP-C3988
89 23 18	UVP-E15	Porty Lotnicze	SP-TPA
89 23 19	UVP-E16	Van Air Europe	SP-TXA OK-UBA
89 23 20	UVP-E8	Eagle Air	OK-UDA 5X-GNF
89 23 21	UVP-E13	Icar Airlines	OK-UDS T9-AAK E7-AAK
89 23 22	UVP-E	Arkhangelsk 2nd Aviation Enterprise	CCCP-67606 RA-67606
89 23 23	UVP-E9	Blue Sky Aviation	CCCP-67607 OK-UDC 5Y-BSA
89 23 24	UVP-E17	Budapest Air Service	HA-YFD
89 23 25	UVP-E3	Kin Avia	2325+ S9-TBJ S9-TBG OY-PAF 3D-DEF^ 3D-DEN 9Q-CEN [+ Soviet] [^ not confirmed]
89 23 26	UVP-E3	DOSAAF	2326+ 19 red^ RF-49415 RF-49921 [+ Soviet] [^ Russia]
89 23 27	UVP-E3	Russian Air Force	2327+ 2327^ 83 red [+ Soviet] [^ Russia]
89 23 28	UVP-E3	unknown	2328+ 2328^ RA-1976K RA-0152G [+ Soviet] [^ Russia]
89 23 29	UVP-E15	Porty Lotnicze	SP-TPB
89 23 30	UVP-E3	Russian Air Force/VVS Rossii	2330+ 2330^ RF-892330# RF-94667" [+ Soviet; ^ Russia; # non-standard marks; " also carries 14 blue]
89 23 31	UVP-E3	Russian Air Force	2331+ 2331^ 86 red [+ Soviet] [^ Russia]
89 23 32	UVP-E3	Russian Air Force	2332+ 2332^ 74 red [+ Soviet] [^ Russia]
89 23 33	UVP-E3	Russian Air Force	2333+ 2333^ 10 red [+ Soviet] [^ Russia]
89 23 34	UVP-E	(Tuva Airlines)	CCCP-67608 [DBR Apr94 Kyzyl, Russia was hit by An-2P CCCP-07308; canx 24Dec96; used for fire training until b/u probably in 2007]
89 23 35	UVP-E3	Di Air	CCCP-67609 RA-67609 LY-AVV ES-PLC 3D-AFH 4O-OOI
89 23 36	UVP-E	Apatas Airlines	CCCP-67610 LY-AVZ
89 23 37	UVP-E	Bulgarian Air Force	066
89 23 38	UVP-E	Bulgarian Air Force	067
89 23 39	UVP-E	Kazair West	CCCP-67611 RA-67611 OM-111(2) OM-UDX UN-67611 UP-L4103
89 23 40	UVP-E	Aircraft Systems South Africa (Pty)	CCCP-67612 RA-67612 ST-CAU ZS-ATB
89 23 41	UVP-E	Transporte Aereo de Colombia	CCCP-67613 HP-1326 YV-986C HK-4147X HK-4147

LET 410 AND 420 TURBOLET

C/n	Model	Last known Owner/Operator	Identities/fates/comments (where appropriate)
89 23 42	UVP-E	Tri-M G Airlines	CCCP-67614 UR-67614 RP-C748 PK-YGL [CofA expired 19Oct10; fate/status unknown]
89 23 43	UVP-E	C S Turisticos C.A.	CCCP-67615 UR-67615 RP-C749 YV-875CP YV1704 YV2144
89 24 01	UVP-E	(Aero Ferinco)	CCCP-67616 LY-AZP TG-AZP+ XA-ACM [+ not fully confirmed; w/o 13Sep01 Chichen Itza, Mexico]]
90 24 02	UVP-E3	Business Aviation	CCCP-67620 RA-67620 9Q-CYM
90 24 03	UVP-E	Aircraft Systems South Africa	CCCP-67621 RA-44477 OK-VDA 5A-DMR ST-DMR ZS-ATF
90 24 04	UVP-E	Ilin	CCCP-67622 RA-67622
90 24 05	UVP-E	Polyarnye Avialinii	CCCP-67623 RA-67623
90 24 06	UVP-E	(Millenium Air)	CCCP-67624 RA-67624 OK-JOB 5N-BFL [w/o 01Dec03 Kano, Nigeria when hit by wing of Boeing 747 5N-EEE; canx 26Oct06]
90 24 07	UVP-E3	Russian Air Force	2407+ 2407^ 60 red [+ Soviet] [^ Russia]
90 24 08	UVP-E3	Kazan 2nd Aviation Enterprise	2408+ RA-67667 [+ Soviet]
90 24 09	UVP-E3	Aircraft Systems South Africa (Pty)	2409+ 73^ RA-67669 OK-VDV F-OTKE ZS-ATI [+ Soviet] [^ Russia; colour unknown]
90 24 10	UVP-E3	Aerograd Kolomna	2410+ 18^ RA-67671 RF-00752 [+ Soviet] [^ Russia; colour unknown]
90 24 11	UVP-E3	Russian Air Force	2411+ 2411 99 red^ [+ Soviet] [^ 2411 also on rear fuselage]
90 24 12	UVP-E3	Russian Air Force	2412+ 98 red^ [+ Soviet] [^ 2412 also on rear fuselage]
90 24 13	UVP-E3	Aircraft Systems South Africa (Pty)/UN	2413+ 24^ RA-67668 OK-VDO F-ORTE ZS-EPB [+ Soviet] [^ Russia; colour unknown]
90 24 14	UVP-E16A	Sprint Air	SP-TXB SP-KTL
90 24 15	UVP-E3	Russian Air Force	2415 114 red [2415 on rear fuselage]
90 24 16	UVP-E3	Polyarnye Avialinii	2416+ 48^ RA-67670 ES-LLA RA-67670 [+ Soviet] [^ Russia; colour unknown]
90 24 17	UVP-E3	Russian Air Force	2417+ 2417^ 09 red [+ Soviet] [^ Russia]
90 24 18	UVP-E	Aero Ruta Maya/Jungle Flying	CCCP-67625 TG-TJH
90 24 19	UVP-E	Aero Ruta Maya/Jungle Flying	CCCP-67626 TG-TJG
90 24 20	UVP-E	Colombian Air Force/SATENA	CCCP-67627 RA-67627 S9-BOZ HK-4224 FAC1103
90 24 21	UVP-E	Slovak Air Force	CCCP-67628 RA-67628 2421
90 24 22	UVP-E	FilAir	CCCP-67629 RA-67629 YU-BXX 9Q-CDN+ [+ see c/n 90 25 19 apparent duplication of marks]
90 24 23	UVP-E	SEARCA	CCCP-67630 S9-BAD HK-4235 [damaged 12Dec08 Capurgana, Colombia]
90 24 24	UVP-E	ex Atlantic Airlines	CCCP-67631 LY-ARA TG-ARE [derelict/wfu by Nov06 Managua, Nicaragua; l/n Mar08; canx by Jun08]
90 24 25	UVP-E	Heli Air Services/UN	CCCP-67632 RA-67632 SP-KTC 3D-EER LZ-CCS
90 24 26	UVP-E	(West Caribbean Airways)	CCCP-67633 UR-67633+ YV-988C HP-1325 HK-4146X HK-4146 [+ not confirmed; w/o 27Dec04 Providencia Island, Colombia; canx 18Oct05]]
90 24 27	UVP-E	Rus Aviation	CCCP-67634 RA-67634
90 24 28	UVP-E	Rus Aviation	CCCP-67635 [stored by May95 Khabarovsk-Two, Russia; reported 2006 on overhaul in Czech Republic for Sasovo Flying School]
90 24 29	UVP-E	Vostok Aviakompania	CCCP-67636 RA-67636
90 24 30	UVP-E	Transaven	CCCP-67637 RA-67637 N28RZ YV-1175C YV2082
90 24 31	UVP-E	Van Air/Manx2	CCCP-67638 RA-67638 OK-VDE SP-KPZ OK-TCA
90 24 32	UVP-E	West Caribbean Airways	CCCP-67639 RA-67639 HA-LAT HK-4187X
90 24 33	UVP-E	ex SA Profesionales	CCCP-67640 HK-4071X HI-665CT HI-665 [hulk by 31Dec06 at Santo Domingo-Herrera, Dominican Republic]
90 24 34	UVP-E	Tri-M G Airlines	CCCP-67641 RA-67641 RP-C728 PK-YGN [CofA expired 22Nov10; fate/status unknown]
90 24 35	UVP-E	Ambjek Air Services	CCCP-67642 RA-67642 OK-VDT 5N-BEA
90 24 36	UVP-E	Feeder Airlines	CCCP-67643 RF-49409 OK-VDB 5A-DMS ST-DMS
90 24 37	UVP-E	Lao Capricorn Air	CCCP-67644 RA-67644 "REG-67644" ER-67644+ ER-LID RDPL-34158 [+ not confirmed]
90 24 38	UVP-E	Petropavlovsk Kamchatsky Air Enterprise	CCCP-67645 RA-67645
90 24 39	UVP E	Van Air/Manx2	CCCP-67646 RA-67646 OK-VDF SP-KPY OK-ASA
90 24 40	UVP-E	Nizhnudinsk Air	CCCP-67647 RA-67647
90 25 01	UVP-E	Indicator Airlines	CCCP-67648 HA-LAO TL-AEE
90 25 02	UVP-E	Easy Link	CCCP-67649 RA-67649 XA-SXX(1) TG-TJI HI-692CT 5N-BCM
90 25 03	UVP-E20	Silver Air	CCCP-67650 RA-67650 S5-BAE LZ-CCG OK-SLD
90 25 04	UVP-E	ABC Air Hungary	CCCP-67651 RA-67651 HA-LAZ SP-KTB HA-LAZ
90 25 05	UVP-E	Ruiban & Duran CA	CCCP-67652 RA-67652 HK-4082X YV-605C YV-1060C [w/o en-route 13Jly03 near San Cristobal, Venezuela]

LET 410 AND 420 TURBOLET

C/n	Model	Last known Owner/Operator	Identities/fates/comments (where appropriate)
90 25 06	UVP-E3	Sky Pasada	CCCP-67653 LZ-KLA 9A-BTB RP-C3779
90 25 07	UVP-E3	Eastern Airways	CCCP-67654 LZ-KLB 9A-BTC OK-VAA 3D-PAT
90 25 08	UVP-E	Aeropacifico	CCCP-67655 N19RZ XA-AFE
90 25 09	UVP-E	(Sakha Avia)	CCCP-67656 RA-67656 [w/o 26Aug96 near Aldan, Yakutia, Russia; canx 21Feb96]
90 25 10	UVP-E	Zest Airways	CCCP-67657 RA-67657 9L-LCL(1) 9A-BNZ RP-C2918
90 25 11	UVP-E10	Cabo Verde Express	SP-TAD SP-FGL 9Q-CUM D4-CBL
90 25 12	UVP-E	Zhezkazgan Air	CCCP-67658 UR-67658 UR-SVI UP-L4102
90 25 13	UVP-E	South Airlines	CCCP-67659 UR-67659 UR-YAM
90 25 14	UVP-E	TEAM Brazil	CCCP-67660 LZ-KLC LZ-CCK OK-VDP PR-CRA
90 25 15	UVP-E10	KIN Avia	SP-TAE SP-FGI SP-FTN(2) 3D-FTN 9Q-CMA
90 25 16	UVP-E8A	ex Farnair Air Transport	HA-LAD [probably wfu by May10 Bruno, Czech Republic; l/n Jly12]
90 25 17	UVP-E8A	Air Max	HA-LAE LZ-RMW
90 25 18	UVP-E8A	Budapest Air Services	HA-LAF
90 25 19	UVP-E	ITAB	CCCP-67661 RA-67661 9L-LBW(2) 9L-LCL(2) 9Q-CDP+ [+ see c/n 90 24 22 apparent duplication of marks]
90 25 20	UVP-E	Petropavlovsk Kamchatsky Air Enterprise	CCCP-67662 RA-67662
90 25 21	UVP-E10A	(Nacional de Aviacion)	SP-FTC SP-FGG S9-TAX HK-4055X HK-4055 [w/o en-route 22Feb07 between Villavicencio and Uribe, near Cubarral, Colombia]
90 25 22	UVP-E3	Bulgarian Air Force	068
90 25 23	UVP-E3	Bulgarian Air Force	069+ LZ-RMA 069 [+ Bulgaria]
90 25 24	UVP-E3	Bulgarian Air Force	064+ LZ-RME 064 [+ Bulgaria]
90 25 25	UVP-E	unknown	CCCP-67663 UR-67663 UR-IBE ST-RAS
90 25 26	UVP-E	Ilin	CCCP-67664 RA-67664
90 25 27	UVP-E	Aircraft Systems South Africa	CCCP-67665 UR-67665 YV-984C(1)+ SP-FGM ST-CAT ZS-ATD [+ probably not officially taken up]
91 25 28	UVP-E20	Heli Air Services/UN	SP-FTH SP-FGH ST-DND LZ-CCT [reported for sale in Brazil]
91 25 29	UVP-E10	SADI	SP-FTI 5H-ZAT S9-TBB HK-4109
91 25 30	UVP-E10	Aero Este	SP-FTK OY-LET S9-TBM CP-2349
91 25 31	UVP-E8D	Silver Air	OK-WDC
91 25 32	UVP-E	(TEAM)	OK-WDJ PT-WLS OK-WDJ OY-TCM PT-FSE [w/o en-route 31Mar06 between Rio Bonito & Saquarema, Brazil]
91 25 33	UVP-E10	Cabo Verde Express	OK-WDL OY-TCL D-CLED D4-CBR
91 25 34	UVP-E	Aerosur	CCCP-67666 OK-WDD CP-2244
91 25 35	UVP-E	Aerosur	CCCP-67667 OK-WDE CP-2245
91 25 36	UVP-E20	Aero Este	CCCP-67668 OK-WDS S9-TAY CP-2328
91 25 37	UVP-E	(Djibouti Airlines)	CCCP-67669 J2-KBC [w/o 17Mar02 Djibouti, Djibouti]
91 25 38	UVP-E19A	(Trade Air)	CCCP-67670 OK-WDO J2-KBE OK-WDO 9A-BTA [w/o 30Oct05 Bergamo, Italy]
91 25 39	UVP-E9	Aero Kenya/UN	OK-WDB OM-WDB (9J-EAL) 9J-EAZ 5X-DIV 5X-UAY 5Y-BRU
91 25 40	UVP-E8C	Heli Air Services/UN	OK-WDA OM-WDA S5-BAF 3D-BAF LZ-CCP
91 26 01	UVP-E	Czech Air Force	CCCP-67671 2601
91 26 02	UVP-E	Czech Air Force	CCCP-67672 2602
91 26 03	UVP-E20	(Central American Airways)	CCCP-67673 OK-WDP J2-KBF OK-WDP LV-WYV S9-TBY D-CLET HH-AVP HR-AUQ [w/o 14Feb11 Cerro de Hula, Tegucigalpa, Honduras]
91 26 04	UVP-E20	Cabo Verde Express	CCCP-67674 OK-WDU OK-006 N4248Y S9-TBN OY-PEY D4-JCA (ZS-PIP)
91 26 05	UVP-E	West Caribbean Airways	CCCP-67675 OK-WDZ HK-4125
91 26 06	UVP-E	Slovenian Air Force	CCCP-67676 S5-BAD L4-01
91 26 07	UVP-E	KIN Avia	CCCP-67677 OK-WDR 3D-WDR 9Q-CEG
91 26 08	UVP-E20C	(FilAir)	CCCP-67678 OK-WDG ES-LLB 9Q-CCN [w/o 25Aug10 Bandundu, Democratic Republic of Congo]
91 26 09	UVP-E	Heli Air Services/UN	CCCP-67679 OK-WDH ES-LLC LZ-CCW
09 26 10	UVP-E20	Ural Mining & Metallurgical Company	OK-UGM RA-67003 [originally reserved with c/n 91 26 10; c/n amended to reflect year of completion]
91 26 11	UVP-E20	ex TEAM Brazil	CCCP-67680 PR-AIA [stored by 28Mar11 Jacarepagua, Brazil; unmarked]
91 26 12	UVP-E	Aerograd	CCCP-67681 UN-67666 RF-00373 RA-67680
91 26 13	UVP-E	Aircraft Systems South Africa (Pty)/ICRC	CCCP-67682 OK-WDM UR-67715 OK-2613 7Q-YKV ZS-MWM
91 26 14	UVP-E19A	Tatarstan Police	CCCP-67683 UR-67716 UR-UTN RF-67571
91 26 15	UVP-E	Elba Fly	CCCP-67684 OK-WDT E7-WDT
91 26 16	UVP-E	Czech Government	CCCP-67685 OK-WYI
91 26 17	UVP-E20	NHT Linhas Aereas	CCCP-67686 OK-2617 PR-CRX

LET 410 AND 420 TURBOLET

C/n	Model	Last known Owner/Operator	Identities/fates/comments (where appropriate)
91 26 18	UVP-E	(Parabat Airlines)	CCCP-67687 OK-WDV S2-ADD [w/o near Dhaka, Bangladesh; by May00 to GIA Dhaka-Tejgaon, Bangladash]
91 26 19	UVP-E19	Mombasa Air Safari/Kush Air	CCCP-67688 OK-WDW 5Y-NIK
91 26 20	UVP-E	(Malindi Air Services)	CCCP-67689 OK-164(3) OK-WDX 5Y-LET [w/o 29May99 Ol Kiombo Air Strip, Kenya]
07 26 21	UVP-E20	Heli Air Service	CCCP-67690 OK-KIM HL5235 OK-KIM LZ-CCQ
09 26 22	UVP-E	Ural Mining & Metallurgical Company	CCCP-67691 OK-UFA RA-67004
95 26 23	UVP-E	Operadora de Turismo Castillo Mourra	CCCP-67692 OK-ADS TI-AVU TG-TJL HR-AVI
95 26 24	UVP-E	Polyarnye Avialinii	CCCP-67693 OK-ADT(2)RA-67693
95 26 25	UVP-E	Polyarnye Avialinii	CCCP-67694 OK-ADU RA-67694
91 26 26	UVP-E	SEARCA	CCCP-67695 OK-146 OM-111(3) HK-4048
91 26 27	UVP-E9	(Mombasa Air Safari)	CCCP-67696 OK-WDY 5Y-UVP [proably w/o 22Aug12 Ngerende Airstrip, Masai Mara, Kenya]
07 26 28	UVP-E20	Ace Air	CCCP-67697 OK-AIS(1) HL5234
08 26 29	UVP-E20	Air Express Algeria	CCCP-67698 7T-VAF
08 26 30	UVP-E20	Aircraft Systems South Africa (Pty)/ICRC	CCCP-67699 OK-2630 ZS-DIH
98 26 31	UVP-E20	Zanzibar Airline Company	OK-DDE 5H-PAE 5H-ZAA
96 26 32	UVP-E9	Eagle Air	VT-ETW OK-BDK (5H-PAH) 5Y-BPX 5X-EIV
96 26 33	UVP-E9	Bluebird Aviation	VT-ETX OK-BDL S2-ABL OK-BDL 5Y-VVA
02 26 34	UVP-E9	Heli Air Services/UN	OK-SLD LZ-CCJ
09 26 35	UVP-E	Air Guyane Express	OK-2635 F-OIXF
06 26 36	UVP-E20	NHT Linhas Aereas	PR-NHA
06 26 37	UVP-E20	NHT Linhas Aereas	PR-NHB
01 26 38	UVP-E	South Korean Forestry Aviation Office	FP502+ HL5236 [+ South Korea]
07 26 39	UVP-E20	NHT Linhas Aereas	PR-NHC
07 26 40	UVP-E20	NHT Linhas Aereas	PR-NHD
92 27 01	UVP-E20	TEAM Brazil	OK-XDJ VT-ETA OK-XDJ PR-IMO
93 27 02	UVP-E9	(Archana Airways)	OK-XDK VT-ETB [w/o 18May96 Kanpur, India]
93 27 03	UVP-E9	(Archana Airways)	OK-ZDE VT-ETC [w/o 11Jly96 in Himalayas, India]
96 27 04	UVP-E9	(Safari Link)	OK-BDG (VT-JVG) VT-ETD OK-BDG S2-ABM OK-BDG 5Y-VVB [w/o 05Mar11 Kichwa Tembo airstrip, Kenya; canx 05Mar10]
94 27 05	UVP-E20	Tunisian Air Force	OK-ZDF Z94041//TS-OTA [dual marks]
94 27 06	UVP-E20	Tunisian Air Force	OK-ZDA Z94043//TS-OTC+ [dual marks; + Z94042 also reported]
94 27 07	UVP-E20	Tunisian Air Force	OK-ZDB Z94045//TS-OTE+ [dual marks]
96 27 08	UVP-E20	Tunisian Air Force	OK-ADN(2) Z94047//TS-OTG [dual marks]
96 27 09	UVP-E20	Tunisian Air Force	OK-BDH Z94049//TS-OTI [dual marks]
92 27 10	UVP-E20D	Czech Air Force	OK-BYF 2710
92 27 11	UVP-E20D	(Precision Air Service)	OK-XDI OK-BYG OK-XDI ZS-OAW OK-XDI 5H-PAC [w/o 16Nov04 Kilimanjaro, Kenya; canx]
08 27 12	UVP-E20	SOMAGEC Guinea Ecuatorial	OK-2712 3C-LLO
09 27 13	UVP-E20	Office of the President of Equatorial Guinea	OK-2713 3C-LLP
08 27 14	UVP-E20	NHT Linhas Aereas	OK-2714 PR-NHE
96 27 15	UVP-E9	(Precision Air Service)	OK-BDJ RP-C8787 OK-BDJ 5H-PAB [w/o 26Jly99 Arusha, Tanzania; l/n 04Feb02; canx]
09 27 16	UVP-E20	Sasovo Flying School	OK-2716 (PR-SLA) OK-UGS RA-67001 [originally reserved with c/n 08 27 16; c/n amended to reflect year of completion]
09 27 17	UVP-E20	Sasovo Flying School	OK-UFB RA-67002
09 27 18	UVP-E20	Slovak Air Force	OK-2718 2718
09 27 19	UVP-E20	Nordeste Linhas Aereas Regionais	OK-SLP PR-NOA
27 20	UVP-E20	Heli Air Services/UN	OK-SLT LZ-CCV
27 21	UVP-E20	Slovak Air Force	OK-SLU 2721
27 22	UVP-E20	(Nordeste Linhas Aereas Regionais)	OK-SLR PR-NOB [w/o 13Jly11 Recife, Brazil]
27 23	UVP-E20	Petropavlovsk-Kamchatsky Avia	OK-SLV RA-67007
27 24	UVP-E20	Petropavlovsk-Kamchatsky Avia	OK-SDT RA-67008

LET 410 AND 420 TURBOLET

C/n	Model	Last known Owner/Operator	Identities/fates/comments (where appropriate)
27 25	UVP-E20	Petropavlovsk-Kamchatsky Avia	OK-SDU RA-67009(2)
92 27 26	UVP-E20	Bluebird Aviation	OK-XDN ZS-NIK 5Y-TTT(1) 5Y-VVG+ 5Y-VVE [+ not fully confirmed]
98 27 27	UVP-E	Blue Sky Aviation	OK-DDF 5Y-BOD
92 27 28	UVP-E20	ex Bluebird Aviation	OK-XDM ZS-NIJ 5Y-VVC [dbr by Jly10 Kichwa Tembo airstrip, Masai Mara, Kenya; l/n Jun12]
92 27 29A	L420	Aircraft Systems South Africa (Pty)/ICRC	OK-XYA (N420LW) N420Y ZS-OSE [model developed for US market with Ayers]
92 27 30	UVP-E20	Aircraft Systems South Africa (Pty)/UN	OK-YDB OK-CDB 5H-HSA ZS-OXR [operated for UN]
92 27 31	UVP-E20	Aircraft Systems South Africa (Pty)	S9-TBA ZS-OBS 5Y-YYY 5Y-TTT(2) 5Y-BXV ZS-ATE
27 32	UVP-E20	Djibouti Air Force	OK-SDV J2-MBE
27 33	UVP-E	Ural Mining & Metallurgical Company	OK-AIT RA-67012
27 34	UVP-E20	Air Guyane Express	OK-AIS(2) F-OIXG
27 35	UVP-E	Aircraft Industries	[stored by Jly97 Kunovice, Czech Republic; never registered; l/n May00]
01 27 35A	L420	Air Express Algeria	OK-GDM ZS-OUE [model developed for US market with Ayers]
97 27 36	UVP-E20	Benair	OK-DDC OK-EDA OY-PBH
27 37	UVP-E20	Russian Air Force	OK-SDY [unknown]
27 38	UVP-E20	Russian Air Force	OK-ODJ [unknown]
27 39	UVP-E20	Aircraft Industries	OK-ODK [for Russian Air Force]
27 40	UVP-E20	Russian Air Force	OK-ODL [unknown]
27 41	UVP-E	Aircraft Industries	[stored by Jly97 Kunovice, Czech Republic; never registered; l/n May00]
28 01	UVP-E20	ex Aircraft Industries	OK-BEK [canx 01Aug11 reported for Kazakhstan customer]
28 02	UVP-E20	Russian Air Force	OK-SDZ [unknown]
28 03	UVP-E20	ex Aircraft Industries	OK-SDS(2) [canx 08Mar12 fate/status unknown]
28 04	UVP-E20	Yamal Airlines	OK-ODO RA-
28 05	UVP-E20	Yamal Airlines	OK-ODM RA-
28 06	UVP-E20	Sasovo Flying School	OK-ODN RA-67014
28 07	UVP-E20	Air Guyane Express	OK-ODR F-OIXI
28 08	UVP-E20	Russian Air Force	OK-ODP 15 blue+ [+ not confirmed]
28 09	UVP-E20	Aircraft Industries	OK-SBB
28 10	UVP-E20	Aircraft Industries	OK-SBA
28 11	UVP-E20	Aircraft Industries	OK-SLW
28 12	UVP-E20	Krasavia	OK-SLZ (unknown)
28 13	UVP-E20	Krasavia	OK-ODJ (unknown)
28 14	UVP-E20	Krasavia	OK-ODS (unknown)
Unidentified			
unkn	UVP-E	Aerotaxi	CU-T1195 [reported 26Oct99 Havana, Cuba]
unkn	UVP-E	Aerotaxi	CU-T1196 [reported 21Oct99 Havana, Cuba]
unkn		unknown	C9-AUR [reported 12Sep12 Nelspruit, South Africa wearing c/n plate of 3D-KIM 851416 also present at same time]
unkn		unknown	C9-AUS [reported 04Jan12 Nelspruit, South Africa]
unkn	UVP	Heritage Aviation	D6-CAQ [reported Jun07 Goma, Democratic Republic of Congo]
unkn		Borki Air Club	FLARF01235 [on TV show]
unkn		unknown	FLARF02835 [reported 18Aug03 & 24Aug07 St Petersburg-Rzhevka, Russia]
unkn		unknown	HA-LAK(1) [reserved for unspecified LET410; marks to c/n 86 16 06]
unkn		(Wodoil Kft)	HA-LAM [reserved for unspecified LET410]
unkn		Business Air	HA-LAP(2) [reported 07Sep99 Budapest, Hungary, not c/n 84 13 28]
unkn		(Business Air)	HA-LAW [reserved for unspecified LET410]
unkn		unknown	HH-TRA [reported derelict 15Apr10 Port-au-Prince, Haiti]
unkn		unknown	HR-ADQ [reported 22Jan11 Roatan-Juan Manuel Galvez Airport, Honduras]
unkn		unknown	HR-ANO [reported 14May94 Opa-locka, FL]
unkn		Islena Airlines	HR-AQW [reported May97 Fort Lauderdale-Executive, FL]
unkn		unknown	HR-AST [reported 26Oct01 Bogota, Colombia]
unkn		unknown	HR-ATK [reported 20Mar04 Caracas-Simon Bolivar, Venezuela & in 2006 Vallemi, Paraguay; l/n Jan09 as abandoned]

LET 410 AND 420 TURBOLET

C/n	Model	Last known Owner/Operator	Identities/fates/comments (where appropriate)	
unkn	UVP-E	Central American Airways	HR-AWC	[reported 04Apr10 San Pedro Sula, Honduras]
unkn			LY-ARR	[unknown aircraft built 28Apr90; CofA expired 09Dec99]
unkn			LY-AZB	[unknown aircraft built 06Jun86; CofA expired 20Apr00]
unkn			LY-AZC	[unknown aircraft built 15May86; CofA expired 27Apr00]
unkn			LY-AZD	[unknown aircraft built 30May86; CofA expired 04Aug99]
unkn			LY-AZE	[unknown aircraft built 20Jun86; CofA expired 04Aug99]
unkn			LY-AZG	[unknown aircraft built 08May86; CofA expired 07Sep99]
unkn			LY-AZJ	[unknown aircraft built Jan86; CofA expired 22Oct99]
unkn			LY-AZL	[unknown aircraft built 29Feb88; CofA expired 24Sep99]
unkn			LY-AZS	[unknown aircraft built 20Sep90; CofA expired 14May00]
unkn			LY-AZT	[unknown aircraft built 29May00; CofA expired 09Jun00]
unkn		Air Max	LZ-MAN	[reported 03Mar97 Knovice, Czech Republic; not in fleet list assumed never delivered]
unkn		unknown	LZ-RMG	[reported]
unkn		unknown	OM-MDF(1)	[reported 26Jun94; not c/n 82 08 01]
unkn		unknown	RA-0152G	[from photo dated 12Jun10]
unkn		unknown	RA-3732K	[from photo]
unkn	UVP	Omsk Aeroclub	RF-00434	[reported 14May06]
unkn		Sokol-Nizhny Novgorod Aviation Factory	RF-01010	[reported 22Jan12 Nizhny Novrorod-somovo, Russia]
unkn	UVP-E3	unknown	RF-49407	[from photo; ex Soviet Air Force]
unkn		Tatarstan Police	RF-67571	[delivered Jan10; reported 16Jun10 Kazan, Russia]
unkn	UVP-E3	DOSAAF	RF-94589	[reported 25Sep11 Kirzhach, Russia]
unkn	UVP-E3	DOSAAF	RF-94591	[reported 08Sep11 based Izhevsk-Pirogovo, Russia]
unkn		DOSAAF	RF-94593	[reported 10Jly11 Sivoritsy-Nikolskoye, Russia]
unkn		Russian Air Force	RF-94595	[reported Nov/Dec10 to a unit at Loginovo, Russia]
unkn		DOSAAF	RF-94596	[reported 08Sep11 based Gatchina-Sivoritsy, Russia]
unkn	UVP-E3	DOSAAF	RF-94597	[reported 01Oct11 Bolshoye-Grylovo, Russia]
unkn	UVP-E3	DOSAAF	RF-94599	[reported 08Sep11 based Izhevsk-Pirogovo, Russia]
unkn	UVP-E3	DOSAAF	RF-94603	[reported 17Sep11 Tanai, Russia]
unkn		unknown	RP-C2910	[reported 27Jly06 Mactan Airport, Cebu, Philippines]
unkn		unknown	RP-C8259	[from photo]
unkn		unknown	ST-CAV	[reported 24Jun08 & 31Mar09 Khartoum, Sudan]
unkn		unknown	ST-DMR	[reported 02Jun08 Kiev-Zhulyany, Ukraine & 31Mar09 Khartoum, Sudan]
unkn		unknown	ST-RAT	[reported 01Jly11 Nairobi-Jomo Kenyatta, Kenya]
unkn		unknown	S9-CAL	[2000-2003 photo at unknown location alongside S9-CAD c/n 841139]
unkn	UVP-E20	unknown	S9-TBV	[reported 16Sep99 Bratislava, Slovakia & 31Oct99 Gosselies, Belgium]
unkn		unknown	S9-TBZ	[reported 13Mar98 Opa-locka, FL]
unkn		unknown	TG-AJM	[reported 19Mar03 Guatemala, City, Guatemala]
unkn		unknown	TG-ALA	[marks reserved 2011 for unidentified LET410]
unkn		unknown	TG-SRO	[marks reserved 2011 for unidentified LET410]
unkn		Minair	TL-AEE	[reported 25Apr10 routing Pescara, Italy – Cagliari, Italy]
unkn		unknown	TN-AHN	[reported 02Aug10 Brazzaville, People's Republic of Congo; these marks also reported on MA60 c/n 0406 but no sightings]
unkn		Komandor	YL-ACF	[reported May96 Riga-Skulte, Latvia; but never officially registered]
unkn		unknown	YS-405P	[reported 14Mar93 Ostend, Belgium on delivery]
unkn		unknown	YV-1000CP	[reported 24Jan98 Lanzarote, Spain; not on Venezuelan register]
unkn		unknown	YV-1097CP	[reported 01Apr04 Hato, Netherlands Antilles]
unkn		Tramas Textiles SA/Rainbow Air	YV220T	[routed 06Mar09 Kharkov, Ukraine to Thessaloniki, Greece; 08/10Mar09 Lanzarote, Spain]
unkn		unknown	YV-2605P	[reported 10Dec02 & 18Dec02 Hato, Netherlands Antilles; not on Venezuelan register]
unkn	UVP	unknown	YV-2669P	[reported 28Apr02 Miranda-La Carlota, Venezuela; not on register]
unkn		unknown	YV328T	
unkn	UVP-E	unknown	3C-DDE	[reported 01Nov07 Bratislava, Slovakia]
unkn		unknown	3C-ZZE	[reported 07May00 Johannesburg-Rand, South Africa]
unkn		unknown	3D-ADR	[reported 17Nov01 Vereeniging, South Africa]
unkn		Sena	3D-ENG	[reported Jan03 & 23May03 Beira, Ukraine & 20Jan06 Kakira, Uganda]
unkn		Pilot Air	3D-ETY	[reported 07May04 Khartoum; flew to Beni & Kinshasa, Democratic Republic of Congo next day]
unkn		Sena	3D-FTI	[reported 05Sep05 Sofia-Vrazhdebna, Bulgaria]
unkn	UVP-E	S T A Mali	3D-KKT	
unkn		Tropical Airways	5H-CRY	[reported Oct11 Zanizibar, Tanzania]

LET 410 AND 420 TURBOLET

C/n	Model	Last known Owner/Operator	Identities/fates/comments (where appropriate)
unkn		unknown	9J-AEN [reported 25Feb99 Lusaka, Zambia]
unkn		Blue Sky Aviation	5Y-BPH
unkn		Bluebird Aviation	5Y-VVF
unkn	UVP	unknown	9L-LBF [reported 06Apr06 La Valletta-Luqa, Malta]
unkn	UVP-E	unknown	9L-LBU(1) [reported 22Dec99 Bratislava, Slovakia & 03Feb00 Prestwick, Scotland, UK on delivery; not c/n 87 19 21]
unkn		S T A Mali	9L-LCV [in TV news programme on 11Jan05]
unkn		unknown	9L-LFX [reg'd 10Dec01 & reported 12Jun08 Nairobi-Wilson, Kenya]
unkn		unknown	9Q-CEM
unkn		(African Air Services Commuter)	9Q-CIF [w/o 14Feb11 Mount Biega, Democratic Republic of Congo en-route Bukavu to Lusenge]
unkn		ITAB	9Q-CMD [reported 12Jan11 Lubumbashi, Democratic Republic of Congo]
unkn		unknown	9Q-CQX
unkn		unknown	9Q-CVZ
unkn		Mango Airlines	9Q-CXG [reported 03Apr10 Larnaca, Cyprus]
unkn		unknown	9Q-CXX
unkn		unknown	9Q-CYI
unkn		unknown	9Q-CZN
unkn		unknown	9XR-DC [w/o 06May04 Jiech, Sudan; but also reported as 9XR-EF]
unkn		Congo Fret Espair	9XR-EF [reported early 2006 Goma, Democratic Republic of Congo but also w/o 06May04 Jiech, Sudan; but also reported as 9XR-DC]
unkn		unknown	2641K [reported active 10Jly10 Gryazi, Russia]

LET 610

C/n	Line No.	Model	Last known Owner/Operator	Identities/fates/comments (where appropriate)
88 00 01?	X01	M	(LET)	OK-130 OK-TZB OK-130 [prototype ff 28Dec88; canx 13Dec89; May11 to Stare Mesto, Czech Republic, for preservation]
89 00 02?	X02	M	(VZLU)	[static test airframe; [tested to destruction]]
90 00 03?	X03	M	ex LET	OK-132 OK-024 OK-132 OK-024 OK-UZB [last flight 23Oct97; stored Kunovice, Czech Republic; 26Apr11 to Olomouc, Czech Republic for preservation]
91 00 04?	X04	M		[static test airframe]
91 00 05?	X05	M	Slovacke Letecke Muzeum	OK-134 OK-VZC OK-134 0005+ [+ Czech Repubilc; preserved 16Jun06 Kunovice, Czech Republic; l/n Jun08]
91 01 01		M	(LET)	OK-136 OK-WZA OK-136 [last flight 28Jun91; fate unknown]
92 01 02			LET	OK-136 OK-XZA [last flight 28Jun91; fate unknown]
92 01 03				[noted on production line Feb94, again Jly97]
92 01 04				[noted on production line Feb94, again Jly97]
02 01				[noted on production line Feb94]
02 02				[noted on production line Feb94, renumbered 03 09]
02 03				[noted on production line Feb94, again Jun96]
02 04		G		[noted on production line Feb94, renumbered 03 08]
02 05		G		[noted on production line Feb94, renumbered 03 07]
97 03 01		G	(LET)	OK-CZD [ff 13May00; last flight 15May06 & wfu Albany, GA, USA; l/n 18Nov06 – noted Jly08]
03 02		M		[noted on production line Feb94]
03 03		GE		[noted on production line Feb94, again Aug98]
03 04		GE		[noted on production line Jun96, again Aug98]
03 05		GE		[noted on production line Jun96, again Aug98]
03 06		GE		[noted on production line Jly97, again Aug98]
03 07		GE		[noted on production line Jly97, again Aug98]
03 08		GE		[noted on production line Jly97, again Aug98]
03 09		GE		[noted on production line Jly97, again Aug98]
03 10		GE		[noted on production line Jly97, again Sep97]
04 01		GE		[noted on production line Sep97]

Production complete

LOCKHEED C-130/L-100 HERCULES

Notes: Unknown, as noted, Vietnamese Air Force serials were probably either the former USAF serial or a corruption of it
AMARC Codes are given in a separate table on page 631 of Volume 2.

C/n	Model	Last known Owner/Operator	Identities/fates/comments (where appropriate)
1001	NC-130	(USAF)	53-3396 [prototype ff 23Aug54; b/u Oct60 Robins AFB, GA]
1002	NC-130	(USAF)	53-3397 [b/u Apr62 Indianapolis, IN]
3001	AC-130A	USAF	53-3129 [preserved Nov96 USAF Armament Museum, Eglin AFB, FL]
3002	JC-130A	(USAF)	53-3130 [tested to destruction 20Feb58 (never flown); b/u Marietta, GA]
3003	JC-130A	USAF	53-3131 [GIA 1978 Sheppard AFB, TX, derelict Mar90; fuselage only by May95 as evacuation trainer]
3004	C-130A	Mexican Air Force	53-3132+ 10601^ 3601 [+ USAF; ^ Mexico]
3005	NC-130A	National Aircraft	53-3133 [wfu AMARC Jun76; fuselage only Oct91; sold Oct97 National Aircraft, Tucson, AZ]
3006	C-130A	(USAF)	53-3134 [wfu AMARC May76; fuselage only Oct90; b/u Jan02]
3007	C-130A	Mexican Air Force	53-3135+ 10602^ 3602 [+ USAF; ^ Mexico]
3008	GC-130A	(USAF)	54-1621 [GIA May67 Sheppard AFB, TX; dumped 1981; b/u May86]
3009	NC-130A	USAF	54-1622 [wfu AMARC May76; fuselage to Western International Aviation Salvage Yard, Tucson, AZ Oct90]
3010	AC-130A	USAF	54-1623 [preserved Dobbins Air Reserve Base, GA; reported for Lockheed Museum, Marietta, GA]
3011	C-130A	(USAF)	54-1624 [wfu AMARC May76; stripped by Jul01]
3012	AC-130A	(USAF)	54-1625 [shot down 22Apr70 near Dak Seang, Laos]
3013	AC-130A	USAF	54-1626 [preserved May76 USAF Museum, Wright-Patterson AFB, OH]
3014	AC-130A	(USAF)	54-1627 [wfu AMARC 01Jun76; sold for scrap Dec04]
3015	AC-130A	USAF	54-1628 [wfu AMARC 28Sep95]
3016	AC-130A	(USAF)	54-1629 [shot at over Laos on 24May69 and crash-landed at Ubon, Thailand]
3017	AC-130A	USAF	54-1630 [preserved Sep95 USAF Museum, Wright-Patterson AFB, OH; in storage Apr97]
3018	C-130A	International Air Response	54-1631+ [unknown]^ 54-1631+ N117TG [+ USAF; ^ S Vietnam AF]
3019	RC-130A	(USAF)	54-1632 [wfu AMARC Jun76; being scrapped Apr97 AirPro International; b/u by Dec05; l/n 09Mar09]
3020	C-130A	(Chad Air Force)	54-1633+ TT-PAB [+ USAF] [w/o 07Mar86 on take-off in Chad]
3021	C-130A	USAF	54-1634+ [unknown]^ 54-1634+ [+ USAF; ^ S Vietnam AF] [wfu AMARC Mar92; fire dump Sep94 Davis-Monthan, AZ; l/n AMARC Jul98]
3022	C-130A	Honduran Air Force	54-1635+ 560 [+ USAF] [stored Sep99 Tegucigalpa-Toncontin, Honduras; l/n 24Nov07]
3023	C-130A	Bolivian Air Force	54-1636+ TAM-64 [+ USAF] [wfu Jly96 La Paz, Bolivia; used for spare parts; l/n Oct07]
3024	GC-130A	USAF	54-1637 [GIA 1992 Goodfellow AFB, TX]
3025	C-130A	(Mexican Air Force)	54-1638+ 10603^ 3603 [+ USAF; ^ Mexico] [w/o 19Sep03 near La Quemada, Mexico]
3026	C-130A	(TBM Inc)	54-1639+ [+ USAF] [b/u for spares Nov90 Dinuba-Sequoia Field, CA]
3027	C-130A	US Army	54-1640+ [unknown]^ 54-1640+ [+USAF; ^ S Vietnam AF; wfu at AMARC Jun90; to US Army as ZF007 Jun92 Fort Bragg, NC as ground trainer]
3028	C-130A	(Vietnamese People's Air Force)	55-0001+ 001/0-50001 [+ USAF] [badly corroded & wfu May88; l/n derelict Feb90 Tan Son Nhut, Vietnam]
3029	C-130A	(USAF)	55-0002+ [unknown]^ 55-0002 [+ USAF; ^ S Vietnam AF; DBR 06Apr75 Bien Hoa, South Vietnam]
3030	C-130A	Honduran Air Force	55-0003+ 557 [+ USAF] [stored Sep99 Tegucigalpa-Toncontin, Honduras; l/n 24Nov07]
3031	C-130A	USAF	55-0004 [wfu AMARC Apr90]
3032	C-130A	(Vietnamese People's Air Force)	55-0005+ 003^ [+ USAF; ^ also reported as 002 which was hijacked to Singapore-Peya Lebar around 01Dec79; wfu with badly corroded wings; derelict May88 Tan Son Nhut, Vietnam]
3033	C-130A	(USAF)	55-0006 [captured by North Vietnamese troops in Apr75; reported w/o]
3034	C-130A	Bolivian Air Force	55-0007+ TAM-65 [+ USAF] [wfu Feb97 & stored La Paz, Bolivia; used for spare parts; l/n Oct07]
3035	C-130A	Digital C-130A LLC	55-0008+ [unknown]^ 55-0008+ AT-530# N2127W N130SA [+ USAF; ^ S Vietnam AF; # Peru]
3036	C-130A	(USAF)	55-0009 [DBR 15Jly67 Da Nang, South Vietnam]
3037	C-130A	(OGMA)	55-0010+ TT-PAE [+ USAF] [confiscated by Portuguese Government Feb90; b/u Jan91 Alverca, Portugal; remains to scrapyard Arranho, Vila Franca de Xira, Lisbon, Portugal]

LOCKHEED C-130/L-100 HERCULES

C/n	Model	Last known Owner/Operator	Identities/fates/comments (where appropriate)
3038	AC-130A	USAF	55-0011 [wfu AMARC 15Nov94]
3039	C-130A	(USAF)	55-0012+ [unknown]^ 55-0012 [+ USAF; ^ S Vietnam AF; wfu AMARC Aug76; to Equipment Supply, NC Nov84; b/u Feb98 with nose to Ontario, CA]
3040	C-130A	(South Vietnam Air Force)	55-0013+ 006 [+ USAF] [wfu as badly corroded & cockpit damaged May88; derelict Feb90 Tan Son Nhut, Vietnam]
3041	AC-130A	ex USAF	55-0014 [preserved Mar96 Robins AFB Museum, GA; l/n 16Oct10]
3042	C-130A	Honduran Air Force	55-0015+ 558 [+ USAF]
3043	C-130A	(South Vietnam Air Force)	55-0016+ [unknown]^ [+ USAF] [shot down 25Dec74 landing Song Be, South Vietnam]
3044	C-130A	(South Vietnam Air Force)	55-0017+ [unknown]^ [+ USAF] [captured by North Vietnam troops in Apr75, fate unknown]
3045	C-130A	ex USAF	55-0018 [wfu AMARC Mar90; fuselage to GIA Oct94 Centre d'Essais Aeronautique de Toulouse, France, l/n Toulouse-Balma 25Apr09]
3046	GC-130A	(USAF)	55-0019 [wfu AMARC May76; GIA Sep82 Hanscom AFB, MA; b/u 1985]
3047	C-130A	(USAF)	55-0020 [w/o 08Mar62 near Alencon, France]
3048	DC-130A	(US Navy)	55-0021+ 158228 [+ USAF; wfu AMARC 02Jun79]
3049	NC-130A	(USAF)	55-0022 [wfu Oct03 Eglin, FL AFB]
3050	NC-130A	Linear Air Park	55-0023+ [+ USAF] [preserved Oct89 Dyess AFB, TX]
3051	NC-130A	(USAF)	55-0024 [wfu AMARC Nov86; sold for scrap 2000, noted with DMI Aviation Mar05; l/n 09Mar09]
3052	C-130A	Central African Republic AF	55-0025+ 381//OB-1394^ N2144F N266LS (N130HL) TL-KNK [+ USAF; ^ Peru; dual marks]
3053	C-130A	(USAF)	55-0026 [wfu AMARC Apr90; to US Army as ZF008 in Jun94; returned to AMARC Jun94; l/n in scrap yard 09Mar09]
3054	C-130A	Mexican Air Force	55-0027+ [unknown]^ 55-0027+ 10608 [+ USAF; ^ S Vietnam AF; wfu by May97; to GIA Santa Lucia AFB, Mexico]
3055	C-130A	Mexican Air Force	55-0028+ 10604^ 3604 [+ USAF; ^ Mexico]
3056	AC-130A	(USAF)	55-0029 [wfu AMARC 15Nov94]
3057	KC-130A	(Peruvian Air Force)	55-0030+ 385 [+ USAF] [b/u Dec01 Lima, Peru]
3058	C-130A	Mexican Air Force	55-0031+ 10605^ 3605 [+ USAF; ^ Mexico]
3059	C-130A	(USAF)	55-0032 [wfu AMARC Jly87; to US Army as ZF004 in Dec88; derelict range target Dec89 near Fort Lewis, WA]
3060	C-130A	(USAF)	55-0033 [wfu AMARC Jan89; to National Aircraft Mar02]
3061	C-130A	(USAF)	55-0034+ [unknown]^ 55-0034 [+ USAF; ^ S Vietnam AF; wfu at AMARC Feb76; to Kirtland AFB, NM Mar85; b/u]
3062	C-130A	(Mexican Air Force)	55-0035+ 10607 [+ USAF] [wfu by May97; b/u Santa Lucia, Mexico; nose preserved]
3063	C-130A	(USAF)	55-0036 [wfu AMARC Aug87; to National Aircraft as scrap Oct02]
3064	GC-130A	Octave Chanute Museum	55-0037+ [+ USAF] [GIA May84 Chanute TTC, IL; preserved Nov95 Rantoul Aviation Complex, IL]
3065	C-130A	(USAF)	55-0038 [w/o in water 18Sep65 near Qui Nhon, South Vietnam]
3066	C-130A	(USAF)	55-0039 [DBR 01Jly65 in mortar attack Da Nang, South Vietnam]
3067	AC-130A	(USAF)	55-0040 [wfu AMARC 03Jun76; fuselage only by Oct90]
3068	C-130A	(USAF)	55-0041 [wfu AMARC Oct87; to National Aircraft Mar02]
3069	C-130A	(USAF)	55-0042 [DBR 01Jly65 in mortar attack Da Nang, South Vietnam]
3070	AC-130A	(USAF)	55-0043 [shot down 18Jun72 by SA-7 missile in Shan Valley, SW of Hue, South Vietnam]
3071	AC-130A	(USAF)	55-0044 [hit by shell 28Mar72 over Ho Chi Minh trail; crew jumped 13m south of Saravane, Laos]
3072	C-130A	(USAF)	55-0045 [captured by North Vietnamese troops in Apr75; fate unknown]
3073	AC-130A	(USAF)	55-0046 [wfu AMARC 15Nov94; b/u May05]
3074	C-130A	US Army	55-0047 [wfu AMARC May87; Dec88 to US Army as ZF003 Fort Benning, GA as GIA]
3075	C-130A	USAF	55-0048 [wfu AMARC May76; Dec83 to Camp Bullis, TX as "C4 Task Force"]
3076	C-130A	(USAF)	56-0468 [w/o 09Aug86 Fort Campbell, KY]
3077	AC-130A	USAF	56-0469 [wfu Hurlburt Field, FL Nov98; to GIA for AC-130U gun trainer; no wings]
3078	C-130A	(USAF)	56-0470 [wfu AMARC Jly87; to National Aircraft Mar02; l/n 09Mar09]
3079	C-130A	(USAF)	56-0471 [wfu AMARC Apr90; to National Aircraft Mar02; l/n 09Mar09]
3080	C-130A	(USAF)	56-0472 [shot down 27May69 landing Phouc Vinh, South Vietnam; SOC 05Jun69]
3081	C-130A	TBM Inc	56-0473+ N473TM^ [+ USAF; ^coded 63]
3082	C-130A	(USAF)	56-0474 [DBF 27Aug63 Naha AB, Okinawa, Japan; fuselage paratrooper trainer Camp Sukiran, Okinawa, Japan]
3083	GC-130A	(USAF)	56-0475 [DBR; GIA Nov90 Chicago-O'Hare AFB, IL; to Lockheed Martin Aircraft Center, Greenville, SC Oct96 with wings and tail removed]

LOCKHEED C-130/L-100 HERCULES

C/n	Model	Last known Owner/Operator	Identities/fates/comments (where appropriate)
3084	C-130A	(South Vietnam Air Force)	56-0476+ 005 [wfu May88; derelict Feb90 Tan Son Nhut, Vietnam]
3085	C-130A	(USAF)	56-0477 [shot down 22May68 E of Ban Thoun, Laos]
3086	C-130A	(T&G Aviation)	56-0478+ N116TG [+ USAF] [w/o 06Sep00 NW of Aubenas, France, operating for Securite Civile, coded 82]
3087	C-130A	Mexican Air Force	56-0479+ [unknown]^ 56-0479+ 10609# TP-300//XC-UTP 3609 [+ USAF; ^ S Vietnam AF; # Mexico]
3088	C-130A	(USAF)	56-0480 [w/o 16Apr68 Camp Bernard, 50m north of Bien Hoa, South Vietnam]
3089	C-130A	(USAF)	56-0481+ [unknown]^ 56-0481 [+ USAF; ^ S Vietnam AF; wfu AMARC Oct87; to National Aircraft Mar02]
3090	C-130A	(USAF)	56-0482+ [unknown]^ 56-0482 [+ USAF; ^ S Vietnam with code HC-K; derelict May88 Tan Son Nhut, Vietnam]
3091	C-130A	(Peruvian Air Force)	56-0483+ [unknown]^ 56-0483+ 390# [+ USAF; ^ S Vietnam AF; # probably ntu; used for spares; serial used by F-28 c/n 11100]
3092	C-130A-II	(Mace Aviation)	56-0484+ N137FF [+ USAF] [wfu AMARC May89; for scrap 1998; l/n 2005]
3093	C-130A	(USAF)	56-0485 [wfu AMARC Jly90; to National Aircraft 2000; l/n 09Mar09]
3094	C-130A	(USAF)	56-0486 [w/o 09Sep86 overran runway Fort Campbell, KY; to AMARC; to National Aircraft 2000; l/n 09Mar09]
3095	C-130A	Chani Enterprises	56-0487+ N6585H N120TG N487UN 9J-AFV 9J-BTM [+ USAF] [stored 1999 Alverca, Portugal; l/n Jan06]
3096	C-130A	(USAF)	56-0488 [w/o 26Nov62 Stewart AFB, NY]
3097	C-130A	(South Vietnam Air Force)	56-0489+ [unknown]^ [+ USAF] [captured by North Vietnam forces in Apr75; fate unknown]
3098	AC-130A	(USAF)	56-0490 [shot down 21Dec72 40kms NE of Pakse, Laos]
3099	C-130A	(Carib Air Transport)	56-0491+ 158229^ N9724V J6-SLQ [+ USAF; ^ USN] [w/o 10Jun91 after take-off from Luanda, Angola]
3100	C-130A	(USAF)	56-0492 [w/o 02May64 Le Shima, Ryukyu Islands, Japan; fuselage to GIA Sukiran, Okinawa, Japan]
3101	C-130A	Davis-Monthan Heritage Park	56-0493+ [+ USAF] [wfu AMARC Aug93; preserved Davis-Monthan AFB, AZ]
3102	C-130A	(USAF)	56-0494 [wfu AMARC Oct91]
3103	C-130A	(USAF)	56-0495+ [unknown]^ 56-0495 [+ USAF; ^ S Vietnam AF; wfu at AMARC; to National Aircraft Mar02; l/n 09Mar09]
3104	C-130A	Aero Firefighting Service	56-0496+ N8053R N45R N134FF [+ USAF] [wfu 2007; to GIA Yuma Proving Ground, Yuma, AZ]
3105	C-130A	US Army	56-0497 [wfu AMARC Oct87; later to US Army as ZF002; to Hunter AAF/Fort Stewart, GA Feb92]
3106	C-130A	USAF	56-0498 [GIA damage repair trainer Mar92 Robins AFB, GA]
3107	C-130A	(USAF)	56-0499 [w/o 13Dec69 Bu Dop, South Vietnam]
3108	C-130A	ex Military Acft Restoration Corp	56-0500+ [unknown]^ 56-0500+ N223MA [+USAF; ^ S Vietnam] [stored derelict Sep95 Luanda, Angola; l/n 28Mar09]
3109	C-130A	(USAF)	56-0501 [w/o 22Jan85 into the Caribbean Sea on approach to Trujillo, Honduras]
3110	C-130A	(USAF)	56-0502 [w/o 08Dec65 An Khe, South Vietnam]
3111	C-130A	(USAF)	56-0503 [wfu AMARC Dec91; to National Aircraft Mar02; l/n 09Mar09]
3112	C-130A	(USAF)	56-0504 [w/o 02Oct80 McMinnville, SE of Nashville, TN]
3113	C-130A	(South Vietnam Air Force)	56-0505+ [unknown] [+ USAF] [captured by North Vietnam forces in Apr75]
3114	C-130A	(USAF)	56-0506 [DBR 26Mar66 Tuy Hoa, South Vietnam]
3115	C-130A	Pride Capital Group	56-0507+ N8055R N45S N4172Q N132HP [+ USAF] [stored 2000 Greybull, WY; l/n 14Oct06]
3116	C-130A	ex Mexican Air Force	56-0508+ 10606^ 3606 [+ USAF; ^ Mexico] [wfu Santa Lucia, Mexico & preserved by gate]
3117	AC-130A	Hurlburt Field Memorial Air Park	56-0509+ [+ USAF] [preserved Nov96 Hurlburt Field, FL]
3118	C-130A	(USAF)	56-0510 [w/o 10Apr70 mountain near Long Tieng, Laos]
3119	C-130A	International Air Response	56-0511+ N132FF^ N121TG [+ USAF; ^ code 83] [stored Mar06 Coolidge, AZ; l/n Feb09]
3120	GC-130A	(USAF)	56-0512 [wfu AMARC May76; GIA Dec84 Richards-Gebaur AFB, MO; b/u Dec95; tail with NASM, MD, fuselage noted El Mirage, CA May05]
3121	C-130A	(USAF)	56-0513 [wfu AMARC Oct87; Jly91 fuselage to GIA Kirtland AFB, NM]
3122	DC-130A	(US Navy)	56-0514+ 560514 [+ USAF] [wfu Dec93, Mojave, CA for spares, fuselage noted El Mirage, CA Nov99]
3123	C-130A	(USAF)	56-0515 [w/o 12Dec65 Bitburg AFB, West Germany]
3124	C-130A	(USAF)	56-0516 [ditched 10Apr70 Gushikawa near Okinawa, Japan]
3125	GC-130A	(USAF)	56-0517 [GIA Oct90 Homestead AFB, FL; destroyed by Hurricane Andrew 24Aug92]

LOCKHEED C-130/L-100 HERCULES

C/n	Model	Last known Owner/Operator	Identities/fates/comments (where appropriate)
3126	GC-130A	USAF	56-0518+ [unknown]^ 56-0518 [+ USAF; ^ S Vietnam AF with code HCM; by Mar93 gate guardian Little Rock AFB, AR; l/n Jan08]
3127	C-130A	(South Vietnam Air Force)	56-0519+ [unknown]^ [+ USAF; code HCP] [derelict May88 Tan Son Nhut, Vietnam]
3128	C-130A	(USAF)	56-0520 [GIA Mar90 Scott AFB, IL; b/u 1992]
3129	C-130A	(South Vietnam Air Force)	56-0521+ [unknown] [+ USAF] [destroyed 18Dec74 on ground at Song Be, South Vietnam]
3130	C-130A	(USAF)	56-0522 [wfu Oct94 Kelly AFB, TX; GIA Lackland AFB; wfu for sale May07 as scrap]
3131	C-130A	(USAF)	56-0523 [wfu AMARC Oct90; to National Aircraft Mar02; l/n 09Mar09]
3132	GC-130A	USAF	56-0524+ [unknown]^ 56-0524 [+ USAF; ^ S Vietnam AF; GIA Oct90 Goodfellow AFB, TX]
3133	C-130A	(Rome Laboratory)	56-0525+ [+ USAF] [wfu & tail removed; used for ECM/EMP tests at Rome, NY]
3134	C-130A	(USAF)	56-0526 [w/o 19Sep58 in mid-air collision with French AF Super Mystere fighter over France]
3135	DC-130A	(USAF)	56-0527 [wfu AMARC 02Jun86,]
3136	C-130A	(USAF)	56-0528 [shot down 02Sep58 by Soviet MiG-17s 30 miles N of Yerevan, Armenia, USSR; remains on display at National Cryptology Museum, MD by Jun99]
3137	C-130A	(USAF)	56-0529 [wfu AMARC Oct90; to National Aircraft Mar02]
3138	C-130A	International Air Response	56-0530+ N131FF N125TG [code 81] [+ USAF]
3139	C-130A	TBM Inc	56-0531+ N531BA [code 67]
3140	C-130A	(South Vietnam Air Force)	56-0532+ 004^ [+ USAF; ^ code GZN] [derelict May88 Tan Son Nhut, Vietnam]
3141	C-130A	(USAF)	56-0533 [shot down 24Nov69 near Ban Salou, Laos]
3142	C-130A	International Air Response	56-0534+ N132FF N131HP^ N126TG [+ USAF] [^ code 131; reported stored after Feb09 Coolidge, AZ]
3143	C-130A	(D&D Enterprises)	56-0535+ N133FF (N132HP) [+ USAF] [b/u 1995 near AMARC/Tucson; fuselage to Greybull, WY for spares]
3144	C-130A	ex Bolivian Air Force	56-0536+ TAM-66 CP-2187 [+ USAF] [wfu Jan97 La Paz, Bolivia; l/n Oct07]
3145	C-130A	(Aero Corporation)	56-0537+ N537TM N130RR N119TG XA-RSG N537UN [+ USAF] [stored Jan99 Marana, AZ; b/u Oct99 for parts to DMI Tucson, AZ]
3146	C-130A	(Hawkins & Powers Aviation)	56-0538+ N134FF N130HP^ [+ USAF, ^ code 130] [w/o 17Jun02 near Walker, CA; wing detached during fire fighting drop]
3147	GC-130A	(USAF)	56-0539 [wfu AMARC Jun76; GIA Apr81 Little Rock AFB, AR; b/u Oct00]
3148	C-130A	(Hemet Valley Flying Service)	56-0540+ N135FF [+ USAF] [w/o 13Aug94 Pearblossom, CA when b/u in mid-flight]
3149	C-130A	(Hemet Valley Flying Service)	56-0541+ N136FF [+ USAF] [b/u Minden/AMARC for spares; fuselage only noted 2000; wings to Chandler, AZ by Mar05]
3150	C-130A	(South Vietnam Air Force)	56-0542+ [unknown] [+ USAF] [captured by North Vietnam forces in Apr75]
3151	C-130A	(USAF)	56-0543+ [unknown]^ 56-0543 [+ USAF; ^ S Vietnam AF; wfu AMARC Oct90; GIA 1995 Davis-Monthan, AZ; Oct02 to National Aircraft]
3152	C-130A	(USAF)	56-0544 [wfu AMARC Oct90; to National Aircraft Mar02]
3153	GC-130A	USAF	56-0545+ [unknown]^ 56-0545 [+ USAF; ^ S Vietnam AF; wfu AMARC Jun76; GIA Dobbins AFB, GA]
3154	C-130A	(USAF)	56-0546 [w/o 17May62 flew into mountains near Nairobi, Kenya]
3155	C-130A	USAF	56-0547 [GIA Jan92 Robins AFB, GA]
3156	C-130A	(USAF)	56-0548 [w/o 12May68 Kham Duc, South Vietnam]
3157	C-130A	(USAF)	56-0549 [w/o 02Mar68 Phu Bai, South Vietnam]
3158	GC-130A	ex USAF	56-0550 [wfu Aug89; fuselage to Quonset State Airport, RI, load trainer]
3159	C-130A	(Chad Air Force)	56-0551+ TT-PAC [+ USAF] [w/o 16Nov87 on landing in Chad]
3160	C-130A	National Vigilance Park	57-0453 [wfu AMARC Dec91; preserved Jly97 Fort George Meade, MD; painted as 60528 to represent aircraft shot down over USSR; l/n 14May09]
3161	C-130A	(USAF)	57-0454 [w/o 27Jly75 after prop separated N of Imlay City, MI]
3162	C-130A	(Peruvian Air Force)	57-0455+ 393 [+ USAF] [wfu by Feb97; stored Lima, Peru; l/n Oct03 with no wings]
3163	C-130A	(USAF)	57-0456 [wfu AMARC Oct87; to National Aircraft Jun00; l/n 09Mar09]
3164	C-130A	Pima Air Museum	57-0457+ [+ USAF] [wfu AMARC May90; preserved Pima County, AZ]
3165	C-130A	(USAF)	57-0458 [wfu AMARC Oct87; to National Aircraft Mar02]
3166	C-130A	Pride Capital Group	57-0459+ N135HP [+ USAF] [stored Jly95 Greybull, WY; 14Oct06]
3167	C-130A	National Air & Space Museum	57-0460+ 70460^ 57-0460+ [+ USAF; ^ S Vietnam AF; preserved Washington-Dulles, VA; l/n 21Sep09]
3168	DC-130A	US Navy	57-0461+ 570461 [+ USAF] [wfu Jan01 NAS China Lake, CA]
3169	GC-130A	USAF	57-0462 [wfu AMARC Jun76; GIA Oct88 MacDill AFB, FL; fuselage only by Feb91]
3170	C-130A	(USAF)	57-0463 [wfu AMARC Jan92; to National Aircraft Jun00; l/n 09Mar09]

LOCKHEED C-130/L-100 HERCULES

C/n	Model	Last known Owner/Operator	Identities/fates/comments (where appropriate)
3171	GC-130A	USAF	57-0464 [GIA May92 Fort McCoy, WI]
3172	C-130A	(South Vietnam Air Force)	57-0465+ [unknown]^ [+ USAF] [captured by North Vietnam forces in Apr75]
3173	C-130A	TBM Inc	57-0466+ N466TM^ [+ USAF; ^ code 64] [avionics test bed used by ASB Avionics at Mojave, CA]
3174	C-130A	(USAF)	57-0467 [DBR 12Oct67 hit vehicle on take-off from Dak Ta, & landed Cam Ranh Bay, South Vietnam]
3175	C-130A	(USAF)	57-0468 [w/o 20May59 on take-off from Ashiya, Japan]
3176	GC-130A	USAF	57-0469 [GIA by Jun95 Pittsburgh Airport, PA]
3177	C-130A	(Peruvian Air Force)	57-0470+ 396//OB-1395^ [+ USAF; ^ dual marks; wfu Nov94 Lima, Peru; b/u Dec01; cockpit preserved with Grupo 8]
3178	GC-130A	USAF	57-0471 [GIA by Oct89 Sheppard AFB, TX]
3179	C-130A	US Army	57-0472+ [unknown]^ 57-0472+ [+ USAF; ^ S Vietnam AF; wfu AMARC Mar76; to US Army as ZF001 & to Fort Bragg, NC Jul86 as GIA]
3180	C-130A	(Chad Air Force)	57-0473+ TT-PAD [+ USAF] [b/u Jan91 Alverca, Portugal]
3181	C-130A	Bolivian Air Force	57-0474+ TAM-61 [+ USAF] [wfu Jul96 La Paz, Bolivia]
3182	C-130A	(USAF)	57-0475 [w/o 24Apr65 near Khorat, Thailand]
3183	C-130A	(Honduran Air Force)	57-0476+ 559 [+ USAF] [wreck on dump La Ceiba, Honduras; l/n Mar03]
3184	GC-130A	USAF	57-0477 [GIA by Apr90 Savannah, GA]
3185	GC-130A	Museum of Aviation	57-0478+ [+ USAF] [GIA Robins AFB, GA; fuselage preserved there Apr97]
3186	C-130A	ex TBM Inc	57-0479+ N479TM [+ USAF] [wfu for spares 22Sep08 Visalia, CA; l/n 13Sep09]
3187	C-130A	(Bolivian Air Force)	57-0480+ TAM-62 [+ USAF] [w/o 21Dec89 Guayaramerin, Bolivia]
3188	C-130A	Bolivian Air Force	57-0481+ TAM-63 [+ USAF] [wfu by May96 La Paz, Bolivia]
3189	C-130A	International Air Response	57-0482+ N8026J N133HP [+ USAF] [stored Greybull, WY; l/n 14Oct06]
3190	GC-130A	USAF	57-0483 [wfu AMARC Apr87, GIA 1987 Norfolk, VA; by Jan99 to Cheatham Naval Annex, Williamsburg, VA]
3191	C-130D	(Peruvian Air Force)	57-0484+ 383 [+ USAF] [b/u Dec01 Lima, Peru]
3192	C-130D	Minnesota Air Guard Museum	57-0485 [wfu AMARC Jan86; preserved Apr88 Minneapolis-St Paul, MN; marked as "55-016/MN"]
3193	GC-130D	USAF	57-0486 [GIA Oct85 Sheppard AFB, TX; fuselage only by May95]
3194	C-130D	(Honduran Air Force)	57-0487+ 556 [+ USAF] [w/o 14Aug86 near Wampusirpi, Honduras]
3195	C-130D	(USAF)	57-0488 [wfu AMARC Jun76]
3196	GC-130D	US Army	57-0489+ [+ USAF] [GIA Oct85 Sheppard AFB, TX; by Nov98 to US Army Quartermaster School, Fort Lee, VA]
3197	GC-130D	ex USAF	57-0490 [GIA Jan86 Chanute AFB, IL; gate guardian Oct94 Stratton ANGB, Schenectady County, NY; l/n 28Aug08]
3198	C-130D	(Peruvian Air Force)	57-0491+ 399 [+ USAF] [derelict by Oct88, Lima, Peru; b/u by Aug93]
3199	C-130D	(USAF)	57-0492 [wfu AMARC Mar85]
3200	C-130D	Pima Air Museum	57-0493+ [+ USAF] [wfu AMARC; preserved Jun88 Pima County, AZ]
3201	C-130D	(USAF)	57-0494 [wfu AMARC Feb85]
3202	C-130D	(USAF)	57-0495 [w/o 05Jun72 Dye III, 200m east of Sondrestrom, Greenland]
3203	DC-130A	(US Navy)	57-0496+ 570496 [+USAF] [wfu for spares 2000 NAS China Lake, CA; SOC Jun01]
3204	DC-130A	(US Navy)	57-0497+ 570497 [+ USAF] [wfu Jun07 AMARC]
3205	C-130A	(Fowler Aeronautical Service)	57-0498+ A97-205^ N22660 N205FA [+ USAF; ^ Australia] [canx 21May90; by May91 RAAF Museum; fuselage Holsworthy Barracks, NSW, Australia Oct93; b/u in 2000]
3206	C-130A	(Aboitiz Air Transport)	57-0499+ A97-206^ (N22669) RP-C3206 [+ USAF; ^ Australia] [wfu Mar91 Manila, Philippines; canx for spares use, parts to Total Aerospace Miami, FL Nov98]
3207	C-130A	OGMA	57-0500+ A97-207^ (N2267B) N22FV EL-AJM N207GM [+ USAF; ^ Australia] [wfu Nov97 NASA Dryden, CA; canx 05May98; stored Apr00 Alverca, Portugal]
3208	C-130A	(Chad Government)	57-0501+ A97-208^ (N2267N) "(SH3017X)" (HK-3017X) N4445V TT-PAA [+ USAF; ^ Australia] [reported wfu Jun93]
3209	C-130A	(Royal Australian Air Force)	57-0502+ A97-209^ (N2267P) [+ USAF; ^ Australia] [GIA Oct79 Richmond, QLD, Australia; damaged in storm Dec01 & b/u]
3210	C-130A	(Aboitiz Air Transport)	57-0503+ A97-210^ (N2267U) N12FV RP-C3210 [+ USAF; ^ Australia] [wfu Apr93 Manila, Philippines; canx for spares use, parts to Total Aerospace Miami, FL Nov98]
3211	C-130A	(Aboitiz Air Transport)	57-0504+ A97-211^ (N2267W) N5394L RP-C3211 [+ USAF; ^ Australia] [wfu Mar91 Manila, Philippines; canx for spares use, parts to Total Aerospace Miami, FL Nov98]
3212	C-130A	Cherry Air Services	57-0505+ A97-212^ (N2268A) "(SK3017X)" (HK-3016X) N13FV N213DW N130PS N131EC [+USAF; ^ Australia]

LOCKHEED C-130/L-100 HERCULES

C/n	Model	Last known Owner/Operator	Identities/fates/comments (where appropriate)
3213	C-130A	(Aboitiz Air Transport)	57-0506+ A97-213^ (N2268G) RP-C3213 3213# RP-C3213 [+ USAF; ^ Australia; # Philippines; wfu by 1995; b/u, parts to Total Aerospace, Miami, FL]
3214	C-130A	Royal Australian AF Museum	57-0507+ A97-214^ (N2268N) [+ USAF; ^ Australia] [wfu 1978 Laverton, WA; preserved May94, Point Cook, VIC Australia]
3215	C-130A	(Airline Marketing Consultants)	57-0508+ A97-215^ (N2268V) N4469P [+ USAF; ^ Australia] [wfu Dec91 Fort Lauderdale, FL; b/u Dec97; canx 18Mar98]
3216	C-130A	OGMA	57-0509+ A97-216^ (N2268W) (HK-3017X) N15FV N216CR [+ USAF; ^ Australia] [stored Jly95 Portugal; canx 05May98; stored Apr00 Alverca, Portugal]
3217	C-130A	(Mexican Air Force)	57-0510+ 10610^ 3610 [+ USAF; ^ Mexico] [w/o 17Sep99 during test-flight into Mount Hidalgo, Cerro la Paila, nr Sahagin, Mexico]
3218	C-130A	(Pride Capital Group)	57-0511+ N134HP [+USAF] [stored by Oct03 Greybull, WY; l/n 14Oct06; canx 06Sep12, probably b/u]
3219	C-130A	International Air Response	57-0512+ N118TG [code 32] [+ USAF]
3220	C-130A	(Pride Capital Group)	57-0513+ N8230H [+ USAF] [sold for spares ex Pope AFB, NC by 1998; wfu Greybull, WY; parts to Total Aerospace, Miami, FL in 2001; b/u]
3221	C-130A	Selfridge Military Air Museum	57-0514+ [+ USAF] [preserved Sep89 Selfridge AFB, MI]
3222	C-130A	(USAF)	57-0515 [wfu by 1996 Eglin AFB, FL; believed b/u for spares]
3223	C-130A	US Army	57-0516 [wfu by 1993 Duke Field, FL; to US Army Aberdeen Proving Ground, MD by 2000]
3224	C-130A	Aeropostal de Mexico	57-0517+ "N9539Q"^ N9539G (N3224B) N3226B HP-1162TLN N3226B HP-1162TLN XA-RSH [+ USAF; ^ painted in error; wfu by 2000 Mexico City-Benito Juarez, Mexico; l/n 04Oct08]
3225	C-130A	Aeropostal de Mexico	57-0518+ N9691N XA-RYZ [+ USAF] [wfu by 2000 Mexico City-Benito Juarez, Mexico; l/n 04Oct08]
3226	RC-130A	(USAF)	57-0519 [wfu Jan89 Langley AFB, VA; SOC Oct89]
3227	C-130A	International Air Response	57-0520+ N138FF^ N119TG [+ USAF; ^ code 88] [stored Coolidge Municipal, AZ; l/n Feb09]
3228	C-130A	Transportes Aereos Bolivianos	57-0521+ TAM-69//CP-2184 CP-2184 [+ USAF; ^ dual marks]
3229	C-130A	USAF	57-0522 [derelict Sep89 Wright-Patterson AFB, OH; l/n Apr09]
3230	DC-130A	(Humberto Montano)	57-0523+ N3149B^ N3226A [+ USAF] [b/u Jan87 Davis-Monthan AFB, AZ; noted Apr97 Sam's scrapyard, AZ; ^ marks not canx until 12Sep12]
3231	GC-130A	(USAF)	57-0524 [wfu Sep89; GIA Mildenhall AFB, UK; b/u; nose to avionics trainer CFB Trenton, ON, Canada]
3501	C-130B	Ecuadorean Air Force	57-0525+ 894 [+ USAF]
3502	C-130B	Hill Aerospace Museum	57-0526 [wfu Jan94; preserved Ogden-Hill AFB, UT]
3503	C-130B	Turkish Air Force	57-0527+ 70527 [+ USAF]
3504	JC-130B	US Army	57-0528 [wfu AMARC; by Oct98 wfu at England AFB, LA; GIA Fort Polk, LA; l/n Mar07]
3505	C-130B	Ecuadorean Air Force	57-0529+ 895 [+ USAF]
3506	C-130B	Botswana Defence Force	58-0711+ OM1 [+ USAF]
3507	NC-130B	ex NASA	58-0712+ N707NA N929NA N707NA [+ USAF] [wfu & stored by Jan01 AMARC; l/n Dec08]
3508	JC-130B	(USAF)	58-0713 [wfu AMARC Jly91; b/u about 1998, nose to Hurlburt Field, FL as simulator]
3509	C-130B	(USAF)	58-0714 [wfu AMARC Oct91; b/u 2005; wing box to Polish AF C-130 rebuild]
3510	C-130B	Tunisian Air Force	58-0715+ Z21120//TS-MTJ^ [+ USAF; ^ dual marks]
3511	NC-130B	(USAF)	58-0716 [wfu AMARC 26Sep94]
3512	C-130B	(Colombian Air Force)	58-0717+ 1006 [+ USAF] [wfu by Mar03 Bogota, Colombia; b/u Oct05]
3513	C-130B	(USAF)	58-0718 [destroyed in explosion 06Oct69 over Chu Lai, South Vietnam]
3514	JC-130B	(USAF)	58-0719 [DBF 11Jan65 Forbes Field, KS, collided on ground with C-130B c/n 3525]
3515	C-130B	Argentine Air Force	58-0720+ TC-56 [+ USAF] [wfu by Apr08 El Palomar AFB, Argentina]
3516	C-130B	(USAF)	58-0721 [w/o 01Feb75 on take-off from New Orleans, LA]
3517	C-130B	(USAF)	58-0722 [w/o 16Apr67 cargo exploded on ground Bao Lac, South Vietnam]
3518	C-130B	Greek Air Force	58-0723+ 723 [+ USAF]
3519	KC-130B	Republic of Singapore Air Force	58-0724+ 720 [+ USAF]
3520	C-130B	Philippine Air Force	58-0725+ 0725 [+ USAF] [wfu May95 Mactan-Cebu, Philippines; l/n 03Aug07]
3521	C-130B	Colombian Air Force	58-0726+ 1010 [+ USAF]
3522	GC-130B	USAF	58-0727 [GIA Mar90 Sheppard AFB, TX]
3523	C-130B	Tunisian Air Force	58-0728+ Z21116//TS-MTF^ [+ USAF; ^ dual marks]
3524	C-130B	(USAF)	58-0729 [wfu & stored AMARC Mar91; sold for scrap 2000; b/u Feb05]
3525	C-130B	(USAF)	58-0730 [DBF 11Jan65 Forbes Field, KS; hit by C-130B c/n 3514 on ground]
3526	C-130BZ	(South African Air Force)	58-0731+ N6541C N8037 580731^ 408 [+ USAF; ^ USN] [reported b/u 2009 but not confirmed]
3527	C-130B	(USAF)	58-0732 [w/o 06Feb82 stalled near Evansville, IN]

LOCKHEED C-130/L-100 HERCULES

C/n	Model	Last known Owner/Operator	Identities/fates/comments (where appropriate)
3528	C-130B	ex Ecuadorean Air Force	58-0733+ 896 [+ USAF] [stored by 2000 Quito-Marescal Sucre AFB, Ecuador; wfu by Oct04]
3529	C-130B	(US Coast Guard)	58-5396+ 1339 [+ USAF] [wfu AMARC Oct83; noted Apr97 National Aircraft scrapyard, AZ; b/u]
3530	C-130BZ	(South African Air Force)	58-0734+ 409 [+ USAF] [reported b/u 2009 but not confirmed]
3531	C-130B	(Colombian Air Force)	58-0735+ 1007 [+ USAF] [DBR in Sep89 in heavy landing in Colombia; l/n 02Feb95 Bogota, Colombia; b/u]
3532	C-130B	Turkish Air Force	58-0736+ 80736 [+ USAF]
3533	C-130B	(US Coast Guard)	58-5397+ 1340 [+ USAF] [wfu AMARC Oct82; b/u Mar97]
3534	C-130B	(USAF)	58-0737 [w/o after structural failure 09Jun67 near Tan Son Nhut, South Vietnam]
3535	C-130B	Philippine Air Force	58-0738+ 738 [+ USAF] [wfu by 2004 Mactan-Cebu, Philippines; l/n 03Aug07]
3536	C-130B	Pakistan Air Force	58-0739+ 58739 [+ USAF]
3537	GC-130B	(USAF)	58-0740 [GIA Homestead AFB, FL; destroyed 24Aug92 by Hurricane Andrew]
3538	C-130B	Argentine Air Force	58-0741+ TC-58 [+ USAF] [wfu by 2000 El Palomar AFB, Argentina for spares; l/n Apr08]
3539	C-130B	Botswana Defence Force	58-0742+ OM3 [+ USAF]
3540	C-130B	(USAF)	58-0743 [DBR 18Feb68 in rocket attack Tan Son Nhut, South Vietnam]
3541	C-130B	ex Uruguayan Air Force	58-0744+ 593 [+ USAF] [wfu since delivery Montevideo, Uruguay; l/n 05Apr08 as derelict]
3542	HC-130B	ex US Coast Guard	58-6973+ 1341 [+ USAF] [by 1998 to GIA Lackland AFB, TX; in USAF c/s marked as 58-1341; 18Jun11 moved to Fort Lee, VA]
3543	C-130B	(USAF)	58-0745 [DBF Oct61 Evreux, France; front part of fuselage used to repair c/n 3530; remains to Spangdahlem, West Germany for spares]
3544	C-130B	Botswana Defence Force	58-0746+ OM2 [+ USAF]
3545	C-130B	ex Philippine Air Force	58-0747+ 3545 [+ USAF] [wfu by 2004 Mactan-Cebu AFB, Philippines]
3546	C-130B	Indonesian Air Force	58-0748+ T-1301^ PK-VHD A-1301 [+ USAF; ^ Indonesia] [wfu by 1987 & preserved Lanud Sulaiman, Indonesia]
3547	C-130B	ex Philippine Air Force	58-0749+ 0749 [+ USAF] [wfu by 1995 Mactan-Cebu AFB, Philippines]
3548	HC-130B	(US Coast Guard)	58-6974+ 1342 [+ USAF] [wfu AMARC Jul82; b/u Mar97]
3549	C-130B	ex Bolivian Air Force	58-0750+ FAB61 [+ USAF] [wfu by Jun04 La Paz, Bolivia]
3550	C-130B	Tunisian Air Force	58-0751+ Z21115//TS-MTE^ [+ USAF; ^ dual marks]
3551	C-130B	Chilean Air Force	58-0752+ 997 [+ USAF]
3552	C-130B	ex Philippine Air Force	58-0753+ 3552 [+ USAF] [wfu by 2004 Mactan-Cebu AFB, Philippines]
3553	C-130B	Bangladesh Defence Force	58-0754+ 80754//S3-AGA^ [+ USAF; ^ dual marks]
3554	KC-130F	(US Marine Corps)	147572 [wfu AMARC Jun04]
3555	KC-130F	(US Marine Corps)	147573 [wfu AMARC 27Feb08; SOC 08Aug08]
3556	C-130B	US Army	58-0755 [wfu AMARC Feb91; to US Army ZF006; to England AFB, LA by Aug95]
3557	KC-130B	Republic of Singapore Air Force	58-0756+ 721 [+ USAF]
3558	C-130B	(USAF)	58-0757 [wfu AMARC Feb93]
3559	C-130B	(Bolivian Air Force)	58-0758+ TAM-60 [+ USAF] [w/o 14Jan00 Chimore Airport, Bolivia]
3560	C-130B	Bolivian Air Force	59-1524+ TAM-66 [+ USAF] [possible w/o 21Apr11 Guayaramerin, Bolivia]
3561	C-130B	(USAF)	59-1525 [wfu AMARC Oct91; 2006 wing centre section to support Polish AF aircraft rebuild]
3562	LC-130F	(US Navy)	59-5922+ 148318 [+ USAF] [DBF 15Feb71 Williams Field, McMurdo, Antarctica]
3563	C-130B	Argentine Air Force	59-1526+ TC-57 [+ USAF] [wfu by 2000 El Palomar AFB, Argentina; l/n Apr08]
3564	LC-130F	(US Navy)	59-5923+ 148319 [+ USAF] [wfu & stored AMARC 10Mar99]
3565	LC-130F	ex US Navy	59-5924+ 148320 [wfu AMARC Jan05; on display celebrity row by Mar03]
3566	KC-130F	(US Navy)	148246 [SOC Nov05, for scrap in 2006; tail to c/n 3725]
3567	LC-130R	ex US Navy	59-5925+ 148321 [+ USAF] [wfu & stored AMARC 29Mar99]
3568	C-130B	Romanian Air Force	59-1527+ 5927 [+ USAF]
3569	C-130B	ex USAF	59-1529 [wfu AMARC Apr92]
3570	C-130B	(USAF)	59-1534 [w/o 27May61 skidded off runway Ramstein AFB, West Germany]
3571	C-130B	Tunisian Air Force	59-1528+ Z21117//TS-MTG^ [+ USAF; ^ dual marks]
3572	C-130B	(Colombian Air Force)	60-5450+ 10301^ N4652 1003 [+ USAF; ^ Canada] [ditched 16Oct82 Atlantic Ocean 300kms east of Cape May, NJ]
3573	KC-130F	ex US Navy	148247 [wfu AMARC Feb07]
3574	KC-130F	ex US Navy	148248 [wfu AMARC Oct04]
3575	C-130B	Colombian Air Force	60-5451+ 10302^ N4653 1001 [+ USAF; ^ Canada]
3576	C-130B	Romanian Air Force	59-1530+ 5930 [+ USAF]
3577	KC-130F	ex US Navy	148249 [wfu AMARC Jul06]

LOCKHEED C-130/L-100 HERCULES

C/n	Model	Last known Owner/Operator	Identities/fates/comments (where appropriate)
3578	C-130B	(Indonesian Air Force)	T-1302+ A-1302 [+ Indonesia] [w/o 11May09 Wamena, West Papua, Indonesia]
3579	C-130B	USAF	59-1531 [wfu 1994 GIA Homestead AFB, FL; to Kelly AFB, TX by 1999; preserved Lackland AFB, TX by Jly05]
3580	C-130B	Indonesian Air Force	N9298R T-1303+ A-1303 [+ Indonesia]
3581	C-130B	(Bolivian Air Force)	59-1532+ TAM-67 [+ USAF] [w/o 31Dec94 Trinidad, Bolivia]
3582	C-130B	ex Indonesian Air Force	N9297R T-1304+ A-1304 [+ Indonesia] [wfu by 2000]
3583	C-130B	ex Indonesian Air Force	N9296R T-1305+ A-1305+ PK-VHC A-1305 [+ Indonesia] [wfu by 1998]
3584	C-130B	(USAF)	59-5957 [wfu AMARC Aug93; 2006 wing centre section to support Polish AF aircraft rebuild
3585	C-130B	Colombian Air Force Museum	59-1535+ 1011^ [+ USAF; ^ Colombia] [wfu by Jun97 Bogota; on display by May04]
3586	C-130B	Tunisian Air Force	59-1533+ Z21114//TS-MTD^ [+ USAF; ^ dual marks]
3587	C-130B	(Colombian Air Force)	60-5452+ 10303^ N4654 1002 [+ USAF; ^ Canada] [DBF 26Aug69 Bogota, Colombia]
3588	C-130B	Bolivian Air Force	59-1536+ FAB65 [+ USAF]
3589	C-130B	Bangladesh Defence Force	59-1537+ 91537//S3-AGB^ [+USAF; ^ dual marks]
3590	CC-130E	(Royal Canadian Air Force)	60-5453+ 10304 [+ USAF] [belly-landed 15Apr66 in field North Battleford, SK, Canada; SOC 12Oct66]
3591	C-130B	(USAF)	60-0293 [w/o 17Jun67 An Khe AFB, South Vietnam]
3592	KC-130F	ex US Marine Corps	148890 [wfu; fuselage to GIA 1996 Hill AFB, UT]
3593	C-130B	ex Philippine Air Force	60-0294+ 0294 [+ USAF] [stored/wfu by 1996]
3594	HC-130B	(US Coast Guard)	60-0311+ 1344 [+ USAF] [wfu AMARC Jly82; noted Apr97 National Aircraft scrapyard, AZ; b/u by 2000]
3595	HC-130B	(US Coast Guard)	60-0312+ 1345 [+ USAF] [wfu AMARC Jun83; b/u by Oct95; cockpit to Austin, TX for BAe C-130X mock-up]
3596	C-130B	ex Uruguayan Air Force	60-0295+ 592//CX-BQX^ [+ USAF; ^ dual marks]
3597	C-130B	ex Greek Air Force	60-0296+ 296 [+ USAF] [wfu Nov96 Elefsis, Greece; l/n 05Nov11]
3598	C-130B	(Indonesian Air Force)	T-1306 [w/o 16Sep65 forced down by RAF Javelin over Malaysia]
3599	C-130B	(Indonesian Air Force)	T-1307 [w/o 01Sep64 in jungle on west coast of Malaysia]
3600	C-130B	(USAF)	60-0297 [shot down 12May68 on take-off from Kham Duc, South Vietnam]
3601	C-130B	Indonesian Air Force	T-1308+ PK-VHA A-1308 [+ Indonesia]
3602	C-130B	(USAF)	60-0298 [w/o 26Apr68 A Loui Valley, 20m SW of Hue, South Vietnam]
3603	C-130B	Tunisian Air Force	60-0299+ Z21119//TS-MTI^ [+USAF; ^ dual marks]
3604	C-130B	ex Greek Air Force	60-0300+ 300 [+ USAF] [wfu Nov96 Elefsis, Greece]
3605	KC-130F	US Marine Corps	148891 [code 403]
3606	KC-130F	ex US Marine Corps	148892 [wfu due to corrosion Sep97 NAS Fort Worth, TX; GIA, outer wings to c/n 3740]
3607	KC-130F	US Marine Corps	148893
3608	KC-130F	US Marine Corps	148894 [code 402] [reported Dec09 to AMARC]
3609	C-130E	ex USAF	61-2358 [wfu 01May12 Edwards AFB, CA; for preservation at base museum]
3610	C-130B	Royal Jordanian Air Force	60-0301+ 141^ 341 [+ USAF; ^ Jordan] [wfu Jun95 Amman-Marka, Jordan; l/n 10May08, GIA]
3611	KC-130B	Republic of Singapore Air Force	60-0302+ 142^ 724 [+ USAF; ^ Jordan]
3612	C-130B	Royal Jordanian Air Force	60-0304+ 140^ 340 [+ USAF; ^ Jordan] [wfu Jun95 Amman-Marka, Jordan; l/n 10May08, GIA]
3613	C-130B	Greek Air Force	60-0303+ 303 [+ USAF]
3614	C-130B	(Indonesian Air Force)	60-0305+ T-1311^ A-1311 [+ USAF; ^ Indonesia] [wfu for spares by 2004]
3615	KC-130B	Indonesian Air Force	T-1309+ A-1309 [+ Indonesia]
3616	KC-130B	Indonesian Air Force	T-1310+ A-1310 [+ Indonesia]
3617	C-130B	Indonesian Air Force	60-0306+ T-1312^ A-1312 [+ USAF; ^ Indonesia]
3618	C-130B	(USAF)	60-0307 [w/o 17Feb67 Tay Ninh, South Vietnam]
3619	KC-130F	(US Marine Corps)	148895 [w/o 12Feb02 Twenty Nine Palms, CA]
3620	KC-130B	Singapore Air Force	60-0308+ 143^ 725 [+ USAF; ^ Jordan]
3621	C-130B	Indonesian Air Force	60-0309+ T-1313^ A-1313 [+ USAF; ^ Indonesia]
3622	C-130B	ex Chilean Air Force	60-0310+ 994 [+ USAF] [by 31Mar08 wfu Santiago de Chile, Chile; only fuselage present]
3623	KC-130F	ex US Marine Corps	148896 [wfu AMARC Jun06]
3624	C-130B	Greek Air Force	61-0948+ 948 [+ USAF]
3625	C-130B	Tunisian Air Force	61-0949+ Z21113//TS-MTC^ [+ USAF; ^ dual marks]
3626	C-130B	Romanian Air Force	61-0950+ 6150 [+ USAF]
3627	KC-130F	US Marine Corps	148897

LOCKHEED C-130/L-100 HERCULES

C/n	Model	Last known Owner/Operator	Identities/fates/comments (where appropriate)
3628	C-130B	Lockheed	61-0951+ [+ USAF] [wfu AMARC Mar92; to Lockheed, Marietta, GA 1992; used in C-130J development programme]
3629	C-130B	ex USAF	61-0952 [wfu AMARC Jan93]
3630	C-130B	(USAF)	61-0953 [w/o 29Mar66 Ple Ku, South Vietnam]
3631	KC-130F	(US Marine Corps)	148898 [wfu AMARC Dec03; SOC 2004]
3632	KC-130F	ex US Marine Corps	148899 [wfu AMARC May06]
3633	C-130B	Philippine Air Force	61-0954+ 0954^ 3633 [+ USAF; ^ Philippines]
3634	C-130B	(USAF)	61-0955 [w/o 25Oct66 Fort Campbell, KY]
3635	C-130B	(Colombian Air Force)	61-0956+ 1012 [+ USAF] [wfu Mar03 Bogota, Colombia; b/u 2005]
3636	C-130F	(South African Air Force)	149787+ 410 [+ USN] [to spares by Aug99 Waterkloof AFB, South Africa; b/u]
3637	C-130B	(Chilean Air Force)	61-0957+ 993 [+ USAF] [wfu 1996 Santiago/Pudahuel, Chile; b/u 2004]
3638	HC-130B	(US Coast Guard)	61-2081+ 1346 [+ USAF] [wfu by 1985; GIA Nov86 Cherry Point MCAS, NC; b/u 2002]
3639	C-130B	(USAF)	61-0958 [wfu AMARC May92; 2006 wing centre section to support Polish AF aircraft rebuild]
3640	KC-130F	(US Marine Corps)	149788 [wfu AMARC May04; SOC Apr05]
3641	HC-130B	(US Coast Guard)	61-2082+ 1347 [+ USAF] [wfu AMARC Jun83; noted Apr97 National Aircraft scrapyard, AZ; b/u by 2000]
3642	C-130B	(USAF)	61-0959 [wfu AMARC Jan93; b/u 2005]
3643	C-130B	Turkish Air Force	61-0960+ 10960 [+ USAF]
3644	KC-130F	ex US Marine Corps	149789 [stored AMARC 27Mar07]
3645	C-130F	(US Navy)	149790 [wfu AMARC Jun92; b/u for spares]
3646	C-130B	Philippine Air Force	61-0961+ 0961 [+ USAF] [wfu Mar96 Mactan-Cebu AFB, Philippines]
3647	C-130B	Bangladesh Defence Force	61-0962+ 10962//S3-AGC^ [+ USAF; ^ dual marks]
3648	C-130B	Turkish Air Force	61-0963+ 10963 [+ USAF]
3649	C-130B	ex Argentine Air Force	61-0964+ TC-59 [+ USAF] [wfu by Sep00 El Palomar AFB, Argentina; l/n Apr08]
3650	HC-130B	(US Coast Guard)	61-2083+ 1348 [+ USAF] [wfu AMARC Jun84; fuselage to Long Beach, CA by 2000]
3651	C-130E	ex USAF	61-2359 [wfu AMARC Jly04]
3652	C-130B	(USAF)	61-0965 [shot down 23Jun69 NW of Saigon, near Suoi Nuoc Trong, South Vietnam]
3653	C-130B	Romanian Air Force	61-0966+ 6166 [+ USAF]
3654	C-130B	(USAF)	61-0967 [w/o 13Apr68 Khe Sanh, South Vietnam]
3655	C-130B	ex Bolivian Air Force	61-0968+ TAM-68 [+ USAF] [wfu by Sep97 La Paz, Bolivia; l/n Oct07]
3656	C-130B	ex Argentine Air Force	61-0969+ TC-60 [+ USAF] [wfu 15Sep11 Moron, Argentina for preservation]
3657	KC-130F	(US Marine Corps)	149791 [wfu San Diego/NAS Miramar, CA; SOC Apr05]
3658	KC-130F	(US Marine Corps)	149792 [wfu AMARC Nov04; SOC Apr05]
3659	WC-130E	(USAF)	61-2360 [wfu AMARC Dec93; b/u Sep01]
3660	C-130F	(South African Air Force)	149793+ 411 [+ USN] [wfu Jun99 Waterkloof AFB, South Africa; Oct09 to be b/u for spares]
3661	C-130F	(US Navy)	149794 [DBR 27Aug92 by typhoon Omar at NAF Agana, Guam; to spares; b/u 14Aug94]
3662	GC-130E	ex USAF	61-2361 [wfu Aug01; GIA Sheppard AFB, TX]
3663	GC-130E	ex USAF	61-2362 [wfu 1994; GIA Little Rock AFB, AR]
3664	KC-130F	ex US Marine Corps	149795 [wfu AMARC Jun06]
3665	KC-130F	US Marine Corps	149796
3666	C-130F	ex US Navy	149797 [wfu AMARC May92]
3667	C-130B	(USAF)	61-0970 [w/o 09Jan66 An Khe, South Vietnam]
3668	C-130B	Uruguayan Air Force	61-0971+ 591//CX-BQW^ [+ USAF; ^ dual marks]
3669	C-130B	(USAF)	61-0972 [shot down 06Jan66 and crashed near Plei Ku, South Vietnam]
3670	C-130B	Turkish Air Force	61-2634+ 12634 [+ USAF]
3671	C-130B	Ethiopian Air Force	61-2635+ 1562 [+ USAF]
3672	C-130B	Ethiopian Air Force	61-2636+ 1563 [+ USAF]
3673	C-130B	(USAF)	61-2637 [DBF 29Apr69 Loc Ninh, South Vietnam]
3674	C-130B	Colombian Air Force	61-2638+ 1014 [+ USAF]
3675	C-130B	Colombian Air Force	61-2639+ 1008 [+ USAF]
3676	C-130B	Bangladesh Defence Force	61-2640+ 12640//S3-AGD^ [+ USAF; ^ dual marks]
3677	C-130B	(USAF)	61-2641 [w/o 19Mar66 Svanfjellet, on approach to Bardufoss, Senja Island, Norway]
3678	C-130B	(USAF)	61-2642 [DBR 21Feb71 in rocket attack on Da Nang, South Vietnam]
3679	C-130B	(USAF)	61-2643 [wfu AMARC May93; 2006 wing centre section to support Polish AF aircraft rebuild]
3680	KC-130F	National Museum of Naval Avn	149798+ [+ USN] [wfu Mar05 Pensacola, FL & preserved]

LOCKHEED C-130/L-100 HERCULES

C/n	Model	Last known Owner/Operator	Identities/fates/comments (where appropriate)
3681	C-130E	ex USAF	61-2363 [wfu 1994 Little Rock AFB, AR; to Apr97 Pope AFB, NC; b/u 2003, fuselage to Malaysia as GIA]
3682	C-130B	(USAF)	61-2644 [w/o 28Nov68 Tonle Cham, South Vietnam]
3683	C-130B	Museo Aeronautico Park	61-2645+ 897^ [+ USAF; ^ Ecuador] [wfu for spares by Jan99; preserved Quito, Ecuador by Oct04]
3684	KC-130F	ex US Marine Corps	149799 [stored AMARC 13Nov06]
3685	KC-130F	ex US Marine Corps	149800 [wfu AMARC Jun04]
3686	C-130F	(US Navy)	149801 [wfu 1991; fuselage at Cherry Point MCAS, NC; sunk as sea reef off NC Mar95]
3687	GC-130E	ex USAF	61-2364 [wfu 1994; GIA Sheppard AFB, TX; to Goodfellow AFB, TX]
3688	C-130E	Snow Aviation International	61-2365+ N5024E 61-2365+ N131EV N307SA [+USAF] [cvtd with NP2000 eight-bladed propellers and wing tip tanks]
3689	C-130B	Pakistan Air Force	61-2646+ 12646//AK-MOB^ [+ USAF; ^ dual marks]
3690	C-130B	Chilean Air Force	61-2647+ 998 [+ USAF]
3691	C-130B	(Pakistan Air Force)	61-2648+ 12648 [+ USAF] [w/o 18Aug65 after skidding off runway in Pakistan]
3692	C-130B	(USAF)	61-2649 [w/o 08Oct67 into mountain near Hue/Phu Bai, South Vietnam]
3693	KC-130F	(US Marine Corps)	149802 [w/o 24Aug65 hit sea wall on take-off from Kai Tak, Hong Kong]
3694	KC-130F	US Marine Corps	149803 [code GR-803]
3695	KC-130F	ex US Marine Corps	149804 [wfu Sep00 due to corrosion MCAS Cherry Point, NC; to GIA]
3696	C-130F	(South African Air Force)	149805+ 412 [+ USN] [used as spares by Aug99 Waterkloof AFB, South Africa; reported Oct09 to be b/u]
3697	C-130B	ex Colombian Air Force	62-3487+ 1009 [+ USAF] [wfu by Jun97 Bogota, Colombia; for spares use]
3698	C-130B	(Pakistan Air Force)	62-3488+ 5-101^ 23488//AQ-ACP# 23488//AS-HFP# [+ USAF; ^ Iran; # Pakistan dual marks; DBR Feb79 Lahore, Pakistan, ground collision with C-130 10687 c/n 4117]
3699	C-130B	(Pakistan Air Force)	62-3489+ 5-102^ 23489 [+ USAF; ^ Iran] [w/o 04Mar70 in Pakistan]
3700	C-130B	(Pakistan Air Force)	62-3490+ 5-103^ 23490//AS-HFQ# [+ USAF; ^ Iran; # Pakistan dual marks; DBF 08Jly69 during refuelling Islamabad, Pakistan; noted dumped Oct86]
3701	C-130B	(Pakistan Air Force)	62-3491+ 5-104^ 23491//AQ-ACV# [+ USAF; ^ Iran; # Pakistan dual marks; DBF 10Sep98 Rawalpindi, Pakistan, ground collision with C-130 24143 c/n 3781]
3702	C-130B	Pakistan Air Force	62-3492+ 23492 [+ USAF]
3703	KC-130F	(US Marine Corps)	149806 [wfu AMARC Dec04; SOC Apr05]
3704	KC-130F	(US Marine Corps)	149807 [DBR 1998 in ground-running incident; b/u; cockpit to MCAS Futenma, Okinawa as GIA]
3705	KC-130F	US Marine Corps	149808
3706	WC-130E	(USAF)	61-2366 [wfu AMARC Sep94; sold for scrap Jun04]
3707	C-130B	ex USAF	62-3493 [wfu by Dec93; to GIA Hill AFB, UT]
3708	C-130B	(Pakistan Air Force)	62-3494+ 23494 [+ USAF] [blown up by bomb 17Aug88 & w/o near Bahawalpur, Pakistan]
3709	KC-130F	(US Marine Corps)	149809 [shot down 01Feb66 & w/o in Gulf of Tonkin, 40m E of Dong Hoi, North Vietnam]
3710	KC-130F	(US Marine Corps)	149810 [DBF 15Jan72 on ground Lake City, FL; tail section at MCAS Cherry Point, NC by Sep84]
3711	KC-130F	(US Marine Corps)	149811 [to NAS China Lake, CA for fire test; SOC 2004]
3712	C-130E	ex USAF	61-2367 [wfu late 2010 Charlotte, NC for preservation at base museum]
3713	C-130E	ex USAF	61-2368 [GIA Aug95 Minneapolis-St Paul Airport, MN; minus wings & tail by Apr98]
3714	C-130E	ex USAF	61-2369 [wfu Dobbins ARB, GA; fuselage only, no tail; GIA; l/n 09Sep08; by Jun12 preserved Pope Field, NC]
3715	C-130E	USAF	61-2370
3716	GC-130E	ex USAF	61-2371 [wfu 2001;GIA Sheppard AFB, TX]
3717	C-130E	USAF	61-2372
3718	KC-130F	(US Marine Corps)	149812 [wfu AMARC Dec04; SOC Apr05]
3719	KC-130F	(US Marine Corps)	149813 [w/o 10Feb68 Khe Sanh, South Vietnam]
3720	C-130E	(USAF)	61-2373 [w/o 08Jun88 near Greenville Airport, MS]
3721	C-130B	Tunisian Air Force	62-3495+ Z21118//TS-MTH^ [+ USAF; ^ dual marks]
3722	C-130B	Turkish Air Force	62-3496+ 23496 [+ USAF]
3723	KC-130F	(US Marine Corps)	149814 [w/o 18May69 over South Vietnam, mid-air collision with F-4B Phantom (BuA151456)]
3724	C-130B	South African Air Force	401
3725	KC-130F	US Marine Corps	149815
3726	KC-130F	ex US Marine Corps	149816 [wfu AMARC Apr04]

LOCKHEED C-130/L-100 HERCULES

C/n	Model	Last known Owner/Operator	Identities/fates/comments (where appropriate)
3727	KC-130F	(US Marine Corps)	150684 [wfu 1995 MCAS Cherry Point NAS, NC; sunk as a reef off NC]
3728	KC-130F	(US Marine Corps)	150685 [w/o 30Jly70 El Toro, CA]
3729	C-130E	ex USAF	62-1784 to AMARC DEc11]
3730	C-130E	(USAF)	62-1785 [shot down 06Sep68 Bao Loc, South Vietnam]
3731	C-130E	USAF	62-1786 [stored AMARC 15Sep09]
3732	C-130E	USAF	62-1787 [wfu 18Aug11 & preserved USAF Museum, Wright-Patterson AFB, OH]
3733	KC-130F	US Marine Corps	150686
3734	KC-130F	(US Marine Corps)	150687 [wfu AMARC Jan02; SOC Jly03]
3735	C-130E	ex USAF	62-1788 [wfu AMARC Nov10]
3736	C-130E	ex USAF	62-1789 [stored Dec08 McChord AFB, WA; Mar10 to be prepared for base museum]
3737	GC-130E	USAF	62-1790 [wfu 2001; GIA Sheppard AFB, TX]
3738	EC-130E	USAF	62-1791
3739	C-130E	Royal Jordanian Air Force	62-1792+ 351^ [+ USAF; ^ assumption only]
3740	KC-130F	(US Marine Corps)	150688 [wfu AMARC Apr02; SOC Jly03]
3741	KC-130F	ex US Marine Corps	150689 [wfu AMARC 26Apr07]
3742	KC-130F	ex US Marine Corps	150690 [wfu AMARC Feb06]
3743	C-130E	USAF	62-1793
3744	GC-130E	ex USAF	62-1794 [wfu 1995; GIA Sheppard AFB, TX; to Goodfellow AFB, TX]
3745	HC-130B	(US Coast Guard)	62-3753+ 1349 [+ USAF] [wfu AMARC Oct82; b/u Mar93]
3746	GC-130E	ex USAF	62-1795 [wfu 2001; GIA Sheppard AFB, TX]
3747	C-130E	Israel Defence Force/Air Force	62-1796+ 304//4X-FBE^ [+ USAF; ^ dual marks]
3748	C-130E	(USAF)	62-1797 [shot down 03May72 near An Loc, South Vietnam]
3749	C-130BZ	South African Air Force	402
3750	C-130B	South African Air Force	403
3751	C-130B	Pakistan Air Force	62-4140+ 24140 [+ USAF]
3752	C-130E	ex USAF	62-1798 [wfu by 2004 Alpena CRTC, MI; GIA]
3753	C-130E	Royal Jordanian Air Force	62-1799+ 349^ [+ USAF; ^ assumption only]
3754	C-130E	(USAF)	62-1800 [w/o 15Dec69 on landing in Taiwan]
3755	C-130E	Polish Air Force	62-1801 1508
3756	C-130E	(USAF)	62-1802 [w/o 31Jly70 near Piggott, AR]
3757	C-130E	(USAF)	62-1803 [wfu AMARC Dec94; sold for scrap Jly04]
3758	C-130E	USAF	62-1804 [stored AMARC 15Sep09]
3759	C-130E	(USAF)	62-1805 [ditched & sank 05Jun72 near Makung AFB, Pescadores Islands, Taiwan Strait]
3760	C-130E	USAF	62-1806
3761	GC-130E	ex USAF	62-1807 [wfu 1997; GIA Sheppard AFB, TX]
3762	C-130E	ex USAF	62-1808 [stored 13Jun08 AMARC]
3763	HC-130B	(US Coast Guard)	62-3754+ 1350 [+ USAF] [wfu AMARC; fuselage at Westover AFB, MA Jun86; b/u Nov95]
3764	C-130B	ex South African Air Force	404 [probably w/o 25Jan10 Waterkloof AFB, South Africa]
3765	C-130BZ	South African Air Force	405
3766	C-130B	Pakistan Air Force	62-4141+ 24141 [+ USAF]
3767	C-130BZ	South African Air Force	406
3768	C-130B	(Pakistan Air Force)	62-4142+ 24142 [+ USAF] [w/o 15Jly66 in mountains in Pakistan]
3769	C-130BZ	ex South African Air Force	407 [reported stored Feb05; wings removed by Oct09]
3770	EC-130E	(USAF)	62-1809 [w/o 24Apr80 after collision with RH-53D (BuA158761) Posht-i-Badam (Desert One), Iran]
3771	C-130E	ex USAF	62-1810 [stored 27May08 AMARC]
3772	C-130E	ex USAF	62-1811 [to AMARC Dec11]
3773	HC-130B	(US Coast Guard)	62-3755+ 1351 [+ USAF; wfu AMARC; b/u Sep88 AirPro International, Tucson, AZ; cockpit to simulator at Reflectone, Tampa, FL]
3774	C-130E	ex USAF	62-1812 [wfu 2001; GIA Sheppard AFB, TX]
3775	C-130E	(USAF)	62-1813 [w/o 09Feb72 after mid-air collision with a T-37B near Little Rock, AR]
3776	C-130E	(USAF)	62-1814 [w/o after electrical fire 03Mar68 Cam Ranh Bay, South Vietnam]
3777	EC-130E	(USAF)	62-1815 [DBR 15Jul67 in rocket attack on Da Nang, South Vietnam]
3778	C-130E	ex USAF	62-1816 [stored 27May08 AMARC]
3779	C-130E	USAF	62-1817
3780	EC-130E	USAF	62-1818
3781	C-130B	(Pakistan Air Force)	62-4143+ 24143//AS-HFO^ [+ USAF; ^ dual marks] [DBF 10Sep98 Rawalpindi, Pakistan; ground collision with C-130 hitting 23491 c/n 3701]
3782	C-130E	(USAF)	62-1819 [wfu & stored AMARC May98; sold for scrap Dec04]
3783	C-130E	USAF	62-1820
3784	C-130E	ex USAF	62-1821 [wfu & stored AMARC Aug97]

LOCKHEED C-130/L-100 HERCULES

C/n	Model	Last known Owner/Operator	Identities/fates/comments (where appropriate)	
3785	C-130E	(USAF)	62-1822	[wfu & stored AMARC Sep97; sold for scrap 2005]
3786	C-130E	ex USAF	62-1823	[for AMARC 2011]
3787	C-130E	ex USAF	62-1824	[stored Sep11 AMARC]
3788	EC-130E	ex USAF	62-1825	[wfu & stored AMARC Oct02]
3789	C-130E	Iraqi Air Force	62-1826+	YI-302 [+ USAF]
3790	C-130E	(USAF)	62-1827	[wfu & stored AMARC Sep97; sold for scrap Dec04]
3791	C-130E	ex USAF	62-1828	[wfu & stored AMARC May98]
3792	C-130E	ex USAF	62-1829	[wfu by Oct03; GIA, Little Rock AFB, AR; to gate City of Jacksonville Joint Education Center]
3793	C-130E	(USAF)	62-1830	[wfu by May94 ; GIA, Little Rock AFB, AR; b/u for scrap Aug02]
3794	C-130E	(USAF)	62-1831	[DBR 30May69 in ground accident St Petersburg, FL]
3795	HC-130P	USAF	62-1832	[stored AMARC 23Sep10]
3796	C-130E	ex USAF	62-1833	[stored Aug11 AMARC]
3797	C-130E	ex USAF	62-1834	[preserved May12 Oklahoma City, OK]
3798	C-130E	ex USAF	62-1835	[stored Aug11 AMARC]
3799	HC-130P	USAF	62-1836	[stored AMARC 23Sep10]
3800	C-130E	ex USAF	62-1837	[stored 12May08 AMARC]
3801	C-130E	(USAF)	62-1838	[w/o 13May95 Bliss Canyon, 30 miles W of Mountain Home AFB, ID]
3802	C-130E	Iraqi Air Force	62-1839+	YI-301 [+ USAF]
3803	C-130E	(USAF)	62-1840	[shot down 02Oct66 over Nha Trang, 19m S of Cam Rahn, South Vietnam]
3804	C-130E	(USAF)	62-1841	[DBF 20Apr74 Andersen AFB, Guam]
3805	C-130E	USAF	62-1842	
3806	C-130E	(USAF)	62-1843	[w/o 20Dec65 into mountain 10m S of Tuy Hoa, South Vietnam; serial re-used on c/n 3990]
3807	C-130E	USAF	62-1844	[stored AMARC 09Sep10]
3808	C-130E	(USAF)	62-1845	[w/o 15Oct73 into Sugar Loaf Mountain, AR]
3809	C-130E	Idaho Military Museum	62-1846+	[+ USAF] [wfu Apr04; preserved Gowen Field-Boise, ID]
3810	C-130E	USAF	62-1847	[stored AMARC 03Sep10]
3811	C-130E	USAF	62-1848	
3812	C-130E	ex USAF	62-1849	[stored Aug11 AMARC]
3813	C-130E	USAF	63-7764	[wfu by Jly11 Little Rock, AR; GIA]
3814	C-130E	ex USAF	62-1850	[wfu AMARC Sep08]
3815	C-130E	USAF	62-1851	
3816	C-130E	USAF	62-1852	[stored AMARC 01Sep10]
3817	C-130E	(USAF)	62-1853	[shot down 12Aug72 on take-off from Soc Trang, South Vietnam]
3818	C-130E	(USAF)	62-1854	[DBR 23May72 in rocket attack on Kontum, South Vietnam]
3819	C-130E	ex USAF	62-1855	[wfu 20Sep11 AMARC]
3820	C-130E	Polish Air Force	62-1856+	1507 [wfu 2011 for GIA use; + USAF]
3821	EC-130E	USAF	62-1857	
3822	C-130E	USAF	62-1858	
3823	C-130E	Royal Jordanian Air Force	62-1859+	350^ [+ USAF; ^ assumption only]
3824	C-130E	ex USAF	62-1860	[wfu AMARC Aug94; GIA Apr97 Brooks AFB, TX]
3825	C-130E	(USAF)	62-1861	[DBF 25Jun68 Tay Ninh, South Vietnam]
3826	C-130E	USAF	62-1862	
3827	HC-130P	USAF	62-1863	
3828	C-130E	ex USAF	62-1864	[stored 21May08 AMARC]
3829	C-130E	(USAF)	62-1865	[DBR 15Nov67 in mortar attack on Dak To, South Vietnam]
3830	C-130E	ex USAF	62-1866	[wfu AMARC Sep08]
3831	C-130E	USAF	63-7765	
3832	C-130E	(USAF)	63-7766	[w/o 28Apr78 Sparrevohn AFS, AK, 160 miles W of Anchorage, AK]
3833	C-130E	ex USAF	63-7767	[wfu AMARC Nov06]
3834	C-130E	ex USAF	63-7768	[wfu Dec03; GIA Sheppard AFB, TX]
3835	C-130E	USAF	63-7769	
3836	C-130E	ex USAF	63-7770	[stored 27May08 AMARC]
3837	C-130E	(USAF)	63-7771	[wfu AMARC May95; sold for scrap Jul04]
3838	C-130E	(USAF)	63-7772	[w/o 12Mar67 An Khe, South Vietnam]
3839	EC-130E(RR)	ex USAF	63-7773	[wfu Oct06; preserved Fort Indiantown Gap, PA]
3840	C-130E	Israel Defence Force/Air Force	63-7774+	301//4X-FBF^ 314//4X-FBI^ [+ USAF; ^ Israel dual marks]
3841	C-130E	(USAF)	63-7775	[shot at & crash-landed 18Apr72 near Lai Khe, South Vietnam]
3842	C-130E	ex USAF	63-7776	[wfu AMARC Jan07]
3843	C-130E	ex USAF	63-7777	[wfu AMARC Jun03; Jan05 to AFRL Kirtland AFB, NM]
3844	C-130E	ex USAF	63-7778	[wfu AMARC Mar03]
3845	GC-130E	ex USAF	63-7779	[wfu by Mar95; GIA Sheppard AFB, TX]

LOCKHEED C-130/L-100 HERCULES

C/n	Model	Last known Owner/Operator	Identities/fates/comments (where appropriate)
3846	C-130E	(USAF)	63-7780 [destroyed in mortar attack 02Jan69 Tonle Cham, South Vietnam]
3847	C-130E	ex USAF	63-7781 [wfu AMARC Jan07]
3848	C-130E	ex USAF	63-7782 [stored 19May08 AMARC]
3849	TC-130G	(Airplane Sales International)	151888+ N93849 [+ USN] [to AMARC & b/u Jun06]
3850	EC-130E(RR)	(USAF)	63-7783 [wfu Apr01 Palmdale, CA; b/u Sep03]
3851	C-130E	USAF	63-7784
3852	C-130E	(USAF)	63-7785 [w/o 17Jun66 in sea SE of Tuy Hoa, South Vietnam; serial re-used on c/n 3991]
3853	C-130E	USAF	63-7786
3854	C-130E	(USAF)	63-7787 [w/o 15Apr78 in Nelson Lake, Fort Irwin, CA]
3855	C-130E	ex USAF	63-7788 [wfu AMARC Feb03]
3856	C-130E	(USAF)	63-7789 [shot down 23May69 into the sea off Alderney, Channel Islands, UK after illegal flight by crew chief]
3857	C-130E	ex USAF	63-7790 [wfu AMARC Nov06]
3858	TC-130G	(US Navy)	151889 [wfu; used for spares 1992 Cherry Point MCAS, NC; b/u Mar94]
3859	C-130E	USAF	63-7791
3860	C-130E	USAF	63-7792 [stored AMARC 26Aug10]
3861	GC-130E	ex USAF	63-7795 [wfu May94; GIA Little Rock AFB, AR; to Boeing Long Beach, CA for tests; fuselage stored by Oct05]
3862	C-130E	ex USAF	63-7796 [stored Aug11 AMARC]
3863	C-130E	(USAF)	63-7797 [w/o 25Mar65 near Alencon, France]
3864	C-130E	(USAF)	63-7798 [w/o 17May72 hit by rocket on take-off from Kontum, South Vietnam]
3865	C-130E	USAF	63-7799
3866	C-130E	USAF	63-7800 [stored AMARC 30Mar10]
3867	GC-130E	(USAF)	63-7801 [DBR 22Jun67 Pope AFB, NC; GIA Little Rock, AR; b/u 99]
3868	C-130E	(USAF)	63-7802 [w/o 30Sep74 Kadena AB, Japan]
3869	C-130E	(USAF)	63-7803 [wfu AMARC Sep94; nose to Tunisia Oct99 to repair c/n 5020]
3870	C-130E	ex USAF	63-7804 [wfu AMARC Aug07]
3871	EC-130G	(US Navy)	151890 [DBR 15Jan72 by in-flight fire in left wing fuel tank, landed at Patuxent River, MD]
3872	C-130E	(USAF)	63-7793 [wfu AMARC Feb96; sold for scrap Aug04]
3873	C-130E	(USAF)	63-7794 [wfu AMARC Dec97; b/u; nose to Minneapolis IAP, MN]
3874	C-130E	ex USAF	63-7805 [wfu AMARC Feb03]
3875	C-130E	ex USAF	63-7806 [wfu AMARC Feb96; fuselage to GIA by Mar00 Fort Monmouth, NJ]
3876	C-130E	ex USAF	63-7807 [wfu AMARC Feb96]
3877	C-130E	ex USAF	63-7808 [wfu AMARC Jun03]
3878	TC-130G	National Museum of Naval Avn	151891+ [+ USN] [wfu Nov02 Pensacola, FL; preserved in Blue Angels colours]
3879	C-130E	ex USAF	63-7809 [wfu at AMARC Jly07]
3880	C-130E	Israel Defence Force/Air Force	63-7810+ 310//4X-FBG^ [+ USAF; ^ dual marks]
3881	C-130E	USAF	63-7811 [stored AMARC 27Sep10]
3882	C-130E	ex USAF	63-7812 [wfu AMARC Aug10]
3883	GC-130E	ex USAF	63-7813 [wfu Apr00; GIA Sheppard AFB, TX]
3884	C-130E	ex USAF	63-7818 [stored 12May08 AMARC]
3885	C-130E	ex USAF	63-7819 [by Jly12 preserved Little Rock AFB, AR]
3886	C-130E	ex USAF	63-7820 [wfu Jan95; GIA Little Rock AFB, AR]
3887	C-130E	ex USAF	63-7821 [wfu AMARC Dec06]
3888	C-130E	USAF	63-7814
3889	EC-130E	USAF	63-7815
3890	C-130E	ex USAF	63-7822 [wfu AMARC Feb03]
3891	C-130E	ex USAF	63-7823 [reported at AMARC 09Mar09; to GIA Hurlburt Field, FL]
3892	C-130E	USAF	63-7824 [stored AMARC 10Sep10]
3893	C-130E	USAF	63-7825
3894	EC-130E	USAF	63-7816
3895	C-130E	USAF	63-7817
3896	EC-130E(RR)	(USAF)	63-7828 [wfu Feb03 Palmdale, CA; b/u Jan05]
3897	C-130E	ex USAF	63-7829 [stored Jly11 AMARC]
3898	C-130E	ex USAF	63-7830 [wfu AMARC Sep07]
3899	C-130E	ex USAF	63-7831 [stored Sep08 AMARC]
3900	C-130E	USAF	63-7832 [stored AMARC 04Oct10]
3901	C-130E	ex USAF	63-7833 [stored Sep11 AMARC]
3902	C-130E	ex USAF	63-7834 [for AMARC 2011]
3903	C-130E	Iraqi Air Force	63-7826+ YI-303 [+ USAF]
3904	C-130E	(USAF)	63-7827 [DBR 15Nov67 in mortar attack on Dak To, South Vietnam]

LOCKHEED C-130/L-100 HERCULES

C/n	Model	Last known Owner/Operator	Identities/fates/comments (where appropriate)
3905	C-130E	ex USAF	63-7835 [wfu AMARC Nov06]
3906	C-130E	(USAF)	63-7836 [wfu AMARC Oct94; sold for scrap Dec04]
3907	C-130E	ex USAF	63-7837 [stored 12May08 AMARC]
3908	C-130E	ex USAF	63-7838 [wfu Dec03 GIA Sheppard AFB, TX]
3909	C-130E	ex USAF	63-7839 [wfu AMARC Nov06]
3910	C-130E	USAF	63-7840 [stored AMARC 05Oct10]
3911	C-130E	ex USAF	63-7841 [wfu AMARC Dec06]
3912	C-130E	ex USAF	63-7842 [wfu AMARC Mar05]
3913	C-130E	Israel Defence Force/Air Force	63-7843+ 312//4X-FBH^ 305//4X-FBJ^ [+ USAF; ^ Israel dual marks]
3914	C-130E	Israel Defence Force/Air Force	63-7844+ 014//4X-FBI^ 314//4X-FBI^ 302 314 [+ USAF; ^ Israel dual marks]
3915	C-130E	ex USAF	63-7845 [stored Aug11 AMARC]
3916	C-130E	ex USAF	63-7846 [wfu AMARC Aug07]
3917	C-130E	ex USAF	63-7847 [wfu AMARC 08Jly08]
3918	C-130E	ex USAF	63-7848 [stored Aug11 AMARC]
3919	C-130E	ex USAF	63-7849 [wfu by Oct05; GIA Sheppard AFB, TX]
3920	C-130E	ex USAF	63-7850 [wfu AMARC Sep07]
3921	C-130E	(USAF)	63-7851 [b/u Jly10 Hill AFB, UT]
3922	C-130E	(USAF)	63-7852 [wfs & b/u Elgin AFB, FL; wings used on others USAF C-130s; tail preserved Little Rock AFB, AR]
3923	C-130E	USAF	63-7853 [seriously damaged 17Jly06 Al Asad Air Base, Iraq; reported returned to service]
3924	C-130E	ex USAF	63-7854 [stored AMARC by Dec00]
3925	C-130E	Mexican Air Force	63-7855+ 318//4X-FBK^ 3612 [+ USAF; ^ Israel dual marks; see c/n 3940, tie up unconfirmed]
3926	C-130E	USAF	63-7856
3927	C-130E	ex USAF	63-7857 [wfu AMARC Dec06]
3928	C-130E	ex USAF	63-7858 [wfu AMARC Mar07]
3929	C-130E	ex USAF	63-7859 [stored Aug11 AMARC]
3930	C-130E	ex USAF	63-7860 [wfu AMARC Mar07]
3931	C-130E	ex USAF	63-7861 [wfu Jan05 Cheyenne, WY]
3932	C-130E	Israel Defence Force/Air Force	63-7862+ 313//4X-FBL^ [+ USAF; ^ Israel dual marks]
3933	C-130E	Lockheed	63-7863+ [+ USAF] [wfu; centre & aft fuselage to C-130J structural testing Marietta, GA Aug95, foward fuselage to Tullahoma, TN]
3934	C-130E	ex USAF	63-7864 [wfu AMARC Sep07]
3935	C-130E	ex USAF	63-7865 [stored 09Jun08 AMARC]
3936	C-130E	ex USAF	63-7866 [wfu AMARC Aug07]
3937	C-130E	ex USAF	63-7867 [for AMARC 2011]
3938	C-130E	Museum of Aviation	63-7868 [preserved 06Sep11 Warner-Robins AFB, GA]
3939	EC-130H	(USAF)	63-7869 [wfu Sep02 Palmdale, CA; b/u Sep03]
3940	C-130E	Mexican Air Force	63-7870+ 316//4X-FBM^ 3613 [+ USAF; ^ Israel dual marks; see c/n 3925, tie up unconfirmed]
3941	C-130E	ex USAF	63-7871 [stored 03Jun08 AMARC]
3942	C-130E	USAF	63-7872
3943	C-130E	Israel Defence Force/Air Force	63-7873+ 307//4X-FBN^ [+ USAF; ^ Israel dual marks]
3944	C-130E	ex USAF	63-7874 [wfu AMARC Sep07]
3945	C-130E	(USAF)	63-7875 [w/o 15May68 at Song Be, South Vietnam]
3946	L-100-20	ex Philippine Air Force	N1130E N50FW PI-97 RP-97 RP-C97 3946 [wfu by Apr04 Mactan-Cebu AFB, Philippines]
3947	C-130E	ex USAF	63-7876 [wfu AMARC 07]
3948	C-130E	ex USAF	63-7877 [by Jun12 preserved Greater Peoria Airport, IL]
3949	C-130E	(USAF)	63-7878 [w/o 06Sep66 in mountains in Taiwan]
3950	C-130E	ex USAF	63-7879 [wfu AMARC 27Jun08]
3951	C-130E	ex USAF	63-7880 [wfu AMARC Dec06]
3952	C-130E	(USAF)	63-7881 [w/o 07Oct92 at Berkeley Springs, WV]
3953	C-130E	ex USAF	63-7882 [wfu AMARC Aug07]
3954	C-130E	USAF	63-7883 [stored AMARC 04Oct10]
3955	C-130E	USAF	63-7884
3956	C-130E	ex USAF	63-7885 [stored 13Jun08 AMARC]
3957	C-130E	(USAF)	63-7886 [w/o 12Oct66 into high ground Aspermont, TX]
3958	C-130E	ex USAF	63-7887 [wfu AMARC Jan07]
3959	C-130E	ex USAF	63-7888 [wfu AMARC Dec06]
3960	C-130E	ex USAF	63-7889 [wfu AMARC 17Jun08]

LOCKHEED C-130/L-100 HERCULES

C/n	Model	Last known Owner/Operator	Identities/fates/comments (where appropriate)
3961	C-130E	ex USAF	63-7890 [wfu AMARC Sep08]
3962	C-130E	(USAF)	63-7891 [wfu AMARC Mar95; sold for scrap Jly04]
3963	C-130E	ex USAF	63-7892 [wfu AMARC Jun07]
3964	C-130E	ex USAF	63-7893 [wfu AMARC Nov06]
3965	C-130E	ex USAF	63-7894 [wfu AMARC Sep08]
3966	C-130E	ex USAF	63-7895 [wfu AMARC Jun10]
3967	C-130E	ex USAF	63-7896 [for AMARC 2011]
3968	C-130E	USAF	63-7897
3969	C-130E	ex USAF	63-7898 [wfu AMARC Sep07]
3970	C-130E	ex USAF	63-7899 [wfu AMARC Sep07]
3971	C-130E	ex USAF	63-9810 [by Nov11 preserved Moody AFB, GA]
3972	C-130E	(USAF)	63-9811 [wfu AMARC Dec94; sold for scrap Jul04]
3973	C-130E	USAF	63-9812
3974	C-130E	USAF	63-9813 [stored AMARC 01Jly10]
3975	C-130E	ex USAF	63-9814 [wfu AMARC Dec06]
3976	C-130E	USAF	63-9815
3977	EC-130E	ex USAF	63-9816 [wfu AMARC Jan07]
3978	EC-130E(RR)	ex USAF	63-9817 [wfu AMARC Jly04]
3979	C-130E	ex USAF	64-0495 [wfu AMARC Apr05]
3980	C-130E	ex USAF	64-0496 [wfu 2005 Robins AFB, GA; GIA; by 16Oct10 on display]
3981	C-130E	(USAF)	64-0497 [wfu AMARC Sep93; to scrap 2004; l/n 09Mar09 Willmott Road scrapyard]
3982	C-130E	ex USAF	64-0498 [wfu AMARC Dec06]
3983	C-130E	ex USAF	64-0499 [wfu AMARC Sep05]
3984	GC-130E	(USAF)	64-0500 [wfu by 1999 Sheppard AFB, TX, GIA; b/u Mar01]
3985	C-130E	(USAF)	64-0501 [w/o 28Apr92 in Blewitt Falls Lake, NC]
3986	C-130E	ex USAF	64-0502 [wfu 23Jun08 AMARC]
3987	C-130E	(USAF)	64-0503 [wfu AMARC Nov93; sold for scrap 2000]
3988	C-130E	ex USAF	64-0504 [wfu AMARC Jly07]
3989	C-130E	(USAF)	64-0505 [DBF 09Dec72 Andersen AFB, Guam]
3990	MC-130E-Y	USAF	64-0506 62-1843 [SOC 31Dec64 to Air America/CIA; used c/n from c/n 3806 on return in 1972]
3991	MC-130E-Y	USAF	64-0507 63-7785 [SOC 24Dec65 to Air America/CiA; used c/n from c/n 3852 on return in 1972; stored Jly07 March AFB, CA]
3992	C-130E-1	(USAF)	64-0508 [shot down 25Apr72 Binh Long, South Vietnam]
3993	C-130E	Israel Defence Force/Air Force	64-0509+ 203//4X-FBO^ [+ USAF; ^ Israel dual marks; stored Sep89 in Israel]
3994	C-130E	USAF	64-0510
3995	C-130E	(USAF)	64-0511 [w/o 31May66 near Thanh Hoa bridge, Song Ma river, South Vietnam]
3996	C-130E	ex USAF	64-0512 [wfu AMARC 24Jun08]
3997	C-130E	(USAF)	64-0513 [wfu AMARC May95; sold for scrap Jly04]
3998	C-130E	ex USAF	64-0514 [wfu AMARC Feb02]
3999	C-130E	USAF	64-0515
4000	C-130E	Israel Defence Force/Air Force	64-0516+ 208//4X-FBP^ [+ USAF; ^ Israel dual marks; stored Tel Aviv-Lod, Israel]
4001	C-130E	ex USAF	64-0517 [wfu AMARC May07]
4002	C-130E	ex USAF	64-0518 [wfu AMARC Apr07]
4003	C-130E	USAF	64-0519
4004	C-130E	USAF	64-0520
4005	C-130E	USAF	64-0521
4006	C-130E	(USAF)	64-0522 [shot down 29Feb68 on take-off from Song Ba, South Vietnam]
4007	MC-130E-C	ex USAF	64-0523 [preserved 25Jun12 Cannon AFB, NM]
4008	C-130E	USAF	64-0524 [GIA Oct94 Little Rock AFB, AR]
4009	C-130E	82nd Airborne Museum	64-0525+ [+ USAF] [wfu Jan05; preserved Fort Bragg, NC]
4010	C-130E	(USAF)	64-0526 [wfu Robins ALC, GA; b/u 2001]
4011	C-130E	Turkish Air Force	63-13186+ ETI-186^ 13186 [+ USAF; ^ Turkey]
4012	C-130E	Turkish Air Force	63-13187+ ETI-187^ 13187 [+ USAF; ^ Turkey]
4013	C-130E	(USAF)	64-0527 [wfu early 2009 Petersburg, VA; 18Apr10 fuselage only to Fort Lee, VA]
4014	C-130E	Israel Defence Force/Air Force	64-0528+ 311//4X-FBQ^ 311//4X-FBD^ [+ USAF; ^ Israel dual marks]
4015	C-130E	Turkish Air Force	63-13188+ ETI-188^ 13188 [+ USAF; ^ Turkey]
4016	C-130E	Turkish Air Force	63-13189+ ETI-189^ 13189 [+ USAF; ^ Turkey]
4017	C-130E	ex USAF	64-0529 [wfu AMARC Dec06]
4018	C-130E	(USAF)	64-0530 [wfu AMARC May94; sold for scrap Dec04]
4019	C-130E	ex USAF	64-0531 [wfu AMARC Jan07]
4020	CC-130E	Canadian Armed Forces	64-17624+ 10305^ 130305 [+ USAF; ^ Canada]

LOCKHEED C-130/L-100 HERCULES

C/n	Model	Last known Owner/Operator	Identities/fates/comments (where appropriate)
4021	C-130E	(USAF)	64-0532 [w/o 08Sep78 in mountains Conway, AR]
4022	C-130E	ex USAF	64-0533 [wfu & preserved May04 Elmendorf AFB, AK]
4023	C-130E	(USAF)	64-0534 [DBR Dec93 Elmendorf AFB, AK; b/u Oct99]
4024	GC-130E	ex USAF	64-0535 [wfu Sheppard AFB, TX; GIA]
4025	C-130E	(USAF)	64-0536 [w/o 02Oct72 in Cha Tien Shan mountains after take-off from Taipei, Taiwan]
4026	CC-130E	ex Canadian Armed Forces	64-17625+ 10306^ 130306 [+ USAF; ^ Canada; wfu Jly11 Abbotsford, BC, Canada]
4027	C-130E	ex USAF	64-0537 [wfu AMARC Nov06]
4028	C-130E	ex USAF	64-0538 [wfu AMARC Feb07]
4029	C-130E	ex USAF	64-0539 [wfu & preserved Nov04 Minneapolis IAP, MN]
4030	C-130E	ex USAF	64-0540 [wfu AMARC Apr07]
4031	C-130E	USAF	64-0541
4032	GC-130E	ex USAF	64-0542 [wfu Sheppard AFB, TX; GIA]
4033	C-130E	(USAF)	64-0543 [w/o 12May82 after wing snapped in formation flight near Judsonia, AR]
4034	C-130E	USAF	64-0544
4035	C-130E	(USAF)	64-0545 [w/o 08Mar69 short of runway in Taiwan]
4036	HC-130P	USAF	64-14852
4037	HC-130P	USAF	64-14853
4038	MC-130P	USAF	64-14854
4039	C-130H	Royal Swedish Air Force	(64-0546)+ 84001^ SE-XBT 84001 [+ USAF; ^ Sweden]
4040	C-130E-1	(USAF)	64-0547 [w/o 28Dec67 near Lai Chau, North Vietnam]
4041	CC-130E	Canadian Armed Forces	64-17626+ 10307^ 130307 [+ USAF; ^ Canada] [wfu Sep11 Abbotsford, BC, Canada]
4042	CC-130E	Canadian Armed Forces	64-17627+ 10308^ 130308 [+ USAF; ^ Canada]
4043	C-130E	(USAF)	64-0548 [w/o short of runway 15Oct67 Khe Sanh, South Vietnam]
4044	C-130E	(USAF)	64-0549 [w/o 12Mar85 at Rapido Drop Zone, Fort Hood, TX]
4045	C-130E	ex USAF	64-0550 [wfu AMARC Feb03]
4046	MC-130E-C	USAF	64-0551
4047	C-130E	Belgian Air Force	64-0552+ N130EV CH-14^ CH-13 [+ USAF; ^ Belgium]
4048	C-130E	(USAF)	64-0553+ [+ USAF] [b/u 2001; nose preserved South Utah Air Museum, Washington, UT]
4049	WC-130E	USAF	64-0554 [wfu AMARC 28Sep93]
4050	CC-130E	(Royal Canadian Air Force)	64-17628+ 10309^ 130309 [+ USAF; ^ Canada] [w/o 28Apr67 Trenton, ON, Canada; SOC 11Jly67]
4051	CC-130E	Canadian Armed Forces	64-17629+ 10310^ 130310 [+ USAF; ^ Canada]
4052	C-130H	Royal New Zealand Air Force	64-15094+ NZ7001 [USAF]
4053	C-130H	Royal New Zealand Air Force	64-15095+ NZ7002 [USAF]
4054	C-130H	Royal New Zealand Air Force	64-15096+ NZ7003 [USAF]
4055	HC-130P	USAF	64-14855
4056	MC-130E-C	ex USAF	64-0555 [stored Jly07 March AFB, CA]
4057	C-130E	ex USAF	64-0556 [GIA Jly93 Hurlburt Field, FL]
4058	GC-130E	(USAF)	64-0557 [wfu 2004 Sheppard AFB, TX GIA ; Jly08 sunk Mammoth Lake Scuba Park, Lake Jackson, TX]
4059	C-130E-1	(USAF)	64-0558 [w/o 05Dec72 near Myrtle Beach, SC; mid-air collision with a F-102A]
4060	CC-130E	Canadian Armed Forces	64-17630+ 10311^ 130311 [+ USAF; ^ Canada]
4061	CC-130E	(Canadian Armed Forces)	64-17631+ 10312^ 130312 [+ USAF; ^ Canada] [w/o 15Oct80 near Chibougamau, QC, Canada]
4062	MC-130E-C	USAF	64-0559
4063	C-130E	(USAF)	64-0560 [wfu AMARC Dec94; sold for scrap Dec04]
4064	GC-130E	USAF	64-17680 [wfu Sheppard AFB, TX; GIA]
4065	MC-130E-C	USAF	64-0561
4066	CC-130E	RCAF Memorial Museum	64-17632+ 10313^ 130313^ [+ USAF; ^ Canada] [wfu & preserved Feb11 CFB Trenton, ON, Canada until replaced by c/n 4067]
4067	CC-130E	RCAF Memorial Museum	64-17633+ 10314^ 130314^ [+ USAF; ^ Canada] [wfu Dec07 CFB Trenton, ON, Canada; preserved Jun09; to be b/u]
4068	MC-130E-C	USAF	64-0562
4069	C-130E	ex USAF	64-17681 [stored 29May08 AMARC]
4070	CC-130E	ex Canadian Armed Forces	64-17634+ 10315^ 130315 [+ USAF; ^ Canada; wfu Jly11 Abbotsford, BC, Canada]
4071	C-130E-1	(USAF)	64-0563 [DBR 25Nov67 in mortar attack on Nha Trang, South Vietnam]
4072	HC-130P	(USAF)	64-14856 [w/o 22Nov96 in sea Humboldt Bay, 60 miles W of Cape Mendocino, CA]
4073	HC-130H	(USAF)	64-14857 [w/o 26Jly00 Al-Mafraq AFB, Jordan]

LOCKHEED C-130/L-100 HERCULES

C/n	Model	Last known Owner/Operator	Identities/fates/comments (where appropriate)
4074	MC-130E-Y	(USAF)	64-0564 [w/o 26Feb81 in sea near Tabones Island, Philippines]
4075	CC-130E	Canadian Armed Forces	64-17635+ 10316^ 10316 [+ USAF; ^ Canada]
4076	C-130E	Turkish Air Force	N9258R 451+ 65-451 [+ Saudi Arabia]
4077	MC-130E-Y	USAF	64-0565
4078	C-130E	(Royal Saudi Air Force]	452 [stored by 2007; b/u]
4079	GC-130E	ex USAF	64-0569 [GIA Mar98 Hill AFB, UT]
4080	MC-130E-C	USAF	64-0566 [wfu Dec11 Dobbins AFB, GA; for testing to destruction]
4081	MC-130P	USAF	64-14858
4082	C-130H	USAF	64-14859
4083	MC-130E-C	ex USAF	64-0567 [wfu 07May11 Hurlburt Field, FL and displayed on base]
4084	HC-130P	USAF	64-14860
4085	C-130E	ex USAF	64-0570 [wfu AMARC Feb03]
4086	MC-130E-C	USAF	64-0568
4087	MC-130E-S	USAF	64-0571
4088	C-130H	USAF	64-14861
4089	EC-130H	USAF	64-14862
4090	MC-130E-C	ex USAF	64-0572 [stored Feb08 March JARB, CA]
4091	C-130E	(Brazilian Air Force)	2450 [w/o 21Dec69 Recife, Brazil]
4092	C-130H	Brazilian Air Force	2451
4093	C-130E	(Brazilian Air Force)	2452 [w/o 26Oct66 on approach in Brazil]
4094	HC-130P	USAF	64-14863
4095	CC-130E	Canadian Armed Forces	64-17638+ 10319^ 130319 [+ USAF; ^ Canada]
4096	CC-130E	ex Canadian Armed Forces	64-17639+ 10320^ 130320 [+ USAF; ^ Canada; wfu Jly11 Abbotsford, BC, Canada]
4097	HC-130P	USAF	64-14864
4098	HC-130P	USAF	64-14865
4099	WC-130H	USAF	64-14866
4100	C-130E	(Turkish Air Force)	64-17949+ ETI-949^ 17949 [+ USAF; ^ Turkey] [w/o 19Oct68 hit mountain on approach to Izmir, Turkey]
4101	L-100-30	(Transamerica Airlines)	N9260R 9J-RCV N920NA N24ST [DBR 29Dec84 on ground by UNITA attack at Cafunfo, Angola]
4102	EC-130E	USAF	65-0962
4103	C-130H	USAF	65-0963
4104	HC-130P	USAF	65-0964
4105	C-130E	USAF	64-18240
4106	WC-130H	(USAF)	65-0965 [vanished 13Oct74 whilst penetrating typhoon Bess, near Taiwan]
4107	C-130H	USAF	65-0966
4108	C-130H	USAF	65-0967
4109	L-100	(Zambian Air Cargoes)	N9261R 9J-RCY [DBR 11Apr68 Ndola, Zambia, ground collision with L-100-20 9J-RBX c/n 4137]
4110	C-130H	USAF	65-0968
4111	C-130H	Canadian Armed Forces	65-0969+ [+ USAF] [wfu Sep98 Robins ALC, GA; 2000 fuselage to GIA CFB Trenton, ON, Canada]
4112	HC-130P	USAF	65-0970
4113	C-130H	Brazilian Air Force	2453
4114	C-130H	Brazilian Air Force	2454
4115	C-130E	Iranian Air Force	65-10686+ 5-105^ 5-101^ 5-8501 [+ USAF; ^ Iran]
4116	MC-130P	USAF	65-0971
4117	C-130E	(Pakistan Air Force)	65-10687+ 5-106^ 5-102^ 10687 [+USAF; ^ Iran] [DBR Feb79 Lahore, Pakistan, after ground collision with C-130 AS-HFP c/n 3698; fuselage l/n Lahore Jun81]
4118	C-130E	(Iranian Air Force)	65-10688+ 5-107 [+ USAF] [destroyed by lightning strike on 18Apr67 in Iran]
4119	C-130E	Pakistan Air Force	65-10689+ 5-108^ 5-103^ 10689 [+ USAF; ^ Iran]
4120	C-130H	(USAF)	65-0972 [wfu & stored AMARC Dec97; sold for scrap Jly04]
4121	HC-130P	USAF	65-0973
4122	CC-130E	Canadian Armed Forces	64-17636+ 10317^ 130317 [+ USAF; ^ Canada]
4123	HC-130P	USAF	65-0974
4124	CC-130E	(Canadian Armed Forces)	65-17637+ 10318^ 130318 [+USAF; ^ Canada] [w/o 29Jan89 Fort Wainwright AAF, AK]
4125	MC-130P	USAF	65-0975
4126	HC-130P	USAF	65-0976
4127	C-130H	USAF	65-0977
4128	C-130E	(Royal Saudi Air Force]	453 [w/o 14Sep80 Medina, Saudi Arabia]

LOCKHEED C-130/L-100 HERCULES

C/n	Model	Last known Owner/Operator	Identities/fates/comments (where appropriate)
4129	L-100-20	(Tepper Aviation)	9J-RBW CF-PWN N109AK C-FPWN J6-SLO N920SJ [w/o 27Nov89 Kamina Air Base, Jamba, Angola]
4130	HC-130P	USAF	65-0978
4131	NC-130H	NASA	65-0979 N439NA
4132	WC-130H	ex USAF	65-0980
4133	HC-130P	USAF	65-0981
4134	L-100-30	(Transafrik/National Air Cargo)	N9263R N16ST N916SJ S9-BAT [w/o 04Jun10 Sharana AFB, Afghanistan]
4135	HC-130P	USAF	65-0982
4136	C-130E	(Royal Saudi Air Force)	454 [w/o 01Jan69 Paris-Le Bourget, France]
4137	L-100-20	(Zambian Air Cargoes)	9J-RBX [DBR 11Apr68 Ndola, Zambia, ground collision with L-100 9J-RCY c/n 4109]
4138	HC-130P	USAF	65-0983
4139	C-130H	USAF	65-0984
4140	C-130H	USAF	65-0985
4141	HC-130P	USAF	65-0986
4142	HC-130P	USAF	65-0987+ 1451^ 65-0987 [+ USAF; ^ USCG]
4143	HC-130P	USAF	65-0988
4144	L-100	Pakistan Air Force	AP-AUT 64144
4145	L-100	(Pakistan Air Force)	AP-AUU 64145 [broke up in turbulence 30Apr68 & crashed near Chaklala, Pakistan]
4146	L-100	(Aerovias Ecuatorianas)	N9267R [DBF 16May68 Macuma, Ecuador]
4147	L-100-30	(Wells Fargo Bank)	N9268R N19ST N919SJ [stored May97 Marana, AZ; b/u Oct98 for spares; fuselage noted Marana Mar03; canx 13Jun06 to Sao Tome]
4148	C-130E	Pakistan Air Force	66-4310+ 5-109^ 5-104^ 64310 [+ USAF; ^ Iran]
4149	C-130E	Iranian Air Force	66-4311+ 5-110^ 5-105^ 5-8502 [+ USAF; ^ Iran]
4150	EC-130H	USAF	65-0989
4151	HC-130H	(USAF)	65-0990 [ditched 04Feb69 while searching for survivors of a Japanese freighter, off Taiwan]
4152	MC-130P	USAF	65-0991
4153	C-130E	Pakistan Air Force	66-4312+ 5-111^ 5-106^ 64312# 4153~ [+ USAF; ^ Iran; # Pakistan; ~ also still carries 64132]
4154	C-130E	(Iranian Air Force)	66-4313+ 5-112 [+ USAF] [w/o 07Apr69 Shiraz, Iran]
4155	MC-130P	USAF	65-0992
4156	MC-130P	USAF	65-0993
4157	MC-130P	USAF	65-0994
4158	EC-130E	(US Coast Guard)	66-4299+ 1414 [+ USAF] [wfu AMARC Oct84; b/u by 2000]
4159	C-130E	Pakistan Air Force	65-12896+ A97-159^ N50848 4159 [+ USAF; ^ Australia]
4160	C-130E	Royal Australian AF Museum	65-12897+ A97-160^ [+ USAF; ^ Australia] [preserved RAAF Point Cook, VIC, Australia]
4161	HC-130P	(USAF)	66-0211 [w/o 02Apr86 after wing broke in turbulence near Magdalena, NH]
4162	MC-130P	USAF	66-0212
4163	MC-130P	(USAF)	66-0213 [w/o 13Feb02 within Afghanistan]
4164	HC-130P	(USAF)	66-0214 [DBR by bomb 29Jul68 Tuy Hoa, South Vietnam]
4165	MC-130P	USAF	66-0215
4166	MC-130P	USAF	66-0216
4167	C-130E	ex Royal Australian Air Force	65-12898+ A97-167 [+USAF] [by Nov00 to battle damage repair training RAAF Richmond, NSW, Australia]
4168	C-130E	ex Royal Australian Air Force	65-12899+ A97-168 [Nov00 to GIA RAAF Richmond, NSW, Australia; no fin or outer wings]
4169	C-130K C.3P	(Lockheed Martin)	65-13021+ XV176^ [+ USAF; ^ RAF] [stored Mar01 Sussex Co/ Georgetown, DE; b/u Feb03]
4170	L-100-20	(Northwest Territorial Airways)	N9258R CF-PWK [DBF 11Apr82 Paulatuk, NT, Canada]
4171	C-130E	Pakistan Air Force	65-12900+ A97-171^ N9022F 4171 [+ USAF; ^ Australia]
4172	C-130E	Australian Army	65-12901+ A97-172 [+ USAF] [Mar03 GIA Holsworthy Army Base, NSW, Australia]
4173	MC-130P	USAF	66-0217
4174	HC-130P	(USAF)	66-0218 [DBR by bomb 29Jly68 Tuy Hoa, South Vietnam]
4175	MC-130P	USAF	66-0219
4176	L-100-20	(TAAG-Angola Airlines)	N9259R N105AK D2-FAF [w/o 15May79 on ground at Sao Tome after overshooting runway]
4177	C-130E	Pakistan Air Force	65-12902+ A97-177^ N9022U 4177 [+ USAF; ^ Australia]
4178	C-130E	Pakistan Air Force	65-12903+ A97-178^ N90220 4178 [+ USAF; ^ Australia]
4179	MC-130P	USAF	66-0220

LOCKHEED C-130/L-100 HERCULES

C/n	Model	Last known Owner/Operator	Identities/fates/comments (where appropriate)
4180	C-130E	Pakistan Air Force	65-12904+ A97-180^ N9023U 4180 [+ USAF; ^ Australia]
4181	C-130E	(Lockheed Martin)	65-12905+ A97-181^ [+ USAF; ^ Australia] [stored Jly00 Sussex Co/Georgetown, DE; b/u for spares for Pakistan AF]
4182	C-130K C.3P	Royal Air Force	65-13022+ XV177 [+ USAF]
4183	HC-130P	USAF	66-0221
4184	HC-130P	USAF	66-0222
4185	MC-130P	USAF	66-0223
4186	HC-130P	ex USAF	66-0224 [stored Dec11 AMARC]
4187	MC-130P	USAF	66-0225
4188	C-130K C.1P	(Lockheed Martin)	65-13023+ XV178^ [+ USAF; ^ RAF] [stored Nov00 Sussex Co/ Georgetown, DE; b/u May03]
4189	C-130E	Pakistan Air Force	65-12906+ A97-189^ N51495 4189 [+ USAF; ^ Australia]
4190	C-130E	ex Royal Australian Air Force	65-12907+ A97-190 [+ USAF] [Nov00 GIA RAAF Richmond, NSW, Australia; no fin]
4191	CC-130E	(Canadian Armed Forces)	65-12766+ 10321^ 130321 [+ USAF; ^ Canada] [w/o 22Jly93 Wainwright, AB, Canada]
4192	CC-130E	(Canadian Armed Forces)	65-12767+ 10322^ 130322 [+ USAF; ^ Canada] [w/o 30Oct91 Point Alert, Ellesmere Island, NT, Canada]
4193	CC-130E	Canadian Armed Forces	65-12768+ 10323^ 130323 [+ USAF; ^ Canada]
4194	CC-130E	ex Canadian Armed Forces	65-12769+ 10324^ 130324 [+ USAF; ^ Canada] [wfu Nov10 CFB Trenton, ON, Canada; l/n Jly11 Abbotsford, BC, Canada]
4195	C-130K C.1P	(Royal Air Force)	65-13024+ XV179 [+ USAF] [w/o 30Jan05 Al Taji, Iraq; shot down]
4196	C-130K C.1	(Royal Air Force)	65-13025+ XV180 [+ USAF] [w/o 24Mar69 RAF Fairford, UK]
4197	L-100	(Trans Mediterranean Airways)	N9269R CF-PWO [w/o 16Jly69 Cayaya, Peru]
4198	C-130K C.1P	Austrian Air Force	65-13026+ XV181^ 8T-CA [+USAF: ^ RAF]
4199	C-130K C.1P	(Lockheed Martin)	65-13027+ XV182^ [+ USAF; ^ RAF] [Sep01 stored Sussex Co/ Georgetown, DE; b/u Feb03]
4200	C-130K C.3P	(Lockheed Martin)	65-13028+ XV183^ [+ USAF; ^ RAF] [17Jly02 stored Sussex Co/ Georgetown, DE; for Polish AF but ntu due to corrosion]
4201	C-130K C.3P	(Royal Air Force)	65-13029+ XV184 [+ USAF] [stored by 28Jly08 Cambridge, UK; by 27Jan09 wings removed; b/u May09]
4202	C-130H	(Brazilian Air Force)	2455 [w/o 27Sep01 near Rio de Janeiro, Brazil]
4203	C-130K C.1P	(Lockheed Martin)	65-13030+ XV185^ N73232 [+ USAF; ^ RAF] [Jan03 stored Sussex Co/ Georgetown, DE; for Polish AF but ntu due to corrosion; sold for scrap Sep05]
4204	C-130K C.1P	(Lockheed Martin)	65-13031+ XV186^ [+ USAF; ^ RAF] [Jun01 stored Sussex Co/ Georgetown, DE; b/u Feb03]
4205	C-130K C.1P	(Lockheed Martin)	65-13032+ XV187^ [+ USAF; ^ RAF] [Jan01 stored Sussex Co/Georgetown, DE; b/u May05]
4206	C-130K C.3P	Royal Air Force	65-13033+ XV188 [+ USAF]
4207	C-130K C.3P	(Lockheed Martin)	65-13034+ XV189^ [+ USAF; ^ RAF] [stored Sussex Co/Georgetown, DE; b/u Mar05]
4208	L-100-30	Safair Freighters	N9227R N18ST N918SJ S9-CAY ZS-ORA
4209	L-100	(Alaska International Air)	9J-REZ N921NA N100AK [DBR 30Aug74 after cargo exploded on ground Galbraith Lake airport, AK; canx 22Jan75]
4210	C-130K C.3P	(Lockheed Martin)	65-13035+ XV190^ N73230 [+ USAF; ^ RAF] [27Jun02 stored Greenville, SC; for Polish AF but ntu due to corrosion; sold for scrap Sep05]
4211	C-130K C.1P	Mexican Air Force	65-13036+ XV191^ 3614 [+ USAF; ^ RAF]
4212	C-130K C.1K	(Lockheed Martin)	65-13037+ XV192^ N73238 [+ USAF; ^ RAF] [May02 stored Greenville, SC; for Polish AF but ntu due to corrosion; sold for scrap Sep05]
4213	C-130K C.3P	(Royal Air Force)	65-13038+ XV193 [+ USAF] [w/o 27May93 into mountain near Blair Athol, Scotland, UK]
4214	C-130K C.1	(Royal Air Force)	65-13039+ XV194 [+ USAF] [w/o 12Sep72 Tromso, Norway]
4215	C-130E	Turkish Air Force	455+ 67-455 [+ Saudi Arabia]
4216	C-130K C.1P	(Lockheed Martin)	65-13040+ XV195^ [+ USAF; ^ RAF] [Jan01 stored Sussex Co/Georgetown, DE; b/u May05]
4217	C-130K C.1P	Royal Air Force	65-13041+ XV196 [+ USAF]
4218	C-130K C.3P	ex Royal Air Force	65-13042+ XV197 [+ USAF] [stored May09 Boscombe Down, UK; Feb11 hulk to Hixon, UK for disposal]
4219	C-130K C.1	(Royal Air Force)	65-13043+ XV198 [+ USAF] [w/o 10Sep73 RAF Colerne, UK]
4220	C-130K C.3P	[Royal Air Force)	65-13044+ XV199 [+ USAF] [wfu Nov05 Cambridge, UK; b/u May09)
4221	L-100-20	(Saturn Airways)	N9248R [w/o 11Oct70 on approach to McGuire AFB, NJ]
4222	L-100-30	(Angola Air Charter)	N9254R N13ST N103AK D2-FAG D2-THB [hit by missile 05Jan90 & crash-landed at Menonque, Angola]

LOCKHEED C-130/L-100 HERCULES

C/n	Model	Last known Owner/Operator	Identities/fates/comments (where appropriate)
4223	C-130K C.1P	Royal Air Force	66-8850+ XV200 [+ USAF]
4224	C-130K C.1K	(Royal Air Force)	66-8851+ XV201 [+ USAF] [wfu Cambridge, UK by Jun95; b/u 2006; cockpit to GIA, centre fuselage to Porton Down, UK; b/u 14May09]
4225	L-100-30	(Saturn Airways)	N759AL N14ST [DBR 23May74, wing broke in turbulence Springfield, IL; canx 11Apr95]
4226	C-130K C.3P	ex Royal Air Force	66-8852+ XV202 [+ USAF] [ferried 12Aug11 Cosford, UK for preservation by RAF Museum]
4227	C-130K C.1K	Sri Lankan Air Force	66-8853+ XV203^ CR880# SCH-3402# SCH-880~ [+ USAF; ^ RAF; # Sri Lanka; ~ assumption only]
4228	C-130K C.1K	(Royal Air Force)	66-8854+ XV204 [+ USAF] [wfu Jun95 Cambridge, UK; b/u Aug98]
4229	L-100	(Airlift International)	N760AL [w/o 24Dec68 Prudhoe Bay, AK]
4230	C-130K C.1P	(Royal Air Force)	66-8855+ XV205 [+ USAF] [w/o 24Aug07 near Kabul or Helmand Province, Afghanistan]
4231	C-130K C.1P	(Royal Air Force)	66-8856+ XV206 [+ USAF] [DBF 24May06 Lashkar Gar, Afghanistan]
4232	C-130K C.3P	(Lockheed Martin)	66-8857+ XV207^ [+ USAF; ^ RAF] [Nov00 stored Sussex Co/Georgetown, DE; b/u May05]
4233	C-130K W.2	ex Marshalls of Cambridge	66-8858+ XV208^ [+ USAF; ^ RAF/MOD] [2008 converted to A400 powerplant testbed; wfu & stored Mar10 Cambridge, UK, for possible spares use]
4234	L-100	(Alaska International Air)	N7999S N102AK [w/o 27Jan74 on approach to Old Man's Camp, AK; canx 05May09]
4235	C-130K C.3P	Royal Air Force	66-8859+ XV209 [+ USAF]
4236	C-130K C.1P	(Lockheed Martin)	66-8860+ XV210^ [+ USAF; ^ RAF] [Dec00 stored Sussex Co/Georgetown, DE; b/u May03]
4237	C-130K C.1P	(Lockheed Martin)	66-8861+ XV211^ [+ USAF; ^ RAF] [Jun01stored Sussex Co/Georgetown, DE; b/u May05]
4238	C-130K C.3P	ex Royal Air Force	66-8862+ XV212 [+ USAF] [stored 21Jan09 Cambridge, UK]
4239	TC-130Q	(Airplane Sales International)	156170+ N15674 [+ USN] [stored & wfu AMARC; b/u by 2003]
4240	C-130K C.1	Sri Lankan Air Force	66-8863+ XV213^ CR881# SCH-3401# SCH-881~ [+ USAF; ^ RAF; # Sri Lanka; ~ assumption only]
4241	C-130K C.3P	Royal Air Force	66-8864+ XV214 [+ USAF]
4242	C-130K C.1P	Mexican Air Force	66-8865+ XV215^ 3615 [+ USAF; ^ RAF]
4243	C-130K C.1	(Royal Air Force)	66-8866+ XV216 [+ USAF] [w/o 09Nov71 in Ligurian Sea off Pisa, Italy]
4244	C-130K C.3P	(Royal Air Force)	66-8867+ XV217 [+ USAF] [stored circa 2007 RAF Lyneham, UK; b/u Nov10; hulk 23Jan11 to Hixon, UK for disposal]
4245	C-130K C.1P	(Lockheed Martin)	66-8868+ XV218^ [+ USAF; ^ RAF] [Dec00 stored Sussex Co/Georgetown, DE; b/u May05]
4246	C-130K C.3P	(Lockheed Martin)	66-8869+ XV219^ [+ USAF; ^ RAF] [Nov00 stored Sussex Co/Georgetown, DE; b/u May04]
4247	C-130K C.3P	(Royal Air Force)	66-8870+ XV220 [+ USAF] [stored circa 2007 RAF Lyneham, UK; b/u Nov10; hulk 16Jan11 to Hixon, UK for disposal]
4248	L-100-30	Safair Freighters	N9262R N101AK N37ST N907SJ S9-CAX ZS-ORB PK-YRW ZS-ORB
4249	EC-130Q	Airplane Sales International	156171+ N34249 [canx 03Dec03; to Tulsa, OK as C-130J GIA]
4250	L-100-20	(Southern Air Transport)	N9266R N22ST N521SJ [w/o 02Sep91, blown up by mine on take-off from Wau, 625m S of Khartoum, Sudan; canx 27Nov91]
4251	C-130K C.3P	ex Royal Air Force	66-8871+ XV221 [+ USAF] [wfu & stored Apr11 RAF Lyneham, UK; ferried 29Jly11 Bruntingthorpe, UK to be b/u for parts]
4252	C-130K C.3P	Mexican Air Force	66-8872+ XV222^ 3616 [+ USAF; ^ RAF]
4253	C-130K C.3P	Mexican Air Force	66-8873+ XV223^ 3617 [+ USAF; ^ RAF]
4254	C-130K C.3P	(Royal Air Force)	66-13533+ XV290 [wfu 2010 RAF Lyneham, UK; b/u circa Nov10]
4255	HC-130H	(USAF)	67-7183+ 1452^ 67-7183+ PNP-023?# 67-7183 [+ USAF; ^ USCG; # Peru; might have been PNP-025; DBR 24Apr92 in Peru; wfu AMARC Jan93; storage code CF119; sold for scrap Jly04]
4256	C-130K C.1P	Austrian Air Force	66-13534+ XV291^ 8T-CB [+ USAF; ^ RAF]
4257	C-130K C.1P	Austrian Air Force	66-13535+ XV292^ 996# XV292^ 8T-CC [+ USAF; ^ RAF; # Chile – flown as such]
4258	C-130K C.1P	(Lockheed Martin)	66-13536+ XV293^ [+ USAF; ^ RAF] [Mar01 stored Greenville, SC; for Polish AF but ntu due to corrosion; sold for scrap Sep05]
4259	C-130K C.3P	(Royal Air Force)	66-13537+ XV294 [+ USAF] [stored by Dec08 Cambridge, UK; b/u Feb12]
4260	C-130H	(USAF)	67-7184+ 1453^ 67-7184+ PNP-025?# 67-7184 [+ USAF; ^ USCG; # Peru might have been PNP-023; GIA Robins AFB, GA; fuselage only 2001]
4261	C-130K C.1P	Royal Air Force	66-13538+ XV295 [+ USAF]
4262	C-130K C.1K	(Royal Air Force)	66-13539+ XV296 [+ USAF] [wfu by Jun95 Cambridge, UK; b/u Jul03]

LOCKHEED C-130/L-100 HERCULES

C/n	Model	Last known Owner/Operator	Identities/fates/comments (where appropriate)
4263	C-130K C.1P	(Lockheed Martin)	66-13540+ XV297^ [+ USAF; ^ RAF] [04Sep01 stored Greenville, SC; for Polish AF but ntu due to corrosion; sold for scrap Sep05]
4264	C-130K C.1P	(Royal Air Force)	66-13541+ XV298 [+ USAF] [DBF 11Jun99 Kukes airstrip, northern Albania]
4265	HC-130H	USAF	67-7185+ 1454^ 67-7185 [+ USAF; ^ USCG] [GIA Jan93 Kirtland AFB, NM]
4266	C-130K C.3P	(Royal Air Force)	66-13542+ XV299 [+ USAF] [stored by Dec08 Cambridge, UK; b/u Dec11]
4267	C-130K C.1P	(Lockheed Martin)	66-13543+ XV300^ [+ USAF; ^ RAF] [Jan01 stored Sussex Co/Georgetown, DE; b/u 2004]
4268	C-130K C.3P	ex Royal Air Force	66-13544+ XV301 [+ USAF] [wfu & stored Apr11 RAF Lyneham, UK; ferried 29Jly11 Bruntingthorpe, UK to be b/u for parts]
4269	EC-130Q	(Airplane Sales International)	156172+ N42699 [+ USN] [wfu AMARC; for scrap]
4270	C-130K C.3P	Marshalls of Cambridge	66-13545+ XV302 [+ USAF; ^ RAF] [wfu Nov02, for fatigue testing, Cambridge Airport, UK]
4271	C-130K C.3P	Royal Air Force	66-13546+ XV303 [+ USAF]
4272	C-130K C.3P	ex Royal Air Force	66-13547+ XV304 [+ USAF] [w/o 06May10 Brize Norton, UK & stored there]
4273	C-130K C.3P	(Royal Air Force)	66-13548+ XV305 [+ USAF] [stored RAF Lyneham, UK; b/u Nov10; hulk 09Jan11 to Hixon, UK for disposal]
4274	C-130K C.1P	(Lockheed Martin)	66-13549+ XV306^ [+ USAF; ^ RAF] [Mar01 stored Sussex Co/ Georgetown, DE; b/u 2004]
4275	C-130K C.3P	Royal Air Force	66-13550+ XV307 [+ USAF]
4276	C-130E	Iranian Air Force	67-14726+ 5-113^ 5-107^ 5-8503 [+ USAF; ^ Iran]
4277	EC-130Q	(Airplane Sales International)	156173+ N34277 [+ USN] [wfu AMARC; for scrap]
4278	TC-130Q	(Airplane Sales International)	156174+ N14278 [+ USN] [wfu AMARC; for scrap]
4279	EC-130Q	(Airplane Sales International)	156175+ N14279 [+ USN] [wfu AMARC; for scrap]
4280	EC-130Q	(US Navy)	156176 [w/o into sea 21Jun77 after take-off from Wake Island, North Pacific, USA]
4281	EC-130Q	(Airplane Sales International)	156177+ N54281 [+ USN] [wfu AMARC; for scrap]
4282	C-130E	Pakistan Air Force	67-14727+ 5-114^ 5-108^ 14727 [+ USAF; ^ Iran]
4283	C-130E	Iranian Air Force	67-14728+ 5-115^ 5-109^ 5-8504 [+ USAF; ^ Iran]
4284	C-130E	Iranian Air Force	67-14729+ 5-116^ 5-110^ 5-8505 [+ USAF; ^ Iran]
4285	CC-130E	Canadian Armed Forces	10325+ 130325 [+ Canada]
4286	CC-130E	Canadian Armed Forces	10326+ 130326 [+ Canada] [wfu Mar08 Abbotsford, BC, Canada; l/n 08Aug08, without outer wings and engines]
4287	C-130H	Brazilian Air Force	2456
4288	CC-130E	Canadian Armed Forces	10327+ 130327 [+ Canada]
4289	CC-130E	Canadian Armed Forces	10328+ 130328 [+ Canada]
4290	C-130E	(Brazilian Air Force)	2457 [w/o 24Jun85 on approach to Santa Maria, Brazil]
4291	SC-130E	ex Brazilian Air Force	N7983R 2458 [stored Nov11 Parque Matrerial Aeronautico Galeao, Brazil]
4292	SC-130E	Brazilian Air Force	2459
4293	SC-130E	(Brazilian Air Force)	2460 [w/o 14Oct94 in the state of Bahia, Brazil after mid-air explosion]
4294	C-130E	Pakistan Air Force	69-7706+ 5-117^ 5-111^ 5-8506^ 97706 [+ USAF; ^ Iran]
4295	C-130E	Iranian Air Force	69-7707+ 5-118^ 5-112^ 5-8507 [+ USAF; ^ Iran]
4296	C-130E	Iranian Air Force	69-7708+ 5-119^ 5-113^ 5-8508 [+ USAF; ^ Iran]
4297	C-130E	Iranian Air Force	69-7709+ 5-120^ 5-114^ 5-8509 [+ USAF; ^ Iran]
4298	C-130E	Iranian Air Force	69-7710+ 5-121^ 5-115^ 5-8510 [+ USAF; ^ Iran]
4299	L-100-30	Transafrik/United Nations	N9232R N520SJ N901SJ S9-DBF 5X-TUD
4300	L-100-30	Transafrik/United Nations	N9265R N104AK N38ST N908SJ S9-CAW 5X-TUB
4301	L-100-30	Transafrik	N7951S N23ST N923SJ S9-CAV 5X-TUA
4302	L-100-20	Libyan Arab Air Cargo	N7952S N30FW PI-99 RP-C99 5A-DJR
4303	L-100-20	(Transafrik)	N9237R N40FW PI-98 C-FDSX N39ST S9-NAI [w/o 09Apr89 Luena, Zambia]
4304	C-130E	Turkish Air Force	479+ 1606+ 68-1606 [+ Saudi Arabia]
4305	LC-130R	(US Navy)	155917 [w/o 28Jan73 Amundsen-Scott, South Pole Station, Antarctica]
4306	C-130E	(Royal Saudi Air Force)	480+ 1607+ [stored by 2007; b/u] [+ Saudi Arabia]
4307	C-130E	Turkish Air Force	481+ 1608+ 68-1608 [+ Saudi Arabia]
4308	C-130H	Argentine Air Force	TC-61
4309	C-130E	(Argentine Air Force)	TC-62 [w/o 28Aug75 after bomb explosion Tucuman, Argentina]
4310	C-130H	(Argentine Air Force)	TC-63 [shot down 01Jun82 by Sea Harrier XZ451 90kms N of Pebble Island, Falklands]
4311	C-130E	Turkish Air Force	N7994S 1609+ 68-1609 [Saudi Arabia]
4312	C-130H	Royal New Zealand Air Force	68-8218+ NZ7004 [+ USAF]
4313	C-130H	Royal New Zealand Air Force	68-8219+ NZ7005 [+ USAF]
4314	C-130E	ex USAF	68-10934 [stored AMARC Apr05]
4315	C-130E	ex USAF	68-10935 [wfu Aug09 & wings removed, Martinsburg, WV; to be used as GIA]

LOCKHEED C-130/L-100 HERCULES

C/n	Model	Last known Owner/Operator	Identities/fates/comments (where appropriate)
4316	C-130E	(USAF)	68-10936 [w/o 30Nov78 35m W of Charleston, SC after being hit by lightning]
4317	C-130E	ex USAF	68-10937 [wfu 2004 Dobbins AFB, GA; for testing to destruction; l/n 17Oct10]
4318	C-130E	ex USAF	68-10938 [stored AMARC Feb03]
4319	C-130E	ex USAF	68-10939 [stored AMARC Apr05]
4320	C-130E	ex USAF	68-10940 [Mar03 GIA Pope AFB, NC]
4321	C-130E	ex USAF	68-10941 [Jan01 GIA Dyess AFB, TX; l/n 28Jly09]
4322	C-130E	(USAF)	68-10942 [damaged 23Mar94 mid-air collision over Pope AFB, NC with GD F-16D 88-0171; b/u 04 Ogden ALC, UT]
4323	C-130E	ex USAF	68-10943 [Aug05 GIA Robins ALC, GA]
4324	C-130E	(USAF)	68-10944 [w/o 28Feb84 into mountains 2½ miles NW of Borja, Spain]
4325	C-130E	(USAF)	68-10945 [w/o 01Jly 87 Fort Bragg, NC]
4326	C-130E	(USAF)	68-10946 [w/o 02Nov84 Giebelstadt AAF, West Germany; nose section used to repair c/n 4029]
4327	C-130E	ex USAF	68-10947 [stored AMARC Jlyl07]
4328	C-130E	USAF	68-10948
4329	C-130E	ex USAF	68-10949 [Dec95 GIA Little Rock AFB, AR; by Oct03 fuselage only]
4330	GC-130E	(USAF)	68-10950 [Oct94 GIA Little Rock AFB, AR; b/u Jan05]
4331	C-130E	(USAF)	68-10951 [w/o 10Dec78 on approach Fort Campbell, KY]
4332	C-130H	Royal Swedish Air Force	84002 [code 842]
4333	L-100-30	(Transamerica Airlines)	N7957S N17ST [w/o 27Aug83 into mountain 31 miles S of Dundo, Angola; canx unknown date]
4334	C-130H	ex Royal Norwegian Air Force	68-10952+ 952^ LN-SUW 952# [+ USAF; ^ Norway, code BW-A; code UN952 for period; # Norway code BW-A; by Nov08 stored AMARC]
4335	C-130H	Forsvarets Flysamling	68-10953+ 953^ (LN-SUR) 953# [+ USAF; ^ Norway; code BW-B; code UN953 for period; # Norway code BW-B; wfu 10Jun07 preserved Oslo-Gardermoen, Norway]
4336	C-130H	ex Royal Norwegian Air Force	68-10954+ 954^ [+ USAF; ^ Norway, code BW-C; code UN954 for period; by Dec08 stored AMARC]
4337	C-130H	ex Royal Norwegian Air Force	68-10955+ 955^ [^ code BW-D] [Oct08 stored AMARC]
4338	C-130H	ex Royal Norwegian Air Force	68-10956+ 956^ [^ code BW-E] [Oct08 stored AMARC]
4339	C-130H	ex Royal Norwegian Air Force	68-10957+ 957^ [^ code BW-F] [Oct08 stored AMARC]
4340	C-130E	ex USAF	69-6566 [stored AMARC Feb03]
4341	AC-130H	(USAF)	69-6567 [shot down 31Jan91 into sea 69 miles SSE of Kuwait City, Kuwait]
4342	AC-130H	USAF	69-6568
4343	AC-130H	USAF	69-6569
4344	AC-130H	USAF	69-6570
4345	AC-130E	(USAF)	69-6571 [shot down 30Mar72 near An Loc, South Vietnam]
4346	AC-130H	USAF	69-6572
4347	AC-130H	USAF	69-6573
4348	AC-130H	USAF	69-6574
4349	AC-130H	USAF	69-6575
4350	L-100-20	(Kuwait Air Force)	N7954S 317 [w/o 05Sep80 near Montelimar, France after lightning strike]
4351	AC-130H	(USAF)	69-6576 [w/o 14Mar94 in sea near Malindi, Kenya]
4352	AC-130H	USAF	69-6577
4353	C-130E	(USAF)	69-6578 [w/o 12Nov71 Little Rock AFB, AR]
4354	GC-130E	ex USAF	69-6579 [Mar98 GIA Dyess AFB, TX]
4355	L-100-20	ex Libyan Arab Air Cargo	N7960S CF-PWR C-FPWR (LX-GCV) 5A-DHJ 5A-DHI 5A-DHO [wfu by 05Oct09 Tripoli-Mitiga, Libya]
4356	C-130E	Air Mobility Command Museum	69-6580+ [+ USAF] [preserved Feb04 Dover AFB, DE]
4357	C-130E	(USAF)	69-6581 [w/o 14Jan81 Ramstein AFB, West Germany]
4358	L-100-20	ex Peruvian Air Force	N7985S N60FW N7985S 394+ OB-R-1188 394//OB-1376^ 394//OB-1374^ [+ Peru; ^ Peru dual marks; wfu by 2001 Lima, Peru]
4359	C-130E	ex USAF	69-6582 [stored AMARC Feb03]
4360	C-130E	ex USAF	69-6583 [stored AMARC Feb03]
4361	L-100-20	(Pacific Western Airlines)	N7982S CF-PWK [w/o 21Nov76 near Eastville, Zaire]
4362	L-100-20	(Transafrik/National Air Cargo)	N7984S N522SJ S9-BOR 5X-TUC [w/o 12Oct10 en-route Bagram AFB to Kabul Airport, Afghanistan, 30km E of Kabul Airport]
4363	MC-130P	USAF	69-5819
4364	L-100-20	(Peruvian AF/SATCO)	N7986S N70FW N7986S 395//OB-R-1004+ [+ dual marks] [w/o 19Feb78 on take-off from Tarapoto, Peru]
4365	C-130E	Iranian Air Force	71-0213+ 5-122^ 5-116^ 5-8511 [+ USAF; ^ Iran]
4366	C-130H	ex Libyan Arab Republic Air Force	111 [wfu by 05Oct09 Tripoli-Mitiga, Libya, no wings]

LOCKHEED C-130/L-100 HERCULES

C/n	Model	Last known Owner/Operator	Identities/fates/comments (where appropriate)
4367	MC-130P	USAF	69-5820
4368	MC-130P	USAF	69-5821
4369	C-130H	Libyan Arab Republic Air Force	112 [stored by Nov04 Tripoli-Mitiga AFB, Libya; l/n 07Oct09]
4370	MC-130P	USAF	69-5822
4371	MC-130P	USAF	69-5823
4372	HC-130N	USAF	69-5824
4373	C-130H	Libyan Arab Republic Air Force	113 [stored by 05Oct09 Tripoli-Mitiga, Libya]
4374	MC-130P	USAF	69-5825
4375	MC-130P	USAF	69-5826
4376	MC-130P	USAF	69-5827
4377	MC-130P	USAF	69-5828
4378	HC-130N	USAF	69-5829
4379	HC-130N	USAF	69-5830
4380	MC-130P	USAF	69-5831
4381	MC-130P	USAF	69-5832
4382	HC-130N	USAF	69-5833
4383	L-100-30	Transafrik/National Airlines	N10ST N910SJ 5X-TUF
4384	L-100-30	(Southern Air Transport)	N11ST N911SJ [w/o 12Aug90 Juba, Sudan; canx 24Aug94]
4385	L-100-20	Transafrik	ZS-GSK A2-AEG ZS-GSK 9Q-CHZ S9-NAL 5X-TUE
4386	C-130E	Iranian Air Force	71-0214+ 5-123^ 5-117^ 5-8512 [+ USAF; ^ Iran]
4387	C-130E	Iranian Air Force	71-0215+ 5-124^ 5-118^ 5-8513 [+ USAF; ^ Iran]
4388	L-100-30	Safair Freighters	N7988S N12ST N912SJ S9-BOQ ZS-ORC
4389	C-130E	Iranian Air Force	71-0216+ 5-125^ 5-119^ 5-8514 [+ USAF; ^ Iran]
4390	C-130E	Iranian Air Force	71-0217+ N7927S 5-126^ 5-120^ 5-8515 [+ USAF; ^ Iran]
4391	L-100-30	(Southern Air Transport)	N15ST [w/o 04Oct86 Kelly AFB, TX; canx 04Jan89]
4392	C-130E	Iranian Air Force	71-0218+ I5-127^ 5-121^ 5-8516 [+ USAF; ^ Iran]
4393	C-130E	(Iranian Air Force)	71-0219+ 5-128^ 5-122 [+ USAF; ^ Iran] [w/o 28Feb74 in a mountain near Mehrabad, Iran]
4394	C-130E	Iranian Air Force	71-0220+ 5-129^ 5-123^ 5-8517 [+ USAF; ^ Iran]
4395	C-130H	Libyan Arab Republic Air Force	114
4396	C-130H	Turkish Air Force	1610+ 476+ 70-1610 [+ Saudi Arabia]
4397	C-130H	(Royal Saudi Air Force)	1611 [b/u by 23Sep06]
4398	C-130E	Iranian Air Force	71-0221+ 5-130^ 5-124^ 5-8518 [+ USAF; ^ Iran]
4399	C-130E	Iranian Air Force	71-0222+ 5-131^ 5-125^ 5-8519 [+ USAF; ^ Iran]
4400	C-130H	Free Libya Air Force	115
4401	C-130H	Libyan Arab Republic Air Force	116 [DBF 08Apr79 Entebbe, Uganda]
4402	C-130E	(Iranian Air Force)	71-0223+ 5-132^ 5-126^ 5-8520 [+ USAF; ^ Iran] [w/o 19Sep79 after loss of control near Shiraz, Iran]
4403	C-130H	Libyan Arab Republic Air Force	117 [stored by 05Oct09 Tripoli-Mitiga AFB, Libya]
4404	C-130E	ex USAF	70-1259 [stored AMARC Apr05]
4405	C-130H	Libyan Arab Republic Air Force	118
4406	C-130H	(Venezuelan Air Force)	3556 [w/o 04Nov80 Caracas Airport, Venezuela]
4407	C-130H	Venezuelan Air Force	4951
4408	C-130H	(Venezuelan Air Force)	7772 [w/o 27Aug76 Lajes, Azores]
4409	C-130H	Venezuelan Air Force	9508
4410	C-130E	USAF	70-1260
4411	C-130H	EADS Sogerma	71-1067+ 9T-TCA^ [stored/on rebuild Bordeaux, France]
4412	L-100-20	(Lockheed)	318+ N4174M N130X [+ Kuwait] [used as technology testbed; w/o 03Feb93 Dobbins AFB, GA; canx 05Feb97]
4413	C-130E	ex USAF	70-1261 [stored AMARC Apr07]
4414	C-130E	Polish Air Force	70-1262+ (1503)^ 1502 [+ USAF; ^ Poland]
4415	C-130E	Polish Air Force	70-1263+ 1505 [+ USAF]
4416	C-130H	Zaire Air Force	71-1068+ 9T-TCB [+ USAF] [substantial damage on landing 14Apr06 Kinshasa, DRC; l/n 08Nov10 not repaired]
4417	C-130E	USAF	70-1264
4418	C-130E	ex USAF	70-1265 [stored AMARC Nov06]
4419	C-130E	ex USAF	70-1266 [stored AMARC Dec06]
4420	C-130E	ex USAF	70-1267 [stored AMARC Dec06]
4421	C-130E	ex USAF	70-1268 [stored AMARC Apr05]
4422	C-130H	(Zaire Air Force)	71-1069+ 9T-TCD [+ USAF] [w/o 18Aug74 Kisangani, Zaire]
4423	C-130E	ex USAF	70-1269 [gate guardian Pope AFB, IL]
4424	C-130E	ex USAF	70-1270 [stored AMARC Nov06]
4425	C-130E	USAF	70-1271

LOCKHEED C-130/L-100 HERCULES

C/n	Model	Last known Owner/Operator	Identities/fates/comments (where appropriate)
4426	C-130E	Polish Air Force	70-1272+ 1503 [+ USAF]
4427	C-130E	Turkish Air Force	70-1947+ ETI-947^ 01947 [+ USAF; ^ Turkey]
4428	C-130E	Polish Air Force	70-1273+ 1501 [+ USAF]
4429	C-130E	ex USAF	70-1274 [stored AMARC Jly07]
4430	C-130H	Israel Defence Force/Air Force	71-1374+ 02//4X-JUA^ 102//4X-FBA^ [+ USAF; ^ Israel; dual marks]
4431	C-130H	Israel Defence Force/Air Force	71-1375+ 06//4X-JUB^ 106//4X-JUB^ 106//4X-FBB^ 4X-EBB 106//4X-FBB^ [+ USAF; ^ Israel; dual marks]
4432	C-130H	(Iranian Air Force)	5-133+ 5-127+ 5-8521 [+ Iran] [shot down 17Mar94 by Armenian rebels near Stepanakert, Armenia]
4433	C-130H	Iranian Air Force	5-134+ 5-128+ 5-8522 [+ Iran]
4434	C-130E	ex USAF	70-1275 [stored AMARC Dec06]
4435	C-130E	Polish Air Force	70-1276+ 1504 [+ USAF]
4436	C-130H	Argentine Air Force	TC-64
4437	C-130H	Argentine Air Force	TC-65 [stored by 2005 El Palomar AFB, Argentina; l/n Apr08]
4438	C-130H	Iranian Air Force	5-135+ 5-129+ 5-8523 [+ Iran]
4439	C-130H	Iranian Air Force	5-136+ 5-130+ 5-8524 [+ Iran]
4440	C-130H	Iranian Air Force	5-137+ 5-131+ 5-8525 [+ Iran]
4441	C-130M	Brazilian Air Force	MM61988//46-02+ 2470 [+ Italy]
4442	C-130H	Iranian Air Force	5-138+ 5-132+ 5-8526 [+ Iran]
4443	C-130H	ex Brazilian Air Force	MM61989//46-03+ 2478 [+ Italy] [stored Nov11 Parque Matrerial Aeronautico Galeao, Brazil]
4444	C-130H	Iranian Air Force	5-139+ 5-133+ 5-8527 [+ Iran]
4445	C-130H	Iranian Air Force	5-140+ 5-134+ 5-8528 [+ Iran]
4446	C-130H	ex Brazilian Air Force	MM61990//46-04+ 2471 [+ Italy] [stored Nov11 Parque Matrerial Aeronautico Galeao, Brazil]
4447	C-130H	Romanian Air Force	MM61991//46-05+ 6191 [+ Italy]
4448	C-130H	Iranian Air Force	5-141+ 5-135+ 5-8529 [+ Iran]
4449	C-130H	Brazilian Air Force	MM61992//46-06+ 2479 [+ Italy]
4450	L-100-20	(Peruvian Air Force)	396//OB-R-956 [dual marks] [w/o 24Apr81 near San Juan, Peru]
4451	C-130H	Brazilian Air Force	MM61993//46-07+ 2473 [+ Italy]
4452	C-130H	Brazilian Air Force	MM61994//46-08+ 2472 [+ Italy]
4453	C-130H	Chilean Air Force	995
4454	C-130H	Iranian Air Force	5-142+ 5-136+ 5-8530 [+ Iran]
4455	C-130H	Belgian Air Force	71-1797+ CH-01 [+ USAF]
4456	C-130H	Iranian Air Force	5-143+ 5-137+ 5-8531 [+ Iran]
4457	C-130H	(Iranian Air Force)	5-144+ 5-138+ 5-8532 [+ Iran] [w/o 19Sep78 Doshan Tappah AFB, Tehran, Iran]
4458	C-130H	Iranian Air Force	5-145+ 5-139+ 5-8533 [+ Iran]
4459	C-130H	Iranian Air Force	5-146+ 5-140+ 5-8534 [+ Iran]
4460	C-130H	(Belgian Air Force)	71-1798+ CH-02 [+ USAF] [w/o 04May06 Brussels Airport, Belgium in hangar fire]
4461	C-130H	Belgian Air Force	71-1799+ CH-03 [+ USAF]
4462	C-130H	Iranian Air Force	5-147+ 5-141+ 5-8535 [+ Iran]
4463	C-130H	(Iranian Air Force)	5-148+ 5-142+ 5-8536 [+ Iran] [w/o 21Dec76 on approach to Shiraz, Iran]
4464	C-130H	Argentine Air Force	TC-66
4465	C-130H	Iranian Air Force	5-149+ 5-143+ 5-8537 [+ Iran]
4466	C-130H	Iranian Air Force	5-150+ 5-144+ 5-8538 [+ Iran]
4467	C-130H	Belgian Air Force	71-1800+ CH-04 [+ USAF]
4468	C-130H	Iranian Air Force	5-151+ 5-145+ 5-8539 [+ Iran]
4469	C-130H	Iranian Air Force	5-152+ 5-146+ 5-8540 [+ Iran]
4470	C-130H	Belgian Air Force	71-1801+ CH-05 [+ USAF]
4471	C-130H	Iranian Air Force	5-153+ 5-147+ 5-8541 [+ Iran]
4472	L-100-30	(Transafrik)	ZS-RSB N107AK N905SJ S9-BAS [w/o 10Jun05 Lokichoggio, Kenya, hit Andover 3C-KKC that was blocking the runway; hulk l/n Jan06]
4473	C-130H	(Belgian Air Force)	71-1802+ CH-06 [+ USAF] [w/o 15Jly96 Eindhoven, Netherlands]
4474	C-130H	Iranian Air Force	5-154+ 5-148+ 5-8542 [+ Iran]
4475	L-100-30	Safair Freighters	ZS-RSC 9Q-CZS(1) ZS-RSC (A2-) ZS-RSC 9Q-CZS(1) S9-NAD ZS-RSC S9-NAD ZS-RSC D2- ZS-RSC
4476	C-130H	Belgian Air Force	71-1803+ CH-07 [+ USAF]
4477	L-100-30	(Transafrik)	ZS-RSD N106AK N906SJ S9-BOP [w/o 28Dec99 Luzamba Airport, Angola]

LOCKHEED C-130/L-100 HERCULES

C/n	Model	Last known Owner/Operator	Identities/fates/comments (where appropriate)
4478	C-130H	Belgian Air Force	71-1804+ CH-08 [+ USAF]
4479	C-130H	Belgian Air Force	71-1805+ CH-09 [+ USAF]
4480	C-130H	Iranian Air Force	5-155+ 5-149+ 5-8543 [+ Iran]
4481	C-130H	Belgian Air Force	71-1806+ CH-10 [+ USAF]
4482	C-130H	Belgian Air Force	71-1807+ CH-11 [+ USAF]
4483	C-130H	Belgian Air Force	71-1808+ CH-12 [+ USAF]
4484	C-130H	Iranian Air Force	5-156+ 5-150+ 5-8544 [+ Iran]
4485	C-130H	Iranian Air Force	5-157+ 5-151+ 5-8545 [+ Iran]
4486	C-130H	Iranian Air Force	5-158+ 5-152+ 5-8546 [+ Iran]
4487	C-130H	Iranian Air Force	5-159+ 5-153+ 5-8547 [+ Iran]
4488	C-130H	Iranian Air Force	5-160+ 5-154+ 5-8548 [+ Iran]
4489	C-130H	Iranian Air Force	5-161+ 5-155+ 5-8549 [+ Iran]
4490	C-130H	Iranian Air Force	5-162+ 5-156+ 5-8550 [+ Iran]
4491	C-130H	Brazilian Air Force	MM61995//46-09 2475 [+ Italy]
4492	C-130H	(Italian Air Force)	MM61996//46-10 [w/o 03Mar77 into Monte Serra, 10m E of Pisa, Italy]
4493	C-130H	Brazilian Air Force	MM61997//46-11 2476 [+ Italy]
4494	C-130H	Brazilian Air Force	MM61998//46-12 2474 [+ Italy]
4495	C-130H	ex Brazilian Air Force	MM61999//46-13 2477 [+ Italy] [stored Nov11 Parque Matrerial Aeronautico Galeao, Brazil]
4496	C-130H	Chilean Air Force	996
4497	C-130H	(Italian Air Force)	MM62000//46-14 [DBR 23Jan79 Milan-Malpensa, Italy; Feb80 parts used for MM61995 c/n 4491]
4498	C-130H	Colombian Air Force	MM62001//46-15 1015 [+ Italy]
4499	C-130E	ex USAF	72-1288 [stored AMARC Mar07]
4500	C-130E	USAF	72-1289
4501	HC-130H	US Coast Guard	72-1300+ 1500 [+ USAF]
4502	C-130E	ex USAF	72-1290 [stored AMARC Jly10]
4503	KC-130H	Royal Saudi Air Force	N7992S 456+ 3201 [+ Saudi Arabia]
4504	C-130E	ex USAF	72-1291 [stored AMARC Sep07]
4505	C-130E	ex USAF	72-1292 [stored AMARC 01May08]
4506	C-130E	ex USAF	72-1293 [stored AMARC Sep07]
4507	HC-130H	US Coast Guard	72-1301+ 1501 [+ USAF]
4508	LC-130H	USAF	73-0839+ 159129^ 73-3300 [+ USAF; ^ USN]
4509	C-130E	ex USAF	72-1294 [stored AMARC May07]
4510	C-130E	ex USAF	72-1295 [stored AMARC Jan07]
4511	KC-130H	Royal Saudi Air Force	457+ 3202 [+ Saudi Arabia]
4512	L-100-20	ex Philippine Air Force	N7967S RP-C100 4512 [wfu Aug91 Mactan-Cebu, Philippines, for spares use; l/n 03Aug07]
4513	HC-130H	US Coast Guard	72-1302+ 1502^ 72-1302+ 1502 [+ USAF; ^ USCG]
4514	C-130E	Turkish Air Force	71-1468+ ETI-468^ 01468 [+ USAF;^ Turkey]
4515	C-130H	Libyan Arab Republic Air Force	119 [export embargoed 1974; stored Marietta, GA; to be b/u]
4516	LC-130R	ex US Navy	73-0840+ 159130 [+ USAF] [stored AMARC 08Mar99]
4517	C-130E	ex USAF	72-1296 [stored AMARC 08May08]
4518	C-130H	Libyan Arab Republic Air Force	120 [export embargoed 1974; stored Marietta, GA; b/u]
4519	C-130E	(USAF)	72-1297 [DBR by shelling 28Apr75 Tan Son Nhut, South Vietnam]
4520	C-130H	(Spanish Air Force)	T.10-1//311-01 [w/o 28May80 into mountain in central Gran Canaria, Spain]
4521	GC-130E	ex USAF	72-1298 [GIA 1998 Sheppard TTC, TX; stored dismantled by Oct07]
4522	LC-130R	(US Navy)	73-0841+ 159131 [+ USAF] [w/o 09Dec87 site D59, 862 miles NE of McMurdo Sound, Antarctica; later stripped for spares & used for c/n 3567]
4523	C-130H	Libyan Arab Republic Air Force	121 [export embargoed 1974; stored Marietta, GA; to be b/u]
4524	C-130E	Turkish Air Force	73-0991+ ETI-991^ 00991 [+ USAF;^ Turkey]
4525	C-130H	Libyan Arab Republic Air Force	122 [export embargoed 1974; stored Marietta, GA; to be b/u]
4526	C-130H	Spanish Air Force	T.10-2//311-02+ T.10-2/31-02 [+ Spain]
4527	C-130E	Polish Air Force	72-1299 1506 [grounded 05Feb10 Mazar-e-Sharif AFB, Afghanistan, following in-flight structural failure]
4528	HC-130H	US Coast Guard	72-0844+ 1503 [+ USAF]
4529	HC-130H	US Coast Guard	72-0845+ 1504 [+ USAF]
4530	C-130H	Israel Defence Force/Air Force	73-1600+ 009//4X-FBC^ 109# 309//4X-FBC^ [+ USAF; ^ Israel dual marks; # Israel]
4531	C-130H	Spanish Air Force	T.10-3//31-03 [Open Skies aircraft]
4532	KC-130H	Royal Saudi Air Force	458+ 3203 [+ Saudi Arabia]
4533	C-130H	(Israel Defence Force/Air Force)	73-1601+ 011//4X-FBD^ [+ USAF; ^ Israel dual marks] [w/o 25Nov75 into mountain Gebel Hala, 35 miles SSE of El Arish, Israel]

LOCKHEED C-130/L-100 HERCULES

C/n	Model	Last known Owner/Operator	Identities/fates/comments (where appropriate)
4534	C-130H	Spanish Air Force	T.10-4//31-04
4535	C-130H	Royal Moroccan Air Force	4535/CNA-OA [dual marks]
4536	C-130H	Libyan Arab Republic Air Force	123 [export embargoed 1974; stored Marietta, GA; to be b/u]
4537	C-130H	(Royal Moroccan Air Force)	4537/CNA-OB [dual marks] [shot down 04Dec76 over Sahara Desert, Morocco]
4538	C-130H	Libyan Arab Republic Air Force	124 [export embargoed 1974; stored Marietta, GA; to be b/u]
4539	KC-130H	Royal Saudi Air Force	459+ 3204 [+ Saudi Arabia]
4540	C-130H	Libyan Arab Republic Air Force	125 [export embargoed 1974; stored Marietta, GA; to be b/u]
4541	C-130H	Libyan Arab Republic Air Force	126 [export embargoed 1974; stored Marietta, GA; to be b/u]
4542	EC-130H	USAF	73-1580
4543	EC-130H	USAF	73-1581
4544	C-130H	USAF	73-1582
4545	EC-130H	USAF	73-1583
4546	EC-130H	USAF	73-1584
4547	EC-130H	USAF	73-1585
4548	EC-130H	USAF	73-1586
4549	EC-130H	USAF	73-1587
4550	EC-130H	USAF	73-1588
4551	C-130H	Royal Moroccan Air Force	4551/CNA-OC [dual marks]
4552	C-130H	Royal Saudi Air Force	1612
4553	CC-130H	(Canadian Armed Forces)	73-1589+ 130329 [+ USAF] [w/o 06Nov82 near CFB Namao, Edmonton, AB, Canada]
4554	EC-130H	USAF	73-1590
4555	CC-130H	(Canadian Armed Forces)	73-1591+ 130330 [+ USAF] [w/o 29Mar85 after mid-air collision with 130331 (c/n 4559) over CFB Namao, AB, Canada]
4556	C-130H	Venezuelan Air Force	4224
4557	EC-130H	USAF	73-1592
4558	L-100-30	(Globe Air)	ZS-RSE N46965 N517SJ [w/o 08Apr87 Travis AFB, CA]
4559	CC-130H	(Canadian Armed Forces)	73-1593+ 130331 [+ USAF] [w/o 29Mar85 after mid-air collision with 130330 (c/n 4555) over CFB Namao, AB, Canada]
4560	C-130H	Royal Saudi Air Force	1614+ 477+ 1614 [+ Saudi Arabia]
4561	L-100-30	(Transafrik)	N20ST N920SJ S9-CAO [shot down 26Dec98 by UNITA rebels Vila Nova, Angola]
4562	L-100-30	Safair Freighters/UN	ZS-RSF C-FNWF ZS-RSF N519SJ N904SJ S9-CAI ZS-RSF
4563	EC-130H	USAF	73-1594
4564	EC-130H	USAF	73-1595
4565	L-100-30	Safair Freighters/Air Contractors	ZS-RSG N250SF N515SJ N902SJ S9-CAJ ZS-RSG
4566	C-130H	Royal Saudi Air Force Museum	460+ [+ Saudi Arabia] [damaged Dec89 in ground fire Jeddah, Saudi Arabia; restored as GIA; preserved by 2002 Riyadh, Sauda Arabia]
4567	C-130H	Royal Saudi Air Force	461+ 1627 [+ Saudi Arabia]
4568	CC-130H	Canadian Armed Forces	73-1596+ 130332 [+ USAF]
4569	C-130H	(Zaire Air Force)	9T-TCE [w/o 14Sep80 Kindu, Zaire]
4570	C-130H	Brazilian Air Force	2463
4571	C-130H	USAF	73-1597
4572	C-130H	Egyptian Air Force	73-1678+ B-678^ 1296 [+ USAF; ^ Denmark]
4573	C-130H	USAF	73-1598
4574	CC-130H	Canadian Armed Forces	73-1599+ 130333 [+ USAF]
4575	C-130H	Royal Moroccan Air Force	4575/CNA-OD [dual marks]
4576	C-130H	(Argentine Air Force)	TC-67 [damaged landing 1996 Tandil AFB, Argentina; sold 2005 to Pakistan for spares use]
4577	C-130H	Venezuelan Air Force	5320
4578	C-130H	Argentine Air Force	TC-68 [stored Oct96 El Palomar, Argentina]
4579	C-130H	USAF	74-1658
4580	CC-130H	Canadian Armed Forces	1211+ N4246M G-52-18 N4246M 130336 [+ Abu Dhabi]
4581	C-130H	Royal Moroccan Air Force	4581/CNA-OE [dual marks]
4582	L-100-30	Tepper Aviation/JJS&D	TR-KKA+ N2189M N2731G [+ Gabon]
4583	C-130H	Royal Moroccan Air Force	4583/CNA-OF [dual marks]
4584	CC-130H	Canadian Armed Forces	1212(1)+ N4247M G-52-17 N4247M 130337 [+ Abu Dhabi]
4585	C-130H	USAF	74-1659
4586	L-100-30	(Transafrik)	N21ST N921SJ S9-BOF [w/o 12Jly06 Kigoma, Tanzania]
4587	C-130H	Egyptian Air Force	73-1679+ B-679+ 1297 [+ USAF; ^ Denmark]
4588	C-130H	French Air Force	9T-TCF+ F-ZJEP 4588//61-PM//F-RAPM [+ Zaire]

LOCKHEED C-130/L-100 HERCULES

C/n	Model	Last known Owner/Operator	Identities/fates/comments (where appropriate)
4589	C-130H	French Air Force	9T-TCG+ 9T-TCC 4589//61-PN//F-RAPN [+ Zaire]
4590	L-100-30	Lynden Air Cargo	ZS-RSH N251SF N516SJ N903SJ N403LC
4591	C-130H	Iranian Air Force	5-157+ 5-8551 [+ Iran]
4592	C-130H	USAF	74-1660
4593	L-100-20	(Philippine Air Force)	RP-C101 4593 [w/o 25Aug08 near Davao, Philippines]
4594	C-130H	(Iranian Air Force	5-158+ 5-8552 [+ Iran] [w/o 29Sep81 near Kahrizak, Iran]
4595	TC-130Q	(Derco Aerospace Inc)	159469+ N54595 [+ USN] [stored AMARC; sold to the Royal Netherlands AF for spares; canx 03Jly12]
4596	C-130H	USAF	74-1661
4597	C-130H	(USAF)	74-1662 [w/o 17Aug96 into Gros Ventre mountain range, 15 miles SE of Jackson Hole, WY]
4598	C-130H	USAF	74-1663
4599	C-130H	Egyptian Air Force	73-1680+ B-680^ 1298 [+ USAF; ^ Denmark]
4600	L-100-30	Bradley Air Services	ZS-RSI C-FNWY ZS-RSI F-WDAQ F-GDAQ TN- ZS-RSI F-GIMV ZS-RSI C-GUSI
4601	TC-130Q	ex US Navy	159348 [wfu by 1995; displayed inside Tinker AFB, OK; l/n 25Jly09]
4602	C-130H	Brazilian Air Force	2464
4603	C-130H	USAF	74-1664
4604	C-130H	USAF	74-1665
4605	VC-130H	Royal Saudi Air Force	HZ-102 HZ-111
4606	L-100-30	Lynden Air Cargo	ZS-RSJ 9Q-CZA ZS-RSJ F-GFAS ZS-RSJ 9Q-CZH ZS-RSJ S9-NAJ ZS-RSJ N401LC
4607	C-130H	Royal Saudi Air Force	463+ 1629 [+ Saudi Arabia]
4608	C-130H	Royal Saudi Air Force	464
4609	C-130H	Royal Saudi Air Force	465
4610	L-100-30	Uganda Govt/Uganda Air Cargo	(N108AK) 5X-UCF (PH-AID) 5X-UCF
4611	C-130H	USAF	74-1666
4612	C-130H	Royal Saudi Air Force	1601
4613	C-130H	USAF	74-1667
4614	C-130H	Royal Saudi Air Force	1602
4615	KC-130R	(US Marine Corps)	74-1654+ 160013 [+ USAF] [stored 07Jan08 AMARC; SOC 08Aug08]
4616	C-130H	USAF	74-1668
4617	C-130H	USAF	74-1669
4618	C-130H	Royal Saudi Air Force	1603+ 478 [+ Saudi Arabia]
4619	C-130H	ex Nigerian Air Force	910+ AT619+ AT450+ AT619+ 910 [+ Nigeria] [stored by Apr10 Lagos, Nigeria]
4620	C-130H(ECM)	USAF	74-1670
4621	C-130H	USAF	74-1671
4622	C-130H	Greek Air Force	741
4623	C-130H	(USAF)	74-1672 [w/o 21Sep81 short of runway at desert strip near Indian Springs AFB, NV]
4624	C-130H	(Nigerian Air Force)	911+ AT634+ AT624+ 624+ [+ Nigeria] [w/o 26Sep92 near Ejigbo, Nigeria]
4625	KC-130H	Brazilian Air Force	2461
4626	KC-130R	US Marine Corps	74-1655+ 160014 [+ USAF] [stored AMARC Jun06]
4627	C-130H	USAF	74-1673
4628	C-130H	Royal Swedish Air Force	84003 [code 843]
4629	KC-130R	(US Marine Corps)	74-1656+ 160015 [+ USAF] [stored AMARC 11Sep07; SOC 04Jan08]
4630	C-130M	Brazilian Air Force	2465
4631	C-130H	USAF	74-1674
4632	C-130H	Greek Air Force	742
4633	C-130H	Royal Saudi Air Force	1604
4634	C-130H	Royal Saudi Air Force	1605
4635	KC-130R	(US Marine Corps)	74-1657+ 160016 [+ USAF] [stored AMARC 06Feb08; SOC 08Aug08]
4636	KC-130H	Brazilian Air Force	2462
4637	C-130H	Royal Saudi Air Force	462+ 1628 [+ Saudi Arabia]
4638	C-130H	ex Nigerian Air Force	912+ AT744+ AT638+ 638+ 912 [+ Nigeria] [stored by Apr10 Lagos, Nigeria]
4639	C-130H	Nigerian Air Force	913+ AT639+ 639913+ 913 [+ Nigeria]
4640	C-130H	USAF	74-1675
4641	C-130H	USAF	74-1676
4642	KC-130H	Spanish Air Force	TK.10-5//31-50
4643	C-130H	USAF	74-1677
4644	C-130H	USAF	74-2061

LOCKHEED C-130/L-100 HERCULES

C/n	Model	Last known Owner/Operator	Identities/fates/comments (where appropriate)
4645	C-130H	(USAF)	74-1678 [w/o 13Apr82 after wing broke 40m W of Erzurum, Turkey]
4646	C-130H	USAF	74-1679
4647	C-130H	USAF	74-2062
4648	KC-130H	Spanish Air Force	TK.10-6//31-51
4649	C-130H	ex Nigerian Air Force	914+ AT649+ 649914+ 914 [+ Nigeria] [wfu Lagos, Nigeria; derelict by Apr95; l/n Apr10]
4650	C-130H	ex Nigerian Air Force	915+ AT450+ AT650915+ 915 [+ Nigeria] [wfu Feb85 Lagos, Nigeria; l/n Apr10]
4651	C-130H	USAF	74-1680
4652	KC-130H	Spanish Air Force	TK.10-7//31-52
4653	KC-130H	Israel Defence Force/Air Force	75-0534+ 420//4X-FBQ^ [+ USAF; ^ dual marks]
4654	C-130H	(USAF)	74-1681 [w/o 09Aug89 whilst dropping an artillery piece at Sicily drop zone, Fort Bragg, NC]
4655	C-130H	USAF	74-2063
4656	KC-130H	Royal Malaysian Air Force	FM2401+ M30-01 [+ Malaysia]
4657	C-130H	USAF	74-1682
4658	YMC-130H	(USAF)	74-1683 [w/o 29Oct80 during rocket assisted take-off/landing trials at an Eglin AFB auxiliary field, FL]
4659	C-130H	(USAF)	74-2064 [w/o 14Mar80 25kms W of Incirlik, Turkey]
4660	KC-130H	Israel Defence Force/Air Force	75-0540+ 422//4X-FBY^ 522//4X-FBY^ [+ USAF; ^ Israel; dual marks]
4661	C-130H	Royal Malaysian Air Force	FM2402+ M30-02 [+ Malaysia]
4662	C-130H	Israel Defence Force/Air Force	75-0535+ 427//4X-FBS^ [+ USAF; ^ Israel; dual marks]
4663	C-130H	USAF	74-1684
4664	KC-130H	Israel Defence Force/Air Force	75-0541+ 445//4X-FBZ^ 545//4X-FBZ^ [+ USAF; ^ Israel; dual marks]
4665	C-130H	Greek Air Force	743
4666	C-130H	USAF	74-1685
4667	C-130H	USAF	74-2065
4668	C-130H	Israel Defence Force/Air Force	75-0536+ 435//4X-FBT [+ USAF; ^ Israel; dual marks]
4669	YMC-130H	Museum of Aviation	74-1686 [preserved 1988, Robins AFB, GA; l/n 16Oct10]
4670	C-130H	USAF	74-1687
4671	C-130H	USAF	74-2066
4672	C-130H	Greek Air Force	744
4673	L-100-30	Air Contractors (Ireland) Ltd	ZS-JIV D2-THE ZS-JIV EI-JIV
4674	C-130H	(Royal Malaysian Air Force)	FM2403+ M30-03 [+ Malaysia] [w/o 25Aug90 Sibu, Sarawak, Malaysia]
4675	C-130H	USAF	74-1688
4676	L-100-30	Lynden Air Cargo/Airlines of PNG	ZS-JVL D2-TAA ZS-JVL (PH-) ZS-JVL PH-RMH ZS-JVL EI-JVL ZS-JVL N406LC P2-LAC
4677	KC-130R	US Marine Corps	75-0550+ 160017 [+ USAF] [stored AMARC 17May06]
4678	C-130H	USAF	74-2067
4679	L-100-30	(Angola Air Charter)	ZS-JIW D2-THC [DBF 07Apr94 at Malange, Angola]
4680	C-130H	Israel Defence Force/Air Force	75-0537+ 448//4X-FBU^ [+ USAF; ^ dual marks] [stored by 2001 Tel Aviv-Lod, Isreal]
4681	C-130H	USAF	74-1689
4682	C-130H	USAF	74-1690
4683	KC-130R	US Marine Corps	75-0551+ 160018 [+ USAF] [stored AMARC Jun06]
4684	L-100-30	Tepper Aviation?	ZS-JIX D2-THZ ZS-JIX PK-MMA ZS-JIX N3867X
4685	C-130H	Royal Malaysian Air Force	FM2404+ M30-04 [+ Malaysia]
4686	C-130H	Israel Defence Force/Air Force	75-0538+ 436//4X-FBW^ 116//4X-FBW^ 436//4X-FBW [+ USAF; ^ Israel; dual marks]
4687	C-130H	USAF	74-1691
4688	C-130H	USAF	74-1692
4689	KC-130R	US Marine Corps	75-0552+ 160019 [+ USAF] [stored AMARC Oct05]
4690	C-130H-30	Royal Malaysian Air Force	FM2405+ M30-05 [+ Malaysia]
4691	L-100-30	United Arab Air Force	ZS-JIY A2-ABZ ZS-JIY 9Q-CZS(1) ZS-JIY D2-THS ZS-JIY 1217
4692	C-130H	Israel Defence Force/Air Force	75-0539+ 428//4X-FBX^ [+ USAF; ^ Israel; dual marks]
4693	C-130H	USAF	74-1693 [DBF 13Feb83 Pope AFB, NC; fuselage to GIA Pope AFB, NC]
4694	C-130H	(USAF)	74-2068 [w/o 28Jun83 at range complex, 100 miles NW of Nellis AFB, NV]
4695	L-100-30	Safair Freighters	ZS-JIZ S9-NAT ZS-JIZ D2-TAD ZS-JIZ 9Q-CPX ZS-JIZ F-GNMM ZS-JIZ
4696	KC-130R	US Marine Corps	75-0553+ 160020 [+ USAF] [stored AMARC Sep05]
4697	C-130H-30	Royal Malaysian Air Force	FM2406 M30-06 [+ Malaysia]

LOCKHEED C-130/L-100 HERCULES

C/n	Model	Last known Owner/Operator	Identities/fates/comments (where appropriate)
4698	L-100-30	Lynden Air Cargo/Airlines of PNG	ZS-JJA F-GFAR ZS-JJA HB-ILG F-GFZE HB-ILG ZS-JJA TU-TNV ZS-JJA D2-TAB ZS-JJA N402LC P2-LAD
4699	C-130H	USAF	74-2069
4700	C-130H	USAF	74-2070
4701	L-100-30	(Zimex Aviation)	ZS-JVM A2-ACA HB-ILF [w/o 14Oct87 after take-off from Kuito, Angola]
4702	KC-130R	(US Marine Corps)	75-0554+ 160021 [+ USAF] [w/o 09Jan02 into mountain near Shamsi, Pakistan]
4703	C-130H	USAF	74-2071
4704	C-130H	Philippine Air Force	4704
4705	C-130H	USAF	74-2072
4706	L-100-20	Peruvian Air Force	382//OB-R-1183+ 382//OB-1377+ [+ Peru dual marks]
4707	C-130H	(Egyptian Air Force)	76-1598+ 1270//SU-BAA^ [+ USAF; ^ dual marks] [DBF on ground 19Feb78 on raid against hijackers Larnaca, Cyprus]
4708	L-100-20	(Peruvian Air Force)	383 [w/o 09Jun83 Puerto Maldonado, Peru]
4709	C-130H	Egyptian Air Force	76-1599+ 1271//SU-BAB^ [+ USAF; ^ dual marks]
4710	L-100-20	ex Gabon Air Force	TR-KKB [reported wfu 24Jan11 Libreville, Gabon]
4711	C-130H	USAF	74-2130
4712	KC-130R	US Marine Corps	75-0555+ 160240 [+ USAF] [stored AMARC Jun06]
4713	C-130H	Royal Moroccan Air Force	4713/CNA-OG [dual marks]
4714	C-130H	(Egyptian Air Force)	76-1600+ 1272//SU-BAC^ [+ USAF; ^ dual marks] [w/o 24Feb09 unknown location in Egypt]
4715	L-100-20	Peruvian Air Force	384//OB-1378 [dual marks]
4716	C-130H	Greek Air Force	75-0542+ 745 [+ USAF]
4717	C-130H	(Royal Moroccan Air Force)	4717/CNA-OH [dual marks] [shot down 12Oct81 Guelta Zemmour, Morocco]
4718	C-130H	USAF	74-2131
4719	C-130H	Egyptian Air Force	76-1601+ 1273//SU-BAD^ [+ USAF; ^ dual marks]
4720	C-130H	Greek Air Force	75-0543+ 746 [+ USAF]
4721	C-130H	Egyptian Air Force	76-1602+ 1274//SU-BAE^ [+ USAF; ^ dual marks]
4722	C-130H	USAF	74-2132
4723	C-130H	Greek Air Force	75-0544+ 747 [+ USAF]
4724	C-130H	(Greek Air Force)	75-0545+ 748 [+ USAF] [w/o 05Feb91 into Mount Othris, Greece; wreck found 4 days later]
4725	LC-130H	USAF	76-0491+ 160740^ 76-3301 [+ USAF; ^ USN]
4726	C-130H	Philippine Air Force	4726
4727	C-130H	Greek Air Force	75-0546+ 749 [+ USAF]
4728	C-130H	Egyptian Air Force	76-1603+ 1275//SU-BAF^ [+ USAF; ^ dual marks]
4729	C-130H	(Greek Air Force)	75-0547+ 750 [+ USAF] [w/o 20Dec97 near Pastra Mountain (Agios Meletios), Greece]
4730	C-130H	USAF	74-2133
4731	LC-130H	USAF	76-0492+ 160741^ 76-3302 [+ USAF; ^ USN]
4732	C-130H	Greek Air Force	75-0548+ 751 [+ USAF]
4733	C-130H	Royal Moroccan Air Force	4733/CNA-OI [dual marks]
4734	C-130H	Greek Air Force	75-0549+ 752 [+ USAF]
4735	C-130H	USAF	74-2134
4736	C-130H	(Zaire Air Force)	9T-TCG+ [+ Zaire] [w/o 19Apr90 near Kinshasa, Zaire]
4737	VC-130H	Royal Saudi Air Force	112
4738	C-130H	Royal Moroccan Air Force	4738/CNA-OJ [dual marks]
4739	C-130H	Royal Moroccan Air Force	4739/CNA-OK [dual marks]
4740	C-130H	Royal Saudi Air Force	466
4741	C-130H	Royal Saudi Air Force	467
4742	C-130H	Royal Moroccan Air Force	4742/CNA-OL [dual marks]
4743	C-130H	(Ecuadorean Air Force)	HC-BEF 743 [w/o 29Apr82 into mountain, Marisal Sucre, Quito, Ecuador]
4744	C-130H	(Bolivian Air Force)	TAM-90//CP-1375+ [+ dual marks] [w/o 28Sep79 into sea after take-off from Panama-Tocumen Airport, Panama]
4745	C-130H	Royal Saudi Air Force	1615
4746	KC-130H	Royal Saudi Air Force	1616+ 3205 [+ Saudi Arabia]
4747	C-130H	Cameroon Air Force	TJX-AC+ TJX-CF [+Cameroons]
4748	C-130H	(Ecuadorean Air Force)	748 [w/o 12Jul78 into Pichincha mountains, Ecuador]
4749	C-130H-30	Portuguese Air Force	6801+ 16801 [+ Portugal]
4750	KC-130H	Royal Saudi Air Force	1617+ 3206 [+ Saudi Arabia]
4751	C-130H	Royal Saudi Air Force	468
4752	C-130H	Cameroon Air Force	TJX-AD+ TJ-XAD TJX-CD [+Cameroons]
4753	C-130H-30	Portuguese Air Force	6802+ 16802 [+ Portugal]

LOCKHEED C-130/L-100 HERCULES

C/n	Model	Last known Owner/Operator	Identities/fates/comments (where appropriate)
4754	C-130H	(Royal Saudi Air Force)	469 [w/o 21Mar91 near Khafji, Ras-al-Mishab, Saudi Arabia; hulk noted Dhahran AFB]
4755	C-130H	Royal Saudi Air Force	1618+ 482 [+ Saudi Arabia]
4756	C-130H	(Royal Saudi Air Force)	470 [w/o 27Mar89 Jeddah, Saudi Arabia]
4757	HC-130H	(US Coast Guard)	77-0317+ 1600 [+ USAF] [w/o 30Jly82 3 miles S of Attu, Aleutian Islands, AK]
4758	C-130H	Royal Saudi Air Force	1619+ 483 [+ Saudi Arabia]
4759	C-130H	Transportes Aereos Bolivianos	TAM-69+ TAM-91//CP-1376^ CP-1376 [+ Bolivia; ^ dual marks]
4760	HC-130H	US Coast Guard	77-0318+ 1601 [+ USAF] [stored AMARC Aug01]
4761	C-130H	(Philippine Air Force)	4761 [w/o 15Dec93 Mount Barnase, Camarines Sur, Southern Luzon, Philippines]
4762	HC-130H	US Coast Guard	77-0319+ 1602 [+ USAF] [stored AMARC Aug01]
4763	L-100-30	Lynden Air Cargo	N108AK VH-CYO N108AK N909SJ N404LC
4764	HC-130H	US Coast Guard	77-0320+ 1603 [+ USAF] [wfu 2003 Elizabeth City, NC, GIA]
4765	C-130H	Gabon Air Force	TR-KKC
4766	C-130H	Sudan Air Force	78-0745+ 1100^ ST-AHR ST-AIF 1100 [+ USAF; ^ Sudan]
4767	C-130H	Sudan Air Force	78-0746+ 1101^ ST-AHN 1101 [+ USAF; ^ Sudan]
4768	KC-130R	US Marine Corps	75-0321+ 160625 [+ USAF] [stored AMARC 15Feb08]
4769	C-130H	Sudan Air Force	78-0747+ 1102 [+ Sudan]
4770	KC-130R	US Marine Corps	75-0322+ 160626 [+ USAF]
4771	C-130H	Sudan Air Force	78-0748+ 1103 [+ USAF]
4772	C-130H	Portuguese Air Force	77-1741+ 6803^ 16803 [+ USAF; ^ Portugal]
4773	KC-130R	US Marine Corps	75-0323+ 160627 [+ USAF]
4774	C-130H	Sudan Air Force	78-0749+ 1104 [+ USAF]
4775	C-130H	Sudan Air Force	78-0750+ 1105^ ST-AHO 1105 [+ USAF; ^ Sudan]
4776	KC-130R	US Marine Corps	75-0324+ 160628 [+ USAF]
4777	C-130H	Portuguese Air Force	77-1742+ 6804^ 16804 [+ USAF; ^ Portugal]
4778	C-130H	Portuguese Air Force	78-0726+ 6805^ 16805 [+ USAF; ^ Portugal]
4779	C-130H	Royal Jordanian Air Force	144+ 744+ 344 [+ Jordan]
4780	C-130H	ex Royal Australian Air Force	A97-001 [wfu & stored Feb10 Richmond, NSW, Australia]
4781	C-130H	Royal Netherlands Air Force	160608+ N14781 G-781 [+ USN]
4782	C-130H	Royal Australian Air Force	A97-002
4783	C-130H	ex Royal Australian Air Force	A97-003 [wfu & stored Richmond, NSW, Australia]
4784	C-130H	Royal Australian Air Force	A97-004
4785	C-130H	Royal Australian Air Force	A97-005
4786	C-130H	Royal Australian Air Force	A97-006
4787	C-130H	Royal Australian Air Force	A97-007
4788	C-130H	Royal Australian Air Force	A97-008
4789	C-130H	Royal Australian Air Force	A97-009
4790	C-130H	ex Royal Australian Air Force	A97-010 [wfu & stored by Apr08 Richmond, NSW, Australia]
4791	C-130H	Royal Australian Air Force	A97-011
4792	C-130H	(Egyptian Air Force)	78-0755+ 1276//SU-BAH^ [+ USAF; ^ dual marks; w/o 29May81 Cairo West, Egypt]
4793	C-130H	ex Royal Australian Air Force	A97-012 [wfu & stored by Apr08 Richmond, NSW, Australia]
4794	C-130H	Egyptian Air Force	78-0756+ 1277//SU-BAI^ [+ USAF; ^ dual marks]
4795	C-130H	Egyptian Air Force	78-0757+ 1278//SU-BAJ^ [+ USAF; ^ dual marks]
4796	L-100-30	Tepper Aviation	9Q-CBJ N123GA N8183J N2679C
4797	C-130H	Egyptian Air Force	78-0758+ 1279//SU-BAK^ [+ USAF; ^ dual marks]
4798	L-100-30	Libyan Arab Air Cargo	N4301M N501AK 5A-DJQ
4799	L-100-30	Bradley Air Services	C-GHPW
4800	L-100-30	Indonesian Air Force	N4304M A-1314
4801	C-130H	Venezuelan Air Force	3134
4802	C-130H	Egyptian Air Force	78-0759+ 1280//SU-BAL^ [+ USAF; ^ dual marks]
4803	VC-130H	Egyptian Air Force	78-0760+ 1281//SU-BAM^ [+ USAF; ^ dual marks]
4804	C-130H	Egyptian Air Force	78-0761+ 1282//SU-BAN^ [+ USAF; ^ dual marks]
4805	C-130H	Egyptian Air Force	78-0762+ 1283//SU-BAP^ [+ USAF; ^ dual marks]
4806	C-130H	Egyptian Air Force	78-0763+ 1284//SU-BAQ^ [+ USAF; ^ dual marks]
4807	C-130H	Egyptian Air Force	78-0764+ 1285//SU-BAR^ [+ USAF; ^ dual marks]
4808	C-130H	Egyptian Air Force	78-0765+ 1286//SU-BAS^ [+ USAF; ^ dual marks]
4809	C-130H	Egyptian Air Force	78-0766+ 1287//SU-BAT^ [+ USAF; ^ dual marks]
4810	C-130H	Egyptian Air Force	78-0767+ 1288//SU-BAU^ [+ USAF; ^ dual marks]
4811	C-130H	Egyptian Air Force	78-0768+ 1289//SU-BAV^ [+ USAF; ^ dual marks]
4812	C-130H	Ecuadorean Air Force	HC-BGO 812+ 892 [+ Ecuador]
4813	C-130H	Royal Jordanian Air Force	345

LOCKHEED C-130/L-100 HERCULES

C/n	Model	Last known Owner/Operator	Identities/fates/comments (where appropriate)
4814	KC-130H	Argentine Air Force	TC-69 [wfu El Palomar, Argentina]
4815	C-130H	USAF	78-0806
4816	KC-130H	Argentine Air Force	TC-70
4817	C-130H	USAF	78-0807
4818	C-130H	USAF	78-0808
4819	C-130H	USAF	78-0809
4820	C-130H	USAF	78-0810
4821	C-130H	USAF	78-0811
4822	C-130H	USAF	78-0812
4823	C-130H	USAF	78-0813
4824	L-100-30	(Indonesian Air Force)	PK-PLU A-1329+ [+ not fully confirmed; w/o 20Dec01 Malikul Saleh, Indonesia]
4825	C-130H	Yemen Airways	1150+ 7O-ADE [+ Yemen]
4826	L-100-30	(Pelita Air Service)	PK-PLV [w/o 23Sep94 into Kowloon Bay after take-off from Kai Tak, Hong Kong]
4827	C-130H	Yemen Airways	1160+ 7O-ADD [+ Yemen] [possibly w/o mid-Nov10 Sana'a, Yemen]
4828	L-100-30	Indonesian Air Force	PK-PLW A-1328
4829	C-130H	(Republic of Niger)	5U-MBD [w/o 16Apr97 near Sorei, Niamey, Niger]
4830	L-100-20	(TAAG-Angola Airlines)	N4080M D2-EAS [shot down 16May81 by missile near Menongue, Angola]
4831	C-130H	Republic of Niger	5U-MBH
4832	L-100-20	(TAAG-Angola Airlines)	N4081M D2-THA [DBF 08Jun86 after belly-landing Dondo, Angola]
4833	L-100-30	(Transportes Aereos Bolivianos)	N4083M TAM-92+ CP-1564 [+ Bolivia] [shot down 16Mar91 by missile near Malanje, Angola while operating for Transafrik]
4834	L-100-30	United Arab Emirates Air Force	N4085M 311+ A6-QFY 311 [+ UAE]
4835	C-130H	Spanish Air Force	T.10-08//311-05 T.10-08/31-05
4836	C-130H	Spanish Air Force	T.10-09//311-06 T.10-09/31-06
4837	C-130H	Royal Saudi Air Force	N4098M HZ-MS19 1632
4838	C-130H	Indonesian Air Force	A-1315
4839	L-100-30	(Transafrik)	N4110M D-ACWF N3847Z D2-EHD [shot down 02Jan99 by UNITA rebels, near Bailundo, 50 miles N of Huambo, Angola, whilst searching for C-130 S9-CAO]
4840	C-130H	Indonesian Air Force	A-1316
4841	C-130H	Spanish Air Force	T.10-10//312-04 T.10-10/31-07
4842	C-130H	Republic of Singapore Air Force	730
4843	VC-130H	Saudi Royal Flight	N4099M HZ-HM5 HZ-114
4844	C-130H	Republic of Singapore Air Force	731
4845	VC-130H	Royal Saudi Air Force	N4101M HZ-HM6 HZ-115 485
4846	C-130H	Republic of Singapore Air Force	N4108M 732
4847	KC-130H	Royal Malaysian Air Force	FM2451 M30-07
4848	C-130H	Republic of Singapore Air Force	N4113M 733
4849	KC-130H	Royal Malaysian Air Force	N4123M FM2452+ M30-08 [+ Malaysia]
4850	L-100-20	Peruvian Air Force	N4115M 397//OB-1377+ 397//OB-1375+ [Peru; dual marks]
4851	L-100-30	Mexican Air Force	N4116M XC-EXP 10611+ 3611 [+ Mexico]
4852	C-130H	USAF	79-0473
4853	L-100-20	Peruvian Air Force	N4119M 398//OB-1376+ [+ dual marks] [wfu Lima, Peru]
4854	C-130H	USAF	79-0474
4855	C-130H	USAF	79-0475
4856	C-130H	USAF	79-0476
4857	C-130H	USAF	79-0477
4858	C-130H	USAF	79-0478
4859	C-130H	USAF	79-0479
4860	C-130H	USAF	79-0480
4861	C-130H	Royal Thai Air Force	79-1714+ L.8-1/23//60101 [+ USAF] [serial followed by code after double slash; damaged in floods Oct11 Don Muang, Thailand]
4862	C-130H	Royal Thai Air Force	79-1715+ L.8-2/23//60102 [+ USAF] [serial followed by code after double slash]
4863	C-130H	Royal Thai Air Force	79-1716+ L.8-3/23//60103 [+ USAF] [serial followed by code after double slash]
4864	C-130H-30	Indonesian Air Force	A-1317 [first stretched production military Hercules]
4865	C-130H-30	Indonesian Air Force	A-1318
4866	KC-130H	Royal Malaysian Air Force	FM2453+ M30-09 [+ Malaysia]
4867	EC-130Q	US Navy	161223 [stored Cherry Point MCAS, NC; for scrap 2005?]
4868	C-130H-30	Indonesian Air Force	A-1319
4869	C-130H-30	Indonesian Air Force	A-1320
4870	C-130H-30	Indonesian Air Force	A-1321+ A-1341 [+ Indonesia]
4871	KC-130H	Spanish Air Force	TK.10-11//312-05 TK.10-11/31-53

LOCKHEED C-130/L-100 HERCULES

C/n	Model	Last known Owner/Operator	Identities/fates/comments (where appropriate)
4872	KC-130H	(Royal Saudi Air Force)	1620 [w/o 24Feb85 Riyadh, Saudi Arabia]
4873	KC-130H	Royal Saudi Air Force	1621+ 3207 [+ Saudi Arabia]
4874	KC-130H	Spanish Air Force	TK.10-12//312-06 TK.10-12/31-54
4875	C-130H	Royal Moroccan Air Force	N4130M+ 4875/CNA-OM^ [+ marks not confirmed; ^dual marks]
4876	C-130H	Royal Moroccan Air Force	N4133M 4876/CNA-ON^ [^ dual marks]
4877	C-130H	Royal Moroccan Air Force	N4137M+ 4877/CNA-OO [+ marks not confirmed; ^dual marks]
4878	C-130H	Oman Air Force	N4138M 81-0001+ 501 [+ USAF]
4879	C-130H	Abu Dhabi Air Force	N4140M 1213
4880	L-100-30T	(Air Algerie)	N4148M 7T-VHG [w/o 13Aug06 nr Piacenza, Italy]
4881	C-130H	Royal Swedish Air Force	84004 [code 844]
4882	C-130H	Abu Dhabi Air Force	N4147M 1214
4883	L-100-30	(Air Algerie)	N4152M 7T-VHK [DBR 01Aug89 Tamanrasset, Algeria]
4884	C-130H	Royal Swedish Air Force	84005 [code 845]
4885	C-130H	Royal Swedish Air Force	84006 [code 846]
4886	L-100-30	Air Algerie	N4160M 7T-VHL
4887	C-130H	Royal Swedish Air Force	84007 [code 847]
4888	C-130H	Royal Moroccan Air Force	N4162M 4888/CNA-OP+ [+ dual marks]
4889	L-100-30	Indonesian Air Force	PK-PLR A-1327
4890	C-130H	Royal Swedish Air Force	84008 [code 848]
4891	L-100-30	Argentine Air Force	N4170M LQ-FAA LV-APW TC-100
4892	C-130H	(Royal Moroccan Air Force)	4892/CNA-OQ+ [+ dual marks; w/o 26Jly11 Goulimime, Morocco]
4893	L-100-30	Ecuadorean Air Force	N4175M 893
4894	C-130H-30	Algerian Government	7T-VHN 7T-WHN
4895	L-100-30	United Arab Air Force	TR-KKD PH-SHE TR-KKD 1216+ A6-MAX 1216 [+UAE]
4896	EC-130Q	(NASA)	161494 [wfu 1995 Wallops Island, VA; used for spares; b/u Oct00]
4897	C-130H-30	Algerian Government	7T-VHO 7T-WHO
4898	C-130H-MP	(Indonesian Air Force)	AI-1322+ A-1322 [+ Indonesia] [w/o 21Nov85 near Berastagi, North Sumatra, Indonesia]
4899	C-130H-30	Indonesian Air Force	A-1323
4900	C-130H	USAF	80-0320
4901	EC-130Q	Kenosha Military Museum	161495+ N427NA [+ USN] [wfu Oct04; preserved Pleasant Prairie, WI; 2012 to Coulson for converstion to fire fighter]
4902	C-130H	USAF	80-0321
4903	C-130H	USAF	80-0322
4904	EC-130Q	ex NASA	161496 [wfu May97 for spares Tucson, AZ; by 09Mar09 at E Nebraska scrapyard]
4905	C-130H	USAF	80-0323
4906	C-130H	USAF	80-0324
4907	KC-130H	Royal Moroccan Air Force	N4216M 4907/CNA-OR+ [+ dual marks]
4908	C-130H	USAF	80-0325
4909	KC-130H	Royal Moroccan Air Force	N4221M 4909//CNA-OS+ [+ dual marks]
4910	C-130H	USAF	80-0326
4911	C-130H	Algerian Air Force	4911//7T-WHT+ [+ dual marks]
4912	C-130H	Algerian Air Force	4912//7T-WHS+ [+ dual marks]
4913	C-130H	Algerian Air Force	4913//7T-WHY+ [+ dual marks]
4914	C-130H	Algerian Air Force	4914//7T-WHZ+ [+ dual marks]
4915	VC-130H	Saudi Royal Flight	N4185M HZ-116
4916	C-130H	Oman Air Force	82-0050+ 502 [+ USAF]
4917	L-100-30	(Indonesian Air Force)	PK-PLS PK-MLS A-1325 [w/o 20May09 near Madiun-Iswahyudi AFB, Indonesia]
4918	C-130H	Saudi Medical Services	N4240M HZ-MS21 HZ-MS2 HZ-MS21
4919	C-130H-30	Algerian Government	7T-VHM 7T-WHM
4920	C-130H	Royal Jordanian Air Force	346
4921	C-130H-30	Algerian Government	7T-VHP 7T-WHP
4922	C-130H	Saudi Medical Services	N4190M HZ-MS7
4923	L-100-30	Indonesian Air Force	PK-PLT PK-MLT A-1326
4924	C-130H	Algerian Air Force	4924//7T-WHR+ [+ dual marks]
4925	C-130H-30	Indonesian Air Force	A-1321
4926	C-130H	(Algerian Air Force)	4926//7T-WHQ+ [+ dual marks] [w/o 30Jun03 near Boufarik, Algeria]
4927	C-130H-30	(Indonesian Air Force)	A-1324 [w/o 05Oct91 Jakarta-Halim, Indonesia]
4928	C-130H	Algerian Air Force	4928//7T-WHJ+ [+ dual marks]
4929	C-130H	Royal Jordanian Air Force	N4202M 347
4930	C-130H	Algerian Air Force	4930//7T-WHI+ [+ dual marks]
4931	HC-130H	US Coast Guard	81-0999+ 1790 [+ USAF]

LOCKHEED C-130/L-100 HERCULES

C/n	Model	Last known Owner/Operator	Identities/fates/comments (where appropriate)
4932	EC-130Q	(National Center for Atmospheric Research)	161531 N41RF (N4086L) N41RF [b/u Apr97 by AirPro International, Tucson, AZ]
4933	C-130H-30	Cameroon Air Force	N4206M TJX-CE+ TJ-XCE [Cameroons]
4934	C-130H	Algerian Air Force	4934//7T-WHF+ [+ dual marks]
4935	C-130H	Algerian Air Force	4935//7T-WHE+ [+ dual marks]
4936	C-130H	Egyptian Air Force	82-0086+ 1290//SU-BEW^ [+ USAF; ^ dual marks]
4937	C-130H	Egyptian Air Force	82-0087+ 1291//SU-BEX^ [+ USAF; ^ dual marks]
4938	C-130H	Egyptian Air Force	82-0088+ 1292//SU-BEY^ [+ USAF; ^ dual marks]
4939	C-130H	USAF	81-0626
4940	KC-130H	Republic of Singapore Air Force	N4237M 734
4941	C-130H	USAF	81-0627
4942	C-130H	USAF	81-0628
4943	C-130H	USAF	80-0332
4944	C-130H	USAF	81-0629
4945	C-130H	USAF	81-0630
4946	C-130H	USAF	81-0631
4947	HC-130H	US Coast Guard	82-0081+ 1700 [+ USAF]
4948	C-130H	Oman Air Force	82-0053+ 503 [+ USAF]
4949	L-100-30	(Kuwait Air Force)	N4107F 322 [captured by Iraqi forces & shot down 27Feb91 by RAF Buccaneer S.2B XX901 at Shayka Mayhar AB, Iraq]
4950	L-100-30	Saudi Royal Flight	N4253M HZ-MS05 HZ-128
4951	L-100-30	Kuwait Air Force	N4249Y 323
4952	L-100-30	Saudi Medical Services	N4254M HZ-MS06
4953	L-100-30	Kuwait Air Force	N4242N 324
4954	L-100-30	Saudi Royal Fllght	HZ-117
4955	L-100-30	Kuwait Air Force	N4232B 325
4956	L-100-30	Saudi Medical Services	N4255M HZ-MS09
4957	L-100-30	Saudi Royal Flight	N4261M HZ-MS10 HZ-129
4958	HC-130H	US Coast Guard	82-0082+ 1701 [+ USAF]
4959	C-130H-30	Royal Thai Air Force	82-0666+ L.8-4/26?//60104 [+ USAF] [serial followed by code after double slash]
4960	L-100-30	Saudi Royal Flight	N4266M HZ-MS14 HZ-132
4961	C-130H-30	Dubai Air Force	312
4962	C-130H-30	ex Nigerian Air Force	N4081M 916 [wfu Lagos, Nigeria; l/n Sep11]
4963	C-130H-30	Nigerian Air Force	N4099R 917
4964	C-130H	Colombian Air Force	N4080M 1004
4965	C-130H	Colombian Air Force	N41030 1005
4966	HC-130H	US Coast Guard	82-0083+ 1702 [+ USAF]
4967	HC-130H	US Coast Guard	82-0084+ 1703 [+ USAF]
4968	C-130H	USAF	82-0054
4969	HC-130H	US Coast Guard	82-0085+ 1704 [+ USAF]
4970	C-130H	USAF	82-0055
4971	C-130H	USAF	82-0056
4972	KC-130T	US Marine Corps	82-0077+ 162308 [+ USAF]
4973	C-130H	USAF	82-0057
4974	KC-130T	US Marine Corps	82-0078+ 162309 [+ USAF]
4975	C-130H	USAF	82-0058
4976	C-130H	Japan Air Self Defense Force	82-0051+ 35-1071 [+ USAF]
4977	C-130H	USAF	82-0059
4978	KC-130T	US Marine Corps	82-0079+ 162310 [+ USAF]
4979	C-130H	USAF	82-0060
4980	C-130H	Japan Air Self Defense Force	82-0052+ 35-1072 [+ USAF]
4981	KC-130T	US Marine Corps	82-0080+ 162311 [+ USAF]
4982	C-130H	USAF	82-0061
4983	C-130H-30	Abu Dhabi Air Force	N4161T 1211
4984	EC-130Q	National Science Foundation	162312+ N130AR [+ USN]
4985	C-130H-30	(Abu Dhabi Air Force)	N4249Y 1212(2) [w/o 05Aug08 Kabul International, Afghanistan]
4986	C-130H-30	Royal Saudi Air Force	N4243M HZ-MS8 1631
4987	C-130H-30	Algerian Air Force	4987//7T-WHD+ [+ dual marks]
4988	C-130H	Royal Netherlands Air Force	162313+ N9239G G-988 [+ USN]
4989	C-130H-30	Algerian Air Force	4989//7T-WHL+ [+ dual marks]
4990	C-130H	Brazilian Air Force	N4187W 2466
4991	C-130H	Brazilian Air Force	N4187W 2467

LOCKHEED C-130/L-100 HERCULES

C/n	Model	Last known Owner/Operator	Identities/fates/comments (where appropriate)
4992	L-100-30	Libyan Arab Air Cargo	N4268M (TY-BBV) 5A-DOM
4993	HC-130H	(US Coast Guard)	83-0007+ 1705 [+ USAF] [w/o 29Oct09 in Pacific Ocean, 24km E of San Clemente, CA after mid-air collision with Bell AH-1 Super Cobra]
4994	CC-130H	Canadian Armed Forces	130334
4995	CC-130H	Canadian Armed Forces	130335
4996	HC-130H	US Coast Guard	83-0505+ 1706 [+ USAF]
4997	C-130H-30	Algerian Air Force	7T-VHA 4997//7T-WHA+ [+ dual marks] [damaged 19Nov10 Paris-Le Bourget, France; 11May11 airfreighted out]
4998	C-130H	(Brazilian Air Force)	2468 [w/o 14Dec87 into sea during approach to Fernando de Noronha Island, Brazil]
4999	HC-130H	US Coast Guard	83-0506+ 1707 [+ USAF]
5000	L-100-30	Libyan Arab Air Cargo	N4269M (TY-BBU) 119+ 5A-DOO [+ Libya]
5001	C-130H-30	Nigerian Air Force	918
5002	HC-130H	US Coast Guard	83-0507+ 1708 [+ USAF]
5003	C-130H-30	Spanish Air Force	N73230 TL.10-1//31-01
5004	MC-130H	USAF	83-1212
5005	HC-130H	US Coast Guard	83-0508 1709
5006	C-130H-30	South Korean Air Force	N4080M 5006+ 45-006 [+ South Korea]
5007	LC-130R	USAF	83-0490
5008	C-130H	USAF	83-0486
5009	KC-130T	US Marine Corps	83-0503+ 162785 [+ USAF]
5010	LC-130R	USAF	83-0491
5011	KC-130T	US Marine Corps	83-0504+ 162786 [+ USAF]
5012	C-130H	USAF	83-0487
5013	LC-130R	USAF	83-0492
5014	C-130H	USAF	83-0488
5015	C-130H	Japan Air Self Defense Force	83-0001+ 45-1073 [+ USAF]
5016	LC-130R	USAF	83-0493
5017	C-130H	Japan Air Self Defense Force	83-0002+ 45-1074 [+ USAF]
5018	C-130H	USAF	83-0489
5019	C-130H-30	South Korean Air Force	N73232 5019+ 45-019 [+ South Korea]
5020	C-130H	Tunisian Air Force	N4249Y Z21011//TS-MTA+ [+ dual marks] [damaged 1995; late 2008 to Derco/Airod Malaysia for rebuild; reported for Philippines AF]
5021	C-130H	Tunisian Air Force	N41030 'TS-MTA' Z21012//TS-MTB+ [+ dual marks]
5022	L-100-30	Ethiopian Airlines	N4272M ET-AJK [unconfirmed report transferred to Ethiopian Air Force]
5023	HC-130H	US Coast Guard	N73235 85-1360+ 1716 [+ USAF]
5024	L-100-30	United Arab Air Force	N4274M TR-LBV G-52-23 1215+ A6-MAC 1215 [+ UAE]
5025	L-100-30	Lynden Air Cargo	N4276M B-3002 ZS-OLG N405LC
5026	MC-130H	USAF	N4278M 86-1699
5027	L-100-30	Northcap LLC/Tepper Aviation	N4278M B-3004 ZS-JAG N4557C N3796B
5028	HC-130H	(US Coast Guard)	84-0479+ 1710 [+ USAF] [w/o 28Jun06 Kodiak, AK]
5029	L-100-30	(Ethiopian Airlines)	N4232B ET-AJL [w/o 17Sep91 Mount Arey, near Djibouti City, Ethiopia]
5030	C-130H-30	South Korean Air Force	N4249Y 5030+ 55-030 [+ South Korea]
5031	HC-130H	US Coast Guard	84-0480 1711
5032	L-100-30	APA Leasing LLC	N4281M N898QR N3755P 41901+ [+ at Bullhead City, AZ 11Jan08 lease to the CIA]
5033	HC-130H	US Coast Guard	84-0481+ 1712 [+ USAF]
5034	HC-130H	US Coast Guard	84-0482+ 1713 [+ USAF]
5035	HC-130H	US Coast Guard	85-0051+ 1714 [+ USAF]
5036	C-130H-30	South Korean Air Force	N4161T 5036+ 55-036 [South Korea]
5037	HC-130H	US Coast Guard	85-0052 1715 [+ USAF]
5038	C-130H	USAF	84-0204
5039	C-130H	USAF	84-0205
5040	KC-130T	US Marine Corps	84-0477 163022 [+ USAF]
5041	MC-130H	(USAF)	84-0475 [w/o 12Jun02 near Gardez, Afghanistan]
5042	MC-130H	USAF	84-0476
5043	C-130H	USAF	84-0206
5044	C-130H	USAF	84-0207
5045	KC-130T	US Marine Corps	84-0478 163023 [+ USAF]
5046	C-130H	USAF	84-0208
5047	C-130H	USAF	84-0209
5048	L-100-30	Transadvaree	N82178
5049	C-130H	USAF	84-0210

LOCKHEED C-130/L-100 HERCULES

C/n	Model	Last known Owner/Operator	Identities/fates/comments (where appropriate)
5050	C-130H	(USAF)	84-0211 [DBR 28Sep04 New Castle County, DE by tornado; b/u]
5051	C-130H	USAF	84-0212
5052	C-130H	USAF	84-0213
5053	MC-130H	USAF	85-0011
5054	MC-130H	(USAF)	85-0012 [DBR 29Dec04 Qayyarah, Iraq]
5055	L-100-30	Prescott Support	N8213G
5056	L-100-30	Ruftberg Company	N8218J
5057			[not built]
5058	C-130H	Taiwan Air Force	85-0013+ 1301 [+ USAF]
5059	C-130H	Taiwan Air Force	85-0014+ 1302 [+ USAF]
5060	C-130H	Taiwan Air Force	85-0015+ 1303 [+ USAF]
5061	C-130H	Taiwan Air Force	85-0016+ 1304 [+ USAF]
5062	C-130H	Taiwan Air Force	85-0017+ 1305 [+ USAF]
5063	C-130H	Taiwan Air Force	85-0018+ 1306 [+ USAF]
5064	C-130H	Taiwan Air Force	85-0019+ 1307 [+ USAF]
5065	C-130H	Taiwan Air Force	85-0020+ 1308 [+ USAF]
5066	C-130H	Taiwan Air Force	85-0021+ 1309 [+ USAF]
5067	C-130H	(Taiwan Air Force)	85-0022+ 1310 [w/o 10Oct97 Taipei-Sungshang, Taiwan]
5068	C-130H	Taiwan Air Force	85-0023+ 1311 [+ USAF]
5069	C-130H	Taiwan Air Force	85-0024+ 1312 [+ USAF]
5070	C-130H	Republic of Singapore Air Force	N73233 735
5071	C-130H	USAF	85-1361
5072	C-130H	USAF	85-1362
5073	C-130H	USAF	85-0035
5074	C-130H	USAF	85-0036
5075	C-130H	USAF	85-1363
5076	C-130H	USAF	85-1364
5077	C-130H	USAF	85-0037
5078	C-130H	USAF	85-1365
5079	C-130H	USAF	85-0038
5080	C-130H	USAF	85-0039
5081	C-130H	USAF	85-1366
5082	C-130H	USAF	85-1367
5083	C-130H	USAF	85-0040
5084	C-130H	USAF	85-1368
5085	KC-130T	US Marine Corps	85-0045+ 163310 [+ USAF]
5086	C-130H	USAF	85-0041
5087	KC-130T	US Marine Corps	85-0046+ 163311 [+ USAF]
5088	C-130H	Japan Air Self Defense Force	85-0025+ 75-1075 [+ USAF]
5089	C-130H	USAF	85-0042
5090	C-130H	Japan Air Self Defense Force	85-0026+ 75-1076 [+ USAF]
5091	MC-130H	USAF	87-0023
5092	MC-130H	USAF	87-0024
5093	C-130H	USAF	86-1391
5094	C-130H	USAF	86-0410
5095	C-130H	USAF	86-1392
5096	C-130H	USAF	86-1393
5097	C-130H	USAF	86-0411
5098	C-130H	(USAF)	86-0412 [crash-landed 27Jun08 on a landing strip NE of Baghdad International Airport, Iraq; later blown up by US forces]
5099	C-130H	USAF	86-1394
5100	C-130H	USAF	86-0413
5101	C-130H	USAF	86-1395
5102	C-130H	USAF	86-0414
5103	C-130H	USAF	86-1396
5104	HC-130H	US Coast Guard	86-0420+ 1717 [+ USAF]
5105	C-130H	USAF	86-0415
5106	HC-130H	US Coast Guard	86-0421+ 1718 [+ USAF]
5107	HC-130H	US Coast Guard	86-0422+ 1719 [+ USAF]
5108	C-130H	Japan Air Self Defense Force	86-0372+ 75-1077 [+ USAF]
5109	C-130H	Japan Air Self Defense Force	86-0373+ 75-1078 [+ USAF]
5110	C-130H	USAF	86-0418
5111	C-130H	USAF	86-1397

LOCKHEED C-130/L-100 HERCULES

C/n	Model	Last known Owner/Operator	Identities/fates/comments (where appropriate)
5112	C-130H	USAF	86-1398
5113	C-130H	USAF	86-0419
5114	C-130H	French Air Force	5114/61-PA//F-RAPA
5115	MC-130H	USAF	87-0125
5116	C-130H	French Air Force	5116/61-PB//F-RAPB
5117	MC-130H	USAF	87-0126
5118	MC-130H	(USAF)	87-0127 [w/o 31Mar05 Driza mountain, SE of Tirana, Albania]
5119	C-130H	French Air Force	5119/61-PC//F-RAPC
5120	HC-130H	US Coast Guard	87-0156+ 1720 [+ USAF]
5121	NC-130H	US Navy	87-0157+ 1721^ 870157# [+ USAF; ^ USN; # E-2C 2000 rotordome testbed]
5122	C-130H	USAF	87-9281
5123	C-130H	USAF	87-9282
5124	C-130H	USAF	87-9283
5125	MC-130W	USAF	87-9284
5126	C-130H	USAF	87-9285
5127	MC-130W	USAF	87-9286
5128	C-130H	USAF	87-9287
5129	MC-130W	USAF	87-9288
5130	MC-130H	USAF	88-0191
5131	MC-130H	USAF	88-0192
5132	MC-130H	USAF	88-0193
5133	MC-130H	USAF	88-0194
5134	MC-130H	USAF	88-0195
5135	MC-130H	USAF	88-0264
5136	C-130H	Japan Air Self Defense Force	87-0137+ 85-1079 [+ USAF]
5137	C-130H	Venezuelan Air Force	2716
5138	KC-130H	Japan Air Self Defense Force	87-0138+ 85-1080 [+ USAF]
5139	AC-130U	USAF	87-0128
5140	C-130H	French Air Force	5140/61-PD//F-RAPD
5141	C-130H	(Chad Air Force)	N73238 TT-PAF [w/o 11Jun06 Abeche, Chad]
5142	C-130H-30	French Air Force	5142/61-PE//F-RAPE
5143	KC-130T	US Marine Corps	86-1973+ 163591 [+ USAF]
5144	C-130H-30	French Air Force	5144/61-PF//F-RAPF
5145	KC-130T	US Marine Corps	86-1974+ 163592 [+ USAF]
5146	C-130H-30	Royal Thai Air Force	L.8-5/31//60105 [serial followed by code after double slash]
5147	KC-130T	US Marine Corps	87-1976+ 164105 [+ USAF]
5148	C-130H-30	Royal Thai Air Force	L.8-6/31//60106 [serial followed by code after double slash]
5149	KC-130T	US Marine Corps	87-1977+ 164106 [+ USAF]
5150	C-130H-30	French Air Force	N4242N 5150/61-PG//F-RAPG
5151	C-130H-30	French Air Force	5151/61-PH//F-RAPH
5152	C-130H-30	French Air Force	5152/61-PI//F-RAPI
5153	C-130H-30	French Air Force	N7323S 5153/61-PJ//F-RAPJ
5154	C-130H	USAF	88-4401
5155	C-130H	USAF	88-4402
5156	C-130H	USAF	88-4403
5157	C-130H	USAF	88-4404
5158	C-130H	USAF	88-4405
5159	C-130H	USAF	88-4406
5160	C-130H	USAF	88-4407
5161	C-130H	(USAF)	88-4408 [w/o 01Apr97 Tegucigalpa, Honduras]
5162	MC-130W	USAF	88-1301
5163	MC-130W	USAF	88-1302
5164	MC-130W	USAF	88-1303
5165	MC-130W	USAF	88-1304
5166	MC-130W	USAF	88-1305
5167	MC-130W	USAF	88-1306
5168	MC-130W	USAF	88-1307
5169	MC-130W	USAF	88-1308
5170	C-130H	Japan Air Self Defense Force	88-1800+ 95-1081 [+ USAF]
5171	C-130H	Japan Air Self Defense Force	88-1801+ 95-1082 [+ USAF]
5172	C-130H	Japan Air Self Defense Force	88-1802+ 95-1083 [+ USAF]
5173	MC-130H	USAF	88-1803
5174	KC-130T	US Marine Corps	88-1806+ 164180 [+ USAF]

LOCKHEED C-130/L-100 HERCULES

C/n	Model	Last known Owner/Operator	Identities/fates/comments (where appropriate)
5175	KCC-130H	Canadian Armed Forces	130338 [designation not confirmed but is tanker]
5176	KC-130T	US Marine Corps	88-1807+ 164181 [+ USAF]
5177	KCC-130H	Canadian Armed Forces	N4080M 130339 [designation not confirmed but is tanker]
5178	C-130H	South Korean Air Force	5178+ 95-178 [+ South Korea]
5179	C-130H	South Korean Air Force	5179+ 95-179 [+ South Korea]
5180	C-130H	South Korean Air Force	5180+ 95-180 [+ South Korea]
5181	C-130H	South Korean Air Force	5181+ 95-181 [+ South Korea]
5182	C-130H	South Korean Air Force	5182+ 05-182 [+ South Korea]
5183	C-130H	South Korean Air Force	N73233 5183+ 05-183 [+ South Korea]
5184	C-130H-30	Chad Air Force	TT-AAH TT-PAH
5185	C-130H	South Korean Air Force	N41030 5185+ 05-185 [+ South Korea]
5186	C-130H	South Korean Air Force	5186+ 05-186 [+ South Korea]
5187	C-130H-30	Egyptian Air Force	1293//SU-BKS [dual marks]
5188	C-130H	USAF	89-1181
5189	KCC-130H	Canadian Armed Forces	130340 [designation not confirmed but is tanker]
5190	C-130H	USAF	89-1182
5191	C-130H-30	Egyptian Air Force	1294//SU-BKT [dual marks]
5192	C-130H	USAF	89-1183
5193	C-130H	USAF	89-1184
5194	C-130H	USAF	89-1185
5195	C-130H	USAF	89-1186
5196	C-130H	USAF	89-1187
5197	C-130H	USAF	89-1188
5198	MC-130W	USAF	89-1051
5199	AC-130U	USAF	89-1052
5200	KCC-130H	Canadian Armed Forces	130341 [designation not confirmed but is tanker]
5201	AC-130U	USAF	89-1053
5202	HC-130N(R)	USAF	88-2101
5203	C-130H	USAF	89-1054 [for conversion to AC-130U]
5204	C-130H	USAF	89-1055 [for conversion to AC-130U]
5205	C-130H	USAF	89-1056 [for conversion to AC-130U]
5206	C-130H-30	Egyptian Air Force	1295//SU-BKU [dual marks]
5207	KC-130H	Canadian Armed Forces	130342 [extensive damage by fire 21Feb12 NAS Key West, FL]
5208	C-130H-30	Royal Thai Air Force	L.8-7/33//60107 [serial followed by code after double slash]
5209	C-130H	Royal Thai Air Force	L.8-8/33//60108 [serial followed by code after double slash]
5210	HC-130(N)	USAF	88-2102
5211	C-130H-30	Royal Saudi Air Force	471+ 1630 [+ Saudi Arabia]
5212	C-130H-30	Royal Saudi Air Force	1622
5213	C-130H	Japan Air Self Defense Force	89-0118+ 05-1084 [+ USAF]
5214	C-130H	Japan Air Self Defense Force	89-0119+ 05-1085 [+ USAF]
5215	C-130H	Taiwan Air Force	90-0176+ 1351 [+ USAF]
5216	C-130H	USAF	89-9101
5217	C-130H	USAF	89-9102
5218	C-130H	USAF	89-9103
5219	KC-130T	US Marine Corps	164441
5220	C-130H	USAF	89-9104
5221	C-130H	USAF	89-9105
5222	KC-130T	US Marine Corps	164442
5223	C-130H	USAF	89-9106
5224	C-130H-30	Algerian Air Force	7T-VHB 5224//7T-WHB [dual marks]
5225	L-100-30	Lynden Air Cargo	N4161T PJ-TAC T-312+ PJ-TAC F-WCDL N425GF N407LC P2-LAE [+ Angola]
5226	C-130H-30	French Air Force	5226/61-PK//F-RAPK
5227	C-130H-30	French Air Force	5227//61-PL//F-RAPL
5228	AC-130U	USAF	89-0509
5229	AC-130U	USAF	89-0510
5230	AC-130U	USAF	89-0511
5231	AC-130U	USAF	89-0512
5232	AC-130U	USAF	89-0513
5233	AC-130U	USAF	89-0514
5234	C-130H	Royal Saudi Air Force	N4099R 472
5235	C-130H	Royal Saudi Air Force	473
5236	MC-130H	USAF	89-0280

LOCKHEED C-130/L-100 HERCULES

C/n	Model	Last known Owner/Operator	Identities/fates/comments (where appropriate)		
5237	MC-130H	USAF	89-0281		
5238	C-130H	USAF	90-9107		
5239	C-130H	USAF	90-9108		
5240	MC-130W	USAF	90-1057		
5241	C-130H	USAF	90-1058		
5242	C-130H	USAF	90-1791		
5243	MC-130H	USAF	89-0282		
5244	MC-130H	USAF	89-0283		
5245	C-130H	USAF	90-1792		
5246	C-130H	USAF	90-1793		
5247	C-130H	USAF	90-1794		
5248	C-130H	USAF	90-1795		
5249	C-130H	USAF	90-1796		
5250	C-130H	USAF	90-1797		
5251	C-130H	USAF	90-1798		
5252	C-130H	Royal Saudi Air Force	474		
5253	C-130H	Royal Saudi Air Force	475		
5254	C-130H	Royal Saudi Air Force	1623		
5255	C-130T	US Navy	164762		
5256	MC-130H	USAF	90-0163		
5257	AC-130U	USAF	90-0164		
5258	C-130T	US Navy	164763	[Blue Angels support aircraft]	
5259	AC-130U	USAF	90-0165		
5260	KC-130T-30	US Marine Corps	164597		
5261	AC-130U	USAF	90-0166		
5262	AC-130U	USAF	90-0167		
5263	KC-130T-30	US Marine Corps	164598		
5264	C-130H-30	Portuguese Air Force	6806+	16806	[+ Portugal]
5265	MC-130H	(USAF)	90-0161	[w/o 07Aug02 near San Salvador, Puerto Rico]	
5266	MC-130H	USAF	90-0162		
5267	C-130H	Royal Saudi Air Force	1624		
5268	C-130H-30	Royal Malaysian Air Force	M30-10		
5269	C-130H	Royal Saudi Air Force	1625		
5270	C-130H	Royal Saudi Air Force	1626		
5271	C-130H	Taiwan Air Force	93-1313+	1313	[+ USAF]
5272	C-130H	Royal Thai Air Force	L.8-9/35//60109	[serial followed by code after double slash; damaged in floods Oct11 Don Muang, Thailand]	
5273	C-130H-30	Royal Netherlands Air Force	N4080M	G-273	
5274	C-130H	Royal Thai Air Force	L.8-10/35//60110	[serial followed by code after double slash]	
5275	C-130H-30	Royal Netherlands Air Force	N4080M	G-275	
5276	C-130H	Taiwan Air Force	93-1314+	1314	[+ USAF]
5277	C-130H-30	Royal Malaysian Air Force	M30-12		
5278	C-130H	USAF	91-1231	[2,000th Hercules delivered]	
5279	AC-130U	USAF	92-0253		
5280	C-130H-30	Royal Thai Air Force	L.8-11/35//60111	[serial followed by code after double slash]	
5281	C-130H-30	Royal Thai Air Force	L.8-12/35//60112	[serial followed by code after double slash]	
5282	C-130H	USAF	91-1232		
5283	C-130H	USAF	91-1233		
5284	C-130H	USAF	91-1234		
5285	C-130H	USAF	91-1235		
5286	C-130H	USAF	91-1236		
5287	C-130H	USAF	91-1237		
5288	C-130H	USAF	91-1238		
5289	C-130H	USAF	91-1239		
5290	C-130H	USAF	91-1651		
5291	C-130H	USAF	91-1652		
5292	C-130H	USAF	91-1653		
5293	C-130H	USAF	91-9141		
5294	HC-130H(N)	USAF	90-2103		
5295	C-130H	USAF	91-9142		
5296	C-130H	USAF	91-9143		
5297	C-130H	USAF	91-9144		
5298	C-130T	US Navy	164993		

LOCKHEED C-130/L-100 HERCULES

C/n	Model	Last known Owner/Operator	Identities/fates/comments (where appropriate)
5299	C-130T	US Navy	164994
5300	C-130T	US Navy	164995
5301	C-130T	US Navy	164996
5302	KC-130T	US Marine Corps	164999 [coded AX-999 then QH-999]
5303	KC-130T	US Marine Corps	165000
5304	C-130T	US Navy	164997
5305	C-130T	US Navy	164998
5306	L-100-30	Ethiopian Airlines	ET-AKG
5307	CC-130H-30	Canadian Armed Forces	N41030 130343
5308	C-130H	Taiwan Air Force	1315
5309	C-130H-30	Royal Malaysian Air Force	M30-11
5310	C-130H	USAF	92-1531
5311	C-130H-30	Royal Malaysian Air Force	M30-14
5312	C-130H	USAF	92-3021
5313	C-130H	USAF	92-3022
5314	C-130H	USAF	92-3023
5315	C-130H	USAF	92-3024
5316	C-130H-30	Royal Malaysian Air Force	M30-15
5317	C-130H	Taiwan Air Force	97-1316+ 1316 [+ USAF]
5318	C-130H	Taiwan Air Force	97-1317+ 1317 [+ USAF]
5319	C-130H-30	Royal Malaysian Air Force	M30-16
5320	CC-130H-30	Canadian Armed Forces	N4080M 130344
5321	C-130H	USAF	92-0550
5322	C-130H	USAF	92-1533
5323	C-130H	USAF	92-1534
5324	C-130H	USAF	92-1535
5325	C-130H	USAF	92-1536 [8-bladed propeller test bed, 2008]
5326	C-130H	USAF	92-1537
5327	C-130H	USAF	92-1538
5328	C-130H	USAF	92-1532
5329	C-130H	USAF	92-1452
5330	C-130H	USAF	92-1453
5331	C-130H	USAF	92-3281
5332	C-130H	USAF	92-0547
5333	C-130H	USAF	92-1454
5334	C-130H	USAF	92-3282
5335	C-130H	USAF	92-0548
5336	C-130H	USAF	92-3283
5337	C-130H	USAF	92-0549
5338	C-130H	USAF	92-3284
5339	KC-130T	US Marine Corps	165162
5340	KC-130T	US Marine Corps	165163
5341	C-130T	US Navy	165158
5342	C-130T	US Navy	165159
5343	C-130H	USAF	92-1451
5344	C-130T	US Navy	165160
5345	C-130T	US Navy	165161 [code BD]
5346	C-130H	USAF	92-0551
5347	C-130H	USAF	92-3285 [stored 17Jun08 AMARC]
5348	C-130H	USAF	92-0552
5349	C-130H	USAF	92-3286
5350	C-130H	USAF	92-0553
5351	C-130H	USAF	92-3287
5352	C-130H	USAF	92-0554
5353	C-130H	USAF	92-3288
5354	C-130H	Taiwan Air Force	97-1318+ 1318 [+ USAF]
5355	C-130H	Taiwan Air Force	97-1319+ 1319 [+ USAF]
5356	Not built		
5357	Not built		
5358	C-130H	Taiwan Air Force	97-1320+ 1320 [+ USAF]
5359	Not built		
5360	C-130H	USAF	93-1455
5361	C-130H	USAF	93-1456

LOCKHEED C-130/L-100 HERCULES

C/n	Model	Last known Owner/Operator	Identities/fates/comments (where appropriate)
5362	C-130H	USAF	93-1457
5363	C-130H	USAF	93-1458 [w/o 01Jly12 near Edgemont, SD]
5364	C-130H	USAF	93-1459
5365	C-130H	USAF	93-1561
5366	C-130H	USAF	93-1562
5367	C-130H	USAF	93-1563
5368	C-130H	USAF	93-1036
5369	C-130H	USAF	93-1037
5370	C-130H	USAF	93-2041
5371	C-130H	USAF	93-2042
5372	C-130H	USAF	93-1038
5373	C-130H	USAF	93-1039
5374	C-130H	USAF	93-7311
5375	C-130H	USAF	93-1040
5376	C-130H	USAF	93-1041
5377	C-130H	USAF	93-7312
5378	C-130H	USAF	94-6701
5379	C-130H	USAF	93-7313
5380	C-130H	USAF	93-7314
5381	HC-130H(N)	USAF	93-2104
5382	C-130H	USAF	94-6702
5383	C-130T	US Navy	165313
5384	C-130T	US Navy	165314
5385	KC-130T	US Marine Corps	165315
5386	KC-130T	US Marine Corps	165316
5387	HC-130H(N)	USAF	93-2106
5388	HC-130H(N)	USAF	93-2105
5389	C-130H	USAF	94-7315
5390	C-130H	USAF	94-7316
5391	C-130H	USAF	94-7317
5392	C-130H	USAF	94-7318
5393	C-130H	USAF	94-6703
5394	C-130H	USAF	94-6704
5395	C-130H	USAF	94-7319
5396	C-130H	USAF	94-7310
5397	C-130H	USAF	94-6705
5398	C-130H	USAF	94-6706
5399	C-130H	USAF	94-6707
5400	C-130H	USAF	94-6708
5401	C-130H	USAF	94-7320
5402	LC-130H	USAF	92-1094
5403	C-130H	USAF	94-7321
5404	C-130T	US Navy	165348
5405	LC-130H	USAF	92-1095
5406	C-130T	US Navy	165349 [coded BD-349 then RU-349]
5407	C-130T	US Navy	165350
5408	C-130J-30 C.4	Royal Air Force	N130JA ZH865 [C-130J-30 prototype, r/o 18Oct95; f/f 05Apr96]
5409	C-130T	US Navy	165351
5410	LC-130H	USAF	93-1096
5411	KC-130T	US Marine Corps	165352
5412	KC-130T	US Marine Corps	165353
5413	C-130J	USAF	N130JC 94-3026+ 94-8151 [+ USAF] [C-130J prototype, r/o 20Oct95; f/f 06Jun96]
5414	C-130J-30 C.4	Royal Air Force	N130JE ZH866
5415	C-130J	USAF	N130JG 94-3027+ 94-8152 [+ USAF]
5416	C-130J-30 C.4	Royal Air Force	N130JJ ZH867
5417	C-130H	USAF	95-6709
5418	C-130H	USAF	95-6710
5419	C-130H	USAF	95-6711
5420	C-130H	USAF	95-6712
5421	C-130H	USAF	95-1001
5422	C-130H	USAF	95-1002
5423	C-130H	USAF	96-1003

LOCKHEED C-130/L-100 HERCULES

C/n	Model	Last known Owner/Operator	Identities/fates/comments (where appropriate)			
5424	C-130H	USAF	N4249Y	96-1004		
5425	C-130H	USAF	N78235	96-1005		
5426	C-130H	USAF	96-1006			
5427	C-130H	USAF	96-1007			
5428	C-130H	USAF	96-1008			
5429	C-130T	US Navy	165378			
5430	C-130T	US Navy	165379			
5431	C-130H	USAF	96-7322			
5432	C-130H	USAF	96-7323			
5433	C-130H	USAF	96-7324			
5434	C-130H	USAF	96-7325			
5435	C-130H	Japan Air Self Defense Force	'75-1016'+	75-1086+	85-1086	[+ Japan]
5436			[not built]			
5437			[not built]			
5438			[not built]			
5439			[not built]			
5440	C-130J-30	Royal Australian Air Force	N130JQ	A97-440		
5441	C-130J-30	Royal Australian Air Force	N130JV	A97-441		
5442	C-130J-30	Royal Australian Air Force	N130JR	A97-442		
5443	C-130J-30 C.4	Royal Air Force	N130JN	ZH868		
5444	C-130J-30 C.4	Royal Air Force	N130JV	ZH869		
5445	C-130J-30 C.4	Royal Air Force	N73235	N78235	ZH870	
5446	C-130J-30 C.4	Royal Air Force/QinetiQ	N73238	ZH871		
5447	C-130J-30	Royal Australian Air Force	N73232	A97-447		
5448	C-130J-30	Royal Australian Air Force	N73230	A97-448		
5449	C-130J-30	Royal Australian Air Force	N73233	A97-449		
5450	C-130J-30	Royal Australian Air Force	N4187W	A97-450		
5451	WC-130J	USAF	N4232B	96-5300		
5452	WC-130J	USAF	N4107F	96-5301		
5453	WC-130J	USAF	N4161T	96-5302		
5454	C-130J	USAF	N4099R	96-8153		
5455	C-130J	USAF	96-8154			
5456	C-130J-30 C.4	Royal Air Force	N4249Y	ZH872		
5457	C-130J-30 C.4	Royal Air Force	N4242N	ZH873		
5458	C-130J-30 C.4	Royal Air Force	N41030	ZH874		
5459	C-130J-30 C.4	Royal Air Force	N4099R	ZH875		
5460	C-130J-30 C.4	(Royal Air Force)	N4080M	ZH876	[damaged 12Feb07 N of Al-Amarah, Iraq, destroyed by Allied Forces on site]	
5461	C-130J-30 C.4	Royal Air Force	N4081M	ZH877		
5462	C-130J-30 C.4	Royal Air Force	N73232	ZH878		
5463	C-130J-30 C.4	Royal Air Force	N4080M	ZH879		
5464	C-130J-30	Royal Australian Air Force	A97-464			
5465	C-130J-30	Royal Australian Air Force	A97-465			
5466	C-130J-30	Royal Australian Air Force	N4107F	A97-466		
5467	C-130J-30	Royal Australian Air Force	N73235	A97-467		
5468	C-130J-30	Royal Australian Air Force	A97-468			
5469	C-130J	USAF	97-1351			
5470	C-130J	USAF	97-1352			
5471	C-130J	USAF	97-1353			
5472	C-130J	USAF	97-1354			
5473	WC-130J	USAF	97-5303			
5474	WC-130J	USAF	97-5304			
5475	WC-130J	USAF	97-5305			
5476	WC-130J	USAF	97-5306			
5477	EC-130J	USAF	97-1931			
5478	C-130J C.5	Royal Air Force	N73238	ZH880		
5479	C-130J C.5	Royal Air Force	N4249Y	ZH881		
5480	C-130J C.5	Royal Air Force	N4081M	ZH882		
5481	C-130J C.5	Royal Air Force	N4242N	ZH883		
5482	C-130J C.5	Royal Air Force	N4249Y	ZH884		
5483	C-130J C.5	Royal Air Force	N41030	ZH885		
5484	C-130J C.5	Royal Air Force	N73235	ZH886		
5485	C-130J C.5	Royal Air Force	N4187W	ZH887		

LOCKHEED C-130/L-100 HERCULES

C/n	Model	Last known Owner/Operator	Identities/fates/comments (where appropriate)		
5486	WC-130J	USAF	98-5307		
5487	WC-130J	USAF	98-5308		
5488	KC-130J	US Marine Corps	165735		
5489	KC-130J	US Marine Corps	165736		
5490	EC-130J	USAF	98-1932		
5491	C-130J	USAF	98-1355		
5492	C-130J	USAF	98-1356		
5493	C-130J	USAF	98-1357		
5494	C-130J	USAF	98-1358		
5495	C-130J	Italian Air Force	N4099R	MM62175//46-40	
5496	C-130J C.5	Royal Air Force	N4187	ZH888	
5497	C-130J	(Italian Air Force)	MM62176//46-41		[w/o 23Nov09 Le Rene, near Coltano, Italy; ex Pisa-Galileo Galilei Airport, Italy]
5498	C-130J	Italian Air Force	MM62177//46-42		
5499	KC-130J	US Marine Corps	165737		
5500	C-130J C.5	Royal Air Force	N4099R	ZH889	
5501	WC-130J	USAF	99-5309		
5502	EC-130J	USAF	99-1933		
5503	C-130J	Italian Air Force	MM62178//46-43		
5504	C-130J	Italian Air Force	MM62179//46-44		
5505	C-130J	Italian Air Force	MM62180//46-45		
5506	KC-130J	US Marine Corps	165738		
5507	KC-130J	US Marine Corps	165739	[code QB-739]	
5508	KC-130J	US Marine Corps	165809		
5509	KC-130J	US Marine Corps	165810		
5510	C-130J	Italian Air Force	MM62181//46-46		
5511	C-130J	Italian Air Force	MM62182//46-47		
5512	C-130J	Italian Air Force	MM62183//46-48		
5513	C-130J	Italian Air Force	MM62184//46-49		
5514	C-130J	Italian Air Force	MM62185//46-50		
5515	KC-130J	US Marine Corps	165957		
5516	KC-130J	US Marine Corps	166380	[code BH-380]	
5517	C-130J-30	USAF	99-1431		
5518	C-130J-30	USAF	99-1432		
5519	C-130J-30	USAF	99-1433		
5520	C-130J	Italian Air Force	MM62186//46-51		
5521	C-130J-30	Italian Air Force	MM62187//46-53		
5522	EC-130J	USAF	00-1934		
5523	C-130J-30	Italian Air Force	MM62188//46-54		
5524	HC-130J	US Coast Guard	2001		
5525	C-130J-30	USAF	01-1461		
5526	C-130J-30	USAF	01-1462		
5527	KC-130J	US Marine Corps	166381	[code BH-381]	
5528	KC-130J	US Marine Corps	166382		
5529	C-130J-30	Italian Air Force	MM62189//46-55		
5530	C-130J-30	Italian Air Force	MM62190//46-56		
5531	C-130J-30	Italian Air Force	MM62191//46-57		
5532	EC-130J	USAF	01-1935		
5533	HC-130J	US Coast Guard	2002		
5534	HC-130J	US Coast Guard	2003		
5535	HC-130J	US Coast Guard	2004		
5536	C-130J-30	Royal Danish Air Force	B-536		
5537	C-130J-30	Royal Danish Air Force	B-537		
5538	C-130J-30	Royal Danish Air Force	B-538		
5539	C-130J-30	Italian Air Force	MM62192//46-58		
5540	C-130J-30	Italian Air Force	MM62193//46-59		
5541	HC-130J	US Coast Guard	2005		
5542	HC-130J	US Coast Guard	2006		
5543	KC-130J	US Marine Corps	166472		
5544	KC-130J	US Navy	166473		
5545	C-130J-30	USAF	02-0314		
5546	C-130J-30	USAF	02-8155		
5547	C-130J-30	USAF	02-1434		

LOCKHEED C-130/L-100 HERCULES

C/n	Model	Last known Owner/Operator	Identities/fates/comments (where appropriate)		
5548	C-130J-30	Italian Air Force	MM62194//46-60		
5549	C-130J-30	Italian Air Force	N51004	MM62195//46-61	
5550	C-130J-30	Italian Air Force	MM62196//46-62		
5551	C-130J-30	USAF	02-1463		
5552	C-130J-30	USAF	02-1464		
5553	KC-130J	US Marine Corps	166511		
5554	KC-130J	US Marine Corps	166512		
5555	KC-130J	US Marine Corps	166513	[code BH-513]	
5556	KC-130J	US Marine Corps	166514	[code QD-514]	
5557	C-130J-30	USAF	03-8154		
5558	C-130J-30	USAF	04-3142		
5559	C-130J-30	USAF	04-3143		
5560	C-130J-30	USAF	04-3144		
5561	C-130J-30	USAF	04-8153		
5562	KC-130J	US Marine Corps	166762		
5563	KC-130J	US Marine Corps	166763		
5564	KC-130J	US Marine Corps	166764		
5565	KC-130J	US Marine Corps	166765		
5566	C-130J-30	USAF	05-8152		
5567	C-130J-30	USAF	05-3146		
5568	C-130J-30	USAF	05-3147		
5569	C-130J-30	USAF	05-3145		
5570	C-130J-30	USAF	05-8157		
5571	C-130J-30	USAF	05-8156		
5572	C-130J-30	USAF	05-1435		
5573	C-130J-30	USAF	05-8158		
5574	C-130J-30	USAF	05-1465		
5575	C-130J-30	USAF	05-1436		
5576	C-130J-30	USAF	05-1466		
5577	KC-130J	US Marine Corps	167108		
5578	KC-130J	US Marine Corps	167109		
5579	KC-130J	US Marine Corps	167110		
5580	KC-130J	US Marine Corps	167111		
5581	C-130J-30	USAF	06-8159		
5582	C-130J-30	USAF	06-4631		
5583	C-130J-30	Royal Danish Air Force	B-583		
5584	C-130J-30	USAF	06-1438		
5585	C-130J-30	USAF	06-1467		
5586	C-130J-30	USAF	06-1437		
5587	C-130J-30	USAF	06-4632		
5588	C-130J-30	USAF	06-4633		
5589	C-130J-30	USAF	06-4634		
5590	KC-130J	US Marine Corps	167923		
5591	KC-130J	US Marine Corps	167924		
5592	KC-130J	US Marine Corps	167925		
5593	KC-130J	US Marine Corps	167926		
5594	C-130J-30	USAF	07-1468		
5595	C-130J-30	USAF	07-4635		
5596	C-130J-30	USAF	07-4636		
5597	C-130J-30	USAF	07-4637		
5598	C-130J-30	USAF	07-4638		
5599	C-130J-30	USAF	07-4639		
5600	C-130J-30	USAF	(07-4640)+	07-46310	[+ USAF]
5601	C-130J-30	Royal Norwegian Air Force	(08-5601)+	601	[+ USAF]
5602	KC-130J	US Marine Corps	167112	[code BH-7112]	
5603	KC-130J	US Marine Corps	167982		
5604	KC-130J	US Marine Corps	167983		
5605	KC-130J	US Marine Corps	167984		
5606	KC-130J	US Marine Corps	167985		
5607	C-130J-30	Royal Norwegian Air Force	5607		
5608	C-130J-30	USAF	07-46311		
5609	C-130J-30	USAF	08-8601		
5610	C-130J-30	[not yet known]			

LOCKHEED C-130/L-100 HERCULES

C/n	Model	Last known Owner/Operator	Identities/fates/comments (where appropriate)	
5611	C-130J-30	USAF	08-8602	
5612	C-130J-30	USAF	08-8604	
5613	C-130J-30	USAF	08-8603	
5614	C-130J-30	USAF	08-8606	
5615	C-130J-30	USAF	08-8605	
5616	C-130J-30	USAF	08-8607	
5617	C-130J	[not yet known]		
5618	KC-130J	US Marine Corps	167927	
5619	C-130J-30	USAF	06-8611	
5620	C-130J-30	USAF	06-8610	
5621	C-130J-30	USAF	06-8612	
5622	C-130J-30	USAF	07-8608	
5623	C-130J-30	USAF	07-8609	
5624	C-130J-30	USAF	07-8613	
5625	C-130J-30	USAF	07-8614	
5626	C-130J-30	Canadian Armed Forces	130601	[CC-130J]
5627	C-130J-30	Canadian Armed Forces	130602	[CC-130J]
5628	C-130J	USAF	07-3170	
5629	C-130J	Royal Norwegian Air Force	629	
5630	C-130J	(Royal Norwegian Air Force)	630	[w/o 15Mar12 en-route near Mount Kebnekaise, Sweden]
5631	C-130J	US Marine Corps	168074	
5632	C-130J	US Marine Corps	168075	
5633	HC-130J	USAF	09-0108	
5634	HC-130J	USAF	09-0109	
5635	C-130J-30	Canadian Armed Forces	130603	[CC-130J]
5636	C-130J-30	Canadian Armed Forces	130604	[CC-130J]
5637	C-130J-30	Canadian Armed Forces	130605	[CC-130J]
5638	C-130J-30	Indian Air Force	KC3801	
5639	C-130J-30	Indian Air Force	KC3802	[used US military hex code AE2736 30Jan11 whilst on delivery]
5640	C-130J-30	Indian Air Force	KC3803	
5641	C-130J-30	USAF	06-3171	
5642	C-130J	USAF	08-3172	
5643	C-130J	USAF	08-3173	
5644	KC-130J	USMC	168065	
5645	KC-130J	USMC	168066	
5646	KC-130J	USMC	168067	
5647	KC-130J	USMC	168068	
5648	C-130J-30	USAF	08-3174	
5649	C-130J-30	Canadian Armed Forces	130606	
5650	C-130J-30	Canadian Armed Forces	130607	
5651	C-130J-30	Canadian Armed Forces	130608	
5652	C-130J-30	for Canadian Armed Forces	130609	
5653	C-130J-30	Indian Air Force	KC3804	
5654	C-130J-30	Indian Air Force	KC3805	
5655	C-130J-30	Indian Air Force	KC3806	
5656	MC-130J	USAF	09-6207	
5657	MC-130J	USAF	09-6208	
5658	MC-130J	USAF	09-6209	
5659	MC-130J	USAF	09-6210	
5660	KC-130J	US Marine Corps	168069	
5661				
5662	C-130J-30	Qatar Air Force	211/MAH	reported 211 might be truncated 08-0211]
5663	C-130J-30	Qatar Air Force	212/MAI	reported 212 might be truncated 08-0212]
5664	C-130J-30	Canadian Armed Forces	130610	
5665	C-130J-30	Canadian Armed Forces	130611	
5666	C-130J-30	Canadian Armed Forces	130612	
5667	C-130J-30	Canadian Armed Forces	130613	
5668	C-130J-30	Qatar Air Force	213/MAJ	[reported 213 might be truncated 08-0213]
5669	C-130J-30	Qatar Air Force	214/MAK	[reported 214 might be truncated 08-0214]
5670	C-130J-30	USAF	08-3175	
5671	C-130J-30	USAF	08-3176	
5672	C-130J-30	USAF	08-3177	
5673	C-130J-30	USAF	08-3178	

LOCKHEED C-130/L-100 HERCULES

C/n	Model	Last known Owner/Operator	Identities/fates/comments (where appropriate)	
5674	C-130J-30	USAF	08-3179	
5675	C-130J-30	USAF	08-5675	
5676	KC-130J	US Marine Corps	168071	
5677	KC-130J	US Marine Corps	168072	
5678	C-130J-30	USAF	08-5678	
5679	C-130J-30	USAF	08-5679	
5680	MC-130J-30	USAF	08-6201	
5682	MC-130J-30	USAF	08-6203	
5683	C-130J-30	USAF	08-5683	
5684	C-130J-30	USAF	08-5684	
5685	C-130J-30	USAF	08-5685	
5686	C-130J-30	USAF	08-5686	
5687	C-130J-30	Canadian Armed Forces	130614	
5688	C-130J-30	Canadian Armed Forces	130615	
5689	C-130J-30	Canadian Armed Forces	130616	
5690	C-130J-30	Canadian Armed Forces	130617	
5691	C-130J-30	USAF	08-5691	
5692	C-130J-30	USAF	08-5692	
5693	C-130J-30	USAF	N51008	08-5693
5694	MC-130J	USAF	08-6204	
5695	MC-130J	USAF	08-6205	
5696				
5697				
5698	C-130J-30	Oman Air Force	525	[was reported as to be 504]
5698	C-130J-30	for Oman as 504		
5699				
5700	C-130J-30	USAF	10-5700	
5701	C-130J-30	USAF	10-5701	
5702				
5702	C-130J-30		[for Iraqi Air Force with c/ns 5703, 5704, 5722, 5723 & 5724]	
5703				
5704				
5705	C-130J-30		[for UAE Air Force with c/ns 5715, 5716, 5721, 5726, 5727, 5728, 5729, 5734, 5735, 5736 & 5737]	
5706				
5707				
5708				
5709				
5710				
5711	MC-130J	USAF	10-5711	
5712				
5713				
5714				
5715				
5716				
5717				
5718				
5719				
5720				
5721				
5722				
5723				
5724				
5725				
5726				
5727				
5728				
5729				
5730				
5731				
5732				
5733				
5734				

LOCKHEED C-130/L-100 HERCULES

C/n	Model	Last known Owner/Operator	Identities/fates/comments (where appropriate)	
5735				
5736				
5737				
5738				
5739				
5740	KC-130J	for Kuwait Air Force		
5741	KC-130J	for Kuwait Air Force		
5742	KC-130J	for Kuwait Air Force		

Unidentified

unkn		UN/World Food	S9-AJO	[reported 09Jan98 Mombasa, Kenya]
unkn		Iranian Air Force		[w/o 02Nov86 or 04Nov86 Zahedan, Iran]
unkn		Iranian Air Force		[w/o 12Mar97 or 14Mar97 Binalub Heights, 24 miles NE of Mashhad, Iran]
unkn		Iranian Air Force		[w/o 02Feb00 Tehran, Iran]
unkn		Iranian Air Force		[w/o 25Jun03 near Rudshour, Iran]
unkn		South Vietnamese Air Force	016	[reported wfu Tan Son Nhut, Vietnam]
unkn		South Vietnamese Air Force	820	[reported wfu Tan Son Nhut, Vietnam]
unkn	C-130H	Sudanese Air Force		[w/o 08Feb90 en route from Harare to Madridi, Sudan, shot down by a missile]
unkn	C-130H	Sudanese Air Force		[w/o 25Jly92 in Sudan]
unkn	C-130H	Sudanese Air Force		[w/o 26Feb96 25 miles south of Khartoum, Sudan[
unkn	C-130J	USAF	06-5586	[undated image on internet with 41st AS 463rd AG markings; possibly c/n 5582 later re-serialled 06-4631]
unkn	C-130H	United Arab Air Force	1212(3)	[reported Nov11 Al Bateen AFB, UAE]

LOCKHEED L.188 ELECTRA

C/n	Model	Last known Owner/Operator	Identities/fates/comments (where appropriate)
1001	188A	(Holiday Airlines)	N1881 N174PS N974HA [prototype ff 06Dec57] [b/u 1975 Oakland, CA; not canx until 21Sep09]
1002	188A	(TAME Ecuador)	N1882 VR-HFN HC-AMS FAE-1002/HC-AMS [dual marks] [b/u 1981 Quito, Ecuador]
1003	188A	National Museum of Naval Avn	N1883 148276+ NASA 927 N927NA N428NA [cvtd YP3V-1 then YP-3A then NP-3A; + USN; by Sep93 preserved Pensacola NAS, FL; l/n 21Oct06]]
1004	188A	(TAME Ecuador)	N1884 N7144C VR-HFO N16816 HC-ANQ FAE-1004/HC-ANQ [dual marks] [b/u 1981 Quito, Ecuador]
1005	188A	(Eastern Air Lines)	N5501 HK-554 N5501E [sold to Argentine Navy for spares; b/u Jun77; but reported stored BAN Almirante Zar, Argentina still as HK-554 & still extant in Apr02]
1006	188A	Air Spray (1967) Ltd	N5501V N1R N1432 N90700 N1006T N125AC PK-RLF C-FVFH [tanker code 489]
1007	188A	(Air Manila International)	N5502 PI-C1061 RP-C1061 [w/o 04Jun76 Agana, Guam]
1008	188A	(Air Manila International)	N5503 PI-C1062 [wfu Jan75 Manila, Philippines; b/u Jan78]
1009	188AF	(Zantop International Airlines)	N5504 [w/o 21Mar82 in hangar collapse Macon, GA]
1010	188A	(Gulfstream American Corp)	N5505 HK-1274 N5585 N5505 N5505C [wfu and stored Oct77 Mojave, CA; b/u Jan82]
1011	188A	(Copa Panama)	N5506 HP-579 [wfu & stored Jly86 Mojave, CA; canx 17Jly86; b/u Oct96]
1012	188AF	(Turboprop Ventures)	N5507 [stored May97 Detroit-Willow Run, MI; l/n 01Nov06; probably b/u by Apr07]
1013	188A	(Gulfstream American Corp)	N5509 HK-553 N5509Y [b/u Jan80 Van Nuys, CA]
1014	188AF	(Turboprop Ventures)	N5510 HK-557 N5510L [stored by 29Sep05 Detroit-Willow Run, MI; l/n 01Nov06; probably b/u by Apr07; but change of ownership 21Oct09 to Rockland Aerospace]
1015	188A	(American Airlines)	N6101A [w/o 03Feb59 New York-La Guardia, NY]
1016	188A	(Morgan Rourke Aircraft Sales)	N5511 [wfu and b/u Jan80 Tucson, AZ]
1017	188AF	Rockland Aerospace	N5512 [stored May97 Detroit-Willow Run, MI; l/n 04Jan08]
1018	188A	(SAHSA)N5513	B-3057 N5513 N5513 HR-SAW [w/o 08Jan81 Guatemala City, Guatemala]
1019	188A	(American Airlines)	N6102A [w/o 06Aug62 Knoxville, TN]
1020	188AF	(Gulfstream American Corp)	N5514 N301FA N5514 [b/u Jan81 Mojave, CA]
1021	188A	(Air Manila International)	N5515 PI-C1060 [w/o 09Jan72 Pasay City, Philippines]
1022	188AF	(Zantop International Airlines)	N5516 [w/o 21Mar82 in hangar collapse Macon, GA]
1023	188AF	(Zantop International Airlines)	N5517 [w/o 14Apr93 Detroit-Willow Run, MI; canx Apr96]
1024	188A	ex Blue Airlines	N6103A (PP-YJG) PP-VJL 9Q-CDK [wfu and stored derelict Nov95 Kinshasa-N'Djili, Zaire]
1025	188A	Museu Aeroespacial	N6104A (PP-YJH) PP-VJM [preserved 1995 Campo dos Afonsos, Rio de Janeiro, Brazil; l/n 23Aug07]
1026	188A	(Mandala Airlines)	N5518 PK-RLH [wfu by 12Feb85 & stored Jakarta-Soekarno-Hatta, Indonesia; b/u May04]
1027	188A	(California Airmotive Corp)	N6105A N5016K [b/u Feb74 Miami, FL]
1028	188A	Air Spray (1967) Ltd	N6106A 555+ HR-EMA 555+ C-GNPB [+ Honduras]
1029	188A	(Gulfstream American Corp)	N5519 HK-555 N5519E [b/u Jan81 Mojave, CA; parts l/n Nov96]
1030	188A	(Eastern Air Lines)	N5520 HK-1275 [repossessed by Eastern and wfu Mar77; b/u; location not reported]
1031	188AF	(Trans Cargo Service)	N6107A N5017K HC-AYL N5017K [wfu Jun76; b/u Nov78 Miami, FL]
1032	188A	ex LAPSA	N5521 ZP-CBX [wfu & stored Nov88 Asuncion-Campo Grande, Paraguay; l/n Jly06 derelict]
1033	188AF	(Turboprop Ventures)	N5522 [wfu & stored May02 Detroit-Willow Run, MI; l/n 10Nov07; b/u by 04Jan08; but change of ownership 21Oct09 to Rockland Aerospace]
1034	188AF	(Zantop International Airlines)	N5523 [w/o 30May84 Chalkhill, PA]
1035	188PF	(Turboprop Ventures)	N5001K CF-PWG N415MA 8R-GEW N415MA N341HA [wfu and stored Apr97 Detroit-Willow Run, MI; l/n 01Nov06; fully b/u by Jan08; but change of ownership 21Oct09 to Rockland Aerospace; canx 12Sep12]
1036	188AF	Air Spray (1967) Ltd	N5524 XA-FAM N83MR C-FNWY G-FNWY N3209A VH-IOB N351Q C-GZVM [tanker code 85]
1037	188A	(Blue Airlines)	N6108A (PP-YJF) PP-VJN 9Q-CDI [w/o 08Feb99 Mbanza-Lemba District, Zaire]
1038	188AF	Air Spray (1967) Ltd	N5525 N344HA C-GKIL C-FDTH
1039	188AF	Buffalo Airways	VH-RMA N356Q N355WS N356Q OE-ILB C-FBAQ [substantial damaged 05Mar12 Yellowknife, NWT, Canada]
1040	188A	(Air Spray (1967) Ltd)	N9701C FAE-1040/HC-AZT+ PP-VNK 9Q-CDU C-GBKT C-GFQA [+ Ecuador; dual marks; tanker code 86; w/o 16Jly03 near Cranbrook, BC, Canada]
1041	188A	ex Filair N6109A	PP-VJO 9Q-CXU [wfu 1998 Kinshasa-N'Djili, Zaire]

LOCKHEED L.188 ELECTRA

C/n	Model	Last known Owner/Operator	Identities/fates/comments (where appropriate)
1042	188A	(Ecuatoriana)	N5526 HC-AQF [wfu May72; b/u Feb75 Miami, FL]
1043	188AF	Rockland Aerospace	N5527 HK-691 N99583 XA-SAM N61AJ N346HA [stored by 29Sep05 Detroit-Willow Run, MI; l/n Aug10]
1044	188AF	(TPI International Airways)	N1883 VH-RMC N357Q [w/o 09Jan85 Kansas City, MO]
1045	188AF	(Groupe Litho Moboti Aviation)	N5528 9Q-CWT [w/o 05Feb86 near Kasongo, Zaire]
1046	188A	(Reeve Aleutian Airways)	N7135C [b/u for spares Jan86 Anchorage, AK; canx Nov90]
1047	188AF	(JBQ Aviation Corp)	VH-RMB N358Q N358WS N358Q [b/u Nov96 Opa-locka, FL; canx Jan97]
1048	188AF	(TRAMACO)	N5529 9Q-CWR [wfu & stored 1987 Kinshasa-N'Djili, Zaire; b/u circa 1989]
1049	188A	(VARIG) N6110A	PP-VJP [w/o 05Feb70 Porto Alegre, Brazil]
1050	188A	(Amerer Air)	N6111A N278AC FAE-1050/HC-AZL+ PP-VNJ HR-AML EL-WWS [+ Ecuador/dual marks] [b/u for spares Dec97 Linz, Austria]
1051	188APF	(Mexican Air Force)	N6112A XC-HDA XC-UTA TP-04+ TP-0201+ XC-UTA [+ Mexico] [wfu & stored Dec87 Seletar, Singapore; assumed b/u there]
1052	188A	(TAME Ecuador)	N9702C FAE-1052/HC-AZY+ [+ Ecuador; dual marks] [w/o 04Sep89 near Lago Agrio, Ecuador]
1053	188AF	Air Spray (1967) Ltd	N5530 HK-692 N5530E TI-ALK N429MA N343HA C-GOIZ
1054	188A	(American Jet Industries)	N6113A N5015K [b/u Apr74 Miami, FL]
1055	188A	(Eastern Air Lines)	N5531 [DBR by bomb 02Jly76 Boston, MA]
1056	188PF	Transafrik	N6114A XC-GIA XC-CFE XC-HEB S9-NAH
1057	188C	(Northwest Orient Airlines)	N121US [w/o 17Mar60 near Tell City, IN]
1058	188A	(Overseas National Airways)	N6115A [b/u Sep75 Wilmington, OH]
1059	188AF	(Great Northern Airlines)	N5002K N401FA [w/o 12Mar76 Lake Udrivik, AK]
1060	188AF	Air Spray (1967) Ltd	N5532 HR-SAV HR-TNT HR-SHN C-FZCS [tanker code 87]
1061	188AF	(American Jet Industries)	VH-TLA N188LA XW-PKA N188LA [b/u Mar76 Seletar, Singapore]
1062	188A	(Eastern Air Lines)	N5533 [w/o 04Oct60 Boston, MA]
1063	188A	(Air Spray (1967) Ltd)	N6116A HK-1416 PP-VLX C-FQYB [tanker code 88; DBF 16Nov00 in hangar Red Deer, AB, Canada]
1064	188AF	(Fairbanks Air Service)	N5003K CF-PWQ N5003K N400FA [w/o 11Dec74 Prudhoe Bay-Deadhorse Airstrip, AK]
1065	188A	(McCulloch Airmotive)	N6117A [b/u Mar71 for spares Tulsa, OK]
1066	188AF	(Integrity Aircraft Sales)	N5534 N664F [b/u Greenville-Donaldson Center, SC; canx Mar93; fuselage only noted Jun93]
1067	188E	ex Argentine Navy	N9703C HR-TNN 0791//6-P-102 [wfu 1991; preserved/stored Trelew-Almirante Naval Base, Chubut Province, Argentina; l/n May08; late 2009 for sale as scrap]
1068	188AF	(Channel Express)	N5535 (G-CHNX) EI-CHO G-CHNX [wfu & stored Oct01 Bournemouth, UK; b/u by 18Sep03]
1069	188AF	(TACA International Airlines)	VH-TLB N188LB XW-PKB N188LB YS-07C [w/o 02Feb80 San Salvador-Comalapa, El Salvador]
1070	188E	ex Argentine Navy	N7136C N5536 0790//6-P-103 [wfu; preserved/stored Trelew-Almirante Naval Base, Chubut Province, Argentina; l/n May08; late 2009 for sale as scrap]
1071	188E	ex Argentine Navy	N5536 HP-654 N511PS 0792//2-P-101 [preserved by May96 Museo de la Aviacion Naval, Bahia Blanca, Buenos Aires, Argentina; l/n May08]
1072	188E	Museo de la Aviacion Naval	N6118A N5534 0793//6-P-104 [+ Argentina] [wfu 28Oct02 Bahia Blanca, Buenos Aires, Argentina; preserved May08]
1073	188A	(ATO – Air Transport Office)	N6119A HK-775 PP-VLY 9Q-CRM 9Q-CTO [wfu by 11Jly08 Kinshasa, Democratic Republic of Congo; l/n 08Nov11]
1074	188AF	(Evergreen International Airlines)	N7137C N5558 [b/u May83 Marana, AZ, for spares]
1075	188CF	(Channel Express)	N5537 SE-FGC N64405 N23AF N423MA N347HA G-OFRT [wfu and b/u Apr01 Coventry, UK; canx 12May03]
1076	188AF	(Fleming International Airways)	N5004K N280F [w/o 06Jly77 St Louis, MO]
1077	188CF	(Aerocondor Colombia)	N122US N300GA N300FA N42FM HK-1809 HK-1845 [wfu and stored Nov87 Barranquilla, Colombia; assumed subsequently b/u]
1078	188C	ex LAPSA	N5538 ZP-CBY [wfu & stored Nov88 Asuncion-Campo Grande, Paraguay; l/n Jly06 derelict]
1079	188AF	Anchorage Airport Fire Dept	N5005K N281F [wfu Feb99 Anchorage, AK; acquired by fire dept; l/n Jun12]
1080	188C	(Trans Service Airlift)	N5539 ZP-CBZ 9Q-CRR [w/o 18Dec95 near Jamba (Kahengula) Airport, Angola]
1081	188A	ex Aerocondor Colombia	N6120A HK-1415 [wfu & stored Apr79 Barranquilla, Colombia; b/u]
1082	188C	Air Spray (1967) Ltd	N123US N123AC PK-PLD C-FVFI [purchased Jly95 for spares use; stored Red Deer, AB, Canada; l/n 26Oct10 with tail of C-FLXT c/n 1130]
1083	188A	(Aerocondor Colombia)	N6121A HK-774 [wfu & stored Apr79 Barranquilla, Colombia; b/u]
1084	188AF	Rockland Aerospace	N5006K N282F [stored by 29Sep05 Detroit-Willow Run, MI; l/n Aug10]

LOCKHEED L.188 ELECTRA

C/n	Model	Last known Owner/Operator	Identities/fates/comments (where appropriate)
1085	188CF	(Spirit of America Airlines)	N124US N402FA N402GN [wfu; canx Mar93; derelict by Jun93 Greenville-Donaldson Center, SC; reported used as fire trainer; assumed now b/u]
1086	188A	(LANSA) N9704C	OB-R-941 [w/o 24Dec71 Puerto Inka, Peru]
1087	188AF	(Aerocondor Colombia)	N7138C HK-1976 [w/o 10Jly75 Bogota, Colombia]
1088	188CF	(Trans Union Leasing Corp)	N5540 SE-FGA N5540 N11VG N5540 TI-LRO N5540 [wfu and stored circa Jan84 Miami, FL; assumed then b/u]
1089	188AF	(Zantop International Airlines)	N5007K N283F [w/o 30Apr75 Prudhoe Bay-Deadhorse Airstrip, AK]
1090	188A	(Braniff Airways)	N9705C [w/o 29Sep59 near Buffalo, TX]
1091	188CF	Air Spray (1967) Ltd	N171PS N971HA N171PS N5539 G-CEXS C-GZCF [tanker code 90; later code 490]
1092	188CF	(Integrity Aircraft Sales)	N5008K N666F [wfu & stored 1990; location not reported but might have been Greenville-Donaldson Center, SC]
1093	188A	(Blue Airlines)	N6122A PP-VLC 9Q-CDL [derelict by Nov95 Kinshasa-N'Djili, Zaire; no recent reports; assumed b/u]
1094	188AF	(Integrity Aircraft Sales)	N7139C CF-IJY N7139C N405GN [wfu & b/u Jun93 Greensboro-Donaldson Center, SC; canx Mar93]
1095	188A	(LANSA) N9706C	OB-R-945 [wfu & stored Dec71 Lima, Peru; fuselage only by Feb97]
1096	188CF	(JBQ Aviation Corp)	N5009K PI-C1063 RP-C1063 N62AJ TF-ISC TF-VLN N4465F [b/u Oct90 Aruba, Lesser Antilles; canx Mar92]
1097	188A	(California Airmotive Corp)	N5010K [b/u 1974 Miami, FL]
1098	188CF	(World Aviation Services)	N5541 SE-FGB N5541 N12VG N5541B N345HA LN-FOO N590HG [stored Jan05 Opa-locka, FL; b/u by 04Feb08]
1099	188A	(Braniff Airways)	N9707C [w/o 03May68 near Dawson, TX]
1100	188C	Atlantic Airlines	N6123A N289AC N665F G-LOFC
1101	188CF	(TPI International Airways)	N125US [b/u Dec89 Miami, FL; canx Aug95]
1102	188PF	ex Argentine Navy	N6124A 0691//5-T-1 [wfu 14May98; preserved/stored Trelew-Almirante Naval Base, Chubut Province, Argentina; l/n Sep98; for sale late 2009 as scrap]
1103	188C	Air Spray (1967) Ltd	N9725C N111 N97 N429NA C-FLJO [tanker code 82]
1104	188AF	(Turboprop Ventures)	N5011K N284F [stored by 29Sep05 Detroit-Willow Run, MI; l/n 01Nov06; b/u by Nov07; but change of ownership 21Oct09 to Rockland Aerospace; canx 27Aug12]
1105	188CF	(Cooperativa de Montecillos)	N126US [w/o 30Jun77 in sea offshore Bocas del Toro, Panama]
1106	188A	(LANSA) N9708C	OB-R-939 [w/o 09Aug70 near Cuzco, Peru]
1107	188AF	(JBQ Aviation Corp)	N5012K N285F [w/o 01Mar99 Shannon, Ireland; b/u]
1108	188C	(California Airmotive Corp)	N127US CF-IJM [b/u 1974 Van Nuys, CA]
1109	188CF	Rockland Aerospace	N172PS TI-LRN N172PS N340HA (VH-CHD) N340HA [stored by Sep05 Detroit-Willow Run, MI; l/n Aug10]
1110	188CF	ex Segers Aviation	N173PS N862U N289F [stored by Nov99 Roswell, NM; change of ownership May02, disappeared from Roswell; fate/status unknown]
1111	188C	(New Air Charter Service)	N128US N25AF C-GNDZ 9Q-CRY [w/o Aug92 in Democratic Republic of Congo; no further details known]
1112	188CF	ex Air Spray (1967) Ltd	N129US N777DP PT-DZK N8LG N360Q N360WS N360Q (VH-CHD) C-GYVI [tanker code 83] [reported wfu by Oct10 Red Deer, AB, Canada]
1113	188C	ex Legion Express	N130US CF-NAY C-FNAY N130US (XA-) N188LE [wfu & stored Oct97 Opa-locka, FL; l/n 16Oct06]
1114	188A	(Mandala Airlines)	N9709C OB-R-946 N9709C N972HA N124AC PK-RLE [wfu & stored Sep89 Jakarta-Soekarno-Hatta, Indonesia; gone by May04, assumed b/u]
1115	188A	(Aerocondor Colombia)	N6125A HK-777 [w/o 27Aug73 near Bogota, Colombia]
1116	188AF	(Atlantic Air Transport)	N6126A N404GN N669F LN-FOL G-LOFG [used for spares Coventry, UK; canx 16Jun04; hulk to fire dump still marked as LN-FOL; 25Jly11 hulk moved to unknown location]
1117	188A	(American Airlines)	N6127A [w/o 14Sep60 near New York-La Guardia, NY]
1118	188PF	(Reeve Aleutian Airways)	N7140C [w/o 05Nov74 in hangar fire Anchorage, AK]
1119	188A	(Blue Airlines)	N6128A PP-VJU 9Q-CDG [w/o 13Mar95 Kinshasa-N'Djili, Zaire]
1120	188MR	Museo de la Aviacion Naval	N6129A 0692//5-T-2+ 0692//6-P-106+ [+ Argentina] [wfu 14May98; preserved by 1998 Museo de la Aviacion Naval, Bahia Blanca, Buenos Aires, Argentina; l/n May08]
1121	188A	(Galaxy Airlines)	N6130A N5532 [w/o 21Jan85 near Reno, NV]
1122	188PF	Mr Jorge O Ramirez	N6131A 0693//5-T-3+ [+ Argentina] [wfu Feb96 Buenos Aires-Ezeiza, Argentina; moved to Buenos Aires city area, in scrapyard; l/n 28Mar09]
1123	188E	(Argentine Navy)	N6132A VH-RMG N2251A N5538 0789//6-P-101 [w/o 23Sep89 Almirante Zar, Argentina]
1124	188A	ex Air Spray (1967) Ltd	N6133A PP-VJW HR-AMM C-GZYH [wfu Dec02 Red Deer, AB, Canada; l/n 26Oct10 still marked HR-AMM]

LOCKHEED L.188 ELECTRA

C/n	Model	Last known Owner/Operator	Identities/fates/comments (where appropriate)
1125	188A	ex Bolivian Air Force	N6134A CP-853 TAM-69+ TAM-01+ [+ Bolivia] [stored by Nov96 La Paz-El Alto, Bolivia; l/n Oct08]
1126	188A	(Trans Service Airlift)	N6135A PP-VJV 9Q-CRS 5H-ARM 9Q-CCV [w/o 21Jan94 Kinshasa, Zaire; stripped for spares Jan95]
1127	188PF	(Great Northern Airlines)	N7141C CF-ZSR N74191 CF-PAK N206AJ N403GN [w/o 05Jan79 Inigok, North Slope, AK]
1128	188PF	(Atlantic Airlines)	N7142C CF-ZST N417MA HP-684 OB-R-1138 N417MA N342HA LN-FON (G-LOFF) [stored Jun00 Coventry, UK; b/u around 13Feb08; canx 02Jun08; remains still present 09Aug08]
1129	188CF	ex Atlantic Airlines	N7143C CF-IJV C-FIJV(1) G-FIJV EI-HCE G-FIJV [last flew 04Jan07; Cof A expired 27Sep07; stored no engines Coventry, UK; l/n 26Sep10]
1130	188C	Air Spray (1967) Ltd	N181H N175PS N595KR N308D C-FLXT [stored May07 Red Deer, AB, Canada; l/n 26Oct10 still with National Science Foundation titles and colours on overhaul]
1131	188CF	ex Atlantic Airlines	N131US CF-IJW N133AJ N667F G-LOFB [DBR 28Jan10 during maintenance Coventry, UK; l/n 26Sep10]
1132	188C	(Nordair)	N132US CF-NAZ [w/o 31Mar77, hit by landing CAF CL-28 Argus serial 10737 c/n 28 at Summerside AFB, PE, Canada; fuselage used to rebuild c/n 1111]
1133	188CF	Air Spray (1967) Ltd	N182H N181H N376PS N863U N290F C-GJTZ
1134	188CF	(TAN Airlines)	N183H N9710C HR-TNL [w/o 21Mar90 Las Mesitas, near Tegucigalpa-Toncontin Airport, Honduras]
1135	188CF	(JBQ Aviation Corp)	N184H N182H N8355C N864U N357WS N355Q [b/u for spares Nov96 Opa-locka, FL; canx Jan97]
1136	188C	(American Flyers Airline)	(N185H) N183H [w/o 22Apr66 near Ardmore Municipal Airport, OK; canx 09Jly09]
1137	188PF	ex Filair N133US	PP-VLB 9Q-CUU [wfu 1998 Kinshasa-N;Djili, Zaire; reported still present 2007]
1138	188PF	Conair Group	N134US CF-IJR C-FIJR G-FIJR (EI-HCF) C-GYCG
1139	188PF	(Filair) N135US	PP-VLA 9Q-CVK 9Q-CGD [reported w/o Jly94 somewhere in Angola, no futher details known]
1140	188PF	Buffalo Airways	N9744C G-LOFH N4HG C-FIJV(2)
1141	188PF	(Panarctic Oils)	N136US CF-PAB [w/o 29Oct74 Rea Point, Melville Island, NT/NU, Canada]
1142	188C	(Northwest Orient Airlines)	N137US [w/o 16Sep61 near Chicago-O'Hare, IL]
1143	188AF	Conair Group	N9745C CF-IJC N9745C LN-MOD LN-FOG G-LOFD C-FYYJ [code 60]
1144	188CF	Atlantic Airlines	N138US N24AF N668F (G-FIJF) EI-CET G-LOFE
1145	188AF	Buffalo Airways	N9746C CF-IJJ N5767 N9746C LN-MOI LN-FOH OE-ILA C-GLBA
1146	188AF	Rockland Aerospace	N5013K N286F [stored by 29Sep05 Detroit-Willow Run, MI; l/n Aug10]
1147	188AF	Mex-Jet Cargo	VH-TLC N188LC YS-06C N188LC OB-M-1328 OB-1328 HK-3642X HK-3706X HK-3706 XA-AEG [damaged 29Mar07; stored following minor damage Panama City-Tocumen International, Panama; l/n 12Dec08]
1148	188AF	(Renown Aviation)	N5014K N287F [bought for spares by Air Spray; b/u Abbotsford, BC, Canada; l/n derelict Jly08]
2001	188CF	(Universal Airlines)	N6934C PH-LLA N6934C N851U [w/o 19Mar72 Hill AFB near Odgen, UT; remains used to rebuild c/n 2010]
2002	188CF	(Atlantic Air Transport)	VH-ECA N359AC HC-AVX N359AC TI-LRM N359AC N359Q F-OGST N359Q G-LOFA [damaged & wfu Jun98 Coventry, UK; used for spares, canx 29Sep98; remains to fire section; l/n Nov02]
2003	188CF	(Hunting Cargo Airlines)	PH-LLB N852U (N852ST) C-GNWD SE-IVS EI-CHW [wfu & stored Dec96 East Midlands Airport, UK; b/u Aug98; canx 20Mar98]
2004	188C	(TAME Ecuador)	VH-ECB N358AC FAE-2004//HC-AZJ [w/o 04Sep89 Taura AFB, Ecuador]
2005	188CF	(Fred Olsen Flyselskap)	N9724C (ZK-BMP) ZK-TEA N31231 LN-FOI [stored Aug97 Coventry, UK; b/u Jly04; nose section reported to Ferrymead Aeronautical Society, Christchurch, New Zealand]
2006	188CF	(Dart Group)	PH-LLC N853U SE-IVR EI-CHX G-BYEF [wfu Dec98 Bournemouth, UK; UK marks not used; b/u Dec01]
2007	188C	Air Spray (1967) Ltd	VH-ECC ZK-CLX N1968R C-GHZI [tanker code 84]
2008	188C	(Mandala Airlines)	VH-ECD ZK-TED N836E PK-RLG [w/o 30Nov85 Medan-Polonia Airport, Indonesia]
2009	188CF	(Galaxy Airlines)	PH-LLD N854U [w/o 29Jan85 Dobbins AFB, Marietta, GA]

LOCKHEED L.188 ELECTRA

C/n	Model	Last known Owner/Operator	Identities/fates/comments (where appropriate)
2010	188PF	Buffalo Airways	(ZK-BMQ) ZK-TEB N33506 CF-NAX N63AJ N178RV C-GNWC N178RV N2RK (G-LOFI) CF-IJX+ C-FIJX [+ applied by sticker in error at Coventry, UK; amended before delivery]
2011	188C	(Tasman Empire Airways)	(ZK-BMR) ZK-TEC [w/o 27Mar65 Whenuapai Airport, New Zealand]
2012	188CF	(Universal Airlines)	PH-LLE N855U [w/o 24Aug70 Hill AFB, Odgen, UT]
2013	188CF	(Transcargo)	PH-LLF N856U N107DH [wfu Jan93 Tucson, AZ; reported b/u by 07Apr03]
2014	188CF	ex Atlantic Airlines	PH-LLG N857U (N857ST) SE-IZU G-FIZU EI-CHY G-FIZU [stored in UK marks by Conair Abbotsford, BC, Canada; l/n 16Jly12]
2015	188CF	(Hunting Cargo Airlines)	PH-LLH N858U C-GNWC SE-IVT EI-CHZ [stored Jun98 East Midlands Airport, UK; b/u Aug98; canx 15Dec98]
2016	188C	(Transamerica Airlines)	PH-LLI N859U [w/o 18Nov79 near Granger, Salt Lake City, UT ex Hill AFB, Ogden, UT]
2017	188CF	(TPI International Airways)	PH-LLK N860U N361WS [b/u for spares Tinker AFB, OK; canx Sep91]
2018	188CF	(JBQ Aviation Corp)	PH-LLL N861U N359WS N354Q [b/u for spares Nov96 Opa-locka, FL; canx Jan97]
2019	188C	(KLM Royal Dutch Airlines)	PH-LLM [w/o 12Jun61 Cairo-International, Egypt]
2020	188C	Mandala Airlines	PK-GLA N320CA HP-640 N511PS N188DM N807DM PK-RLI [wfu & stored Sep89 Jakarta-Soekarno-Hatta, Indonesia; gone by May04; assumed b/u]
2021	188C	(Garuda Indonesian Airways)	PK-GLB [w/o 16Feb67 Menado-Sam Ratulangi Airport, Indonesia]
2022	188C	Transapel	PK-GLC N322CA FAP-400+ HP-1042 S9-NAF TG-ANP (HK-3707X) HK-3716 HK-3716X HK-3716 [+ Panama] [stored in hangar Mar96 Bogota, Colombia]

Production complete

LOCKHEED P-3 ORION SERIES

C/n	Model	Last known Owner/Operator	Identities/fates/comments (where appropriate)

Notes: A South Korean aircraft used test marks N4161T in Apr95.
An Iranian aircraft was w/o prior to 1979, one between 1979 and 1984; two have been used for spares.
AMARC Codes are given in a separate table on page 633 of Volume 2.

C/n	Model	Last known Owner/Operator	Identities/fates/comments (where appropriate)
9998	P3V-1	(Lockheed)	[static test airframe; b/u]
1003	NP-3A	National Museum of Naval Avn	148276+ N927NA N428NA [+ USN] [cvtd from L188 Electra; preserved by Aug96 Pensacola NAS, FL; canx Apr06; l/n 21Oct06]
185.5001	NP-3D	ex US Navy	148883 [stored Patuxent River NAS, MD]
185.5002	P-3A	(US Navy)	148884 [DBR 06Aug77; b/u Jacksonville, FL]
185.5003	UP-3A	(US Navy)	148885 [wfu Jul91; b/u Jacksonville, FL]
185.5004	P-3A	(US Navy)	148886 [wfu & stored AMARC May83; coded 2P0005; b/u for spare parts]
185.5005	EP-3E	ex US Navy	148887 [wfu & stored AMARC 13Dec94; coded 2P0159]
185.5006	EP-3E	(US Navy)	148888 [b/u Alameda NAS, CA]
185.5007	UP-3A	ex US Navy	148889 [wfu & stored AMARC Jan09]
185.5008	RP-3A	(US Navy)	149667 [DBF & b/u Jacksonville, FL]
185.5009	EP-3E	(US Navy)	149668 [b/u Jacksonville, FL]
185.5010	EP-3B	(US Navy)	149669 [b/u Greenville, SC]
185.5011	RP-3A	ex US Navy	149670 [wfu & stored AMARC 19Dec94; coded 2P0147]
185.5012	EP-3A	ex US Navy	149671 [wfu China Lake NAWC, CA]
185.5013	P-3A	(US Navy)	149672 [w/o 30Jan63 near Patuxent River, MD]
185.5014	UP-3A	ex US Navy	149673 [wfu & stored AMARC 31Mar92; coded 2P0078]
185.5015	NP-3D	ex US Navy	149674 [wfu & stored AMARC 26Sep05; coded 2P0240; SOC 17Jan06]
185.5016	VP-3A	ex US Navy	149675 [SOC Sep05]
185.5017	VP-3A	ex US Navy	149676 [wfu & stored AMARC 14Dec06; coded 2P0245]
185.5018	UP-3A	(Chilean Navy)	149677+ 403 [+ USN] [stored AMARC with code 2P0072] [wfu & dumped Vina del Mar AFB, Chile; used for spares]
185.5019	EP-3B	(US Navy)	149678 [b/u Greenville, SC]
185.5020	EP-3E	(US Navy)	150494 [b/u Aug92 Greenville, SC]
185.5021	UP-3A	ex US Navy	150495 [wfu & stored AMARC 28Jan04; coded 2P0199]
185.5022	VP-3A	(US Navy)	150496 [wfu & stored; SOC Dec04]
185.5023	EP-3E	(US Navy)	150497 [b/u Jun92 Alameda NAS, CA]
185.5024	EP-3E	(US Navy)	150498 [b/u Aug92 Alameda NAS, CA]
185.5025	NP-3D	(US Navy)	150499 [wfu & stored AMARC Apr06; coded 2P0243; SOC 19Jly06]
185.5026	RP-3A	(US Navy)	150500 [wfu Oct92 Jacksonville, FL; b/u Macon, GA]
185.5027	EP-3E	(US Navy)	150501 [b/u 1991 Alameda NAS, CA]
185.5028	EP-3E	(US Navy)	150502 [b/u Jun90 Greenville, SC]
185.5029	EP-3E	(US Navy)	150503 [b/u Jun90 Greenville, SC; fuselage to China Lake NAS, CA]
185.5030	UP-3A	(US Navy)	150504 [b/u Whidbey Island NAS, WA]
185.5031	EP-3E	(US Navy)	150505 [b/u Nov95 Jacksonville, FL]
185.5032	P-3A	(US Navy)	150506 [wfu & stored AMARC Mar83; coded 2P0001; b/u]
185.5033	UP-3A	Chilean Navy	150507+ P.3-4^ 402 [+ USN; stored AMARC with code 2P0070; ^ Spain]
185.5034	P-3A	(US Navy)	150508 [DBF 04Dec64 Cubi Point NAS, Philippines]
185.5035	P-3A	Moffett Field Museum	150509+ [+ USN] [preserved Moffett Field, CA]
185.5036	P-3A	Aero Union	150510+ P.3-5^ 150510+ N917AU# [+ USN; ^ Spain; # Aerostar Firebomber]
185.5037	VP-3A	Pima Air & Space Museum	150511+ [+ USN] [wfu & stored AMARC 13May03; coded 2P0190; preserved Pima, AZ]
185.5038	RP-3A	(US Navy)	150512 [wfu Alameda NAS, CA; b/u]
185.5039	P-3A	Aero Union	150513+ P.3-6^ N920AU# [+ USN; ^ Spain; # Aerostar Firebomber]
185.5040	UP-3A	US Customs Service	150514+ N18314 [+ USN]
185.5041	VP-3A	ex US Navy	150515 [wfu & stored AMARC 20Oct04; coded 2P0229]
185.5042	P-3A	Museo del Aire	150516+ P.3-7//22-26^ [+ USN; ^ Spain; preserved Aug94 Jerez, Spain; later Moron, Spain; moved Nov99 to Cuatro Vientos, Spain]
185.5043	P-3A	ex US Navy	150517 [wfu; GIA, Jacksonville NAS, FL]
185.5044	UP-3A	Museo de la Aviacion Naval	150518+ 401^ [+ USN; stored AMARC with code 2P0045; ^ Chile; wfu, preserved Vina del Mar AB, Chile]
185.5045	UP-3A	ex US Navy	150519 [wfu & stored AMARC 06Jan93; coded 2P0088]
185.5046	RP-3A	Western Aerospace Museum	150520+ [+ USN] [wfu; preserved Oakland, CA]
185.5047	NP-3D	US Navy	150521 [code 341]
185.5048	NP-3D	US Navy	150522
185.5049	P-3A	(US Navy)	150523 [wfu & stored AMARC Apr83; coded 2P0003; trials aircraft; b/u]
185.5050	NP-3D	US Navy	150524 [code 335]

LOCKHEED P-3 ORION SERIES

C/n	Model	Last known Owner/Operator	Identities/fates/comments (where appropriate)
185.5051	NP-3D	US Navy	150525
185.5052	UP-3A	Misawa Aviation & Science Museum	150526+ [+ USN] [wfu, preserved Misawa, Japan]
185.5053	UP-3A	ex US Navy	150527 [wfu & stored AMARC 18Apr90; coded 2P0041]
185.5054	UP-3A	ex US Navy	150528 [wfu & stored AMARC 18Apr90; coded 2P0043]
185.5055	EP-3A	(Hawkins & Powers Aviation)	150529+ [+ USN] [wfu; used for spares, Greybull, WY]
185.5056	P-3A	ex US Navy	150604 [wfu & stored AMARC 07Aug85; coded 2P0021; fuselage only]
185.5057	UP-3A	ex US Navy	150605 [wfu & stored AMARC 29Sep05; coded 2P0241; SOC 17Jan06]
185.5058	P-3A	(US Navy)	150606 [wfu & stored AMARC Apr83; coded 2P0004; b/u]
185.5059	UP-3A	ex Chilean Navy	150607+ 406 [+ USN] [stored AMARC with code 2P0058] [stored Vina del Mar AFB, Chile]
185.5060	P-3A	(US Navy)	150608 [wfu & stored AMARC 20Mar84; coded 2P0006; fuselage only, removed from inventory Jan05]
185.5061	P-3A	(US Navy)	150609 [wfu & stored AMARC Apr83; coded 2P0002; b/u]
185.5062	P-3A	(US Navy)	151349 [wfu & stored AMARC Oct84; coded 2P0016; b/u]
185.5063	P-3A	(US Navy)	151350 [w/o 05Apr68 in South China Sea]
185.5064	P-3A	ex US Navy	151351 [wfu & stored AMARC Nov84; coded 2P0019; to systems mock-up at Waco, TX]
185.5065	TP-3A	ex US Navy	151352 [wfu & stored AMARC 05Jun97; coded 2P0180]
185.5066	UP-3A	ex US Navy	151353 [wfu & stored AMARC 29Apr91; coded 2P0060]
185.5067	UP-3A	ex Chilean Navy	151354+ 405 [+ USN; stored AMARC with code 2P0074; wfu & dumped Vina del Mar AFB, Chile; used for spares]
185.5068	P-3A	(Aero Union)	151355+ [+ USN] [used for spares]
185.5069	P-3A	(Brazilian Air Force)	151356+ [+ USN; wfu & stored AMARC 09Jan86; coded 2P0025; to Brazil, believed for spares use only]
185.5070	TP-3A	Vintage Aircraft Holdings	151357+ [+ USN; wfu & stored AMARC 11Aug98; coded 2P0187; exchanged Dec04 by National Museum of Naval Aviation for a Brewster Buffalo]
185.5071	P-3A	ex US Navy	151358 [wfu & stored AMARC 25Apr85; coded 2P0020; fuselage only]
185.5072	P-3A	(Aero Union)	151359+ N184AU N924AU# [+ USN; stored AMARC with code 2P0024; # Aerostar Firebomber; w/o 17Oct91 near Missoula, MT]
185.5073	P-3A	ex US Navy	151360 [wfu & stored AMARC 17Apr91; coded 2P0059]
185.5074	P-3A	Aero Union	151361+ N183AU N925AU# [+ USN; stored AMARC with code 2P0011; # Aerostar Firebomber]
185.5075	P-3A	(US Navy)	151362 [w/o 17Nov64 Argentia, off Newfoundland, Canda]
185.5076	P-3A	(US Navy)	151363 [w/o 02Jun69 Adak NAS, Aleutian Islands, AK]
185.5077	TP-3A	(US Navy)	151364 [wfu & stored AMARC 22Aug95; coded 2P0167; b/u]
185.5078	P-3A	(US Navy)	151365 [w/o 28Apr67 South China Sea]
185.5079	UP-3A	(Greek Air Force)	151366+ 151366 [+ USN; stored AMARC with code 2P0015; used for spares Tanagra, Greece]
185.5080	UP-3A	ex US Navy	151367 [preserved Keflavik NAS, Iceland]
185.5081	UP-3A	ex US Navy	151368 [wfu & stored AMARC 26Dec91; coded 2P0073]
185.5082	P-3A	Aero Union	151369+ N182AU N927AU# [+ USN; stored AMARC with code 2P0014; # Aerostar Firebomber]
185.5083	TP-3A	(US Navy)	151370 [wfu & stored AMARC 27Apr95; coded 2P0161; b/u]
185.5084	TP-3A	ex US Navy	151371 [wfu & stored AMARC 30May97; coded 2P0179]
185.5085	P-3A	Aero Union	151372+ N185AU N923AU# [+ USN; stored AMARC with code 2P0022]; # Aerostar Firebomber]
185.5086	P-3A	(US Navy)	151373 [to fire dump Mar89 Alameda NAS, CA; b/u]
185.5087	P-3A	Jacksonville NAS Collection	151374+ [+ USN] [preserved Jacksonville NAS, FL]
185.5088	TP-3A	(US Navy)	151375 [wfu & stored AMARC 16May95; coded 2P0162; b/u]
185.5089	TP-3A	ex US Navy	151376 [wfu & stored AMARC 21Jun95; coded 2P0163]
185.5090	P-3A	ex Aero Union	151377+ [+ USN] [wfu for spares use May96 Chico, CA]
185.5091	P-3A	ex US Navy	151378 [wfu & stored AMARC 02Sep86; coded 2P0028]
185.5092	TP-3A	ex US Navy	151379 [wfu & stored AMARC 15Dec97; coded 2P0183]
185.5093	P-3A	(US Navy)	151380 [w/o 27Jul65 Kindley AFB, Bermuda]
185.5094	P-3A	(US Navy)	151381 [w/o 23Feb78 Jacksonville International, FL]
185.5095	TP-3A	(US Navy)	151382 [wfu & stored AMARC 21Jun95; coded 2P0164; b/u]
185.5096	P-3A	ex US Navy	151383 [wfu & stored AMARC 06Dec85; coded 2P0023]
185.5097	UP-3A	Chilean Navy	151384+ 407 [+ USN; stored AMARC with code 2P0042]
185.5098	P-3A	Aero Union	151385+ N921AU# [+ USN; # Aerostar Firebomber]
185.5099	UP-3A	ex US Navy	151386 [wfu & stored AMARC 15Jun84; coded 2P0010; fuselage only]

LOCKHEED P-3 ORION SERIES

C/n	Model	Last known Owner/Operator	Identities/fates/comments (where appropriate)
185.5100	P-3A	Aero Union	151387+ N181AU N922AU# [+ USN; stored AMARC with code 2P0017; # Aerostar Firebomber]
185.5101	UP-3A	ex US Navy	151388 [wfu & stored AMARC 07Nov84; coded 2P0018; fuselage only]
185.5102	UP-3A	(Greek Air Force)	151389+ 151389 [+ USN; stored AMARC with code 2P0013; used for spares Tanagra, Greece]
185.5103	UP-3A	US Customs Service	151390+ N15390 [+ USN]
185.5104	P-3A	Aero Union	151391+ N180AU N406TP N900AU# [+ USN; stored AMARC with code 2P0027; # Aerostar Firebomber]
185.5105	TP-3A	ex US Navy	151392 [preserved Kaneohe Bay MCAS, HI]
185.5106	P-3A	ex US Navy	151393 [wfu & stored AMARC 05Feb86; coded 2P0026; fuselage only]
185.5107	TP-3A	(US Navy)	151394 [wfu & stored AMARC 27Apr95; coded 2P0160; b/u]
185.5108	UP-3A	US Customs Service	151395+ N16295 [+ USN]
185.5109	UP-3A	(US Navy)	151396 [wfu & stored AMARC 26Mar84; coded 2P0007; removed from inventory Mar05]
185.5110	P-3A	Brazilian Air Force	152140+ [unknown] [+ USN; stored AMARC with code 2P0051; awaiting conversion to P-3AM standard & delivery]
185.5111	UP-3A	Chilean Navy	152141+ 408 [+ USN; stored AMARC with code 2P0061]
185.5112	P-3T	ex Royal Thai Navy	152142+ 42^ 1202^ 1204 [+ USN; stored AMARC with code 2P0040; ^ Thailand; stored by 01Oct07 U-Tapao, Thailand]
185.5113	P-3T	Royal Thai Navy	152143+ 43^ 1204^ 1205 [+ USN; stored AMARC with code 2P0056; ^ Thailand]
185.5114	P-3A	(US Navy)	152144 [w/o 16Jan68 Shikoku Island, Japan]
185.5115	P-3A	Spanish Air Force	152145+ P.3-03//22-22 [+ USN]
185.5116	P-3A	Brazilian Air Force	152146+ 7211 [+ USN]; stored AMARC with code 2P0046]
185.5117	P-3A	ex US Navy	152147 [wfu & stored AMARC 06Jan93; coded 2P0089]
185.5118	P-3A	ex US Navy	152148 [wfu & stored AMARC 14Dec89; coded 2P0029; fuselage only]
185.5119	P-3A	(Spanish Air Force)	152149+ P.3-2 [w/o 08Jul77 Jerez, Spain]
185.5120	NP-3D	US Navy	152150 [USN; stored for a period AMARC with code 2P0012]
185.5121	P-3A	(US Navy)	152151 [w/o 05Dec71 near Cubi Point NAS, Philippines]
185.5122	P-3A	National Museum of Naval Avn	152152+ [+ USN] [preserved Oct90 Pensacola NAS, FL]
185.5123	P-3A	Spanish Air Force	152153+ P.3A-01//22-21 [+ USN]
185.5124	P-3A	ex US Navy	152154 [wfu & stored AMARC 18Dec89; coded 2P0031]
185.5125	P-3A	(US Navy)	152155 [w/o 26May72; missing in the Pacific off California, USA]
185.5126	P-3A	ex US Navy	152156 [preserved Brunswick NAS, ME]
185.5127	P-3A	ex US Navy	152157 [wfu & stored AMARC 24Jul90; coded 2P0052]
185.5128	P-3A	US Navy	152158 [allegedly marked with different identity, flying special operations]
185.5129	P-3A	(US Navy)	152159 [w/o 03Aug70 after mid-air explosion en-route Nellis AFB, NV to North Island NAS, CA]
185.5130	P-3A	(US Navy)	152160 [preserved as gate guard Kindley NAS, Bermuda; left by USN 1995 following closure of base; to fire trainer until reported b/u in Mar98]
185.5131	P-3A	(US Navy)	152161 [w/o 18Jan81 Whidbey Island NAS, WA]
185.5132	P-3AM	Brazilian Air Force	152162+ 7205 [+ USN] [stored AMARC with code 2P0053]
185.5133	P-3A	ex Royal Thai Navy	152163+ [+ USN; stored AMARC 2P0055; for spares use U-Tapao, Thailand; l/n 01Oct07]
185.5134	P-3A	(US Navy)	152164 [b/u Alameda NAS, CA]
185.5135	UP-3A	Chilean Navy	152165+ 404 [+ USN; stored AMARC with code 2P0054]
185.5136	P-3A	(US Navy)	152166 [w/o Jan89; scrapped Whidbey Island NAS, WA]
185.5137	P-3A	Brazilian Air Force	152167+ 7208^ [+ USN; stored AMARC with code 2P0039; ^ awaiting conversion to P-3AM standard & delivery]
185.5138	P-3A	Brazilian Air Force	152168+ 7209 [+ USN; stored AMARC with code 2P0034; ^ awaiting conversion to P-3AM standard & delivery]
185.5139	UP-3A	The Hawaii Museum of Flying	152169+ [+ USN] [preserved Barbers Point NAS, HI]
185.5140	UP-3A	US Customs Service	152170+ N16370 [+ USN]
185.5141	P-3A	(US Navy)	152171 [w/o 09Apr66 off Isla de Guadalupe, Mexico]
185.5142	P-3A	(US Navy)	152172 [w/o 04Jul66 Battle Creek, MI in a ground collision]
185.5143	P-3AM	Brazilian Air Force	152173+ 7206 [+ USN; stored AMARC with code 2P0038]
185.5144	P-3A	Brazilian Air Force	152174+ 7201 [+ USN; stored AMARC with code 2P0048; also reported as 7207]
185.5145	P-3A	Brazilian Air Force	152175+ [unknown] [+ USN; stored AMARC with code 2P0033; awaiting conversion to P-3AM standard and delivery]
185.5146	P-3A	ex US Navy	152176 [wfu & stored AMARC 18Apr90, coded 2P0044]

LOCKHEED P-3 ORION SERIES

C/n	Model	Last known Owner/Operator	Identities/fates/comments (where appropriate)
185.5147	P-3A	Royal Thai Navy Museum	152177+ [+ USN; stored AMARC with code 2P0049; for spares use U-Tapao, Thailand; l/n 01Oct07; by Oct09 preserved U-Tapao, Thailand]
185.5148	P-3A	(US Navy)	152178 [wfu & stored AMARC Apr84; coded 2P0008; b/u]
185.5149	P-3A	ex US Navy	152179 [wfu & stored AMARC 05Apr84; coded 2P0009]
185.5150	P-3A	Brazilian Air Force	152180+ 7200 [+ USN; stored AMARC with code 2P003]
185.5151	P-3A	(Greek Air Force)	152181+ 152181 [+ USN; stored AMARC with code 2P0047; used for spares Tanagra, Greece]
185.5152	P-3A	(US Navy)	152182 [w/o 03Jun72 Mediterranean off N coast of Morocco]
185.5153	P-3A	ex Greek Air Force	152183+ 152183 [+ USN; stored AMARC with code 2P0030; GIA/spares use Elefsis AFB, Greece]
185.5154	UP-3T	Royal Thai Navy	152184+ 1206 [USN; stored AMARC with code 2P0050]
185.5155	P-3A	ex US Navy	152185 [wfu & stored AMARC 25Sep90; coded 2P0057]
185.5156	P-3AM	Brazilian Air Force	152186+ 7202 [+ USN; stored AMARC with code 2P0032]
185.5157	P-3A	Brazilian Air Force	152187+ [unknown] [+ USN; stored AMARC with code 2P0035; awaiting conversion to P-3AM standard & delivery]
185.5158	P-3B LW	Argentine Navy	152718+ 0867//6-P-51 [+ USN; stored AMARC with code 2P0095; by Mar12 stored Trewlew, Argentina]
185.5159	EP-3J	ex US Navy	152719 [wfu & stored AMARC 13Sep99; code 2P0188]
185.5160	P-3B HW	(US Navy)	152720 [w/o 16Jun83 Kauai, HI]
185.5161	P-3B LW	South Korean Navy	152721+ 152721 [+ USN; stored AMARC with code 2P0069]
185.5162	P-3AEW	US Customs Service	152722 N147CS [+ USN]
185.5163	P-3B LW	South Korean Navy	152723+ 152723 [+ USN; stored AMARC with code 2P0063]
185.5164	P-3B LW	(US Navy)	152724 [w/o 26Apr78 in Atlantic Ocean 20 miles off Lajes, Azores]
185.5165	P 3B LW	South Korean Navy	152725+ 152725 [+ USN; stored AMARC with code 2P0099]
185.5166	P-3B LW	South Korean Navy	152726+ 152726 [+ USN; stored AMARC with code 2P0091]
185.5167	UP-3B	ex US Navy	152727 [wfu & stored AMARC 30Oct95; code 2P0173]
185.5168	P-3B LW	South Korean Navy	152728+ 152728 [+ USN] [stored AMARC with code 2P00185]
185.5169	P-3B LW	US Customs Service	152729+ N729SK [+ USN] [stored AMARC with code 2P00112]
185.5170	P-3B LW	ex US Navy	152730 [wfu & stored AMARC 27Aug92; code 2P0083]
185.5171	P-3B LW	(Aero Union)	152731+ N926AU [w/o 20Apr05 near Chico, CA; canx 13May05]
185.5172	P-3B LW	Argentine Navy	152732+ 0868//6-P-52 [+ USN; stored AMARC with code 2P0096; by Mar12 stored Trewlew, Argentina]]
185.5173	P-3B HW	(US Navy)	152733 [DBR 17May83 Barbers Point NAS, HI]
185.5174	P-3B LW	ex US Navy	152734 [wfu & stored AMARC 27Aug91; code 2P0068]
185.5175	P-3B HW	NASA	152735+ N426NA [+ USN]
185.5176	P-3B LW	ex US Navy	152736 [wfu & stored AMARC 20Aug91; code 2P0066]
185.5177	P-3B LW	ex US Navy	152737 [wfu & stored AMARC 30Apr92; code 2P0080]
185.5178	RP-3D	ex US Navy	152738 [wfu & stored AMARC 01Dec93; code 2P0110]
185.5179	NP-3B	US Navy	152739
185.5180	UP-3B	Vintage Aircraft Holdings	152740+ [wfu & stored AMARC 16Mar94; code 2P0133; exchanged Apr05 by National Museum of Naval Aviation for a Brewster Buffalo]
185.5181	P-3B LW	US Customs Service	152741+ N741SK [+ USN; stored AMARC with code 2P0107]
185.5182	P-3B LW	ex US Navy	152742 [wfu & stored AMARC 23Feb94; code 2P0125]
185.5183	P-3B LW	ex US Navy	152743 [wfu & stored AMARC 01Apr92; code 2P0079]
185.5184	P-3B LW	Greek Air Force	152744+ 152744 [+ USN; stored AMARC with code 2P0092]
185.5185	EP-3J	(US Navy)	152745 [DBF 24Apr98 Brunswick NAS, ME; b/u Aug99]
185.5186	P-3B LW	Argentine Navy	152746+ 0869//6-P-53 [+ USN; stored AMARC with code 2P0093]
185.5187	P-3B LW	Greek Air Force	152747+ 152747 [+ USN; stored AMARC with code 2P0135]
185.5188	P-3B LW	ex US Navy	152748 [preserved Selfridge ANGB, MI]
185.5189	P-3B LW	(US Navy)	152749 [w/o 15Mar73 off Brunswick NAS, ME]
185.5190	P-3K	Royal New Zealand Air Force	152886+ NZ4201 [+ USN]
185.5191	P-3B LW	ex US Navy	152750 [wfu & stored AMARC 16Dec92; code 2P0086]
185.5192	P-3K	Royal New Zealand Air Force	152887+ NZ4202 [+ USN]
185.5193	P-3B LW	ex US Navy	152751 [wfu & stored AMARC 06Jan94; code 2P0117]
185.5194	P-3B LW	(US Navy)	152752 [wfu & stored AMARC 15Dec93; code 2P0113; Nov99 b/u for spares for Argentine Navy]
185.5195	P-3B LW	South Korean Navy	152753+ 152753 [+ USN; stored AMARC with code 2P0084]
185.5196	P-3B LW	ex US Navy	152754 [wfu & stored AMARC 06Jan94; code 2P0118]
185.5197	UP-3B	ex US Navy	152755 [wfu & stored AMARC 09Sep93; code 2P0100]
185.5198	P-3B LW	ex US Navy	152756 [wfu & stored AMARC 13Aug91; code 2P0064]
185.5199	P-3B LW	(US Navy)	152757 [w/o 22Sep78 Portland, ME]

LOCKHEED P-3 ORION SERIES

C/n	Model	Last known Owner/Operator	Identities/fates/comments (where appropriate)
185.5200	P-3K	Royal New Zealand Air Force	152888+ NZ4203 [+ USN]
185.5201	P-3B LW	US Navy	152758 [wfu & stored AMARC 19Feb93; code 2P0094; allocated to RAAF as A9-201 but NTU, due to severe wing corrosion]
185.5202	P-3K2	Royal New Zealand Air Force	152889+ NZ4204 [+ USN]
185.5203	P-3B LW	ex US Navy	152759 [wfu & stored AMARC 21Mar94; code 2P0134]
185.5204	P-3B LW	(Royal Australian Navy)	152760+ [+ USN][stored AMARC with code 2P0081; to Australian Navy for spares use Jun95; at RAAF Edinburgh, SA, Australia; cockpit for simulator, fuselage for BDR training]
185.5205	P-3B LW	Argentine Navy	152761+ 0870//6-P-54 [+ USN; stored AMARC with code 2P0103]
185.5206	P-3B LW	South Korean Navy	152762+ 152762 [+ USN; stored AMARC with code 2P0071]
185.5207	P-3B LW	Argentine Navy	152763+ 0871//6-P-55 [+ USN; stored AMARC with code 2P0111]
185.5208	P-3K	Royal New Zealand Air Force	152890+ NZ4205 [+ USN]
185.5209	P-3B LW	ex US Navy	152764 [preserved Whidbey Island NAS, WA]
185.5210	P-3B LW	(US Navy)	152765 [w/o 06Mar69 Lemoore NAS, CA]
185.5211	P-3B LW	Vintage Aircraft Holdings	153414+ [+USN; wfu & stored AMARC 28Sep93; code 2P0101; exchanged Apr05 by National Museum of Naval Aviation for a Brewster Buffalo]
185.5212	P-3B LW	Greek Air Force	153415+ 153415 [+ USN; stored AMARC with code 2P0136]
185.5213	P-3B LW	South Korean Navy	153416+ 153416 [+ USN; stored AMARC with code 2P0146]
185.5214	P-3B LW	ex US Navy	153417 [wfu & stored AMARC 20Aug91; code 2P0067]
185.5215	P-3B LW	ex US Navy	153418 [wfu & stored AMARC 23Feb90; code 2P0036]
185.5216	P-3B LW	Argentine Navy	153419+ 0872// 6-P-56 [+ USN; stored AMARC with code 2P0120; sale to Greek AF ntu]
185.5217	P-3B LW	ex US Navy	153420 [wfu & stored AMARC 13Jan94; code 2P0121]
185.5218	P-3B LW	ex US Navy	153421 [wfu & stored AMARC 14Jan94; code 2P0122]
185.5219	P-3B LW	South Korean Navy	153422+ [Argentine Navy] 153422 [+ USN; stored AMARC with code 2P0114]
185.5220	P-3B LW	US Customs Service	153423+ N423SK [+ USN; stored AMARC with code 2P0065]
185.5221	P-3B LW	Greek Air Force	153424+ 153424 [+ USN; stored AMARC with code 2P0124]
185.5222	UP-3B	(US Navy)	153425 [b/u Alverca AFB, Portugal]
185.5223	P-3B LW	ex US Navy	153426 [wfu & stored AMARC 24Nov92; code 2P0085]
185.5224	P-3B LW	Greek Air Force	153427+ 153427 [+ USN; stored AMARC with code 2P0144]
185.5225	P-3B LW	(US Navy)	153428 [w/o 11Dec77 Hierro Island, Canary Islands, Spain]
185.5226	P-3B LW	(NASA)	153429 [wfu & stored AMARC, code PB001, then AXNB0001; 14Mar94 to NASA for spares use]
185.5227	P-3B LW	ex US Navy	153430 [wfu & stored AMARC 17Dec92; code 2P0087]
185.5228	P-3B LW	US Customs Service	153431+ N431SK [+ USN; stored AMARC with code 2P0109]
185.5229	P-3B LW	ex US Navy	153432 [wfu & stored AMARC 24Jul91; code 2P0062]
185.5230	UP-3B	ex NASA	153433 [wfu & stored AMARC 06Dec99; coded 2P0189; to NASA Sep01 with code AXNB0002]
185.5231	TAP-3B	Royal Australian Navy	153434+ (A9-231) A9-434 [+ USN; stored AMARC with code 2P0082]
185.5232	P-3B LW	ex US Navy	153435 [wfu & stored AMARC 27Jan94; coded 2P0123]
185.5233	P-3B LW	ex US Navy	153436 [wfu & stored AMARC 25Mar94; coded 2P0142]
185.5234	P-3B LW	ex US Navy	153437 [wfu & stored AMARC 30Jun93; coded 2P0097]
185.5235	TAP-3B	Royal Australian Navy	153438+ A9-438 [+ USN; stored AMARC with code 2P0116]
185.5236	TAP-3B	Royal Australian Navy	153439+ (A9-236) A9-439 [+ USN; stored AMARC with code 2P0090]
185.5237	P-3B LW	(US Navy)	153440 [w/o 06Feb68 near Phu Quoc Island, Gulf of Thailand, Vietnam]
185.5238	P-3B LW	Greek Air Force	153441+ 153441 [+ USN; stored AMARC with code 2P0104]
185.5239	NP-3D	US Navy	153442 [Rotordome AEW testbed]
185.5240	P-3B HW	ex US Navy	153444 [preserved New Orleans Joint Reserve Base NAS, LA]
185.5241	P-3B HW	(US Navy)	153445 [w/o 01Apr68 in sea off Vietnam, shot down]
185.5242	P-3AEW	US Customs Service	153446+ N144CS [+ USN; stored AMARC with code 2P0141]
185.5243	P-3AEW	US Customs Service	153447+ N143CS [+ USN; stored AMARC with code 2P0126]
185.5244	P-3B HW	ex US Navy	153448 [wfu & stored AMARC 15Mar94; code 2P0132]
185.5245	P-3B HW	ex US Navy	153449 [wfu & stored AMARC 24Mar94; code 2P0139]
185.5246	P-3B HW	US Navy	153450
185.5247	P-3B HW	ex US Navy	153451 [wfu & stored AMARC 21Dec93; coded 2P0115]
185.5248	P-3AEW	US Customs Service	153452+ N142CS [+ USN; stored AMARC with code 2P0130]
185.5249	P-3B HW	(US Navy)	153453 [stored AMARC with code 2P0131; Jly00 to Lockheed at Marietta, GA; b/u for spares, wings to c/n 5505]
185.5250	P-3B HW	(US Navy)	153454 [b/u Jun91 Alameda NAS, CA]
185.5251	P-3B HW	ex US Navy	153455 [wfu & stored AMARC 23Mar94; code 2P0138]

LOCKHEED P-3 ORION SERIES

C/n	Model	Last known Owner/Operator	Identities/fates/comments (where appropriate)
185.5252	P-3B HW	ex US Navy	153456 [wfu & stored AMARC 13Oct94; code 2P0155]
185.5253	P-3B HW	ex US Navy	153457 [wfu & stored AMARC 29Mar94; code 2P0143]
185.5254	P-3B HW	ex US Navy	153458 [wfu & stored AMARC 20Oct94; code 2P0156]
185.5255	P-3B HW	ex US Navy	154574 [wfu after cracks found; preserved Willow Grove NAS, PA]
185.5256	P-3AEW	US Customs Service	154575+ N148CS [+ USN]
185.5257	P-3N	Royal Norwegian Air Force	154576+ 576^ 4576 [+ USN; ^ Norway]
185.5258	P-3B HW	(US Navy)	154577 [SOC 17Sep02]
185.5259	P-3B HW	ex US Navy	154578 [wfu & stored AMARC 22Mar94; code 2P0137]
185.5260	P-3B HW	ex US Navy	154579 [wfu & stored AMARC 20Sep94; code 2P0154]
185.5261	P-3B HW	ex US Navy	154580 [wfu & stored AMARC 28Feb94; code 2P0127]
185.5262	P-3AEW	US Customs Service	154581+ N149CS [+ USN; stored AMARC with code 2P0149]
185.5263	P-3B HW	ex US Navy	154582 [wfu & stored AMARC 17Nov93; code 2P0106]
185.5264	P-3B HW	Spanish Air Force	154583+ 583^ P.3-8//22-31# P.3B-08//22-31 P.3M-08//22-31 [+ USN; ^ Norway; # Spain]
185.5265	P-3B HW	ex US Navy	154584 [wfu & stored AMARC 27Jul93; code 2P0098]
185.5266	P-3B HW	(US Navy)	154585 [b/u Jun94 Jacksonville NAS, FL]
185.5267	P-3B HW	ex US Navy	154586 [wfu & stored AMARC 19Nov93; code 2P0108]
185.5268	NP-3D	US Navy	154587 [code RL-589]
185.5269	P-3B HW	ex US Navy	154588 [wfu & stored AMARC 28Oct94; code 2P0157]
185.5270	NP-3D	US Navy	154589
185.5271	P-3B HW	ex US Navy	154590 [wfu & stored AMARC 03Nov94; code 2P0158]
185.5272	P-3B HW	(US Navy)	154591 [DBR 05Sep80 Kauai, HI]
185.5273	P-3B HW	ex US Navy	154592 [wfu & stored AMARC 10Nov93; code 2P0105]
185.5274	P-3B HW	ex US Navy	154593 [wfu & stored AMARC 28Apr94; code 2P0145]
185.5275	P-3B HW	ex US Navy	154594 [wfu & stored AMARC 24May94; code 2P0148]
185.5276	P-3B HW	ex US Navy	154595 [wfu & stored AMARC 29Aug94; code 2P0150]
185.5277	P-3B HW	(US Navy)	154596 [w/o 27Jun79 Subic Bay, Philippines]
185.5278	P-3B HW	ex US Navy	154597 [wfu & stored AMARC 14Sep94; code 2P0153]
185.5279	P-3B HW	ex US Navy	154598 [wfu & stored AMARC 13Sep94; code 2P0151]
185.5280	P-3B HW	ex US Navy	154599 [wfu & stored AMARC 13Sep94; code 2P0152]
185.5281	RP-3D	ex US Navy	154600 [wfu & stored AMARC 15Oct93; code 2P0102]
185.5282	P-3B HW	ex US Navy	154601 [wfu & stored AMARC 24Mar94; code 2P0140]
185.5283	P-3B HW	ex US Navy	154602 [wfu & stored AMARC 09Mar94; code 2P0129]
185.5284	P-3B HW	ex US Navy	154603 [wfu & stored AMARC 07Jan94; code 2P0119]
185.5285	P-3B HW	ex US Navy	154604 [wfu & stored AMARC 09Mar94; code 2P0128]
185.5286	P-3AEW	US Customs Service	154605+ A9-605^ N96LW N146CS [+ USN; ^ Australia]
185.5287	P-3B	(US Navy)	154606 [canx, not built]
185.5288	P-3B	(US Navy)	154607 [canx, not built]
185.5289	P-3B	(US Navy)	154608 [canx, not built]
185.5290	P-3B	(US Navy)	154609 [canx, not built]
185.5291	P-3B	(US Navy)	154610 [canx, not built]
185.5292	P-3B	(US Navy)	154611 [canx, not built]
185.5293	P-3B	(US Navy)	154612 [canx, not built]
185.5294	P-3B	(US Navy)	154613 [canx, not built]
185.5295	P-3B	[canx, not built]	
185.5296	P-3B	[canx, not built]	
185.5297	P-3B	[canx, not built]	
185.5298	P-3B	[canx, not built]	
185.5299	P-3B	[canx, not built]	
185.5300	P-3B	[canx, not built]	
185C.5301	P-3B HW	Spanish Air Force	156599+ 599//KK-L^ P.3-9//22-32# P.3B-09//22-32 [+ USN; ^ Norway; # Spain]
185C.5302	P-3B HW	Spanish Air Force	156600+ 600//KK-M^ P.3-10//22-33# P.3B-10//22-33 [+ USN; ^ Norway; # Spain]
185C.5303	P-3B HW	Spanish Air Force	156601+ 601//KK-N^ P.3-11//22-34 [+ USN; ^ Norway] [stored Nov10 Moron de la Frontera, Spain]
185C.5304	P-3B HW	Spanish Air Force	156602+ 602//KK-O^ P.3-12//22-35# P.3B-12//22-35 [+ USN; ^ Norway; # Spain]
185C.5305	P-3N	Royal Norwegian Air Force	156603+ 603//KK-P^ 6603 [+ USN; ^ Norway]
185B.5401	P-3K	Royal New Zealand Air Force	155291+ A9-291^ NZ4206 [+ USN; ^ Australia]
185B.5402	P-3P	(Portuguese Air Force)	155292+ A9-292^ N4003X 4801# 14801 [+ USN; ^ Australia; # Portugal; wfu BA Montijo, Portugal, b/u Mar06]

LOCKHEED P-3 ORION SERIES

C/n	Model	Last known Owner/Operator	Identities/fates/comments (where appropriate)
185B.5403	P-3P	Portuguese Air Force	155293+ A9-293^ N4005X 4802# 14802 [+ USN; ^ Australia; # Portugal; wfu BA Montijo, Portugal]
185B.5404	P-3P	Portuguese Air Force	155294+ A9-294^ N4006S 4803# 14803 [+ USN; ^ Australia; # Portugal; stored Jly08 Beja, Portugal]
185B.5405	P-3P	Portuguese Air Force	155295+ A9-295^ N4003G 4804# 14804 [+ USN; ^ Australia; # Portugal; wfu Jul95 Alverca, Portugal; to GIA BA Ota, Portugal]
185B.5406	P-3B HW	(Royal Australian Air Force)	155296+ A9-296 [+ USN] [w/o 11Apr68 Moffett Field NAS, CA]
185B.5407	P-3P	Portuguese Air Force	155297+ A9-297^ N4008B 4805# 14805 [wfu Mar11 Beja, Portugal] [+ USN; ^ Australia; # Portugal]
185B.5408	P-3P	Museu do Ar	155298+ A9-298^ N64854 4806# 14806# [+ USN; ^ Australia; # Portugal; wfu May05, preserved Sintra, Portugal]
185B.5409	P-3AEW	US Customs Service	155299+ A9-299^ N91LC N145CS [+ USN; ^ Australia]
185B.5410	P-3B HW	Royal Australian Air Force	155300+ A9-300 [+ USN] [DBF 27Jan84 RAAF Edinburgh, SA, Australia; used as simulator]
285A.5500	NP-3D	US Navy	153443
285A.5501	EP-3E	US Navy	156507 [Aries II]
285A.5502	P-3C	(US Navy)	156508 [b/u 1998; SOC Sep99]
285A.5503	P-3C	ex US Navy	156509 [wfu & stored AMARC 11Dec07; code 2P0246]
285A.5504	P-3C-IIIR	US Navy	156510
285A.5505	EP-3E	US Navy	156511 [Aries II]
285A.5506	P-3C	ex US Navy	156512 [wfu & stored AMARC 20Sep95; code 2P0169]
285A.5507	P-3C	ex US Navy	156513 [wfu & stored AMARC 20Sep95; code 2P0170]
285A.5508	EP-3E	US Navy	156514 [Aries II]
285A.5509	P-3C-IIIR	US Navy	156515
285A.5510	P-3C-IIIR	ex US Navy	156516 [wfu & stored AMARC 08Apr04; code 2P0213]
285A.5511	EP-3E	US Navy	156517 [Aries II]
285A.5512	P-3C-IIIR	ex US Navy	156518 [wfu & stored AMARC 11Feb04; code 2P0203]
285A.5513	EP-3E	US Navy	156519 [Aries II]
285A.5514	P-3C	(US Navy)	156520 [wfu & stored AMARC; SOC Apr04]
285A.5515	P-3C-IIIR	US Navy	156521
285A.5516	P-3C-IIIR	(US Navy)	156522 [SOC Jan05]
285A.5517	P-3C-IIIR	ex US Navy	156523 [wfu & stored AMARC 20Jul04; code 2P0223]
285A.5518	P-3C	ex US Navy	156524 [wfu & stored AMARC 11Sep96; code 2P0177]
285A.5519	P-3C	ex US Navy	156525 [wfu & stored AMARC 23Oct03; code 2P0191]
285A.5520	P-3C	ex US Navy	156526 [wfu & stored AMARC 29Sep95; code 2P0172]
285A.5521	P-3C-IIIR	US Navy	156527
285A.5522	EP-3E	US Navy	156528 [Aries II]
285A.5523	EP-3E	US Navy	156529 [Aries II]
285A.5524	P-3C-IIIR	(US Navy)	156530 [wfu & stored AMARC 28Jun04; code 2P0220; SOC Nov04]
285A.5525	P-3C-IIIR	US Navy	157310
285A.5526	P-3C-IIIR	(US Navy)	157311 [SOC Jan04]
285A.5527	P-3C-IIIR	(US Navy)	157312 [SOC Dec04]
285A.5528	P-3C-IIIR	(US Navy)	157313 [wfu & stored AMARC 14Dec04; code 2P0232; SOC Apr05]
285A.5529	P-3C-IIIR	Taiwanese Navy	157314 3306+ [was AMARC; code 2P0193]
285A.5530	P-3C-IIIR	ex US Navy	157315 [wfu & stored AMARC 08Mar04; code 2P0207]
285A.5531	EP-3E	US Navy	157316 [Aries II]
285A.5532	P-3C-IIIR	ex US Navy	157317 [wfu & stored AMARC 12Jul04; code 2P0222]
285A.5533	EP-3E	US Navy	157318 [Aries II]
285A.5534	P-3C-IIIR	US Navy	157319
285A.5535	EP-3E	(US Navy)	157320 [Aires II] [DBR 22Sep97 Souda Bay, Crete, Greece; fuselage to Waco, TX]
285A.5536	P-3C-IIIR	Taiwanese Navy	157321 3312 [was stored AMARC; code 2P0202]
285A.5537	P-3C-IIIR	US Navy	157322
285A.5538	P-3C-IIIR	(US Navy)	157323 [wfu & stored AMARC 11May04; code 2P0216; SOC Nov04]
285A.5539	P-3C-IIIR	ex US Navy	157324 [wfu & stored AMARC 31Aug04; code 2P0226]
285A.5540	EP-3E	US Navy	157325 [Aries II]
285A.5541	EP-3E	US Navy	157326 [Aries II]
285A.5542	P-3C-IIIR	ex US Navy	157327 [code LD-327] [stored May08 Whidbey Island NAS, WA]
285A.5543	P-3C-IIIR	(US Navy)	157328 [SOC Jan04]
285A.5544	P-3C-IIIR	US Navy	157329
285A.5545	P-3C-IIIR	US Navy	157330
285A.5546	P-3C-IIIR	US Navy	157331

LOCKHEED P-3 ORION SERIES

C/n	Model	Last known Owner/Operator	Identities/fates/comments (where appropriate)
285A.5547	P-3C	(US Navy)	157332 [w/o 12Apr73 Moffett Field NAS, CA, after mid-air collision with NASA Convair 990-30A-5 N711NA, c/n 30-10-1]
285A.5548	NP-3C	US Navy	158204
285A.5549	P-3C-IIIR	ex US Navy	158205 [wfu & stored AMARC 31Mar04; code 2P0212]
285A.5550	P-3C	US Navy	158206
285A.5551	NP-3D	US Navy	158227 [stored for period AMARC with code 2P0194]
285A.5552	P-3C-IIIR	Taiwanese Navy	158207 3311 [was stored AMARC; code 2P0198]
285A.5553	P-3C-IIIR	(US Navy)	158208 [SOC Nov04]
285A.5554	P-3C-IIIR	(US Navy)	158209 [SOC Nov04]
285A.5555	P-3C-IIIR	US Navy	158210
285A.5556	P-3C-IIIR	ex US Navy	158211 [wfu & stored AMARC 11Feb04; code 2P0204]
285A.5557	P-3C-IIIR	ex US Navy	158212 [wfu & stored AMARC 16Mar04; code 2P0210]
285A.5558	P-3C	(US Navy)	158213 [w/o 17Apr80 Pago Pago Harbour, Samoa]
285A.5559	P-3C-IIIR	US Navy	158214
285A.5560	P-3C-IIIR	US Navy	158215
285A.5561	P-3C-IIIR	(US Navy)	158216 [wfu & stored AMARC 07Dec04; code 2P0230; SOC Apr05]
285A.5562	P-3C-IIIR	ex US Navy	158217 [w/o 25Mar95 Oman Sea; remains to fire dump Fujairah, UAE; l/n 2009]
285A.5563	P-3C-IIIR	ex US Navy	158218 [wfu & stored AMARC 09Mar04; code 2P0208]
285A.5564	P-3C-IIIR	ex US Navy	158219 [wfu & stored AMARC 13Jan04; code 2P0197]
285A.5565	P-3C-IIIR	(US Navy)	158220 [wfu & stored AMARC 30Jun04; code 2P0221; SOC Jan04]
285A.5566	P-3C-IIIR	ex US Navy	158221 [wfu & stored AMARC 06Jan04; code 2P0195]
285A.5567	P-3C-IIIR	US Navy	158222
285A.5568	P-3C-IIIR	(US Navy)	158223 [wfu & stored AMARC 08Jun04; code 2P0218; SOC Jan04]
285A.5569	P-3C-IIIR	US Navy	158224
285A.5570	P-3C-IIIR	US Navy	158225 [code LD-225]
285A.5571	P-3C-IIIR	ex US Navy	158226 [wfu & stored AMARC 24Aug04; code 2P0224]
285A.5572	P-3C-IIIR	US Navy	158563
285A.5573	P-3C-IIIR	US Navy	158564
285A.5574	P-3C-IIIR	ex US Navy	158565 [wfu & stored AMARC 20Apr04; code 2P0214]
285A.5575	P-3C-IIIR	Taiwanese Navy	158566 3302 [was stored AMARC; code 2P0205]
285A.5576	P-3C-IIIR	US Navy	158567
285A.5577	P-3C-IIIR	US Navy	158568
285A.5578	P-3C-IIIR	(US Navy)	158569 [wfu & stored AMARC; SOC Jun04]
285A.5579	P-3C-IIIR	US Navy	158570
285A.5580	P-3C-IIIR	US Navy	158571
285A.5581	P-3C-IIIR	Taiwanese Navy	158572 3310 [was stored AMARC; code 2P0192]
285A.5582	P-3C-IIIR	(US Navy)	158573 [w/o 21Oct08 Bagram AFB, Afghanistan; another report suggests c/n 5756 BuA 161585]]
285A.5583	P-3C-IIIR	US Navy	158574
285A.5584	P-3C-III	US Navy	158912
285A.5585	P-3C-IIIR	Taiwanese Navy	158913+ 3301 [was stored AMARC; code 2P0196]
285A.5586	P-3C-IIIR	US Navy	158914 [code 914]
285A.5587	P-3C-IIIR	US Navy	158915
285A.5588	P-3C-IIIR	US Navy	158916 [code 916]
285A.5589	P-3C-IIIR	US Navy	158917 [code 917]
285A.5590	P-3C-IIIR	US Navy	158918
285A.5591	P-3C-IIIR	US Navy	158919
285A.5592	P-3C-IIIR	Taiwanese Navy	158920 3305 [was stored AMARC; code 2P0215]
285A.5593	P-3C-IIIR	US Navy	158921 [code LD-921]
285A.5594	P-3C-IIIR	US Navy	158922 [code LD-922]
285A.5595	P-3C-IIIR	US Navy	158923 [code RD-923]
285A.5596	P-3C-IIIR	US Navy	158924
285A.5597	P-3C-IIIR	US Navy	158925
285A.5598	P-3C-IIIR	US Navy	158926
285A.5599	P-3C-IIIR	US Navy	158927 [code LD-927]
285A.5600	P-3C-IIIR	US Navy	158928 [stored for period AMARC with code 2P0186]
285A.5601	P-3C-IIIR	US Navy	158929
285A.5602	P-3C	(US Navy)	158930 [w/o 21Mar91 60m NW of San Diego, CA after colliding with P-3C 159325 (c/n 5615)]
285A.5603	P-3C-IIIR	ex US Navy	158931 [wfu & stored AMARC 03Sep04; code 2P0227]
285A.5604	P-3C-IIIR	ex US Navy	158932 [wfu & stored AMARC 20Sep04; code 2P0228]
285A.5605	P-3C-IIIR	Taiwanese Navy	158933 3309 [was stored AMARC; code 2P0219]
285A.5606	P-3C-IIIR	US Navy	158934

LOCKHEED P-3 ORION SERIES

C/n	Model	Last known Owner/Operator	Identities/fates/comments (where appropriate)
285A.5607	P-3C-IIIR	US Navy	158935
285A.5608	P-3C-IIIR	US Navy	159318
285A.5609	P-3C-IIIR	Taiwanese Navy	159319 3308 [was stored AMARC; code 2P0201]
285A.5610	P-3C-IIIR	US Navy	159320
285A.5611	P-3C-IIIR	Taiwanese Navy	159321 3307 [was stored AMARC; code 2P0209]
285A.5612	P-3C-IIIR	US Navy	159322
285A.5613	P-3C-IIIR	US Navy	159323
285A.5614	P-3C-IIIR	ex US Navy	159324 [wfu & stored AMARC 16Mar04; code 2P0211]
285A.5615	P-3C	(US Navy)	159325 [w/o 21Mar91 60m NW of San Diego, CA after colliding with P-3C 158930 (c/n 5602)]
285A.5616	P-3C-IIIR	US Navy	159326
285A.5617	P-3C-IIIR	Taiwanese Navy	159327 3303 [was AMARC; code 2P0206]
285A.5618	P-3C-IIIR	(US Navy)	159328 [wfu & stored AMARC 28Jan04; code 2P0200; SOC Jan04]
285A.5619	P-3C-IIIR	US Navy	159329
285A.5620	P-3C-IIIR	US Navy	159503
285A.5621	P-3C-1	US Navy	159504
285A.5622	WP-3D	US Dept of Commerce/ NOAA	159773+ N42RF [+ USN]
285A.5623	P-3C-1	Pakistan Navy	159505+ 85 [+ USN; stored AMARC with code 2P0174]
285A.5624	P-3C-1	US Navy	159506
285A.5625	P-3C-IIIR	US Navy	159507
285A.5626	P-3C-1	Pakistan Navy	159508 88 [+USN; stored AMARC 17Sep96, coded 2P0178]
285A.5627	P-3C-1	Pakistan Navy	159509+ [+ USN; wfu & stored AMARC 06Aug96; code 2P0176; awaiting conversion & delivery]
285A.5628	P-3C-1	(Pakistan Navy)	159510+ 87 [+ USN; wfu & stored AMARC 30May96; code 2P0175; w/o 27May11 Karachi-Mehran, Pakistan]
285A.5629	P-3C-1	Pakistan Navy	159511+ 86 [+ USN; wfu & stored AMARC 13Jul95; code 2P0165]
285A.5630	P-3C-1	US Navy	159512 [code 512]
285A.5631	P-3C-1	US Navy	159513
285A.5632	P-3C-1	US Navy	159514
285A.5633	WP-3D	US Dept of Commerce/ NOAA	159875+ N43RF [+ USN]
285A.5634	P-3C-1	(Pakistan Navy)	159883+ 84 [+ USN; stored AMARC with code 2P0171; w/o 27May11 Karachi-Mehran, Pakistan]
285A.5635	P-3C-1	US Navy	159884
285A.5636	P-3C-IIIR	US Navy	159885
285A.5637	P-3C-1	(US Navy)	159886 [wfu & stored AMARC 25Oct05; code 2P0242; SOC 17Jan06]
285A.5638	P-3C-IIIR	US Navy	159887
285A.5639	P-3C-1	US Navy	159888 [stored for period AMARC with code 2P0168]
285A.5640	P-3C-IIIR	US Navy	159889
285A.5641	P-3C-1	Pakistan Navy	159890+ 90 [+ USN; wfu & stored AMARC 10Aug95; coded 2P0166; May11 awaiting conversion & delivery]
285A.5642	P-3C-IIIR	(US Navy)	159891 [SOC Nov04]
285A.5643	P-3C-1	(US Navy)	159892 [w/o 26Oct78 in Pacific Ocean, 200 miles SW of Attu Island, Aleutians, AK]
285A.5644	P-3C-1	(US Navy)	159892 [wfu & stored AMARC 28Oct97; code 2P0181; to Raytheon at Waco, TX May00 for spares]
285A.5645	P-3C-IIIR	US Navy	159894
285A.5646	P-3C-IIIR	US Navy	160283
285A.5647	P-3C-1	ex US Navy	160284 [wfu & stored AMARC 31Oct06; code 2P0244]
285A.5648	P-3C-1	(US Navy)	160285 [wfu & stored AMARC 03Dec97; code 2P0182; to Raytheon at Waco, TX Sep00; SOC 29Nov06]
285A.5649	P-3C-IIIR	Taiwanese Navy	160286 3315 [was stored AMARC; code 2P0231]
285A.5650	P-3C-IIIR	US Navy	160287
285A.5651	P-3C-1	US Navy	160288 [wfu & stored Barbers Point NAS, HI]
285A.5652	P-3C-1	Pakistan Navy	160289+ 89 [+ USN; wfu & stored AMARC 16Dec97; code 2P0184]
285A.5653	P-3C-IIIR	US Navy	160290 [code LL-290]
285A.5654	EP-3C-II	US Navy	160291
285A.5655	P-3C-IV	US Navy	160292
285A.5656	P-3C-II	US Navy	160293
285D.5657	AP-3C	Royal Australian Air Force	(160294)+ 160751+ A9-751 [+ USN; Sea Sentinel conversion]
285D.5658	AP-3C	Royal Australian Air Force	160752+ A9-752 [+ USN; Sea Sentinel conversion]
285A.5659	P-3C-II	US Navy	160610
285D.5660	AP-3C	Royal Australian Air Force	160753+ A9-753 [+ USN; Sea Sentinel conversion]

LOCKHEED P-3 ORION SERIES

C/n	Model	Last known Owner/Operator	Identities/fates/comments (where appropriate)
285A.5661	P-3C-II	(US Navy)	160611 [SOC Aug05]
285D.5662	P-3C-II	(Royal Australian Air Force)	160754+ A9-754 [+ USN; w/o 26Apr91 West Island, Cocos Islands; wreck b/u & sunk locally as an artificial reef]
285A.5663	P-3C-II	US Navy	160612
285D.5664	P-3C-II	Royal Australian Air Force	160755+ A9-755 [+ USN]
285A.5665	P-3C-II	US Navy	160761
285D.5666	P-3C-II	Royal Australian Air Force	160756+ A9-756 [+ USN]
285A.5667	P-3C-II	(US Navy)	160762 [wfu 11Apr92 due to corrosion]
285D.5668	AP-3C	Royal Australian Air Force	160757+ A9-757 [+ USN; Sea Sentinel conversion]
285A.5669	P-3C-II	US Navy	160763
285A.5670	P-3C-II	US Navy	160764
285A.5671	P-3C-II	US Navy	160765
285D.5672	P-3C-II	Royal Australian Air Force	160758+ A9-758 [+ USN]
285A.5673	P-3C-II	US Navy	160766
285D.5674	AP-3C	Royal Australian Air Force	160759+ A9-759 [+ USN; Sea Sentinel conversion]
285A.5675	P-3C-II	US Navy	160767
285D.5676	AP-3C	Royal Australian Air Force	160760+ A9-760 [+ USN; Sea Sentinel conversion]
285A.5677	P-3C-II	(US Navy)	160768 [wfu & stored AMARC 01Sep05; code 2P0238; SOC 17Jan06]
285A.5678	P-3C-II	ex US Navy	160769 [wfu & stored AMARC 26Sep07; code 2P0247]
285A.5679	P-3C-II	US Navy	160770
285A.5680	P-3C-II	US Navy	160999
285A.5681	P-3C-II	(US Navy)	161000 [SOC Jan04]
285B.5682	CP-140	Canadian Armed Forces	N64996 140101
285A.5683	P-3C-II	US Navy	161001
285A.5684	P-3C-II	US Navy	161002
285A.5685	P-3C-II	(US Navy)	161003 [wfu & stored AMARC 25Aug04; code 2P0225; SOC Nov04]
285A.5686	P-3C-II	ex US Navy	161004 [wfu & stored AMARC 19May04; code 2P0217]
285A.5687	P-3C-II	US Navy	161005
285A.5688	P-3C-II	US Navy	161006
285B.5689	CP-140	Canadian Armed Forces	N64959 140102
285A.5690	P-3C-II	German Navy	161007^ [^ USN; wfs 25Jly11 to GIA at Nordholz, Germany]
285A.5691	P-3C-II	NASA	161008 N102Z N436NA [tail code NASA830 reported]
285A.5692	P-3C-II	(US Navy)	161009 [SOC Aug05]
285B.5693	CP-140	Canadian Armed Forces	N64854 140103
285A.5694	P-3C-II	US Navy	161010
285A.5695	P-3C-II	US Navy	161011
285A.5696	P-3C-II	US Navy	161012
285B.5697	CP-140	Canadian Armed Forces	N48354 140104
285A.5698	P-3C-II	US Navy	161013 [stored AMARC Nov10]
285A.5699	P-3C-II	US Navy	161014
285A.5700	P-3C-II	US Navy	161121
285A.5701	P-3C-II.3	US Navy	161122
285A.5702	P-3C-II	(US Navy)	161123 [wfu & stored AMARC 12Sep05; code 2P0239; SOC 17Jan06]
285A.5703	P-3C-II	US Navy	161124
285B.5704	CP-140	Canadian Armed Forces	N4007A 140105
285A.5705	P-3C-II	US Navy	161125
285B.5706	CP-140	Canadian Armed Forces	N40035 140106
285A.5707	P-3C-II	US Navy	161126
285B.5708	CP-140	Canadian Armed Forces	N4006S 140107
285B.5709	CP-140	Canadian Armed Forces	N4008R 140108
285A.5710	P-3C-II	US Navy	161127
285B.5711	CP-140	Canadian Armed Forces	N4009K 140109
285B.5712	CP-140	Canadian Armed Forces	N48354 140110
285A.5713	P-3C-II	(US Navy)	161128 [wfu & stored AMARC 04Aug05; code 2P0234; SOC Oct05]
285B.5714	CP-140	Canadian Armed Forces	N64996 140111
285B.5715	CP-140	Canadian Armed Forces	N64854 140112
285A.5716	P-3C-II	US Navy	161129 [code L]
285B.5717	CP-140	Canadian Armed Forces	N4007A 140113
285A.5718	P-3C-II	(US Navy)	161130 [wfu & stored AMARC 06Sep05; code 2P0237; SOC 17Jan06]
285B.5719	CP-140	Canadian Armed Forces	N40035 140114
285B.5720	CP-140	Canadian Armed Forces	N64959 140115
285A.5721	P-3C-II	ex US Navy	161131 [wfu & stored AMARC 31Aug05; code 2P0236; SOC 17Jan06; reported on display in Celebrity Row, Davis-Monthan, AZ]

LOCKHEED P-3 ORION SERIES

C/n	Model	Last known Owner/Operator	Identities/fates/comments (where appropriate)
285B.5722	CP-140	Canadian Armed Forces	N4006S 140116
285B.5723	CP-140	Canadian Armed Forces	N4008R 140117
285A.5724	P-3C-II.5	US Navy	161132
285B.5725	CP-140	Canadian Armed Forces	N4009K 140118
285A.5726	P-3C-II.5	US Navy	161329
285A.5727	P-3C-II.5	US Dept of Commerce/ NOAA	161330+ N44RF [+ USN; stored AMARC with code 2P0233]
285A.5728	P-3C-II.5	(US Navy)	161331 [over-stressed in flight & probably w/o 22Jly08; ex NAS Whidbey Island NAS, WA]
285A.5729	P-3C-II.5	US Navy	161332 [code 332]
285A.5730	P-3C-II.5	US Navy	161333
285A.5731	P-3C-II.5	US Navy	161334 [code LL-334]
285A.5732	P-3C-II.5	ex US Navy	161335 [stored AMRC Nov10]
285E.5733	P-3C-II.5	Portuguese Air Force	161368+ 300^ 14807 [+ USN, ^ Netherlands]
285A.5734	P-3C-II.5	US Navy	161336 [code 336]
285A.5735	P-3C-II.5	US Navy	161337
285A.5736	P-3C-II.5	US Navy	161338
285E.5737	P-3C-II.5	German Navy	161369+ 301^ 60+01 [+ USN, ^ Netherlands]
285A.5738	P-3C-II.5	US Navy	161339
285A.5739	P-3C-II.5	(US Navy)	161340 [wfu & stored AMARC 09Aug05; code 2P0235; SOC Oct05]
285A.5740	P-3C-II.5	US Navy	161404 [code 404]
285E.5741	P-3C-II.5	German Navy	161370+ 302^ 60+02 [+ USN, ^ Netherlands]
285A.5742	P-3C-II.5	US Navy	161405
285A.5743	P-3C-II.5	US Navy	161406
285A.5744	P-3C-II.5	US Navy	161407
285E.5745	P-3C-II.5	German Navy	161371+ 303^ 98+01# 60+03 [+ USN, ^ Netherlands, # Germany]
285A.5746	P-3C-II.5	US Navy	161408
285A.5747	P-3C-II.5	US Navy	161409
285A.5748	P-3C-III	US Navy	161410
285A.5749	P-3C-II.5	US Navy	161411
285E.5750	P-3C-II.5	Portuguese Air Force	161372+ 304^ 14808 [+ USN, ^ Netherlands]
285A.5751	P-3C-II.5	US Navy	161412
285A.5752	P-3C-II.5	US Navy	161413
285A.5753	P-3C-II.5	US Navy	161414
285E.5754	P-3C-II.5	German Navy	161373+ 305^ 60+04 [+ USN, ^ Netherlands]
285A.5755	P-3C-II.5	US Navy	161415
285A.5756	P-3C-II.5	US Navy	161585
285A.5757	P-3C-II.5	US Navy	161586
285E.5758	P-3C-II.5	Portuguese Air Force	161374+ 306^ 14809 [+ USN, ^ Netherlands]
285A.5759	P-3C-II.5	US Navy	161587
285A.5760	P-3C-II.5	US Navy	161588
285A.5761	P-3C-II.5	US Navy	161589
285E.5762	P-3C-CUP+	Portuguese Air Force	161375+ 307^ 14810 [+ USN, ^ Netherlands]
285A.5763	P-3C-II.5	US Navy	161590
285A.5764	P-3C-II.5	US Navy	161591
285E.5765	P-3C-II.5	German Navy	161376+ 308^ 60+05 [+ USN, ^ Netherlands]
285A.5766	P-3C-II.5	US Navy	161592
285A.5767	P-3C-II.5	US Navy	161593
285A.5768	P-3C-II.5	US Navy	161594
285E.5769	P-3C-II.5	German Navy	161377+ 309^ 60+06 [+ USN, ^ Netherlands]
285A.5770	P-3C-II.5	US Navy	161595
285A.5771	P-3C-II.5	US Navy	161596 [code 596]
285G.5772	P-3C-III	(US Navy)	161762 [w/o 25Sep90 Crows Landing, near San Jose, CA]
285E.5773	P-3C-II.5	Portuguese Air Force	161378+ 310^ 14811 [+ USN, ^ Netherlands]
285E.5774	P-3C-II.5	German Navy	161379+ 311^ 60+07 [+ USN, ^ Netherlands]
285G.5775	P-3C-III	US Navy	161763
285E.5776	P-3C-II.5	German Navy	161380+ 312^ 60+08 [+ USN, ^ Netherlands]
285G.5777	P-3C-III	US Navy	161764 [code LD-764]
285D.5778	AP-3C	Royal Australian Air Force	162656+ N64854 A9-656 [+ USN; Sea Sentinel conversion]
285G.5779	P-3C-III	US Navy	161765
285D.5780	AP-3C	Royal Australian Air Force	162657+ N64911 A9-657 [+ USN; Sea Sentinel conversion]
285G.5781	P-3C-III	US Navy	161766
285D.5782	AP-3C	Royal Australian Air Force	162658+ N4009K A9-658 [+ USN; Sea Sentinel conversion]

LOCKHEED P-3 ORION SERIES

C/n	Model	Last known Owner/Operator	Identities/fates/comments (where appropriate)			
285G.5783	P-3C-III	US Navy	161767			
285D.5784	AP-3C	Royal Australian Air Force	162659+	N64996	A9-659	[+ USN; Sea Sentinel conversion]
285D.5785	AP-3C	Royal Australian Air Force	162660+	N64854	A9-660	[+ USN; Sea Sentinel conversion]
285G.5786	P-3C-III	US Navy	162314			
285D.5787	P-3W	Royal Australian Air Force	162661+	N64911	A9-661	[+ USN]
285G.5788	P-3C-III	US Navy	162315			
285D.5789	AP-3C	Royal Australian Air Force	162662+	N64996	A9-662	[+ USN; Sea Sentinel conversion]
285G.5790	P-3C-III	US Navy	162316			
285D.5791	P-3W	Royal Australian Air Force	162663+	N4009K	A9-663	[+ USN]
285G.5792	P-3C-III	US Navy	162317			
285D.5793	AP-3C	Royal Australian Air Force	162664+	N64854	A9-664	[+ USN; Sea Sentinel conversion]
285G.5794	P-3C-III	US Navy	162318			
285D.5795	P-3W	Royal Australian Air Force	162665+	N4009H	A9-665	
285G.5796	P-3C-III	US Navy	162770	[code LN-770]		
285G.5797	P-3C-III	US Navy	162771			
285G.5798	P-3C-III	US Navy	162772			
285G.5799	P-3C-III	US Navy	162773			
285G.5800	P-3C-III	US Navy	162774			
285G.5801	P-3C-III	US Navy	162775			
285G.5802	P-3C-III	US Navy	162776			
285G.5803	P-3C-III	US Navy	162777	[code LK-777]		
285G.5804	P-3C-III	US Navy	162778			
285G.5805	P-3C-III	US Navy	162998			
285G.5806	P-3C-III	US Navy	162999	[code 999]		
285G.5807	P-3C-III	US Navy	163000	[code 000]		
285G.5808	P-3C-III	US Navy	163001	[code LD-001]		
285G.5809	P-3C-III	US Navy	163002			
285G.5810	P-3C-III	US Navy	163003			
285G.5811	P-3C-III	US Navy	163004			
285G.5812	P-3C-III	(US Navy)	163005	[DBR 10Jul03 Jacksonville NAS, FL; cockpit fire]		
285G.5813	P-3C-III	US Navy	163006			
285G.5814	P-3C-III	US Navy	163289			
285G.5815	P-3C-III	US Navy	163290			
285G.5816	P-3C-III	US Navy	163291			
285H.5817	P-3C-III	Royal Norwegian Air Force	163296+	3296	[+ USN]	
285H.5818	P-3C-III	Royal Norwegian Air Force	163297+	3297	[+ USN]	
285H.5819	P-3C-III	Royal Norwegian Air Force	163298+	3298	[+ USN]	
285H.5820	P-3C-III	Royal Norwegian Air Force	163299+	3299	[+ USN]	
285G.5821	P-3C-III	US Navy	163292			
285G.5822	P-3C-III	US Navy	163293			
285G.5823	P-3C-III	US Navy	163294			
285G.5824	P-3C-III	US Navy	163295			
285D.5825	P-3C-II.75	Pakistan Navy	164467+	25^	81	[+ USN]; stored AMARC with code 2P075; ^ Pakistan]
285D.5826	P-3C-II.75	Pakistan Navy	164468+	26^	82	[+ USN; stored AMARC with code 2P076; ^ Pakistan]
285D.5827	P-3C-II.75	(Pakistan Air Force)	164469+	27^	83	[+ USN; stored AMARC with code 2P077: ^ Pakistan; w/o 29Oct99 into the sea near Pasni, 55 miles west of Karachi, Pakistan]
285B.5828	CP-140A	(Canadian Armed Forces)	N6563L	140119	[wfu Jly05 CFB Greenwood , NS, Canada]	
285B.5829	CP-140A	ex Canadian Armed Forces	N6564K	140120	[wfu& stored 28Feb11 AMARC]	
285B.5830	CP-140A	ex Canadian Armed Forces	N65672	140121	[wfu & stored 07Feb11 AMARC]	
285D.5831	P-3C-III+	South Korean Navy	165098+	N4080M	950901	[+ USN]
285D.5832	P-3C-III+	South Korean Navy	165099+	N4081M	950902	[+ USN]
285D.5833	P-3C-III+	South Korean Navy	165100+	N4099R	950903	[+ USN]
285D.5834	P-3C-III+	South Korean Navy	165101+	N4107F	950905	[+ USN]
285D.5835	P-3C-III+	South Korean Navy	165102+	950906	[+ USN]	
285D.5836	P-3C-III+	South Korean Navy	165103+	950907	[+ USN]	
285D.5837	P-3C-III+	South Korean Navy	165104+	950908	[+ USN]	
285D.5838	P-3C-III+	South Korean Navy	165105+	950909	[+ USN]	
685A.6001	P-3F	Iranian Navy	159342+	5-256^	5-8701	[+ USN; ^ Iran]

LOCKHEED P-3 ORION SERIES

C/n	Model	Last known Owner/Operator	Identities/fates/comments (where appropriate)
685A.6002	P-3F	(Iranian Navy)	159343+ 5-257^ 5-8702 [+ USN; ^ Iran] [w/o 15Feb85 Shiraz AB, Iran]
685A.6003	P-3F	Iranian Navy	159344+ 5-258^ 5-8703 [+ USN; ^ Iran]
685A.6004	P-3F	Iranian Navy	159345+ 5-259^ 5-8704 [+ USN; ^ Iran]
685A.6005	P-3F	Iranian Navy	159346+ 5-260^ 5-8705 [+ USN; ^ Iran]
685A.6006	P-3F	Iranian Navy	159347+ 5-261^ 5-8706 [+ USN; ^ Iran]
785A.7001	P-3C-II.5	Japanese Maritime Self Defense Force	161267+ 5001 [+ USN]
785A.7002	P-3C-II.5	(Japanese Maritime Self Defense Force)	161268+ 5002 [+ USN] [wfu Oct08 Atsugi, Japan; b/u 20Oct09]
785A.7003	P-3C-II.5	Japanese Maritime Self Defense Force	161269+ 5003 [+ USN] [cvtd to P-3C-III] [wfu for spares Nov11 Atsugi, Japan]

PRODUCTION BY KAWASAKI HEAVY INDUSTRIES IN JAPAN

1001	EP-3	Japanese Maritime Self Defense Force	9171
1002	EP-3	Japanese Maritime Self Defense Force	9172
1003	EP-3	Japanese Maritime Self Defense Force	9173
1004	EP-3	Japanese Maritime Self Defense Force	9174
1005	EP-3	Japanese Maritime Self Defense Force	9175
2001	UP-3C	Japanese Maritime Self Defense Force	9151
3001	UP-3D	Japanese Maritime Self Defense Force	9161
3002	UP-3D	Japanese Maritime Self Defense Force	9162
3003	UP-3D	Japanese Maritime Self Defense Force	9163
9001	P-3C-II.5	Japanese Maritime Self Defense Force	5004 [cvtd to P-3C-III]
9002	P-3C-II.5	Japanese Maritime Self Defense Force	5005 [wfu & stored Mar11 Atsugi AFB, Japan]
9003	P-3C-II.5	Japanese Maritime Self Defense Force	5006
9004	P-3C-II.5	Japanese Maritime Self Defense Force	5007 [cvtd to P-3C-III; reported 2011 stored]
9005	P-3C-II.5	Japanese Maritime Self Defense Force	5008
9006	P-3C-II.5	Japanese Maritime Self Defense Force	5009
9007	P-3C-II.5	Japanese Maritime Self Defense Force	5010
9008	P-3C-II.5	Japanese Maritime Self Defense Force	5011 [cvtd to P-3C-III]
9009	P-3C-II.5	Japanese Maritime Self Defense Force	5012 [cvtd to P-3C-III]
9010	P-3C-II.5	Japanese Maritime Self Defense Force	5013
9011	P-3C-II.5	Japanese Maritime Self Defense Force	5014
9012	P-3C-II.5	Japanese Maritime Self Defense Force	5015
9013	P-3C-II.5	Japanese Maritime Self Defense Force	5016 [b/u Mar11 Atsugi AFB, Japan]
9014	P-3C-II.5	Japanese Maritime Self Defense Force	5017 [cvtd to P-3C-III]
9015	P-3C-II.5	Japanese Maritime Self Defense Force	5018
9016	P-3C-II.5	Japanese Maritime Self Defense Force	5019
9017	P-3C-II.5	Japanese Maritime Self Defense Force	5020
9018	P-3C-II.5	Japanese Maritime Self Defense Force	5021
9019	P-3C-II.5	Japanese Maritime Self Defense Force	5022
9020	P-3C-II.5	Japanese Maritime Self Defense Force	5023
9021	P-3C-II.5	Japanese Maritime Self Defense Force	5024
9022	P-3C-II.5	Japanese Maritime Self Defense Force	5025
9023	P-3C-II.5	Japanese Maritime Self Defense Force	5026
9024	P-3C-II.5	Japanese Maritime Self Defense Force	5027
9025	P-3C-II.5	Japanese Maritime Self Defense Force	5028
9026	P-3C-II.5	Japanese Maritime Self Defense Force	5029
9027	P-3C-II.5	Japanese Maritime Self Defense Force	5030
9028	P-3C-II.5	Japanese Maritime Self Defense Force	5031
9029	P-3C-II.5	(Japanese Maritime Self Defense Force)	5032 [DBR 31Mar92 Iwo Jima, Japan]
9030	P-3C-II.5	Japanese Maritime Self Defense Force	5033
9031	P-3C-II.5	Japanese Maritime Self Defense Force	5034
9032	P-3C-II.5	Japanese Maritime Self Defense Force	5035
9033	P-3C-II.5	Japanese Maritime Self Defense Force	5036
9034	P-3C-II.5	Japanese Maritime Self Defense Force	5037
9035	P-3C-II.5	Japanese Maritime Self Defense Force	5038
9036	OP-3C	Japanese Maritime Self Defense Force	5039+ 9133 [+ Japan]

LOCKHEED P-3 ORION SERIES

C/n	Model	Last known Owner/Operator	Identities/fates/comments (where appropriate)		
9037	P-3C-II.5	Japanese Maritime Self Defense Force	5040		
9038	P-3C-II.5	Japanese Maritime Self Defense Force	5041		
9039	P-3C-II.5	Japanese Maritime Self Defense Force	5042		
9040	OP-3C	Japanese Maritime Self Defense Force	5043+	9131	[+ Japan]
9041	P-3C-II.5	Japanese Maritime Self Defense Force	5044		
9042	P-3C-II.5	Japanese Maritime Self Defense Force	5045		
9043	P-3C-II.5	Japanese Maritime Self Defense Force	5046		
9044	P-3C-II.5	Japanese Maritime Self Defense Force	5047		
9045	P-3C-II.5	Japanese Maritime Self Defense Force	5048		
9046	P-3C-II.5	Japanese Maritime Self Defense Force	5049		
9047	P-3C-II.5	Japanese Maritime Self Defense Force	5050		
9048	P-3C-II.5	Japanese Maritime Self Defense Force	5051		
9049	P-3C-II.5	Japanese Maritime Self Defense Force	5052		
9050	P-3C-II.5	Japanese Maritime Self Defense Force	5053		
9051	P-3C-II.5	Japanese Maritime Self Defense Force	5054		
9052	P-3C-II.5	Japanese Maritime Self Defense Force	5055		
9053	P-3C-II.5	Japanese Maritime Self Defense Force	5056		
9054	P-3C-II.5	Japanese Maritime Self Defense Force	5057		
9055	OP-3C	Japanese Maritime Self Defense Force	5058+	9134	[+ Japan]
9056	P-3C-II.5	Japanese Maritime Self Defense Force	5059		
9057	P-3C-II.5	Japanese Maritime Self Defense Force	5060		
9058	P-3C-II.5	Japanese Maritime Self Defense Force	5061		
9059	P-3C-II.5	Japanese Maritime Self Defense Force	5062		
9060	P-3C-II.5	Japanese Maritime Self Defense Force	5063		
9061	P-3C-II.5	Japanese Maritime Self Defense Force	5064		
9062	P-3C-II.5	Japanese Maritime Self Defense Force	5065		
9063	P-3C-II.5	Japanese Maritime Self Defense Force	5066		
9064	P-3C-II.5	Japanese Maritime Self Defense Force	5067		
9065	OP-3C	Japanese Maritime Self Defense Force	5068+	9135	[+ Japan]
9066	OP-3C	Japanese Maritime Self Defense Force	5069+	9132	[+ Japan]
9067	P-3C-III	Japanese Maritime Self Defense Force	5070		
9068	P-3C-III	Japanese Maritime Self Defense Force	5071		
9069	P-3C-III	Japanese Maritime Self Defense Force	5072		
9070	P-3C-III	Japanese Maritime Self Defense Force	5073		
9071	P-3C-III	Japanese Maritime Self Defense Force	5074		
9072	P-3C-III	Japanese Maritime Self Defense Force	5075		
9073	P-3C-III	Japanese Maritime Self Defense Force	5076		
9074	P-3C-III	Japanese Maritime Self Defense Force	5077		
9075	P-3C-III	Japanese Maritime Self Defense Force	5078		
9076	P-3C-III	Japanese Maritime Self Defense Force	5079		
9077	P-3C-III	Japanese Maritime Self Defense Force	5080		
9078	P-3C-III	Japanese Maritime Self Defense Force	5081		
9079	P-3C-III	Japanese Maritime Self Defense Force	5082		
9080	P-3C-III	Japanese Maritime Self Defense Force	5083		
9081	P-3C-III	Japanese Maritime Self Defense Force	5084		
9082	P-3C-III	Japanese Maritime Self Defense Force	5085		
9083	P-3C-III	Japanese Maritime Self Defense Force	5086		
9084	P-3C-III	Japanese Maritime Self Defense Force	5087		
9085	P-3C-III	Japanese Maritime Self Defense Force	5088		
9086	P-3C-III	Japanese Maritime Self Defense Force	5089		
9087	P-3C-III	Japanese Maritime Self Defense Force	5090		
9088	P-3C-III	Japanese Maritime Self Defense Force	5091		
9089	P-3C-III	Japanese Maritime Self Defense Force	5092		
9090	P-3C-III	Japanese Maritime Self Defense Force	5093		
9091	P-3C-III	Japanese Maritime Self Defense Force	5094		
9092	P-3C-III	Japanese Maritime Self Defense Force	5095		
9093	P-3C-III	Japanese Maritime Self Defense Force	5096		
9094	P-3C-III	Japanese Maritime Self Defense Force	5097		
9095	P-3C-III	Japanese Maritime Self Defense Force	5098		
9096	P-3C-III	Japanese Maritime Self Defense Force	5099		
9097	P-3C-III+	Japanese Maritime Self Defense Force	5100		
9098	P-3C-III+	Japanese Maritime Self Defense Force	5101		

LOCKHEED P-3 ORION SERIES

C/n	Model	Last known Owner/Operator	Identities/fates/comments (where appropriate)	
Unidentified				
unkn		Pakistan Navy	86	[reported May09 Greenville, SC]
unkn	P-3C	Pakistan Navy	87	[reported handed over 07Jan10]
unkn	P-3CK	South Korean Navy	90910	[ex USN; delivered 23Feb10]
unkn	P-3CK	South Korean Navy	90912	[ex USN; delivered 23Feb10]
unkn	P-3CK	South Korean Navy	90913	[ex USN; delivered 23Feb10]
unkn	P-3CK	South Korean Navy	90915	[photo image]
unkn	P-3CK	South Korean Navy	90917	[ex USN; noted Sacheon, South Korea]
unkn	P-3AM	Brazilian Air Force	7203	[delivered 03Dec10 Salvador AFB, Brazil; report of c/n being 5220 appears to be incorrect]
unkn	P-3AM	Brazilian Air Force	7204	[not c/n 5137 as once reported]
unkn	P-3AM	Brazilian Air Force	7207	[reported 09Mar09 E Nebraska scrapyard, Davis-Monthan AFB, AZ]
unkn	P-3AM	Brazilian Air Force	7210	[delivered 24Mar08 Salvador AFB, Brazil; possibly one of the aircraft noted above awaiting conversion. Also reported by Nov07 as being used for spares Rio-Galeao AFB, Brazil; l/n 24Mar08]

NIHON NAMC YS-11

C/n	Model	Last known Owner/Operator	Identities/fates/comments (where appropriate)
1001/2001		NAMC	JA8611 [prototype ff 30Aug62; preserved Jly82 Tokyo-Narita, Japan; l/n 02Oct08]
1003/2002		(Naka Nihon Koku)	JA8612 [wfu 05Nov79 Osaka-Itami, Japan; canx 12Nov79; b/u by Nov80]
2003	104	National Science Museum	JA8610 [wfu 08Dec98 Tokyo-Haneda, Japan; preserved Ueno, Tokyo, Japan; canx 24Jun99 as wfu]
2004	101	(Robinson Air Crane)	JA8639 HL5219 RP-C1414 N102MP XA-RPC N602GL [stored Apr99 Opa-locka, FL, still marked as XA-RPC; b/u Nov06]
2005	A-101	(Venada Aviation)	JA8641 N205VA [wfu & stored Mar90 Las Vegas-Henderson, NV; canx Jan94; b/u after Jly94]
2006	A-106	(Kingsley Aviation)	JA8640 N206VA [wfu & stored Mar90 Las Vegas-Henderson, NV; canx Jan94; b/u after Jly94]
2007	106	(Air Aruba)	JA8643 N102LM P4-YSD [wfu & stored 1991 Banjul, Gambia; derelict by Mar04; b/u by Jly05]
2008	103	Japan Air Self-Defense Force	52-1151
2009	103	Japan Air Self-Defense Force	52-1152
2010	102	(Aboitiz Air Transport)	JA8644 PK-MYP JA8644 RP-C3205 [wfu by 26Mar02 Manila, Philippines; b/u by May07]
2011	102	(Merpati Nusantara Airlines)	JA8645 PK-MYN [w/o 01Apr71 Jakarta, Indonesia]
2012	107	(Aerosierra de Durango)	PI-C962 RP-C962 N103MP XA-RQU [b/u for spares 1999 Durango, Mexico]
2013	102	ex Asian Spirit	(JA8646) JA8650 PK-MYT JA8650 RP-C2014 [wfu Jun01 Manila, Philippines]
2014	108	(Air Aruba)	JA8648 N991CL P4-YSE P4-KFC [stored Jly96 Tucson, AZ; b/u by Jly02]
2015	107	(Donald Maier)	PI-C963 RP-C963 N105MP [wfu by Feb88 Honolulu International, HI; b/u Jly89 ; canx 03Jun11]
2016	108	(Aboitiz Air Transport)	JA8651 RP-C3204 [wfu & stored 2002 Manila, Philippines; l/n Apr05; assumed b/u]
2017	108	(Air Philippines)	JA8653 P4-KFE RP-C1930 (RP-C2721) [wfu late 2000 Subic Bay Airport, Philippines; Mar03 sunk in Subic Bay for use by scuba divers]
2018	105	Japan Air Self-Defense Force	62-1153
2019	105	Japan Air Self-Defense Force	62-1154
2020	109	ex Aboitiz Air Transport	JA8656 P4-KFF RP-C1936 RP-C2253 (RP-C3215) [wfu Jan06 Manila, Philippines; l/n 04Dec07 with no engines]
2021	110	(Aboitiz Air Transport)	JA8700 RP-C3215 [wfu & stored 2002 Manila, Philippines; l/n Jun03; assumed b/u]
2022	109	(Toa Domestic Airlines)	JA8662 [w/o 10Jan88 Lake Nakaumi, Japan]
2023	111	(All Nippon Airways)	JA8658 [w/o 13Nov66 in sea near Matsuyama Airport, Japan]
2024	111	ex Gambia International Airlines	JA8660 C5-GAB [wfu by Mar98 Banjul, Gambia; l/n 15Jly05]
2025	111	ex Windward Islands Airways	JA8661 RP-C1420 N107MP PJ-WIK [wfu Dec91; by Jun99 moved Philipsburg, near St Maarten, Netherlands Antilles; used as bar "Air Lekkerbek"; l/n 12Feb12]
2026	109	(Air Philippines)	JA8665 OB-R-893 JA8665 P4-KFJ RP-C1960 [stored Jun01 Manila, Philippines; b/u Jly02]
2027	116	(Donald Maier)	PI-C964 RP-C964 N108MP [wfu by Aug89 Purdue University Airport, Lafayette, IN; b/u by Dec93; canx 01Jly11]
2028	114	(Donald Maier)	JA8666 N116MP [wfu & stored Jly89 Purdue University Airport, Lafayette, IN; canx Sep89; 25Mar05 parts of fuselage and wings sunk off Oahu, HI as artificial reef]
2029	117	(Aboitiz Air Transport)	JA8706 N1145H JA8706 PK-MYA JA8706 RP-C3207 [stored by Aug98 Manila, Philippines; no recent reports; assumed b/u]
2030	117	ex Gambia International Airlines	JA8707 N1146H JA8707 C5-CGA C5-GAA [wfu by 08Mar02 Banjul, Gambia]
2031	A-117	(Robinson Air Crane)	JA8686 N1147H JA8686 N118MP XA-RPB N603GL [stored Apr99 Opa-locka, FL, l/n 16Oct06; b/u by Nov06]
2032	109	(Air Philippines)	JA8667 P4-KFK RP-C1981 [w/o 24Jun96 Naga Airport, Philippines]
2033	M-112	Japan Maritime Self-Defense Force	9041
2034	111	(Aboitiz Air Transport)	JA8668 RP-C3203 [wfu for spares May94 Manila, Philippines; l/n Jun03; assumed b/u]
2035	120	Grissom Air Museum	JA8676 OB-R-857 JA8676 P4-KFD [preserved by 17Aug97 Grissom AFB, Peru, IN; l/n 21Jly08]

NIHON NAMC YS-11

C/n	Model	Last known Owner/Operator	Identities/fates/comments (where appropriate)
2036	111	(Aerosierra de Durango)	JA8672 N119MP JA8672 PK-RYY (N119MP) N121MP XA-RPF [b/u 1999 Durango, Mexico]
2037	124	(Air Philippines)	JA8675 P4-KFL RP-C1983 [stored by Jun03 Subic Bay Airport, Philippines; no recent reports; assumed b/u]
2038	114	(Mandala Airways)	JA8678 PK-RYZ [b/u Nov88 at Tokyo-Haneda, Japan]
2039	121	(Philippine Airlines)	JA8679 PI-C965 RP-C965 [wfu 1980 Manila, Philippines, later b/u; canx by 1984]
2040	120	(Piedmont Airlines)	OB-R-895 N264P [wfu 1978 Winston-Salem, NC; b/u 1982]
2041	125	(Toa Domestic Airlines)	JA8680 PP-CTA JA8680 [w/o 28May75 Osaka-Itami, Japan]
2042	125	(Airborne Express)	JA8681 PP-CTB JA8681 HL5207 RP-C1415 N112PH N902TC [stored Wilmington, OH; l/n Dec90; probably b/u; canx 15Aug94 as destroyed; location also reported as being Tucson, AZ]
2043	125	(Korean Airlines)	JA8682 PP-CTC PP-SMX HL5208 [hijacked 11Dec69 to Pyongyang, North Korea & damaged on landing; fate unknown]
2044	125	(Lynrise Aircraft)	JA8683 PP-CTD PP-SMZ JA8683 HL5215 RP-C1416 N113PH N903TC [wfu & stored May90 Tucson, AZ; b/u between Aug98 & Sep01; canx 30Dec92]
2045	128	(Mid Pacific Airlines)	JA8684 N109MP [wfu & stored Jun91 Purdue University Airport, Lafayette, IN; l/n Nov91; report not b/u until Jun98]
2046	128	(Piedmont Airlines)	JA8685 JQ2046 OB-R-907 N265P [wfu 1978 Winston-Salem, NC; b/u 1982]
2047	118	(Japan Civil Aviation Bureau)	JA8720 [wfu 24Apr07 Tokyo-Haneda, Japan and stored; canx 25Apr07; l/n 06Oct08]
2048	115	(Japan Civil Aviation Bureau)	JA8711 [wfu Oct02 Tokyo-Haneda, Japan; b/u Nov02, sections removed by road]
2049	115	Sojo University	JA8712 N4047C [never left Japan; US marks canx 13Aug03; to GIA Kumamoto, Japan; l/n11Aug03]
2050	A-205	(Airborne Express)	JA8685 N156P N910AX [by 11Nov10 derelict Laredo, TX; canx 07Mar12]
2051	A-205	Trans Air Congo	JA8687 N158P N911AX 3C-QRM 3D-DYS 9Q-CYS [stored by Jun11 Rand, South Africa; l/n Aug11]
2052	A-205	ex Airborne Express	JA8688 N162P N912AX [stored Jly97 Fort Lauderdale International, FL; l/n 21Feb11]
2053	A-205	ex Airborne Express	JA8689 N164P N913AX [canx 26Jan06 sold in Mexico; l/n 11Nov10 Laredo, TX still as N913AX]
2054	A-202	Michinoku Traditional Boat Museum	PP-CTE JA8809 [wfu & canx 07Jly03; preserved Aomori, Japan]
2055	A-202	Japan Aviation Academy	PP-CTF JA8805 [wfu Jly03 to GIA Wajima School, near Noto Airport, Japan]
2056	A-205	ex Airborne Express	JA8690 N169P N914AX [stored Jly97 Fort Lauderdale International, FL; l/n 21Feb11]
2057	A-205	(Gus & Associates)	JA8691 N159P [b/u Jly93 Hyannis, MA; canx 08Aug12]
2058	M-113	Japanese Maritime Self-Defense Force	9042
2059	A-211	(VASP)	JA8692 PP-SMI [w/o 12Apr72 mountain 50km north of Rio de Janeiro, Brazil]
2060	A-208	(Nihon Kinkyori Airways)	JA8693 [w/o 11Mar83 Nakashibetsu Airport, Japan]
2061	A-205	(Gus & Associates)	JA8694 N187P [b/u Jly93 Hyannis, MA; canx 14Aug12]
2062	A-205	ex Airborne Express	JA8695 N189P N915AX [stored Jly97 Fort Lauderdale International, FL; l/n 21Feb11]
2063	A-202	(Cruzeiro do Sul)	PP-CTG [w/o 18Oct72 Sao Paulo-Congonhas, Brazil]
2064	A-202	(Air Caribbean)	JQ2064 PP-CTH JA8795 N993CL 9Y-TIH [stored Oct00 Port of Spain, Trinidad; subsequently b/u]
2065	A-209	(Air Caribbean)	JA8696 N990CL 9Y-TIZ [stored Oct00 Port of Spain, Trinidad; subsequently b/u]
2066	A-208	ex Aerolitoral	JA8697 N907TC XA-RRG [stored Apr91 Greenwood-Leflore, MS; l/n Apr06]
2067	A-211	ex Asian Spirit	JA8698 RP-C2015 [stored 11Aug04 Manila, Philippines; l/n 04Dec07 derelict]
2068	A-211	(VASP)	JA8699 PP-SMJ [w/o 23Oct73 Rio de Janeiro-Santos Dumont, Brazil]
2069	A-209	ex Astro Air/South Phoenix Airlines	JA8715 P4-YSC P4-KFA RP-C3587 [stored by 18May06 Manila, Philippines; l/n 04Dec07]

NIHON NAMC YS-11

C/n	Model	Last known Owner/Operator	Identities/fates/comments (where appropriate)
2070	A-310	ex Alcon Servicios Aereos	JA8714 HL5206 RP-C1417 N125MP (SE-KTV) P4-GLC S9-CAP XA-TQP [not on register since 2003; stored Saltillo, Mexico; l/n 18Aug09]
2071	A-607	Aero JBR	JA8713 N171RV (SE-KTX) N171RV XA-TTY XA-UFJ
2072	A-306	(Mid-Pacific Cargo)	CF-TAK C-FTAK N4989S N110PH [wfu & stored Nov94 Purdue University Airport, Lafayette, IN; l/n Jly97; b/u Jun98]
2073	A-306	Alcon Servicios Aereos	CF-TAM C-FTAM N5592M N111PH XA-TND [reported flying with "Rush" Oct08]
2074	EB-305	Japanese Air Self-Defense Force	82-1155 [cvtd 1995 to YS-11EB by installation of GE CT-64 engines; ELINT]
2075	A-205	(Airborne Express)	JA8718 N214P N916AX [wfu & b/u for spares Jan85 Wilmington, OH]
2076	A-212	(VASP)	JA8719 PP-SML [DBF 07Nov71 Aragaras Airport, Brazil]
2077	A-205	Aerodan	JA8721 N218P N917AX XA-YYS
2078	A-213	ex Aboitiz Air Transport	JA8722 RP-C3589 [sale to Phuket Air fell through, not delivered; by 14May07 derelict Manila, Philippines; l/n 04Dec07 still in Phuket Air c/s]
2079	A-212	Air Link International Airways	JA8723 PP-SMM JA8723 N995CL P4-KFG RP-C1931 RP-C2252
2080	A-202	ex Cruzeiro do Sul	PP-CTI [w/o 29Apr77 Navegantes-Itajai Airport, Brazil; hulk noted 14Jan10 Tijucas, Brazil, in Pepsi Cola c/s]
2081	A-202	(TCA Ltd)	PP-CTJ JA8804 N994CL [wfu Jly96 Tucson, AZ; l/n Jun02; b/u by Jly02]
2082	A-202	(Pacific Southwest Airlines)	PP-CTK N208PA [w/o 05Mar74 near Borrego Springs, CA]
2083	A-202	ex Astro Air/South Phoenix Airlines	PP-CTL JA8794 (RP-C2084) RP-C3217 [wfu 18May06 Manila, Philippines; l/n 04Dec07]
2084	A-212	(Japan Civil Aviation Bureau)	JA8709 PP-SMN JA8709 [wfu 24Apr07 Tokyo-Haneda, Japan & stored; canx 25Apr07; l/n 29May12]
2085	A-213	(All Nippon Airways)	JA8708 [w/o 20Oct69 Miyazaki Airport, Japan]
2086	A-309	(KFS Aviation Aruba NV)	LV-JII N114MP [stored by Aug93 Purdue University Airport, Lafayette, IN; canx Dec97; b/u summer 98]
2087	A-309	(KFS Aviation Aruba NV)	LV-JIJ N115MP [stored by Nov94 Purdue University Airport, Lafayette, IN; canx Dec97; b/u summer 98]
2088	A-309	(KFS Aviation Aruba NV)	JQ2088 LV-JLJ JA8832 N124MP [stored by Nov94 Purdue University Airport, Lafayette, IN; canx Dec97; b/u summer 98]
2089	A-609	ex Aboitiz Air Transport	JQ2089 JA8756 TR-LPG TU-TID JA8756 RP-C3201 [wfu 2002 Manila, Philippines; l/n 04Dec07]
2090	A-214	ex Aboitiz Air Transport	JA8710 RP-C2739 [wfu Jan03 Manila, Philippines; l/n 04Dec07]
2091	A-212	(Aerolitoral)	JA8716 PP-SMO N209PA JA8716 N908TC XA-RPU [stored Apr91 Greenwood-Leflore, MS; b/u Sep96]
2092	A-217	ex Aboitiz Air Transport	JA8717 RP-C2677 [wfu 30Oct06 for spares use Manila, Philippines; l/n 04Dec07]
2093	A-207	ex Japan Maritime Safety Agency	JA8701 [code LA701] [wfu May10; departed 12Jun10 Tokyo-Haneda, to Miho AFB, Japan; canx 31Jan11]
2094	A-213	(Air Nippon Airways)	JA8726 [wfu & canx 16Jly96; b/u 19Jly96 Osaka-Itami, Japan; canx 16Jly96]
2095	A-213	(ANK-Air Nippon)	JA8727 [w/o 16Feb00 Sapporo-Okadama Airport, Japan; canx 19Oct00]
2096	A-213	(Air Nippon Airways)	JA8728 [canx 04Apr95 as wfu & b/u on that day Osaka-Itami, Japan]
2097	A-213	ex Phuket Airlines	JA8729 HS-KVU [wfu & stored Jun05 Bangkok-Don Muang, Thailand; canx by 31Aug09; l/n 20Oct11; probably destroyed in floods Nov11]
2098	A-213	(Asian Spirit)	JA8730 RP-C3209 [wfu 2003 Manila, Philippines; l/n Jun03; assumed b/u]
2099	A-213	Kakamigahara Aerospace Museum	JA8731 [canx 07Dec95; preserved Gifu, Japan; l/n 04Oct08]
2100	T-216	ex Japanese Maritime Self- Defense Force	6901 [wfs 18May11 Shimofusa, Japan; l/n Jly]
2101	A-213	Tokorozawa Aviation Museum	JA8732 [canx 02Jun97; preserved Air Nippon c/s, Saitama, Japan; l/n 04Oct08]
2102	A-213	Saga Airport	JA8733 [canx 10Aug98 as wfu; on display Saga Airport, Japan; l/n Jun07]
2103	A-213	Tajima Airport	JA8734 [wfu 31Jan99 and put on display Tajima Airport, Hyogo, Japan; l/n Jun07]

NIHON NAMC YS-11

C/n	Model	Last known Owner/Operator	Identities/fates/comments (where appropriate)
2104	A-658	(KFS Aviation Aruba NV)	JQ2104 JA8751 JA8757 SX-BBJ LN-MTA JA8757 PK-IYE JA8757 N113MP [stored by Aug93 Purdue University Airport, Lafayette, IN; b/u summer 98; canx 15Jly11]
2105	A-313	(KFS Aviation Aruba NV)	JQ2105 JA8750 N112MP [stored by May94 Purdue University Airport, Lafayette, IN; b/u summer 98]
2106	A-301	ex Aboitiz Air Transport	JQ2106 JA8758 SX-BBM (LN-MTB) JA8758 HL5216 RP-C1418 JA8758 N219LC P4-KFB RP-C3590 [w/o 16Nov06 Manila, Philippines; l/n 04Dec07]
2107	A-301	(Philippine Airlines)	JQ2107 JA8759 JA8774 HL5221 RP-C1419 [w/o 17Jly77 in sea near Mactan-Cebu International Airport, Philippines]
2108	A-213	Zest Airways	JA8735 RP-C3592 [damaged 02Jan08 Masbate, Philippines]
2109	A-205	(Gus & Associates)	JA8740 N219P [wfu by 1988 Hyannis, MA; b/u Jly93; canx 27Aug12]
2110	A-219	(China Airlines)	JQ2110 JA8762 B-156 [w/o 12Aug70 near Grand Hotel, Yuan Shan, near Sung Shan Airport, Taipei, Taiwan]
2111	A-213	(Asian Spirit)	JA8736 RP-C3212 [wfu & canx Apr02 Manila, Philippines; reported b/u Dec02; not noted May07]
2112	A-205	(Airborne Express)	JA8741 N224P N918AX [w/o 06Mar92 Wilmington, OH; used for spares, fully b/u by May97]
2113	A-205	(Airborne Express)	JA8742 N245P N919AX [stored by Apr98 Fort Lauderdale International, FL; b/u Apr98; canx Aug98]
2114	A-205	(Airborne Express)	JA8745 N247P N920AX [stored 04Mar96 Wilmington, OH; b/u for scrap; l/n Apr97; canx Apr98]
2115	A-513	Sanuki Kodomonokuni Park	JA8743 [wfu & canx 26Jan98; on display amusement park near Takamatsu Airport, Japan; l/n Jun07]
2116	A-513	ex Phuket Airlines	JA8744 HS-KVO [stored Nov05 Bangkok-Don Muang,Thailand; canx by 31Aug09; l/n 20Oct11; probably destroyed in floods Nov11]
2117	A-205	(Airborne Express)	JA8746 N254P N921AX [stored Wilmington, OH; b/u for spares; l/n Jly93; canx Aug98]
2118	A-205	(Air Aruba)	JA8747 N257P P4-YSB [stored Dec91 Oranjestad Airport, Aruba; by Feb97 in poor condition; b/u by 02Oct02]
2119	A-205	(Gus & Associates)	JA8748 N259P [b/u Jly93 Hyannis, MA]
2120	A-205	ex Airborne Express	JA8749 N268P N922AX [stored Jly97 Fort Lauderdale International, FL; taxied 13Jan11; l/n 21Feb11]
2121	A-205	(Aerolitoral)	JA8751 N4646K N269P XA-ROL N4646K [wfu Apr91 Greenwood-Leflore, MS still marked as XA-ROL; l/n Nov96; b/u by Dec96]
2122	A-500	(Gus & Associates)	JA8752 N273P [wfu by 1988 Hyannis, MA; b/u Jly93]
2123	T-206	ex Japanese Maritime Self-Defense Force	6902 [wfu by 2010 Simofusa, Japan; l/n Jly11 with no engines]
2124	A-402	Japanese Air Self-Defense Force	92-1156 [cvtd to navigation trainer]
2125	EB-402	Japanese Air Self-Defense Force	92-1157 [cvtd 1998/99 to YS-11EB by installation of GE CT-64 engines; ELINT]
2126	A-205	(Aerolitoral)	JA8754 N274P XA-ROV [wfu Apr91 Greenwood-Leflore, MS; l/n Oct; b/u by Dec96]
2127	A-213	(Air Nippon Airways)	JA8755 [b/u late Aug96 Osaka-Itami, Japan; canx 19Aug96]
2128	A-614	(Aboitiz Air Transport)	JQ2128 TR-LPJ TU-TIE JA8821 RP-C3202 [wfu & stored Jun97 Manila, Philippines; b/u by May07]
2129	A-318	(GUs & Associates)	JQ2129 TR-KIA N924 [b/u Jly93 Hyannis, MA]
2130	A-219	(Mid Pacific Airlines)	B-158 JA8823 N905TC [stored by Dec90 Purdue University Airport, Lafayette, IN; l/n Nov91; subsequently b/u]
2131	A-213	SuperClubs Breezes	JA8760 N904TC P4-YSA [wfu Mar90 Oranjestad Airport, Aruba; Nov03 moved next to Breeze Hotel, Willemstad, Curacao, Netherlands Antilles, in use as restaurant; l/n Mar12]
2132	T-206	ex Japanese Maritime Self-Defense Force	6903 [wfu by 2010 Shimofusa, Japan; l/n Jly11 with no engines]
2133	A-513	ex Phuket Airlines	JA8761 HS-KVA [wfu & stored by Aug05 Bangkok-Don Muang, Thailand; canx by 31Aug09; l/n 20Oct11; probably destroyed in floods Nov11]
2134	A-217	(Toa Domestic Airlines)	JA8764 [w/o 03Jly71 Mount Yokotsu-dake, Hokkaido, Japan]
2135	A-227	Jesada Technik Museum	JQ2135 JA8763 RP-C3586 HS-APA [canx 17Aug09; dismantled 19Sep10 Bangkok-Don Muang, Thailand; preserved Nakhon Chai Si, Thailand]
2136	A-520	ex Greek Air Force	SX-BBG 2136 [wfu & stored Dec95 Elefsis AFB, Greece; l/n Apr08]

NIHON NAMC YS-11

C/n	Model	Last known Owner/Operator	Identities/fates/comments (where appropriate)
2137	A-520	ex Greek Air Force	SX-BBH 2137 [wfu Jly98; preserved Elefsis AFB Heritage Park, Greece, opposite main gate; l/n Apr08]
2138	A-523	(Aboitiz Air Transport/Asian Spirit)	JA8769 RP-C3208 [stored by Jun03 Manila, Philippines; gone by May07; assumed b/u]
2139	A-300	(Mid Pacific Airlines)	JQ2139 JA8779 HL5222 RP-C1421 N128MP [w/o 15Mar89 Purdue University Airport, Lafayette, IN]
2140	A-627	(Tramaco)	(TR-LPM) 9Q-CWL [wfu Jan90 Kinshasa, Zaire; b/u Jly93]
2141	A-227	(Air Caribbean)	JQ2141 JA8765 N992CL 9Y-TII [stored Oct00 Port of Spain, Trinidad; subsequently b/u]
2142	A-227	Interisland Airlines	JQ2142 JA8766 RP-C3338
2143	A-520	Greek Air Force	SX-BBI 2143 [cvtd to calibrator; active Sep08]
2144	A-520	(Greek Air Force)	SX-BBK 2144 [stored Nov94 Athens-Hellinikon, Greece; derelict by Apr96; l/n Jly01; moved 2004 before Olympic Games; probably now b/u]
2145	A-520	Greek Air Force	SX-BBL 2145 [stored Mar00 Elefsis AFB, Greece; l/n Apr08]
2146	A-523	ex Phuket Airlines	JQ2146 JA8772 HS-KUO [wfu & stored Aug05 Bangkok-Don Muang, Thailand; canx by 31Aug09; l/n 20Oct11; probably destroyed in floods Nov11]
2147	A-222	Aero Majestic	(JA8768) PK-IYS JA8768 RP-C3339 RP-C3591 [stored circa 2008 Manila, Philippines]
2148	T-206	ex Japanese Maritime Self-Defense Force	6904 [wfu by Jly11 Shimofusa, Japan; l/n with no engines]
2149	A-227	ex Aboitiz Air Transport	JA8771 RP-C3585 [stored by 04Dec07 Manila, Philippines]
2150	P-402	Japanese Air Self-Defense Force	02-1158
2151	EB-402	Japanese Air Self-Defense Force	02-1159 [cvtd 1996 to YS-11EB by installation of GE CT-64 engines; ELINT]
2152	A-227	ex Phuket Airlines	JQ2152 JA8759 HS-KAO [wfu & stored Aug05 Bangkok-Don Muang, Thailand; canx by 31Aug09; l/n 20Oct11;probably destroyed in floods Nov11]
2153	A-520	Greek Air Force	SX-BBP 2153 [stored Dec94 Elefsis AFB, Greece; l/n Apr08]
2154	A-213	(Mid Pacific Airlines)	JA8773 N906TC [w/o 13Jan87 near Lafayette, IN]
2155	A-520	(Olympic Airways)	SX-BBQ [w/o 21Oct72 in sea near Athens-Hellinikon Airport, Greece]
2156	A-520	(Olympic Airways)	SX-BBR [w/o 23Nov76 Savantoporos Mountains, near Kozani, Greece]
2157	A-227	Misawa Aviation & Science Museum	JA8776 [canx 25Nov02; preserved Misawa, Japan; l/n Nov07]
2158	A-213	(Asian Spirit)	JA8775 N107SD JU-9050 RP-C3214 [wfu & stored Jun03 Manila, Philippines; not seen May07; assumed b/u]
2159	A-402	Japanese Air Self-Defense Force	12-1160
2160	EB-402	Japanese Air Self-Defense Force	12-1161 [cnvd 1997 to YS-11EB by installation of GE CT-64 engines; ELINT]
2161	EA-402	Japanese Air Self-Defense Force	12-1162 [cnvd 2001 to YS-11EA by installation of GE CT-64 engines; ECM trainer]
2162	EA-402	Japanese Air Self-Defense Force	12-1163 [cnvd 1997 to YS-11EA by installation of GE CT-64 engines; ECM trainer]
2163	A-227	Japan Aviation Academy	JA8777 [wfu 09Apr04 to GIA at Wajima School, near Noto Airport, Japan]
2164	A-213	ex Japan Maritime Safety Agency	JA8780+ RP-C [+ code LA780] [canx 16Nov09 to Philippines; but May10 still at Shimofusa, Japan]
2165	A-214	(Trygon Ltd)	JA8778 (N108SD) N996CL 9Y-TJB 9U-BHP [DBF 03Nov01 Southend Airport, UK]
2166	A-217	Japan Aviation Academy	JA8781 [wfu 28Feb05 to GIA at Wajima School, near Noto Airport, Japan]
2167	A-213	(Japanese Air Self-Defense Force)	JA8782 [code LA782] [wfu 18Dec09 Shimofusa AFB, Japan; canx 02Mar10 as wfu]
2168	A-214	ex Asian Spirit	JA8787 N12035 RP-C3588 [wfu & stored Manila, Phillippines]
2169	A-621	Piarco Fire Service	(TR-LPN) TR-KIB N169RV 9Y-THO [stored Nov98 Port of Spain, Trinidad; donated to airport fire service; l/n 04Mar10]
2170	A-623	(Gordon B Hamilton)	PK-PYA PK-PYV JA8806 N217LC [wfu Jly96 Tucson, AZ; l/n Jun02; b/u Jly02; canx 09Feb08 as destroyed/scrapped]
2171	A-623	(KFS Aviation Inc)	PK-PYW JA8807 N218LC [wfu Sep91 Tucson, AZ; l/n Jun02; b/u by Jun02]
2172	A-623	(Reeve Aleutian Airways)	JA8786 N172RV [DBF 06Nov74 Anchorage, AK]
2173	A-626	Barker Airmotive	JA8789 N173RV [stored out of hours Anchorage AK; l/n 15Feb07; by 16Aug09 at Laredo, TX; l/n 11Nov10]
2174	A-404	Japanese Air Self-Defense Force	9043

NIHON NAMC YS-11

C/n	Model	Last known Owner/Operator	Identities/fates/comments (where appropriate)
2175	A-207	(Japan Maritime Safety Agency)	JA8702 [code LA702] [wfu for spares Shimofusa AFB, Japan, canx 02Mar10 as wfu]
2176	A-217	Japan Aerospace Exploration Agency	JA8788 [wfu 24Oct06 and used for non-flying research Kagoshima, Japan]
2177	A-213	ex Japan Maritime Safety Agency	JA8791+ RP-C [+ code LA791] [canx 16Nov09 to Philippines; but Apr10 still at Shimofusa, Japan]
2178	A-513	Piarco Fire Service	JA8792 N4206V 9Y-TIK [stored Nov98 Port of Spain, Trinidad; donated to airport fire service; l/n 04Mar10]
2179	A-523	Philippines Air Force Museum	JA8785 PI-67 RP-77 (N129MP) [stored by Jly96 Manila, Philippines; later preserved Villamor, Manila, Philippines; but reported 25Nov09 as derelict]
2180	T-320	ex Japanese Air Self-Defense Force	6905 [wfs 18May11 Shimofusa, Japan]
2181	T-320	ex Japanese Air Self-Defense Force	6906 [wfs 18May11 Shimofusa, Japan]
2182	M-320	Japanese Air Self-Defense Force	9044 [DBR 28Sep09 Ozuki NAS, Shimonoseki, Japan; to be used for parts at Yokota, Japan]
Unidentified			
unkn		Colombian Army	EJC-122 [stored/impounded by 02Jly01 Bogota-El Dorado, Colombia; l/n Mar08; reports of being either c/n 2070 or c/n 2073 disproved]

Production complete

NORD 260/262 (formerly Max Holste MH.250/MH.260 Super Broussard)

C/n	Model	Last known Owner/Operator	Identities/fates/comments (where appropriate)

Note: Known French military codes and or call signs follow the serial after two forward slashes

C/n	Model	Last known Owner/Operator	Identities/fates/comments (where appropriate)
001	MH-250	(Max Holste Aviation)	F-WJDA [f/f 20May59 with piston engines; re-engined with turbine engines as the MH.260 f/f Jly60 and re-engined again as MH.260-01
01	MH-260	(French Air Force)	F-WJDV 01//GG [ff 27Jly60; nose section preserved Musee de L'air et de L'Espace, Paris-Le Bourget, France]
1		(Nord Aviation)	F-WJSN [f/f 29Jan62; wfu]
2		(Nord Aviation)	F-WKRB? F-BKRB [CofA expired Feb65; b/u]
3		Association Antilope	F-BKRH F-AZRH [preserved Montpellier, France; l/n 28Dec09]
4		(Nord Aviation)	F-BKRS [CofA expired Nov64; b/u]
5		(Nord Aviation)	F-BLEA LN-LMB F-BLEA [wfu; fate unknown]
6		(French Air Force)	F-WLGP F-BLGP LN-LMG 6/MA [reported b/u 1994 Cuers, France]
7		(French Air Force)	F-BLHN 7//MB [wfu to GIA Rochefort-Soubise, France; l/n May96; subsequently b/u]
8		A.M.P.A.A.	F-BLHO? LN-LME F-BLHO 8//MC+ (F-GNMH) [+ France; preserved by l'Association des Mecaniciens Pilotes D'Aeronefs Anciens, Melun-Villaroche, France]
9		(French Air Force)	F-WLHP 9//ME [wfu to GIA Rochefort-Soubise, France; l/n May96 subsequently b/u]
10			[completed but never flew; used for spares Melun-Villaroche, France]

Production complete

NORD 262 FREGATE/MOHAWK 298*

C/n	Model	Last known Owner/Operator	Identities/fates/comments (where appropriate)
01	262	J C Calabuig	F-WKVR 01//F-ZADM+ F-WHTT [prototype ff 24Dec62] [+ code DM] [wfu & stored Coulommiers-Voisins, France; l/n 21May05]
1	262CS	(French Navy)	F-WLKA F-BLKA F-BLKE F-WLKE F-BLKE 1//F-SCCS [wfu & b/u Toulon-Hyeres, France; fuselage stored; l/n 23Jun07]
2	262E	(Nord Aviation)	F-WLHQ F-BLHQ 5R-MCC F-WOFU F-BNGB [w/o 31Dec70 in Mediterranean en-route Algiers-Dar el Beida, Algeria to Menorca-Mahon, Spain]
3	262A	ex French Air Force	F-WLHR F-BLHR F-WLHR 3//F-ZVOH F-BLHF 3//F-ZVOH [preserved Jun95 La Ferte-Alais, France; l/n 17Jun07]
4	262B-11	Trans Service Airlift	F-WLHS F-BLHS HB-ABD F-GBEI 9Q-CCR
5	262B-11	(Air Inter)	F-WLHT F-BLHT [w/o 12Nov73 near Craon, Mayenne, France]
6	262B-11	(Rebecca S Ruccius)	F-WLHU F-BLHU ZS-IZX N37680 [wfu 1984 Tulsa, OK; l/n Feb92; assumed b/u]
7	262B-11	ex Air Littoral	F-WLHV F-BLHV HB-ABC F-GBEJ [wfu Oct91 to GIA with ESMA Aviation Academy, Montpellier, France; canx 15Oct91]
8	262A-14	(Aligiulia)	F-WNDE F-BNDE JA8646 PI-C967 RP-C967 N87TC N420SA I-ALGM [wfu May86 for spares Dinard, France; l/n Dec95; b/u]
9	262A-44	(Pocono Airlines)	F-WLHX N26201 CF-BCU N26201 N411SA [wfu Wilkes-Barre Scanton International, PA; l/n Jly97; assumed b/u]
10	262A-44	(Industrie Air Charter)	F-WNDA N26202 7T-VSR F-BVFG [wfu by Aug90; stored derelict 1995 Dinard, France; l/n Oct96; assumed b/u]
11	262A-44	(Trans Service Airlift)	F-WNDB N26203 F-GBEK 9Q-CJK [w/o 27Jan93 Kinshasa-N'Dolo, Zaire]
12	262A-44	ex Transafrik	F-WNDC N26207 7T-VSS F-BVFH S9-NAR [wfu & stored 1992 Sao Tome, Sao Tome & Principe; l/n Dec95]
13	262A-44	(Tradco Inc)	F-WNDD N26208 N343PL [wfu Nov99 Wilkes-Barre Scanton International, PA; l/n Oct94; assumed b/u]
14	262A-44	ex ITAB Cargo of Zaire	F-WNDA N26209 7T-VSQ F-BVFI 9Q-CVC [wfu 1997; l/n Mar94]
15	262A-14	Aerolineas Sosa	F-WNDD JA8652 PI-C968 RP-C968 N88TC N417SA HR-ARJ [stored by Mar99 La Ceiba, Honduras]
16	262A-44	Musee de L'Air et de L'Espace	F-WNDB N26210 CF-BCR N26210 16//F-Y... [wfu May99 & preserved Le Bourget, France]
17	262A-12 *	ex Majestic Airways	F-WNDC N26211 N29812 VH-HKS [Mohawk 298 prototype; wfu May94 Bundaberg, QLD, Australia; canx 13Nov95 as wfu; 30Sep98 moved to vacant lot opposite airfield]
18	262A-44	ex Air Affaires Afrique	F-WNDA N26212 7T-VST F-BVFJ S9-TAD TJ-AID [wfu Oct 96 Douala, Cameroon; by 12Oct07 derelict]
19	262A-44	(Air Algerie)	F-WNDB N26213 7T-VSU [w/o 24Jan79 Bechar-Leger Airport, Algeria]
20	262A-37	ex Air Affaires Afrique	F-WLHX F-BLHX TJ-AHU [stored at Douala, Cameroon; l/n Dec97]

NORD 260/262 (formerly Max Holste MH.250/MH.260 Super Broussard)

C/n	Model	Last known Owner/Operator	Identities/fates/comments (where appropriate)
21	262A-21	ex Aerolineas Sosa	F-WNLI F-BNLI F-WOFQ F-BOFQ OY-BDD N7885A OY-BDD TG-ANP HR-ARU [stored by Dec04 La Ceiba, Honduras]
22	262A-14	(Aligiulia)	F-WNDC JA8663 PI-C966 RP-C966 N89TC N419SA I-ALGR [wfu & stored by 10Sep86 Trieste, Italy; b/u 1992]
23	262A-44	ex Transafrik	F-WNDD N26215 CF-BCS N26215 N108TA S9-NAX [wfu; by Jun00 fuselage dumped off airport near Sao Tome Airport, Sao Tome & Principe]
24	262A-44	(Tradco Inc)	F-WNDB N26217 CF-BCT N26217 N345PL [wfu by Nov90 Wilkes-Barre Scanton International, PA; assumed b/u]
25	262A-21	(National Aircraft Systems)	F-WNDA I-SARL OY-BDL D-CIMB OY-BDL N481A [wfu by Dec93; derelict by Nov96 Panama City, FL; assumed b/u]
26	262A-24	(Rousseau Aviation)	F-WNTT F-BNTT [w/o 29Dec73 Dole, Jura mountains, France]
27	262A-25	(Rousseau Aviation)	F-BNMO [w/o 05Dec71 Lannion-Servel Airport, Cote de Granit, France]
28	262A-29	ex French Navy	F-WNMP 28//F-YCKY [stored by Jan07 Lorient-Lann-Bihoue, France]
29	262AG-43 *	(Pennsylvania Commuter Airlines)	F-BNKX 4R-ACL F-WNDD G-AYFR F-BTDQ N26227 N26227 N29808 [Mohawk 298 conversion; wfu Dec87 Harrisburg, PA; l/n Oct90; assumed b/u]
30	262A-32	ex SFA	F-WNDA F-BPNS [wfu & used as GIA St-Yan, France; later moved to fire dump]
31	262A-26 *	(SJF Aviation Holdings)	F-WNDB SE-CCR N26224 N29802 [Mohawk 298 conversion; canx Mar00 as destroyed/scrapped]
32	262A-26	ex RACSA	SE-CCS N26225 N344PL TG-NTR [wfu Guatemala City-La Aurora, Guatemala; by 23Nov07 wings & tail section removed]
33	262A-27	ex Aerolineas Sosa	F-WNDD OY-BCO N274A HR-ARP [stored by Mar99 La Ceiba, Honduras; by 11Sep11 wfu San Pedro Sula, Honduras]
34	262A-21	ex Tempelhof Airways	I-SARP OY-BDM (D-CAMY) D-CIMA OY-BDM N488A N106TA N106TA [wfu by Feb92; derelict by May96 Berlin-Tempelhof, Germany; l/n 08May12]
35	262A-32	ITAB Cargo of Zaire	F-WNDB F-BPNT 9Q-CAP
36	262C-50P	ITAB Cargo of Zaire	F-WPXA F-BPXA XT-MAJ XT-OAG 9Q-CDH
37	262A-30	RACSA	F-WNDC D-CADY OY-BLV N275A HK-3878X TG-JSG
38	262A-32	(Business Aviation)	F-WOFA F-BPNU (F-GJSY) 9Q-CPM [reported crashed whilst operated by Malu Aviation during Feb09 somewhere in Democratic Republic of Congo]
39	262A-32	(SFA)	F-WNDC F-BPNV [w/o 14Aug75 St-Yan, France]
40	262A-32	ex SFA	F-WNDD F-BPNX [wfu by Nov89; derelict by Sep96 Toulouse-Blagnac, France]
41	262A-33	(Swift Aire)	F-WOFC 5R-MCU F-BVPP N418SA [w/o 10Mar79 into sea Marina del Rey, near Los Angeles Airport, CA]
42	262A-36 *	Queensland Air Museum	F-WOFD F-BPNY N26228 N29811 VH-HIX [Mohawk 298 conversion; wfu 05Apr93 Bundaberg, QLD, Australia; canx 13Nov95 as wfu; 22Feb96 preserved Caloundra, QLD, Australia]
43	262A-28	ex French Navy	F-WOFE 43//F-YCKB [wfu & by Sep06 to GIA Rochefort-St Agnant, France]
44	262A-34	(French Air Force)	F-ZKJL 44//F-RBOA [w/o 21Jan71 near Privas, Ardeche, France]
45	262A-34	ex French Navy	45//F-RBOB 45//F-Y... [wfu by Feb09; Dec10 stored Chateaudun France; l/n 18Jun11 fuselage only]
46	262A-34	ex French Navy	46//F-RBOC 46//F-Y... [wfu by Feb09; stored Chateaudun, France; l/n 18Jun11 fuselage only]
47	262A-27	(Altair Airlines)	OY-BKR (N276A) N7886A [w/o 08Apr77 nr Reading, PA, after mid-air collision with Cessna 195 N4377N]
48	262A-36 *	(Allegheny Airlines)	F-WOFZ F-OCOG F-BSTN TN-ACS N29824 N29824 [Mohawk 298 conversion; w/o 12Feb79 Clarksburg, WV; canx]
49	262A-32	(Business Aviation of Congo)	F-WOFX F-BOHH 9Q-CUM [reported w/o in August 2008 Namoya, Democratic Republic of Congo]
50	262A-38 *	(Majestic Airways)	F-WOFC F-OCNQ TS-LIP N29817 VH-HKT [Mohawk 298 conversion; canx 13Nov95 as wfu; stored Jan96 Bundaberg, QLD, Australia; fuselage sunk as an artificial reef off Bundaberg in the Great Barrier Reef, Australia]
51	262A-34	ex French Navy	51//F-RBOD 51//F-YDCA [wfu by 18Jun11 Chateaudun, France; fuselage only]
52	262A-34	ex French Navy	52//F-RBOE 52//F-Y... [by 22Jun07 stored & wfu by Feb09 Nimes-Garons, France; Dec10 stored Chateaudun, France; l/n 18Jun11 fuselage only]
53	262A-34	ex French Navy	53//F-RBOF 53//F-Y... [by Jly10 stored Chateaudun, France; l/n 18Jun11 fuselage only]
54	262A-30	Lycee Tristan Corbiere	F-WNDA D-CIFG OY-TOV N487A OY-TOV (N91205) OY-TOV [canx 22Nov94 to GIA Oct95 with Brit'Air at Morlaix, France; l/n 07Apr08]
55	262A-40	ex CEV	55//F-ZVMH [code MH] [wfu & stored 2009 Istres, France; reported will go to St Yan, France as GIA]
56	262A-26 *	(Richmor Aviation)	F-WNDA SE-CCT N26226 N29813 [Mohawk 298 conversion; canx 27Nov02; b/u at unknown location by Oct05]

NORD 260/262 (formerly Max Holste MH.250/MH.260 Super Broussard)

C/n	Model	Last known Owner/Operator	Identities/fates/comments (where appropriate)
57	262A-42	(Business Aviation/Malu Aviation)	OY-IVA 9Q-CBA [w/o 02Oct06 Kikwit Airport, Democratic Republic of Congo]
58	262A-41	ex CEV/EPNER	58//F-ZVMJ [code MJ] [wfu & stored 2009 Istres, France]
59	262A-29	ex French Navy	59//F-Y... [wfu & to GIA Rochefort-St Agnant, France]
60	262A-29	ex French Navy	F-WOFB 60//F-Y... [stored Nimes-Garons, France; wfu by Feb09]
61	262A-29	(French Navy)	61//F-Y... [stored by Sep99 Nimes-Garons, France; b/u by Feb05]
62	262A-29	ex French Navy	62//F-Y... [stored Mar00 Lorient-Lann-Bihoue, France; l/n Jan07]
63	262A-29	ex French Navy	63//F-Y... [wfu by Feb09; by 18Jun11 stored Chateaudun, France fuselage only]
64	262D-51	ex French Air Force	F-ZJYV 64//F-SDIT 64//F-RBAA [code AA] [wfu Chateaudun, France; l/n 04Jun07]
65	262A-29	(French Navy)	65//F-Y... [dumped by Nov98 Nimes-Garons, France; gone by Feb05]
66	262D-51	ex French Air Force	66//F-RBAB [code AB] [wfu Chateaudun, France; l/n 04Jun07]
67	262A-41	CEV/EPNER	67//F-ZVMI [code MI] [wfu 2004 Istres-Le Tube, France; l/n 05Jun05]
68	262D-51	ex French Air Force	68//F-RBAC 68//F-SCCR 68//F-RBAC [code AC] [wfu Chateaudun, France; l/n 04Jun07]
69	262A-26	ex French Navy	SE-FUA N26222 F-WJAK 69//F-Y... [wfu by Feb09; by Jly10 stored Chateaudun, France; l/n 18Jun11 fuselage only]
70	262A-29	ex French Navy	70//F-Y... [code AN] [wfu by Feb09; by 18Jun11 stored Chateaudun, France fuselage only]
71	262A-29	ex French Navy	71//F-Y... [wfu by Feb09; Dec10 stored Chateaudun France; l/n 18Jun11 fuselage only]
72	262A-29	Musee de L'Air et de L'Espace	72//F-Y... [wfu Feb99; operated last operational flight by a French Navy Nord 262; preserved 23Jun09 Paris-Le Bourget, France]
73	262A-29	ex French Navy	73//F-Y... [wfu by Feb09; by 18Jun11 stored Chateaudun, France fuselage only]
74	262C-61	Malu Aviation	F-BSUF (F-OHRB) 9Q-CKN
75	262A-29	ex French Navy	75//F-Y... [wfu; by Dec10 stored Chateaudun, France; l/n 18Jun11 fuselage only]
76	262D-51	ex French Air Force	76//F-RBAD 76//F-TEDA [code 316-DA] [wfu & to GIA Chateaudun, France; l/n 04Jun07]
77	262D-51	ex French Air Force	77//F-RBAE 77//F-SCCS 77//F-RBAK [code AK] [wfu Chateaudun, France; l/n 03Jun07]
78	262D-51	(French Air Force)	78//F-RBAF [code AF] [DBR 26Dec99 by storm 'Lothar' at Villacoublay, France]
79	262A-29	ex French Navy	79//F-Y... [wfu by Feb09; by Jly10 stored Chateaudun, France; l/n 18Jun11 fuselage only]
80	262D-51	ex French Air Force	80//F-RBAG 80//F-SCCT 80//F-RBAW [code AW] [wfu Chateaudun, France; l/n 04Jun07]
81	262D-51	ex CEV/EPNER	81//F-RBAH 81//F-SDMA 81//F-RBAH [code AH] [wfu Chateaudun, France; l/n 04Jun07]
82	262C-62	(Gabon Air Force)	F-WNDC TR-KJA [stored by Sep97 Libreville-Leon M'Ba, Gabon; l/n Sep00; probably now b/u]
83	262D-51	ex French Air Force	83//F-RBAI 83//DB//F-TEDB [code 316-DB] [wfu Jly00 Chateaudun, France; l/n 04Jun07]
84	262A-27	(Leasing Finance Corp)	OY-BDR N486A [wfu & stored Apr95 Fort Lauderdale International, FL; assumed b/u; canx 30Aug12]
85	262A-29	(French Navy)	85//F-Y... [DBR 17Jan79 Cherbourg, France; b/u Dinard-Pleurtuit, France]
86	262D-51	ex French Air Force	86//F-RBAJ 86//F-TEDD + 86//F-RABJ [+ code 316-DD] [wfu 2000; by 15Oct07 at Toulouse-Francazal, France, minus parts; Feb12 front fuselage to Chateaudun, France]
87	262D-51	ex French Air Force	87//F-RBAK 87//F-SCCU 87//F-TEDC [code 316-DC] [wfu Jly00 Chateaudun, France; l/n 04Jun07]
88	262D-51	ex French Air Force	88//F-RBAL [code AL] [wfu Chateaudun, France; l/n 04Jun07]
89	262D-51	French Air Force	89//F-RBAM 89//F-RBAZ [Code AZ] [wfu & preserved by Jan06 Collection de la Base Aerienne de Chateaudun, Chateaudun, France; l/n Jun10]
90	262C-62	(Gabon Air Force)	TR-KJB [w/o 29Nov90 near Libreville, Gabon]
91	262D-51	ex French Air Force	91//F-RBAN 91//F-RBAT [code AT] [wfu Chateaudun, France; l/n 04Jun07]
92	262D-51	ex French Air Force	92//F-RBAO 92//F-TEDE [code 316-DE] [wfu Chateaudun, France]
93	262D-51	ex French Air Force	93//F-RBAP 93//F-SDMB 93//F-RBAP [code AP] [wfu Chateaudun, France; l/n 04Jun07]
94	262D-51	ex French Air Force	94//F-RBAQ 94//F-RBAU [code AU] [wfu Chateaudun, France; l/n 04Jun07]
95	262D-51	ex French Air Force	95//F-RBAR [code AR] [wfu Metz-Frescaty, France; l/n Dec04; by Jly12 stored Chateaudun, France]
96	262C-63	(Kenyan DCA)	F-WNDA 5Y-DCA [b/u Nairobi, Kenya; canx by 30Sep08]
97	262C-64	(Gabon Air Force)	TR-KJC [wfu by Jan00 & l/n Sep00 Libreville-Leon M'Ba, Gabon; assumed b/u]
98	262C-65	ex Burkina Faso Air Force	XT-MAK [wfu Ouagadougou, Burkina Faso; l/n Feb05]

NORD 260/262 (formerly Max Holste MH.250/MH.260 Super Broussard)

C/n	Model	Last known Owner/Operator	Identities/fates/comments (where appropriate)
99	262A *	(Majestic Airways)	N29814 N29814 VH-HEI [Mohawk 298 conversion; stored Jan96 Bundaberg, QLD, Australia; canx 13Nov95 as wfu; fuselage sunk as an artificial reef off Bundaberg in the Great Barrier Reef, Australia]
100	262A-45	ex French Navy	F-WNDA F-BVRV N26224 F-GBEH 100//F-Y... [wfu by Feb09; by Jly10 stored Chateaudun, France; l/n 18Jun11 fuselage only]
101	262A *	(Richmor Aviation)	N29816 [Mohawk 298 conversion; l/n Oct89; b/u no details known]
102	262A-20	(French Navy)	N26202 102//F-YDCY [sold as scrap Jun96]
103	262C-66	(Congolese Air Force)	F-WNDB TN-216 TN-230 [w/o 28Jan90 near Kinkala, Congo]
104	262C-67	(French Navy)	F-ODBT F-BYCT 104//F-Y... [dumped by Nov98 Nimes-Garons, France; gone by Feb05; assumed b/u]
105	262D-51	ex French Air Force	105//F-RBHL 105//F-RBAE [code AE] [wfu Chateaudun, France; l/n 04Jun07]
106	262D-51	ex French Air Force	106//F-RBHM 106//F-RBAY [code AY] [wfu Chateaudun, France; l/n 04Jun07]
107	262D-51	ex French Air Force	107//F-RBHN 107//F-RBAX [code AX] [wfu Chateaudun, France; l/n 04Jun07]
108	262D-51	ex French Air Force	108//F-RBHO 108//F-RBAG [code AG] [wfu Chateaudun, France; l/n 04Jun07]
109	262D-51	ex French Air Force	109//F-RBHP 109//F-RBAM [code AM] [wfu Chateaudun, France; l/n 04Jun07]
110	262D-51	ex French Air Force	110//F-RBHQ 110//F-RBAS [code AS] [wfu Chateaudun, France; l/n 04Jun07]

Production complete

QUEST KODIAK 100

C/n	Model	Last known Owner/Operator	Identities/fates/comments (where appropriate)			
K0101		Quest Aircraft Co	N490KQ	[pre-production aircraft; f/f 22Oct04]		
100-0001		Spokane Turbine Center	N491KQ	[production prototype; f/f 16Mar07]		
100-0002		Spirit Air	N838SA			
100-0003		MAS Ventures 1 Inc	N493KQ	N719MS	[floatplane]	
100-0004		Jansair LLC	N494KQ			
100-0005		Mercy Air	N495KQ			
100-0006		Tyler Aviation	N55PY			
100-0007		US Department of the Interior	N708	[floatplane]		
100-0008		Summer Institute of Linguistics	N498KQ	P2-SIB		
100-0009		Townes Aircraft Sales	N525AH			
100-0010		Emirates Star Aviation	N522CM			
100-0011		Mission Aviation Fellowship Indonesia	N58NH	PK-MEA		
100-0012		Quest Aircraft Co	N500KQ			
100-0013		SC Meridian	N461JH	N879JG		
100-0014		Brice Inc	N974JB			
100-0015		Samaritan's Purse	N466SP			
100-0016		Open Door Aviation	N959WB			
100-0017		Mission Aviation Fellowship Indonesia	N102MF			
100-0018		MHOC LLC/Mary Help of Christens	N497BH			
100-0019		US Department of the Interior	N736	[floatplane]		
100-0020		Mission Aviation Fellowship Indonesia	N9710M	PK-MEB		
100-0021		US Department of the Interior	N710			
100-0022		US Department of the Interior	N745	[floatplane]		
100-0023		US Department of the Interior	N769	[floatplane]		
100-0024		MAC Aircraft Sales	N917CM			
100-0025		Town & Country Aviation	N505KQ			
100-0026		Mission Aviation Fellowship Indonesia	N103MF	PK-MEC		
100-0027		Telus Communications	N492KQ	C-FTEL		
100-0028		ICM Inc	N504KQ	HZ-SBS2+	N504KQ	[+ painted as such but not delivered]
100-0029		US Department of the Interior	N700FW			
100-0030		Brandebury Tool Company	N444BT			
100-0031		ex New Tribes Mission	N498KK+	PK-	[+ canx 06Aug11 to Indonesia]	
100-0032		Centurion Eye Hospital	N219EM	ZS-XUP		
100-0033		US Department of the Interior	N758	[floatplane]		
100-0034		Mission Aviation Fellowship Indonesia	N104MF	PK-MED		
100-0035		US Department of the Interior	N702FW			
100-0036		US Department of the Interior	N723	[floatplane]		
100-0037		Simon P Coffin	N669LG			
100-0038		Summer Institute of Linguistics	N497KQ	P2-SIR		
100-0039		Missionary Aviation Fellowship	N106MF			
100-0040		Paxton Aviation Inc	N10PZ			
100-0041		CLY Aviation	N856TC			
100-0042		Denali Leasing	N31JA	N195WK*	[* marks reserved 20Aug12]	
100-0043		Richard G Sugden	N726RS			
100-0044		LON Aviation	N23EG			
100-0045		Aircraft Guaranty Corp	N63DR			
100-0046		Air Choini	N501KQ			
100-0047		Royal Canadian Mounted Police	N496KQ	C-GMPI		
100-0048		SIL Aviation	N499KQ	P2-SID		
100-0049		ex General Conference Corp	N506KQ+	PK-	[+ canx 01Aug11 to Indonesia]	
100-0050		P W Feenstra Construction	N458TP			
100-0051		Jackson 50 LLC	N150K			
100-0052		Win Win Aviation	N509KQ			
100-0053		Kodiak Leasing	N1232H			
100-0054		Specialized Aircraft Services	(N951CM)	N54KQ		
100-0055		Boomerang Pastoral Pty	N502KQ	VH-KKW		
100-0056		Skate One Corp	N564BB			
100-0057		ex Mission Aviation Fellowship	N67MF+	PK-	[cancelled 17Aug12 to Indonesia]	
100-0058		ex Mission Aviation Fellowship	N68MF+	PK-	[cancelled 17Aug12 to Indonesia]	
100-0059		Redtail Partners	(N499KQ)	N771RT		
100-0060		Quest Aircraft Co	N60KQ			
100-0061		Kuwinda Air	N621TX			
100-0062		Superior Airways	C-GNTJ			

QUEST KODIAK 100

C/n	Model	Last known Owner/Operator	Identities/fates/comments (where appropriate)		
100-0063		Hoyt Aviation Consultants	N63HC		
100-0064		Quest Aircraft Co	N64KQ		
100-0065		Banyan Aircraft Sales	N65HA		
100-0066		Quest Aircraft Co	N66KQ		
100-0067		ex Aircraft Guaranty Corp	N67KQ+	XA-	[cancelled 30Aug12 to Mexico]
100-0068		Iris Ministries	N68KQ		
100-0069		Quest Aircraft Co	N69KQ		
100 0070		Kodiak Flyers	N557HD		
100-0071		Quest Aircraft Co	N71KQ		
100-0072		Quest Aircraft Co	N72KQ		
100-0073		Aircraft Guaranty Corp	N73KQ		
100-0074		Quest Aircraft Co	N74KQ		
100-0075		Quest Aircraft Co	N572SG		
100-0076					
100-0077					
100-0078					
100-0079					
100-0080					
100-0081					
100-0082					
100-0083					
100-0084					

SAAB SF.340

C/n	Model	Last known Owner/Operator	Identities/fates/comments (where appropriate)
001	340A	SAAB-Scania	SE-ISF [prototype ff 25Jan83; wfu Jan87 and stored; canx 27Jan87; by 21Oct06 displayed on pole Linkoping, Sweden; l/n Jun09]
002	340B	Flygtekniska Skolar i Nykoping	SE-ISA [SF.340A cvtd SF.340B prototype f/f 09Sep87; wfu 11May96 donated to technical training school at Nykoping, Sweden; l/n 23Sep09]
003	340A	(Fairchild Industries Inc)	SE-ISB N9668N [wfu; used as mockup for SAAB 2000; fate unknown]
004	340A	Pacific Coastal Airlines	SE-E04 N340CA N340SZ C-GPCE
005	340A	(Crossair)	SE-E05 HB-AHA [w/o 21Feb90 Zurich, Switzerland; used as cabin trainer]
006	340A	Pacific Coastal Airlines	SE-E06 N360CA C-GPCJ [possibly wfu by 10May09 Vancouver, BC, Canada]
007	340AF	ABC Air Hungary	SE-E07 HB-AHB SE-LBP YL-BAG OH-SAG SE-LBP (OY-GMS) OY-SCF SE-LBP EC-JPH G-CDYE S5-BAN S5-BAT HA-TAE
008	340AF	Pel-Air Express	SE-E08 G-BSFI SE-ISC G-HOPP SE-ISC PH-KJK VH-KDB
009	340A	(Raslan Air Service)	SE-E09 HB-AHC SU-PAB [stored 19Jly00; wfu by 04Aug05; b/u May07, remains left by road]
010	340A (QC)	SprintAir (Sky Express)	SE-E10 N370CA N107PX SE-LTI SP-KPO
011	340A	Air Scorpio	SE-E11 N342AM 9M-NSB VH-KEQ S5-BAO LZ-SAC
012	340A	Sol Lineas Aereas	SE-E12 N380CA N108PX LV-CEI
013	340A	First Kuwait General Trading & Contracting	SE-E13 SE-ISO LV-PHW LV-WLD N13UV 9K-XXX + OD-IST [+ probably false registration; badly damaged 12Mar07 Kuwait City, Kuwait and stored; l/n 20May08]
014	340A	Sol Lineas Aereas	SE-E14 N340SF N14XS LV-BEX [reported wfu Feb12]
015	340A (QC)	SprintAir (Sky Express)	SE-E15 SE-ISP SP-KPH
016	340AF	Pel-Air Express	SE-E16 VH-KDK
017	340A	Citilink	SE-E17 SE-ISR LY-ISR SE-ISR 9G-CTS
018	340A	Ryjet	SE-E18 HB-AHD OK-PEP SE-LMV (OE-LXA) EC-JHE
019	340AF	Pen Air	SE-E19 N343AM VH-OLG N343AM N19CQ C-GYQM N340AQ
020	340A	Air Scorpio	SE-E20 HB-AHE OK-RGS HB-AHE G-GNTC S5-BAM LZ-SAB
021	340A	SkyBahamas Airline	SE-E21 N341CA N109PX N776SB C6-SBD
022	340A	Overland Airways	SE-E22 N19M N53LB N39MB N804CE N340SS [stored by 01Mar11 Rand, South Africa
023	340A	ex SkyBahamas Airline	SE-E23 N342CA N110PX N778SB C6-SBC [wfu early 2011 Nassau, Bahamas, for spares use]
024	340A	(Riverhawk Aviation)	SE-E24 N343CA N111PX [wfu May06 for spares San Antonio, TX; l/n Jan07]
025	340A	(Sol Lineas Aereas)	SE-E25 N344CA N112PX LV-CEJ [w/o 18May11 near Prahuaniyeu, Rio Negro, Argentina]
026	340AF	SprintAir (Sky Express)	SE-E26 HB-AHF D-CDIE HB-AHF VH-ZLY SP-KPK
027	340A	Pacific Coastal Airlines	SE-E27 N320PX N27XJ C-GPCN
028	340A	Provincial Airlines	SE-E28 N347CA N336BE C-FPAG
029	340A	Blake Air	SE-E29 N100PM N108PM N77A N747P N98AL N184K N541BC
030	340A	Vigo Jet	SE-E30 N344AM XA-UGM XA-UIT
031	340A	(Mesaba Airlines/Northwest Airlink)	SE-E31 N321PX N31XJ [Jan06 to IBC Airways for spares use; canx 07Feb06; l/n May05 Loring-Limestone, ME; assumed b/u]
032	340A	(Mesaba Airlines/Northwest Airlink)	SE-E32 N346AM [to Worthington Aviation Parts for spares; by Dec02 stored Grand Rapids, MI, assumed b/u; canx 28May03]
033	340A	Regions Bank	SE-E33 SE-ISS LV-YOB (N33CQ) N441EA N460BA [repossessed 16Dec09 by bank; stored Fort Lauderdale-Executive, FL; l/n 20Oct11]
034	340A	ex Compagnie Aerienne du Mali	SE-E34 N356CA N338BE ZS-PML [wfu by Dec11 Bamako, Mali; to C & L Aerospace for spares]
035	340A	(Colgan Air/US Airways Express)	SE-E35 SE-IST N35CQ N35SZ [stored by 04Oct09 Bangor, ME; wfu & sold to C & L for spares; canx 28May10; hulk l/n Feb12]
036	340A	Aircraft Guaranty Corp	SE-E36 N200PM N260PM N77M ZS-ABM N727DL
037	340AF	Avion Express	SE-E37 LN-NVD PH-KJL SE-KPD LY-NSC
038	340A	SprintAir (Sky Express)	SE-E38 HB-AHG D-CDIF HB-AHG VH-ZLZ ZK-NLM VH-ZRX SP-KPL

SAAB SF.340

C/n	Model	Last known Owner/Operator	Identities/fates/comments (where appropriate)
039	340A	(Express Airlines/Northwest Airlink)	SE-E39 N347AM [b/u Dec02 Nashville, TN for spares; canx 31Dec02]
040	340A	(Shuttle America/United Express)	SE-E40 HB-AHH D-CDIG SE-E40 N40CQ N40SZ [w/o 08Jun05 Washington-Dulles, DC]
041	340AF	IBC Airways	SE-E41 N322PX N41XJ XA-BML N691BC
042	340A	Aircraft Guaranty Corp	SE-E42 SE-ISU ZK-NLP VP-CRC N632RF
043	340A	Pacific Coastal Airlines	SE-E43 HB-AHI D-CDIH SE-E43 N43CQ N43SZ C-GPCQ
044	340A	CTK Network Aviation	SE-E44 N357CA N339BE ZS-PMJ 9G-CTL
045	340AF	Avion Express	SE-E45 SE-ISV LY-NSB
046	340A	Aeko Kula Inc/Aloha Air Cargo	SE-E46 N323PX N46XJ XA-STX N843KH
047	340A	Provincial Airlines	SE-E47 N358CA N337BE C-FPAI
048	340A	ex Mesaba Airlines/Northwest Airlink	SE-E48 N324PX N48XJ [stored 13May05 Bangor, ME; l/n 16Sep07; b/u due to corrosion; canx 06Aug08; hulk l/n Feb12]
049	340A	Air Rarotonga	SE-E49 HB-AHK G-GNTA ZK-EFS E5-EFS
050	340A	Creole VA LLC	SE-E50 N340SA N44KS
051	340A	ex Mali Air Express	SE-E51 N325PX ZS-PMN 3X-GED [by Jly12 wfu Orebro, Sweden]
052	340AF	RAF-Avia	SE-E52 VH-KDP SE-E52 YL-RAG
053	340A	(Baron International Aviation)	SE-E53 N359CA [b/u Jun01 Nashville, TN; canx 17Apr03]
054	340A	(Mesaba Airlines/Northwest Airlink)	SE-E54 N326PX (ZS-PMO) [canx 21Apr05 as exported to South Africa, but never delivered; b/u Nov06 Nashville, TN]
055	340AF	Avion Express	SE-E55 LN-NVE PH-KJH SE-KPE LY-NSA
056	340A	(Avion Express)	SE-E56 N361CA (TF-) N456EA 9N-AGK SE-LMX LY-ISA [sold May11 to SprintAir, Poland; b/u for parts: canx]
057	340A	ex Quebecair Express	SE-E57 N401BH C-GQXF N57AD [stored by 13May05 Bangor, ME; canx 30Nov07 sold in Canada for spares; by 04May08 Vancouver, BC, Canada with Pacific Coastal; b/u end May12]
058	340A	(Mesaba Airlines/Northwest Airlink)	SE-E58 N402BH [stored 31Jly03 Bangor, ME; wfu 11May05 for spares; l/n Jan06; canx 10Apr06]
059	340A	ex Nationale Regionale Transport	SE-E59 N327PX ZS-PMS [wfu by Feb11 Lanseria, South Africa; l/n Aug11]
060	340AF	IBC Airways	SE-E60 N403BH N611BC
061	340AF	IBC Airways	SE-E61 N404BH N631BC
062	340A	(Business Express Airlines)	SE-E62 N340BE [stored 12Dec00 Nashville, TN; b/u for spares Jan03]
063	340A	(Business Express Airlines)	SE-E63 N341BE [stored 12Dec00 Nashville, TN; b/u for spares Dec02]
064	340AF	Solinair	SE-E64 N320CA N464EA 9N-AGM SE-E64 S5-BBS
065	340A (QC)	SprintAir	SE-E65 OH-FAA SE-KCR SP-KPG
066	340A (QC)	NEX Time Jet	SE-E66 OH-FAB SE-KCS (SP-KPH)
067	340A	Western Air	SE-E67 SE-ISX ZK-NLE N712MG C6-HBW
068	340A	ex Aircraft Africa Contracts	SE-E68 (HS-SHF) N328PX N68XJ ZS-CTK [sold to C & L Aerospace for parts]
069	340AF	IBC Airways	SE-E69 (N340CL) N69LP VH-OLH ZK-FXC N69LP LV-PMZ LV-WYS N69LP N340SL N641BC
070	340A (QC)	SprintAir	SE-E70 OH-FAC SE-KCT SP-KPC
071	340A	SprintAir (Sky Express)	SE-E71 D-CDIA SE-E71 OK-REK SE-LGS SP-KPV
072	340A	Bimini Island Air/Sunvest	SE-E72 (N341CL) N72LP LV-PMO LV-WXE N72LP N4340P N72VN N325SV
073	340A	Worthington Aviation Parts	SE-E73 N935MA [stored by 03Mar10 Springfield, MO; parts use]
074	340A	Danu Oro Transportas	SE-E74 N406BH SE-E74 SE-LTO LY-RAS
075	340A	ex Corporate Express	SE-E75 D-CDIB SE-E75 LV-PLP LV-WON N75UW C-GXPS [stored by Jan1o Calgary, AB, Canada; l/n 03Sep11]
076	340AF	IBC Airways	SE-E76 N329PX N76XJ N651BC
077	340A	ex Nationale Regionale Transport	SE-E77 N922MA C-GQXD ZS-DOA [wfu Feb11 Lanseria, South Africa; l/n Aug11]
078	340A	ex Central Connect Airlines	SE-E78 N407BH SE-LSR LY-NSE+ OK-CCK^ [+ painted on aircraft 10Sep07, but not delivered; ^ canx 07Sep11 on return to lessor]
079	340A	(Mesaba Airlines/Northwest Airlink)	SE-E79 (N343CL) N340PX N79XJ [wfu Apr05 Orebro, Sweden and used for spares; canx 22Apr05; l/n 09Mar09]
080	340A	NEX Time Jet/Air Aland	SE-E80 SE-ISY
081	340AF	RAF-Avia	SE-E81 F-GELG N374DC OH-SAC EC-IRD YL-RAH
082	340AF	Loganair	SE-E82 HB-AHL G-GNTB
083	340A	Fleet Air International	SE-E83 F-GFBZ N376DC OH-SAD EC-IUP HA-TAB
084	340A	IBC Airways	SE-E84 HB-AHM ZK-NSK N163PW N671BC

SAAB SF.340

C/n	Model	Last known Owner/Operator	Identities/fates/comments (where appropriate)
085	340AF	Pel-Air Express	SE-E85 F-GGBJ VH-EKT
086	340A	Danu Oro Transportas	SE-E86 F-GGBV G-RUNG LY-RUN
087	340A	Sprint Air	SE-E87 LN-NVF N110TA SE-KUT OK-SGY LN-NVF SE-KUT OK-CCB D-COPS SE-KUT SP-KPZ
088	340A	IBC Airways	SE-E88 HB-AHN ZK-FXD N88XW XA-MDG N901BC
089	340A	Exec Direct Aviation	SE-E89 N360MA N753BA N360MA N89MQ N89XJ SE-LJK 6Y-JXD
090	340A	(Business Express Airlines)	SE-E90 N741BA [to spares Oct05 by White Industries, Bates City, MO; canx 13Feb08; b/u by 28Jly10]
091	340A	Direct Aero Services/Blue Air	SE-E91 N361MA N752BA N361MA N91MQ N991XJ SE-LJL YR-DAH
092	340A	Tropical Transport Services	SE-E92 N742BA N792BA [stored by 09Aug98 Fort Lauderdale-International, FL; change of marks 17Feb10; l/n 21Feb11]
093	340A	Tropical Transport Services	SE-E93 N743BA N793BA [stored by 09Aug98 Fort Lauderdale-International, FL; change of marks 17Feb10; l/n 21Feb11]
094	340A	Pacific Coastal Airlines	SE-E94 LV-AXV N94BN N107EA C-GPCG
095	340A	US Naval Research Laboratory	SE-E95 N362MA N95MQ N95CQ [reported wfu]
096	340A	(Chautauqua Airlines)	SE-E96 N342BE N96CN [wfu Mar03 Lancing, MI; b/u for spares by Worthington Aviation Parts; canx 19Dec03]
097	340A	Mars RK/MRK Airlines	SE-E97 SE-ISZ ZK-NLR N177DF UR-CGQ
098	340A	Western Air	SE-E98 N363MA N98MQ N98XJ C6-VIP
099	340A	(SkyBahamas Airline)	SE-E99 N364MA N99RZ N99XJ C-FLPC N99VC C6-SBE [dbr 07Jan10 Nassau-Pindling International, Bahamas; b/u Feb12]
100	340A (QC)	Sky Taxi	SE-E01 SE-ISK G-GNTD OE-GIF SP-MRB
101	340A	Central Connect Airlines	SE-F01 N343BE N101CN OK-CCF
102	340A	Astars LLC/United States Navy TPS	SE-F02 N365MA N102AE N102XJ N384MA N304ST
103	340A	(Mesaba Airlines/Northwest Airlink)	SE-F03 N366MA N103AE N103XJ N103VN [wfu Mar03 Bangor, ME, due to corrosion; b/u 10Apr04; remains still present 11May05; canx 23Feb06]
104	340A	Central Connect Airlines	SE-F04 N344BE N104CQ OK-CCG
105	340A	Air Sunshine	SE-F05 N744BA
106	340A	ex Mesaba Airlines/Northwest Airlink	SE-F06 LV-AXW SE-F06 SE-KSV N106PX N106XJ [stored & wfu 13May05 Bangor, ME; derelict hulk by Feb12]
107	340A	ex Mesaba Airlines/Northwest Airlink	SE-F07 N367MA N107AE N107XJ [stored by 31Jly03 Bangor, ME; to be b/u; l/n 11May05]
108	340A	Aeko Kula Inc/Aloha Air Cargo	SE-F08 N345BE N108CQ OK-CCE N844KH
109	340AF	Pen Air	SE-F09 N368MA N109AE N109XJ N662PA
110	340A	SkyBahamas Airline	SE-F10 N369MA N110MQ N110XJ C6-SBE+ C6-SBG [+ [painted in error]
111	340A	Avitrans Nordic	SE-F11 N745BA C-GQXK N30NC SE-F11 SE-KXE LY-KXE SE-KXE SP-MRD* [* marks reserved 2011 for Sky Taxi]
112	340A	Avitrans/Skyways Express	SE-F12 N370MA N112AE N112XJ (SE-LJM) SE-F12 LY-RIK SE-LJM
113	340A (QC)	Loganair/Flybe	SE-F13 HB-AHO G-GNTF SE-F13 G-GNTF
114	340A	NEX Time Jet/Air Aland	SE-F14 N371MA N114SB N114XJ (SE-LJN) SE-F14 LY-DIG SE-LJN (4L-EUI)
115	340A	Solar Air	SE-F15 N372MA N115SB N115XJ SE-LJO SE-F15 HS-HPY SE-LJO HS-SAC [probably destroyed in floods Nov11 Bangkok-Don Muang, Thailand]
116	340A	Direct Aero Services/Air Batumi	SE-F16 (HB-AHP) D-CDIC ZK-NLT N601SE SE-F16 YR-DAA
117	340A	Direct Aero Services/Blue Air	SE-F17 F-GHDB N378DC OH-SAE EC-INU EC-IVD SE-F17 YR-DAC
118	340A	SprintAir (Sky Express)	SE-F18 N373MA N118AE N118CQ N118SD SE-F18 SP-KPN
119	340A	Taby Air Maintenance	SE-F19 N374MA N119AE N119XJ SE-LJP [reported 09Mar09 stored still as N119XJ Orebro-Bofors, Sweden]
120	340A	Western Air	SE-F20 HB-AHP ZK-FXA N418MW C6-JAY
121	340A	Western Air	SE-F21 N109TA D-CDIJ SE-F21 N121CQ C6-RMW
122	340A	Western Air/Cat Island Air	SE-F22 HB-AHQ ZK-FXB N379KB C6-CAA
123	340A	Sol Lineas Aereas	SE-F23 N375MA N123MQ N123CQ N123XS LV-BMD
124	340A	Mars RK/MRK Airlines	SE-F24 D-CDID ZK-NLQ N340JW UR-CGR
125	340AF	IBC Airways	SE-F25 N125CH N661BC

SAAB SF.340

C/n	Model	Last known Owner/Operator	Identities/fates/comments (where appropriate)
126	340A (QC)	Fleet Air International	SE-F26 HB-AHR G-GNTG SE-LSP HA-TAD
127	340A	NEX Time Jet	SE-F27 B-12200 SE-LEP
128	340A	Plus International Bank	SE-F28 N128CH HI-848 N128CH [stored Fort Lauderdale Executive, FL: l/n 20Feb12]
129	340A	(Golden Air)	SE-F29 B-12299 SE-LES [wfu by 30Nov08 Trolhattan, Sweden; canx 26Aug11 as b/u]
130	340A (QC)	Sky Express/Direct Fly	SE-F30 (SE-ISL) LN-SAA SE-ISL SP-KPE
131	340A	Sol Lineas Aereas	SE-F31 VH-KDI LV-BTP
132	340A	Estonian Air Regional	SE-F32 HB-AHS SE-F32 EC-229 EC-GGK SE-KFA OK-TOP OM-BAA OK-TOP SE-LMT ZK-NLC SE-LMT ES-ASM
133	340A	Transwest Air	SE-F33 SE-ISM G-GNTE SE-ISM C-GKCY
134	340A	Robin Hood Aviation	SE-F34 HB-AHT ZK-NLS SE-F34 OE-GIR
135	340A (QC)	Sky Express/Direct Fly	SE-F35 OH-FAD SE-KCU SP-KPF
136	340A	ex Mali Air Express	SE-F36 F-GHMJ N136AN ZK-NLN 3X-GEJ [by Jly12 wfu Orebro, Sweden]
137	340A	CTK Network Aviation	SE-F37 SE-ISN ZK-NLH N662RH SE-ISN YR-DAB 9G-CTQ
138	340A	Plus International Bank	SE-F38 N746BA N138CQ N138SD HI-866 N138SD
139	340A (QC)	SprintAir (Sky Express)	SE-F39 OH-FAE SP-KPR
140	340A	Pacific Coastal Airlines	SE-F40 N140N N140CG (N140XJ) C-GCPU
141	340A	NextJet	SE-F41 D-CHBA SE-KRS ZK-NSL OK-UFO SE-LMR
142	340A	Transportes Aereos Guatemaltecos	SE-F42 N341PX N142XJ TG-BJO
143	340A	Sky Taxi	SE-F43 F-GHMK N375DC OH-SAF EC-IRR SP-MRC
144	340A	OLT – Ostfriesische Lufttransport	SE-F44 D-CHBB SE-KRT ZK-NSM LV-PMG LV-WTF D-COLE
145	340AF	SprintAir (Sky Express)	SE-F45 SE-ISD ZK-FXQ SE-ISD SP-KPU
146	340A	SF340A-146 Holding Inc	SE-F46 N146CA N335BE N146CQ SU-FLE 3D-FCP N146PJ
147	340A	(Mesaba Airlines/Northwest Airlink)	SE-F47 N342PX [DBR 02Jan93 Hibbing, MN; sold to White Industries for parts; fuselage by Jan96 Bates City, MO; canx 17Jan02; nose to Flight Safety as simulator; l/n 25Apr07]
148	340A	Maxfly Aviation	SE-F48 N747BA N148CQ N148SD C-GCPZ N334MA
149	340A	SkyBahamas Airline	SE-F49 N748BA N149CQ N149SZ N779SB C6-SBB
150	340A	Sol Lineas Aereas	SE-F50 N346BE N150CN LV-BEW
151	340A	Estonian Air Regional	SE-F51 (OY-BZU) N120TA SE-KUU 9M-NSC VH-LPI ZK-NLG SE-KUU ES-ASN
152	340A	(Worthington Aviation Parts)	SE-F52 N749BA N152CQ (N152SD) [wfu Aug06; reported to Fort Wayne, IN for parts recovery]
153	340A	Purple Moon	SE-F53 F-GHMI N153AN ZK-NLO OE-GOD
154	340A	(Formosa Airlines)	SE-F54 B-12266 [sold to Golden Air, Sweden, arrived Trollhattan, Sweden 11Jly04; wing corrosion; wfu and used for spares; l/n 18Jun06]
155	340A	Pel-Air Express	SE-F55 VH-EKD
156	340A	Golden Air/NextJet	SE-F56 SE-ISE ZK-NLF SE-ISE YL-BAP SE-ISE
157	340A	ex Lynx Air International	SE-F57 N751BA N157CQ N157SD [stored 21Jan11 St Petersburg, FL]
158	340A	(Lynx Air International)	SE-F58 N158CA N334BE N158CQ N158SD [stored Jan07 Fort Lauderdale-International, FL; l/n 20Feb11, later b/u for parts]
159	340A	Central Connect Airlines	SE-F59 (SE-ISI) D-CHBC SE-KRN ZS-NLI LY-NSD OK-CCL [reported sold to Alandia Air for parts use]
160	340B	Loganair/Flybe	SE-F60 HB-AKA ER-SGC SE-F60 G-LGNI
161	340B	Central Connect Airlines	SE-F61 HB-AKB XA-AEM SE-KXH OK-CCD
162	340B	Golden Air	SE-F62 SE-ISG
163	340B	South Airlines	SE-F63 (OO-RXL) HB-AHZ (F-GGZM) OO-RXL OK-UGU OM-UGU (SE-KCG) (SE-KCX) 5Y-FLA 4L-EUI UR-IMF
164	340B	NextJet	SE-F64 HB-AKC XA-AAO SE-KXG
165	340B	Transwest Air	SE-F65 N586MA C-GTJX
166	340B	PL2 LLC	SE-F66 N587MA C-GTJY N327SA
167	340B	Finnaviation/Golden Air	SE-F67 OH-FAF
168	340B	Sol Lineas Aereas	SE-F68 F-GKLA HB-AKP ER-ASA ER-SGA HB-AKP YR-VGS D-CDAU SE-LJR LV-CSK
169	340B	Loganair/Flybe	SE-F69 N588MA G-GNTH G-LGND
170	340B	Swedish Air Force	SE-F70 100001 [type TP 100A; code 001]

SAAB SF.340

C/n	Model	Last known Owner/Operator	Identities/fates/comments (where appropriate)
171	340B	ex Kenya Flamingo Airways	SE-F71 HB-AHY OO-RXM OK-UGT OM-UGT (SE-KCY) SE-KCH 5Y-FLB (4L-GIA) [stored Mar10 Ostrava, Czech Republic; reported sold in Sweden to Golden Air & in Ukraine]
172	340B	Loganair/Flybe	SE-F72 N589MA G-GNTI G-LGNE
173	340B	Loganair/Flybe	SE-F73 HB-AKD F-GPKD SE-F73 G-LGNJ
174	340B	(Flagship Airlines/American Eagle)	SE-F74 N174AE [wfu 08Aug03 Abilene, TX; l/n 21Oct04; canx 01Feb05]
175	340B	REX – Regional Express	SE-F75 PH-KSA N143NC VH-OLL
176	340B	NEX Time Jet	SE-F76 HB-AKE XA-AFR SE-KXI
177	340B	(Flagship Airlines/American Eagle)	SE-F77 N177AE [stored 07Dec02 Abilene, TX; l/n 21Oct04; canx 12Aug05]
178	340B	REX – Regional Express	SE-F78 PH-KSB N141NC XA-ADH N178CT VH-YRX
179	340B	REX – Regional Express/Pel Air	SE-F79 PH-KSC (XA-) N145NC XA-ACB N179CT VH-XRX HS-GBB HS-HPE VH-ZXS
180	340B	(Flagship Airlines/American Eagle)	SE-F80 N180AE [wfu 10Aug03 Abilene, TX; canx 11May05 due to corrosion; to Colgan Air for parts; b/u Jun05]
181	340B	Pen Air	SE-F81 N590MA N665PA
182	340B	REX – Regional Express	SE-F82 HB-AKF ER-SGB VH-ZLX
183	340B	Aeromexico Connect	SE-F83 PH-KSD N144NC XA-ACK
184	340B	Colgan Air/United Express	SE-F84 N184AE N300CE N184CJ
185	340B	Loganair/Flybe	SE-F85 HB-AKG F-GPKG (YR-VGT) SE-F85 G-LGNK
186	340B	REX – Regional Express	SE-F86 PH-KSE N142NC XA-ACR N186CT VH-JRX HS-GBA HS-HPI VH-ZJS
187	340B	Loganair/Flybe	SE-F87 N347BE XA-TUN N347BE SE-F87 G-LGNM
188	340B	Central Connect Airlines	SE-F88 PH-KSF XA-TJI OK-CCO
189	340B	Eril Thun AB/NEX Time Jet	SE-F89 PH-KSG XA-TKT SE-KXJ
190	340B	Transwest Air	SE-F90 N348BE XA-TUQ C-GTWK
191	340B	Colgan Air/United Express	SE-F91 N191AE N301CE N191MJ
192	340B	Loganair/Flybe	SE-F92 N591MA G-GNTJ N192JE G-LGNF
193	340B	Colgan Air/United Express	SE-F93 N193AE N302CE N193CJ
194	340B	Colgan Air/United Express	SE-F94 N194AE N303CE N194CJ
195	340B	(KLM Cityhopper)	SE-F95 PH-KSH [w/o 04Apr94 Amsterdam-Schiphol, Netherlands]
196	340B	Colgan Air/United Express	SE-F96 N349BE XA-TUC N196JW N196CJ
197	340B	Loganair/Flybe	SE-F97 N350BE XA-ASM N350BE SE-F97 G-LGNN
198	340B	Colgan Air/United Express	SE-F98 N198AE N304CE N198CJ
199	340B	Loganair/Aer Arann	SE-F99 N592MA G-LGNA
200	340B	REX – Regional Express	SE-E02 HB-AKH YR-VGN VH-RXQ
201	340B	Colgan Air/United Express	SE-G01 N201AE N309CE
202	340B	Colgan Air	SE-G02 N202KD N305CE N202SR
203	340B	Colgan Air	SE-G03 N203NE N306CE N203CJ
204	340B	Colgan Air/United Express	SE-G04 N204NE N307CE N204CJ
205	340B	REX – Regional Express	SE-G05 VH-OLM
206	340B	Pen Air	SE-G06 N593MA N675PA
207	340B	ex REX – Regional Express	SE-G07 VH-OLN "VH-PBS"+ [+ last service 08Feb08; wfu Wagga Wagga, NSW, Australia; to Australian Airline Pilot Academy as GIF off airport, with false marks; canx 03Jun10 as retired]
208	340B	Central Connect Airlines	SE-G08 HB-AKI YR-VGM OK-CCC
209	340B	REX – Regional Express	SE-G09 N355BE VH-RXX
210	340B	Colgan Air	SE-G10 N210AE N308CE N210CJ
211	340B	Polet Aviakompania	SE-G11 N211NE VQ-BGB
212	340B	Pen Air	SE-G12 N594MA N685PA
213	340B	(Crossair)	SE-G13 HB-AKK [w/o 10Jan00 near Niederhasli, Switzerland]
214	340B	Aerocentury Corp	SE-G14 N214DA N311CE [stored by May11 Springfield, MO; for sale]
215	340B	Avitrans Nordic/NEX Time Jet	SE-G15 HB-AKL YR-VGO D-CDEO SE-LJS
216	340B	Loganair/Flybe	SE-G16 N595MA G-LGNB
217	340B	Argentine Air Force	SE-G17 PH-KSI XA-TKL N217JJ T-34
218	340B	Polet Aviakompania	SE-G18 N218AE VQ-BGF
219	340B	ex Flagship Airlines/American Eagle	SE-G19 N219AE [stored 02Sep08 Kingman, AZ; l/n 10Oct11]
220	340B	Colgan Air/United Express	SE-G20 N360PX N220MJ
221	340B	NEX Time Jet	SE-G21 HB-AKM F-GPKM D-CASD SE-LJT
222	340B	(Flagship Airlines/American Eagle)	SE-G22 N222NE [stored 27Sep05 Abilene, TX; b/u late 2005; canx 14Oct05]

SAAB SF.340

C/n	Model	Last known Owner/Operator	Identities/fates/comments (where appropriate)
223	340B	Estonian Air Regional	SE-G23 SE-KSI VH-EKK SE-KSI D-CASB SE-KSI ES-ASO
224	340B	Lakeshore Express	SE-G24 N224TH N9CJ
225	340B	South Airlines	SE-G25 HB-AKN YR-VGR UR-IMX
226	340B	Argentine Air Force	SE-G26 PH-KSK XA-TJR N285DC T-32
227	340B	(Flagship Airlines/American Eagle)	SE-G27 N227AE [wfu May00; canx 19Apr04 wfu; fuselage to Texas State Technical College West Texas, Abilene, TX; l/n 27Sep05]
228	340B	South Airlines	SE-G28 HB-AKO YR-VGP UR-IMS
229	340B	REX – Regional Express	SE-G29 SE-KSK VH-KDR SE-KSK D-CASC SE-KSK LY-ESM SE-KSK VH-ZLR
230	340B	Business Aviation Centre	SE-G30 F-GHVS SE-KTE XA-TQY SE-KTE OK-CCN SE-KTE UR-APM
231	340B	Wings West Airlines/American Eagle	SE-G31 N231LN [stored 26Jan04 Abilene, TX; l/n12Oct11]
232	340B	Polet Aviakompania	SE-G32 N232AE VQ-BGC
233	340B	S3B Leasing LLC	SE-G33 N233CH N233CJ N702RS
234	340B	(Wings West Airlines/American Eagle)	SE-G34 N234AE [canx 03Oct06; ferried after canx 19May07 to Waco-Regional, TX]
235	340B	Aviation Inventory Resources	SE-G35 N235AE
236	340B	ex Simmons Airlines/American Eagle	SE-G36 N236AE [stored 08Aug08 Abilene, TX; 28Sep08 to Kingman, AZ; l/n 10Oct11]
237	340B	Colgan Air/United Express	SE-G37 N351BE N237MJ
238	340B	ex Simmons Airlines/American Eagle	SE-G38 N238AE [stored 01Oct08 Kingman, AZ; l/n 10Oct11]
239	340B	Colgan Air/United Express	SE-G39 N352BE N239CJ
240	340B	ex Simmons Airlines/American Eagle	SE-G40 N240DS [stored 02Nov08 Kingman, AZ; l/n 10Oct11]
241	340B	(Simmons Airlines/American Eagle)	SE-G41 N241AE [wfu 24Dec04 Abilene, TX; l/n Sep05; canx 02Aug06 for parts]
242	340B	Colgan Air/United Express	SE-G42 N353BE N242CJ
243	340B	(Simmons Airlines/American Eagle)	SE-G43 N243AE [stored 09Apr03 Abilene, TX; l/n 27Sep05; canx 03Oct06 as wfu]
244	340B	ex Simmons Airlines/American Eagle	SE-G44 N244AE [stored 06Mar03 Abilene, TX; l/n 12Oct11]
245	340B	ex Simmons Airlines/American Eagle	SE-G45 N245AE [stored 22Sep02 Abilene, TX; l/n 12Oct11]
246	340B	Loganair/Flybe	SE-G46 N354BE XA-TUM N869DC SE-G46 G-LGNL
247	340B	Simmons Airlines/American Eagle	SE-G47 N247AE [stored 27Aug03 Abilene, TX; l/n 12Oct11]
248	340B	Lambert Leasing/"MBV"	SE-G48 EI-CFA N248PX EC-349 SE-G48 LY-SBA SE-KXD XA-TUB N248DP C6-LSR N248DP
249	340B	Colgan Air	SE-G49 N361PX N249CJ
250	340B	Polet Aviakompania	SE-G50 N250AE VQ-BGD
251	340B	ex Colgan Air	SE-G51 EI-CFB N251PX HK-4088X XA-TQO N251CJ [stored 13Jly12 Bangor, ME]
252	340B	S3B Leasing LLC	SE-G52 N252CH N252CJ N703RS
253	340B	ex Simmons Airlines/American Eagle	SE-G53 N253AE [stored 03Nov08 Kingman, AZ; l/n10Oct11]
254	340B	ex Simmons Airlines/American Eagle	SE-G54 N254AE [stored 18Mar04 Abilene, TX; l/n 12Oct11]
255	340B	Happy Air	SE-G55 EI-CFC (N255PX) OH-FAH LY-SBB SE-G55 XA-TTW N255AJ HS-HPA
256	340B	ex Simmons Airlines/American Eagle	SE-G56 N256AE [stored 26Jan04 Abilene, TX; l/n 12Oct11]
257	340B	REX – Regional Express	SE-G57 EI-CFD N257PX (F-GNVQ) VH-EKX
258	340B	ex Colgan Air/US Airways Express	SE-G58 N362PX
259	340B	Eznis Airways	SE-G59 N259AE JU-9901
260	340B	IBC Airways	SE-G60 N363PX N431BC
261	340B	ex Simmons Airlines/American Eagle	SE-G61 N261AE [stored by 27Sep05 Abilene, TX; l/n 12Oct11]
262	340B	Pen Air/Island Air Hawaii	SE-G62 N364PX
263	340B	ex Simmons Airlines/American Eagle	SE-G63 N263AE [stored 01Oct08 Kingman, AZ; l/n 11Oct11]
264	340B	ex Simmons Airlines/American Eagle	SE-G64 N264AE [stored 26Jan04 Abilene, TX; l/n 12Oct11]
265	340B	Pen Air	SE-G65 N365PX
266	340B	ex Simmons Airlines/American Eagle	SE-G66 N266AE [stored 25Sep08 Kingman, AZ; l/n 11Oct11]
267	340B	Aerolineas SOSA	SE-G67 N366PX+ HR- [+ canx 10Sep12 to Honduras]
268	340B	(Simmons Airlines/American Eagle)	SE-G68 N268AE [stored 09Apr03 Abilene, TX; l/n Aug07; canx 12Sep07]
269	340B	ex Simmons Airlines/American Eagle	SE-G69 N269AE N902AE [stored 03Oct08 Kingman, AZ; l/n 10Oct11]
270	340B	Argentine Air Force	SE-G70 PH-KSL XA-TIU XA-CGO N284DC T-31
271	340B	IBC Airways	SE-G71 N367PX
272	340B	ex Simmons Airlines/American Eagle	SE-G72 N272AE [stored 27Oct04 Abilene, TX; l/n 12Oct11]
273	340B	Polet Aviakompania	SE-G73 N273AE VQ-BGE

SAAB SF.340

C/n	Model	Last known Owner/Operator	Identities/fates/comments (where appropriate)
274	340B	IBC Airways	SE-G74 N368PX N481BC
275	340B	REX – Regional Express	SE-G75 N356BE N275CJ VH-RXE
276	340B	Business Aviation Centre	SE-G76 F-GHVT SE-KTK UR-ARO
277	340B	Colgan Air/United Express	SE-G77 N357BE N277MJ
278	340B	ex Simmons Airlines/American Eagle	SE-G78 N278AE [stored 21Oct04 Abilene, TX; l/n 12Oct11]
279	340B	REX – Regional Express	SE-G79 N358BE VH-RXN
280	340B	ex Simmons Airlines/American Eagle	SE-G80 N280AE [stored 18Mar04 Abilene, TX; l/n 12Oct11]
281	340B	Japan Air Commuter	SE-G81 JA8886
282	340B	ex Simmons Airlines/American Eagle	SE-G82 N282AE N903AE [stored Abilene, TX; l/n 12Oct11]
283	340B	Aviation Inventory Resources	SE-G83 N283AE VH-UYI N283AE [reported for Western Air, Bahamas]
284	340B	ex Simmons Airlines/American Eagle	SE-G84 N284AE [stored 21Oct04 Abilene, TX; l/n 12Oct11]
285	340B	REX – Regional Express	SE-G85 N359BE VH-RXS
286	340B	ex Simmons Airlines/American Eagle	SE-G86 N286AE [stored 01Oct08 Kingman, AZ; l/n 10Oct11]
287	340B	REX – Regional Express	SE-G87 N360BE VH-TRX
288	340B	Argentine Air Force	SE-G88 PH-KSM XA-TKA N288JJ T-33
289	340B	ex Norse Air Charter	SE-G89 B-3651 ZS-PDP
290	340B	REX – Regional Express	SE-G90 N361BE VH-KRX
291	340B	REX – Regional Express	SE-G91 N362BE VH-NRX
292	340B	ex Norse Air Charter	SE-G92 B-3652 ZS-PDR 9N-AHK ZS-PDR [stored Rand, South Africa; l/n Feb11 in poor condition]
293	340B	REX – Regional Express	SE-G93 N363BE VH-ORX
294	340B	Turbo Lease LLC/Air Panama	SE-G94 N364BE N294CJ HP-1671PST
295	340B	Turbo Lease LLC/Peninsula Airways	SE-G95 N369PX
296	340B	(Norse Air Charter/Catovair)	SE-G96 B-3653 ZS-PDO 9N-AHM ZS-PDO [wfu by 24Sep09 Rand, South Africa still marked as 9N-AHM; b/u Nov10; canx 30Nov10 to USA]
297	340B	Eznis Airways	SE-G97 N297AE JU-9903
298	340B	ex Simmons Airlines/American Eagle	SE-G98 N298AE [stored 02Oct08 Kingman, AZ; l/n 10Oct11]
299	340B	Turbo Lease LLC/Air Panama	SE-G99 N365BE N299CJ HP-1670PST
300	340B	ex Turbo Lease LLC	SE-E03 N370PX [stored by 21Sep10 Bangor, ME; Oct11 wfu for parts; l/n Feb12]
301	340B	Vincent Aviation	SE-C01 N301AE VH-UYN ZK-VAA
302	340B	(Yeti Airlines)	SE-C02 B-3654 ZS-PDS 9N-AHL [stored 24Oct06 Kathmandu, Nepal; b/u for parts Mar12]
303	340B	REX – Regional Express	SE-C03 N366BE VH-PRX
304	340B	ex Simmons Airlines/American Eagle	SE-C04 N304AE [stored 10Sep08 Kingman, AZ; l/n 10Oct11]
305	340B	ex Simmons Airlines/American Eagle	SE-C05 N305AE [stored 27Sep05 Abilene, TX; l/n 12Oct11]
306	340B	ex Simmons Airlines/American Eagle	SE-C06 N306AE [stored Abilene, TX; L/n 12Oct11]
307	340B	ex Simmons Airlines/American Eagle	SE-C07 N307AE [stored 02Oct08 Kingman, AZ; l/n 10Oct11]
308	340B	Japan Air Commuter	SE-C08 JA8887
309	340B	ex Simmons Airlines/American Eagle	SE-C09 N309AE [stored 09Jan03 Abilene, TX; l/n 12Oct11]
310	340B	Sol Lineas Aereas?	SE-C10 F-GHVU SE-KCV N695PA SE-C10 SE-KCV VH-UYC N470LH LV-CYC
311	340B	REX – Regional Express	SE-C11 SE-KXA VH-SBA
312	340B	ex Simmons Airlines/American Eagle	SE-C12 N312AE [stored 11Apr04; Abiline, TX; l/n 12Oct11]
313	340B	ex Simmons Airlines/American Eagle	SE-C13 N313AE [stored 03Nov08 Kingman, AZ; l/n 10Oct11]
314	340B	ex Simmons Airlines/American Eagle	SE-C14 N314AE N904AE [stored 03Oct08 Kingman, AZ; l/n 10Oct11]
315	340B	(Regional Lineas Aereas)	SE-C15 SE-KXB F-GMVQ EC-158 EC-GFM [w/o 14May97 Oporto, Spain; by 15May98 fuselage in use as GIA Rouen-Boos, France]
316	340B	SkyBahamas Airline	SE-C16 VH-LIH N676PA+ C6- [+ canx 27May11 to Bahamas]
317	340B	ex Simmons Airlines/American Eagle	SE-C17 N317AE [stored 02Nov08 Kingman, AZ; l/n 10Oct11]
318	340B	Loganair/Flybe	SE-C18 SE-KXC F-GMVZ EC-GMI F-GTSF SE-KXC G-LGNC
319	340B	ex Simmons Airlines/American Eagle	SE-C19 N319AE N905AE [stored Abilene, TX; l/n 12Oct11]
320	340B	ex Simmons Airlines/American Eagle	SE-C20 N320AE [stored 05Sep08 Kingman, AZ; l/n 10Oct11]
321	340B	ex Colgan Air	SE-C21 N321TH OE-GAS HK-4115X XA-TQX N321CJ [stored 19Apr12 Bangor, ME]
322	340B	REX – Regional Express	SE-C22 SE-KVN VH-KDV
323	340B	ex Simmons Airlines/American Eagle	SE-C23 N323AE [stored 04Nov08 Kingman, AZ; l/n 10Oct11]
324	340B	ex Simmons Airlines/American Eagle	SE-C24 N324AE [stored 03Nov08 Kingman, AZ; l/n 10Oct11]
325	340B	REX – Regional Express	SE-C25 SE-KVO VH-KDQ

SAAB SF.340

C/n	Model	Last known Owner/Operator	Identities/fates/comments (where appropriate)
326	340B	ex Simmons Airlines/American Eagle	SE-C26 N326AE [stored 10Apr03 Abilene, TX; l/n 12Oct11]
327	340B	Loganair/Flybe	SE-C27 VH-CMH SE-C27 G-LGNG
328	340B	Pen Air	SE-C28 F-GMVV VH-XDZ N677PA
329	340B	ex Simmons Airlines/American Eagle	SE-C29 N329AE [stored 22Jly08 Abilene, TX; 06Jly09 to Kingman, AZ; l/n 10Oct11]
330	340B	ex Simmons Airlines/American Eagle	SE-C30 N330AE [stored 27Sep05 Abilene, TX; l/n 12Oct11]
331	340B	Japan Air Commuter	SE-C31 JA8888
332	340B	ex Simmons Airlines/American Eagle	SE-C32 N332AE [by 29Mar04 stored Abilene, TX; l/n 12Oct11]
333	340B	Loganair/Flybe	SE-C33 F-GMVX VH-XDA SE-C33 G-LGNH
334	340B	Colgan Air/United Express	SE-C34 N334AE N312CE N334CJ
335	340B	Royal Thai Air Force	SE-C35 N335AE N314CE [unknown]
336	340B	Bearskin Airlines	SE-C36 B-12233 B-3655 SE-C36 C-FTLW
337	340B	(Formosa Airlines)	SE-C37 B-12255 [w/o 18Mar98 in sea 11km off Hsinchu, Taiwan]
338	340B	Colgan Air/US Airways Express	SE-C38 N338SB N338CJ
339	340B	Colgan Air	SE-C39 N339SB N339CJ
340	340B	ex Simmons Airlines/American Eagle	SE-C40 N340RC [stored Nashville, TN; l/n 04Nov11]
341	340B	Colgan Air/US Airways Express	SE-C41 N341SB N341CJ
342	340B	Swedish Air Force	SE-C42 100002 [AEW prototype – S.100B Argus; code 002]
343	340B	Colgan Air/United Express	SE-C43 N343SB N315CE N343CJ
344	340B	Colgan Air/US Airways Express	SE-C44 N344SB N344CJ
345	340B	Pen Air	SE-C45 N345SB N345CV N679PA
346	340B	Colgan Air/US Airways Express	SE-C46 N346SB N346CJ
347	340B	Colgan Air/US Airways Express	SE-C47 N347SB N347CJ
348	340B	(Aero South Pacific Pty)	SE-C48 N348SB N906AE N316CE VH-UYH [b/u 15Dec10 Townsville, QLD, Australia by C&L Aerospace; canx 19Jan11]
349	340B	ex Worthington Aviation Parts	SE-C49 N349SB [donated Mar03 by American Airlines to Illinois Aviation Academy, Du Page, Chicago, IL as training airframe; ferried 10Apr07 to Quebec, QC, Canada; assumed for spares use; canx 19Mar09]
350	340B	Colgan Air/US Airways Express	SE-C50 N350CF N350CJ
351	340B	Calm Air International	SE-C51 B-12261 B-3656 C-FSPB
352	340B	Colgan Air/United Express	SE-C52 N352SB N317CE N352CJ
353	340B	(Flagship Airlines/American Eagle)	SE-C53 N353SB [DBR 21Mar00 Killeen, TX; l/n Mar00 Dallas-Fort Worth, TX; canx 19Apr04 for spares use]
354	340B	(Wings West Airlines/American Eagle)	SE-C54 N354SB [stored by Mar00 Lawton-Fort Sill Regional, OK; canx 25Oct03 as destroyed, no further reports]
355	340B	Japan Air Commuter	SE-C55 JA8703
356	340B	Colgan Air/United Express	SE-C56 N356SB N356CJ
357	340B	Vincent Aviation	SE-C57 B-12262 B-3657 B-615L SE-C57 SX-BTE SE-C57 VH-UYA ZK-VAB
358	340B	(REX – Regional Express)	SE-C58 N358RZ N318CE VH-UYF [b/u 15Dec10 Townsville, QLD, Australia by C&L Aerospace; canx 19Jan11]
359	340B	Eznis Airways	SE-C59 N359SB LY-ESK JU-9905
360	340B	Air Partner Leasing USA	SE-C60 B-12263 B-3658 B-616L SE-C60 SX-BTD SE-C60 VH-UYE N875PC
361	340B	Japan Air Commuter	SE-C61 JA8704
362	340B	Japan Maritime Safety Agency	SE-C62 VH-TCH N362JE N678PA SE-C62 JA953A
363	340B	Japan Maritime Safety Agency	(B-12264) SE-C63 F-GMVY SE-KCZ XA-ADY N363JJ SE-KCZ JA954A
364	340B	Calm Air International	SE-C64 B-12265 SE-LHO C-GMNM
365	340B	Japan Air Commuter	SE-C65 JA8642
366	340B	Calm Air International	SE-C66 C-FTJV
367	340B	Swedish Air Force	SE-C67 VH-EKG SE-C67 100008 [AEW conversion S.100B Argus; code 008]
368	340B	Japan Air Commuter	SE-C68 JA8649
369	340B	REX – Regional Express	SE-C69 VH-EKH
370	340B	REX – Regional Express	SE-C70 N370AM VH-ZLQ
371	340B	REX – Regional Express	SE-C71 N371AE VH-ZLA
372	340B	Royal Thai Air Force	SE-C72 VH-EKN SE-C72 100009+ 70202 [+ Sweden; AEW conversion S.100B Argus, had code 009; with Thai AF in passenger role]
373	340B	REX – Regional Express	SE-C73 N373AE VH-ZLC
374	340B	REX – Regional Express	SE-C74 N374AE VH-ZLF
375	340B	REX – Regional Express	SE-C75 N375AE VH-ZLG
376	340B	REX – Regional Express	SE-C76 N376AE VH-ZLH

SAAB SF.340

C/n	Model	Last known Owner/Operator	Identities/fates/comments (where appropriate)
377	340B	Calm Air International	SE-C77 C-FTJW
378	340B	Japan Air Commuter	SE-C78 JA8900
379	340B	Swedish Air Force	SE-C79 100003 [AEW conversion S.100B Argus; code 003]
380	340B	REX – Regional Express	SE-C80 N380AE VH-ZLJ
381	340B	REX – Regional Express	SE-C81 N381AE VH-ZLK
382	340B	REX – Regional Express	SE-C82 N382AE VH-ZLO
383	340B	REX – Regional Express	SE-C83 N383AE VH-ZLS
384	340B	REX – Regional Express	SE-C84 N384AE VH-LKH+ VH-REX [+ unofficial marks painted on for publicity purposes]
385	340B	Japan Maritime Safety Agency	SE-C85 JA8951 [code MA951]
386	340B	REX – Regional Express	SE-C86 N386AE VH-ZLV
387	340B	REX – Regional Express	SE-C87 N387AE VH-ZLW
388	340B	REX – Regional Express	SE-C88 N388AE VH-ZRZ
389	340B	REX – Regional Express	SE-C89 N389AE VH-ZRB
390	340B	REX – Regional Express	SE-C90 N390AE VH-ZRC
391	340B	REX – Regional Express	SE-C91 N391AE VH-ZRE
392	340B	REX – Regional Express	SE-C92 N392AE VH-ZRH
393	340B	REX – Regional Express	SE-C93 N393AE VH-ZRN
394	340B	REX – Regional Express	SE-C94 N394AE VH-ZLI
395	340B	Swedish Air Force	SE-C95 100004 [AEW conversion S.100B Argus; code 004]
396	340B	REX – Regional Express	SE-C96 N396AE VH-ZRJ
397	340B	REX – Regional Express	SE-C97 N397AE VH-ZRK
398	340B	REX – Regional Express	SE-C98 N398AM VH-ZRL
399	340B	Japan Air Commuter	SE-C99 JA8594
400	340B	REX – Regional Express	SE-400 N400BR VH-ZRM
401	340B	REX – Regional Express	SE-B01 N901AE VH-ZRY
402	340B	ex Mesaba Airlines/US Airways Express	SE-B02 N402XJ [reported leased to Silver Air]
403	340B	Pen Air	SE-B03 N403XJ
404	340B	Pen Air	SE-B04 N404XJ
405	340B	Japan Maritime Safety Agency	SE-B05 JA8952
406	340B	Pen Air	SE-B06 N406XJ
407	340B	ex Mesaba Airlines/US Airways Express	SE-B07 N407XJ [stored 09Apr12 Bangor, ME]
408	340B	Vincent Aviation	SE-B08 N408XJ VH-VNX
409	340B	United Arab Air Force	SE-B09 100005+ SE-B09+ 1332 [+ Sweden; AEW conversion S.100B Argus; code 005]
410	340B	Pen Air	SE-B10 N410XJ
411	340B	ex Mesaba Airlines/Northwest Airlink	SE-B11 N411XJ [stored 21Dec11 Bangor, ME]
412	340B	ex Mesaba Airlines/US Airways Express	SE-B12 N412XJ [wfs by 15Feb12 to be stored at Bangor, ME]
413	340B	ex Mesaba Airlines/US Airways Express	SE-B13 N413XJ [reported for Silver Airways]
414	340B	ex Mesaba Airlines/US Airways Express	SE-B14 N414XJ [wfs by 15Feb12; stored 11May12 Bangor, ME]
415	340B	ex Mesaba Airlines/Delta Connection	SE-B15 N415XJ [stored 18Feb10 Bangor, ME; l/n Feb12]
416	340B	Provincial Airlines	SE-B16 N416XJ C-GPAJ
417	340B	ex Mesaba Airlines/Delta Connection	SE-B17 N417XJ [stored 19Nov10 Bangor, ME; l/n Feb12]
418	340B	Silver Airways	SE-B18 N418XJ [wfs by 15Feb12 stored Bangor, ME; 24May12 to Nashville, TN]
419	340B	Japan Air Commuter	SE-B19 JA001C
420	340B	Colgan Air	SE-B20 N420XJ [reported for Silver Airways]
421	340B	ex Mesaba Airlines/Delta Connection	SE-B21 N421XJ [stored by Feb12 Bangor, ME; reported for Vincent Aviation, New Zealand]
422	340B	Nok Mini	SE-B22 N422XJ HS-GBC
423	340B	Nok Mini	SE-B23 N423XJ HS-GBD
424	340B	for Vincent Aviation	SE-B24 N424XJ (LV-CJU) VH- [now reported Jun12 for Pen Air]
425	340B	Eznis Airways	SE-B25 N425XJ JU-9907+ [+ marks not fully confirmed]
426	340B	Nok Mini	SE-B26 N426XJ (LV-CJT) HS-GBE
427	340B	Silver Airways	SE-B27 N427XJ N327AG
428	340B	ex Mesaba Airlines/Delta Connection	SE-B28 N428XJ [stored 03Feb11 Bangor, ME; l/n Feb12]
429	340B	Lambert Leasing	SE-B29 N429XJ [stored 31Jan11 Bangor, ME; by 05Nov11 stored Nashville, TN]
430	340B	Lambert Leasing	SE-B30 N430XJ [stored 17Feb11 Bangor, ME; l/n Feb12]
431	340B	United Arab Air Force	SE-B31 100006+ SE-B31 1331 [+ Sweden; AEW conversion S.100B Argus; code 006]
432	340B	Hokkaido Air System	SE-B32 JA01HC

SAAB SF.340

C/n	Model	Last known Owner/Operator	Identities/fates/comments (where appropriate)			
433	340B	Sliver Airways	SE-B33	N433XJ	N353AG*	[* marks reserved 21May12]
434	340B	Silver Airways	SE-B34	N434XJ	N334AG	
435	340B	ex Mesaba Airlines/Delta Connection	SE-B35	N435XJ	[reported for Nok Mini, Thailand]	
436	340B	Lambert Leasing	SE-B36	N436XJ	[stored 21Apr11 Bangor, ME]	
437	340B	Silver Airways	SE-B37	N437XJ	N341AG	
438	340B	ex Mesaba Airlines/Delta Connection	SE-B38	N438XJ	[stored 29Jun11 Bangor, ME; l/n Feb12]	
439	340B	Lambert Leasing	SE-B39	N439XJ	[stored 25May11 Bangor, ME; l/n Feb12]	
440	340B	Hokkaido Air System	SE-B40	JA02HC		
441	340B	SAAB AB	SE-B41	N441XJ	SE-MCG	[MSA (maritime security aircraft) demonstrator]
442	340B	Silver Airways	SE-B42	N442XJ	N352AG*	[* marks reserved 11Sep09]
443	340B	Silver Airways	SE-B43	N443XJ	N343AG*	[* marks reserved 15Aug12]
444	340B	Silver Airways	SE-B44	N444XJ	N344AG	
445	340B	Silver Airways	SE-B45	N445XJ	N351AG	
446	340B	Silver Airways	SE-B46	N446XJ	N346AG	
447	340B	Silver Airways	SE-B47	N447XJ		
448	340B	Silver Airways	SE-B48	N448XJ	N348AG	
449	340B	Nok Mini	SE-B49	N449XJ	HS-GBF	
450	340B	ex Mesaba Airlines/Delta Connection	SE-B50	N450XJ	[stored 08Feb12 Bangor, ME]	
451	340B	ex Mesaba Airlines/Delta Connection	SE-B51	N451XJ	[stored by 09Apr12 Bangor, ME]	
452	340B	ex Mesaba Airlines/Delta Connection	SE-B52	N452XJ	[stored early Feb12 Bangor, ME]	
453	340B	ex Mesaba Airlines/Delta Connection	SE-B53	N453XJ	[stored by 09Apr12 Bangor, ME]	
454	340B	ex Mesaba Airlines/Delta Connection	SE-B54	N454XJ	[stored by 09Apr12 Bangor, ME]	
455	340B	Royal Thai Air Force	SE-B55	100007+	70201	[+ Sweden; AEW conversion S.100B Argus had code 007]
456	340B	ex Mesaba Airlines/Delta Connection	SE-B56	N456XJ	[wfs by 15Feb12 to be stored at Bangor, ME]	
457	340B	ex Mesaba Airlines/Delta Connection	SE-B57	N457XJ	[stored by 09Apr12 Bangor, ME]	
458	340B	Hokkaido Air System	SE-B58	JA03HC		
459	340B	Japan Air Commuter	SE-B59	JA002C		

Production complete

SAAB 2000

C/n	Model	Last known Owner/Operator	Identities/fates/comments (where appropriate)
001		ex SAAB-Scania	SE-001 (SE-LSI) [prototype ff 26Mar92; wfu & stored Sep95 Linkoping, Sweden; canx 26Jun96; l/n Apr00 shortly after b/u; hulk to fire dump l/n Jun09]
002		ex SAAB Aircraft	SE-002 [canx 31Mar00 as wfu; to GIA Nykoping-Skavsta, Sweden; l/n 08Sep09]
003		ex SAAB Aircraft	SE-003 [canx 26Jun06; wfu Mar01; used for fire training Halmstad, Sweden; l/n 13Jun07]
004		Swiss International/Carpatair	SE-004 HB-IZA YR-SBD
005		OLT Express	SE-005 HB-IZB SE-005 D-AOLB
006		Eastern Airways	SE-006 HB-IZC SE-006 OH-SRC SE-006 G-CDKA
007		Golden Air Flyg	SE-007 (D-ADIA) HB-IZD SE-007 G-CCTJ SE-007 LY-SBQ SE-LXH
008		Eastern Airways	SE-008 (D-ADIB) HB-IZE SE-008 D-AOLA G-CERY
009		Eastern Airways	SE-009 (HB-IZD) (D-ADIC) HB-IZF SE-009 SE-LOX SE-009 G-CDEA
010		Darwin Airline	SE-010 (D-ADIC) (HB-IZD) HB-IZG
011		Darwin Airline	SE-011 (D-ADID) HB-IZH
012		Golden Air Flyg	SE-012 HB-IZI (YR-SBB) F-GOZI SE-KXK
013		Golden Air Flyg	SE-013 D-ADSA F-GTSA EI-CPQ F-GTSL SE-LOT YR-SBL
014		Swedish Aircraft Holdings	SE-014 (D-ADIB) D-ADSB F-GTSB SE-014 CS-TLK SE-014 YR-SBM SE-LRA
015		Darwin Airline	SE-015 (F-GOZJ) HB-IZJ
016		OLT-Ostfriesische Lufttransport	SE-016 D-ADSC F-GTSC EI-CPW F-GNEH SE-016 CS-TLN SE-016 D-AOLC
017		Joe Gibbs Racing	SE-017 V7-9508 F-GJIG LX-DBR F-GOAJ (VH-UYA) SE-017 N519JG
018		Swiss International/Carpatair	SE-018 HB-IZK YR-SBJ
019		Pakistan Air Force	SE-019 F-GMVB SE-019 J-019
020		Hendrick Motorsports	SE-020 N5123L N5123 N511RH
021		Joe Gibbs Racing	SE-021 F-GMVC SE-021 N157JG
022		Moldavian Airlines/Carpatair	SE-022 HB-IZL ER-SFB
023		Air Kilroe/Eastern Airways	SE-023 D-ADSD F-GTSD LY-SBD SE-023 G-CFLV
024		Golden Air Flyg	SE-024 HB-IZM SE-LTX
025		Pakistan Air Force	SE-025 D-ADSE F-GTSE LY-SBC SE-025 10025 [AEW aircraft]
026		Swiss International/Carpatair	SE-026 HB-IZN YR-SBB
027		Hendrick Motorsports	SE-027 N5124 N508RH
028		US Department of Justice	SE-028 (V7-9509) F-GMVR SE-KCF EI-CPM F-GNEI SE-KCF N92225 [US Marshalls – Justice Prisoner & Alien Transportation System]
029		Polet Aviakompania	SE-029 HB-IZO VP-BPL
030		Hendrick Motorsports	SE-030 N5125 N500PR N5125 N509RH
031		Darwin Airline	SE-031 HB-IZP SE-LOG N168GC HB-IZP
032		Eastern Airways/Air Southwest	SE-032 HB-IZQ LY-SBG SE-032 G-CDKB
033		Carpatair	SE-033 HB-IZR YR-SBK
034		Meregrass	SE-034 F-GMVD SE-034 N512RH N166GC N814BB
035		Golden Air Flyg	SE-035 HB-IZS SE-LOM LY-SBK SE-LOM
036		Eastern Airways/British Airways	SE-036 HB-IZT SE-036 G-CDEB
037		OLT Express	SE-037 HB-IZU D-AOLT
038		Golden Air Flyg	SE-038 HB-IZV YR-SBA SE-MFF
039		Swiss International/Carpatair	SE-039 HB-IZW YR-SBC
040		Pakistan Air Force	SE-040 F-GMVE SE-040 10040 [AEW aircraft]
041		Carpatair	SE-041 HB-IZX YR-SBE
042		Air Kilroe/Eastern Airways	SE-042 SE-LSA OH-SAT SE-LSA G-CERZ
043		Golden Air Flyg	SE-043 SE-LSB OH-SAU SE-LSB
044		Carpatair	SE-044 SE-LSC OH-SAS SE-LSC LY-SBY SE-LSC YR-SBN D-AOLX* [marks reserved for OLT]
045		Pakistan Air Force	SE-045 F-GMVF LX-RAC F-GMVU SE-045 LY-SBW SE-045 10045 [AEW aircraft]
046		Golden Air Flyg	SE-046 SE-LSE OH-SAW SE-LSE
047		ex Swiss Air Lines	SE-047 HB-IZY [w/o 10Jly02 Werneuchen, Berlin, Germany; fuselage moved to Alton, Hants, UK; by 10Jan10 to Angelholm, Sweden, for spares recovery by Golden Air]
048		Darwin Airline	SE-048 HB-IZZ
049		Pakistan Air Force	SE-049 F-GMVG SE-049 10049 [AEW aircraft]
050		Swedish Aircraft Holdings	SE-050 (OM-DGA) SE-051 SE-LSI YR-SBH SE-LSI [stored by Aug10 Linkoping, Sweden for AEW conversion]

SAAB 2000

C/n	Model	Last known Owner/Operator	Identities/fates/comments (where appropriate)
051		Japan Civil Aviation Board	SE-051 (OM-EGA) JA003G
052		ex Carpatair	SE-052 SE-LSH (I-MEDD) YR-SBI [stored by Aug10 Linkoping, Sweden]
053		(SAS Commuter)	SE-053 SE-LSF [DBR 08Oct99 Stockholm-Arlanda, Sweden; b/u Apr00 for spare parts; canx 24Nov00; remains shipped to Dodson International Parts, Rantoul, KS]
054		Japan Civil Aviation Board	SE-054 JA004G
055		Air Kilroe/Eastern Airways	SE-055 SE-LSG OH-SAX SE-LSG G-CFLU
056		Golden Air Flyg	SE-056 HB-IYA ER-SFA SE-LXK
057		Polet Aviakompania	SE-057 HB-IYB VP-BPM
058		Polet Aviakompania	SE-058 HB-IYC VP-BPN
059		Darwin Airline	SE-059 HB-IYD VP-BPP HB-IYD
060		Polet Aviakompania	SE-060 HB-IYE VP-BPQ
061		Polet Aviakompania	SE-061 HB-IYF VP-BPR
062		Golden Air Flyg	SE-062 HB-IYG SE-LTU
063		Golden Air Flyg	SE-063 HB-IYH SE-LTV [last SAAB airliner built]

Production complete

SAUNDERS ST-27 and ST-28

Note: Only registrations known to have been allotted since conversion to turbo-prop power are given below. c/n 101 reported to be new-build aircraft.

C/n	Old c/n	Model	Last known Owner/Operator	Identities/fates/comments (where appropriate)
001	14058	ST-27	(Air Atonabee)	CF-YBM-X CF-YBM HK-1286X HK-1286 C-GYCQ [f/f 28May69; wfu & stored Dec80 Peterborough, ON, Canada; later b/u]
002	14129	ST-27	(City Express)	CF-XOK-X C-FXOK [wfu 14Aug88 London, ON, Canada; later b/u; canx 05Oct89]
003	14050	ST-27	(Voyageur Airways)	CF-FZR-X HK-1299 (C-GTFN) C-FFZR [wfu & stored North Bay, ON, Canada; probably used for spares]
004	14059	ST-27	(City Express)	CF-YAP HK-1287X HK-1287 C-FYAP C-GYCR [wfu & stored Aug88 Toronto-Island Airport, ON, Canada; later b/u; canx Oct89]
005	14087	ST-28	(Air Atonabee)	CF-YBM-X C-FYBM [prototype ST-28; ff 17Jly74; reported b/u Peterborough, ON, Canada]
006	14054	ST-27	Western Canada Avn Museum???	CF-LOL C-FLOL [wfu Aug88; stored Toronto-Island Airport, ON, Canada; canx Jan90; 2007 report stored St Andrews, Winnipeg, MB, Canada; Oct94 preserved Winnipeg, MB]
007	14141	ST-27	(Air Atonabee)	CF-CNT C-FCNT [w/o 25Aug84 St Johns, NL, Canada; canx Oct87]
008	14137	ST-27	(City Express)	CF-CNX C-FCNX [wfu & stored May88 Sudbury, ON, Canada; used as GIA by Sault College of Applied Arts & Technology, Sault Ste Marie, ON, Canada; canx Nov94]
009	14095	ST-27	Canadian Bushplane Museum	C-GCML [wfu & stored Toronto-Island Airport, ON, Canada; canx Aug93; preserved Sault Ste Marie, ON, Canada]
010	14070	ST-27	(City Express)	CF-FZP C-FFZP [wfu & stored Aug88 Toronto-Island Airport, ON, Canada; later b/u; canx Nov89]
011	14097	ST-27	(City Express)	CF-JFH C-FJFH [wfu & stored Aug88 Toronto-Island Airport, ON, Canada; later b/u; canx 05Oct89]
012	14112	ST-27	(City Express)	CF-HMQ C-FHMQ 8P-GWP C-FHMQ [wfu & stored Aug88 Toronto-Island Airport, ON, Canada; later b/u; canx Oct89]
013	14051	ST-27	On Air	C-GCAT [wfu & stored Jun84 Toronto-Island Airport, ON; canx 13Nov96 as "inactive"; later reported at Thunder Bay, ON, Canada minus wings]
101		ST-28	Saunders Aircraft Corp	C-GYAP-X [last flight 28Apr76; Jun96 wfu & stored semi-derelict Gimli Airport, MB, Canada; l/n 2008; aircraft owned by Western Canada Aviation Museum on loan to Gimli Air Base Historical Society]

Production and Conversions Complete.

SHAANXI (AVIC II) Y-8

C/n	Model	Last known Owner/Operator	Identities/fates/comments (where appropriate)
00 18 01		AVIC	B-181L [possibly first prototype; current status unknown]
00 18 02	C	AVIC	182+ B-504L [+ China] [c/n not confirmed; current status unknown]
02 08 03		Xian Aeronautical Institute	31041+ 31046+ [+ China] [31041 not confirmed]
03 08 05		Chinese Air Force	31140
06 08 02		(Sri Lankan Air Force)	CP701+ CR871+ [+ Sri Lanka] [w/o 18Nov95 shot down near Paly, Sri Lanka]
06 08 04		(Sri Lankan Air Force)	CP702+ CR872+ [w/o 05Jly92 Jaffna province, Sri Lanka; possibly shot down]
07 08 02		(Sri Lankan Air Force)	B-3105+ CR873^ 4R-HVC CR873^ [+ c/n not confirmed] [^ Sri Lanka] [w/o 15Aug02 Ratmalana, Sri Lanka]
07 08 04		ex Sudan Air Force	ST-ALU [derelict by 2001 Wau, Sudan; l/n 04Apr07]
08 08 03	D	Myanmar Air Force	5815 [c/n not confirmed]
08 08 04	D	Myanmar Air Force	5816
09 08 01	D	Myanmar Air Force	5817
09 08 02	D	Myanmar Air Force	5818
10 (08) 01	8F100	Universal Airlines	B-3101 [Chinese AF]B-3101
10 (08) 02?	8F100	Chinese Air Force	B-3102 (unknown)
10 (08) 05?	8F100	Chinese Air Force	B-3103 (unknown)
11 08 01	F100	Payam Air	EP-BOA+ EP-TPQ [+ c/n not confirmed]
11 08 02	F100	Payam Air	EP-BOB+ EP-TPX [+ c/n not confirmed]
11 (08) 04?	F200	Tanzanian Air Force	JW9034 [delivered 26Oct03; subsequently reported Dar-es-Salaam, Tanzania]
12 (08) 01?	F200	Tanzanian Air Force	JW9035 [delivered 26Oct03; subsequently reported Dar-es-Salaam, Tanzania; l/n 12Dec11 Mtwara, Tanzania]
13 08 02		Chinese Navy	9382
13 (08) 03?	8F100	(China Postal Airlines)	B-3109 [also reported as a Y8B c/n 10 08 09; canx by 30Dec08; fate/status unknown]
13 (08) 04?	8F100	(China Postal Airlines)	B-3110 [canx by 30Dec08 fate/status unknown]
15 08 05	JB	Chinese Navy	9331
18 18 01		Chinese Air Force	6682
20 18 01	KJ200	Chinese Air Force	30171
20 18 02	XZ	Chinese Air Force	21110
20 18 03	GX4	Chinese Air Force	[unknown]
21 18 03	KJ200	Chinese Air Force	30173
21 18 04	KJ200	Chinese Air Force	30174
21 18 05	KJ200	Chinese Air Force	30175
28 (08) 05	T		[reported on production line Sep09]
Unidentified – Civil			
unkn	F-200	Tanzanian Air Force	B-069L [reported 17Mar10 Kunmimg, China on overhaul; possibly JW9034]
unkn	F400	AVIC	B-575L [prototype Y-8F400; f/f 25Aug01]
unkn	KJ200	AVIC	B-576L [prototype Y-8F200 converted to KJ200; f/f 08Nov01; reported 09Nov00 Zhuhai, China as former & 22Oct04 Hefei, China]
unkn	Y-8B	(Civil Aviation Administration of China)	B-3104 [not current 2008; fate/status unknown]
unkn		(Civil Aviation Administration of China)	B-3196 [not current 2008; fate/status unknown]
unkn		(Civil Aviation Administration of China)	B-3198 [not current 2008; fate/status unknown]
unkn		(Civil Aviation Administration of China)	B-3199 [not current 2008; fate/status unknown]
unkn		OK Air	B-4071 [from photo & noted 06Oct09 Kaifeng, China; marks also on Y7G c/n 0201]
unkn		OK Air	B-4072 [noted 06Oct09 Kaifeng, China; marks also on Y7G c/n 0204]
unkn		China Aviation Museum	B-4101 [preserved Changping, Beijing, China]
unkn	8D	unknown	EP-ARF [reported 22Jun00 Sharjah, UAE; fate/status unknown]
Unidentified– Military			
unkn		Chinese Flight Test Establishment	076 [from 2003 photo]
unkn	CB	Chinese Flight Test Establishment	079 [radar testbed]
unkn		Chinese Air Force	181 [photo at Lhasa, China]
unkn		China Flight Test Establishment	728 from photo; rader test bed]
unkn		China Flight Test Establishment	729 [reported 13Oct09 Yanliang, China]

SHAANXI (AVIC II) Y-8

C/n	Model	Last known Owner/Operator	Identities/fates/comments (where appropriate)	
unkn		China Flight Test Establishment	730	[reported 13Oct09 Yanliang, China]
unkn		Chinese Air Force	980	[from photo]
unkn		Chinese Air Force	982	[reported 12Oct09 Hanzhong, China; CAAC c/s]
unkn		Chinese Air Force	983	[reported Sep01 Lhasa, China]
unkn		Chinese Air Force	987	
unkn		Chinese Air Force	989	
unkn	E	Xian Aeronautical Institute	4139	[drone carrier]
unkn	CB	Chinese Air Force	5121	[from photo]
unkn	CB	Chinese Air Force	5123	[reported 03Sep09 in China]
unkn	G	Chinese Air Force	5125	[from photo]
unkn	G	Chinese Air Force	5126	[from late 2009 photo]
unkn	G	Chinese Air Force	5128	[from late 2009 photo]
unkn		Chinese Air Force	5321	[from 2008 photo]
unkn	E	Chinese Air Force	5322	[reported 18Feb10 Dalian, China]
unkn	E	Chinese Air Force	5328	[from 2009 photo]
unkn		Chinese Air Force	6681	[from 2008 photo]
unkn		Chinese Navy	8331	[reported 11Sep07 Shanghai-Hongqiao, China]
unkn	X	Chinese Navy	9231	[from Oct08 photo]
unkn	J	Chinese Navy	9261	[+ MPA was Y-8X then Y-8J c/n 0408..?; based Dachang, China]
unkn	X+	Chinese Navy	9271	[+ MPA] [reported 08Oct09 Laiyang, China]
unkn	J	Chinese Navy	9281	[+ was Y-8X; reported 08Oct09 Laiyang, China]
unkn	X	Chinese Navy	9291	
unkn	J	Chinese Navy	9301	[based Dachang, China]
unkn	J	Chinese Navy	9311	[reported 08Oct09 Laiyang, China
unkn	J	Chinese Navy	9321	[reported 08Oct09 Laiyang, China
unkn		Chinese Navy	9322	[reported May08 Liangxiangzhen, China]
unkn		Chinese Navy	9332	[reported May08]
unkn		Chinese Navy	9341	[reported 08Oct09 Laiyang, China
unkn		Chinese Navy	9342	[reported May08]
unkn	DZ	Chinese Navy	9351	[ELINT aircraft; reported summer 2004 near Shanghai, China]
unkn	DZ	Chinese Navy	9361	[ELINT aircraft]
unkn		Chinese Navy	9362	[reported May08]
unkn	KJ200	Chinese Navy	9371	[reported 12Nov10 at factory Shaanxi, China]
unkn	WH	Chinese Navy	9381	[reported Oct11]
unkn	C	Chinese Navy	9372	[reported 31May08 Chengdu, China & May08 Liangxiangzhen, China]
unkn	KJ200	Chinese Navy	9391	[from photo]
unkn	KJ200	Chinese Navy	9421	[from photo]
unkn	CH	Chinese Navy	9512	[reported preserved 29Sep09 Liangxiangzhen, China]
unkn		Chinese Navy	9522	[reported 29Sep09 Liangxiangzhen, China]
unkn		Chinese Navy	9532	[reported 29Sep09 Liangxiangzhen, China]
unkn	GXX4	Chinese Air Force	10015	[ECM aircraft][from Mar08 photo which could be faked]
unkn		Chinese Air Force	10252	[from photo dated 07Feb10]
unkn		Chinese Air Force	10253	[from photo dated 07Feb10]
unkn		Chinese Air Force	10254	[from photo dated 07Feb10]
unkn		Chinese Air Force	10255	[from 2011 photo]
unkn	C	Chinese Air Force	10257	[from photo]
unkn	C	Chinese Air Force	10258	[from photo]
unkn	C	Chinese Air Force	10259	[reported 02Mar11 Kunming, China]
unkn		Chinese Air Force	10352	[reported 21Nov11 Kunming, China]
unkn		Chinese Air Force	10356	[reported 09Apr12 Kunming, China]
unkn		Chinese Air Force	10357	[from 2011 photo]
unkn		Chinese Air Force	20041	[from Sep09 photo; weather research aircraft]
unkn		Chinese Air Force	20042	[from Aug07 photo]
unkn		Chinese Air Force	20044	[reported 06Oct09 Kaifeng, China]
unkn		Chinese Air Force	20046	[reported 18May08 Chengdu, China]
unkn		Chinese Air Force	20048	[weather research aircraft; reported 07Aug07 Hohhot, China & May08 Chengdu, China]
unkn		Chinese Air Force	20049	[reported 16May08 Chengdu, China]
unkn		Chinese Air Force	20088	[weather research aircraft; photo 06Aug07 Hohhot, China; possible photo retouched from 20048]
unkn		Chinese Air Force	20142	[reported 06Oct09 Kaifeng, China]
unkn		Chinese Air Force	20144	[reported 06Oct09 Kaifeng, China]

SHAANXI (AVIC II) Y-8

C/n	Model	Last known Owner/Operator	Identities/fates/comments (where appropriate)	
unkn	C	Chinese Air Force	20145	[reported 18Nov10 Zhuhai, China]
unkn		Chinese Air Force	20146	[reported 18May08 Chengdu, China]
unkn		Chinese Air Force	20148	[from May08 photo]
unkn		Chinese Air Force	20240	
unkn		Chinese Air Force	20241	[reported 06Oct09 Kaifeng, China]
unkn		Chinese Air Force	20242	[reported 06Oct09 Kaifeng, China]
unkn		Chinese Air Force	20243	[reported 06Oct09 Kaifeng, China]
unkn		Chinese Air Force	20244	[from photo]
unkn		Chinese Air Force	20245	[reported 06Oct09 Kaifeng, China]
unkn		Chinese Air Force	20246	[from 2008 photo & reported 06Oct09 Kaifeng, China]
unkn		Chinese Air Force	20247	[reported 06Oct09 Kaifeng, China]
unkn		Chinese Air Force	20141	[reported 16May08 Chengdu, China]
unkn		Chinese Air Force	20142	[reported 06Oct09 Kaifeng, China]
unkn		Chinese Air Force	20778	[reported May12]
unkn	CB	Chinese Air Force	21011	[electronic warfare aircraft; from photo]
unkn	CB	Chinese Air Force	21013	[electronic warfare aircraft; from photo]
unkn	G	Chinese Air Force	21014	[from photo]
unkn	T	Chinese Air Force	21015	[electronic warfare aircraft; from photo]
unkn	CB	Chinese Air Force	21018	[reported 16May08 Chengdu, China]
unkn	CB	Chinese Air Force	21019	[from photo]
unkn	XZ	Chinese Air Force	21111	[from 2010 photo]
unkn	C3I	Chinese Air Force	30271	[from Mar07 photo]
unkn	T	Chinese Air Force	30272	[from photo]
unkn	T	Chinese Air Force	30273	
unkn		Chinese Air Force	31042	[from photo]
unkn		China Aviation Museum	31045	[preserved Changping, Beijing, China]
unkn		Chinese Air Force	31048	[from photo]
unkn	KJ200	Chinese Air Force	30172	[from photo]
unkn	KJ200	Chinese Air Force	30177	[reported May09 Beijing-Capital, China]
unkn	T?	Chinese Air Force	30273	[from photo]
unkn		ex Chinese Air Force	31141	[by 1988 reported in Beijing Aeronautical Institute, China]
unkn		Chinese Air Force	31145	[reported 26Oct96 Shahe AFB, China; possibly was a An-12]
unkn		Chinese Air Force	31146	[from photo]
unkn		Chinese Air Force	31147	[photo in Xian Aeronautical Institute, China]
unkn		(Chinese Air Force)	31242	[w/o 04Jan02 Zheng Zou Air Base, China; see also 31243 which was separate accident]
unkn		(Chinese Air Force)	31243	[w/o 04Jan02 Zheng Zou Air Base, China; see also 31242 which was separate accident]
unkn		Chinese Air Force	31248	[reported 26Feb98 Beijing-Capital, China]
unkn		Chinese Air Force	31341	[from photo]
unkn		Chinese Army	94001	
unkn		Chinese Army	94003	[reported in 2008]
unkn		Chinese Army	94006	[reported in 2008]
unkn		Chinese Army	94008	[reported in 2008]
unkn		Chinese Army	94009	[reported in 2008]
unkn	ZDK-03	Pakistan Air Force	11-001	[reported Nov11]
unkn	ZDK-03	Pakistan Air Force	11-002	[reported Nov11]
unkn	AEW	China Flight Test Establishment	T0518	[reported 2005 & May06 Nanjing, China]
unkn		Chinese Army	LH00001	[from photo]
unkn		Chinese Army	LH4002	[from photo]

SHORT SC.5 BELFAST

C/n	Model	Last known Owner/Operator	Identities/fates/comments (where appropriate)
SH1816	C.1	(Heavylift Aviation Holdings)	XR362 G-ASKE XR362 G-52-14 G-BEPE [ff 05Jan64; wfu 26Oct84; b/u Feb94; gone by 25Feb94 Southend, UK; canx 01Mar94]
SH1817	C.1	(Heavylift Cargo Airlines)	XR363 G-OHCA [wfu 01Mar79 still marked as XR363; b/u Feb94; gone by 25Feb94 Southend, UK; canx 01Mar94]
SH1818	C.1	(Royal Air Force)	XR364 [wfu Aug78 to Rolls-Royce (1971) Ltd; b/u 11Jun79 Hucknall, UK]
SH1819	C.1	Heavylift Cargo Airlines	XR365 G-HLFT 9L-LDQ RP-C8020 [converted to Mk2] [stored since 2010 Cairns, QLD, Australia; l/n Jun12 no regn]
SH1820	C.1	(Royal Air Force)	XR366 [wfu Aug78 to Rolls-Royce (1971) Ltd; b/u 08Aug79 Hucknall, UK]
SH1821	C.1	(Heavylift Aviation Holdings)	XR367 G-52-15 G-BFYU [canx 27Jun92; used for spares; hulk scrapped at Southend, UK Apr/Jun01]
SH1822	C.1	(Heavylift Aviation Holdings)	XR368 G-52-13 G-BEPS [canx 09Nov00 stored Southend, UK; usable parts removed Sep08 for use on c/n SH1819; b/u started 23Oct08, completed 30Oct08]
SH1823	C.1	(Euro Latin Commercial Co)	XR369 G-BEPL [wfu Nov78; canx 20Nov78; b/u 10Jly79 Hucknall, UK]
SH1824	C.1	(Royal Air Force)	XR370 [wfu Aug78 to Rolls-Royce (1971) Ltd; b/u 04Jly79 Hucknall, UK]
SH1825	C.1	Royal Air Force Museum	XR371 [preserved 06Oct78 Cosford, UK; l/n Nov09]
SH1826		[allocated for possible civil order, not built]	
SH1827		[allocated for possible civil order, not built]	

Production complete

SHORT SC.7 SKYVAN (SKYLINER*)

C/n	Model	Last known Owner/Operator	Identities/fates/comments (where appropriate)
SH1828	1A	(Short Bros & Harland Ltd)	G-ASCN [ff 17Jan63] [wfu 15Aug66 Belfast-Sydenham, UK; used as GIA; b/u Nov76]
SH1829	2-100	(Short Bros & Harland Ltd)	G-ASCO [wfu 21May68 Belfast-Sydenham, UK; b/u Oct72; canx 05Mar73]
SH1830	3	(Short Bros & Harland Ltd)	G-ASZI [wfu 30Dec68 Belfast-Sydenham, UK; canx 11Jan71; dumped 18Mar72; dismantled & removed to Mallusk scrapyard 19Oct72]
SH1831	3A-100	Swala Airlines	G-ASZJ (OY-JRI) 9U-BHJ ZS-ORN 9Q-CSD [converted to Skyliner standard]
SH1832	2-100	(Aeralpi)	I-TORE [w/o 06Mar67 Venice-Marco Polo, Italy; canx]
SH1833	2-100	(Short Bros & Harland Ltd)	G-ATPF [wfu 27Jan69 Belfast-Sydenham, UK; canx 05Mar73; b/u Nov76]
SH1834	2-100	(Short Bros & Harland Ltd)	I-CESA G-AXCS [b/u 19Oct72 Belfast-Sydenham, UK; canx 05Mar73]
SH1835	2-200	(AiResearch)	G-ATPG N731R [b/u Nov76 Belfast, UK; canx]
SH1836	2		[not completed and fuselage used in SH1898]
SH1837	2-200	(St Louis University)	N4906 G-AVGO N4906 N14909+ N4909 [+ marks not confirmed; wfu 1973; used as GIA St Louis, MO; b/u Nov76]
SH1838	3-200	(RV Aviation)	(VH-EJR) G-AVJX VH-FSG N10TC N40GA OH-SBB [w/o 01Nov89 off Mariehamn Archipelago, Finland; canx; noted Apr91 Helsinki-Malmi, Finland; later used by Sotilas Ja Lentotex-Nikkan Museo]
SH1839	3-200	(North Star Air Cargo)	(VH-EJS) G-AWCS N33VC N30GA [w/o 01Sep95 near Farewell, AK; canx 21Nov95]
SH1840	3-300	(Ansett Airlines of PNG)	VH-PNI [w/o 01Sep72 Mount Giluwe, Papua New Guinea; canx 01Sep72]
SH1841	3-300	(Viking International Air Freight)	(VH-PNJ) N725R [w/o 14Apr72 La Crosse, WI; canx]
SH1842	3-100	Vertical Air/Skydive DeLand	(VH-EJT) G-AWCT CR-LJF D2-EJF N3126W 90-0042+ N3126W N101UV (N931MA) [+ US Army]
SH1843	3-200	ex North Star Air Cargo	N729R N20DA N51NS [stored by Dec99 Milwaukee, WI; l/n Nov07]
SH1844	3-200	Ten Barrel Inc	(G-14-1) N732R G-14-16 N732R N30DA N430NA C-FUMC C-GTBU
SH1845	3-100	(North Star Air Cargo)	N734R CF-GSC C-FGSC N101FX [canx 21Aug09; probably wfu]
SH1846	3-200	ex Aire Express	N4916 P2-BAG N4916 N1846 [reported at Eloy, AZ Aug08 as fuselage on pallets with no wings; l/n 26Nov11]
SH1847	3-200	Ten Barrel Inc	G-AWKV N735R N3419 4X-AYZ N3419 SX-BBW N3419 N80DA C-GDRG PT-WKU C-GDRG PT-WYA C-GDRG N64HB C-FTBI
SH1848	3-200	(Gifford Aviation)	(6Y-JFL) N3201 XW-PEK XW-PGL N70DA [w/o 15May81 Slate Creek, AK; reported used for spares but reg'd 30May82 to Ben Lomond Inc; canx 15Apr09]
SH1849	3-200	(Gifford Aviation)	VH-PNJ N30P N64AC [w/o 31Dec77 Toksook Bay, AK; canx]
SH1850	3-200	(Island Airlines)	N4917 [w/o 25Aug77 Kona-Keahole Airport, HI; canx]
SH1851	3-200	Kavalair/Skydive Arizona	G-14-1 G-AWSG (PK-PSB) PK-XSA PK-PSE PK-ESA PK-WSA PK-TRQ N28LH
SH1852	3-200	North Star Air Cargo	G-14-1 G-AWVM PP-SDO N33BB G-AWVM N50DA
SH1853	3-200	Alaska Air Taxi	G-AWJM VH-FSH G-AWJM N60DA N80JJ N731E
SH1854	3-200	ex Transway Air Services	G-14-2 G-AWWS CF-VAN N7978 G-AWWS EI-BNN OY-JRL EL-ALH 3D-AER [stored by 21Sep09 Nairobi-Wilson, Kenya, in damaged condition]
SH1855	3M-400	ex Austrian Air Force	G-14-27 5S-TA [SOC 30Nov07; preserved Zeltweg, Austria; l/n 01Jly11]
SH1856	3-200	North Star Air Cargo	G-14-28 G-AWYG N28TC N50GA N50NS
SH1857	3-200	(Delaware Air Freight)	G-14-29 G-AXAD N20CK N40DA [DBR 28Nov73 in tornado Huntsville, AL; canx]
SH1858	3-200	(Jetco Aviation International)	G-14-30 G-AXAE (N3748) N21CK [w/o 02Jly70 into Potomac River, MD on approach Washington-National; canx]
SH1859	3-200	Perris Valley Aviation	G-14-31 G-AXAF N22CK N101WA C-GHBQ N101WA (9M-AXB) N101WA (PH-BOX) (PH-DAF) N101WA
SH1860	3M-400	Swala Airlines	G-14-32 5S-TB 9Q-CST
SH1861	3-200	(Pan Alaska Airways)	G-14-33 G-AXAG N123PA [w/o en-route 22Oct70 near Bettles, AK; canx; wings used in rebuild of c/n SH1853]
SH1862	3-200	ex Troy Air	G-14-34 G-AXCT CF-YQY HC-AXH CF-WCY C-GWCY (N406TH) N70854 N406TH [accident 21Oct86 Nightmute, AK; status unclear, no sightings; still current]
SH1863	3-200	(Malaysia Air Charter)	G-14-35 G-AXCU N100LV 9M-AXA [l/n operational 16Nov96; no reports since 2000; canx]
SH1864	3-200	(Wirakris Udara)	G-14-36 CF-TAI G-14-36 G-AYYR 9M-AQG 9M-AXO [reported sold to USA 16Feb89; not traced]
SH1865	3-200	(Gulf Air)	G-14-37 (G-AXFI) N200LV G-AXFI A4O-SI [w/o 22Nov76 off Das Island, Abu Dhabi, UAE; canx]

SHORT SC.7 SKYVAN (SKYLINER*)

C/n	Model	Last known Owner/Operator	Identities/fates/comments (where appropriate)
SH1866	3M-400	(Royal Air Force of Oman)	G-14-38 G-AXWU SX-BBT G-AXWU G-14-38 912 [converted 1982 to Seavan; wfu 06Jun98; SOC 27Aug08; fate unknown]
SH1867	3M-400	(Royal Air Force of Oman)	G-14-39 G-AXPT G-14-39 911 [wfu 06Jun98; 11Apr04 hulk to Masirah AFB, Oman]
SH1868	3M-400	Malaysia Air Charter	G-14-40 (N23CK) G-AXNV SAE-10-100+ SAE-T-100+ SAE-T-2011+ SAE-T-189+ HC-AXN HP-856 N5592Y 9M-AXN [+ Ecuador; dual marks with HC-AXN; l/n 16Nov96 Miri, Sarawak, Malaysia]
SH1869	3-400	(Pink Aviation Services)	G-14-41 G-AXLB SX-BBN OE-FDI(1) [w/o 16Jun96 near Hoogeveen, Netherlands; b/u for spares; canx Oct96; fuselage at various locations until l/n Dec04 Assen, Netherlands]
SH1870	3-400	Malu Aviation	G-14-42 G-AXLC SX-BBO SE-LDK 9Q-CLD
SH1871	3M-400	(Indonesian Air Force)	G-14-43 (G-AXMO) T-701 [w/o 01Feb71 in sea off Biak, Indonesia]
SH1872	3-200	(Companhia de Diamantes de Angola)	G-14-44 G-AXLD CF-NAS D2-EOH [reportedly w/o Mar94, no details known]
SH1873	3-200	(North Star Air Cargo)	G-14-45 G-AXLE N10DA [w/o 16Sep96 near Findlay, PA; canx 25Mar98]
SH1874	3-100	ex North Star Air Cargo	G-14-46 G-AYDO VR-H PK-PSD PK-HME PK-TRS N52NS (N68SH) N52NS [by 24Apr04 at Eloy, AZ, fuselage noted cut in pieces, no wings & no marks; for spares use; c/n from plate in cockpit; restored 09Jan09 to Stephen L Hill (Skydive AZ)]
SH1875	3M-400	(Royal Air Force of Oman)	G-14-47 902 [stored Jly94 Muscat-Seeb AFB, Oman; SOC 02Sep06]
SH1876	3M-400	Royal Air Force of Oman	G-14-48 G-AYCS 903
SH1877	3M-400	Oman Armed Forces Museum	G-14-49 904 [wfu & stored Jly94; SOC 02Sep06; preserved Muscat City, Oman; l/n 04Nov10]
SH1878	3M-400	(Royal Air Force of Oman)	G-14-50 905 [wfu 06Jun98; reported b/u 1999 for spares; SOC 02Sep06]
SH1879	3M-400	(Royal Air Force of Oman)	(G-14-51) G-AYDP 901 [stored Jly94 Muscat-Seeb AFB, Oman; l/n no wings Dec98]
SH1880	3M-400	(Royal Air Force of Oman)	(G-14-52) 906 [DBR Feb76 Muscat-Seeb AFB, Oman; stored no wings Dec98; b/u for spares 1999; by 01Jly09 derelict hulk]
SH1881	3M-400	Pink Aviation Services	G-14-53 T-702+ A-0702+ AF-0702+ PK-DSF N12LH OE-FDV [+ Indonesia]
SH1882	3M-400	(Indonesian Air Force)	G-14-54 T-703 [w/o 19Dec72 Celebes, Indonesia]
SH1883	3-100	(Collier Mosquito Control District)	G-14-55 CF-QSL C-FQSL N410AC [b/u Naples-Municipal, FL; canx 21Nov06 as wfu]
SH1884	3A-100	(Royal Nepalese Army)	G-14-56 G-AYIX 9N-RAA RAN-19 [wfu & stored post 2001 Kathmandu Airport, Nepal; by 05Sep08 moved to Nairobi-Wilson, Kenya; l/n 07Oct08]
SH1885	3-100	Perris Valley Aviation	G-14-57 G-AYJN A4O-SN G-BKME N4280Y YV-802CP N4NE
SH1886	3-100	Air America SRL (Italy)	G-14-58 G-AYJO A4O-SO G-BKMF C9-ASN OE-FDE
SH1887	3M-400	(Argentine Coast Guard)	G-14-59 PA-50 [w/o 01May82 Port Stanley, Falklands]
SH1888	3M-400	GB Airlink	G-14-60 PA-51+ LX-ABC N80GB [+ Argentina]
SH1889	3A-400	Babcock Support Services	G-14-61 PA-52+ LX-DEF G-BVXW [+ Argentina] [wfu 30Jan03; b/u for spares Kidlington, UK; l/n May04; canx 06Apr06]
SH1890	3M-400	CAE Aviation	G-14-62 PA-53 LX-GHI F-GTHI
SH1891	3M-100	(Argentine Coast Guard)	G-14-63 PA-54 [w/o 14May82 Pebble Island, Falklands; wreckage l/n 2004]
SH1892	3-100	(Peterborough Parachute Centre)	G-14-64 G-AYZA (PK-PSC) PK-PSA PK-ESD G-OVAN [w/o 28Dec93 Empuriabrava, Spain; canx 17Jun94]
SH1893	3-100	Ayeet Aviation & Tourism	G-14-65 G-AYZB PK-PSA N8189J 9M-BAM VH-IBS 4X-AGP
SH1894	3M-400	Royal Nepalese Army	G-14-66 G-AYZD RA-N14 9N-RF14 RAN-14 [derelict by Oct06 Kathmandu, Nepal; not noted Feb09]
SH1895	3M-400	(Royal Air Force of Oman)	G-14-67 907 [SOC 02Sep08; fate unknown]
SH1896	3M-400	Royal Air Force of Oman	G-14-68 908
SH1897	3M-400	ex Royal Thai Border Police	G-14-69 G-AZKL 21897 [stored by 26Nov09 Bangkok-Don Muang, Thailand; probably DBR Nov11 in floods Don Muang, Thailand]
SH1898	3M-400	(Royal Nepal Air Force)	G-14-70 G-AZHP RA-RF15+ RA-N15+ RAN-15 [+ Nepal] [w/o 07Apr78 at Rukumkot, Nepal]
SH1899	3M-400	(Sultan of Oman's Air Force)	G-14-71 909 [w/o 17Sep74 Tawi Atair, Dhofar, Oman; wreck l/n Muscat-Seeb AFB, Oman 17May79]
SH1900	3M-400	Royal Air Force of Oman	G-14-72 910 [Seavan conversion]
SH1901	3A-100*	Pink Aviation Services	G-14-73 G-AZRY LN-NPA SE-GEX 9M-AXT N8117V OY-JRK OE-FDK
SH1902	3M-400	ex Royal Thai Border Police	G-14-74 G-AZSR 21902 [stored by 26Nov09 Bangkok-Don Muang, Thailand; probably DBR Nov11 in floods Don Muang, Thailand]

SHORT SC.7 SKYVAN (SKYLINER*)

C/n	Model	Last known Owner/Operator	Identities/fates/comments (where appropriate)
SH1903	3A-100*	Swala Airlines?	G-14-75 G-AZYW LN-NPG 9Q-CDA [reported shot down in 1998 en-route Nairobi-Wilson, Kenya to Dirico, Democratic Republic of Congo; more recent reports suggest still active]
SH1904	3-100	(Pink Aviation Services)	G-14-76 PK-PSF (G-BMFR) OE-FDL(1) [w/o 07Jun95 Hohenems, Austria; canx Aug95; hulk reported to Klatovy, Czech Republic; l/n 30May08]
SH1905	3-100	Summit Air Charters	G-14-77 PK-PSG (G-BMFS) N8190U C-GKOA N52NS C-GKOA
SH1906	3A-100	Ryan Air	G-14-78 G-AZWX 1906+ U-01+ HS-DOH^ HS-DOA HS-DCC N1906 [+ Thailand] [^ marks reported in error]
SH1907	3A-100*	North Star Air Cargo	G-14-79 G-BAHK A4O-SK G-BKMD EI-BUB G-BKMD N754BD
SH1908	3A-100*	ex ScanWings	G-14-80 G-BAIT LN-NPC SE-GEY OH-SBA [report sold 08Mar05 Helsinki University of Technology, then 19Apr08 ferried to Valencia, Spain]
SH1909	3-100	ex Summit Air Charters	G-14-81 G-BAID (XC-TAP) XC-GAY XA-SRC N56NS C-GJGS [reported wfu by late 2010 Chilliwack, BC, Canada; l/n 19Oct11]
SH1910	3-100	(Deraya Air Taxi)	G-14-82 PK-PSH PK-DSV [stored by 25Oct06 Jakarta-Halim, Indonesia; b/u Feb07 by IAP Group Australia for spares]
SH1911	3-100	North Star Air Cargo	G-14-83 G-BAIE XC-GAZ XA-SRD N549WB
SH1912	3M-400	Collier Mosquito Control District	G-14-84 703+ VH-IBR VH-JIM+ VH-IBR N644M [+Singapore] [+ marks applied on 15Jly97]
SH1913	3M-400	(Pullout Skydiving Club)	G-14-85 700+ VH-WGG (OY-CLM) VH-WGG [+ Singapore; DBF 12Dec01 in hangar Ravenna, Italy; arson suspected]
SH1914	3M-400	(Pullout Skydiving Club)	G-14-86 701+ 9V-BNJ 701+ VH-WGL [+ Singapore; DBF 12Dec01 in hangar Ravenna, Italy; arson suspected]
SH1915	3M-400	Swala Airlines	G-14-87 702+ VH-WGQ 5Y- 9Q-CXF [+ Singapore]
SH1916	3M-400	ex Sydney Skydiving Centre	G-14-88 704+ VH-IBO 4X- [+ Singapore; wfu by 21Oct08 Bankstown, NSW, Australia; l/n 13Oct09; canx 22May12 to Israel, for possible use as parts]
SH1917	3M-400	Collier Mosquito Control District	G-14-89 705+ VH-IBS N642M [+ Singapore]
SH1918	3A-100*	(Arctic Circle Air)	G-14-90 G-BBEZ JA8793 9M-AXC N20086 [w/o 13Jly92 Bethel, AK; canx 27Oct02]
SH1919	3M-400	Royal Thai Border Police	G-14-91 G-BBFA 21919
SH1920	3-100	Kavalair/Skydive Arizona	G-14-92 G-BBPL TP0213//XC-UTI+ N53NS C-FPSQ N53NS N39LH [+ Mexico; also reported as Mexican AF TP-213 & TP-210/XC-UTI & TP-210/XC-UTL]
SH1921	3M-400	Yemen Air Force	G-14-93 G-BBRR 1153
SH1922	3M-400	Yemen Air Force	G-14-94 G-BBRU 1155
SH1923	3-100	(Eastindo Air Taxi)	G-14-95 G-BBUR PK-PSI PK-ESC [w/o 03Oct86 Mount Tarawera, near Manado Airport, Indonesia]
SH1924	3-100	Pink Aviation Services	G-14-96 G-BBUS PK-PSJ PK-DSU 4R- VH-CHK OE-FDP(2)
SH1925	3A-100*	Kavalair/Skydive Arizona	G-14-97 G-BBYC PK-PSK PK-HMF PK-TRT N26LH
SH1926	3A-100*	North Star Air Cargo	G-14-98 G-BBYD PK-PSL PK-FCD PK-TRR N114LH
SH1927	3A-100*	Skyventure Arizona	G-14-99 G-BBYF PK-PSM PK-DJK N46LH
SH1928	3M-400	(Ghana Air Force)	G-14-100 G-BCFG G451 [code B] [reported wfu 1986 & b/u Apr91 by Airwork, Hurn, UK]
SH1929	3M-400	Pink Aviation Services	(G-14-101) G-BCFH G452+ OE-FDP(1) [+ Ghana] [code C+] [wfs circa Dec03, at some time dismantled; by 17Apr12 fuselage at Klatovy, Czech Republic still marked as G-452]
SH1930	3M-400	Pink Aviation Services	(G-14-102) G-BCFI G450+ OE-FDL(2) [+ Ghana] [code A+] [stored 14Jun08 Takoradi, Ghana
SH1931	3M-400	Pink Aviation Services	G-14-103 G-BCFJ G453+ [code D] [+ Ghana] [reported wfu 1986 & b/u Apr91by Airwork, Hurn, UK]
SH1932	3M-400	Pink Aviation Services	G-14-104 G-BCFK G454+ OE-FDI(2) [+ Ghana] [code E+] [Dec03 subject to ownership dispute with Ghanaian authorities; reported as of 14Jun08 still stored Takoradi, Ghana]
SH1933	3M-400	Accra Trade Training School	G-14-105 G-BCFL G455+ OE-FDX [+ Ghana] [code F+] [Dec03 subject to ownership dispute with Ghanaian authorities; reported in use as GIA Accra-Kotoka, Ghana; l/n Feb08]
SH1934			[completed as SD.3-30 c/n SH3000 (G-BSBH)]
SH1935			[completed as SD.3-30 c/n SH3001 (G-BDBS)]
SH1936			[completed as SD.3-30 c/n SH3002 (G-BDMA)]
SH1937			[completed as SD.3-30 c/n SH3003 (G-BDSU)]
SH1938	3-100	ex Sociedade de Aviacao Ligeira	(G-14-106) G-BCMI CR-LOD D2-EOD [wfu by 22Jly06 Luanda, Angola; l/n 28Mar09]

SHORT SC.7 SKYVAN (SKYLINER*)

C/n	Model	Last known Owner/Operator	Identities/fates/comments (where appropriate)
SH1939	3-200	Collier Mosquito Control District	G-14-107 G-BCIB JA8800 VH-IBT N643M
SH1940	3M-400	(Royal Air Force of Oman)	G-14-108 913 [stored Jly94 Muscat-Seeb AFB, Oman; l/n Feb08 no wings; wfu 13Jly98]
SH1941	3M-400	Royal Air Force of Oman	G-14-109 914
SH1942	3M-400	Royal Air Force of Oman	G-14-110 915 [Seavan conversion]
SH1943	3A-100	Invicta Aviation	(G-14-111) 5T-MAM G-14-1943 LX-JUL G-PIGY
SH1944	3M-400	Royal Air Force of Oman	G-14-112 G-BDBT 916 [Seavan conversion] [stored Jly94 Muscat-Seeb AFB, Oman]
SH1945	3M-400	(CAE-Aviation)	G-14-113 5T-MAN LX-UGO [w/o 02Dec93 Vahun, Liberia]
SH1946	3-100	(Mexican Air Force)	G-14-114 G-BDVM XC-BOD TP-0214+ TP-214^ XB-VLR TP-214# [+ Mexico; used marks/call signs XC-UTJ, XC-UTM, XC-UTQ; ^ Mexico; used XC-UTN; # Mexico XC-UTQ; w/o 23Jly98 Pico de Orizaba, Veracruz, Mexico]
SH1947	3-100	(Venezuela Ministry of Transportation)	G-14-115 G-BDSV YV-O-MC-8 YV-O-MTC-8 YV-O-SAR-3+ [DBR 14Oct98 Caracas-Simon Bolivar, Venezuela; hit by Aeropostal 727 N280US; + marks allocated but not used before w/o]
SH1948	3-100	(Venezuela Ministry of Transportation)	G-14-116 G-BDVN YV-O-DAC-3 YV-O-MTC-3 YV-O-SAR-2+ [DBR 14Oct98 Caracas-Simon Bolivar, Venezuela; hit by Aeropostal 727 N280US; + marks allocated but not used before w/o]
SH1949	3-100	Museo del Transporte	G-14-117 G-BDVO YV-O-MC-9 YV-O-MTC-9 YV-489C [wfu 1991; preserved Caracas-Miranda, Venezuela as YV-O-MTC-9]
SH1950	3-100	Desert Sand Aircraft Leasing Co	G-14-118 G-BDVP XC-BOT TP-0210+ TP-215^ XB-ICT HK-4383 N78LA [+ Mexico; used marks/call sign XC-UTI; ^ Mexico; used XC-UTM]
SH1951	3-100	Skylift Taxi Aereo/Azul do Vento	G-14-119 G-BEHZ TP-0215+ N52NS C-FSDZ PT-PQD [+ Mexico; used marks/call sign XC-UTN]
SH1952	3-100	(Mexican Air Force)	G-14-120 G-BELY TP-0216+ TP-212^ [+ Mexico; used marks/call sign XC-UTI] [^ Mexico; used XC-UTK] [stored Apr90 to 1992 – unconfirmed sold to Troy Air; but also reported Jly98 Mexico City Airport, Mexico]
SH1953	3-100	Summit Air Charters	(G-14-121) G-BELZ TP-0217+ TP-213^ N38314 XC-UTJ N38314 N504FS C-FSDZ [+ Mexico; used marks/call sign XC-UTJ; ^ Mexico; used XC-UTL; w/o en-route 08Oct00 near Echo Lake, near Port Radium, NT, Canada; canx 03Oct02]
SH1954	3-100	Invicta Aviation	G-14-122 G-BEOL JA8803 VH-IBA ZS-OIO G-BEOL
SH1955	3-100	Compania Aerea de Viajes Expresos – CAV	G-14-123 G-BEOM YV-O-MC-10YV-O-MTC-10 YV-O-MTC-11 YV-O-SAR-1
SH1956	3-100	Saudi Ministry of Petroleum & Minerals	(G-14-124) G-BERZ HZ-ZAL
SH1957	3-100	Saudi Ministry of Petroleum & Minerals	(G-14-125) G-BFHZ HZ-ZAP
SH1958	3M-400	(Pink Aviation Services)	G-14-126 G-BFIA "7O7P-AAB" 7P-AAB PMU-1+ N981GA ZS-MJP^ OE-FDF [+ Lesotho] [^ for a period had UN code UN473] [w/o 17Oct98 Zell am See, Austria]
SH1959	3M-100	(Trans Guyana Airways)	G-14-127 G-BFUI FAP-300+ HP-300 N1959S OY-SUY 8R-GMC [+ Panama] [w/o 08Nov03 Georgetown-Ogle Airport, Guyana]
SH1960	3M-100	World Geoscience Corp	G-14-128 G-BFUJ 7P-AAC PMU-2+ N982GA ZS-MJS ZS-MJS ZS-MJS VH-WGT [+ Lesotho] [^ used UN code UN472]
SH1961	3A-100	(Pan-Malaysian Air Transport)	G-14-129 G-BFUL A4O-SM 9M-AXX 9M-PID [w/o 31Jan93 (or 30Jan93) flew into Mount Kapur, Indonesia]
SH1962	3M-400	Pan-Malaysian Air Transport	(G-14-130) G-BFUM OC1+ N6196P G-BFUM 9M-PIH [+ Botswana; code Z1]
SH1963	3A-100	(Artic Circle Air)	G-14-131 G-BGFP A4O-SP 9M-AYB 9M-PIF N2088Z [w/o 20Sep07 Mystic Lake Lodge Airstrip, AK; canx 15Apr09]
SH1964	3M-400	Pink Aviation Services	(G-14-132) G-BGFR OC2+ 9M-FAT OE-FDN [+ Botswana; code Z2]
SH1965	3-100	Wirakris Udara	G-14-133 G-BGRY G-14-133 ZS-KMX 9M-WKB
SH1966	3-100	(Guyana Defence Force)	G-14-134 G-BGWB 8R-GFF [w/o 18Jan81flew into mountain en-route in Guyana; another report states 02Jan81; canx]
SH1967	3-100	(Hornbill Skyways)	G-14-1967 G-BHHS 9M-AXM [w/o 30Jly93 in jungle, near Miri Airport, Sarawak, Malaysia]
SH1968	3-100	Ten Barrel Inc	G-14-136 G-BHPH (9M-AXU) 7Q-YMA N7009X OY-SUT 9M-AZT N491AS C-FYSQ
SH1969	3-100	Saudi Ministry of Petroleum & Minerals	(G-14-137) G-BHCH HZ-ZAS
SH1970	3-100	Saudi Ministry of Petroleum & Minerals	(G-14-138) G-BHHT HZ-ZAT

SHORT SC.7 SKYVAN (SKYLINER*)

C/n	Model	Last known Owner/Operator	Identities/fates/comments (where appropriate)
SH1971	3-100	(Air Malawi)	(G-14-139) G-BHPI 7Q-YMB [shot down 06Nov87 near Ulongwe, Malawi close to Mozambique border]
SH1972	3-100	(Arctic Circle Air)	G-14-140 G-BHVJ 7Q-YMU N7009Y N451SA [w/o 25Mar97 mid-air collision with Cessna 207A N800GA (c/n 00495) Nunapitchuk, AK; canx 10Aug98]
SH1973	3-100	(Malawi Police Air Wing)	(G-14-141) G-BHVK 7Q-YAY [w/o 24Apr86 south of Mombasa, Kenya]
SH1974	3-100	(Guyana Defence Force)	(G-14-142) G-BIFL 8R-GFK [wfu 1987; damaged at unknown location reported as "KAN", patched up flown to Georgetown-Timehri, Guyana & scrapped]
SH1975	3-100	(Airtech Rajawali Udara)	(G-14-143) G-BIOH 8Q-CA001 8Q-AMA 9M-AZB [w/o 03Sep91 near Long Seridan, Miri, Sarawak, Malaysia]
SH1976	3-100	(Guyana Defence Force)	(G-14-1976) G-BJDA 8R-GRR [probably wfu by 12Oct08 Georgetown-Cheddi Jagan, Guyana]
SH1977	3-100	Skydive Arizona	(G-14-145) G-BJDB ZS-LFG 9M-LLA N41LH
SH1978	3-100	(Royal Nepal Army)	G-14-1978 G-BJDC RAN-23 [w/o 30Dec85 near Dhangarhi, Nepal]
SH1979	3-100	Desert Eagle Aviation	(G-14-147) G-BJDD HK-3011X HK-3011 HK-3011P HK-3011W N9040U HK-3011 N58LA
SH1980	3-100	Guyana Defence Force	G-14-1980 G-BLLI G-14-1980 (8P-SKY) 8P-ASG 8R-GGK
SH1981	3-100	Dubai Men's College	G-14-1981 G-BMHH AGAW-121+ T332 + 320+ [+ United Arab Emirates; wfu by Nov04 used as GIA with serial 320 in Arabic numerals; l/n 27Jan11]
SH1982	3-100		(G-14-150) [not completed; fuselage scrapped; left Belfast-Sydenham, UK 13Feb89]

Production complete

SHORT SD.3-30

C/n	Model	Last known Owner/Operator	Identities/fates/comments (where appropriate)
SH1937	–	structural test airframe	[TA-1/003] [structural trials at Weybridge]
SH3000	100	(Short Brothers & Harland Ltd)	G-BSBH [prototype f/f 22Aug74; wfu by 13Apr81 Sydenham, Northern Ireland; canx 08Dec88; used for non-destructive fire training; l/n Apr95; 1999 b/u & hulk to scrap yard in Portadown, Northern Ireland until fully b/u]
SH3001	UTT	Ulster Aviation Society	G-14-3001 G-BDBS [wfu by 28Sep92; canx 01Jly93; preserved Langford Lodge then Long Kesh, Northern Ireland]
SH3002	100	(Corporate Air)	G-14-3002 G-BDMA (N335GW) N330US N789US [canx 05Oct09; fate/status unknown]
SH3003	100	ex Command Airways	G-14-3003 G-BDSU D-CBVK N57DD [wfu 1994; to White Industries, Bates City, MO for parts; dismantled by Jun96; canx 17Dec03; l/n 04Oct07]
SH3004	100	ex Command Airways	G-14-3004 N51DD [wfu Dec90; to White Industries, Bates City, MO for parts; still extant 6Nov98; l/n 25Apr07]
SH3005	100	Serco International Fire Training	G-14-3005 C-GTAS G-BKIE G-METO G-METP G-SLUG G-BKIE [wfu by 22Aug93; used for spares Jly94 Newcastle, UK; canx 16Sep97; hulk to Teesside for fire training; l/n 19Jan09 marked "G-JON"]
SH3006	100	ex Air BVI	G-14-3006 G-BEEO C-GTAM G-BEEO VP-LVR [w/o 02May93 Beef Island Airport, BVI; by 07Nov06 hulk to Dodson International Parts, Rantoul, KS for parts; l/n Oct11]
SH3007	100	(Air Cargo Carriers)	G-14-3007 C-GTAV G-NICE G-BLTD G-BMTD C-GSKW N330AC [canx 26Jan12 as wfu; l/n Milwaukee, MI]
SH3008	100	(Air Cargo Carriers)	G-14-3008 G-BENB D-CDLT G-14-3008 N330SB N58DD TG-TJA N58DD [canx 17Feb12; probably wfu Milwaukee, MI]
SH3009	100	(White Industries)	G-14-3009 N52DD N309SB [stored Apr88 until Nov94; wfu to White Industries, Bates City, MO for parts; canx 26Feb93; dismantled by Jun96; l/n 25Apr07]
SH3010	100	(K & K Aircraft Inc)	G-14-3010 G-BETN N330GW 85-25342+ N8154G [canx 03Aug11 as wfu fate/status unknown; + US Army C-23C]
SH3011	100	Millville Army Airfield Museum	G-14-3011 G-BEWT N331GW 85-25343+ [+ US Army C-23C; preserved Millville, NJ; l/n Oct07]
SH3012	100	(Allegheny Commuter Airlines)	G-14-3012 G-BEZX N696HA [by Oct99 to FAA Technical Center, Atlantic City, NJ for tests until DBR; l/n 15Mar05]
SH3013	100	Corporate Air	G-14-3013 G-BFDX D-CODO N241CA N330SB (N277CC) N330SB
SH3014	100	(Henson Aviation)	G-BFDY N796HA [wfu 22Oct91 for spares by Space Age Aviation; canx 09Nov91]
SH3015	100	ex Corporate Air	G-14-3015 G-BFHY D-CDLA N331CA N331SB [by 15Aug07 stored Honolulu, HI]
SH3016	100	(Freedom Air)	G-14-3016 G-BFMA D-CDLB N412CA N74NF [w/o 28Aug93 Guam-A B Won Pat International Airport, Guam; canx 26Feb03]
SH3017	100	(Air Cargo Carriers)	G-14-3017 G-BFMB PJ-DDA N335MV [b/u Milwaukee, WI; l/n 28Jan04; canx 25Feb05]
SH3018	100	Air Cargo Carriers	G-14-3018 G-BFMD PJ-DDB N336MV
SH3019	100	(US Army)	G-BFSW N332GW 85-25344 [C-23C] [stored 1992 Lakehurst, NJ; by Jly98 derelict Redstone Arsenal, Huntsville, AL]
SH3020	100	(Crown Airways/USAir Express)	G-BFSX N371HA N58AN [used for spares; canx 06Dec93]
SH3021	100	ex Airways International	G-BFTP D-CDLC N115CA VR-CBS N5132T N166RC [by 26Jly02 fuselage only at Milwaukee, MI; assumed used for spares]
SH3022	100	ex Starlight Express	G-14-3022 G-BFUH N372HA [wfu & stored Mojave, CA; derelict by Oct93; no recent reports]
SH3023	100	(Titan Airways)	G-14-3023 G-BFZW D-CDLD G-RNMO G-ZAPC [w/o 03Jan97 Liverpool, UK; canx 14Feb97]
SH3024	100	(Allegheny Commuter Airlines)	G-14-3024 G-BFZX N724SA [wfu 04Dec91 for spares by Space Age Aviation; probably b/u]
SH3025	100	(Air Cargo Carriers)	G-BFZY N373HA N55AN [b/u Milwaukee, WI; l/n 27Sep04; canx 27Sep04]
SH3026	100	Win Win Aviation	G-BGEY N330L C-FYBO N330E
SH3027	100	ex US Army	G-BGEZ N334GW 85-25345 [C-23C] [by Apr00 stored Milwaukee, WI]
SH3028	100	(Space Age Aviation)	G-BGMZ N896HA [canx 25Aug93 to Canada but reported b/u spares West Nyack, NY]
SH3029	100	Air Cargo Carriers	G-14-3029 G-BGNA G-BTJR SE-IVX G-BTJR VH-LSI N334AC
SH3030	100	(Emerald Airways)	G-14-3030 G-BGNB N330MV G-BGNB 5N-OJU CS-DBY G-SSWP [wfu by 2003 Southend, UK; b/u 14May04; nose to RAF Manston History Museum; canx 08Oct04]
SH3031	100	(Dynamic Aviation Group)	G-BGNC N799SA [status unknown; probably b/u for spares by Space Age Aviation]

SHORT SD.3-30

C/n	Model	Last known Owner/Operator	Identities/fates/comments (where appropriate)
SH3032	100	ex Metro Express	G-BGNE N330SD N935MA [w/o 20May83 Beaumont-Municipal Airport, TX; by 1994 to White Industries, Bates City, MO; dismantled by Jun96; l/n 25Apr07]
SH3033	100	ex Labrador Airways	G-BGNF N996HA C-GLAP [canx 24Feb00 as wfu; reported stored location not known]
SH3034	100	(Gill Air)	G-BGNG N331MV N330FL G-BGNG [wfu Jun96 Bournemouth, UK; b/u Jly96; canx 16Aug96; by 2010 fuselage in use as shed Canford Heath, Poole, UK]
SH3035	100	(Gill Air)	G-BGNH N331L (G-BGNH) [wfu May92 for spares, Newcastle, UK; canx 11Nov92; fuselage Mar96 to fire service; b/u circa 2001]
SH3036	100	Air Cargo Carriers	G-14-3036 G-BGNI N936MA
SH3037	100	ex Mountain Air Cargo	G-14-3037 G-BGNJ N50AN [canx 25Sep95; to Dodson International Parts, Rantoul, KS for spares; by 09Nov06 in two parts; l/n 16Jly10]
SH3038	100	Air Cargo Carriers	G-BGZV (N332L) N690RA N167RC
SH3039	100	(Freedom Air)	G-BGZU N51AN [canx 17Aug92 as destroyed; probably b/u by Turbine Conversions Inc]
SH3040	100	(Air Cargo Carriers)	G-BGZT N937MA [DBR 18May06 Myrtle Beach, SC; b/u for spares; by 05Mar09 hulk only at Milwaukee-General Mitchell International, WI; canx 16Jun09]
SH3041	100	(Suburban Airlines)	G-14-3041 (G-BHCG) N844SA [DBR 03Jun80 Allentown, PA; canx; returned to Shorts & rebuilt as Short SD.3-60 c/n SH.3600]
SH3042	100	ex Emerald Airways	G-14-3042 G-BHHU N332MV N181AP G-BHHU OY-MUC G-BHHU D-CTAG G-SSWA [wfu 04May06 Blackpool, UK; canx 13 Dec 06; hulk on dump l/n 25Aug07; b/u Nov07; wings & parts to RAF Millom Museum, UK]
SH3043	100	(Olympic Aviation)	G-14-3043 (G-BHJL) (G-BHJM) SX-BGA [wfu & stored 18Mar94 Athens, Greece; b/u Jun97]
SH3044	100	(Freedom Air)	G-14-3044 G-BHHV N53DD N344SB N76NF [DBR 08Dec02 Guam, by typhoon; b/u for spares]
SH3045	100	(Suburban Airlines)	G-14-3045 G-BHHW N846SA [stored Sep90; wfu & b/u Dec91 Fort Lauderdale-Executive, FL]
SH3046	100	ex Air Cargo Carriers	G-BHJJ N938MA [wfu by 22Jan09; to Dodson International Parts, Rantoul, KS; b/u 16Jly10]
SH3047	100	(Air Cargo Carriers)	G-BHSH N939MA [reported wfu Dec03 Milwaukee, WI; l/n 25Jly10; canx 15Feb12]
SH3048	100	(Olympic Aviation)	(G-14-3048) G-BHVL SX-BGB [wfu & stored 18Mar94 Athens, Greece; b/u Jun97]
SH3049	100	(Short Brothers/British Air Ferries)	G-BHWT N333MV G-BHWT [w/o 11Jan88 Southend, UK; taxied into Viscount 806 G-APIM; canx 15Dec88; b/u]
SH3050	100	ex Aeronaves del Centro	G-BHWU YV-373C [stored by Jan94 Caracas, Venezuela; by 01 Dec 07 wfu Valencia, Venezuela]
SH3051	100	(Victoria Air)	G-14-3051 G-BHWV N140CN [sold to Atlanta Air Salvage; b/u Sep94 Miami, FL for parts]
SH3052	100	(Space Age Aviation)	G-14-3052 G-BHYJ N304CA [probably b/u for parts; l/n Sep03]
SH3053	100	(Space Age Aviation)	G-14-3053 G-BHYK N847SA [probably b/u for parts; l/n Sep03]
SH3054	100	ex Aeronaves del Centro	G-14-3054 G-BHYL (N695RA) YV-374C [wfu by Jan92 Caracas, Venezuela; derelict by 06Feb95]
SH3055	100	(SkyWay Enterprises)	G-14-3055 G-BHYM N141CN C-FLAC N805SW [w/o 09Apr03 DuBois-Regional, PA; hulk to MTW Aerospace, Montgomery, AL for parts; l/n 24Jan06]
SH3056	100	Deraya Air Taxi	G-BIFG LV-OJG N487NS VH-HUS DQ-SUN PK-DSB
SH3057	100	(Air Tabernacle)	G-BIFH LV-OJH N488NS G-BIFH G-IOCS [wfu & stored Apr98 Southend, UK; DBF 14May99; canx 11Apr01]
SH3058	100	(Space Age Aviation)	G-BIFI N848SA [probably b/u for parts; l/n Sep03]
SH3059	100	(Freedom Air)	G-14-3059 G-BIFJ N54DD N9241Q [believed b/u by 04Oct05; canx 01Nov05]
SH3060	200	Deraya Air Taxi	G-14-3060 G-BIFK VH-KNN G-BIFK N58MM G-BIFK DQ-FIJ PK-DSR
SH3061	100	(Chartair)	G-14-3061 G-BIGA (YV-375C) VH-KNO [wfu & stored Oct01 Alice Springs, NT, Australia; l/n 27Apr03 with parts missing]
SH3062	100	(Command Airways)	G-BIOD (SU-BCP) N335GW N156DD [wfu & stored by Sep90 Fort Lauderdale-Executive, FL; l/n Dec91 part b/u; canx 04Feb92]
SH3063	200	(Gill Aviation)	G-14-3063 G-BIOE VH-KNP G-BIOE N59MM G-BIOE [stored May97 Newcastle, UK; canx 01Dec97; b/u May98]
SH3064	100	(Streamline Aviation)	G-14-3064 G-BIOF N4270A N280VY EI-BNM G-14-3064 G-BIOF (N334SB) 5N-AOX G-LEDN G-SSWN [w/o 25May00 Paris-Charles de Gaulle, France; canx 05Oct00; fuselage to MTW Aerospace, Montgomery, AL; l/n 24Jan06]
SH3065	100	(Olympic Aviation)	G-14-3065 G-BIOG SX-BGC [wfu & stored 18Mar94 Athens, Greece; b/u Jun97]

SHORT SD.3-30

C/n	Model	Last known Owner/Operator	Identities/fates/comments (where appropriate)
SH3066	100	(Olympic Aviation)	G-14-3066 G-BITU SX-BGD [wfu & stored 18Mar94 Athens, Greece; b/u Jun97]
SH3067	100	ex Gill Aviation	G-14-3067 G-BIRN G-BPMA [w/o 13Feb89 Glasgow, UK; canx 12May89; hulk to White Industries, Bates City, MO for spares; l/n 25Apr07]
SH3068	100	North East Aircraft Museum	G-14-3068 G-BITV G-OGIL [DBR 01Jly92 Newcastle, UK; canx 12Nov92; preserved Sunderland, UK; l/n 23Oct08]
SH3069	100	(Muk Air)	G-14-3069 G-BITX OY-MUB [canx 08May01; dismantled 21May01 Bournemouth, UK; fuselage to Pocklington, UK as glider launch control cabin]
SH3070	100	(Air Cavrel)	G-14-3070 G-EASI G-BITW [wfu & stored 09Jun98 Coventry, UK; canx 20Jly99; b/u late Jly99 fuselage to Hillside Nurseries, Alton, UK]
SH3071	200	Mountain Air Cargo	G-14-3071 G-BIYA N330AE N2679U
SH3072	200	M & N Aviation	G-BIYD N2678G C-GLAT N106SW
SH3073	200	(Sunstate Airlines)	G-BIYE VH-KNQ [wfu & stored Jly95 Townsville, QLD, Australia; canx 24Oct95 as wfu; b/u for spares; l/n Sep96]
SH3074	200	Mountain Air Cargo	G-14-3074 G-BIYF N26288
SH3075	100	(SAFT Air Express)	G-14-3075 G-BIYG N337MV N182AP G-BIYG TR-WEH TR-LEH [w/o 02Apr98 La Lope, Gabon]
SH3076	200	(Streamline Aviation)	G-14-3076 G-BIYH N338MV N183AP G-BIYH C-FYXF G-SSWU [DBR 18Sep99 on ground, Luton, UK, hit by landing AA-5B G-BDLR; dismantled & taken to unknown location 03Mar03; canx 23Sep03]
SH3077	200	Air Cargo Carriers	G-14-3077 G-BJFK 4X-CSP N390GA
SH3078	100	(Streamline Aviation)	G-14-3078 G-BJLK EI-BLP G-BJLK N5369X G-14-3078 G-BJLK [stored Jan97 Southend, UK; b/u in Dec97; canx 28Jan98]
SH3079	200	Air Cargo Carriers	G-14-3079 G-BJLL N2629P
SH3080	200	(SkyWay Enterprises)	G-14-3080 G-BJLM N2629Y [DBR 02Feb98 Miami, FL; 03Feb00 hulk moved to Kissimmee, FL; l/n 12Nov05; gone by Feb06]
SH3081	200	(SkyWay Enterprises)	G-14-3081 G-BJUJ N2630A [DBR 02Feb98 Miami, FL; 03Feb00 hulk moved to Kissimmee, FL; l/n 12Nov05; gone by Feb06]
SH3082	100	(Lynrise Aircraft Financing)	G-14-3082 G-BJUK G-OCAS G-14-3082 G-BJUK [wfu & stored May94 Exeter, UK; b/u 19Jun95; canx 02Dec96]
SH3083	200	(Olympic Aviation)	G-14-3083 G-BJUL SX-BGE [w/o 03Aug89 Samos, Greece]
SH3084	200	(Olympic Aviation)	G-BJWA SX-BGF [wfu Jan94 Athens, Greece; b/u Jun97]
SH3085	200	ex Bangkok Airways	G-14-3085 G-BJXF HS-TSA HS-SKP [stored by Dec94 Bangkok-Don Muang, Thailand; b/u Jun95; by Aug03 displayed restaurant Sam Khok, near Pathum Thani, Thailand]
SH3086	200	ex Thai Airways	G-14-3086 G-BJXG HS-TSB [sold 1992 to Bangkok Airways for spares; stored Bangkok-Don Muang, Thailand; b/u Jun95; by Oct01 hulk at Marukatalyan Place, Hua Hin, Thailand; l/n Jan08]
SH3087	200	(Thai Airways)	G-14-3087 G-BJXH HS-TSC [sold 1992 to Bangkok Airways for spares; stored Bangkok-Don Muang, Thailand; b/u Jun95]
SH3088	200	(Thai Airways)	G-BKDL HS-TSD [sold 1992 to Bangkok Airways for spares; stored Bangkok-Don Muang, Thailand; b/u Jun95]
SH3089	200	(Block Air)	G-14-3089 G-BKDM N330CA C-GLAL G-DACS [wfu & stored May02 Southend, UK; b/u Jun03; hulk to Hanningfield Metals, Stock, UK; canx 15Aug03; l/n 11Aug06]
SH3090	200	(Lynrise Aircraft Financing)	G-14-3090 G-BKDN G-BNTX [wfu 12Jan90 Exeter, UK & to fire dump; canx 23Jun98; remains removed by 09Feb00]
SH3091	200	(Lynrise Aircraft Financing)	G-14-3091 G-BKDO G-BNTY [wfu & stored Mar90 Exeter, UK; b/u early 1995; canx 11Jun98]
SH3092	100	(Ireland Airways)	G-14-3092 G-BKMU EI-BEG EI-BEH G-14-3092 G-BKMU SE-IYO G-BKMU EI-EXP [stored 13Feb98 Exeter, UK; b/u Mar99; Apr 99 fuselage to Valley Nurseries, Beech, near Alton, Hants, UK]
SH3093	200	(Freedom Air)	G-14-3093 G-BKMV (EI-BNM) N155DD N92417 [wfu & b/u May05 Guam; canx 01Nov05]
SH3094	200	(Short Brothers)	G-14-3094 G-BKMW [converted Dec88 to C-23 Sherpa; b/u Mar96 Belfast City, Northern Ireland, UK; canx 14Nov96]
SH3095	100	(Streamline Aviation)	G-14-3095 G-BKSU G-BNYA 4X-CSQ G-SSWT [wfu & stored Oct00 Southend, UK; b/u Aug01; canx 21Oct02]
SH3096	100	(Short Brothers PLC)	G-14-3096 G-BKSV N332SB G-14-3096 G-OATD [DBR by bomb 27Nov89 Belfast Harbour, Northern Ireland, UK; canx 10Apr90; fuselage l/n Dec94]
SH3097	200	(Flying Enterprise)	G-14-3097 G-BLGG SE-INZ [canx 30Jun99; b/u for spares Aug99 Axamo, Sweden; to fire training airframe Jonkoping, Sweden; l/n Jun02]

SHORT SD.3-30

C/n	Model	Last known Owner/Operator	Identities/fates/comments (where appropriate)
SH3098	UTT	ex Royal Thai Army	G-14-3098 G-BLJA 3098 [wfu Feb03 Bangkok-Don Muang, Thailand; l/n Jan09 with wings cut off; by mid-2009 to Pranburi Infantry Centre, Hua Hin, Thailand, for static exhibition]
SH3099	UTT	ex Royal Thai Police	G-14-3099 G-BLJB 43099+ 25099 [+ Thailand] [l/n Jan07 active; by 26Nov09 stored Bangkok-Don Muang, Thailand; DBR Nov11 in floods]
SH3100	C-23A	(SkyWay Enterprises)	G-14-3100 G-BLLJ 83-0512+ N118SW [+ USAF; stored AMARC with code CD0001: canx 13Aug12 as wfu; fate/status unknown]
SH3101	C-23A	Semirara Mining Corp	G-14-3101 G-BLLK 83-0513+ N46JH RP-C1099 [+ USAF; stored AMARC with code CD0003]
SH3102	UTT	ex Royal Thai Army	G-14-3102 G-BLLL 3102 [wfu Feb03 Bangkok-Don Muang, Thailand; l/n Jan09; by mid-2009 to Pranburi Infantry Centre, Hua Hin, Thailand, for static exhibition]
SH3103	C-23A	Air Cargo Carriers	G-14-3103 84-0458+ N264AG N264AC [+ USAF stored AMARC with code CD0002; stored by Mar02 Milwaukee, MI, for spares use; l/n Aug08 still marked as 40458/ED; l/n 27/7/10]
SH3104	C-23A	Era Alaska	G-14-3104 84-0459+ N174Z N168LM [+ USAF]
SH3105	UTT	Royal Thai Police	G-14-3105 G-BLRR 43105+ 25105 [+ Thailand; probably DBR Nov11 in floods Don Muang, Thailand]
SH3106	C-23A	(Bureau of Land Management)	G-14-3106 84-0460+ N176Z N178LM [+ USAF] [canx 28Feb00; used as ground trainer Redmond, OR; l/n 01May03 & probably b/u]
SH3107	C-23A	(Air Cargo Carriers)	G-14-3107 84-0461+ N260AG [wfu & stored for parts Jun01 Milwaukee, MI; l/n 28May06 still as 40461; l/n 27Jly10; canx 15Feb12]
SH3108	UTT	(Royal Thai Army)	-3108 [order cancelled, not completed; fuselage used in c/n SH3124]
SH3109	C-23A	(USDA Forest Service)	G-14-3109 84-0462+ N179Z [+ USAF]
SH3110	C-23A	US Army	G-14-3110 84-0463
SH3111	C-23A	US Army	G-14-3111 84-0464
SH3112	C-23A	Aviation Services/Freedom Air	G-14-3112 84-0465+ N172Z N188LM N330FA [+ USAF]
SH3113	JC-23A	(US Army)	G-14-1113 G-14-3113 G-BLZG 84-0466 [w/o 16Jly92 near Fort Rucker, AL]
SH3114	C-23A	US Army	G-14-3114 84-0467
SH3115	C-23A	USDA Forest Service	G-14-3115 84-0468+ N175Z [+ USAF]
SH3116	C-23A	USDA Forest Service	G-14-3116 84-0469+ N173Z [+ USAF]
SH3117	C-23A	Icecap LLC	G-14-3117 84-0470+ N261AG [+ USAF]
SH3118	JC-23A	ex US Army	G-14-3118 84-0471 [reported by Sep07 GIA Enterprise Community College, Enterprise-Municipal, AL]
SH3119	C-23A	USDA Forest Service	G-14-3119 84-0472+ N178Z [+ USAF]
SH3120	C-23A	McNeely Charter Service	G-14-3120 84-0473+ N262AG [+ USAF]
SH3121	UTT	(Tanzanian People's DF)	G-BMGX 131+ 331^ JW9036 [+ Amiri Guard Air Wing; ^ UAE; w/o 01Jun07 Kizota, Tanzania]
SH3122	UTT	(Short Brothers)	G-BMLF [not completed; b/u Feb89; canx 22Jly91]
SH3123	UTT	Industria Venezolana de Aluminio	G-14-3123 G-BMLG YV-O-GUR-1
SH3124	100	(Government of Quebec)	G-14-3124 G-BPYU C-FPQE [built with parts from c/n SH3108]; w/o 01Dec93 Umiujaq, PQ, Canada; canx 10Apr97]
SH3201	C-23B	NASA	G-BSJI 88-1861 N435NA
SH3202	C-23B	NASA	G-BSJJ 88-1862 N423NA
SH3203	C-23B	US Army	G-BSJK 88-1863
SH3204	C-23B	NASA	G-BSJL 88-1864 N430NA
SH3205	C-23B	US Army	G-BSJM 88-1865
SH3206	C-23B	US Army	G-BSJN 88-1866
SH3207	C-23B	NASA	G-BSJO 88-1867 N428NA
SH3208	C-23B	US Army	G-BSJP 88-1868
SH3209	C-23B	US Army	G-BSJR 88-1869
SH3210	C-23B	West Virginia ANG	G-BSJS 88-1870 N5078T
SH3211	C-23C	US Army	G-14-3211 G-BUCU 90-7011
SH3212	C-23B	US Army	G-14-3212 G-BUCV 90-7012
SH3213	C-23B	US Army	G-BUCW 90-7013
SH3214	C-23B	US Army	G-BUCX 90-7014
SH3215	C-23C	US Army	G-14-3215 G-BUCY 90-7015
SH3216	C-23B	US Army	G-14-3216 G-BUCZ 90-7016
Unidentified		HP-1403APP (these marks used on Cessna 208B c/n B0790) and HP-1404APP both reported 14Mar00 at San Jose, Costa Rica; probably both ntu	

Production complete

SHORT SD3.60

C/n	Model	Last known Owner/Operator	Identities/fates/comments (where appropriate)
SH3600	100	(Short Brothers PLC)	(G-BSBL) G-ROOM [prototype built from SD3-30 c/n 3041; ff 01Jun81; DBR by bomb 27Nov89 Belfast City, Northern Ireland; used for spares; canx 24May90]
SH3601	100	Air Cargo Carriers	G-14-3601 G-WIDE N360SA
SH3602	200	Mayair	G-14-3602 G-BKJC N360MQ HP-1317APP YN-CGF XA-MYI
SH3603	100	(Associated Aviation)	G-14-3603 G-BKKT N368MQ G-OJSY 5N-BBZ [reported wfu by early 2006,canx late 2006; no other details]
SH3604	100	(BAC Express Airlines)	G-14-3604 G-BKKU G-RMSS G-BPCO G-OLAH EI-CWG G-ROND [wfu & stored Nov06 Edinburgh, UK; to fire service Nov07; b/u Jun08; canx 19Jan09]
SH3605	100	ex Air Wisconsin/United Express	G-14-3605 G-BKKV N342MV [wfu & stored Jan91 Hagerstown, MA; Aug93 to White Industries, Bates City, MO, for spares; canx 07Oct05; l/n 04Oct07]
SH3606	100	(Gill Aviation)	G-BKKW G-14-3606 G-DASI [wfu & b/u 28-30Oct00 Guernsey, Channel Islands, UK; canx 18Feb02]
SH3607	200	Aeroperlas	G-14-3607 G-BKKX N361MQ HP-1319APP
SH3608	100	(Engage Aviation LLC)	G-14-3608 G-BKMX N161EA+ [+ reg'd for spares recovery, not worn; stored by 03Jun09 Edinburgh, UK; b/u and left by road 09Jun09; canx 16May11]
SH3609	100	John the Baptist School	G-14-3609 (G-BKMY) N343MV SE-KLO G-SSWO [wfu & stored 2006 Blackpool, UK; canx 06Jun07; preserved 10Apr08 RAF Millom, UK; 10Dec10 to Colwick, UK for use as classroom]
SH3610	100	Great Lakes Turbines Inc	G-14-3610 (G-BKMZ) N715NC HP-1251APP N476RW
SH3611	100	Air Cargo Carriers	(G-BKPO) G-14-3611 G-BMAJ G-WACK C-GPCE N642AN
SH3612	200	ITAB	G-14-3612 G-BKPP N362MQ HP-1318APPYN-CGG 9Q-CAP
SH3613	100	Air Cargo Carriers	G-14-3613 G-BKPR N601A C-FCRB N360RW
SH3614	200	Tiara Air	G-14-3614 G-BKSL N363MQ HP-1315APP P4-TIC [reported for spares use]
SH3615	100	ex Air Wisconsin/United Express	G-14-3615 G-BKSM N344MV [wfu & stored Jan91 Hagerstown, MA; Aug93 to White Industries, Bates City, MO, for spares; canx 11Oct05; l/n 04Oct07]
SH3616	100	Islena Airlines	G-14-3616 G-BKSN N345MV HR-IAP
SH3617	100	Air Cargo Carriers	G-14-3617 N617FB G-BKUF N617FB
SH3618	100	(Air Cargo Carriers)	G-14-3618 G-BKUG N691A [probably DBR 25Nov97 Billings, MT; canx 7Sep04 as destroyed; assumed b/u]
SH3619	100	Tiara Air	G-14-3619 G-BKUH N364MQ C-GPCG P4-TIA
SH3620	100	Pacific Coastal Airlines	G-14-3620 G-BKWJ VH-MVX (N366AC) C-GPCF
SH3621	100	Tiara Air	G-14-3621 G-BKWK N365MQ C-GPCN P4-TIB
SH3622	300	Pacific Coastal Airlines	G-14-3622 N622FB C-GPCW
SH3623	100	Air Cargo Carriers	G-14-3623 G-BKWM N601CA
SH3624	C-23B+	US Army	G-14-3624 G-BKWN N912SB N418SA+ 93-1317 [+ cvtd Sep95 to C-23B+ with new c/n SH3401]
SH3625	100	Air Cargo Carriers	G-14-3625 G-BKZN N4498Y (N133CA)
SH3626	100	Air Cargo Carriers	G-14-3626 G-BKZO VH-MVW N367AC VH-MVW+ N367AC [+ marks restored but not reapplied]
SH3627	100	Air Cargo Carriers	G-14-3627 G-BKZP N701A
SH3628	C-23B+	US Army	G-14-3628 G-BKZR OY-MMC G-SALU (SE-IXO) G-OAEX G-BKZR N424SA + 93-1320 [+ cvtd Dec96 to C-23B+ with new c/n SH3404]
SH3629	C-23B+	US Army	G-14-3629 N913SB N403SA+ N913SB 93-1319 [+ cvtd Dec96 to C-23B+ with new c/n SH3403]
SH3630	100	(Sunstate Airlines)	G-14-3630 G-BLCN VH-FCU [wfu for spares 26Mar97 Townsville, QLD, Australia; l/n as hulk Jun98; canx 22Mar99]
SH3631	100	ex Aeroperlas	G-14-3631 G-BLCO N914SB N131DA C-FTAZ N360MM HP-1326APP [wfu by 05Sep10 Panama City-Gelabert, Panama, painted as HP-AOPA; fuselage only by Nov10]
SH3632	100	(Aerocondor)	G-14-3632 G-BLCP OY-MMA EI-BYU OY-MMA (SE-KSU) OY-MMA G-BLCP CS-TMY [wfu & stored 13Jly04; b/u Jly06]
SH3633	100	Air Cargo Carriers	G-14-3633 G-BLCR G-BMAR C-GPCJ N688AN
SH3634	C-23B+	US Army	G-14-3634 G-BLCS N132DA N405SA+ 93-1321 [+ cvtd Dec96 to C-23B+ with new c/n SH3405]
SH3635	200	(HD Air)	G-14-3635 G-BLED EI-BEK G-CLAS [b/u Edinburgh, UK & left by road 08Jun09 reportedly to be used for spares in USA; canx 09Jun09 to USA]
SH3636	C-23B+	US Army	G-14-3636 G-BLEE EI-BEL G-SBAC N408SA+ 93-1324 [+ cvtd Mar97 to C-23B+ with new c/n SH3408]
SH3637	100	(Associated Aviation)	G-14-3637 G-BLEF G-LEGS 5N-BBL [reported wfu by early 2006, no other details]
SH3638	100	ex Aerocondor	G-14-3638 G-BLEG G-ISLE CS-TMN [airline ceased operations Apr08; status unknown]
SH3639	100	Jim Hankins Air Service	G-14-3639 G-BLEH N366MQ

SHORT SD3.60

C/n	Model	Last known Owner/Operator	Identities/fates/comments (where appropriate)
SH3640	100	SkyWay Enterprises	G-14-3640 G-BLGA N367MQ
SH3641	100	(British Regional Airlines)	G-14-3641 G-BLGB [w/o 09Feb98 Stornoway, UK; canx 19Nov98; 23Mar99 fuselage to Lasham, UK fire training; l/n 06Apr05]
SH3642	100	(Aer Lingus Commuter)	G-14-3642 G-BLGC EI-BEM [w/o 31Jan86 near East Midlands airport, UK; canx 28Aug86]
SH3643	C-23B+	US Army	G-14-3643 G-BLGD N631KC N407SA+ 93-1323 [+ cvtd Mar97 to C-23B+ with new c/n SH3407]
SH3644	C-23B+	US Army	G-14-3644 G-BLGE N632KC C-GLAJ G-BLGE (SE-KGV) C-GLAJ N418SA + 94-0311 [+ cvtd Mar98 to C-23B+ with new c/n SH3425]
SH3645	C-23B+	US Army	G-14-3645 G-BLGF N633KC N406SA+ 93-1322 [+ cvtd Dec96 to C-23B+ with new c/n SH3406]
SH3646	C-23B+	US Army	G-14-3646 G-BLIJ N634KC N409SA+ 93-1325 [+ cvtd Sep97 to C-23B+ with new c/n SH3409]
SH3647	C-23B+	US Army	G-14-3647 G-BLIU N635KC VH-TAO N427SA + N635KC 93-1333 [+ cvtd Sep97 to C-23B+ with new c/n SH3417]
SH3648	100	(BAC Express Airlines)	G-14-3648 G-BLIL OY-MMB G-OAAS SE-KCI G-SSWM [stored 04May06 Coventry, UK; canx 06Jun07; b/u by Jly08]
SH3649	C-23B+	US Army	G-14-3649 G-BLIM N346MV N410SA+ 93-1326 [+ cvtd Apr97 to C-23B+ with new c/n SH3410]
SH3650	C-23B+	US Army	G-14-3650 G-BLIN N347MV N432SA+ 93-1327 [+ cvtd Apr97 to C-23B+ with new c/n SH3411]
SH3651	100	Air Cargo Carriers	G-14-3651 G-BLJR 9M-KGN VH-BWO N368AC
SH3652	100	Air Cargo Carriers	G-14-3652 G-BLJS N124CA
SH3653	100	Air Cargo Carriers	G-14-3653 G-BLJT N151CA
SH3654	C-23B+	US Army	G-14-3654 G-BLJU N369MQ+ 93-1334 [+ cvtd Oct97 to C-23B+ with new c/n SH3418]
SH3655	100	(SkyWay Enterprises)	G-14-3655 G-BLJV N370MQ [wfu & stored Jan95 Opa-locka, FL; b/u May08]
SH3656	100	(Aer Arann)	G-14-3656 G-BLPU EI-BPD G-RMCT EI-BPD [w/o 04Feb01 Sheffield, UK; canx 13Jul01; fuselage to Leeds-Bradford, UK for fire training; l/n Sep04]
SH3657	C-23B+	US Army	G-14-3657 G-BLPV SE-KEX G-BLPV N412SA+ 93-1328 [+ cvtd Jun97 to C-23B+ with new c/n SH3412]
SH3658	C-23B+	US Army	G-14-3658 G-BLPW N371MQ+ 93-1335 [+ cvtd Nov97 to C-23B+ with new c/n SH3419]
SH3659	100	(Executive Airlines/American Eagle)	G-14-3659 G-BLPX N372MQ [wfu & stored Jan95 Opa-locka, FL; derelict by 28May96; b/u by May08]
SH3660	C-23B+	US Army	G-14-3660 G-BLPY SE-KEY G-MAXW N413SA+ 93-1329 [+ cvtd Oct97 to C-23B+ with new c/n SH3413]
SH3661	100	(Engage Aviation LLC)	G-14-3661 G-BLRT SE-KRV G-BLRT TC-AOA G-EXPS EI-SMB G-EXPS N162EA+ [+ reg'd for spares recovery, not worn; b/u started by 03Jun09 Edinburgh, UK; remains left by road 08Jun09; canx 16May11]
SH3662	C-23B+	US Army	G-14-3662 N362SA+ 94-0312 [+ cvtd 1997 to C-23B+ with new c/n SH3426]
SH3663	C-23B+	US Army	G-14-3663 N360SE+ 94-0313 [+ cvtdJun98 to C-23B+ with new c/n SH3427]
SH3664	C-23B+	US Army	G-14-3664 G-BLTO EI-BSM G-BLTO SE-KKZ G-BLTO N426SA+ 93-1330 [+ cvtd Sep95 to C-23B+ with new c/n SH3416]
SH3665	100	ex IAL Corp	G-14-3665 G-BLUC N190SB HP-1280APP HR-ATT N391RC [by 16Jly10 with Dodson International Parts, Rantoul, KS, dismantled]
SH3666	C-23B+	US Army	G-14-3666 G-BLUD N191SB C-GLAO N403SA+ 94-0310 [+ cvtd Mar98 to C-23B+ with new c/n SH3424]
SH3667	100	(Tyr Aviation)	G-14-3667 G-BLRU B-3601 C-FRIZ [canx 01Mar95 to USA but b/u and to fire dump Feb00 Calgary, AB, Canada]
SH3668	100	(Aeroperlas)	G-14-3668 G-BLUR N360SY HP-1257APP [reported derelict by Mar98 Panama City-Albrook, Panama; l/n Mar02; assumed b/u]
SH3669	100	Islena Airlines	G-14-3669 G-BLUU B-3602 N361PA HR-IAW
SH3670	100	(BAC Express Airlines)	G-14-3670 G-BLWJ B-3603 N108PS(1) HR-IAQ SE-KGV G-SSWR [wfu & stored Nov06 Coventry, UK; canx 06Aug07; l/n Nov07; b/u by Jly08]
SH3671	100	Islena Airlines	G-14-3671 G-BLWK B-3604 N108PS(2) HR-IAT
SH3672	100	Servicios Aereos Profesionales	G-14-3672 G-BLWN B-3605 8P-SCD HI-657CT HI-657
SH3673	100	(CAAC)	G-14-3673 G-BLYF B-3606 [w/o 22Oct85 Enshi, China]
SH3674	100	ex SAPSA	G-14-3674 G-BLYG B-3607 8P-SCE HI-658CT [wfu by Dec06 Santo Domingo-Herrera, Dominican Republic; spares use]
SH3675	200	(BAC Express)	G-14-3675 G-BLYH B-3608 G-CBAC [stored Guangzhou, China; not delivered & wfu by Mar98; canx 28Feb02]

SHORT SD3.60

C/n	Model	Last known Owner/Operator	Identities/fates/comments (where appropriate)
SH3676	100	(BAC Express)	G-14-3676 G-BLZT [stored 20Nov00 Exeter, UK; wfu & to Sunshine Airspares (Florida) by Feb01 for parts; canx 11Mar02; cut up by 27Mar02; hulk to Southend, UK until left Sep03]
SH3677	100	(Canadian Regional Airlines)	G-14-3677 G-BLZU C-GTAU [wfu & stored Oct96 Vancouver, BC, Canada; canx Apr97 to USA but b/u Sep99]
SH3678	100	ex Liberty Express/US Air Express	G-14-3678 G-BLZV N342SB [wfu by 26Jly05; to White Industries, Bates City, MO for parts; l/n Jly10]
SH3679	100	(Canadian Regional Airlines)	G-14-3679 G-BMEN C-GTAX [wfu & stored Oct96 Vancouver, BC, Canada; canx Apr97 to USA but b/u Oct99]
SH3680	200	ex Bangkok Airways	G-14-3680 G-BMEO HS-TSE HS-SKN [wfu 1994 Bangkok-Don Muang, Thailand; b/u Apr96; by Jan00 fuselage at Naresuan Camp, Hua Hin, Thailand as parachute trainer; l/n Jan08]
SH3681	200	ex Bangkok Airways	G-14-3681 G-BMEP HS-TSF HS-SKO [wfu 1994 Bangkok-Don Muang, Thailand; b/u Apr96; by Jan00 hulk Maruektayawan Place, Hua Hin, Thailand; l/n Jan08]
SH3682	C-23B+	US Army	G-14-3682 G-BMER N373MQ+ 94-0307 [+ cvtd Jan98 to C-23B+ with new c/n SH3421]
SH3683	C-23B+	US Army	G-14-3683 G-BMES N374MQ+ 94-0308 [+ cvtd Feb98 to C-23B+ with new c/n SH3422]
SH3684	C-23B+	US Army	G-14-3684 G-BMHV N375MQ+ 93-1336 [+ cvtd Dec97 to C-23B+ with new c/n SH3420][w/o 03Mar01 en-route to Hulburt AFB, Norfolk, VA to Unadilla, GA]
SH3685	C-23B+	US Army	G-14-3685 G-BMHW N376MQ+ 94-0309 [+ cvtd Jun97 to C-23B+ with new c/n SH3423]
SH3686	100	(Engage Aviation LLC)	G-14-3686 G-BMHX SE-LGE G-SSWC G-TMRA N163EA+ [+ regd for spares recovery, not worn; b/u started by 03Jun09 Edinburgh, UK; remains taken away before 09Jun09; canx 16May11]
SH3687	C-23B+	US Army	G-14-3687 G-BMHY G-OREX N428SA+ 93-1332 [+ cvtd Jun97 to C-23B+ with new c/n SH3414]
SH3688	200	(BAC Express Airlines)	G-14-3688 G-BMLC SE-LDA G-BMLC [wfu by 24May05 Coventry, UK; canx 06Jun07; b/u by Jly08; nose preserved in bar in Barrow, UK]
SH3689	C-23B+	US Army	G-14-3689 G-BMLD (EI-BSN) EI-BSP G-UBAC SE-KXU G-UBAC N6368X+ 94-0314 [+ cvtd Jun97 to C-23B+ with new c/n SH3428]
SH3690	200	HD Air	G-14-3690 G-BMLE N690PC C6-BFT G-SSWB G-TMRB
SH3691	200	Air Cargo Carriers	G-14-3691 G-BMNG (N691PC) N360PC C6-BFW N881BC N618AN
SH3692	200	ex Aerocondor	G-14-3692 G-BMNH N693PC OY-MUD CS-TLJ [stored Sep07 Cascais-Tires, Portugal; l/n 05Oct10 being worked on]
SH3693	200	Great Lakes Turbines Inc	G-14-3693 G-BMNI N695PC C6-BFK A3-BFK N429AS 5W-SPX N693GL
SH3694	200	ex Aerocondor	G-14-3694 G-BMNJ N694PC G-BMNJ CS-TMH [wfu by 24Apr05 Cascais-Tires, Portugal; l/n 05oct10 in poor condition]
SH3695	C-23B+	US Army	G-14-3695 G-BMNK (5N-AOX) G-14-3695 (EI-BVJ) EI-BVM G-TBAC N419SA+ 93-1318 [+ cvtd Dec96 to C-23B+ with new c/n SH3402]
SH3696	200	ex Pacific Island Aviation	G-14-3696 G-BMUV N711PK [wfu & stored Feb05 Saipan, Northern Mariana Islands; by Mar06 to MAS Aviation, FL for parts; l/n 19Feb06]
SH3697	200	ex Pacific Island Aviation	G-14-3697 G-BMUW N711HJ [wfu & stored Feb05 Saipan, Northern Mariana Islands; by Mar06 to MAS Aviation, FL for parts; l/n 19Feb06]
SH3698	200	Great Lakes Turbines Inc	G-14-3698 G-BMUX N711MP 5W-SPE N711MP
SH3699	200	SkyWay Enterprises	G-14-3699 G-BMUY N377MQ (N699AE)
SH3700	200	SkyWay Enterprises	G-14-3700 G-BMXP N378MQ
SH3701	200	ex SkyWay Enterprises	G-14-3701 G-BMXR N379MQ [wfu by 05Jun01 Kissimmee, FL; used for parts, by15Aug08 fuselage only; l/n 09Nov11]
SH3702	200	SkyWay Enterprises	G-14-3702 G-BMXS N380MQ
SH3703	200	SkyWay Enterprises	G-14-3703 G-BMXT N381MQ (N703AE) [stored by 08Nov11 Kissimmee, FL]
SH3704	200	SkyWay Enterprises	G-14-3704 G-BMXU N382MQ (N704AM) [stored by 12May00 Kissimmee, FL; l/n 08Nov11]
SH3705	200	Kingsland Primary School	G-14-3705 G-BNBA SE-IXE G-SSWE [wfu by 22Aug05 Coventry, UK; canx 06Jun07; to school in Bucknall, Stoke on Trent, UK, used as classroom; l/n 30Aug12]
SH3706	200	SkyWay Enterprises	G-14-3706 G-BNBB N383MQ (N706AM)
SH3707	200	SkyWay Enterprises	G-14-3707 G-BNBC N385MQ (N707JN)
SH3708	C-23B+	US Army	G-14-3708 G-BNBD G-OGCI N435SA+ 93-1331 [+ cvtd Aug97 to C-23B+ with new c/n SH3415]
SH3709	200	M & N Aviation Enterprises	G-14-3709 G-BNBE N386MQ (N709AE)
SH3710	200	(SkyWay Enterprises)	G-14-3710 G-BNBF N387MQ (N710AE) [stored by Apr02 Kissimmee, FL; l/n May05; probably b/u by Feb06]

SHORT SD3.60

C/n	Model	Last known Owner/Operator	Identities/fates/comments (where appropriate)
SH3711	200	(SkyWay Enterprises)	G-14-3711 G-BNBG N384MQ (N711AE) [stored by Apr02 Kissimmee, FL; l/n May05; probably b/u by Feb06]
SH3712	200	(Engage Aviation LLC)	G-14-3712 G-BNDI G-OBLK G-BNDI G-OBLK EI-SMA G-TMRO N164EA+ [wfu by 21Jly06 Cascais-Tires, Portugal; l/n 19Jly08; + reg'd 20May09 for probable spares recovery; canx 16May11]
SH3713	200	Comeravia	G-14-3713 G-BNDJ G-OBOH EI-CPR G-XPSS YV396T
SH3714	200	(ACL Aviation Support)	G-14-3714 G-BNDK G-OBHD G-BNDK G-OBHD [stored by 05Mar06 Blackpool, UK; b/u by Nov80 & fuselage to Retro Aviation, Market Drayton, UK; canx 27Jan11]
SH3715	200	(Engage Aviation LLC)	G-14-3715 G-BNDL N711PM G-SSWX G-JEMX (N165EA) [stored by 02Dec06 Southend, UK; regd 22May09 for spares recovery; regn not applied; fully b/u by 23Oct09; canx 16May11]
SH3716	300	Ben Air	G-14-3716 G-BNDM N360AR EI-CMG G-BNDM OY-MUG
SH3717	300	not yet known	G-14-3717 G-BNFA G-14-3717 EI-BTH G-BNFA G-BWMZ 5Y-BKW ZS-PBB 5Y-BVC+ ZS- [+ canx 19Nov08 to South Africa]
SH3718	300	Trans Executive Airlines of Hawaii/Trans Air	G-14-3718 G-BNFB G-14-3718 EI-BTI G-BNFB VQ-TSK N808TR
SH3719	300	(Philippine Airlines)	G-14-3719 G-BNFC G-14-3719 EI-BTJ [w/o 13Dec87 Mount Munay near Iligan, Philippines]
SH3720	300	ex Air Cargo Carriers	G-14-3720 G-BNFD G-14-3720 EI-BTK G-BNFD VH-SUM N372AC [DBR 05Feb06 mid-air collision with N3735W (SH3735) ex Milwaukee WI; made emergency landing Juneau-Dodge County Airport, WI]
SH3721	300	Freedom Air	G-14-3721 G-BNFE N121PC F-OHQG N121PC N74NF
SH3722	300	Trans Executive Airlines of Hawaii	G-14-3722 G-BNMS N722PC F-OHQH N722PC N221LM
SH3723	300	(Loganair)	G-14-3723 G-BNMT N160DD G-BNMT [w/o 27Feb01 near Granton Harbour, Firth of Forth, near Edinburgh-Turnhouse, UK]
SH3724	300	Air Seychelles	G-14-3724 G-BNMU N161DD (F-OHQP) G-BNMU S7-PRI
SH3725	300	Potomac Aviation	G-14-3725 G-BNMV N162DD D-CFDX N162DD N151PR [by Dec11 fuselage only San Juan, PR, still with Roblex titles]
SH3726	300	ex Roblex Aviation	G-14-3726 G-BNMW EI-BTO G-BNMW SE-LCC G-BNMW N411ER [by Dec11 stored San Juan, PR]
SH3727	300	(Fuerza Aerea Venezolana)	G-14-3727 G-BNYE YV-O-GUR-2 YV-O-GUR-0-12 1952 [w/o 21Aug04 Mount El Perico near Maracay-El Libertador AFB, Venezuela]
SH3728	300	MAS Inc	G-14-3728 G-BNYF EI-BTP G-14-3728 EI-BTP G-BNYF VH-SUR VH-SEO (OY-PBV) 3C-SEO+ 3C-LGQ N522LJ [+ not confirmed]
SH3729	300	Trans Executive Airlines of Hawaii/Trans Air	G-14-3729 G-BNYG N729PC 6Y-JMX(1) N729PC
SH3730	300	(CC Air/US Air Express)	G-14-3730 G-BNYH N730CC [w/o 20Aug90 Charlotte, NC]
SH3731	300	Trans Executive Airlines of Hawaii	G-14-3731 G-BNYI N360CC G-BNYI N360CC 5N-BFT N4476F
SH3732	300	Air Cargo Carriers	G-14-3732 G-BOEF VR-BKM VP-BKM D-CMAX HH-PRX N3732X PK-DSN N3732X
SH3733	300	Air Cargo Carriers	G-14-3733 G-BOEG N133PC N163DD D-CFXE G-BOEG CS-TLS G-BOEG N569FU N733CH
SH3734	300	Trans Executive Airlines of Hawaii/Trans Air	G-14-3734 G-BOEL N134PC N164DD D-CFAO N808KR
SH3735	300	(Air Cargo Carriers)	G-14-3735 G-BOEI VR-BKL VP-BKL D-CFLX HH-PRY G-BOEI N3735W [w/o 05Feb06 near Watertown, WI after mid-air collision with N372AC (SH3720) ex Milwaukee WI; canx 18Apr06]
SH3736	300	Air Cargo Carriers	G-14-3736 G-BOEJ VH-MJU G-VBAC N376AC
SH3737	300	Nightexpress	G-14-3737 G-BOFG G-OLBA D-CCAS
SH3738	300	(Air Manos)	G-14-3738 G-BOFH G-OLTN G-ZAPF 4X-CSL SX-BFN [canx 22Jun01 to USA as to spares; stored by 26Oct01 West Memphis, AR; l/n Jun02; wings used to rebuild N165DD (SH3740)]
SH3739	300	Freedom Air (Aviation Services)	G-14-3739 G-BOFI G-CPTL G-ZAPG EI-COR SX-BFW N2843F
SH3740	300	ex Roblex Aviation	G-14-3740 G-BOFJ N165DD D-CFXF N165DD [rebuilt with wings from c/n SH3738; by Dec11stored San Juan, PR]
SH3741	300	Roblex Aviation	G-14-3741 G-BOFK "G-LOGW"+ G-OLGW G-ZAPD N875RR [+ marks painted on aircraft in error]
SH3742	300	Air Cargo Carriers	G-14-3742 G-BOWF N742CC D-CFXH N742CC N974AA
SH3743	300	Deraya Air Taxi	G-14-3743 G-BOWG N743CC N824BE F-OHQF N743RW PK-DSS
SH3744	300	Nightexpress	G-14-3744 G-BOWH N744CC N825BE D-CRAS
SH3745	300	ex Air Jamaica Express	G-14-3745 G-BOWI N745CC N826BE N261GA 6Y-JMX(2) [stored by 25May02 Fort Lauderdale International, FL; later Oklahoma City, OK; l/n Jun07]

SHORT SD3.60

C/n	Model	Last known Owner/Operator	Identities/fates/comments (where appropriate)
SH3746	300	Trans Executive Airlines of Hawaii/Trans Air	G-14-3746 G-BOWJ N746SA N827BE
SH3747	300	Albedo Corporation/Ben Air	G-14-3747 G-BPFN N747SA N747HH G-BPFN G-GPBV OY-PBV
SH3748	300	(Air Cargo Carriers)	G-14-3748 G-BPFO N748SA N748CC D-CFXC N748CC [w/o 16Dec04 Oshawa-Municipal Airport, ON, Canada; canx 15Feb08]
SH3749	300	Air Cargo Carriers	G-BPFP N828BE N262GA D-CFXD N749JT N973AA
SH3750	300	ex Aircraft Africa Contracts	G-14-3750 G-BPFR B-12277 G-BPFR G-BWMW 5Y-BKP ZS-OXU [reported wfu by 13Oct09 Lanseria, South Africa; gone by 2010]
SH3751	300	Roblex Aviation	G-BPFS G-OCIA G-REGN G-BPFS G-BVMX N948RR
SH3752	300	Air Cargo Carriers	G-BPKV D-CAAS VH-SUL N136LR
SH3753	300	(Mario's Air)	G-BPKW N753CN N153CC D-CFXG G-BPKW N173DM [May06 to MTW Aerospace, Montgomery, AL for spares; canx 12Jly06; l/n 02Jly06]
SH3754	300	Air Cargo Carriers	G-BPKX N754CN N829BE N263GA D-CFXA N263GA N972AA
SH3755	300	Roblex Aviation	G-BPKY G-OEEC G-BVMY SE-LHY N377AR
SH3756	300	Air Cargo Carriers	G-BPKZ (B-) N830BE N264GA D-CFXB G-BPKZ N360AB
SH3757	300	Deraya Air Taxi	G-BPXK (B-) N831BE N265GA N350TA P4-AVF N350TA PK-DSH
SH3758	300	Ayit Aviation & Tourism	G-BPXL VH-MJH G-KBAC S7-PAL 4X-AVP
SH3759	300	Trans Executive Airlines of Hawaii /Trans Air	G-BPXM N159CC N351TA
SH3760	300	Ben Air	G-BPXN B-8811 RP-C3319 VH-SEG OY-PBW
SH3761	300	Fuerza Aerea Venezolana	G-BPXO N161SB N161CN G-CEAL 4113
SH3762	300	Fuerza Aerea Venezolana	G-BRMX N162SB N162CN G-OCEA 4112 + 2358 [+ Venezuela]
SH3763	300	(Avisto (Overseas)/Sirte Oil Co)	G-BRMY HB-AAM [w/o 13Jan00 ditched off Marsa el-Brega, Libya]
SH3764	300	Air Cargo Carriers	G-BRMZ D-CBAS VH-SUF N764JR
SH3765	100	(Short Brothers PLC)	(G-BRNA) [not built; canx 08Oct93]
SH3766	100	(Short Brothers PLC)	(G-BRNB) [not built; canx 08Oct93]
SH3767	100	(Short Brothers PLC)	(G-BRWI) [not built; canx 08Oct93]
SH3768	100	(Short Brothers PLC)	(G-BRWJ) [not built; canx 08Oct93]
SH3769	100	(Short Brothers PLC)	(G-BRWK) [not built; canx 08Oct93]
SH3770	100	(Short Brothers PLC)	(G-BRWL) [not built; canx 08Oct93]
SH3771	100	(Short Brothers PLC)	(G-BRWM) [not built; canx 08Oct93]
Unidentified			
unkn			N690SB [operated by US government dept; first noted Jun95 & Dec96 Felker Army Airfield & 23Jan99 at Marana, AZ; has never entered USCAR register; is a C-23B Sherpa]
unkn		Tiara Air	P4-TIC [reported Jly10 wfu for spares Oranjestad, Aruba; probably not flown as such]
unkn			YV2358 [reported 19Feb11 Caracas, Venezuela]
unkn		ITAB	9Q-CAP [reported ferried across Atlantic 26-27Aug11 to Accra, Ghana]

US ARMY NATIONAL GUARD C-23B+ SHERPA CONVERSION C/N BREAKDOWN; HISTORIES INCLUDED UNDER ORIGINAL C/N ABOVE

New c/n & build no	Old c/n	US Army serial
SH3401/AK001	SH3624	93-1317
SH3402/AK002	SH3695	93-1318
SH3403/AK003	SH3629	93-1319
SH3404/AK004	SH3628	93-1320
SH3405/AK005	SH3634	93-1321
SH3406/AK006	SH3645	93-1322
SH3407/AK007	SH3643	93-1323
SH3408/AK008	SH3636	93-1324
SH3409/AK009	SH3646	93-1325
SH3410/AK010	SH3649	93-1326
SH3411/AK011	SH3650	93-1327
SH3412/AK012	SH3657	93-1328
SH3413/AK013	SH3660	93-1329
SH3414/AK016	SH3687	93-1332
SH3415/AK015	SH3708	93-1331
SH3416/AK014	SH3664	93-1330
SH3417/AK017	SH3647	93-1333
SH3418/AK018	SH3654	93-1334

SHORT SD3.60

C/n	Model	Last known Owner/Operator	Identities/fates/comments (where appropriate)
SH3419/AK019		SH3658	93-1335
SH3420/AK020		SH3684	93-1336
SH3421/AK021		SH3682	94-0307
SH3422/AK022		SH3683	94-0308
SH3423/AK023		SH3685	94-0309
SH3424/AK024		SH3666	94-0310
SH3425/AK025		SH3644	94-0311
SH3426/AK026		SH3662	94-0312
SH3427/AK027		SH3663	94-0313
SH3428/AK028		SH3689	94-0314

Production complete

SWEARINGEN (FAIRCHILD) SA.226TC METRO II

Notes: SA226TA Merlin IV/IVA aircraft in the range AT-001 to AT-685B are included in our sister publication *Business Turboprops International.* Registration history prior to conversion from Merlins not included. For details please refer to *Business Turboprops International.* The "B" suffix after a c/n indicates aircraft that have been converted to a higher Maximum Take-Off Weight (MTOW)

C/n	Model	Last known Owner/Operator	Identities/fates/comments (where appropriate)
TC-200	S226	(Swearingen)	N226TC [cvtd to SA.226AT Merlin IV c/n AT-003E; later history in Business Turboprops International]
TC-201	S226	(Provincial Airlines)	N21RM N5302M N525LB C-FSDS [canx 27Jly96 as wfu, fate unknown]
TC-202	S226	(Air-Lift Commuter)	9Q-CFV N505LB [w/o 23Apr87 Wilmington-New Hanover County Airport, NC; canx 09Aug89]
TC-202E +	S226	ex Aviation Materials	N5291M [+ cvtd from SA.226AT c/n AT-001; canx 13Mar91 as wfu; stored Aviation Warehouse, El Mirage, CA; l/n 19May07]
TC-203	S226	ex Top Fly	N5303M OY-BYH EC-701 EC-GAN [wfu by 22Apr08 Barcelona, Spain; l/n 21Apr11]
TC-204	S226	ex North American Airlines	N5304M OY-BYN N81969 C-GSWB [canx 18Jun99 on sale to White Industries, Bates City, MO; used for spares; l/n 25Apr07]
TC-205	S226	ex Martinaire	N260S N511SS [DBR 07Dec84 Harrison, AR & wfu for spares; by Jan 93 to OK Aircraft Parts, Gilroy, GA; later to Aviation Warehouse, El Mirage, CA]
TC-206	S226	Key Lime Air	N261S N509SS
TC-207	S226	(Grand Aire Express)	N262S N514SS N501AB N168GA [wfu Jly01; used as GIA Winnipeg, MB; l/n May05; not present 11Jly08]
TC-208	S226	(Transportation Systems Inc)	N303BG N18SL D-IHRB N18SL C-FIDB C-GEMM N161WA [canx 29Sep04 fate/reason unknown]
TC-208E +	S226	SITCO Mine	N5336M 9Q- [+ cvtd from SA.226AT c/n AT-019; nothing known, possibly b/u in USA]
TC-209	S226	ex Martinaire	N423S N512SS [wfu; by Jan93 to OK Aircraft Parts, Gilroy GA; later to Aviation Warehouse, El Mirage, CA]
TC-210	S226	(Air Vendee)	N424S N510SS F-GERV [w/o 01Feb88 Rouen, France; canx 11Mar91]
TC-211	S226	1802 Lima	N425S N516SS [status unknown; probably wfu or b/u]
TC-211E +	S226	ex Regional Airlines	N5356M F-GGSV [+ cvtd from SA.226AT c/n AT-021; wfu Jan92; b/u Sep94 location unknown]
TC-211EE +	S226	(Air Niagara Express)	N5355M C-GJDX [+ cvtd from SA.226AT c/n AT-022; w/o 11Feb88 into Lake Ontario, Canada; canx 15Aug88]
TC-211EEE +	S226	ex Martinaire	N426S N515SS [+ cvtd from SA.226AT c/n AT-023; wfu; by Jan93 to OK Aircraft Parts, Gilroy, GA; later to Aviation Warehouse, El Mirage, CA; l/n 02Mar12]
TC-211EEEE +	S226	Skyway International	CC-ECC C-04^ N2685B C-GJWS N200PT JA22PT N200PT [+ cvtd from SA.226AT c/n AT-024; ^ Chile]
TC-212 +	S226	White Industries	CC-ECD C-05^ N2683U C-GGRX N654DW [+ cvtd from SA.226AT c/n AT-026; ^ Chile; wfu for spares; by Jan96 fuselage only Bates City, MO; l/n Jun06; canx 04Feb09]
TC-213	S226	Venexcargo	CC-ECE C-06^ CC-ECL N2684S C-GDAU N213PT N617DM YV-852CP YV1442+ [^ Chile; + not fully confirmed]
TC-214	S226	ex Hunter Aviation Support Services	CC-ECN C-07^ CC-CBL CC-PMS N26836 N333FA [^ Chile] [canx 26Apr99 as sold in Australia; reported used as GIA Wagga Wagga, NSW, Australia]
TC-215	S226	Berry Aviation	N5364M N62SA N911HF N165BA
TC-215E +	S226	(Propair)	N5365M N302TL C-GKFS [+ cvtd from SA.226AT c/n AT-038E; w/o 23Oct96 Puvirnituq Airport, PQ, Canada; canx 14Nov96]
TC-217	S226	(Worldwide Aircraft Services)	N5366M N61SA N86RA [canx 29 Oct99 as destroyed/scrapped; fate unknown]
TC-218	S226	Argentine Gendarmerie	N442JA N21SL SE-IOH N622SP GN-711 [by apr12 wfu Campo de Mayo, Argentina]
TC-219	S226	(Grand Aire Express)	N538S N167GA [b/u Jan00 Toledo, OH]
TC-220	S226	(Ibertrans Aerea)	N5370M N443JA C-GFAP N220AT EC-930 EC-GDG [w/o 18Feb98 near Barcelona-El Prat, Spain]
TC-221	S226	ex Pirinair Express	N5372M OO-JPI EC-666 EC-FZB [wfu by 02Apr11 Barcelona, Spain]
TC-222	S226	(Fairchild Acquisition)	N5369M N63SA [wfu Oct90 probably b/u San Antonio, TX; canx 09Jly93]

SWEARINGEN (FAIRCHILD) SA.226TC METRO II

C/n	Model	Last known Owner/Operator	Identities/fates/comments (where appropriate)
TC-222E +	S226	ex Key Lime Air	N639S N332BA^ [+cvtd from SA.226AT c/n AT-047; ^ canx Apr98 to Argentina, sale not completed, restored Aug98; w/o 18Nov03 Grand Junction-Walker Field, CO; still current]
TC-222EE +	S226	Perimeter Airlines	N5379M A4O-AI N104GS C-FSLZ N104GS C-FSLZ [+ cvtd from SA.226AT c/n AT-046; substantial damage 03Mar09 Winnipeg, MB, Canada]]
TC-223 +	S226	Key Lime Air	(N224AM) N2MM EC-421(2) EC-GNM N81418 [+ cvtd from SA.226AT c/n AT-048]
TC-224 +	S226	(Candler & Associates)	(N225AM) N5302M N6SS N502SS [+ cvtd from SA.226AT c/n AT-049; canx 18Feb92 as destroyed; fate unknown]
TC-225 +	S226	(1802 Lima)	(N226AM) N223AM [+ cvtd from SA.226AT c/n AT-050; canx 11Mar93 as destroyed; reported wfu Dallas, TX; to Aviation Warehouse, El Mirage, CA; l/n Dec09]
TC-226	S226	(Swearingen)	N5386M [cvtd to SA.226AT c/n AT-051]
TC-227 +	S226	(Superior Aviation)	N224AM [+ cvtd from SA.226AT c/n AT-052; w/o 19Aug97 Des Moines International Airport, IA; canx 15Jan99]
TC-227E +	S226	(Bimini Island Air)	A4O-AU N90459 N222AM N677SP [+ cvtd from SA.226AT c/n AT-053; DBR 15Jun02 Fort Lauderdale-Executive, FL; l/n 16Oct06; assumed b/u by Aug08]
TC-228	S226	(Air Wisconsin)	N650S [w/o 12Jun80 near Valley, 24 kms west of Omaha, NE]
TC-228E +	S226	(Worldwide Aircraft Services)	N225AM C-GJTK N510TN [+ cvtd from SA.226AT c/n AT-054; canx 09Nov95 reason unknown]
TC-229 +	S226	(Candler & Associates)	N226AM [+ cvtd from SA.226AT c/n AT-055; wfu Fort Lauderdale-Executive, FL; assumed b/u by Aug08; canx 04Nov08]
TC-229E +	S226	(Scheduled Skyways)	N227AM N7SS N503SS [+ cvtd from SA.226AT c/n AT-056; w/o 27Aug83 Hot Springs-Memorial Field, AR]
TC-230	S226	GAS Wilson/Aero Coasta Sol	N64SA C-GBXE N4206M [stored by Jun03 Springfield-Branson National, MO; l/n 06Nov05; by 10Mar10 fuselage only]
TC-231	S226	(Aviation Services Inc)	N65SA ZK-MES N220KC [w/o 17Aug93 near Hartford-Brainard Airport, CT; canx 30Jun94]
TC-232	S226	(Key Lime Air)	N5389M N60U [w/o 03Dec03 Denver-International, CO – collided with N340AE Metro III c/n AC-510; canx 31Oct06]
TC-233	S226	(Propair)	N101UR C-GQAL [w/o 18Jun98 Montreal-Mirabel, QB, Canada; canx 30Aug10]
TC-234	S226	(Superior Aviation)	N160MA N220AM [canx 30Oct07 for spares to White Industries, Bates City, MO; l/n 25Apr07]
TC-234E +	S226	(Candler & Associates)	N162MA [+ cvtd from SA.226AT c/n AT-059; canx 26Oct00 b/u for spares]
TC-235	S226	Carson Air	N5394M N61Z N235BA C-GSKC
TC-236	S226	(Candler & Associates)	N163MA [canx 01Dec00 as destroyed]
TC-237	S226	Key Lime Air	N5437M N62Z
TC-237E +	S226	(Airman)	N752S XA-RYM N766AS LV-WSD [+ cvtd from SA.226AT c/n AT-060; DBR 27Nov01 Bahia Blanca, Argentina]
TC-238	S226	Superior Aviation	N5436M LV-MDD N5436M N329BA [status unknown]
TC-238E +	S226	(Tejas Airlines)	N300TL [+ cvtd from SA.226AT c/n AT-06; w/o 3Aug78 Austin-Municipal, TX]
TC-239	S226	(Hulas Kanodia)	N301TL N603AS [reported stored by May95 Winnipeg, MB, Canada; not noted 11Jly08, assumed b/u; canx 22Aug12]
TC-239E +	S226	(Perimeter Airlines)	N227AM C-FTNV [+ cvtd from SA.226AT c/n AT-062(1); w/o 08Nov06 Norway House Airport, MB, Canada; canx 17Jly08]
TC-240	S226	(Britt Airways)	N63Z [w/o 30Jan84 near Terre Haute-Hulman Regional, IN]
TC-241	S226	(J W Duff Aircraft)	N70A [wfu & stored Aug84 Tucson, AZ; b/u Mar91 by Hamilton Aircraft]
TC-242	S226	(Britt Airways)	N65Z [wfu Sep91 & sold to Perimeter Airlines for spares use; canx 02Oct91 as sold in Canada]
TC-243	S226		[cvtd to SA.226AT c/n AT-062(2)]
TC-244	S226		[cvtd to SA.226AT c/n AT-062E]
TC-245	S226	Clingenpeel Inc	N71Z
TC-246	S226	(Swearingen)	N5650M [cvtd to SA.226AT c/n AT-064E]
TC-247	S226	not yet known	N5448M OO-JPK HZ-SN9 N5448M YV-940C N247ML+ XA- [+ canx 05Mar12 to Mexico]
TC-248	S226	Key Lime Air	N770S
TC-249	S226	Perimeter Airlines	N5451M LV-MGE N5451M N327BA C-FFDB

SWEARINGEN (FAIRCHILD) SA.226TC METRO II

C/n	Model	Last known Owner/Operator	Identities/fates/comments (where appropriate)
TC-250	S226	(Perimeter Airlines)	N5452M C-GYPA [w/o 11Oct01 near Shamattawa Airport, MB, Canada; canx 13Feb02]
TC-251	S226	(Pel-Air/Royal Australian Air Force)	N102UR N335BA VH-IAR VH-EEQ [wfu Apr99 Wagga Wagga, NSW, Australia; used by RAAF as GIA; canx 23Sep99]
TC-252	S226	(BinAir Aero Service)	N5456M OY-AZW D-IBCF OY-AZW PH-RAZ D-IBIN [canx 16Nov11 as wfu]
TC-253	S226	Carson Air	N5457M LV-MGF N5457M N328BA C-GKLN
TC-254	S226	unknown	N5451M N67X+ XA- [+ canx 18Aug93 to Mexico]
TC-255	S226	(Superior Aviation)	N5458M HK-2121 N255AV N265AM N731AC [w/o 09Nov00 Fort Wayne International, IN]
TC-256	S226	(Hardy Aviation)	N5460M VH-SWN (ZK-MAA) ZK-SWA VH-WGY VH-ANJ VH-MMY [w/o 16Jly02 on ground Darwin Airport, NT, Australia when hit by runaway Cessna 182; canx 28Jan03; l/n basically intact Aug08]
TC-257	S226	Museo Nacional de Aeronautica	N5462M LV-PAO LQ-MLV LV-MLV+ LQ-MLV [preserved on gate by May10 Moron, Argentina] [+ marks not fully confirmed]
TC-258	S226	Blue City Aviation/Highland Airways	N5463M 4X-CSA C-GBDF OY-NPA G-CEGE
TC-259	S226	(Toll Aviation Pty)	N781S C-FEPZ VH-UZQ [canx 31Mar09 as "destroyed/ scrapped in 2007"; nothing else known]
TC-260	S226	(AVAir/Nashville Eagle)	N23AZ [w/o 18Dec87 Washington-Dulles, DC; canx 30Apr91]
TC-261	S226	(Britt Airways)	N322BA [canx 30May90 probably as a result of damage 16Oct88 Cleveland, OH]
TC-262	S226	Hardy Aviation	N24AZ YV-472C N49GW VH-MKS
TC-263	S226	Perimeter Airlines	N103UR C-GQAP
TC-264	S226	2080061 Ontario Inc	N5470M D-IFAM F-GBTO SX-BSD N5470M C-GKPX
TC-265	S226	(Superior Aviation)	N5471M N245AM [canx 30Oct07 for spares to White Industries, Bates City, MO; l/n 25Apr07]
TC-266	S226	(The Memphis Group)	N25AZ [b/u for spares, Greenwood, MS; canx 04Feb91]
TC-267	S226	ex Mapiex Aero	N101GS HP-1348MAM [wfu by May09 Panama City-Gelabert, Panama; l/n 05Sep10 b/u]
TC-268	S226	(The Memphis Group)	N5664M HK-2176 N268AV [b/u for spares, Greenwood, MS; canx 07Feb91]
TC-269	S226	CBG LLC/Key Lime Air	N43RA N326BA C-GYXC N326BA
TC-270	S226	Queensland Air Museum	N5467M VH-BPV ZK-SWC VH-BIF [canx 12Oct93 as wfu; preserved Caloundra, QLD, Australia, painted as "VH-BPV" of Bush Pilots; l/n 10Mar07]
TC-271	S226	ex Kaiken Lineas Aereas	N102GS LV-WDV [wfu by 04Mar09 Rio Grande, Argentina; l/n Dec10]
TC-272	S226	(Bush Pilots Airways)	N5492M VH-BPL [w/o 02Apr81 Emerald, QLD, Australia & canx same date]
TC-273	S226	(Zorex)	N5472M OY-JER EC-GPE [b/u 20Sep10 Zaragoza, Spain for spares; hulk l/n 11Jly11]
TC-274	S226	Caribe Rico Inc	N5499M C-FSWC N7774H C-FTJC N274FS
TC-275	S226	(Skywest Airlines)	N5490M VH-SWO [w/o 13May80 nr Esperance, WA, Australia & canx same date]
TC-276	S226	CBG LLC/Key Lime Air	N103GS N276CA
TC-277	S226	National Aerospace Laboratory	N5651M PH-NLZ
TC-278	S226	Perimeter Airlines	N5493M C-GYRD
TC-279	S226	Perimeter Airlines	N5694M YU-ALH OO-VGE F-GFGE C-GIQF
TC-280	S226	Berry Aviation	N303TL N323BA
TC-281	S226	Aeronaves TSM	(N781S) N5473M N164GA N396RY XA-UFO
TC-282	S226	IBC Airways	N45RA N248AM N841BC
TC-283	S226	(Perimeter Airlines)	N5474M C-FHOZ [w/o 01Nov96 Gods River, MB, Canada; canx 29Jly98]
TC-284	S226	(Pel-Air/Royal Australian Air Force)	N5468M VH-BIS VH-WGW VH-EER [wfu Apr99 Wagga Wagga, NSW, Australia; used by RAAF as GIA; canx 23Sep99]
TC-285	S226	Perimeter Airlines	N5653M YU-ALI OO-VGA F-GFGD C-GIQG
TC-286	S226		[cvtd to SA.226AT c/n AT-071E]
TC-287	S226	Casair	N5657M VH-BPG ZK-SWD VH-WGV VH-NGX
TC-288	S226	Perimeter Airlines	N5655M YU-ALJ OO-VGG F-GFGF C-GIQK
TC-289	S226	Nachang Aviation	N5659M VH-KDR VH-IAU
TC-290	S226	Holli Aero Leasing	N5660M EC-DGU 4X-CSB C-GGSW N751AA N41LH N4090M

SWEARINGEN (FAIRCHILD) SA.226TC METRO II

C/n	Model	Last known Owner/Operator	Identities/fates/comments (where appropriate)
TC-291	S226	(Magnum Airlines)	N5662M HB-LLA ZS-LKG [w/o 18Nov88 Johannesburg, South Africa; canx 31Aug92]
TC-292	S226	RG International Aircraft Corp	N5663M CP-1516 N2510R
TC-293	S226	Western Cape Ferries	N161SW C-GBXX N393AA ZS-ZOC [major damage 13Jun10 Lanseria, South Africa]
TC-294	S226	(North American Airlines)	N5666M N47RA N168SW C-FEPW [w/o 13Jun97 Ottawa, OT, Canada; canx 16Oct98]
TC-295	S226	Perimeter Airlines	N104UR C-GQAJ N104UR C-FUIF+ C-GQAJ [+ possibly ntu]
TC-296	S226	(Perimeter Airlines)	N5475M C-FNKN N139PA C-FNKN [damaged 02Nov97 Island Lake, MB, Canada; ferried to Winnipeg & declared DBR; canx 18Dec98]
TC-297	S226	(Delta Air)	N5667M HB-LLB D-IASN [w/o 04Jun85 Friedrichshafen, West Germany; used for spares; by Mar04 remains to Liege-Bierset, Belgium]
TC-298	S226	Tellico Air Service	N324BA N324TA
TC-299	S226	(Eagle Aviation)	N105GS F-GFIJ 5Y-DNT [w/o 25Oct92 Mogadishu, Somalia; by Aug99 stored Nairobi-Wilson, Kenya; no recent reports]
TC-300	S226	(GAS Wilson)	N228AM [canx 27Jun06 sold in Canada for spares; l/n wfu 12Jly09 Kelowna, BC, Canada]
TC-301	S226	Flightline	N5666M F-GCFE SX-BSC N5FY EC-JIP
TC-302	S226	Carson Air	N501SS N240AM C-FJTQ N151SA C-GDLK
TC-303	S226	Zorex	N5681M TU-TXV N235AM C-FIIC N9U C-FWWP VH-MYD N117AR EC-JYC
TC-304	S226	Worldwide Aircraft Services	N325BA [status unknown]
TC-305	S226	(Superior Aviation)	N229AM [w/o 15Apr03 Denver-International, CO; canx 17Jly03; hulk to Dodson International Parts, Rantoul, KS; l/n Jun06]
TC-306	S226	(Superior Aviation)	N48RA N246AM C-FJTJ N152SA [by 25Apr07 wfu for spares; canx 25Oct07; with White Industries, Bates City, MO]
TC-307	S226	(Kaiken Lineas Aereas)	N1005Y VH-BPA N1005Y N334BA LV-WIY [wfu 1999 for spares]
TC-308	S226	Carson Air	N106GS F-GFIK 5Y-CNT N91452 N300GL C-FKKR
TC-309	S226	C & L Systems	N1006A 4X-CSC D-ICRJ N9751X [sale reported in Mexico but not canx]
TC-310	S226	(Kaiken Lineas Aereas)	N504SS N242AM LV-WDU [wfu 1999 for spares]
TC-311	S226	Aeronaves TSM	N303TL N116BS N226FA XA- N226FA+ XA- [+ canx 15Dec09 to Mexico; possibly for spares use, stored since about 2001; reported for Aeronaves TSM; restored 15Apr10; canx again 14May10 to Mexico]
TC-312	S226	Casair	N1015B VH-WGX
TC-313	S226	ex Trader Air Line	N230AM LV-WNY [wfu by Nov01 derelict San Fernando, Buenos Aires, Argentina; l/n 22Apr08]
TC-314	S226	ex Swiftair/DHL	N232AM EC-488 EC-EZD [wfu by 22Apr08 Barcelona, Spain; l/n 12Jly11]
TC-315	S226	Osterreichisches Luftfahrtmuseum	N1014X OE-LSA [w/o 19Sep84 Vienna, Austria; preserved Graz, Austria; l/n 22Apr07]
TC-316	S226	ex Superior Aviation	N505SS N250AM [wfu for spares by White Industries, Bates City, MO; l/n 25Apr07; b/u by 12Jly10]
TC-317	S226	(Muk Air Taxi)	N1006G OY-ARI C-GFBF OY-ARI [w/o 01Jan89 Ornskoldsvik, Sweden; b/u for spares 1992 Roskilde, Denmark]
TC-318	S226	Zorex	N5476M OY-JEO (EC-) EC-HJC
TC-319	S226	ex Swiftair/DHL	N223AM EC-487 EC-EZE [wfu by 22Apr08 Barcelona, Spain; l/n 12Jly11]
TC-320	S226	(Jetcraft Air Cargo)	N1006L VH-EPB VH-UZS [w/o 16Apr93 Mackay, QLD, Australia; canx 16Dec94]
TC-321	S226	Berry Aviation	N1006N N105UR C-GQAX N105UR N226BA
TC-322	S226	(GAS Wilson)	N57RA N167SW YV-468C N43GW [reported wfu & b/u Jun01; canx 11Feb03]
TC-323	S226	(Aerovan Ejecutivos)	N1006W D2-EDT N31261 N888LB SE-IVU N323GW N323LB+ [+ canx 30Aug12 fate/status unknown]
TC-324	S226	(Mapiex Aero)	N115BS HP-1364MAM [reported DBR Bocas del Toro, Panama; fuselage used within Costa Verde Hotel, Manuel Antonio, Costa Rica]
TC-325	S226	Carson Air	N162SW C-GLSC

SWEARINGEN (FAIRCHILD) SA.226TC METRO II

C/n	Model	Last known Owner/Operator	Identities/fates/comments (where appropriate)
TC-326	S226	Casair	N1007G VH-KDQ VH-UUK VH-KGX
TC-327	S226	(Skywest Airlines)	N163SW [w/o 16Jan87 Salt Lake City, UT after mid-air collision with Mooney N6485U; deregistered]
TC-328	S226	(Muk Air Taxi)	N10110 OE-LSB D-IKOO ZS-LJH N917MM OY-BZW [w/o 16Jan91 Copenhagen, Denmark; hulk to fire dump]
TC-329	S226	Perimeter Airlines	N236AM C-FIIA
TC-330	S226	Fly Logic	N1007Y HB-LLC ZS-LJC N30TR (F-GEJX) ZS-LJC N7217N SE-KCP
TC-331	S226	(Magnum Airlines)	N116BS ZS-KYA [w/o14Apr82 location unknown; canx 11Jun82]
TC-331E +	S226	Carson Air	N1006U VH-EEF N1006U N255AM C-GCAU [+ cvtd from SA.226AT c/n AT-075]
TC-332	S226	(Perimeter Airlines)	N237AM C-FKEX [w/o 10May05 Thompson, MB, Canada; canx 15Apr08]
TC-333	S226	(BinAir Aero Service)	N1007A 4X-CSD D-ICRK [canx 16Nov11 as wfu]
TC-334	S226	ex Western Air Express	N341PL C-GBWF N341PL N159WA [reported wfu & dumped by 30Apr07 Kamloops, BC, Canada; l/n 08Aug08]
TC-334E +	S226	(Air Littoral)	(N235AM) F-GCPG [+ cvtd from SA.226AT c/n AT-076; w/o 18Nov88 Montlucon-Gueret (Lepaud), France]
TC-337	S226	Aeronaves TSM	N1008F N256AM N166GA N851LH+ XA- [+ canx 03Oct07 to Mexico for possible spares use]
TC-338	S226	Regio Air	N1008K H4-SIA N90141 D-IESS
TC-340	S226	Aero Sudpacifico	N58RA N247AM XA-SJY
TC-343	S226	Perimeter Airlines	N342PL VH-UZY C-FUZY
TC-344	S226	Baires Fly	(N242AM) OE-LSC OO-XGF F-GFJU (OO-MMM) OO-III N44CS LV-WHG
TC-346	S226	ex Air Tango	N1007W N107GG N1007W N52EA LV-WEO XA-UHW+ [+ not confirmed]
TC-347	S226	Sunwest Aviation	N1008T OO-LAW N330BA C-FGEW
TC-349	S226	(Ryan Blake Air Charter)	N1007N VH-EEG N26583 F-GDMR N100ED C-GIQI ZS-OYI [w/o 19Jly03 Point Lenana, Mount Kenya, Kenya]
TC-350	S226	Aero Davinci Internacional	N1008G D-IHCW N4254Y XA-TGV
TC-352	S226	Perimeter Airlines	N506SS N167MA C-FJNW
TC-353	S226	Aerofuturo	N1009B XC-KUO N4981H D-IKBB OE-LSE OO-XGO F-GFJV OO-NNN N53CS XA-SFS XA-UGN
TC-355	S226	(Swiftair)	N241AM EC-780 EC-FHB [w/o 19Oct93 Madrid-Barajas, Spain; hulk burnt 16Apr02]
TC-356	S226	(Turbine Group Inc)	N243AM XA-HAO N356TC [w/o 04Feb97 Lazaro Cardenas, Mexico; canx 03Jan11]
TC-358	S226	Carson Air	N1009R C-FBWN N1009R C-GCAW
TC-359	S226	(Servicio Aereos Vargas Espana)	N1009T CP-1635 [w/o 13Dec97 near La Veriente, Bolivia]
TC-361	S226	Perimeter Airlines	N13RA N166SW C-FIHB
TC-362	S226	ex Conquistadair	N117BS YV-469C N51GW+ C- [+ canx 18Nov09 to Canada]
TC-364	S226	(Candler and Associates)	N124AV [w/o 19Dec86 Billings, MT; canx 22Jly93]
TC-365	S226	(Compagnie Aerienne du Languedoc)	N1009W F-GCTE [w/o 22Nov87 Le Puy-Loudes Airport, France; canx 29Mar88]
TC-367	S226	(Perimeter Airlines)	N10095 C-FGEP [w/o 10Feb90 Winnipeg, MB, Canada; canx 29Jly98]
TC-368	S226	Sunwest Aviation	N10099 VH-BPK N368SA F-GEBU C-GSWK
TC-370	S226	Carson Air	N125AV C-GKKC
TC-371	S226	ex Intermediacion Aerea	N1010B OY-BJT SE-IMD OY-BJT EC-GMG [l/n Aug03 stored Cuatro Vientos, Spain; canx in 01Nov09 register]
TC-373	S226	Perimeter Airlines	N1010Z C-FIHE
TC-374	S226	Top Fly	N10104 OY-AUO LN-SAP SE-IKP OY-AUO D-IAEF OY-AUO EC-GXJ
TC-376	S226	Aeronaves TSM	N508SS N251AM N169GA N637PJ XA-UKP
TC-377	S226	TSM Air Logistics	N1009J C-GIZG N5052H C-FJTD N616GA N742ES [wfu Toledo-Express, OH; probable spares use]
TC-379	S226	Carson Air	N1011U C-FBWQ
TC-380	S226	Carson Air	N10110 (D-IHUV) D-IHUC HB-LPG I-FSAG C-GMET C-GKLJ
TC-382	S226	Perimeter Airlines	N1011N (N112GG) C-FSWT
TC-383	S226	BES Operations Pty	D-IBAN SE-IKZ VH-SSV

SWEARINGEN (FAIRCHILD) SA.226TC METRO II

C/n	Model	Last known Owner/Operator	Identities/fates/comments (where appropriate)
TC-385	S226	Perimeter Airlines	N10116 N126AV YV-471C N46GW XA-TGG C-FBTL
TC-386	S226	Aero Sudpacifico	N10117 HK-2561X N10117 EI-BRI N32AG
TC-389	S226	Aero Cuahonte	N507SS N257AM XA-STV XA-GUU
TC-390	S226	Vuelos Mediterraneo	N1012B N244AM C-FBWY N19WP EC-HCU [damaged 2004; stored non-airworthy Reus, Spain; l/n 17Jly10]
TC-392	S226	Flamingo Accent (USA)	N1012K ZS-LAA N392CA (ZS-JDB) D2-FJM N392CM
TC-393	S226	Cedma Aviacion	N1012N 4X-CSE OO-JPY D-ICRL N867MA LV-ZEB
TC-395	S226	Casair	N1012U (D-IJHB) F-GFVS N20849 VH-TFQ VH-OGX
TC-396	S226	(TriCoastal Air)	N1012Z N369AV N165GA N629EK [w/o 08Feb06 near Paris, TN en-route Dayton, OH to Harlingen, TX; canx 27Feb07; hulk to Atlanta Air Salvage, Griffin, GA; l/n 02Oct06]
TC-398	S226	Berry Aviation	N10115 N601AS N54EA
TC-399	S226	Western Air Express	N10125 N602AS N56EA N160WA
TC-401	S226	(Aero Cuahonte)	N10RA N137WW C-GGKM N137WW XA-SLU [w/o 13Jun94 Uruapan, Mexico]
TC-402	S226	Museo dell'Aviazione	N10129 OE-LSD OO-XGI F-GFJX OO-JJJ I-SWAB [wfu Jan00; preserved Rimini, Italy; l/n 23May08]
TC-404	S226	Aeronaves TSM	N1013B C-FGPW XA-ADS
TC-406	S226		N5478M [cvtd to SA.227AC c/n AC-406]
TC-408	S226	ex Tadair	N1013F N252AM EC-243 EC-FPC [wfu by 16Aug03 Barcelona, Spain; l/n 21Apr11]
TC-409	S226	Aeronaves TSM	N1013G C-FLNG XA-ADQ
TC-411	S226	Western Air Express	N1013P N16RA N138WW C-FAIP N8116V SX-BSG N5974V N158WA
TC-412	S226	Aeronaves TSM	N1013S N253AM XA-SAK N253AM XA-SXB XA-TSM
TC-413	S226	Aero Cuahonte	N18RA N139WW C-GJWM N139WW XA-SER
TC-415	S226		N173MA [cvtd to SA.227AC c/n AC-415]
TC-416	S226		N177MA [cvtd to SA.227AC c/n AC-416]
TC-418	S226	Western Air Express	N1013Z N500WN N500WJ N58AE C-GRET N162WA
TC-419	S226	Hawk Air	N1014A D-IJHB ZS-LBR N7205L LV-WXW

SWEARINGEN (FAIRCHILD) MODEL 227

C/n	Model	Last known Owner/Operator	Identities/fates/comments (where appropriate)
SWEARINGEN (FAIRCHILD) SA.227AC METRO III			
AC-406 +	S227	(Candler & Associates)	N5478M N379PH N227FA [+ cvtd from SA.226T c/n TC-406; wfu for parts; canx 19Feb04]
AC-415 +	S227	Servicios Aereos Patagonicos	N173MA LV-RBP N173MA LV-RBP [+ cvtd from SA.226T c/n TC-415]
AC-416 +	S227	Servicios Aereos Patagonicos	N177MA LV-RBR N177MA LV-RBR [+ cvtd from SA.226T c/n TC-416]
AC-420	S227	(North Flying/Air Norway)	N1014D N67TC (N568G) OY-NPB [w/o 02Mar11 Oslo-Gardermoen, Norway; canx 26Apr11]
AC-421B +	S227	River City Aviation	N5498M 88003^ SE-LIM D-COLD N211RH [+ cvtd from SA.226AT c/n AT-070; ^ Sweden with code 883]
AC-422B	S227	(Fairchild Corp)	N1014P N422AC C-GSLA N2183A [w/o 18Sep92 San Antonio, TX]
AC-425	S227	Baires Fly	N1014G HB-LLD EC-DXT HB-LLD N721MA LV-ZMG
AC-429	S227	Baires Fly	N1014N HB-LLE N429M C-FJLF LV-WRA
AC-430B	S227	Aeronaves TSM	N1014S XB-AEE N1014S N344AE N788C SX-BMO N430PF XA-SUS
AC-432B	S227	International Business Air	N1014T TC-FAB N33042 F-GLPE SE-LIL
AC-437	S227	(Merlin Express)	N30008 4X-CSF N2671V [w/o 16Aug99 San Antonio, TX; canx 25Feb00]
AC-442	S227	Texas Air Charters	N3005J N442BA [wfu & stored Feb02 Fort Lauderdale-International, FL; to White Industries, Bates City, MO for spares; l/n 25Apr07]
AC-443	S227	Ameriflight	N182MA N443NE N443AF
AC-445	S227	(Comair)	N3005U HB-LLF N445AC [w/o 08Nov90 Greater Cincinnati Airport, KY; canx 08Nov90]
AC-448	S227	Flying America	N3009F HB-LNA N448CA C-FJLE LV-PNF LV-YIC
AC-449	S227	(Pioneer Air Lines)	N30093 [w/o 07Dec82 near Pueblo, CO]
AC-451B	S227	Farnair Hungary	N211CA VH-NEM SE-LEF HA-FAO
AC-455 +	S227	Ameriflight	N69CS N356AE N155AF [+ cvtd from SA.227AT c/n AT-455]
AC-457	S227	(Trans-Colorado Airlines)	N68TC [w/o 19Jan88 8 kms east of Durango-La Plata County Airport, CO; canx 18May89]
AC-458	S227	(Regional Airlines)	N3025R SE-GSO F-GILN [w/o 19Sep93 Troyes, France]
AC-460	S227	Transportes Aereos Neuquen	N3029F LV-AOP
AC-461B +	S227	Union Air	N120FA EC-437 EC-FSV N25LD EC-HXY LV-BGR [+ cvtd from SA.227AT c/n AT-461]
AC-463	S227	(IBC Airways)	N3033F N630PA N811BC [w/o 30Mar05 Miami-Dade Collier Airport, FL; canx 27Feb06]
AC-466	S227	(Avline Metro/Aerodinos Ltda)	N3044J [w/o 12Nov92 Trinidad Airport, Bolivia]
AC-467	S227	Flying America	N3046L TF-JMK LV-BGH
AC-470	S227	Itali Airlines	N30486 HB-LNB N470A (N470CA) C-FJLX C-FAFM N581BT (D-CBST) I-BSTI
AC-472	S227	US Dept of Justice/Locair	N604AS N345AE XA-SFU N345PA XA-SFU XB-GGJ+ XB-RFQ N345PA N227ML N672KS [+ marks not fully confirmed]
AC-473	S227	Ameriflight	N180MA N473NE N473AF
AC-475	S227	Ameriflight	N191MA N475NE N475AF
AC-476	S227	Ameriflight	N192MA N476NE N476AF
AC-478	S227	(Transportes Aereos Neuquen)	LV-AOR [w/o 25Jan96 Rincon de los Sauces Airport, Argentina]
AC-479	S227	ex GAS Wilson	N188MA N479NE C-GERW N479GW [stored by 12May08 San Marcos-Municipal, TX; l/n 04Jan09]
AC-481	S227	(Skylink Airlines)	N3055Q D-CABA C-GSLB [w/o 26Sep89 Terrace, BC, Canada]
AC-482	S227	(Air Class/DHL)	N482SA N610PA N784C CX-LAS [w/o 06Jun12 near Flores Island, Montevideo-Carrasco, Uruguay]
AC-484	S227	Vigo Jet	N606AS N341AE XA-TXX
AC-485	S227	Joda LLC	N3049D C-GIQN N890MA 4R-SEN N890MA
AC-487B +	S227	IBC Airways	N550TD XA-SYW N550TD N861BC [+ cvtd from SA.227AT c/n AT-487]
AC-488	S227	Ameriflight	N190MA N488NE N488AF
AC-490	S227	Toll Aviation Pty	N30693 VH-UZD
AC-491	S227	Ameriflight	N209CA C-FJTB N209CA N191AF
AC-494	S227	(Pel-Air Express/TNT)	N605AS VH-SSM VH-EET [wfu for parts Darwin, NT, Australia; canx 12Oct10 as pwfu]

SWEARINGEN (FAIRCHILD) MODEL 227

C/n	Model	Last known Owner/Operator	Identities/fates/comments (where appropriate)
AC-496	S227	Joda LLC	N3107P
AC-497	S227	Aeronaves TSM	N3107N F-GHVA N110AV N98EB XA-UKJ(1) XA-DCX
AC-498	S227	Toll Aviation Pty	N3102C 4X-CSG N2685P OY-BPL VH-UZP
AC-499	S227	Ben-Air AG	N3106D OY-BJP LN-HPF SE-KHH F-GHVG OY-BJP
AC-500	S227	(Nurnberger Flugdienst-NFD)	N3107K (D-CABB) D-IABB D-CABB [w/o 08Feb88 Dusseldorf, West Germany]
AC-503	S227	Aeronaves TSM	N607AS N164SW C-FJLO(1) N530AV N102GS XA-EEE
AC-504 +	S227	Hardy Aviation	N31072 VH-TFG [+ cvtd from SA.227AT c/n AT-504]
AC-505B	S227	BinAir Aero Service	N31074 HB-LND EC-DXS HB-LND F-GHVC TF-BBG D-CNAF
AC-506 +	S227	Martinaire	N370AE [cvtd from SA.227AT c/n AT-506]
AC-508	S227	CBG LLC/Key Lime Air	N31077 HK-2891X N31077 ZK-NSW N508FA
AC-509	S227	Business Aviation Courier	N3108B XA-TAK N3108B
AC-510	S227	(Key Lime Air)	N3108E N340AE [canx 28Jly10 as wfu, location unknown]
AC-513 +	S227	Brindabella Airlines	N3108H ZK-NSV N513FA VH-TAO [+ cvtd from SA.227AT c/n AT-513]
AC-514	S227	(FNG Aviation/Skylink Air Charter)	N3108K N165SW [w/o 05Jan97 near Bullhead City, AZ; canx 28Mar00; to White Industries, Bates City, MO for spares; l/n 25Apr07]
AC-516	S227	Provincia de Catamarca	N3108N HB-LNC D-CFEP N45ML LV-WEE
AC-517	S227	Toll Aviation Pty	N3108X (4X-CSH) VH-UUG VH-UZS
AC-519	S227	ex Aeromecanic SAS	N31083 HB-LNE F-GHVE EC-GJV F-GTRB [GIA Marseille-Marignane, France; l/n 09May08; canx 04Nov11 as wfu]
AC-520	S227	Ameriflight	N31088 HP-1141TLN HC-BQR TG-DHL N152AF
AC-522	S227	Metro-Jet LLC/Berry Aviation	N3109B N227LJ [by 15Oct07 derelict Hawthorne-Municipal, CA]
AC-523	S227	(Rijnmond Air Services)	N3109C D-CABE PH-DYM (D-CNAS) [w/o 19Sep05 Rotterdam Airport, Netherlands; canx 02Dec05]
AC-524 +	S227	(Norcanair)	N4442F C-FIPW [+ cvtd from SA.227AT c/n AT-524; w/o 21Sep04 La Ronge, SK, Canada]
AC-525	S227	DES LLC	N31078 N782C
AC-526	S227	Toll Aviation Pty	N3109H OY-GAW 88001+ SE-IVP OY-GAW VH-UZW [+ Sweden]
AC-528 +	S227	North Delaware Co	N5441F [+ cvtd from SA.227AT c/n AT-528]
AC-530	S227	Toll Aviation Pty	N3109Y D-CABD N224AV ZK-NST VH-UUO
AC-531	S227	Business Aviation Courier	N31094 N387PH
AC-532 +	S227	Aeronaves TSM	N3110B N372PH XA-UKJ(2) [+ cvtd from SA.227AT c/n AT-532]
AC-533	S227	(Career Aviation Company)	N3110H N620PA [w/o 17Aug06 near Grain Valley Airport, KS; hulk to White Industries, Bates City, MO for spares; canx 10Oct08; l/n 16Jly10]
AC-535	S227	(Coast Aviation Credit/L C Busre)	N3110J N781C [w/o 13Nov10 Andahuaylas, Peru]
AC-537	S227	(Air Tango)	N3110S HB-LNO F-GHVD N715BC LV-WIL [w/o 03Jun99 Santa Fe-Sauce Viejo Airport, Argentina]
AC-538	S227	Berry Aviation	N373PH (N732C)
AC-540	S227	Berry Aviation	N3110W N389PH N789C
AC-542	S227	KCBG LLC/Key Lime Air	N3110Y (YV-498CP)+ OY-BPD LN-NVA N7063X ZK-NSX N542FA [+ marks not fully confirmed]
AC-543B +	S227	(Servicios Aereos Patagonicos)	D-CKVW N107AS LV-WAG [+ cvtd from SA.227AT c/n AT-543; canx 04Jun98; fate unknown]
AC-545	S227	(Lone Star Airlines)	N31107 N342AE [w/o 25Aug92 Hot Springs, AR; canx 20Nov92]
AC-546 +	S227	ex Eagle Airways	N31108 ZK-OAA [+ cvtd from SA.227AT c/n AT-546; reported by Nov01 stored/preserved in garden Hamilton, New Zealand; canx 01Mar02]
AC-547 +	S227	ex Eagle Airways	N3111D ZK-PBA [+ cvtd from SA.227AT c/n AT-547; wfu Oct01 Hamilton, New Zealand; dismantled; fuselage reported at golf course entrance Palmerston North, New Zealand]
AC-550	S227	Key Lime Air	N31110 N787C
AC-551	S227	(Airwork New Zealand)	N3111H D-CABF ZK-POA [broke up in flight 02May05 en-route Auckland – Blenheim, New Zealand]
AC-552	S227	(Infra Limited SE)	N31113 C-GJTB N398GM [stored by 22Oct08 Tamiami, FL; l/n 04Feb10; canx 31Aug12 fate unknown]
AC-553	S227	Toll Aviation Pty	N3112X D-CABH N220CT VH-UZG
AC-554	S227	ex Air Demand LLC/Skylink Charter	(D-CABF) N3112K N343AE [DBR 29Sep02 Hawthorne-Municipal, CA; derelict by 15Oct07; l/n 16Jun08]
AC-558	S227	ex Texas Air Charters	N3112Y N169SW N558BA [wfu & stored Feb02 Fort Lauderdale-International, FL; to White Industries, Bates City, MO for spares; l/n 25Apr07]

SWEARINGEN (FAIRCHILD) MODEL 227

C/n	Model	Last known Owner/Operator	Identities/fates/comments (where appropriate)
AC-559	S227	Worthington Aviation Parts	N559SA N170SW N766C
AC-565	S227	Aeronaves TSM	N3113G HZ-SN7 N163WA XA-UNQ
AC-571	S227	Berry Aviation	N3113Z N374PH N729C
AC-572	S227	GAS Wilson	N3114C N375PH N718C C-GYXA N572GW
AC-573	S227	ex Swazi Express Airways	N376PH ZS-OWK 3D-SEA [wfu by Aug11 Lanseria, South Africa]
AC-574	S227	Ameriflight	(D-CABG) N377PH
AC-575	S227	Vent Airlines	N3114X N378PH N575EG
AC-576	S227	GAS Wilson	N3119W N371PH
AC-578	S227	Ameriflight	N31137 C-FJLE N578AF
AC-579	S227	(Chautauqua Airlines/US Air Express)	N31138 [w/o 04Jan90 Hagerstown, MD; hulk sold to White Industries, Bates City, MO; by Jan96 fuselage only; canx 13Jun96; l/n 25Apr07]
AC-580	S227	(North Flying)	N3115A OY-BPH TC-FBU OY-BPH [w/o 24Dec02 Aberdeen-Dyce, UK]
AC-581	S227	Aeropacifico	N3115H C-FAFE XA-AFT
AC-582	S227	Airwork Flight Operations	N3113S N380PH ZK-PAA ZK-LFT
AC-583	S227	Trans Northern Aviation	N3114G (N505TN)
AC-584	S227	Baires Fly	N3114H (N381PH) LV-PMF LV-WTE
AC-586	S227	Aeropacifico	N3115K C-GNAV N911EJ XA-UAJ
AC-587	S227	Carson Air	N3115T C-GAMI
AC-588	S227	Western Air	N3115M C-FAMH N892MA C6-JER [major damage 20Dec09 Cap Haitien International Airport, Haiti; l/n 15Apr10]
AC-589	S227	Berry Aviation	N3115U N382PH N589BA XA-TSF (N589BA) [stored by 2005 San Marcos-Municipal, TX; canx 18Jun11; l/n 02Nov11 still marked XA-TSF]
AC-590	S227	Berry Aviation	N3115Y N383PH N590BA XA-TSG (N590BA) [stored by May08 San Marcos-Municipal, TX; canx 18Jun11; l/n 02Nov11 still marked XA-TSG]
AC-591 +	S227	ex FS Air Service	N3116B N176SW N505FS [+ cvtd from SA.227AT c/n AT591; wfu for spares; canx 22Nov05; to MTW Aerospace, Montgomery, AL; l/n 01Mar06]
AC-592	S227	Martinaire	N3116D N384PH N592BA
AC-594	S227	Helitec	N3116F (LV-) N3116F N16GA YV-1000C YV171T
AC-595	S227	Career Aviation Co	N3116L N385PH LV-ZPH N385PH C6-KER N446GL
AC-596	S227	Business Aviation Courier	N3116N
AC-597	S227	(MTW Aerospace)	N3116T N386PH [stored by Aug11 Fort Lauderdale International, FL; canx 16Jly12 for parts]
AC-598	S227	Western Air	N3116Z C6-SAR
AC-599	S227	(Western Air)	N31168 C6-SAW [w/o 07Sep02 Andros Town Airport, Bahamas; by Dec03 remains to MTW Aerospace, Montgomery, AL; l/n 22Oct06]
AC-600	S227	(Airtex Air Services)	N3117A VH-IAW VH-OZA [w/o 09Apr08 dived into sea near Bundeena, NSW, Australia; canx 02Jly08]
AC-601	S227	BinAir Aero Service	N3117K OY-BPJ N90AG I-FSAH D-CSAL
AC-603	S227	Air Columbia/Itali Airlines	N3117S I-BSTS
AC-604	S227	(Flying Carpet Air Transport Services)	N3117V C-FNAL OD-MAB [CofA expired 06Sep09 fate/status unknown]
AC-605	S227	Superior Aviation	N31171
AC-606B	S227	Airwork Flight Operations	D-CABG ZK-POB
AC-610B	S227	Brindabella Airlines	N3118K N610AV VH-ANW VH-CUZ VH-UUZ VH-TGQ VH-OZV
AC-611B	S227	Bemidji Aviation Services	N3118N N611AV VH-NEL VH-EEX N611BA
AC-612	S227	Winrye Aviation Pty	N3119B N347AE VH-SST VH-EEQ
AC-613	S227	(Peninsula Airways/PenAir)	N3119H N348AE N670PA [w/o 03May96 Saint Paul Island, AK; canx 13Dec97]
AC-614	S227	Career Aviation Co	N614AV VH-SSZ VH-EES N614TR
AC-615B	S227	Swiftair Hellas	N615AV VH-NEK N972GA EC-HJO SX-BGU
AC-616	S227	Perimeter Airlines	N3119U N349AE VH-UZS VH-UUF C-FMAV
AC-617	S227	Career Aviation Co	N2683B N350AE VH-SSV VH-EER VH-SSV VH-EEJ N617BT
AC-619B	S227	Bemidji Aviation Services	N619AV VH-UZA VH-OYC VH-EEU N619BA
AC-620	S227	ex Tadair	N174SW EC-GKR [w/o 12Apr02 Palma de Mallorca, Majorca, Spain; wreck l/n 25May09]
AC-621	S227	Flight International Aviation	N175SW

SWEARINGEN (FAIRCHILD) MODEL 227

C/n	Model	Last known Owner/Operator	Identities/fates/comments (where appropriate)
AC-622	S227	(AvAir)	N622AV [w/o 19Feb88 Cary, NC near Raleigh-Durham Airport, NC; canx30 Oct96]
AC-623B	S227	Air Chathams/Chathams Pacific	N623AV ZK-CIC
AC-627B	S227	Aeronaves TSM	N627AV SP-ZMA N627AV XA-AAT N799BW XA-TYX
AC-628B	S227	Aeronaves TSM	N628AV SP-ZMB N628AV XA-TRH N280EM XA-SLW
AC-629B	S227	(Tamair Charter)	N629AV VH-NEJ [w/o 16Sep95 Tamworth, NSW, Australia & canx same day]
AC-632	S227	Sierra West Airlines	N2680V N346AE VH-SSW VH-EER N632TR
AC-633+	S227	Martinaire	N3113C N354AE [+ cvtd from SA.226T c/n TT-555]
AC-634	S227	Ameriflight	N3119Q N421MA
AC-635	S227	Ameriflight	N3119T N422MA
AC-636	S227	Ameriflight	N26823 N423MA
AC-637B	S227	Sunshine Express	N1637 N352AE ZK-RCA VH-SEZ
AC-638	S227	(Provincial Airlines)	N638AV N353AE C-FITW [canx 10Sep02 for spares use; to Dodson International Aircraft Parts, Rantoul, KS; l/n Jun06]
AC-639	S227	Ameriflight	N424MA
AC-640	S227	CBG LLC	N425MA (N640KL)
AC-641	S227	Brindabella Airlines	N2683U N351AE ZK-SDA VH-SEF
AC-642	S227	Aero VIP/Air Class	N2684S N355AE N821BC CX-CSS
AC-643	S227	(AeroSur)	N643AV N179SW CP-2321 [w/o 31Dec97 Trinidad, Bolivia]
AC-644B	S227	Bearskin Airlines	LX-LGL OO-FFF N644VG C-GYQT
AC-645	S227	Ameriflight	N426MA
AC-646	S227	Ameriflight	N428MA
AC-647	S227	CBG LLC/Key Lime Air	N2685B N184SW CX-TAA N184SW
AC-648	S227	AeroNova	N2685L EC-GUS
AC-649	S227	Kolob Canyons Air Services	N26861 C6-REX N649KA
AC-650B	S227	Perimeter Airlines	N26863 (N650AV) C-GFWX
AC-651B	S227	(SEUR/Swiftair)	N2687U (N651AV) D-CABI LV-WAH N97HG EC-583 EC-FXD [w/o 28Jly98 Barcelona, Spain]
AC-652B	S227	Kolob Canyons Air Services	N26877 (N652AV) 4R-SEK N26877 C6-FPO N652KA
AC-653	S227	(Horizon Airlines)	N2689E [w/o 29Sep87 Twin Falls, ID; canx 23Apr91]
AC-654B	S227	IBC Airways	N26906 N831BC
AC-655B	S227	CBG LLC	N2691W (N655KL)
AC-656	S227	(KAL Aviation)	N26895 SX-BGG [w/o in sea 28Jly99 near Rhodes-Diagoras Airport, Greece]
AC-657	S227	J P Air Cargo	N26902 SX-BBX ES-JFA
AC-658B	S227	AeroNova	N2692P EC-HCH
AC-659B	S227	IBC Airways	N2693C N871BC
AC-660	S227	Martinaire	N26932 (N660AV)
AC-661B	S227	Western Air	N26952 (N661AV) N661FA C6-SAQ [stolen 26Apr07 Lynden Pindling Airport, Nassau, Bahamas; still missing 01Sep08]
AC-662B	S227	Air One Express	N26959 (N662AV)
AC-663B	S227	(Corporate Air)	N2697V VH-VEH [w/o 01Jly06 Canberra, ACT, Australia; canx 10Oct06]
AC-664	S227	not yet known	N26974+ CP- [+ canx 30May12 to Bolivia]
AC-665	S227	Brindabella Airlines	N2698C VH-OZN VH-TAM
AC-666	S227	McNeely Charter Service	N2699Y [reported damaged 31Aug08 & stored by 03Jan09 New Braunfels, TX]
AC-667B	S227	Hardy Aviation (NT) Pty	N357AE C-FAFS VH-TGD
AC-668B	S227	Provincial Airlines	N358AE C-FAFI N668JS C-GMEW
AC-669	S227	AeroNova	N2702Z EC-GVE
AC-670B	S227	Bearskin Airlines	N2704J LX-LGM OO-GGG N670VG C-FYAG
AC-671	S227	Ameriflight	N671AV (N671AF)
AC-672	S227	Ameriflight	N672AV
AC-673	S227	Ameriflight	N673AV (N673AF)
AC-674B	S227	Carson Air	N359AE C-FAFM C-FTSK
AC-675	S227	Ameriflight	N360AE
AC-676	S227	(Aerotransporte Petrolero)	N361AE C-FAFZ HK-4275X [w/o 05May04 Carepa-Antonio Roldan Betancourt Airport, Colombia]
AC-677B	S227	Ameriflight	N362AE
AC-678B	S227	Perimeter Airlines	N363AE (N941BC) C-FJLO(2)
AC-679B	S227	AeroNova	N364AE VH-UUC N6UB EC-JCU
AC-680	S227	Berry Aviation	N365AE N680AX

SWEARINGEN (FAIRCHILD) MODEL 227

C/n	Model	Last known Owner/Operator	Identities/fates/comments (where appropriate)
AC-681B	S227	Business Aviation Courier	N366AE
AC-682	S227	Sierra West Airlines	N682AV N921BC N681TR
AC-683	S227	(Skywest Airlines)	N683AV [w/o 01Feb91 Los Angeles, CA; Boeing 737-3B7 N388US (c/n 23310) landed on top of it on the runway; canx 13Oct94]
AC-684B	S227	Carson Air	N2718C C-FAFR N585MA C-FAFR N585MA C-FAFR
AC-685	S227	Business Aviation Courier	N685AV N685BA
AC-686B	S227	Sharp Aviation Pty	N686AV VH-UUN
AC-687B	S227	Aeronaves TSM	N2701D N455AM N445MA XA-PNG
AC-688	S227	Artac Aviacion	N2701X N688NE N727C EC-126 EC-GEN
AC-689B	S227	AeroNova	N2705F N689NE N706C D-COLC EC-IXL [reported by 11Oct08 on fire storage ramp at Las Palmas, Gran Canaria, Spain]
AC-690B	S227	GAS Wilson	N2706B N690NE N715C D-COLT N690WW
AC-691	S227	Berry Aviation	N27060 N367AE N691AX
AC-692B	S227	Airwork Flight Operations	N2707D G-BOJN N2707D ZK-NSS
AC-693B	S227	Aeronaves TSM	N456AM N446MA XA-MIO
AC-694B	S227	Swiftair Hellas	N457AM EC-GXE SX-BKW SX-BKZ
AC-696B	S227	Perimeter Aviation	N368AE N748JA ZS-JAM N227LD C-FJTS
AC-697B	S227	GAS Wilson	N369AE N730C N697AX
AC-698	S227	Ameriflight	N2711R N698AF
AC-699B	S227	Mediterranean Air Freight	N458AM EC-GYB SX-BMT
AC-700	S227	Perimeter Airlines	N459AM C-FFJM
AC-701	S227	Ameriflight	N27119 C-GWXZ N801AF
AC-702	S227	(IBC Airways)	N2712B N702M [canx 21Jan05; wfu Fort Lauderdale-Executive, FL for spares; l/n 30Apr05]
AC-703	S227	Promotora Industrial Totopala	N2713V N703CA XA-ACQ
AC-704	S227	Aeronaves TSM	N704C XA-UAL
AC-705	S227	Brindabella Airlines	N2717K EI-BWU ZK-NSU VH-TAG
AC-706B	S227	Bearskin Airlines	N27185 G-BUKA N27185 ZK-NSQ G-BUKA C-GYRL
AC-707B	S227	Bemidji Aviation Services	N27186 N84GM N227LC
AC-708B	S227	Merlin Airways	N27188 N708EG
AC-709B	S227	IBC Airways	N2708D N891BC
AC-710B	S227	GAS Wilson	N2710T N430MA
AC-711	S227	(Air Nelson)	N2719B EI-BWV ZK-NSY [b/u by Jly03 Nelson, New Zealand; canx 30Sep04; nose section used as mobile exhibit; l/n 15Apr06]
AC-712	S227	(Air Nelson)	N2719C EI-BWW ZK-NSZ [b/u by Jly03 Nelson, New Zealand]
AC-713B	S227	Carson Air	N2719H C-FJKK
AC-714B	S227	Perimeter Airlines	N2719L N433MA VH-UUQ C-GWVH
AC-715	S227	(Coast Aviation Credit/L C Busre)	N2720B CP-2301 N115GS [w/o 05Nov10 Huanuco, Peru]
AC-716	S227	(Skywest Airlines)	N2721M [w/o 15Jan90 Elko, NV]
AC-717	S227	Aeronaves TSM	N27213 N434MA XA-UMW
AC-718	S227	(Westair de Mexico)	N27220 XA-TKK [wfu Jly02 for spares; to MTW Aerospace, Montgomery, AL; l/n 22Oct06]
AC-719B	S227	Bearskin Airlines	N27239 N436MA C-FAMC
AC-720	S227	AeroNova	N2724S XA-TGD N2724S EC-HZH
AC-721B	S227	Arcraft Propulsion Leasing	N438MA
AC-722	S227	ex Euro Continental Air/Manx 2	N439MA EC-GPS [wfu by 03Aug11 Isle of Man, UK; l/n 07Aug12]
AC-723	S227	Westair de Mexico	N2725D XA-TLA
AC-724	S227	Aeronaves TSM	N27240 CP-2297 N106GS XA-EGC
AC-725B	S227	Bearskin Airlines	N442MA N227FA C-GYXL
AC-726B	S227	GAS Wilson	N158MC
AC-727	S227	Ryan Blake Air Charter	N2726N CP-2296 N110GS ZS-OJH
AC-728B	S227	GAS Wilson	N159MC
AC-729	S227	Baires Fly	N27283 LV-VDJ
AC-730	S227	ex Ibertrans Aerea	N2727B EC-GKK [w/o 11Jan97 Djerba-Zarzis, Tunisia; by Jan99 fuselage dumped Madrid-Barajas, Spain; l/n 21Jan06]
AC-731	S227	Key Lime Air	N2728G (N731KY)
AC-732	S227	(MTW Aerospace)	N27278 XA-TGD? XA-TKE N139LC [stored by Jan12 Fort Lauderdale International, FL; canx 16Jly12, for parts]
AC-733B	S227	Aerocon	N160MC CP-2500
AC-734B	S227	Colombian National Police	N27244 86-0450+ PNC-0221 [+ USAF; C-26A]
AC-735	S227	not yet known	N27297 XA-TJQ N523WA N239LC+ CP- [+ canx 20Mar12 to Bolivia]
AC-736	S227	Aero VIP/Air Class	N2730P XA-TOH N339LC CX-CLA

SWEARINGEN (FAIRCHILD) MODEL 227

C/n	Model	Last known Owner/Operator	Identities/fates/comments (where appropriate)
AC-737B	S227	Colombian National Police	N2728F 86-0451+ PNC-0222 [+ USAF; C-26A]
AC-738	S227	Ameriflight	N2734X C-GWXX N838AF
AC-739B	S227	Bearskin Airlines	N27341 I-ORIS N227JH C-GYHD
AC-740B	S227	Venezuelan Air Force	N2730M 86-0452+ 1964 [+ USAF; C-26A]
AC-741B	S227	Carson Air	N161MC C-FNAM N301NE N41NE C-GKLK
AC-742B	S227	ex USAF	N2731M 86-0453 [C-26A] [possibly RSS-A2 with Barbados Air National Guard]
AC-743B	S227	Barbados Air National Guard	N27310 86-0454+ RSS-A1 [+ USAF; C-26A]
AC-744B	S227	not yet known	N2734B XB-EVL N8170E N32TJ N345TJ (P4-) YV-947CP YV147T
AC-745B	S227	Venezuelan Air Force	N2731B 86-0455+ 0009 [USAF; C-26A]
AC-746B	S227	Kolob Canyons Air Services	N2735Y N162MC N46NE LV-YBL N46NE C6-SAD N746KA
AC-747B	S227	USAF	N27364 86-0456 [C-26A] [reported stored San Antonio, TX]
AC-748B	S227	(Ryan Blake Air Charter)	N2741A I-SASR OE-GMT OY-FCM OE-LIZ OY-NPC ZS-OLS [DBR 10Sep04 George Airport, South Africa; 20Sep04 fuselage to Wonderboom, South Africa]
AC-749B	S227	Western Air	N2741Q 86-0457+ C6-ASD [+ USAF; C-26A]
AC-750B	S227	Berry Aviation	N27442
AC-751B	S227	USAF	N2743N 86-0458 [C-26A] [reported stored San Antonio, TX]
AC-752	S227	Ameriflight	N27444 XA-TML N529AF
AC-753B	S227	USAF	N2744A 86-0459 [C-26A] [reported stored San Antonio, TX]
AC-754B	S227	ex Career Aviation Co	N2746Z N54NE D-COLB N754TR+ F- [+ canx 06Aug12 to France]
AC-755B	S227	Aero VIP/Air Class	N27465 CX-CLS
AC-756B	S227	Perimeter Aviation	N27330 C-FAFW N575MA C-FAFW ZS-SDM C-FLRY
AC-757B	S227	BinAir Aero Service	N57NE F-GJPN D-CPSW
AC-758B	S227	BinAir Aero Service	N58NE F-GPSN D-CAVA
AC-759B	S227	Worthington Aviation Parts	N306NE N640PA
AC-760B	S227	Aeronaves TSM	N307NE N60NE N760TR+ XA- [+ canx 09Nov10 to Mexico]
AC-761B	S227	ex Lynx Air International	N61NE+ XA- [+ canx 13Feb12 to Mexico; restored 14Sep12]
AC-763B	S227	Sierra West Airlines	N63NE
AC-765	S227	CBG LLC/Key Lime Air	N2751N ZK-NSI N765FA
AC-767B	S227	FLI-HI LLC	N27521 ZK-NSJ N767FA N3531Q
AC-769B	S227	Key Lime Air	N27541 HZ-SN1 HZ-SN10 N769KL
AC-775B	S227	ex Peninsula Airways	N650PA+ C- [+ canx 17Dec08 to Canada; at Kelowna, BC, Canada 10Apr09 being used for spares by Carson Air]
AC-776B	S227	Baires Fly	N27640 N776NE VH-NEF N776NE LV-WJT
AC-782B	S227	Bearskin Airlines	N3000S C-FYWG
AC-785B	S227	Bearskin Airlines	N30019 C-FFZN
AC-788B	S227	Key Lime Air	N3003M A9C-DHL1 A9C-DHA N788KL

SWEARINGEN (FAIRCHILD) SA.227BC METRO III

C/n	Model	Last known Owner/Operator	Identities/fates/comments (where appropriate)
BC-762B	S227	(Colombian Air Force)	N2749D 89-0460+ 1242^ 5742 [+ USAF; C-26B; ^ Colombia; w/o 10Aug06 Medellin-Jose Maria Cordova, Colombia; used for spares; l/n 29Jun08]
BC-764B	S227	Museo Aeroespacial	N2749X 87-1000+ 1240^ [+ USAF; C-26B; ^ Colombia; preserved Bogota-El Dorado, Colombia; l/n Jly08]
BC-766B	S227	Colombian Air Force	N2750V 87-1001+ 1241?^ 5741?^ [+ USAF; C-26B; ^ Colombia; serials not confirmed]
BC-768B	S227	(Aerocon)	N27531 XA-SBN N768ML CP-2548 [w/o 06Sep11 near Trinidad, Bolivia]
BC-770B	S227	Career Aviation Co	N27556 XA-RWS N770ML [derelict by 13Jun10 Opa-locka, FL in scapping area]
BC-771B	S227	Epsilon Aviation	(N71NE) XA-RVR N771MW SX-BNN
BC-772B	S227	Artac Aviacion	N2756T XA-RWK N702AM EC-307 EC-GJM
BC-773B	S227	Aerocon	N2757A XA-RVS ZS-OMV AP-BHL N773US CP-2590 [major damage 27Dec09 Ernesto Roca Airport, Guayaramerin, Bolivia]
BC-774B	S227	Ver-Avia	N27617 XA-RXH N774MW SX-BMM
BC-777B	S227	(Aerolitoral/Aeromexico)	N27644 XA-RXM [b/u by 29Jun03 Mena-Intermountain Municipal, AR]

SWEARINGEN (FAIRCHILD) MODEL 227

C/n	Model	Last known Owner/Operator	Identities/fates/comments (where appropriate)
BC-778B	S227	(Aerolitoral/Aeromexico)	N2775J XA-SBD [b/u during 2003 Mena-Intermountain Municipal, AR]
BC-779B	S227	CBG LLC/Key Lime Air	N27787 XA-RXW N779BC
BC-780B	S227	Aerocon	N27779 XA-SCI ZS-CAC AP-BHK N780AL CP-2602 [major damage 01Dec09 Trinidad, Bolivia]
BC-781B	S227	Airlift USA LLP	N3000R XA-RYY N781ML [reported for Aerocon, Bolivia]
BC-783B	S227	Aerocon	N3001H XA-RSB N783ML CP-2563
BC-786B	S227	Top-Fly	N3002K XA-SCS N768ML N61AJ EC-IRS
BC-787B	S227	Key Lime Air	N3003A XA-SAQ N787KL
BC-789B	S227	(Flightline/Manx 2)	N3003T XA-SES ZS-PDW EC-ITP [w/o 10Feb11 Cork, Ireland]

SWEARINGEN (FAIRCHILD) SA.227CC METRO 23

C/n	Model	Last known Owner/Operator	Identities/fates/comments (where appropriate)
CC-827B	S227	(Bearskin Airlines)	N3033A C-GYYB [w/o 01May95 near Sioux Narrows/Nestor Falls, ON, Canada after mid-air collision with PA-31-350 C-GYPZ (c/n 31-7652168); canx 08May98]
CC-829B	S227	Bearskin Airlines	N30154 C-GYTL
CC-841B	S227	Bearskin Airlines	N3022R (N841MW) N456LA C-FXUS
CC-842B	S227	Amaszonas/Aerocon	N30220 VH-NEO N510FS CP-2473
CC-843B	S227	Airwork Flight Operations	N30228 ZK-POE
CC-844B	S227	Airwork Flight Operations	N30229 ZK-POF

NOTE: These were orginally SA.227DCs with c/ns starting with "DC-"

SWEARINGEN (FAIRCHILD) SA.227DC METRO 23

C/n	Model	Last known Owner/Operator	Identities/fates/comments (where appropriate)
DC-557B	S227	(Fairchild Aircraft)	N400FA [cvtd from SA.227AT c/n AT-557; wfu for spares San Antonio, TX; canx 23Mar00 as scrapped]
DC-784M	S227	Peruvian Air Force	N3003F 90-0523+ 342 [+ USAF; C-26B]
DC-790M	S227	Peruvian Air Force	N3003U 90-0524+ 343 [+ USAF; C-26B]
DC-791M	S227	USAF	N3004D 90-0529+ N529CD^ N90956^ 90-0529 [+ USAF; RC-26B; ^ marks allocated to government bodies, but probably never used]
DC-792M	S227	Peruvian Air Force	N3004K 90-0525 344 [+ USAF; C-26B]
DC-793M	S227	US Army	N3004T 90-0526 [C26B]
DC-794M	S227	US Army	N3004V 90-0527 [C26B]
DC-795M	S227	US Navy	N3004W 90-0528+ 900528 [+ USAF; C-26B]
DC-796M	S227	US Navy	N3004X 90-0530+ 900530 [+ USAF; C-26B]
DC-797B	S227	Vee H Aviation/Corporate Air	N30042 VH-KDJ VH-VEU
DC-798M	S227	US Navy	N30046 90-0531+ 900531 [+ USAF; C-26B]
DC-799M	S227	US Army	N30047 89-0515 [C26B]
DC-800B	S227	(Sunshine Express Airlines)	N3005U VH-KDT [DBR Jun06 in hangar Brisbane Airport, QLD, Australia whilst undergoing maintenance; canx 19Apr07]
DC-801M	S227	US Navy	N3005W 91-0502+ 910502 [+ USAF; C-26D]
DC-802M	S227	US Army	N3006M 91-0503 [C26B]
DC-803M	S227	USAF	N3007C 91-0504+ N459DF^ N6131Z^ 91-0504 [+ USAF; RC-26B; ^ marks allocated to government bodies, but probably never used]
DC-804M	S227	US Army	N3007H 91-0505 [C26B]
DC-805B	S227	BinAir Aero Service	N3008L XA-SFC N715MQ D-CKPP
DC-806M	S227	US Army	N3007R 91-0506 [C26B]
DC-807M	S227	US Army	N3008G 91-0507 [C26B]
DC-808B	S227	IAP Group/Toll Aviation	N3008M XA-SFX N8085K VH-HPB
DC-809M	S227	Colombian National Police	N3008Q 91-0508+ PNC-0224 [+ USAF; C-26B; used AMARC code CB0001]
DC-810M	S227	US Army	N3008M 91-0509 [C26B]
DC-811M	S227	Colombian National Police	N3009B 91-0510+ PNC-0226 [+ USAF; C-26B; used AMARC code CB0002]
DC-812B	S227	ex Aircraft Consultants	N3008T XA-TCJ N812GS VH-HPG N812LD+ YV [+ marks canx 23Sep08 to Venezuela]
DC-813M	S227	US Army	N3009P 91-0511 [C26B]
DC-814M	S227	Trinidad Defence Force/Coast Guard	N3009Z 91-0512+ 910512 215 [C-26D] [+ used AMARC code CB0003]
DC-815M	S227	US Army	N30099 91-0513 [C26B]
DC-816M	S227	US Navy	N3010P 91-0514 910514 [C-26D]
DC-817B	S227	Aerocon	N3010S XA-SGH N817JE VH-UUD CP-2485

SWEARINGEN (FAIRCHILD) MODEL 227

C/n	Model	Last known Owner/Operator	Identities/fates/comments (where appropriate)
DC-818B	S227	(Aero-Tropics Air Services)	N3012Q XA-SGG N818GL VH-TFU [w/o 07May05 South Pap Ridge, near Lockhart River Airport, QLD, Australia; canx 15Nov05]
DC-819B	S227	Aerocon	N3012U XA-SGV N819SK LV-BYL N819SK CP-2655
DC-820B	S227	Key Lime Air/Denver Air Connection	N3013B XA-SHD (ZS-PBT) N820DC
DC-821B	S227	EP Aviation LLC	N3013L XA-SHE N821JB N955BW [operated by Presidential Airways for US Government bodies]
DC-822B	S227	IAP Group Australia	N3013Q XA-SVA N822MM VH-HAN HL5237 VH-YUZ
DC-823B	S227	Toll Aviation Pty	N30137 XA-SVB N823MM VH-HPE
DC-824B	S227	Aerocon	N30134 XA-SVC N824GL VH-UUA N471Z CP-2527
DC-825B	S227	AeroSur	N3021A CP-2253
DC-826B	S227	Sharp Aviation Pty	N3025A XA-SNF ZS-PBU N52ML VH-SWK
DC-828M	S227	US Army	N3015F 91-0572 [C26B]
DC-830B	S227	Aerocon	N3016X CP-2257 N1119K XA-TFF N1119K CP-2477
DC-831M	S227	USAF	N3017R 92-0369+ N3017R^ N203CD^ N6105L^ 92-0369 [+ USAF; RC-26B; ^ marks allocated to government bodies, but probably never used]
DC-832M	S227	Trinidad Defence Force/Coast Guard	N3018C 92-0370+ 920370 216 [C-26D] [stored AMARC code CB0004]
DC-833M	S227	US Navy	N3018P 92-0371 920371 [C-26D]
DC-834M	S227	USAF	N3019S 92-0372+ N372CD^ N61050^ 92-0372 [+ USAF; RC-26B; ^ J580 marks allocated to government bodies, but probably never used]
DC-835M	S227	USAF	N30193 92-0373+ N30193 92-0373 [+ USAF; C-26B]
DC-836M	S227	US Navy	N30196 90-7038 907038 [RC-26D]
DC-837B	S227	Bearskin Lake Air Service	N3021N VH-KDO C-GSOQ
DC-838B	S227	Bearskin Lake Air Service	N3021U VH-KAN C-GSNP
DC-839B	S227	Pearl Aviation	N3022F VH-DMI VH-OYI
DC-840B	S227	Airnorth Regional	N3022L (N840MW) (N455LA) VH-ANY
DC-845B	S227	Vee H Aviation	N3023Q VH-KED VH-VEK
DC-846B	S227	Bearskin Lake Air Service	N30236 VH-KEU C-GJVO
DC-847B	S227	Amaszonas	N3024B N847LS CP-2459
DC-848B	S227	Pearl Aviation	N3024U N452LA VH-OYB
DC-849B	S227	not yet known	N3024V N451LA I-VICY D-CICY
DC-850B	S227	Colombian National Police	N3025B N850LS PNC-0229
DC-851B	S227	Sharp Aviation	N3025T VH-HWR
DC-852B	S227	Perimeter Airlines	N3025W N453LA EC-421 EC-GLI N453LA C-GMWW
DC-853B	S227	Colombian National Police	N3025Y N853LS PNC-0227
DC-854B	S227	Colombian National Police	N3026R N854LS PNC-0228
DC-855B	S227	ex Top-Fly	N3026U N454LA EC-395 EC-GJX [reported derelict at Las Palmas, Gran Canaria, Spain; l/n Jan06]
DC-856B	S227	American Jet	N3027B OE-LIA N3027B LV-BYM
DC-857M	S227	US Army	N3027N 94-0259+ N3027N^ 94-0259 [+ USAF; C-26B; ^ marks allocated to government bodies, but probably never used]
DC-858M	S227	USAF	N3027W 94-0260+ N402CD^ N6091F^ 94-0260 [+ USAF; RC-26B; ^ marks allocated to government bodies, but probably never used]
DC-859M	S227	USAF	N30273 94-0261+ N261CD^ N6135Y^ 94-0261 [+ USAF; RC-26B; ^ marks allocated to government bodies, but probably never used]
DC-860M	S227	USAF	N3028F 94-0262+ N262CD^ N61045^ 94-0262 [USAF; RC-26B ^ marks allocated to government bodies, but probably never used]
DC-861M	S227	USAF	N3028L 94-0263+ N3028L^ N60947^ N70753^ 94-0263 [+ USAF; RC-26B; ^ marks allocated to government bodies, but probably never used]
DC-862M	S227	USAF	N3028S 94-0264+ N264CD^ N9089V^ 94-0264 [+ USAF; RC-26B; ^ marks allocated to government bodies, but probably never used]
DC-863M	S227	USAF	N3028T 94-0265+ N265CD^ N9117A^ 94-0265 [+ USAF; RC-26B; ^ marks allocated to government bodies, but probably never used]
DC-864B	S227	EP Aviation	N3028U B-3950 C-GKAF N956BW [operated by Presidential Airways for US Government bodies]
DC-865B	S227	North Flying	N30289 9M-BCH OY-NPD
DC-866B	S227	Alta Flights	N3029F B-3951 C-GSAF
DC-867B	S227	North Flying	N3029R 9M-APA VH-MYE N23VJ OY-NPE
DC-868B	S227	EP Aviation	N30296 B-3952 C-FAFI ZK-JSV C-FAFI N654AR
DC-869B	S227	Sharp Aviation	N3030N 9M-APB VH-MYI

SWEARINGEN (FAIRCHILD) MODEL 227

C/n	Model	Last known Owner/Operator	Identities/fates/comments (where appropriate)					
DC-870B	S227	Pearl Aviation	N3030S	VH-DMO	VH-OYN			
DC-871B	S227	Airnorth Regional	N3030T	VH-HCB	VH-ANA			
DC-872B	S227	Bearskin Airlines	N3030X	VH-KEX	C-GJVW			
DC-873B	S227	Airnorth Regional	N3031Q	VH-ANW				
DC-874B	S227	Skippers Aviation	N3032L	VH-WAI				
DC-875B	S227	Pearl Aviation	N3033B	VH-SWM	VH-OYG			
DC-876B	S227	Skippers Aviation	N3033U	VH-WAJ				
DC-877B	S227	Skippers Aviation	N30337	VH-WAX				
DC-878B	S227	M7 Aviation Services	N3034D	SU-UAB	N5LN			
DC-879B	S227	Helitec	N3034P	SU-UAC	N6ER	YV221T		
DC-880B	S227	North Flying	N3002K	TF-JME	OY-NPF			
DC-881B	S227	Toll Aviation Pty	N3004D	TF-JML	N6BN	VH-UZN		
DC-882B	S227	CBG LLC/Key Lime Air	N3004X	B-3953	C-GAFQ	N882DC		
DC-883B	S227	Skippers Aviation	N30042	VH-WBA				
DC-884B	S227	Skippers Aviation	N30046	VH-WBQ				
DC-885B	S227	Bearskin Airlines	N30047	N885ML	C-GJVC			
DC-886B	S227	Hardy & Sons Pty	N3006M	N886ML	VH-HVH			
DC-887B	S227	Sunwest Aviation	N3007C	C-GSHZ				
DC-888B	S227	American Jet	N3007H	B-3955	C-GIAF	ZK-JSJ	C-GIAF	N332AJ
			LV-BYN					
DC-889B	S227	American Jet	N3007R	B-3957	C-FDMR	N889AJ	LV-BYJ	
DC-890B	S227	Bearskin Airlines	N30135	B-3959	C-GAFQ	N30135	C-GAFQ	N211SA
			C-GAFQ					
DC-891B	S227	Alta Flights	N3018T	B-3956	C-GAAF			
DC-892B	S227	Worthington Aviation Parts	N3031Z	B-3958	C-GAFO	N892DC		
DC-893B	S227	FLM Aviation	N3032A	D-CNAG				
DC-894B	S227	Sharp Aviation Pty	N3032F	VH-UUB				
DC-895B	S227	FLM Aviation?	N30384	D-CNAC				
DC-896B	S227	Hardy Aviation	N3042E	D-CSWF	VH-TWL			
DC-897B	S227	Sunwest Aviation	N3051Q	C-GSHY				
DC-898B	S227	Bearskin Airlines	N3054D	N898ML	C-GJVH			
DC-899B	S227	Hardy Aviation (NT) Pty	N3060H	D-CEBR	N3217P	YV-1084CP? YV256T		VH-CNH
DC-900B	S227	Sunwest Aviation	N30666	D-CJKO	C-GSHV			
DC-901B	S227	American Jet	N3070F	LV-PIR	LV-ZXA			
DC-902B	S227	Bearskin Airlines	N3084W	9H-AEU	N902WB	C-GJVB		
DC-903B	S227	US Army Corp of Engineers	N3086H	N903NJ	N55CE			
DC-904B	S227	Helitec	N3094W	N904NJ	YV185T			

SWEARINGEN (FAIRCHILD) SA.227PC METRO 23

C/n	Model	Last known Owner/Operator	Identity	Comments
PC-436	S227	(Fairchild Aircraft)	N3114F	[b/u May86 San Antonio, TX; canx 14Jan88]
PC-562	S227	(Fairchild Aircraft)	N3113H	[b/u Sep86 San Antonio, TX; canx 17Sep86]

Unidentified

C/n	Model	Last known Owner/Operator	Identity	Comments
unkn	S227		LV-WRT	[reported Nov09 Santa Cruz-International, Bolivia]
unkn	S227	Barbados Air National Guard	RSS-A2	[ex USAF C-26A; white c/s; possibly c/n AC-742B]
unkn	S227	Aero Davinci Internacional	XA-AFL	
unkn	S227		XA-BLM	[reported 24Sep09 Mexico City, Mexico]
unkn	S227	Enrique Cuahonte Delgado	XA-HUO	
unkn	S227	Consorcio Helitec	YV394T	[reported 2009]
unkn	S227		YV2363	[reported 01Dec07 Ocumare del Tuy, Venezuela]
unkn	S227	Peruvian Air Force	PNC-223	[reported; probably former C-26]
unkn	S227	Mexican Air Force	3901	[reported; probably former C-26]
unkn	S227	Mexican Air Force	3902	[reported; probably former C-26]
unkn	S227	Mexican Air Force	3903	[reported; probably former C-26]
unkn	S227	Mexican Air Force	3904	[reported; probably former C-26]

Production complete

TUPOLEV Tu-114 and variants

C/n	Model	Last known Owner/Operator	Identities/fates/comments (where appropriate)
5611		Central Russian Air Force Museum	CCCP-L5611 [ff 15Nov57][preserved 16Mar72 Monino, Russia; l/n Nov08]
88401		(Aeroflot/Moscow)	CCCP-76458 [canx 1975; fate unknown]
88402		(Aeroflot/Moscow)	CCCP-76459 [wfu & displayed early 1977 near Novgorod Airport, USSR, until destroyed by arson in spring 1990; hulk b/u]
88411		(Tupolev OKB)	[static test airframe]
88412		(Aeroflot/Moscow)	CCCP-76460 [canx 20Jly76 as time expired; l/n 14Nov77 Moscow-Domodedovo, USSR]
98413		(Aeroflot/Moscow)	CCCP-76464 [canx 1976; by Aug77 preserved Moscow-Domodedovo, Russia; until b/u 28Jly/05Aug06]
98421		(Aeroflot/Moscow)	CCCP-76465 [canx 30Apr76 as time expired; fate unknown]
98422		(Aeroflot/Moscow)	CCCP-76466 [canx 1975; fate unknown]
98423		(Aeroflot/Moscow)	CCCP-76467 [canx 1975; fate unknown]
98424		(Aeroflot/Moscow)	CCCP-76468 [canx 1975; fate unknown]
608425		(Aeroflot/Moscow)	CCCP-76469 [canx 1975; fate unknown]
608431		(Aeroflot/Moscow)	CCCP-76470 [canx 1976; preserved Moscow-Vnukovo, Russia until b/u Jun06]
608432		(Aeroflot/Moscow)	CCCP-76471 [canx 1975; fate unknown]
818433		(Aeroflot/Moscow)	CCCP-76472 [canx 1976; fuselage stored Moscow-Domodedovo, Russia; l/n 1995]
618434		(Aeroflot/Moscow)	CCCP-76473 [canx 1976; fate unknown]
618435		(Aeroflot/Moscow)	CCCP-76474 [canx 1976; fate unknown]
618441		(Aeroflot/Moscow)	CCCP-76475 [canx 1976; l/n Nov77 Moscow-Domodedovo, USSR; fate unknown]
618442		(Aeroflot/Moscow)	CCCP-76476 [canx 1976; fate unknown]
618443		(Aeroflot/Moscow)	CCCP-76477 [canx 1976; derelict Moscow-Domodedovo, Russia, gone by 1991]
628444		(Aeroflot/Moscow)	CCCP-76478 [canx 25Feb76, fuselage stored 1991-1999 Moscow-Domodedovo, Russia; b/u]
628445	D	(Aeroflot/Moscow)	CCCP-76479 [w/o mid Aug62 Moscow-Vnukovo, USSR in ground accident; canx 31Aug62; fuselage to local scrapyard for about 20 years]
62M451	D	(Soviet Air Force)	CCCP-76480 [canx 13Feb73 to Soviet AF; wfu spring 1981; fate unknown]
62M452	D	(Aeroflot/Moscow)	CCCP-76481 [canx 1976; fate unknown]
62M453	D	(Aeroflot/Moscow)	CCCP-76482 [canx 1976; fate unknown]
62M454	D	(Aeroflot/Moscow)	CCCP-76483 [canx 1975; fate unknown]
63M455	D	(Aeroflot/Moscow)	CCCP-76484 [canx 1976; fate unknown]
63M461	D	(Aeroflot/Moscow)	CCCP-76485 [canx 06Jul77; spring 1977 to Krivoy Rog Technical School, Ukraine; l/n May08]
63M462	D	(Aeroflot/Moscow)	CCCP-76486 [canx 1976; preserved 09Sep76 Tyumen-Roshchino, USSR; b/u 1986]
63M463	D	(Aeroflot/Moscow)	CCCP-76487 [canx 1976; fate unknown]
64M464	D	(Aeroflot/Moscow)	CCCP-76488 [canx 1976; fate unknown]
64M465	D	(Aeroflot/Moscow)	CCCP-76489 [canx 1976; fate unknown]
64M471	D	Civil Aviation Board Museum	CCCP-76490 [preserved May83 Ulyanovsk, USSR/Russia; l/n Jly08]
64M472	D	(Aeroflot/International)	CCCP-76491 [w/o 17Feb66 Moscow-Sheremetyevo, USSR; canx 18Apr66]
6800402	Tu-116	Civil Aviation Board Museum	7801+ CCCP-76462 [+ Soviet] [preserved 1989 Ulyanovsk, USSR/Russia; l/n Jun07]
7800409	Tu-116	(Soviet Air Force)	7802 CCCP-76463 [wfu Apr91 Uzin, USSR; and b/u]

TUPOLEV Tu-126

61M601	Tu-126LL	(Soviet Air Force)	618601 [wfu 1990; on dump Zhukovski, Russia by Aug92, b/u]
65M611	Tu-126	(Soviet Air Force)	[not known] [canx 1984; probably b/u 1990]
65M612	Tu-126	(Soviet Air Force)	[not known] [canx 1984; probably b/u 1990]
66M613	Tu-126	(Soviet Air Force)	[not known] [canx 1984; probably b/u 1990]
66M621	Tu-126	(Soviet Air Force)	[not known] [canx 1984; probably b/u 1990]
66M622	Tu-126	(Soviet Air Force)	[not known] [canx 1984; probably b/u 1990]
67M623	Tu-126	(Soviet Air Force)	[not known] [canx 1984; probably b/u 1990]
67M624	Tu-126	(Soviet Air Force)	[not known] [canx 1984; probably b/u 1990]
67M625	Tu-126	(Soviet Air Force)	[not known] [canx 1984; probably b/u 1990]

Production complete

VICKERS-ARMSTRONGS VISCOUNT

C/n	Model	Last known Owner/Operator	Identities/fates/comments (where appropriate)
1	630	(Ministry of Supply)	VX211 G-AHRF [prototype ff 16Jly48; w/o 27Aug52 landing in Sahara Desert, near Khartoum, Sudan; canx 21Nov53]]
2	663	(Royal Air Force)	VX217 (G-AHRG) VX217 [DBF 1958; b/u 1959 Seighford, UK]
3(1)	640	(Vickers-Armstrongs)	(G-AJZW) [project canx, airframe not built; canx 09Apr48]
3(2)	700	(Vickers-Armstrongs)	G-AMAV [wfu & stored Oct60; fuselage to Stansted fire school, UK Aug63; canx 11Oct60]
4	701	(British European Airways)	G-ALWE [w/o 14Mar57 Wythenshawe on approach to Manchester-Ringway, UK; canx 18Mar57]
5	701	Duxford Aviation Society	G-ALWF [wfu 16Apr72 & preserved 1975 Duxford, UK]; canx 18Apr72]
6	701	(British European Airways)	G-AMNY [w/o 05Jan60 Luqa Airport, Malta; canx 15Jan60]
7	701	Museum of Flight	(G-AMNZ) G-AMOG [wfu May76 & canx 17May76; preserved RAF Cosford, UK; moved by road 17Aug06 East Fortune, Scotland]
8	708	(Air France)	F-BGNK [w/o 12Dec56 Milly-la-Foret, France]
9	701	(Cambrian Airways)	G-AMOA [w/o 19Jan70 Bristol-Lulsgate, UK; canx 06May71]
10	708	(Alidair)	F-BGNL G-ARBY F-BOEC G-ARBY [w/o 17Jly80 Ottery St Mary, near Exeter Airport, Devon, UK; canx 01Feb82]
11	701	(Aeroclube do Brasil)	G-AMOB PP-SRI [wfu & stored Apr70; Apr75 donated to Aeroclube do Brazil, Rio de Janeiro-Jacarepagua, Brazil; b/u Jun79]
12	708	(Air Inter)	F-BGNM G-ARER F-BOEA [w/o 28Dec71 Aulnat, Clermont Ferrand, France; fuselage noted 08Sep97 at "Concorde" supermarket, Lempdes France, Clermont-Ferrand, France]
13	701	(Cambrian Airways)	G-AMOC (PP-SRK) G-AMOC VP-BCH G-AMOC [wfu & stored 09Oct70; canx 19Jly71; b/u Oct71 Cardiff-Rhoose, Wales]
14	708	(MMM Aero Services)	F-BGNN G-ARGR F-BOEB G-ARGR 9Q-CAN(2) [b/u Jan87 Kinshasa, Zaire]
15	701	ex VASP	G-AMOD PP-SRJ [wfu & stored Feb69; preserved in playground Piracicaba, Brazil; l/n 14Aug11]
16	708	(Air Inter)	F-BGNO [wfu & stored Sep74; b/u Apr75 Paris-Orly, France]
17	701	(Cambrian Airways)	G-AMOE [wfu 06Jan72; canx 03Sep73; to cabin crew trainer Newcastle Airport, UK; Apr77 on display at Lambton Pleasure Park, UK using tail from c/n 159, painted as "G-WHIZ"; moved 1982 moved to Saltwell Park, Gateshead, UK; b/u Mar93]
18	708	(Air Inter)	F-BGNP [wfu & stored Feb74 Paris-Orly, France; b/u Apr75]
19	701	(VASP)	G-AMOF PP-SRM [w/o 31Oct66 Rio de Janeiro-Santos Dumont, Brazil]
20	701	(Cambrian Airways)	(G-AMOG) G-AMNZ [wfu & stored Jun71 Cardiff-Rhoose, Wales; b/u Oct71; canx 05Oct71]
21	701	(Cambrian Airways)	G-AMOH [wfu & stored Nov71 Cardiff-Rhoose, Wales; canx 01Sep72; b/u Sep72]
22	701	Museu de Bebedouro	G-AMOI (PP-SRK) PP-SRL [wfu & stored Jly69 San Paulo-Congonhas, Brazil; donated to Bebedouro Museum, Brazil; reported by mid-96 dismantled & stored]
23	701	(Cambrian Airways)	G-AMOJ [wfu & stored Feb71 Cardiff-Rhoose, Wales; canx 19Jly71; b/u Dec71]
24	701X	(Linea Aeropostal Venezolana)	G-AMOK YV-C-AMB (YV-10C) [wfu & stored 13Oct75 Caracas, Venezuela; assumed later b/u]
25	701	(Cambrian Airways)	G-AMOL [w/o 20Jly65 Speke Airport, Liverpool, UK; canx 20Jly65]
26	701	(British European Airways)	G-AMOM [w/o 20Jan56 Blackbushe, Hampshire, UK; canx 20Jan56]
27	701	(Cambrian Airways)	G-AMON [wfu & stored 31Mar76 Cardiff-Rhoose, Wales; canx 10May76 as wfu; flew 17Jun76, after canx, Southend, UK for parts recovery; hulk b/u May79]
28	701	(Cambrian Airways)	G-AMOO [wfu & stored Dec70 Cardiff-Rhoose, Wales; canx 12Aug71; b/u Oct71]
29	701	(Cambrian Airways)	G-AMOP [wfu & stored Aug71 Cardiff-Rhoose, Wales, canx 13Apr72; b/u Sep72]
30	707	(Channel Airways)	EI-AFV G-APZB [wfu 12May68 Southend, UK; b/u Feb70; canx 26Feb70]
31	707	(Go Group)	EI-AFW VR-BBJ G-ARKH VR-BBJ G-ARKH VP-BCF (N7972) [b/u by late 1983; in scrap yard south of Mojave, CA]
32	707	(James Carter)	EI-AFY VR-BBH G-ARKI VR-BBH G-ARKI VP-BCE N7973 [wfu Fort Lauderdale-International, FL; b/u Jan77]
33	708	(Air Inter)	F-BGNQ [wfu Nov74; b/u in 1975; canx]
34	707	(Channel Airways)	EI-AGI G-APZC [wfu & stored 29Sep68; CofA expired 24Jun69; b/u Jan70 Southend, UK; canx 23Feb70]
35	708	Viscount 35 Association	F-BGNR (OY-AFN) (OY-AFO) F-BGNR [GIA Perth, Scotland 08Oct73, with Airwork; latterly preserved by Viscount 35 Association at Midland Air Museum, Baginton, Coventry, UK; arrived 06Sep07]
36	708	(MMM Aero Services)	F-BGNS G-ARIR F-BLHI G-ARIR 9Q-CAH [not delivered; wfu & stored Nov84 Ostend, Belgium; b/u Dec88]
37	708	(Alidair)	F-BGNT G-BDIK [wfu & stored Oct76 East Midlands Airport, UK; b/u 1979; canx 24Mar83]

VICKERS-ARMSTRONGS VISCOUNT

C/n	Model	Last known Owner/Operator	Identities/fates/comments (where appropriate)
38	708	Auto und Technik Museum	F-BGNU [preserved 26Mar75 Mulhouse-Habsheim, France; Sep94 moved to Sinsheim, Germany; l/n Apr08]
39	708	(Air Inter)	F-BGNV [w/o 12Aug63 24kms N of Lyon, France]
40	744	Pima Air & Space Museum	CF-TGI N22SN [canx Oct91; preserved Pima County, Tucson, AZ]
41	744	ex Guila Air	CF-TGJ N117H N81RR N240RC XA-RJC 9Q-CGA [stored Brazzaville, Republic of Congo; l/n late 2010 in poor condition]
42	724	(Air Canada)	CF-TGK [b/u Jly70 St Malo, MB, Canada]
43	724	(Trans-Canada Air Lines)	CF-TGL [10Nov58 New York-Idlewild, NY after collision with L-1049D Super Constellation N6503C c/n 4165]
44	720	(Trans Australia Airlines)	VH-TVA [w/o 31Oct54 Mangalore, VIC, Australia; canx 19Nov54]
45	720	(MacRobertson Miller Airlines)	VH-TVB VH-RMQ [w/o 31Dec68 48kms south of Port Headland, WA, Australia; canx 31Dec68]
46	720	(Ansett-ANA)	VH-TVC [w/o 30Nov61 into Botany Bay, Sydney, NSW, Australia; canx 30Nov61]
47	720	(Flight Spares Ltd)	VH-TVD [wfu Aug67 Southend, UK; canx 30Sep67; b/u Feb70]
48	720	(Trans Australia Airlines)	VH-TVE [wfu Apr67; b/u Dec69 Melbourne-Essendon, VIC, Australia; canx 30Jan70]
49	720	(Flight Spares Ltd)	VH-TVF [wfu Aug67; b/u Feb70 Southend, UK; canx]
50	724	(Air Inter)	CF-TGM F-BMCH [w/o 27Oct72 into Mount Pic du Picon, 60kms west of Lyon, France]
51	744	(James Stanley Leasing Co)	CF-TGN N744W N1898M N1898S N180RC [wfu Tucson, AZ; b/u Jly93]
52	724	(Janus Airways)	CF-TGO F-BMCG G-BDRC [wfu at Exeter; canx 09Oct84 as wfu; moved May86 to fire school Manston, Kent, UK; DBR 16Oct87 by high winds & b/u]
53	724	(Canadian Dept of Transport)	CF-TGP [wfu & b/u Oct70 Montreal-Dorval, QC, Canada; remains used for parts for c/n 218]
54	724	Institut Aeronautique Amaury de la Grange	CF-TGQ F-BMCF [preserved Jly75 Merville, France]
55	724	(Air Inter)	CF-TGR N911H F-BNAX [wfu & stored Oct74; b/u in 1975 Paris-Orly, France]
56	724	(Chiswick Scrap Metal)	CF-TGS [wfu & stored Apr71; b/u Jun73 Winnipeg, MB, Canada]
57	724	(Goulet Enterprises)	CF-TGT [wfu & stored Jan69; b/u Jly70 Winnipeg, MB, Canada]
58	724	(Chiswick Scrap Metal)	CF-TGU [wfu & stored Jan69; b/u Jun73 Winnipeg, MB, Canada]
59	724	(Chiswick Scrap Metal)	CF-TGV [wfu & stored May71; b/u Jun73 Winnipeg, MB, Canada]
60	724	(Chiswick Scrap Metal)	CF-TGW [wfu & stored May70; b/u Jun73 Winnipeg, MB, Canada]
61	701C	(Aeroclube Rio Claro)	G-ANHA PP-SRP [wfu & stored Feb69; preserved 1975 Rio Claro, Brazil until b/u date unknown]
62	701C	(Aeroclube de Sao Paulo)	G-ANHB PP-SRN [wfu & stored Feb69; preserved 1972 Sao Paulo-Campo de Marte Airport, Sao Paulo, Brazil; 16May93 DBF]
63	701C	(British European Airways)	G-ANHC [w/o 22Oct58 Anzio, Italy, after mid-air collision with an Italian AF F-86K; canx 11Nov58]
64	701C	Museu de Bebedouro	G-ANHD PP-SRO [wfu & stored Feb69; preserved 1974 Bebedouro, Brazil; l/n Dec96 in poor condition]
65	701C	(VASP)	G-ANHE PP-SRQ [w/o 03Mar65 Rio de Janeiro-Galeao, Brazil]
66	701C	(VASP)	G-ANHF PP-SRR [w/o 04Sep64 en-route Pico da Caledonia, Nova Friburgo, Brazil]
67	735	(Alidair)	YI-ACK G-BFMW [wfu & stored Jan82 East Midlands Airport, UK; CofA expired 15Jun82; 27Oct83 to airport fire service; b/u; canx 05Dec83]
68	735	(Iraqi Airways)	YI-ACL [w/o 17Apr73 Mosul, Iraq; remains sold for spares]
69	735	(Guernsey Airlines)	YI-ACM G-BFYZ [w/o 25Oct79 Kirkwall, Scotland; canx 24Mar83]
70	737	(Uplands Airport)	CF-GXK [wfu & stored Jly82 Ottawa-Uplands, ON, Canada; canx Jan84; used for spares; remains donated to fire dept until b/u]
71	702	(Channel Airways)	VP-TBK G-APTA VP-BBW G-APTA VP-BBW G-APTA [wfu & stored Jly69 Southend, UK; b/u Jan70; canx 24Feb70]
72	702	(Field Aircraft Services)	VP-TBL G-APOW VP-BCD G-APOW [wfu & stored May69; b/u Feb70 Castle Donington, UK; canx 06Apr70]
73	702	(Field Aircraft Services)	VP-TBM G-APPX VP-BBV G-APPX [wfu & stored Aug75 East Midlands Airport; canx 20Aug75; b/u Oct77]
74	732	(Hunting-Clan Air Transport)	G-ANRR OD-ACF G-ANRR [w/o 02Dec58 Frimley, Surrey, UK; canx 08Jun60]
75	732	(Cambrian Airways)	G-ANRS OD-ACH G-ANRS OD-ACH G-ANRS SU-AKY G-ANRS [wfu 10Jly69 Cardiff-Rhoose, Wales & canx 05Nov69; used as cabin trainer painted with false regn G-WHIZ; to Wales Aircraft Museum used as shop; Feb93 to fire service; b/u Feb96]
76	732	(United Arab Airlines)	G-ANRT OD-ACG G-ANRT YI-ADM G-ANRT SU-AKX [w/o 23Mar64 Beirut, Lebanon; remains to MEA for spares, fuselage used for crew training]

VICKERS-ARMSTRONGS VISCOUNT

C/n	Model	Last known Owner/Operator	Identities/fates/comments (where appropriate)
77	736	(British Midland Airways)	(LN-FOF) G-AODG OD-ACR G-AODG [w/o 20Feb69 Castle Donington, UK; canx 07Mar69]
78	736	(British United Airways)	(LN-FOL) G-AODH VP-TBY G-AODH [w/o 30Oct61 Frankfurt, West Germany; canx 02Jan62]
79	723	(Indian Airlines Corporation)	IU683+ VT-DWI [+ India] [wfu & stored Jan71; b/u Delhi, India]
80	730	(Indian Airlines Corporation)	IU684+ VT-DWJ [+ India] [wfu & stored Oct73; b/u Dec73 Delhi, India]
81	702	(Linea Aeropostal Venezolana)	VP-TBN 9Y-TBN VP-TCI 9Y-TBN YV-C-AMT (YV-09C) [wfu Jan76 Caracas,Venezuela; used as cabin trainer until Aug85; subsequently b/u]
82	763D	(TACA International Airlines)	YS-09C [w/o 05Mar59 Managua-Las Mercedes, Nicaragua]
83	734	(Chinese Air Force)	J-751+ 414^ B-414 B-5114 [+ Pakistan Air Force; ^ China; wfu & stored Beijing-Nan Yuan, China; later b/u]
84	720	(Trans Australia Airlines)	VH-TVG [wfu Oct69; b/u Dec69 Melbourne-Essendon, VIC, Australia; canx 30Jan70]
85	739	(Misrair – Egyptian Airlines)	SU-AIC [w/o 01Oct56 in Royal Air Force air raid on Almaza, Egypt]
86	739	(United Arab Airlines)	SU-AID [w/o 6Mar62 near Wadi Halfa Airport, Sudan]
87	739	(British Eagle Int'l Airlines)	SU-AIE G-ATDU [b/u Apr69 Liverpool-Speke, UK; canx 10Jly69 as wfu]
88	744	(All Nippon Airways)	N7402 G-APKJ (YV-C-ANJ) G-APKJ [w/o 12Jun61 Osaka-Itama Airport, Japan; remains to Ansett-ANA & b/u for spares; canx 12Jun61 but CAA not advised until 18Sep63]
89	744	(Shackleton Aviation)	N7403 G-APKK (YV-C-ANK) G-APKK XR801 [stored 25Oct71 Hurn, UK; 18May72 ferried to Baginton, Coventry, UK; 1973 moved to Bolsover, UK until b/u circa 1975]
90	744	(Capital Airlines)	N7404 [heavy landing 20Feb56 Chicago-Midway, IL; parts used to build c/n 301]
91	755D	(Cubana)	(G-AOCA) CU-C603 CU-T603 [w/o 01Nov58 Nipe Bay, Cuba]
92	755D	(British Midland Airways)	(G-AOCB) CU-C604 CU-T604 VR-BBL G-AOCB [wfu 31Oct69; Castle Donington, UK; canx 16Apr70; b/u May70]
93	755D	(British Midland Airways)	(G-AOCC) CU-C605 CU-T605 VR-BBM G-AOCC [wfu & canx 21Apr69; b/u Aug69 Castle Donington, UK]
94	749	(Linea Aeropostal Venezolana)	YV-C-AMV [w/o 25Jan71 Merida, Venezuela]
95	749	(Linea Aeropostal Venezolana)	YV-C-AMX [w/o 14Aug74 on Isla de Margarita, near Porlamar, Venezuela]
96	749	(Linea Aeropostal Venezolana)	YV-C-AMY YV-C-AMZ [w/o 01Nov71 Maracaibo, Venezuela]
97	747	(Ansett Airways)	G-ANXV VH-BAT VH-RMO [wfu & stored Dec68; b/u Oct76 Melbourne-Essendon, VIC, Australia; canx 26Mar70]
98	748D	Zimbabwe Military Museum	VP-YNA 7Q-YDK VP-YNA Z-YNA [wfu 31May85; Aug86 preserved Gweru, Zimbabwe; l/n Feb06]
99	748D	(Air Zimbabwe)	VP-YNB Z-YNB [wfu Dec85 Harare, Zimbabwe; used for ground training; b/u 2001]
100	748D	(Air Zimbabwe)	VP-YNC Z-YNC [wfu 20Oct83 Harare, Zimbabwe; b/u Mar85]
101	748D	(Air Rhodesia)	VP-YND [w/o 12Feb79 east of Kariba, Rhodesia, hit by missile]
102	748D	(Central African Airways)	VP-YNE [w/o 09Aug58 east of Benghazi, Libya]
103	745	(United Air Lines)	N7405 [w/o 09Jly64 near Newport, TN]
104	745	(Da Vu Aviation Inc)	N7406 N764C N764E [wfu & stored Feb72 possibly at Sarasota, FL; canx; final fate unknown]
105	745	(Airgo Air Freight)	N7407 [canx 18Aug81 due to accident; believed DBR by tropical storm "Dennis" somewhere in Florida, possibly at Homestead AFB]
106	745	(Bobby K Green)	N7408 [stored 11Jan69 Sussex County Airport, Georgetown, DE; l/n Jan88; circa Jan96 sold to Mid Atlantic Air Museum, Reading, PA for spares to support c/n 233]
107	745	(Robert Kivett)	N7409 [stored 11Jan69 Sussex County Airport, Georgetown, DE; l/n 29Sep91; b/u mid-90s]
108	745	(Capital Airlines)	N7410 [w/o 20May58 near Point of Rocks, Brunswick, MD, after mid-air collision with North American T-33A 53-5966]
109	745	(Morgan Rourke Aircraft Sales)	N7411 [stored 11Jan69 Sussex County Airport, Georgetown, DE; by 06May82 in poor condition Salt Lake City, UT; used for spares 1995 by White Industries, Bates City, MO; l/n Aug96; final fate unknown]
110	745	(Ronald J Clark)	N7412 [wfu & stored Jly85 Tucson, AZ; used for spares in support of Go Group Viscounts; b/u around 1993]
111	745	(California Airmotive)	N7413 [wfu & stored Fox Field, Lancaster, CA; b/u 1971]
112	745D	(Aeropesca Colombia)	N7414 OE-LAN N7414 HK-1320 [w/o 26Aug81 Mount Santa Elena, Colombia]
113	745D	(Aloha Airlines)	N7415 OE-LAO N7415 [DBF 18Aug71 Honolulu, HI]
114	745D	(Somali Airlines)	N7416 I-LIRC 6OS-SAN 6O-SAN [wfu & b/u for spares Mogadishu, Somalia; derelict shell l/n Feb93]
115	745D	(Kearney & Trecker Corporation)	N7417 [b/u for spares Feb69; location not recorded]

VICKERS-ARMSTRONGS VISCOUNT

C/n	Model	Last known Owner/Operator	Identities/fates/comments (where appropriate)
116	745D	(British Midland Airways)	N7418 I-LIRE G-AWGV [wfu Apr70; used for training Teesside, UK until b/u; canx 16Apr70 as wfu]
117	745D	(Turbo Aire Holdings Inc)	N7419 N460RC [b/u Aug93 Tucson, AZ; canx Oct01]
118	745D	(Aerolineas TAO)	N7420 G-ARHY PI-C773 N745HA PI-C773 I-LIRT HK-1057 [wfu & stored Bogota-El Dorado, Colombia; l/n 22Sep78; assumed b/u]
119	745D	(Alitalia)	N7421 I-LITS [wfu & stored Sep69; b/u for spares Jly71 Rome-Ciampino, Italy]
120	745D	(California Airmotive)	N7422 [wfu & stored; b/u Nov73 Santa Barbara, CA]
121	745D	(Pittsburgh Institute of Aeronautics)	N7423 [wfu Jan69; donated by United Air Lines & used for ground training; assumed subsequently b/u]
122	745D	(Southern Illinois University)	N7424 [wfu; Jan69; donated by United Air Lines & used for ground training; b/u circa 1986/87]
123	745D	(Lindsay Newspapers)	N7425 [wfu Nov71 and b/u Sarasota, FL]
124	745D	(BKS Air Transport)	N7426 G-ATTA [wfu & stored Jan70 Leeds-Yeadon, UK; canx 24Apr70 as wfu; b/u Nov71]
125	745D	(Associated Products of America)	N7427 [wfu & stored 1975 Wildwood, NJ; b/u1983; canx Apr86]
126	745D	(Servicios Aereos Nacionales)	N7428 [wfu & b/u Oct75 Guayaquil, Ecuador; some derelict parts still present in 1979]
127	745D	(Capital Airlines)	N7429 [w/o 01Dec67 Akron, OH]
128	745D	(United Air Lines)	N7430 [w/o 23Nov62 nr Ellicott City, 16 miles SW of Baltimore, MD]
129	745D	(United Air Lines)	N7431 [w/o 09Jan67 Norfolk, VA]
130	745D	(PLUNA)	N7432 I-LIFS CX-BHA-F CX-BHA [wfu & b/u in 1977 Montevideo, Uruguay]
131	745D	(PLUNA)	N7433 I-LINS CX-BHB-F CX-BHB [wfu & used for spares Jan75 Montevideo, Uruguay]
132	745D	(California Airmotive)	N7434 [wfu & stored Jun68; b/u Nov73 Santa Barbara, CA]
133	745D	(Ronald J Clark)	N7435 [wfu & stored Jly85 Tucson, AZ; canx Jly85 b/u around 1993]
134	745D	(Ronald J Clark)	N7436 [wfu & stored Apr82 Tucson, AZ; canx Dec85; b/u circa 1983]
135	745D	(Capital Airlines)	N7437 [w/o 06Apr58 Tri-City Airport, Saginaw, MI]
136	745D	(Oral Roberts Evangelistic Association)	N7438 [wfu & b/u Dec68 location not recorded; remains to Aero Jet Services]
137	745D	(Ronald J Clark)	N7439 [b/u Tucson, AZ; canx Oct94; Sep99 fuselage donated to Mid Atlantic Air Museum, Reading, PA & used in restoration of c/n 233]
138	745D	Comfama Recreation Park	N7440 HK-1708 [wfu 31Mar91 Medellin, Colombia after being overstressed on flight from Bogota to San Andres Island; donated to Comfama Recreation Park, Rionegro, Colombia; l/n 21Jly05]
139	745D	(Embry-Riddle Aeronautical University)	N7441 [wfu & b/u in 1975 Santa Barbara, CA]
140	759D	(Icelandair)	G-AOGG TF-ISN [wfu & b/u May70 Reykjavik, Iceland]
141	742D	(Brazilian Air Force)	(LN-SUN) FAB-2100+ C-92-2100 [+ Brazil] [w/o 08Dec67 Rio de Janeiro-Santos Dumont, Brazil]
142	757	(Beaver Enterprises)	CF-TGX [wfu & stored Apr73 Winnipeg, MB, Canada; b/u Jun75, location not recorded]
143	757	(Trans-Canada Air Lines)	CF-TGY [w/o 03Oct59 Toronto, ON, Canada]
144	757	Confederate Air Force	CF-TGZ N3832S [arrived in 1982 & preserved Apr97 Confederate Air Force Museum, Brownsville, TX painted as "CF-TGZ"; l/n Jan11]
145	747	(Ansett-ANA)	G-ANYH VH-BUT VH-RMP [wfu & b/u Feb71 Melbourne-Essendon, VIC, Australia]
146	756D	(Trans Australia Airlines)	VH-TVH [wfu & b/u May70 Melbourne-Essendon, VIC, Australia]
147	756D	(Trans Australia Airlines)	VH-TVI [wfu & stored Apr69; b/u May70 Sydney-Mascot, NSW, Australia; canx 13May70]
148	756D	(Trans Australia Airlines)	VH-TVJ [wfu & stored Oct68; b/u Jun70; nose preserved 1999 Caloundra, QLD, Australia]
149	759D	(Icelandair)	G-AOGH TF-ISU [w/o 14Apr63 Nesoy Island, on approach to Oslo-Fornebu, Norway]
150	802	(British European Airways)	(G-AOHA) G-AOJA [w/o 23Oct57 Belfast-Nutts Corner, Northern Ireland; canx 23Oct57]
151	802	(Liverpool Airport Fire Service)	(G-AOHB) G-AOJB [wfu & stored Apr76 Liverpool-Speke Airport, Liverpool, UK; canx 07May76 as wfu; to fire service 19Oct76; b/u Jan89]
152	802	(Wales Aircraft Museum)	(G-AOHC) G-AOJC [wfu & stored Oct75; canx 31Oct75 as wfu; b/u 1996 Cardiff-Rhoose, Wales; fuselage only to Enstone Jly96; subsequently believed moved to unknown location in Leicestershire, UK]

VICKERS-ARMSTRONGS VISCOUNT

C/n	Model	Last known Owner/Operator	Identities/fates/comments (where appropriate)
153	802	(Jersey Airport Fire Service)	(G-AOHD) G-AOJD [to fire service Jersey Airport, Channel Islands, UK in 1976; canx 07May76 as wfu; b/u between Jan-Mar03]
154	802	(British Airways)	(G-AOHE) G-AOJE [wfu & stored Mar80 Cardiff-Rhoose, Wales; used by fire section until b/u Aug81; canx 11Jly84]
155	802	(British Airways)	(G-AOHF) G-AOJF [wfu & stored Feb80 Cardiff-Rhoose, Wales; b/u Aug81; canx 11Jly84]
156	802	(British Airways)	G-AOHG [wfu & stored Apr75 Cardiff-Rhoose, Wales; canx 30May75; used by fire section until b/u Oct75]
157	802	(British Airways)	G-AOHH [wfu & stored 20Nov75 Yeadon, (Leeds-Bradford), UK; canx 12Dec75; b/u 1976]
158	802	(British European Airways)	G-AOHI [w/o 19Jan73 Ben More, Perth, Scotland; canx 12Feb73]
159	802	(British Airways)	G-AOHJ [wfu & stored Apr76 Newcastle, UK; canx 07May76 as wfu; b/u Jly76; tail used in rebuld of c/n 17]
160	802	(British Airways)	G-AOHK [wfu & stored Apr76 Yeadon, (Leeds-Bradford), UK; b/u 1976; canx 07May76 as wfu; forward fuselage sold to Hotel de France, Jersey, Channel Islands & mated to c/n 164]
161	802	(Southend Airport Authority)	G-AOHL [wfu & stored 02Apr80 Cardiff-Rhoose, Wales; Feb81 to cabin service trainer at Southend, UK; canx 27Mar81; by 1989 wfu & dumped, to fire dump by Dec03; remains to Hanningfield Metals, Stock, Essex, UK 11Aug06]
162	802	(Transtel)	G-AOHM (5V-TTI) 3D-OHM [w/o 24Jly01 N'Djamena, Chad; reported b/u late 03]
163	802	(British Airways)	G-AOHN [wfu & stored Aug75 Cardiff-Rhoose, Wales; canx 01Oct75 as wfu; subsequently b/u]
164	802	(Hotel de France)	G-AOHO [wfu May76 Cardiff-Rhoose, Wales; fuselage to Hotel de France, St Helier, Jersey, UK; canx 07May76; b/u early 1984]
165	802	(British European Airways)	G-AOHP [w/o 17Nov57 near Hellerup, Copenhagen, Denmark; canx 04Dec57]
166	802	(British Airways)	G-AOHR [wfu & stored Aug75 Cardiff-Rhoose, Wales; canx as wfu 01Oct75; b/u Jun76; fuselage to St Athan, Wales fire dump, gone by 1988; nose to 192 Sqdn ATC, TAVR Centre, Bridgend, Wales]
167	802	(British Airways)	G-AOHS [wfu & b/u Jun75 Cardiff-Rhoose, Wales; remains to fire dump; canx 11Jly75]
168	802	(British Air Ferries)	G-AOHT ZS-SKY G-AOHT [wfu & stored Southend, UK Jly87; b/u Mar91; canx 21Jly94; later cockpit reported at Stock, Essex, UK]
169	802	(British European Airways)	G-AOHU [w/o 07Jan60 London-Heathrow, London, UK; canx 19Jan60]
170	802	Mango Airlines	G-AOHV G-BLNB G-OPFI 3D-PFI 5V-TTP 3D-PFI+ "TU-TAB"^ 3D-PFI+ 9Q-COD [+ illegal use of marks; ^ at one time reported as TU-VAB, these marks also used on a F-28; reported in good condition 25Nov09 Lubumbashi, Democratic Republic of Congo]
171	802	(Birmingham Airport Fire Service)	(G-AOHW) G-AORD [wfu Dec75 Birmingham-Elmdon, UK; used by local fire service, until 1976; canx 19Jan76]
172	803	(Aer Lingus)	PH-VIA EI-AOG [wfu & stored Oct69 Dublin, Ireland; b/u Jly72; canx 26Jly72]
173	803	(Aer Lingus)	PH-VIB EI-AOJ [wfu & stored Nov70 Dublin, Ireland; b/u Jan73; canx 22Jan73]
174	803	(Aer Lingus)	PH-VIC (EI-AOK) EI-APD [wfu & stored Oct70 Dublin, Ireland; canx 31Oct70; b/u May71]
175	803	(Airwork Services)	PH-VID EI-AOL G-AYTW (506)+ [+ Oman; canx 21Jan72 to Ireland but sold in Oman & not delivered; wfu 1973 for spares Bournemouth-Hurn, UK; DBF 12Oct75 in fire fighting exhibition]
176	803	(Aer Lingus)	PH-VIE EI-AOF [w/o 22Jun67 2 miles N of Ashbourne, Dublin, Ireland]
177	803	(Aer Lingus)	PH-VIF EI-AOE HB-ILP EI-AOE [wfu & stored Nov69 Dublin, Ireland; canx Nov69; b/u Jly72]
178	803	(Aer Lingus)	PH-VIG EI-AOM [w/o 24Mar68 into Irish Sea, 80kms from Tuskar Rock, off the Wexford Coast, Ireland; canx 24Mar68]
179	803	(Aer Lingus)	PH-VIH EI-AOI [wfu & stored Oct71 Dublin, Ireland; canx 03Jan7]; b/u Dec72]
180	803	Irish Aviation Museum	PH-VII EI-AOH [wfu & stored Nov70 Dublin, Ireland; canx 03Jan72; b/u Dec72, nose & cockpit preserved by Irish Aviation Museum, Dublin; nose section l/n 28Nov08 Castlemoate House, Dublin, in barn in bad condition]
181	756D	(Trans Australia Airlines)	VH-TVK [wfu & b/u May70 Sydney-Mascot, NSW, Australia; canx 13May70]
182	701C	Fundacao Museu da Tecnologia	G-AOFX PP-SRS [wfu & stored Feb69; preserved Jan71 Sao Paulo, Brazil; no recent reports]
183	764D	(Servicios Aereos Nacionales)	N905 N905G HC-BEM [w/o 29Dec77 near Cuenca, Ecuador]
184	764D	(Viscount Unlimited Inc)	N906 N906RB [wfu & stored Apr93 Tucson, AZ; b/u for spares; canx Jan98 as scrapped]
185	764D	(Servicios Aereos Nacionales)	N907 XB-WOW N907G HC-BCL [w/o 04Sep77 in mountains near Cuenca, Ecuador]

VICKERS-ARMSTRONGS VISCOUNT

C/n	Model	Last known Owner/Operator	Identities/fates/comments (where appropriate)
186	760D	(British Midland Airways)	VR-HFI (VR-RCH) 9M-ALY (VR-AAU) VR-AAW G-AWCV [wfu & stored 28Nov69; 16 Apr70 ferried Newcastle, UK; canx 16Apr70 as wfu; b/u for spares May70]
187	760D	(Aden Airways)	VR-HFJ VR-SEE 9M-AMS VR-AAV [DBR by bomb 30Jun67 Khormaksar Airport, Aden]
188	761D	(Union of Burma Airways)	XY-ADF [w/o 24Aug72 Akyab, Burma]
189	761D	(MMM Aero Services)	XY-ADG ZS-JVY A2-ABY 3D-ACV ZS-JVY 9Q-CVL [wfu and b/u Mar93 Kinshasa, Zaire]
190	761D	(Southern International Air Transport)	XY-ADH G-APZN XY-ADH 9Q-CRH XY-ADH G-APZN [UK marks not officially restored; stored 31Jly79 Eastleigh, UK, wfu Nov79; b/u 21Jan80]
191	765D	(Walter L. Cole)	N306 N140RA [stored Jun86 Tucson, AZ; b/u mid-1997; canx Aug97]
192	768D	(Indian Airlines)	(VT-DIE) VT-DIO [w/o 11Sep63 51kms south of Agra, India]
193	768D	(Indian Airlines)	VT-DIF [wfu & stored Aug70 Delhi-Palam, India; b/u 1971]
194	768D	(Indian Airlines)	VT-DIG [wfu & stored 09Feb71 Delhi-Palam, India; b/u 1971]
195	768D	(Indian Airlines)	VT-DIH [w/o 15Nov61 Colombo-Ratmalana Airport, Ceylon]
196	768D	(Lane Xang Airlines)	VT-DII XW-PNG [wfu & stored Bangkok-Don Muang, Thailand; by Sep92 b/u]
197	756D	(Toowoomba Aviation Museum)	VH-TVL [wfu & stored Aug69 ; donated & preserved Oct71 Toowoomba, QLD, Australia; by Apr89 moved to local timber yard; l/n 06Oct08 – fuselage only]
198	745D	(Shackleton Aviation)	N7442 G-ARUU XR802 [wfu & stored May72; b/u Feb73 Coventry-Baginton, UK; b/u Feb73]
199	745D	(California Airmotive)	N7443 [wfu & b/u Feb68 Burbank, CA]
200	745D	(California Airmotive)	N7444 [wfu & b/u Mar68 Burbank, CA]
201	745D	(Wings of History – California Antique Aircraft Museum)	N7445 N923RC N923RA N500TL N220RC XA-MOS N220RC [preserved Mar92 San Martin, CA part b/u; Oct93 parts except front fuselage to Davis-Monthan AFB, AZ]
202	745D	(California Airmotive)	N7446 [wfu & b/u Feb68 Burbank, CA]
203	745D	(California Airmotive)	N7447 [wfu & b/u Feb68 Burbank, CA]
204	745D	(SAETA)	N7448 HC-AYZ [wfu & sold to Aeropesca Colombia for spares; b/u Feb80 Quito, Ecuador]
205	745D	(Aerolineas Condor)	N7449 HC-BHB [w/o 14Jly80 Loja-Camilo Ponce Enriquez Airport, Ecuador]
206	745D	(Trans Florida Airlines)	N7450 [wfu & stored Jly88 Daytona Beach, FL; subsequently b/u]
207	745D	(Aero Flite)	N7451 [wfu & b/u May70 Twin Falls, OH]
208	745D	(Aero Flite)	N7452 [wfu & b/u May70 Cody, NY; remains to Westernair, Albuquerque, NM]
209	745D	(California Airmotive)	N7454 [wfu & b/u Jan68 Burbank, CA]
210	745D	(California Airmotive)	N7455 [wfu & b/u Apr68 Burbank, CA]
211	745D	(Kearney & Trecker Corporation)	N7456 N1898K [wfu & stored Aug76 Milwaukee, WI; b/u Nov03]
212	745D	(Aeropesca Colombia)	N7457 YS-28C HK-1773 HK-2382 [w/o 26Mar82 in mountains, 130kms SE of Bogota, Colombia]
213	745D	(James Stanley Leasing)	N7458 XA-CIN XA-COT (N7458) [wfu & stored Mar89 Tucson, AZ; b/u Oct93 still as XC-COT]
214	745D	(McKinnon Enterprises)	N7459 [wfu & stored Apr68 Victoria, BC, Canada; b/u Jan69]
215	745D	(Essex Wire Corp)	N7460 [wfu & b/u Jly72 Fort Wayne, IN]
216	745D	(California Airmotive)	N7461 [wfu & b/u Feb68 Burbank, CA]
217	745D	(Capital Airlines)	N7462 [w/o 18Jan60 Holdcroft, Charles City, VA]
218	757	(Wabush Mines)	CF-THA [wfu & b/u for spares Sep76; location not recorded]
219	757	Mr Don Fyk	CF-THB [stored Jun75 Teulon, MB, Canada; 1982 dismantled & by road to Garland, MB, Canada & preserved; canx Jan86; l/n 07Apr07]
220	757	(Beaver Enterprises)	CF-THC [b/u after Jun75, location not recorded]
221	757	(Air Canada)	CF-THD [wfu & stored Teulon, MB, Canada Jun69; b/u Sep71]
222	757	(R Wiklund)	CF-THE [wfu & stored Winnipeg, MB, Canada Jun69; b/u Sep71]
223	757	(Beaver Enterprises)	CF-THF [wfu & stored Teulon, MB, Canada Jun75; in 1980s without outer wings marked as "B-LAMM" and "Ontario Central"; subsequently b/u]
224	757	British Columbia Aviation Museum	CF-THG C-FTHG [wfu & stored Sep79 Vancouver, BC, Canada; 10Jun80 to Pacific Vocational Institute as GIA; preserved Apr05 Victoria, BC, Canada]
225	745D	(Northeast Airlines)	(N7463) G-16-4 EI-AJW G-APNF 9K-ACD G-APNF [wfu & stored Apr70 Leeds-Bradford, UK; canx 23Apr70; Sep70 b/u & burnt Newcastle-Woolsington, UK]
226	745D	(SAETA)	(N7464) G-APBH N6599C N1298 N1298G XC-POV [wfu & used for spares Apr76 Quito, Ecuador]
227	745D	(Skyline Sweden)	(N7465) VH-TVO PI-C772 SE-CNK [wfu & stored Aug76 Malmo-Sturup, Sweden; b/u Nov77 to Mar78; canx 11Nov77; front fuselage preserved Malmo Tekniska Museet, Malmo, Sweden]

VICKERS-ARMSTRONGS VISCOUNT

C/n	Model	Last known Owner/Operator	Identities/fates/comments (where appropriate)
228	745D	(Turbo Aire Holdings Inc)	(N7466) G-16-3 EI-AJV G-16-3 G-APNG CF-RBC N505W N24V [wfu & stored Jun86 Tucson, AZ; canx Dec91; b/u post Dec96]
229	745D	(Turbo Aire Holdings Inc)	(N7467) G-APFR CF-DTA N660RC [wfu Jun90 Tucson, AZ; b/u Aug93; canx Oct01]
230	745D	(James Stanley Leasing Corp)	(N7468) G-16-6 G-APLX N6595C N776M N27DH N776M [wfu & stored Aug88 Tucson, AZ; b/u Aug93]
231	745D	(United Air Lines)	(N7469) N7465 [w/o 28Nov67 Raleigh-Durham, NC]
232	745D	(Aeropesca Colombia)	(N7470) N6590C N7416 HK-1319X HK-1319 [wfu & stored Jan82 Bogota-El Dorado, Colombia; b/u Nov82]
233	745D	Mid-Atlantic Air Museum	(N7471) N6591C N820BK N1898T N98KT N555SL N7471 [preserved May92, Reading, PA]
234	745D	(Northeast Airlines)	(N7472) N6592C [w/o 15Nov61 Boston, MA after collision with National Airlines DC-6B N8228H c/n 43821]
235	772	(Commerce International)	VP-TBS 9Y-TBS YV-C-AMU 9Y-TBS [wfu & stored Sep70 Port of Spain, Trinidad; b/u Dec72]
236	772	(Commerce International)	VP-TBT 9Y-TBT [wfu Sep70; used by Port of Spain, Trinidad fire service; DBF by 1974]
237	772	(Commerce International)	VP-TBU 9Y-TBU [wfu & stored Sep70 Port of Spain, Trinidad; b/u by 1974]
238	772	(Commerce International)	VP-TBX 9Y-TBX [wfu & stored Sep70 Port of Spain, Trinidad; b/u by Sep73]
239	754D	(Middle East Airlines-Air Liban)	OD-ACT [destroyed on ground in military action 28Dec68 Beirut, Lebanon]
240	754D	(Air Zimbabwe)	OD-ACU JY-ACI OD-ACU VP-WAR ZS-JPU 3D-AAL ZS-JPU VP-WAR Z-WAR [wfu & b/u Mar85 Harare, Zimbabwe]
241	754D	(Air Zimbabwe)	OD-ACV VP-YTE(1) 7Q-YDL ZS-KJG VP-WJI Z-WJI [wfu & stored Jun84 Harare, Zimbabwe; subsequently b/u]
242	754D	(Aloha Airlines)	OD-ACW N7410 [w/o 27Jun69 Honolulu, HI in ground collision with Hawaiian Airlines DC-9-31 N906H c/n 47171]
243	754D	Trans Service Airlift	(G-APCD) OD-ADD JY-ACK OD-ADD VP-YTE(2) ZS-JUJ A2-ABD ZS-JUJ VP-YTE(2) Z-YTE 9Q-CVF [active until mid-90s; not in 2004 official register; presumably b/u]
244	754D	(Middle East Airlines)	(G-APCE) OD-ADE [w/o 01Feb63 near Ankara, Turkey, after mid-air collision with Turkish AF C-47, 43-6028, c/n 19668]
245	754D	(Middle East Airlines-Air Liban)	OD-ACX [w/o 21Apr64 El Arish, Gaza Strip]
246	754D	(Turkish Air Force)	OD-ACY TC-SEC 246 [wfu & stored Jly88 Etimesgut, Ankara, Turkey; later moved to fire dump; b/u by Oct01]
247	779D	(Indian Airlines)	LN-FOM OE-LAE LN-FOM G-ARBW LN-FOM VT-DOD [wfu & stored Jly71 Delhi-Palam, India; subsequently b/u]
248	804	(British World Airlines)	G-AOXU SP-LVC ZK-NAI VQ-GAB G-CSZB (N141RA) [wfu & stored 15Oct96 Southend, UK; CofA expired 24Jan97; canx 19Aug98; b/u Sep98; parts to Moorabbin Air Museum, VIC, Australia to assist in restoration of VH-TVR c/n 318; cockpit preserved East Midlands Aeropark, UK]
249	804	(LOT-Polish Airlines)	G-AOXV SP-LVA [w/o 20Aug65 St Trond, 26kms W of Liege, Belgium]
250	779D	(Huns Air)	LN-FOH OE-LAB LN-FOH G-APZP LN-FOH VT-DOE [wfu & used for spares in 1980, probably at Bombay-Santa Cruz, India]
251	779D	(Huns Air)	LN-FOI OE-LAC LN-FOI VT-DOH [wfu & stored Apr71 Bombay-Santa Cruz, India; b/u post Jan86]
252	779D	(Indian Airlines)	LN-FOK OE-LAD LN-FOK VT-DOI [wfu & stored Mar71 Delhi-Palam, India; subsequently b/u]
253	802	(Newcastle Airport Fire Service)	(G-AORC) G-AOHW [wfu Nov75; canx 17Nov75 as wfu; to fire service 18 May76 Newcastle, UK; l/n in 1986 derelict]
254	802	(British European Airways)	(G-AORD) G-AORC [w/o 28Apr58 Craigie, 4½ miles ENE of Prestwick, Scotland; canx 02May58]
255	806	(British European Airways)	G-AOYF [DBR 20Oct57 Johannesburg, South Africa; some of the remains used in the building of c/n 418 G-APOX; canx 04Sep58]
256	806	(British Air Ferries)	G-AOYG [wfu Feb92 Southend, UK; b/u Jan94; canx 07Mar94]
257	806	(Caicos International Airways)	(G-AOYH) G-AOYI G-LOND G-AOYI G-LOND [wfu & stored 20Jun88 Southend, UK; canx 17Jun92; b/u Feb93; remains noted Feb94 at Stock, Essex, UK]
258	805	(Aer Lingus)	(G-AOYI) G-APDW VR-BAX CF-MCJ EI-AMA [wfu & stored Jan70 Dublin, Ireland; b/u May72]
259	806	(British World Airlines)	G-AOYJ G-BLOA [wfu & stored Jly93 Southend, UK; derelict by Jan94; b/u Aug96; canx 07Jly98]
260	806	(Mandala Airlines)	G-AOYK PK-RVK [w/o 07Jan76 Manado, Sulawesi, Indonesia]
261	806	(British Air Ferries)	G-AOYL [wfu for spares Sep87 Southend, UK; b/u Feb93; canx 22Jun94]

VICKERS-ARMSTRONGS VISCOUNT

C/n	Model	Last known Owner/Operator	Identities/fates/comments (where appropriate)
262	806	(Lineas Aereas Canarias)	G-AOYM EC-DYC [wfu & stored May89 Tenerife (North) Los Rodeos Airport, Canary Islands, Spain; later to La Granja Park, Santa Cruz, Canary Islands as a night club; b/u in 1995]
263	806	(British World Airlines)	G-AOYN G-OPAS [wfu & stored Jun96 Southend, UK; b/u Feb97, forward fuselage to Duxford Museum; canx 28Jly97; loaned Dec06 to Bournemouth Aviation Museum]
264	806	ex Lineas Aereas Canarias	G-AOYO EC-DXU [wfu & stored May89 Tenerife (North) Los Rodeos Airport, Canary Islands, Spain; l/n 07Jun12]
265	806	(Heli-Jet Aviation Ltd)	G-AOYP G-PFBT 3D-PBH [wfu & stored Lanseria Airport, Johannesburg, South Africa; b/u Apr06]
266	806	(British World Airlines)	G-AOYR [wfu & stored 20Apr94 Southend, UK; b/u Jun96; canx 07Jly98]
267	806	(British Air Ferries)	G-AOYS [wfu & stored Jan84 Southend, UK; b/u Feb85; canx 30Nov88]
268	806	Mandala Airlines	G-AOYT B-3001 B-2035 PK-RVT [w/o 13Jan85 Yogyakarta-Adisutjipto Airport, Indonesia; subsequently b/u for spares]
269	757	(Air Canada)	CF-THH [wfu & stored Sep68 Manitoba, MB, Canada; b/u Jly70 by Gaulet Enterprises, of St Malo, MB, Canada]
270	757	Canada Aviation Museum	CF-THI [preserved Nov69 Rockcliffe, Ottawa, ON, Canada]
271	757	(Air Canada)	CF-THK [w/o 07Apr69 Sept-Iles Airport, QC, Canada]
272	757	(Zaire Aero Service)	CF-THL [b/u for spares 1979 in Canada, probably at Winnipeg, MB]
273	757	(National Research Council)	CF-THM [wfu & stored Winnipeg, MB, Canada; b/u Aug84]
274	757	(Beaver Enterprises)	CF-THN [wfu & stored 10Jun75 Winnipeg, MB, Canada; b/u Aug84]
275	757	(Beaver Enterprises)	CF-THO [b/u post Jun75 Winnipeg, MB, Canada]
276	757	(Beaver Enterprises)	CF-THP [wfu & stored 04Dec73 Winnipeg, MB, Canada; b/u Aug84]
277	757	ex Bazair	CF-THQ 9Q-CTU [wfu & stored 1998 Boende, Democratic Republic of the Congo; l/n 09Sep04]
278	757	(Beaver Enterprises)	CF-THR [wfu & stored Jun75 Winnipeg, MB, Canada; subsequently b/u]
279	757	Western Canada Aviation Museum	CF-THS [preserved Nov82 Winnipeg, MB, Canada]
280	781D	(Bazair)	150+ ZS-LPR 9Q-CWL [+ South Africa] [w/o 06Jun97 40kms west of Bunia, Democratic Republic of Congo]
281	807	(Gibraltar Airways)	ZK-BRD G-BBVH [w/o 23Nov88 Tangier, Morocco; canx 07Feb89]
282	807	(Southern International)	ZK-BRE VP-LKA VP-LAU G-CSZA (N140RA) [wfu & stored 22Dec80 Stansted, UK; b/u Sep82 for spares; canx 04Oct82]
283	807	Ferrymead Aeronautical Society	ZK-BRF [wfu 15Jly74; donated for preservation 10Apr75; moved 28Jan00 to Ferrymead Historic Park, Christchurch, New Zealand; l/n 17Mar08]
284	745D	Francesco de Pinedo Technical College	(N7473) N6594C I-LIRG [wfu & stored 14Jan70 Rome-Ciampino, Italy; Jly71 to GIA in Rome, Italy; l/n 08Apr12]
285	745D	(Heslin & Associates)	(N7474) N7464 [b/u late 1968 Trenton, NJ]
286	745D	(BKS Air Transport)	(N7475) N6593C N746HA YS-07C G-AVED [wfu & stored Apr70; canx 22Apr70; b/u Nov70 Newcastle-Woolsington, UK]
287	745D	(Capital Airlines)	(N7476) N7463 [w/o 12May59 Chase, MD]
288	745D	(SAETA)	(N7477) N6596C I-LIRM HC-ART [w/o 03Jun70 Cuenca, Ecuador]
289	808	(Aer Lingus)	EI-AJI [wfu & stored Oct69 Dublin, Ireland; canx 31Oct69; b/u May72]
290	808	(Aer Lingus)	EI-AJJ [wfu & stored Dec69 Dublin, ireland; canx 31Oct69; b/u May72]
291	808	(British World Airlines)	EI-AJK HB-ILR G-BBDK G-OPFE [w/o 24Mar96 Belfast-Aldergrove, Northern Ireland; canx 10May96; wreck b/u May96]
292	768D	(Indian Airlines)	VT-DIX [w/o 09Aug71 Jaipur, India]
293	768D	(Indian Airlines)	VT-DIZ [wfu & stored 13Jan72 Delhi-Palam, India; subsequently b/u]
294	768D	(J D Melvin)	VT-DJA XW-TFK+ XU-LAM RDPL-34016 N92622 [+ marks not confirmed; US marks probably ntu; stored 1985 Bangkok, Thailand, then b/u; canx 28Mar11]
295	768D	(Royal Air Lao)	VT-DJB XW-PNJ+ [+ marks not confirmed; fate not clear; also reported as wfu & stored Feb71 Delhi-Palam, India; reported painted in camouflage before b/u]
296	768D	(Huns Air)	VT-DJC [w/o 28Aug80 Vijayawada, Andhra Pradesh, India]
297	782D	(Air Rhodesia)	EP-AHA VP-WAS [w/o 03Sep78 when hit by missile in Whamira Hills, near Karoi, 16kms from Lake Kariba, Rhodesia]
298	782D	(Trans Service Airlift)	EP-AHB VP-WAT Z-WAT 9Q-CKK [wfu & stored Dec93 Kinshasa-N'Djili Airport, Democratic Republic of Congo; 1994 b/u]
299	782D	(Iran Airlines)	EP-AHC [w/o 15Feb65 Isfahan, Iran; subsequently b/u]
300	784D	ex Malmo Aero	PI-C770 SE-CNL [wfu & b/u for spares Oct72 Malmo-Bulltofta, Sweden; remains moved to Stockholm-Arlanda, Sweden for fire training; l/n 21Apr05]
301	757	(Air Canada)	CF-THJ [built using parts from c/n 90; wfu & stored 21Jan69 Winnipeg, MB, Canada; b/u Jly71]
302	757	(Air Canada)	CF-THT [w/o 13Jun64 Toronto-Malton, Canada]
303	757	(Zaire Aero Service)	CF-THU 9Q-CPD [w/o 28Aug84 Kinshasa-N'Djii Airport, Zaire]

VICKERS-ARMSTRONGS VISCOUNT

C/n	Model	Last known Owner/Operator	Identities/fates/comments (where appropriate)
304	757	(Zaire Aero Service)	CF-THV 9Q-CKB [wfu & stored 1982 Kinshasa-N'Dolo Airport, Zaire; subsequently b/u]
305	757	(Zaire Aero Service)	CF-THW 9Q-CPJ [wfu & stored Mar84 Kinshasa-N'Dolo Airport, Zaire; b/u Sep84]
306	757	(Pratt & Whitney Canada)	CF-THX [wfu & b/u for spares in 1977; location not recorded]
307	757	(Zaire Aero Service)	CF-THY 9Q-CKS [wfu & stored 1985 Kinshasa-N'Dolo Airport, Zaire; presumed b/u]
308	757	(Aero Leasing & Sales)	CF-THZ C-FTHZ [wfu & stored 1982 Montreal-Dorval, QC, Canada; canx Nov96; l/n Mar97; b/u; nose & tail reported in downtown Montreal]
309	757	(Air Canada)	CF-TIA [wfu & stored 23Aug72; b/u Jun73 Winnipeg, MB, Canada]
310	757	(Air Charter Service)	CF-TIB 9Q-CPP C-FTIB 9Q-CTS [w/o 1988 Tshikapa, Zaire; l/n derelict Apr92]
311	806	(British Air Ferries)	G-AOYH C-GWPY G-BNAA [wfu & stored May87 Southend, UK; derelict by Feb90; canx 26Feb91; b/u 11Jly91 by Hanningfield Metals; nose section noted Feb94 Stock, Essex, UK]
312	805	(Aer Lingus)	G-APDX VR-BAY EI-ALG [wfu & stored Nov69 Dublin, Ireland; canx 31Oct69; b/u May72]
313	821		[not built; ordered by Eagle Aviation; canx before construction]
314	821		[not built; ordered by Eagle Aviation; canx before construction]
315	821		[not built; ordered by Eagle Aviation; canx before construction]
316	827	(PLUNA)	G-AOYV PP-SRH CX-BIZ (N460RC) [wfu & stored; canx01Mar82; preserved 1986 Montevideo-Carrasco Airport, Uruguay; by Nov95 moved to fire dump; l/n 2003 in local scrap yard]
317	818	(South African Airways)	CU-N621 CU-T621 ZS-CVA [w/o 13Mar67 into sea 35kms from East London, South Africa]
318	816	Australian National Avn Museum	CU-N622 CU-T622 (ZS-CVB) VH-TVR(2) [wfu & stored 04 Apr70 Melbourne-Essendon, VIC, Australia; donated & preserved Jun70 Melbourne-Moorabbin, VIC, Australia]
319	818	ex Asian Aviation Services	CU-N623 CU-T623 VH-RML B-2019 PK-MVK [wfu & stored Feb83; last known preserved in bad condition in closed Tienyuantzium Amusement Park, T'u Lou, Taiwan]
320	835	(Ray Charles Enterprises)	CU-N624 CU-T624 N500T N500TL N923RC [w/o 19Oct85 Monroe County Airport, IN; remains sold to Go Group for spares]
321	769D	Jadepoint USA	CX-AQN N410RC [wfu & stored Jan88 Tucson, AZ; b/u 1990]
322	769D	(PLUNA)	CX-AQO [w/o 11May75 Buenos Aires-Jorge Newbery Airport, Argentina]
323	769D	(PLUNA)	CX-AQP [wfu & stored 11Jan67 Montevideo-Carrasco, Uruguay; b/u Jly69; remains l/n Apr74]
324	784D	(Malmo Aero)	PI-C771 YS-06C PI-C771 SE-CNM [wfu & stored Aug71; b/u Oct71 Malmo-Bulltofta, Sweden]
325	785D	Somalia Airlines	I-LIFE 6OS-AAK 6O-SAK [wfu & stored Jun77 Mogadishu, Somalia; b/u Nov79]
326	785D	(Alitalia)	I-LIFT [b/u Jly71 Rome-Ciampino, Italy; remains to Aerolineas TAO for spares use]
327	785D	(Aerolineas TAO)	I-LILI HK-1061X HK-1061 [wfu & stored Jan75 Bogota-El Dorado, Colombia; b/u; l/n Nov79]
328	785D	(Alitalia)	I-LAKE [w/o 28Mar64 into Mount Somma on approach to Naples, Italy]
329	785D	(SAETA)	I-LARK HC-AVP [w/o 23Apr79 Pastaza Province, en-route Quito to Cuenca, Ecuador]
330	785D	(Alitalia)	I-LOTT [b/u Jly71 Rome-Ciampino, Italy; remains to Aerolineas TAO for spares use; remains l/n 03Oct72]
331	773	(Iraqi Airways)	YI-ACU [w/o 09Mar65 Cairo, Egypt]
332	786D	(Aeropesca Colombia)	HK-943X HK-943 (CU-P633) YS-08C (VT-DNR) YS-08C [wfu & b/u for spares Jan76 San Salvador, El Salvador]
333	786D	(BKS Air Transport)	(HK-946X) AN-AKP YS-11C (VT-DNS) G-AVIY [wfu & stored Yeadon (Leeds-Bradford), UK Apr70; canx 24Apr70; b/u Jun70 Wymeswold, UK]
334	786D	(Go Group Unlimited)	(HK-947X) AN-AKQ N200Q HC-BDL XA-MOS (N65337) [wfu & stored Jun84 Tucson, AZ; b/u Aug93; canx 03Mar11]
335	815	(Pakistan International Airlines)	AP-AJC [w/o 18May59 Rawalpindi, Pakistan]
336	815	(British Midland Airways)	AP-AJD G-AVJA (LX-LGE) [w/o 20Mar69 Manchester-Ringway, UK; canx 11Apr69]
337	815	(Pakistan International Airlines)	AP-AJE [w/o 14Aug59 Karachi, Pakistan]
338	814	Home Office	D-ANUN G-BAPF SE-FOY G-BAPF [wfu & canx 17Jun92; to the Home Office Fire Training Centre, Moreton-in-Marsh, UK for non-destructive training; l/n 08Sep07]

VICKERS-ARMSTRONGS VISCOUNT

C/n	Model	Last known Owner/Operator	Identities/fates/comments (where appropriate)
339	814	(British Midland Airways)	D-ANOL G-AWXI [w/o 22Jan70 London-Heathrow, UK; canx 16Mar70; remains to East Midlands Airport, UK Mar70 for use as spares; front fuselage to National Diving Centre, Stoney Cove, Leicestershire & sunk for dive training; l/n Feb07]
340	814	(British Midland Airways)	D-ANAD G-BAPD SE-FOX G-BAPD [wfu & stored Sep78 East Midlands Airport, UK; b/u Jan79; wings used in rebuild of G-BMAT c/n 349; canx 02Jly81]
341	814	(Viscount Unlimited Inc)	D-ANIP G-BAPE 4X-AVI G-BAPE N401RA N145RA [wfu & stored Feb88 Tucson, AZ; in poor condition by Aug97; l/n 26May01; b/u Mar02]
342	814	(West African Air Cargo)	D-ANUR G-AZNH 503+ G-AZNH 9G-ACL [+ Oman] [w/o 10Jun78 Monrovia-Payne Field, Liberia]
343	814	(Airwork Services)	D-ANEF (G-AZNP) (504)+ [+ Oman] [w/o 28Jan72 Bournemouth-Hurn, UK whilst on delivery; canx 24Feb72]
344	814	(Ali Finance Ltd)	D-ANIZ G-BAPG 4X-AVH G-BAPG (SE-KBU) G-BAPG [wfu & stored 01Aug89 Southend, UK; canx 17Jun92; b/u Jun97]
345	789D	Museu Aeroespacial	2101+ C-92-2101+ [+ Brazil] [wfu 1970; preserved Delio Jardim de Mattos Airfield, Rio de Janeiro, Brazil; l/n Mar07]
346	813	CAA Fire School	ZS-CDT (ZS-SBT) G-AZLP [wfu & stored Nov83 Teesside, UK; 1986 to local CAA fire school; canx 19Dec86]
347	813	(British Midland Airways)	ZS-CDU (ZS-SBU) G-AZLR [wfu 1983; canx 26Apr90; Dec96 to cabin services trainer East Midlands Airport, UK; b/u Mar97]
348	813	CAA Fire School	ZS-CDV (ZS-SBV) G-AZLS [wfu & stored Nov82 Teesside, UK; 1986 to local CAA fire school; canx 19Dec86]
349	813	(British Air Ferries)	ZS-CDW (ZS-SBW) G-AZLT G-BMAT+ G-OHOT [+ rebuilt using wings from c/n 340; w/o 25Feb94 Stowe-by-Chartley, near Uttoxeter, UK; canx 07Jly94]
350	813	ex British Midland Airways	ZS-CDX (ZS-SBX) ZS-CDX (G-AZLU) G-AZNA [wfu & stored Oct90 Southend, UK; canx 17Jun92; by Sep92 preserved outside night club Zomergem, near Ghent, Belgium; l/n 2007]
351	813	(British Midland Airways)	ZS-CDY (ZS-SBY) ZS-CDY (G-AZLV) G-AZNB [CofA expired 08May83; canx 19Dec88 as wfu; b/u 1987 Teesside. UK]
352	813	CAA Fire School	ZS-CDZ (ZS-SBZ) ZS-CDZ (G-AZLW) G-AZNC [wfu & stored Feb82 Teesside, UK; 1986 used for non-destructive training; canx 27Oct88; l/n Mar02]
353	812	(Bouraq Indonesia Airlines)	N240V N501T N501TL B-2037 PK-IVS [w/o 26Aug80 25kms NE of Jakarta, Indonesia]
354	812	(Continental Airlines)	N243V [w/o 08Jly62 Amarillo, TX]
355	812	(Merpati Nusantara Airlines)	N241V VH-RMK B-2021 PK-MVO [wfu 1983 Jakarta-Soekamo Hatta, Indonesia; reported Oct05 b/u]
356	812	(Continental Airlines)	N242V [w/o 28Jan63 Kansas City-Salina Municipal Airport, KS]
357	812	(Alidair)	N244V G-ATUE [wfu & stored May72 East Midlands Airport, UK; b/u Jly77; canx 17Jan78; nose section extant in local scrap yard until Mar78]
358	812	(Far Eastern Air Transport)	N245V G-AVIW B-2031 PK-IVR B-2031 [b/u post Feb83 Kaohsiung, Gaoxiong, Taiwan]
359	812	(Channel Airways)	N246V G-AVHK [wfu & stored May70 Southend, UK; b/u Jun72; canx 21Mar73]
360	812	(Channel Airways)	N248V G-AVJZ [w/o 03May67 Southend, UK; canx 13Jun67]
361	812	(Channel Airways)	N249V G-AVNJ [wfu & stored Oct69 Southend, UK; b/u Jun72; canx 22Nov72]
362	812	(Channel Airways)	G-APPC N250V G-APPC [wfu & stored Sep68 Southend, UK; b/u Jun72; canx 21Mar73]
363	812	(Channel Airways)	N251V (G-AVGY) G-AVHE [wfu & stored 30May70 Southend, UK; b/u Jun72; canx 14Feb73; nose section preserved Albatros Flugmuseum, Stuttgart, Germany; l/n Jly07]
364	812	(Channel Airways)	(N252V) G-APPU N252V G-APPU [w/o 04May68 Southend, UK; canx 04May68]
365	812	(Stansted Fire School)	N253V G-ATVR [wfu & stored 30Sep72 Stansted, UK; Jly72 to May80 used by local fire school; canx 14Mar77]
366	812	(Channel Airways)	N254V G-ATVE [wfu & stored 26Oct69 Southend, UK; b/u Jun72; canx 22Nov72]
367	800		[aircraft not built]
368	814	Flugausstellung Junior	D-ANAM [wfu Jly70 Hamburg, Germany & used for apprentice training; Oct76 preserved Hermeskeil, Germany, marked as "814"; l/n Apr08]
369	814	Flugzeug Restaurant Silbervogel	D-ANAB [wfu & stored Dec69; circa 1970 in use as cafe Eschershausen, Hanover, Germany; 2002 moved to Ricklingen, Hanover, Germany; l/n Jun07]
370	814	(British Midland Airways)	D-ANAC G-AYOX 4X-AVA G-AYOX [wfu & stored Jan84 Teesside, UK; dismantled 04Sep86 & by road to Southend, UK for use as cabin trainer; b/u May92 by Hanningfield Metals, remains to Stock, Essex, UK; canx 24Feb87]
371	838	(Royal Air Force)	9G-AAV XT661 [wfu Feb89; sold for scrap Jly93; b/u at DRA Bedford, UK, remains to Hanningfield Metals, Stock, Essex, UK]

VICKERS-ARMSTRONGS VISCOUNT

C/n	Model	Last known Owner/Operator	Identities/fates/comments (where appropriate)
372	838	(Skyline Sweden)	9G-AAW G-BDKZ (PK-RVO) G-BDKZ SE-FOZ [w/o 15Jan77 Stockholm-Bromma, Sweden]
373	756D	(Trans Australia Airlines)	VH-TVM [wfu & b/u May70 Melbourne-Essendon, VIC, Australia; canx 13May70]
374	756D	(Air Zimbabwe)	VH-TVN A2-ZEL VP-YNI Z-YNI [wfu & stored Jly84; used by fire service, Harare Airport, Zimbabwe]
375	815	(Baltic Aviation)	AP-AJF G-AVJB (LX-LGD) G-AVJB SE-IVY [wfu Apr89; Jan90 to High Chaparal Wild West Theme Park, Hillerstorp, Sweden; 2003 DBF]
376	815	(Luxair)	AP-AJG LX-LGC [w/o 22Dec69 Luxembourg-Findel, Luxembourg; wreck b/u May70]
377	785D	(SAETA)	I-LIRS HC-ARS [w/o 15Aug76 near peak of Chimborazo Volcano en-route from Quito to Cuenca, Ecuador]
378	785D	(Alitalia)	I-LIZT [w/o 21Dec59 Rome-Ciampino, Italy]
379	785D	(Somali Airlines)	I-LIRP 6OS-AAJ 6O-AAJ [w/o 06May70 Mogadishu, Somalia]
380	785D	(Aerolineas TAO)	I-LIZO HK-1058 [w/o 08Jun74 Monte San Isidro, W of Cucuta, Colombia]
381	806	(British Air Ferries)	G-APEX [wfu & stored 26Mar84 Southend, UK; canx 14Feb90; b/u 1994]
382	806	ex Global Airways	G-APEY 3C-PBH 3D-JAP 9Q-CON [stored after 2005 Kinshasa-N'Djili Airport, Democratic Republic of Congo; b/u started 14Jly08]
383	757	(Air Charter Service)	CF-TIC 9Q-CGQ [wfu & stored 1988 Kinshasa-N'Djili, Democratic Republic of Congo; b/u 1994]
384	757	Fondation Aerovision Quebec	CF-TID C-FTID-X "N6225C" [used as engine testbed with test engines fitted in nose; wfu & preserved Oct89 St Hubert, Montreal, QC, Canada; circa May99 painted in false US marks for movie; Aug11 moved to College Montmorency, Laval, PQ, Canada, reported for fire training use]
385	757	(Western Canada Avn Museum)	CF-TIE [wfu Apr73; preserved Jly75 Winnipeg, MB, Canada; DBF 12Apr80]
386	757	(Zairean Airlines)	CF-TIF 9Q-CPY [wfu in 1989 Kinshasa-N'Djili, Democratic of Congo; l/n Apr96; b/u 1997]
387	757	Tony Hammerling	CF-TIG [wfu & stored Mar73 Winnipeg, MB, Canada; Jun75 moved to Summerland, MB, Canada; by 26Apr82 to Golden Acres Trailer Camp, Winnipeg, MB, Canada; l/n 04lJly82]
388	825		[ordered for Black Lion Aviation; completed as c/n 424]
389	812	(Mandala Airlines)	N247V G-AVJL B-2033 PK-RVW [wfu & stored 12Sep95 Jakarta-Soekarno Hatta, Indonesia; b/u 1997]
390	800		[aircraft not built]
391	798D	ex General John Numbi	N6597C N3939V N8989V N150RC XA-RJL 9Q-CUW [possibly wfu circa 2002; l/n in poor condition 12May09 Kinshasa-N'Djili, Democratic Republic of Congo]
392	798D	(Aero Eslava)	N6598C N98CR N200RC XA-SCM [w/o 27Jly92 into mountains 20 miles E of Mexico City, Mexico en-route from Puebla to Mexico City]
393	739A	(British Eagle Int'l Airlines)	SU-AKN G-ATDR [wfu & b/u May70 Blackbushe, UK; canx 19Feb73]
394	739A	(British Eagle Int'l Airlines)	SU-AKO G-ATFN [w/o 09Aug68 near Langenbruck, N of Munich, West Germany; canx 09Aug68]
395	804	(LOT-Polish Airlines)	G-APKG SP-LVB [w/o 19Dec62 Warsaw-Okecie, Poland]
396	806	(Royal Air Lao)	G-APKF XW-TDN [w/o Mar75 Phnom Penh, Cambodia]
397	827	(Jadepoint USA Inc)	PP-SRC CX-BIY N480RC [wfu & stored 1987 Tucson, AZ; b/u Mar92]
398	827	(VASP)	PP-SRD [w/o 15May73 Salvador, Brazil]
399	827	(VASP)	PP-SRE [w/o 15Sep68 Sao Paulo, Brazil]
400	827	ex PLUNA	PP-SRF CX-BJA (N490RC) [wfu Jun97; used as GIA Montevideo, Uruguay; l/n 07Sep11]
401	827	(VASP)	PP-SRG [w/o 22Dec59 after mid-air collision with Brazilian AF AT-6 Harvard on approach to Rio de Janeiro-Galeao, Brazil]
402	831	(Arkia)	G-APND JY-ADB G-APND (4X-AVF) G-APND G-16-20 4X-AVF [wfu by 01Apr84 Tel Aviv, Israel; 04/05Mar89 shipped in sections to Stansted, UK & to Southend, UK for spares recovery; remains to Stock, Essex, UK; Sep89 nose stored Coggeshall, Essex; l/n Apr91]
403	831	(Pima Community College)	G-APNE JY-ADA G-APNE 4X-AVE [wfu & stored May82 Tucson, AZ; b/u circa 2000; rear fuselage still with college Apr04]
404	823		[not built; ordered by California Eastern Airways; canx before construction]
405	823		[not built; ordered by California Eastern Airways; canx before construction]
406	823		[not built; ordered by California Eastern Airways; canx before construction]
407	823		[not built; ordered by California Eastern Airways; canx before construction]
408	823		[not built; ordered by California Eastern Airways; canx before construction]
409	823		[not built; ordered by California Eastern Airways; canx before construction]
410	823		[not built; ordered by California Eastern Airways; canx before construction]
411	823		[not built; ordered by California Eastern Airways; canx before construction]

VICKERS-ARMSTRONGS VISCOUNT

C/n	Model	Last known Owner/Operator	Identities/fates/comments (where appropriate)
412	806	Brooklands Aviation Museum	G-APIM [w/o 11Jan88 Southend, UK after collision with Short SD.3-30 G-BHWT (c/n SH3049); remains preserved Weybridge, UK; canx 01Mar91]
413	806	(Mandala Airlines)	G-APJU PK-RVM [w/o 01Feb75 Taipei-Sung Shan Airport, Taiwan; b/u for scrap]
414	832	(Mandala Airlines)	VH-RMG B-2015 PK-RVP [wfu & stored Oct94 Jakarta-Soekarno Hatta, Indonesia; l/n in 2002 b/u]
415	832	(Mandala Airlines)	VH-RMH B-2023 9M-AQE B-2023 PK-RVN [w/o 01May81 Semerang, Indonesia]
416	832	(Ansett-ANA)	VH-RMI [w/o 22Sep66 16kms from Winton, QLD, Australia]
417	832	(Merpati Nusantara Airlines)	VH-RMJ B-2017 PK-MVN [wfu & stored early 1984 Jakarta-Soekarrno Hatta, Indonesia; l/n 27Oct85; subsequently b/u]
418	806	(Mandala Airlines)	[built using some parts from c/n 255] G-APOX PK-RVL [wfu & stored Jakarta-Soekarano Hatta, Indonesia; assumed subsequently b/u]
419	831	(Tucson Airport Authority)	ST-AAN G-ASED EC-WZK EC-AZK G-ASED 4X-AVG [wfu & stored Oct94 Tucson, AZ; gone by Jun99; assumed b/u]
420	800		[aircraft not built]
421	808C	MMM Aero Services	EI-AKJ EI-AKO D-ADAN 505+ 9Q-CBT 9Q-CGM [+ Oman] [wfu 1985 Kinshasa, Zaire]
422	808	(Aer Lingus)	EI-AKK [w/o 21Sep67 Bristol-Lulsgate, UK]
423	808C	(MMM Aero Services)	EI-AKL D-ADAM 504+ 9Q-CBS 9Q-CAN(1) [+ Oman] [wfu Nov84 Kinshasa, Zaire; subsequently b/u]
424	833	(Arkia)	G-APTB 4X-AVB [wfu & b/u for spares for British Air Ferries Mar89 Tel Aviv, Israel]
425	833	(Arkia)	G-APTC 4X-AVC [w/o 26Oct69 Tel Aviv, Israel]
426	833	(Arkia)	G-APTD JY-ADC G-APTD 4X-AVD [wfu & stored Nov79 East Midlands Airport, UK; b/u between 1982 and 1984]
427	739B	(United Arab Airlines)	SU-AKW [w/o 29Sep60 into sea off Elba, Italy]
428	807A	(Australian Aircraft Sales)	(ZK-BRG) ZK-BWO (VP-LAU) (G-CSZC) [stored circa 1975 Seletar, Singapore; canx 22Jan76; l/n 21Nov80; assumed subsequently b/u]
429	794D	(Turk Hava Yollari)	TC-SEV [w/o 17Feb59 near Gatwick Airport, UK]
430	794D	Havacilik Muzesi	TC-SEL 430 [wfu 1990 preserved Istanbul-Yesilkoy, Turkey; l/n 17Feb10]
431	794D	Turkish Police	TC-SES 431 [wfu 1990 GIA Eskisehir-Anadolu, Turkey; on display by Apr99]
432	794D	(Turk Hava Yollari)	TC-SET [w/o 02Feb69 Ankara, Turkey]
433	816	(Mandala Airlines)	VH-TVP B-2025 PK-RVS [wfu & stored Apr93 Jakarta/Soekarno-Hatta, Indonesia; l/n Nov95; subsequently b/u]
434	816	(Mandala Airlines)	VH-TVQ B-2027 PK-MVL PK-RVU [w/o 24Jly92 Mount Liliboi en-route from Jakarta to Ambon, Indonesia]
435	836	(Trans Intair)	VH-TVR(1) N40N A6-435+ N40NA VH-EQP 501^ (3D-ACM) G-BFZL ZS-NNI 9Q-CGL [+ Australia; ^ Oman] [w/o 15 or 27Apr03 at gravel airstrip in Democratic Republic of Congo]
436	816	ex Air Zimbabwe	VH-TVS EP-MRS A6-436+ N40NB VH-EQQ 502^ 3D-ACN G-BGLC VP-WGB Z-WGB [+ Australia; ^ Oman] [wfu & stored Dec90 Harare, Zimbabwe; moved 1991 Chegutu, Zimbabwe in use as bar/restaurant, with c/n 446]
437	837	(Austrian Airlines)	OE-LAF [w/o 26Sep60 11kms W of Moscow-Sheremetyevo, USSR]
438	837	Brooklands Museum	OE-LAG XT575 [wfu Jly93 Bruntingthorpe, UK; dismantled 1996, forward fuselage preserved Weybridge, UK; l/n 07Feb07]
439	837	(Far Eastern Air Transport)	OE-LAH G-AZOV B-2029 [w/o 31Jly75 near Taipei, Taiwan]
440	837	ex TAC Colombia	OE-LAK HK-1412 [wfu & stored in 1980; location not recorded]
441	837	ex TAC Colombia	OE-LAL HK-1267 [DBR 14Dec77 Bucaramanga-Palo Negro, Colombia; wreck still present 12Dec07]
442	837	(Lineas Aereas la Urraca)	OE-LAM OE-IAM HK-1347 [w/o 21Jan72 near Funza, 32kms from Bogota, Colombia]
443	828	(Merpati Nusantara Airlines)	G-ARKX JA8201 PK-MVT [wfu & b/u 1973 Jakarta-Soerkarno Hatta, Indonesia]
444	828	(All Nippon Airways)	G-ARKY JA8202 [w/o 19Nov62 near Nagoya, Japan]
445	828	(Merpati Nusantara Airlines)	G-ARKZ JA8203 (PK-MVU) PK-MVG [wfu & stored by 29Jly89 Jakarta/Soekarno Katta, Indonesia; l/n May94; assumed b/u]
446	838	ex Air Zimbabwe	9G-AAU G-BCZR (PK-RVN) G-BCZR VP-WGC Z-WGC [wfu & stored Dec90 Harare, Zimbabwe; moved 1991 Chegutu, Zimbabwe in use as bar/restaurant, in Coca Cola c/s; with c/n 436]
447	814	Lufthansa	D-ANAF [wfu 1970 Hamburg, West Germany; Apr72 to Frankfurt Airport, Germany as ground trainer; wfu Dec11]
448	828	(Merpati Nusantara Airlines)	G-ARWT JA8205 PK-MVS [w/o 10Nov71 near Padang, West Sumatra, Indonesia]
449	828	(All Nippon Airways)	G-ARWU JA8206 [wfu & stored Apr69 Tokyo-Haneda, Japan; b/u Dec70]

VICKERS-ARMSTRONGS VISCOUNT

C/n	Model	Last known Owner/Operator	Identities/fates/comments (where appropriate)
450	828	(All Nippon Airways)	G-ARWV JA8207 [wfu & stored Apr69 Tokyo-Haneda, Japan; b/u Dec70]
451	843	(Bouraq Indonesia Airlines)	G-ASDP 402 RP-C792 PK-IVZ [wfu & stored Aug93 Jakarta/Soekarno Hatta, Indonesia; assumed b/u]
452	843	(Bouraq Indonesia Airlines)	G-ASDR 404 RP-C794 PK-IVW [w/o 04Jly88 Balikpapan-Sepinggan Airport, Indonesia]
453	843	Chinese Air Force	G-ASDS 406 50258 [wfu & preserved Datangshan Museum, Beijing, China]
454	843	(Bouraq Indonesia Airlines)	G-ASDT 408 RP-C793 PK-IVX [w/o 28Aug92 Banjarmasin, Indonesia]
455	843	(Bouraq Indonesia Airlines)	G-ASDU 410 RP-C795 PK-IVY [wfu & stored Feb96 Jakarta/Soekarno Hatta, Indonesia, with cracked wingspar; b/u by May04]
456	843	(Bouraq Indonesia Airlines)	G-ASDV 412 50259+ PK-IVU [+ China] [wfu & stored Oct94 Jakarta/Soekarno Hatta, Indonesia, l/n Nov97; subsequently b/u]
457	828	ex Intercontinental de Aviacion	G-ASBM JA8208 HK-2404X HK-2404 [wfu & stored Oct94 Bogota-El Dorado, Colombia; l/n (less wings) Mar08]
458	828	(SAN Ecuador)	G-ASBO JA8209 [w/o 08Oct82 Cuenca, Ecuador]
459	828	(Merpati Nusantara Airlines)	G-ASBR JA8210 [wfu & stored 22Oct89 Jakarta/Soekarno Hatta, Indonesia; b/u Nov92]

Production complete

VICKERS-ARMSTRONGS VANGUARD/MERCHANTMAN

C/n	Model	Last known Owner/Operator	Identities/fates/comments (where appropriate)
701	950		[Static test airframe]
702	950		[Static test airframe]
703	951	(Vickers-Armstrongs)	G-AOYW [ff 20Jan59] [wfu & stored Oct64; b/u 1964 Wisley, UK; canx 29Oct64; always quoted as a 951 in UK ARB published registers, but elsewhere has been quoted as a series 950]
704	951	(British European Airways)	G-APEA [wfu Dec72; canx19Dec72; b/u May73 London-Heathrow, UK]
705	951	(British European Airways)	G-APEB [wfu 31Mar73; b/u Jun73 London-Heathrow, UK; canx 04Jun73]
706	951	(British European Airways)	G-APEC [w/o en-route 02Oct71 near Aarsele, 30kms SW of Ghent, Belgium; canx 02Oct71]
707	951	(British European Airways)	G-APED [wfu 24Feb71; canx 05Jan73; b/u May73 London-Heathrow, UK]
708	951	(British European Airways)	G-APEE [w/o 27Oct65 London-Heathrow, UK; canx 27Oct65]
709	951	(Merpati Nusantara Airlines)	G-APEF PK-MVJ [wfu & stored by 26Nov73 Jakarta-Kemayoran, Indonesia; b/u]
710	953C	(Hunting Cargo Airlines)	G-APEG [wfu & stored Jun83 East Midlands Airport, UK; canx 18Feb92; Apr96 moved to fire dump; gone by 19Jun97]
711	953	(Merpati Nusantara Airlines)	G-APEH PK-MVF [wfu & stored Jan81 Jakarta-Kemayoran, Indonesia; b/u in 1982]
712	953	(Merpati Nusantara Airlines)	G-APEI PK-MVD [wfu & stored 1980 Jakarta-Kemayoran, Indonesia; l/n Nov91; b/u in 1992]
713	953C	(Hunting Cargo Airlines)	G-APEJ [wfu 24Dec92 East Midlands Airport, UK; b/u 01Jun95; canx 15Nov96; nose preserved Brooklands Museum, Weybridge, UK]
714	953C	(Hunting Cargo Airlines)	G-APEK [wfu & stored by Dec89 Perpignan, France; later b/u; canx 07Nov96]
715	953C	(Inter Cargo Service)	G-APEL F-BYCF TR-LZA F-GEJF [w/o 29Jan88 Toulouse-Blagnac, France]
716	953C	(Hunting Cargo Airlines)	G-APEM F-BYCE G-APEM [wfu 06Jan94 East Midlands Airport, UK; b/u 11Nov95; canx 07Nov96]
717	953	(Merpati Nusantara Airlines)	G-APEN PK-MVE [wfu & stored Jan82 Jakarta-Kemayoran, Indonesia; l/n Jan82; b/u by 1994]
718	953C	(British Airways)	G-APEO [b/u Nov77 London-Heathrow, UK; canx 05Dec77]
719	953C	Brooklands Museum	G-APEP [preserved Oct96 Weybridge, UK; canx 28Feb97 as wfu; l/n 31Oct09]
720	953	(British Airways)	G-APER [wfu & stored Dec74 London-Heathrow, UK; b/u Apr75; canx 25Apr75]
721	953C	(Hunting Cargo Airlines)	G-APES [wfu 04Feb95 East Midlands Airport, UK; canx 28Feb97; b/u 24May97; nose section preserved East Midlands Aeropark; l/n 11Oct08]
722	953C	(Hunting Cargo Airlines)	G-APET [wfu 06Jly91 East Midlands Airport, UK; Dec92 donated to fire service; canx 07Nov96; hulk b/u May97]
723	953	(British Airways)	G-APEU [wfu & stored Nov74 London-Heathrow, UK; canx 25Apr75; b/u Jun75]
724	952	(Interamericana Export-Import)	CF-TKA [wfu & b/u Aug73 Montreal-Dorval, QC, Canada, by Invicta International]
725	952F	(Europe Aero Service)	CF-TKB G-AYFN TF-JES G-AYFN G-41-172 SE-FTK (G-AYFN) F-BXAJ [wfu Jly79 Perpignan, France; derelict by Aug85; b/u late 1989]
726	952	(Europe Aero Service)	CF-TKC F-BTOX [wfu Jan77 Perpignan, France; l/n Jly80; b/u late 1982]
727	952	(Europe Aero Service)	CF-TKD G-AXOY TF-AVA G-AXOY TF-JEJ G-AXOY F-BXOH [wfu Nov75 Perpignan, France; l/n Jly80; b/u late 1982]
728	952	(Air Holdings)	CF-TKE PK-MVW G-BAMX [wfu 06Jun73 Southend, UK; canx 10Jly74; b/u 29Apr75]
729	952	(Europe Aero Service)	CF-TKF G-AZRE F-BXOF [wfu Sep75 Perpignan, France; l/n Jly80; b/u late 1982]
730	952F	(Inter Cargo Service)	CF-TKG G-AYLD SE-FTH G-AYLD F-BUFT TR-LBA F-GEJE [w/o 06Feb89 Marseille-Marignane, France]
731	952	(Europe Aero Service)	CF-TKH F-BTOU [wfu Nov75 Perpignan, France; l/n Jly80; b/u late 1982]
732	952	(Air Holdings)	CF-TKI [stored Dec69 Cambridge Airport, UK; 1972 used for structural tests; b/u 25Jan74 Southend, UK]
733	952	(Invicta International Airlines)	CF-TKJ G-AXOO PK-ICC (G-AXOO) [wfu & stored May73 Manston Airport, UK; b/u by 03May76; canx 05Dec77]
734	952F	(Europe Aero Service)	CF-TKK F-BTYB [wfu Jan77 Perpignan, France; l/n Jly80; b/u by late 1982]
735	952	(Europe Aero Service)	CF-TKL F-OCUA [wfu 1975 Perpignan, France; l/n Jly80; b/u by late 1982]
736	952	(Interamericana Export-Import)	CF-TKM [wfu & b/u Aug73 Montreal-Dorval, QC, Canada, by Invicta International]
737	952F	(Europe Aero Service)	CF-TKN G-AXNT F-BXOO [wfu Oct75 Perpignan, France; l/n Jly80; b/u by late 1982]
738	952	(Air Trader)	CF-TKO [bought for spares; wfu & stored May72 Stockholm-Bromma, Sweden; Oct73 in use for fire practice; b/u Mar78]
739	952	(Europe Aero Service)	CF-TKP G-BAFK PK-MVR G-BAFK F-BXOG [wfu Dec79 Perpignan, France; l/n Jly80; b/u by late 1982]
740	952	(Merpati Nusantara Airlines)	CF-TKQ (G-AZUI) [wfu & b/u Feb74 Jakarta-Kemayoran, Indonesia; canx 20Mar74]
741	952	(Europe Aero Service)	CF-TKR F-OCUB F-BVRZ [wfu Nov80 Perpignan, France; derelict by Aug85; later b/u]

VICKERS-ARMSTRONGS VANGUARD/MERCHANTMAN

C/n	Model	Last known Owner/Operator	Identities/fates/comments (where appropriate)
742	952	(Interamericana Export-Import)	CF-TKS [wfu & b/u Aug73 Montreal-Dorval, QC, Canada, by Invicta International]
743	952	(Europe Aero Service)	CF-TKT F-BTYC [wfu Jan77 Perpignan, France; l/n Jly80; b/u by late 1980]
744	952	(Merpati Nusantara Airlines)	CF-TKU G-AZNG SE-FTI G-AZNG PK-MVC G-AZNG F-BVUY PK-MVA [wfu by Nov85 Jakarta-Kemayoran, Indonesia; b/u by 1994]
745	952	(Invicta International Airlines)	CF-TKV G-AXOP [w/o 10Apr73 Jura mountains, 15km S of Basel-Mulhouse Airport, France; canx 08Jun73]
746	952	(Merpati Nusantara Airlines)	CF-TKW F-BTOV PK-MVH [wfu & dismantled Dec87 Perpignan, France; hulk by road to Porthus, Pyrenees, France as rescue trainer; no subsequent reports]

Production complete

YUNSHUJI/AVIC II Y-7/MA60

C/n	Model	Last known Owner/Operator	Identities/fates/comments (where appropriate)

Note: Aircraft are listed in the order Y-7-100, Y-7-200 and then Y-7H, Y-7G and MA-60.

C/n	Model	Last known Owner/Operator	Identities/fates/comments (where appropriate)
01 7 01			[possible static test airframe]
01 7 02		Chinese Air Force	12608
01 7 03		Chinese Air Force	B-421 B-3433(1) 3179
01 7 04		Chinese Air Force	B-423 B-3434 8192
01 7 05			[possibly not built]
02 7 01			[possibly not built]
02 7 02		(China Eastern Airlines)	B-3451(1) [converted 1982 to Y-7H (MA60) c/n 00 7H 02]
02 7 03		(China Southern Airlines)	B-3452(1) [wfu Nanyang, China; probably b/u; canx]
02 7 04	100C	CAAC Aeronautical Institute Collection	B-3453(1) [preserved Tianjin, China; l/n 17Sep09]
02 7 05		(China Southern Airlines)	B-3454 [wfu & stored 1995 Nanyang, China; canx]
03 7 01		(China Southern Airlines)	B-3455(1) [wfu & stored 1995 Nanyang, China; canx]
03 7 02	100	ex Air Guinee	B-3499 3X-GCL+ [+ c/n not confirmed; reported wfu/stored Conakry, Guinea]
03 7 03		Beijing Aviation Enthusiasts Club	B-3456(1) [wfu 1995; preserved by Oct07 Jicha Fulu, near Beijing, China; l/n 17Sep09]
03 7 04		Guangzhou Civil Aviation College	B-3457 [wfu 1995 Nanyuan, China; to GIA Guangzhou, Pudong, China; l/n 19Sep09]
03 7 05		(Air Guangzhou)	B-3458 [wfu by Oct96 Chengdu, China; probably b/u but current Apr09]
04 7 01		(China Eastern Airlines)	B-3459 [wfu & stored by 1994 Nanyang, China; canx]
04 7 02		(China Eastern Airlines)	B-3460 [wfu post Nov91 Hefei, China; canx]
04 7 03		(Air China)	B-3461 [canx; fate/status unknown]
04 7 04	100C	(Air China)	B-3462 [wfu 1998 Hohhot, China; l/n Apr00; fate unknown; canx]
04 7 05	100C	(Air China)	B-3463 [wfu 1998 Hohhot, China; l/n Apr00; fate unknown; canx]
04 7 06	100C	ex Air Guizhou	B-3464 [wfu; possibly b/u but still current Apr09]
04 7 07	100C	(China Northern Airlines)	B-3466 [canx; fate/status unknown]
04 7 08			[possibly not built]
04 7 09			[possibly not built]
04 7 10			[possibly not built]
05 7 01	100C	(China Northern Airlines)	B-3467 [canx; fate/status unknown]
05 7 02	100C	ex Air China	B-3465 [canx by Jan09; fate/status unknown; l/n May08 Chengdu, China]
05 7 03	100	Guangzhou Civil Aviation College	B-3468 [wfu by 05Oct05 Harbin, China; canx; to GIA Guangzhou, Pudong, China; l/n 19Sep09]
05 7 04	100	ex CAAC Flying College	B-3469 [canx 2009 fate/status unknown]
05 7 05	100	ex CAAC Flying College	B-3470 [canx 2009 fate/status unknown]
05 7 06	100	Beijing Aviation Enthusiasts Club	B-3471 [wfu 26Oct06; by Oct07 preserved CAAC Museum, Jicha Fulu, near Beijing, China; canx; l/n 17Sep09]
05 7 07	100	ex Wuhan Airlines	B-3472 [stored by May01 Wuhan-Hankou, China; l/n Oct05; canx; fate/status unknown]
05 7 08	100	(China Eastern Airlines)	B-3473 [stored by Apr00 Taiyuan, China; canx]
05 7 09	100C	(Sichuan Airlines)	B-3496 [stored/wfu Apr99 Chengdu, China; canx]
05 7 10	100	China Flight Test Establishment	072 [c/n not confirmed]
06 7 01	100	(China Eastern Airlines)	B-3474 [stored/wfu by Apr00 Taiyuan, China; canx]
06 7 02	100C	Sichuan Airlines	B-3497 [preserved by Apr99 Sichuan A/L, Chengdu Airport, China; l/n Nov08; canx]
06 7 03	100C	ex Air Changan	B-3475 "1226" [stored/wfu by 24Oct02 Xian, China; canx; by Sep09 preserved Shilihe market, Beijing, China; c/n not confirmed]
06 7 04	100	(Fujian Airlines)	B-3476(1) [canx; fate/status unknown]
06 7 05	100C	(China Northern Airlines)	B-3477 [canx; fate/status unknown]
06 7 06	100C	(Sichuan Airlines)	B-3498 [l/n 27Sep99 Chengdu, China; canx; fate/status unknown]
06 7 07	100	(China Northern Airlines)	B-3478 [canx; fate/status unknown]
06 7 08	100	(Wuhan Airlines)	B-3479 [w/o 04Nov93 Wangjiadun, China; canx]
06 7 09	100	ex CAAC Flying College	B-3480 [canx during 2011; fate/status unknown]
06 7 10	100	(China Eastern Airlines)	B-3481 [stored/wfu by Apr00 Taiyuan, China; canx]
07 7 01	100C	(China Eastern Airlines)	B-3482 [stored Hefei, China; canx; fate/status unknown]
07 7 02	100	(Nanjing Airlines)	6051+ B-3717 [+ China] [canx; fate/status unknown]
07 7 03	100C	(China Northern Airlines)	B-3484 [canx; fate/status unknown]
07 7 04	100	(Nanjing Airlines)	6061+ B-3718 [+ China] [canx; fate/status unknown]
07 7 05	100C	Guangzhou Civil Aviation College	B-3486 [wfu by 05Oct05 Harbin, China; canx; to GIA Guangzhou, Pudong, China; l/n 19Sep09]
07 7 06	100	Nanjing University of Aeronautics	B-3487 [by 23Feb06 GIA Nanjing, China; canx; l/n Apr08]

YUNSHUJI/AVIC II Y-7/MA60

C/n	Model	Last known Owner/Operator	Identities/fates/comments (where appropriate)
07 7 07	100	Guangzhou Civil Aviation College	B-3488 [wfu by 05Oct05 Harbin, China; canx; to GIA Guangzhou, Pudong, China; l/n 19Sep09]
07 7 08	100C	Chinese Navy	B-3489 [not known] [Coast Guard Surveillance]
07 7 09	100C	ex Wuhan Airlines	B-3490 [stored/wfu by May01 Wuhan-Hankou, China; l/n 10Oct05; canx]
07 7 10	100C	ex Wuhan Airlines	B-3491 [stored/wfu by May01 Wuhan-Hankou, China; l/n 10Oct05; canx]
08 7 01	100C	ex Wuhan Airlines	B-3442 [stored/wfu by May01 Wuhan-Hankou, China; l/n 10Oct05; canx]
08 7 02	100C	ex Wuhan Airlines	B-3443 [stored/wfu by 10Oct05 Wuhan-Hankou, China; canx]
08 7 03	100C	ex Air China	B-3492 [wfu 1999 Hohhot, China; canx; l/n 14Apr00; reported returned to factory, no further news]
08 7 04	100C	Chinese Navy	B-3493 [not known] [Coast Guard Surveillance]
08 7 05	100C	(PMT Air)	B-3494 XU-072 [w/o 21Nov05 Ratanakiri, Cambodia]
08 7 06	100C	(China Northern Airlines)	B-3495 [canx; fate/status unknown]
08 7 07	100	(Fujian Airlines)	6071+ B-3715 [+ China] [canx; fate/status unknown]
08 7 08	100C	ex Royal Phnom Penh	B-3449 XU-071 [by 03Apr08 stored Phnom Penh-Pochentong, Cambodia]
08 7 09	100C	(Sichuan Airlines)	B-3441 [stored/wfu by 11Apr99 Chengdu, China; canx]]
08 7 10	100C	(Air China)	B-3450 [reported wfu 2000; canx; fate/status unknown]
09 7 01	100C	(Air Changan)	B-3444 [canx; fate/status unknown; l/n 27May00 active Xian, China]
09 7 02	100C	Chinese Military	B-3447 [not known]
09 7 03	100C	(China Northern Airlines)	B-3446 [canx; fate/status unknown]
09 7 04			[possibly not built]
09 7 05	100C	(Sichuan Tri-Star)	B-3445 [canx; fate/status unknown; l/n 20Oct06 Guanghan, China]
09 7 06	100C	ex Royal Phnom Penh	B-3448 XU-070 [by 03Apr08 stored Phnom Penh-Pochentong, Cambodia]
09 7 07	100	(Fujian Airlines)	6081+ B-3716 [+ China] [by 03Apr08 stored Phnom Penh-Pochentong, Cambodia]
09 7 08	100C	(Zhongyuan Airlines)	B-3439 [canx; fate/status unknown; l/n 16May01 Zhengzhou, China]
09 7 09	100C	(Zhongyuan Airlines)	B-3438 [canx; fate/status unknown; l/n 15Aug04 Zhengzhou, China]
09 7 10	100C	(Sichuan Airlines)	B-3437 [stored/wfu by 11Apr99 Chengdu, China; canx]
10 7 01	100	ex CAAC Flying College	B-3436 [stored/wfu by Mar03 Guanghan, China; l/n Mar08; canx]
10 7 02	100	ex CAAC Flying College	B-3435 [flew last Y-7 civil operational flight in China on 26Mar11; reported for training use at Guanghan, China]
10 7 03	100	Chinese Air Force	9032
10 7 04	100	Chinese Air Force	9042
10 7 05	100	Chinese Air Force	5066
10 7 06	100	Chinese Air Force	5813
10 7 07	100C	ex Lao Aviation	RDPL-34119 [stored/wfu by Feb02 Vientiane-Wattay, Laos; l/n 07Nov09]
10 7 08	100	Chinese Air Force	5010
10 7 09	100	Chinese Air Force	3418
10 7 10	100	Chinese Air Force	4510
11 7 01	100	Chinese Air Force	5011
11 7 02	100	Chinese Air Force	9052 [c/n not confirmed]
11 7 03			[test airframe ?]
11 7 04	100C	(Shandong Airlines)	B-3704 [wfu 1996; canx; fate/status unknown]
11 7 05	100C	(Air Changan)	B-3708 [stored/wfu by Oct02 Xian, China; l/n Oct05; gone by Apr07; canx]
12 7 01	100C	(Air Changan)	B-3707 [stored/wfu by Oct02 Xian, China; l/n Oct05; gone by Apr07; canx]
12 7 02	100	Chinese Air Force	9062 [c/n not confirmed]
12 7 03	100C	ex Lao Army Air Force	RDPL-34015 [derelict by Jan06 Xieng Khouang, China; l/n Jan09]
12 7 04	100C	Lao Army Air Force	RDPL-34016
12 7 05	100	ex Shanxi Airlines	B-3701 [stored/wfu by 16Apr07 Taiyuan, China; canx]
12 7 06	100	ex Lao Aviation	RDPL-34127 [stored/wfu by 07Nov09 Vientiane-Wattay, Laos]
12 7 07	100C	ex Shanxi Airlines	B-3702 [stored/wfu by 16Apr07 Taiyuan, China; marked as just B-; canx; by 13Jly11 at Haikou China as GIA]
12 7 08	100	ex Shanxi Airlines	B-3703 [stored/wfu by 16Apr07 Taiyuan, China; marked as just B-; canx; by 13Jly11 at Haikou China as GIA]
12 7 09	100C	CAAC Flying College	9030+ B-82700 [+ China] [non-standard four number Chinese marks]
12 7 10	100C	CAAC Flying College	9040+ B-82701 [+ China] [non-standard four number Chinese marks]
13 7 01	100C	Lao Aviation	RDPL-34128
13 7 02	100	Chinese Air Force	60021
13 7 03		Chinese Air Force	[not known]
13 7 04	100C	CAAC Flying College	9050+ B-89050 [+ China] [non-standard four number Chinese marks]
13 7 05	100C	CAAC Flying College	9060+ B-89060 [+ China] [non-standard four number Chinese marks]

YUNSHUJI/AVIC II Y-7/MA60

C/n	Model	Last known Owner/Operator	Identities/fates/comments (where appropriate)
200-0001	200A	ex Air Changan	B-570L+ B-3720 [+ might be same aircraft as c/n 00 7A 01 below; Chinese Register gives c/n as 0001; canx 2009, for sale as spares]
200-0002			[nothing known]
200-0003	200A	ex Air Changan	B-3721 [Chinese Register gives c/n as 0003; canx 2009, for sale as spares]
00 7A 01	200A	AVIC	B-570L+ [+ might be same aircraft as c/n 200-0001]
00 7H 02	Y-7H	China Flight Test Establishment	B-3451(1) 073+ [converted from Y-7 c/n 02702 above; + c/n not confirmed]
00 7H 03	Y-7H-500	(Mauritanian Air Force)	B-546L B-3719 5T-MAG [w/o 12May98 Nema, Mauritania]
02 7H 02	Y-7H	Chinese Air Force	4520
05 7H 02	Y-7H	Chinese Air Force	33140
01 01	MA60	AVIC	B-559L B-3425+ [+ marks previously used by An-24RV c/n 4 73 09]
01 02	MA60	Joy Air	B-3430
01 03	MA60	Joy Air	B-3431
01 04	MA60	Chinese Air Force	[not known]
01 05	MA60	Joy Air	B-3432
02 01	Y-7G	China United Airlines	B-4071 [marks also noted on Y-8]
02 02	MA60	ex Sichuan Airlines	B-3426+ [+ marks previously used by An-24RV c/n 4 74 01; canx by Jan09 fate/status unknown]
02 03	MA60	Xian Aircraft Company	B-3429+ B-651L^ [+ marks previously used by An-24RV c/n 4 74 07; ^ c/n not confirmed]
02 04	Y-7G	China United Airlines	B-4072 [marks also noted on Y-8]
02 05	Y-7G	China United Airlines	B-4073 [c/n and operator to be confirmed]
02 06	Y-7G	China United Airlines	B-4074 [c/n and operator to be confirmed]
02 07	Y-7G	China United Airlines	B-4075 [c/n and operator to be confirmed]
02 08	Y-7G	China United Airlines	B-4076 [c/n and operator to be confirmed]
02 09	Y-7G	China United Airlines	B-4077 [c/n and operator to be confirmed]
03 01	MA60	Air Zimbabwe	B-674L Z-WPJ [damaged 03Nov09 Bulawayo, Zimbabwe]
03 02	MA60	Air Zimbabwe	Z-WPK
03 03	MA60	Air Zimbabwe	Z-WPL
04 01	MA60	Zambian Air Force	AF607
04 02	MA60	Lao Aviation	B-761L RDPL-34168
04 03	MA60	Lao Aviation	RDPL-34169
04 04	MA60	Zambian Air Force	B-692L 9J-ZAA+ AF608 [+ for ferry flight only?]
04 05	MA60	Air Congo International	B-762L TN-AHL
04 06	MA60	Air Congo International	B-800L TN-AHN+ [+ no sightings, by 02Aug10 marks reported on LET410; possibly ntu/delivered]
04 07	MA60	Merpati Nusantara	B-799L PK-MZA
04 08	MA60	Air Congo International	B-???L TN-AHO [stored Brazzaville, Democratic Republic of Congo]
04 09	MA60	Merpati Nusantara Airlines	B-803L PK-MZC
04 10	MA60	Merpati Nusantara Airlines	B-???L PK-MZD
05 01	MA60	Merpati Nusantara Airlines	B-???L PK-MZE
05 02	MA60	Merpati Nusantara Airlines	B-???L PK-MZF
05 03	MA60	Bolivian Air Force	B-850L FAB-96 [was reported as c/n 0411 in error; damaged extent unknown 18Mar11 Rurrenabaque, Bolivia]
05 04	MA60	Bolivian Air Force	B-858L FAB-97 [was reported as c/n 0412 in error]
05 05	MA60	Merpati Nusantara Airlines	B-???L PK-MZG
05 06	MA60	Merpati Nusantara Airlines	B-???L PK-MZH
05 07	MA60	Lao Aviation	RDPL-34171
05 08	MA60	Lao Aviation	RDPL-34172
05 09	MA60	OK Air	B-3709
05 10	MA60	OK Air	B-895L B-3710
06 01	MA60	Merpati Nusantara Airlines	B-???L PK-MZI
06 02	MA60	Merpati Nusantara Airlines	B-???L PK-MZJ
06 03	MA60	(Merpati Nusantara Airlines)	B-???L PK-MZK [w/o 07May11 Kaimana, Indonesia]
06 04	MA60	Merpati Nusantara Airlines	B-???L PK-MZL
06 05	MA60	Merpati Nusantara Airlines	B-???L PK-MZM
06 06	MA60	Merpati Nusantara Airlines	B-???L PK-MZN
06 07	MA600	Civil Aviation Flight University of China	B-971L B-3457 [rolled out 29Jun08; ff 09Oct08; is a new variant with main entry door moved to the front fuselage and improved avionics; also reported as c/n 067107]
06 08	MA60	Merpati Nusantara Airlines	B-???L PK-MZO
06 09	MA60	Merpati Nusantara Airlines	B-???L PK-MZP

YUNSHUJI/AVIC II Y-7/MA60

C/n	Model	Last known Owner/Operator	Identities/fates/comments (where appropriate)		
06 10	MA60	Yunnan Dacite General Aviation	B-3421		
07 01			[nothing known]		
07 02			[nothing known]		
07 03	MA60	Zest Airways	B-956L	RP-C8892	[damaged 25Jun09 Catican, Philippines]
07 04	MA60	(Zest Airways)	B-957L	RP-C8893	[w/o 11Jan09 Caticlan-Malay Airport, Philippines]
07 05	MA60	Happy Aviation Co	B-3451(2)		
07 06	MA60	Happy Aviation Co/Joy Air	B-3452(2)		
07 07	MA60	Happy Aviation Co/Joy Air	B-3453(2)		
07 08	MA60	Helitours	4R-HTN		
07 09	MA60	Helitours	4R-HTO		
07 10	MA60	Zest Airways	B-956L	RP-C8894	
07 11	MA60	Zest Airways	B-963L	RP-C8895	
07 12	MA60	Zest Airways	B-964L	RP-C8896	
07 14	MA60	OK Air	B-3440		
07 15	MA60	OK Air	B-3433(2)		
08 03	MA60	Joy Air	B-3455(2)		
08 04	MA60	Joy Air	B-3459		
08 05	MA60	Joy Air	B-3476(2)		
08 06	MA60	Myanma Airways	XY-AIO		
08 07	MA60	Myanma Airways	XY-AIP		
08 08	MA60	Myanma Airways	XY-AIQ		
08 09	MA60	OK Air	B-3711		
09 06	MA600	China Civil Aviation Flight Centre	B-3456(2)		
097III07	MA600	AVIC	B-015L		[reported Nov11 displayed at Dubai Airshow; note Roman style 3 in middle of c/n]

Unidentified – Civil Prefix

C/n	Model	Last known Owner/Operator	Identities	Comments
unkn	Y-7H-200	AVIC	B-502L	[reported 16Nov98 Zhahai, China]
unkn	MA60	for Merpati	B-851L	[reported Kunming, China; not PK-MZG, MZI, MZJ or MZK]
unkn	MA600	ex Merpati	B-864L	[reported stored 13Oct09 Xian, China & flying 01Dec10 Kunming, China; probably one of the above undelivered aircraft]
unkn	MA60	ex Merpati	B-867L	[reported 01Dec10 Kunming, China; probably one of of the above undelivered aircraft]
unkn	MA600	AVIC 1	B-871L	[reported 13Oct09 Xian, China]
unkn	MA60	for Merpati	B-949L	[reported Kunming, China; not PK-MZG, MZI, MZJ or MZK]
unkn	MA60	for Air Burundi	B-1019L	[reported delivered 18Jun12 via Kunming, China]
unkn	Y-7G	unknown	B-6015	[reported 08Apr12 Shahe AFB, China; marks current on China Eastern A320]
unkn	Y-7G	unknown	B-6016	[reported 08Apr12 Shahe AFB, China; marks current on China Eastern A320]
unkn	Y-7G	unknown	B-6017	[reported 08Apr12 Shahe AFB, China; marks current on China Eastern A320]
unkn	Y-7G	unknown	B-6018	[reported 08Apr12 Shahe AFB, China; marks current on China Southern A319]
unkn	Y-7G	unknown	B-6019	[reported 08Apr12 Shahe AFB, China; marks current on China Southern A319]
unkn	Y-7-200A		B-6111	[reported 20Mar95 Yanglang, China; regn incorrect series]
unkn	MA60	Tajik Air	EY-201	[reported handed over 23Dec11 Dushanbe, Tajikstan]
unkn	MA60	Laos Government/Air Force	RDPL-34026	[reported delivered 10Apr12 via Kunming, China]
unkn	MA60	Laos Government/Air Force	RDPL-34028	[reported delivered 10Apr12 via Kunming, China]
unkn	Y-7-100C	Lao Aviation	RDPL-34120	[reported 18Apr99 Chiang Mai, Thailand]

Unidentified – Military

C/n	Model	Last known Owner/Operator	Identities	Comments
unkn	Y-7	Qinqdao Naval Museum	028	[preserved by Sep07 Qinqdao, China; Chinese Navy c/s]
unkn	Y-7	China Flight Test Establishment	711	[reported 13Oct09 Xian-Yanliang, China]
unkn	Y-7	China Flight Test Establishment	712	[reported 13Oct09 Xian-Yanliang, China]
unkn	Y-7	Chinese Air Force	5628	[from photo; a passenger aircraft]
unkn	Y-7H	Chinese Air Force	5823	[from photo]
unkn	Y-7H	Chinese Air Force	5833	[from photo]
unkn	Y-7H	Chinese Air Force	5853	[reported 15May01 Wuhan-Nanhu, China]
unkn	Y-7H	Chinese Air Force	5863	[reported 15May01 Wuhan-Nanhu, China]
unkn	Y-7-100	Chinese Air Force	6011	[reported Apr12 with Shenyang Flight]
unkn	Y-7-100	Chinese Air Force	9038	[from photo]
unkn	Y-7-100	Chinese Air Force	10051	[reported 25Oct10 Kunming, China]
unkn	Y-7-100	Chinese Air Force	10052	[from 2007 photo]
unkn	Y-7H	Chinese Air Force	10054	[from photo]

YUNSHUJI/AVIC II Y-7/MA60

C/n	Model	Last known Owner/Operator	Identities/fates/comments (where appropriate)	
unkn	Y-7H	Chinese Air Force	10055	[from 2010 photo]
unkn	Y-7H	Chinese Air Force	10056	[from 2010 photo]
unkn	Y-7H	Chinese Air Force	10650	[from 2010 photo]
unkn	Y-7-100	Chinese Air Force	11350	[reported May12]
unkn	Y-7	Chinese Air Force	20044	[reported 06Oct09 Keifeng, China]
unkn	Y-7	Chinese Air Force	20142	[reported 06Oct09 Keifeng, China]
unkn	Y-7	Chinese Air Force	20144	[reported 06Oct09 Keifeng, China]
unkn	Y-7	Chinese Air Force	20241	[reported 06Oct09 Keifeng, China]
unkn	Y-7	Chinese Air Force	20242	[reported 06Oct09 Keifeng, China]
unkn	Y-7	Chinese Air Force	20243	[reported 06Oct09 Keifeng, China]
unkn	Y-7	Chinese Air Force	20245	[reported 06Oct09 Keifeng, China]
unkn	Y-7	Chinese Air Force	20246	[reported 06Oct09 Keifeng, China]
unkn	Y-7	Chinese Air Force	20247	[reported 06Oct09 Keifeng, China]
unkn	Y-7H	Chinese Air Force	20541	[reported 17Oct09 Zhengzhou, China]
unkn	Y-7H	Chinese Air Force	20542	[from 2007 photo]
unkn	Y-7H	Chinese Air Force	20543	[from photo]
unkn	Y-7H	Chinese Air Force	20545	[version not confirmed; from photo]
unkn	Y-7H	Chinese Air Force	20640	[from 2009 photo]
unkn	Y-7H	Chinese Air Force	20641	[from photo]
unkn	Y7-100	Chinese Air Force	21678	[from early 2012 photo]
unkn	Y-7	Chinese Air Force	30578	[reported during 2006]
unkn	Y-7G	Chinese Air Force	30579	[from photo]
unkn	Y-7H	Chinese Air Force	33041	[exact type unconfirmed] [reported 19Mar96 Beijing-Nan Yuan, China]
unkn	Y-7H	Chinese Air Force	33042	[exact type unconfirmed] [reported 02Oct99 & 15May01 Wuhan-Hankou, China]
unkn	Y-7H	Chinese Air Force	33043	[exact type unconfirmed] [reported 02Oct99 & 15May01 Wuhan-Hankou, China]
unkn	Y-7H	Chinese Air Force	33044	[exact type unconfirmed] [reported 29Sep99 Guangzhou, China]
unkn	Y-7H	Chinese Air Force	33045	[exact type unconfirmed] [reported 02Oct99 Wuhan-Hankou, China]
unkn	Y-7H	Chinese Air Force	33046	[exact type unconfirmed] [reported 02Oct99 & 15May01 Wuhan-Hankou, China]
unkn	Y-7H	Chinese Air Force	33047	[exact type unconfirmed] [reported 02Oct99 Wuhan-Hankou, China]
unkn	Y-7H	Chinese Air Force	33048	[exact type unconfirmed] [reported 02Oct99 & 15May01 Wuhan-Hankou, China]
unkn	Y-7H	Chinese Air Force	33049	[exact type unconfirmed] [reported 02Oct99 Wuhan-Hankou, China]
unkn	Y-7H	Chinese Air Force	33141	[exact type unconfirmed] [reported 02Oct99 Wuhan-Hankou, China]
unkn	Y-7H	Chinese Air Force	33142	[exact type unconfirmed] [reported 02Oct99 & 15May01 Wuhan-Hankou, China]
unkn	Y-7	Chinese Air Force	40551	[reported Sep05 Shane, China & 15Apr07 Beijing-Nan Yuan, China]
unkn	Y-7	Chinese Air Force	40552	[reported Sep05 & May08 Shane, China]
unkn	Y-7	Chinese Air Force	40553	[reported Sep05 & May08 Shane, China]
unkn	Y-7-100	China United Airlines?	51055	[reported Sep05 Shane, China; serial noted in Oct88 on An-24 c/n unknown]
unkn	Y-7-100?	China United Airlines	51057	[reported 05Apr00 Foshan, China; exact type unconfirmed]
unkn	Y-7-100?	China United Airlines?	51058	[reported 05Apr00 Foshan, China & Sep05 Shane, China; exact type unconfirmed]
unkn	Y-7-100	China United Airlines	51059	[reported 01Jun93 Beijing-Nan Yuan, China]
unkn	Y-7-100	Chinese Air Force	60022	[reported 13May & 14Oct09 Tongzhou, China]
unkn	Y-7-100	Chinese Air Force	70025	[from photo]
unkn	Y-7	Chinese Air Force	71025	[from photo; 105 on nose based at Chengdu-Pengshan, China]
unkn	Y-7	Chinese Air Force	71026	[from photo; large "106" on fuselage]
unkn	HYJ7	Chinese Air Force	71116	[in TV programme during Jun07 with code 16 red]
unkn	HYJ7	Chinese Air Force	71126	[from photo; 116 on nose based at Chengdu-Pengshan, China]
unkn	HYJ7	Chinese Air Force	71223	[from photo, based at Chengdu-Pengshan, China]
unkn	Y-7	Chinese Air Force	71229	[from photo "129" on fuselage]
unkn	HYJ7	Chinese Air Force	71315	[from photo]
unkn	Y-7	Chinese Air Force	71320	[from photo "130" on fuselage]

YUNSHUJI/AVIC II Y-7/MA60

C/n	Model	Last known Owner/Operator	Identities/fates/comments (where appropriate)	
unkn	HYJ7	Chinese Air Force	71322	[from photo, "132" on nose; based at Chengdu-Pengshan, China]
unkn	Y-7H	Chinese Navy	82500?	[photo with code 50 on fuselage]
unkn	Y-7H	Chinese Navy	82506?	[photo with code 56 on fuselage]
unkn	Y-7H	Chinese Navy	82507?	[photo with code 57 on fuselage]
unkn	Y-7H	Chinese Navy	82508?	[photo with code 58 on fuselage]
unkn	Y-7H	Chinese Navy	82509?	[photo with code 59 on fuselage]
unkn	Y-7	Chinese Navy	86208	[from photo]
unkn	Y-7H	Chinese Navy	82701	[from photo]
unkn	Y-7-100	Chinese Navy	9010	[reported]
unkn	Y-7	Chinese Navy	9017	[from photo]
unkn	Y-7-100C	Chinese Navy	9020	[reported 19May09 Changzhi-Wangcun, China]
unkn	Y-7	Chinese Navy	9027	[from early 2004 photo]
unkn	Y-7	Chinese Navy	9030	[reported]
unkn	Y-7-100	Chinese Navy	9037	[from photo]
unkn	Y-7	Chinese Navy	9040	[reported]
unkn	Y-7	Chinese Navy	9050	[reported]
unkn	Y-7	Chinese Navy	9070	[reported 18May09 Changzhi-Wangcun, China]
unkn	Y-7	Chinese Navy	9080	[reported 18May09 Changzhi-Wangcun, China]
unkn	Y-7	Chinese Navy	9090	[reported 18May09 Changzhi-Wangcun, China]
unkn	Y-7H	Chinese Navy	9112	[reported in 2008]
unkn	Y-7H	Chinese Navy	9122	[reported in 2008]
unkn	Y-7H	Chinese Navy	9132	[reported in 2008]
unkn	Y-7H	Chinese Navy	9142	[reported in 2008]
unkn	Y-7H	Chinese Navy	9152	[reported in 2008]
unkn	Y-7H	Chinese Navy	9162	[reported in 2006 & 2008]
unkn	?	Chinese Army	LH94003	[reported in 2008]
unkn	Y-7H	Chinese Army	LH94004	[from photo]
unkn	?	Chinese Army	LH94005	[from photo]
unkn	?	Chinese Army	LH94006	[reported in 2008]
unkn	?	Chinese Army	LH94008	[reported in 2008]
unkn	?	Chinese Army	LH94009	[reported in 2008]
unkn	MA60	Cambodian Air Force	MT-301	[reported 31May12 Kunmimg, China; also reported without MT prefix]
unkn	Y-7H	(Mauritanian Air Force)	5T-MAF	[w/o 05Apr96 Atlantic Ocean, near Mauritanian coast]
unkn	Y-7	Zambian Air Force	AF-607	[reported 16Oct09 Livingstone, Zambia]
unkn	Y-7	Zambian Air Force	AF-608	[reported 16Oct09 Livingstone, Zambia]

EXPERIMENTAL AND LIMITED PRODUCTION AIRCRAFT

AEROPROGRESS T-101 GRATCH

C/n	Model	Last known Owner/Operator	Identities/fates/comments (where appropriate)
unkn		Federation of Light Aviation	FLARF-01466 [fate/status unknown]
unkn		North Express	RA-01777 [fate/status unknown]
008?		North Express	RA-02555 [fate/status unknown]

AERO SPACELINES GUPPY

Note: Except first aircraft built from Boeing Stratocruiser/C-97 components with new c/ns.

C/n	Line No.	Model	Last known Owner/Operator	Identities/fates/comments (where appropriate)
15938	41	SG	Pima Air & Space Museum	N1038V N940NA N940NS [f/f 31Aug65; preserved Pima, Tucson, AZ]
0001		101/SG	(Aero Spacelines Inc)	N111AS [f/f 13Mar70; w/o 12May70 Mojave, CA: but location also reported as Edwards AFB, CA]
0002		101	(Aero Spacelines Inc)	N112AS [on register dated Jan70 until at least Jly75 as a 337MGT-1; but assumed either not built or completed]
001		201/SGT	British Aviation Heritage	N211AS F-BTGV [f/f 24Aug70; preserved Jly96 Bruntingthorpe, UK; l/n 03May09]
002		201/SGT	Ailes Anciennes	N212AS F-BPPA [canx 05Dec96; preserved Toulouse-Blagnac, France; l/n 25Apr09]
003		201/SGT	EADS	F-WDSG F-GDSG [canx 20Oct97; preserved Hamburg-Finkenwerder, Germany; l/n 30Jan09]
004		201/SGT	NASA	F-WEAI F-GEAI N941NA

AHRENS AR 404

C/n	Model	Last known Owner/Operator	Identities/fates/comments (where appropriate)
0001X		Ahrens Aircraft Corp	N404AR [f/f 01Dec76; fate/status unknown]
001		ex Bromon Aircraft	N1028G [canx 06Aug02 destroyed; fuselage stored east of Las Vegas-McCarran, NV]
002		(Bromon Aircraft)	(N1028K) [assumed not built and marks ntu]
003		(Ahrens Aircraft Corp)	(N1028N) [assumed not built and marks ntu]
004		(Ahrens Aircraft Corp)	(N1028S) [assumed not built and marks ntu]

AIR METALL AM-C111

C/n	Model	Last known Owner/Operator	Identities/fates/comments (where appropriate)
V-1	400SP	(Air Metal)	[never registered; dismantled 1977 without flying; stored by Sep93 Landshut, Germany; rediscovered late 2009, presented to Deutsches Technikmuseum for preservation]

AMECO-HAWK GAFHAWK 125

C/n	Model	Last known Owner/Operator	Identities/fates/comments (where appropriate)
001	200	Hawk Industries Inc	N101GH [re-engined with piston engine; reported stored by 11Jun06 Delta Junction, AK; fate/status unknown]

ANTONOV An-70

C/n	Model	Last known Owner/Operator	Identities/fates/comments (where appropriate)
01 01		(Antonov Design Bureau)	UR- [only wore UR-] [prototype ff 16Dec94; w/o 10Feb95 near Kiev-Gostomel, Ukraine, collided with chase plane An-72 72966]
77 01 02		Antonov Design Bureau	UR- UR-NTK [second prototype ff 24Apr97; was to be static airframe but built as flying example; seriously damaged 27Jan01 & rebuilt; report has line number 01-03 might reflect this rebuild]

AVIATION TRADERS ATL.90 ACCOUNTANT I

C/n	Model	Last known Owner/Operator	Identities/fates/comments (where appropriate)
01	1	(Aviation Traders Ltd)	G-41-1 G-ATEL [f/f 09Jly57; wfu Jan58; canx 08Oct59; b/u Feb60 Southend, UK]

BERIEV Be-30

C/n	Model	Last known Owner/Operator	Identities/fates/comments (where appropriate)
none	Be-30		CCCP-23166 [full scale mock-up only]
none	Be-30A		CCCP-30170 [full scale mock-up only]
01	Be-30	(Taganrog Mashinostroitelny Zavod)	CCCP-30 CCCP-30167 [prototype ff 08Jly68] [fate unknown]
02	Be-30+	(Taganrog Mashinostroitelny Zavod)	CCCP-02 CCCP-67204+ [+ tie-up assumed; reg'n from photo only as Be32; fate unknown]
03		(Taganrog Mashinostroitelny Zavod)	CCCP-03 CCCP-48978 [fate unknown]
01 OS	Be-32K+	(Taganrog Aviatsionnaya Nauchno-Technicjeskikompleks)	CCCP-67205 RA-67205 [+ converted from Be30: l/n wfu Jun99 Taganrog-Yuzhny, Russia Jun99]
02 OS	Be-30	(Taganrog Mashinostroitelny Zavod)	CCCP-67206 [fate unknown]
03 OS	Be-30	(Taganrog Mashinostroitelny Zavod)	CCCP-67207 [fate unknown]
04 OS	Be-30	(Taganrog Mashinostroitelny Zavod)	CCCP-67208 [fate unknown]
05 OS	Be-32+	Central Russian Air Force Museum	CCCP-67209 [+ converted from Be-30; preserved by Apr83 Monino, Russia; l/n Nov08]

BREGUET 940/941

C/n	Model	Last known Owner/Operator	Identities/fates/comments (where appropriate)
01	940	(Breguet)	F-ZWVF [f/f 21May58; wfu 1961; fate/status unknown]
01	941	(Breguet)	F-WJSD F-ZWVZ [wfu; fate/status unknown]
1	941S	(French Air Force)	F-ZJRK F-SDIX//118-IX F-RANA//62-NA [wfu Apr74; by Aug91 b/u Cloyes-sur-le-Loir, France]
2	941S	(French Air Force)	F-ZJRL F-RANB//62-NB [wfu Apr74; by Aug91 b/u Cloyes-sur-le-Loir, France]
3	941S	ex French Air Force	F-ZJRM F-SDIH//118-IH F-RANC//62-NC [wfu Jly64; preserved by 18May08 Aubenas, France]
4	941S	Musee de l'Air et de l'Espace	F-SDIY//118-IY F-RAND//62-ND [wfu Jly74; preserved Paris-Le Bourget, France; l/n 20Sep09]

DASSAULT MD.320 HIRONDELLE

C/n	Model	Last known Owner/Operator	Identities/fates/comments (where appropriate)
01		(Musee de l'Air et de l'Espace)	F-WPXB [f/f 11Sep68; stored Paris-Le Bourget, France until DBF 11May90]
02		(Avions M Dassault)	[not completed; still intact Jly76 Bordeaux, France]

DASSAULT MD.410 SPIRALE

C/n	Model	Last known Owner/Operator	Identities/fates/comments (where appropriate)
01		(Avions M Dassault)	01 [f/f 08Apr60; wfu; fate/status unknown]

DASSAULT MD.415 COMMUNAUTE

C/n	Model	Last known Owner/Operator	Identities/fates/comments (where appropriate)
01		(Avions M Dassault)	F-WJDN [f/f 10May59; wfu; b/u 1967]

DE HAVILLAND CANADA DHC-4 CARIBOU

C/n	Model	Last known Owner/Operator	Identities/fates/comments (where appropriate)
1	X	(de Havilland of Canada)	CF-KTK-X 5303+ [+ Canada] [fitted with GE T64 engines, at request of GE, for testing of proposed turbine development of the Caribou called Caribou II; ff 22Sep61, TT 300 hours; refitted with piston engines. The Caribou II was eventually developed as the DHC-5 Buffalo]
237	T	Palm Beach Aviation	N600NC [converted to PT6A power by Pen Aero Aviation]
238	T	Aughrim Holding Co	N238PT [converted to turbine power& f/f in May10; USCAR still has with P & W R-2000 engines]
240	T	(New Cal Aviation Inc)	N400NC [converted to prototype PT6A powered DHC-4T f/f 06Nov91; w/o 27Aug92 Gimli Airport, MB, Canada]
303	T	Pen Turbo	N303PT [registered as a turbo conversion 22Nov11 ex N300NC]

FAIRCHILD C-123T PROVIDER

C/n	Model	Last known Owner/Operator	Identities/fates/comments (where appropriate)
20241	C-123T	(Mancro Aircraft Co)	56-4357 N6828 [converted by Mancro Aircraft: f/f 24Oct80; project abandoned and reverted to piston power]

IPTN 250

C/n	Model	Last known Owner/Operator	Identities/fates/comments (where appropriate)
PA-1	50	IPTN PK-XNG	[f/f 10Aug95; presumed wfu Bandung, Indonesia late 1990s]
PA-2	100	IPTN PK-XNH	[presumed wfu Bandung, Indonesia late 1990s]

ROKS-AERO T108 ORYOL

C/n	Model	Last known Owner/Operator	Identities/fates/comments (where appropriate)
unkn		Roks-Aero	RA-93108 [possible full size mock-up; stored or preserved by May94 Moscow-Khodynka (Frunze), Russia]

SUKHOI Su-80

C/n	Model	Last known Owner/Operator	Identities/fates/comments (where appropriate)
0101	GP	(Sukhoi OKB)	[static test frame; wfu after wing unexpectedly broke]
0102	GP	Sukhoi OKB	[l/n 20Aug05 Zhukovsky, Russia; status/fate unknown]
0103	GP	Sukhoi OKB	[mock-up]
0104	GP	Sukhoi OKB	[production test frame]
0105	GP	Sukhoi OKB	82912 [f/f 28Jun06; wfu autumn 2006 & stored Komsomolsk-na-Amure, Russia]
0106	GP	Sukhoi OKB	[reported nearing completion in 2005; l/n Komsomolsk-na-Amure, Russia]
0107	GP	Sukhoi OKB	[reported nearing completion in 2005]

Flight testing suspended in 2006; no further developments known.

TECHNOAVIA RYSACHOK

C/n	Model	Last known Owner/Operator	Identities/fates/comments (where appropriate)
00-01		Technoavia Rysachok	777 red
00-03		Technoavia Rysachok	778 red